Australia

**Darwin &
the Northern
Territory**
p796

Queensland
p267

**Perth &
Western Australia**
p878

**Adelaide &
South Australia**
p714

**Sydney &
New South Wales**
p66

**Canberra &
Around**
p252

**Melbourne &
Victoria**
p453

Tasmania
p629

Brett Atkinson, Anthony Ham, Paul Harding, Kate Morgan, Charles Rawlings-Way,
Andy Symington, Kate Armstrong, Carolyn Bain, Cristian Bonetto,
Peter Dragicevich, Trent Holden, Virginia Maxwell, Tamara Sheward, Tom Spurling,
Benedict Walker, Steve Waters, Donna Wheeler

PLAN YOUR TRIP

BRISBANE P270

KINGS CANYON, WATARRKA
NATIONAL PARK P870

ON THE ROAD

Contents

ON THE ROAD

NGILGI CAVE P933

NICKICHEN / SHUTTERSTOCK ©

Contents

Aboriginal and Torres Strait
Islander people should be
aware that this book may
contain images of or refer-
ences to deceased people.

Welcome to Australia

Australia is a wild and beautiful place, a land whose colour palette of red outback sands and Technicolor reefs frames sophisticated cities and soulful Indigenous stories.

Hip Cities

Most Australians live along the coast, and most of these folks live in cities – 89% of Australians, in fact. It follows that cities here are a lot of fun. Sydney is the glamorous poster child with world-class beaches. Melbourne is all arts, alleyways and stellar food. Brisbane is a subtropical town on the rise; Adelaide has festive grace and pubby poise. Perth breathes west coast optimism and Canberra showcases many cultural treasures, while tropical northern Darwin and the chilly southern sandstone city of Hobart couldn't be more different.

Wild Lands & Wildlife

Australia is an extraordinarily beautiful place, as rich in rainforest (from Far North Queensland to far-south Tasmania) as it is in remote rocky outcrops like Uluru, Kakadu and the Kimberleys. The coastline – beset with islands and deserted shores – is wild and wonderful, too. Animating this splendour is wildlife like nowhere else on the planet – a place of kangaroos and crocodiles, of wombats and wallabies, platypus, crocodiles, dingoes and so much more. Tracking these, and Australia's 700-plus bird species, is enough to unleash your inner David Attenborough.

Epicurean Delights

Australia plates up a multicultural fusion of European techniques and fresh Pacific-rim ingredients – aka 'Mod Oz' (Modern Australian). Seafood plays a starring role, from succulent Moreton Bay bugs to delicate King George whiting. Of course, beer in hand, you'll still find beef, lamb and chicken at Aussie barbecues. Don't drink beer? Australian wines are world-beaters: punchy Barossa Valley shiraz, Hunter Valley semillon and cool-climate Tasmanian sauvignon blanc. Tasmania produces outstanding whisky too. Need a caffeine hit? You'll find cafes pretty much everywhere these days.

The Open Road

There's a lot of tarmac across this wide brown land. From Margaret River to Cooktown, Jabiru to Dover, the best way to appreciate Australia is to hit the road. Car hire is relatively affordable, and road conditions are generally good, and beyond the big cities traffic fades away. If you're driving a campervan, you'll find well-appointed caravan parks in most sizeable towns. Or, hire a 4WD and go off-road: camp in Australia's national parks and secluded corners, or head off down a classic desert track.

Why I Love Australia

By Anthony Ham, Writer

God I love this place. There is something in the wild lands of the outback that call to me in ways I only partly understand. It happens out on the lonely Carpentaria Hwy or down by the Victoria River near Timber Creek or watching platypus on the Bombala River. It is the possibility, even if I never see it, that a fabulous sighting of wildlife could happen at any moment. Boiled down to its essence: this is a wild land whose natural and human history are writ large on an impossibly beautiful canvas.

For more about our writers, see p1104

Above: Kings Canyon (p870), Watarrka National Park

Australia

INDONESIA

SAVU SEA

TIMOR-LESTE

TIMOR SEA

Cobourg Peninsula

Melville Island

Bathurst Island

Darwin

Jabiru

Kakadu National Park
Ancient culture and tropical wilderness (p821)

Cape Londonderry

Joseph Bonaparte Gulf

Katherine

Matarank

INDIAN OCEAN

Kakadu National Park

Wyndham

Kununurra

Daly Waters

Cape Leveque

The Kimberley

Derby

Fitzroy Crossing

Broome

Halls Creek

Broome & the Kimberley
Miraculous colours of desert and sea (p992)

Tennant Creek

NORTHERN TERRITORY

Port Hedland

Dampier

Karratha

The Pilbara

North West Cape

Exmouth

Uluru-Kata Tjuta NP
Seriously big and beautiful rocks (p871)

MacDonnell Ran

Newman

Gibson Desert

Alic Sprin

Yulara

Little Sandy Desert

WESTERN AUSTRALIA

Uluru-Kata Tjuta National Park

Carnarvon

Shark Bay

Marla

SOUTH AUSTRALIA

Great Victoria Desert

Mt Magnet

South Australian Wine Regions
Top drops down south (p744-77)

Coobe Pedy

INDIAN OCEAN

Geraldton

Kalgoorlie–Boulder

Nullarbor Plain

Eucla

Cedu

Perth
Fremantle

Norseman

Great Australian Bight

Bunbury

Wagin

Esperance

Melbourne
Hipsters, arts and Australia's best coffee (p456)

Busselton

Margaret River

Cape Leeuwin

Albany

Great Ocean Road
World-class road trip and great surf (p538)

ELEVATION

2000m
1500m
1000m
750m
500m
250m
0

Margaret River Region
Top-notch vineyards and wild coastline (p932)

Cradle Mountain
Amazing views from Tassie's famous peak (p709)

SOUTHERN OCEAN

MONA
Unique, challenging and unmissable arts (p639)

10°S
15°S
20°S
25°S
30°S
35°S
40°S

110°E 115°E 120°E 125°E 130°E 135

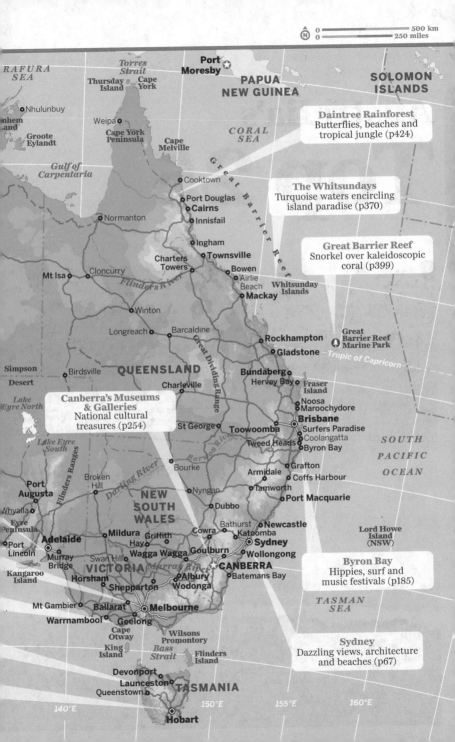

0 / 500 km
0 / 250 miles

ARAFURA SEA

Torres Strait
Thursday Island
Cape York

Port Moresby
PAPUA NEW GUINEA

SOLOMON ISLANDS

Nhulunbuy

Arnhem Land

Groote Eylandt

Weipa
Cape York Peninsula
Cape Melville

CORAL SEA

Daintree Rainforest
Butterflies, beaches and tropical jungle (p424)

Gulf of Carpentaria

Cooktown
Port Douglas
Cairns
Innisfail

Great Barrier Reef

The Whitsundays
Turquoise waters encircling island paradise (p370)

Normanton

Ingham
Townsville
Bowen
Airlie Beach
Whitsunday Islands
Mackay

Great Barrier Reef
Snorkel over kaleidoscopic coral (p399)

Mt Isa
Cloncurry
Charters Towers

Flinders River

Winton

Longreach
Barcaldine

Rockhampton
Gladstone

Great Barrier Reef Marine Park
Tropic of Capricorn

Simpson Desert

Lake Eyre North

Birdsville

QUEENSLAND

Charleville

Great Dividing Range

Bundaberg
Hervey Bay
Fraser Island

Canberra's Museums & Galleries
National cultural treasures (p254)

St George
Toowoomba

Noosa
Maroochydore
Brisbane
Surfers Paradise
Coolangatta
Byron Bay

Lake Eyre South

Flinders Ranges

Bourke

Balonne River

Tweed Heads

SOUTH PACIFIC OCEAN

Broken Hill

Darling River

NEW SOUTH WALES

Nyngan

Armidale
Grafton
Coffs Harbour
Tamworth
Port Macquarie

Port Augusta

Whyalla

Eyre Peninsula

Port Lincoln

Adelaide

Mildura
Hay
Griffith

Murray Bridge

Swan Hill

Kangaroo Island

VICTORIA

Horsham

Shepparton

Dubbo

Bathurst
Cowra
Goulburn

Wagga Wagga

Albury
Wodonga

Katoomba
Newcastle
Sydney
Wollongong
CANBERRA
Batemans Bay

Lord Howe Island (NSW)

Byron Bay
Hippies, surf and music festivals (p185)

Murray River

Mt Gambier
Ballarat
Warrnambool
Geelong
Melbourne

Cape Otway

King Island

Wilsons Promontory

Bass Strait

Flinders Island

TASMAN SEA

Sydney
Dazzling views, architecture and beaches (p67)

Devonport
Launceston
Queenstown
TASMANIA

Hobart

140°E   150°E   155°E   160°E

Australia's
Top 25

Sydney

1 The big-ticket sights are all in Sydney (p66) – the Sydney Opera House, the Rocks and Sydney Harbour Bridge are at the top of most people's lists – but to really catch Sydney's vibe, spend a day at the beach. Stake out a patch of sand at Bondi Beach, lather yourself in sunscreen and plunge into the surf; or hop on a harbour ferry from Circular Quay to Manly for a swim, a surf or a walk along the sea-sprayed promenade to Shelly Beach. Ahhh, this is the life! Below left: Bondi Beach (p87)

Great Barrier Reef

2 The Great Barrier Reef (p399) – described by Sir David Attenborough as one of the most beautiful places on the planet – is as fragile as it is beautiful. Stretching more than 2000km along the Queensland coastline, it's a complex ecosystem populated with dazzling coral, languid sea turtles, gliding rays, timid reef sharks and tropical fish of every colour and size. Whether you dive on it, snorkel over it or explore it via scenic flight or glass-bottomed boat, this vivid undersea kingdom and its coral-fringed islands is unforgettable.

RYAN PIERSE / GETTY IMAGES ©

JEFF HUNTER / GETTY IMAGES ©

2

Uluru-Kata Tjuta National Park

3 Australia's most recognised natural wonder, Uluru (p875), draws pilgrims from around the world like moths to a big red flame. No matter how many postcard images you have seen, nothing prepares you for the Rock's immense presence and spiritual gravitas. Not far away is a mystical clutch of stone siblings known as Kata Tjuta (the Olgas). Deeply cleaved with gorges and decorated with tufts of vegetation, these 36 pink-red domes majestically flaunt their curves and blush intensely at sunset.

MONA

4 Occupying an improbable riverside location a ferry ride from Hobart's harbourfront, the Museum of Old & New Art (p639) is an innovative, world-class institution. Described by its owner, Hobart philanthropist David Walsh, as a 'subversive adult Disneyland', three levels of astounding underground galleries showcase more than 400 challenging and controversial artworks. You might not like everything you see, but a visit here is a sure-fire conversation starter and one of Australia's unique arts experiences.

Melbourne

5 Why the queue? Oh, that's just the line to get into the latest 'no bookings' restaurant in Melbourne (p456). The next best restaurant, chef, cafe, barista, food truck may be the talk of the town, but there are things locals would never change: the leafy parks and gardens in the inner city; the crowded trams that whisk creative 'northerners' to sea-breezy St Kilda; and the allegiances that living in such a sports-mad city brings. The city's world-renowned street-art scene expresses Melbourne's fears, frustrations and joys.

Great Ocean Road

6 The Twelve Apostles – craggy formations jutting out of wild waters – are one of Victoria's most vivid sights, but it's the 'getting there' road trip that doubles their impact. Drive slowly along roads that curl beside Bass Strait beaches, then whip inland through rainforest studded with small towns and big trees. The secrets of the Great Ocean Road (p538) don't stop there; further along is maritime treasure Port Fairy and hidden Cape Bridgewater. For the ultimate in slow travel, walk the Great Ocean Walk from Apollo Bay to the Apostles.

Byron Bay

7 Up there with kangaroos and Akubra hats, big-hearted Byron Bay (p185) – just Byron to its mates – is one of the enduring icons of Australian culture. Families on school holidays, surfers and sun-seekers from across the globe gather by the foreshore at sunset, drawn to this spot on the world map by fabulous restaurants, a chilled pace of life and an astonishing range of activities on offer. But mostly they're here because this is one of the most beautiful stretches of coast in the country.

The Whitsundays

8 You can hop around a whole stack of tropical islands in this seafaring life and never find anywhere with the sheer beauty of the Whitsundays (p370). Travellers of all monetary persuasions launch yachts from Airlie Beach and drift between these lush green isles in a slow search for paradise (you'll probably find it in more than one place). Don't miss Whitehaven Beach (p374) – one of Australia's (and the world's) best. Wish you were here?

AUSTRALIANCAMERA / SHUTTERSTOCK ©

LOUISE DENTON PHOTOGRAPHY / GETTY IMAGES ©

Australian Wildlife

9 Native wildlife (p1036) brings Australia's wild regions to life. You'll never forget seeing your first kangaroo bounding across an outback plain, or encountering your first wombat in the bush. From the crocs of Kakadu to whale watching off Western Australia, sea turtles on Queensland beaches and adorable little penguins and fur seals on Victoria's Phillip Island, you'll take great delight in crossing these off your must-see list – also dingoes, wallabies, platypuses, goannas and more! And with more than 700 bird species to track down, don't forget your binoculars.

Daintree Rainforest

10 Lush green rainforest replete with fan palms, ferns and twisted mangroves tumble down towards a white-sand coastline in the World Heritage–listed Daintree (p424) rainforest. Upon entering the forest, you'll be enveloped in a cacophony of birdsong, frog croaking and the buzz of insects. Explore the area via night tours, mountain treks, interpretive boardwalks, canopy walks, self-guided walking trails, 4WD trips, horse riding, kayaking, croc-spotting cruises, tropical-fruit orchard tours and tastings… If you're lucky, you might even spot a cassowary.

Kakadu National Park

11 Kakadu (p821) is more than a nature reserve: it's an adventure into a unique natural and cultural landscape. The sandstone ramparts of Kakadu and neighbouring Arnhem Land have sheltered humans for aeons, and an extraordinary legacy of rock art remains. Represented are figures of the Dreaming, hunting stories, zoological diagrams, and 'contact art' – records of visitors from Indonesia and more recent European colonists. Kakadu's Ubirr and Nourlangie galleries are of World Heritage significance and accessible to all. Bottom right: Jim Jim Falls (p827)

South Australian Wine Regions

12 Adelaide is drunk on the success of its three world-famous wine regions, all within two hours' drive: the Barossa Valley (p759) to the north, with its gutsy reds and German know-how; McLaren Vale (p743) to the south, a Mediterranean palette of sea and shiraz; and the Clare Valley (p764), known for riesling and wobbly bike rides (in that order). Better-kept secrets are the cool-climate stunners from the Adelaide Hills and the country cab sauv from the Coonawarra. Top: Barossa Valley

Canberra's Museums & Galleries

13 Though Canberra is only a century old, Australia's capital has always been preoccupied with history. The major drawcard here is a portfolio of lavishly endowed museums and galleries focused on interpreting the national narrative. Institutions such as the National Gallery of Australia (p254), National Museum of Australia (p257), National Portrait Gallery (p254) and Australian War Memorial (p254) offer visitors a fascinating insight into the country's history and culture.

Cradle Mountain

14 Carved out by millennia of ice and wind, crescent-shaped Cradle Mountain (p709) is Tasmania's most recognisable – and spectacular – mountain peak. It's an all-day walk (and boulder scramble) to the summit and back, for unbelievable panoramas over Tasmania's alpine heart. Or you can stand in awe below and take in the perfect views across Dove Lake to the mountain. If the peak has disappeared in clouds or snow, warm yourself by the fire in one of the nearby lodges...and come back tomorrow. Top: Dove Lake

Broome & the Kimberley

15 Australia's northwestern frontier is one of its most beautiful corners. In Broome (p992), every evening a searing crimson sun slips into the turquoise Indian Ocean over beaches that never seem to end. The far-flung Dampier Peninsula is all about extraordinary cliffs, Indigenous cultural experiences, outdoor adventures and luxury camping. And then there's the Kimberley, a world of blood-red rock formations, remote trails and unrelenting beauty, not to mention that mysterious call of the outback. Bottom: Cable Beach (p992)

GERARD SOURY / GETTY IMAGES ©

Ningaloo Reef

16 Swim beside 'gentle giant' whale sharks, snorkel among pristine coral, surf off seldom-visited reefs and dive at one of the world's premier locations at this World Heritage–listed marine park (p982), which sits off the North West Cape on the Coral Coast in Western Australia. Rivalling the Great Barrier Reef for beauty, Ningaloo has more accessible wonders: shallow, turquoise lagoons are entered straight from the beach for excellent snorkelling. Development is very low-key, so be prepared to camp, or take day trips from the access towns of Exmouth and Coral Bay.

Top left: Whale shark

The Outback & Broken Hill

17 Whether you're belting a station-wagon along South Australia's Oodnadatta Track or depreciating your 4WD on the Birdsville Track in Queensland, you'll know you're not just visiting the outback, you've become part of it. Out here, the sky is bluer and the dust redder. Days are measured in kilometres, spinifex mounds and tyre blowouts. Nights are spent in the five-zillion-star hotel, waiting for one to fall... If time is not on your side, a road trip to the outback mining town of Broken Hill (p211) may be as far from the coast as you can get.

Top right: Broken Hill

Indigenous Art

18 Immersed in the Dreaming – a vast unchanging network of life tracing back to spiritual ancestors – Aboriginal art is a conduit between past and present, people and land. Central Australian dot paintings (p1032) are exquisite, as are Tiwi Island carvings and fabrics, Arnhem Land bark paintings, Torres Strait Islander prints, weavings and carvings, and creations from Aboriginal-owned art cooperatives in the Kimberley. You can make an informed purchase at commercial galleries or (even better) direct from Aboriginal communities.

Bottom right: Aboriginal art from the Northern Territory

Nitmiluk (Katherine Gorge) National Park

19 While paddling a canoe upstream through one gorge and then another and leaving the crowds behind, you will be drawn into the silence of these towering cliffs, which squeeze the waters of the Katherine River (p836). Take a break on a sandy river beach, walk up to a viewpoint or take a helicopter flight for an eagle-eye view. The surrounding Nitmiluk National Park has even more to offer such as the Jatbula Trail, a five-day walk from the Gorge to the wonderful Leliyn (Edith Falls).

Pinnacles Desert

20 It could be mistaken for the surface of Mars – scattered among the dunes of Nambung National Park (p923), thousands of ghostly limestone pillars rise from the plain like a petrified alien army. One of the West's most bizarre landscapes, the Pinnacles Desert attracts thousands of visitors each year. Although it's easily enjoyed as a day trip from Perth, stay overnight in nearby Cervantes for multiple visits to experience the colour changes at dawn, sunset and full moon, when most tourists are back in their hotels.

19

20

Margaret River Region

21 The decadent joy of drifting from winery to winery along eucalypt-shaded country roads is just one of the delights of Western Australia's southwest. There are caves to explore, historic towns to visit and spring wildflowers to ogle. Surfers bob around in the world-class breaks near Margaret River (p937), but it's not unusual to find yourself on a white-sand beach where the only footprints are your own. In late winter and early spring, cast an eye offshore to spot whales migrating along the 'Humpback Highway'.

Arnhem Land

22 Visiting Arnhem Land (p828) in the Top End is a fantastic opportunity to get beyond the crowds. The Injalak Arts & Crafts Centre at Gunbalanya is a terrific place to start, while the remote Cobourg Peninsula has a certain earth's-first-morning quality. The beaches are pristine (and very often deserted) and the wildlife, both on land and in the sea, is abundant in a way rarely seen in the Territory. And at every turn there's that exhilarating feeling that comes from being hours beyond the end of the nearest paved road. Bottom: Injalak Hill rock art (p830)

Wilsons Promontory

23 Victoria's southernmost point and finest coastal national park, Wilsons Promontory (p586; known as Wilsons Prom) is heaven for bushwalkers, wildlife-watchers and surfers. The bushland and coastal scenery here is out of this world; even short walks from the main base at Tidal River will take you to beautiful beaches and bays. But with more than 80km of walking trails through forests, marshes and valleys of tree ferns, over low granite mountains and along beaches backed by sand dunes, the best of the Prom requires some serious footwork. Top left: Tidal River

Fraser Island

24 The world's largest sand island, Fraser Island (p346) is home to dingoes, shipwrecks and all manner of birdlife. Four-wheel drive vehicles – regular cars aren't allowed – fan out around epic camp spots and long white beaches. The wild coastline curbs any thoughts of doing much more than wandering between pristine creeks and freshwater lakes. Beach camping under the stars will bring you back to nature. A short ferry trip away is Hervey Bay, where humpback whales shoot along the coast in winter and spring. Top right: Wreck of the *Maheno* (p348)

The Ghan

25 The legendary *Ghan* (p45) – named after central Australia's pioneering Afghan cameleers – is one of the world's great railway journeys. Begun in 1877, the old line from Marree to Alice Springs suffered from wash outs and shoddy construction before a shiny new line replaced it in 1980. The Alice-to-Darwin section followed in 2004: now there's 2979km and 42 hours of track between Adelaide and Darwin. The *Ghan* isn't cheap or fast, but the experience of rolling through the vast, flat expanse of central Australia's deserts is magical.

Need to Know

For more information, see Survival Guide (p1049)

Currency
Australian dollar ($)

Language
English

Visas
All visitors to Australia need a visa, except New Zealanders. Apply online for an ETA or eVisitor visa, each allowing a three-month stay: www.border.gov.au.

Money
ATMs widely available in cities and larger towns. Credit cards accepted for hotels, restaurants, transport and activity bookings.

Mobile Phones
European phones work on Australia's network, but most American and Japanese phones don't. Use global roaming or a local SIM card and a prepaid account.

Time
Australia has three main time zones: Australian Eastern, Central and Western Standard Time. Sydney is on AEST, which is GMT/UCT plus 10 hours.

When to Go

- Darwin GO Jun–Aug
- Cairns GO Jul–Sep
- Perth GO Oct–Dec
- Sydney GO Dec–Feb
- Hobart GO Jan–Mar

Desert, dry climate
Dry climate
Tropical climate, wet/dry seasons
Warm to hot summers, mild winters

High Season
(Dec–Feb)

➡ Summertime: local holidays, busy beaches and cricket; wet season in the Top End.

➡ Prices rise 25% for big-city accommodation.

➡ Outdoor rock concerts, film screenings and food festivals abound.

Shoulder Season
(Mar–May & Sep–Nov)

➡ Warm sun, clear skies, shorter queues.

➡ Easter (late March or early April) is busy with Aussie families on the loose.

➡ Autumn leaves are atmospheric in Victoria, Tasmania and South Australia.

Low Season
(Jun–Aug)

➡ Cool rainy days down south; mild days and sunny skies up north.

➡ Low tourist numbers; attractions keep slightly shorter hours.

➡ Head for the desert, the tropical north or the snow.

Useful Websites

Lonely Planet (www.lonely planet.com/australia) Destination information, hotel bookings, traveller forum and more.

Tourism Australia (www.australia.com) Glossy main government tourism site with visitor info.

Bureau of Meteorology (www.bom.gov.au) Nationwide weather forecasts.

Guardian Australia (www.theguardian.com/au) Local online edition of the Guardian with nationwide news.

Parks Australia (www.environment.gov.au/topics/national-parks) Australia's national parks and reserves.

Important Numbers

Regular Australian phone numbers have a two-digit area code followed by an eight-digit number. Drop the initial 0 if calling from abroad.

Australia's country code	✓61
International access code	✓0011
Emergency (ambulance, fire, police)	✓000
Directory assistance	✓1223

Exchange Rates

Canada	C$1	$1.05
China	Y1	$0.19
Euro	€1	$1.40
Japan	¥100	$1.17
New Zealand	NZ$1	$0.94
South Korea	W100	$0.11
UK	UK£1	$1.64
US	US$1	$1.31

For current exchange rates see www.xe.com

Daily Costs

Budget: Less than $150

➡ Hostel dorm bed: $28–40

➡ Double room in a basic motel: $80–130

➡ Simple main meal: $10–15

➡ Short bus or tram ride: $4

Midrange: $150–300

➡ Double room in a motel, B&B or hotel: $130–250

➡ Brunch in a good cafe: $25–40

➡ Door charge at gig: $10–20

➡ Short taxi ride: $25

Top End: More than $300

➡ Double room in a top-end hotel: from $250

➡ Three-course meal in an upmarket restaurant: $100 per person

➡ Theatre tickets: from $50 per person

➡ Domestic flight between two main cities: from $100

Opening Hours

Business hours vary from state to state, but the following is a guide.

Banks 9.30am-4pm Monday to Thursday; until 5pm on Friday

Cafes 7am-5pm

Petrol stations 8am-10pm; some 24 hours

Pubs 11am-midnight, bars 4pm till late

Restaurants noon-2.30pm and 6pm-9pm

Shops 9am-5pm Monday to Saturday

Supermarkets 7am-8pm; some 24 hours

Arriving in Australia

Sydney Airport (p1067) AirportLink trains run to the city centre every 10 minutes from around 5am to 1am (20 minutes). Prebooked shuttle buses service city hotels. A taxi into the city costs $55 (30 minutes).

Melbourne Airport (p1067) SkyBus services run to the city (20 minutes), leaving every 10 to 30 minutes around the clock. A taxi into the city costs around $40 (25 minutes).

Brisbane Airport (p1067) Airtrain trains run into the city centre (20 minutes) every 15 to 30 minutes from 5am (6am weekends) to 10pm. Prebooked shuttle buses service city hotels. A taxi into the city costs $35 to $45 (25 minutes).

Getting Around

Australia is the sixth-largest country in the world: how you get from A to B requires some thought.

Car Travel at your own tempo, explore remote areas and visit regions with no public transport. Hire cars in major towns; drive on the left.

Plane Fast track your holiday with affordable, frequent, fast flights between major centres. Carbon offset your flights if you're feeling guilty.

Bus Reliable, frequent long-haul services around the country. Not always cheaper than flying.

Train Slow, expensive and infrequent...but the scenery is great! Opt for a sleeper carriage rather than an 'overnighter' seat.

For much more on **getting around**, see p1068

What's New

Camping on Farms

A host of new websites have launched in Australia enabling travellers to book a night on rural properties, camping or staying in a 'tiny house'. Check out youcamp. com and unyoked.co to get started.

Barangaroo Reserve

Sydney Harbour has a brand new park, occupying a former industrial dockland adjacent to Darling Harbour and the Rocks. It boasts sandstone blocks, lovely trees and showstopping harbour views. (p71)

Great Ocean Road Breweries

Australia's craft-beer obsession continues along the GOR. New brewers here include Prickly Moses' new Brewhouses at Apollo Bay (p556) and Queenscliff (p547), Rogue Wave Brewing (p552) at Aireys Inlet and Blackman's Brewery (p549) in Torquay.

Parramatta

It's an exciting time to be in Sydney's geographical heart. The plan is to turn Parramatta into a second 'city centre' for the metropolis. It's a buzzing place to visit. (p99)

Royal Flying Doctor Service

Darwin's best new museum is all high tech in a worthy tribute to this outback institution. (p800)

Djakanimba Pavilions

Beswick's Ghunmarn Culture Centre is already world-class but now you can stay overnight. (p843)

The Ghan

It may not be to everyone's liking, but the Ghan, the legendary north–south train that crosses central Australia's desert, has gone upmarket and become a truly exclusive experience. (p45)

Elizabeth Quay

Perth's riverfront is enlivened with new public spaces, cafes, restaurants and hotels at this development linking the Swan River with the CBD. (p882)

Albany's Spectacular New Viewing Platform

Experience the incredible energy of the Southern Ocean from this vertiginous viewing platform in Torndirrup National Park near Albany. (p953)

Kalbarri National Park

Improvements from late 2017 include a fully sealed road to Nature's Window and the Z-Bend, plus trails, a new 'Skywalk', and interpretive signage. (p965)

Adelaide Oval

The development of this iconic stadium promises to bring the Oval into the elite of Australian sporting venues, befitting its gorgeous looks. (p718)

For more recommendations and reviews, see lonelyplanet. com/australia

If You Like...

Beaches

Bondi Beach An essential Sydney experience: carve up the surf or just laze around and people-watch. (p87)

Wineglass Bay It's worth the scramble up and over the saddle to visit this gorgeous goblet of Tasmanian sand. (p673)

Whitehaven Beach The jewel of the Whitsundays in Queensland, with powdery white sand beaches and crystal-clear waters. (p374)

Bells Beach Australia's best-known surf beach is near Torquay on Victoria's Great Ocean Road. (p548)

Hellfire Bay Talcum-powder sand in Western Australia's Cape Le Grand National Park, which is precisely in the middle of nowhere. (p958)

Avalon The most photogenic of Sydney's gorgeous northern beaches. (p99)

Fraser Island The world's largest sand island is basically one big beach. (p346)

Cape Tribulation The rainforest sweeps down to smooch the reef at empty stretches of sand. (p425)

Shark Bay Around 1500km of remote beaches and towering limestone cliffs. (p966)

Cable Beach Surely the most famous, camel-strewn, sunset-photographed beach in WA. (p992)

Islands

Kangaroo Island A great spot in South Australia (SA) for wildlife-watching and super-fresh seafood. (p750)

Bruny Island A windswept, sparsely populated retreat south of Hobart, with magical coastal scenery. (p655)

Fraser Island The world's largest sand island has giant dunes, freshwater lakes and abundant wildlife. (p346)

The Whitsundays Check yourself into a resort or go sailing around this pristine Queensland archipelago. (p370)

North Stradbroke Island Brisbane's holiday playground, with surf beaches and passing whales. (p303)

Rottnest Island A ferry ride from Fremantle in Western Australia (WA) is this atmospheric atoll with adorable quokkas but a chequered history. (p911)

Lizard Island A real get-away-from-it-all isle in Far North Queensland: splash out on a resort or rough it with some camping. (p428)

Lady Elliot Island Ringed by the Great Barrier Reef, this remote Queensland island is the place to play castaway. (p355)

Wilderness

Blue Mountains National Park The closest true wilderness to Sydney: spectacular canyons, cliffs and dense eucalypt forests. (p150)

Flinders Ranges National Park Treading a line between desolation and beauty, the ancient outcrops of SA's Ikara (Wilpena Pound) are mesmerising. (p788)

Limmen National Park Remote park with two 'lost cities' of bizarre and very beautiful rock pinnacles. (p844)

Cobourg Peninsula Watch for sea turtles and whales (and crocs!) at this isolated stretch of paradise. (p830)

Nitmiluk (Katherine Gorge) National Park Tackle the epic five-day Jatbula Trail in this rugged Northern Territory (NT) wilderness, with plenty of cooling swim-spots on the way. (p832)

Cradle Mountain–Lake St Clair National Park Immerse yourself in Tasmania's sometimes forbidding, ever-photogenic landscape. (p709)

The Kimberley In northern WA you'll find pounding waterfalls, spectacular gorges, barren

peaks and an empty coastline. (p992)

Daintree Rainforest Explore Far North Queensland's ancient forest with abundant activities and few tourists. (p424)

Wine Regions

Barossa Valley Home to Australia's greatest reds, with 80-plus cellar doors around historic German-settled villages, in SA. (p759)

McLaren Vale An hour south of Adelaide, this is Mediterranean-feeling shiraz heaven. (p743)

Tamar Valley Tasmania's key cool-climate wine area, a short hop from Launceston. (p686)

Clare Valley SA's Clare Valley makes riesling that rocks – enough said. (p764)

Yarra Valley An hour from Melbourne, the Yarra Valley is the place for syrupy whites and complex cabernets. (p523)

Hunter Valley Dating back to the 1820s, the Hunter Valley is Australia's oldest wine region – super semillon. (p151)

Granite Belt Queensland's high-altitude wine region produces some surprisingly good wines. (p308)

Mornington Peninsula Southeast of Melbourne and centred on Red Hill, this wine region is super scenic. (p530)

Margaret River Known for its Bordeaux-style varietals, chardonnay and sauvignon blanc, as well as a growing number of craft breweries. (p932)

Pubs & Live Music

Venue 505 Sydney's best little jazz bar features top-notch performers in an edgy underground space. (p134)

Top: Ikara (Wilpena Pound), Flinders Ranges National Park (p788)
Bottom: Clare Valley (p764)

Governor Hindmarsh Hotel A sprawling old Adelaide rocker with decent pub grub and all kinds of live tunes. (p734)

Palace Hotel An extravagantly muralled old Broken Hill pub enjoying a revival. (p214)

The Tote The battered old Tote remains an essential Melbourne rock room. (p508)

Corner Legendary live-music pub in Richmond, Melbourne. (p509)

Zoo Grungy, alternative and unfailingly original: the best spot in Brisbane for rock acts on the rise. (p297)

Courthouse Hotel A raffish Sydney backstreet boozer in equally raffish Newtown. (p130)

Apollonian Hotel Historic Gympie pub, relocated to Boreen Point, complete with lush garden and a legendary Sunday spit roast. (p336)

Art Galleries

National Gallery of Australia This superb Canberra museum houses 7500-plus works by Aboriginal and Torres Strait Islander artists. (p254)

MONA Australia's most thematically challenging art museum is the talk of Hobart town. (p639)

National Gallery of Victoria International Home to travelling exhibitions par excellence (Monet, Dali, Caravaggio): queue up with the rest of Melbourne to get in. (p466)

Art Gallery of NSW This old-stager keeps things hip with ever-changing exhibitions, including the always-controversial Archibald Prize for portraiture. (p75)

Art Gallery of South Australia On Adelaide's North Terrace, this art gallery does things with progressive style. (p715)

Art Gallery of Ballarat Australia's oldest and largest regional gallery, crammed with works by noted Australian artists. (p566)

Museum & Art Gallery of the Northern Territory Darwin's classy art gallery is packed full of superb Indigenous art. (p801)

Ghunmarn Culture Centre One of the Northern Territory's best, with an exceptional collection of art and culture from West Arnhem Land. (p843)

Pro Hart Gallery In Broken Hill, NSW, there is a collection of works by this miner-turned-world-renowned painter. (p212)

Indigenous Culture

Kuku-Yalanji Dreamtime Walks Guided walks through Mossman Gorge in Queensland with Indigenous guides. (p424)

Uluru-Kata Tjuta Cultural Centre Understand local Aboriginal law, custom and religion on Uluru's doorstep. Book an Indigenous guide for the Rock. (p876)

Ngurrangga Tours Cultural expeditions from Karratha in WA to nearby petroglyphs and waterholes. (p986)

Dampier Peninsula Interact with remote WA communities and learn how to spear fish and catch mudcrabs. (p1001)

Kakadu Animal Tracks Tours through Kakadu's famous Aboriginal rock-art galleries and wetlands, departing Darwin or Jabiru. (p824)

Barunga Festival Aboriginal cultural and sports festival near Katherine. Music, dance, arts, storytelling, crafts, football and spear throwing. (p836)

Injalak Arts & Crafts Centre Terrific gallery, shop and a chance to sit with the artists while they paint. (p830)

Garma Festival One of Australia's best Aboriginal festivals out in Eastern Arnhem Land. (p831)

Uptuyu Personalised cultural tours taking in wetlands, rock art, fishing and Indigenous Kimberley communities. (p1004)

Outback Adventure

4WD to Cape York One of the country's great wilderness adventures is the off-road journey to mainland Australia's northern tip: take a tour or go it alone. (p431)

The Red Centre Explore Uluru and Kata Tjuta in Australia's desert heart on a tour from Alice Springs. (p871)

Karijini National Park Scramble, abseil, slide and dive through gorges on an adventure tour in this remote WA park. (p989)

Oodnadatta Track Tackle this historic former rail route in SA, passing Kati Thanda (Lake Eyre), remote pubs and skittery emus and lizards. (p794)

Mungo National Park A wonderful outback destination in NSW, with amazing land formations, wildlife and Aboriginal cultural tours. (p215)

Arnhem Land Take a tour of remote Arnhem Land from Kakadu National Park, NT. (p828)

Purnululu National Park Wander through these ancient eroded beehive domes in WA. (p1013)

Month by Month

January

January yawns into action as Australia recovers from its Christmas hangover. The festival season kicks in with sun-stroked outdoor music festivals; Melbourne hosts the Australian Open tennis. Wet season in the Top End.

Sydney Festival

'It's big' says the promo material. Indeed, sprawling over three summer weeks, this fab affiliation of music, dance, talks, theatre and visual arts – much of it free and family-focused – is an artistic behemoth. (p107)

MONA FOMA

In Hobart, MONA FOMA is MONA's Festival of Music & Art. Under the auspices of Brian Ritchie, the bass player from Violent Femmes, it's as edgy, progressive and unexpected as the museum itself. (p643)

Australia Day

The date when the First Fleet landed in 1788, 26 January, is Australia's 'birthday'. Australians celebrate with picnics, barbecues, fireworks and, increasingly, nationalistic flag-waving, drunkenness and chest-beating. In less mood to celebrate are Indigenous Australians, who refer to it as Invasion Day or Survival Day.

Australian Open

Held at Melbourne Park in late January, the Australian Open draws tennis fanatics from around the planet as the world's best duke it out on the courts. Invariably it's baking hot. (p1048)

February

February is usually Australia's warmest month: hot and sticky up north as the wet season continues, but divine in Tasmania and Victoria. Locals go back to work or to the beach.

Adelaide Fringe

All the acts that don't make the cut (or don't want to) for the more highbrow Adelaide Festival end up in the month-long Fringe, second only to Edinburgh's version. Comedy, music and circus spill from the Garden of Unearthly Delights in the parklands. (p723)

Sydney's Gay & Lesbian Mardi Gras

Mardi Gras is a month-long arts festival that runs deep into March and culminates in a flamboyant parade along Sydney's Oxford St that attracts 300,000 spectators. Gyms empty out and waxing emporiums tally their profits. After-party tickets are gold. (p1056)

Tropfest

The world's largest short-film festival happens in Parramatta in February, with satellite links to locations in Melbourne, Canberra and Surfers Paradise. A compulsory prop must appear in each entry: a kiss, sneeze, balloon... (p107)

March

March is harvest time in Australia's vineyards and recently it has been as hot as January and February. Melbourne's streets jam up with the Formula One Grand Prix.

☆ WOMADelaide

This annual festival of world music, arts, food and dance is held over four days in Adelaide's luscious Botanic Park, attracting crowds from around Australia. Eight stages host hundreds of acts. It's very family friendly and you can get a cold beer too. (p723)

☆ Australian Formula One Grand Prix

Melbourne's normally tranquil Albert Park explodes with four days of Formula One rev-head action in late March. The 5.3km street circuit around the lake is known for its smooth, fast surface. (p473)

🎭 Adelaide Festival

Culture vultures absorb international and Australian dance, drama, opera and theatre performances at this ultra-classy annual event. Australia's biggest multi-arts event. (p723)

April

Melbourne and the Adelaide Hills are atmospheric as European trees turn golden then maroon. Up north the rain is abating and the desert temperatures are becoming manageable. Easter means pricey accommodation everywhere.

☆ Byron Bay Bluesfest

Music erupts over the Easter weekend when 20,000 festival-goers swamp Byron Bay to hear blues-and-roots bands from all over the world (Ben Harper, Neil Young, Bonnie Raitt). Held on Tyagarah Tea Tree Farm, 11km north of Byron. Some folks camp. (p187)

🎭 Tjungu Festival

The otherwise in-between month of April in the Red Centre sees the dynamic Tjungu Festival take over Yulara, with a focus on local Aboriginal culture. (p873)

May

The dry season begins in the Northern Territory (NT), northern Western Australia (WA) and Far North Queensland: relief from humidity. A great time to visit Uluru (Ayers Rock), before the tour buses arrive in droves.

🐟 Whale Watching

Between May and October, migrating southern right and humpback whales come close to shore to feed, breed and calf. See them at Hervey Bay (New South Wales), Warrnambool (Victoria), Victor Harbor (South Australia), Albany (WA) and North Stradbroke Island (Queensland). (p1041)

🍴 Noosa Food & Wine

One of Australia's best regional culinary fests, with cooking demonstrations, wine tastings, cheese exhibits, feasting on gourmet fare and live concerts at night. Over three days in mid-May. (p324)

☆ Alice Springs Cup Carnival

Five days of racing and an abundance of social activities is as good an excuse as any to dust off the old suit or frock and sink a few cold ones under a shady marquee while the horses do their stuff. (p854)

June

Winter begins: snow falls across the southern Alps ski resorts and football season fills grandstands across the country. Peak season in the tropical north: waterfalls and outback tracks are accessible (accommodation prices less so).

🎭 Laura Aboriginal Dance Festival

Sleepy Laura, 330km north of Cairns on the Cape York Peninsula in Far North Queensland, hosts the largest traditional Indigenous gathering in Australia. Communities from the region come together for dance, song and ceremony. The Laura Races and Rodeo happen the following weekend. (p435)

🐟 Ski Season

When winter blows in (June to August), snow bunnies and powder hounds dust off their skis and snowboards and make for the mountains. Victoria and New South Wales (NSW) have the key resorts; there are a couple of small runs in Tasmania too. See www.ski.com.au. (p55)

July

Pubs with open fires, cosy coffee shops and empty beaches down south; packed markets, tours and accommodation up north.

Bring warm clothes for anywhere south of Alice Springs. Don't miss MIFF.

☆ Beer Can Regatta

The NT festival calendar is studded with quirky gems like this one at Darwin's Mindil Beach, where hundreds of 'boats' constructed from empty beer cans race across the shallows. Much drinking and laughter: staying afloat is a secondary concern. (p803)

☆ Melbourne International Film Festival

Right up there with Toronto and Cannes, MIFF has been running since 1952 and has grown into a wildly popular event. Myriad short films, feature-length spectaculars and documentaries flicker across city screens from late July into early August.

August

August is when southerners, sick of winter's grey-sky drear, head to Queensland for some sun. Approaching the last chance to head to the tropical Top End and outback before things get too hot and wet.

✵ Cairns Festival

Running for three weeks from late August to early September, this massive art-and-culture fest brings a stellar program of music, theatre, dance, comedy, film, Indigenous art and public exhibitions. Outdoor events held in public plazas, parks and gardens make good use of Cairns' tropical setting. (p405)

September

Spring heralds a rampant bloom of wildflowers across outback WA and SA, with flower festivals happening in places such as Canberra and Toowoomba. Football finishes and the spring horse-racing carnival begins.

✵ Brisbane Festival

One of Australia's largest and most diverse arts festivals runs for 22 days in September and features an impressive line-up of concerts, plays, dance performances and fringe events. It finishes off with Riverfire, an elaborate fireworks show over the river. (p279)

☆ AFL Grand Final

The pinnacle of the Australian Football League (AFL) season is this spectacle in Melbourne, watched (on TV) by millions of impassioned Aussies. Tickets to the game are scarce, but at half-time neighbourhood BBQs move into the local park for a little amateur kick-to-kick. (p1047)

October

The weather avoids extremes everywhere: a good time to go camping or to hang out at some vineyards (it's a dirty job, but someone's gotta do it...). The build-up to the rains begins in the Top End – *very* humid.

✵ Melbourne Festival

This annual arts festival offers some of the best of opera, theatre, dance and visual arts from around Australia and the world. It starts in early October and runs through to early November.

November

Northern beaches may close due to 'stingers' – jellyfish in the shallow waters off north Queensland, the NT and WA. Outdoor events ramp up; the surf life-saving season flexes its muscles on beaches everywhere.

♟ Margaret River Gourmet Escape

The culinary world's heavy hitters descend on Margaret River for four days of culinary inspiration; Nigella Lawson and Rick Stein headlined the event in 2016. Australia's growing crew of celebrity chefs usually attend as well. (p933)

☆ Melbourne Cup

On the first Tuesday in November, Australia's (if not the world's) premier horse race chews up the turf in Melbourne (www.melbour necup.com). Country towns schedule racing events to coincide with the day and the country does actually pause to watch the 'race that stops a nation'. (p481)

✵ Sculpture by the Sea

From late October to early November, the cliff-top trail from Bondi Beach to Tamarama in Sydney transforms

into an exquisite sculpture garden. Serious prize money is on offer for the most creative, curious or quizzical offerings from international and local sculptors. (p107)

🎆 Fremantle Festival

Ten days of parades, music, dance, comedy, visual arts, street theatre and workshops. Founded in 1905, it's Australia's longest-running festival. Highlights include the Kite Extravaganza and the Wardarnji Indigenous Festival. (p907)

December

Ring the bell, school's out! Holidays begin two weeks before Christmas. Cities are packed with shoppers and the weather is desirably hot. Up north, monsoon season is under way: afternoon thunderstorms bring pelting rain.

🏃 Sydney to Hobart Yacht Race

Pack a picnic and join the Boxing Day (26 December) crowds along Sydney's waterfront to watch the start of the Sydney to Hobart, the world's most arduous open-ocean yacht race. (p107)

☆ Sydney Harbour Fireworks

A fantastic way to ring in the New Year: join the crowds overlooking the harbour as the Sydney Harbour Fireworks light up the night sky. There's a family display at 9pm; the main event erupts at midnight. (p107)

Top: An AFL game at the Melbourne Cricket Ground (p466)
Bottom: New Year's Eve fireworks over Sydney Harbour

Itineraries

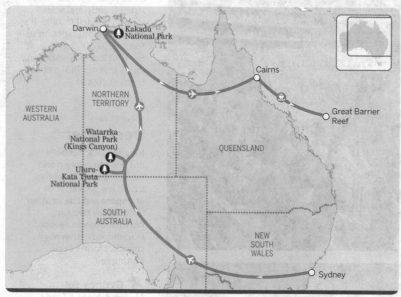

 Best of Australia

Two weeks to explore one of the largest countries on the planet will never be enough, but if you plan carefully and don't mind flying between stops, you can get a taste for Australia's greatest hits.

Fly into **Sydney** to explore one of the world's most charismatic cities – wander about the long and lovely waterfront, tour the Sydney Opera House and take a ferry to Manly, all the while enjoying outstanding museums and great food. After a minimum of three nights, fly directly to Yulara to spend four days exploring **Uluru-Kata Tjuta National Park** – both Uluru and Kata Tjuta (The Olgas) deserve as much time as you can give them – including a night in **Watarrka (Kings Canyon) National Park**.

With a week left, you're headed for the Top End. Fly to **Darwin** and head straight out to **Kakadu National Park** – three days is a minimum to see the rock art, take the river cruises and enjoy the fabulous wildlife. Return to Darwin, then jump on a plane to **Cairns**, from where you can spend your last few days diving or snorkelling the **Great Barrier Reef**.

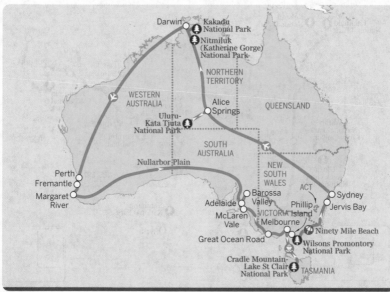

The Giant Loop

4 WEEKS

From Sydney to the outback, all the way out west and back again – this route is something of an Australian epic and covers many of the country's highlights in one busy month.

Bid a fond *au revoir* to the bright lights, bars and boutiques of **Sydney** and take an flight to **Alice Springs** in desert-hot central Australia. Check out the outstanding Alice Springs Desert Park, then tour south to the astonishing **Uluru-Kata Tjuta National Park**. Uluru gets all the press, but Kata Tjuta's boulders are just as stunning (and less crowded).

Back in Alice, hire a car and scoot north along the Stuart Hwy to emerging, rough-and-ready **Darwin**. En route, paddle a canoe or take a cruise at gorgeous **Nitmiluk (Katherine Gorge) National Park**, and check out some crocodiles and ancient Aboriginal rock-art galleries at **Kakadu National Park**.

From Darwin, hop on another flight to visit **Perth** and the soulful old port town of **Fremantle** nearby. Continuing south, wine away some hours around **Margaret River** until you're ready to tackle the flat immensity of the **Nullarbor Plain** – if you're not up for the epic drive to festival-frenzied **Adelaide**, the *Indian Pacific* train ride is unforgettable.

Check out the world-class wine regions around Adelaide (the **Barossa Valley** and **McLaren Vale** are both an easy drive), or head east along the impossibly scenic **Great Ocean Rd** to sports-mad **Melbourne**. Don't miss a game of Australian Rules football or cricket at the cauldron-like Melbourne Cricket Ground.

If you have a few extra days, take the car ferry across to **Tasmania**. The island state preserves some of the country's oldest forests and World Heritage–listed mountain ranges: **Cradle Mountain–Lake St Clair National Park** is accessible and absolutely beautiful.

Back in Melbourne, continue along the Victorian coast to the penguins and koalas on **Phillip Island** and white-sand seclusion of **Wilsons Promontory National Park**. Spend a couple of days somewhere along **Ninety Mile Beach** then cruise up the southern NSW coast to idyllic **Jervis Bay** (spot any whales?). Back in Sydney, there are so many beaches you're sure to find a patch of sand with your name on it.

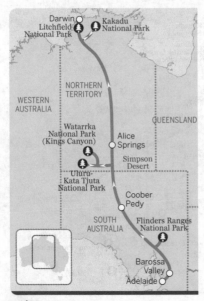

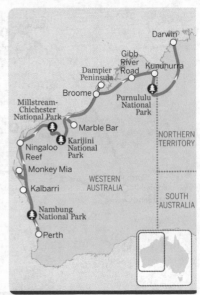

Adelaide to Darwin
2 WEEKS

Perth to the Kimberley
3-4 WEEKS

This classic 3000km dash up the Stuart Hwy takes you into Australia's desert heart.

From the old stone pubs of **Adelaide**, head north to the **Barossa Valley** for world-class red wines. Next stop is **Flinders Ranges National Park**: Ikara (Wilpena Pound) jags up from the semidesert.

Just off the Stuart Hwy are the opal-tinted dugouts of unique **Coober Pedy**. Continuing north into the desert, the Lasseter Hwy delivers you to iconic **Uluru-Kata Tjuta National Park**. The chasm of **Watarrka National Park (Kings Canyon)** is 300km further north.

Overnight in the desert oasis of **Alice Springs**, then continue north (consider flying) to the wetlands and rock-scapes of World Heritage–listed **Kakadu National Park** and the waterfalls and swimming holes of **Litchfield National Park**.

Gone are the days when **Darwin** was just an outpost: these days the city is very multicultural, as a visit to the fabulous Mindil Beach Sunset Market will confirm. Don't miss the quirky Deckchair Cinema and excellent Museum & Art Gallery of the Northern Territory.

Feeling adventurous? Steer your 4WD north from Perth...and keep going till you hit Darwin! You'll need your own wheels.

After exploring the west's capital of **Perth**, the next stop is otherworldly **Nambung National Park**, followed by **Kalbarri** with its sea cliffs and incredible gorges. Commune with dolphins at Shark Bay's **Monkey Mia**, then hug the coast for superb snorkelling at **Ningaloo Reef**.

Inland are the ironstone hues of the Pilbara. Cool off at tranquil **Millstream-Chichester National Park** then plunge into the gorges at **Karijini National Park**. Down a beer at **Marble Bar**, then follow a coastline known as the Big Empty northeast to **Broome**: watch the camels on Cable Beach at sunset. Nearby **Dampier Peninsula** beckons with pristine beaches and camping in Indigenous communities. From here, veer east into the Kimberley along legendary **Gibb River Road**.

Restock in **Kununurra** before heading south to the sandstone domes of **Purnululu National Park**. Take the lonely Duncan Road into the Northern Territory: once you're on asphalt, **Darwin** isn't far away.

ANDREW WATSON / GETTY IMAGES ©

AMOPHOTO.AU / SHUTTERSTOCK ©

Top: Brisbane (p270)

Bottom: Henley Beach, Adelaide (p715)

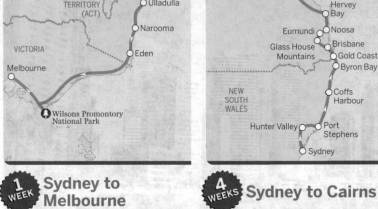

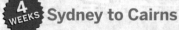

1 WEEK — Sydney to Melbourne

Most people fly into Sydney, Australia's biggest city. But don't miss Melbourne, Sydney's arty rival, approximately 1000km to the south.

Check out **Sydney** from its sparkling harbour: the gorgeous Sydney Opera House and colossal Sydney Harbour Bridge are unmissable. Feel like a swim? Bondi Beach's backpackers, beach breaks and bikinis make for a quintessential Australian experience.

Heading south, zip through **Royal National Park** to the elevated **Grand Pacific Drive**, continuing to **Wollongong** and the lovely coastal town of **Kiama**. Nearby, the Illawarra Fly Tree Top Walk and Zipline traverse the rainforest canopy.

Continuing south, meander through **Ulladulla**, **Narooma** and the aptly named **Eden** near the Victorian border. The road from here to Melbourne is low-key: throw in some blissful bushwalks and beaches at **Wilsons Promontory National Park**.

Melbourne is a vibrant city famous for the arts, Australian Rules football and coffee. Wander the laneways, mooch around the galleries, grab a pub dinner and catch a live band.

4 WEEKS — Sydney to Cairns

Hugging the east coast between Sydney and Cairns for 2864km, this is the most well-trodden path in Australia. You could do it in two weeks, but why not take four and really chill out.

Start with a few days immersed in the bright lights and glitz of **Sydney**, then meander north along the Pacific Hwy through central and northern New South Wales (NSW). Hang out in the **Hunter Valley** for some fine vino-quaffing, and stop to splash in the sea at family-friendly **Port Stephens** and **Coffs Harbour,** home of the iconic, kitsch Big Banana. Skip up to **Byron Bay** for New Age awakenings and superb beaches, then head over the Queensland border to the party-prone, surf-addled **Gold Coast**. Pause in hip **Brisbane** then amble up through the **Glass House Mountains** and hippie **Eumundi** to affluent **Noosa** on the Sunshine Coast.

The Bruce Hwy traces the stunning coast into Far North Queensland. Spot some passing whales off the coast of **Hervey Bay** and track further north to the blissful **Whitsundays** archipelago, the coral charms of the **Great Barrier Reef** and the scuba-diving nexus of **Cairns**.

Plan Your Trip
Your Reef Trip

The Great Barrier Reef, stretching over 2000km from just south of the Tropic of Capricorn (near Gladstone) to just south of Papua New Guinea, is the most extensive reef system in the world. There are numerous ways to experience this magnificent spectacle. Diving and snorkelling are the best methods of getting close to the menagerie of marine life and dazzling corals. You can also surround yourself with fabulous tropical fish without getting wet on a semi-submersible or a glass-bottomed boat, or see the macro perspective on a scenic flight.

When to Go

High season on the reef is from June to December. The best overall underwater visibility is from August to January.

From December to March, **northern Queensland** (north of Townsville) has its wet season, bringing oppressive heat and abundant rainfall (it's cooler from July to September). Stinger (jellyfish) season is between November and May; most reef operators offer Lycra stinger suits to snorkellers and divers, or bring your own.

Anytime is generally good to visit the **Whitsundays**. Winter (June to August) can be pleasantly warm, but you will occasionally need a jumper. South of the Whitsundays, summer (December to March) is hot and humid.

Southern and central Queensland experience mild winters (June to August) – pleasant enough for diving or snorkelling in a wetsuit.

Picking Your Spot

There are many popular and remarkable spots from which to access the 'GBR', but bear in mind that individual areas change over time, depending on the weather or recent damage.

Best for...

Wildlife
Sea turtles around Lady Elliot Island or Heron Island.

Looking for reef sharks and rays while kayaking off Green Island.

Spotting wild koalas on Magnetic Island.

Snorkelling
Getting underwater at Knuckle, Hardy and Fitzroy Reefs.

Offshore at Magnetic Island or the Whitsunday Islands.

Views from Above
Scenic chopper or plane rides from Cairns or the Whitsunday Islands.

Skydiving over Airlie Beach.

Sailing
Sailing from Airlie Beach through the Whitsunday Islands.

Exploring Agincourt Reef from Port Douglas.

Mainland Gateways

There are several mainland gateways to the reef, all offering slightly different experiences and activities. Here's a brief overview, ordered from south to north.

Agnes Water & Town of 1770 Small towns and good choices if you want to escape the crowds. Tours head to Fitzroy Reef Lagoon, one of the most pristine sections of the reef, where visitor numbers are still limited. The lagoon is excellent for snorkelling, but also spectacular viewed from the boat.

Gladstone A bigger town but still a relatively small gateway. It's an excellent choice for avid divers and snorkellers, being the closest access point to the southern or Capricorn reef islands and innumerable cays, including Lady Elliot Island.

Airlie Beach A small town with a full rack of sailing outfits. The big attraction here is spending two or more days aboard a boat and seeing some of the Whitsunday Islands' fringing coral reefs. Whether you're a five- or no-star traveller, there'll be a tour to match your budget.

Townsville Renowned among divers. Whether you're learning or experienced, a four- or five-night diving safari around the numerous islands and pockets of the reef is a great choice. Kelso Reef and the wreck of the SS *Yongala* are teeming with marine life. There are also a couple of day-trip options on glass-bottomed boats, but for more choice you're better off heading to Cairns. The gigantic Reef HQ Aquarium is also here.

Mission Beach Closer to the reef than any other gateway destination, this small town offers a few boat and diving tours to sections of the outer reef. The choice isn't huge, but neither are the crowds.

Cairns The main launching pad for reef tours, with a staggering number of operators offering everything from relatively inexpensive day trips on large boats to intimate five-day luxury charters. Tours cover a wide section of the reef, with some operators going as far north as Lizard Island. Inexpensive tours are likely to travel to inner, less pristine reefs. Scenic flights also operate out of Cairns.

Port Douglas A swanky resort town and a gateway to the Low Isles and Agincourt Reef, an outer ribbon reef featuring crystal-clear water and stunning corals. Diving, snorkelling and cruising trips tend to be classier, pricier and less crowded than in Cairns. You can also take a scenic flight from here.

Cooktown Close to Lizard Island, but most tour operators here shut down between November and May for the wet season.

Islands

Speckled throughout the reef is a profusion of islands and cays that offer some of the most stunning access. Here is a list of some of the best islands, travelling from south to north.

Lady Elliot Island The coral cay here is twitcher heaven, with 57 resident bird species. Sea turtles also nest here and it's possibly the best spot on the reef to see manta rays. It's also a famed diving location. There's a resort here, but you can also visit Lady Elliot on a day trip from Bundaberg.

Heron Island A tiny, tranquil coral cay sitting amid a huge spread of reef. It's a diving mecca, but the snorkelling is also good and it's possible to do a reef walk from here. Heron is a nesting ground for green and loggerhead turtles and home to 30 bird species. The sole resort on the island charges accordingly.

Hamilton Island The big daddy of the Whitsundays, Hamilton is a sprawling, family-friendly resort laden with infrastructure. While the atmosphere isn't exactly intimate, there's a wealth of tours going to the outer reef. It's also a good place to see patches of the reef that can't be explored from the mainland.

Hook Island An outer Whitsunday island surrounded by fringing reefs. There's excellent swimming and snorkelling here, and the island's sizeable bulk provides plenty of good bushwalking. There's affordable accommodation on Hook and it's easily accessed from Airlie Beach, making it a top choice for those on a modest budget.

Orpheus Island A national park and one of the reef's most exclusive, tranquil and romantic hideaways. Orpheus is particularly good for snorkelling – you can step right off the beach and be surrounded by colourful marine life. Clusters of fringing reefs also provide plenty of diving opportunities.

REEF RESOURCES

Dive Queensland www.dive-queens land.com.au

Tourism Queensland www.queens landholidays.com.au

Great Barrier Reef Marine Park Authority www.gbrmpa.gov.au

Department of National Parks, Sport & Racing www.nprsr.qld.gov.au

Australian Bureau of Meteorology www.bom.gov.au

Reef Highlights

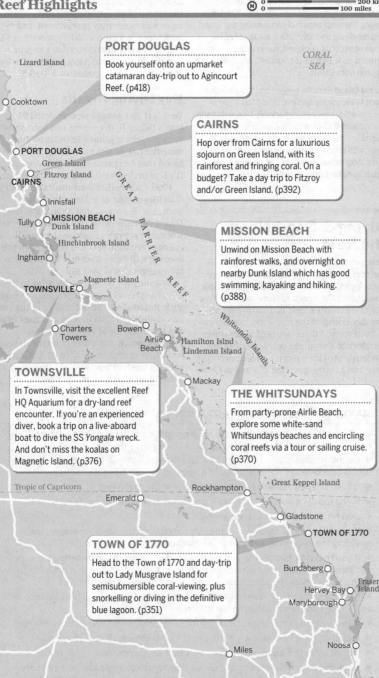

Ⓝ 0 —— 200 km
0 —— 100 miles

CORAL SEA

Lizard Island

Cooktown

PORT DOUGLAS

Book yourself onto an upmarket catamaran day-trip out to Agincourt Reef. (p418)

PORT DOUGLAS

Green Island

Fitzroy Island

CAIRNS

CAIRNS

Hop over from Cairns for a luxurious sojourn on Green Island, with its rainforest and fringing coral. On a budget? Take a day trip to Fitzroy and/or Green Island. (p392)

Innisfail

Tully

MISSION BEACH
Dunk Island

Hinchinbrook Island

Ingham

GREAT BARRIER REEF

Magnetic Island

TOWNSVILLE

MISSION BEACH

Unwind on Mission Beach with rainforest walks, and overnight on nearby Dunk Island which has good swimming, kayaking and hiking. (p388)

Charters Towers

Bowen

Airlie Beach

Hamilton Islnd

Lindeman Island

Whitsunday Islands

TOWNSVILLE

In Townsville, visit the excellent Reef HQ Aquarium for a dry-land reef encounter. If you're an experienced diver, book a trip on a live-aboard boat to dive the SS *Yongala* wreck. And don't miss the koalas on Magnetic Island. (p376)

Mackay

THE WHITSUNDAYS

From party-prone Airlie Beach, explore some white-sand Whitsundays beaches and encircling coral reefs via a tour or sailing cruise. (p370)

Tropic of Capricorn

Great Keppel Island

Emerald

Rockhampton

Gladstone

TOWN OF 1770

TOWN OF 1770

Head to the Town of 1770 and day-trip out to Lady Musgrave Island for semisubmersible coral-viewing, plus snorkelling or diving in the definitive blue lagoon. (p351)

Bundaberg

Hervey Bay

Fraser Island

Maryborough

Miles

Noosa

Green Island Another of the reef's true coral cays. The fringing reefs here are considered to be among the most beautiful surrounding any island, and the diving and snorkelling are spectacular. Covered in dense rainforest, the entire island is national park. Bird life is abundant. Accessible as a day trip from Cairns.

Lizard Island Remote, rugged and the perfect place to escape civilisation, Lizard has a ring of talcum-white beaches, remarkably blue water and few visitors. It's home to the Cod Hole, arguably Australia's best-known dive site, where you can swim with docile potato cod weighing as much as 60kg. Accommodation here has no grey areas: it's either five-star luxury or bush camping.

Diving & Snorkelling the Reef

Much of the diving and snorkelling on the reef is boat-based, although there are some excellent reefs accessible by walking straight off the beach of some islands. Free use of snorkelling gear is usually part of any day cruise to the reef – you can typically fit in around three hours of underwater wandering. Overnight or liveaboard trips obviously provide a more in-depth experience and greater coverage. If you don't have a diving certificate, many operators offer the option of an introductory dive, where an experienced diver conducts an underwater tour. A lesson in safety procedures is given beforehand and you don't require a five-day Professional Association of Diving Instructors (PADI) course or a 'buddy'.

Key Diving Details

Your last dive should be completed 24 hours before flying – even in a balloon or for a parachute jump – in order to minimise the risk of residual nitrogen in the blood that can cause decompression injury. It's fine to dive soon after arriving by air.

Find out whether your insurance policy classifies diving as a dangerous-sport exclusion. For a nominal annual fee, the Divers Alert Network (www.diversalertnetwork.org) provides insurance for medical or evacuation services required in the event of a diving accident. DAN's hotline for emergencies is ☎+1 919 684 9111.

Visibility for coastal areas is 1m to 3m, whereas several kilometres offshore visibility is 8m to 15m. The outer edge of the reef has visibility of 20m to 35m and the Coral Sea has visibility of 50m and beyond.

In the north, the water is warm all year round, from around 24°C to 30°C. Going south it gradually gets cooler, dropping to a low of 20°C in winter.

MAKING A POSITIVE CONTRIBUTION TO THE REEF

The Great Barrier Reef is incredibly fragile and it's worth taking some time to educate yourself on responsible practices while you're there.

➡ No matter where you visit, take all litter with you – even biodegradable material such as apple cores – and dispose of it back on the mainland.

➡ It is an offence to damage or remove coral in the marine park.

➡ If you touch or walk on coral you'll damage it and get some nasty cuts.

➡ Don't touch or harass marine animals.

➡ If you have a boat, be aware of the rules in relation to anchoring around the reef, including 'no anchoring areas' to avoid coral damage.

➡ If you're diving, check that you are weighted correctly before entering the water and keep your buoyancy control well away from the reef. Ensure that equipment such as secondary regulators and gauges aren't dragging over the reef.

➡ If you're snorkelling (especially if you're a beginner), practise your technique away from coral until you've mastered control in the water.

➡ Hire a wetsuit rather than slathering on sunscreen, which can damage the reef.

➡ Watch where your fins are – try not to stir up sediment or disturb coral.

➡ Do not enter the water near a dugong, whether you're swimming or diving.

➡ Note that there are limits on the amount and types of shells that you can collect.

Top: Snorkelling the
Great Barrier Reef
(p399)

Bottom: Port Douglas
(p418)

PANORAMIC IMAGES / GETTY IMAGES ©

TOP SNORKELLING SITES

Some nondivers may wonder if it's really worth going to the Great Barrier Reef 'just to snorkel'. The answer is a resounding yes! Much of the rich, colourful coral lies just underneath the surface (coral needs bright sunlight to flourish) and is easily viewed by snorkellers. Here's a round-up of some top snorkelling sites.

➡ Fitzroy Reef Lagoon (Town of 1770)
➡ Heron Island (Capricorn Coast)
➡ Keppel Island (Capricorn Coast)
➡ Lady Elliot Island (Capricorn Coast)
➡ Lady Musgrave Island (Capricorn Coast)
➡ Hook Island (Whitsundays)
➡ Hayman Island (Whitsundays)
➡ Border Island (Whitsundays)
➡ Lizard Island (Cairns)
➡ Hardy Reef (Whitsundays)
➡ Knuckle Reef (Whitsundays)
➡ Michaelmas Reef (Cairns)
➡ Hastings Reef (Cairns)
➡ Norman Reef (Cairns)
➡ Saxon Reef (Cairns)
➡ Opal Reef (Port Douglas)
➡ Agincourt Reef (Port Douglas)
➡ Mackay Reef (Port Douglas)

Top Reef Dive Spots

The Great Barrier Reef is home to some of the world's best diving sites. Here are a few of our favourite spots to get you started:

SS Yongala A sunken shipwreck that has been home to a vivid marine community for more than 90 years.

Cod Hole Go nose-to-nose with a potato cod.

Heron Island Join a crowd of colourful fish straight off the beach.

Lady Elliot Island With 19 highly regarded dive sites.

Wheeler Reef Massive variety of marine life, plus a great spot for night dives.

Boat Excursions

Unless you're staying on a coral-fringed island, you'll need to join a boat excursion to experience the reef's real beauty. Day trips leave from many places along the coast, as well as from resorts, and typically include the use of snorkelling gear, snacks and lunch, with scuba diving an optional extra.

On some boats, naturalists or marine biologists give talks on the reef's ecology.

Boat trips vary dramatically in passenger numbers, type of vessel and quality – which is reflected in the price – so get all the details before committing. When selecting a tour, consider the vessel (motorised catamaran or sailing ship), the number of passengers (from six to 400), what extras are offered and the destination. The outer reefs are usually more pristine. Inner reefs often show signs of damage from humans and coral-eating crown-of-thorns starfish. Coral bleaching is a major issue in far northern sections of the reef.

Many boats have underwater cameras for hire, although you'll save money by hiring these on land (or using your own waterproof camera or underwater housing). Some boats also have professional photographers on board who will dive and take high-quality shots of you in action.

Liveaboards

If you want to do as much diving as possible, a liveaboard is an excellent option as you'll do three dives per day, plus some night dives, in more remote parts of the Great Barrier Reef. Trip vary from one to 12 nights. The three-day/three-night voyages, which allow up to 11 dives (nine day and two night dives), are the most common.

It's worth checking out the various options as some boats offer specialist itineraries, following marine life and events such as minke whales or coral spawning, or offer trips to less-visited spots like the far northern reefs, Pompey Complex, Coral Sea Reefs or Swain Reefs.

It's recommended to go with operators who are Dive Queensland (www.dive-queensland.com.au) members: this ensures they follow a set of guidelines. Ideally, they'll also be accredited by Ecotourism Australia (www.ecotourism.org.au).

Popular departure points for liveaboard dive vessels, along with the locales they visit are:

Bundaberg The Bunker Island group, including Lady Musgrave and Lady Elliot Islands, possibly Fitzroy, Llewellyn and the rarely visited Boult Reefs or Hoskyn and Fairfax Islands.

Town of 1770 Bunker Island group.

Gladstone Swains and Bunker Island group.

Mackay Lihou Reef and the Coral Sea.

Airlie Beach The Whitsundays, Knuckle Reef and Hardy Reef.

Townsville SS *Yongala* wreck, plus canyons of Wheeler Reef and Keeper Reef.

Cairns Cod Hole, Ribbon Reefs, the Coral Sea and possibly far northern reefs.

Port Douglas Osprey Reef, Cod Hole, Ribbon Reefs, Coral Sea and possibly the far northern reefs.

Dive Courses

In Queensland, there are numerous places where you can learn to dive, take a refresher course or improve your skills. Courses here are generally of a high standard, and all schools teach either PADI or Scuba Schools International (SSI) qualifications. Which certification you choose isn't as important as choosing a good instructor, so be sure to seek recommendations and meet with the instructor before committing.

One of the most popular places to learn is Cairns, where you can choose between courses for the budget-minded (four-day courses cost between $520 and $765) that combine pool training and reef dives, to

longer, more intensive courses that include reef diving on a liveaboard (five-day courses, including three-day/two-night liveaboard, cost between $800 and $1000).

Other places where you can learn to dive, and then head out on the reef, include Bundaberg, Mission Beach, Townsville, Airlie Beach, Hamilton Island, Magnetic Island and Port Douglas.

Camping on the Great Barrier Reef

Pitching a tent on an island is a fun and affordable way to experience the Great Barrier Reef. Campers enjoy an idyllic tropical setting at a fraction of the cost of the five-star island resort down the road. Campsite facilities range from extremely basic (read: nothing) to fairly flash, with showers, flush toilets, interpretive signage and picnic tables. Most islands are remote, so ensure you're prepared for emergencies.

Wherever you stay, you'll need to be self-sufficient, bringing your own food and drinking water (5L per day per person is recommended). Weather can prevent pick-ups, so have enough supplies to last an extra few days in case you get stranded.

Camp only in designated areas, keep to trails and take out all that you brought in. Fires are banned, so you'll need a gas stove or similar. National park camping permits must be booked online through the Queensland government's Department of National Parks, Sport & Racing (www.nprsr.qld.gov.au). Here are our picks:

Whitsunday Islands Nearly a dozen beautifully sited camping areas, scattered on the islands of Hook, Whitsunday and Henning.

Capricornia Cays Camping available on three separate coral cays – Masthead Island, North West Island and Lady Musgrave Island, a fantastic, uninhabited island with a maximum limit of 40 campers.

Dunk Island Easy to get to, with good swimming, kayaking and hiking.

Fitzroy Island Resort and national park with walking trails through bush, and coral off the beaches.

Frankland Islands Coral-fringed islands with white-sand beaches off Cairns.

Lizard Island Magnificent beaches, coral and wildlife; visitors mostly arrive by plane.

Plan Your Trip

Your Outback Trip

Exactly where Australia's outback starts and ends is hard to pin down on a map. But you'll know you're there when the sky yawns enormously wide, the horizon is unnervingly empty, and the sparse inhabitants you encounter are incomparably resilient and distinctively Australian. Out here, enduring Indigenous culture, unique wildlife and intriguing landscapes await the modern-day adventurer.

Best...

For Indigenous Culture
Kakadu National Park in the tropical Top End wilderness offers ancient rock art and cultural tours run by Indigenous guides.

Outback National Park
Iconic Uluru in Uluru-Kata Tjuta National Park is simply unmissable, while nearby Kata Tjuta is less well known but just as impressive.

Outback Track
Oodnadatta Track: 620km of red dust, emus, lizards, salt lakes and historic railroad remnants.

Outback Road Trip
The Stuart Hwy from Darwin to Port Augusta is an epic journey from the tropical north to the parched central deserts.

Season to Visit
June to October, with mild temperatures and generally dry weather early in the season, and wildflowers in spring.

Things to Pack
Sunscreen, sunglasses, a hat, insect repellent, plenty of water and some good tunes for the car stereo.

About the Outback

The Australian outback is a vast region, radiating out from the centre of the continent. While most Australians live on the coast, that thin green fringe is hardly typical of this enormous land mass. Inland is the desert soul of Australia.

Weather patterns vary from region to region – from sandy arid desert to semi-arid scrubland to tropical savannah – but you can generally rely on hot sunny days, starry nights and kilometre after kilometre of unbroken horizon.

When to Go
Best Times

Winter June through August is when southeastern Australia (where most of the population lives) is sniffling through rainy and cloudy winter days, and the outback comes into its own. Rain isn't unheard of in outback Australia – in fact there's been a whole lot of it over recent years, including in December 2016 when they had to briefly close Uluru-Kata Tjuta National Park to visitors and several outback communities flooded. But moderate daytime temperatures, cold nights and good driving conditions are the norm. Winter is also the best time to visit the tropical Top End, with low humidity, dry days and mild temperatures.

Spring September and October is springtime, and prime time to head into the outback, especially if you're into wildflowers. The MacDonnell Ranges near Alice Springs and the Flinders Ranges in northern South Australia erupt with colourful blooms, all the more dazzling in contrast with red-orange desert sands.

Avoid

Summer Central Australia heats up over summer (December through February) – temperatures approaching 50°C have been recorded in some desert towns – but that's just part of the picture. With the heat comes dusty roads, overheating cars, driver fatigue, irritating flies and the need to carry extra water everywhere you go. In the Top End the build-up to the wet season is uncomfortably humid, and the eventual monsoon can see many a road cut and dirt roads made impassable for weeks at a time.

Planes, Trains or Automobiles

Air If you want to access the outback without a long drive, the major airlines fly into Alice Springs and Yulara (for the central deserts) and Darwin (for the tropical Top End), departing from Perth, Adelaide and the major east-coast cities. From Darwin or Alice you can join a guided tour or hire a 4WD and off you go.

Train Unlike much of the world, train travel in Australia is neither affordable nor expedient. It's something you do for a special occasion or for the sheer romance of trains, not if you want to get anywhere in a hurry. That said, travelling on the *Indian Pacific* between Perth and Sydney or the legendary *Ghan* between Adelaide and Darwin takes you through parts of the country you wouldn't see otherwise, and it certainly makes for a leisurely holiday. Train travel is also a good way to beat the heat if you're travelling in summer. So if you have time on your side and you can afford it, train travel could be perfect for you.

Car You can drive through the Red Centre from Darwin to Adelaide with detours to Uluru and Kakadu and more without ever leaving sealed roads. However, if you really want to see outback Australia, there are plenty of side routes that breathe new life into the phrase 'off the beaten track' (bring a 4WD). Driving in the outback has its challenges – immense distances and occasionally difficult terrain – but it's ultimately the most rewarding and intimate way to experience Australia's 'dead heart' (rest assured, it's alive and kicking!).

Essential Outback

The Red Centre: Alice Springs, Uluru & Kings Canyon

Alice is a surprising oasis: big enough to have some great places to eat and stay, as well as some social problems. Nearby, the East and West MacDonnell Ranges are classic outback landforms: red rocks, dramatic canyons and plenty of wildlife. Palm Valley in Finke National Park is one of the outback's least-known gems. Uluru is to tourists what half a watermelon is to ants at a picnic: people from all over the globe swarm to and from this monolith at all times of the day. But it's still a remarkable find. The local Anangu people would prefer that you didn't climb it. Watarrka (Kings Canyon), about 300km north of Uluru, is a spectacular chasm carved into the rugged landscape.

The Stuart Highway: Adelaide to Darwin

In either direction, from the north or south, the paved Stuart Hwy is one of Australia's greatest road trips: 2834km of red desert sand, flat scrubland and galloping roadside emus. Heading north, make sure you stop at spookily pock-marked Coober Pedy – the opal-mining capital of the world – and detour to Uluru on your way to the Alice. Nitmiluk (Katherine Gorge) National Park is also en route, a photogenic series of sheer rocky gorges and waterholes. Kakadu National Park is next, with World Heritage-listed tropical wetlands. When you get to Darwin, reward yourself with a cold beer and some nocturnal high jinks on Mitchell St.

The Tropics: Darwin, Kakadu & Katherine

The outback in the tropical Top End is a different experience to the deserts further south. Here, the wet and dry seasons determine how easy it is to get from A to B. In the Wet, roads become impassable and crocodiles move freely through the wetlands. But before you cancel your plans, this is also a time of abundance and great natural beauty in the national parks – plus Kakadu resorts can go down to half the price! Darwin isn't technically in the outback, but it still feels like a frontier town, especially in the Dry when backpackers from around the world fill the bars and Mindil Beach market. Katherine, three hours to the south, is much more 'country', and the jumping-off point for the astonishing Nitmiluk (Katherine Gorge) National Park.

The Victoria Highway: Katherine to the Kimberley

The Victoria Hwy is a significant section of the epic Savannah Way from Cairns to Broome, the classic 'across-the-top' route. Leaving Katherine it winds through classic cattle country, where farms can be as big as small European countries. It also passes some lovely river-and-escarpment country around Victoria River Crossing and there are 4WD and hiking opportunities, outback camp sites, rock art, national parks, red gorges and crocodiles. And this region boasts some of the Top End's best barramundi fishing. The immense Gregory National Park, a former cattle station, is best explored with a 4WD (some tracks may be accessible in a 2WD in the Dry), while Keep River

On the Oodnadatta Track (p794)

National Park is also worth exploring. Exploring the Kimberley requires a 4WD to tackle trails like the epic Gibb River road.

OUTBACK CYCLING

Pedalling your way through the outback is certainly not something to tackle lightly, and certainly not something you'd even consider in summer. But you do see the odd wiry, suntanned soul pushing their panniers along the Stuart Hwy between Adelaide and Darwin. Availability of drinking water is the main concern: isolated water sources (bores, tanks, creeks etc) shown on maps may be dry or undrinkable. Make sure you've got the necessary spare parts and bike-repair knowledge. Check with locals if you're heading into remote areas, and always tell someone where you're headed. And if you make it through, try for a book deal – this is intrepid travel defined.

Facilities

Outback roadhouses emerge from the desert-heat haze with surprising regularity. It always pays to calculate the distance to the next fuel stop, but even on the remote Oodnadatta Track or Tanami Road you'll find petrol and cold beer every few hundred kilometres. Most roadhouses (many of them open 24 hours) sell fuel and have attached restaurants where you can get a decent steak and a fry-up feed. Just don't expect an epicurean experience. There's often accommodation for road-weary drivers out the back, including camp sites, air-conditioned motel-style rooms, often with shared bathrooms, and basic cabins.

ROAD TRAINS

On many outback highways you'll see thundering road trains: huge trucks (a prime mover plus two, three or four trailers), some more than 50m long. These things don't move over for anyone: it's like a scene from *Mad Max* having one bear down on you at 120km/h.

A few tips: when you see a road train approaching on a narrow bitumen road, slow down and pull over – if the truck has to put its wheels off the road to pass you, the resulting barrage of stones will almost certainly smash your windscreen. When trying to overtake one, allow plenty of room (about a kilometre) to complete the manoeuvre. Road trains throw up a lot of dust on dirt roads, so if you see one coming it's best to just pull over and stop until it's gone past.

And while you're on outback roads, don't forget to give the standard bush greeting to oncoming drivers – it's simply a matter of lifting the index finger off the steering wheel to acknowledge your fellow explorer.

Resources

Department of Environment, Water & Natural Resources (www.environment.sa.gov.au/parks/Home) South Australian national parks info.

Bureau of Meteorology (www.bom.gov.au) Weather forecasts and warnings.

Parks & Wildlife (www.nt.gov.au/leisure/parks-reserves) NT national parks info; click through to fact-sheet PDFs for each park.

Parks Australia (www.environment.gov.au/topics/national-parks) Extensive information about the federally administered Kakadu and Uluru-Kata Tjuta National Parks.

South Australian Tourism Commission (www.southaustralia.com) Accommodation, activities, events, tours and transport.

Travel NT (www.northernterritory.com) NT travel guide with excellent high-level coverage.

Organised Tours

If you don't feel like doing all the planning and driving, a guided tour is a great way to experience the Aussie outback. These range from beery backpacker jaunts between outback pubs, to Indigenous cultural tours and multiday bushwalking treks into remote wilderness.

Outback Tracks

The Australian outback is criss-crossed by sealed highways, but one of the more interesting ways to get from A to B is by taking a detour along historic cattle and rail routes. While you may not necessarily need a 4WD to tackle some of these roads, the rugged construction of these vehicles makes for a much more comfortable drive. But whatever your wheels of choice, you will need to be prepared for the isolation and lack of facilities.

Don't attempt the tougher routes during the hottest part of the year (December to February, inclusive); apart from the risk of heat exhaustion, simple mishaps can lead to tragedy in these conditions. There's also no point going anywhere on outback dirt roads if there has been recent flooding.

Unpaved Tracks

Most outback tracks are unsealed, although there may be some sections paved with tarmac.

Mereenie Loop Road

Starting in Alice Springs this well-used track is an alternative route to the big attractions of the Red Centre. The route initially follows the sealed Larapinta and Namatjira Drives skirting the magnificent MacDonnell Ranges to Glen Helen Gorge. Beyond Glen Helen the route meets the Mereenie Loop Rd. This is where things get interesting. The Mereenie Loop Rd requires a permit ($5) and is usually so heavily corrugated that it will rattle a conventional 2WD until it finds its weak spot. This is the rugged short cut to Watarrka (Kings Canyon) National Park; from Watarrka the sealed

Outback Tracks: Off the Beaten Path

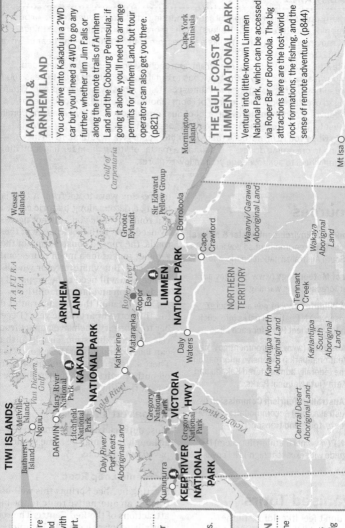

KAKADU & ARNHEM LAND

You can drive into Kakadu in a 2WD car but you'll need a 4WD to go any further, whether Jim Falls or along the remote trails of Arnhem Land and the Cobourg Peninsula; if going it alone, you'll need to arrange permits for Arnhem Land, but tour operators can also get you there. (p821)

THE GULF COAST & LIMMEN NATIONAL PARK

Venture into little-known Limmen National Park, which can be accessed via Roper Bar or Borroloola. The big attractions here are the lost-world rock formations, the fishing, and the sense of remote adventure. (p844)

TIWI ISLANDS

Leave the car far behind and venture across the waters to Bathurst Island to experience Tiwi Island culture, with its fascinating history and unique art. (p812)

KEEP RIVER NATIONAL PARK

A little-visited yet rewarding detour on the way to northern WA, Keep River National Park features Aboriginal art, wildlife, short walks and stunning sandstone formations. (p841)

VICTORIA RIVER REGION

Detours lead off the highway into the isolated sandstone escarpment country of Judbarra/Gregory National Park and onto 4WD tracks and wilderness camp sites under big skies. (p840)

DESERT TRACKS

The famous cross-desert routes – the Birdsville, Oodnadatta and Strzelecki Tracks – should not be taken lightly. Well-prepared travellers are rewarded with pioneering history, big skies and unparalleled solitude. (p794-5)

FLINDERS RANGES

Getting off the tarmac is the best way to explore the Flinders and the only way to get into the Gammon Ranges. Experience Aboriginal heritage, mining relics and magnificent scenery. (p785)

RED CENTRE WAY

Traverse Australia's Red Centre – the gorges of the MacDonnell Ranges, the gape of Kings Canyon, and the splendor of Uluru and Kata Tjuta – by taking this road less travelled. (p865)

WESTERN AUSTRALIA

Gibson Desert

Lake Mackay Aboriginal Land

Lake Mackay

Haasts Bluff   MacDonnell Ranges   Alice Springs

Aboriginal Land

Finke Gorge National Park

Kings Canyon

Petermann Aboriginal Land

RED CENTRE WAY

Uluru-Kata Tjuta National Park

Atnetye Aboriginal Land

Pmere Nyente Aboriginal Land

Pmer Ulperre Ingwemirne Aboriginal Land

Simpson Desert

Pitjantjatjara Aboriginal Land

Conservation Park

Maralinga Tjarutja Aboriginal Land

Great Victoria Desert

Nullarbor Plain

Eucla

Great Australian Bight

Nullarbor National Park

Yalata Aboriginal Land

Nullarbor Regional Reserve

Ceduna

Yellabinna Regional Reserve

Lake Gairdner

Tallaringa Conservation Park

Marla

Coober Pedy

SOUTH AUSTRALIA

OODNADATTA TRACK

Simpson Desert Regional Reserve

BIRDSVILLE TRACK

Birdsville

Innamincka Regional Reserve

Strzelecki Regional Reserve

STRZELECKI TRACK

Lake Eyre North

Lake Eyre National Park

Lake Eyre South

Lake Torrens

Wulkathunha-Gammon Ranges National Park

FLINDERS RANGES

Port Augusta

OUTBACK DRIVING & SAFETY CHECKLIST

Due to the lack of water, long distances between fuel stops and isolation, you need to be particularly organised and vigilant when travelling in the outback, especially on remote sandy tracks.

Communication

➡ Report your route and schedule to the police, a friend or relative.

➡ Mobile phones are useless if you go off the highway. Consider hiring a satellite phone, high-frequency (HF) radio transceiver equipped to pick up the Royal Flying Doctor Service bases, or emergency position-indicating radio beacon (EPIRB).

➡ In an emergency, stay with your vehicle; it's easier to spot than you are, and you won't be able to carry a heavy load of water very far.

➡ If you do become stranded, consider setting fire to a spare tyre (let the air out first). The pall of smoke will be visible for kilometres.

Your Vehicle

➡ Have your vehicle serviced and checked before you leave.

➡ Load your vehicle evenly, with heavy items inside and light items on the roof rack.

➡ Consider carrying spare fuel in an appropriate container.

➡ Carry essential tools: a spare tyre (two is preferable), fan belt, radiator hose, tyre-pressure gauge and air pump, and a shovel.

➡ An off-road jack might come in handy, as will a snatch strap or tow rope for quick extraction when you're stuck (useful if there's another vehicle to pull you out).

Supplies & Equipment

➡ Carry plenty of water: in warm weather allow 5L per person per day and an extra amount for the radiator, carried in several containers.

➡ Bring plenty of food in case of a breakdown.

➡ Carry a first-aid kit, a torch with spare batteries, a compass and a GPS.

Weather & Road Conditions

➡ Check road conditions before travelling: roads that are passable in the Dry (March to October) can disappear beneath water during the Wet.

➡ Don't attempt to cross flooded bridges or causeways unless you're sure of the depth, and of any road damage hidden underwater.

Dirt-Road Driving

➡ Inflate your tyres to the recommended levels for the terrain you're travelling on; on desert sand, deflate your tyres to 20–25psi to avoid getting bogged. Don't forget to re-inflate them when you leave the sand.

➡ Reduce speed on unsealed roads, as braking distances increase.

➡ Dirt roads are often corrugated: keeping an even speed is the best approach.

➡ Dust on outback roads can obscure your vision, so stop and wait for it to settle.

➡ Choose a low gear for steep inclines and the lowest gear for steep declines. Use the brake sparingly and don't turn sideways on a hill.

Road Hazards

➡ Take a rest every few hours: driver fatigue is an all-too-common problem.

➡ Wandering cattle, sheep, emus, kangaroos, camels etc make driving fast a dangerous prospect. Take care and avoid nocturnal driving, as this is often when native animals come out. Many car-hire companies prohibit night-time driving.

➡ Road trains are an ever-present menace on the main highways and even on some unsealed roads. Give them a wide berth – they're much bigger than you!

Outback road signs

Luritja Rd connects to the Lasseter Hwy and Uluru-Kata Tjuta National Park. There has been talk for years of sealing this track, but it remains just talk.

Oodnadatta Track

Mostly running parallel to the old *Ghan* railway line through outback SA, this iconic track is fully bypassed by the sealed Stuart Hwy to the west. Using this track, it's 429km from Marree in the northern Flinders Ranges, to Oodnadatta, then another 216km to the Stuart Hwy at Marla. As long as there is no rain, any well-prepared conventional vehicle should be able to manage this fascinating route, but a 4WD will do it in style.

Birdsville Track

Spanning 517km from Marree in SA to Birdsville just across the border of Queensland, this old droving trail is one of Australia's best-known outback routes – although it's not known for spectacular and varying scenery. It's often feasible to travel it in a well-prepared, conventional vehicle but not recommended.

Strzelecki Track

This track covers much of the same territory through SA as the Birdsville Track. Starting south of Marree at Lyndhurst, it reaches Innamincka 460km northeast and close to the Queensland border. It was close to Innamincka that the hapless explorers Burke and Wills died. A 4WD is a safe bet, even though this route has been much improved due to work on the Moomba gas fields.

Nathan River Road

This road, which resembles a farm track in parts, is a scenic section of the Savannah Way, a cobbled-together route which winds all the way from Cairns to Broome. This particular section traverses some remote country along the western edge of the Gulf of Carpentaria between Roper Bar and Borroloola, much of it protected within Limmen National Park. A high-clearance vehicle is a must and carrying two spare tyres is recommended because of the frequent sharp rocks. Excellent camping beside barramundi- and crocodile-filled streams and waterholes is the main attraction here.

Tanami Track

Turning off the Stuart Hwy just north of Alice Springs, this 1055km route runs northwest across the Tanami Desert to Halls Creek in Western Australia. The road has received extensive work so conventional vehicles are often OK, although there are sandy stretches on the WA side and it can be very corrugated if it hasn't been graded recently. Get advice on road conditions in Alice Springs.

Plenty & Sandover Highways

These remote routes run east from the Stuart Hwy, north of Alice Springs, to Boulia or Mt Isa in Queensland. The Plenty Hwy skirts the northern fringe of the Simpson Desert and offers the chance of gem fossicking in the Harts Range. The Sandover Hwy offers a memorable if monotonous experience in remote touring. It is a novelty to see another vehicle. Both roads are not to be taken lightly; they are often very rough going with little water and with sections that are very infrequently used. Signs of human habitation are rare and facilities are few and far between.

Finke & Old Andado Tracks

The Finke Track (the first part of which is the Old South Rd) follows the route of the old *Ghan* railway (long since dismantled) between Alice Springs and the Aboriginal settlement of Finke (Aputula). Along the

---

> ### PERMITS FOR ABORIGINAL LANDS
>
> ➡ In the outback, if you plan on driving through pastoral stations and Aboriginal communities you may need to get permission first. This is for your safety; many travellers have tackled this rugged landscape on their own and required complicated rescues after getting lost or breaking down.
>
> ➡ Permits are issued by various Aboriginal land-management authorities. Processing applications can take anywhere from a few minutes to a few days.

---

way you can call into Chambers Pillar Historical Reserve to view the colourful sandstone tower. From Finke the road heads east along the Goyder Creek, a tributary of the Finke River, before turning north towards Andado Station and, 18km further, the homestead. At Old Andado the track swings north for the 321km trip to Alice. The Old Andado Track winds its way through the Simpson Desert to link the Homestead with Alice Springs. On the way you pass the Mac Clark Conservation Reserve, which protects a stand of rare waddy trees. A high-clearance 4WD is definitely recommended and you should be equipped with high-frequency (HF) radio or emergency position-indicating radio beacon (EPIRB).

Simpson Desert

The route crossing the Simpson Desert from Mt Dare, near Finke, to Birdsville is a real test of both driver and vehicle. A 4WD is definitely required on the unmaintained tracks and you should be in a party of at least three vehicles equipped with sat phones, HF radio and/ or EPIRB.

Paved Roads

Stuart Highway

The Stuart Hwy is one of the world's truly epic road trips, covering 2834km from Darwin in the north to Port Augusta. It's paved all the way, offering gateways to the outback's major attractions, and punctuated by roadhouses at regular intervals like outback opals on a chain.

Lasseter Highway

From Alice Springs it's a six-hour drive to Uluru-Kata Tjuta National Park along the paved Stuart and then Lasseter Hwys. The road is also paved from Lasseter Hwy up to Kings Canyon along the Luritja Rd.

Victoria Highway

The Victoria Hwy runs from Katherine to Kununurra (515km). It's the only paved road connecting the NT with WA and passes through Victoria River and Timber Creek en route.

Plan Your Trip

Australia Outdoors

Australia serves up plenty of excuses to just sit back and roll your eyes across the landscape, but that same landscape lends itself to boundless outdoor pursuits – whether it's getting active on the trails and mountains on dry land, or on the swells and reefs offshore.

On the Land

Bushwalking is a major pastime in all Australian states and territories. Cycling is a great way to get around, despite the mammoth distances sometimes involved. There's also skiing in the mountains and wildlife-watching pretty much everywhere.

Bushwalking

Bushwalking (also known as hiking, trekking or tramping, depending on where you're from) is supremely popular in Australia, with vast swathes of untouched scrub and forest providing ample opportunity. Hikes vary from 20-minute jaunts off the roadside to week-long wilderness epics. The best time to head into the bush varies from state to state, but as a general rule the further north you go the more tropical and humid the climate gets: June to August are the best walking months up north; down south, summer and early autumn (December to March) are better.

Notable walks include the Overland Track (p710) and the South Coast Track (p661) in Tasmania, and the Australian Alps Walking Track, Great Ocean Walk (p556) and Great South West Walk (p565) in Victoria. The Bibbulmun Track (p951) in Western Australia (WA) is epic, as is the

When to Go

September & October

Spring brings the climax of the football season, which means a lot of yelling from the grandstands. The more actively inclined rejoice in sunnier weather and warmer days, perfect for bushwalking, wildlife watching and rock climbing.

December–February

Australians hit the beach in summer: prime time for surfing, sailing, swimming, fishing, snorkelling, skydiving, paragliding…

March–May

Autumn is a nostalgic time in Australia, with cool nights and wood smoke: perfect weather for a bushwalk or perhaps a cycling trip – not too hot, not too cold.

June–August

When winter hits, make a beeline for the outback, the tropical Top End or the snow. Pack up your 4WD and head into the desert for a hike or scenic flight, or grab your snowboard and head into the mountains for some powdery fun.

Thorsborne Trail (p386) across Hinchinbrook Island and the Gold Coast Hinterland Great Walk in Queensland.

In New South Wales (NSW) you can trek between Sydney and Newcastle on the Great North Walk, tackle the Coast Track in **Royal National Park** (☏02-9542 0648; www.nationalparks.nsw.gov.au; cars $12, pedestrians & cyclists free; ⊘side roads 7am-8.30pm), the Six Foot Track (p148) in the Blue Mountains, or scale Mt Kosciuszko (p241), Australia's highest peak. In South Australia (SA) you can bite off a chunk of the 1200km Heysen Trail (p747), while in the Northern Territory (NT) there's the majestic 233.5km Larapinta Trail (p855) and remote tracks in Kakadu National Park (p821) and Nitmiluk (Katherine Gorge) National Park (p832).

Most visitor information centres have information sheets on local national parks, and these invariably include an overview of bushwalks in the area – a good way to start planning. Most are also available online as pdfs through the relevant state or federal national park authority.

Bushwalking Safety

Before you lace up your boots, make sure you're walking in a region – and on tracks – within your realm of experience, and that you feel healthy and comfortable walking for a sustained period. Check with local authorities for weather and track

RESPONSIBLE BUSHWALKING

To help preserve the ecology and beauty of Australia, consider the following tips when bushwalking:

➡ Carry out all your rubbish, including sanitary napkins, tampons, condoms and toilet paper. Never bury your rubbish: digging disturbs soil and ground cover and encourages erosion. Buried rubbish will likely be dug up by animals, who may be injured or poisoned by it.

➡ Where there is a toilet, use it. Where there is none, bury your waste. Dig a small hole 15cm (6in) deep and at least 100m (320ft) from any watercourse. Cover the waste with soil and a rock. In snow, dig down to the soil.

➡ Don't use detergents or toothpaste in or near watercourses, even if they are biodegradable.

➡ For personal washing, use biodegradable soap and a water container at least 50m (160ft) away from the watercourse. Disperse the waste water widely to allow the soil to filter it fully.

➡ Wash cooking utensils 50m (160ft) from watercourses using a scourer, sand or snow instead of detergent.

➡ Stick to existing tracks and avoid short cuts. Walking around a muddy bog only makes it bigger – plough straight through.

➡ Don't depend on open fires for cooking. Cook on a lightweight kerosene, alcohol or Shellite (white gas) stove and avoid those powered by disposable butane gas canisters.

➡ In alpine areas, ensure that everyone is outfitted with enough clothing so that fires are not a necessity for warmth.

➡ If you light a fire, use an existing fireplace. Don't surround fires with rocks. Use only dead, fallen wood. In huts, leave wood for the next person.

➡ Do not feed the wildlife as this can lead to animals becoming dependent on hand-outs; unbalanced populations; and diseases.

➡ Study-up on local laws, regulations and etiquette about local wildlife and the environment.

➡ Pay any requisite track fees and obtain permits.

➡ Seek advice from environmental organisations such as the **Wilderness Society** (www.wilderness.org.au) the **Australian Conservation Foundation** (www.acf online.org.au) and **Planet Ark** (www.planetark.org).

updates: be aware that weather conditions and terrain can vary significantly within regions, and that seasonal changes can considerably alter any track.

Cycling

Cyclists in Australia have access to plenty of cycling routes and can tour the country for days, weekends or even multiweek trips. Or you can just rent a bike for a few hours and cycle around a city.

Standout longer routes include the **Murray to the Mountains Rail Trail** (www. murraytomountains.com.au) and the **East Gippsland Rail Trail** (www.eastgippslandrail trail.com.au) in Victoria. In WA the Munda Biddi Trail offers 900km of mountain biking, or you can rampage along the same distance on the Mawson Trail in SA. The 480km Tasmanian Trail (p635) is a north-south mountain-bike route across the length of the island state.

Rental rates charged by most outfits for road or mountain bikes start at around $25/50 per hour/day. Deposits range from $50 to $250, depending on the rental period. Most states have bicycle organisations that can provide maps and advice.

Wildlife Watching

The local wildlife is one of Australia's top selling points, and justifiably so. National parks are the best places to meet the residents, although many species are nocturnal so you may need to hone your torch (flashlight) skills to spot them. Camping in national parks greatly increases your chances of seeing something interesting. Tracking down the numerous iconic and charismatic species can be like a treasure hunt – you just have to know where to look. To get things started, here's five of the top wildlife encounters from around the country:

➡ **Whales** Hervey Bay, Queensland

➡ **Grey kangaroos** Namadgi National Park, Australian Capital Territory

➡ **Penguins** Phillip Island, Victoria

➡ **Tasmanian devils** Maria Island, Tasmania

➡ **Wombats** Cradle Mountain–Lake St Clair National Park, Tasmania

Skiing & Snowboarding

Australia has a small but enthusiastic skiing industry, with snowfields straddling

---

> ### BEST BUSHWALKS
> ➡ **Thorsborne Trail** (p386), Queensland
>
> ➡ **Great Ocean Walk** (p556), Victoria
>
> ➡ **Overland Track** (p710), Tasmania
>
> ➡ **Heysen Trail** (p747), Deep Creek Conservation Park, South Australia
>
> ➡ **Larapinta Trail** (p855), Northern Territory

the NSW–Victoria border. The season is relatively short, however, running from about mid-June to early September, and snowfalls can be unpredictable. The top places to ski:

➡ **Thredbo, NSW** (p242)

➡ **Perisher Valley, NSW** (p243)

➡ **Mt Buller, Victoria** (p600)

➡ **Falls Creek, Victoria** (p616)

➡ **Mt Hotham, Victoria** (p617)

On the Water

As Australia's national anthem will melodiously inform you, this land is 'girt by sea'. Surfing, fishing, sailing, diving and snorkelling are what people do here – national pastimes one and all. Marine-mammal-watching trips have also become popular in recent years. Inland there are vast lakes and meandering rivers, offering rafting, canoeing, kayaking and (yet more) fishing opportunities.

Surfing

Bells Beach, Cactus, Margaret River, the Superbank...mention any of them in the right company and stories of surfing legend will undoubtedly emerge. The Superbank and Bells Beach are mainstays on the Association of Surfing Professionals (ASP) World Tour calendar each year, with Bells the longest-serving host of an ASP event. Cactus dangles the lure of remote mystique, while Margaret River is a haunt for surfers chasing bigger waves.

While the aforementioned might be jewels, they're dot points in the sea of stars that Australia has to offer. Little wonder – the coastline is vast, touching the Indian, Southern and South Pacific Oceans. With that much potential swell, an intricate coastal architecture and the right conditions, you'll find anything from innocent breaks to gnarly reefs not far from all six Australian state capitals.

Here's a run-down of the key surfing spots around the country:

New South Wales

➡ Manly through to Avalon, otherwise known as Sydney's northern beaches.

➡ Byron Bay, Lennox Head and Angourie Point on the far north coast.

➡ Nambucca Heads and Crescent Head on the mid-north coast.

➡ The areas around Jervis Bay and Ulladulla on the south coast.

Queensland

➡ The Superbank (a 2km-long sandbar stretching from Snapper Rocks to Kirra Point).

➡ Burleigh Heads through to Surfers Paradise on the Gold Coast.

➡ North Stradbroke Island in Moreton Bay.

➡ Caloundra, Alexandra Heads, near Maroochydore, and Noosa on the Sunshine Coast.

South Australia

➡ Cactus Beach, west of Ceduna on remote Point Sinclair – internationally recognised for quality and consistency.

➡ Greenly Beach on the western side of the Eyre Peninsula.

➡ Pennington Bay – the most consistent surf on Kangaroo Island.

➡ Pondalowie Bay and Stenhouse Bay on the Yorke Peninsula, part of Innes National Park.

➡ Victor Harbor, Port Elliot and Middleton Beach south of Adelaide.

Tasmania

➡ Marrawah on the exposed northwest coast – can offer huge waves.

➡ St Helens and Bicheno on the east coast.

➡ Eaglehawk Neck on the Tasman Peninsula. Legendary Shipstern Bluff isn't far from here – Australia's heaviest wave.

➡ Closer to Hobart, Cremorne Point and Clifton Beach.

Victoria

➡ Bells Beach, the spiritual home of Australian surfing (...when the wave is on, few would argue, but the break is notoriously inconsistent).

➡ Smiths Beach on Phillip Island.

➡ Point Leo, Flinders, Gunnamatta, Rye and Portsea on the Mornington Peninsula.

➡ On the southwest coast, Barwon Heads, Point Lonsdale, Torquay and numerous spots along the Great Ocean Rd.

Western Australia

➡ Margaret River, Gracetown and Yallingup in the southwest.

➡ Trigg Point and Scarborough Beach, just north of Perth.

➡ Further north at Geraldton and Kalbarri.

➡ Down south at Denmark on the Southern Ocean.

Diving & Snorkelling

The Great Barrier Reef (p399) has more dazzling diving and snorkelling sites than you can poke a fin at. Put simply, the reef is one of the world's best places for diving and snorkelling.

In Western Australia, Ningaloo Reef (p982) is every bit as interesting as the east-coast reefs, without the tourist numbers. There are spectacular artificial reefs here too, created by sunken ships at Albany and Dunsborough.

The Rapid Bay jetty off the Gulf St Vincent coast (p746) in SA is renowned for its abundant marine life, and in Tasmania the Bay of Fires (p676) and Eaglehawk Neck (p662) are popular spots. In NSW head for Jervis Bay (p226) and Fish Rock Cave off South West Rocks.

Fishing

Barramundi fishing is hugely popular across the Top End. In the NT, these are the best fishing spots:

➡ **Daly River** (p820)

➡ **Cobourg Peninsula** (p830)

➡ **Eastern Arnhem Land** (p831)

➡ **Mary River National Park** (p817)

➡ **Borroloola** (p845)

Over on the Queensland coast of the Gulf of Carpentaria, try Karumba (p441) and Lake Tinaroo in Queensland.

Humpback whale, Hervey Bay (p337)

Ocean fishing is possible right around the country, from pier or beach, or you can organise a deep-sea charter. There are magnificent glacial lakes and clear highland streams for trout fishing in Tasmania.

Before casting a line, be warned that strict limits to catches and sizes apply in Australia, and many species are threatened and therefore protected. Check local guidelines via fishing equipment stores or through the relevant state-government fishing bodies for information.

Whale-, Dolphin- & Marine-Life-Watching

Southern right and humpback **whales** pass close to Australia's southern coast on their migratory route between the Antarctic and warmer waters. The best spots for whale-watching cruises are Hervey Bay in Queensland, Eden in southern NSW, the mid-north coast of NSW, Warrnambool in Victoria, Albany on WA's southwest cape, and numerous places in SA. Whale-watching season is roughly May to October. For whale sharks and manta rays try WA's Ningaloo Marine Park.

Dolphins can be seen year-round along the east coast at Jervis Bay, Port Stephens and Byron Bay in NSW; off the coast of WA at Bunbury and Rockingham; off North Stradbroke Island in

Queensland; and you can swim with them off Sorrento in Victoria. You can also see **little penguins** in Victoria on Phillip Island. In WA, **fur seals** and **sea lions** can be seen at Rottnest Island, Esperance, Rockingham and Green Head, and all manner of beautiful sea creatures inhabit Monkey Mia (including **dugongs**). Sea lions also visit the aptly named (though not technically correct) Seal Bay on SA's Kangaroo Island.

Resources

➡ **Bicycles Network Australia** (www.bicycles.net.au) Information, news and links.

➡ **Bushwalking Australia** (www.bushwalking australia.org) Website for the national body, with links to state and territory bushwalking clubs and federations.

➡ **Coastalwatch** (www.coastalwatch.com) Surf-cams, reports and weather charts for all the best breaks.

➡ **Dive-Oz** (www.diveoz.com.au) Online scuba-diving resource.

➡ **Fishing Australia** (www.fishingaustralia.com.au) Comprehensive fishing coverage.

➡ **Ski Online** (www.ski.com.au) Commercial site with holiday offers plus snow-cams, forecasts and reports.

1. Sydney Harbour Bridge (p70) 2. Degraves St, Melbourne (p467)
3. Mossman River, Daintree National Park (p424) 4. Noosa (p321)

PISAPHOTOGRAPHY / SHUTTERSTOCK ©

Australia's Eastern States

Hit the road, Jack: Australia's eastern states – Queensland, New South Wales, the Australian Capital Territory (ACT) and Victoria – are road-tripping nirvana, with picture-perfect beaches, rainforests, hip cities and the Great Barrier Reef.

Into the Wild

Strung out for more than 18,000km, Australia's east coast is a rippling ribbon of beaches and rampant wildlife. Offshore, the astonishing Great Barrier Reef is a 2000km-long hyper-coloured haven for tropical marine life. Fringing the land are myriad islands and brilliant beaches, with Australia's best surf peeling in. Inland are bewitching national parks, lush rainforests, jagged peaks and native critters aplenty.

City Scenes

Home to Indigenous Australians for millennia, Sydney was also Australia's first European settlement. Sassy and ambitious yet unpretentious, the city remains a honey-pot lure for anyone looking for a good time. To the south, Melbourne is Australia's arts and coffee capital; boomtown Brisbane is a glam patchwork of inner-city neighbourhoods. And don't forget Australia's capital, Canberra – so much more than a political filing cabinet!

Action Stations

Exploring Australia's eastern states is an exercise in, well...exercise! The sun is shining and fit-looking locals are outdoors – jogging, swimming, bushwalking, surfing, cycling, kayaking, snorkelling... Why not join in? Or just head for the beach, where the locals let it all hang out.

Eat, Drink & Celebrate

Australia's big east-coast cities lift the lid on a rich culinary experience, with fantastic cafes, sprawling food markets and world-class restaurants. After dark, moody wine bars, student-filled speakeasies and boisterous Aussie pubs provide plenty of excuses to bend an elbow, chew the fat and maybe watch a bit of football.

DAVID KIRKLAND / TOURISM NT ©

1. Artist, Injalak Arts & Crafts Centre (p830) 2. McLaren Vale (p743)
3. Kata Tjuta (the Olgas; p877) 4. Perth (p879)

Australia's Centre & West

MILTON WORDLEY / GETTY IMAGES ©

Welcome to Australia's epic centre, South Australia and the Northern Territory – wild and beautiful country and the nation's Indigenous heartland. Further west is (surprise, surprise) Western Australia, a vast state framed by 12,500km of spectacular coastline.

The Desert & the Tropics

Call that Australia? *This* is Australia. Ever since *Crocodile Dundee* brought Kakadu to the world's attention, the outback and Top End have been on the radar for their impressive portfolio of quintessentially Aussie land forms. From Uluru and Kata Tjuta rising improbably from the desert to the pristine coastline of Arnhem Land, it's hard to escape the feeling that in this land lies eternity...

Aboriginal Connections

In the Northern Territory it's relatively easy to cross the cultural frontier and meet Indigenous Australians on their terms: on an intimate exploration of country led by an Indigenous guide, in quiet conversation with artists at work, or in the timeless rituals of a festival.

South Australia Awaits

South Australia is home to Australia's premier wine regions: the Barossa Valley, McLaren Vale, Clare Valley, Adelaide Hills and the Coonawarra. Also here is wonderful Kangaroo Island and underrated Adelaide, a hip city with amazing festivals, a simmering arts scene and great pubs, bars and foodie culture.

The Wild West

If the huge expanse of Western Australia (WA) was a separate nation, it would be the world's 10th-largest country. Most West Australians live on the coast – Perth and neighbouring Fremantle are cosmopolitan cities – yet you can wander along a WA beach without seeing another footprint, engage with abundant wildlife, or camp alone and stargaze in a national park.

Regions at a Glance

Sydney & New South Wales

Surf Beaches
Food
Wilderness

Bondi & Beyond
Sydney's surf beaches can't be beaten. Bondi is the name on everyone's lips, but the waves here get crowded. Head south to Maroubra or Cronulla, or north to Manly, for more elbow room.

Culinary Sydney
Modern Australian (aka Mod Oz) is the name of the culinary game here – a pan-Pacific fusion of styles and ingredients with plenty of Sydney seafood. Serve it up with a harbour view and you've got a winning combo.

Sydney's Hinterland Parks
New South Wales (NSW) has some of the best national parks in Australia. Around Sydney there's the Royal National Park, with fab walks and beaches; waterways and wildlife in Ku-ring-gai Chase National Park; and vast tracts of native forest in Wollemi National Park in the Blue Mountains.

p66

Canberra & the ACT

History & Culture
Wineries
Politics

National Treasures
Canberra offers the National Gallery of Australia, with its magnificent collections of Australian, Asian and Aboriginal and Torres Strait Islander art; the National Museum of Australia, whose imaginative exhibits provide insights into the Australian heart and soul; the moving and fascinating Australian War Memorial; and the entirely impressive National Portrait Gallery.

Capital Wines
Canberra's wine industry is relatively new, but it is winning admirers with a consistent crop of fine cool-climate wines. The Canberra vineyards are an easy and picturesque drive from downtown.

The National Debate
Politics is what really makes Canberra tick: find out for yourself at a rigorous session of Question Time at Parliament House, or visit Old Parliament House and check out the Museum of Australian Democracy.

p252

Queensland

Diving & Snorkelling
Beaches & Islands
Urban Culture

Great Barrier Reef

Blessed with the fish-rich, Technicolor Great Barrier Reef, Queensland is the place for world-class diving and snorkelling. Take a day trip, bob around in a glass-bottom boat, or just paddle out from the beach on a reef-fringed island.

Explore the Coast

There's great surf along Queensland's south coast, and reefs and rainforest-cloaked islands further north, but for picture-perfect white-sand beaches and turquoise seas, the Whitsundays are unmissable: get on a yacht and enjoy.

Brisbane Rising

Watch out Sydney and Melbourne, Brisbane is on the rise! Hip bars, fab restaurants, a vibrant arts culture and good coffee everywhere: 'Australia's new world city' is an ambitious, edgy, progressive place to be.

p267

Melbourne & Victoria

History
Sports
Surf Beaches

Golden Days

Walk the boom-town streets of 1850s gold-rush towns. With their handsome, lace-fringed buildings, Melbourne, Bendigo and Ballarat are rich reminders of how good Victoria had it in those days.

Footy & Cricket

Melbourne is the spiritual home of Australian Rules football: grab some friends and boot a ball around a wintry city park. Summer means cricket: local kids are either watching it on TV, talking about it or out in the streets playing it.

The Surf Coast

With relentless Southern Ocean swells surging in, there's plenty of quality (if chilly) surf along Victoria's Great Ocean Road. Bells Beach is Australia's most famous break, and home to the Rip Curl Pro surf comp every Easter.

p453

Tasmania

Food
Wildlife
History

Culinary Excellence

Tasmania produces larders full of fine food and drink. Chefs from all over Australia are increasingly besotted with Tasmania's excellent fresh produce, including briny fresh salmon and oysters, cool-climate wines, hoppy craft beers and plump fruit and vegetables.

Wombats, Whales & Devils

You might not spy a thylacine, but on a Tassie bushwalk you can see wallabies, possums, pademelons, iconic Tasmanian devils and possibly a snake or two. There's also whale-, seal- and penguin-spotting along the coast.

Colonial Stories

Tasmania's bleak colonial history is on display in Port Arthur and along the Heritage Hwy, made all the more potent by dramatic landscapes seemingly out of proportion with the state's compact footprint.

p629

Adelaide & South Australia

Wine
Festivals
National Parks

Australia's Best Wines

We challenge you to visit South Australia (SA) without inadvertently driving through a wine region. You may have heard of the Barossa Valley, Clare Valley and McLaren Vale, but what about the lesser-known Langhorne Creek, Mt Benson, Currency Creek or the Adelaide Hills regions? All top drops worth pulling over for.

A Full Summer Calendar

At the end of every summer Adelaide erupts with festivals: visual arts, world music, theatre, busking and the growl of V8 engines. The only question is, why do it all at the same time?

Coorong to Flinders Ranges

The dunes and lagoons of Coorong National Park are amazing, but for sheer geologic majesty visit Ikara (Wilpena Pound), part of the craggy, rust-red Flinders Ranges National Park in central South Australia.

p714

Darwin & the Northern Territory

Landscapes
Wildlife
Indigenous Culture

The Drama of the Outback

Many of Australia's most dramatic landscapes – Uluru, Kata Tjuta (The Olgas), Kings Canyon, Nitmiluk (Katherine Gorge), Kakadu – are found here. And then there's the sheer immensity of the outback...

Mammals, Birds & Crocs

The Northern Territory outback is brilliant for wildlife, from dingoes to kangaroos, wallabies to emus, while up north Kakadu has brilliant wildlife (crocs!) and even better birding.

Indigenous Meeting Places

Nowhere in Australia can you get quite this connected to Australia's Indigenous people and their culture, from wonderful community art centres to festivals and Indigenous guides.

p798

Perth & Western Australia

Coastal Scenery
Adventure
Wildlife

A Beautiful Coast

There are boundless beaches along Western Australia's spectacular 12,500km-long coastline. But for sheer sandy delight, visit the isolated beaches leading down to the shallow lagoons and reefs of the World Heritage–listed Ningaloo Marine Park.

Explore the Wild

Bring it on: take the ride of your life along the bone-shaking Gibb River Road, to the exceptional Mitchell Falls and remote Kalumburu. Jump on a speedboat and head full throttle for the Horizontal Waterfalls, then grab a canoe and paddle down the mighty Ord River.

Animals Galore

You can spy sharks, rays, turtles and migrating whales along WA's central west coast. Inland, birds flock to the oasis pools of Millstream-Chichester National Park, and pythons and rock wallabies hide in the shadows of Karijini National Park.

p878

On the Road

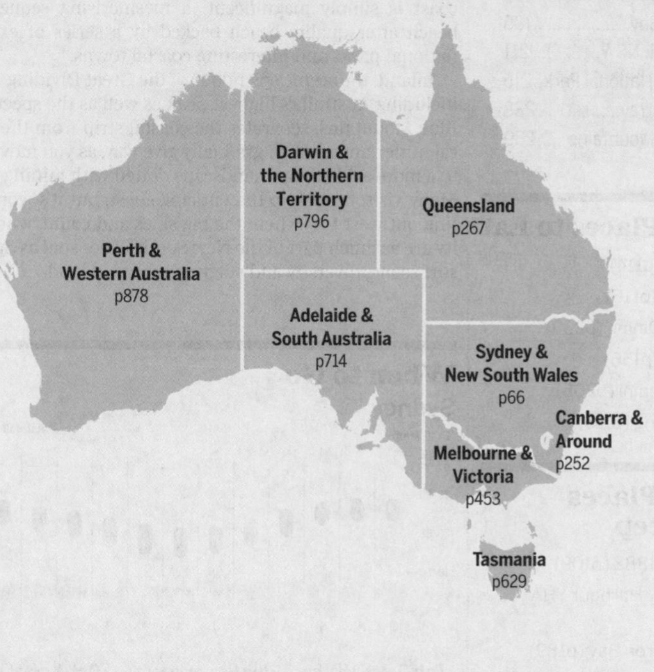

**Darwin &
the Northern
Territory**
p796

Queensland
p267

**Perth &
Western Australia**
p878

**Adelaide &
South Australia**
p714

**Sydney &
New South Wales**
p66

**Canberra &
Around**
p252

**Melbourne &
Victoria**
p453

Tasmania
p629

Sydney & New South Wales

POP 7.7 MILLION / 🗐 02

Best Places to Eat

➜ Quay (p114)

➜ Sepia (p116)

➜ Biota Dining (p239)

➜ Muse (p156)

➜ Lolli Redini (p205)

➜ Mr Wong (p115)

Best Places to Sleep

➜ Ovolo 1888 (p109)

➜ Sydney Harbour YHA (p108)

➜ 28° Byron Bay (p189)

➜ ADGE Boutique Apartment Hotel (p111)

➜ Bannisters by the Sea (p229)

Why Go?

Australia's most populous state is home to its largest city: glitzy, vibrant, intoxicating Sydney, an unforgettable metropolis in a privileged natural setting. Bondi Beach and the harbour are justly famous, but in reality the whole NSW coast is simply magnificent: a mesmerising sequence of beach after quality beach backed by a series of excellent national parks and interesting coastal towns.

Inland, the scenic splendour of the Great Dividing Range, including Australia's highest peak as well as the spectacular Blue Mountains, separates the coastal strip from the pastoral hinterlands, which gradually give way, as you move west, to a more arid outback landscape dotted with mining towns. Many visitors stick to the enticing coast, but it's worth getting out west too, where the big skies and country hospitality are as much part of the New South Wales soul as Sydney's surf scene, diversity and staggeringly good food.

When to Go
Sydney

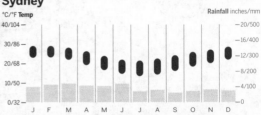

Feb Great weather but less crowded beaches, plus Mardi Gras gearing up in Sydney.

Jun Bearable temperatures out west; cosy snuggling in ski lodges and Blue Mountains guesthouses.

Oct A great month for whale watching up and down the east coast.

ⓘ Transport

Sydney has Australia's busiest airport, and domestic flights, many operated by **Regional Express** (REX; ☎ 13 17 13; www.rex.com.au) radiate out to numerous NSW airports.

Trains reach many towns in northern and central NSW, and there's a line out west to Broken Hill and onwards.

Bus services may not be frequent, but they are reliable and cover most of the places that you can't reach by train.

NSW TrainLink (☎ 13 22 32; www.nswtrainlink. info) connects Sydney with northern and country NSW, Melbourne, Brisbane and Canberra.

SYDNEY

POP 5.1 MILLION / ☎ 02

More laid-back than any major metropolis should rightly be, Australia's largest settlement is one of the great international cities. Blessed with outstanding natural scenery across its magnificent harbour, stunning beaches and glorious national parks, Sydney is home to three of the country's major icons – the Harbour Bridge, the Opera House and Bondi Beach. But the attractions definitely don't stop there. This is the country's oldest and most diverse city, a sun-kissed settlement that is characterised by a wonderful food culture, hedonistic attitudes, intriguing history and the brash charm of its residents.

History

What is now Greater Sydney is the ancestral home of at least three distinct Aboriginal peoples, each with their own language. Ku-ring-gai was generally spoken on the northern shore, Dharawal along the coast south of Botany Bay, and Dharug from the harbour to the Blue Mountains. The coastal area around Sydney is the ancestral home of the Eora people (which literally means 'from this place'), who were divided into clans such as the Gadigal and the Wangal.

In 1770 Lieutenant (later Captain) James Cook dropped anchor at Botany Bay. The ship's arrival alarmed the local people, and Cook noted in his journal: 'All they seem'd to want was for us to be gone.'

In 1788 the British came back, this time for good. Under the command of naval captain Arthur Phillip, the 'First Fleet' included a motley crew of convicts, marines and livestock. Upon arriving at Botany Bay, Phillip was disappointed by what he saw – particularly the lack of a fresh water source – and ordered the ships to sail north, where he found 'the finest harbour in the world'. The date of the landing at Sydney Cove was 26 January, an occasion that is commemorated each year with the Australia Day public holiday (known to many Indigenous members of the community as 'Invasion Day').

Armed resistance to the British was led by Indigenous warriors including Pemulwuy (c 1750–1802), a member of the Dharug-speaking Bidjigal clan from around Botany Bay, and Musquito (c 1780–1825), an Eora man from the north shore of Port Jackson. The Indigenous fighters were eventually crushed and the British colony wrested control. The fleet brought with them European diseases such as smallpox, which devastated the Eora people (only three of the Gadigal clan are said to have survived).

The early days of settlement were difficult, with famine a constant threat, but gradually a bustling port was established with stone houses, warehouses and streets. The surrounding bushland was gradually converted into farms, vegetable gardens and orchards.

In 1793 Phillip returned to London and self-serving military officers took control of Government House. Soon, the vigorous new society that the first governor had worked so hard to establish began to unravel. Eventually London took action, dispatching a new governor, Lachlan Macquarie, to restore the rule of law. Under his rule many grand buildings were constructed (most of which still stand today), setting out a vision for Sydney that would move it from its prison-camp origins to a worthy outpost of the British Empire.

In 1813 the Blue Mountains were penetrated by explorers Blaxland, Lawson and Wentworth, opening the way for the colony to expand onto the vast fertile slopes and plains of the west. By the 1830s the Lachlan, Macquarie, Murrumbidgee and Darling river systems had been explored and the NSW colony started to thrive.

The 20th century saw an influx of new migrants from Europe (especially after WWII), Asia and the Middle East, changing the dynamics of the city as it spread westwards and became the multicultural metropolis that it is today.

QUEENSLAND

Lightning Ridge
Tibooburra
Milparinka
Wanaaring
Brewarrina
Walgett
Bourke
Mt Oxley (309m)
Macquarie Marshes Nature Reserve
White Cliffs
Gunderbooka National Park
A71
Coonamble
Tilpa
Darling River
Mt Grenfell Historic Site
Mutawintji National Park
Cobar
A32
Mundi Mundi Plain
Umberumberka Reservoir
A32
Wilcannia
B87
Silverton
Broken Hill
Menindee Lakes
Menindee
B75
Condobolin
Parkes
A39
Kinchega National Park
Willandra National Park
Forbes
B79
Mungo National Park
10
Hillston
Lachlan River
B64
Wentworth
Cocoparra National Park
Young
B64
Mildura
Griffith
Leeton
Temora
Robinvale
Balranald
Hay
Murrumbidgee River
Junee
Jugiong
A20
Narrandera
M31
SOUTH AUSTRALIA
B400
Colambeyan National Park
Newell
Hwy
Wagga Wagga
Gundag
Deniliquin
Jerilderie
Tocumwal
A39
Corowa
Albury
Snowy Mountains
Moama
Wodonga
Echuca
Kosciuszko National Park
8
VICTORIA
Thre
Bendigo
Murray River

Sydney & New South Wales Highlights

1 **Sydney** (p67) Living it up beachside and harbourside in this captivating, diverse city.

2 **Blue Mountains** (p142) Gazing out over sandstone cliffs to blue-tinged eucalypt forests below.

3 **Hunter Valley** (p151) Sipping semillon and enjoying the finer things in life in boutique vineyards.

4 **Lord Howe Island** (p249) Climbing Mount Gower for an unforgettable view way out in the Pacific.

5 **Waterfall Way** (p175) Driving this route through some of the North Coast's most enchanting landscapes.

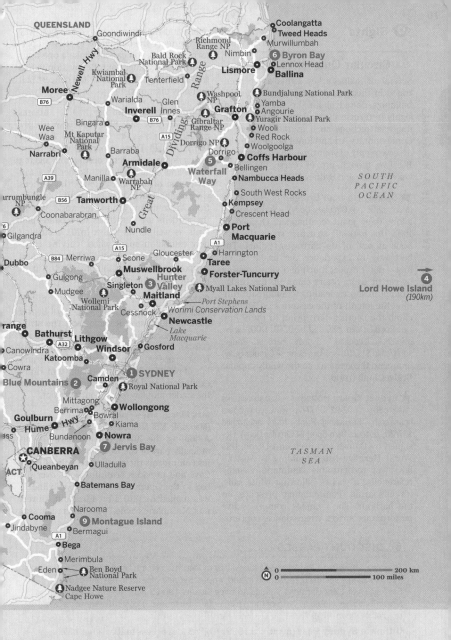

QUEENSLAND
Goondiwindi
Coolangatta
Tweed Heads
Murwillumbah
Richmond
Range NP   Nimbin
Bald Rock
National Park   6 Byron Bay
Lismore   Lennox Head
Tenterfield   Ballina

Kwiambal
National
Park

Moree
B76

Warialda
Glen
Inverell Innes
B76

Washpool
NP   Bundjalung National Park
Grafton   Yamba
Angourie
Yuragir National Park
Wooli
Red Rock
Woolgoolga

Wee
Waa
Bingara

Mt Kaputar
National
Park
Barraba

Gibraltar
Range NP

Dorrigo NP
Dorrigo

Narrabri

Armidale   Coffs Harbour
Bellingen
5 Waterfall
Way   Nambucca Heads

A39
Manilla
Warrabah
NP

South West Rocks

Kempsey
Crescent Head

Tamworth
B56

Coonabarabran

Nundle

Port
Macquarie
A1

Gilgandra

A15
Gloucester   Harrington

Dubbo
B84 Merriwa   Scone
Taree
Forster-Tuncurry

Muswellbrook
Hunter
Gulgong   Singleton 3 Valley
Maitland
Myall Lakes National Park

Mudgee
Wollemi
National Park   Cessnock

Port Stephens
Worimi Conservation Lands

range
Bathurst   Lithgow
A32
Canowindra

Newcastle
Lake
Macquarie

Gosford

Katoomba
Windsor

Cowra

Blue Mountains 2

Camden 1 SYDNEY

Mittagong
Berrima
Goulburn   Bowral
Hume   Hwy

Royal National Park

Wollongong
Kiama

Bundanoon   Nowra
CANBERRA   7 Jervis Bay

ACT
Queanbeyan   Ulladulla

Batemans Bay

Narooma
Cooma   9 Montague Island
Jindabyne   Bermagui
A1
Bega

Merimbula
Eden   Ben Boyd
National Park
Nadgee Nature Reserve
Cape Howe

SOUTH
PACIFIC
OCEAN

4
Lord Howe Island
(190km)

TASMAN
SEA

N   0   200 km
    0   100 miles

6 **Byron Bay** (p185)
Unwinding into the unique vibe
of this iconic coastal town.

7 **Jervis Bay** (p226)
Marvelling at the white white
sands and sparkling waters of
this large, idyllic bay.

8 **Kosciuszko National Park**
(p241) Walking the trails in
this highland park so beautiful
it makes the heart sing.

9 **Montague Island**
(p231) Watching seals,

penguins, dolphins and whales
at this marvellous wildlife spot.

10 **Mungo National Park**
(p215) Appreciating the Indigenous history and stirring
scenery of an accessible slice
of outback.

👁 Sights

SYDNEY & NEW SOUTH WALES SYDNEY

◉ Circular Quay & The Rocks

Several of Sydney's key sights are concentrated in this area. Museums and venerable buildings dotted about the Rocks give insights into Australia's colonial history, while major attractions such as the Museum of Contemporary Art and Royal Botanic Garden deserve plenty of your time. The indisputable Big Two, though, are, of course, the Sydney Opera House and Sydney Harbour Bridge.

★**Sydney Harbour Bridge**　　　BRIDGE
(Map p80; 🚇Circular Quay) Sydneysiders adore their giant 'coathanger'. Opened in 1932, this majestic structure spans the harbour at one of its narrowest points. The best way to experience the bridge is on foot – don't expect much of a view crossing by car or train. Stairs climb up the bridge from both shores, leading to a footpath running the length of the eastern side. You can climb the southeastern pylon to the **Pylon Lookout** (Map p80; 🚲02-9240 1100; www. pylonlookout.com.au; Sydney Harbour Bridge; adult/child $15/10; ⊗10am-5pm; 🚇Circular Quay) or ascend the great arc on the wildly popular BridgeClimb (p106).

★**Sydney Opera House**　　NOTABLE BUILDING
(Map p80; 🚲02-9250 7777; www.sydneyopera house.com; Bennelong Point; tours adult/child $37/20; ⊗tours 9am-5pm; 🚇Circular Quay) Designed by Danish architect Jørn Utzon, this World Heritage–listed building is Australia's most recognisable landmark. Visually referencing a yacht's billowing white sails, it's a soaring, commanding presence on the harbour. The complex comprises five performance spaces where dance, concerts,

opera and theatre are staged. The best way to experience the building is to attend a performance, but you can also take a one-hour multilingual guided tour. Renovation works from 2017 to 2019 will close the concert hall and may disrupt visits.

★**Royal Botanic Garden**　　GARDENS
(Map p80; 🚲02-9231 8111; www.rbgsyd.nsw.gov. au; Mrs Macquaries Rd; ⊗7am-dusk; 🚇Circular Quay) 🌿**FREE** These expansive gardens are the city's favourite picnic destination, jogging route and snuggling spot. Bordering Farm Cove, east of the Opera House, the gardens were established in 1816 and feature plant life from Australia and around the world. Within the gardens are hothouses with palms and ferns as well as the Calyx (p70), a striking new exhibition space whose curving glasshouse gallery features a wall of greenery and temporary plant-y exhibitions. Grab a park map at any of the main entrances.

Calyx　　GALLERY
(Map p80; www.rbgsyd.nsw.gov.au; Royal Botanic Garden; ⊗10am-4pm; 🚇Martin Place) This striking new exhibition pavilion in the Botanic Garden incorporates a cool, curving glasshouse space with a living wall of greenery and lots of plants. It hosts high-quality temporary exhibitions on botanical themes. Check out the spider monkey topiary out the front.

Mrs Macquaries Point　　PARK
(Map p74; Mrs Macquaries Rd; 🚇Circular Quay) Adjoining the Royal Botanic Gardens but officially part of the Domain, Mrs Macquaries Point forms the northeastern tip of Farm Cove and provides beautiful views over the bay to the Opera House and city skyline. It was named in 1810 after Elizabeth, Governor Macquarie's wife, who ordered a seat

---

ℹ DISCOUNT PASSES

Sydney Museums Pass (www.sydneylivingmuseums.com.au; adult/child $24/16) Allows a single visit to 12 museums in and around Sydney, including the Museum of Sydney, Hyde Park Barracks, Justice & Police Museum and Susannah Place. It's valid for a month and available at each of the participating museums. It costs the same as two regular museum visits.

Ultimate Sydney Pass (adult/child $99/70) Provides access to the high-profile, costly attractions operated by British-based Merlin Entertainment: Sydney Tower Eye (including the Skywalk), Sydney Sea Life Aquarium, Wild Life Sydney Zoo, Madame Tussauds and Manly Sea Life Sanctuary. It's available from each of the venues, but is often considerably cheaper online through the venue websites. If you plan on visiting only some of these attractions, discounted Sydney Attractions Passes are available in any combination you desire.

SYDNEY IN...

Two Days

Start your first day by getting a train to Milsons Point and walking back to the Rocks across the **Harbour Bridge**. Then explore the Rocks area, delving into all the narrow lanes. Next, follow the harbour past the **Opera House** to the **Royal Botanic Garden** and on to the **Art Gallery of NSW** (p75). That night, enjoy a performance at the **Opera House** (p133) or check out the action in Chinatown or Darlinghurst. Next day, spend some time soaking up the sun and scene at **Bondi** (p87) – be sure to take the clifftop walk to Coogee and then make your way back to Bondi for a sunset dinner at **Icebergs Dining Room** (p121).

Four Days

On day three, board a ferry and sail through the harbour to Manly, where you can swim at the beach or follow the **Manly Scenic Walkway** (p104). That night, head to Surry Hills for drinks and dinner. On day four, learn about Sydney's convict heritage at the **Hyde Park Barracks Museum** (p75) and then spend the afternoon shopping in Paddington or Newtown.

One Week

With a week, you can spare a couple of days to visit the majestic **Blue Mountains** (p142), fitting in a full day of bushwalking before rewarding yourself with a gourmet dinner. Back in Sydney, explore Watsons Bay, Darling Harbour and **Taronga Zoo** (p95).

chiselled into the rock from which she could view the harbour. **Mrs Macquarie's Chair**, as it's known, remains to this day.

⭐ **Rocks Discovery Museum**   MUSEUM
(Map p80; ☑ 02-9240 8680; www.therocks.com; Kendall Lane; ⊙ 10am-5pm; ⛴ Circular Quay) FREE Divided into four chronological displays – Warrane (pre-1788), Colony (1788–1820), Port (1820–1900) and Transformations (1900 to the present) – this small, excellent museum, tucked away down a Rocks laneway, digs deep into the area's history and leads you on an artefact-rich tour. Sensitive attention is given to the Rocks' original inhabitants, the Gadigal (Cadigal) people, and there are interesting tales of early colonial characters.

⭐ **Sydney Observatory**   OBSERVATORY
(Map p80; ☑ 02-9217 0111; http://maas.museum/sydney-observatory; 1003 Upper Fort St; ⊙ 10am-5pm; ⛴ Circular Quay) FREE Built in the 1850s, Sydney's copper-domed, Italianate sandstone observatory squats atop pretty **Observatory Hill**, overlooking the harbour. Inside is a collection of vintage apparatus, including Australia's oldest working telescope (1874), as well as background on Australian astronomy and transits of Venus. Also on offer are entertaining tours (adult/child $10/8), which include a planetarium show. Bookings are essential for night-time star-gazing sessions (adult/child $22/17), which run Monday to Saturday, and Aboriginal sky storytelling sessions (adult/child $18/12). All tours are great for kids.

⭐ **Walsh Bay**   WATERFRONT
(Map p80; www.walshbaysydney.com.au; Hickson Rd; ⛴ 324, 325, 998, ⛴ Wynyard) This section of Dawes Point waterfront was Sydney's busiest before the advent of container shipping and the construction of new port facilities at Botany Bay. The last decade has seen the Federation-era wharves here gentrified beyond belief, morphing into luxury hotels, apartments, theatre spaces, power-boat marinas, cafes and restaurants. It's a picturesque place to stroll, combining the wharves and harbour views here with nearby Barangaroo Park.

Barangaroo Reserve   PARK
(Map p80; www.barangaroo.com; Hickson Rd; ⊙ 24hr; ⛴ 324, 325, ⛴ Circular Quay) Part of Barangaroo, the major redevelopment project of what was a commercial port, this park sits on a headland with wonderful harbour perspectives. It only opened in 2015, so still looks a bit bare in parts as the native trees and plants have got some growing to do among the quarried sandstone blocks. A lift connecting the park's three levels is good for weary legs. There is underground parking and a cultural space to come.

Sydney Harbour

←NORTH

Manly

North Head

South Head

Middle Head

Georges Head

Camp Cove

Chowder Head

Balmoral Beach

Hunters Bay

Taronga Zoo
Even if you've hired a car, the best way to reach this excellent zoo is by ferry. Zip to the top in a cable car then wind your way back down to the wharf.

Taronga Zoo

Manly
Catch a ferry to Manly to explore the outer harbour. Stroll to the beach, drink at the wharf and make sure you're well positioned on your return journey for any photos you missed earlier.

Little Sirius Cove

Mosman Bay

Cremorne Point

Kirribilli
Unless the prime minister or governor-general invite you into their homes for tea, the best views you'll get of Kirribilli House and Admiralty House are from the water. Keep your eyes peeled.

Neutral Bay

Kirribilli House

Kirribilli

Admiralty House

Sydney Harbour Bridge

Luna Park

North Sydney Olympic Pool

Sydney Harbour Bridge
As you pass by the bridge, keep an eye out for the hardy souls trudging along the top on their bridge climb. Head here at sunrise or sunset for golden harbour views.

TOP TIP
Don't forget that the harbour continues west of the bridge. Back up a Manly trip with a river ferry service.

Watsons Bay
Imagine Watsons Bay as the isolated fishing village it once was as you pull into its sheltered wharf. Stroll around South Head for views up the harbour and over ocean-battered cliffs.

Fort Denison
Known as Pinchgut, this fortified speck was once a place of fearsome punishment. The bodies of executed convicts were left to hang here as a grisly warning to all; the local Aborigines were horrified.

DINOZZAVER/SHUTTERSTOCK ©

FERRIES
Circular Quay is the hub for state-run Sydney Ferries; nine separate routes leave from here, journeying to 38 different wharves.

Watsons Bay

Macquarie Lighthouse

Vaucluse Bay

Shark Bay

Rose Bay

Point Piper

Bradleys Head

Shark Island

Double Bay

Darling Point

Clark Island

Garden Island

Naval Base

Elizabeth Bay

Fort Denison

Mrs Macquaries Point

Potts Point

Woolloomooloo Finger Wharf

Sydney Opera House

Government House

Farm Cove

Royal Botanic Garden

Circular Quay

The Rocks

Sydney Opera House
You can clamber all over it and walk around it, but nothing beats the perspective you get as your ferry glides past the Opera House's dazzling sails. Have your camera at the ready.

Circular Quay
Circular Quay has been at the centre of Sydney life since the First Fleet dropped anchor here in 1788. Book your ferry ticket, check the indicator boards for the correct pier and get on board.

Sydney

Lane Cove National Park

NORTH BALGOWLAH

CASTLE COVE

Ku-ring-gai Chase National Park (15km)

SEAFORTH

CLONTARF

CHATSWOOD

Chatswood

CASTLECRAG

28

Clontarf Beach

WILLOUGHBY

Artarmon

Manly Rd

Epping Rd

NORTHBRIDGE

Middle

Gore Hill Fwy

LANE COVE

NAREMBURN

Pacific Hwy

CAMMERAY

Long Bay

Spit Rd

BALMORAL

Hunters Bay

RIVERVIEW

St Leonards

CROWS NEST

CREMORNE

Military Rd

5

GREENWICH

Wollstonecraft

Falcon St

NEUTRAL BAY

MOSMAN

Bradleys Head Rd

Chowder Bay

LONGUEVILLE

67

54

Waverton

45

64

Taronga Zoo

Taylors Bay

Lane Cove River

73

North Sydney

68

70

WOOLWICH

Mosman Bay

71

Robertsons Point

Bradleys Head

56

Milsons Point

65

61

32

55

Balls Head

62

12

KIRRIBILLI

35

60

57

Cockatoo Island Visitor Centre

9

BIRCHGROVE

63

Snails Bay

McMahons Point

1

Mrs Macquaries Point

Sydney Harbour (Port Jackson)

41

52

53

See Central Sydney Map (p80)

48

13

Clarke Island

POINT PIPER

BALMAIN

BALMAIN EAST

22

58

40

See Darling Harbour & Pyrmont Map (p86)

27

76

40

PYRMONT

See Kings Cross, Darlinghurst & Woolloomooloo Map (p88)

59

DOUBLE BAY

Balmain Rd

Rozelle Bay

34

38

Edgecliff

Jubilee Park

50

See Haymarket & Chinatown Map (p84)

46

Lilyfield

43

Glebe

39

ULTIMO

ANNANDALE

GLEBE

44

Bondi Junction

51

See Newtown & the Inner West Map (p98)

See Surry Hills Map (p101)

See Paddington & Centennial Park Map (p96)

BONDI JUNCTION

Blue Mountains (90km)

WAVERLEY

Queens Park

Stanmore

54

St Peters

Green Square

WATERLOO

ZETLAND

Centennial Park

49

Alison Rd

RANDWICK

St Peters

ALEXANDRIA

KENSINGTON

COOGEE

Sydenham

47

Botany Rd

Australian Golf Club

University of NSW

Coogee Bay Rd

33

TEMPE

66

Princes Hwy

MASCOT

Mascot

Gardeners Rd

ROSEBERY

Anzac Pde

KINGSFORD

Sydney (3km)

Mahon Pool (2.4km)

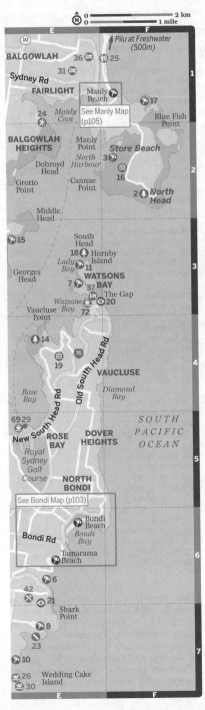

Museum of Contemporary Art GALLERY
(MCA; Map p80; ☑02-9245 2400; www.mca.
com.au; 140 George St; ☉10am-5pm Fri-Wed, to
9pm Thu; ℞Circular Quay) **FREE** By the harbour, the MCA is a showcase for Australian
and international contemporary art, with a
rotating permanent collection and temporary exhibitions. Aboriginal art often features prominently. The Gotham City–style
art-deco building has had a modern gallery
space grafted on to it, the highlight of which
is the rooftop cafe, a stunning spot for a bite
or drink with views. There are free guided
tours daily, with several languages available.

Susannah Place Museum MUSEUM
(Map p80; ☑02-9241 1893; www.sydneyliving
museums.com.au; 58-64 Gloucester St; adult/child
$12/8; ☉tours 2pm, 3pm & 4pm; ℞Circular Quay)
Dating from 1844, this terrace of four houses
and a shop selling historical wares is a fascinating time capsule of life in the Rocks since
colonial times. After a short film about the
people who lived here, a guide will take you
through the claustrophobic homes, which
are decorated to reflect different periods in
their histories. The visit lasts an hour. It's
worth ringing to book at weekends.

◉ City Centre & Haymarket

★**Art Gallery of NSW** GALLERY
(Map p88; ☑1800 679 278; www.artgallery.nsw.
gov.au; Art Gallery Rd; ☉10am-5pm Thu-Tue, to
10pm Wed; ◻441, ℞St James) **FREE** With its
neoclassical Greek frontage and modern
rear end, this much-loved institution plays
a prominent role in Sydney society. Blockbuster touring exhibitions arrive regularly
and there's an outstanding permanent collection of Australian art, including a substantial Indigenous section. The gallery also
hosts lectures, concerts, screenings, celebrity talks and children's activities. A range
of free guided tours is offered on different
themes and in various languages; enquire at
the desk or check the website.

Hyde Park Barracks Museum MUSEUM
(Map p80; ☑02-8239 2311; www.sydneyliving
museums.com.au; Queens Sq, Macquarie St; adult/
child $12/8; ☉10am-5pm; ℞St James) Convict
architect Francis Greenway designed this
squarish, decorously Georgian structure
(1819) as convict quarters. Fifty thousand men
and boys sentenced to transportation passed
through here in 30 years. It later became an
immigration depot, a women's asylum and
a law court. These days it's a fascinating

Sydney

museum, focusing on the barracks' history and the archaeological efforts that helped reveal it. Entry includes a good audio guide.

Museum of Sydney   MUSEUM
(MoS; Map p80; ☎02-9251 5988; www.sydney livingmuseums.com.au; cnr Phillip & Bridge Sts; adult/child $12/8; ⊙10am-5pm; ⌂Circular Quay) Built on the site of Sydney's first Government House, the MoS is a fragmented, storytelling museum, which uses installations to explore the city's history. The area's long Indigenous past is highlighted, plus there's interesting coverage of the early days of contact between the Gadigal and the colonists. Key figures in Sydney's planning and architecture are brought to life, while there's a good section on the First Fleet itself, with scale models.

Martin Place SQUARE
(Map p80; ⓇWynyard, ⓇMartin Place) Studded with imposing edifices, long, lean Martin Place was closed to traffic in 1971, forming a terraced pedestrian mall complete with fountains and areas for public gatherings. It's the closest thing to a main civic square that Sydney has.

Sydney Tower Eye TOWER
(Map p80; ☑1800 258 693; www.sydneytower eye.com.au; level 5, Westfield Sydney, 188 Pitt St; adult/child $26.50/17, Skywalk $70/49; ⊘9am-9.30pm May-Sep, to 10pm Oct-Apr; ⓇSt James) The 309m-tall Sydney Tower (finished in 1981 and still known as Centrepoint by many Sydneysiders) offers unbeatable 360-degree views from the observation level 250m up – and even better ones for the daredevils braving the Skywalk on its roof. The visit starts with the 4D Experience – a short 3D film giving you a bird's-eye view (a parakeet's to be exact) of city, surf, harbour and what lies beneath the water, accompanied by mist sprays and bubbles; it's actually pretty darn cool.

Hyde Park PARK
(Map p84; Elizabeth St; ⓇSt James, Museum) Formal but much-loved Hyde Park has manicured gardens and a tree-formed tunnel running down its spine, which looks particularly pretty at night, illuminated by fairy lights. The park's northern end is crowned by the richly symbolic art-deco **Archibald Memorial Fountain** (Map p80; ⓇSt James), while at the other end is the Anzac Memorial.

Anzac Memorial MEMORIAL
(Map p84; ☑02-9267 7668; www.anzacmemorial .nsw.gov.au; Hyde Park; ⊘9am-5pm; ⓇMuseum) **FREE** Fronted by the Pool of Remembrance, this dignified art-deco memorial (1934) commemorates the soldiers of the Australia and New Zealand Army Corps (Anzacs) who served in WWI. The interior dome is studded with 120,000 stars – one for each New South Welshman and -woman who served. These twinkle above Rayner Hoff's poignant sculpture *Sacrifice*. A major project is adding a new Hall of Service, to feature names and soil samples of all the NSW places of origin of WWI soldiers.

Queen Victoria Building HISTORIC BUILDING
(QVB; Map p80; ☑02-9264 9209; www.qvb. com.au; 455 George St; tours $15; ⊘9am-6pm Mon-Wed, Fri & Sat, 9am-9pm Thu, 11am-5pm Sun; ⓇTown Hall) Unbelievably, this High Victorian Gothic masterpiece (1898) was repeatedly slated for demolition before it was restored in the mid-1980s. Occupying an entire city block on the site of the city's first markets, the QVB is a Venetian Romanesque-inspired temple to the gods of retail.

★**Chinatown** AREA
(Map p84; www.sydney-chinatown.info; ⓇPaddy's Markets, ⓇTown Hall) With a discordant soundtrack of blaring Canto pop, Dixon St is the heart of Chinatown: a narrow, shady pedestrian mall with a string of restaurants and insistent spruikers. The ornate dragon gates *(paifang)* at either end have fake bamboo tiles, golden Chinese calligraphy and ornamental lions to keep evil spirits at bay. Chinatown is a fabulous eating district, which effectively extends for several blocks north and south of here, and segues into Koreatown and Thaitown to the east.

◉ Darling Harbour & Pyrmont

Unashamedly tourist-focused, Darling Harbour will do its best to tempt you to its shoreline bars and restaurants with fireworks displays and a sprinkling of glitz. The eastern side unfurls three strips of bars and restaurants at Cockle Bay, King Street Wharf and the new South Barangaroo development. On its western flank, Pyrmont, though it appears to be sinking under the weight of its casino and motorway flyovers, still has a historic feel in parts, and strolling its harbourside wharves is a real pleasure.

★**Australian National Maritime Museum** MUSEUM
(Map p86; ☑02-9298 3777; www.anmm.gov.au; 2 Murray St; permanent collection free, temporary exhibitions adult/child $20/free; ⊘9.30am-5pm, to 6pm Jan; ♿; ⓇPyrmont Bay) **FREE** Beneath a soaring roof, the Maritime Museum sails through Australia's inextricable relationship with the sea. Exhibitions range from Indigenous canoes to surf culture, immigration to the navy. The worthwhile 'big ticket' (adult/child $30/18) includes entry to some of the vessels moored outside, including the atmospheric submarine HMAS *Onslow* and the destroyer HMAS *Vampire*. The high-production-value short film *Action Stations* sets the mood with a re-creation of a mission event from each vessel. Excellent free guided tours explain each vessel's features.

ALFONSO FERNANDEZ / SHUTTERSTOCK ©

1. Queen Victoria Building (p138)
Shop in style at this High Victorian Gothic masterpiece, which now boasts nearly 200 shops.

2. Sydney Opera House (p70)
Book tickets to a dance, music or theatre performance to experience this remarkable building up close.

3. Bondi Icebergs Pool (p102)
For a natural saltwater wave pool, head to this Bondi institution.

4. Sydney cityscape
Sydney's privileged position on the stunning NSW coast makes it Australia's most photogenic city.

Central Sydney, Circular Quay & The Rocks

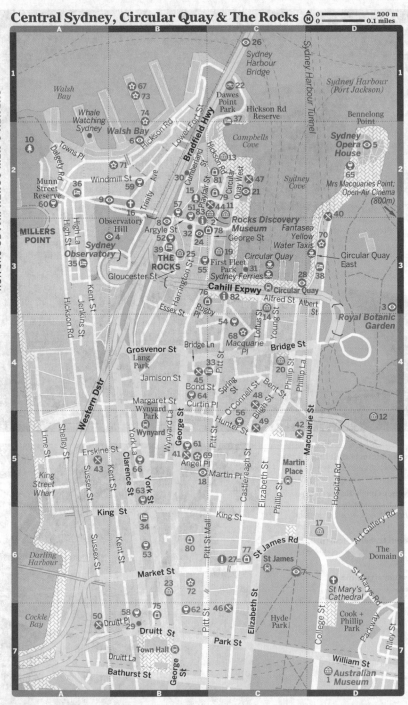

0 ———— 200 m
0 ———— 0.1 miles

Walsh Bay

Walsh Bay

Whale Watching Sydney

Sydney Harbour Bridge

Dawes Point Park

Hickson Rd Reserve

Campbells Cove

Sydney Harbour Tunnel

Sydney Harbour (Port Jackson)

Bennelong Point

Sydney Opera House

Mrs Macquaries Point; Open-Air Cinema (800m)

Sydney Cove

MILLERS POINT

Munn Street Reserve

Windmill St

Observatory Hill

Sydney Observatory

Argyle St

THE ROCKS

Rocks Discovery Museum

George St

Fantasea Yellow Water Taxis

Circular Quay East

Circular Quay

First Fleet Park

Sydney Ferries

Cahill Expwy

Alfred St

Albert St

Royal Botanic Garden

Rugby Pl

Essex St

Macquarie Pl

Bridge St

Grosvenor St

Lang Park

Bridge Ln

Jamison St

Bond St

Curtin Pl

Spring St

O'Connell St

Bligh St

Bent St

Phillip La

Phillip St

Macquarie St

Margaret St

Wynyard Park

Wynyard

Hunter St

George St

Pitt St

Castlereagh St

Elizabeth St

Phillip St

Hospital Rd

Martin Place

Art Gallery Rd

King Street Wharf

Erskine St

Clarence St

York St

Angel Pl

Martin Pl

King St

Shelley St

Lime St

Kent St

Sussex St

St James Rd

St James

The Domain

Darling Harbour

King Street Wharf

Market St

Pitt St Mall

King St

St Mary's Cathedral

Cook + Phillip Park

Cockle Bay

Druitt Pl

Druitt St

Town Hall

Druitt La

Bathurst St

George St

Park St

Hyde Park

Elizabeth St

College St

St Marys Rd

Riley St

William St

Australian Museum

Central Sydney, Circular Quay & The Rocks

★ **Chinese Garden of Friendship** GARDENS (Map p84; ☏02-9240 8888; www.chinesegarden. com.au; Harbour St; adult/child $6/3; ◷9.30am-5pm Apr-Sep, 9.30am-5.30pm Oct-Mar; ⓐTown

Hall) Built according to Taoist principles, the Chinese Garden of Friendship is usually an oasis of tranquillity – although construction noise from Darling Harbour's redevelopment can intrude from time to time. Designed by architects from Guangzhou (Sydney's sister city) for Australia's bicentenary in 1988, the garden interweaves pavilions, waterfalls, lakes, paths and lush plant life. There's also a teahouse.

★ **Sydney Sea Life Aquarium** AQUARIUM

(Map p86; ☎02-8251 7800; www.sydneyaquarium.com.au; Aquarium Pier; adult/child $40/28; ◷9.30am-6pm Mon-Thu, to 7pm Fri-Sun & school holidays, last entry 1hr earlier; ⊠Town Hall) ◢ As well as regular wall-mounted tanks and ground-level enclosures, this impressive complex has two large pools that you can walk through, safely enclosed in Perspex tunnels, as an intimidating array of sharks and rays pass overhead. Other highlights include a pair of dugongs, clownfish (howdy Nemo), platypuses, moon jellyfish (in a disco-lit tube), sea dragons and the swoonworthy finale: the two-million-litre Great Barrier Reef tank.

Wild Life Sydney Zoo ZOO

(Map p86; ☎02-9333 9245; www.wildlifesydney.com.au; Aquarium Pier; adult/child $40/28; ◷9.30am-5pm Apr-Sep, to 7pm Oct-Mar, last entry 1hr before close; ⊠Town Hall) Complementing its sister and neighbour, Sea Life, this large complex houses an impressive collection of Australian native reptiles, butterflies, spiders, snakes and mammals (including kangaroos and koalas). The nocturnal section is particularly good, bringing out the extrovert in the quolls, potoroos, echidnas and possums. As interesting as Wild Life is, it's not a patch on Taronga Zoo. Still, it's worth considering as part of a combo with Sea Life, or if you're short on time. Tickets are cheaper online.

The Star CASINO

(Map p86; ☎02-9777 9000; www.star.com.au; 80 Pyrmont St, Pyrmont; ◷24hr; ⊠The Star) Sydney's first casino complex includes hotels, high-profile restaurants, bars, a nightclub, an excellent food court, a light-rail station and the kind of high-end shops that will ensure that, in the unlikely event that you do happen to strike it big, a large proportion of your winnings will remain within the building.

★ **Sydney Fish Market** MARKET

(Map p86; ☎02-9004 1108; www.sydneyfishmarket.com.au; Bank St; ◷7am-4pm; ⊠Fish Market) This precinct on Blackwattle Bay shifts over 15 million kilograms of seafood

---

🏃 City Walk
The Rocks & Circular Quay

START CADMAN'S COTTAGE
END ROYAL BOTANIC GARDEN
LENGTH 3.5KM; TWO HOURS

Start outside ❶ **Cadman's Cottage**, inner-city Sydney's oldest house. It was built on a now-buried beach for Government Coxswain John Cadman (a boat and crew superintendent) in 1816. The Sydney Water Police detained criminals here in the 1840s and it was later converted into a home for retired sea captains.

Head north along Circular Quay West past the ❷ **Overseas Passenger Terminal**, where multistorey luxury cruise ships regularly dock. For a killer harbour view, if there's no ship to block it, head up to the level-four observation deck in the turret on the northern end.

Further along the quay are ❸ **Campbell's Storehouses**, built in 1839 by Scottish merchant Robert Campbell to house his stash of tea, alcohol, sugar and fabric. Construction of the 11 warehouses didn't finish until 1861, and a brick storey was added in 1890. Such buildings were common around Circular Quay into the early 20th century, but most have been demolished since. These survivors now sustain a string of touristy restaurants.

Play spot-the-bridal-party as you loop past the ❹ **Park Hyatt** (p108) and into the small park at the end of Dawes Point. Couples jet in from as far away as China and Korea to have photos taken here in front of the perfect Opera House background.

As you pass under the harbour bridge, keep an eye out for Luna Park on the opposite shore. Stroll around Walsh Bay's gentrified ❺ **Edwardian wharves** and then cross the road and cut up the stairs (marked 'public stairs to Windmill St') just before the Roslyn Packer Theatre. Continue up the hill on teensy Ferry Lane. Near the top you'll find the foundations of ❻ **Arthur Payne's house**; he was the first victim of the 1900 bubonic plague outbreak.

At the corner of Windmill St is the ❼ **Hero of Waterloo** (p125), a contender for the title of Sydney's oldest pub. Turn right on Lower Fort St and head to ❽ **Argyle Place**, a quiet, English-style village green lined with terraced houses.

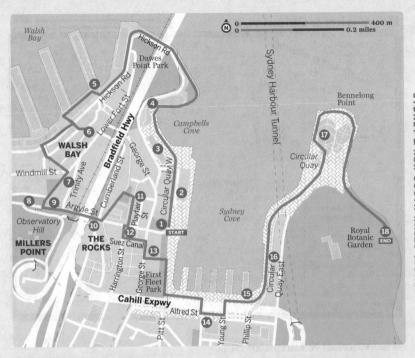

Across the road is the handsome
9 Garrison Church. Hook left into Argyle St
and stroll down through the **10 Argyle Cut**.
Convict labourers excavated this canyonlike
section of road clear through the sandstone
ridge that gave the Rocks its name. The work
began in 1843 with hand tools, and was completed (with the aid of dynamite) in 1867.

Just past the Cut take the stairs to the left
and head along Gloucester Walk to
11 Foundation Park, which evokes the
area's cramped past. Take the stairs down
through the park, duck around the building
at the bottom and exit onto Playfair St where
there's a row of historic terraced houses.

Cross Argyle St into Harrington St then jag
left into **12 Suez Canal**. One of few remaining
such lanes, it tapers as it goes downhill until
it's less than a metre wide (hence the name,
which is also a pun on the word 'sewers').
Constructed in the 1840s, it was notorious
as a lurking point for members of the Rocks
Push, a street gang that relieved many a drunk
of their wallet in the latter part of the 19th century. Where it intersects Nurses Walk look for
the hoist jutting out of the building, once used
for hauling goods to the upper floors.

Turn right into George St and cut through
the **13 Museum of Contemporary Art**

(p75), Sydney's major showcase for big-
name exhibitions. Exit onto Circular Quay and
follow the waterline past the ferry wharves.

Cut underneath the train station to the
fabulously renovated **14 Customs House**.
Stroll back to the water to check out the bad
buskers and the plaques of the **15 Sydney
Writers Walk**. This series of metal discs, set
into the Circular Quay promenade, holds rumi-
nations from prominent Australian writers and
the odd literary visitor. The likes of Mark Twain,
Germaine Greer, Peter Carey, Umberto Eco
and Clive James wax lyrical on subjects ranging from Indigenous rights to the paradoxical
nature of glass. Genres range from eloquent
poems addressing the human condition to a
ditty about a meat pie by Barry Humphries.

Continue past the **16 Opera Quays**
(p133) apartment and entertainment
complex on Circular Quay East, which is
disparagingly referred to by Sydneysiders as
'The Toaster'.

The heaven-sent sails of the **17 Sydney
Opera House** (p70) are directly in front of
you, adjacent to an unmissable perspective
of the Sydney Harbour Bridge off to the left.
Circumnavigate Bennelong Point, then follow
the water's edge to the gates of the **18 Royal
Botanic Garden** (p70).

Haymarket & Chinatown

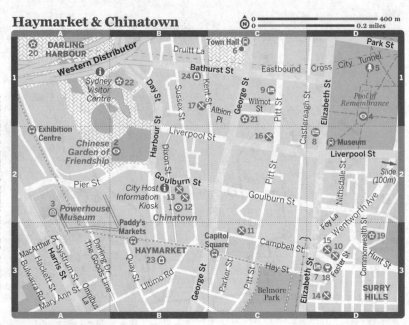

Haymarket & Chinatown

annually, and has retail outlets, restaurants, a sushi bar, an oyster bar, and a highly regarded cooking school. Chefs, locals and overfed seagulls haggle over mud crabs, Balmain bugs, lobsters and slabs of salmon at the daily fish auction, which kicks off at 5.30am weekdays. Check it out on a behind-the-scenes tour (adult/child $35/10).

◎ Kings Cross & Potts Point

Traditionally Sydney's seedy red-light zone, the Cross has changed markedly in recent years. Lockout laws have killed the late-night bar life, and major building programs have accelerated gentrification in this so-close-to-the-city district. The area's blend of backpackers and quirky locals is still enticing though, and its leafy streets and good eateries make for surprisingly pleasant daytime meanders. Below, by the water, the old sailors' district of Woolloomooloo is a great spot for glitzy wharf restaurants or a handful of pubs of some character.

★**Elizabeth Bay House**   HISTORIC BUILDING
(Map p88; ☑ 02-9356 3022; www.sydneyliving museums.com.au; 7 Onslow Ave, Elizabeth Bay; adult/child $12/8; ☺ 11am-4pm Fri-Sun; ⊠ Kings Cross) Now dwarfed by 20th-century apartments, Colonial Secretary Alexander Macleay's elegant Greek Revival mansion was one of the finest houses in the colony when it was completed in 1839. The architectural highlight is an exquisite oval saloon with a curved and cantilevered staircase. There are lovely views over the harbour from the upstairs rooms. Drop down to the twin cellars for an introductory audiovisual with a weird beginning.

Woolloomooloo Wharf   HISTORIC BUILDING
(The Finger Wharf; Cowper Wharf Roadway, Woolloomooloo; ☐ 311, ⊠ Kings Cross) A former wool and cargo dock, this beautiful Edwardian wharf faced oblivion for decades before a 2½-year demolition-workers' green ban on the site in the late 1980s saved it. It received a huge sprucing up in the late 1990s and has emerged as one of Sydney's most exclusive eating, sleeping and marina addresses.

◉ **Surry Hills & Darlinghurst**

Sydney's hippest and gayest neighbourhood is also home to its most interesting dining and bar scene. The plane trees and up-and-down of increasingly chic Surry Hills merge into the terraces of vibrant Darlinghurst. They are pleasant, leafy districts appealingly close to the centre.

★**Australian Museum**   MUSEUM
(Map p80; ☑ 02-9320 6000; www.australian museum.net.au; 6 College St, Darlinghurst; adult/child $15/free; ☺ 9.30am-5pm; ⊠ Museum) Under an ongoing process of modernisation, this museum, established just 40 years after the First Fleet dropped anchor, is doing a brilliant job of it. A standout is the Indigenous Australians section, covering Aboriginal history and spirituality, from Dreaming stories to videos of the Freedom Rides of the 1960s. The stuffed animal gallery of the natural history section manages to keep it relevant, while the excellent dinosaur

THE CHANGING CROSS

Kings Cross is a bizarre, densely populated dichotomy: strip joints, tacky tourist shops and backpacker hostels bang heads with classy restaurants, boozy bars and gorgeous guesthouses. A weird cross-section of society is drawn to the bright lights: buskers, beggars, junkies, tourists, prostitutes, pimps, groomed metrosexuals, horny businessmen and underfed artists roam the streets on equal footing. But things are changing as 'lockout laws', which restricted opening hours until 1.30am for bars and 3am for music venues, have taken the kick out of the nightlife and development is steering the Cross towards its likely destiny as just another posh eastern suburb. But its villagey, bohemian inclusive feel still makes it intriguing for now.

SYDNEY & NEW SOUTH WALES SYDNEY

gallery features the enormous Jobaria as well as local bruisers like Muttaburrasaurus.

There are also interesting displays on extinct megafauna (giant wombats – simultaneously cuddly and terrifying), current Australian creatures, a kids section and more. We're looking forward to the new Long Gallery exhibition, due to open in October 2017, focusing on 100 objects and 100 key people from Australia's past, and new Oceania galleries that will incorporate the colourful Pacific Island collection.

Don't miss heading up to the cafe, which has brilliant views of St Mary's Cathedral and down to Woolloomooloo.

★**Brett Whiteley Studio**   GALLERY
(Map p101; ☑ 02-9225 1881; www.artgallery. nsw.gov.au/brett-whiteley-studio; 2 Raper St, Surry Hills; ☺ 10am-4pm Fri-Sun; ⊠ Central) **FREE** Acclaimed local artist Brett Whiteley (1939–1992) lived fast and without restraint. His hard-to-find studio (look for the signs on Devonshire St) has been preserved as a gallery for some of his best work. Pride of place goes to his astonishing *Alchemy*, a giant multi-panel extravaganza that could absorb you for hours with its broad themes, intricate details and humorous asides. The studio room upstairs also gives great insight into the character of this masterful draughtsman and off-the-wall genius.

Darling Harbour & Pyrmont

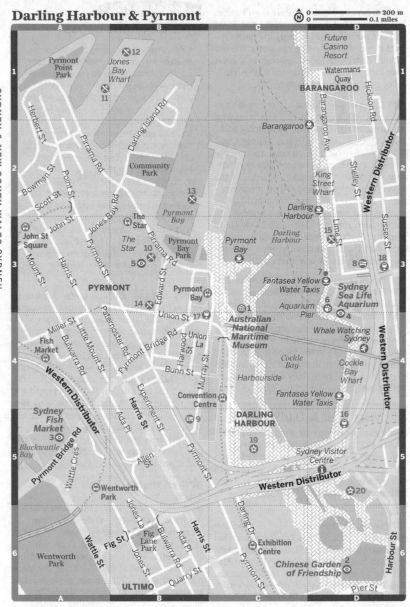

Sydney Jewish Museum MUSEUM
(Map p88; ☎02-9360 7999; www.sydneyjewish
museum.com.au; 148 Darlinghurst Rd, Darlinghurst; adult/child $10/7; ⊙1-4pm Mon-Thu, noon-
2pm Fri, 10am-4pm Sun; ☒Kings Cross) This
museum examines Australian Jewish history, culture and tradition, from the time
of the First Fleet (which included 16 known
Jews), to the immediate aftermath of WWII
(when Australia became home to the greatest number of Holocaust survivors per
capita, after Israel), to the present day. The

Darling Harbour & Pyrmont

centrepiece is a new permanent exhibition on the Holocaust, with sobering personal testimonies; another examines the role of Jews in Australia's military, while temporary exhibitions are always excellent. There's a kosher cafe upstairs.

⊙ Paddington & Centennial Park

Alwyas a byword for eastern-suburbs elegance, this band of suburbs is distinctly well-heeled – and in Paddington's case, the heels are probably Manolo Blahniks. This is still Sydney's fashion and art heartland, full of pretty green corners and eye-catching boutiques.

Centennial Park PARK
(Map p96; ☑02-9339 6699; www.centennial parklands.com.au; Oxford St, Centennial Park; ☒Bondi Junction) Scratched out of the sand in 1888 in grand Victorian style, Sydney's biggest park is a rambling 189-hectare expanse full of horse riders, joggers, cyclists and in-line skaters. During the summertime the resident Moonlight Cinema (p133) attracts the crowds.

⊙ Bondi, Coogee & the Eastern Beaches

Sydney sheds its suit and tie, ditches the strappy heels and chills out in the eastern beaches. Beach after golden-sand beach, alternating with sheer sandstone cliffs, are the classic vistas of this beautiful, laid-back and egalitarian stretch of the city.

★**Bondi Beach** BEACH
(Map p103; Campbell Pde, Bondi Beach; ☒333, 380-2) Definitively Sydney, Bondi is one of the world's great beaches: ocean and land collide, the Pacific arrives in great foaming swells, and all people are equal, as democratic as sand. It's the closest ocean beach to the city centre (8km away), has consistently good (though crowded) waves, and is great for a rough-and-tumble swim (the average water temperature is a considerate 21°C). If the sea's angry, try the child-friendly saltwater sea baths at either end of the beach.

Bronte Beach BEACH
(Map p74; Bronte Rd, Bronte; ▣; ☒378) A winning family-oriented beach hemmed in by sandstone cliffs and a grassy park, Bronte lays claims to the title of the oldest surf lifesaving club in the world (1903). Contrary to popular belief, the beach is named after Lord Nelson, who doubled as the Duke of Bronte (a place in Sicily), and not the famous literary sorority. There's a kiosk and a changing room attached to the surf club, and covered picnic tables near the public barbecues.

Waverley Cemetery CEMETERY
(Map p74; ☑02-9083 8899; www.waverley cemetery.com; St Thomas St, Bronte; ⊙7am-5pm May-Sep, 7am-7pm Oct-Apr; ☒378) Many Sydneysiders would die for these views...and that's the only way they're going to get them. Blanketing the clifftops between Bronte and Clovelly beaches, the white marble gravestones here are dazzling in the sunlight. Eighty thousand people have been interred here since 1877, including writers Henry

Kings Cross, Potts Point & Darlinghurst

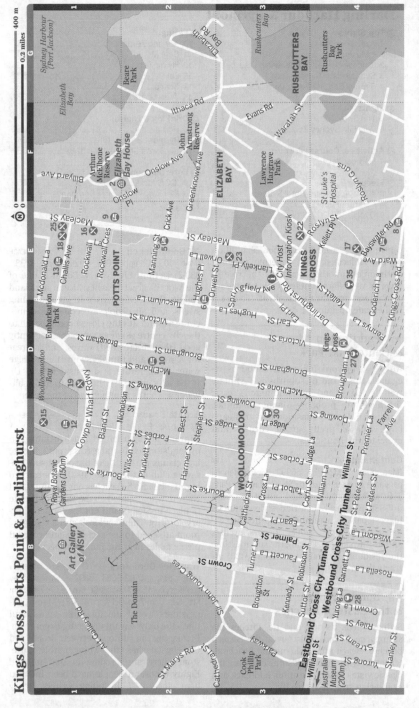

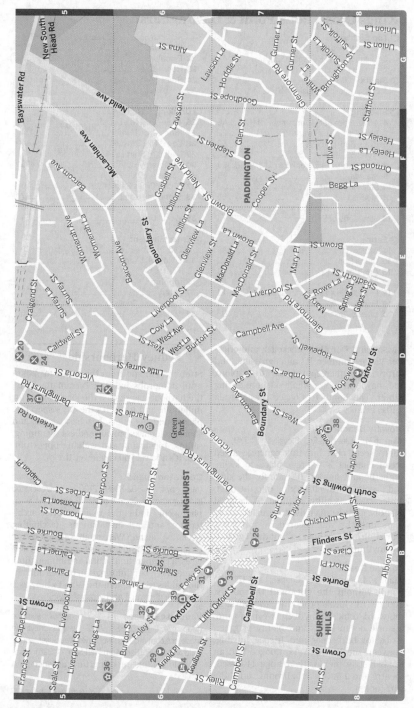

Kings Cross, Potts Point & Darlinghurst

Lawson and Dorothea Mackellar, and cricketer Victor Trumper. It's an engrossing (and surprisingly uncreepy) place to explore, and maybe to spot a whale offshore during winter. The Bondi to Coogee coastal walk (p104) heads past it.

Clovelly Beach   BEACH
(Map p74; Clovelly Rd, Clovelly; 🚌339) It might seem odd, but this concrete-edged ocean channel is a great place to swim, sunbathe and snorkel. It's safe for the kids, and despite the swell surging into the inlet, underwater visibility is great. A beloved friendly grouper fish lived here for many years until he was speared by a reckless tourist. Bring your goggles, but don't go killing anything...

Coogee Beach   BEACH
(Map p74; Arden St, Coogee; 🚌372-373) Bondi without the glitz and the posers, Coogee (tip: locals pronounce the 'oo' as in the word 'took') has a deep sweep of sand, historic ocean baths and plenty of green space for barbecues and frisbee hurling. Between the World Wars, Coogee had an English-style pier, with a huge 1400-seat theatre and a 600-seat ballroom...until the surf took it.

◎ Sydney Harbourside

Stretching inland from the heads for 20km until it morphs into the Parramatta River, the harbour has shaped the local psyche for millennia, and today it's the city's sparkling playground. Its inlets, beaches, islands and shorefront parks provide endless swimming, sailing, picnicking and walking opportunities. It's a jewel you can never tire of.

Cockatoo Island   ISLAND
(Map p74; 🗗02-8969 2100; www.cockatoo island.gov.au; 🛳Cockatoo Island) Studded with photogenic industrial relics, convict architecture and art installations, fascinating Cockatoo Island (Wareamah) opened to the public in 2007 and now has regular ferry services, a campground, rental accommodation, a cafe and a bar. Information boards and audio guides ($5) explain the island's time as a prison, a shipyard and a naval base.

Vaucluse House   HISTORIC BUILDING
(Map p74; 🗗02-9388 7922; www.sydneyliving museums.com.au; Wentworth Rd, Vaucluse; adult/ child $12/8; ⊙10am-4pm Wed-Sun; 🚌325) Construction of this imposing, turreted specimen

(Continued on page 95)

AL YOSHI / GETTY IMAGES ©

Sydney's Beaches

Whether you join the procession of the bronzed and the beautiful at Bondi, or surreptitiously slink into a deserted nook hidden within Sydney Harbour National Park, the beach is an essential part of the Sydney experience. Even in winter, watching the rollers break while you're strolling along the sand is exhilarating. Sydney's beaches broadly divide into the eastern beaches, south of the harbour, running from Bondi southwards, and the northern beaches, north of the harbour, starting at Manly.

Contents

➡ **Beach Culture**

➡ **Need to Know**

➡ **Beaches by Neighbourhood**

➡ **Lonely Planet's Top Choices**

Above Mahon Pool (p92)

Beach Culture

In the mid-1990s an enthusiastic businesswoman obtained a concession to rent loungers on Tamarama Beach and offer waiter service. Needless to say, it didn't last long. Even at what was considered at the time to be Sydney's most glamorous beach, nobody was interested in that kind of malarkey.

For Australians, going to the beach is all about rolling out a towel on the sand with a minimum of fuss. And they're certainly not prepared to pay for the privilege. Sandy-toed ice-cream vendors are acceptable; martini luggers are not. In summer one of the more unusual sights is the little ice-cream boat pulling up to Lady Bay (and other harbour beaches) and a polite queue of nude gentlemen forming to purchase their icy poles.

Surf lifesavers have a hallowed place in the culture and you'd do well to heed their instructions, not least of all because they're likely to be in your best interest. It's not coincidental that the spark for racist riots in Cronulla a few years back was an attack on this oh-so-Australian institution.

Ocean Pools

If you have children or shark paranoia, or surf just isn't your thing, you'll be pleased to hear that Sydney's blessed with a string of 40 man-made ocean pools up and down the coast, most of them free. Some, like **Mahon Pool** (www.randwick.nsw.gov. au; Marine Pde, Maroubra; 376-377) FREE, are what are known as bogey holes – natural-looking rock pools where you can safely splash about and snorkel, even while the surf surges in. Others are more like swim-

1. Bondi Beach (p87)
2. Camp Cove
3. Tamarama Beach

ming pools; Bondi's Icebergs (p102) is a good example of this kind. They normally close a day a week so they can clean the seaweed out.

Need to Know

If you're not used to swimming at surf beaches, you may be unprepared for the dangers.

➡ Always swim between the red-and-yellow flags on lifesaver-patrolled beaches. Not only are these areas patrolled, they're positioned away from dangerous rips and underwater holes. Plus you're much less likely to get clobbered by a surfboard.

➡ If you get into trouble, hold up your hand to signal the lifesavers.

➡ Never swim under the influence of alcohol or other drugs.

➡ Due to pollution from stormwater drains, avoid swimming in the ocean for a day and in the harbour for three days after heavy rains. And on a related topic, don't drop rubbish – including cigarette butts – on the streets unless you don't mind swimming with it come the next rainfall.

Beaches by Neighbourhood

Sydney Harbour Lots of hidden coves and secret sandy spots; the best are out near the Heads and around Mosman.

Eastern Beaches High cliffs frame a string of surf beaches, with excellent coffee and cold beer just a short stumble away.

Northern Beaches A steady succession of magical surf beaches stretching 30km north from Manly to Palm Beach.

Bronte Baths at Bronte Beach (p87)

Best for Snorkelling

➡ Gordons Bay (p100)

➡ North Bondi (p87)

➡ Camp Cove (Cliff St, Watsons Bay; ⊚Watsons Bay)

➡ Shelly Beach (p97)

➡ Clovelly Beach (p90)

Lonely Planet's Top Choices

Bondi Beach (p87) Australia's most iconic ocean beach.

Nielsen Park (p95) The pick of the harbour beaches, surrounded by beautiful national park.

Bronte Beach (p87) Family-friendly and backed by park, this is an Eastern Beaches gem.

Whale Beach (p99) Peachy-coloured sand and crashing waves; you've really left the city behind at this stunning Northern Beaches haven.

Murray Rose Pool (p104) The closest beach to the city is also one of Sydney's finest.

Harbour Beaches & Pools

The pick of Sydney's harbour beaches include Camp Cove and Lady Bay near South Head (the latter of which is mainly a gay nude beach), Shark Beach at Nielsen Park in Vaucluse, and Balmoral Beach on the north shore. Also popular are the netted swimming enclosures at Cremorne Point on the North Shore and Murray Rose Pool near Double Bay. There are plenty of little sandy gems scattered about that even Sydneysiders would be hard pressed to find, including Parsley Bay and Milk Beach right in the heart of residential Vaucluse.

of Gothic Australiana, set amid 10 hectares of lush gardens, began in 1805, but the house was tinkered with into the 1860s. Atmospheric, and decorated with beautiful European period pieces, the house offers visitors a rare glimpse into early Sydney colonial life, as lived by the well-to-do. The history of the Wentworths who occupied it, is fascinating, and helpful guides give great background on them. In the grounds is a popular tearoom.

Nielsen Park   PARK, BEACH

(Map p74; Vaucluse Rd, Vaucluse; ⊙national park area 5am-10pm; ☐325) Something of a hidden gem, this gorgeous harbourside park with a sandy beach was once part of the then 206-hectare Vaucluse House estate. Secluded beneath the trees is Greycliffe House, a gracious 1851 Gothic sandstone pile (not open to visitors), which serves as the headquarters of Sydney Harbour National Park. Despite its ominous name, there's really nothing to worry about at **Shark Beach** – it has a net to put paranoid swimmers at ease.

Visit on a weekday when it's not too busy: just mums with kids, retirees and slackers taking sickies from work.

Watsons Bay   AREA

(Map p74; ☑Watsons Bay) Watsons Bay, east of the city centre and north of Bondi, was once a small fishing village, as evidenced by the tiny heritage cottages that pepper the suburb's narrow streets (and now cost a fortune). While you're here, tradition demands that you sit in the beer garden at the Watsons Bay Hotel at sunset and watch the sun dissolve behind the disembodied Harbour Bridge, jutting up above Bradley's Head.

On the ocean side, **The Gap** is a dramatic clifftop lookout where proposals and suicides happen with similar frequency.

South Head   NATIONAL PARK

(Map p74; www.nationalparks.nsw.gov.au; Cliff St, Watsons Bay; ⊙5am-10pm; ☑Watsons Bay) At the northern end of Camp Cove, the **South Head Heritage Trail** kicks off, leading into a section of Sydney Harbour National Park distinguished by harbour views and crashing surf. It passes old fortifications and a path heading down to **Lady Bay** (Map p74; Cliff St), before continuing on to the candy-striped **Hornby Lighthouse** and the sandstone **Lightkeepers' Cottages** (1858). Between April and November, look out to sea to where the whale-watching boats have congregated and you'll often see cetaceans.

★**McMahons Point**   VIEWPOINT

(Map p74; ☑McMahons Point) Is there a better view of the Bridge and the Opera House than from the wharf at this point, a short hop by ferry northwest of the centre? It's all unfolded before you and is a stunning spot to be when the sun is setting.

★**Taronga Zoo**   ZOO

(Map p74; ☑02-9969 2777; www.taronga.org.au; Bradleys Head Rd, Mosman; adult/child $46/26; ⊙9.30am-5pm Sep-Apr, 9.30am-4.30pm May-Aug; ☑; ☐247, ☑Taronga Zoo) A 12-minute ferry ride from Circular Quay, this bushy harbour hillside is full of kangaroos, koalas and similarly hirsute Australians, plus numerous imported guests. The zoo's critters have million-dollar harbour views, but seem blissfully unaware of the privilege. Encouragingly, Taronga sets benchmarks in animal care and welfare. Highlights include the nocturnal platypus habitat, the Great Southern Oceans section and the Asian elephant display. Feedings and encounters happen throughout the day, while in summer, twilight concerts jazz things up (see www.twilightattaronga.org.au).

Tours include **Nura Diya** (www.taronga.org.au; 90min tour adult/child $99/69; ⊙9.45am Mon, Wed & Fri); **Roar & Snore** (☑02-9978 4791; www.taronga.org.au; adult/child $335/215) is an overnight family experience.

Catching the ferry is part of the fun. From the wharf, the Sky Safari cable car or a bus

LOCAL KNOWLEDGE

RIDING THE 389

A good introduction to Sydney's eastern suburbs is a ride on the 389 bus, as it generally avoids major roads in favour of smaller suburban streets. Catch it near the Maritime Museum (p77) and take in the Pyrmont harbour foreshore in a long loop that eventually brings you into the city centre across Darling Harbour. Crossing the city from west to east, it zigzags its way through characterful Darlinghurst streets before cruising the prettiest parts of upmarket Paddington. After a dose of urban ugliness at Bondi Junction bus interchange, it then approaches Bondi Beach via the interesting back streets, ending up at North Bondi with the beach just down the hill ahead of you.

Paddington & Centennial Park

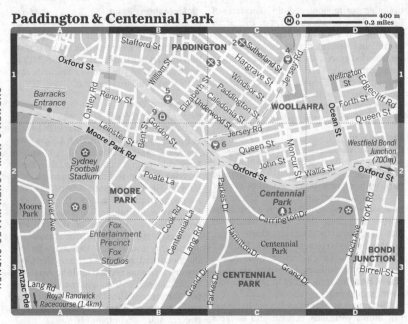

Paddington & Centennial Park

will whisk you to the main entrance, from which you can traverse the zoo downhill back to the ferry. Disabled access is good, even when arriving by ferry.

If you are driving and staying a while, note that the zoo car park ($18 per day) is much cheaper than the metered parking on the streets around (weekdays/weekends $4.20/7 per hour). Getting here by bus is the cheapest option; the 247 heads here from Wynyard.

Luna Park   AMUSEMENT PARK
(Map p74; ☑ 02-9922 6644; www.lunapark sydney.com; 1 Olympic Dr, Milsons Point; ⊙ 11am-10pm Fri & Sat, 10am-6pm Sun, 11am-4pm Mon; 🚇 Milsons Point) FREE A sinister chip-toothed clown face (50 times life-sized) forms the entrance to this old-fashioned amusement

park overlooking Sydney Harbour. It's one of several 1930s features, including the Coney Island funhouse, a pretty carousel and the nausea-inducing rotor. You can purchase a two-ride pass ($20), or buy a height-based unlimited-ride pass (adults $52, kids $22 to $45, cheaper if purchased online). Hours are complex, and extended during school and public holidays. It also functions as a concert venue.

◉ Newtown & the Inner West

The bohemian sweep of the inner west is an array of suburbs packed with great places to eat and drink. The quiet streets of Glebe and louder Newtown, grouped around the University of Sydney, are the most well-known of these tightly packed suburbs, but Enmore,

Marrickville, Summer Hill, Petersham and more are all worth investigating. All the essential hang-outs for students – bookshops, cafes and pubs – are present in abundance, but the Inner West is a lifestyle choice for a whole swathe of Sydney society.

★**Powerhouse Museum** MUSEUM
(Museum of Applied Arts & Sciences (MAAS); Map p84; ☑02-9217 0111; www.powerhousemuseum. com; 500 Harris St, Ultimo; adult/child $15/8; ☺10am-5pm; ♠; ☒Exhibition Centre) A short walk from Darling Harbour, this cavernous science and design museum whirs away inside the former power station for Sydney's defunct, original tram network. The collection and temporary exhibitions cover everything from robots and life on Mars to steam trains to climate change to atoms to fashion, industrial design and avant-garde art installations. There are great options for kids of all ages but it's equally intriguing for adults. Grab a map of the museum once you're inside. Disabled access is good.

The Powerhouse is due to move to a new location in Parramatta that is set to be completed in 2022.

★**White Rabbit** GALLERY
(Map p98; www.whiterabbitcollection.org; 30 Balfour St, Chippendale; ☺10am-5pm Wed-Sun, closed Feb & Aug; ☒Redfern) FREE If you're an art lover or a bit of a Mad Hatter, this particular rabbit hole will leave you grinning like a Cheshire Cat. There are so many works in this private collection of cutting-edge, contemporary Chinese art that only a fraction can be displayed at one time. Who knew that the People's Republic was turning out work that was so edgy, funny, sexy and idiosyncratic? It's probably Sydney's best contemporary art gallery.

Central Park AREA
(Map p98; www.centralparksydney.com; Broadway; ☺10am-8pm; ☒Central) Occupying the site of an old brewery, this major residential and shopping development is a striking sight. Most impressive is Jean Nouvel's award-winning, vertical-garden-covered tower, One Central Park. The cantilevered platform high above has been designed to reflect sunlight onto the greenery below. Its lower floors have plenty of food options, ping pong, shops, a supermarket and gallery spaces, while adjacent Kensington St and Spice Alley (p122) offer further gastronomic pleasure. Two new Norman Foster–designed apartment towers, Duo, are under construction.

★**Nicholson Museum** MUSEUM
(Map p98; ☑02-9351 2812; www.sydney.edu. au/museums; University Pl, University of Sydney; ☺10am-4.30pm Mon-Fri, noon-4pm 1st Sat of month; ☒412, 413, 436, 438-40, 461, 480, 483, M10) FREE Within the University of Sydney's quadrangle, this is one of the city's great under-the-radar attractions. Combining modern ideas with ancient artefacts, it's an intriguing collection of Greek, Roman, Cypriot, Egyptian and Western Asian antiquities. Attic vases and Egyptian mummies take their place alongside themed cross-cultural displays, plus there's a fabulous Pompeii made from Lego that features toga-clad citizens alongside the likes of Pink Floyd rocking the amphitheatre. The museum is to be incorporated into the new **Chau Chak Wing Museum** (Map p98; ☑02-9351 2222; http:// sydney.edu.au; University Pl, University of Sydney; ☒412, 413, 436, 438-40, 461, 480, 483, M10) FREE by 2019.

◉ **Manly**

With both a harbour side and a glorious ocean beach, Manly is Sydney's only ferry destination with surf. Capping off the harbour with scrappy charm, it's a place worth visiting for the ferry ride alone. The surf's good, there are appealing contemporary bars and eateries and, as the gateway to the Northern Beaches, it makes a popular base for the board-riding brigade.

★**Manly Beach** BEACH
(Map p105; ☒Manly) Sydney's second most famous beach stretches for nearly two golden kilometres, lined by Norfolk Island pines and scrappy midrise apartment blocks. The southern end of the beach, nearest The Corso, is known as South Steyne, with North Steyne in the centre and Queenscliff at the northern end; each has its own surf lifesaving club.

Shelly Beach BEACH
(Map p74; ☒Manly) This sheltered north-facing ocean cove is just a short 1km walk from the busy Manly beach strip. The tranquil waters are a protected haven for marine life, so it offers wonderful snorkelling.

Manly Sea Life Sanctuary AQUARIUM
(Map p105; ☑1800 199 742; www.manlysea lifesanctuary.com.au; West Esplanade; adult/child $25/17; ☺9.30am-5pm; ☒Manly) Not the place to come if you're on your way to Manly Beach

Newtown & the Inner West

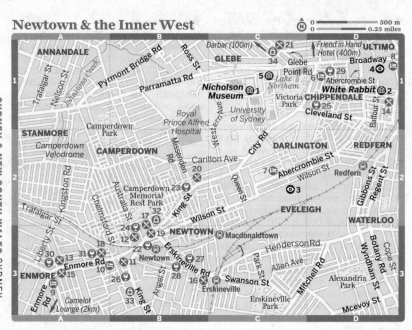

Newtown & the Inner West

for a surf. Underwater glass tubes enable you to become alarmingly intimate with 3m grey nurse sharks. Want to text if they're not hungry? **Shark Dive Xtreme** (Map p105; dives from $299; ⊙ Fri-Wed) enables you to enter their world. Upstairs, the adorable residents of the penguin enclosure have lawless amounts of fun.

★ **Store Beach** BEACH
(Map p74; ☺dawn-dusk) A hidden jewel on North Head, magical Store Beach can only be reached by kayak or boat. It's a fairy-penguin breeding ground, so access is prohibited from dusk, when the birds waddle in.

★ **North Head** NATIONAL PARK
(Map p74; North Head Scenic Dr, Manly; ☐135) About 3km south of Manly, spectacular, chunky North Head offers dramatic cliffs, lookouts and sweeping views of the ocean, the harbour and the city; hire a bike and go exploring.

North Head is believed to have been used as a ceremonial site by the native Camaraigal people. These days, most of the headland is part of Sydney Harbour National Park.

The 9km, four-hour Manly Scenic Walkway (p104) loops around the park; pick up a brochure from the visitor centre. Also here is the historic **Quarantine Station** (Q Station; Map p74; ☑02-9466 1551; www. quarantinestation.com.au; 1 North Head Scenic Dr, Manly; ☺museum 10am-4pm Sun-Thu, to 8pm Fri & Sat; ☐135) FREE.

◉ **Northern Beaches**

Wilder and harder to get to than Sydney's eastern strands, the Northern Beaches are a must-see, especially for surfers. Although you'll most likely approach them as a day trip, they're very much a part of the city, with the suburbs pushing right up to the water's edge. Some neighbourhoods are more ritzy than others, but what they all have in common is a devotion to the beach.

Palm Beach BEACH
(Ocean Rd, Palm Beach; ☐L90, 190) Long, lovely Palm Beach is a meniscus of bliss, famous as the setting for cheesy TV soap *Home & Away*. The 1881 Barrenjoey Lighthouse punctuates the northern tip of the headland. The suburb Palm Beach has two sides, the magnificent ocean beach, and a pleasant strip on Pittwater, where the calmer strands are good for young kids. From here you can get ferries to other picturesque Pittwater destinations.

Barrenjoey Lighthouse LIGHTHOUSE
(☑02-9451 3479; www.nationalparks.nsw.gov.au; Palm Beach; ☐L90, 190) This historic sandstone lighthouse (1881) sits at the northern tip of the Northern Beaches in an annexe of Ku-ring-gai Chase National Park. You've got two route options, shorter stairs or a wind-ing track, for the steep hike to the top (no toilets!), but the majestic views across Pittwater and down the peninsula are worth the effort. On Sundays short tours run half-hourly from 11am to 3pm; no need to book. The top is also a good spot for a bit of whale watching.

Whale Beach BEACH
(Whale Beach Rd, Whale Beach; ☐L90, 190) Sleepy Whale Beach, 3km south of Palm Beach, is well worth seeking out – a paradisaical slice of deep, orange-tinted sand backed by pines and flanked by steep cliffs; it's a good beach for surfers and families. There's a sea pool at its southern end.

Avalon BEACH
(Barrenjoey Rd, Avalon; ☐L88, L90, 188-190) Caught in a sandy '70s time warp, Avalon is the mythical Australian beach you always dreamt of but could never find. Challenging surf and sloping, gold-tangerine sand have a boutique headland for a backdrop. There's a sea pool at the southern end. Good cheap eating options abound in the streets behind.

◉ **Parramatta**

The district of Parramatta, 23km west of central Sydney, was founded in 1788 by Governor Phillip, who needed a place to grow grain to supply the colony. The Indigenous Darug people named it Burramatta for the plentiful eels that are still the symbol and nickname of Parramatta's famous rugby league team.

Parramatta is an important commercial and administrative centre, with an ambitious development program to grow it into a real alternative to the CBD. Originally a separate city, it now is roughly the geographical midpoint of Sydney's immense urban sprawl.

Experiment Farm Cottage HISTORIC BUILDING
(☑02-9635 5655; www.nationaltrust.org.au; 9 Ruse St, Harris Park; adult/child $9/4; ☺10.30am-3.30pm Wed-Sun; ☒Harris Park) This colonial bungalow stands on the site of Australia's first official land grant. In 1789 Governor Phillip allocated 12 hectares to emancipated convict James Ruse as an experiment to see how long it would take Ruse to wean himself off government supplies. The experiment was a success, and Ruse became Australia's first private farmer. He sold the land to surgeon John Harris, who built this house around 1835. It's furnished in period style with lovely early-colonial furniture.

Entrance is by very informative guided tour; the last one begins at 3pm.

Elizabeth Farm   HISTORIC BUILDING
(☑02-9635 9488; www.sydneylivingmuseums.com.au; 70 Alice St, Rosehill; adult/child $12/8; ☺10am-4pm Wed-Sun; ⎗Rosehill) Elizabeth Farm contains part of Australia's oldest surviving European home (1793), built by renegade pastoralist and rum trader John Macarthur. Heralded as the founder of Australia's wool industry, Macarthur was a ruthless capitalist whose politicking made him immensely wealthy and a thorn in the side of successive governors. The pretty homestead is now a hands-on museum where you can recline on the reproduction furniture and thumb voyeuristically through Elizabeth Macarthur's letters.

Old Government House   HISTORIC BUILDING
(☑02-9635 8149; www.nationaltrust.org.au; Parramatta Park, Parramatta; ☺10am-4pm Tue-Sun; ⎗Parramatta) The country residence of the early governors, this elegant Georgian Palladian building is now a preciously maintained museum furnished with original colonial furniture. It dates from 1799, making it the oldest remaining public building in Australia. Temporary exhibitions add to the building's interest and there's a vine-draped courtyard restaurant. The park itself is great, a pretty riverside community space with a democratic feel.

⊙ Outer Sydney

Lane Cove National Park   NATIONAL PARK
(www.nationalparks.nsw.gov.au; Lady Game Dr, Chatswood West; per car $8; ☺9am-6pm; ⎗North Ryde) This 601-hectare park, surrounded by North Shore suburbia, is a great place to stretch out on some middle-sized bushwalks. It's home to dozens of critters, including some endangered owls and toads. If you visit in spring, the water dragons will be getting horny and the native orchids and lilies will be flowering.

There's a boat shed on Lane Cove River that rents out rowboats and kayaks, but swimming isn't a good idea. You can also cycle and camp, and some sections are wheelchair accessible.

Wet'n'Wild Sydney   AMUSEMENT PARK
(☑13 33 86; www.wetnwildsydney.com.au; 427 Reservoir Rd, Prospect; over/under 110cm tall $80/70; ☺Sep-Apr, hours & days vary; ⎙; ⎗shuttle from Parramatta Station) The famous Gold Coast theme park has opened in Sydney with more than 40 slides, including a 360-degree loop slide that hits speeds of up to 60km/h. At the heart of the park is Australia's largest wave pool.

⚡ Activities

Cycling

Manly Bike Tours   CYCLING
(Map p105; ☑02-8005 7368; www.manlybiketours.com.au; Belgrave St, Manly; hire per hr/day from $16/33; ☺9am-6pm Oct-Mar, 9am-5pm Apr-Sep; ⛴Manly) 🚲 Hires bikes and provides maps and routes for self-guided tours. There's a big variety of bikes available and it's right across from the ferry wharf. It's got lockers for you to store gear while you ride.

Sydney Bike Tours   CYCLING
(Map p80; ☑02-8005 5724; www.sydneybiketours.com.au; shop 25, 12 Playfair St; bikes per hr/day from $21/38; ☺9am-6pm Oct-Mar, to 5pm Apr-Sep) Hires city and road bikes and supplies you with maps and suggested routes for self-guided tours.

Diving

Dive Centre Bondi   DIVING
(Map p103; ☑02-9369 3855; www.divebondi.com.au; 198 Bondi Rd, Bondi; ☺9am-6pm Mon-Fri, 8am-6pm Sat & Sun; ⎙333) Friendly and professional, this centre offers guided dives from shore ($155 for two) or boat ($185 for two) as well as equipment hire. It is PADI certified and offers dive courses (including $395 Open Water, $495 Advanced).

Dive Centre Manly   DIVING
(Map p105; ☑02-9977 4355; www.divesydney.com.au; 10 Belgrave St, Manly; ☺8.30am-6pm; ⛴Manly) Offers snorkel safaris ($50), two-day learn-to-dive PADI courses (from $495), guided shore dives (one/two dives $125/145) and boat dives (two dives $195).

**Gordons Bay Underwater
Nature Trail**   DIVING
(Map p74; www.gordonsbayscubadivingclub.com.au; Victory St, Clovelly; ⎙339) Accessed from beyond the car park just south of Clovelly Beach, this is a 500m underwater chain guiding divers around reefs, sand flats and kelp forests.

Kayaking

Sydney Harbour Kayaks   KAYAKING
(Map p74; ☑02-9960 4590; www.sydneyharbourkayaks.com.au; Smiths Boat Shed, 81 Parriwi Rd, Mosman; ☺9am-5pm Mon-Fri, 7.30am-

Surry Hills

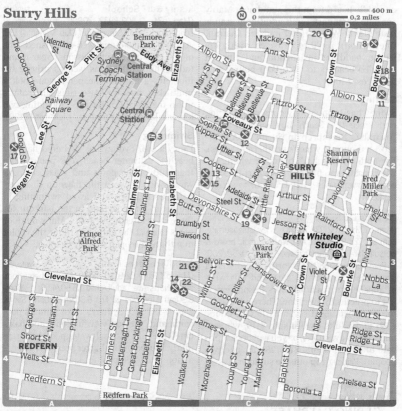

SYDNEY & NEW SOUTH WALES SYDNEY

Surry Hills

5pm Sat & Sun; 📱173-180) Rents kayaks (from $20 per hour) and stand-up paddleboards (from $25), and leads excellent four-hour ecotours ($125) from near the Spit Bridge.

Manly Kayak Centre　　　　KAYAKING
(Map p105; ☎02-9976 5057; www.manlykayakcen tre.com.au; West Esplanade, Manly; 1/2/4/8hr from $25/40/50/70; ⊘9am-5pm; 🚢Manly) As long as you can swim, you can hire a kayak

or paddle board from this stand near Manly Sea Life Sanctuary (with additional stands near Manly Wharf Hotel and the Quarantine Station). You'll be provided with a life jacket, paddling instruction and tips on secluded beaches to visit. Four-hour kayak tours cost $109.

Surfing

Sydney has been synonymous with surfing ever since the Beach Boys effused about 'Australia's Narrabeen' in 'Surfin' USA' (Narrabeen is one of Sydney's northern beaches). For updates on what's breaking where, see www.coastalwatch.com, www.surf-forecast.com, www.magicseaweed.com or www.realsurf.com.

★ **Let's Go Surfing**   SURFING
(Map p103; ☎02-9365 1800; www.letsgosurfing.com.au; 128 Ramsgate Ave, North Bondi; board & wetsuit hire 1hr/2hr/day/week $25/30/50/200; ⏰9am-5pm; ☐380-2) North Bondi is a great place to learn to surf, and this well-established surf school offers lessons catering to practically everyone. There are classes for grommets aged seven to 16 (1½ hours, $49) and adults (two hours, $110, women-only classes available), or you can book a private tutor (1½ hours, $195/284 for one/two people). Prices drop outside summer.

Manly Surf School   SURFING
(Map p74; ☎02-9932 7000; www.manlysurfschool.com; North Steyne Surf Club, Manly; ☐139, ☺Manly) Reliable and well-established, this offers two-hour surf lessons year-round (adult/child $70/55), as well as private tuition. It's a fair bit cheaper if you book a multi-class package. Also runs surf safaris up to the Northern Beaches, including two lessons, lunch, gear and city pick-ups ($120).

Swimming

Fancy a dip? Sydney has sheltered harbour beaches, saltwater beach rock pools, more than 100 public pools and crazy surf. Always swim between the flags on lifesaver-patrolled beaches, and avoid swimming in the ocean for a day and in the harbour for three days after heavy rains. Many outdoor pools close at the end of April for the cooler months and reopen in early October.

Bondi Icebergs Pool   SWIMMING
(Map p103; ☎02-9130 4804; www.icebergs.com.au; 1 Notts Ave; adult/child $6.50/4.50; ⏰6am-6.30pm Mon-Wed & Fri, 6.30am-6.30pm Sat & Sun; ☐333, 380) Sydney's most famous pool commands the best view in Bondi and has a cute little cafe. It's a saltwater pool that's regularly doused by the bigger breakers. There's a more sheltered pool for kids.

DON'T MISS

KU-RING-GAI CHASE

Spectacular 14,928-hectare **Ku-ring-gai Chase National Park** (☎02-9472 8949; www.nationalparks.nsw.gov.au; Bobbin Head Rd, North Turramurra; per car per day $12, landing fee by boat adult/child $3/2; ☐Mt Colah), 24km from the city centre, forms Sydney's northern boundary. It's a classic mix of sandstone, bushland and water vistas, taking in over 100km of coastline along the southern edge of Broken Bay, where it heads into the Hawkesbury River.

Ku-ring-gai takes its name from its original inhabitants, the Guringai people, who were all but wiped out just after colonisation through violence at the hands of British settlers and introduced disease. It's well worth reading Kate Grenville's Booker-nominated *The Secret River* for an engrossing but harrowing telling of this story.

Remnants of Aboriginal life are visible today thanks to the preservation of more than 800 sites, including rock paintings, middens and cave art. To learn more, enter the park through the Mt Colah entrance and visit the **Kalkari Discovery Centre** (☎02-9472 9300; Ku-ring-gai Chase Rd, Mt Colah; ⏰9am-5pm), which has displays and videos on Australian fauna and Aboriginal culture.

Elevated park sections offer glorious water views over Cowan Creek, Broken Bay and Pittwater. The view from West Head across Pittwater to Barrenjoey Lighthouse is a winner. This whole section of the park is a fabulous wilderness with sensational views all around. Tracks drop down to perfect little coves.

If you are arriving by car, enter the park off Pacific Hwy, Mt Colah; Bobbin Head Rd, North Turramurra; or, for the West Head, Cottage Point and Pittwater section, McCarrs Creek Rd, Terrey Hills. You can also reach the latter section by ferry from Palm Beach.

Bondi

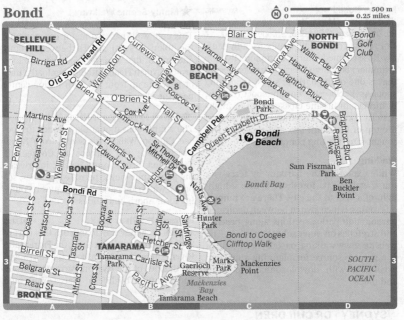

Bondi

◎ Top Sights

✛ Activities, Courses & Tours

⊜ Sleeping

⊗ Eating

⊖ Drinking & Nightlife

⊕ Shopping

Andrew (Boy) Charlton Pool   SWIMMING
(Map p74; ☎02-9358 6686; www.abcpool.org;
1c Mrs Macquaries Rd; adult/child $7.40/5.60;
☻6am-8pm; ⛲; ⊠Martin Place) Sydney's best
saltwater pool – smack bang next to the
harbour – is a magnet for water-loving gays,
straights, parents and fashionistas. Serious
lap swimmers rule the pool, so maintain
your lane. Wheelchair accessible.

Wylie's Baths   SWIMMING
(Map p74; ☎02-9665 2838; www.wylies.com.
au; 4b Neptune St, Coogee; adult/child $5/2.40;
☻7am-7pm Oct-Mar, 7am-5pm Apr-Sep; ⊠372-
374) On the rocky coast south of Coogee
Beach, this superb sea-water pool (1907) is

targeted at swimmers more than splash-
abouts. After your swim, take a yoga class
($18), enjoy a massage, or have a coffee at
the kiosk, which has magnificent views.

McIvers Baths   SWIMMING
(Map p74; www.randwick.nsw.gov.au; Beach St,
Coogee; donation 20c; ☻sunrise-sunset; ⊠372-
374) Perched against the cliffs south of
Coogee Beach and well-screened from passers-by, McIvers Baths has been popular for
women's bathing since before 1876. Its strict
women-only policy has made it popular with
an unlikely coalition of nuns, Muslim women
and lesbians. Small children of either gender
are permitted.

Murray Rose Pool SWIMMING

(Redleaf Pool; Map p74; 536 New South Head Rd, Double Bay; 🚌324-326, 🚢Double Bay) FREE
Not really a pool at all, family-friendly Murray Rose (named after a champion Olympic swimmer) is a large, shark-netted enclosure that is one of the harbour's best swimming spots. As the closest swimming spot to the city, it attracts an urbane cross-section of inner-eastern locals. A boardwalk runs around the top of the shark net, and there are two sought-after floating pontoons.

Walking

While exploring the harbour by ferry is a must, walking its foreshore is also a highlight of a visit to the city. There are numerous routes, which switch between dedicated harbourside paths, sections along beaches and stretches on quiet suburban roads. The website www.walkingcoastalsydney.com.au is a great resource for planning your own excursion, with downloadable brochures and maps.

★**Manly Scenic Walkway** WALKING

(Map p74; www.manly.nsw.gov.au; 🚢Manly)
This epic walk has two major components: the 10km western stretch between Manly and Spit Bridge, and the 9.5km eastern loop around North Head. Either download a map or pick one up from the information centre near the wharf.

★**Bondi to Coogee Clifftop Walk** WALKING

The simply sensational 6km Bondi to Coogee Clifftop Walk leads south from Bondi Beach along the clifftops to Coogee via Tamarama, Bronte and Clovelly, interweaving panoramic views, patrolled beaches, sea baths, waterside parks and plaques recounting local Aboriginal stories.

Parramatta River Walk WALKING

There's no better way to explore this part of Sydney than by walking along the Parramatta River. There's a path on both the north and south sides of the river in Parramatta itself, and plenty of birdlife in places. You could

---

SYDNEY FOR CHILDREN

With boundless natural attractions and relaxed, outdoor living, Sydney is great for kids.

The calm waters of Sydney's harbour beaches are tops for youngsters. If you're particularly paranoid about sharks, head to the netted areas at **Murray Rose Pool** (p104), **Nielsen Park** (p95), **Balmoral** (Map p74; The Esplanade, Balmoral; 🚌238, 245, 257) and **Manly Cove** (Map p105; 🚢Manly). Most of Sydney's surf beaches have saltwater ocean pools, such as the spectacular **Bondi Icebergs** (p102) and **McIvers Baths** (p103). There are also some excellent indoor public pools complete with slides and other watery attractions. Or make a summer's day of it at **Wet'n'Wild** (p100). Most surf schools also cater for kids and have special holiday packages.

Most beaches have superb playgrounds and right in the middle of the city at Darling Harbour there's an incredible adventure park with water games, swings, slides and flying foxes. Once you're done you can stroll up to **Wild Life Sydney** (p82) and the **Sydney Aquarium** (p82) or pop into the fascinating **Maritime Museum** (p77) to see its excellent collection of boats and ships. The fascinating collection of the **Powerhouse Museum** (p97) is also (for now) close by. Across town, the **Australian Museum** (p85) is a real hit with the younger crowd, especially its excellent dinosaur exhibition.

A certain winner is the ferry ride to the excellent **Taronga Zoo** (p95) or combine a trip to Manly with a visit to the penguins at the **Sea Life Sanctuary** (p97). Across the Harbour Bridge from the centre, **Luna Park** (p96) has been thrilling kids for more than 80 years.

If the thought of dragging the kids around a gallery fills you with dread, you'll be surprised by the child-friendly **Art Gallery of NSW** (p75). Its dynamic program includes free shows most Sundays, tailored discovery trails and self-guided, child-focused audio tours. There are also regular art safaris and creative workshops at the **Museum of Contemporary Art** (p75).

The delights of the **Opera House** (p70) aren't restricted to adults. Catch the best in international children's theatre, school-holiday shows and free Creative Play sessions. There's also a junior version of the popular Opera House Tour.

Little astronomers might want to do some stargazing or see the Time Ball drop at the very kid-focused **Sydney Observatory** (p71).

Manly

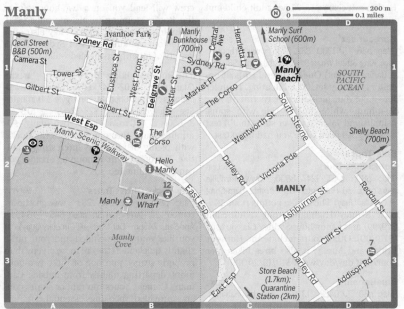

head towards Sydney, or go upstream and discover Lake Parramatta. The excellent resources on www.walkingcoastalsydney.com. au are helpful for planning.

🕝 Tours

Boat Tours

There's a wide range of harbour cruises available, from paddle steamers to maxi yachts. If you're pinching pennies, take the return ferry trip to Manly and consider yourself very clever.

★ **Whale Watching Sydney**   WILDLIFE
(Map p80; ☎02-9583 1199; www.whalewatching sydney.com.au; ⏱mid-May–early Dec) Humpback and southern right whales habitually shunt up and down the Sydney coastline, sometimes venturing into the harbour. WWS runs three-hour (adult/child $97/60) or 2½-hour ($60/40) tours beyond the Heads. For a faster ride that also offers a more intimate whale experience, there are two-hour jet-boat expeditions ($65/45). Boats depart from Jetty 6, Circular Quay or from Cockle Bay Wharf, Darling Harbour.

Captain Cook Cruises   CRUISE
(Map p80; ☎02-9206 1111; www.captaincook. com.au; Wharf 6, Circular Quay; 🚢Circular Quay) As well as ritzy lunch and dinner cruises and

Manly

whale watching, this crew offers an aquatic version of a hop-on, hop-off bus tour, stopping at Watsons Bay, Taronga Zoo, Fort Denison, Garden Island, Shark Island, Manly, Circular Quay, Luna Park and Darling

Harbour. It costs $45/25 per adult/child and includes some commentary.

Harbour Jet
BOATING
(Map p86; ☎1300 887 373; www.harbourjet.com; King Street Wharf 9; adult/child from $80/50; ☑Darling Harbour) One of several jet-boat operators (Sydney Jet, Oz Jet Boating, Thunder Jet – take your pick), these guys run a 35- or 50-minute white-knuckle ride with spins, fishtails and 75km/h power stops that'll test how long it's been since you had breakfast.

Bike Tours

Bonza Bike Tours
CYCLING
(Map p80; ☎02-9247 8800; www.bonzabiketours.com; 30 Harrington St; ⏱office 9am-5pm; ☑Circular Quay) These bike boffins run a 2½-hour Sydney Highlights tour (adult/child $79/99) and a four-hour Sydney Classic tour ($119/99). Other tours include the Harbour Bridge and Manly. It also hires bikes (per hour/half-day/day/week $10/19/29/125).

BlueBananas
CYCLING
(Map p80; ☎0422 213 574; www.bluebananas.com.au; 281 Clarence St; ☑Town Hall) Take some of the puff out of a guided cycling tour on an electric bike. Options include the 1½-hour Bike the Bridge tour ($59) and the 2½-hour Sydney City Tour ($99). The office is in a little arcade of shops.

Bike Buffs
CYCLING
(☎0414 960 332; www.bikebuffs.com.au; adult/child $95/70; ☑Circular Quay) Offers daily four-hour, two-wheeled tours around the harbourside sights, departing from Argyle Place opposite the Garrison Church. It also offers other tours and hires bikes (per half-day/day/week $35/60/295).

Walking Tours

Sydney Architecture Walks
WALKING
(☎0403 888 390; www.sydneyarchitecture.org; adult walks $49-59, cycle incl bike $120) These bright young archi-buffs run two 3½-hour cycling tours and five themed two-hour walking tours (The City; Utzon and the Sydney Opera House; Harbourings; Art, Place and Landscape; and Modern Sydney). There's an excellent focus on explaining modern architectural principles and urban design. It's cheaper if you book in advance.

Peek Tours
WALKING
(☎0420 244 756; www.peektours.com.au; ☑Circular Quay) If you find that a cool beverage makes local history easier to digest, this crew will lead you on a two-hour tour of the Rocks, stopping in historic pubs ($80, including a drink at each). They also offer three-hour walking tours of Sydney and a variety of other beer-themed walks.

The Rocks Walking Tours
WALKING
(Map p80; ☎02-9247 6678; www.rockswalkingtours.com.au; Shop 4a, cnr Argyle & Harrington Sts; adult/child/family $28/12/68; ⏱10.30am & 1.30pm; ☑Circular Quay) Two daily 90-minute tours through the historic Rocks, with plenty of tales and interesting minutiae. The office is in a shopping arcade; you can book online too.

The Rocks Ghost Tours
WALKING
(Map p80; ☎02-9241 1283; www.ghosttours.com.au; 28 Harrington St; adult $45; ⏱6.45pm Apr-Sep, 7.45pm Oct-Mar; ☑Circular Quay) If you like your spine chilled and your pulse slightly quickened (they're more creepy than properly scary), join one of these two-hour tours, departing nightly from outside Cadman's Cottage. Tours run rain or shine (ponchos provided); bookings essential.

I'm Free
WALKING
(Map p84; ☎0405 515 654; www.imfree.com.au; 483 George St; ⏱10.30am & 2.30pm; ☑Town Hall) FREE Departing twice daily from the square off George St between the Town Hall and St Andrew's Cathedral (no bookings taken – just show up), these highly rated three-hour tours are nominally free but are run by enthusiastic young guides for tips. The route takes in the Rocks, Circular Quay, Martin Place, Pitt St and Hyde Park.

Other Tours

★ BridgeClimb
WALKING
(Map p80; ☎02-8274 7777; www.bridgeclimb.com; 3 Cumberland St; adult $248-383, child $168-273; ☑Circular Quay) Don headset, safety cord and a dandy grey jumpsuit and you'll be ready to embark on an exhilarating climb to the top of Sydney's famous harbour bridge. The priciest climbs are at dawn and sunset. A cheaper, 90-minute 'sampler' climb (heading only halfway up) is also available, as is an 'express climb', which ascends to the top via a faster route.

Sydney Seaplanes
SCENIC FLIGHTS
(Map p74; ☎1300 732 752; www.seaplanes.com.au; Seaplane Base, Lyne Park, Rose Bay; 15/30min flights per person $200/265; ☑Rose Bay) Based very near Rose Bay ferry wharf, this company offers scenic flights around Sydney

Harbour and beaches. Aerial excitement meets epicurean delight when you take a seaplane flight to a secluded seafood restaurant such as the Berowra Waters Inn. Rose Bay has a long seaplane tradition; in fact it was Australia's first international airport.

✪ Festivals & Events

★ Sydney Festival   CULTURAL
(www.sydneyfestival.org.au; ⊘ Jan) Sydney's premier arts and culture festival showcases three weeks of music, theatre and visual art.

Chinese New Year   CULTURAL
(www.sydneychinesenewyear.com) Seventeen-day, Chinatown-based festival featuring food, fireworks, dragon dancers and drag-on-boat races to see in the lunar new year. Actual dates vary slightly, but it's always in late January and early February.

★ Tropfest   FILM
(www.tropfest.org.au) The world's largest short-film festival is enjoyed from picnic blankets in Parramatta Park on one day in early February.

St Jerome's Laneway Festival   MUSIC
(www.sydney.lanewayfestival.com; ⊘ Feb) A one-day music festival held in early February at the Sydney College of the Arts, Rozelle, which reliably and presciently schedules the world's hippest new indie acts, just as they're breaking (past headliners have included Florence + The Machine, Lorde and St Vincent).

★ Sydney Gay & Lesbian Mardi Gras   LGBT
(www.mardigras.org.au; ⊘ Feb-Mar) A two-week cultural and entertainment festival culminating in the world-famous massive parade and party on the first Saturday in March.

Sydney Royal Easter Show   FAIR
(www.eastershow.com.au) Ostensibly an agricultural show, this wonderful Sydney tradition is a two-week fiesta of carnival rides, kiddie-centric show bags and sugary horrors. Crowds are massive.

Biennale of Sydney   CULTURAL
(www.biennaleofsydney.com.au) High-profile festival of art and ideas held between March and June in even-numbered years.

★ Sydney Writers' Festival   LITERATURE
(www.swf.org.au; ⊘ May) The country's preeminent literary shindig is held over a week in May, in various prime locations around the central city.

Vivid Sydney   CULTURAL
(www.vividsydney.com) Immersive light installations and projections in the city, plus performances from local and international musicians, and public talks and debates with leading global creative thinkers; held over 18 days from late May.

★ Sydney Film Festival   FILM
(www.sff.org.au; ⊘ Jun) Held (mostly) at the magnificent State Theatre (p136), this excellent, highly regarded film festival screens art-house gems from Australia and around the world.

City2Surf   SPORTS
(www.city2surf.com.au) On the second Sunday in August, over 80,000 people run (or walk) the 14km from Hyde Park to Bondi Beach. The fastest runners reach the beach in a little over 40 minutes. Their athletic seriousness is counterbalanced by family activities, silly outfits and the odd cardiac scare.

Good Food Month   FOOD & DRINK
(www.goodfoodmonth.com) October-long celebration of food and wine, with dining events, cooking classes and night noodle markets in Hyde Park.

Sculpture by the Sea   ART
(www.sculpturebythesea.com) For 17 days from late October, the clifftop trail from Bondi Beach to Tamarama transforms into a sculpture garden. Serious prize money is on offer for the most creative, curious or quizzical offerings from international and local sculptors.

Sydney to Hobart Yacht Race   SPORTS
(www.rolexsydneyhobart.com; ⊘ Dec) On 26 December Sydney Harbour is a sight to behold as hundreds of boats crowd its waters to farewell the yachts competing in this gruelling race.

★ New Year's Eve   FIREWORKS
(www.sydneynewyearseve.com; ⊘ 31 Dec) The biggest party of the year, with flamboyant firework displays on the harbour. There's a family-friendly display at 9pm then the main event at midnight. There are also any number of other events on and around the harbour. There's a variety of regulated zones to watch the fireworks from, some ticketed, some alcohol-free.

🛏 Sleeping

There are hotels scattered throughout Sydney, but you'll find the international chains with all their bells and whistles in Circular Quay and the city centre. The suburbs and beaches host a diverse bunch of boutique escapes, from heritage-listed terrace houses to sleek apartments and beach bungalows.

Nearly all hotels operate flexible pricing, so be sure to book your stay well in advance for the best rates.

🛏 Circular Quay & the Rocks

★ **Sydney Harbour YHA** HOSTEL $$
(Map p80; ☑02-8272 0900; www.yha.com. au; 110 Cumberland St; dm $55-75, d $200-240; ❄✱@🛜; ᴿCircular Quay) 🏊 Any qualms about the unhostel-like prices will be shelved the moment you head up to the ample rooftop space of this sprawling, modern hostel and see the superb views of Circular Quay. All of the spacious rooms, including the dorms, have en suites and there are a host of sustainability initiatives in place.

Lord Nelson Brewery Hotel PUB $$
(Map p80; ☑02-9251 4044; www.lordnelson brewery.com; 19 Kent St; r $180-200; ❄✱🛜; ᴿCircular Quay) Built in 1836, this atmospheric sandstone pub has a tidy set of upstairs rooms, with exposed stone walls and dormer windows with harbour glimpses. Most of the eight light-filled rooms have en suites; there's also one with a private exterior bathroom. The downstairs microbrewery is a welcoming place for a pint and a meal. Rates include continental breakfast.

★ **Harbour Rocks** BOUTIQUE HOTEL $$$
(Map p80; ☑02-8220 9999; www.harbour rocks.com.au; 34 Harrington Street; r $300-550; ❄✱@🛜; ᴿCircular Quay) This deluxe boutique hotel on the site of Sydney's first hospital has undergone a chic and sympathetic transformation from colonial warehouse and workers' cottages to a series of New York loft-style rooms, with high ceilings, distressed brick and elegant furnishings. It maintains a historic feel, offers relaxed personable service and has a great little garden balcony terrace.

Pullman Quay Grand
Sydney Harbour APARTMENT $$$
(Map p80; ☑02-9256 4000; www.pullman quaygrandsydneyharbour.com; 61 Macquarie St; apt $450-800; ᴾ❄✱@🛜✉; ᴿCircular Quay) With the Opera House as its neighbour, the building known locally as 'The Toaster' has a scorching-hot location. These well-designed contemporary apartments, large and well-equipped, set you in Sydney's glitzy heart, encircled by top restaurants, cocktail bars and that attention-seeking harbour. The small number of rooms and blend of residents and visitors gives it a quiet ambience away from its lively bar Hacienda.

Park Hyatt HOTEL $$$
(Map p80; ☑02-9256 1234; www.sydney.park. hyatt.com; 7 Hickson Rd; r $1150-1600; ᴾ❄✱@🛜✉; ᴿCircular Quay) At Sydney's most expensive hotel the impeccable service levels and facilities are second to none. With full frontal views across Circular Quay, you can catch all the action from your bed, balcony or bathtub. From the rooftop pool you feel you can almost touch the Harbour Bridge. And with 24-hour butler service for all, it's not like you need to be anywhere else.

Langham HOTEL $$$
(Map p80; ☑02-9256 2222; www.langham hotels.com; 89-113 Kent St; r $500-700; ᴾ❄✱@🛜✉; ᴿWynyard) This opulent hotel eschews excessive glitz in favour of an elegant antique ambience. The result is a true five-star stay, featuring afternoon turn-down service, in-house pastry kitchen, a page-long pillow menu and an extravagant pool and day spa experience, where guests can swim under a star-dazzled ceiling. Carefully selected works of art dot the building, giving it quite a different feel to other CBD hotels.

🛏 City Centre & Haymarket

★ **Railway Square YHA** HOSTEL $
(Map p101; ☑02-9281 9666; www.yha.com.au; 8-10 Lee St; dm $39-52, d from $142, without bathroom from $132; ✱@🛜✉; ᴿCentral) A lovely piece of industrial renovation has converted Central station's former parcel shed into a really appealing hostel, in a great location but away from the bustle. Dorms with corrugated roofs and underfloor-heated bathrooms are spotless; some are actually in converted train carriages. There's a cafe and laundry facilities, plus the pool was being upgraded at time of research.

Sydney Central YHA HOSTEL $
(Map p101; ☑02-9218 9000; www.yha.com.au; 11 Rawson Pl; dm $44-55, d from $150, without bathroom from $130; ᴾ❄✱@🛜✉; ᴿCentral) 🏊 Near Central station, this 1913 heritage-listed monolith is the mother of all Sydney YHA proper-

ties. The renovated hostel includes everything from a travel agency to an in-house cinema. The rooms are brightly painted and the kitchens are great but the highlight is sweating it out in the sauna, then cooling off in the rooftop pool. There's a 10% HI discount.

Grace Hotel HOTEL $$

(Map p80; ☑02-9272 6888; www.gracehotel. com.au; 77 York St; r $200-300; P🐾❄🏋🛜; 🚇Wynyard) The sumptuous neo-Gothic exterior makes this 1920s building a Sydney landmark, and its stylish art-deco interior adds impact. By comparison the rooms are bland, but they are pleasant and commodious, and facilities are excellent. Best is the atmosphere downstairs, with a decent Irish pub, piano lounge and busy eateries; it's a real hub of activity.

Hyde Park Inn HOTEL $$

(Map p84; ☑02-9264 6001; www.hydeparkinn. com.au; 271 Elizabeth St; r $198-286; P🐾❄🛜; 🚇Museum) Right on the park, this relaxed place offers brightly decorated studio rooms with kitchenettes, deluxe rooms with balconies and full kitchens, and some two-bedroom apartments. All have flat-screen TVs with cable access and some have microwaves and kitchenettes. Breakfast and parking is included in the rate, making it great value for central Sydney.

★ QT Sydney BOUTIQUE HOTEL $$$

(Map p80; ☑02-8262 0000; www.qtsydney. com.au; 49 Market St; r $350-450; P🐾❄🛜; 🚇Town Hall) Fun, sexy and relaxed, this ultra-theatrical, effortlessly cool hotel is located in the historic State Theatre. Art-deco eccentricity is complemented by quirky extras in the rooms, which are distinct and decorated with real style and flair; there's a definite wow factor. There's also a luxurious spa plus a bar and grill operated by one of the city's most fashionable restaurateurs.

Establishment Hotel BOUTIQUE HOTEL $$$

(Map p80; ☑02-9240 3100; www.merivale.com. au; 5 Bridge Lane; r $350-500; 🐾❄@🛜; 🚇Wynyard) In a discreet laneway, this designer boutique hotel in a refurbished 19th-century warehouse invokes Asia with its incense aromas and dark-wood fittings. There are two principal room styles: 'light', all white-and-tan contemporary colouring; and sexier 'dark', with wooden floorboards and a nocturnal feel. Decadent nights out are assured with a posse of the company's acclaimed bars and restaurants right around you.

ⓘ HOTEL PRICES

These days, all but the smallest hotels vary their prices depending on the season, special events, day of the week (weekends tend to be more expensive) and, most importantly, occupancy. Where prices vary widely, we've listed a 'from' amount, basing this on the cheapest room available given a reasonable amount of notice in the high (but not necessarily peak) season. If you leave booking until the last minute, you may find yourself paying considerably more.

The summer high season lasts from around December to March, with the absolute peak being between Christmas and New Year (especially New Year's Eve). Prices also shoot up again in late February/early March in the lead up to Mardi Gras.

Primus Hotel Sydney HOTEL $$$

(Map p84; ☑02-8027 8000; www.primus hotelsydney.com; 339 Pitt St; r $290-380; P🐾❄🛜; 🚇Town Hall) In the former Water Board building, this slick conversion has a magnificent lobby space with red pillars and glorious art-deco details. There's space to spare here, with wide corridors and ample, commodious rooms; excellent service is a noteworthy feature. Though the pool itself is tiny, the deck surrounding it is a fabulous spot that may open to the public.

🏨 Darling Harbour & Pyrmont

★ Ovolo 1888 BOUTIQUE HOTEL $$$

(Map p86; ☑02-8586 1888; www.ovolohotels. com; 139 Murray St; shoebox d $239-299, d $299-349; 🐾❄@🛜; 🚇Convention Centre) In a heritage-listed wool store, this stylish gem combines industrial minimalism with the warmth of ironbark wood beams, luxury appointments and engaged staff. Rooms range from the aptly named shoebox to airy lofts and attic suites with harbour views. The minibar is complimentary, and if you book direct you get to enjoy free drinks and canapes at the daily happy hour.

Adina Apartment Hotel Sydney Harbourside APARTMENT $$$

(Map p86; ☑02-9249 7000; www.adinahotels. com.au; 55 Shelley St; apt $229-500; P❄🛜; 🚇Darling Harbour) Heaven is a swish, spacious apartment where people clean up after you. That's exactly what happens at this low-rise development just off King St Wharf. All apartments have kitchens, and all but the studios have laundry facilities and balconies. They are all very spacious, and there's a great atrium pool and gym area.

🛏 Kings Cross & Potts Point

★ **Blue Parrot Backpackers**   HOSTEL $
(Map p88; ☑ 02-9356 4888; www.blueparrot. com.au; 87 Macleay St, Potts Point; dm $39-45; ⊖@🛜; ☒ Kings Cross) If Polly wanted a cracker of a hostel she'd head to this brilliant, colourful spot run with real enthusiasm by a pair of sisters. It's a personal experience that feels more like a share house (but much cleaner!). There's a great back courtyard and high-ceilinged dorms with good bunks and mattresses. Movies, Playstation and a barbecue add points. For 18- to 35-year-olds.

Eva's Backpackers   HOSTEL $
(Map p88; ☑ 02-9358 2185; www.evasbackpack ers.com.au; 6-8 Orwell St, Kings Cross; dm $34-40, d $97-107; ⊖❄@🛜; ☒ Kings Cross) Likeable Eva's is a long-time favourite and a secure, clean welcoming hostel that belies the building's intriguingly shady history. The great roof terrace has a super view of the city skyline and there's a new common-kitchen area being built up there in 2017, along with a major renovation of bathrooms and dorms that should leave it looking very spruce.

Kings Cross Backpackers   HOSTEL $
(Map p88; ☑ 02-8705 3761; www.kingscross backpackers.com.au; 79 Bayswater Rd, Kings Cross; dm $35-43; ⊖❄@🛜; ☒ Kings Cross) Nicely set in a quieter part of the Cross, this is a well-run place with renovated air-conditioned, clean dorms that sleep four to 12 and come with lockers and under-bed storage. The

---

ℹ THE HOSTEL SCENE

Sydney's hostels range from the sublime to the sublimely grotty. A clump of flash-packer-style blocks encircling Central station have raised the bar, offering en suites, air-conditioning, rooftop decks and, in one case, a pool. Private rooms in such places are often on par with midrange hotels – and in many cases the prices aren't all that different either. You'll find smaller, cheaper hostels in Kings Cross (still the backpacker capital). Many hostels have weekly rates and some have specific areas for long-stayers.

---

downstairs kitchen-lounge and sweet roof terrace are the places to hang out. Security is good and the price is fair. Breakfast is included, but it's a couple of blocks away.

Macleay   APARTMENT $$
(Map p88; ☑ 02-9357 7755; www.themacleay. com; 28 Macleay St, Elizabeth Bay; r $180-250; 𝗣⊖❄@🛜; ☒ Kings Cross) At the posh end of Kings Cross, surrounded by fabulous restaurants, is this understated place. The studios are a little faded but all have small kitchenettes and there's a laundry on each floor. An added plus is the rooftop pool and gym. Staff are welcoming and helpful; ask for a room on a higher floor for city and harbour views.

Hotel 59   B&B $$
(Map p88; ☑ 02-9360 5900; www.hotel59.com. au; 59 Bayswater Rd, Kings Cross; s $105, d $135-145; ⊖❄🛜; ☒ Kings Cross) With just nine simple, spotless comfortable rooms, family-run Hotel 59 offers great bang for your buck on the quiet but still very convenient part of Bayswater Rd. The owners are genuinely helpful and attentive and the cafe downstairs does whopping cooked breakfasts (included in the price) for those barbarous Kings Cross hangovers.

Mariners Court   HOTEL $$
(Map p88; ☑ 02-9320 3888; www.mariners court.com.au; 44-50 McElhone St, Woolloomooloo; r $110-160; 𝗣⊖❄@🛜; ☐ 311, ☒ Kings Cross) Once a naval retirement home, this is now an under-the-radar hotel on a quiet street. It hasn't been modified much, so is solid rather than flash, but offers excellent value for this location and simple, comfortable rooms with jug, fridge and either balcony or courtyard. Other pluses are the complimentary hot breakfast buffet, pool table and sun deck. Good wheelchair access.

★ **Ovolo Hotel Woolloomooloo**   HOTEL $$$
(Map p88; ☑ 02-9331 9000; www.ovolohotels. com; 6 Cowper Wharf Roadway, Woolloomooloo; r $400-700; 𝗣⊖❄@🛜; ☐ 311, ☒ Kings Cross) Superbly set in Woolloomooloo Wharf, this excellent smart-casual hotel has extremely friendly young staff and a very likeable set of features. 'Superoo' rooms are mostly either road-facing or skylit, so for water views upgrade to a deluxe, facing east, or city, facing west. It's ultra-characterful with long corridors, industrial machinery and unusually shaped, artfully designed rooms, some split-level. A Sydney standout.

Simpsons of Potts Point BOUTIQUE HOTEL **$$$**
(Map p88; ☑02-9356 2199; www.simpsons hotel.com; 8 Challis Ave, Potts Point; r $255-355; [P][☺][✳][@][🛜]; [🚉]Kings Cross) At the quiet end of a busy cafe strip, this 1892 villa has been affectionately restored with decorative flourishes of yesteryear. The interior is a stunner, with art, elegance and cosy luxury right through the handsome public areas and dozen guest rooms. The downstairs lounge is perfect for a game of chess and a complimentary sherry. Service is personalised and highly competent.

🛏 Surry Hills & Darlinghurst

★Bounce HOSTEL **$**
(Map p101; ☑02-9281 2222; www.bouncehotel. com.au; 28 Chalmers St, Surry Hills; dm $40-48, d $149-159; [☺][✳][@][🛜]; [🚉]Central) 🏃 Right by Central, this hostel offers boutique budget accommodation. Dorms (various configurations) are modern and very spacious, with extra-large lockers. Private rooms are hotel-quality; it's a value-packed option. The place is really well run, catering to the needs of the party crew and those who want a quieter stay. The huge kitchen is a plus and the fabulous roof terrace is a show-stealer. Top marks.

Big Hostel HOSTEL **$**
(Map p84; ☑02-9281 6030; www.bighostel. com; 212 Elizabeth St, Surry Hills; dm $32-36, s/d $89/110; [☺][✳][@][🛜]; [🚉]Central) A great, no-frills hostel experience with a rooftop terrace and a crowded but decent communal area and kitchen. Dorms do the job, with lockers, high ceilings and enough space. The four-bed ones cost a little more but have a bathroom and small TV. The price is good for central Sydney too. Continental breakfast is included. Wi-fi is free downstairs only.

57 Hotel HOTEL **$$**
(Map p101; ☑02-9011 5757; www.57hotel.com.au; 57 Foveaux St, Surry Hills; s $219-299, d $229-449; [☺][✳][🛜]; [🚉]Central) Converted from a technical college, this hotel goes to town on modish grey, black and chocolate colouring. Rooms vary widely, from the extremely compact shoebox twins to large, light king-bedded rooms on the corners of the building. We love the doggie towel rails. There is free coffee and morning pastries in the lobby lounge.

Medusa BOUTIQUE HOTEL **$$**
(Map p88; ☑02-9331 1000; www.medusa.com. au; 267 Darlinghurst Rd, Darlinghurst; r $245-405; [☺][✳][@][🛜][✳]; [🚉]Kings Cross) Winding across two back-to-back terraces, Medusa has a curious interior layout and eye-catching rooms in three sizes with large beds, art-deco features and regal furnishings (the best face the courtyard). You are guaranteed warm personal service from the excellent staff. Small touches such as the Aesop toiletries and Lindt chocolates add points, and the tremendous location is a real plus.

★ADGE Boutique Apartment Hotel APARTMENT **$$$**
(Map p88; ☑02-8093 9888; www.adgehotel. com.au; 222 Riley St, Surry Hills; apt $400-800; [P][☺][✳][🛜]; [🚌]333, 380) Modern, catchy and bold, ADGE puts a clever, upbeat twist on the ubiquitous serviced apartment experience. The idiosyncratic but extremely comfortable two-bedroom apartments have gloriously striped liquorice-allsort carpets, floor-to-ceiling windows, quality kitchens with Smeg fridge and appealing balconies. Little extras, including a welcome drink and turn-down service, add points. It's an ideal urban experience and great value for two couples.

🛏 Bondi, Coogee & the Eastern Beaches

Bondi Beachouse YHA HOSTEL **$**
(Map p103; ☑02-9365 2088; www.yha.com.au; 63 Fletcher St, Tamarama; dm $33-37, tw & d without bathroom $90, d/f $110/180; [☺][🛜]; [🚌]361) Perched on a hillside between Bondi and Tamarama Beaches, this 95-bed art-deco hostel is the best in Bondi. Dorms sleep four to eight and come with wooden floors and spacious lockers; some of the private rooms have ocean views – all are clean and well maintained. Facilities include a cinema room, spacious common areas, a courtyard barbecue and a rooftop deck with top views.

Bondi Beach House GUESTHOUSE **$$**
(Map p103; ☑02-9300 0369; www.bondibeach house.com.au; 28 Sir Thomas Mitchell Rd, Bondi Beach; s $130, d $195-320; [P][☺][✳][🛜]; [🚌]380-2) In a tranquil pocket behind Campbell Pde, this charming place offers a homely atmosphere with rustic-chic furnishings and a well-equipped communal kitchen. Though only a two-minute walk from the beach, you may well be tempted to stay in all day – the courtyard and terrace are great spots for relaxing, and the breezily arty rooms are conducive to long sleep-ins.

Dive Hotel
BOUTIQUE HOTEL **$$**

(Map p74; ☑02-9665 5538; www.divehotel. com.au; 234 Arden St, Coogee; r $210-380; [P][⊕][❄]@[⟨⟩][☻]; ☐372-374) In a cracking location right across the road from the beach, this relaxed, family-run affair is thankfully very inaccurately named. Simple, likeable contemporary rooms come with fridge, microwave and small stylish bathrooms fitted out with mosaic tiles and stainless steel sinks. Sociable continental buffet breakfast in an appealing indoor-outdoor area is a highlight, as are the personable owners and their friendly dogs.

★ QT Bondi
APARTMENT **$$$**

(Map p103; ☑02-8362 3900; www.qtbondi.com. au; 6 Beach Rd, Bondi Beach; apt $399-720; [P][⊕][❄][⟨⟩][☻]; ☐333, 380-2) Colourful, chic and appropriately beachy, this newish apartment hotel is steps from the beach and offers a very appealing combination of facilities, location and attitude. All the rooms and suites are exceedingly spacious, with light-coloured furniture and an airy feel. King Deluxe and above have balconies, but there are no ocean views here. All rooms have kitchenette, bathtub and laundry facilities.

🛏 Sydney Harbourside

★ Cockatoo Island
CAMPGROUND **$**

(Map p74; ☑02-8969 2111; www.cockatoo island.gov.au; camp sites from $45, 2-bed tents $150-175, apt from $250, houses from $595; [⟨⟩]; 🛥Cockatoo Island) Waking up on an island in the middle of the harbour is an extraordinary Sydney experience. Bring your own tent (or just sleeping bags) or 'glamp' in a two-person tent complete with a double bed on the water's edge. Non-campers will enjoy the elegant houses and apartments. For self-caterers, there's a well-equipped camp kitchen; for everyone else, there are two cafes and bars. Note that you can't take alcohol onto the island unless you are staying in one of the houses.

Watsons Bay
Boutique Hotel
BOUTIQUE HOTEL **$$**

(Map p74; ☑02-9337 5444; www.watsonsbay hotel.com.au; 10 Marine Pde, Watsons Bay; r $259-559; [P][⊕][❄][⟨⟩]; 🛥Watsons Bay) The ferry pulls up to the doorstep of this chic, Hampton's-inspired hotel in a charming beachside hamlet. Expect luxuries such as crisp linen, trendy bathroom accessories and slick glassed-in en suites. The hotel's multilevel Beach Club hums on weekends, and noise can be an issue despite double glazing. Rates include breakfast.

Glenferrie Lodge
GUESTHOUSE **$$**

(Map p74; ☑02-9955 1685; www.glenferrie lodge.com; 12a Carabella St, Kirribilli; s/d without bathroom $88/128, d $152; [P][⊕]@[⟨⟩][☻]) ✎ Set in a grand 19th-century house in a peaceful Kirribilli location very close to the ferry (or a pleasant stroll to the city across the bridge), this lodge offers excellent Sydney value for its modern rooms, most of which share gym-style bathrooms. It's a sizeable, slightly chaotically run complex with a kitchen-cafe area and a garden with a playground. If you book direct, breakfast is included.

The location is lovely, and the PM's Sydney residence is just at the end of the street. Prices vary widely by the day; check the website. Saturdays are significantly more expensive.

🛏 Newtown & the Inner West

Mad Monkey Backpackers
HOSTEL **$**

(Map p98; ☑02-8705 3762; www.madmonkey broadway.com.au; 20 City Rd, Chippendale; dm $38-48; [⊕][❄][⟨⟩]; ☐412, 413, 422, 423, 🚊Central) There's a lot to like about this friendly, well-equipped hostel in a top location. Dorms are tight but have very decent mattresses, while bathrooms are above average with hairdryers and straighteners on hand. There's a guaranteed social life with party buses and free entry to major Saturday nightclubs, plus free comfort food to aid recovery the next day. Breakfast and Netflix included.

Mandelbaum House
GUESTHOUSE **$**

(Map p98; ☑02-9692 5200; www.mandelbaum. usyd.edu.au; 385 Abercrombie St, Darlington; s/d without bathroom $75/98, d/apt $135/170; ☉late Nov–mid-Feb; [P][⊕][❄]@[⟨⟩]; 🚊Redfern) ✎ One of the University of Sydney's residential colleges, this sweet spot makes a great place to stay in summer. It's a small, genuinely friendly place with a personal welcome, a not-for-profit ethos and a range of comfortable rooms, some of which share excellent bathrooms. The location is great for exploring Redfern and Newtown.

★ Tara Guest House
B&B **$$**

(Map p98; ☑02-9519 4809; www.taraguest house.com.au; 13 Edgeware Rd, Enmore; d with/ without bathroom $225/195; [⊕][⟨⟩]; ☐426) A couple who engages with and really appreciates their guests have created a wonderful place here in a character-packed 1880 house. The striking rooms are luminous, soaring spaces with fabulous features. Avant-garde art adds character, while Oscar the dog, free airport transfers and gourmet communal breakfasts are other highlights. Standout hospitality makes this one of Sydney's best options.

★ Forsyth Bed & Breakfast B&B $$

(Map p74; ☑02-9552 2110; www.forsythbnb. com; 3 Forsyth St, Glebe; d $195-235; ⊜✳☎; ▣431, ▣Glebe) This boutique hideaway in a lovely part of Glebe is an enticing spot with just two stunning designer rooms: modern, uncluttered and graced with well-chosen art. Rozelle has a lovely balcony and spacious en suite, while Asian-inflected Blackwattle has a tiny bathroom and its own sitting room. The owner provides faultless hospitality, solicitous advice and quality breakfasts in the Japanese-inspired garden.

Urban Hotel BOUTIQUE HOTEL $$

(Map p98; ☑02-8960 7800; www.theurbanhotel. com.au; 52-60 Enmore Rd, Newtown; r $199-299; ⊜✳@☎; ▣Newtown) A couple of minutes' walk from Newtown station and surrounded by great bars and eats, this casual hotel in a former RSL Club offers edgy industrial-styled studio accommodation. The Urban stands out from the crowd with a slew of extras such as free landline calls Australia-wide and relaxed check-in and -out options. Kitchens include coffee-pod machine and minibars stocked with local craft beers.

The huge mural on the facade is by noted street artist Fintan Magee and is a commentary on the rising cost of housing in Sydney.

Old Clare Hotel BOUTIQUE HOTEL $$$

(Map p98; ☑02-8277 8277; www.theoldclarehotel. com.au; 1 Kensington St, Chippendale; r $300-600; ▣⊜✳☎✉; ▣Central) A sensitive brewery-office conversion is now a 62-room hotel in a primo Chippendale location. Rooms are well back from noisy Broadway, and high-ceilinged and easy-on-the-eye, with artful bespoke details such as the lamps made of salvaged toolshed paraphernalia. Superior categories are appreciably larger but the cheapest rooms still have king beds, attractive amenities and a good sense of space.

⌷ Manly

Manly Bunkhouse HOSTEL $

(Map p74; ☑02-9976 0472; www.bunkhouse. com.au; 35 Pine St, Manly; dm $42, d $105; ▣⊜@☎; ▣151, 158, 169, ⛴Manly) An easy walk from the beach, this laid-back hostel in a nice old house has a distinct surf vibe. High-ceilinged, en-suite dorms have plenty of room to move and lots of storage space, making them popular with long-termers. The renovated private rooms also have bathrooms and are a good deal. There's a great backyard with BBQ and funky paintings on the walls.

101 Addison Road B&B $$

(Map p105; ☑02-9977 6216; www.bb-manly.com; 101 Addison Rd, Manly; r $165-200; ▣⊜☎; ⛴Manly) This sumptuously decorated 1880s cottage is perched on a quiet street close to the beach and ferry wharf. Two rooms are available but the delightful host only takes one booking at a time (from one to four people), meaning you'll have free rein of the antique-strewn accommodation, including a private lounge with piano and open fire.

Cecil Street B&B B&B $$

(Map p74; ☑02-9977 8036; www.cecilstreetbb. com.au; 18 Cecil St, Fairlight; s $120-160, d $140-200; ▣⊜☎; ▣142, ⛴Manly) This low-key bed and breakfast is in a handsome Federation-style brick home on a hill above Manly. The two simple but tastefully decorated rooms make the most of high ceilings, lead-light windows and polished timber floors. They share a modern bathroom and little sitting room. The only downside is the steep hike back from the beach.

Quest Manly APARTMENT $$$

(Map p105; ☑02-9976 4600; www.questmanly. com.au; 54a West Esplanade, Manly; apt $340-445; ▣⊜✳☎; ⛴Manly) Superbly located for all of Manly's beachy delights as well as a speedy escape to the city (the ferry couldn't be closer), the Quest's smart, self-contained apartments are a great option. It's worth paying extra for the harbour view.

⌷ Northern Beaches

Sydney Lakeside Holiday Park CAMPGROUND $

(☑02-9913 7845; www.sydneylakeside.com.au; 38 Lake Park Rd, North Narrabeen; sites $47-102, d $140-170, cabins $204-299; ▣⊜✳☎✉; ▣L84, L87, L90, 184, 187, 188, 190) This superbly equipped holiday park has a wide range of cabins and several choices of camp site, including ones with private bathrooms. It's a great one for the kids, with its location near the beach and lake, and an on-site water-park and games.

✗ Eating

Sydney's cuisine rivals that of any great world city. Sydney truly celebrates Australia's place on the Pacific Rim, marrying the freshest local ingredients with the flavours of Asia, the Americas and, of course, its colonial past.

Sydney's top restaurants are properly pricey, but eating out needn't be expensive. There are plenty of ethnic eateries where you can grab a cheap, zingy pizza or a bowl of noodles. Cafes are a good bet for a solid, often adventurous and usually reasonably priced meal. And the numerous BYO (bring your own wine) restaurants offer a substantially cheaper eating experience; the Inner West is brimful of them.

✗ Circular Quay & the Rocks

The charismatic back lanes of the Rocks are dotted with little eateries, from 24-hour pancake joints to white-linen palaces. Around the horseshoe from the Harbour Bridge to the Opera House you'll find dozens of up-market restaurants, all with winning water views. It should come as no surprise that this most touristy of precincts is also the priciest. If at all possible, budget for at least one night where you can throw on your glad rags and let Sydney's showiness seduce you.

★ Fine Food Store   CAFE $
(Map p80; ☑ 02-9252 1196; www.finefoodstore. com; cnr Mill Lane & Kendall Lane; light meals $9-15; ◉ 7am-4.30pm Mon-Sat, 7.30am-4.30pm Sun; ☜ ✍; ⓡ Circular Quay) The Rocks some-times seems all pubs, so it's a delight to find this tucked-away contemporary cafe that works for a sightseeing stopover or a better, cheaper breakfast than your hotel. Staff are genuinely welcoming, make very respectable coffee, and offer delicious panini, sandwiches and other breakfast and lunch fare. The outside tables on this narrow lane are the spot to be.

★ Quay   MODERN AUSTRALIAN $$$
(Map p80; ☑ 02-9251 5600; www.quay.com.au; L3, Overseas Passenger Terminal; 4/8 courses $175/235; ◉ 6-9.30pm Mon-Thu, noon-1.30pm & 6-9.30pm Fri-Sun; ⓡ Circular Quay) Quay is shamelessly guilty of breaking the rule that good views make for bad food. Chef Peter Gilmore never rests on his laurels, consistently delivering the exquisitely crafted, adventurous cuisine that has landed Quay on the prestigious World's Best Restaurants list. And the view? Like dining in a postcard. Book online well in advance, but it's always worth phoning just in case.

Aria   MODERN AUSTRALIAN $$$
(Map p80; ☑ 02-9240 2255; www.ariarestau rant.com; 1 Macquarie St; 2-/3-/4-course dinner $115/145/170, degustation $205; ◉ noon-2.15pm & 5.30-10.30pm Mon-Fri, noon-1.45pm & 5-10.30pm Sat, noon-2.15pm & 5.30-8.30pm Sun; ⓡ Circular Quay) Aria is a star in Sydney's fine-dining firmament, an award-winning combination of chef Matt Moran's stellar dishes, Opera House views, a stylishly renovated interior and faultless service. A pre- and post-theatre à la carte menu is available before 7pm and

---

BREKKIE & BRUNCH IN SYDNEY

It might be something to do with long nights of partying, but breakfast and brunch is something Sydney cafes do particularly well. Many locals prefer to conduct business over a morning latte instead of a power lunch or an upmarket dinner, and friends often launch the day with scrambled eggs, carrot juice and a few laughs. The prime break-fasting 'hoods are Potts Point, Surry Hills and the beaches, but it'd be weird not to find a decent brekky cafe in any inner-city 'burb. Yum cha in Chinatown is also a hugely popular weekend brunch option (expect to queue).

It's in the caffeine stakes that Sydney wipes the floor with London and Los Angeles (as do most Australasian cities). You won't have to settle for wussy drip-filtered pap here – it's espresso all the way. The big international chains have sprouted up, but they're generally considered the last refuge of the unimaginative. Choose a local cafe instead and order a flat white (espresso with milk that's been perfectly warmed but not bubbled – it's an art all of its own), caffe latte (similar but milkier, often served in a glass), a cappuccino (espresso topped with frothed milk and chocolate or cinnamon), a long or short black (espresso without milk and with varying amounts of water), a macchiato (a short black with a tiny splash of milk) or a ristretto (very concentrated espresso). Nearly all cafes also offer soy or 'skinny' (skim) milk.

after 10pm, perfect for a special meal before or after a special night at the Opera House (one/two/three courses $55/90/110).

✕ City Centre & Haymarket

Without harbour views, central-city restaurants tend to be discreet, upmarket spots – perfect for secret handshakes over million-dollar deals. Some have beaten geography by perching themselves atop towers. Chinatown is your best bet for a cheap, satisfying meal – especially after midnight. Chinese food dominates, but you'll also find Vietnamese, Malaysian, Korean and Thai. There's also a Little Korea along Pitt St near Liverpool St; and Thaitown on Campbell St.

Mamak   MALAYSIAN $
(Map p84; ☑02-9211 1668; www.mamak.com. au; 15 Goulburn St; mains $6-17; ☺11.30am-2.30pm & 5.30-10pm Mon-Thu, to 1am Fri, 11.30am-1am Sat, to 10pm Sun; ☑; ⓡTown Hall) Get here early (from 5.30pm) if you want to score a table without queuing, because this eat-and-run Malaysian joint is one of the most popular cheapies in the city. The satays are cooked over charcoal and are particularly delicious when accompanied by a flaky golden roti.

Central Baking Depot   BAKERY $
(Map p80; www.centralbakingdepot.com.au; 37-39 Erskine St; items $5-13; ☺7am-4pm Mon-Fri, 8am-4pm Sat; ☑; ⓡWynyard) CBD produces quality baked goods right in the heart of the CBD (central business district). Drop by for a savoury snack (pies, quiche, sausage rolls, croissants, pizza slices, sandwiches), or a sweet treat with coffee. Seating is limited to a modest scattering of tables and a window bench.

★ Mr Wong   CHINESE $$
(Map p80; ☑02-9240 3000; www.merivale. com.au/mrwong; 3 Bridge Lane; mains $26-38; ☺noon-3pm & 5.30-11pm Mon-Wed, noon-3pm & 5.30pm-midnight Thu & Fri, 10.30am-3pm & 5.30pm-midnight Sat, 10.30am-3pm & 5.30-10pm Sun; ☎☑; ⓡWynyard) Classy but comfortable in an attractive low-lit space on a CBD laneway, this has exposed-brick colonial warehouse chic, a huge team of staff and hanging ducks in the open kitchen. Lunchtime dim sum offerings bristle with flavour and the 'textured' chicken and jellyfish salad is a mouth-freshening sensation. Mains such as crispy pork hock are sinfully sticky, while Peking duck rolls are legendary.

An impressive wine list and attentive, sassy service seals the deal.

★ Restaurant Hubert   FRENCH $$
(Map p80; ☑02-9232 0881; www.restaurant hubert.com; 15 Bligh St; dishes $15-42; ☺5pm-1am Mon-Sat; ⓡMartin Place) The memorable descent into the sexy old-time ambience plunges you straight from suity Sydney to some 1930s cocktail movie. Delicious French fare comes in old-fashioned portions – think terrine, black pudding or duck plus a few more avant-garde creations. Candlelit tables and a long whisky-backed counter provide seating. There are no bookings for small groups so wait it out in the bar area. This is one of few quality Sydney venues that serve food this late. Check out the vast collection of miniature bottles on your way down.

★ Azuma   JAPANESE $$
(Map p80; ☑02-9222 9960; www.azuma.com. au; Level 1, Chifley Plaza, Hunter St; mains $22-48; ☺noon-2.30pm & 6-10pm Mon-Fri, 6-10pm Sat; ⓡMartin Place) Tucked away upstairs in Chifley Plaza, this is one of Sydney's finest Japanese restaurants. Sushi and sashimi are of stellar quality and too pretty to eat – almost. Other options include sukiyaki and hot-pot DIY dishes and an excellent tasting menu ($110 per person). It's a great place to get acquainted with high-class modern Japanese fare. It also has some moreish sake by the carafe.

★ Pablo & Rusty's   CAFE $$
(Map p80; ☑02-9283 9543; www.pabloand rustys.com.au; 161 Castlereagh St; light meals $10-25; ☺6.30am-5pm Mon-Fri, 8am-3pm Sat; ☎☑; ⓡTown Hall) One of central Sydney's best cafes, this place is always buzzy. The inviting wood-and-brick decor and seriously good coffee (several single origins available daily) is complemented by a range of appealing breakfast and lunch specials ranging from sandwiches to wholesome Mediterranean- and Asian-influenced combos such as tuna poke with brown rice or lychee and ginger tapioca.

Ash St Cellar   MODERN AUSTRALIAN $$
(Map p80; ☑02-9240 3000; www.merivale. com.au/ashstcellar; 1 Ash St; large plates $18-26; ☺8.30am-11pm Mon-Fri; ☎; ⓡWynyard) One of the many tendrils of the Ivy complex, Ash St Cellar is an urbane lane-side wine bar that does excellent cheese, charcuterie and shared plates. Sit outside, if it's not too gusty, and agonise over the 200-plus wines on the list. Despite the suits sweeping through, the vibe is relaxed and unhurried.

Chat Thai
THAI **$$**

(Map p84; ☑02-9211 1808; www.chatthai.com.au; 20 Campbell St; mains $10-20; ⊙10am-2am; ☑; ⚐Capitol Square, ⚐Central) Cooler than your average Thai joint, this Thaitown linchpin is so popular that a list is posted outside for you to affix your name to should you want a table. Expat Thais flock here for the dishes that don't make it onto your average suburban Thai restaurant menu – particularly the more unusual sweets.

Sydney Madang
KOREAN **$$**

(Map p84; ☑02-9264 7010; 371a Pitt St; mains $13-23; ⊙11.30am-2am; ⚐Museum) Down a teensy Little Korea lane is this backdoor gem – an authentic BBQ joint that's low on interior charisma but high on quality and quantity. Noisy, cramped and chaotic, yes, but the chilli seafood soup will have you coming back.

★ Sepia
JAPANESE, FUSION **$$$**

(Map p80; ☑02-9283 1990; www.sepiarestaurant.com.au; 201 Sussex St; degustation $215, matching wines $135; ⊙noon-3pm Fri & Sat, 6-10pm Tue-Sat; ⚐Town Hall) A Japanese sensibility permeates the boundary-pushing menu at what is sometimes said to be Australia's best restaurant, while molecular cuisine and the forage ethos play their part in the creation and presentation of the stunning morsels. Sensational seafood and exquisite bursts of flavour make the palate sing. The atmosphere is plush, low-lit and fairly formal; there's also a wine bar.

★ Tetsuya's
FRENCH, JAPANESE **$$$**

(Map p84; ☑02-9267 2900; www.tetsuyas.com; 529 Kent St; degustation $230, matching wines $110; ⊙5.30-10pm Tue-Fri, noon-3pm & 5.30-10pm Sat; ⚐Town Hall) Concealed in a villa behind a historic cottage amid the high-rises, this extraordinary restaurant is for those seeking a culinary journey rather than a simple stuffed belly. Settle in for 10-plus courses of French- and Japanese-inflected food from the creative genius of Japanese-born Tetsuya Wakuda. It's all great, but the seafood is sublime. Book way ahead.

★ Rockpool Bar & Grill
STEAK **$$$**

(Map p80; ☑02-8078 1900; www.rockpool.com; 66 Hunter St; mains $45-59, bar mains $18-32; ⊙noon-3pm & 6-11pm Mon-Fri, 6-11pm Sat, 5.30-10.30pm Sun; ⚐Martin Place) You'll feel like a 1930s Manhattan stockbroker when you dine at this sleek operation in the art-deco City Mutual Building. The bar is famous for its dry-aged, full-blood Wagyu burger (make sure you order a side of the hand-cut fat chips), but carnivores will be equally enamoured with the succulent steaks, stews and fish dishes served in the grill.

Golden Century
CHINESE, SEAFOOD **$$$**

(Map p84; ☑02-9212 3901; www.goldencentury.com.au; 393-399 Sussex St; mains $28-44; ⊙noon-4am; ☑; ⚐Town Hall) The fish tank at this frenetic Cantonese place, a Chinatown classic, forms a window-wall to the street, full of a whole lot of nervous fish, crabs, lobsters and abalone. Splash out on the whole lobster cooked in ginger and shallots: tank–net–kitchen–you. It's open very late but is also wildly popular for weekend yum cha.

Mercado
MODERN AUSTRALIAN **$$$**

(Map p80; ☑02-9221 6444; www.mercadorestaurant.com; 4 Ash St; small plates $21-32; ⊙noon-2.30pm Mon-Thu, noon-2.30pm & 5.30-10pm Fri, 5.30-10.30pm Sat; ⚐Wynyard) Set in a busy, buzzy basement, Mercado riffs on Spanish themes to produce an excellent menu of tapas-style dishes backed up by succulent spit-roasted meats. The chef produces cheeses and smoked meats on-site, and generous depth of flavour in things like smoked eggplant or 'fish and chips' roe dip is truly impressive. An interesting selection of Spanish wine adds points.

✕ Darling Harbour & Pyrmont

Rows of restaurants line Darling Harbour, many of them pairing their sea views with seafood. Most are pricey tourist-driven affairs that are good but not outstanding. The Star has sought to assert itself as a fine-dining mecca, luring many a gifted restaurateur. There are some truly excellent restaurants here, but the shopping-mall atmosphere won't be for everyone. On the wharves in Pyrmont are a couple of excellent restaurants.

Adriano Zumbo
SWEETS **$**

(Map p86; www.zumbo.com.au; the Star, 80 Pyrmont St; 6 zumbarons $16.50; ⊙11am-10pm Mon, to 11pm Tue-Thu, to midnight Fri & Sat, to 9pm Sun; ⚐The Star) The man who introduced Sydney to the macaron keeps indulging his Willy Wonka fantasies in this shop in the Star complex, where baked treats are artfully displayed. The macarons (or zumbarons, as they're known here), tarts, pastries and cakes are as astonishing to look at as they are to eat. It's just outside the Lyric Theatre.

The Malaya
MALAYSIAN $$

(Map p86; ☎02-9279 1170; www.themalaya.com.au; 39 Lime St; mains $24-36; ☺noon-3pm & 6-10pm Mon-Fri, noon-3pm & 5.30-10pm Sat, 5.30-10pm Sun; ☜☑; ☺Darling Harbour) There's something really life-affirming about quality Malaysian cooking, and what you get here is certainly that. Dishes bursting with flavour and spice make it a very authentic experience, while fabulous views over Darling Harbour (fireworks on Saturday nights) add romance. The atmosphere is a very Sydney blend of upmarket and casual. À la carte is better than the set menu.

Cafe Morso
CAFE $$

(Map p86; ☎02-9692 0111; www.cafemorso.com.au; Jones Bay Wharf; breakfast $12-20, lunch mains $18-25; ☺7am-3.30pm Mon-Fri, 9am-2.30pm Sat, 8am-3.30pm Sun; ☜☑; ☺The Star) On pretty Jones Bay Wharf, this makes a fine venue for breakfast or lunch, though it gets pretty busy so you may want to book. There's a mixture of Channel 7 workers and yacht skippers. Sassy breakfasts – try the bacon gnocchi – morph into proper cooked lunches, or you can just grab a sandwich.

★ LuMi
ITALIAN $$$

(Map p86; ☎02-9571 1999; www.lumidining.com; 56 Pirrama Rd, Pyrmont; 8 courses $115, 3-/5-course lunches Fri & Sat $55/75; ☺6.30-10.30pm Wed & Thu, noon-2.30pm & 6-10.30pm Fri & Sat, noon-2.30pm & 6.30-10.30pm Sun; ☜; ☺Pyrmont Bay) This wharf spot sits right alongside the bobbing boats, though views aren't quite knock-me-down. Hidden but just steps from Darling Harbour and the Star, it offers casual competence and strikingly innovative Italian-Japanese fusion cuisine. The degustation is a tour de force, with memorable creations including extraordinary pasta dishes. The open kitchen is always entertaining, service is smart and both wine and sake lists are great.

★ Sokyo
JAPANESE $$$

(Map p86; ☎02-9657 9161; www.star.com.au/sokyo; the Star, 80 Pyrmont St; breakfast $23-39, mains $32-65; ☺7-10.30am & 5.30-10pm daily, noon-2pm Fri & Sat; ☜☑; ☺The Star) Bringing Toyko glam to the edge of the casino complex, Sokyo serves well-crafted sushi and sashimi, delicate tempura, tasty robata grills and sophisticated mains. It also dishes up Sydney's best Japanese-style breakfast. Solo travellers should grab a counter seat by the sushi kitchen to watch all the action unfurl.

Flying Fish
SEAFOOD $$$

(Map p86; ☎02-9518 6677; www.flyingfish.com.au; Jones Bay Wharf; mains $40-50; ☺6-10.30pm Mon, noon-2.30pm & 6-10.30pm Tue-Sat, noon-2.30pm Sun; ☺The Star) On a lovely Pyrmont wharf, this is everything a seafood restaurant should be, with crisp white tablecloths to stain with crustacean juice, gleaming glasses and water views. Romance and city lights work their magic here, aided by excellent food and an indulgent cocktail list. It also has the coolest toilets in town – the clear-glass stalls frost over when you close the door.

✕ Kings Cross & Potts Point

Room 10
CAFE $

(Map p88; ☎02-8318 0454; www.facebook.com/room10espresso; 10 Llankelly Pl, Kings Cross; mains $8-14; ☺7am-4pm Mon-Fri, 8am-4pm Sat & Sun; ☒☑; ☺Kings Cross) Genuinely warm and welcoming, this tiny cafe is the sort of place where staff know all the locals by name. The coffee is delicious and the food's limited to sandwiches, salads and such – tasty and uncomplicated. Perch inside at impossibly tiny tables or do some people-watching on this lovable laneway.

Piccolo Bar
CAFE $

(Map p88; ☎02-9368 1356; www.piccolobar.com.au; 6 Roslyn St, Kings Cross; light meals $5-10; ☺8am-2.30pm Mon-Fri; ☜; ☺Kings Cross) A surviving slice of the old bohemian Cross, this tiny cafe hasn't changed much in over 60 years. The walls are covered in movie-star memorabilia, and Vittorio Bianchi still serves up strong coffee, omelettes and abrasive charm, as he's done for over 40 years.

Harry's Cafe de Wheels
FAST FOOD $

(Map p88; ☎02-9357 3074; www.harryscafedewheels.com.au; Cowper Wharf Roadway, Woolloomooloo; pies $5-8; ☺8.30am-2am Mon & Tue, 8.30am-3am Wed & Thu, 8.30am-4am Fri, 9am-4am Sat, 9am-1am Sun; ☒311, ☺Kings Cross) Open since 1938 (except for a few years when founder Harry 'Tiger' Edwards was on active service), Harry's has been serving meat pies to everyone from Pamela Anderson to Frank Sinatra and Colonel Sanders. You can't leave without trying a Tiger: a hot meat pie with sloppy peas, mashed potato, gravy and tomato sauce.

★ Cho Cho San
JAPANESE $$

(Map p88; ☎02-9331 6601; www.chochosan.com.au; 73 Macleay St, Potts Point; mains $18-38; ☺5.30-11pm Mon-Thu, noon-11pm Fri-Sun; ☺Kings Cross)

Glide through the shiny brass sliding door and take a seat at the communal table that runs the length of this stylish Japanese restaurant, all polished concrete and blond wood. The food is just as artful as the surrounds, with tasty *izakaya*-style bites emanating from both the raw bar and the *hibachi* grill. There's a good sake selection too.

★**Yellow** VEGETARIAN $$
(Map p88; ☑02-9332 2344; www.yellowsydney. com.au; 57 Macleay St, Potts Point; degustation menu $70; ☺6-11pm Mon-Fri, 8am-3pm & 6-11pm Sat & Sun; ☑; ☒Kings Cross) Once a sunflower-yellow symbol of all things Bohemian, this former artists' residence is now a top-notch contemporary vegetarian restaurant. Dishes are prepared with real panache, and exquisitely presented. The tasting menus (including a vegan one) take the Sydney non-meat scene to new levels. Weekend brunch is also a highlight, as is the wine list.

Farmhouse MODERN AUSTRALIAN $$
(Map p88; ☑0448 413 791; www.farmhouse kingscross.com.au; 4/40 Bayswater Rd, Kings Cross; set menu $60; ☺sittings 6.30pm & 8.30pm Wed-Sat, 2pm & 6.30pm Sun; ☒Kings Cross) Occupying a space between restaurant and supper club, this narrow sliver of a place has a tiny kitchen and a charming host. Diners sit at one long table and eat a set menu that features uncomplicated, delicious dishes from high-quality produce. There are good wines and a buzzy, fun atmosphere. Prebooking is essential.

Fratelli Paradiso ITALIAN $$
(Map p88; ☑02-9357 1744; www.fratelliparadiso. com; 12-16 Challis Ave, Potts Point; breakfast $12-14, mains $22-38; ☺7am-11pm Mon-Sat, to 10pm Sun; ☒Kings Cross) This underlit trattoria has them queuing at the door (especially on weekends). The intimate room showcases seasonal Italian dishes cooked with Mediterranean zing. Lots of busy black-clad waiters, lots of Italian chatter, lots of oversized sunglasses. No bookings.

China Doll ASIAN $$$
(Map p88; ☑02-9380 6744; www.chinadoll.com. au; 4/6 Cowper Wharf Roadway, Woolloomooloo; mains $35-54; ☺noon-3pm & 6-10.30pm; ☐311, ☒Kings Cross) Gaze over the Woolloomooloo marina and city skyline as you tuck into deliciously inventive dishes drawing inspiration from all over Asia. The setting is memorable, but the food keeps up, with delicious textures and flavour combinations. Plates are

designed to be shared, although waiters can arrange half-serves for solo diners.

Otto Ristorante ITALIAN $$$
(☑02-9368 7488; www.ottoristorante.com.au; 8/6 Cowper Wharf Roadway, Woolloomooloo; mains $38-49; ☺noon-10.30pm; ☐311, ☒Kings Cross) Forget the glamorous waterfront location and the A-list crowd – Otto will be remembered for single-handedly dragging Sydney's Italian cooking into the new century with dishes such as *strozzapreti con gamberi* (artisan pasta with fresh Yamba prawns, tomato, chilli and black olives). Its opening hours mean you can often grab a table here on spec midafternoon, but booking at meal times is essential.

✗ Surry Hills & Darlinghurst

Scruffy Surry Hills' transformation into Sydney's foodie nirvana means that it's an ever-changing array of wonderful eateries inhabiting surprising nooks amid terrace houses and former warehouses, with new places opening all the time.

★**Bourke Street Bakery** BAKERY $
(Map p101; ☑02-9699 1011; www.bourkestreet bakery.com.au; 633 Bourke St, Surry Hills; items $5-14; ☺7am-6pm Mon-Fri, to 5pm Sat & Sun; ☑; ☐301, ☒Central) Queuing outside this teensy bakery is an essential Surry Hills experience. It sells a tempting selection of pastries, cakes, bread and sandwiches, along with sausage rolls that are near legendary in these parts. There are a few tables inside but on a fine day you're better off on the street.

★**Le Monde** CAFE $
(Map p101; ☑02-9211 3568; www.lemondecafe. com.au; 83 Foveaux St, Surry Hills; dishes $10-16; ☺6.30am-4pm Mon-Fri, 7am-2pm Sat; ☎; ☒Central) Some of Sydney's best breakfasts are served between the demure dark wooden walls of this small street-side cafe. Top-notch coffee and a terrific selection of tea will gear you up to face the world, while dishes such as truffled poached eggs or confit pork belly make it worth walking up the hill for.

Reuben Hills CAFE $
(Map p101; ☑02-9211 5556; www.reubenhills. com.au; 61 Albion St; mains $9-22; ☺7am-4pm Mon-Sat, 7.30am-4pm Sun; ☎☑; ☒Central) An industrial fitout and Latin American menu await here at Reuben Hills (aka hipster central), set in a terrace and its former garage. Fantastic single-origin coffee and fried

chicken, but the eggs, tacos and *baleadas* (Honduran tortillas) are no slouches, either.

Messina
ICE CREAM $

(Map p88; 02-9331 1588; www.gelatomessina. com; 241 Victoria St; 1/2/3 scoops $4.80/6.80/8.80; noon-11pm Sun-Thu, to 11.30pm Fri & Sat; ; Kings Cross) Join the queues of people who look like they never eat ice cream at the counter of Sydney's most popular gelato shop. Clearly even the beautiful people can't resist quirky flavours such as figs in marsala and salted caramel. It's all delicious, and there are several dairy-free options. The attached dessert bar serves sundaes.

Infinity Bakery
BAKERY $

(Map p88; 02-9380 4320; www.infinitybakery. com.au; 274 Victoria St, Darlinghurst; loaves €4-9; 5.30am-9.30pm Mon-Fri, to 10pm Sat, to 9pm Sun; ; Kings Cross) One of Sydney's standout artisan bakers, Infinity has heroic opening hours and delicious sourdough and Turkish breads, as well as coffee and a small selection of cafe fare: rolls, pies, croissants and the like.

Spice I Am
THAI $

(Map p84; 02-9280 0928; www.spiceiam. com; 90 Wentworth Ave, Surry Hills; mains $15-20; 11.30am-3.30pm & 5-10pm Tue-Sun; ; Central) Once the preserve of expat Thais, this red-hot spot now has queues out the door. No wonder, as every one of the 70-plus dishes on the menu is superfragrant and superspicy. It's been so successful that it's opened the upmarket version in **Darlinghurst** (Map p88; 02-9332 2445; 296-300 Victoria St, Darlinghurst; mains $19-22; 5.30-10.30pm Mon-Wed, 11.30am-3.30pm & 5.30-10.30pm Thu-Sun; ; Kings Cross). The sign is unobtrusive so it's easy to walk past: don't.

Nada's
LEBANESE $

(Map p101; 02-9690 1289; 270 Cleveland St, Surry Hills; dishes $8-16; noon-3pm & 5.30-10pm Wed-Mon, 5.30-10pm Tue; ; 372, Central) There are swisher Lebanese restaurants around, but for a no-frills delicious feed at a very fair price, it's hard to beat this old family-run favourite. The set meal at $29 a head is a bargain; just don't fill up too much on the bread and dips or you won't manage the sizeable chunks of Turkish delight at the end.

★ Porteño
ARGENTINE $$

(Map p101; 02-8399 1440; www.porteno.com. au; 50 Holt St, Surry Hills; sharing plates $20-50; 6pm-midnight Tue-Sat; Central) In a new location, this upbeat and deservedly acclaimed Argentine restaurant is a great place to eat. The 'animal of the day' is slow-roasted for eight hours before the doors even open and is always delicious. Other highlights include the homemade chorizo and morcilla, but lighter touches are also in evidence, so it's not all meat-feast. There's a decent Argentine wine list too.

★ Dead Ringer
TAPAS $$

(Map p101; 02-9331 3560; http://deadringer. wtf; 413 Bourke St, Surry Hills; dishes $18-33; 5pm-midnight Mon-Fri, noon-midnight Sat & Sun; ; 333, 380) This charcoal-fronted terrace is a haven of quality eating and drinking in a laid-back format. Barstool it or grab an outdoor table and graze on the short menu that changes slightly daily and runs from bar snacks through tapas to mains. Though well-presented, the food's all about flavour combinations rather than airy artistry. There's always something interesting by the glass to accompany.

★ Gratia & Folonomo
CAFE, FUSION $$

(Map p101; 02-8034 3818; www.gratia.org.au; 370 Bourke St, Surry Hills; cafe dishes $12-21, restaurant mains $21-34; 8am-3pm & 6-10.30pm; ; 374, 397, 399) Not-for-profit eateries often score higher on good intentions than cooking, but this is the real deal. A great cafe, Gratia, with genuinely friendly staff and a pleasant, light feel, does juices and eclectic brunchy fare, while the restaurant part, Folonomo (from 'for love not money') serves brilliant modern Australian fare. All profits go to charitable organisations, which diners can help choose. Applause.

There's a gallery space upstairs too, and they actively help and train refugees.

Chaco
JAPANESE $$

(Map p88; 02-9007 8352; www.chacobar. com.au; 238 Crown St, Darlinghurst; skewers €4-7; ramen 5.30-9pm Mon, noon-2pm Wed-Sun, yakitori 6-10pm Tue-Sat; Museum) This little place has a simple, effortless Japanese cool and some seriously good food. The ramen are good, and there are very succulent gyoza and delicious meatball sticks to dip in egg. The yakitori skewers are available Tuesday to Saturday nights and are a highlight, bursting with flavour. Don't be afraid to try the more unusual ones...

Malabar
SOUTH INDIAN $$

(Map p88; 02-9332 1755; www.malabarcuisine. com.au; 274 Victoria St, Darlinghurst; mains $22-26; 5.30-10.30pm Mon & Tue, noon-2.30pm &

5.30-10.30pm Wed-Sun; ⚲; ⛔Kings Cross) Delicious dosas, piquant Goan curries and the soft seductive tastes of India's south make this sizeable, well-established Darlinghurst restaurant a standout. The open kitchen and decor, with large black-and-white photos on the walls, add atmosphere. Owner and staff are very genial and will guide you through the substantial menu. You can BYO wine.

Muum Maam
THAI **$$**

(Map p101; ☑02-9318 0881; www.muummaam. com.au; 50 Holt St, Surry Hills; lunch dishes $14-16, dinner mains $24-32; ⊙11.30am-3pm & 6-10pm Mon-Fri, 6-10pm Sat; ⚲; ⛔Central) Packing a punch for the eyes and tastebuds, this is a buzzy spot beloved of those creative types who work hereabouts. It has a double identity that really works, with a food cart doling out lunch specials before the open kitchen turns to more serious, lavishly presented Thai creations in the evening. There's a big communal table but you can also go solo.

Bar H
ASIAN FUSION **$$**

(Map p84; ☑02-9280 1980; www.barhsurryhills. com; 80 Campbell St, Surry Hills; dishes $14-42; ⊙6-10pm Mon-Thu, to midnight Fri & Sat; ⛔Central) Marrying Chinese and Japanese dishes with native Australian bush ingredients, this sexy, shiny, black-walled corner eatery is completely unique and extremely impressive. Dishes range considerably in size and are designed to be shared; confer with your waiter about quantities. There's a $68 tasting menu that offers a fine experience of the quality and diversity on offer.

Single O
CAFE **$$**

(Single Origin Roasters; Map p84; ☑02-9211 0665; www.singleo.com.au; 60-64 Reservoir St, Surry Hills; mains $14-21; ⊙6.30am-4pm Mon-Fri, 7.30am-3pm Sat; ⚲⚲; ⛔Central) ⚲ Unshaven graphic designers roll cigarettes at little outdoor tables in the bricky hollows of deepest Surry Hills, while inside impassioned, bouncing-off-the-walls caffeine fiends prepare their beloved brews, along with a tasty selection of cafe fare. Something of a trendsetter a few years back, this place still does coffee as good as anywhere in Sydney. The hole-in-the-wall alongside does takeaways.

El Loco
MEXICAN **$$**

(Excelsior Hotel; Map p101; ☑02-9240 3000; www.merivale.com.au/elloco; 64 Foveaux St, Surry Hills; mains $10-18; ⊙noon-midnight Mon-Thu, to 3am Fri & Sat, to 10pm Sun; ⚲⚲; ⛔Central) As much as we lament the passing of live rock

at the Excelsior Hotel, we have to admit that the hip, colourful Mexican cantina that's taken over the band room is pretty darn cool. The food's tasty, inventive, and, at $6 per taco, fantastic value. The party kicks on till late on weekends with DJs in a social, fun atmosphere.

Devonshire
MODERN EUROPEAN **$$$**

(Map p101; ☑02-9698 9427; www.thedevonshire. com.au; 204 Devonshire St, Surry Hills; degustation $95, matching wines $55, mains $37; ⊙noon-2.30pm Fri, 6-10pm Tue-Sat; ⛔Central) It's a long way from a two-Michelin-starred Mayfair restaurant to grungy old Devonshire St for chef Jeremy Bentley, although cuisinewise, perhaps not as far as you'd think. His food is simply extraordinary – complex, precisely presented and full of flavour. And while there's white linen on the tables, the atmosphere isn't the least bit starchy.

Bodega
TAPAS **$$$**

(Map p101; ☑02-9212 7766; www.bodegatapas. com; 216 Commonwealth St; tapas $12-24, share plates $22-30; ⊙noon-2pm Fri, 6-10pm Tue-Sat; ⛔Central) The coolest progeny of Sydney's tapas explosion, Bodega has a casual vibe, good-lookin' staff and a funky matador mural. Dishes vary widely in size and price and are very loosely rooted in Central American and Spanish cuisine. Wash 'em down with Spanish and South American wine, sherry, port or beer, and plenty of Latin gusto.

⚲ Paddington & Centennial Park

Four in Hand
MODERN AUSTRALIAN **$$**

(Map p96; ☑02-9326 2254; www.fourinhand. com.au; 105 Sutherland St, Paddington; mains $28-38; ⊙5.30-9.30pm Mon-Wed, noon-3pm & 5.30-9.30pm Thu-Sun; ☐389) You can't go far in Paddington without tripping over a beautiful old pub with amazing food. This is among the best: quality meats and seafood are given confident treatment and exotic garnishes, never losing sight of the gastropub idea. That hill back up to Oxford St after a heavy lunch is a killer.

Lucio's
ITALIAN **$$$**

(Map p96; ☑02-9380 5996; www.lucios.com.au; 47 Windsor St, Paddington; mains $39-48; ⊙12.30-3pm & 6.30-10.30pm Tue-Sat; ☐389) Among all the cutting-edge Italian cuisine, there's still a lot of love for this expensive but gloriously welcoming neighbourhood favourite. Much of it is likely from owners of Paddington galleries, as it seems to have bought all their stock over the years: you couldn't fit a postcard on the bright walls.

✖ Bondi, Coogee & the Eastern Beaches

Lox, Stock & Barrel   CAFE, JEWISH $

(Map p103; ✆02-9300 0368; www.loxstockand barrel.com.au; 140 Glenayr Ave, Bondi Beach; breakfast & lunch dishes $10-22, dinner $18-29; ⊙7am-3.30pm Sun-Tue, 7am-3.30pm & 6-10pm Wed & Thu, 7am-3.30pm & 6-11pm Fri & Sat; 🛜🖉🖩; 🚌389) Stare down the barrel of a smoking hot bagel and ask yourself one question: Wagyu corned-beef Reuben, or homemade pastrami and Russian coleslaw? In the evening the menu sets its sights on steak, lamb shoulder and slow-roasted eggplant. It's always busy, even on a wet Monday.

Three Blue Ducks   CAFE $$

(Map p74; ✆02-9389 0010; www.threeblueducks. com; 141-143 Macpherson St, Bronte; breakfast $14-22, lunch $20-32, dinner $28-38; ⊙6.30am-2.30pm Sun-Tue, 6.30am-2.30pm & 5-11pm Wed-Sat; 🛜🖉; 🚌378) 🖉 These ducks are a fair waddle from the water, but that doesn't stop queues forming outside the graffiti-covered walls for weekend breakfasts across two seating areas. The adventurous chefs have a strong commitment to using local, organic and fair-trade food whenever possible.

Trio   CAFE $$

(Map p103; ✆02-9365 6044; www.triocafe.com. au; 56 Campbell Pde, Bondi Beach; dishes $18-27; ⊙7am-3pm Mon-Fri, 7.30am-3.30pm Sat & Sun; 🛜🖉; 🚌333, 380-2) Brunch in Bondi has become de rigueur in Sydney in recent years, and this friendly, unpretentious cafe is one of the top spots to do it. The menu covers several global influences, from Mexican chilaquiles to Middle Eastern shakshouka via some Italian bruschetta. It's a great way to start a day by the sea.

Icebergs Dining Room   ITALIAN $$$

(Map p103; ✆02-9365 9000; www.idrb.com; 1 Notts Ave, Bondi; mains $46-52; ⊙noon-3pm & 6.30-11pm Tue-Sun; 🚌333, 380) 🖉 Poised above the famous Icebergs swimming pool, Icebergs' views sweep across the Bondi Beach arc to the sea. Inside, bow-tied waiters deliver fresh, sustainably sourced seafood and steaks cooked with élan. There's also an elegant cocktail bar. In the same building, the Icebergs club has a bistro and bar with simpler, cheaper fare.

✖ Sydney Harbourside

Harvest   VEGETARIAN $$

(Map p74; ✆02-9818 4201; www.harvestveg etarianrestaurant.com; 71 Evans St, Rozelle; mains $22-26; ⊙6-10pm Tue-Sat; 🖉; 🚌441-5) In business for nearly half a century, this place offers inventive, rich and satisfying vegetarian fare in a warm and upbeat atmosphere. There are several vegan dishes too, and global influences are fruitfully combined in the dishes. BYO and licensed.

Riverview Hotel & Dining   MODERN AUSTRALIAN $$

(Map p74; ✆02-9810 1151; www.theriverview hotel.com.au; 29 Birchgrove Rd, Balmain; bar mains $20-32, restaurant mains $36-52; ⊙bar meals noon-9pm, restaurant 6-9pm Mon-Thu, noon-2.30pm & 6-9pm Fri-Sun; 🛜; 🚢Balmain) Foodies flock here to try the excellent fish dishes and nose-to-tail meat creations in the elegant upstairs dining room, while locals are equally keen on the pizzas served in the downstairs bar. It's a lovely pub in itself, with hanging baskets and a characterful interior.

Dunbar House   CAFE $$

(Map p74; ✆02-9337 1226; www.dunbarhouse. com.au; 9 Marine Pde, Watsons Bay; breakfast $12-18, lunch $18-27; ⊙8am-3.30pm; 🚢Watsons Bay) This meticulously restored 1830s mansion is a gorgeous spot for brunch, particularly if you can score one of the harbour-view tables on the verandah. Bookings recommended on weekends. It's named after a famous 19th-century shipwreck that occurred near here.

Catalina   MODERN AUSTRALIAN $$$

(Map p74; ✆02-9371 0555; www.catalinarosebay. com.au; Lyne Park, Rose Bay; mains $49-52; ⊙noon-3pm & 6-10.30pm Mon-Sat, noon-3pm Sun; 🚢Rose Bay) Named after the flying boats that were based here, this excellent Rose Bay restaurant has marvellous views, a buzzy eastern suburbs vibe and an impressive wine list. With this location, you expect some seafood on the menu, and it doesn't disappoint. Quality offerings are sourced from around the country, but meaty options are available, with roast suckling pig a speciality.

Doyles on the Beach   SEAFOOD $$$

(Map p74; ✆02-9337 2007; www.doyles.com. au; 11 Marine Pde, Watsons Bay; mains $40-50; ⊙noon-3pm & 5.30-8.30pm Mon-Thu, to 9pm Fri, noon-4pm & 5.30-9pm Sat, noon-4pm & 5.30-8.30pm Sun; 🚢Watsons Bay) There may well be better places for seafood, but few can

MARRICKVILLE

Once the slightly frumpy western neighbour of Newtown and Enmore, the suburb of Marrickville has gradually attracted bohemians, artists, students and kooks forced out of Newtown by rising rents. Alongside a great set of pubs and bars (some of which host live music), cafes are Marrickville's new claim to fame. We suggest you explore the neighbourhood under your own steam. Jump off the train at Marrickville station, turn right and head up Illawarra Rd.

compete with Doyles' location or its history – this restaurant first opened in 1885. Catching the harbour ferry to Watsons Bay for a seafood lunch is a quintessential Sydney experience. If the prices make you think twice, grab fish 'n' chips ($13 to $20) from its takeaway outlet at the ferry wharf.

✕ Newtown & the Inner West

Newtown's King St and Enmore Rd are among the city's most diverse eat streets, with Thai restaurants sitting alongside Vietnamese, Greek, Lebanese and Mexican, but the scene is replicated on a smaller scale in nearly every inner west suburb. And when it comes to coffee culture, all roads point this way too.

Tramsheds Harold Park FOOD HALL
(Map p74; ☑02-8398 5695; www.tramsheds haroldpark.com.au; Maxwell Rd, Glebe; ☺7am-10pm; ✿❅; ☑Jubilee Park) Sydney's latest foodie hangout is this refurbished centenarian brick tram depot at the northern end of Glebe. It's a handsome redevelopment with a supermarket, providores and a selection of modern-thinking eateries, including one specialising in fresh pasta, another in organic meats, a sustainable fish restaurant, a contemporary Middle Eastern, a Spanishy tapas place from the Bodega team and Messina gelati.

Wedge CAFE $
(Map p98; ☑02-9660 3313; www. thewedgeglebe.com; cnr Cowper St & Glebe Point Rd; light meals $8-18; ☺7am-4pm Mon-Sat, 8am-3pm Sun; ❅❆; ☑Glebe) Cut a corridor out of the side of a building, open it to the street and add artful industrial decor and you have

the Wedge, which is wowing Glebe with its delicious single-origin espressos and cold brews as well as delicious, artfully presented breakfasts, sandwiches and lunch specials. The quality and atmosphere are great, but it's popular, so lingering feels selfish.

Black Star Pastry BAKERY $
(Map p98; ☑02-9557 8656; www.blackstar pastry.com.au; 277 Australia St, Newtown; snacks $4-10; ☺7am-5pm; ✐; ☑Newtown) Wise folks follow the black star to pay homage to excellent coffee, a large selection of sweet things and a few very good savoury things (gourmet pies and the like). There are only a few tables; it's more a snack-and-run or picnic-in-the-park kind of place. Prepare to queue.

Cow & the Moon ICE CREAM $
(Map p98; ☑02-9557 4255; 181 Enmore Rd; small gelati $5.50; ☺8.30am-10.30pm Sun-Thu, 8.30am-11.30pm Fri & Sat; ❅✐❆; ☑Newtown) Forget the diet and slink into this cool corner cafe, where an array of sinful truffles and tasty tarts beckons seductively. Ignore them and head straight for the world's best gelato – the title this humble little place won in 2014 at the Gelato World Tour title in Rimini, Italy. There's decent coffee too.

Faheem Fast Food PAKISTANI $
(Map p98; ☑02-9550 4850; www.faheem fastfood.com.au; 194 Enmore Rd; dishes $12-14; ☺5pm-midnight Mon-Fri, noon-midnight Sat & Sun; ✐; ☑426) This Enmore Rd stalwart offers a totally no-frills dining atmosphere but very tasty and authentic curry and tandoori options served until late. Its Haleem lentil and beef curry is memorably tasty, while the brain *nihari* is another standout, and not as challenging as it sounds.

Spice Alley ASIAN $
(Map p101; www.kensingtonstreet.com.au; Kensington St, Chippendale; dishes $8-16; ☺11am-9.30pm; ✐; ☑Central) This little laneway off Kensington St by Central Park is a picturesque outdoor eating hub serving street-foody dishes from several different Asian cuisines. Grab your noodles, dumplings or pork belly and fight for a stool. Quality is reasonable rather than spectacular, but prices are low and it's fun. It's cashless: pay by card or load up a prepay card from the drinks booth.

Mary's BURGERS $
(Map p98; www.facebook.com/marysnewtown; 6 Mary St, Newtown; mains $13-18; ☺4pm-midnight Mon-Thu, noon-midnight Fri & Sat, noon-10pm Sun;

🛜 🏊; 🚇 Newtown) Not put off by the grungy aesthetics, the ear-splitting heavy metal or the fact that the graffiti-daubed building was previously a sexual health clinic and a Masonic Temple? Then head up to the mezzanine of this dimly lit hipster bar for some of the best burgers and fried chicken in town.

★Thanh Binh
VIETNAMESE $$

(Map p98; ✆02-9557 1175; www.thanhbinh. com.au; 111 King St; mains $18-28; ⏱5-11pm Mon-Fri, noon-11pm Sat & Sun; 🏊; 🚇 Macdonaldtown) This old Vietnamese favourite isn't top of the trendmeter any more, but it should be for its wide range of consistently delicious dishes. Favourites are soft-shell crab on papaya salad or sinful pork belly and quail eggs in stock. Other dishes get you launching into a wrapping, rolling, dipping and feasting frenzy. Service is always friendly.

Maggie's
THAI $$

(Map p98; ✆02-9516 5270; 75 Erskineville Rd, Erskineville; mains $18-26; ⏱5-9pm, closed Mon Jun-Sep; 🏊; 🚇 Erskineville) Worth the short stroll downhill from the Newtown strip, or as the focus of a night out in pleasant Erskineville itself, this small neighbourhood Thai restaurant is a real gem. A short menu and blackboard specials offer intense, flavour-packed dishes from the open kitchen with great presentation and some unusual flavours. Intelligent service adds to the experience, as does outdoor seating.

3 Olives
GREEK $$

(Map p98; ✆02-9557 7754; 365 King St, Newtown; mains $24-27, meze dishes $13-16; ⏱5.30pm-midnight Wed-Sun; 🚇 Newtown) There's something very life-affirming about a good Greek restaurant, and this family-run taberna ticks all the boxes. The decor is restrained, with olive-coloured walls, but there's nothing restrained about the portions or aromas: mounds of perfectly textured BBQ octopus, big chunks of melt-in-the-mouth lamb kleftiko, warm flatbread, hearty meatballs and more-ish olives. It's an excellent celebration of traditional eating.

Timbah
TAPAS $$

(Map p74; ✆02-9571 7005; www.timbahwine bar.com.au; 375 Glebe Point Rd, entrance on Forsyth St; tapas $12-17; ⏱5.30-9pm Tue-Thu, 5pm-9.30pm Fri, 4.30-9.30pm Sat; 🚇 Glebe) 🍷 Quite a way down Glebe Point Rd is an excellent independent bottleshop; turn right to find this convivial wine bar it runs downstairs.

There's always something interesting available by the glass, and staff are open to cracking something on demand. Food is tasty, with Australian native flavours and home-grown herbs. The bar is open for drinks from 4pm and also opens Sundays.

Thai Pothong
THAI $$

(Map p98; ✆02-9550 6277; www.thaipothong. com.au; 294 King St, Newtown; mains $18-31; ⏱noon-3pm daily, plus 6-10.30pm Mon-Thu, 6-11pm Fri & Sat, 5.30-10pm Sun; 🅿 🏊; 🚇 Newtown) The menu at this crowd-pleasing restaurant is full of long-time favourites and people still queue for them. The army of staff are efficient and friendly, and the food reliably excellent. Top choice is a window seat to watch the Newtowners pass by. If you pay cash, you get a discount, paid in a local currency only redeemable in the gift shop.

Stinking Bishops
CHEESE $$

(Map p98; ✆02-9007 7754; www.thestinking bishops.com; 63 Enmore Rd, Newtown; 2-/3-/4-cheese boards $21/29/37; ⏱5-10pm Tue & Wed, 11am-10pm Thu-Sat, 11am-6pm Sun; 🏊; 🚇 Newtown) A pungent array of artisanal cheeses is the raison d'être of this popular shop and eatery. Choose the varieties you want, pick a wine or craft beer to accompany, and off you go. There are also very tasty charcuterie boards. All its wares are sourced from small producers and available to take home, too.

Darbar
INDIAN $$

(Map p74; ✆02-9660 5666; www.darbar.com. au; 134 Glebe Point Rd; mains $18-25; ⏱5.30-10pm Mon & Tue, noon-2.30pm & 5.30-10pm Wed-Sun; 🏊; 🚌 431,433) Head through the gates to leave Glebe behind and venture into a brick grotto of glorious spice and flavour. This has a strong local following and is strong on presentation, quality and value for money. There are lots of veggie options.

★Ester
MODERN AUSTRALIAN $$$

(Map p98; ✆02-8068 8279; www.ester-restau rant.com.au; 46/52 Meagher St; mains $32-49; ⏱6-10pm Mon-Thu, noon-3pm & 6-11pm Fri, 6-11pm Sat, noon-5pm Sun; 🏊; 🚇 Redfern) Ester breaks the trend for hip eateries by accepting bookings, but in other respects it exemplifies Sydney's contemporary dining scene: informal but not sloppy; innovative without being overly gimmicky; hip, but never try-hard. Influences straddle continents and dishes are made to be shared. If humanly possible, make room for dessert.

★**Boathouse on**
Blackwattle Bay SEAFOOD $$$
(Map p74; ☑02-9518 9011; www.boathouse.net.
au; 123 Ferry Rd, Glebe; mains $42-48; ☺6-10pm
Tue-Thu, noon-3pm & 6-11pm Fri-Sun; ♒Glebe)
The best restaurant in Glebe, and one of the
best seafood restaurants in Sydney. Offer-
ings range from oysters so fresh you'd think
you shucked them yourself, to a snapper pie
that'll go straight to the top of your favour-
ite-dish list. The views over the bay and An-
zac Bridge are stunning. Arrive by water taxi
for maximum effect.

Glebe Point Diner MODERN AUSTRALIAN $$$
(Map p74; ☑02-9660 2646; www.glebepoint
diner.com.au; 407 Glebe Point Rd; mains $29-48;
☺6-10pm Mon & Tue, noon-3pm & 6-10pm Wed &
Thu, noon-3pm & 5.30-11pm Fri & Sat, noon-3pm
Sun; ♒Jubilee Park) A sensational neighbourhood diner, where only the best local
produce is used and everything – from the
home-baked bread and hand-churned
butter to the nougat finale – is made from
scratch. The food is creative and comforting
at the same time: a rare combination. The
menu and specials change regularly.

✗ Manly

Jah Bar TAPAS $$
(Map p105; ☑02-9977 4449; www.jahbar.com.
au; Shop 7, 9-15 Central Ave, Manly; tapas $14-22;
☺5-11pm Tue-Thu, noon-11pm Fri & Sat, noon-
10pm Sun; ☎; ♒Manly) With indoor tables
squeezed around the large open kitchen and
a small courtyard area, it pays to book ahead
here. A breezy array of tapas has shot off at
tangents from their Spanish and Mexican
ancestors and are really delicious – the raw
fish crispy tacos have appealing zing, the
calamari bursts with spicy flavours and the
scallops with braised pork cheek are sensa-
tional. Service is very engaged.

Boathouse Shelly Beach CAFE $$
(Map p74; ☑02-9934 9977; www.theboathous
esb.com.au; 1 Marine Pde, Manly; kiosk mains $12-
19, restaurant mains $18-29; ☺7am-4pm Mon-Sat,
7am-8pm Sun; ☎☑) This sweet little spot on
picturesque Shelly Beach makes a top venue
for breakfast juices, brunches, fish 'n' chips,
oysters or daily fish specials, served either
in the restaurant section or from the kiosk.

★**Pilu at Freshwater** SARDINIAN $$$
(☑02-9938 3331; www.pilu.com.au; Moore Rd,
Freshwater; 3/5/7 courses $95/110/125; ☺noon-
2.30pm Tue-Sun, plus 6-11pm Tue-Sat; ♒139)

Housed within a heritage-listed beach
house overlooking the ocean, this multi-
award-winning Sardinian restaurant serves
specialities such as oven-roasted suckling
pig and traditional flatbread. Your best
bet is to plump for the tasting menu (from
$105) and thereby eliminate any possible or-
der envy. There are some excellent wines on
offer here, beautifully decanted and served.

✗ Northern Beaches

Boathouse Palm Beach CAFE $$
(☑02-9974 5440; www.theboathousepb.com.au;
Governor Phillip Park, Palm Beach; mains $17-29;
☺7am-4pm; ☎☑; ♒L90, 190) Sit on the large
deck facing Pittwater or grab a table on the
lawn out front – either option is alluring at
Palm Beach's most popular cafe. The food
(try the legendary fish and chips or the vibrant salads) is nearly as impressive as
the views, and that's really saying something.

★**Jonah's** MODERN AUSTRALIAN $$$
(☑02-9974 5599; www.jonahs.com.au; 69 Bynya
Rd, Whale Beach; 2/3/4 courses $88/115/130;
☺7.30-9am, noon-2.30pm & 6.30-11pm; ☎;
♒L90, 190) On the hill above Whale Beach,
luxurious Jonah's has fabulous perspectives
over the ocean. The food is easy on the eye
too, with immaculate presentation and ex-
cellent fish dishes. For the ultimate Sydney
indulgence, take a seaplane from Rose Bay,
order the seafood platter for two, and stay
overnight in one of the ocean-view rooms
($499 per person, including dinner and
breakfast).

◗ Drinking & Nightlife

In a city where rum was once the main cur-
rency, it's little wonder that drinking plays a
big part in the Sydney social scene – whether
it's knocking back some tinnies at the beach,
schmoozing after work or warming up for a
night on the town. Sydney offers plenty of
choice in drinking establishments, from the
flashy to the trashy.

◗ Circular Quay & the Rocks

★**Glenmore** PUB
(Map p80; ☑02-9247 4794; www.theglenmore.
com.au; 96 Cumberland St; ☺10am-midnight Sun-
Thu, to 1am Fri & Sat; ☎; ♒Circular Quay) Down-
stairs it's a predictably nice old Rocks pub,
but head up to the rooftop and the views
are beyond fabulous: Opera House (until
a cruise ship docks), harbour and city sky-

LOCAL KNOWLEDGE

NIGHTLIFE KNOW-HOW

Sydney's bouncers are often strict, arbitrary and immune to logic. They are usually contracted by outside security firms so have no problem in turning away business. Being questioned and searched every time you want a drink after 8pm on a weekend can definitely mar a Sydney night out.

➡ It is against the law to serve people who are intoxicated and you won't be admitted to a venue if you appear drunk. Expect to be questioned about how much you've had to drink that night: it's more to see if you're slurring your words than actual interest.

➡ If security staff suspect that you're under the legal drinking age (18), you'll be asked to present photo ID with proof of your age. Some bars scan ID for everyone entering.

➡ Some gay bars have a 'no open-toed shoes' policy, ostensibly for safety (to avoid broken glass), but sometimes invoked to keep straight women out.

➡ Some pubs have smoking areas, but you aren't allowed to take food into that area – even if you're happy to do so.

line all present and accounted for. It gets rammed up here on the weekends, with DJs, good food and plenty of wine by the glass. The food's decent too.

★ Hero of Waterloo   PUB
(Map p80; ☎02-9252 4553; www.heroofwaterloo. com.au; 81 Lower Fort St; ☺10am-11.30pm Mon-Wed, 10am-midnight Thu-Sat, 10am-10pm Sun; ﷽Circular Quay) Enter this rough-hewn 1843 sandstone pub to meet some locals, chat up the Irish bar staff and grab an earful of the swing, folk and Celtic bands (Friday to Sunday). Downstairs is a dungeon where, in days gone by, drinkers would sleep off a heavy night before being shanghaied to the high seas via a tunnel leading straight to the harbour.

★ Opera Bar   BAR
(Map p80; ☎02-9247 1666; www.operabar. com.au; lower concourse, Sydney Opera House; ☺9am-midnight Sun-Thu, 9am-1am Fri & Sat; ﷽Circular Quay) Right on the harbour with the Opera House on one side and the Harbour Bridge on the other, this perfectly positioned terrace manages a very Sydney marriage of the laid-back and the sophisticated. It's an iconic spot for visitors and locals alike. There's live music or DJs most nights and a decent selection of food (dishes $12 to $28).

Hotel Palisade   PUB
(Map p80; ☎02-9018 0123; www.hotelpalisade. com; 35 Bettington St; ☺noon-midnight Mon-Fri, 11am-midnight Sat & Sun; ﷽; ﷽Circular Quay) Reopened with hipster flair, this historic Millers Point pub preserves its tea-coloured tiles, faded brick and nostalgia-tinted downstairs

bar. On top of the venerable building, however, there's a shiny new glass section with super bridge views, pricey drinks and posh food. It often fills up or books out, but there's a less glitzy, more comfy perch on the little 4th-floor balcony.

Bulletin Place   COCKTAIL BAR
(Map p80; www.bulletinplace.com; 10 Bulletin Pl; ☺4pm-midnight Mon-Wed, 4pm-1am Thu-Sat, 4-10pm Sun; ﷽Circular Quay) A discreet entrance on this little street of cafes and bars conceals the staircase up to one of Sydney's most talked-about cocktail bars. Personable, down-to-earth staff shake up great daily creations that are high on zinginess and freshness and low on frippery. It's a small space, so get there early. Cocktails are about 20 bucks each.

Australian Hotel   PUB
(Map p80; ☎02-9247 2229; www.australianher itagehotel.com; 100 Cumberland St; ☺11am-midnight; ﷽; ﷽Circular Quay) With its wide verandah shading lots of outdoor seating, this handsome early-20th-century pub is a favoured pitstop for a cleansing ale; they were doing microbrewed beer here long before it became trendy and have a great selection. The kitchen also does a nice line in gourmet pizzas ($18 to $28), including ever-popular toppings of kangaroo, emu and crocodile.

Lord Nelson Brewery Hotel   BREWERY
(Map p80; ☎02-9251 4044; 19 Kent St; ☺11am-11pm Mon-Sat, noon-10pm Sun; ﷽Circular Quay) Built in 1836 and converted into a pub in 1841, this atmospheric sandstone boozer is one of three claiming to be Sydney's oldest (all using slightly different criteria). The on-site

brewery cooks up its own natural ales (try the Old Admiral). A pint of dark, stout-y Nelson's Blood is a fine way to partake.

Fortune of War
PUB

(Map p80; ☎02-9247 2714; www.fortuneofwar.com.au; 137 George St; ☺9am-midnight Sun-Thu, to 1am Fri & Sat; ⓇCircular Quay) Operating right here since 1828, this pub was rebuilt in the early 20th century and retains much charm from that era in its characterful bar. It has a solid mix of locals and tourists and features cheerful covers of classic Aussie rock hits on Thursday, Friday and Saturday nights and on weekend afternoons.

Argyle
BAR

(Map p80; ☎02-9247 5500; www.theargylerocks.com; 18 Argyle St; ☺11am-midnight Sun-Wed, to 3am Thu-Sat; ⓇCircular Quay) This mammoth conglomeration of five bars is spread through the historic sandstone Argyle Stores buildings, including a cobblestone courtyard and underground cellars resonating with DJ beats. The decor ranges from rococo couches to white extruded plastic tables, all offset with kooky chandeliers and moody lighting. During the day the courtyard is a pleasant place for a drink or a spot of lunch.

🍸 City Centre & Haymarket

The city centre has long been known for upmarket, after-work booze rooms, none of which you would describe as cosy locals. Much more interesting is the wide network of 'small bars', which are speakeasy-style places lurking in the most unlikely back alleys and basements.

Most small bars have been subject to a midnight closure due to lockout laws, but a trial allowing them to open until 2am was due to begin at the time of writing, so expect some opening hours to be extended.

★ Frankie's Pizza
BAR

(Map p80; www.frankiespizzabytheslice.com; 50 Hunter St; ☺4pm-3am Sun-Thu, noon-3am Fri & Sat; ⓕ; ⓇMartin Place) Descend the stairs and you'll think you're in a 1970s pizzeria, complete with plastic grapevines, snapshots covering the walls and tasty pizza slices ($6). But open the nondescript door in the corner and an indie wonderland reveals itself. Bands play here at least four nights a week (join them on Tuesdays for live karaoke) and there's another bar hidden below.

★ Uncle Ming's
COCKTAIL BAR

(Map p80; www.unclemings.com.au; 55 York St; ☺noon-midnight Mon-Fri, 4pm-midnight Sat; ⓇWynyard) We love the shadowy, romantic opium-den atmosphere of this small bar secreted away in a basement by a shirt shop. It's an atmospheric spot for anything from a quick beer before jumping on a train at Wynyard to a leisurely exploration of the cocktail menu. It also does an excellent line in dumplings and usually has very welcoming bar staff.

Grandma's
COCKTAIL BAR

(Map p80; ☎02-9264 3004; www.grandmasbarsydney.com; basement, 275 Clarence St; ☺3pm-midnight Mon-Fri, 5pm-1am Sat; ⓇTown Hall) Billing itself as a 'retrosexual haven of cosmopolitan kitsch and faded granny glamour', Grandma's hits the mark. A stag's head greets you on the stairs and ushers you into a tiny subterranean world of parrot wallpaper and tiki cocktails. It's very quirky, and very relaxed and casual for a CBD venue. Toasted sandwiches provide sustenance. Look for it behind the Fender shop.

Baxter Inn
BAR

(Map p80; www.thebaxterinn.com; 152-156 Clarence St; ☺4pm-1am Mon-Sat; ⓇTown Hall) Yes, it really is down that dark lane and through that unmarked door (there are two easily

---

LOCKOUT LAWS

In an effort to cut down on alcohol-fuelled violence, tough licensing laws have been introduced to a large area of the central city bounded by the Rocks, Circular Quay, Woolloomooloo, Kings Cross, Darlinghurst, Haymarket and the eastern shores of Darling Harbour.

Within this zone, licensed venues are not permitted to admit people after 1.30am. However, if you arrive before then, the venue is permitted to continue serving you alcohol until 3am, or 3.30am in the case of venues with live entertainment, which you can enter until 2am. This latter amendment was announced in late 2016 after widespread protest from the public and industry over the severity of the laws. The change was too little, too late for many venues, which had already closed down.

spotted bars on this courtyard, but this is through a door to your right). Whisky's the main poison and the friendly bar staff really know their stuff. There's an elegant speakeasy atmosphere and a mighty impressive choir of bottles behind the bar.

O Bar
COCKTAIL BAR

(Map p80; 📞02-9247 9777; www.obardining.com.au; Level 47, Australia Square, 264 George St; ⊙5pm-late Sat-Thu, noon-late Fri; 🚇; 🚉Wynyard) The cocktails at this 47th-floor revolving bar aren't cheap, but they're still substantially cheaper than admission to Sydney Tower – and it's considerably more glamorous. The views are truly wonderful; get up there shortly after opening time, and kick back to enjoy the sunset and transition into night.

Mojo Record Bar
BAR

(Map p80; 📞02-9262 4999; www.mojorecord bar.com; 73 York St; ⊙4pm-midnight Mon-Wed, 4pm-1am Thu-Sat; 🚉Wynard) This dark and easygoing basement bar is curiously combined with a record shop, so you can browse the vinyl (if the shop part is still open) with a drink in hand. You're pretty much guaranteed good music too: it was pretty blues-y at last visit.

Ivy
BAR, CLUB

(Map p80; 📞02-9254 8100; www.merivale.com/ivy; L1, 330 George St; ⊙noon-late Mon-Fri, 6.30pm-3.30am Sat; 🚇; 🚉Wynyard) Hidden down a lane off George St, Ivy is the HQ of the all-pervading Merivale Group. It's a fashionable complex of bars, restaurants... even a swimming pool. It's also Sydney's most hyped venue; expect lengthy queues of suburban kids teetering on unfeasibly high heels, waiting to shed $40 on a Saturday for entry to Sydney's hottest club night, Pacha.

At other times, the main club space is Palings, a good bar and popular eatery, with Thai street food on the menu alongside steaks, grilled fish, salads and other well-prepared meals. It's a buzzy, open space that's good for leisurely lunch once the office crowd disperses around 2pm.

Marble Bar
BAR

(Map p80; 📞02-9266 2000; www.marble barsydney.com.au; basement, 488 George St; ⊙4pm-midnight Sun-Thu, to 2am Fri & Sat; 🚇; 🚉Town Hall) Built for a staggering £32,000 in 1893 as part of the Adams Hotel on Pitt St, this ornate underground bar is one of the best places in town for putting on the Ritz (even if this is the Hilton). The over-the-top late-Victorian decor is staggering, and the atmosphere great. Musos play anything from jazz to funk, Thursday to Saturday.

Slip Inn & Chinese Laundry
PUB, CLUB

(Map p86; 📞02-8295 9999; www.merivale.com.au/chineselaundry; 111 Sussex St; club $20-30; ⊙11am-late Mon-Fri, 4pm-late Sat, Chinese Laundry 9pm-3am Fri & Sat; 🚇; 🚉Wynyard) Slip in to this warren of rooms on the edge of Darling Harbour and bump hips with the kids. There are bars, pool tables, a beer garden and Mexican food, courtesy of El Loco. On Friday and Saturday nights the bass cranks up at the long-running Chinese Laundry nightclub, accessed via Slip St.

Darling Harbour & Pyrmont

Home
BAR, CLUB

(Map p86; www.homesydney.com; 1 Wheat Rd, Cockle Bay Wharf; ⊙club 9pm-late Thu-Sat; 🚇; 🚉Town Hall) Welcome to the pleasuredome: a three-level, 2100-capacity timber and glass 'prow' that's home to a dance floor, countless bars, outdoor balconies, and sonics that make other clubs sound like transistor radios. You can catch live music most nights at the attached Tokio Hotel bar downstairs (www.tokiohotellive.com.au), and the club is normally open Thursday to Saturday, and often features big-name DJs.

Pyrmont Bridge Hotel
PUB

(Map p86; 📞02-9660 6996; www.pyrmont bridgehotel.com; 96 Union St; ⊙24hr; 🚇; 🚉Pyrmont Bay) Standing like a guardian of tradition at the entrance to Pyrmont, this solid centenarian pub is a bastion of no-frills Sydney drinking culture. With an island bar and rooftop terrace, there are plenty of handsome features; there's also lots of character and regular live music. But its biggest selling point is its 24-hour license...the CBD lockout zone ends a few metres away.

In practice, they usually close for an hour or two around 5am so they can hose the place down and begin again.

Kings Cross & Potts Point

Traditionally Sydney's premier party precinct, this neighbourhood has had the life sucked out of it by the central Sydney licensing laws introduced in 2014. Most of the late-night clubs have closed. On the upside, the streets look less like a war zone in the wee hours. Woolloomooloo has some great old pubs near the water.

★**Old Fitzroy Hotel** PUB
(Map p88; ☑02-9356 3848; www.oldfitzroy. com.au; 129 Dowling St, Woolloomooloo; ⊙11am-midnight Mon-Fri, noon-midnight Sat, 3-10pm Sun; ☎; ⓡ Kings Cross) Islington meets Melbourne in the backstreets of Woolloomooloo: this totally unpretentious **theatre pub** (Map p88; www.oldfitztheatre.com) is also a decent old-fashioned boozer in its own right, with a great variety of beers on tap and a convivial welcome. Prop up the bar, grab a seat at a stree-tside table or head upstairs to the bistro, pool table and couches.

Kings Cross Hotel PUB
(Map p88; ☑02-9331 9900; www.kingscross hotel.com.au; 244-248 William St, Kings Cross; ⊙noon-1am Sun-Thu, to 3am Fri & Sat; ☎; ⓡ Kings Cross) This grand old brick building guards the entrance to the Cross and is one of the area's best pubs, with several levels of boozy entertainment. The balcony bar is a very pleasant spot for lunch, while the rooftop that opens weekend evenings has the drawcard vistas. Saturdays are good, with DJs on all levels.

World Bar BAR, CLUB
(Map p88; ☑02-9357 7700; www.theworld bar.com; 24 Bayswater Rd, Kings Cross; ⊙2pm-midnight Sun & Mon, 2pm-3am Tue-Sat; ☎; ⓡ Kings Cross) ✿ World Bar (a reformed bordello) is an unpretentious grungy club with three floors to lure in the backpackers and cheap drinks to loosen things up. DJs play indie, hip hop, power pop and house nightly. Wednesday (The Wall) and Saturday (Cakes) are the big nights. In the earlier evening, it's a pleasant place for a quiet drink on the foliage-rich verandah.

⬚ Surry Hills & Darlinghurst

Once upon a time this neighbourhood was known for its grungy live-music pubs and high-octane gay scene. Many of the music venues have subsequently been converted into chic bar-restaurants and the gay bars have eased up on the gas, but this area still contains some of Sydney's best nightspots. You just have to look harder to find them. The 'small bar' phenomenon has taken off here, with many of Sydney's best lurking down the most unlikely lanes.

★**Love, Tilly Devine** WINE BAR
(Map p88; ☑02-9326 9297; www.lovetillydevine. com; 91 Crown Lane, Darlinghurst; ⊙5pm-midnight Mon-Sat, 5-10pm Sun; ⓡ Museum) This split-level laneway bar is pretty compact, but the wine list certainly isn't. It's an extraordinary document, with some exceptionally well-chosen wines and a mission to get people away from their tried-and-tested favourites and explore. Take a friend and crack open a leisurely bottle of something.

★**Wild Rover** BAR
(Map p84; ☑02-9280 2235; www.thewildrover. com.au; 75 Campbell St, Surry Hills; ⊙4pm-midnight Mon-Sat; ⓡ Central) Look for the unsigned wide door and enter this supremely cool brick-lined speakeasy, where a big range of craft beer is served in chrome steins and jungle animals peer benevolently from the green walls. The upstairs bar opens for trivia and live bands.

★**Shakespeare Hotel** PUB
(Map p101; ☑02-9319 6883; www.shakespeare hotel.com.au; 200 Devonshire St, Surry Hills; ⊙10am-midnight Mon-Sat, 11am-10pm Sun; ⓡ Central) This is a classic Sydney pub (1879) with art nouveau tiled walls, skuzzy carpet, the horses on the TV and cheap bar meals. There are plenty of cosy hidey-holes upstairs and a cast of local characters. It's a proper convivial all-welcome place that's the antithesis of the more gentrified Surry Hills drinking establishments.

Beresford Hotel PUB
(Map p101; ☑02-9240 3000; www.merivale. com.au/theberesfordhotel; 354 Bourke St, Surry Hills; ⊙noon-1am; ☒374, 397, 399) The well-polished tiles of the facade and interior are a real feature at this elegantly refurbished historic pub. It's a popular pre-club venue for an upmarket mixed crowd at weekends but makes for a quieter retreat midweek. The front bar is as handsome as they come; out the back is one of the area's best beer gardens, while upstairs is a schmick live-music and club space.

Shady Pines Saloon BAR
(Map p88; ☑0405 624 944; www.shadypines saloon.com; shop 4, 256 Crown St, Darlinghurst; ⊙4pm-midnight; ⓡ Museum) With no sign or street number on the door and entry via a shady back lane (look for the white door before Bikram Yoga on Foley St), this subterranean honky-tonk bar caters to the urban boho. Sip whisky and rye with the good ole hipster boys amid Western memorabilia and taxidermy.

121BC

WINE BAR

(Map p101; ☑02-9699 1582; www.121bc.com.au; 4/50 Holt St; ⊗5pm-midnight Tue-Sat; ☎; ⊠Central) The first challenge is finding it (enter from Gladstone St) and the second is scoring a spot. After that, it's easy – seat yourself at the communal table under the bubbly light fixture and ask the waitstaff to suggest delicious drops from their tasty, pricey Italian wine selection and snacks to suit your inclinations. Everything's good, so you can't really go wrong.

Winery

WINE BAR

(Map p101; ☑02-9331 0833; www.thekeystone group.com.au; 285a Crown St, Surry Hills; ⊗noon-midnight; ☎; ⊠Central) Beautifully situated back from the road in the leafy grounds of a historic water reservoir, this oasis serves dozens of wines by the glass to the swankier Surry Hills set. Sit for a while and you'll notice all kinds of kitsch touches lurking in the greenery: headless statues, upside-down parrots, iron koalas. It's a very fun, boisterous scene on weekend afternoons.

Palms on Oxford

GAY, CLUB

(Map p88; ☑02-9357 4166; 124 Oxford St, Darling hurst; ⊗8pm-midnight Thu & Sun, to 3am Fri & Sat; ⊠333, 380) No one admits to coming here, but the lengthy queues prove they are lying. In this underground dance bar, the heyday of Stock Aitken Waterman never ended. It may be uncool, but if you don't scream when Kylie hits the turntables, you'll be the only one. Lots of fun and a friendly place.

Midnight Shift

GAY, CLUB

(The Shift; Map p88; ☑02-9358 3848; www. themidnightshift.com.au; 91 Oxford St, Darlinghurst; ⊗noon-1am Sun-Thu, noon-3am Fri & Sat; ⊠Museum) The grand dame of the Oxford St gay scene, known for its lavish drag productions, has been forced into something of a change of identity by the lockout laws. The downstairs bar is much improved and appeals for early-in-the-night drinks; the upstairs club, which charges an entrance fee some nights, can still get seriously tits-to-the-wind.

Stonewall Hotel

GAY, BAR

(Map p88; ☑02-9360 1963; www.stonewallho tel.com; 175 Oxford St, Darlinghurst; ⊗noon-3am; ⊠333,380) Nicknamed 'Stonehenge' by those who think it's archaic, Stonewall has three levels of bars and dance floors, and attracts a younger crowd. Cabaret, karaoke and quiz nights spice things up; Wednesday's Malebox is an inventive way to bag yourself a boy.

Arq

GAY, CLUB

(Map p88; ☑02-9380 8700; www.arqsydney. com.au; 16 Flinders St, Darlinghurst; ⊗9pm-3am Thu-Sun; ⊠333, 380) If Noah had to fill his Arq with groovy gay clubbers, he'd head here with a big net and some tranquillisers. This flash megaclub has a cocktail bar, a recovery room and two dance floors with high-energy house, drag shows and a hyperactive smoke machine.

🍷 Paddington & Centennial Park

Paddington

BAR

(Map p96; ☑02-9240 3000; www.merivale. com.au/thepaddington; 384 Oxford St, Paddington; ⊗noon-midnight Mon-Thu, noon-3am Fri & Sat, noon-10pm Sun; ☎; ⊠333, 380) There's a new kick to Paddington's weekend nightlife, and this bar-restaurant is a key player. Drinks and service are excellent, while succulent chickens spinning on the rotisserie provide a simple but very high class eating choice. The design, all white tiles, distressed brick and black-and-white photos of ancestors brandishing haunches of meat, deliberately recalls a butcher's shop, a little cynically, as it wasn't one.

Unicorn

PUB

(Map p88; www.theunicornhotel.com.au; 106 Oxford St, Paddington; ⊗11am-midnight Sun, 11am-1am Mon & Tue, 11am-3am Wed-Sat; ☎; ⊠333, 380) This spacious art-deco pub is casual and unpretentious, a fine place to sink a few craft beers, sip some Australian wines or try out the pool table atop a Persian-style rug. Burgers are the highlight of the OK eating offerings. There's a cosy downstairs bistro and small beer garden off it. More than the sum of its parts.

Wine Library

WINE BAR

(Map p96; ☑02-9360 5686; www.wine-library. com.au; 18 Oxford St, Woollahra; ⊗4-11.30pm Mon-Thu, noon-11.30pm Fri & Sat, noon-10pm Sun; ☎; ⊠333, 380) An impressive range of wines by the glass, a smart-casual ambience and a Mediterranean-inclined menu make this the most desirable library in town. There's courtyard seating out the back and very helpful service.

Lord Dudley Hotel

PUB

(Map p96; ☑02-9327 5399; www.lorddudley. com.au; 236 Jersey Rd, Paddington; ⊗11am-11pm Sun-Wed, to midnight Thu-Sat; ☎; ⊠389) Popular with rich older geezers and block-shouldered rugby union types, the Lord Dudley is as close to an English country pub as Sydney gets. The exterior is festooned with hanging baskets; the interior features dark woody walls and 18 quality beers on tap, served by the pint.

Bondi, Coogee & the Eastern Beaches

★ Coogee Pavilion   BAR
(Map p74; ☑02-9240 3000; www.merivale. com.au/coogeepavilion; 169 Dolphin St, Coogee; ⊙7.30am-midnight; 🛜👶; 🚌372-374) With numerous indoor and outdoor bars, a kids' play area and a glorious adults-only rooftop, this vast complex has brought a touch of inner-city glam to Coogee. Built in 1887, the building originally housed an aquarium and swimming pools. Now, space, light and white wood give a breezy feel. Great eating options run from Mediterranean-inspired bar food to fish 'n' chips and sashimi.

Anchor   BAR
(Map p103; ☑02-8084 3145; www.anchor barbondi.com; 8 Campbell Pde, Bondi Beach; ⊙5pm-midnight Tue-Fri, 12.30pm-midnight Sat & Sun; 🛜; 🚌333, 380-382) Surfers, backpackers and the local cool kids slurp down icy margaritas at this bustling bar at the south end of the strip. It sports a dark-wood nautical, piratey feel and is also a great spot for a late snack. The two-hour happy hour from 5pm weekdays is a great way to start the post-surf debrief.

North Bondi RSL   BAR
(Map p103; ☑02-9130 3152; www.northbondirsl. com.au; 120 Ramsgate Ave, North Bondi; ⊙noon-10pm Mon-Fri, 10am-midnight Sat, 10am-10pm Sun; 👶; 🚌380-382, 389) This Returned & Services League bar ain't fancy, but with views no one can afford and drinks that everyone can, who cares? The kitchen serves good cheap nosh, including a dedicated kids' menu. Bring ID, as nonmembers need to prove that they live at least 5km away. Grab a balcony seat for the perfect beach vistas.

Coogee Bay Hotel   PUB
(Map p74; ☑02-9665 0000; www.coogeebay hotel.com.au; 253 Coogee Bay Rd, Coogee; ⊙7am-4am Mon-Sat, to midnight Sun; 🛜; 🚌372-374) This enormous, rambling, rowdy complex packs in the backpackers for live music, open-mic nights, comedy and big-screen sports in the beaut beer garden, sports bar and Selina's nightclub. Sit on a stool at the window overlooking the beach and sip on a cold one.

Sydney Harbourside

★ Sheaf   PUB
(Golden Sheaf Hotel; Map p74; ☑02-9327 5877; www.thesheaf.com.au; 429 New South Head Rd, Double Bay; ⊙10am-1am Mon-Wed, to 2am Thu-Sat, to midnight Sun; 🛜; 🚌324-327, 🚢Double Bay, 🚆Edgecliff) A cracking pub, especially at weekends when it thrums with life all day, this is a real eastern suburbs favourite whose recent makeover has only enhanced it. The beer garden is among Sydney's best: large, with good wines by the glass, heaters, evening entertainment and solid food (all day from Friday to Sunday). Lots of other spaces mean there's something for all.

★ Watsons Bay Beach Club   PUB
(Map p74; ☑02-9337 5444; www.watsons bayhotel.com.au; 1 Military Rd, Watsons Bay; ⊙10am-midnight Mon-Sat, to 10pm Sun; 🚢Watsons Bay) One of the great pleasures in life is languishing in the rowdy beer garden of the Watsons Bay Hotel, mere metres from the ferry wharf, after a day at the beach. It goes off here at weekends, with food options and a rowdy good time had by all. Stay to watch the sun go down over the city.

Rag & Famish   PUB
(Map p74; ☑02-9955 1257; www.ragandfamish. com.au; 199 Miller St, North Sydney; ⊙10am-midnight Mon-Thu, to 1am Fri & Sat, to 10pm Sun; 🛜; 🚆North Sydney) This classic old Australian pub once stood virtually alone, wide verandah providing the shade for contemplating another slow-paced north-of-the-harbour day. These days, however, it's dwarfed by steel-and-glass office buildings and surrounded by busy traffic. Nevertheless, it's a fine spot for quality craft beers or pub grub from pies to generously proportioned burgers and sandwiches. There's a beer garden, lounge and a posher upstairs dining area.

Newtown & the Inner West

★ Courthouse Hotel   PUB
(Map p98; ☑02-9519 8273; 202 Australia St; ⊙10am-midnight Mon-Sat, to 10pm Sun; 🚆Newtown) A block back from the King St fray, the 150-year-old Courthouse is one of Newtown's best pubs, the kind of place where everyone from pool-playing goth lesbians to magistrates can have a beer and feel right at

home. It packs out for Sydney Swans games. The beer garden is one of Sydney's best: spacious, sheltered and cheerful, with decent pub food available.

★ Young Henry's
BREWERY

(Map p98; ☑ 02-9519 0048; www.younghenrys. com; 76 Wilford St, Newtown; ☺ noon-7pm Mon-Fri, 10am-7pm Sat, 11am-7pm Sun; ☒ Newtown) Conviviality is assured in this craft brewery bar, where the beer is as fresh as you'll get. Basically, it's filled a bit of warehouse with high tables, a loud stereo system and a counter to serve its delicious beer, opened the roller door and filled it with happy locals. It doesn't do eats, but there's a different food truck option outside each weekend.

★ Earl's Juke Joint
BAR

(Map p98; www.facebook.com/earlsjukejoint; 407 King St, Newtown; ☺ 4pm-midnight; ☒ Newtown) The current it-bar of the minute, swinging Earl's serves craft beers and killer cocktails to the Newtown hiperati. It's hidden behind the facade of the butcher's shop it used to be, but once in, you're in swinging New Orleans, with a bar as long as the Mississippi.

Duck Inn
PUB

(Map p98; ☑ 02-9319 4415; www.theduckinnpub andkitchen.com; 74 Rose St, Chippendale; ☺ 11am-11pm Mon-Sat, noon-10pm Sun; ☎; ☒ 422, 423, 426, ☒ Redfern) What Chippendale does best is a real feeling of neighbourhood despite its proximity to central Sydney. This backstreet pub takes food and drink seriously but is as convivial as they come, spacious with a comfortable buzz and sociable beer garden. There's an interesting, changing selection of tap beers, 18 wines by the glass and a nice line in shared roast platters: try the duck.

Erskineville Hotel
PUB

(Map p98; ☑ 02-9565 1608; www.theerko. com.au; 102 Erskineville Rd, Erskineville; ☺ 11am-midnight Mon-Sat, 11am-10pm Sun; ☎; ☒ Erskineville) The Erko's art-deco glory is something to behold, and it also happens to be one of the area's best pubs. The wood-lined beer garden, local characters, range of curious spaces to drink in, and good pub food served in generous portions makes it a real gem of the community. Unusually for Sydney pubs, it's even got some street-side tables.

Knox Street Bar
BAR

(Map p98; ☑ 02-8970 6443; www.knoxstreetbar. com; cnr Knox & Shepherd Sts, Chippendale; ☺ 6-10pm Mon, 4-10pm Tue-Thu, 4pm-midnight Fri &

Sat; ☒ Central) A curious semi-underground layout, offbeat decor and an appealingly louche ambience have put this spot firmly on many Inner Westies' favourites list. DJs keep the crowd ticking, and there are regular events in a little performance space to one side. Homemade sausages, cocktails and hipsters drive the party. Spin the wheel and play cocktail roulette.

Corridor
COCKTAIL BAR

(Map p98; ☑ 0405 671 002; www.corridorbar. com.au; 153a King St; ☺ 5pm-midnight Mon, 4pm-midnight Tue-Thu, 3pm-midnight Fri & Sat, 3-10pm Sun; ☒ Macdonaldtown) The name exaggerates this bar's skinniness, but not by much. Downstairs the bartenders serve old-fashioned cocktails and some zingy, fruity ones – the passionfruit mojito is a great palate-cleanser – and a good range of wine, while upstairs there's interesting art (for sale) and a tiny deck. There's live music some nights.

Bank Hotel
PUB

(Map p98; ☑ 02-8568 1900; www.bankhotel. com.au; 324 King St; ☺ 11am-1am Mon-Wed, 11am-2am Thu, 11am-4am Fri & Sat, 11am-midnight Sun; ☎; ☒ Newtown) The Bank didn't always sport the artful heritage-wood look that it has now but has consistently been a Newtown classic in its central railway-side position. Its large retractable-roofed beer garden at the back is a highlight, as is the craft beer bar above it, which always has interesting guest ales on tap. Food is based around Mexican-style barbecue options.

Lockout laws in the CBD have increased the Bank's popularity markedly, so prepare to queue on Friday and Saturday night.

Imperial Hotel
GAY & LESBIAN

(Map p98; ☑ 02-9516 1766; www.imperialsyd ney.com.au; 35 Erskineville Rd, Erskineville; admission free-$15; ☺ 3pm-midnight Sun, Wed & Thu, to 5am Fri & Sat; ☒ Erskineville) The art-deco Imperial is legendary as the starting point for *The Adventures of Priscilla, Queen of the Desert*. The front bar is a lively place for pool-shooting and cruising, with the action shifting to the cellar club late on a Saturday night. But it's in the cabaret bar that the legacy of Priscilla is kept alive.

Sly Fox
PUB

(Map p98; ☑ 02-9557 2917; www.slyfox.syd ney; 199 Enmore Rd, Enmore; ☺ 2pm-midnight Sun & Tue, 2pm-3am Wed & Thu, 2pm-6am Fri & Sat; ☒ Newtown) This crafty canine has several

LGBTIQ SYDNEY

LGBTIQ folk have migrated to Oz's Emerald City from all over Australia, New Zealand and the world, adding to a community that is visible, vibrant and an integral part of the city's social fabric. Partly because of that integration, partly because of smartphone apps facilitating contact, and partly because of lockout laws, the gay nightlife scene has died off substantially. But the action's still going on and Sydney is indisputably one of the world's great queer cities.

The famous **Sydney Gay & Lesbian Mardi Gras** (p107) is now the biggest annual tourist-attracting date on the Australian calendar. While the straights focus on the parade, the gay and lesbian community throws itself wholeheartedly into the entire festival, including the blitzkrieg of partying that surrounds it. There's no better time for the gay traveller to visit Sydney than the two-week lead-up to the parade and party, held on the first Saturday in March.

Darlinghurst and Newtown have traditionally been the gayest neighbourhoods, although all of the inner suburbs have a higher than average proportion of gay and lesbian residents. Most of the gay venues are on the Darlinghurst section of Oxford St, with classic spots like the **Stonewall** (p129), **Midnight Shift** (p129), **Palms** (p129) and, around the corner, **Arq** (p129). However, some of the best events are held at mixed pubs, such as the **Sly Fox** (p131) and the legendary Sunday afternoon session at the **Beresford** (p128).

Beach scenes include the north end of Bondi, **Lady Bay** (p95), a pretty nudist beach tucked under South Head, **Obelisk** (Map p74; Chowder Bay Rd; 244), a secluded nude beach with a bush hinterland and **Murray Rose Pool** (p104), another harbour beach. Women-only **McIvers Baths** (p103) is extremely popuar with the Sapphic set.

Free gay and lesbian media includes LOTL (www.lotl.com), the Star Observer (www.starobserver.com.au) and SX (www.gaynewsnetwork.com.au).

shifts of mood through the week, from hipster haunt to local drinking hole and, on Wednesday nights, a transformation into Sydney's premier lesbian bar. As the week slides to an end it reinvents itself yet again, this time as a live-music venue. DJs take up the baton until everyone's booted out into the dawn.

Marlborough Hotel   PUB
(Map p98; 02-9519 1222; www.marlborough hotel.com.au; 145 King St, Newtown; ◷10am-4am Mon-Sat, 10am-midnight Sun; Macdonaldtown) One of many great old art-deco pubs in Newtown, the Marly has a front sports bar with live bands on weekends and a shady beer garden. Head upstairs for a great balcony, soul food and rockabilly bands at Miss Peaches, or downstairs for all sorts of kooky happenings at the Tokyo Sing Song nightclub on Friday and Saturday nights.

Friend in Hand Hotel   PUB
(Map p74; 02-9660 2326; www.friendinhand. com.au; 58 Cowper St, Glebe; ◷8am-midnight Mon-Sat, 10am-10pm Sun; ; Glebe) At heart Friend in Hand is still a working-class pub with a resident loud-mouth cockatoo and

a cast of grizzly old-timers and local larrikins propping up the bar. But then there's all the other stuff: live music, life drawing, poetry readings, crab racing, comedy nights. Strewth Beryl, bet you weren't expecting that.

🍸 Manly

★ Manly Wharf Hotel   PUB
(Map p105; 02-9977 1266; www.manlywharfhotel. com.au; East Esplanade, Manly; ◷11.30am-midnight Mon-Fri, 11am-midnight Sat, 11am-10pm Sun; ; Manly) Just along the wharf from the ferry, this remodelled pub is all glass and water vistas, with loads of seating so you've a good chance of grabbing a share of the view. It's a perfect spot for sunny afternoon beers. There's good pub food, too (mains $18 to $26), with pizzas, fried fish and succulent rotisserie chicken all worthwhile.

Donny's   COCKTAIL BAR
(Map p105; 02-9977 1887; www.donnys.com. au; 7 Market Pl, Manly; ◷6-11pm Mon, 4pm-midnight Tue-Fri, noon-midnight Sat, noon-10pm Sun; Manly) Tucked away on a side street,

this two-level bar-restaurant is an atmospheric spot for a great night-time cocktail if you can read the menu in the low-lit speakeasy ambience. Sweet-toothers will love the sugar-and-coffee hit that is the Sticky Date Espresso, while the ginned-up 'detox' option is served to look like you're having a healthy pot of tea in case your personal trainer drops by. It does some smart fusion food too and has regular live bands.

Hotel Steyne   PUB
(Map p105; ☑02-9977 4977; www.hotelsteyne.
com.au; 75 The Corso, Manly; ⊙9am-2am Mon-Sat, to midnight Sun; ☎; ⛴Manly) With something for everyone, the Steyne is a Manly classic that's big enough to get lost in: it's like a village of its own with various bars and eating areas around the sociable central courtyard, which goes loud and late most nights. The rum-focused Moonshine bar has a balcony with beach views.

 Northern Beaches

Newport   PUB
(Newport Arms Hotel; ☑02-9997 4900; www.
merivale.com.au/thenewport; cnr Beaconsfield & Kalinya Sts, Newport; ⊙11am-midnight Mon-Sat, 11am-11pm Sun; ☎📶; 🚌187-190) This legendary Northern Beaches pub actually overlooks not the ocean but the Pittwater side, with bobbing boats and quiet strands the outlook. It's an absolutely enormous complex, with acres of appealing outdoor seating, several bars, good food, table tennis and all sorts of stuff going on. It's a great, family-friendly place to while away a sunny afternoon.

☆ Entertainment

Take Sydney at face value and it's tempting to unfairly stereotype its good citizens as shallow and a little narcissistic. But take a closer look: the arts scene is thriving, sophisticated and progressive – it's not a complete accident that Sydney's definitive icon is an opera house!

Cinema

★**Golden Age Cinema & Bar**   CINEMA
(Map p84; ☑02-9211 1556; www.ourgoldenage.
com.au; 80 Commonwealth St, Surry Hills; tickets $20; ⊙4pm-midnight Wed-Fri, 2.30pm-midnight Sat & Sun; 🚇Central) In what was once the Sydney HQ of Paramount pictures, a heart-warming small cinema has taken over the former screening room downstairs. It

shows old favourites, art-house classics and a few recherché gems. There's a great small bar here too; it's a fabulous place for a night out. The separate cafe at ground level is an attractive coffee-stop too.

Moonlight Cinema   CINEMA
(Map p96; www.moonlight.com.au; Belvedere Amphitheatre, cnr Loch & Broome Aves, Centennial Park; adult/child $19/14.50; ⊙sunset Dec-Mar; 🚇Bondi Junction) Take a picnic and join the bats under the stars in magnificent Centennial Park; enter via the Woollahra Gate on Oxford St. A mix of new-release blockbuster, art-house and classic films is screened.

OpenAir Cinema   CINEMA
(Map p74; www.stgeorgeopenair.com.au; Mrs Macquarie's Rd; tickets $38; ⊙Jan & Feb; 🚇Circular Quay) Right on the harbour, the outdoor three-storey screen here comes with surround sound, sunsets, skyline and swanky food and wine. Most tickets are purchased in advance, but a limited number go on sale at the door each night at 6.30pm; check the website for details.

Dendy Opera Quays   CINEMA
(Map p80; ☑02-9247 3800; www.dendy.com.au; 2 Circular Quay East; adult/child $20/14; ⊙sessions 9.30am-9.30pm; 🚇Circular Quay) When the harbour glare and squawking seagulls get too much, follow the scent of popcorn into the dark folds of this plush cinema. Screening first-run, independent world films, it's augmented by friendly attendants and a cafe-bar.

Classical Music

★**Sydney Opera House**   PERFORMING ARTS
(Map p80; ☑02-9250 7777; www.sydneyopera house.com; Bennelong Point; 🚇Circular Quay) The glamorous jewel at the heart of Australian performance, Sydney's famous Opera House has five main stages. Opera may have star billing,

---

ⓘ WHAT'S ON LISTINGS

Sydney Morning Herald Friday's 'Shortlist' section, also online at www.
smh.com.au.

What's On Sydney (www.whatson
sydney.com)

What's On City of Sydney (http://
whatson.cityofsydney.nsw.gov.au)

Time Out Sydney (www.timeout.
com/sydney)

ℹ️ BOOKING WEBSITES

Moshtix (☑ 1300 438 849; www.moshtix. com.au)

Ticketek (☑ 132 849; www.ticketek. com.au)

Ticketmaster (☑ 136 100; www.ticket master.com.au)

but it's also an important venue for theatre, dance and classical concerts, while big-name bands sometimes rock the forecourt. Renovation will close the concert hall until 2019, and may disrupt other performances.

★ **City Recital Hall**   CLASSICAL MUSIC
(Map p80; ☑ 02-8256 2222; www.cityrecitalhall. com; 2 Angel Pl; ⊗ box office 9am-5pm Mon-Fri; 🚇 Wynyard) Based on the classic configuration of the 19th-century European concert hall, this custom-built 1200-seat venue boasts near-perfect acoustics. Catch top-flight companies such as Musica Viva, the Australian Brandenburg Orchestra and the Australian Chamber Orchestra here.

Dance

Bangarra Dance Theatre   DANCE
(Map p80; ☑ 02-9251 5333; www.bangarra.com. au; Pier 4/5, 15 Hickson Rd; 🚌 324, 325, 998, 🚇 Circular Quay) Bangarra is hailed as Australia's finest Aboriginal performance company. Artistic director Stephen Page conjures a fusion of contemporary themes, Indigenous traditions and Western technique. When not touring internationally, the company performs at the Opera House or at its own small theatre in Walsh Bay.

Sydney Dance Company   DANCE
(SDC; Map p80; ☑ 02-9221 4811; www.sydney dancecompany.com; Pier 4/5, 15 Hickson Rd; 🚌 324, 325, 998, 🚇 Circular Quay) Australia's number-one contemporary-dance company has been staging wildly modern, sexy, sometimes shocking works for nearly 40 years. Performances are usually held across the street at the Roslyn Packer Theatre (p136), or at **Carriageworks** (Map p98; ☑ 02-8571 9099; www.carriageworks.com.au; 245 Wilson St, Eveleigh; ⊗ 10am-6pm; 🚇 Redfern) **FREE**.

Live Music

★ **Metro Theatre**   LIVE MUSIC
(Map p84; ☑ 02-9550 3666; www.metrotheatre. com.au; 624 George St; 🚇 Town Hall) The Metro is easily Sydney's best venue for catching lo-

cal and alternative international acts in intimate, well-ventilated, easy-seeing comfort. Other offerings include comedy, cabaret and dance parties.

Oxford Art Factory   LIVE MUSIC
(Map p88; ☑ 02-9332 3711; www.oxfordartfactory .com; 38-46 Oxford St, Darlinghurst; 🚇 Museum) Indie kids party against an arty backdrop at this two-room multipurpose venue modelled on Andy Warhol's NYC creative base. There's a gallery, a bar and a performance space that often hosts international acts and DJs. Check the website for what's on.

Venue 505   LIVE MUSIC
(Map p101; ☑ 0419 294 755; www.venue505. com; 280 Cleveland St, Surry Hills; ⊗ doors open 6pm Mon-Sat; 🚌 372, 🚇 Central) Focusing on jazz, roots, reggae, funk, gypsy and Latin music, this small, relaxed venue is artist-run and thoughtfully programmed. The space features comfortable couches and murals by a local artist. It does pasta, pizza and share plates so you can munch along to the music.

Basement   LIVE MUSIC
(Map p80; ☑ 02-9251 2797; www.thebasement. com.au; 7 Macquarie Pl; tickets $5-80; ⊗ noon-1am; 🚇 Circular Quay) Once solely a jazz venue, the Basement now hosts international and local musicians working across many disciplines and genres. Dinner-and-show tickets net you a table by the stage, guaranteeing a better view than the standing-only area just by the bar.

The upstairs bar is a decent spot for a beer with the after-work crowd.

Camelot Lounge   LIVE MUSIC
(Map p74; ☑ 02-9550 3777; www.camelot lounge.com; 19 Marrickville Rd, Marrickville; ⊗ 6pm-late Thu-Sun, plus shows other nights; 🚇 Sydenham) In ever-increasingly hip Marrickville, this eclectic little venue hosts jazz, world music, blues, folk, comedy, cabaret and all manner of other weird stuff. It's very close to Sydenham station.

ICC Sydney   LIVE MUSIC
(Map p84; ☑ 02-8297 7600; www.iccsydney. com.au; Darling Dr; 🚇 Convention Centre) The shiny new International Convention Centre at Darling Harbour has three theatres, including a large one that seats 8000 people, and principally holds big touring bands, replacing the former Entertainment Centre.

Spectator Sport

⭐ **Sydney Cricket Ground** SPECTATOR SPORT

(SCG; Map p96; ☎02-9360 6601; www.sydney cricketground.com.au; Driver Ave, Moore Park; ☒373-377) During the cricket season (October to March), the stately SCG is the venue for interstate cricket matches (featuring the NSW Blues), and sell-out international five-day Test, one-day and 20/20 limited-over matches. As the cricket season ends, the Australian Rules (AFL) season starts, and the stadium becomes a blur of red-and-white-clad Sydney Swans (www.sydney-swans.com.au) fans. The atmosphere for international cricket and Swans games is excellent. Book via Ticketek.

Sydney Football Stadium SPECTATOR SPORT

(Allianz Stadium; Map p96; ☎02-9360 6601; www.sydneycricketground.com.au; Moore Park Rd, Moore Park; ☒373-377) It's now officially named after an insurance company, but these naming rights change periodically, so we'll stick with the untainted-by-sponsorship moniker for this elegant 45,500-capacity stadium. It's home to local heroes the Sydney Roosters rugby league team (www.roosters.com.au), the NSW Waratahs rugby union team (www.waratahs.

WORTH A TRIP

SPORTS-CRAZY SYDNEY

Sydneysiders are sports crazy. Getting to a match is a great way to absorb some local culture and atmosphere.

Rugby League Sydney's all-consuming passion is rugby league, a superfast, super-macho game with a frenzied atmosphere for spectators. The **National Rugby League** (NRL; www.nrl.com) comp runs from March to October, climaxing in the sell-out Grand Final at ANZ Stadium. You can catch games every weekend during the season, played at the home grounds of Sydney's various tribes. The easiest ground to access is the 45,500-seat Sydney Football Stadium, home of the Sydney Roosters. Tickets start around $25 via www.tickets.nrl.com.

Rugby Union Despite its punishing physical component, Union (www.rugby.com.au) has a more upper-class rep than rugby league and a less fanatical following in Sydney. The annual southern hemisphere Rugby Championship (formerly the Tri-Nations) between Australia's Wallabies, New Zealand's All Blacks, South Africa's Springboks and Argentina's Pumas provokes plenty of passion – particularly the matches against New Zealand, which determine the holders of the ultimate symbol of Trans-Tasman rivalry, the Bledisloe Cup (the Aussies haven't won it since 2002). In the SuperRugby competition, the NSW Waratahs bangs heads with other teams from Australia, New Zealand, Argentina, Japan and South Africa. Most big matches are at **ANZ Stadium** (☎02-8765 2300; www.anzstadium.com.au; Olympic Blvd; tours adult/child $29/19; ⊙tours 11am, 1pm & 3pm daily, gantry 9am Fri-Wed; ☒Olympic Park).

Australian Football League (AFL) See the Sydney Swans in their red and white splendour from March to September at the Sydney Cricket Ground or ANZ Stadium at Sydney Olympic Park. Sydney's other team, the Greater Western Sydney Giants, play most home games at another stadium in the Olympic Park complex. Tickets start at around $25, available via www.afl.com.au.

Soccer The A-League bucks convention, playing games from late August to February rather than through the depths of winter. Sydney FC (www.sydneyfc.com) won the championship in 2006 and 2010. The newer Western Sydney Wanderers haven't won a grand final yet but landed an even bigger prize in 2014, the Asian Champions League. The W-League is the parallel women's equivalent, and is garnering rapidly increasing support. The same two Sydney clubs participate.

Cricket Major international Test, one-day and T20 matches take place at the Sydney Cricket Ground in summer. New South Wales play sparsely supported four-day Sheffield Shield matches here and at other Sydney grounds, while the all-action **Big Bash** (www.bigbash.com.au) draws huge crowds.

com.au) and the Sydney FC A-league football (soccer) team (www.sydneyfc.com).

All of these teams have passionate fans (possibly the most vocal are the crazies in the Roosters' 'chook pen'), so a home game can be a lot of fun. Book through Ticketek.

Royal Randwick Racecourse HORSE RACING
(Map p74; ☑ 02-9663 8400; www.australianturf club.com.au; Alison Rd, Randwick; ☐ 339) The action at Sydney's most famous racecourse peaks in April with several high-profile races, including the $4 million Queen Elizabeth Stakes; check the online calendar for race days, which are normally every second Saturday. It's always a fun day out, with Sydney fashion on show. On race days, special shuttle buses run from Chalmers St outside of Central station.

Wentworth Park GREYHOUND RACING
(Map p74; ☑ 02-9649 7166; www.wentworth park.com.au; Wentworth Park Rd, Glebe; entry $6; ☺ 5.30-11pm Wed & Sat; ☐ Wentworth Park) Wentworth Park is Australia's premier greyhound-racing complex, where the fast, skinny mutts tear around the track after tin hares. Dog races have been happening here since 1932, and there's a lovely old-fashioned vibe about the place. In 2016 the NSW government announced a ban on dog racing in the state, but went back on it after an adverse public reaction. Bars and bistro on site.

Theatre

★ Belvoir St Theatre THEATRE
(Map p101; ☑ 02-9699 3444; www.belvoir.com. au; 25 Belvoir St, Surry Hills; ☐ 372, ☐ Central) In a quiet corner of Surry Hills, this intimate venue, with two small stages, is the home of an often-experimental and consistently excellent theatre company that specialises in quality Australian drama. It often commissions new works and is a vital cog in the Sydney theatre scene.

★ State Theatre THEATRE
(Map p80; ☑ 02-9373 6655; www.statetheatre. com.au; 49 Market St; ☐ Town Hall) The beautiful 2000-seat State Theatre is a lavish, giltridden, chandelier-dangling palace. It hosts the Sydney Film Festival, concerts, comedy, opera, musicals and the odd celebrity chef.

Sydney Theatre Company THEATRE
(STC; Map p80; ☑ 02-9250 1777; www.sydney theatre.com.au; Pier 4/5, 15 Hickson Rd; ☺ box office 9am-7.30pm Mon, 9am-8.30pm Tue-Fri, 11am-8.30pm Sat, 2hr before show Sun; ☐ 324, 325, 998, ☐ Circular Quay) Established in 1978, the STC is Sydney theatre's top dog and has played an important part in the careers of many famous Australian actors (especially Cate Blanchett, who was co-artistic director from 2008 to 2013). You can book tours of the company's Wharf and Roslyn Packer Theatres ($10). Performances are also staged at the Opera House. The Wharf Theatre's bar is great, too; well worth a stop even without a show.

Roslyn Packer Theatre THEATRE
(Map p80; ☑ 02-9250 1999; www.roslynpacker theatre.com.au; 22 Hickson Rd; ☐ 324, 325, 998, ☐ Circular Quay) Opened in 2004, this is the most significant theatre built in the city since the Sydney Opera House. The state-of-the-art facility seats 850 and is managed by Sydney Theatre Company. Sydney Dance Company and a host of other troupes also perform here.

Monkey Baa Theatre Company THEATRE
(Map p84; ☑ 02-8624 9340; www.monkeybaa. com.au; 1 Harbour St; tickets around $25; ☐ Town Hall) If you can drag them away from the neighbouring playground, bring your budding culture vultures here to watch Australian children's books come to life. This energetic company devises and stages its own adaptations.

🔒 Shopping

Sydney's city centre is brimming over with department, chain and international fashion stores and arcades – shopping here is about as fast and furious as Australia gets. Paddington is the place for art and fashion, while new and secondhand boutiques around Newtown and Surry Hills cater to a hipper, more alternative crowd. Double Bay, Mosman and Balmain are a bit more 'mother of the bride', and if you're chasing bargains, head to Chinatown or the Alexandria factory outlets.

Newtown and Glebe have the lion's share of book and record stores. For surf gear, head to Bondi or Manly. Woollahra, Newtown (around St Peters station) and Surry Hills are good for antiques. For souvenirs – from exquisite opals to tacky T-shirts – try the Rocks, Circular Quay and Darling Harbour.

Artery ART
(Map p88; ☑ 02-9380 8234; www.artery.com. au; 221 Darlinghurst Rd, Darlinghurst; ☺ 10am-6pm Mon-Fri, 10am-4pm Sat & Sun; ☐ Kings Cross) 🍃 Step into a world of mesmerising dots and swirls at this gallery devoted to Aboriginal art. Artery's motto is 'ethical, contemporary,

affordable', and while canvases by more established artists cost in the thousands, small, unstretched canvases start at around $35.

Gannon House Gallery ART
(Map p80; ☑ 02-9251 4474; www.gannonhouse gallery.com; 45 Argyle St; ⏰ 10am-6pm; ☒ Circular Quay) Specialising in contemporary Australian and Aboriginal art, Gannon House purchases works directly from artists and Aboriginal communities. You'll find the work of prominent artists such as Gloria Petyarre here, alongside lesser-known names. There are always some striking and wonderful pieces.

Makery ARTS & CRAFTS
(Map p88; ☑ 0419 606 724; www.work-shop.com. au; 106 Oxford St, Darlinghurst; ⏰ 10.30am-6.30pm Tue-Fri, 10am-5pm Sat, 11am-4pm Sun; ☒ 333, 380) 𝄟 This ample corner space is an innovative idea that lets local artisans and designers sell their products in a single space. There's an excellent range of everything from jewellery to candles to clothing; it's always worth a browse.

★ Abbey's BOOKS
(Map p80; ☑ 02-9264 3111; www.abbeys.com. au; 131 York St; ⏰ 8.30am-6pm Mon-Wed & Fri, 8.30am-8pm Thu, 9am-5pm Sat, 10am-5pm Sun; ☒ Town Hall) Easily central Sydney's best bookshop, Abbey's has many strengths. It's good on social sciences and has excellent resources for language learning, including a great selection of foreign films on DVD. There's also a big sci-fi and fantasy section.

Gleebooks BOOKS
(Map p98; ☑ 02-9660 2333; www.gleebooks. com.au; 49 Glebe Point Rd, Glebe; ⏰ 9am-7pm Sun-Wed, to 9pm Thu-Sat; ☒ Glebe) One of Sydney's best bookshops, Gleebooks' aisles are full of politics, arts and general fiction, and staff really know their stuff. Check its calendar for author talks and book launches.

Better Read Than Dead BOOKS
(Map p98; ☑ 02-9557 8700; www.betterread. com.au; 265 King St, Newtown; ⏰ 9.30am-9pm Sun-Thu, 9.30am-10pm Fri & Sat; ☒ Newtown) This is our favourite Newtown bookshop, and not just because of the pithy name and the great selection of Lonely Planet titles. Nobody seems to mind if you waste hours perusing the beautifully presented aisles, stacked with high-, middle- and deliciously low-brow reading materials.

Berkelouw Books BOOKS
(Map p88; ☑ 02-9360 3200; www.berkelouw. com.au; 19 Oxford St, Paddington; ⏰ 9.30am-9pm Sun-Thu, to 10pm Fri & Sat; ☒ 333, 380) Expecting the dank aroma of secondhand books? Forget it! Follow your nose up to the cafe, then browse through three floors of preloved tomes, new releases, antique maps and Australia's largest collection of rare books. The Berkelouws have specialised in secondhand books and printed rarities over six generations since setting up shop in Holland in 1812.

Opal Minded JEWELLERY
(Map p80; ☑ 02-9247 9885; www.opalminded. com; 55 George St; ⏰ 9am-6.30pm; ☒ Circular Quay) This shop in the Rocks is one of several spots around here where you can stock up on the opal, that quintessential piece of Aussie bling. Quality and service are both excellent.

Faster Pussycat FASHION & ACCESSORIES
(Map p98; ☑ 02-9519 1744; www.facebook.com/ fasterpcat; 431a King St, Newtown; ⏰ 11am-6pm Tue-Fri, 11am-5pm Sat & Sun; ☒ Newtown) Inspired by 'trash pop culture, hot rods and rock and roll', this cool cat coughs up retro clothing and accessories for all genders and ages (including punk babywear) in several shades of leopard print.

★ Carriageworks
Farmers Market MARKET
(Map p98; http://carriageworks.com.au; Carriageworks, 245 Wilson St, Eveleigh; ⏰ 8am-1pm Sat; ☒ Redfern) 𝄟 Over 70 regular stallholders sell their goodies at Sydney's best farmers market, held in a heritage-listed railway workshop. Food and coffee stands do a brisk business and vegetables, fruit, meat and seafood from all over the state are sold in a convivial atmosphere.

Paddington Markets MARKET
(Map p96; ☑ 02-9331 2923; www.paddington markets.com.au; 395 Oxford St, Paddington; ⏰ 10am-4pm Sat; ☒ 333, 380) Originating in the 1970s, when they were drenched in the scent of patchouli oil, these markets are considerably more mainstream these days. They're still worth exploring for their new and vintage clothing, crafts and jewellery. Expect a crush.

Glebe Markets MARKET
(Map p98; www.glebemarkets.com.au; Glebe Public School, cnr Glebe Point Rd & Derby Pl; ⏰ 10am-4pm Sat; ☒ 431, 433, ☒ Glebe) The best of the west; Sydney's dreadlocked, shoeless, inner-city contingent beats a course to this

crowded hippy-ish market. There are some great handcrafts and design on sale, as well as an inclusive, community atmosphere.

The Rocks Markets MARKET
(Map p80; www.therocks.com; George St; ⌚9am-3pm Fri, 10am-5pm Sat & Sun; 🚆Circular Quay) Under a long white canopy, the stalls at this sizeable weekend market are a focus for tourists, but there's not too much koala tat at all, and some excellent handicrafts. It's a good place to shop for gifts for the folks back home. It takes up the top end of George St, and winds through to Argyle St, where there are food options. The Friday 'Foodies Market' offers more tasty treats.

Bondi Markets MARKET
(Map p103; www.bondimarkets.com.au; Bondi Beach Public School, Campbell Pde, Bondi Beach; ⌚9am-1pm Sat, 10am-4pm Sun; 🚌380-382) On Sundays, when the kids are at the beach, their school fills up with Bondi characters rummaging through tie-dyed secondhand clothes, original fashion, books, beads, earrings, aromatherapy oils, candles, old records and more. There's a farmers market here on Saturdays.

Paddy's Markets MARKET
(Map p84; www.paddysmarkets.com.au; 9-13 Hay St; ⌚10am-6pm Wed-Sun; 🚊Paddy's Markets, 🚆Central) Cavernous, 1000-stall Paddy's is the Sydney equivalent of Istanbul's Grand Bazaar, but swap the hookahs and carpets for mobile-phone covers, Eminem T-shirts and cheap sneakers. Pick up a VB singlet for Uncle Bruce or wander the aisles in capitalist awe.

Red Eye Records MUSIC
(Map p80; ☎02-9267 7440; www.redeye.com.au; 143 York St; ⌚9am-6pm Mon-Wed, Fri & Sat, 9am-9pm Thu, 10am-5pm Sun; 🚆Town Hall) Partners of music freaks beware: don't let them descend the stairs into this shop unless you are prepared for a lengthy delay. The shelves are stocked with an irresistible collection of new, classic, rare and collectable LPs, CDs, crass rock T-shirts, books, posters and music DVDs.

Utopia Records MUSIC
(Map p84; ☎02-9571 6662; www.utopia.com.au; 511 Kent St; ⌚10am-6pm Mon-Wed, Fri & Sat, 10am-8pm Thu, noon-4pm Sun; 🚆Town Hall) This well-established spot is Sydney's best music store for metal of all genres and hard rock. Horns up! The entrance is on Bathurst St.

Revolve Records MUSIC
(Map p98; ☎02-9519 9978; www.revolverecords.com.au; 65 Erskineville Rd, Erskineville; ⌚noon-6pm Mon-Wed, 11.30am-7pm Thu & Fri, 10am-6pm Sat & Sun; 🚆Erskineville) Vinyl hounds should head here, just up from Erskineville station for a treasure-trove of secondhand records of all types.

★ **Queen Victoria Building** SHOPPING CENTRE
(QVB; Map p80; ☎02-9265 6800; www.qvb.com.au; 455 George St; ⌚9am-6pm Mon-Wed, Fri & Sat, 9am-9pm Thu, 11am-5pm Sun; 🚆Town Hall) The magnificent QVB takes up a whole block and boasts nearly 200 shops on five levels. It's a High Victorian Gothic masterpiece – without doubt Sydney's most beautiful shopping centre.

★ **Strand Arcade** SHOPPING CENTRE
(Map p80; www.strandarcade.com.au; 412 George St; ⌚9am-5.30pm Mon-Wed & Fri, 9am-9pm Thu, 9am-4pm Sat, 11am-4pm Sun; 🚆Town Hall) Constructed in 1891, the Strand rivals the QVB in the ornateness stakes. The three floors of designer fashions, Australiana and old-world coffee shops will make your short-cut through here considerably longer. Some of the top Australian designers have stores here.

Westfield Sydney MALL
(Map p80; www.westfield.com.au/sydney; 188 Pitt St Mall; ⌚9.30am-6.30pm Mon-Wed, Fri & Sat, 9.30am-9pm Thu, 10am-6pm Sun; 📶; 🚆St James) The city's most glamorous shopping mall is a bafflingly large complex gobbling up Sydney Tower and a fair chunk of Pitt St Mall. The 5th-floor food court is close to Sydney's best.

David Jones DEPARTMENT STORE
(Map p80; ☎02-9266 5544; www.davidjones.com.au; 86-108 Castlereagh St; ⌚9.30am-7pm Sun-Wed, 9.30am-9pm Thu & Fri, 9am-7pm Sat; 🚆St James) DJs is Sydney's premier department store, occupying two enormous city buildings. The Castlereagh St store has women's and children's clothing; Market St has menswear, electrical goods and a high-brow food court. David Jones also takes up a sizeable chunk of **Westfield Bondi Junction** (Map p74; ☎02-9947 8000; www.westfield.com.au; 500 Oxford St, Bondi Junction; ⌚9am-6pm Mon-Wed & Sat, 9am-9pm Thu, 9am-7pm Fri, 10am-6pm Sun; 🚆Bondi Junction) and is scheduled to open at Barangaroo.

★ **Australian Wine Centre** WINE
(Map p80; ☑ 02-9247 2755; www.australianwine
centre.com; Goldfields House, 1 Alfred St; ⊙ 10am-
7pm Sun & Mon, 9.30am-8pm Tue-Thu & Sat,
9.30am-9pm Fri; ☒ Circular Quay) This multilingual basement store is packed with quality
Australian wine, beer and spirits. Despite its
location, it's no tourist trap: smaller producers are well represented, along with a staggering range of prestigious Penfolds Grange
wines and other bottle-aged gems. International shipping can be arranged.

ℹ Information

MEDICAL SERVICES

Call ☑ 000 in all emergencies.

Kings Cross Clinic (☑ 02-9358 3066; www.
kingscrossclinic.com.au; 13 Springfield Ave,
Kings Cross; ⊙ 9am-1pm & 2.30-6pm Mon-Fri,
10am-1pm Sat; ☒ Kings Cross) General and
travel-related medical services.

Royal Prince Alfred Hospital (RPA; ☑ 02-9515
6111; www.slhd.nsw.gov.au/rpa; Missenden Rd,
Camperdown; ☐ 412)

St Vincent's Hospital (☑ 02-8382 1111; www.
svhs.org.au; 390 Victoria St, Darlinghurst;
☒ Kings Cross)

POST

Australia Post (☑ 13 76 78; www.auspost.com.
au) Has branches throughout the city.

TOURIST INFORMATION

Sydney Visitor Centre (Map p80; ☑ 02-
8273 0000; www.sydney.com; cnr Argyle &
Playfair Sts; ⊙ 9.30am-5.30pm; ☒ Circular
Quay) In the heart of the Rocks, this branch has
a wide range of brochures, and staff can book
accommodation, tours and attractions.

Sydney Visitor Centre (Map p84; ☑ 02-
8273 0000; www.sydney.com; Palm Grove,
Darling Harbour; ⊙ 9.30am-5.30pm; ☒ Town
Hall) Under the highway overpass, this branch
has a wide range of brochures and events
guides, and staff can book accommodation,
tours and attractions. You will likely find it
moved to a temporary location nearby while a
major new Darling Harbour development is built
on this site.

City Host Information Kiosk (Map p80;
www.cityofsydney.nsw.gov.au; cnr Pitt & Alfred
Sts; ⊙ 9am-5pm; ☒ Circular Quay)

City Host Information Kiosk (Map p84;
www.cityofsydney.nsw.gov.au; Dixon St;
⊙ 11am-5pm; ☒ Town Hall) Under a pagoda-
style roof in the heart of Chinatown.

City Host Information Kiosk (Map p88;
www.cityofsydney.nsw.gov.au; cnr Darlinghurst
Rd & Springfield Ave, Kings Cross; ⊙ 9am-5pm;
☒ Kings Cross)

Hello Manly (Map p105; ☑ 02-9976 1430;
www.hellomanly.com.au; East Esplanade, Manly;
⊙ 9am-5pm Mon-Fri, 10am-4pm Sat & Sun;
☒ Manly) This helpful visitors centre, just outside the ferry wharf and alongside the bus interchange, has free pamphlets covering the **Manly
Scenic Walkway** (p104) and other Manly
attractions, plus loads of local bus information.
Staff can book a variety of tours, including quick
20-minute walking tours of Manly ($5).

**Parramatta Heritage & Visitor Information
Centre** (☑ 02-8839 3311; www.discover
parramatta.com; 346a Church St, Parramatta;
⊙ 9am-5pm; ☒ Parramatta) Knowledgeable
staff will point you in the right direction with
loads of brochures and leaflets, info on access
for visitors with impaired mobility, and details on
local Aboriginal cultural sites. Runs free walking
tours on Tuesdays and Fridays; phone to book.

ℹ Getting There & Away

AIR

The vast majority of visitors to Sydney arrive at
Sydney Airport, 10km south of the city centre.
Numerous airlines fly here from destinations
throughout Australia, Asia, Oceania, Europe
(with a stopover), North America and elsewhere.

Sydney Airport (Kingsford Smith Airport; ☑ 02-
9667 9111; www.sydneyairport.com.au; Airport
Dr, Mascot), 10km south of the city centre, is
Australia's busiest airport, handling flights from
all over the country and the world. The international (T1) and domestic (T2 and T3) terminals
are 4km apart on either side of the runway.

Airlines

Virgin Australia (☑ 13 67 89; www.virgin
australia.com), **Qantas** (☑ 13 13 13; www.
qantas.com.au), **Tigerair** (☑ 1300 174 266;
https://tigerair.com.au) and Qantas' budget
alternative, **Jetstar** (☑ 131 538; www.jetstar.
com), run frequent flights to and from other
Australia capitals. **Regional Express** (REX; ☑ 13
17 13; www.rex.com.au), **AirLink** (☑ 02-6884
2435; www.airlinkairlines.com.au) and **FlyPelican** (☑ 02-4965 0111; www.flypelican.com.au)
connect smaller centres.

For international airlines, see www.sydney
airport.com.au (click on 'Flight Information').

BUS

Long-distance coaches arrive at Sydney Coach
Terminal, underneath Central station. From here
you can walk along Eddy Ave for the suburban
trains or turn left onto Pitt St for the major bus
stop on Railway Sq.

Sydney Coach Terminal (Map p101; ☑ 02-
9281 9366; www.sydneycoachterminal.com.
au; Eddy Ave; ⊙ 8am-6pm, from 6am summer;
☒ Central) There's a tour desk here, internet
terminals and same-day bag storage.

Australia Wide Coaches (☑ 02-9516 1300; www.austwidecoaches.com.au) Services to Orange and Bathurst.

Firefly (☑ 1300 730 740; www.fireflyexpress. com.au) Runs Sydney to Melbourne and on to Adelaide.

Greyhound (☑ 1300 473 946; www.greyhound. com.au) Has the most extensive nationwide network.

Murrays (☑ 13 22 51; www.murrays.com.au) Runs from Canberra to Sydney and the South Coast.

Port Stephens Coaches (☑ 02-4982 2940; www.pscoaches.com.au) Coaches to Newcastle and Nelson Bay.

Premier Motor Service (☑ 133 410; www. premierms.com.au) Runs Cairns to Eden, via Brisbane, Gold Coast and Sydney.

TRAIN

Trains chug into Sydney's Central station from as far north as Brisbane (13½ hours), as far south as Melbourne (11½ hours) and as far west as Perth (four days!); see NSW TrainLink and the Indian Pacific for details.

NSW TrainLink (☑ 13 22 32; www.nswtrainlink. info) The government-owned train network, connecting Sydney to Canberra, Melbourne, Griffith, Broken Hill, Dubbo, Moree, Armidale and Brisbane.

Sydney Trains (☑ 13 15 00; www.sydneytrains. info) Connects Sydney with the Blue Mountains, South Coast and Central Coast.

Indian Pacific (☑ 1800 703 357; www.great southernrail.com.au) The famous train that heads clear across the continent from Perth to Sydney.

❶ Getting Around

TO/FROM THE AIRPORT
Bus

Service from the airport is limited to the 400 route between Burwood and Bondi Junction (55 minutes), which departs roughly every 20 minutes.

Shuttle

Airport shuttles head to hotels and hostels in the city centre, and some reach surrounding suburbs and beach destinations. Operators include **KST Airporter** (☑ 02-8339 0155; www. kst.com.au; airport to CBD adult/child $17/12), **Airport Shuttle North** (☑ 02-9997 7767; www.asntransfers.com; to Manly 1/2/3 people $41/51/61) and **Manly Express** (☑ 02-8068 8473; www.manlyexpress.com.au; airport to Manly 1/2/3 people $40/55/65).

Taxi

Fares from the airport are approximately $45 to $55 to the city centre, $55 to $65 to North Sydney and $90 to $100 to Manly.

Train

Trains from both the domestic and international terminals, connecting into the main train network, are run by **Airport Link** (www.airportlink. com.au; adult/child $13.40/12 plus normal rail fare; ⊗ 5am-11.45pm, extended on Fri & Sat night). They're frequent (every 10 minutes), quick (13 minutes to Central) and easy to use, but airport tickets are charged at a hefty premium. If there are a few of you, it's cheaper to catch a cab. The cheapest alternative is to catch the bus to Rockdale station (route 400, 12 minutes) and then catch the regular train to Central (15 minutes).

CAR & MOTORCYCLE

Avoid driving in central Sydney if you can: there's a confusing one-way street system, parking's elusive and expensive (even at hotels), and parking inspectors, tolls and tow-away zones proliferate. Conversely, a car is handy for accessing Sydney's outer reaches (particularly the beaches) and for day trips.

Car Hire

Car-rental prices vary depending on season and demand. Read the small print to check age restrictions, exactly what your insurance covers and where you can take the car.

If you take a small car for a few days, you can hope to find deals around the $25 a day mark.

The big players have airport desks and city offices (mostly around William St, Darlinghurst). Local companies also compete on rates and quality.

For motorbike hire, try **Bikescape** (☑ 02-8123 0917; www.bikescape.com.au; cnr Parramatta Rd & Young St, Annandale; tours from $195; ⓡ Stanmore).

Car-rental companies:

Ace Rentals (☑ 02-9222 2595; www.acerental cars.com.au)

Avis (☑ 02-9246 4600; www.avis.com.au; 200 William St, Woolloomooloo; ⊗ 7.30am-6pm; ⓡ Kings Cross)

Bayswater Car Rental (☑ 02-9360 3622; www.bayswatercarrental.com.au; 180 William St, Woolloomooloo; ⊗ 7am-6.30pm Mon-Fri, 8am-3.30pm Sat, 9am-3.30pm Sun; ⓡ Kings Cross)

Budget (☑ 02-8255 9600; www.budget.com. au; 93 William St, Darlinghurst; ⊗ 7.30am-5.45pm Mon-Fri, to 3.45pm Sat & Sun; ⓡ Kings Cross)

Europcar (☑ 02-8255 9050; www.europcar. com.au)

Hertz (☑ 02-9360 6621; www.hertz.com.au; 65 William St, Darlinghurst; ⊗ 7.30am-5.30pm Mon-Fri, 8am-1pm Sat & Sun; ⓡ St James)

Jucy Rentals (☑ 1800 150 850; www.jucy. com.au)

Thrifty (⏀ 02-8374 6177; www.thrifty.com.au; 85 William St, Darlinghurst; ⏀7.30am-5.30pm Mon-Fri, 7.30-11.30am Sat & Sun; ⏀ Kings Cross)

Toll Roads

There are hefty tolls on most of Sydney's motor-ways and major links (including the Harbour Bridge, Harbour Tunnel, Cross City Tunnel and Eastern Distributor). The tolling system is electronic, meaning that it's up to you to organise an electronic tag or visitors' pass through any of the following websites: www.roam.com.au, www.roamexpress.com.au, www.tollpay.com.au or www.myetoll.com.au. Note that most car-hire companies can supply e-tags.

Vehicle Purchase

Sydney Travellers Car Market (⏀ 02-9331 4361; www.sydneytravellerscarmarket.com. au; level 2, Kings Cross Car Park, Ward Ave, Kings Cross; ⏀10am-5pm Mon-Sat; ⏀ Kings Cross) In a car park, this is a useful forum for travellers looking to buy and sell vehicles for Australian road trips.

PUBLIC TRANSPORT

Sydneysiders love to complain about their public transport system, but visitors should find it surprisingly easy to navigate. The train system is the linchpin, with lines radiating out from Central station. Ferries head all around the harbour and up the river to Parramatta; light rail is useful for Pyrmont and Glebe; and buses are particularly useful for getting to the beaches.

Transport NSW (⏀ 131 500; www.transport nsw.info) is the body that coordinates all of the state-run bus, ferry, train and light-rail services. You'll find a useful journey planner on its website.

The TripView app is very useful for real-time public transport info and journey planning.

Bus

➞ **Sydney Buses** (⏀ 131 500; www.sydney buses.info) has an extensive network, operating from around 5am to midnight, when less frequent NightRide services commence.

➞ Bus routes starting with an X indicate limited-stop express routes; those with an L have limited stops.

➞ There are several bus hubs in the city centre; these include Wynyard Park by Wynyard train station, Railway Square by Central train station, the QVB close to Town Hall station, and Circular Quay by the ferry and train stop of the same name.

➞ Use your Opal card to ride buses; tap on when you board, and remember to tap off when you alight, or you'll be charged maximum fare.

Ferry

➞ Most **Sydney Ferries** (Map p80; ⏀ 131 500; www.transportnsw.info) operate between 6am and midnight. The standard Opal Card single fare for most harbour destinations is $5.74; ferries to Manly, Sydney Olympic Park and Parramatta cost $7.18.

➞ Private company **Manly Fast Ferry** (⏀ 02-9583 1199; www.manlyfastferry.com.au; adult one-way off-peak/peak $8.70/7.80) offers boats that blast from Circular Quay to Manly in 18 minutes.

Light Rail

➞ Trams run between Central station and Dulwich Hill, stopping at Chinatown, Darling Harbour, The Star casino, Sydney Fish Market, Glebe and Leichhardt en route.

➞ Opal card fares cost $2.10 for a short journey and $3.50 for a longer one.

➞ A second light rail line is being built and is due to open in 2019. It will run from Circular Quay down a now car-free George St right

---

OPAL CARD

Sydney's public transport network now runs on a smartcard system called Opal (www. opal.com.au).

The card can be obtained (for free) and loaded with credit (minimum $10) at numerous newsagencies and convenience stores across Sydney. When commencing a journey you'll need to touch the card to an electronic reader, which are located at the train station gates, near the doors of buses and light rail carriages, and at the ferry wharves. You then need to touch a reader when you complete your journey so that the system can deduct the correct fare. You get a discount when transferring between services, after a certain number of journeys in the week, and daily charges are capped at $15 ($2.50 on Sundays). You can use the Opal card at the airport train stations, but none of the aforementioned bonuses apply.

You can still buy single tickets (Opal single trip tickets) from machines at train stations, ferry wharves and light rail stops, or from the bus driver. These are more expensive than the same fare using the Opal card, so there's not much point unless you don't think you'll use $10 worth during your Sydney stay.

You can purchase a child/youth Opal card for those aged four to 15 years; they travel half-price. For student and pensioner discount Opal cards, you have to apply online.

through the city centre to Central station, then veer east through Surry Hills, head past the SCG and Sydney Football Stadium and on to Kingsford, with a branch veering to Randwick.

Train

Sydney Trains (p140) has a large suburban railway web with relatively frequent services, although there are no lines to the northern or eastern beaches.

Trains run from around 5am to midnight: check timetables for your line. They run a little later at weekends. Trains are replaced by NightRide buses in the small hours. These mostly leave from Town Hall station or Central station.

Trains are significantly more expensive at peak hours, which are from 7am to 9am and 4pm to 6.30pm, Monday to Friday.

A short one-way trip costs $3.38 with an Opal card, or $2.36 off-peak.

TAXI

Metered taxis are easy to flag down in the central city and inner suburbs, except at changeover times (3pm and 3am).

Fares are regulated, so all companies charge the same. Flagfall is $3.60, with a $2.50 'night owl surcharge' after 10pm on a Friday and Saturday until 6am the following morning. After that the fare is $2.19 per kilometre, with an additional surcharge of 20% between 10pm and 6am nightly. There's also a $2.50 fee for bookings.

The ride-sharing app Uber operates in Sydney and is very popular. Other apps such as GoCatch offer ride-sharing and normal taxi bookings; which can be very handy on busy evenings.

For more on Sydney's taxis, see www.nswtaxi. org.au.

Major taxi companies:

Legion Cabs (☑13 14 51; www.legioncabs. com.au)

Premier Cabs (☑13 10 17; www.premiercabs. com.au)

RSL Cabs (☑02-9581 1111; www.rslcabs.com.au)

Silver Service (☑133 100; www.silverservice. com.au)

Taxis Combined (☑133 300; www.taxiscom bined.com.au)

WATER TAXI

Water taxis are a fast way to shunt around the harbour (Circular Quay to Watsons Bay in as little as 15 minutes). Companies will quote on any pick-up point within the harbour and the river, including private jetties, islands and other boats. All have a quote generator on their website. It's much better value for groups than couples.

Fantasea Yellow Water Taxis (Map p86; ☑1800 326 822; www.yellowwatertaxis. com.au; Cockle Bay Wharf; ⊗7.30am-10pm, prebooking required for service outside these hours) Set price for up to four passengers, then $10 per person for additional people. Sample fares from King Street Wharf: to Manly for $195, Cockatoo Island $100, Watsons Bay $135. There are shared services for closer destinations, which include Taronga Zoo ($30), the Fish Market ($25), Fort Denison ($25) and Luna Park ($15).

AROUND SYDNEY

Blue Mountains

With stunning natural beauty, the World Heritage region of the Blue Mountains is an Australian highlight. The slate-coloured haze that gives the mountains their name comes from a fine mist of oil exuded by the huge eucalypts that form a dense canopy across the landscape of deep, often inaccessible valleys and chiselled sandstone outcrops.

The foothills begin 65km inland from Sydney, rising to an 1100m-high sandstone plateau riddled with valleys eroded into the stone. There are eight connected conservation areas in the region, offering truly fantastic scenery, excellent bushwalks (hikes), Aboriginal engravings and all the canyons and cliffs you could ask for.

Although it's possible to day-trip from Sydney, consider staying a night (or longer) so you can explore the towns, do at least one bushwalk and eat at some of the excellent restaurants. The hills can be surprisingly cool throughout the year, so bring warm clothes.

Activities & Tours

The mountains are a popular cycling destination, with many people taking their bikes on the train to Woodford and then cycling downhill to Glenbrook, a ride of two to three hours. Cycling maps are available from the visitor centres.

Blue Mountains Explorer Bus BUS (☑1300 300 915; www.explorerbus.com.au; 283 Bathurst Rd; adult/child $44/22; ⊗departures 9.45am-4.45pm) Significantly better than its average city equivalents, this is a useful way to get around the most popular Blue Mountains attractions. It offers hop-on, hop-off service on a Katoomba–Leura loop and also

has a route taking in Wentworth Falls. Buses leave from Katoomba station every 30 to 60 minutes and feature entertaining live commentary. Various packages include admission to attractions. You can buy tickets on board, from the office at Katoomba station or from a variety of participating shops.

Trolley Tours BUS
(☑ 02-4782 7999; www.trolleytours.com.au; 76 Bathurst St; adult/child $25/15) This company runs a hop-on, hop-off bus barely disguised as a trolley, looping around 29 stops in Katoomba and Leura. The same company, located opposite Katoomba station, runs buses to the Jenolan Caves (p152) and various combination packages.

Blue Mountains Adventure Company ADVENTURE
(☑ 02-4782 1271; www.bmac.com.au; 84a Bathurst Rd; abseiling from $150, canyoning $230, bushwalking from $30) Located opposite Katoomba station, this set-up offers abseiling, canyoning, combinations of the two, bushwalking and rock climbing.

River Deep Mountain High ADVENTURE
(☑ 02-4782 6109; www.rdmh.com.au; abseiling $165-230, canyoning $230) ✍ A professional outfit rigorous about comfort and safety, these guys offer abseiling, canyoning and a combination of the two. Other options include a range of hiking and mountain-biking tours.

Australian School of Mountaineering ADVENTURE
(☑ 02-4782 2014; http://climbingadventures.com.au; 166 Katoomba St) Professional and reliable, this company, based in an equipment store, offers guided excursions as well as training courses. It tackles rock climbing, abseiling and canyoning as well as bushcraft, mountaineering and cross-country skiing.

Blue Mountains

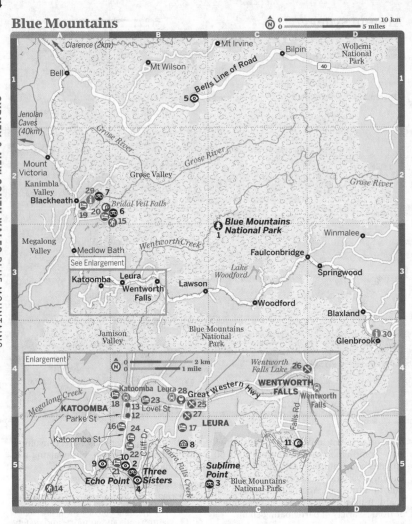

✨ Festivals & Events

Yulefest CHRISTMAS
(www.yulefest.com) These Christmas-style celebrations between June and August are held in hotels and restaurants across the region. While you can't expect snow and reindeer, it's as wintry as things get in this part of Australia.

🛏 Sleeping

There's a good range of accommodation in the Blue Mountains, but book ahead during winter and for Friday and Saturday nights.

Leafy Leura is your best bet for romance, while Blackheath is a good base for hikers; Katoomba is more built-up, although it does have excellent hostels.

Caravan parks dot the area, and there are bush campsites in the parks – some free. Tourist offices have a comprehensive list.

ℹ Information

For more information on the national parks (including walking and camping), contact the **NPWS Visitors Centre** at **Blackheath** (p150), about 2.5km off the Great Western Hwy and 10km north of Katoomba.

Blue Mountains

There are information centres on the Great Western Hwy at **Glenbrook** (☑1300 653 408; www.bluemountainscitytourism.com.au; Great Western Hwy; ☉8.30am-4pm Mon-Sat, to 3pm Sun; ☎) and at Echo Point in **Katoomba** (p149). Both can provide plenty of information and will book accommodation, tours and attractions.

❶ Getting There & Away

Trains (☑13 15 00; www.sydneytrains.info) run hourly from Sydney's Central Station to Katoomba and beyond via a string of Blue Mountains towns. The journey takes two hours to Katoomba and costs $8.30 on an Opal card.

To reach the Blue Mountains by road, leave Sydney via Parramatta Rd. At Strathfield detour onto the toll-free M4, which becomes the Great Western Hwy west of Penrith and takes you to all of the Blue Mountains towns. It takes approximately 1½ hours to drive from central Sydney to Katoomba. A scenic alternative is the Bells Line of Road (p147).

❶ Getting Around

There are limited local bus services run by **Blue Mountains Bus** (☑02-4751 1077; www.bmbc. com.au), but it's often easiest to get the train between towns. In Katoomba and Leura, two competing hop-on, hop-off bus services are a good way to get around the main sights with little fuss, but walking between most of them isn't too burdensome either.

Wentworth Falls

As you head into the town of Wentworth Falls, you'll get your first real taste of Blue Mountains scenery: views to the south open out across the majestic Jamison Valley. The village itself is pleasant for a short potter along the main street.

Wentworth Falls Reserve   WATERFALL, PARK
(Falls Rd; ☒Wentworth Falls) The falls that lend the town its name launch a plume of spray over a 300m drop. This is the starting point of several walking tracks, which delve into the sublime Valley of the Waters, with waterfalls, gorges, woodlands and rainforests. Be sure to stretch your legs along the 1km return to Princes Rock, which offers excellent views of Wentworth Falls and the Jamison Valley. The reserve is 2.5km from Wentworth Falls station on the other side of the highway.

Nineteen23
MODERN AUSTRALIAN **$$$**

(📞 0488 361 923; www.nineteen23.com.au; 1 Lake St; mains $30-40; ⊙ 6-10pm Thu & Fri, noon-3pm & 6-10pm Sat & Sun; 🍷📶) Wearing its 1920s ambience with aplomb, this elegant dining room is a favourite with loved-up couples happy to gaze into each other's eyes over a lengthy degustation. While the food isn't particularly experimental, it's beautifully cooked and bursting with flavour. There's also upmarket B&B and self-catering accommodation here.

Leura

Leura is the Blue Mountains' prettiest town, fashioned around undulating streets, well-tended gardens and sweeping Victorian verandahs. Leura Mall, the tree-lined main street, offers rows of country craft stores and cafes for the daily tourist influx. Leura adjoins Katoomba, slightly higher into the range.

⊙ Sights

★ Sublime Point
VIEWPOINT

(Sublime Point Rd) Southeast of Leura, this sharp, triangular outcrop narrows to a dramatic lookout with sheer cliffs on each side. It's much, much quieter than Katoomba's more famous Echo Point, and on sunny days cloud shadows dance across the vast blue valley below.

Leuralla NSW Toy & Railway Museum
MUSEUM, GARDENS

(📞 02-4784 1169; www.toyandrailwaymuseum.com. au; 36 Olympian Pde; adult/child $15/5, gardens only $10/5; ⊙ 10am-5pm) The striking art deco mansion that was once home to HV 'Doc' Evatt, the third president of the UN General Assembly, is jam-packed with an incredible array of collectables – from grumpy Edwardian baby dolls to *Dr Who* figurines to a rare set of Nazi propaganda toys. Railway memorabilia is scattered throughout the handsome gardens.

🛌 Sleeping

★ Greens of Leura
B&B **$$**

(📞 02-4784 3241; www.thegreensleura.com.au; 24-26 Grose St; r $175-220; 🅿️ ❄️ 📶) On a quiet street parallel to the Mall, this pretty centenarian house set in a lovely garden offers genuine hospitality and five rooms named after British literary figures. All are individually decorated; some have four-poster beds and spas. There's a great lounge with attached courtyard. Rates include breakfast as well as afternoon tea with sparkling wine and other goodies.

★ Broomelea
B&B **$$**

(📞 02-4784 2940; www.broomelea.com.au; 273 Leura Mall; r $175-225; 🅿️ ❄️ @ 📶) A consummately romantic Blue Mountains B&B, this fine Edwardian house offers a cheery welcome, four-poster beds, lovely gardens, a great verandah, an open fire and a snug lounge. There's also a self-contained cottage for families and plenty of other comforts. There's a two-night minimum stay at weekends.

🍴 Eating & Drinking

Leura Garage
MEDITERRANEAN **$$**

(📞 02-4784 3391; www.leuragarage.com.au; 84 Railway Pde; dishes $15-29; ⊙ noon-9pm or later; 📶) In case you were in any doubt that this hip cafe-bar was once a garage, the suspended mufflers and stacks of old tyres press the point. At dinner the menu shifts gears to rustic shared plates served on wooden slabs, including deli-treat-laden pizza.

Silk's Brasserie
MODERN AUSTRALIAN **$$$**

(📞 02-4784 2534; www.silksleura.com; 128 Leura Mall; 2-/3-course dinner midweek $59/69, weekends $65/75; ⊙ noon-3pm & 6-10pm) A warm welcome awaits at Leura's long-standing fine diner. Despite its contemporary approach, it's a brasserie at heart, so the serves are generous and flavoursome. It's a comfortable space, its chessboard tiles and parchment-coloured walls creating an inviting semiformal atmosphere. Make sure you save room for the decadent desserts.

Alexandra Hotel
PUB

(📞 02-4782 4422; www.alexandrahotel.com.au; 62 Great Western Hwy; ⊙ 10am-10pm Sun-Thu, to midnight Fri & Sat; 📶) On the main road, the Alex is a gem of an old pub, with lots of character. Join the locals at the pool table or listening to DJs and live bands on the weekend. There's also a more-than-decent line in pub food.

Katoomba

Swirling, otherworldly mists, steep streets lined with art deco buildings, astonishing valley views, and a quirky miscellany of restaurants, buskers, artists, bawdy pubs and classy hotels – Katoomba, the biggest town in the mountains, manages to be bohemian and bourgeois, embracing and distant all at once. It's got a great selection of accommodation and is a logical base, particularly

WORTH A TRIP

BELLS LINE OF ROAD

This stretch of road between North Richmond and Lithgow is the most scenic route across the Blue Mountains and is highly recommended if you have your own transport. It's far quieter than the highway and offers bountiful views.

Bilpin, at the base of the mountains, is known for its apple orchards. The Bilpin Markets are held at the district hall every Saturday from 10am to noon.

Midway between Bilpin and Bell, the **Blue Mountains Botanic Garden Mount Tomah** (☑ 02-4567 3000; www.rbgsyd.nsw.gov.au; ⊘ 9am-5.30pm Mon-Fri, 9.30am-5.30pm Sat & Sun) ✔ **FREE** is a cool-climate annexe of Sydney's Royal Botanic Garden where native plants cuddle up to exotic species, including some magnificent rhododendrons.

To access Bells Line from central Sydney, head over the Harbour Bridge and take the M2 and then the M7 (both have tolls). Exit at Richmond Rd, which becomes Blacktown Rd, then Lennox Rd, then (after a short dog-leg) Kurrajong Rd and finally Bells Line of Road.

if you're on a budget or travelling by public transport.

◉ Sights & Activities

★ Echo Point   VIEWPOINT
(Echo Point Rd) Echo Point's clifftop viewing platform offers a magical prospect of the area's most visited sight, the Three Sisters. Warning: the point draws vast, serenity-spoiling tourist gaggles, their idling buses farting fumes into the mountain air – arrive early or late to avoid them. The surrounding parking is expensive, so park a few streets back and walk. There's a tourist office (p149) here.

➡ Three Sisters
The Blue Mountains' essential sight is a rocky trio called the Three Sisters. The story goes that the sisters were turned to stone by a sorcerer to protect them from the unwanted advances of three young men, but the sorcerer died before he could turn them back into humans. A 500m trail leads to more lookouts and a bridge across to the first Sister.

Scenic World   CABLE CAR
(☑ 02-4780 0200; www.scenicworld.com.au; cnr Violet St & Cliff Dr; adult/child $39/21; ⊘ 9am-5pm) This long-time favourite, the Blue Mountains' most touristy attraction, offers spectacular views. Ride the glass-floored Skyway gondola across the gorge and then ride the vertiginously steep Scenic Railway, billed as the steepest railway in the world, down the 52-degree incline to the Jamison Valley floor. From here you can wander a 2.5km forest boardwalk (or hike the 12km, six-hour-return track to the Ruined Castle rock formation) before catching a cable car back up the slope.

The 686 bus stops at Echo Point and here, and this is on both the hop-on, hop-off bus routes, but it's only a 2.5km walk from Echo Point, and quite a pleasant one too.

Waradah Aboriginal Centre   CULTURAL CENTRE
(☑ 02-4782 1979; www.waradahaboriginalcentre.com.au; 33-37 Echo Point Rd; show adult/child $20/15; ⊘ 9am-5pm) This gallery and shop displays some exceptional examples of Aboriginal art alongside tourist tat such as painted boomerangs. However, the main reason to visit is to catch one of the 15-minute shows. Held throughout the day, they provide an interesting and good-humoured introduction to Indigenous culture.

★ Golden Stairs Walk   HIKING
(Glenraphael Dr) If you have your own transport, tackle the Golden Stairs Walk, a less congested route down to the Ruined Castle (a famous rock formation) than the track from Scenic World. It's a steep, exhilarating trail leading down into the valley (about 8km, five hours return). Take plenty of water.

To get there, continue along Cliff Dr from Scenic World for 1km and look for Glenraphael Dr on your left. It quickly becomes rough and unsealed. Watch out for the signs to the Golden Stairs on the left after a couple of kilometres.

🛏 Sleeping

No 14   HOSTEL $
(☑ 02-4782 7104; www.no14.com.au; 14 Lovel St; dm $28, r with/without bathroom $79/69; ⊜ @ 🖛) Resembling a cheery share house, this small hostel has a friendly vibe, colourful bedding and helpful managers. There's no TV, so guests tend to talk to actually each other. A basic breakfast is included. The verandah deck is a top spot to chill out.

DON'T MISS

BLUE MOUNTAINS BUSHWALKING

For tips on walks to suit your level of experience and fitness, call the National Parks' Blue Mountains Heritage Centre (p150) in Blackheath, or the information centres in Glenbrook (p145) or Katoomba (p149). All three sell a variety of walk pamphlets, maps and books.

Note that the bush here is dense and that it can be easy to become lost – there have been deaths. Always leave your name and walk plan with the Katoomba police or at the national parks centre. The police and the national parks and information centres all offer free personal locator beacons and it's strongly suggested you take one with you, especially for longer hikes. Remember to carry lots of clean drinking water and plenty of food.

The two most popular bushwalking areas are the Jamison Valley, south of Katoomba, and the Grose Valley, northeast of Katoomba and east of Blackheath. Top choices include the Golden Stairs Walk (p147) and the Grand Canyon Walk (p149).

One of the most rewarding long-distance walks is the 45km, three-day **Six Foot Track** from Katoomba along the Megalong Valley to Cox's River and on to the Jenolan Caves. It has camp sites along the way.

Flying Fox HOSTEL $

(☑ 02-4782 4226; www.theflyingfox.com.au; 190 Bathurst Rd; camp sites per person $21, dm $32, r $82-84; P ⊝ ⊛) 🍽 The owners are travellers at heart and have endowed this hostel with an endearing home-away-from-home feel. There's no party scene here – just mulled wine and Tim Tams in the lounge, free breakfasts and a weekly pasta night. Dorms are high-ceilinged and spacious; private rooms are pleasant and a decent deal. The garden has spaces to pitch tents and a nice outlook.

★ Blue Mountains YHA HOSTEL $$

(☑ 02-4782 1416; www.yha.com.au; 207 Katoomba St; dm $32-37, d with/without bathroom $134/119; P ⊝ @ ⊛) Behind the austere brick exterior of this popular 200-bed hostel are dorms and family rooms that are comfortable, light filled and spotlessly clean. Facilities include a lounge (with an open fire), a pool table, an excellent communal kitchen and an outdoor space with BBQ. Staff can book activities and tours for you. HI discounts apply.

Lurline House B&B $$

(☑ 02-4782 4609; www.lurlinehouse.com.au; 122 Lurline St; r $160-200; P ⊝ ⊛ ⊛) Handsome, spacious rooms with four-poster beds and dark wood furniture are true to the Federation features of this sizeable, excellently run guesthouse. Other rooms come with spa bath, and there's a lounge where guests can help themselves to fruit or drinks. Rooms are immaculately presented, but it's a cheerful, laid-back place. Breakfast is an impressive event, with an open kitchen.

Shelton-Lea B&B $$

(☑ 02-4782 9883; www.sheltonlea.com; 159 Lurline St; r $170-275; P ⊝ ⊛) 🍽 This sweet bungalow has four spacious suites, all with their own entrance and sitting area, some with spa bathtub and three with kitchenette. There's a hint of art deco in the decor and lots of plush furnishings. There's a two-night minimum stay at weekends, when you get a cooked breakfast (midweek it's continental).

Lilianfels HOTEL $$$

(☑ 02-4780 1200; www.lilianfels.com.au; 5-19 Lilianfels Ave; r $330-525; P ⊝ ⊛ @ ⊛ ⊛ ⊛) Very close to Echo Point and enjoying spectacular views, this luxury resort has 85 rooms, the region's top-rated restaurant (Darley's; dinner Tuesday to Sunday, three courses $125) and an array of facilities including a spa, heated indoor and outdoor pools, a tennis court, a billiards/games room, a library and a gym. Rooms come in a variety of categories; some have excellent vistas. Decor is classically plush.

✖ Eating

True to the Bean CAFE $

(☑ 0438 396 761; www.facebook.com/truetothe bean; 123 Katoomba St; waffles $3-6; ⊙ 6.30am-4pm Mon-Sat, 8am-4pm Sun; ⊛ 🍽) The Sydney obsession with single-estate coffee has made its way to Katoomba's main drag in the form of this tiny espresso bar. There's a small but sweet selection of food, with the likes of bircher muesli, baked potatoes and waffles. In good old milk-bar style, it also does a variety of shakes in unusual flavours.

Station Bar & Woodfired Pizza PIZZA $$
(☑ 02-4782 4782; www.stationbar.com.au; 287 Bathurst Rd; pizzas $18-26; ⊙ noon-midnight; 🛜) Bringing visitors and locals together, this is an upbeat space that combines three happy things – craft beer, pizza and live music – in a very likeable space next to the train station. It only does pizzas (plus a couple of salads), but they're delicious, with offbeat gourmet toppings. The compact trackside courtyard is great for a summer pint in good company.

ℹ Information

Echo Point Visitors Centre (☑ 1300 653 408; www.bluemountainscitytourism.com.au; Echo Point; ⊙ 9am-5pm) A sizeable centre with can-do staff and a gift shop.

Blackheath

The crowds and commercial frenzy fizzle considerably 10km north of Katoomba in neat, petite Blackheath. The town measures up in the scenery stakes, and it's an excellent base for visiting the Grose and Megalong Valleys. There are several memorable lookouts around town, and trailheads for some top hikes.

◉ Sights & Activities

Evans Lookout VIEWPOINT
(Evans Lookout Rd) Signposted 4km from the highway in Blackheath, this lookout presents a magnificent perspective of sandstone cliffs dropping to the valley and canyon below. It's one of the most scenic of the Blue Mountains lookouts, and is also a trailhead for the majestic Grand Canyon bushwalk, perhaps the area's best half-day excursion.

Govetts Leap Lookout VIEWPOINT
(Govetts Leap Rd) This popular lookout is a focal point for visitors to Blackheath. It offers great views up the valley of the Grose River, with an interesting explanatory panel on the geology that has created such an impressive landscape.

★ Grand Canyon Walk HIKING
(Evans Lookout Rd) This spectacular 5km circuit plunges you from Evans Lookout into the valley for a memorable walk along the 'Grand Canyon' before looping back up to the road about 1.5km short of the lookout. Though strenuous on the descent and ascent, it's one of the area's shadier walks and takes most people around three hours.

🛏 Sleeping

Sports Bunkhouse HOSTEL $
(☑ 02-4787 6688; www.sportsbunkhouse.com.au; 60 Govetts Leap Rd; dm/s/d/tw $35/60/75/80; 🅿 ⊜ 🛜) Around the back of Glenella Guesthouse, this purpose-built modern bunkhouse is aimed at walkers and cyclists. It offers good-value private rooms and a very comfortable bunk room, as well as a kitchen, a great verandah and a garden area. Rates drop for multi-night stays.

★ Glenella Guesthouse GUESTHOUSE $$
(☑ 02-4787 8352; www.glenella.com.au; 56 Govetts Leap Rd; r $140-195, f $230-270; 🅿 ⊜ ❋ 🛜) Gorgeous Glenella has been functioning as a guesthouse since 1912 and is now operated with enthusiasm and expertise by a young British couple who make guests feel very welcome. There are seven comfortable bedrooms, an attractive lounge and a stunning dining room where a truly excellent breakfast (included in rates) is served. Marvellous period features include ceiling mouldings and lead lighting. The owners also operate the Sports Bunkhouse around the back.

Jemby-Rinjah Eco Lodge CABIN $$
(☑ 02-4787 7622; www.jemby.com.au; 336 Evans Lookout Rd; cabins $225-265; 🅿 ⊜ 🛜) 🍃 Near Evans Lookout, these attractive, rustic eco-cabins are lodged so deeply in the gums and bottlebrush that it feels as though you're in very remote bushland, with just the rustle of leaves and the chirp of birds for company. All the one- and two-bedroom weatherboard cabins are equipped with kitchenette and crockery; the deluxe model has a Japanese hot tub.

🍴 Eating

Vesta BISTRO $$$
(☑ 02-4787 6899; www.vestablackheath.com.au; 33 Govetts Leap Rd; mains $29-38; ⊙ 5-10pm Wed-Fri, 12.30-3pm & 5-10pm Sat & Sun, closed Wed summer; ☑) Feeling the sting of a Blue Mountains cold snap? It's easy to warm up with Vesta's century-old wood-fired bakery oven roaring in the background, serving up hearty plates of roasted meats (all free range, grass fed and local), accompanied by share plates of homemade charcuterie and bottles of Aussie wine, to a boisterous local crowd.

Ashcrofts MODERN AUSTRALIAN $$$
(☑ 02-4787 8297; www.ashcrofts.com; 18 Govetts Leap Rd; mains dinner $37-40, lunch $20-23; ⊙ 6-10pm Thu, 11.30am-2.30pm & 6-10pm Fri,

> ### NATIONAL PARKS OF THE BLUE MOUNTAINS REGION
>
> Part of the Greater Blue Mountains World Heritage Area, the vast **Blue Mountains National Park** (www.nationalparks.nsw.gov.au) has more than 140km of walking trails. Adjoining it, and stretching between Katoomba and the Jenolan Caves, **Kanangra-Boyd National Park** (www.nationalparks.nsw.gov.au) covers 68,000 hectares of plateau and valley separated by the region's trademark sandstone cliffs. There are several long-distance walks in the park, but make sure you take the requisite precautions (p148). Other shorter walks leave from Kanangra Wells, accessed by road south of Jenolan.

8am-2.30pm & 6-10pm Sat & Sun) This acclaimed restaurant is a long-time Blue Mountains favourite. The snug dining room is a charming spot to dip into the short but polished menu, which changes seasonally and favours creative pairings and delicious, generous textures. Weekend breakfasts are a great time to drop by, too.

❶ Information

Blue Mountains Heritage Centre (📞 02-4787 8877; www.nationalparks.nsw.gov.au; ⊘9am-4.30pm) The helpful, official NPWS visitor centre has information about local walks and national parks. It's at the end of Govetts Leap Rd, near the Govetts Leap viewpoint, and has a small gallery attached.

NEWCASTLE & THE CENTRAL COAST

Central Coast

The largest town along the coast between Sydney and Newcastle is the transport and services hub of **Gosford**. Nearby, relaxed **Avoca** has a lovely beach and an old cinema, while **Terrigal** has a beautiful crescent-shaped beach with good surf, a bustling town centre and a variety of top spots to refuel. A series of saltwater 'lakes' spreads north up the coast between Bateau Bay and Newcastle, including deep, placid **Lake Macquarie**.

⊙ Sights

Bouddi National Park NATIONAL PARK
(📞 02-4320 4200; www.nationalparks.nsw.gov.au; vehicle access $8) At this spectacular park, short walking trails lead to isolated beaches and dramatic lookouts from where you can experience the annual whale migration between June and November. There are camp sites ($24 to $33 for two people) at Little Beach,

Putty Beach and Tallow Beach; book ahead. Only the Putty Beach site has drinkable water.

Australian Reptile Park ZOO
(📞 02-4340 1022; www.reptilepark.com.au; Pacific Hwy, Somersby; adult/child $35/19; ⊘9am-5pm) Get up close to koalas and pythons, and watch funnel-web spiders being milked (for the production of antivenin) and a Galapagos tortoise being fed. There are wonderful tours for kids. It's signposted off the M1 Pacific Motorway, or you could get a cab from Gosford station.

Brisbane Water National Park NATIONAL PARK
(📞 02-4320 4200; www.nationalparks.nsw.gov.au; Woy Woy Rd, Kariong; vehicle access at Girrakool & Somersby Falls picnic areas $8) Bordering the Hawkesbury River, 9km southwest of Gosford, this park, despite its name, is mostly sandstone outcrops and forest, with only a short Brisbane Water frontage. It's famed for its explosions of spring wildflowers and Guringai stone engravings, the most impressive gallery of which is the Bulgandry Aboriginal Engraving Site, 3km south of the Pacific Hwy on Woy Woy Rd. A favourite retreat for Sydneysiders is the pretty village of **Pearl Beach**, on the southeastern edge of the park.

⮕ Sleeping

There are numerous holiday lets right up and down the coast, as well as a wide selection of hotel and motel accommodation. National parks offer rustic camping.

✗ Eating

Woy Woy Fishermen's Wharf SEAFOOD $$
(📞 02-4341 1171; www.woywoyfishermenswharf.com.au; The Boulevarde, Woy Woy; restaurant mains $18-30; ⊘takeaway 11am-4pm Sun-Wed, 11am-7pm Thu-Sat, restaurant 8-11am & noon-3pm Mon-Wed, 8-11am & noon-8.30pm Thu-Sat, noon-3pm Sun) The Cregan family has been serving its outstanding fish and chips since 1974. Grab

them takeaway and enjoy in the park (like the pelicans, who are fed daily at 3pm) or take a table at the smart restaurant, which dangles over the mangrove-y water. There's also a good fish shop here. It's just a couple of minutes from the train station.

Pearls on the Beach MODERN AUSTRALIAN $$$
(02-4342 4400; www.pearlsonthebeach.com.au; 1 Tourmaline Ave, Pearl Beach; mains $41; noon-2.30pm & 6-10pm Thu-Sun) Share tasty, unpretentious, flavourful Modern Australian dishes at this highly rated restaurant, housed in a comfortable whitewashed cottage right on the sand at idyllic little Pearl Beach. Save room for the very tempting dessert menu. Opening hours extend in January and reduce in winter.

❶ Information
Central Coast Visitor Centre (02-4343 4444; www.visitcentralcoast.com.au; 52 The Avenue, Kariong; 9am-5pm Mon-Fri, 9.30am-3.30pm Sat, 10am-2pm Sun)

❶ Getting There & Away
Driving from Sydney, you can choose to head straight up the M1 Pacific Motorway towards Newcastle (via various Central Coast exits) or meander along the coast.

Gosford is a stop on the Newcastle and Central Coast line, with frequent trains from Sydney and Newcastle (both: adult/child $8.30/4.15, 1½ hours). There are several other Central Coast stops, including Woy Woy. Trains also stop at Wondabyne within Brisbane Water National Park upon request (rear carriage only).

Local buses connecting the various towns and beaches are operated by **Busways** (02-4368 2277; www.busways.com.au) and **Redbus** (02-4332 8655; www.redbus.com.au).

The Hunter Valley
A filigree of narrow lanes criss-crosses this verdant valley, but a pleasant country drive isn't the main motivator for visitors – sheer decadence is. The Hunter is one big gorge fest: fine wine, gourmet restaurants, boutique beer, chocolate, cheese, olives, you name it. Bacchus would surely approve.

The Hunter wineries are refreshingly attitude free and welcoming to novices. They nearly all have a cellar door with free or cheap tastings.

The Hunter Valley is exceedingly hot during summer, so – like its shiraz – it's best enjoyed in the cooler months.

◉ Sights
Most attractions lie in an area bordered to the north by the New England Hwy and to the south by Wollombi/Maitland Rd, with the main cluster of wineries and restaurants in Pokolbin. For spectacular views and a more chilled-out pace, head to the vineyards northwest around Broke and Singleton.

Lake's Folly WINERY
(02-4998 7507; www.lakesfolly.com.au; 2416 Broke Rd, Pokolbin; redeemable tasting fee $5; 10am-4pm) Try the highly acclaimed cabernet blend and chardonnay, which are both grown, vintaged and bottled on the estate. These small-production wines tend to sell out, so the cellar door is closed for four to six months of the year, normally from mid-December. Call ahead.

First Creek Wines WINERY
(02-4998 7293; www.firstcreekwines.com.au; 600 McDonalds Rd, Pokolbin; 9.30am-5pm Mon-Sat, to 4pm Sun) Very centrally located, this winery has an exciting team of winemakers who produce elegant, age-worthy styles. The expertly crafted drops offer great value. Tastings are free and the staff is super friendly.

Petersons WINERY
(02-4990 1704; www.petersonswines.com.au; 552 Mt View Rd, Mt View; 9am-5pm Mon-Sat, 10am-5pm) Though this winery has a cellar door on the main road in Pokolbin, it's worth heading up to this location, where the ultra-friendly staff have more time for

WORTH A TRIP

HAWKESBURY RIVER
Less than an hour from Sydney, the tranquil Hawkesbury River flows past honeycomb coloured cliffs, historic townships and riverside hamlets into bays and inlets and between a series of national parks, including **Ku-ring-gai Chase** (p102) and **Brisbane Water** (p150).

Accessible by train, the riverside township of **Brooklyn** is a good place to hire a houseboat and explore the river. Further upstream, a narrow forested waterway diverts from the Hawkesbury and peters down to the chilled-out river town of **Berowra Waters**, where a handful of businesses, boat sheds and residences cluster around the free, 24-hour ferry across Berowra Creek.

a chat and to guide you through the tasty, classically styled wines. It's a very welcoming experience. The Back Block shiraz is particularly delicious.

Small Winemakers Centre
WINERY

(☑ 02-4998 7668; www.smallwinemakers.com.au; 426 McDonalds Rd, Pokolbin; redeemable tasting fee $5; ⊙10am-5pm) With a sweet location by a little dam, this has a good attitude and showcases more than 30 varieties of wine from five great little estates, some of which don't have cellar doors. Generous tasting sessions.

Audrey Wilkinson Vineyard
WINERY

(☑ 02-4998 1866; www.audreywilkinson.com.au; 750 DeBeyers Rd, Pokolbin; ⊙10am-5pm) Enjoy the expansive views with a picnic at this hilltop cellar door. It's a sublime setting for one of the valley's oldest vineyards (first planted in 1866) and there's an interesting historic display. An extensive range of wines is available for tasting, with a free list, a $5 list and a $10 one. There are cottages here (weekend rates $500 to $850) if you want to stay.

Piggs Peake Winery
WINERY

(☑ 02-6574 7000; www.piggspeake.com; 697 Hermitage Rd, Pokolbin; ⊙10am-5pm) Priding itself on nontraditional winemaking practices, this winery is one to watch, producing limited-edition, unwooded wines that are causing quite a stir in the viniculture world. The names of the wines come straight from the pig-pun: try the prosecco-style Prosciutto or, for those on a tight budget, the $10-a-bottle Swill.

WORTH A TRIP

JENOLAN CAVES
....

Far from other Blue Mountains attractions, the limestone **Jenolan Caves** (☑ 02-6359 3911; www.jenolancaves.org.au; Jenolan Caves Rd, Jenolan; adult/child from $35/24; ⊙tours 9am-5pm) is one of the most extensive, accessible and complex systems in the world – a vast network that's still being explored. Several caves are open to the public, and tours cycle between them. There are various multi-tour packages and discounts.

Named Binoomea (Dark Places) by the Gundungurra tribe, the caves took shape 400 million years ago. White explorers first passed through in 1813 and the area was protected from 1866.

Glandore Estate
WINERY

(☑ 02-4998 7140; www.glandorewines.com; 1595 Broke Rd, Pokolbin; redeemable tasting fee $5; ⊙10am-5pm) This sweet spot has a smartly kitted out tasting area and some under-the-radar but rather tasty whites and reds, including a couple with the unusual white grape savagnin. Staff members are knowledgeable. Try to book one of the wine and chocolate matchings in the afternoon.

Keith Tulloch Winery
WINERY

(☑ 02-4998 7500; www.keithtullochwine.com.au; cnr Hermitage & Deasys Rds, Pokolbin; tastings $5; ⊙10am-5pm) Keith Tulloch is a fourth-generation winemaker who creates small-batch, ultrapremium drops. His estate has one of the most inviting tasting settings in the region: upstairs overlooking the vineyard. There's also the option of staying over in a lovely two-bedroom apartment (from $590 to $890 per night). There's also a chocolate shop and the excellent Muse Kitchen (p156) restaurant.

Tamburlaine
WINERY

(☑ 02-4998 4200; www.tamburlaine.com.au; 358 McDonalds Rd, Pokolbin; ⊙9am-5pm) 🍷 Australia's largest producer of certified organic wines, Tamburlaine has an attractively rustic cellar door. It does a full range of white varietals, some tasty cabernet and shiraz, and a couple of dessert wines.

Moorebank Vineyard
WINERY

(☑ 02-4998 7610; www.moorebankvineyard.com; 150 Palmers Lane, Pokolbin; ⊙10am-5pm) 🍷 Sustainable winemaking practices and delicious homemade condiments. It does an interesting Gewürztraminer among other varietals.

Hunter Beer Co
BREWERY

(Potters Resort; ☑ 02-4991 7922; www.hunter beerco.com; Wine Country Dr, Nulkaba; tours $10; ⊙10am-5pm, tours 4pm daily plus noon Sat & Sun) This is the Hunter's first microbrewery, just on the northern outskirts of Cessnock near the YHA. Join a tour to see how it all works and get three tastings. The tasting room has 10 beers on tap and the complex's pub also has the company's beers on draught.

🏃 Activities

Balloon Aloft
BALLOONING

(☑ 02-4990 9242; www.balloonaloft.com; $339) Take to the skies for a sunrise hot-air-balloon ride over the vineyards. The jaunt lasts for about an hour and is followed up with bubbles and breakfast at Peterson House Winery.

Hunter Valley

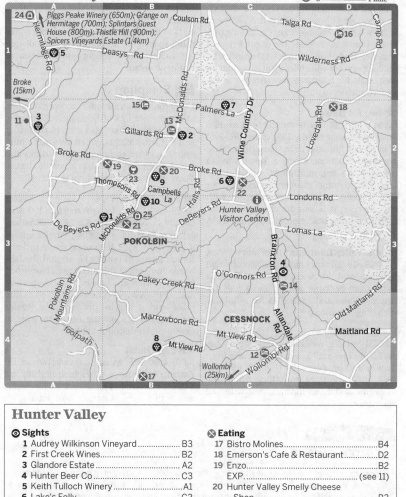

Hunter Valley

☞ Tours

If no one's volunteering to stay sober enough to drive, don't worry: there are plenty of winery tours available, ranging from minibuses that just do basic transport between wineries to full-on gourmet extravaganzas. Some operators will collect you in Sydney or Newcastle for a lengthy day trip. See www.winecountry.com.au.

★ Two Fat Blokes   FOOD, WINE

(☑ 0414 316 859; www.twofatblokes.com.au; 1616 Broke Rd, Pokolbin; half-day $69, full day $165-249) A barrel of fun and taste, these immersive gourmet experiences are a great way to discover the region. Upbeat guided tours take you to some excellent vineyards, but there's plenty more besides the wine, with cheese, beer, delicious lunches and plenty of entertaining background information. A standout.

Hunter Valley Boutique Wine Tours   WINE

(☑ 0419 419 931; www.huntervalleytours.com.au) Reliable and knowledgeable small-group tours from $80 per person for a half-day (three cellars) and from $115 for a full day including lunch.

Kangarrific Tours   WINE

(☑ 0431 894 471; www.kangarrifictours.com; full-day $129) This small-group tour departs from Sydney and promises the Hunter's most diverse itinerary. Taste everything from wine to gelato and have morning tea with the eponymous roos.

✵ Festivals & Events

Big international names (think Springsteen, Stones) regularly drop by for weekend concerts at the larger vineyards. If there's something special on, accommodation books up well in advance. Check for info at www.winecountry.com.au.

🛏 Sleeping

Numerous wineries offer accommodation, and there are lots of boutique self-catering places. Prices shoot up savagely on Friday and Saturday nights, when two-night minimum stays are common and weddings also put a strain on available accommodation. Many places don't accept children.

★ Hunter Valley YHA   HOSTEL $

(☑ 02-4991 3278; www.yha.com.au; 100 Wine Country Dr, Nulkaba; dm $35-37, r with/without bathroom $108/94; P ❄ 🛜 🛂) At the end of a long day's wine tasting or grape picking, there's plenty of bonhomie around the barbecue and pool at this attractive refurbished hostel. Dorms are four-berth and spotless, and there's a sweet verandah, as well as hire bikes and a nearby brewery-pub. Rooms can get hot. It's on the northern edge of Cessnock. HI discount applies.

Australia Hotel   PUB $

(☑ 02-4990 1256; www.australiahotel.com.au; 136 Wollombi Rd, Cessnock; s/tw with shared bathroom $45/60, r weekends $95; P ❄ 🛜) The rooms above this local watering hole look a bit

---

DON'T MISS

HUNTER WINE TRAILS

Home to some of the oldest vines (dating from the 1860s) and biggest names in Australian wine, the Hunter is known for its semillon, shiraz and, increasingly, chardonnay.

The valley's 150-plus wineries range from small-scale, family-run affairs to massive commercial operations. Most offer free tastings, although some charge a small fee, usually redeemable against a purchase.

Grab a copy of the free *Hunter Valley Official Map & Touring Guide* from the **visitor centre** (p157) at Pokolbin and use its handy map to plot your course, or just follow your nose, hunting out the tucked-away small producers.

If you're buying cases, be prepared to negotiate a little. Thirteen for the price of twelve is common, as is throwing in a six-pack of a previous vintage. Most wineries offer significant discounts if you join their wine club, which means you have to buy another case or two in the next year.

DrinkWise Australia recommends that to comply with the blood-alcohol limit of 0.05%, men who are driving should drink no more than two standard drinks in the first hour and then no more than one per hour after that. Women, who tend to reach a higher blood-alcohol concentration faster than men, should drink only one standard drink in the first hour. Wineries usually offer 20mL tastes of wine – five of these equal one standard drink.

weary but are perfectly adequate for resting your woozy wine head. The sparkling new bathrooms will make you feel much better in the morning.

Grange on Hermitage
B&B $$
([☎] 02-4998 7388; www.thegrangeonhermitage.com.au; 820 Hermitage Rd, Pokolbin; r $195-260, cottages $390-460; [P][⊖][✳][☎]) Spacious grounds, eucalypts and vines make this a most appealing place to relax. Rooms are enormous, with modern amenities, kitchenette and spa bath, and there are lots of lovely touches by the friendly owners, like fresh flowers and just-baked muffins delivered to your door as part of breakfast. There are also two cottages sleeping four to six.

Thistle Hill
B&B $$
([☎] 02-6574 7217; www.thill.com.au; 591 Hermitage Rd, Pokolbin; r $285; [P][✳][☎][✖]) This idyllic 8-hectare property features rose gardens, a lime orchard, a vineyard, a self-contained cottage sleeping five and a luxurious guesthouse with six double rooms. Rooms and common areas have an elegant French provincial sensibility and are strikingly attractive. There's a great lounge and deck by the pool. Breakfast (continental midweek, cooked at weekends), wine and cheese are all supplied.

★ Tonic
BOUTIQUE HOTEL $$$
([☎] 02-4930 9999; www.tonichotel.com.au; 251 Talga Rd, Lovedale; d incl breakfast $270-350, apt $500-700; [P][⊖][✳][☎][✖]) The polished-concrete floors and urban minimalist style of this handsome complex work a treat in the vivid Hunter light. There's a lovely outlook over a dam into the sunset from the impressive rooms and two-bedroom apartment. Bathrooms and beds are great, breakfast supplies are placed in your room, and an excellent common area and genial host make for an exceptional experience.

No children under 15 years.

Longhouse
APARTMENT $$$
([☎] 0402 101 551; www.thelonghouse.com.au; 385 Palmers Lane, Pokolbin; apt $650-850; [P][⊖][✳][☎]) 🌿 More than 50 architecture students designed this chic avant-garde pad, based on a traditional Australian wool shed. Made from concrete, corrugated iron and reclaimed timber, it is divided into three enormous, stylishly furnished two-bed apartments with an incredible 48m deck.

Splinters Guest House
B&B $$$
([☎] 02-6574 7118; www.splinters.com.au; 617 Hermitage Rd, Pokolbin; cottages $370-550; [P][⊖][✳][☎][✖]) These handsome cottages are some of the Hunter's best, with beautiful decor and smart furniture. The owners care for their guests very well, with a generous breakfast in the fridge plus wine and cheese, a dessert wine and other details. Cottages sleep six; some smaller ones were being built in late 2016.

Hermitage Lodge
CABIN $$$
([☎] 02-4998 7639; www.hermitagelodge.com.au; 609 McDonalds Rd, Pokolbin; r $250-475; [P][⊖][✳][☎][✖]) Ideally located within walking distance of a variety of cellar doors, this well run spot has rooms ranging from fairly basic motel-style doubles to bright, modern, spacious studios and suites, with sunny decks overlooking a shiraz vineyard; two have a secluded upstairs deck with spa bath. There's a good northern Italian restaurant on site as well as a guest laundry.

As everywhere, rooms are significantly cheaper midweek.

Spicers Vineyards Estate
RESORT $$$
([☎] 02-6574 7229; www.spicersretreats.com; 555 Hermitage Rd, Pokolbin; ste $599-699; [P][✳][☎][✖]) 🌿 Surrounded by bushland, these 12 modern high-end spa suites have king-size beds and cosy lounge areas with open fireplace: perfect for sipping shiraz in winter. The luxury suites are worth the extra $100 a night, with balconies (most) and particularly stunning bathrooms. Unwind at the day spa or in the pool before a meal at the top-notch **Restaurant Botanica** (2/3 courses $69/79; [🕙] 6-8.30pm Wed-Fri, noon-3pm & 6-8.30pm Sat & Sun; [☎]) 🌿.

Service is cheerful and excellent and there are nice touches like a free bottle of bubbles in your room. No children.

✕ Eating

There's some excellent eating to be done in the Hunter, which has a reputation as a gourmet destination. Many restaurants don't open midweek. Bookings are essential. Many wineries have restaurants.

Hunter Valley Smelly Cheese Shop
DELI $
([☎] 02-4998 6713; www.smellycheese.net.au; Roche Estate, 2144 Broke Rd, Pokolbin; mains $12-18; [🕙] 10am-5pm Sun-Thu, to 5.30pm Fri & Sat) Along with the great range of stinky desirables filling the cheese counter, there are deli

platters, pizzas, burgers and baguettes to go, as well as a freezer of superb gelato. There are good daily specials and a cheery attitude despite the besieging hordes. There's another branch in Pokolbin Village.

Enzo
CAFE $$

(☑02-4998 7233; www.enzohuntervalley.com.au; cnr Broke & Ekerts Rds, Pokolbin; breakfast mains $16-31, lunch $23-37; ☉9am-4pm Mon-Fri, 8.30am-4pm Sat & Sun; ☎☑) Claim a table by the fireside in winter or in the garden in summer to enjoy the rustic dishes served at this popular Italian-inflected cafe in a lovely setting. The food is reliably excellent, and David Hook winery is here, so you can add a tasting to your visit.

★Muse Restaurant
MODERN AUSTRALIAN $$$

(☑02-4998 6777; www.musedining.com.au; 1 Broke Rd, Pokolbin; 2/3 courses $75/95; ☉noon-3pm Sat & Sun, 6.30-10pm Wed-Sat; ☑) Inside the dramatic Hungerford Hill winery complex is the area's highest-rated restaurant, offering sensational contemporary fare and stellar service in an attractive modern space. Presentation is exquisite, especially for dishes on the degustation menu, which is compulsory on Saturday ($125, with wine $185). Vegetarians get their own menu (two/three courses $60/80).

★Muse Kitchen
EUROPEAN $$$

(☑02-4998 7899; www.musedining.com.au; Keith Tulloch Winery, cnr Hermitage & Deasys Rds, Pokolbin; mains $34-36; ☉noon-3pm Wed-Sun, plus 6-9pm Sat; ☎☑) For a fabulous lunch, head to this relaxed incarnation of the Hunter's top restaurant, Muse. Dine outside on a seasonal menu of European bistro food inspired by the vegetables, fruit and herbs grown up the road. Save room for the exquisite dessert selection and wine tasting at the Keith Tulloch (p152) cellar door.

Hunters Quarter
MODERN AUSTRALIAN $$$

(☑02-4998 7776; www.huntersquarter.com; Cockfighter's Ghost, 576 De Beyers Rd, Pokolbin; mains $36-44; ☉6-11pm Mon, noon-3.30pm & 6-11pm Thu-Sat, noon-3.30pm Sun; ☎) With a lovely outlook over the vines from the array of floor-to-ceiling windows, this place is bustling but intimate. Flavoursome dishes are produced from high-quality ingredients; the house-smoked salmon is a taste sensation. A good range of wines by the glass lets you taste your way around this and nearby vineyards. Monday is 'locals' night', when two/three courses are $60/75.

EXP.
MODERN AUSTRALIAN $$$

(☑02-4998 7264; www.exprestaurant.com.au; 1596 Broke Rd, Pokolbin; 5/8 courses $85/110; ☉noon-2.30pm & 6-9pm Wed-Sat, noon-2.30pm Sun) Local lad Frank Fawkner had an impressive restaurant career in the region and elsewhere before opening his own place in Oakvale winery. His subtle, fresh, texture-rich degustation menus are wowing the Sydney food mafia, and with good reason. You'll need to book ahead.

Emerson's Cafe & Restaurant
MODERN AUSTRALIAN $$$

(☑02-4930 7029; www.emersonsrestaurant.com.au; 492 Lovedale Rd, Lovedale; mains $35-42; ☉11am-3pm Wed, 11am-3pm & 6-10pm Thu & Fri, 8am-3pm & 6-10pm Sat & Sun; ☎) Set in Adina winery, this is run by a chef who has had a notable Hunter trajectory and offers hearty weekend breakfast choices to set you up for a day of tasting, and exquisitely presented lunch and dinner options sourced primarily from local producers.

Margan
MODERN AUSTRALIAN $$$

(☑02-6579 1317; www.margan.com.au; 1238 Milbrodale Rd, Broke; 2/3/5 courses $65/80/100; ☉noon-3pm & 6-9.30pm Fri & Sat, noon-3pm Sun) ✐ There's a tempting array of dishes at this rammed-earth restaurant, where much of the produce is sourced from the kitchen garden and farm; the rest comes from local providores whenever possible. The luscious food is beautifully accompanied by the excellent estate-made wines. Views stretch across the vines to the Brokenback Range.

Bistro Molines
FRENCH $$$

(☑02-4990 9553; www.bistromolines.com.au; Tallavera Grove, 749 Mt View Rd, Mt View; mains $38-44; ☉noon-3pm Thu, Sun & Mon, noon-3pm & 7-9pm Fri & Sat) Set in the Tallavera Grove winery, this French restaurant run by the Hunter Valley's most storied chef has a carefully crafted, seasonally driven menu that is nearly as impressive as the vineyard views. There's lovely seating in the paved courtyard, and an elegant exterior. Daily specials supplement the menu.

🍷 Drinking & Nightlife

Wollombi Tavern
PUB

(☑02-4998 3261; www.wollombitavern.com.au; 2994 Great North Rd, Wollombi; ☉10am-10pm Mon-Thu, 10am-midnight Fri, 9.30am-midnight Sat, 9am-10pm Sun) This fabulous little pub at the road junction in Wollombi is the home of the potent Dr Jurd's Jungle Juice, a dangerous brew of port, brandy and wine. On the weekends, the tavern is a favourite pit stop for motorbike clubs (the nonscary sort). You can camp for free in the meadow (no showers).

Goldfish Bar & Kitchen BAR
(www.thegoldfish.com.au; Roche Estate, cnr Broke & McDonalds Rds, Pokolbin; ☺noon-11pm Mon-Thu, to 1am Fri & Sat, to 10pm Sun; ☏) All wined out? Try a classic cocktail on the spacious terrace or in the lounge of this popular bar, a great place to hang out. There's an impressive spirit selection and it also does a decent line in food. There's live music most Saturday nights.

Harrigan's PUB
(☑02-4998 4300; www.harrigansirishpub.com.au; 2090 Broke Rd, Pokolbin; ☺9am-10pm or later, bistro from 7am; ☏) A comfortable Irish pub with beef-and-Guinness pies on the menu, a sprawling beer garden and live bands most weekends. Sitting on the deck here is a convivial Hunter Valley pleasure.

🛍 Shopping

Binnorie Dairy CHEESE
(☑02-4998 6660; www.binnorie.com.au; cnr Hermitage Rd & Mistletoe Lane, Pokolbin; ☺10am-5pm Tue-Sat, to 4pm Sun) Offers an exceptional range of handcrafted creamy soft cheeses from a stylish shopfront in a little complex with a winery and cafe. The goat's-cheese log, labne and marinated feta are particularly moreish.

Hunter Olive Centre FOOD
(☑02-4998 7524; www.pokolbinestate.com.au; 298 McDonalds Rd, Pokolbin; ☺9am-5pm, tastings 10am-4pm) Hidden behind Pokolbin Estate Vineyard, this stone cottage offers dozens of local gourmet products to buy or try on little squares of bread – oil, tapenade, chutney, jam etc. You buy a bag of bread for 50¢, then help yourself from the tasting samples arrayed around the room.

🛈 Information

Hunter Valley Visitor Centre (☑02-4993 6700; www.huntervalleyvisitorcentre.com.au; 455 Wine Country Dr, Pokolbin; ☺9am-5pm Mon-Sat, to 4pm Sun; ☏) Has a huge stock of leaflets and info on valley accommodation, attractions and dining.

🛈 Getting There & Away

From Sydney, you can head straight up the M1 motorway, then head to the valley via the exit near Gosford (which allows you to take the scenic route up through Wollombi), the Cessnock turnoff, or the Hunter Expressway (which begins near Newcastle).

Bus Rover Coaches (☑02-4990 1699; www.rovercoaches.com.au) has five buses heading between Newcastle and Cessnock (1¼ hours) on weekdays and two on Saturday; no Sunday service. Other buses head to Cessnock from the train stations at Morisset (one hour, two daily) and Maitland (50 minutes, hourly or better Monday to Saturday, six Sunday).

Sydney Trains has a line heading through the Hunter Valley from Newcastle ($4.82, 50 minutes). Branxton is the closest station to the vineyards, although only Maitland has bus services to Cessnock.

🛈 Getting Around

There are several options for exploring without a car. The **YHA hostel** (p154) hires bikes, as do **Grapemobile** (☑02-4998 7660; www.grapemobile.com.au; 307 Palmers Lane, Pokolbin; per 8hr $45; ☺10am-6pm) and **Hunter Valley Cycling** (☑0418 281 480; www.huntervalleycycling.com.au; per 1/2 days $35/50). **Sutton Estate** (☑0448 600 288; www.suttonestateelectricbikehire.com; 381 Deasys Rd, Pokolbin; half/full day $50/65) rents electric bikes. The other choices are to take a tour (p154) or a **taxi** (☑02-6572 1133; www.taxico.com.au).

Vineyard Shuttle (☑02-4991 3655; www.vineyardshuttle.com.au; ☺6pm-midnight Tue-Sat) Offers a door-to-door service between Pokolbin accommodation and restaurants.

Newcastle
POP 308,300

The port city of Newcastle may be one-10th the size of Sydney, but Australia's second-oldest city punches well above its weight. Superb surf beaches, historical architecture and a sun-drenched climate are only part of its charm. Fine dining, hip bars, quirky boutiques, a diverse arts scene and a laid-back attitude combine to make it well worth a couple of days of your time.

Newcastle had a rough trot at the end of the 20th century, with a major earthquake and the closure of its steel and shipbuilding industries. Its other important industry, shipping coal, has a decidedly sketchy future too, but Novocastrians always seem to get by with creative entrepreneurship and a positive attitude.

◉ Sights

Newcastle has a constantly evolving and morphing small-gallery scene; check at the tourist office (p163) for the latest pop-up.

★ Newcastle Maritime Museum   MUSEUM

(☑ 02-4929 2588; www.maritimecentrenewcastle. org.au; Lee Wharf, 3 Honeysuckle Dr, Honeysuckle Precinct; adult/child $10/5; ⊘ 10am-4pm Tue-Sun) Newcastle's nautical heritage is on show at this museum, appropriately located on the harbour. The intriguing exhibition provides an insight into the soul of the city, and there's a good dose of local history, covering shipwrecks (including the 2007 grounding of the *Pasha Bulker*, on which there's a film), lifeboats and the demise of the steelworks and shipbuilding industries. A quick intro by the staff is great for setting the scene.

★ Newcastle Art Gallery   GALLERY

(☑ 02-4974 5100; www.nag.org.au; 1 Laman St; ⊘ 10am-5pm Tue-Sun) FREE Ignore the brutalist exterior, as inside this remarkable regional gallery are some wonderful works. There's no permanent exhibition; displays rotate the gallery's excellent collection, whose highlights include art by Newcastle-born William Dobell and John Olsen as well as Brett Whiteley and modernist Grace Cossington Smith.

Olsen's works, in particular, bring an explosive vibrancy to the gallery, with his generative organic swirls flamboyantly representing water-based Australian landscapes. Look out for his ceiling painting by the central stairwell and his brilliant *King Sun and the Hunter*, a tribute to the essence of his native city, painted at age 88 in 2016.

★ Merewether Aquarium   PUBLIC ART

(Henderson Pde, Merewether) Not an aquarium in the traditional sense, this pedestrian underpass has been charmingly transformed into a pop-art underwater world by local artist Trevor Dickinson. There are numerous quirky details, including the artist himself as a diver. Find it at the southern end of Merewether Beach, opposite the Surfhouse top entrance.

Newcastle Museum   MUSEUM

(☑ 02-4974 1400; www.newcastlemuseum.com. au; 6 Workshop Way; ⊘ 10am-5pm Tue-Sun, plus Mon school holidays; ⊕) FREE This attractive museum in the restored Honeysuckle rail workshops tells a tale of the city from its Indigenous Awabakal origins to its rough-and-tumble social history, shaped by a cast of convicts, coal miners and steelworkers. Exhibitions are interactive and engaging, ranging from geology to local icons like Silverchair and the Newcastle Knights. If you're travelling with kids, check out hands-on science centre Supernova and the hourly sound-and-light show on the steelmaking process. There's also a cafe.

Fort Scratchley   FORT

(☑ 02-4974 5033; www.fortscratchley.com.au; Nobbys Rd; tunnel tour adult/child $12.50/6.50, full tour $16/8; ⊘ 10am-4pm Wed-Mon, last tour 2.30pm) FREE Perched above Newcastle Harbour, this intriguing military site was constructed during the Crimean War to protect the city against a feared Russian invasion. During WWII the fort returned fire on a Japanese submarine, making it the only Australian fort to have engaged in a maritime attack. It's free to enter, but the guided tours are worth taking, as you venture into the fort's labyrinth of underground tunnels. Head to the shop for tickets or for a self-guided-tour brochure.

Nobby's Head   VIEWPOINT

Originally an island, this headland at the entrance to Newcastle's harbour was joined to the mainland by a stone breakwater built by convicts between 1818 and 1846; many of those poor souls were lost to the wild seas during construction. The walk along the spit towards the lighthouse and meteorological station is exhilarating.

King Edward Park   PARK

(Reserve Rd) This magnificently landscaped ocean-side park offers sweeping views, lots of grass and plenty of shady spots for lounging around. The best views are from the **obelisk** at the top.

🏃 Activities

★ Bathers Way   WALKING

(www.visitnewcastle.com.au) This scenic coastal path from Nobby's Beach to Glenrock Reserve winds past swathes of beach and fascinating historical sites including Fort Scratchley and the Convict Lumber Yard. Interpretative signs describing Indigenous, convict and natural history dot the 5km trail. North of Bar Beach, it connects with the high, swirling **Memorial Walk**, which offers magical sea views.

DON'T MISS

NEWCASTLE'S BEACHES

At the eastern end of town, surfers and swimmers adore **Newcastle Beach**; the **ocean baths** (www.newcastle.nsw.gov.au; Shortland Esplanade) FREE are a mellow alternative, encased in wonderful multicoloured art deco architecture. There's a shallow pool for toddlers and a backdrop of heaving ocean and chugging cargo ships. Surfers should goofy-foot it to **Nobby's Beach**, just north of the baths – the fast left-hander known as the Wedge is at its northern end.

South of Newcastle Beach, below King Edward Park, is Australia's oldest ocean bath, the convict-carved **Bogey Hole**. It's an atmospheric place to splash about in when the surf's crashing over its edge. The most popular surfing breaks are at **Bar Beach** and **Merewether Beach**, two ends of the same beach a bit further south.

The city's famous surfing festival, **Surfest** (www.surfest.com; Merewether Beach), takes place in February each year.

🛏 Sleeping

Newcastle has a good choice of midrange accommodation, from remodelled pub rooms to B&Bs and business hotels. Hostels and camping are also available.

Newcastle Beach YHA HOSTEL $
(📞 02-4925 3544; www.yha.com.au; 30 Pacific St; dm/s/d $39/70/94; 🌐@🏠) It may have the look of a grand English mansion, but this sprawling, brick, heritage-listed YHA has the ambience of a laid-back beach bungalow, with great common spaces and airy, comfortable dorms. Just a minute away from the surf, it offers complimentary bodyboard use, surfboard hire, and BBQ nights and weekly pub meals for free. HI discount.

Stockton Beach Holiday Park CAMPGROUND $
(📞 1800 778 562; www.stocktonbeach.com; 3 Pitt St, Stockton; unpowered/powered sites Feb-Dec $37/45, Jan $51/65, cabins $180-320; P🌐 🏠🌊) 🏄 The beach is at your doorstep (or should that be tent flap?) at this tourist park behind the dunes in Stockton, a short ferry ride from Newcastle (or 20km by road). With large, grassy camp sites, en suites for vans and smart, modern villas, it's a flash place to park yourself. There's a public pool next door.

★ Junction Hotel BOUTIQUE HOTEL $$
(📞 02-4962 8888; www.junctionhotel.com.au; 204 Corlette St, The Junction; r $139-189; 🌐🏠🌊) The upstairs of this suburban pub has been transformed with nine flamboyantly appointed rooms featuring African-animal themes and wacky colours. All have generous-sized beds and flashy bathrooms with disco lights and little privacy. Well located among the Junction's boutiques and cafes, it's just a 10-minute walk to the beach.

★ Crown on Darby APARTMENT $$
(📞 02-4941 6777; www.crownondarby.com.au; 101 Darby St; apt midweek $176-205, weekend $194-286; P🌐🏠🌊) Close to cafes and restaurants, this excellent modern complex of 38 apartments is right on Newcastle's coolest street. Studios are reasonably sized and have kitchenettes. One-bedroom apartments are a worthwhile upgrade, with interconnecting options, full kitchens and huge living rooms; some have spa baths. Both open and closed balconies are available, so request your preference. Parking is a reasonable $15.

★ Lucky Hotel BOUTIQUE HOTEL $$
(📞 02-4925 8888; www.theluckyhotel.com.au; 237 Hunter St; r $145-180; 🌐🏠🌊) A slick but sympathetic revamp has turned this grand old 1880s dame into an upbeat, modern place to stay above a great pub. The 28 light-filled rooms are small but tastefully decorated, with mod touches like luxe bedding and toiletries, not to mention a hand-painted quote about luck in case you need the inspiration. Corridors showcase black-and-white photos of old Newcastle.

Hamilton Heritage B&B B&B $$
(📞 02-49611242; www.accommodationinnewcastle.com.au; 178 Denison St, Hamilton; r $140-170; P🌐🏠🌊) Offering courtesy and a cosy atmosphere, this Federation-era home near the Beaumont St cafe strip makes for a characterful stay. The house has some beautiful original features, and the three rooms (including a family suite sleeping six) have en suites and tea- and coffee-making facilities. Guests can use the kitchen and back deck overlooking a lovely subtropical garden.

Newcastle

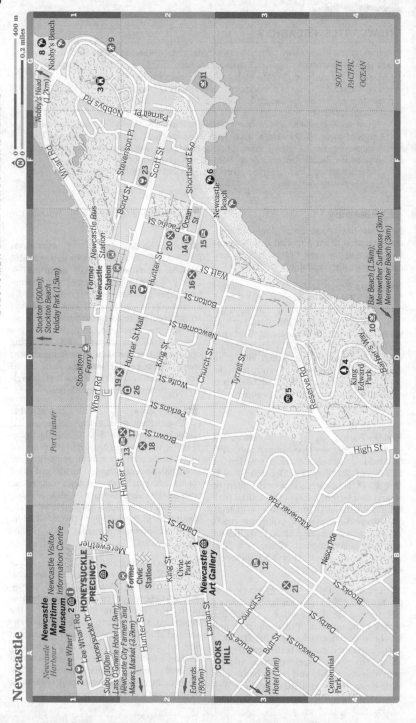

SOUTH PACIFIC OCEAN

Port Hunter

COOKS HILL

King Edward Park

Nobby's Head (1.2km)

Nobby's Beach

Stockton (500m);
Stockton Beach
Holiday Park (1.5km)

Bar Beach (1.5km);
Merewether Surfhouse (3km);
Merewether Beach (3km)

Subo (100m);
Lass O'Gowrie Hotel (1.5km);
Newcastle City Farmers and
Makers Market (3.2km)

Lee Wharf Rd

Honeysuckle Dr

HONEYSUCKLE PRECINCT

Newcastle Harbour

Newcastle Maritime Museum

Newcastle Visitor Information Centre

Former Civic Station

Newcastle Art Gallery

Junction Hotel (1km)

Edwards (800m)

Nobbys Rd

Parnell Pl

Wharf Rd

Stevenson Pl

Scott St

Shortland Esp

Newcastle Beach

Pacific St

Ocean St

Watt St

Hunter St

Bolton St

Newcomen St

King St

Church St

Tyrrell St

Reserve Rd

Bathers Way

Baths Rd

High St

Kitchener Pde

Nesca Pde

Brooks St

Darby St

Dawson St

Bull St

Bruce St

Council St

Laman St

King St

Civic Park

Darby St

Hunter St

Wolfe St

Perkins St

Brown St

Hunter St Mall

Merewether St

Bond St

Former Newcastle Station

Newcastle Bus Station

Stockton Ferry

Wharf Rd

Centennial Park

400 m
0.2 miles

Newcastle

Novotel Newcastle Beach HOTEL **$$$**
(☑02-4037 0000; www.novotelnewcastlebeach. com.au; 5 King St; r $279-334; [P][⊝][✳][@][⊚]) Ideally situated for Newcastle Beach, this breezy hotel seamlessly checks out the business guests on Friday morning and welcomes families that afternoon. Rooms are moderately sized but stylishly furnished. It's worth the upgrade to the superior rooms, which offer floor-to-ceiling windows and better views. Accommodation and breakfast are free for under-16s.

✗ Eating

Newcastle has a thriving eating scene. Darby St is a local icon for cafes, Thai and Vietnamese restaurants and pizza, while the harbourfront has lots of options, particularly in the Honeysuckle Precinct near the tourist office. In Hamilton, eateries cluster along Beaumont St, and the beaches have plenty of nearby options too.

One Penny Black CAFE **$**
(☑02-4929 3169; www.onepennyblack.com.au; 196 Hunter St; mains $14-18; ⊙6.30am-4.30pm; [⊚][✎]) It's perpetually popular for a reason – here you'll probably have to queue for an excellent espresso or filter coffee, served by staff who know their stuff. Devotees also rave about the toasties and fabulous breakfast platters.

★ Edwards MODERN AUSTRALIAN **$$**
(☑02-4965 3845; www.theedwards.com.au; 148 Parry St; breakfast & lunch dishes $14-21, dinner plates for 2 $41-60; ⊙7am-midnight Tue-Sat, to

10pm Sun; [⊚]) If new Newcastle had a beating heart, it would be found at this happening West End bar-cafe-diner, stylishly flaunting its warehouse chic on this light-industrial street. It's the place to be at all hours, for delicious egg breakfasts, casual lunches, late-night bar snacks, great wines by the glass and succulent roast meats from the wood-fired oven.

Co-owned by Silverchair bass player Chris Joannou, this used to be a drive-through dry cleaners (you can still drop off your dirty clothes, or chuck them in the coin laundry). The complex also includes a motorcycle workshop and a music shop.

Momo CAFE **$$**
(☑02-4926 3310; www.facebook.com/momowhole food.newcastle; 227 Hunter St; dishes $12-22; ⊙7.30am-3pm; [⊚][✎]) In a striking, high-ceilinged former bank building that at first seems too big for it, this friendly cafe specialises in wholefoods, offering mostly vegetarian and vegan choices. Textures, colours and flavours make the dishes very appealing, and influences range from Himalayan to local. The owners are considering opening some evenings.

Three Monkeys CAFE **$$**
(☑02-4926 3779; www.threemonkeyscafe.com.au; 131 Darby St, Cooks Hill; dishes $14-24; ⊙7.30am-3pm Mon & Tue, to 10pm Wed-Sat, to 5pm Sun; [⊚][✎]) It's difficult to go wrong on the Darby St strip, but this place stands out for its quality coffee, colourful juice and food creations – try the

smashed avocado with beetroot hummus – streetside seating and little backyard.

Merewether Surfhouse CAFE, STEAK $$

(☑ 02-4918 0000; www.surfhouse.com.au; Henderson Pde, Merewether; mains cafe $15-20, bar $18-24, restaurant $32-39; ☺ cafe 7am-4pm, pizza 4-11pm Mon-Fri, 11.30am-11pm Sat & Sun, restaurant 11.30am-late Wed-Sat, to 4pm Sun) Watch the action on Merewether Beach from one of the many spaces in this architecturally notable complex. The swanky promenade cafe offers coffee and lazy breakfasts, and later in the day there's pizza and gelato. Head to the top-floor restaurant, which has floor-to-ceiling windows, and nails surf or turf at fine-dining prices; it's also a top spot for a sundowner.

Napoli Centrale PIZZA $$

(☑ 02-4023 2339; www.napolicentrale.com.au; 173 King St; pizzas $15-30; ☺ 5-10pm Mon-Thu, 11am-3pm & 5-10pm Fri-Sun; ☑) This understated pizza and pasta joint is a real hot spot for locals craving wood-fired pizza. The sparsely topped, crisply based pizzas are so authentic they feature imported Neapolitan flour and San Marzano tomatoes. Bookings are essential, or you can grab a takeaway from the window and eat on the beach.

★ Subo MODERN AUSTRALIAN $$$

(☑ 02-4023 4048; www.subo.com.au; 551d Hunter St; 5 courses $88; ☺ 6-10pm Wed-Sun; ☑) Book in advance for a table at tiny Subo, an innovative, highly lauded restaurant serving light, exquisite food with a contemporary French influence. The restaurant exclusively serves a five-course menu that changes seasonally.

Restaurant Mason MODERN AUSTRALIAN $$$

(☑ 02-4926 1014; www.restaurantmason.com; 3/35 Hunter St; set menus $80-125, mains $46; ☺ 6-9pm Tue & Wed, noon-3pm & 6-10pm Thu-Sat; ☑) There's a summery feel to this fine-dining restaurant, with tables placed under the plane trees outside and a dining space that opens to the elements. There's a modern-French feel to the menu, though a variety of other regional and avant-garde influences are present. Dishes make the most of fresh produce, including wild-foraged local herbs. There are separate tasting menus for vegetarians.

Bocados SPANISH $$$

(☑ 02-4925 2801; www.bocados.com.au; 25 King St; tapas $16-24, raciones $25-35; ☺ 6-11pm Tue-Sun) A block away from Newcastle Beach, Bocados (the name means 'mouthfuls') has a menu featuring *tapas* (small plates) and *raciones* (larger plates) that trawl the Iberian peninsula for their inspiration. There are some pretty authentic ingredients as well as plenty of Spanish drops on the menu. It's BYO on Tuesday and Wednesday.

♥ Drinking & Nightlife

★ Coal & Cedar COCKTAIL BAR

(☑ 0499 345 663; www.coalandcedar.com; 380-382 Hunter St; ☺ 4pm-midnight Mon-Sat, to 10pm Sun) Pull up a stool at the long wooden bar in this Prohibition-style speakeasy; early on it was so underground it didn't even publish the address. Now the secret's out, you'll find Newcastle's finest drinking old-fashioneds to the blues. The door can be tough to spot; it's to the right of the stairs. If it's shut, text them to open up.

Reserve Wine Bar WINE BAR

(☑ 02-4929 3393; www.reservewinebar.com.au; 102 Hunter St; ☺ 5-9pm Tue, noon-11pm or midnight Wed-Fri, 3pm-midnight Sat; ☎) Calling itself a 'grape emporium', this bar, in a former bank, has more than 350 wines in the vault, including many from Newcastle's Hunter Valley backyard. Enjoy your tipple with a bite from the decadent grazing menu.

Lucky Hotel PUB

(☑ 02-4925 8888; www.theluckyhotel.com.au; 237 Hunter St; ☺ 11am-11pm Mon-Thu, to 1am Fri & Sat, to 10pm Sun; ☎) With a genuinely convivial vibe and a handsome interior of exposed brick and wooden fittings, this is a successfully characterful refurbishment of an old pub. On offer are a decent line in smoked meats, good drinks, pleasant outdoor high tables and comfy rooms upstairs.

Grain Store BREWERY

(☑ 02-4023 2707; www.grainstorenewcastle.com.au; 64 Scott St; ☺ 11am-10pm Tue-Thu, to 1am Fri & Sat, to 9.30pm Sun; ☎) Once the grain and keg store for the old Tooheys beer factory, this rustic brewery-cafe is an atmospheric place to refresh yourself with one of the 21 eclectic Australian-brewed craft beers on tap. There's all-day food, with pizzas, burgers and American-style meat dishes featuring prominently.

Honeysuckle Hotel PUB

(☑ 02-4929 1499; www.honeysucklehotel.com.au; Lee Wharf, Honeysuckle Dr, Honeysuckle Precinct; ☺ 10am-11pm Mon-Thu, to midnight Fri & Sat, to 10pm Sun; ☎) The deck at this waterfront place, located in a cavernous but cool converted warehouse looking across at the port, is a perfect spot for a sundowner. Sip Caribbean flavours under the rafters in the Rum Bar upstairs on Friday and Saturday, and there's usually live music at the weekends too.

☆ Entertainment

Newcastle Knights SPECTATOR SPORT
(☑ 02-4028 9100; www.newcastleknights.com.au; McDonald Jones Stadium, Turton Rd, New Lambton) The pride of Newcastle, the Knights are the local rugby-league side. They've had a rough trot of late, but there's plenty of passion around them here, and a game is a great experience. In summer, the stadium is used by the Newcastle Jets A-league soccer team.

Lass O'Gowrie Hotel LIVE MUSIC
(☑ 02-4962 1248; www.lassogowriehotel.com.au; 14 Railway St, Wickham; ☎) Built in 1877, this is the oldest pub in Newcastle and has been the heart of the local music scene for the last 15 years. See local original acts here from Wednesday to Sunday nights. It's just north of the new main train station at Wickham.

🛍 Shopping

Emporium ARTS, FASHION
(www.renewnewcastle.org; 185 Hunter St; ⊙10am-4pm Wed & Sat, to 5pm Thu & Fri) 🖉 On the ground floor of the former David Jones department store are boutiques and galleries filled with a treasure trove of locally made art, fashion, furniture and design.

Newcastle City Farmers & Makers Market MARKET
(☑ 02-4934 3013; www.newcastlecityfarmers market.com.au; Newcastle Showground, Griffiths Rd; ⊙8am-1pm Sun) A fabulous showcase of Hunter Valley gourmet produce, plus international delights like Tibetan dumplings and buttery French pastries.

ℹ Information

Newcastle Visitor Information Centre
(☑ 02-4929 2588; www.visitnewcastle.com. au; Lee Wharf, 3 Honeysuckle Dr, Honeysuckle Precinct; ⊙10am-4pm Tue-Sun) Shares the Maritime Museum building by the water.

ℹ Getting There & Away

AIR

Port Stephens Coaches (p163) has frequent buses stopping at the **airport** (NTL; ☑ 02-4928 9800; www.newcastleairport.com.au; 1

Williamtown Dr, Williamtown) en route between Newcastle (40 minutes) and Nelson Bay (one hour). A taxi from the airport to Newcastle city centre costs about $60. **Fogg's** (☑ 0410 581 452; www.foggsshuttle.com.au), **Hunter Valley Day Tours** (☑ 02-4951 4574; www.huntervalley daytours.com.au) and **Newcastle Airport Transfers** (☑ 02-4928 9822; www.newcastle airport.com.au; 1/2/4 people $45/50/65) operate shuttles to Newcastle and the surrounding region.

Jetstar (☑ 13 15 38; www.jetstar.com) flies to/from Melbourne, the Gold Coast and Brisbane; **Qantas** (☑ 13 13 13; www.qantas.com.au) flies to/from Brisbane; **Regional Express** (REX; ☑ 13 17 13; www.rex.com.au) flies to/from Sydney and Taree; and **Virgin Australia** (☑ 13 67 89; www.virginaustralia.com) flies to/from Brisbane and Melbourne.

BUS

Nearly all long-distance buses stop at **Newcastle Bus Station**, at the eastern end of town, but most will only stop at the new **transport interchange** at Wickham once it opens in 2017.

Busways (☑ 02-4983 1560; www.busways. com.au) At least two buses daily to Tea Gardens ($20.50, 1½ hours), Hawks Nest ($20.90, 1¾ hours), Bluey's Beach ($28, two hours), Forster ($32, 3¼ hours) and Taree ($35, four hours).

Greyhound (☑ 1300 473 946; www.greyhound. com.au) Two to three daily coaches to/from Sydney ($32 to $35, 2¾ hours), Port Macquarie ($57 to $62, four hours), Coffs Harbour ($79 to $86, six to seven hours), Byron Bay ($140, 10½ hours) and Brisbane ($171, 13½ to 15 hours).

Port Stephens Coaches (☑ 02-4982 2940; www.pscoaches.com.au) Regular buses to Anna Bay (1¼ hours), Nelson Bay (1½ hours), Shoal Bay (1½ hours) and Fingal Bay (two hours).

Premier Motor Service (☑ 13 34 10; www.pre miermms.com.au) Daily coaches to/from Sydney ($34, three hours), Port Macquarie ($47, 3¾ hours), Coffs Harbour ($58, six hours), Byron Bay ($71, 11 hours) and Brisbane ($76, 14½ hours).

Rover Coaches (☑ 02-4990 1699; www.rover coaches.com.au) Four buses to/from Cessnock (1¼ hours) on weekdays and two on Saturday.

TRAIN

Sydney Trains (p140) will run regular services to Newcastle's new transport interchange at Wickham (scheduled to open in 2017) from Gosford ($8.30, 1½ hours) and Sydney ($8.30, 2¾ hours). Meanwhile, trains stop at Hamilton, with connecting buses into the centre. A line also heads to the Hunter Valley; Branxton ($6.50, 50 minutes) is the closest stop to wine country.

ⓘ Getting Around

BICYCLE

Swipe 'n' Ride (www.swipeandride.com.au; per 1hr/4hr/day $11/22/33) This no-fuss scheme means you just swipe your credit card and grab a bike. There are only two, close-together stations: at the Crowne Plaza Hotel and by the tourist office. Both have helmets and locks available.

BUS

Newcastle has an extensive network of **local buses** (☑ 13 15 00; www.newcastlebuses.info). There's a fare-free bus zone in the inner city between 7.30am and 6pm. Otherwise you need to tap on and off with an Opal card or pay the fare to the driver. The main depot is next to the former Newcastle train station in the east of the city.

FERRY

Stockton Ferry (www.transportnsw.info; adult/child $2.60/1.30) Leaves every half-hour from Queens Wharf from 5.15am to about 11pm to the suburb of Stockton.

TRAIN

From mid-2017, all train services to Newcastle will terminate at the new station at Wickham. From here, shuttle bus 110 (in future, a light-rail service) runs into the centre, stopping at the former train stations of Civic and Newcastle. Until the Wickham station is finished, trains are stopping at Hamilton.

NORTH COAST NSW

Lovely, lazy beach towns and pristine national parks leapfrog each other all the way up this stupendous stretch of coast. Inland, lush farmland and ancient tracts of World Heritage–listed rainforest do the same.

Providing a buffer between New South Wales' capital city sprawl to the south and Queensland's Gold Coast strip up over the border, Northern NSW offers an altogether simpler way of life. Farmers rub shoulders with big-city seachangers and post-hippie alternative lifestylers here: if you're looking for stellar local produce, a single origin coffee or a psychic reading, you won't be disappointed. And if you're searching for a surf break, rest assured there will be an awesome one, right around the next corner.

Port Stephens

POP 69,730

An hour's drive north of Newcastle, the sheltered harbour of Port Stephens is blessed with near-deserted beaches, extraordinary national parks and a unique sand-dune system. The main centre, Nelson Bay, is home to both a fishing fleet and an armada of tourist vessels, the latter trading on the town's status as the 'dolphin capital of Australia'.

◎ Sights

Worimi Conservation Lands   NATURE RESERVE (www.worimiconservationlands.com; 3-day entry permits $10) Located at Stockton Bight, these are the longest moving sand dunes in the southern hemisphere, stretching more than 35km. Thanks to the generosity of the Worimi people, the traditional owners of the area, you're able to roam around and drive along the beach (4WD only, and always check conditions). Get your permits from the visitor centre or NPWS office in Nelson Bay, the Anna Bay BP service station, or the 24-hour Metro service station near the Lavis Lane entry.

Tomaree National Park   NATIONAL PARK (www.nationalparks.nsw.gov.au/tomaree-national-park) This wonderfully wild expanse offers beautiful hiking in an area that can feel far more remote than you actually are. The park harbours angophora forests and several threatened species, including the spotted-tailed quoll and powerful owl, and you can spot outcrops of the rare volcanic rock rhyodacite. In spring, the Morna Point trail is strewn with wildflowers.

🏃 Activities

Just east of Nelson Bay is slightly smaller Shoal Bay, which has a long swimming beach; a short drive south is Fingal Bay, with another lovely beach on the fringes of Tomaree National Park. The park stretches west around the clothing-optional Samurai Beach, a popular surfing spot, and One Mile Beach, a gorgeous semicircle of the softest sand and bluest water.

Port Stephens Surf School   SURFING (☑ 0411 419 576; www.portstephenssurfschool.com. au; 2hr group surf lessons $60 1hr group stand-up paddleboarding lessons $45) Offers both group and private surf and stand-up paddleboarding lessons at One Mile and Fingal Beaches. Board hire is also available (one/two hours $20/30).

👉 Tours

Port Stephens 4WD Tours   TOURS (☑ 02-4984 4760; www.portstephens4wd.com.au; James Patterson St, Anna Bay) Offers a 1½-hour Beach & Dune tour (adult/child $52/31), a three-hour Sygna Shipwreck tour ($90/50) and a sandboarding experience ($28/20) out on the magnificent dunes of the Worimi Conservation Lands. You can stay as long as you like if sandboarding; just jump on the shuttle when you want to go home.

Port Stephens Paddlesports KAYAKING
(☑ 0405 033 518; www.paddleportstephens.com.au; 35 Shoal Bay Rd, Shoal Bay; kayak/paddleboard hire per hr $25/30; ☺ Sep-May) Offers a range of kayak and stand-up-paddleboard hire as well as excursions, including 1½-hour sunset tours (adult/child $40/30) and 2½-hour discovery tours ($50/40).

🛏 Sleeping

Melaleuca Surfside Backpackers HOSTEL $
(☑ 02-4981 9422; www.melaleucabackpackers.com.au; 2 Koala Pl, One Mile Beach; sites $20, dm per person $32-36, d tent/cabin $70/100; @🛜) Architect-designed cabins are set amid peaceful scrub inhabited by koalas, kookaburras and sugar gliders at this friendly, well-run place. You can also pitch your own tent among bushland (the whole site is blissfully car-free) or book one of the bed-equipped tents. There's a welcoming lounge area and kitchen, and the owners offer sandboarding and other excursions.

Marty's at Little Beach HOTEL $$
(☑ 02-4981 9100; www.martys.net.au; cnr Gowrie Ave & Intrepid Close, Nelson Bay; r $120, apt $200-260; ✳🛜🏊🐾) This popular, low-key motel is an easy stroll to Little Beach and Shoal Bay, and has simple beach-house-inspired rooms and modern, self-contained apartments. Families with kids older than babes in cots are only accommodated in the two-bedroom executive suites.

O'Carrollyn's BUNGALOW $$
(☑ 02-4982 2801; www.theoasisonemile.com.au; 5 Koala Pl; bungalows $190-310; ✳🛜🏊) Nine two-bedroom, self-contained loft bungalows (two with Jacuzzis and some designed for families; all wheelchair-accessible) nestle around a billabong in 5 acres of landscaped garden. Guests also have use of garden BBQs and outdoor dining tables. Various wellness therapists can be booked to come and give treatments in the on-site wellness area, which also has an infrared sauna.

⭐**Anchorage** RESORT $$$
(☑ 02-4984 2555; www.anchorageportstephens.com.au; Corlette Point Rd, Corlette; d $245-415; P✳🛜🏊) Facing an expansive sweep of bay, this marina-fronted resort is Port Stephens' most stylish place to stay. Rooms have a crisp, coastal charm, with super-comfortable, relaxed interiors, and all have either a balcony or terrace. There are larger suites and apartments for those after the added luxury of space or for families.

The great pool area, excellent restaurant and Barbor spa will have you lingering. Come evening there's fine dining at Wild Herring and the cosy lure of a bay-window seat in the moody Hamptons-esque upstairs bar.

Bali at the Bay APARTMENT $$$
(☑ 02-4981 5556; www.baliatthebay.com.au; 1 Achilles St, Shoal Bay; apt $250-300; ✳) Two self-contained apartments – chock-full of flower-garlanded Buddhas and carved wood – do a good job of living up to the name here. It's the extras that make these private retreats really special: bathrooms are super luxe; there's complimentary sparkling wine and Bintang beer (naturally) in the fridge; and Nespresso machines. Spa treatments are also available.

🍴 Eating & Drinking

Red Ned's Gourmet Pie Bar FAST FOOD $
(www.redneds.com.au; 17-19 Stockton St, Nelson Bay; pies $6; ☺ 6.30am-5pm) More than 50 varieties of weird and wonderful pies from crocodile in mushroom-and-white-wine sauce to macadamia-nut Thai satay chicken. There's also the absolute classic, savoury mince, or old-school lamb's fry and bacon. The beef is sourced from nearby Stroud and the chickens are free range.

Little Beach Boathouse SEAFOOD $$
(☑ 02-4984 9420; www.littlebeachboathouse.com.au; Little Beach Marina, 4 Victoria Pde; mains $28-38; ☺ 12-2pm & 5.30-9pm Tue-Sat, 11.30am-2.30pm Sun) In an airy but intimate dining room, right on the water, you can order fabulously fresh salads, local seafood share plates, and truffle and parmesan fries. It's hard to concentrate on the food when there are views of diving dolphins and majestic pelicans coming in to land.

Nice at Nelson Bay CAFE $$
(☑ 02-4981 3001; www.niceatnelsonbay.com.au; Nelson Towers Arcade, 71a Victoria Pde; breakfast mains $18.80; ☺ 8am-2pm) Breakfast heaven is hidden in an arcade near the waterfront, where this cafe serves up no less than six variations of eggs Benedict, a couple of groaning pancake dishes and thick-cut French toast served with savoury sides.

★ **Wild Herring**   MODERN AUSTRALIAN **$$$**
(📞02-4984 2555; www.anchorageportstephens.
com.au; Corlette Point Rd, Corlette Point; mains
$40-46; ⏰6-10pm) The Anchorage resort's
Galley Kitchen morphs into a fine-dining
restaurant in the evening, but the simple
waterfront space still vibes holiday calm.
Dishes range from simply done kingfish with
broccoli and vinaigrette made from a beau-
tiful shellfish reduction, to more ambitious
plates of langoustine and scallops doused
in sea-vegetable butter. Staff, attentive but
chilled, can advise on the excellent wine list.

Point   SEAFOOD **$$$**
(📞02-4984 7111; www.thepointrestaurant.com.au;
Ridgeway Ave, Soldiers Point; mains $26-40, seafood
platters $149; ⏰noon-3pm Tue-Sun, 6-9pm Tue-
Sat) The locals' favourite go-to restaurant for
a romantic milestone, this marina spot has
lovely views from the balcony and dining
room. It serves up loads of seafood choices,
including oysters from local farm Holberts,
plus steaks, duck and vegetarian options.

★ **Swell**   CAFE, BAR
(📞02-4982 1378; www.swellkiosks.com.au; 10a
Hannah Pde, One Mile; ⏰6.30am-11pm) What
every perfect beach needs: a year-round,
all-day hangout. Come for the well-made
flat-white coffee on the way to a dawn surf,
for cheese toasties and milkshakes at lunch,
and finish the day here with beers on tap
and hand-cut hot chips. There's even live
music on Sunday afternoons. Don't miss
the prawn baguettes and 'bloke's burger' –
an extra-large specimen with absolutely no
salad or vegetable matter.

ℹ Information

Visitor Information Centre (📞1800 808 900;
www.portstephens.org.au; 60 Victoria Pde, Nelson Bay; ⏰9am-5pm) Has interesting displays
about the marine park, lots of other information and a range of 'PS I love you' merchandise.

ℹ Getting There & Away

Port Stephens Coaches (📞02-4982 2940;
www.pscoaches.com.au) zips around Port
Stephens' townships heading to Newcastle and
Newcastle Airport ($4.50, 50 minutes). A daily
service runs to/from Sydney (one way/return
$39/61, four hours) stopping at Anna Bay,
Nelson Bay and Shoal Bay.

Port Stephens Ferry Service (📞0412 682 117;
www.portstephensferryservice.com.au; adult/
child return $24/13) and the **MV Wallamba**
(📞0408 494 262; www.teagardens.nsw.

au/index_files/wally.htm; adult/child return
$20/10) chug from Nelson Bay to Tea Gardens
(stopping at Hawks Nest) and back two to three
times a day.

Myall Lakes National Park

On an extravagantly pretty section of the
coast that feels deliciously remote, this large
national park incorporates a patchwork of
lakes, islands, dense littoral rainforest and
beaches. **Seal Rocks**, a bush-clad hamlet
hugging Sugarloaf Bay, is one of Australia's
most epic surf destinations. Further south,
the lakes support an incredible quantity
and variety of bird life, including bowerbirds, white-bellied sea eagles and tawny
frogmouths. The coastal rainforest is cut
through with fire trails and beach tracks
that lead to the beach dunes at **Mungo
Brush**, perfect territory for spotting wildflowers and surprising dingoes.

⊙ Sights

Seal Rocks   BEACH
(www.nationalparks.nsw.gov.au/myall-lakes-
national-park; vehicles $8) This remarkably un-
developed town and its collection of beaches
has long held mythic status among the
global surfing community. There's plenty to
enjoy even if you're not here for the idyllic,
secluded breaks. Number One Beach has
beautiful rock pools, usually mellow waves
and beautiful sand. Or take the short walk
to the Sugarloaf Point Lighthouse for epic
ocean views, with a detour to lonely Lighthouse Beach, a popular surfing spot.

Broughton Island   BIRD SANCTUARY
(www.nationalparks.nsw.gov.au/myall-lakes-
national-park) This island is uninhabited except for muttonbirds and little penguins,
and its surrounding waters are home to an
enormous diversity of fish. The diving is excellent, and the beaches are secluded.

Moonshadow (📞02-4984 9388; www.
moonshadow.com.au; 35 Stockton St, Nelson Bay)
⛵ runs full-day trips to the island from Nelson Bay on Sundays between October and
Easter (more frequently over the summer
school holidays), which include snorkelling
and boom-net rides (adult/child $95/55).
Basic camping (no power or water) at the island's Little Poverty Beach is operated by the
NSW National Parks & Wildlife service, and
must be prebooked online. If you have your
own vessel (and have registered with Marine Rescue Port Stephens), you can arrange

WORTH A TRIP

DETOUR: OLD BAR TO LAKE CATHIE

Beyond the increasingly urban Forster, whose **visitor centre** (🖉02-6554 8799; www.greatlakes.org.au; Little St, Forster; ⊙9am-5pm) has info on this area, the coast reverts to a series of atmospheric little towns and long stretches of unspoilt beach and lush forest that are wonderful to explore.

Just back from the Pacific Hwy, Taree (population 17,800) is the rural centre that serves the fertile Manning Valley. Head a little west from here to the nearby town of Wingham for English county cuteness with a rugged lumberjack history.

But the coast beckons. Old Bar, at the southern head of the Manning River, is a longtime surfing favourite but now has what might be the midcoast's first destination hotel, the marvellous **Boogie Woogie Beach House** (🖉02-6557 4224; www.boogiewoogie beachhouse.com.au; 31 David St, Old Bar; d $189-280; ⓟ ❋ 🛜).

Further north, you can head east down the estuary to the sprawling beach town of Harrington, sheltered by a spectacular rocky breakwater and watched over by pelicans.

A short drive northeast of Harrington is Crowdy Head, a small fishing and surfing town at the edge of Crowdy Bay National Park. The views of deserted beaches and wilderness from the 1878 lighthouse are extraordinary. There are a number of beautifully remote campgrounds in the park. Little Dooragan National Park is immediately north of Crowdy Bay National Park, on the shores of Watson Taylor Lake and is dominated by North Brother Mountain. A sealed road leads to the lookout at the top, which offers incredible views of the coast. Heading north you'll pass through Laurieton. Turn left here and cross the bridge to North Haven, an absolute blinder of a surf beach. Continuing north the road passes Lake Cathie (*cat*-eye), a shallow body of water that's perfect for kids to have a paddle in.

transfers – see the national parks website for current operators.

🛏 Sleeping

⭐**Treachery Camp**　　　CAMPGROUND $
(🖉02-4997 6138; www.treacherycamp.com.au; 166 Thomas Rd, Seal Rocks; sites adult $17-22, child $10-13 cabins $105-260) Tree-shaded free camping set behind the dunes and coastal scrub of Treachery Beach. Campers have access to a large amenities block for hot showers and cooking, as well as a great on-site cafe. Book well ahead for the cabins, which range from basic but pretty to architect designed.

Seal Rocks Holiday Park　　CAMPGROUND $
(🖉02-4997 6164; www.sealrocksholidaypark.com. au; Kinka Rd, Seal Rocks; sites $45, cabins $110-200; 🛜) Offers a range of budget accommodation, including 14 cabins and grassed camping and caravan sites that are right on the water. The cabins sleep up to six and some include private bathrooms and overlook the sea.

NPWS Campgrounds　　CAMPGROUND $
(🖉1300 072 757; www.nationalparks.nsw.gov.au/ myall-lakes-national-park; sites per 2 people $25-35) There are 19 basic camping grounds dotted around the park; only some have drinking water and flush toilets. All locations can be booked on website.

⭐**Bombah Point Eco Cottages**　　COTTAGE $$$
(🖉02-4997 4401; www.bombah.com.au; 969 Bombah Point Rd, Bombah Point; cottages $275-325; 🐕) 🌿 In the heart of the national park, these architect-designed glass-fronted cottages sleep up to six guests. The 'eco' in the name is well deserved: sewage is treated onsite using a bio-reactor system; electricity comes courtesy of solar panels; and filtered rainwater tanks provide water. Cottages are quietly luxurious with huge rainwater spa baths and stylish cast-iron fireplaces.

Sugarloaf Point Lighthouse　　COTTAGE $$$
(🖉02-4997 6590; www.sealrockslighthouseaccom modation.com.au; cottages from $340; 🛜) Watch the crashing waves and wandering wildlife from one of three fully renovated 19th-century lighthouse-keeper's cottages. Each is self-contained and has two or three bedrooms and a barbecue. Ceilings are high and the heritage-style interiors are mercifully unfussy. The location, as you might imagine, is extraordinary.

🍴 Eating

This is self-catering country, with some great options for fresh seafood. Otherwise, head down to Port Stephens, up to Pacific Palms or inland for restaurants.

❶ Getting There & Away

From the town of Hawks Nest the scenic Mungo Brush Rd heads through the park to Bombah Broadwater, where the Bombah Point ferry makes the five-minute crossing every half-hour from 8am to 6pm ($6 per car). Continuing north, a 10km section of Bombah Point Rd heading to the Pacific Hwy at Bulahdelah is unsealed.

Port Macquarie

POP 44, 340

Making the most of its position at the entrance to the subtropical coast, Port, as it's commonly known, might be a minimetropolis but it remains overwhelmingly holiday focused. A string of beautiful beaches fans out either side of town, all a short driving distance from the centre. Most are great for swimming and surfing, and they seldom get crowded.

◉ Sights

Koala Hospital　　　　　　WILDLIFE RESERVE
(www.koalahospital.org.au; Lord St; by donation; ◎8am-4.30pm) Chlamydia, traffic accidents and dog attacks are the biggest causes of illness and injury for koalas living near urban areas; about 250 end up in this shelter each year. You can walk around the open-air enclosures any time, but you'll learn more on a tour (3pm). Signs detail the stories of some of the longer-term patients. Check the website for volunteer opportunities.

Sea Acres National Park　　　NATIONAL PARK
(☑02-6582 3355; www.nationalparks.nsw.gov.au/sea-acres-national-park; 159 Pacific Dr; adult/child $8/4; ◎9am-4.30pm) This 72-hectare pocket of national park protects the state's largest and most diverse strand of coastal rainforest. It's alive with birds, goannas, brush turkeys and diamond pythons. The Rainforest Centre has an excellent **cafe** (☑02-6582 4444; www.rainforestcafe.com.au; mains breakfast $10-15, lunch $12-22; ◎9am-4pm; ☑) ✿ and audiovisual displays about the local Birpai people. The highlight is the wheelchair-accessible 1.3km-long boardwalk through the forest. Fascinating one-hour guided tours by knowledgeable volunteers are run during high season.

Glasshouse Regional Gallery　　GALLERY
(☑02-65818888; www.glasshouse.org.au/regional-gallery; cnr Clarence & Hay Sts; ◎10am-4pm Tue-Sun) FREE This dynamic multilevel space provides an interesting overview of local cre-

ativity, and hosts regular touring exhibitions from Australia's top museums and galleries.

Port Macquarie
Historical Museum　　　　　　MUSEUM
(☑02-6583 1108; www.port-macquarie-historical-museum.org.au; 22 Clarence St; adult/child $5/2; ◎9.30am-4.30pm Mon-Sat) An 1836 house has been transformed into this surprisingly interesting little museum. Aboriginal and convict history are given due regard before more eclectic displays take over, including a 'street of shops' and a display of beautiful old clothes, which includes a whole section on underwear.

Maritime Museum　　　　　　MUSEUM
(www.maritimemuseumcottages.org.au; 6 William St; adult/child/family $5/2/12; ◎10am-4pm) The old pilot station (1882) above Town Beach has been converted into a small maritime museum, which is full of character. Allow a good hour to pore over its fascinating collection.

🏃 Activities

Surfing is particularly good at **Town**, **Flynn's** and **Lighthouse** beaches, all of which are patrolled in summer. The rainforest runs down to the sand at **Shelly** and **Miners** beaches, the latter of which is an unofficial nudist beach.

Whale season is from May to November; there are numerous vantage points around town, or you can get a closer look on a whale-watching cruise.

It's possible to walk all the way from the **Town Wharf** to Lighthouse Beach.

★**Port Macquarie**
Coastal Walk　　　　　　　WALKING
This wonderful coastal walk begins at Town Green foreshore and winds for about 9km along the coast to **Tracking Point Lighthouse** (Lighthouse Rd) in Sea Acres National Park. There are plenty of opportunities for swimming (it takes in eight beaches) and between May and November you can often view the whale migration. The walk can be divided into shorter 2km sections.

Soul Surfing　　　　　　　　SURFING
(☑02-6582 0114; www.soulsurfing.com.au; classes from $50) A family-run school that is particularly good for nervous beginners. Also runs school-holiday intensives and day-long women's workshops that include yoga, relaxation and food along with the surf lessons.

🛏 Sleeping

Port Macquarie

Backpackers
HOSTEL $

(☑ 02-6583 1791; www.portmacquariebackpackers. com.au; 2 Hastings River Dr; dm/s/d from $36/72/82; @ 🛜 🌊) This heritage-listed house has pressed-tin walls, colourful murals and a leafy backyard with a small pool. Traffic can be noisy, but the freebies (including wi-fi, bikes, beach shuttles and bodyboards) and a relaxed attitude more than compensate.

Sundowner Breakwall Tourist Park
HOSTEL $

(☑ 02-6583 2755; www.sundownerholidays.com; 1 Munster St; dm $28, sites per 2 people $38-45, cabins $98-310) With extensive facilities and a roomy feel, this quality place is right by the river mouth. There's a backpackers' area with a separate kitchen and lounge.

Flynns on Surf
VILLA $$

(☑ 02-6584 2244; www.flynns.com.au; 25 Surf St; 1-/2-/3-bedroom villas $180/240/300; P🌊🛜🌊) These smart one-, two- and three-bedroom villas are set on their own private estate. Each has a gorgeous bush outlook and is fully self-contained, with extra comforts such as Nespresso machines and iPod docks. The surf is 200m away, and it's a three-minute walk into town.

Beachport
B&B $$

(☑ 0423 072 669; www.beachportbnb.com.au; 155 Pacific Dr; d $70-200; 🌊🛜) At this excellent B&B the two downstairs rooms open onto private terraces, while the upstairs unit is more spacious. A basic do-it-yourself breakfast is provided, and Rainforest Cafe is just across the road. Prices include afternoon tea on arrival.

🍴 Eating

Social Grounds
CAFE $

(151 Gordon St; mains $7-14; ⊙6am-2.30pm Mon-Fri, to noon Sat, 7am-noon Sun) Pull up a chair at the shared tables on the deck of this hip, super-stylish local hang-out. The wall menu wanders from eggs and bagels to towering Reuben sandwiches and gutsy salads. The coffee is dependably good.

★ Latin Loafer
TAPAS $$

(☑ 02-6583 9481; www.latinloafer.com.au; 74 Clarence St; dishes $10-20; ⊙noon-3pm & 5-10pm Tue-Thu, noon-11pm Fri-Sun) Specialising in Spanish and South American wines, this fabulously atmospheric place has a spot overlooking the river. Salted-cod croquettes and beef empanadas make for good aperitivo snacks or combine with Peruvian spiced potatoes, kingfish ceviche and grilled octopus to make a meal.

★ Bill's Fishhouse
MODERN AUSTRALIAN $$

(☑ 02-6584 7228; www.billsfishhouse.com.au; 2/18-20 Clarence St; mains $22-32; ⊙6-10pm Tue-Sun & noon-2.30pm Fri-Sun) A super light and pretty space to escape the heat and eat the freshest of seafood (and lovely local poultry and beef, too). A brief menu – fish and chips, salmon with beets and greens, sirloin with bernaise – is augmented daily with chef's pick from the fish market. The wine list is similarly tight. Bookings are advised at night.

★ Stunned Mullet
MODERN AUSTRALIAN $$$

(☑ 02-6584 7757; www.thestunnedmullet.com. au; 24 William St; mains $36-42; ⊙noon-2.30pm & 6-10pm) This fresh, seaside spot is one serious dining destination. The inspired contemporary menu features classic dishes such as confit duck with truffled polenta, alongside exotic listings such as Patagonian toothfish. Note, all fish is wild caught. The extensive international wine list befits Port's best restaurant and there's a small but super-impressive wine-by-the-glass and half-bottle selection.

Fusion 7
FUSION $$$

(☑ 02-6584 1171; www.fusion7.com.au; 124 Horton St; mains $32-37; ⊙6-9pm Tue-Sat) Chef-owner Lindsey Schwab has worked in London with the father of fusion cuisine, Peter Gordon, and in some of Sydney's top restaurants. He now oversees a short but innovative menu where local produce features prominently and desserts are particularly wow-factor. Call ahead for bookings.

ⓘ Information

Visitor Information Centre (☑ 02-6581 8000; www.portmacquarieinfo.com.au; Glasshouse, cnr Hay & Clarence Sts; ⊙9am-5.30pm Mon-Fri, to 4pm Sat & Sun)

ⓘ Getting There & Away

AIR

Port Macquarie Airport (☑ 02-6581 8111; www.portmacquarieairport.com.au; Oliver Dr) is 5km from the centre of town; a taxi will cost $20 and it's served by regular local buses. Regular flights run to Sydney and Brisbane on

Port Macquarie

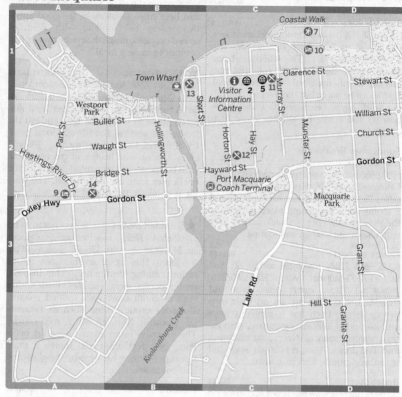

Port Macquarie

◎ Top Sights

◎ Sights

◎ Activities, Courses & Tours

◎ Sleeping

◎ Eating

Qantaslink (☑ 13 13 13; www.qantas.com.au) and **Virgin** (☑ 13 67 89; www.virginaustralia. com). **JetGo** (☑ 1300 328 000; www.jetgo. com) flies to Melbourne's Essendon Airport four times a week.

BUS

Regional buses depart from **Port Macquarie Coach Terminal** (Gordon St).

Busways (☑ 02-6583 2499; www.busways. com.au) Runs local bus services to Port Macquarie Airport ($5.50, 28 minutes) and Kempsey ($18, one hour).

Greyhound (☑ 1300 473 946; www.greyhound. com.au) Two daily buses head to/from Sydney (6½ hours), Newcastle (four hours), Coffs Harbour (2½ hours), Byron Bay (six hours) and Brisbane (10 hours).

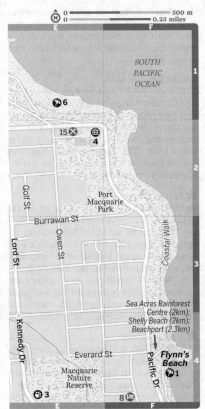

Premier (☑13 34 10; www.premierms.com.au)
Daily coaches to/from Sydney ($60, 6½ hours),
Newcastle ($47, 3¾ hours), Coffs Harbour ($47,
2¼ hours), Byron Bay ($66, 7½ hours) and
Brisbane ($67, 11 hours).

TRAIN

The closest train station is at Wauchope, 18km
west of Port Macquarie. Buses connect with
arriving trains.

Crescent Head

POP 1070

This beachside hideaway has one of the
best right-hand surf breaks in the country. Many people come to the area simply
to watch the longboard riders surf the epic
waves of **Little Nobby's Junction**. There's
also good shortboard riding off Plomer Rd.
Untrammelled **Killick Beach** stretches
14km north.

🛏 Sleeping

Surfari HOSTEL, MOTEL **$**
(☑02-6566 0009; www.surfaris.com; 353 Loftus
Rd; sites $20, dm/d $40/150; @🛜📶) Surfari
started the original Sydney–Byron surf tours
and now base themselves in Crescent Head
because 'the surf is guaranteed every day'.
The rooms are clean and comfortable, and
surf-and-stay packages are a speciality. It's
located 3.5km along the road to Gladstone.

**Sun Worship
Eco Apartments** APARTMENT **$$$**
(☑1300 664 757; www.sunworship.com.au; 9 Bel-
more St; apt $230-320; 🛜) 🌿 Stay in guilt-
mitigated luxury in one of five rammed-
earth villas featuring sustainable design,
including flow-through ventilation and solar
hot water. They have everything you need,
but the decor doesn't quite live up to the ex-
cellence of the architecture.

ⓘ Getting There & Away

Busways (☑02-6562 4724; www.busways.
com.au) runs between Crescent Head and
Kempsey ($10.50, 25 minutes) two to three
times a day; no Sunday services.

Hat Head National Park

Covering almost the entire coast from
Crescent Head to South West Rocks, this
74-sq-km **national park** (vehicle entry $8)
protects scrubland, swamps and some amaz-
ing beaches, backed by one of the largest
dune systems in NSW.

The isolated beachside village of **Hat
Head** (population 325) sits at its centre. At
the far end of town, behind the holiday park,
a picturesque wooden footbridge crosses the
Korogoro Creek estuary. The water is so
clear you can see fish darting around.

Stop off at Gladstone's **Heritage Hotel**
(www.heritagehotel.net.au; 21 Kinchela St, Glad-
stone; mains from $16; ⊙10am-midnight Mon-Sat,
to 9pm Sun), around a 20-minute drive inland
and along the river.

The best views can be had from **Smoky
Cape Lighthouse**, at the northern end of
the park. During the annual whale migration
it's a prime place from which to spot them.

🛏 Sleeping

NPWS Camp Sites CAMPGROUND **$**
(www.nationalparks.nsw.gov.au/hat-head-national-
park; sites per adult/child $6/3.50) Camp at
Hungry Gate, 5km south of Hat Head, for

a beautifully back-to-basics holiday among native figs and paperbarks. The site operates on a first-in basis and does not take bookings; a ranger will come around and collect fees. There are nonflush toilets and a BBQ area, but you'll need to bring your own drinking water. Kangaroos provide entertainment.

South West Rocks

POP 4810

One of many pretty seaside towns on this stretch of coast, South West Rocks has spectacular beaches and enough interesting diversions for at least a night or two.

The lovely curve of **Trial Bay**, stretching east from the township, takes its name from the *Trial*, a boat that sank here during a storm in 1816 after being stolen by convicts fleeing Sydney. The eastern half of the bay is now protected by **Arakoon National Park**, centred on a headland that's popular with kangaroos, kookaburras and campers. On its eastern flank, **Little Bay Beach** is a small grin of sand sheltered from the surf by a rocky barricade. It's both a great place for a swim and also the starting point for some lovely walks.

Sights

Trial Bay Gaol MUSEUM
(02-6566 6168; www.nationalparks.nsw.gov.au/arakoon-national-park; Cardwell St; adult/child $10/7; 9am-4.30pm) Occupying Trial Bay's eastern headland, this sandstone prison was built between 1877 and 1886 to house convicts brought in to build a breakwater. When nature had other ideas and the breakwater washed away, the imposing structure fell into disuse, aside from a brief, rather tragic, interlude in WWI when men of German and Austrian heritage were interned. Today it contains a museum devoted to its unusual history; even if you don't visit within, it's worth a detour for the views.

It's a pleasant 4km dawdle along the beach from South West Rocks.

Sleeping & Eating

Trial Bay Gaol Campground CAMPGROUND $
(02-6566 6168; www.nationalparks.nsw.gov.au/arakoon-national-park; Cardwell St; sites $35, summer & school holidays $60) Behind the Trial Bay Gaol, this stunning NPWS camping ground affords generous beach views from most camp sites and hosts ever-present kanga-

roos. Amenities include drinking water and flush toilets, and coin-slot hot showers and gas BBQs. Online bookings for this camping ground must be made at least two days prior to your stay.

Smoky Cape Retreat B&B $$
(02-6566 7740; www.smokycaperetreat.com.au; 1 Cockatoo Pl, Arakoon; d $130-220;) This cosy retreat in bushland near Arakoon has three private spa suites and rambling gardens that house a saltwater pool and a tennis court. The owners run a charming cafe on their deck where they serve a complimentary hot breakfast.

★ **Smoky Cape Lighthouse B&B** B&B, COTTAGE $$$
(02-6566 6301; www.smokycapelighthouse.com; Lighthouse Rd; s/d $150/220, 3-bedroom cottages per 2 nights $500-580;) Romantic evenings can be spent gazing out to sea while the wind whips around the historic lighthouse-keeper's residence and kangaroos come out to graze high up on the headland. Views are ridiculously beautiful; rooms are trad. Rates jump on weekends.

★ **Malt & Honey** CAFE $
(02-6566 5200; 5-7 Livingstone St; mains $10-16; 7.30am-4pm Tue-Sun) An urban sensibility combines with beach-town warmth and charm at this busy cafe. Pick up an early-morning latte (made with Toby's Estate beans) or grab a seat for crumpets with macadamia crumble, house-made muesli or the big breakfast of lamp chops, chorizo, eggs and bacon. Big salads and other healthy but satisfying options appear on the lunch menu.

Information

Visitor Information Centre (02-6566 7099; www.macleayvalleycoast.com.au; 1 Ocean Ave; 9am-4pm)

Getting There & Away

Busways (02-6562 4724; www.busways.com.au) Runs two to four times a day to/from Kempsey from Monday to Saturday (adult/child $13.60/6.80, 46 minutes).

Nambucca Heads

POP 6220

Nambucca Heads is languidly strewn over a dramatically curling headland interlaced with the estuaries of the glorious Nambucca

River. It's a quiet and rather unglamorous place, evoking sun-soaked holidays of the 1970s and '80s.

Sights

Yarriabini National Park   NATIONAL PARK
(www.nationalparks.nsw.gov.au/yarriabini-national-park) The highlight of this lush, rainforest-filled park is the dramatic coastal view from the summit of Mt Yarriabini, which is accessible via scenic Way Way Creek Rd.

Captain Cook Lookout   VIEWPOINT
Of the area's numerous viewpoints, Captain Cook Lookout, set on a high bluff, is the best to ponder the swathe of beaches, and to look for whales during the migration season. A road here leads down to the tide pools of Shelly Beach.

V-Wall   LANDMARK
For decades residents and holidaymakers have decorated the rocks of Nambucca's breakwater with vivacious multicoloured artwork, and with notes to lovers, families and new-found friends. Visitors are encouraged to paint their own messages, if they can find some space on the boulders.

Activities

Nambucca Boatshed   BOATING
(Beachcomber Marine; 02-6568 6432; www.nambuccaboatshed.com.au/activities; Riverside Dr; boat hire per 2hr/day $80/220, kayak hire per hr $25; 7am-4.45pm Mon-Sat, to 3pm Sun) Book online, or have the friendly staff rent you a motor boat, kayak or stand-up paddleboard and assist with local fishing advice. Conveniently, you can also stock up on lunch at the attached cafe.

Sleeping & Eating

White Albatross Holiday Park   CAMPGROUND $
(02-6568 6468; www.whitealbatross.com.au; 52 Wellington Dr; sites $66, cabins $145-215; ❄ 🛜 ⛱ 🐕) Located near the river mouth, this large holiday park is laid out around a sheltered lagoon. The cabins are kept fastidiously clean and have full kitchens. There is a jolly on-site tavern with a great deck.

Riverview Boutique Hotel   GUESTHOUSE $$
(02-6568 6386; www.riverviewlodgenambucca.com.au; 4 Wellington Dr; s $169 d $179-225; P ❄ 🛜) This former pub, built in 1887, is a wooden, two-storey charmer with eight neat, smart rooms; all have private balconies and some rooms have views.

★ **Taverna Six**   GREEK $$
(02-6569 0000; www.facebook.com/TavernaSix; 405 Grassy Head Rd, Grassy Head; mains $22-28; 6.30-9pm Thu-Sat, lunch from 11am Sun) Relax in the courtyard while an affable staff serves up mezze, herb-strewn salads, fresh seafood and local lamb. Fabulously authentic dishes utilise beautiful coastal produce along with some nice Greek imports, such as Peloponnese bottarga. Greek music plays and the surf rolls in across the road in a perfect Greek–Australian pairing.

Matilda's   SEAFOOD $$$
(02-6568 6024; 6 Wellington Dr; mains $35; 6-9pm Mon-Sat) This cute shack has old-fashioned beachfront character and serves up a menu of mostly seafood, including oysters. Locals rave about the cheesecake and pavlova desserts. BYO ($4 corkage).

Information

Nambucca Heads Visitor Information Centre (1800 646 587; www.nambuccatourism.com.au; cnr Riverside Dr & Pacific Hwy; 9am-5pm)

Getting There & Away

BUS
Long-distance buses stop at the visitor centre.
Busways (02-6568 3012; www.busways.com.au) Six buses to/from Bellingen ($9.70, 1¼ hours) and Coffs Harbour ($11.90, 1¼ hours) on weekdays, and one or two on Saturday.
Greyhound (1300 473 946; www.greyhound.com.au) Coaches run daily to Sydney ($100, eight hours), Port Macquarie ($22, 1¾ hours), Coffs Harbour ($13, 45 minutes), Byron Bay ($60, 4½ hours) and Brisbane ($106, 8¼ hours).
Premier (13 34 10; www.premierms.com.au) Daily coaches to/from Sydney ($63, eight hours), Port Macquarie ($38, 1¾ hours), Coffs Harbour ($34, 40 minutes), Byron Bay ($58, 5¾ hours) and Brisbane ($63, 9¼ hours).

TRAIN
NSW TrainLink (13 22 32; www.nswtrainlink.info) Three daily trains to/from Sydney ($66, eight hours), Wingham ($25, three hours), Kempsey ($8, one hour) and Coffs Harbour ($5, 40 minutes), and two to Brisbane ($62, 6¼ hours).

Bellingen
POP 3040

Buried in deep foliage on a hillside above the Bellinger River, this gorgeous town dances to the beat of its own bongo drum.

'Bello' is flush with organic produce, and the switched-on community has an urban sensibility. Located between the spectacular rainforest of Dorrigo National Park and a spoiled-for-choice selection of beaches, it is definitely a jewel on the East Coast route.

It's also the beginning of the iconic Waterfall Way, which continues past Dorrigo and then winds west to Armidale.

◉ Sights

Bellingen Island
WILDLIFE RESERVE

(www.bellingen.com/flyingfoxes) This little semi-attached island on the Bellinger River (it's only completely cut off when the river is in flood) is home to a huge colony of grey-headed flying foxes. For a closer look, take the steep path onto the island from Red Ledge Lane, on the northern bank. The best months to visit are from October to January, when the babies are being born and nursed. Wear long trousers and use inset repellent to ward off stinging nettles, leaches, ticks and mosquitoes.

At dusk the flying foxes fly out in their thousands to feed, though this impressive sight is best viewed from the bridge in the centre of town.

✯ Festivals & Events

Bellingen Readers & Writers Festival
LITERATURE

(www.bellingenwritersfestival.com.au; ☉Jun) Established and emerging writers appear at talks, panels, readings, poetry slams and workshops over the Queen's Birthday long weekend in June.

Bello Winter Music
MUSIC

(www.bellowintermusic.com; ☉early Jul) A nicely chilled music festival with local and international folk, roots, blues, world, hip-hop and pop acts. There's great food, and both free and ticketed events.

⌷ Sleeping

Much of the region's accommodation is in small B&Bs and cottages scattered across the hillsides. Breakfast is generally included in overnight prices.

Bellingen YHA
HOSTEL $

(Belfry Guesthouse; ☎02-6655 1116; www.yha.com.au; 2 Short St; dm $30, r with/without bathroom $135/80; @☎) A tranquil, homey atmosphere pervades this renovated weatherboard house, with impressive views from the broad verandah. Pick-ups from the bus

stop and train station in Urunga are sometimes possible if you call ahead.

Federal Hotel
HOTEL $

(☎02-6655 1003; www.federalhotel.com.au; 77 Hyde St; d with shared bathroom $80; ☎) This beautiful old country pub has renovated weatherboard rooms, some of which open onto a balcony facing the main street. Downstairs, the sprawling bars offer food and live music.

Bellingen Riverside Cottages
CABIN $$

(☎02-6655 9866; www.bellingenriversidecottages.com.au; 224 North Bank Rd; cottages $195-300; ✳✳) These polished mountain cabins have cosy interiors with country furnishings and big, sunny windows. Timber balconies overlook the river, which you can tackle on a complimentary kayak. Your first night includes a sizeable DIY breakfast hamper.

★ Lily Pily
B&B $$$

(☎02-6655 0522; www.lilypily.com.au; 54 Sunny Corner Rd; d $280; ✳☎) Set on a knoll five minutes drive south of the centre, this beautiful architect-designed complex has three bedrooms overlooking the river. It's aesthetically undemanding but designed to pamper, with champagne and nibbles on arrival, lavish breakfasts served until noon, luxurious furnishings and more. It has a beautiful garden setting and mountain views.

★ Promised Land Retreat
CABIN $$$

(☎02-6655 9578; www.promisedlandretreat.com.au; 934 Promised Land Rd, Gleniffer; cabins $320; ℗✳☎) A 10-minute drive from town over the evocatively named Never Never River, these three stylish and private cottages feature open-plan living areas attached to decks with dramatic views to the Dorrigo escarpment. Facilities include a tennis court, a games room and complimentary mountain bikes.

✗ Eating

Eating in Bellingen is a pleasure: it has a large and ever-growing number of cafes and casual restaurants, most of which make use of local and organic produce.

★ Hearthfire Bakery
BAKERY $

(☎02-6655 0767; www.hearthfire.com.au; 73 Hyde St; lunch mains $9-16; ☉7am-5pm Mon-Fri, to 2pm Sat & Sun) Follow the smell of hot-from-the-woodfire organic sourdough and you'll find this outstanding country bakery and cafe. Try the famous macadamia fruit loaf

DON'T MISS

WATERFALL WAY

Considered New South Wales' most scenic drive, the 190km Waterfall Way links a number of beautiful national parks between Coffs Harbour and Armidale, taking you through pristine subtropical rainforest, Edenic valleys, and, naturally, spectacular waterfalls. As you emerge into the tablelands, there is green countryside and wide plains. Bellingen is the natural starting point; even a short foray from Dorrigo will reward with stunning views. Some destinations to consider:

➡ **Guy Fawkes River National Park** (www.nationalparks.nsw.gov.au/guy-fawkes-river-national-park) and the stunning Ebor Falls are 50km past Dorrigo.

➡ Make your way into the **Cathedral Rock National Park** (www.nationalparks.nsw.gov.au/cathedral-rock-national-park) or take a detour down Point Lookout Rd to **New England National Park** (www.nationalparks.nsw.gov.au/new-england-national-park), a section of the Gondwana Rainforests World Heritage Area.

➡ Further west **Oxley Wild Rivers National Park** (www.nationalparks.nsw.gov.au/oxley-wild-rivers-national-park) is home to the towering plunge waterfall beauty of Wollomombi Falls.

or settle in with a coffee and a beautiful savoury pie. There is a full breakfast menu daily, and lunch dishes – including mezze plates, soups and salads – are served during the week.

Bellingen Gelato Bar ICE CREAM $
(www.bellingengelato.com.au; 101 Hyde St; single/double scoops $4/6; ⊙10am-6pm daily Oct-Apr, closed Mon & Tue May-Sep) Robert Sebes, the former owner of a legendary inner-Sydney cafe, has been scooping out stellar gelato in Bellingen since 2006. It's all made from scratch, with minimal added sugar. Traditional Italian flavours, such as zabaglione and pistacchio, are fabulously distinct, while Sebes' own creations – perhaps halva or spiced plum – are inventive but never faddish or overloaded.

Purple Carrot CAFE $$
(☑02-6655 1847; 105 Hyde St; mains $15-18; ⊙8am-3pm) The breakfast-biased menu offers eggs galore alongside dishes such as brioche French toast, smoked trout on a potato rösti and creamy pesto mushrooms. Get in early for Sunday brunch.

Oak Street Food & Wine MODERN AUSTRALIAN $$$
(☑02-6655 9000; www.oakstreetfoodandwine.com.au; 2 Oak St; mains $30-37; ⊙6-10pm Wed-Sat) This much-loved restaurant continues to turn out sophisticated, accessible dishes that make the most of the Bellinger Valley bounty in a beautifully atmospheric setting. A pre-dinner wine on the verandah is a quintessential hinterland experience.

 Drinking & Nightlife

People of Coffee CAFE
(☑1300 720 799; www.ameliafranklin.com.au; 3/44 Hyde St; ⊙6am-3pm Mon-Fri, to 2pm Sat) ✦ While there's no shortage of good coffee in Bellingen, Amelia Franklin roasts onsite with beans that are not only organic, but bird-friendly, rainforest-alliance and fair- and direct-trade certified. Come for top-quality coffee (espresso or cold drip). Her not-for-profit shopfront cafe also trains baristas. The toasties and healthy cakes are also delicious.

Bellingen Brewery & Co MICROBREWERY
(3/5 Church St; ⊙5-11pm Wed-Fri, from noon Sat & Sun) From English-style bitters to a summer drinking ale, cider and an in-house 3.5% ginger beer. Excellent pub food, such as buffalo and barra burgers.

No 5 Church St BAR
(www.5churchstreet.com; 5 Church St; mains $16-20; ⊙8am-8pm; ☎) Morphing effortlessly from cafe to bar, this vibrant venue stages an eclectic roster of live music, movie nights and community gatherings. The menu, be it breakfast, lunch or dinner, comes with a directory of local growers who have produced the ingredients for the egg dishes, pizzas, salads and burgers.

 Shopping

Bellingen Growers' Market MARKET
(www.bellingengrowersmarket.com; Bellingen Showgrounds, cnr Hammond & Black Sts; ⊙8am-1pm 2nd & 4th Sat of month) Most of the produce

here is organic and comes from surrounding farms. There are also plenty of secondhand clothes, as well as a cafe, a story-teller for the kids and roving musicians.

Bellingen Community Market MARKET
(www.bellingenmarkets.com.au; Bellingen Park, Church St; ⊙9am-3pm 3rd Sat of the month) A regional sensation, with more than 250 stalls selling fresh produce, artisan food products, craft, clothing and plants.

❶ Information

Waterfall Way Information Centre (✆02-6655 1522; www.visitnsw.com/visitor-information-centres/waterfall-way-visitor-centre-bellingen; 29-31 Hyde St; ⊙9am-5pm) Stocks brochures on scenic drives, walks and an arts trail.

❶ Getting There & Away

Bellingen is a short drive inland from the coast along the spectacular Waterfall Way. Local **buses** (✆02-6655 7410; www.busways.com.au) service the town from Nambucca and Coffs, via Sawtell, and **coaches** (✆02-6732 1051; www.new englandcoaches.com.au) run from Tamworth.

Dorrigo

POP 1070

Arrayed around the T-junction of two wider-than-wide streets, Dorrigo is a pretty little place. One gets the sense that this might be the next Bellingen in terms of food and wine, but it hasn't quite happened yet. The winding roads that lead here from Armidale, Bellingen and Coffs Harbour, however, reveal rainforests, mountain passes and waterfalls – some of the most dramatic scenery in NSW.

◉ Sights

The town's main attraction is Dangar Falls, 1.2km north of town, which cascades over a series of rocky shelves before plummeting into a basin. You can swim if you have a yen for glacial bathing. A partly sealed road continues north past here and swings east into Coffs Harbour via beautiful winding rainforest roads and a huge tallow-wood tree, 56m high and more than 3m in diameter.

★**Dorrigo National Park** NATIONAL PARK
(✆02-6657 2309; www.nationalparks.nsw.gov.au; Dome Rd) This 119-sq-km park is part of the Gondwana Rainforests World Heritage Area and home to a huge diversity of vegetation

and more than 120 species of bird. The **Rainforest Centre** (✆02-9513 6617; www.national parks.nsw.gov.au/dorrigo-national-park; Dome Rd; adult/child $2/1; ⊙9am-4.30pm; 🛜), at the park entrance, has displays and a film about the park's ecosystems, as well as information on walks. There's free wi-fi, a wonderful cafe (p177), and a charging station for phones and cameras. The Skywalk, a platform that juts out over the rainforest, provides wonderful views across the valleys below.

Starting from the Rainforest Centre, the Wonga Walk is a two-hour, 6.6km-return walk on a bitumen track through the depths of the rainforest. Along the way it passes a couple of very beautiful waterfalls, one of which you can walk behind.

🛏 Sleeping

★**Mossgrove** B&B $$
(✆02-6657 5388; www.mossgrove.com.au; 589 Old Coast Rd; d $225) Set on 2.5 hectares, 8km from Dorrigo, this lovely federation-era home has two traditionally furnished rooms, a cosy guest lounge and a private guest bathroom, all tastefully renovated while echoing the house's heyday. A continental breakfast is included.

★**Tallawarra Retreat B&B** B&B $$
(✆02-6657 2315; www.tallawalla.com; 113 Old Coramba Rd; s/d $130/160; 🐕) This peaceful B&B is set amid picturesque gardens and forest around 1km from Dorrigo town centre. The hosts are friendly and the four rooms are comfortable and blissfully quiet. The complimentary afternoon teas (homemade scones, jam and cream, and pots of tea or coffee) and the hearty, hot English breakfast, make for great value.

Lookout Mountain Retreat B&B $$
(✆02-6657 2511; www.lookoutmountainretreat. com.au; 15 Maynards Plains Rd; d $140-190; 🅿🛜) Spectacular views and a blissfully quiet location make this 26-room place rather special. Exposed bricks and beams give the rooms a cosy feel, and they are spotless and surprisingly stylish. The suite has a kitchenette if you'd like to self-cater.

🍽 Eating

Dorrigo Wholefoods CAFE $
(✆02-6657 1002; www.dorrigowholefoods.com.au; 28 Hickory St; mains with salad $14-16; ⊙6.30am-5pm Mon-Fri, 8am-2pm Sat) Head past the bulk legumes and make up a plate from a cabinet of salads, cakes and savoury morsels such as

lobster pot pie, Thai fish cakes and zucchini-ricotta fritters. The staff whips up super juice combinations, too.

Canopy Cafe CAFE $$
(☑ 02-6657 1541; www.canopycafedorrigo.com.au; Dome Rd; mains $13-22; ☺ 9am-4.30pm) The food is as impressive as the view at this cafe within the Dorrigo National Park Rainforest Centre. The rather sophisticated menu runs from hearty breakfast dishes to spicy laksa and tasty open sandwiches, which can be eaten out on the sunny terrace.

ℹ Information

Dorrigo Information Centre (☑ 02-6657 2486; www.dorrigo.com; 36 Hickory St; ☺ 10am-3pm Mon-Fri) Located in the middle of what passes for the main drag, this is run by volunteers who share a passion for the area. Pick up the useful scenic drives brochure ($1).

Rainforest Centre (p176) This park visitor centre, at the western entrance to Dorrigo National Park, has a shop, exhibits and a cafe.

ℹ Getting There & Away

Three New England Coaches per week head to Coffs Harbour ($48, 1½ hours)

Coffs Harbour

POP 71,800

Despite its inland city centre, Coffs has a string of fabulous beaches. Equally popular with families and backpackers, the town offers plenty of water-based activities, action sports and wildlife encounters, not to mention the kitsch yellow beacon that is the Big Banana. It also makes an easy base for exploring the quaint towns and beautiful drives of the hinterland.

⊙ Sights

Park Beach is a long, lovely stretch of sand backed by dense shrubbery and sand dunes, which conceal the buildings beyond. **Jetty Beach** is somewhat more sheltered. **Diggers Beach**, reached by turning off the highway near the Big Banana, is popular with surfers, with swells averaging 1m to 1.5m. Naturists let it all hang out at **Little Diggers Beach**, just inside the northern headland.

★ Muttonbird Island ISLAND
(www.nationalparks.nsw.gov.au/muttonbird-island-nature-reserve) The Gumbaynggirr people knew this island as Giidany Miirlarl,

meaning Place of the Moon. It was joined to Coffs Harbour by the northern breakwater in 1935. The walk to the top (which is quite steep at the end) provides sweeping vistas. From late August to early April this eco-treasure is occupied by some 12,000 pairs of mating wedge-tailed shearwaters, with their cute offspring visible in December and January.

Solitary Islands Aquarium AQUARIUM
(www.solitaryislandsaquarium.com; Bay Dr, Charlesworth Bay; adult/child $12/8; ☺ 10am-4pm Sat & Sun, daily in school holidays) On weekends this small aquarium belonging to Southern Cross University's Marine Science Centre is open to the public. Touch-tanks and enthusiastic, well-qualified guides provide close encounters with fish, coral and an octopus (try visiting at feeding time) that frequent the waters of the Solitary Islands Marine Park.

Bunker Cartoon Gallery GALLERY
(www.bunkercartoongallery.com.au; John Champion Way; adult/child $3/2; ☺ 10am-4pm) Displays rotating selections from its permanent collection of 18,000 cartoons in a WWII bunker.

Big Banana AMUSEMENT PARK
(www.bigbanana.com; 351 Pacific Hwy; ☺ 9am-5pm) **FREE** Built in 1964, the Big Banana started the craze for 'Big Things' in Australia. Admission is free, with charges for the associated attractions such as ice skating, toboggan rides, mini-golf, the waterpark, plantation tours and the (irresistibly named) 'World of Bananas Experience'. But beyond the kitsch appeal, there's not really much to see.

🏃 Activities

Canoes, kayaks and stand-up paddleboards can be hired from Mangrove Jack's cafe (p179). Keen hikers should pick up a copy of the *Solitary Islands Coastal Walk* brochure ($2) from the visitor centre.

Coffs Creek Walk & Cycleway WALKING
A lovely 8km bush circuit links the central business district (CBD) with the harbour. We recommend starting at the Pet Porpoise Pool, Orlando St, or the Memorial Olympic Pool, Coffs St.

East Coast Surf School SURFING
(☑ 02-6651 5515; www.eastcoastsurfschool. com.au; Diggers Beach; lessons from $55) A

Coffs Harbour

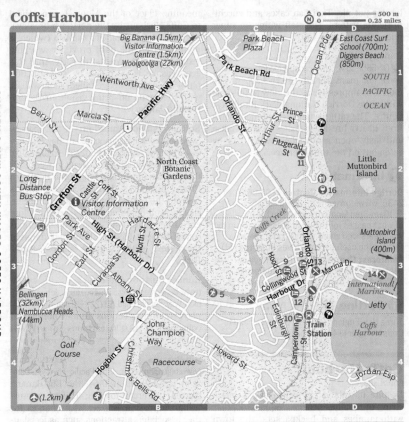

Coffs Harbour

◎ Sights

✦ Activities, Courses & Tours

🛏 Sleeping

✕ Eating

☕ Drinking & Nightlife

particularly female-friendly outfit run by former pro surfer Helene Enevoldson.

Lee Winkler's Surf School SURFING
(☎02-6650 0050; www.leewinklerssurfschool. com.au; Park Beach; from $55) One of the oldest surf schools in Coffs.

Valery Trails HORSE RIDING
(☎02-6653 4301; www.valerytrails.com.au; 758 Valery Rd, Valery; 2hr rides adult/child $65/55) A stable of more than 75 horses and plenty of acreage to explore; located 15km northeast of town.

Coffs City Skydivers
SKYDIVING

(☑02-6651 1167; www.coffsskydivers.com.au; Coffs Harbour Airport; tandem jumps $269-359) Throw yourself out of a plane from 4572m in the highest beach skydive in Australia.

Jetty Dive
DIVING

(☑02-6651 1611; www.jettydive.com.au; 398 Harbour Dr) The Solitary Islands Marine Park is a meeting place of tropical waters and southern currents, making for a wonderful combination of corals, reef fish and seaweed. This dive shop offers spectacular diving and snorkelling trips (double boat dives $170), PADI certification ($445), and, from June to October, whale watching (adult/child $59/49).

🎉 Festivals & Events

Sawtell Chilli Festival
FOOD & DRINK

(www.sawtellchillifestival.com.au; ⊙early Jul) The hottest food festival on the Coffs Coast draws thousands of visitors for spicy food, cooking demonstrations, street entertainment and dancing off the (mild) winter chill.

🛏 Sleeping

Coffs Harbour YHA
HOSTEL $

(☑02-6652 6462; www.yha.com.au; 51 Collingwood St; dm $30-33, d $90-140; @🆒) A super-friendly and nicely positioned hostel with spacious dorms. Private rooms have bathrooms, and the TV lounge and kitchen are clean and colourful. You can hire surfboards and bikes. A favourite with both families and young travellers on the fruit-picking circuit.

Park Beach Holiday Park
CAMPGROUND $

(☑02-6648 4888; www.coffsholidays.com.au; Ocean Pde; camp sites $35-45, cabins $89-140; 🆒🆒) This holiday park is massive but has an ideal location at the beach. Kids are well catered for with a shaded jumping pillow and an action-packed pool featuring slides and fountains.

★ Coffs Jetty BnB
B&B $$

(☑02-6651 4587; www.coffsjetty.com.au; 41a Collingwood St; d $130-170; ❄🆒) A cut above your average B&B, this townhouse has private, tastefully decorated, spacious rooms with walk-in wardrobes and terrific bathrooms. Enjoy your breakfast on the balcony, then make the easy stroll to the beach and jetty restaurants. One of the suites has a kitchenette, while all have microwaves and fridges.

Pier Hotel
PUB $$

(☑02-6652 2110; www.pierhotelcoffs.com.au; 356 Harbour Dr; s without bathroom $69-129, d $129-179, without bathroom $99-135; 🅿🆒) The Pier reinvigorates the Australian tradition of the upstairs pub room. A mix of shared and en suite accommodation occupies the lovely, airy 1st floor, all of which is simple but smartly furnished and comfortable. Downstairs the pub has both an unreconstructed public bar as well as an atmospheric wine cellar. Complimentary airport pick-ups and drop-offs are a nice bonus.

Observatory Apartments
APARTMENT $$

(☑02-6650 0462; www.theobservatory.com.au; 30-36 Camperdown St; apt $177-190; ❄🆒🆒) The studio, two- and three-bedroom apartments in this attractive modern complex are bright and airy, with cook-up-friendly kitchens. All have balconies, with views to the ocean across the road and parkland, and some have spa baths.

🍴 Eating & Drinking

Old John's
CAFE $

(www.facebook.com/oldjohns; 360 Harbour Dr; mains $10-17; ⊙6.30am-3.30pm daily, 5.30-9pm Wed) Coffs' cool kid enclave, with the town's best coffee and a menu of healthy hipster favourites, from breakfast chia 'pud' and superfood bowls or lunch salads of salt-roasted beets, Bellingen greens and goat's curd. Wednesday, and occasionally other, evenings see live music, cocktails, sliders and pasta.

Fishermen's Coop
FISH & CHIPS $

(☑02-6652 2811; www.coffsfishcoop.com.au; Marine Dr; mains $10-17; ⊙11am-7pm) Grab some excellent fish and chips and devour them right beside the fishing trawlers of Coffs' sizeable fleet. You can call ahead for takeaways, too.

★ Lime Mexican
MEXICAN $$

(☑0421 573 570; www.limemexican.com.au; 366 Harbour Dr; dishes $14-18; ⊙5-10pm Tue-Sun; 🆒) Lime does modern Mexican tapas-style, designed to share. The taco line-up includes the usual favourites as well as grilled salmon, seared scallops and braised lamb, and there are big plates with pork belly on spicy rice, cheese-stuffed jalapeño peppers and smoky paprika corn.

Mangrove Jack's
CAFE $$

(☑02-6652 5517; www.mangrovejackscafe.com.au; Promenade Centre, Harbour Dr; mains breakfast $10-18, lunch $18-32, dinner $25-36; ⊙7.30am-3pm daily, 5-9pm Fri & Sat; ☏) The attraction here is the wonderful location on a quiet bend of Coffs Creek and the balcony where you can enjoy a coffee or beer.

★ **Fiasco** ITALIAN $$$
(☑ 02-6651 2006; www.fiascorestaurant.com.au; 22 Orlando St; pizzas $19-24, mains $29-39; ⊘ 5-9pm Tue-Sat) Upmarket Italian fare is prepared in an open kitchen using produce from the best local suppliers and herbs from the restaurant's own garden. Expect authentic delights such as organic Angus beef with celeriac purée, homemade egg pasta with pesto and ricotta, and well-done pizzas from the simple margherita to those embellished with buffalo mozzarella or Roman-style pork belly.

You can also choose to sit at the bar for antipasti and a glass of Italian vermentino or barbera

Latitude 30 SEAFOOD $$$
(☑ 02-6651 6888; www.latitude30.com.au; 1 Marina Dr; mains $30-40; ⊘ 8am-9pm) So much to choose from at this seafood spot on the Marina: will it be shared plates of Thai-style soft-shell crab, gravlax and braised octopus, or a main of fish pie or seafood paella? With a view of the charming working harbour to the jetty and Muttonbird Island, or across to Little Park Beach and the Pacific Ocean?

The deck makes a table here one of the most sought-after in town.

Surf Club Park Beach PUB
(☑ 02-6652 9870; www.surfclubparkbeach.com; 23 Surf Club Rd, Park Beach; ⊘ 7am-11pm) A Sunday-afternoon session on the beach deck listening to local musicians is a top Coffs experience. Drinks can take you into a seafood or tapas dinner.

ⓘ Information

Visitor Information Centre (☑ 02-6651 1629; www.coffscoast.com.au; Coffs Central, 35-61 Harbour Dr; ⊘ 9am-5pm)

ⓘ Getting There & Away

AIR

Qantas (☑ 13 13 13; www.qantas.com.au), **Virgin** (☑ 13 67 89; www.virginaustralia.com) and **Tigerair** (☑ 02-8073 3421; www.tigerair.com.au) all fly to **Coffs Harbour Airport** (☑ 02-6648 4767; www.coffscoast.com.au/airport; Airport Dr), 3km southwest of town. There are Fly Corporate services to Brisbane.

BUS

Long-distance and regional buses operated by **Greyhound** (☑ 1300 473 946; www.greyhound.com.au), **Premier** (☑ 13 34 10; www.premierms.com.au) and **New England Coaches** (☑ 02-6732 1051; www.newenglandcoaches.com.au) leave from the **bus stop** on the corner of McLean St and the Pacific Hwy.

TRAIN

NSW CountryLink (☑ 13 22 32; www.nswtrainlink.info) runs three daily trains to Casino, which connect to Brisbane ($84.15, 5½ hours) by either train or coach, and south to Sydney ($95, nine hours).

North of Coffs Harbour

The Pacific Hwy runs near the coast – but not in sight of it – for 30km north of Coffs. Look for turn-offs to small beaches that are often quite uncrowded.

Around 25km north of Coffs, **Woolgoolga** (locally known as Woopi) is famous for its surf and its Sikh community. It's worth stopping by, particularly when the **Bollywood Beach Bazaar** (☑ 02-6654 7673; www.facebook.com/bollywoodmarket; ⊘ 1st & 4th Sat of month) or **Curryfest** (www.curryfest.com.au; ⊘ Sep) are on.

The village of Red Rock is set between a beautiful beach and a glorious fish-filled river inlet. **Yuraygir National Park** (www.nationalparks.nsw.gov.au/yuraygir-national-park; vehicle entry $8) is the state's longest stretch of undeveloped coastline, covering a 65km stretch of pristine coastal ecosystems stretching north from Red Rock. The isolated beaches are outstanding and there are bushwalking paths where you can view endangered coastal emus.

You can bush-camp at six basic camp sites (adult/child $10/5 per night).

Grafton

POP 18,700

The small city of Grafton on the Clarence River marks the start of the Northern Rivers region, which stretches all the way to the Queensland border. It's an area defined as much by its beaches and clement weather as it is by its three major waterways (the Richmond and Tweed Rivers are the others). Don't be fooled by the franchises along the highway – Grafton's grid of gracious streets has grand pubs and some splendid old houses.

◎ Sights

Victoria Street Precinct AREA
Victoria St is the city's main heritage precinct, with some fine examples of 19th-century architecture, including the **courthouse** (1862) at No 47, the **Anglican Cathedral** (commenced 1884) on the corner of Duke St and **Roches Family Hotel** (1871) at No 85.

✺ Festivals & Events

Jacaranda Festival CULTURAL
(www.jacarandafestival.org.au; ☉ late Oct) For two weeks from late October, Australia's longest-running floral festival paints the town mauve.

⊨ Sleeping

Annie's B&B B&B $$
(☎ 0421 914 295; www.anniesbnbgrafton.com; 13 Mary St; s/d $145/160; ❀ ☞ ☞) This beautiful Victorian house on a leafy corner has private rooms with an old-fashioned ambience, set apart from the rest of the family home. A continental breakfast is provided.

✗ Eating & Drinking

Heart & Soul Wholefood Cafe CAFE $
(☎ 02-6642 2166; 124a Prince St; mains $8-15; ☉ 7.30am-5pm, to 2pm Sat, 8am-noon Sun; ☞) This beautifully styled cafe is the work of two couples who love plant-based eating. Expect ceramic bowls filled with warming Asian soups and stir fries, bright salads, and sweet treats such as the choc-mint 'cheese-fake'.

Roches Family Hotel PUB
(☎ 02-6642 2866; www.roches.com.au; 85 Victoria St; ☉ 10am-11pm Mon-Thu, to midnight Fri & Sat, 11am-10pm Sun) Breaking the rule that states regional pubs must be cavernous and starkly lit, this historic corner hotel is a cosy spot for a drink or a reasonably priced bite. It's worth calling in just for a peek at the beer-can collection and the croc in the public bar.

❶ Information

Clarence River Visitor Information Centre
(☎ 02-6642 4677; www.clarencetourism.com; cnr Spring St & Pacific Hwy; ☉ 9am-5pm; ☞) South of the river.

❶ Getting There & Away

AIR
Regional Express (Rex; ☎ 13 17 13; www.rex. com.au) flies to Sydney on weekdays from the

Clarence Valley Regional Airport (GFN; ☎ 02-6643 0200; www.clarence.nsw.gov.au), 12km south of town.

BUS
Busways (☎ 02-6642 2954; www.busways. com.au) Runs local services including four to eight buses to Maclean (one hour), Yamba (1¼ hours) and Angourie (1½ hours) daily; all $12.30.

Greyhound (☎ 1300 473 946; www.greyhound. com.au) Coaches to/from Sydney (10½ hours, three daily), Nambucca Heads (2½ hours, two daily), Coffs Harbour (one hour, three daily), Byron Bay (three hours, three daily) and Brisbane (6½ hours, three daily).

Northern Rivers Buslines (☎ 02-6626 1499; www.nrbuslines.com.au) One bus to/from Maclean ($6, 43 minutes) and Lismore ($6, three hours) on weekdays.

Premier (☎ 13 34 10; www.premierms.com.au) Daily coaches to/from Sydney ($67, 9½ hours), Nambucca Heads ($34, 1¾ hours), Coffs Harbour ($34, one hour), Byron Bay ($47, 4¼ hours) and Brisbane ($52, 7½ hours).

Ryans Bus Service/Forest Coach Lines North (☎ 02-6652 3201; www.ryansbusservice. com.au) Weekday buses to/from Woolgoolga ($21, 1½ hours), Red Rock ($20, 50 minutes) and Coffs Harbour ($21.80, two hours).

TRAIN
There are good **train** (☎ 13 22 32; www. nswtrainlink.info) links to Sydney as well as Kempsey, Nambucca Heads, Coffs Harbour and also, less frequently, Brisbane.

Yamba & Angourie

At the mouth of the Clarence River, the fishing town of Yamba is rapidly growing in popularity thanks to its gently bohemian lifestyle, splendid beaches, and excellent cafes and restaurants. Oft heard descriptions such as 'Byron Bay 20 years ago' are not unfounded. Neighbour Angourie, 5km to the south, is a tiny, chilled-out place that has long been a draw for experienced surfers and was proudly one of Australia's first surf reserves.

◎ Sights

Angourie Blue Pools SPRING
(The Crescent) These springwater-fed waterholes south of Spooky Beach are the remains of the quarry used for the breakwater. Daring folk climb the cliff faces and plunge to the depths. The saner can slip silently into the water, surrounded by bush, only metres from the surf.

Bundjalung National Park NATIONAL PARK
(www.nationalparks.nsw.gov.au/bundjalung-nation
al-park; vehicle entry $8) Stretching for 25km
along the coast north of the Clarence River
to South Evans Head, this national park is
largely untouched. Most of it is best explored
with a 4WD. However, the southern reaches
can be easily reached from Yamba via the
passenger-only **Clarence River Ferries**
([📞]0408 664 556; www.clarenceriverferries.com.
au; adult/child return $8.30/4.20; [◷]11am-3pm)
to Iluka (at least four daily). This section of
the park includes Iluka Nature Reserve, a
stand of rainforest facing Iluka Beach, part
of the Gondwana Rainforests World Heritage Area.

On the other side of Iluka Bluff the literally named Ten Mile Beach unfurls.

🏃 Activities

Yamba Kayak KAYAKING
([📞]02-6646 0065; www.yambakayak.com; adult/
child per 3hr $70/60, per 5hr $100/80) Half- and
full-day kayaking adventures are the speciality, with forays into nearby wilderness areas.
Hire also available.

Xtreme Cycle & Skate CYCLING
([📞]02-6645 8879; www.facebook.com/YambaCycle
Skate; 34 Coldstream St, Yamba; bike hire per
half/full day $22/30; [◷]9.30am-4.30pm Mon-Fri,
9am-noon Sat, noon-2pm Sun) Great family-
run shop that offers cycle hire (including
dual-suspension mountain bikes), sales and
repairs. Ask or check the Facebook page for
details of its casual trail-ride convoy out in
the state forest (they can of course rent you
a bike if you don't have your own with you).

🛌 Sleeping

Pacific Hotel PUB $
(www.pacifichotelyamba.com.au/accommodation;
18 Pilot St, Yamba; dm $30-40, d with/without
bathroom $130/80; [P][🛜]) 'Motel-style' rooms
in this lovely old pub have a lot of charm
and satisfyingly clean lines. If you can put
up with sharing a bathroom and manage to
snare a corner cheapie, you've hit the view
jackpot of a lighthouse out one window and
the sea out the other. En suite rooms have
balconies as well as fridges and TVs.

Yamba YHA HOSTEL $
([📞]02-6646 3997; www.yha.com.au; 26 Coldstream
St, Yamba; dm $32-36, d $95; [@][🛜][🐾][🏊]) This welcoming, family-run hostel has light-filled
dorms, a popular bar and restaurant, and a
barbecue area with a tiny pool on the roof.

**Seascape Ocean Front
Apartments** APARTMENT $$
([📞]0429 664 311; www.seascapeunits.com.au;
4 Ocean St, Yamba; apt $175-250; [P][🛜]) Two
ocean-view apartments, a small bungalow
and a riverside cottage are all furnished in
bright, contemporary nautical style. Apart-
ment views are spectacular and each space
has retained its '50s Australian coastal
bones. As you can imagine, given the views,
the location is the best. Prices are cheaper
for mutiple-night stays.

🍴 Eating & Drinking

⭐ Beachwood Cafe TURKISH $$
([📞]02-6646 9781; www.beachwoodcafe.com.au;
22 High St, Yamba; mains breakfast $12-18, lunch
$18-26; [◷]7am-2pm Tue-Sun) Cookbook author
Sevtap Yüce steps out of the pages to deliver
her bold *Turkish Flavours* to the plate at
this wonderful little licensed cafe. Most of
the tables are outside, where the grass verge
has been commandeered for a kitchen garden. From the organic mandarin juice and
passionfruit polenta cake to the Turkish-
style sardines and dolmades for lunch, it's a
surprising delight.

⭐ Leche Cafe CAFE $$
([📞]0401 471 202; www.facebook.com/LecheCafe;
27 Coldstream St, Yamba; mains $14-25; [◷]6am-
2pm) After some backyard yoga at Leche
Cafe you might want to tuck into coconut
bread and Byron Bay–based Marvell cof-
fee. The sophisticated lunch menu is just
as wholesome, with beetroot burgers, cau-
liflower curries and fish tacos. And it gets
better: Leche hosts Saturday-night live gigs,
DJs and parties, such as a midsummer Ha-
waiian luau.

Pacific Hotel PUB
([📞]02-6646 2466; www.pacifichotelyamba.com.au;
18 Pilot St, Yamba; [◷]10am-midnight Mon-Thu, to
1.30am Fri & Sat) Perched on the the cliffs over-
looking Yamba Beach, this 1930-built hotel
really does have some of the best pub views
in Australia. There are regular live music
and DJ nights, and the food's tasty, too.

ℹ️ Getting There & Away

Yamba is 15km east of the Pacific Hwy; turn off
at the Yamba Rd intersection just south of the
Clarence River. There are four to eight **Bus-
ways buses** ([📞]02-6645 8941; www.busways.
com.au) from Yamba to Angourie ($3.40, nine
minutes), Maclean ($9.30, 19 minutes) and
Grafton ($12.30, 1¼ hours) daily. **Greyhound**

(⏰ 1300 473 946; www.greyhound.com.au) runs coach services up and down the coast to all the big towns and cities; **NSW Trainlink** (⏰ 13 22 32; www.nswtrainlink.info) looks after the others.

Ballina

POP 14,070

At the mouth of the Richmond River, Ballina is spoilt for white sandy beaches and crystal-clear waters. In the late 19th century it was a rich lumber town; a scattering of gracious historic buildings can still be found on its backstreets. These days Ballina is popular with family holidaymakers and retirees, and home to the region's airport.

⊙ Sights

For a good sampling of local history, stroll the length of **Norton Street**, which boasts a number of impressive late 19th-century buildings from Ballina's days as a rich lumber town.

Northern Rivers Community Gallery   GALLERY
(NRCG; ⏰ 02-6681 6167; www.nrcgballina.com; 44 Cherry St) An excellent regional gallery representing the strong creative community that is an essential part of this region. Housed in the historic former Ballina Municipal Council Chambers, built in 1927, it hosts a rota of shows that showcase local artists and craftspeople, and also includes edgy, contemporary works and interesting events.

Big Prawn   LANDMARK
(Ballina Bunnings, 507 River St) Ballina's big prawn was nearly thrown on the BBQ in 2009, but no one had the stomach to dispatch it. After a 5000-signature pro-prawn petition and a $400,000 restoration in 2013, the 9m, 35-tonne, 30-year-old crustacean is looking as fetching as ever.

⏱ Tours

Aboriginal Cultural Concepts   CULTURAL
(⏰ 0405 654 280; www.aboriginalculturalconcepts. com; half-/full-day tours per person $80/160; ⊙ Wed-Sat) Gain an Indigenous Australian perspective on the local area with heritage tours exploring mythological sites along the Bundjalung coast. You can also do a self-drive tour meeting up with your guide at middens, former camping grounds, contact sites, fertility sites, fish traps and hunting areas along the way.

Kayak Ballina   KAYAKING
(⏰ 02-6681 4000; www.kayakballina.com; tours $70) Kayak Ballina's beautiful waterways on these three-hour guided tours; you may pass dolphins and migratory birds.

🛏 Sleeping

Ballina Travellers Lodge   MOTEL $
(⏰ 02-6686 6737; www.ballinatravellerslodge.com. au; 36-38 Tamar St; d without bathroom $75, with bathroom $115-125; ❄✳🛜🏊) The motel rooms here are surprisingly plush, with feature walls, pretty bedside lamps and nice linen. Super-saver rooms (that is, the ones that share a bathroom) are a rung down in the decor stakes but represent good value.

Shaws Bay Holiday Park   CARAVAN PARK $
(⏰ 02-6686 2326; www.northcoastholidayparks. com.au; 1 Brighton St; camp sites/cabins from $42/143; ✳@🛜) Manicured and well positioned, this park is on the lagoon and an easy walk from the centre. The range of self-contained units includes three deluxe villas.

Ballina Palms Motor Inn   MOTEL $$
(⏰ 02-6686 4477; www.ballinapalms.com; cnr Bentinck & Owen Sts; s $125, d $135-160; ✳🛜🏊) With its lush garden setting and carefully considered decor, this little place is a standout motel. The rooms aren't overly large, but they all have kitchenettes, floorboards, marble tops in the super-fresh bathrooms and high comfort levels.

Ballina Heritage Inn   MOTEL $$
(⏰ 02-6686 0505; www.ballinaheritageinn.com. au; 229 River St; d $120-165; ✳🛜🏊) Near the centre of town, this tidy inn has neat, bright and comfortable rooms that are a significant leap up in quality from most of the other motels on this strip.

🍴 Eating

★ Belle General   CAFE $
(⏰ 0411 361 453; www.bellegeneral.com; 12 Shelly Beach Rd; dishes $12-19; ⊙8am-3pm) Eggs on kale; coconut and date loaf; blueberry hotcakes. Lamb burgers, paleo veggie lasagne, nasi goreng...everything is gluten-free, unless you're having something on sourdough toast, but even then you can sub in some quinoa loaf if you prefer.

Ballina Gallery Cafe   CAFE $$
(⏰ 02-6681 3888; www.ballinagallerycafe.com.au; 46 Cherry St; mains breakfast $12-18, lunch $14-26; ⊙7.30am-3pm Wed-Sun) Ballina's 1920s

former council chambers are home to the town's best cafe. Interesting breakfasts such as saganaki baked eggs and green fritters are offered with a side serve of contemporary art. Dine inside or outside on the verandah.

La Cucina di Vino   ITALIAN $$
(☑ 02-6618 1195; www.lacucinadivino.com; 2 Martin St; mains $24-35, pizzas $17-19; ☺ 5-9pm Mon & Tue, 11am-3pm & 5-9pm Wed-Sun) Water views and carefully prepared dishes make this old-school Italian restaurant beneath the Ramada hotel a choice for a long lunch or dinner.

ℹ Information

Ballina Visitor Information Centre (☑ 02-6686 3484; www.discoverballina.com; 6 River St; ☺ 9am-5pm)

ℹ Getting There & Away

AIR

Ballina Byron Gateway Airport (☑ 02-6681 1858; www.ballinabyronairport.com.au; Southern Cross Dr) is 5km north of the centre of town. Qantas flies from Sydney only, but **Jetstar** (☑ 13 15 38; www.jetstar.com.au) and **Virgin** (☑ 13 67 89; www.virginaustralia.com) also run services to/from Melbourne. A taxi to the centre of Ballina should cost roughly $12 to $15. There are regular buses and shuttle services and rental-car options for Ballina and beyond.

BUS

A number of bus lines service local towns and beyond, linking to Sydney and Brisbane, including NSW TrainLink buses that link to rail services in Casino.

Blanch's (☑ 02-6686 2144; www.blanchs.com.au)

Greyhound (☑ 1300 473 946; www.greyhound.com.au)

NSW TrainLink (☑ 13 22 32; www.nswtrainlink.info)

Premier (☑ 13 34 10; www.premierms.com.au)

Lennox Head

POP 7340

A protected National Surfing Reserve, Lennox Head's picturesque coastline has some of the best surf on the coast, with a world-class point break. Its village atmosphere and laid-back locals make it a mellow alternative to its boisterous and well-touristed neighbour, Byron, 17km north, and you can also get well-made coffee and a rather good feed.

◉ Sights

Seven Mile Beach   BEACH
Long and lovely Seven Mile Beach starts at the township and stretches north. It's accessible to 4WDs, but you will need a permit from the Caltex Service Station. The best place for a dip is near the surf club, at the northern end of town.

⌂ Sleeping & Eating

Lake Ainsworth Holiday Park CAMPGROUND $
(☑ 02-6687 7249; www.northcoastholidayparks.com.au; Pacific Pde; camp sites $34-39, cabins $95-130; ☜) By the lake and near the beach, this family-friendly holiday park has a wide range of units, from rustic cabins without bathrooms to a deluxe villa sleeping six. There are fresh amenities and a kitchen for campers.

Lennox Point Holiday Apartments   APARTMENT $$
(☑ 02-6687 5900; www.lennoxholidayapartments.com; 20-21 Pacific Pde; apt $195-250; ❋ ☜ ☒) Gaze at the surf from your airy apartment in this new complex, then take a splash with a borrowed board from reception. The one-bedroom apartments are the same size as the two-bedrooms, so they feel more spacious.

★**Cafe Marius**   LATIN AMERICAN $$
(☑ 02-6687 5897; www.cafemarius.com.au; 90-92 Ballina St; mains $16-24; ☺ 7am-3.30pm Mon-Thu, to 9pm Fri & Sat, 8am-3.30pm Sun) Hip kids serve and consume a super-tasty selection of Latin American and Spanish dishes, excellent coffee and jugs of sangria from morning to late in this cool little licensed cafe, nestled down the back of an arcade. Fridays and Saturdays between 5pm and 7pm are 'lazy arvo' hours, when buckets of Corona beer go for $20.

Foam   MODERN AUSTRALIAN $$
(☑ 02-6687 7757; www.foamlennox.com; 41 Pacific Pde; mains lunch $18-24, dinner $28-38; ☺ noon-3pm & 6-10pm Wed-Fri, 7.30am-3pm & 6-10pm Sat, 7.30am-3pm Sun) With its Seven Mile Beach views and the atmosphere of a luxury beach house, the deck at Foam is the spot to fuel up over breakfast (even the bread is house-made) or a share a bottle of well-sourced wine over a long lunch. There's a Saturday dinner service with both à la carte and a five-course tasting menu ($85).

ℹ Getting There & Away

Ballina airport is around 14km away and is serviced by local bus company **Blanch's** (☑ 02-6686 2144; www.blanchs.com.au) as well as local taxis.

Byron Bay

POP 4960

The intense popularity of Byron Bay can be, at first, a mystery. Sure, the beaches are sublime, but there are spectacular beaches all along this coast. Its locals have come to symbolise an Australian haute-boho lifestyle, yet much of the town is a squat, architectural mishmash and has a traffic problem. So why the legions of global fans? As they say in Byron, it's the vibe.

Come to surf epic breaks at dawn, paddle through hazy beach afternoons and sigh at the enchanting sunsets. Come to do reiki, refine your yoga practice, do a raw fast and hang with the fire-twirlers by the beach at sunset. Idle with the striped T-shirt set at the town's excellent restaurant tables, then kick on with backpackers, musicians, models, young entrepreneurs, ageing hippies and property developers at one of its beery, shouty pubs. Or, because it's Byron, do all of the above, then repeat.

◉ Sights

★ **Cape Byron State Conservation Park**　　STATE PARK
(www.nationalparks.nsw.gov.au/cape-byron-state-conservation-area) Spectacular views reward those who climb up from the **Captain Cook Lookout** (Lighthouse Rd) on the **Cape Byron Walking Track**. Ribboning around the headland, the track dips and (mostly)

soars its way to the lighthouse. Along the way, look out for dolphins (year-round) and migrating whales during their northern (June to July) and southern (September to November) migrations. You're also likely to encounter bold brush turkeys and shyer wallabies. Allow about two hours for the entire 3.7km loop.

You can also drive right up to the lighthouse (parking costs $7).

Cape Byron Lighthouse　　LIGHTHOUSE
(www.nationalparks.nsw.gov.au; Lighthouse Rd; ⊙10am-4pm) FREE This 1901 lighthouse is Australia's most easterly and also its most powerful shipping beacon. Inside there are maritime and nature displays. If you want to venture to the top, you'll need to take one of the volunteer-run tours, which operate from 10am to 3pm (with gold-coin donation). There's also a cafe and self-contained accommodation in the lighthouse-keeper's cottages. Parking $7.

The Farm　　FARM
(www.thefarmbyronbay.com.au; 11 Ewingsdale Rd, Ewingsdale; tours adult/child/family $10/5/25; ⊙7am-4pm) FREE A community of growers and producers share this photogenic, 80-acre green oasis just outside Byron, along with the Three Blue Ducks (p189) restaurant, a produce store, a bakery and a florist. The dedication to traditional and sustainable practices here is both a working ethos and an educational mission. Feel free to roam and picnic between veggie plots and

DON'T MISS

BYRON BEACHES

West of the town centre, wild **Belongil Beach** with its high dunes avoids the worst of the crowds and is clothing-optional in parts. At its eastern end lies the **Wreck**, a powerful right-hand surf break.

Immediately in front of town, lifesaver-patrolled **Main Beach** is busy from sunrise to sunset with yoga classes, buskers and fire dancers. As it stretches east it merges into **Clarkes Beach**. The most popular surf break is at the **Pass** near the eastern headland.

Around the rocks is gorgeous **Watego's Beach**, a wide crescent of white sand surrounded by rainforest. A further 400m walk brings you to secluded **Little Watego's** (inaccessible by car), another lovely patch of sand directly under rocky Cape Byron. Head here at sunset for an impressive moonrise. Tucked under the south side of the Cape (entry via Tallow Beach Rd) is **Cosy Corner**, which offers a decent-sized wave and a sheltered beach when the northerlies are blowing elsewhere.

Tallow Beach is a deserted sandy stretch that extends for 7km south from Cape Byron. This is the place to flee the crowds. Much of the beach is backed by **Arakwal National Park**, but the suburb of **Suffolk Park** sprawls along the sand near its southern end. **Kings Beach** is a popular gay-friendly beach, just off Seven Mile Beach Rd past the Broken Head Holiday Park.

Byron Bay

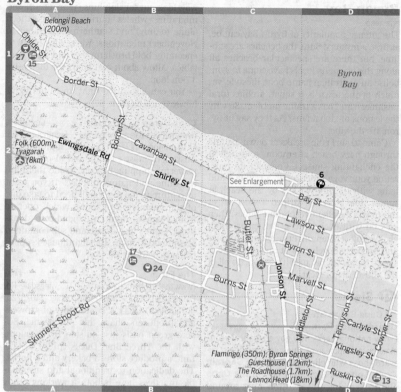

cattle-dotted fields. Tours happen twice daily (9am and 1pm) during January and mornings the rest of the year.

🏃 Activities

Adventure sports abound in Byron Bay and most operators offer a free pick-up service from local accommodation. Surfing and diving are the biggest draws.

Skydive Byron Bay SKYDIVING
(☑ 02-6684 1323; www.skydivebyronbay.com; Tyagarah Airfield; tandem jumps $200-350) Hurtle to earth from 4267m with young, fun and well-trained instructors.

Be Salon & Spa SPA
(☑ 0413 432 584; www.besalonspa.com.au; 14 Middleton St; 30min massages $60) Manicures, pedicures, facials and waxing are offered alongside 'metaphysical' healing, massage, re-balancing and naturopathy.

Go Sea Kayaks KAYAKING
(☑ 0416 222 344; www.goseakayakbyronbay.com.au; adult/child $69/59) 🌊 Sea kayak tours in Cape Byron Marine Park led by a team of local surf lifesavers.

Byron Bay Ballooning BALLOONING
(☑ 1300 889 660; www.byronbayballooning.com.au; Tyagarah Airfield; adult/child $350/175) One-hour sunrise flights including champagne breakfast; Byron's a wonderful place to balloon over.

Surf & Bike Hire CYCLING
(☑ 02-6680 7066; www.byronbaysurfandbikehire.com.au; 31 Lawson St; ⏰ 9am-5pm) Rents bikes and surfboards (from $10 per day) plus other active gear.

Dive Byron Bay DIVING
(☑ 02-6685 8333; www.byronbaydivecentre.com.au; 9 Marvell St; dives $60, snorkelling tours $69; ⏰ 9am-5pm) Introductory ($165), freediving

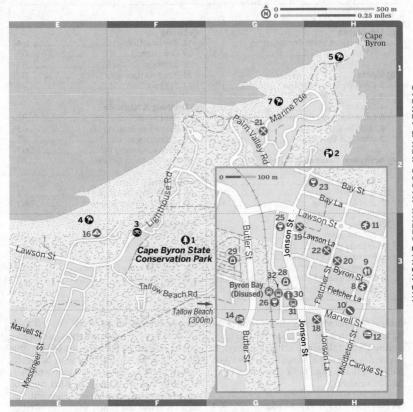

($550) and Professional Association of Diving Instructors (PADI; from $1595) courses.

Black Dog Surfing SURFING
(☑ 02-6680 9828; www.blackdogsurfing.com; 11 Byron St; 3½hr lessons $65) Intimate (seven people max) group lessons, including women's and kids' courses. Highly rated.

☞ Tours

★ Mountain Bike Tours MOUNTAIN BIKING
(☑ 0429 122 504; www.mountainbiketours.com.au; half-/full-day tours $79/119) 🍃 Environmentally aware bike tours into the rainforest and along the coast.

Aboriginal Cultural Concepts CULTURAL
(☑ 0405 654 280; www.aboriginalculturalconcepts.com; half-/full-day tours $80/160; ⊙ 10am-1pm Wed-Sat) Heritage tours exploring mythological sights along the Bundjalung coast. Includes bush-tucker tour.

★ Festivals & Events

Byron Bay Writers' Festival LITERATURE
(www.byronbaywritersfestival.com.au; ⊙ early Aug) Gathers together big-name writers and literary followers from across Australia.

Splendour in the Grass MUSIC
(www.splendourinthegrass.com; North Byron Parklands; ⊙ late Jul) Three-day festival featuring big-name indie artists. Huge.

Byron Bay Bluesfest MUSIC
(www.bluesfest.com.au; Tyagarah Tea Tree Farm; ⊙ Easter; 🐾) Held over Easter, this jam attracts high-calibre international performers (Neil Young and Barry Gibb in recent years) and local heavyweights.

⌷ Sleeping

By any standards, Byron beds are expensive. Many locals rent out their own places, but even Airbnb and holiday lets are inflated. If you're in the market for 'barefoot

Byron Bay

luxury' – relaxed but stylish – you're in luck. Book well in advance for January, during festival time and school holidays. If you're not a teenager, avoid Schoolies Week (which actually runs for a few weeks from mid-November).

★**Nomads Arts Factory Lodge** HOSTEL $
(☎02-6685 7709; www.nomadsworld.com/arts-factory; Skinners Shoot Rd; dm $35-43, d $85-115; ❋@✆☎) ✐ For an archetypal Byron experience, try this rambling mini-city next to a picturesque swamp, 15-minutes' walk from town. Choose from colourful six- to 10-bed dorms, a female-only lakeside cottage, or a tepee village. Couples can opt for aptly titled 'cube' rooms, island-retreat canvas huts or the pricier 'love shack' with bathroom.

Byron Beach Resort HOSTEL $
(☎02-6685 7868; www.byronbeachresort.com.au; 25 Childe St; dm $32-52, d $105-160, 2-bed cottages $260; ℗❋☎) This fabulous, well-managed resort opposite Belongil Beach is a terrific and affordable alternative to staying in central Byron. Attractive dorms, cottages and self-contained apartments are scattered through the hammock-filled gardens. There's daily yoga, free bikes and the fun Treehouse (p190) pub next door. It's a 15-minute walk (or free shuttle ride) down Belongil Beach into town.

Clarkes Beach Holiday Park CAMPGROUND $
(☎02-6685 6496; www.northcoastholidayparks.com.au; 1 Lighthouse Rd; camp sites $47-67, cabins $165-345; ❋☎) The cabins might be tightly packed but they, along with shady tent sites, sit within attractive bush in what must be one of the town's most spectacular settings, high up above the beach and overlooked by the Capy Byron lighthouse.

★**Barbara's Guesthouse** GUESTHOUSE $$
(☎0401 580 899; www.byronbayvacancy.com; 5 Burns St; d $160-250; ☎) This pretty 1920s family home, in a quiet residential street, has four simple but elegant guest rooms. Lofty ceilings, smart beachy style and thoughtful hosts make this a great easygoing choice. There's a communal kitchen where breakfast supplies and a coffee machine greet you each morning, and there's an airy back deck for an early evening drink and catch up.

Flamingo GUESTHOUSE $$
(☎02-6680 9577; www.flamingobyronbay.com.au; 32 Bangalow Rd; ste $139-179, cottages $249-299; ℗❋☎) The Flamingo offers a choice of suites, a four-bedroom house or a super-stylish barn. All feature polished timber floors, fully equipped kitchens, modern bathrooms and large open verandahs, creating a perfect combination of rustic Byron charm and on point design.

Arcadia House
B&B **$$**

(☑02-6680 8699; www.arcadiahousebyron.com. au; 48 Cowper St; d $145-375; ❄️🛜) Amid a large garden on a quiet street, this delightful old Queenslander has airy verandahs and six traditionally furnished rooms with four-poster beds and cushion-strewn sofas. It's about a 10-minute walk to the beach, or jump on a complimentary bike.

Byron Springs Guesthouse
GUESTHOUSE **$$**

(☑0457 808 101; www.byronsprings.com.au; 2 Oodgeroo Garden; s without bathroom $95-125, d $175-235, d without bathroom $150-175; P🛜) Polished floorboards, crisp white linen, big verandahs and a leafy setting a couple of kilometres south of town make this a lovely choice if you like to be removed from the throng. A continental breakfast is included and there are complimentary bikes.

★28° Byron Bay
BOUTIQUE HOTEL **$$$**

(☑02-6685 7775; www.28byronbay.com.au; 12 Marvell St; d from $460; P❄️🛜🏊) A perfect combination of absolute privacy and personal warmth make this a rare find. An effortless, relaxed luxury lends each of the four rooms a bolthole appeal (especially with their deep baths and individual plunge pools), but you're also just a short amble to Byron's favourite upmarket eating options and, of course, the beach.

Elements
RESORT **$$$**

(☑02-6639 1500; www.elementsofbyron.com.au; 144 Bayshore Dr; 1-bedroom villa $380; P❄️🛜🏊) 🌿 Behind 2km of Belongil dunes, this is Byron's newest and most luxurious resort. One hundred or so private villas nestle in coastal bushland and, while there are no ocean views, the sound of the surf, and cicadas, is ever present. Split-level villas are spacious, tasteful and soothing. The main pavilion, pool and restaurant have a relaxed, almost ironic Australian glamour.

Byron Beach Abodes
VILLA **$$$**

(☑0419 490 010; www.byronbeachabodes.com.au; cottages & apt $295-995) A handpicked collection of Byron's best design-driven properties, Byron Beach Abodes attracts overseas guests, honeymooners and Sydney's fashion set. Each has its own unique style and is nestled in the town's most upmarket enclave. You're close to the beach and lighthouse walks.

Our pick is the Chapel, the smallest and least expensive but with an eclectic allure (100-year-old exposed bricks, recycled timber beams) and a palette of black and white.

✗ Eating

Byron is a darling destination for food-focused travellers. This could well be the clean-eating capital of the country: golden lattes are ubiquitous; juices are always cold-pressed; and breakfast bowls are more common than bacon and eggs. Weekly markets overflow with farm-fresh produce. Plenty of upmarket restaurants serve climate-appropriate Modern Australian dishes, and more casual eateries do global favourites such as tacos, tapas and sushi. Ingredients are usually local and sourced from small, or-ganic producers. Book ahead for dinner.

★Bay Leaf Café
CAFE **$**

(www.facebook.com/bayleafcoffee; 2 Marvell St; mains $14-22; ⊙7am-2pm) You might be tempted to snigger at the raft of Byron clichées on offer at this always busy cafe (golden lattes, coconut cold brew, kombucha, tousle-haired locals, a '70s psych rock soundtrack etc), but that would mean missing out on food and drinks that are made with love and a remarkable attention to detail.

Chichuahua
MEXICAN **$**

(☑02-6685 6777; Feros Arcade, 25 Jonson St; tacos $6.50-7.50; ⊙11am-8.30pm) Follow the holy Virgin to this arcade hole-in-the-wall taqueria that serves up Byron's most authentic and good-value Mexican. It's ripe for takeaway (and also delivers within central Byron), but you can eat in if there's a spare fold-out chair and table available. The slow-roast brisket and chilli-coconut prawn tacos are hard to go past.

Combi
CAFE **$**

(www.wearecombi.com.au; 21-25 Fletcher St; ⊙7am-4pm) Melbourne clean-eating icons Combi have brought their signature raw, organic and highly Instagrammable drinks, cakes and breakfast and lunch bowls to Byron. House-made mylk (coconut or almond milk) can be had in coffee, or made into fruit, matcha or turmeric lattes, and in matcha or raw cacao mylkshakes or superfood smoothies.

The raw extends to pizza, pad Thai and pasta, and there's slow-cooked soup or gluten-free sandwiches.

★Three Blue Ducks at the Farm
FARM RESTAURANT **$$**

(☑02-6684 7888; www.thefarmbyronbay.com.au; 11 Ewingsdale Rd, Ewingsdale; ⊙7.30am-3pm Mon-Sun, 5-10pm Fri-Sun) The legendary Sydney team behind Three Blue Ducks moved up north to showcase its paddock-to-plate food philosophy. Their rustic barn cafe and restaurant forms the beating heart of The Farm (p185). The breakfast menu does typical Byron healthy, but also surprises with 'spanner crab scramble' or black sausage and roast potatoes. Lunch and dinner menus are simple, but there's a gentle sophistication to the cooking.

★ St Elmo
SPANISH $$

(☑02-6680 7426; www.stelmodining.com; cnr Fletcher St & Lawson Lane; dishes $14.50-28; ⊙5-11pm Mon-Sat, to 10pm Sun) Perch on a stool at this moody modern tapas restaurant, where rock-star bar staff create wicked cocktails or can pour you one of the better wines by the glass found in this part of the world (including natural and minimal intervention drops). The solidly Iberian menu is bold and broad, with traditional favourites mixing it up with contemporary flourishes.

★ Folk
CAFE $$

(www.folkbyronbay.com; 399 Ewingsdale Rd; mains $15-18; ⊙7.30am-2.30pm) This delightful wooden-cottage cafe sits beside a busy caravan park but is a world unto itself. The barista may pause while making your organic cow, soy, macadamia, coconut or almond latte to wander out and flip over the James Taylor vinyl, and you'll settle in with the menu of incredibly pretty and super-healthy drinks, salads and gluten-free cakes.

The Roadhouse
MODERN AUSTRALIAN, CAFE $$

(☑0403 355 498; www.roadhousebyronbay.com; 6/142 Bangalow Rd; mains $14-29; ⊙6.30am-2.30pm & 6-10pm Tue-Sat, 6.30am-2.30pm Sun & Mon) A short trip out of town will find you at Byron's most atmospheric night spot. Rocking incredible, locally sourced wholefoods and coffee, Roadhouse also transforms into a dimly lit, blues-infused bar late into the night, with more than 500 types of whisky on the menu and refreshing cocktails.

Rae's Restaurant
SEAFOOD $$$

(☑02-6685 5366; www.raesonwategos.com; 8 Marine Pde, Wategos Beach; mains $38-45; ⊙noon-3pm & 6-11.30pm) The sound of the surf perfectly sets off the excellent seafood, poultry and vegetarian dishes at this exclusive little retreat in Watego's. Dishes are simple, clear flavoured and use wonderful local produce. The seafood degustation ($115; or $175 with matched wines) is a super way to while away an afternoon or evening.

Byron at Byron Restaurant
MODERN AUSTRALIAN $$$

(☑02-6639 2111; www.thebyronatbyron.com.au; 77-97 Broken Head Rd; mains $34-58; ⊙8am-9pm) With flickering candles and a rainforest backdrop 4km south of town, this intimate resort restaurant offers light, Mediterranean-style dishes created around the best of the Northern Rivers region produce, such as sweet Bangalow pork and Yamba prawns. If you don't want to commit to a long lunch or dinner, the casual snack menu from 3pm to 9pm uses the same stellar produce.

🍷 Drinking & Nightlife

★ Treehouse on Belongil
PUB

(☑02-6680 9452; www.treehouseonbelongil.com; 25 Childe St; ⊙7.30am-11pm) A homespun beach bar where wooden decks spill out among the trees, afternoons are for drinking, and live, original music is played all weekend. Most of the food comes from the wood-fired oven.

Byron Bay Brewing Co
BREWERY

(www.byronbaybrewery.com.au; 1 Skinners Shoot Rd; ⊙11am-midnight) At this old piggery turned booze barn you can drink frosty glasses of house pale lager in a light, louvered space by the brewing vats or outside in the tropical courtyard shaded by a giant fig tree.

Beach Hotel
PUB

(www.beachhotel.com.au; cnr Jonson & Bay Sts; ⊙11am-late) Soak up the atmosphere and the views in the iconic beachfront beer garden. Surf movies are screened out the back, and even though the one-time owner, '70s comedy star Strop, has moved on, the original Crocodile Dundee hat adorns the bar.

Railway Friendly Bar
PUB

(The Rails; ☑02-6685 7662; www.therailsbyronbay.com; 86 Jonson St; ⊙11am-late) 'The Rails' indoor-outdoor mayhem draws everyone from lobster-red British tourists to high-on-life earth mothers and babyboomer tourists. The front beer garden, conducive to long, beery afternoons, has live music. Excellent burgers, with variants including roo, fish and tofu.

Cocomangas
CLUB

(www.cocomangas.com.au; 32 Jonson St; ⊙9pm-late Wed-Sat) Byron's longest-standing nightclub, with regular backpacker nights. No entry after 1.30am.

🔒 Shopping

★ Byron Farmers' Market
MARKET

(www.byronfarmersmarket.com.au; Butler Street Reserve; ⊙8-11am Thu) Both a market and a symbol of the strength of the local community, this weekly market has a wide variety of mainly organic stalls, with both fresh produce and all manner of local products. Come early and hang with the locals for great coffee and breakfast, then linger for live music.

Arts & Industry Estate
ARTS & CRAFTS

(www.byronartstrail.com) A booming mini-city around 3km inland from Byron proper, the Arts & Industry Estate is home to Byron's ever-growing community of creative businesses. Check the website or grab the *Industry Trail* map available from the tourist office or your accommodation, and explore its many homewares, vintage, fashion, jewellery and gourmet businesses. There are also good cafes and a brewery for rest stops.

Byron Bay Artisan Market
MARKET

(www.byronmarkets.com.au; Railway Park, Jonson St; ⊙4-9pm Sat Nov-Mar) Local artists and designers show their wares at this popular night market. Expect leather goods, jewellery and clothing, plus live entertainment.

ℹ️ Information

Byron Central Hospital (☑02-6639 9400; www.ncahs.nsw.gov.au; 54 Ewingsdale Rd; ⊙24hr)

Byron Visitor Centre (☑02-6680 8558; www.visitbyronbay.com; Old Stationmaster's Cottage, 80 Jonson St; ⊙9am-5pm) The place for accurate tourist information, and last-minute accommodation and bus bookings.

ℹ️ Getting There & Away

AIR

Byron Bay Shuttle (www.byronbayshuttle.com.au; adult/child $20/12) and **Xcede** (☑02-6620 9200; www.byronbay.xcede.com.au) serve both Coolangatta (Gold Coast; $37) and Ballina ($18) airports. The former airport has more flights.

BUS

Coaches stop on **Jonson St** near the tourist office. Operators include **Premier** (☑13 34 10; www.premierms.com.au), **Greyhound** (☑1300 473 946; www.greyhound.com.au) and **NSW TrainLink** (☑13 22 32; www.nswtrainlink.info; Jonson St).

Blanch's (☑02-6686 2144; www.blanchs.com.au) Regular buses to/from Ballina Byron Gateway Airport ($9.60, one hour), Ballina ($9.60, 55 minutes), Lennox Head ($7.60, 35 minutes), Bangalow ($6.40, 20 minutes) and Mullumbimby ($6.60, 25 minutes).

Brisbane 2 Byron Express Bus (☑1800 626 222; www.brisbane2byron.com; one way/return $38/76) Two daily buses to/from Brisbane ($38, two hours) and Brisbane Airport ($54, three hours); one service only on Sundays.

Byron Bay Express (www.byronbayexpress.com.au; one way/return $30/55) Five buses a day to/from Gold Coast Airport (1¾ hours) and Surfers Paradise (2¼ hours) for $30/55 one way/return.

Byron Easy Bus (☑02-6685 7447; www.byronbayshuttle.com.au) Minibus service to Ballina Byron Gateway Airport ($20, 40 minutes), Gold Coast Airport ($39, two hours), Brisbane ($40, 3½ hours) and Brisbane Airport ($54, four hours).

Northern Rivers Buslines (☑02-6626 1499; www.nrbuslines.com.au) Weekday buses to/from Lismore (1½ hours; $12), Bangalow (30 minutes) and Mullumbimby (20 minutes), both $9.70.

TRAIN

People still mourn the loss of the popular CountryLink train service that ran from Sydney. Nsw TrainLink now has buses connecting to trains at the Casino train station (70 minutes). Get full details from the rather forlorn former train station.

NORTH COAST HINTERLAND

Away from the coast, the lush scenery, organic markets and a large population that embraces alternative lifestyles make this one of Australia's most alluring regions – for locals and visitors alike (real-estate prices are now as common an overhear as chakra cleansing once was). Stay up here for deep relaxation, good food and access to numerous healing practitioners. Or day-trip from the coast, visiting beautiful towns such as Bangalow or hitting the hiking trails and swimming holes of one of the region's extraordinary national parks.

Bangalow

POP 2160

Surrounded by subtropical forest and rolling green farmland 14km from Byron, Bangalow (Bangers to friends) is home to a flourishing creative community, a dynamic, sustainable food scene and a range of urbane boutiques. A new arts precinct, which houses community arts organisations plus a number of cute shops and a lovely cafe, is but a stroll up the hill on Station St. The little town heaves during the monthly **Bangalow Market** (www.bangalowmarket.com.au; Bangalow Showgrounds; ⊙ 9am-3pm 4th Sun of month), but it's well worth making trip at any time for a dose of its languid sophistication.

🛏 Sleeping

Bungalow 3   GUESTHOUSE **$$**
(🖉 0401 441 582; www.messengerproperty.com.au/bungalow3; 3 Campbell St; studios $130-165, houses $230-320; ❋) This pretty weatherboard cottage in central Bangalow has two simply decorated rooms, and French doors opening to the deck and edible garden. There is an additional one-bedroom studio; larger groups can hire out the whole place.

★**Bangalow Guesthouse**   B&B **$$$**
(🖉 02-6687 1317; www.bangalowguesthouse.com.au; 99 Byron St; r $195-285; 🕾) This stately old wooden villa sits on the river's edge, so guests can spot platypuses and oversized lizards as they enjoy breakfast. It's the stuff of B&B dreams, with spacious private rooms and elegant, soulful decor that works well with the original architecture.

🍴 Eating & Drinking

★**Woods**   CAFE **$**
(www.folkbyronbay.com; 10 Station St; mains $12-19; ⊙ 7.30am-3pm Tue-Sun) A hinterland outpost of Byron's Folk cafe, this place forms the heart of the arts precinct. It's as indie and folky as you might imagine, a lovely place of whitewash and wood that serves up good coffee, the healthiest of sweets, drinks, and beautiful lunches such as soba noodles or local spiced rice and quinoa with kale, pickles, watercress and toasted seeds.

Italian Diner   ITALIAN **$$**
(www.theitaliandiner.com.au; 37-39 Byron St; mains $24-36, pizzas $20-26; ⊙ noon-3pm & 6-10pm) Sitting on the verandah of this buzzy bistro, enjoying a Campari and a bowl of *linguine gamberi* made with local prawns, it's hard not to imagine that you're enjoying a long lunch somewhere by the Med. There are also fabulous wood-fired pizzas and desserts.

Town Restaurant
& Cafe   MODERN AUSTRALIAN **$$$**
(🖉 02-6687 2555; www.townbangalow.com.au; 33 Byron St; cafe mains $16-24, restaurant degustation $85; ⊙ cafe 8am-3pm Mon-Sat, 9am-3pm

Sun, restaurant 7-9.30pm Thu-Sat) Upstairs (Uptown, if you will) is one of northern NSW's perennially excellent restaurants, serving a six-course degustation menu carefully and imaginatively constructed from seasonal local produce. Never fear - there's a vegetarian option too. Both of the menus can be had with matched wines (an additional $55). Head Downtown for simple but beautifully done cafe breakfasts, light lunches and a counter that's heavy with sweet baked things.

Bangalow Hotel   PUB
(www.bangalowhotel.com.au; 1 Byron St; ⊙ 10am-midnight Mon-Sat, noon-10pm Sun) Sit on the deck of this much-loved and nicely preserved pub for a drink; listen to live music; and order gourmet burgers. Alternatively, reserve a table at its more-upmarket **Bangalow Dining Rooms** (🖉 02-6687 1144; www.bangalowdining.com; mains $20-34; ⊙ noon-3pm & 5.30-9pm).

🛍 Shopping

★**Little Peach**   ARTS & CRAFTS, ANTIQUES
(🖉 02-6687 1415; www.littlepeach.com.au; 17 Byron St; ⊙ 10am-5pm Mon-Fri, to 4pm Sat & Sun) This little piece of Japan has been a Bangalow favourite for years. Regular buying trips to Tokyo mean a never-ending stock of stunning wooden *kokeshi* dolls, kimonos and other beautiful pieces made from vintage Japanese silks, as well as beautifully chosen French accessories and globally sourced homewares.

Bangalow Farmers Market   MARKET
(Bangalow Hotel Car Park, 1 Byron St; ⊙ 8-11am Sat) One of the most favoured of the farmers markets, because of its pretty setting.

ⓘ Getting There & Away

Blanch's (🖉 02-6686 2144; www.blanchs.com.au) Weekday bus 640 goes to/from Byron Bay ($6.60, 20 minutes) and Ballina ($7.60, 30 minutes).

Byron Easy Bus (🖉 02-6685 7447; www.byronbayshuttle.com.au) Operates shuttles to/from Ballina Byron Gateway Airport.

Northern Rivers Buslines (🖉 02-6626 1499; www.nrbuslines.com.au; 🕾) Weekday buses to/from Lismore (1¼ hours, $6).

NSW TrainLink (🖉 13 22 32; www.nswtrainlink.info) Daily coaches to/from Murwillumbah ($9.70, 1¼ hours), Tweed Heads ($11.30, two hours), Burleigh Heads ($13.70, 1½ hours) and Surfers Paradise ($15.30, two hours).

Lismore

POP 29,410

Lismore is the unassuming commercial centre of the Northern Rivers region, chock full of heritage buildings and a country-town saunter. A vibrant community of creatives, the Southern Cross University student population and a larger than average gay and lesbian presence provide the town with an unexpected eclecticism. It's an interesting place to visit, though most travellers prefer to stay on the coast or deeper in the hinterland.

◉ Sights

Koala Care Centre WILDLIFE RESERVE
(☑02-6621 4664; www.friendsofthekoala.org; Rifle Range Rd; adult/family $5/10; ☺tours 10am & 2pm Mon-Fri, 10am Sat) This centre takes in sick, injured and orphaned koalas; visits are only possible by guided tour at the designated times. It's a great way to both meet koalas and to support this volunteer service that help's them. To see koalas in the wild, head to **Robinson's Lookout** (Robinson Ave, Girard's Hill), immediately south of the town centre.

Lismore Regional Gallery GALLERY
(www.lismoregallery.org; 131 Molesworth St; ☺10am-4pm Tue, Wed & Fri, to 6pm Thu, to 2pm Sat & Sun) FREE Lismore's diminutive gallery has long been a cultural force in the town and a real centre of creative life in the region. At the end of 2017 it's set to relocate to a large new site on the corner of Keen and Magellan Sts, with more than five gallery spaces and exciting new programs in the works.

☆彡 Festivals & Events

Tropical Fruits LGBT
(www.tropicalfruits.org.au; ☺31 Dec) This legendary New Year's bash is country NSW's biggest gay and lesbian event. There are also parties at Easter and on the Queen's Birthday holiday in June.

Lismore Lantern Parade PARADE
(www.lanternparade.com; ☺Jun) More than 30,000 people line the streets to watch giant illuminated creatures glide past on the Saturday closest to the winter solstice.

🛏 Sleeping

Karinga MOTEL $
(☑02-6621 2787; www.karingamotel.com; 258 Molesworth St; d $120-145; ✳ 🛜 ✳) The pick of the litter, the Karinga has had a tasteful

facelift: rooms have been fully refurbished and there's a good lap pool and spa.

★Melville House B&B $$
(☑02-6621 5778; www.melvillehouselismore.com; 267 Ballina St; s $40-140, d $50-165; ⊛ ✳ ✳ ✳) This grand country home was built in 1942 by the owner's grandfather and features the area's largest private swimming pool. The six rooms offer superb value and are decorated with local art, cut glass and antiques. Some have external bathrooms but even the small 'struggling writer's room' has its own. Breakfast is included for the larger rooms; otherwise it's $10 extra.

✖ Eating & Drinking

★Republic of Coffee CAFE $
(☑0403 570 503; www.facebook.com/republicof coffee; 98 Magellan St; ☺6.30am-2pm Mon-Fri) The most serious-about-coffee cafe in town. You can also pick up good pies, donuts and other pastries. But you're here for the coffee, right?

★Palate
at the Gallery MODERN AUSTRALIAN $$
(☑02-6622 8830; www.palateatthegallery.com; 133 Molesworth St; breakfast $15-19, mains $16-32; ☺11.30am-2.30pm Tue-Fri, 8am-2.30pm Sat & Sun, 6-10pm Wed-Sat; 🔊) This slick pavilion has French doors opening onto a sunny, shrub-lined terrace. It morphs seamlessly from a smart daytime cafe into one of Lismore's best night-time dining options, serving elegant dishes such as mussels in white wine and roast chicken in a tarragon and cream sauce.

Deck BAR
(SCU Unibar; ☑02-6626 9602; www.unibarand cafe.scu.edu.au; 1 Military Rd; ☺9am-midnight university term time) A university bar that has great gigs due to Southern Cross University's unique 'Bachelor of Rock'n'Roll' program. Upcoming gigs are listed on the website. It's a student bar, so can get messy.

🛍 Shopping

Farmers Market MARKET
(Lismore Showground; ☺8-11am Sat) Lismore stages its farmers market at the showground, off Nimbin Rd.

ℹ Information

Lismore Visitor Information Centre (☑02-6626 0100; www.visitlismore.com.au; 207 Molesworth St; ☺9.30am-4pm)

ℹ️ Getting There & Away

AIR

Regional Express (Rex; ☑️13 17 13; www.regionalexpress.com.au) Flies to/from Sydney.
Lismore Regional Airport (☑️02-6622 8296; www.lismore.nsw.gov.au; Bruxner Hwy) Three kilometres south of the city.

BUS

Buses stop at the **Lismore City Transit Centre** (cnr Molesworth & Magellan Sts).
Northern Rivers Buslines (☑️02-6622 1499; www.nrbuslines.com.au) Local buses plus services to Grafton (three hours), Ballina (1¼ hours), Lennox Head (one hour), Bangalow (1¼ hours) and Byron Bay (1½ hours); all fares are $12.
NSW TrainLink (☑️13 22 32; www.nswtrainlink.info) Coaches to/from Byron Bay ($9.25, one hour), Mullumbimby ($11.55, one hour), Brunswick Heads ($13.85, 1½ hours) and Brisbane ($40.35, three hours).
Waller's (☑️02-6622 6266; www.wallersbus.com) Three buses weekdays to/from Nimbin ($9.50, 30 minutes).

Nimbin

POP 1670

Welcome to Australia's alternative-lifestyle capital, a little town set in an impossibly pretty valley that almost drowns under the weight of its own clichés. Once an unremarkable Northern Rivers dairy village, Nimbin was changed forever in May 1973. Thousands of counter-culture kids and back-to-earth-movement types descended on the town for the Aquarius Festival. Many stayed on and created new communities in the beautiful countryside around the town, hoping to continue the ideals of the 10-day celebration.

Today the psychedelic murals of the rainbow-serpent Dreaming and marijuana bliss that line Nimbin's main street are fading, and the dreadlocked locals are weathered. While genuine remnants of the peace-and-love generation remain, the town has become much darker since the '80s. The brazen weed dealers who make a living from the bus tours that barrel up from Byron are known to also peddle harder drugs, and alcohol-fueled violence is on the rise. See it once, but you'll probably not come back.

👁️ Sights

⭐ **Djanbung Gardens** GARDENS
(☑️02-6689 1755; www.permaculture.com.au; 74 Cecil St; tours $5, with guide $20; ⏰10.30am-4pm Wed-Sun, guided tours 11am Sat) **FREE** Nimbin has been at the forefront of the organic gardening movement and this world-renowned permaculture education centre, created out of a degraded cow pasture, is home to food forests, vegetable gardens, a drought-proof system of dams, ponds and furry farm animals. There's a range of short courses available and you can book ahead for guided tours on Saturday mornings ($20).

Hemp Embassy CULTURAL CENTRE
(☑️02-6689 1842; www.hempembassy.net; 51 Cullen St; ⏰9am-5pm) Part shop, part stronghold for minor political group the Hemp Party, this colourful place raises consciousness about impending marijuana legalisation, and provides all the tools and fashion items you'll need to attract police attention. The embassy organises the **MardiGrass festival** in May (www.nimbinmardigrass.com).

🛏️ Sleeping & Eating

Nimbin Rox YHA HOSTEL $
(☑️02-6689 0022; www.nimbinrox.com.au; 74 Thorburn St; sites/teepees/dm/d from $14/26/30/68; @🛜🏊) Escape the coastal crowds at this hostel and camping ground perched on a lush hill at the edge of town. You'll find plenty of spots to unwind, with hammocks strung among the trees, a lovely heated pool and a nearby swimming creek. Friendly managers go out of their way to please with free pancake breakfasts and a regular shuttle run into town.

Grey Gum Lodge GUESTHOUSE $
(☑️02-6689 1713; www.greygumlodge.com; 2 High St; d $85-135; @🛜) The valley views from the front verandah of this palm-draped wooden Queenslander-style house are gorgeous. All the rooms are comfortable, tastefully furnished and have their own bathrooms.

Black Sheep Farm GUESTHOUSE $$
(☑️02-6689 1095; www.blacksheepfarm.com.au; 449a Gungas Rd; d $220; 🏊) Guests might struggle to leave this self-contained cabin with a saltwater pool and a Finnish sauna on the edge of a rainforest. It sleeps up to seven people ($20 per extra person). There's also a smaller and cheaper cottage available.

Nimbin Hotel PUB FOOD $
(☑️02-6689 1246; www.nimbinhotel.com.au; Cullen St; mains $11-22; ⏰11am-10pm) This classic boozer has a vast back porch overlooking a verdant valley. The Hummingbird Bistro

HINTERLAND NATIONAL PARK

The spectacular waterfalls, the sheer cliff of solidified lava and the dense rainforest of 80-sq-km **Nightcap National Park** (www.nationalparks.nsw.gov.au/nightcap-national-park; vehicles $8), around 25km west of Mullumbimby, are perhaps to be expected in an area with the highest annual rainfall in NSW. It's part of the Gondwana Rainforests World Heritage Area and home to many native birds and protected creatures. From Nimbin, a 10km drive via Tuntable Falls Rd and Newton Dr leads to the edge of the park and then on to Mt Nardi (800m).

The **Historic Nightcap Track** (16km, 1½ days), which was stomped out by postal workers in the late 19th century, runs from Mt Nardi to **Rummery Park**, a picnic spot and camping ground. **Peate's Mountain Lookout**, just on from Rummery Park, offers a panoramic view all the way to Byron. The **Minyon Loop** (7.5km, four hours) is a terrific half-day hike around the spectacular Minyon Falls, which are good for an icy splash. A largely unsealed but very scenic road leads from the Channon to the Terania Creek Picnic Area, where an easy track heads to **Protestor Falls** (1.4km return).

The vast **Border Ranges National Park** (www.nationalparks.nsw.gov.au/border-ranges-national-park; vehicles $8) covers 317 sq km on the NSW side of the McPherson Range, which runs along the NSW–Queensland border. It's part of the Gondwana Rainforests World Heritage Area and it's estimated that representatives of a quarter of all bird species in Australia can be found here.

The eastern section of the park can be explored on the 44km **Tweed Range Scenic Drive** (gravel, and usable in dry weather), which loops through the park from Lillian Rock (midway between Uki and Kyogle) to Wiangaree (north of Kyogle on Summerland Way). The signposting on access roads isn't good (when in doubt take roads signposted to the national park), but it's well worth the effort.

The road runs through mountain rainforest, with steep hills and lookouts over the Tweed Valley to Wollumbin (Mt Warning) and the coast. The short walk out to the **Pinnacle Lookout** is a highlight and one of the best places to see the silhouette of Wollumbin against a rising sun. At **Antarctic Beech** there is a forest of 2000-year-old beech trees. From here, a walking track (about 5km) leads down to lush rainforest, swimming holes and a picnic area at **Brindle Creek**.

Northwest of Uki, 41-sq-km **Wollumbin National Park** (www.nationalparks.nsw.gov.au/wollumbin-national-park) surrounds Wollumbin (Mt Warning; 1156m), the most dramatic feature of the hinterland, towering over the valley. Its English name was given to it by James Cook in 1770 to warn seafarers of offshore reefs. Its far older Aboriginal name, Wollumbin, means 'cloud catcher', 'fighting chief of the mountain' or 'weather maker'.

The summit is the first part of mainland Australia to see sunlight each day, a drawcard that encourages many to make the trek to the top. You should be aware that, under the law of the local Bundjalung people, only certain people are allowed to climb the sacred mountain; they ask you not to climb it, out of respect for this law. Instead, you can get an artist's impression of the view from the 360-degree mural at the **Murwillumbah Visitor Information Centre** (☑1800 118 295, 02-6672 1340; www.tweedtourism.com.au; 271 Tweed Valley Way; ☺9am-4.30pm).

Wollumbin is part of the Gondwana Rainforests World Heritage Area. Keep an eye out for the Albert's lyrebird on the Lyrebird Track (300m return).

serves up everything from a 'treehugger's salad' to curries and grilled barramundi. There's live music most weekends, and backpacker rooms upstairs.

ℹ Information

Nimbin Visitor Information Centre (☑02-6689 1388; www.visitnimbin.com.au; 46 Cullen St; ☺10am-4pm)

ℹ Getting There & Away

Various operators including **Gosel's** (p196), **Grasshoppers** (☑0438 269 076; www.grasshoppers.com.au) and **Waller's** (p196) offer day tours or shuttles to Nimbin from Byron Bay, sometimes including stops at surrounding sights. Most leave at 10am and return around 6pm.

Gosel's (☑ 02-6677 9394) Two buses on weekdays to Uki (40 minutes) and Murwillumbah (one hour).

Waller's (☑ 02-6622 6266; www.wallersbus. com) At least three buses on weekdays to/from Lismore (30 minutes).

CENTRAL & OUTBACK NSW

Trust us, there is life beyond Sydney and the NSW coast – and it's worthy of attention. Epicurean retreats like Mudgee and Orange send a siren call to city slickers, Broken Hill's mining heritage is rich and nation-defining, and national parks offer sand dunes, ancient rock art, wildlife-filled forests and glorious walking trails.

From the rolling green hills of New England to the red-dirt glow of the outback, there are some beautifully Australian moments to savour: stargazing into pristine skies, sharing a yarn with eccentrics in mining communities, marvelling over art in unlikely places. Festivals mark the region's calendars with excuses to party. Inland NSW is a rich slice of the nation that it's well worth getting to know.

ⓘ Getting There & Away

A vast network of highways criss-cross central and outback NSW, as well as a rail-and-bus network, operated by **NSW TrainLink** (☑ 13 22 32; www.nswtrainlink.info), that is sadly only half what it once was.

Qantas (QF; ☑ 13 13 13; www.qantas.com. au) operates domestic services from Sydney to Dubbo, Orange, Armidale and Tamworth.

Rex (☑ 13 17 13; www.rex.com.au) matches those routes with the exception of Tamworth, but adds Broken Hill into the mix.

New England

Verdant scenery prompted the first British settlers to name this area New England in 1839. In the northern 'highlands' especially, images of Britain still spring to mind, especially when mist settles in the cool-climate hilltops and fertile valleys, little churches sit in oak-studded paddocks and winding roads navigate impossibly green landscapes. Lest you're lulled into a false sense of rural genteelness, the cowboy flavour of Tamworth will set you straight.

Tamworth
POP 61,121

It's not quite the Wild West, but Tamworth sits in prime farming country and the town is not so much a regional centre as a holy land: a pilgrimage destination for many music-loving Australians. The religion is country music, the god Slim Dusty, and the holy grail is the world's biggest golden guitar. If you're in the market for bona fide Aussie cowboys and cowgirls, you've come to the right place.

◉ Sights

★**Tamworth Marsupial Park** PARK
(Endeavour Dr; ⊙8am-4.45pm; 🚼) FREE Over-friendly cockatoos, showy peacocks and a mob of native animals live here alongside a playground, barbecues and picnic shelters. There are lovely short walks to the neighbouring botanic gardens. Take Brisbane St east.

Oxley Scenic Lookout VIEWPOINT
(Scenic Rd; ⊙7am-10pm) FREE Follow Tamworth's jacaranda-lined White St to the very top, where you'll reach this viewpoint. It's the best seat in the house as the sun sets.

Big Golden Guitar MUSEUM
(☑02-6765 2688; www.biggoldenguitar.com.au; New England Hwy; ⊙9am-5pm; 🅿🚼) Behind the 12m-high golden guitar, this building is home to the Tamworth Visitor Information Centre (p198), a cafe, and a gift shop peddling local tunes and souvenirs. There's also the cheesy **Gallery of Stars Wax Museum** (adult/child $10/5) honouring Australian country-music legends. It's one for the true fans (or true fans of kitsch). It's on the southern stretch of the highway leading into town, about 5km from the city centre.

Country Music Hall of Fame MUSEUM
(☑02-6766 9696; www.countrymusichalloffame. com.au; cnr Peel & Murray Sts; adult/child $7/ free; 🅿🚼) At this museum, you can track Tamworth's musical heritage across two exhibitions: the memorabilia-filled Walk a Country Mile, and the Country Music Hall of Fame, both housed inside a building shaped like a guitar – do you spot a theme here...?

✦ Festivals & Events

★**Tamworth Country Music Festival** MUSIC
(www.tcmf.com.au; ⊙mid-Jan) Held over 10 rollicking days from mid-January, this festival is billed as the biggest music fes-

tival in the Southern Hemisphere. Recent stats show the festival featured more than 700 performers across 120 venues, with around 2800 single events entertaining some 55,000 visitors!! That's an awful lot of boot-scooting!

Many acts are free, otherwise most tickets range from $5 to $50 (see the festival website). The Festival Express bus ($5/20 for a day/entire festival) connects the various venues and most hotels.

Hats Off To Country   MUSIC

(◷Jul) If you missed the Tamworth Country Music Festival (p196), get along to this smaller version, with around 100 acts, held over four days in July.

🛏 Sleeping

Golf Links Motel   MOTEL **$**

(☑02-6762 0505; http://go.golflinksmotel.com. au; 260 Bridge St, West Tamworth; d from $110; [P][✳][🛜][🛝]) This neat and tidy motel has large, tidy, updated rooms, a convenient West Tamworth location, opposite the Tamworth Golf Club, a small pool and great rates: best in class.

Rex Tamworth   HOSTEL **$**

(☑02-6766 1030; www.rextamworth.com; 32 White St; d from $60; [P][🛜]) Tamworth's friendliest hostel, with a hotch-potch of colourful, quirky rooms that have eclectic cheapo and vintage furnishings, sits on a quiet, leafy street away from the main drag.

★CH on Peel   BOUTIQUE HOTEL **$$**

(☑02-6766 7260; www.chonpeel.com.au; cnr Peel & Brisbane Sts; d from $169; [P][@][🛜]) Tamworth's newest and swankiest digs occupy a delightful art deco building in the centre of town and are priced well for the quality of inclusions. Fresh, bright, rooms feature simple but stylish designer decor and downy pillow-top mattresses with quality linens. Dining downstairs is decent.

Quality Hotel Powerhouse   HOTEL **$$**

(☑02-6766 7000; www.powerhousetamworth. com.au; 248 Armidale Rd, East Tamworth; r/apt from $185/205; [P][✳][🛜][🛝]) Home to classy, well-equipped hotel rooms, suites and serviced apartments, and a host of on-site amenities, this smart motel is well suited to travelling solo professionals, with its quality business amenities, comfortable beds and good bathrooms, and families, who appreciate the extra space afforded by family rooms and apartments. It's adjacent to the

Powerhouse Motorcycle Museum (☑02-6766 7000; www.powerhousemotorcyclemuseum. com.au; 250 Armidale Rd, East Tamworth; adult/child $8/4; ◷9am-5pm; [P]).

Retreat at Frog-Moore Park   B&B **$$$**

(☑02-6766 3353; www.froogmoorepark.com.au; 78 Bligh St; r incl breakfast from $225; [🛜]) Five individually styled suites (with names like Moroccan Fantasy and The Dungeon) make this avant-garde B&B one of Tamworth's quirkier and more luxurious options. Rooms are large, the gardens are delightful, and the breakfasts might just be the best in town.

🍴 Eating

★Ruby's Cafe & Gift Store   CAFE **$**

(☑02-6766 9833; 494 Peel St; ◷8am-5pm Tue-Sat; [✳][🛜]) This fabulous, funky cafe with sprawling courtyard could be straight out of Melbourne's inner west, serving inner-city breakfast treats like Moroccan eggs, avocado smash and a particularly noteworthy take on the humble eggs benedict. Oh...and Melbourne-grade coffee.

★Pig and Tinder Box   MODERN AUSTRALIAN **$$**

(☑02-6766 1541; www.thepigandtinderbox.com.au; 429 Peel St; mains $12-28; [✳][🛜]) In the heart of Tamworth, 'the Pig' is the consistent go-to for tasty small plates, delicious wood-fired pizzas, killer cocktails and a bustling vibe.

Hopscotch   MODERN AUSTRALIAN **$$**

(☑02-6766 8422; www.hopscotchrestaurant.com. au; Bicentennial Park, cnr Kable Ave & Hill St; ◷7am-3pm Mon-Tue, to 10pm Wed & Thu, to midnight Fri & Sat, to 9pm Sun; [P][✳][🛜][♿]) Almost always open and just as frequently popular, the polished concrete floors amplify the din of the delighted diners in this modern parkside establishment in Tamworth, but there's no denying one of the better all-day breakfast menus for miles, which is why they keep on coming through the doors. It's a decent spot for a casual lunch, dinner and drinks as well.

Le Pruneau   FRENCH **$$**

(☑02-6765 3666; www.lepruneau.com.au; 83 Bridge St; lunch mains $10-22, dinner $32-36; ◷7.30am-10pm Tue-Sat, to 3pm Sun; [P][✳][🍴]) 🍴 This French-owned cottage-style cafe and restaurant in West Tamworth is worth seeking out for its creative, delicious cooking. There's a local **organic market** behind the cottage on Saturday mornings. Dinner bookings advised.

ℹ Information

Tamworth Visitor Information Centre (☑ 02-6767 5300; www.destinationtamworth.com.au; New England Hwy; ☺ 9am-5pm; 🛜) To get into the string of things, drop into this font of local knowledge on all things New England and country music, at the **Big Golden Guitar** (p196).

ℹ Getting There & Away

Tamworth is 115km southwest of Armidale on the New England Hwy, and 282km northwest of Newcastle.

Qantas (p196) has at least two flights a day between Tamworth and Sydney. New low-cost airline **Jetgo** (☑ 1300 328 000; www.jetgo.com) operates a direct, daily service to/from Brisbane.

Greyhound (☑ 1300 473 946; www.greyhound.com.au) has nightly bus services along the New England Hwy between Sydney and Brisbane – these stop at Tamworth, Armidale, Tenterfield and Toowoomba en route. Tamworth to Brisbane is 9½ hours ($128), to Sydney is 6½ hours ($78).

New England Coaches (☑ 02-6732 1051; www.newenglandcoaches.com.au) runs some useful services: Tamworth to Coffs Harbour (from $92) and Tamworth to Brisbane (from $117). Both services run three times a week.

NSW TrainLink (p196) runs a daily Xplorer rail service between Sydney and Tamworth (from $59, six hours) that continues on to Armidale.

Armidale

ELEV 980M / POP 23,674

Australia's highest city, situated atop the Northern Tablelands, is surrounded by some of Australia's best grazing country. With a wealth of attractive heritage buildings, gardens and moss-covered churches, Armidale looks like the stage set for a period drama.

It's a four-season town: summers are mild and clear, autumnal foliage is spectacular, crisp winters often see light snowfalls, and manicured gardens burst to life in an explosion of bright spring colours.

◉ Sights

Saumarez Homestead HISTORIC BUILDING
(☑ 02-6772 3616; www.nationaltrust.org.au/places/saumarez-homestead; 230 Saumarez Rd; adult/child $12/6; ☺ 10am-5pm; 🅿) Explore the lovely grounds and sumptuous rooms of this lavish Edwardian mansion built between 1888 and 1906, once the former residence of Armidale landowner Henry Dumaresq. Guided tours (10.30am, 2pm, 3.30pm Saturday and Sunday) are highly recommended.

**New England
Regional Art Museum** MUSEUM
(NERAM; ☑ 02-6772 5255; www.neram.com.au; 106-114 Kentucky St; ☺ 10am-4pm Tue-Sun; 🅿 ♿) **FREE** At the southern edge of Armidale, NERAM has a sizeable permanent collection and good contemporary exhibitions. The *Yellow Room Triptych* by Margaret Olley is a highlight.

**Aboriginal Cultural Centre
& Keeping Place** GALLERY
(☑ 02-6771 3606; www.acckp.com.au; 128 Kentucky St; ☺ 9am-4pm Mon-Fri, 10am-2pm Sat; 🅿 ♿) **FREE** Down the road from the New England Regional Art Museum, this cultural centre will broaden your perception of Indigenous art. There's a small sweet cafe here serving up some imaginative examples of bush tucker.

🍽 Sleeping & Eating

⭐**Lindsay House** B&B $$
(☑ 02-6771 4554; www.lindsayhouse.com.au; 128 Faulkner St; s/d from $140/190; 🛜) Immerse yourself in a time when beds were four-poster, ceilings were ornate, furniture was beautifully crafted and port was served in the evening. This lovely old home in Armidale is as restful and recuperative as it is grand.

Petersons Guesthouse GUESTHOUSE $$$
(☑ 02-6772 0422; www.petersonsguesthouse.com.au; Dangarsleigh Rd; r from $200; ❄🛜) Restored to its former opulence, this 1911 estate has seven large, characterful suites and magnificent grounds (popular for wedding parties), although the rooms could do with a refresh. Dining packages come highly recommended and can include cool-climate wine tastings and Sunday picnic lunches (call ahead for hours, as the estate is closed to visitors when functions are held).

⭐**Goldfish Bowl** BAKERY, CAFE $
(☑ 02-6771 5533; 160 Rusden St; lunch $8-20; ☺ 7am-4pm Mon-Fri, to 1pm Sat; ❄) First-rate coffee and delectable baked goods pulled from the wood-fired oven make this a worthy pit stop while in Armidale. Load up on pastries, sourdough bread or gourmet pizza for carb-loaded heaven.

Bistro on Cinders FUSION $$
(☑ 02-6772 4273; www.bistrooncinders.com; 14 Cinders Lane; mains $14-28; ☺ 11am-3pm Tue-Wed, 11am-3pm & 5-9pm Thu-Sat; 🅿❄🍽) Behind Armidale's post office is this cool,

contemporary, family-run bistro *à la mode* focused around a small courtyard. The ever-changing menu fuses a variety of Asian and Western styles to create inventive dishes like cauliflower and thyme butter soup, Moroccan spiced lamb pies and Thai calamari salad.

ⓘ Information

Armidale Visitor Information Centre (☑ 02-6770 3888; www.armidaletourism.com.au; 82 Marsh St; ☺ 9am-5pm; ☎) Runs tours and is the font of knowledge for all things Armidale.

ⓘ Getting There & Away

Armidale is approximately 485km north of Sydney via the Pacific Motorway and New England Hwy. It's also possible to take the Pacific Hwy to Coffs Harbour and then scoot inland for 190km along the wonderfully scenic Waterfall Way.

Qantas (p196) and **Rex** (p196) both fly the Sydney-to-Armidale route at least once per day.

Greyhound (☑ 1300 473 946; www.greyhound.com.au) has nightly services along the New England Hwy between Sydney and Brisbane – these stop at Tamworth, Armidale, Tenterfield and Toowoomba. Armidale to Sydney is eight hours ($116).

New England Coaches (☑ 02-6732 1051; www.newenglandcoaches.com.au) runs some useful services: Armidale to Coffs Harbour (from $72, 3 hrs); and Armidale to Brisbane (from $106, 9½ hours). Both services run three times a week.

NSW TrainLink (p196) operates daily direct Xplorer rail services from Sydney (from $66, eight hours).

Tenterfield

ELEV 850M / POP 3300

Loosely regarded as the birthplace of the Australian nation, it was at the Tenterfield School of Arts in 1889 that Sir Henry Parkes delivered the speech that led to the Federation of all Australian states in 1901. Its other claim to fame is that entertainer Peter Allen (the 'Boy from Oz'), was born here: golden oldies may remember his famous song 'Tenterfield Saddler'.

With its roost of charming heritage buildings, the sleepy, attractive town, atop the Northern Tablelands, serves as the regional hub for a smattering of villages surrounded by picturesque national parks. High altitude means cooler climes in summer, and occasional ground-snow accumulations of up to 30cm, in winter.

◉ Sights

Sir Henry Parkes Memorial School of Arts   HISTORIC BUILDING
(☑ 02-6736 6100; www.henryparkestenterfield.com; 201-205 Rouse St; ☺ 10am-4pm) Australian-history boffins will enjoy the museum (adult/child $5/2) in this beautifully restored old hall. It's notable as the place where Sir Henry Parkes, the 'Father of Federation', delivered the 1889 Tenterfield Oration, a speech proposing that the six separate British colonies in Australia should unite. Others may simply appreciate the library, cinema and cafe.

Bald Rock National Park   NATIONAL PARK
(☑ 02-6736 4298; www.nationalparks.nsw.gov.au; Naas Rd; per car per day $8; P ♿) About 35km northeast of Tenterfield (take Naas Rd, signposted 'Woodenbong' – really), you can hike to the top of Australia's largest exposed granite monolith (which looks like a stripy little Uluru). There are lovely walks in the area (including two routes up the rock for great views), plus picnic sites and a camping area (adult/child $10/5) near the base. Kangaroos and birdsong are highlights.

Richmond Range National Park   NATIONAL PARK
(Gorge Creek; P) **FREE** Off the beaten track, 117km east of Tenterfield, this 15,712-hectare park contains some of the best-preserved old-growth rainforest in NSW. It's part of a World Heritage–listed preserve showing off what this part of Australia looked like before settlement.

🛏 Sleeping & Eating

Tenterfield Lodge & Caravan Park   CARAVAN PARK $
(☑ 02-6736 1477; www.tenterfieldlodgecaravanpark.com.au; 2 Manners St; unpowered/powered sites $26/29, dm from $36, cabins from $70; P @) This friendly place has a range of accommodation from camp sites and on-site vans to small cabins. There's a picnic area and a neat little playground for kids.

★ **Commercial Boutique Hotel**   BOUTIQUE HOTEL $$
(☑ 02-6736 4870; www.thecommercialboutiquehotel.com; 288 Rouse St; r from $170; P ❋ ☎) A glorious 1940s art-deco pub has found a new lease of life, reinvented as a glamorous boutique hotel (with eight monochrome rooms). The dining area has had a makeover, too, and is now a handsome bar showcasing local wine and craft beers.

Tenterfield Gourmet Pizza PIZZA **$$**
(☑ 02-6736 5500; www.tenterfieldgourmetpizza. com; 236 Rouse St; pizza $13-23; ⊘ noon-2pm & 5-8.30pm; ❈ ☑) Tenterfield's only pizza joint just happens to be an excellent one. Fans of the genre will not be disappointed. Tasty homestyle pastas are also available.

❶ Information

Tenterfield Visitor Information Centre (☑ 02-6736 1082; www.tenterfieldtourism.com.au; 157 Rouse St; ⊘ 9.30am-5pm Mon-Sat, to 4pm Sun; ☎) Has helpful bushwalking guides and can assist with arranging tours to the many national parks dotted around the surrounding terrain.

❶ Getting There & Away

Tenterfield is somewhat inconveniently tucked away in the High Country near the Queensland border. It's 93km north of Glen Innes, in NSW, and 112km south of Warwick, in Queensland. Gone are the golden days of domestic rail, when Tenterfield was once a significant station on the line.

NSW TrainLink (p196) operates a daily bus to/from Armidale ($25, 2½ hours) which connects to the daily Xplorer train between Armidale and Sydney (from $66, eight hours).

New England Coaches (☑ 02-6372 1051; www.newenglandcoaches.com.au) operate a service three times a week to Armidale ($60, 2½ hours) and Brisbane ($80, 5½ hours).

Northern Rivers Buslines (☑ 02-6626 1499; www.nrbuslines.com.au) has three weekly buses to Lismore ($6, two hours), with connections to Byron Bay.

Buses depart and arrive from the Tenterfield Community Centre on Manners St.

NORTHERN NEW SOUTH WALES

People tend to race through northern NSW and its archetypal Australian landscape, possibly with Queensland beaches on their minds. If Queensland's not on the itinerary, chances are Lightning Ridge is. Like other mining communities, the town throws up as many characters as it does gems.

Coonabarabran

ELEV 505M / POP 3200

Coonabarabran ('Coona' to locals) is widely recognised as an ideal place for stargazing thanks to its pristine air, high altitude (505m) and low humidity. It's an old-fashioned, respectable sort of a country town, where people still have good manners and seem to respect and care for their environment.

Perhaps the best reason to visit is for the town's proximity to the extraordinary Warrumbungle National Park, which in 2016 was declared Australia's first Dark Sky Park. To find out what that means, check out: http://darksky.org/idsp.

◉ Sights

★ **Warrumbungle National Park** NATIONAL PARK
(☑ 02-6825 4364; www.nationalparks.nsw.gov.au/ visit-a-park/parks/Warrumbungle-National-Park; John Renshaw Pkwy; per car per day $8; ⊘ 24hr; ℗) Sitting 35km west of Coonabarabran, this 232-sq-km park has spectacular granite domes, ample bushwalking trails, plentiful wildlife and brilliant wildflower displays during spring. It's one of NSW's most beautiful parks, although a bushfire swept through in 2013; some areas will take years to fully recover.

Park fees are payable at the **Warrumbungle National Park NWPS Visitor Centre** (☑ 02-6825 4364; www.nationalparks.nsw.gov.au/ things-to-do/Visitor-centres/Warrumbungle-Visitor-Centre/visitor-info; off John Renshaw Parkway, Warrambungle National Park; ⊘ 9am-4pm; ☎); there are excellent camp sites nearby at Camp Blackman (adult/child from $6/3.50). Walking tracks include the peerless 12.5km Breadknife and Grand High Tops Walk.

Siding Spring Observatory OBSERVATORY
(☑ 02-6842 6211; www.sidingspringobservatory. com.au; Observatory Rd; adult/child $5.50/3.50; ⊘ 9.30am-4pm Mon-Fri, 10am-4pm Sat & Sun; ℗ ❸) Coonabarabran's skies are so clear, the Australian National University chose to set up this research facility some 27km west of the town, on the edge of Warrumbungle National Park. The site is home to telescopes belonging to national and international institutions and includes the 3.9m Anglo-Australian Telescope, the largest optical (visible light) telescope in Australia. There are no public stargazing facilities here, but there's a **visitor centre** where you can boggle your mind with solar-system facts and figures.

Milroy Observatory OBSERVATORY
(☑ 0428 288 244; www.milroyobservatory.com.au; Morrisseys Rd; adult/child $30/15; ⊘ tours 8.30pm in summer, 6pm & 8pm in Winter; ℗) Milroy Observatory offers the largest public-access telescope in the southern hemisphere (it's a 40-in device that sits on a hilltop about

10km outside Coona). They run regular 90-minute stargazing sessions. Bookings essential: see the homepage for full details.

🛏 Sleeping

All Travellers Motor Inn   MOTEL $
(✆ 02-6842 1133; www.alltravellers.com.au; Newell Hwy; r from $100; 🅿❄🐾🛜🏊) Coonabarabran's nicest motel has cool, double-brick retro rooms that have been consistently maintained and updated, as well as a lovely pool to cool off in during those hot summer days.

ℹ Information

Coonabarabran Visitor Information Centre
(✆1800 242 881; www.warrumbungleregion. com.au; Newell Hwy; ⊙9am-5pm; 🐾) As well as providing maps and information on the Warrumbungle National Park and surrounds, there's a small, free dinosaur museum and local art and history displays.

Lightning Ridge

POP 2492

This strikingly imaginative outback mining town (one of the world's few sources of valuable black opals) has real frontier spirit, and is home to eccentric artisans, true-blue bushies and a generally unconventional collective.

👁 Sights

★Chambers of the Black Hand   GALLERY
(✆02-6829 0221; www.chambersoftheblackhand. com.au; 3 Mile Rd, Yellow Car Door 5; adult/child $35/10; ⊙tours from 9.30am & 3pm Apr-Oct, 10.30am Nov-Mar; 🅿♿) This place is remarkable, and symbolises the crazy and creative sides of the Ridge. Artist and miner Ron Canlin has turned a 40ft-deep mining claim into a cavernous gallery of carvings and paintings: superheroes, celebrities, pharaohs, Buddhas, animals, you name it. Call to confirm tour times; courtesy-bus pickup from your accommodation is offered.

Opal Mine Adventure   MINE
(✆02-6829 0473; www.opalmineadventure.com. au; Lot 45, Angledool Rd via Gem St; adult/child $20/8; ⊙9am-5pm Apr-Oct, 8.30am-12.30pm Nov-Mar; 🅿♿) The most easily accessible mine experience in Lightning Ridge, in a former working mine, lets visitors get a feel for the type of cramped environment encountered by the average opal miner working underground. That said, the aver-

age miner wouldn't have to fossick past the ubiquitous gift shop and tourist hype, nor benefit from the user-friendly wide stairways and flood-lighting, as you will.

🏃 Activities

★Lightning Ridge Bore Baths   SWIMMING
(Pandora St; ⊙noon-10am) 🆓 Enjoy scenic vistas while soaking in these unique open-air baths. The hot (41.5°C), mineral-rich water is drawn from 1200m below ground. Sunrise or sunset here can be magnificent, and chatting with the locals is a treat. Note: it's usually closed for two hours a day, from 10am to noon, for cleaning. The water's high temperatures aren't suitable for small children.

🛏 Sleeping

★Opal Caravan Park   CARAVAN PARK $
(✆02-6829 1446; www.opalcaravanpark.com.au; 142 Pandora St; camp sites $27-45, cabins from $110; 🅿❄🛜🏊) This new, well-planned bushland park almost opposite the Lightning Ridge Bore Baths offers excellent modern facilities: self-contained cabins, a swimming pool, wi-fi, camp sites with en suite, and a camp kitchen with pizza oven. There's even a small area for fossicking. Go for the brand new Executive cabins, if available.

ℹ Information

Lightning Ridge Visitor Information Centre
(✆02-6829 1670; www.lightningridgeinfo.com. au; Morilla St; ⊙9am-5pm; 🐾)

CENTRAL NSW

Central NSW's relative proximity to Sydney and its bucolic landscapes have recently seen the region's agricultural communities gain popularity among weekenders, grey nomads on tour and city slickers seeking a tree-change. Getting here by road or rail, traversing the iconic Blue Mountains across the Great Dividing Range, is half the fun.

Both Orange and Mudgee are must-dos for foodies and winos alike, while travelling families love Dubbo, Parkes and Bathurst for their selection of kid-friendly museums and attractions.

Keep heading west and soon enough, things start drying up and the rich, red outback soil takes over.

Bathurst

ELEV 650M / POP 42,231

Bathurst is Australia's oldest inland settlement, boasting European trees, a cool climate and a beautiful, manicured central square where formidable Victorian buildings can snap you back to the past. And then, in a dramatic change of pace, it's also the bastion of Australian motor sport, hosting numerous events.

⊙ Sights

★ Australian Fossil & Mineral Museum
MUSEUM

(☑02-6331 5511; www.somervillecollection.com.au; 224 Howick St; adult/child $14/7; ⊙10am-4pm Mon-Sat, to 2pm Sun) Don't let the dry name fool you – this place is a treasure chest full of wonder. It's home to the internationally renowned Somerville Collection: rare fossils, plus gemstones and minerals in every colour of the rainbow (amethysts, diamonds, rubies, ancient insects frozen in amber). The museum also houses Australia's only complete *Tyrannosaurus rex* skeleton.

Mt Panorama
LANDMARK

(www.mount-panorama.com.au; Mountain Straight, Mt Panorama) FREE Rev-heads will enjoy the 6.2km **Mount Panorama Motor Racing Circuit**, venue for the epic Bathurst 1000 V8 race each October (which sees crowds of up to 200,000). It's a public road, so you can drive around the circuit – but only up to an unthrilling 60km/h. There's a lookout and racing-themed children's playground at the top.

All roads lead to the track, including southwest along William St.

Abercrombie House
HISTORIC BUILDING

(☑02-6331 4929; www.abercrombiehouse.com.au; 311 Ophir Rd; adult/child $15/10; ⊙10.30am-3pm Wed-Fri, until 4pm Sat & Sun Sep-Mar; ℗) This astonishing Tudor Gothic confection and 52-room mansion lies 7km northwest of Bathurst town centre. Admission to the heritage-listed private home is by self-guided tour. The house and gardens frequently hosts special events: check the website for hours and the event calendar.

National Motor Racing Museum
MUSEUM

(☑02-6332 1872; www.nmrm.com.au; 400 Panorama Ave; adult/child $15/7; ⊙9am-4.30pm) With a focus on the history of Mt Panorama and the Bathurst 1000, this museum at the base of Mt Panorama celebrates the achievements of

Australian motor racing and features plenty of souped-up hot rods to get you all revved up.

★☆ Festivals & Events

Bathurst 1000
SPORTS

(www.supercars.com/bathurst1000; Mt Panorama; ⊙early Oct) Over four days in October, petrol-heads throng to Bathurst for this 1000km touring-car race, considered the pinnacle of Australian motor sport.

⎚ Sleeping

Governor Macquarie Motor Inn
MOTEL $

(☑02-6331 2211; www.governormacquarie.com.au; 19 Charlotte St; r from $90; ℗❋☲) This smart, freshly refurbished motel boasts one of central Bathurst's quieter locations, set back from the busy main drag. King Executive suites, a free guest laundry and saltwater pool add value.

Rydges Mount Panorama
HOTEL $$

(☑02-6338 1888; www.rydges.com/bathurst; 1 Conrod Straight; r from $159; ☎☲) Boasting a trackside location at Mt Panorama, Rydges' 129 stylish studios and apartments sell out months in advance when the vroom-vrooms are in town: every room has a view over the racetrack. For the rest of the year, the location is blissfully quiet, although a little inconvenient.

✗ Eating & Drinking

Church Bar
PIZZA $$

(☑02-6334 2300; www.churchbar.com.au; 1 Ribbon Gang Lane; pizzas $17-25; ⊙noon-10pm Sun-Thu, to midnight Fri & Sat; ❋) This restored 1850s church now attracts punters praying to a different deity: the god of wood-fired pizza. The soaring ceilings and verdant courtyard off Bathurst's William St make it one of the town's best eating and socialising venues.

9inety 2wo
MODERN AUSTRALIAN $$$

(☑02-6332 1757; www.9inety2wo.com; 92 Bentinck St; mains $42; ⊙6-9pm Tue-Sat; ❋) The former Temperance Hall of Bathurst (1877) sets the stage for this smart dinner-only restaurant serving Modern Australian dishes influenced by global cuisine. Spatchcock, barramundi, lamb, duck and scallops all make an appearance.

Two Heads Brewing
CRAFT BEER

(☑02-6331 5369; www.twoheadsbrewing.com; 2a Piper St; ⊙5-10pm Wed, 11.30am-10pm Thu-Sat, to 4pm Sun; ☎) Lovers of craft beers will want to check out the local brews of this trendy

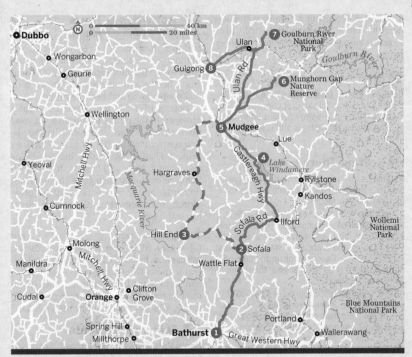

Driving Tour
Bathurst to Gulgong

START BATHURST
END GULGONG
LENGTH 265 KM (WITHOUT DETOUR)

The region north of Bathurst is good driving territory with beautiful scenery, parks and reserves and a handful of quaint little towns.

Follow the signs towards Lithgow from ❶ **Bathurst** city centre, then take the turn-off for Sofala. An easy drive through increasingly rolling country dips down into a valley 43km northeast of Bathurst. Just before crossing the bridge, detour along the charming, ramshackle main street of ❷ **Sofala**, a pretty hangover from the region's gold-mining days. If you've endless time, consider the long, partially unpaved 105km detour to Mudgee via ❸ **Hill End**, another old gold-mining village. Otherwise, from Sofala continue for 28km to Ilford where you join the main Lithgow–Mudgee road. As you head northwest, you'll pass pretty ❹ **Lake Windamere** before reaching ❺ **Mudgee**. Ignore the town's untidy outskirts and head for the centre, taking Church St which becomes Ulan Rd, which in turn heads northwest of town past some of the best wineries. Consider a detour to the ❻ **Munghorn Gap Nature Reserve**, where there's the popular 8km-return Castle Rock walking trail; the reserve is home to the endangered bird, the regent honeyeater.

Back on the main Ulan road, around 29km after leaving Mudgee, ignore for now the turn-off for Gulgong, and do the same for the national park another 3km on. Pass the scarred landscape of an open-cut mine for 10km, then take the turn-off for 'The Drip' in ❼ **Goulburn River National Park**. This 3km-return walk along a narrow river valley is one of the prettier short walks in regional New South Wales. The trail begins at the car park around 200m down off the road, next to a popular swimming hole, and passes between a steepish escarpment and the riverbank; there are some Aboriginal rock paintings on the overhanging rocks across the creek around halfway along. Watch also for wallabies, kangaroos and wombats.

Return to your car and to Ulan, then follow the signs for historic ❽ **Gulgong**, which lies 24km away through dense, fire-scarred forest.

brewhouse occupying a former warehouse near the station. It's an equally worthy place to grab a casual bite from the gourmet beer-paired menus.

ℹ️ Information

Bathurst Visitor Information Centre (📞 02-6332 1444; www.visitbathurst.com.au; 1 Kendall Ave; ⏰ 9am-5pm) Provides information about wineries, hiking trails and scenic drives in the region.

ℹ️ Getting There & Away

Bathurst is just over 200km from Sydney on the Great Western Hwy. The route crosses the picturesque Blue Mountains.

Australia Wide Coaches (📞 02-6362 7963; www.austwidecoaches.com.au; ⏰ phone reservations 6am-7pm) run a daily express service between Sydney and Orange that stops in Bathurst ($40, 3½ hours). Coaches pick up and drop off at the Bathurst Bus Interchange at the corner of William and Howick Sts.

NSW Trainlink (p196) operates a daily XPT rail service from Sydney (from $32, 3½ hours) and at least four daily coach services from Lithgow ($8.80, one hour) to Bathurst Station.

Orange

ELEV 863M / POP 40,075

Orange might just be the prettiest regional centre in NSW. It has fine heritage architecture, a mild, high-elevation climate and just enough going on to make it a great place to visit, or live. Now a city, Orange has become a convivial, fast-growing regional centre with a booming food-and-wine scene.

◎ Sights

★ Mt Canobolas   NATURE RESERVE
(🅿️ 🚻) Southwest of Orange, this conservation area encompasses waterfalls, views, walking trails and bike paths. Swimmer-friendly **Lake Canobolas** is a great place to start with plenty of picnic areas and a lakeside children's playground – the turn-off to the lake is on the extension of Coronation Rd, 8km west of town.

Orange Regional Museum   MUSEUM
(📞 02-6393 8444; www.orangemuseum.com.au; 151 Byng St; ⏰ 9am-5pm; 👶) **FREE** This fabulous free museum – in a brand new architecturally designed building with a sloping grass roof – is the city's cultural pride and joy, with permanent exhibits on local history, as well as visiting exhibitions.

🏃 Activities & Tours

Orange is a delicious destination for wine-and-food tourism. The region has a reputation for distinctive cool-climate wines (see www.winesoforange.com.au). Orchard fruits, berries and nuts are also grown here, and quality lamb and beef are raised.

Dozens of cellar doors and farm gates are open to the public in this area – a good place to begin your exploration is the visitor centre. Pick up the *Orange & District Wine & Food Guide*, with a map outlining six routes in town and beyond. It also highlights cellar doors, farm gates (berry farms, orchards) and local-produce outlets (providores, microbrewers), plus picnic areas along the way.

Orange Wine Tours   WINE
(📞 02-5310 6818; www.orangewinetours.com.au; half-day tours from $85) This popular local operator knows Orange's myriad of cellar doors and farm gates better than anyone. If you can't be fussed with all the driving and navigating, why not leave it to the professionals?

🎊 Festivals & Events

Banjo Patterson Poetry Festival   LITERATURE
(www.brandorange.com.au/orange-nsw/banjo-paterson-festival; ⏰ end Feb) This festival celebrates the works of Banjo Patterson, one of Australia's best-known bush poets, famous for his iconic 'The Man from Snowy River' (first published in 1890). You'll find readings, competitions and various literary events held throughout Orange.

Orange Wine Festival   WINE
(http://brandorange.com.au; ⏰ Oct) This popular boozy festival celebrating the region's excellent vineyards is held each October.

F.O.O.D Week   FOOD
(Food of Orange District; www.orangefoodweek.com.au; ⏰ late Mar–mid-Apr) Book your accommodation in advance if you plan to visit for this foodie fest highlighting local produce.

🛏️ Sleeping

Duntryleague   GUESTHOUSE $
(📞 02-6362 3466; www.duntryleague.com.au; Woodward St; d from $125; 🅿️ 📶) Orange's most stunning heritage building (built in 1876), is home to a 14-room guesthouse, function centre and golf course. Rooms have been modernised but retain their period charm, with continual upgrades taking place. It's

worth popping by just to see this beautiful building.

★ **de Russie Boutique Hotel** BOUTIQUE HOTEL **$$**

(☑ 02-6360 0973; www.derussiehotels.com.au; 72 Hill St; d from $175; ✱ ☎ ☎) As good as anything in Sydney, this little slice of hotel heaven in Orange has boutique written all over it. It has luxe mod cons, including kitchenettes in every studio (a hamper of breakfast supplies is included).

Arancia B&B B&B **$$$**

(☑ 02-6365 3305; www.arancia.com.au; 69 Wrights Lane, Nashdale; s/d from $180/250; ✱ ☎) Set in rolling green hills, this Orange B&B has hotel-worthy facilities on a smaller scale: five spacious rooms with big beds, en suites and classy furnishings. Breakfasts here are renowned. It's adults only, with a two-night minimum on weekends. Packages are available.

✖ Eating & Drinking

Bodhi Garden VEGETARIAN **$**

(☑ 02-6360 4478; www.bodhigardenvegetarian. com.au; 341 Summer St; meals $7-19; ☉ 11.30-2pm & 5.30-9pm Mon-Sat; ✱ ☑) This popular Asian-style vegetarian restaurant has a huge menu that is sure to tempt even the hardiest of carnivores, with lots of 'not-meat' products like soy fish, crispy nuggets and gluten slices. Of course there's plenty of plain and simple tofu, veggies and noodles on offer as well.

★ **Agrestic Grocer** CAFE **$$**

(☑ 02-6360 4604; www.facebook.com/theagrestic grocer; 426 Molong Rd; lunch $16-28; ☉ 8.30am-5.30pm Mon-Fri, to 4pm Sat & Sun; ✱ ☎) 'This is what happens when shopkeepers and farmers unite,' says the flyer. The results are pretty wonderful. This rustic cafe-grocer celebrates local produce a few kilometres north of town on the Mitchell Hwy (known as Molong Rd at this point). Breakfast on house-made crumpets, lunch on Italian panzanella salad or Korean barbecue burger. It's all delicious.

★ **Lolli Redini** MODERN AUSTRALIAN **$$$**

(☑ 02-6361 7748; www.lolliredini.com.au; 48 Sale St; 2/3 courses $70/90; ☉ 6-9pm Tue-Sat & noon-2pm Sat; ✱ ☑) See Orange's finest produce wrapped in all its glory at this much-lauded restaurant (bookings essential). The matching of food with wines is well-thought-out,

the setting and service are exemplary, and the kitchen creations (including many for vegetarians) sing with flavour.

Eighteen 70 MODERN AUSTRALIAN **$$$**

(☑ 02-6361 9020; www.eighteen70.com.au; 85 March St; set lunches $20, dinner mains $34-40; ☉ noon-2pm & 6-9pm Tue-Fri, 6-9pm Sat & Mon; ✱ ☎) Housed in an elegant restored cottage and garden, this fabulous modern Australian restaurant is one for the romantics, with white starched tablecloths, dim lighting and beautifully prepared cuisine, perfect for date night in Orange. It's famous for a unique dessert: the sweet burger, featuring a jam bun, coconut, chocolate ice cream, banana marshmallow and berry jelly. It actually works!

★ **Ferment** WINE BAR

(☑ 02-6360 4833; www.orangewinecentre.com.au; 87 Hill St; ☉ 11am-7pm) Inside a gorgeous heritage building, Ferment shines a spotlight on local wines (it's the cellar door for a handful of small producers around Orange). You can talk wine, graze on platters or just admire the stylish fit-out. Ferment's clever offer: half-day bike hire and lunchtime picnic for two for $55.

ⓘ Information

Orange Visitor Information Centre (☑ 02-6393 8226; www.visitorange.com.au; 151 Byng St; ☉ 9am-5pm) One of NSW's top visitor centres, located inside the iconic building housing the Orange Regional Museum, is a font of information on all things Orange – and a decent chunk of the rest of NSW. Its friendly, exceptionally helpful staff will have no trouble answering any query you can throw about their town.

ⓘ Getting There & Away

Located on the Mitchell Highway, 54km west of Bathurst and 257km west of Sydney, Orange is well connected to the outside world by road, rail and air.

Qantas (p196) and Rex (p196) operate daily flights to/from Sydney.

NSW TrainLink (p196) has two direct daily rail services from Orange station to Sydney (from $37, 4¾ hours) as well as at least four coach services per day to Lithgow ($18.50, 1¾ hours) where you can connect to regular interurban trains to Sydney.

Also departing from Orange station, **Australia Wide Coaches** (☑ 02-6362 7963; www.aust widecoaches.com.au; 12 Ash St; ☉ 9am-4pm) have one bus a day to Sydney ($40, four hours), via Bathurst.

Millthorpe

ELEV 960M / POP 1109

Only 20 minutes from Orange, the pioneering village of Millthorpe, with its heritage architecture, is a little slice of the mid-1800s. Its cuteness is such that the National Trust has classified the whole place. It's a quieter alternative to staying in Orange, although the town comes alive with weekenders and Sunday drivers.

For more information, check out www.millthorpevillage.com.au.

◉ Sights

Golden Memories
Millthorpe Museum   MUSEUM
(✆ 02-6366 3980; www.millthorpemuseum.com; 37 Park St; $8; ⊙10am-4pm Mon-Fri; ⊞) This wonderful rural museum has eight buildings housing a diverse collection of artefacts on a range of themes from local and Aboriginal history, farming and Australian inventions. Allow about two hours to get around.

⊨ Sleeping

Millthorpe Bed & Breakfast   B&B $$
(✆ 02-6366 3967; www.millthorpebedandbreakfast.com.au; 11 Morley St; r from $175; ⊞) For a touch of the modern in rustic Millthorpe, this compact B&B at the edge of town has three hotel-standard rooms with crisp, minimalist decor and luxury touches like a heated floor and fine linens. There's a two-night minimum stay on weekends.

Hockeys   COTTAGE $$$
(✆ 0421 121 937; www.hockeysaccommodation.com.au; 28 Park St; r $260-300; P⊞⊞) Perfect for those seeking a little privacy and perhaps a dash of romance, this popular, beautifully restored and updated self-contained accommodation in the old Millthorpe Chemist building, boasts all the comforts of home and then some – like a jetted tub, luxurious linens and underfloor heating.

✗ Eating

★ Tonic   MODERN AUSTRALIAN $$
(✆ 02-6366 3811; www.tonicmillthorpe.com.au; cnr Pym & Victoria Sts; 2/3 courses $65/75; ⊙dinner Thu-Sat, brunch & lunch Sat & Sun; ⊞⊠) Classy Tonic is highly lauded for its sophisticated contemporary food that celebrates the region. Perhaps you'll start with roasted quail, followed by the Cowra lamb rack with roasted tomato tortellini? Be sure to save room for drool-worthy original desserts the likes of warm rhubarb-and-ginger minestrone! Book ahead.

Old Mill Cafe   CAFE $$
(✆ 02-6366 3188; www.theoldmillcafe.com.au; 12 Pym St; mains $15-20; ⊙9am-4pm Thu-Mon; ⊞⊞) Coffee and cakes in a designer-rustic setting is the staple here. Lunchtime deliciousness comes in the form of beef-and-shiraz pies, or flathead fillets with hand-cut chips. Save room for dessert – the lemon meringue tarts are worth travelling for.

Cork & Fork   MODERN AUSTRALIAN $$
(✆ 02-6366 3999; www.commercialhotelmillthorpe.com.au; 29 Park St; mains $20-32; ⊙noon-2.30pm & 5-9pm Wed-Sat, noon-2.30pm Sun; ⊞) This bistro in the gorgeous Commercial Hotel has fabulous pub food, fireplaces, local wines and not a TV or poker machine in sight.

ⓘ Getting There & Away

Orange Buslines (✆ 02-6362 3197; www.buslinesgroup.com.au/orange; 120 Canobolas Rd) operate regular scheduled services from Orange to Millthorpe ($6, 30 minutes). Take the 530 bus towards Bathurst.

Cowra

POP 9730

Lovely little Cowra is synonymous with being the site of the only land battle fought on Australian soil during WWII, when, in August 1944, more than 1000 Japanese prisoners attempted to break out of a prisoner-of-war camp here. During the surprise attack, 231 Japanese were killed or committed ritual suicide; four Australians were also killed.

Cowra has since aligned itself with Japan and the causes of reconciliation and world peace, and there are some poignant and worthwhile sites here to explore. An overnight visit is recommended.

◉ Sights

★ Japanese Garden   GARDENS
(✆ 02-6341 2233; www.cowragarden.com.au; Ken Nakajima Pl; adult/child $15/8; ⊙8.30am-5pm; P) Built as a token of Cowra's connection with Japanese POWs (but with no overt mention of the war or the breakout), this tranquil 5-hectare garden and attached cultural centre are superbly presented and well worth visiting (albeit with a steep entry fee). Audio guides ($2) explain the plants, history and design of the garden.

You can buy food for the koi (carp), or feed yourself at the on-site cafe (which serves mostly Australian fare, with a small nod to Japanese cuisine).

POW Campsite & Guard Tower MEMORIAL

(Evans St) FREE From the war cemeteries on Doncaster Road north of Cowra, signs lead to the site of the Japanese breakout. A voice-over from the watchtower recounts the story. You can still see the camp foundations, and info panels explain the military and migrant camps of wartime Cowra.

✤ Festivals & Events

Sakura Matsuri CULTURAL

(Cherry Blossom Festival) Cowra's pretty and hugely popular *sakura matsuri* is held over a week in late September, with Japanese food, culture and thousands of delicate pink cherry blossoms on show.

⌂ Sleeping

Cowra Crest Motel MOTEL $

(✏02-6342 2799; www.cowracrestmotel.com.au; 133 Kendal St; r from $120; P✷☎) Tucked away off Cowra's main drag, this spotlessly clean, solid-brick motel has tastefully and recently refurbished rooms and an excellent location near a supermarket.

Cowra Services Club Motel MOTEL $$

(✏02-6341 1999; www.cowraservicesclubmotel.com.au; 105/111 Brisbane St; r from $130; P✷☎) New in 2015, Cowra's fanciest digs are light-filled, airy and adjacent to 'the Club'. Suitable for the more discerning road-tripper, perky rooms are tastefully furnished in neutral tones with bright accents and shiny, large, flat-screen TVs.

✖ Eating & Drinking

The Quarry Restaurant & Cellar Door MODERN AUSTRALIAN $$

(✏02-6342 3650; www.thequarryrestaurant.com.au; 7191 Boorowa Rd; lunch mains $22-33, dinner mains $34; ⊙noon-2.30pm Thu-Sun, 6.30-10pm Fri & Sat; P✷) Four kilometres out of Cowra, the Quarry restaurant is handsomely set amid the vineyards, and the kitchen output wins regular praise (especially the puddings!). There's a sizeable wine list, too – the Quarry is the cellar door for a number of local vineyards.

Oxley Wine Bar WINE BAR

(✏02-6341 4100; http://theoxley.com.au; 9-11 Kendal St; ⊙noon-9pm Wed-Thu, 8am-midnight Fri & Sat, 8am-3pm Sun) The Oxley is where the good stuff happens in Cowra: live music on Friday nights, Saturday DJs and retro stylings to accompany your craft beers, local wines and pizzas.

ℹ Information

Cowra Visitor Information Centre (✏02-6342 4333; www.cowratourism.com.au; Olympic Park, Mid Western Hwy; ⊙9am-5pm) Be sure to come here to check out the excellent nine-minute holographic film about the Cowra Breakout and get the latest local news from the friendly staff.

ℹ Getting There & Away

Cowra is 108km southwest of Bathurst along the Mid Western Hwy.

NSW TrainLink (p196) operates daily bus services from Cowra to Orange (from $13, 1½ hours) onwards to Bathurst ($20, 1¾ hours), where you can connect to Sydney-bound trains (from $32, 3½ hours).

Dubbo

POP 36,941

An important rural centre on the north-south Newell Highway, what Dubbo lacks in visual charm, it makes up for in a variety of interesting, kid-friendly, educational and cultural attractions. Parents will appreciate the area's vineyards and an up-and-coming dining scene.

◉ Sights

★ Taronga Western Plains Zoo ZOO

(✏02-6881 1400; www.taronga.org.au; Obley Rd; 2-day passes adult/child $47/26; ⊙9am-4pm) This is Dubbo's star attraction, not to mention one of the best zoos in regional Australia. You can walk the 6km circuit, ride a hire bike ($15) or drive your car, getting out at enclosures along the way. Guided walks (adult/child $15/7.50) start at 6.45am on weekends (additional days in school holidays). Book ahead for special animal encounters or the glorious accommodation packages – spend a night at a bush camp, in family-sized cabins, or in safari-style lodges, overlooking savannah. See website for details.

Dubbo Regional Botanic Garden GARDENS

(✏02-6801 4000; www.drbg.com.au; Coronation Drive, East Dubbo; ⊙9am-4pm Mon-Fri, 9.30am-4.30pm Sat & Sun) FREE This beautiful and educational botanical garden is divided into four parts: the stunning Shoyoen Japanese

Garden, the Sensory Gardens, Biodiversity Garden and the Oasis Valley, offering a real glimpse of botanical diversity thriving on the fringe of the Australian outback. Best of all, admission is free!

Old Dubbo Gaol   MUSEUM
(☑ 02-6801 4460; www.olddubbogaol.com.au; 90 Macquarie St; adult/child $17.50/5.50; ⊙ 9am-4pm) This is a museum where 'animatronic' characters tell their prison stories. There are also characters in costume and guided tours on weekends (daily in school holidays); twilight tours are possible, too. Creepy but authentic.

RFDS Visitor Centre   MUSEUM
(☑ 02-6841 2555; Dubbo City Regional Airport, Cooreena Rd; adult/child $4/2; ⊙ 1-4pm Tue-Sat) Come to learn about Australia's unique and essential Royal Flying Doctor Service (RFDS), by way of a short documentary, historical memorabilia and a tour of parts of the base. There's even a flight simulator you can try (when it's not in official use).

🛌 Sleeping

Akuna Motor Inn & Apartments   MOTEL $
(☑ 02-6885 4422; www.akunamotorinn.com.au; 109 Whylandra St; r from $139; P 🛜 🌊) This spotless, pleasantly refurbished, centrally located motel is a great choice for travelling families who can spread out in its selection of family rooms and newly built apartments. Kids love the pool, while adults enjoy added extras like jetted tubs (in some rooms), free Foxtel TV and drive-up access.

★ Best Western Bluegum   MOTEL $$
(☑ 02-6882 0900; www.bluegummotorinn.com; 109 Cobra St; r from $169; P 🛜 🌊) Boasting a central location, set back from the Mitchell Hwy, across from a park, and fresh from a top-notch renovation, this excellent motel hasn't cut corners. Choose from seven room types ranging from standard to executive and family rooms: all feature 50-inch smart TVs with Foxtel, pillow-top mattresses, whisper-quiet air-conditioners, quality linen and excellent high-speed wi-fi.

Westbury Guesthouse   GUESTHOUSE $$
(☑ 02-6881 6105; www.westburydubbo.com.au; cnr Brisbane & Wingewarra Sts; s/d from $130/160; ❄ 🛜) This lovely old heritage home (1915) has six spacious, en-suite rooms furnished in period style with mod-cons like flat-screen TVs, bar fridges, DVD players and reverse-cycle air-conditioning.

Breakfast is served in the attached restaurant, which serves spicy, aromatic Thai cuisine by night.

🍴 Eating & Drinking

CSC Restaurant
and Bar   MODERN AUSTRALIAN $
(☑ 02-6884 0790; www.cscdubbo.com.au; 15 Church St; breakfast $6-16, tapas $12-24; ⊙ 7am-10pm Wed-Sat, 8am-12pm Sun, 7am-5pm Mon & Tue; ❄ 🛜 🍴) Using fresh, seasonal ingredients, this smart and funky former cafe has expanded its premises and menu to meet demand and offer an evening dinner service and fully stocked bar. Excellent breakfasts, light lunches and evening pizza and tapas come highly recommended.

Two Doors Tapas & Wine Bar   WINE BAR $$
(☑ 02-6885 2333; www.twodoors.com.au; 215 Macquarie St; dishes $8-24; ⊙ 4pm-late Tue-Fri, from 10am Sat; ❄) Dine in style in cool, subterranean sandstone rooms or have a drink in the leafy courtyard with Dubbo's handful of hipsters as they dream of Portland and Paris, while munching on tasty *arancini*, soft-shell crab and *patatas bravas*.

Old Bank   BAR
(☑ 02-6884 7728; www.oldbankdubbo.com; 232 Macquarie St; ⊙ noon-midnight Mon-Sat) Occupying the former Bank of NSW building (1876), this bar-restaurant is ineffably stylish and a cut above the rest of Dubbo's offerings, with plenty of nooks and crannies in which to wine and/or dine.

ℹ Information

Dubbo Visitor Information Centre (☑ 02-6801 4450; www.dubbo.com.au; cnr Macquarie St & Newell Hwy; ⊙ 9am-5pm)

ℹ Getting There & Away

Dubbo City Regional Airport (☑ 02-6801 4560; www.dubboairport.com; Cooreena Rd) has daily direct flights to Sydney with Qantas (p196) and Rex (p196), the latter also offering less-frequent services to Broken Hill.

NSW TrainLink (p196) operates one daily XPT train service between Dubbo and Sydney (from $45, 6½ hours).

By road, the city is a regional hub for transport, with these major highways meeting here:
➡ A32 Mitchell Hwy between Sydney and Adelaide
➡ A39 Newell Hwy between Melbourne and Brisbane
➡ B84 Golden Hwy from Newcastle.

WORTH A TRIP

PARKES

The sleepy inland rural town of Parkes has two wildly different claims to fame.

The **CSIRO Parkes Observatory** (☑02-6861 1777; www.csiro.au/parkes; 585 Telescope Rd; ☺visitor centre 8.30am-4.15pm) FREE is a massive radio telescope (about 20km north of Parkes) that was glorified on film in *The Dish* (2000). The complex includes a visitor centre with space info, a 3D theatre (adult/child $7.50/6) and oodles of information on radio astronomy.

Secondly, hundreds of Elvis impersonators descend in January for one of the most unique, baffling and, some would say, fun, festivals in the land. The **Parkes Elvis Festival** (www.parkeselvisfestival.com.au; ☺Jan) celebrates the King's birthday with five days of mania.

Parkes is located on the Newell Hwy, 124km south of Dubbo and 33km north of Forbes. Trains run from Sydney to Parkes (from $52, 6½ hours) and there are two daily buses from Orange ($14, 2½ hours).

Mudgee

POP 9830

Situated in the fertile Cudgegong Valley, Mudgee is a handsome town with wide streets, fine old homes and historic buildings, surrounded by vineyards and rolling hills. It takes its name from the Indigenous Wiradjuri word 'moothi', meaning 'nest in the hills'.

The wineries come hand-in-hand with excellent food and plenty of decent accommodation, making Mudgee a stellar weekend getaway. It's just under four hours' drive from Sydney, each way, so you might want to take an extra day.

◉ Sights

★**Lowe Vineyard**   WINERY
(☑03-6372 0800; www.lowewine.com.au; Tinja Lane; ☺10am-5pm; P) You can follow a walking and cycling trail through the orchards and vines of this idyllic organic farm, past donkeys and chickens to picnic grounds. The cellar door has tastings and a superb grazing platter ($30) of local flavours, and Zin House (p210) is on the grounds. Check the website for events, too.

Robert Stein Winery & Vineyard   WINERY
(☑02-6373 3991; www.robertstein.com.au; Pipeclay Lane; ☺10am-4.30pm; P) The small, rustic cellar door of this established vineyard has an eclectic and interesting range of wines to sample, including a sparkling shiraz and a semillon liqueur. There's also a quaint vintage motorcycle museum (free) and an excellent paddock-to-plate restaurant, Pipeclay Pumphouse (p210).

Burnbrae Winery   WINERY
(☑02-6373 3504; www.burnbraewines.com.au; 548 Hill End Rd; ☺10am-4pm; P) Established in 1968, this multi-award-winning winery has a historic winemaker's cottage where you can spend an evening (from $200 per night); but you'll likely be here to sample its wide variety of *cuvées* from the cellar door, which also prepares fabulous antipasto boards for you to sample under the winery's wise old peppercorn tree.

⛟ Tours

Mudgee Wine & Country Tours   TOURS
(☑02-6372 2367; www.mudgeewinetours.com.au; half-/full-day wine tours $50/80) This local operator has been running cellar-door and sightseeing tours in the area for over 15 years. Better known wineries like **di Lusso Estate** (☑02-6373 3125; www.dilusso.com.au; 162 Eurunderee Lane; ☺cellar door 10am-5pm Mon-Sat, to 4pm Sun; trattoria 12-3pm; P) and **Pieter van Gent** (☑02-6373 3030; www.pvgwinery.com. au; 141 Black Springs Rd; ☺9am-5pm Mon-Sat, 10.30am-4pm Sun; P) as well as lesser-known vineyards are frequently visited, though custom tours are also available.

🎉 Festivals & Events

Mudgee Wine Festival   FOOD & DRINK
(www.mudgeewine.com.au; ☺Sep) This popular festival celebrating the region's 35 wineries, local farms and paddock-to-plate restaurants runs through the month of September and features live music, cellar-door events, tastings and special lunches and dinners. Check the website for full details and book accommodation well in advance.

🛏 Sleeping

Comfort Inn Aden
MOTEL $

(☑ 02-6372 1122; adenmudgee.com.au; 1 Sydney Rd; r from $120; P 🗱 🛜 🌊) Choose from ultramodern rooms that have recently been completely renovated in a clean, minimalist style with colourful accents (from $140), and cheaper standard rooms ($120) that have been updated but retain some older motel-style furnishings. Enjoy free wi-fi and Foxtel throughout. There's even a gym and pool.

★ Perry Street Hotel
BOUTIQUE HOTEL $$

(☑ 02-6372 7650; www.perrystreethotel.com.au; cnr Perry & Gladstone Sts; ste from $175; 🗱 🛜) Stunning apartment suites make a sophisticated choice in town. The attention to detail is outstanding, right down to the kimono bathrobes, Nespresso machine and free gourmet snacks.

Wildwood Guesthouse
GUESTHOUSE $$

(☑ 02-6373 3701; www.wildwoodmudgee.com. au; Henry Lawson Dr; r incl breakfast from $210; P 🗱 🛜) This rustic homestead has four comfortable bedrooms, individually styled with big downy beds, fine linens and an eclectic mix of antiques. Each opens out onto the wrap-around verandah overlooking the tranquil countryside.

Mudgee Homestead Guesthouse
GUESTHOUSE $$$

(☑ 02-6373 3786; www.mudgeehomestead.com. au; 3 Coorumbene Court; s/d incl breakfast from $210/240, cottages from $340; P 🗱 🛜) Set amid 40 acres replete with resident kangaroos, just five minutes from town, this classic country homestead boasts sweeping rural views from its big, country-style rooms that don't skimp on comforts, with luxurious bedding, attractive antiques and fabulous bathrooms. There's a two-night minimum stay on weekends, but packages generally include fine dinners.

There's a fully self-contained cottage suitable for families, but the main house is adults only. Book ahead.

🍴 Eating

Butcher Shop Café
CAFE $

(☑ 02-6372 7373; 49 Church St; mains $11-19; ⏰ 8am-5pm Mon-Fri, to 4pm Sat & Sun; 🗱 🛜) A hip eatery in an old butchery, with stained glass, vintage decor and contemporary artwork on the walls. The delicious fare is understated and includes salads and gourmet burgers, and the coffee is roasted in-house.

★ Alby & Esthers
CAFE $$

(☑ 02-6372 1555; www.albyandesthers.com.au; 61 Market St; mains $12-22; ⏰ 8am-5pm Mon-Thu, to late Fri & Sat; 🗱) Down an alleyway is this supremely pretty courtyard cafe, serving up fine local produce and good coffee. It morphs into a wine bar on Friday and Saturday nights.

★ Pipeclay Pumphouse
MODERN AUSTRALIAN $$$

(☑ 02-6373 3998; www.pipeclaypumphouse.com. au; 1 Pipeclay Lane; lunch $10-25, dinner 2/3 courses $55/70; ⏰ noon-3pm & 6-9pm Thu-Fri, 8.30am-3pm & 6-9pm Sat-Sun; P 🗱) On the grounds of the Robert Stein Winery (p209), this farm-to-table (paddock-to-plate) stunner is the talk of Mudgee, serving to-die-for weekend breakfasts, light lunches as well as two-to-three-course and degustation dinners. Dinner bookings essential.

★ Zin House
MODERN AUSTRALIAN $$$

(☑ 02-6372 1660; www.zinhouse.com.au; 329 Tinja Lane; 5-course set menus from $85; ⏰ noon-3pm & 5-10pm Fri-Sat, noon-3pm Mon; P 🗱) 🍃 The glorious Lowe Vineyard (p209) is home to this weekend highlight: long, leisurely six-course lunches of simply prepared local produce (either home-grown, or impeccably sourced). Diners share farmhouse tables in a beautifully designed home. Gather your friends, book ahead.

🍷 Drinking & Nightlife

★ Roth's
WINE BAR

(☑ 02-6372 1222; www.rothswinebar.com.au; 30 Market St; ⏰ 5pm-midnight Wed-Sat) The oldest wine bar in NSW (built in 1923) sits behind a small heritage facade, and serves up great local wines (by the glass from $6), fine bar food and excellent live music. Bliss.

Mudgee Brewing Company
MICROBREWERY

(☑ 02-6372 6726; www.mudgeebrewery.com.au; 4 Church St; ⏰ 8am-5.30pm Mon-Wed, to 10pm Thu-Sun; 🛜) In addition to fine meals throughout the day, this airy space hosts live music on Thursday and Friday nights, and Sunday afternoons (from 4.30pm). Signature beers on tap include Mudgee Mud imperial stout and Mudgee Pale Ale.

ℹ Information

Mudgee Visitor Information Centre (☑ 02-6372 1020; www.visitmudgeeregion.com.au; 84 Market St; ⏰ 9am-5pm; 🛜) The visitor centre, near the post office, can help with wine-tasting jaunts.

ℹ Getting There & Away

Mudgee is 128km north of Lithgow along the Castlereagh Hwy. From Sydney, it's a pretty drive through the Blue Mountains and over the Great Dividing Range.

NSW TrainLink (p196) operates one morning and one afternoon bus service from the former Mudgee train station to Lithgow train station ($26.50, 2¼ hours), where you can connect to regular scheduled trains to Sydney.

OUTBACK NSW

NSW is rarely credited for its far-west outback corner, but it should be. Out here, grey saltbush and red sand make it easy to imagine yourself superimposed onto the world's biggest Aboriginal dot painting, a canvas reaching as far as the eye can see.

Bourke

POP 2047

Australian poet Henry Lawson once said, 'If you know Bourke, you know Australia.' Immortalised by Australians in the expression 'back of Bourke' (meaning, in the middle of nowhere), this town sits on the edge of the outback, miles from anywhere and sprawled along the Darling River.

◉ Sights

Back O' Bourke Exhibition Centre   MUSEUM
(☑ 02-6872 1321; www.visitbourke.com.au; Kidman Way; adult/child $22/10; ☺9am-5pm Apr-Oct, to 4pm Mon-Fri Nov-Mar; ℙ) This highly worthwhile exhibition space follows the legends of the back country (both Indigenous and settler) through interactive displays. The centre also houses the Bourke Visitor Information Centre and sells packages that include one or all of the town's major attractions – a river cruise on the **PV Jandra** (☑02-6872 1321; departs Kidman Camp; adult/child $16/10; ☺9am & 3pm Mon-Sat, 2.30pm Sun Apr-Oct), an entertaining outback show (staged at 11am) and a bus tour of the town and surrounds. (Note that the cruise and show operate April to October only.)

Bourke NPWS Office   TOURIST INFORMATION
(☑ 02-6872 2744; 51 Oxley St; ☺9am-5pm) Contact the NPWS office for visits to the Aboriginal art sites at **Gundabooka National Park**, the newest outback national park. There,

you can camp at Dry Tank (adult/child $6/4) or try the shearer's quarters (doubles $80).

🛏 Sleeping & Eating

Kidman's Camp   CAMPGROUND, CABINS $$
(☑ 02-6872 1612; www.kidmanscamp.com.au/bourke; Cunnamulla Rd, North Bourke; camp sites from $32, cabins from $109; 🛜🈂) An excellent place to base yourself, on river frontage about 8km out of Bourke. The PV Jandra cruise departs from here, and Poetry on a Plate is staged in the grounds. Plus there are lush gardens, swimming pools and cabins – family-sized with shared bathrooms, or comfy log cabins with bathroom, kitchenette and verandah.

Bourke Riverside Motel   MOTEL $$
(☑ 02-6872 2539; www.bourkeriversidemotel.com.au; 3-13 Mitchell St; s/d from $115/130; 🈂🛜🈂) This rambling motel has riverside gardens and a range of well-appointed rooms and suites: some have heritage overtones and antique furniture, some have kitchen, some are family-sized. A fine choice.

★ Poetry on a Plate   AUSTRALIAN $$
(☑0427 919 964; www.poetryonaplate.com.au; Kidman's Camp; adult/child $25/12; ☺from 6.30pm Tue, Thu, Sun Apr-Oct) A heart-warmingly unique offering here in Bourke: a well-priced night of bush ballads and storytelling around a campfire under the stars, with a simple, slow-cooked meal and dessert to boot. Dress warmly and bring your own drinks. Camp chairs and cutlery are provided.

ℹ Information

Bourke Visitor Information Centre (☑ 02-6872 1321; www.visitbourke.com.au; Kidman Way; ☺9am-5pm; 🛜) While at first glance it may appear that there's not much to see and do here in Bourke, the friendly staff at this well-stocked visitor centre will set you straight with what's on and can assist with booking things in. It's also home to the unmissable-when-in-town, Back O' Bourke Exhibition Centre.

Broken Hill

☑08 / POP 18,517

The massive mullock heap (of mine residue) that forms a backdrop for Broken Hill's town centre accentuates the unique character of this desert frontier town. For all its remoteness, the fine facilities and high-quality attractions can feel like an oasis somewhere close to the end of the earth. Some of the state's most impressive national parks are nearby, as is an intriguing near-ghost town, and everywhere there is an impressive spirit of community and creativity.

History

The area around Broken Hill was traditionally occupied by the Wiljakali people. A boundary rider, Charles Rasp, laid the foundations here that took Australia from an agricultural country to an industrial nation. In 1883 he discovered a silver lode and formed the Broken Hill Proprietary Company (which now goes by the name of BHP Billiton). It ultimately became Australia's largest company and an international giant.

Today the world's richest deposits of silver, lead and zinc are still being worked here, although mining operations are winding down, leading to a declining population.

◉ Sights

★ **Broken Hill Regional Art Gallery** GALLERY
(www.bhartgallery.com.au; 404-408 Argent St; gold-coin donation; ☺10am-5pm Mon-Fri, to 4pm Sat & Sun) This impressive gallery is housed in the beautifully restored Sully's Emporium from 1885. It's the oldest regional gallery in NSW and holds 1800 works in its permanent collection. Artists featured include Australian masters such as John Olsen, Sidney Nolan and Arthur Streeton, plus there is strong Indigenous representation.

★ **Royal Flying Doctor Service Museum** MUSEUM
(☑08-8080 3714; www.flyingdoctor.org.au; Airport Rd; adult/child $8.50/4; ☺9am-5pm Mon-Fri, 10am-3pm Sat & Sun; Ⓟ) This iconic Australian institution has a visitor centre at the airport. There are stirring displays and stories of health innovation and derring-do in the service of those who live and work in remote places (note: this base serves a staggeringly vast area of 640,000 sq km). It's a real eye-opener, and the video is guaranteed to stir emotions.

Line of Lode Miners Memorial MEMORIAL
(Federation Way; ☺6am-9pm) FREE Teetering atop the silver skimp dump is this moving memorial with memorable views. It houses the impressively stark Cor-Ten steel memorial to the 900 miners who have died since Broken Hill first became a mining town; it's an appalling litany of gruesome deaths. To

get here, travel south along Iodide St, cross the railway tracks then follow the signs.

Pro Hart Gallery GALLERY
(www.prohart.com.au; 108 Wyman St; adult/child $6/4; ☺10am-5pm Mar-Nov, to 4pm Dec-Feb) Kevin 'Pro' Hart (1928–2006) was a former miner and is widely considered one of outback Australia's premier painters. His iconic work is spread over three storeys, his studio has been re-created, and there's a fascinating video presentation about his life and work. You can also admire his Rolls Royce collection.

Kinchega National Park NATIONAL PARK
(www.nationalparks.nsw.gov.au; River Dr; $8 per car per day; Ⓟ) There are three well-marked driving trails through this park surrounding the Menindee Lakes: the River Drive (20km), Lake Drive (18km) and Woolshed Drive (6.5km). Accommodation is available at the shearers' quarters (beds $20), which can be booked at **Broken Hill NPWS office** (☑08-8080 3200; 183 Argent St; ☺8.30am-4.30pm Mon-Fri). There are also riverside and lakeside camping areas (adult/child $6/4).

Living Desert State Park NATURE RESERVE
(www.stateparks.nsw.gov.au/living_desert; adult/child $6/3; ☺walking trails 9am-5pm Mar-Nov, 6am-2pm Dec-Feb) One of the most memorable experiences of Broken Hill is viewing the sunset from the **Living Desert Sculpture Symposium** (Nine Mile Rd; ☺9am-sunset Mar-Nov, from 6am Dec-Feb), on the highest hilltop 12km from town. The sculptures are the work of 12 international artists who carved the huge sandstone blocks on-site, part of this 24-sq-km state park. The park is also home to a **flora and fauna sanctuary** featuring a 2.2km Cultural Walk Trail and a 1km Flora Trail.

🏃 Activities

★ **Outback Astronomy** ASTRONOMY
(☑0427 055 225; www.outbackastronomy.com. au; 18817 Barrier Hwy; ♿) Broken Hill is surrounded by desert, making it a great place to experience inky black skies and celestial splendour. This fabulous operator runs one-hour night-sky-viewing shows from its desert base. The presenter points out constellations and various features visible to the naked eye, and through powerful binoculars (provided).

The website lists a calendar of forthcoming shows.

Broken Hill

Broken Hill

👉 Tours

Tri State Safaris — DRIVING

(☎08-8088 2389; www.tristate.com.au; 422 Argent St; day tours from $220) Well-regarded Broken Hill operator offering one- to 15-day tours to remote outback places like Mutawintji, Kinchega or Mungo National Parks, Corner Country, Birdsville and the Simpson Desert. The most popular is the one-day tour

($220) of Broken Hill and Silverton. You can also tag-along with some tours in your own 4WD at reduced rates.

🛏 Sleeping

★ Palace Hotel — HISTORIC HOTEL **$**

(☎08-8088 1699; www.thepalacehotelbrokenhill.com.au; 227 Argent St; dm/s/d with shared bathroom from $30/45/65, d from $125; ❄) Star of

ℹ PHONES, TIMES & FOOTBALL

When the NSW government refused to give Broken Hill the services it needed, saying the town was just a pinprick on the map, the council replied that Sydney was also a pinprick from where it was, and Broken Hill would henceforth be part of South Australia (SA). Since the town was responsible for much of NSW's wealth, Broken Hill was told it was to remain part of NSW. In protest, the town adopted SA time, phone area code, and football, playing Australian Rules from then on.

Tourists beware: time in Broken Hill is Central Standard Time (CST), 30 minutes later than the surrounding area on Eastern Standard Time (EST); you're in the 08 phone-code region; and don't talk about rugby in the pub.

the hit Australian movie *The Adventures of Priscilla, Queen of the Desert,* this huge and ageing icon won't be to everyone's taste, but a stay here is one of the outback's most unique sleeping experiences. Newer rooms have balcony access and en suites, but most are proudly retro. For the full experience, try the Priscilla Suite (from $135).

Caledonian B&B
B&B $

(🖉 08-8087 1945; www.caledonianbnb.com.au; 140 Chloride St; d with shared bathroom incl breakfast from $89, cottages from $140; ❋🤶) This fine Broken Hill B&B is in a refurbished pub (1898) known as 'the Cally' – it also has three self-contained cottages, each sleeping up to six. Hugh and Barb are welcoming hosts and the rooms are lovingly maintained. Wake up and smell Hugh's espresso coffee and you'll be hooked.

★ Emaroo Cottages
COTTAGE $$

(🖉 08-8595 7217; http://brokenhillcottages.com.au; cottages from $175; 🅿❋🤶) Staying in one of these three fabulous, fully self-contained, renovated two-bedroom miners cottages is a great way to experience the Hill. Each cottage is located in a different part of town, and has excellent security, undercover parking, air conditioning, wi-fi, a full kitchen, bathroom and laundry, and the price can't be beat. Go for Emaroo Oxide, if you can.

Red Earth Motel
MOTEL $$

(🖉 08-8087 5694; www.redearthmotel.com.au; 469 Argent St; studio apt from $160, 2-/3-bedroom apt from $230/270; 🅿❋🤶📶) One of the better motels in rural NSW, this outstanding family-run place in Broken Hill has large, stylish rooms – each has a separate sitting area and kitchen facilities, making them ideal for longer stays. There's a guest laundry, plus pool and barbecue area.

✖ Eating & Drinking

★ Silly Goat
CAFE $

(🖉 08-8088 4774; 360 Argent St; dishes $8-18; ⏲ 7.30am-5pm Tue-Fri, 8am-2pm Sat, 8am-1pm Sun; ❋🤶) What's this? Pour-overs and single-origin coffee in the outback? Nice work, Silly Goat. The menu here would be at home in any big-city cafe, the array of cakes is tempting, the coffee is great, and the vibe is busy and cheerful.

Thom, Dick & Harry's
CAFE $

(🖉 08-8088 7000; http://thomdickharrys.com.au; 354 Argent St; light lunches $9-14; ⏲ 8am-5.30pm Mon-Thu, to 6pm Fri, 9am-2pm Sat; ❋) A narrow shop cluttered with stylish kitchenware and gourmet produce. Sit in among it (or on the street) for a decent coffee and delicious baguette.

The Astra
MODERN AUSTRALIAN $$

(🖉 08-8087 5428; www.theastra.com.au; 393 Argent St; mains $16-36; ❋🖉) Dining at the Astra is a classy affair, with a varied menu of Modern Australian cuisine and upscale pub fare from juicy steaks, seafood dishes including oysters, to pizza, pasta, generous burgers and nightly chef's specials.

★ Palace Hotel
PUB

(🖉 08-8088 1699; http://thepalacehotelbroken hill.com.au; 227 Argent St; ⏲ from 3pm Mon-Wed, from noon Thu-Sat) Built in 1889, Broken Hill's most famous pub, of *Priscilla, Queen of the Desert* fame, has an elaborate cast-iron verandah, plus wonderfully kitsch landscape murals covering almost every inch of the public areas. There's excellent pub-grub in the **Sidebar restaurant** (mains $17 to $36), but at the very least, a drink in the front bar or on the upstairs balcony is essential.

If you're partial to a flutter, play the iconic Aussie game of 'two-up' (gambling on the fall of two coins) on Fridays from 9pm.

❶ Information

Broken Hill Visitor Information Centre (☑ 08-8088 3560; www.visitbrokenhill.com.au; cnr Blende & Bromide Sts; ⏰ 8.30am-5pm Mar-Nov, to 3pm Dec-Feb; ☎) This should be considered a first stop when you get to town. Broken Hill has so much to do (surprising, we know) and a lot of it is on dusty, dangerous roads, so talk to the genuinely friendly staff and help yourself to brochures and maps to get your head around the city's outlying attractions.

❶ Getting There & Away

Broken Hill is a long way away – wherever you are. By road, it's 1144km east, to Sydney, and 512km southwest to Adelaide, in South Australia.

Rex (REX; ☑ 13 17 13; www.rex.com.au) offers the quickest way to get to Broken Hill from Sydney and Adelaide, but flights are expensive.

NSW TrainLink (p196) runs a daily Xplorer train service from Sydney to Broken Hill (from $66, 13½ hours).

Broken Hill is a stop on the iconic **Indian Pacific** (☑ 1800 703 357; www.greatsouthernrail. com.au) train between Sydney and Perth. For those who don't wish to take the full four-day trek, returning to Sydney from Broken Hill on the overnight service is a great way to experience the journey. You can travel from Sydney to Broken Hill, also, but in that direction you'll miss the sunset views over the desert.

Buses R Us (☑ 08-8285 6900; www.busesrus. com.au) operate two to three buses per week to Adelaide ($120, seven hours) from the Broken Hill Visitor Information Centre.

Mungo National Park

The remote, beautiful and important **Mungo National Park** (☑ 03-5021 8900; $8 per vehicle per day) covers 278.5 sq km of the Willandra Lakes Region World Heritage Area. A site of global archaeological and anthropological significance, it is one of Australia's most accessible slices of the outback, although the term 'accessible' is used loosely here.

Within the park, Lake Mungo is a dry lake and the site of the oldest archaeological finds in Australia. It also has the longest continual record of human culture: the world's oldest-recorded cremation site – thought to be 42,000 years old – has been found here!

⊙ Sights

★ **Walls of China**   ARCHAEOLOGICAL SITE
(☑ 03-5021 8900; Mungo National Park; ⏰ 24hr) A 33km semicircle ('lunette') of sand dunes, the fabulous Walls of China has been created by the unceasing westerly wind. From the visitor centre (p217) a road leads across the dry lakebed to a car park, then it's a

---

WORTH A TRIP

SILVERTON

Quirkiness overflows at Silverton, a former silver-mining town, now ghost town-cum-living museum. It's located 25km west of Broken Hill along a sealed road. Silverton's fortunes peaked in 1885, when it had a population of 3000, but in 1889 the mines closed and the people (and some houses) moved to Broken Hill. Visiting is like walking into a Russell Drysdale painting. The town's unique appearance lends itself well to the silver screen – astute viewers will recognise locations used in films such as *Mad Max II* and *A Town Like Alice*.

When you're here, it's impossible to get lost. History buffs should beeline to the fascinating **Silverton Gaol and Historical Museum** (☑ 08-8088 5317; cnr Burke & Layard Sts; adult/child $4/2; ⏰ 9.30am-4pm), followed by the **Silverton School Museum** (☑ 08-8088 7481; http://silverton.org.au/silverton-school-museum; Layard St; adult/child $2.50/1; ⏰ 9.30am-3.30pm Mon, Wed, Fri-Sun): both are crammed with artefacts from another age. Considerably more offbeat is the **Mad Max 2 Museum** (☑ 08-8088 6128; http://silverton.org.au/mad-max-museum; Stirling St; adult/child $7.50/5; ⏰ 10am-4pm), the culmination of Englishman Adrian Bennett's lifetime obsession with the theme. It's then worth driving another 5km to **Mundi Mundi Lookout** (Wilangee Rd), from where the horizon is so vast you can see the curvature of the Earth.

After all that, you'll need to stop for a beer and a pub meal at the fabulous **Silverton Hotel** (☑ 08-8088 5313; Layard St; d $120, extra person $25; ❄☎). If you enjoy the beer garden so much that you can't drive back to the Hill, you can always spend the night in comfy, refurbished motel rooms.

The **Silverton Visitor Information Centre** (☑ 08-8088 7566; Loftus St; ⏰ 9am-4pm Mon-Fri) can answer all your questions about this dusty, endearing little ghost town.

① MUNGO NATIONAL PARK AT A GLANCE

When to Visit Year-round, but best April to October (summer temperatures are scorching)

Gateway Towns Mildura, Wentworth, Balranald, Broken Hill

Main Attractions Walls of China land formations; outback isolation; wildlife; Aboriginal sites

Transport Unsealed roads into the park are accessible in 2WD vehicles except after rains

short walk to the **viewing platform**. Getting up close to the formations is by guided tour only.

Lake Mungo   LAKE

(Mungo National Park) One of 17 lakes in the Willandra Lakes Region World Heritage Area, the dry lake bed of Lake Mungo is home to many significant archaeological finds, including the discovery of the oldest human remains in Australia (nicknamed 'Mungo Man') and the site of the oldest ritual cremation in the world ('Mungo Lady').

🏃 Activities

⭐ Mungo Track   SCENIC DRIVE

The Mungo Track is a 70km signposted loop road around the heart of Mungo, linking the park's main attractions – you'll pass diverse landscapes, lookouts, short walks and plenty of emus and kangaroos.

Although it's unsealed, the road is generally fine for 2WD cars in dry weather; in good weather (ie, not too hot), mountain-bikers may be tempted.

Beyond the Walls of China parking area, the road continues to the pretty **Red Top Lookout**, which boasts fine views over the deeply eroded ravines of the lunette sand dunes. After that point, the Mungo Track is a one-way road that loops all the way back to the visitor centre.

Pick up a map from the visitor centre before setting out, and be sure to come equipped with enough petrol, a spare tyre, and plenty of drinking water. You can break the journey with an overnight stay at **Belah Campground** (📞03-5021 8900; adult/child $8/4).

👉 Tours

Aboriginal Discovery Tours   CULTURAL

(📞03-5021 8900; www.visitmungo.com.au/discovery-tours; adult/child $50/35) For those who visit the park independently, the NPWS conducts tours from the visitor centre led by Indigenous rangers, with the most popular option being the walk to the Walls of China. Check online for schedules: tours generally run daily in school holidays, weekends the rest of the year. Departure times depend on weather forecast, sunset time etc.

Discover Mildura   TOURS

(📞03-5024 7448; www.discovermildura.com; 14 Stockmans Drive, Mildura; tours per person $165) An excellent way to explore Mungo National Park, from Mildura, day trips include pick-up from and drop-off at your Mildura accommodation, morning tea, lunch, all transport, entry fees, experienced guides and an escorted walk to the Walls of China.

🛏 Sleeping

Mungo Shearers' Quarters   HOSTEL $

(📞1300 072 757; www.nationalparks.nsw.gov.au/camping-and-accommodation/accommodation/Mungo-Shearers-Quarters; Mungo National Park; adult/child $30/10; ❄) The former shearers' quarters comprises five neat, good-value rooms (each sleeping up to six in various configurations; BYO bedding). Rooms share a communal kitchen and bathroom, and a barbecue area. Bookings can be made online.

Main Campground   CAMPGROUND $

(📞03-5021 8900; www.nationalparks.nsw.gov.au/camping-and-accommodation/campgrounds/main-campground; Mungo National Park; adult/child $8/4) Located 2km from the Mungo National Park Visitor Centre, where you self-register and pay. Free gas barbecues and pit toilets are available; there are flush toilets and showers at the visitor centre. BYO drinking water.

Mungo Lodge   LODGE $$$

(📞1300 663 748; www.mungolodge.com.au; 10142 Arumpo Road, Arumpo; dm $25, cabins $199-279; ❄🛜) 🌿 This privately managed ecoresort on the outskirts of Mungo National Park offers a range of accommodation types from camp sites ($25) and dorm beds, to budget and deluxe, self-contained cabins: the latter being the plushest lodgings within cooee of the park. The lodge houses an inviting bar, lounge and restaurant area open for breakfast, lunch and dinner (mains $22 to $32).

ℹ️ Information

Mungo National Park Visitor Centre (📞 03-5021 8900; www.visitmungo.com.au; Mailbox Rd, Mungo National Park; ⏰ 8.30am-4.30pm Mon-Fri) Has displays on the park's cultural and natural history, and it's here that you can pick up maps, pay park and camping fees, and enquire about tours. Next door are the Shearers' Quarters (p216) accommodation and the Historic Woolshed, dating from 1869 and well worth a look. All park entry ($8 per person, per day) and camp fees (adult/child $6/4) are payable here.

ℹ️ Getting There & Away

Mungo National Park is 110km from Mildura and 150km from Balranald on good, unsealed roads that become instantly impassable after rain – a sturdy 2WD vehicle is generally fine in dry weather, but most rental-car companies prohibit taking their vehicles on unsealed roads. Be sure to check before setting out.

From Wentworth the route is about 150km, and the road is sealed for 100km. The remaining 50km is slow-going without a 4WD. Contact the tourist offices in the gateway towns to see if the roads into Mungo are open and accessible.

The closest places selling fuel are Balranald, Mildura, Wentworth, Pooncarie and Menindee.

There is no public transport in the area, and by far the safest, easiest and most rewarding way to explore the park is by guided tour, with the added benefit of knowledgeable guides.

Tibooburra & Corner Country

Out here, it's a different world; both harsh and peaceful, stretching forever to the endless sky. This far-western corner of NSW is a semidesert of red plains, heat, dust and flies – somewhere to fall off the map.

Tiny Tibooburra, the hottest town in the state, is a quintessential frontier town, with two rough-around-the-edges sandstone pubs and a landscape of large red rock formations known as 'gibbers'. It's the gateway to Sturt National Park – be sure to visit the **NPWS Sturt Visitor Centre** (📞 08-8091 3308; www.nationalparks.nsw.gov.au; 52 Briscoe St; ⏰ 8.30am-4.30pm Mon-Fri; 📶) before setting out.

North and northwest of Tibooburra, vast **Sturt National Park** (📞 08-8091 3308; www.nationalparks.nsw.gov.au/visit-a-park/parks/Sturt-National-Park; Tibooburra; per vehicle per day $8; 🅿️) encompasses over 3400 sq km of classic outback terrain. There are camping grounds and picnic areas in four locations; note that only untreated water is available

in the park, so come prepared with fuel, food and water to ensure you travel safely in this hot, remote country.

SOUTH COAST NEW SOUTH WALES

There's something special about the NSW coastline south of Sydney: something about the light, about the region's under-the-radar little-sibling status, about the oysters, about the inlets and estuaries and national parks and marine mammals frolicking offshore.

While it can't compare weather-wise to the more-visited North Coast – rain is fairly regular – its scenic beauty is staggering. Rough, rustic national parks and traditional fishing towns harbour some of the nation's most idyllic beaches, from the white sands and calm turquoise water of amazing Jervis Bay to big surf strands along the whole stretch from the Royal National Park on Sydney's southern edge to Eden, near the Victorian border.

Eden is known for its great whale-watching, but you can see these migrating leviathans all along the coast in this region. Dolphins are ubiquitous and the seals and penguins at Montague Island make it a brilliant wildlife-watching destination.

Royal National Park

This prime stretch of wilderness is at the city's doorstep, and encompasses secluded beaches, vertiginous cliffs, scrub, heath, rainforest, swamp wallabies, lyrebirds and raucous flocks of yellow-tailed black cockatoos.

This wonderful coastal park, protecting 15,091 hectares and stretching inland from 32km of beautiful coast, is the world's second-oldest national park (1879).

👁️ Sights

Wattamolla Beach   BEACH
(www.nationalparks.nsw.gov.au; Wattamolla Rd) About halfway along the coast, Wattamolla Beach is one of the park's favourite picnic spots and gets pretty busy in summer. It has the great advantage of having both a surf beach and a lagoon, allowing for safe swimming. There's also a waterfall; jumping is popular but strictly prohibited. The beach is 3.3km from the main road, accessed from very near the Bundeena turn-off.

Garie Beach   BEACH
(www.nationalparks.nsw.gov.au; Garie Beach Rd)
Three kilometres down a turn-off from the main road, this excellent surf beach is a picturesque spot. Like all of the Royal National Park surf beaches, swimming can be treacherous. There's a toilet block but no other facilities despite the large building complex, though the beach is patrolled on summer weekends.

🛏 Sleeping

Bonnie Vale Campground   CAMPGROUND $
(☎1300 072 757; www.nationalparks.nsw.gov.au; Sea Breeze Lane, Bundeena; sites for 2 $33; P ♒) This campground is 1.5km west of central Bundeena and has pleasant, flat, grassy sites. It's right by the water, with both sheltered bay beach and river estuary for swimming. It is well equipped, with toilets, hot showers, electric barbecues and picnic tables.

★Beachhaven   B&B $$$
(☎02-9544 1333; www.beachhavenbnb.com.au; 13 Bundeena Dr, Bundeena; r $300-350; P ♒ ❄ 🛜) Right on gorgeous Hordens Beach, this classy B&B is run by a welcoming couple who offer two fabulous rooms. Both have a kitchenette, a king bed with plush fabrics, and some fine antique furnishings, as well as a generously stocked fridge and lovely patio area. Beach House is right by the sand, while Tudor Cottage is tucked away in a little subtropical garden.

Other highlights include a romantic outdoor spa bath overlooking the beach, kayak and stand-up paddleboard on hand, and a friendly tame possum family. Prices drop markedly for multinight stays.

❶ Information

Royal National Park Visitor Centre (☎02-9542 0648; www.nationalparks.nsw.gov.au; 2 Lady Carrington Dr, Audley; ⏰8.30am-4.30pm) Entrance fees, camping permits, maps and bushwalking information. The centre is at Audley, 2km inside the park's northeastern entrance, off the Princes Hwy. There's also a cafe here with very pleasant verandah seating.

❶ Getting There & Away

Cronulla Ferries (☎02-9523 2990; www.cronullaferries.com.au; adult/child $6.40/3.20) travels to **Bundeena** from Cronulla, accessible by train from Sydney.

You can also get a train to Waterfall and hike into the park from there.

Wollongong & Around

POP 292,400
The 'Gong', 80km south of Sydney, has the laid-back ambience of a sizeable country town and is very likeable for just that reason. A small but enjoyable bar and restaurant scene adds to the charm of two excellent city beaches and a pretty harbour. The university gives it a youthful feel and the laid-back surfie lifestyle makes it easy to relax.

A spectacular forested sandstone escarpment runs south from the Royal National Park past Wollongong, overlooking a wonderful series of beaches, all with their own rail stop.

❂ Sights

★North Beach   BEACH
Stretching north from the harbour, North Beach has breaks suitable for all visitors and is conveniently close to the city centre. It's the main centre of Wollongong beach action. For the most challenging waves head to the Acids Reef break near the rocks opposite Stuart Park. North Beach has lifesavers all year round at its southern end.

Wollongong City Beach   BEACH
The southern of Wollongong's two city beaches is a lovely stretch of whiteish sand with good swimming and, depending on the wind, surfing. Looking north it's a romantic vista of headland and lighthouse, but turn around and the view of the massive Port Kembla steelworks will banish any tropical island fantasies.

Wollongong Botanic Garden   GARDENS
(☎02-4227 7667; www.wollongong.nsw.gov.au/botanicgarden; 61 Northfields Ave, Keiraville; ⏰7am-5pm Apr-Sep, 7am-6pm Mon-Fri, 7am-6.45pm Sat & Sun Oct-Mar; 🚌55A/55C) 🆓 FREE Northwest of the centre, but easily accessed on the free 55 shuttle bus from the station, which has a stop here, this has habitats including tropical, temperate and woodland. It's a nice break from the beach and a top spot for a picnic lunch. In summer there's an outdoor cinema (www.sunsetcinema.com.au).

Belmore Basin   HARBOUR
Wollongong's fishing fleet is based at this harbour's southern end. The basin was cut from solid rock in 1868. There's a fishing cooperative and the old **Breakwater Light-**

Wollongong

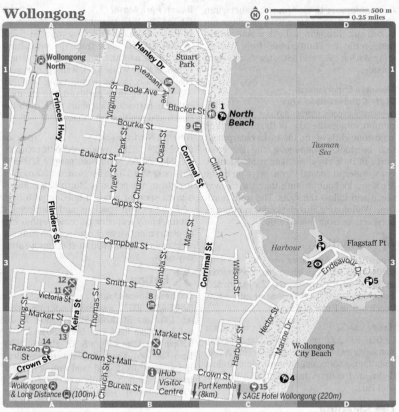

Wollongong

house (built in 1872) on the point. Nearby, on the headland, is the newer **Wollongong Head Lighthouse** (Flagstaff Hill Lighthouse). The harbour beach is great for young children, with sand and gentle waves. Between here and North Beach there are both swimming pools and a swimmable rock pool.

Science Centre & Planetarium MUSEUM
(☏ 02-4286 5000; www.sciencecentre.com.au; 60 Squires Way, North Wollongong; adult/child $14/10; ☺10am-4pm Thu-Tue, daily Jan) Quizzical kids of all ages can indulge their senses here. The museum is operated by the University of Wollongong and covers everything

from dinosaurs to electronics. Planetarium shows ($4.50, or $3 extra with an admission ticket) run throughout the day. You can get here on the free shuttle buses from Wollongong station (55A and 55C); they stops right outside.

Illawarra Escarpment State Conservation Area
PARK

(www.nationalparks.nsw.gov.au) Spectacular rainforest hugs the edge of the ever-eroding sandstone cliffs of the Illawarra escarpment that overlooks Wollongong and the coast north of it. It rises to 534m at Mt Kembla. For wonderful coastal views, drive up to the Mt Keira lookout (464m); take the freeway north and follow the signs. The train north from Wollongong also gives good rainforesty perspectives from down below.

🏃 Activities

Pines Surfing Academy
SURFING

(📞 0410 645 981; www.pinessurfingacademy.com.au; 1a Cliff Rd, North Wollongong; 2hr lessons $50, 3-day course $120) Surf lessons at either City Beach or the Farm Beach.

HangglideOz
ADVENTURE SPORTS

(📞 0417 939 200; www.hangglideoz.com.au; tandem flights midweek/weekends $245/295) A reliable hang-gliding operator offering tandem flights and courses from Bald Hill in Stanwell Park.

🛌 Sleeping

Keiraleagh
HOSTEL $

(📞 02-4228 6765; www.backpack.net.au; 60 Kembla St; dm $25-38, s/d without bathroom $75/85, d $140; 🌐@🛜) This welcoming and rambling heritage house has a bohemian surf hippy vibe, basic cleanliness and a genuinely friendly atmosphere. The dorms could do with thicker mattresses, but it's the great garden and barbecue area that make it such a relaxing spot. It only takes cash.

SAGE Hotel Wollongong
HOTEL $$

(📞 02-4201 2111; www.sagewollongong.com; 60-62 Harbour St; r $199-299; P🌐❄🛜❄) Handy for the sports precinct and the city beach, this airy modern hotel has tastefully designed rooms and pretty good facilities. Rooms are a good size and come with coffee machine and other mod-cons. Try for one near the top of the building for ocean or golf-course views. The higher-grade rooms come with balcony. Good pubs and restaurants are a short walk away.

Beach Park Motel
MOTEL $$

(📞 02-4226 1577; www.beachparkmotel.com.au; 10 Pleasant Ave, North Wollongong; r $125-210; P🌐❄🛜) Just back from the beachfront park, this is a solid, friendly option. A variety of rooms have white brick walls, good space, colourful doors and comfortable facilities. Most look out onto parkland, the cheapest onto the carpark. It's a short walk from the beach and pretty good value.

Novotel Northbeach
HOTEL $$$

(📞 02-4224 3111; www.novotelnorthbeach.com.au; 2-14 Cliff Rd, North Wollongong; r $299-379; P🌐❄@🛜❄) This renovated 200-roomer is right by the action at North Beach and is a great spot for a beach holiday, with bags of facilities and spacious and comfortable rooms, many featuring balconies with ocean or escarpment views. Prices soar on summer weekends – think $400 to $600 for a Saturday room.

🍴 Eating

Balinese Spice Magic
INDONESIAN $

(📞 02-4227 1033; www.balinesespicemagic.com.au; 130 Keira St; lunch $10-18, dinner $17-26; ⊙ 5.30-9.30pm Tue & Wed, 11am-2.30pm & 5.30-9.30pm Thu, 11am-2.30pm & 5.30-11pm Fri, 5.30-11pm Sat; 📶) Look forward to excellent Indonesian food and welcoming service from the friendly family owners. Thai and Vietnamese eateries also line Keira St, but this is our pick of the best flavours to remind you of your time drifting aimlessly around Southeast Asia. There are lots of vegan options.

⭐ Caveau
MODERN AUSTRALIAN $$$

(📞 02-4226 4855; www.caveau.com.au; 122-124 Keira St; 7-course degustation menu $110, with wine $160; ⊙ 6-11pm Tue-Sat; 📶) This lauded restaurant serves gourmet treats such as kingfish tartare and poached scampi. The menu changes seasonally and there's a three-course menu ($85) available from Tuesday to Thursday. There's a separate degustation for vegetarians. The ambience is Gong-casual with great spotty chairs and sleek dark decor.

⭐ Babyface
JAPANESE, AUSTRALIAN $$$

(📞 02-4295 0903; www.burnsburyhospitality.com.au; 179 Keira St; mains $24-40; ⊙ 6-10pm Mon, 6-11pm Wed & Thu, noon-3pm & 6pm-midnight Fri & Sat, noon-3pm & 6-10pm Sun) Buzzy and loud, this relative Wollongong newcomer combines Japanese ideas with some wild

Australian herbs and berries to create a satisfying blend of flavours. Salmon and kingfish are the backbones of the menu, which features a sashimi section, smaller plates and large ones. There are some very interesting wines by the glass and upbeat, friendly staff. Sit at the bar if no tables.

🍸 Drinking & Nightlife

★ His Boy Elroy
BAR

(☑02-4244 8221; www.hisboyelroy.com.au; 176 Keira St; burgers $12-19; ⊙5-10pm Mon & Tue, 11am-10pm Wed, Thu & Sun, 11am-midnight Fri & Sat) Recently re-opened in new premises, this excellent bar is now more burgers, cocktails and spirits than the cafe it began as. Offering outdoor seating, a revamped cocktail list and a great selection of interesting whiskies, it's great for a drink. The burgers are reliably excellent, and the new smoked meat choices should be great too.

Humber
BAR

(☑02-4263 0355; www.humber.bar; 226 Crown St; ⊙6.30am-midnight Mon-Fri, 7.30am-midnight Sat, 7.30am-10pm Sun; 🛜) This relative newcomer occupies an unusually shaped building, once the Humber car dealership. Downstairs does coffees and lunches in the morning, then the place morphs into a stylish cocktail bar in the evening. The 1st-floor art deco–inspired bar is a beautiful space, while the rooftop feels like the deck of a yacht. Palms, parasols and fresh coconuts add to the carnival cruise feel.

Illawarra Brewery
BAR

(☑02-4220 2854; www.thebrewery.net.au; cnr Crown & Harbour Sts; ⊙11am-11pm Mon-Thu, 10am-1am Fri & Sat, 10am-10pm Sun) This slick bar attached to the entertainment centre, with ocean views, has its own craft beers on tap, plus occasional seasonal brews. Guest beers from around Australia complete a happy and hoppy picture, and there's decent food on tap as well. The outdoor terrace is a great spot to sit. It's a popular one with sports fans too.

ℹ Information

IHub Visitor Centre (☑1800 240 737; www.visitwollongong.com.au; 93 Crown St; ⊙9am-5pm Mon-Sat, 10am-4pm Sun; 🛜) Bookings and information.

ℹ Getting There & Away

Trains on the **South Coast Line** (☑13 15 00; www.sydneytrains.info) run to/from Sydney's

Central Station ($8.30, 90 minutes), and continue south as far as Nowra/Bomaderry via Kiama and Berry.

All long-distance buses leave from the eastern side of the railway station. **Premier** (☑13 34 10; www.premierms.com.au) has two daily buses to Sydney ($18, two hours) and Eden ($69, seven to eight hours). **Murrays** (☑13 22 51; www.murrays.com.au) has buses to Canberra ($48.40, 3¼ hours).

ℹ Getting Around

A free shuttle bus, the Gong Shuttle (routes 55A and 55C), runs every 10 to 20 minutes on a loop from the station to the university, and North Wollongong, useful for reaching North Beach, the Botanic Garden and Science Centre.

Kiama & Around

POP 12,800

Kiama's sculpted coastline includes numerous beaches and crazy rock formations, including a famous but often underwhelming blowhole. The town is characterised by its likeably daggy, laid-back vibe and magnificent mature Norfolk pines. Inland are viewpoints and outdoor activities in the forested highlands.

◉ Sights

Kiama Blowhole
LANDMARK

Kiama's famous blowhole sits on the point by the centre of town. It's fairly underwhelming except when the surf's up and a southeaster's blowing: then, water explodes high up out of the fissure. It's floodlit at night. The **Little Blowhole** (off Tingira Cres, Marsden Head) along the coast to the south is less impressive but much more regular.

Minnamurra Rainforest Centre
NATURE RESERVE

(☑02-4236 0469; www.nationalparks.nsw.gov.au; Minnamurra Falls Rd, via Jamberoo; car $12; ⊙9am-5pm, last entry 4pm) On the eastern edge of **Budderoo National Park**, 15km inland from Kiama, this is a surprisingly lush subtropical rainforest. A 2.6km loop walk transits through the rainforest following a cascading stream. Look out for water dragons and lyrebirds. A secondary 1.6km walk on a steepish track leads to the **Minnamurra Falls**. The helpful visitor centre can supply park and ecosystem information. There's a worthwhile cafe here, open 10am to 4pm at busy times, 11.30am to 2.30pm on quieter days.

A weekday bus from Kiama station gets up here, but there's six hours between arrivals.

★ **Seven Mile Beach** BEACH
(www.nationalparks.nsw.gov.au) Backed by national park, this magnificent curved stretch of white-ish sand lives up to its name (and a bit more). It runs from Shoalhaven Heads in the south to Gerroa in the north, and can also be accessed via a series of turn-offs to beachside national park picnic areas.

🛏 Sleeping & Eating

Bellevue Accommodation APARTMENT $$
(☑ 02-4232 4000; www.bellevueaccommodation. com.au; 21 Minnamurra St; r $150-250; P ❄ ✳ 🛜) This charming place hosts guests in modern comfort within a two-storey 1890s heritage manor. The apartments are equipped with a full kitchen, laundry facilities, lovely verandah space and ocean views. It's a short walk to the main street. There's usually a two-night minimum stay, but it's always worth a call just in case.

★ **Kiama Harbour Cabins** CABIN $$$
(☑ 02-4232 2707; www.kiamacoast.com.au; Blowhole Point; cottages $300-400; P ❄ ✳ 🛜) In the best position in town, these cottages are neat as a pin and well equipped with barbecues on verandahs overlooking the beach and the nearby ocean pool. Prices are for the January high season, when there's a seven-night minimum stay. At other times it's only two nights and rates are at least 25% lower.

Hungry Monkey CAFE $
(☑ 0403 397 353; http://thehungrymonkeyyy.com; 5/32 Collins St; dishes $12-20; ⊙ 6.30am-4pm Mon-Wed, 6.30am-9pm Thu-Sat, 7.30am-4pm Sun; 🛜 🍴) One of a row of cute cottages, this is a very likeable cafe doing burgers, wraps, salads and breakfast plates with great combos of ingredients and plenty of zing and taste. It serves food all day and is licensed too: a good all-rounder.

Kabari Bar BISTRO $$
(☑ 02-4233 0572; www.kabaribar.com; 78 Manning St; mains $18-30; ⊙ food 8am-3pm Sun & Mon, to 10pm Wed-Sat) By the lively surf beach in town, this likeable shack has a takeaway kiosk that's busy all day but also puts on more sophisticated fare in its two-level restaurant section. It offers water views and competently presented plates running from seafood to better meat dishes and pizzas. There's live music at the bar at weekends.

❶ Information

Visitor Centre (☑ 02-4232 3322; www. kiama.com.au; Blowhole Point Rd; ⊙ 9am-5pm) On Blowhole Point. Helpful with finding accommodation.

❶ Getting There & Away

Kiama is most easily reached by train, with frequent **Sydney Trains** (☑ 13 15 00; www. sydneytrains.info) departures to Wollongong, Sydney and Nowra (Bomaderry) via Berry.

Premier (☑ 13 34 10; www.premierms.com.au) buses run twice daily to Eden ($69, 7½ hours) and Sydney ($25, 2½ hours). **Kiama Coaches** (☑ 02-4232 3466; www.kiamacoaches.com. au) runs to Gerroa, Gerringong and Minnamurra (via Jamberoo).

If you're driving, take the beach detour via Gerringong and Gerroa and rejoin the highway either in Berry or just north of Nowra.

Kangaroo Valley

POP 300

From either Nowra or Berry, a shaded forested road meanders to pretty Kangaroo Valley. This lovely historic town is cradled by mountains, and the sleepy main street has cafes, craft shops, a historic sandstone bridge and a great pub. It's a sort of idealised rural Australia, with a vibrant palette of colours. Activities in the surrounding area include biking, hiking, canoeing and camping. See www.visitkangaroovalley.com.au for operators and B&B accommodation.

⊙ Sights

★ **Cambewarra Lookout** VIEWPOINT
(⊙ 7.30am-9pm) Signposted off the Cambewarra Mountain between Kangaroo Valley and Nowra, this lookout offers a stupendous perspective over the winding Shoalhaven River and the alluvial agricultural lands far below, and right along the coast. There's a cafe here whose deck takes full advantage of the vista.

Pioneer Village Museum MUSEUM
(☑ 02-4465 1306; www.kangaroovalleymuseum. com; 2029 Moss Vale Rd; adult/child $10/5; ⊙ 10am-4pm Fri-Mon & Wed, daily Jan & other school holidays) Next to the picturesque Hampden bridge, the walkabout Pioneer Museum Park provides a visual encounter with rural life in the late 19th century. There's a range of buildings, as well as bushwalks and barbecue/picnic facilities, so it's a good spot to take the kids on an excursion.

Fitzroy Falls
WATERFALL

(www.nationalparks.nsw.gov.au; Morton National Park; per vehicle $4) Though the summers and reservoir requirements frequently reduce the actual torrent to a trickle, this 81m-high waterfall is worth a visit for the views alone. A spectacular outlook has views over forest-clad hills and juxtaposed with bare sandstone escarpment – a classic NSW scene. The visitor centre here is the best resource for wildlife and walking information in the area and has a cafe. The falls are about 17km northwest of the bridge in Kangaroo Valley, up a steep mountain road.

🏃 Activities

Kangaroo Valley Canoes
KAYAKING, CANOEING

(Kangaroo Valley Safaris; ☑ 02-4465 1502; www.kangaroovalleycanoes.com.au; 2031 Moss Vale Rd) North of the Hampden Bridge, this well-established operator offers a range of guided or self-guided canoeing and kayak trips, including multiday options. It also does canoe, kayak and bike hire.

Kangaroo Valley Adventure Co
ADVENTURE SPORTS

(☑ 02-4465 1372; www.kvac.com.au; Glenmack Park Campground) Friendly Kangaroo Valley Adventure Co offers combined hiking and biking (half-day $60), canoeing and camping (overnight $85), kayaking (half-day $80 to $90) and biking, hiking and kayaking (full day $100).

🛏 Sleeping & Eating

Boutique B&Bs and farmstays cluster in and around town, and along the road to Berry. There are a couple of camping parks in the centre of the village; for a bush-camping experience head north out of town to Bendeela picnic spot. It's signed.

Glenmack Park
CAMPGROUND $

(www.glenmack.com.au; 215 Moss Vale Rd; camp sites per adult/child $18/14, powered sites $44, cabins $75-205; 🅿🗗❄🐾🐕🐕) Genially run and central, this campground covers a lot of bases. There's plenty of shade and a range of sweet cabins including some budget ones without bathroom. A big pool, a jumping pillow, and an on-site activities operator means that this is an appealing family option too.

★ Laurels B&B
B&B $$$

(☑ 02-4465 1693; www.thelaurelsbnb.com.au; 2501 Moss Vale Rd; r $265-295; 🗗🐾) Five kilometres northwest of the bridge, this is a privileged spot to find yourself. Your delightful and cultured hosts offer a warmly personal welcome, and the four rooms in this lovely centenarian bungalow are sumptuous spaces with king beds, elegant antique furniture and high comfort levels. Books, wine and cheese in the late afternoon, peaceful surrounding countryside: a delightfully civilised retreat.

Cloud Song
B&B $$$

(☑ 02-4465 1194; www.cloudsonginkangaroovalley.com.au; 170 Moss Vale Rd; d $250; 🅿🗗❄🐾) These beautiful modern cabins are stylishly designed and located right in the centre of town. Nevertheless, it feels like a real retreat, set in a verdant garden. They are fabulously relaxing spaces with their own decks, upstairs bedroom with balcony, and standout in-room breakfast. Your host is extremely welcoming.

Bistro One46
BISTRO $$

(☑ 02-4465 2820; www.bistro146.com.au; 146 Moss Vale Rd; mains $26-34; ⏱ 5.30-9pm Fri, 11am-3pm & 5.30-9pm Sat, 11am-3pm & 5.30-8.30pm Sun, 11am-2.30pm & 5.30-8.30pm Mon & Tue) In the centre of the village, this vine-swathed beauty has a pleasantly cosy interior and a sweet little verandah. The food is well presented, colourful and not overly complicated. It covers a range of bases, including kangaroo carpaccio, seafood and Italian, and it's all pretty tasty.

ℹ Information

Fitzroy Falls Visitor Centre (☑ 02-4887 7270; www.nationalparks.nsw.gov.au; Nowra Rd, Fitzroy Falls; per vehicle $4; ⏱ 9am-5pm May-Aug, 9am-5.30pm Sep-Apr) This visitor centre by the Fitzroy Falls is a good source of walking and nature information for the Morton National Park. There's a cafe here.

ℹ Getting There & Away

Kennedy's (☑ 02-4421 7596; www.kennedystours.com.au) runs a few buses a week between Bomaderry train station and Kangaroo Valley.

Shoalhaven Coast

Well in weekender range from Sydney, this striking region features wonderful sandy beaches backed by a luscious green interior dotted with heritage towns, state forests and national parks. The white sands and turquoise waters of Jervis Bay are a highlight.

SYDNEY & NEW SOUTH WALES SHOALHAVEN COAST

Berry

POP 1700

Berry, a slightly mannered but undeniably lovely heritage town, is a popular inland stop on the South Coast. Look forward to a smattering of antique and design stores, and a thriving foodie scene with good cafes and restaurants. Currently choked by its main-street highway traffic, Berry should become a much more tranquil, appealing place when the bypass is finished around early 2018.

◉ Sights

The town's short main street features National Trust–classified buildings and there are good-quality vineyards in the rolling countryside around Berry.

★ Silos Estate   WINERY
(☑ 02-4448 6082; www.silosestate.com; B640 Princes Hwy, Jaspers Brush; ⊙ tastings 11am-5pm) ❋ Beautifully set on a green hillside overlooking the pretty countryside between Berry and Nowra, this lovely winery is well worth a visit. It makes a range of tasty drops under two labels and also offers cheese and alpaca ham. There's an excellent restaurant here too, lots of forward-thinking environmental initiatives and four utterly relaxing boutique rooms ($205 to $275).

⌱ Sleeping

Conjuring up images of cosy wood fires, Berry is a popular weekender in winter as well as summer. There are lots of fairly up-market choices across here and Kangaroo Valley.

Berry Hotel   HOTEL $
(☑ 02-4464 1011; www.berryhotel.com.au; 120 Queen St; s/d $80/110; 🅟 ☕ 🛜) This popular local watering hole has standard but large fan-cooled pub bedrooms with bathrooms down the hall. Mattresses could be firmer, but it's a pretty authentic place to stay, with its own style and plenty of value. There's a shared balcony space and, downstairs, decent food served in the pub's rear dining room and courtyard.

Berry Village Boutique Motel   MOTEL $$
(☑ 02-4464 3570; www.berrymotel.com.au; 72 Queen St; r $185-275; 🅟 ☕ ❄ 🛜 ⛌) On the main road, this is an exceedingly well run, upmarket place with a gourmet restaurant and large, comfortable rooms. They're modern and attractively carpeted with new king

beds in some. Standard ones face the front, while those behind have a more tranquil park lookout. Higher-grade rooms have spa facilities. Constant improvements here are the sign of a quality establishment.

Bellawongarah at Berry   B&B $$$
(☑ 02-4464 1999; www.accommodation-berry.com.au; 869 Kangaroo Valley Rd, Bellawongarah; r $250-260; 🅟 ☕ ❄ 🛜) Rainforest surrounds this wonderful place, 8km from Berry on the mountain road to Kangaroo Valley. There are two rooms, one a sumptuous loft space in the main house, which features Asian art, a large spa bath overlooking the greenery, and a cosy lounge and sleeping area under the eaves. The other is a cute 1868 Wesleyan cottage-church with an airy, French provincial feel.

✖ Eating

Famous Berry Donut Van   CAFE $
(☑ 0435 297 530; 73 Princes Hwy; doughnuts $1.80; ⊙ 9am-6pm; 🚗) For generations now, parents driving the family down the South Coast for the holidays have bribed the kids by promising a stop at this food truck if they were good along the way. The doughnuts are made fresh and, hot and sugary, are delicious. It also does coffee and other snacks.

★ Silos Restaurant   MODERN AUSTRALIAN $$
(☑ 02-4448 6160; www.silos.com.au; B640 Princes Hwy, Jaspers Brush; 5-/8-course tasting menu $70/95; ⊙ noon-2pm & 6-10pm Thu-Sat, noon-2pm Sun, open daily in Jan) The former grain silos that give this winery its name overlook this loveable restaurant, which has a sweet verandah space and dining room with dreamy views over the vineyard's grassy slopes. It's a sort of rural idyll but the cuisine would bear up in any urban gastro-street. Confident and innovative flavour combinations, local produce (including estate-farmed alpacas) and friendly staff make this a standout.

★ Hungry Duck   ASIAN $$
(☑ 02-4464 2323; www.hungryduck.com.au; 85 Queen St; mains $16-35, 5-/9-course banquet $55/85; ⊙ 6-9.30pm Mon, Wed & Thu, noon-2pm & 6-9.30pm Fri-Sun; 🚗) ❋ A contemporary Asian menu is served tapas-style, although larger mains are also available. There's a rear courtyard and kitchen garden where herbs are plucked for the plate. Fresh fish, meat and eggs are all sourced locally. Look for it near the BP station in the centre of town.

Berry Woodfired Sourdough
BAKERY, CAFE **$$**

(☑02-4464 1617; www.berrysourdoughcafe.com. au; cnr Prince Alfred & Princess Sts; pies $6.80, mains $16-26; ☺8am-3pm Wed-Sun) Stock up on bread or dine in at this bakery that's beloved by foodies. Try the delicious gourmet pies or go for a more substantial dish, with daily fish and meat specials adding to a short, quality menu. The owners also run **Milkwood Bakery** (☑02-4464 3033; 109 Queen St; pies $6.80; ☺6am-5.30pm Mon-Fri, 7am-5pm Sat & Sun) on Berry's main drag.

South on Albany
MODERN AUSTRALIAN **$$**

(☑02-4464 2005; www.southonalbany; 3/65 Queen St; mains $29-33; ☺6-10pm Wed-Fri, noon-2.30pm & 6-10pm Sat, noon-2.30pm Sun) Just off the main drag, this has solid wooden tables and a sound philosophy of seasonal ingredients highlighted in a short, excellent menu. It's a notably welcoming place, with cheerful service, a pleasant outlook and an interesting wine list.

🛍 Shopping

Treat Factory
FOOD

(☑02-4464 1112; www.treatfactory.com.au; 6 Old Creamery Lane; ☺9.30am-4.30pm Mon-Fri, 10am-4pm Sat & Sun) Well worth the short detour off the highway, this factory shop is an old-school place chock-full of nostalgic lollies such as rocky road and liquorice. It also does a nice line in pickles and sauces.

ⓘ Getting There & Away

Trains run every hour or two to Nowra/Bomaderry ($3, 10 minutes) and to Kiama ($3.40, 30 minutes), where you change to trains heading north to Wollongong ($4.50, 1¼ hours) and Sydney ($6, 2¾ hours).

Premier (☑13 34 10; www.premierms.com. au) has buses to Sydney ($25, three hours, twice daily) via Kiama, and south to Eden via all coastal towns.

Nowra

POP 28,000

Nowra, around 17km from the coast, is the largest town in the Shoalhaven area. Although there are prettier South Coast towns, it's a solid, laid-back regional centre and can be a decent base for the surrounding attractions of Berry, Kangaroo Valley and Jervis Bay. Nowra's conjoined twin, Bomaderry, is the southern terminus of the South Coast rail line.

👁 Sights

Meroogal
MUSEUM

(☑02-4421 8150; www.sydneylivingmuseums.com. au; cnr West & Worrigee Sts; adult/child $12/8; ☺10am-4pm Sat, plus Thu & Fri Jan & other school holidays) Intriguingly, this historic 1885 house contains the artefacts accumulated by four generations of women who have lived there. Entrance is by guided tour, which leaves on the hour (last tour 3pm). It's a lovely building in a tranquil setting near the oval some three blocks west of central Nowra.

Coolangatta Estate
WINERY

(☑02-4448 7131; www.coolangattaestate.com. au; 1335 Bolong Rd, Shoalhaven Heads; ☺winery 10am-5pm) **FREE** On the north side of the estuary, 13km east of Bomaderry and just before Shoalhaven Heads, is this atmospheric and historic winery on an estate first established in 1822. There's cellar door tasting of its praiseworthy wines, a 'wine garden' and restaurant that makes a fine lunch spot, and tours of the estate on **Segways** (☑0402 000 222; www.segwaytourssouthcoast.com.au; tours $75-100) or in a large **'Bigfoot' vehicle** (☑0428 244 229; www.bishopsadventures.com.au; Coolangatta Estate, Shoalhaven Heads; adult/child $25/15) that takes you up the hill for tremendous views. The estate also offers excellent accommodation in convict-built buildings.

🛏 Sleeping

Coolangatta Estate
B&B **$$**

(☑02-4448 7131; www.coolangattaestate.com. au; 1335 Bolong Rd, Shoalhaven Heads; r $140-220; P✳☎☎☀) Staying on this venerable wine-producing estate is a real treat. Rooms, spread across different buildings, vary widely, from a cute convict-built timber cottage with a high bed and historic feel, to cosy rooms in the servants' quarters or separate lodge building. Room-only rates are available, and prices are significantly lower midweek. It's a popular wedding venue, so weekends are often booked out.

The estate is 13km east of the Bomaderry Princes Hwy junction.

Quest Nowra
APARTMENT **$$**

(☑02-4421 9300; www.questnowra.com.au; 130 Kinghorne St; studio apt $189-216, 1-bedroom apt $209-236; P☺✳☎) A welcome addition to Nowra's somewhat limited accommodation scene, these jazzy modern apartments are run in an upbeat, amiable way in the centre of town. Studios have a big bed, a hotplate, a proper fridge and a microwave, while the apartments add a full kitchen and laundry. Space and facilities are excellent, and there's an on-site smokehouse cafe-restaurant. Rates can drop sharply off-season depending on demand.

🍴 Eating & Drinking

★ Wharf Rd   MODERN AUSTRALIAN $$
(☑ 02-4422 6651; www.wharfrd.com.au; 10 Wharf Rd; small/large plates $17/32; ⊘ noon-3pm & 6-10pm Wed-Sat, noon-3pm Sun, extended hours Dec & Jan) Right on the river, this restaurant is in Nowra's nicest corner, especially when the jacarandas are blooming alongside. Despite the roar of traffic, the dining room is a romantic venue for quality, cosmopolitan cuisine Shared plates include alpaca sirloin, blue-eye trevalla with chilli, or avocado and squid tacos. It's a likeable, unpretentious place that's easily the best restaurant in town.

★ Hop Dog Beerworks   CRAFT BEER
(☑ 0428 293 132; www.hopdog.com.au; Unit 2, 175 Princes Hwy; ⊘ tastings & sales 10am-4pm Tue-Thu & Sat, 10am-6pm Fri) In an industrial estate 4km south of central Nowra, Hop Dog's beautifully balanced hoppy brews have iconic status with beerhounds across the country. There's always something new on offer, and, despite the unromantic retail barn surrounds, it's great to drop by for a chat and a sip of something. Bottles and growlers are available to take away. It's near the big Bunnings Warehouse.

ℹ Information

Nowra Visitor Centre (☑ 1300 662 808; www.shoalhaven.nsw.gov.au; 42 Bridge Rd; ⊘ 9am-5pm Mon-Thu & Sat, 9am-6pm Fri, 10am-2pm Sun) Just west of the Princes Hwy in a theatre complex.

ℹ Getting There & Away

Premier (☑ 13 34 10; www.premierms.com.au) has buses to Sydney ($25, three hours) and Eden ($57, five to six hours) via Ulladulla ($18, one hour) and other coastal towns.

Sydney Trains (☑ 13 15 00; www.sydneytrains.info) run from Sydney to Kiama, where you change to a train on the same platform for the onward connection to Nowra (Bomaderry) via Berry. The total journey takes around 2¾ hours. There's a train every hour or two.

Local buses connect Bomaderry station with the centre of town and run to Jervis Bay, Berry and surrounding towns.

Jervis Bay

This large, sheltered bay combines snow-white sand, crystalline waters, national parks and frolicking dolphins. Seasonal visitors include Sydney holidaymakers (summer and most weekends), and migrating whales (May to November).

In 1995 the Aboriginal community won a land claim in the Wreck Bay area and now jointly administers Booderee National Park at the southern end of the bay. By a strange quirk this area is actually part of the Australian Capital Territory, not NSW.

Most development is around Huskisson and Vincentia, and the northern shore has less tourist infrastructure. Beecroft Peninsula forms the northeastern side of Jervis Bay, ending in the dramatic sheer cliffs of Point Perpendicular. Most of the peninsula is navy land but is usually open to the public and harbours some beautiful, secluded beaches.

◉ Sights

Jervis Bay Maritime Museum   MUSEUM
(☑ 02-4441 5675; www.jervisbaymaritimemuseum.asn.au; Woollamia Rd, Huskisson; adult/child $10/free; ⊘ 10am-4pm) With a historic collection, the 1912 *Lady Denman* ferry and **Timbery's Aboriginal Arts & Crafts** gallery and shop. There's a growers' market on the first Saturday of the month, and a visitor information centre.

🏃 Activities

Huskisson is the centre for most activities, which include whale watching, dolphin watching, kayaking and kitesurfing. South of Huskisson, the sand of gorgeous **Hyams Beach** is reputedly the world's whitest.

Jervis Bay Kayaks   KAYAKING
(☑ 02-4441 7157; www.jervisbaykayaks.com.au; 13 Hawke St, Huskisson; kayak hire 2hr/4hr/day $39/59/69, sea kayak hire 3hr/day $60/75, bike hire 2hr/day $29/50, tours $96-145) This friendly spot offers rentals of simple sit-on-top kayaks and stand-up paddleboards as well as of single and double sea kayaks on St Georges Basin or Jervis Bay (with experience). It can organise guided sea-kayaking trips, and self-guided camping and kayaking expeditions. It also hires bikes.

Dive Jervis Bay   DIVING, SNORKELLING
(☑ 02-4441 5255; www.divejervisbay.com; 64 Owen St, Huskisson; 2 dives $199) The marine park is popular with divers: the clear water offers

good visibility, and there are lots of fruitful sites. Snorkellers can visit a nearby seal colony (May to October). This set-up offers PADI courses and guided dives, as well as equipment rental and bike hire.

⌲ Tours

Jervis Bay Wild   WILDLIFE, BOATING
(☑ 02-4441 7002; www.jervisbaywild.com.au; 58 Owen St, Huskisson; trips $35-95) This operator offers 90-minute dolphin-watching trips and longer trips that offer whale watching in season and a circuit of the bay's beautiful beaches at other times. Another trip buses you to Currarong for a cruise back to Huskisson exploring the cliffscapes around the Beecroft Peninsula.

Dolphin Watch Cruises   WILDLIFE, BOATING
(☑ 02-4441 6311; www.dolphinwatch.com.au; 50 Owen St, Huskisson; ⊙ dolphin-/whale-/seal-watching tour $35/65/85) This well-established set-up on the main street in Huskisson offers tours in a small, fast boat and a larger, more sedate triple-decker. Whale watching is great in season (September to November). It also has a 38ft catamaran available for sailing charters.

⌸ Sleeping

Prices increase on weekends and in January. Huskisson is the principal accommodation hub, but there are options in many of the settlements. Booderee National Park offers campsites, as does the Beecroft Peninsula.

Huskisson B&B   B&B $$
(☑ 02-4441 7551; www.huskissonbnb.com.au; 12 Tomerong St, Huskisson; r $225-255; P ⊕ ❋ ☎ ☎) This sweet centenarian timber cottage with a verandah, near the entrance to town, offers four bright, airy and colourful rooms containing comfy beds, stylish bathrooms with freestanding bathtubs and fluffy towels, and lots of little facilities that ease your stay. Breakfast is a quality affair that extends into cooked territory at weekends.

★ Paperbark Camp   LODGE $$$
(☑ 02-4441 6066; www.paperbarkcamp.com.au; 571 Woollamia Rd, Woollamia; d $395-620; P ⊕ ☎) ✦ Camp in ecofriendly style in these 12 super-luxurious safari tents with en suites and wraparound decks. It's set in dense bush 4km from Huskisson; borrow kayaks to paddle up the creek to the bay, or grab a bike for the ride into town. There's an excellent restaurant here exclusively for guests, and an impressive breakfast is included.

There's no power in the tents except for solar lighting, but there are chargers and a guest fridge in the reception complex.

✖ Eating & Drinking

Huskisson is a trendy weekend spot for Sydneysiders and has a couple of excellent cafes, good pub food and a classy Asian fusion restaurant. Eating is much more limited in the Bay's other settlements, though there are options in Vincentia, Callala Bay and elsewhere.

5 Little Pigs   CAFE $
(☑ 02-4441 7056; www.5littlepigs.com.au; 64 Owen St, Huskisson; dishes $12-19; ⊙ 7am-4pm Sun-Thu, to 5pm Fri & Sat; ☎ ☑) Likeable and upbeat, this main-street cafe opens early and offers decent coffee and a range of excellent breakfasts and lunches. Blackboard specials add options and the friendly owners are good for a chat.

Wild Ginger   ASIAN $$
(☑ 02-4441 5577; www.wild-ginger.com.au; 42 Owen St, Huskisson; mains $31.50; ⊙ 3-11pm Tue-Sun; ☎) By some distance Huskisson's most sophisticated restaurant, Wild Ginger is a relaxed showcase of flavours from Thailand, across Southeast Asia and Japan. Look forward to tasty local seafood featuring in delicately treated, aroma-packed dishes. It also does cocktails, which are only $10 until 6pm.

Huskisson Hotel   PUB
(Husky Pub; ☑ 02-4441 5001; www.thehuskisson.com.au; 73 Owen St, Huskisson; ⊙ 11am-midnight Mon-Sat, to 10pm Sun; ☎) The social centre of Huskisson and indeed the whole Jervis Bay area is this light and airy pub that offers fabulous bay views and decent food, running from pizzas and burgers to fish and steak dishes, with daily specials in each category. The sizeable outside deck here packs out over summer and there's live music most weekends.

❶ Information

Jervis Bay Visitor Information Centre (Woollamia Rd, Huskisson; ⊙ 10am-4pm) Helpful tourist information within the Jervis Bay Maritime Museum building.

❶ Getting There & Away

Nowra Coaches (☑ 02-4423 5244; www.nowracoaches.com.au) runs buses around the Jervis Bay area, with connections to Nowra and the train station at Bomaderry.

Booderee National Park

Overlooking the crystal-clear waters of the southernmost part of Jervis Bay, this is a standout national park offering excellent beaches with adjacent camp sites, an interesting botanic garden, short walking trails and Indigenous heritage.

◉ Sights

Booderee Botanic Gardens　　　　　GARDENS
(www.booderee.gov.au; ⊙ 8am-4pm) With enormous rhododendrons and coastal plant species once used for food and medicine by local Indigenous groups, these botanic gardens are within the park off the road to Cave Beach.

⌂ Sleeping

Bristol Point　　　　　CAMPGROUND $
(☏ 02-4443 0977; www.booderee.gov.au; camp sites $22, plus per adult/child $11/5; ℗⊜) This sweet rustic national park camp site has forested sites with a short walking track down to a beach on Jervis Bay. It's for tents only and there's no power. It's a lot cheaper outside of school holidays. You can walk to the Green Patch beach and camp site at low tide.

Cave Beach　　　　　CAMPGROUND $
(☏ 02-4443 0977; www.booderee.gov.au; camp sites $22, plus per adult/child $11/5; ℗) A grassy camping area near a majestic ocean beach means this is prime territory for surfers. There are toilets and cold-water showers. It's walk-in, so tents only. It's a 500m walk from the car park down to the sites, so don't leave valuables in your vehicle.

Green Patch　　　　　CAMPGROUND $
(☏ 02-4443 0977; www.booderee.gov.au; camp sites $22, plus per adult/child $11/5; ℗) The largest of the Booderee campsites and the only one where campervans are allowed, this site is divided into two sections on either side of a lagoon. It's a short walk to the beach on Jervis Bay. There's no power but there's water, toilets, showers and barbecue facilities.

❶ Information

Booderee Visitor Centre (☏ 02-4443 0977; www.booderee.gov.au; Jervis Bay Rd; ⊙ 9.30am-3pm Sun-Thu, 9am-4pm Fri & Sat, 9am-4pm daily in Jan) Get maps and info from Booderee visitor centre at the Booderee National Park entrance.

❶ Getting There & Away

Buses get as far as Hyams Beach, but not to the park itself.

Ulladulla & Mollymook

POP 12,100

Ulladulla is a fishing-focused town with a picturesque coastal location. Adjoining it to the north, Mollymook has a gorgeous beach and is a favourite summer destination for Sydneysiders. There are some excellent places to stay and eat in town and other great beaches nearby.

◉ Sights & Activities

Milton　　　　　VILLAGE
The characterful 19th-century town of Milton, 6km north of Ulladulla on the Princes Hwy, is a pleasant spot to visit, with craft shops, heritage buildings and an up-and-coming hipster vibe. There are good places to eat and stay here too.

Murramarang National Park　　　NATIONAL PARK
(www.nationalparks.nsw.gov.au; per car per day $8) Stretching along a secluded section of coastland, this scenic park offers excellent beaches, Indigenous heritage and plentiful animal and bird life. Surfing is good at several beaches and marked walking trails give scope for land-based activity.

★ Pigeon House Mountain　　　　HIKING
(Didthul) Some 33km west of Ulladulla by road, this iconic mountain in the Morton National Park section of the Budawang range is an excellent walk. It involves two climbs through bush separated by a flat phase, then an ascent up a series of ladders to a summit with magnificent views. It's 5.3km return from the car park; allow three to four hours.

⌂ Sleeping

Ulladulla Lodge　　　　　HOSTEL $
(☏ 02-4454 0500; www.ulladullalodge.com.au; 63 Princes Hwy, Ulladulla; dm $35, d $80-85; ℗⊜) This guesthouse-style place has a surf vibe and laid-back feel. It's clean, comfy, and pretty close to the beach. The owners hire surfboards, wetsuits and kayaks. There's a common kitchen and barbecues, though limited wi-fi reception.

Mollymook Shores　　　　　MOTEL $$
(☏ 02-4455 5888; www.mollymookshores.com.au; 11 Golf Ave, Mollymook; r $145-235; ℗⊜❋☎) Right by the beachfront in Mollymook,

this is more hotel than motel in style, with rooms arranged around a leafy courtyard. They've all been recently renovated and are spacious and well-equipped. Owners and staff are helpful and this makes an excellent coastal base. Seven different room types offers slightly different facilities. There's room-service breakfast but no restaurant.

★ **Bannisters Pavilion**　　　　HOTEL $$$
(☑ 02-4455 3044; www.bannisters.com.au; 87 Tallwood Ave, Mollymook; r $275-430; P ⊜ ❋ 🐾 ➳) Just back from Mollymook beach, this new hotel is visually striking but designed with great subtlety, blending in well with its surroundings. There's space to spare here, with wide hallways, plush, light rooms with pleasant woody outlooks and private patio or balcony space. The top deck is a lot of fun, with a bar, a heated pool and a restaurant creating a very casual-chic space.

★ **Bannisters by the Sea**　　　HOTEL $$$
(☑ 02-4455 3044; www.bannisters.com.au; 191 Mitchell Pde, Mollymook; r $365-510, ste $430-925; P ⊜ ❋ 🐾 ➳) The bones of a 1970s motel provide the basis of this hip, unassumingly luxurious place. Rooms are effortlessly stylish, with light, appropriately beachy decor. Balconies with lovely coastal views and the sound of the rolling surf are highlights, as are the can-do staff and quality restaurant. Furled umbrellas outside every door are a nice touch: this is the South Coast, after all.

Breakfast is included in all rates.

✕ Eating

Hayden's Pies　　　　　　　BAKERY $
(☑ 02-4455 7798; 166 Princes Hwy, Ulladulla; pies $4-7; ⊙ 6am-5pm Mon-Sat, 7am-5pm Sun) With traditional ones and a range of innovative gourmet pies – think Peking Duck or goat curry – this excellent bakery is awash with crusty goodness and delicious aromas. There's a daily pie special, gluten-free options and other home baking treats. Are these the South Coast's best pies? It's hard to think of a tastier one.

★ **Tallwood**　　　MODERN AUSTRALIAN, CAFE $$
(☑ 02-4455 5192; www.tallwoodeat.com.au; 2/85 Tallwood Ave, Mollymook; breakfast $12-26, dinner mains $28-36; ⊙ 6-10pm Wed-Fri & Mon, 8am-2.30pm & 6-10pm Sat & Sun, open for coffee at other times, longer hours Jan; ☑) Tallwood kicks off the day with excellent coffee and delicious breakfasts such as ricotta hotcakes, before segueing into more innovative dishes at weekend brunches and dinner. Highlights to be enjoyed in the colourful and modern surroundings include Portuguese fish cakes with saffron mayo, Balinese-spiced duck, and *dukkah*-spiced eggplant. There are good vegetarian options, and Australian craft beers and wines are proudly featured.

★ **Cupitt's Winery**
& Restaurant　　　MODERN AUSTRALIAN $$$
(☑ 02-4455 7888; www.cupitt.com.au; 58 Washburton Rd, Ulladulla; mains $30-40; ⊙ food noon-2pm Wed-Sun & 6-8.30pm Fri & Sat, winery 10.30am-5pm Wed-Sun; 🐾) Enjoy respected cuisine and wine tasting in this restored 1851 creamery, 3km west of town and well signposted. It's a pleasantly rural location with relaxing views over a lake and cattle grazing in a green valley. There's boutique vineyard accommodation (one/two nights $330/575) and a craft brewery. The restaurant is focused on quality ingredients and slow food principles. Book ahead.

Rick Stein at Bannisters　　　SEAFOOD $$$
(☑ 02-4455 3044; www.bannisters.com.au; 191 Mitchell Pde, Mollymook; mains $36-48; ⊙ 12.30-3pm & 6-10pm Wed, Sat & Sun, 6-10pm Thu & Fri; 🐾) Elegantly situated on Bannister's Point, 1km north of town. Celebrity chef Rick Stein's excellently selected and presented seafood fare matches the fine views. There's a touch of French and a touch of Asian to the menu, which usually includes oysters, local snapper and seafood pie.

ⓘ Information

Shoalhaven Visitor Centre (☑ 02-4444 8819; www.shoalhavenholidays.com.au; Princes Hwy, Ulladulla; ⊙ 9am-5pm Mon-Sat, 9am-4pm Sun) Bookings and information in the civic centre and library on the highway.

ⓘ Getting There & Away

Premier (☑ 13 34 10; www.premierms.com.au) runs between Sydney ($35, 4¼ to five hours) and Eden ($50, four hours), via Batemans Bay ($14, 45 minutes) and Nowra ($18, one hour).

Eurobodalla Coast

Meaning 'Land of Many Waters', this southern coastline celebrates all things blue. Swathes of green also punctuate the area's sprawling Eurobodalla National Park.

Batemans Bay

POP 11,300

Good nearby beaches and a sparkling estuary make this fishing port one of the South Coast's most popular holiday centres. The town sits at the point where the Clyde River becomes the sea and has a somewhat old-fashioned summer resort feel. Batemans Bay is a good base for watery activities.

◉ Sights

Closest to town is **Corrigans Beach**, and longer beaches north of the bridge lead into Murramarang National Park. Surfers flock to **Pink Rocks**, **Surf Beach**, **Malua Bay**, **McKenzies Beach** and **Bengello Beach**. **Broulee** has a wide crescent of sand, but there's a strong rip at the northern end.

☆ Activities

Batemans Bay is a fine base for getting out on the water. Numerous operators offer lessons, hire and guided excursions with kayaks, surfboards, snorkels or stand-up paddleboards. Some are based in other towns but operate right along this section of coast.

Total Eco Adventures   WATER SPORTS
(☑02-4471 6969; www.totalecoadventures.com.au; 7/77 Coronation Dr, Broulee) This set-up offers kayaking, with various river excursions around the region, as well as hire. It also does snorkelling and stand-up paddling excursions and rents out surfboards.

Surf the Bay Surf School   SURFING
(☑0432 144 220; www.surfthebay.com.au; group/private lesson $40/90) This surfing and paddleboarding school operates at Batemans, Broulee and Narooma and has special courses for kids during school holidays. It also hires equipment.

Region X   KAYAKING
(☑1300 001 060; http://regionx.com.au; kayak rental 1hr $30, tours $75-95) Rent a kayak to explore nearby waterways or take one of several paddling tours around Batemans Bay and the coast to the south. It also offers cycle hire. The hire station is at Mossy Point, south of Batemans.

⌂ Sleeping

Zorba Waterfront Motel   MOTEL $$
(☑02-4472 4804; www.zorbamotel.com.au; Orient St; r $130-180; P❄✳🅿) Handily located right by the string of bayside eateries, this is a friendly, family-run place that has been a solid option for years. The blue trim is true to its Greek name and rooms are spacious and comfortable, with balconies or terrace space. It's worth the small extra cost to get one with water views.

Bay Breeze   MOTEL $$
(☑02-4472 7222; www.baybreezemotel.com.au; 21 Beach Rd; r $175-300; P❄✳🅿) Very centrally located, this upmarket motel has a super position overlooking the bay. It's very professionally run, and with just seven rooms, it has the attention to detail of a boutique hotel. There's a subtle Balinese theme in the attractive rooms, which are equipped with coffee machines and stylish bathrooms.

✖ Eating

Innes' Boatshed   FISH & CHIPS $
(☑02-4472 4052; 1 Clyde St; fish & chips $14, 6 oysters $9; ⊙9am-8pm Sun-Thu, 9am-8.30pm Fri & Sat) Since the 1950s this has been one of the South Coast's best-loved fish-and-chip and oyster joints. This is arguably the centre of the town. Head out to the spacious deck but mind the pelicans. It's cash only and there's no alcohol served or BYO arrangement.

Blank Canvas   CAFE $$
(☑02-4472 5016; Annetts Arcade, Orient St; dishes $14-32; ⊙8.30am-2pm & 5.30-8.30pm Wed-Mon Feb-Dec, 8.30am-9pm daily Jan; 🅿) Right on the water with a pleasant shady terrace, this cafe by day morphs into a more intimate modern Australian dining experience in the evenings. It takes coffee seriously, with cold drip and various single origins available, making this the town's best stop for breakfast or brunch.

On the Pier   SEAFOOD $$$
(☑02-4472 6405; www.onthepier.com.au; 2 Old Punt Rd; mains $29-35; ⊙6-8.30pm Thu, noon-2pm & 6-8.30pm Fri & Sat, 9am-3pm Sun) With a lovely waterside location, this friendly Batemans favourite has magical views over the river and hills behind, especially at sunset. Local fish are a highlight, but it also does tasty meat dishes. Service is cheery and the ambience fairly casual. Opening hours vary somewhat through the year.

❶ Information

Batemans Bay Visitor Centre (☑02-4472 6900; www.eurobodalla.com.au; cnr Princes Hwy & Beach Rd; ⊙9am-5pm Sep-Apr, 9am-4pm May-Aug) Covering town and the wider Eurobodalla area.

WORTH A TRIP

MOGO

Mogo is a historic strip of wooden houses with cafes and souvenir shops 9km south of Batemans Bay. It was originally a gold-rush town and **Gold Rush Colony** (☑02-4474 2123; www.goldrushcolony.com.au; 26 James St; adult/child $20/12; ☺10am-4pm) is a re-creation of a pioneer village of that era, complete with free gold panning and cabins for accommodation.

Mogo Zoo (☑02-4474 4930; www.mogozoo.com.au; 222 Tomakin Rd; adult/child $31/16; ☺9am-5pm), 2km east off the highway, is a small but interesting zoo with rare white lions and an enthralling troop of gorillas.

❶ Getting There & Away

The scenic Kings Hwy climbs the escarpment and heads to Canberra from just north of Batemans Bay.

Premier (☑13 34 10; www.premierms.com.au) runs buses to Sydney ($45, six hours) and Eden ($46, three to four hours) via Ulladulla ($16, 45 minutes) and Moruya ($11, 30 minutes).

Murrays (☑13 22 51; www.murrays.com.au) runs buses to Canberra ($37.60, 2½ hours), Moruya ($13.60, 40 minutes) and Narooma ($20.90, 1¾ hours).

V/Line (☑1800 800 007; www.vline.com.au) runs a bus-train combination to Melbourne via Bairnsdale ($60.60, 11½ hours) on Tuesdays, Fridays and Sundays.

Priors (☑02-4472 4040; www.priorsbus.com.au) runs regional services, including a bus to Broulee and Moruya via various surf beaches.

Moruya

POP 2500

Moruya ('black swan') has Victorian buildings gathered around a broad river. There's a popular Saturday market and a couple of great places for a bed and a meal.

🛏 Sleeping & Eating

★ **Post & Telegraph B&B**   B&B $$
(☑02-4474 5745; www.postandtelegraphbb.blogspot.com; cnr Page & Campbell Sts; s/d incl breakfast $125/155; ⓟ☺🛜) This 19th-century post and telegraph office is now an enchanting four-room B&B with great historical character. High ceilings, period features and antique furnishings and objects are allied with friendly, genuine hospitality and numerous thoughtful details. There's a lovely shared verandah, decanters of sherry and port and an excellent common lounge. You couldn't ask for a lovelier spot to stop.

The River   MODERN AUSTRALIAN $$$
(☑02-4474 5505; www.therivermoruya.com.au; 16b Church St; mains $30-36, 5-course degustation $85, with matching wines $115; ☺noon-2.30pm Wed-Sun, 6-9.30pm Wed-Sat; ✸) Perched right over the river in a position just west of the bridge in downtown Moruya, The River combines local and seasonal ingredients with international flavours. There's a short, quality modern Australian menu with a five-course tasting menu option. Book ahead.

❶ Getting There & Away

Moruya Airport (MYA; ☑0409 037 520; www.esc.nsw.gov.au; George Bass Dr) is 7km from town, near North Head. **Rex** (☑13 17 13; www.rex.com.au) flies from Merimbula and Sydney.

Murrays (☑13 22 51; www.murrays.com.au) buses head to Canberra ($40.80, 3½ hours), Batemans Bay ($13.30, 40 minutes) and Narooma ($14.80, 45 minutes).

Premier (p231) runs buses to Sydney ($49, six to seven hours) via Batemans Bay ($11, 30 minutes) and in the other direction to Eden ($46, 2½ to three hours) via all coastal towns.

V/Line (p231) runs a bus-train combination to Melbourne via Bairnsdale ($60.60, 11½ hours) on Tuesdays, Fridays and Sundays.

Narooma

POP 2400

At the mouth of a tree-lined river estuary and flanked by surf beaches, Narooma is a pretty seaside town. It is also the jumping-off point for Montague Island, a very rewarding offshore excursion.

◎ Sights

★ **Montague Island
(Baranguba)**   NATURE RESERVE
(www.montagueisland.com.au) Nine kilometres offshore from Narooma, this small, pest-free island is home to seabirds and fur seals. Little penguins nest here, especially from September to February, while seals (and offshore whales) are most numerous from September to November.

Various guided tours (p232) conducted by park rangers are number- and weather-dependent; book ahead through the visitor centre. The morning tours are longer and the evening tours wait for the penguins to come ashore. Boat operators can combine the island visit with snorkelling and whale watching.

You can stay at the island's beautifully renovated **lighthouse keepers' cottages** (☑02-4476 0800; www.nationalparks.nsw.gov.au; Montague Island; cottages $1200-1800; ☻☎) ☝, but you'll need to book well ahead.

🏃 Activities

Narooma Marina BOATING
(☑02-4476 2126; www.naroomamarina.com.au; 30 Riverside Dr; boat per hour/half-day/day $55/145/265, surfboard half/full day $20/40, kayak $25 1st hour then $20 per hour) This friendly set-up on the river hires out canoes, kayaks, pedalos, fishing boats, surfboards and stand-up paddleboards. Basically, it's a one-stop shop for getting you out on the water. Note that you aren't allowed to land at Montague Island except on an approved tour.

Underwater Safaris DIVING
(☑0415 805 479; www.underwatersafaris.com. au; 1/2 dives $80/120) This diving operator runs PADI courses and guided dives around Montague Island and elsewhere along the coast. It also runs snorkelling and whale-watching excursions.

☞ Tours

Montague Island Nature Reserve Tours WALKING, BOATING
(☑02-4476 2881; www.montagueisland.com.au; per person $90-125) A number of operators run boat trips to Montague Island, where you link up with a national parks guide to show you over the island, visiting the seal colonies, lighthouse and more. Evening tours in season let you watch the penguins march back onshore. You can book via the visitor centres at Narooma or Batemans Bay (p230).

🛏 Sleeping

Narooma Motel HOSTEL, MOTEL $
(☑02-4476 3287; www.naroomamotel.com.au; 243 Princes Hwy; dm $35-40, d $100-130; ℗☻@☎) Offering a genuine welcome and very fair prices, this motel is a likeable place that offers compact budget motel-style rooms and dormitory accommodation. There's a sizeable common kitchen, a lovely conservatory lounge and a peaceful garden area with barbecue. Heather and Les are kind hosts who go out of their way to make you feel welcome.

Lynch's Hotel HOTEL $
(☑02-4476 2001; 135 Wagonga St; s/d without bathroom $70/100; ℗☻☎) This old-school timber pub in the heart of town offers simple but rather endearing rooms with shared kitchen and bathroom facilities. Try to grab a room on one of the verandahs. It's a place without pretensions but with plenty of character. The pub and restaurant downstairs are also worthwhile.

★**Whale Motor Inn** MOTEL $$
(☑02-4476 2411; www.whalemotorinn.com; 104 Wagonga St; d $143-231; ℗☻❄☎❄❄) ☝ Excellently run by a friendly couple, this is a standout place to stop that offers a lot even in the lower categories: the Premier rooms are a real bargain, capacious and modern. The range of suites ramps it up another notch, with sophisticated facilities and lots of thoughtful extras. There's a small pool, a quality restaurant and a lovely panoramic outlook.

Anchors Aweigh B&B $$
(☑02-4476 4000; www.anchorsaweigh.com.au; 5 Tilba St; s $105, d $149-225; ℗☻❄☎) ☝ Five very commodious and light rooms, two with spa bath and king-sized beds and one with a private verandah, make great South Coast bases at this cordially run B&B on a central side street. Public areas are great too; check out the teddy bear and other collections and the model train running through the breakfast room.

🍴 Eating

Quarterdeck Marina CAFE $$
(☑02-4476 2723; www.quarterdecknarooma.com. au; 13 Riverside Dr; mains $15-29; ☉10am-4pm Thu, 10am-8pm Fri, 10am-3pm & 6-8pm Sat, 8am-3pm Sun; ☎) Enjoy excellent seafood lunches and Sunday breakfasts in this red shed under the gaze of dozens of tikis and autographed photos of 1950s TV stars. Great inlet views and regular live music. It's a real good-times Narooma hub.

Whale Restaurant MODERN AUSTRALIAN $$$
(☑02-4476 2411; www.whalemotorinn.com; 104 Wagonga St; mains $31-36; ☉6-9pm Tue-Sat; ☎) ☝ The dining at this motel restaurant is as good as the dreamy coastal views. A philosophy of using quality local ingredients, some from its own vegetable garden, inspires a

menu that showcases the magnificent local oysters, homemade pasta, foraged ingredients, Tilba cheeses, sustainable fish and aged beef. There's a pleasant lounge for a pre-dinner drink.

ⓘ Information

Narooma Visitor Centre and Gallery (☑ 02-4476 2881; www.narooma.org.au; Princes Hwy; ☉ 9am-5pm Oct-Easter, 10am-4pm Easter-Sep) This friendly volunteer-run visitor centre is great for local information and also includes a gallery stocked by the local arts and crafts society and a free historical museum. You can buy bus tickets here too.

ⓘ Getting There & Away

Premier (☑ 13 34 10; www.premierms.com.au) runs buses to Eden ($41, 2½ hours) and Sydney ($58, seven hours) via Wollongong ($56, five hours).

V/Line (p231) runs a daily bus-train combination from Narooma to Melbourne ($60.60, 11 hours) via Bairnsdale.

Murrays (☑ 13 22 51; www.murrays.com.au) has daily buses to Moruya ($14.80, one hour), Batemans Bay ($20.90, two hours) and Canberra ($48.40, 4½ hours).

Local buses do circuits around the immediate Narooma area.

Tilba Tilba & Central Tilba

POP 400

The coastal road north from Bermagui rejoins the Princes Hwy just before the loop road to these National Trust villages in the shadow of Gulaga.

Tilba Tilba is tiny compared to its not-very-large neighbour, 2km down the road.

Central Tilba has remained virtually unchanged since it was a 19th-century gold-mining boom town. Cafes and craft shops fill the heritage buildings along touristy Bate St. Behind the Dromedary pub, walk up to the water tower for terrific views of Gulaga (formerly called Mt Dromedary, hence the name).

⊙ Sights

Foxglove Gardens　　　　　GARDENS
(☑ 02-4473 7375; www.foxglovegardens.com; Corkhill Dr, Tilba Tilba; adult/child $9/2; ☉ 9.30am-5pm Oct-Mar, 10am-4pm Apr-Sep) At the southern end of Tilba Tilba, this is a magical 3½-acre private garden. It offers a surprising and peaceful retreat into a secluded world of hidden avenues, a rose garden, bowers, a duck pond and other Victorian touches. The heritage cottage alongside was being prepped to offer B&B accommodation at time of research and should be well worth investigating.

🛏 Sleeping

★ **Bryn at Tilba**　　　　　　B&B $$
(☑ 02-4473 7385; www.thebrynattilba.com.au; 91 Punkalla-Tilba Rd, central Tilba; r $235-265; P ➲ 🞰) Follow central Tilba's main street a kilometre out of town to this fabulous building that sits on a green-lawned hillside. It's a lovely, peaceful spot with wide-arching views from the rooms and wide verandah. Three rooms with hardwood floors, a light, airy feel and characterful bathrooms share sumptuous common spaces; there's also a separate self-contained cottage.

ⓘ Information

Bates Emporium (Bate St, Central Tilba; ☉ 8am-5pm Mon-Fri, 8.30am-4.30pm Sat, 9am-4.30pm Sun; 🞰) There's information and fuel at Bates Emporium, at the start of the main street of central Tilba.

ⓘ Getting There & Away

Premier (☑ 13 34 10; www.premierms.com.au) runs a daily bus to Sydney ($59, eight hours) via Narooma ($8, 25 minutes), and Eden ($36, two hours) via Merimbula ($28, 90 minutes).

OFF THE BEATEN TRACK

MAGICAL MYSTERY BAY TOUR

South of Narooma, just before the turn-off to the Tilbas, take the road to gorgeously undeveloped **Mystery Bay** and the southernmost pocket of **Eurobodalla National Park**. At the southern end of the main surf beach, a rock formation has created an idyllic **natural swimming pool**. There's a council-run **campground** (☑ 0428 622 357; www.mysterybaycampground.com.au; Mystery Bay Rd, Mystery Bay; adult/child $16/4) under the trees. It's so close to the beach you could boil a billy with your tootsies in the sand – well, almost.

Sapphire Coast

The southernmost stretch of the NSW coast is one of its most memorable. Take virtually any road east of the Princes Hwy for mainly unblemished coast set amid rugged spectacular surroundings. Excellent national parks offer beaches, wildlife and rustic camping, the towns have an authentic feel and interesting heritage, and the whale watching from September to November is some of Australia's best. Another highlight is the local oysters, one of the world's great seafood treats.

Bermagui

POP 1500

South of bird-filled Wallaga Lake, Bermagui ('Bermie') is a laid-back fishing port with fisherfolk, surfers, alternative lifestylers and Indigenous Australians. Bermagui is off the highway, so it has a more tranquil vibe than some of the towns on it.

🛏 Sleeping

Harbourview Motel   MOTEL **$$**
(☑ 02-6493 5213; www.harbourviewmotel.com.au; 56-58 Lamont St; s $160-185, d $180-205; P ❄ ✳ 🛜) Run in very shipshape fashion, this motel has high-standard, spacious exemplary rooms that are kept spotless by the enthusiastic owner, who is a top source of local information. Each room has a private barbecue area, a full kitchenette and excellent facilities. There's an on-site Japanese restaurant and the place is very well located for the beach or Fishermen's Wharf.

Bermagui Motor Inn   MOTEL **$$**
(☑ 02-6493 4311; www.bermaguimotorinn.com.au; 38 Lamont St; s/d $120/130 deluxe d $165; P ❄ ✳ 🛜) With an excellent location right at Bermagui's principal intersection, this is run by an amiable couple and has spacious, upgraded modern rooms with comfortable beds and decent facilities, including a laundry. Rooms in the budget category have just a double bed, while queen rooms offer more space and amenities.

✕ Eating

★**Il Passaggio**   ITALIAN **$$**
(☑ 02-6493 5753; www.ilpassaggio.com.au; Fishermen's Wharf, 73 Lamont St; pizzas $18-24, mains $26-36; ⊙ 6-9pm Wed & Thu, noon-2pm & 6-11pm Fri-Sun) Cheerfully located on the top deck of the building by the fishing harbour, Il Passaggio has winning outdoor seating where you can look over the boats that brought your catch. Tasty proper-Italian pizzas are popular, and the short menu of quality mains, homemade pasta and antipasti bursts with flavour. Good wines by the glass and cheerful staff make this a winner.

🍷 Drinking & Nightlife

★**Horse & Camel Wine Bar**   WINE BAR
(☑ 02-6493 3410; www.horseandcamel.com.au; Fishermen's Wharf, 73 Lamont St; ⊙ 3-10pm Thu-Sun Mar-Nov, 2pm-late Wed-Mon Dec-Feb) On the top level of the Fishermen's Wharf complex, this amiably run wine bar is a top spot to relax with a glass of something interesting while pondering the views over the boats from the balcony seating. Inside is cosy, and there's a pleasing array of deli share plates and chunky weekend pizzas ($17 to $26). Hours vary slightly according to demand.

ℹ️ Information

Visitor Centre (☑ 02-6493 3054; www.visitbermagui.com.au; Bunga St; ⊙ 10am-4pm) The purpose-built information centre near the town's main intersection has a museum and discovery centre.

ℹ️ Getting There & Away

Premier (☑ 13 34 10; www.premierms.com.au) runs daily between Sydney ($60, 8½ hours) and Eden ($31, 1¾ hours).

V/Line (p231) runs four coaches a week to Bairnsdale, Victoria, connecting with a train to Melbourne (total $60.60, 10½ hours)

Merimbula & Pambula

POP 7700

Arrayed along a long, golden beach and an appealing inlet, Merimbula hosts both holidaymakers and retirees. In summer, this is one of the few places on the far South Coast that gets crowded.

Merimbula and nearby Pambula are deservedly famous for their wonderful oysters – make sure you try some.

👁 Sights

Potoroo Palace   ZOO
(☑ 02-6494 9225; www.potoroopalace.com; 2372 Princes Hwy, Yellow Pinch; adult/child $20/12; ⊙ 10am-4pm; 🚼) Warmly run Potoroo Palace, a not-for-profit animal sanctuary, has echidnas, kangaroos, dingoes, koalas, potoroos

and native birds. There's also a cafe here, with daily lunch specials. It's 9km northwest of Merimbula on the road to Bega.

Merimbula Aquarium
AQUARIUM

(☑ 02-6495 4446; www.merimbulawharf.com.au; Lake St; adult/child $22/15; ⏰ 10am-5pm) Right at the end of the road southeast of the centre, this is accessed through a restaurant with super views and has mostly local and tropical Australian fish species; there's also a turtle and some small sharks. Fish feeding sessions take place Monday, Wednesday and Friday at 11.30am. Entry usually includes a guided tour.

🏃 Activities

Cycle 'n' Surf
CYCLING, SURFING

(☑ 02-6495 2171; www.cyclensurf.com.au; 1b Marine Pde; bicycle hire per hr/half-day/full day $12/25/35) Reliable and friendly operator near the beach who specialises in bikes but also hires out bodyboards and surfboards.

Coastlife Adventures
SURFING, KAYAKING

(☑ 02-6494 1122; www.coastlife.com.au; Fishpen Rd; group/private surf lessons $65/120, kayak tours from $65, kayak & stand-up paddleboards rental per hour $25) Offer surfing and stand-up paddleboarding lessons and hire, plus sea kayak tours and kayak hire. It also has bases at Pambula Beach and Tathra.

Merimbula Marina
WILDLIFE WATCHING

(☑ 02-6495 1686; www.merimbulamarina.com; Merimbula jetty, Market St) This operator runs popular whale-watching tours (adults $60 to $69) three times daily from September to November, as well as dolphin-watching cruises ($35) and fishing trips ($90 for four hours). You can also hire a 'tinnie' boat and a rod and go for it yourself.

Merimbula Divers Lodge
DIVING

(☑ 02-6495 3611; www.merimbuladiverslodge.com. au; 15 Park St; 1/2 boat dives $69/120, equipment for 1/2 dives $55/99) Offers basic instruction, PADI courses and snorkelling trips – good for beginners. It runs guided dives to nearby wrecks, which include the *Empire Gladstone*, which sank in 1950. There are accommodation packages available too.

🛏 Sleeping

NRMA Merimbula Beach Holiday Park
CAMPGROUND $

(☑ 02-6499 8999; www.nrmaholidayparks.com.au; 2 Short Point Rd; camp sites $40-60, cabins & villas $150-360; 🅿️ 🐾 🛜 🏊 👶) A little away from the town centre but close to the surf action and vistas of Short Point Beach, this is a great spot with both powered and unpowered camp sites, some with clifftop views, and a range of cabins and villas, many of them quite upmarket.

Wandarrah Lodge
HOSTEL $

(☑ 02-6495 3503; www.wandarrahlodge.com.au; 8 Marine Pde; dm/s/d $32/60/70; 🅿️ 🐾 🛜) This clean, casual place, with friendly owners, a good kitchen and spacious shared areas, is near the surf beach and the bus stop. Rooms are simple, spotless and homey, with shared bathrooms, and there's a pool table, and kayak and surfboard hire. It was up for sale at time of research, so things may change.

Coast Resort
APARTMENT $$$

(☑ 02-6495 4930; www.coastresort.com.au; 1 Elizabeth St; 1-/2-/3-bedroom apt $320/520/740; 🅿️ 🐾 ❄️ 🛜 👶) This huge upmarket apartment-style complex is ultramodern and commodious. Facilities are great and the two pools, tennis court and proximity to the beach are all very appealing. Prices halve outside the January high season.

🍴 Eating

Dulcie's Cottage
BURGERS $

(www.dulcies.com.au; 60 Main St; burgers $12-17; ⏰ noon-midnight Mon-Sat, noon-10pm Sun; 🛜) Inner-city Sydney hipsterdom has arrived on the Sapphire Coast in the form of this bar and burger joint by the RSL club. A cute weatherboard cottage and casual outdoor seating makes a comfortable venue for convivial drinks and tasty burgers whipped up in a food truck out front (for licensing reasons apparently).

Merimbula Wharf
SEAFOOD $$

(☑ 02-6495 4446; www.merimbulawharf.com.au; Lake St; mains $18-31; ⏰ 10am-5pm year-round plus 6-9pm some nights Dec-Apr; 🛜) The views over bay and beach are just stunning from the windows of this friendly restaurant that incorporates an aquarium at the wharf southeast of central Merimbula. Lunch fish dishes are uncomplicated and tasty; ring for summer dinner opening hours as they are a little variable.

★ Wheelers
SEAFOOD $$$

(www.wheelersoysters.com.au; 162 Arthur Kaine Dr, Pambula; 12 oysters from shop $12-15, restaurant mains $34-42; ⏰ shop 10am-5pm Sun-Thu, 10am-6pm Fri & Sat, restaurant noon-2.30pm daily, 6pm-late Mon-Sat; 🚗) Come here on the way to Merimbula from Pambula, to enjoy totally delicious fresh oysters – either takeaway or from the shop or enjoyed in the relaxing restaurant. The menu features oysters prepared loads of ways and other great seafood and steak dishes. Tours showcasing some people's favourite bivalve depart at 11am Monday to Saturday ($12.50).

ℹ Information

Merimbula Visitor Information Centre
(☑ 02-6495 1129; www.sapphirecoast.com.au; 4 Beach St; ☉ 9am-5pm Mon-Fri, 9am-4pm Sat, 10am-4pm Sun) In the centre of town by the lake.

ℹ Getting There & Away

AIR

Merimbula Airport (MIM; ☑ 02-6495 4211; www.merimbulaairport.com.au; Arthur Kaine Dr) is 1km out of town on the road to Pambula. **Rex** (☑ 13 17 13; www.rex.com.au) flies daily to Melbourne and Sydney, some via Moruya. At time of research, **Free Spirit** (☑ 03-9994 6121; www.freespiritairlines.com.au) was flying between Melbourne and Merimbula three times a week.

BUS

Premier (☑ 13 34 10; www.premierms.com.au) has two daily buses to Sydney ($69, 8½ hours) and Eden ($11, 30 minutes). **NSW TrainLink** (☑ 13 22 32; www.nswtrainlink.info) runs a daily bus to Canberra ($40, four hours). **V/Line** (p231) runs buses to Bairnsdale in Victoria, where you can connect to Melbourne by train.

Local **buses** (Market St) run Mondays to Fridays to Eden and Bega at schoolkid-friendly hours.

Eden

POP 3000

Eden's a sleepy, appealing place with real local character set on magnificent Twofold Bay. Often the only bustle is down at the harbour when the fishing boats and cruise ships come in. When the wharf extension project is complete, the town will be even busier. Around the surrounding area are stirring beaches, national parks and wilderness areas.

Eden's began as a whaling town from as early as 1791. Now that the migrating humpback whales and southern right whales are left in peace, they pass so close to the coast that this is one of Australia's best whale-watching locations.

◎ Sights

Killer Whale Museum   MUSEUM
(☑ 02-6496 2094; www.killerwhalemuseum.com.au; 94 Imlay St; adult/child $10/2.50; ☉ 9.15am-3.45pm Mon-Sat, 11.15am-3.45pm Sun) Established in 1931, the museum's main purpose is to preserve the skeleton of Old Tom, a killer whale and local legend. His is an extraordinary story: this cetacean Judas used to round up humpbacks for the local whaling fleet. A theatrette screens a cetacean documentary, while other exhibits include one on wartime – a surprising number of vessels were sunk by German mines around here.

☞ Tours

Ocean Wilderness   KAYAKING
(☑ 0405 529 214; www.oceanwilderness.com.au; 4/6hr tours from $85/130) This professional set-up runs sea-kayaking trips through Twofold Bay and to Ben Boyd National Park, and a full-day excursion to Davidson Whaling Station.

Cat Balou Cruises   WILDLIFE
(☑ 0427 962 027; www.catbalou.com.au; Main Wharf, 253 Imlay St; adult/child $85/65) This crew operates 3½-hour whale-spotting voyages from September to November; there are also shorter budget trips (adult/child $60/45). At other times of the year, dolphins and seals can usually be seen during the three-hour bay cruise (adult/child $75/50).

Kiah Wilderness Tours   KAYAKING
(☑ 0429 961 047; www.kiahwildernesstours.com.au; 1167 Princes Hwy, Kiah) On the Towamba River 12km south of Eden, these offer guided kayak tours on a coastal estuary. Birdlife is great. There are two-hour tasters ($70) and half-day ($85 to $105) and full-day ($150) excursions.

✿ Festivals & Events

Whale Festival   STREET CARNIVAL
(www.edenwhalefestival.com.au; ☉ late Oct or early Nov) Eden comes alive for this festival, with a carnival, street parade and stalls plus guided whale watching and documentary screenings.

⌂ Sleeping

Great Southern Inn   PUB $
(☑ 02-6496 1515; www.greatsoutherninn.com.au; 121 Imlay St; basic/standard r $40/100; 🅿 ❄ 🛜) The pub in the heart of town offers great

value for its basic en suite rooms. The cheapest just has a bunk bed and a fan, but the price is appealingly low.

Seahorse Inn
BOUTIQUE HOTEL **$$**

(📞 02-6496 1361; www.seahorseinnhotel.com. au; Boydtown Park Rd, Boydtown; r $205-349; P ⊝ ✳ 🛜) At Boydtown, 8km south of Eden, the Seahorse Inn has a majestic waterside position with lawns running to the beach on Twofold Bay. It's a lavish boutique hotel with all the trimmings, and there's a good restaurant and garden bar, which are open to nonguests. Rooms are modern and very amply proportioned, with king-sized beds in all. Most have a balcony with water views.

All room rates include a continental breakfast.

Twofold Bay Motor Inn
MOTEL **$$**

(📞 02-6496 3111; www.twofoldbaymotorinn. au; 164-166 Imlay St; r $165-205; P ⊝ ✳ 🛜 ≋) Right in the centre of town, this cheerily run motel offers spacious modern hotel-standard rooms, some with water views. All have a kitchenette; there's also a tiny indoor pool.

★ Crown & Anchor Inn
B&B **$$$**

(📞 02-6496 1017; www.crownandanchoreden. au; 239 Imlay St; r $190-230, multinight stay $160-190; ⊙ Sep-May; P ⊝ 🛜) A real labour of love has gloriously restored this 1845 coaching inn, with period detail and original features throughout. It's a place of extraordinary character and historic authenticity. Rooms are small, cosy and delightful, with curious bathrooms hidden behind mirrors. There are lovely common areas too, including a back patio with a marvellous view over Twofold Bay. An excellent locally sourced breakfast is included.

The welcoming owners prefer guests to make reservations, and don't accept bookings that include young children.

✖ Eating

Sprout
CAFE **$**

(📞 02-6496 1511; www.sprouteden.com.au; 134 Imlay St; mains $12-18; ⊙ 7.30am-4pm Mon-Fri, 8am-3pm Sat & Sun; 🛜 🅿) 🍃 On the main street, this shop and cafe showcases lots of organic and sustainable produce, top-notch burgers and the best coffee in town. The back garden area is a pleasant spot in which to eat on a sunny day.

★ Wharfside Café
CAFE **$$**

(📞 02-6496 1855; Main Wharf, 253 Imlay St; dishes $15-26, dinner mains $28-33; ⊙ 8am-3pm daily year-round, plus 6-10pm Fri & Sat Nov-Mar; 🛜) Decent breakfasts, tasty coffee and great outdoor tables by the harbour make this handsome, friendly cafe-restaurant a good way to start the day. Try some local seafood with a glass of wine for lunch; dinner options are more elaborate creations around fresh fish, big steaks and rich, tasty sauces. The main wharf is downhill from town.

Great Southern Inn
PUB FOOD **$$**

(📞 02-6496 1515; www.greatsoutherninn.com.au; 158 Imlay St; mains $15-30; ⊙ food noon-2pm & 6-8pm; 🛜 🅗) Among some run-of-the-mill pub favourites, this spacious bistro out the back of the town's best pub does some really excellent local seafood, including delicious oysters and a reliably tasty catch of the day. Portions are generous and they're usually pretty good about serving a bit later than closing time too.

ℹ Information

Eden Visitor Centre (📞 02-6496 1953; www. visiteden.com.au; Mitchell St; ⊙ 9am-5pm Mon-Fri, 10am-4pm Sat & Sun) Bookings and information. By the main road roundabout in the centre. It also runs minibus tours to surrounding attractions.

ℹ Getting There & Away

Premier (📞 13 34 10; www.premierms.com. au) runs north to Sydney ($71, nine to 10 hours) twice daily via all major coastal towns. **NSW TrainLink** (📞 13 22 32; www.nswtrainlink.info) runs a daily bus service to Canberra ($42, 4½ hours). For Melbourne ($51, 8¼ hours), **V/Line** (p231) runs a bus and train combination via Bairnsdale.

Local buses have limited service to Merimbula and Bega on weekdays.

Ben Boyd National Park

With two sections either side of Eden, the 10,485-hectare **Ben Boyd National Park** (www.nationalparks.nsw.gov.au; vehicle in southern/northern section $8/free) is an excellent spot. The southern section has more to see, with some heritage buildings, a long coastal walk and top wildlife-spotting opportunities. It is accessed by mainly gravel roads leading off sealed Edrom Rd, which leaves the Princes Hwy 19km south of Eden.

◉ Sights

Green Cape Lightstation   LIGHTHOUSE
(☑ 02-6495 5000; www.nationalparks.nsw.gov.
au; Green Cape Rd; 2-/4-person cottage
$280/350) At the southern tip of the southern section of the Ben Boyd National Park,
elegant 1883 Green Cape Lightstation offers awesome views. There are hour-long
tours (available 10am to 2pm, adult/child
$10/5) and three lavishly restored keepers'
cottages. This is a great spot to see whales
in season, and you may well see wombats
nibbling the grass in the late afternoon.
On the way here, stop at the viewpoint for
majestic vistas over Disaster Bay and Wonboyn Beach.

Boyd's Tower   HISTORIC BUILDING
FREE At the end of Edrom Rd is the turn-off
for Boyd's Tower, built in the late 1840s with
Sydney sandstone. It was intended to be a
lighthouse, but the government wouldn't
give Boyd permission to operate it. It's an
impressive structure, and one of the trailheads for the Light to Light walk.

🏃 Activities

★ Light to Light Walk   HIKING
This excellent 30km coastal walk links
Boyd's wannabe lighthouse to the real one
at Green Cape. There are camp sites along
the route at Saltwater Creek and Bittangabee Bay.

🛏 Sleeping

Ben Boyd National Park
Campgrounds   CAMPGROUND $
(☑ 02-6495 5000; www.nationalparksnsw.gov.au;
adult/child $12/6, minimum $24) If you are
walking the 30km Light to Light Walk, there
are camp sites along the route at Saltwater
Creek and Bittangabee Bay, which can be
booked ahead online or by phone. They can
also be accessed by road.

SOUTHERN NSW & THE MURRAY

Just south of Sydney, the Southern Highlands offer the chance for a wonderful weekend getaway, best enjoyed with someone
special. Beyond, the 900km Hume Hwy is
the fastest way to travel between Sydney and
Melbourne, but the road is dull and it's notoriously easy to get a speeding fine.

Further down the Great Dividing Range
are the Snowy Mountains, Australia's highest sierra, with winter skiing and great summer walking and riding.

The Murray and Murrumbidgee Rivers
defining the Riverina district offer respite in
a harsh landscape, with irrigation harnessed
for agriculture, and a growing food-tourism
scene around Griffith.

Southern Highlands

With a lush, cool climate (even in summer),
a wealth of historical attractions, some seriously posh nosh and luxe lodgings, the compact area known as the Southern Highlands
makes for a wonderful day trip or weekend
break from Sydney – for the lowdown, see
www.southern-highlands.com.au.

Mittagong & Bowral

POP 8103 (MITTAGONG), 12,154 (BOWRAL)
While the twinned towns of Mittagong and
Bowral are separate entities (as locals would
be keen to declare), they're so inextricably
intertwined that it makes sense to look at
them as a pair.

Mittagong is the smaller of the two, 5km
to the north, and has a more down-to-
earth vibe. Big brother Bowral has a loftier,
classier feel, with some top-notch restaurants, stately heritage homes and luxury
accommodation.

◉ Sights

★ International Cricket
Hall of Fame   MUSEUM
(☑ 02-4862 1247; www.internationalcrickethall.
com.au; St Jude St, Bowral; adult/child $20/11;
⊙ 10am-5pm; P) Bowral is where the late,
great cricketer Sir Donald Bradman, Australia's most legendary sporting hero, spent
his boyhood. Incorporating the **Bradman
Museum of Cricket** (www.bradman.com.
au), which has an engrossing collection of
Ashes and Don-centric memorabilia, the
complex has a pretty cricket oval and boasts
an ever-expanding collection showcasing
the international game.

Mt Gibraltar Reserve   PARK
(☑ 02-4871 2888; 250 Oxley Dr, Mittagong; P) A
drive up to this fabulous reserve (at 863m)
with picnic areas and no fewer than three
lookouts, offering stunning views of the valley below, is a must.

WORTH A TRIP

BERRIMA

Just over 7km west of Bowral is heritage-classified Berrima, founded in 1829. Today it's like a living museum, featuring galleries, antique shops, and good food and wine. It's extremely popular with Sydney day-trippers at weekends and during public holidays.

Around 3km north of Berrima, **Berkelouw's Book Barn & Café** (☑02-4877 1370; www.berkelouw.com.au; Old Hume Hwy, Bendooley; ⊙9am-5pm) stocks more than 200,000 secondhand tomes and the attached **Bendooley Bar & Grill** (☑02-4877 2235; www.ben dooleyestate.com.au; 3020 Old Hume Hwy, Berrima; pizza $22-28, mains $28-38; ⊙10am-3pm; ❋☑) showcases local produce. Try the prawn-and-chilli pizza with an Aussie craft beer.

If you have some cash to splash and fancy yourself a foodie, a degustation at **Eschalot** (☑02-4877 1977; www.eschalot.com.au; 24 Old Hume Hwy, Berrima; mains $36-40, 7-course de-gustation $110; ⊙noon-2.30pm Thu-Sun, 6-9pm Wed-Sat; P ❋) will round out the perfect day.

Morton National Park   NATIONAL PARK

(☑02-4887 7270; www.nationalparks.nsw.gov.au/ visit-a-park/parks/Morton-National-Park; $8 per vehicle per day; P) Morton National Park, one of NSW's largest, features the deep gorges and high sandstone plateaus of the Budawang Range. It's easily accessible from Bundanoon, its northern gateway. Follow the well-marked bushwalking trails, admiring waterfalls that plunge into valleys below.

✦✦ Festivals & Events

★ **Bowral Tulip Time Festival**   CULTURAL
(www.tuliptime.net.au; ⊙Sep) Bowral explodes with colour during the beautiful spring flower festival.

🛏 Sleeping & Eating

Imperial Hotel & Motel   MOTEL $
(☑02-4861 1779; www.theimperial.com.au; 228-234 Bong Bong St, Bowral; r from $125; P❋🛜) This fabulous motel, set back from the eponymous and popular hotel, has stylish, modern, oversized rooms offering excellent value in pricey Bowral.

★ **Links House Hotel**   BOUTIQUE HOTEL $$$
(☑02-4861 1977; www.linkshouse.com.au; 17 Links Rd, Bowral; r from $210; P❋🛜) This boutique guesthouse has a drawing room and garden courtyard straight out of *Remains of the Day*. Prices are highest on Friday and Saturday.

Raw & Wild   CAFE $$
(☑02-4861 3129; 250 Bong Bong St, Bowral; mains $14-24; ⊙8am-5.30pm Sun-Thu, to 9pm Fri & Sat; ☑) ✐ Enter through the health-food shop to reach Bowral's best cafe, with a focus on all things organic, local, wild and sustainable. It's all very tasty too, and quality beers and wines mean you don't need to be too

virtuous. The weekend tapas nights are very popular.

★ **Biota Dining**   MODERN AUSTRALIAN $$$
(☑02-4862 2005; http://biotadining.com; 18 Kangaloon Rd, Bowral; brunch mains $19, degustation from $110; ⊙6-9.30pm Tue-Thu, noon-2.30pm & 6-9.30pm Fri & Mon, 9-11am & 6-9.30pm Sat & Sun) Innovative seasonal menus include dishes such as salted cucumber with oysters and beach plants, and the wine list is as good as the weekend brunch. Try the crab and creamed egg sliders with a restorative pepperberry Bloody Mary.

ℹ Information

Southern Highlands Visitors Centre (☑02-4871 2888; www.southern-highlands.com.au; 62-70 Main St, Mittagong; ⊙9am-5pm Mon-Fri, to 4pm Sat & Sun; 🕾) Comprehensive information on the area.

ℹ Getting There & Away

Mittagong is 110km from Sydney, just off the Hume Motorway. Bowral is 5km further south.

Sydney Trains (☑13 15 00; www.sydney trains.info) operates regular services from both towns to Sydney ($8.30, 1¾ hours).

Snowy Mountains

The 'Snowies' form part of the Great Dividing Range where it straddles the NSW–Victoria border. They include the highest peak on the Australian mainland, Mt Kosciuszko (2228m), and its vast national park. This is Australia's only true alpine area; snow falls from early June to late August and skiing is usually possible until October. Summer is also a very pleasant time to visit, with ample opportunities for hiking, cycling, kayaking and horse riding.

ℹ Getting There & Away

AIR

Regional Express (www.rex.com.au) flies week-days between Sydney and **Snowy Mountains Airport** (☑ 02-6452 5999; 1611 Kosciuszko Rd), which is 17km southwest of Cooma on the road to Jindabyne.

BUS

NSW TrainLink (☑ 13 22 32; www.nswtrainlink.info) Operates coaches on the Canberra–Cooma–Merimbula–Eden (daily) and Canberra–Cooma–Jindabyne (three per week) routes; from Canberra you can connect by train to Sydney.

V/Line (☑ 1800 800 007; www.vline.com.au) Coaches from Canberra stop in Cooma before continuing to Lakes Entrance and Bairnsdale, where you can connect by train to Melbourne.

Greyhound (☑ 1300 473 946; www.greyhound.com.au) During the ski season, Greyhound operates a coach service between Sydney and Thredbo, stopping in Canberra, Cooma, Jindabyne and at the Perisher Skitube.

Murrays (☑ 13 22 51; www.murrays.com.au) Operates a seasonal Snow Express coach (July and August) between Canberra and Thredbo, stopping in Cooma and Jindabyne.

Snoexpress (☑ 1800 642 112; www.snoexpress.com.au; ⊙ mid-Jun–mid-Sep) Runs a coach from Canberra to both Thredbo and Perisher on Fridays and Sundays during the ski season, also stopping in Jindabyne.

Other operators provide package trips, from as far away as Sydney and Port Stephens.

Cooma

ELEV 800M / POP 6300

Ringed by hills, Cooma is a nice-enough small town with some attractive 19th-century buildings scattered along its main

---

HORSING ABOUT

Perhaps due to the deep impression that Banjo Paterson's acclaimed poem 'The Man From Snowy River' has left on the Australian psyche, horse riding is a popular pursuit in these parts. You can channel your inner jackaroo on a multi-day back-country trek with **Reynella Rides** (☑ 02-6454 2386; www.reynellarides.com.au; 669 Kingston Rd, Adaminaby; 3-/4-/5-day treks from $1300/1600/1990) or **Snowy Wilderness** (☑ 1800 218 171; www.snowywilderness.com.au; Barry Way, Ingebirah; 2/3/4hr ride $110/165/220, 1-/3-/4-/5-day treks $315/990/1290/1590).

---

streets. It's laid-back and sleepy in summer, but its proximity to the snowfields keeps it busy during winter. Sydney-based skiers often stop here for an affordable night's accommodation before hitting the slopes the next day.

◉ Sights

NSW Corrective Services Museum   MUSEUM
(☑ 02-6452 5974; www.correctiveservices.justice.nsw.gov.au; 1 Vagg St; gold coin donation; ⊙ 9am-3pm Mon-Sat) Next to the still-functioning Cooma Gaol, this interesting museum exhibits artefacts from convict days through to the present, following the theme *Crime Through Time*. Jump-suited inmates conduct tours and sell their art and crafts.

Snowy Hydro Discovery Centre   MUSEUM
(☑ 1800 623 776; www.snowyhydro.com.au; Yulin Ave; ⊙ 8am-5pm Mon-Fri, 9am-2pm Sat & Sun) **FREE** You don't have to be an engineering tragic to be fascinated by the gargantuan feat of human endeavour that is the Snowy Mountains Scheme. This centre, 2km north of town, tells the story of its creation by way of a short introductory video and in-depth displays. Commenced in 1949, the hydroelectric scheme's seven powerstations, 16 major dams and 145km of tunnels took 25 years and more than 100,000 people to complete.

🛏 Sleeping & Eating

Cooma Snowy Mountains Tourist Park   CARAVAN PARK $
(☑ 02-6452 1828; www.coomatouristpark.com.au; 286 Sharp St; sites from $28, cabin with/without bathroom from $79/60; P ❀) On the highway, 1.5km west of town, this big place has basic units ranging from 'shearers' huts' (no bathrooms) to cabins with en suites. Prices shoot up in winter.

Ellstanmor   B&B $$
(☑ 02-6452 2402; www.ellstanmor.com.au; 32 Massie St; r from $150; P ❀) Built in 1875, this charming old two-storey house has four simply decorated but elegant en suite rooms. Guests are encouraged to spread out in the Victorian parlour and dining room. Rates include a continental breakfast, or you can order a cooked version.

Kettle & Seed   CAFE $
(☑ 02-6452 5882; www.snowymountainscoffee.com.au; 47 Vale St; mains $4.50-8.50; ⊙ 7am-4pm Mon-Fri, 8am-noon Sat) A coffee shop that

wouldn't be out of place in an upmarket Sydney suburb, this place roasts its own beans. The light meals (sandwiches, wraps, ham-and-cheese croissants and spinach pies) are good, but almost incidental when the coffee is this great.

ℹ️ Information

Cooma Visitor Centre (📞1800 636 525; www.visitcooma.com.au; 119 Sharp St; ⏰9am-3pm) Information and souvenirs.

Jindabyne

ELEV915M / POP 1730

Jindabyne is the closest town to Kosciuszko National Park's major ski resorts, and more than 20,000 visitors pack in over winter. In summer, it assumes a sluggish vibe, paced around paddling and fishing in its large lake. Lake Jindabyne was created in 1967 after the completion of a dam on the Snowy River as part of the vast hydroelectric Snowy Mountains Scheme; the original town of Jindabyne lies beneath the placid waters.

👁️ Sights & Activities

Snowy Region Visitor Centre   TOURIST INFORMATION
(📞02-6450 5600; www.nationalparks.nsw.gov.au; Kosciuszko Rd; ⏰8.30am-4.30pm) This large National Parks & Wildlife Service-run centre has displays on Kosciuszko National Park (look out for the tank of DayGlo critically endangered southern corroboree frogs), a cinema (screening a short film about the park during the day and blockbusters by night) and a cafe. Buy vehicle passes here and pick up locator beacons for back-country hikes (free with $400 deposit).

Mountain Adventure Centre   ADVENTURE SPORTS
(📞1800 623 459; www.mountainadventurecentre.com.au; Snowline Centre, 6532 Kosciuszko Rd; ⏰9am-4pm Nov-May, 8am-6pm Jun-Oct) Outdoor gear for sale and hire, and guided activities can be arranged. Try mountain biking, canoeing or hiking in summer, and cross-country skiing, telemarking or snowshoeing in winter.

Sacred Ride   ADVENTURE SPORTS
(📞02-6456 1988; www.sacredride.com.au; 6 Thredbo Tce; ⏰10am-4pm) These are the people to see for mountain biking. Gear hire and activities including wakeboarding, mountain biking, sailing, water skiing, canoeing and kayaking.

🛏️ Sleeping & Eating

Jindy Inn   GUESTHOUSE $
(📞02-6456 1957; www.jindyinn.com.au; 18 Clyde St; r from $99; 🅿️🐾📶) It doesn't look like much from the outside but this friendly guesthouse has spacious, nicely decorated motel-style rooms with comfy beds; some rooms have lake views. A continental breakfast is included and there's also a guest kitchen.

Snowy Mountains Backpackers   HOSTEL $
(📞02-6456 1500; www.snowybackpackers.com.au; 2/3 Gippsland St; dm/r from $30/65; @📶) Set above a popular cafe in the town centre, this little hostel has a large central lounge and a sunny deck. The rooms range from dorms to private rooms, all with shared facilities, and there's also a family room with an en suite.

Red Door Roastery   CAFE $
(📞02-6457 1122; www.reddoorroastery.com.au; Town Centre Complex, 33 Kosciuszko Rd; mains $7.50-16; ⏰7.30am-3pm daily Jun-Oct, Thu-Tue Nov-May) Grab an outdoor table with lake views and plan your day's adventure over Jindy's best coffee and an all-day menu that includes a terrific breakfast wrap.

Takayama   JAPANESE $$
(📞02-6456 1133; www.takayama.com.au; L1, Nuggets Crossing Shopping Centre, Snowy River Ave; mains $15-24; ⏰6-10pm Tue-Sat) Takayama isn't your typical small-town Japanese restaurant; for starters there's very little sushi on the menu. Instead, expect heartier, weather-appropriate dishes such as *gyoza* (dumplings), *karaage* (fried chicken), beef *tataki* (seared, marinated and finely sliced), whole fish and a truly excellent ramen soup.

Café Darya   PERSIAN $$$
(📞02-6457 1867; www.cafedarya.com.au; L1, 3 Kosciuszko Rd; mains $30-34; ⏰6-9pm Tue-Sat Dec-Oct) Fill up on slow-cooked lamb shank in Persian spices and rose petals or a rustic trio of dips at this long-standing eatery. BYO beer and wine. Cash only.

Kosciuszko National Park

Covering 694,000 hectares and stretching for 150km, this alpine park contains Australia's highest peak and is the source of two of the country's most legendary rivers:

SYDNEY & NEW SOUTH WALES SNOWY MOUNTAINS

the Murray and the Snowy. In winter it's a major ski destination, while in summer travellers come to walk the alpine tracks, drive the leafy back roads, explore the limestone caves and engage in some serious mountain biking.

The mountains have long been an important ceremonial destination for Aboriginal people, with large intertribal gatherings held here during summer, coinciding with the annual migration of the large edible Bogong moth.

⊙ Sights

Yarrangobilly Caves   CAVE
(☑ 02-6454 9597; www.nationalparks.nsw.gov.au; Snowy Mountains Hwy; site fee $3, 1/2/3 caves $18/30/45, guided tours adult/child $22/17; ⊙ 9am-4pm) Yarrangobilly Caves is a complex of three caves, with the requisite stalactites, helictites and a remarkable 4m stalagmite, known as Cleopatra's Needle. At the site there is also a blissfully located 20m mineral thermal pool, its green waters maintaining a constant temperature of 27°C year-round. We spotted kangaroos here last time we visited. The caves are 6km off the Snowy Mountains Hwy, which stretches from Cooma northwest to the Hume Hwy, cutting a meandering path through the beautiful highlands of Kosciuszko's north.

Activities

The main ski resorts are Thredbo, on the southern slopes of Kosciuszko, and Perisher on the eastern side. The much smaller Charlotte Pass resort is approached from the Perisher side and sits higher up the slopes.

The ski season officially lasts from Queen's Birthday weekend (early June) to Labour Day (early October). Snow-making machines ensure that there's usually some snow during these months, although it's not guaranteed. The most consistent actual snowfall is from June to August.

Off the slopes there's lively nightlife, excellent restaurants, and a plethora of facilities and activities catering to families. Both Thredbo and Perisher have a designated kids' skiing program, crèches and day care.

On the downside, the resorts tend to be particularly crowded at weekends and the limited season means operators have to get their returns quickly, so costs are high.

Thredbo Alpine Village   SNOW SPORTS
(☑ 1300 020 589; www.thredbo.com.au; ski-lift passes adult/child $120/69) The only ski resort in Australia that even remotely resembles a year-round village, Thredbo is a pleasant settlement in a wooded cleft on Kosciuszko's southern slopes. Not content with being the nation's number-one skiing spot (and with the longest runs), it has garnered a reputation as an events and mountain-biking

---

LOCAL KNOWLEDGE

CLIMBING KOSCIUSZKO

Australia's highest mountain, Mt Kosciuszko (2228m) is relatively easy to climb, although getting to the top can nevertheless be a strenuous exercise. Hiking is possible when there's no snow, but weather conditions can be changeable throughout the year, so check at one of the national park offices before setting out. You won't want to be up on the mountain if a thunderstorm is brewing as much of the track is covered in a metal grille.

From November until April Thredbo Alpine Village (p242) offers a range of guided walks of between four and six hours, either by day ($50), at sunset ($110) or under the full moon ($110); check the website for dates and times.

Solo options include the following:

Mt Kosciuszko Track From Thredbo, take the Kosciuszko Express Chairlift (p243). From the top of the lift it's a straightforward 13km hike to the summit and back.

Summit Walk Drive to the end of the paved road above Charlotte Pass, then follow a wide gravel track. It's a 9km climb to the summit (18km return), including a steep final climb.

Main Range Track Also beginning above Charlotte Pass, this strenuous 20km loop includes a river crossing. Check conditions before setting out, as the water level can rise quickly when it rains.

destination, and as a convenient base for climbing Australia's highest mountain.

Perisher
SNOW SPORTS

(☑ 1300 655 822; www.perisher.com.au) Of Perisher's numerous ski runs, 22% are suitable for beginners, 60% for intermediate skiers and 18% for advanced, with most of the action in Perisher Valley. Guthega (1640m) and Mt Blue Cow (1890m) are mainly day resorts, so they're smaller and less crowded.

From Guthega, cross-country skiers head to the Main Range or Rolling Ground. Blue Cow is accessible via the **Skitube** (☑ 1300 655 822; www.perisher.com.au; same-day return adult/child $52/29, open return $79/40), and features alpine and cross-country runs, bowl skiing and snowboarding. Boarders should head for the half-pipe park at Perisher Valley's Front Valley, where there are rails, boxes, kickers etc.

Thredbo Mountain Bike Park
MOUNTAIN BIKING

(www.thredbo.com.au; day pass adult/child $75/53, rental $144/121; ☉ mid-Nov–Apr) Three gravity-fuelled tracks start from the top of the Kosciuszko Express chairlift: the 10km All-Mountain Trail, the steeper 4.5km Kosciuszko Flow Trail and the full-throttle 3.3km Cannonball Downhill Trail. There are also a couple of tracks around the village, six cross-country routes, and a skills park, a jump park and a pump track.

Kosciuszko Express Chairlift
SKIING

(day pass adult/child return $35/18; ☉ 9am-4pm) Thredbo's main chairlift ascends 560m over the course of its 1.8km length, taking a lot of the legwork out of an ascent of Mt Kosciuszko. It operates almost year-round, and for the brief times it's closed the slightly shorter Snowgums chairlift next to it takes up the slack.

🛏 Sleeping

Kosciuszko Tourist Park
CAMPGROUND $

(☑ 02-6456 2224; www.kosipark.com.au; 1400 Kosciuszko Rd; sites from $26, cabins with/without bathroom from $118/79) The only commercial camping ground in the national park, this tranquil place is set amid the gums at Sawpit Creek along the road to Perisher. Cabins are basic, with bunk beds and kitchenettes.

Lake Crackenback
RESORT $$

(☑ 02-6451 3000; www.lakecrackenback.com.au; 1650 Alpine Way; r from $199; ✴ @ ✺) Sprawling over 60 hectares just outside Kosciuszko

National Park, this massive complex has apartments jutting over a lake and mountain-view chalets dotted about the grounds. The restaurants are excellent; there's a luxurious spa centre; and plenty of activities are on offer (canoeing, kayaking, mountain biking, golf and archery). It's handy to both Thredbo and the Skitube to Perisher.

Heidi's Chalet
APARTMENT $$$

(☑ 02-9743 0911; www.heidis.com.au; Link Rd, Smiggin Holes, Perisher; apt from $600; ☉ Jun-Sep; P) Four-person apartments in a smart stone and corrugated-iron block that's only a short snowy shuffle from the ski lifts.

Thredbo YHA
HOSTEL $

(☑ 02-6457 6376; www.yha.com.au; 2 Buckwong Pl, Thredbo; dm from $33, r with/without bathroom from $93/81; ☎) Thredbo's best budget option has spacious common areas and tidy bedrooms. Rates surge in winter.

Snowgoose Apartments
APARTMENT $$

(☑ 02-6457 6415; www.snowgooseapartments. com.au; 25 Diggings Tce, Thredbo; apt from $155; P) Just above the shops but set back from the road, this luxurious set of contemporary apartments offers gas-log fireplaces, good kitchens, underfloor heating, balconies and views galore. All but the studios have a dedicated parking spot.

Ski In Ski Out
LODGE $$$

(☑ 02-6457 7030; www.skiinskiout.com.au; Crackenback Dr, Thredbo; houses from $400; P ☎) Like it says on the tin, you can literally ski down to this cluster of luxurious modern chalets set at the end of a quiet cul-de-sac, a short shuffle from the chairlifts. Most have balconies.

✗ Eating

Central Road 2625
CAFE $$

(☑ 02-6457 7271; www.facebook.com/centralroad 2625; Village Sq, Thredbo; mains $24-29; ☉ 8am-3.30pm Wed-Sun) Occupying a prime spot on the Village Square, this cool corner cafe serves up an eclectic menu of hearty dishes, including buttered mushrooms with kim chi, breakfast burritos, curries and laksa. The coffee is excellent, too.

Bernti's
PUB FOOD $$

(☑ 02-6457 6332; www.berntis.com.au; 4 Mowamba Pl, Thredbo; mains $14-16; ☉ 5pm-late daily May-Oct, Tue-Sat Nov-Apr) Top-notch pub grub is served in the pleasant little wood-lined bar beneath this well-regarded midrange lodge. Only a handful of dishes are offered at a time; Bernti's is known for its steaks but we'd also highly recommend the beef *rendang*. Grab a seat by the windows and take in the views.

❶ Information

NPWS Perisher Valley Information Centre (☏02-6457 4444; www.nationalparks.nsw. gov.au; 9914 Kosciuszko Rd; ⊗8am-4pm daily Jun-Oct, Mon-Fri Nov-May) Offers information and advice on walks and other activities, including up-to-date weather forecasts. Sells vehicle passes and provides locator beacons for back-country walks (free, deposit $400).

Thredbo Information Centre (☏02-6459 4294; www.thredbo.com.au; 6 Fri Dr; ⊗9am-4.30pm) Bookings, national-park passes, showers, and weather and track information.

Riverina

The Riverina is NSW's most productive and agriculturally diverse region, due to its warm climate, vast plains and ample supply of water for irrigation. Its characterful towns are well worth exploring.

Gundagai

POP 1926

Straddling the banks of the Murrumbidgee River, almost halfway between Sydney and Melbourne, little Gundagai is replete with Aussie folklore – gold rushes and bushrangers form part of its colourful history.

Immortalised in 'Along the Road to Gundagai', a folk song written by Jack O'Hagan in 1922 and made famous by country legend Slim Dusty, Gundagai today is an almost forgotten country town, but it's worth a stop here to see the Dog on the Tuckerbox and just to say that you've 'been to Gundagai'.

◉ Sights

Mt Parnassus Lookout VIEWPOINT (🅿) It's easy to see how the landscapes of the Riverina won the hearts of so many iconic Australian poets and songwriters, as you savour the sweeping 360-degree views from this lofty viewpoint.

Dog on the Tuckerbox MONUMENT (37 Annie Pyers Dr; 🅿) About 7km north of town, the famous Dog on the Tuckerbox is a poignant sculpture of a dog from the 19th-century bush ballad.

🛌 Sleeping

Gundagai River Caravan Park CARAVAN PARK $ (☏02-6944 1702; www.gundagairivercaravanpark. com.au; 67 Middleton Dr; powered/unpowered sites $29/26, cabins from $90; 🅿❄) This pleasant campground and caravan park boasts a lovely riverside location on the banks of the Murrumbidgee and has a selection of comfortable cabins, a kids playground and good shared facilities.

Old Bridge Inn INN $$ (☏02-6944 4250; 1 Tumut St, South Gundagai; s/d $80/130; 🅿❄🐾) In south Gundagai, this lovely 1850s building has relaxed B&B accommodation, an excellent restaurant that's open for lunch and dinner (mains $16 to $32), and amiable owners.

Lanigan Abbey B&B $$$ (☏02-6944 2852; www.laniganabbey.com.au; 72 First Ave; r from $250; 🅿❄🐾) This heritage-listed former convent has been painstakingly restored and filled to the brim with priceless antiques, furnishings and art (over 700 pieces) to make it one of the most individual B&Bs in the state, complete with a full silver-service hot breakfast. It won't be to everyone's taste, but it's well worth a look.

❶ Information

Gundagai Visitor Information Centre (☏02-6944 0250; www.visitgundagai.com.au; 249 Sheridan St; ⊗8.30am-5pm; 🐾) Housed within the centre is **Rusconi's Marble Masterpiece** (admission $5), an intricate marble model that relentlessly plays 'Along the Road to Gundagai', so that you'll likely hum it mindlessly for days.

Albury

POP 51,082

This major regional centre on the Murray River sits on the state border opposite its Victorian twin, Wodonga. It's a good launch pad for trips to the snowfields and high country of both Victoria and NSW and for exploring the upper Murray River.

The town is often overlooked by busy motorists in a hurry to get back to the big smoke, but visitors might be surprised and delighted by its pleasant layout, variety of accommodation and handful of interesting attractions.

◎ Sights

★ MAMA   GALLERY
(Murry Art Museum Albury; ☑ 02-6043 5800; www.
alburycity.nsw.gov.au; 546 Dean St; ⊙ 10am-5pm
Mon-Fri, to 4pm Sat, noon-4pm Sun) **FREE** After
a $10.5-million makeover, Albury's fabulous
art gallery reopened in mid-2015 as arguably the finest NSW gallery outside Sydney.
Highlights include the Indigenous and contemporary galleries.

Albury Library Museum   MUSEUM
(☑ 02-6023 8333; www.alburycity.nsw.gov.au; cnr
Kiewa & Swift Sts; ⊙ 10am-7pm Mon, Wed & Thu, to
5pm Tue & Fri, to 4pm Sat, noon-4pm Sun) **FREE**
An excellent, state-of-the-art museum with
displays on local history, including Indigenous culture and 20th-century migration
into the area.

⎚ Sleeping

Albury Wodonga YHA   HOSTEL $
(☑ 02-6040 2999; www.yha.com.au; 372 Wagga
Rd; dm/d from $32/74; @ ⊛ ⊠) About 4.5km
north of central Albury, with cabins, vans
and backpacker dorms.

★ Briardale B&B   B&B $$
(☑ 02-6025 5131; www.briardalebnb.com.au; 396
Poplar Dr; r from $160; ⊛) This elegant North
Albury B&B has beautiful rooms with an
understated antique style. The property ad-
joins a spacious park.

✗ Eating & Drinking

Green Zebra   CAFE $
(☑ 02-6023 1100; www.greenzebra.com.au; 484
Dean St; mains $12-19; ⊙ 8am-6.30pm Mon-Fri,
7.30am-3pm Sat & Sun; ⊛ �⌂) ⌖ Homemade
pasta, salads and other organic dishes are
all winners at this excellent main-street cafe.

Mr Benedict   CAFE $$
(☑ 02-6041 1840; www.mrbenedict.com.au; 664
Dean St; mains $12-22; ⊙ 7.30am-3pm Wed-Sun;
⊛ ☎) Well-regarded Mr Benedict combines the best coffee in town, a concise but

well-chosen beer and wine list, and interesting breakfast and lunch blackboard specials.

Kinross Woolshed   PUB FOOD $$
(☑ 02-6043 1155; www.kinrosswoolshed.com.au;
Old Sydney Rd, Thurgoona; mains $14-32; ⊙ 9am-
late Mon-Fri, from 7am Sat, from 8am Sun; ℗ ⊛)
Drive (or get the shuttle bus) to this country
pub in an 1890s woolshed. Country music
kicks off on Saturday night after budget-
friendly $2 bacon-and-egg rolls.

ZedBar   COCKTAIL BAR
(☑ 02-6021 2622; www.zedbar.com.au; 586 Dean
St; ⊙ 11am-10pm Tue-Thu, to 2am Fri & Sat) Al-
bury's classiest bar has nightly drink spe-
cials, killer cocktails, great tunes and bar
food, bringing a taste of the big smoke to the
country.

❶ Information

Albury Visitor Information Centre (☑ 1300
252 879; www.visitalburywodonga.com; Rail-
way Pl; ⊙ 9am-5pm; ☎) Opposite the railway
station.

❶ Getting There & Away

Albury is well connected to NSW and Victoria by
road, rail and air. It's 553km from Sydney and
326km from Melbourne.

    Qantas (QF; ☑ 13 13 13; www.qantas.com.au),
Rex (ZL; ☑ 13 17 13; www.rex.com.au) and **Vir-
gin Australia** (DJ; ☑ 13 67 89; www.virginaus
tralia.com) operate domestic flights to Sydney,
Melbourne and smaller centres from **Albury
Airport** (ABX; ☑ 02-6043 5865; www.flyalbury.
com.au; 121 Airport Dr), which is 4km out of
town; taxis are available (fares about $15), but
there is no public transport to the airport.

    Greyhound Australia (☑ 1300 473 946; www.
greyhound.com.au) operates buses between
Sydney ($101, nine hours) and Melbourne ($55,
3¾ hours) that stop in Albury.

    NSW TrainLink (☑ 13 22 32; www.nswtrain-
link.info) operates a daily and overnight XPT
train service from Sydney to Albury (from $66,
7½ hours) and Melbourne ($47, 3¼ hours). **V/
Line** (☑ 13 61 96; www.vline.com.au) has regular

---

❶ BORDER-HOPPING ALONG THE MURRAY

Most of the major towns along the great Murray River are on the Victorian side, but it's
easy to hop back and forth across the river at towns like Albury, Corowa, pretty Tocum-
wal, just south of Deniliquin, and Moama.

    The Echuca/Moama Visitor Information Centre serves both towns and is located in
Echuca beside the bridge that crosses into NSW. Ask about trips on the paddle steamers
that ply these waters (reminders of when the Murray and Darling Rivers were the main
conduits of communication and trade).

trains between Albury and Melbourne (from $38, four hours).

Wagga Wagga

POP 55,820

The Murrumbidgee River squiggles around Wagga Wagga's northern end, and riverside eucalypts complement tree-lined streets and lovely gardens. Known as 'place of many crows' to the Wiradjuri people, 'Wagga' is NSW's largest inland city and it's a gem.

Although Wagga isn't Australia's best-known winegrowing area, there are some excellent places worth checking out.

◎ Sights

Museum of the Riverina   MUSEUM
(☑ 02-6926 9655; www.museumriverina.com.au; cnr Baylis & Morrow Sts; ⊙ 10am-4pm Tue-Sat, to 2pm Sun) FREE This interesting museum is split over two sites: this one, in the historic Council Chambers building, and the second, adjacent to the **Wagga Wagga Botanic Gardens** (Macleay St; ⊙ sunrise-sunset; P); the latter site focuses on Wagga's people, places and events.

Charles Sturt University Winery   WINERY
(☑ 02-6933 2435; http://winery.csu.edu.au; Charles Sturt Cellar Door, Mambarra Dr, CSU Campus; ⊙ 11am-4pm; P) In 1893 the university vineyard at Wagga Wagga was planted. A viticulture teaching program was established in 1976 and the winery has been under professional management since 1990. Come for tastings and warehouse sales.

Wagga Wagga Art Gallery   GALLERY
(☑ 02-6926 9660; www.wagga.nsw.gov.au/gallery; Civic Centre, Morrow St; ⊙ 10am-4pm Tue-Sat, to 2pm Sun; P) The highlight of this regional gallery showcasing the works of local and national artists is the wonderful **National Art Glass Gallery**.

🏃 Activities

★ Wagga Beach   SWIMMING
(Tarcutta St) With brand-new public facilities, Wagga Beach is a beautiful spot for a lazy float or a picnic with friends. Best at sunset on a hot day. It's at the end of Tarcutta St.

🛏 Sleeping

**Wagga Wagga Beach
Caravan Park**   CARAVAN PARK $
(☑ 02-6931 0603; www.wwbcp.com.au; 2 Johnston St; sites per person $25, cabins from $120; P✳🐾🅰) Adjacent to the wonderful Wagga Beach, this van park includes its own swimming beach fashioned from the riverbank and a range of inexpensive cabins.

★ Houston   BOUTIQUE HOTEL $$
(☑ 02-5908 1321; www.thehoustonwagga.com.au; 44 Kincaid St; r from $150; P✳🐾) This centrally located, eight-room all-suite boutique hotel is country NSW's finest new offering, with sumptuous original decor, luxurious linens and staff who make you feel special. The excellent website gives a good indication of what to expect. The best thing: affordable and reasonable pricing.

Townhouse Hotel   BOUTIQUE HOTEL $$
(☑ 02-6921 4337; http://townhousewagga.com. au; 70 Morgan St; r from $129; ✳🐾🅰) Fun, funky and full of flair, the Townhouse has a mish-mash of generally stylish rooms and apartments in a variety of configurations, furnished in a range of styles. The cheapest rooms lack exterior windows. If that bothers you, check with the friendly, professional staff.

🍴 Eating

Pot 'n' Kettle   CAFE $$
(☑ 02-6921 3340; 10 Blake St; mains $6-22; ⊙ 7am-4pm; ✳🐾) This fabulous little cafe doing great breakfasts and healthy (and

---

WORTH A TRIP

JUNEE

Featuring a high concentration of impressive heritage architecture, Junee makes an excellent day trip from Wagga Wagga, 43km to the south.

A highlight is the **Roundhouse Railway Museum** (☑ 02-6924 2909; www.roundhouse museum.com.au; Harold St; adult/child $6/4; ⊙ noon-4.30pm Mon-Fri, from 9.30am Sat & Sun; P). Built in 1947, the Roundhouse, a giant turntable with 42 train-repair bays, is the only surviving, working one of its kind in Australia.

Afterwards, drop in to the **Commercial Hotel** (☑ 02-6924 4224; cnr Lorne & Waratah Sts; ⊙ 11am-10pm), one of the town's magnificent old verandah pubs, for a schooner.

delicious) lunches including vibrant salads, pastas and risottos (as well as great coffee and decadent cakes) is, as one would expect, usually humming with activity.

Oak Room Kitchen & Bar
BISTRO $$$

(☑02-6921 4337; www.townhousewagga.com/the-oakroom; Townhouse Hotel, 70 Morgan St; bar snacks $8-19, mains $28-39; ☺6pm-late Mon-Sat; ✷) The bustling Oak Room combines small plates, like seared Queensland scallops, with larger meals, including house-made gnocchi and roast lamb from the nearby Riverina region. The bar is open for drinks and snacks from 5pm.

Magpies Nest
BISTRO $$$

(☑02-6933 1523; www.magpiesnestwagga.com; 20 Pine Gully Rd; set menu $55; ☺5.30pm-late Tue-Sat; ✷) A delightfully informal restaurant set in a well restored 1860s stone stable overlooking the Murrumbidgee River flats and surrounded by olive groves and vineyards.

🍷 Drinking & Nightlife

Union Club Hotel
PUB

(☑02-6921 2236; http://unionhotelwagga.com.au; 122 Baylis St; ☺10am-11pm Sun-Thu, to 1am Fri & Sat) One of Wagga's favourite watering holes is loved for its enormous wraparound verandah upstairs.

Thirsty Crow Brewing Co
CRAFT BEER

(www.thirstycrow.com.au; 31 Kincaid St; ☺4-10pm Mon & Tue, 11am-11.30pm Wed-Sat, noon-9.30pm Sun; ☎) Come for the tasty beer – the hoppy Dark Alleyway IPA is a good choice – and stay for the wood-fired pizzas ($19 to $27).

ℹ️ Information

Wagga Visitor Information Centre (☑1300 100 122; www.visitwagga.com; 183 Tarcutta St; ☺9am-5pm; ☎)

ℹ️ Getting There & Away

Wagga Wagga is midway between Young and Albury on the Olympic Hwy.

Qantas (p245) and Rex (p245) have direct flights to Sydney; Rex flights are on smaller planes and (usually) cost more.

Wagga Wagga is a stop on the twice-daily NSW TrainLink (p245) XPT service between Sydney ($62, 6½ hours) and Melbourne ($62, 4½ hours). The train also stops in Albury ($19, 1¼ hours). Connecting buses to a variety of rural destinations depart from the station.

Griffith
POP 43,181

Welcome to Little Italy in the heart of NSW, where it's estimated that 60% of the town's residents have Italian ancestors. Griffith's restaurant scene makes it the food-and-wine capital of the Riverina, with two points to note: food means Italian food, and wine means cellar-door tastings – few wineries have restaurants.

👁 Sights

Hermit's Cave Lookout
VIEWPOINT

(℗) This panoramic lookout is located above the fascinating **Hermit's Cave**, which was inhabited by an Italian-born man for decades in the early 20th century; watch out for snakes.

De Bortoli
WINERY

(www.debortoli.com.au; De Bortoli Rd, Bilbul; ☺9am-5pm Mon-Sat, to 4pm Sun; ℗) Visit the cellar door of this well-known Australian winery and be sure to try the astounding Black Noble dessert wine.

McWilliam's Hanwood Estate
WINERY

(☑02-6963 3404; www.mcwilliams.com.au; Jack McWilliam Rd, Hanwood; ☺tastings 10am-4pm Tue-Sat; ℗) Don't miss a visit to the region's oldest (1913) and best-known winery. It's really hard not to taste everything you possibly can!

🎉 Festivals & Events

UnWINEd
FOOD & DRINK

(www.unwined-riverina.com; ☺Oct) A festival of local wine and produce featuring wine tastings, lunches and live music.

🛏 Sleeping

Yambil Inn
MOTEL $

(☑02-6964 1233; www.yambilinn.com.au; 155 Yambil St; s/d $110/$122; ℗✷☎☒) The owners of this little motel keep the place immaculate. Its large, tidy, renovated rooms have all that you need for a good night's sleep.

Shearer's Quarters Backpackers
HOSTEL $

(☑0423 852 134; www.shearersquarters.com. au; Remembrance Dr; 2-bed dm per person per night/week $35/170; ℗) This basic hostel has everything a working backpacker needs after a hard day's labour, from hammocks to game consoles and pool tables around the shady communal courtyard.

✕ Eating

Bertoldo's Bakery   BAKERY $
(☑ 02-6964 2514; www.bertoldos.com; 324 Banna Ave; desserts from $6; ⊗ 8.30am-5pm; ✳) This Italian patisserie and panetteria will have you drooling, if not coming back for more.

★ Zecca   ITALIAN $$
(☑ 02-6964 4050; www.zeccagriffith.com.au; 239 Banna Ave; mains $16-36; ⊗ 11am-4pm Tue-Wed, to 11pm Thu & Fri, 6-11pm Sat; ✳) New to the Griffith dining scene, Zecca serves up handmade pasta and Italian meals in the funky modern setting of a converted 1940s Rural Bank building. The kitchen uses local ingredients where possible, working with farmers to showcase the best regional produce.

Roastery   CAFE $$
(www.facebook.com/TheRoasteryGriffith; 232 Banna Ave; mains $12-26; ⊗ 7am-5pm Mon-Fri, 8am-3pm Sat & Sun; ✳) The Roastery sources its own beans from around the world and combines Griffith's best coffee and local Riverina wines with cafe favourites and counter food.

La Scala   ITALIAN $$
(☑ 02-6962 4322; 455b Banna Ave; mains $26-32; ⊗ 6-9.30pm Tue-Sat; ✳) Expect old-school recipes, mural-covered walls and cheap house white by the glass. Just brilliant.

❶ Information

Griffith Visitor Information Centre (☑ 02-6962 4145; www.visitgriffith.com.au; cnr Banna & Jondaryan Aves; ☎)

❶ Getting There & Away

Rex (p245) has daily flights to Sydney from Griffith Airport, 3km north of town.

Local and regional buses stop at the **Griffith Travel & Transit Centre** (☑ 02-6962 7199; Banna Ave).

NSW TrainLink (p245) operates two daily bus services to Wagga Wagga ($19, three hours), where you can connect to XPT train services to Sydney ($62, 6½ hours) and Melbourne ($62, 4½ hours).

Deniliquin

POP 7494

A quintessential inland Australian town, Deniliquin, also known as 'Deni', lies along a wide, lazy bend of the Edwards River. Here you'll find an attractive river beach and some appealing riverside walks amid the red gums. There's also a famed and ever-growing festival dedicated to that curious Aussie obsession, the ute.

❍ Sights

★ McLean Beach   BEACH
At the northern end of town, McLean Beach is one of Australia's finest river beaches, with sand, picnic facilities and a walking track.

Island Sanctuary   WILDLIFE RESERVE
FREE The 16-hectare Island Sanctuary, at the junction of the Edwards River and Tarrangle Creek, has a fine walking track among the river red gums. It's home to plenty of wildlife, including eastern grey kangaroos, and almost one-fifth of all bird species recorded in Australia have been seen here. Enter via a footbridge off the southeastern end of Cressy St.

✦ Festivals & Events

★ Deniliquin Ute Muster   CULTURAL
(www.deniutemuster.com.au; ⊗ late Sep) Held on the NSW Labour Day long weekend, the muster attracts people (and their utes) from across the country. Events include a rodeo, chainsaw sculpting, wood chopping, helicopter rides and kids' activities. The festival also draws big names in Australian music: Cold Chisel, the Hoodoo Gurus and Crowded House have all appeared in recent years.

🛏 Sleeping & Eating

★ Mclean Beach
Holiday Park   CARAVAN PARK $
(☑ 03-5881 2448; www.mcleanbeach.com.au; 1 Butler St; powered sites $34, cabins $120-180; P ☎) Friendly staff and a great position adjacent to McLean Beach, with its own long river frontage, make this holiday park an excellent choice. Try for one of the sparkling new Riverview villas.

Cottages on Edward   B&B $$
(☑ 0407 815 641; www.cottagesonedward.com.au; 304 River St; cottages incl breakfast Sun-Thu $145, Fri & Sat $175; ✳) These two charming cottages, across the Edward River at the eastern end of town, are overseen by the equally charming Richard and Pat. The rooms have understated antique furnishings, spa baths and a real sense of being a home away from home.

Crossing Café
MODERN AUSTRALIAN $$

(☑03-5881 7827; www.thecrossingcafe.com.au; 295 George St; mains $14-28; ⊙8am-4pm Tue-Thu, 8am-late Fri, 8.30am-late Sat, 8.30am-4pm Sun; ▣) With a deck overlooking an idyllic riverside view, Crossing offers such dishes as Thai beef salad or salt-and-pepper calamari. The menu's focus is on quality rather than quantity.

❶ Information

Deniliquin Visitor Information Centre
(☑1800 650 712; www.visitdeni.com.au; George St; ⊙9am-4pm; ☎) Bookings and information.

❶ Getting There & Away

NSW TrainLink (p245) buses run to Wagga Wagga ($37, 3½ hours), where you can connect to the XPT train to Sydney ($62, 6½ hours).

LORD HOWE ISLAND

POP 350, PLUS UP TO 400 VISITORS

Rising from the Pacific a remote 600km from the New South Wales mainland, little Lord Howe's tropical, World Heritage–listed beauty is under the radar given the jaw-dropping spectacle of this former volcano that you see as you fly in. It looks like a Bond villain's lair with two lofty mountains overlooking an idyllic lagoon, perfect crescents of beach and a verdant rainforest-y interior criss-crossed with walking trails.

Lord Howe's isolation and comparatively recent appearance – it was formed by hotspot volcanic activity around seven million years ago – lends it a unique ecology, with many plant and insect species found only here. Birds rule the roost, with nesting terns noisily present and the eerie cries of muttonbirds in their burrows punctuating the night. Ongoing ecological projects are seeking to remove introduced species.

The island's restricted accommodation and flight capacity mean that a visit here doesn't come cheap, but relaxation is guaranteed with limited internet and no mobile signal.

◉ Sights

★ Mount Gower
MOUNTAIN

The southernmost of the two magnificent peaks dominating the island, Mt Gower (875m) is a spectacular sight. Though it looks sheer at first glance, it's actually a rel-

atively straightforward climb. You must go with a guide – Jack Shick (☑02-6563 2218; www.lordhoweislandtours.net) and Dean Hiscox (☑02-6563 2260; www.lordhoweislandtours.com; Boatsheds, Lagoon Rd) both offer this – but you won't need any special skills, just moderate fitness. Climbs must be booked ahead. The trip takes eight to 10 hours return.

Lord Howe Island Museum
MUSEUM

(☑02-6563 2111; www.lhimuseum.com; cnr Lagoon & Middle Beach Rds; ⊙9am-3pm Mon-Fri, 10am-2pm Sat & Sun) FREE At what passes on Lord Howe for a major road junction, the town's museum has an interesting if somewhat random display on local history, taking in whaling, wars and the flying boat service, and an engaging, more modern room on the local environment, presented with colourful flair. There's also a souvenir shop and tourist information desk. Donations are appreciated.

North Beach
BEACH

This pretty crescent of sand is reached by a thigh-straining up-and-down walk over a ridge from town but it's worth it, with barbecue facilities and the clamour of nesting sooty terns. Don't fancy the stairs? Get your arms working instead and paddle here in a kayak.

Intermediate Hill
HILL

Another star exhibit for the Australian love of no-bullshit names, this hill (250m) offers some of the island's better views of Ball's Pyramid and a spectacular perspective over Mt Lidgbird from the platform at the top. The main access trail starts opposite the airport turn-off.

Ned's Beach
BEACH

A short stroll from town, Ned's Beach offers good snorkelling – you can hire wetsuits and gear from a little stall. Feeding the fish in the shallows here is an old Lord Howe favourite – take dollar coins to operate the fish-food machine.

★ Ball's Pyramid
MOUNTAIN

Sticking out of the middle of the ocean some 20km southeast of Lord Howe Island, the memorably jagged silhouette of this crag stands 561m high. A volcano caused by the same hot spot that threw up Lord Howe, its ascent is for very serious climbers only. But a boat trip out here is a memorable experience, and the diving and birdwatching are excellent. Several Lord Howe operators can get you out here, weather permitting.

ⓘ LORD HOWE LOWDOWN

Flights

If your flight is fully loaded, your checked-in bag might be bumped to the next day's flight, so pack necessaries for the first night in your carry-on. Weather means boat trips are often cancelled, and flights can be too. Don't book anything important for the same day you are meant to fly back from Lord Howe.

Insurance

Travel insurance is recommended due to the possibility of cancelled flights. If you're stuck on the island, the airline will pay one night's accommodation but no more.

Internet

Wi-fi is available at a handful of hotspots around the island and at many of the accommodation options. It's unreliable. There are various access packages, starting at 100MB over three days for $4.95.

Telephone

There's no mobile coverage on the island and many locals are keen to keep it that way, as it's an appealing feature to many visitors after the first-day out-of-contact nerves. Payphones dot the island, and there are a few free phones around to make local calls.

Time

Lord Howe Island is half an hour ahead of NSW in winter (UTC plus 10½ hours). When daylight savings time operates on the mainland, Lord Howe shifts half an hour only, so it's the same as NSW (UTC plus 11 hours).

Tourist Information

There's a tourist desk in the Lord Howe Island Museum. The website www.lordhowe island.info is very useful.

🏃 Activities & Tours

There's great scope for outdoors fun on Lord Howe Island. On land, walking is the main attraction, with the guided hike up Mount Gower the highlight. A network of well-marked trails covers the rest of the island, offering super viewpoints and secluded beaches.

On the water, you can grab a kayak or paddleboard to explore the lagoon, go snorkelling or surfing, or take a turtle-spotting boat trip. Other boat excursions include fishing trips, circumnavigations of the island or journeys to magnificent Ball's Pyramid.

Diving is also good here, with a couple of operators offering a variety of trips. The standout diving experience is the day's trip to Ball's Pyramid.

🛏 Sleeping

Pinetrees Lodge   RESORT $$$

(☑ Lord Howe Island 02-6563 2177, reservations 02-9262 6585; www.pinetrees.com.au; Lagoon Rd; d all-inclusive 5 nights $3550; ☺ Sep-May; ℗ ⊜) In business since 1842, and taking guests for well over a century, this venerable Lord Howe institution has had a recent renovation leaving rooms and cottages comfortable, light and contemporary without diminishing the charm of this relaxing resort. No wi-fi or phone signal means a real de-stressing experience, while excellent service extends to the restaurant – casual buffet lunches and gourmet dinners – and spa.

Beachcomber Lodge   APARTMENT $$$

(☑ 02-6563 2032; www.beachcomberlhi.com. au; Anderson Rd; d May-Sep $170, Oct-Apr $375; ⊜ ☎) Set in a handsome centenarian bungalow on the hill above 'downtown', this is run by a fifth-generation islander family and offers a casual vibe. Most apartments open off the verandah and offer appealing beds and a small kitchen. In summer there's an on-site restaurant; winter rates are among the island's most affordable. The owner has a boat available for trips.

Leanda Lei Apartments   APARTMENT $$$

(☑ 02-6563 2195; www.leandalei.com.au; Middle Beach Rd; high/shoulder season d from $355/300; ℗ ⊜ ☎) 🖉 Run by a friendly, efficient family, this place has competitive rates, a central location and more rooms than most so it's a reliable option. Spacious, bland and comfortable apartments make a likeable island base; many look over the grassy garden. There's a shop opposite and bikes and BBQs on-site. Restaurant and airport transfers are included.

✖ Eating

Coral Café   CAFE **$$**
(☑02-6563 2488; cnr Middle Beach & Lagoon Rds; light meals $8-18, dinner mains $27-30; ⊙9am-3pm & 6-8pm Mon, Wed & Fri, 9am-3pm Tue & Thu, 9am-2pm & 6-8pm Sat & Sun; 🖥🍴) This likeable spot at the museum has decent lunch fare – think focaccias, wraps and sandwiches – with rice-paper rolls and sushi-style creations as other options. There are also hot specials. It opens most evenings for fusion- or roast-oriented dinners. It's got the best wi-fi around too, and the staff are happy for you to lounge around on the deck using it when the cafe's not open.

Golf Club   AUSTRALIAN **$$**
(☑02-6564 2179; www.lordhowegolf.com.au; Lagoon Rd; mains $26-32; ⊙6-8pm Thu-Tue) Near the airport, this nine-holer offers beautiful views for a round but is also one of the island's simple but reliable places to eat. Tuesday nights it fries up locally caught fish, while Thursdays and Fridays have BBQ options including kingfish, and a curry special.

There are great sunset views; the bar opens a little earlier.

★ Anchorage
Restaurant   MODERN AUSTRALIAN **$$$**
(☑02-6563 2287; www.earlsanchorage.com; Ned's Beach Rd; dinner mains $30-45; ⊙8am-8pm; 🖥) Open all day, this is the island's go-to spot for a morning coffee or post-walk pick-me-up. It's also an excellent place to eat. Genuinely friendly management and an attractive, welcoming indoor-outdoor space, with a light nautical themed, provide a venue for sophisticated, beautifully presented modern Australian dishes with local kingfish a regular highlight. Service is sparky and the quality is reliably sky-high.

❶ Getting There & Away

Qantaslink flies to Lord Howe from Sydney, Brisbane and Port Macquarie. Flights are expensive for the distance, typically costing over $1000 return, a little cheaper off-season. One way around this is to fly on points: there aren't many dates available, but you don't need many points to get here as it's just a domestic flight.

❶ Getting Around

Just about everything is within walking distance on Lord Howe, and there are also lots of places hiring or lending bikes. All accommodation providers meet incoming flights. There are hire cars available, but you won't need one unless mobility is an issue.

Canberra & the ACT

POP 358,000 / 🖉 02

Best Places to Eat

➡ Cupping Room (p261)

➡ Morks (p262)

➡ Akiba (p261)

➡ Aubergine (p262)

➡ Courgette (p262)

Best Places to Sleep

➡ East Hotel (p260)

➡ Hotel Hotel (p261)

➡ Little National Hotel (p260)

➡ Hyatt Hotel Canberra (p261)

➡ Blue & White Lodge (p260)

Why Go?

Carved out of New South Wales (NSW) in 1911 and transferred into the direct control of the federal government, the Australian Capital Territory (ACT) was created solely to provide a neutral location for a national capital. The rivalry between the two most powerful states, NSW and Victoria, was even more pronounced back then than it is now. It made sense for the capital to be situated somewhere between Sydney and Melbourne, and it was deemed important that the new city should have its own water supply, so as not to be held hostage by any state government.

Effectively the ACT is just Greater Canberra, along with a chunk of mountainous wilderness to the south (which provides that all-important water source). Come here to explore Australia's interesting little capital, and perhaps take a walk in the bush while you're at it.

When to Go
Canberra

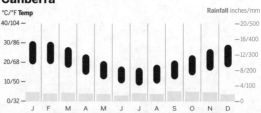

Apr Cellar doors beckon during the Canberra District Wine Week.

Sep The Floriade festival fills the capital with flowers and fun.

Dec & Jan School holidays and a lack of parliamentary sittings minimises crowds and hotel prices.

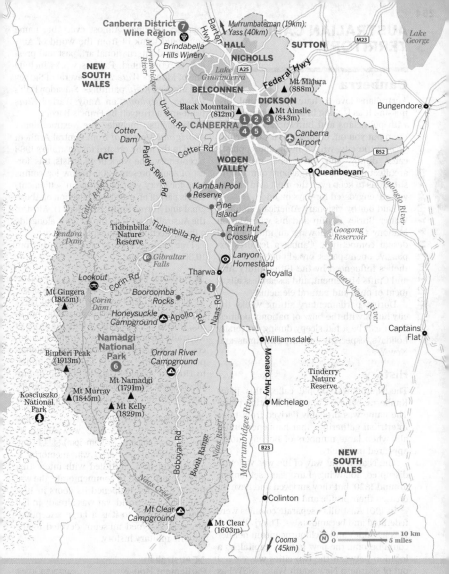

Canberra & the ACT Highlights

1 National Gallery of Australia (p254) Delving into a vast treasure trove of Australian and international art.

2 National Portrait Gallery (p254) Pondering the eclectic array of faces that have shaped Australian culture.

3 Australian Parliament House (p254) Witnessing democracy in action within symbolism-laden walls.

4 Australian War Memorial (p254) Learning about how Australia's chequered military history helped to define the national psyche.

5 Lake Burley Griffin (p257) Paddling, cycling, skating or strolling around Canberra's central lake.

6 Namadgi National Park (p266) Spotting kangaroos and Aboriginal rock art on a walk through the wilderness.

7 Canberra District Wine Region (p266) Sampling the award-winning cold-climate drops being produced at the region's wineries.

AUSTRALIAN CAPITAL TERRITORY

Canberra

Australians love to hate their capital, dismissing it as lacking in soul and being filled with politicians and bureaucrats. Don't let them put you off. Canberra is a wonderfully green little city, with a lively and sophisticated dining and bar scene, interesting architecture and a smorgasbord of major institutions to keep even the most avid culture vulture engrossed for days on end.

Laid out by visionary American architect Walter Burley Griffin and his wife Marion Mahony Griffin following an international design competition, Canberra features expansive open spaces, broad boulevards, aesthetics influenced by the 19th-century Arts and Crafts Movement, and a seamless alignment of built and natural elements.

During parliamentary sitting weeks the city hums with the buzz of national politics, but it can be a tad sleepy during university holidays, especially around Christmas and New Year.

History

The Ngunnawal people called this place Kanberra, believed to mean 'meeting place'. The name was probably derived from huge intertribal gatherings that happened annually when large numbers of Bogong moths appeared in the city.

The Ngunnawal way of life was violently disrupted following European settlement around 1820, but they survived and have increased their profile and numbers.

In 1901 Australia's separate colonies were federated and became states. The rivalry between Sydney and Melbourne meant neither could become the new nation's capital, so a location between the two cities was carved out of southern New South Wales (NSW) as a compromise. This new city was officially named Canberra in 1913, and replaced Melbourne as the national capital in 1927.

⊙ Sights

★ **National Gallery of Australia**   GALLERY
(Map p258; ☑ 02-6240 6502; www.nga.gov.au; Parkes Pl, Parkes; costs vary for special exhibitions; ⊙ 10am-5pm) **FREE** The nation's extraordinary art collection is showcased in a suitably huge purpose-built gallery within the parliamentary precinct. Almost every big name you could think of from the world of Australian and international art, past and present, is represented. Famous works include one of Monet's *Waterlilies,* several of Sidney Nolan's *Ned Kelly* paintings, Salvador Dali's *Lobster Telephone,* an Andy Warhol *Elvis* print and a triptych by Francis Bacon.

Highlights include the extraordinary *Aboriginal Memorial* from Central Arnhem Land in the lobby, created for Australia's 1988 bicentenary. The work of 43 artists, this 'forest of souls' presents 200 hollow log coffins (one for every year of European settlement) and is part of an excellent collection of Aboriginal and Torres Strait Islander art. Most of the Australian art is on the 1st floor, alongside a fine collection of Asian and Pacific art.

Free guided tours are offered hourly from 10.30am to 2.30pm.

★ **National Portrait Gallery**   GALLERY
(Map p258; ☑ 02-6102 7000; www.portrait.gov. au; King Edward Tce, Parkes; ⊙ 10am-5pm) **FREE** Occupying a flash new purpose-built building, this wonderful gallery tells the story of Australia through its faces – from wax cameos of Indigenous Australians to colonial portraits of the nation's founding families, to Howard Arkley's DayGlo portrait of musician Nick Cave. There is a good cafe for post-exhibition coffee and reflection.

★ **Australian War Memorial**   MUSEUM
(Map p258; ☑ 02-6243 4211; www.awm.gov.au; Treloar Cres, Campbell; ⊙ 10am-5pm) **FREE** Canberra's glorious art deco war memorial is a highlight in a city filled with interesting architecture. Built to commemorate 'the war to end all wars', it opened its doors in 1941 when the next world war was already in full swing. Attached to it is a large, exceptionally well designed museum devoted to the nation's military history.

★ **Australian Parliament House**   NOTABLE BUILDING
(Map p258; ☑ 02-6277 5399; www.aph.gov.au; ⊙ 9am-5pm) **FREE** Opened in 1988, Australia's national parliament building is a graceful and deeply symbolic piece of architecture. The building itself is embedded in the Australian soil, covered with a turf roof and topped by a spindly but soaring 81m-high flagpole. The same detailed thought has been applied to the interior and there's plenty to see inside, whether the politicians are haranguing each other in the chambers or not.

Canberra

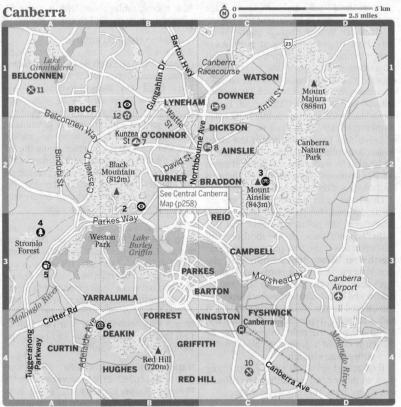

Canberra

⊙ Sights
1 Australian Institute of Sport B1
2 Australian National Botanic Gardens .. B2
3 Mt Ainslie C2
4 National Arboretum............................. A3
5 National Zoo & Aquarium A3
6 Royal Australian Mint B4

⊜ Sleeping
7 Alvio Tourist Park B2

⊗ Eating
10 Aubergine C4
11 Malaysian Chapter A1

8 Aria Hotel..C2
9 Blue & White Lodge C1

✪ Entertainment
12 GIO Stadium Canberra B1

See Central Canberra Map (p258)

After passing through airport-style security, visitors are free to explore large sections of the building and watch parliamentary proceedings from the public galleries. The only time that tickets are required is for the high theatre of Question Time in the House of Representatives (2pm on sitting days); tickets are free but must be booked through the Sergeant at Arms. See the website for a calendar of sitting days.

After entering through the Marble Foyer, pop into the Great Hall to take a look at the vast tapestry, which took 13 weavers two years to complete. Upstairs in the corridors surrounding the hall, there are interesting displays including temporary exhibits from the Parliamentary art collection. Look out for a 1297 edition of the Magna Carta and the original of Michael Nelson Tjakamarra's *Possum & Wallaby Dreaming*, which features both on the $5 note and writ large as the mosaic you passed in Parliament's forecourt.

There are further displays in the Members' Hall, ringed with august portraits of former prime ministers. From the hall, corridors branch off towards the two debating chambers. Australia has a Westminster-style democracy and its chambers echo the colour scheme of the famous 'Mother of Parliaments' in London, with a subtle local twist. Rather than the bright red of the House of Lords and the deep green of the lower house, Australia's parliament house uses a dusky pink for its Senate and a muted green for the House of Representatives, inspired by the tones of the local eucalypts.

Lifts head up to the roof where there are lawns designed for people to walk on – a reminder to the politicians below that this is the 'people's house'. As the focal point of Canberra, this is the best place to get a perspective on Walter Burley Griffin's city design. Your eyes are drawn immediately along three axes, with the Australian War Memorial backed by Mt Ainslie directly ahead, the commercial centre on an angle to the left and Duntroon (representing the military) on an angle to the right. Interestingly, the church is denied a prominent place in this very 20th-century design.

Free guided tours (30 minutes on sitting days, 45 minutes on nonsitting days) depart at 9.30am, 11am, 1pm, 2pm and 3.30pm.

Museum of Australian Democracy   MUSEUM
(Map p258; ☑ 02-6270 8222; www.moadoph.gov. au; Old Parliament House, 18 King George Tce, Parkes; adult/child/family $2/1/5; ☺ 9am-5pm) The seat of government from 1927 to 1988, this elegantly proportioned building offers visitors a whiff of the political past. Displays cover Australian prime ministers, the roots of democracy and the history of local protest movements. You can also visit the old Senate and House of Representative chambers, the parliamentary library and the prime minister's office. Kids will love the dress up and

---

ⓘ WILDLIFE ON THE HOP

Canberra is one of the best cities in Australia for spotting wild kangaroos. Some of the best places include Weston Park on the shores of Lake Burley Griffin northwest of Parliament House, Government House, Mount Ainslie and Namadgi National Park.

---

play rooms, while those with a thing for bling will enjoy the replica crown jewels.

Australian National Botanic Gardens   GARDENS
(Map p255; ☑ 02-6250 9588; www.nationalbotanic gardens.gov.au; Clunies Ross St, Acton; ☺ 8.30am-5pm) FREE On Black Mountain's lower slopes, these large gardens showcase Australian floral diversity over 35 hectares of cultivated garden and 50 hectares of remnant bushland. Various themed routes are marked out, with the best introduction being the 30-to-45 minute main path, which takes in the eucalypt lawn (70 species are represented), rock garden, rainforest gully and Sydney Region garden. A 3.2km bushland nature trail leads to the garden's higher reaches.

National Zoo & Aquarium   ZOO
(Map p255; ☑ 02-6287 8400; www.nationalzoo. com.au; 999 Lady Denman Dr, Weston Creek; adult/child $40/23; ☺ 9.30am-5pm) It's certainly not the biggest in Australia but Canberra's zoo is well laid out and animal friendly, with plenty of big cats and cute critters to keep the kids amused. It also offers various behind-the-scenes experiences where you can help to feed the sharks, lions, tigers and bears, and interact with rhinos and cheetahs.

National Library of Australia   LIBRARY
(Map p258; ☑ 02-6262 1111; www.nla.gov.au; Parkes Pl, Parkes; ☺ gallery 10am-5pm) FREE This institution has accumulated more than 10 million items since being established in 1901 and has digitised more than nine billion files. Don't miss the **Treasures Gallery**, where artefacts such as Captain Cook's *Endeavour* journal and Captain Bligh's list of mutineers are among the regularly refreshed displays; free 30-minute tours are held at 11.30am daily.

National Arboretum   PARK
(Map p255; ☑ 02-6207 8484; www.national arboretum.act.gov.au; Forest Dr, Weston Creek; ☺ 6am-8.30pm Oct-Mar, 7am-5.30pm Apr-Sep) FREE Located on land previously affected by bush fires, Canberra's National Arboretum is an ever-developing showcase of trees from around the world. It is early days for many of the plantings, but it's still worth visiting for the spectacular visitor centre and the excellent views over the city. Regular guided tours are informative, and there is a brilliant adventure playground for kids.

To get here, catch bus 81 (weekdays) or bus 981 (weekends) from platform 10 at the Civic bus interchange.

Questacon
MUSEUM

(Map p258; ☑ 02-6270 2800; www.questacon. edu.au; King Edward Tce, Parkes; adult/child $23/18; ⏱ 9am-5pm; ⓘ) This kid-friendly science centre has educational and fun interactive exhibits. Explore the physics of sport, athletics and fun parks; cause tsunamis; and take shelter from cyclones and earthquakes. Exciting science shows, presentations and puppet shows are all included.

National Museum of Australia
MUSEUM

(Map p258; ☑ 02-6208 5000; www.nma.gov.au; Lawson Cres, Acton Peninsula; tours adult/child $15/10; ⏱ 9am-5pm) FREE Perhaps it's the disconcerting angular nature of the building itself or the disjointed layout of the displays, but there's something about this celebration of all things Australian that doesn't quite gel in the way that Canberra's other national cultural institutions do. That said, the room jam-packed with Aboriginal artefacts is fascinating, and the museum often plays host to blockbuster touring exhibitions. Don't miss the 12-minute introductory film, shown in the small rotating Circa Theatre.

National Capital Exhibition
MUSEUM

(Map p258; ☑ 02-6272 2902; www.nationalcapital. gov.au; Barrine Dr, Commonwealth Park; ⏱ 9am-5pm) FREE This small but fascinating museum tells the story of how Canberra came to be Australia's capital. Displays include reproductions of the drawings entered in the international competition to design the city, including the exquisite watercolour renderings of the winning design created by Marion Mahony Griffin, the often overlooked wife and creative partner of Walter Burley Griffin.

Lake Burley Griffin
LAKE

(Map p258) This ornamental lake was created in 1963 when the 33m-high Scrivener Dam was erected on the Molonglo River. It's lined with important institutions and monuments, including the National Carillon and **Captain Cook Memorial Water Jet** (Map p258). You can cycle the entire 28km perimeter in two hours or walk it in seven. Alternatively, you can split the route into smaller chunks by judicious use of the two main bridges.

National Carillon
TOWER

(Map p258; ☑ 02-6257 1068; www.nationalcapital. gov.au; Aspen Island, Lake Burley Griffin) This 50m-high bell tower was opened in 1970 as a gift from Britain on Canberra's 50th anniversary. The tower has 55 bells, weighing from 7kg to 6 tonnes each, making it one of the world's largest musical instruments. The bells mark the hour and there's usually a recital at 12.30pm from Wednesday through Sunday.

Royal Australian Mint
MUSEUM

(Map p255; ☑ 02-6202 6999; www.ramint.gov.au; Denison St, Deakin; ⏱ 8.30am-5pm Mon-Fri, 10am-4pm Sat & Sun) FREE The Royal Australian Mint is Australia's biggest money-making operation. Its gallery showcases the history of Australian coinage; here you can learn about the 1813 'holey dollar' and its enigmatic offspring, the 'dump'.

Mt Ainslie
VIEWPOINT

(Map p255; Ainslie Dr) Northeast of the city, 843m-high Mt Ainslie has fine views day and night. You can drive to the summit or take the walking track that starts behind the Australian War Memorial.

Aboriginal Tent Embassy
HISTORIC SITE

(Map p258; King George Tce, Parkes) First erected in 1972, this protest camp on the lawn in front of Old Parliament House came and went over the following 20 years but has been a constant presence since then, providing a continuing reminder of Indigenous dispossession for those visiting the symbolic heart of Australian democracy.

🏃 Activities

Canberra has an extensive network of dedicated cycle paths. The Canberra & Region Visitors Centre is a good source of information, as is Pedal Power ACT (www.pedal power.org.au).

Manuka Swimming Pool
SWIMMING

(Map p258; ☑ 02-6295 1910; www.manukapool. com.au; NSW Cres, Griffith; adult/child $6/4.50; ⏱ 6am-7pm Mon-Fri, 8am-7pm Sat & Sun) Art deco–era 30m outdoor pool.

☞ Tours

Balloon Aloft
BALLOONING

(Map p258; ☑ 02-6249 8660; www.canberra balloons.com.au; 120 Commonwealth Ave, Yarralumla; adult/child from $330/240) Meet in the foyer of the Hyatt for a flight over Canberra – the ideal way to understand the city's unique design.

Lake Burley Griffin Cruises
CRUISE

(Map p258; ☑ 0419 418 846; www.lakecruises. com.au; Barrine Dr, Acton; adult/child $20/9; ⏱ mid-Sep–May) Informative one-hour lake cruises.

Central Canberra

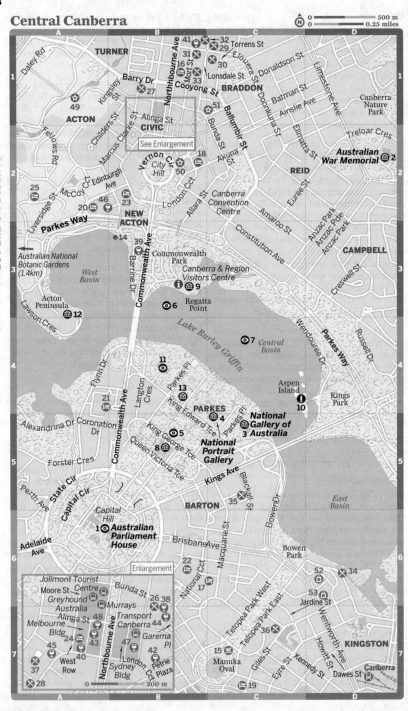

N
0 — 500 m
0 — 0.25 miles

TURNER

Daley Rd

Kingsley St

Barry Dr

27

Childers St

49

ACTON

Fellows Rd

Marcus Clarke St

Northbourne Ave

41 32 Torrens St
31 29
16 30
Mort St
33 Lonsdale St
Cooyong St
Elouera St
Donaldson St

BRADDON

Batman St

Ainslie Ave

Limestone Ave

Canberra
Nature
Park

Treloar Cres

Australian
War Memorial 2

Alinga St
CIVIC
See Enlargement

51

Ballumbir St

Bunda St

Akuna St

Vernon Cir
City
Hill
18
50

Edinburgh Ave

McCoy

St

25

20 46 23

NEW
ACTON

Liversidge St

Parkes Way

London Cct

Allara St

Canberra
Convention
Centre

REID

Euree St

Elimatta St

Anzac Park

Anzac Pde

Anzac Park

CAMPBELL

Amaroo St

Constitution Ave

Creswell St

Australian National
Botanic Gardens
(1.4km)

West
Basin

14

39

Barrine Dr

Commonwealth Ave

Commonwealth
Park

Canberra & Region
Visitors Centre

9

Acton
Peninsula

Lawson Cres

12

6 Regatta
Point

Lake Burley Griffin

7 Central
Basin

Wendouree Dr

Parkes Way

Russell Dr

Flynn Dr

11

21

Langton Cres

13

Parkes Pl

King Edward Tce

PARKES

4

Parkes Pl

National
Gallery of
3 Australia

Aspen
Island

10

Kings
Park

Alexandrina Dr

Coronation
Dr

King George Tce

5

8

Queen Victoria Tce

National
Portrait
Gallery

Forster Cres

Kings Ave

Blackall St

Bowen Dr

East
Basin

Perth Ave

State Cir

Capital Cir

Capital
Hill

1 Australian
Parliament
House

BARTON

35

Brisbane Ave

Macquarie St

Bowen
Park

Adelaide
Ave

22

National Cct

17

52 34

53

Jardine St

Telopea Park West

Telopea Park East

Wentworth Ave

Enlargement

Jolimont Tourist
Centre
Moore St
Greyhound
Australia
Alinga St
Melbourne
Bldg
24
45
40
37
West
Row
28

Bunda St

26 38

Murrays
Australia
Transport
Canberra 44
Garema
Pl
47 42
London
Sydney
Bldg
Petrie

48

43

Northbourne Ave

15 Manuka
Oval

Giles St

Eyre St

Kennedy St

Howitt St

36

KINGSTON

19

Dawes St

Canberra

0 — 200 m

Central Canberra

✦ Festivals & Events

National Multicultural Festival CULTURAL
(www.multiculturalfestival.com.au; ⊕Feb) Three days of art, culture and food.

Royal Canberra Show AGRICULTURAL SHOW
(www.canberrashow.org.au; ⊕late Feb) The country comes to town.

Enlighten CULTURAL
(www.enlightencanberra.com.a) For 10 days in early March various Canberra institutions are bathed in projections and keep their doors open late, while a night noodle market fills bellies and live music fills the air.

Canberra Balloon Spectacular AIR SHOW
(www.balloonspectacular.com.au; ⊕Mar) Hot-air balloons lift off from the lawns in front of Old Parliament House during this nine-day festival.

National Folk Festival MUSIC
(www.folkfestival.org.au; ⊕Easter) One of Australia's largest folk festivals, running for five days in Exhibition Park.

Canberra International Music Festival MUSIC
(www.cimf.org.au; ⊕late Apr-early May) Eleven days of classical music in significant Canberra locations and buildings.

Floriade FAIR
(www.floriadeaustralia.com) This elaborate display of spring flowers is one of the city's biggest events, drawing the crowds to Commonwealth Park from mid-September to mid-October.

🛏 Sleeping

Canberra's accommodation is at its busiest and most expensive during parliamentary sitting days. Hotels charge peak rates mid-week, but reduced rates at weekends. Peak rates also apply during the Floriade festival in September and October.

⭐ **Blue & White Lodge** MOTEL **$**
(Map p255; ☎ 02-6248 0498; www.blueandwhite lodge.com.au; 524 Northbourne Ave, Downer; s/d $95/100; 🅿 ❄ 🛜) On the main approach into Canberra from the north, this long-standing motel-style place and its indistinguishable sister, the Canberran Lodge, are reliable budget options in what can be a pricey city. It's a long walk into town but there's a bus stop nearby.

Alvio Tourist Park CARAVAN PARK **$**
(Map p255; ☎ 02-6247 5466; www.aliviogroup. com.au; 20 Kunzea St, O'Connor; sites with/without bathroom from $75/60, cabins with/without bathroom from $143/134; 🅿 ❄ @ 🛜 ⛱) Hidden in Canberra's bushy fringes, this well equipped tourist park has a range of tidy cabins in various configurations and an excellent outdoor swimming pool. While it's a fair way out of town, it's on a bus route that heads straight through the heart of Civic and the parliamentary precinct.

⭐ **Little National Hotel** HOTEL **$$**
(Map p258; ☎ 02-6188 3200; www.littlenational hotel.com.au; 21 National Circuit, Barton; r from $119; 🅿 ❄ @ 🛜) Housed within a stark black-metal cube, this brilliant boutique hotel delivers affordable style by way of small but well designed rooms. Compensating for the lack of cat-swinging space is an appealing 'library' and a bar offering panoramic views of the city. Book early; advance bookings are a steal but prices can more than double when it's busy.

⭐ **East Hotel** HOTEL **$$**
(Map p258; ☎ 02-6295 6925; www.easthotel. com.au; 69 Canberra Ave, Kingston; apt from $220; 🅿 ❄ @ 🛜) Straddling the divide between boutique and business, East offers stylishly executed spaces and smile-inducing extras such as free lollies and design magazines for loan in the lobby. Even the studios have work desks, iPod docks, espresso machines and kitchenettes, and there are one- and two-bedroom suites if you need to spread out. Plus there's an exceedingly cool bar and a bookshop-restaurant downstairs.

Aria Hotel HOTEL **$$**
(Map p255; ☎ 02-6279 7000; www.ariahotel. com. au; 45 Dooring St, Dickson; r/apt from $159/191; 🅿 ❄ @ 🛜) The standard rooms aren't overly large in this new block but they have comfy beds, excellent rainfall showers, balconies and everything else you'd expect from a smart business hotel. There are some good deals to be had if you book ahead.

Avenue HOTEL **$$**
(Map p258; ☎ 02-6246 9500; www.avenuehotel. com.au; 80 Northbourne Ave, Braddon; r/apt from $143/219; 🅿 ❄ 🛜) Raw concrete offset with angled glass provides a striking if somewhat brutal introduction to this large, contemporary hotel. Rooms are spacious and schmick; ask for one facing the central courtyard to avoid the traffic noise. Parking is free if you book directly.

University House HOTEL **$$**
(Map p258; ☎ 02-6125 5211; http://unihouse. anu.edu.au; 1 Balmain Cres, Acton; s/tw/d/apt from $101/135/150/195; 🅿 ❄ 🛜) This 1950s-era building, with original custom-built furniture, resides in the bushy grounds of the Australian National University (ANU) and is favoured by research students, visiting academics and the occasional politician. The spacious rooms and two-bedroom apartments are unadorned but comfortable. There's also a peaceful central courtyard and a friendly little cafe downstairs.

QT Canberra BOUTIQUE HOTEL **$$**
(Map p258; ☎ 02-6247 6244; www.qtcanberra. com.au; 1 London Circuit, New Acton; r/ste from $184/379; ❄ 🛜) A playful irreverence towards politics underscores the lobby, and very comfortable rooms are trimmed with cool design touches such as retro postcards of past Aussie prime ministers. Service can be hit or miss. Downstairs the country's political movers and shakers do their finest *House of Cards* impressions in the Capitol Bar & Grill.

Burbury Hotel HOTEL **$$**
(Map p258; ☎ 02-6173 2700; www.burburyhotel. com.au; 1 Burbury Close, Barton; r/apt from $142/175; 🅿 ❄ 🛜) This business hotel offers rooms and one- and two-bedroom suites. The decor is neutral and relaxing, and rooms are pleasantly light-filled. Adjacent apartments are excellent for families, and the complex includes two impressive Asian restaurants. Guests can use the spa and pool at the Hotel Realm across the road.

Quest
APARTMENT $$

(Map p258; ☑02-6243 2222; www.questapart
ments.com.au; 28 West Row, Civic; apt from $169;
❄ 🤏) These tidy apartments are within easy
walking distance of all of the bars and eater-
ies of Civic, Acton and Braddon. Each comes
with a comfortable lounge, big TV and mod-
ern kitchenette; some have balconies and
laundry facilities.

Canberra City YHA
HOSTEL $$

(Map p258; ☑02-6248 9155; www.yha.com.au;
7 Akuna St, Civic; dm $38-41, d with/without bath-
room $140/125; ❄ @ 🤏 ≋) You can't beat the
position of this hostel, smack-bang in the
city centre, although be warned: it's popular
with school groups. Amenities include bike
hire, a small indoor pool, a sauna, a kitchen,
an outdoor terrace with a barbecue, and a
cafe.

★ Hotel Hotel
HOTEL $$$

(Map p258; ☑02-6287 6287; www.hotel-hotel.
com.au; 25 Edinburgh Ave, New Acton; r from $266;
❄ 🤏) Hotel Hotel's spectacular exterior
translates to an equally hip interior. Rooms
are quirkily decorated, and while the (very)
subdued lighting isn't to everyone's taste,
we're big fans of the hotel's audacious and
dramatic ambience. Reception is filled with
nooks, crannies and mini-libraries, and Ho-
tel Hotel's **Monster Kitchen & Bar** (Map
p258; breakfast $16-19, shared plates $20-35;
☺6.30am-1am) is just as interesting.

★ Hyatt Hotel Canberra
HOTEL $$$

(Map p258; ☑02-6270 1234; www.canberra.park.
hyatt.com; 120 Commonwealth Ave, Yarralumla; r
from $295, ste from $690; P ❄ @ 🤏 ≋) Spotting visiting heads of state is a popular activity in the foyer of Canberra's most luxurious
and historic hotel. More than 200 rooms,
well used meeting spaces and a popular tea
lounge mean that a constant stream of visitors passes through the building. Rooms are
large and extremely well equipped, and facilities include an indoor pool, a spa, a sauna
and a gym.

✖ Eating

Canberra has a sophisticated dining scene,
catering to political wheelers and dealers
and locals alike. Established dining hubs include Civic, Kingston and Griffith, and there
are good Asian eateries in Dickson. New
Acton, the Kingston Foreshore development
and Lonsdale St in Braddon are the hippest
new areas.

Hamlet
STREET FOOD $

(Map p258; www.broddogs.com.au; 16 Lonsdale
St, Braddon; mains $5-20; ☺noon-late) Sympto-
matic of the enviable hipsterisation of Braddon, the Hamlet is a wonderfully ramshackle
village of food trucks and hole-in-the-wall
eateries, accompanied by a bar, a gallery
and plenty of outdoor seating. Our current
favourite outlet is BrodDogs, a tasty offshoot
of Kingston's Brodburger, which sells nothing but good-quality, tasty hot dogs. If that
doesn't appeal, there's Italian, Greek, Vietnamese, Indian...

Two Before Ten
CAFE $

(Map p258; www.twobeforeten.com.au; 1 Hobart
Pl, Civic; mains $11-18; ☺7am-4pm Mon-Fri, 8am-
2pm Sat & Sun) Breaking from the Australian
tradition that says good cafes should be
bohemian and battered looking, this airy
eatery brings a touch of Cape Cod to the
centre of a city block. The serves are perhaps a little too fashionably petite but the
coffee is excellent.

Lonsdale Street Roasters
CAFE $

(Map p258; www.lonsdalestreetroasters.com; 7
Lonsdale St, Braddon; mains $8-12; ☺6.30am-4pm
Mon-Fri, 8am-4pm Sat & Sun) In hip Braddon,
this grungy-chic cafe serves up damn fine
coffee along with tasty pastries and rolls.
There's a bigger **branch** (Map p258; 23 Lonsdale St; mains $15-17; ☺7am-4pm) just up the
road with a large terrace; it has more of an
emphasis on eating, but the food's better
here at the original.

★ Cupping Room
CAFE $$

(Map p258; ☑02-6257 6412; www.thecupping
room.com.au; 1 University Ave, Civic; mains $11-24;
☺7am-4pm; 🍴) Queues often form outside
this airy corner cafe, drawn by the prospect
of Canberra's best coffee and an interesting
menu, including vegetarian and vegan op-
tions. The seasonal chia pudding is extraor-
dinary, but if you prefer something a little
more familiar, the burgers are equally as
epic. Choose your coffee blend from the tast-
ing notes and prepare to be amazed.

★ Akiba
ASIAN $$

(Map p258; ☑02-6162 0602; www.akiba.com.
au; 40 Bunda St, Civic; noodle & rice dishes $12-15,
share plates $18-33; ☺11.30am-midnight Sun-Wed,
to 2am Thu-Sat) A high-octane vibe pervades
this super-slick pan-Asian eatery, fuelled by a
hip young crew that effortlessly splashes together cocktails, dispenses food recommendations and juggles orders without breaking

a sweat. A raw bar serves up delectable sashimi, freshly shucked oysters and zingy ceviche. Salt-and-Sichuan-pepper squid and pork-belly buns are crowd pleasers, and we love the Japanese-style eggplant.

★ Morks
THAI $$

(Map p258; ☑02-6295 0112; www.morks.com.au; 19 Eastlake Pde, Kingston; mains $24-30; ⊙noon-2pm & 6-10pm Tue-Sat, noon-2pm Sun) Our favourite of the restaurants along the Kingston foreshore, Morks offers a contemporary spin on Thai cuisine, with Chinese and Malay elements added to the mix. Ask for a table outside to watch the passing promenade, and tuck into multiple serves of the starters; the sweet potato dumplings in Penang curry are staggeringly good.

Malaysian Chapter
MALAYSIAN $$

(Map p255; ☑02-6251 5670; www.malaysian chapter.com.au; 8 Weedon Close, Belconnen; mains $18-23; ⊙noon-2pm Tue-Fri & 5.30-9pm Mon-Sat; ☑) Fans of authentic Kuala Lumpur hawker cuisine should make the trek around 8km northwest from Civic to this unassuming, family-run spot in the surprisingly large commercial centre of Belconnen. Highlights includes *nasi goreng* (fried rice; served either as a *rendang, sambal* or curry), zingy tamarind fish, excellent satay and a cooling sago dessert.

Eightysix
MODERN AUSTRALIAN $$

(Map p258; ☑02-6161 8686; www.eightysix. com.au; cnr Elouera & Lonsdale St, Braddon; dishes $18-48) Prepare to share at this zippy contemporary eatery, where dishes range from delectable steamed duck buns to a whole lamb shoulder. Solo travellers should opt to sit at the kitchen counter and watch the precision of the kitchen in full swing. If you're part of a visiting sumo wrestling team or just a shameless glutton, opt for the $86 all-you-can-eat option.

Elk & Pea
LATIN AMERICAN $$

(Map p258; ☑0436 355 732; www.elkandpea. com.au; 21 Lonsdale St, Braddon; breakfast & lunch $11-25, tacos $8, shared plates $39-45; ⊙7.30am-2.30pm Mon, to 11pm Tue-Sun) Mexican influences pervade the menu and cocktail list of this hip little anytime eatery, which includes spicy eggs for brekkie, burgers and wraps for lunch, and Canberra's best tacos for dinner. In the evening there's also a menu of substantial Latin American–influenced dishes designed to be split between two or three people.

★ Courgette
MODERN AUSTRALIAN $$$

(Map p258; ☑02-6247 4042; www.courgette. com.au; 54 Marcus Clarke St, Civic; 3-course lunch $66, 4-course dinner $88; ⊙noon-3pm & 6.30-11pm Mon-Sat) With its crisp white linen, impeccable service and discreet but expensive ambience, Courgette is the kind of place to bring someone you want to impress, like a date or, perhaps, the Finnish ambassador. The exacting standards continue with the precisely prepared, exquisitely plated and flavour-laden food.

★ Aubergine
MODERN AUSTRALIAN $$$

(Map p255; ☑02-6260 8666; www.aubergine.com. au; 18 Barker St, Griffith; 4-course menu $90; ⊙6-10pm Mon-Sat) You'll need to travel out to the southern suburbs to find Canberra's top-rated restaurant. While the location may be unassuming, the same can't be said for the menu, which is exciting, innovative and seasonally driven. Although only a four-course menu is offered, you can choose between a handful of options for most courses. Service and presentation are assured.

Les Bistronomes
FRENCH $$$

(Map p258; ☑02-6248 8119; www.lesbistronomes. net; cnr Mort & Elouera Sts, Braddon; mains $31-36; ⊙noon-2pm & 6-9pm Tue-Sat) Wine bottles line the wall and melodious French language radiates from the kitchen at this excellent little bistro. At $50, the five-course Saturday set lunch is terrific value; expect a succession of perfectly cooked, beautifully presented dishes that will leave you comfortably full without straining your belt.

Lilotang
JAPANESE $$$

(Map p258; ☑02-6273 1424; www.lilotang.com. au; 1 Burbury Close, Barton; mains $29-38; ⊙noon-2.30pm Tue-Fri & 6-11pm Tue-Sat) Artfully strung rope distracts from an industrial-looking ceiling at this upmarket Japanese restaurant in the Burbury Hotel. Highlights include steamed oysters wrapped in beef *tataki* (seared and thinly sliced beef) and basically anything barbecued on the *robata*.

Pomegranate
MEDITERRANEAN $$$

(Map p258; ☑02-6295 1515; www.pomegranate kingston.com; 31 Giles St, Kingston; mains $30-34; ⊙noon-2pm & 6-9pm Tue-Sat) Techniques from France combine with the traditions of the eastern Mediterranean, adding finesse to rustic dishes that burst with flavour. Despite the white-linen ambience, the serves are generous and the service is friendly and relaxed.

Ottoman   TURKISH $$$

(Map p258; ☑ 02-6273 6111; www.ottomancuisine.com.au; 9 Broughton St, Barton; mains $32-36; ⊘ noon-2.30pm & 6-10pm Tue-Fri, 6-10pm Sat) Set in an elegant garden pavilion, Ottoman has long been a favourite dining destination for Canberra's power brokers. Familiar dishes (meze, dolma, kofte) are given subtle contemporary twists, but for the most part they're left deliciously traditional.

 Drinking & Nightlife

Pubs and bars are concentrated in Civic and around Lonsdale and Mort Sts in Braddon. New Acton is also worth a look.

Aviary Rooftop   ROOFTOP BAR

(Map p258; ☑ 0421 552 417; www.aviaryrooftop.com; 3 Barrine Dr, Acton; ⊘ 5pm-late Thu, noon-late Fri-Sun) Perched on top of a stack of shipping containers by the shore of Lake Burley Griffin, this large open-sided space offers drinks in plastic glasses and has regular DJ sets. If you're peckish, head to one of the food stalls downstairs by the popular basketball court.

Bar Rochford   WINE BAR

(Map p258; ☑ 02-6230 6222; www.barrochford.com; L1, 65 London Circuit, Civic; ⊘ 5pm-late Tue-Thu, noon-1am Fri, 5pm-1am Sat) Bearded barmen concentrate earnestly on their cocktail constructions and wine recommendations at this sophisticated but unstuffy bar in the Melbourne Building. Dress up and hope for a table by one of the big arched windows.

Joe's Bar   COCKTAIL BAR

(Map p258; ☑ 02-6178 0050; www.joesateast.com; East Hotel, 69 Canberra Ave, Kingston; ⊘ noon-late) Colourful glass and draped metal beads add to the glitzy boho ambience at this attractive Italian food and wine bar attached to the East Hotel. The extensive cocktail list includes a whole page of speciality gin and tonics, and the bar staff really knows its Italian wines, too. Pace yourself with a serve of polenta chips, arancini balls or antipasti.

Molly's   COCKTAIL BAR

(Map p258; www.molly.net.au; Rear, 37 London Circuit, Civic; ⊘ 4pm-midnight Mon-Wed, to 2am Thu-Sat) The prohibition shtick is a now well worn trope but who doesn't love the thrill of wandering back lanes and discovering subterranean drinking dens? Molly's offers an eight-page whisky list, sorted by country (Indian whisky anyone?). To find it, turn off London Circuit at Gozleme Cafe, turn right and look for a lightbulb above an open wooden door.

Highball Express   COCKTAIL BAR

(Map p258; www.highballexpress.com.au; L1, 82 Alinga St, Civic; ⊘ 4pm-late Tue-Sat) There's no sign, so take a punt and climb the fire escape in the lane behind Smith's Alternative to this louche tropical take on a 1920s Cuban rum bar. The highball cocktails are excellent and often come served with banana chips.

BentSpoke Brewing Co   MICROBREWERY

(Map p258; ☑ 02-6257 5220; www.bentspokebrewing.com.au; 38 Mort St, Braddon; ⊘ 11am-midnight) With 16 excellent beers and ciders on tap, BentSpoke is one of Australia's best craft brewers. Sit at the bike-themed bar or relax outside and kick things off with a tasting tray of four beers ($16). Our favourite is the Barley Griffin Ale, subtly tinged with a spicy Belgian yeast. Good pub food, too.

Smith's Alternative   BAR

(Map p258; ☑ 0401 084 773; www.smithsalternative.com; 76 Alinga St, Civic; ⊘ 8am-midnight Mon-Thu, to 3am Fri & Sat, noon-midnight Sun) When the legendary Smith's Alternative Bookshop closed down, it turned out that the name worked just as well for its successor. The new Smith's is an artsy cafe-bar and performance space, with a makeshift stage in one corner and cakes in the cabinet. In the evenings, except to be bemused by anything from live music to slam poetry to theatre.

Parlour Wine Room   WINE BAR

(Map p258; ☑ 02-6257 7325; www.parlour.net.au; 16 Kendall Lane, New Acton; ⊘ noon-late Tue-Sun) Modern banquettes share the polished wooden floor with well stuffed chesterfield lounges in this contemporary take on the Victorian smoking lounge. Views over the lake complement the list of local, Australian and international wines, and killer cocktails.

Hippo Co   BAR

(Map p258; ☑ 02-6247 7555; www.facebook.com/hippococbr; level 1, 17 Garema Pl, Civic; ⊘ 5pm-2am) This cosy lounge-bar is popular with young whisky and cocktail slurpers who file in for Wednesday-night jazz – the turntable rules other evenings.

Cube   GAY & LESBIAN

(Map p258; ☑ 02-6257 1110; www.cubenightclub.com.au; 33 Petrie Plaza, Civic; ⊘ 10pm-late Thu-Sun) Canberra's one and only gay club has been lurking in this basement for practically forever. These days it seems to attract as many straight women as gay men. Expect cheap drinks on Thirsty Thursdays.

Academy CLUB
(Map p258; ☑02-6253 2091; www.academy club.com.au; 50 Bunda St, Civic; admission varies; ☺9pm-late Thu-Sat) The original movie screen of this former cinema lights up the crowded dance floor with frenetic, larger-than-life visuals. Head to the Candy Bar cocktail lounge if you want to take it easy.

Phoenix PUB
(Map p258; ☑02-6169 5092; www.lovethephoenix. com; 23 East Row, Civic; ☺5pm-1am Mon-Wed, to 3am Thu-Sat) The studenty Phoenix is a staunch supporter of local music, with bands playing around four nights a week. On other nights you might strike a comedian, a poet or a pub quiz.

☆ Entertainment

Entertainment listings appear in Thursday's *Canberra Times* and on the BMA website (www.bmamag.com).

GIO Stadium Canberra STADIUM
(Map p255; ☑02-6256 6700; www.giostadium canberra.com.au; Battye St, Bruce) The Canberra Raiders (www.raiders.com.au) is the home-town rugby league side, and in season (from March to September) the team plays here

---

KIDS IN THE CAPITAL

Kids like Canberra because there's lots of cool stuff for them to do. Most of the museums and galleries have kids programs, and many offer dedicated tours and events – check websites for details.

For hands-on fun, visit **Questacon** (p257), the **National Museum of Australia** (p257) and the **Australian Institute of Sport** (AIS; Map p255; ☑02-6214 1010; www.experienceais.com; Leverrier St, Bruce; adult/child $20/12; ☺tours 10am, 11.30am, 1pm & 2.30pm). It's even possible to cuddle a cheetah and pat a red panda at the **National Zoo & Aquarium** (p256).

For fresh air and exercise, go for a bike ride around Lake Burley Griffin or head to the **Tidbinbilla Nature Reserve** (p266) or **Namadgi National Park** (p266).

---

regularly. Also laying tackles at Canberra Stadium is the ACT Brumbies (www.brumbies. com.au) rugby union team, which plays in the international Super Rugby competition (February to August).

Dendy Canberra CINEMA
(Map p258; ☑02-6221 8900; www.dendy.com.au; 2nd fl, Canberra Centre, 148 Bunda St, Civic; adult/child $20/15) Independent and art-house cinema. Tuesday is discount day.

ANU Bar LIVE MUSIC
(Map p258; ☑02-6125 3660; www.anuunion.com. au; University Ave, Acton; gigs $5-20) The Uni Bar (on the Australian National University campus) has live gigs regularly during semester. Up-and-coming bands that have played here in the past include a little Seattle three-piece called Nirvana.

Canberra Theatre Centre THEATRE
(Map p258; ☑02-6275 2700; www.canberratheatre centre.com.au; London Circuit, Civic Sq, Civic; ☺box office 9am-5pm Mon-Fri, 10am-2pm Sat) Canberra's live theatre hub.

🛍 Shopping

Old Bus Depot Markets MARKET
(Map p258; ☑02-6295 3331; www.obdm.com. au; 21 Wentworth Ave, Kingston; ☺10am-4pm Sun) A veritable Sunday institution in Canberra, this large, bustling market has one big hall completely devoted to food and another to crafts.

Canberra Glassworks ARTS & CRAFTS
(Map p258; ☑02-6260 7005; www.canberra glassworks.com; 11 Wentworth Ave, Kingston; ☺10am-4pm Wed-Sun) Call in to this converted Edwardian power station, the young city's oldest public heritage building, to watch glass being blown in the 'hot shop' and to peruse the exquisite results in the adjacent gallery and shop.

ℹ Information

Most of central Canberra is covered by a free wi-fi service.

Canberra Hospital (☑02-6244 2222; www. health.act.gov.au; Yamba Dr, Garran; ☺emergency 24hr)

Canberra & Region Visitors Centre (Map p258; ☑02-6205 0044; www.visitcanberra. com.au; Regatta Point, Barrine Dr, Commonwealth Park; ☺9am-4pm) Dispenses masses of information, including its own quarterly *Canberra Events* brochure.

ℹ️ Getting There & Away

AIR

Canberra Airport (Map p255; ☎ 02-6275 2222; www.canberraairport.com.au; 2 Brindabella Circuit) is within the city itself, only 7km southeast of Civic.

The only international flights are operated by **Singapore Airlines** (www.singaporeair.com), which flies to/from Singapore and Wellington.

Qantas (www.qantas.com) and associated QantasLink partners fly to/from Adelaide, Brisbane, Melbourne, Perth and Sydney. Virgin Australia (www.virginaustralia.com.au) flies to/from Adelaide, Brisbane, Gold Coast, Melbourne and Sydney. **Tigerair Australia** (www.tigerair.com. au) also heads to Melbourne, while **FlyPelican** (www.flypelican.com.au) services Newcastle and Dubbo.

BUS

The interstate bus terminal is at the **Jolimont Tourist Centre** (Map p258; 67 Northbourne Ave, Civic; ⊙ 5am-10.30pm), where you'll find booking desks for the major bus companies.

Greyhound Australia (p1070) Coaches to Sydney ($42, 3½ hours), Yass ($15, 55 minutes), Wagga Wagga ($40, three hours), Albury ($58, 4½ hours) and Melbourne ($88, eight hours), along with seasonal buses to the ski resorts.

Murrays (Map p258; ☎ 13 22 51; www. murrays.com.au; 65 Northbourne Ave; ⊙ 7am-7pm) Express services to Sydney ($45, 3½ hours), Wollongong ($49, 3¼ hours), Batemans Bay ($38, 2½ hours), Moruya ($41, 3¼ hours) and Narooma ($49, 4½ hours), as well as the ski fields.

NSW TrainLink (☎ 13 22 32; www.nswtrainlink. info) Coaches depart Canberra Railway Station on the Canberra–Cooma–Merimbula–Eden (daily) and Canberra–Cooma–Jindabyne (three per week) routes.

CAR & MOTORCYCLE

The Hume Hwy connects Sydney and Melbourne, passing 50km north of Canberra. The Federal Hwy runs north to connect with the Hume near Goulburn, and the Barton Hwy (Rte 25) meets the Hume near Yass. To the south, the Monaro Hwy connects Canberra with Cooma.

TRAIN

NSW TrainLink Services from Sydney ($56, four hours), Bowral ($34, 2½ hours), Bundanoon ($30, two hours) and Bungendore ($7, 40 minutes) pull into Kingston's **Canberra Railway Station** (Wentworth Ave, Kingston) three times daily.

V/Line (☎ 1800 800 007; www.vline.com.au) A daily service combines a train from Melbourne to Albury Wodonga with a bus to Canberra ($108, nine hours).

ℹ️ GETTING TO AND FROM THE AIRPORT

A taxi to the city centre costs from around $50 to $55.

Airport Express (☎ 1300 368 897; www.royalecoach.com.au; one way/return $12/20) runs between the airport and the city roughly hourly during the day.

Transport Canberra (Map p258; ☎ 13 17 10; www.transport.act.gov.au; East Row, Civic; adult/child $4.70/2.30, day pass $9/4.50; ⊙ information centre 6.30am-10pm Mon-Sat, 8am-7pm Sun) bus 11 runs between city platform 9 and Brindabella Business Park (right next to the airport) at least hourly between 6am and 6pm.

ℹ️ Getting Around

The bus network, operated by **Transport Canberra** (p265), will get you to most places of interest in the city. It recommends you use Google Maps as your travel planner, or call into the Civic office for maps and timetables.

A smart-card system operates, but if you're only here for a week or so, you're better off paying the driver in cash; a day pass costs less than two single tickets, so purchase one on your first journey of the day.

What is referred to as the city bus station is actually a set of 11 bus stops scattered along Northbourne Ave, Alinga St, East Row and Mort St.

At the time of writing, a new light rail track running north from Civic along Northbourne Ave, was under construction. The first stage is scheduled to be completed in late 2018.

Around Canberra

There are plenty of opportunities for day trips from Canberra, whether you're seeking bushwalking, cycling or relaxation. The bushy, hilly southern section of the ACT has scope for walking and makes a good break from the capital's museums. Just across the border in NSW, 35km east of Canberra, is Bungendore, an attractive village that bustles on weekends but slumbers during the week. There are galleries and antique stores aplenty.

◎ Sights

Lanyon Homestead HISTORIC BUILDING
(☎ 02-6235 5677; www.historicplaces.com.au; Tharwa Dr, Tharwa; adult/child $7/5; ⊙ 10am-4pm Tue-Sun) In 1834, when convicts were sent in to clear this land on the edge of Murrumbidgee River for grazing, this truly

WORTH A TRIP

CANBERRA DISTRICT WINE REGION

Canberra's wine region produces high-country cool-climate wines, with riesling and shiraz the star varietals. Most of the best wineries are actually across the border in NSW, north of the city.

Heading north on the Barton Hwy (A25), turn left near Hall onto Wallaroo Rd to get to **Brindabella Hills Winery** (☑ 02-6161 9154; www.brindabellahills.com.au; 156 Woodgrove Close, Wallaroo; ⊙ 10am-5pm Sat & Sun). Back on the highway continue north and turn off to the right towards Springrange to visit **Wily Trout Vineyard** (☑ 02-6230 2487; www.wilytrout.com.au; 431 Nanima Rd, Springrange; ⊙ 10am-5pm), home to the popular smokehouse deli-restaurant **Poachers Pantry** (p266). Further north still there's a cluster of acclaimed wineries near Murrumbateman, including **Eden Road** (☑ 02-6226 8800; www.edenroadwines.com.au; 3182 Barton Hwy, Murrumbateman; ⊙ 11am-4pm Wed-Sun), **Clonakilla** (☑ 02-6227 5877; www.clonakilla.com.au; 3 Crisps Lane, Murrumbateman; ⊙ 10am-5pm) and **Helm** (☑ 02-6227 5953; www.helmwines.com.au; 19 Butts Rd, Murrumbateman; ⊙ 10am-5pm Thu-Mon).

For further options, visit www.canberrawines.com.au.

was a wild frontier. Now it's a pretty slice of rural landscape, ringed by hills and with a garden that wouldn't be out of place in the Cotswolds. It's well worth the trip 25km south from Canberra to explore the gracious Victorian homestead, outbuildings and flowerbeds and to ponder the improbability of it all.

Namadgi National Park NATIONAL PARK
(☑ 02-6207 2900; www.environment.act.gov.au; Naas Rd, Tharwa; ⊙ visitor centre 9am-4pm) FREE
Namadgi is the Ngunnawal word for the mountains southwest of Canberra, and this national park includes eight of those peaks higher than 1700m. It offers good bushwalking, mountain biking, fishing and horse riding, along with the opportunity to view Aboriginal rock art. Make camping bookings online ($8 per person) or at the visitor centre, 2km south of Tharwa. While you're there, say gidday to Spencer, the resident carpet python.

Tidbinbilla Nature Reserve NATURE RESERVE
(☑ 02-6205 1233; www.tidbinbilla.act.gov.au; Tidbinbilla Reserve Rd; entry per car $12; ⊙ 7.30am-6pm Apr-Nov, to 8pm Oct-Mar, visitor centre 9am-5pm) Abutting the Namadgi National Park, 40km southwest of Canberra, this reserve is rich in Australian wildlife including kangaroos and emus, and platypuses and lyrebirds at dusk. Check online for ranger-guided activities.

✷ Festivals & Events

Canberra District Wine Week WINE
(www.canberrawines.com.au; ⊙ Apr) The 'week' stretches for 10 days during this harvest festival that features wine tastings, food and tours.

🛏 Sleeping & Eating

Old Stone House B&B $$
(☑ 02-6238 1888; www.theoldstonehouse.com.au; 41 Molonglo St, Bungendore; r $220; ❋ 🛜) Set behind a large oak tree on Bungendore's main road, this charismatic 1867 granite-block house offers four antique-furnished rooms, all of which have private bathrooms, although one is just across the corridor. Start your day with a three-course breakfast and a wander through the garden.

Poachers Pantry DELI $$
(☑ 02-6230 2487; www.poacherspantry.com.au; Nanima Rd, Springrange; mains breakfast $18-22, lunch $38; ⊙ noon-3pm Mon-Fri, 9.30am-3pm Sat & Sun) This deli-restaurant at Wily Trout Vineyard is renowned for smoked meats and fish, best enjoyed as part of a platter ($28 to $36).

🔒 Shopping

Bungendore Wood Works Gallery ARTS & CRAFTS
(☑ 02-6238 1682; www.bungendorewoodworks.com.au; 22 Malbon St, Bungendore; ⊙ 9am-5pm) Showcases superb works crafted from Australian timber, as well as changing art exhibitions.

Queensland

POP 4.84 MILLION / 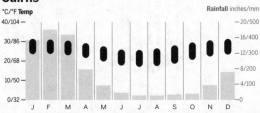 07

Best Places to Eat

➜ Gauge (p285)

➜ Wasabi (p326)

➜ Prawn Star (p407)

➜ On the Inlet (p422)

➜ Borough Barista (p317)

Best Places to Sleep

➜ New Inchcolm Hotel & Suites (p283)

➜ Tryp (p283)

➜ Vacy Hall (p307)

➜ Bellview (p405)

➜ Coral Beach Lodge (p421)

➜ 1770 Getaway (p354)

Why Go?

From the surf-soaked Gold Coast beaches and buzzing Brisbane to the tropical Daintree rainforest, the Sunshine State offers a dizzying array of distractions and outdoor adventures. Queensland's big-ticket lure is the 2000km-long submarine kingdom of the Great Barrier Reef, an underwater wonderland of colourful marine life and corals. Tropical islands are also a speciality, where you can charter a yacht or just laze on a near-deserted beach.

Even away from the surfing, snorkelling and diving, Queensland delivers on adventure: go white-water rafting on grade-IV rapids, kayak the coastline, skydive onto the beach or bushwalk through rainforests and gorges. Wildlife-watching is superb here too, with tropical birds, whales, cassowaries and crocs filling your photo album. And don't discount the wonders of the vast inland Outback or the remote 4WD territory of Cape York Peninsula – some of Australia's most rugged and exhilarating travel.

When to Go
Cairns

°C/°F Temp	Rainfall inches/mm

A temperature and rainfall chart for Cairns, months J F M A M J J A S O N D. Temperature axis 0/32, 10/50, 20/68, 30/86, 40/104. Rainfall axis 0, 4/100, 8/200, 12/300, 16/400, 20/500.

Jun–Sep Crowds and higher prices in the north, cooler in the south. Best time to spot migrating whales.

Apr–May & Oct–Nov Warm, with long beach days. Fewer crowds; resort prices drop slightly.

Dec–Mar The wet season: hot with torrential rain in the north. Party season on the Gold Coast.

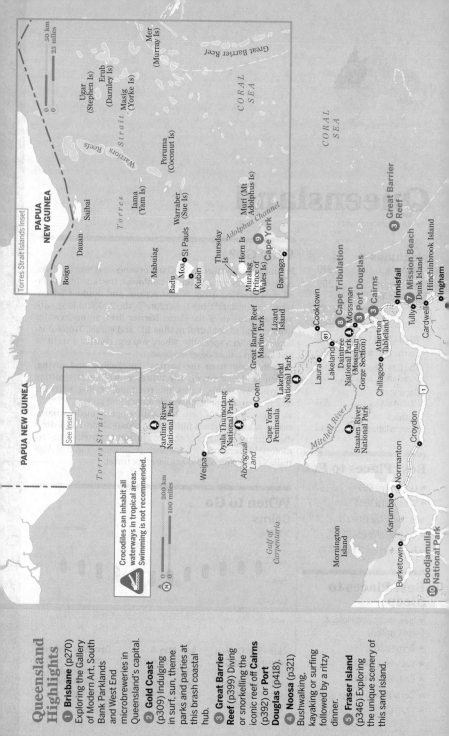

Queensland Highlights

1 Brisbane (p270)
Exploring the Gallery of Modern Art, South Bank Parklands and West End microbreweries in Queensland's capital.

2 Gold Coast (p309) Indulging in surf, sun, theme parks and parties at this brash coastal hub.

3 Great Barrier Reef (p399) Diving or snorkelling the iconic reef off **Cairns** (p392) or **Port Douglas** (p418).

4 Noosa (p321) Bushwalking, kayaking or surfing followed by a ritzy dinner.

5 Fraser Island (p346) Exploring the unique scenery of this sand island.

Crocodiles can inhabit all waterways in tropical areas. Swimming is not recommended.

Torres Strait Islands Inset

PAPUA NEW GUINEA

Boigu
Dauan
Saibai
Ugar (Stephen Is)
Erub (Darnley Is)
Mabuiag
Iama (Yam Is)
Poruma (Coconut Is)
Mer (Murray Is)
Badu
Moa
St Pauls
Warraber (Sue Is)
Kubin
Thursday Is
Horn Is
Muri (Mt Adolphus Is)
Muralag (Prince of Wales Is)
9 Cape York
Bamaga
Adolphus Channel

Torres Strait
Warrior Reefs
CORAL SEA
Great Barrier Reef

PAPUA NEW GUINEA

Torres Strait

See Inset

6 Jardine River National Park
Weipa
Aboriginal Land
Coen
Cape York Peninsula
Ovala Thumotang National Park
Lakefield National Park
Laura
Lakeland
Cooktown
Great Barrier Reef Marine Park
Lizard Island
Daintree National Park (Mossman Gorge Section)
8 Cape Tribulation
Mossman
3 Port Douglas
3 Cairns
Atherton Tableland
Chillagoe
Mareeba
3 Great Barrier Reef
7 Mission Beach
Innisfail
Dunk Island
Tully
Cardwell
Hinchinbrook Island
Ingham

Mitchell River
Staaten River National Park
Croydon
Normanton
Karumba
Gulf of Carpentaria
Mornington Island
Burketown
10 Boodjamulla National Park

CORAL SEA

0 — 50 km
0 — 25 miles

0 — 200 km
0 — 100 miles

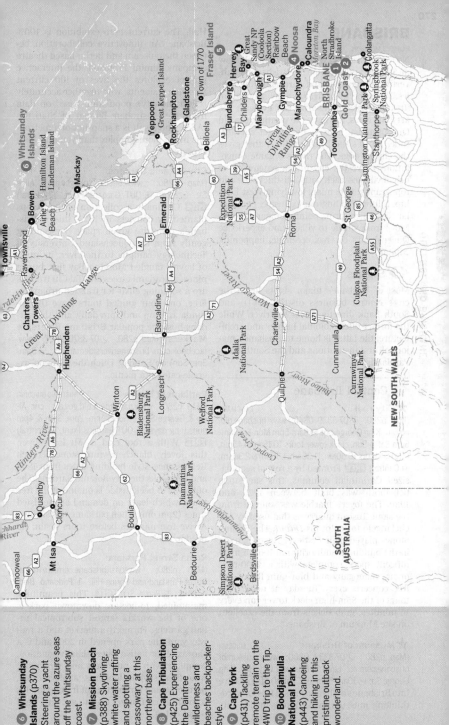

6 Whitsunday Islands (p370)
Steering a yacht around the azure seas off the Whitsunday coast.

7 Mission Beach (p388)
Skydiving, white-water rafting and spotting a cassowary at this northern base.

8 Cape Tribulation (p425)
Experiencing the Daintree wilderness and beaches backpacker-style.

9 Cape York (p431)
Tackling remote terrain on the 4WD trip to the Tip.

10 Boodjamulla National Park (p443)
Canoeing and hiking in this pristine outback wonderland.

Camooweal
Mt Isa
Cloncurry
Quamby
Boulia
Bedourie
Birdsville
Simpson Desert National Park
Diamantina National Park
Winton
Bladensburg National Park
Longreach
Barcaldine
Welford National Park
Idalia National Park
Quilpie
Charleville
Cunnamulla
Currawinya National Park
Culgoa Floodplain National Park
St George
Roma
Expedition National Park
Bioela
Gladstone
Town of 1770
Rockhampton
Great Keppel Island
Yeppoon
Mackay
Bowen
Airlie Beach
Ravenswood
Townsville
Charters Towers
Hughenden
Emerald
Biloela
Bundaberg
Childers
Maryborough
Gympie
Maroochydore
Caloundra
Noosa
BRISBANE
Gold Coast
Coolangatta
Springbrook National Park
Stanthorpe
Lamington National Park
Toowoomba

Hervey Bay
Great Sandy NP (Cooloola Section)
Rainbow Beach
Fraser Island

North Stradbroke Island
Moreton Bay

Whitsunday Islands
Hamilton Island
Lindeman Island

Great Dividing Range

Flinders River
Burdekin River
Leichhardt River
Warrego River
Bulloo River
Paroo River
Cooper Creek
Diamantina River

SOUTH AUSTRALIA

NEW SOUTH WALES

A1
A2
A4
A5
A6
A7
A55
A71
66
78
63
62
55
60
39
17
54
49
85
46
71
83
1
49
55

BRISBANE

POP 2.3 MILLION

No longer satisfied with being in the shadow of Sydney and Melbourne, Brisbane is subverting stereotypes and surprising the critics. Welcome to Australia's new subtropical 'It kid'. Brisbane's charms are evident: the arts, the cafes, the bars, the weather, the old Queenslander houses, the go-get-'em attitude. But it's the Brisbane River that gives the city its edge. The river's organic convolutions carve the city into a patchwork of urban villages, each with a distinct style and topography: bohemian, low-lying West End; hip, hilltop Paddington; exclusive, peninsular New Farm; prim, pointy Kangaroo Point. Move from village to village and experience Queensland's diverse, eccentric, happening capital.

◉ Sights

Most of Brisbane's major sights lie in the city's central business district (CBD) and South Bank directly across the river. While the former offers colonial history and architecture, the latter is home to Brisbane's major cultural institutions and the South Bank Parklands.

◉ Central Brisbane

★ **City Hall**   LANDMARK
(Map p280; ☑07-3339 0845; www.brisbane.qld. gov.au; King George Sq; ☺8am-5pm Mon-Fri, 9am-5pm Sat & Sun, clock tower tours 10.15am-4.45pm, City Hall tours 10.30am, 11.30am, 1.30pm & 2.30pm; 🚉Central) FREE Fronted by a row of sequoia-sized Corinthian columns, this sandstone behemoth was built between 1920 and 1930. The foyer's marble was sourced from the same Tuscan quarry as that used by Michelangelo to sculpt his *David*. The Rolling Stones played their first-ever Australian gig in the building's auditorium in 1965, a magnificent space complete with a 4300-pipe organ, mahogany and blue-gum floors and free concerts every Tuesday at noon. Free tours of the 85m-high clock tower run every 15 minutes; grab tickets from the excellent on-site Museum of Brisbane.

★ **Museum of Brisbane**   MUSEUM
(Map p280; ☑07-3339 0800; www.museumof brisbane.com.au; Level 3, Brisbane City Hall, King George Sq; ☺10am-5pm; 🚉Central) FREE Delve into Brisbane's highs and lows at this forward-thinking museum, tucked away inside City Hall. The current hero exhibition is 100% Brisbane. An innovative collaboration between the museum and Berlin-based theatre company Rimini Protokoll, the interactive project explores the lives of 100 current Brisbane residents, who together accurately reflect the city's population based on data from the Australian Bureau of Statistics (ABS). The result is a snapshot of a metropolis much more complex than you may have expected.

City Botanic Gardens   PARK
(Map p280; www.brisbane.qld.gov.au; Alice St; ☺24hr; 🚌QUT Gardens Point, 🚉Central) FREE Originally a collection of food crops planted by convicts in 1825, this is Brisbane's favourite green space. Descending gently from the Queensland University of Technology campus to the river, its mass of lawns, tangled Moreton Bay figs, bunya pines, macadamia trees and Tai Chi troupes are a soothing elixir for frazzled urbanites. Free, one-hour guided tours leave the rotunda at 11am and 1pm daily, and the gardens host the popular **Brisbane Riverside Markets** (Map p280; ☑07-3870 2807; www. facebook.com/brisbaneriversidemarkets; ☺8am-3pm Sun) on Sunday. Ditch the gardens' average cafe for a picnic.

Parliament House   HISTORIC BUILDING
(Map p280; www.parliament.qld.gov.au; cnr Alice & George Sts; ☺tours 1pm, 2pm, 3pm & 4pm nonsitting days; 🚌QUT Gardens Point, 🚉Central) FREE With a roof clad in Mt Isa copper, this lovely blanched-white stone, French Renaissance–style building dates from 1868 and overlooks the City Botanic Gardens. The only way to peek inside is on one of the free tours, which leave on demand at the listed times (2pm only when parliament is sitting). Arrive five minutes before tours begin; no need to book.

Roma Street Parkland   PARK
(Map p280; www.visitbrisbane.com.au/Roma-Street-Parkland-and-Spring-Hill; 1 Parkland Blvd; ☺24hr; 🚉Roma St) FREE This beautifully maintained, 16-hectare downtown park is one of the world's largest subtropical urban gardens. Formerly a market and a railway yard, the park opened in 2001 and is a showcase for native Queensland vegetation, complete with a rainforest and fern gully, waterfalls, skyline lookouts, a playground, barbecues and no shortage of frangipani. It's something of a maze: easy to get into, hard to get out of.

Shrine of Remembrance   LANDMARK
(Map p280; Anzac Sq, Ann St; 🚇Central) Designed in the Greek Revival style, this graceful monument honours the Australian men
and women who have served in conflicts
around the world. Its 18 columns symbolise
1918, the end of WWI, while the structure itself is made of prized Queensland sandstone
from Helidon, a town to the west of Brisbane.

Old Government House   HISTORIC BUILDING
(Map p280; ☑07-3138 8005; www.ogh.qut.edu.
au; 2 George St; ⊙9am-4pm, 1hr guided tours
10.30am Tue-Thu; 🚊QUT Gardens Point, 🚇Central)
FREE Hailed as Queensland's most important historic building, this 1862 showpiece
was designed by estimable government architect Charles Tiffin as a plush residence
for Sir George Bowen, Queensland's first
governor. The lavish innards were restored
in 2009 and the property now offers free
podcast and guided tours; the latter must be
booked by phone or email. The building also
houses the William Robinson Gallery, dedicated to the Australian artist and home to an
impressive collection of his works, including
two Archibald Prize–winning paintings.

St John's Cathedral   CHURCH
(Map p280; ☑07-3835 2222; www.stjohns
cathedral.com.au; 373 Ann St; ⊙9.30am-4.30pm;
🚇Central) A magnificent fusion of stone,
carved timber and stained glass just west
of Fortitude Valley, St John's Cathedral is a
beautiful example of 19th-century Gothic
Revival architecture. The building is a true
labour of love: construction began in 1906
and wasn't finished until 2009, making it
one of the world's last cathedrals of this architectural style to be completed.

Commissariat Store Museum   MUSEUM
(Map p280; www.queenslandhistory.org; 115
William St; adult/child/family $6/3/12; ⊙10am-
4pm Tue-Fri; 🚊North Quay, 🚇Central) Built by
convicts in 1829, this former government
storehouse is the oldest occupied building
in Brisbane. Inside is an immaculate little
museum devoted to convict and colonial
history. Don't miss the convict 'fingers' and
the exhibit on Italians in Queensland.

⊙ South Bank & West End

★**Queensland
Cultural Centre**   CULTURAL CENTRE
(Map p280; Melbourne St, South Bank; 🚊South
Bank Terminals 1 & 2, 🚇South Brisbane) On South
Bank, just over Victoria Bridge from the
CBD, the Queensland Cultural Centre is the
epicentre of Brisbane's cultural confluence.
Surrounded by subtropical gardens, the
sprawling complex of architecturally nota-
ble buildings includes the Queensland Per-
forming Arts Centre (p298), the Queensland
Museum & Sciencentre, the Queensland Art
Gallery, the State Library of Queensland,
and the particularly outstanding Gallery of
Modern Art (GOMA).

★**Gallery of Modern Art**   GALLERY
(GOMA; Map p280; www.qagoma.qld.gov.au;
Stanley Pl, South Bank; ⊙10am-5pm; 🚊South
Bank Terminals 1 & 2, 🚇South Brisbane) **FREE**

QUEENSLAND BRISBANE

WORTH A TRIP

D'AGUILAR NATIONAL PARK

Suburban malaise? Slake your wilderness cravings at this 36,000-hectare **national
park** (www.nprsr.qld.gov.au/parks/daguilar; 60 Mount Nebo Rd, The Gap), just 10km northwest of the city centre but worlds away (it's pronounced 'dee-ag-lar'). At the park's
entrance the **Walkabout Creek Visitor Information Centre** (☑07-3164 3600; www.
walkaboutcreek.com.au; wildlife centre adult/child/family $7.20/3.50/18.25; ⊙9am-4.30pm)
has maps. There's an on-site wildlife centre, home to a number of local critters, including
reptiles and nocturnal marsupials.

Walking trails in the park range from a few hundred metres to a 24km-long loop.
Among them is the 6km-return Morelia Track at the Manorina day-use area and the
4.3km Greenes Falls Track at Mt Glorious. Mountain biking and horse riding are also
options. You can camp in the park too, in remote, walk-in bush **camp sites** (☑137 468;
www.npsr.qld.gov.au/parks/daguilar/camping.html; per person/family $6.15/24.60). There are
a couple of walks (1.5km and 5km return) kicking off from the visitor centre, but other
walks are a fair distance away (so you'll need your own wheels).

To get here catch bus 385 ($5.70, 25 minutes) from Roma St Station to The Gap
Park'n'Ride, then walk a few hundred metres up the road.

Greater Brisbane

Gallipoli Barracks
Military Area

Enoggera Creek

D'Aguilar National
Park (3km)

31

Waterworks Rd

ASHGROVE

31

5

Wardell St

13

KELVIN
GROVE

Coopers Camp Rd

Jubilee Tce

5

BARDON

Boundary St

16
Latrobe Tce

PADDINGTON

See West End &
Petrie Terrace
Map (p286)

Mt Coot-tha
Reserve

7

AUCHENFLOWER

32
Milton

MT COOT-THA

9

3

M5

Frederick St

Milton Rd

Auchenflower

Coronation Dr

Sir Samuel Griffith Dr

Western Fwy

21 33

6

TOOWONG

Toowong

TARINGA

Moggill Rd

33
Taringa

Coronation Dr

ST
LUCIA

M5

Moggill Rd

CHAPEL
HILL

33

20

Indooroopilly

INDOOROOPILLY

St Lucia
Golf Links

Coonan St

Chelmer

Brisbane River

Lone Pine Koala
Sanctuary (5km)

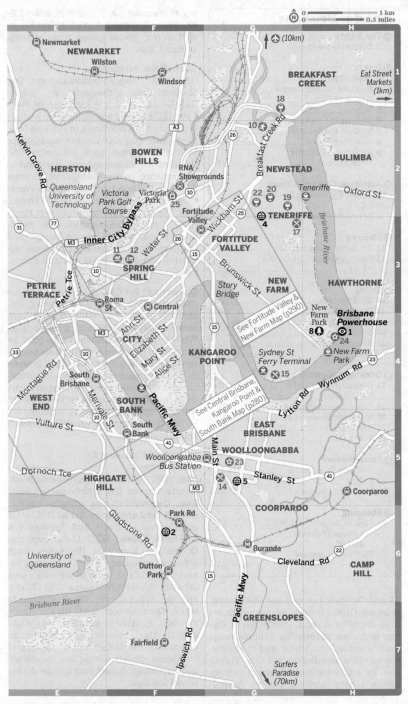

Greater Brisbane

All angular glass, concrete and black metal, must-see GOMA focuses on Australian art from the 1970s to today. Continually changing, and often confronting, exhibits range from painting, sculpture and photography to video, installation and film. There's also an arty bookshop, children's activity rooms, a **cafe** (p287), a Modern Austral-ian **restaurant** (☎07-3842 9916; mains $39-47; ⊙noon-2pm Wed-Sun, plus 5.30-8pm Fri), as well as free guided gallery tours at 11am, 1pm and 2pm.

South Bank Parklands PARK
(Map p280; www.visitbrisbane.com.au; Grey St, South Bank; ⊙dawn-dusk; ⊛; ⊠South Bank Terminals 1, 2 & 3, ⊠South Brisbane, South Bank) FREE Should you sunbake on a sandy beach, chill in a rainforest, or eye-up a Nepalese peace pagoda? You can do all three in this 17.5-hectare park overlooking the city centre. Its canopied walkways lead to performance spaces, lush lawns, eateries and bars, public art and regular free events ranging from yoga sessions to film screenings. The star attractions are Streets Beach (p277), an artificial, lagoon-style swimming beach (packed on weekends); and the near-60m-high Wheel of Brisbane, delivering 360-degree views on its 10-minute rides.

Queensland Art Gallery GALLERY
(QAG; Map p280; www.qagoma.qld.gov.au; Melbourne St, South Bank; ⊙10am-5pm; ⊠South Bank Terminals 1 & 2, ⊠South Brisbane) FREE While current construction works (due for completion in September 2017) have temporarily limited its gallery space, QAG is home to a fine a permanent collection of Australian and international works. Australian art dates from the 1840s to the 1970s: check out works by celebrated masters including Sir Sydney Nolan, Arthur Boyd, William Dobell and George Lambert.

**Queensland Museum &
Sciencentre** MUSEUM
(Map p280; ☎07-3840 7555; www.southbank.qm.qld.gov.au; cnr Grey & Melbourne Sts, South Bank; Queensland museum admission free, Sciencentre adult/child/family $14.50/11.50/44.50; ⊙9.30am-5pm; ⊠South Bank Terminals 1 & 2, ⊠South Brisbane) FREE Dig deeper into Queensland history at the state's main historical repository, where intriguing exhibits include a skeleton of the state's own dinosaur *Muttaburrasaurus* (aka 'Mutt'), and the *Avian Cirrus,* the tiny plane in which Queenslander Bert Hinkler made the first England-to-Australia solo flight in 1928. Also on-site is the Sciencentre, an educational fun house with a plethora of interactive exhibits delving into life science and technology. Expect long queues during school holidays.

Queensland Maritime Museum   MUSEUM

(Map p280; ☑ 07-3844 5361; www.maritime museum.com.au; Stanley St; adult/child/family $16/7/38; ⊙ 9.30am-4.30pm, last admission 3.30pm; 🚢 Maritime Museum, 🚉 South Bank) On the southern edge of the South Bank Parklands is this sea-salty museum, the highlight of which is the gigantic HMAS *Diamantina*, a restored WWII frigate that you can clamber aboard and explore.

Wheel of Brisbane   FERRIS WHEEL

(Map p280; ☑ 07-3844 3464; www.thewheel ofbrisbane.com.au; Grey St, South Bank; adult/ child/family $19/13.50/55; ⊙ 10am-10pm Sun-Thu, to 11pm Fri & Sat; 🚢 South Bank Terminals 1 & 2, 🚉 South Brisbane) Don't have wings but pining for a lofty view of the city? Then consider a ride on the riverside Wheel, a few steps from the Queensland Performing Arts Centre (p298). The enclosed gondolas rise to a height of nearly 60m, which while not spectacularly high, still offers a revealing, 360-degree panorama of the booming skyline. Rides last 10 to 12 minutes and include audio commentary of Brisbane sights. Online bookings offer a nominal discount.

⊙ Fortitude Valley & New Farm

Brisbane Riverwalk   BRIDGE

(Map p290; 🚌 195, 196, 🚢 Sydney St) Jutting out over the city's big, brown waterway, the Brisbane Riverwalk offers a novel way of surveying the Brisbane skyline. The 870m-long path – divided into separate walking and cycling lanes – runs between New Farm and the Howard St Wharves, from where you can continue towards the central Brisbane itself. The Riverwalk replaces the original floating walkway, sadly washed away in the floods of 2011.

★ Brisbane Powerhouse   ARTS CENTRE

(Map p272; ☑ box office 07-3358 8600, reception 07-3358 8622; www.brisbanepowerhouse. org; 119 Lamington St, New Farm; ⊙ 9am-9pm Tue-Sun; 🚌 195, 196, 🚢 New Farm Park) On the eastern flank of New Farm Park stands the Powerhouse, a once-derelict power station superbly transformed into a contemporary arts centre. Its innards pimped with graffiti remnants, industrial machinery and old electrical transformers turned lights, the centre hosts a range of events, including art exhibitions, theatre, live music and comedy. You'll also find two buzzing riverside restaurants. Check the website to see what's on.

Chinatown   AREA

(Map p290; Duncan St, Fortitude Valley; ⊙ 24hr; 🚉 Fortitude Valley) Punctuated by a replica Tang dynasty archway at its western end, Duncan St is Brisbane's rather modest Chinatown. The pedestrianised strip (and the stretch of Ann St between Duncan St and Brunswick Street Mall) is home to a handful of Chinatown staples, including glazed flat ducks hanging behind steamy windows, Asian grocery stores and the aromas of Thai, Chinese, Vietnamese and Japanese cooking. The area is at it most rambunctious during Chinese New Year (p278) festivities.

New Farm Park   PARK

(Map p272; www.newfarmpark.com.au; Brunswick St, New Farm; ⊙ 24hr; 🚌 195, 196, 🚢 New Farm Park) On the tail end of Brunswick St by the river, New Farm Park will have you breathing deeply with its jacaranda trees, rose gardens and picnic areas. It's a perfect spot to spend a lazy afternoon, with gas barbecues and free wi-fi (near the rotunda at the river end of the park). Younger kids will especially love the playground – a Crusoe-esque series of platforms among vast Moreton Bay fig trees. **Jan Powers Farmers Market** (Map p272; www.janpowersfarmers markets.com.au; Brisbane Powerhouse, 119 Lamington St; ⊙ 6am-noon Sat) and the **Moonlight Cinema** (p298) happen here too.

⊙ Greater Brisbane

Brisbane Botanic Gardens   GARDENS

(Map p272; ☑ 07-3403 2535; www.brisbane. qld.gov.au/botanicgardens; Mt Coot-tha Rd, Mt Coot-tha; ⊙ 8am-5.30pm, to 5pm Apr-Aug; 🚌 471) **FREE** At the base of Mt Coot-tha, this 52-hectare garden houses a plethora of mini-ecologies, from cactus, bonsai and herb gardens, to rainforests and arid zones. Free guided walks are held at 11am and 1pm Monday and Saturday, and self-guided tours can be downloaded from the website. To get here via public transport, take bus 471 from Adelaide St in the city, opposite King George Sq ($4.60, 25 minutes).

Mt Coot-tha Reserve   NATURE RESERVE

(Map p272; www.brisbane.qld.gov.au; Mt Coot-tha Rd, Mt Coot-tha; ⊙ 24hr; 🚌 471) **FREE** A 15-minute drive or bus ride from the city, this huge bush reserve is topped by 287m Mt Coot-tha, Brisbane's highest point. On the hillsides you'll find the Brisbane Botanic Gardens, the **Sir Thomas Brisbane**

Planetarium (Map p272; ☑07-3403 2578; www.brisbane.qld.gov.au/planetarium; Mt Coot-tha Rd; admission free, shows adult/child/family/concession $15.80/9.60/43/13; ⊙10am-4pm Tue-Fri, 11am-8.15pm Sat, 11am-4pm Sun), walking trails and the eye-popping **Mt Coot-tha Lookout** (Map p272; ☑07-3369 9922; www.brisbanelookout.com; 1012 Sir Samuel Griffith Dr; ⊙24hr), the latter offering a bird's-eye view of the city skyline and greater metro area. On a clear day you'll even spot the Moreton Bay islands.

Lone Pine Koala Sanctuary WILDLIFE RESERVE (☑07-3378 1366; www.koala.net; 708 Jesmond Rd, Fig Tree Pocket; adult/child/family $36/22/85; ⊙9am-5pm; ☐430) About 12km south of the city centre, Lone Pine Koala Sanctuary occupies a patch of parkland beside the river. It's home to over 130 koalas, plus kangaroos, possums, wombats, birds and other Aussie critters. The koalas are undeniably cute – most visitors readily cough up the $18 to have their picture snapped hugging one.

BRISBANE'S GALLERY SCENE

While the **Gallery of Modern Art** (p271), aka GOMA, and the **Queensland Art Gallery** (p274) might steal the show, Brisbane also has a growing array of smaller private galleries and exhibition spaces where you can mull over both the mainstream and the cutting-edge.

The Pillars Project (Map p280; www.thepillarsproject.com; Merrivale St, South Brisbane; ⊙24hr; ☐198, ☒South Bank Terminals 1 & 2, ☒South Brisbane) One of Brisbane's most unexpected art spaces. A series of pillars under the South Brisbane Rail Underpass have been transformed into arresting street-art murals by numerous artists. Among these is the internationally acclaimed, Brisbane-raised Fintan Magee.

Institute of Modern Art (IMA; Map p290; ☑07-3252 5750; www.ima.org.au; 420 Brunswick St, Fortitude Valley; ⊙noon-6pm Tue, Wed, Fri & Sat, to 8pm Thu; ☒Fortitude Valley) Located in the Judith Wright Centre of Contemporary Arts in Fortitude Valley is this excellent noncommercial gallery with an industrial vibe and regular showings by both local and international names working in mediums as diverse as installation art, photography and painting.

TW Fine Art (Map p290; ☑0437 348 755; www.twfineart.com; 181 Robertson St, Fortitude Valley; ⊙10am-5pm Tue-Sat, to 3pm Sun; ☐470, ☒Fortitude Valley) Easy-to-miss, this Fortitude Valley gallery eschews the 'keep it local' mantra for intellectually robust, critically acclaimed contemporary art from around the world. It also runs an innovative online gallery of limited-edition prints, which you can browse at the gallery and have couriered straight to your home.

Fireworks Gallery (Map p272; ☑07-3216 1250; www.fireworksgallery.com.au; 52a Doggett St, Newstead; ⊙10am-6pm Tue-Fri, to 4pm Sat; ☐300, 302, 305, 306, 322, 393, 470) A fabulous warehouse space showcasing mainly painting and sculpture by both Indigenous and non-Indigenous contemporary Australian artists. It's just a short stroll from James St in Fortitude Valley.

Milani (Map p272; ☑07-3391 0455; www.milanigallery.com.au; 54 Logan Rd, Woolloongabba; ⊙11am-6pm Tue-Sat; ☐174,175, 204) **FREE** A superb gallery with cutting-edge Aboriginal and confronting contemporary artwork. It's in an industrial corner of Woolloongabba, surrounded by car yards and hairdressing equipment suppliers – if it looks closed, simply turn the door handle.

Suzanne O'Connell Gallery (Map p290; ☑07-3358 5811; www.suzanneoconnell.com; 93 James St, New Farm; ⊙11am-4pm Wed-Sat; ☐470) **FREE** This New Farm gallery specialises in Indigenous art, with brilliant works from artists all across Australia. Check the website for regular exhibition openings.

Jan Murphy Gallery (Map p290; ☑07-3254 1855; www.janmurphygallery.com.au; 486 Brunswick St, Fortitude Valley; ⊙10am-5pm Tue-Sat; ☐195, 196, 199, ☒Fortitude Valley) Fronted by a strip of Astroturf, this charcoal-grey gallery is another leading exhibition space for contemporary Australian talent in the thick of Fortitude Valley's gallery district.

There are animal presentations scheduled throughout the day.

Activities

You'll find a plethora of excellent art and heritage walking trails around town at www. brisbane.qld.gov.au/facilities-recreation/ sports-leisure/walking/walking-trails.

CityCycle CYCLING
(☑1300 229 253; www.citycycle.com.au; hire per hour/day $2.20/165, 1st 30min free; ☺24hr) To use Brisbane's bike-share, subscribe via the website ($2/11 per day/week), then hire a bike (additional fee) from any of the 150 stations around town. It's pricey to hire for more than an hour, so make use of the free first 30 minutes per bike and ride from station to station, swapping bikes as you go. Only a quarter of bikes include a helmet (compulsory to wear) so you may need to purchase one from shops such as Target or Kmart.

Spring Hill Baths SWIMMING
(Map p272; ☑1300 332 583; www.cityaquatics andhealth.com.au; 14 Torrington St, Spring Hill; adult/child/family $5.40/3.90/16.40; ☺6.30am-7pm Mon-Thu, to 6pm Fri, 8am-5pm Sat, 8am-1pm Sun; ☐30, 321) Opened in 1886, this quaint heated 25m pool was the city's first in-ground pool. Still encircled by its cute timber change rooms, it's one of the oldest public baths in the southern hemisphere.

Streets Beach SWIMMING
(Map p280; ☑07-3156 6366; ☺daylight hours; ☒South Bank Terminals 1, 2 & 3, ☒South Bank) A central spot for a quick (and free) dip in Australia's only artificial, inner-city beach at South Bank. Lifeguards, hollering kids, beach babes, strutting gym-junkies, palm trees, ice cream carts – it's all here.

Urban Climb CLIMBING
(Map p286; ☑07-3844 2544; www.urbanclimb. com.au; 2/220 Montague Rd, West End; adult/child $20/18, once-off registration fee $5; ☺noon-10pm Mon-Fri, 10am-6pm Sat & Sun; ☐60, 192, 198) An indoor climbing wall with one of the largest bouldering walls in Australia. Suitable for both beginners and advanced climbing geeks.

Pinnacle Sports CLIMBING
(☑07-3368 3335; www.pinnaclesports.com.au; 2hr abseiling from $80, 3hr climbing from $90) Climb the Kangaroo Point Cliffs or abseil down them: either way it's a lot of fun! Options include a two-hour sunset abseil, as well as full-day rock-climbing trips to the Glass House Mountains.

**Story Bridge
Adventure Climb** ADVENTURE SPORTS
(Map p280; ☑1300 254 627; www.sbac.net. au; 170 Main St, Kangaroo Point; climb from $100; ☐234, ☒Thornton St, Holman St) Scaling Brisbane's most famous bridge is nothing short of thrilling, with unbeatable views of the city – morning, twilight or night. The two-hour climb scales the southern half of the structure, taking you 80m above the twisting, muddy Brisbane River below. Dawn climbs are run on the last Saturday of the month. Minimum age 10 years.

Riverlife ADVENTURE SPORTS
(Map p280; ☑07-3891 5766; www.riverlife.com. au; Naval Stores, Kangaroo Point Bikeway, Kangaroo Point; hire bikes/in-line skates per 4hr $35/40, kayaks per 2hr $35; ☺9am-5pm; ☒Thornton St) Based at the bottom of the Kangaroo Point Cliffs, Riverlife offers numerous active city thrills. Rock climb (from $55), abseil ($45) or opt for a kayak river trip (from $45). The latter includes a booze-and-food 'Paddle and Prawns' option ($85) on Friday and Saturday nights. Also rents out bikes, kayaks and in-line skates.

Q Academy MASSAGE
(Map p290; ☑1300 204 080; www.qacademy. com.au; 20 Chester St, Newstead; 1hr massage $30; ☐300, 302, 305, 306, 322, 470) Q Academy offers one of Brisbane's best bargains: one-hour relaxation or remedial massage for $30. Although the practitioners are massage students at the accredited academy, all have extensive theoretical training and enough experience to leave you feeling a lot lighter. It's a very popular spot, so book online at least a week in advance.

Skydive Brisbane SKYDIVING
(☑1300 663 634; www.skydive.com.au; from $300) Offers tandem skydives over Brisbane, landing on the beach in Redcliffe. See the website for specials.

Fly Me to the Moon BALLOONING
(☑07-3423 0400; www.brisbanehotairballooning. com.au; adult/child incl transfers from $250/330) One-hour hot-air balloon trips over the hinterland. Flights are followed by a champagne breakfast at a vineyard in the Scenic Rim region west of the Gold Coast. Return transfers to Brisbane are available.

☞ Tours

CityCat
BOATING

(☑13 12 30; www.translink.com.au; one-way $5.60; ⊙5.25am-11.25pm) Ditch the car or bus and catch a CityCat ferry along the Brisbane river for a calmer perspective. Ferries run every 15 to 30 minutes between the Northshore Hamilton terminal northeast of the city to the University of Queensland in the southwest, stopping at 16 terminals in between, including Teneriffe, New Farm Park, North Quay (for the CBD) and South Bank (also handy for West End).

Brisbane Greeters
TOURS

(Map p280; ☑07-3156 6364; www.brisbane greeters.com.au; Brisbane City Hall, King George Sq; ⊙10am) Free, small-group, hand-held introductory tours of Brizzy with affable volunteers. Book at least three days in advance, either online or by phone. Booking online allows you to opt for a 'Your Choice' tour, based on your personal interests and schedule. Note that 'Your Choice' tours should be booked at least five days in advance.

River City Cruises
CRUISE

(Map p280; ☑0428 278 473; www.rivercity cruises.com.au; South Bank Parklands Jetty A; adult/child/family $29/15/65) River City runs 1½-hour cruises with commentary from South Bank to New Farm and back. They depart from South Bank at 10.30am and 12.30pm (plus 2.30pm during summer).

XXXX Brewery Tour
TOURS

(Map p286; ☑07-3361 7597; www.xxxx.com.au; cnr Black & Paten Sts, Milton; adult/child $32/18; ☑375, 433, 475) Feel a XXXX coming on? This 1½-hour brewery tour includes a few humidity-beating ales (leave the car at home). Tours run four times daily Monday to Friday and nine times Saturday; check the website. Also on offer are combined brewery and Suncorp Stadium (p298) tours (adult/child $48/28) at 10.30am Thursday. Book tours in advance, and wear enclosed shoes. There's also an alehouse here if you feel like kicking on.

Brisbane Ghost Tours
TOURS

(☑07-3344 7265; www.brisbaneghosttours.com. au; walking tours adult/child/family $20/13/55, bus tours adult/child $50/40) 'Get creeped' on these 1½-hour guided walking tours or 2½-hour bus tours of Brisbane's haunted heritage: murder scenes, cemeteries, eerie arcades and the infamous **Boggo Road Gaol** (Map p272; ☑07-3844 0059, 0411 111 903; www.boggo roadgaol.com; Annerley Rd, Dutton Park; history tour adult/child/family $26.50/13.75/52, ghost tour adult/child over 12yr $45/30; ⊙1½hr historical tours 11am Thu-Sun, plus 10am Sun, 2hr ghost tours 7.30pm Wed & Fri-Sun, also 8.30pm Fri; ☑112, 116, 202). Offers several tours a week; bookings essential.

☞ Courses

Golden Pig Cooking School & Cafe
COOKING

(Map p272; ☑07-3666 0884; www.goldenpig. com.au; 38 Ross St, Newstead; 4hr cooking class $165; ⊙cafe 7.30am-noon Mon, to 2pm Tue-Fri; ☑300, 302, 305) In a warehouse on the edge of Newstead, chef Katrina Ryan runs a series of popular cooking classes, with themes ranging from modern Greek, Vietnamese and South American, to Middle Eastern, brunch and sourdough baking. Ryan's background is impressive, having worked at some of Australia's top restaurants. See the website for class times and types, which also include 'singles' classes for foodies sick of Tinder.

✯ Festivals & Events

Brisbane International
SPORTS

(www.brisbaneinternational.com.au; ⊙Jan) Running over eight days in early January, this pro tennis tournament is a prologue to Melbourne's Grand-Slam Australian Open, held later in the month. Featuring the world's top players, it takes place at the Queensland Tennis Centre in the riverside suburb of Tennyson.

BrisAsia Festival
CULTURAL

(www.brisbane.qld.gov.au; ⊙Jan/Feb) Running for three weeks in late January and February, this festival celebrates both traditional and modern Asian cultures with over 80 events across the city. The festival program includes dance, music and theatre performances, film screenings, interactive community events and no shortage of Asian cuisines.

Chinese New Year
CULTURAL

(www.chinesenewyear.com.au; ⊙Jan/Feb) Held in Fortitude Valley's Chinatown Mall (Duncan St) in January/February. Firecrackers, whirling dragons and fantastic food.

Brisbane Street Art Festival
ART

(www.bsafest.com.au; ⊙Feb) The hiss of spray cans underscores this booming two-week festival, which sees local and international street artists transform city walls into arresting art works. Live mural art aside, the program includes exhibitions, music, theatre, light shows, workshops and street-art masterclasses.

Brisbane Comedy Festival COMEDY
(www.briscomfest.com; ☻ Feb/Mar) Feeling blue? Check yourself into this month-long laugh-fest, usually running from late February to March. Showcasing almost 70 comedy acts from Australia and beyond, festival gigs take place at the riverside Brisbane Powerhouse (p298) arts hub as well as at Brisbane City Hall (p270).

CMC Rocks Queensland MUSIC
(www.cmcrocks.com; ☻ Mar) The biggest country and roots festival in the southern hemisphere, taking place over three days and nights in March at Willowbank Raceway in the southwest outskirts of Brisbane. Expect big-name international acts like Dixie Chicks, Little Big Town and Kip Moore as well as homegrown country A-listers.

Anywhere Theatre Festival PERFORMING ARTS
(www.anywherefest.com; ☻ May) For over two weeks in May, all of Brisbane becomes a stage as hundreds of performances pop up across the city in the most unexpected of places. Expect anything from theatre in laneways to cabaret in antique shops and bellowing sopranos in underground reservoirs.

Queensland Cabaret Festival PERFORMING ARTS
(www.queenslandcabaretfestival.com.au; ☻ Jun) Come June, the Brisbane Powerhouse (p298) cranks up the sass and subversion for the 10-day Queensland Cabaret Festival. Expect a mix of both local and international acts, with past performers including US actor and singer Molly Ringwald and British *chansonnière* Barb Jungr.

Queensland Music Festival MUSIC
(QMF; www.queenslandmusicfestival.org.au; ☻ Jul) Renowned singer-songwriter Katie Noonan is the current artistic director of this biennial statewide festival, which serves up an eclectic program of music ranging from classical to contemporary. Held over three weeks in July in odd-numbered years. Most events are free.

'Ekka' Royal Queensland Show CULTURAL
(www.ekka.com.au; ☻ Aug) Country and city collide at this epic 10-day event in August. Head in for fireworks, showbags, theme-park rides, concerts, shearing demonstrations and prize-winning livestock by the truck load. There's also a cooking stage, with demonstrations and the odd celebrity chef.

Bigsound Festival MUSIC
(www.bigsound.org.au; ☻ Sep) Held over three huge days in September, Australia's premier new music festival draws buyers, industry experts and fans of fresh Aussie music talent. With the Judith Wright Centre of Contemporary Art (p298) as its heart, the fest features around 150 up-and-coming artists playing around 15 venues.

Brisbane Festival PERFORMING ARTS
(www.brisbanefestival.com.au; ☻ Sep) One of Australia's largest and most diverse arts festivals, running for three weeks in September and featuring an impressive schedule of concerts, plays, dance and fringe events. The festival ends with the spectacular 'Riverfire', an elaborate fireworks show over the Brisbane River.

Brisbane Pride Festival LGBT
(www.brisbanepride.org.au) Spread over four weeks in September, Australia's third-largest LGBT+ festival includes the popular Pride March and Fair Day, which sees thousands march from Fortitude Valley to New Farm Park in a celebration of diversity. Pride's fabulous Queen's Ball takes place in June.

Brisbane Writers Festival LITERATURE
(BWF; www.uplit.com.au; ☻ Sep) Queensland's premier literary event has been running for over five decades. Expect a five-day program of readings, discussions and other thought-provoking events featuring both Australian and international writers and thinkers.

Oktoberfest CULTURAL
(www.oktoberfestbrisbane.com.au; ☻ Oct) Brisbanites don their *Lederhosen* and *Dirndl* for Australia's biggest German shindig, held at the Brisbane Showgrounds over two weekends in October. It's a sud-soaked blast, with traditional German grub, yodelers, oompah bands and a dedicated 'Kinder Zone' with rides, Deutsch lessons and more for little aspiring Germans.

Park Sounds MUSIC
(www.parksounds.com.au; ☻ Nov) Hip-hop rules at Brisbane's newest music festival, held at Pine Rivers Park in suburban Strathpine. The 2016 line-up included ARIA-winning A-listers Bliss n Eso, as well as other

Central Brisbane, Kangaroo Point & South Bank

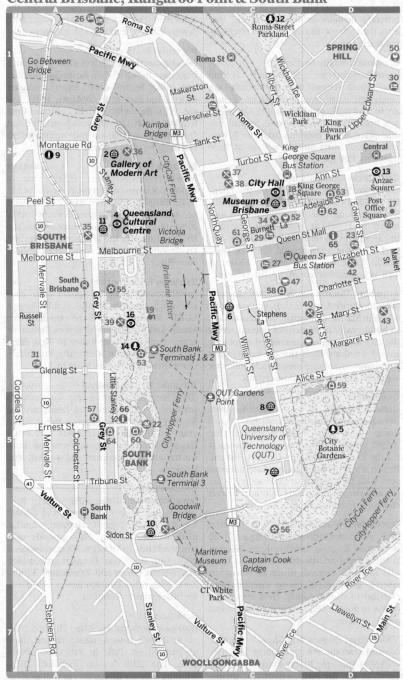

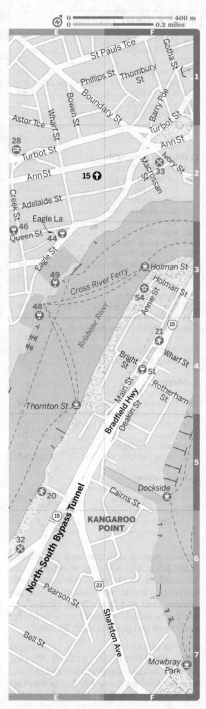

of-the-moment Aussie acts like Drapht and Pon Cho (of Thundamentals). Held over an afternoon in November.

Brisbane Asia Pacific Film Festival   FILM (BAPFF;brisbaneasiapacificfilmfestival.com; ☺ Nov/ Dec) A 16-day celebration of cinema from Oceania and Asia, with around 80 films from countries as diverse as Australia, New Zealand, China, Korea, Phillipines, Afghanistan, India, Russia and Iran. The program includes feature films, shorts and documentaries, as well as panel discussions and other special events.

🛏 Sleeping

Prices do not generally abide by any high- or low-season rules; wavering rates usually reflect demand. Rates are often higher mid-week, as well as during major events and holiday periods.

🛏 Central Brisbane

Base Brisbane Embassy   HOSTEL **$** (Map p280; ☎ 07-3014 1715; www.stayatbase. com; 214 Elizabeth St; dm/d/tw from $35/100/130; ❄ @ ☎; ⋒ Central) A city branch of the Base chain, this spruced-up place is quieter than other hostels despite being just behind the bustling Queen Street Mall. While it feels a little soulless, it does have its draws, among them a large screening room for films, and a sun deck with barbecue and city views. Slurp craft beers at the **Embassy Hotel** (Map p280; www.embassybar.com.au; ☺ 11am-10pm Mon-Wed, to 11pm Thu, to late Fri, noon-late Sat) downstairs.

Base Brisbane Uptown   HOSTEL **$** (Map p280; ☎ 07-3238 5888; www.stayatbase. com; 466 George St; dm/tw & d from $21/145; ❄ @ ☎; ⋒ Roma St) This purpose-built hostel near Roma St Station flaunts its youth with mod interiors, decent facilities and overall cleanliness. Each room has air-con, a bathroom and individual lockers, and it's wheelchair-accessible. The bar downstairs is a party palace, with big-screen sports, DJs and open-mic nights.

Next   HOTEL **$$** (Map p280; ☎ 07-3222 3222; www.snhotels. com/next/brisbane; 72 Queen St; r from $180; ❄ ☎ ≋; ⋒ Central) Right above the Queen Street Mall, Next delivers stylish, central, affordable accommodation. Rooms are generic though svelte and contemporary, with high-tech touchscreen technology and

Central Brisbane, Kangaroo Point & South Bank

decent beds. The outdoor lap pool flanks a buzzing bar, itself adjacent to a handy traveller lounge (complete with massage chairs and showers) for guests who check-in early or want a place to relax before a late flight. There's an on-site gym too.

Ibis Styles HOTEL **$$**
(Map p280; ☑07-3337 9000; www.ibisstylesbrisbaneelizabeth.com.au; 40 Elizabeth St; d from $140; ❄@☎; 圓Central) Smart, contemporary, budget digs is what you get at the world's largest Ibis hotel. Multicoloured carpets and

striking geometric shapes set a playful tone in the lobby, and while the standard rooms are smallish, all are comfortable and fresh, with fantastic mattresses, smart TVs and impressive river and South Bank views. Property perks include a small gym with quality equipment and guest laundry facilities.

Punthill Brisbane HOTEL **$$**
(Map p280; ☑07-3055 5777, 1300 731 299; www.punthill.com.au/property/brisbane/punthill-brisbane; 40 Astor Tce, Spring Hill; 1-/2-bedroom apt from $150/185; ℗❄☎; 圓Central) Its lobby

graced with retro bicycles (for hire), Punthill offers smart, contemporary suites in muted colours. Digs include comfy king beds, kitchenette or full kitchen, balcony and millennial details like flat-screen TV and iPod dock. On-site facilities include a small pool, gym and guest laundry. A good all-round option, with competitive rates and a central location. Parking $25.

**New Inchcolm
Hotel & Suites**   HISTORIC HOTEL **$$$**
(Map p280; ☑ 07-3226 8888; www.inchcolm. au; 73 Wickham Tce; d from $210; P ✳ ☎; ☒ Central) Built in the 1920s as doctors' suites, the heritage-listed Inchcolm (complete with oak-clad vintage elevator) is fabulously plush and intimate. Rooms in the newer wing have more space and light; in the heritage wing there's more character. All feature thoughtful touches, including coffee machines, Ridel stemware and minibars with locally sourced treats. There's also an in-house restaurant. Parking $40.

🛏 South Bank & West End

GoNow Family Backpacker   HOSTEL **$**
(Map p286; ☑ 0434 727 570, 07-3472 7570; www. gonowfamily.com.au; 147 Vulture St, West End; dm $19-30, d $70; P ✳ ☎; ☐ 198, 199) These have to be the cheapest beds in Brisbane, and GoNow is doing a decent job of delivering a clean, respectful, secure hostel experience despite the bargain-basement pricing. It's not a party place: you'll be better off elsewhere if you're looking to launch into the night with drunken forays. The upstairs rooms have more ceiling height.

Brisbane Backpackers   HOSTEL **$**
(Map p286; ☑ 1800 626 452, 07-3844 9956; www.brisbanebackpackers.com.au; 110 Vulture St, West End; dm $21-34, d/tw/tr from $100/110/135; P ✳ @ ☎ ☒; ☐ 198, 199) If you're looking to party, you're in the right place. This hulking hostel comes with a great pool and bar area, and while rooms are basic, they're generally well maintained. An easy walk from West End's buzzing eateries, bars and live-music venues.

Rydges South Bank   HOTEL **$$**
(Map p280; ☑ 07-3364 0800; www.rydges.com; 9 Glenelg St, South Brisbane; r from $180; ✳ ☎ ☒; ☒ South Brisbane) Fresh from a recent refurbishment, this 12-floor winner is within walking distance of South Bank Parklands and major galleries. In rich hues of silver,

grey and purple, standard rooms are large and inviting (try to get one facing the city), with sublimely comfortable beds, smart TVs, free wi-fi, motion-sensor air-con and small but modern bathrooms.

🛏 Fortitude Valley & New Farm

Bunk Backpackers   HOSTEL **$**
(Map p290; ☑ 1800 682 865, 07-3257 3644; www.bunkbrisbane.com.au; 11-21 Gipps St, Fortitude Valley; dm from $25, s $60, tw/apt from $85/190; P ✳ @ ☎ ☒; ☒ Fortitude Valley) This old arts college was reborn as a backpackers over a decade ago – and the party hasn't stopped! It's a huge, five-level place with dozens of rooms (mostly eight-bed dorms), just staggering distance from the Valley nightlife. Facilities include a large communal kitchen, pool and Jacuzzi, and in-house bar, Birdees (Map p290; ☑ 07-3852 5000; www.katarzyna. com.au/venues/birdees; 608 Ann St; ⏰ 3pm-late Mon-Wed, noon-late Thu-Sun), as well as a few great five-bed apartments. Not for bed-by-10pm slumberers. Parking $12.

Bowen Terrace   GUESTHOUSE **$**
(Map p290; ☑ 07-3254 0458; www.bowenterrace. com.au; 365 Bowen Tce, New Farm; dm from $34, s/d without bathroom from $70/80, d/f with bathroom from $95/145; P @ ☎ ☒; ☐ 196, 195, 199) In a restored, century-old Queenslander, Bowen Terrace offers modestly priced lodging in a real-estate hot spot. Simple rooms include TV, bar fridge, quality linen and lofty ceilings with fans (no air-con). There's a communal kitchen, as well as laundry facilities and a pool. Sound-proofing between the rooms isn't great, but the place is good value for money, with more class than your average hostel.

Tryp   BOUTIQUE HOTEL **$$**
(Map p290; ☑ 07-3319 7888; www.trypbrisbane. com; 14-20 Constance St, Fortitude Valley; r $160-340; ✳ ☎; ☒ Fortitude Valley) Fans of street art will appreciate this hip 65-room slumber pad, complete with a small gym, a rooftop bar and a glass-panelled elevator affording views of the graffiti-strewn shaft. Each of the hotel's four floors features work by a different Brisbane street artist, and while standard rooms are small, all are comfy and feature coffee machines and fab marshmallow beds.

Limes   BOUTIQUE HOTEL **$$**
(Map p290; ☑ 07-3852 9000; www.limeshotel. com.au; 142 Constance St, Fortitude Valley; d from $180; P ✳ ☎; ☒ Fortitude Valley) Although

the rooms at trendy Limes are tight, they do make good use of limited space, with plush bedding, kitchenette and work space. Thoughtful extras include coffee machines, free wi-fi and gym passes. While we love the rooftop hot tub, bar and cinema, it can make for noisy nights; bring ear plugs if you're a light sleeper. Parking nearby for $20.

Greater Brisbane

Brisbane City YHA
HOSTEL $

(Map p280; ☑07-3236 1004; www.yha.com.au; 392 Upper Roma St; dm from $34, tw & d with/without bathroom from $125/107, f from $145; P❄@🛜🏊; 🚌375, 380, 🚇Roma St) This immaculate, well-run hostel has a rooftop pool and a sundeck with eye-popping river views. The maximum dorm size is six beds (not too big); most have bathrooms. Big on security, kitchen space (lots of fridges) and activities, the place runs film nights as well as weekly city walking tours and barbecues. That said, this is a YHA, not a nonstop party palace. Parking $12.

Brisbane City Backpackers
HOSTEL $

(Map p280; ☑1800 062 572, 07-3211 3221; www.citybackpackers.com; 380 Upper Roma St; dm $19-33, d/tr from $80/105; P❄@🛜🏊; 🚌375, 380, 🚇Roma St) On the Upper Roma St hostel row, this hyperactive, low-frills party palace makes good use of its limited outdoor space, including a viewing tower and pool. The on-site bar has something happening every night: DJs, pool comps, quiz nights, karaoke… Free wi-fi too. Cheaper rooms have no air-con. If you came to party, you're in the right place.

Newmarket Gardens Caravan Park
CAMPGROUND $

(Map p272; ☑07-3356 1458; www.newmarketgardens.com.au; 199 Ashgrove Ave, Newmarket; powered/unpowered sites $43/41, on-site vans $57, budget r $68, cabins $135-160; P❄@🛜; 🚌390, 🚇Newmarket) Just 4km north of the city and dotted with mango trees, this place offers a row of five simple budget rooms (no aircon), five tidy cabins (with air-con) and a sea of van and tent sites. Not much in the way of distractions for kids. From central Brisbane, bus 390 stops around 200m east of the caravan park (alight at stop 20).

Art Series – The Johnson
HOTEL $$

(Map p272; ☑07-3085 7200; www.artserieshotels.com.au/johnson; 477 Boundary St, Spring Hill; r from $165; P❄🛜🏊; 🚌301, 321, 411) Opened in 2016, this is Brisbane's first Art Series hotel. It's dedicated to abstract artist Michael Johnson, whose big, bold brushstrokes demand attention in the svelte lobby. Framed works by Johnson also grace the hotel's uncluttered contemporary rooms, each with heavenly AH Beard mattresses, designer lighting and free wi-fi. There's an on-site gym as well as a sleek 50m rooftop pool designed by Olympic gold-medalist Michael Klim.

✗ Eating

Brisbane's food scene is flourishing – a fact not lost on the nation's food critics and switched-on gluttons. From Mod Oz degustations to curbside food trucks, the city offers an increasingly competent, confident array of culinary highs.

✗ Central Brisbane

Miel Container
BURGERS $

(Map p280; ☑07-3229 4883; www.facebook.com/mielcontainer; cnr Mary & Albert Sts; burgers from $12; ⏰11am-10pm Mon-Thu & Sat, to 11pm Fri; 🚇Central) Planted in a nook below Brisbane's skyscrapers, this rude-red shipping container flips outstanding burgers. Choose your bun, your burger, your veggies, cheese and sauces, then search for a spare seat by the footpath. If it's all too hard, opt for the classic Miel grass-fed beef-pattie burger with onion jam, bacon and bush tomato. Succulent, meaty bliss.

Felix for Goodness
CAFE $

(Map p280; ☑07-3161 7966; www.felixforgoodness.com; 50 Burnett La; mains lunch $12-22, dinner $23-24; ⏰7am-2.30pm Mon & Tue, to 9.30pm Wed-Fri, 8am-2pm Sat; 🛜🍴; 🚇Central) 🌱 Felix channels Melbourne with its arty laneway locale, industrial fit-out and effortlessly cool vibe. Sip espresso or chow down decent brunch grub like spelt poppy seed pikelets with vanilla cream, saffron cardamom and poached pears, or pumpkin, ricotta and caramelised onion frittata. A short evening menu focuses on bar bites (best paired with a creative cocktail), with the odd pasta or risotto main.

Strauss
CAFE $

(Map p280; ☑07-3236 5232; www.straussfd.com; 189 Elizabeth St; dishes $6.50-13.50; ⏰6.30am-3pm Mon-Fri; 🛜; 🚇Central) Strauss bucks its corporate surrounds with low-key cool and a neighbourly vibe. Head in for pastries or a short, competent, locavore menu of creative salads, thick-cut toasted sandwiches (go for the pastrami, sauerkraut, cheese and pickle combo) and upgraded classics like French toast paired with lemon curd and labna. The place takes its coffee seriously, with cold brew and rotating espresso and filtered options.

Govinda's
VEGETARIAN $

(Map p280; ☑07-3210 0255; www.brisbane govindas.com.au; 358 George St; all-you-can-eat $12.90; ⊙7am-8pm Mon-Fri, from 11am Sat; ☑; ▣Roma St) Grab a plate and pile it high with the likes of vegetarian curry, koftas (veggie puffs), salads, pappadams, chutneys and semolina fruit pudding at this no-frills budget eatery, run by the Hare Krishnas. You'll find another branch at West End (Map p286; ☑0404 173 027; 82 Vulture St; ⊙11am-3pm & 5-8pm Mon-Fri, 11am-3pm Sat; ▣199).

Greenglass
FRENCH $$

(Map p280; www.facebook.com/greenglass336; 336 George St; lunch $12-30, dinner mains $18-35; ⊙7am-9pm Mon-Fri; ▣Roma St) Up a flight of stairs wedged between a discount chemist and a topless bar is this pared-back, loft-style newcomer. Head up for novel breakfast items like charcoal bun filled with fried egg, avocado and thinly sliced pork belly, French-centric bistro lunch dishes and an enlightened wine list that favours small-batch Australian drops.

⭐Urbane
MODERN AUSTRALIAN $$$

(Map p280; ☑07-3229 2271; www.urbane restaurant.com; 181 Mary St; 5-course menu $110, 7-course menu $145; ⊙6-10.30pm Tue-Sat; ☑; ▣Eagle St Pier, ▣Central) Argentinian chef Alejandro Cancino heads intimate Urbane, the apotheosis of Brisbane fine dining. If the budget permits, opt for the eight-course degustation, which does more justice to Cancino's talents. Needless to say, dishes intrigue and delight, whether it's corn 'snow' (made by dropping corn mousse into liquid nitrogen) or pickled onion petals filled with tapioca pearls and regional macadamia nuts. The wine list is smashing.

🍴 South Bank & West End

Plenty West End
CAFE $

(Map p286; ☑07-3255 3330; www.facebook. com/plentywestend; 284 Montague Rd, West End; dishes $5.50-23.50; ⊙6.30am-3pm, kitchen closes 2.25pm; ☎☑; ▣60, 192, 198) 🥐 In the far west of West End lies this graphics-factory-turned-cafe, a rustic, industrial backdrop for farm-to-table edibles. Scan the counter for freshly made panini and cakes, or the blackboard for headliners like caramelised Brussels sprouts with pumpkin purée, feta, raisins and pumpkin seeds. Libations include fresh juices, kombucha on tap and fantastic, organic coffee. When you're done, pick up some pineapple hot sauce at the in-store providore.

Morning After
CAFE $

(Map p286; ☑07-3844 0500; www.morningafter. com.au; cnr Vulture & Cambridge Sts, West End; breakfast $9-19, lunch mains $15-21; ⊙7am-4pm; ☎☑; ▣199) Decked out in contemporary blonde-wood furniture, gleaming subway tiles and bold green accents, this new-school West End cafe is crisper than an apple. Join the effortlessly cool for vibrant, revamped cafe fare such as zucchini fritters with fried eggs, carrot and ginger purée and Vietnamese salad, and bucatini pasta with kale pesto, spinach purée and pistachio. Alas, the coffee is a little less consistent.

Kiss the Berry
HEALTH FOOD $

(Map p280; ☑07-3846 6128; www.kisstheberry. com; 65/114 Grey St, South Bank; bowls $10.50-16; ⊙7am-5pm; ☑; ▣South Bank Terminals 1 & 2, ▣South Brisbane) Overlooking South Bank Parklands is this youthful, upbeat açaí bar serving fresh, tasty bowls of the organic super food in various combinations. Our favourite is the naughty-but-nice Snickers Delight (with banana, strawberries, raw cacao powder, peanut butter, coconut water, almond milk, granola, raw cocoa nibs and coconut yoghurt and flakes). For a liquid açaí fix, opt for one of the meal-in-a-cup smoothies.

⭐Gauge
MODERN AUSTRALIAN $$

(Map p280; ☑07-3852 6734; www.gaugebrisbane. com.au; 77 Grey St, South Brisbane; breakfast $12-19, mains $26-33; ⊙7am-3pm Mon-Wed, 7am-3pm & 5.30-9pm Thu & Fri, 8am-3pm & 5.30-9pm Sat, 8am-3pm Sun; ▣South Bank Terminals 1 & 2, ▣South Brisbane) Forget Hansel. Cafe-style Gauge is so hot right now. In a sparse space punctuated by black-spun aluminum lamps, native flora and a smashing wine list, contemporary dishes burst with Australian confidence. Signatures include a provocative 'blood taco' packed with roasted bone marrow, mushroom and native thyme, and a brilliant twist on banana bread – garlic bread with burnt vanilla and brown butter.

West End & Petrie Terrace

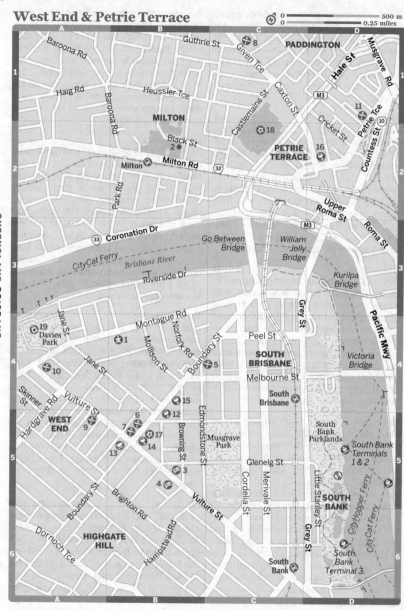

Julius   ITALIAN $$

(Map p280; ☎07-3844 2655; www.juliuspizzeria.com.au; 77 Grey St, South Brisbane; pizzas $21-24.50; ☺noon-9.30pm Sun, Tue & Wed, to 10pm Thu, to 10.30pm Fri & Sat; 🚢South Bank Terminals 1 & 2, ☒South Brisbane) Suited up in polished concrete and the orange glow of Aperol, this svelte Italian fires up superlative pizzas, divided into *pizze rosse* (with tomato sauce) or *pizze bianche* (without). The former includes a simple, beautiful marinara, cooked the proper Neapolitan way (sans seafood).

West End & Petrie Terrace

QUEENSLAND BRISBANE

The pasta dishes are also solid, with *fritelle di ricotta* (fried ricotta dumplings filled with custard) making a satisfying epilogue.

GOMA Cafe Bistro CAFE **$$**
(Map p280; ☏07-3842 9906; www.qagoma.qld. gov.au; Gallery of Modern Art, Stanley Pl, South Bank; lunch $15-34; ☺10am-3pm Mon-Fri, from 8.30am Sat & Sun; ⛴South Bank Terminals 1 & 2, ⛐South Brisbane) The casual, indoor-outdoor Goma Cafe Bistro serves high-quality burgers, salads and modern bistro mains, with both breakfast and lunch served on the weekends.

Billykart West End MODERN AUSTRALIAN **$$**
(Map p286; ☏07-3177 9477; www.billykart.com. au; 2 Edmondstone St, West End; breakfast $6-23.50, dinner mains $26-36; ☺restaurant 7am-2.30pm Mon & Sun, 7am-9.30pm Tue-Sat, shop 11am-5pm Mon, 11am-9pm Tue-Fri, 9am-9pm Sat, 9am-5pm Sun; ⛐192, 196, 198, 199) Celeb chef Ben O'Donoghue heads Billykart, a slick yet casual eatery where billy-kart blueprints and faux Queenslander veneers salute local childhood memories. Dishes are beautifully textured and flavoured, from the cult-status breakfast Aussie-Asian eggs (tiger prawn, bacon, deep fried egg, oyster sauce, chilli and shizu cress) to a smashing lunch-and-dinner spanner crab spaghettini. Weekend breakfast is popular; head in by 9am.

Sea Fuel FISH & CHIPS **$$**
(Map p286; ☏07-3844 9473; www.facebook. com/seafuel; 57 Vulture St, West End; meals $14-26; ☺11.30am-8.30pm; 🖋; ⛐199) The only thing missing is a beach at Sea Fuel, one of Brisbane's best fish-and-chip peddlers. It's

a polished, modern spot, with distressed timber tabletops and blown-up photos of coastal scenes. The fish is fresh and sustainably caught in Australian and New Zealand waters, and the golden chips flawlessly crisp and sprinkled with chicken salt. Alternatives include fresh oysters, Thai fish cakes and sprightly salads.

Chop Chop Chang's ASIAN **$$**
(Map p286; ☏07-3846 7746; www.chopchop changs.com.au; 185 Boundary St, West End; mains $18-32, banquet menus $38-55; ☺11.30am-3pm & 5.30-9.30pm; ⛐199) 'Happiness never decreases by being shared.' So said the Buddha. And the hungry hordes at Chop Chop Chang's seem to concur, passing around bowls of flavour-packed, pan-Asian street food like caramelised pork with tamarind, star anise and cassia bark, Isaan-style larb (ground-pork with pak chi farung, hot mint and dry chilli) and cooling watermelon and pomelo salad. Open later on Friday and Saturday nights.

★Stokehouse Q MODERN AUSTRALIAN **$$$**
(Map p280; ☏07-3020 0600; www.stokehouse. com.au; River Quay, Sidon St, South Bank; mains $36-42; ☺noon-late Mon-Thu, 11am-late Fri-Sun; ⛴South Bank Terminal 3, ⛐South Bank) Sophisticated Stokehouse guarantees a dizzying high, its confident, locally sourced menu paired with utterly gorgeous river and city views. At crisp, linen-clad tables, urbanites toast to inspired creations like chicken liver and Madeira brûlée with fruit toast, pear and native cranberry chutney. Next door, Stoke Bar offers similar views for a more casual (albeit pricey) drinking session.

✖ Fortitude Valley

★ King Arthur Cafe
MODERN AUSTRALIAN $

(Map p290; 07-3358 1670; www.kingarthur cafe.com; 164c Arthur St, Fortitude Valley; meals $11.50-21; 7am-3pm Tue-Fri, to 2pm Sat-Mon; ; 470, Fortitude Valley) Just off James St, King Arthur is never short of eye-candy creatives, guzzling gorgeous coffee (including batch brew), nibbling on just-baked goods and tucking into revamped cafe classics like scrambled eggs with kale, broccoli, fermented chilli and goats curd, or warm smoked local fish with horseradish cream, potato hash and pickled seasonal veggies. Best of all, it's all made using local produce and ethically sourced meats.

Nodo Donuts
CAFE $

(Map p290; 07-3852 2230; www.nodo.com. au; 1 Ella St, Newstead; dishes $7.50-16; 7am-3pm Tue-Fri, from 8am Sat & Sun; ; 300, 302, 305, 306, 322, 470) Light-washed, hip-kid Nodo serves up Brisbane's poshest doughnuts (usually sold out by 2pm), with combos like blueberry and lemon and Valrhona chocolate with beetroot. They're baked (not fried), gluten-free and even include a raw variety, dehydrated for nine hours. The rest of the cafe menu is equally focused on natural, unrefined ingredients, from the green breakfast bowl to the activated almond-milk Magic Mushroom shake. Great coffee too.

Ben's Burgers
BURGERS $

(Map p290; 07-3195 3094; www.bensburgers. com.au; Winn Ln, 5 Winn St; burgers $11; 7am-late; Fortitude Valley) Prime ingredients drive Ben's, a small, pumping joint in the Valley's coolest laneway. Roll out of bed for a breakfast Elvis (bacon, peanut butter, banana, maple syrup), or head in later for the lunch and dinner burgers, among them a meat-free option. Sides are straight forward – fries or chilli cheese fries – with brownies and pecan pie making for a fitting epilogue.

Thai Wi-Rat
THAI, LAOTIAN $

(Map p290; 07-3257 0884; 270-292 Brunswick St, Fortitude Valley; dishes $12-19; 11am-3pm & 5-9.30pm Mon-Thu, to 10pm Fri-Sun; Fortitude Valley) Under the watchful eyes of Thai royalty, locals sit at easy-wipe tables and tuck into chilli-heavy Thai and Laotian dishes at this lo-fi Chinatown eatery. Ditch the lunch specials for main-menu items like crunchy, tangy *som tum* (green paw paw salad) or classic *larb* (spicy minced-meat salad). The wines on offer aren't great, so consider bringing your own bottle of plonk. Takeaway available.

James Street Market
MARKET $

(Map p290; www.jamesst.com.au/james-st-market; 22 James St, Fortitude Valley; 8-piece sashimi $17, hot dishes $10-28; 8.30am-7pm Mon-Fri, 8am-6pm Sat & Sun; 470, Fortitude Valley) Local gourmands drop by this small, contemporary, lavishly stocked market for sophisticated fridge and pantry fare, including pesto-stuffed olives, stinky cheeses, dips, freshly baked bread, pastries and tubs of homemade gelato. If you're feeling a little peckish, the fresh seafood counter serves good sushi, sashimi and warming dishes like Japanese noodle soup with Moreton Bay bug.

★ Longtime
THAI $$

(Map p290; 07-3160 3123; www.longtime.com. au; 610 Ann St; mains $15-45; 5.30-10pm Tue-Thu & Sun, to 10.30pm Fri & Sat; ; Fortitude Valley) Blink and you'll miss the alley leading to this dim, kicking hot spot. The menu is designed for sharing, with a banging repertoire of sucker-punch, Thai-inspired dishes that include a must-try soft shell crab bao with Asian slaw. Reservations are only accepted for 5.30pm, 6pm and 6.30pm sittings, after which it's walk-ins only (Tuesday and Sunday are the easiest nights to score a table).

Les Bubbles
STEAK $$

(Map p290; 07-3251 6500; www.lesbubbles. com.au; 144 Wickham St, Fortitude Valley; steak frites $30; noon-11pm Sun-Thu, to midnight Fri & Sat; Fortitude Valley) From the red-neon declaration – 'Quality meat has been served here since 1982' – to the photos of crooks and cops, this sassy steakhouse relishes its former brothel days. Today the only thing on the menu is superb steak frites, served with unlimited fries and salad. Simply choose your sauce (try the green peppercorn and cognac option) and your libation.

Tinderbox
ITALIAN $$

(Map p290; 07-3852 3744; www.thetinderbox. com.au; 7/31 James St, Fortitude Valley; pizzas $20-24, mains $28; 5pm-late Tue-Sun; 470, Fortitude Valley) Popular with on-point James St peeps, this modern, mosaic-clad bistro straddles a leafy laneway by the Palace Centro cinemas. The menu is a share-friendly, Italian affair, spanning spicy 'nduja arancini and seared cuttlefish with chilli and rocket, to perfectly charred wood-fired pizzas like a

FOOD TRUCKS & NIGHT MARKETS

When it comes to food trucks and street food, Brisbane's crush has turned into a full-blown affair. There's an ever-growing number of food vans roaming city streets, serving up good-quality fast food, from tacos, ribs, wings and burgers, to wood-fired pizza, Brazilian hot dogs and Malaysian saté. You'll find a list of Brisbane food trucks (with respective menus) at www.bnefoodtrucks.com.au, a website that also includes a handy, interactive map showing the current location of food trucks across town.

From Tuesday to Sunday, Fish Lane (opposite the Queensland Museum & Sciencentre on Grey St) is the setting for **Eating at Wandering Cooks** (www.facebook.com/wanderingcooks), a rotating mix of quality food trucks and stalls open for lunch and dinner.

Further east along the Brisbane River, in suburban Hamilton, is the hugely popular **Eat Street Markets** (p292). Easily reached on the CityCat (alight at Bretts Wharf) it's the city's hipsterish take on the night street-food market, with a maze of upcycled shipping containers pumping out everything from freshly shucked oysters to smoky American barbecue and Turkish gözleme, all to the sound of live, rocking bands.

standout *funghi* (porcini mushrooms, mozzarella and roasted onion). Wash it all down with an innovative cocktail.

★ **E'cco**   MODERN AUSTRALIAN **$$$**
(Map p280; ☑07-3831 8344; www.eccobistro.com.au; 100 Boundary St; mains $36-42, 5-course tasting menu $89; ⊗noon-2.30pm Tue-Fri, 6pm-late Tue-Sat; ☑; ☑174, 230, 300) Years on, E'cco remains one of the state's gastronomic highlights. Polished yet personable staff deliver beautifully balanced, visually arresting dishes, which might see cured ocean trout flavoured with oyster emulsion or perfect suckling pig meet its match in smoked carrot purée, kimchi and spicy 'nduja (spreadable pork salumi). The kitchen offers a smaller, dedicated vegetarian menu (mains $30 to $38) as well as a highly recommended, good-value tasting menu for the full effect.

✕ New Farm

New Farm Confectionery   SWEETS **$**
(Map p290; ☑07-3139 0964; www.newfarmconfectionery.com.au; 14 Barker St, New Farm; sweets from $3; ⊗10am-6pm Wed & Thu, to 9.30pm Fri & Sat; ☑195, 196, 199) For a locavore sugar rush, squeeze into this tiny confectioner, located on the side of the New Farm Six Cinemas. From the macadamia brittle and chocolate-coated Madagascan vanilla marshmallow, to the slabs of blackberry-infused white chocolate, all of the products are made using natural, top-tier ingredients. Nostalgic types shouldn't miss the sherbet powder, made with actual fruit and paired with lollipops for gleeful dipping.

Sourced Grocer   MODERN AUSTRALIAN **$**
(Map p272; ☑07-3852 6734; www.sourcedgrocer.com.au; 11 Florence St, Teneriffe; dishes $7-23; ⊗7am-3pm Mon-Sat, 8am-3pm Sun, shop 7am-8pm Mon-Thu, to 7pm Fri, to 5pm Sat, to 4pm Sun; ☑199, 393, ☑Teneriffe) You can have your avocado on sourdough (with smoked labna, naturally) *and* buy your local Bee One Third honey at Sourced Grocer, a understatedly cool warehouse turned cafe-providore. Decked out with cushioned milk crates, a vertical garden and native flora in recycled tins, its open kitchen smashes it with seasonal, locavore dishes like standout cabbage pancakes with crispy Brussels sprout leaves, soft egg and shaved goats-milk cheese.

Little Loco   CAFE **$**
(Map p290; ☑07-3358 5706; www.facebook.com/littlelococafe; 121 Merthyr Rd, New Farm; breakfast $8-17, lunch $14.50-17; ⊗6am-3pm Mon-Fri, 6.30am-2.30pm Sat & Sun; ☑; ☑196, 199, 195) A white space speckled green with plants, this little New Farm local keeps peeps healthy like with dishes the Green Bowl, a tasty, feel-great combo of kale, spinach, broccolini, feta, pomegranate seeds, avocado and dukkah. There's no shortage of vegetarian and paleo bites, as well as dairy- and gluten-free options. Such salubrious credentials make sense given that the cafe's owner is Brisbane soccer player Daniel Bowles.

Double Shot   CAFE **$**
(Map p272; ☑07-3358 6556; www.facebook.com/doubleshotnewfarm; 125 Oxlade Dr, New Farm; mains $11.50-19.50; ⊗7am-3pm Wed, Thu & Sat, to 9pm Fri, 8am-3pm Sun; ☑196, ☑Sydney St) With its button-cute wooden porch, manicured hedge and upbeat furniture,

Fortitude Valley & New Farm

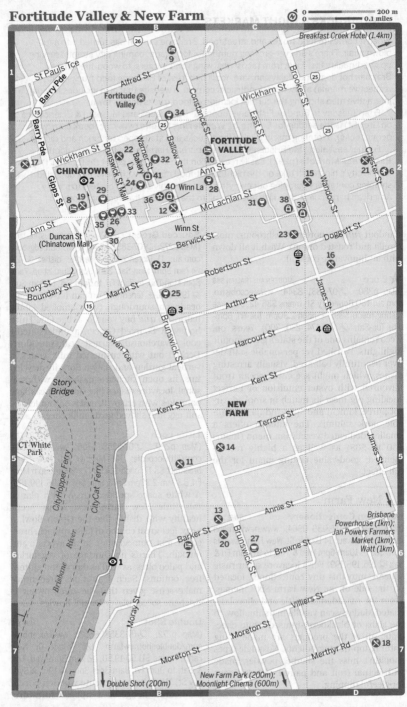

Breakfast Creek Hotel (1.4km)

Double Shot (200m)

New Farm Park (200m);
Moonlight Cinema (600m)

Brisbane
Powerhouse (1km);
Jan Powers Farmers
Market (1km);
Watt (1km)

QUEENSLAND BRISBANE

Fortitude Valley & New Farm

⊙ Sights
1 Brisbane Riverwalk	B6
2 Chinatown	A2
Institute of Modern Art	(see 37)
3 Jan Murphy Gallery	B3
4 Suzanne O'Connell Gallery	D4
5 TW Fine Art	C3

⊙ Activities, Courses & Tours
6 Q Academy	D2

⊙ Sleeping
7 Bowen Terrace	B6
8 Bunk Backpackers	A2
9 Limes	B1
10 Tryp	C2

⊗ Eating
11 Balfour Kitchen	B5
12 Ben's Burgers	B2
13 Chouquette	C6
14 Himalayan Cafe	C5
15 James Street Market	D2
16 King Arthur Cafe	D3
17 Les Bubbles	A2
18 Little Loco	D7
19 Longtime	A2
20 New Farm Confectionery	C6
21 Nodo Donuts	D2
22 Thai Wi-Rat	B2
23 Tinderbox	C3

⊙ Drinking & Nightlife
24 APO	B2
Birdees	(see 8)
25 Bloodhound Corner Bar & Kitchen	B3
26 Cloudland	B2
27 Death Before Decaf	C6
28 Eleven	C2
29 Elixir	A2
30 Family	B3
31 Gerard's Bar	C2
32 Holey Moley Golf Club	B2
33 Press Club	B2
34 Wickham Hotel	B1
35 Woolly Mammoth Alehouse	A2

⊙ Entertainment
36 Beat MegaClub	B2
37 Judith Wright Centre of Contemporary Arts	B3
The Zoo	(see 36)

⊙ Shopping
38 Camilla	C2
39 James Street	C2
40 Miss Bond	B2
Outpost	(see 40)
41 Stock & Supply	B2
Tym Guitars	(see 12)
Winn Lane	(see 12)

QUEENSLAND BRISBANE

petite Double Shot is a hit with brunching mums, dog-walkers and polished, suit-clad realtors. Join the New Farm crew for good coffee and staples like coconut bread with whipped ricotta, Spanish sardines on sourdough or refreshing green papaya, coconut and chicken salad. Tapas served from 3pm on Friday.

Chouquette BAKERY $
(Map p290; ☎ 07-3358 6336; www.chouquette.com.au; 19 Barker St, New Farm; items $2.50-11; ⊙ 6.30am-4pm Wed-Sat, to 12.30pm Sun; 🅿; 🚌 195, 196, 199) The best patisserie this side of Toulouse? Something to think about as you grab a nutty coffee and a bag of the namesake *chouquettes* (small choux pastries topped with granulated sugar), a shiny slice of *tarte au citron,* or a filled baguette. Charming French-speaking staff are the glacé cherry on the torte.

Balfour Kitchen MODERN AUSTRALIAN $$
(Map p290; ☎ 1300 597 540; www.spicersretreats.com/spicers-balfour-hotel/dining; Spicers Balfour Hotel, 37 Balfour St, New Farm; breakfast $14-25, dinner mains $32-38; ⊙ 6.30-11am, noon-2.30pm & 5.30-8.30pm Mon-Fri, from 7.30am Sat & Sun; 🚌 195, 196, 199) Should you nosh in the dining room, on the verandah or among the frangipani in the courtyard? This polished cafe-restaurant creates a very Queensland conundrum. Wherever you may land a linen-covered table, swoon over nuanced, sophisticated dishes, from morning brioche French toast with hazelnut, chocolate ganache and sour cherries, to evening hot-smoked barramundi paired with charred cauliflower and pil-pil sauce. Live tunes accompany Sunday lunch.

Himalayan Cafe NEPALI $$
(Map p290; ☎ 07-3358 4015; 640 Brunswick St, New Farm; mains $16-27; ⊙ 5.30-9.30pm Tue-Thu & Sun, to 10.30pm Fri & Sat; 🅿; 🚌 195, 196, 199) Awash with prayer flags, this free-spirited, karma-positive restaurant pulls in the punters with authentic Tibetan and Nepalese dishes like tender *fhaiya deakau* (lamb with veggies, coconut milk, sour cream and spices). Repeat the house mantra: 'May positive forces be with every single living thing that exists'.

Watt
MODERN AUSTRALIAN **$$**

(Map p272; ☑07-3358 5464; www.wattbrisbane.com.au; Brisbane Powerhouse, 119 Lamington St, New Farm; bar food $10-29, restaurant $25-34; ⏰10.30am-6pm Mon, to 10pm Tue-Fri, 8am-10pm Sat & Sun; ☐195, 196, ☒New Farm Park) On the riverbank level of the Brisbane Powerhouse is Watt, a breezy, contemporary space made for long, lazy vino sessions and people watching. Keep it casual with bar bites like Cuban fish tacos and manchego croquettes, or book a table in the restaurant for farm-to-table options like wild Bendigo rabbit pappardelle with smoked speck, hazelnut, watercress pesto and parmesan.

Kangaroo Point & Woolloongabba

Cliffs Cafe
CAFE **$**

(Map p280; ☑07-3391 7771; www.cliffscafe.com.au; 29 River Tce, Kangaroo Point; dishes $6.50-19.50; ⏰7am-5pm; ☐234) Looking straight out at the river, skyline and City Botanic Gardens, lofty Cliffs offers what is arguably the best view of Brisbane. It's a casual, open-air pavilion, serving big breakfasts, panini, burgers, fish and chips, salads and sweet treats. While the food won't necessarily blow your socks off, the unobstructed, postcard panorama will. Kick back with a coffee or beer and count your blessings.

Pearl Cafe
CAFE **$$**

(Map p272; ☑07-3392 3300; www.facebook.com/pearl.cafe.brisbane; 28 Logan Rd, Woolloongabba; mains $16-34; ⏰7am-8pm Tue-Sat, to 3pm Sat & Sun; ☐125, 175, 204, 234) Channeling Melbourne and Paris with its Euro flair, Pearl is one of Brisbane's best-loved weekend brunch spots. There are freshly baked cakes on the counter, a sophisticated selection of spirits on the shelf, and beautiful cafe dishes on the menu. Snub the underwhelming avocado on toast for more inspiring options, among them the popular daytime pork cotoletta. Sandwiches are chunky and generously filled.

★1889 Enoteca
ITALIAN **$$$**

(Map p272; ☑07-3392 4315; www.1889enoteca.com.au; 10-12 Logan Rd, Woolloongabba; pasta $21-42, mains $32-49; ⏰noon-2.30pm & 6-10pm Tue-Fri, 6-10pm Sat, noon-2.30pm Sun; ☐125, 175, 204, 234) Italian purists rightfully adore this moody, sophisticated bistro and wine store, where pasta is *not* served with a spoon (unless requested) and a Roman-centric menu

delivers seductive dishes like *carciofi alla Giuda* (Jewish-Roman-style fried artichoke with parsley and lemon mascarpone) and melt-in-your-mouth gnocchi with pork and fennel sausage, Parmesan cream and black truffle tapenade. Superlative wines include drops from lauded, smaller Italian producers.

Greater Brisbane

Eat Street Markets
STREET FOOD **$**

(☑07-3358 2500; www.eatstreetmarkets.com; 99 MacArthur Ave, Hamilton; admission adult/child $2.50/free, meals from $10; ⏰4-10pm Fri & Sat; ☒Bretts Wharf) What was once a container wharf is now Brisbane's hugely popular take on the night food market. Its maze of shipping-containers-turned-kitchens peddle anything from freshly shucked oysters to smoky American barbecue and Turkish gözleme. Add craft brews, festive lights and live music and you have one of Brisbane's coolest nights out. To get here, catch the CityCat ferry to Brett's Wharf.

Scout
CAFE **$**

(Map p286; ☑07-3367 2171; www.scoutcafe.com.au; 190 Petrie Tce, Petrie Terrace; mains $14-18; ⏰7am-3pm; ☐375, 380) This vintage neighbourhood shopfront was vacant for 17 years before Scout showed up and started selling bagels. The vibe is downbeat, affable and creative, with a short, clean menu of healthy salads and bagels stuffed with combos like roasted rosemary potatoes, gorgonzola, mozzarella and chilli jam.

★Shouk Cafe
MIDDLE EASTERN **$$**

(Map p272; ☑07-3172 1655; www.shoukcafe.com.au; 14 Collingwood St, Paddington; dishes $15.50-22; ⏰7.30am-2.30pm; ☎☑; ☐375) Shouk wins on many levels: affable staff, laid-back vibe, verdant views from the backroom and – most importantly – generous portions of fresh, gorgeous dishes inspired by the Middle East. Swoon over sardines on toasted rye with roasted capsicum, chopped olives, raisins, orange-pickled fennel and labna, or the beautiful *kusheri* (spiced brown rice with lentils, chickpeas and caramelised onion on a beetroot and tahini purée).

Kettle & Tin
CAFE **$$**

(Map p286; ☑07-3369 3778; www.kettleandtin.com.au; 215 Given Tce, Paddington; mains $14-32; ⏰7am-4pm Mon & Sun, to 9pm Tue-Thu, to 10pm Fri & Sat; ☐375) Behind its picket fence, cute-as-a-button Kettle & Tin serves up solid, scrumptious cafe grub. Breakfast standouts include thick-cut Kassler bacon with sautéed kale, white beans, celeriac purée and roasted apple, while Paddo's lunching ladies fawn over the daikon and carrot salad with toasted sesame, nori seaweed and puffed rice. Come dinner, cross the Pacific with the ever-popular smoked-duck-breast fajitas.

Drinking & Nightlife

Brisbane's bar scene has evolved into a sophisticated entity, with sharp, competent drinking holes pouring everything from natural wines and locally made saisons, to G&Ts spiked with native ingredients. The city's live-music scene is equally robust, with cult-status venues in Fortitude Valley, West End and the city itself pumping out impressive local and international talent. Tip: always carry some photo ID.

Central Brisbane

★ Super Whatnot   BAR
(Map p280; ☑ 07-3210 2343; www.superwhatnot. com; 48 Burnett La; ⊙ 3-11pm Mon-Thu, noon-1am Fri, 3pm-1am Sat, 3-8pm Sun; ⊠ Central) Trailblazing Super Whatnot remains one of Brisbane's coolest drinking holes, an industrial, split-level playpen in a former beauty school. Slip inside for cognoscenti craft beers, decent vino and crafty cocktails, served to a pleasure-seeking mix of indie kids and thirsty suits. Bar bites include cheeky hot dogs and nachos.

Coffee Anthology   CAFE
(Map p280; ☑ 07-3210 1881; www.facebook.com/ coffeeanthology; 126 Margaret St; ⊙ 7am-3.30pm Mon-Fri, to noon Sat; ☎; ⊠ Central) True to its name, Coffee Anthology keeps caffeine geeks hyped with a rotating selection of specialist blends from cult-status roasters like Padre and Industry Beans. Tasting notes guide the indecisive, and you can even buy a bag or two if you like what's in your cup. Friendly, breezy and contemporary, the place also serves simple breakfast and lunch bites, from porridge and muffins to bagels.

Brooklyn Standard   BAR
(Map p280; ☑ 0405 414 131; www.facebook.com/ brooklynstandardbar; Eagle Ln; ⊙ 4pm-late Mon-Fri, 6pm-late Sat; ⊠ Riverside, ⊠ Central) The red neon sign sets the tone: 'If the music is too loud, you are too old'. And loud, live, nightly tunes are what you get in this rocking cellar bar, decked out in NYC paraphernalia and buzzing with a mixed-age crowd. Stay au-

thentic with a Brooklyn lager or knock back a kooky cocktail (either way, the pretzels are on the house).

Gresham Bar   BAR
(Map p280; www.thegresham.com.au; 308 Queen St; ⊙ 7am-3am Mon-Fri, 4pm-3am Sat & Sun; ☎; ⊠ Central) Tucked into one corner of a noble, heritage-listed bank building, the Gresham evokes the old-school bars of New York; we're talking pressed-metal ceiling, Chesterfields and a glowing cascade of spirit bottles behind a handsome timber bar (complete with library-style ladder). It's a dark, buzzing, convivial spot, with an especially robust selection of whiskies and a snug side room you'll find difficult to leave.

John Mills Himself   CAFE, BAR
(Map p280; ☑ bar 0421 959 865, cafe 0434 064 349; www.johnmillshimself.com.au; 40 Charlotte St; ⊙ cafe 6.30am-3.30pm Mon-Fri, bar 4-10pm Tue-Thu, to midnight Fri; ⊠ Central) No doubt Mr Mills would approve of this secret little coffee shop, occupying the very building in which he ran a printing business last century. Accessible from both Charlotte St and an alley off Elizabeth St, its marble bar and penny-tile floors set a very Brooklyn scene for top third wave coffee. Later in the day, cafe becomes intimate bar, pouring craft Australian beers and spirits.

Mr & Mrs G Riverbar   BAR
(Map p280; ☑ 07-3221 7001; www.mrandmrsg. com.au; Eagle Street Pier, 1 Eagle St; ⊙ 3-10pm Mon & Tue, noon-11pm Wed & Thu, noon-midnight Fri & Sat, noon-10pm Sun; ⊠ Eagle St Pier, ⊠ Central) Mr & Mrs G spoils guests with curving floor-to-ceiling windows overlooking the river, skyline and Story Bridge. It's a casually chic affair, with vibrantly coloured bar stools, cushy slipper chairs and hand-painted Moroccan side tables on which to rest your glass of chenin blanc. If you're feeling peckish, generous tapas dishes include succulent *keftethes* (Greek-style meatballs), cheese and charcuterie.

Riverbar & Kitchen   BAR
(Map p280; ☑ 07-3211 9020; www.riverbarand kitchen.com.au; 71 Eagle St; ⊙ 7am-11.30pm; ⊠ Riverside, ⊠ Central) A chilled-out spot for an afternoon ale or barrel-aged cocktail, Riverbar & Kitchen is true to its name, down by the muddy Brisbane River at the base of the Eagle Street Pier complex. Decked-out like a boat shed, with coiled ropes, white-painted timber and booths, the vibe is

QUEENSLAND BRISBANE

LGBTIQ BRISBANE

While Brisbane's LGBTIQ scene is significantly smaller than its Sydney and Melbourne counterparts, the city has an out-and-proud queer presence.

Major events on the calendar include **Melt** (www.brisbanepowerhouse.org/festivals; ☉ Jan/Feb), a 12-day feast of queer theatre, cabaret, dance, comedy, circus acts and visual arts held at the Brisbane Powerhouse in January and February. In March, the Powerhouse also hosts the **Queer Film Festival** (www.brisbanepowerhouse.org/festivals/brisbane-queer-film-festival; ☉ Mar), a showcase for gay, lesbian, bisexual and transgender films. September heralds the **Brisbane Pride Festival** (p279), which peaks during Pride Fair Day, held at New Farm Park.

Fortitude Valley's **Wickham Hotel** (Map p290; ☎ 07-3852 1301; www.thewickham.com.au; 308 Wickham St; ☉ 6.30am-late Mon-Fri, 10am-late Sat & Sun; ☒ Fortitude Valley) attracts a mainly mixed crowd these days, though it remains a staunchly queer-friendly pub. The Valley is also home to gay-friendly clubs **Beat MegaClub** (Map p290; www.thebeatmegaclub.com.au; 677 Ann St, Fortitude Valley; ☉ 8pm-5am Mon-Sat, from 5pm Sun; ☒ Fortitude Valley) and the scenier **Family** (p295); on Sunday the latter hosts 'Fluffy', Brisbane's biggest gay dance party. Closer to the city centre, the **Sportsman Hotel** (Map p280; ☎ 07-3831 2892; www.sportsmanhotel.com.au; 130 Leichhardt St, Spring Hill; ☉ 1pm-1am Sun-Thu, to 2.30am Fri & Sat; ☒ Central) is another perennially busy gay venue: a blue-collar, orange-brick pub with pool tables, drag shows and a rather eclectic crowd. In general, you'll find a significant local gay presence in the inner suburbs of Fortitude Valley, New Farm, Newstead, West End and Paddington.

For current entertainment and events listings, interviews and articles, check out *Q News* (www.qnews.com.au) and *Blaze* (www.gaynewsnetwork.com.au). Tune in to *Queer Radio* (9pm to 11pm every Wednesday; www.4zzzfm.org.au), a radio show on 4ZZZ (aka FM102.1) – another source of Brisbane info. For lesbian news and views, *Dykes on Mykes* precedes it (7pm to 9pm Wednesday).

casual, breezy and free-flowing. Decent food too, from morning staples to burgers, pizzas and surf-and-turf bistro mains.

🍸 South Bank

Maker　　　　　　　COCKTAIL BAR
(Map p280; ☎ 0437 338 072; 9 Fish Ln, South Brisbane; ☉ 4pm-midnight Tue-Sun; ☒ South Bank Terminals 1 & 2, ☒ South Brisbane) Intimate, black-clad and spliced by a sexy brass bar, Maker crafts seamless, seasonal cocktails using house liqueurs, out-of-the-box ingredients and a splash of whimsy. Here, classic negronis are made with house-infused vermouth, while gin and tonics get Australian with native quandong and finger lime. Other fortes include a sharp edit of boutique wines by the glass and beautiful bar bites prepared with award-winning restaurant Gauge (p285).

Cobbler　　　　　　　BAR
(Map p286; www.cobblerbar.com; 7 Browning St, West End; ☉ 5pm-1am Mon, 4pm-1am Tue-Thu & Sun, 4pm-2am Fri & Sat; ☒ 60, 192, 198, 199) Whisky fans will weep tears of joy at the sight of Cobbler's imposing bar, graced with over 400 whiskies from around the globe. Channeling a speakeasy vibe, this dimly lit West End wonder also pours a cognoscenti selection of rums, tequilas and liqueurs, not to mention a crafty selection of cocktails that add modern twists to the classics. Bottoms up!

Catchment Brewing Co　　　　　BREWERY
(Map p286; ☎ 07-3846 1701; www.catchmentbrewingco.com.au; 150 Boundary St, West End; ☉ 4-10pm Mon, 11am-10pm Tue-Thu & Sun, 11am-1am Fri & Sat; ☒ 199) Sink local suds at Catchment, a hip, two-level microbrewery with notable, seasonal nosh and live music in the courtyard. House brews include Pale Select, a nod to the signature beer of the defunct West End Brewery, while guest taps showcase other local beers. The best seats in the house are the two, tiny, 1st-floor balconies, serving up afternoon sun and Boundary St views.

Jungle　　　　　　　BAR
(Map p286; ☎ 0449 568 732; www.facebook.com/junglewestend; 76 Vulture St, West End; ☉ noon-midnight Thu-Sun; ☒ 199) Aloha and welcome to paradise… Well, at least to Brisbane's

only proper tiki bar. An intimate, hand-built bamboo hideaway pimped with wood-carved stools, a green-glowing bar and DJ-spun Hawaiian tunes, it's an apt place to cool down with a tropical libation. Keep it classic with a rumalicious piña colada (served in a pineapple, naturally), or neck a Red Stripe lager from Jamaica.

Blackstar Coffee Roasters   CAFE
(Map p286; www.blackstarcoffee.com.au; 44 Thomas St, West End; ⊙7am-5pm; 🚲; 🚌199) One of Brisbane's top coffee roasters, laidback Blackstar is never short of West End hipsters, hippies and laptop-tapping creatives. Slurp a single-origin espresso or cool down with a bottle of cold-pressed coffee. Food options (lunch dishes $10 to $17) include brownies, eggs and spanakopita, while its string of special events includes a ukulele night on the last Friday of the month.

Archive Beer Boutique   BAR
(Map p286; ☑07-3844 3419; www.archivebeer boutique.com.au; 100 Boundary St, West End; ⊙11am-late; 🚌198,199) A foaming juggernaut, Archive serves up a dizzying choice of craft suds. Whether you're hankering for a Brisbane chilli-choc porter, a Melbourne American IPA or a Sydney guava gose, chances are you'll find it pouring here. There are over 20 rotating beers on tap, as well as hundreds of Aussie and imported bottled brews. Decent bar grub includes grilled meats, burgers and pizzas.

🍺 Fortitude Valley

★ Gerard's Bar   WINE BAR
(Map p290; ☑07-3252 2606; www.gerardsbar. com.au; 13a/23 James St; ⊙3-10pm Mon-Thu, noon-late Fri & Sat; 🚌470, 🚇Fortitude Valley) A stylish, grown-up bar that's one of Brisbane's best. Perch yourself at the polished concrete bar, pick an unexpected drop from the sharply curated wine list, and couple with standout bar snacks that include flawless croquettes and prized Jamón Iberico de Belotta. If you're craving a cocktail, try the signature 'Gerard The Drunk', an intriguing, climate-appropriate medley of vodka, passionfruit, pomegranate and rose water.

APO   COCKTAIL BAR
(Map p290; ☑07-3252 2403; www.theapo.com. au; 690 Ann St; ⊙3pm-1am Tue, noon-1am Wed, Thu & Sun, noon-3am Fri & Sat; 🚇Fortitude Valley) A smart, quality-driven establishment, the APO was once an apothecary (hence the name). It's a dark, moody, two-level space, where Victorian brickwork contrasts with polished concrete floors and the odd marble feature wall. Drinks are sharp, sophisticated and include bottled single-batch cocktails such as a rhubarb-and-vanilla negroni. Topping it off is a smashing menu of French-Lebanese inspired bites, including a not-be-missed Lebanese taco.

Eleven   ROOFTOP BAR
(Map p290; ☑07-3067 7447; www.elevenrooftop bar.com.au; 757 Ann St; ⊙noon-midnight Tue-Thu & Sun, to 3am Fri & Sat; 🚇Fortitude Valley) Slip into your slinkiest threads for Brisbane's finest rooftop retreat, its marble bar pouring a competent list of libations, including pickled-onion-pimped martinis and high-flying French champagnes. Drink in the multi-million-dollar view, which takes in the city skyline and Mt Coot-tha beyond, and schmooze to DJ-spun tunes later in the week. The dress code is especially strict on Friday and Saturday evenings; see the website.

Cloudland   BAR
(Map p290; ☑07-3872 6600; www.katarzyna. com.au/venues/cloudland; 641 Ann St; ⊙4pm-late Tue-Thu, 11.30am-late Fri-Sun; 🚇Fortitude Valley) Jaws hit the floor at this opulent, multilevel bar, club and Pan-Asian restaurant. Named for a much-loved, long-demolished 1940s Brisbane dance hall, Cloudland has birdcage booths, lush foliage and vast chandeliers that are best described as enchanted forest meets sheikh palace meets Addams Family gothic. Free salsa lessons on Thursday from 9pm.

Family   CLUB
(Map p290; ☑07-3852 5000; www.thefamily. com.au; 8 McLachlan St; ⊙9pm-3.30am Fri-Sun; 🚇Fortitude Valley) Queue up for one of Brisbane's biggest and mightiest clubs. The music here is phenomenal, pumping through four levels with myriad dance floors, bars, themed booths and elite DJs from home and away. Running on Sunday, the 'Fluffy' dance party is a big hit with Brisbane's younger, hotter gay party peeps.

Holey Moley Golf Club   COCKTAIL BAR
(Map p290; ☑1300 727 833; www.holeymoley. com.au; 25 Warner St; 9-hole mini golf game per person $16.50; ⊙noon-late Mon-Fri, 10am-late Sat & Sun; 🚇Fortitude Valley) Mini golf, in a church, with cocktails is what awaits at Holey Moley (best booked ahead). Order a Putty Professor (rum, milk, chocolate sauce, peanut butter, Reese's Peanut Butter Cup,

crushed Maltesers) and tee off on one of two courses. Each of the 18 holes is themed; the standout Game of Thrones–themed Iron Throne is by local artist Cezary Stulgis. Kids welcome until 5pm.

Bloodhound Corner Bar & Kitchen BAR

(Map p290; ☑ 07-3162 6402; www.bloodhound cornerbar.com.au; 454 Brunswick St; ⊙ 3pm-late Mon-Wed, noon-late Thu-Sun; ☒ Fortitude Valley) Starting life as a grocery store, this 19th-century pile is now a new-school Valley bar. Vintage brick walls, mottled floorboards and open fireplaces share the space with street art, a pinball machine and plenty of hipster beards. Guzzle international beers, well-mixed cocktails, or get experimental with one of the craft spirit flights. Decent bar snacks nod to South America, with live music upstairs on Saturday.

Woolly Mammoth Alehouse BAR

(Map p290; ☑ 07-3257 4439; www.woollymam moth.com.au; 633 Ann St; ⊙ 4pm-late Tue-Thu, from noon Fri-Sun; ☒ Fortitude Valley) The combination of craft beer, giant Jenga and 14-foot shuffleboard table is not lost on Gen Y and Millennials, who stream into this big, polished playpen to let the good times roll. Brew types include IPAs, saisons and goses, most of which hail from Australian microbreweries. Check the website to see what's playing on the Mane Stage, which could be anything from comedy to UK hip-hop.

Elixir ROOFTOP BAR

(Map p290; ☑ 07-3363 5599; www.elixirrooftop. com.au; 646 Ann St; ⊙ 4pm-late Wed-Fri, 1pm-late Sat & Sun; ☒ Fortitude Valley) What rooftop Elixir lacks in views it makes up for in ambience. Hurry up the stairs for a sultry, tropical playpen of lush leaves, flickering tealights, DJ-spun beats and languid play beds. Refresh with craft beers or Elixir's Fresh Market martini, a twist on the classic using hand-picked market fruits. Check the website for drinks and food promotions.

Press Club COCKTAIL BAR

(Map p290; ☑ 07-3852 5000; www.pressclub. net.au; 339 Brunswick St; ⊙ 7pm-2.30am Tue-Thu, 6pm-3am Fri & Sat, 6pm-2am Sun; ☒ Fortitude Valley) Looking more like a hangout for aliens than journos (picture sci-fi bar stools and glowing chandeliers), Press Club sets an off-beat scene for cocktails, ciders and smooth live tunes. Head in Tuesday and Saturday for R&B, Wednesday for jazz, Thursday for swing, or Friday for funk and soul. Tuesday

nights are especially huge while Sunday's DJ sets are popular with local 'hospo' (hospitality) peeps.

New Farm

★ The Triffid BAR

(Map p272; ☑ 07-3171 3001; www.thetriffid.com. au; 7-9 Stratton St, Newstead; ☒ 300, 302, 305, 306, 322, 393) Not only does the Triffid have an awesome beer garden (complete with shipping-container bars and a cassette-themed mural honouring Brisbane bands), it's also one of the city's top live-music venues. Music acts span local, Aussie and international talent, playing in a barrel-vaulted WWII hangar with killer acoustics. It's hardly surprising given that the place is owned by former Powderfinger bassist John Collins.

★ Green Beacon Brewing Co MICROBREWERY

(Map p272; ☑ 07-3252 8393; www.greenbeacon. com.au; 26 Helen St, Teneriffe; ⊙ noon-late; ☎; ☒ 393, 470, ☒ Teneriffe) In a cavernous warehouse in post-industrial Teneriffe, Green Beacon brews some of Brisbane's best beers. The liquid beauties ferment in vast stainless-steel vats behind the long bar before flowing through the taps and onto your grateful palate. Choose from six core beers or seasonal specials like blood-orange IPA. Peckish? Decent bites include fresh local seafood, and there's always a guest food truck parked out front.

Newstead Brewing Co MICROBREWERY

(Map p272; ☑ 07-3172 2488; www.newsteadbrew ing.com.au; 85 Doggett St, Newstead; ⊙ 11am-midnight; ☒ 60, 393, 470, ☒ Teneriffe) What was once a bus depot is now a pumping microbrewery, its 12 taps pouring six standard house brews, one cider and five seasonal beers (dubbed the 'fun stuff' by one staffer). For an enlightening overview, order the paddle board of four different brews. If beer doesn't rock your boat, knock back cocktails, craft spirits or wine from a small, engaging list of smaller producers.

On the food front, ditch the so-so pizzas for the deliciously spicy, tangy buffalo wings.

Death Before Decaf COFFEE

(Map p290; 3/760 Brunswick St; ⊙ 24hr; ☒ 195, 196, 199) Kick-ass specialty coffee, brewed all day and all through the night: this ink-loving, headbanging legend is a Godsend for people craving a decent cup after 4pm. Death Before Decaf, we salute you.

🍷 Kangaroo Point & Woolloongabba

Canvas Club
COCKTAIL BAR

(Map p272; ☑07-3891 2111; www.canvasclub.com. au; 16b Logan Rd, Woolloongabba; ⊙noon-midnight Tue-Fri, from 10am Sat & Sun; ☐125, 175, 204, 234) Slap bang on Woolloongabba's main eating, drinking and shopping strip, Canvas sets a hip, arty scene for cheeky cocktail sessions. Debate the symbolism of the street-art mural while downing seasonal libations like the Don Pablo (rum, amaro and apple-and-cinnamon foam) or the silky smooth Bangarang (tequila, watermelon, chilli, coriander, lime and condensed milk). Smashing.

Story Bridge Hotel
PUB

(Map p280; ☑07-3391 2266; www.storybridge hotel.com.au; 200 Main St, Kangaroo Point; ⊙6.30am-midnight Sun-Thu, to 1.30am Fri & Sat; ☐234, 🚢Thornton St, Holman St) Beneath the bridge at Kangaroo Point, this beautiful 1886 pub and beer garden is perfect for a pint after a long day exploring. Regular live music (see the website for upcoming acts) and a good choice of drinking and eating areas.

🍷 Greater Brisbane

★ Lefty's Old Time Music Hall
BAR

(Map p286; www.leftysoldtimemusichall.com; 15 Caxton St, Petrie Tce; ⊙5pm-late Tue-Sun; ☐375) Paint the town and the front porch too, there's a honky-tonk bar in Brisvegas! Tarted up in chandeliers and mounted moose heads (yep, those are bras hanging off the antlers), scarlet-hued Lefty's keeps the good times rolling with close to 200 whiskies and the sweet twang of live country-and-western. A short, star-spangled food menu includes chilli cheese fried and southern fried chicken.

Regatta Hotel
PUB

(Map p272; ☑07-3871 9595; www.regattahotel. com.au; 543 Coronation Dr, Toowong; ⊙6.30am-1am; 🚢Regatta) Dressed in iron lacework and prettier than a wedding cake, this 1874 pub is a Brisbane institution. Directly opposite the Regatta CityCat ferry terminal, its revamped drinking spaces include a polished, contemporary main bar, a chi-chi outdoor courtyard and a basement speakeasy called The Walrus Club (open 5pm to late Thursday to Saturday). Check the website for weekly events, which often include live music.

Breakfast Creek Hotel
PUB

(Map p272; ☑07-3262 5988; www.breakfast creekhotel.com; 2 Kingsford Smith Dr, Albion; ⊙10am-late; ☐300, 302, 305) Built in 1889 and sporting an eclectic French-Renaissance style, the Breakfast Creek Hotel is a Brisbane icon. The pub offers various bars and dining areas, including a beer garden and an art deco 'private bar' where the wooden kegs are spiked daily at noon. A converted electricity substation on-site is now home to Substation No 41, an urbane bar with over 400 rums in its inventory.

☆ Entertainment

Most big-ticket international bands have Brisbane on their radar, and the city regularly hosts top-tier DJ talent. World-class cultural venues offer a year-round program of theatre, dance, music and comedy.

Qtix (☑13 62 46; www.qtix.com.au) is a booking agency, usually for more high-brow entertainment.

Riverstage
LIVE MUSIC

(Map p280; ☑07-3403 7921; www.brisbane.qld. gov.au/facilities-recreation/arts-and-culture/river stage; 59 Gardens Point Rd; 🚢QUT Gardens Point, 🚆Central) Evocatively set in the Botanic Gardens, this outdoor arena hosts no shortage of prolific national and international music acts. Past performers include U2, 5 Seconds of Summer, Ellie Goulding and Flume.

Lock 'n' Load
LIVE MUSIC

(Map p286; ☑07-3844 0142; www.locknload bistro.com.au; 142 Boundary St, West End; ⊙3pm-late Mon-Thu, from noon Fri, from 7am Sat & Sun; ☎; ☐199) Ebullient and woody, this two-storey gastropub lures an upbeat crowd of music fans, here to watch jazz, acoustic, roots, blues and soul acts take to the small front stage. Catch a gig, then show up for breakfast or lunch the next day (the brekkie of craft-beer baked beans with fat bacon, sour cream, jalapeños and corn bread tames a hangover). Check the website for upcoming gigs.

The Zoo
LIVE MUSIC

(Map p290; ☑07-3854 1381; www.thezoo.com.au; 711 Ann St, Fortitude Valley; ⊙7pm-late Wed-Sun; 🚆Fortitude Valley) Going strong since 1992, the Zoo has surrendered a bit of musical territory to the Hi-Fi and Brightside, but it is still a grungy spot for indie rock, folk, acoustic, hip-hop, reggae and electronic acts, with no shortage of raw talent. Recent acts have included Gold Coast garage rockers Bleeding Knees Club and American indie pop artist Toro y Moi.

Brisbane Jazz Club
JAZZ

(Map p280; ☎ 07-3391 2006; www.brisbanejazz club.com.au; 1 Annie St, Kangaroo Point; adult/ under 18yr $31/11; ⏱ 6.30-11pm Thu-Sat, 5.30-10pm Sun; ☻ Holman St) Straight out of the bayou, this tiny riverside jazz shack has been Brisbane's jazz beacon since 1972. Anyone who's anyone in the scene plays here when they're in town.

South Bank Cineplex
CINEMA

(Map p280; ☎ 07-3829 7970; www.cineplex.com. au; cnr Grey & Ernest Sts, South Bank; adult/child from $6.50/4.50; ⏱ 10am-late; ☻ South Bank Terminals 1, 2 & 3, ☒ South Bank) The cheapest complex for the mainstream releases: wade through a sea of popcorn aromas and teenagers.

Queensland Performing Arts Centre
PERFORMING ARTS

(QPAC; Map p280; ☎ guided tours 07-3840 7444, tickets 136 246; www.qpac.com.au; Queensland Cultural Centre, cnr Grey & Melbourne Sts, South Bank; tours adult/child $15/10; ⏱ box office 9am-8.30pm Mon-Sat; ☻ South Bank Terminals 1 & 2, ☒ South Brisbane) Brisbane's main performing arts centre comprises four venues and a small exhibition space focused on aspects of the performing arts. The centre's busy calendar includes ballet, concerts, theatre and comedy, from both Australian and international acts. One-hour backstage tours run on Friday from 10.30am; book tickets by phone or email, or purchase them on the day from the ground-floor QPAC cafe.

Judith Wright Centre of Contemporary Arts
PERFORMING ARTS

(Map p290; ☎ 07-3872 9000; www.judithwright centre.com; 420 Brunswick St, Fortitude Valley; ⏱ box office 11am-4pm Mon-Fri; ☎; ☒ Fortitude Valley) Home to both a medium-sized and intimate performance space, this free-thinking arts incubator hosts an eclectic array of cultural treats, including contemporary dance, circus and visual arts. It's also the hub for the hugely popular Bigsound Festival (p279), a three-day music fest in September. Scan the website for upcoming performances and exhibitions.

Brisbane Powerhouse
PERFORMING ARTS

(Map p272; ☎ box office 07-3358 8600; www. brisbanepowerhouse.org; 119 Lamington St, New Farm; ☒ 195, 196, ☻ New Farm Park) What was a 1920s power station is now a buzzing hub of nationally and internationally acclaimed theatre, music, comedy, dance and more. There are loads of happenings at the Powerhouse – some free – as well as popular in-house bars and restaurants with standout views over the Brisbane River. See the website for upcoming events.

Suncorp Stadium
STADIUM

(Map p286; www.suncorpstadium.com.au; 40 Castlemaine St, Milton; ☒ 375, 379) In winter, rugby league is the big spectator sport here and local team the Brisbane Broncos call this stadium home.

The Gabba
STADIUM

(Brisbane Cricket Ground; Map p272; www. thegabba.com.au; 411 Vulture St, Woolloongabba; ☒ 174, 175, 184, 185, 200) You can cheer both AFL football and interstate and interna-

---

OUTDOOR CINEMA

One of the best ways to spend a warm summer night in Brisbane is with a picnic basket and some friends at an outdoor cinema. **Moonlight Cinema** (www.moonlight.com.au; Brisbane Powerhouse, 119 Lamington Rd, New Farm; adult/child $17/12.50; ⏱ 7pm Wed-Sun; ☒ 195, 196, ☻ New Farm Park) runs between December and early March at New Farm Park near the Brisbane Powerhouse. Films, which include current mainstream releases and the odd cult classic, screen from Wednesday to Sunday, flickering into life around 7pm.

A parallel option is **Ben & Jerry's Openair Cinemas** (Map p280; www.openaircine mas.com.au; Rainforest Green, South Bank Parklands, South Bank; adult/child online $17/12, at the gate $22/17; ⏱ from 5.30pm Tue-Sat, from 5pm Sun; ☻ South Bank Terminals 1 & 2, ☒ South Brisbane) at South Bank, where from late September to mid-November you can watch big-screen classics and recent releases under the stars (or clouds) at the Rainforest Green at South Bank Parklands. Hire a beanbag or deckchair, or bring a picnic rug. Note that most sessions sell out online prior to the night of the screening, so book in advance. Live music (which sometimes includes prolific Australian acts) runs beforehand.

tional cricket at the Gabba in Woolloong-abba, south of Kangaroo Point. If you're new to cricket, try and get along to a Twenty20 match, which sees the game in its most explosive form. The cricket season runs from late September to March; the football from late March to September.

Shopping

Brisbane's retail landscape is deliciously eclectic, stretching from Vogue-indexed high-end handbags to weekend-market arts and craft.

🖺 Central Brisbane

Noosa Chocolate Factory   FOOD
(Map p280; www.noosachocolatefactory.com.au; 144 Adelaide St; ⊗8am-7pm Mon-Thu, to 9pm Fri, 9am-6pm Sat, 10am-5pm Sun; 🚇Central) 🍴 Don't delude yourself: the small batch, artisanal chocolates from this Sunshine Coast Willy Wonka will override any self control. Best sellers include generous, marshmallowy Rocky Road and a very Queensland concoction of unroasted macadamias covered in Bowen mango–flavoured chocolate. Best of all, the chocolate here is palm-oil free. A second branch at No 156 also serves specialty coffee and hot chocolate.

Maiocchi   FASHION & ACCESSORIES
(Map p280; ☑07-3012 9640; www.maiocchi.com.au; Brisbane Arcade, 117 Adelaide St; ⊗9am-5.30pm Mon-Thu, 8.30am-8pm Fri, 9am-4pm Sat, 11am-4pm Sun; 🚇Central) Homegrown label Maiocchi is well known for its gorgeous, vintage-inspired frocks, simple in cut but rich in little details and quirks. Expect custom prints, '50s silhouettes and the Japanese influences. Your next summery cocktail dress aside, the boutique also stocks tops, pants and shoes, as well as a thoughtfully curated selection of Australian-made jewellery, bags and homewares. You'll find it in the heritage-listed Brisbane Arcade.

Jan Powers Farmers Market   MARKET
(Map p280; www.janpowersfarmersmarkets.com.au; Reddacliff Place, George St; ⊗8am-6pm Wed; 🚢North Quay, 🚇Central) Central Brisbane lives out its bucolic village fantasies when local growers and artisans descend on Reddacliff Place to sell their prized goods. Fill your shopping bags with just-picked fruit and vegetables, meats and seafood, fresh pasta, fragrant breads, pastries and more. Stock up for a picnic in the City Botanic Gardens,

or simply grab a coffee and a ready-to-eat, multiculti bite.

Archives Fine Books   BOOKS
(Map p280; ☑07-3221 0491; www.archivesfinebooks.com.au; 40 Charlotte St; ⊗9am-6pm Mon-Thu, to 7pm Fri, to 5pm Sat; 🚇Central) Rickety bookshelves and squeaky floorboards set a nostalgic scene at this sprawling repository of pre-loved pages. While the true number of books on offer is a little less than the one million claimed (our little secret), the place is a veritable sea of engaging titles. The oldest book on our last visit – by the canonised Roberto Francesco Romolo Bellarmino – dated back to 1630.

🖺 South Bank & West End

Where The Wild Things Are   BOOKS
(Map p286; ☑07-3255 3987; www.wherethewildthingsare.com.au; 191 Boundary St, West End; ⊗8.30am-6pm Mon-Sat, to 5pm Sun; 👶; 🚌199) Little brother to Avid Reader next door, Where The Wild Things Are stocks a whimsical collection of books for toddlers, older kids and teens. The bookshop also runs regular activities, from weekly story-time sessions to book launches, signings and crafty workshops covering themes like book illustration. Scan the bookshop's website and Facebook page for upcoming events.

Jet Black Cat Music   MUSIC
(Map p286; ☑0419 571 299; www.facebook.com/jetblackcatmusic; 72 Vulture St, West End; ⊗10.30am-5pm Tue-Fri, 10am-4pm Sat; 🚌199) Serious music fans know all about Shannon Logan and her little West End record shop. She's usually behind the piano-cum-counter, chatting with a loyal fan base who drop in for an in-the-know, hard-to-find booty of indie vinyl and CDs. Logan only sells what she's passionate about, and the place also hosts occasional in-store gigs showcasing well-known local and international indie talent.

🖺 Fortitude Valley

Camilla   FASHION & ACCESSORIES
(Map p290; ☑07-3852 6030; www.camilla.com.au; 1/19 James St; ⊗9.30am-5pm Mon-Wed, Fri & Sat, to 7pm Thu, 10am-4pm Sun; 🚌470, 🚇Fortitude Valley) Fans of Camilla's statement-making silk kaftans include Beyoncé and Oprah Winfrey. And while the label may be Bondi based, its wildly patterned, resort-style creations – which also include frocks,

tops, jumpsuits and swimwear – are just the ticket for languid lounging in chi-chi Brisbane restaurants and bars. Fierce and fabulous, these pieces aren't cheap, with kaftans starting from $500 and bikinis at around $300.

Stock & Supply
FASHION & ACCESSORIES

(Map p290; ☎07-3061 7530; www.stockand supply.com.au; 4/694 Ann St; ☒Fortitude Valley) Technically on Bakery Lane, just off Ann St, this youthful, unisex bolthole serves up a cool selection of smaller surf and streetwear brands. Pick up anything from graphic tees to beachwear from the likes of skater outfit Crawling Death and surf-meets-art label The Critical Slide Society. The store also stocks wallets, jewellery, caps and footwear.

James Street
FASHION & ACCESSORIES

(Map p290; www.jamesst.com.au; James St; ☒470, ☒Fortitude Valley) Channeling LA with its low-slung architecture, sports cars and chic eateries is the Valley's glamtastic stretch of James St. Slip under its colonnade of fig trees for high-end boutiques, including celebrated Aussie fashion labels Scanlan & Theodore and Sass & Bide, homegrown designer Camilla Franks and Melbourne skincare brand Aesop.

Winn Lane
FASHION & ACCESSORIES

(Map p290; www.winnlane.com.au; Winn La; ☒Fortitude Valley) Duck behind Ann St (off Winn St) and discover this arty congregation of boutiques, bookshops, jewellers and casual eats. Spangled with street art, the lane has a vibe that is emerging and quirky. Don't miss **Miss Bond** (Map p290; ☎0410 526 082; www.facebook.com/missbond.com.au; 5g Winn Ln; ☺10am-4pm Wed-Sat, to 3pm Sun) for contemporary, locally designed jewellery, **Outpost** (Map p290; ☎07-3666 0306; www. theoutpoststore.com.au; 5 Winn St; ☺10am-6pm Tue-Thu & Sat, to 8pm Fri, 9.30am-4.30pm Sun) for in-the-know men's labels and accessories and, just off Winn Lane, **Tym Guitars** (Map p290; ☎07-3161 5863; www.tymguitars.com.au; 5 Winn St; ☺10am-5pm Tue-Thu & Sat, to 7pm Fri, 11am-4pm Sat), famed for its handmade guitar pedals, vintage guitars and punk-heavy vinyl collection.

TO MARKET, TO MARKET

Beyond the weekly farmers markets that feed the masses in **central Brisbane** (p299), **New Farm** (p275) and **West End** (p301) is a string of other fantastic local markets, peddling anything from handmade local fashion and bling, to art, skincare and out-of-the-box giftware. Hit the stalls at the following options.

Young Designers Market (Map p280; www.youngdesignersmarket.com.au; Little Stanley St, South Bank; ☺10am-4pm, 1st Sun of the month; ☒South Bank Terminal 3, ☒South Bank) Explore the work of up to 80 of the city's best emerging designers and artists, selling fashion and accessories, contemporary jewellery, art, furniture and homewares. Held beside South Bank Parklands, the market generally runs on the first Sunday of the month.

Collective Markets South Bank (Map p280; www.collectivemarkets.com.au; Stanley St Plaza; ☺5-9pm Fri, 10am-9pm Sat, 9am-4pm Sun; ☒South Bank Terminal 3, ☒South Bank) It might draw the tourist hordes, but this thrice-weekly event by South Bank Parklands peddles some great items, from artisan leather wallets and breezy summer frocks, to handmade jewellery, skincare, homewares and art.

Finders Keepers Markets (Map p272; www.thefinderskeepers.com/brisbane-markets; Old Museum, 480 Gregory Tce, Bowen Hills; adult/child $2/free; ☺hours vary; ☒370, 375, ☒Fortitude Valley) A biannual market with over 100 art and design stalls held in a 19th-century museum that's now a concert hall in inner-suburban Bowen Hills. Complete with live music and food, it's a great spot to score high-quality, one-off fashion pieces, jewellery and more from local and interstate design talent.

Brisbane Riverside Markets (p270) Come Sunday, chilled-out crowds gather at the northern end of the City Botanic Gardens for this weekly city-centre market. Scan the stalls for pretty, handmade frocks, scented candles, colourful ceramics and a plethora of street food from all corners of the globe. Live music keeps the mood festive and the peeps grooving.

Greater Brisbane

Paddington Antique Centre ANTIQUES
(Map p272; ☎ 07-3369 8088; www.paddington
antiquecentre.com.au; 167 Latrobe Tce, Paddington; ⊙ 10am-5pm Mon-Sat, to 4pm Sun; 🚌 375)
Built in 1929, this former theatre is now
a sprawling antiques emporium. Over 50
dealers sell all manner of treasure and trash
under a peeling, midnight-blue ceiling,
from flouncy English crockery, to retro fashion, lamps, toys, film posters, even the odd
17th-century Chinese vase. Take your time
and pay attention – you never know what
you might find.

Davies Park Market MARKET
(Map p286; www.daviesparkmarket.com.au; Davies
Park, West End; ⊙ 6am-2pm Sat; 🚌 199, 192, 198)
Under a grove of huge Moreton Bay fig
trees, this popular, laid-back Saturday market heaves with fresh produce, not to mention a gut-rumbling booty of multicultural
food stalls. Grab an organic coffee from The
Gyspy Vardo, sip it on a milk crate, then
scour the place for organic fruit and veggies,
artisanal provisions, herbs, flowers, handmade jewellery and even the odd bonsai.

ℹ️ Information

INTERNET ACCESS

Brisbane City Council offers free wi-fi access in
much of central Brisbane (the CBD), and you will
also find free wi-fi hot spots at South Bank Parklands, Roma Street Parkland, the State Library
of Queensland, James St in Fortitude Valley and
New Farm Park.

Brisbane Square Library (www.brisbane.qld.
gov.au; 266 George St; ⊙ 9am-6pm Mon-Thu,
to 7pm Fri, 10am-3pm Sat & Sun; 📶; 🚤 North
Quay, 🚉 Central) Free wi-fi access.

MEDICAL SERVICES

CBD Medical Centre (☎ 07-3211 3611; www.
cbdmedical.com.au; Level 1, 245 Albert St;
⊙ 7am-7pm Mon-Fri, 8.30am-5pm Sat, 9.30am-
5pm Sun; 🚉 Central) General medical services
and vaccinations.

Royal Brisbane & Women's Hospital (☎ 07-
3646 8111; www.health.qld.gov.au/rbwh; Butterfield St, Herston; 🚌 370, 375, 333) Located
3km north of the city centre. Has a 24-hour
casualty ward.

Travellers' Medical & Vaccination Centre
(TMVC; ☎ 07-3815 6900; www.traveldoctor.
com.au; 75a Astor Tce, Spring Hill; ⊙ 8.30am-
4.30pm Mon-Fri; 🚉 Central) Travellers' medical
services.

MONEY

American Express (☎ 1300 139 060; www.
americanexpress.com; 261 Queen St; ⊙ 9am-
5.30pm Mon-Fri; 🚉 Central) Foreign exchange
bureau.

Travelex (☎ 07-3210 6325; www.travelex.
com.au; Shop 149F, Myer Centre, Queen St
Mall; ⊙ 8am-6pm Mon-Thu, to 8pm Fri, 9am-
5pm Sat, 10am-4pm Sun; 🚉 Central) Money
exchange.

POST

Main Post Office (GPO; Map p280; ☎ 13
13 18; www.auspost.com.au; 261 Queen St;
⊙ 7am-6pm Mon-Fri, 10am-1.30pm Sat; 🚉 Central) Brisbane's main post office.

TOURIST INFORMATION

**Brisbane Visitor Information & Booking
Centre** (Map p280; ☎ 07-3006 6290; www.
visitbrisbane.com.au; The Regent, 167 Queen
St Mall; ⊙ 9am-5.30pm Mon-Thu, to 7pm Fri,
to 5pm Sat, 10am-5pm Sun; 🚉 Central) Terrific
one-stop info counter for all things Brisbane.

South Bank Visitor Information Centre (Map
p280; ☎ 07-3156 6366; www.visitbrisbane.
com.au; Stanley St Plaza, South Bank; ⊙ 9am-
5pm; 🚤 South Bank Terminal 3, 🚉 South Bank)
One of Brisbane's official tourist information
hubs, with brochures, maps and festival guides,
plus tour and accommodation bookings, and
tickets to entertainment events.

ℹ️ Getting There & Away

AIR

Sixteen kilometres northeast of the city centre,
Brisbane Airport (p1067) is the third-busiest
airport in Australia and the main international
airport serving Brisbane and southeastern
Queensland.

It has separate international and domestic terminals about 2km apart, linked by the **Airtrain**
(p302), which runs every 15 to 30 minutes
from 5am (6am on weekends) to 10pm (between
terminals $5/free per adult/child).

It's a busy hub, with frequent domestic connections to other Australian capital cities and
regional towns, as well as nonstop international
flights to New Zealand, the Pacific islands, North
America and Asia (with onward connections to
Europe and Africa).

BUS

Brisbane's main bus terminus and booking office
for long-distance buses is the **Brisbane Transit
Centre** (Roma St Station; www.brisbane
transitcentre.com.au; Roma St), about 500m
northwest of the city centre. It also incorporates
Roma St train station, which services both
long-distance and suburban trains.

Booking desks for **Greyhound** (📱 1300 473 946, 07-4690 9850; www.greyhound.com.au) and **Premier Motor Service** (📱 13 34 10; www. premierms.com.au) are here.

Long-haul routes include Cairns, Darwin and Sydney though it's usually just as affordable to fly, not to mention a lot quicker.

CAR & MOTORCYCLE

Brisbane has an extensive network of motor-ways, tunnels and bridges (some of them tolled) run by **Transurban Queensland** (📱 13 33 31; www.govianetwork.com.au). The Gateway Motor-way (M1) runs through Brisbane's eastern suburbs, shooting north towards the Sunshine Coast and northern Queensland and south towards the Gold Coast and Sydney. See the Transurban Queensland website for toll details and fees.

Major car rental companies have offices at Brisbane Airport and in the city. Smaller rental companies with branches near the airport (and shuttles to get you to/from there) include **Ace Rental Cars** (📱 1800 620 408; www.acerental cars.com.au; 330 Nudgee Rd, Hendra), **Apex Car Rentals** (📱 1800 558 912; www.apexrentacar. com.au; 400 Nudgee Rd, Hendra) and **East Coast Car Rentals** (📱 1800 327 826; www.eastcoast carrentals.com.au; 504 Nudgee Rd, Hendra).

TRAIN

Brisbane's main station for long-distance trains is Roma St Station (essentially the same complex as the Brisbane Transit Centre). For reservations and information contact **Queensland Rail** (📱 13 16 17; www.queenslandrail.com.au).

NSW TrainLink Brisbane to Sydney

Spirit of Queensland Brisbane to Cairns

Spirit of the Outback Brisbane to Longreach via Bundaberg, Gladstone and Rockhampton

Tilt Train Brisbane to Rockhampton via Bundaberg and Gladstone

Westlander Brisbane to Charleville

ℹ Getting Around

Brisbane's excellent public-transport network – bus, train and ferry – is run by TransLink, which runs a Transit Information Centre at Roma St Station (Brisbane Transit Centre). The tourist offices in the **city centre** (p301) and **South Bank** (p301) can also help with public transport information. Complimenting the network is a nifty network of bike paths.

TO/FROM THE AIRPORT

Airtrain (📱 1800 119 091; www.airtrain.com. au; adult one-way/return $17.50/33) services run every 15 to 30 minutes from 5am (6am on weekends) to 10pm, connecting Brisbane airport's two terminals to central Brisbane. Handy stops include Fortitude Valley, Central Station, Roma St Station (Brisbane Transit Centre),

South Brisbane and South Bank (one-way/return $17.50/33). Trains continue to the Gold Coast (one-way from $33.70).

Con-X-ion (📱 1300 370 471; www.con-x-ion. com) runs regular shuttle buses between the airport and hotels in the Brisbane city centre (one-way/return $20/36). It also connects Brisbane Airport to Gold Coast hotels and private residences (one-way/return $49/92), as well as to Sunshine Coast hotels and private residences (one-way/return from $52/96). Book tickets online.

A taxi to central Brisbane costs $50 to $60.

CAR & MOTORCYCLE

Ticketed two-hour parking is available on many streets in the CBD and the inner suburbs. Heed the signs: Brisbane's parking inspectors are pretty ruthless. During the day, parking is cheaper around South Bank and the West End than in the city centre, but it's free in the CBD in the evening from 6pm weekdays (from noon on Saturday). For more detailed information on parking, see www.visitbrisbane.com.au/parking.

PUBLIC TRANSPORT

Buses, trains and ferries operate on an eight-zone system: all of the inner-city suburbs are in Zone 1, which translates into a single fare of $4.60/2.30 per adult/child. If travelling into Zone 2, tickets are $5.70/2.85.

If you plan to use public transport for more than a few trips, you'll save money by purchasing a **Go Card** (www.translink.com.au/tickets-and-fares/go-card; starting balance adult/child $10/5). Purchase the card, add credit and then use it on city buses, trains and ferries, and you'll save more than 30% off individual fares. Go Cards are sold (and can be recharged) at transit stations, 7-Eleven convenience stores, newsagents, by phone or online. You can also top-up on CityCat ferry services (cash only).

Boat

CityCat (p278) catamarans service 18 ferry terminals between the University of Queensland in St Lucia and Northshore Hamilton. Handy stops include South Bank, the three CBD terminals, New Farm Park (for Brisbane Powerhouse) and Bretts Wharf (for Eat Street Markets). Services run roughly every 15 minutes from 5.20am to around midnight. Tickets can be bought on board or, if you have one, use your Go Card.

Free **CityHopper ferries** zigzag back and forth across the water between North Quay, South Bank, the CBD, Kangaroo Point and Sydney St in New Farm. These additional services start around 6am and run till about 11pm.

TransLink also runs **Cross River Ferries**, connecting Kangaroo Point with the CBD, and New Farm Park with Norman Park on the adjacent shore (and also Teneriffe and Bulimba further north). Ferries run every 10 to 30 minutes from around 6am to around 11pm. Fares/zones apply as per all other Brisbane transport.

For more information, including timetables, see www.brisbaneferries.com.au.

Bus

Brisbane's bus network is extensive and especially handy for reaching West End, Kangaroo Point, Woolloongabba, Fortitude Valley, Newstead, as well as Paddington.

In the city centre, the main stops for local buses are the underground **Queen Street Bus Station** (Map p280) and **King George Square Bus Station** (Map p280). You can also pick up many buses from the stops along Adelaide St, between George and Edward Sts.

Buses generally run every 10 to 30 minutes, from around 5am (around 6am Saturday and Sunday) till about 11pm.

CityGlider and BUZ services are high-frequency services along busy routes. Tickets cannot be purchased on board CityGlider and BUZ services; use a Go Card (p302).

Free, hop-on, hop-off City Loop and Spring Hill Loop bus services circle the CBD and Spring Hill, stopping at key spots like QUT, Queen Street Mall, City Botanic Gardens, Central Station and Roma Street Parkland. Buses run every 10 minutes on weekdays between 7am and 6pm.

Brisbane also runs dedicated nocturnal Night-Link bus, train and fixed-rate taxi services (the latter from specified taxi ranks) from the city and Fortitude Valley. See translink.com.au for details.

Train

TransLink's **Citytrain network** has six main lines, which run as far north as Gympie on the Sunshine Coast and as far south as Varsity Lakes on the Gold Coast. All trains go through Roma St Station, Central Station and Fortitude Valley Station; there's also a handy South Bank Station.

The **Airtrain** service integrates with the Citytrain network in the city centre and along the Gold Coast line.

Trains run from around 4.30am, with the last train on each line leaving Central Station between 11.30pm and midnight (later on Friday and Saturday). On Sunday the last trains run at around 11pm or 11.30pm.

Single train tickets can be bought at train stations, or use your Go Card.

For timetables and a network map, see www.translink.com.au.

TAXI

There are numerous taxi ranks in the city centre, including at Roma St Station, Treasury (corner of George and Queen Sts), Albert St (corner of Elizabeth St) and Edward St (near Elizabeth St). You might have a tough time hailing one late at night in Fortitude Valley: there's a rank near the corner of Brunswick St and Ann St, but expect long queues. The main taxi companies are **Black & White** (☎13 32 22; www.blackandwhitecabs.com.au) and **Yellow Cab Co** (☎13 19 24; www.yellowcab.com.au).

NightLink flat-fare taxis run on Friday and Saturday nights, with dedicated ranks at Elizabeth Street (corner of George St) in the city and on Warner St in Fortitude Valley.

AROUND BRISBANE

North Stradbroke Island

POP 2030

An easy 30-minute ferry chug from the Brisbane suburb of Cleveland, this unpretentious holiday isle is like Noosa and Byron Bay rolled into one. There's a string of glorious powdery white beaches, great surf and some quality places to stay and eat. It's also a hot spot for spying dolphins, turtles, manta rays and, between June and November, hundreds of humpback whales. 'Straddie' also offers freshwater lakes and 4WD tracks.

At Point Lookout, the eye-popping **North Gorge Headlands Walk** is an absolute highlight. It's an easy 20-minute loop around the headland along boardwalks, with the thrum of cicadas as your soundtrack. Keep an eye out for turtles, dolphins and manta rays offshore. The view from the headland down Main Beach is a showstopper.

About 8km east of Dunwich on Alfred Martin Way is the car park for **Naree Budjong Djara National Park** (www.nprsr.qld.gov.au/parks/naree-budjong-djara; Alfred Martin Way). From here, take the 2.6km walking track to Straddie's glittering centrepiece, **Blue Lake (Kaboora)**: keep an eye out for forest birds, skittish lizards and swamp wallabies along the way. There's a wooden viewing platform at the lake, which is encircled by a forest of paperbarks, eucalypts and banksias. You can cool off in the water, if you don't mind the spooky unseen depths.

North Stradbroke Island Historical Museum (☎07-3409 9699; www.stradbrokemuseum.com.au; 15-17 Welsby St, Dunwich; adult/child $5/1; ⊙10am-2pm Tue-Sat, 11am-3pm Sun) describes shipwrecks and harrowing voyages, and gives an introduction to the island's rich Aboriginal history (the Quandamooka are

the traditional owners of Minjerribah, aka Straddie).

Activities

Manta Lodge & Scuba Centre
DIVING

(07-3409 8888; www.mantalodge.com.au; 132 Dickson Way, Point Lookout; wetsuit/surfboard hire $20/30, diving course from $500) Based at the YHA (p305), Manta Scuba Centre offers a broad range of options. You can hire a wetsuit, mask, snorkel and fins ($25 for 24 hours) or a surfboard, or take the plunge with a diving course. Snorkelling trips (from $60) include a boat trip and all gear.

North Stradbroke Island Surf School
SURFING

(07-3409 8342; www.northstradbrokeislandsurf school.com.au; lessons from $50) Small-group, 1½-hour surf lessons in the warm Straddie waves. Solo lessons available if you're feeling bashful.

Straddie Adventures
KAYAKING

(0433 171 477; www.straddieadventures.com.au; adult/child sea-kayaking trips from $75/40, sandboarding $35/30) Operated by the area's traditional Aboriginal owners, this outfit runs insightful sea-kayaking trips with an Indigenous cultural bent. Sandboarding sessions are also offered.

Sleeping & Eating

Straddie Camping
CAMPGROUND $

(07-3409 9668; www.straddiecamping.com. au; 1 Junner St, Dunwich; 4WD sites from $16.55, powered/unpowered sites from $39/32, cabins from $120; booking office 8am-4pm Mon-Sat) There are eight island campgrounds operated by this outfit, including two 4WD-only fore-shore sites (permits required – $43.75). The best of the bunch are grouped around Point Lookout: **Cylinder Beach**, **Adder Rock** and **Home Beach** all overlook the sand. **Amity**

Point campground has new eco-cabins. Good weekly rates; book well in advance.

Manta Lodge YHA HOSTEL $

(☑ 07-3409 8888; www.mantalodge.com.au; 132 Dickson Way, Point Lookout; dm/d/tw/f from $35/90/90/115; @ �Ⓡ) This affable, three-storey hostel has clean (if unremarkable) rooms and a great beachside location. There's a communal firepit out the back, a curfew-free kitchen, cosy communal spaces, plus a dive school downstairs. Rental options include surfboards, bodyboards, stand-up paddleboards, bikes and snorkelling gear. Wi-fi is free in communal area and $5 for 24 hours in the dorms.

★Allure APARTMENT $$$

(☑ 1800 555 200, 07-3415 0000; www.allurestrad broke.com.au; 43-57 East Coast Rd, Point Lookout; bungalows/villas from $175/250; ✸ �Ⓡ ☒) Set in a leafy compound with a pool, a gym and a kitchen garden for guests, Allure offers large, spotless, contemporary bungalows and villas. Bungalows are a studio-style affair with kitchenette and mezzanine bedroom, while villas offer full kitchens and separate bedrooms. All have private laundry facilities and outdoor deck with barbecues. While there isn't much space between the shacks, they're cleverly designed with privacy in mind.

★Island Fruit Barn CAFE $

(☑ 07-3409 9125; 16 Bingle Rd, Dunwich; mains $10-16; ☺ 7am-5pm Mon-Fri, to 4pm Sat, 8am-4pm Sun; ☑) On the main road in Dunwich, Island Fruit Barn is a casual little congregation of tables with excellent breakfasts, smoothies, salads, sandwiches, winter soups and cakes, many gluten free or vegan, and all made using top-quality ingredients. Order the scrumptious spinach-and-feta roll, then stock up on fresh produce and gourmet condiments in the super-cute grocery section.

Blue Room Cafe CAFE $

(☑ 0438 281 666; 27 Mooloomba Rd, Point Lookout; dishes $10-18; ☺ 7.30am-2.30pm, providore to 5.30pm Mon-Sat, to 2pm Sun; ☑) A youthful, beach-shack-chic cafe, with a small alfresco terrace and fresh, feel-good dishes like red papaya filled with kiwi fruit and strawberries and topped with granola and cacao crunch; organic-egg omelette with spinach and goats-milk cheese; and generous fish tacos jammed with grilled fish and house-made Mexican black-bean corn salsa. Small bites include cookies and yummy vegan

snacks. The adjoining providore is aptly named the Green Room.

❶ Getting There & Away

The hub for ferries to North Stradbroke Island is the Brisbane seaside suburb of Cleveland. From here, **Stradbroke Ferries** (☑ 07-3488 5300; www.stradbrokeferries.com.au; return per vehicle incl passengers from $110, walk-on adult/child $10/5; ☺ 5.30am-8pm) offers passenger/vehicle services to Dunwich and back (45 minutes, 12 to 17 times daily). Cheaper online fares are available for vehicles. **Gold Cats Stradbroke Flyer** (☑ 07-3286 1964; www.flyer. com.au; Middle St, Cleveland; return adult/ child/family $19/10/50; ☺ 5am-7.30pm) runs passenger-only trips daily between Cleveland and One Mile Jetty at Dunwich (30 minutes, 13 to 14 daily). A free Stradbroke Flyer courtesy bus picks up water-taxi passengers from the Cleveland train station 10 minutes prior to most water taxi departures (see the website for exclusions).

Regular Citytrain (www.translink.com.au) services run from Brisbane's Central and Roma St Stations (as well as the inner-city stations of South Bank, South Brisbane and Fortitude Valley) to Cleveland station ($8.60, one hour). Buses to the ferry terminal meet the trains at Cleveland station (seven minutes).

❶ Getting Around

Straddie is big: it's best to have your own wheels to explore it properly. If you plan to go off-road, you can get information and buy a 4WD permit ($43.75) from **Straddie Camping** (p304).

Alternatively, **Stradbroke Island Buses** (☑ 07-3415 2417; www.stradbrokeislandbuses. com.au) meet the ferries at Dunwich and run to Amity and Point Lookout (one-way/return $4.70/9.40). Services run roughly every hour and the last bus to Dunwich leaves Point Lookout at 6.20pm. Cash only.

There's also the **Stradbroke Cab Service** (☑ 0408 193 685), which charges around $60 from Dunwich to Point Lookout.

Straddie Super Sports (☑ 07-3409 9252; www.straddiesupersports.com.au; 18 Bingle Rd, Dunwich; hire per hr/day mountain bikes $10/50, kayaks $15/60, SUP board $10/50; ☺ 8am-4.30pm Mon-Fri, to 3pm Sat, 9am-2pm Sun) in Dunwich hires out mountain bikes (per hour/day $10/50).

Moreton Island

POP 300

If you're not going further north in Queensland than Brisbane but want a fix of tropical bliss, sail over to Moreton Island. Its prelapsarian beaches, dunes, bushland and lagoons are protected, with 95% of the isle comprising the **Moreton Island National Park & Recreation Area** (www.nprsr.qld. gov.au/parks/moreton-island). Apart from a few rocky headlands, it's all sand, with Mt Tempest, the highest coastal sand hill in the world, towering high at a lofty 280m. Off the west coast are the rusty, hulking Tangalooma Wrecks, which provide excellent snorkelling and diving.

The island has a rich history, from early Aboriginal settlements to the site of Queensland's first and only whaling station at Tangalooma, which operated between 1952 and 1962.

🔘 Sights & Activities

Around half a dozen dolphins swim in from the ocean and take fish from the hands of volunteer feeders each evening. You have to be a guest of the Tangalooma Island Resort to participate, but onlookers are welcome. Also at the resort is the **Tangalooma Marine Education & Conservation Centre** (☑1300 652 250; www.tangalooma.com; Tangalooma Island Resort; ⊙10am-noon & 1-4pm), which has a display on the diverse marine and bird life of Moreton Bay.

Island bushwalks include a desert trail (two hours) leaving from Tangalooma Island Resort, as well as the strenuous trek up Mt Tempest, 3km inland from Eagers Creek – worthwhile, but you'll need transport to reach the start.

Cape Moreton Lighthouse offers great views when the whales are passing by.

Moreton Bay Escapes (☑1300 559 355; www.moretonbayescapes.com.au; 1-day tour adult/child from $200/140, 2-day camping tours from $360/250) 🢒 runs informative one-, two- and three-day 4WD tours that will have you snorkelling or kayaking, sandboarding, marine wildlife-watching and hiking. **Adventure Moreton Island** (☑07-3410 6927; www. adventuremoretonisland.com; 1-day tours from $145) runs a day tours, among them an Island Adrenaline Tour ($189), allowing you to choose four activities from a list that includes quad-bike riding, sandboarding, and snorkelling at the Tangalooma Wrecks.

Tangalooma hosts the island's sole **resort** (☑1300 652 250, 07-3637 2000; www.tangalooma. com; Tangalooma; d from $210, 2-/3-/4-bedroom apt from $480/510/550; 🅿️@🛜🏊). There are also five national-park **camping areas** (☑13 74 68; www.nprsr.qld.gov.au/experiences/camping;

sites per person/family $6.15/24.60) on Moreton Island, all with water, toilets and cold showers. Book online or by phone before you get to the island.

ℹ️ Getting There & Away

Several ferries operate from the mainland. To explore once you get to the island, bring a 4WD or take a tour. Most tours are ex-Brisbane, and include ferry transfers.

Micat (☑07-3909 3333; www.micat.com.au; Tangalooma; return adult/child from $52/35, standard 4WD incl 2 people $200-300) Vehicle ferry services from Port of Brisbane to Tangalooma around eight times weekly (75 to 90 minutes); see the website for directions to the ferry terminal.

Tangalooma Flyer (☑07-3637 2000; www.tangalooma.com; return adult/child $80/45) Fast passenger catamaran operated by Tangalooma Island Resort. It makes the 75-minute trip to the resort three to four times daily from Holt St Wharf in the Brisbane suburb of Pinkenba (see the website for directions).

Amity Trader (☑07-3820 6557; www.amity trader.com; 4WD/walk-on passengers return $270/40) Runs vehicle barges for 4WD vehicles and walk-on passengers from the Brisbane suburb of Victoria Point to Kooringal on Moreton Island several times monthly. See the website for the current timetable.

Toowoomba

POP 114,620

Squatting on the edge of the Great Dividing Range, 700m above sea level, Toowoomba is a sprawling country hub with wide tree-lined streets and stately homes. While it isn't a see-it-before-you-die kind of place, it does have a few surprises up its sleeve for those who stay a day or two.

Along with some fine heritage buildings and gardens, Toowoomba has also become a hub for street art, with several outstanding **murals** and the annual **First Coat Art & Music Festival** (www.firstcoat.com.au; ⊙May).

🔘 Sights

Cobb & Co Museum   MUSEUM
(☑07-4659 4900; www.cobbandco.qm.qld.gov.au; 27 Lindsay St; adult/child/family $12.50/6.50/32; ⊙10am-4pm) Immediately north of Queens Park, this engaging, child-friendly museum houses Australia's finest collection of horse-drawn vehicles, including beautiful 19th-century Cobb & Co Royal Mail coaches and an omnibus used in Brisbane until 1924.

Hands-on displays depict town life and outback travel during the horse-powered days, and the museum also houses a blacksmith forge and an interesting Indigenous section, with shields, axe heads, boomerangs, plus animated films relating Dreaming stories. Look for the spinning windmills out the front.

Picnic Point   PARK
(www.picnic-point.com.au; Tourist Rd; ☺24hr, cafe-restaurant 8.30am-5pm Mon-Thu, to 9pm Fri, 8am-9pm Sat, 8am-5pm Sun) **FREE** Riding high on the rim of the Great Dividing Range and strung along the eastern edge of town are Toowoomba's Escarpment Parks, the pick of which is Picnic Point. You'll find walking trails, plenty of namesake picnic spots, a playground for kids, as well as a cafe-restaurant (mains $14 to $35). That said, what everyone really comes for are the eye-popping views over the Lockyer Valley. It's from here that you can really appreciate just how lofty Toowoomba really is.

Toowoomba Regional Art Gallery   GALLERY
(☑07-4688 6652; www.tr.qld.gov.au/facilities-recreation/theatres-galleries/galleries; 531 Ruthven St; ☺10am-4pm Tue-Sat, 1-4pm Sun) **FREE** Toowoomba's modestly sized art gallery houses an interesting collection of paintings, ceramics and drawings. Its permanent exhibition of Australian art includes works by late 19th- and early 20th-century greats such as Tom Roberts, Arthur Streeton and Rupert Bunny, while the adjacent room showcases mainly European decorative arts from the 17th to 19th centuries. Call ahead to view the gallery's notable library, a treat of rare books, maps and manuscripts. The venue also hosts regular touring exhibitions.

Queens Park Botanic Gardens   GARDENS
(www.tr.qld.gov.au; cnr Lindsay & Campbell Sts; ☺24hr) **FREE** Toowoomba's showpiece botanical gardens are a blaze of colour in the spring and autumn. Graced with parterre gardens, neat English flower beds, palms and conifers, they're a perfect spot for a picnic or a lazy read-and-snooze. You'll find the gardens in the northeast corner of Queens Park, across the street from the Cobb & Co Museum.

🛏 Sleeping & Eating

Toowoomba Motor Village   CARAVAN PARK $
(☑1800 675 105; www.toowoombamotorvillage. com.au; 821 Ruthven St; powered/unpowered sites $38/32, cabins & units $72-130; ❄☎) This trim-and-tidy hillside park is a 2.5km hike south

of the centre, but it is well equipped and offers views over the suburbs.

★**Vacy Hall**   GUESTHOUSE $$
(☑07-4639 2055; www.vacyhall.com.au; 135 Russell St; d $135-245; ☎) Uphill from the town centre, this magnificent 1873 mansion (originally a wedding gift from a cashed-up squatter to his daughter) offers 12 heritage-style rooms with no shortage of authentic charm. A wide verandah wraps around the house, all rooms have en suites or private bathrooms, and most have working fireplaces. Super-high ceilings make some rooms taller than they are wide. Free wi-fi.

Junk Asian   ASIAN $
(☑0474 744 425; www.junkboat.com.au; 5/476 Ruthven St; dishes $10-20; ☺11am-10pm) One of several trendy eateries at the Walton Stores redevelopment, this casually hip Pan-Asian eatery is the brainchild of two-hatted chef Tony Kelly. Under a slithering Chinese dragon, young and old get chin and fingers messy over street-food staples like ramen with slow-cooked egg and pork, green papaya salad, and addictive Chinese bao stuffed with soft shell crab, chipotle, burnt lime kewpie and pickled slaw.

Firefly   CAFE $$
(☑07-4564 9197; www.thefireflycafe.com.au; 100 Russell St; mains lunch $16.50-22, dinner $26-29; ☺7am-3pm Tue-Sat, plus 5.30-8pm Fri; ☑) With street art on the wall and plastic farm animals on the tables, warm, kooky Firefly occupies a former car-detailing workshop on the edge of the city centre. High-quality, seasonal produce drives generous, honest dishes like toasted brioche with grilled peaches, sweet dukkah and whipped coconut cream, not to mention a lusty Brekky Burger (with bacon, fried eggs, spinach and onion jam). Great coffee too.

ℹ Information

Toowoomba Visitor Information Centre
(☑1800 331 155, 07-4639 3797; www.southern queenslandcountry.com.au; 86 James St; ☺9am-5pm; ☎) Located southeast of the centre, at the junction with Kitchener St. Peel yourself off a vast bed-sheet-sized map of town. Also stocks self-guided *Toowoomba Tourist Drive* maps.

ℹ Getting There & Away

Toowoomba is 126km west of Brisbane on the Warrego Hwy. **Greyhound** (p302) services

QUEENSLAND TOOWOOMBA

run eight times daily between Brisbane Airport, central Brisbane and Toowoomba ($35, two hours), and once daily to Stanthorpe ($47, 2½ hours) further south. **Murrays** ([☎]132 251; www.murrays.com.au) also runs services between Brisbane Airport, central Brisbane and Toowoomba (from $24, four daily), though less frequently. Toowoomba's **main bus station** (cnr Neil St & Bell St Mall) serves both city and long-distance routes.

From Brisbane Airport, the **Airport Flyer** ([☎]1300 304 350, 07-4630 1444; www.theairportflyer.com.au; one-way/return $75/140) runs six daily door-to-door services to/from Toowoomba. The cost is cheaper for more than one passenger.

Granite Belt

Dappling the western flanks of the Great Dividing Range about 210km southwest of Brisbane, the Granite Belt is Queensland's only real wine region, where hillsides are lined with cool-climate vineyards, olive groves and orchards growing apples, pears, plums and peaches.

Stanthorpe

POP 5385

Queensland's coolest town (literally), Stanthorpe is one of the state's lesser-known tourist drawcards. Today, functional Stanthorpe and the tiny village of Ballandean, about 20km to the south, claim a flourishing wine industry, with cellar-door sales, on-site dining, vineyard events and boutique accommodation.

But it's not all wine and song: the Granite Belt's changing seasons also make it a prime fruit-growing area, with plenty of fruit picking available for backpackers who don't mind chilly mornings.

Most of the Granite Belt wineries are located south of Stanthorpe around Ballandean. Pick up a map and brochure from the **Stanthorpe Visitor Information Centre** ([☎]1800 762 665, 07-4681 2057; www.granitebeltwinecountry.com.au; 28 Leslie Pde, Stanthorpe; [⊙]9am-4pm).

Aside from local wineries you can visit the **Granite Belt Brewery** ([☎]07-4681 1370; www.granitebeltbrewery.com.au; 146 Glenlyon Dr, Stanthorpe; [⊙]10am-midnight, restaurant noon-2.30pm & 5.30pm-late), or delve into history at the **Stanthorpe Heritage Museum** ([☎]07-4681 1711; www.halenet.com.au/~jvbryant/museum.html; 12 High St, Stanthorpe; adult/child/family $7/3.50/20; [⊙]10am-4pm Wed-Fri, 1-4pm Sat, 9am-1pm Sun).

[🛏] Sleeping & Eating

Backpackers of Queensland HOSTEL $
([☎]0429 810 998; www.backpackersofqueensland.com.au; 80 High St, Stanthorpe; dm per week $195; [❄]) The management here helps young fruit pickers find work, and accommodates them in utilitarian comfort. There's a minimum one-week stay in five-bed dorms with en suites. No booze, drugs, smoking or monkey business.

Top of the Town Tourist Park CARAVAN PARK $
([☎]07-4681 4888; www.topoftown.com.au; 10 High St, Stanthorpe; powered sites $48, cabin/motel d from $120/125; [❄][@][🐾][⛱]) A bushy site on the northern side of Stanthorpe, this is a serviceable option if you're here for seasonal work in the vineyards and orchards.

[★]Diamondvale B&B Cottages COTTAGE $$
([☎]07-4681 3367; www.diamondvalecottages.com.au; 26 Diamondvale Rd, Stanthorpe; 1-/2-/4-bedroom from $160/320/650; [🐾]) In atmospheric bushland outside of Stanthorpe (expect to see kangaroos, koalas and echidnas), Diamondvale consists of four lovely private cottages and a four-bedroom lodge, each with old-fashioned details, a wood-burning fireplace, kitchen and verandah. The communal barbecue hut is a winner, as is the hospitality of owners Tony and Kerryn. Walk 2km along the creek into town or simply jump in for a swim.

Aussie Beef Steakhouse STEAK $$
([☎]07-4681 1533; www.aussiebeefsteakhouse.com.au; 1 High St, Stanthorpe; mains $20-38; [⊙]6-7.30pm Tue-Thu, to 8pm Fri & Sat) A modest, family-friendly eatery serving impressive bits of beef (rib, rump, eye or porterhouse fillets), plus other meaty mains like beef-cheek and shiraz pie or pork loin with a maple and paprika glaze. The steakhouse is tacked onto the side of a motel on the northern edge of town.

Brass Monkey Brew House MICROBREWERY
([☎]0488 967 401; www.brassmonkeybrewhouseptyltd.com; 106 Donges Rd, Severnlea; [⊙]10am-6pm Thu-Mon) Just south of Stanthorpe is this award-winning, family-run microbrewery. Occupying a humble tin shed scattered with communal tables and a fireplace, its small-batch beers (made using local hops) are listed on blackboards along the wall. Slurp on anything from German pilsner to English brown ale, best paired with the family's celebrated Bratwurst sausage. Other bites might

include decent beef-cheek pie and a stout-soaked burger (naturally).

ℹ Getting There & Away

Crisps Coaches (☑ 07-4661 8333; www.crisps.com.au) runs services from Brisbane to Stanthorpe ($69, 3¼ hours, one to three daily) via Warwick. One daily service continues on to Tenterfield in NSW (except on Saturday), stopping in Glen Alpin and Ballandean en route. The company also runs three daily services from Toowoomba to Stanthorpe ($49, two to 3½ hours) on weekdays, reduced to one service daily on weekends.

GOLD COAST

Built for pleasure, and remaining a place utterly dedicated to sun, surf and the body beautiful, this strip of coast is possibly Australia's most iconic holiday destination. Its shimmering high-rises can, when glimpsed from afar, appear like a make-believe city, and its reputation for tackiness is occasionally deserved. But this is far outstripped by a booming, youthful spirit and startling physical beauty: some 52km of pristine sand and countless epic surf breaks, heartbreakingly hazy sunsets, blissful water temperatures and 300 sunny days a year.

ℹ Getting There & Away

AIR

Gold Coast Airport (p1067) is in Coolangatta, 25km south of Surfers Paradise. All the main Australian domestic airlines fly here. **Scoot** (www.flyscoot.com), **Air Asia** (☑ 1300 760 330; www.airasia.com) and **Air New Zealand** (☑ 13 24 76; www.airnewzealand.com.au) fly in from overseas.

Brisbane Airport (p1067) is 16km northeast of Brisbane city centre and accessible by train. It is a useful arrival point for the Gold Coast, especially for international visitors.

BUS

Premier Motor Service (☑ 13 34 10; www.premierms.com.au) A couple of daily services head to Brisbane (from $21, 1½ hours), Byron Bay (from $29, 2½ hours) and other coastal areas.

Greyhound (www.greyhound.com.au) Has frequent services to/from Brisbane ($23, 1½ hours), Byron Bay ($35, 2½ hours) and beyond.

TRAIN

TransLink (☑ 13 12 30; https://translink.com.au) Citytrain services connect Brisbane with Nerang, Robina and Varsity Lakes stations on

the Gold Coast (75 minutes) roughly every half hour. The same line extends north of Brisbane to Brisbane Airport.

ℹ Getting Around

TO/FROM THE AIRPORT

Gold Coast Tourist Shuttle (☑ 1300 655 655, 07-5574 5111; www.gcshuttle.com.au; one way per adult/child $22/13) Meets flights into Gold Coast Airport and transfers to most Gold Coast accommodation. Also runs to Gold Coast theme parks.

Con-X-ion Airport Transfers (☑ 1300 266 946; www.con-x-ion.com) Transfers to/from Gold Coast Airport (one way adult/child from $22/13), Brisbane airport (one way from adult/child $49/25) and Gold Coast theme parks.

Byron Bay Xcede (www.byronbay.xcede.com.au) Transfers from Gold Coast Airport to hotels and private addresses in Byron Bay, prebooking advised (adult/child $37/18.50)

BUS

Surfside Buslines (☑ 13 12 30; www.surfside.com.au), a subsidiary of Brisbane's main TransLink operation, runs regular buses up and down the Gold Coast, plus shuttles from the Gold Coast train stations into Surfers Paradise and beyond (including the theme parks).

Surfside, in conjunction with Gold Coast Tourist Shuttle, also offers a Freedom Pass, which includes return Gold Coast Airport transfers, unlimited theme-park transfers and local bus travel for $78/39 per adult/child. It's valid for

Gold Coast & Hinterland

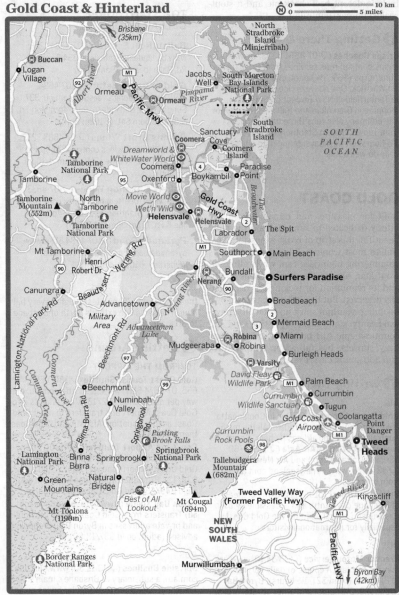

three days; five-, seven- and 10-day passes are also available.

TRAM

G:link (Gold Coast Light Rail; ☑ 13 12 30; http://translink.com.au) is a handy if rather pricey light rail and tram service connecting Southport and Broadbeach with stops along the way. It's worth buying a Go Explore day pass (adult/child $10/5; available only from 7-Eleven shops) if you're doing more than one very short trip. Otherwise you can buy single-trip tickets (from $4.80) from a machine on the tram platform.

Surfers Paradise

POP 22,150

Some may mumble that paradise has been lost, but there's no denying that Surfers' frenetic few blocks and its glorious strip of sand attracts a phenomenal number of visitors – 20,000 per day at peak. Party-hard teens and early-20-somethings come here for a heady dose of clubs, bars, malls and perhaps a bit of beach-time as a hangover remedy before it all starts again. Families like the ready availability of big apartments, loads of kid-friendly eating options and, yes, that beautiful beach.

◎ Sights & Activities

SkyPoint Observation Deck   VIEWPOINT
(www.skypoint.com.au; Level 77, Q1 Bldg, Hamilton Ave, Surfers Paradise; adult/child/family $24/14/62; ⊙ 7.30am-8.30pm Sun-Thu, to 11.30pm Fri & Sat) Surfers Paradise's best sight is best observed from your beach towel, but for an eagle-eye view of the coast and hinterland, zip up to this 230m-high observation deck near the top of Q1, one of the world's notably tall buildings. You can also tackle the **SkyPoint Climb** up the spire to a height of 270m (adult/child from $74/54).

Cheyne Horan School of Surf   SURFING
(☎ 1800 227 873; www.cheynehoran.com.au; 2hr lessons $49; ⊙ 10am & 2pm) Learn to carve up the waves at this school, run by former pro surfer Cheyne Horan. Multilesson packages reduce the cost.

Balloon Down Under   BALLOONING
(☎ 07-5500 4797; www.balloondownunder.com; 1hr flights adult/child $279/225) Up, up and away on sunrise flights over the Gold Coast, ending with a champagne breakfast.

✲ Festivals & Events

★ Bleach Festival   CULTURAL
(www.bleachfestival.com.au; ⊙ early Apr) Visual-art shows, contemporary dance, music of all genres, theatre and performances, held in a variety of indoor and outdoor spaces. There's a late-summer party vibe, with the occasional superstar performer heading the bill, as well as some edgy and provocative work.

Gold Coast 600   SPORTS
(www.v8supercars.com.au) For three days in October the streets of Surfers are transformed into a temporary race circuit for high-speed racing cars.

⌂ Sleeping

Budds in Surfers   HOSTEL $
(☎ 07-5538 9661; www.buddsinsurfers.com.au; 6 Pine Ave, Surfers Paradise; dm $32-34, d $95-110; @ 중 ☒) Laid-back Budds features tidy bathrooms, clean tiles, a sociable bar and a nice pool, all just a short hop from calm Budds Beach. Bike hire available. Female-only dorms are available on request and there's one double with en suite.

Sleeping Inn Surfers   HOSTEL $
(☎ 1800 817 832, 07-5592 4455; www.sleepinginn.com.au; 26 Peninsular Dr, Surfers Paradise; dm $30-34, d $78-92; @ 중 ☒) This backpackers occupies an old apartment block away from the centre, so, as the name suggests, there's a chance you may get to sleep in. Larger dorms come with their own kitchen and bathroom and most have a private living area. Note, no children allowed, and guests in dorm rooms must have an international passport. An adjoining apartment block offers some renovated private rooms.

Chateau Beachside Resort   APARTMENT $
(☎ 07-5538 1022; www.chateaubeachside.com.au; cnr Elkhorn Ave & Esplanade, Surfers Paradise; studio/1-bedroom apt $99/119; ❉ @ 중 ☒) Less Loire Valley, more Las Vegas, this seaside 'chateau' (actually an 18-storey tower) has studios and apartments that are individually furnished, and all but the very cheapest have ocean views. The 18m pool is a bonus. Minimum two-night stay.

★ Island   HOTEL $$
(☎ 07-5538 8000; www.theislandgoldcoast.com.au; 3128 Surfers Paradise Blvd; d $180-250; P ❉ 중 ☒) The fabulously faded Islander Hotel has been reborn as the Island and it's indeed an island of contemporary style in this corner of Surfers. Rooms have standard low ceilings but their natural timber, whitewash and monochromatic palette makes for a soothing bolthole. Plus they're spacious – doubles are 27 sq metres, suites 45 sq metres – and have king-sized beds.

★ QT   HOTEL $$
(☎ 07-5584 1200; www.qtgoldcoast.com.au; 7 Staghorn Ave, Surfers Paradise; d $185-280; ❉ 중 ☒) Acapulco chairs, retro bikes and preppy-styled staff are a deliberate take on the mid-century-design glory days of Surfers. The clever transformation of what was yet another bland '80s tower really does work, with an airy lobby you'll be happy to

Surfers Paradise

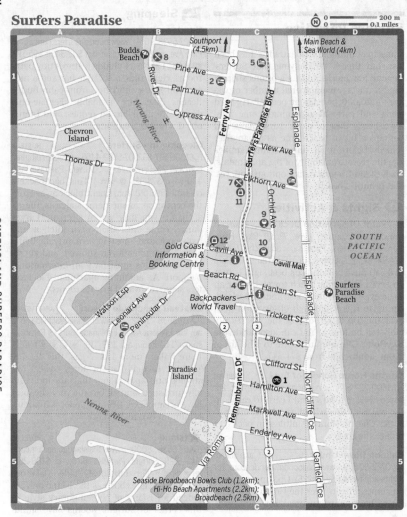

hang about in. Room interiors are less nostalgic, but have plenty of colour pops.

Eating

Self-caterers will find supermarkets in the **Chevron Renaissance Shopping Centre** (www.chevronrenaissanceshoppingcentre.com. au; cnr Elkhorn Ave & Surfers Paradise Blvd, Surfers Paradise; ⊙9am-5.30pm Mon-Sat, 10am-4pm Sun) and **Circle on Cavill** (www.circleoncavill. com.au; cnr Cavill & Ferny Aves, Surfers Paradise; ⊙9am-5.30pm Mon-Sat, 10am-4pm Sun).

★ **Bumbles Café**   CAFE **$$**
(☑07-5538 6668; www.bumblescafe.com; 21 River Dr, Budds Beach, Surfers Paradise; mains $14-24; ⊙7.30am-4pm) This gorgeous spot – a converted house (actually, at one stage, a brothel) – is the place for breakfast, sweet treats and coffee. It comprises a series of rooms, from the pink Princess Room (perfect for afternoon tea) to a library. Serves up some very desirable cakes.

Surfers Sandbar   MODERN AUSTRALIAN **$$**
(☑07-5526 9994; www.facebook.com/sandbargc; 52 Esplanade, Surfer Paradise; mains $18-29; ⊙6.30am-midnight) After a staggering 19 years in beachside business, the owners here handed over the reigns to their son. Back from serious hospitality work in Bali, he transformed Sandbar into a Riviera-meets-Canggu hot spot, full of intriguing interior details, happy locals and creative, globally inflected dishes.

Baritalia   ITALIAN **$$**
(☑07-5592 4700; www.baritaliagoldcoast.com.au; Shop 15, Chevron Renaissance Centre, cnr Elkhorn Ave & Surfers Paradise Blvd, Surfers Paradise; pizzas $20-28, lunch specials $14-16, mains $20-38; ⊙8am-late; 🛜) A thoroughly Italian place with a fab outdoor terrace and friendly, European staff. Go for the Byron Bay slow-roasted pork belly, or excellent pastas, pizzas and risotto (including gluten-free choices). Decent Australian and Italian wines by the glass and good coffee.

Drinking & Nightlife

★ **Elsewhere**   CLUB
(☑07-5592 6880; www.elsewherebar.com; 23 Cavill Ave, Surfers Paradise; ⊙9pm-4am Thu-Sun) A Saturday Night Fever–style dance floor always bodes well for good times, and this little bar-to-club venue features DJs who know their electronica, including cracking live sets from the soon-to-be-famous. Crowds

ⓘ SCHOOLIES ON THE LOOSE

Every year in November, thousands of teenagers flock to Surfers Paradise to celebrate the end of their high-school education in a raging three-week party known as Schoolies Week. Although local authorities have stepped in to regulate excesses, boozed-up and drug-addled teens are still the norm. It's not pretty.

For more info, see www.schoolies.com.

are cooler than elsewhere but it's a friendly, conversation-filled place until DJs seriously turn up the volume.

Black Coffee Lyrics   BAR, CAFE
(☑0402 189 437; www.facebook.com/blackcoffee lyrics; 40/3131 Surfers Paradise Blvd, Surfers Paradise; ⊙5pm-late Tue-Fri, from 8am Sat & Sun) Upstairs and hidden in an unexpected location – within a nondescript arcade – this is the antithesis to Surfers shiny. Filled with vintage furniture and bordering on grungy, it's a dark oasis where locals come for coffee and tapas-style dishes, for steaks, and for bourbon, boutique brews and espresso martinis until late. Weekend breakfasts are hearty and there's the option of beer or bloody Marys from 10am.

ⓘ Information

Backpackers World Travel (☑07-5561 0634; www.backpackerworldtravel.com; 3063 Surfers Paradise Blvd, Surfers Paradise; ⊙10am-4pm; 🛜) Accommodation, tour and transport bookings and internet access.

Gold Coast Information & Booking Centre (☑1300 309 440, 07-5536 4709; www.visit goldcoast.com; 2 Cavill Ave, Surfers Paradise; ⊙8.30am-5pm Mon-Fri, 9am-6pm Sat, 9am-4pm Sun) The main Gold Coast tourist information booth; also sells theme-park tickets and has public transport info.

Main Beach & The Spit
POP 3970

North of Surfers Paradise, Main Beach makes for a serene base if you're here for views, beach time and generally taking it easy. Further north the Spit separates the Southport Broadwater from the Pacific Ocean, stretching 5km to almost meet South Stradbroke Island.

⦿ Sights & Activities

Main Beach Pavilion
ARCHITECTURE

(Macarthur Pde; ⊙9am-5pm) FREE The lovely Spanish Mission–style Main Beach Pavilion (1934) is a remnant from pre-boom days. Inside are some fabulous old photos of the Gold Coast before the skyscrapers.

★ Federation Walk
WALKING

(www.federationwalk.org) This pretty 3.7km trail takes you through patches of fragrant littoral rainforest, flush with beautiful bird life, and runs parallel to one of the world's most beautiful strips of surf beach. Along the way it connects to the Gold Coast Oceanway, which heads 36km to Coolangatta. Federation Walk begins and finishes at the entrance to Sea World, in the car park of Phillip Park.

Australian Kayaking Adventures
KAYAKING

(☑0412 940 135; www.australiankayakingadven tures.com.au; half-day tours adult/child $85/75, sunset tours $55/45) Paddle out to underrated South Stradbroke Island, or take a dusk paddle around Chevron Island in the calm canals behind Surfers.

Island Adventures
WHALE WATCHING

(☑07-5532 2444; www.goldcoastadventures.com. au; Mariner's Cove, 60-70 Sea World Dr, Main Beach; cruises incl lunch adult/child $129/69) Alternatively gawp at wildlife and the Broadwater's sprawling McMansions on this catamaran cruise that includes water sports and a BBQ lunch on Mclaren's Landing Eco Resort.

🛏 Sleeping & Eating

Surfers Paradise YHA at Main Beach
HOSTEL $

(☑07-5571 1776; www.yha.com.au; 70 Sea World Dr, Main Beach; dm $33-36, d & tw $85; @🛜) Despite the Surfers Paradise of the name, this is a great 1st-floor position overlooking the marina. There's a free shuttle bus, BBQ nights every Friday, and the hostel is within wobbling distance of the Fisherman's Wharf Tavern. Sky-blue dorms; very well organised. Can also arrange tours and activities.

Main Beach Tourist Park
CARAVAN PARK $

(☑07-5667 2720; www.goldcoasttouristparks.com. au; 3600 Main Beach Pde, Main Beach; powered sites $62, cabins & villas from $165; P❄🛜🏊) Just across the road from the beach and surrounded by a phalanx of high-rise apartments, this caravan park is a family favourite. It's a tight fit between sites, but the facilities are good and the location is iconic.

Pacific Views
APARTMENT $$

(☑07-5527 0300; www.pacificviews.com.au; cnr Main Beach Pde & Woodroffe Ave, Main Beach; 1-bedroom apt $140-210; P❄🛜🏊) If you can cope with decor surprises, these individually owned and furnished apartments have amazing floor-to-ceiling views, living-room sized balconies and helpful staff. They're just one block back from the beach, and there's a cafe downstairs that will make you coffee at 5.30am if you're up for an early beach wander.

Peter's Fish Market
SEAFOOD $

(☑07-5591 7747; www.petersfish.com.au; 120 Sea World Dr, Main Beach; meals $9-16; ⊙9am-7.30pm) A no-nonsense fish market–cum–fish and chip shop selling fresh and cooked seafood. It's fresh from the trawlers, in all shapes and sizes, and at great prices. Kitchen opens at noon.

★ Pier
MODERN AUSTRALIAN, PIZZA $$

(☑07-5527 0472; www.piermarinamirage.com. au; Ground fl, Marina Mirage, Sea World Dr, Main Beach; pizzas $18-24; ⊙noon-11.30pm) An easy but super-stylish marina-side spot, with upstairs and downstairs seating, both perfect for yachtie views. The mostly European staff is winning and the menu is flexible. Wood-fired pizzas can be combined with arancini (which get their own menu), or there are small and large dishes that tick a number of culinary boxes without being faddish.

★ Bar Chico
MODERN AUSTRALIAN $$

(☑07-5532 9111; www.barchico.com.au; 26-30 Tedder Ave, Main Beach; dishes $12-22; ⊙4pm-midnight Mon-Wed, from noon Thu-Sun) A welcome addition to the Tedder strip, this dark and moody European-style bar does fabulous cheese and charcuterie plates, fish or meat tapas-style dishes and big, beguiling salads. Displays a chef-like attention to detail, with in-house fermenting and curing, and lots of high-end ingredients. Wine is similarly thoughtful, with some particularly nice Spanish drops.

Providore
CAFE $$

(☑07-5532 9390; www.providoremirage.com.au; Marina Mirage, 74 Sea World Dr, Main Beach; mains $16-29; ⊙7am-6pm) Floor-to-ceiling windows rimmed with Italian mineral-water bottles, inverted desk lamps dangling from the ceiling, good-looking Euro tourists, wines by the glass, perfect patisserie goods, cheese fridges, and baskets overflowing with fresh produce: this excellent deli-cafe gets a lot of things right.

★ **Gourmet Farmers Market** MARKET
(☑07-5555 6400; www.facebook.com/Marina MirageFarmersMarket; Marina Mirage, 74 Sea World Dr, Main Beach; ⊙7-11am Sat) On Saturday mornings the open spaces of the Marina Mirage mall fill with stalls selling seasonal fruit and veg, baked goods, pickles, oils, vinegars, seafood, pasta and more, all from small-scale producers and makers.

Broadbeach, Mermaid & Nobby Beach

POP 19,890

Directly south of Surfers Paradise, Broadbeach may be all about apartment towers and pedestrian malls, but it's decidedly more upmarket than its neighbour, with carefully landscaped streets and smart places to eat, drink and shop.

Miami Marketta (www.miamimarketta.com; 23 Hillcrest Pde, Miami; ⊙cafe 6am-2pm Tue-Sat, street food 5-10pm Wed, Fri & Sat) is a permanent street market with food, fashion and live music, a smidge south of Mermaid in just-as-cool Miami.

🛏 Sleeping & Eating

Hi-Ho Beach Apartments APARTMENT $$
(☑07-5538 2777; www.hihobeach.com.au; 2 Queensland Ave, Broadbeach; 1-/2-bedroom apt $175/275; P❋☎❆) A top choice for location, close to the beach and cafes. You're not paying for glitzy lobbies here, but rooms are

---

GOLD COAST THEME PARKS

The gravity-defying roller-coasters and water slides at the Gold Coast's American-style parks offer some seriously dizzying action and, although recently beset with a number of accidents, still attract huge crowds. Discount tickets are sold in most of the tourist offices on the Gold Coast or can be bought online (☑13 33 86; www.themeparks.com.au). The Mega Pass ($110 per person for 14-day entry) grants unlimited entry to Sea World, Warner Bros. Movie World, Wet'n'Wild and the little-kid-friendly farm-park Paradise Country (all owned by Village Roadshow). Dreamworld and WhiteWater World have a Summer Season Pass giving unlimited entry (adult/child $99/79).

A couple of tips: the parks can get insanely crowded, so arrive early or face a long walk from the car park. Also note that the parks don't let you bring your own food or drinks.

Dreamworld (☑07-5588 1111, 1800 073 300; www.dreamworld.com.au; Dreamworld Pkwy, Coomera; adult/child $65/55; ⊙10am-5pm) Touts itself as Australia's 'biggest' theme park. There are the 'Big 9 Thrill Rides', plus Wiggles World and the DreamWorks experience, both for younger kids. Other attractions include Tiger Island, and a range of interactive animal encounters. A one-day pass (adult/child $65/55) gives you entry to both Dreamworld and WhiteWater World.

Sea World (www.seaworld.com.au; adult/child $80/70; ⊙9.30am-5pm) Continues to attract controversy for its marine shows, where dolphins and sea lions perform tricks for the crowd. While Sea World claims the animals lead a good life, welfare groups argue that keeping such sensitive sea mammals in captivity is harmful, and is especially exacerbated when mixed with human interaction. The park also displays penguins and polar bears, and has water slides and roller-coasters.

Movie World (☑07-5573 3999, 13 33 86; www.movieworld.com.au; Pacific Hwy, Oxenford; adult/child $79/69; ⊙9.30am-5pm) Movie-themed shows, rides and attractions, including the Batwing Spaceshot, Justice League 3D Ride and Scooby-Doo Spooky Coaster. Batman, Austin Powers, Porky Pig et al roam through the crowds.

Wet'n'Wild (☑07-5556 1660, 13 33 86; www.wetnwild.com.au; Pacific Hwy, Oxenford; adult/child $79/69; ⊙10am-5pm) The ultimate water slide here is the Kamikaze, where you plunge down an 11m drop in a two-person tube at 50km/h. This vast water park also has pitch-black slides, white-water rapids and wave pools.

WhiteWater World (☑1800 073 300, 07-5588 1111; www.dreamworld.com.au/whitewater-world; Dreamworld Pkwy, Coomera; adult/child $65/55; ⊙10am-4pm Mon-Fri, to 5pm Sat & Sun) This park features the Cave of Waves, Pipeline Plunge and more than 140 wet and watery activities and slides.

comfortable and it's well managed, clean and quiet. And, hey, the Vegas-esque sign!

★ **Sparrow**

Eating House MODERN AUSTRALIAN $

(☑ 07-5575 3330; www.sparroweatinghouse.com. au; 2/32 Lavarack Rd, Nobby Beach; sharing dishes $11-22; ⊙ 5pm-midnight Wed-Fri, from 7am Sat & Sun) This lovely clean-lined monochrome industrial space with green accents has a low-key glamour and a kitchen that loves what it does. Come for a casual lunch of spring gnocchi with hazelnuts and herbs; enjoy a blood-orange margarita and some tequila prawns; or pop in for a glass of small-producer wine.

Cardamom Pod VEGETARIAN $

(www.cardamompod.com.au; 1/2685 Gold Coast Hwy, Broadbeach; 1/2/3/4 dishes with rice $10/16/24/31; ⊙ 11.30am-9.30pm; ☑) 🔗 Vegetarians rejoice! This magical Krishna-inspired, vegan-friendly eatery conjures up some of the best vegetarian cuisine around. Choose from curry, vegan bake or cheesy bake of the day. Finish off with a trademark dessert: raw, gluten- and sugar-free (and delicious). Everything is made from scratch on the premises.

★ **Glenelg Public House** STEAK $$

(☑ 07-5575 2284; www.theglenelgpublichouse. com.au; 2460 Gold Coast Hwy, Mermaid Beach; mains $22-32; ⊙ 5pm-midnight Mon-Thu, from noon Fri-Sun) A passionate little place, this atmospheric eating and drinking den uses premium produce and has a light hand with accompaniments. The epic steak list ($22 to $68, sharing $80 to $90) takes in local breeds, the best of New Zealand and New South Wales tablelands and both grass- and grain-fed cuts. There's also an 'early tea' dinner special before 6.30pm.

★ **BSKT Cafe** MODERN AUSTRALIAN $$

(☑ 07-5526 6565; www.bskt.com.au; 4 Lavarack Ave, Mermaid Beach; mains $10-27; ⊙ 7am-4pm Mon-Thu, to 10pm Fri & Sat, to 5pm Sun; ☑ 👶) This satisfyingly industrial cafe is 100m from the beach, but that's far from its only charm. It's the brainchild of four buddies whose focus is organic produce, and the dishes and service punch well above cafe level. Vegans and paleos will be equally at home here, as will kids – there's a fenced play area – and yogis – there's an upstairs yoga school.

🍷 Drinking & Nightlife

★ **Cambus Wallace** COCKTAIL BAR

(www.thecambuswallace.com.au; 4/2237 Gold Coast Hwy, Nobby Beach; ⊙ 5pm-midnight Tue-Thu, from 4pm Fri-Sun) Dark, moody, maritime-themed bar that attracts a good-looking but relaxed local crew. Settle in with something from its long, long list of bottled beer and cider, or try a Gold Coast take on cocktail classics (there's no Dark 'n' Stormy but a coconut, lime and rum Maiden Voyage could not be better suited to the climate).

Seaside Broadbeach Bowls Club CLUB

(☑ 07-5531 5913; www.broadbeachbowlsclub.com; 169 Surf Pde, Broadbeach; ⊙ 11.30am-8pm) Home to the best bowling greens in Australia – some say, the world. Far from a tired old space, this traditional club has had a modern makeover with its bars and restaurants bright, breezy and beachy. Come for a sunset beer on the huge terrace, and barefoot bowls.

Burleigh Heads

POP 9580

The super-chilled surfie enclave of Burleigh (drop the 'Heads', you're already fond friends, right?) has long been a family favourite, but is currently having its moment in the sun. The town's gently retro vibe and palpable youthful energy epitomise both the Gold Coast's timeless appeal and its new, increasingly interesting, spirit. You'll find some of the region's best cafes and restaurants dotted around its little grid and, yes, that famous right-hand point break still pumps while the beautiful pine-backed beach continues to charm everyone who lays eyes on it.

🅾 Sights

Burleigh Head National Park PARK

(www.npsr.qld.gov.au/parks/burleigh-head; Goodwin Tce, Burleigh Heads; ⊙ 24hr) FREE Walk the headland through Burleigh Head National Park, a 27-hectare rainforest reserve with plenty of bird life and several walking trails. Gives great views of the Burleigh surf.

★ **Village Markets** MARKET

(☑ 0487 711 850; www.thevillagemarkets.co; Burleigh Heads State School, 1750 Gold Coast Hwy, Burleigh Heads; ⊙ 8.30am-1pm 1st & 3rd Sun of month) A long running market that highlights local designers, makers and collectors,

GOLD COAST'S BEST SURF

The Gold Coast possesses some of the longest, hollowest and best waves in the world, and is lauded for its epic consistency. The creation of the Superbank – a sand bar that's formed as part of anti-erosion efforts and stretches 2km from the Queensland–New South Wales border up to Kirra – has made for a decade of even better waves, even more often.

Snapper Rocks A highly advanced point break at Coolangatta's far south; home to the Quiksilver Pro World Surfing League, and home break to Australian pro surfers Stephanie Gilmore and Joel Parkinson.

Duranbah Universally known as D-bah, this point and peaky beach break is good for those who like their waves technical and punchy.

Greenmount Classic beach break that benefits from a southerly swell – sightings of pro surfers Mick Fanning and Joel Parkinson are not uncommon.

Kirra Beautiful beach break that doesn't work that often, but, oh when it does.

Burleigh Heads Strong currents and boulders to watch out for, but a perfect break that's more often on than not.

The Spit One of north Goldie's stalwarts, this peaky beach break can work even when the surf is small.

with fashion and lifestyle stalls, lots of live music and a strong local following.

David Fleay Wildlife Park WILDLIFE RESERVE
(☑ 07-5576 2411; www.npsr.qld.gov.au/parks/david-fleay; cnr Loman Lane & West Burleigh Rd, West Burleigh; adult/child/family $22/10/55; ⊗ 9am-5pm) Opened by the doctor who first succeeded in breeding platypuses, this wildlife park has 4km of walking tracks through mangroves and rainforest, and plenty of informative native wildlife shows throughout the day. It's around 3km inland from Burleigh Heads.

Jellurgal Cultural Centre CULTURAL CENTRE
(☑ 07-5525 5955; www.jellurgal.com.au; 1711 Gold Coast Hwy, Burleigh Heads; ⊗ 8am-3pm Mon-Fri) ✐ FREE This Aboriginal cultural centre at the base of Burleigh's headland sheds some light on life here hundreds and thousands of years ago. There's a collection of artefacts and a number of different tours (various prices) of the local areas available – all include walks to the headland (Jellurgal, the Dreaming Mountain), past middens and important Aboriginal sites.

🛏 Sleeping & Eating

Burleigh Break MOTEL $
(www.burleighbreak.com.au; 1935 Gold Coast Hwy, Burleigh Heads; d $120-160; P �3) A progressive renovation has seen one of the Gold Coast's beloved mid-century motels transformed into a friendly and great-value place to stay. Classic motel design means highway views but you're still just a minute's amble from the beach. Rooms have retained vintage features where possible, but otherwise are fresh and simple. Ask about long-stay discounts.

**Burleigh Beach
Tourist Park** CARAVAN PARK $
(☑ 07-5667 2750; www.goldcoasttouristparks.com.au; 36 Goodwin Tce, Burleigh Heads; powered sites $46-60, cabins $140-210; ❄ @ �3 ⛴) This council-owned park is snug, but it's well run and in a great spot near the beach. Aim for one of the three blue cabins at the front of the park. There's a minimum two-night stay for cabins.

★ **Borough Barista** CAFE $
(14 Esplanade, Burleigh Heads; mains $5-19; ⊗ 5.30am-2.30pm) It's all cool tunes and friendly vibes at this little open-walled espresso shack. Join local surfers for their dawn piccolo lattes and post-surf for a chia bowl or breakfast salad on a footpath bench. Lunches revolve around good proteins with burgers or big salads.

Paddock Bakery BAKERY $
(☑ 0419 652 221; www.paddockbakery.com; Hibiscus Haven, Miami; dishes $9-17; ⊗ 7.30am-2.30pm) An antique wood-fired oven sits in the heart of this beautiful old weatherboard cottage and turns out wonderful bread, croissants,

granola and pastries. The semi-sourdough donuts have a devoted fan base, as do the Nutella doughboats – spherical shaped so as to fit more goo. There's a full breakfast and lunch menu, too, as well as top coffee and cold-pressed juices.

Burleigh Social CAFE $
(2 Hibiscus Haven, Burleigh Heads; dishes $12-19; ⏱6am-2pm) This backstreet cafe has a party vibe from early morning at its picnic-table seating. There's paleo granola or the big paleo breakfast (salmon, bacon or ham with kale, eggs and avocado) or nicely done versions of Australian cafe staples such as smashed avocado, eggs on sourdough and bacon-and-egg rolls. Brisket subs and veggie burgers take it into lunch.

★**Rick Shores** MODERN ASIAN $$
(⏱07-5630 6611; www.rickshores.com.au; 43 Goodwin Tce, Burleigh Heads; mains $32-52; ⏱noon-11pm Tue-Sun) Feet-in-the-sand dining can often play it safe, and while this Modern Asian newcomer sends out absolute crowd-pleasing dishes, it's also pleasingly inventive. The space is all about the view, the sound of the nearby waves, the salty breeze and communal-table conviviality. Serves are huge, which can allay the menu price if you're not dining solo and are into sharing.

★**Harry's Steak Bistro** STEAK $$
(⏱07-5576 8517; www.harryssteakbistro.com.au; 1744 Gold Coast Hwy, Burleigh Heads; mains $20-40; ⏱5-11pm Wed & Thu, noon-11pm Fri-Sun) Don't misread the menu – a mix and match steak-and-sauce affair, plus unlimited fries – as belonging to a chain restaurant. Harry's, a stylish, sparse paean to 'beef, booze and banter', is super-serious about its steaks, with each accredited with the name of its farm and region.

★**Justin Lane Pizzeria & Bar** PIZZA $$
(⏱07-5576 8517; www.justinlane.com.au; 1708 Gold Coast Hwy, Burleigh Heads; pizzas $19-24; ⏱5pm-late) One of the seminal players in Burleigh's food and drinking scene, Justin Lane has now colonised most of an old shopping arcade. Yes, the fun stretches upstairs, downstairs and across the hall. Great pizzas, simple but flavour-packed pasta dishes and possibly the coast's best regional Italian wine list make it a must, even if you're not here for the party vibe.

🍷 Drinking & Nightlife

Black Hops Brewing BREWERY
(www.blackhops.com.au; 15 Gardenia Grove, Burleigh Heads; ⏱10am-6pm Mon-Fri, noon-4pm Sat) The Black Hops boys run a friendly and fun tap room where you can enjoy a paddle or whatever craft delight they've currently got on tap. There are eight poetically named beers – from the Bitter Fun pale ale to the Flash Bang white IPA – to choose from, or you can purchase whatever they have bottled.

Burleigh Brewing Company BREWERY
(⏱07-5593 6000; www.burleighbrewing.com.au; 17a Ern Harley Dr, Burleigh Heads; monthly tours $50; ⏱3-6pm Wed & Thu, to 8.30pm Fri, 2-8pm Sun) Hang out in this light, woody and blokey space with fellow beer lovers. There's live music and local food trucks, not to mention a 24 tap line-up of Burleigh brews, including its main line and pilot project beers. Tours run on Wednesday nights mid-month and need to be booked through the website.

Currumbin & Palm Beach
POP 16,310

Around the point from Burleigh, Palm Beach has a particularly lovely stretch of sand, backed with a few old-style beach shacks. Its numbered streets are also home to some great coffee stops and dining ops. Further south again, Currumbin is a sleepy family-focused town, with a beautiful surf beach, safe swimming in Currumbin Creek and some evocative mid-century architecture worth clocking. It's also home to the iconic eponymous wildlife sanctuary.

◎ Sights & Activities

Kids will enjoy a swim at **Currumbin Rock Pools** (Currumbin Creek Rd, Currumbin Valley).

The **Currumbin Wildlife Sanctuary** (⏱07-5534 1266, 1300 886 511; www.cws.org.au; 28 Tomewin St, Currumbin; adult/child/family $49/35/133; ⏱8am-5pm) includes Australia's biggest rainforest aviary, where you can hand-feed a Technicolor blur of rainbow lorikeets. There's also kangaroo feeding, photo ops with koalas and crocodiles, reptile shows and Aboriginal dance displays. Entry is reduced after 3pm, and there's often an adults-at-kids-prices special during school holidays.

✗ Eating & Drinking

Feather & Docks
CAFE $

(☑07-5659 1113; www.featheranddocks.com.au; 1099 Gold Coast Hwy, Palm Beach; dishes $12-18; ☺5.30am-3pm; ☑) Given the witness-the-fitness early-to-rise lifestyle round these parts, the notion of breakfast burgers and lunch that starts at 10.30am makes a lot of sense. That said, most things on the menu work for either breakfast or lunch, from the French toast to the brekky tortilla to the stacked pastrami melts.

★ Bstow
MODERN AUSTRALIAN $$

(☑0410 033 380; www.bstow.com.au; 8th Ave Plaza, 1176 Gold Coast Hwy, Palm Beach; mains $18-24) Best-of-both-worlds Bstow is somewhere you'll want to hang with a drink – it does very special cocktails; think house-infused gin and freshly pressed, muddled or juiced mixers – but also warrants a leisurely dinner – the sharing-plate-style dishes are seriously considered, easy on the eye and a creative mix of tastes and textures.

Collective
MODERN AUSTRALIAN $$

(www.thecollectivepalmbeach.com.au; 1128 Gold Coast Hwy, Palm Beach; mains $17-24; ☺noon-9pm) Locals' favourites come together here, with five kitchens serving one great, rambling indoor-outdoor communal dining space, strung with fairy lights, flush with pot plants and packed with up to 300 happy eaters. There are two bars, one of them a balmy rooftop affair. Choose from burgers, pizza, tapas, Asian fusion, Mexican and Mod Oz share plates. You can even head here for a post-surf breakfast at 7am.

★ Balter
BREWERY

(☑07- 5525 6916; www.balter.com.au; 14 Traders Way, Currumbin; tasting paddles $12; ☺3-9pm Fri, 1-8pm Sat & Sun) Local surf star Mick Fanning (the man who punched a shark, right?) and his fellow circuit legends Joel Parkinson, Bede Durbidge and Josh Kerr are all partners in this wonderful new brewery, hidden away at the back of a Currumbin industrial estate. Come and sample the already sought-after Balter XPA or a special such as the German-style Keller pilsner.

Coolangatta

POP 5710

A down-to-earth beach town on Queensland's far southern border, 'Coolie' has quality surf beaches, including the legend-ary Superbank, and a tight-knit, very real community that makes it feel less touristy than it otherwise could. The legendary **Coolangatta Gold** (www.sls.com.au/cool angattagold) surf-lifesaving comp happens here every October and the **Quicksilver and Roxy Pro** (www.aspworldtour.com) kicks off surfing's most prestigious world tour at Snapper Rocks each March. Follow the boardwalk north around Kirra Point for another beautiful long stretch of beach, sometimes challenging surf, and locally loved indie-atmosphere cafes and bars.

Point Danger Light, the lighthouse on the headland between Coolangatta and Tweed Heads, marks the border between Queensland and New South Wales and offers amazing views along the coast.

For local surfing lessons, try **Gold Coast Surfing Centre** (☑0417 191 629; www.gold coastsurfingcentre.com; group lessons $45) or **Cooly Surf** (☑07-5536 1470; 25 Griffith St, Coolangatta; 2hr surfing lessons $45; ☺9am-5pm).

🛏 Sleeping & Eating

Coolangatta Sands Backpackers
HOSTEL $

(☑07-5536 7472; www.taphousegroup.com.au/coolangatta-sands-backpackers; cnr Griffith & McLean Sts, Coolangatta; dm $17-25, d $68-80; ❄@🖙) Above the boozy Coolangatta Sands Hotel, this hostel is a warren of rooms and corridors, but there's a fab wrap-around balcony above the street (no booze allowed unfortunately – go downstairs to the pub) and red chesterfields in the TV room for when it's raining.

Kirra Beach Tourist Park
CARAVAN PARK $

(☑07-5667 2740; www.goldcoasttouristparks.com.au; 10 Charlotte St, Kirra; powered/unpowered sites $39/35, s/d $65/140, cabins $125-140; ❄@🖙⛱) A large council-run park with plenty of trees, wandering ibises and a camp kitchen and heated swimming pool. Good-value self-contained cabins (with or without bathroom), all a few hundred metres from the beach.

★ La Costa Motel
MOTEL $$

(☑07-5599 2149; www.lacostamotel.com.au; 127 Golden Four Dr, Bilinga; d $130-185; ❄🖙) One of the few motels of 1950s 'highway heritage', this mint-green weatherboard, located just off the Gold Coast Hwy, has stayed true to its roots on the outside, while the interiors are neat, comfortable and include kitchenettes. A lovely apartment with a private deck suits longer stays. Prices are significantly lower outside high season.

★ **Hotel Komune**   HOTEL, HOSTEL $$
(☑ 07-5536 6764; www.komuneresorts.com; 146 Marine Pde, Coolangatta; dm $38-45, 1-bedroom apt $140-180, 2-bedroom apt $185-300; 🛜🕸) With a palm-laden pool area and an ultra laid-back vibe, this 10-storey converted apartment tower is the ultimate surf retreat. It has budget dorms, apartments and a hip penthouse begging for a party. That said, the party is usually to be found downstairs, at the on-site bar (well, nightclub) from around 9pm, with music Fridays to Sundays.

Cafe Dbar   MODERN AUSTRALIAN $$
(☑ 07-5599 2031; www.cafedbar.com.au; 275 Boundary St, Coolangatta; mains $19-27; ⊙ 11.15am-3pm Mon-Thu, to 8pm Fri-Sun) This lovely spot is perched above the cliffs of Point Danger, at the easternmost point of two states, almost on top of the NSW–Queensland border. You can deliberate on any number of fabulous breakfast options, grab a good takeaway coffee, or stay for share plates and salads. There's also a stylish little shop attached for a postprandial browse.

★ **Black Sheep Espresso Baa**   CAFE
(☑ 07-5536 9947; www.tbseb.com.au; 72-80 Marine Pde, Coolangatta; ⊙ 5am-3pm) A passionate crew of coffee obsessives run this cute little cafe right in the heart of the Marine Pde shopping strip. Perfect espresso, filter coffee and that Gold Coast necessity, iced lattes, are joined by a small but creative breakfast and lunch menu.

🍷 **Drinking & Nightlife**

★ **Eddie's Grub House**   BAR
(☑ 07-5599 2177; www.eddiesgrubhouse.com; 171 Griffith St, Coolangatta; ⊙ noon-10.30pm Tue-Thu & Sun, to midnight Fri & Sat) An old-school rock-and-roll bar, with dirty blues and best-of rock soundtrack, Eddie's is emblematic of the new Gold Coast: indie, ironic and really fun. Yes, there's grub to be had, and Eddie's 'dive bar comfort food' is exactly that. But this is a place for drinking, dancing, chatting and chilling (as they say themselves).

Coolangatta Hotel   PUB
(www.thecoolyhotel.com.au; cnr Marine Pde & Warner St, Coolangatta; ⊙ 10am-late) The hub of Coolangatta's sometimes boisterous nocturnal scene, this huge pub, right across from the beach, pumps with live bands (Grinspoon, The Rubens), sausage sizzles, pool comps, trivia nights, acoustic jam nights, surprisingly sophisticated pub-meal deals (pasta and rosé, anyone?) – basically, the works. Big Sunday sessions.

Gold Coast Hinterland

Inland from the surf and sand of the Gold Coast, the densely forested mountains of the McPherson Range feel a million miles away. There are some brilliant national parks here, with subtropical jungle, waterfalls, lookouts and rampant wildlife.

Tamborine Mountain

The squat, mountain-top rainforest community of Tamborine Mountain – comprising Eagle Heights, North Tamborine and Mt Tamborine – is 45km inland from the Gold Coast beaches, and has cornered the arts-and-craft, Germanic-kitsch, package-tour, chocolate-fudge-liqueur market in a big way. If this is your bag, **Gallery Walk** (☑ 07-5545 2006; 197 Long Rd, Eagle Heights) in Eagle Heights is the place to stock up.

OFF THE BEATEN TRACK

SOUTH STRADBROKE ISLAND

This narrow, 21km-long sand island is largely undeveloped and full of wildlife – the perfect antidote to the Gold Coast's busyness. At its northern end, the narrow channel separating it from North Stradbroke Island is a top fishing spot; at its southern end, where the Spit is only 200m away, you'll find breaks so good they have Gold Coast's surfers braving the swim over.

South Stradbroke was once attached to North Stradbroke, until a huge storm in 1896 blasted through the isthmus that joined them. You can charter a boat or do a day tour with **Water'bout** (☑ 0401 428 004; www.waterbout.com.au; Waterways Dr Boat Ramp, Proud Park, Main Beach; tours per adult $125).

Campers should head to North Currigee, South Currigee or Tipplers **campgrounds** (www.goldcoasttouristparks.com.au/straddie-park-home; camp sites/cabins/huts $26/149/68).

Tamborine National Park (www.nprsr.qld.gov.au/parks/tamborine) comprises 13 sections stretching across the 8km plateau, offering waterfalls and super views of the Gold Coast. Accessed via easy-to-moderate walking trails are Witches Falls, Curtis Falls, Cedar Creek Falls and Cameron Falls. Pick up a map at the visitor centre in North Tamborine.

With **Skywalk** (☑07-5545 2222; www.rainforestskywalk.com.au; 333 Geissman Dr, North Tamborine; adult/child/family $20/10/49; ⊙9.30am-4pm) you can take a 1.5km walk descending down into the forest floor to pretty Cedar Creek, with spectacular elevated steel viewpoints and bridges cutting through the upper canopy along the way. Look out for rare Richmond birdwing butterflies en route.

Lamington National Park

Australia's largest remnant of subtropical rainforest cloaks the deep valleys and steep cliffs of the McPherson Range, reaching elevations of 1100m on the Lamington Plateau. Here, the 200-sq-km **Lamington National Park** (www.nprsr.qld.gov.au/parks/lamington) is a Unesco World Heritage Site and has more than 160km of walking trails.

The two most accessible sections of the park are **Binna Burra** and **Green Mountains**, both reached via long, narrow, winding roads from Canungra (not great for big campervans). Binna Burra can also be accessed from Nerang.

Green Mountains Campground (☑13 74 68; www.nprsr.qld.gov.au/parks/lamingtoncamping.html; Green Mountains; site per person/family $6.15/24), at the end of Lamington National Park Rd, is adjacent to the day-use visitor car park. There are plenty of spots for tents and caravans (and a toilet-and-shower block); book in advance.

Binna Burra Mountain Lodge (☑1300 246 622, 07-5533 3622; www.binnaburralodge.com.au; 1069 Binna Burra Rd, Beechmont; powered/unpowered sites $35/28, safari tents $105, d with/without bathroom $290/175; ℙ) is an atmospheric mountain retreat and the closest thing to a ski lodge in the bush. You can stay in rustic log cabins, well-appointed apartments (known as 'sky lodges') with spectacular scenic rim views, or in a tent surrounded by forest. There's a good restaurant and teahouse.

The famous 1926 **O'Reilly's Rainforest Retreat** (☑07-5502 4911, 1800 688 722; www.oreillys.com.au; Lamington National Park Rd, Green

Mountains; s $80-99, d $149-188, 1-bedroom villas $360-375; @🔊🏊) has lost much of its original grandeur but retains a rustic charm – and sensational views! There are plenty of organised activities, plus a day spa, a cafe, a bar and a restaurant.

Springbrook National Park

About a 40-minute drive west of Burleigh Heads, **Springbrook National Park** (☑13 74 68; www.nprsr.qld.gov.au/parks/springbrook) is a steep remnant of the huge Tweed Shield volcano that centred on nearby Mt Warning in NSW more than 20 million years ago. It's a wonderland for hikers, with excellent trails through cool-temperate, subtropical and eucalypt forests offering a mosaic of gorges, cliffs and waterfalls.

Excellent viewpoints in the park include the appropriately named **Best of All Lookout** (Repeater Station Rd), **Canyon Lookout** (Canyon Pde), which is also the start of a 4km circuit walk to Twin Falls, and the superb lookout beside the 60m **Goomoolahra Falls** (Springbrook Rd), giving views across the plateau and all the way back to the coast.

There are 11 grassy sites at pretty **Settlement Campground** (☑13 74 68; www.nprsr.qld.gov.au/parks/springbrook/camping.html; 52 Carricks Rd, Springbrook; sites per person/family $6/24), the only one at Springbrook. There are toilets and gas BBQs but no showers. Book ahead.

NOOSA & THE SUNSHINE COAST

The Sunshine Coast – the 100 golden kilometres stretching from the tip of Bribie Island to the Cooloola Coast – is aglow with perfect beaches, coveted surf and a laid-back, sun-kissed populace who will quickly tell you how lucky they are. Resort towns dot the coast, each with its own appeal and vibe, from upmarket, cosmopolitan Noosa to newly hip, evolving Caloundra.

Further inland is the lush, cool hinterland. It's here that you'll find the ethereal Glass House Mountains, looming over the land- and seascapes, and the iconic Australia Zoo. Further north, the Blackall Range offers a change of scenery with thick forests, lush pastures and quaint villages dotted with artisan food shops, cafes and crafty boutiques.

QUEENSLAND NOOSA & THE SUNSHINE COAST

Sunshine Coast

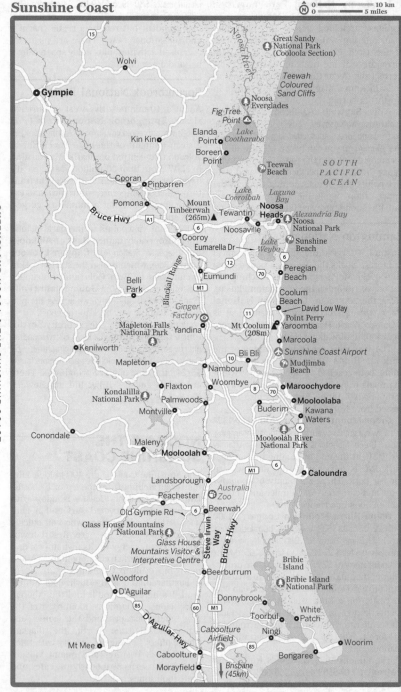

0 — 10 km
0 — 5 miles

Wolvi

Gympie

Great Sandy
National Park
(Cooloola Section)

Teewah
Coloured
Sand Cliffs

Kin Kin

Noosa
Everglades

Fig Tree
Point

Elanda
Point

Lake
Cootharaba

Boreen
Point

Teewah
Beach

SOUTH
PACIFIC
OCEAN

Cooran   Pinbarren

Lake
Cooroibah

Laguna
Bay

Pomona

Mount
Tinbeerwah
(265m)

Tewantin

**Noosa
Heads**

Alexandria Bay

Bruce Hwy

A1

Noosaville

Noosa
National Park

Cooroy

Eumarella Dr

Lake
Weyba

Sunshine
Beach

Belli
Park

Blackall Range

Eumundi

12

M1

70

Peregian
Beach

Ginger
Factory

Coolum
Beach

David Low Way

Mapleton Falls
National Park

Yandina

Mt Coolum
(208m)

Point Perry
Yaroomba

Kenilworth

Mapleton

Nambour

10

Bli Bli

Marcoola

Sunshine Coast Airport

Mudjimba
Beach

Woombye

8

70

Maroochydore

Kondalilla
National Park

Flaxton

Palmwoods

Buderim

Mooloolaba

Montville

Kawana
Waters

6

Conondale

Maleny

Mooloolah River
National Park

Mooloolah

M1

6

Caloundra

Landsborough

Australia
Zoo

Peachester

Old Gympie Rd

6

Beerwah

Glass House Mountains
National Park

Steve Irwin Way

Bruce Hwy

Glass House
Mountains Visitor &
Interpretive Centre

Bribie
Island

Bribie Island
National Park

Woodford

Beerburrum

D'Aguilar

85

D'Aguilar Hwy

60

M1

Donnybrook

White
Patch

Toorbul

Caboolture
Airfield

Ningi

Mt Mee

Caboolture

85

Bongaree

Woorim

Morayfield

Brisbane
(45km)

ⓘ Getting There & Around

AIR

Sunshine Coast Airport (Maroochydore Airport; ☑ 07-5453 1500; www.sunshinecoastairport. com; Friendship Ave, Marcoola) is at Marcoola, 10km north of Maroochydore and 26km south of Noosa. **Jetstar** (☑ 13 15 38; www.jetstar.com) and **Virgin Australia** (☑ 13 67 89; www.virgin australia.com) have daily direct flights from Sydney and Melbourne; **Qantas** (☑ 13 13 13; www. qantas.com.au) flies direct from Sydney eight times weekly. Jetstar also runs direct flights from Adelaide three times weekly.

From July to October, **Air New Zealand** (www. airnewzealand.com) flies direct from Auckland three to four times weekly.

BUS

Greyhound Australia (☑ 1300 473 946; www.greyhound.com.au) has several daily services from Brisbane to Caloundra (from $19, two hours), Maroochydore (from $23, two hours) and Noosa (from $24, 2½ to 3¼ hours). **Premier Motor Service** (☑ 13 34 10; www.premierms.com.au) also runs buses to Maroochydore ($23, 1½ to 1¾ hours) and Noosa ($23, 2½ hours) from Brisbane.

Several companies offer transfers from Sunshine Coast Airport and Brisbane to points along the coast. Fares from Brisbane cost from around $40 to $60 and from Sunshine Coast Airport between $25 and $35. (Fares are around half-price for children.)

Con-X-ion (p302) Does airport transfers from the Sunshine Coast and Brisbane Airports.

Henry's (☑ 07-5474 0199; www.henrys.com. au) Runs a door-to-door service from Sunshine Coast Airport to points north as far as Noosa Heads and Tewantin.

Sunbus (TransLink; ☑ 13 12 30; www.sunbus. com.au) This local TransLink-operated bus buzzes between Caloundra and Noosa, and from Noosa to the train station at Nambour ($8.60, 1¼ hours) via Eumundi.

Noosa

POP 39,380

Noosa is one of Australia's most fashionable resort towns, a salubrious hub backing onto crystalline waters and pristine subtropical rainforest. The town is located within the **Noosa Biosphere Reserve**, a Unesco-recognised area famous for its highly diverse ecosystem.

While the designer boutiques, polished restaurants and canal-side villas draw the beach-elite sophisticates, the beach and bush are free, leading to a healthy intermingling of urbane fashionistas and laid-back surfers and beach bods. Noosa encompasses three main zones: upmarket Noosa Heads (around Laguna Bay and Hastings St), the more relaxed Noosaville (along the Noosa River) and the administrative hub of Noosa Junction.

On long weekends and school holidays, the shopping and dining strip of Hastings St becomes a slow-moving file of traffic; the rest of the time, it's delightfully low(er) key.

◉ Sights & Activities

Covering the headland, **Noosa National Park** (www.noosanationalpark.com; Noosa Heads) is one of Noosa's top sights; the most scenic way to reach it is to follow the boardwalk along the coast from town. The park's walking tracks lead to stunning coastal scenery, idyllic bays and great surfing. Pick up a walking-track map from the Noosa National Park Information Centre (p327) at the park's entrance.

For a panoramic view that takes in Noosa, its densely wooded national park, the ocean and distant hinterland, walk or drive up to **Laguna Lookout** (Viewland Dr, Noosa Junction).

For surfing lessons and watersports try **Merrick's Learn to Surf** (☑ 0418 787 577; www.learntosurf.com.au; Beach Access 14, Noosa Main Beach, Noosa Heads; 2hr lessons $65; ⊙9am & 1.30pm), **Foam and Resin** (53 Hastings St, Noosa Heads; surfboard rental 2hr/full-day $25/35, stand-up paddleboard rental 2hr $30; ⊙9am-5pm), **Noosa Ocean Rider** (☑ 0438 386 255; www.facebook.com/NoosaOceanrider; Jetty 17, 248 Gympie Tce, Noosaville; 1hr per person/family $70/$250) and **Kayak Noosa** (☑ 07-5455 5651; www.kayaknoosa.com; 194 Gympie Tce, Noosaville; 2hr sunset kayak adult/child $60/45).

Noosa Ferry (p327) runs an informative hop-on, hop-off Classic Tour (all-day pass adult/child $25/7) between Tewantin and the Sofitel Noosa Pacific Resort jetty in Noosa Heads.

☞ Tours

Noosa Woody Hire   DRIVING
(☑ 0475 587 385; www.noosawoodyhire.com; driving tour 1/2/4hr $190/290/590) Cruise around in an attention-stealing 1946 Ford Woody. Accommodating four to five passengers, the vehicle was lovingly restored by young, affable local Tim Crabtree. With his wife, Kim, the surfboard shaper offers tailored tours; all include refreshments. The four-hour tour includes a gourmet picnic lunch

and can take in hinterland foodie stops; they can also visit the Eumundi Markets (p336).

Bike On Australia MOUNTAIN BIKING
(07-5474 3322; www.bikeon.com.au; guided mountain-bike tours from $65, bike hire per day $25) Runs a variety of tours, including self-guided and adventurous eco-jaunts. The fun, half-day Off the Top Tour – downhill on a mountain bike – costs $79. Also rents out road bikes (three/seven days from $120/250).

✷ Festivals & Events

Noosa Festival of Surfing SURFING
(www.noosafestivalofsurfing.com) A week of wave-riding action in March. There's a huge range of competition divisions, from invite-only pros to amateur competitions spanning all age brackets – there's even a dog surfing category! Water action aside, events include surf talks and workshops as well as film screenings and live music.

Noosa Food & Wine FOOD & DRINK
(www.noosafoodandwine.com.au; ☺May) A four-day tribute to all manner of gastronomic delights, featuring prolific chefs, master-classes, special lunches and dinners, as well as themed food and wine tours.

Noosa Long Weekend CULTURAL
(www.noosalongweekend.com) A 10-day festival of music, dance, theatre, film, visual arts, literature and food in July.

🛏 Sleeping

For an extensive list of short-term holiday rentals, try Noosa Visitor Centre (p327) and the privately run **Accom Noosa** (07-5447 3444, 1800 072 078; www.accomnoosa.com.au; Shop 5/41 Hastings St, Noosa Heads).

★**YHA Halse Lodge** HOSTEL $
(07-5447 3377; www.halselodge.com.au; 2 Halse Lane, Noosa Heads; dm $33.50, d $88; @ 🛜) This splendid, colonial-era Queenslander is a legendary backpacker stopover and well worth the clamber up its steep drive. There are four-to-six-bed dorms, twins, doubles and a lovely wide verandah. Popular with locals, the bar is a mix-and-meet bonanza, offering great meals (mains $16.50 to $26.50), cheap happy-hour beers, and live music on Thursdays. Close to the Main Beach action.

Flashpackers HOSTEL $
(07-5455 4088; www.flashpackersnoosa.com; 102 Pacific Ave, Sunshine Beach; mixed dm from $38, female dm $45, d from $100; ❀ 🛜 ⊠) Flash-packers challenges the notion of hostels as flea-bitten dives. Thoughtful touches to its neat dorms include full-length mirrors, personal reading lights, ample wall sockets and the free use of surfboards and bodyboards.

Noosa River Holiday Park CARAVAN PARK $
(07-5449 7050; www.noosaholidayparks.com.au; 4 Russell St, Noosaville; unpowered/powered sites $38/46; 🛜) This park is especially appealing for its location on the banks of the Noosa River, right between Noosa Heads and Noosaville. The latter's eateries and bars are within walking distance and the site itself has lovely spots to take a dip in the river. It's a seriously popular place: reservations open nine months in advance and it usually books out soon after.

★**10 Hastings** MOTEL $$
(07-5455 3350; www.10hastingsstreet.com.au; 10 Hastings St, Noosa Heads; studio from $199, studio ste from $250, 2-bedroom apt from $400; P ❀ 🛜 ⊠) A rarity along Noosa's central Hastings Street, this renovated boutique motel is a refreshing option from the resorts. Clean, fresh, beach-chic rooms come as compact two-person studios and larger studio suites (sleeping two adults and two children). Larger still are the two-bedroom apartments (sleeping up to six). Perks include complimentary beach towels and mini-bar items. Check for minimum stays.

Hotel Laguna APARTMENT $$
(07-5447 3077; www.hotellaguna.com.au; 6 Hastings St, Noosa Heads; studios/ste from $165/230; P ❀ 🛜 ⊠) Neatly wedged between the river and Hastings St, Hotel Laguna consists of self-contained apartments and smaller studios. All apartments are privately owned and each individually decorated, but all are smart and pleasant (if not always spotless). There's a communal guest laundry and courtyard-style pool area. The location means you are only a roll-out-of-bed to the beach and a coffee whiff from great cafes.

★**Fairshore** APARTMENT $$$
(07-5449 4500; www.fairshorenoosa.com.au; 41 Hastings St, Noosa Heads; 4-person apt from $495; P ❀ 🛜 ⊠) A smart, family-friendly apartment resort with direct access to Noosa Main Beach and buzzing Hastings St, Fairshore comes with a magazine-worthy, palm-fringed pool area. Two-bedroom apartments offer one or two bathrooms; though each apartment varies in style, all have laundry facilities and most are contemporary.

Noosa Heads

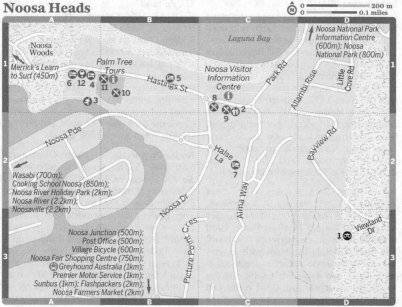

Noosa Heads

There's also a small gym. Parking is free (vehicle height restriction 1.85m).

✗ Eating

Noosa prides itself on being a culinary destination, with global and local flavours on offer from fine restaurants to beachside takeaways. In Noosa Heads, eateries clutter Hastings St; in Noosaville, head to Thomas St and Gympie Tce.

Self-caterers can stock up on groceries at **Noosa Fair Shopping Centre** (☏07-5447 3788; www.noosafairshopping.com.au; 3 Lanyana Way, Noosa Junction; ⊘supermarket 8am-9pm Mon-Fri, to 5.30pm Sat, 9am-6pm Sun) in Noosa Junction. Altogether more atmospheric is the Sunday **Noosa Farmers' Market**

(☏0418 769 374; www.noosafarmersmarket.com. au; Noosa Australian Football Club Grounds, 155 Weyba Rd, Noosaville; ⊘7am-noon Sun).

Betty's Burgers &
Concrete Co   BURGERS $

(☏07-5455 4378; www.bettysburgers.com.au; 2/50 Hastings St, Noosa Heads; burgers $10-16; ⊘10am-9pm) Betty's has achieved cult status all the way down Australia's East Coast, which explains the queues at its lush, semi-alfresco Noosa outlet – but the burgers are worth the wait for pillowy soft buns and flawlessly grilled, premium-meat patties (veggie option available). The perfect fries are wonderfully crispy and the moreish concretes (frozen custard drinks) come in flavours like lemon-raspberry cheesecake. Bliss.

Bordertown BBQ & Taqueria
AMERICAN, MEXICAN $

(☑ 07-5442 4242; www.facebook.com/bordertown barbeque; 1/253 Gympie Tce, Noosaville; burgers $12-17, tacos $7-9; ⊙ 8am-9pm Sun-Thu, to 10.30pm Fri & Sat; ☜☝) Pimped with murals by Queensland artists Mitch 13 and Thom Stuart, clued-in Bordertown rocks great burgers and succulent tacos (with authentic shells made by a Mexican family in Melbourne). Libations at the concrete bar include craft beers, creative cocktails and an alcoholic Bordertown Cola, made in-house using sassafras, vermouth and Fernet-Branca. Check their Facebook page for DJ sessions.

Hard Coffee
CAFE $

(☑ 0410 673 377; 18 Hastings St, Noosa Heads; mains $10-16; ⊙ 7am-3pm) One of the cheaper options on Hastings St, super-casual Hard Coffee lurks inside a nondescript food court. The food is simple but tasty, with options like smoked-salmon focaccia, steak sandwich BLAT, and a basic but satisfying avo smash for a bargain $10. Good coffee and no shortage of regulars chatting about the morning surf.

Tanglewood Organic Sourdough Bakery
BAKERY $

(☑ 07-5473 0215; www.facebook.com/tanglewood organicsourdough; Belmondos Organic Market, 59 Rene St, Noosaville; pastries from $5; ⊙ 8am-5pm Mon-Fri, to 4pm Sat; ☜) Part of the upmarket Belmondos Organic Market, Tanglewood will have you oohing and aahing over its just-made, buttery pastries, artfully displayed on timber logs. If you can't make up your mind, opt for the standout pecan tart or their famous bread-and-butter pudding. Then there are the chocolate sea-salt cookies, not to mention those gorgeous loaves of artisan bread...

★ Thomas Corner
MODERN AUSTRALIAN $$

(☑ 07-5470 2224; www.thomascorner.com.au; cnr Thomas St & Gympie Tce, Noosaville; mains $16-33; ⊙ 11.30am-8pm Mon-Fri, 8am-8pm Sat & Sun; ☜) Lunching ladies rightfully adore this casually chic, alfresco nosh spot. It's run by locally renowned chef David Rayner, whose vibrant, beautifully plated creations might see locally smoked fish paired with endive, apple, labne and pancetta crumbs, or parmesan-and-sage gnocchi happily married with mushrooms, spinach, truffle paste and poached egg. The popular weekend breakfast menu is equally as inspired.

El Capitano
PIZZA $$

(☑ 07-5474 9990; www.elcapitano.com.au; 52 Hastings St, Noosa Heads; pizzas $22-25; ⊙ 5-9.30pm) Down an easy-to-miss path and up a set of stairs is Noosa's best pizzeria, a hip, swinging hot spot with bar seating (good for solo diners), louvred windows and marine-themed street art. The light, fluffy pizzas here are gorgeous, made with sourdough bases and topped with artisan ingredients. Check the blackboard for pizza and cocktail specials – and always book ahead.

Noosa Boathouse
MODERN AUSTRALIAN $$

(☑ 07-5440 5070; www.noosaboathouse.com. au; 194 Gympie Tce, Noosaville; mains $20-38; ⊙ restaurant 11.30am-3pm & 5-8pm Tue-Sun, cafe 6am-6pm daily, rooftop bar 4.30-7pm Tue-Sun) This modern, floating nosh spot has numerous sections: cafe, fish 'n' chip kiosk, rooftop bar (open for sunset drinks) and a Cape Cod–style restaurant. While the latter's menu – think Mod Oz with Italian and Asian touches – isn't quite as ambitious as it sounds, the place is a fantastic option for great-tasting food and killer views sans the eye-watering price tag.

★ Noosa Beach House
MODERN AUSTRALIAN $$$

(☑ 07-5449 4754; www.noosabeachhousepk.com. au; 16 Hastings St, Noosa Heads; dinner mains $39-46, 6-course tasting menu $100; ⊙ 6.30-10.30am & 5.30-9.30pm daily, also noon-2.30pm Sat & Sun) An uncluttered mix of white walls, glass and timber, this effortlessly chic restaurant belongs to globe-trotting celebrity chef Peter Kuravita. Seasonal ingredients and fresh local seafood underscore a contemporary menu whose deeply seductive Sri Lankan snapper curry with tamarind and *aloo chop* (potato croquette) nods to Kuravita's heritage. Weekends see a good-value five-curry lunch, served family-style for $38 per person.

★ Wasabi
JAPANESE $$$

(☑ 07-5449 2443; www.wasabisb.com; 2 Quamby Pl, Noosa Heads; 3 courses $80, 7-/9-course omakase menu $134/157; ⊙ 5-9.30pm Wed, Thu & Sat, noon-9.30pm Fri & Sun) An award-winning, waterside destination restaurant, Wasabi is on the lips of every local gourmand. Premium produce from the region and Wasabi's own farm sings in delicate yet thrilling dishes like handmade duck-egg noodles and fresh fish in burnt-onion broth with fish-crackling and legumes, or tempura-style spanner crab and *yama imo* (mountain potato) dumpling with kombu salt and *yuzu* zest.

Drinking & Nightlife

★ **Clandestino Roasters** COFFEE
(☑1300 656 022; www.clandestino.com.au; Belmondos Organic Market, 59 Rene St, Noosaville; ⊙7am-4pm Mon-Fri, to 3pm Sat; 🗢) It might be off the tourist radar, but this trendy warehouse microroastery packs in hipsters, surfers and suits, all here for Noosa's top coffee. Choose from two blends and eight single origins served a number of ways, including espresso-style, cold-drip, clover, V60 pour-over and siphon. Communal tables and free wi-fi make it a popular spot with the laptop brigade.

★ **Village Bicycle** BAR
(☑07-5474 5343; 2/16 Sunshine Beach Rd, Noosa Junction; ⊙4pm-midnight Mon-Sat, from 12.30pm Sun) Noosa's coolest local drinking spot by far, Village Bicycle is run by young mates Luke and Trevor. Splashed with street art, it's a convivial space, packed nightly with loyal regulars here to knock back some beers, tuck into quality bar grub – think tacos and burgers – and listen to live tunes.

Miss Moneypenny's COCKTAIL BAR
(☑07-5474 9999; www.missmoneypennys.com; 6 Hastings St, Noosa Heads; ⊙11.30am-midnight; 🗢) Dashing, award-winning Miss Moneypenny sets a sophisticated scene for languid toasts. Well-crafted cocktails fall into numerous categories, from Seasonals and Sours to tongue-in-cheek '80s Cruise Ship Drinks. Not that irony gets in the way of quality: even the piña colada is shaken with original Coco Lopez coconut cream. Nosh includes posh bar bites and pizzas ($16 to $30).

ℹ Information

Noosa Visitor Information Centre (☑07-5430 5000; www.visitnoosa.com.au; 61 Hastings St, Noosa Heads; ⊙9am-5pm; 🗢) Official tourist office.

Palm Tree Tours (☑07-5474 9166; www.palmtreetours.com.au; Bay Village Shopping Centre, 18 Hastings St, Noosa Heads; ⊙9am-5pm) Long-standing tour desk.

Noosa National Park Information Centre (☑07-5447 3522; ⊙8.45am-4.15pm) At the entrance to Noosa National Park.

ℹ Getting There & Away

Long-distance bus services stop at the **Noosa Junction Bus Station** on Sunshine Beach Rd in Noosa Junction. **Greyhound Australia** (☑1300 473 946; www.greyhound.com.au) has several daily bus connections from Brisbane to Noosa

(from $24, 2½ to 3¼ hours), while **Premier Motor Service** (p302) has one ($23, 2½ hours).

Most hostels have courtesy pick-ups.

Sunbus (TransLink; ☑13 12 30; www.sunbus.com.au) operates frequent services from Noosa to Maroochydore ($10.50, one hour to 1¼ hours) and Nambour train station ($10.50, 1¼ hour).

ℹ Getting Around

BICYCLE

Bike On Australia (p324) rents out bicycles from several locations in Noosa, including **Flashpackers** (p324) in Sunshine Beach. Alternatively, bikes can be delivered to and from your door for $35 (or free if the booking is over $100).

BOAT

Noosa Ferry (☑07-5449 8442; www.noosaferry.com) operates ferries between Noosa Heads and Tewantin several times a day (all-day pass adult/child $25/7). **Noosa Water Taxi** (☑0411 136 810; www.noosawatertaxi.com; one-way per person $10) operates a water taxi service around Noosa Sound (Friday to Sunday), and is also available for private charters and water-taxi hire by appointment.

BUS

Sunbus (p327) has local services that link Noosa Heads, Noosaville, Noosa Junction and Tewantin.

CAR & MOTORCYCLE

All the major car-rental brands can be found in Noosa; rentals start at about $55 per day.

Noosa Car Rentals (☑0429 053 728; www.noosacarrentals.com.au)

Scooter Hire Noosa (☑07-5455 4096; www.scooterhirenoosa.com; 13 Noosa Dr, Noosa Heads; 4/24hr $39/59; ⊙8.30am-5pm)

Bribie Island

POP 18,135

This slender island at the northern end of Moreton Bay is linked to the mainland by bridge and is popular with young families, retirees and those with a cool million (or three) to spend on a waterfront property. While it's far more developed than Stradbroke or Moreton Islands, there are still secluded spots to be found.

The **Abbey Museum** (☑07-5495 1652; www.abbeymuseum.com; 63 The Abbey Pl, off Old Toorbul Point Rd, Caboolture; adult/child $12/7, family from $19.80; ⊙10am-4pm Mon-Sat) houses an extraordinary collection of art and archaeology, once the collection of Englishman

'Reverend' John Ward. The Abbey Medieval Festival is held here in June or July.

The nearby **Caboolture Warplane Museum** (☑ 07-5499 1144; www.cabooltoruewarplane museum.com; Hangar 104, Caboolture Airfield, Mc-Naught Rd, Caboolture; adult/child/family $10/5/30; ⊙ 9am-3pm) houses a booty of restored WWII planes, including a P51D Mustang, CAC Wirraway and Cessna Bird Dog.

Pick up maps and information at **Bribie Island Visitor Information Centre** (☑ 07-3408 9026; www.tourismbribie.com.au; Benabrow Ave, Bellara; ⊙ 9am-4pm).

🛌 Sleeping & Eating

Bribie Island National Park Camping   CAMPGROUND **$**
(☑ 13 74 68; www.npsr.qld.gov.au/parks/bribie-island; camp sites per person/family $6.15/24.60) On the island's west coast, **Poverty Creek** is a large, grassy camping site. Facilities here include toilets, a portable toilet/waste disposal facility and screened cold showers. Just south, **Ocean Beach** offers similar facilities. On the east coast, the **Gallagher Point** camping area harbours a limited number of bush camping sites, with no toilets or other facilities. All three sites are accessible by 4WD.

Bribie Island SLSC   PUB FOOD **$$**
(☑ 07-3408 2141; www.thesurfclubbribieisland.com. au; First Ave, Woorim; mains $18-30; ⊙ 11.30am-2.30pm & 5.30pm-late) While the pub grub here won't blow you away, it's tasty enough and comes with a beachside deck for chilled wave-watching sessions. Expect all the surf-club staples, from garlic prawns and beer-battered barramundi to pasta dishes and golden schnitzel.

ℹ Getting There & Away

There is no 4WD hire on Bribie, and you'll need a vehicle access permit ($46.25 per week) for the island's more off-track spots. Pick up one at **Gateway Bait & Tackle** (☑ 07-5497 5253; www. gatewaybaitandtackle.com.au; 1383 Bribie Island Rd, Ningi; ⊙ 5.30am-5pm Mon, Tue, Thu & Fri, to 2pm Wed, 4.30am-5pm Sat, 4.30am-3pm Sun) or online (www.npsr.qld.gov.au).

Frequent Citytrain services run from Brisbane to Caboolture, from where **Bribie Island Coaches** (☑ 07-3408 2562; www.bribiecoaches.com. au) route 643 runs to Bribie Island via Ningi and Sandstone Point. Buses run roughly every hour, stopping in Bongaree and continuing through to Woorim. Regular Brisbane Translink fares apply (one-way from central Brisbane $11.40).

Glass House Mountains

The breathtaking volcanic plugs of the Glass House Mountains rise abruptly from the sub-tropical plains 20km northwest of Caboolture. In Dreaming legend, these curious rocky peaks belong to a family of mountain spirits. To British explorer James Cook, their shapes recalled the industrial, conical glass-making furnaces of his native Yorkshire. It's worth diverting off the Bruce Hwy onto the slower Old Gympie Rd to snake your way through dense bush, scattered with old Queenslander shacks and offering arresting views of these spectacular magma intrusions.

The **Glass House Mountains National Park** is broken into several sections, with picnic grounds and lookouts but no camping grounds. The peaks are reached by a series of sealed and unsealed roads that head inland from Steve Irwin Way, which itself is home to the blockbuster Australia Zoo, founded by the world-famous Crocodile Hunter himself.

Glass House Mountains Ecolodge (☑ 07-5493 0008; www.glasshouseecolodge.com; 198 Barrs Rd, Glass House Mountains; r $125-220; ✳ 🛜) 🅿, near Australia Zoo, offers a range of wonderful, good-value sleeping options, including cosy Orchard Rooms ($125), the reformed Church Loft ($220), and converted railway carriages. Mt Tibrogargan can be seen from the gorgeous garden.

The **Glasshouse Mountains Tavern** (www.glasshousemountainstavern.com.au; 10 Reed St, Glass House Mountains; mains $14-32.50; ⊙ 10am-9pm Sun-Thu, to midnight Fri, to 9.30pm Sat, kitchen closes around 8pm) cooks up tasty, no-nonsense pub nosh, including steaks, bangers (sausages), burgers and salads.

Caloundra

POP 77,600

Straddling a headland at the southern end of the Sunshine Coast, Caloundra has shaken off the quaint 'Valium Coast' cliches and reinvented itself as an unexpected centre of cool. Beyond its golden beaches, water sports and beautiful Coastal Pathway walking track is a burgeoning creative scene, spanning everything from top-notch coffee shops and bars to street art and a microbrewery, not to mention the coast's most sharply curated regional art galleries. The cherry on the proverbial cake is the Caloundra Music Festival, one of Queensland's biggest, best-loved annual music events.

⊙ Sights & Activities

On Sunday mornings, crowds flock to Bulcock St to browse the market stalls at **Caloundra Street Fair** (www.caloundrastreetfair.com.au; Bulcock St; ⊙8am-1pm Sun).

Caloundra Regional Gallery   GALLERY
(☑07-5420 8299; http://gallery.sunshinecoast.qld.gov.au; 22 Omrah Ave; ⊙10am-4pm Tue-Fri, to 2pm Sat & Sun) **FREE** When you're done with catching rays and waves, side-step to this small, sophisticated gallery. Rotating exhibitions showcase quality local and national artists, with a number of outstanding Art Prize shows each year. The gallery stays up late for **Friday³Live** on the third Friday of the month, with music, talks, performances, drinks and bites.

Queensland Air Museum   MUSEUM
(☑07-5492 5930; www.qam.com.au; 7 Pathfinder Dr; adult/child/family $13/7/30; ⊙10am-4pm) Occupying two hangers beside Caloundra Airport, the volunteer-run QAM houses circa 70 civilian and military aircraft, including a mid-century Douglas DC-3 (the world's first mass-produced all-metal airliner) and a supersonic F-111 fighter jet belonging to the Royal Australian Air Force. Displays shed light on various aspects of Australian and international aviation history, including wartime battles and women in aviation, and there's a small collection of fabulously retro brochures, cabin bags and in-flight crockery from Australian airlines past and present.

Caloundra Surf School   SURFING
(☑0413 381 010; www.caloundrasurfschool.com.au; 1½hr lessons from $50) The pick of the local surf schools, with board hire also available.

Deluxe Kombi Service   DRIVING
(☑07-5491 5432, 0402 615 126; www.deluxekombiservice.com.au; ⊙1hr tour $77) What better way to explore the area than in a 1960s Kombi with a cool surfer dude? Local Michael Flocke has meticulously restored two rare vans (complete with sunroof and seating for eight), which he uses for insightful, anecdote-rich tours of the town and surrounding region. Book a one-hour town tour or longer, bespoke tours of the Sunshine Coast hinterland.

Sunshine Coast Skydivers   SKYDIVING
(☑07-5437 0211; www.sunshinecoastskydivers.com.au; Caloundra Aerodrome, Pathfinder Dr; tandem jumps from $279) Send your adrenalin into overdrive as you scan Caloundra

---

DON'T MISS

AUSTRALIA ZOO

Just north of Glass House Mountains is one of Queensland's, if not Australia's, most famous tourist attractions. **Australia Zoo** (☑07-5436 2000; www.australiazoo.com.au; 1638 Steve Irwin Way, Beerwah; adult/child/family $59/35/172; ⊙9am-5pm) is a fitting homage to its founder, zany wildlife enthusiast Steve Irwin. The park has an amazing menagerie, with a Cambodian-style Tiger Temple, the famous Crocoseum and a dizzying array of critters, including native dingoes, Tasmanian devils and hairy-nosed wombats.

Various companies offer tours from Brisbane and the Sunshine Coast. The zoo operates a free bus to/from the Beerwah train station.

---

and the Pacific Ocean from a brain-squeezing 4570m up (or even just 2130m, if you prefer).

Blue Water Kayak Tours   KAYAKING
(☑07-5494 7789; www.bluewaterkayaktours.com; half-day tours minimum 4 people $100, twilight tours $55; ⊙half-day tours 8.30am Tue-Sun; twilight tours Wed-Sun) Energetic kayak tours across the channel to the northern tip of Bribie Island National Park; single and double kayaks are available. All tours must be booked in advance.

🎉 Festivals & Events

Caloundra Music Festival   MUSIC
(www.caloundramusicfestival.com; ⊙Sep-Oct) A four-day, family-friendly music festival held at Kings Beach, with 40,000-strong crowds and a diverse line-up of entertainment, featuring prolific current and veteran Australian rock and indie pop acts, as well as international guests.

🛏 Sleeping & Eating

**Dicky Beach Family
Holiday Park**   CARAVAN PARK $
(☑07-5491 3342; www.sunshinecoastholidayparks.com.au; 4 Beerburrum St; powered/unpowered site $46/41, cabins from $118; ❄ ⑤ ☒) You can't get any closer to Dicky, one of Caloundra's most popular beaches. The brick cabins are as ordered and tidy as the grounds and there's a small swimming pool for the kids.

WOODSTOCK DOWNUNDER

The famous **Woodford Folk Festival** (www.woodfordfolkfestival.com; ⊘ Dec/Jan) features a huge diversity of over 2000 national and international performers playing folk, traditional Irish, Indigenous and world music, as well as buskers, belly dancers, craft markets, visual-arts performances, environmental talks and Tibetan monks. The festival is held on a property near the town of Woodford from 27 December to 1 January each year. Camping grounds are set up on-site with toilets, showers and a range of foodie marquees, but prepare for a mud bath if it rains. The festival is licensed so leave your booze at home. Tickets cost $137 per day ($168 with camping) and can be bought online or at the gate. Check online for updated programs.

Woodford is 35km souththwest of **Caboolture**. Shuttle buses run regularly from the Caboolture train station to and from the festival grounds.

Caloundra Backpackers   HOSTEL **$**
(☑07-5499 7655; www.caloundrabackpackers.com.au; 84 Omrah Ave; dm from $26, d with/without bathroom from $75/60; ☎) Caloundra's only hostel is a no-nonsense budget option with a sociable courtyard, book exchange, and weekly BBQ, pizza and wine-and-cheese nights. Dorms won't inspire, but they're clean and peaceful.

Monaco   APARTMENT **$$**
(☑07-5490 5490; www.monacocaloundra.com.au; 12 Otranto Ave; 1-/2-/3-bedroom apts from $159/240/329; ⓟ❄☎☒) Modern, good-sized apartments one block from Bulcock Beach. Apartments are individually owned, so styles vary; the more expensive apartments offer full water vistas. Wi-fi is free but capped, and apartments are serviced every eight days. Property perks include a stylish, heated lap pool, separate kids' pool, spa, sauna, gym and games rooms. Minimum two-night stay, with cheaper rates for longer stays.

★ **Baci Gelati**   GELATO **$**
(49 Bulcock St; gelato from $4.50; ⊘9am-5pm Mon-Fri, 9.30am-5pm Sat, 10am-4pm Sun) Baci scoops out some of the best gelato in Queensland, made by an Italian expat, his Hungarian wife and a fellow Italian mate. The secret: top-quality ingredients, from fresh fruit and Bronte pistachios to Belgian chocolate and local Maleny milk. Creative flavours include ginger beer, chai, salted caramel and an extraordinary Sicilian hazelnut. Take-home packs are available (0.5/1L $12/23).

Green House Cafe   VEGETARIAN **$**
(☑07-5438 1647; www.greenhousecafe.com.au; 5/8 Orumuz Ave; mains $13-17; ⊘8am-3pm Mon-Fri, to 2pm Sat & Sun; ☑) A showcase for local ingredients, this chilled, light-filled laneway spot serves up fresh, organic and filling vegetarian grub such as avocado on toast with cashew cheese, shakshouka eggs and *nasi goreng*. For a serious health kick, down a smoothie with kale and seasonal greens paired with banana, coconut-milk yoghurt, kiwi, chia seeds, coconut water and supergreens powder. Mama will approve.

Cptn   INTERNATIONAL **$$**
(☑07-5341 8475; www.cptnkingsbeach.com.au; 1/8 Levuka Ave, Kings Beach; mains lunch $18-29, dinner $26-29; ⊘6am-6pm Mon-Thu, to 9.30pm Fri-Sun, kitchen to 3pm Mon-Thu & 8pm Fri-Sun; ☎) Beachside Cptn beats the competition with its crisp, contemporary fit-out and beautiful, honest nosh. Don't expect culinary acrobatics, just well-executed, thoughtful dishes like barramundi fish 'n' chips, grilled halloumi with roasted vegetables, or grilled chicken breast with mixed Mediterranean vegetables, roast potatoes, goats cheese and red-wine jus. Good coffee, well-priced wines by the glass and a young, friendly team.

🍷 Drinking & Nightlife

Lamkin Lane Espresso Bar   CAFE
(www.facebook.com/lamkinlane; 31 Lamkin Ln; ⊘6am-4pm Mon-Fri, 7am-noon Sat & Sun) The hearts of coffee snobs will sing at Lamkin Lane, where affable, knowledgeable baristas like nothing better than chatting about the week's pair of special blends and trio of single-origins. The team here have a strong relationship with their coffee farmers, which means your brew is as ethical as it is smooth and aromatic. Cash only.

Moffat Beach Brewing Company   MICROBREWERY
(☑07-5491 4023; 12 Seaview Tce, Moffat Beach; ⊘7am-4pm Mon & Tue, to late Wed-Sat, to 8pm Sun) Just up from hipster-staple Moffat

Beach, this cafe-cum-microbrewery has both guest and house brews on tap (look out for the cult-status double IPA Iggy Hop). Bottled beers span Oz and the globe; the four-brew paddle ($20) will help the indecisive. Nod away to live tunes on Fridays from 5pm and on weekends from 3pm (the latter sessions are especially pumping).

26 Degrees
COCKTAIL BAR

(☑07-5492 0555; www.facebook.com/26degrees Bar; 10 Leeding Tce, Rumba Beach Resort; ☺10am-late; 🛜) Twenty-six degrees is both the average temperature in Caloundra and the town's degree of latitude – it's now also one of Caloundra's most fashionable spots to imbibe. Located inside the Rumba Resort, the poolside bar is a beach-chic affair, with white louvres, white-washed timber bar and lush green foliage. Dirty martini lovers will appreciate their funky version, made with marinated olives.

ℹ️ Information

Sunshine Coast Visitor Centre (☑07-5458 8846; www.visitsunshinecoast.com; 7 Caloundra Rd; ☺9am-4pm Mon-Fri, to 3pm Sat & Sun; 🛜) On the roundabout at the town's entrance; there's also a centrally located kiosk on **Bulcock St** (☑07-5458 8847; 77 Bulcock St; ☺9am-3pm; 🛜). Both branches offer free wi-fi.

ℹ️ Getting There & Away

Greyhound Australia (☑1300 473 946; www.greyhound.com.au) buses run one daily morning service from Brisbane to Noosa, stopping in Caloundra (from $19, two hours) en route. There is also one morning service to Brisbane.

Sunbus (TransLink; ☑13 12 30; www.sunbus.com.au) has frequent services to Maroochydore ($5.70, one hour). Transfer in Maroochydore for buses to Noosa.

The **Caloundra Transit Centre** (23 Cooma Tce) is the main bus station for both long-distance and local buses, located a quick walk south of Bulcock St. (At the time of research the building itself was closed, though buses continue to stop here.)

Mooloolaba & Maroochydore

POP 12,550 (MOOLOOLABA), 18,300 (MAROOCHYDORE)

Mooloolaba has seduced many with its sublime climate, golden beach and laid-back lifestyle. Eateries, boutiques and pockets of resorts and apartments have spread along Mooloolaba Esplanade, transforming this once-humble fishing village into one of Queensland's most popular holiday destinations.

Further north, booming Maroochydore takes care of the business end, with a brand new city centre under construction and a string of buzzing eateries, as well as its own stretch of sandy beachfront.

👁️ Sights & Activities

Sea Life Sunshine Coast
AQUARIUM

(☑1800 618 021; www.underwaterworld.com.au; Wharf Marina, Parkyn Pde, Mooloolaba; adult/child/family $39/26/130; ☺9am-5pm) Kids will love this popular tropical oceanarium, complete with an 80m-long transparent underwater tunnel for close-up views of rays, reef fish and eight species of shark. There's a touch tank, live shows, presentations and – during school holidays – the option of sleeping at the aquarium overnight ($90 per person).

While visitors can also swim with seals and dive with sharks, it's worth considering that animal-welfare groups believe that captivity is debilitating and stressful for marine animals and exacerbated by human interaction.

Wildlife HQ
ZOO

(☑0428 660 671; www.whqzoo.com; adult/child/family $29/15/79; ☺9am-4pm) Located at the **Big Pineapple** (www.bigpineapple.com.au; 76 Nambour Connection Rd, Woombye; FREE), this 20-acre zoo houses native Australian, African, South American and rare Asian critters, among them red pandas and tahrs (Himalayan mountain goats).

Sunreef
DIVING

(☑07-5444 5656; www.sunreef.com.au; Wharf Marina, Parkyn Pde, Mooloolaba; dives from $165; ☺8am-5pm Mon-Sat, to 4pm Sun) Offers two dives (from $165) on the wreck of sunken warship HMAS *Brisbane*. Also runs a day trip to Flinders Reef (from $229), including two dives, equipment, lunch and snacks. A PADI Open Water Diver course is $495.

Hire Hut
WATER SPORTS

(☑07-5444 0366; www.hirehut.com.au; Wharf, Parkyn Pde, Mooloolaba) Hires out kayaks (two hours $25), giant stand-up paddleboards (two hours $350, up to 10 people per board), jet skis (one hour $180) and boats (per hour/half-day from $42/75). Also hires out bicycles (two/four hours $19/25).

Robbie Sherwell's
XL Surfing Academy
SURFING

(📞07-5478 1337, 0423 039 505; www.xlsurfing academy.com; 1hr private/group lessons $95/45) Dip a toe into Aussie surf culture at this long-established school, which caters to all levels, from rookie to advanced.

🥾 Tours

Coastal Cruises Mooloolaba
CRUISE

(📞0419 704 797; www.cruisemooloolaba.com. au; Wharf Marina, Parkyn Pde, Mooloolaba) Sunset ($25) and seafood lunch cruises ($35) through Mooloolaba Harbour, the river and canals.

Whale One
WILDLIFE

(📞1300 942 531; www.whaleone.com.au; Wharf Marina, Parkyn Pde, Mooloolaba; whale-watching tours adult/child/family $59/39/196) Between June and November, Whale One runs cruises that get you close to the spectacular acrobatic displays of humpback whales, which migrate north from Antarctica to mate and give birth.

🎉 Festivals & Events

Big Pineapple Music Festival
MUSIC

(www.bigpineapplemusicfestival.com; ⊙May) The one-day 'Piney Festival' is one of the region's top music events, with four stages showcasing titans of the current Aussie music scene. Past acts have included alternative rockers John Butler Trio and Birds of Tokyo, alt-electronica acts Rüfüs and Hermitude, and even Brisbane's own progressive-pop twins The Veronicas. Camp sites are available and sell out quickly.

Maroochy Music &
Visual Arts Festival
MUSIC

(www.mmvaf.com; ⊙Sep; 🛜) Headliners at this annual, one-day fest in Maroochydore have included of-the-moment Australian music acts Peking Duk and Matt Corby; alt-indie talent such as Boo Seeka, George Maple and Ngaiire have also taken the stage. The visual-arts side of the fest includes specially commissioned works from local and international artists.

🛏 Sleeping & Eating

Cotton Tree Holiday Park
CAMPGROUND $

(📞07-5459 9070; www.sunshinecoastholidayparks. com.au; Cotton Tree Pde, Cotton Tree, Maroochy-dore; powered/unpowered sites from $48/41 villas from $157) In Cotton Tree, a popular area of Maroochydore, this holiday park enjoys direct access to the beach and Maroochy River.

Mooloolaba Beach Backpackers
HOSTEL $

(📞07-5444 3399; www.mooloolababackpackers. com; 75 Brisbane Rd, Mooloolaba; dm with/without bathroom $34/30, d $75; P🛜🏊) Some dorms have en suites, and although the rooms are a little drab, the number of freebies (bikes, surfboards, stand-up paddleboards and breakfast) more than compensates. Besides, it's only 500m from beachside activities and nightlife.

Dockside Apartments
APARTMENT $$

(📞07-5478 2044; www.docksidemooloolaba.com. au; 50 Burnett St, Mooloolaba; 2-/3-bedroom apt from $290/375; P❄🛜🏊) While the fully equipped apartments here are all different (all are privately owned and rented out), each is neat, clean and comfortable. The property sits in a quiet spot away from the hubbub, but is an easy walk from Mooloolaba's main restaurant and bar strip, surf club, beach and wharf precinct. Discounted rates for longer stays.

Maroochydore Beach Motel
MOTEL $$

(📞07-5443 7355; www.maroochydorebeachmotel. com; 69 Sixth Ave, Maroochydore; s/d/f from $120/135/180; P❄🛜🏊) A quirky, spotless, themed motel with 18 different rooms, including the Elvis Room (naturally), the Egyptian Room, and the Aussie Room (complete with toy wombat). Although on a main road, it's less than a 200m walk to the beach.

★ Oceans
RESORT $$$

(📞07-5444 5777; www.oceansmooloolaba.com.au; 101-105 Mooloolaba Esp, Mooloolaba; 2-bedroom apt from $500; P❄🛜🏊) Cascading water and contemporary art greet guests at this upmarket apartment resort directly across from the beach. Ocean views are de rigueur in the apartments, which are sleek and immaculately clean, with Nespresso machines, standalone spa and quality appliances. Apartments are serviced daily and there's also adult's and children's pools, a gym and a sauna. Parking and wi-fi are free.

★ Velo Project
CAFE $

(📞07-5444 8693; www.theveloproject.com.au; 19 Careela St, Mooloolaba; dishes $6-22.50; ⊙7am-2pm; 🛜) In-the-know Velo sits on a Mooloolaba side street. A mishmash of recycled furniture and vintage ephemera, it's an easy, breezy affair, where locals play retro board games while munching on smashed avo with red onion, roasted garlic, corn and fresh herbs, or housemade toasted banana, macadamia and date bread with mascarpone and an orange-cardamon syrup. Great, locally roasted coffee too.

Good Bar
AMERICAN $

(☑07-5477 6781; www.thegoodbar.com.au; 5/19-23 First Ave, Mooloolaba; burgers $12-20, hot dogs $12-16; ⊙11am-late Tue-Sun, kitchen closes 10.30pm) Clad in concrete floors and red-and-black tiles, trendy Good Bar serves quality American grub, including succulent burgers and epic *haute dawgs* with combos like house-smoked Weiner with Asian slaw, peanuts, crispy noodles and *nam jim* sauce. Other standouts include a 20-hour smoked Cape Grim brisket. There's a French-Mex breakfast menu on weekends, plus craft spirits and beers behind the bar.

Piano Bar
MEDITERRANEAN $$

(☑0422 291 249; www.thepianobar.com.au; 22-24 Ocean St, Maroochydore; bar snacks $4-9, tapas $9-20; ⊙5-10pm Mon & Tue, to 11pm Wed & Thu, noon-11pm Fri-Sun) Bohemian down to its tasseled lampshades, Liberace tomes and fedora-clad barkeeps, Piano Bar peddles generously sized, pan-Mediterranean tapas (order one or two at a time). The charred marinated octopus is pillow-soft, while the glazed beetroot with feta is beautifully textured. Less ubiquitous wine varietals and live blues, funk or jazz Wednesday to Monday seal the deal.

★ Spice Bar
FUSION $$$

(☑07-5444 2022; www.spicebar.com.au; 1st fl, 123 Mooloolaba Esplanade, Mooloolaba; small plates $7-18, large plates $28-36; ⊙6pm-late Tue, noon-3pm & 6pm-late Wed-Sun) Local gourmands swoon over this slick, contemporary eatery dishing up superb Asian-fusion fare. The menu is a share-plates affair, with options ranging from Hervey Bay scallops with a soy-ginger *sabayon* to butter-soft beef cheek *rendang* with sweet potato, snake beans and curry leaf. For the best experience, opt for one of the fantastic degustation menus (five/seven/10 courses $55/75/90).

🍷 Drinking & Nightlife

Pallet Espresso Bar
COFFEE

(☑0487 342 172; www.facebook.com/thepallet espressobar; 2/161-163 Brisbane Rd, Mooloolaba; ⊙6.30am-3pm Mon-Fri, to 1pm Sat) You'll find (upcycled) pallets here, along with chatty locals, a communal table and a couple of soccer balls, in case you feel the urge to have a kick on the lawn. Not a lot of food options (think raisin toast and some sweet baked treats), but what it does do well is full-bodied, velvety, espresso-based coffee. Just off Brisbane Rd.

Taps@Mooloolaba
BAR

(☑07-5477 7222; www.tapsaustralia.com.au; cnr Esplanade & Brisbane Rd, Mooloolaba; ⊙noon-late) A beer fiend's nirvana, Taps lets you pull your own suds. Seriously. It may sound gimmicky, but it's serious business: there are around 20 craft and other brews to quench the most serious of post-surf thirsts. Beer-friendly bites include cream-cheese-stuffed jalapeños, burgers, loaded fries and a taco salad.

SolBar
CLUB

(☑07-5443 9550; www.solbar.com.au; 10/12-20 Ocean St, Maroochydore; ⊙7.30am-late) SolBar is a godsend for city-starved indie fans. A constantly surprising line-up takes to the stage here, and budding singer-songwriters can try their own luck at the open-mic night on Wednesdays. The venue doubles as a swinging cafe-bar-restaurant, serving everything from smashed avo, pancakes and zucchini-and-corn fritters at brekkie to lunch and dinner grub such as burgers, pizzas and salads.

ⓘ Information

The **Mooloolaba Visitor Information Centre** (☑07-5458 8844; www.visitsunshinecoast. com.au; cnr Brisbane Rd & First Ave, Mooloolaba; ⊙9am-3pm; 🛜) is located a block away from the esplande in the heart of town. The **Maroochydore Visitor Information Centre** (☑07-5458 8842; www.visitsunshinecoast. com.au; cnr Sixth Ave & Melrose St, Maroochydore; ⊙9am-4pm Mon-Fri, to 3pm Sat & Sun; 🛜) also lies one block from the beach.

Further north in Marcoola, Sunshine Coast Airport also houses a **tourist information centre** (☑07-5448 9088; www.visitsunshinecoast. com.au; Sunshine Coast Airport, Friendship Drive, Marcoola; ⊙9am-3pm).

ⓘ Getting There & Away

AIR

Sunshine Coast Airport (p323) Gateway airport for the Sunshine Coast, with direct daily flights to Sydney and Melbourne and thrice-weekly direct flights to Adelaide. Seasonal non-stop flights to Auckland, New Zealand.

BUS

Long-distance buses stop in front of the Sunshine Coast Visitor Information Centre in Maroochydore and beside Underwater World –

Sea Life in Mooloolaba. **Greyhound** (☑1300 473 946; www.greyhound.com.au) buses stop in both Maroochydore and in Mooloolaba, running several times daily to Brisbane (one-way departing Mooloolaba/Maroochydore from $21/22, around two hours). **Premier Motor Services** (☑13 34 10; www.premierms.com. au) runs buses once daily to and from Brisbane (one-way $23, 1½ to 1¾ hours).

Sunbus (TransLink; ☑13 12 30; www.sunbus. com.au) has frequent services between Mooloolaba and Maroochydore ($4.60, 15 minutes) and on to Noosa ($8.60, one to 1½ hours). The **local bus interchange** (Horton Pde, Maroochydore) is at Sunshine Plaza shopping centre.

Coolum & Peregian

POP 7905 (COOLUM); 3530 (PEREGIAN)

Rocky headlands create a number of secluded coves before spilling into the fabulously long stretch of golden sand and rolling surf of Coolum Beach. Like much of the coast along here, the backdrop is spreading suburbia, but thanks to a reasonable cafe society and easy access to the coast's hot spots, it's a useful escape from the more popular and overcrowded holiday scenes at Noosa, Mooloolaba and Maroochydore.

Peregian is the place to indulge in long, solitary beach walks, surfing excellent breaks, and the not-so-uncommon spotting of whales breaking offshore.

Skydive Ramblers (☑07-5448 8877; www.skydiveforfun.com; Sunshine Coast Airport, Kittyhawk Cl, Marcoola; jump from 1830/4570m $299/429) will throw you out of a plane at a ridiculous height. Soak up the coastal view before a spectacular beach landing.

Coolum Surf School (☑0438 731 503; www.coolumsurfschool.com.au; 2hr lesson $60, 5-lesson package $225) will have you riding the waves in no time with surfing lessons; they also hire out surfboards/bodyboards ($50/25 for 24 hours).

🛏 Sleeping & Eating

Coolum Beach Caravan Park CARAVAN PARK $
(☑07-5446 1474; www.sunshinecoastholidayparks. com.au; 1827 David Low Way, Coolum Beach; powered sites $46, cabins from $157; 🐾) Location, location, location: the park not only has absolute beach frontage, but is also just across the road from Coolum's main strip.

Villa Coolum MOTEL $
(☑07-5446 1286; www.villacoolum.com; 102 Coolum Tce, Coolum Beach; 1-bedroom units $99-159, 2-bedroom units $129-180; 🐾❄) Hidden behind a verandah, these good-value '70s-style units offer a warm, friendly welcome. While they show signs of wear and tear, they're spacious and upbeat, with tropical accents and comfy beds. Adding appeal is a pool, pleasant garden and walking distance to one of the area's in-the-know beaches, First Bay.

The Caf CAFE $
(☑07-5446 3564; www.thecafcoolum.com; 21 Birtwill St, Coolum Beach; mains $14-19; ⊗6.30am-4pm; 🐾) Complete with cable-reel-turned-table, cockatoo wallpaper and laid-back vibe, this is arguably Coolum's coolest little cafe. The place whips up great gourmet salads and sandwiches, pies, fresh juices and feel-good smoothies.

Le Bon Delice CAFE $
(☑07-5471 2200; www.lebondelice.com.au; cnr Heron St & David Low Way, Peregian Beach; cakes from $3, meals $9-14; ⊗7am-4pm Mon & Wed-Sat, to 3pm Sun) From the *mille feuille* (French vanilla slice), tarts and pillowy mousse cakes to the *dacquoises* and eclairs, the calorific concoctions from French-born owner and *pâtissier* Jean Jacques at this corner patisserie are as beautiful to look at as they are to devour. If you're hankering for something savoury, nibble on the quiche. Also opens on Tuesdays during the school holidays.

Hand of Fatima CAFE $$
(☑0434 364 328; www.facebook.com/handoffatima cafe; 2/4 Kingfisher Dr, Peregian Beach; mains $17-18.50; ⊗5.30am-2.30pm) A friendly, lo-fi cafe where barefoot beach-goers banter with the staff while waiting for their impeccable macchiatos. In one corner is the tiny open kitchen, pumping out Middle Eastern–inspired dishes like breakfast Persian rice pudding with roasted fruits and nuts, or lunchtime braised *cotechino* sausage with lentils, caramelised onion and Turkish bread. Cash only.

★**Embassy XO** CHINESE $$$
(☑07-5455 4460; www.embassyxo.com.au; 56 Duke St, Sunshine Beach; mains $29-42; ⊗restaurant 6-9pm Wed-Sun, also noon-2pm Fri & Sat, noon-3pm Sun, bar menu 3-6pm Wed-Sun) Smart, sophisticated Embassy XO is not your average suburban Chinese joint. Local produce drives smashing Asian dishes like Hinterland zucchini flowers stuffed with tofu and Sichuan chill caramel and Moreton Bay bug wontons with *tobiko* and coconut miso bisque. Other options include gorgeous banquets (vegetarian/nonvegetarian $55/80),

yum cha lunch Friday to Sunday and moreish bar snacks from 3pm to 6pm.

Pitchfork　　　　　MODERN AUSTRALIAN **$$$**
(☑07-5471 3697; www.pitchforkrestaurant.com.au; 5/4 Kingfisher Dr, Peregian Beach; mains $32-45; ⊗noon-2pm & 5pm-late Tue-Sun) The award-winning chefs at this bright, summery restaurant pump out a concise, contemporary menu where crispy soft-shell crab might get fresh peppercorn *nam jim* and green apple, or where roasted pork belly goes sultry in a smoked pork *jus*. Allow time for a meal here: sip on an Italian *soave* and soak up the action on the lush, green square.

Cooloola Coast

Stretching for 50km between Noosa and Rainbow Beach, the Cooloola Coast is a remote strip of long sandy beach backed by the Cooloola Section of the **Great Sandy National Park**. Although it's undeveloped, the 4WD and tin-boat set flock here in droves, so it's not always as peaceful as you might imagine. If you head off on foot or by canoe along one of the many inlets or waterways, however, you'll soon escape the crowds. The coast is famous for the **Teewah coloured sand cliffs**, estimated to be about 40,000 years young.

Great Sandy National Park: Cooloola Section

Extending from Lake Cootharaba north to Rainbow Beach, this 54,000 hectare section of national park offers wide ocean beaches, soaring cliffs of richly coloured sands, pristine bushland, heathland, mangroves and rainforest, all of which are rich in bird life, including rarities such as the red goshawk and the grass owl. One of the most extraordinary experiences here is driving along the beach from Noosa North Shore to Double Island Point, around 50km to the north.

The route is only accessible to 4WDs with a vehicle permit (available from www.npsr.qld.gov.au) and forms part of the Great Beach Drive, a spectacular coastal touring route linking Noosa and Hervey Bay. At Double Island Point, a 1.1km-long walking trail leads up to spectacular ocean views and a lighthouse dating back to 1884. From June to October, it's also a prime place for spotting majestic humpback whales.

From the Double Island Point section of the beach, a 4WD track cuts across the point to the edge of a large tidal lake (perfect for kids and less confident swimmers) and then along Rainbow Beach to the town of Rainbow Beach, passing along the way spectacular coloured cliffs made of ancient, richly oxidised sands in over 70 earthy shades. According to local Indigenous legend, the sands obtained their hues when Yiningie (a spirit represented by a rainbow) plunged into the cliffs after fighting an evil tribesman. The black sand is rutile, once locally mined to make titanium for American space technology.

Great Beach Drive 4WD Tours (☑07-5486 3131; www.greatbeachdrive4wdtours.com; full-day tour adult/child/family $165/95/475) offers intimate, eco-centric 4WD tours of the spectacular Great Beach Drive from Noosa to Rainbow Beach. **Epic Ocean Adventures** (☑0408 738 192; www.epicoceanadventures.com.au; 1/6 Rainbow Beach Rd, Rainbow Beach; 3hr surfing/kayaking trip $65/75; ⊗shop 8am-5pm) runs adventure tours departing both Rainbow Beach and Noosa, and including dolphin- and turtle-spotting kayaking trips.

Hoof it along the beach with **Rainbow Beach Horse Rides** (☑0412 174 337; www.rainbowbeachhorserides.com.au; Clarkson Dr, Rainbow Beach; 90min beach ride $140), including an evocative, two-hour Full Moon Ride ($200).

The most popular (and best-equipped) **camping grounds** (☑13 74 68; www.npsr.qld.gov.au; sites per person/family $6.15/24.60) are Fig Tree Point (at the northern end of Lake Cootharaba), Harry's Hut (about 4km upstream) and Freshwater (about 6km south of Double Island Point) on the coast. You can also camp at designated zones on the beach if you're driving up to Rainbow Beach.

Rainbow Beach Ultimate Camping (☑07-54868633; www.rainbow-beach-hire-a-camp.com.au; 2-/3-/5-night camping experience for 1-4 people from $580/690/820) takes all the hard work out of camping by providing most of the equipment and setting it up for you, from the tent, mattresses, stretchers and crockery, to the dining table, BBQ, private toilet and shower.

For park information contact the **QPWS Great Sandy Information Centre** (☑07-5449 7792; 240 Moorindil St, Tewantin; ⊗8am-4pm).

Lake Cooroibah

A couple of kilometres north of Tewantin, the Noosa River widens into Lake Cooroibah. Surrounded by lush bushland,

WORTH A TRIP

EUMUNDI

Adorable Eumundi is a quaint highland village with a quirky New Age vibe that's greatly amplified during its famous market days. Fig trees, weatherboard pubs and tin-roof cottages line its historic streetscape, which is dotted with cafes, galleries, eclectic boutiques and crafty folk.

Eumundi Markets (☎07-5442 7106; www.eumundimarkets.com.au; 80 Memorial Dr; ⊙8am-1.30pm Wed, 7am-2pm Sat) is one of Australia's most famous and atmospheric artisan markets, attracting over 1.6m visitors a year to its 600-plus stalls. Dive into a leafy, bohemian wonderland of hand-crafted furniture, jewellery, clothing and accessories, art, fresh local produce, gourmet provisions and more.

Internationally renowned surfboard shaper **Tom Wegener** (www.tomwegenersurfboards.com; Cooroy) offers homestays where you can spend a day or two learning about the craft of surfboard shaping. The homestay costs $500 per day (excluding materials) and includes eight hours in the studio, plus meals and surfing sessions.

The **Imperial Hotel** (☎07-5442 8811; www.imperialhoteleumundi.com.au; 1 Etheridge St; mains $18-34; ⊙10am-late) is a gorgeous colonial-style pub with kooky bohemian touches,much-loved for its beer garden, extensive menu and live music acts.

One of Queensland's top dining destinations (book three weeks ahead for weekends), **Spirit House** (☎07-5446 8994; www.spirithouse.com.au; 20 Nindery Rd, Yandina; share plates $14-49; ⊙noon-3pm daily & 6-9pm Wed-Sat) evokes the deep jungles of Southeast Asia with Thai flavours propelling confident dishes like fried soft-shell crab with curry powder and garlic, and braised duck leg with fish sauce, watermelon, ginger and mint. It's also home to a cooking school (four-hour classes $150). It's 11km south of Eumundi.

the glassy lake feels a world away from the bustle of Noosa and makes for a soothing day trip.

From the end of Moorindil St in Tewantin, cash-only **Noosa North Shore Ferries** (☎07-5447 1321; www.noosanorthshoreferries.com.au; one-way per pedestrian/car $1/7; ⊙5.30am-10.20pm Sun-Thu, to 12.20am Fri & Sat) shuttle across the river to Noosa North Shore. Ferries depart approximately every 10 minutes.

The refreshingly feral **Gagaju Bush Camp** (☎07-5474 3522; http://gagaju.tripod.com; 118 Johns Rd, Cooroibah; dm $15; @) is a riverside eco-wilderness camp with basic dorms constructed out of recycled timber.

Noosa North Shore Retreat (☎07-5447 1225; www.noosanorthshoreretreat.com.au; Beach Rd, Noosa North Shore; powered/unpowered camp sites from $42/32, cottages/r from $170/220; ✳@✳) has everything from camping and vinyl 'village tents' to shiny motel rooms and cottages, and the **Great Sandy Bar & Restaurant** (mains $19-28).

Lake Cootharaba & Boreen Point

Cootharaba is the largest lake in the Cooloola Section of Great Sandy National Park, measuring about 5km across and 10km in length. On the western shores of the lake and

at the southern edge of the national park, **Boreen Point** is a relaxed little community and home to one of Queensland's oldest and most atmospheric pubs. The lake is the gateway to the glassy **Noosa Everglades**, which lure with the offer of bushwalking, canoeing and bush camping.

From Boreen Point, a road leads another 5km to **Elanda Point** (unsealed for half the way).

Kanu Kapers (☎07-5485 3328; www.kanukapersaustralia.com; 11 Toolara St, Boreen Point; guided tour adult/child from $155/80, 2-/3-day kayaking & camping tour $395/595) offers fantastic half-day and full-day guided tours of the Noosa Everglades, as well two- and three-day kayaking and camping adventures to Cooloola National Park. Self-guided tours are also available.

On Lake Cootharaba, stunning little **Boreen Point Camping Ground** (☎07-5485 3244; www.noosaholidayparks.com.au; Esplanade, Boreen Point; powered/unpowered sites from $31/25) is crowd-free and provides you with your own secluded patch of lake-front, native bush.

Framed by palms, jacarandas, quandong trees and the odd bush turkey, the adorable old **Apollonian Hotel** (☎07-5485 3100; www.apollonianhotel.com.au; 19 Laguna St, Boreen Point; mains $18-28; ⊙kitchen 10am-8pm Sun-Thu, to

10pm Fri & Sat, bar 10am-10pm Sun-Thu, to midnight Fri & Sat; 📶), complete with shady verandahs and a beautifully preserved interior, dates back to the late 19th century. It's famous for its Sunday spit-roast lunch.

Sunshine Coast Hinterland

Inland from Nambour, the **Blackall Range** forms a stunning backdrop to the Sunshine Coast's beaches a short 50km away. A relaxed half- or full-day circuit drive from the coast follows a winding road along the razorback line of the escarpment, passing through quaint mountain villages and offering spectacular views of the coastal lowlands.

The one standout village is bohemian **Maleny** (population 3440), which offers an intriguing melange of artists, musicians and other creative souls; ageing hippies; rural 'tree-changers' and co-op ventures.

There are many ye olde lolly shops in this neck of the woods, but **Sweets on Maple** (📞 07-5494 2118; www.sweetsonmaple.com.au; 39 Maple St, Maleny; homemade fudge 100g from $5; ⊙ 9.30am-4.30pm Mon-Fri, to 4pm Sat & Sun) licks them all.

Maleny is on the craft-beer radar thanks to hip **Brouhaha Brewery**, sporting an industrial fit-out and outdoor deck. Its nine brews include IPAs, stouts, saisons and sours, some made with local produce. At **Big Barrel** (📞 07-5429 6300; www.malenymountain wines.com.au; 787 Landsborough-Maleny Rd, Maleny; ⊙ 10am-5pm) wines include a smooth Maleny rosé (made using locally grown Chambourcin grapes), while the microbrewery uses local rainwater to produce some unusual drops, from malt-forward Scotch ale to a mango cider.

The hinterland's real appeal, however, is its natural beauty: lush green pastures, softly folded valleys, waterfalls, swimming holes, rainforests and trail-laced national parks.

FRASER COAST

The Fraser Coast runs the gamut from coastal beauty, beachfront national parks and tiny seaside villages to agricultural farms and sugar-cane fields surrounding old-fashioned country towns.

Hervey Bay

POP 52,288

Hervey Bay is an unassuming seaside community with an endless beachfront esplanade ideal for extensive lingering – Pialba, Torquay and Scarness all claim a section. Here patrons of beer gardens and cafes dust off their sandy feet after a dip in the warm, gentle waters surrounding the town. Young travellers with an eye on Fraser Island rub shoulders with grey nomads passing languidly through camp sites and serious fisherfolk recharging in pursuit of the one that got away. Throw in the chance to see majestic humpback whales frolicking in the water and the town's convenient access to the World Heritage–listed Fraser Island, and it's easy to understand how Hervey Bay has become an unflashy, yet undeniably appealing, tourist hot spot.

Fraser Island shelters Hervey Bay from the ocean surf and the sea here is shallow and completely flat – perfect for kiddies and summer holiday pics.

◉ Sights

Reef World AQUARIUM
(📞 07-4128 9828; Pulgul St, Urangan; adult/child $20/10, shark dives $55; ⊙ 9.30am-4pm) In operation since 1979, this small aquarium is popular with families for its interactive feeding sessions at 11am and 2.30pm. You can also take a dip with lemon, whaler and other nonpredatory sharks.

Fraser Coast Discovery Sphere MUSEUM
(📞 07-4191 2610; www.frasercoastdiscoverysphere. com.au; 166 Old Maryborough Rd, Pialba; goldcoin donation; ⊙ 10am-4pm) The stalwart of family-centred Hervey Bay tourism is a little tired, but still a very informative way to learn about the region's geography and marine life.

Wetside Water Park PARK
(📞 1300 79 49 29; www.frasercoast.qld.gov.au/Wetside; The Esplanade, Scarness; ⊙ 10am-6pm Wed-Sun, daily during school holidays) On hot days, this spot on the foreshore can't be beaten. There's plenty of shade, fountains, and a boardwalk with water infotainment. Opening hours vary so check the website for updates.

🏃 Activities & Tours

Whale-watching

Whale-watching tours operate out of Hervey Bay every day (weather permitting) during the annual migrations between late July and

Hervey Bay

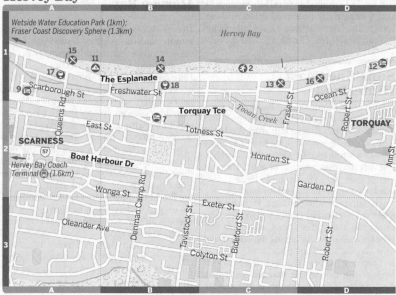

early November. Sightings are guaranteed from August to the end of October (with a free subsequent trip if the whales don't show). Outside of the peak season, many boats offer dolphin-spotting tours. Boats cruise from **Urangan Harbour** out to Platypus Bay and then zip around from pod to pod to find the most active whales. Most vessels offer half-day tours for around $120 for adults and $60 for children, and most include lunch and/or morning or afternoon tea. Tour bookings can be made through your accommodation or the information centres.

Whale-watching outfits include:

Spirit of Hervey Bay (☑ 1800 642 544; www.spiritofherveybay.com; Urangan Harbour; adult/child $120/60; ⊗ 8.30am & 1.30pm)

Freedom Whale Watch (☑ 1300 879 960; www.freedomwhalewatch.com.au; Urangan Harbour)

Blue Dolphin Marine Tours (☑ 07-4124 9600; www.bluedolphintours.com.au; Urangan Harbour; adult/child $150/120)

Tasman Venture (☑ 1800 620 322; www.tasmanventure.com.au; Urangan Harbour; whale-watching adult/child $115/60; ⊗ 8.30am & 1.30pm)

Other Activities

Hervey Bay Ecomarine Tours CRUISE (☑ 07-4124 0066; www.herveybayecomarinetours.com.au; Urangan Marina; 5hr tour adult/child $85/45) Cruise on a 12m glass-bottomed boat, the only one in Hervey Bay. Includes snorkelling, coral viewing and an island barbecue. It's a wonderful day out with family or friends. The new owners also run peaceful 90-minute cruises at 7am and 5pm daily.

Air Fraser Island SCENIC FLIGHTS (☑ 1300 172 706; www.airfraserisland.com.au) Air Fraser's 'Day Away' ($150) is terrific value for those looking to land on the island and explore a little on foot. Add a 4WD on arrival for another $100. Price includes return flight from Hervey Bay or Sunshine Coast.

Aquavue WATER SPORTS (☑ 07-4125 5528; www.aquavue.com.au; 415a The Esplanade, Torquay) In the prime spot on the Torquay foreshore is this long-running aquatic-sports operator. They hire out paddle boards and kayaks ($20 per hour), catamarans ($50 per hour), and jet skis ($50 per 15 minutes). More adventurous souls who perhaps don't have time to visit Fraser properly can take a very fun 90-minute run

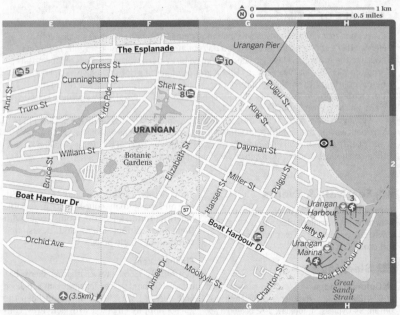

Hervey Bay

to gorgeous Moon Point, which includes lunch ($260).

Susan River Homestead HORSE RIDING
(☑ 07-4121 6846; www.susanriver.com; Maryborough–Hervey Bay Rd) Horse-riding packages (adult/child $250/160) including accommodation, all meals and use of the on-site swimming pool and tennis courts. Day-trippers can canter off on two-hour horse rides (adult/child $85/75).

Skydive Hervey Bay SKYDIVING
(☑ 0458 064 703; www.skydiveherveybay.com.au) Tandem skydives from $325 at 4270m, with up to 45 mouth-flapping seconds of free fall, the highest legal altitude in Australia. Or get a taste of the plummet from 1830m for $189.

Fraser Explorer Tours TOURS
(☑ 07-4194 9222; www.fraserexplorertours.com. au; 1-/2-day tours from $179/330) Very experienced drivers; frequent departures.

A WHALE OF A TIME

Every year, from July to early November, thousands of humpback whales cruise into Hervey Bay's sheltered waters for a few days before continuing their arduous migration south to the Antarctic. Having mated and given birth in the warmer waters off northeastern Australia, they arrive in Hervey Bay in groups of about a dozen (known as pulses), before splitting into smaller groups of two or three (pods). The new calves utilise the time to develop the thick layers of blubber necessary for survival in icy southern waters by consuming around 600L of milk daily.

Viewing these majestic creatures is simply awe-inspiring. You'll see these showy aqua-acrobats waving their pectoral fins, tail slapping, breaching or simply 'blowing', and many will roll up beside the whale-watching boats with one eye clear of the water...making those on board wonder who's actually watching whom.

✯✯ Festivals & Events

Hervey Bay Ocean Festival   CULTURAL
(www.herveybayoceanfestival.com.au; ⊙ Aug) The newly crowned Ocean Festival blesses boats and croons to the whales.

🛏 Sleeping

★ **Colonial Lodge**   APARTMENT $
(☑ 07-4125 1073; www.herveybaycoloniallodge.com.au; 94 Cypress St, Torquay; 1-/2-bedroom apt $95/140; ❄❂🐾) Only nine apartments at this hacienda-style lodge in the middle of Torquay mean that guests can hang out by the pool with a level of exclusivity. Staff are friendly and the apartments are bigger than average, with a lovely seating out front. It's a short walk to the shallows across the road.

Emeraldene Inn   INN $
(☑ 07-4124 5500; www.emeraldene.com.au; 166 Urraween Rd; d from $110) The Emeraldene has been around for a while, but the 10 rooms deserve more attention given the very reasonable price tag and the lovely bush setting just a few blocks from the shore.

Scarness Beachfront Tourist Park   CARAVAN PARK $
(☑ 07-4128 1274; www.beachfronttouristparks.com.au; The Esplanade, Scarness; powered/unpowered sites from $41/34; 🐾) Fronting Hervey Bay's exquisitely long sandy beach, all of Beachfront's three shady parks live up to their name, with fantastic ocean views.

Colonial Village YHA   HOSTEL $
(☑ 07-4125 1844; www.yha.com.au; 820 Boat Harbour Dr, Urangan; dm/d/cabins from $22.50/52/81; ❄@🐾❂) This excellent YHA is set on 8 hectares of tranquil bushland, close to the marina and only 50m from the beach. It's a lovely spot, thick with ambience, possums and parrots. Facilities include a pool, tennis and basketball courts, and a sociable bar-restaurant. All dorm rooms come with their own dining tables and desks, and stand-alone single beds.

Flashpackers   HOSTEL $
(☑ 07-4124 1366; www.flashpackersherveybay.com; 195 Torquay Tce, Torquay; dm $26-32, d $80; ❄❂🐾) Very hospitable staff keep the guests happily engaged with activities, contests and movies when they are not lounging by the excellent pool, or fixing a snack from the walk-in fridge. The dorm rooms are decent enough and the en-suite rooms are quite posh by hostel standards. It's set just back from the beach, but this is a positive as the street has ample parking and there's a little more discretion for late-night revelers stumbling back to bed.

Mango Tourist Hostel   HOSTEL $
(☑ 07-4124 2832; www.mangohostel.com; 110 Torquay Rd, Scarness; dm/d $28/60; P❄❂) Small and discerning hostel run by knowledgeable local Phil, who communicates clearly and directly, and his lovely wife, who balances the act. Intimate and loaded with character (and geckos), the old Queenslander, set on a quiet street away from the beach, sleeps guests in a four-bed dorm room and two very homey doubles.

Shelly Bay Resort   APARTMENT $$
(☑ 07-4125 4533; www.shellybayresort.com.au; 466 The Esplanade, Torquay; 1-/2-bedroom units $139/170; ❄@🐾) The bright, breezy beach-facing apartments at Shelly Bay Resort are some of the best value in town, especially the two-bedroom ones, which have prime corner locations overlooking the pool. Customer service is first class, whether staying for work or pleasure; there's a lot to like about this one.

Pier One
RESORT $$

(☑07-4125 4965; www.herveybaywaterfrontapts.
com.au; 569 The Esplanade; 1-/2-bedroom apt
$189/259) The latest large-scale project on
the Esplanade, Pier One sits alongside Pier
Apartments and suits short-term travellers
looking for a view of the sea in the back-
ground and the pool in the foreground. The
apartments are bigger than most, come with
two bathrooms, Ikea furniture and a very
reasonable price tag.

Grange Resort
RESORT $$$

(☑07-4125 2195; www.thegrange-herveybay.com.
au; 33 Elizabeth St, Urangan; 1-/2-bedroom villas
from $235/305; ✱� ☂ ☒) Reminiscent of a styl-
ish desert resort with fancy split-level condos and filled with life's little luxuries, the
Grange is thriving under new management
and is close to the beach and to town. Pets
are very welcome – a rarity in these parts –
except in the fabulous pool bar where am-
phibious creatures sink beers until the sun
goes down.

✖ Eating

Bayaroma Cafe
CAFE $

(☑07-4125 1515; 428 The Esplanade, Torquay;
breakfast $10-22, mains $9.50-20; ☺6.30am-
3.30pm; ☑) Famous for its coffee, all-day
breakfasts and people-watching position,
Bayaroma has a jam-packed menu that truly
has something for everyone – even vegetarians! Attentive, chirpy service is an added
bonus.

Enzo's on the Beach
CAFE $

(www.enzosonthebeach.com.au; 351a The Esplanade, Scarness; mains $8-20; ☺6.30am-5pm)
This shabby-chic beachside cafe is the place
to go to fill up on sandwiches, wraps, salads
and coffees before working them off on a
hired kayak or kite-surfing lesson.

★ Paolo's Pizza Bar
ITALIAN $$

(☑07-4125 3100; www.paolospizzabar.com.au;
2/446 The Esplanade; mains $14-27; ☺5-9pm)
Hordes of locals come for a slice of Naples
from the pizza oven or in the form of fine
pasta (the spaghetti marinara at $22 was
amazing), and relish the attentive family-run
service. It's the best Italian in the region, but
you can't book, so get here early to avoid the
shoulder shrug.

★ Coast
FUSION $$

(☑07-4125 5454; 469 The Esplanade, Torquay;
mains $21-60; ☺5pm-late Tue & Wed, 11.30am-late
Thu-Sun) A local restaurateur and a red-hot

English chef have teamed up to deliver an outstanding Australian venture in the unlikely
locale of Hervey Bay. Almost all meals are
prepared to be shared, and span the Asian–
Middle Eastern cuisine range. Not hungry?
Share a cocktail pitcher (from $30) and nib-
ble on bar snacks more akin to hors d'oeuvres.

Black Dog Café
MODERN AUSTRALIAN $$

(☑07-4124 3177; 381 The Esplanade, Torquay;
mains $12-35; ☺lunch & dinner) Black Dog de-
livers a variety of contemporary Australian
staples to all parts of Hervey Bay. Its relaxed
diner down the Torquay end of the Espla-
nade serves up burgers, seafood, salads and
the like without fuss and at very fair prices.

☙ Drinking & Nightlife

Beach House Hotel
PUB

(344 The Esplanade) The Beach House has
been reborn, thanks to a shed load of cash,
a prime viewpoint on Scarness Beach and
a willingness to give the people what they
want: beer taps at every turn, gambling
dens, a huge courtyard, decent food and ac-
cessible live music most nights of the week.

Hoolihan's
PUB

(382 The Esplanade, Scarness; ☺11am-2am) Like
all good Irish pubs, Hoolihan's is wildly pop-
ular, especially with the backpacker crowd.
This one is pretty basic, but the kerbside
seating is ideal for people-watching, or for
being watched by people, whichever comes
first.

ⓘ Information

Hervey Bay Visitor Information Centre

(☑1800 811 728; www.visitfrasercoast.com;
cnr Urraween & Maryborough Rds) Helpful and
well-stocked with brochures and information.
On the outskirts of town.

Marina Kiosk (☑07-4128 9800; Buccaneer Ave,
Urangan Boat Harbour, Urangan; ☺6am-6pm)

ⓘ Getting There & Away

AIR

Hervey Bay airport is on Don Adams Dr, just off
Booral Rd. **Qantas** (☑13 13 13; www.qantas.
com.au) and **Virgin** (☑13 67 89; www.virgin
australia.com.au) have daily flights to/from
destinations around Australia.

BOAT

Boats to Fraser Island leave from River Heads,
about 10km south of town, and from **Uran-
gan Marina**. Most tours leave from **Urangan
Harbour**.

BUS

Buses depart **Hervey Bay Coach Terminal** (☎ 07-4124 4000; Central Ave, Pialba). **Greyhound** (☎ 1300 473 946; www.greyhound.com.au) and **Premier Motor Service** (☎ 13 34 10; www.premierms.com.au) have several services daily to/from Brisbane ($72, 6½ hours), Maroochydore ($91, six hours), Bundaberg ($29, two hours) and Rockhampton ($92, six hours).

Tory's Tours (☎ 07-4128 6500; www.torystours.com.au) has twice daily services to Brisbane airport (adult/child $80/68). **Wide Bay Transit** (☎ 07-4121 3719; www.widebaytransit.com.au) has hourly services from Urangan Marina (stopping along The Esplanade) to Maryborough ($8, one hour) every weekday, with fewer services on weekends.

ⓘ Getting Around

Hervey Bay is the best place to hire a 4WD for Fraser Island.

Aussie Trax (☎ 07-4124 4433; www.fraserisland4wd.com.au; 56 Boat Harbour Dr, Pialba)

Fraser Magic 4WD Hire (☎ 07-4125 6612; www.fraser4wdhire.com.au; 5 Kruger Ct, Urangan)

Hervey Bay Rent A Car (☎ 07-4194 6626; www.herveybayrentacar.com.au; 5 Cunningham St, Torquay)

Safari 4WD Hire (☎ 07-4124 4244; www.safari4wdhire.com.au; 102 Boat Harbour Dr, Pialba)

Rainbow Beach

POP 1142

Rainbow Beach is an idyllic Australian beach town at the base of the Inskip Peninsula, which is best known for its colourful sand cliffs and easy access by barge to Fraser Island. It's a decidedly low-key place, half-secret to non-4WD lovers who know little of the dramatic approach possible along the Cooloola Section of the Great Sandy National Park. It's a great place to try your hand at different outdoor activities, tap into the backpacker party scene, or just chill out with family and friends.

🏃 Activities

Rainbow Paragliding PARAGLIDING
(☎ 07-5486 3048, 0418 754 157; www.paraglidingrainbow.com; glides $200) If ever there was a place worthy of leaping from, then the colourful cliffs of Rainbow Beach may just be it. Jean Luc has been paragliding here with exhilarated customers for 20 years. Better value than skydiving and a more mellow thrill.

Wolf Rock Dive Centre DIVING
(☎ 07-5486 8004, 0438 740 811; www.wolfrockdive.com.au; 20 Karoonda Rd; double dive charters from $240) Wolf Rock, a congregation of volcanic pinnacles off Double Island Point, is regarded as one of Queensland's best scuba-diving sites. The endangered grey nurse shark is found here all year.

Epic Ocean Adventures SURFING
(☎ 0408 738 192; www.epicoceanadventures.com.au; 3hr surf lessons $65, 3hr kayak tours $75) Rainbow Beach can throw up some challenging breaks for beginners, but the instructors here are first class. They also offer dolphin-spotting sea-kayak tours.

Fraser's on Rainbow ADVENTURE SPORTS
(☎ 07-5486 8885; www.frasersonrainbow.com) Rainbow Beach is a smart alternative to Hervey Bay as a gateway to Fraser Island. These three-day tag-along tours cost $479 and are seriously fun.

Surf & Sand Safaris ADVENTURE SPORTS
(☎ 07-5486 3131; www.surfandsandsafaris.com.au; half-day tours adult/child $75/40) Half-day 4WD tours through the Great Sandy National Park and along the beach to the coloured sands and lighthouse at Double Island Point. Full-day trips can also be arranged through a partner operator.

Pippies Beach House DRIVING
(☎ 07-5486 8503; www.pippiesbeachhouse.com.au) Departs Rainbow Beach; well-organised, small convoys to Fraser Island ($417) with high safety standards. Maximum of 34 guests and highly recommended by the party set filling out Pippies' dorm rooms.

🛏 Sleeping

Rainbow Beach Hire-a-Camp CAMPGROUND $
(☎ 0419 464 254 07-5486 8633; all-inclusive camping 4 people $145) Camping on the beach is one of the best ways to experience this part of the coast; if you don't have camping gear, Rainbow Beach Hire-a-Camp can hire out equipment, set up your tent, provide food and cooking equipment and camp site, organise camping permits and break camp for you when you're done. Too easy!

Dingo's Backpacker's Resort HOSTEL $
(☎ 1800 111 126; www.dingosresort.com; 20 Spectrum St; dm $30; ✳ @ 🛜 🏊) This party hostel with a busy bar is not for those in need of a good rest. It has loud music (live or otherwise) and karaoke most nights, a chill-out

gazebo, free pancake breakfasts and cheap meals nightly. Dorms are clean and adequate, and excellent tours can be arranged.

Rainbow Beach Holiday Village CARAVAN PARK $
(📞07-5486 3222; www.rainbowbeachholidayvillage. com; 13 Rainbow Beach Rd; powered/unpowered sites from $43/36, villas from $120; ❄ ⬛) Popular beachfront park with a range of villas if you want the vibe but not the hassle.

Pippies Beach House HOSTEL $
(📞07-5486 8503; www.pippiesbeachhouse.com. au; 22 Spectrum St; dm/d $24/65; ❄ @ 🛜 ⬛) This five-bedroom beach house has been converted into a relaxed hostel – the party is elsewhere in Rainbow – where you can catch your breath between outdoor pursuits. Free breakfast, wi-fi and boogie boards, and lots of organised group activities, sweeten the stay. Pippies has expanded, but insist on staying in the main house if you can.

★ Debbie's Place B&B $$
(📞07-5486 3506; www.rainbowbeachaccom modation.com.au; 30 Kurana St; d/ste from $150/180, 3-bedroom apt from $340; ❄ 🛜 ⬛) Greenery abounds at Debbie's meticulously kept Queenslander, which has become the standard bearer for Rainbow Beach holiday accommodation. The charming rooms are fully self-contained, with private entrances and verandahs. The effervescent Debbie is a mine of information and makes this a cosy home away from home. You can leave your car here if taking a tour to Fraser.

✖ Eating

Rainbow Fruit CAFE $
(📞07-5486 3126; 2 Rainbow Beach Rd; wraps from $9; ⏱8am-5pm) Rainbow fresh fruit and vegetables are sliced, diced and puréed for a range of juices, wraps and salads at this humble cafe on the main strip.

★Waterview Bistro MODERN AUSTRALIAN $$
(📞07-5486 8344; Cooloola Dr; mains $26-35; ⏱11.30am-11.30pm Wed-Sat, to 6pm Sun) Sunset drinks are a must at this swish restaurant with sensational views of Fraser Island from its hilltop perch. Get stuck into the signature seafood chowder, steaks and seafood, or have fun cooking your own meal over hot stones.

Rainbow Beach Surf Lifesaving Club PUB FOOD $$
(📞07-5486 3249; Wide Bay Esp; mains from $15; ⏱11am-10pm) The food is fairly standard pub fare, served quickly, with huge slabs of meat, pasta and sides of chips, but the view and the accompanying beer are the reason you come to places like Rainbow Beach in the first place. The strong community spirit is palpable, even if the odd resident boozer makes for a sad mid-afternoon.

ℹ Information

Rainbow Beach Visitor Centre (📞07-5486 3227; www.rainbowbeachinfo.com.au; 8 Rainbow Beach Rd; ⏱7am-5.30pm) Despite the posted hours, it's open sporadically.
Shell Tourist Centre (36 Rainbow Beach Rd; ⏱6am-6pm) At the Shell service station; arranges tour bookings and barge tickets for Fraser Island.

ℹ Getting There & Away

Greyhound (📞1300 473 946; www.grey hound.com.au) has several daily services from Brisbane ($51, five hours), Noosa ($34, three hours) and Hervey Bay ($28, two hours). **Premier Motor Service** (📞13 34 10; www.pre mierms.com.au) has less expensive services. **Active Tours and Transfers** (📞07 5313 6631; www.activetransfers.com.au) runs a shuttle bus to Rainbow Beach from Brisbane Airport ($135, three hours) and Sunshine Coast Airport ($95, two hours).

Most 4WD-hire companies will also arrange permits and barge costs to Fraser Island ($100 per vehicle return), and hire out camping gear. Try **All Trax** (📞07-5486 8767; www.fraser island4x4.com.au; Rainbow Beach Rd, Shell service station; per day from $165) or **Rainbow Beach Adventure Centre** (📞07-5486 3288; www.adventurecentre.com.au; 13 Spectrum St; per day from $180).

Maryborough
POP 23,113
Founded in 1847, Maryborough is one of Queensland's oldest towns, and its port saw the first shaky step ashore for thousands of 19th-century free settlers looking for a better life in the new country. Heritage and history are Maryborough's specialities; the pace of yesteryear is reflected in its beautifully restored colonial-era buildings and gracious Queenslander homes.

This charming old country town is also the birthplace of Pamela Lyndon (PL) Travers, creator of the umbrella-wielding Mary Poppins. The award-winning film Saving Mr Banks tells Travers' story, with early-1900s Maryborough in a starring role.

There's a life-sized statue of Ms Poppins on the corner of Richmond and Wharf Sts. Mary Poppins groupies should schedule their trips for the Mary Poppins Festival in June/July.

In the historic area beside the Mary River, **Portside** (101 Wharf St; ⊙10am-4pm Mon-Fri, to 1pm Sat & Sun) has 13 heritage-listed buildings, parkland and museums. The Portside Centre, located in the former Customs House, has interactive displays on Maryborough's history. **Brennan & Geraghty's Store** (☑07-4121 2250; 64 Lennox St; adult/family $5.50/13.50; ⊙10am-3pm) is now a museum crammed with tins, bottles and packets, including early Vegemite jars and curry powder from the 1890s.

Standy's B&B (50 Ferry Rd; 1-/2-bedroom studios $150/180), a white beauty on the banks of the Mary River, is set on 15 acres of prime land. Guests can choose from two spacious, country-style studios, with white walls and polished floorboards. The food, service and surrounds are all excellent. **Pop In** (203 Bazaar St; sandwiches $8.50; ⊙7am-3pm Mon-Fri, to 1pm Sat) is a popular local cafe with a rotating fresh salad menu and a reputation for fine sandwiches and cakes. Service is efficient and friendly – it's the place to go for a quick meal if you're passing through Maryborough.

Gympie

POP 18,360

Gympie is a pleasant former gold-rush town with some fine heritage architecture, lush parkland and a good ol' country feel. Come in August for the **Gympie Music Muster** (www.muster.com.au), one of the finest country music festivals in Australia.

The **Gympie Gold Mining & Historical Museum** (☑07-5482 3995; www.gympiegoldmuseum.com.au; 215 Brisbane Rd; adult/child/family $10/5/25; ⊙9am-4pm) holds a diverse collection of mining equipment and steam engines, while the **Woodworks Forestry & Timber Museum** (☑07-5483 7691; www.woodworksmuseum.com.au; cnr Fraser Rd & Bruce Hwy; $5; ⊙10am-4pm Mon-Sat) displays memorabilia from the region's old logging days.

If you can't muster up the energy to drive any further, the **Gympie Muster Inn** (☑07-5482 8666; www.gympiemusterinn.com.au; 21 Wickham St; d from $140) is a friendly motel.

Childers

POP 1570

Surrounded by lush green fields and rich red soil, Childers is a charming little town, its main street lined with tall, shady trees and lattice-trimmed historical buildings. The lovely, 100-year-old Federal Hotel has swingin' saloon doors, while a bronze statue of two romping pig dogs sits outside the Grand Hotel. Backpackers flock to Childers for fruit-picking and farm work.

There's a moving memorial to the 15 backpackers who were tragically killed in a hostel fire in 2000, and fantastic art at the **Childers Palace Memorial & Art Gallery** (☑07-4130 4660; 72 Churchill St; ⊙9am-5pm Mon-Fri, to 3pm Sat & Sun) FREE.

The **Old Pharmacy** (☑0400 376 359; 90 Churchill St; adult/child $5/3; ⊙9am-3.30pm Mon-Fri, 9am-1pm Sat) was an operational apothecary's shop between 1894 to 1982, and also functioned as the town dentist, vet, optician and local photographer.

Sugarbowl Backpackers (☑07-4126 1521; www.sugarbowlchilders.com; Bruce Hwy; powered site $29, cabin $90; @≋) is well-maintained and welcoming for those seeking farm labour. Near the Woolworths supermarket, **Drunk Bean** (☑07-4126 1118; Childers Shopping Centre, Bruce Hwy; mains $8-14; ⊙7am-4pm) is an excellent cafe that doubles as an arts-and-craft store. Breakfast, smoothies, light lunches and a stretch of the legs.

ⓘ Getting There & Away

Childers is 50km south of Bundaberg. **Greyhound Australia** (☑1300 473 946; www.greyhound.com.au) and **Premier Motor Service** (☑13 34 10; www.premierms.com.au) both stop at the Shell service station north of town and have daily services to/from Brisbane ($91, 6½ hours), Hervey Bay ($19, one hour) and Bundaberg ($27 1½ hours).

Bundaberg

POP 70,590

Bundaberg is the largest town in the Fraser Coast region and is known across the land more for its eponymous dark rum and fruit-farming backpackers than its coral-fringed beach hamlets. The town proper is an agricultural centre with some friendly pubs and a decent regional art gallery. However, in many people's eyes, the beach hamlets around Bundaberg are more attractive than the town itself. Some 25km north of the centre is Moore Park with wide, flat beaches. To the south is the very popular Elliott Heads with a nice beach, rocky foreshore and good fishing.

⊙ Sights & Activities

★ Bundaberg Rum Distillery   DISTILLERY
(☎07-4131 2999; www.bundabergrum.com.au; Hills St; self-guided tours adult/child $19/9.5, guided tours $28.50/14.25; ⊙10am-3pm Mon-Fri, to 2pm Sat & Sun) Bundaberg's biggest claim to fame is the iconic Bundaberg Rum: you'll see the Bundy Rum polar bear on billboards and bumper stickers all over town. Choose from either a self-guided tour through the museum, or a guided tour of the distillery – tours depart on the hour. Both include a tasting for those over 18. Wear closed shoes.

Bundaberg Barrel   BREWERY
(☎07-4154 5480; www.bundaberg.com; 147 Bargara Rd; adult/child $12/5; ⊙9am-4.30pm Mon-Sat, 10am-3pm Sun) Bundaberg's nonalcoholic ginger beer and other soft drinks aren't as famous as Bundy Rum, but they are very good. Visit the Barrel to take an audio tour of the small museum. Tastings are included and it's geared towards families.

Bundaberg Regional Arts Gallery   GALLERY
(☎07-4130 4750; www.bundabergregionalgalleries.com.au; 1 Barolin St; ⊙10am-5pm Mon-Fri, 11am-3pm Sat & Sun) FREE This small (and vividly purple) gallery has surprisingly good exhibitions.

Hinkler Hall of Aviation   MUSEUM
(☎07-4130 4400; www.hinklerhallofaviation.com; Mt Perry Rd, Botanic Gardens; adult/child $18/10, family $28-40; ⊙9am-4pm) This modern museum has multimedia exhibits, a flight simulator and informative displays chronicling the life of Bundaberg's famous son Bert Hinkler, who made the first solo flight between England and Australia in 1928.

Bundaberg Aqua Scuba   DIVING
(☎07-4153 5761; www.aquascuba.com.au; 239 Bourbong St; diving courses from $349) Leads dives to nearby sites around Innes Park.

Burnett River Cruises   CRUISE
(☎0427 099 009; www.burnettrivercruises.com.au; School Lane, East Bundaberg; 2½hr tours adult/child $26.50/10) The *Bundy Belle*, an old-fashioned ferry, chugs at a pleasant pace

---

TURTLE TOTS

Mon Repos, 15km northeast of Bundaberg, is one of Australia's most accessible turtle rookeries. From November to late March, female loggerheads lumber laboriously up the beach to lay eggs in the sand. About eight weeks later, the hatchlings dig their way to the surface, and, under cover of darkness, emerge en masse to scurry as quickly as their little flippers allow down to the water.

The **Bundaberg Visitor Centre** (p346) has information on turtle conservation and organises nightly **tours** (adult/child $12/6.25) from 7pm during the season. Bookings are mandatory and need to be made through the visitor centre or online at www.bundabergregion.org. The Bundaberg Visitor Centre also has reports of how many turtles have been seen through the season.

---

to the mouth of the Burnett River. See website or call for tour times.

🛏 Sleeping & Eating

Bundaberg Spanish Motor Inn   MOTEL $
(☎07-4152 5444; www.bundabergspanishmotorinn.com; 134 Woongarra St; s/d $115/120; ✸🖳⊠) A Spanish hacienda-style motel does not feel out of place in the dry Bundaberg climate, and this old-fashioned motor inn in a quiet side street off the main drag is *muy bueno* (very good). Spotless units are self-contained and all rooms overlook the central pool. Breakfast is *deliciosa*.

Bigfoot Backpackers   HOSTEL $
(☎07-4152 3659; 66 Targo St; dm from $24; 🅿✸) Pretty grim, bare-bones dorm rooms at this central hostel, but it's an excellent place to arrange fruit-picking jobs and to meet other travellers in the spacious games-room area.

★ Inglebrae   B&B $$
(☎07-4154 4003; www.inglebrae.com; 17 Branyan St; r incl breakfast $130-150; ✸) For old-world English charm in a glorious Queenslander, this delightful B&B is just the ticket. Polished timber and stained glass seep from the entrance into the rooms, which come with high beds and small antiques.

★ **Alowishus Delicious** CAFE $
(☑ 07-4154 2233; 176 Bourbong St; coffees from $3, mains $10-22; ⊙ 7am-5pm Mon-Wed, 7am-9pm Thu, 7am-11pm Fri, 8am-11pm Sat, 8am-5pm Sun) Finally! A cafe open at night! This creative catering company is a great place to type that blog, meet a friend for a late-night pastry, or bang in a coffee between shifts picking mangoes.

Spicy Tonight FUSION $
(☑ 07-4154 3320; 1 Targo St; dishes $12-20; ⊙ 11am-2.30pm & 5-9pm Mon-Sat, 5-9pm Sun) What do you get when you cross Thai and Indian? Spices you never knew could coexist. Bundaberg's saucy little secret serves hot curries, vindaloo, tandoori and a host of vegetarian dishes.

Indulge CAFE $
(80 Bourbong St; dishes $9-18; ⊙ 8.30am-4.30pm Mon-Fri, 7.30am-12.30pm Sat) Much of the local Bundaberg sugar must go into the incredible cakes and pastries at this cafe, which promotes local produce.

★ **Oodies Cafe** CAFE $$
(☑ 07-4153 5340; www.oodies.com.au; 103 Gavin St; ⊙ 6.30am-4pm) A double garage on the edge of Bundaberg's CBD is the unlikely venue for the town's coolest cafe. Oodies is an oddity where you can lounge on leather armchairs with the hipcats sipping chai lattes, or dine from the healthy, well-priced breakfast and lunch menus. Sandwiches, burgers, cakes and more are served.

Cool Banana's Cafe CAFE $$
(☑ 07-4198 1182; 91 Bourbong St; meals from $10; ⊙ 8am-8.30pm) Cheap and cheerful cafe run by the same crowd as **Les Chefs** (☑ 07-4153 1770; 238 Bourbong St; mains $27; ⊙ lunch Tue-Fri, dinner Mon-Sat). Daily specials include fish and chips, kebabs and lamb roasts. Coffee and breakfast is decent too.

🍸 Drinking & Nightlife

Spotted Dog Tavern BAR
(☑ 07-4198 1044; 217 Bourbong St) Bundaberg's most popular bar-restaurant is busy all day. Food is nothing special – standard pub fare without much fuss – but the music, live sports, and air of permanent celebration on the spacious patio make it a local favourite.

Bargara Brewing Company CRAFT BEER
(☑ 07-4152 1675; 10 Tantitha St; ⊙ 11am-10pm Wed-Sat, 5-10pm Sun) Bundaberg has a buzzing new rival to the rum monopoly in the form of a craft brewery that serves fine platters of nibbles to accompany pints of Drunk Fish, Great Barrier Beer and Hip Hop.

ℹ Information

Bundaberg Visitor Centre (☑ 07-4153 8888, 1300 722 099; www.bundabergregion.org; 271 Bourbong St; ⊙ 9am-5pm) This reliable information centre serves the region admirably. Definitely stop by if you are driving through the area.

ℹ Getting There & Away

AIR
Bundaberg is served daily by **Virgin** (p341) and **Qantas** (☑ 13 13 13; www.qantas.com.au).

BUS
The **coach terminal** (☑ 07-4153 2646; 66 Targo St) is on Targo St. Both **Greyhound** (☑ 1300 473 946; www.greyhound.com.au) and **Premier Motor Service** (☑ 13 34 10; www.premierms.com.au) have daily services connecting Bundaberg with Brisbane ($94, seven hours), Hervey Bay ($29, two hours) and Rockhampton ($54, five hours).
Duffy's Coaches (☑ 1300 383 397) has numerous services every weekday to Bargara ($5, 35 minutes), leaving from the back of Target on Woongarra St.

TRAIN
The **Queensland Rail** (☑ 1800 872 467; www.traveltrain.com.au) Tilt Train stops at Bundaberg train station en route to Brisbane ($49, 4½ hours, Sunday to Friday). Queensland Rail's Sunlander ($89, seven hours, three weekly) also travels from Brisbane to Bundaberg on its route to Cairns and Rockhampton.

Fraser Island

The local Butchulla people call it K'Gari – paradise – and for good reason. Sculpted from wind, sand and surf, the striking blue freshwater lakes, crystalline creeks, giant dunes and lush rainforests of this gigantic sandbar form an enigmatic island paradise unlike anywhere else. Fraser Island is the largest sand island in the world (measuring 120km by 15km), and is the only known place where rainforest grows on sand.

Inland, the vegetation varies from dense tropical rainforest and wild heath to wetlands and wallum scrub, with sandblows, mineral streams and freshwater lakes opening onto long sandy beaches. The island, most of which is protected as part of the Great Sandy National Park, is home to a profusion of bird life and wildlife, including the

Fraser Island

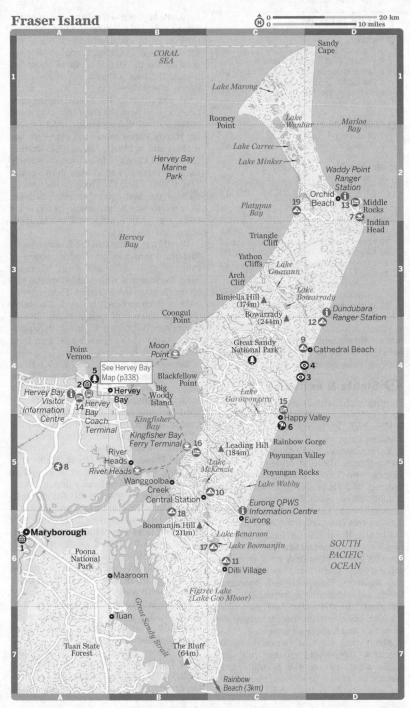

Fraser Island

famous dingo, while offshore waters teem with dugong, dolphins, manta rays, sharks and migrating humpback whales.

◎ Sights & Activities

Starting at the island's southern tip, where the ferry leaves for Inskip Point on the mainland, a high-tide access track cuts inland, avoiding dangerous Hook Point, and leads to the entrance of the Eastern Beach's main thoroughfare. The first settlement is **Dilli Village**, the former sand-mining centre; **Eurong**, with shops, fuel and places to eat, is another 9km north. From here, an inland track crosses to Central Station and Wanggoolba Creek (for the ferry to River Heads).

Right in the middle of the island is the ranger centre at **Central Station**, the starting point for numerous walking trails. From here you can walk or drive to the beautiful **McKenzie, Jennings, Birrabeen** and **Boomanjin Lakes**. Lake McKenzie is spectacularly clear and ringed by white-sand beaches, making it a great place to swim; Lake Birrabeen sees fewer tour and backpacker groups.

About 4km north of Eurong along the beach, a signposted walking trail leads across sandblows to the beautiful **Lake Wabby**, the most accessible of Fraser's lakes. An easier route is from the Lake Wabby Lookout, off Cornwell's Break Rd from the inland side. Lake Wabby is surrounded on three sides by eucalyptus forest, while the fourth side is a massive sandblow that encroaches on the lake at a rate of about 3m a year. The lake is deceptively shallow and diving is very dangerous.

As you drive up the beach, during high tide you may have to detour inland to avoid Poyungan and **Yidney Rocks**, before reaching **Happy Valley**, which has places to stay, a shop and a bistro. About 10km further north is **Eli Creek**, a fast-moving waterway that will carry you effortlessly downstream. About 2km from Eli Creek is the rotting hulk of the **Maheno**, a former passenger liner which was blown ashore by a cyclone in 1935 as it was being towed to a Japanese scrap yard.

Roughly 5km north of the *Maheno* you'll find the **Pinnacles**, an eroded section of coloured sand cliffs, and about 10km beyond, **Dundubara**, with a ranger station and an excellent camping ground. Then there's a 20km stretch of beach before you come to the rock outcrop of **Indian Head**. Sharks, manta rays, dolphins and (during the migration season) whales can often be seen from the top of this headland.

Between Indian Head and Waddy Point, the trail branches inland, passing **Champagne Pools**, which offers the only safe saltwater swimming on the island. There are good camping areas at **Waddy Point** and **Orchid Beach**, the last settlement on the island. Many tracks north of here are closed for environmental protection.

The **Fraser Island Great Walk** is a stunning way to experience this enigmatic island. The trail undulates through the island's interior for 90km from Dilli Village to Happy Valley. Broken up into seven sections of around 6km to 16km each, plus some side trails, it follows the pathways of Fraser Island's original inhabitants, the Butchulla people. En route, the walk passes underneath rainforest canopies, circles around some of the island's vivid lakes, and courses through shifting dunes.

It's imperative that you visit www.npsr.qld.gov.au for maps, detailed information and updates on the track, which can close when conditions are bad.

Air Fraser Island (p351) has a terrific value 'Day Away' tour ($150) for those looking to land on the island and explore on foot. Depart from Hervey Bay or Sunshine Coast.

SAND SAFARIS

The only way to explore Fraser Island (besides walking) is with a 4WD. For most travellers, there are three transport options: tag-along tours, organised tours or 4WD hire; the fourth option is to stay at one of the island's accommodations and take day tours from there. This is a fragile environment; bear in mind that the greater the number of individual vehicles driving on the island, the greater the environmental damage. With an average of 1000 people per day visiting the island, Fraser can sometimes feel like a giant sandpit with its own peak hour and congested beach highway.

Tag-Along Tours

Popular with backpackers, tag-along tours see groups of travellers pile into a 4WD convoy and follow a lead vehicle with an experienced guide and driver. Travellers take turns driving the other vehicles, which can be great fun, but has also led to accidents. Rates hover around $400 to $430; be sure to check if your tour includes food, fuel, alcohol, etc. Accommodation is often in tents.

Advantages: you can make new friends fast; driving the beaches is exhilarating. Disadvantages: if food isn't included, you'll have to cook; groups can be even bigger than on bus tours.

Dropbear Adventures (☑1800 061 156; www.dropbearadventures.com.au) Lots of departures from Hervey Bay, Rainbow Beach and Noosa to Fraser Island; easy to get a spot.

Fraser's on Rainbow (p342) Departs from Rainbow Beach.

Pippies Beach House (p342) Departs Rainbow Beach; well-organised, small convoys with high safety standards.

Organised Tours

Most organised tours cover Fraser's hot spots: rainforests, Eli Creek, Lakes McKenzie and Wabby, the coloured Pinnacles and the *Maheno* shipwreck.

Advantages: expert commentary; decent food and comfortable accommodation; often the most economical choice. Disadvantages: day-tour buses often arrive en masse at the same place at the same time; less social.

Cool Dingo Tours (☑07-4120 3333; www.cooldingotour.com; 2-/3-day tours from $360/415) Overnight at lodges with the option to stay extra nights on the island. The party option.

Fraser Explorer Tours (p339) Very experienced drivers; lots of departures.

Fraser Experience (☑07-4124 4244; www.fraserexperience.com; adult/child from $180/130) Small group tours offer greater freedom with the itinerary.

Remote Fraser (☑07-4124 3222; www.tasmanventure.com.au; tours $150) Day tours to the less-visited west coast.

4WD Hire

You can hire a 4WD from Hervey Bay, Rainbow Beach or on Fraser Island itself. All companies require a hefty bond, usually in the form of a credit-card imprint, which you will lose if you drive in salt water – don't even think about running the waves!

When planning your trip, reckon on covering 20km an hour on the inland tracks and 40km an hour on the eastern beach. Most companies will help arrange ferries, permits and camping gear. Rates for multiday rentals start at around $185 a day.

Advantages: complete freedom to roam the island and escape the crowds. Disadvantages: you may encounter beach and track conditions that even experienced drivers find challenging; expensive.

There are rental companies in Hervey Bay (p342) and Rainbow Beach (p343). On the island, **Aussie Trax** (☑07-4124 4433; www.fraserisland4wd.com.au) hires out 4WDs from $283 per person, per day.

🛏 Sleeping

Camping permits are required in order to camp at NPSR camping grounds and any public areas (ie along the beach). The most developed **NPSR camping grounds** (☑13 74 68; www.npsr.qld.gov.au; per person/family $6.15/24.60), with coin-operated hot showers, toilets and BBQs, are at **Waddy Point**, **Dundubara** and **Central Station**. Campers with vehicles can also use the smaller camping grounds with fewer facilities at **Lake Boomanjin**, and at **Ungowa** and **Wathumba** on the western coast. Walkers' camps are set away from the main camping grounds, along the Fraser Island Great Walk trail. The trail map lists the camp sites and their facilities. Camping is permitted on designated stretches of the eastern beach, but there are no facilities. Fires are prohibited except in communal fire rings at Waddy Point and Dundubara – bring your own firewood in the form of untreated, milled timber.

Supplies on the island are limited and costly. Stock up well before arriving, and be prepared for mosquitoes and March flies.

Dilli Village Fraser Island   CAMPGROUND $
(☑07-4127 9130; www.usc.edu.au; sites per person $10, dm/cabins $50/120) Managed by the University of the Sunshine Coast, which uses this precinct as a base for research purposes, Dilli Village offers good sites on a softly sloping camping ground. Great value for the space.

Cathedrals on Fraser   CARAVAN PARK $
(☑07-4127 9177; www.cathedralsonfraser.com.au; Cathedral Beach; powered/unpowered sites $39/29, 2-bed cabins with/without bathroom $200/180; ⌨) New owners have kept up the standard and lowered the prices at this spacious dingo-fenced park with abundant, flat, grassy sites. It's a hit with families.

★**Kingfisher Bay Resort**   RESORT $$
(☑1800 072 555, 07-4194 9300; www.kingfisherbay.com; Kingfisher Bay; d from $178, 2-bedroom villas $329; ❄@♨) 🕭 This elegant eco-resort has hotel rooms with private balconies, and sophisticated two- and three-bedroom timber villas that are elevated to limit their environmental impact. There's a three-night minimum stay in high season. The Seabelle Restaurant is terrific (mains from $18), while the three bars are great fun in summer at sunset, especially the Dingo Bar.

Fraser Island Retreat   CABIN $$
(☑07-4127 9144; www.fraserisretreat.com.au; Happy Valley; d/apt from $140/200; @♠♨) Located in the relatively remote Happy Valley, halfway along the east coast of the island, this retreat's nine timber cabins (each sleeping up to four people) are great for a comfortable nature experience. The cabins are airy, nestled in native foliage and close to the beach. On-site there's a camp kitchen, a licensed restaurant and a shop that sells fuel.

★**Eliza Fraser Lodge**   LODGE $$$
(☑0418 981 610; www.elizafraserlodge.com.au; per person $375) Located at a stunning house up at Orchid Beach in the northeast of the island, Eliza Fraser is the finest lodging available. Serviced directly by Air Fraser (regular ferry transfers also available), the two-level house is exquisite for families or

---

ℹ DEALING WITH DINGOES

Despite its many natural attractions and opportunities for adventure, there's nothing on Fraser Island that gives a thrill comparable to your first glimpse of a dingo. Believed to be among the most genetically pure in the world, the dingoes of Fraser are sleek, spry and utterly beautiful. They're also wild beasts that can become aggressive at the drop of a hat (or a strong-smelling food sack). While attacks are rare, there are precautions that must be taken by every visitor to the island.

➡ However skinny they appear, or whatever woebegone look they give you, never feed dingoes. Dingoes that are human-fed quickly lose their shyness and can become combative and competitive. Feeding dingoes is illegal and carries heavy fines.

➡ Don't leave any food scraps lying around, and don't take food to the lakes: eating on the shore puts your food at 'dingo level', an easy target for scrounging scavengers.

➡ Stay in groups, and keep any children within arm's reach at all times.

➡ Teasing dingoes is not only cruel, but dangerous. Leave them alone, and they'll do same.

➡ Dingoes are best observed at a distance. Pack a zoom lens and practise some silence, and you'll come away with some brilliant photographs…and all your limbs intact.

small groups. The hosts are expert guides and will organise fishing trips, nature hikes and 4WD adventures, or let you enjoy the run of the house and spectacular surrounds.

ℹ️ Information

You must purchase permits from **NPSR** (☎13 74 68; www.npsr.qld.gov.au) for vehicles (less than a month $48.25) and to camp in the NPSR camping grounds ($6.15/24.60 per person/family) before you arrive. Permits aren't required for private camping grounds or resorts. Buy permits online or check with visitors centres for up-to-date lists of where to buy them.

Eurong QPWS Information Centre (☎07-4127 9128) is the main ranger station. Others can be found at **Dundubara** (☎07-4127 9138) and **Waddy Point** (☎07-4127 9190). Offices are often unattended as the rangers are out on patrol.

ℹ️ Getting There & Away

Before crossing via ferry from either Rainbow Beach or Hervey Bay, ensure that your vehicle has suitably high clearance (if you're one of the few not visiting on a tour, that is) and, if camping, that you have adequate food, water and fuel.

AIR

Air Fraser Island (☎1300 172 706, 07-4125 3600; www.airfraserisland.com.au) charges from $150 for a return flight (30-minute round trip) to the island's eastern beach, departing Hervey Bay airport.

BOAT

Vehicle ferries connect Fraser Island with **River Heads**, about 10km south of Hervey Bay, or further south at **Inskip Point**, near Rainbow Beach. Ferries from Hervey Bay dock at **Moon Point**.

Fraser Venture Barge (☎1800 227 437, 07-4194 9300; www.fraserislandferry.com. au) Makes the crossing (pedestrian adult/child return $58/30, vehicle and four passengers $175 return, 30 minutes) from River Heads to Wanggoolba Creek on the western coast of Fraser Island. It departs daily from River Heads at 8.30am, 10.15am and 4pm, and returns from the island at 9am, 3pm and 5pm.

Kingfisher Bay Ferry (☎1800 227 437, 07-4194 9300; www.fraserislandferry.com) Operates a daily vehicle and passenger ferry (pedestrian adult/child return $58/30, vehicle and four passengers return $175, 50 minutes) from River Heads to Kingfisher Bay, departing at 6.45am, 9am, 12.30pm, 3.30pm, 6.45pm and 9.30pm (Friday and Saturday only) and returning at 7.50am, 10.30am, 2pm, 5pm, 8.30pm and 11pm (Friday and Saturday only).

Manta Ray (☎07-5486 3935; www.mantaray fraserislandbarge.com.au) Coming from Rainbow Beach, Manta Ray has two ferries making the 15-minute crossing from Inskip Point to Hook Point on Fraser Island, continuously from about 6am to 5.30pm daily (vehicle return $120).

ℹ️ Getting Around

A 4WD is necessary if you're driving on Fraser Island; you'll need a permit. Expensive fuel is available from stores at Cathedral Beach, Eurong, Kingfisher Bay, Happy Valley and Orchid Beach. If your vehicle breaks down, call the **tow-truck service** (☎0428 353 164, 07-4127 9449) in Eurong.

The 4WD **Fraser Island Taxi Service** (☎07-4127 9188; www.fraserservice.com.au) operates all over the island. Bookings are essential, as there's only one cab for the whole island!

If you want to hire a 4WD while on the island, **Aussie Trax** (p349) has a medium-sized fleet, from Suzuki Sierras to LandCruisers, available at the **Kingfisher Bay Resort**.

CAPRICORN COAST & THE SOUTHERN REEF ISLANDS

The stretch of coastline that straddles the tropic of Capricorn is one of the quietest and most lovely lengths of the east coast. While local families flock to the main beaches during school holidays, the scene is uncrowded for most of the year, and even in high season you needn't travel far to find a deserted beach.

Agnes Water & Town Of 1770

POP 1650

Agnes Water is the east coast's most northerly surf beach, a long, glorious point break rolling into an idyllic shoreline by a friendly strip of shops. A 6km jaunt down the road is the site of Captain Cook's first landing in Queensland in, you guessed it, 1770. The short bluff walks are outstanding, and the camping ground is one of the most dreamy in the state, a launching point for kayaking and paddleboarding and fishing excursions around the inlets of the 'Discovery Coast'.

👁️ Sights & Activities

Miriam Vale Historical Society Museum   MUSEUM
(☎07-4974 9511; www.agneswatermuseum.com; Springs Rd, near cnr Captain Cook Dr, Agnes Water; adult/child $3/free; ⊙1-4pm Mon & Wed-Sat, 10am-4pm Sun) The museum displays extracts from Cook's journal and the original

Capricorn Coast

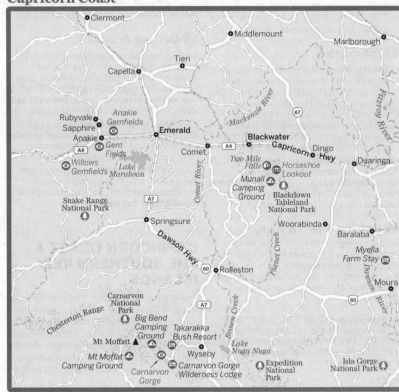

telescope from the first lighthouse built on the Queensland coast.

★ Scooter Roo Tours   ADVENTURE SPORTS
(☑ 07-4974 7697; www.scooterrootours.com; 2694 Round Hill Rd, Agnes Water; 3hr rides $85) You don't need to be a petrol head to absolutely love this hilarious and informative 50km-tour of the Agnes Water area. Better yet, you only need a car licence to get low and dirty on a real 'chopper' bike. Wear long pants and closed-in shoes; they'll supply the tough-guy leather jackets (with flames, of course).

1770 SUP   WATER SPORTS
(☑ 0421 026 255; www.1770sup.com.au; 1½/2hr tours $45/50) Explore the calm waters and sandy banks of 1770 with a top notch stand-up paddleboarding (SUP) instructor. Tours include an intro lesson, or rent your own board for $25/30 for one/two hours. The roving SUP trailer can often be found on the 1770 waterfront across from Tree Bar.

1770 Liquid Adventures   KAYAKING
(☑ 0428 956 630; www.1770liquidadventures. com.au) Paddle off on a spectacular twilight kayak tour. For $55 you ride the waves off 1770, before retiring to the beach for drinks and snacks as the sun sets – keep an eye out for dolphins. You can also rent kayaks (from $20/30 per one/two hours). Family tours ($30 per person) focus on bird and marine life and will appeal to any child who is comfortable paddling alone.

1770 Larc Tours   TOURS
(☑ 07-4974 9422; www.1770larctours.com.au; day trip adult/child $155/95) 🛥 The ex-military Lighter Amphibious Resupply Cargo (LARC) vehicle makes a comfortable ride for exploring the natural joys of Bustard Head and Eurimbula National Park. Guides know their stuff and will entertain all ages. Aside from the signature seven-hour day trip (lunch included), they also run hour-long afternoon

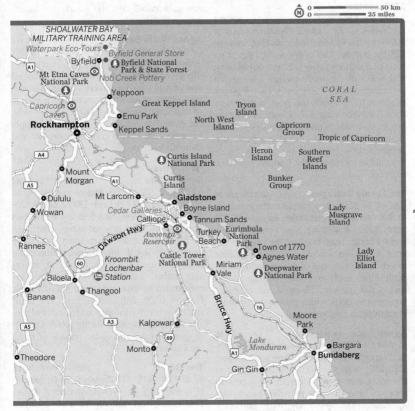

tours (adult/child $38/17) and sandboarding safaris ($120).

✿ Festivals & Events

Agnes Blues & Roots Festival　MUSIC
(www.agnesbluesandroots.com.au; SES Grounds, Agnes Water) Top names and up-and-coming Aussie acts crank it up in the last weekend of February.

⏏ Sleeping

★Cool Bananas　HOSTEL **$**
(☑1800 227 660, 07-4974 7660; www.coolbananas. net.au; 2 Springs Rd, Agnes Water; dm $29; @ 🛜) The young and free go bananas for this funky, open-minded backpacker hangout, with a questionable colour scheme but an irresistible vibe cultivated by the friendly owners. Roomy six- and eight-bed dorms are functional, and management does not allow rooms to be locked in order to en-courage mingling. Funnily enough, it works

(smiles all round when we visited!). It's only a five-minute walk to the beach and shops.

Backpackers @ 1770　HOSTEL **$**
(☑0408 533 851; www.backpackers1770.com.au; 22 Grahame Colyer Dve; dm $26/60) The most established hostel in 1770 is a beauty. The upsides are obvious: easy interactions between staff and guests, spotless dorms, three smart doubles at a good price point and a lush communal garden where meals are taken and stories are shared. For many young travellers, this hostel is an east coast must.

1770 Camping Ground　CARAVAN PARK **$**
(☑07-4974 9286; www.1770campingground.com. au; Captain Cook Dr, Town of 1770; powered/ unpowered sites from $39/35, beachfront sites $44) This camping ground, 1770's favourite, must challenge for best location on the east coast. Fall into the shallow water from your tent strung among plenty of shady trees.

1770 Southern Cross Backpackers
HOSTEL $

(☑07-4974 7225; www.1770southerncross.com; 2694 Round Hill Rd, Agnes Water; dm/d incl breakfast $25/85; @ 🎧 🛋) The large eucalypt-forest re-treat of Southern Cross is 2.5km out of town and will suit the more mellow backpacker (or one in search of time out!). There's plenty of space to lie about the pool, play games, cook a BBQ or sling a hammock. A courtesy bus takes revellers and beach-goers into the 'action' of Agnes, but most guests just roam between their bare four-bed dorms, pleasant double rooms and the Buddha Bar come nightfall.

The Lovely Cottages
GUESTHOUSE $$

(☑07-4974 9554; www.thelovelycottages.com.au; 61 Bicentennial Dr, Agnes Water; cottages $155, 2 nights $300; P ❄ 🎧 🛋) New owners and a name change have boosted the creative energy at this eco-retreat and outdoor gallery, which is the epitome of Queensland casual bush chic. Each colourful cottage sleeps up to five people. There is an excellent lagoon-style pool, which makes for thrilling swimming in the bush scrub.

Agnes Water Beach Club
APARTMENT $$

(☑07-4974 7355; www.agneswaterbeachclub.com. au; 3 Agnes St, Agnes Water; 1-/2-bedroom apt from $180/280; ❄@🎧🛋) The Beach Club has the most convenient location for access to shops in Agnes and the patrolled beach. The apartments themselves are bright and comfortable, facing onto a good-sized pool. Very much a family atmosphere permeating the communal areas.

★1770 Getaway
RESORT $$$

(☑07-4974 9323; www.1770getaway.com.au; 303 Bicentennial Dve, Agnes Water; d from $170; P 🎧 🛋) The much-loved Getaway Garden Cafe (p354) has expanded its repertoire with a delightful series of villas running across four acres of bush onto an empty stretch of beach. Each villa has an airy, open feel and luxury bathrooms. Breakfast by the pond can be included and there's a hip little boutique on-site.

✖ Eating

Sol Foods
VEGAN $

(☑07-4974 9039; 1 Round Hill Rd; salads from $10, cakes from $6; ⏺8am-4.30pm) This wholefoods grocer doubles as a cafe and an enlightened source of local knowledge. The vegan cakes

are unbeatable and the salads are hearty and good value.

Agnes Water Bakery
BAKERY $

(☑07-4974 9500; Round Hill Rd; pies $5.50; ⏺6am-4pm Mon-Sat, to 2pm Sun) Don't dawdle if you want to get your mouth around one of this popular bakery's killer pies. Expect gourmet stuffings, including a couple of vegetarian selections. On the sweet side, the chocolate eclairs, jam scrolls and apple turnovers are usually gone by noon. Oh, and there's bread, too.

★Getaway Garden Café
MODERN AUSTRALIAN $$

(☑07-4974 9323; 303 Bicentennial Dr, Agnes Water; breakfast $7-19, lunch $10-22, dinner $20-25; ⏺8am-4pm Sun-Thu & 5.30-late Wed & Sun) The region's most revered eatery continues to impress due to its culinary simplicity using only local ingredients, impeccable family-oriented service and natural, waterside setting. Breakfasts are healthy and accompanied by fine coffee and juices. Lunch features pizza, fish and burgers. The lamb spit roasts on Wednesday and Sunday nights are very popular with locals (book ahead). Stop in for cake and coffee outside of main meal times.

Tree Bar
MODERN AUSTRALIAN $$

(☑07-4974 7446; 576 Captain Cook Dr, Town of 1770; mains $16-34; ⏺breakfast, lunch & dinner) This is the best outlook for a sun-downer and a steak sandwich in 1770. This little salt-encrusted waterfront diner and bar is no award-winner, but it marvellously catches sea breezes from the beach through the trees. Prices are a little steep for the quality, but you couldn't paint a better view.

Agnes Water Tavern
PUB FOOD $$

(☑07-4974 9469; 1 Tavern Rd, Agnes Water; mains $15-30; ⏺from 11.30am) A broad snapshot of Australian life is found in the huge Tavern just outside town, where you can drink, gamble, play games, watch sport, party, eat, meet and enjoy the sunshine in the ample outdoor seating. The backpacker set keep it lively some nights. Lunch and dinner specials daily.

❶ Information

Agnes Water Visitors Centre (☑07-4902 1533; 71 Springs Rd, Town of 1770; ⏺9am-5pm Mon-Fri, to 4pm Sat & Sun) Staffed by above-and-beyond volunteers who even leave out information and brochures when it's closed, just in case a lost soul blows into town.

Discover 1770 (07-4974 7557; www.discover 1770.com.au; next to Shell service station) With so many different operators plying the Discovery Coast – and often changing hands or merging businesses – the friendly folk at Discover 1770 can help to guide your decision making. At the time of research, it was the only outlet for arranging boats to Lady Musgrave Island.

ℹ Getting There & Away

A handful of **Greyhound** (1300 473 946; www. greyhound.com.au) buses detour off the Bruce Hwy to Agnes Water; daily services include Bundaberg ($28, 1½ hours) and Cairns ($210, 21 hours). **Premier Motor Service** (13 34 10; www.premierms.com.au) also goes in and out of town.

Eurimbula & Deepwater National Parks

Deepwater National Park (www.nprsr.qld. gov.au/parks/deepwater), south of Agnes Water, is an unspoiled coastal landscape with long beaches, freshwater creeks, good fishing spots and two camping grounds. It's also a breeding ground for loggerhead turtles, which dig nests and lay eggs on the beaches between November and February.

The 78-sq-km Eurimbula National Park (http://www.npsr.qld.gov.au/parks/eurimbula), on the northern side of Round Hill Creek, has a landscape of dunes, mangroves and eucalypts. Both offer delightful beaches, hikes and splendid, relatively accessible isolation in the Australia bush.

Camping permits are available from the **NPSR** (13 74 68; www.npsr.qld.gov.au; permit per person/family $6.15/24.60). **Wreck Rock Campground** has a sizeable picnic area, rain and bore water, and composting toilets.

Gladstone

POP 37,940

Gladstone is middle-sized town known nationwide, for better or worse, as a major port for the mining industry, and an industrial town with a power station and an incongruous outlook on the Great Barrier Reef. You might want to head straight for the marina (Bryan Jordan Dr), the main departure point for boats to the southern coral cay islands of Heron, Masthead and Wilson on the Great Barrier Reef. If there's anything happening in town, it's on at the port end of Gondoon St.

Lake Awoonga Boat Hire (07-4975 0930; tinnies half-day $80, kayaks per hour $15) is an unofficial tourist guide and friendly boat hire place, or you can charter the **MV Mikat** (0427 125 727; www.mikat.com.au).

Located at the marina, the **visitor centre** (07-4972 9000; Bryan Jordan Dr; 8.30am-4.30pm Mon-Fri, 9.30am-4.30pm Sat & Sun) is the departure point for boats to Heron Island.

Gladstone Backpackers (07-4972 5744; www.gladstonebackpackers.com.au; 12 Rollo St; dm/tw $28/66; @ 🛜 🐕) is the budget bolthole in town.

The **Gladstone Yacht Club** (07-4972 2294; www.gyc.com.au; 1 Goondoon St; mains from $22; noon-2pm & 6-8.30pm Mon-Thu, 11.30am-2.30pm & 5.30-9pm Fri & Sat, 11.30am-2pm & 6-8.30pm Sun) is a welcoming place where burgers and seafood are the best bets. You can also eat on the deck overlooking the water.

Southern Reef Islands

While much fuss is made about the Great Barrier Reef's northern splendour, Southern Reef Island is the place of 'castaway' dreams: tiny coral atolls fringed with sugary white sand and turquoise-blue seas, and hardly anyone within flipper-flapping reach. From beautiful Lady Elliot Island, 80km northeast of Bundaberg, secluded and uninhabited coral reefs and atolls dot the ocean for about 140km up to Tryon Island. Lady Musgrave is essentially a blue lagoon in the middle of the ocean, while Heron Island is a discerning natural escape for adventurous families and world-class scuba diving.

Several cays in this part of the reef are excellent for snorkelling, diving and just getting back to nature – though reaching them is generally more expensive than reaching islands nearer the coast. Some of the islands are important breeding grounds for turtles and seabirds, and visitors should be aware of precautions to ensure the wildlife's protection.

Lady Elliot Island

Set on the southern rim of the Great Barrier Reef, Lady Elliot is a 40-hectare vegetated coral cay populated with nesting sea turtles and an impressive number of seabirds. It's considered to have the best snorkelling in the southern Great Barrier Reef and the diving is good too: explore an oceanbed of shipwrecks, coral gardens, bommies (coral pinnacles or outcroppings) and blowholes, and abundant marine life, including barracuda, giant manta rays and harmless leopard sharks.

Lady Elliot Island Eco Resort (☑1800 072 200; www.ladyelliot.com.au; r $175-420, children $95) has been around for a few decades now, but it has fortunately lost little of its ramshackle charm. The cabins are a great deal for groups of four on a budget, while the garden suites offer a little more protection from the wind and more space to stretch out at night.

Heron Island

Part of the smaller Capricornia Cays group, Heron Island is ranked among the finest scuba diving regions in the world, particularly in terms of ease of access. Visitors to Heron generally know what they are coming for – underwater paradise – but the island's rugged beauty is reason enough to stay above the surface. A true coral cay, it is densely vegetated with pisonia trees and surrounded by 24 sq km of reef. There's a resort and research station on the northeastern third of the island; the remainder is national park. Note that 200,000 birds call the island home at different stages of the year, so there can be a lot of guano at times.

The island has excellent beaches, superb snorkelling and, during the season, turtle watching.

Heron Island Resort (☑1300 863 248; www.heronisland.com; d/ste from $330/572) is not particularly glamorous, despite the hefty price tag for a room, however the interaction with an incredible natural environment is difficult to find elsewhere in the world, and the resort itself should not be the reason you visit. Great deals are often available on its website. Meal packages are extra, and guests will pay $62/31 (one way) per adult/child for launch transfer, $338 by seaplane from Gladstone.

The Heron Islander (☑1800 837 168; www.heronisland.com; adult/child one-way $62/31) departs Gladstone daily at 2pm (adult/child one-way $62/31, 2½ hours).

For a more glamorous approach, take a seaplane (☑1300 863 248; www.heronisland.com; $338 one-way). Departures are daily subject to demand, and times can vary.

Rockhampton & Around

POP 66,190

Welcome to Rockhampton ('Rocky' to its mates), where the hats, boots and utes are big...but the bulls are even bigger. With over 2.5 million cattle within a 250km radius of Rockhampton, it's called Australia's Beef Capital for a reason. This sprawling country town is the administrative and commercial centre of central Queensland, its wide streets and fine Victorian-era buildings (take a stroll down Quay St) reflecting the region's prosperous 19th-century heyday of gold and copper mining and beef-cattle industry.

Straddling the tropic of Capricorn, Rocky can be aptly scorching. It's 40km inland and lacks coastal sea breezes; summers are often unbearably humid. The town has a smattering of attractions but is best seen as a gateway to the coastal gems of Yeppoon and Great Keppel Island, and the Byfield National Park to the north.

◉ Sights

★ Botanic Gardens   GARDENS
(☑07-4932 9000; Spencer St; ◷6am-6pm) FREE Just south of town, these gardens are a beautiful oasis, with tropical and subtropical rainforest, landscaped gardens and lily-covered lagoons. The formal Japanese garden is a zone of tranquillity, there's a cafe (open 8am to 5pm), and small, well-kept zoo (open 8.30am to 4.30pm, admission free) has koalas, wombats, dingoes, monkeys, a walk-through aviary and tonnes more.

Dreamtime Cultural Centre   CULTURAL CENTRE
(☑07-4936 1655; www.dreamtimecentre.com.au; Bruce Hwy; adult/child $15.50/7.50; ◷10am-3.30pm Mon-Fri, tours 10.30am & 1pm) The story of the local Dharumbal people is well conveyed in this easily accessible insight into Aboriginal and Torres Strait Islander heritage and history. The excellent 90-minute tours are hands on – throw your own boomerangs! – and appeal to all ages. It's about 7km north of the city centre.

Kershaw Gardens   GARDENS
(☑07-4936 8254; via Charles St; ◷6am-6pm) FREE Just north of the Fitzroy River, this excellent botanical park is devoted to Australian native plants. Its attractions include artificial rapids, a rainforest area, a fragrant garden and heritage architecture.

Mt Archer   MOUNTAIN
This mountain (604m) has walking trails weaving through eucalypts and rainforest abundant in wildlife. A brochure to the park is available from the visitor centres.

Rockhampton Art Gallery   GALLERY
(☑07-4936 8248; www.rockhamptonartgallery.com.au; 62 Victoria Pde; ◷10am-4pm) FREE Boasting an impressive collection of Austral-

CAPRICORN CAVES

The **Capricorn Caves** (☑ 07-4934 2883; www.capricorncaves.com.au; 30 Olsens Caves Rd; adult/child/family $30/15/75; ☺ 9am-5pm) are a rare acoustic and visual treat found deep beneath the Berserker Range 24km north of Rockhampton near the Caves township. The most popular one-hour tour includes listening to a classical music recording and, around mid-morning, a sunlit refraction of stunning natural beauty. These ancient caves honeycomb a limestone ridge where you'll see cave coral, stalactites, dangling fig-tree roots and, less likely, little insectivorous bats.

In December, around the summer solstice (1 December to 14 January), sunlight beams directly through a 14m vertical shaft into Belfry Cave, creating an electrifying light show. If you stand directly below the beam, reflected sunlight colours the whole cavern with whatever colour you're wearing.

Daring spelunkers can book a two-hour 'adventure tour' ($75; reserve a day or more in advance), which takes you through tight spots with names such as 'Fat Man's Misery'. You must be at least 16 years old for this tour.

The Capricorn Caves complex has barbecue areas, a pool, a kiosk, and accommodation (powered sites $35, cabins $150 to $180).

ian paintings, this gallery includes works by Sir Russell Drysdale and Sir Sidney Nolan. Contemporary Indigenous artists are also on display.

Archer Park Rail Museum MUSEUM
(☑ 07-4936 8191; www.rockhamptonregion.qld.gov.au; 51-87 Denison St; adult/child/family $8/5/26; ☺ 10am-3pm Mon-Thu, 10am-1pm Sun) This museum is housed in a former train station built in 1899. Through photographs and displays it tells the station's story, and that of the unique Purrey steam tram. Take a ride on the restored tram – the only remaining one of its kind in the world! – every Sunday from 10am to 1pm.

🛏 Sleeping

Southside Holiday Village CARAVAN PARK $
(☑ 07-4927 3013; www.sshv.com.au; Lower Dawson Rd; powered/unpowered sites $38/30, cabins $93, villas $98-125; ✻ @ 🛜 🏊) This is one of the city's best caravan parks, with neat, self-contained cabins and villas, large grassy camp sites and a good kitchen. Prices are for two people. It's about 3km south of the centre on a busy main road.

Rockhampton Backpackers HOSTEL $
(☑ 07-4927 5288; www.rockhamptonbackpackers.com.au; 60 MacFarlane St; dm/d $23.50/60; ✻ @ 🛜 🏊) A very fluid, unpretentious YHA hostel that at times resembles an employment agency, Rocky Backpackers has an industrial-sized communal kitchen, open-plan living areas where travellers share information on cattle stations and fruit farms,

and basic four-bed dorms. The pool is small but you'll take a cold puddle in Rocky's brutal summers.

Criterion HOTEL $$
(☑ 07-4922 1225; www.thecriterion.com.au; 150 Quay St; pub r $65-90, motel r $130-160; ✻ 🛜) The Criterion is Rockhampton's grandest old pub, with an elegant foyer, a friendly bar and a well-respected steakhouse. For travellers – or heavy drinkers – its top two storeys have dozens of dated period rooms, some in original heritage style, and all exceptional value for money. All rooms have showers, although the toilets are down the hall. If it's a little raw, or noisy, you can find a number of bland, though modern motel rooms next door.

⭐ **Denison**
Boutique Hotel BOUTIQUE HOTEL $$$
(☑ 07-4923 7378; www.denisonboutiquehotel.com.au; 233 Denison St; d $200) The newest hotel in Rockhampton is also the finest: a gorgeous white building constructed in 1885. Surrounded by rose gardens and hedges, Denison rooms have king-sized four-poster beds, high ceilings and large plasma TVs. Discounts are available online, which make the experience very accessible.

🍴 Eating & Drinking

Ginger Mule STEAK $
(☑ 07-4927 7255; 8 William St; mains from $10; ☺ noon-midnight Tue-Thu, noon-2am Fri, 4pm-2am Sat) Rocky's coolest eatery bills itself as a tapas bar, but everyone's here for one thing: steak! The steak sandwich ($11) has to be

WORTH A TRIP

MYELLA FARMSTAY

Myella Farm Stay (☑ 07-4998 1290; http://myella.weebly.com; Baralaba Rd; d/tr from $90/130, 2/3 days $250/390, powered sites $22; ✴ @ ✈), 125km southwest of Rockhampton, gives you a taste of the outback on its 10.6-sq-km farm. Lots of options are available, including comfortable camping and bush meals ($10 to $20) for those who are just passing through. The best experience though is engaging in the many activities on offer in a package deal. The package includes bush explorations by horseback, motorcycle and 4WD, all meals, accommodation in a renovated homestead with polished timber floors and a wide veranda, farm clothes and free transfers from Rockhampton.

among the best bargain meals in Queensland, while the $12 sirloin flies out of the busy kitchen late into the night. Morphs into a cocktail bar late in the evening.

Pacino's   ITALIAN **$$**
(☑ 07-4922 5833; cnr Fitzroy & George Sts; mains $25-40; ☉ lunch & dinner) Run by the same family for 30 years, Pacino's is a riverside favourite and the best Italian for miles. Pricey, though consistently popular for enormous pasta dishes and many regional specialities. The lamb's brains and lobster ravioli are well above what you'd expect from such a small city, though avoid the pizza.

Restaurant 98   SEAFOOD **$$**
(☑ 07-4920 1000; www.98.com.au; 98 Victoria Pde; mains $18-46; ☉ breakfast daily, lunch Mon-Fri, dinner Mon-Sat) Oysters, steak and flagons of fine red wine are the signature order at this licensed dining room attached to **Motel 98** (d from $124). Sit inside or on the terrace overlooking the Fitzroy River.

★ Great Western Hotel   PUB
(☑ 07-4922 1862; www.greatwesternhotel.com. au; cnr Stanley & Denison Sts; ☉ 10am-2am) The GWH is part country pub, part concert venue, and part of Rockhampton's social fabric. Try to time your visit to Rocky for a Wednesday or Friday night when you can watch brave cattlefolk being tossed in the air by bucking bulls and broncos. The pub is a jocular place with enough memorabilia to stuff a B-grade western. Touring bands

occasionally rock here, alongside bouts of Ultimate Fighting and stand-up comedy; you can get tickets online. The food is all about great steak.

❶ Information

Tropic of Capricorn Visitor Centre (☑ 1800 676 701; Gladstone Rd; ☉ 9am-5pm) Helpful centre on the highway right beside the tropic of Capricorn marker, 3km south of the centre.

❶ Getting There & Away

AIR

Qantas (☑ 13 13 13; www.qantas.com.au) and **Virgin** (☑ 13 67 89; www.virginaustralia.com) connect Rockhampton with various cities. The airport is about 6km from the centre of town.

BUS

Greyhound (☑ 1300 473 946; www.greyhound. com.au) buses run from Rockhampton to Brisbane ($168, 12 hours) and Mackay ($65, four hours), among other destinations.

TRAIN

Queensland Rail (☑ 1800 872 467; www. queenslandrailtravel.com.au) runs a daily service to Brisbane ($135, 12 hours) and Gladstone ($39, three hours).

Yeppoon
POP 17,241

Yeppoon has slowly evolved from a tiny village known as a launching pad for trips to Great Keppel Island to today's more established seaside town. The long, beautiful beach serves as a holiday destination or residential highlight for many graziers, miners and other folk from nearby Rockhampton seeking to beat the heat. A hinterland of volcanic outcrops and pineapple patches and (a short drive north) the wonderful Byfield National Park, give Yeppoon a rich diversity often overlooked by travellers from other parts of Australia. The broad, quiet streets, sleepy motels and beachside cafes are the setting for a nightly migration of black-and-red flying foxes, which pass over the main beach and beyond in a startling sunset display.

🏃 Activities

Sail Capricornia   CRUISE
(☑ 0402 102 373; www.sailcapricornia.com.au; full-day cruises incl lunch adult/child $115/75) Sail Capricornia offers snorkelling cruises on board the *Grace* catamaran, as well as sunset ($55) and three-day ($499) cruises.

Funtastic Cruises CRUISE
(📞 0438 909 502; www.funtasticcruises.com; full-day cruises adult/child/family $98/80/350) Funtastic Cruises operates full-day snorkelling trips on board its 17m catamaran, with a two-hour stopover on Great Keppel Island, morning and afternoon tea, and all snorkelling equipment included. It can also organise camping drop-offs to islands en route.

🛏 Sleeping & Eating

Beachside Caravan Park CARAVAN PARK $
(📞 07-4939 3738; Farnborough Rd; powered sites $31-34, unpowered sites $28) This basic, neat little camping ground, north of the town centre, commands a wonderful, totally beachfront location. It has good amenities and grassed sites with some shade, but no cabins or on-site vans. Rates are for two people.

★ Surfside Motel MOTEL $$
(📞 07-4939 1272; www.yeppoonsurfsidemotel.com.au; 30 Anzac Pde; r from $140; ❄ @ 🛜 🏊) Location and service lift the Surfside to the top of the tree in Yeppoon. Across the road from the beach and close to town, this 1950s strip of lime-green motel units epitomises summer holidays at the beach. And it's terrific value – the rooms are spacious and unusually well equipped, complete with toaster, hair dryer and free wi-fi. Prices go down for three or more nights.

While Away B&B B&B $$
(📞 07-4939 5719; www.whileawaybandb.com.au; 44 Todd Ave; s $115, d $140-155, incl breakfast; ❄) Perenially popular B&B, While Away has good-sized, immaculately clean rooms with wheelchair access and a quiet location back from the beach. The bubbly owners offer complimentary nibbles, tea, coffee, port and sherry as well as generous breakfasts.

Coral Inn Yeppoon HOSTEL $$
(📞 07-4939 2925; www.coralinn.com.au; 14 Maple St; d/q from $129/149; ❄ ❄ @ 🛜 🏊) Beautiful lawns and reef-bright colours in the rooms, all with en suites and mod-cons, make Coral Inn a great find, just back from the beach. Families and discerning groups in particular will enjoy enjoy the quad rooms, communal kitchen, and mini 'beach' area with hammocks and an inviting pool. Note that management do enforce a number of rules to deter rowdy backpackers.

Strand Hotel PUB FOOD $
(📞 07-4939 1301; www.thestrandyeppoon.com.au; 2 Normanby St; mains from $16; ⏱ noon-2.30pm & 6-9pm Mon-Fri, 11.30am-2.30pm & 5.30-9pm Sat & Sun) There has been a welcome refurb in the form of glass frontage and faux-leather furniture at this grand old pub facing the sea. The food is dependable, ranging from pizzas ($16 to $24) to fantastic steaks ($29 to $42). There's live music most weekends, and the odd random weeknight.

★ Megalomania FUSION $$$
(📞 07-4939 2333; www.megalomaniabarandbistro.com.au; cnr James & Arthur Sts; mains $26-40; ⏱ noon-2pm & 6pm-late Tue-Sat) An Oz-Asian fusion beast, with a stylish ambience that's hard to replicate anywhere, let alone a small coastal town, by head chef Callan Crigan. Panko-crumbed tiger prawns and red sea

---

WORTH A TRIP

BYFIELD

Byfield is a village 40km north of Yepoon in Byfield National Park, a well-concealed landscape of rare diversity: empty sand dunes running up to rocky pinnacles, wetlands and semitropical rainforests. A 4WD will get you to remote hiking paths and isolated beaches beautiful enough to warrant a much longer stay.

Nob Creek Pottery (📞 07-4935 1161; www.nobcreekpottery.com.au; 216 Arnolds Rd; ⏱ 10am-4pm Thu-Mon) **FREE** is a working pottery and gallery nestled in leafy rainforest. The gallery showcases hand-blown glass, woodwork and jewellery; the handmade ceramics are outstanding. Take a boat trip through the rainforest with **Waterpark Eco-Tours** (📞 07-4935 1171; www.waterparkecotours.com; 201 Waterpark Creek Rd; 2-3hr tour $27.50, cabins $150), keeping an eye out for bright blue kingfishers, baby turtles and big daddy eels.

There are five **camping grounds** (📞 13 74 68; www.nprsr.qld.gov.au; per person/family $6.15/24.60) to choose from (bookings essential). Nine Mile Beach and Five Rocks are on the beach and you'll need a 4WD to access them.

salt soft shell crab were our starters ($18 each), and Byron Bay pork belly and white miso barramundi came in for mains ($36 each). You get the idea. Loll beneath the fig tree with your stiff cocktail, or clink silverware in the indoor woodsy surrounds.

ℹ Information

Capricorn Coast Information Centre (☑1800 675 785; www.capricorncoast.com.au; Ross Creek Roundabout; ⊙9am-5pm) Has plenty of information on the Capricorn Coast and Great Keppel Island, and can book accommodation and tours.

ℹ Getting There & Away

Yeppoon is 43km northeast of Rockhampton. **Young's Bus Service** (☑07-4922 3813; www.youngsbusservice.com.au) runs frequent buses from Rockhampton ($6.70 one way) to Yeppoon and down to the Rosslyn Bay Marina.

If you're driving, there's a free daytime car park at the marina. For longer, secure undercover parking, the **Great Keppel Island Security Car Park** (☑07-4933 6670; 422 Scenic Hwy; per day from $15) is on the Scenic Hwy south of Yeppoon, by the turn-off to the marina.

Keppel Konnections (www.keppelkonnections.com.au) and **Funtastic Cruises** (p359) both leave from Yeppoon daily to Great Keppel Island and the Great Keppel National Park.

Great Keppel Island

This jewel of the Capricorn Coast is synonymous the with deserted-island fantasies of the urban travel set. Once home to one of Australia's most iconic resorts, the 4-sq-km island, with natural bushland covering 90% of the interior, has 17 beaches, all in the category of 'bloody beautiful'. A new mega-resort, environmental research centre and golf course are on the way, so get here soon if you prefer to do your islands in solitude.

🏃 Activities

Freedom Fast Cats   CRUISE
(☑07-4933 6888; www.freedomfastcats.com; Keppel Bay Marina, Rosslyn Bay; tours adult/child from $78/50) Operates a range of island tours, from glass-bottomed boat reef-viewing to snorkelling and boom-netting.

Great Keppel Cruises   BOATING
(☑0401 053 666; www.greatkeppelcruises.com.au; half-/full-day trip $65/125) *Keppel Dreams* departs from Fisherman's Beach for snorkelling forays around the island. Departures

are scheduled to fit in with **Keppel Konnections** arrival from Yeppoon.

Watersports Hut   WATER SPORTS
(☑07-0415076644; Putney Beach; ⊙Sat, Sun & school holidays) This outfit on the main beach hires out snorkelling equipment, kayaks and catamarans, and runs tube rides.

🛏 Sleeping & Eating

⭐ **Svendsen's Beach**   CABIN $$
(☑07-4938 3717; www.svendsensbeach.com; d from $115) 🌱 The three-night minimum stays are barely enough at this secluded boutique retreat on the 'other' side of Great Keppel. Run by knowledgeable Carl and Lindy, the retreat is an ecofriendly operation, run on solar and wind power; there's even a bush-bucket shower. It's the perfect place for snorkelling, bushwalking and romantic getaways. Guests can choose from luxury tent-bungalows (doubles $115) on elevated timber decks, plus a colourful studio ($150) and house (from $220; sleeps up to four people), all within a turtle shuffle of the beach.

Great Keppel Island Hideaway   RESORT $$
(☑07-4939 2050; www.greatkeppelislandhideaway.com.au; safari tents $90 r $140-200, cabins $200-360) This hideaway is set across massive grounds on a sublime bend of Fisherman's Beach. The distance between the various cabins, houses and safari tents lends an air of rugged isolation to a family holiday. The reality is there's a beachfront restaurant (mains $12 to $25) nearby where guests compare their lodgings, sip on sundowners and half-contemplate a nature walk somewhere not too far away.

Keppel Lodge   GUESTHOUSE $$
(☑07-4939 4251; www.keppellodge.com.au; Fisherman's Beach; d per person $65-75, houses $520-600; @🤚) Keppel Lodge is terrific value and sandy stumbling distance to Fisherman's Beach. The pleasant open-plan house has four large bedrooms (with bathrooms) branching from a large communal lounge and kitchen. It's available in its entirety – ideal for a group booking – or as individual suites.

Island Pizza   PIZZA $
(☑07-4939 4699; The Esplanade; dishes $6-30; ⊙varies) You'll be doing better than us if you can figure out exactly when this incongruously located pizza house is open, but if you hang around long enough, someone will let you know. The pizzas are huge and delicious. Get anything with pineapple on it.

ℹ️ Getting There & Away

Great Keppel is a 30-minute ferry trip from Roslyn Bay Marina in Yeppoon. **Keppel Konnections** (www.keppelkonnections.com.au) has twice daily services to the island departing Yeppoon at 9am and 3pm and returning at 10am and 4pm. **Freedom Fast Cats** (☑ 07-4933 6888; www.freedomfastcats.com; return adult/child/family $55/35/160) leave Yeppoon at 9.15am and return at 2.30pm or 3.45pm depending on the day and the season.

Capricorn Hinterland

The central highlands, west of Rockhampton, are home to two excellent national parks. Blackdown Tableland National Park is a brooding, powerful place, while visitors to Carnarvon National Park will be gobsmacked by the spectacular gorge.

At Emerald, 270km inland, try fossicking for gems in the heat and rubble – you'll be surrounded by the good people and vibe of the outback. Try to stick to the cooler months between April and November.

Carnarvon National Park

Carnarvon Gorge is a dramatic rendition of Australian natural beauty. The 30km-long, 200m-high gorge was carved out over millions of years by Carnarvon Creek and its tributaries twisting through soft sedimentary rock. What was left behind is a lush, other-worldly oasis, where life flourishes, shielded from the stark terrain. You'll find giant cycads, king ferns, river oaks, flooded gums, cabbage palms, deep pools, and platypuses in the creek. Escaped convicts often took refuge here among ancient rock paintings. The area was made a national park in 1932 after defeated farmers forfeited their pastoral lease.

For most people, Carnarvon Gorge *is* the Carnarvon National Park, because the other sections – including Mt Moffatt (where Indigenous groups lived some 19,000 years ago), Ka Ka Mundi and Salvator Rosa – have long been difficult to access.

Coming from Rolleston the road is bitumen for 75km and unsealed for 20km. From Roma via Injune and Wyseby homestead, the road is good bitumen for about 215km, then unsealed and fairly rough for the last 30km. After heavy rain, both these roads can become impassable.

The main walking track also starts here, following Carnarvon Creek through the gorge, with detours to various points of interest. These include the Moss Garden (3.6km from the picnic area), Ward's Canyon (4.8km), the Art Gallery (5.6km) and Cathedral Cave (9.3km). Allow at least a whole day for a visit.

Sunrover Expeditions (☑ 1800 353 717; www.sunrover.com.au; safaris per person incl all meals

---

OFF THE BEATEN TRACK

GEM FIELDS

The gem fields of central Queensland are a tough landscape drawing prospectors who eke out a living until a jackpot (or sunstroke) arrives. Fossickers descend in winter – in the hot summers the towns are nearly deserted. Sapphires are the main haul, but zircons are also found and, very rarely, rubies. Sapphire and Rubyvale are two of the main towns on the fields.

To go fossicking you need a licence, which can be bought online (www.dnrm.qld.gov.au; adult/family $7.75/11.15) or at a few places in the area – the **Central Highlands Visitors Centre** (www.centralhighlands.com.au; 3 Clemont St, Emerald; ⊘10am-4.30pm) in Emerald has a list. If you just wish to dabble, you can buy a bucket of 'wash' (mine dirt in water) from one of the fossicking parks to hand-sieve and wash.

Bobby Dazzler Mine Tours (☑ 07- 4981 0000) will help you get your hands dirty in the right way, and throw in a fair whack of local history and colour to boot.

Pat's Gems (☑ 07-4985 4544; 1056 Rubyvale Rd, Sapphire; ⊘8.30am-4pm) is a quirky shop and fossicking station where regular visitors and travelling prospectors can rent equipment and pick up tips on how to find that precious gem.

The superclean and friendly **Sapphire Caravan Park** (☑ 07-4985 4281; www.sapphirecaravanpark.com.au; 57 Sunrise Rd, Sapphire; powered/unpowered sites $29/25, cottages $115), set on four hilly acres with sites and cabins tucked into the eucalyptus forest, is great for fossickers.

$940) runs a five-day camping safari into Carnarvon Gorge between August and October.

There is national parks **camping** (☑13 74 68; www.qld.gov.au/camping; sites per person/family $6.15/24.60) at **Big Bend** and **Mt Moffat**, as well as the excellent **Takarakka Bush Resort** (☑07-4984 4535; www.takarakka.com.au; Wyseby Rd; powered/unpowered sites from $45/38, cabins $195-228), with safari tents, cottages and cabins.

WHITSUNDAY COAST

Many travellers to Australia, especially those with a sailing pedigree, head straight for the Whitsunday Islands and barely leave. This white-fringed archipelago, a stunning feature of the Coral Sea coast, can be easily seen from shore. Opal-jade waters and pure-white beaches fringe the forested isles; around them, tropical fish swarm through the world's largest coral garden in the Great Barrier Reef Marine Park. The gateway to the islands, Airlie Beach, is a backpacker hub with a parade of tanned faces zinging between boats, beaches and nightclubs. This is as close to the islands as some budget travellers will get.

Mackay

POP 82,500

Once home to opera star Dame Nellie Melba, this workaday, midsized Queensland city puts tourism a distant second to the machinations of the sugar and agricultural industries, but there's nonetheless plenty to like about Mackay's tropical suburbia. For starters, it's an incongruously impressive art-deco destination, and even better is its location between protected mangroves and a smart, beachy marina. Mackay is a convenient base for excursions out of town, but when the backpacker shuffle and island-hopping overwhelms, its alfresco cafes provide a quick urban fix. It's only a 1½-hour drive to Airlie Beach and boats to the Whitsundays, and a scenic jaunt past the sugarcane fields to Eungella National Park.

⊙ Sights & Activities

Mackay Marina (Mackay Harbour) is worth the trip to wine and dine with a waterfront view, while the artificial **Bluewater Lagoon** (☉9am-5.45pm) **FREE** near Caneland Shop-

ping Centre has water fountains, water slides, grassed picnic areas, free wi-fi and a cafe.

Mackay Regional Botanical Gardens GARDENS
(Lagoon St) On 33 hectares, 3km south of the city centre, these gardens are a must-see for flora fans. Home to five themed gardens and the Lagoon cafe-restaurant (open Wednesday to Sunday).

Tours

Reeforest Adventure Tours CULTURAL TOUR
(☑07-4959 8360, 1800 500 353; www.reeforest.com) The Mackay region's most experienced operator offers a wide range of junkets, including a platypus and rainforest eco-safari, two-day Eungella tours, and a Cape Hillsborough expedition in the footsteps of the Juipera mob. In the cane-crushing season (June to December), you can see how sugar cane is turned into sweet crystals with its two-hour tour of the Farleigh Sugar Mill (adult/child $28/14); long pants and enclosed shoes are required.

Heritage Walk WALKING
(☑07-4944 5888; ☉8.45am Tue & Wed May-Sep) **FREE** Weekly wandering (1½ to two hours) that takes in the sights and secrets of ye olde Mackay. Leaves from Paxton's Warehouse on the corner of River and Carlyle Sts.

🛏 Sleeping

★ **Stoney Creek Farmstay** FARMSTAY $
(☑07-4954 1177; www.stoneycreekfarmstay.com; Peak Downs Hwy; dm/stables/cottages $25/130/175) 🌿 This bush retreat 32km south of Mackay is a down 'n' dirty option in the best possible way. Stay in an endearingly ramshackle cottage, the rustic livery stable or the charismatic Dead Horse Hostel, and forget all about the mod-cons: this is dead-set bush livin'. Three-hour horse rides cost $105 per person and lots of other activities are available. Free dorm room if you ride for two consecutive days.

Mackay Marine Tourist Park CARAVAN PARK $
(☑07-4955 1496; www.mmtp.com.au; 379 Harbour Rd; powered/unpowered sites $35/32, villas $110-180; ❄@🛜🐕) A step up from the usual caravan parks: all cabins and villas come with private patios and widescreen TVs, and you've gotta love anywhere with a giant jumping pillow.

Whitsunday Coast

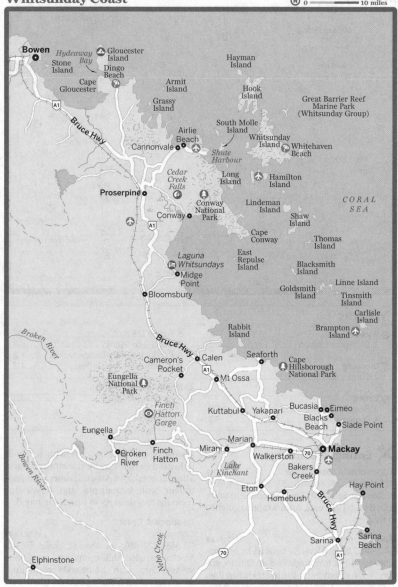

Coral Sands Motel MOTEL **$$**
(☎ 07-4951 1244; www.coralsandsmotel.com.au; 44 Macalister St; r from $115; ✳❀✉) One of Mackay's better midrange options, the Coral Sands boasts ultrafriendly management and large rooms in a central location. Popular with the transient workforce, it's a bit tropi-kitsch, but with the river, shops, pubs and cafes so close to your doorstep, you won't care. Great value.

Mackay

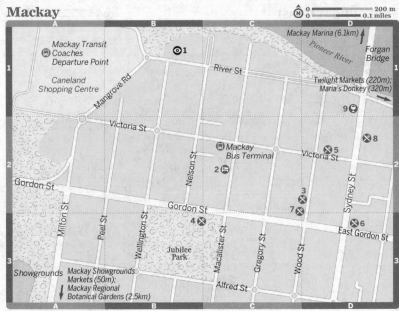

Mackay

◉ Sights
1 Bluewater Lagoon.....................................B1

🛏 Sleeping
2 Coral Sands Motel C2

✖ Eating
3 Burp Eat Drink...D2
4 Foodspace B3

5 Fusion 128...D2
6 Oscar's on Sydney D3
7 Paddock & Brew Company.....................C2
8 Woodsman's Axe Coffee........................D2

🍷 Drinking & Nightlife
9 Ambassador Hotel D1

✖ Eating & Drinking

Woodsman's Axe Coffee　　　CAFE $
(41 Sydney St; coffee from $4.30; ☺ 6am-2pm Mon-Fri, 7am-2pm Sat & Sun) The best coffee in town paired with light eats, from wraps to quiches to muffins.

Maria's Donkey　　　TAPAS $
(☑ 07-4957 6055; 8 River St; tapas $8-15; ☺ noon-10pm Wed & Thu, to midnight Fri-Sun) Quirky, energetic riverfront joint dishing up tapas, jugs of sangria, occasional live music and general good times. Service is erratic, but somehow, that's part of the charm.

Fusion 128　　　MODERN AUSTRALIAN $$
(☑ 07-4999 9329; 128 Victoria St; mains $13.50-33; ☺ 11.30am-2pm & 5.30pm-10pm) The latest foodie instalment in Mackay is Fusion 128, a superb, casual restaurant with a low-lit industrial design run by the effusive David Ming. It combines Asian flavours with Australian bush ingredients, and serves fine cocktails and desserts to match the mood.

Paddock & Brew Company　　　AMERICAN $$
(☑ 0487 222 880; 94 Wood St; mains $18-30) Mackay needed this upmarket, craft-beer-soaked, American home-style restaurant, which serves up amazing burgers ($25). Part of the new breed of north Queensland culinary creatives, the team at Paddock & Brew whiz between the wooden tables at this happening pre-party venue.

Oscar's on Sydney　　　FUSION $$
(☑ 07-4944 0173; cnr Sydney & Gordon Sts; mains $10-23; ☺ 7am-5pm Mon-Fri, to 4pm Sat, 8am-4pm

Sun) The delicious *poffertjes* (Dutch pancakes with traditional toppings) are still going strong at this very popular corner cafe, but don't be afraid to give the other dishes a go. Top spot for breakfast.

Foodspace CAFE $$
(www.artspacemackay.com.au; Gordon St; mains $16-26; ⊙9am-3pm Tue-Sun) You can graze on impressive salads, sandwiches and light meals prepared by beginning chefs at Foodspace, the licensed cafe inside Artspace Mackay.

Burp Eat Drink MODERN AUSTRALIAN $$$
(☑07-4951 3546; www.burp.net.au; 86 Wood St; mains from $33; ⊙11.30am-3pm & 6pm-late Tue-Fri, 6pm-late Sat) Run by the enterprising NE Food mob, this swish Melbourne-style restaurant in the tropics has a small but tantalising menu. Sophisticated selections include pork belly with scallops, Kaffir-lime-crusted soft-shell crab, plus some serious steaks.

Ambassador Hotel BAR
(☑07-4953 3233; www.ambassadorhotel.net.au; 2 Sydney St; ⊙5pm-late Thu, 4pm-late Fri-Sun) Both a social and historical landmark, the Ambassador is art deco outside, wild 'n' crazy inside. There's multilevel carousing on weekends, including Mackay's only rooftop bar. Remarkably, you will soon be able to sleep here in renovated dorms and double rooms.

🛍 Shopping

They like their markets in Mackay; try the **Mackay Showgrounds Markets** (Milton St; ⊙6.30am-10am Sat), **Twilight Markets** (Northern Beaches Bowls Club; ⊙5pm-9pm 1st Fri of the month) and the **Troppo Market** (Mt Pleasant Shopping Centre car park; ⊙from 7.30am 2nd Sun of the month).

ⓘ Information

Mackay Visitor Centre (☑1300 130 001; www.mackayregion.com; 320 Nebo Rd; ⊙9am-5pm; 🛜) About 3km south of the centre. Internet access and wi-fi.

ⓘ Getting There & Away

AIR
The airport is about 3km south of the centre of Mackay.

Jetstar (☑13 15 38; www.jetstar.com.au), **Qantas** (☑13 13 13; www.qantas.com.au) and **Virgin** (☑13 67 89; www.virginaustralia.com) have flights to/from Brisbane.

BUS
Buses stop at the **Mackay Bus Terminal** (cnr Victoria & Macalister Sts), where tickets can also be booked. **Greyhound** (☑1300 473 946; www.greyhound.com.au) travels up and down the coast. Sample one-way adult fares and journey times: Airlie Beach ($33, two hours), Townsville ($72, 6½ hours), Cairns ($127, 13 hours) and Brisbane ($227, 17 hours).

Premier (☑13 34 10; www.premierms.com.au) is less expensive than Greyhound but has fewer services.

TRAIN
The *Spirit of Queensland*, operated by **Queensland Rail** (☑1800 872 467; www.queenslandrail.com.au), runs from Mackay to Brisbane ($199, 13 hours) and Cairns ($159, 14 hours). The train station is at Paget, 5km south of the city centre.

ⓘ Getting Around

Major car-rental firms have desks at Mackay Airport; see www.mackayairport.com.au/travel/car-hire for listings. **NQ Car & Truck Rental** (☑07-4953 2353; www.nqcartruckrentals.com.au; 6 Malcolmson St, North Mackay) is a reliable local operator.

Mackay Transit Coaches (☑07-4957 3330; www.mackaytransit.com.au) has several services around the city, and connects the **city** with the harbour and northern beaches; pick up a timetable at the **visitor centre** (p365) or look online.

For a taxi, call **Mackay Taxis** (☑13 10 08).

Airlie Beach

POP 9165

Aside from being the obvious departure point for most trips to the unparalleled Whitsunday Islands, Airlie Beach has long been a destination par excellence on the east coast road-trip and binge-drink adventure trail. Its multiple hostels and massive beer gardens sit opposite a lawn-surrounded swimming lagoon where nothing much happens but the passing of carefree youth and the rhythm of unskilled sailors, taking to the sparkling seas and jungle-clad isles with bleary-eyed wonder.

🏃 Activities

Lagoon SWIMMING
(Shute Harbour Rd) **FREE** Take a dip year-round in the stinger-croc-and-tropical-nasties-free lagoon in the centre of town.

Airlie Beach

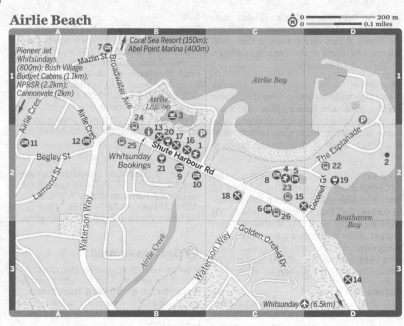

Airlie Beach

Red Cat Adventures　　　　BOATING
(☎1300 653 100, 07-4940 2000; www.redcatad
ventures.com.au) Excellent family-owned operation with three distinct crafts and tours.
Our pick is the Ride to Paradise ($569), a
two-night adventure to a 'secret' resort, as
well as many highlights of the Whitsundays.

Airlie Beach Skydivers　　　SKYDIVING
(☎1300 759 348; www.airliebeachskydivers.com.
au; 2/273 Shute Harbour Rd; 4270m jumps from

$249) The only beach landing in Airlie Beach
is provided by this passionate team with a
shopfront on Shute Harbour Rd.

Skydive Airlie Beach　　　SKYDIVING
(☎07-4946 9115; www.skydive.com.au/airlie-beach;
skydives from $199) Jump out of a plane from
1830m, 2440m or 4270m and land in front of
the cafe set on Airlie Beach. Fabulous group
and there is not a more beautiful view in the
world for a death-defying plummet.

Whitsunday Sailing Adventures BOATING
(☑ 07-4946 4999; www.whitsundayssailing
adventures.com.au; The Esplanade) This
well-connected agency can book seats on
every sailing boat in town, plus a few decent dive operators.

Pioneer Jet Whitsundays BOATING
(☑ 1800 335 975; www.pioneerjet.com.au; Abel
Point Marina; adult/child $69/49) The Ultimate
Bay Blast is a thunderous 30-minute spin
in a jet boat. Fun and informative guides
round off the experience. Expect to get very
wet.

Just Tuk'n Around GUIDED TOUR
(www.justtuknaround.com.au; tours per person
$30) Fun and informative 30-minute tours
around the 'secrets' of Airlie Beach reveal
more than you'd think possible in a small
coastal town.

Lady Enid BOATING
(☑ 0407 483 000; www.ladyenid.com.au; boat trips
from $225) High-end bespoke sailing trips for
couples aboard a heritage yacht.

Illusions BOATING
(☑ 0455 142 021; www.illusion.net.au; day tours
$125) A 12m catamaran that offers the least
expensive, yet consistently good, sailing
tours to the islands.

Solway Lass BOATING
(☑ 1800 355 377; www.solwaylass.com; 3-day,
3-night trips from $589) You get a full three
days and nights on this 28m tall ship – the
only authentic tall ship in Airlie Beach. Popular with backpackers.

☞ Tours

Cruise Whitsundays CRUISE
(☑ 07-4846 70602; www.cruisewhitsundays.com;
Shingley Dr, Abel Point Marina; full-day cruises from
$99) As well as operating a ferry to the Whit-
sunday Islands, Cruise Whitsundays offers
trips to Hardy Reef, Whitehaven Beach and
islands, including Daydream and Long. Or
grab a daily Island Hopper pass (adult/child
$125/65) and make your own itinerary. It
also operates a popular day trip aboard the
Camira ($195).

Air Whitsunday SCENIC FLIGHTS
(☑ 07-4946 9111; www.airwhitsunday.com.au; Terminal 1, Whitsunday Airport) Offers a range of
tours, including day trips to Whitehaven
($255) and scenic-flight-plus-snorkelling
tours of the Great Barrier Reef ($375).

Whitsunday Crocodile Safari TOURS
(☑ 07-4948 3310; www.crocodilesafari.com.au;
adult/child $120/60) Spy on wild crocs, explore
secret estuaries and eat real bush tucker.

✱☆ Festivals & Events

Airlie Beach Race Week SAILING
(www.airlieraceweek.com; ☉ Aug) The town's
sailing pedigree is tested every August when
sailors from across the world descend on
Airlie for the town's annual regatta.

Airlie Beach Music Festival MUSIC
(airliebeachfestivalofmusic.com.au; ☉ Nov) This
festival has really taken off since its inception
into the Whitsunday social calendar back in
2012. Party to three days of Australian and
international rock, folk and electronic music,
with plenty of local talent on show.

⇞ Sleeping

Airlie Beach is a backpacker haven, but
with so many hostels, standards vary and
bedbugs are a common problem. There
is also a remarkable variety of midrange
accommodation particularly suitable for
families. Not a lot at the very top end though.

★ Kipara RESORT $
(☑ 07-4946 6483; www.kipara.com.au; 2614 Shute
Harbour Rd; r/cabins/villas from $85/105/130;
❈@☎☝) Tucked away in the lush, green
environs of Jubilee Pocket, this budget resort makes it easy to forget you're only 2km
from the frenzy of town (it's next to the bus
stop so you don't need a car). It's mega-clean
and offers outstanding value, with helpful
staff, cooking facilities and regular wildlife
visits – one of Airlie's best options. Huge
discounts available online. There's a fab pool
with surrounding deck.

★ Sunlit Waters APARTMENT $
(☑ 07-4946 6352; www.sunlitwaters.com; 20
Airlie Cres; studios from $95, 1-bedroom apt
$115; ❈☎☝) Just so affordable for a tour-
ist town like Airlie Beach! We expected
the studio apartments to be tiny or run
down, but they are beautifully presented
and have everything you need, including
a self-contained kitchenette and stunning
views from the long balconies. There's even
a good swimming pool.

Flametree Tourist Village CARAVAN PARK $
(☑ 07-4946 9388; www.flametreevillage.com.au;
2955 Shute Harbour Rd; powered/unpowered
site $40/30, cabin from $109; ❈@☝☝) Our

ⓘ CYCLONE WARNING

In Queensland's far north, between November and April each year, cyclones – known in the northern hemisphere as hurricanes – are a part of life, with an average of four or five forming each season. It's rare for these cyclones to escalate into full-blown destructive storms, however in March 2017 Severe Tropical Cyclone Debbie made landfall near Airlie Beach, causing significant damage and flooding in South East Queensland and the Northern Rivers area of New South Wales. Airlie Beach and Bowen were affected as well.

Bringing torrential rain, strong winds and ferocious seas, the storm killed at least twelve people in Australia, primarily as a result of extreme flooding. At the time of writing the clean-up was in full swing. We recommend checking ahead before you travel to ensure that accommodation is available and .confirm the state of the beaches.

During the season, keep a sharp ear out for cyclone predictions and alerts. If a cyclone watch or warning is issued, stay tuned to local radio and monitor the Bureau of Meteorology website (www.bom.gov.au) for updates and advice. Locals tend to be complacent about cyclones, but will still buy out the bottle shop when a threat is imminent!

favourite camping ground and caravan park in the region has been thoroughly scrubbed up and is a top alternative to the chaos of Airlie Beach. Spacious sites are scattered through lovely, bird-filled gardens and there's a good camp kitchen and BBQ area. It's 6.5km west of Airlie.

Airlie Beach YHA   HOSTEL $
(☑ 07-4946 6312; www.yha.com.au; 394 Shute Harbour Rd; dm $33, d from $85; ❊@☎☳) Trust YHA to provide a genuine alternative for young budget travellers to sordid hostels and inconvenient bush dumps. Central and reasonably quiet with a sparkling pool and great kitchen facilities, this is our favourite hostel in Airlie Beach, though the double rooms are pretty grim.

Airlie Waterfront Backpackers   HOSTEL $
(☑ 1800 089 000; www.airliewaterfront.com; 6 The Esplanade; dm from $22, d from $74; ❊☎) Basic hostel, with coveted ocean views and a very central location. A little less hectic than other downtown options.

Bush Village Budget Cabins   HOSTEL $
(☑ 07-4946 6177, 1800 809 256; www.bushvillage.com.au; 2 St Martins Rd; dm from $33, d with/without bathroom from $97/82; ℙ❊@☎☳) Not for those looking for a party, this budget place suits travellers who have their own vehicle and enjoy having a village to return to after a long day on the reef or a night on the tiles. The dorms and doubles are in a clutch of self-contained cabins and it's licensed so you can sit and drink a beer by the pool. It's a five-minute walk to Abel Point Marina and about a half-hour stroll to central Airlie Beach. Reception closes early so communicate clearly.

Beaches Backpackers   HOSTEL $
(☑ 07-4946 6244; www.beaches.com.au; 356 Shute Harbour Rd; dm/d from $20/85; ❊@☎☳) The hostel scene in Airlie is pretty fickle, but Beaches is consistent in its bubbly customer service and unwavering desire to crank the party to maximum (and fair enough given the awesomeness of the open-air bar). Dorms are sufficient, but could be cleaner.

Note that the hostel sustained some damage from Cyclone Debbie; check ahead that they are taking guests.

Waterview   APARTMENT $$
(☑ 07-4948 1748; www.waterviewairliebeach.com.au; 42 Airlie Cres; studios from $140, 1-bedroom units from $155; ❊☎) Waterview's small units are an excellent choice for location and comfort. You can enjoy glimpses of the main street and gorgeous views of the bay. The rooms are modern, airy and spacious, and have kitchenettes for self-caterers. Top value for a couple in Airlie who can do without a pool.

Airlie Beach Hotel   HOTEL $$
(☑ 07-4964 1999; www.airliebeachhotel.com.au; cnr The Esplanade & Coconut Gr; motel from $145, hotel r $195-295; ❊☎☳) The ABH has seen it all in Airlie. The sea-facing hotel rooms are some of the best in town at this price point. With three restaurants and a bottle shop on site and a perfect downtown location, you could do far worse than stay here.

The hotel was damaged during Cyclone Debbie and had to close temporarily: it is due to reopen in January 2018.

Coral Sea Resort   RESORT $$$
(☑ 07-4964 1300; www.coralsearesort.com; 25 Ocean View Ave; d from $275; ❊@☎☳) Coral Sea Resort is an excellent option for families

and older folk wanting quality service, spacious tiled rooms, and one of the best pool settings in Queensland. An easy stroll to the marina, it's located at the end of a low headland just west of the town centre. Many rooms have stunning views, but you'll save plenty of dosh by going for a garden view and then lingering poolside.

Airlie Waterfront B&B   B&B $$$
(☑ 07-4946 7631; http://airliewaterfrontbnb.com.au; cnr Broadwater Ave & Mazlin St; 1-/2-bedroom apt from $209/252; ❄ @ ☎ ☎) Karen and Malcolm are gregarious hosts at this misnamed property, which is more like a small resort. Views are superb from the position slightly above town, accessed by a five-minute stroll along the boardwalk. The two-bedroom apartments are the best value in town. Some rooms have a spa.

✗ Eating

The strip facing the port at the new Port of Airlie is a good hunting ground for sophisticated, upmarket dining options, while downtown Airlie Beach has a mishmash of everything from cheap takeaway kebab shops to fancier restaurants with outdoor patios. There's a massive **Woolworths supermarket** (Shute Harbour Rd; ❄ 8am-9pm) conveniently located in the centre of town for self-caterers.

Harry's Corner   CAFE $
(☑ 07-4946 7459; 273 Shute Harbour Rd; mains $7-18; ❄ 7am-3pm) Locals are wild about Harry's, which serves tea in quaint European tea sets, Danish sandwiches, filled bagels and good-sized salads. The all-day breakfasts are a must for a hangover.

Wisdom Health Lab   CAFE $
(1b/275 Shute Harbour Dr; toasties from $5.50, juices from $7; ❄ 7.30am-3.30pm; ☑) Mostly a takeaway place, this rightfully busy corner cafe does have a few indoor and outdoor tables. It serves healthy toasties, sandwiches (including lots of vegetarian options such as a tasty lentil burger), and a huge array of fresh smoothies and juices.

★ Mr Bones   PIZZA $$
(☑ 0413 017 331; Lagoon Plaza, 263 Shute Harbour Rd; shared plates $12-17, pizzas $15-23; ❄ 9am-9pm Tue-Sat) Carefully curated play lists and creative thin-based pizzas have made Mr Bones the coolest place to eat in Airlie since it opened six years ago. Overlooking the lagoon, the small, sunny restaurant also has

an extensive 'not pizzas' menu of appetisers to play around with. Service is upbeat and interested. Great coffee, too.

Airlie Beach
Treehouse   MODERN AUSTRALIAN $$
(☑ 07-4946 5550; www.airlietreehouse.com/; 6/263-265 Shute Harbour Rd; mains $18-36; ❄ 8.30am-9.30pm) This new restaurant by the lagoon is making ripples for its uncomplicated service and quality food in a shady setting.

Denman Cellars Beer Cafe   TAPAS $$
(☑ 07-4948 1333; Shop 15, 33 Port Dr; tapas $10, mains $18-38; ❄ 11am-10pm Mon-Fri, 8am-11pm Sat & Sun) Regular live music and a convivial mood are found in this tapas bar that stocks more boutique beers – 700 brews! – than the rest of the town combined. The food – such as a shared seafood platter ($57), and 'beer bites' such as zucchini balls ($14) and duck pancakes ($17) – is decent. Larger meals are available.

Fish D'vine   SEAFOOD $$
(☑ 07-4948 0088; 303 Shute Harbour Rd; mains $17-33; ❄ 5pm-late) Pirates were definitely onto something: this fish-and-rum bar is shiploads of fun, serving up all things nibbly from Neptune's realm and lashings and lashings of rum (over 200 kinds of the stuff). Yo-ho-ho! Sport eaters can take on the 'Seafood Indulgence', a mountain of shells and claws for a whopping $149.

♟ Drinking & Nightlife

It's said that Airlie Beach is a drinking town with a sailing problem. The bars at **Magnums** (☑ 07-4964 1199, 1800 624 634; www.magnums.com.au; 366 Shute Harbour Rd; camp sites/van sites $24/26, dm/d from $24/56; ❄ @ ☎) and Beaches, the two big backpackers in the centre of town, are always crowded, and are popular places to kick off a ribald evening.

Mama Africa   CLUB
(263 Shute Harbour Rd; ❄ 9pm-5am) Mama's is a jumping African-style safari nightclub throbbing with a beat that both hunter and prey find hard to resist. Themed nights and all kinds of promotions aimed at the backpacker party set ensure spontaneous all-nighters any day of the week.

Just Wine & Cheese   WINE BAR
(Shop 8, 33 Port Dr; wines by the glass $7-18; ❄ 3-10pm) Run by two astute wine afficionados, this glamorous bottle shop and bar serves

fine examples of what it promises, with a view of the Port of Airlie marina.

Paddy's Shenanigans   IRISH PUB
(352 Shute Harbour Rd; ⊙5pm-3am) Live music every night, but otherwise the usual sports-watching, hard-drinking venue.

❶ Information

Whitsunday Bookings (☑07-4948 2201; www.whitsundaybooking.com.au; 346 Shute Harbour Rd) Tina has been helping travellers book the right tour for years. For a while this office was even the default tourist information office, although now it looks like many of the other information booking centres along the strip.

Whitsundays Central Reservation Centre (☑1800 677 119; www.airliebeach.com; 259 Shute Harbour Rd) To take the hassle out of finding the right accommodation, Whitsundays Central Reservation Centre can be of enormous assistance.

❶ Getting There & Away

AIR

The closest major airports are Whitsunday Coast (Proserpine) and Hamilton Island.

Whitsunday Airport (☑07-4946 9180) is a small airfield 6km east of Airlie Beach, midway between Airlie Beach and Shute Harbour.

BOAT

Transfers between the **Port of Airlie** (www.portofairlie.com.au) and Hamilton, Daydream and Long Islands are run by **Cruise Whitsundays** (p367).

BUS

Greyhound (☑1300 473 946; www.greyhound.com.au) and **Premier Motor Service** (☑13 34 10; www.premierms.com.au) buses detour off the Bruce Hwy to Airlie Beach. There are buses between Airlie Beach and all of the major centres along the coast, including Brisbane ($248, 19 hours), Mackay ($31, two hours), Townsville ($49, four hours) and Cairns ($100, nine hours).

Long-distance buses stop on The Esplanade, between the sailing club and the Airlie Beach Hotel.

Whitsunday Transit (☑07-4946 1800; www.whitsundaytransit.com.au) connects Proserpine (Whitsunday Airport), Cannonvale, Abel Point, Airlie Beach and Shute Harbour. There are **several stops** along **Shute Harbour Rd**.

The Whitsundays

Seen from above, the Whitsundays are like a stunning organism under the microscope. Indigo, aqua, yellow and bottle-green cellu-lar blobs mesmerise the senses. Sheltered by the Great Barrier Reef, the waters are particularly perfect for sailing. Seen from afloat in the Coral Sea, any of the 74 islands will hypnotise on approach and leave you giddy with good fortune.

Some of the oldest archaeological sites on the east coast are found here and you can only imagine the displeasure of the Ngaro people at losing such land to sawmills.

Five of the islands have resorts but most are uninhabited, and several offer back-to-nature beach camping and bushwalking. Whitehaven Beach is the finest beach in the Whitsundays and, many claim, the world. Airlie Beach, on the mainland, is the coastal hub and major gateway to the islands, where you can book myriad tours and activities, or just party hard.

⚡ Activities

Sailing & Cruising

Atlantic Clipper   BOATING
(www.atlanticclipper.com.au; 2-day, 2-night trips from $460) Young, beautiful and boozy crowd... and there's no escaping the antics. Snorkelling (or recovering) on Langford Island is a highlight.

Derwent Hunter   BOATING
(☑1800 334 773; www.tallshipadventures.com.au; day trips $195) A deservedly popular sailing safari on a beautiful timber gaff-rigged schooner. A good option for couples and those more keen on wildlife than the wild life.

SV Domino   BOATING
(www.aussieyachting.com; day trips $180) Takes a maximum of eight guests to Bali Hai Island, a little-visited 'secret' of the Whitsundays. Includes lunch and a good two-hour snorkel. The boat is also available for custom, private charters.

Prima Sailing   BOATING
(☑0447 377 150; www.primasailing.com.au; 2-day/2-night tours from $390) Fun tours with a 12-person maximum. Ideal for couples chasing style and substance.

Whitehaven Xpress   BOATING
(☑07-4946 1585; www.whitehavenxpress.com.au; day trip $160) Various boat excursions, but best known for its daily trip to Whitehaven Beach.

Diving

Most dives in this area visit the easy-to-reach fringing reefs around the Whitsundays, but you can also dive further afield on the Great Barrier Reef.

Costs for open-water courses with several ocean dives start at around $900. **Whitsunday Diving Academy** (📞1300 348 464; www.whitsundaydivingacademy.com.au; 2579 Shute Harbour Rd, Jubilee Pocket) is a good place to start.

A number of sailing cruises include diving as an optional extra. Prices start from $95 for introductory or certified dives. Ferry operator Cruise Whitsundays (p367) offers dives (from $119) on day trips to their reef pontoon.

Most of the island resorts also have dive schools and free snorkelling gear.

Kayaking

Paddling with dolphins and turtles is one of the best ways to experience the Whitsundays. **Salty Dog Sea Kayaking** (📞07-4946 1388; www.saltydog.com.au; Shute Harbour; half-/full-day trips $80/130) offers guided tours and kayak rental ($50/80 per half-/full day), plus a brilliant six-day kayak and camping expedition ($1650) that's suitable for beginners.

👉 Tours

Ocean Rafting   BOATING
(📞07-4946 6848; www.oceanrafting.com.au; adult/child/family from $134/87/399) Visit the 'wild' side of the islands in a very fast, big yellow speedboat. Swim at Whitehaven Beach, regain your land legs with a guided national park walk, or snorkel the reef at Mantaray Bay and Border Island.

Ecojet Safari   TOURS
(📞07-4948 2653; tours per person $195) Explore the islands, mangroves and marine life of the northern Whitsundays on these three-hour, small-group jet-ski safaris (two people per jet ski).

Big Fury   BOATING
(📞07-4948 2201; www.magicwhitsundays.com; adult/child/family $130/70/350) Speed out to Whitehaven Beach on an open-air sports boat, and follow up with lunch and snorkelling at a secluded reef nearby. Great value and bookable through Airlie Beach travel agencies.

HeliReef   SCENIC FLIGHTS
(📞07-4946 9102; www.helireef.com.au) Scenic helicopter flights from $135.

🛌 Sleeping

NPSR (www.npsr.qld.gov.au) manages the Whitsunday Islands National Park camping grounds on several islands for both

TOP BEACHES

The Whitsundays boast some of the finest beaches in the country full of them. Our top picks:

Whitehaven Beach (p374) With azure-blue waters lapping the pure-white, silica sand, Whitehaven on Whitsunday Island is absolutely stunning.

Chalkies Beach Opposite Whitehaven Beach, on Haslewood Island, this is another idyllic, white-sanded beach.

Langford Island At high tide, Langford is a thin strip of sand on the rim of a ludicrously picturesque coral-filled turquoise lagoon.

Butterfly Bay On the northern side of Hook Island is this protected bay, which flutters with butterfly song each winter.

Catseye Beach (p373) Hamilton Island's Catseye Beach is a busy-ish spot by Whitsunday standards, but its palm-shaded sand and turquoise waters are social-media ready.

independent campers as well as groups on commercial trips. Camping permits ($6.15/24.60 per person/family) are available online or at the **NPSR booking office** (📞13 74 68; www.npsr.qld.gov.au; cnr Shute Harbour & Mandalay Rds; ⊙9am-4.30pm Mon-Fri) in Airlie Beach.

You must be self-sufficient and are advised to take 5L of water per person per day plus three days' extra supply in case you get stuck. You should also have a fuel stove as wood fires are banned on all islands.

Whitsunday Island Camping Connections – Scamper (📞07-4946 6285; www.whitsundaycamping.com.au) leaves from Shute Harbour and can drop you at South Molle, Denman or Planton Islands ($65 return); Whitsunday Island ($105 return); Whitehaven Beach ($155 return); and Hook Island ($160 return).

Long Island

Long Island has secluded, pretty white beaches, lots of adorable wild rock wallabies and 13km of walking tracks.

Camp at Long Island's **Sandy Bay** (www.nprsr.qld.gov.au; sites per person/family $6.15/24.60).

SAILING THE WHITSUNDAYS

The Whitsundays are the place to skim across fantasy-blue waters on a tropical breeze. If you're flexible with dates, last-minute stand-by rates can considerably reduce the price and you'll also have a better idea of weather conditions. Many travellers hang out in Airlie Beach for a few days for this exact purpose, although you may end up spending your savings in the pub!

Most vessels offer snorkelling on the fringing reefs, where the colourful soft corals are often more abundant than on the outer reef. Diving and other activities nearly always cost extra.

Once you've decided, book at one of the many booking agencies in Airlie Beach.

Other than the superfast **Camira** (p367), sailing boats aren't able to make it all the way to destinations such as Whitehaven Beach on a day trip from Airlie Beach. Instead they usually go to the lovely Langford Reef and Hayman Island; check before booking.

Bareboat Sailing

Rent a boat without skipper, crew or provisions. You don't need formal qualifications, but you (or one of your party) have to prove that you can competently operate a vessel.

Expect to pay between $500 and $1000 a day in high season (September to January) for a yacht sleeping four to six people, plus a booking deposit and a security bond (refunded when the boat is returned undamaged). Most companies have a minimum hire period of five days.

There are a number of bareboat charter companies around Airlie Beach, including the following:

Charter Yachts Australia (☑1800 639 520; www.cya.com.au; Abel Point Marina; 4 people from $495)

Cumberland Charter Yachts (☑1800 075 101; www.ccy.com.au; Abel Point Marina)

Queensland Yacht Charters (☑1800 075 013; www.yachtcharters.com.au; Abel Point Marina)

Whitsunday Escape (☑1800 075 145; www.whitsundayescape.com; Abel Point Marina)

Whitsunday Rent A Yacht (☑1800 075 000; www.rentayacht.com.au; 6 Bay Tce, Shute Harbour)

Crewing

In return for a free bunk, meals and a sailing adventure, crewing will see you hoisting the mainsail and cleaning the head. Look for 'Crew Wanted' signs around the marina, and at restaurants and hotels. Your experience will depend on the vessel, skipper, other crew members (if any) and your own attitude. Be sure to let someone know where you're going, with whom and for how long. Aside from safety precautions, it may make them bitterly jealous.

Palm Bay Resort (☑1300 655 126; www.palmbayresort.com.au; villas from $229, bures from $249, bungalows from $329) is Long Island's luxury self-catering resort where guests can choose from a variety of secluded housing options. The pool is huge and the camaraderie between guests is understated given there is no dining area. The resort store sells gourmet groceries and a rustic bar provides the booze. If you want your own supplies delivered, contact **Whitsundays Provisions** (☑07-4946 7344; www.whitprov.com.au). This is a model for sustainable tourism that could have some legs.

Cruise Whitsundays (☑07-4946 4662; www.cruisewhitsundays.com) connects Palm Bay Resort to the Port of Airlie by frequent daily services ($48 each way).

Hook Island

The 53-sq-km Hook Island, the second-largest island in the Whitsundays group, is predominantly national park and rises to 450m at Hook Peak. There are a number of good beaches dotted around the island, and some of the region's best diving and snorkelling locations.

There are national park **camping grounds** (www.npsr.qld.gov.au; sites per person/family $6.15/24.60) at Maureen Cove, Steen's Beach, Curlew Beach and Crayfish Beach. Although basic, they provide some wonderful back-to-nature opportunities.

South Molle Island

The largest of the Molle group of islands at 4 sq km, South Molle is virtually joined to Mid and North Molle Islands. Apart from the private residence area and golf course at Bauer Bay in the north, the island is all national park and is criss-crossed by 15km of walking tracks, with some superb lookout points.

There are national park **camping grounds** ($\square$ 13 74 68; www.npsr.qld.gov.au; sites per person/family $6.15/24.60) at Sandy Bay in the south, and at Paddle Bay near the resort.

Daydream Island

Daydream Island is the closest resort to the mainland and perfectly located to attract the tourist hordes. At just over 1km long and 200m wide, the island can be explored in an hour or two; one strength is its marine biology program, which allows visitors to encounter much of the region's wildlife in a short space of time. Unfortunately, it does feel overwhelming at times, more sterile than natural. Recently sold to an investment group that plans to make it a 'luxury' destination, it will likely retain its popularity as a day-trip destination and is suitable for everybody, especially busy families, or travellers with little time to explore the 'real' Whitsundays. Damage from Cyclone Debbie in early 2017 has meant the redevelopment has been brought forward, and the resort is expected to reopen in 2018.

Daydream Island Resort & Spa ($\square$ 1800 075 040; www.daydreamisland.com; d from $245; $\ast$ $\widehat{\gg}$ $\underline{\approx}$) has a monopoly on the accommodation on the island. Rooms are reasonably priced and many face out to the glorious Coral Sea. Tennis courts, a gym, catamarans, windsurfing, three swimming pools and an open-air cinema are all included in the tariff. There's also a club with constant activities to keep children occupied.

Hamilton Island

POP 1350

Welcome to a little slice of resort paradise where the paved roads are plied with golf buggies, steep, rocky hills are criss-crossed by walking trails, and the white beaches are buzzing with water-sports action. Though it's not everyone's idea of a perfect getaway, it's hard not to be impressed by the selection of high-end accommodation, restaurants, bars and activities – if you've got the cash, there's something for everyone.

Day trippers can use some resort facilities – including tennis courts, a golf driving range and a minigolf course – and enjoy the island on a relatively economical budget.

A few shops by the harbour organise dives and certificate courses, and just about everyone can sign you up for a variety of cruises to other islands and the outer reef.

If you only have time for one walk, make it the clamber up to Passage Peak (239m) on the northeastern corner of the island.

$\bowtie$ Sleeping & Eating

★Qualia   RESORT $$$
($\square$ 1300 780 959; www.qualia.com.au; d from $1100; $\ast$ $@$ $\widehat{\gg}$ $\underline{\approx}$) Stunning, ultraluxe Qualia is set on 30 secluded acres, with modern villas materialising like heavenly tree houses in the leafy hillside. The resort has a private beach, two restaurants, a spa and two swimming pools. It remains our favourite luxury resort for miles.

Reef View Hotel   HOTEL $$$
($\square$ 02-9007 0009; www.hamiltonisland.com.au/reef-view-hotel; d from $370; $\ast$ $@$ $\underline{\approx}$) Aptly named, this hilltop resort has spectacular views over the green hills out to turquoise seas. It's central and popular with families and groups. It's a slightly more manageable price for long-ish stays, and the mood is more low-key.

Popeye's Fish n' Chips   FISH & CHIPS $
(Front St; fish & chips $11.50; $\odot$ 10am-9pm Sun-Thu, 11.30am-9pm Fri & Sat) Massive boxes of fish and chips that can comfortably feed two people. Also sells burgers, chicken...and fishing bait.

Manta Ray Cafe   CAFE $$
($\square$ 07-4946 8213; Marina Village; mains $17-30; $\odot$ 10.30am-9pm) Wood-fired gourmet pizzas are a favourite here, but you can also settle in for an afternoon of drinks and oysters. It's popular with families and day visitors.

$\oplus$ Getting There & Away

AIR

Hamilton Island Airport is the main arrival centre for the Whitsundays, and is serviced by **Qantas** ($\square$ 13 13 13; www.qantas.com.au), **Jetstar** ($\square$ 13

15 38; www.jetstar.com.au) and **Virgin** (☑ 13 67 89; www.virginaustralia.com.au).

BOAT
Cruise Whitsundays (☑ 07-4946 4662; www. cruisewhitsundays.com) Connects Hamilton Island Airport and the marina with the Port of Airlie in Airlie Beach ($48).

Hayman Island

The most northern of the Whitsunday group, little Hayman is just 4 sq km in area and rises to 250m above sea level. It has forested hills, valleys and beaches, and a luxury five-star resort. Hayman Island has long been a stage for the lifestyles of the rich and famous. It is Australia's most celebrated island resort, first conceived by an airline magnate, and ever since then the enviable playground of celebrities and dignitaries of every stripe. Sadly, the average punter will have to settle for the other 73 islands; Hayman is for resort guests only.

An avenue of stately date palms leads to the entrance of **One&Only Hayman Island Resort** (☑ 07-4940 1838; www.hayman.com.au; r incl breakfast $730-12,300; ❄ @ ☎ ☎), one of the most gilded playgrounds on the Great Barrier Reef, with its hectare of swimming pools (open around the clock), landscaped gardens and exclusive boutiques. The rooms vary from well-appointed poolside cabins to deluxe three-bedroom suites and stand-alone villas; all are huge. Unfortunately the resort will be unable to take bookings until mid-2018 due to Cyclone Debbie.

Lindeman Island

Situated 15km southeast of the luxurious Hamilton Island, Lindeman was once a flashy resort but has since been returned to nature by liquidators. For the past decade, only nature photographers and hikers have provided any semblance of bustle, making independent treks for the varied island tree life and the sublime view from Mt Oldfield (210m). The mood is poised to change however, as a $600m redevelopment is set to commence in 2017. Lindeman is still mostly national park, with empty bays and 20km of impressive walking trails. Get here while you can.

Boat Port (sites per person/family $6.15/ 24.60) is an open campground on a sandy beach area backed by rainforest. There are basic toilet and picnic facilities. It was once a bay used to clean sailing vessels, hence the name.

Whitsunday Island

Long proclaimed by talking heads of tourism as one of Australia's most beautiful beaches, **Whitehaven Beach**, on Whitsunday Island, is a pristine 7km-long stretch of blinding sand (at 98% pure silica, the sand is some of the whitest in the world), bounded by lush tropical vegetation and a brilliant blue sea. From Hill Inlet at the northern end of the beach, the swirling pattern of dazzling sand through the turquoise and aquamarine water paints a magical picture. There's excellent snorkelling from its southern end.

There are national park **camping grounds** (sites per person/family $6.15/24/60) at Dugong, Nari's and Joe's Beaches in the west, at Chance Bay in the south, at the southern end of Whitehaven Beach, and Peter Bay in the north.

Other Whitsunday Islands

The northern islands are undeveloped and seldom visited by cruise boats or water taxis. Several of these – Gloucester, Saddleback and Armit Islands – have national park camping grounds.

Bona Bay on Gloucester Island has the largest **camping ground** (☑ 13 74 68; www. npsr.qld.gov.au; sites per adult/family $6.15/24.60), with toilets, picnic tables and good shelter. Armit Island's basic camping ground has a toilet and picnic tables, while Saddleback has a modest site, which is close to the mainland and has picnic tables.

Cumberland Islands

There are about 70 islands in the Cumberland group, sometimes referred to as the southern Whitsundays. Almost all the islands are designated national parks. **Brampton Island** is well-known for its nature walks, and will soon be home to a 'seven-star' resort. Facilities on all islands, aside from **Keswick Island**, are very limited and access can be difficult unless you have your own boat or can afford to charter one (or a seaplane); ask for more info at the Mackay visitor centre (p365).

Keswick Island Campground (☑ 1300 889 290; unpowered sites from $20, ste from $80) has a number of unpowered sites within a very easy walking distance of pristine Basil Bay and is a real secret among the camping community.

CONWAY NATIONAL PARK

There's enough diverse beauty in Conway National Park to lure travellers to Airlie Beach away from the Whitsundays, deep into the rainforest hills and remote beaches that were once the hunting grounds of the Giru Dala. The mountains of this national park and the Whitsunday Islands are part of the same coastal mountain range. Rising sea levels following the last ice age flooded the lower valleys, leaving only the highest peaks as islands, now cut off from the mainland.

Several walking trails start from near the picnic and day-use area. Further along the main road, towards Coral Point and before Shute Harbour, there's a 1km track leading down to Coral Beach and The Beak lookout.

About 1km past the day-use area, there's a 2.4km walk up to the **Mt Rooper lookout**, with good views of the Whitsunday Passage and islands.

To reach the beautiful **Cedar Creek Falls**, turn off the Proserpine–Airlie Beach road onto Conway Rd, 18km southwest of Airlie Beach. It's then about 15km to the falls; the roads are well signposted.

The **Beach House** (☑ 1300 889 290; www.keswickisland.com.au; 6 Coral Passage Dr, Keswick Island; houses $275) is a good way to enjoy Keswick's beauty without any hassle. The modern, stylish property sleeps six comfortably and has direct beach access to Basil Bay.

Bowen

POP 9277

Bowen is a small coastal town set on a hill just north of Airlie Beach, and is famous for its mangoes – Bowen gets busy during fruit-picking season – but known locally for its secret bays and inlets. Its wide, quiet streets, wooden Queenslander houses and laid-back, friendly locals encourage a gentle pace of life. The foreshore, with its landscaped esplanade, picnic tables and BBQs, is a focal point, but there are some truly stunning – and little-visited – beaches and bays northeast of the town centre.

Keep an eye out for the 'Bowenwood' sign on the town's water tower; Baz Luhrmann's epic movie *Australia* was shot here in 2007 and the locals are still a little star-struck.

🛏 Sleeping & Eating

Bowen Backpackers　　　　HOSTEL $
(☑ 07-4786 3433; www.bowenbackpackers.com.au; Herbert St; dm night/week from $40/190; ❄ @ ☎) Located at the pretty beach end of Herbert St (past the Grandview Hotel), this is the place to stay if you're working in the surrounding fruit farms. New management has a stellar reputation around town. Rooms are neat and reasonably spacious.

Barnacles Backpackers　　　　HOSTEL $
(☑ 07-4786 4400; www.barnaclesbackpackers.com; 18 Gordon St; dm from $30; ☎) New management has taken over this 84-room hostel, which has close links to the fruit-picking industry. The communal areas have a clinical feel, but it's highly functional and quiet. Jury is out on the direction it will take, so listen to the backpacker grapevine for the latest.

Rose Bay Resort　　　　RESORT $$
(☑ 07-4786 9000; www.rosebayresort.com.au; 2 Pandanus St; r $160-300; ❄ @ ☎) Rose Bay is a seriously underrated beach, especially for snorkelling, and guests at this friendly resort have it pretty much all to themselves. Spacious studios and comfy units all sleep four guests quite comfortably. You'll need a car to reach the Bowen strip. Minimum two-night stay.

Jochheims Pies　　　　BAKERY $
(49 George St; pies $5; ☺ 5.30am-3.30pm Mon-Fri, to 12.30pm Sat) Jochheims has been keeping Bowen bellies full of homemade pies and baked treats since 1963. Try a Hugh Jackman (hunky beef) pie – the actor was a regular here during the filming of *Australia*.

✈ Getting There & Away

Greyhound (☑ 1300 473 946; www.greyhound.com.au) and **Premier** (☑ 13 34 10; www.premierms.com.au) are two companies that have frequent bus services running to/from Airlie Beach ($26, 1½ hours) and Townsville ($29, four hours).

Eungella National Park

Mystical, mountainous Eungella National Park covers nearly 500 sq km of the lofty Clarke Range, but is largely inaccessible except for the walking tracks around Broken River and Finch Hatton Gorge. The large tracts of tropical and subtropical vegetation have been isolated from other rainforest areas for thousands of years and now boast several unique species, including the orange-sided skink and the charming Eungella gastric-brooding frog, which incubates its eggs in its stomach and gives birth by spitting out the tadpoles.

Finch Hatton Gorge

Finch Hatton Gorge is a remarkable, prehistoric place set in a rugged subtropical rainforest. Hills of farmland disappear into a lush gorge dotted with volcanic boulders and buzzing with bird and insect life. It can feel like you've stepped through a geographical black hole into another physical dimension.

A gorgeous 1.6km walking trail leads to **Araluen Falls**, with its tumbling waterfalls and swimming holes, and a further 1km hike takes you to the **Wheel of Fire Falls**, another cascade with a deep swimming hole. Both these falls tend to be busy with locals on weekends.

Rainforest Scuba (☑ 0434 455 040; www. rainforestscuba.com; 55 Anzac Pde, Finch Hatton) claims the dubious title of the world's first rainforest dive operator; submerge in crystal-clear creeks where eels, platypus, turtles and fish share the habitat.

A brilliantly fun and informative way to explore the rainforest here is to glide through the canopy with **Forest Flying** (☑ 07-4958 3359; www.forestflying.com; $60). The sky-high guided tours see you harnessed to a 350m-long cable and suspended up to 25m above the ground; you control your speed via a pulley system.

Platypus Bushcamp (☑ 07-4958 3204; www.bushcamp.net; Finch Hatton Gorge; sites/dm/ huts $7.50/25/75; ☀) ✿ is a true-blue bush retreat hand-built by Wazza, the eccentric owner. The three basic huts are surrounded by rainforest. A creek with platypuses and great swimming holes runs next to the camp, and the big, open-air communal kitchen and eating area is the heart of the place.

Broken River

Cool and sometimes misty, Broken River is worth a detour inland from Mackay for its high-elevation rainforest where hilly cattle ranches house some very happy cows and prolific bird life. Broken River has some of the best walking tracks in the region and you may spot a few marsupials hiding in the brush.

Fern Flat Camping Ground (www.npsr. qld.gov.au/camping; sites per person/family $6.15/24.60) is a lovely place to camp, with shady sites adjacent to the river where the platypuses play. This is a walk-in camping ground and is not vehicle accessible, but it's an easy 500m past the information centre and kiosk. Register online.

Crediton Hall Camping Ground (www. npsr.qld.gov.au; sites per person/family $6.15/24.60), 3km after Broken River, is accessible to vehicles. Turn left into Crediton Loop Rd and turn right after the Wishing Pool circuit track entrance.

❶ Getting There & Away

The park is 84km west of Mackay. There are no buses to Eungella or Finch Hatton, but **Reeforest Adventure Tours** (p362) runs day trips from Mackay and will drop off and pick up those who want to linger; however, tours don't run every day so your stay may wind up being longer than intended.

TOWNSVILLE TO CAIRNS

Spread out between the tourist darlings of Cairns and the Whitsunday Islands, this lesser-known, stretch of quiet, palm-edged beaches is where giant endangered cassowary graze for seeds, and koalas nap in gum trees on turquoise encircled islands.

Townsville

POP 174,797

Northern Queensland's less-visited major city is easy on the eye: at Townsville's heart is its handsome, endless esplanade, an ideal viewing platform to fabulous Magnetic Island offshore. It's a pedestrian-friendly city, and its grand, refurbished 19th-century buildings offer loads of landmarks. If in doubt, join the throngs marching up bright red Castle Hill to gaze across the city's dry environs.

GREAT BARRIER REEF TRIPS FROM TOWNSVILLE

The Great Barrier Reef lies further offshore from Townsville than it does from Cairns and Port Douglas; the extra fuel costs push up prices. On the upside, it's less crowded (and the reef suffers less from the effects of crowds). Trips from Townsville are generally dive-oriented; if you only want to snorkel, take a day trip that just goes to the reef – the *Yongala* wreck is for diving only. The *Yongala* is considerably closer to Alva Beach near Ayr than to Townsville, so if your main interest is wreck diving, you may want to consider a trip with Alva Beach–based **Yongala Dive** (p383).

The **visitor centre** (p381) has a list of Townsville-based operators offering PADI–certified learn-to-dive courses with two days' training in the pool, plus at least two days and one night living aboard the boat. Prices start at $600, and you'll need to obtain a dive medical (around $60).

Adrenalin Dive (✆07-4724 0600; www.adrenalinedive.com.au; 252 Walker St) Day trips to the Yongala (from $264) and Lodestone Reef (from $229), both including two dives. Also offers live-aboard trips and dive-certification courses.

Remote Area Dive (RAD; ✆07-4721 4424; www.remoteareadive.com.au; 16 Dean St) Runs day trips (from $225) to Orpheus and Pelorus islands. Also live-aboard trips and dive courses.

Townsville has a lively, young populace, with thousands of students and members of the armed forces intermingling with old-school locals, fly-in-fly-out mine workers, and summer-seekers lapping up the average 320 days of sunshine per year. Needless to say, the nightlife is often full throttle.

◉ Sights

★ Reef HQ Aquarium

AQUARIUM

(www.reefhq.com.au; Flinders St E; adult/child $28/14; ⊙9.30am-5pm) A staggering 2.5 million litres of water flow through the coral-reef tank here, home to 130 coral and 120 fish species. Kids will love seeing, feeding and touching turtles at the turtle hospital. Talks and tours (included with admission) throughout the day focus on different aspects of the reef and the aquarium.

★ Museum of Tropical Queensland

MUSEUM

(✆07-4726 0600; www.mtq.qm.qld.gov.au; 70-102 Flinders St E; adult/child $15/8.80; ⊙9.30am-5pm) An absolute must for school-age children and grown-up science and history fans, the Museum of Tropical Queensland reconstructs scenes using detailed models with interactive displays. At 11am and 2.30pm you can load and fire a cannon, 1700s-style. Galleries include the kid-friendly MindZone science centre, and displays on North Queensland's history from the dinosaurs to the rainforest and reef.

Australian Institute of Marine Science

RESEARCH INSTITUTE

(AIMS; ✆07-4753 4444; www.aims.gov.au) Scheduled to re-commence free two-hour tours (10am Fridays from March through November) in mid-2017 after extensive renovations, this marine-research facility at Cape Ferguson conducts crucial research into issues such as coral bleaching and management of the Great Barrier Reef, and how it relates to the community; advance bookings are essential. The turn-off from the Bruce Hwy is 35km southeast of Townsville.

Billabong Sanctuary

WILDLIFE RESERVE

(www.billabongsanctuary.com.au; Bruce Hwy; adult/child $35/22; ⊙9am-5pm) Just 17km south of Townsville, this eco-certified wildlife park offers up-close encounters with Australian wildlife – from dingoes to cassowaries – in their natural habitat. You could easily spend all day at the 11-hectare park, with feedings, shows and talks every half-hour or so.

Botanic Gardens

GARDENS

(⊙sunrise-sunset) **FREE** Townsville's botanic gardens are spread across three locations: each has its own character, but all have tropical plants and are abundantly green. Closest to the centre, the formal, ornamental Queens Gardens (p378) are 1km northwest of town at the base of Castle Hill.

Townsville

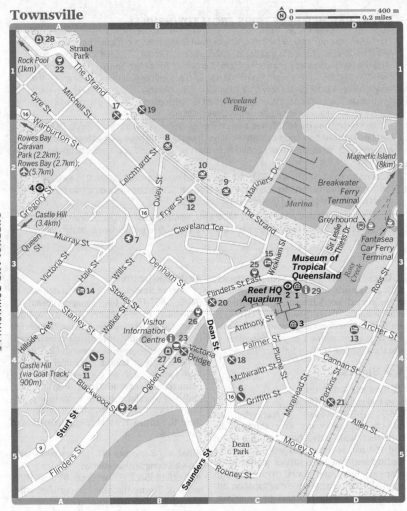

Castle Hill
VIEWPOINT

FREE Much of Townsville's fit and fabulous hoof it up this striking 286m-high red hill (an isolated pink granite monolith) that dominates Townsville's skyline for stunning views of the city and Cleveland Bay. Walk up via the rough 'goat track' (2km one way) from Hillside Cres. Otherwise, drive via Gregory St up the narrow, winding 2.6km Castle Hill Rd. A signboard up top details short trails.

Cultural Centre
CULTURAL CENTRE

(📞 07-4772 7679; www.cctownsville.com.au; 2-68 Flinders St E; adult/child $5/2; ⏰ 9.30am-4.30pm) Showcases the history, traditions and cus-

toms of the local Wulgurukaba and Bindal peoples. Call for guided-tour times.

Queens (Botanic) Gardens
GARDENS

(cnr Gregory & Paxton Sts; ⏰ sunrise-sunset) **FREE** If you fancy a lazy picnic, head to these ornamental gardens at the base of Castle Hill.

Maritime Museum of Townsville
MUSEUM

(📞 07-4721 5251; www.townsvillemaritimemuseum. org.au; 42-68 Palmer St; adult/child/family $6/3/15; ⏰ 10am-3pm Mon-Fri, noon-3pm Sat & Sun) One for the boat buffs, with a gallery dedicated to the wreck of the *Yongala* and

Townsville

exhibits on North Queensland's naval industries. Tours of decommissioned patrol boat HMAS *Townsville* are available.

🏃 Activities

Strand   SWIMMING
Stretching 2.2km, Townsville's waterfront is interspersed with parks, pools, cafes and playgrounds – with hundreds of palm trees providing shade. Its golden-sand beach is patrolled and protected by two stinger enclosures.

At the northern tip is the **rock pool** (The Strand; ⊘24hr) FREE, an enormous artificial swimming pool surrounded by lawns and sandy beaches. Alternatively, head to the chlorinated safety of the heritage-listed, Olympic-sized swimming pool, **Tobruk Memorial Baths** (www.townsville.qld.gov.au; The Strand; adult/child $5/3; ⊘5.30am-7pm Mon-Thu, to 6pm Fri, 7am-4pm Sat, 8am-5pm Sun). There's also a fantastic **water playground** (The Strand; ⊘10am-8pm Dec-Mar, to 6pm Sep-Nov, Apr & May, to 5pm Jun-Aug) FREE for the kids.

Skydive Townsville   SKYDIVING
(☑07-4721 4721; www.skydivetownsville.com.au; 182 Denham St; 3050/4270m tandem dives from $395/445) Hurl yourself from a perfectly good plane and land right on the Strand, or over on Magnetic Island.

🎎 Festivals & Events

The city has a packed calendar of festivals and events, including the home games of its cherished **North Queensland Cowboys** National Rugby League team (www.cowboys.com.au).

Townsville 500   SPORTS
(www.v8supercars.com.au; ⊘Jul) Racing cars roar through a purpose-built street circuit each July during the V8 Supercar Championship.

Australian Festival of Chamber Music   MUSIC
(www.afcm.com.au; ⊘Aug) Townsville gets cultural during this internationally renowned festival each August at various venues across the city.

🛏 Sleeping

★**Civic Guest House**   HOSTEL **$**
(☑07-4771 5381; www.civicguesthousetownsville.com.au; 262 Walker St; dm/d from $20/56; @ 🛜) This old-fashioned hostel respects the independent traveller's needs for cleanliness, comfort, security and easy company. The mustard-coloured, colonial-tinged Civic is a welcome change from the boisterous backpacker trend. Free transport to/from the ferry or bus station.

Orchid Guest House
GUESTHOUSE $

(📱07-4771 6683, 0418 738 867; www.orchidguesthouse.com.au; 34 Hale St; dm $28, d with/without bathroom $90/65; ❄) The Orchid has really bloomed since our last visit. In a quiet hillside location within walking distance of town, the old suburban inner-city home is now wonderfully kept in that quaint Queensland fashion, with a peaceful flow of guests looking for a place to make plans for Magnetic Island or find temporary work.

Reef Lodge
HOSTEL $

(📱07-4721 1112; www.reeflodge.com.au; 4 Wickham St; dm $23-35, d with/without bathroom $80/62; ❄@📶) The only downtown hostel worth bothering with is a warren of room configurations, but the staff are very capable of creating a sense of community in the games room, chill-out zone and hammock-strewn garden area. Jobs can be found in the region here, if you've spent all your dough at the nearby nightclubs.

Rowes Bay Caravan Park
CARAVAN PARK $

(📱07-4771 3576; www.rowesbaycp.com.au; Heatley Pde; powered/unpowered sites $36/28, cabins with/without bathroom from $110/75, villas $115-140; ❄@📶🏊) Leafy park directly opposite Rowes Bay's beachfront. The villas are smaller than cabins, but spiffier.

Historic Yongala Lodge Motel
MOTEL $

(📱07-4772 4633; www.historicyongala.com.au; 11 Fryer St; motel r $79-139, 1/2-bedroom apt $115/159; ❄🏊🐕) Built in 1884, this lovely historic building with gingerbread-house-style balustrades, is but a short stroll from the Strand and city centre. The rooms and apartments are small but good value. Long-term 'tenants' and noisy party-goers can detract from the overall feel of the place, but there's enough variety and space to make it work.

Oaks M on Palmer
BOUTIQUE HOTEL $$

(📱07-4753 2900; 81 Palmer St; d from $100; 🅿❄🏊🐕) Perfect for an after-party or pre-dinner in-room drinks, Oaks M is right at the end of the Palmer St shuffle. The rooms are small, but stylish and bright. Popular with single professionals. Parking is free, service is discrete, and there's a small gym.

🍴 Eating

Perpendicular to the Strand, Gregory St has a clutch of cafes and takeaway joints. The Palmer St dining strip offers a diverse range of cuisines: wander along and take your pick. Many of Townsville's bars and pubs also serve food.

Harold's Seafood
SEAFOOD $

(cnr The Strand & Gregory St; meals $4-10; ⏰8am-9pm Mon-Thu, to 9.30pm Fri-Sun) The big fish-and-chip joint on the corner whips up fish burgers ($12) and large-sized barramundi and salad ($11).

★Longboard Bar & Grill
MODERN AUSTRALIAN $$

(📱07-4724 1234; www.longboardbarandgrill.com; The Strand, opp Gregory St; mains $15-37; ⏰11.30am-3pm & 5.30pm-late) The coolest place in Townsville for a light meal and a light party overlooking the water is this surf-themed pub-restaurant, which does terrific nightly specials including tacos and buffalo wings. The regular steak, seafood and pasta menu is very reliable. Orders are taken at the bar, but that's not a problem as the vibe is right most nights, and staff are fast and efficient.

Jam
MODERN AUSTRALIAN $$

(📱07-4721 4900; 1 Palmer St; mains $15-30; ⏰7am-10pm) This neat midrange restaurant, on happening Palmer St, understands its casual northern Queensland clientele and serves a wide menu with celebratory breakfasts and desserts.

Wayne & Adele's Garden of Eating
MODERN AUSTRALIAN $$

(📱07-4772 2984; 11 Allen St; mains from $19; ⏰6.30-10.30pm Mon, to 11pm Thu-Sat, noon-3pm Sun) Irreverence at every turn in this husband-and-wife-run gourmet restaurant situated in an Aussie backyard (well courtyard, at least). Those who like a side serving of quirky with their grub shouldn't miss mains including Safety Net (crocodile pattie with an eggnet Asian salad) or Bounce Back (tandoori kangaroo fillet with lime pickle yoghurt).

Summerie's Thai Cuisine
THAI $$

(📱07-4420 1282; www.summeriesthaicuisine.com.au; 232 Flinders St; lunch specials $13, dinner mains from $17; ⏰11.30am-2.30pm & 5.30-10pm) A wildly successful local Thai restaurant with a prime downtown location and a new branch in the suburbs, Summerie's adapts traditional dishes to the Aussie palate and incorporates Coral Sea produce in dishes such as Barrier Reef (fish sauce, coriander and chilli jam-spiced seafood), Heaven on Earth (slow-cooked coconut prawns with crunchy greens) and Summer Sunset (sweet-and-sour pineapple sauce).

A Touch of Salt
MODERN AUSTRALIAN **$$$**

(☑07-4724 4441; www.atouchofsalt.com.au; 86-124 Ogden St; mains $35-37; ⊙noon-3pm & 6-11.30pm) Although the favoured high-end dining experience for Townsville's posh set doesn't look very stylish upon entry, the bar is slick, the service is fussy and the sophisticated Asian-fusion cuisine is ambitious (though can overreach at times).

Drinking & Nightlife

Townsville Brewery
BREWERY

(252 Flinders St; ⊙11.30am-midnight Mon-Sat) Brews are made on-site at this hopping, stunningly restored 1880s former post office. Soak up a Townsville Bitter or Bandito Loco.

Beach Bar
BAR

(Watermark Hotel, 72-74 The Strand) The place to be seen in Townsville. Well, if it's good enough for Missy Higgins and Silverchair, then it's good enough for the rest of us. Some serious Sunday sessions take place in the tavern bar with prime ocean views down the flash end of The Strand.

Coffee Dominion
CAFE

(www.coffeedominion.com.au; cnr Stokes & Ogden Sts; ⊙6am-5pm Mon-Fri, 7am-1pm Sat & Sun) 🍃 An eco-conscious establishment roasting beans sourced from Atherton Tableland to Mombasa. If you don't find a blend you like, invent your own and they'll grind it fresh.

Grand Northern Hotel
PUB

(☑07-4771 6191; 500 Flinders St) This historic 1901 pub in Townsville's bustling centre is not exactly a tranquil haven, but it's great for a beer at any time. For those who like to be in the thick of it all, the GN can't be beat.

Heritage Bar
BAR

(☑07-4724 1374; www.theheritagetownsville.com; 137 Flinders St E; bar snacks from $11; ⊙5pm-2am Tue-Sat) A surprisingly chic craft bar. Suave 'mixologists' deliver creative cocktails ($18) to a cool crowd looking for more than a beer-barn swillfest. Also has a sophisticated bar menu for meals (think BBQ bourbon pork, and scallop and chorizo gnocchi), as well as nibbles such as coconut prawns.

🛍 Shopping

Check out the weekly **Cotters Market** (www.townsvillerotarymarkets.com.au; Flinders St Mall; ⊙8.30am-1pm Sun) or monthly **Strand**

Night Market (www.townsvillerotarymarkets.com.au; The Strand; ⊙5-9.30pm 1st Fri of month May-Dec).

ℹ️ Information

Great Barrier Reef Marine Park Authority (☑07-4750 0700; www.gbrmpa.gov.au) National body overseeing the Great Barrier Reef.

Visitor Information Centre (☑07-4721 3660; www.townsvilleholidays.info; 280 Flinders St; ⊙9am-5pm) Extensive visitor information on Townsville, Magnetic Island and nearby national parks. There's another branch on the Bruce Hwy 10km south of the city.

ℹ️ Getting There & Away

AIR

From **Townsville Airport** (www.townsvilleairport.com.au), **Virgin** (☑13 67 89; www.virginaustralia.com), **Qantas** (☑13 13 13; www.qantas.com.au), **Air North** (☑1800 627 474; www.airnorth.com.au) and **Jetstar** (☑13 15 38; www.jetstar.com.au) fly to Cairns, Brisbane, the Gold Coast, Sydney, Melbourne, Mackay and Rockhampton, with connections to other major cities.

BOAT

SeaLink (☑07-4726 0800; www.sealinkqld.com.au) runs a ferry service to Magnetic Island from Breakwater in Townsville (return adult/child including all-day bus pass $35/17.50, 25 minutes). There's one trip per hour between 5.30am and 11.30pm. Ferries arrive and depart Magnetic Island from the terminal at Nelly Bay.

BUS

Greyhound (☑1300 473 946; www.greyhound.com.au; The Breakwater, Sealink Travel Centre, Sir Leslie Thiess Dr) has three daily services to Brisbane ($249, 24 hours), Rockhampton ($129, 12 hours), Airlie Beach ($49, 4½ hours), Mission Beach ($44, 3¾ hours) and Cairns ($64, six hours). Buses pick up and drop off at the **Breakwater Ferry Terminal** (2/14 Sir Leslie Thiess Dr; lockers per day $4-6).

Premier Motor Service (☑13 34 10; www.premierms.com.au) has one service a day to/from Brisbane ($184, 23 hours) and Cairns ($55, six hours), stopping in Townsville at the **Fantasea car ferry terminal** (Ross St, South Townsville).

TRAIN

Townsville's **train station** (Charters Towers Rd) is 1km south of the centre.

The Brisbane–Cairns *Spirit of Queensland* travels through Townsville five times a week. Journey time between Brisbane and Townsville is 25 hours (one-way from $189), while tickets to Cairns (6½ hours) start from $79. Contact **Queensland Rail** (☑1800 872 467; www.queenslandrail.com.au).

ⓘ Getting Around

Townsville Airport is 5km northwest of the city centre in Garbutt. A taxi to town costs about $22.

Sunbus (☏ 07-4771 9800; www.sunbus.com.au) runs local bus services around Townsville. Route maps and timetables are available at the visitor information centre and online.

Taxis congregate at ranks across town, or call **Townsville Taxis** (☏ 13 10 08; www.tsvtaxi.com.au).

Magnetic Island

POP 2500

Sitting within shouting distance of Townsville, Magnetic Island is a verdant island and one of Queensland's most laid-back residential addresses. The local population, who mostly commute to Townsville or cater for the tourist trade, must pinch themselves as they come home to the stunning coastal walking trails, gum trees full of dozing koalas (you're likely to spot some), and surrounding bright turquoise seas.

Over half of this mountainous, triangular island's 52 sq km is national park, with scenic walks and abundant wildlife, including a large (and adorable) rock wallaby population. Inviting beaches offer adrenalin-pumping water sports, and the chance to just bask in the sunshine. The granite boulders, hoop pines and eucalyptus are a fresh change from the clichéd tropical-island paradise.

◉ Sights

There's one main road across the island, which goes from Picnic Bay, past Nelly and Geoffrey Bays, to Horseshoe Bay. Local buses ply the route regularly. Walking trails through the bush also link the main towns. Maps are available at the ferry terminal ticket desk.

◉ Picnic Bay

Picnic Bay is one of the most low-key spots on the island, dominated more by a community of friendly locals than anything else. There's a stinger net during the season (November to May) and the swimming is superb. There's also a fine jetty if you like to throw in a line.

◉ Nelly Bay

Magnetic Harbour in Nelly Bay is your first taste of life on the island. There's a wide range of busy but relaxing eating and sleep-

ing options and a decent beach. There's also a children's playground towards the northern end of the beach, and good snorkelling on the fringing coral reef.

◉ Arcadia Bay

Arcadia village is a conglomerate of shops, eateries and accommodation. Its main beach, **Geoffrey Bay**, has a reef at its southern end (reef walking at low tide is discouraged). By far its prettiest beach is the cove at **Alma Bay** with huge boulders tumbling into the sea. There's plenty of shade here, along with picnic tables and a children's playground.

If you head to the end of the road at **Bremner Point**, between Geoffrey Bay and Alma Bay, at around 5pm you can have wild rock wallabies – accustomed to being fed at the same time each day – literally eating out of the palm of your hand. For those who make it out here, this can be a trip highlight.

◉ Radical Bay & the Forts

Townsville was a supply base for the Pacific during WWII, and the forts were designed to protect the town from naval attack. If you're going to do just one walk, then the **forts walk** (2.8km, 1½ hours return) is a must. It starts near the Radical Bay turn-off, passing lots of ex-military sites, gun emplacements and false 'rocks'. At the top of the walk is the observation tower and command post, which have spectacular coastal views, and you'll almost certainly spot koalas lazing about in the treetops. Return the same way or continue along the connecting paths, which deposit you at Horseshoe Bay (you can catch the bus back).

Nearby Balding Bay is Maggie's unofficial nude beach.

◉ Horseshoe Bay

Horseshoe Bay, on the north coast, is the best of Maggie's accessible beaches and attracts its share of young, hippie-ish nature lovers and older day-trippers. You'll find water-sports gear for hire, a stinger net, a row of cafes and a fantastic pub. Bungalow Bay Koala Village has a **wildlife park** (☏ 07-4778 5577, 1800 285 577; www.bungalowbay.com.au; 40 Horseshoe Bay Rd, Horseshoe Bay; adult/child $29/13; ⊙ 2hr tours 10am, noon & 2.30pm), where you can cuddle crocs and koalas. Pick up local arts and crafts at Horseshoe Bay's market (⊙9am-2pm 2nd & last Sun of month), which sets up along the beachfront.

🏃 Activities

Big Mama Sailing
BOATING

(☑0437 206 360; www.bigmamasailing.com; full-day cruise adult/child $195/110) Hit the water on an 18m ketch with passionate boaties Stu, Lisa and Fletcher, who recently moved the Big Mama down from Mission Beach.

Pro Dive Magnetic
DIVING

(☑0424 822 450; www.prodivemagnetic.com; 43 Sooning St, Nelly Bay) This Nelly Bay dive school offers splashing Magnetic Island day trips for both snorkellers ($149) and scuba divers ($199). PADI courses cost $299.

Tropicana Tours
DRIVING

(☑07-4758 1800; www.tropicanatours.com.au; full day adult/child $198/99) Ziggy and co run magnificent island tours that take in the island's best spots in their stretch 4WD. Prices include close encounters with wildlife, lunch at a local cafe and a sunset cocktail. Shorter tours are also available, but the eight-hour version is a hit.

Horseshoe Bay Ranch
HORSE RIDING

(☑07-4778 5109; www.horseshoebayranch.com. au; 38 Gifford St, Horseshoe Bay; 2hr rides $120) Gallop dramatically into the not-so-crashing surf on this popular bushland-to-beach two-hour tour. Pony rides for littlies are available too (20 minutes, $20).

Magnetic Island Sea Kayaks
KAYAKING

(☑07-4778 5424; www.seakayak.com.au; 93 Horseshoe Bay Rd, Horseshoe Bay; morning/evening tour $85/60) 🌿 Magnetic Island is a perfect destination for sea kayaking, with plenty of launching points, secret beaches, marine life, and laid-back cafes to recharge in after your paddle. Join an eco-certified morning or sunset tour, or go it alone on a rented kayak (single/double per day $85/160).

Pleasure Divers
DIVING

(☑07-4778 5788; www.pleasuredivers.com.au; 10 Marine Pde, Arcadia; open-water courses per person from $300; ⊙8.30am-5pm) A snorkel tour with these guys based in Arcadia is a good-value way to get an appreciation of the ecology around Geoffrey Bay. Deep-water thinkers can do three-day PADI open-water courses to kick-start their scuba skills, as well as advanced courses and *Yongala* wreck dives for regular plungers.

DIVING THE YONGALA WRECK

Yongala Dive (☑07-4783 1519; www.yongaladive.com.au; 56 Narrah St, Alva Beach) offers dive trips ($259 including gear) out to the *Yongala* wreck from Alva Beach, 17km northeast of Ayr. It only takes 30 minutes to get out to the wreck from here, instead of a 2½-hour boat trip from Townsville. Book ahead for backpacker-style accommodation at its onshore **dive lodge** (☑07-4783 1519; www.yongaladive.com.au; 56 Narrah St; dm/d $29/68; @), with free pick-ups from Ayr.

🛏 Sleeping

★ Base Backpackers
HOSTEL $

(☑1800 242 273; www.stayatbase.com; 1 Nelly Bay Rd, Nelly Bay; camping per person $15, dm $32-37, d from $110; @ 🕏 ⛱) Away from any semblance of holidaymakers to disrupt your natural state, Base has to be one of the best-located hostels in Australia, situated between Nelly and Picnic Bays. It's famous for wild full-moon parties, and things can get raucous at any time at the infamous on-site Island Bar. Sleep, food and transport package deals are available.

Arcadia Beach Guest House
GUESTHOUSE $

(☑07-4778 5668; www.arcadiabeachguesthouse. com.au; 27 Marine Pde, Arcadia; dm from $35, safari tents $65, r with bathroom $135-170, r without bathroom $75-85; ❄ 🕏 ⛱) Well-priced and staffed by effusive professionals, Arcadia Beach Guest House does a lot right, including providing an enormous variety of sleeping quarters. Will you stay in a bright, beachy room (named after Magnetic Island's bays), a safari tent or a dorm? Go turtle-spotting from the balcony, rent a canoe, a Moke or a 4WD...or all of the above?

Magnetic Island B&B
B&B $$

(☑07-4758 1203; www.magneticislandbedand breakfast.com; 11 Dolphin Ct, Horseshoe Bay; d $150) The double rooms here book out quickly, but a new Bush Retreat ($190) sleeps four and is a great deal for some natural seclusion. Rooms are bright and breezy, and the hosts are astutely professional. There's a neat saltwater pool, and the inclusive breakfasts are wholesome and delicious. Minimum two-night stay applies.

Shambhala Retreat BUNGALOW $$
(☏ 0448 160 580; www.shambhala-retreat-mag
netic-island.com.au; 11 Barton St, Nelly Bay; d from
$105; ✱☀☷) 🏄 With some of the best-value,
self-contained, tropical units on the island,
Shambhala is a green-powered property
with distinct Buddhist influences evident in
the wall hangings and water features. Two
units have outdoor courtyard showers; all
have fully equipped kitchens, large bath-
rooms and laundry facilities. Local wildlife
is often drawn to the patios. Minimum stay
is two nights.

Arcadia Village Motel HOTEL $$
(☏ 07-4778 5481; www.arcadiavillage.com.au; 7 Ma-
rine Pde, Arcadia; r from $120; ✱☀☷) Situated
down the quiet end of Marine Pde (which is
saying something in a chilled-out place like
Maggie), this family-friendly motel has an
on-site bistro and bar, which can get a little
rowdy on weekends. There are two awesome
pools, and a great beach a short stroll across
the street.

Island Leisure Resort RESORT $$
(☏ 07-4778 5000; www.islandleisure.com.au; 4
Kelly St; buré d from $197, buré f from $247;
✱☀☷) Self-contained, Polynesian-style
cabins (burés) give this by-the-beach spot
an extra-tropical feel. Private patios allow
guests to enjoy their own piece of paradise:
a lagoon pool and BBQ area beckon social
souls.

Magnetic Sunsets APARTMENT $$
(☏ 07-4778 1900; www.magneticsunsets.com.au;
7 Pacific Dr; 1-/2-/3-bedroom apt $195/295/395,
B&B s/d $115/159; ✱☀☷) These great-value,
self-contained apartments are just a literal
stagger from the beach. Private balconies
overlook the bay; inside, they're cool, clean

WORTH A TRIP

RAVENSWOOD & CHARTERS TOWERS

Detour inland from the coast to taste a bit of Queensland's outback character at these
two old gold towns.

Ravenswood is a tiny gold-mining town whose fortunes have fluctuated over the
past century. It's now best known for its two grand hotels, one of which supposedly
houses one of Queensland's most active resident ghosts.

Accommodation, food and of course drinks can be found in the town's two pubs, the
Imperial Hotel (☏ 07-4770 2131; 23 Macrossan St; s/d $39/65; P☀✱☷) and the **Rail-
way Hotel** (☏ 07-4770 2144; 1 Barton St; s/tw/d $42/79/90; P✱☀☷).

The 19th-century gold-rush settlement of **Charters Towers** (pop 8500) is about
140km southwest of Townsville on the Flinders Hwy. William Skelton Ewbank Melbourne
(WSEM) Charters was the gold commissioner during the rush, when the town was the
second-largest, and wealthiest, in Queensland. The 'towers' are its surrounding tors
(hills). With almost 100 mines, some 90 pubs and a stock exchange, the town became
known simply as 'the World'.

The **Stock Exchange Arcade** (☏ 07-3223 6666; www.nationaltrust.org.au/places/stock-
exchange-building-and-arcade; 76 Mosman St; ☉ 9am-5pm), with its barrel-vaulted portico,
was the commercial hub of town in Queensland in the late 19th century. Today it features
a breezy, sun-filtered cafe and a fine art gallery.

Come nightfall, panoramic **Towers Hill**, the site where gold was first discovered, is
the atmospheric setting for an open-air cinema showing the 20-minute film *Ghosts After
Dark* – check seasonal screening times and buy tickets ($10) at the visitor centre.

Staying at the atmospheric and friendly old **Royal Private Hotel** (☏ 07-4787 8688;
www.royalprivate-hotel.com; 100 Mosman St; r from $60; ✱☀) feels like something between
time travel and visiting a museum.

For those looking for a real-life cattle station experience, contact the friendly Rhonda
at **Bluff Downs** (☏ 07-4770 4084; dm $20, d $90-300, camp sites $20). The vast majority
of guests are looking for medium-term employment, but passers-by are welcome. It's
110km northwest of Charters Towers.

The excellent **Charters Towers Visitor Centre** (☏ 07-4761 5533; www.charterstowers.
qld.gov.au; 74 Mosman St; ☉ 9am-5pm) books all tours in town, including those to the
reputedly haunted Venus Gold Battery, where gold-bearing ore was crushed and processed from 1872 to 1973.

and welcoming. Smart, new B&B rooms are good alternatives.

✕ Eating & Drinking

★ Cafe Nourish   CAFE $
(📞07-4758 1885; 3/6 Pacific Dr, Horseshoe Bay; wraps from $9; ⊗8am-4pm) Horseshoe Bay has become the hip cafe strip and our favourite cafe on the island does the small things well: fresh, healthy wraps, breakfasts, smoothies and energy balls. And don't even get us started on the coffee. Service is energetic and heartfelt.

Noodies on the Beach   MEXICAN $
(📞07-4778 5786; 2/6 Pacific Dr, Horseshoe Bay; mains from $10; ⊗10am-10pm Mon-Wed & Fri, 8am-10pm Sat, 8am-3pm Sun; 🅿) An integral part of the Horseshoe Bay food scene, Noodies is an irreverent Mexican-themed cafe with a book exchange and a licence to serve killer margaritas.

Arcadia Night Market   MARKET $
(RSL Hall, Hayles Ave, Arcadia; ⊗5.30-8pm Fri) Small but lively night market with licensed bar and plenty of cheap eats to chow through.

Gilligan's Cafe   CAFE $$
(Arcadia Village; burgers $14-18; ⊗8am-4pm) Fun, licensed cafe in Arcadia that pumps out massive breakfasts and the finest burgers on Maggie. The owners have a *Gilligan's Island* thing going on. Get stranded while you enjoy the decent booze selection over lunch.

Marlin Bar   PUB FOOD $$
(📞07-4758 1588; 3 Pacific Dr, Horseshoe Bay; mains $16-24; ⊗11am-8pm) Marlin Bar is popular with sailing crews dropping anchor in Horseshoe Bay and locals looking for some live music in the evenings. Meals are on the large side and (surprise!) revolve around seafood. Dogs are welcome.

Picnic Bay Hotel   PUB FOOD $$
(📞07-4778 5166; www.picnicbayhotel.com.au; 1 The Esplanade, Picnic Bay; mains $11-26; ⊗9.30am-10pm) There are worse places to settle in at for a drink than the very quiet Picnic Bay, with Townsville's city lights sparkling across the bay. There's an all-day grazing menu and huge salads.

❶ Getting There & Away

SeaLink (p381) runs an excellent ferry service to Magnetic Island from Townsville (return adult/child including all-day bus pass $35/17.50, 25 minutes). There's roughly one trip per hour between 5.30am and 11.30pm. All ferries arrive and depart Maggie from the terminal at Nelly Bay. Car parking is available in Townsville.

Fantasea (📞07-4796 9300; www.magnetic islandferry.com.au; Ross St, South Townsville) operates a car ferry crossing eight times daily (seven on weekends) from the south side of Ross Creek, taking 35 minutes. It costs $178 (return) for a car and up to three passengers, and $29/17 (adult/child return) for foot passengers only. Bookings are essential and bicycles are transported free.

❶ Getting Around

Sunbus (www.sunbus.com.au/sit_magnetic_ island) ploughs between Picnic and Horseshoe Bays, meeting all ferries and stopping at major accommodation places. A day pass covering all zones is $7.20, or you can include it in your ferry ticket price. Be sure to talk to the bus drivers, who love chatting about everything Maggie.

Moke- ('topless' car) and scooter-rental places abound. You'll need to be over 21 years old, have a current driver's licence and leave a credit-card deposit. Scooter hire starts at around $40 per day, Mokes at about $75. Try **MI Wheels** (📞07-4758 1111; www.miwheels.com.au; 138 Sooning St, Nelly Bay) for a classic Moke, or **Roadrunner Scooter Hire** (📞07-4778 5222; 3/64 Kelly St, Nelly Bay) for scooters and trail bikes.

Ingham & Around

POP 4681

Ingham is a cane-cutting centre with a proud Italian heritage. It's also the guardian of the 120-hectare **Tyto wetlands** (Tyto Wetlands Information Centre; 📞07-4776 4792; www.tyto.com. au; cnr Cooper St & Bruce Hwy; ⊗8.45am-5pm Mon-Fri, 9am-4pm Sat & Sun), which has 4km of walking trails and attracts around 230 species of birds, including far-flung guests from Siberia and Japan. The locals – hundreds of wallabies – love it too, converging at dawn and dusk. The town is the jumping-off point for the majestic **Wallaman Falls**; at 305m, it's the longest single-drop waterfall in Australia.

Mungalla Station (📞07-4777 8718; www. mungallaaboriginaltours.com.au; 2hr tours adult/ child $70/35) 🌿, 15km east of Ingham, runs insightful tours led by Aboriginal people, which include boomerang throwing and stories from the local Nywaigi culture, plus a traditional Kupmurri lunch. Minimum of 10 needed, so call ahead to check. Basic camping sites also available.

In August the **Australian Italian Festival** (www.australianitalianfestival.com.au) celebrates the fact that 60% of Ingham residents are of Italian descent. The motto is 'eat, drink and celebrate'.

You can camp at **Wallaman Falls Campground** (www.npsr.qld.gov.au; sites per person/family $6.15/24.60).

The poem that inspired the iconic Slim Dusty hit 'Pub With No Beer' (1957) was written in the **Lees Hotel** (☑ 07-4776 1577; www.lees hotel.com.au; 58 Lannercost St, Ingham; s/d from $90/105, meals from $14; ☺ lunch & dinner Mon-Sat; ✳ ᗏ) by Ingham cane-cutter Dan Sheahan, after American soldiers drank the place dry. The en-suite rooms here are very comfortable, while the busy bistro does fine steak and pasta dishes. Oh, and there's plenty of beer.

The award-winning **Hinchinbrook Marine Cove Resort** (☑ 07-4777 8395; www. hinchinbrook-marine-cove-resort.com.au; 54 Dungeness Rd; d $135, bungalows $150; ✳ ᗏ) is terrific value given the bright, spacious bungalows sleep up to five, management is hands-on and there's easy access to Hinchinbrook Island.

Cardwell

POP 1300

It's no wonder the truck drivers make Cardwell a must-stop destination. Given the Bruce Hwy runs inland for most of the east coast, it's a rare blessing to see and hear the sea lapping right outside your vehicle window; the uninterrupted views of Hinchinbrook Island don't hurt either. Most travellers merely linger here for seasonal fruit picking (check at the backpackers if you're looking for work), but there are worse places in the world to slow down.

The **Rainforest & Reef Centre** (☑ 07-4066 8601; www.greatgreenwaytourism.com/rain forestreef.html; 142 Victoria St; ☺ 8.30am-5pm Mon-Fri, 9am-1pm Sat & Sun), next to Cardwell's jetty, has a truly brilliant interactive rainforest display, and detailed info on Hinchinbrook Island and other nearby national parks.

Cardwell Beachcomber Motel & Tourist Park (☑ 07-4066 8550; www.cardwellbeach comber.com.au; 43a Marine Pde; powered/unpowered sites $38/29, motel d $98-125, cabins & studios $120-130; ✳ @ ᗏ) has a good variety of options and a small restaurant.

Cardwell Central Backpackers (☑ 07-4066 8404; www.cardwellbackpackers.com.au; 6 Brasenose St; dm $24; @ ᗏ) can both arrange regular work and host in a heartfelt, secure way. They also accept overnighters.

Hinchinbrook Island

Australia's largest island national park (399 sq km) is a holy grail for walkers, but it's not easy to get to and advance planning is essential. Granite mountains rise dramatically from the sea and wildlife creeps through the foliage. The mainland side is dense with lush tropical vegetation, while long sandy beaches and tangles of mangrove curve around the eastern shore.

Hinchinbrook Island Cruises (☑ 07-4066 8601; www.hinchinbrookislandcruises.com.au) runs a service from Cardwell's Port Hinchinbrook Marina to Hinchinbrook's Ramsay Bay boardwalk ($99 per person one way, 1½ hours). It also operates a four-hour, two-island tour (adult/child $110/99) that includes a cruise between Goold and Garden Islands spotting dolphins, dugongs and turtles, before docking at Ramsay Bay boardwalk for a walk on the 9km-long beach and a picnic lunch.

NPSR **camp sites** (☑ 13 74 68; www.npsr.qld. gov.au; sites per person $6.15) are interspersed along the wonderful 32km Thorsborne Trail (or East Coast Trail).

Tully

POP 2350

It may look like just another sleepy sugarcane village, but Tully is a burg with a boast, calling itself the 'wettest town in Australia'. A gigantic golden gumboot at Tully's entrance is as high as the waters rose (7.9m) in 1950: climb the spiral staircase to the viewing platform up top to get a sense of just how much that is! And while boggy Babinda challenges Tully's claim, the fact remains that all that rain ensures plenty of raftable rapids on the nearby Tully River (p389), and shimmering fruit farms in need of travelling labour.

The **Golden Gumboot Festival** (☺ May) celebrates the soak with a parade and lashings of entertainment.

Book at the visitor centre for 90-minute tour of **Tully Sugar Mill** (adult/child $17/11; ☺ daily late Jun-early Nov).

The Indigenous operators of **Ingan Tours** (☑ 07-4068 0189; www.ingan.com.au; 5 Blackman St) visit sacred story places on their full-day Spirit of the Rainforest tours (Tuesdays,

PALUMA RANGE NATIONAL PARK

It's worth making time to venture off the Bruce Hwy via the Paluma Range National Park, southern gateway to the Wet Tropics World Heritage Area. The park is divided into two parts, the Mt Spec section and the northern Jourama Falls section, with both offering a variety of waterholes, inland beaches, hiking trails and a gentle entrée into tropical north Queensland. This glorious parallel universe, running alongside the Bruce Hwy from roughly Ingham to Townsville, is also prime platypus-spotting territory.

Mt Spec

The Mt Spec part of the park (61km north of Townsville or 40km south of Ingham) is a misty Eden of rainforest and eucalypt trees criss-crossed by a variety of walking tracks. This range of habitats houses an incredibly diverse population of birds, from golden bowerbirds to black cockatoos.

From the northern access route of the Bruce Hwy, take the 4km-long partially-sealed Spiegelhauer Rd to **Big Crystal Creek**; from there, it's an easy 100m walk from the car park to **Paradise Waterhole**, a popular spot with a sandy beach and lofty mountain views.

The southern access route (Mt Spec Rd) is a sealed, albeit twisty, road that writhes up the mountains to **Paluma Village**. Beware: though you may have come up here 'just for a drive', the village's cool air and warm populace may change your mind.

En route to Paluma, be sure to stop off at **Little Crystal Creek**, a picturesque swimming hole with a cute stone bridge, picnic area and waterfalls.

In Paluma village the cool **Rainforest Inn** (☑ 07-4770 8688; www.rainforestinnpaluma. com; 1 Mt Spec Rd; d $125; ❄) has well-designed rooms and a nearby restaurant-bar.

Jourama Falls

Waterview Creek tumbles down these eponymous falls and other cascades past palms and umbrella trees, making this section a fine place for a picnic and a perambulation. It's a steep climb to the lookout; keep your eyes peeled for kingfishers, freshwater turtles and endangered mahogany gliders on the way up. The **NPSR camping ground** (www. npsr.qld.gov.au; sites per person/family $6.15/24.60) has cold showers, gas BBQs, water (treat before drinking) and composting toilets.

This part of the park is reached via a 6km sealed road (though the creek at the entrance can be impassable in the Wet), 91km north of Townsville and 24km south of Ingham. Be sure to fuel up before veering off the highway.

Thursdays and Saturdays) and offer powerful, authentic insights into the lives of the area's first people.

🛏 Sleeping & Eating

Banana Barracks   HOSTEL $
(☑ 07-4068 0455; www.bananabarracks.com; 50 Butler St; weekly 8-/4-bed dm $135/165; @ 🛜 🏊) Banana Barracks is the go-to backpackers for wannabe fruit pickers in the Tully region. The hostel is also the hub of Tully's nightlife, Rafters Bar, with an on-site nightclub.

Mount Tyson Hotel   PUB $
(☑ 07-4068 1088; www.mttysonhotel.com.au; s/d $60/105) This newly renovated pub is a bit bland in terms of ambience, but the motel rooms are fresh and clean, and provide good value for a short stay.

★ **Redgates Steakhouse**   DINER $$
(☑ 0400 773 315; 99 Butler St) A top bloke runs this spacious diner on the way into town. The menu is long and ever-changing, but the mainstays are the burgers – both the fish and beef ($12) get a massive thumbs up, while the thickshakes and coffee come in a close second. Wi-fi is fast and free.

ℹ Information

Tully Visitor & Heritage Centre (☑ 07-4068 2288; Bruce Hwy; ⏰ 8.30am-4.45pm Mon-Fri, 9am-2pm Sat & Sun) The Tully Visitor & Heritage Centre has a brochure outlining a self-guided heritage walk around town, with 17 interpretative panels (including one dedicated to Tully's UFO sightings), and walking-trail maps for the nearby national parks. The centre also has free internet and a book exchange.

WORTH A TRIP

ORPHEUS ISLAND

Orpheus is a heavenly 1300-hectare island 80km north of Townsville, with a protected national park and surrounding ocean that is part of the Great Barrier Reef Marine Park. Its dry sclerophyll forest is a geographical anomaly this far north, where bandicoots, green tree frogs, echidnas, ospreys and a peculiar number of goats roam free, the latter as part of a madcap 19th-century scheme to provide food for potential shipwreck survivors. Visitors gravitate towards the eucalypt-scented hiking trails and crystal-clear snorkelling.

Part of the Palm Islands group, Orpheus is surrounded by magnificent fringing reef that's home to a mind-blowing collection of fish (1100 species) and a mammoth variety of both hard and soft corals. While the island is great for snorkellers and divers year-round (pack a stinger suit in summer), seasonal treats such as manta-ray migration (August to November) and coral spawning (mid-November) make the trip out here all the more worthwhile.

Orpheus Island Lodge (✆ 07-4839 7937; www.orpheus.com.au; Orpheus Island; d incl meals from $1500) is arguably the finest five-star resort in Queensland, rivalling the more famous Hayman Island for sheer tropical splendour, food, service and prestige.

Nautilus Aviation (✆ 07-4034 9000; www.nautilusaviation.com.au; one way from Townsville $275) runs helicopters from Townsville at 2pm daily for $275 one way. The spectacular trip takes 30 minutes. Otherwise, ask around the town of Lucinda to arrange a boat ride over.

Mission Beach

The rainforest meets the Coral Sea at Mission Beach, a tropical enclave of beach hamlets that has long threatened to take the Australian getaway circuit by storm. Yet this Coral Sea bolt-hole has maintained a beautiful balance between yoga living, backpacker bravado and eco-escape, plus it has Australia's highest density of cassowaries and is the gateway to Dunk Island.

Collectively referred to as Mission Beach, or just 'Mission', the area comprises a sequence of individual, very small and laid-back villages strung along the coast. Bingil Bay lies 4.8km north of Mission Beach proper (sometimes called North Mission). Wongaling Beach is 5km south; from here it's a further 5.5km south to South Mission Beach. Most amenities are in Mission proper and Wongaling Beach.

🏃 Activities

There's a **stinger enclosure** for swimming during stinger season (January through March).

Skydive Mission Beach　　　SKYDIVING
(✆ 1300 800 840; www.skydivemissionbeach.com.au; 1 Wongaling Beach Rd; 1830/4270m tandem dives $199/334) Mission Beach is rightfully one of the most popular spots in Australia for skydiving, with views over gorgeous islands and blue water, and a soft landing on a white-sand beach. Skydive Australia, known locally as Skydive Mission Beach, runs several flights per day.

Altitude Skydivers　　　SKYDIVING
(✆ 07-4088 6635; www.altitudeskydive.com.au; 4/46 Porter Promenade; 4270m $299) The new boys in town are a small, highly experienced and fun-loving jump team, with very competitive pricing.

Coral Sea Kayaking　　　KAYAKING
(✆ 07-4068 9154; www.coralseakayaking.com; half-/full-day tours incl lunch $80/136) Knowledgeable full-day guided tours to Dunk Island; easygoing bob-arounds on the half-day option. Longer three-day journeys to the Barnard and Family Islands can be arranged.

🛏 Sleeping

⭐ **Jackaroo Hostel**　　　HOSTEL $
(✆ 07-4068 7137; www.jackaroohostel.com; 13 Frizelle Rd; sites $12-15, dm/d incl breakfast from $25/58; 🅿@🛜🏊) Oh to be young enough again to justify whiling away the days in a timber pole-frame retreat deep in the rainforest by a huge jungle pool overlooking the Coral Sea. Bugger it: just drive inland past Clump Mountain, find a quiet double room and wander around the communal areas granting silent, wise nods to those young rascals bronzing in the tropical sun.

Dunk Island View Caravan Park
CARAVAN PARK $

(07-40688248; www.dunkislandviewcaravanpark.com; 21 Webb Rd; sites $30-32, 1-/2-bedroom units $105/135; ❄️ 🛜 🏊 🐕) One of the best caravan parks we visited in northern Queensland, its views of Dunk Island are stupendous and the grounds are impeccably kept. The small pool is welcome in stinger season, and there's also an on-site cafe (fish and chips, $9).

Mission Beach Ecovillage
CABIN $

(07-4068 7534; www.ecovillage.com.au; Clump Point Rd; d $119-150, 2-bedroom bungalows $180; ❄️ 🛜 🏊) With its own banana and lime trees scattered around its tropical gardens, and a direct path through the rainforest to the beach, this 'ecovillage' makes the most of its environment. Clustered around a rocky pool, the bungalows are a little worn, but there's a licensed restaurant and bubbly enough service to compensate.

Mission Beach Retreat
HOSTEL $

(07-4088 6229; www.missionbeachretreat.com.au; 49 Porter Promenade; dm $22-25, d $56; ❄️ @ 🛜 🏊) Bang in the centre of town, with the bonus of being beachfront, this is an easy, breezy backpacker spot that's hard not to like. YHA-accredited, this place fills up quickly. Extras include a shuttle service to the supermarket and free wi-fi. Staff insist on friendly interaction with guests.

Rainforest Motel
MOTEL $

(07-4088 6787; www.rainforestmotel.com; 9 Endeavour Ave; d/tw $95/105; ❄️ @ 🛜 🏊) Though not about to gain plaudits for contemporary luxury, this hidden motel off Mission's humble main street is nonetheless great value and is very well serviced. Rooms are cool and clean, and the communal sitting areas near the tiny pool feel like you've been dropped in a rainforest garden. Free bikes available.

Sanctuary
CABIN $

(1800 777 012, 07-4088 6064; www.sanctuaryatmission.com; 72 Holt Rd; dm $40, huts s/d from $75/80, cabins $185; ⏱ mid-Apr–mid-Dec; @ 🛜 🏊) 🍃 This popular group retreat centre is reached by a steep 600m-long rainforest walking track from the car park (4WD pick-up available). At Sanctuary you can sleep surrounded only by flyscreen on a platform in a simple hut, or opt for an en-suite cabin whose shower has floor-to-ceiling rainforest views. Yoga, night walks and massage are all available to guests at a cost.

Scotty's Mission Beach House
HOSTEL $

(07-4068 8676, 1800 665 567; www.scottysbeachhouse.com.au; 167 Reid Rd; dm $24-29, d $71; ❄️ @ 🛜 🏊) Dropped right on a quiet stretch of beach, Scotty's is a YHA hostel with modest rooms grouped around a grassy pool area. Management is tapped into the east coast circuit and is keen to help guests capitalise on their adventure. Out front, Scotty's Bar & Grill ($12-24; ⏱ 5pm-12am), open to nonguests, has something happening virtually every night, from fire-twirling shows to pool comps to live music.

Hibiscus Lodge B&B
B&B $$

(07-4068 9096; www.hibiscuslodge.com.au; 5 Kurrajong Cl; r from $145; 🛜) The main homestead of this charming Mission Beach property forms the backdrop for a local fauna roll-call. Hibiscus Lodge is a discerning choice; you can taste the self-satisfaction at the breakfast table. With only three (very private) rooms, bookings are essential. Generous online discounts are available. No kids.

Licuala Lodge
B&B $$

(07-4068 8194; www.licualalodge.com.au; 11 Mission Circle; d incl breakfast from $135; 🛜 🏊) You'll need your own car and a willingness to sit still at this peaceful B&B located 1.5km from the beach and pretty much everything else. Guests alternate between the wonderful verandah, where breakfast can be taken overlooking landscaped gardens, and the swimming pool surrounded by a rock garden. Cassowaries pop by regularly to check out the scene.

TULLY RIVER RAFTING

The Tully River provides thrilling white water year-round thanks to Tully's trademark bucket-downs and the river's hydroelectric floodgates. Rafting trips are timed to coincide with the daily release of the gates, resulting in Grade IV rapids foaming against a backdrop of stunning rainforest scenery.

Day trips with **Raging Thunder Adventures** (07-4030 7990; www.ragingthunder.com.au; full-day rafting $189) or **R'n'R White Water Rafting** (07-4041 9444; www.raft.com.au; full-day rafting from $179) include a BBQ lunch and transport from Tully or nearby Mission Beach.

Nautilus B&B B&B $$

(1 Nautilus St; 2-bedroom apt from $180) While bookings are technically only available on-line, it's worth popping past Nautilus B&B and asking Dena if she can help you out. Two newly built, pristine white-tiled apartments sit side-by-side atop a hill overlooking the town, offering a smooth stay. The one large shared bathroom has a powerful shower, while each room has its own small courtyard.

★ **Sejala on the Beach** CABIN $$$

(☑07-4088 6699; www.sejala.com.au; 26 Pacific Pde; d $275; ❀ ❀) Choose from 'Waves', 'Coral' and 'Beaches', three self-contained beach 'huts' within snoring sound of the coconut palms. Each one comes with rainforest shower, deck with private BBQ and loads of character. Perfect for hiding away with a partner.

✖ Eating

Early Birds Cafe CAFE $

(Shop 2, 46 Porter Promenade; mains $7-18; ☺6am-3pm Thu-Tue; ☑) The only joint open first thing in the morning, Early Birds wins return customers with its honest, cheap, cafe-style breakfasts (veggie $14) and famous, bigger-than-average fresh juices.

Fish Bar SEAFOOD $

(☑07-4088 6419; Porter Promenade; mains $10-17; ☺10am-midnight) Very affordable fish and other ocean creatures are served up in a casual atmosphere. A small courtyard has views of the sea. Takeaway available.

★ **Bingil Bay Cafe** CAFE $$

(☑07-4068 7146; 29 Bingil Bay Rd; mains $14-23; ☺6.30am-10pm; ☑) Sunshine, rainbows, coffee and gourmet grub make up the experience at this lavender landmark with a great porch for watching the world drift by. Breakfast is a highlight, but it's open all day. Regular art displays and live music ensure a creative clientele.

Caffe Rustica ITALIAN $$

(☑07-4068 9111; 24 Wongaling Beach Rd; mains $13-25, pizzas $10-25; ☺5pm-late Wed-Sat, 10am-9pm Sun; ☑) Traditional pizza and pasta are the staples at this evening haunt set inside a corrugated-iron beach shack; they also make their own gelato and sorbet. Bookings are encouraged as it's popular with locals year-round.

Garage Bar & Grill MODERN AUSTRALIAN $$

(☑07-4088 6280; 41 Donkin Lane; meze plates $17; ☺9am-late; ❀ ☑) The hot spot in Mission with the 20-something set, the Garage is famous for its delicious 'sliders' (mini

---

THE CASSOWARY: ENDANGERED NATIVE

Like something out of *Jurassic Park*, this flightless prehistoric bird struts through the rainforest. It's as tall as a grown man, has three razor-sharp, dagger-style clawed toes, a bright-blue head, red wattles (the lobes hanging from its neck), a helmet-like horn, and shaggy black feathers similar to an emu's. Meet the cassowary, an important link in the rainforest ecosystem. It's the only animal capable of dispersing the seeds of more than 70 species of trees whose fruit is too large for other rainforest animals to digest and pass (which acts as fertiliser). You're most likely to see cassowaries in the wild around Mission Beach, Etty Bay and the Cape Tribulation section of the Daintree National Park. They can be aggressive, particularly if they have chicks. Do not approach them; if one threatens you, don't run – give the bird right-of-way and try to keep something solid between you and it, preferably a tree.

It is estimated that there are 1000 or less cassowaries in the wild north of Queensland. An endangered species, the cassowary's biggest threat is loss of habitat, and most recently the cause has been natural. Tropical Cyclone Yasi stripped much of the rainforest around Mission Beach bare, threatening the struggling population with starvation. The cyclone also left the birds exposed to the elements, and more vulnerable to dog attacks and cars as they venture out in search of food.

Next to the **Mission Beach visitor centre**, there are cassowary conservation displays at the **Wet Tropics Environment Centre**, staffed by volunteers from the **Community for Cassowary & Coastal Conservation** (www.cassowary conservation.asn.au). Proceeds from gift-shop purchases go towards buying cassowary habitat. The website www.savethecassowary.org.au is also a good source of info.

burgers) and free-pour cocktails ($14). The hard-working chef mixes up the menu regularly and the management ensure there's a festive vibe in the beer garden with an eclectic playlist and tapas specials.

Millers Beach Bar & Grill PUB FOOD $$
(☑07-4068 8177; www.millersbeachbar.com.au; 1 Banfield Pde; mains $14-38; ⊗3pm-late Tue-Fri, noon-late Sat & Sun) Wongaling Beach's evening star, Millers is so close to the beach you'll be picking sand out of your beer. It's a popular function space, but the occasional crowd only adds to the ambience, especially at sunset with Dunk Island calling in the distance. The fish burger ($18) was a hit when we visited.

★**PepperVine** MODERN AUSTRALIAN $$$
(☑07-4088 6538; 2 David St; mains $16-32; ⊗4.30pm-11pm) On the Village Green, PepperVine is an uncomplicated contemporary restaurant borrowing from Italian, Spanish and Mod-Oz culinary influences, but nailing the atmosphere and service. Wood-fired pizza and a glass of Australian wine is the early evening staple, but the fine dining announces itself after sunset as the crowd descends.

🛍 Shopping

Between them, **Mission Beach Markets** (Porter Promenade; ⊗8am-1pm 1st & 3rd Sun of month) and **Mission Beach Rotary Monster Market** (Marcs Park, Cassowary Dr, Wongaling Beach; ⊗8am-12.30pm last Sun of month Apr-Dec) operate three Sundays a month.

❶ Information

Mission Beach Visitor Centre (☑07-4068 7099; www.missionbeachtourism.com; Porters Promenade, Mission Beach; ⊗9am-4.45pm Mon-Sat, 10am-4pm Sun) The main visitor centre in town has reams of information in multiple languages.

Wet Tropics Environment Centre (☑07-4068 7197; www.wettropics.gov.au; Porter Promenade; ⊗10am-4pm) Next door to the Mission Beach Visitor Centre you'll find displays and movies about the local environment, including, of course, the cassowary.

❶ Getting There & Away

Greyhound (☑1300 473 946; www.greyhound.com.au) and **Premier** (☑13 34 10; www.premierms.com.au) buses stop in Wongaling Beach next to the 'big cassowary'. Fares with

PARONELLA PARK

Set beside a series of creeks and waterfalls 50km northwest of Mission Beach (with at least one resident croc), **Paronella Park** (☑07-4065 0000; www.paronellapark.com.au; Japoonvale Rd, Mena Creek; adult/child $44/23) is a whimsical tropical retreat and a romantic, Dali-esque escape from reality. Moss-covered steps, lush tropical foliage and huge palatial structures appear straight from some Victorian-Mayan movie set. Nearby camping and quaint on-site cabins ($90) are available.

Greyhound/Premier are $25/19 to Cairns (two hours), $44/46 to Townsville (3½ hours).

Dunk Island

Dunk is known to the Djiru Aboriginal people as Coonanglebah (the island of peace and plenty). They're not wrong: this is pretty much your ideal tropical island, with lush jungle, white-sand beaches and impossibly blue water.

Walking trails criss-cross (and almost circumnavigate) Dunk: the circuit track (9.2km) is the best way to have a proper stickybeak at the island's interior and abundant wildlife. There's snorkelling over bommies (coral pinnacles or outcroppings) at Muggy Muggy and great swimming at truly beautiful Coconut Beach. On weekends in high season there are often special events such as bongo lessons or a ukulele band – check with the Mission Beach Visitor Centre.

Dunk Island was hammered by Cyclone Yasi in 2011, but has since mostly recovered, although part of the old resort remains off limits and a veritable eyesore.

Mission Beach Charters (☑07-4068 7009; adult/child return $35/18; 3hr tour $50) runs a shuttle as well as a range of fishing, diving and camping trips, or you can stay at the **Dunk Island campground** (☑0417 873 390; per person/family $6.15/24.60).

Innisfail & Around

POP 7500

Innisfail is a handsome, unhurried north Queensland town known for fishing, plantation farming and a remarkable collection of art-deco edifices.

In March, the **Feast of the Senses** (www.feastofthesenses.com.au) is a highlight of the northern Queensland culinary calendar.

About 27km along the Palmerston Hwy (signposted 4km northwest of Innisfail), the **Mamu Tropical Sky Walk** (www.mamutropicalskywalk.com.au; Palmerston Hwy; adult/child/family $23/12/64; ◷9.30am-5.30pm, last entry 4.30pm) 🚲 gives you eye-level views of the fruits, flowers and birds, and a bird's-eye perspective from its 100-step, 37m-high tower. Allow at least an hour to complete the 2.5km, wheelchair-accessible circuit.

Backpackers Shack (📞0499 042 446, 07-4061 7760; www.backpackersshack.com; 7 Ernest St; dm per week $195; P⚒@) has dormitory-style accommodation and acts as an unofficial employment agency for seasonal fruit workers.

Travellers with their own wheels will love **Flying Fish Tourist Park** (📞07-4061 3131; www.ffpvanpark.com.au; 39 Elizabeth St, Flying Fish Point; powered sites $32-39, cabins $50-99, villa $119-125; ⚒@🛜🏊) from where you can fish right off the beach across the road.

Oliveri's Continental Deli (www.oliverisdeli.com.au; 41 Edith St; sandwiches $8.50-11; ◷8.30am-5.15pm Mon-Fri, to 12.30pm Sat; 🍴) is an Innisfail institution offering goodies including 60-plus varieties of European cheese, ham and salami, and scrumptious sandwiches. Fantastic coffee, too.

Innisfail to Cairns

Part of the Wet Tropics World Heritage Area, steamy, dreamy **Wooroonooran National Park** brims with stunning natural spectacles, including Queensland's highest peak (Mt Bartle Frere, 1622m), dramatic falls, tangled rainforest, unusual flora and fauna and blissfully cool swimming holes. Camping permits are available through NPSR.

Babinda is a small working-class town that leads 7km inland to the **Babinda Boulders**, where a photogenic creek rushes between 4m-high granite rocks. It's croc-free, but here lurks an equal danger: highly treacherous waters. Aboriginal Dreaming stories say that a young woman threw herself into the then-still waters after being separated from her love; her anguish caused the creek to become the surging, swirling torrent it is today. Almost 20 visitors have lost their lives at the boulders. Swimming is permitted in calm, well-marked parts of the creek, but pay careful heed to all warning signs. Walking tracks give you safe access for obligatory gasps and photographs.

There's free camping at **Babinda Boulders Camping Area** FREE.

CAIRNS & AROUND

Tropical Far North Queensland between Cairns and Cooktown is a highlight on any east coast traveller's itinerary. As well as coastal Cairns, Port Douglas and the Great Barrier Reef, this region boasts the highland Atherton Tablelands and the unsurpassed wilderness of the Unesco World Heritage–listed Daintree rainforest. Look out for crocs and cassowaries, but don't miss it!

Cairns

POP 160,285

Cairns (pronounced 'cans') has come a long way since its beginnings as a boggy swamp and rollicking goldfields port. Heaving under the weight of countless resorts, tour agencies, souvenir shops and a million reminders of its proximity to the Great Barrier Reef, Cairns is unabashedly geared towards tourism.

Old salts claim Cairns has lost its soul, but it does have an infectious holiday vibe. The city centre is more boardshorts than briefcases, and you'll find yourself throwing away all notions of speed and schedules here, thanks to heady humidity and a hearty hospitality that can turn a short stroll into an impromptu social event. Fittingly, Cairns is awash with bars, clubs, eateries and cafes suiting all budgets. There's no beach in town, but the magnificent Esplanade Lagoon more than makes up for it; otherwise, the northern beaches are but a local bus ride or short drive away.

◎ Sights

Cairn's newest attraction, the state-of-the-art **Cairns Aquarium** (📞07-4044 7300; www.cairnsaquarium.com.au; 163 Abbott St; adult/child/family $42/28/126; ◷9am-5.30pm), was due to open in mid-2017.

★**Cairns Esplanade, Boardwalk & Lagoon**　　　　　WATERFRONT
(www.cairns.qld.gov.au/esplanade; ◷lagoon 6am-9pm Thu-Tue, noon-9pm Wed; 👪) FREE
Sunseekers and fun-lovers flock to Cairns Esplanade's spectacular **swimming lagoon**

on the city's reclaimed foreshore. The artificial, sandy-edged, 4800-sq-metre saltwater pool is lifeguard patrolled and illuminated nightly. The adjacent 3km foreshore **boardwalk** has picnic areas, birdwatching vantage points, free barbecues and fitness equipment. Follow the signposts for the excellent **Muddy's** (www.cairns.qld.gov.au/esplanade/facilities/playgrounds/muddys; Esplanade; ⊕) **FREE**, which has playgrounds and water fun for little kids, and the skate ramp, beach volleyball courts, bouldering park and Fun Ship playground.

★**Flecker Botanic Gardens**   GARDENS
(☑ 07-4032 6650; www.cairns.qld.gov.au/cbg; 64 Collins Ave; ⊙ grounds 7.30am-5.30pm, visitor centre 9am-4.30pm Mon-Fri, 10am-2.30pm Sat & Sun) **FREE** These gorgeous gardens are an explosion of greenery and rainforest plants. Highlights include a section devoted to Aboriginal plant use, the **Gondwana Heritage Garden**, and an excellent conservatory filled with butterflies and exotic flowers. Staff at the made-of-mirrors visitor centre can advise on free guided garden walks (daily from 10am).

Follow the **Rainforest Boardwalk** to **Saltwater Creek** and **Centenary Lakes**, a birdwatcher's delight. Uphill from the gardens, **Mt Whitfield Conservation Park** (www.cairns.qld.gov.au/facilities-sport-leisure/sport-and-recreation/active-living/red-and-green-arrow-walking-tracks; Edge Hill) has walking tracks through the rainforest to city viewpoints.

★**Reef Teach**   CULTURAL CENTRE
(☑ 07-4031 7794; www.reefteach.com.au; 2nd fl, Mainstreet Arcade, 85 Lake St; adult/child/family $23/14/60; ⊙ lectures 6.30-8.30pm Tue-Sat) ✎ Take your knowledge to new depths at this fun, informative centre, where marine experts explain how to identify specific species of fish and coral, and how to approach the reef respectfully.

Mangrove Boardwalk   NATURE RESERVE
(Airport Ave) **FREE** Explore the swampier side of Cairns on this revelatory wander into the wetlands. Eerie snap-crackle-slop noises provide a fitting soundtrack to the spooky surrounds, which are signposted with informative guides to the weird life forms scurrying in the mud below you. Slather yourself in mosquito repellent. The boardwalk (and its car park) is just before Cairns Airport (p1067).

Tjapukai Aboriginal Cultural Park   CULTURAL CENTRE
(☑ 07-4042 9999; www.tjapukai.com.au; Cairns Western Arterial Rd, Caravonica; adult/child/family $62/42/166; ⊙ 9am-5pm) Managed by the area's original custodians, this award-winning cultural extravaganza tells the story of creation using bot giant holograms and actors. There's a dance theatre, a gallery, boomerang- and spear-throwing demonstrations and turtle-spotting canoe rides. The **Nightfire** dinner-and-show package (adult/child/family $123/75/321, from 7pm to 9.30pm) culminates in a fireside corroboree.

Crystal Cascades   WATERFALL
(via Redlynch) About 14km from Cairns, the Crystal Cascades are a series of beautiful waterfalls and idyllic, croc-free swimming holes that locals would rather keep to themselves. The area is accessed by a 1.2km (30-minute) pathway. Crystal Cascades is linked to Lake Morris (the city's reservoir) by a steep rainforest **walking trail** (allow three hours return); it starts near the picnic area.

There is no public transport to the pools. Drive to the suburb of Redlynch, then follow the signs.

CAIRNS GALLERIES

Cairns Regional Gallery (☑ 07-4046 4800; www.cairnsregionalgallery.com.au; cnr Abbott & Shields Sts; adult/child $5/free; ⊙ 9am-5pm Mon-Fri, 10am-5pm Sat, 10am-2pm Sun) The permanent collection of this acclaimed gallery has an emphasis on local and Indigenous work.

Canopy Art Centre (☑ 07-4041 4678; www.canopyartcentre.com; 124 Grafton St; ⊙ 10am-5pm Tue-Sat) Showcases prints, paintings, sculptures and weavings of Indigenous artists from Cairns and communities as far north as the Torres Strait.

Tanks Arts Centre (☑ 07-4032 6600; www.tanksartscentre.com; 46 Collins Ave; ⊙ 9.30am-4.30pm Mon-Fri) Three gigantic, ex-WWII fuel-storage tanks have been transformed into art galleries; it's also an inspired performing-arts venue.

KickArts (www.kickarts.org.au; CoCA, 96 Abbott St; ⊙ 10am-5pm Mon-Sat) **FREE** Showcases cutting-edge local and regional artworks, plus touring exhibitions.

Cairns

QUEENSLAND CAIRNS

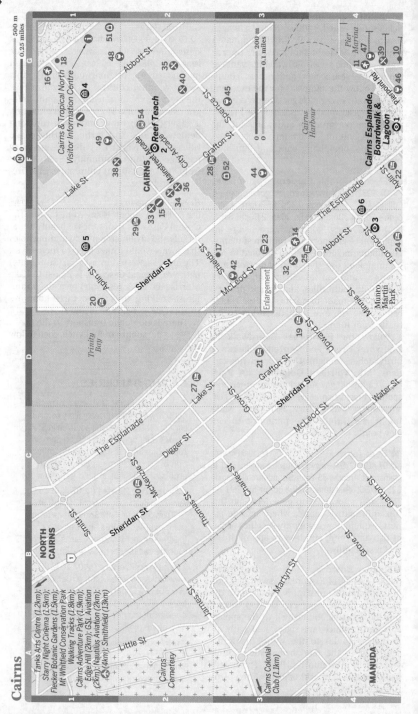

NORTH CAIRNS

MANUDA

Trinity Bay

Cairns Harbour

Pier Marina

Cairns Esplanade, Boardwalk & Lagoon

CAIRNS

Reef Teach

Mainstreet Arcade

City Arcade

Cairns & Tropical North Visitor Information Centre

Tanks Arts Centre (1.2km);
Starry Night Cinema (1.5km);
Flecker Botanic Gardens (1.5km);
Mt Whitfield Conservation Park
  Walking Tracks (1.8km);
Cairns Adventure Park (1.9km);
Edge Hill (2km); GSL Aviation
  (2km); Nautilus Aviation (2km);
  (4km); Smithfield (13km)

Cairns Colonial Club (1.1km)

Munro Martin Park

Enlargement

Abbott St
Spence St
Grafton St
Lake St
Aplin St
Shields St
McLeod St
Sheridan St
Sheridan St
Sheridan St
Sheridan St
The Esplanade
The Esplanade
Smith St
Digger St
McKenzie St
Thomas St
Charles St
Grove St
Grove St
Lake St
Grafton St
Upward St
Minnie St
Abbott St
Florence St
Aplin St
Aplin St
McLeod St
Water St
Gatton St
James St
Martyn St
Little St
Pierpoint Rd

Cairns Cemetery

500 m
0.25 miles

200 m
0.1 miles

🏃 Activities

Innumerable tour operators run adventure-based activities from Cairns, most offering transfers to/from your accommodation.

★ Cairns Zoom & Wildlife Dome
ADVENTURE SPORTS, WILDLIFE

(☎ 07-4031 7250; www.cairnszoom.com.au; Wharf St; wildlife entry $24, wildlife & zoom $45; ⏱ 9am-6pm) Cards, croupiers and...crocodiles? On top of the Reef Hotel Casino (p409), this unusual park brings the best of Far North Queensland's outdoors inside, with a native-creatures zoo, aviary and recreated rainforest. The complex is criss-crossed with ziplines, swings, obstacle courses and more; the truly adventurous can even venture outside for a nerve-testing dome climb.

★ Behana Days Canyoning
OUTDOORS

(☎ 0427 820 993; www.behanadays.com; tours $179) Give the salty stuff a break and join this fantastic freshwater expedition to beautiful Behana Gorge, a rainforest oasis of pools, waterfalls and canyons 45 minutes south of Cairns. The all-day tours include abseiling, ziplining, cliff jumping, snorkelling and swimming; you'll be shown the ropes (literally) on the day. Transfers and lunch included.

★ Rapid Boarders
WATER SPORTS

(☎ 0427 364 311; www.rapidboarders.com.au; tour $235) If you'd rather ride in the rapids than on them, this utterly exhilarating full-day adventure is for you. Thrill seekers ride river-boards down the mighty Tully, taking on pumping Grade 3 rapids at eye level. It's the only tour of its kind in Australia. This is not for the water-shy; participants must be good swimmers and relatively fit.

★ Aussie Drifterz
OUTDOORS

(☎ 0401 318 475; www.facebook.com/aussiedrifterz; adult/child $75/55) Scenic and serene (and virtually guaranteed to kick a hangover), a relaxing bob down the beautiful Behana Gorge on an inner tube is tough to beat. The crystal-clear river runs through natural tree tunnels, and you'll almost certainly catch glimpses of curious wildlife (don't fret; crocs not included).

Cairns Adventure Park
ADVENTURE SPORTS

(☎ 07-4053 3726; www.cairnsadventurepark.com.au; 82 Aeroglen Dr, Aeroglen; packages from $39; ⏱ 9am-5pm) Zipline, rock climb or abseil in rainforest surrounds with views to the sea

Cairns

as breathtaking as the high-energy activities themselves. For something more sedate, the park also offers bushwalks and birdwatching. Contact the office about pick-ups from your accommodation; if you're driving, get there by taking the Aeroglen turn-off opposite Cairns Airport (p1067).

Flyboard Cairns WATER SPORTS
(📞0439 386 955, 0487 921 714; www.flyboard cairns.com.au; 30/60min session $169/299) Billed as a combination of waterskiing, wakeboarding and snowboarding, flyboarding gives thrill seekers the chance to surf the sky while attached to a water jetpack – and cop some bird's-eye views while you're up there. It looks tricky, but the experienced instructors here guarantee even beginners will get airborne; no fly, no pay.

AJ Hackett Bungy & Minjin ADVENTURE SPORTS
(📞07-4057 7188; www.ajhackett.com/cairns; McGregor Rd, Smithfield; bungee $169, minjin $129, combos from $259; ⊙from 10am) Bungy jump from the 50m rainforest tower or drop 45m and swing through the trees at 120km/h in the Minjin harness swing. Pricing includes return transfers from Cairns.

👉 Tours

An astounding 800-plus tours drive, chug, sail and fly out of Cairns daily, making the selection process almost overwhelming. We recommend operators with the benefit of years of experience, and who cover the bases of what visitors are generally looking for, and then some.

Great Barrier Reef

Reef trips generally include transport, lunch, stinger-suits and snorkelling gear. When choosing a tour, consider the vessel type, its capacity, inclusions and destination: outer reefs are more pristine but further afield; inner reefs can be patchy and show signs of decay.

Almost all boats depart from the Marlin Wharf, with check-in and booking facilities located inside the Reef Fleet Terminal (p410), around 8am, returning at about 6pm. Smaller operators may check-in boatside at their berth on the wharf itself; check with your operator.

⭐ Falla Reef Trips   BOATING
(☑ 0400 195 264; www.fallareeftrips.com.au; D-Finger, Marlin Marina; adult/child/family from $145/90/420, intro dives $85) Reach the reef in inimitable style on this graceful 1950s pearl lugger. The tours, which spend time at Coral Gardens and Upolu Cay, have an exclusive feel. There's a maximum of 22 guests (who can help with the sailing), personalised snorkel tours and the old-school boat is the polar opposite of the sleek fibreglass vessels bobbing elsewhere on the reef.

⭐ Reef Magic   DIVING, SNORKELLING
(☑ 07-4031 1588; www.reefmagiccruises.com; Reef Fleet Terminal; adult/child/family day trips from $210/105/525) A long-time family favourite, Reef Magic's high-speed cat sails to its all-weather Marine World pontoon moored on the edge of the outer reef. If you're water shy, try a glass-bottomed boat ride, chat with the marine biologist or have a massage!

Reef Encounter   DIVING, SNORKELLING
(☑ 07-4037 2700; http://reefencounter.com.au; 100 Abbott St; 2-day liveaboard from $450) If one day isn't enough, try an overnight 'reef sleep' with Reef Encounter. Twenty-seven air-conditioned en-suite cabins accommodate a maximum of 42 guests; you don't even have to snorkel or dive to appreciate this floating hotel. A wide range of programs, including meals and daily departures from Cairns, make this excellent value for those wanting something a little different.

Scenic Flights

Great Barrier
Reef Helicopters   SCENIC FLIGHTS
(☑ 07-4081 8888; www.gbrhelicopters.com.au; Helipad, Pierpoint Rd; flights per person from $175) Offers a range of scenic helicopter flights, from a 10-minute soar above Cairns city to an hour-long hover over the reef and rainforest ($699).

GSL Aviation   SCENIC FLIGHTS
(☑ 1300 475 000; www.gslaviation.com.au; 3 Tom McDonald Dr, Aeroglen; 40min flights per person from $179) Those wanting to see the reef from above would do well to consider these scenic flights; they are cheaper than chopper tours, and offer more time in the air.

White-water Rafting

Raging Thunder   ADVENTURE SPORTS
(☑ 07-4030 7990; www.ragingthunder.com.au; 59-63 Esplanade) These experienced folks offer rafting, canyoning ($169) and hot-air ballooning ($250) trips and tours. Foam-hounds can choose between full-day Tully River rafting trips (standard trip $209, 'xtreme' trip $250)

SEX ON THE REEF

If you're a keen diver or just a romantic at heart, try to time your visit with the annual coral spawning, an all-in orgy in which reef corals simultaneously release millions of eggs and sperm into the water. The ejaculatory event has been described as looking like a psychedelic snowstorm, with trails of reproductive matter streaking the sea in rainbow colours visible from miles away.

The spawning occurs sometime in November or December; the exact date depends on factors including water temperature (must be 26°C or above), the date of the full moon, the stillness of the water and the perfect balance between light and dark (who doesn't appreciate a bit of mood lighting?). Most Cairns-based diving outfits offer special spawning night dives for those looking to get in on the action. Even if you're on land, you may notice an, um, 'amorous' aroma on the night of the mass love-in.

DIVE COURSES & TRIPS

Cairns, scuba-dive capital of the Great Barrier Reef, is a popular place to attain Professional Association of Diving Instructors (PADI) open-water certification. A staggering number of courses (many multilingual) are available; check inclusions thoroughly. All operators require you to have a dive medical certificate, which they can arrange (around $60). Reef taxes ($20 to $80) may apply.

Keen, certified divers should look for specialised dive opportunities such as night diving, annual coral spawning, and trips to Cod Hole, near Lizard Island, one of Australia's premier dive locations. Recommended dive schools and operators include:

Mike Ball Dive Expeditions (☑07-4053 0500; www.mikeball.com; 3 Abbott St; liveaboards from $1827, PADI courses from $395)

Cairns Dive Centre (CDC; ☑07-4051 0294; www.cairnsdive.com.au; 121 Abbott St; liveaboard 1-/2-nights from $435/555, day trips from $120, dive courses from $520)

Deep Sea Divers Den (☑07-4046 7333; www.diversden.com.au; 319 Draper St; day trips from $165)

Pro-Dive (☑07-4031 5255; www.prodivecairns.com.au; cnr Grafton & Shields Sts; day trips adult/child from $195/120, PADI courses from $765)

Tusa Dive (☑07-4047 9100; www.tusadive.com; cnr Shields St & Esplanade; adult/child day trips from $205/130) 🕊

and half-day Barron trips ($133). They also run transfers (adult/child/family $75/48/205) to/from and activities on Fitzroy Island.

Foaming Fury   RAFTING
(☑07-4031 3460; www.foamingfury.com.au; half-/full-day trip from $138/200) Full-day trips on the Russell River, and half-day trips down the Barron. Prices include transfers. Family rafting and multiday package options are also available.

Ballooning & Skydiving

Hot Air Cairns   BALLOONING
(☑07-4039 9900; www.hotair.com.au/cairns; Reef Fleet Terminal; 30min flight adult/child from $250/219) Balloons take off from Mareeba to float through dawn over the Atherton Tablelands. Prices include return transfers from Cairns. These trips are worth the 4am wake-up call.

Skydive Cairns   ADVENTURE
(☑1300 663 634; www.skydive.com.au/cairns; 47 Shields St; tandem jumps from $334) Scream from 4270m up at otherwise serene views of the reef and rainforest.

Cape Tribulation & the Daintree

Billy Tea Safaris   OUTDOORS
(☑07-4032 0077; www.billytea.com.au; day trips adult/child/family $220/165/665) 🕊 This reliable bunch offers exciting small-group day trips to Cape Trib in purpose-built 4WD vehicles. They also run multiday safaris head-ing as far north as Cape York and over to the islands of the Torres Strait.

Atherton Tablelands

Barefoot Tours   OUTDOORS
(☑07-4032 4525; www.barefoottours.com.au; tour $105) Backpackers love this fun, full-day jaunt around the Tablelands, with swimming stops at waterfalls and a natural water slide.

Free pick-ups from central accommodation from 7am; tours arrive back in town by 7pm to 8pm. Minimum age 13.

On the Wallaby   OUTDOORS
(☑07-4033 6575; www.onthewallaby.com; day tour $99, overnight tours $139-189) Excellent activity-based tours of the Tablelands' rainforests and waterfalls including swimming, cycling, hiking and canoeing. Daily pick-ups from Cairns at 8am.

City Tours

⭐**Segway Tours**   OUTDOORS
(☑0451 972 997; www.cairnsninebottours.com; tour $79; ⊙tours 9.30am & 3.30pm) Glide through some of Cairns' most beautiful natural surrounds on an easy-to-master Segway. The 90-minute tours start at the Esplanade and run past mangroves, Centenary Lakes and the Botanic Gardens (p393); they're a peaceful and immersive way to check out local flora and fauna (including the ever-present possibility of a croc or two).

(Continued on page 405)

SUPERJOSEPH / SHUTTERSTOCK ©

The Great Barrier Reef

Each year, more than 1.5 million visitors come to this World Heritage–listed area that stretches across 2000km of coastline. Diving and snorkelling are just some of the ways to experience this wonderful and rich ecosystem. There's also sailing, scenic flights and idyllic days exploring the reef's gateway towns and stunning islands.

Contents
- ➡ **Gateways to the Reef**
- ➡ **Top Reef Encounters**
- ➡ **Nature's Theme Park**

Above Aerial view of the Great Barrier Reef

Gateways to the Reef

There are numerous ways to approach Australia's massive undersea kingdom. You can head to a popular gateway town and join an organised tour, sign up for a multiday sailing or diving trip exploring less-travelled outer fringes of the reef, or fly out to a remote island, where you'll have the reef largely to yourself.

Southern Reef Islands

For an idyllic getaway off the beaten path, book a trip to one of several remote reef-fringed islands on the southern edge of the Great Barrier Reef. You'll find fantastic snorkelling and diving right off the island.

Port Douglas

An hour's drive north of Cairns, Port Douglas is a laid-back beach town with dive boats heading out to over a dozen sites, including more pristine outer reefs, such as Agincourt Reef.

The Whitsundays

Home to turquoise waters, coral gardens and palm-fringed beaches, the Whitsundays offer many options for reef-exploring: base yourself on an island, go sailing, or stay on Airlie Beach and island-hop on day trips.

Townsville

Australia's largest tropical city is far from the outer reef (2½ hours by boat) but has some exceptional draws: access to Australia's best wreck dive, an excellent aquarium, marine-themed museums, plus multiday liveaboard dive boats departing from here.

Cairns

The most popular gateway to the reef, Cairns has dozens of boat operators offering day trips with snorkelling, as well as multiday reef explorations on liveaboard vessels. For the uninitiated, Cairns is a good place to learn to dive.

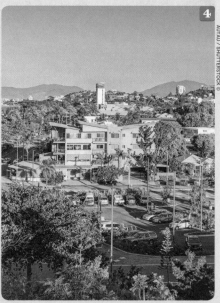

1. Clownfish 2. Port Douglas (p418)
3. Palm Cove (p413) 4. Townsville (p376)

TANYA ANN PHOTOGRAPHY / GETTY IMAGES ©

1. Whitehaven Beach (p374) **2.** Helicopter flight over Whitsunday Islands (p370) **3.** Snorkelling, Cairns (p397)

Top Reef Encounters

Donning a mask and fins and getting an up-close look at this aquatic marvel is one of the best ways to experience the Great Barrier Reef. You can get a different take aboard a glass-bottomed boat tour, on a scenic flight or on a land-based reef walk.

Diving & Snorkelling

The classic way to see the Great Barrier Reef is to board a catamaran and visit several different coral-rich spots on a long day trip. Nothing quite compares to that first underwater glimpse, whether diving or snorkelling.

Semi-Submersibles & Boats

A growing number of reef operators (especially around Cairns) offer semi-submersible or glass-bottomed boat tours, which give cinematic views of coral, rays, fish, turtles and sharks – without you ever having to get wet.

Sailing

You can escape the crowds and see some spectacular reef scenery aboard a sailboat. Experienced mariners can hire a bareboat, others can join a multiday tour – both are easily arranged from Airlie Beach or Port Douglas.

Reef Walking

Many reefs of the southern Great Barrier Reef are exposed at low tide, allowing visitors to walk on the reef top (on sandy tracks between living coral). This can be a fantastic way to learn about marine life, especially if accompanied by a naturalist guide.

Scenic Flights

Get a bird's-eye view of the vast coral reef and its cays and islands from a scenic flight. You can sign up for a helicopter tour or a seaplane tour (particularly memorable over the Whitsundays).

Nature's Theme Park

Home to some of the greatest biodiversity of any ecosystem on earth, the Great Barrier Reef is a marine wonderland. You'll find 30-plus species of marine mammals along with countless species of fish, coral, molluscs and sponges. Above the water, 200 bird species and 118 butterfly species have been recorded on reef islands and cays.

Common fish species include dusky butterfly fish, which are a rich navy blue with sulphur-yellow noses and back fins; large graphic turkfish, with luminescent pastel coats; teeny neon damsels, with darting flecks of electric blue; and six-banded angelfish, with blue tails, yellow bodies and tiger stripes. Rays, including the spotted eagle ray, are worth looking out for.

The reef is also a haven to many marine mammals, such as whales, dolphins and dugongs. Dugongs are listed as vulnerable, and a significant number of them live in Australia's northern waters; the reef is home to around 15% of the global population. Humpback whales migrate from Antarctica to the reef's warm waters to breed between May and October, and minke whales can be seen off the coast from Cairns to Lizard Island in June and July. Porpoises and killer and pilot whales also make their home here.

One of the reef's most-loved inhabitants is the sea turtle. Six of the world's seven species (all endangered) live on the reef and lay eggs on the islands' sandy beaches in spring or summer.

Fishing

Catcha Crab Tours FISHING

(☎ 07-4051 7992; www.cairnscatchacrab.com.au; adult/child $95/75) These long-running tours not only offer visitors the chance to catch some tasty tucker, but are a simultaneously thrilling and relaxing way to take in the mangroves and mudflats of Trinity Inlet. The four-hour tours, which include morning or afternoon tea plus a fresh crab lunch, depart at 8.30am and 1pm. There are free pickups if you're staying in the city centre.

✯✯ Festivals & Events

Cairns Ukulele Festival MUSIC

(www.cairnsukulelefestival.net) Uke players from around the world descend on Cairns every August to plinka-plinka in paradise. Events include workshops, jams and parties.

Cairns Festival FAIR

(www.cairns.qld.gov.au/festival; ⊙ end Aug-early Sep) The Cairns Festival takes over the city with a packed program of performing arts, visual arts, music and family events.

🛏 Sleeping

Cairns is a backpacker hot spot, with hostels ranging from intimate, converted houses to hangar-sized resorts. Holiday apartment complexes are dotted across the city. Dozens of drive-in motels line Sheridan St.

Families and groups should check out **Cairns Holiday Homes** (☎ 07-4045 2143; www.cairnsholidayhomes.com.au). If you plan to stick around for a while, **Cairns Sharehouse** (☎ 07-4041 1875; www.cairns-sharehouse.com; 17 Scott St; per week from $120-260; ❄🛜❄) has around 200 long-stay rooms strewn across the city. The **Accommodation Centre** (☎ 1800 807 730, 07-4051 4066; www.accomcentre.com.au) has information on a wide range of sleeping options.

★**Bellview** HOSTEL $

(☎ 07-4031 4377; www.bellviewcairns.com.au; 85-87 Esplanade; dm/s/d $22/35/55, motel units $59-75; P❄🛜❄) This low-key hostel has been on the radars of discerning backpackers since – seemingly – time eternal. There's little surprise it's lasted so long, thanks to a perfect position looming over the most bustling slice of the Esplanade, basic but well-maintained rooms and a staff that knows its stuff; the lovely pool helps too. Despite its central location, noise doesn't seem to travel to the rooms.

★**Cairns Coconut Holiday Resort** CARAVAN PARK $

(☎ 07-4054 6644; www.coconut.com.au; cnr Bruce Hwy & Anderson Rd, Woree; powered sites/cabins/units/villas/condos from $43/115/135/155/245; P❄✻🛜❄) If you're travelling with kids and don't mind being a bit (8km) out of town, this holiday park is a destination unto itself. It's got a massive water park, two pools with slides, playgrounds, a humungous jumping pillow, tennis courts, minigolf, spas, an outdoor cinema and much more, all spread over 11 immaculate hectares. Accommodation choices are as varied as the facilities.

★**Cairns Plaza Hotel** HOTEL $

(☎ 07-4051 4688; www.cairnsplaza.com.au; 145 Esplanade; d/studios/ste from $124/150/170; P❄@🛜❄) One of Cairns' original high-rise hotels, the Plaza is – thanks to a full makeover and professional staff – one of the best. Rooms have crisp, clean decor, and functional kitchenettes; many enjoy stunning views over Trinity Bay. A guest laundry, friendly round-the-clock reception staff and great rates make it an excellent choice. Kids will be thrilled by its location, directly across from Muddy's (p393).

★**Travellers Oasis** HOSTEL $

(☎ 07-4052 1377; www.travellersoasis.com.au; 8 Scott St; dm/s/d from $28/57/68; P❄@🛜❄) Folks love this little hippy hostel, hidden away in a side street behind **Cairns Central Shopping Centre** (☎ 07-4041 4111; www.cairnscentral.com.au; cnr McLeod & Spence Sts; ⊙9am-5.30pm Mon-Wed, Fri & Sat, to 9pm Thu, 10.30am-4pm Sun). It's intimate, inviting and less party-centric than many of Cairns' other offerings. A range of room types – from three-, four- and six-bed dorms, to single, twin and deluxe double rooms – are available. Air conditioning is $1 for three hours.

★**Tropic Days** HOSTEL $

(☎ 07-4041 1521; www.tropicdays.com.au; 28 Bunting St, Bungalow; camping per person $14, tents $18, dm/d from $26/64; P❄✻🛜❄) Tucked behind the showgrounds (with a courtesy bus into town), this popular hostel has a tropical garden with hammocks, pool table, bunk-free dorms, fresh linen and towels, free wi-fi and a relaxed vibe. Its Monday night croc, emu and roo barbecues are legendary. Air conditioning is $1 for three hours.

Tropic Days and the equally awesome Travellers Oasis are sister hostels.

★Gilligan's Backpacker's Hotel & Resort
HOSTEL **$**

(☎07-4041 6566; www.gilligans.com.au; 57-89 Grafton St; dm/r from $24/120; 🅿@🛜🏊) There's nothing quite like Gilligan's: a loud, proud, party-hardy flashpacker resort, where all rooms have en suites and most have balconies. Higher-priced rooms come with fridges and TVs. Guests get $4 dinners. The mammoth bar and adjacent lagoon pool is the place to be seen, and there's more nightly entertainment than you can poke a stick at. Pick-up central.

★Lake Placid Tourist Park
CARAVAN PARK **$**

(☎07-4039 2509; www.lakeplacidtouristpark. com; Lake Placid Rd; powered sites from $37, bungalows from $60, en-suite cabins from $85, cottages from $110; 🅿🛜🏊) Just a 15-minute drive from the city centre, but far enough away to revel in rainforesty repose, this delightful spot overlooks the aptly named Lake Placid: it's an excellent alternative to staying downtown if you're driving. Camping and a variety of well-priced, tasteful accommodation options are available. It's within striking distance of a wide range of attractions and the northern beaches.

★Northern Greenhouse
HOSTEL **$**

(☎07-4047 7200; www.northerngreenhouse.com. au; 117 Grafton St; dm/apt from $26/95; 🅿@🛜🏊) It fits into the budget category, but this friendly, relaxed place is a cut above, with tidy dorms and neat studio-style apartments with kitchens and balconies. The central deck, pool and games room are great for socialising. Free breakfast and Sunday BBQ seal the deal.

Cairns Central YHA
HOSTEL **$**

(☎07-4051 0772; www.yha.com.au; 20-26 McLeod St; dm/s/d from $27.50/59.50/71; 🅿@🏊) Opposite Cairns Central Shopping Centre (p405), this award-winning YHA is bright, spotlessly clean and professionally staffed. En-suite rooms are available and there are free pancakes for breakfast!

Floriana Guesthouse
GUESTHOUSE **$**

(☎07-4051 7886; www.florianaguesthouse.com; 183 Esplanade; s/d $79/89, studios $130-150; 🅿@🛜🏊) The Cairns-of-old still exists at this quirky guesthouse, which retains its original polished floorboards and art-deco fittings. The swirling staircase leads to 10 individually decorated rooms; all have en suites.

Cairns Girls Hostel
HOSTEL **$**

(☎07-4051 2016; www.cairnsgirlshostel.com.au; 147 Lake St; dm/tw $20/48; 🛜) Sorry lads! This white-glove-test-clean, female-only hostel is one of the most accommodating budget stays in Cairns.

Cairns Colonial Club
RESORT **$$**

(☎07-4053 8800; www.cairnscolonialclub.com.au; 18-26 Cannon St, Manunda; r $95-175; 🅿🛜🏊) A stalwart on the Cairns accommodation map since 1986, this Queenslander-style resort has a little something for everyone; families, businessfolk and solo travellers all love it here. Tucked away in a leafy suburb, the 11-acre complex boasts three pools, playgrounds, bars, a popular restaurant and gorgeous gardens. It's 4km from the centre of town; a shuttle bus runs regularly.

Bay Village Tropical Retreat
APARTMENT **$$**

(☎07-4051 4622; www.bayvillage.com.au; cnr Lake & Gatton Sts; d $135, apt $165-275; 🅿🛜🏊) Sleek, shiny and ever-so-slightly removed from the Cairns hubbub, this complex offers large, cool apartments (one to three bedrooms) and spacious serviced rooms. It's a lovely place to hang your hat, and perhaps an even better spot for filling your stomach; it's attached to the award-winning Bayleaf Balinese Restaurant.

Reef Palms
APARTMENT **$$**

(☎07-4051 2599; www.reefpalms.com.au; 41-47 Digger St; apt from $120; 🅿@🛜🏊) Couples and families love the excellent value and friendly service at this quiet complex. The squeaky-clean apartments have cooking facilities and balconies or courtyards; larger apartments include a lounge area and spa.

★201 Lake Street
HOTEL **$$$**

(☎07-4053 0100, 1800 628 929; www.201lake street.com.au; 201 Lake St; r from $205, apt $270-340; 🛜🏊) Lifted from the pages of a trendy magazine, this gorgeous apartment complex has a stellar pool and a whiff of exclusivity. Grecian white predominates and guests can choose from a smooth hotel room or contemporary apartments with an entertainment area, a plasma-screen TV and a balcony.

✖ Eating

The **Night Markets** (www.nightmarkets.com. au; Esplanade; dishes $10-15; ⏱10am-11pm) have a cheap, busy Asian-style food court; despite the name, the eateries here are open all day.

For fresh fruit, veg and other local treats, hit Rusty's Markets (p409) on the weekend; for groceries, try the Cairns Central Shopping Centre (p405).

★ Ganbaranba   JAPANESE $

(☎07-4031 2522; 12 Spence St; mains $8-12; ⏰11.30am-2.30pm & 5-8.30pm) You'll recognise this tiny place by the queues outside, and the beatific faces of the customers inside. This is a cult joint, and without a doubt the best place for ramen in Cairns. Slurpers can watch the chefs making noodles; if the view proves too tempting, you can ask for a refill for a mere $1.50. Absolutely worth the wait.

Cafe Fika   SWEDISH $

(☎07-4041 1150; www.swedishshop.com.au; 111-115 Grafton St; meals $9.50-15; ⏰7am-4pm Mon-Fri, 9am-2pm Sat) From meatballs with lingonberry jam to toast topped with *skagen* (prawn, dill and sour cream), this little Euro-haven serves up Swedish classics to hungry hordes of homesick Scandinavians and locals looking for something new. There's an excellent gourmet grocery store attached, stocked with treats from Sweden (of course), Germany, Hungary, Estonia, France and elsewhere.

Pineapple Cafe   HEALTH FOOD $

(www.facebook.com/pineapplecafecairns; 92 Lake St; mains $10-18; ⏰7am-3pm Mon-Sat) Healthy, fresh and creative cuisine is dished up by the ladleful at this adorable cafe; think acai and smoothie bowls, super-food salads, grass-fed beef burgers and all-day breakfasts that are actually good for you. The feel-good vibes don't end with what you put in your mouth: the cafe itself is adorned with happy-making murals and the staff always have a smile.

Bagus   INDONESIAN $

(☎07-4000 2051; www.baguscafe.info; 149 Esplanade; mains $10-20; ⏰6.45am-2.30pm & 5.30-8.30pm Mon, Tue, Thu & Sat, 6.45am-2.30pm Wed & Fri, noon-3pm & 5.30-8.30pm Sun) The heady aromas of traditional Indonesian street food waft from this friendly little hole-in-the-wall; the nasi goreng could be straight from a beach cafe in Bali. Breakfasts ($4.50 to $11.50) are good value. Opposite Muddy's (p393) playground.

Tokyo Dumpling   JAPANESE $

(☎07-4041 2848; www.facebook.com/tokyodumpling46; 46 Lake St; dumplings from $4.50, bowls from $13.80; ⏰11.30am-9.30pm) Come to this spotless little takeaway for ludicrously more-ish homemade dumplings and exceptional rice and noodle dishes. Lunch specials are between 11am and 2pm. We predict you won't be able to eat here just once.

Meldrum's Pies in Paradise   BAKERY $

(☎07-4051 8333; 97 Grafton St; pies $5.30-6.80; ⏰7am-4.30pm Mon-Fri, to 2.30pm Sat; ☑) Multi-award-winning Meldrum's deserves the accolades bestowed upon its seemingly innumerable renditions of the humble Aussie pie; it's been at it since 1972, an achievement that speaks volumes in a transient tourist town like Cairns. For something different, try the chicken and macadamia satay or tuna mornay with spinach pies; the many vegetarian options are delicious, and they sell out quickly.

★ Spicy Bite   INDIAN, FUSION $$

(☎07-4041 3700; www.spicybitecairns.com; cnr Shields St & Esplanade; mains $15.50-35; ⏰5-10pm; ☑) Cairns has plenty of good Indian restaurants, but none are quite as innovative as this unassuming place, where fusion food has been turned into a write-home-about-it experience: where else on earth could you try crocodile masala or kangaroo tikka? The classic curries are divine, and there are loads of vegetarian and vegan options.

★ Prawn Star   SEAFOOD $$

(☎0456 421 172; www.facebook.com/prawnstarcairns; E-Finger, Berth 31, Marlin Marina; seafood from $20; ⏰10am-8pm) Trawler restaurant Prawn Star is tropical dining perfection: clamber aboard and fill yourself with prawns, mud crabs, oysters and whatever else was caught that day, while taking in equally delicious harbour views. A second boat – Prawn Star Too – was added to the eat-fleet in mid-2017, but seating is still limited and much in-demand: get there early. Why the Cairns waterfront isn't lined with restaurants like this is a mystery for the ages.

★ Bayleaf Balinese Restaurant   BALINESE $$

(☎07-4051 4622; www.bayvillage.com.au/bayleaf; Bay Village Tropical Retreat, cnr Lake & Gatton Sts; mains $14-25; ⏰noon-2pm Mon-Fri, 6pm-late nightly) One of Cairns' best restaurants isn't along the waterfront or in the lobby of a flash hotel, but rather, attached to a mid-range apartment complex. Completely unexceptional from the outside, the Balinese food that is created inside by specialist chefs is outrageously good and wholly authentic. Order a ton of starters, go for the banquet or share a heap of mains.

★**Perrotta's
at the Gallery**   MEDITERRANEAN **$$**
(🕿 07-4031 5899; www.perrottasatg.com; 38 Abbott St; breakfast $7-23, mains $19-37; ⊙6.30am-10pm; 🍴) This unmissable eatery, connected to the Cairns Regional Gallery (p393), tempts you onto its covered deck with splendid gourmet breakfasts – until 3pm! – fresh juices, barista coffees and an inventive Mediterranean-inspired lunch and dinner menu. It's a chic spot with an interesting crowd and ideal people-watching perches.

Fetta's Greek Taverna   GREEK **$$**
(🕿 07-4051 6966; www.fettasgreektaverna.com.au; 99 Grafton St; mains $26.50-28.50, set menu $35; ⊙11.30am-3pm Mon-Fri, 5.30pm-late daily) The white walls and blue-accented windows do a great job evoking Santorini, but it's the classic Greek dishes that are the star of the show here. The set menu goes the whole hog – dip, saganaki, moussaka, salad, grilled meats, calamari, baklava and coffee. Yes, you can break your plate.

★**Ochre**   MODERN AUSTRALIAN **$$$**
(🕿 07-4051 0100; www.ochrerestaurant.com.au; Marlin Pde; mains $28-40; ⊙11.30am-2.30pm & 5.30-9.30pm) The menu at this innovative waterfront restaurant utilises native Aussie fauna (such as croc with native pepper, or roo with quandong-chilli glaze) and flora (try wattle-seed damper loaf or Davidson plum mousse). It also cooks Tablelands steaks to perfection. Can't decide? Order a tasting plate.

Dundees   SEAFOOD **$$$**
(🕿 07-4051 0399; www.dundees.com.au; Marlin Pde; mains $25-82; ⊙11.30am-late) This tried-and-true waterfront restaurant comes up trumps for ambience, generous portions and friendly service. The varied menu of appealing appetisers includes chunky seafood chowder, tempura soft-shell crab and lightly dusted calamari strips; main-meal highlights include barbecued lobster, wagyu eye fillets and enormous seafood platters.

🍷 **Drinking & Nightlife**

★**Three Wolves**   BAR
(🕿 07-4031 8040; www.threewolves.com.au; Red Brick Laneway, 32 Abbott St; ⊙4pm-midnight Thu-Sat & Mon, 2-10pm Sun) Intimate, understated and bang-on-trend (think Edison bulbs, copper mugs and mixologists in old-timey barkeep aprons), this new laneway bar has delivered a very welcome dash of Melbourne. It's got an excellent selection of speciality spirits, cocktails and beers, plus a bar menu including hip faves like pulled-pork tortillas, sliders and New York–style hot dogs. Small but superb.

★**Green Ant Cantina**   BAR
(🕿 07-4041 5061; www.greenantcantina.com; 183 Bunda St; ⊙4pm-late Tue-Sun) Behind the railway station, this grungy, rockin' Tex-Mex bar is an ace and arty alternative hang-out. Smothered in bright murals and peopled by friendly folks, the Green Ant brews its own beers and hosts regular music events. It also does fab food, including pulled-pork quesadillas, jambalaya and the infamous, blistering Wings of Death.

★**Salt House**   BAR
(🕿 07-4041 7733; www.salthouse.com.au; 6/2 Pierpoint Rd; ⊙11am-2am Mon-Fri, 7am-2am Sat & Sun) By the yacht club, Cairns' coolest, classiest bar caters to a hip and happy crowd. With killer cocktails, tremendous views, occasional live music and DJs, and a superb mod-Oz nibbles-and-mains menu, the Salt House is absolutely not to be missed.

★**Conservatory Bar**   WINE BAR
(🕿 0467 466 980; www.theconservatorybar.com.au; 12-14 Lake St; ⊙4-10pm Wed-Thu, to midnight Fri & Sat, to 9pm Sun) Tucked away in a little room in a little laneway, this is Cairns' best wine bar, and one of the city's top places for a low-key tipple, whatever your flavour. It also makes fabulous cocktails and has loads of craft beers. It's relaxed, friendly and oozes a tropical sophistication all its own. The Conservatory regularly hosts exhibitions and live (mellow) music.

★**Lyquid Nightlife**   CLUB
(🕿 07-4028 3773; www.lyquid.com.au; 33 Spence St; ⊙9pm-3am) Lyquid is the hottest ticket in town: dress to impress and party the night away with top DJs, professional bartenders and a happy, hyped-up young crowd.

★**Jack**   PUB
(🕿 07-4051 2490; www.thejack.com.au; cnr Spence & Sheridan Sts; ⊙10am-late) The Jack is a kick-arse pub by any standards, housed in an unmissable heritage Queenslander with an enormous shaded beer garden. There are nightly events, including live music and DJs, killer pub grub, and an adjacent hostel (dorm from $26) for those who just can't tear themselves away.

Pier Bar
BAR

(☎07-4031 4677; www.thepierbar.com.au; Pier Shopping Centre, 1 Pierpoint Rd; ◔11.30am-late) This local institution is much loved for its killer waterfront location and daily happy hour (5pm to 7pm). Its Sunday sessions are the place to see and be seen, with live music, food and drink specials and an always-happening crowd.

Grand Hotel
PUB

(☎07-4051 1007; www.grandhotelcairns.com; 34 McLeod St; ◔10am-9pm Mon-Wed, to 11pm Thu, to midnight Fri & Sat, to 8pm Sun) Established in 1926, this laid-back haunt is worth visiting just to rest your beer on the bar – an 11m-long carved crocodile! There's usually live music on the weekend. It's a great place to loiter with the locals.

Woolshed
BAR

(☎07-4031 6304; www.thewoolshed.com.au; 24 Shields St; ◔7pm-3am Sun-Thu, to 5am Fri & Sat) An eternal backpacker magnet and meat market, where young travellers, dive instructors and living-it-up locals get happily hammered and dance on tables. The classier Cotton Club speakeasy-style cocktail bar is downstairs.

☆ Entertainment

Pop & Co Tapas & Music Bar
LIVE MUSIC

(☎07-4019 6132; 92 Abbott St; ◔5pm-late Wed-Sun) Live jazz, blues and croony tunes share the limelight with a good nibbles menu and some of the cheapest on-tap beers in town. It's a diminutive diamond, and its local popularity means it sometimes gets crowded. You'll find it next to the giant jelly babies at the Centre of Contemporary Arts as you head north down Abbott St.

Starry Night Cinema
CINEMA

(www.starrynightcinema.com.au; Flecker Botanic Gardens, Collins Ave, Edge Hill; adult/child from $13/5) Enjoy classic films amid the foliage and finery of the Botanic Gardens (p393). Check the website for upcoming showings (there are usually one or two a month).

Reef Hotel Casino
CASINO

(☎07-4030 8888; www.reefcasino.com.au; 35-41 Wharf St; ◔9am-5am Fri & Sat, to 3am Sun-Thu) In addition to table games and pokies, Cairns' casino has four restaurants and four bars, including the enormous Casino Sports Arena bar.

Centre of Contemporary Arts
GALLERY, THEATRE

(CoCA; www.centre-of-contemporary-arts-cairns. com.au; 96 Abbott St; ◔10am-5pm Mon-Sat) CoCA houses the KickArts (p393) galleries of local contemporary visual art, as well as the JUTE Theatre (www.jute.com.au). Look for the jelly babies out the front.

🛍 Shopping

★ Rusty's Markets
MARKET

(☎07-4040 2705; www.rustysmarkets.com.au; 57-89 Grafton St; ◔5am-6pm Fri & Sat, to 3pm Sun) No weekend in Cairns is complete without a visit to this busy and vibrant multicultural market. Weave (and taste) your way through piles of seasonal tropical fruits, veggies and herbs, plus farm-fresh honey, locally grown flowers, excellent coffees, curries, cold drinks, antiques and more.

Doongal Aboriginal Art
ART

(☎07-4041 4249; www.doongal.com.au; 49 Esplanade; ◔9am-6pm) Authentic artworks, boomerangs, didgeridoos and other traditional artefacts by local and central Australian Indigenous artists. Worldwide shipping available.

❶ Information

Cairns 24 Hour Medical Centre (☎07-4052 1119; cnr Grafton & Florence Sts; ◔24hr) Centrally located medical centre; it also does dive medicals.

Cairns & Tropical North Visitor Information Centre (☎07-4051 3588; www.tropicalnorth queensland.org.au; 51 Esplanade; ◔8.30am-6pm Mon-Fri, 10am-6pm Sat & Sun) This is the only government-run visitor information centre in town offering impartial advice. Hundreds of free brochures, maps and pamphlets are available. Friendly staff can help with booking accommodation and tours. Look for the yellow 'i' on the blue background.

Cairns Base Hospital (☎07-4226 0000; 165 Esplanade) Largest hospital in Far North Queensland.

Post Office (☎13 13 18; www.auspost.com. au; 38 Sheridan St; ◔8.30am-5.30pm Mon-Fri, 9am-12.30pm Sat)

❶ Getting There & Away

AIR

Qantas (p1067), **Virgin Australia** (☎13 67 89; www.virginaustralia.com) and **Jetstar** (☎13 15 38; www.jetstar.com.au), and a handful of international carriers, arrive in and depart from **Cairns Airport** (p1067), located approximately

6km from the city centre, with direct services to all Australian capital cities except Canberra and Hobart, and to regional centres including Townsville, Weipa and Horn Island. Direct international connections include Bali, Singapore, Manila, Tokyo and Port Moresby.

Hinterland Aviation (☑ 07-4040 1333; www. hinterlandaviation.com.au)

Skytrans (☑ 1300 759 872; www.skytrans. com.au)

BOAT

Almost all reef trips from Cairns depart the Marlin Wharf (sometimes called the Marlin Jetty), with booking and check-in facilities located inside the **Reef Fleet Terminal** (Pierpoint Rd). A handful of smaller operators may have their check-in facilities boat-side, on the wharf itself. Be sure to ask for the correct berth number.

International cruise ships and **SeaSwift** (☑ 1800 424 422, 07-4035 1234; www.seaswift. com.au; 41-45 Tingira St, Portsmith; one way/return from $650/1166) ferries to Seisia on Cape York dock at and depart from the **Cairns Cruise Terminal** (☑ 07-4052 3888; www. cairnscruiselinerterminal.com.au; cnr Wharf & Lake Sts).

BUS

Long-distance buses arrive at and depart from the **Interstate Coach Terminal** (Reef Fleet Terminal), **Cairns Central Railway Station**, the **airport** (p1067) and the **Cairns Transit Mall** (Lake St).

Cairns Cooktown Express (☑ 07-4059 1423; www.cairnsbuscharters.com/services/cairns-cooktown-express)

Greyhound Australia (☑ 1300 473 946; www. greyhound.com.au)

John's Kuranda Bus (☑ 0418 772 953)

Premier Motor Service (☑ 13 34 10; www. premierms.com.au)

Sun Palm (☑ 07-4087 2900; www.sunpalm transport.com.au)

Tablelands Tours & Transfers (☑ 07-4045 1882; www.tablelandstoursandtransfers. com.au)

Trans North (☑ 07-4095 8644; www.trans northbus.com; Cairns Central Railway Station)

CAR & MOTORCYCLE

Major car-rental companies have airport and downtown (usually on Sheridan St) branches. Daily rates start at around $40 for a compact auto and $80 for a 4WD. **Cruising Car Rental** (☑ 07-4041 4666; www.hirecarcairns.com; 196 Sheridan St; per day from $39) and **Rent-a-Bomb** (☑ 07-4031 4477; www.rentabomb. com.au; 144 Sheridan St; per day from $33) have cheap rates on older model vehicles. If you're looking for a cheap campervan, **Jucy** (☑ 1800 150 850; www.jucy.com.au; 55 Dutton St, Portsmith; per day from $40), **Spaceships** (☑ 1300 132 469; www.spaceshipsrentals.com. au; 3/52 Fearnley St, Portsmith; per day from $40) and **Hippie Camper Hire** (☑ 1800 777 779; www.hippiecamper.com; 432 Sheridan St; per day from $44) have quality wheels at budget prices. **Bear Rentals** (☑ 1300 462 327; www. bearrentals.com.au; cars per day from $127) has top-notch Land Rover Defenders that make bush-bashing a breeze.

If you're in for the long haul, check hostels, www.gumtree.com.au and the big notice-board on Abbott St for used campervans and ex-backpackers' cars.

If you prefer two wheels to four, try **Choppers Motorcycle Tours & Hire** (☑ 07-4051 6288; www.choppersmotorcycles.com.au; 150 Sheridan St; rental per day from $90) or **Cairns Scooter & Bicycle Hire** (☑ 07-4031 3444; www.cairnsbicyclehire.com.au; 47 Shields St; scooters/bikes per day from $87/11).

TRAIN

The **Kuranda Scenic Railway** (☑ 07-4036 9333; www.ksr.com.au; adult/child one way from $50/25, return from $76/38) runs daily; the **Savannahlander** (☑ 07-4053 6848; www. savannahlander.com.au) offers a miscellany of rail journeys into the outback from **Cairns Central Railway Station** (Bunda St).

Queensland Rail (☑ 1300 131 722; www. queenslandrailtravel.com.au) For services between Brisbane and Cairns.

ⓘ Getting Around

TO/FROM THE AIRPORT

The airport is about 6km north of central Cairns; many hotels and hostels offer courtesy pick-up. **Sun Palm** meets all incoming flights and runs a shuttle (adult/child $15/7.50) directly to your accommodation; its **Airport Connect Shuttle** ($4) runs between the airport and a **Sunbus** (☑ 07-4057 7411; www.sunbus.com. au/cairns; single/daily/weekly ticket from $2.40/4.80/19.20) stops on Sheridan St just north of town. **Cairns Airport Shuttle** (☑ 0432 488 783; www.cairnsairportshuttle.com.au) is a good option for groups; the more passengers, the cheaper the fare.

Taxis to the city centre are around $25 (plus $4 airport surcharge).

Some travellers choose to walk between the airport and town to save on bus or taxi fares, but keep in mind, these are busy roads: a pedestrian was hit by a car and killed in 2015. Also, crocodiles have been known to cross Airport Ave, which is bordered by mangrove swamps, so...

BICYCLE

Cairns is criss-crossed with cycling paths and circuits; some of the most popular routes take in the Esplanade, **Botanic Gardens** (p393) and Centenary Lakes. There's a detailed list of routes and maps at www.cairns.qld.gov.au/region/tourist-information/things-to-do/cycle.

Cairns Scooter & Bicycle Hire (p410)
Pro Bike Rental (📞 0438 381 749; www.probikerental.com.au; bikes per day from $120)

BUS

Sunbus (📞 07-4057 7411; www.sunbus.com)

TAXI

Cairns Taxis (📞 13 10 08; www.cairnstaxis.com.au)

Around Cairns

Green Island

Showing some of the scars that come with fame and popularity, this pretty coral cay (45 minutes from Cairns) nevertheless retains much of its beauty. The island has a rainforest interior with interpretive walks, a fringe of white-sand beach, and superb snorkelling just offshore; it's great for kids. You can walk around the island (which, along with its surrounding waters, is protected by national- and marine-park status) in about 30 minutes.

The star attraction at family-owned aquarium **Marineland Crocodile Park** (📞 07-4051 4032; www.greenislandcrocs.com.au; adult/child $19/9; ⏰ 9.30am-4pm) is Cassius, the world's largest croc in captivity at 5.5m. Believed to be over 110 years old, he's fed daily at 10.30am and 1.30pm.

Luxurious **Green Island Resort** (📞 07-4031 3300; www.greenislandresort.com.au; ste from $580; ❄@≋) maintains a sense of privacy and exclusivity despite having sections opened to the general public, including restaurants, bars, an ice-cream parlour and water-sports facilities. Spacious split-level suites feature tropical themes, timber furnishings and inviting balconies.

Big Cat (📞 07-4051 0444; www.greenisland.com.au; adult/child/family from $90/45/225) has transfers and day-return tours to Green Island.

Fitzroy Island

A steep mountaintop rising from the sea, fabulous Fitzroy Island has clinking coral beaches, giant boulders and rainforest walking tracks, one of which ends at a now inactive lighthouse. It's a top spot for swimming and snorkelling; one of the best places to lay your towel is Nudey Beach, which, despite its name, is not officially clothing-optional.

The **Cairns Turtle Rehabilitation Centre** (www.saveourseaturtles.com.au; adult/child $8.80/5.50; ⏰ tours 1pm & 2pm) looks after sick and injured sea turtles before releasing them back into the wild. Daily educational tours (45 minutes, maximum 15 guests) take visitors through the turtle hospital to meet recovering residents. Bookings through the Fitzroy Island Resort are essential.

Fitzroy Island Resort (📞 07-4044 6700; www.fitzroyisland.com; studios/cabins from $185/445, ste/apt from $300/350; ❄🌐≋) has tropi-cool accommodation ranging from sleek studios, suites and beachfront cabins through to luxurious apartments. The restaurant, bar and kiosk are open to day trippers. Budgeteers can book here for a site at the **Fitzroy Island Camping Ground** (📞 07-4044 6700; www.fitzroyisland.com; sites $35).

Fast Cat (www.fitzroyisland.com/getting-here; adult/child/family $78/39/205) departs Cairns' Marlin Wharf (berth 20) at 8am, 11am and 1.30pm (bookings essential) and whisks you to Fitzroy Island in just 45 minutes. It returns to Cairns at 9.30am, 12.15pm and 5pm.

Frankland Islands

If the idea of hanging out on one of five uninhabited, coral-fringed islands with excellent snorkelling and stunning white-sand beaches appeals, cruise out to the Frankland Group National Park. These continental islands are made up of High Island to the north, and Normanby, Mabel, Round and Russell Islands to the south.

Frankland Islands Cruise & Dive (📞 07-4031 6300; www.franklandislands.com.au; adult/child from $169/99) runs excellent day trips that include a cruise down the Mulgrave River, snorkelling gear, tuition and lunch.

Cairns' Northern Beaches

Yorkeys Knob

POP 2770

Yorkeys Knob is a laid-back beach community best known for its marina and **golf course** (📞 07-4055 7933; www.halfmoonbaygolf.com.au; 9/18 holes $26/42, clubs hire $25), and the cheeky crocs that frequent it. The 'Knob'

Around Cairns

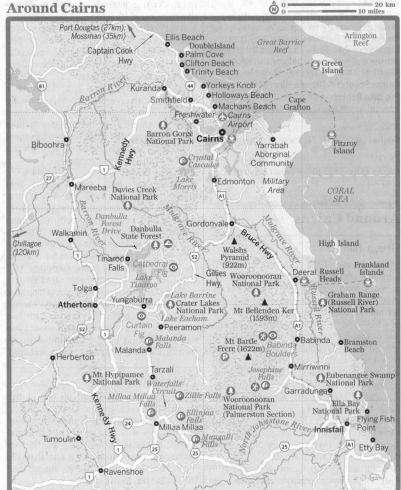

part of the name elicits chortles from easily amused locals; others wonder where the apostrophe went. Yorkeys has a stinger net in summer.

Blazing Saddles (📞 07-4055 7400; www.blazingsaddles.com.au; 154 Yorkeys Knob Rd; horse rides from $125) has half-day horse-riding tours that meander through rainforest, mangroves and sugar-cane fields.

For fresh seafood and delightful views of the marina's expensive floating toys from the expansive dining deck, **Yorkeys Knob Boating Club** (📞 07-4055 7711; www.ykbc.com.au; 25-29 Buckley St; mains $18-30; ⊙ 10am-midnight Mon-Thu, to 2am Fri & Sat, 8am-midnight Sun; 🖉) is worth the trip from Cairns.

Trinity Beach

One of the region's better-kept secrets, Trinity Beach, with its gorgeous stretch of sheltered sand, pretty esplanade and sensibly priced dining and accommodation, has managed to stave off the tourism vibe, despite being a holiday hot spot and popular dining destination for locals in the know. There's not much to do here except eat, sleep and relax, but Trinity Beach's central position makes it easy to get out and about if you're feeling active.

One of the most handsome blocks on the beachfront, **Sea Point on Trinity Beach** (☑ 07-4057 9544; www.seapointontrinity beach.com; 63 Vasey Esplanade; apt $165-230; P ❄ 🛜 ☲) offers indoor-outdoor balconies, tiled floors and breezy outlooks.

Don't let the easy-breezy beach-shack vibe fool you into thinking the food at **Fratelli on Trinity** (☑ 07-4057 5775; www.fratelli.net.au; 47 Vasey Esplanade; mains $20-35; ⊙ 7am-10pm Wed-Sun, from 5.30pm Mon & Tue) is anything less than top-class. Pastas are superb, and dishes like pistachio prawns and soft-shell crab with pomegranate and saffron aioli might even distract you from the million-dollar views.

Blue Moon Grill (☑ 07-4057 8957; www. bluemoongrill.com.au; Shop 6, 22-24 Trinity Beach Rd; mains $22-40; ⊙ 4-10pm Mon-Thu, 7-11am & 4-10pm Fri-Sun) wows with a creative, original menu presented with passion. Where else can you try crocodile popcorn?

Palm Cove

POP 1215

The best known of Cairns' northern beaches, Palm Cove has grown into a destination in its own right. More intimate than Port Douglas and more upmarket than its southern neighbours, Palm Cove is a cloistered coastal community with a beautiful promenade along the paperbark-lined Williams Esplanade. Its gorgeous stretch of white-sand beach and its sprinkling of fancy restaurants do their best to lure young lovers from their luxury resorts; inevitably, they succeed.

If you can drag yourself off the beach or poolside, Palm Cove has some excellent water-sports operators, including **Beach Fun Co** (☑ 0411 848 580; www.beachfunco.com; cnr Williams Esplanade & Harpa St), **Palm Cove Watersports** (☑ 0402 861 011; www.palmcove watersports.com; 149 Williams Esplanade; kayak hire per hr from $20) and **Pacific Watersports** (☑ 0413 721 999; www.pacificwatersports.com. au; 41 Williams Esplanade), which offers turtle tours by SUP or kayak.

🛏 Sleeping & Eating

⭐ **Cairns Beaches Flashpackers**　HOSTEL $
(☑ 07-4055 3797; www.cairnsbeachesflashpackers. com; 19 Veivers Rd; dm/d $45/120; P ❄ 🛜 ☲) Though technically a hostel – the first and only in Palm Cove – this splendid, spotless place 100m from the beach is more restful retreat than party palace. The bunk-free

dorms are tidy and comfortable; the private rooms have en suites and sliding-door access to the pool. Cook in the immaculate communal kitchen, or scout for restaurants further afield on a Piaggio scooter.

Palm Cove Holiday Park　CAMPGROUND $
(☑ 07-4055 3824; www.palmcovehp.com.au; 149 Williams Esplanade; powered/unpowered sites from $36/29; P 🛜) For cheap, alfresco Palm Cove accommodation, stake out your spot at this modern, well-run beachfront camping ground near the jetty. It has tent and van sites, a new camp kitchen, a barbecue area and a laundry.

⭐ **Sarayi**　BOUTIQUE HOTEL $$
(☑ 07-4059 5600; www.sarayi.com.au; 95 Williams Esplanade; d $115-240; P ❄ 🛜 ☲) White, bright and perfectly located among a grove of melaleucas across from the beach, Sarayi is a wonderful choice for couples, families and the growing number of visitors choosing to get married on its rooftop terrace. The name means 'palace' in Turkish, and it's an apt one: the laid-back but efficient management here does everything to ensure you're treated like royalty.

⭐ **Reef House Resort & Spa**　BOUTIQUE HOTEL $$$
(☑ 07-4080 2600; www.reefhouse.com.au; 99 Williams Esplanade; d from $300; P ❄ 🛜 ☲) Once the private residence of an army brigadier, Reef House is more intimate and understated than most of Palm Cove's resorts. The whitewashed walls, wicker furniture and big beds romantically draped in muslin add to the air of refinement. The Brigadier's Bar works on an honesty system; complimentary punch is served by candlelight at twilight.

⭐ **Chill Cafe**　CAFE $$
(☑ 0439 361 122; www.chillcafepalmcove.com.au; 41 Williams Esplanade; mains from $19; ⊙ 6am-late) The *primo* position on the corner of the waterfront Esplanade, combined with fun, friendly and attentive service, sexy tunes and a huge airy deck are all great reasons to try the oversized, tasty treats (think fish tacos and chunky club sandwiches) offered by this hip cafe. You can also just soak up some sunshine with a juice or a beer.

Seafarer's Oyster Bar & Restaurant　SEAFOOD $$
(☑ 07-4059 2653; 45 Williams Esplanade; oysters per dozen from $20, mains from $19; ⊙ noon-3pm & 5-8.30pm Mon-Thu, noon-8.30pm Fri-Sun) Come

for the delicious oysters and the freshest seafood in town; stay for the beach breezes and social buzz.

★ **Vivo** MODERN AUSTRALIAN $$$
(☑07-4059 0944; www.vivo.com.au; 49 Williams Esplanade; mains from $30; ⊘7.30am-9pm) The most beautiful-looking restaurant on the Esplanade is also one of the finest. Menus (breakfast, lunch and dinner) are inventive and well-executed using fresh local ingredients, service is second to none, and the outlook is superb. Daily set menus are excellent value.

★ **Beach Almond** SEAFOOD $$$
(☑07-4059 1908; www.beachalmond.com; 145 Williams Esplanade; mains from $27; ⊘5-11pm Mon-Sat, noon-3pm & 5-11pm Sun) The rustic, ramshackle, beach-house-on-sticks exterior belies the exceptional fine dining experience that awaits within. Black-pepper prawns, Singaporean mud crab and banana-leaf barramundi are among the fragrant innovations here, combining Asian flavours and spices.

🍷 **Drinking & Nightlife**

Apres Beach Bar & Grill BAR
(☑07-4059 2000; www.apresbeachbar.com.au; 119 Williams Esplanade; ⊘8am-11pm) The most happening place in Palm Cove, with a zany interior of old motorcycles, racing cars, and a biplane hanging from the ceiling, plus regular live music. Big on steaks of all sorts, too.

Surf Club Palm Cove BAR
(☑07-4059 1244; www.surfclubpalmcove.com.au; 135 Williams Esplanade; ⊘11am-10pm Mon & Tue, to midnight Wed-Sat, 8am-midnight Sun) This local hang-out is great for a drink in the sunny garden bar, bargain-priced seafood and decent kids' meals.

Ellis Beach

Little Ellis Beach is the last – and arguably the best – of Cairns' northern beaches and the closest to the highway, which runs right past it. The long sheltered bay is a stunner, with a palm-fringed, patrolled swimming beach, and a stinger net in summer. Cairns' only (unofficial) clothing-optional beach, **Buchans Point**, is at the southern end of Ellis; there's no stinger net here, so consider your valuable assets before diving in in your birthday suit.

North of Ellis Beach towards Port Douglas, **Hartley's Crocodile Adventures**

(☑07-4055 3576; www.crocodileadventures.com; Captain Cook Hwy, Wangetti Beach; adult/child/family $37/18.50/92.50; ⊘8.30am-5pm) offers a daily range of squeal-inducing events including croc farm tours, feedings, 'crocodile attack' and snake shows, and croc-infested lagoon cruises.

Ellis Beach Oceanfront Bungalows (☑1800 637 036, 07-4055 3538; www.ellisbeach. com; Captain Cook Hwy; powered/unpowered sites from $41/34, cabins with shared bathroom from $115, bungalow d from $170, oceanfront bungalows from $190; ❄@☀) has camping, cabins and contemporary bungalows, the best of which have direct ocean views. Just try to drive past **Ellis Beach Bar 'n' Grill** (☑07-4055 3534; www.ellisbeachbarandgrill.com.au; Captain Cook Hwy; mains $10-30; ⊘8am-8pm) and not stop for a beer and a burger.

ATHERTON TABLELANDS

Climbing back from the coast between Innisfail and Cairns is the fertile food bowl of the far north, the Atherton Tablelands. Quaint country towns, eco-wilderness lodges and luxurious B&Bs dot greener-than-green hills between patchwork fields, pockets of rainforest, spectacular lakes, waterfalls, and Queensland's highest mountains, Bartle Frere (1622m) and Bellenden Ker (1593m).

The Tablelands make for a great getaway from the swelter of the coast; they're almost always a few degrees cooler than Cairns, and on winter nights things get downright chilly.

❶ Getting There & Away

Trans North (p410) has regular bus services connecting Cairns with various spots on the Tablelands, including Kuranda ($6.70, 30 minutes), Mareeba ($19.60, one hour), Atherton ($25.30, 1¾ hours) and Herberton/Ravenshoe ($32/37.40, two/2½ hours, Monday, Wednesday, Friday).

Kuranda

POP 2970

Tucked away in thick rainforest, arty, alternative Kuranda is one of Cairns' most popular day trips. During the day, this hippie haven swarms with tourists soaking up the vibe, visiting animal sanctuaries and poking around its famous markets; come evening, you can almost hear the village sigh as the streets and pubs are reclaimed by mellow

QUEENSLAND KURANDA

locals (and the occasional street-hopping wallaby).

Just getting here is an experience in itself: choose between driving a winding forest road, chugging up on a train or soaring over the treetops on Australia's longest gondola cableway (p416).

◎ Sights & Activities

★ Kuranda Original Rainforest Markets
MARKET

(☏07-4093 9440; www.kurandaoriginalrainforest market.com.au; Therwine St; ◎9.30am-3pm) Follow the clouds of incense down to these atmospheric, authentic village markets. Operating since 1978, they're still the best place to see artists at work and hippies at play. Pick up everything from avocado ice cream to organic lingerie and sample local produce such as honey and fruit wines.

BatReach
WILDLIFE RESERVE

(☏07-4093 8858; www.batreach.com; 13 Barang St; by donation; ◎10.30am-2.30pm Tue, Wed, Thu & Sun) Visitors are welcome at this rescue and rehabilitation centre for injured and orphaned bats, possums and gliders. Passionate volunteers are more than happy to show folks around and explain the work they do. It's located next to the fire station.

Rainforestation
PARK

(☏07-4085 5008; www.rainforest.com.au; Kennedy Hwy; adult/child/family $47/23.50/117.50; ◎9am-4pm) You'll need a full day to properly explore this enormous complex, divided into three sections: a **koala and wildlife park**, the interactive **Pamagirri Aboriginal Experience** and a **river and rainforest tour** aboard the amphibious Army Duck boat-truck.

The park is 3km east of Kuranda. Shuttles (adult one-way/return $7/12, child $3.50/6) run every half hour between the park and Kuranda village.

Rainforestation is included in the Capta 4 Park Pass (www.capta.com.au), which offers discounted entry to four Far North Queensland attractions.

Heritage Markets
MARKET

(☏07-4093 8060; www.kurandamarkets.com.au; Rob Veivers Dr; ◎9.30am-3.30pm) This is Kuranda's more touristy market, hawking Australiana souvenirs – think emu oil, kangaroo-skin bow ties and Akubra hats – by the busload. It's also home to Frogs (www.frogsrestaurant. com.au; mains $12.40-35; ◎9.30am-4pm; ☏🍴)

cafe and a handful of wildlife sanctuaries, including **Kuranda Koala Gardens** (☏07-4093 9953; www.koalagardens.com; adult/child $18/9, koala photos extra; ◎9am-4pm), **Australian Butterfly Sanctuary** (☏07-4093 7575; www.australianbutterflies.com; adult/child/family $19.50/9.75/48.75; ◎9.45am-4pm) and **Birdworld** (☏07-4093 9188; www.birdworldkuranda. com; adult/child $18/9; ◎9am-4pm).

Kuranda Riverboat
CRUISE

(☏07-4093 0082; www.kurandariverboat.com.au; adult/child/family $18/9/45; ◎hourly 10.45am-2.30pm) Hop aboard for a 45-minute calm-water cruise along the Barron River, or opt for an hour-long interpretive rainforest walk in a secluded spot accessible only by boat.

You'll find Kuranda Riverboat on the jetty behind the train station; buy tickets (cash only) for the cruise on board, or book online for the walk.

🛏 Sleeping & Eating

Kuranda Rainforest Park
CARAVAN PARK $

(☏07-4093 7316; www.kurandarainforestpark.com. au; 88 Kuranda Heights Rd; powered/unpowered sites $32/30, s/d without bathroom $35/70, cabins $90-110; ☞🅿🌀🛜🏊) This well-tended park lives up to its name, with grassy camp sites enveloped in rainforest. The basic but cosy 'backpacker rooms' open onto a tin-roofed timber deck, cabins come with poolside or garden views, and there's an excellent restaurant (p416) serving local produce on-site. It's a 10-minute walk from town via a forest trail.

Fairyland House
B&B $

(☏07-4093 9194; www.fairylandhouse.com.au; 13 Fairyland Rd; r per person from $60; 🅿) With a vegan raw-food restaurant, tarot readings, yoga classes, abundant fruit garden and wellness workshops, this bush retreat is about as 'Kuranda' as they come. All rooms are airy and open onto the garden. It's a 4km walk to the village; no cooked or animal food products, cigarettes, alcohol, pets or drugs allowed.

★ Cedar Park Rainforest Resort
RESORT $$

(☏07-4093 7892; www.cedarparkresort.com.au; 250 Cedar Park Rd, Koah; s/d incl breakfast from $165/175; 🅿🌀🛜) 🌿 Set deep in the bush (a 20-minute drive from Kuranda towards Mareeba), this unusual property is part Euro-castle, part Aussie-bush-retreat. In lieu of TV, visitors goggle at wallabies, peacocks and dozens of native birds; there are hammocks aplenty, creek access, a fireplace, and a gourmet restaurant with well-priced meals and free port.

German Tucker
GERMAN $

(www.germantucker.com; Therwine St; sausages $7.50-9; ⊙10am-3pm) Fill up on classic *Würste* or try the tasty emu and crocodile sausages at this amusing eatery, where they blast oompah music and splash out steins of top-notch German beer.

Petit Cafe
CRÊPES $

(www.petitcafe.com.au/kuranda; Original Kuranda Rainforest Markets, 7 Therwine St; crêpes $10-17; ⊙8am-3pm) Duck out the back of the Original Kuranda Rainforest Markets (p415) for a mouth-watering range of crêpes with savoury or sweet fillings. Winning combinations such as macadamia pesto and feta cheese will entice *le* drool.

★ Kuranda Veranda
INTERNATIONAL $$

(www.kurandarainforestpark.com.au; Kuranda Rainforest Park, 88 Kuranda Heights Rd; mains $13-27; ⊙5.30-9.30pm Mon, Tue & Thu-Sat, 11.30am-9.30pm Sun; ⊘⊕) Hidden away in the foliage at the Kuranda Rainforest Park (p415), this superb restaurant serves up massive portions of steaks, stir-fries and salads. Kids will have fun ticking off the ingredients for their very own 'create-a-tayta' (loaded baked potato) and the build-your-own sundaes. The restaurant has a no-phones rule, so put 'em away and enjoy the sound of real tweets for a change.

DON'T MISS

TABLELANDS MARKETS

As is seemingly obligatory for any quaint country region, the tiny towns of the Tablelands host a miscellany of monthly markets. Kuranda's blockbuster bazaars are legendary, but for something a bit more down-home, check out these:

Yungaburra Markets (www.yungaburra markets.com; Gillies Hwy; ⊙7.30am-12.30pm 4th Sat of month)

Malanda Markets (Malanda Showgrounds; ⊙7am-noon 3rd Sat of month)

Atherton Undercover Markets (Merriland Hall, Robert St; ⊙7am-noon 2nd Sun of month)

Tumoulin Country Markets (63 Grigg St; ⊙8am-noon 4th Sun of month)

ⓘ Information

Kuranda Visitor Information Centre (☑07-4093 9311; www.kuranda.org; Centenary Park; ⊙10am-4pm) The knowledgeable staff at the unmissable, map-laden visitor centre in Centenary Park are happy to dish out advice.

ⓘ Getting There & Away

Kuranda is as much about the journey (from Cairns) as the destination: choose between the **Skyrail Rainforest Cableway** (☑07-4038 5555; www.skyrail.com.au; cnr Cook Hwy & Cairns Western Arterial Rd, Smithfield; adult/child one way from $50/25, return $75/37.50; ⊙9am-5.15pm) and the **Kuranda Scenic Railway** (p410), or do both with a combination return ticket (adult/child from $109.50/$54.75). Fares to Kuranda from Cairns are $6.70 with **Trans North** (p410), $16 on the **Cairns Cooktown Express** (p410) and $5 with **John's Kuranda Bus** (p410).

Kuranda is a 25km drive up the Kuranda Range from Cairns.

Mareeba

POP 10,180

Mareeba revels in a Wild West atmosphere, with local merchants selling leather saddles, handcrafted bush hats and the oversized belt buckle of your bronco-bustin' dreams; unsurprisingly, it hosts one of Australia's biggest **rodeos** (www.mareebarodeo.com.au; ⊙Jul).

Once the heart of Australia's main tobacco-growing region, Mareeba has since turned its soil to more wholesome produce, with fruit orchards, coffee plantations and distilleries in abundance. There is also a handful of unusual natural attractions in the region that differ dramatically from those found in the higher-altitude central Tablelands.

Mareeba Tropical Savanna & Wetland Reserve (☑07-4093 2514; www.mareebawet lands.org; adult/child/family $10/5/25; ⊙8.30am-4.30pm Apr-Dec) is a wonderful 20-sq-km reserve that includes woodlands, grasslands, swamps and the expansive Clancy's Lagoon, a birdwatchers' nirvana. **Granite Gorge Nature Park** (☑07-4093 2259; www.granite gorge.com.au; adult/child $10/3; 12km from Mareeba, occupies an alien landscape of humungous granite boulders, caves, turtle-inhabited swimming holes and wildlife galore.

Campers can use the **rodeo camping grounds** (☑07-4092 1654; www.mareebarodeo. com.au; Kerribee Park; powered/unpowered sites for 2 people $18/15) year-round.

Atherton

POP 7287

The largest settlement and unofficial capital of the Atherton Tablelands, Atherton is a spirited country town that makes a decent base for exploring the region's highlights.

Many backpackers head up to the Tablelands for year-round fruit picking work; the **Atherton Visitor Information Centre** (07-4091 4222; www.itablelands.com.au; cnr Main & Silo Sts; 9am-5pm) can help with up-to-date work info.

Thousands of Chinese migrants came to the region in search of gold in the late 1800s. All that's left of Atherton's Chinatown is corrugated-iron **Hou Wang Miau Temple** (07-4091 6945; www.houwang.org.au; 86 Herberton Rd; adult/child $10/5; 11am-4pm Wed-Sun). Admission includes a guided tour.

Crystal Caves (07-4091 2365; www.crystal caves.com.au; 69 Main St; adult/child/family $22.50/10/55; 9am-5pm Mon-Fri, to 4pm Sat & Sun;) is a gaudy mineralogical museum that houses the world's biggest amethyst geode (more than 3m high and weighing 2.7 tonnes).

Millaa Millaa

Evocatively nicknamed the 'Village in the Mist', charming Millaa Millaa is a small and gloriously green dairy community famous for its wonderful waterfalls. Surrounded by rolling farmland dotted with black-and-white cows, it's a picturesque spot to stop for lunch or to spend a few quaint and quiet nights.

There's accommodation at **Millaa Millaa Tourist Park** (07-4097 2290; www.millaa caravanpark.com.au; cnr Malanda Rd & Lodge Ave; powered/unpowered sites $29/24, cabins $65, with bathroom $75-110;) and the **Millaa Millaa Hotel** (07-4097 2212; www.millaa millaahotel.info; 15 Main St; s/d $85/95;). Stop in sat the **Falls Teahouse** (07-4097 2237; www.fallsteahouse.com.au; 6 Theresa Creek Rd; meals from $10; 9am-4pm, closed Wed) for a Devonshire tea.

Malanda & Around

Malanda has been a byword for 'milk' in north Queensland ever since 560 cattle made the 16-month overland journey from New South Wales in 1908; there's still a working dairy here. Rainforest-shrouded Malanda and its surrounds – including the other-worldly **Mt Hypipamee** crater – are also home to shy, rare Lumholtz's tree-kangaroos; bring a low-wattage torch for an evening of spotlighting.

The **Malanda Dairy Centre** (07-4095 1234; www.malandadairycentre.com; 8 James St; 9am-3pm Wed-Sun) **FREE** has a family-friendly museum that highlights the region's bovine history. Spot a platypus or fish for barramundi at the **Australian Platypus Park & Tarzali Lakes Aquaculture Centre** (07-4097 2713; www.tarzalilakes.com; Millaa Millaa-Malanda Rd, Tarzali; 10am-4pm;).

Malanda Falls Visitor Centre (07-4096 6957; www.malandafalls.com; 132 Malanda-Atherton Rd; 9.30am-4.30pm) has thoughtful displays and **guided rainforest walks** (www.malanda falls.com; adult/child/family $20/10/50; 9.30am & 11am Fri, Sat & Sun).

Yungaburra

Wee, winsome Yungaburra ticks every box on the country-cute checklist; within one lap of its tree-lined streets, you'll find 19 heritage-listed sites, a welcoming 1910 pub populated by local larrikins, boho-boutiques and cafes, and a dedicated platypus-watching platform. Its proximity to Lake Tinaroo and some of the region's top natural attractions makes Yungaburra a contender for best base on the Tablelands.

The sacred, 500-year-old Curtain Fig tree (p418), signposted 3km out of town, is a must-see for its gigantic, otherworldly aerial roots that hang down to create an enormous 'curtain'. If you're very quiet, you might catch a glimpse of a timid monotreme at the **platypus-viewing platform** (Gillies Hwy) **FREE** on Peterson Creek.

Explore the wilds around Yungaburra with **Alan's Wildlife Tours** (07-4095 3784; www.alanswildlifetours.com.au; day tours $90-500, multiday tours from $1790), led by a passionate local naturalist.

Tablelands Folk Festival (www.table landsfolkfestival.org.au; Oct) is a fabulous community event held in Yungaburra and neighbouring Herberton featuring music, workshops, performances and a market.

Sleeping & Eating

★ **On the Wallaby**   HOSTEL $
(07-4095 2031; www.onthewallaby.com; 34 Eacham Rd; sites per person $15, dm/d with shared bathroom $25/60;) This cosy hostel

features handmade timber furniture and mosaics, spotless rooms and no TV! Nature-based tours ($40) include night canoeing; tour packages and transfers are available from Cairns. Cook for yourself in the communal kitchen, or indulge in the nightly barbecue ($12).

★ **Yungaburra Hotel** PUB FOOD **$$**
(Lake Eacham Hotel; ☑ 07-4095 3515; www.yunga burrahotel.com.au; 6-8 Kehoe Pl; mains from $23; ⊙ restaurant 11am-8pm, pub to 11pm) This wonderful, welcoming, original-timber country pub ranks as one of the best in the state, let alone on the Tablelands. It often hosts live jams and bands; even if there's nothing on, it's an ideal place to sink a schooner, meet the locals and soak up the old-school atmosphere. The restaurant does huge, wholesome meals.

ℹ Information

Yungaburra Information Centre (☑ 07-4095 2416; www.yungaburra.com; Maud Kehoe Park; ⊙ 9am-5pm Mon-Sat, 10am-4pm Sun) The utterly delightful volunteers at this immaculate centre can help recommend accommodation, provide info on walks and tours and generally yarn about all things Yungaburra.

Lake Tinaroo

Lake Tinaroo, also known as Tinaroo Dam, was allegedly named when a prospector stumbled across a deposit of alluvial tin and, in a fit of excitement, shouted 'Tin! Hurroo!' The excitement hasn't died down since, with locals fleeing the swelter of the coast for boating, waterskiing and shoreline lolling. **Barramundi fishing** (☑ 0438 012 775; www.tinaroobarra.com; full-/half-day fishing $600/350) is permitted year-round, though if you're not joining a charter, you'll need to pick up a permit from local businesses.

The 28km **Danbulla Forest Drive** winds its way through rainforest and softwood plantations along the north side of the lake. The unsealed but well-maintained road passes the pretty **Lake Euramoo** and the boardwalk-encircled **Cathedral Fig**, a gigantic 500-year-old strangler fig similar to the **Curtain Fig** (Fig Tree Rd, East Barron) in nearby Yungaburra; it's also accessible via a signposted road off the Gillies Hwy.

There are five NPSR **camping grounds** (☑ 13 74 68; www.npsr.qld.gov.au/parks/danbulla; camping permits per person/family $6.15/24.60)

in the Danbulla State Forest. All have water, barbecues and toilets; advance bookings are essential.

Lake Tinaroo Holiday Park (☑ 07-4095 8232; www.laketinarooholidaypark.com.au; 3 Tinaroo Falls Dam Rd, Tinaroo Falls; powered/unpowered sites $37/27, cabins from $90; P ✿ ☞ ☎) is a modern, well-equipped and shady camping ground with tinnies, canoes and kayaks for rent.

Crater Lakes National Park

Part of the Wet Tropics World Heritage Area, the two mirrorlike, rainforest-fringed croc-free volcanic crater lakes of Lake Eacham and Lake Barrine are popular for swimming.

There's info at the **Rainforest Display Centre** (McLeish Rd, Lake Eacham; ⊙ 9am-1pm Mon, Wed & Fri).

Spot water dragons and tortoises or simply relax and soak up the views on a 45-minute **cruise** (www.lakebarrine.com.au/cruises; adult/child/family $18/8/40; ⊙ 9.30am, 11.30am & 1.30pm) around Lake Barrine; book and board at the excellent **Lake Barrine Teahouse** (☑ 07-4095 3847; www.lakebarrine.com.au; Gillies Hwy; mains from $8.50; ⊙ 9am-3pm).

The pretty **Lake Eacham Tourist Park** (☑ 07-4095 3730; www.lakeeachamtouristpark. com; Lakes Dr; powered/unpowered sites $27/22, cabins $110-130; @ ☞), 1km down from Lake Eacham, has shady sites, cosy cabins, a general store, and cafe.

PORT DOUGLAS TO COOKTOWN

Port Douglas

POP 3205
From its early days as a fishing village, Port Douglas has grown into a sophisticated and upmarket resort town that's quite a contrast to Cairns' hectic tourist scene. The outer Great Barrier Reef is less than an hour offshore, the Daintree Rainforest is practically in the backyard, and there are more resorts than you can poke a snorkel at: a growing number of flashpackers, cashed-up couples and fiscally flush families choose Port Douglas as their Far North base.

Apart from easy access to the reef and daily sunset cruises on the inlet, the town's main attraction is Four Mile Beach a broad strip of palm-fringed, white sand that begins at the eastern end of Macrossan St, the main drag for shopping, wining and dining. On the western end of Macrossan you'll find the picturesque Dickson Inlet and Reef Marina, where the rich and famous park their aquatic toys.

⊙ Sights

★ Wildlife Habitat Port Douglas   ZOO
(☑ 07-4099 3235; www.wildlifehabitat.com.au; Port Douglas Rd; adult/child/family $34/17/85; ⊕ 8am-5pm) This sanctuary endeavours to keep and showcase native animals in enclosures that mimic their natural environment, while allowing you to get up close to koalas, kangaroos, crocs, cassowaries and more. Tickets are valid for three days. For an extra special experience book for **Breakfast with the Birds** (adult/child/family breakfast incl admission $53/26.50/132.50; ⊕ 8-10.30am) or **Lunch with the Lorikeets** (adult/child incl admission $56/28; ⊕ noon-2pm). It's 5km from town ($5 by shuttle bus).

Trinity Bay Lookout   VIEWPOINT
(Island Point Rd) Head up to Flagstaff Hill for sensational views over **Four Mile Beach** and the Coral Sea. Drive or walk up via Wharf St, or there's a walking path leading up from the north end of Four Mile Beach.

Court House Museum   MUSEUM
(☑ 07-4098 1284; www.douglashistory.org.au; Wharf St; adult/child $2/free; ⊕ 10am-1pm Tue, Thu, Sat & Sun) The 1879 Court House contains historical exhibits, including the story of Ellen Thompson, who was tried for murder in 1887 and the only woman ever hanged in Queensland.

🏃 Activities

Port Douglas is best known for its smorgasbord of activities and tours, both on water and land. For golfers the **Mirage Country Club** (☑ 07-4099 5537; www.miragecountryclub.com.au; 9/18 holes $55/85) and **Palmer Sea Reef** (☑ 07-4087 2222; http://palmergolf.com.au; 9/18 holes with cart $85/145) are two of north Queensland's top resort courses.

Several companies offer PADI open-water certification as well as advanced dive certificates, including **Blue Dive** (☑ 0427 983 907; www.bluedive.com.au; 32 Macrossan St; reef intro diving courses from $300). For one-on-one instruction, learn with **Tech Dive Academy**

(☑ 0422 016 517; www.tech-dive-academy.com; 4-day open-water courses from $1290).

★ Wind Swell   WATER SPORTS
(☑ 0427 498 042; www.windswell.com.au; Barrier St; lessons from $50) Kitesurfing and stand-up paddleboarding for everyone from beginners to high flyers. Kitesurfing lessons and paddleboarding tours from the beach start at $50, but there are also plenty of advanced options. Find them in action at the southern end of Four Mile Beach.

Port Douglas Yacht Club   BOATING
(☑ 07-4099 4386; www.portdouglasyachtclub.com.au; 1 Spinnaker Close; ⊕ from 4pm Wed) Free sailing with club members every Wednesday afternoon: sign on from 4pm. Those chosen to go sailing are expected to stay for dinner and drinks in the club afterwards.

Aquarius Sunset Sailing   CRUISE
(☑ 07-4099 6999; www.tropicaljourneys.com; adult/child $60/50; ⊕ cruises depart 4.45pm) Twilight sailing is practically de rigueur in Port Douglas. This 1½-hour catamaran cruise includes canapés, and BYO alcohol is allowed.

Ballyhooley Steam Railway   RAIL
(☑ 07-4099 1839; www.ballyhooley.com.au; 44 Wharf St; adult/child day pass $12/6; ⊕ Sun; ⊞) Kids will get a kick out of this cute miniature steam train. Every Sunday (and some public holidays), it runs from the little station at Reef Marina to St Crispins Station four times between 10am and 4pm. A round trip takes about one hour; discounts are available for shorter sections.

☞ Tours

The outer reef is closer to Port Douglas than it is to Cairns, and the unrelenting surge of visitors has had a similar impact on its condition here. You will still see colourful corals and marine life, but it is patchy in parts.

Most day tours depart from Reef Marina. Tour prices usually include reef tax, snorkelling, transfers from your accommodation, lunch and refreshments.

★ Quicksilver   CRUISE
(☑ 07-4087 2100; www.quicksilver-cruises.com; Reef Marina; adult/child/family $238/119/535) Major operator with fast cruises to its own pontoon on Agincourt Reef. Try an 'ocean walk' helmet dive ($166) on a submerged platform or snorkelling with a marine biologist (from $60). Also offers 10-minute

Port Douglas

scenic helicopter flights ($175, minimum two passengers).

Reef Sprinter
SNORKELLING

(☎ 07-4099 6127; www.reefsprinter.com.au; Shop 3, Reef Marina; adult/child from $130/110) The fastest way to the reef, this 2¼-hour snorkelling trip gets to the Low Isles in just 15 minutes for one to 1½ hours in the water. Half-day outer reef trips are also available (from $200).

Poseidon
TOURS

(☎ 07-4087 2100; www.poseidon-cruises.com.au; Reef Marina; adult/child $240/171) This luxury catamaran specialises in snorkelling trips to the Agincourt Ribbon Reefs, as well as scuba diving (one/two dives an additional $46/66).

Sailaway
SAILING, SNORKELLING

(☎ 07-4099 4200; www.sailawayportdouglas.com; Shop 18, Reef Marina; adult/child $255/178; 🖼) Runs a popular catamaran sailing and snor-

kelling trip to the Low Isles that's great for families. The afternoon and sunset cruises are for adults only.

★ Tony's Tropical Tours
TOURS

(☎ 07-4099 3230; www.tropicaltours.com.au; day tours from $185) This luxury, small-group (eight to 10 passengers) tour operator specialises in trips to out-of-the-way sections of the Mossman Gorge and Daintree Rainforest (adult/child $185/160), and Bloomfield Falls and Cape Trib (adults only $215 – good mobility required). A third tour heads south to the Tablelands. Highly recommended.

Bike N Hike
CYCLING

(☎ 0477 774 443; www.bikenhiketours.com.au; tours $120-128) Mountain bike down the aptly named Bump Track on a cross-country bike tour, or take on an action-packed berserk night tour. Also does half-day cycling and hiking trips.

Port Douglas

◎ Sights
1 Court House Museum............................B1
2 Four Mile Beach.................................D4
3 Trinity Bay Lookout.............................D2

✈ Activities, Courses & Tours
4 Aquarius Sunset Sailing......................A3
5 Ballyhooley Steam Railway.................B3
6 Blue Dive..C2
7 Lady Douglas.....................................A3
8 Port Douglas Yacht Club.....................A4
9 Poseidon..A3
Quicksilver.....................................(see 4)
10 Reef Sprinter.....................................A2
11 Sailaway..A3

🛏 Sleeping
12 Mantra Aqueous on Port.....................C3
13 Martinique on Macrossan...................D3
14 Peppers Beach Club...........................C4
15 Port Douglas Backpackers.................C3
16 Tropic Breeze Caravan Park...............C4

✖ Eating
17 2 Fish Restaurant Port Douglas...........C3
18 Cafe Fresq...B2
19 Cafe Ziva...B2
20 Coles Supermarket.............................B2
21 Harrisons Restaurant.........................B2
22 Little Larder.......................................C2
23 Mocka's Pies......................................B2
24 On the Inlet..A3
25 Seabean..B2
Yachty...(see 8)

🍸 Drinking & Nightlife
26 Hemingway's......................................A3
27 Iron Bar...B2
28 Tin Shed..A2

🛍 Shopping
29 Port Douglas Markets.........................B1
30 Reef Marina Sunset Market................A3

Back Country Bliss Adventures ADVENTURE
(☑07-4099 3677; www.backcountryblissadventures.com.au; tours $99-249) Go with the flow as you drift-snorkel down the Mossman River. Also small-group sea-kayaking, hiking and mountain-biking trips.

Lady Douglas BOATING
(☑0408 986 127; www.ladydouglas.com.au; Reef Marina, Wharf St; 1½hr cruises adult/child/family $35/15/90; ⊙cruises 10.30am, 12.30pm, 2.30pm & 4.30pm) Lovely paddle steamer running four daily croc-spotting river tours (including a sunset cruise) along the Dickson Inlet.

✪ Festivals & Events

Port Douglas Carnivale CARNIVAL
(www.carnivale.com.au; ⊙May) Port is packed for this 10-day festival, which includes a colourful street parade featuring live music, and lashings of good food and wine.

Portoberfest BEER
(Reef Marina; ⊙late Oct) The tropical take on Oktoberfest, with live music, German food and, *natürlich,* beer is held at Lure Restaurant in the Reef Marina.

🛏 Sleeping

Although it has a few backpacker resorts and caravan parks, Port Douglas isn't a true budget destination like Cairns – five-star resorts and boutique holiday apartments are more a part of the PD experience. Much of

the accommodation is some distance from town off the 5km-long Port Douglas Rd, while most restaurants, bars, pubs and the marina are around the main drag, Macrossan St.

★Coral Beach Lodge HOSTEL $
(☑07-4099 5422; www.coralbeachlodge.com; 1 Craven Close; dm $25-39, d $114; ❄@🛜🏊) ✈ A cut above most backpacker places, this fabulous, chilled-out hostel has well-equipped en-suite dorms (with four or five beds) and double or triple rooms that put many motels in the shade – flat-screen TVs, new bathrooms and comfy beds. Each room has an outdoor area with hammocks, and there's a lovely pool, games room, kitchen and helpful owners. Highly recommended.

Dougies HOSTEL $
(☑07-4099 6200, 1800 996 200; www.dougies.com.au; 111 Davidson St; tent s/tw $25/40, sites per person $25, dm $30, d $75; ❄@🛜🏊) It's easy to hang about Dougies' sprawling grounds in a hammock by day and move to the bar at night. If you can summon the energy, bikes and fishing gear are available for rent and the beach is a 300m walk east. Free pick-up from Cairns on Monday, Wednesday and Saturday.

Port Douglas Backpackers HOSTEL $
(☑07-4099 5011; http://portdouglasbackpackers.com.au; 37 Warner St; dm $20-28, d $85; ❄🏊) For a cheap bed close to the centre of town, this brand-new place will suit travellers looking for action. There's a lively bar at

the front, clean four- to eight-bed dorms, a few private rooms at the rear and a pool in between. Free transfer to Cairns Tuesday, Thursday and Sunday.

Tropic Breeze Caravan Park　CARAVAN PARK $
(☑ 07-4099 5299; www.tropicbreeze.com.au; 24 Davidson St; powered/unpowered sites $48/37, cabins $120; ❋ ❄) This small park is beautifully located a short walk to the beach and town. Grassy sites, and units with kitchenette but no bathroom.

★**Pink Flamingo**　BOUTIQUE HOTEL $$
(☑ 07-4099 6622; www.pinkflamingo.com.au; 115 Davidson St; d $145-205; ❋ @ ❄ ❄) Flamboyantly painted rooms, private walled courtyards and a groovy alfresco pool-bar make the Pink Flamingo Port Douglas' hippest gay-friendly digs. With just two studios and 10 villas, it's an intimate stay in a sea of mega-resorts. Heated pool, a gym and bike rental are also on offer.

Mantra Aqueous on Port　APARTMENT $$
(☑ 07-4099 0000; www.mantraaqueousonport. com.au; 3-5 Davidson St; d from $180, 1-/-2-bed apt from $280/415; ❋ ❄ ❄) You can't beat the location of this unique resort with four individual pools. The pricier ground-floor rooms have swim-up balconies, and all rooms have outdoor Jacuzzi tubs! Studio and one- and two-bedroom apartments are available. Longer stays attract cheaper rates.

Martinique on Macrossan　APARTMENT $$
(☑ 07-4099 6222; www.martinique.com.au; 66 Macrossan St; apt $215; ❋ ❄ ❄) This terracotta boutique block contains lovely tiled one-bedroom apartments, each with a small kitchen, a private balcony, colourful accents and plantation shutters. Wonderful hosts and an excellent main street location near the beach seal the deal. The pool has six coves and is supervised by a lavish elephant and dolphin shrine. Good value.

★**Peppers Beach Club**　RESORT $$$
(☑ 1300 737 444; www.peppers.com.au/beach-club; 20-22 Davidson St; spa ste from $309, 1-/2-bedoom ste from $409/566; ❋ ❄ ❄) A killer location and an exceptional, enormous, sandy lagoon-pool, combined with luxurious, airy apartments with high-end furnishings and amenities, put Peppers right up there with Port Douglas' best. Some rooms have balcony spas, others swim-up decks or full kitchens. Family friendly, but recommended for young romantics.

Thala Beach Nature Reserve　RESORT $$$
(☑ 07-4098 5700; www.thalabeach.com.au; Captain Cook Hwy; d $255-668; ❋ ❄ ❄) On a private coastal headland 15km south of Port Douglas, Thala Beach is an upmarket eco-retreat so relaxing that even locals come here to chill for the weekend. Luxurious treehouse-style bungalows are scattered throughout the jungle with easy access to a private stretch of beach, two pools, walking trails and a quality restaurant.

 Eating

Port Douglas' compact centre is awash with sophisticated cafes and restaurants, many with a tropical alfresco setting. All of the resorts also have restaurants.

Self-caterers can stock up on supplies at the large **Coles Supermarket** (11 Macrossan St; ⏰7am-6pm) in the Port Village shopping centre.

Cafe Fresq　CAFE $
(☑ 07-4099 6111; 27 Macrossan St; mains $6-19; ⏰7am-3pm) Fresq is always busy at breakfast with tables spilling out onto the footpath. Good coffee, gourmet breakfasts, pancakes and lunch items such as soft-shell crab burgers.

Cafe Ziva　FRENCH $
(20 Macrossan St; mains $7.50-22; ⏰12.30-10pm; ❄) Ziva specialises in French-style pancakes with a range of savoury galettes (such as ham and cheese) and sweet crêpes, along with sandwiches, smoothies and fresh juice. The open-fronted cafe is good for people-watching.

Mocka's Pies　BAKERY $
(☑ 07-4099 5295; 9 Grant St; pies $4.50-6; ⏰8am-4pm) Local institution serving classic Aussie pies with exotic fillings such as crocodile, kangaroo and barramundi.

★**Yachty**　MODERN AUSTRALIAN $$
(☑ 07-4099 4386; www.portdouglasyachtclub.com. au; 1 Spinnaker Close; mains $22-34; ⏰noon-2.30pm & 5.30-8pm) One of the best-value nights out is the local yacht club, where well-crafted meals, from Moroccan spiced lamb to lobster tail, are served nightly with sunset views over Dickson Inlet. The lunch menu is similar but cheaper.

★**On the Inlet**　SEAFOOD $$
(☑ 07-4099 5255; www.ontheinlet.com.au; 3 Inlet St; mains $26-42; ⏰noon-11.30pm) You'll feel like you're floating over Dickson Inlet here,

with tables spread out along a huge deck from where you can await the 5pm arrival of George, the 250kg groper that comes to feed most days. Take up the bucket-of-prawns-and-a-drink deal ($18 from 3.30pm to 5.30pm) and watch the reef boats come in.

Seabean
TAPAS $$

(☏07-4099 5558; www.seabean.com.au; 3/28 Wharf St; tapas $9-15, paella from $35; ☺3-9pm Mon-Thu, noon-9pm Fri-Sun) This cool little tapas bar with bright red stools and attentive staff brings quality Spanish plates and paella to PD.

Little Larder
CAFE $$

(☏07-4099 6450; Shop 2, 40 Macrossan St; mains $10-19; ☺7.30am-3pm) Brekky until 11.30am then gourmet sandwiches and killer cocktails from noon. Good coffee, or try freshly brewed and super healthy kombucha tea.

★Harrisons Restaurant
MODERN AUSTRALIAN $$$

(☏07-4099 4011; www.harrisonsrestaurant.com.au; 22 Wharf St; lunch $19-26, dinner mains from $38; ☺noon-2pm & 5-10pm) Marco Pierre White-trained chef-owner Spencer Patrick whips up culinary gems that stand toe-to-toe with Australia's best. Fresh locally sourced produce is turned into dishes such as smoked duck breast and tamarind beef cheeks. Possibly the only place in Port where diners bother ditching their thongs for shoes.

★Flames of the Forest
MODERN AUSTRALIAN $$$

(☏07-4099 3144; www.flamesoftheforest.com.au; Mowbray River Rd; dinner with show, drinks & transfers from $219; ☺Tue, Thu & Sat) This unique experience goes way beyond the traditional concept of 'dinner and a show', with diners escorted deep into the rainforest for a truly immersive night of theatre, culture and gourmet cuisine. Transport provided from Port Douglas or Cairns (no self-drive). Bookings essential.

2 Fish Restaurant Port Douglas
SEAFOOD $$$

(☏07-4099 6350; www.2fishrestaurant.com.au; Shop 11, 56 Macrossan St; mains $32-44; ☺noon-10pm) In a town where seafood is plentiful, 2 Fish stands out for its upmarket innovative dishes, over a dozen types of fish, from coral trout to red emperor and wild barramundi, along with locally caught oysters, prawns and sea scallops. In between lunch and dinner, tapas plates are available.

🍷 Drinking & Nightlife

Pubs turn into clubs later in the night and Port has a **Moonlight Cinema** (www.moonlight.com.au/port-douglas; QT Resort, 87-109 Port Douglas Rd; adult/child $17.50/13; ☺Thu-Sun Jun-Oct) in season.

★Hemingway's
MICROBREWERY

(☏07-4099 6663; www.hemingwaysbrewery.com; Reef Marina, 44 Wharf St) Port Douglas deserves its own brewery and Hemingway's makes the most of a fabulous location on the Reef Marina with a broad deck, a long bar and Dickson Inlet views. There are currently six brews on tap, including Hard Yards dark lager and Pitchfork Betty's pale ale. Naturally, food is available, but this is one for the beer connoisseurs.

Tin Shed
CLUB

(☏07-4099 5553; www.thetinshed-portdouglas.com.au; 7 Ashford Ave; mains $22-29; ☺10am-10pm) Port Douglas' Combined Services Club (sign in as a guest member) has gone a bit fancy since its days of being dubbed the Tin Shed, but the over-water deck, good-value meals and reasonably priced drinks make this an inviting spot at any time of day.

Iron Bar
PUB

(☏07-4099 4776; www.ironbarportdouglas.com.au; 5 Macrossan St; ☺11am-3am) Wacky outback meets Wild West decor of corrugated iron and old timber, setting the scene for a wild night out. Don't miss the nightly 8.30pm cane-toad races ($5).

🛍 Shopping

The weekly **Reef Marina Sunset Market** (Reef Marina, Wharf St; ☺noon-6.30pm Wed) and **Port Douglas Markets** (Anzac Park, Macrossan St; ☺8am-2pm Sun) are both good for crafts, souvenirs and local produce.

ℹ Information

There are many tour booking agents in PD masquerading as tourist information offices, but no official tourist office.

Post Office (☏07-4099 5210; 5 Owen St; ☺8.30am-5pm Mon-Fri, 9am-noon Sat)

Port Douglas Tourist Information Centre (☏07-4099 5599; www.infoportdouglas.com.au; 23 Macrossan St; ☺8am-6.30pm) Not a government tourist office, but a reliable private booking agency; pick up brochures here and book tours.

ℹ️ Getting There & Away

Port Douglas Bus (📞 070-4099 5665; www.portdouglasbus.com.au) and **Sun Palm** (📞 07-4087 2900; www.sunpalmtransport.com.au; adult/child $35/17.50) operate daily between Port Douglas, Cairns and the airport.

Trans North (📞 07-4095 8644; www.transnorthbus.com.au) picks up in Port Douglas on the coastal drive between Cairns and Cooktown.

ℹ️ Getting Around

Hire bikes at the **Bicycle Centre** (📞 07-4099 5799; www.portdouglasbikehire.com.au; 3 Warner St; half-/full-day from $16/20; ⏱️ 8am-5pm).

Minibuses, such as those run by **Coral Reef Coaches** (📞 07-4098 2800; www.coralreefcoaches.com.au), shuttle between town and the highway for around $5.

Major car-rental chains have branches here, or try **Comet Car Hire** (📞 07-4099 6407; http://cometcarhire.com.au; 3/11 Warner St) and keep it local.

Mossman

POP 1730

Surrounded by sugar-cane fields, the workaday town of Mossman, 20km north of Port Douglas, is best known for beautiful Mossman Gorge, part of Daintree National Park. The town itself is worth a stop to get a feel for a Far North Queensland working community and to stock up if you're heading further north.

⊙ Sights & Activities

★ Mossman Gorge
GORGE

In the southeast corner of Daintree National Park, 5km west of Mossman town, Mossman Gorge forms part of the traditional lands of the Kuku Yalanji people. The gorge is a boulder-strewn valley where sparkling water washes over ancient rocks. It's 3km by road from the **visitor centre** (📞 07-4099 7000; www.mossmangorge.com.au; ⏱️ 8am-6pm) to a viewpoint and refreshing swimming hole – take care as the currents can be swift. You can walk the 3km but visitors are encouraged to take the shuttle (adult/child return $9.10/4.55, every 15 minutes).

There are several kilometres of walking trails on boardwalks and a picnic area at the gorge, but no camping.

★ Kuku-Yalanji Dreamtime Walks
OUTDOORS

(adult/child $62/31; ⏱️ 10am, 11am, noon, 1pm & 3pm) These unforgettable 1½-hour Indigenous-guided walks of Mossman Gorge include a smoking ceremony, bush tea and damper. Book through the Mossman Gorge Centre.

The Daintree & Cape Tribulation

The Daintree represents many things: Unesco World Heritage–listed **rainforest** (www.daintreerainforest.com), a river, a reef, laid-back villages and the home of its traditional custodians, the Kuku Yalanji people. It encompasses the coastal lowland area between the Daintree and Bloomfield Rivers, where the rainforest tumbles right down to the coast. It's a fragile, ancient ecosystem, once threatened by logging, but now protected as a national park.

Part of the Wet Tropics World Heritage Area, the spectacular region from the Daintree River north to Cape Tribulation features ancient rainforest, sandy beaches and rugged mountains. North of the Daintree River, electricity is supplied by generators or, increasingly, solar power. Shops and services are limited, and mobile-phone reception is patchy at best. The **Daintree River Ferry** (www.douglas.qld.gov.au/community/daintree-ferry; car one-way/return $14/26, motorcycle $5/10, pedestrian & bicycle $1/2; ⏱️ 6am-midnight) carries wanderers and their wheels across the river every 15 minutes or so.

Cow Bay & Around

Tiny Cow Bay is the first community you reach after the Daintree ferry crossing. On the steep, winding road between Cape Kimberley and Cow Bay, the **Walu Wugirriga Lookout** (Alexandra Range Lookout) offers sweeping views beyond the Daintree River inlet; it's especially breathtaking at sunset.

The white-sand **Cow Bay Beach**, at the end of Buchanan Creek Rd, rivals any coastal paradise.

The award-winning **Daintree Discovery Centre** (📞 07-4098 9171; www.discoverthedaintree.com; Tulip Oak Rd; adult/child/family $32/16/78; ⏱️ 8.30am-5pm) features an aerial walkway leading you high into the forest canopy. A theatre screens films on cassowaries, crocodiles, conservation and climate change.

DAINTREE VILLAGE

For wildlife lovers and birdwatchers, it's well worth taking the 20km each-way detour from the Mossman-Daintree Rd to tiny Daintree village, set on a plateau of farmland on the Upper Daintree River. Croc-spotting cruises are the main event. Try long-running **Crocodile Express** (☑ 07-4098 6120; www.crocodileexpress.com; 1hr cruises adult/child/family $28/14/65; ◷ cruises 8.30am), **Daintree River Wild Watch** (☑ 0447 734 933; www.daintreeriverwildwatch.com.au; 2hr cruises adult/child $60/35), which has informative sunrise birdwatching cruises and sunset photography nature cruises, or **Daintree River Cruise Centre** (☑ 07-4098 6115; www.daintreerivercruisecentre.com.au; 2914 Mossman-Daintree Rd; adult/child $28/14; ◷ 9.30am-4pm).

The boutique 'banyans' (treehouses) of **Daintree Eco Lodge & Spa** (☑ 07-4777 7377; www.daintree-ecolodge.com.au; 3189 Mossman-Daintree Rd; treehouses $325-425; ❋ @ ☞ ☎) 🗡 sit high in the rainforest a few kilometres south of the village. Nonguests are welcome at its superb **Julaymba Restaurant** (☑ 07-4098 6100; mains $28-32; ◷ dinner from 4.30pm), where the menu makes expert use of local produce.

In the village, **Big Barramundi Garden** (☑ 07-4098 6186; www.bigbarra.daintree.info; 12 Stewart St; mains $18-22, burgers from $9; ◷ 10am-4pm) serves exotic burgers (barra, crocodile and kangaroo) and smoothies or fruit juices (black sapote, paw paw) as well as Devonshire teas.

Get closer to nature on a boat trip with **Cape Tribulation Wilderness Cruises** (☑ 0457 731 000; www.capetribcruises.com; Cape Tribulation Rd; adult/child from $30/22) or a walking tour with **Cooper Creek Wilderness** (☑ 07-4098 9126; http://coopercreek.com.au; 2333 Cape Tribulation Rd; guided walks $60-170).

🛌 Sleeping & Eating

★ **Epiphyte B&B**   B&B $
(☑ 07-4098 9039; www.rainforestbb.com; 22 Silkwood Rd; s/d/cabins from $80/110/150) This lovingly built, laid-back place is set on a lush 3.5-hectare property. Individually styled rooms are of varying sizes, but all have their own verandah. A spacious, private cabin features a patio, kitchenette and sunken bathroom. Minimum two-night stay.

Lync-Haven Rainforest Retreat   CAMPGROUND $
(☑ 07-4098 9155; www.lynchaven.com.au; Lot 44, Cape Tribulation Rd; camp sites per person $14, powered sites $32, d from $150; ❋) This family-friendly retreat is set on a 16-hectare property on the main road, about 5km north of Cow Bay, and has walking trails, hand-reared kangaroos, well-grassed sites and comfy en-suite rainforest cabins. The restaurant serves robust steaks, good pasta and fish.

Daintree Ice Cream Company   ICE CREAM $
(☑ 07-4098 9114; www.daintreeicecream.com.au; Lot 100, Cape Tribulation Rd; ice creams $6.50; ◷ 11am-5pm) We dare you to drive past this all-natural ice-cream producer with a palette of flavours that changes daily. You might get macadamia, black sapote and wattleseed – they're all delicious.

Cow Bay Hotel   PUB FOOD $$
(☑ 07-4098 9011; 1480 Cape Tribulation Rd; mains $18-24; ◷ noon-2pm & 6-8pm, bar 10am-10pm) If you're craving a decent counter meal, a coldie and that Aussie country pub atmosphere, the Cow Bay is the only real pub this side of the Daintree River.

Cape Tribulation
POP 330

Cape Trib is at the end of the winding sealed road from the Daintree River and, with its two magnificent beaches, laid-back vibe, rainforest walks and compact village, it's a little slice of paradise.

Despite the backpacker bars and tour operators (jungle surfing, anyone?), Cape Trib still retains a frontier quality, with road signs alerting drivers to cassowary crossings, and croc warnings making evening beach strolls a little less relaxing. The fact that there's no reliable mobile phone reception or network internet adds to the remoteness – and freaks a few travellers out!

The rainforest skirts beautiful **Myall** and **Cape Tribulation** beaches, which are separated by a knobby cape. The village here marks the end of the sealed road: beyond, the strictly 4WD-only Bloomfield Track continues north to Wujal Wujal.

Cape Tribulation Area

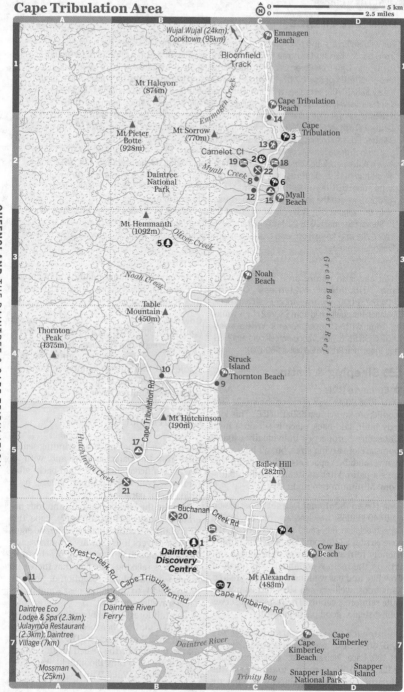

N
0 — 5 km
0 — 2.5 miles

Wujal Wujal (24km);
Cooktown (95km)

Bloomfield
Track

Emmagen
Beach

Mt Halcyon
(874m)

Emmagen Creek

Cape Tribulation
Beach
14

Mt Pieter
Botte
(928m)

Mt Sorrow
(770m)

Cape
Tribulation

13
3

Camelot Cl

Myall Creek

19 2
22
18

Daintree
National
Park

8
6

12
15

Myall
Beach

Mt Hemmanth
(1092m)

Oliver Creek

5

Noah Creek

Noah
Beach

Table
Mountain
(450m)

Great Barrier Reef

Thornton
Peak
(1375m)

Struck
Island

10
9

Thornton Beach

Hutchinson Creek

Mt Hutchinson
(190m)

Cape Tribulation Rd

17

Bailey Hill
(282m)

21

Buchanan Creek Rd

20

16

4

Cow Bay
Beach

Forest Creek Rd

1

Daintree
Discovery
Centre

Mt Alexandra
(483m)

Cape Tribulation Rd

7

Cape Kimberley Rd

Daintree Eco
Lodge & Spa (2.3km);
Julaymba Restaurant
(2.3km); Daintree
Village (7km)

11

Daintree River
Ferry

Cape
Kimberley

Cape
Kimberley
Beach

Snapper
Island

Mossman
(25km)

Daintree River

Snapper Island
National Park

Trinity Bay

Cape Tribulation Area

⊙ Sights & Activities

Good access points for Cape Trib and Myall beaches are the signposted Kulki and Dubuji boardwalks, respectively.

Bat House WILDLIFE RESERVE
(☑07-4098 0063; www.austrop.org.au; Cape Tribulation Rd; $5; ☉10.30am-3.30pm Tue-Sun) A nursery for injured or orphaned fruit bats (flying foxes), run by conservation organisation Austrop.

Mt Sorrow Ridge Walk WALKING
Mt Sorrow is a demanding day hike for fit walkers. The ridge-walk trail starts about 150m north of the Kulki picnic area car park, just off the Bloomfield Rd. The strenuous walk (7km, five to six hours return, start no later than 10am), offers spectacular views over the rainforest and reef.

⟱ Tours

Most tours offer free pick-ups from local accommodation.

★ Ocean Safari TOURS
(☑07-4098 0006; www.oceansafari.com.au; Cape Tribulation Rd; adult/child/family $139/89/415; ☉8am & noon) Ocean Safari leads small groups (25 people maximum) on morning and afternoon snorkelling cruises to the Great Barrier Reef, just half an hour offshore. Wetsuit hire ($8) available.

Paddle Trek Kayak Tours KAYAKING
(☑07-4098 1950; www.capetribpaddletrek.com.au; Lot 7, Rykers Rd; half-day guided trips $75-85) Guided sea-kayaking trips (morning/afternoon 2½/3½ hours) depart from Cape Trib Beach House (p428).

Mason's Tours WALKING, DRIVING
(☑07-4098 0070; www.masonstours.com.au; Mason's Store, Cape Tribulation Rd) Long-timer Lawrence Mason conducts enlightening rainforest walks (groups of up to five people two hours/half day $300/500), including a night walk; 4WD tours up the Bloomfield Track to Cooktown are also available (groups up to five people half/full day $800/1250).

Jungle Surfing Canopy Tours OUTDOORS
(☑07-4098 0043; www.junglesurfing.com.au; ziplines $95, night walks $45, combo $130; ☉7.45am-3.30pm, night walks 7.30pm) Get right up into the rainforest on an exhilarating two-hour flying-fox (zipline) surf through the canopy. Guided night walks follow biologist-guides who shed light on the dark jungle. Rates include pick-up from Cape Trib accommodation (self-drive not permitted).

D'Arcy of the Daintree DRIVING
(☑0402 849 249; www.darcyofdaintree.com.au; 116 Palm Rd, Diwan; tours adult/child from $146/108) Local Mike D'Arcy offers entertaining small-group 4WD trips up the Bloomfield Track to Wujal Wujal Falls (half day) and as far as Cooktown (full day).

Cape Trib Horse Rides
HORSE RIDING

(☑ 07-4098 0043; www.capetribhorserides.com.au; rides per person from $99; ☺ 8am & 2.30pm) Leisurely morning and afternoon rides along the beach and into the forest.

🛏 Sleeping & Eating

Restaurants at Cape Trib's resorts are all open to nonguests. There's a **supermarket** (☑ 07-4098 0015; Cape Tribulation Rd; ☺ 8am-6pm) stocking basic supplies for self-caterers.

★ Cape Trib Beach House
HOSTEL, RESORT $

(☑ 07-4098 0030; www.capetribbeach.com.au; 152 Rykers Rd; dm $29, cabin $150-180; ❋ @ ☎ ⛱) The Beach House is everything that's great about Cape Trib – a secluded patch of rainforest facing a pristine beach and a friendly vibe that welcomes backpackers, couples and families. Clean dorms and romantic almost-beachfront cabins make the most of the location. The open-deck licensed **restaurant** (mains $18-30) and bar is so good many locals eat and drink here. HI affiliated.

Cape Tribulation Camping
CAMPGROUND $

(☑ 07-4098 0077; www.capetribcamping.com.au; Lot 11, Cape Tribulation Rd; powered sites adult/child $20/10, unpowered sites $15/10) Myall Beach is just steps away from this lovely laid-back camping ground. Grassy sites with good facilities (unless you want a pool) and the Sand Bar is a sociable verandah restaurant serving Cape Trib's best wood-fired pizzas.

PK's Jungle Village
HOSTEL $

(☑ 07-4098 0040; www.pksjunglevillage.com; Cape Tribulation Rd; unpowered sites per person $15, dm $25-32, cabin d $70-125; ❋ @ ☎ ⛱) With the giant **Jungle Bar** (mains $11-25; ☺ 7.30am-10pm) restaurant-pool area, a boardwalk to Myall Beach and a range of budget accommodation, PK's has long been a favourite with backpackers. Camp sites and dorms are a little cramped but the place is well-maintained and sociable.

Rainforest Hideaway
B&B $

(☑ 07-4098 0108; www.rainforesthideaway.com; 19 Camelot Close; d $135-149) ✎ This colourful B&B, consisting of one room in the main house and a separate cabin, was single-handedly built by its owner, artist and sculptor 'Dutch Rob' – even the furniture and beds are handmade. A sculpture trail winds through the property.

★ Whet
AUSTRALIAN $$

(☑ 07-4098 0007; www.whet.net.au; 1 Cape Tribulation Rd; mains $16.50-33; ☺ 11am-4pm & 6-8.30pm) Whet is regarded as Cape Trib's most sophisticated place to eat, with a loungy cocktail-bar feel and romantic, candlelit, alfresco dining. Tempura wild barramundi and house chicken-curry grace the menu; all lunch dishes are under $20. You'll often find locals at the bar.

★ Mason's Store & Cafe
CAFE $$

(☑ 07-4098 0016; 3781 Cape Tribulation Rd; mains $9-18, tasting plates from $29; ☺ 10am-4pm) Everyone calls into Mason's for tourist info, the liquor store, or to dine out on exotic meats. Pride of place on the menu at this laid-back alfresco cafe goes to the croc burger, but you can also try camel, emu and kangaroo in burgers or tasting plates. A short walk away is a crystal-clear, croc-free swimming hole ($1).

WORTH A TRIP

LIZARD ISLAND

The five islands of the Lizard Island Group lie 33km off the coast about 100km north of Cooktown. Lizard, the main island, has rocky, mountainous terrain, glistening white beaches and spectacular fringing reefs for snorkelling and diving. Most of the island is national park and teeming with wildlife. Sumptuous accommodation and dining epitomise five-star luxury at the ultra-exclusive **Lizard Island Resort** (☑ 1300 863 248; www.lizardisland.com.au; Anchor Bay; d $1900-2900; ❋ @ ☎ ⛱), decimated by Cyclone Ita in April 2014 and exquisitely rebuilt and refurbished in 2015. There's limited bush camping at the island's **camp site** (☑ 13 74 68; www.npsr.qld.gov.au/parks/lizard-island/camping.html; Watsons Bay; per adult/family $6.15/24.60) ✎. There are no shops on the island. Book air transfers to/from Cairns through the resort.

Daintree Air Services (☑ 07-4034 9300; www.daintreeair.com.au; day tours from $740) offers spectacular full-day tours from Cairns including gourmet lunch, snorkelling gear, transfers and a local guide to take you to some of the most magnificent spots in this pristine ecosystem.

ℹ️ Information

Mason's Store (📞 07-4098 0070; Cape Tribulation Rd; ⊙ 8am-6pm) The best place for regional info including Bloomfield Track conditions.

North to Cooktown

Aside from flying in, there are two routes to Cooktown from the south: the coastal route from Cape Tribulation via the 4WD-only Bloomfield Track, and the inland route, which is sealed all the way via the Peninsula and Cooktown Developmental Rds.

Bloomfield Track

It's a little over 100km from Cape Trib to Cooktown on the Bloomfield Track and all but 32km of it is sealed – however, that section is strictly 4WD only.

Starting at Cape Trib, it's 8km to the first water crossing at **Emmagen Creek**. From here the road climbs and dips steeply, and turns sharp corners, then follows the broad Bloomfield River before reaching it 24km further in at the Indigenous community of Wujal Wujal. Here you'll find the **Bana Yirriji Art Centre** (📞 07-4060 8333; www.wujalartcentre.com.au; Bloomfield Rd, Wujal Wujal; ⊙ 9am-4pm Mon-Fri; 🅿️) **FREE**. Continue along the river for 1km to the impressive **Bloomfield Falls**. Crocs inhabit the river and the site is significant to the Wujal Wujal community. The half-hour **Walker Family Walking Tours** (📞 07-4040 7500; adult/child $25/12.50; ⊙ by reservation) 🌿 of the falls and surrounding forest are highly recommended.

About 7km north of Wujal Wujal is the small community of **Ayton**, with a store, cafes, beach access and some great places to stay, including **Bloomfield Beach Camp** (📞 07-4060 8207; www.bloomfieldbeach.com.au; 20 Bloomfield Rd, Ayton; powered/unpowered sites $30/25, cabin d & safari tents $85, cottages $165) and **Bloomfield Escape** (📞 07-4060 8346; www.bloomfieldescape.com.au; 9 Weary Bay Rd; cabins from $125; ❄️📶).

The sealed road continues for another 25km north to Rossville, where a rough 3km driveway leads to **Home Rule Rainforest Lodge** (📞 07-4060 3925; www.home-rule.com.au; Rossville; unpowered sites per adult/child $10/5, r $35/20). Spotless facilities include shared cabins and a communal kitchen; walk to waterfalls or canoe on Wallaby Creek. Home Rule is ground zero for the **Wallaby Creek**

Festival (www.wallabycreekfestival.org.au; ⊙ end Sep), a three-day, multicultural, family friendly event featuring roots, blues and Indigenous music.

It's another 9km to the iconic **Lion's Den Hotel** (📞 07-4060 3911; www.lionsdenhotel.com.au; 398 Shiptons Flat Rd, Helenvale; camping per person $12, powered sites $30, s/d $50/60, safari tents $90; ❄️⛺), a legendary oasis with a tangible history dating back to 1875. You'll find fuel, ice-cold beer, strong coffee, awesome pizzas, pub grub and live music. Spend a night camping or staying in one of the pole-tent cabins. Don't miss a swim in the croc-free creek.

Nearby, explore the surrounding rainforest and waterfall of **Mungumby Lodge** (📞 07-4060 3158; www.mungumby.com; Helenvale; d/f $260/279; 📶⛺) 🌿, where en-suite bungalows are scattered among the lawns and mango trees. Rates include breakfast and nature tours are available. About 4km further north, the road meets the sealed Mulligan Hwy, from where it's 28km to Cooktown.

Cooktown

POP 2340

At the southeastern edge of Cape York Peninsula, coastal Cooktown is a small place with a big history: for thousands of years, Waymbuurr was the place the local Guugu Yimithirr and Kuku Yalanji people used as a meeting ground, and it was here that on 17 June 1770, Lieutenant (later Captain) Cook beached the *Endeavour,* which had earlier struck a reef offshore from Cape Tribulation. Cook's crew spent 48 days here repairing the damage, making Cooktown Australia's first (albeit transient) non-Indigenous settlement.

Today, Cooktown makes the most of its history and pristine natural environment and is a starting base for tours to the Cape and serious fishing trips.

👁️ Sights & Activities

James Cook Museum   MUSEUM
(📞 07-4069 6004; www.nationaltrust.org.au/places/james-cook-museum; 50 Helen St; adult/child $10/3; ⊙ 9am-4pm) Cooktown's finest building (an 1899 convent), this National Trust museum houses well-preserved relics including journal entries, the cannon and anchor from the *Endeavour,* and displays on local Indigenous culture, as well as a brand new visitor centre (p431).

Cooktown Botanic Gardens GARDENS

(off Walker St; ⊘24hr; P⛟) FREE The 62-hectare botanical gardens contain a large number of plant species, including the Cooktown orchid. Marked walking trails lead to the beaches at Finch Bay and Cherry Tree Bay. Download the free smartphone app Cook 1770, which provides a self-guided audio tour.

Grassy Hill Lookout VIEWPOINT

(P) FREE Captain Cook climbed this 162m-high hill looking for a passage through the reefs. The 360-degree views of the town, river and ocean are truly spectacular, especially at sunset. Easy vehicle access is up a steep sealed road (Hope St) from town. Walkers can ascend via a bush trail from Cherry Tree Bay.

There's a small working lighthouse at the summit, along with interpretive boards.

Nature's Powerhouse CULTURAL CENTRE

(☑07-4069 5763; off Walker St; ⊘10am-4pm; P) FREE At the entrance to Cooktown Botanic Gardens (p430), this environmental centre is home to the inviting **Kindred Cafe** (mains $8-18; ⊘10am-4pm; 🅿) and the **Vera Scarth-Johnson Gallery**, displaying botanical illustrations of the region's native plants.

Bicentennial Park PARK

(Charlotte St; ⛟) This waterfront park is home to a much-photographed bronze **Captain Cook statue** and nearby **Milbi Wall** – a 12m-long mosaic depicting the history of the local Gungarde (Guugu Yimithirr) people, from Creation stories through to attempts at reconciliation. Out in the water is a rock marking the spot where Cook ran aground.

☞ Tours

Maaramaka Walkabout Tours CULTURAL

(☑07-4060 9389; 2 McIvor Rd, Hopevale; 1/2hr tours from $42/84) 🖉 Aboriginal cultural stories, rainforest walks, bush tucker, home cooking and a camping ground in a gorgeous setting near Hopevale; call for arrangements.

✼ Festivals & Events

Cooktown Discovery Festival CULTURAL

(www.cooktowndiscovery.com; ⊘early Jun) This exuberant festival commemorates Cook's landing in 1770 with a costumed reenactment, fancy-dress parade and Indigenous events.

🛏 Sleeping

★Pam's Place Hostel & Cooktown Motel HOSTEL, MOTEL $

(☑07-4069 5166; www.cooktownhostel.com; cnr Charlotte & Boundary Sts; dm $30, s & d $60, motel d from $95; ❊@🛜🏊) Cooktown's YHA-associated hostel is also part motel, but it ticks all the backpacker boxes with its big kitchen, free lockers and relaxing tropical garden. The 'dorms' are more like private rooms with one or two beds, fridge and small TV. Friendly management can help find harvest work.

Cooktown Orchid Travellers Park CARAVAN PARK $

(☑07-4069 6400; cnr Walker & Charlotte Sts; powered/unpowered sites $36/33; 🛜🏊) The smallest and most central of Cooktown's van parks, Orchid is basic and a little cramped but welcoming, with a pool and camp kitchen and direct access to The Italian restaurant.

Cooktown Holiday Park CARAVAN PARK $

(☑07-4069 5417; www.cooktownholidaypark.com.au; 31-41 Charlotte St; powered sites $45, cabins from $105; ❊🛜🏊) Built for caravans and motorhomes with all sites powered and a decent size. Also a range of cabins, units and impressive camp facilities.

★Milkwood Lodge COTTAGE $$

(☑07-4069 5007; www.milkwoodlodge.com; Annan Rd; d $145; P❊🏊) The six split-level pole cabins here have a wonderfully secluded rainforest feel. Beautifully designed with large balconies and modern amenities, they make the ultimate romantic getaway, 2.5km south of Cooktown.

✗ Eating & Drinking

Charlotte St has pubs, cafes and a few restaurants.

Capers CAFE $

(☑07-4069 5737; 160 Charlotte St; meals $6.50-19; ⊘7am-2pm Mon-Fri, 7am-noon Sat; 🛜) The most convivial cafe in Cooktown serves fine coffee and smoothies and excels in breakfast and light lunches. Eat inside or on the small street-front deck.

The Italian ITALIAN $$

(☑07-4069 6338; 95 Charlotte St; pizza $22-26, mains $21-34; ⊘4-10pm Tue-Sat; ⛟) The name says it all really: great pizzas and a wide-ranging Italian menu from pasta and risotto to thoughtful veal and seafood dishes, all served in a convivial atmosphere complete with red-and-white-check table-cloths. Semi-alfresco dining room with occasional live music and efficient service.

★ Balcony
Restaurant
MODERN AUSTRALIAN **$$$**

(☑ 07-4069 5400; 128 Charlotte St; mains $28-45; ⊙ 7-10am & 5.30-10pm; 🖥🛜) Sovereign Resort's formal Balcony Restaurant serves Mod Oz cuisine such as Atherton eye fillet and crispy skinned coral trout, as well as share plates such as seafood and bush-tucker platters. Its less formal Cafe-Bar (mains $12 to $23; open 10am to 10pm) has reasonably priced fish and chips, steak and burgers, as well as pool tables and free internet.

Top Pub
PUB

(☑ 07-4069 5308; 96 Charlotte St; ⊙ 10am-midnight) Also known as the Cooktown Hotel, the Top Pub is a classic weatherboard corner pub and the most alluring drinking spot for locals. Live music on weekends, big beer garden and meals and pizza available.

ℹ Information

Cooktown Visitor Centre (☑ 07-4069 6004; www.cooktownandcapeyork.com; 50 Helen St; ⊙ 9am-4pm) The brand new visitor centre is an impressive addition to the **James Cook Museum** (p429).

ℹ Getting There & Away

Cooktown's airfield is 7.5km west of town along McIvor Rd. **Hinterland Aviation** (☑ 07-4040 1333; www.hinterlandaviation.com.au) has up to three flights daily (Monday to Saturday) to Cairns (one way from $175, 40 minutes).

Cairns Bus Charters operates the daily **Cairns Cooktown Express** (☑ 07-4059 1423; www.cairnsbuscharters.com/services/cairns-cooktown-express; adult/child $80/40) along the inland route to Cairns ($79, five hours). **Trans North** (p424) travels to Cooktown on both the inland route ($84, 5¼ hours) and the more interesting coastal route ($85, 5½ hours).

CAPE YORK PENINSULA

Rugged, remote, Cape York Peninsula has one of the wildest tropical environments on the planet. The Great Dividing Range forms the spine of the Cape: tropical rainforests and palm-fringed beaches flank its eastern side, sweeping savannah woodlands, eucalyptus forests and coastal mangroves its west. This untamed landscape undergoes a spectacular transformation each year when the torrential rains of the monsoonal wet season set in: rough, dry earth turns to rich, red mud; quenched, the tinder-dry bush awakens in vibrant greens, and trickling creek-beds swell to raging rivers teeming with barramundi and menaced by saltwater crocodiles.

Generally only possible in the Dry, the overland pilgrimage to the Tip is an exhilarating 4WD trek into one of Australia's last great frontiers, but this is not just the preserve of hard-core off-roaders. If they stick to the main track, anyone with a 4WD and a sense of adventure can travel to the Tip.

☞ Tours

If you're travelling solo or nervous about hiring a 4WD and going it alone, a tour is probably your best option for exploring the Cape.

Tour operators run Cape expeditions from Cairns and Cooktown; most run between April and October and range from 10 to 14 days with no more than 20 passengers. An early or late wet season may affect dates. Places typically visited include Laura, Rinyirru (Lakefield) National Park, Coen, Weipa, the Eliot River system (including Twin Falls), Bamaga, Somerset and Cape York. Thursday and Horn Islands are usually optional extras. Transport can be by land, air and/or sea, while accommodation is camping or basic motels. Meals and hotel transfers are usually included.

★ Cape York Day Tour
TOURS

(☑ 07-4034 9300; www.daintreeair.com.au; per person $1590; ⊙ Apr-Jan) Operated by Daintree Air Services, the world's longest scenic flight takes you, at low-level, along the outer Great Barrier Reef and Daintree Rainforest. A 4WD collects you in Bamaga and takes you to the tip of the Australian continent before returning to Cairns. Meals are included. Operates on demand, outside the Wet.

Cape York Motorcycle
Adventures
TOURS

(☑ 07-4059 0220; www.capeyorkmotorcycles.com. au; 8-day tours from $5550) Fully supported dirt-bike adventures range from one- or two-day safaris (from $509) to the eight-day trips from Cairns to the Tip ($5550). The trip is cheaper if you bring your own dirt bike (from $3950).

QUEENSLAND

Cape York Peninsula

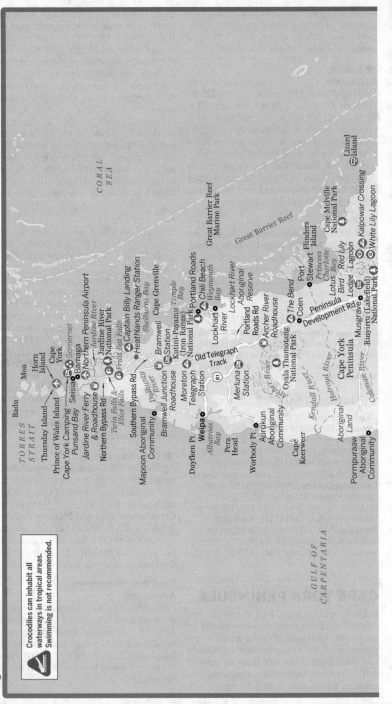

Crocodiles can inhabit all waterways in tropical areas. Swimming is not recommended.

100 km
50 miles

CORAL SEA

GULF OF CARPENTARIA

TORRES STRAIT

Badu
Moa
Horn Island
Thursday Island
Prince of Wales Island
Cape York Camping
Pansand Bay
Jardine River Ferry & Roadhouse
Northern Bypass Rd
Seisia
Bamaga
Somerset
Cape York
Northern Peninsula Airport
Jardine River
Jardine River National Park
Twin Falls & Eliot Falls
Fruit Bat Falls
Captain Billy Landing
Southern Bypass Rd
Heathlands Ranger Station
Shelburne Bay
Bramwell
Cape Grenville
Bramwell Junction Roadhouse
Dulhunty River
Mapoon Aboriginal Community
Kutini-Payamu (Iron Range) National Park
Temple Bay
Moreton Telegraph Station
Old Telegraph Track
Portland Roads
Chili Beach
Weymouth Bay
Lockhart River
Duyfken Pt
Weipa
Albatross Bay
Pera Head
Worbody Pt
Aurukun Aboriginal Community
Cape Keerweer
Merluna Station
Oyala Thumotang National Park
Archer River
Archer River Roadhouse
Portland Roads Rd
Lockhart River Aboriginal Reserve
Lockhart River
The Bend
Coen
Port Stewart
Princess Charlotte Bay
Flinders Island
Red Lily Lagoon
Bird Lagoon
Lotus Lodge
Peninsula Development Rd
Cape York Peninsula
Musgrave
Rinyirru (Lakefield) National Park
White Lily Lagoon
Kalpowar Crossing
Cape Melville National Park
Lizard Island
Great Barrier Reef Marine Park
Great Barrier Reef
Holroyd River
Kendall River
Coleman River
Aboriginal Land
Pormpuraaw Aboriginal Community

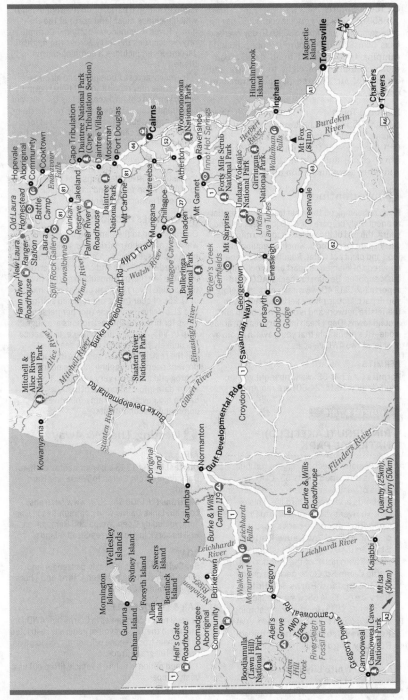

Oz Tours Safaris TOURS

(☑ 1800 079 006; www.oztours.com.au; 10-day fly-drive camping tours from $3090, 16-day overland tours from $3790) Numerous tours include camping trips from 10 to 16 days, accommodated tours from eight to 10 days and a range of air, sea and overland transport options.

Heritage Tours TOURS

(☑ 1800 775 533; www.heritagetours.com.au; 7-day fly-drive $2550, 12-day camping $2880; ☺ May-Oct) Big range of Cape tours, including fly-drive, cruise and overland, with camping and other accommodation options.

ⓘ Information

If you're heading off the main track, it's essential to adequately prepare for 4WD journeys beyond Laura, the end of the sealed road. You must carry spare tyres, tools, winching equipment, food and plenty of water. Roadhouses can be hundreds of kilometres apart and stock only basic supplies. Be sure to check **RACQ road reports** (☑ 13 19 40; www.racq.com.au) before you depart. Mobile phone service is limited to the Telstra network and is only available in and around towns. Don't head into very remote areas alone – it's preferable that you travel in a convoy of at least two 4WD vehicles.

PERMITS

Permits (☑ 13 74 68; www.npsr.qld.gov.au; adult/family $6.15/24.60) are required to

---

WORTH A TRIP

RINYIRRU (LAKEFIELD) NATIONAL PARK

Queensland's second-largest national park is renowned for its 537,000 hectares of vast river systems, spectacular wetlands and prolific bird life. This extensive river system drains into Princess Charlotte Bay on the park's northern perimeter. The **New Laura Ranger Station** (☑ 07-4060 3260) is located about 25km north of the junction with Battle Camp Rd. Book permits online via **Queensland Parks & Wildlife Service** (☑ 13 74 68; www.npsr.qld.gov.au; permits $6.15) for the best camping facilities (with toilets and showers) at **Kalpowar Crossing**. The picturesque **Red Lily Lagoon**, with its red lotus lilies (best appreciated in the morning), and **White Lily Lagoon** attract masses of bird life.

---

camp in national parks or on Aboriginal land, which includes most land north of the Dulhunty River. The Injinoo Aboriginal Community, which runs the ferry across the mighty Jardine River, includes a camping permit in the ferry fee.

Travelling across Aboriginal land elsewhere on the Cape may require an additional permit, which you can obtain by contacting the relevant community council. See the Cape York Sustainable Futures website (www.cysf.com.au) for details. Permits can take up to six weeks to be issued.

Refer to the Cape York Land Council (www.cylc.org.au) for a comprehensive overview of the historic native title claims that have seen up to 30% of Cape York's land handed back to its traditional owners in recent years.

ALCOHOL RESTRICTIONS

On the way up to the Cape you'll see signs warning of alcohol restrictions, which apply to all visitors. In some communities alcohol is banned completely and cannot be carried in. In the Northern Peninsula Area (north of the Jardine River) you can carry a maximum of 11.25L of beer (or 9L of premixed spirits) and 2L of wine per vehicle (not per person). Fines for breaking the restrictions are huge – up to $45,712 for a first offence. In practice it's unlikely your vehicle will be searched, but the restrictions and fines are in place to prevent people smuggling in large quantities of grog and are taken very seriously. For up-to-date information see https://www.datsip.qld.gov.au/programs-initiatives/community-alcohol-limits.

ⓘ Getting There & Away

AIR

QantasLink (☑ 13 13 13; www.qantas.com.au) Daily flights from Cairns to Weipa and Horn Island.

Skytrans (☑ 1300 759 872; www.skytrans.com.au) Links Cairns with communities in Cape York, including Coen, Weipa and Bamaga, as well as servicing the Torres Strait Islands.

BOAT

SeaSwift (p410) is a weekly passenger and cargo ferry running between Cairns and Thursday Island (and Seisia).

CAR & MOTORCYCLE

Several rental companies in Cairns hire 4WDs for the trip to the Tip, but you're generally restricted to the main track – none will permit you to go on the Old Telegraph Track.

A good option is to hire a vehicle fitted out as a bush camper.

Bear Rentals (☑1300 462 327; https://bear rentals.com.au; rentals per day $130-230)
Captain Billy's Bushranger (☑07-4041 2191; www.captainbilly4wdhire.com.au)
Cairns 4WD Hire (☑1300 360 339; www. cairns4wdhire.net.au)

Laura

POP 120

Since 2013, when the Peninsula Developmental Rd (PDR) was sealed as far as Laura, visitor numbers have been on the increase, but not much else has changed in this sleepy community. It's known for its proximity to Quinkan Country rock art – listed by Unesco in the world's top 10 rock-art sites – and the three-day **Laura Aboriginal Dance Festival** (☑07-4019 6212; www.laura dancefestival.com; ⊙ Jun odd years), Australia's largest celebration of Indigenous dance and culture.

The **Quinkan & Regional Cultural Centre** (☑07-4060 3457; www.quinkancc.com.au; Lot 2, Peninsula Developmental Rd; exhibition adult/child $5.50/3; ⊙8.30am-3pm; P) ✎ covers the history of the region. Insightful tours of Quinkan Country rock-art sites with an Indigenous guide (price on application) can be booked here.

You can camp at the basic **Quinkan Hotel** (☑07-4060 3393; www.quinkanhotel.com.au; Deighton Rd; camping per person $10, power $4, s/d $79/99; ⊙10am-midnight; P❀), which is where you'll be drinking and eating dinner if you stay at the tidy **Laura Motel** (☑07-4060 3238; Terminus St; d from $120; P❀), opposite.

Fuel up at the **Laura Roadhouse** (☑07-4060 2211; Peninsula Developmental Rd; powered/unpowered sites $22/20, meals from $10; ⊙6am-8pm), which does good breakfasts, or the **Laura Store & Post Office** (☑07-4060 3238; Deighton Rd; ⊙8am-6pm). Both sell ice and basic groceries.

About 12km south of Laura look out for the badly signposted turn-off to the **Split Rock Gallery** (Peninsula Developmental Rd; by donation; P) ✎, the only rock-art site open to the public without a guide. The sandstone escarpments here are covered with paintings thought to date back 14,000 years. If there are no tour groups, it can be quite a surreal experience to walk the path up the hillside in silence, solitude and isolation, before coming upon the various other-worldly 'galleries' in the rock faces.

Laura to Coen

North of Laura, some of the (dry) creek crossings, such as at the Little Laura and Kennedy Rivers, are great places to camp. For a scenic alternative route to Musgrave, take the turn-off for Rinyirru (Lakefield) National Park, about 28km north of Laura.

Staying on the Peninsula Developmental Rd (PDR) brings you to a food-and-fuel pit stop, the **Hann River Roadhouse** (☑07-4060 3242; Peninsula Developmental Rd; ⊙7.30am-10pm), 76km north of Laura. From here on, the flat, featureless landscape is spectacular monotony, broken only by sweeping grasslands and giant termite mounds. **Musgrave Roadhouse** (☑07-4060 3229; www.musgrave roadhouse.com.au; sites adult/child $10/5, r $110; ⊙7.30am-9pm; ❀) is a welcome stop after 80km. Coen is another rugged 109km further north.

Coen

Coen, the unofficial 'capital' of the central Cape, is a tiny township 108km north of Musgrave, with a history of gold mining (gold was first discovered here in 1876) and as a stop on the Telegraph Line. Wash down the bull dust with a beer at the legendary **Exchange Hotel** (☑07-4060 1133; Regent St; ⊙10am-11pm): after a boozy prank, the 'S' was added to the sign, creating the S'Exchange Hotel!

Apart from the pub you'll find a couple of general stores and camping areas. The turn-off to the remote Oyala Thumotang National Park (formerly known as the Mungkan Kandju National Park) is 25km north.

Call into the **Wunthulpu Visitor Centre** (⊙7am-8pm Mon-Sat, 8am-1pm Sun) FREE and **Cape York Heritage House** (Regent St; by donation; ⊙10am-5pm) for a taste of Indigenous and colonial history.

North of Coen

Coen is the last town before either Weipa (260km) or Bamaga (440km), so to some degree this is where the Cape trip really begins. It's reasonably easy going (and partly sealed) along the Peninsula Developmental Rd to Weipa, but things get more interesting at the turn-off to the Telegraph Rd and the journey north to Bramwell Junction. Along the way is the turn-off to Iron Range National Park and Chilli Beach (p437).

The **Archer River Roadhouse** (07-4060 3266; sites adult/child $10/5, s/d $100/150, meals $11-36; 8am-8pm;), 66km north of Coen, serves the best burgers on the Cape and is the last fuel before Bramwell Junction (170km north on Telegraph Rd) or Weipa (197km west on the Peninsula Developmental Rd).

North of Archer River, it's easy going as the road is now sealed almost all the way to the junction with the Telegraph Rd. If heading to Weipa, consider calling in at **Merluna Station** (07-4060 3209; www.merlunastation.com.au; camping adult/child $13/5, s/d without bathroom $90/100, units from $130;), one of the Cape's few farmstays.

Follow the Telegraph Rd north for a rough and bumpy 22km stretch to the Wenlock River crossing. There's a bridge, but flood waters can reach over 14m here. It's worth stopping at the welcoming and historic **Moreton Telegraph Station** (07-4060 3360; www.moretonstation.com.au; camping adult/child $10/5, safari tents $140, cabins $180; 8am-6pm), where there's good camping and bushwalking.

The turn-off to **Bramwell Station** (07-4060 3300; www.bramwellstationcapeyork.com.au; camping per person $10), Australia's northernmost cattle station, is 5km before the **Bramwell Junction Roadhouse** (07-4060 3230; unpowered sites adult/child $10/5; 7am-7pm), which marks the intersection of the Southern Bypass Rd and the rugged 4WD-only Old Telegraph Track. The roadhouse has the last fuel and supplies before the Jardine River Ferry.

Weipa

The largest town on the Cape, Weipa is essentially a mining town – the site of the world's largest bauxite mine (the ore from which aluminium is processed). Don't let that put you off though: many Cape travellers venture out this way for a taste of the Gulf waters, for the legendary barramundi fishing and to explore camping opportunities north to Mapoon.

Surprisingly for such a remote region, Weipa is a full-service town (thanks largely to Rio Tinto), with a large **supermarket** (Kerr Point Dr; 8am-7pm Mon-Wed & Fri, 8am-9pm Thu, 8am-5pm Sat) and a **golf course**

(07-4069 7332; www.carpentariagolfclub.com; 1 Tom Morrison Dr; from 8am).

The 2½-hour Town & Mine Tour gives a historical overview of Weipa and visits the mind-blowingly massive bauxite mining operation, where 22,000 tonnes of bauxite is mined every 24 hours and promptly sent onto waiting ships in the harbour.

At Evans Landing, the Western Cape Cultural Centre is worth a look for its historical and environmental displays.

Sleeping & Eating

Weipa Caravan Park & Camping Ground CAMPGROUND $
(07-4069 7871; www.campweipa.com.au; Lot 172, Kerr Point Dr; powered/unpowered sites $38/30, cabins $70-145, villas & lodge r $170-190;) This shady spot on the waterfront operates as the town's informal tourist office, organising mine and fishing tours, including the popular **Town & Mine Tours** (adult/child $40/15; 8.30am & 2.30pm). Facilities are good and the camping is complemented by a range of cabins, villas and beachfront lodge rooms. Easy access to the beach.

Heritage Resort MOTEL $$
(07-4069 8000; www.heritageresort.com.au; Kerr Point Dr; s/d $150/165;) The spacious rooms and comfy beds are a welcome surprise at this friendly motel-style resort next to the shopping complex. There's a restaurant serving everything from Thai to pizzas and an inviting palm-shaded pool.

★ **Bauxite Bill's** BISTRO $$$
(07-4090 6666; 10 Duyfken Cres; mains $28-40; noon-2pm & 6-8.30pm;) The seafood and grill restaurant at **Albatross Bay Resort** (1800 240 663; www.albatrossbayresort.com.au; 10 Duyfken Cres; d $165-235;) is the top place to eat in town and prices reflect that. Dine on local barramundi and big steaks in the air-con restaurant or out on the deck. The attached Sports Bar has cheaper bar meals all day from noon.

Bramwell Junction to Jardine River

Bramwell Junction marks the intersection of the two routes north to the **Jardine River Ferry** (07-4069 1369; return with/without trailer $129/99, motorbike $39; 8am-5pm). The longer route on the regularly graded and partly sealed Southern and Northern Bypass

Rds is quicker, avoiding the difficult creek crossings between the Wenlock and Jardine Rivers.

The more direct but extreme 4WD route along the **Old Telegraph Track** (OTT) is for serious adventurers only; it has deep corrugations, powdery sand and difficult creek crossings, especially the Palm Creek and Dulhunty River crossings and notorious Gunshot Creek. The OTT follows the remnants of the Overland Telegraph Line, constructed during the 1880s to allow communication between Cairns and the Cape.

Roughly halfway along its northern trajectory, the Old Telegraph Track (OTT) reconnects with the Southern Bypass Rd for about 9km, until the Northern Bypass Rd heads west (then north) to the Jardine River Ferry crossing. Follow the signposts and hit the OTT for just a few easily negotiated kilometres to reach the turn-off to stunning **Fruit Bat Falls**, with its crystal-clear swimming hole and picnic area (no camping). It's a further 7km from this turn-off along the OTT to the turn-off for **Eliot and Twin Falls**. The falls and the deep, emerald-green swimming holes are spectacular, but getting here requires crossing Scrubby Creek, so check conditions in advance. It's worth a long sojourn at the extremely popular **Eliot Falls Campground** (☑ 13 74 68; www.npsr.qld.gov.au; per person/family $6.15/24.60), for which you must book.

After Eliot Falls, between Sam Creek and Mistake Creek, a rugged track heads west, rejoining the Northern Bypass Rd for about 45km to the Jardine River Ferry. This route requires a couple of tricky creek crossings, but avoids the need to backtrack via Scrubby Creek.

When you reach the croc-infested Jardine, Queensland's largest perennial river, there's a roadhouse, camping and the Jardine River Ferry, run by the Injinoo Community Council. A bridge across the Jardine has been proposed and partly funded, but is yet to get the green light.

Bamaga & Seisia

Bamaga, 45km north of the Jardine River, is home to Cape York Peninsula's largest Torres Strait Islander community. Five kilometres northwest of Bamaga, coastal Seisia looks out across the Torres Strait and is the

IRON RANGE NATIONAL PARK

Roughly 36km north of the Archer River Roadhouse (p436), a turn-off leads 135km through the Iron Range National Park – comprising Australia's largest area of lowland rainforest, with animals found no further south in Australia – to the tiny coastal settlement of **Portland Roads**. Camp just south of here at **Chilli Beach** (www.npsr.qld.gov.au; adult/family $6.15/24.60), or savour a little comfort in **Portland House** (☑ 07-4060 7193; www.portlandhouse.com.au; cottages per person from $95), a self-contained beachside cottage.

About 40km south of Portland Roads is the Lockhart River Aboriginal Community, where you can get fuel and groceries (no alcohol) or visit the gallery at **Lockhart River Art** (☑ 07-4060 7341; http://lockhartriverart.com.au; 1 Piiramo Rd, Lockhart; ⊙ hours vary).

ideal tropical base from which to explore the Tip.

Cape York Adventures (☑ 07-4069 3302; www.capeyorkadventures.com.au; boat charter per day $800, 5-day fishing/camping trips $2999) offers half-/full-day fishing trips ($125/250 per person) and a day trip to Thursday and Horn Islands ($199).

Seisia Holiday Park (☑ 07-4203 0992; www.seisiaholidaypark.com; Koraba Rd, Seisia; sites adult/child $12/6, powered sites $20/12, s/d from $85/125; ❄) is a popular camping ground with cabins, A-frame villas, self-contained cottages and a kiosk serving meals ($12 to $28) daily except Monday. The park is also the booking agent for the ferry to Thursday Island and a range of local tours.

The beachfront outlook is fine from laid-back **Loyalty Beach Campground & Fishing Lodge** (☑ 07-4069 3372; www.loyalty beach.com; 1 Loyalty Beach Rd; unpowered sites adult/child $12/6, powered sites per vehicle extra $5, budget d $95, lodge s/d $145/165; ❄), 4km by road from Seisia wharf or a 1.5km walk along the beach. It's a pick-your-own-site sort of place, but there are also simple rooms and a self-contained beach house for those who want to sleep in style. There's a decent restaurant and bar – book ahead for evening meals.

The Tip

You're almost there! It's only 33km and a relatively easy drive from Bamaga to the Tip of Australia.

From Bamaga the road north passes Lockerbie Homestead. The **Croc Tent** (☑ 07-4069 3210; www.croctent.com.au; cnr Punsand Bay & Pajinka Rds; ◷8am-6pm), across the road, sells souvenirs and provides an unofficial tourist information service. Turning left here, it's 11km on a rough road to the idyllic oasis of **Cape York Camping** (☑ 07-4069 1722; www.capeyorkcamping.com.au; Punsand Bay Rd; powered/unpowered sites per person $33/17, d from $190; ▣▣) on beautiful Punsand Bay.

Back on the main road to the Tip you'll pass through **Lockerbie Scrub**, the northernmost rainforest in Australia, before reaching a Y-junction.

The track right leads to the pretty foreshore and campground at **Somerset**. The inviting lodge you see across the water on Pabaju (Albany) Island awaits you at the end of a serious day's fishing with the friendly folk at **CY Fishing Charters** (☑ 07-4069 2708; www.cyfishingcharters.com.au; Pabaju Island; day charters per person from $200, d per person from $150).

The left track leads 10km past the now derelict Pajinka Wilderness Lodge to a car park, from where a 1km walk along the beach or over the headland takes you to the Tip of Cape York, the northernmost point of mainland Australia.

Thursday Island & Horn Island

POP 2610 (THURSDAY ISLAND), 539 (HORN ISLAND)

The Torres Strait Islands, Australia's most northern frontier, consist of more than 100 islands stretching like stepping stones for 150km from the top of Cape York Peninsula to Papua New Guinea. The islands vary from the rocky, northern extensions of the Great Dividing Range to small coral cays and rainforest-covered volcanic mountains.

Horn Island is the air hub for the islands and the Cape, connected by regular ferries to nearby Thursday Island (TI). **Prince of Wales Island** is the largest of the group, but tiny TI (only 3 sq km) is the administrative capital, 30km off the Cape. Although it lacks its own freshwater supply, the island was selected for its deep harbour, sheltered port and proximity to major shipping channels.

Permission to visit outer islands may be required; contact the **Torres Strait Regional Council** (☑ 07-4034 5700; www.tsirc.qld. gov.au; 46 Victoria Pde, Thursday Island; ◷9am-5pm Mon-Fri).

◉ Sights & Activities

★**Torres Strait**
Heritage Museum   MUSEUM
(☑ 07-4090 3333; www.torresstraitheritage.com; 24 Outie St, Horn Island; museum adult/child $7/3.50, tours from $45/22.50; ◷9am-5pm) Fascinating tours revealing the island's significant and all-but-forgotten military history, including fixed gun sites and aircraft wrecks, are run by the friendly folk at this wonderful local history museum on Horn Island. Book ahead from June to September.

Gab Titui Cultural Centre   GALLERY
(☑ 07-4069 0888; www.gabtitui.com.au; cnr Victoria Pde & Blackall St, Thursday Island; ◷9am-4.30pm Mon-Fri, 10am-3pm Sat) FREE On Thursday Island, the Gab Titui Cultural Centre houses a modern gallery displaying the cultural history of the Torres Strait, and hosts cultural events and changing exhibitions by local artists. Tours ($8 per person) by appointment.

LAX Tours   CULTURAL
(☑ 07-4069 1356, 0427 691 356; www.laxcharters andtours.com.au; Thursday Island; tours per person from $60) Friendly Thursday Island local Dirk will show you around his island, including Green Hill Fort and the Japanese Pearl Divers Memorial, on personalised one-hour tours. Charter fishing trips are also available.

Peddells Tours   BUS
(☑ 07-4069 1551; www.peddellsferry.com.au; adult/child from $32/16; ◷8.30am-5pm) Peddells runs 90-minute bus tours of Thursday Island, taking in all the major tourist sites. Also offers Cape York 4WD day trips and Horn Island WWII tours.

🛏 Sleeping & Eating

Gateway Torres Strait Resort   RESORT $$
(☑ 07-4069 2222; www.torresstrait.com.au; 24 Outie St, Horn Island; r from $230; ▣@▣) This friendly resort has 22 self-contained retro units, a saltwater pool and a licensed restaurant. It's a five-minute walk from the Horn Island wharf.

Grand Hotel   HOTEL $$

(☎ 07-4069 1557; www.grandhotelti.com.au; 6 Victoria Pde, Thursday Island; s $150-230, d $190-310; ❇ @) On the hill behind TI wharf, the Grand has a range of modern rooms from budget ones at the back to front rooms with ocean and mountain views. Rates include breakfast. The **restaurant** (mains $15-25; ⊘ noon-2pm & 6-8pm) serves some of TI's best meals.

❶ Getting There & Away

QantasLink (www.qantas.com.au) flies twice daily from Cairns to Horn Island, while **Skytrans** (☎ 1300 759 872; www.skytrans.com.au) flies there from Cairns on weekdays.

Peddells Ferry Service (☎ 07-4069 1551; www.peddellsferry.com.au; Engineers Jetty, Thursday Island; adult/child each way $58/29) runs regular ferries from the Seisia jetty to Thursday Island, and **McDonald Charter Boats** (☎ 1300 664 875; www.tiferry.com.au; adult/child return ferry $15/7.50; ⊘ office 9am-4pm Mon-Fri) operates a ferry service between the islands.

GULF SAVANNAH

The epic Savannah Way runs all the way from Cairns to Broome, skirting the top of the country. The Queensland section, linking the east coast with the Gulf of Carpentaria, from Cairns to Burketown, is one of the state's great road trips. With detours to Karumba and Boodjamulla (Lawn Hill) National Park, this is a real outback adventure, and you don't even need a 4WD to explore most of this route in the Dry. Check www.gulf-savannah.com.au and www.savannah way.com.au for more info.

❶ Getting There & Away

Rex (☎ 13 17 13; www.rex.com.au) flies on weekdays between Cairns and Normanton (from $380) and twice weekly from Cairns to Burketown (from $460).

Trans North (☎ 07-4096 8644; www.trans northbus.com) runs a bus three times a week between Cairns and Karumba ($156, 11 hours), stopping at all towns, including Undara turn-off ($68, 4½ hours) and Normanton ($150, 10 hours). It departs at 6.30am from Cairns Monday, Wednesday and Friday, and Karumba Tuesday, Thursday and Saturday.

No public buses link Normanton with Mt Isa or Burketown.

Undara Volcanic National Park

About 190,000 years ago, the Undara shield volcano erupted, sending waves of molten lava coursing through the surrounding landscape. While the surface of the lava cooled and hardened, hot lava continued to race through the centre of the flows, eventually leaving the world's longest continuous (though fragmented) lava tubes from a single vent.

A worthwhile detour is the signposted drive to **Kalkani Crater**. The crater rim walk is an easy 2.5km circuit from the day-use car park, with good views over the surrounding countryside.

Opera in the Outback (www.undara.com. au; Undara Experience; tickets from $53, 3-day pass $267; ⊘ Oct) and **Outback Rock & Blues** (Undara Experience; weekend pass $154; ⊘ Apr) are two annual very different music events staged at Undara Experience Resort in October.

Undara is 15km south of the Savannah Way on a sealed road.

The Undara lava tubes can only be visited by guided tour with **Undara Experience** (☎ 07-4097 1900, 1800 990 992; www.undara. com.au; tours adult/child/family from $58/29/174) and there are three main daily tours leaving from the resort.

🛏 Sleeping & Eating

In rustic bushland just outside the national park, **Undara Experience Resort** (☎ 1800 990 992; www.undara.com.au; Undara Rd; powered/unpowered sites per adult $18.50/15, swag tent d $75, railway carriage d $175; ❇ ❇) has a super range of accommodation, from a shady campground to nifty little swag tents on raised platforms and modern en-suite rooms. Pride of place goes to the restored railway carriages, charmingly fitted out, some with en suite. Lots of bushwalks and easy access to the lava tubes.

The resort is something of an oasis, with a pool, a store, a good **restaurant** (dinner mains $22-31; ⊘ noon-2pm & 6-8pm) and bar, barbecue areas and campfire activities.

Undara to Croydon

About 32km west of the tiny gem-fossicking centre of **Mt Surprise**, the partly sealed **Explorers' Loop** (check road conditions) takes you on a 150km circuit through old gold-mining towns. At **Einasleigh**, have a drink at the only pub before visiting the Copperfield gorge. Beyond the small town of **Forsayth** is the real reason to venture out to this remote location - the private spring-fed oasis of **Cobbold Gorge**, one of those unexpectedly beautiful outback finds. **Cobbold Gorge Village** (☑ 1800 669 922, 07-4062 5470; www.cobboldgorge.com.au; Cobbold Gorge; powered/unpowered sites $38/28, with en suite $52, cabins $120-145; ☺ Apr-Oct; ✽🛜🛝) runs three-hour bushwalking **tours** (☑ 07-4062 5470, 1800 669 922; www.cobboldgorge.com.au; Cobbold Gorge; adult/child/family $86/43/216; ☺ 10am Apr-Oct, plus 1.30pm Jun-Aug) that culminate in a boat cruise through the stunning gorge. The infinity pool with a swim-up bar, restaurant and lush camp sites at the resort are a welcome find out here.

Georgetown (population 244) is the endpoint of the loop, back on the Savannah Way. The only real attraction here is the flash **Terrestrial Centre** (☑ 07-4062 1485; Low St, Georgetown; ☺ 8am-4.30pm Mon-Fri, 9.30am-3.30pm Sat & Sun), home to a visitor centre and the **Ted Elliot Mineral Collection** (☑ 07-4062 1485; Low St, Georgetown; $5; ☺ 8am-4.30pm Mon-Fri, 9.30am-3.30pm Sat & Sun), a shimmering collection of more than 4500 minerals, gems and crystals from all over Australia.

Croydon

POP 310

Incredibly, little Croydon was once the biggest town in the Gulf thanks to a short but lucrative gold rush. Gold was discovered in Croydon in 1885, but by the end of WWI it had run out and the place became little more than a ghost town.

Today there's a small but well-preserved historic precinct; Croydon's **visitor information centre** (☑ 07-4748 7152; Samwell St; ☺ 9am-4.30pm daily Apr-Sep, 9am-4.30pm Mon-Fri Oct-Mar) has a map of the main sights. **Lake Belmore** (Lake Belmore Rd), 4km north of the centre, is stocked with barramundi if you feel like fishing - or swimming.

At the timber **Croydon General Store** (☑ 07-4745 6163; 95 Sircom St; ☺ 7am-6.30pm Mon-Fri, 9am-7.30pm Sat & Sun) the sign declares this the 'oldest store in Australia, established 1894'. The interior is definitely a throwback to ye olde days: wooden floorboards and the small collection of historical curios are worth checking out.

For an overnight stay, try the friendly **Croydon Caravan Park** (☑ 07-4745 6238; www.croydon.qld.gov.au/croydon-caravan-park; cnr Brown & Alldridge Sts; powered/unpowered sites $30/20, cabins d/f $100/120; ✽🛝) or the town's only remaining pub, the **Club Hotel** (☑ 07-4745 6184; www.croydonclubhotel.com; cnr Brown & Sircom Sts; d $80, units $115; ✽🛝), with self-contained units and poolside rooms. The bar and bistro serve up huge meals ($23 to $30) and pizza ($18 to $20), ice-cold beer, and sunset views from the streetside verandah.

Normanton

POP 1470

The port for Croydon's gold rush, Normanton boasts a broad and rather long main street lined with some colourful old buildings. These days it's a tourist junction for Karumba- and Burketown-bound travellers, and the terminus for the *Gulflander* train. The Norman River produces whopping barramundi; every Easter the **Barra Bash** lures big crowds, as do the **Normanton Rodeo**

HISTORIC GULF TRAINS

Two nostalgic train trips operate in the Gulf. The historic **Savannahlander** (☑ 07-4053 6848, 1800 793 848; www.savannahlander.com.au; one-way/return $250/426, child half-price), aka the 'Silver Bullet', chugs along a traditional mining route from Cairns to Forsayth and back, departing from Cairns on Wednesday at 6.30am and returning on Saturday at 6.40pm. A range of tours (including side trips to Chillagoe, Undara and Cobbold Gorge) and accommodation can be booked online.

The snub-nosed **Gulflander** (☑ 07-4745 1391, 1800 577 245; www.gulflander.com.au; adult one way/return $69/115, child half-price) runs once weekly in each direction between Normanton and Croydon on the 1891 gold-to-port railway line alongside the Gulf Developmental Rd. It leaves Normanton on Wednesday at 8.30am, and leaves Croydon on Thursday at 8.30am.

& **Show** (mid-June) and the **Normanton Races** (September).

Everyone stops to take a photo of **Krys the Crocodile** on Landsborough St. It's a supposedly life-sized statue of an 8.64m saltie shot by croc hunter Krystina Pawloski on the Norman River in 1958 – the largest recorded croc in the world.

The **Normanton Train Station** (☑07-4745 1391; Matilda St) `FREE` has a small museum and is home to the *Gulflander* when it's not journeying out to Croydon.

In the historic Burns Philp building, Normanton's excellent **visitor information & heritage centre** (☑07-4745 8444; www.carpentaria.qld.gov.au; cnr Caroline & Landsborough Sts; ◷9am-4pm Mon-Fri, to noon Sat & Sun Apr-Sep, closed Sun Oct-Mar) has a library, historical displays and lots of regional information.

Normanton Tourist Park (☑07-4745 1121, 1800 193 469; www.normantontouristpark.com.au; 14 Brown St; powered/unpowered sites $34/26, cabin d $120; ❄�﹖☀) has a shady setting, a huge pool and an artesian spa to soak in.

An impossible-to-miss main-street icon is the **Purple Pub** (☑07-4745 1324; cnr Landsborough & Brown Sts; s/d $100/120, mains $16-25; ❄), painted lurid aubergine because it was the only cheap paint available. Comfortable motel rooms congregate in the Brolga Palms motel out back.

Karumba

POP 590

Aaah, Karumba: fishing mecca and winter base of many a southern retiree. When the sun sinks into the Gulf of Carpentaria in a fiery ball of burnt ochre, this is a little piece of outback paradise. Even if you don't like fishing, Karumba is the only town accessible by sealed road on the entire Gulf coast, and it's a great place to kick back for a few days.

The actual town is on the Norman River, while Karumba Point – the better option for accommodation – is about 6km away by road on the beach. The two communities are also linked by a hot, exposed 3km walking path. Karumba's **visitor information centre** (☑07-4747 7522; www.carpentaria.qld.gov.au; Walker St, Karumba Town; ◷9am-4.30pm Mon-Fri, 10am-3pm Sat & Sun Apr-Sep, closed Sat & Sun Oct-Mar; �﹖) has details of fishing charters and cruises.

◉ Sights & Activities

Barramundi Discovery Centre HATCHERY
(☑07-4745 9359; 148 Yappar St, Karumba Town; adult/child $17.50/8.50; ◷tours 10.30am & 1.30pm Mon-Fri, 9.30am Sat & Sun, shop 9.30am-3pm Mon-Fri & 9am-noon Sat & Sun) Everything you ever wanted to know about the barramundi can be learnt on the fascinating guided tours at this hatchery and breeding centre, where you can also hand-feed 'barra'. The gift shop stocks locally made bags and wallets fashioned from barramundi, crocodile and cane-toad leather.

★**Croc & Crab Tours** TOURS
(☑0417-011 411; www.crocandcrab.com.au; half-day tours adult/child $120/60, cruises adult/child $80/40) These excellent half-day tours include crab-catching and croc-spotting on the Norman River, and a lunch of mud crabs and local prawns. Also offers sunset cruises to Sand Island.

Ferryman CRUISE
(☑07-4745 9155; www.ferryman.net.au; Gilbert St; sunset cruise adult/child $50/25, wildlife cruise $75/30) A sunset cruise on the Norman River and Gulf is de rigueur in Karumba. During the Dry, Ferryman operates regular sunset cruises that include cold drinks and prawn, fruit and cheese platters. Boats depart from Gilbert St pontoon in Karumba Town.

⌷ Sleeping & Eating

Karumba Point Sunset Caravan Park CARAVAN PARK $
(☑07-4745 9277; www.sunsetcp.com.au; 53 Palmer St, Karumba Point; powered/unpowered sites $43/37, cabins $127; ❄�﹖☀) Pricey sites and a bit cramped, but for location alone – right next to the boat ramp – this is the most popular of the five caravan parks in the Karumba region. Shady palm trees, clean amenities and free wifi (near reception) are bonuses.

Karumba Point Tourist Park CARAVAN PARK $
(☑07-4745 9306; www.karumbapoint.com.au; 2 Col Kitching Dr; powered/unpowered sites $36/26, onsite vans $60; ☀) This friendly van park on the road into Karumba Point has spacious sites and new cabins with en suites are planned. Activities, including bingo and the free fish fry on Saturday nights, keep visitors happy.

End of the Road Motel
MOTEL $$

(☑ 07-4745 9599; www.endoftheroadmotel.com.au; 26 Palmer St, Karumba Point; d $165-210; ❇ 🌐 ❄) Karumba's best all-round motel has a range of rooms from studios to self-contained one- and two-bedroom apartments, and sunset views from the garden. The best rooms have Gulf views, of course.

Ash's Holiday Units
MOTEL $$

(☑ 07-4745 9132; www.ashsholidayunits.com.au; 21 Palmer St, Karumba Point; s/d/tr $108/117/123, cottage d/tr $150/180; ❇ @ 🌐 ❄) The six self-contained motel-style cabins surround a small pool and sleep up to six people each. There's also a great-value two-bedroom cottage. The attached cafe serves great fish and chips, plus the 'barra' burger ($10).

The Boat Shed
SEAFOOD $

(☑ 07-4745 9501; dishes $7-15; ☺ 8am-7pm) Also called the Karumba Point Fishing Seafood Market, you know the fish is fresh here as the owners catch it themselves. Buy local seafood to go, or dine in on some of the best fish and chips around.

★ Sunset Tavern
PUB FOOD, SEAFOOD $$

(☑ 07-4745 9183; www.sunsettavern.com.au; The Esplanade, Karumba Point; mains $15-35; ☺ 10am-10pm) This big open-sided place is the hub of Karumba Point at sunset. It's the place to watch the sun sink into the Gulf over a glass of wine and a seafood platter. The food is reasonably good, but the view is better – arrive early for a seat at an outdoor table for the sweetest sunset experience.

Northwest Corner

The remote Northwest Corner will take you to one of Queensland's most beautiful national parks. The road from Normanton to Burketown is sealed for about 30km, then it's a well-maintained dirt road with concrete flood ways for about 120km to the Leichhardt River – usually passable to all vehicles in the Dry. The final 70km to Burketown is sealed. About 37km out of Normanton, turn off at the signposted stop by eerie **Burke & Wills Camp 119**, the northernmost camp of the ill-equipped explorers' wretched 1861 expedition – they came within just 5km of reaching the Gulf.

The alternative route south from Normanton is the Burke Developmental Rd (also called the Matilda Hwy), which is

sealed all the way to Cloncurry (380km), where it joins the Barkly and Flinders Hwys. Flood-way signs give you an idea of how big the waters get in the Wet.

Everyone stops at the **Burke & Wills Roadhouse** (☑ 07-4742 5909; sites per person $10, s/d $70/80, meals $8-30; ☺ 5.30am-10pm; ❇) to down a cold drink or refuel. From here the sealed Wills Developmental Rd shoots west to Gregory, from where you can continue north to Burketown or west to Boodjamulla National Park.

If you're travelling from outback Queensland to the Northern Territory (NT), there are two main routes. The easy way is the sealed Barkly Hwy from Mt Isa to Three Ways (640km), from where you can head south to Alice Springs or north to Darwin on the sealed Stuart Hwy. The more adventurous route is the continuation of the Savannah Way west of Burketown. It's almost 500km of partly sealed, but occasionally rough, 4WD territory from Burketown to Borroloola (NT) and beyond. This road is usually impassable in the Wet. Along the way you'll pass the **Doomadgee Aboriginal Community** (☑ 07-4745 8351), where you're welcome to buy fuel and supplies; village access is subject to council permission, and alcohol is restricted. It's another mostly sealed 80km of Melaleuca scrub to **Hell's Gate Roadhouse** (☑ 07-4745 8258; www.hells gateroadhouse.com.au; camping per person $10, powered sites $45, cabins from $70; ❇), 50km from the NT border. The roadhouse has fuel, camping, cabins and meals.

Burketown

POP 200

Burketown is isolated but accessible – the road in from Gregory is sealed and the road from Normanton is in good condition in the Dry. It's satisfyingly remote, endearingly friendly, and the fishing, either on the Albert River or 30km north at the Gulf, is legendary. This is also the best place in the world to witness the extraordinary 'morning glory' cloud phenomenon, a series of giant tubular clouds that roll in when conditions are right between August and November.

Burketown has a small **visitor centre** (☑ 07-4745 5111; cnr Musgrave & Burke St; ☺ 11am-4pm Mon-Fri Apr-Oct), a **caravan park** (☑ 07-4745 5118; www.burketowncaravanpark.net. au; Sloman St; powered sites s/d $29/35, cabins d $86-130; ❇), a cafe and the excellent

Burketown Pub (07-4745 5104; www.burke townpub.com; cnr Beames St & Musgrave; unit s/d $135/145, mains $17-38; ⊙ Wed-Sat from 10am, Sun-Tue from 11am; ❋), rebuilt after burning down in 2012.

Burketown to Boodjamulla National Park

The 120km road south from Burketown to one-pub Gregory is sealed but from there it's around 100km of partly unsealed road to the entrance to beautiful Boodjamulla (Lawn Hill) National Park.

Fuel is available at the **Gregory Downs Hotel** (07-4748 5566; Gregory; s/d camp sites $10/12, d units $100; ❋), a laid-back spot for a beer or pub meal (dinner Monday to Friday, a barbecue on Saturday night and lunch Sunday). From Gregory, the sealed Wills Development Rd leads 147km east to join the Matilda Hwy at Burke & Wills Roadhouse.

Boodjamulla National Park

Boodjamulla is simply one of the most beautiful and pristine places in all of outback Queensland. A series of deep flame-red sandstone gorges tower above the spring-fed, luminous green Lawn Hill Creek. Lush vegetation, including cabbage-leaf palms, pandanus and turkey bush line the gorge, providing a haven for wildlife at this outback oasis. The Waanyi Aboriginal people have inhabited the area for some 30,000 years, leaving traces of rock art.

In the southern part of the park is the World Heritage–listed **Riversleigh fossil field**, with a small **camping ground** (13 74 68; www.npsr.qld.gov.au; sites per person/family $6.15/24.60; ⊙ Mar-Oct), 4km south of the Riversleigh D site (the only part of the fossil field open to the public). This is thought to be the richest fossil mammal site in Australia with everything from giant snakes and carnivorous kangaroos to pocket-sized koalas. Campers must book ahead, and be totally self-sufficient.

🛏 Sleeping & Eating

There's an excellent national parks **camping ground** (13 74 68; www.npsr.qld.gov.au; sites per person/family $6.15/24.60) right next to Lawn Hill Gorge. While it has no power, there is running water, showers, toilets and a ranger office.

The main hub for accommodation is **Adel's Grove** (07-4748 5502; www.adelsgrove. com.au; camping d/f $36/50, safari tents with dinner, bed & breakfast $255-290, cabins $260-320), 10km east of the park entrance. It's an excellent mini-resort on the banks of Lawn Hill Creek with an on-site bar and **restaurant** (mains $10-18, 2-course dinner $35; ⊙ 7-8am, noon-2pm & 4-10pm) that has a big open-air deck. There's a shady riverside camping area (no power) separated from the main accommodation area. Other options are safari tents on raised platforms (riverside ones are more expensive), simple air-con cabins and new en-suite cabins. Most of the accommodation (other than camping) is on a dinner, bed and breakfast basis, but ask about bed-only if you prefer to self-cater. Fuel, food packs and basic groceries are available.

OUTBACK QUEENSLAND

Beyond the Great Dividing Range the outback sky opens up over tough country, both relentless and beautiful. Travellers come for the exotic and intimate Australian experience, their restlessness tamed by the sheer size of the place, its luminous colours and its silence.

This a region of rodeos and bush races, country pubs and characters, caravanning nomads, backpackers tending bars and burnt-orange sunsets. In the dry season, endless blue skies hover over stony deserts, matched only by the brilliant velvety clarity of the Milky Way at night.

Queensland's outback is an eye-wateringly vast region, but it's surprisingly accessible, criss-crossed by sealed roads and peppered with towns small and slightly smaller.

ⓘ Getting There & Away

The main driving routes include Townsville to Mt Isa on the Overlanders Way and Brisbane to Mt Isa on the Matilda Hwy.

Bus Queensland (1300 287 537; http://busqld.com.au) and **Greyhound Australia** (1300 473 946; www.greyhound.com.au) cover the major routes from Brisbane and Townsville.

Queensland Rail (13 16 17; www.queenslandrail.com.au) operates three major rail routes from the coast into the outback. *Spirit of the Outback* runs from Brisbane to Longreach, *Westlander* from Brisbane to Charleville, and *Inlander* from Townsville to Mt Isa.

Charters Towers to Cloncurry

The Flinders Hwy runs a gruelling but sealed and straight 775km from Charters Towers west to little Cloncurry. The highway was originally a Cobb & Co coach run, and along its length are small towns established as coach stopovers. The main towns are Prairie, Hughenden, Richmond and Julia Creek.

In Hughenden, drop into the **Flinders Discovery Centre** (☑07-4741 2970; www.visit hughenden.com.au; 37 Gray St; adult/child $5/2; ☺9am-5pm daily Apr-Oct, 9am-5pm Mon-Fri & 9am-2pm Sat & Sun Nov-Mar) to see the replica Muttaburrasaurus skeleton, whose fossils were found south of here. **Porcupine Gorge National Park** (☑07-4741 1113; www.npsr.qld. gov.au/parks/porcupine-gorge; sites per person/ family $6.15/24.60), 70km north of Hughenden, is a fine place for remote camping and bushwalking.

In tiny Richmond, don't miss the excellent **Kronosaurus Korner** (☑07-4741 3429; www.kronosauruskorner.com.au; 91-93 Goldring St; adult/child/family $20/10/40; ☺8.30am-5pm Apr-Oct, to 4pm Nov-Mar), a museum housing Australia's best collection of marine fossils, most found by local landholders. Pride of place goes to an almost complete 4.25m pliosaur skeleton – one of Australia's best-preserved vertebrate fossils – and a partial skeleton of *Kronosaurus queenslandicus*, the largest known marine reptile to have lived here. You can hire maps and fossil-finding equipment, or join one of the two-hour guided digs (adult/child $30/25) at 3pm on Tuesday and Thursday from May to September.

Cloncurry

POP 2310

The 'Curry' is renowned as the birthplace of the Royal Flying Doctor Service, and **John Flynn Place** (☑07-4742 4125; www.johnflynn place.com.au; cnr Daintree & King Sts; admission by donation; ☺9am-4pm Mon-Fri year round, 9am-3pm Sat & Sun May-Sep) is a must-see museum celebrating Dr Flynn's work setting up this invaluable outback service. It's the only town of any real size between Charters Towers and Mt Isa. In the 19th century Cloncurry was the largest producer of copper in the British Empire. Today it's a busy pastoral centre with a reinvigorated mining industry.

There's information and historical displays at **Cloncurry Unearthed** (☑07-4742 1361; www.cloncurry.qld.gov.au; Flinders Hwy; museum admission by donation; ☺8.30am-4.30pm Mon-Fri year-round, 9am-4.30pm Sat & Sun May-Oct, to 2pm Sat & Sun Nov-Apr; ☎) in the Mary Kathleen Memorial Park.

The historic main building at the **Wagon Wheel Motel** (☑07-4742 1866; 54 Ramsay St; s/d from $95/105; ❄☎✸), with a restaurant and bar, is said to be the oldest licensed premises in northwest Queensland. At the back, the motel rooms are clean and comfortable with TV and fridge. It's worth paying the few extra dollars for the larger and newer deluxe rooms.

Constructed of rammed red earth, the **Gidgee Inn** (☑07-4742 1599; www.gidgeeinn. com.au; McIlwraith St; d $165-185; ❄☎✸) is Cloncurry's most upmarket accommodation with reasonably plush and comfortable rooms for these parts, a pool and a good restaurant and bar.

Mt Isa

POP 22,500

You can't miss the smelter stacks from the zinc mine as you drive into Mt Isa, one of Queensland's longest-running mining towns and a travel and lifestyle hub for outback Queensland. Whether you've come to work, play or just pass through, a night spent in one of Isa's clubs may cause you to forget you're in the remote outback.

At night the surrounding cliffs glow and zing with industry; the view from City Lookout of the twinkling mine lights and silhouetted smokestacks is strangely pretty. The surrounding country has a stark red beauty, too. Strange rock formations – padded with olive-green spinifex – line the perimeter of town, and deep-blue sunsets eclipse all unnatural light.

Proud locals share life in the dusty heat and the geographic isolation – often over multiple beers – and the sense of community is palpable. Try to visit in mid-August for Australia's largest rodeo.

◉ Sights & Activities

★**City Lookout** VIEWPOINT
(Lookout Rd; ☺24hr) FREE Everyone should make the short trip up to the city lookout for excellent 360-degree views of Mt Isa. The best time is sunset, when the smelter stacks

are silhouetted and the mine lights begin to twinkle.

★ Outback at Isa
MUSEUM

(📞07-4749 1555; www.experiencemountisa.com.au; 19 Marian St; ⊙8.30am-5pm) The award-winning Outback at Isa combines the visitor centre (p446) and booking office with three of Isa's major attractions. The **Hard Times Mine** (adult/child/family $76/35/199; ⊙tours daily) is an authentic underground trip to give you the full Isa mining experience. **Isa Experience & Outback Park** (adult/child/family $20/10/50; ⊙8.30am-5pm) is a hands-on museum providing a colourful and articulate overview of mining, pioneering and local history. The fascinating **Riversleigh Fossil Centre** (adult/child/family $12/8/33; ⊙8.30am-5pm) recreates finds from the world-renowned fossil fields at Boodjamulla National Park.

There are various combination packages, including the two-day pass (adult/child $99/45), which includes admission to all of the attractions.

Underground Hospital
MUSEUM

(📞07-4749 0281; Joan St; guided tours adult/child $16/free; ⊙10am-2pm) With the threat of Japanese bombing raids in 1942, and a ready supply of miners and equipment, Mt Isa Hospital went underground. The bombs never came but the underground hospital was preserved. You can also see an example of a tent house, once common in Mt Isa, here.

School of the Air
TOURS

(📞07-4744 8333; www.mtisasde.eq.edu.au; 137-143 Abel Smith Pde; tours $2; ⊙tours 10am Mon-Fri) These one-hour tours during school term demonstrate the outback's isolation and innovation.

✦✦ Festivals & Events

Mt Isa Rodeo
RODEO

(www.isarodeo.com.au; ⊙2nd weekend in Aug) Mt Isa is the rodeo capital of Australia and this is the biggest event of the year. Don't miss it if you're in town, and book ahead for accommodation.

🛏 Sleeping

Mt Isa Caravan Park
CARAVAN PARK $

(📞07-4743 3252; www.mtisacaravanpark.com.au; 112 Marian St; powered/unpowered sites $35/28, cabins $90-140; 🅿🏊) The closest caravan park to the town centre is an impressive

tourist village with a swag of sleeping options, including self-contained units. There's also a small pool, shady grassed areas and friendly management.

Travellers Haven
HOSTEL $

(📞07-4743 0313; www.travellershaven.com.au; 75 Spence St; dm/s/d $30/60/75; 🆒@🛜🏊) The rooms are fairly modest but this is the only genuine backpacker hostel in Isa – and most of outback Queensland – so it's a great meeting place and has the essentials like a pool, a kitchen and free wi-fi. The owners offer informal tours and may be able to help you find work locally.

It's a short walk from Outback at Isa (p445), or you can call ahead for pick-up.

Fourth Avenue Motor Inn
MOTEL $$

(📞07-4743 3477; www.fourthavemotorinn.com; 14 Fourth Ave; d/f from $140/160; 🆒🛜🏊) This friendly, colourful motor inn, in a quiet residential zone, has a large saltwater pool in a neat outdoor area. Rooms are a touch above the town average for the price.

Spinifex Motel
MOTEL $$

(📞07-4749 2944; www.spinifexmotel.com.au; 79-83 Marian St; r $175-195, apt $395; 🆒@🛜) A brilliant little four-star establishment with large, tiled rooms, tasteful furniture, writing desks and private outdoor patios. The new serviced apartments are three-bedroom townhouses perfect for groups or families.

★ Red Earth Hotel
BUSINESS HOTEL $$$

(📞1800 603 488; www.redearth-hotel.com.au; Rodeo Dr; d $239-269; 🆒@🛜) The boutique Red Earth is undoubtedly Mt Isa's top address (unless you want a pool), with period-style furniture, claw-foot bath-tubs and uniformed staff. It's worth paying the little extra for a private balcony, spa and huge TV. There's a cocktail bar, and an excellent restaurant in the lobby. Online discounts available.

✕ Eating & Drinking

Brew & Scoop
CAFE $

(📞07-4743 3353; 13a West St; dishes $7-20; ⊙6am-9pm) Great coffee and ice cream, but this fine all-day cafe also offers super breakfast fare along with burgers, wraps and fish and chips.

Happy Box Noodles
ASIAN $

(📞07-4743 0889; 32 Miles St; mains $11-13; ⊙11.30am-9.30pm Sun-Wed, to 10pm Thu-Sat) Quick and tasty takeaway pan-Asian noodle

Mt Isa

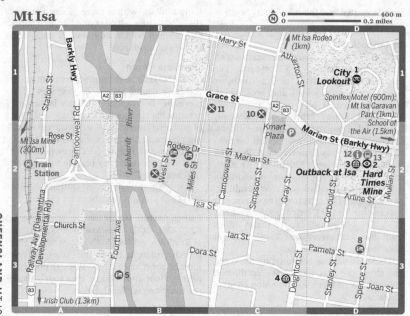

and rice dishes, including sushi, laksa and chow mein.

Frog & Toad Bistro
AUSTRALIAN $$

(☑07-4743 2365; Buffs Club, 35 Simpson St; mains $14-35; ⊙11.30am-2pm & 6-9pm Mon-Fri, 7.30am-2pm & 6-9pm Sat & Sun; 🚼) In Buffs Club (p446), the Frog & Toad serves up generous portions of pasta, pizza, steak and schnitzel in true Aussie style. Kids' menu available.

Rodeo Bar & Grill
STEAK $$

(☑07-4749 8888; cnr Miles St & Rodeo Dr; lunch $15-20, mains $20-32; ⊙6.30am-11.30am, noon-5pm & 6-9pm) Booth seating brings a touch of intimacy to this cavernous bar-restaurant with open kitchen inside the renovated Isa Hotel. The menu offers something for everyone, from pizzas and tapas-style snacks to outback-sized steaks. Breakfast in a booth is surprisingly good, too.

Buffs Club
BAR

(☑07-4743 2365; www.buffs.com.au; 35 Simpson St; ⊙8am-3am Mon-Fri, 7.30am-3am Sat & Sun, bars open 10am) The most central and enduringly popular of Isa's clubs, Buffs has the Blue Tongue sports bar, Boomerang coffee shop, cocktail bar, sun deck and live entertainment on weekends. You can eat well at the Frog & Toad Bistro.

Irish Club
BAR

(☑07-4743 2577; www.theirishclub.com.au; 1 19th Ave; ⊙10am-2am, to 3am Fri & Sat) A couple of kilometres south of town, the Irish Club feels a bit more sophisticated than Isa's other clubs and is a truly multipurpose venue. There's a gaming room, piano bar, the cavernous Blarney Bar, coffee, the slightly tacky but heaving Rish nightclub, a decent restaurant and even a gym.

ℹ Information

Mt Isa Visitor Information Centre (☑07-4749 1555; www.experiencemountisa.com.au; 19 Marian St; ⊙8.30am-5pm) The helpful visitor and booking centre is inside Outback at Isa (p448).

ℹ Getting There & Away

AIR

Rex (☑13 17 13; www.rex.com.au) flies direct from Mt Isa to Townsville daily and services many outback destinations, including Birdsville and Burketown. **Qantas** (☑13 13 13; www.qantas.com.au) has flights to Brisbane and Townsville, while **Virgin Australia** (☑13 67 89) has a daily flight to Brisbane.

The **airport** (☑07-4409 3000; www.mountisaairport.com.au; Barkly Hwy) is 8km north of the town centre.

Mt Isa

⊚ **Top Sights**
1 City Lookout D1
2 Hard Times Mine........................... D2
3 Outback at Isa D2

⊚ **Sights**
Isa Experience & Outback
Park.. (see 3)
Riversleigh Fossil Centre .... (see 3)
4 Underground Hospital C3

🛏 **Sleeping**
5 Fourth Avenue Motor Inn................ B3
6 Isa Hotel B2
7 Red Earth Hotel.............................. B2
8 Travellers Haven............................. D3

✖ **Eating**
9 Brew & Scoop................................. B2
10 Frog & Toad Bistro C1
11 Happy Box Noodles......................... C1
Rodeo Bar & Grill .... (see 6)

⊙ **Drinking & Nightlife**
Buffs Club .... (see 10)

ℹ **Information**
12 Mt Isa Visitor Information
Centre... D2

ℹ **Transport**
13 Bus Queensland.............................. D2
Greyhound Australia .... (see 13)

BUS

Bus Queensland (p443) has a daily service from Mt Isa to Brisbane ($220, 21 hours) via Charleville and Longreach, and travels three times a week to Townsville ($133, 10 hours) via Charters Towers.

Greyhound Australia (p443) offers twice-weekly services to Townsville ($132, 11½ hours) and Alice Springs ($225, 15 hours).

Both companies have depots at **Outback at Isa** (p445).

TRAIN

The **Queensland Rail** (☎1800 872 467; www. queenslandrailtravel.com.au) *Inlander* train runs between Mt Isa and Townsville twice a week.

Mt Isa to Charleville

The Barkly and Landsborough Hwys dissect central Queensland, encompassing a large area of largely flat cattle farming country. For travellers it's by turns dinosaur country, Waltzing Matilda country, Qantas country and even Crocodile Dundee country.

The first place to stop after the Cloncurry turn-off is tiny McKinlay. It's 30 years since *Crocodile Dundee* hit the screens, but the McKinlay pub, aka **Walkabout Creek Hotel** (☎07-4746 8424; Landsborough Hwy, McKinlay; ⊙10am-midnight), is still today trading off its success. Stop in for a cold beer or pizza and check out the old photos and movie memorabilia. There's a camping ground out the back.

Further along, Kynuna is also worth a stop for the atmospheric **Blue Heeler Hotel** (☎07-4746 8683; Landsborough Hwy, Kynuna; ⊙6am-9pm). Banjo Paterson is said to have performed 'Waltzing Matilda' here after visiting nearby Combo Waterhole, possibly the inspiration for the song's billabong.

Winton

POP 950

Winton is a satisfying and friendly country town in the heart of cattle, sheep and dinosaur country – this is the best base from which to explore central Queensland's remarkable prehistoric fossil finds. The town also does its best to make the most of its 'Waltzing Matilda' connections. Banjo Paterson reputedly wrote the Aussie anthem after a visit here, and it was first performed at the North Gregory Hotel (p448).

Elderslie St is a colourful streetscape of old timber pubs, historic buildings and opal shops, so there's plenty of photogenic period charm here.

Winton's tribute to Banjo Paterson, the **Waltzing Matilda Centre**, burned down in 2015, but should be rebuilt and open by the time you read this.

⊙ Sights

Royal Theatre   THEATRE
(73 Elderslie St; Opal Walk $5, screening $7; ⊙9am-5pm, screenings 8pm Wed Apr-Sep) There's an old-movie-world charm in the canvas chairs, corrugated tin walls and star-studded ceiling at this classic semi-outdoor theatre (1918), complete with the world's biggest deckchair. Enter via the Opal Walk gallery or come for the nostalgic film on Wednesday night.

Musical Fence   PUBLIC ART
(off Kennedy Developmental Rd; ⊙24hr) This quirky bit of outback art features a musical wire fence and other bits of steel to bang on to your heart's content.

DINOSAUR TRAIL

Fossil fiends, amateur palaeontologists and those who are simply fans of *Jurassic Park* will love outback Queensland's triangular Dinosaur Trail. The northern points are Richmond, home of Australia's richest collection of marine dinosaur fossils, and Hughenden, home of Muttaburrasaurus. But it's the Winton region that offers two of the best prehistoric attractions.

About 95 million years ago – give or take a few million – a herd of small dinosaurs got spooked by a predator and scattered. The resulting stampede left thousands of footprints in the stream bed, which nature remarkably conspired to fossilise and preserve. The **Dinosaur Stampede National Monument** (☑ 07-4657 0078; www.dinosaurtrackways.com.au; Winton-Jundah Rd, Lark Quarry; guided tours adult/child $25/12.50; ☺ 8.30am-5pm, tours 9.30am, 11am, noon, 1pm, 2pm & 3pm), at Lark Quarry 110km southwest of Winton, is outback Queensland's mini Jurassic Park, where you can see the remnants of the prehistoric stampede. Protected by a sheltered walkway, the site can only be visited by guided tour where guides will explain what scientists have deduced happened that day. There are no facilities to stay or eat, but it's a well-signposted drive on the partly unsealed Winton–Jundah road, suitable for 2WD vehicles in the Dry (allow 1½ hours).

The **Australian Age of Dinosaurs Museum** (☑ 07-4657 0712; www.australianageofdinosaurs.com; Lot 1, Dinosaur Dr; adult/child/family $33/18/75; ☺ 8.30am-5pm, guided tours hourly 9am-3pm, closed Sun Oct-Apr), 15km east of Winton on the Landsborough Hwy, is a fascinating interactive dinosaur research museum housed on a local cattle station atop a rugged plateau known as the 'Jump Up'. There are two sides to the museum – the laboratory and the collection, the latter comprising original dinosaur fossils found in the region that make up the incomplete skeletons of 'Matilda' and 'Banjo'. The latest discovery, announced in 2016, is a new species and genus of titanosaur named *Savannasaurus elliottorum*. Each side is visited on a 30-minute tour with a half-hour break in between. Fossil enthusiasts can book in advance for two days of working with technicians cleaning dinosaur bones ($164), or book well in advance for one of the annual three-week digs ($3700 per week).

Matilda Country Tours (☑ 07-4657 1607; www.matildacountrytouristpark.com; 43 Chirnside St; tours $45-85; ☺ 8am daily) offers daily bus transport to both sites.

Ask at visitor centres in the region about the **Dino Pass**, which gives reduced admission to all attractions on the Dinosaur Trail.

Arno's Wall SCULPTURE

(Vindex St) **FREE** Arno's Wall is one of Winton's quirky outback attractions – a 70m-long work-in-progress by artist Arno Grotjahn, featuring a huge range of industrial and household items, from TVs to motorcycles, ensnared in mortar.

Diamantina Heritage Truck & Machinery Museum MUSEUM

(☑ 0429 806 140; www.wintontruckmuseum.com; Kennedy Developmental Rd; $5; ☺ 8am-5pm) Fans of big trucks and old vehicles will love the historic collection of old Macks, Chevys and Model T Fords in this large shed. A special exhibit is the MAN truck belonging to the legendary Cape York female trucker 'Toots' Holzheimer, who drove long-haul for three decades from the 1960s.

🛏 Sleeping & Eating

There are three caravan parks in town, as well as a few motels.

★ North Gregory Hotel HOTEL $$

(☑ 07-4657 0647; www.northgregoryhotel.com; 67 Elderslie St; d $120-150; 🖳 🖵) This historic art-deco beauty has plenty of stories and is the pick of the town's pubs for accommodation in pub-style or en-suite rooms. The lobby is like a glamorous film-noir set and the rooms are styled somewhere between the pub's heyday and 20th-century Brisbane. 'Waltzing Matilda' was allegedly first performed by Banjo Paterson in the hotel on 6 April 1895.

Tattersalls Hotel PUB FOOD $$

(☑ 07-4657 1309; 78 Elderslie St; mains $17-30; ☺ noon-2pm & 6-8pm) This friendly corner pub is an incongruous foodie destination, with generous reasonably priced pub food best devoured on the wooden verandah facing the street. There are rooms upstairs and a **van park** (Werna St; powered sites $30) across the road.

ⓘ Getting There & Away

Bus Queensland (☑1300 287 537; http://busqld.com.au) stops at Winton on the daily run between Brisbane ($185, 20 hours) and Mt Isa ($108, 4½ hours).

Longreach

POP 3200

A prosperous, pioneering outback town, Longreach was the home of Qantas early last century, but these days it's equally famous for the Australian Stockman's Hall of Fame & Outback Heritage Centre, one of Queensland's best museums, and Cobb & Co stagecoach tours. The tropic of Capricorn passes through here – look for the marker near the **visitor centre** (☑07-4658 3555; 99 Eagle St; ☺9am-4.45pm Mon-Fri, 9am-noon Sat & Sun), which points to the torrid (north) and temperate (south) zones.

◉ Sights & Activities

★**Australian Stockman's Hall of Fame & Outback Heritage Centre** MUSEUM
(☑07-4658 2166; www.outbackheritage.com.au; Landsborough Hwy; adult/child/family $32/15.50/80; ☺9am-5pm) In a beautifully conceived building with an impressive multi-arched design, this is a fine museum, and also a tribute to outback pioneers, early explorers, stockmen and Indigenous Australians. Five themed galleries, some featuring interactive touch-screen displays, cover: Aboriginal culture; European exploration (there's a nifty map showing the trails of Burke and Wills, Ludwig Leichhardt, Ernest Giles and co); pioneers and pastoralists; 'Life in the Outback'; and the stockman's gallery.

★**Qantas Founders Outback Museum** MUSEUM
(☑07-4658 3737; www.qfom.com.au; Landsborough Hwy; adult/child/family $28/18/78; ☺9am-5pm, to 4pm Dec-Mar) Qantas Founders Outback Museum houses a life-sized replica of an Avro 504K, the first aircraft owned by the fledgling airline. Interactive multimedia and working displays tell the history of Qantas. Next door, the original 1921 Qantas hangar houses a mint-condition DH-61. Towering over everything outside is a bright and shiny retired 1979 **Boeing 747-200B Jumbo** (museum & jet tour adult/child/family $63/43/180, wing walks adult/child $65/55; ☺jet tours 9.30am, 11am, 1pm & 2.30pm, wing walks 11am, 12.30pm & 2.30pm). The tour of the Jumbo Jet and nearby Boeing 707 is fascinating, and you can do a wing-walk with safety harness (bookings essential).

Outback Pioneers TOURS
(☑07-4658 1776; www.outbackpioneers.com.au; 128 Eagle St; ☺8am-5pm Mon-Sat) The main tour operator in Longreach runs a sunset paddle-wheeler cruise, followed by dinner under the stars and campfire entertainment (adult/child/family $94/64/284). The Cobb & Co Stagecoach Experience ($94/64/284) is a highlight, combining a 45-minute horse-drawn stagecoach ride with a theatre show, lunch and a film, or you can opt for just the stagecoach ride ($74/49/221). Book ahead.

If you're short on time, Harry Redford's Old Time Tent Show is an entertaining hour from noon Monday to Friday (adult/child $15/10).

🛏 Sleeping & Eating

Longreach Tourist Park CARAVAN PARK $
(☑07-4658 1781; www.longreachtouristpark.com.au; 12 Thrush Rd; powered/unpowered sites $37/28, sites with bathroom $49, cabins from $115; ✳✳) This large, spacious park lacks grass but has a small grotto of spa pools, a new swimming pool and the Woolshed restaurant and bar.

★**Kinnon & Co Outback Lodges** LODGE $$
(☑07-4658 3811; www.outbackpioneers.com.au; 63-65 Ilfracombe Rd; self-contained cabins $130-160, slab huts $180; ✳✳) The comfortable self-contained lodges here are excellent value – a step up from the town's motels – and the timber slab huts and homestead stables offer a rustic pioneer outback feel with modern styling. There's a palm-shaded pool, native gardens and a large covered communal area. It's opposite the Qantas Founders Outback Museum (p449).

Longreach Motor Inn MOTEL $$
(☑07-4658 2322; www.outbacklongreach.com.au; 84 Galah St; d $145-180; ✳🛜✳) Huge rooms with corresponding balconies and professional staff are the features of this popular motel on the edge of the shopping strip. The gated pool and shady garden kill an afternoon with ease. The on-site restaurant, **Harry's** (☑07-4658 1996; mains $28-36; ☺5.30-8.30pm Mon-Sat), is among the best in Longreach.

Merino Bakery   BAKERY $
(☑ 07-4658 1715; 120 Eagle St; dishes $2-11; ⊙ 5am-
5pm Mon-Fri, 5am-1pm Sat, 7am-1pm Sun) There's
often a weekend queue for coffee, cakes and
fresh bread at this busy corner bakery. Delicious baked good, pies and sandwiches.

CCD Restaurant & Beer Garden   BISTRO $$
(☑ 07-4658 2798; 110 Eagle St; mains $15-35, ta-
pas $8-11; ⊙ 11am-2pm & 5.30-9.30pm daily, from
7.30am Fri-Sun) The narrow, darkened dining
room gives way to a shady beer garden out
the back at this stylish main-street bistro.
Steaks, pasta dishes and calamari salad are
complemented by tapas plates such as chilli
prawns and mini hot dogs.

🛍 Shopping

**Kinnon & Co
Station Store**   FASHION & ACCESSORIES
(☑ 07-4658 2006; www.outbackpioneers.com.au;
126 Eagle St; ⊙ 8.30am-5pm Mon-Fri, 9am-noon
Sat) The fabulous Station Store is crammed
with Aussie outback fashion – boots, akubra
hats, leather bags, clothing, saddles and
stockman's whips, along with unusual gifts
and souvenirs. Worth a look even if you're
not buying. Cafe attached.

ⓘ Getting There & Away

Bus Queensland (p451) stops daily on its run
between Brisbane ($160, 18 hours) and Mt Isa
($125, seven hours).

Greyhound Australia (☑ 1300 473 946; www.
greyhound.com.au) has a bus service between
Longreach and Rockhampton ($105, 9½ hours)
on Tuesday and Thursday. All buses stop outside
the Commercial Hotel.

Queensland Rail (☑ 13 16 17; www.queens
landrail.com.au) operates the twice-weekly
Spirit of the Outback service between Longreach
and Brisbane via Rockhampton.

Barcaldine

POP 1655

Barcaldine (bar-*call*-din), a historic little
outback pub town at the junction of the
Landsborough and Capricorn Hwys (Rte
66), gained its place in Australian history
in 1891 when it became the headquarters
of a major shearers' strike. The confronta-
tion led to the formation of the Australian
Workers' Party, forerunner of the Australian
Labor Party. The organisers' meeting place
was the Tree of Knowledge, a ghost gum that
was planted near the train station and long

stood as a monument to workers and their
rights. It was mysteriously poisoned in 2006
but a radical and impressive **memorial** (Oak
St) now stands as a testament to those days.

The original inhabitants of Barcaldine
were the Inningai, encountered by explorer
Thomas Mitchell when he passed through
in 1824. Coming into conflict with European
settlers, they were forced off their lands by
the time the Barcaldine township was estab-
lished in the mid-19th century.

The excellent **Australian Workers Her-
itage Centre** (☑ 07-4651 1579; www.australian
workersheritagecentre.com.au; Ash St; adult/child/
family $17/10/42; ⊙ 9am-5pm Mon-Sat, 10am-
4pm Sun) is dedicated to Australian social,
political and industrial movements so inter-
twined with Barcaldine's past.

Oak St is lined with photogenic old timber
pubs. Try the **Shakespeare Hotel** (☑ 07-4651
1111; 95 Oak St; s/d without bathroom $30/40, cabin
d $60) for cheap rooms or a counter meal.

The compact little **Homestead Caravan
Park** (☑ 07-4651 1308; www.homesteadcvpark.
com.au; 24 Box St; powered/unpowered sites
$28/18, cabins $55-75, units $90; ❄ 🔊), with
grassy sites, is only a short walk to the town
centre and pubs. The friendly management
also runs the local roadhouse and a Chinese
takeaway.

Barcaldine Country Motor Inn (☑ 07-
4651 1488; www.barcaldinecountrymotorinn.com.
au; 1 Box St; s/d $110/120; ❄) is central, clean
and guests can use the pool at nearby **Bar-
caldine Motel** (☑ 07-4651 1244; www.barcaldine
motel.com.au; 5 Box St; s/d $80/90, villa s/d
$120/130; ❄ 🖵).

ⓘ Information

Barcaldine Visitor Information Centre (☑ 07-
4651 1724; cnr Oak & Willow Sts; ⊙ 8.15am-
4.30pm Mar-Oct, 9am-2pm Sat & Sun Nov-Feb)
Barcaldine's flash new visitor centre is in the
refurbished former Globe Hotel. Local informa-
tion and historical exhibits.

Charleville

POP 3500

Charleville is the grand old dame of central
Queensland. It's the largest town in Mulga
country, and the gateway to the outback
from the south. Due largely to its prime
locale on the Warrego River, the town was
an important centre for early explorers –
Cobb & Co had its largest coach-making
factory here. Despite a debilitating four-year

drought, the town has maintained its prosperity as a major Australian wool centre and has some fascinating attractions for travellers involving the night sky and the rare bilby.

⊙ Sights

Charleville

Bilby Experience   WILDLIFE RESERVE
(☑07-4654 7771; www.savethebilbyfund.com; King St; ⊗11am-6pm Tue-Sat, 3-6pm Sun & Mon) **FREE** The new bilby experience interpretive centre at the railway station offers a rare opportunity to learn about the native marsupial bilby and the long-running captive breeding and conservation program here. Book ahead for one of the guided tours (adult/child $15/10) or the more intimate 'Up Close and Personal Encounters' ($30/20).

Cosmos Centre   OBSERVATORY
(☑07-4654 7771; www.cosmoscentre.com; 1 Milky Way Rd; night observatory adult/child $28/19, sun viewing $12/9; ⊗10am-4pm, observatory from 7.30pm) See the outback night sky in all its glory at the Cosmos Centre via a high-powered telescope and an expert guide. The 90-minute sessions start at 7.30pm, soon after sunset. There's also a solar telescope here for daytime sun viewing. Both are dependent on cloudless skies, which are frequent out here.

🛏 Sleeping & Eating

★**Evening Star**   FARMSTAY $
(Thurlby Station; ☑07-4654 2430; www.eveningstar.com.au; 818 Adavale Rd; powered/unpowered sites $33/26, cabins $110; ⊗Apr-Oct) This welcoming station property, one of the few station-stays left in outback Queensland, is only 8km west of Charleville but feels a world away. There's plenty of space for camping, a single en-suite cabin, a rustic bar and regular music around the campfire. Station tours ($50 per person) are run on Wednesday and Saturday.

Hotel Corones   HOTEL $
(☑07-4654 1022; www.hotelcorones.net.au; 33 Wills St; s/d without bathroom $60/80, motel d $110, heritage rooms d $150; ❄) Majestic Hotel Corones is a classic country pub with basic rooms upstairs, renovated heritage rooms featuring fireplaces and stained-glass windows, and neat motel rooms at the side. Eat in the grandiose dining room, beer garden or old-school public bar.

ⓘ Information

Charleville Visitor Centre (☑07-4654 7771; www.murweh.qld.gov.au; 1 Milky Way Rd; ⊗9am-5pm, closed Sun Nov-Mar) At the Cosmos Centre; can book tours in the region.

ⓘ Getting There & Away

Bus Queensland (☑1300 287 537; http://busqld.com.au) has a direct overnight service from Brisbane to Charleville; a second bus stops here on the Brisbane–Mt Isa run.

The *Westlander* train (www.queenslandrail.com.au) links Brisbane with Charleville (from $90, 17 hours), departing Brisbane at 7.15pm on Tuesday and Thursday, and leaving Charleville at 6.15pm on Wednesday and Friday.

Channel Country

Named for the channels carved out by summer rains further north, this vast, sparsely populated region stretches south from Mt Isa to Birdsville via Boulia and Bedourie.

The road is sealed from Mt Isa to Bedourie, then a rugged but passable 200km gravel track to Birdsville. Approaching Birdsville from the south (Birdsville Track from Marree) or east from Charleville is all dirt and a 4WD is recommended.

Boulia

POP 230
The unofficial 'capital' of the Channel Country is a peaceful little outpost on the cusp of the great Simpson Desert. The world's longest mail run ends here, having travelled some 3000km from Port Augusta in South Australia. If you're here for the third weekend in July, the **Boulia Camel Races** (day/weekend pass from $10/40) is one of Australia's premier camel racing events.

The most famous residents of Boulia are the mysterious min-min lights, a supposedly natural phenomenon that occurs when the temperature plummets after dark, and erratic lights appear on the unusually flat horizon. They're out there, perhaps, or at least there's sci-fi animatronic gadgetry and eerie lighting in an hourly 'alien' show at the **Min Min Encounter** (☑07-4746 3386; Herbert St; adult/child/family $20/16/50; ⊗9am-5pm daily Apr-Sep, reduced hours Sat & Sun Oct-Mar). Doubling as the information centre, this is classic travel kitsch.

The **Stone House Museum** (cnr Pituri & Hamilton Sts; adult/child $5/3; ⊗8.30am-5pm Mon-Fri, 10am-2pm Sat & Sun) has sheds full of

DON'T MISS

BIRDSVILLE BENDERS

During the first weekend in September, the annual **Birdsville Cup** (www.birdsvilleraces.com; general entry $25-30) horse races draw up to 7000 fans from all over the country to drink, dance and punt on the horses for three dusty days. Parking is free for all light aircraft.

The awesome three-day outback rock festival **Birdsville Big Red Bash** (☉early Jul) started in 2012 and has grown to be almost as well attended as the Birdsville Cup! Expect a line-up of well-known Aussie artists.

outback stuff, space junk, local history, Aboriginal artefacts and the preserved 1888 home of the pioneering Jones family.

Boulia Caravan Park (☎07-4746 3320; Diamantina Developmental Rd; camp sites per person $10, powered sites $27, cabins $75-95), on the banks of the Burke River, has some shady sites, surprisingly grassy areas and just a few cabins, while the **Desert Sands Motel** (☎07-4746 3000; www.desertsandsmotel.com.au; 50 Herbert St; s/d $132/142; ❄☎) has modern and spacious air-con units. Boulia's only pub, the **Australian Hotel** (☎07-4746 3144; 22 Herbert St; s/d $50/60, motel units $130; ❄) is a classic outback watering hole with cold beer and a decent restaurant (mains $18 to $25).

Bedourie

POP 280

Bedourie is the administrative centre for the huge Diamantina Shire, and a friendly outback outpost. Coming from Boulia, it's 200km south on a sealed road. A big attrac-

tion is the free public swimming pool and **artesian spa** (Nappa St; ☉7am-7pm) **FREE**.

Drop in to the **visitor centre** (☎07-4746 1040; 13 Herbert St; ☉8.30am-4.30pm Mon-Fri) for local information. Next door is the historic Mud Hut.

Accommodation and meals are available from **Simpson Desert Oasis** (☎07-4746 1291; www.simpsondesertoasis.com.au; 1 Herbert St; powered/unpowered sites with bathroom $35/15, cabin s/d $120/140, motel s/d $140/150; ❄@) and at the **Royal Hotel** (☎07-4746 1201; www.bedouriehotel.com; Herbert St; r from $88; ❄).

Birdsville

POP 120

Aspiring off-the-beaten-track travellers can't claim the title until they visit Birdsville, an iconic Australian settlement on the fringe of the Simpson Desert, and in the most inland corner of outback Queensland.

Birdsville is remote, but it's as much a destination as a place to pass through on a trans-outback journey. For many the main reason to visit is the annual Birdsville Cup (p452) in September (parking free for all light aircraft), but a beer in the **Birdsville Hotel** (☎07-4656 3244; www.theoutback.com.au; Adelaide St; d $170; ❄) and a 4WD trip to the **Big Red** dune are good enough reasons to visit.

Birdsville has a caravan park and a bakery but the standout is the Birdsville Hotel, built in 1884, a great place to sip a cold beer on the verandah or enjoy a hearty pub meal.

Before heading out on the Birdsville Track, check in at the **Wirrarri Centre** (☎07-4656 3300; 29 Burt St; ☉8.30am-5pm Mon-Fri, 9am-noon Sat & Sun).

Melbourne & Victoria

POP 6.07 MILLION / 🗂 03

Best Places to Eat

➡ Brae (p554)

➡ Attica (p499)

➡ IGNI (p543)

➡ Stefano's Restaurant (p624)

➡ Royal Mail Hotel (p582)

Best Places to Sleep

➡ Clifftop at Hepburn (p529)

➡ Treasury on Collins (p482)

➡ Lighthouse Keepers' Cottages (p588)

➡ Kilns (p612)

➡ Beacon Point Ocean View Villas (p555)

Why Go?

Melbourne is food-obsessed, marvellously multicultural and a showpiece for Australian culture. Beyond the city limits, Victoria offers rich history, stunning wilderness and culinary excellence.

Spread throughout the state, many of these small towns' epicurean credentials go from strength to strength with local-produce-driven restaurants, craft-beer breweries, coffee roasters and excellent wineries. Victorians are also spoiled for scenery and wilderness. From the Great Ocean Road snaking along one of the world's most spectacular coastlines, and wildlife-rich Wilsons Promontory to the picturesque mountains of the High Country, ethereal landscape of the Grampians and desert-like national parks of the northwest – opportunities to explore are endless, whether on two legs or skis, two wheels or four.

When to Go
Melbourne

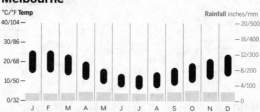

Dec–Jan Beaches are packed with holidaymakers; book months ahead for coastal accommodation.

Feb–Mar Quieter, more accommodation options. Late summer weather can be particularly hot.

Apr–Nov Whale watching July to September in Warrnambool; ski season is June to August.

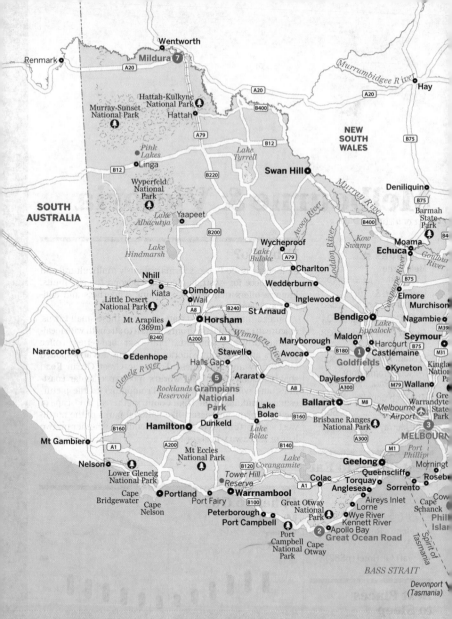

Melbourne & Victoria Highlights

1 **Goldfields** (p566)
Exploring the streetscapes of gold-rush towns with eateries, galleries and markets.

2 **Great Ocean Road** (p538) Taking it slow on a road that curls beside spectacular beaches then whips inland through rainforests.

3 **Melbourne** (p456)
Seeking out cool cafes, hidden bars and the hottest restaurants.

4 **Wilsons Promontory** (p586) Strapping on your hiking boots to admire the sheer natural beauty.

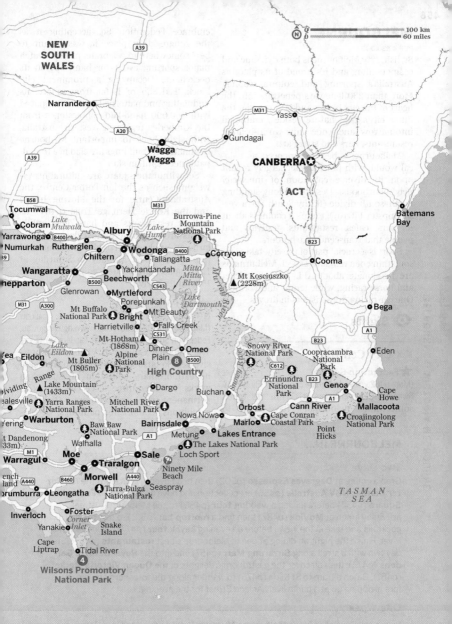

NEW SOUTH WALES

Narrandera

Tocumwal
Cobram
Yarrawonga
Numurkah
Rutherglen
Chiltern
Wangaratta
Shepparton
Glenrowan
Myrtleford
Porepunkah
Mt Buffalo
National Park
Harrietville
Bright
Mt Beauty
Falls Creek

Wagga Wagga
Gundagai

Albury
Wodonga
Tallangatta
Yackandandah
Beechworth
Corryong

Mt Hotham
(1868m)
Alpine
National Park
Mt Buller
(1805m)
Dinner
Plain
Omeo

High Country

Mt Kosciuszko
(2228m)

Lake Hume
Burrowa-Pine
Mountain
National Park

Mitta Mitta River
Lake Dartmouth

Murray River

CANBERRA

ACT

Yass

Cooma

Bega

Batemans
Bay

Lake Mulwala
Lake Mountain
(1433m)
Eildon
Lake Eildon

Dividing Range
Yarra Ranges
National Park
Warburton
Baw Baw
National Park
Walhalla
Moe
Warragul
Morwell
Traralgon
Tarra-Bulga
National Park
Leongatha
Inverloch
Foster
Yanakie

Dargo
Mitchell River
National Park
Bairnsdale
Metung
Sale
Loch Sport

Buchan
Nowa Nowa
Orbost
Marlo
Lakes Entrance
The Lakes National Park
Ninety Mile Beach
Seaspray

Snowy River
National Park
Errinundra
National Park
Genoa

Cann River
Cape Conran
Coastal Park
Point Hicks

Mallacoota
Croajingolong
National Park

Coopracambra
National Park
Eden
Cape Howe

Snake Island
Cape Liptrap
Tidal River

Corner Inlet

Wilsons Promontory National Park

TASMAN SEA

100 km
60 miles

⑤ **Grampians National Park** (p578) Rock climbing, abseiling or bushwalking the stunning sandstone and granite outcrops.

⑥ **Phillip Island** (p534) Spying the nightly parade of penguins.

⑦ **Mildura** (p619) Cruising on the Murray to a winery

lunch on a restored paddle steamer.

⑧ **High Country** (p599) Skiing the slopes on a high-adrenalin adventure.

MELBOURNE

POP 4,530,000

Stylish, arty Melbourne is both dynamic and cosmopolitan, and it's proud of its place as Australia's sporting and cultural capital. More than 230 laneways penetrate into the heart of the city blocks and it's here that the inner city's true nature resides, crammed into narrow lanes concealing world-beating restaurants, bars and street art.

Melbourne is best experienced as a local would, with its character largely reliant upon its diverse collection of inner-city neighbourhoods. Despite a long-standing north–south divide (flashy South Yarra versus hipster Fitzroy), there's a coolness about its bars, cafes, restaurants, festivals and people that transcends the borders.

Sport is a crucial part of the city, taking on something of a religious aspect. Melburnians are passionate about AFL football, cricket and horse racing, while tennis and Formula One car racing draw visitors in droves.

⊙ Sights

◎ City Centre

★**Federation Square** SQUARE
(Map p462; www.fedsquare.com; cnr Flinders & Swanston Sts; 圓Flinders St) While it's taken some time, Melburnians have come to embrace Federation Sq, accepting it as the congregation place it was meant to be – somewhere to celebrate, protest, watch major sporting events or hang out on its deckchairs. Occupying a prominent city block, 'Fed Square' is far from square: its undulating and patterned forecourt is paved with 460,000 hand-laid cobblestones from the Kimberley region in Western Australia, with sight lines to important Melbourne landmarks. Its buildings are clad in a fractal-patterned reptilian skin.

Set within the square are cultural heavyweights such as the Ian Potter Centre, the Australian Centre for the Moving Image and the Koorie Heritage Trust (p464), as well as restaurants and bars. Free public events are staged here most days, particularly at weekends. Highly recommended free tours depart Monday to Saturday at 11am; spaces are limited, so get there 10 to 15 minutes early.

★**Ian Potter Centre:**
NGV Australia GALLERY
(Map p462; 🖉03-8620 2222; www.ngv.vic.gov.au; Federation Sq; ⊙10am-5pm; 圓Flinders St) FREE
The National Gallery of Victoria's impressive Fed Sq offshoot was set up to showcase its extraordinary collection of Australian works. Set over three levels, it's a mix of permanent (free) and temporary (ticketed) exhibitions, comprising paintings, decora-

---

MELBOURNE IN...

Two Days

Grab a coffee at **Degraves Espresso** (p502) then head over to check out the **Ian Potter Centre: NGV Australia** (p456) art collection and have a look around **Federation Square** (p456) before joining a **walking tour** (p480) to see Melbourne's street art. Enjoy lunch at **MoVida** (p487) then find a **rooftop bar** (p501) to test the city's cocktails and take in the views before an evening **kayak tour** (p477) down the Yarra River. Finish the night off dining at one of Melbourne's best **restaurants** (p487). Start day two with a stroll along **Birrarung Marr** (p457) and into the **Royal Botanic Gardens** (p473), then discover the gastronomic delights of the **Queen Victoria Market** (p461). Catch a tram to St Kilda (p476) to wander along the foreshore and pier before propping up at a bar in lively Acland Street for the evening.

One Week

Spend a couple of hours at **Melbourne Museum** (p469) then head into Fitzroy to boutique-shop along Gertrude Street (p513) and grab lunch and coffee at **Proud Mary** (p503) in Collingwood. Back in the city centre, wander through **Chinatown** (p460) and check out Ned Kelly's armour at the **State Library** (p461) before grabbing some dumplings at **HuTong** (p488) for dinner. Spend the rest of the week exploring the shopping and cafe-hopping in hip Windsor and Prahran (p496), hitting the market in **South Melbourne** (p473) and heading out to the **Abbotsford Convent** (p468). Be sure to fit in a meal at **Supernormal** (p487) and a drink at **Bar Americano** (p500).

tive arts, photography, prints, sculpture and fashion. Free tours are conducted daily at 11am, noon, 1pm and 2pm.

Australian Centre for the Moving Image
MUSEUM

(ACMI; Map p462; ☑03-8663 2200; www.acmi. net.au; Federation Sq; ☺10am-5pm; ◉Flinders St) FREE Managing to educate, enthrall and entertain in equal parts, ACMI is a visual feast that pays homage to Australian cinema and TV, offering an insight into the modern-day Australian psyche perhaps as no other museum can. Its screens don't discriminate against age, with TV shows, games and movies on call, making it a great place to spend a day watching TV and not feel guilty about it. Free tours are conducted daily at 11am and 2.30pm.

Birrarung Marr
PARK

(Map p462; Batman Ave; ◉Flinders St) Multi-terraced Birrarung Marr is a welcome addition to Melbourne's patchwork of parks and gardens, featuring grassy knolls, river promenades, thoughtful planting of indigenous flora, and great viewpoints of the city and the river. There's also a scenic route to the MCG (p466) via the 'talking' William Barak Bridge – listen out for songs, words and sounds representing Melbourne's cultural diversity as you walk.

★Hosier Lane
PUBLIC ART

(Map p462; ◉Flinders St) Melbourne's most celebrated laneway for street art, Hosier Lane's cobbled length draws camera-wielding crowds snapping edgy graffiti, stencils and art installations. Subject matter runs to the mostly political and countercultural, spiced with irreverent humour; pieces change almost daily (not even a Banksy is safe here). Be sure to see Rutledge Lane (which horseshoes around Hosier), too.

Flinders Street Station
HISTORIC BUILDING

(Map p462; cnr Flinders & Swanston Sts; ◉Flinders St) If ever there were a true symbol of the city, Flinders St station would have to be it. Built in 1854, it was Melbourne's first railway station, and you'd be hard-pressed to find a Melburnian who hasn't uttered the phrase 'Meet me under the clocks' at one time or another (the popular rendezvous spot is located at the front entrance of the station). Stretching along the Yarra, it's a beautiful neoclassical building topped with a striking octagonal dome.

St Paul's Cathedral
CHURCH

(Map p462; ☑03-9653 4333; www.cathedral. org.au; cnr Flinders & Swanston Sts; ☺7.30am-7.30pm Sun, 8am-6pm Mon-Fri, 9am-4pm Sat; ◉Flinders St) Services were celebrated on this prominent site from the city's first days, but work on Melbourne's Anglican cathedral wasn't commenced until 1880. Consecrated in 1891, the present Gothic Revival church is the work of distinguished ecclesiastical architect William Butterfield (a case of architecture by proxy, as he did not condescend to visit Melbourne, instead sending drawings from England). It features ornate stained-glass windows, Victorian-era tiling, and stripes of cream and grey stone.

Melbourne Town Hall
NOTABLE BUILDING

(Map p462; ☑03-9658 9658; www.thatsmelb ourne.com.au; 90-130 Swanston St; ☺tours 11am & 1pm Mon-Fri; ◉Flinders St) FREE Since it opened in 1870, this grand neoclassical civic building has welcomed everyone from Queen Elizabeth II, who took tea here in 1954, to the Beatles, who waved to thousands of screaming fans from the balcony in 1964. Take the free one-hour tour to see the Grand Organ (built in 1929, and the largest grand romantic organ in the southern hemisphere), sit in the Lord Mayor's chair or tickle the keys of the same piano that Paul McCartney played.

Old Treasury Building
MUSEUM

(Map p462; ☑03-9651 2233; www.oldtreasury building.org.au; 20 Spring St; ☺10am-4pm Sun-Fri; ◉Parliament) FREE The fine neoclassical architecture of the Old Treasury (1862), designed by JJ Clarke, is a telling mix of hubris and functionality. The basement vaults were built to house the millions of pounds' worth of loot that came from the Victorian goldfields and now feature multimedia displays telling stories from that era. Also downstairs is the 1920s caretaker's flat and a reproduction of the 70kg *Welcome Stranger* nugget, found in 1869.

Parliament House
HISTORIC BUILDING

(Map p462; ☑03-9651 8568; www.parliament.vic. gov.au; Spring St; ☺8.30am-5.30pm Mon-Fri; ◉Parliament) FREE The grand steps of Victoria's parliament (1856) are often dotted with slow-moving, tulle-wearing brides smiling for the camera, or placard-holding protesters doing the same. On sitting days the public is welcome to view proceedings from

Melbourne

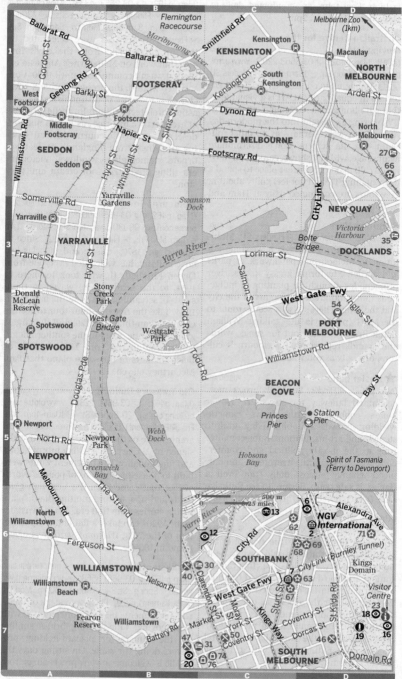

A **B** **C** **D**

Ballarat Rd
Gordon St
Droop St
Geelong Rd
Ballarat Rd
Flemington Racecourse
Maribyrnong River
Smithfield Rd
KENSINGTON
Kensington
Macaulay
Melbourne Zoo (1km)
NORTH MELBOURNE
Arden St
West Footscray
Barkly St
FOOTSCRAY
Kensington Rd
South Kensington
Williamstown Rd
Middle Footscray
Footscray
Napier St
Sims St
Dynon Rd
North Melbourne
SEDDON
Hyde St
Whitehall St
WEST MELBOURNE
27
66
Seddon
Somerville Rd
Yarraville Gardens
Footscray Rd
Swanson Dock
CityLink
NEW QUAY
Victoria Harbour
35
Yarraville
YARRAVILLE
Hyde St
Yarra River
Lorimer St
Bolte Bridge
DOCKLANDS
Francis St
Salmon St
Donald McLean Reserve
Stony Creek Park
West Gate Bridge
West Gate Fwy
54
Ingles St
PORT MELBOURNE
Spotswood
Westgate Park
Todd Rd
SPOTSWOOD
Douglas Pde
Todd Rd
Williamstown Rd
Bay St
Newport
North Rd
Newport Park
Webb Dock
BEACON COVE
Princes Pier
Station Pier
NEWPORT
Greenwich Bay
Hobsons Bay
Spirit of Tasmania (Ferry to Devonport)
Melbourne Rd
North Williamstown
The Strand
Ferguson St
WILLIAMSTOWN
Nelson Pl
Williamstown Beach
Fearon Reserve
Williamstown
Battery Rd

500 m
0.25 miles
Yarra River
6
13
NGV International
Alexandra Ave
71
12
62
2
SOUTHBANK
City Rd
68
69
CityLink (Burnley Tunnel)
Kings Domain
30
7
63
40
Clarendon St
West Gate Fwy
Moray St
Sims St
67
Visitor Centre
23
Market St
York St
Kings Way
Coventry St
St Kilda Rd
18
16
47
31
50
Coventry St
Dorcas St
46
19
20
76
74
SOUTH MELBOURNE
Domain Rd

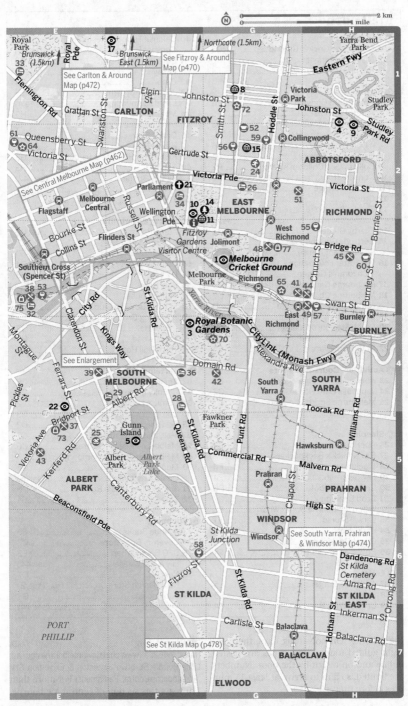

MELBOURNE & VICTORIA

Melbourne

the galleries. On nonsitting days, there are eight guided tours a day; times are posted online and on a sign by the door. Numbers are limited, so aim to arrive at least 15 minutes before time.

★Chinatown   AREA
(Map p462; www.chinatownmelbourne.com.au; Little Bourke St, btwn Swanston & Exhibition Sts; 🚇 Melbourne Central, Parliament) For more than 150 years this section of central Melbourne,

now flanked by five traditional arches, has been the focal point for the city's Chinese community and it remains a vibrant neighbourhood of historic buildings filled with Chinese (and other Asian) restaurants. Come here for yum cha (dim sum) or to explore the attendant laneways for late-night dumplings or cocktails. Chinatown also hosts the city's **Chinese New Year** (www.china townmelbourne.com.au; Little Bourke St; ⊘ Jan or Feb) celebrations.

Chinese miners arrived in Victoria in search of the 'new gold mountain' in the 1850s and started to settle in this strip of Little Bourke St from the 1860s. To learn more about the Chinese Australian story, visit the excellent **Chinese Museum** (⌨ 03-9662 2888; www.chinesemuseum.com.au; 22 Cohen Pl; adult/child $10/8.50; ⊘ 10am-4pm; 🚇 Parliament).

Royal Arcade   HISTORIC BUILDING
(Map p462; www.royalarcade.com.au; 335 Bourke St Mall; 🚊 86, 96) Built between 1869 and 1870, this Parisian-style shopping arcade is Melbourne's oldest and it's managed to retain much of its charming 19th-century detail. A black-and-white chequered path leads to the mythological figures of giant brothers Gog and Magog, perched with hammers within the domed exit to Little Collins St. They've been striking the hour here since 1892.

State Library of Victoria   LIBRARY
(Map p462; ⌨ 03-8664 7002; www.slv.vic.gov. au; 328 Swanston St; ⊘ 10am-9pm Mon-Thu, to 6pm Fri-Sun, galleries 10am-5pm; 🚇 Melbourne Central) This grand neoclassical building has been at the forefront of Melbourne's literary scene since it opened in 1856. When its epicentre, the gorgeous octagonal **La Trobe Reading Room**, was completed in 1913, its reinforced-concrete dome was the largest of its kind in the world; its natural light illuminates the ornate plasterwork and the studious Melbourne writers who come here to pen their works. For visitors, the highlight is the fascinating collection showcased in the **Dome Galleries**.

Start on the dome viewing balcony on the 6th floor and then work your way down to the Dome Galleres, spread over the next two floors. The 5th floor has the *Changing Face of Victoria* exhibition. Its most notable items are the armour and death mask of Ned Kelly, Australia's most infamous bushranger; the menacing helmet was cobbled together from a plough with a slit cut out for the eyes. There's also numerous original Burke

and Wills memorabilia and John Batman's controversial land treaty (read: land grab), in which he's believed to have forged the signatures of the Wurundjeri people.

Bibiliophiles won't want to miss the *Mirror of the World* exhibition on the 4th floor, featuring a weird and wonderful collection of books through the ages, including a 4000-year-old Sumerian cuneiform tax receipt, significant religious tomes and beautifully rendered nature studies. There are also a couple of galleries on the ground floor near the main entrance.

For more information, join a free hourlong themed tour (departing at 11.30am, 1pm and 2pm).

The lawns in front of the library are a popular lunching and blogging spot; protests and free events are often held here.

Old Melbourne Gaol   HISTORIC BUILDING
(Map p462; ⌨ 03-8663 7228; www.oldmelbourne gaol.com.au; 337 Russell St; adult/child/family $25/14/55; ⊘ 9.30am-5pm; 🚇 Melbourne Central) Built in 1841, this forbidding bluestone prison was in operation until 1929. It's now one of Melbourne's most popular museums, where you can tour the tiny, bleak cells. Around 135 people were hanged here, including Ned Kelly, Australia's most infamous bushranger, in 1880; one of his death masks is on display. Visits include the Police Watch House Experience, where you get 'arrested' and thrown in the slammer (more fun than it sounds).

Queen Victoria Market   MARKET
(Map p462; www.qvm.com.au; 513 Elizabeth St; ⊘ 6am-2pm Tue & Thu, to 5pm Fri, to 3pm Sat, 9am-4pm Sun; 🚇 Flagstaff) With over 600 traders, the Vic Market is the largest open-air market in the southern hemisphere and attracts thousands of shoppers. It's where Melburnians sniff out fresh produce among the booming cries of spruiking fishmongers and fruit-and-veg vendors. The wonderful deli hall (with art-deco features) is lined with everything from soft cheeses, wines and Polish sausages to Greek dips, truffle oil and kangaroo biltong.

Hellenic Museum   MUSEUM
(Map p462; ⌨ 03-8615 9016; www.hellenic.org. au; 280 William St; adult/child $10/5; ⊘ 10am-4pm Tue-Sun; 🚇 Flagstaff) Housed in a beautiful neoclassical building, formerly the Royal Mint, this museum is dedicated to Greek immigrants who moved here in the 1950s and the contribution they've made to the city – Melbourne has the largest Greek population

Central Melbourne

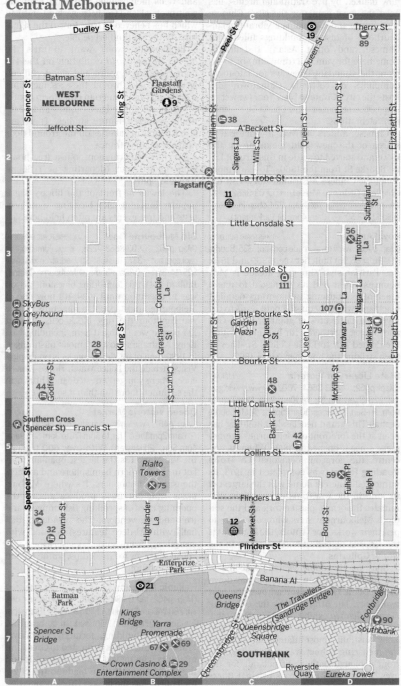

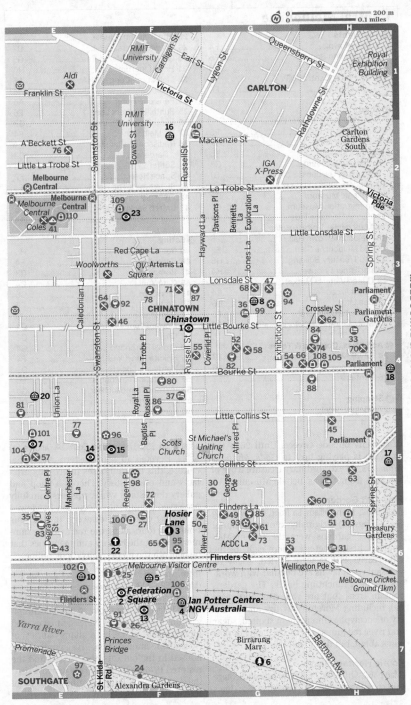

MELBOURNE & VICTORIA

Central Melbourne

of any city outside Greece. Until 2024 the museum is playing host to *Gods, Myths & Monsters*, an extraordinary treasure trove of artefacts from Athens' Benaki Museum.

Flagstaff Gardens PARK
(Map p462; btwn William, La Trobe, Dudley & King Sts; ⊠Flagstaff) Originally known as Burial Hill, these gardens were the site of Melbourne's first cemetery, where eight of the city's early settlers were buried. Today its pleasant open lawns are popular with workers taking a lunchtime break. The gardens contain trees that are well over 100 years old, including Moreton Bay figs and a variety of eucalypts, among them spotted, sugar and river red gums. There are plenty of possums about, but don't feed them.

Koorie Heritage Trust CULTURAL CENTRE
(Map p462; ☑03-8662 6300; www.koorieheritage trust.com; Yarra Building, Federation Sq; tours adult/child $33/17; ⊙10am-5pm; ⊠Flinders St) **FREE** Devoted to southeastern Aboriginal culture, this centre houses interesting artefacts and oral history. There's a shop and gallery downstairs while, upstairs, carefully preserved significant objects can be viewed in display cases and drawers. It also runs hour-long tours along the Yarra during summer, evoking the history and memories that lie beneath the modern city (book online).

Immigration Museum MUSEUM
(Map p462; ☑13 11 02; www.museumvictoria.com. au/immigrationmuseum; 400 Flinders St; adult/child $14/free; ⊙10am-5pm; ⊠55) The Immigration Museum uses voices, images and memorabilia to tell the many stories of Australian immigration. It's symbolically housed in the old Customs House, and the restored 1876 building alone is worth a visit: the Long Room is a magnificent piece of Italian Renaissance–revival architecture.

Sea Life AQUARIUM
(Map p462; ☏1800 026 576; www.melbourne aquarium.com.au; cnr Flinders & King Sts; adult/ child/family $46/26/99; ◷9.30am-6pm; ♿; 🚊35, 70, 75) This interesting but extremely pricey aquarium is home to giant rays, gropers and sharks, all of which cruise around a 2.2-million-litre tank, watched closely by visitors in a see-through tunnel. Gentoo and king penguins potter about in icy 'Antarctica', while one of Australia's largest saltwater crocs casts a menacing eye over his lair. Divers are thrown to the sharks three times a day; for a mere $299 you can join them. Tickets are cheaper online.

St Patrick's Cathedral CHURCH
(Map p458; ☏03-9662 2233; www.stpatricks cathedral.org.au; 1 Cathedral Pl, East Melbourne; ◷9am-5pm Mon-Fri; 🚊Parliament) Designed by William Wardell, Melbourne's Catholic cathedral is among the world's finest examples of Gothic Revival architecture and the largest church building in Australia. Building began in 1858 and continued until the spires were added in 1939. The imposing bluestone exterior and grounds are but a preview of its contents: inside are several tonnes of bells, an organ with 4500 pipes, ornate stained-glass windows, and exquisite mosaics in the Blessed Sacrament chapel.

◉ Southbank & Docklands

The reinvention of Southbank as a glitzy tourist precinct is so complete that it's hard to imagine that, before the 1980s, it was a gritty industrial zone supporting a major port. Now its pleasant riverside promenade is peppered with famous restaurants and hotels, while the presence of some of the city's top arts institutions makes it an essential part of any Melbourne itinerary. To the city's west, the once working wharves of

Docklands have given birth to a mini city of apartments, offices, restaurants, plazas, public art and parks.

★ **NGV International**   GALLERY
(Map p458; ☑03-8662 1555; www.ngv.vic.gov. au; 180 St Kilda Rd, Southbank; ☉10am-5pm; ☒Flinders St) FREE Housed in a vast, brutally beautiful, bunkerlike building, the international branch of the National Gallery of Victoria has an expansive collection that runs the gamut from the ancient to the bleeding edge. Regular blockbuster exhibitions (prices vary) draw the crowds, and there are free 45-minute highlights tours at 11am and 1pm daily, and hour-long tours at midday and 2pm.

Eureka Skydeck   VIEWPOINT
(Map p458; ☑03-9693 8888; www.eurekasky deck.com.au; 7 Riverside Quay, Southbank; adult/ child $20/12, Edge extra $12/8; ☉10am-10pm; ☒Flinders St) Melbourne's tallest building, the 297m-high Eureka Tower was built in 2006, and a wild elevator ride takes you to its 88 floors in less than 40 seconds (check out the photo on the elevator floor if there's time). The Edge – a slightly sadistic glass cube – cantilevers you out of the building; you've got no choice but to look down.

**Australian Centre
for Contemporary Art**   GALLERY
(ACCA; Map p458; ☑03-9697 9999; www.accaon line.org.au; 111 Sturt St, Southbank; ☉10am-5pm Tue-Sun; ☒1) FREE ACCA is one of Australia's most exciting and challenging contemporary galleries, showcasing the work of a range of local and international artists. The building is, fittingly, sculptural, with a rusted exterior evoking the factories that once stood on the site, and a soaring interior designed to house often massive installations.

Arts Centre Melbourne   ARTS CENTRE
(Map p458; ☑1300 182 183; www.artscentre melbourne.com.au; 100 St Kilda Rd, Southbank; ☉box office 9am-8.30pm Mon-Fri, 10am-5pm Sat; ☒Flinders St) The Arts Centre is made up of two separate buildings, Hamer Hall and the **Theatres Building** (under the spire, including a free gallery space with changing exhibitions), linked by a series of landscaped walkways. Tours of the theatres and exhibitions leave daily at 11am (adult/child $20/15); the Sunday tour includes the backstage areas.

⊙ Richmond & East Melbourne

Melbourne is one of the world's great sporting cities, and Richmond and East Melbourne are the nexus for all things active. The neighbourhood's southeastern skyline is dominated by the angular shapes of sporting stadia, none more hulking than the mighty Melbourne Cricket Ground. North from here are the genteel streets of East Melbourne, centred on pretty Fitzroy Gardens. Richmond is a part-gentrified, part-gritty residential and commercial expanse peppered with interesting eateries.

★ **Melbourne Cricket Ground**   STADIUM
(MCG; Map p458; ☑03-9657 8888; www.mcg. org.au; Brunton Ave, East Melbourne; tour adult/ child/family $23/12/55, incl museum $32/16/70; ☉tours 10am-3pm; ☒Jolimont) With a capacity of 100,000 people, the 'G' is one of the world's great sporting venues, hosting cricket in summer and AFL (Australian Football League; Aussie rules) footy in winter. For many Australians it's considered hallowed ground. Make it to a game if you can (highly recommended), but otherwise you can still make your pilgrimage on nonmatch-day **tours** that take you through the stands, media and coaches' areas, change rooms and members' lounges. The MCG houses the state-of-the-art **National Sports Museum** (☑03-9657 8879; www.nsm.org.au; Gate 3; adult/ child/family $23/12/55; ☉10am-5pm).

Fitzroy Gardens   PARK
(Map p458; www.fitzroygardens.com; Wellington Pde, East Melbourne; ☒Jolimont) The city drops away suddenly just east of Spring St, giving way to Melbourne's beautiful backyard, Fitzroy Gardens. The park's stately avenues are lined with English elms, flowerbeds, expansive lawns, strange fountains and a creek. A highlight is Cooks' Cottage, which belonged to the parents of navigator Captain James Cook. The cottage was shipped brick by brick from Yorkshire and reconstructed here in 1934. Nearby is a **visitor centre** (☑03-9658 9658; www.thatsmelbourne.com.au; ☉9am-5pm) with a cafe attached and the delightful 1930s **conservatory** (Fitzroy Gardens, Wellington Pde, East Melbourne; ☉9am-5pm).

Cooks' Cottage   HISTORIC BUILDING
(Map p458; Fitzroy Gardens, Wellington Pde, East Melbourne; adult/child/family $6.50/3.50/18; ☉9am-5pm; ☒Jolimont) Built in 1755, this humble family cottage can lay claim to being

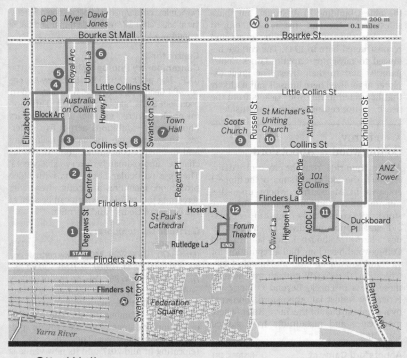

🏃 City Walk
Arcades & Laneways

START DEGRAVES ST
END MOVIDA
LENGTH 3KM; 2½ HOURS

Central Melbourne is a warren of 19th-century arcades and cobbled bluestone laneways featuring street art, basement restaurants, boutiques and bars.

Start on **①** **Degraves St**, an archetypal Melbourne side street lined with interesting shops and cafes. Grab a coffee at Degraves Espresso, then continue north, crossing over Flinders Lane to cafe-filled **②** **Centre Place**, good for spotting street art.

Cross Collins St, turn left and enter the **③** **Block Arcade**; built in 1891, it's based on Milan's Galleria Vittorio Emanuele II arcade. Ogle the window display at the Hopetoun Tea Rooms before continuing through the arcade, turning left and exiting right onto Elizabeth St.

At the next corner cross the road and turn right into Little Collins St. Consider stopping for an afternoon tipple at kooky **④** **Chuckle Park** (p501), then continue on and turn left into wonderfully ornate **⑤** **Royal Arcade**

(p461); look out for Gog and Magog, hammering away under the dome. Wander through to Bourke St Mall, then turn right and continue until you find street-art-covered **⑥** **Union Lane** on the right.

Follow Union Lane to the end, turn left onto Little Collins St, then take a right on Swanston St. Walk past **⑦** **Melbourne Town Hall** (p457) on the other side of Swanston St, and pop into the 1932 **⑧** **Manchester Unity Building** to snoop around its impressive foyer, then cross Swanston St and head up the hill to the 'Paris End' of Collins St. Along the way you'll pass the 1873 Gothic **⑨** **Scots Church** (the first Presbyterian church in Victoria) and the 1866 **⑩** **St Michael's Uniting Church**.

Turn right into Exhibition St, then right into Flinders Lane, and continue until you see **⑪** **Duckboard Place**. Head down the laneway and take your time to soak up the street art before horseshoeing around into AC/DC Lane, past rock 'n' roll dive bar Cherry.

Continue on down Flinders Lane to the street-art meccas of **⑫** **Hosier Lane** (p457) and Rutledge Lane before finishing with tapas and a hard-earned drink at MoVida.

the oldest building in Australia, but that's sidestepping the fact that it was shipped from Yorkshire in 253 packing cases and reconstructed here in 1934. The cottage belonged to navigator Captain James Cook's parents later in their lives. The great explorer never lived here himself, but it's likely that he visited it. Buy your tickets from the nearby visitor centre to take a look inside.

👁 Fitzroy, Collingwood & Abbotsford

A short tram ride from the city centre delivers you to the doorstep of some of the hippest enclaves in Melbourne, where up-to-the-minute eateries and midcentury furniture stores sit comfortably next to century-old classic pubs and divey live-music venues. Fitzroy, Melbourne's first suburb, and Collingwood have long had a reputation for vice and squalor and, despite ongoing gentrification, there's still enough grit holding these areas in check. Beyond Collingwood is largely industrial Abbotsford, bordered by a scenic stretch of the Yarra River, where more cafes and restaurants have started sprouting.

Abbotsford Convent HISTORIC SITE
(Map p458; ☑03-9415 3600; www.abbotsford convent.com.au; 1 St Heliers St, Abbotsford; tours $15; ⊘7.30am-10pm; 🚌200, 207, 🚉Victoria Park) FREE The nuns are long gone at this former convent, which dates to 1861, but today its rambling collection of ecclesiastical architecture is home to a thriving arts community of galleries, studios, eateries including the **Convent Bakery** (☑03-9419 9426; www.conventbakery.com; mains $10-20; ⊘7am-5pm) and vegetarian **Lentil as Anything** (☑03-9419 6444; www.lentilasanything. com; by donation; ⊘9am-9pm; ☑), and a bar, spread over nearly 7 hectares of riverside land. Tours of the complex run at 2pm Sunday.

Collingwood Children's Farm FARM
(Map p458; www.farm.org.au; 18 St Heliers St, Abbotsford; adult/child/family $10/5/20; ⊘9.15am-4.30pm; 🚌200, 207, 🚉Victoria Park) The inner city melts away at this rustic riverside retreat that's beloved not just by children. There's a range of frolicking farm animals that kids can help feed, as well as cow milking and guinea-pig cuddles! The cafe opens at 9am and can be visited without entering the farm itself, and the monthly **farmers market**

(www.mfm.com.au/markets/collingwood-childrens-farm; adult/child $2/free; ⊘8am-1pm 2nd Sat of month) is a local highlight.

Centre for Contemporary Photography GALLERY
(CCP; Map p470; ☑03-9417 1549; www.ccp.org. au; 404 George St, Fitzroy; ⊘11am-5pm Wed-Fri, noon-5pm Sat & Sun; 🚌86) FREE This not-for-profit centre exhibits contemporary photography exhibitions across five galleries. Shows traverse traditional techniques and the highly conceptual, and exhibitions change approximately every six weeks. There's a particular fascination with video projection, including a nightly after-hours screening in a window, which can be seen at the corner of George and Kerr Sts.

Gertrude Contemporary Art Space GALLERY
(Map p470; ☑03-9419 3406; www.gertrude.org. au; 200 Gertrude St, Fitzroy; ⊘11am-5.30pm Tue-Fri, to 4.30pm Sat; 🚌86) This nonprofit gallery and studio complex has been going strong for nearly 30 years; many of its alumni are now certified famous artists. The monthly exhibition openings often see crowds spilling out onto the street. The gallery will be relocating in mid-2017, and its new venue is yet to be confirmed. Also check out its new space nearby, **Glasshouse** (Map p458; 44 Glasshouse Rd, Collingwood; ⊘noon-5pm Tue-Sat; 🚌109, 86).

Alcaston Gallery GALLERY
(Map p470; ☑03-9418 6444; www.alcastongallery. com.au; 11 Brunswick St, Fitzroy; ⊘10am-6pm Tue-Fri, 11am-5pm Sat; 🚌11) FREE Set in an imposing boom-style terrace, the Alcaston showcases international and Australian art, with a focus on the work of living Indigenous artists. The gallery works directly with Indigenous communities and is particularly attentive to cultural sensitivities; it shows a wide range of styles from traditional to contemporary. Check the website for exhibitions.

Backwoods Gallery GALLERY
(Map p458; ☑03-9041 3606; www.backwoods. gallery; 25 Easey St, Collingwood; ⊘noon-6pm Tue-Sun; 🚌86) Set up in 2010 by a team of Melbourne street artists, the Backwoods Gallery promotes and exhibits works by Australian and international artists, with a focus on urban contemporary art, stencil, street art and illustration in its warehouse space in a Collingwood backstreet.

Australian Galleries
GALLERY

(Map p470; ☑03-9417 4303; www.australiangal leries.com.au; 35 Derby St, Collingwood; ⊙10am-6pm; 🚊86) Around since the 1950s, this gallery in the backstreets of Collingwood showcases contemporary Australian art with monthly-changing exhibitions. Across the road is its stock room, with a huge, varied collection (also open 10am to 6pm).

👁 Carlton & Brunswick

Home to Melbourne's Italian community and the University of Melbourne, Carlton dishes up a heady mix of intellectual activity, espresso and excellent food – the same things that lured bohemians to the area in the 1950s. You'll see the *tricolori* unfurled with characteristic passion come soccer finals and the Grand Prix.

Head west to multicultural-meets-hipster Brunswick to feast on Middle Eastern cuisine on Sydney Rd before bar-hopping home.

★Melbourne Museum
MUSEUM

(Map p472; ☑13 11 02; www.museumvictoria. com.au; 11 Nicholson St, Carlton; adult $14, child & student free, exhibitions extra; ⊙10am-5pm; 🚋 Tourist Shuttle, 🚋City Circle, 86, 96, 🚊Parliament) This museum provides a grand sweep of Victoria's natural and cultural histories, incorporating dinosaur fossils, giant-squid specimens, a taxidermy hall, a 3D volcano and an open-air forest atrium of Victorian flora. Become immersed in the legend of champion racehorse and national hero Phar Lap. The excellent Bunjilaka, on the ground floor, presents Indigenous Australian stories and history told through objects and Aboriginal voices with state-of-the-art technology. There's also an IMAX cinema.

★Royal
Exhibition Building
HISTORIC BUILDING

(Map p472; ☑13 11 02; www.museumvictoria. com.au/reb; 9 Nicholson St, Carlton; tours adult/child $10/7; 🚋 Tourist Shuttle, 🚋City Circle, 86, 96, 🚊Parliament) Built for the 1880 International Exhibition, and winning Unesco World Heritage status in 2004, this beautiful Victorian edifice symbolises the glory days of the Industrial Revolution, the British Empire and 19th-century Melbourne's economic supremacy. It was the first building to fly the Australian flag, and Australia's first parliament was held here in 1901; it now hosts everything from trade fairs to car shows,

as well as the biennial Melbourne Art Fair. Tours of the building leave from Melbourne Museum (opposite) at 2pm.

Melbourne General Cemetery
CEMETERY

(Map p458; ☑03-9349 3014; www.mgc.smct.org. au; College Cres, Parkville; ⊙8am-6pm Apr-Sep, to 8pm Oct-Mar; 🚋1, 6) Melbourne has been burying its dead in this cemetery since 1852. It's worth a stroll to see the final resting place of three Australian prime ministers, the ill-fated explorers Burke and Wills, Walter Lindrum's billiard-table tombstone and a shrine to Elvis erected by fans. Check the website about guided day and night tours.

University of Melbourne
UNIVERSITY

(Map p472; ☑03-8344 4000; www.unimelb.edu. au; Grattan St, Carlton; 🚋1, 6, 72) The esteemed University of Melbourne was established in 1853 and remains one of Australia's most prestigious universities. Its blend of Victorian Gothic stone buildings, midcentury international-style towers and postmodern showpieces provides a snapshot of changing architectural aspirations. The campus sprawls from Carlton through to the neighbouring suburb of Parkville, and its extensive grounds house the university colleges. Most notable is the Walter Burley Griffin–designed **Newman College**. Pick up a *Sculpture on Campus* map from the **Ian Potter Museum of Art** (Map p472; ☑03-8344 5148; www.art-museum.unimelb.edu.au; 800 Swanston St, Parkville; ⊙10am-5pm Tue-Fri, noon-5pm Sat & Sun; 🚋1, 6, 72) **FREE**.

Museo Italiano
MUSEUM

(Map p472; ☑03-9349 9000; www.museoitaliano. com.au; 199 Faraday St, Carlton; ⊙10am-5pm Tue-Fri, noon-5pm Sat; 🚋 Tourist Shuttle, 🚋1, 6) **FREE** Telling the story of Melbourne's Italian community, this museum offers a good starting point to put the history of Lygon St into both historical and contemporary context.

Ceres
CULTURAL CENTRE

(☑03-9389 0100; www.ceres.org.au; cnr Roberts & Stewart Sts, East Brunswick; ⊙9am-5pm, cafe 9am-3pm Mon-Fri, to 4pm Sat & Sun; 🚋96) 🌿**FREE** Ceres, the name of the Roman goddess of agriculture and fertility, also stands for Centre for Education & Research in Environmental Strategies, a two-decades-old community environment built on a former rubbish tip. Stroll around the permaculture and bush-food nursery before refuelling with an organic homemade chai and lunch at Merri Table cafe.

Fitzroy & Around

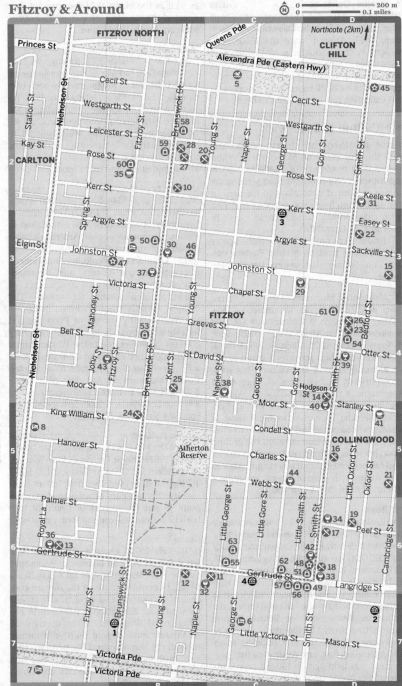

Fitzroy & Around

There's a grocery store and community market where you can find piles of organic and backyard-produced goodies, and the info centre has a great bookstore on sustainability-related matters and organic gardening.

◎ North Melbourne & Parkville

This strip of central Melbourne stretches from the shabby railway yards and gridlocked thoroughfares of West Melbourne, through the surprisingly quiet Victorian neighbourhood of North Melbourne and into the ample green spaces of Parkville.

The big attraction here is the zoo, but it's also worth stopping by to sample the low-key neighbourhood pubs, eateries and shops of North Melbourne's Victoria, Errol and Queensberry Sts.

★ **Melbourne Zoo** ZOO
(☎ 1300 966 784; www.zoo.org.au; Elliott Ave, Parkville; adult/child $33/17, children weekends & holidays free; ☺ 8am-5pm; ☑; ☒ Royal Park) 🖉 Established in 1861, this compact zoo is the oldest in Australia and the third oldest in the world. It remains one of the city's most popular attractions and it continues to innovate, recently becoming the world's first carbon-neutral zoo. Set in landscaped gardens, the zoo's enclosures aim to simulate the animals' natural habitats and give them the option to hide if they want to (the gorillas and the tigers are particularly good at playing hard to find).

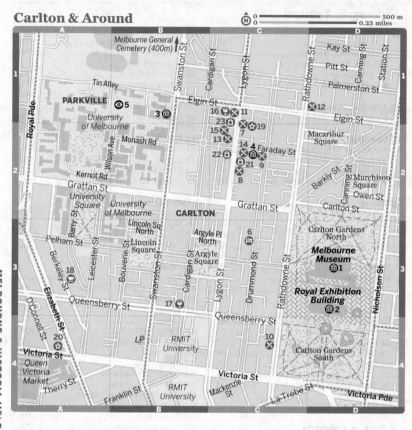

Carlton & Around

HEIDE MUSEUM OF MODERN ART

The former home of John and Sunday Reed, **Heide Museum of Modern Art** (☑ 03-9850 1500; www.heide.com.au; 7 Templestowe Rd, Bulleen; adult/child $22/18; ☺ 10am-5pm Tue-Sun; ☐ 903, ☒ Heidelberg) is a prestigious not-for-profit art gallery with a sculpture garden in its wonderful grounds. It holds regularly changing exhibitions, many of which include works by the famous artists that called Heide home, including Sir Sidney Nolan and Albert Tucker. The collection is spread over three buildings: a large purpose-built gallery, the Reeds' original farmhouse and the wonderful modernist house they built in 1963 as 'a gallery to be lived in'.

There's a cafe, or you can pack a picnic to eat by the Yarra. The free tours (Tuesday 2pm) are a great introduction to Melbourne's 20th-century painting scene.

Bulleen is 14km northeast of the city centre.

👁 South Melbourne, Port Melbourne & Albert Park

The well-heeled trio of South Melbourne, Port Melbourne and Albert Park isn't short on lunching ladies, AFL stars and Porsche-steering Lotharios living it up in grandiose Victorian terraces and bayside condos. Leafy and generally sedate, the area boasts some of Melbourne's most beautiful heritage architecture, both civic and domestic. South Melbourne is the busiest neighbourhood, with a bustling market, cult-status cafes and sharply curated design stores. Albert Park offers culture in a former gasworks, while Port Melbourne's home to Station Pier, from where ferries shoot south to Tasmania.

South Melbourne Market   MARKET
(Map p458; ☑ 03-9209 6295; www.southmelbournemarket.com.au; cnr Coventry & Cecil Sts, South Melbourne; ☺ 8am-4pm Wed, Sat & Sun, to 5pm Fri; ☐ 12, 96) Trading since 1864, this market is a neighbourhood institution, its labyrinthine guts packed with a brilliant collection of stalls selling everything from organic produce and deli treats to hipster specs, art and crafts. The place is famous for its dim sims (sold here since 1949), and there's no shortage of atmospheric eateries. From early January to late February, there's a lively night market on Thursday. The site is also home to a cooking school – see the website for details.

Albert Park Lake   LAKE
(Map p458; btwn Queens Rd, Fitzroy St, Aughtie Dr & Albert Rd, Albert Park; ☐ 96) Elegant black swans give their inimitable bottoms-up salute as you jog, cycle or walk the 5km perimeter of this constructed lake. Lakeside Dr was used as an international motor-racing circuit in the 1950s, and since 1996 the revamped track has been the venue for the **Australian Formula One Grand Prix** (☑ 1800 100 030; www.grandprix.com.au; tickets from $55) each March. Also on the periphery is the Melbourne Sports & Aquatic Centre (p479), with an Olympic-size pool and child-delighting wave machine.

St Vincent Place   ARCHITECTURE
(Map p458; St Vincent Pl, Albert Park; ☐ 1) For a taste of Victorian-era finery, take a stroll in St Vincent Pl, a heritage precinct in Albert Park. Consisting of a long, arch-shaped street skirting a central landscaped garden, it's considered Australia's finest example of a 19th-century residential square. The street itself is flanked by some of Melbourne's grandest Victorian terraces, many of which date to the 1860s. Such elegance and boldness reflect Melbourne's blooming confidence during the gold rush. The precinct is 700m south of South Melbourne Market.

👁 South Yarra, Prahran & Windsor

★ **Royal Botanic Gardens**   GARDENS
(Map p458; www.rbg.vic.gov.au; Birdwood Ave, South Yarra; ☺ 7.30am-sunset; ☐ Tourist Shuttle, ☐ 1, 3, 5, 6, 16, 64, 67, 72) FREE From the air, Melbourne's 94-acre Royal Botanical Gardens evokes a green lung in the middle of the city. Drawing over 1.5 million visitors annually, the gardens are considered one of the finest examples of Victorian-era landscaping in the world. You'll find a global selection of plantings and endemic Australian flora. Mini ecosystems, such as a cacti and succulents area, a herb garden and an indigenous rainforest, are set amid vast lawns.

South Yarra, Prahran & Windsor

South Yarra, Prahran & Windsor

MELBOURNE & VICTORIA MELBOURNE

In summer the gardens play host to Moonlight Cinema (p508) and theatre performances. Other features include the 19th-century **Melbourne Observatory** (☑03-9252 2429; adult/child/family $24/20/70; ☉tours by appointment 9pm Mon;) for tours of the night sky, and the excellent, nature-based **Ian Potter Foundation Children's Garden** (☑03-9252 2300; www.rbg.vic. gov.au/visit-mel bourne/attractions/children-garden; ☉10am-dusk Wed-Sun, daily Victorian school holidays), a whimsical, child-scaled place that invites kids and their parents to explore, discover and imagine.

The **visitor centre** (☑03-9252 2429; Observatory Gate, Birdwood Ave; ☉9am-5pm Mon-Fri, from 9.30am Sat & Sun) is the departure point for tours, some of which are free and all of which should be booked by calling ahead (see the website for details). Close by, the National Herbarium, established in 1853, contains over a million dried botanical specimens used for plant-identification purposes.

For visitors who can't get enough, the Royal Botanical Gardens has recently developed the **Australian Garden** (☑03-5990 2220; 1000 Ballarto Rd, Cranbourne; ☉9am-5pm; ☒796, ☒Cranbourne) **FREE** in the outlying suburb of Cranbourne, around 40km from the city centre.

Shrine of Remembrance   MONUMENT
(Map p458; ☑03-9661 8100; www.shrine.org.au; Birdwood Ave, South Yarra; ☉10am-5pm; ☒Tourist Shuttle, ☒3, 5, 6, 16, 64, 67, 72) **FREE** One of Melbourne's icons, the Shrine of Remembrance is a commanding memorial to Victorians killed in WWI. Built between 1928 and 1934, much of it with Depression-relief, or 'susso' (sustenance), labour, its stoic, classical design is partly based on the Mausoleum of Halicarnassus, one of the seven ancient wonders of the world. The shrine's upper balcony affords epic panoramic views of the Melbourne skyline and all the way up tram-studded Swanston St.

This unobstructed view isn't coincidental; planning regulations continue to restrict any building that would encroach on the view of the shrine from Swanston St as far back as Lonsdale St.

The shrine itself draws thousands to its annual Anzac Day (25 April) dawn service, while the Remembrance Day service at 11am on 11 November commemorates the signing of the 1918 Armistice marking the formal end to WWI. At this precise moment a shaft of light shines through an opening in the ceiling, passing over the Stone of Remembrance and illuminating the word 'love'; on all other days this effect is demonstrated using artificial lighting on the hour.

With its cenotaph and eternal flame (lit by Queen Elizabeth II in 1954), the forecourt was built as a memorial to those who died in WWII, and several other specific memorials surround the shrine. Below the shrine, a stunningly conceived architectural space houses the Galleries of Remembrance, a museum dedicated to telling the story of Australians at war via its 800-plus historical artefacts and artworks.

The complex is under 24-hour police guard; during opening hours the police are quaintly required to wear uniforms resembling those worn by WWI light-horsemen. Download the free Shrine of Remembrance app for a self-guided tour, or consider joining the **free guided tours** daily at 11am and 2pm, often conducted by returned soldiers.

Government House HISTORIC BUILDING
(Map p458; ☑03-9656 9889; www.national trust.org.au; Kings Domain, South Yarra; tours $18; ⊙tours 10am Mon & Thu; ☐Tourist Shuttle, ☐1, 3, 5, 6, 16, 64, 67, 72) On the outer edge of the Botanic Gardens, the Italianate Government House dates to 1872. A replica of Queen Victoria's Osborne House on England's Isle of Wight, it has served as the residence of all Victorian governors, as well as being the royal pied-à-terre. Unfortunately, the two-hour tour of the property is only available to groups of 10 or more. Tours should be booked at least two weeks ahead, by phone or email.

Como House HISTORIC BUILDING
(Map p474; ☑03-9827 2500, tour bookings 03-9656 9889; www.nationaltrust.org.au; cnr Williams Rd & Lechlade Ave, South Yarra; adult/child/family $15/9/35; ⊙gardens 9am-5pm Mon-Sat, from 10am Sun, house tours 11am, 12.30pm & 2pm Sat & Sun) A wedding cake of Australian Regency and Italianate architecture, this elegant colonial residence is among Melbourne's heritage royalty. Dating to 1840, it houses belongings of the high-society Armytage family, the last and longest owners, who lived in the house for 95 years. House tours run every Saturday and Sunday and tickets can be purchased online or by phone.

Prahran Market MARKET
(Map p474; ☑03-8290 8220; www.prahran market.com.au; 163 Commercial Rd, South Yarra; ⊙7am-5pm Tue & Thu-Sat, 10am-3pm Sun; ☐72, 78, ☐Prahran) Prahran Market is a Melbourne institution, whetting appetites since 1881. While much of the current structure dates to the 1970s and '80s, the Commercial Rd facade – designed by Charles D'Ebro in a Queen Anne–revival style – dates to 1891. Grab a speciality coffee from Market Lane (p506) and trawl stalls heaving with organic produce, seafood, meat, handmade pasta, gourmet deli items and more. The market is also home to culinary store and cooking school **Essential Ingredient** (Map p474; ☑03-9827 9047; www.essentialingredient. com.au; classes $175-275).

★**Justin Art House Museum** GALLERY
(JAHM; Map p474; ☑0411 158 967; www.jahm. com.au; cnr Williams Rd & Lumley Ct, Prahran; adult/child $25/free; ⊙by appointment; ☐5, 6, 64) The geometric, zinc-clad home of Melbourne art collectors Charles and Leah Justin doubles as the Justin Art House Museum. Book ahead for a private tour of the couple's dynamic collection of contemporary art, consisting of more than 250 pieces amassed over four decades. There's a strong emphasis on video and digital art, with the works rotated regularly. Guided tours take around two hours. The house was designed by the couple's daughter, Elisa.

Artists Lane PUBLIC ART
(Map p474; Artists Lane, Windsor; ☐5, 6, 64, 78, ☐Windsor) Running parallel to Chapel St is Artists Lane (Aerosol Alley to south-siders), a long bluestone alley soaked in street art. The project was initiated by artist Wayne Tindall, who started by painting himself and his wife outside his studio in the laneway before getting other artists involved, with the blessing of the local council. In the corner of the car park that spills off the laneway, look out for childlike human-animal hybrids by internationally renowned Melbourne artist Kaff-eine.

◉ **St Kilda**

St Kilda is Melbourne's slightly tattered bohemian heart, a place where a young Nick Cave played gloriously chaotic gigs at the George Hotel (formerly the Crystal Ballroom) and a place featured in countless songs, plays, novels, TV series and films.

Starting life as a 19th-century seaside resort, the neighbourhood has played many roles: post-war Jewish enclave, red-light district, punk-rocker hub and real-estate hot spot. It's a complex, hypnotic jumble of boom-style Victorian mansions, raffish Spanish Moorish apartments, seedy side streets, cosmopolitan wine bars, crusty pubs, rickety roller coasters and nostalgia-inducing theatres.

St Kilda Foreshore   BEACH
(Map p478; Jacka Blvd, St Kilda; 3, 12, 16, 96) Despite the palm-fringed promenades and golden stretch of sand, St Kilda's seaside appeal is more Brighton, England, than Venice, LA. The kiosk at the end of St Kilda Pier is as much about the journey as the destination: the pier offers a knockout panorama of the Melbourne skyline.

During summer Port Phillip EcoCentre (Map p478; 03-9534 0670; www.ecocentre.com; 55a Blessington St, St Kilda) runs a range of tours, including urban wildlife walks and coastal discovery walks, and offers information on the little-penguin colony that lives in the breakwater behind the pier's kiosk.

Linden New Art   GALLERY
(Map p478; 03-9534 0099; www.lindenarts. org; 26 Acland St, St Kilda; 11am-4pm Tue & Thu-Sun, to 8pm Wed; 3, 12, 16, 96) Housed in a wrought iron-clad 1870s mansion, Linden mainly champions new contemporary art by midcareer artists. The annual postcard show (generally held from late October to January) is a highlight.

Luna Park   AMUSEMENT PARK
(Map p478; 03-9525 5033; www.lunapark. com.au; 18 Lower Esplanade, St Kilda; single ride adult/child $11/10, unlimited rides $50/40; hrs vary; 3, 16, 96) Luna Park opened in 1912 and still has the feel of an old-style amusement park, with creepy Mr Moon's gaping mouth swallowing you up as you enter. There's a heritage-listed 'scenic railway' (the oldest operating roller coaster in the world), a beautifully baroque carousel with hand-painted horses, swans and chariots, as well as the full complement of gut-churning rides.

St Kilda Botanical Gardens   GARDENS
(Map p478; 03-9209 6777; www.portphillip.vic. gov.au; cnr Blessington & Tennyson Sts, St Kilda; sunrise-sunset, conservatory 10.30am-3.30pm Mon-Fri, sunrise-sunset Sat & Sun; 96.) Taking pride of place on the southern line of the Barkly, Carlisle and Blessington St triangle, the Botanical Gardens are an unexpected haven from the St Kilda hustle. Wide gravel paths invite a leisurely stroll, and there are plenty of shady spots to sprawl on the open lawns. Features include local indigenous plants, a subtropical-rainforest conservatory and a giant chessboard for large-scale plotting.

Jewish Museum of Australia   MUSEUM
(Map p478; 03-9834 3600; www.jewishmuseum. com.au; 26 Alma Rd, St Kilda; adult/child/family $10/5/20; 10am-4pm Tue-Thu, to 3pm Fri, to 5pm Sun, closed Jewish holy days; 3, 67) Interactive displays tell the history of Australia's Jewish community from the earliest days of European settlement, while permanent exhibitions celebrate Judaism's rich cycle of festivals and holy days. The museum also has a good curatorial reputation for its contemporary art exhibitions. By car, follow St Kilda Rd from St Kilda Junction, then turn left at Alma Rd.

Jewish Holocaust Centre   MUSEUM
(03-9528 1985; www.jhc.org.au; 13-15 Selwyn St, Elsternwick; by donation; 10am-4pm Mon-Thu, to 2pm Fri, noon-4pm Sun; 67, Elsternwick) FREE Dedicated to the memory of the six million Jews who lost their lives during the Holocaust, this well-presented museum was set up by survivors as a sobering reminder of the atrocities they endured. Guided tours are often led by Holocaust survivors.

Activities

Kayak Melbourne   KAYAKING
(Map p462; 0418 106 427; www.kayakmelbourne.com.au; Alexandra Gardens, Boathouse Dr, Southbank; tours $82-110; 11, 48) Ninety-minute City Sights tours paddle past Southbank to Docklands, while two-hour River to Sky tours include entry to the Eureka Skydeck (p466). You can also start your day saluting the sun on a two-hour Yoga Sunrise tour, or end it with a 2½-hour Moonlight tour starting from Docklands.

Royal Melbourne Yacht Squadron   BOATING
(RMYC; Map p478; 03-9534 0227; www. rmys.com.au; Pier Rd, St Kilda; 3, 16, 96) Here anyone can have a go on a yacht ($20) on Wednesday night during daylight-saving time (October to April); arrive by 4.30pm. Wear nonmarking shoes (with white soles) and bring sunscreen and waterproof gear. In

St Kilda & Around

0 500 m
0 0.25 miles

MELBOURNE & VICTORIA MELBOURNE

Alma Park East
Alma Park West

Westbury St
Blenheim St
Raglan St
Nelson St

ST KILDA EAST

Chapel St
Chapel St

Redan St
Crimea St
Odessa St
Argyle St
Lambeth Pl
Alma Rd
Crimea St

Charnwood Cres
Waterloo Cres

St Kilda Rd

Charles St
Inkerman St
Blanche St

Queen St
Inkerman St
Camden St

Pakington St
Martin St
Duke St

BALACLAVA
Balaclava
William St
Marlborough St
Nightingale St

Carlisle St
27

16
19

25
30
34

Brighton Rd

Greeves St
Vale St
Carlisle St
Mitchell St
Smith St
Blessington St

28
Irymple Ave
Mozart St
Tennyson St

ELWOOD

St Kilda Botanical Gardens
4
Herbert St
22

Barkly St
26
39
8
33

Dalgety St
Burnett St
Gurner St
Grey St
Little Grey St

St Kilda Sports Club (100m)
35
14
11
31
21
15

ST KILDA WEST

Mary St
Park St
Fitzroy St
Jackson St
Victoria St
Acland St
Eldon Rd
Neptune St
St Leonards Ave
Alfred Pl
Robe St
Clyde St
Hawker St
Havelock St

38
2

ST KILDA

Alfred Square
41

The Esplanade
Lower Esplanade
Cavell St
Shakespeare Gr
O'Donnell Gardens
3
37

Peanut Farm Reserve
Spenser St
Acland St
Barkly St
Belford St
Foster St
Charles St

12
23
32
36
24
17
18

Chaucer St
40
20
Mitford St

Elwood Beach (1.5km)

Marine Pde
Jacka Blvd
29

Catani Gardens
Beaconsfield Pde
Pier Rd

9
10
7
5

6

Hobsons Bay

Port Phillip

St Kilda & Around

winter, races take place on Wednesday afternoon, so you'll need to arrive by noon. Races also take place most Saturdays, though times vary; call ahead.

Japanese Bath House BATHHOUSE
(Map p458; ☎03-9419 0268; www.japanese
bathhouse.com; 59 Cromwell St, Collingwood; bath $32, shiatsu 30/60min $48/82; ⊙11am-last entry 8pm Tue-Fri, last entry 6pm Sat & Sun; ⊕109) Urban as the setting is, it's as serene as can be inside this authentic *sentō* (bathhouse). Partake in some communal skinship (it's nude, segregated bathing), a shiatsu and a postsoak sake or tea in the tatami lounge. Bookings are recommended and there's a useful how-to guide on the website for the uninitiated.

Aurora Spa Retreat SPA
(Map p478; ☎03-9536 1130; www.auroraspare
treat.com; 2 Acland St, St Kilda; 1hr massage $175; ⊙10am-6pm Mon, Tue, Thu & Fri, 11.30am-7.30pm Wed, 9am-5.30pm Sat, 10am-3pm Sun; ⊕3, 12, 16, 96) Treatments at this chichi oasis inside the Prince hotel (p486) range from body massages and exfoliations to facials, man-

icures and pedicures. The award-winning Kitya Karnu signature treatment ($225) is especially popular, consisting of an hour of scrubbing, rubbing and smoothing in a private steam room. Treatments lasting two or more hours attract a 30% discount Monday to Thursday.

Fitzroy Swimming Pool SWIMMING
(Map p470; ☎03-9205 5180; 160 Alexandra Pde, Fitzroy; adult/child/under 5yr $6.50/3.30/free; ⊙6am-9pm Mon-Thu, to 8pm Fri, 8am-6pm Sat & Sun; ⊕11) Between laps, locals love catching a few rays up in the bleachers or on the lawn; there's also a toddler pool.

Melbourne Sports & Aquatic Centre SWIMMING
(MSAC; Map p458; ☎03-9926 1555; www.msac.
com.au; Albert Rd, Albert Park; adult/child from $8.20/5.60; ⊙5.30am-10pm Mon-Fri, 7am-8pm Sat & Sun; ⊕96, 112) Flanking Albert Park Lake (p473), Melbourne's premier aquatic centre was a venue for the 2006 Commonwealth Games. Facilities include indoor and outdoor 50m pools, an indoor 25m pool, a wave pool, water slides, a spa, sauna and

steam room, and spacious common areas. Childcare is available.

Prahran Aquatic Centre
SWIMMING

(Map p474; ☑ 03-8290 7140; www.facebook.com/prahranaquaticcentre; 41 Essex St, Prahran; adult/child $6.20/3.50; ⏱ 5.45am-7.45pm Mon-Fri, 6am-6.15pm Sat, 7am-6.15pm Sun; ☒ 72, 78, ☒ Prahran) More than just a 50m heated outdoor pool, this place is a total scene in summer, with no shortage of buffed south-side bods soaking up some rays on the poolside lawn. Centre facilities include a spa, a sauna, a steam room and (in summer) a toddler pool.

Kite Republic
KITESURFING

(Map p478; ☑ 03-9537 0644; www.kiterepublic.com.au; St Kilda Sea Baths, 4/10-18 Jacka Blvd, St Kilda; 1hr lesson $90; ⏱ 10am-6pm Mon-Fri, to 5pm Sat & Sun; ☒ 96) Offers kiteboarding lessons, tours and equipment; also a good source of info. In winter it can arrange snow-kiting at Mt Hotham. Also rents stand-up paddleboards (SUPs) and street SUPs.

Stand Up Paddle HQ
WATER SPORTS

(Map p478; ☑ 0416 184 994; www.supb.com.au; St Kilda Pier, St Kilda; hire per hr $30, 1½hr tour $99; ☒ 96) Arrange a lesson or hire SUP equipment from St Kilda Pier, or join its Yarra River tour.

⛵ Tours

Melbourne Street Tours
WALKING

(☑ 03-93285556; www.melbournestreettours.com; tours $69; ⏱ city centre 1.30pm Tue, Thu & Sat, Fitzroy 11am Sat) Three-hour tours exploring the street art of the city centre or Fitzroy. The tour guides are street artists themselves, so you'll get a good insight into this art form.

★Rentabike
CYCLING

(Map p462; ☑ 0417 339 203; www.rentabike.net.au; Federation Wharf; rental per hr/day $15/40, 4hr tour incl lunch adult/child $110/79; ⏱ 10am-5pm; ☒ Flinders St) 🏃 Rents bikes and runs Real Melbourne Bike Tours, offering a local's insight into the city, with a foodie focus.

Melbourne By Foot
WALKING

(Map p462; ☑ 1300 311 081; www.melbournebyfoot.com; departs Federation Sq; tours $40; ⏱ 1pm; ☒ Flinders St) Take a few hours out and experience a mellow, informative three-hour walking tour that covers laneway art, politics, Melbourne's history and diversity. Highly recommended; book online. There's also a Beer Lovers tour ($85).

Hidden Secrets Tours
WALKING

(☑ 03-9663 3358; www.hiddensecretstours.com; tours from $29) Offers a variety of walking tours covering subjects such as lanes and arcades, history, architecture and cafe culture.

Melbourne Visitor Shuttle
BUS

(www.thatsmelbourne.com.au; 2 days $10; ⏱ 9.30am-3.45pm) Hop-on, hop-off bus tour with an audio commentary, stopping at 13 of Melbourne's main sights on a 90-minute loop.

Aboriginal Heritage Walk
CULTURAL

(Map p458; ☑ 03-9252 2429; www.rbg.vic.gov.au; Royal Botanic Gardens, Birdwood Ave, South Yarra; adult/child $31/12; ⏱ 11am Sun-Fri; ☒ 3, 5, 6, 16, 64, 67, 72) 🏃 The Royal Botanic Gardens is on a traditional camping and meeting place of the Kulin people, and this tour takes you through their story – from songlines to plant lore, all in 90 fascinating minutes. The tour departs from the gardens' visitor centre (p475).

City Circle Trams
TOURS

(☑ 13 16 38; www.ptv.vic.gov.au; ⏱ 10am-6pm Sun-Wed, to 9pm Thu-Sat; ☒ 35) 🆓 Designed primarily for tourists, this free tram service travels around the city centre, passing many city sights along the way. It runs every 12 minutes or so and there's a recorded commentary.

Eight refurbished W-class trams operate on this route. Built in Melbourne between 1936 and 1956, they have all been painted a distinctive deep burgundy or green and gold. You can also dine on board the **Colonial Tramcar Restaurant** (Map p458; ☑ 03-9695 4000; www.tramrestaurant.com.au; tram stop 125, Normanby Rd, Southbank; meals $82-140; ⏱ departs 1pm, 5.45pm & 8.35pm; ☑; ☒ 12, 96, 109) while scuttling around Melbourne's streets.

★ Festivals & Events

Australian Open
SPORTS

(www.australianopen.com; Melbourne Park, Olympic Blvd, Melbourne; ⏱ Jan) The world's top tennis players and huge, merry-making crowds descend for Australia's grand-slam tennis championship.

St Jerome's Laneway Festival
MUSIC

(www.lanewayfestival.com; Footscray Community Arts Centre, 45 Moreland St, Footscray; ⏱ Jan) It got its start at St Jerome's bar in the city centre's Caledonian Lane, but this one-day music fest has lost nothing in its move to the

Footscray riverside. Laneway does a brilliant job in scheduling international and local alternative artists just as they're starting to break through.

★ Chinese New Year   CULTURAL
(www.chinatownmelbourne.com.au; Little Bourke St; ☺ Jan or Feb) The lunar new year goes off with a bang in Chinatown, where the world's biggest processional dragon rules the streets.

Midsumma Festival   LGBT
(www.midsumma.org.au) Melbourne's annual gay and lesbian festival features more than 100 events from mid-January to mid-February, bookended by a carnival in Alexandra Gardens and the Pride March along Fitzroy St, St Kilda.

Australian Formula 1 Grand Prix   SPORTS
(☑ 1800 100 030; www.grandprix.com.au; Albert Park Lake, Albert Park; tickets from $55; ☺ Mar) The zippy 5.3km street circuit around the (normally) tranquil Albert Park Lake is known for its smooth, fast surface. The buzz, both on the streets and in your ears, takes over Melbourne for four days of revhead action.

Melbourne Food & Wine Festival   FOOD & DRINK
(www.melbournefoodandwine.com.au; ☺ Mar-Apr) Market tours, wine tastings, cooking classes and presentations by celeb chefs take place at venues across the city (and state).

Melbourne International Comedy Festival   COMEDY
(www.comedyfestival.com.au; ☺ Mar-Apr) An enormous range of local and international comic talent hits town, with four weeks of laughs.

AFL Grand Final   SPORTS
(www.afl.com.au; MCG, Brunton Ave, East Melbourne) It's easier to kick a goal from the boundary line than to pick up random tickets to the Grand Final, usually held on the final Saturday in September, but it's not hard to get your share of finals fever anywhere in Melbourne (particularly at pubs).

Melbourne Cup   SPORTS
(www.springracingcarnival.com.au; Flemington Racecourse) Culminating in the prestigious Melbourne Cup, the Spring Racing Carnival is as much a social event as a sporting one. The Cup, held on the first Tuesday in November, is a public holiday in Melbourne.

🛏 Sleeping

As in any big city, accommodation in Melbourne is relatively expensive and you'll need to book well ahead if your trip coincides with a major event such as the Australian Open (p1048) or the Melbourne Cup. Prices tend to shoot up on Friday and Saturday nights, and are often at their lowest on Sunday night.

🛏 Airport & Around

If you've got an early flight to catch – or you're arriving late and jet-lagged and just need a place to crash – there are some decent options near Melbourne Airport. The **Parkroyal** (☑ 03-8347 2000; www.parkroyal hotels.com; Arrival Dr, Melbourne Airport; r from $323; ❄ @ 🛜 🏊) has all the bells and whistles, and direct 'air-bridge' access to the terminal. The smart but slightly further away **Holiday Inn Melbourne Airport** (☑ 03-9933 5111; www.ihg.com; 10-14 Centre Rd, Melbourne Airport; r from $206; 🅿 ❄ 🛜 🏊) is a cheaper option, with a free shuttle service.

🛏 City Centre

Space Hotel   HOSTEL $
(Map p462; ☑ 03-9662 3888; www.spacehotel. com.au; 380 Russell St; dm from $37, r with/without bathroom from $100/89; ❄ 🛜; 🚇 Melbourne Central) One of Melbourne's few genuine flashpackers, this sleek place walks the line between hostel and budget hotel. The better private rooms have iPod docks and flat-screen TVs, while dorms have thoughtful touches like large lockers equipped with sensor lights and lockable adapters. Some of the doubles have en suites and balconies. The rooftop hot tub is another big tick.

Home @ The Mansion   HOSTEL $
(Map p470; ☑ 03-9663 4212; www.homeatthe mansion.com; 80 Victoria Pde, East Melbourne; dm/r from $33/80; @ 🛜; 🚇 Parliament) Located within a castlelike former Salvation Army building with grand double staircases, this is one of Melbourne's few hostels with genuine character. It has 92 dorm beds and a couple of double rooms; all rooms are light and bright and have lovely high ceilings. There are two small TV areas, a courtyard out the front and a sunny kitchen.

Melbourne Central YHA   HOSTEL $
(Map p462; ☑ 03-9621 2523; www.yha.com.au; 562 Flinders St; dm from $36, d with/without

bathroom $130/107; @ 🛜; 🚉Southern Cross) The former Markillie's Hotel has been transformed by the YHA gang: expect a lively reception, handsome rooms, and kitchens and common areas on each of the four levels. Entertainment's high on the agenda, and there's a cafe on the ground floor and a grand rooftop area. Best of all are the two private en-suite rooms on the roof.

Pensione Hotel
HOTEL $

(Map p462; ☑03-9621 3333; www.pensione. com.au; 16 Spencer St; s/d from $115/125; P ❋ @ 🛜 🛋; 🚉Southern Cross) With refreshing honesty, the lovely, boutique Pensione Hotel names some room categories 'matchbox' and 'shoebox' – but what you don't get in size is more than made up for in style and reasonable rates.

★Treasury on Collins
APARTMENT $$

(Map p462; ☑03-8535 8535; www.treasuryon collins.com.au; 394 Collins St; apt from $198; ❋ 🛜; 🚆11, 12, 48, 109) This imposing stone neoclassical building (1876) once housed a branch of the Bank of Australia. An impressive bar now fills the downstairs space, its impossibly high ceiling supported by gilt-edged columns. The apartments, on the other hand, are modern and restrained, not to mention chic and spacious. Winning extras include coffee machines, laundries and free Netflix.

Alto Hotel on Bourke
HOTEL $$

(Map p462; ☑03-8608 5500; www.altohotel. com.au; 636 Bourke St; r/apt from $176/220; P ❋ 🛜; 🚉Southern Cross) 🌿 Environmentally minded Alto has water-saving showers, energy-efficient lights and double-glazed windows, and in-room recycling is encouraged. Rooms are well equipped, with good light and neutral decoration, and even the 'petite' rooms are a reasonable size. Studios have kitchenettes, while larger apartments have full kitchens. Guests also have access to a full-service gym nearby.

United Backpackers
HOSTEL $$

(Map p462; ☑03-9654 2616; www.unitedback packers.com.au; 250 Flinders St; dm from $40, r with/without bathroom $170/125; ❋ @ 🛜; 🚉Flinders St) Occupying an Edwardian building right in the heart of the action, and opposite Flinders St station, this perpetually buzzing backpackers has been thoughtfully renovated throughout. The prices are steep for a hostel, but it's arguably the best one in the city.

Punthill Flinders Lane
APARTMENT $$

(Map p462; ☑03-9631 1199; www.punthill. com.au; 267 Flinders Lane; apt from $158; ❋ 🛜; 🚉Flinders St) The black-walled lobby sets a schmick tone for this well-positioned apartment hotel. The spacious one-bedroom apartments have full kitchens, while the studios are more like hotel rooms with kitchenettes. Plus there's a communal laundry hidden in a cupboard in the corridor.

Radisson on Flagstaff Gardens
HOTEL $$

(Map p462; ☑03-9322 8000; www.radisson.com/ melbourneau; 380 William St; r from $222; ❋ @ 🛜; 🚉Flagstaff) Directly opposite Flagstaff Gardens, this is a great option for those who enjoy a bit of greenery outside their window while being in striking distance of city sightseeing. The rooftop spa is a huge perk.

Punthill Little Bourke
APARTMENT $$

(Map p462; ☑03-8680 5900; www.punthill.com. au; 11-17 Cohen Pl; apt from $160; ❋ @ 🛜 🛋; 🚉Parliament) Neat and modern open-plan apartments have bright colours, balconies, laundries and stainless-steel kitchens. Lots of light, an indoor lap pool and a heart-of-Chinatown laneway location lift this little place above the ordinary.

Vibe Savoy Hotel
HOTEL $$

(Map p462; ☑03-9622 8888; www.tfehotels.com; 630 Little Collins St; r from $200; ❋ 🛜; 🚉Southern Cross) With 11 floors, the Savoy was the tallest building in Melbourne when it first opened its doors in the 1920s. Although it's been thoroughly made over, period features still show through. It's a concoction of traditional hotel comforts, bright colours and contemporary furnishings.

★QT Melbourne
HOTEL $$$

(Map p462; ☑03-8636 8800; www.qtmelbourne. com.au; 133 Russell St; r from $350; @ 🛜; 🚆86, 96) Rough concrete surfaces, brass trim, lifts with tapestry light boxes that play house music and say random stuff in a Russian accent: this is one of Melbourne's newest, quirkiest and best boutique hotels. The rooms are beautifully kitted out and there's a great plant-draped rooftop bar too.

★Ovolo Laneways
BOUTIQUE HOTEL $$$

(Map p462; ☑03-8692 0777; www.ovolohotels. com.au; 19 Little Bourke St; r from $219; ❋ @ 🛜; 🚉Parliament) This boutique hotel mixes hipster chic with a funky executive vibe. It's friendly, fun and loaded with goodies –

there's a free self-service laundry, a free mini-bar in each room, free booze downstairs at the daily happy hour and a Nespresso machine in the lobby.

Hotel Lindrum BOUTIQUE HOTEL $$$

(Map p462; ☑03-9668 1111; www.hotellindrum. com.au; 26 Flinders St; r from $330; ❋ 🖰; 🚇Parliament) One of the city's most attractive hotels, this was once the snooker hall of the legendary and literally unbeatable Walter Lindrum. Expect minimalist tones, subtle lighting and tactile fabrics. Spring for a deluxe room and you'll snare either arch or bay windows and marvellous Melbourne views. And yes, there's a billiard table – one of Lindrum's originals, no less.

Adelphi Hotel HOTEL $$$

(Map p462; ☑03-8080 8888; www.adelphi.com. au; 187 Flinders Lane; r from $335; ❋🖰➡; 🚇Flinders St) One of Australia's first boutique hotels, this discreet Flinders Lane property has a distinctly glam European feel, with design touches throughout. The lobby looks good enough to eat, although it could just be the dessert-themed Om Nom restaurant and cocktail bar that's making us salivate. You'll also find free lollies and nonalcoholic beverages in the well-stocked minibars.

St Jerome's The Hotel TENTED CAMP $$$

(Map p462; ☑0406 118 561; www.stjeromesthe hotel.com.au; Melbourne Central rooftop, 3/300 Lonsdale St; tents $420-480; 🚇Melbourne Central) Each of the canvas glamping tents here has a double or a queen bed with funky bedspreads, reverse-cycle air-conditioners, a complimentary cooler of craft beer and cider, and free 10-pin bowling at Strike next door. Come morning, there's an on-site barista and brekky box. It's a great experience, but then it would need to be for these prices.

Park Hyatt HOTEL $$$

(Map p458; ☑03-9224 1234; www.melbourne. park.hyatt.com; 1 Parliament Sq, East Melbourne; r from $375; ❋@🖰➡; 🚇Parliament) Resembling a Californian shopping mall from the outside, the Park Hyatt has a luxurious interior with wood panelling, shiny surfaces and miles of marble. Rooms are elegantly subdued, and most have supersized baths, clever layouts that maximise your chance of seeing natural light and lovely treetop-level views. There's a lavish indoor pool, plus a great tennis court.

Sofitel HOTEL $$$

(Map p462; ☑03-9653 0000; www.sofitel-melb ourne.com; 25 Collins St; r from $352; 🅿❋ @🖰➡; 🚇Parliament) Guest rooms at the Sofitel start on the 36th floor, so you're guaranteed views that will make you giddy. The rooms are of a high international style and, though the hotel entrance is relentlessly workaday, you'll soon be a world (or at least 36 floors) away.

Grand Hyatt Melbourne HOTEL $$$

(Map p462; ☑03-9657 1234; www.melbourne. grand.hyatt.com; 123 Collins St; r from $445; ❋@🖰➡; 🚇Flinders St) Plenty grand enough to warrant the name, this famous Collins St five-star has over 500 rooms, with marble bathrooms, designated workspaces and floor-to-ceiling windows looking out to the city centre, Yarra River or MCG.

🛏 Southbank & Docklands

Hilton Melbourne South Wharf HOTEL $$

(Map p458; ☑03-9027 2000; www.hiltonmelbourne. com.au; 2 Convention Centre Pl, South Wharf; r from $200; 🅿❋🖰; 🚍35, 70, 75) Polished wood and natural fibres provide an earthy feel in this luxurious hotel. Suites are huge and some offer dazzling views along the river. There's an in-house Aboriginal art gallery and all of the art in reception is for sale – except for the giant piece above the desk that appears to have been crafted from pot scourers.

Quest Docklands APARTMENT $$

(Map p458; ☑03-9630 1000; www.questdock lands.com.au; 750 Bourke St, Docklands; apt from $220; 🅿❋@🖰; 🚍35, 70, 75, 🚇Southern Cross) Join the new breed of Melburnians on the Docklands frontier. These apartments are well kept and smartly furnished, and, while the studios are small, they have kitchens and laundry facilities; one-bedroom apartments have balconies. It's practically on the doorstep of Etihad Stadium, so it's perfect for big-game visits.

Crown Towers HOTEL $$$

(Map p462; ☑03-9292 6868; www.crownhotels. com.au/crown-towers-melbourne; 8 Whiteman St, Southbank; r from $338; 🅿❋🖰➡; 🚍55) Crown's flashest digs, this oversized hotel shrugs off the gaudy glitziness of its reception by the time you reach the quietly elegant rooms, many of which have extraordinary views. The large bathrooms have separate tubs and shower stalls, and the walk-in wardrobe is something you could easily get used to.

Crown Metropol HOTEL $$$

(Map p458; ☑ 03-9292 8319; www.crownmetropol
melbourne.com.au; 8 Whiteman St, Southbank; r
from $258; **P** ❋ **@** 🛜 ☃; 🛗 12, 96, 109) Welcome
to the biggest hotel in the southern hemi-
sphere, with a staggering 658 rooms spread
over 28 floors. Guests have access to Skybar
on the top floor and the most extraordinary
indoor infinity pool one floor down, offering
views over the city to the Dandenongs in the
distance. Rooms are suitably luxurious.

🛏 Richmond & East Melbourne

Aberlour Court APARTMENT $$

(Map p458; ☑ 03-9039 5310; www.aberlourcourt.
com.au; 462 Victoria Pde, East Melbourne; apt
from $155; **P** ❋ **@** ☃; 🚉 North Richmond) Built
sometime in the latter half of last century,
this three-storey brick residential block has
been thoroughly smartened up and converted into an appealing apartment hotel.
The brand-new bathrooms and kitchens
are decked out in Italian tiles, and every
unit has laundry facilities and separate bedrooms; the better ones have balconies or private terraces too.

🛏 Fitzroy, Collingwood & Abbotsford

★**Nunnery** HOSTEL $

(Map p470; ☑ 1800 032 635; www.nunnery.
com.au; 116 Nicholson St, Fitzroy; dm/s/d from
$34/95/120; **@** 🛜; 🛗 96) Built in 1888, the
Nunnery oozes atmosphere, with sweeping staircases and many original features;
the walls are dripping with religious works
of art and ornate stained-glass windows.
You'll be giving thanks for the big, comfortable lounges and communal areas. The
next-door Nunnery Guesthouse has larger
rooms in a private setting (from $130). It's
popular, so book ahead. All rates include
breakfast.

★**Tyrian Serviced
Apartments** APARTMENT $$

(Map p470; ☑ 03-9415 1900; www.tyrian.com.
au; 91 Johnston St, Fitzroy; apt from $188; **P** ❋ 🛜;
🛗 11) These spacious, self-contained mod-
ern apartments have a certain Fitzroy-celeb
vibe. Big couches, flat-screen TVs, European
laundries and balconies add to the appeal,
and plenty of restaurants and bars are right
at your door. It's rounded off with free wi-fi
and parking. Rooms facing Johnston St can
get noisy.

Brooklyn Arts Hotel B&B $$

(Map p470; ☑ 03-9419 9328; www.brooklynarts
hotel.com.au; 48-50 George St, Fitzroy; s/d from
$115/155; 🛜; 🛗 86) There are seven rooms
in this character-filled hotel owned by film-
maker and artist Maggie Fooke. Set in a
lovely terrace house, rooms vary in size but
are all clean, quirky, colourful and beautifully decorated. Spacious upstairs rooms
with high ceilings and balconies are the pick
(from $220). Expect lively conversation at
the included continental breakfast of local
sourdough bread and homemade jams.

🛏 Carlton & Brunswick

169 Drummond B&B $$

(Map p472; ☑ 03-9663 3081; www.169drummond.
com.au; 169 Drummond St, Carlton; d incl break-
fast $135; ☯ ❋ 🛜; 🛗 1) This privately owned
guesthouse in a renovated 19th-century ter-
race is well located just a block from vibrant
Lygon St. Rooms feature fireplaces and
Persian rugs, and there's a homey dining
area and kitchenette for guests' use. It's gay
friendly and welcoming to all.

🛏 North Melbourne & Parkville

Bev & Mick's Backpackers HOSTEL $

(McMahon's Hotel; Map p458; ☑ 03-9328 2423;
www.facebook.com/BevAndMicksBackpackers; 575
Spencer St, West Melbourne; dm $28-30; **@** 🛜;
🚉 North Melbourne) On the city's fringe, this
rough-around-the-edges backpackers is con-
venient for balancing sightseeing with local
life. Above an appealing pub, it's always so-
cial, with a fantastic beer garden.

Larwill Studio HOTEL $$

(Map p458; ☑ 03-9032 9111; www.thelarwillstudio.
com.au; 48 Flemington Rd, Parkville; r from $189;
P 🛜; 🛗 55, 57, 59) Named after artist David Larwill (1956–2011), whose paintings
brighten the walls, this highly unusual hotel
is within the confines of the Royal Children's
Hospital. Don't let that put you off: the
rooms are fresh, breezy and, despite being
relatively simple, not remotely hospital-like.
It's worth paying $30 more for a park view.

🛏 South Melbourne, Port Melbourne & Albert Park

Drop Bear Inn HOSTEL $

(Map p458; ☑ 03-9690 2220; www.dropbear-
inn.com.au; 115 Cecil St, South Melbourne; dm/d
from $24/50; **@** 🛜; 🛗 96, 12) Named after

Australia's legendary fearsome creature, this hostel is right opposite South Melbourne Market, so it's great for fresh produce – particularly the bargains available at closing time. It's above a pub, so it'll suit those looking to party. Most rooms have good natural light and more charm than is generally found at hostels. Free wi-fi.

★**Coppersmith** BOUTIQUE HOTEL $$
(Map p458; ☑03-8696 7777; http://coppersmith hotel.com.au; 435 Clarendon St, South Melbourne; r from $230; ❋🖥🛜; 🚋12) Low key, contemporary and elegantly restrained, the 15-room Coppersmith has every right to call itself a boutique property. Designer furniture, heavenly beds and fine woollen rugs set a seductive tone in the muted rooms, each with Nespresso machine, work desk, free wi-fi and recordable cable TV. On-site assets include a smart, locavore bistro-bar and a rooftop deck with skyline views.

Blackman BOUTIQUE HOTEL $$
(Map p458; ☑03-9039 1444, 1800 278 468; www. artserieshotels.com.au/blackman; 452 St Kilda Rd, Melbourne; r from $200; ❋🛜; 🚋3, 5, 6, 16, 64, 67, 72) While it may not have any original Charles Blackman paintings (though there are loads of prints and Blackman room decals), it does have a superb outlook – aim for a corner suite for views of Albert Park Lake and the city skyline. Beds are luxurious, though wear-and-tear is a problem in some rooms.

🛏 South Yarra, Prahran & Windsor

Back of Chapel HOSTEL $
(Map p474; ☑03-9521 5338; www.backofchapel. com; 50 Green St, Windsor; dm $32-36, d $80; ⊘reception 8.30am-5pm; @🛜; 🚋6, 78, 🚉Windsor) Literally 20 steps from the cooler end of Chapel St, Back of Chapel offers budget-conscious slumber in an old Victorian terrace. A clean, laid-back spot with four- and six-bed dorms, it also offers private twins, doubles and triples. Facilities include communal kitchen, BBQ and coin-operated laundry. It's especially popular with those on a working holiday. All rates include breakfast.

Hotel Claremont GUESTHOUSE $
(Map p474; ☑03-9826 8000; www.hotelclaremont. com; 189 Toorak Rd, South Yarra; dm/d from $48/88; 🛜; 🚋78, 79, 🚉South Yarra) In a heritage building dating to 1868, the Claremont offers good value on an exclusive strip. Rooms are simple, clean and comfortable, with high ceilings, wooden floorboards and shared bathrooms. There's a guest laundry and 24-hour reception. Best of all, it's steps from Chapel St and South Yarra station (a mere two stations from the city centre). Rates include breakfast.

Cullen BOUTIQUE HOTEL $$
(Map p474; ☑03-9098 1555; www.artserieshotels. com.au/cullen; 164 Commercial Rd, Prahran; r from $209; ❋@🛜; 🚋72, 78, 79, 🚉Prahran) The work of late grunge painter Adam Cullen drives the decor here: his vibrant and often graphic art provides such visions as Ned Kelly shooting you from the opaque bedroom-bathroom dividers. Rooms are stylish and comfy, with handy kitchenettes, though the standard studios are small. Rooms facing north and west from level four and up offer the best views.

Olsen BOUTIQUE HOTEL $$
(Map p474; ☑03-9040 1222; www.artserieshotels. com.au/olsen; 637 Chapel St, South Yarra; r from $199; 🅿❋🛜🏊; 🚋78, 🚉South Yarra) At the top end of Chapel St, steps from svelte South Yarra boutiques and cafes, this 224-suite property honours artist John Olsen. The painter's bold, raw artworks add verve to the open-plan, grey-and-silver rooms, each of which comes with handy kitchenette and sublimely comfortable AH Beard bed. Staff are attentive and the hotel's glass-bottomed pool juts out over Chapel St.

Punthill South Yarra Grand APARTMENT $$
(Map p474; ☑1300 731 299; www.punthill.com. au; 7 Yarra St, South Yarra; studios from $159, 1-/2-bedroom apt from $179/249; 🅿❋🛜; 🚋78, 79, 🚉South Yarra) It's the little things, like a blackboard and chalk in the kitchen for messages, that make this modern, charcoal-accented place a great choice. The smart, contemporary studios and apartments are equipped with kitchens; the one-, two- and three-bedroom apartments also have laundry facilities. The property has a small number of bikes for hire (per hour/day $4/15).

Royce on St Kilda Road BOUTIQUE HOTEL $$
(Map p458; ☑03-9677 9900; www.roycehotels. com.au; 379 St Kilda Rd, Melbourne; r from $189; ❋🛜; 🚋3, 5, 6, 16, 64, 67, 72) Close to the Botanic Gardens, the Royce occupies a Moorish-inspired building from the late 1920s. Originally a Rolls-Royce showroom, it's now a boutique slumber spot, with a mix of period

and modern features and a range of room types. Rooms are comfortable – with good bedding, marble bathrooms and large plasma TVs – if somewhat lacklustre. Facilities include a gym.

Lyall
BOUTIQUE HOTEL $$$

(Map p474; ☑03-9868 8222, 1800 338 234; www.thelyall.com; 16 Murphy St, South Yarra; r from $255; ❄🖧; ⊠South Yarra) Just off Toorak Rd, the 40-suite Lyall, with one- and two-bedroom apartments, is all about the good life: on-site spa and champagne bar, original artwork by French-born Thierry B, even a pillow menu. Suites are plush, if a little worn, with a seductive, textural palette of shantung, taffeta, suede, velvet and brocade. Regular guests include Melbourne-raised singer Olivia Newton-John.

🛏 St Kilda

★ Base
HOSTEL $

(Map p478; ☑03-8598 6200; www.stayatbase.com; 17 Carlisle St, St Kilda; dm/d from $34/145; 🅿❄@🖧; ⊠3, 16, 96) Well-run Base has streamlined en-suite dorms and slick doubles. There's a floor set aside for female travellers, and a bar and live-music nights keep the good times rolling.

Habitat HQ
HOSTEL $

(Map p478; ☑03-9537 3777; www.habitathq.com.au; 333 St Kilda Rd, St Kilda; dm/d from $34/119; 🅿❄@🖧; ⊠3, 67) There's not much this clean, newish hostel doesn't have. Check off open-plan communal spaces, fully equipped kitchen, bar, beer garden, free breakfast, a travel agent and a pool table, for starters. Follow Carlisle St from St Kilda to St Kilda Rd – it's on your left.

Abode St Kilda
MOTEL $$

(Map p478; ☑03-9536 9700; www.easystay.com.au; 63 Fitzroy St, St Kilda; d from $122; 🅿❄🖧; ⊠3, 12, 16, 96) A great choice for those who've outgrown hostels but want an affordable private room in the heart of the action. Although the exterior suggests dodgy motel, the rooms are upbeat, contemporary and comfortable, with free wi-fi and in-house movies, handy kitchenettes, and bathrooms with underfloor heating and rain shower heads.

Prince
HOTEL $$

(Map p478; ☑03-9536 1111; www.theprince.com.au; 2 Acland St, St Kilda; r from $175; 🅿❄🖧❄; ⊠3, 12, 16, 96) The brooding, David Lynch-esque lobby sets a sexy, stylish tone at this fashionable favourite. Rooms are pared back and chic, if a little tired. Also on-site are the celebrated Prince Bandroom (p508) (be prepared for weekend noise) and the Aurora Spa Retreat (p479). Note that the hotel's (unheated) pool is in a private-function space and so isn't always accessible.

Hotel Tolarno
HOTEL $$

(Map p478; ☑03-9537 0200; www.tolarnohotel.com.au; 42 Fitzroy St, St Kilda; s/d/ste from $109/119/169; ❄🖧; ⊠3, 12, 16, 96) Once the site of art dealer Georges Mora's seminal gallery, Tolarno has a range of rooms, all eclectically furnished, with good beds, bright and bold original artworks, Nespresso machine and free wi-fi. Those at the front of the building might get a bit noisy, but they compensate with balconies and enormous windows overlooking Fitzroy St.

🍴 Eating

🍴 City Centre

★ Hakata Gensuke
RAMEN $

(Map p462; ☑03-9663 6342; www.gensuke.com.au; 168 Russell St; mains $13-14; ⏱11.30am-2.45pm & 5-9.30pm Mon-Fri, noon-9.30pm Sat & Sun; ⊠Parliament) Gensuke is one of those places that only does one thing and does it extraordinarily well. In this case it's *tonkotsu* (pork broth) ramen. Choose from three types (signature, sesame-infused 'black' or spicy 'god fire') and then order extra toppings (marinated *cha-shu* pork, egg, seaweed, black fungus). Inevitably there will be a queue, but it's well worth the wait.

Traveller
CAFE $

(Map p462; www.sevenseeds.com.au; 2/14 Crossley St; bagels $7-10; ⏱7am-5pm Mon-Fri; ⊠86, 96) This pocket-sized place is a proper stand-and-lean espresso bar, serving top-notch coffee courtesy of local roastery Seven Seeds. However, there are a couple of stools around the edge if you want to settle in with a newspaper and filled bagel (cream cheese; avocado and lemon; pastrami and Dijon etc). The sweet things displayed at the counter are enticing too.

Wonderbao
CHINESE $

(Map p462; ☑03-9654 7887; www.wonderbaokitchen.com.au; Literature Lane; bao $2.70-5.20; ⏱8am-6pm Mon-Fri, 11am-4pm Sat; ⊠Melbourne Central) Wonderbao does only one thing – no prizes for guessing what. Its *bao* (steamed buns) range from the traditional sticky-barbecue-pork variety to oddities like the breakfast *bao*. There are a few stools by the window but no tables.

Spring Street Grocer
DELI **$**

(Map p462; ☑03-9639 0335; www.springstreet grocer.com.au; 157 Spring St; rolls $12-13, ice cream $5; ☺9am-9pm; ☒Parliament) Join the waiting queue at **Gelateria Primavera** for fresh gelati, with a daily-changing selection scooped from traditional *pozzetti* (metal tubs fitted into the benchtops). Next door, the **sandwich bar** serves coffee and made-to-order rolls. Head down the winding staircase to reach the pungent **cheese cave**, an atmospheric maturation cellar with an impressive selection of international cheeses.

Stalactites
GREEK **$**

(Map p462; ☑03-9663 3316; www.stalactites. com.au; 177-183 Lonsdale St; mains $11-18; ☺24hr; ☒Melbourne Central) What's not to love about a 24-hour 'souva' joint? Especially when it's been doling out late-night lamb souvlakis in Melbourne for nearly 40 years. Located in the heart of what remains of the central city's little Greek precinct, it's an institution for an early-hours feed. The cavelike interior is hilarious too.

★Supernormal
ASIAN **$$**

(Map p462; ☑03-9650 8688; www.supernormal. net.au; 180 Flinders Lane; dishes $16-39; ☺11am-11pm; ☒Flinders St) Drawing on his years spent in Shanghai and Hong Kong, chef Andrew McConnell presents a creative selection of pan-Asian sharing dishes, from dumplings to raw seafood to slow-cooked Sichuan lamb. Even if you don't dine in, stop by for his now-famous takeaway New England lobster roll. No dinner bookings, so get here early to put your name on the list.

★Chin Chin
SOUTHEAST ASIAN **$$**

(Map p462; ☑03-8663 2000; www.chinchinres taurant.com.au; 125 Flinders Lane; mains $20-39; ☺11am-late; ☒Flinders St) Insanely popular, and for good reason, chic Chin Chin serves delicious Southeast Asian hawker-style food designed as shared plates. It's housed in a glammed-up old warehouse with a real New York feel, and while there are no bookings, you can fill in time at the **Go Go Bar** downstairs until there's space.

Hardware Société
CAFE **$$**

(Map p462; ☑03-9078 5992; 120 Hardware St; mains $14-26; ☺7.30am-2.30pm; ☒Melbourne Central) If you're not prepared for a lengthy queue, go elsewhere, as this wonderful little cafe is always heaving. Once you're finally seated – either outdoors under the awnings or beneath the butterfly wallpaper in the cute interior – an inventive menu of mouth-watering French-influenced cafe fare awaits.

Gazi
GREEK **$$**

(Map p462; ☑03-9207 7444; www.gazirestaurant. com.au; 2 Exhibition St; mains $12-28; ☺11.30am-late; ☒Parliament) The latest offering from George Calombaris of *MasterChef* fame, this side project to the fancier Press Club (next door) is set in a designer-industrial space and delivers a menu inspired by Greek street food. Select from authentic shared starters, gourmet mini souvlakis filled with soft-shell crab or duck, chargrilled octopus and spit-roasted meats.

Mamasita
MEXICAN **$$**

(Map p462; ☑03-9650 3821; www.mamasita.com. au; 1st fl, 11 Collins St; tacos $7, quesadillas $15, shared plates $24-27; ☺5-11pm Sun-Wed, noon-midnight Thu-Sat; ☒Parliament) The restaurant responsible for kicking off Melbourne's obsession with authentic Mexican street food, Mamasita is still one of the very best. The chargrilled corn sprinkled with cheese and chipotle mayo is a legendary starter, and there's a fantastic range of corn-tortilla tacos and a mammoth selection of tequila. It doesn't take reservations for dinner, so prepare to wait.

Café Vue
CAFE **$$**

(Map p462; ☑03-9691 3843; www.vuedemonde. com.au; 430 Little Collins St; mains $12-18; ☺7am-4pm Mon-Thu, to late Fri; ☒55, 86, 96) The most affordable outpost of Shannon Bennett's Vue de Monde empire serves excellent coffee and a wondrous range of cakes, pastries, Reuben sandwiches and fancy burgers. Join the cult following the pistachio cupcakes.

MoVida
TAPAS **$$**

(Map p462; ☑03-9663 3038; www.movida.com. au; 1 Hosier Lane; tapas $4-8, raciones $16-34; ☺noon-late; ☒Flinders St) MoVida's location in much-graffitied Hosier Lane is about as Melbourne as it gets. Line up by the bar, cluster around little window tables or, if you've booked, take a seat in the dining area for fantastic Spanish tapas and *raciones*. MoVida Next Door – yes, right next door –

is the perfect place for preshow beers and tapas.

Pellegrini's Espresso Bar ITALIAN $$

(Map p462; ☑ 03-9662 1885; 66 Bourke St; mains $18; ⏰ 8am-11pm Mon-Sat, noon-8pm Sun; ⊠ Parliament) The Italian equivalent of a classic 1950s diner, locally famous Pellegrini's has remained genuinely unchanged for decades. There's no menu with prices; the staff will tell you what's available. Expect classic Italian comfort food: lasagne, spaghetti bolognese and big slabs of cake. Service can be brusque, but that's all part of the experience.

Flower Drum CHINESE $$

(Map p462; ☑ 03-9662 3655; www.flowerdrum. melbourne; 1st fl, 17 Market Lane; mains $18-40; ⏰ noon-3pm & 6-11pm Mon-Sat, 6-10.30pm Sun; ☎; ⊠ Parliament) Established in 1975, Flower Drum continues to be Melbourne's most celebrated Chinese restaurant, imparting a charmingly old-fashioned ambience through its dark wood, lacquerwork and crisp white linen. The sumptuous but ostensibly simple Cantonese food (from a menu that changes daily) is delivered with the top-notch service you'd expect in such elegant surroundings.

Bar Lourinhã TAPAS $$

(Map p462; ☑ 03-9663 7890; www.barlourinha. com.au; 37 Little Collins St; tapas $4-8, raciones $16-30; ⏰ noon-11pm Mon-Thu, to 1am Fri & Sat; ⊠ Parliament) Grab a seat at the bar and let the charming waitstaff lead you through a menu of modern Portuguese and Spanish dishes and a corresponding list of Iberian wine. The zingy kingfish pancetta is a very good place to start.

Mesa Verde MEXICAN $$

(Map p462; ☑ 03-9654 4417; www.mesaverde. net.au; 6th fl, Curtin House, 252 Swanston St; mains $12-20; ⏰ 4pm-late Tue-Sun; ⊠ Melbourne Central) Part of the wonderful Curtin House complex, Mesa Verde does great Mexican food to a backdrop of Sergio Leone screenings. As well as street-food dishes, there's a vast selection of tequilas and mezcals, and an exotic choice of salts for margaritas, including black truffle.

HuTong Dumpling Bar CHINESE $$

(Map p462; ☑ 03-9650 8128; www.hutong.com. au; 14-16 Market Lane; mains $14-31; ⏰ 11.30am-3pm & 5.30-10.30pm; ⊠ Parliament) HuTong's reputation for divine *xiao long bao* means getting a lunchtime seat anywhere in this three-level building isn't easy. Downstairs,

watch chefs make the delicate dumplings, then hope they don't watch you making a mess eating them.

Belleville INTERNATIONAL $$

(Map p462; ☑ 03-9663 4041; www.belleville-melbourne.com; Globe Alley; mains $17-25; ⏰ 11am-1am; ⊠ Melbourne Central) Billing itself as 'the home of worldly eats, drinks and beats', Belleville has an enormous Brazilian rotisserie that barbecues 90 chickens at once. The rest of the sharing-style menu bounces around the globe but centres on Asia, with a few North American dishes (poutine, s'mores) thrown in for good measure.

Seamstress CHINESE $$

(Map p462; ☑ 03-9663 6363; www.seamstress. com.au; 113 Lonsdale St; mains $18-35; ⏰ noon-2.30pm & 5.30-10pm Mon-Fri, 5.30-10pm Sat; ⊠ Parliament) Start off with a cocktail under a canopy of tiny *qipao* dresses on the top floor, then make your way downstairs to the dining room for some contemporary Chinese cooking. The 19th-century warehouse, complete with rickety wooden stairs, is fabulously atmospheric.

Hopetoun Tea Rooms CAFE $$

(Map p462; ☑ 03-9650 2777; www.hopetountea rooms.com.au; Block Arcade, 282 Collins St; mains $18-26; ⏰ 8am-5pm; ⊠ Flinders St) Since 1892 patrons have been nibbling pinwheel sandwiches here, taking tea (with pinkies raised) and delicately polishing off a lamington. Hopetoun's venerable status results in almost perpetual queues. Salivate over the window display while you wait.

★ Lee Ho Fook CHINESE $$$

(Map p462; ☑ 03-9077 6261; www.leehofook. com.au; 11-15 Duckboard Pl; mains $32-42; ⏰ noon-2.30pm & 6-11pm Mon-Fri, 6-11pm Sat & Sun; ⊠ Parliament) Occupying an old brick warehouse down a fabulously skungy laneway, Lee Ho Fook is the epitome of modern Chinese culinary wizardry. The kitchen packs an extraordinary amount of flavour into signature dishes such as crispy eggplant with red vinegar, chicken crackling, liquorice wagyu beef, and crab and scallop rice with homemade XO sauce. The service is terrific too.

Tonka INDIAN $$

(Map p462; ☑ 03-9650 3155; www.tonkarestaurant. com.au; 20 Duckboard Pl; mains $26-40; ⏰ noon-3pm & 6pm-late Mon-Sat; ⊠ Parliament) Tonka's dining room is long, elegant and very white, with billowy white mesh forming clouds overhead. The food, however, is gloriously technicolour. The punchy flavours of Indian cuisine are combined with unexpected elements – burrata, for instance, served with coriander relish and charred roti. Get the clued-up sommelier to recommend some appropriate matches from the extraordinary wine list.

Coda   SOUTHEAST ASIAN **$$$**
(Map p462; ☑03-9650 3155; www.codarestaurant.com.au; basement, 141 Flinders Lane; larger plates $39-46; ☺noon-3pm & 6pm-late; ⍟Flinders St) Coda has a wonderful basement ambience, with exposed light bulbs and roughly stripped walls. Its innovative menu leans heavily towards Southeast Asian flavours, but Japanese, Korean, French and Italian influences are all apparent. While there are larger dishes made for sharing, the single-serve bites – such as the crispy prawn and tapioca betel leaf – are particularly good.

Cumulus Inc   MODERN AUSTRALIAN **$$$**
(Map p462; ☑03-9650 1445; www.cumulusinc.com.au; 45 Flinders Lane; breakfast $14-18, mains $36-44; ☺7am-11pm; ⍟Parliament) This bustling informal eatery focuses on beautiful produce and simple but artful cooking, served at the long marble bar and at little round tables dotted about. Dinner reservations are only taken for groups, so expect to queue. Upstairs is the Cumulus Up wine bar.

Longrain   THAI **$$$**
(Map p462; ☑03-9671 3151; www.longrain.com; 44 Little Bourke St; mains $30-40; ☺6-10pm Mon-Thu, noon-3pm & 5.30pm-late Fri, 5.30pm-late Sat & Sun; ⍟Parliament) Get in early or expect a long wait (sip a drink and relax, they suggest) before sampling Longrain's innovative Thai cuisine. The communal tables don't exactly work for a romantic date, but they're great for checking out everyone else's meals. Dishes are designed to be shared; try the pork-and-prawn eggnet, the amazing seafood dishes and the coconut sorbet.

Vue de Monde   MODERN AUSTRALIAN **$$$**
(Map p462; ☑03-9691 3888; www.vuedemonde.com.au; 55th fl, Rialto, 525 Collins St; set menu $230-275; ☺6-11pm Mon-Wed, noon-2pm & 6-11pm Thu-Sun; ⍟Southern Cross) Surveying the world from the old observation deck of the Rialto tower, Melbourne's favoured spot for occasion dining has views to match its storied reputation. Visionary chef Shannon Bennett, when he's not mentoring on *MasterChef*, produces sophisticated set

menus showcasing the very best Australian ingredients. Book well – months – ahead.

Grossi Florentino   ITALIAN **$$$**
(Map p462; ☑03-9662 1811; www.grossiflorentino.com; 1st fl, 80 Bourke St; 2-course lunch $65, 3-course dinner $140; ☺noon-2.30pm & 6pm-late Mon-Fri, 6pm-late Sat; ⍟Parliament) Over-the-top gilded plasterwork, chandeliers and 1930s Florentine Renaissance murals engender a real sense of occasion at this top-notch Italian restaurant. Decadent set menus are accompanied by exquisite canapés and delicious bread, and the service is extremely slick. The Grill and Cellar Bar below offer more affordable options.

Bomba   TAPAS **$$$**
(Map p462; ☑03-9077 0451; www.bombabar.com.au; 103 Lonsdale St; tapas $3.50-8, mains $26-36; ☺noon-3pm & 5pm-late Mon-Fri, 5pm-late Sat & Sun; ⍟Parliament) Reminiscent of a buzzing Spanish *bodega*, Bomba offers up tasty authentic tapas, *raciones* for those who are hungrier, and Catalan stews and paellas. The wine list is predominantly Spanish and the vermouth flows freely, as does the cold Estrella. Afterwards, head up to the rooftop bar for a nightcap.

Kenzan   JAPANESE **$$$**
(Map p462; ☑03-9654 8933; www.kenzan.com.au; 56 Flinders Lane; mains lunch $33, dinner $38-48; ☺noon-2.15pm & 6-10pm Mon-Sat; ☎; ⍟Parliament) Kenzan has an unpromising setting on the edge of a shopping mall but serves up sublime sashimi and sushi, with the *nabe ryori* (which you cook at your table) another fine option. Can't choose? Lunch or dinner set menus are outstanding..

🍴 Southbank & Docklands

Crown (Map p458; ☑03-9292 8888; www.crownmelbourne.com.au; 8 Whiteman St, Southbank; ⍟12, 55, 96, 109) has done a good job of luring people into its casino complex by installing some of Australia's most famous restaurateurs in glamorous riverside venues. While prices are steep, quality is high – unlike at some other eateries in this touristy stretch. South Wharf also has some interesting dining options right at the river's edge.

Bangpop   THAI **$$**
(Map p458; ☑03-9245 9800; www.bangpop.com.au; 35 South Wharf Promenade, South Wharf; mains $21-29; ☺noon-late; ☑; ⍟35, 70, 75) Bangpop breathes a bit of colour and vibrancy into

the area with its bar made from Lego and dangling filament bulbs. Flavour-packed hawker-style dishes and curries are served at communal cafe tables and accompanied by Thai-inflected cocktails.

★ Spice Temple   CHINESE $$$

(Map p462; ☑ 03-8679 1888; www.rockpool.com; Crown, Yarra Promenade, Southbank; mains $15-52; ☺6-11pm Mon-Wed, noon-3pm & 6-11pm Thu-Sun; ☑; ☑55) When he's not at Rockpool (p490) next door or in one of his Sydney restaurants, well-known chef Neil Perry pays homage to the spicy cuisines of China's central provinces at this excellent waterfront eatery. By day you can gaze at the river while you tuck into the $49 yum cha banquet. By night, descend to the atmospheric darkened tabernacle beneath.

Rockpool Bar & Grill   STEAK $$$

(Map p462; ☑ 03-8648 1900; www.rockpool.com; Crown, Yarra Promenade, Southbank; mains $35-70; ☺noon-2.30pm & 6-11pm Sun-Fri, 6-11pm Sat; ☑55) The Melbourne outpost of Neil Perry's empire offers his signature seafood raw bar, but the star is the dry-aged beef. The masculine space is simple and stylish, as is the menu. The bar offers the same menu and service with the bonus of an additional, cheaper menu ($24 to $29).

✗ Richmond & East Melbourne

Richmond's main draw has traditionally been restaurant-packed Victoria St, with its long strip of cheap Vietnamese and other Asian eateries. However, standards are arguably higher on Swan St, Church St and Bridge Rd.

NO RESERVATIONS

A widespread trend in Melbourne's fine-dining scene has many of the city's hottest restaurants (MoVida, Mamasita, Longrain, Supernormal and Chin Chin, to name a few) adopting a 'no bookings' policy. The move has received its share of love and criticism but is mostly aimed at delivering more flexibility and spontaneity. Most places will take your number and call once a spot has opened so you're not awkwardly hanging around waiting – or else people make a drink at the bar or a predinner stroll part of their night out.

Thy Thy   VIETNAMESE $

(Map p458; ☑ 03-9429 1104; 1st fl, 142 Victoria St, Richmond; mains $9-16; ☺9am-10pm; ☑North Richmond) Head upstairs to this Victoria St original (unchanged since 1987) for cheap and delicious Vietnamese food. No corkage for BYO booze.

Sabai   THAI $$

(Map p458; ☑ 03-8528 6884; www.sabairichmond. com.au; 460 Church St, Richmond; mains $17-24; ☺11.30am-9.30pm Mon-Fri, 4-9.30pm Sat & Sun; ☑East Richmond) The traditional wisdom is that Sydney does Thai and Melbourne does Vietnamese, but this little neighbourhood restaurant bucks that trend, serving a delicious mix of classic and modern Thai dishes in smart surroundings. The service is excellent too.

Meatmother   AMERICAN $$

(Map p458; ☑ 03-9041 5393; www.meatmother. com.au; 167 Swan St, Richmond; mains $20-28; ☺5pm-late Wed & Thu, noon-3pm & 5pm-late Fri-Sun; ☑70) Vegetarians, beware; this eatery is a shrine to the slaughterhouse, as is evident in the meat cleavers hanging on the walls. All meat is smoked over oak, from the 12-hour pulled-pork sandwich to the 20-hour beef brisket. At lunchtime it offers a range of $15 burgers and sandwiches, including a delicious burnt-end bun. Wash it down with some American whiskey.

Demitri's Feast   GREEK $$

(Map p458; ☑ 03-9428 8659; www.demitrisfeast. com.au; 141 Swan St, Richmond; mains $10-24; ☺8am-4pm Tue-Sun; ☑East Richmond) This down-to-earth cafe may be tiny, but it's full of huge Greek flavours in dishes such as spanakopita, souvlaki and meze platters. There's an interesting breakfast menu (the zucchini and feta fritters are a standout), and the coffee is excellent too, especially when paired with a traditional Greek sweet or two.

Richmond Hill Cafe & Larder   CAFE $$

(Map p458; ☑ 03-9421 2808; www.rhcl.com.au; 48-50 Bridge Rd, Richmond; lunch $12-27; ☺7am-5pm; ☑48, 75) Once the domain of well-known cook Stephanie Alexander, this deli-cafe may be looking a little dated, but it's still excellent. It boasts a top-notch cheese room and a menu ranging from the simple (cheesy toast) to little works of art (bircher muesli with chia-seed cubes and raspberry dust). There are breakfast cocktails for the adventurous.

Minamishima
JAPANESE **$$$**

(Map p458; ☎ 03-9429 5180; www.minamishima. com.au; 4 Lord St, Richmond; per person $150; ⊗ 6-10pm Tue-Sat; 🚊 48, 75) Hidden down a side street, Minamishima offers possibly the most unique Japanese dining experience this side of the equator. Sit at the bar seats and watch sushi master Koichi Minamishima prepare seafood with surgical precision and serve it one piece at a time. There's only a handful of seats, so book well in advance.

⚒ Fitzroy, Collingwood & Abbotsford

Smith St's astounding food scene just keeps evolving and has now extended into the surrounding backstreets, with cafes and restaurants setting up shop in converted warehouses. Gertrude St is packed side-by-side with cafes and some excellent fine-dining options, while Brunswick St has a few well-established favourites (the rest is a little hit-and-miss). A good scene is starting to develop on the Abbotsford side of Johnston St, too.

★ Lune Croissanterie
BAKERY **$**

(Map p470; www.lunecroissanterie.com; 119 Rose St, Fitzroy; pastries $5.50-12.50; ⊗ 7.30am-3pm Mon, Thu & Fri, from 8am Sat & Sun; 🚊 11) The queues may have you turning on your heel, but good things come to those who wait, and here they come in the form of some of the best pastries you'll ever taste – from the lemon-curd cruffin to a classic almond croissant. In the centre of this warehouse space sits a climate-controlled glass cube, the Lune Lab, where the magic happens.

★ Smith & Deli
DELI, VEGAN **$**

(Map p470; ☎ 03-9042 4117; www.smithand daughters.com; 111 Moor St, Fitzroy; sandwiches $10-15; ⊗ 8am-6pm Tue-Sat; ✎ ; 🚊 11) Full of '50s-NYC-deli charm with a vegan twist, this little takeaway creates what might be the closest vegetarians will get to eating meat – it's even been known to fool a few carnivores. Sandwiches are made to order and filled with all the favourites; try the Rubenstein, loaded with 'pastrami', sauerkraut and pickles, or opt for the Club Sandwiches Not Seals.

★ Gelato Messina
GELATO **$**

(Map p470; www.gelatomessina.com; 237 Smith St, Fitzroy; 1 scoop $4.80; ⊗ noon-11pm Sun-Thu, to 11.30pm Fri & Sat; 🚊 86) Messina is hyped as

Melbourne's best ice-creamery and its popularity is evident in the queues of people in summer waiting to wrap their smackers around such smooth flavours as salted coconut and mango, poached figs in marsala, or blood-orange sorbet. You can watch the ice-cream makers at work through glass windows inside.

Huxtaburger
BURGERS **$**

(Map p470; ☎ 03-9417 6328; www.huxtaburger. com.au; 106 Smith St, Collingwood; burgers $10-14.50; ⊗ 11.30am-10pm Sun-Thu, to 11pm Fri & Sat; 🚊 86) This American-style burger joint is a hit for its crinkle-cut chips in old-school containers (go the spicy chipotle salt), tasty burgers (veg options available) on glazed brioche buns, and bottled craft beers. Other branches are in the **city** (Map p462; Fulham Pl; burgers $7-14; ⊗ 11.30am-10pm; 🚊 Flinders St) and Prahran (p497).

Babka Bakery Cafe
BAKERY, CAFE **$**

(Map p470; ☎ 03-9416 0091; 358 Brunswick St, Fitzroy; mains $11-19; ⊗ 7am-7pm Tue-Sun; 🚊 11) From borscht to dumplings, Russian flavours infuse the lovingly prepared breakfast and lunch dishes at little local institution Babka. It also has its own bakery, and the heady aroma of cinnamon and freshly baked sourdough bread, pies and cakes makes even just a coffee worth queuing for.

Lazerpig
PIZZA **$$**

(Map p470; ☎ 03-9417 1177; www.lazerpig.com.au; 9-11 Peel St, Collingwood; pizza $16-24; ⊗ 4pm-late Mon-Wed, noon-late Thu-Sun; 🚊 86) From the neon-pink pig sign out the front to the pub-style interior, disco ball and red-gingham tablecloths, hip Lazerpig is a hard one to get your head around. It's a bit rock 'n roll and disco meets trattoria, where people pile in to scoff the excellent wood-fired pizzas and booze on craft beer or cocktails to DJs doin' their thing.

Easey's
BURGERS **$$**

(Map p458; http://easeys.com.au; 48 Easey St, Collingwood; burgers $10-23; ⊗ 11am-10pm Sun-Thu, to 11pm Fri & Sat; 🚊 86) Biting into burgers and gulping back beers in a graffiti-covered old train carriage perched on top of a backstreet rooftop – it doesn't get much more Collingwood than this. Easey's does a handful of no-holds-barred burgers that will have your cholesterol rising faster than you can say 'gimme the side of triple-fried dim sims'.

It also does one of the best veggie burgers around: a potato-and-zucchini rösti with all the usual burger trimmings and not a dollop of hummus or slice of avocado in sight.

Horn
AFRICAN $$

(Map p470; ☑ 03-9417 4670; www.thehorncafe. com.au; 20 Johnston St, Collingwood; mains $16-21; ☺ 6pm-late Wed-Sat, 3-10pm Sun; 🚌 86) Straight outta Addis Ababa, the flavours and feel of this Ethiopian restaurant are as authentic as its homemade *injera* (soft bread; prepared fresh daily). Tear it into your meal using your fingers and wash it down with Ethiopian beer. There's jazz on Thursday evening, and on Sunday the eight-piece Black Jesus Experiment plays traditional Ethiopian music with a modern take.

Charcoal Lane
MODERN AUSTRALIAN $$

(Map p470; ☑ 03-9418 3400; www.charcoallane. com.au; 136 Gertrude St, Fitzroy; mains $19-31; ☺ noon-3pm & 6-9pm Tue-Sat; 🚌 86) 🍴 Housed in an old bluestone former bank, this training restaurant for Indigenous and disadvantaged young people is one of the best places to try native flora and fauna; menu items may include pan-seared emu fillet with lemon-myrtle risotto and wattleseed crème brûlée. The chef's native tasting plate for two ($30) is a great place to start. Weekend bookings advised.

Moroccan Soup Bar
MOROCCAN $$

(☑ 03-9482 4240; www.moroccansoupbar.com.au; 183 St Georges Rd, North Fitzroy; banquet per person $23; ☺ 6-10pm Tue-Sun; 🚭; 🚌 11) Prepare to queue before being seated by stalwart Hana, who will then go through the vegetarian menu verbally while you sip a mint tea (it's an alcohol-free zone). The banquet is great value and the sublime chickpea bake is a favourite, driving locals to queue with their own pots and containers for takeaway.

Horn Please
INDIAN $$

(http://hornplease.com.au; 167 St Georges Rd, North Fitzroy; dishes $12-23; ☺ 6-9pm Sun-Wed, to late Thu-Sat; 🚌 11) The regularly changing menu at this stylish spot spans street food, curries, dal and tandoor dishes. You might find charred trout cooked on the tandoor, creamy black-lentil dal or smoked-lamb curry, and don't miss the homemade *kulfi* (Indian ice cream). The beer fridge is stocked with a great selection of craft brews.

Project Forty Nine
CAFE, DELI $$

(Map p470; ☑ 03-9419 4449; www.projectforty nine.com.au; 107 Cambridge St, Collingwood; cafe mains $13-16, restaurant mains $26-31; ☺ cafe 7am-4pm, deli 9am-6pm Wed-Mon; 🚌 86) Project Forty Nine brings a slice of the country to Collingwood's industrial backstreets with this outpost of its original cafe in Beechworth, regional Victoria. The huge, airy warehouse incorporates deli, cafe, restaurant and wine bar, focusing on a fusion of country Victorian produce and Italian flavours in the cafe and restaurant, while the wine bar showcases northeastern Victorian wines.

Transformer
VEGETARIAN $$

(Map p470; ☑ 03-9419 2022; www.transformer fitzroy.com; 99 Rose St, Fitzroy; mains $16-24; ☺ 5.30-10pm Mon-Thu, 11.30am-11pm Fri, 9am-11pm Sat, 9am-10.30pm Sun; 🛜 🚭; 🚌 11) This is haute vegetarian cuisine (think ricotta and rye gnocchi rather than tofu stir-fry) in a sophisticated, plant-filled warehouse space that's perfect for breakfast, dinner dates or cocktails.

Smith & Daughters
LATIN AMERICAN, VEGAN $$

(Map p470; ☑ 03-9939 3293; www.smithand daughters.com; 175 Brunswick St, Fitzroy; dishes $10-18; ☺ 6pm-1am Tue-Fri, 10am-1am Sat, 10am-11pm Sun; 🚭; 🚌 11) This cosy corner restaurant has an all-vegan menu. Latin flavours are present in tasty dishes such as paella fritters and 'chorizo' tacos, and extend to the cocktail menu, with jalapeño, cucumber and coriander margaritas and sangria by the jug.

Hotel Jesus
MEXICAN $$

(Map p470; www.hoteljesus.com.au; 174 Smith St, Collingwood; dishes $6-16; ☺ noon-late Wed-Sun, Taco Wey shop noon-5pm Tue, to 6pm Wed-Sat; 🚌 86) Set in an old post-office building, this brash retro cantina is going for fun, with gleaming tiles, red folding chairs and a daggy picture menu. Street food is the focus, particularly tostadas, topped with flavours that are a bit hit-and-miss, sadly. The tick-the-box paper ordering system and the service need a little finessing, and the menu could be clearer.

Smith Street Alimentari
CAFE, DELI $$

(Map p470; ☑ 03-9416 1666; www.alimentari. com.au/smith-street; 302 Smith St, Collingwood; panini $9.50-11.50, mains $10-24; ☺ 8am-6pm Mon-Wed & Sat, to 7pm Thu & Fri; 🛜; 🚌 86) A winning Italian deli-cafe combo offering take-home meals, panini, salads, fresh pasta and rotisserie meats. The expansive space extends to a dining area with a Mediterranean inspired menu and lovely rear courtyard.

Belle's Hot Chicken
AMERICAN $$

(Map p470; 03-9077 0788; http://belleshot chicken.com; 150 Gertrude St, Fitzroy; chicken & a side from $17; noon-10pm Sun-Thu, to 11pm Fri & Sat; 86) Chef Morgan McGlone knew he was onto a good thing while honing his kitchen skills in the States. But ever since he brought Nashville fried chicken back to Australia and paired it with natural wine, it's been a finger-lickin' revolution. Launch into tenders, drumsticks or wings with your preference of heat (note: 'Really F**kin Hot' is so named for good reason).

Robert Burns Hotel
SPANISH $$

(Map p470; 03-9417 2233; www.robertburns hotel.com.au; 376 Smith St, Collingwood; paella per person from $20, mains from $27; 5-11pm Mon & Tue, noon-midnight Wed-Sat, noon-11pm Sun; 86) A slick makeover several years back meant the loss of its appealing dingy charm, but thankfully the authenticity of its Spanish flavours remain: the Burns' seafood paella is still one of Melbourne's best. The $17 lunch menu with a drink Wednesday to Saturday is great value.

Vegie Bar
VEGETARIAN $$

(Map p470; 03-9417 6935; www.vegiebar. com.au; 380 Brunswick St, Fitzroy; mains $13-18; 11am-10pm Sun-Thu, to 10.30pm Fri & Sat; ; 11) An oldie but a goodie, this cavernous warehouse eatery has been feeding droves of Melbourne's veggie-loving residents for over 20 years. Expect inventive fare and big servings from its menu of delicious thin-crust pizzas, tasty salads, burgers and curries, as well as great smoothies and fresh juices. Also has a fascinating selection of raw food dishes, and plenty of vegan choices.

★ Cutler & Co
MODERN AUSTRALIAN $$$

(Map p470; 03-9419 4888; www.cutlerandco. com.au; 55 Gertrude St, Fitzroy; mains $36-48; 6pm-late Tue-Sun, lunch from noon Sun; 86) Hyped for all the right reasons, this is Andrew McConnell's flagship Melbourne restaurant and its attentive, informed staff and joy-inducing dishes have quickly made it one of Melbourne's top places for fine dining. The menu strives to incorporate the best seasonal produce across the à la carte offering, the degustation menu (from $150), and the casual Sunday lunch designed for sharing.

Saint Crispin
MODERN AUSTRALIAN $$$

(Map p470; 03-9419 2202; www.saintcrispin. com.au; 300 Smith St, Collingwood; 2/3 courses $50/65; 6pm-late Tue-Thu, noon-late Fri-Sun; 86) The stylish interiors, light-filled space, prompt service and excellent food make this one of the best places for fine dining in the inner city. You can choose from two or three courses, or opt for the chef's tasting menu (from $100). The duo behind the restaurant spent time working together at Michelin-starred The Square in London.

IDES
MODERN AUSTRALIAN $$$

(Map p470; 03-9939 9542; www.idesmelbourne. com.au; 92 Smith St, Collingwood; 6-course degustation $110; from 6pm Wed-Sun; 86) What started as a pop-up is now a permanent restaurant in Smith St. Word spread quickly that Attica (p499) sous chef Peter Gunn had started his own establishment, where he does the term 'creative' justice with a contemporary take on fine dining. It's a six-course, seasonal affair preceded by hot bread with dangerously good house peanut butter.

✕ Carlton & Brunswick

Sydney Rd in Brunswick is Melbourne's Middle Eastern hub, with plenty of bakeries and long-time favourite restaurants spread out along the thoroughfare. Since the arrival of Mediterranean immigrants in the 1950s, Lygon St in Carlton has been synonymous with Italian cuisine. For a mix of both cuisines, head to the East Brunswick end of Lygon St, where a couple of excellent Italian and Middle Eastern restaurants can be found, along with some well-loved cafes.

Heartattack and Vine
ITALIAN $

(Map p472; 03-9005 8674; www.heartattackand vine.com.au; 329 Lygon St, Carlton; 7am-11pm Mon-Fri, from 8am Sat & Sun; ; Tourist Shuttle, 1, 6) Heartattack and Vine is a relaxed space with a neighbourhood feel all centred on a long wooden bar. Drop in for a coffee morning or night, prop up at the bar for an Aperol spritz or glass of wine, grab a brekky pastry or prawn brioche roll for lunch, or spend the evening sampling the *cicchetti*, a Venetian take on tapas.

Very Good Falafel
FALAFEL $

(03-9383 6479; www.shukiandlouisa.com; 626 Sydney Rd, Brunswick; felafel from $8.50; 11am-10pm Mon-Sat; ; 19, Anstey) They started off selling dips at markets and now Louisa and Shuki have set up permanent shop here. Their backgrounds combine perfectly: Shuki grew up on Middle Eastern home cooking in Israel, while Louisa's family has a farm in the Mallee growing chickpeas! On offer are Israeli-style pita with fresh (and indeed very good!) felafel, tasty salads and filter coffee.

Pidapipo
GELATO $

(Map p472; ☑03-9347 4596; http://pidapipo.com.au; 299 Lygon St, Carlton; 1 scoop $4.50; ☉noon-11pm; ☐Tourist Shuttle, ☐1, 6) Pidapipo is the perfect precinema, pretheatre, post-pizza – whenever! – treat when you're hanging out on Lygon St. Owner Lisa Valmorbida learned from the best in the world at the Carpigiani Gelato University and now whips up her own handmade creations on-site from local and imported Italian ingredients.

A1 Lebanese Bakehouse
MIDDLE EASTERN $

(http://a1bakery.com.au; 643-5 Sydney Rd, Brunswick; pastries from $1.40, plates from $7; ☉7am-7pm Sun-Wed, to 9pm Thu-Sat; ☐19, ☐Anstey) This huge, classic Sydney Rd eatery and bakery is perfect for dining in on hearty Lebanese food including falafel and chicken tawouk plates, or takeaway piping-hot pastries and pizzas: spinach-and-cheese triangles, labne pizza and *kaak* (sesame buns filled with halloumi cheese).

Brunetti
ITALIAN $

(Map p472; ☑03-9347 2801; www.brunetti.com.au; 380 Lygon St, Carlton; panini around $10, mains from $17; ☉cafe 6am-11pm Sun-Thu, to midnight Fri & Sat; ☎; ☐Tourist Shuttle, ☐1, 6, 96) Bustling from dawn to midnight, Brunetti is a mini-Roman empire with a drool-inducing display of cakes and sweets. It's famous for its coffee, granitas and authentic *pasticceria* (pastries), and also does a menu of pizzas, pastas and panini.

★ D.O.C. Espresso
ITALIAN $$

(Map p472; ☑03-9347 8482; www.docgroup.net; 326 Lygon St, Carlton; mains $12-20; ☉7.30am-late Mon-Sat, 8am-late Sun; ☐Tourist Shuttle, ☐1, 6) Run by third-generation Italian Australians, authentic D.O.C. has breathed new life into Lygon St. The espresso bar features homemade pasta specials, Italian microbrewery beers and *aperitivo* time (4pm to 7pm), when you can enjoy a negroni with complimentary nibble board.

★ Rumi
MIDDLE EASTERN $$

(☑03-9388 8255; www.rumirestaurant.com.au; 116 Lygon St, East Brunswick; dishes $13-28; ☉6-10pm; ☐1, 6) A fabulously well-considered place that serves up a mix of traditional Lebanese cooking and contemporary interpretations of old Persian dishes. The *sigara*

boregi (cheese and pine-nut pastries) are a local institution, and tasty mains from the charcoal BBQ are balanced with a large and interesting selection of vegetable dishes.

★ D.O.C. Pizza & Mozzarella Bar
PIZZA $$

(Map p472; ☑03-9347 2998; www.docgroup.net; 295 Drummond St, Carlton; pizzas $17-25; ☉5pm-late Mon-Wed, noon-late Fri-Sun; ☐Tourist Shuttle, ☐1, 6) D.O.C. has jumped on the Milanese-led mozzarella-bar trend and serves up the milky-white balls – your choice of local cow or imported *buffala* – as entrees, in salads or atop fabulous pizzas. Pizza toppings include bitter-sweet *cicoria* (chicory) and lemon, and wild mushrooms and truffle oil; the litmus-test margherita gets rave reviews.

Longhorn Saloon
AMERICAN $$

(Map p472; ☑03-9348 4794; www.longhornsaloon.com.au; 118 Elgin St, Carlton; mains $16-44; ☉from 5pm Tue-Thu, noon-late Fri-Sun; ☐1, 6) Longhorn Saloon is an upmarket Wild West saloon-style restaurant-bar with lots of pressed copper, exposed brick, dark wood and low lighting. The menu features Southern-style flavours, from steaks cooked on the wood-fire grill to a brisket Reuben sandwich and a side of jalapeño-spiced mac 'n cheese. Pair it with a hoppy US IPA or a classic Dark 'n' Stormy cocktail.

Milk the Cow
EUROPEAN $$

(Map p472; ☑03-9348 4771; www.milkthecow.com.au; 323 Lygon St, Carlton; cheeseboards from $27, flights & fondue from $17; ☉noon-late; ☐1, 6) When a cheese craving strikes, head to licensed fromagerie Milk the Cow for baked camembert with a crusty baguette or a farmer's board of country-style bites. The electric milking chandeliers are a talking point, as is the giant glass cabinet filled with more than 150 unique, hard-to-find cheeses from all over the world.

Epocha
EUROPEAN $$

(Map p472; ☑03-9036 4949; www.epocha.com.au; 49 Rathdowne St, Carlton; small/large sharing plates from $16/27; ☉noon-3pm & 5.30-10pm Tue-Sat, noon-3pm Sun; ☐City Circle, 30) Set within a Victorian double-storey terrace dating from 1884, elegant Epocha creates an interesting mix of Greek- and English-inspired dishes that's reflective of each of the co-owners' successes in previous restaurants. It all comes together beautifully for the $68 sharing menu. Head upstairs for fantastic cocktails at **Hannah's Bar**.

Pope Joan CAFE $$

(📞03-9388 8858; www.popejoan.com.au; 75-79 Nicholson St, East Brunswick; mains $15; ⏰7.30am-3pm; 🛜; 🚌96) This East Brunswick favourite is the perfect place to drop in, offering a comfort-food menu featuring all-day breakfasts, sensational sandwiches, St Ali coffee and 'liquid breakfasts' of Bloody Marys, as well as craft beer. A few doors up you'll find its bright produce store, Hams & Bacon, where you can grab a takeaway sandwich.

Hellenic Republic GREEK $$

(📞03-9381 1222; www.hellenicrepublic.com.au; 434 Lygon St, East Brunswick; mains $12-32; ⏰5.30-10pm Mon-Thu, noon-10pm Fri-Sun; 🛜; 🚌1, 6) The ironbark grill at George Calombaris' northern outpost works overtime grilling up pita, king prawns, calamari and whole fish, and luscious lamb. The *taramasalata* (white-cod-roe dip) is unbelievably good. Choose from à la carte or sharing menus and wash it all down with a warming ouzo from the long list.

Bar Idda ITALIAN $$

(📞03-9380 5339; www.baridda.com.au; 132 Lygon St, East Brunswick; mains $18-30; ⏰6-10pm Mon-Sat, 5.30-10pm Sun; 🚌1, 6) This cosy Sicilian restaurant is intimate and relaxed, with a share-plates menu ranging from barbecued swordfish to vegetarian layered eggplant, and classic Italian desserts of tiramisu, affogato and cannoli.

Ray CAFE $$

(332 Victoria St, Brunswick; meals $13-21; ⏰7.30am-4pm Mon-Fri, 8.30am-4pm Sat & Sun; 🛜📷; 🚌19, 🚆Brunswick) Its graffitied facade makes it look like an abandoned house...before opening up to reveal the cafe as an inviting space with exposed brick and friendly service. The inspired menu reflects Brunswick by mixing Middle Eastern flavours with classic cafe fare named after bands: Rage Against the Tagine, God Speed You Black Lentil. There's also a vegan menu.

Shakahari VEGETARIAN $$

(Map p472; 📞03-9347 3848; www.shakahari.com.au; 201 Faraday St, Carlton; mains $19-22; ⏰noon-3pm & 6-9.30pm Mon-Fri, 6-10.30pm Sat & Sun; 📷; 🚌Tourist Shuttle, 🚌1, 6, 96) Shakahari's limited, seasonal menu reflects both Asian and European influences, and dishes are made using great produce. Established over 40 years ago, and bedecked with a collection of Asian antiques, Shakahari takes its mission seriously. If the weather is in your favour, ask to be seated in the palm-fringed courtyard.

Tiamo ITALIAN $$

(Map p472; 📞03-9347 5759; www.tiamo.com.au; 303 Lygon St, Carlton; mains $15-26; ⏰6am-10.30pm; 🚌Tourist Shuttle, 🚌1, 6) When you've had enough of pressed, siphoned, Slayer-machined, poured-over, filtered and plunged coffee, head here to one of Lygon St's original Italian cafe-restaurants. There's the laughter and relaxed joie de vivre that only a well-established restaurant can offer. Great pastas and pizza, too. Also has the upmarket Tiamo 2 next door.

🍴 South Melbourne, Port Melbourne & Albert Park

All three neighbourhoods are perfect for casual footpath dining on sunny weekends, with a good number of casual cafes and restaurants. There's a slew of places to eat at on and off Clarendon St in South Melbourne, though not all are especially noteworthy. You'll find fabulous fresh produce, decent coffee and quality sit-down eateries at South Melbourne Market. Restaurants and cafes dot Bridport St and Victoria Ave in Albert Park, as well as Bay St in Port Melbourne. There's a small handful of restaurants overlooking the bay, though many serve nondescript food.

St Ali CAFE $

(Map p458; 📞03-9686 2990; www.stali.com.au; 12-18 Yarra Pl, South Melbourne; dishes $8-25; ⏰7am-6pm; 🚌12) A hideaway warehouse conversion where the coffee's carefully sourced and guaranteed to be good. If you can't decide between house blend, speciality, black or white, there's a six-coffee tasting 'adventure' ($20). The food menu covers all bases with competence and creativity, from virtuous vanilla-and-maple quinoa pudding with baby Thai basil to cult-status corn fritters with poached eggs and grilled halloumi.

Andrew's Burgers BURGERS $

(Map p458; 📞03-9690 2126; www.andrewshamburgers.com.au; 144 Bridport St, Albert Park; burgers from $8.50; ⏰11am-9pm Mon-Sat; 🚌1) Andrew's is a family-run, wildly popular institution that's been around since the '50s. It's walls are still wood-panelled, and now they're covered with photos of local celebs who, like many, drop in for a classic burger with the lot and a big bag of chips to take away. Veg option available.

Jock's Ice-Cream

ICE CREAM $

(Map p458; ☑ 03-9686 3838; 83 Victoria Ave, Albert Park; single cone $4; ☉ noon-8pm Mon-Thu, to 10pm Fri & Sat, to 9pm Sun; 🖪 1) For almost two decades Jock has been scooping up his made-on-site sorbets and ice creams for bay-siders (and the odd Canadian teen-pop icon). Cult-status flavours include hokey-pokey and a star-spangled jam-and-peanut-butter combo. Take-home tubs also available.

Simply Spanish

SPANISH $$

(Map p458; ☑ 03-9682 6100; www.simplyspanish. com.au; South Melbourne Market, cnr Coventry & Cecil Sts, South Melbourne; gourmet paellas from $20.50, tapas $8-16; ☉ 8am-9pm Wed-Sat, to 4pm Sun; 🖪 12, 96) When a Melbourne restaurant wins the title of 'Best Paella Outside of Spain' in Valencia, you know you're on to a good thing. This casual market eatery is *the* place to go for paella, which is available here in numerous combos. While you wait, nibble on a tapas dish or two.

Paco y Lola

MEXICAN $$

(Map p458; ☑ 03-9696 5659; http://pacoylola. com.au; shop 99, South Melbourne Market, cnr Coventry & Cecil Sts, South Melbourne; burritos $13-14, mains $15-30; ☉ 8.30am-10.30pm Wed & Fri, 9am-11pm Thu, 7.30am-11pm Sat, 7.30am-5pm Sun; 🖪 12, 96) Upbeat and casual, Paco y Lola cooks up a storm of zingy, fresh, generous Mexican flavours, from juicy burritos, que-sadillas and tacos to more substantial op-tions like Mexican pork ribs and refreshing soft-shell-crab salad. If there are two of you, don't miss the *caldo de pescado*, a fragrant Mexican fish soup made with super-fresh seafood from the adjoining market.

Orient East

MALAYSIAN $$

(Map p458; ☑ 03-9685 2900; www.orienteast.com. au; 348 St Kilda Rd, Melbourne; mains $17-27; ☉ 6.30am-10pm Mon-Fri, 7-11am & 5-9pm Sat & Sun; 🖪 3, 5, 6, 16, 64, 67, 72) A convenient lunch spot if you're visiting the Shrine of Remem-brance and Botanic Gardens across the road, Orient East whips up British-colonial Straits cuisine in a setting reminiscent of a 1960s foreign-correspondent cafe. Enjoy hawker-style grub such as black-pepper soft-shell-crab buns, prawn *char kuey teow* (fried flat noodles) and fragrant laksas, best washed down with some cold craft suds.

Bellota Wine Bar

ITALIAN $$$

(Map p458; ☑ 03-9078 8381; http://bellota.com. au; 181 Bank St, South Melbourne; mains $28-34; ☉ 11am-11pm Tue-Sat; 🖪 1, 12) This handsome wine bar and bistro is an extension of the adjoining Prince Wine Store, with an ever-changing wine list and beautiful dishes to match. Whether you're dining at the bar or at one of the intimate back tables (the latter require a reservation), expect to swoon over perfect grilled octopus, *vitello tonnato* (thinly sliced veal) and elegant, nuanced pastas.

✖ South Yarra, Prahran & Windsor

The three neighbourhoods are packed with great eateries, spanning all price ranges and countless cuisines. Toorak Rd in South Yarra has a number of fine-dining options, along with trendier cafes and bistros. Chapel St heaves with cafes and hotspot eateries, the best of which lie south of Commercial Rd. Commercial Rd itself is home to Prahran Market, a must for fresh produce, pasta and deli treats. Both Greville and High Sts also host a number of decent nosh spots.

★ Zumbo

DESSERTS $

(Map p474; ☑ 1800 858 611; http://zumbo. au; 14 Claremont St, South Yarra; macarons $2.80, cakes from $6; ☉ 7am-7pm; 🖪 78, 🖪 South Yarra) Aussie pâtissier Adriano Zumbo is hot property, famed for his outrageously cre-ative, technically ambitious concoctions. Here, cheesecake might be made with yuzu-cream-cheese mousse and shaped like a Swiss cheese, and a tart might get spicy with churros-custard crème and Mexican-hot-chocolate crème. And then there's the '70s disco-chamber-like fit-out. Fine print: the coffee's better next door.

Two Birds One Stone

CAFE $

(Map p474; ☑ 03-9827 1228; www.twobirdsone stonecafe.com.au; 12 Claremont St, South Yarra; dishes $14-22.50; ☉ 7am-3.30pm Mon-Fri, from 8am Sat & Sun; 🖪 78, 🖪 South Yarra) Sand-blasted oak stools, whitewashed timber and a wintry forest mural evoke Scandinavia at Two Birds One Stone, a crisp, contemporary cafe with smooth third-wave coffee and a smart, produce-driven menu. Find your happy place tucking into soul-nourishing dishes like ricotta pancakes with figs, mar-malade syrup and pistachio cream, or pan-seared salmon with potato rösti, truffled cauliflower puree and poached eggs.

Uncommon

CAFE $

(Map p474; ☑ 03-9510 6655; www.uncommon food.com; 60 Chapel St, Windsor; dishes $11-23; ☉ 7am-3.30pm Mon-Fri, from 8am Sat & Sun; 🖪 5,

64, 78, 🚻 Windsor) White-on-white interiors and cascading plants await at Uncommon, a cool, light-filled cafe singing the praises of local, seasonal produce and out-of-the-box dishes. Highlights include the sublime sliced salmon with mild green chilli, soft-herb scramble and whipped honey, and the coffee-rubbed short rib with potato croquette, pickled green tomato and egg. Serves are on the smaller size but feel just right.

Tivoli Road Bakery   CAFE $
(Map p474; 🔲 03-9041 4345; http://tiviliroad. com.au; 3 Tivoli Rd, South Yarra; dishes $7-12; ⏲ 7.30am-4pm; 🚌 78, 🚻 South Yarra) Join fashionistas, realtors and upmarket hipsters at this contemporary, side-street bakery-cafe, serving everything from impossibly light custard doughnuts to generously stuffed sandwiches, made-from-scratch pies and sausage rolls, and fashionable salads. Its cult-status artisanal loaves are also on offer, as well as a small selection of other local treats, from jam to nougat.

Huxtaburger   BURGERS $
(Map p474; www.huxtaburger.com.au; 203 High St, Prahran; burgers from $10; ⏲ 11.30am-10pm Sun-Thu, to 11pm Fri & Sat; 🚌 6, 78, 🚻 Prahran) The south-side branch of Fitzroy burger royalty (p497), Huxtaburger is famed for its sweet brioche buns, grass-fed wagyu patties and crinkle-cut chips (best sprinkled with spicy chipotle salt). There are a couple of veggie burgers, too, as well as an ice-cream burger for those who don't know when to stop.

Gilson   MODERN AUSTRALIAN $$
(Map p458; 🔲 03-9866 3120; http://gilsonres taurant.com.au; 171 Domain Rd, South Yarra; pizzas $18-25 , mains $24-34; ⏲ 6am-11pm Mon-Fri, from 7am Sat & Sun) Sassy new kid Gilson straddles the line between cafe and restaurant. Directly opposite the Botanic Gardens, it has a concrete and Italian-marble fit-out inspired by midcentury French modernism and contemporary, Italian-influenced food. Forgo the famous (and underwhelming) grilled cucumber for the outstanding pasta dishes and interesting wood-fired pizzas. Rounding things off are intriguing wines and cocktails, and attentive, knowledgeable staff.

Colonel Tan's   THAI $$
(Map p474; 🔲 03-9521 5985; http://revolverup stairs.com.au/colonel-tans; 229 Chapel St, Prahran; mains $15-29; ⏲ 5-11pm Tue-Thu & Sat, from noon Fri; 🚌 6, 78, 🚻 Prahran) In the back corner of pumping Revolver Upstairs (p507), retro-

licious Colonel Tan's dishes out top-notch Thai-American fusion. Expect such things as corn, coriander and pickled-chilli doughnuts, soft-shell-crab burgers with curried egg, and a Bangkok bolognese that tastes a hell of a lot better than it sounds.

Fonda   MEXICAN $$
(Map p474; 🔲 03-9521 2660; http://fondamexican. com.au; 144 Chapel St, Windsor; tacos from $6.50, burritos from $14; ⏲ 11.30am-10.30pm Sun-Thu, to 11pm Fri & Sat, rooftop from 5.30pm Mon-Wed, from noon Thu-Sun; 🚌 6, 78, 🚻 Windsor) Fun, thumping Fonda serves Mexican-with-a-twist street food. The emphasis is on fresh, local ingredients, from Queen Vic Market produce to authentic, made-from-scratch tacos from La Tortilleria. Order the prawn taco with kimchi and caramelised pineapple and wash it down with a burnt-orange margarita. Dine downstairs or try your luck on the see-and-be-seen rooftop (ridiculously busy at weekends).

Hawker Hall   SOUTHEAST ASIAN $$
(Map p474; 🔲 03-8560 0090; http://hawker hall.com.au; 98 Chapel St, Windsor; dishes $8-34; ⏲ 11am-late; 🚌 5, 6, 64, 78, 🚻 Windsor) Did you hear the one about the turn-of-the-century stable turned hipster take on a Southeast Asian food hall? Decked with playful Chinatown-style signage, ever-popular Hawker Hall serves up spicy, punchy share-style dishes like barbecue pork and lychee salad and fiery Portuguese devil chicken curry. No reservations, so head in before 6pm or after 9.30pm to minimise the wait.

Stables of Como   CAFE $$
(Map p474; 🔲 03-9827 6886; www.thestablesof como.com.au; Como House & Garden, cnr Williams Rd & Lechlade Ave, South Yarra; sandwiches $13-20, mains $23-29; ⏲ 9am-5pm Mon-Sat, from 10am Sun) This studiously rustic cafe occupies the former stables at heritage-listed Como House (p476). Nibble gourmet sandwiches, salads or more substantial creations like corn and zucchini fritters with roasted tomatoes, bacon and herb-spiked ricotta. Afternoon high tea includes a free-flow mimosas option ($65), and the cafe also offers gourmet picnic hampers (per person $60; book at least 48 hours ahead).

WoodLand House   MODERN AUSTRALIAN $$$
(Map p474; 🔲 03-9525 2178; www.woodlandhouse. com.au; 78 Williams Rd, Prahran; tasting menus from $125; ⏲ 6.30-9pm Tue, Wed & Sat, noon-3pm

& 6.30-9pm Thu & Fri, noon-3pm Sun; 🚫6) In a glorious Victorian villa, WoodLand House is home turf for young-gun chefs Thomas Woods and Hayden McFarland, former sous chefs for lauded Melbourne restaurateur Jacques Reymond. The menu spotlights quality locally sourced produce, cooked confidently and creatively in dishes like wood-roasted mussels with asparagus and salted yolk. Thursday and Friday offer a good-value three-course lunch with a glass of wine for $55.

Da Noi
ITALIAN $$$

(Map p474; ☑️03-9866 5975; http://danoi.com.au; 95 Toorak Rd, South Yarra; mains $30-40, 4-course tasting menu $75-95; ⊙noon-10.30pm; 🚊South Yarra) Elegant Da Noi serves up beautiful dishes from Sardinia, the island home of owner-chef Pietro Porcu. Offerings change daily, with the chef's special reinterpreted several times a night on some occasions. Just go with it. For the full effect, opt for the four-course set menu, which sees the chef decide your dishes based on whatever's best that day. Bookings advised.

✖️ St Kilda

Despite having seen better days, Fitzroy St remains a popular eating strip, and you'll find the good, the very good and the downright ugly along its length. Acland and Barkly Sts also hum with dining options, the former also famed for its historic cake shops. Over the Nepean Hwy, Carlisle St in Balaclava has its fair share of hipster cafes and trendy eateries, catering to a mostly local crowd.

St Kilda Dispensary
CAFE $

(Map p478; ☑️03-9077 4989; www.facebook.com/TheStKildaDispensary; 13 Brighton Rd, St Kilda; dishes $6.50-18; ⊙7am-3.30pm Mon-Fri, from 8am Sat & Sun; 🚊16, 67, 79) In what was the first dispensary in the southern hemisphere during the 1940s, this cafe keeps with the medical theme with tiled counters, test tubes and beakers, and a menu that prescribes the good stuff: house-made cold drip, corn fritters and comforting bubble and squeak.

Monk Bodhi Dharma
CAFE $

(Map p478; ☑️03-9534 7250; rear 202 Carlisle St, Balaclava; dishes $9-19; ⊙7am-5pm Mon-Fri, from 8am Sat & Sun; 🥄; 🚊3, 16, 78) Monk Bodhi Dharma's location, down an alley off Carlisle St (next to Woolworths), means it doesn't get

much foot traffic, which is lucky given that this cosy brick cafe has enough devotees as it is. A former 1920s bakehouse, it's now all about transcendental vegetarian food, from house-made bircher muesli to zucchini and mint hotcakes. House-roasted single-estate coffee tops things off.

Si Señor
MEXICAN $

(Map p478; ☑️03-9995 1083; www.sisenor.com.au; 193 Carlisle St, Balaclava; tacos $6-6.50, burritos $13-14.50; ⊙noon-3pm & 5-10pm Mon-Thu, noon-10pm Fri-Sun; 📶; 🚊3, 16, 78, 🚊Balaclava) Si Señor is one of the most authentic Mexican joints in the city. Tasty spit-and-grilled meats are heaped onto soft corn tortillas under the direction of the place's Mexican owner. If you've overdone the hot sauce, cool it down with an authentic *horchata* (a delicious rice-milk and cinnamon drink).

Glick's
BAGELS $

(Map p478; www.glicks.com.au; 330a Carlisle St, Balaclava; bagels from $4; ⊙6am-8pm Sun-Thu, 6am-30min before sunset Fri, 30min after sunset-midnight Sat; 🚊3, 16, 78, 🚊Balaclava) A staple for the local Jewish community, kosher bakery Glick's sells bagels baked and boiled in-house. Stick with the classics and try the 'New Yorker' with cream cheese and egg salad.

Monarch Cake Shop
DESSERTS $

(Map p478; ☑️03-9534 2972; www.monarchcakes.com.au; 103 Acland St, St Kilda; slice of cake from $5; ⊙8am-9.30pm Sun-Thu, to 10pm Fri & Sat; 🚊96) Monarch is a favourite among St Kilda's Eastern European cake shops, and its *Kugelhopf* (marble cake), plum cake and Polish baked cheesecake can't be beaten. In business since 1934, the shop doesn't seem to have changed much, with a soft, old-time atmosphere and wonderful buttery aromas. It also does good coffee.

Lentil as Anything
VEGETARIAN $

(Map p478; ☑️0424 345 368; www.lentilasanything.com; 41 Blessington St, St Kilda; by donation; ⊙noon-9pm; 🥄; 🚊3, 16, 96) Choosing from the vegetarian menu is easy. Deciding what to pay can be hard. This unique not-for-profit operation provides training and educational opportunities for marginalised people, as well as tasty flesh-free grub. Whatever you pay for your meal goes towards helping new migrants, refugees, people with disabilities and the long-term unemployed. There are several branches, including one at Abbotsford Convent (p468).

Claypots SEAFOOD **$$**
(Map p478; ☑03-9534 1282; www.facebook.com/
claypotsstkilda; 213 Barkly St, St Kilda; claypots
$20, mains $24-45; ⏱noon-1am; ➧96) A local
favourite, Claypots serves up fresh, share-
style plates of seafood. Its namesake dish is
available in a number of options, including
a beautifully spiced Moroccan (mussels and
fish fillet cooked with couscous, tomato, egg-
plant, harissa, zaatar and chickpeas). Get in
early to both nab a seat and ensure the good
stuff is still available, as hot items go fast.

Matcha Mylkbar CAFE, VEGETARIAN **$$**
(Map p478; ☑03-9534 1111; www.matchamylk
bar.com; 72a Acland St, St Kilda; dishes $15-22;
⏱8am-3pm; ➧; ➧3, 16, 96) If you've spied
anything from Matcha Mylkbar in your
Instagram feed, it's likely you've been left
green with envy. This small, contemporary
St Kilda cafe is known for its matcha-heavy
menu, which is also 100% plant based and
vegan friendly.

Uncle VIETNAMESE **$$**
(Map p478; ☑03-9041 2668; www.unclestkilda.
com.au; 188 Carlisle St, St Kilda; mains $30-34;
⏱5pm-late Mon & Tue, noon-late Wed-Sun; ➧3,
16, 78, ➧Balaclava) Uncle delivers stellar Viet-
namese cooking in a quintessentially St Kilda
space, complete with popular rooftop din-
ing area. The *pho* (noodle soup) is fragrant
and herbaceous, and best ordered as a small
portion so you have room to try the golden,
crunchy deliciousness of the DIY chicken-
tenderloin steamed *bao*. Wash it all down
with Viet sangria or a can of Vietnamese beer.

Newmarket Hotel AMERICAN **$$**
(Map p478; ☑03-9537 1777; www.newmarketst
kilda.com.au; 34 Inkerman St, St Kilda; sharing
plates from $13; ⏱noon-3pm & 6-10.30pm; ➧3,
16, 67) Sporting interiors by renowned architects Six Degrees, this historic pub channels
the California–Mexico border with tasty
dishes like tacos, smoked-chicken quesadillas and scallop ceviche with salt-water
cream and chilli. There's no shortage of
quality wood-fired meats, and the weekday
lunch specials are excellent value. There's a
top-shelf bar to boot.

I Carusi II PIZZA **$$**
(Map p478; ☑03-9593 6033; 231 Barkly St,
St Kilda; pizza $19-26; ⏱6-10pm Mon-Fri, from
5pm Sat & Sun; ➧3, 16, 96) Located around
the corner from the Acland St chaos, this
casually elegant Italian is well loved for
its thin-based pizzas. While quality isn't

always consistent, when they're done well
the pizzas are smashing. Check the board
for creative pasta specials, and flaunt your
sophistication by ordering a Cynar *spritz* –
Venice's less-sweet take on the ubiquitous
Aperol *spritz*. Bookings advised.

Batch Espresso CAFE **$$**
(Map p478; ☑03-9530 3550; 320 Carlisle St, Bal-
aclava; mains $16; ⏱7am-4.30pm, kitchen to 3pm
Mon-Fri, to 3.30pm Sat & Sun; ➧3, 3a, 16, ➧Bala-
clava) Like a pair of well-worn slippers, Batch
feels snug and familiar. Upcycled artworks
by Melbourne-based artists Joost Bakker
and Peter James Smith share the limelight
with trinkets from loyal regulars, many of
whom keep coming back for the cafe's dark-
roasted coffee, kedgeree (an Indian dish
with house-smoked fish, coriander and egg)
and potato-and-spinach hash.

★**Attica** MODERN AUSTRALIAN **$$$**
(☑03-9530 0111; www.attica.com.au; 74 Glen Eira
Rd, Ripponlea; tasting menu $250; ⏱6pm-late
Tue-Sat; ➧67, ➧Ripponlea) The only Austral-
ian restaurant on the San Pellegrino World's
Top 50 Restaurants list, Attica is home to
prodigious Kiwi import Ben Shewry and his
extraordinary culinary creations. Native in-
gredients shine in dishes like bunya bunya
with salted red kangaroo, or bush-currant
granité with lemon aspen and rosella flower.
Reservations accepted three months ahead,
on the first Wednesday of each month at
9am. Note that tables of two can go within
a couple of hours, especially for Friday and
Saturday nights. You'll have a better chance
with a table for four or more, or trying for
dinner midweek. It's also worth emailing or
calling to check if availability isn't showing
online. If driving, follow Brighton Rd south
and turn left onto Glen Eira Rd.

Lau's Family Kitchen CHINESE **$$$**
(Map p478; ☑03-8598 9880; www.lauskitchen.
com.au; 4 Acland St, St Kilda; mains $26-45;
⏱noon-3pm Mon-Fri, 12.30-3.30pm Sun, dinner
sittings 6pm & 8pm daily; ➧16, 96) This polished
nosh spot serves beautiful, home-style Can-
tonese with a few Sichuan surprises, including a seductive braised eggplant with spiced
minced pork. Reserve for one of the two dinner sittings, and check out the elegant wall
panels, made from 1930s kimonos.

Stokehouse SEAFOOD **$$$**
(Map p478; ☑03-9525 5555; www.stokehouse.
com.au; 30 Jacka Blvd, St Kilda; mains $36-42;
⏱noon-3pm & 6pm-late; ➧3a, 16, 96) After a

devastating fire, the lauded Stokehouse is back, brighter and better than ever. Striking contemporary architecture and floor-to-ceiling bay views set the right tone for fresh, modern, seafood-centric dishes, not to mention a stuff-of-legend bombe Alaska. This is one of Melbourne's hottest restaurants, so always book ahead.

Downstairs at beach level is the Stokehouse's casual, walk-in bar-bistro Pontoon (p507), as well as a fish-and-chip kiosk.

Cicciolina   ITALIAN $$$

(Map p478; ☑03-9525 3333; www.cicciolina stkilda.com.au; 130 Acland St, St Kilda; mains lunch $18-30, dinner $27-45; ☺noon-10pm; ☐3, 16, 96) This hideaway of dark wood, subdued lighting and pencil sketches is a St Kilda institution. The menu is modern Italian, with dishes that might see tortellini paired beautifully with Persian feta, ricotta, pine nuts, lime zest, asparagus and burnt sage butter. Bookings only for lunch; for dinner, eat very early or while away your wait in the moody back bar.

🍷 Drinking & Nightlife

Melbourne's drinking scene is easily the best in Australia and as good as any in the world. There's a huge diversity of venues, ranging from hip basement dives hidden down laneways to sophisticated cocktail bars perched on rooftops. Many pubs have pulled up the beer-stained carpet and polished the concrete, but don't dismiss the character-filled oldies that still exist.

🍸 City Centre

★ Heartbreaker   BAR

(Map p462; ☑03-9041 0856; www.heartbreaker bar.com.au; 234a Russell St; ☺5pm-3am Mon-Sat, to 11pm Sun; ☐Melbourne Central) Black walls, red lights, skeleton handles on the beer taps, random taxidermy, craft beer, a big selection of bourbon, rock and punk on the sound system, and tough-looking sweethearts behind the bar – all the prerequisites, in fact, for a hard-rocking good time.

★ Madame Brussels   ROOFTOP BAR

(Map p462; ☑03-9662 2775; www.madame brussels.com; 3rd fl, 57-59 Bourke St; ☺noon-11pm Sun-Wed, to 1am Thu-Sat; ☐Parliament) Head up to this wonderful rooftop terrace if you've had it with Melbourne-moody and all that dark wood. Although it's named for a famous 19th-century brothel owner, it feels

like a camp 1960s country club, with much Astroturfery and wisteria, and staff dressed for a spot of tennis.

★ Croft Institute   BAR

(Map p462; www.thecroftinstitute.com.au; 21 Croft Alley; ☺5pm-midnight Mon-Thu, 5pm-3am Fri, 8pm-3am Sat; ☐86, 96) Hidden in a graffitied laneway off a laneway, the slightly creepy Croft is a laboratory-themed bar downstairs, while upstairs at weekends the 1950s-themed gymnasium opens as a club. There's a $5 cover charge for DJs Friday and Saturday nights.

★ Bar Americano   COCKTAIL BAR

(Map p462; www.baramericano.com.au; 20 Presgrave Pl; ☺5pm-1am Mon-Sat; ☐Flinders St) A hideaway bar in a lane off Howey Pl, Bar Americano is a teensy standing-room-only affair with black-and-white chequered floors complemented by classic 'do not spit' subway-tiled walls and a subtle air of speakeasy. Once it hits its 14-person max, the grille gets pulled shut. The cocktails here don't come cheap, but they do come superb.

★ Siglo   ROOFTOP BAR

(Map p462; ☑03-9654 6631; www.siglobar.com. au; 2nd fl, 161 Spring St; ☺5pm-3am; ☐Parliament) Siglo's sought-after terrace comes with Parisian flair, wafting cigar smoke and serious drinks. It fills with suits on Friday night, which may lure or horrify you. Regardless, pick a time to mull over a classic cocktail, snack on upper-crust morsels and admire the 19th-century vista over Parliament and St Patrick's Cathedral. Entry is via the similarly unsigned Supper Cl.

Boilermaker House   BAR

(Map p462; www.boilermakerhouse.com.au; 209-211 Lonsdale St; ☺4pm-3am; ☐Melbourne Central) A real surprise on busy, workaday Lonsdale St, this dimly lit haven of urbanity has a phenomenal 850 whiskies on its list, along with 12 craft beers on tap and a further 40 by the bottle. Snack on cheese, charcuterie and jalapeño poppers as you make your way through them.

Cookie   BAR

(Map p462; ☑03-9663 7660; www.cookie.net.au; 1st fl, Curtin House, 252 Swanston St; ☺noon-3am; ☐Melbourne Central) Part bar, part Thai restaurant, this kooky-cool venue with grand bones is one of the more enduring rites of passage of the Melbourne night. The bar is unbelievably well stocked with fine whiskies, wines, and plenty of craft beers among the more than 200 brews on offer. The staff also knows how to make a serious cocktail.

Melbourne Supper Club
BAR

(Map p462; ☑03-9654 6300; www.melbourne supperclub.com.au; 1st fl, 161 Spring St; ☺5pm-4am Sun-Thu, to 6am Fri & Sat; ⓡParliament) Let's face it, late-night bars can be shady places, but that's not the case at this sophisticated hideaway by the Princess Theatre, entered via an unsigned wooden door. It's a favoured after-work destination for performers and hospitality types. Cosy into a chesterfield, browse the encyclopaedic wine menu and relax; the sommeliers will cater to any liquid desire.

Rooftop Bar
ROOFTOP BAR

(Map p462; ☑03-9654 5394; www.rooftopcinema. com.au; 6th fl, Curtin House, 252 Swanston St; ☺noon-1am; ⓡMelbourne Central) This bar sits at dizzying heights atop happening Curtin House. In summer it transforms into an outdoor cinema with striped deckchairs and a calendar of new and classic favourite flicks.

Garden State Hotel
BAR

(Map p462; ☑03-8396 5777; www.gardenstate hotel.com.au; 101 Flinders Lane; ☺11am-late; ☎; ⓡFlinders St) Just as in a grand English garden, there are orderly bits, wild bits and little dark nooks in this so-hot-right-now multipurpose venue. Shuffle past the suits into the main bar area, which is backed by shiny copper vats and a three-storey void filled with mature trees. The best part is the chandelier-festooned Rose Garden cocktail bar in the basement.

Market Lane Coffee
CAFE

(Map p462; www.marketlane.com.au; 109-111 Therry St; ☺7am-4pm; ⓡMelbourne Central) It's all about the super-strong coffee at this branch of Market Lane. It serves a few pastries, too, but as it's right opposite Queen Victoria Market there's no shortage of snacks at hand to enjoy with your takeaway cup. There's another branch in the market's deli hall.

Lui Bar
COCKTAIL BAR

(Map p462; ☑03-9691 3888; www.vuedemonde. com.au; 55th fl, Rialto, 525 Collins St; ☺5.30pm-midnight Mon-Wed, 11.30am-1am Thu, 11.30am-3am Fri & Sat, 11.30am-midnight Sun; ⓡSouthern Cross) Some people are happy to shell out $36 for the view from the 120m-high Melbourne Star, but we'd much rather spend $25 on a cocktail at this sophisticated bar perched 236m up the Rialto tower. Suits and jet-setters cram in most nights, so get there early (and nicely dressed) to claim your table.

Chuckle Park
BAR

(Map p462; ☑03-9650 4494; www.chucklepark. com.au; 322 Little Collins St; ☺11am-1am; ⓡ86, 96) Creating a park out of a narrow laneway and an expanse of astroturf, this kooky crew serves huge jars of cocktails and pulled-pork rolls from a little 1970s caravan parked down one end. Hanging plant jars double as swaying lights, and indie and rock music entertain the in-the-know crowd.

Riverland
BAR

(Map p462; ☑03-9662 1771; www.riverlandbar. com; vaults 1-9, Federation Wharf; ☺8am-late; ⓡFlinders St) Perched below Princes Bridge alongside the Yarra River, this bluestone beauty keeps things simple with good wine, beer on tap and bar meals that hit the mark: burgers, ribs, fish and chips. The outside tables are a treat when the weather is kind. Be prepared for rowdiness before and after footy matches at the nearby MCG.

Carlton Hotel
BAR

(Map p462; ☑03-9663 3246; www.thecarlton. com.au; 193 Bourke St; ☺3pm-late Sun-Wed, noon-late Thu-Sat; ⓡ86, 96) Over-the-top Melbourne rococo gets another workout here and never fails to raise a smile. The tropical deck on the 1st floor is shrouded in jasmine and bougainvillea. Check out the rooftop **Palmz** if you're looking for some Miami-flavoured vice, or just a great view.

Gin Palace
COCKTAIL BAR

(Map p462; ☑03-9654 0533; www.ginpalace. com.au; 10 Russell Pl; ☺4pm-3am; ⓡ86, 96, ⓡFlinders St) With a drinks list to make your liver quiver, Gin Palace is the perfect place to grab a soft couch, secluded alcove or bathtub filled with cushions, sip, and take it slow. The martinis here are legendary and it's open super late most nights.

Double Happiness
COCKTAIL BAR

(Map p462; ☑03-9650 4488; www.double-happiness.com.au; 21 Liverpool St; ☺4pm-1am Mon-Wed, 4pm-3am Thu & Fri, 6pm-3am Sat, 6pm-1am Sun; ⓡ86, 96, ⓡParliament) This stylish hole-in-the-wall is decked out in Chinese propaganda posters and Mao statues, and serves an excellent range of Asian-influenced chilli- and coriander-flavoured cocktails, along with a legendary espresso martini.

Section 8
BAR

(Map p462; www.section8.com.au; 27-29 Tattersalls Lane; ☺noon-11pm Sun, 10am-11pm Mon-Wed, 10am-1am Thu & Fri, noon-1am Sat; ⓡMelbourne Central) Enclosed within a cage full of shipping containers, graffiti and wooden-pallet seating, Section 8 remains one of the city's hippest bars. It's quite a scene, with DJs playing regularly.

Degraves Espresso
CAFE

(Map p462; ☑03-9654 1245; 23-25 Degraves St; ☺7am-10pm Mon-Sat, 8am-5pm Sun; ⓡFlinders St) In atmospheric Degraves St, this institution is a good spot to grab a quick takeaway coffee and wander the laneways.

🍷 Southbank & Docklands

Boatbuilders Yard
BAR

(Map p458; ☑03-9686 5088; www.theboat buildersyard.com.au; 23 South Wharf Promenade, South Wharf; ☺7am-late; ⓖ12, 96, 109) Occupying a slice of South Wharf next to the historic *Polly Woodside* ship, Boatbuilders attracts a mixed crowd of office workers, travellers and Melburnians keen to discover this developing area. It's made up of 'zones' running seamlessly from the indoor cafe-bar to the outdoor BBQ and bocce pit. There are usually live bands or DJs at weekends.

Ponyfish Island
BAR

(Map p462; www.ponyfish.com.au; Southbank Pedestrian Bridge, Southbank; ☺11am-late; ⓡFlinders St) Not content with hiding bars down laneways or on rooftops, Melburnians are finding ever more creative spots to do their drinking. Where better than a little open-air nook on the pylon of a bridge arcing over the Yarra? It's a surprisingly good spot to knock back beers in the sun while snacking on toasted sandwiches or cheese plates.

🍷 Richmond & East Melbourne

Mountain Goat Brewery
MICROBREWERY

(☑03-9428 1180; www.goatbeer.com.au; 80 North St, Richmond; ☺5-10pm Wed & Fri; ⓖ48, 75) This local microbrewery occupies a large warehouse in Richmond's backstreets. Sample its range of beers with an $11 tasting paddle while nibbling pizza. There are free brewery tours at 6.30pm on Wednesday. It's tricky to reach: head east on Bridge Rd, then turn left at Burnley St and right at North St.

DT's Hotel
GAY

(Map p458; ☑03-9428 5724; www.facebook.com/dtspub/; 164 Church St, Richmond; ☺6pm-midnight Tue, 4pm-1am Wed-Sat, 2-11pm Sun; ⓖ78) This long-standing gay pub hosts drag shows, karaoke, pool competitions and happy hours.

Public House
BAR

(Map p458; ☑03-9421 0187; www.publichouse.com.au; 433-435 Church St, Richmond; ☺noon-late Tue-Sun; ⓡEast Richmond) Not in any way resembling a public house from any discernible period in history, this swanky bar has been given a striking fit-out using raw and recycled materials. The food's excellent and DJs set up at weekends, attracting a young, good-looking crowd ready to, uh, mingle.

Touchwood
CAFE

(Map p458; ☑03-9429 9347; www.touchwood cafe.com; 480 Bridge Rd, Richmond; ☺7am-4pm; ⓖ48, 75) There's plenty of space both indoors and in the courtyard of this light, airy cafe housed in a former recycled-furniture store (hence the name). The coffee's single origin and the doughnuts at the counter are difficult to resist.

🍷 Fitzroy, Collingwood & Abbotsford

★ Black Pearl
COCKTAIL BAR

(Map p470; ☑03-9417 0455; www.blackpearlbar.com.au; 304 Brunswick St, Fitzroy; ☺5pm-3am, Attic Bar 7pm-2am Thu-Sat; ⓖ11) After 15 years in the game, Black Pearl goes from strength to strength, winning awards and receiving global accolades along the way. Low lighting, leather banquettes and candles set the mood downstairs. Prop at the bar to study the extensive cocktail list or let the expert bartenders concoct something to your taste. Upstairs is the table-service Attic Bar; book ahead.

★ Marion
WINE BAR

(Map p470; ☑03-9419 6262; www.marionwine.com.au; 53 Gertrude St, Fitzroy; ☺5-11pm Mon-Thu, noon-11pm Fri, 8am-11pm Sat & Sun; ⓖ86) Melbourne's poster-boy chef, Andrew McConnell, knew what he was doing when he opened Marion. The wine list is one of the area's most impressive and the space – catering to both stop-ins and long, romantic chats – is a pleasure to be in. Food changes regularly, but expect charcuterie from McConnell's butcher Meatsmith and specials with a European bent (dishes $10 to $34).

★ **Everleigh** COCKTAIL BAR
(Map p470; www.theeverleigh.com; 150-156 Gertrude St, Fitzroy; ⏰ 5.30pm-1am; 🚇 86) Sophistication and bartending standards are off the charts at this upstairs hidden nook. Settle into a leather booth in the intimate setting with a few friends for conversation, and exclaiming over classic 'golden era' cocktails like you've never tasted before.

★ **Naked for Satan** BAR
(Map p470; ☎ 03-9416 2238; www.nakedforsatan.com.au; 285 Brunswick St, Fitzroy; ⏰ noon-midnight Sun-Thu, to 1am Fri & Sat; 🚇 11) Vibrant, loud and reviving an apparent Brunswick St legend (a man nicknamed Satan who would get down and dirty, naked because of the heat, in an illegal vodka distillery under the shop), this place packs a punch with its popular *pintxos* (Basque tapas; $1 to $2), huge range of beverages, and unbeatable roof terrace (Naked in the Sky) with wraparound balcony.

★ **Proud Mary** CAFE
(Map p470; ☎ 03-9417 5930; 172 Oxford St, Collingwood; ⏰ 7.30am-4pm Mon-Fri, 8.30am-4pm Sat & Sun; 🕿; 🚇 86) A champion for direct-trade, single-origin coffee, this quintessential industrial Collingwood red-brick space takes its caffeine seriously. It's consistently packed, not only for the excellent brew but also for the equally top-notch food, such as ricotta hotcakes or free-range pork with fennel crackling.

For a further coffee education, check out **Aunty Peg's** (Map p458; ☎ 03-9417 1333; www.auntypegsbypmc.com.au; 200 Wellington St, Collingwood; ⏰ 8am-5pm; 🚇 86), its roastery nearby.

**Stomping Ground
Brewery & Beer Hall** BREWERY
(Map p458; ☎ 03-9415 1944; www.stompingground.beer; 100 Gipps St, Collingwood; ⏰ 11.30am-11pm Mon-Thu, to 1am Fri & Sat; 🕿🚻; 🚇 109, 🚈 Collingwood) This inviting brewery set in a former textile factory is a relaxed, leafy retreat with exposed-brick walls, hanging plants, a kids' play area and a large central bar. There are 15 to 25 Stomping Ground beers on tap, as well as rotating guest beers, and a menu of wood-fired pizzas, burgers and salads.

Bar Liberty BAR
(Map p470; http://barliberty.com; 234 Johnston St, Fitzroy; ⏰ 5pm-late Mon-Sat & from noon Sun; 🚇 86) From a team of hospitality heavyweights, Bar Liberty is bringing carefully selected wines (over 300 on the list) and expertly crafted cocktails to Fitzroy minus any pretentiousness. The approach is laid-

back, the atmosphere is relaxed and the dining focus is on bold, refined food. There are monthly wine dinners upstairs and a rear courtyard beer garden, Drinkwell.

Industry Beans CAFE
(Map p470; ☎ 03-9417 1034; www.industrybeans.com; 3/62 Rose St, Fitzroy; ⏰ 7am-4pm Mon-Fri, 8am-4pm Sat & Sun; 🕿; 🚇 96, 11) It's all about coffee chemistry at this warehouse cafe tucked in a Fitzroy side street. The coffee guide takes you through the speciality styles on offer (roasted on -ite), from AeroPress and pourover to cold drip and espresso, and helpful staff take the pressure off deciding. The food menu (brunch $12 to $35) is ambitious but doesn't always hit the mark.

Sircuit GAY
(Map p470; www.sircuit.com.au; 103 Smith St, Fitzroy; ⏰ 7.30pm-late Wed-Sun; 🚇 86) Hugely popular with a big cross section of gay men, Sircuit is an old-school gay bar with pool tables, drag shows, a back room and, as the night progresses, a heaving dance floor.

Noble Experiment BAR
(Map p470; ☎ 03-9416 0058; www.thenobleexperiment.com.au; 284 Smith St, Collingwood; ⏰ 5pm-late Wed & Thu, noon-late Fri-Sun; 🚇 86) If 1920s Prohibition-era cocktails are your tipple then swing by the Noble Experiment for a bottle-aged negroni, a bootleggers iced tea or a Kentucky cobbler. Spread over three levels, the decor hints at New York old-world charm and there's a seriously good food offering, from a chef's menu to slow-cooked meats designed for sharing.

Craft & Co MICROBREWERY
(Map p470; ☎ 03-9417 4755; www.thecraftandco.com.au; 390 Smith St, Collingwood; ⏰ 7am-4pm Mon-Wed, 7am-late Thu & Fri, 8am-late Sat, 8am-6pm Sun; 🚇 86) Take time to explore this two-storey warehouse – there's lots going on, from cafe, coffee roaster, bakery and deli to brewery and distillery. Most of the (daytime) cafe menu's ingredients are produced in-house and are also for sale, among them bread, cheese, charcuterie, coffee, beer, gin and vodka. Come evening the place becomes a bar with an almost exclusively Australian booze list.

Forester's Hall BAR
(Map p470; www.forestershall.com.au; 64 Smith St, Collingwood, cnr Smith & Gertrude Sts; ⏰ 4pm-2am Tue-Thu, 4pm-4am Fri, 2pm-4am Sat, 2pm-2am Sun; 🚇 86) The former nightclub here has

been transformed into a haven for beer lovers, with 32 well-curated taps on offer from Australia and around the world. Pair this with pizzas served till 2am, ping-pong tables, street-side seating, a mezzanine space and an upstairs dive bar, and you've got a winning combo for a night out.

Grace Darling
PUB

(Map p470; ☑ 03-9416 0055; www.thegracedarling hotel.com.au; 114 Smith St, Collingwood; mains $18-30; ⏱ noon-1am Mon-Sat, to 11pm Sun; ☒ 86) Adored by Collingwood football fans as the birthplace of the club, these days the Grace has been given a spit-and-polish and attracts a clientele of pretty young things. The bluestone beauty has a cosy restaurant, streetside tables, and live music, mainly aimed at the young indie crowd.

Peel Hotel
GAY, CLUB

(Map p458; ☑ 03-9419 4762; www.thepeel.com.au; 113 Wellington St, Collingwood; ⏱ 11pm-5am Thu, to 7am Fri & Sat; ☒ 86) The Peel is one of the best-known and most popular gay venues in Melbourne. It's the last stop of a big night.

Panama Dining Room & Bar
BAR

(Map p470; ☑ 03-9417 7663; www.thepanama. com.au; 3rd fl, 231 Smith St, Fitzroy; ⏱ bar 5pm-late, restaurant from 6pm; ☒ 86) Disappear up the stairs to where Smith St's traded in for a Manhattan feel at this warehouse space with huge arched windows. Sip serious cocktails, such as a barrel-aged negroni or a pineapple-and-chipotle daiquiri, while snacking on BBQ king prawns or grilled saganaki. For a more serious feed, park yourself in the dining area for the Euro-inspired menu with an Australian twist.

Napier Hotel
PUB

(Map p470; ☑ 03-9419 4240; www.thenapierhotel. com; 210 Napier St, Fitzroy; ⏱ 3-11pm Mon-Thu, noon-1am Fri, noon-11pm Sat, 1-11pm Sun; ☒ 86, 11) The Napier has stood on this corner for over a century; many pots have been pulled as the neighbourhood has changed, as demonstrated by the memorabilia of the sadly departed Fitzroy footy team. Worm your way around the central bar to the boisterous dining room for an iconic Bogan burger. Head upstairs to check out the gallery, too.

Union Club Hotel
PUB

(Map p470; ☑ 03-9417 2926; www.unionclubhotel. com.au; 164 Gore St, Fitzroy; ⏱ 3pm-late Mon-Wed, noon-late Thu-Sat, noon-11pm Sun; ☒ 86) A die-hard local with a retro feel and happy chatter from a relaxed indie crowd. The large curved bar is one of Melbourne's best spots to park yourself; the food is good, honest pub nosh; and the beer garden and roof deck beg you to make a lazy afternoon of it on a hot day.

Standard Hotel
PUB

(Map p470; ☑ 03-9419 4793; 293 Fitzroy St, Fitzroy; ⏱ 3-10pm Mon, to 11pm Tue, noon-11pm Wed-Sat, noon-10pm Sun; ☒ 96, 11) Flaunting a great beer garden, the Standard is anything but its moniker. The Fitzroy backstreet local has down-to-earth bar staff and a truly eclectic crowd enhancing an atmosphere defined by live music on Sunday, footy on the small screen, and loud and enthusiastic chatter.

🍷 Carlton & Brunswick

Wide Open Road
CAFE

(☑ 03-9010 9298; http://wideopenroad.com.au; 274 Barkly St, Brunswick; ⏱ 7am-4pm Mon-Fri, to 5pm Sat, 8am-5pm Sun; ☎; ☒ 19, ☒ Jewell) Wide Open in name translates to wide open in space at this inviting converted-warehouse cafe-roastery just off hectic Sydney Rd. There's plenty of elbow room at the communal tables, where you can tuck into dishes from a refreshingly inventive menu. Try the fish-finger sandwich with pickled cucumbers while sipping a Bathysphere house-blend espresso or weekly-changing filter coffee.

Seven Seeds
CAFE

(Map p472; ☑ 03-9347 8664; www.sevenseeds. com.au; 114 Berkeley St, Carlton; ⏱ 7am-5pm Mon-Sat, 8am-5pm Sun; ☒ 19, 59) The most spacious location in the Seven Seeds coffee empire, this rather out-of-the-way warehouse cafe has plenty of room to store your bike and sip a splendid coffee. Public cuppings are held 9am Friday. It also owns Traveller (p486) and **Brother Baba Budan** (Map p462; www. sevenseeds.com.au; 359 Little Bourke St; ⏱ 7am-5pm Mon-Sat, 9am-5pm Sun; ☎; ☒ Melbourne Central) cafes in the CBD.

Lincoln
PUB

(Map p472; ☑ 03-9347 4666; http://hotellincoln. com.au/; 91 Cardigan St, Carlton; ⏱ noon-11pm Sun-Thu, to midnight Fri & Sat; ☒ 1, 6) A bit posher than your average old Carlton boozer, the Lincoln hints at historical charm with art-deco features and a dark-wood curved bar. It offers an impressive wine list and a rotating selection of craft beer on tap, alongside the classic Carlton Draught, of course. The

CRAFT BEER & MICROBREWERIES

Until recently, thirsty Melburnians were given the choice of only two or three mainstream beers on tap (and perhaps an interstate lager if they were feeling adventurous). But the last decade has seen the emergence of microbreweries and craft-beer bars, primed to meet the demands of beer geeks who treat their drinking more seriously.

The big event on the Melbourne beer calendar is **Good Beer Week** (www.goodbeer week.com.au; ☺May), held in May, showcasing local, national and foreign craft beers. **Aussie Brewery Tours** (☑1300 787 039; www.aussiebrewerytours.com.au; tour incl transport, lunch & tastings $160; ☺Thu-Mon) will help you get around, offering a tour of several inner-city breweries and prestigious pubs.

kitchen does gastropub meals (coffee-cured salmon, whole baby snapper) and does them well.

Padre Coffee CAFE
(☑03-9381 1881; www.padrecoffee.com.au; 438 Lygon St, East Brunswick; ☺7am-2pm Mon, to 4pm Tue-Sat, 8am-4pm Sun; ☜; ☒1, 6) A big player in Melbourne's coffee movement, this East Brunswick warehouse-style cafe is the original roaster for Padre Coffee and brews its premium single-origins and blends.

Jimmy Watson's WINE BAR
(Map p472; ☑03-9347 3985; www.jimmywatsons. com.au; 333 Lygon St, Carlton; ☺wine bar 11am-11pm, Wolf's Lair rooftop 4-11pm; ☒Tourist Shuttle, ☒1, 6) If this Robin Boyd–designed midcentury building had ears, there'd be a few generations of writers and academics in trouble. Keep it tidy at Watson's wine bar with something nice by the glass, go a bottle of dry and dry (vermouth and ginger ale) and settle in the leafy courtyard, or head up to the Wolf's Lair rooftop for cocktails with a view.

Alderman WINE BAR
(☑03-9380 9003; 134 Lygon St, East Brunswick; ☺5-11pm Tue-Thu, to 1am Fri, 3pm-1am Sat, 3-11pm Sun; ☜; ☒1, 6) A classic East Brunswick local, the Alderman has an inviting traditional heavy wooden bar, an open fireplace, a good beer and cocktail selection, and welcoming staff. There's a small courtyard and you can order from restaurant Bar Idda (p495) next door.

Gerald's Bar WINE BAR
(☑03-9349 4748; http://geraldsbar.com.au; 386 Rathdowne St, North Carlton; ☺5-11pm Mon-Sat; ☒1, 6) Wine by the glass is democratically selected at this neighbourhood favourite, and they spin some fine vintage vinyl from behind the curved wooden bar. Gerald himself is out the back preparing to feed you whatever he feels like on the day with produce sourced mainly from local producers.

Retreat PUB
(☑03-9380 4090; www.retreathotelbrunswick. com.au; 280 Sydney Rd, Brunswick; ☺noon-1am Mon-Thu & Sun, to 3am Fri & Sat; ☒19, ☒Brunswick) This pub is so big that it's a tad overwhelming. Find your habitat – garden backyard, grungy band room or intimate front bar – and settle in for the long haul. A long-time champion of live music, it hosts nightly free gigs, which might include acoustic sets in the front bar earlier in the week or bands in the band room Thursday to Sunday.

🍺 North Melbourne & Parkville

Town Hall Hotel PUB
(Map p458; ☑03-9328 1983; www.townhallhotel northmelbourne.com.au; 33 Errol St, North Melbourne; ☺4pm-1am Mon-Thu, noon-1am Fri & Sat, noon-11pm Sun; ☒57) Sure, it's more than a bit grungy, but that's part of the charm of this endearingly unfussy local that's festooned with rock iconography (Bowie and Iggy feature prominently). Other more traditionally religious figures adorn the rear dining room, and there's a beer garden, too. There's often live music from Thursday to Sunday; otherwise they'll be spinning some classic vinyl.

🍺 South Melbourne, Port Melbourne & Albert Park

Clement CAFE
(Map p458; www.clementcoffee.com; shop 89, South Melbourne Market, cnr Coventry & Cecil Sts, South Melbourne; ☺7am-5pm; ☒12, 96) There's a buzz about this tiny cafe at the perimeter of South Melbourne Market, not only for its expertly crafted brew but also for its homemade salted-caramel or jam-and-custard

doughnuts. Grab a streetside stool or get a takeaway and wander the market stalls.

Colonial Brewery Co   BREWERY
(Map p458; ☑03-8644 4044; www.colonial brewingco.com.au/port-melbourne; 89 Bertie St, Port Melbourne; ⊙noon-11pm Thu & Fri; ☐109) This east coast outpost of Western Australian craft brewery Colonial pours smooth, thirst-crushing suds in a huge warehouse decked out with steel tanks, ping-pong table and food trucks. Staff are passionate and knowledgeable about the beers (which include seasonal drops), and the *Kölsch* goes down especially well.

🍷 South Yarra, Prahran & Windsor

★**Rufus**   COCKTAIL BAR
(Map p474; ☑03-9525 2197; www.rufusbar.com. au; 1st fl, 143 Greville St, Prahran; ⊙4pm-late; ☐6, 72, 78, ☐Prahran) Hidden above Greville St, Rufus is deliciously posh and proper, dripping with chandeliers, tinted mirrors and swagged drapes. That the place is named after Sir Winston Churchill's beloved poodle is no coincidence: the late British prime minister is Rufus' muse, hence the emphasis on quality champagnes, martinis and whiskies, the standout Yorkshire-pudding roll, and your butlerlike waiter. Enter from the laneway.

Woods of Windsor   BAR
(Map p474; ☑03-9521 1900; www.woodsofwindsor. com.au; 108 Chapel St, Windsor; ⊙5.30pm-1am Tue-Sat; ☐78, 5, 6, 64, ☐Windsor) Dark timber, kooky taxidermy and a speakeasy vibe make the Woods a suitable place to hide on those brooding, rainy Melbourne nights. Bunker down for a standout selection of whiskies (including rarer drops), or ditch them altogether for a little Italian subversion: the drinks list includes a string of variations on the classic negroni apéritif. *Cin cin!*

Market Lane Coffee   CAFE
(Map p474; ☑03-9804 7434; www.marketlane. com.au; Prahran Market, 163 Commercial Rd, South Yarra; ⊙7am-5pm Tue & Thu-Sat, to 4pm Wed, 8am-5pm Sun; ☐72, 78, 79, ☐Prahran) This is one of Melbourne's top speciality coffee roasters, hiding away at the back of Prahran Market. The beans here are strictly seasonal, producing cups of joe that are beautifully nuanced...and best paired with one of the scrumptious pastries. Free one-hour cup-

pings run at 10am on Saturday (get in by 9.30am to secure your place).

Emerson   BAR, CLUB
(Map p474; ☑03-9825 0900; www.theemerson. com.au; 143-145 Commercial Rd, South Yarra; ⊙5pm-midnight Thu, noon-5am Fri & Sat, noon-3.30am Sun; ☐72, 78, ☐Prahran) A swanky three-level venue with cocktail bar, club and rooftop bar. On Sunday afternoon the rooftop's a huge hit with gay revellers, who head up to sip skinny bitches (vodka and soda), catch up on the goss and show off all that gym work.

Railway Hotel   BAR
(Map p474; ☑03-9510 4050; www.therailway. com.au; 29 Chapel St, Windsor; ⊙noon-late; ☐5, 64, 78, ☐Windsor) This smart, casual gastropub is divided into numerous design-savvy spaces. The upstairs bar and deck runs one of the area's two gay-oriented Sunday sessions, this one attracting a slightly older, more down-to-earth crowd. Check out the talent (or at least the great skyline view).

Montereys   BAR
(Map p474; ☑03-9525 0980; 218 Chapel St, Prahran; ⊙noon-1am Tue-Sat, 11am-11pm Sun; 🎵; ☐6, 78, ☐Prahran) This corner bar was inspired by a US road trip, a fact reflected in such cocktails as the Palm Beach Paloma (cucumber, jalapeños, smoky Mezcal, grapefruit, lime) and nosh like lobster rolls (which could use a little more lobster). The real draw, however, is the daily happy hour (5pm to 7pm), with $2 freshly shucked oysters and $6 glasses of bubbles.

Windsor Castle Hotel   PUB
(Map p474; ☑03-9525 0239; www.windsorcastle. com.au; 89 Albert St, Windsor; ⊙3pm-late Mon-Thu, from noon Fri-Sun; ☐5, 64, ☐Windsor) What's not to love about a lime-hued pub with a herd of pink elephants on the roof? The Windsor Castle is a backstreet veteran, full of cosy nooks, sunken pits, fireplaces and flocked wallpaper. Top billing goes to the tiki-themed beer garden, especially fun on hot summer weekend nights.

Yellow Bird   BAR
(Map p474; ☑03-9533 8983; www.yellowbird. com.au; 122 Chapel St, Windsor; ⊙7.30am-late Mon-Fri, from 8am Sat & Sun; ☐6, 78, ☐Windsor) This little bird keeps Windsor's cool kids happy with all-day drinks and diner-style food. It's owned by the drummer from Something for Kate, so the loud, dark rock

'n' roll ambience is genuine, with a passing cast of musos, a fantastic playlist of underground bands and one of the most outrageously kitsch bars in town.

Borsch, Vodka & Tears

BAR

(Map p474; ☑ 03-9530 2694; www.borschvodka andtears.com; 173 Chapel St, Windsor; ◷ 8am-late Mon-Fri, from 9am Sat & Sun; ◻ 6, 78, ◻ Prahran) A Chapel St classic, Borsch, Vodka & Tears is a nod to the area's Eastern European influences. The more than 100 vodkas include clear, oak-matured, fruit-infused and traditional *nalewka kresowa* (made according to old Russian and Polish recipes). Staff are clued-up, and the menu includes borscht and blintzes good enough to make your Polish grandpa weep. *Na zdrowie!* (Cheers!)

Revolver Upstairs

CLUB

(Map p474; ☑ 03-9521 5985; www.revolver upstairs.com.au; 229 Chapel St, Prahran; ◷ 5pm-4am Tue & Wed, 5pm-6am Thu, 5pm Fri to noon Sat, 24hr 5pm Sat-9am Mon; ◻ 6, 78, ◻ Prahran) Rowdy Revolver can feel like an enormous version of your lounge room, but with 54 hours of nonstop music come the weekend, you're probably glad it's not. Live music, art exhibitions, not to mention interesting local, national and international DJs, keep the mixed crowd wide awake.

🍷 St Kilda

★ Bar Di Stasio

WINE BAR

(Map p478; ☑ 03-9525 3999; http://distasio. com.au/about/bar-di-stasio; 31 Fitzroy St, St Kilda; ◷ 11.30am-midnight; ◻ 3, 12. 16, 96) Within Pompidou-style scaffolding – the work of artist Callum Morton – lies this buzzing, grown-up bar, dominated by a floor-to-ceiling mural of Caravaggio's *Flagellation of Christ*. Behind the deep marble bar, waiters seemingly plucked from Venice's Caffè Florian mix perfect Campari *spritzes* while dishing out gorgeous bites, from lightly fried local seafood to elegant pastas (available until 11pm). Book: the place is extremely popular.

★ Pontoon

BAR

(Map p478; ☑ 03-9525 5445; http://pontoon stkildabeach.com.au; 30 Jacka Blvd, St Kilda; ◷ noon-midnight; ◻ 3, 16, 96) Beneath the fine-dining Stokehouse (p499) is its casual, buzzing bar-bistro, a light-soaked space with floor-to-ceiling windows and a deck looking right out at the beach and sunset. Slip on the shades and sip craft suds or a local prosecco while eyeing the crowd for the odd local celeb. A shared-plates menu delivers some decent bites, overpriced and undersized pizzas aside.

Misery Guts

BAR

(Map p478; ☑ 03-8590 6431; http://miseryguts bar.com; 19 Grey St, St Kilda; ◷ 4-11pm Wed, to midnight Thu, 2pm-1am Fri & Sat, 2pm-midnight Sun; ◻ 3, 16, 96) There's nothing cantankerous about this unruffled local, a few steps (and a million miles) away from Fitzroy St's backpacker bars. Punctuated with various oddities – including a menacing vintage police sign – it's where the locals actually lounge, gossiping over decent beers, interesting wines by the glass and tweaked cocktails like a limoncello *spritz*. There's live blues or jazz from 6pm Sunday.

Dogs Bar

BAR

(Map p478; ☑ 03-9593 9535; http://dogsbar.com. au; 54 Acland St, St Kilda; ◷ 11.30am-1am; 🛜; ◻ 3, 16, 96) You're guaranteed a good time at this St Kilda veteran, a joint that's rarely short of berets, boozy debates and raucous banter from local old-timers. Soaked in afternoon sunshine, the outdoor tables are a prime people-watching spot (especially at weekends), while the golden-hued interior is the setting for nightly live blues, rock or funk, usually from 9pm.

St Kilda Bowling Club

PUB

(Map p458; ☑ 03-9534 5229; www.stkildasports club.com.au; 66 Fitzroy St, St Kilda; ◷ noon-late; ◻ 12, 16, 96) This fabulously intact old clubhouse is tucked behind a trimmed hedge and a splendid bowling green. The long bar serves drinks at 'club prices' (ie cheap) and you'll be joined by St Kilda's hippest on Sunday afternoons. Kick off your shoes, roll a few bowls, knock back beers and watch the sun go down along with your bowling accuracy.

Local Taphouse

BAR

(Map p478; ☑ 03-9537 2633; www.thelocal.com. au; 184 Carlisle St, St Kilda; ◷ noon-late; ◻ 3, 16, 78, ◻ Balaclava) Reminiscent of an old-school Brooklyn bar, the warm, wooden Local has a rotating cast of craft beers and an impressive bottle list. There's a beer garden upstairs, and a snug drawing-room mix of leather couches and open fires inside. Weekly events include live comedy (including well-established acts) on Monday, and live soul, funk, blues or reggae on Friday and Saturday.

Hotel Barkly
PUB

(Map p478; ☑ 03-9525 3371; www.hotelbarkly. com; 109 Barkly St, St Kilda; ⊙ 4pm-late Tue, from 11.30am Wed-Sun; ☐ 3, 16, 67) The street-level public bar is the place to go if you're up for sinking a few pints, wiggling to whatever comes on the jukebox and snogging a stranger before last drinks. The rooftop bar (open Friday only) feigns a bit of class, but things get messy up there, too. It's worth it for the spectacular sunset views across St Kilda, though.

Vineyard
BAR

(Map p478; www.thevineyard.com.au; 71a Acland St, St Kilda; ⊙ 10.30am-3am Mon-Fri, from 10am Sat & Sun; ☐ 3, 16, 96) An old favourite, the Vineyard has the perfect corner position and outdoor seating to attract crowds of backpackers and scantily clad young locals, who enjoy themselves so much they drown out the neighbouring roller coaster. Sunday-afternoon sessions are big here.

☆ Entertainment

Cinema

Moonlight Cinema
CINEMA

(Map p458; www.moonlight.com.au; Gate D, Royal Botanic Gardens, Birdwood Ave, South Yarra; ☐ 1, 3, 5, 6, 16, 64, 67, 72) Melbourne's original outdoor cinema hits the Royal Botanic Gardens from early December to early April, screening a mix of current mainstream releases and retro classics. Bring your own picnic hamper or buy light eats and booze at the venue; 'Gold Grass' tickets include waitstaff service and a reserved beanbag bed in the premium viewing area.

Astor
CINEMA

(Map p474; ☑ 03-9510 1414; www.astortheatre. net.au; cnr Chapel St & Dandenong Rd, Windsor; tickets $17; ☐ 5, 64, 78, ☒ Windsor) This 1936 art-deco darling has had more ups and downs than a Hollywood diva. Recently saved from permanent closure, it's one of Melbourne's best-loved landmarks, with double features most nights and a mixed bag of recent releases, art-house films and cult classics. Discount tickets ($12 to $13) are available Monday, Wednesday and Thursday.

Cinema Nova
CINEMA

(Map p472; ☑ 03-9347 5331; www.cinemanova. com.au; 380 Lygon St, Carlton; ☐ Tourist Shuttle, ☐ 1, 6) See the latest in art-house, docos and foreign films at this locals' favourite. Cheap Monday screenings ($7 before 4pm, $9 after 4pm).

Live Music

The Tote
LIVE MUSIC

(Map p458; ☑ 03-9419 5320; www.thetotehotel. com; cnr Johnston & Wellington Sts, Collingwood; ⊙ 4pm-late Wed-Sun; ☐ 86) One of Melbourne's most iconic live-music venues, this divey Collingwood pub has a great roster of local and international punk and hardcore bands, and one of the best jukeboxes in the universe. Its temporary closure in 2010 brought Melbourne to a stop, literally: people protested on city-centre streets against the liquor-licensing laws that were blamed for the closure.

Cherry
LIVE MUSIC

(Map p462; www.cherrybar.com.au; AC/DC Lane; ⊙ 6pm-late Mon-Sat, 2pm-late Sun; ☒ Flinders St) Of course Melbourne's most legendary live-rock bar is located in a black-walled, neon-lit basement on AC/DC Lane. There's often a queue, but once you're inside a welcoming, slightly anarchic spirit prevails. Live music and DJs play seven nights a week, and there's a long-standing soul night on Thursday.

Forum
CONCERT VENUE

(Map p462; ☑ 1300 111 011; www.forummelbourne. com.au; 150-152 Flinders St; ☒ Flinders St) One of the city's most atmospheric live-music venues, the Forum does double duty as a cinema during the Melbourne International Film Festival. The striking Moorish exterior (an over-the-top fantasia with minarets, domes and dragons) houses an equally interesting interior, with the southern night sky rendered on the domed ceiling.

Prince Bandroom
LIVE MUSIC

(Map p478; ☑ 03-9536 1168; www.princebandroom. com.au; 29 Fitzroy St, St Kilda; ☐ 12, 16, 96) The Prince is a legendary St Kilda venue, with a solid line-up of local and international acts spanning hip-hop, dance, rock and indie. It's an eclectic mix, with recent guests including UK rapper Tinie Tempah, American roots-rock trio Moreland & Arbuckle and Nordic hardcore-punk outfit Refused.

Toff in Town
LIVE MUSIC

(Map p462; ☑ 03-9639 8770; www.thetoffintown. com; 2nd fl, Curtin House, 252 Swanston St; ⊙ 5pm-3am Sun-Thu, to 5am Fri & Sat; ☒ Melbourne Central) An atmospheric venue well suited to cabaret, the Toff also works for intimate gigs by rock gods, avant-folksters or dance-hall queens. The moody bar next door serves post-set drinks of the French wine and cocktail variety.

Palais Theatre
CONCERT VENUE

(Map p478; ☑03-9525 3240, tickets 136 100; Lower Esplanade, St Kilda; ☒3, 16, 96) Standing gracefully next to Luna Park, the heritage-listed Palais (c 1927) is a St Kilda icon. Scheduled to reopen in May 2017 after a nip and tuck (which includes repainting the building in its original colours), the deco giant hosts some of the biggest names in local and international music and comedy.

Corner
LIVE MUSIC

(Map p458; ☑03-9427 7300; www.cornerhotel. com; 57 Swan St, Richmond; ☺4pm-late Mon-Fri, noon-3am Sat, noon-1am Sun; ☒Richmond) The band room here is one of Melbourne's most popular midsize venues, and it's seen plenty of loud and live action over the years, from Dinosaur Jr to the Buzzcocks. If your ears need a break, there's a friendly front bar. The rooftop has city views but gets packed, and often with a different crowd from the music fans below.

Night Cat
LIVE MUSIC

(Map p470; ☑03-9417 0090; www.thenightcat. com.au; 141 Johnston St, Fitzroy; ☺9pm-3am Fri & Sat, 7pm-3am Sun; ☒11) The Night Cat is a barn-sized space with a dance floor that sees lots of action. Music is generally in the Latin, jazz or funk vein. Offers salsa dance classes ($20) on Sunday night.

Festival Hall
CONCERT VENUE

(Map p458; ☑03-9329 9699; www.festivalhall. com.au; 300 Dudley St, West Melbourne; ☒220, ☒North Melbourne) This former boxing stadium – aka 'Festering Hall' (especially on hot summer nights) – is a fave for live international acts. The Beatles played here in 1964.

Last Chance Rock & Roll Bar
LIVE MUSIC

(Map p472; ☑03-9329 9888; www.thelastchance. com.au; 238 Victoria St, North Melbourne; ☺4pm-late Mon-Thu, noon-7am Fri & Sat, noon-11pm Sun; ☒19, 57, 55) The Public Bar, a much-loved local institution, closed recently and Last Chance took over in the same spirit – it's clear there's been no spit-and-polish here and it's just as perfectly divey as ever. Live bands play most nights and lean towards the punk genre.

Gasometer
LIVE MUSIC

(Map p470; ☑03-9416 3335; www.thegasometer hotel.com.au; 484 Smith St, Collingwood; ☺4pm-midnight Tue & Wed, 4pm-2am Thu, noon-3am Fri & Sat, noon-midnight Sun; ☒86) This corner bluestone pub features a cosy front bar, an ex-

---

TICKETS

Tickets for concerts, theatre, comedy, sports and other events are usually available from one of the following agencies:

Halftix (Map p462; www.halftix melbourne.com; Melbourne Town Hall, 90-120 Swanston St; ☺10am-2pm Mon, 11am-6pm Tue-Fri, 10am-4pm Sat; ☒Flinders St) Discounted theatre tickets are sold on the day of performance.

Moshtix (www.moshtix.com.au)

Ticketek (Map p462; www.ticketek.com. au; 252 Exhibition St; ☺9am-5pm Mon-Fri, 10am-3pm Sat)

Ticketmaster (Map p462; ☑1300 111 011; www.ticketmaster.com.au; Forum, 150-152 Flinders St; ☺9am-6pm Mon-Fri)

---

cellent line-up of bands most nights – from up-and-coming local acts to punk and indie big names – and one of the best band rooms in the city, with a mezzanine level and a retractable roof for open-air gigs.

Howler
LIVE MUSIC

(☑03-9077 5572; https://h-w-l-r.com; 7 Dawson St, Brunswick; ☺noon-1am; ☒19, ☒Jewell, Brunswick) At the back of a car park near the train tracks is not usually a recommendable spot to hang out, but behind a street-art-covered warehouse facade is this leafy oasis of a bar and arts hub. The purpose-built theatre hosts everything from international DJs and stand-up comedy to a great line-up of noise, indie and electronica bands. Opposite the Brunswick Baths.

Old Bar
LIVE MUSIC

(Map p470; ☑03-9417 4155; www.theoldbar. com.au; 74-76 Johnston St, Fitzroy; ☺4pm-3am Mon-Fri, 2pm-3am Sat & Sun; ☎; ☒96, 11) With live bands seven days a week and a licence till 3am, the Old Bar's another reason that Melbourne is the rock 'n' roll capital of Australia. It gets great local bands and a few internationals in its grungy band room with a house-party vibe.

Opera

Melbourne Opera
OPERA

(Map p462; ☑03-9614 4188; www.melbourne opera.com) A not-for-profit company that performs classic and light opera in various venues, including the **Regent Theatre** (Map

GAY & LESBIAN MELBOURNE

While there's still a handful of specifically gay venues scattered around the city, some of the best hangouts are weekly takeovers of mainstream bars (especially Sunday afternoon at the **Railway Hotel** (p506) in Windsor, Sunday evening at the **Emerson** (p506) in South Yarra and Thursday night at **Yah Yah's** (Map p470; http://yahyahs. com.au; 99 Smith St, Fitzroy; ⏰5pm-5am Thu-Sat; 🚋86) in Fitzroy). Semiregular themed gay party nights are also popular, such as **Woof** (www.woofclub.com), **DILF** (www.iwan tadilf.com), **Closet** (www.facebook.com/closetpartyoz), **Fabuland** (www.fabuland.com. au) and **Swagger** (www.facebook.com/swaggerparty). For lesbians, there's **Fannys at Franny's** (www.francescasbar.com.au/fannys-frannys) and **Mother Party** (www.face book.com/sojuicysaturdays).

The big event on the queer calendar is the annual **Midsumma Festival** (www.mid summa.org.au; ⏰Jan-Feb). It has a diverse program of cultural, community and sporting events, including the popular Midsumma Carnival at Alexandra Gardens, St Kilda's Pride March and much more. Australia's largest GLBT film festival, the **Melbourne Queer Film Festival** (www.melbournequeerfilm.com.au; ⏰Mar), screens more than 100 films from around the world.

For more local info, pick up a copy of the free magazines **Star Observer** (www.star observer.com.au), **MCV** (www.gaynewsnetwork.com.au) and **LOTL** (Lesbians on the Loose; www.lotl.com). Gay and lesbian radio station **JOY 94.9FM** (www.joy.org.au) is another important resource for visitors and locals.

p462; ☑1300 111 011; www.marrinertheatres.com. au; 191 Collins St; 🚆Flinders St).

Opera Australia OPERA
(Map p458; ☑03-9685 3777; www.opera.org.au; Arts Centre, 100 St Kilda Rd, Southbank; 🚆Flinders St) The national opera company performs with some regularity at the Arts Centre (p466).

Victorian Opera OPERA
(☑03-9001 6400; www.victorianopera.com.au) Dedicated to innovation and accessibility, this opera company's program, pleasingly, doesn't always play it safe. It performs mainly at the Arts Centre (p466) and the Recital Centre.

Theatre & Arts

Red Stitch Actors Theatre THEATRE
(Map p474; ☑03-9533 8082; www.redstitch.net; rear 2 Chapel St, Windsor; 🚋5, 64, 78, 🚆Windsor) Featuring prolific national talent, Red Stitch is one of Australia's most respected actors' ensembles, staging new international works that are often premieres in Australia. The company's intimate black-box theatre is located opposite the historic Astor cinema, down the end of a driveway.

Theatre Works THEATRE
(Map p478; ☑03-9534 3388; www.theatreworks. org.au; 14 Acland St, St Kilda; 🚋3, 16, 96) Theatre Works is one of Melbourne's veteran independent theatre companies. With award-winning creative director John Sheedy at the helm, the company's focus is firmly on new Australian works.

Melbourne Theatre Company THEATRE
(MTC; Map p458; ☑03-8688 0800; www.mtc. com.au; 140 Southbank Blvd, Southbank; 🚋1) Melbourne's major theatrical company stages around a dozen productions each year, ranging from contemporary (including many new Australian works) to Shakespeare and other classics. Performances take place in its award-winning Southbank Theatre, a striking black building enclosed within angular white tubing.

La Mama THEATRE
(Map p472; ☑03-9347 6948; www.lamama. com.au; 205 Faraday St, Carlton; tickets $10-25; ⏰box office 10.30am-5pm Mon-Fri, 2-3pm Sat & Sun; 🚌Tourist Shuttle, 🚋1, 6) La Mama is historically significant in Melbourne's theatre scene. This tiny, intimate forum produces new Australian works and experimental theatre, and has a reputation for developing emerging playwrights. It's a ramshackle old building with an open-air bar.

Shows also run at its larger **Courthouse theatre** at 349 Drummond St, so check your tickets carefully for the correct location ahead of the show.

Comedy

Comic's Lounge
COMEDY

(Map p458; ☑03-9348 9488; www.thecomics
lounge.com.au; 26 Errol St, North Melbourne; ☺din-
ner/show from 6.30/8pm Mon-Sat; ☒57) There's
stand-up featuring Melbourne's best-known
funny people most nights of the week here.
If you like to live dangerously, Tuesday's
when professional comedians try out new
material. Admission prices vary.

Comedy Theatre
THEATRE

(Map p462; ☑1300 111 011; www.marrinertheatres.
com.au; 240 Exhibition St; ☒Parliament) This
midsize 1920s Spanish–style venue is dedicated to comic theatre, stand-up and
musicals.

Classical Music

Melbourne Recital Centre
CLASSICAL MUSIC

(Map p458; ☑03-9699 3333; www.melbournerecital.
com.au; 31 Sturt St, Southbank; ☺box office 9am-
5pm Mon-Fri; ☎; ☒1) This building may look
like a framed piece of giant honeycomb,
but it's actually the home (or hive?) of the
Melbourne Chamber Orchestra (www.
mco.org.au) and lots of small ensembles. Its
two halls are said to have some of the best
acoustics in the southern hemisphere. Performances range from chamber music to
classical, jazz, world music and dance.

Melbourne Symphony
Orchestra
LIVE PERFORMANCE

(MSO; Map p462; ☑03-9929 9600; www.mso.
com.au; Hamer Hall, 100 St Kilda Rd, Southbank;
☒Flinders St) The MSO has a broad reach:
while not afraid to be populist (it's done
sell-out performances with Burt Bacharach
and Kiss), it usually performs classical sym-
phonic masterworks. It plays regularly at
its **Hamer Hall** (Map p462; ☑1300 182 183;
www.artscentremelbourne.com.au; 100 St Kilda Rd,
Southbank; ☒1, 3, 6, 16, 64, 67, 72, ☒Flinders St)
home, but it also runs a summer series of free
concerts at the **Sidney Myer Music Bowl**
(Map p458; ☑1300 182 183; www.artscentre
melbourne.com.au; Kings Domain, 21 Linlithgow Ave,
Southbank; ☒3, 5, 6, 16, 64, 67, 72).

Dance

Australian Ballet
BALLET

(Map p458; ☑1300 369 741; www.australianballet.
com.au; 2 Kavanagh St, Southbank; ☒1) More
than 50 years old, the Melbourne-based Australian Ballet performs traditional and new
works in the Arts Centre and all around the
country. You can take an hour-long tour of
the Primrose Potter Australian Ballet Cen-

tre ($39, bookings essential) that includes
a visit to the production and wardrobe departments as well as watching the dancers
practise in the studios.

Chunky Move
DANCE

(Map p458; ☑03-9645 5188; www.chunkymove.
com.au; 111 Sturt St, Southbank; ☒1) This acclaimed contemporary-dance company performs mainly at the **Malthouse Theatre**
(Map p458; ☑03-9685 5111; www.malthousethe
atre.com.au; 113 Sturt St, Southbank). It also
runs a variety of public dance classes; check
the website.

Shopping

Melbourne is a city of passionate, dedicated
retailers catering to a broad range of tastes,
whims and lifestyles. It's particularly good
for small, independent clothing boutiques
catering to both women and men. From city
laneways and arcades to suburban shopping
streets and malls, you'll find plenty of places
to loosen your wallet and pick up something
unique.

City Centre

★ Craft Victoria
ARTS & CRAFTS

(Map p462; ☑03-9650 7775; www.craft.org.au;
31 Flinders Lane; ☺11am-6pm Mon-Sat; ☒Parlia-
ment) This retail arm of Craft Victoria showcases handmade goods, mainly by Victorian
artists and artisans. Its range of jewellery,
textiles, accessories, glass and ceramics
bridges the art–craft divide and makes for
some wonderful mementos of Melbourne.
There are also a few galleries with changing
exhibitions; admission is free.

Alpha60
FASHION & ACCESSORIES

(Map p462; ☑03-9663 3002; www.alpha60.
com.au; 2nd fl, 209 Flinders Lane; ☺10am-6pm;
☒Flinders St) Melbourne has a reputation
for top-notch retail spaces, but this place is
just showing off. Alpha60's signature store
is hidden within the Hogwartsian chapter
house of St Paul's Cathedral, where fresh,
casual women's clothing is displayed on a
phalanx of mannequins while giant projections of roosters keep watch. There's another
store below at ground level.

Oscar Hunt Tailors
CLOTHING

(Map p462; ☑03-9670 6303; www.oscarhunt.
com.au; 3rd fl, 43 Hardware Lane; ☺8.30am-
6.30pm Mon-Fri, 9am-5pm Sat; ☒Melbourne Central) Make like a gentleman in this tailoring

showroom and workshop, where you can have a suit designed, pick up ties, pocket squares and alpaca scarves, and enjoy a spot of whisky at the lounge bar while you wait. The tailors use traditional methods, working closely with each client for an approach as tailored as the end result.

Melbournalia
GIFTS & SOUVENIRS

(Map p462; ☑03-9663 3751; www.melbournalia.com.au; 50 Bourke St; ⊗10am-7pm; ⍟Parliament) This is the place to stock up on interesting souvenirs by more than 100 local designers – prints featuring city icons, crazy socks and great books on Melbourne.

Original & Authentic Aboriginal Art
ART

(Map p462; ☑03-9663 5133; www.originaland authenticaboriginalart.com; 90 Bourke St; ⊗10am-6pm; ⍟Parliament) For more than 20 years this centrally located gallery has sourced Indigenous art from the Central and Western Deserts, the Kimberleys and Arnhem Land. It subscribes to the City of Melbourne's code of practice for Indigenous art, ensuring authenticity and ethical dealings with all artists.

NGV Shop
DESIGN

(Map p462; ☑03-8662 1543; www.ngv.vic.gov.au; Ian Potter Centre, Federation Sq; ⊗10am-5pm; ⍟Flinders St) This gallery shop has a wide range of international design magazines, a kids' section and a good selection of artsy objects.

Hill of Content
BOOKS

(Map p462; ☑03-9662 9472; www.hillofcontent bookshop.com; 86 Bourke St; ⊗10am-6pm Sat-Thu, to 8pm Fri; ⍟Parliament) Melbourne's oldest bookshop (established 1922) has a range

---

CAMBERWELL MARKET

Filled with secondhand and handcrafted goods, the **Camberwell Sunday Market** (www.camberwellsundaymarket.org; Market Pl, Camberwell; ⊗6.30am-12.30pm Sun; ⍟Camberwell) is where Melburnians come to offload their unwanted items and where antique hunters come to find them. It's great for discovering preloved (often rarely worn) items of clothing, restocking a bookcase and finding unusual curios.

---

of general titles and an extensive stock of books on art, classics and poetry.

Metropolis
BOOKS

(Map p462; ☑03-9663 2015; www.metropolis bookshop.com.au; 3rd fl, Curtin House, 252 Swanston St; ⍟Melbourne Central) Lovely bookish eyrie with a focus on art, architecture, fashion and film.

Basement Discs
MUSIC

(Map p462; ☑03-9654 1110; www.basementdiscs.com.au; 24 Block Pl; ⊗10am-6pm; ⍟Flinders St) Apart from a range of CD titles across all genres, Basement Discs has regular in-store performances by big-name touring and local acts. Descend to the basement for a browse; you never know who you might find playing.

Wunderkammer
ANTIQUES

(Map p462; ☑03-9642 4694; www.wunderkam mer.com.au; 439 Lonsdale St; ⊗10am-6pm Mon-Fri, to 4pm Sat; ⍟Flagstaff) Surprises abound in this 'Wonder Chamber'. The strangest of shops, it stocks taxidermy, insects in jars, antique scientific tools and surgical equipment.

RM Williams
CLOTHING

(Map p462; ☑03-9663 7126; www.rmwilliams.com; Melbourne Central, cnr La Trobe & Swanston Sts; ⊗10am-7pm Sat-Wed, to 9pm Thu & Fri; ⍟Melbourne Central) An Aussie icon, even for city slickers, this brand will kit you out in stylish essentials for working the land, including a pair of its famous boots. The Melbourne Central branch occupies the historic brick shot tower at the centre of the complex and has a mini museum inside.

Paperback Books
BOOKS

(Map p462; ☑03-9662 1396; www.paperback books.com.au; 60 Bourke St; ⊗9.30am-10pm Mon-Thu, to 11.30pm Fri, 11am-11.30pm Sat, noon-7pm Sun; ⍟Parliament) A small space jam-packed with carefully selected titles, including a good selection of Australian literature – great when you need a novel late at night.

City Hatters
HATS

(Map p462; ☑03-9614 3294; www.cityhatters.com.au; 211 Flinders St; ⊗9am-5pm; ⍟Flinders St) Located beside the main entrance to Flinders St station, this evocatively old-fashioned store is the most convenient place to purchase an iconic Akubra hat, a kangaroo-leather sun hat or something a little more unique.

🔒 Southbank & Docklands

DFO South Wharf
MALL

(Map p458; www.dfo.com.au; 20 Convention Centre Pl, South Wharf; ⊙10am-6pm Sat-Thu, to 9pm Fri; 🚋12, 96, 109) Set over two floors, this large centre offers factory-outlet shopping at its most tempting. Big brands represented include Ben Sherman, Tumi, Lacoste, Victoria's Secret, Vans and Converse.

NGV Design Store
DESIGN

(Map p458; 🕿03-8620 2243; www.ngv.vic.gov.au; NGV International, 180 St Kilda Rd, Southbank; ⊙10am-5pm; 🚉Flinders St) This large store sells well-designed and thoughtful show-based merchandise, arty T-shirts, a beautifully produced range of posters, and a hefty collection of art and design books.

🔒 Richmond & East Melbourne

Pookipoiga
GIFTS & SOUVENIRS

(Map p458; 🕿03-8589 4317; www.pookipoiga.com; 64 Bridge Rd, Richmond; ⊙9.30am-5pm; 🚋48, 75) 🌿 Everything is ethically produced, sustainable and animal friendly at this cute little gift store, packed with interesting things. There's a great selection of quirky greeting cards, loud socks and toiletries.

Lily & the Weasel
GIFTS & SOUVENIRS

(Map p458; 🕿03-9421 1008; www.lilyandtheweasel.com.au; 173 Swan St, Richmond; ⊙11am-5pm Tue-Sun; 🚋70) A mix of beautiful things from around the globe is stocked at this interesting store, alongside the work of local designers such as children's toys, scarves, toiletries and Robert Gordon ceramics.

🔒 Fitzroy, Collingwood & Abbotsford

★ Third Drawer Down
HOMEWARES

(Map p470; www.thirddrawerdown.com; 93 George St, Fitzroy; ⊙10am-6pm; 🚋86) It all started with its signature tea-towel designs (now found in MoMA in New York) at this 'museum of art souvenirs'. It makes life beautifully unusual by stocking absurdist pieces with a sense of humour as well as high-end art by well-known designers. Giant watermelon stools sit next to Yayoi Kusama's ceramic plates and scarves by Ai Weiwei.

Mud Australia
CERAMICS

(Map p470; 🕿03-9419 5161; www.mudaustralia.com; 181 Gertrude St, Fitzroy; ⊙10am-6pm Mon-Fri, to 5pm Sat, noon-5pm Sun; 🚋86) You'll find some of the most aesthetically beautiful – as well as functional – porcelainware at Australian-designed Mud. Coffee mugs, milk pourers, salad bowls and serving plates come in muted pastel colours with a raw matte finish.

Polyester Records
MUSIC

(Map p470; 🕿03-9419 5137; www.polyesterrecords.com; 387 Brunswick St, Fitzroy; ⊙10am-8pm Mon-Thu & Sat, to 9pm Fri, 11am-6pm Sun; 🚋11) This popular record store has been selling Melburnians independent music from around the world for decades, and it also has a great range of local stuff. The knowledgeable staff will help you find what you're looking for and can offer great suggestions.

Happy Valley
GIFTS & SOUVENIRS

(Map p470; 🕿03-9077 8509; www.happyvalleyshop.com; 294 Smith St, Collingwood; ⊙10.30am-6pm Mon-Fri, 10am-6pm Sat, 11am-5pm Sun; 🚋86) It's difficult to pigeonhole Happy Valley: it's an art store, bookshop and gallery of wonderful things you didn't realise you needed, from laugh-out-loud cards to beautiful jewellery and locally designed homewares. The well-curated range of books includes hardback art titles and a great selection of cookbooks from some of the city's top restaurants.

Poison City Records
MUSIC

(Map p470; www.poisoncityrecords.com; 400 Brunswick St, Fitzroy; ⊙noon-5pm Mon, 11am-5.30pm Wed-Fri, to 5pm Sat & Sun; 🚋11) Independent record/skate shop with its own Poison City label releasing excellent indie, punk and fuzz-rock Melbourne bands such as the Nation Blue, the Meanies, White Walls and Smith Street Band.

Obüs
FASHION & ACCESSORIES

(Map p470; 🕿03-9416 0012; www.obus.com.au; 226 Gertrude St, Fitzroy; ⊙10am-6pm Mon-Sat, 11am-5pm Sun; 🚋86) Melbourne-based designer Kylie Zerbst set up Obüs over 15 years ago with this, her first store. Known for bright geometric patterns and soft bamboo-cotton travel essentials, the clothing is sophisticated yet fun and offers pieces that get you from work to going out without a change.

Ess
CLOTHING

(Map p470; 🕿03-9495 6112; www.ess-laboratory.com; 114 Gertrude St, Fitzroy; ⊙11am-5.30pm Mon-Fri, to 5pm Sat, 12.30-4.30pm Sun; 🚋86) Japanese design duo Hoshika Oshimie and her sound-artist collaborative partner,

MAYDAYS / GETTY IMAGES ©

PATJO / SHUTTERSTOCK ©

3

**Southbank pedestrian bridge
over the Yarra River**
roll through Melbourne CBD to experience the
ty's culture and architecture.

Beach huts at Brighton Beach
elbourne's beach suburbs offer the perfect
taway, just a tram ride from the city.

Street art in Hosier Lane (p457)
elbourne's network of laneways and alleys are
decked in colourful street art.

Aerial view of Melbourne's CBD
e city lights up at night and keeps bustling until
e early hours; plunge into its wealth of dining and
ghtlife options.

Tatsuyoshi Kawabata, have created waves in Melbourne since Hoshinka established Ess Laboratory in 2001. The National Gallery of Victoria has Ess designs in its collection, but don't let that stop you claiming one for yourself.

Smith Street Bazaar
VINTAGE, HOMEWARES

(Map p470; ☑ 03-9419 4889; 305 Smith St, Fitzroy; ⊘ 11am-6pm Mon-Fri, noon-6pm Sat, 12.30-5pm Sun; ☐ 86) A great place to find midcentury furniture (the occasional Grant Featherston chair), Danish pottery, lamps of all shades and sizes, as well as vintage clothing and shoes. Best of all, it's well organised.

Aesop
COSMETICS

(Map p470; ☑ 03-9419 8356; www.aesop.com; 242 Gertrude St, Fitzroy; ⊘ 11am-5pm Sun & Mon, 10am-6pm Tue-Fri, 10am-5pm Sat; ☐ 86) This homegrown empire specialises in citrus- and botanical-based aromatic balms, hair masques, scents, cleansers and oils in beautifully simple packaging for both men and women. There are plenty of branches around town (and plenty of opportunities to sample the products in most of Melbourne's cafe bathrooms).

Rose Street Artists' Market
MARKET

(Map p470; www.rosestmarket.com.au; 60 Rose St, Fitzroy; ⊘ 11am-5pm Sat & Sun; ☐ 11) One of Melbourne's most popular art-and-craft markets showcases the best of local designers. Here you'll find up to 70 stalls selling matte silver jewellery, clothing, ceramics and iconic Melbourne screen prints. After shopping, head to the attached Young Blood's Diner (7am to 5pm Wednesday to Sunday) for rooftop cocktails or brunch, or both.

SpaceCraft
HOMEWARES

(Map p470; ☑ 03-9486 0010; www.spacecraftaus tralia.com; 255 Gertrude St, Fitzroy; ⊘ 10am-5.30pm Mon-Sat, 11am-5pm Sun; ☐ 86) An excellent place to find a made-in-Melbourne souvenir that won't end up at the back of the cupboard. Textile artist Stewart Russell's botanical and architectural designs adorn everything from stools to socks to bed linen.

Gorman
FASHION & ACCESSORIES

(Map p470; www.gormanshop.com.au; 235 Brunswick St, Fitzroy; ⊘ 10am-6pm Mon-Sat, 11am-5pm Sun; ☐ 11) Lisa Gorman makes everyday clothes that are far from ordinary and that are cut from bright, vibrant fabrics. Plenty of other branches around town.

Crumpler
FASHION & ACCESSORIES

(Map p470; ☑ 03-9417 5338; www.crumpler. com; 87 Smith St, Fitzroy; ⊘ 10am-6pm Mon-Sat, to 5pm Sun; ☐ 86) Crumpler's bike-courier bags – designed by two former couriers looking for a bag they could hold their beer in while cycling home – are what started it all. The brand's durable, practical designs now extend to bags for cameras, laptops and iPads, and can be found around the world. The original messenger bags start at around $150.

Northside
MUSIC

(Map p470; ☑ 03-9417 7557; www.northside records.com.au; 236 Gertrude St, Fitzroy; ⊘ 11am-6pm Mon-Wed & Sat, to 7pm Thu & Fri, 1-5pm Sun; ☐ 86) Northside's stock is DJ-mash-up eclectic, from NY hard salsa to hip-hop, from straight-up funk to Bollywood soundtrack, much of it on vinyl. Despite appearances to the contrary, staff are never too cool for school, and are happy to track down rare albums on request.

Brunswick Street Bookstore
BOOKS

(Map p470; ☑ 03-9416 1030; www.brunswick streetbookstore.com; 305 Brunswick St, Fitzroy; ⊘ 10am-9pm; ☐ 11) Lovely store with knowledgeable staff and a good selection of children's books.

🔒 Carlton & Brunswick

Mr Kitly
HOMEWARES

(☑ 03-9078 7357; http://mrkitly.com.au; 381 Sydney Rd, Brunswick; ⊘ 11am-6pm Mon & Wed-Fri, to 4pm Sat & Sun; ☐ 19, ☐ Brunswick) Head up the narrow stairs to a treasure trove of carefully curated homewares, indoor plants and accessories with a heavy Japanese influence. Get lost in time in this beautiful store as you covet everything from Hasami porcelain and copper gardening tools to Lithuanian bed linen and self-watering pot plants by Decor in pretty pastel colours.

Readings
BOOKS

(Map p472; www.readings.com.au; 309 Lygon St, Carlton; ⊘ 9am-11pm Mon-Sat, 10am-9pm Sun; ☐ Tourist Shuttle, ☐ 1, 6) A potter around this defiantly prosperous indie bookshop can occupy an entire afternoon if you're so inclined. There's a dangerously loaded (and good-value) specials table and switched-on, helpful staff. Just next door is its speciality children's store.

Also in the city centre (Map p462; ☑ 03-8664 7540; State Library, 328 Swanston

St; ⊙10am-6pm; 🚇Melbourne Central) and St Kilda (p518).

Gewürzhaus
FOOD

(Map p472; ☑03-9348 4815; www.gewurzhaus. com.au; 342 Lygon St, Carlton; ⊙10am-6pm Mon-Sat, 11am-5pm Sun; 🚋Tourist Shuttle, 🚊1, 6) Set up by two enterprising young German girls, this store is a chef's dream with its displays of spices from around the world, including Indigenous Australian blends, flavoured salts and sugars. It has high-quality cooking accessories and gifts, and cooking classes, too. There's a city store inside the **Block Arcade** (Map p462; ☑03-9639 6933; Block Arcade, 282 Collins St; ⊙9.30am-6pm; 🚇Flinders St).

Poppy Shop
TOYS

(Map p472; ☑03-9347 6302; http://poppyshop. com.au; 283 Lygon St, Carlton; ⊙9.30am-5.30pm Mon-Thu, to 6pm Fri, to 5pm Sat, 11am-4pm Sun; 🚋Tourist Shuttle, 🚊1, 6, 16) A Carlton stalwart, tiny Poppy is a riot of intriguing toys, decorative objects and other happy-making paraphernalia. From handcrafted wooden toys to mechanical wind-up robots and tiny kewpie dolls for a few dollars, there's plenty to keep whole families entertained (if you can all fit at the same time).

South Melbourne, Port Melbourne & Albert Park

Coventry Bookstore
BOOKS

(Map p458; ☑03-9686 8200; www.coventry bookstore.com.au; 265 Coventry St, South Melbourne; ⊙9.30am-5.30pm Mon-Fri, 9am-5pm Sat, 9.30am-4.30pm Sun; 🚊1, 12) Despite its modest size, this independent trader packs a punch with a clued-up selection of books. Lose track of time while leafing through local and international fiction and biographies, not to mention beautiful tomes on travel, design, fashion, architecture and more. Little bookworms will appreciate the dedicated children's book room out the back.

Vincent 2
HOMEWARES

(Map p458; ☑03-9686 7702; www.vincentdesign. com.au; 269 Coventry St, South Melbourne; ⊙10am-5pm Mon-Sat, 11am-4pm Sun; 🚊1, 12) Nordic-inspired Vincent 2 ensures that every aspect of your day is aesthetically pleasing. Shop for local and international design objects, from striking takes on placemats, rugs, umbrellas and cognac glasses to stylish leather goods, iPhone docking stations and playfully themed bed linen.

Nest
HOMEWARES

(Map p458; ☑03-9699 8277; www.nesthome wares.com.au; 289 Coventry St, South Melbourne; ⊙9.30am-5.30pm Mon-Sat, to 5pm Sun; 🚊12, 96) In a soothing, light-filled space, Nest stocks a gorgeous range of homewares and gifts, from 100%-linen bedding to soy candles, Aesop skincare and a range of cotton-knit 'comfort wear' that's way too nice to hide at home in. Staff are delightful. From South Melbourne Market head along Coventry St.

Avenue Books
BOOKS

(Map p458; ☑03-9690 2227; www.avenuebook store.com.au; 127 Dundas Pl, Albert Park; ⊙9am-7pm; 🚊1) Everyone needs a neighbourhood bookshop like this one, full of nooks and crannies to perch with literary fiction, cooking, gardening, art and children's books. Cluey staff make spot-on recommendations too.

South Yarra, Prahran & Windsor

ArtBoy Gallery
ART

(Map p474; ☑03-9939 8993; http://artboygallery. com; 99 Greville St, Prahran; ⊙10am-6pm Mon-Thu, to 5pm Sat, 11am-4pm Sun; 🚊6, 72, 78, 🚇Prahran) ArtBoy displays the talent of up-and-coming and established Melbourne artists. Artworks are affordable, unique and edgy, ranging from stencil to abstract, pop and photography. Even the gallery's rear roller door is a showcase for local creativity, with a feline-themed aerosol portrait by street artist Silly Sully. To see it, head around the corner onto Porter St and then into Brenchley Pl.

Lunar Store
DESIGN

(Map p474; ☑03-9533 7668; www.lunarstore. com.au; 2/127 Greville St, Prahran; ⊙11am-5pm Mon-Wed, 10am-6pm Thu & Fri, 10am-5pm Sat, 11am-4pm Sun; 🚊6, 72, 78, 🚇Prahran) This adorable space belongs to Jules Unwin, who fills it up with her favourite things. It's a great place to score quirky, offbeat design objects by both local and foreign artisans. Snoop around and you might find anything from Danish earthenware pencil holders to Melbourne-made ceramic necklaces and pooch-themed pouches from LA. Fun, contemporary, yet strangely nostalgic.

Signed & Numbered
ART

(Map p474; ☑03-9077 6468; http://signed andnumbered.com.au; 153 Greville St, Prahran; ⊙11am-5pm Wed-Fri & Sun, from 10am Sat; 🚊6, 72, 78, 🚇Prahran) Art at its democratic best:

Signed & Numbered deals in affordable limited-edition prints from more than 60 local and international artists, both emerging and established. Displayed pretty much like vinyl in a record store, the works span numerous print mediums, from etchings, letterpress and lino to screen and digital woodblock.

Chapel Street Bazaar VINTAGE
(Map p474; ☑03-9529 1727; www.facebook.com/ChapelStreetBazaar; 217-223 Chapel St, Prahran; ⊗10am-6pm; ☒6, 78, 79, ☒Prahran) Calling this a 'permanent undercover collection of market stalls' won't give you any clue to what's tucked away here. Bluntly, this old arcade is a sprawling, retro-obsessive riot. Whether it's Italian art glass, modernist furniture, classic Hollywood posters or Noddy eggcups that float your boat, you'll find it here. Warning: prepare to lose all track of time.

Third Drawer Down DESIGN
(Map p474; ☑03-9988 2390; www.thirddrawerdown.com; 155 Greville St, Prahran; ⊗11am-5pm Mon-Sat; ☒6, 72, 78, ☒Prahran) Dressed in a head-turning Camille Walala mural, Third Drawer Down is perfect for those who thought they had it all. Expect to step out with the likes of giant pineapple-shaped pool floats, altered ceramic plates featuring bearded ladies, statement-making socks, or a convertible backpack enlivened by an Echo Peaks Pendleton wool-panel print. Shopping was never quite this much fun.

Scanlan Theodore FASHION & ACCESSORIES
(Map p474; ☑03-9824 1800; www.scanlantheodore.com; 566 Chapel St, South Yarra; ⊗10am-6pm Mon-Thu, to 7pm Fri, to 5.30pm Sat, 11am-5pm Sun; ☒78, 79, ☒South Yarra) Scanlan Theodore helped define the Melbourne look in the 1980s and, despite the cut-throat nature of local retail, the label is still going strong with its super-feminine, beautifully tailored everyday and special-occasion wear. Although it's now considered a mature, mainstream label, its creations continue to make a statement, with clean lines and elegant, understated style.

Greville Records MUSIC
(Map p474; ☑03-9510 3012; www.grevillerecords.com.au; 152 Greville St, Prahran; ⊗10am-6pm Mon-Thu & Sat, to 7pm Fri, 11am-5pm Sun; ☒78. 79, ☒Prahran) One of the last bastions of the 'old' Greville St, this banging music shop has such a loyal following that the great Neil Young invited the owners on stage during a Melbourne concert. The forte here is vinyl, with no shortage of eclectic and limited-edition discs (a super-limited Bob Dylan *Live in Sydney 1966* double vinyl has been discovered here...).

🔒 St Kilda

Readings BOOKS
(Map p478; ☑03-9525 3852; www.readings.com.au/st-kilda; 112 Acland St, St Kilda; ⊗10am-9pm; ☒3, 16, 96) Defiantly prospering indie bookshop. There's a dangerously loaded (and good-value) specials table, switched-on staff and everyone from Lacan to Charlie & Lola on the shelves. Best of all, the store supports a string of independent publishers, as well as locally produced journals.

St Kilda Esplanade Market MARKET
(Map p478; www.stkildaesplanademarket.com.au; Esplanade, St Kilda; ⊗10am-4pm Sun May-Sep, to 5pm Oct-Apr; ☒3, 12, 16, 96) Fancy a Sunday stroll shopping by the seaside? Well, here's the place, with a kilometre of trestle tables joined end to end. Pick up anything from locally made ceramics, sculpture, glassware and woodwork to photographic prints, organic soaps and tongue-in-cheek, retro tea towels.

Bitch is Back DESIGN
(Map p478; ☑03-9534 8025; www.thebitchisback.com.au; 100a Barkly St, St Kilda; ⊗closed Mon; ☒3, 16, 67) This bitch offers a fabulous treasure trove of high-end vintage and mid-20th-century furniture and other design objects. There's an emphasis on Danish and Italian pieces from the 1920s to the 1980s, from armchairs and table lamps to glassware and ceramics. You might also stumble across highly sought-after furniture by European-trained, Australian-based designers like the Rosando Brothers, Dario Zoureff and Jakob Rudowski.

Dot Herbey FASHION & ACCESSORIES
(Map p478; ☑03-9593 6309; www.dotandherbey.com; 229 Barkly St, St Kilda; ⊗10.30am-6.30pm Mon-Wed, to 7pm Thu & Fri, 10am-6pm Sat & Sun; ☒96) Grandma Dot and Grandpa Herb smile down upon this tiny corner boutique from a mural-sized photo, right at home among the vintage floral fabrics, Japanese linen and understated bohemian cool. Scan the racks for grandpa tops, cotton overalls, beautiful knits and other pieces in gorgeous, ethical fabrics.

ℹ Information

DANGERS & ANNOYANCES

There are occasional reports of alcohol-fuelled violence in some parts of Melbourne's city centre late on weekend nights – particularly in King St.

INTERNET ACCESS

Free wi-fi is available at central city spots such as Federation Sq, Flinders St station, Crown Casino and the State Library. Free wi-fi is now the norm in most midrange accommodation, although you sometimes have to pay in both budget and top-end places. Many cafes also offer free wi-fi.

If you're not travelling with your own device, there are plenty of libraries around Melbourne with terminals, though you'll need to bring ID to sign up and prebooking is recommended. The **City** (🖉03-9658 9500; 253 Flinders Lane; ⊙8am-8pm Mon-Thu, 8am-6pm Fri, 10am-5pm Sat, noon-5pm Sun; 🚇Flinders St), **St Kilda** (🖉03-9209 6655; http://library. portphillip.vic.gov.au; 150 Carlisle St, St Kilda; ⊙10am-8pm Mon-Thu, to 6pm Fri, to 5pm Sat & Sun; 🚊3, 16, 78, 🚇Balaclava) and **Prahran** (🖉03-8290 3344; www.stonnington.vic.gov. au/library/Visit-us/Prahran-Library; 180 Greville St, Prahran; ⊙10am-6pm Mon-Fri, to 1pm Sat; 🚊78, 79, 🚇Prahran) libraries all offer access.

MEDICAL SERVICES

Royal Children's Hospital (🖉03-9345 5522; www.rch.org.au; 50 Flemington Rd, Parkville; 🚊57)

Royal Melbourne Hospital (🖉03-9342 7000; www.thermh.org.au; 300 Grattan St, Parkville; 🚊19, 55, 59)

La Trobe St Medical (🖉03-9650 0023; Melbourne Central, 211 La Trobe St; ⊙8.30am-5pm Mon-Fri; 🚇Melbourne Central)

QV Medical Centre (🖉03-9662 2256; www. qvmedical.com.au; L1 QV, 292 Swanston St; ⊙9am-5pm Mon-Sat, 10.30am-5.30pm Sun)

Travel Doctor (TVMC; 🖉03-9935 8100; www. traveldoctor.com.au; L2, 393 Little Bourke St; ⊙9am-5pm Mon-Wed & Fri, to 8pm Thu, to 1pm Sat)

Travel Doctor (🖉03-9690 1433; www.travel doctor.com.au; 3 Southgate Ave, Southbank; ⊙8.30am-5.30pm Mon-Fri)

Wellnation Clinic (🖉03-9662 4856; www. wellnationclinics.com.au; 368 Elizabeth St)

POST

Australia Post offers a very reliable service; visit www.auspost.com.au for up-to-date postage rates and the location of post offices.

Melbourne GPO Post Shop (Map p462; 🖉13 13 18; www.auspost.com.au; 250 Elizabeth St; ⊙8.30am-5.30pm Mon-Sat; 🚊19, 57, 59)

Franklin Street Post Shop (Map p462; 🖉13 13 18; www.auspost.com.au; 58 Franklin St; ⊙9am-5pm Mon-Fri)

TOURIST INFORMATION

Melbourne Visitor Centre (Map p462; 🖉03-9658 9658; www.thatsmelbourne.com.au; Federation Sq; ⊙9am-6pm; 🛈; 🚇Flinders St) Comprehensive information on Melbourne and regional Victoria, resources for mobility-impaired travellers, and a travel desk for accommodation and tour bookings. There are power sockets for recharging phones, too. There's a chance the centre might need to move sometime in 2017 due to construction work nearby.

ℹ Getting There & Away

Most travellers to Melbourne arrive via Melbourne Airport, which is well connected to the city by shuttle bus and taxi. There are also interstate trains and buses, a direct boat from Tasmania, and two minor domestic airports nearby.

Flights, cars and tours can be booked online at lonelyplanet.com/bookings.

AIR
Melbourne Airport

Melbourne Airport (MEL; 🖉03-9297 1600; www.melbourneairport.com.au; Departure Rd, Tullamarine) is the city's only international and main domestic airport, located 22km northwest of the city centre in Tullamarine. It has all of the facilities you'd expect from a major airport, including **Baggage Storage** (🖉03-9338 3119; www.baggagestorage.com.au; Terminal 2, International Arrivals, Melbourne Airport; per 24hr $16; ⊙5am-12.30am).

Dozens of airlines fly here from destinations in the South Pacific, Asia, the Middle East and the Americas. The main domestic airlines are **Qantas** (🖉13 11 31; www.qantas.com), **Jetstar** (🖉131 538; www.jetstar.com), **Virgin Australia** (🖉13 67 89; www.virginaustralia.com), **Tiger-air** (🖉1300 174 266; www.tigerair.com) and **Regional Express** (Rex; 🖉131 713; www.rex. com.au).

Avalon Airport

Jetstar (p519) flights to and from Sydney and Brisbane use **Avalon Airport** (🖉03-5227 9100; www.avalonairport.com.au; 80 Beach Rd, Lara), around 55km southwest of Melbourne's city centre.

Essendon Airport

Once Melbourne's main international airport, **Essendon Airport** (MEB; 🖉03-9948 9400; www.essendonairport.com.au; 7 English St,

Essendon Fields; 🚌 59) is only 11km north of the city centre. Now only small operators fly from here to domestic destinations.

Free Spirit Airlines (📞 03-9379 6122; www.freespiritairlines.com.au) flies to/from Merimbula and Burnie.

Jetgo (📞1300 328 000; www.jetgo.com) flies to/from to Port Macquarie, Dubbo and Brisbane.

Sharp Airlines (📞1300 556 694; www.sharpairlines.com) flies to/from Flinders Island, King Island, Portland and Warrnambool.

BOAT

The **Spirit of Tasmania** (Map p458; 📞1800 634 906, 03-6419 9320; www.spiritoftasmania.com.au; Station Pier, Port Melbourne; adult/car 1 way from $99/188) ferry crosses Bass Strait from Melbourne to Devonport, Tasmania, at least nightly; there are also day sailings during peak season. The crossing takes 10 hours.

BUS

The main terminus for long-distance buses is within the northern half of Southern Cross station. Here you'll find counters for all the main bus companies, along with **luggage lockers** (📞03-9619 2588; www.southerncrossstation.net.au; Southern Cross station, 99 Spencer St; per 24hr $10-16; ⊙ during train-service hours).

Firefly (Map p462; 📞1300 730 740; www.fireflyexpress.com.au; Southern Cross station, 99 Spencer St) Overnight coaches to/from Sydney ($65, 12 hours), Wagga Wagga ($65, 5¾ hours), Albury ($65, 3½ hours), Ballarat ($50, 1¾ hours) and Adelaide ($60, 9¾ hours).

Greyhound (Map p462; 📞1300 473 946; www.greyhound.com.au) Coaches to Albury ($55, 3½ hours), Wagga Wagga ($69, 6¼ hours), Gundagai ($75, 7¼ hours), Yass ($85, 8¼ hours) and Canberra ($88, eight hours).

V/Line (📞1800 800 007; www.vline.com.au) Services destinations within Victoria, including Korumburra ($15, two hours), Mansfield ($29, three hours) and Echuca ($29, three hours).

CAR & MOTORCYCLE

The most direct (and boring) route between Melbourne and Sydney is the Hume Hwy (870km). The Princes Hwy hugs the coast and is much more scenic but much longer (1040km). Likewise, the main route to/from Adelaide is the Western/Dukes Hwy (730km), but this misses out on the Great Ocean Road.

TRAIN

Southern Cross station is the terminus for intercity and interstate trains.

Great Southern Rail (📞1800 703 357; www.greatsouthernrail.com.au) Runs the *Overland* between Melbourne and Adelaide ($149, 10½ hours, twice weekly).

NSW TrainLink (📞13 22 32; www.nswtrainlink.info) Twice-daily services to/from Sydney ($92, 11½ hours) via Benalla ($24, 2¼ hours), Wangaratta ($34, 2½ hours), Albury ($47, 3¼ hours) and Wagga Wagga ($63, 4½ hours).

V/Line (p1070) Operates the Victorian train and bus networks; direct services include Geelong ($9, one hour), Warrnambool ($36, 3¾ hours), Ballarat ($15, 1½ hours), Bendigo ($22, two hours) and Albury ($38, four hours).

🛈 Getting Around

TO/FROM THE AIRPORT

Melbourne Airport The **SkyBus** (Map p462; 📞1300 759 287; www.skybus.com.au; Southern Cross station, 99 Spencer St; adult/child $18/9; 🚈 Southern Cross) departs regularly and connects the airport to Southern Cross station 24 hours a day. There are also services to other parts of Melbourne, including St Kilda.

Southern Cross station Long-distance trains and buses arrive at this large station on the Docklands side of the city centre. From here it's easy to connect to metropolitan trains, buses and trams.

Avalon Airport Near the neighbouring city of Geelong, but connected to Melbourne's Southern Cross station by **Sita Coaches** (📞03-9689 7999; www.skybus.com.au; adult/child $22/10).

CAR & MOTORCYCLE

Driving in Melbourne presents its own set of challenges, due to the need to share the road with trams.

Where the trams run along the centre of the road, drivers cannot pass them once they indicate that they're stopping, as passengers board and alight from the street.

In the city centre many intersections are marked 'right turn from left only'. This is the counter-intuitive 'hook turn', devised so as not to block trams or other cars. Right-turning drivers are required to move into the far left of the intersection and then turn right once the lights on that side of the intersection turn green. See www.vicroads.vic.gov.au for further details.

Car Hire

Most car and campervan hire places have offices at Melbourne Airport and in the city or central suburbs.

Aussie Campervans (📞03-9317 4991; www.aussiecampervans.com)

Avis (📞03-8855 5333; www.avis.com.au)

Britz Australia (📞1300 738 087; www.britz.com.au)

ⓘ TICKETS & PASSES

Melbourne's buses, trams and trains use **myki**, a 'touch on, touch off' travel-pass system. It's not particularly convenient for short-term visitors as it requires you to purchase a $6 plastic myki card and then put credit on it before you travel.

Travellers should consider buying a **myki Explorer** ($15), which includes the card, one day's travel and discounts on various sights; it's available from SkyBus terminals, PTV hubs, the **Melbourne Visitor Centre** (p519) and some hotels. Otherwise, standard myki cards can be purchased at 7-Elevens or newsagents.

The myki can be topped up at 7-Eleven stores, machines at most train stations and at some tram stops in the city centre; online top-ups can take some time to process. You can either top up with pay-as-you-go **myki Money** or purchase a seven-day unlimited **myki Pass** ($41); if you're staying more than 28 days, longer passes are available.

For travel within metropolitan Melbourne (zones 1 and 2), the pay-as-you-go fare is $4.10 for two hours, or capped at $8.20 for the day ($6 on weekends). There are large fines for travelling without having touched on a valid myki card; ticket inspectors are vigilant and unforgiving.

For more information, see **PTV** (Public Transport Victoria; ☏ 1800 800 007; www.ptv.vic. gov.au).

Budget (☏ 1300 362 848; www.budget.com. au)

Europcar (☏ 1300 131 390; www.europcar. com.au)

Hertz (☏ 03-9663 6244; www.hertz.com.au)

Rent a Bomb (☏ 03-9428 0088; www.rent abomb.com.au; 452 Bridge Rd, Richmond; ⌂ 48, 75)

Thrifty (☏ 1300 367 227; www.thrifty.com.au)

Travellers Autobarn (☏ 1800 674 374; www. travellers-autobarn.com.au) Hires and sells vehicles.

Parking

Parking inspectors are particularly vigilant in the city centre. Most of the street parking is metered and it's more likely than not that you'll be fined if you overstay your metered time. Also keep an eye out for 'clearway' zones (prohibited kerbside parking indicated by signs), which can result in sizeable fines. There are plenty of parking garages in the city centre; rates vary. Motorcyclists are allowed to park on the footpath except in some parts of the city centre where there are signs.

Toll Roads

Both drivers and motorcyclists will need to purchase a Melbourne Pass ($5.50 start-up fee, plus tolls and a 75c vehicle-matching fee per trip) if they're planning on using one of the two toll roads: **CityLink** (☏ 13 26 29; www.citylink.com.au), from Tullamarine Airport to the city and eastern suburbs, or **EastLink** (☏ 03-9955 1400; www. eastlink.com.au), which runs from Ringwood to Frankston. Pay online or via phone – but pay within three days of using the toll road to avoid a fine.

Rental cars are sometimes set up for automatic toll payments; check when you hire.

TAXI

Melbourne's taxis are metered and require an estimated prepaid fare when hailed between 10pm and 5am (you may need to pay more or get a refund depending on the final fare). Toll charges are added to fares. Two of the largest taxi companies are **Silver Top** (☏ 131 008; www. silvertop.com.au) and **13 Cabs** (☏ 13 22 27; www.13cabs.com.au). **Uber** (www.uber.com) also operates in Melbourne.

TRAIN

Flinders St station is the main city hub for Melbourne's 17 train lines. Trains start around 5am weekdays, run until midnight Sunday to Thursday, and all night on Friday and Saturday nights. Trains generally run every 10-20 minutes during the day and every 20-30 minutes in the evening.

Payment is via myki card; PTV has timetables, maps and a journey planner on its website.

TRAM

Trams are intertwined with the Melbourne identity and an extensive network covers the city. They run roughly every 10 minutes during the day (more frequently in peak periods), and every 20 minutes in the evening. Services run until midnight Sunday to Thursday, 1am Friday and Saturday, and six lines run all night on weekends.

The entire city centre is a free tram zone. The zone is signposted on tram stops, with messages broadcast on board when you're nearing its edge to warn you that you should either hop off or pay with a myki card. Note that there's no need to 'touch off' your myki on the trams, as all zone 1 journeys are charged at the same rate – although it won't matter if you do.

PTV (www.ptv.vic.gov.au) has timetables, maps and a journey planner on their website.

AROUND MELBOURNE

The Dandenongs

The low ranges of the verdant Dandenongs, just 35km from Melbourne, feel a world away from the city and make a fantastic day trip. Mt Dandenong (633m) is the tallest peak and the landscape is a patchwork of exotic and native flora with a lush understorey of tree ferns. Take care driving on the winding roads – apart from other traffic, you might see a lyrebird wandering across.

The consumption of tea and scones is de rigueur in the many cafes in the hills, or you can stop for lunch at some quality restaurants in towns such as Olinda, Sassafras and Emerald.

On summer weekends, the hills are alive with day trippers – visit for midweek for the best experience.

◉ Sights & Activities

Dandenong Ranges National Park NATIONAL PARK
(www.parkweb.vic.gov.au; ⬛ Upper Ferntree Gully, Belgrave) This national park contains the four largest areas of remaining forest in the Dandenongs. The Ferntree Gully Area has several short walks, including the popular **1000 Steps** (Mt Dandenong Tourist Rd, Dandenong Ranges National Park, Ferny Creek) up to **One Tree Hill Picnic Ground** (Lord Somers Rd, Tremont), two hours return, part of the **Kokoda Memorial Track**, which commemorates Australian WWII servicemen who served in New Guinea. Bring sturdy shoes as its steps get slippery.

SkyHigh Mt Dandenong VIEWPOINT
(☎03-9751 0443; www.skyhighmtdandenong.com.au; 26 Observatory Rd, Mt Dandenong; per vehicle $6; ⊙9am-10pm Mon-Thu, to 10.30pm Fri, 8am-11pm Sat & Sun; ⬛688) Drive up to SkyHigh for amazing views over Melbourne and Port Phillip Bay from the highest point in the Dandenongs. The view of the city lights at dusk is spectacular. There's a cafe-restaurant, a garden, picnic areas and a maze (adult/child/family $6/4/16).

Puffing Billy RAIL
(☎03-9757 0700; www.puffingbilly.com.au; Old Monbulk Rd, Belgrave; return adult/child/family to Gembrooke $71.50/36/143; ⬛Belgrave) Holding fond childhood memories for many a Melburnian, popular *Puffing Billy* is an iconic restored steam train that toots its way through the ferny hills from Belgrave to Emerald Lake Park and Gembrook. Kids love to dangle their legs out the sides of the open-air compartments, and you can hopon and hopoff en route to enjoy a picnic or walk. Check its website for various dining packages and themed trips.

Trees Adventure ADVENTURE SPORTS
(☎03-9752 5354; www.treesadventure.com.au; Old Monbulk Rd, Belgrave; 2hr session adult/child $40/35; ⊙11am-5pm Mon-Fri, 9am-5pm Sat & Sun; ⬛Belgrave) Reminiscent of the Ewok village in *Return of the Jedi*, Trees Adventure is a blast of tree climbs, flying foxes and obstacle courses in a stunning patch of old-growth forest made up of sequoia, mountain ash and Japanese oak trees. The safety system ensures you're always attached to a secure line; there are beginner sections suitable for kids as young as five (per two hours $25).

✖ Eating & Drinking

★ Piggery Cafe CAFE $$
(☎03-9691 3858; www.piggerycafe.com.au; 1 Sherbrooke Rd, Sherbrooke; mains $12-25; ⊙10am-5pm Mon-Fri, 9am-5pm Sat & Sun) Set over 23 acres on the 1920s Burnham Beeches estate is this venture by celebrity chef Shannon Bennett. What was a former piggery is now a trendy open-plan cafe-restaurant with chargrilled barbecue dishes, kitchen garden produce and homebaked goods. Expect a menu of wagyu beef burgers, charcoal trout, prawn rolls and pork belly.

Miss Marple's Tearoom TEAHOUSE
(☎03-9755 1610; www.missmarplestearoom.com; 382 Mt Dandenong Tourist Rd, Sassafras; ⊙11am-4pm Mon-Fri, to 4.30pm Sat & Sun) This quaint English tearoom, inspired by the Agatha Christie character, comes with floral tablecloths, Devonshire scones ($9.50 for two) and sticky toffee pudding, as well as lunch mains. It's wildly popular on weekends; two-hour waits are not unusual.

❶ Information

Dandenong Ranges & Knox Visitor Information Centre (☎03-9758 7522; www.visitdandenongranges.com.au; 1211 Burwood Hwy, Upper Ferntree Gully; ⊙11am-3pm Mon, 9.30am-4.30pm Tue-Sat, 10am-2pm Sun; ⬛Upper Ferntree Gully) Outside the Upper Ferntree Gully train station; good for walking maps.

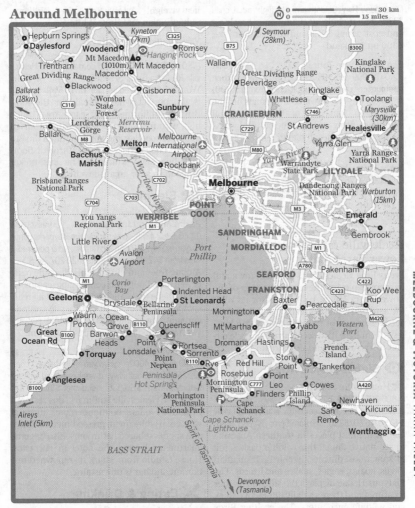

ⓘ Getting There & Away

It's just under an hour's drive from Melbourne's city centre to Olinda, Sassafras or Belgrave. The quickest route is via the Eastern Fwy, exiting on Burwood Hwy or Boronia Rd.

Suburban trains from Melbourne (Belgrave Line) head to Belgrave station.

Yarra Valley

The lush Yarra Valley is Victoria's premier wine region and weekend getaway – partly for its close proximity to Melbourne, but mainly for the 80-plus wineries, superb res-

taurants, national parks and wildlife. This is the place to rise at dawn in a hot-air balloon over patchwork fields and vineyards and kick back with a pinot noir at world-class wineries.

🏃 Activities

Ballooning over the Yarra Valley is a peaceful way to view the hills and vineyards. One-hour dawn flights with operators **Global Ballooning** (☑1800 627 661; www. globalballooning.com.au; 1hr flights adult/child from $285/365) and **Go Wild Ballooning** (☑03-9739 0772; www.gowildballooning.com.au; 621

Maroondah Hwy, Coldstream; 1hr flight adult/child $330/285) include a champagne breakfast and cost about $275 midweek and around $300 on weekends.

Eco Adventure Tours CULTURAL
(📱0418 999 936, 03-5962 5115; www.ecoadventuretours.com.au; walks adult/child from $50/30) A great way to see native animals in the wild is to join one of these nocturnal wildlife-spotting and daytime cultural walks in the Healesville, Toolangi and Dandenongs areas.

Yarra Valley Winery Tours TOURS
(📱1300 496 766; www.yarravalleywinerytours.com. au; tours from Yarra Valley/Melbourne $110/140) Daily tours taking in four or five wineries, plus lunch.

Healesville & the Lower Yarra Valley

Pretty little Healesville is the main town and base for exploring the triangular area of the Lower Yarra Valley. It's famous for its wildlife sanctuary, and perfectly located for easy access to some of the region's finest wineries – from here it's a scenic drive or cycle circuit to Yarra Glen and Coldstream.

◉ Sights & Activities

⭐**Healesville Sanctuary** ZOO
(📱03-5957 2800, 1300 966 784; www.zoo.org.au/ healesville; Badger Creek Rd; adult/child/family $32.50/16.30/82.10; ⊙9am-5pm; 📷685, 686) One of the best places in southern Australia to see native fauna, this wildlife park is full of kangaroos, dingoes, lyrebirds, Tasmanian devils, koalas, eagles, snakes and lizards. The Platypus House displays the shy underwater creatures, and there's a daily interactive show and wildlife encounters. The exciting Birds of Prey presentation features huge wedge-tailed eagles and owls soaring through the air. Check the website for timings. Admission for kids is free on weekends and holidays.

⭐**TarraWarra Museum of Art** GALLERY
(📱03-5957 3100; www.twma.com.au; 311 Healesville-Yarra Glen Rd; adult/child $7.50/free; ⊙11am-5pm Tue-Sun) In a striking contemporary building at TarraWarra Estate, this excellent gallery showcases Australian art from the 1950s onwards and also features regularly changing Australian and international contemporary art exhibitions. The rotating permanent collection includes work from heavyweights Arthur Boyd, Fred Williams, Sidney Nolan and Brett Whiteley.

Yarra Valley Chocolaterie & Ice Creamery FACTORY
(📱03-9730 2777; www.yvci.com.au; 35 Old Healesville Rd, Yarra Glen; ⊙9am-5pm) A bit of Willy Wonka has arrived in the Yarra Valley – this is the perfect winery break for the kids. Brightly uniformed staff carry trays piled high with free samples made with imported Belgian chocolate and you can watch the European chocolatiers at work through floor-to-ceiling glass windows. The Bushtucker range makes for great souvenirs.

🛏 Sleeping

BIG4 Yarra Valley Park Lane Holiday Park CAMPGROUND $
(📱03-5962 4328; www.parklaneholidayparks.com. au/yarravalley; 419 Don Rd; unpowered & powered sites from $42, d cabins & tents $122-207; ❄🐾) Among trees and birdlife, this riverside park is well kitted out with comfortable cabins, luxury belle tents and campsites. It's a great spot for kids with an adventure playground and jumping cushion, as well as bike rental, swimming pool, tennis courts and a gym.

Healesville Hotel HOTEL $$
(📱03-5962 4002; www.yarravalleyharvest.com. au; 256 Maroondah Hwy; d week/weekend without bathroom from $115/135, incl dinner $310; ❄🐱🛜) An iconic Healesville landmark, this restored 1910 hotel offers boutique rooms upstairs with crisp white linen, pressed-metal ceilings and spotless shared bathrooms. Also has chic apartments behind the hotel in Furmston House (studio from $180). Its renowned restaurant and bar is downstairs.

🍴 Eating & Drinking

Healesville Harvest Cafe CAFE $
(📱03-5962 4002; www.yarravalleyharvest.com.au; 256 Maroondah Hwy; snacks $7-20; ⊙8am-4pm; 🛜) Next to the Healesville Hotel, the Harvest is perfect for fresh coffee and light meals made with local produce – salads, sandwiches, cakes, breakfast rolls, sausage rolls and soups. Head next door to its **Kitchen & Butcher** (📱03-5962 2866; ⊙10am-6pm Mon-Fri, 9am-6pm Sat, 10am-4pm Sun) to pick up gourmet picnic goodies and hampers.

⭐**Giant Steps** MODERN AUSTRALIAN, WINE $$
(📱03-5962 6111; www.giantstepswine.com.au; 336 Maroondah Hwy; small/large plates from $16/26; ⊙11am-late Mon-Fri, 9am-late Sat & Sun; 🛜) The

MELBOURNE & VICTORIA YARRA VALLEY

YARRA VALLEY WINERIES

The **Yarra Valley** (http://wineyarravalley.com.au) has more than 80 wineries and 50 cellar doors scattered around its rolling, vine-cloaked hills, and is recognised as Victoria's oldest wine region – the first vines were planted at Yering Station in 1838. The region produces cool-climate, food-friendly drops such as chardonnay, pinot noir and pinot gris, as well as not-half-bad, full-bodied reds.

The smaller family-run wineries are equal to the large-scale producers, offering a less pretentious experience; visit www.yarravalleysmallerwineries.com.au for a list.

Some cellars charge a small fee for tasting, which is redeemable on purchase. Top Yarra Valley wineries with cellar door sales and tastings:

Coldstream Hills (☑ 03-5960 7000; www.coldstreamhills.com.au; 31 Maddens Lane, Coldstream; ⊙ 10am-5pm) Chardonnay, pinot noir and velvety merlot are the prime picks.

Domain Chandon (☑ 03-9738 9200; www.chandon.com; 727 Maroondah Hwy, Coldstream; ⊙ 10.30am-4.30pm) Established by the makers of Moët & Chandon, this slick operation with stunning views is worth a visit for the free guided tours at 11am, 1pm and 3pm, which include a peek at its atmospheric riddling hall.

Medhurst Wines (☑ 03-5964 9022; www.medhurstwines.com.au; 24-26 Medhurst Rd, Gruyere; ⊙ cellar door 11am-5pm Thu-Mon, restaurant 11.30am-5pm Fri-Sun) Polished concrete and glass work well together at this modern winery.

Oakridge (☑ 03-9738 9900; www.oakridgewines.com.au; 864 Maroondah Hwy, Coldstream; ⊙ 10am-5pm) The cellar door affords stunning views at this award-winning winery. Contemporary fare is dished up in its chic restaurant.

Rochford (☑ 03-5957 3333; www.rochfordwines.com.au; 878-880 Maroondah Hwy, cnr Hill Rd, Coldstream; ⊙ 9am-5pm) A huge complex with a restaurant, cafe and regular concerts.

TarraWarra Estate (☑ 03-5957 3510; www.tarrawarra.com.au; 311 Healesville–Yarra Glen Rd, Healesville; tastings $5; ⊙ 11am-5pm Tue-Sun) A convivial bistro and winery in a striking building. Sip away while lazing on the grassy knolls and visit the superb adjoining art gallery.

Yering Farm Wines (☑ 03-9739 0461; www.yeringfarmwines.com; 19-21 St Huberts Rd, Yering; ⊙ 10am-5pm) A rustic, family-owned little cellar door in an old hay shed with lovely views.

Yering Station (☑ 03-9730 0100; www.yering.com; 38 Melba Hwy, Yering; ⊙ 10am-5pm) Victoria's first vineyard, and home to the heady shiraz-viognier blend.

massive, refurbed Giant Steps is known for both its cellar door and buzzing restaurant. The delicious wood-fired dishes – featuring anything from a grilled snapper to chicken and tofu – steal the show, followed by slow-cooked lamb shoulder, duck fat chips and a charcuterie selection.

Healesville Hotel MODERN AUSTRALIAN $$
(☑ 03-5962 4002; www.yarravalleyharvest.com.au; 256 Maroondah Hwy; mains $16-41; ⊙ noon-3pm & 6-10pm) One of the area's culinary showstoppers, historic Healesville Hotel is split into a formal dining room and the inviting front bar for more casual gastropub fare; the latter is a perfect spot for a pint or a glass of red by the fire. It's known for its wood-grilled meats over red-gum coals,

slow-cooked lamb and steaks served with buttermilk-fried onion rings.

Zonzo ITALIAN $$
(☑ 03-9730 2500; www.zonzo.com.au; 957 Healesville-Yarra Glen Rd; pizza $24, share menu per person $50; ⊙ noon-3pm Wed-Sun & 6pm-late Fri-Sun) At the Zonzo Estate Winery is this stylish Italian and traditional pizza restaurant with superb views out over the valley. The thin-crust pizzas just fly off the plate. They also offer tastings of their wines in their cellar door converted from old horse stables. Bookings recommended.

ezard @ Levantine Hill MODERN AUSTRALIAN $$$
(☑ 03-5962 1333; www.levantinehill.com.au; 882 Maroondah Hwy, Coldstream; 5-/8-course degustation menu $135/195; ⊙ 11am-5pm Mon & Wed-Fri,

10am-10pm Sat, 10am-5pm Sun) This restaurant by acclaimed chef Teage Ezard is a collaboration with the Levantine Hill winery. Within its striking contemporary cellar door overlooking the vineyards, it has wine barrel–inspired booth seating to take a long lunch of creative cuisine from a degustation menu designed specifically to match the wines.

Elenore's Restaurant MODERN AUSTRALIAN $$$
(✆03-9237 3333; www.chateauyering.com.au; 42 Melba Hwy, Chateau Yering; 2-/3-course menu $85/98; ⊙6-9pm) Within the historic 1850s Yering chateau and winery is this contemporary fine dining restaurant with a reputation as one of the region's best. Featuring a chef who's worked at Michelin-star restaurants, here you can select multiple courses from its à la carte menu with items such as twice-cooked brisket with betel-leaf farci or smoked duck pie with crispy-skin salad.

★Four Pillars DISTILLERY
(✆03-5962 2791; www.fourpillarsgin.com.au; 2a Lilydale Rd; tastings & tour $10; ⊙10.30am-5.30pm Sun-Thu, to 9.30pm Fri & Sat) One of Victoria's best-run microdistillers is this class operator that specialises in inventive gins that you can watch being made while sampling the goods. Grab a paddle to taste their range, including an Australian gin, Spiced Negroni, Rare Dry and Navy Strength (58.8%). Staff are enthusiastic, friendly and knowledgeable.

★Napoleone Brewery & Ciderhouse BREWERY
(✆03-9738 9100; www.napoleonecider.com.au; 12 St Huberts Rd; ⊙10am-5pm) A welcome variation among the ubiquitous wineries is this stop to sample Napoleone's selection of beers and ciders. Set in a contemporary glass atrium looking on to the brewing equipment, here you can sample the range of ales and ciders available by the tasting paddle ($12). Brewery tours are held at 11am each Saturday ($20 including tasting), or by appointment.

ℹ Information

Yarra Valley Visitor Centre (✆03-5962 2600; www.visityarravalley.com.au; Harker St, Healesville; ⊙9am-5pm) Main info centre for the Lower Yarra Valley with loads of brochures as well as maps for sale.

ℹ Getting There & Away

Healesville is 65km north of Melbourne, an easy one-hour drive via the Eastern Fwy and Maroondah Hwy/B360.

McKenzie's Bus Line (✆03-5962 5088; www.mckenzies.com.au) runs daily from Melbourne's Southern Cross station to Healesville ($4.10, 1½ hours) en route to Marysville and Eildon; check website for schedule.

From Melbourne, suburban trains run to Lilydale, where there are regular buses to Healesville.

Marysville & Lake Mountain

Spread across a valley between Narbethong and Lake Mountain, Marysville is the main base for the cross-country ski fields at Lake Mountain and is reached via a beautiful drive over the Black Spur from Healesville; look out for lyrebirds on the way.

Lake Mountain Alpine Resort (✆03-5957 7222; www.lakemountainresort.com.au; 1071 Lake Mountain Rd; ⊙8am-4.30pm Mon-Fri Oct-May, to 6.30pm Jun-Sep) has ski hire, a ski school, a cafe and undercover barbecue areas.

Marysville was at the epicentre of the tragic 2009 bushfires, during which most of the town's buildings were destroyed and 34 people tragically lost their lives. The town's tight-knit community continues to steadily and courageously rebuild.

⊙ Sights & Activities

Phoenix Museum MUSEUM
(Black Saturday Museum; ✆0418 175 090; www.blacksaturdaymuseum.com; 11 Murchison St; $5; ⊙9am-5pm) A must-see sight for any visitor to Marysville is this sobering exhibition that shows the devastating impact the 2009 bushfires had on the town. It includes photos, video and salvaged items. It shares space with the visitor information centre.

Steavenson Falls WATERFALL
(Falls Rd) Spectacular Steavenson Falls, about 2km from town, is Victoria's highest waterfall (84m). The infrastructure has been rebuilt since the fires, with a viewing platform spanning the river and floodlights illuminating the falls to 11pm.

🛏 Sleeping

Marysville Caravan Park CAMPGROUND $
(✆03-5963 3247; www.marysvillecaravanpark.com.au; 1130 Buxton Rd; powered site from $38, cabins from $99; ❋🐾) At the edge of town, this park has excellent self-contained riverside cabins, camping and a kids play area. Other than the pricier cabins, it's BYO linen and towels.

BLACK SATURDAY

Victoria is no stranger to bushfires. In 1939, 71 people died in the Black Friday fires; in 1983 Ash Wednesday claimed 75 lives in Victoria and South Australia. But no one was prepared for the utter devastation of the 2009 bushfires that became known as Black Saturday.

On 7 February, Victoria recorded its hottest temperature on record with Melbourne exceeding 46°C and some parts of the state topping 48°C. Strong winds and tinder-dry undergrowth from years of drought, combined with the record-high temperatures, created conditions in which the risk of bushfires was extreme. The first recorded fires began near Kilmore and strong winds from a southerly change fanned the flames towards the Yarra Ranges. Within a few devastating hours a ferocious firestorm engulfed the tiny bush towns of Marysville, Kinglake, Strathewen, Flowerdale and Narbethong, while separate fires started at Horsham, Bendigo and an area southeast of Beechworth. The fires virtually razed the towns of Marysville and Kinglake, and moved so quickly that many residents had no chance to escape. Many victims of the fires died in their homes or trapped in their cars, some blocked by trees that had fallen across the road.

Fires raged across the state for more than a month, with high temperatures, winds and practically no rainfall making it impossible for fire crews to contain the worst blazes. New fires began at Wilsons Promontory National Park (burning more than 50% of the park area), Dandenong Ranges and in the Daylesford area.

The statistics tell a tragic tale: 173 people died; more than 2000 homes were destroyed; an estimated 7500 people were left homeless; and more than 4500 sq km were burned. What followed from the shell-shocked state and nation was a huge outpouring of grief, humanitarian aid and charity. Strangers donated tonnes of clothing, toys, food, caravans and even houses to bushfire survivors, while an appeal set up by the Australian Red Cross raised more than $300 million.

Today the blackened forests around Kinglake and Marysville are regenerating, and the communities are rebuilding. Tourism remains a big part of the economy, and visiting the shops, cafes and hotels in the area continues to boost their recovery.

Vibe Hotel HOTEL $$
(☑ 03-5957 7700; www.tfehotels.com; 32-42 Murchison St; r $160-250, ste $260-350; ❇ 🖧 🗩) While it has the best rooms in town by far, a slick business-style hotel along Maryville's sleepy main road still seems a bit out of place. Regardless, it makes for a very comfortable stay with modern rooms and large suites with balconies and kitchenettes. Facilities include a heated pool, gym, tennis court and swish restaurant-cafe next door.

🍴 Eating & Drinking

Fraga's Café CAFE $$
(☑ 03-5963 3216; www.facebook.com/fragascafe; 19 Murchison St; meals $9.50-26.50; ⊙ 9am-4pm Mon-Fri, to 4.30 Sat & Sun) A vibrant, arty cafe serving the town's best coffee, creative mains, pies and cakes, as well as local ciders.

The Duck Inn PUB
(☑ 03-5963 3437; www.facebook.com/theduckinnmarysvillepub; 6 Murchison St; ⊙ Mon & Wed 4-11pm, Thu-Sun 11am-11pm) It's been a long wait in between drinks, but *finally* Marysville has got its pub back. The Duck Inn opened its doors in late 2016 (eight years after the fires) and features local breweries on tap, regional wines and a menu of pub classics ($15 to $34).

ℹ Information

Marysville Lake Mountain Visitor Information Centre (☑ 03-5963 4567; www.marysvilletourism.com; 11 Murchison St; ⊙ 9am-5pm; 🗩) The modern tourist office provides helpful service, wi-fi and bike hire (per two hours/day $15/30). There's also a free app to download.

ℹ Getting There & Away

Marysville is 100km from Melbourne, a 1½-hour drive via the Maroondah Hwy. It's 40 minutes from Healesville.

McKenzie's Bus Line (p526) has a daily service to/from Melbourne ($11.62, two hours) via Healesville.

WORTH A TRIP

ST ANDREWS COMMUNITY MARKET

Sleepily ensconced in the hills 35km north of Melbourne is the township of St Andrews, which is synonymous with its weekly hippy **market** (www.standrews market.com.au; ⊘8am-2pm Sat). Every Saturday morning the scent of eucalypt competes with incense as an alternative crowd comes to mingle and buy hand-made crafts, enjoy a shiatsu massage, sip chai, have their chakra aligned or just listen to the street musos.

To get here, a shuttle bus departs from Hurstbridge train station.

Daylesford & Hepburn Springs

POP 2565 (DAYLESFORD), 459 (HEPBURN SPRINGS)

Daylesford and Hepburn Springs form the 'spa centre of Victoria'. Set among the scenic hills, lakes and forests of the Central Highlands, it's a fabulous year-round destination where you can soak away your troubles and sip wine by the fireside. The local population is an interesting blend of new agers and old-timers, and there's also a thriving gay and lesbian scene here.

The health-giving properties of the area's mineral springs were first claimed back in the 1870s, attracting droves of fashionable Melburnians. The well-preserved and restored buildings show the prosperity of these towns, as well as the lasting influence of the many Swiss-Italian miners who came to work the tunnel mines in the surrounding hills.

Sights & Activities

Pick up a copy of the mineral springs leaflet from the visitor centre for a listing of the 100-odd springs in the region, which details the mineral composition for each.

Good local walks incorporating various mineral spring pumps include Sailors Falls, Tipperary Springs, Central Springs Reserve and the Hepburn Springs Reserve; take a water bottle with you to taste-test the naturally carbonated water. The visitor centre (p530) has maps and walking guides.

Convent Gallery GALLERY
(⊘03-5348 3211; http://conventgallery.com.au; 7 Daly St, Daylesford; $5; ⊘10am-4pm) This beautiful 19th-century convent on Wombat Hill has been brilliantly converted into an art gallery with soaring ceilings, grand archways and magnificent gardens dotted with sculpture. Head up the path in the gardens behind the convent for sweeping views over the town. There's also an atrium cafe, cocktail bar and penthouse apartment (doubles including breakfast $295).

They run evening ghost tours here too (2½ hours, $49 including wine; book ahead).

Wombat Hill Botanic Gardens GARDENS
(Central Springs Rd, Daylesford; ⊘sunrise-sunset) Oak, pine and cypress trees fill these beautiful gardens, which have a picnic area and lookout tower with fine views of the countryside.

Activities

★**Hepburn Bathhouse & Spa** SPA
(⊘03-5321 6000; www.hepburnbathhouse.com; Mineral Springs Reserve Rd, Hepburn Springs; 2hr bathhouse entry $25-44; ⊘9am-6.30pm Sun-Thu, 8am-8pm Sat) Within the **Hepburn Mineral Springs Reserve**, the main bathhouse is a sleek ultramodern building where you can gaze out on the bush setting while soaking in the public pool or lazing on spa couches. The spa offers various treatments or a soak in a private mineral-springs pool in the original historic building (1895). Around the bathhouse are picnic areas, mineral spring pumps (bring an empty bottle to fill) and the historic **Pavilion** cafe.

Shizuka Ryokan SPA
(⊘03-5348 2030; www.shizuka.com.au; 7 Lakeside Dr, Hepburn Springs; treatments from $130) Shiatsu massage and spa treatments with natural sea salts and seaweed extracts feature at this Japanese-style country spa retreat. The speciality here is its indulgent Geisha facial.

Mineral Spa at Peppers SPA
(⊘03-5348 2100; www.mineralspa.com.au; 124 Main Rd, Springs Retreat, Hepburn Springs; 1hr from $65) A complex with indoor and outdoor mineral water spas and plunge pool. Also come for an exfoliation with Australian desert salts before an algae gel wrap, then move into the lavender-infused steam room or take a soft pack float.

Wombat Discovery Tours WILDLIFE WATCHING
(☏0484 792 212; www.wombatdiscoverytours.
com.au; tours adult/child from $35/20) These
highly recommended night tours are a
wonderful opportunity to spot Australian
wildlife in its natural habitat (as opposed
to enclosures) in the Wombat State Forest.
Here you're very likely to see wombats, kangaroos
and wallabies, along with the occasional
koala, echidna and glider. Trips are
mostly Saturday nights, but check its website
for the schedule. Rates include pickup
from Daylesford.

🛏 Sleeping

2 Dukes GUESTHOUSE $
(☏03-5348 4848; www.2dukesdaylesford.com; 2
Duke St, Daylesford; r with shared bathroom from
$99; 🛜) Flying the flag for affordable accommodation
in Daylesford is this well-run,
former doctor's surgery turned guesthouse
kitted out with vintage finds and original
bright artworks. The five rooms each have
their own personalities and share a bathroom
(one room has an en-suite). Light
breakfast is included and there's free wi-fi
rounding out the best offer in town.

★Hepburn Springs Chalet HOTEL $$
(☏03-5348 2344; www.hepburnspringschalet.
com.au; 78 Main Rd, Hepburn Springs; midweek/
weekend r from $110/150; 🛜) If Don Draper
was in town, this is where he'd drop his
briefcase. Originally a 1920s guesthouse, the
owners have retained the original features,
complementing them with retro charm like
deco mirrors and velvet lounges in the sitting
areas and cocktail bar. Rooms are basic,
but comfortable and cosy, and come with
en-suites.

Lake House BOUTIQUE HOTEL $$$
(☏03-5348 3329; www.lakehouse.com.au; 4 King
St, Daylesford; d incl half board from $610; ✻🛜)
Overlooking Lake Daylesford, the famous
Lake House is set in rambling gardens with
bridges and waterfalls. Its 35 rooms are split
into spacious waterfront rooms with balcony
decks, and lodge rooms with private
courtyards. Rates include breakfast and
three-course dinner at its famed restaurant;
two-night minimum on weekends.

★Grande Hotel HERITAGE HOTEL $$$
(☏03-5348 1978; www.thegrandehotel.com.au; 1
Church Ave, Hepburn Springs; r incl half board $325-
405) The recently restored historic Grande
Hotel has been done up superbly with its
boutique rooms delivering a quintessential
Hepburn atmosphere. Room 5 is the pick
with forest views and spa bath. Rates include
breakfast and three-course dinner in
its exquisite fine dining restaurant. It also
has an elegant cocktail bar and a popular
cabaret theatre with shows on Friday nights.

★Clifftop at Hepburn VILLA $$$
(☏1300 112 114; www.clifftopathepburn.com.
au; 209-219 Main Rd; 2-bedroom apt from $350)
The ultimate place to treat yourself are
these rustic-chic designer villas with wrap-
around windows overlooking the forest. Each
two-bedroom villa features a suave decor of
blonde woods, Danish furniture, ceramics,
sun lounge, French wood-fire heaters and
stand-alone stone bathtubs. Rooms have either
a massage chair or arcade-game consoles.

🍴 Eating & Drinking

Cliffy's Emporium DELI, CAFE $
(☏03-5348 3279; www.cliffysemporium.com.au; 30
Raglan St, Daylesford; mains $12-22; ⊗8am-4.30pm
Sun-Fri, till late Sat; 🍴) 🌿 Behind the vine-
covered verandah of this local institution is
an old-world cafe perfect for breakfast, pies
and baguettes, as well as local Malmsbury-
roasted coffee. It's also a provedore crammed
with preserves, meats and cheeses.

Farmers Arms PUB FOOD $$
(☏03-5348 2091; www.thefarmersarms.com.au;
1 East St, Daylesford; mains $22-42; ⊗noon-late)
Modern and rustic surroundings and food
meld tastefully in this classic country red-
brick gastropub. There's a welcoming front
bar and a beer garden for summer days,
featuring local beers by Daylesford Brewery.

★Lake House MODERN AUSTRALIAN $$$
(☏03-5348 3329; www.lakehouse.com.au; 4 King
St, Daylesford; 2-4 course meals midweek/weekend
$95/115; ⊗noon-2.30pm & 6-9pm; 🛜) You can't
talk about Daylesford without waxing on
about the Lake House, long regarded as the
town's top dining experience. It doesn't disappoint
with stylish purple high-back furniture,
picture windows showing off Lake
Daylesford, a superb seasonal menu, an
award-winning wine list and impressive service.
If you can't decide, try the tasting menu
($155, or vegetarian $135). Book well ahead
for weekends.

Kazuki's JAPANESE $$$
(☏03-5348 1218; www.kazukis.com.au; 1 Camp St,
Daylesford; 3-/5-courses $80/110, 7-course tasting
menu $140; ⊗6pm-late Thu-Mon, noon-2pm Sat

HANGING ROCK & THE MACEDON RANGES

A short distance off the Calder Fwy, less than an hour's drive north of Melbourne, the Macedon Ranges is a beautiful area of low mountains, native forest, excellent regional produce and wineries, often enveloped in cloud in winter, but great on a sunny day.

Made famous by the spooky Joan Lindsay novel (and subsequent film by Peter Weir) *Picnic at Hanging Rock*, about the disappearance of a group of 19th-century schoolgirls, **Hanging Rock** (☑ 03-5421 1469, 1800 244 711; www.visitmacedonranges.com; per vehicle $10 or per person $4; ☺ 9am-5pm) is an ancient and captivating place. The volcanic rock formations are the sacred site of the traditional owners, the Wurundjeri people, but you're welcome to clamber up the rocks along the 20-minute path. From the summit there are views of Mt Macedon and the surrounding countryside. It's a 10-minute drive from the pleasant town of **Woodend**, which is easily reached from Melbourne by V/Line train ($8.80, one hour). There's no public transport to Hanging Rock, so if you don't have a car you'll need to arrange a taxi.

Also worth a stop is the small historic township of **Trentham** with Victoria's highest single-drop **waterfalls**, and its quaint streetscape with some excellent new eateries and historic pubs.

& Sun) Kazuki's brings an unexpected twist to Daylesford's dining scene with its fusion of Japanese and French cuisine. The two-room restaurant, incorporating a wine and sake bar, is intimate, and there's an al-fresco courtyard at the side.

Blue Bean Cafe   CAFE
(☑ 03-5348 2297; www.facebook.com/bluebean lovecafe; 115 Main Rd, Hepburn Springs; mains $15-25; ☺ 8am-3pm Mon-Thu, to 9pm Fri-Sun) Taking over from the iconic Red Star Cafe is this equally cool, locally run spot. It does the best coffee in the region, featuring a weekly single-origin coffee to go with tasty breakfasts and lunches. It also has an impressive craft beer selection with 25 varieties, as well as cocktails, local wines, live music on Fridays and a chilled-out courtyard.

★ Old Hepburn Hotel   PUB
(☑ 03-5348 2207; www.oldhepburnhotel.com.au; 236 Main Rd, Hepburn Springs; ☺ 4pm-midnight Mon & Tue, noon-midnight Wed & Thu, noon-1am Fri & Sat, noon-11pm Sun; 🛜) A country pub with both character and taste, the Old Hepburn makes for a great night out with live music on weekends (usually free). The pub food hits the spot, and it has a ripper beer garden and friendly locals. It's a bit out of town, but call ahead for free bus pickup and drop-off service from Hepburn.

☆ Entertainment

★ Grande Hotel   CABARET
(☑ 03-5348 1978; www.thegrandehotel.com.au; 1 Church Ave, Hepburn Springs; tickets $10-30; ☺ Fri evenings) Since the demise of Hepburn's iconic Palais, the Grande has stepped in to fill a much needed-gap by opening its doors as a wonderful theatre hosting anything from cabaret and burlesque to sultry jazz. Shows are on Friday nights in its evocative basement space inside the historic hotel; most folk combine them with dinner and cocktails.

ℹ Tourist Information

Daylesford Visitor Centre (☑ 1800 454 891, 03-5321 6123; www.visitdaylesford.com; 98 Vincent St, Daylesford; ☺ 9am-5pm) Within an old fire station, this excellent tourist centre has good information on the area and mineral springs. They also have a self-guided walking-tour map for Daylesford. There's a history **museum** (☑ 03-5348 1453; www.daylesfordhistory.com.au; 100 Vincent St, Daylesford; adult/child $4/1; ☺ 1.30-4.30pm Sat & Sun) next door too.

ℹ Getting There & Away

Daylesford is 115km from Melbourne, a 1½-hour drive via the Calder Hwy; take the Woodend turn-off, from where it's a 35-minute drive.

Daily **V/Line** (☑ 1800 800 007; www.vline.com.au) train and coach services connect Melbourne by train to Woodend or Ballarat, then bus to Daylesford ($12.80, two to 2½ hours). The buses run from Bridport St opposite the fire station.

Local buses operate the 3km journey between Daylesford (from Bridport St) and Hepburn Springs ($2.40); it's a 10-minute journey.

Mornington Peninsula

The Mornington Peninsula – the boot-shaped area of land between Port Phillip Bay and Western Port Bay – has been Melbourne's summer playground since the 1870s, when paddle steamers ran down to

Portsea. Today, much of the interior farming land has been replaced by vineyards and orchards – foodies love the peninsula, where a winery lunch is a real highlight – but it still retains lovely stands of native bushland.

The calm 'front beaches' are on the Port Phillip Bay side, where families holiday at bayside towns from Mornington to Sorrento. The rugged ocean 'back beaches' face Bass Strait and are easily reached from Portsea, Sorrento and Rye; there are stunning walks along this coastal strip, part of the Mornington Peninsula National Park.

The bay heads are so close that it's just a short hop by ferry across from Sorrento to Queenscliff on the Bellarine Peninsula.

ⓘ Information

Peninsula Visitor Information Centre (☑1800 804 009, 03-5987 3078; www.visitmornington peninsula.org; 359b Nepean Hwy, Dromana; ⊙9am-5pm) The peninsula's main visitor information centre can book accommodation and tours, and stocks an abundance of brochures.

Sorrento & Portsea

POP 1448

Historic Sorrento is the standout town on the Mornington Peninsula for its beautiful limestone buildings, ocean and bay beaches, and buzzing seaside summer atmosphere. This was the site of Victoria's first official European settlement, established by an expedition of convicts, marines, civil officers and free settlers who arrived from England in 1803.

The last village on the peninsula, posh Portsea is a bit like Victoria's equivalent of the Hamptons, where many of Melbourne's wealthiest families have built seaside mansions.

As well as its adjoining Point Nepean National Park, of most interest for tourists are the dive shops here offering a number of tours – from wreck dives and snorkelling to sea kayak trips to visit seals and dolphins.

⊙ Sights & Activities

The calm bay beach is good for families and you can hire paddle boards on the Sorrento foreshore. The 10-minute climb up to Coppins Lookout in Sorrento offers good views.

★ **Bayplay**   DIVING, WATER SPORTS
(☑03-5984 0888; www.bayplay.com.au; 3755 Pt Nepean Rd; dives $68-130) A must for anyone wanting to get out on the water is this dive operator that offers PADI courses as well as guided diving and snorkelling trips to see a heap of marine life. However, it's most popular for its **sea-kayaking tours** (adult/child $99/88), where you can regularly spot dolphins and seals. They also do stand-up paddleboard tours (two hours $75), sailing trips (from $99) and hire out kayaks.

For landlubbers they rent out bikes (per day $30), organise glamping and run tours to visit Fort Nepean.

Moonraker Charters   WILDLIFE
(☑03-5984 4211; www.moonrakercharters.com.au; Esplanade Rd; sightseeing from $45, dolphin & seal swimming from $135) Operates dolphin- and seal-swimming tours from Sorrento Pier.

⚑ Sleeping

Sorrento Foreshore Camping Ground   CAMPGROUND $
(☑03-5950 1011; www.mornpen.vic.gov.au/activ ities/camping; Nepean Hwy; unpowered/powered sites $26/40, peak season $41/48; ⊙Oct-May) Hilly, bush-clad sites between the bay beach and the main road into Sorrento.

Hotel Sorrento   HOTEL $$
(☑03-5984 8000; www.hotelsorrento.com.au; 5-15 Hotham Rd, Sorrento; r weekdays/weekends incl breakfast from $170/210; ☒ ☜) The legendary Hotel Sorrento trades on its famous name and has a swag of accommodation. Its lovely 'On the Hill' double and family apartments have airy living spaces, spacious bathrooms and private balconies. Its pub has fabulous water views and is a good spot for a drink.

✗ Eating & Drinking

All Smiles   MODERN AUSTRALIAN $$
(☑03-5984 5551; www.allsmiles.com.au/morning ton-peninsula; 250 Ocean Beach Rd; mains $22-26; ⊙9.30am-2.30pm Wed-Sun) Literally on the Sorrento back beach, the menu here is decent enough with pizza, fish and chips, and calamari salad, but it's really all about the view. The Sunday buffet breakfasts (adult/child $20/12) are a great way to treat yourself.

Acquolina Ristorante   ITALIAN $$
(☑03-5984 0811; 26 Ocean Beach Rd; mains $25-38; ⊙6-10pm Wed-Mon Oct-Nov & Mar-May, daily in summer) Acquolina set the bar when it opened in Sorrento with its authentic Italian fare. This is hearty, simple food – handmade pasta and ravioli dishes matched with wines sourced first-hand from Italy, grappa and homemade (utterly irresistible) tiramisu.

WORTH A TRIP

MORNINGTON PENINSULA REGIONAL GALLERY

The outstanding **Mornington Peninsula Regional Gallery** (MPRG; ☑ 03-5975 4395; http://mprg.mornpen.vic.gov.au; Dunns Rd; adult/child $4/free; ⊙ 10am-5pm Tue-Sun) has changing exhibitions and a permanent collection of modern and contemporary Australian prints and paintings, representing the likes of Boyd, Tucker and Whiteley. There are free guided tours at 3pm on Wednesday, Saturday and Sunday.

Cakes & Ale Bistro　　　　　FRENCH $$$
(☑ 03-5984 4995; www.cakes-and-ale.com.au; 100-102 Ocean Beach Rd; mains $29-45; ⊙ noon-9pm Mon-Fri, 9am-9pm Sat & Sun) Offering some much needed class on Sorrento's main street is this smart restaurant doing seasonal produce sourced from around Victoria. Its attractive space is fitted out with plants, polished floors and distressed walls, and has a French-inspired menu of fisherman's pot pie, confit Milawa duck leg and roasted spatchcock. It does breakfasts on weekends, with quality coffee by **Little Rebel** (☑ 0418 121 467; www.littlerebel.com.au; 22 Collins Rd, Dromana; ⊙ 8am-2pm Mon-Fri).

Portsea Hotel　　　　　　　　PUB
(☑ 03-5984 2213; www.portseahotel.com.au; 3746 Point Nepean Rd; 🛜) Portsea's pulse is the sprawling, half-timber Portsea Hotel (c 1876), an enormous pub with a great lawn and terrace area looking out over the bay and historic pier. It's where the beautiful people come to be seen (especially come polo season), with regular events and DJs over summer. There's an excellent bistro (mains $24 to $27) and old-style **accommodation** (s/d without bathroom from $75/145, with bathroom from $135/180; 🛜).

ℹ Information

Sorrento Beach Visitors Centre (☑ 03 5984 1478; www.visitmorningtonpeninsula.org; cnr Ocean Beach Rd & George St; ⊙ 10am-4pm) The visitors centre is on the main drag in town, with a whopping selection of brochures and an after-hours info touch screen.

ℹ Getting There & Away

Sorrento and Portsea are accessed from Melbourne, just under a two-hour drive, along Eastlink (M3) and Mornington Peninsula Freeway (M11).

By public transport, from Melbourne take the train to Frankston station from where you can transfer to bus 788 to Sorrento and Portsea. Otherwise the ferry is a great way to get across Queenscliff, from where you can explore the Bellarine Peninsula and Great Ocean Rd.

Point Nepean National Park

At the peninsula's western tip is the scenic **Point Nepean National Park** (☑ 13 19 63; www.parkweb.vic.gov.au; Point Nepean Rd; ⊙ 8am-5pm), a historic site that played an important role as Australia's defence site from the 1880s to 1945. Remarkably, it was from here where the first Allied shots were fired in both WWI and WWII.

The national park is known for its stunning coastal scenery and features a number of lovely walks and cycling paths. A large section of the park is a former range area and still out of bounds due to unexploded ordnance.

You can visit its **Fort Nepean**, as well at the fascinating historic **Quarantine Station precinct**. Dating from 1852, this complex was used to quarantine passengers right until 1979; today it's a museum with interesting displays detailing its history, along with some 50 heritage buildings to explore, including the **Hospital** and **Wash House**.

ℹ Information

Point Nepean Visitor Information Centre (☑ 03-8427 2099; www.parkweb.vic.gov.au; Ochiltree Rd; ⊙ 10am-5pm) Will give you the lowdown on the park, hires bikes for $30.10 per day, as well as self-guided walking maps and iPod audio tours ($13.90). From Portsea you can walk or cycle to the point (12km return), or take the shuttle bus (adult/child return $10/7.50), a hop-on, hop-off bus service that departs the visitor centre every 30 minutes from 10.30am to 4pm.

ℹ Getting There & Away

Point Nepean National Park is at the far western tip of the Mornington Peninsula, facing directly across from Queenscliff and 112km from Melbourne. It's located about 2km west of Portsea.

To get to the national park by public transport take bus 788 from Frankston to the end of the line at Portsea, from where it's a 1km walk to the visitor centre.

Red Hill & Around

POP 731

The undulating hills of the peninsula around Red Hill and Main Ridge are one of the region's undoubted highlights. The centre of the region's viticulture and wine-making industries, it's unsurprisingly a favourite destination for foodies. Full of trees and tumbling hills, you can spend a sublime afternoon hopping around the winery cellar doors, restaurants and producers of local delights.

✖ Eating

Green Olive at Red Hill   MODERN AUSTRALIAN **$$**
(☑ 03-5989 2992; www.greenolive.com.au; 1180 Mornington-Flinders Rd, Main Ridge; tapas $12.95; ⊙9am-5pm; 🐾) Set on a 27-acre farm is this family-run enterprise that revolves around its light-filled restaurant with lovely outdoor tables overlooking the pastoral surrounds. Food is from the farm or locally sourced, with a menu of shared plates, wood-fired pizzas, homemade sausages and slow-cooked meats. They produce their own olive oil, wines and beers, among other homemade goods for purchase.

Merricks General Wine Store   CAFE **$$**
(☑ 03-5989 8088; www.merricksgeneralstore.com. au; 3460 Frankston-Flinders Rd, Merricks; breakfast $10-20, meals $16-36; ⊙8.30am-5pm) Dating back to the 1920s is this iconic stop that's an attractive, sprawling space with wooden floorboards and open fire. The rustic bistro is renowned for using fresh, local produce; a cellar door showcases wines from the Elgee Park and Baillieu Vineyard wineries. There's also an art gallery exhibiting local contemporary works.

The Epicurean   PIZZA **$$**
(☑ 03-5989 4000; www.theepicurean.com.au; 165 Shoreham Rd, Red Hill South; pizzas $20-32, mains $28-47; ⊙8.30am-9pm Wed-Sat, to 4pm Sun; 🐾) Whether you're here for its inviting cafe or slick cavernous restaurant doing wood-fired pizzas, the popular Epicurean is a class act. The restaurant is the main attraction, within its striking atrium 'shed' (a former apple-packing house) with exposed sleepers, polished concrete floors and copper pendant lighting. There's also a cellar room representing local wineries (tastings $9).

Red Hill Cheese   CHEESE
(☑ 03-5989 2035; www.redhillcheese.com.au; 81 William Rd, Red Hill; ⊙11am-5pm Sat & Sun) If you're around on a weekend, stop in for cheese tastings at this picturesque cellar door surrounded by bush. They specialise in artisan cheeses made from sheep, goat and buffalo milk.

Sunny Ridge Strawberry Farm   FOOD
(☑ 03-5989 4500; www.sunnyridge.com.au; cnr Shands & Mornington-Flinders Rds; adult/child $9/4; ⊙9am-5pm Nov-Apr, 11am-4pm Sat & Sun May-Oct) If all this booziness is too much, pick your own strawberries at Sunny Ridge Strawberry Farm. Admission includes 500g of strawberries (250g for kids) and there's a cafe serving all things strawberry – from wines to ice cream.

🍷 Drinking & Nightlife

⭐ **Bass & Flinders**   DISTILLERY
(☑ 0419 548 430, 03-5989 3154; www.bassand flindersdistillery.com; 232 Red Hill Rd, Red Hill; tasting flight $10, class per hr $140; ⊙11am-5pm Fri-Sun) Drop by this boutique distillery to taste its wonderful range of unique gins, from its shiraz grape gin and a truffle varietal to its 'Angry Ant' – distilled using indigenous Australian botanicals sourced from outback Western Australia and infused with bull-ant pheromone! They also offer gin master classes where you can make up your own batch from a choice of botanicals.

⭐ **Red Hill Brewery**   MICROBREWERY
(☑ 03-5989 2959; www.redhillbrewery.com.au; 88 Shoreham Rd, Red Hill South; ⊙11am-6pm Fri-Sun) Established in 2005, this popular microbrewery produces fantastic beers to sample by the pot, pint or tasting paddle ($12),

---

DON'T MISS

PENINSULA HOT SPRINGS

There are lots of spas and massage centres popping up along the peninsula, but none better than **Peninsula Hot Springs** (☑ 03-5950 8777; www. peninsulahotsprings.com; Springs Lane, Fingal; bathhouse adult/child Tue-Thu $35/20, Fri-Mon $45/30; ⊙7.30am-10pm), a large and luxurious complex that utilises hot, mineral-rich waters pumped from deep underground. There's a huge menu of spa, private bathing and massage treatments available, or you can just relax in the bathhouse. It's about 7km inland from Rye, off Browns Rd.

MORNINGTON PENINSULA WINERIES

Most of the peninsula's wineries are in the hills between Red Hill and Merricks, and most have excellent cafes or restaurants attached. Several companies offer winery tours – ask at the **visitor centre** (p531). For an overview, check out **Mornington Peninsula Wineries & Region** (www.mpva.com.au). Wineries to consider include the following:

Montalto (☑03-5989 8412; www.montalto.com.au; 33 Shoreham Rd, Red Hill South; ⊙cellar door & cafe 11am-5pm, restaurant noon-3pm, 6.30-11pm Fri & Sat) One of the Peninsula's best winery restaurants, renowned for its pinot noir and chardonnay. There's also the piazza and garden cafe for casual dining, as well as a beguiling sculpture garden.

Pier 10 (☑03-5989 8849; www.pier10wine.com.au; 10 Shoreham Rd; mains $16-37; ⊙cellar door 11am-5pm, restaurant noon-2.30pm Thu-Sun, 6pm-late Fri & Sat) This scenic, boutique winery is within a converted tin shed that houses both its cellar door and bistro restaurant.

Port Phillip Estate (☑03-5989 4444; www.portphillipestate.com.au; 263 Red Hill Rd, Red Hill South; 2-/3-course meal from $68/85, cellar door mains $15-22; ⊙cellar door 11am-5pm, restaurant noon-3pm Wed-Sun, 6.30-9pm Fri & Sat) A stunning winery inside a building that resembles a Bond villain's lair. It has one of the peninsula's best restaurants with stunning views, a gastronomic menu or lighter meals, and wine tastings ($5).

Red Hill Estate (☑03-5931 0177; www.redhillestate.com.au; 53 Shoreham Rd, Red Hill South; ⊙cellar door 11am-5pm, restaurant noon-5pm, 6-9pm Sat) Sample maritime cool climate pinots and chardonnays or dine at the renowned Max's Restaurant, which in 2017 was about to undergo major redevelopment.

Ten Minutes By Tractor (☑03-5989 6080; www.tenminutesbytractor.com.au; 1333 Mornington-Flinders Rd, Main Ridge; 5-/8-course tasting menu $114/144, 2-/3-course meal $69/92; ⊙cellar door 11am-5pm, restaurant noon-3pm Wed-Sun, 6.30-9pm Thu-Sat) This is one of regional Victoria's best restaurants and you won't find a better wine list on the Peninsula. The unusual name comes from the three vineyards, which are each 10 minutes apart by tractor.

T'Gallant (☑03-5931 1300; www.tgallant.com.au; 1385 Mornington-Flinders Rd, Main Ridge; mains $16-32; ⊙cellar door 9am-5pm, restaurant 11.30am-3pm Mon-Fri, 11am-4pm Sat & Sun) A rustic trattoria with delicious wood-fired pizzas, pork sausages and homemade lasagne. Its cellar door offers free tastings of its luscious pinot gris and prosecco.

accompanied by a plate of southern-style smoked BBQ (from $15) to enjoy on its deck.

ⓘ Getting There & Away

Located in the approximate centre of the peninsula, Red Hill is 84km from Melbourne. Take the Mornington Peninsula Fwy (M11) and exit on to the Nepean Hwy towards Red Hill/Flinders region.

From Frankston, bus 782 passes through Merricks and Point Leo en route to Flinders.

Phillip Island

POP 9406

Famous for the Penguin Parade and Motorcycle Grand Prix racing circuit, Phillip Island attracts a curious mix of surfers, petrolheads and international tourists making a beeline for those little penguins.

At its heart, Phillip Island is still a farming community, but nature has conspired to turn it into one of Victoria's most popular tourist destinations. Apart from the nightly waddling of the penguins, there's a large seal colony, abundant bird life and fauna. The rugged south coast has some fabulous surf beaches, a swag of family attractions and plenty of accommodation. Visit in winter, though, and you'll find a very quiet place where the local population of farmers, surfers and hippies go about their business.

The Boonwurrung people are the traditional inhabitants of the island, though what they'd have made of coachloads of Penguin Parade tourists and biker gangs making their way over the San Remo bridge is anyone's guess.

Phillip Island

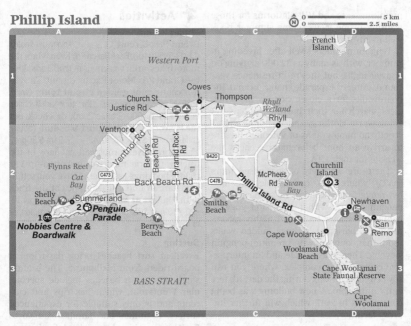

Phillip Island

◉ Top Sights

1 Nobbies Centre & Boardwalk A2
2 Penguin Parade A2

◉ Sights

Antarctic Journey .... (see 1)
3 Churchill Island D2
History of Motorsport Museum .....(see 4)

◉ Activities, Courses & Tours

Grand Prix Guided Circuit
Tours ....(see 4)

Phillip Island Circuit Go Karts .... (see 4)
4 Phillip Island Grand Prix Circuit B2

◉ Sleeping

5 Clifftop C2
6 Cowes Caravan Park...........................B1
7 Glen Isla House B1
8 Island Accommodation YHA.................D2

◉ Eating

9 BEANd...D3
10 Cape Kitchen C2

◉ Sights

★ Nobbies Centre & Boardwalk VIEWPOINT
(☑03-5951 2800; Summerlands) **FREE** At the island's southwestern tip is this dramatic viewpoint for the **Nobbies** offshore rock formations. Here the gigantic cafe and souvenir shop known as the **Nobbies Centre** has incredible ocean vistas and the multimedia Antarctic Journey (p536). In front of the centre, a **boardwalk** winds down to vantage points of the formations, as well the blow hole, and beyond to the Seal Rocks – inhabited by Australia's largest fur-seal colony. There are coin-operated binoculars, but bring your own if you have them.

★ Penguin Parade WILDLIFE RESERVE
(☑03-5951 2800; www.penguins.org.au; 1019 Ventnor Rd, Summerland Beach; admission from adult/child/family $25.10/12.50/62.70, underground viewing $60/30/150; ☉9.30am-dusk, penguins arrive at sunset) The Penguin Parade attracts more than half a million visitors annually to see the little penguins (*Eudyptula minor*), the world's smallest, and cutest of their kind. The main penguin complex includes concrete amphitheatres that hold up to 3800 spectators who come to see the little fellas just after sunset as they waddle from the sea to their land-based nests. There's also an underground viewing section,

premium seats and VIP platforms for those wanting prime views; come summer book well in advance.

Penguin numbers swell after breeding in summer, with as many as 32,000 arriving on a given night, but they're in residence year round. After the parade, hang around the boardwalks for a closer view as the stragglers search for their burrows and mates. Bring warm clothing, and take note there's strictly no photography or videoing. Be sure to arrive an hour beforehand – check the website for their ETA.

There are a variety of specialised tours (p535) where you can be accompanied by rangers to explain the behaviour of penguins, tours with night-vision goggles, behind-the-scenes tours and highly recommended Aboriginal heritage guided walks ($60) that conclude with premium penguin viewing. There's also a cafe and an interpretive centre at the complex, where you can spy penguins nesting during the day; it's free entry until 4pm. A new building was being constructed in 2017, which will further improve facilities.

Antarctic Journey
OBSERVATORY, THEATRE

(☑ 03-5951 2800; www.penguins.org.au/attractions/recreational-areas/the-nobbies; 1320 Ventnor Rd, Nobbies Centre, Summerlands; adult/child/family $18/9/45; ⊙ 9am-5pm) On the southwest tip of the island is this cutting-edge multimedia exhibition space that spotlights the shared waters between here and Antarctica. Its interactive displays are highly informative, with cool augmented reality features. It's located in the Nobbies Centre, a five-minute drive from the Penguin Parade, so aim to visit in mid afternoon if you're seeing the penguins.

Churchill Island
FARM

(☑ 03-5951 2800; www.penguins.org.au; Phillip Island Rd, Newhaven; adult/child/family $12.50/6.25/31.25; ⊙10am-5pm Mon-Fri, from 9am Sat & Sun) Connected to Phillip Island by a bridge near Newhaven, Churchill Island is a delightful working farm where Victoria's first crops were planted. Its historic homestead and garden is surrounded by paddocks of grazing highland cattle and looks out to fabulous ocean views. There are several pleasant walking tracks looping around the island. Time your visit for farm activity demonstrations, including sheep shearing, cow milking and watching working sheep dogs in action.

Activities

Phillip Island

Grand Prix Circuit
ADVENTURE SPORTS

(☑ 03-5952 9400; Back Beach Rd) Even when the motorbikes aren't racing, petrolheads love the Grand Prix Motor Racing Circuit. The visitor centre runs **guided circuit tours** (www.phillipislandcircuit.com.au; 1hr tour adult/child/family $25/15/60; ⊙ tours 2pm), or check out the **History of Motorsport Museum** (adult/child/family $17.50/8.50/42; ⊙ 9am-5.30pm). The more adventurous can cut laps of the track with a racing driver in hotted-up V8s ($360; bookings essential). Drive yourself in a go-kart around a scale replica of the track with **Phillip Island Circuit Go Karts** (per 10-/20-/30-min $35/60/80; ⊙ 9am-5.30pm, longer hr in summer).

Surfing

Excellent surf beaches bring day-tripping board riders from Melbourne. The island's south-side ocean beaches include spectacular **Woolamai**, which has rips and currents and is only suitable for experienced surfers. Beginners and families can go to **Smiths Beach**, where Island Surfboards offers surfing lessons and hires out gear. **Berrys Beach** also has a beautiful wave and is usually quieter than Woolamai or Smiths. Around the Nobbies, Cat Bay and Flynns Reef will often be calm when the wind is blowing onshore at the Woolamai and Smiths areas.

Tours

Wild Ocean Eco Boat
WILDLIFE WATCHING

(☑ 03-5951 2800; www.penguins.org.au; Cowes or Rhyll Jetty; per person adult/child/family Adventure Tour $85/65/235, Island Discovery $130/75/345, Shearwater Sunset $65/49/179; ⊙ Adventure Tour 3pm, Island Discovery 11am Dec-Apr, Shearwater Sunset 7.15-8.30pm Nov-Apr) These boat tours give you the option of visiting various sights around the island: the Australian fur seal colony at Seal Rocks; the scenic coastline of dramatic rock formations; or sunset tours to see shearwaters return to their clifftop nests.

Go West
TOURS

(☑ 03-9485 5290; www.gowest.com.au; tour $135) One-day tour from Melbourne that includes entry to the Penguin Parade, lunch, wildlife encounters and wine-tasting. It has iPod commentary in several languages and wi-fi on the bus.

✳ Festivals & Events

Australian Motorcycle Grand Prix   SPORTS
(☑1800 100 030; www.motogp.com.au) The island's biggest event is the Australian Motorcycle Grand Prix, one of the most scenic circuits on the MotoGP international calendar. Its three days of action are usually held in October, when the the island's population jumps from 8000 people to over 150,000.

🛌 Sleeping

Phillip Island Glamping   TENTED CAMP $$
(☑0404 258 205; www.phillipislandglamping.com.au; d tent hire weekday/weekend from $120/140) A different kind of arrangement to the norm, here you book your camp site (choosing from any of the island's campgrounds), and the staff sets up your bell tent. It'll be ready to go upon your arrival, equipped with mattress, bedding, towels, heater, digital radio, table and chairs, esky and full set of cooking utensils. Once you're done, they'll clean it all up again – lazy camping at its best.

🛌 Cowes

Cowes Caravan Park   CARAVAN PARK $
(☑03-5952 2211; www.cowescaravanpark.com.au; 164 Church St, Cowes; campsites from $40, cabins from $90-130; ✳🐾) The place for beach-side camping is this park that offers a range of campsites and en-suite cabins – the better ones have air-con and beach views. It's 1km from Cowes.

★Clifftop   BOUTIQUE HOTEL $$$
(☑03-5952 1033; www.clifftop.com.au; 1 Marlin St, Smiths Beach; d $235-290; ✳🐾) It's hard to imagine a better location for your island stay than perched above Smiths Beach. Of the seven luxurious suites here, the top four have ocean views and private balconies, while the downstairs rooms open onto gardens – all have fluffy beds and slick contemporary decor.

★Glen Isla House   BOUTIQUE HOTEL $$$
(☑03-5952 1882; www.glenisla.com; 230 Church St, Cowes; d/ste from $255/355; ✳🐾) This brilliant boutique hotel is one of the best addresses on the island. Ensconced in a renovated 1870 homestead and outbuildings, Glen Isla is all about understated, old-world luxury with modern touches such as huge plasma TVs. It has 2 acres of lovely gardens and is only a five-minute walk to the beach. No children under 12.

🛌 Newhaven

★Island Accommodation YHA   HOSTEL $
(☑03-5956 6123; www.theislandaccommodation.com.au; 10-12 Phillip Island Rd, Newhaven; dm $27-50, d $99-155; @🐾) 🐾 This large purpose-built backpackers has huge identical living areas on each floor, complete with table tennis, PlayStations and cosy fireplaces for winter. Its rooftop deck has terrific views and its eco-credentials are excellent. Cheapest dorms sleep 12 and doubles are motel standard. They have bike hire (per day $20), with the cycle path out front leading all the way to Cowes.

✗ Eating

✗ Cowes

BEANd   CAFE $
(☑0407 717 588; www.beand.com.au; 157 Marine Pde, Shop 4; breakfast $8-15; ⊙7am-4pm Thu-Tue) At the bridge heading into Phillip Island is this micro-coffee roaster that does a top-notch brew, using single-origin beans sourced from around Africa, Asia and Latin America. It's a vibrant, friendly little cafe, with all its coffee roasted onsite and prepared as pour overs, aeropress and espresso. All-day breakfasts and burgers for lunch.

Madcowes   CAFE, DELI $
(☑03-5952 2560; www.madcowescafe.com.au; 17 the Esplanade, Cowes; mains $9-18; ⊙6.30am-3pm) This stylish cafe-foodstore looks out to the main beach and cooks up some of the heartiest breakfasts and light lunches on the island. Its quinoa bowl makes for a healthy start to the day, while its deluxe breakfast roll (filled with bacon, fried egg, cheese and a hash brown) is the perfect hangover cure. For lunch it does roast beef sandwiches, tempura squid and local wines.

✗ Newhaven

Cape Kitchen   MODERN AUSTRALIAN $$
(☑03-5956 7200; www.thecapekitchen.com.au; 1215 Phillip Island Rd, Newhaven; breakfast from $19, lunch $27-48; ⊙8.30am-4.30pm Fri-Mon) Grab a window seat to take in all-encompassing ocean vistas while enjoying delicious breakfasts such as house-smoked salmon with scrambled eggs and sourdough. For lunch there's the likes of charcoal trout, red-curry Gippsland mussels or a roasted South Gippsland lamb shoulder to share.

ℹ Information

Phillip Island Visitor Information Centre
(☐ 1300 366 422; www.visitphillipisland.
com; 895 Phillip Island Tourist Rd, Newhaven;
☺ 9am-5pm, to 6pm school holidays; ☎) The
main visitor centre on the island has a wall
of brochures and maps. It sells tickets to the
penguin parade, and sight packages that bring
healthy discounts. It also offers a super-help-
ful accommodation booking service and has
free wi-fi.

Cowes Visitor Information Centre (☐ 1300
366 422; www.visitphillipisland.com; cnr
Thompson & Church Sts, Cowes; ☺ 9am-5pm)
An alternative to the info centre in Newhaven.

ℹ Getting There & Away

About 140km from Melbourne, by car Phillip
Island can only be accessed by crossing the
bridge between San Remo and Newhaven. From
Melbourne take the Monash Fwy (M1) and exit at
Pakenham, joining the South Gippsland Hwy at
Koo Wee Rup.

By public transport you'll need to get a com-
bination of train and bus to Phillip Island. V/Line
runs around eight trips a day from Melbourne's
Southern Cross Station to Cowes via Koo Wee
Rup ($14.40 2½ hours) or a longer journey via
Dandenong (3½ hours).

GREAT OCEAN ROAD

The Great Ocean Road (B100) is one of Australia's most famous road-touring routes.
It takes travellers past world-class surfing
breaks, through pockets of rainforest and
calm seaside towns, and under koala-filled
tree canopies. It shows off sheer limestone
cliffs, dairy farms and heathlands, and gets
you up close and personal with the crashing
waves of the Southern Ocean.

Hunt out the isolated beaches and light-
houses in between the towns and the thick
eucalyptus forests in the Otway hinterlands
to really escape the crowds. Rather than
heading straight to the Great Ocean Road,
a fork in the road at Geelong can take you
the long, leisurely way there, through the
Bellarine Peninsula with visits to charming
Queenscliff and wineries en route.

Day-tripping tourists from Melbourne
rush in and out of the area in less than 12
hours but, in a perfect world, you'd spend at
least a week here.

Geelong

POP 210,875

As Victoria's second-largest city, Geelong is a
proud town with an interesting history and
pockets of charm.

Great Ocean Road & Southwest Coast

It's centred around the sparkling Corio Bay waterfront and the city centre, where heritage buildings from the boom days of the gold-rush era and thriving wool industry have now been converted into swanky restaurants and bars. It's also a footy-mad town, passionate about its home-town AFL team, the Cats.

◉ Sights & Activities

Geelong Waterfront   WATERFRONT

(Beach Rd) Geelong's sparkling revamped waterfront precinct is a great place to stroll, with plenty of good restaurants set on scenic piers, plus historical landmarks, a 19th-century carousel, sculptures, grand homes, swimming areas, playgrounds and grassy sections ideal for picnics. In summer you can jump in and cool off at popular **Eastern Beach**, with an art-deco bathing pavilion complete with diving boards, sunbathing area and a toddler pool. Jan Mitchell's 100-plus famous painted **Bay Walk Bollards** are also scattered the length of the waterfront.

Geelong Art Gallery   GALLERY

(☑03-5229 3645; www.geelonggallery.org.au; 55 Little Malop St; ◷10am-5pm) **FREE** With over 6000 works in its collection, this excellent gallery has celebrated Australian paint-ings such as Eugene von Guérard's *View of Geelong* and Frederick McCubbin's 1890 *A Bush Burial*. Also exhibits contemporary works and has free tours on Sundays at 2pm.

National Wool Museum   MUSEUM

(☑03-5272 4701; www.geelongaustralia.com.au/nwm; 26 Moorabool St; adult/child/family $9/5/30; ◷9.30am-5pm Mon-Fri, 10am-5pm Sat & Sun) More interesting than it may sound, this museum showcases the importance of the wool industry in shaping Geelong economically, socially and architecturally – many of the grand buildings in the area are former wool-store buildings, including the museum's 1872 bluestone building. There's a sock-making machine and a massive 1910 Axminster carpet loom that gets chugging at hourly intervals.

Powerhouse Geelong – City Precinct   GALLERY

(☑0418 526 640; www.powerhousegeelong.com; 20 Brougham St; ◷9.30am-5pm) **FREE** In addition to the **street art park** (40 Mackey St, North Geelong; $5; ◷10am-5pm) in the old power station in North Geelong are these galleries and studio spaces set within a 100-year-old brick wool storing house. Set above the **Brougham Street Markets** (☑03-5221 2490; www.facebook.com/brougham

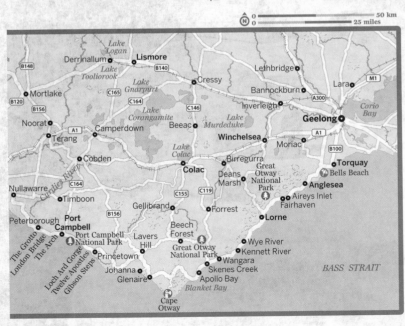

The Great Ocean Road

The Great Ocean Road begins in Australia's surf capital Torquay, swings past Bells Beach, then winds its way along the coast to the wild and windswept koala heaven of Cape Otway. The Twelve Apostles and Loch Ard Gorge are obligatory stops before the road sweeps on towards Warrnambool with its whales, and Port Fairy with its fine buildings and folk festival, and the natural drama peaks again close to the South Australian border.

GORDON BELL / SHUTTERSTOCK ©

Twelve Apostles (p557)
ese dramatic rock formations are a high point of
ctoria's best-known road trip.

Port Fairy (p562)
maritime village with historic charm.

Bells Beach (p549)
is world-famous point break hosts Australia's
emier surf event, the Rip Curl Pro.

Koala, Cape Otway (p556)
eisurely drive along the forested Cape Otway
astline offers an excellent chance of koala sightings.

MAYDAYS / GETTY IMAGES ©

PETE SEAWARD/LONELY PLANET ©

Geelong

Geelong

⊙ Sights
1 Eastern Beach D2
2 Geelong Art Gallery B2
3 Geelong Waterfront C2
4 National Wool Museum B2
5 Old Geelong Gaol C3
6 Powerhouse Geelong – City
   Precinct B2

⊕ Activities, Courses & Tours
Geelong Gaol Ghost Tours .... (see 5)

🛏 Sleeping
7 Devlin Apartments B4
8 Gatehouse on Ryrie C3

⊗ Eating
9 Geelong Boat House B1
10 Hot Chicken Project D1
11 IGNI B3
12 Pistol Pete's Food n Blues D1
13 Tulip A1

🍸 Drinking & Nightlife
14 Cartel Coffee Roaster D1

✪ Entertainment
15 Kardinia Park B4

🛍 Shopping
Brougham Street Markets .... (see 6)

streetmarkets; ⊙10am-6pm), here everything is for sale and features the work of some 300 street artists from the area and beyond. Call ahead for street-art workshops (per hour $25).

Old Geelong Gaol HISTORIC BUILDING
(📞03-5221 8292; www.geelonggaol.org.au; cnr Myers & Swanston Sts; adult/child/family $10/5/22; ⊙1-4pm Sat & Sun, daily school holidays) Built in 1849, HSM Prison Geelong may have closed

its doors in 1991, but this old bluestone jail remains as terrifying as ever. You'll see its grim cells set over three levels, plus the shower block, watchtowers and gallows. Each exhibit is accompanied by audio, explaining anything from contraband or crude homemade weapons to former cellmates such as Chopper Read (cell 39). **Ghost tours** (📞1300 865 800; www.twistedhistory.net. au; adult/child $33/22) are also run here.

Boom Gallery   GALLERY
(📞0417 555 101; www.boomgallery.com.au; 11 Rutland St, Newtown; ⏰9am-4pm Mon-Sat) **FREE** Down an industrial street off Pakington St, Boom's warehouse space in an old wool mill shows contemporary works by Melbourne and local artists. It sells great design objects and jewellery, and the attached cafe does fantastic coffee and seasonal food.

**Narana Aboriginal
Cultural Centre**   CULTURAL CENTRE
(📞03-5241 5700; www.narana.com.au; 410 Torquay Rd, Grovedale; ⏰9am-5pm Mon-Fri, 10am-4pm Sat, cafe 8am-4pm Mon-Fri, to 3pm Sat, gallery Tue-Sat, by appointment Mon) **FREE** The Wathaurung people, the original inhabitants of Geelong, called the area Jillong, and this precinct in its outskirts offers a fascinating insight into their culture. There's a a gallery featuring Victoria's largest collection of Indigenous art; a fusion cafe that offers contemporary dishes using indigenous ingredients; didgeridoo performances (or play it yourself); a boomerang-throwing gallery; and a native garden (by donation) which features emus, wallabies and koalas. Call ahead for daily tours.

🛏 Sleeping

⭐**Devlin Apartments**   APARTMENT $$
(📞03-5222 1560; www.devlinapartments.com.au; 312 Moorabool St; r $160-500; ❄🐾) Geelong's most stylish offerings are these boutique apartments, housed in a 1926 heritage-listed building (the former Gordon Tech school). Each of the apartments has themed designs including 'New Yorker' loft-style apartments with arched windows; 'Modernist', furnished with Danish designer chairs; and 'Industrial', featuring wrought iron, rustic wood and tiled brick bathrooms.

Gatehouse on Ryrie   GUESTHOUSE $$
(📞0417 545 196; www.gatehouseonryrie.com.au; 83 Yarra St; d incl breakfast $110-130; 🅿@🐾) A prime location in the centre of town,

this guesthouse is one of Geelong's best midrange choices. Built in 1897 it features gorgeous timber floorboards throughout, spacious rooms (most with shared facilities) and a communal kitchen and lounge area. Breakfast is in the glorious front room.

🍴 Eating & Drinking

Hot Chicken Project   AMERICAN $
(📞03-5221 9831; 84a Little Malop St; mains from $16; ⏰noon-10pm) Slotting in perfectly along Little Malop is this cosy, welcoming diner specialising in authentic Nashville chicken. Choose from a menu of wings, tenders or dark meats – or hot fish or tofu – in a spectrum of heat levels peaking at 'Evil Chicken', served with a side of slaw or turnip greens.

Geelong Boat House   FISH & CHIPS $
(📞03-5222 3642, 0427 319 019; www.geelongboat house.com.au; Geelong Waterfront, Western Beach; fish & chips from $10; ⏰10am-8pm) Jutting out into the water, this fish-and-chip joint is built on top of a barge once used to dredge the Yarra River. Grab a chair on the deck or rooftop, or laze on one of its picnic blankets on the grassy banks. There's also a seafood restaurant in its attached boat shed.

Tulip   MODERN AUSTRALIAN $$
(📞03-5229 6953; www.tuliprestaurant.com.au; 9/111 Pakington St, Geelong West; smaller/larger dishes from $18/22; ⏰noon-2.30pm Wed-Sat & 5.30-late Mon-Sat) One of only two hatted restaurants in Geelong, unassuming Tulip on 'Pako' St delivers a gastronomic experience with its mix of inventive small and large plates designed to share. Dishes may include native items such as kangaroo tartare with pepperberry oil, cured Spanish leg ham, whole lamb shoulder or poached ocean trout with grilled peas and mussels.

Pistol Pete's Food n Blues   AMERICAN $$
(📞03-5221 0287; www.pistolpetesfoodnblues.com. au; 93a Little Malop St; mains $17-24; ⏰noon-10pm Sun-Thu, to 12.30am Fri & Sat) A divey hang out serving up Cajun-style burgers, shrimp po'boys, southern-style fried chicken, gumbo, swamp fries and baloney sandwiches. Live music is also a feature with regular bluesy, Americana, twang bands to enjoy with US craft beers, Kentucky whiskeys and bourbons.

⭐**IGNI**   MODERN AUSTRALIAN $$$
(📞03-5222 2266; www.restaurantigni.com; Ryan Pl; 5-/8-courses $100/150; ⏰6-10pm Thu & Sun, noon-2.30pm & 6-10pm Fri & Sat) Creating a buzz

among food lovers across Melbourne is this latest venture by well-lauded chef (and local boy) Aaron Turner. The set tasting menus change on a whim, incorporating a mix of indigenous and European flavours from saltbush to oyster leaf, or marron to squab, using a wood-fired grill fuelled by ironbark and red gum.

★ **Cartel Coffee Roaster** COFFEE
(☑ 03-5222 6115; www.coffeecartel.com.au; 1-80 Little Malop St; single-origin coffee $4.50; ⊘ 7am-5pm Mon-Thu, to 5.30pm Fri, to 2pm Sat, 9am-2pm Sun) A big player in Australia's third-wave coffee movement is this single-origin roaster run by a passionate owner who personally forges relations with farmers across Africa, Asia and Latin America. The result is well-sourced beans, expertly roasted and pre-pared in its smart space on happening Little Malop.

★ **Little Creatures & White Rabbit** BREWERY
(☑ Little Creatures 03-5202 4009, White Rabbit 03-5202 4050; www.littlecreatures.com.au; cnr Fyans & Swanston Sts; mains $16-28; ⊘ 11am-5pm Mon-Tue, 11am-9pm Wed-Fri, 8am-9pm Sat, 8am-5pm Sun; ⃕) Sharing space within the historic red-brick wool mill complex are these two separate, well-respected breweries that have come together to create a giant playground for beer lovers. Little Creatures is the bigger operation, a vast indoor/outdoor vibrant space, while White Rabbit, relocated from Healesville in 2015, is the more boutique offering, with a chic set-up among its brewing equipment.

☆ Entertainment

Barwon Club LIVE MUSIC
(☑ 03-5221 4584; www.barwonclub.com.au; 509 Moorabool St; ⊘ 11am-late) The Barwon has long been Geelong's premier live music venue, and has spawned the likes of Magic Dirt, Bored! and Warped, seminal bands in the 'Geetroit' rock scene. As well as catching local and international bands, it's a great pub for a beer.

Kardinia Park STADIUM
(Simonds Stadium; ☑ 03-5224 9111; www.kardinia park.vic.gov.au; 370 Moorabool St, South Geelong; tickets from $25) Recently renovated and fitted with light towers, this AFL stadium is sacred ground for locals as the home of their beloved team, the Cats, who play here in winter.

ℹ Tourist Information

National Wool Museum Visitor Centre (www.visitgreatoceanroad.org.au; 26 Moorabool St; ⊘ 9am-5pm; ⃕) Geelong's main tourist information office has brochures on Geelong, the Bellarine Peninsula and the Otways, as well as free wi-fi. There's also a **visitor centre** (☑ 03-5283 1735; www.visitgreatoceanroad.org.au; Princes Hwy, Little River; ⊘ 9am-5pm) on Geelong Rd, at the service station near Little River, for those heading directly to the Great Ocean Road, and a small **kiosk** (Geelong Waterfront; ⊘ 9am-5pm) on the waterfront.

ℹ Getting There & Away

AIR

Jetstar (p519) has services to/from **Avalon Airport** (p519), around a 20-minute drive from Geelong.

Avalon Airport Shuttle (☑ 03-5278 8788; www.avalonairportshuttle.com.au) meets all flights at Avalon Airport and goes to Geelong (adult/child $22/15, 35 minutes) and along the Great Ocean Road, starting from Torquay ($50/25, one hour).

BUS

Gull Airport Service (☑ 03-5222 4966; www.gull.com.au; 45 McKillop St; ⊘ office 9am-5pm Mon-Fri, 10am-noon Sat) Has 14 services a day between Geelong and Melbourne Airport (adult/child $32/20, 1¼ hours), departing from the city centre and Geelong station.

McHarry's Buslines (☑ 03-5223 2111; www.mcharrys.com.au) Runs frequent buses from Geelong station to Torquay and the Bellarine Peninsula ($3.20, 20 minutes).

V/Line (☑ 1800 800 007; www.vline.com.au; Gordon Ave, Geelong Train Station) Buses run from Geelong station to Apollo Bay ($19, 2½ hours, three daily) via Torquay ($3.20, 25 minutes), Anglesea ($6.40, 45 minutes), Lorne ($11.60, 1½ hours) and Wye River ($14.40, two hours). On Monday, Wednesday and Friday a bus continues to Port Campbell ($33.20, five hours) and Warrnambool ($37.60, 6½ hours), which involves a change at Apollo Bay. The train is a much quicker and cheaper option for those heading direct to Warrnambool ($25.80, 2½ hours), though you'll miss out on the Great Ocean Road experience. Heading inland, there's a bus to Ballarat ($10.20, 1½ hours).

CAR

The 25km Geelong Ring Road runs from Corio to Waurn Ponds, bypassing Geelong entirely. To get to Geelong city, be careful not to miss the Princes Hwy (M1) from the left lanes.

TRAIN

V/Line trains run frequently from **Geelong station** (☑ 03-5226 6525; www.vline.com.au; Gordon Ave) to Melbourne's Southern Cross station (from $8.80, one hour). Trains also head from Geelong to Warrnambool ($25.80, 2½ hours, three daily).

Bellarine Peninsula

Melburnians have been making the drive down the Princes Hwy (Geelong Rd) to the seaside villages along the Bellarine Peninsula for more than a century. It's known for its family and surf beaches, historic towns and its wonderful cool-climate wineries.

As well as linking up with the Great Ocean Road, it's just a short ferry trip from here over to the Mornington Peninsula.

Activities

Bellarine Rail Trail   CYCLING
(www.railtrail.com/au/vic/bellarine) Following the route of the historical train line, this 32.5km bike path links South Geelong station with Queenscliff. It's a mostly flat sealed surface that, other than a few crossings, avoids riding on the main roads, passing through Drysdale en route to Queenscliff.

Information

Bellarine Visitor Information Centre
(☑ 03-5250 6861, 1800 755 611; http://app. geelongbellarineovg.com; 1251 Bellarine Hwy, Wallington; ⊙ 9am-5pm) Located within the premises of **Flying Brick Cider Co.** (p546), this tourist information centre has a heap of brochures and ideas on what to do in the area.

Queenscliff

POP 1418
Historic Queenscliff is a charming seaside town that mixes a salty maritime character with one of Victoria's most picturesque streetscapes. Many of its heritage-listed 19th-century buildings have been converted into hotels, restaurants and art galleries. It's a great base from which to explore the nearby wineries and beaches, along with several historical sites and museums in town. The views across the Port Phillip Heads and Bass Strait are glorious.

Sights

Fort Queenscliff   HISTORIC SITE
(☑ 03-5258 1488; www.fortqueenscliff.com.au; cnr Gellibrand & King Sts; 90-min tours adult/child/family $12/6/30; ⊙ 11am, 1pm & 3pm daily school holidays, 11am Mon-Fri, 1pm & 3pm Sat & Sun non-peak season) Queencliff's fort was first used as a coastal defence in 1882 to protect Melbourne from a feared Russian invasion. It remained a base until 1946, before being used as the Army Staff College until late 2012; today it functions as the defence archive centre. The 90-minute guided tours take in the military museum (not always accessible), the magazine, cells and its twin lighthouses. It's a defence area, so bring ID for entry. Cash only.

Queenscliff Gallery   GALLERY
(☑ 03-5258 4927; www.qgw.com.au; 81 Hesse St; ⊙ 10am-5pm Wed-Mon) **FREE** A lovely space inside a historic stone church (c 1868), this interesting gallery exhibits works by contemporary Australian artists who work on paper. Lithograph is the main focus, and it's all for purchase.

Queenscliff Maritime Museum   MUSEUM
(☑ 03-5258 3440; www.maritimequeenscliffe.org. au; 2 Wharf St; adult/child $8/5; ⊙ 10.30am-4.30pm) Home to the last lifeboat to serve the Rip, this museum has displays on the pilot boat process, shipwrecks, lighthouses and steamships. Don't miss the historic 1895 boat shed with its paintings that served as a record of passing ships in the bay.

Activities

Sea-All Dolphin Swims   WILDLIFE
(☑ 03-5258 3889; www.dolphinswims.com.au; Queenscliff Harbour; sightseeing tours adult/child $75/65, 3½hr snorkel $145/125; ⊙ 8am & 1pm Oct-Apr) Offers sightseeing tours and swims with seals and dolphins in Port Phillip Heads Marine National Park. Seal sightings are guaranteed; dolphins aren't always seen, but there's a good chance. Snorkelling trips take in Pope's Eye (an unfinished military fort), which is home to abundant fish and an Australasian gannet breeding colony, before visiting a permanent Australian fur seal colony at Chinaman's Hat.

Dive Victoria   DIVING
(Queenscliff Dive Centre; ☑ 03-5258 4188; www. divequeenscliff.com.au; Queenscliff Harbour; per dive with/without gear $140/65) Victoria's premier dive operator offers SSI dive courses and trips for all levels, from intro to technical. There are some 200 sites in the area, taking in rich marine life and shipwrecks from the past three centuries, including ex-HMAS *Canberra,* scuttled in 2009, and

BELLARINE WINERIES & PRODUCE

The Bellarine/Geelong area has over 50 wineries, and is a region well known for its cool-climate pinot noir, chardonnay and shiraz. It's also an area famous for its fantastic local produce.

If you don't have your own wheels, consider a winery tour with **For the Love of Grape** (☑ 0408 388 332; www.fortheloveofgrape.com.au; half-/full-day tours from Geelong $75/139, from Melbourne $85/149), or visit during **Toast to the Coast** (www.toasttothe coast.com.au; tickets $45; ☺ early Nov) festival in November.

Most listings here are open daily during summer and on weekends; other times call ahead.

Scotchmans Hill (☑ 03-5251 3176; www.scotchmans.com.au; 190 Scotchmans Rd, Drysdale; ☺ 10.30am-4.30pm) One of the Bellarine's first wineries remains one of its very best.

Jack Rabbit (☑ 03-5251 2223; www.jackrabbitvineyard.com.au; 85 McAdams Lane, Bellarine; ☺ noon-3pm daily, from 6pm Fri & Sat) Come to this boutique winery for stunning bay views enjoyed from its deck with a glass of its pinot and a bowl of mussels.

Flying Brick Cider Co. (☑ 03-5250 6577; www.flyingbrickciderco.com.au; 1251-1269 Bellarine Hwy, Wallington; tasting paddles $13; ☺ bar 10am-5pm Sun-Thu, 10am-late Fri & Sat, restaurant noon-3pm Mon-Thu, noon-3 & 6-9pm Fri & Sat, noon-4pm Sun) A popular stop along the highway is this cider house that produces a range of quality apple and pear alcoholic ciders, enjoyed on its grassy outdoor area.

Basils Farm (☑ 03-5258 4280; www.basilsfarm.com.au; 43-53 Nye Rd, Swan Bay; ☺ 10am-5pm Fri-Sun, daily in Jan) Enjoy a bottle of prosecco and a produce platter while enjoying fabulous views of Swan Bay.

Terindah Estate (☑ 03-5251 5536; www.terindahestate.com; 90 McAdams Lane, Bellarine; mains $26-38; ☺ 10am-4pm) Another winery with incredible views, quality pinots and fine dining in its glasshouse shed.

Drysdale Cheeses (☑ 0437 816 374; www.drysdalecheeses.com; 2140 Portarlington Rd, Bellarine; ☺ 1-4pm 1st Sun of the month) Taste award-winning goats-milk cheese and yogurts on the first Sunday of each month.

Manzanillo Olive Grove (☑ 03-5251 3621, 0438 513 621; www.manzanillogrove.com.au; 150 Whitcombes Rd, Drysdale; ☺ 11am-4.30pm Sat & Sun) Dunk bread into samples of cold-pressed extra virgin and chilli-infused olive oils.

Little Mussel Cafe (☑ 03-5259 1377; www.advancemussel.com.au; 230-250 Queenscliff Rd, Portarlington; mains $16-28; ☺ 10am-5pm Fri-Sun) The place to sample local mussels and oysters, served as chowder, in bowls of tomato and chilli, or on tasting plates.

WWI submarines. Also does snorkel trips and dive lessons.

★ Festivals & Events

Queenscliff Music Festival   MUSIC
(☑ 03-5258 4816; www.qmf.net.au; ☺ last weekend Nov) One of the coast's best festivals features big-name Australian and international musos with a folksy, bluesy bent.

🛏 Sleeping

Queenscliff Dive Centre   HOSTEL $
(☑ 03-5258 4188; www.divevictoria.com.au; 37 Learmonth St; dm divers/nondivers $30/40, s/d $100/120; 🛜🐾) While this hostel-style accommodation is primarily for divers, if there

are rooms available it's a good option for budget travellers too. The modern shared kitchen and lounge facilities are bright and airy, while the simple rooms are out the back. It's BYO linen and towels ($15 to hire). It was built in 1864 when it was used as Cobb & Co horse stables.

Twomey's Cottage   B&B $$
(☑ 0400 265 877; www.classiccottages.com.au; 13 St Andrews St; d $110-140) Just the place to soak up Queenscliff's historical atmosphere, this heritage cottage is fantastic value. Its claim to fame is as the residence of Fred Williams when he painted his Queenscliff series, plus renowned recitalist Keith Humble composed music here, so creative vibes abound.

★ Vue Grand
HOTEL $$$

(☑ 03-5258 1544; www.vuegrand.com.au; 46 Hesse St; r incl breakfast $178-258; ❀ ☎) One of Queenscliff's most elegant historic buildings, the Vue has everything from standard pub rooms to its modern turret suite (boasting 360-degree views) and bay-view rooms (with freestanding baths in the lounge).

Athelstane House
BOUTIQUE HOTEL $$$

(☑ 03-5258 1024; www.athelstane.com.au; 4 Hobson St; r incl breakfast $180-310; ❀ ☎) Dating back to 1860, double-storey Athelstane House is a beautifully kept historic building that's notable as Queenscliff's oldest guesthouse. Its rooms are spotless, and mix period touches with modern comforts such as corner spa baths, iPod docks, DVD players and fast wi-fi. Its front lounge is a good place to hang out, with a vintage record player and a stack of vinyl.

✗ Eating & Drinking

Shelter Shed
CAFE $$

(☑ 03-5258 3604; www.sheltershedqueenscliff.com. au; 25 Hesse St; dishes $15-30; ☺ 8am-3pm; ☎) Within a wonderful light-filled space with a glowing fire in winter, and an inviting garden courtyard for sunny days, this is a great choice for breakfast or lunch. It's popular for the Asian eggs on jasmine rice with abalone sauce, and its prawn watercress roll with dill mayo. There's plenty of grilled seafood and meat dishes too.

360 Q
INTERNATIONAL $$

(☑ 03-5257 4200; www.360q.com.au; 2 Wharf St; breakfast from $15, lunch from $18, dinner $26-39; ☺ 8am-4pm daily, 6-9pm Fri & Sat) Undoubtedly one of Queenscliff's best restaurants, 360 Q features wonderful views overlooking the picturesque marina. It does an original breakfast menu and some light lunch options such as a Vietnamese pork bánh mì, while for dinner try its fragrant chilli-tomato Portarlington mussels with crusty bread.

Athelstane House
MODERN AUSTRALIAN $$$

(☑ 03-5258 1024; www.athelstane.com.au; 4 Hobson St; breakfast $14-22, mains $30-38; ☺ 8-10am & 6-8pm) Come for breakfast or dinner inside this lovely heritage home, or outside on the pretty garden deck. For dinner choose from a daily seasonal menu that may include chargrilled eye fillet or tempura battered fish. In the morning they do homemade oven-baked muesli as well as the usual hot breakfasts.

Vue Grand Dining Room
MODERN AUSTRALIAN $$$

(☑ 03-5258 1544; www.vuegrand.com.au; 46 Hesse St; 2-/3-course meals $59/79, 5-course Bellarine tasting menu without/with wine or beers $95/149; ☺ 6-9pm Wed-Sat) The grande dame of Queenscliff dining, Vue Grand's stately dining room serves up fabulous dishes such as lamb back strap with saffron, fennel, pomegranate and whipped feta, backed up by a splendid wine and beer menu. The Bellarine tasting menu is a fine journey around the peninsula, with local-produce-heavy dishes matched with local wine or beers.

Queenscliff Brewhouse
PUB

(☑ 03-5258 1717; www.queenscliffbrewhouse.com. au; 2 Gellibrand St; ☺ 11am-1am Mon-Sat, to 11pm Sun) Prickly Moses have set up their second brewhouse here in Queenscliff, branching out from their Otways base. Their full range is showcased on tap, as well as a selection of guest brewers, best enjoyed in the beer garden.

❶ Information

Queenscliff Visitor Centre (☑ 03-5258 4843; www.queenscliff.com.au; 55 Hesse St; ☺ 9am-5pm; ☎) Plenty of brochures on the area. Also sells the self-guided walking tour map *Queenscliff – A Living Heritage*. Wi-fi and internet access next door at the library.

❶ Getting There & Away

From Melbourne, Queenscliff (and the rest of the Bellarine Peninsula) is easily accessible via the Princess Fwy (M1) to Geelong. Rather than taking the Geelong bypass, head through Geelong to the Bellarine Hwy (B110).

Queenscliff–Sorrento **ferries** (☑ 03-5257 4500; www.searoad.com.au; 1 Wharf St East, Queenscliff; one-way foot passenger adult/child $11/8, car incl driver $64, bicycle free; ☺ hourly 7am-6pm) take 40 minutes.

Queenscliff is the start or finish point of the 32.5km long **Bellarine Rail Trail** (p545), which links it with South Geelong station.

Torquay

POP 17,105

In the 1960s and '70s Torquay was just another sleepy seaside town. Back then, surfing in Australia was a decidedly countercultural pursuit, its devotees crusty hippy dropouts living in clapped-out Kombis, smoking pot and making off with your daughters. These days it's become unabashedly mainstream and the town's proximity to world-famous Bells Beach, and status as home of two iconic surf brands – Rip Curl and Quiksilver, both initially wetsuit makers – ensures Torquay's place as the undisputed capital of the Australian surf industry. It's one of Australia's fastest growing towns, experiencing a population increase of 67% between 2001 and 2013 that these days makes it feel almost like an outer suburb of Geelong.

◉ Sights & Activities

Torquay's beaches lure everyone from kids in floaties to backpacker surf-school pupils. **Fisherman's Beach**, protected from ocean swells, is the family favourite. Ringed by shady pines and sloping lawns, the **Front Beach** beckons lazy bums, while surf life-savers patrol the frothing **Back Beach** during summer. Famous surf beaches nearby include Jan Juc, Winki Pop and, of course, **Bells Beach** (Great Ocean Rd).

★ Australian National Surfing Museum   MUSEUM
(☑ 03-5261 4606; www.surfworld.com.au; 77 Beach Rd, Surf City Plaza; adult/child/family $12/8/25; ⊙ 9am-5pm) The perfect starting point for those embarking on a surfing safari is this well-curated museum that pays homage to Australian surfing. Here you'll see Simon Anderson's groundbreaking 1981 thruster, Mark Richard's awesome airbrushed board art collection and, most notably, Australia's Surfing Hall of Fame. It's full of great memorabilia (including Duke Kahanamoku's wooden longboard), videos and displays on surf culture through the 1960s to the '80s.

Surfing

Go Ride a Wave   SURFING
(☑ 03-5261 3616, 1300 132 441; www.gorideawave.com.au; 1/15 Bell St; 2hr lessons from adult/child $69/59) Offers lessons for surfing, SUP and kayaking, and hires boards, too. They run camps along the Great Ocean Road and Bellarine Peninsula. Rates are cheaper with advance booking.

Torquay Surf Academy   SURFING
(☑ 03-5261 2022; www.torquaysurf.com.au; 34a Bell St; 2hr group/private lessons $60/180) Offers surf lessons for groups or one-on-one. Also hires surfboards (from $25), SUPs (from $35), body-boards ($20) and wetsuits ($10), as well as bikes (from $20).

🛏 Sleeping

Bells Beach Backpackers   HOSTEL $
(☑ 03-5261 4029; www.bellsbeachbackpackers.com.au; 51-53 Surfcoast Hwy; van s/d $20/24, dm/d from $32/80; @ 🖥) On the main highway in Torquay (not Bells Beach) is this friendly backpackers, which does a great job of fitting into the fabric of this surf town. It has a casual, homely atmosphere with basic rooms that are clean and in good nick, and a large kitchen that 'van packers' can also use.

Torquay Foreshore Caravan Park   CAMPGROUND $
(☑ 03-5261 2496; www.torquaycaravanpark.com.au; 35 Bell St; powered sites $37-89, d cabins $109-295, 2-bedroom units $190-395; 🖥) Just behind the Back Beach is the largest camping ground on the Surf Coast. It has good facilities and premium-priced cabins with sea views. The wi-fi is in the camp kitchen only.

Beachside Accommodation   APARTMENT $$
(☑ 0419 587 445; www.beachsideaccommodationtorquay.com.au; 24 Felix Cres; d $110-160; ❄ 🖥) Only a five-minute stroll to the beach is this relaxed residential-style accommodation owned by a German-English couple, where you'll get a private patio with BBQ and an Aussie backyard atmosphere.

✕ Eating & Drinking

Bottle of Milk   BURGERS $
(☑ 03-5264 8236; www.thebottleofmilk.com; 24 Bell St; burgers from $10; ⊙ noon-9pm) Trading off the success of its **Lorne branch** (☑ 03-5289 2005; 52 Mountjoy Pde; burgers $11-18; ⊙ 8am-8pm), Bottle of Milk's winning formula of burgers, beaches and beers makes it rightfully popular. Inside is decked out with booth seating, polished floorboards and tiled walls, or head out to its beer garden with an open fireplace. Good coffee, too.

Cafe Moby   CAFE $
(☑ 03-5261 2339; 41 The Esplanade; mains $12-18; ⊙ 6.30am-3pm; 🖥 👶) This old weatherboard house on the Esplanade harks back to a time when Torquay was simple, which is not to say its meals aren't modern: fill up on a pork belly burger, wood-fired pizza or honey-roasted lamb souvlaki. There's a whopping great playground out the back for kids, and a little bar out the front doing Forrest brewery beers.

★ **Bomboras Kiosk** CAFE $$
(www.bomboras.com.au; 48 The Esplanade, Fisherman's Beach; meals $5-22; ☺7.30am-5pm) Right on the sand, this is just the place for hungry beachgoers to recharge their batteries with homemade sausage rolls, cakes, salads, milkshakes or locally roasted coffee. During the summer they open the rooftop bar with local brews, ciders, DJs and prime ocean views.

Fisho's SEAFOOD $$
(☑0474342124;www.facebook.com/fishostorquay; 36 The Esplanade; mains from $19; ☺noon-3pm & 5-8pm) Not your average fish and chip shop, instead this oceanfront joint does an original take on the classics such as tempura flake, zesty lime shark popcorn and sweet potato cakes. It's set up on the waterfront in an atmospheric weatherboard house with AstroTurf front seating, and local beers and cider on tap.

★ **Blackman's Brewery** MICROBREWERY
(☑03-5261 5310; www.blackmansbrewery.com.au; 26 Bell St; ☺noon-10pm Wed-Sun, daily in summer) One of Vic's best microbreweries is this brewpub where you can taste all eight of Blackman's beers, which are produced onsite. Go the tasting paddle ($16) to enjoy its range of IPAs, unfiltered lager, pale ale and porters for a roaring fire or in the AstroTurf beer garden. They've also got a smoker for BBQ meats, pizzas and platters. Swing by at 4pm for a free brewery tour.

🛍 Shopping

Rip Curl Surf
Factory Outlet FASHION & ACCESSORIES
(Baines Seconds; 16 Baines Cres; ☺9am-5.30pm) Rips Curl's shiny main outlet is in the Surf City Plaza, but head round the back to the industrial estate for Rip Curl's factory outlet, where you'll get 30% off the price of last season's clothing and wetsuits. A big-name global brand these days, Rip Curl was founded here in Torquay in 1969.

ℹ Information

Torquay Visitor Information Centre (www. greatoceanroad.org; Surf City Plaza, Beach Rd; ☺9am-5pm) The well-resourced tourist office next to the Australian National Surfing Museum makes a good starting point along the Great Ocean Road to fine tune your itinerary. There's free wi-fi and internet available at the library next door.

ℹ Getting There & Away

Torquay is 15 minutes' drive south of Geelong on the B100.

McHarry's Buslines (p544) runs an hourly bus (No 51) from 9am to 8pm (around 5pm weekends) from Geelong to Torquay ($3.20, 40 minutes).

V/Line (p544) buses run four times daily Monday to Friday (two on weekends) from Geelong to Torquay ($3.20, 25 minutes).

Torquay to Anglesea

The Great Ocean Road officially begins on the stretch between Torquay and Anglesea. A slight detour takes you to famous **Bells Beach**, the powerful point break that is part of international surfing folklore; it has hosted Australia's premier surfing event, the Bells Classic (now the Rip Curl Pro), since 1973. (It was here too, in name only, that Keanu Reeves and Patrick Swayze had their ultimate showdown in the film *Point Break*.

Around 3km away, on the outskirts of Torquay, is the surf town of **Jan Juc**, a local hang-out for surfers, with a mellow, sleepy vibe. Nine kilometres southwest of Torquay is the turn-off to spectacular **Point Addis**, a vast sweep of pristine clothing-optional beach that attracts surfers, nudists, hang-gliders and swimmers, as well as those embarking on the recommended Koorie Cultural Walk.

🏃 Activities

Koorie Cultural Walk WALKING
A highly recommended detour signposted off the Great Ocean Road is the fantastic Koorie Cultural Walk, a 2km trail that details how the Indigenous Wathaurung people lived here for millennia. It's a lovely bushwalk through the Great Otway National Park, with echidnas and wallabies, and spectacular coastal outlooks of dramatic cliffs and pristine beaches, including the lovely **Addiscott Beach**.

Surf Coast Walk WALKING
(www.surfcoastwalk.com.au) This epic walk follows the scenic coastline for 30km from Torquay to Moggs Creek, just outside Aireys Inlet. The full route takes 11 hours, but if you don't have that much time, it's also divided into 12 distinct walks, each of which cover a good variety of landscapes.

ⓘ GREAT OCEAN ROAD TOURS

Go West Tours (☑03-9485 5290; www.gowest.com.au; tours $130) Melbourne-based company offering full-day tours taking in Bells Beach, koalas in the Otways, the Twelve Apostles and around, before returning to Melbourne. Free wi-fi on bus.

Otway Discovery Tour (☑03-9629 5844; www.greatoceanroadtour.com.au; 1/2/3-day tours $109/289/380) Very affordable Great Ocean Road tours. The two-day tours include Phillip Island, while the three-day version takes in the Grampians.

Ride Tours (☑1800 605 120, 0427 180 357; www.ridetours.com.au; tours $210) Two-day, one-night minibus trips along the Great Ocean Road. Rates include dorm accommodation and meals.

🎉 Festivals & Events

Rip Curl Pro   SURFING
(www.aspworldtour.com; ⊙Easter) Since 1973, Bells has hosted the Rip Curl Pro every Easter long weekend. The world championship ASP tour event draws thousands to watch the world's best surfers carve up the big autumn swells, where waves have reached 5m during the contest! The Rip Curl Pro occasionally decamps to Johanna Beach, two hours west, when fickle Bells isn't working.

Anglesea

POP 2653

Mix sheer orange cliffs falling into the ocean with hilly, tree-filled 'burbs and a population that booms in summer and you've got Anglesea, where sharing fish and chips with seagulls by the Anglesea River is a decades-long family tradition for many.

🏃 Activities

Anglesea Golf Club   GOLF
(☑03-5263 1582; www.angleseagolfclub.com.au; Golf Links Rd; 20min kangroo tours adult/child $10/5, 9/18 holes from $25/45, club hire 9/18 holes $25/35; ⊙10am-4pm Mon-Fri) Here you can watch kangaroos graze on the fairways on an organised tour, or, even better, pair your sightings with a round of golf. If you don't

want to do a tour, you'll be able to spot kangaroos from the road.

Go Ride a Wave   SURFING
(☑03-5263 2111, 1300 132 441; www.gorideawave.com.au; 143b Great Ocean Rd; 2hr lessons adult/child from $69/59, 2hr board hire from $25; ⊙9am-5pm) Long-established surf school that runs lessons and hires out boards, SUPs and kayaks.

🛌 Sleeping

Anglesea Backpackers   HOSTEL $
(☑03-5263 2664; www.angleseabackpackers.com; 40 Noble St; dm $30-35, d/f $115/150; @🛜) While most hostels like to cram 'em in, this simple, homely backpackers has just two dorm rooms and one double/triple, and is clean, bright and welcoming. In winter the fire glows warmly in the cosy living room. There are free bikes for guests and the owner can pick you up from town or as far away as Torquay.

Anglesea Beachfront
Family Caravan Park   CAMPGROUND $
(☑03-5263 1583; www.angleseabeachfront.com.au; 35 Cameron Rd; powered sites $38-86, d cabins $110-271; @🛜🏊) Beach- and riverfront caravan park with a pool, wi-fi, two camp kitchens, a jumping pillow, an indoor spa and a games room.

🍴 Eating

Coffetti Gelato   GELATO $
(☑0434 274 781; www.facebook.com/coffettigelato; Shop 4, 87-89 Great Ocean Rd, Anglesea Shopping Village; cups from $4; ⊙8am-6pm, to 9.30pm in summer) Run by an Italian-Aussie husband-wife team is this authentic gelateria doing a range of delicious homemade flavours as well as popsicles, granitas and Ugandan coffee. It's just outside the entrance of the supermarket.

Maids Pantry   CAFE $
(☑03-5263 1420; 119 Great Ocean Rd; breakfasts & sandwiches from $8; ⊙7am-5pm) Across from the Anglesea River is this bright, rustic cafe that doubles as a provedore general store stocking a good selection of local produce. It has a wide selection of sandwiches, sliders, pies and brunch specials, and has garden seating round the back.

McGain's Cafe   CAFE $
(☑03-5263 3841; www.mcgains.com.au; 1 Simmons Ct; dishes from $7; ⊙cafe 8.30am-3pm, shop to 5pm; 🛜) 🌿 Snack among the foliage at this

lovely sunlit cafe with an atrium nursery locale. The menu is largely organic using produce from their attached foodstore. As well as delicious breakfasts and lunches, it does great single-origin coffee roasted by Cartel in Geelong. It's left off the Great Ocean Road before you hit the Anglesea shops.

Captain Moonlite   MODERN AUSTRALIAN **$$**
(📞 03-5263 2454; www.captainmoonlite.com.au; 100 Great Ocean Rd; mains from $25; ⏰ 8am-10pm Fri-Sun, 8am-4pm Mon, 5-10pm Thu) Sharing space with the Anglesea Surf Life Saving Club – with unbeatable views over the beach – Captain Moonlite mixes unpretentious decor with a quality, highly seasonal menu, which it describes as 'coastal European'. Expect tasty breakfasts such as ocean trout and soft-boiled egg on rye, mezze-style plates and mains such as slow-roasted lamb and fresh seafood.

ℹ️ Information

Anglesea Visitor Information Centre (www.visitgreatoceanroad.org.au; Great Ocean Rd; ⏰ 9am-5pm; 🐾) Located at the lake, this information centre has a heap of brochures for the area, including walks in the surrounding national park.

ℹ️ Getting There & Away

There are four to six daily V/Line buses to/from Geelong to Anglesea ($6.40, 45 minutes) on weekdays, and two departures on weekends.

The Geelong bypass has reduced the time it takes to drive from Melbourne to Anglesea to around 75 minutes.

Aireys Inlet

POP 1071

Midway between Anglesea and Lorne, Aireys Inlet is an attractive coastal hamlet with a tight-knit community of locals and sea-changers, plus plenty of holidaymakers. It's home to a historic lighthouse which forms the backdrop to glorious stretches of beach, including **Fairhaven** and **Moggs Creek**. Ask at the Anglesea visitor centre for brochures on the great coastal walks around here.

⊙ Sights & Activities

The lovely 3.5km **Aireys Inlet Cliff Walk** begins at Painkalac Creek, rounds Split Point and makes its way to Sunnymead Beach. The Surf Coast Walk (p549) continues along the coast here – pick up a copy of *Walks of Lorne & Aireys Inlet* from visitor centres.

⭐**Split Point Lighthouse**   LIGHTHOUSE
(📞 1800 174 045, 03-5263 1133; www.splitpointlighthouse.com.au; Federal St; 45min tours adult/child/family $14/8/40; ⏰ tours hourly 11am-2pm, summer holidays 10am-5pm) Scale the 136 steps to the top of the beautiful 'White Queen' lighthouse for sensational 360-degree views. Built in 1891, the 34m-high lighthouse is still operational (though now fully automated). During off-peak times a tour guide will accompany you to the top, whereas in summer it's run as a self-guided tour with staff on hand to answer questions.

Blazing Saddles   HORSE RIDING
(📞 0418 528 647, 03-5289 7322; www.blazingsaddlestrailrides.com; Lot 1 Bimbadeen Dr; per person 1¼hr bush rides from $50, 2½hr beach & bush rides $115) People come from around the world to hop on a Blazing Saddles horse and head along stunning Fairhaven Beach or into the bush.

🛏️ Sleeping

Inlet Caravan Park   CABIN **$**
(📞 03-5289 6230; www.aicp.com.au; 19-25 Great Ocean Rd; powered sites $39, cabins d $105-280; @🐾♨) More cabin town than tent city, this neat park is close to the township's few shops.

⭐**Cimarron B&B**   B&B **$$**
(📞 03-5289 7044; www.cimarron.com.au; 105 Gilbert St; d $125-225; 🐾) Built in 1979 from local timbers and using only wooden pegs and shiplap joins, Cimarron is an idyllic getaway with views over Point Roadknight. The large lounge area has book-lined walls and a cosy fireplace, while upstairs are two unique, loft-style doubles with vaulted timber ceilings; otherwise there's a denlike apartment. Out back, it's all state park and wildlife. Two-night minimum stay.

Gay friendly, but no kids.

Pole House   RENTAL HOUSE **$$$**
(📞 03-5220 0200; www.greatoceanroadholidays.com.au; 60 Banool Rd, Fairhaven; from $470) One of the most iconic houses along the Great Ocean Road, the Pole House is a unique architectural piece that, as the name suggests, sits atop a pole, with extraordinary ocean views. Access to the house is via an external pedestrian bridge.

✕ Eating & Drinking

Willows Tea House CAFE $

(☑ 03-5289 6830; 7 Federal St; scones $4, breakfast from $8; ◷ 9am-5pm; 🅰) Soak up Aireys' seafaring atmosphere at this teahouse set up within a historic weatherboard cottage a few steps from the lighthouse. Stop by for morning or afternoon tea to indulge in homemade scones with jam and cream, enjoyed in its cosy interior or at outdoor tables.

Captain of Aireys PIZZA $$

(☑ 03-5297 4024; www.thecaptainofaireys.com. au; 81 Great Ocean Rd; pizzas $15-25; ◷ 11am-8pm Thu-Sun, longer hours in summer) Named after a local seafaring character who resided in the area during the early 20th century is this popular pizzeria doing authentic Neapolitan-style wood-fired pizzas.

★ á la grecque GREEK $$$

(☑ 03-5289 6922; www.alagrecque.com.au; 60 Great Ocean Rd; mains $28-40; ◷ noon-3pm & 6-9.30pm Wed-Sun Aug-Dec, noon-3pm & 6-9.30pm daily Dec-Apr, closed May-Jul) Be whisked away to the Mediterranean at this outstanding modern Greek taverna. Mezze such as seared scallops or braised cuttlefish with apple, celery and a lime dressing, and mains such as grilled pork shoulder, are sensational. So is the wine list.

★ Aireys Pub MICROBREWERY

(☑ 03-5289 6804; www.aireyspub.com.au; 45 Great Ocean Rd; pots from $5; ◷ 11.30am-late; 🅰) Established in 1904, this pub is a survivor, twice burning to the ground before closing its doors in 2011, only to be revived by the efforts of a bunch of locals chipping in to save it. Now it's better than ever, with an on-site brewery, **Rogue Wave**, to go with its fantastic kitchen (mains $20 to $34), meat smoker, roaring fire, live music and sprawling beer garden.

❶ Getting There & Away

From Melbourne count on around a 1¾-hour drive for the 123km trip to Aireys Inlet, and a bit longer if you're heading via Torquay (27km, 25 minutes).

Departing from Geelong Station, V/Line has four to six daily buses (two on weekends) to Aireys Inlet ($8.80, one hour), which continue on to nearby stops at Fairhaven, Moggs Creek and Eastern View for the same fare.

Lorne

POP 1046

One of the Great Ocean Road's original resort towns, Lorne may be a tad overdeveloped these days but it still retains all the charms that have lured visitors here since the 19th century. Beyond its main strip it has an incredible natural beauty: tall old gum trees line its hilly streets, and Loutit Bay gleams irresistibly. It gets busy; in summer you'll be competing with day trippers for restaurant seats and lattes, but, thronged by tourists or not, it's a lovely place to hang out.

◉ Sights & Activities

★ Qdos Art Gallery GALLERY

(☑ 03-5289 1989; www.qdosarts.com; 35 Allenvale Rd; ◷ 9am-5pm Thu-Mon, daily Jan) **FREE** Amid the lush forest that backs on to Lorne, Qdos always has something interesting showing at its contemporary gallery, to go with its open-air sculpture garden. There's also a lovely little cafe doing wood-fired pizzas and *ryokan*-style accommodation.

Great Ocean Road Story MUSEUM

(15 Mountjoy Pde; ◷ 9am-5pm) **FREE** Set up inside the Lorne Visitor Centre is this permanent exhibition of displays, videos and books that offer an informative background to the interesting history of the Great Ocean Road's construction.

Erskine Falls WATERFALL

(Erskine Falls Access Rd) Head out of town to see this lovely waterfall. It's an easy walk to the viewing platform, or 250 (often slippery) steps down to its base, from where you can explore further or head back on up.

✦✦ Festivals & Events

Falls Festival MUSIC

(www.fallsfestival.com; 2-/3-/4-day tickets $249/ 299/339; ◷ 28 Dec – 1 Jan) A four-day knees-up over New Year's on a farm just out of town, this stellar music festival attracts a top line-up of international rock and indie groups. Past headliners include Iggy Pop, Kings of Leon and the Black Keys. Sells out fast (within an hour); tickets include camping.

🛏 Sleeping

Big Hill Track CAMPGROUND $

(☑ 13 1963; www.parkweb.vic.gov.au; 1265 Deans Marsh-Lorne Rd, Benwerrin) A good option for backpackers with tents or a van is this free camping ground located 15km north of Lorne, along the road heading to Birregurra. You'll need to chance your luck, however, as there are no bookings, with the 12 sites filled on a first-come, first-served basis.

Lorne Foreshore Caravan Park
CAMPGROUND **$**

(☑ 03-5289 1382; www.lornecaravanpark.com.au; 2 Great Ocean Rd; unpowered sites $28-55, powered sites $37-89, d cabins $97-189; ☎) Book at the Foreshore Caravan Park for all of Lorne's five caravan parks. Of the five, **Erskine River Caravan Park**, where the booking office is located, is the prettiest, though note there's no swimming in the river. It's on the left-hand side as you enter Lorne, just before the bridge. Book well ahead for peak-season stays. Wi-fi in reception only.

★ Qdos
RYOKAN **$$$**

(☑ 03-5289 1989; www.qdosarts.com; 35 Allenvale Rd; r incl breakfast from $300; ☎) The perfect choice for those seeking a romantic getaway or forest retreat, Qdos' luxury Zen tree houses are fitted with tatami mats, rice-paper screens and no TV. Two-night minimum; no kids.

✖ Eating

HAH
CAFE **$**

(Health and Hire; ☑ 0437 759 469, 0406 453 131; www.hahlornebeach.com.au; 81 Mountjoy Pde; mains from $8; ☉ 8.30am-5pm, longer hours in summer; ☎) Keep that beach body in check and head down to this health-conscious cafe with a prime location on the foreshore. Its menu is loaded with superfoods, protein balls, salads and leafy smoothies, as well as gourmet toasties and homebaked banana bread drizzled with Lorne honey.

Swing Bridge Cafe & Boathouse
CAFE **$**

(☑ 0423 814 770; 30 Great Ocean Rd; meals $10-16; ☉ 8am-2.30pm Fri-Mon, daily in summer) This tiny cafe overlooking the water at the historic swing bridge (c 1934) has an appealing retro beach vibe. It's the place for single-origin coffee, to go with its range of brioches filled with anything from pulled pork and beef brisket to jerk tofu with salsa verde. On summer evenings they do Argentinian-style charcoal barbecues or paella on the lawn.

★ Lorne Beach Pavilion
MODERN AUSTRALIAN **$$**

(☑ 03-5289 2882; www.lornebeachpavilion.com.au; 81 Mountjoy Pde; breakfast $9-23, mains $19-45; ☉ 9am-5pm Mon-Thu, 9am-9pm Fri, 8am-9pm

---

GREAT OCEAN ROAD CHOCOLATERIE & ICE CREAMERY

A sure way to placate those backseat nags of 'are we there yet?' is the roadside **Great Ocean Road Chocolaterie & Ice Creamery** (☑ 03-5263 1588; www.gorci.com.au; 1200 Great Ocean Rd, Bellbrae; ☉ 9am-5pm) , located 11km outside Anglesea. It's a massive site that makes all of its own truffles and chocolates (try its bush-tucker range), as well as 20 flavours of ice cream. There's an on-site cafe, and chocolate-making courses (from $40) most Saturdays; book online.

Sat & Sun) With its location on the foreshore, life here is a beach, especially with a cold drink in hand. Cafe-style breakfasts and lunches hit the spot, while a more upmarket Modern Australian menu of seafood and rib-eye steaks is on for dinner. Come at happy hour for $7 pints, or otherwise swing by at sunset for a bottle of prosecco.

Ipsos
GREEK **$$**

(☑ 03-5289 1883; www.ipsosrestaurant.com.au; 48 Mountjoy Pde; sharing plates $5-29; ☉ noon-3pm & 6-10pm Thu-Mon, longer hours in summer) From the same family that ran Kosta (a Lorne institution that's relocated to Aireys Inlet) comes this smart, casual taverna that's opened in the exact same location where it all started in 1974. Run by the sons, the menu comprises mainly Greek-influenced sharing plates, or you can go its signature slow-roasted lamb shoulder ($66 for two).

ⓘ Information

Lorne Visitor Centre (☑ 03-5289 1152, 1300 891 152; www.lovelorne.com.au; 15 Mountjoy Pde; ☉ 9am-5pm; ☎) Stacks of information (including heaps of ideas for walks in the area), helpful staff, fishing licences, bus tickets and accommodation referrals. Also has a gift shop, internet access, free wi-fi and a charger out the front for electric cars.

ⓘ Getting There & Away

V/Line (p544) buses pass through daily from Geelong ($11.60, 1½ hours) en route to Apollo Bay ($5, from one hour).

If driving from Melbourne allow just under two hours for the 143km journey.

Wye River

POP 140

The Great Ocean Road snakes spectacularly around the cliff-side from Cumberland River before reaching this little town with big ideas. Unfortunately on Christmas Day in 2015, major bush fires destroyed some 116 homes in the area, and the entire town was evacuated; fortunately no deaths were recorded.

🛏 Sleeping & Eating

Big4 Wye River Holiday Park CAMPGROUND $
(www.big4wyeriver.com.au; 25 Great Ocean Rd; unpowered sites $30-45, powered sites $38-50, cabins $120-185, houses $310-395; ✳@) Just back from the beach is this popular caravan park, which sprawls over 10 hectares. Featuring an Otways forest backdrop, its grassy sites are great for camping, and there's a range of comfortable units.

**Wye River Foreshore
Camping Reserve** CAMPGROUND $
(☑03-5289 0412; sites $40; ⊙Nov-Apr) This camping ground offers powered beachside sites during summer.

★**Wye Beach Hotel** PUB FOOD $$
(☑03-5289 0240; www.wyebeachhotel.com.au; 19 Great Ocean Rd; mains from $27; ⊙11.30am-11pm; 🛜) Undoubtedly one of the best coastal pubs in Victoria, if not Australia – the ocean views just don't get much better than this. It has an unpretentious, local vibe and an all-regional craft-beer selection on tap – with brews from Forrest, Torquay and Aireys Inlet. There's pub food too, though it's a bit on the pricey side.

Wye General CAFE $$
(☑03-5289 0247; www.thewyegeneral.com; 35 Great Ocean Rd; mains $15-26; ⊙8am-5pm Mon-Sat, to 4pm Sun) This well-loved general store does provisions and groceries; however it's most noteworthy for its smart indoor-outdoor cafe/bar. Polished concrete floors, timber features and a sophisticated retro ambience, it does old-fashioned cocktails, beer on tap and a menu of breakfasts, burgers and sourdough toasties made in-house.

❶ Getting There & Away

There are several buses a day here from Geelong ($14.40, two hours).

Wye River is located 159km from Melbourne, around a 2½-hour drive. It's positioned approximately halfway between Lorne and Apollo Bay on the Great Ocean Road.

Kennett River

Located 25km east of Apollo Bay is Kennett River, which has some great koala spotting just behind the caravan park. There are also glow worms that shine at night up the same stretch of Grey River Rd (take a torch).

The friendly bush **Kennett River Holiday Park** (☑03-5289 0272, 1300 664417; www.kennettriver.com; 1-13 Great Ocean Rd; unpowered sites $31-58, powered sites $37-68, d cabins from $115; 🛜) is one of the best sites along the coast, equally popular with surfers, families, travellers and young couples.

Kennett River is located directly on the Great Ocean Road, 165km from Melbourne. It's a 30-minute drive to Lorne. From Geelong there are three buses a day ($16, two hours).

Apollo Bay

POP 1095

One of the larger towns along the Great Ocean Road, Apollo Bay has a tight-knit community of fisherfolk, artists, musicians and sea changers. Rolling hills provide a postcard backdrop to the town, while broad, white-sand beaches dominate the foreground. It's

---

DON'T MISS

BRAE

Regarded as one of Australia's best restaurants, **Brae** (☑03-5236 2226; www.braerestaurant.com; 4285 Cape Otway Rd, Birregurra; 8-course tasting plates per person $190-220, plus matched wines $125; ⊙noon-3pm Fri-Mon & from 6pm Thu-Sat) 🌿 was set up in 2012 by owner-chef Dan Hunter, who mostly uses whatever is growing in its 12 hectares of organic gardens to create some delightful gastronomic concoctions. For good reason it's a regular on the list of the World's Best 100 Restaurants. Reservations are essential, and need to be made well in advance. It's located only a 30-minute drive from Lorne in the picturesque town of Birregurra.

FORREST

Tucked away in the hinterland of the Otways, a 30-minute drive from Apollo Bay, the former logging town of Forrest has emerged as one of the new tourist hotspots in the Otways.

Since the closure of the logging industry, it has reinvented itself as one of the best mountain biking destinations in the state. Parks Victoria and the Department of Environment and Primary Industries (DEPI) have opened 16 cross-country trails (adding up to more than 50km) – ranging from beginner to highly advanced. Grab a trail map (www.rideforrest.com.au/trails) from the **Corner Store** (www.thecornerstoreforrest.com.au; cnr Blundy & Station Sts, Forrest; bike hire half-/full day $75/95; ⊘9am-4pm Mon-Thu, 8am-5pm Fri-Sun).

Located 7km from Forrest is scenic **Lake Elizabeth**, famous for its population of platypuses and surreal scenery of dead trees jutting from its glassy water. **Otway Eco Tours** (☑0419 670 985; www.platypustours.net.au; adult/child $85/50) runs guided canoe trips at dusk and dawn to spot platypuses.

The town is also very well known for its microbrewery, the **Forrest Brewing Company** (☑03-5236 6170; www.forrestbrewing.com.au; 26 Grant St, Forrest; 6-beer tasting pallets $12, pots/pints from $5.50/10; ⊘9am-5pm Sun-Wed, to 11pm Thu-Sat, daily Dec-Jan), where you can sample eight different beers brewed on-site and dig into quality pub meals.

For food, **Bespoke Harvest** (☑03-5236 6446; www.bespokeharvest.com.au; 16 Grant St, Forrest; set menu $65; ⊘noon-2.30pm Fri-Mon, 6-8pm Fri & Sat) 🍴 is bringing people into town with its highly seasonal, contemporary Med-inspired cuisine, most of which is sourced from its kitchen garden.

also an ideal base for exploring magical Cape Otway (p556) and Otway National Park. It has some of the best restaurants along the coast and several lively pubs, and is one of the best towns on the Great Ocean Road for budget travellers, with numerous hostels and ready transport access.

◉ Sights & Activities

Mark's Walking Tours   WALKING
(☑0417 983 985; www.greatoceanwalk.asn.au/markstours; tours $50) Take a walk around the area with local Mark Brack, son of the Cape Otway lighthouse keeper. He knows this stretch of coast, its history and its ghosts better than anyone around. Daily tours include shipwreck tours, historical tours, glow-worm tours and Great Ocean Walk treks. Minimum two people – prices drop the more people on the tour.

Apollo Bay Surf & Kayak   ADVENTURE
(☑0405 495 909; www.apollobaysurfkayak.com.au; 157-159 Great Ocean Rd; 2hr kayak tours $70, 2hr surf lessons adult/child $65/60) Head out to an Australian fur seal colony in a double kayak. Tours (with full instructions for beginners) depart from Marengo Beach (to the south of the town centre). Also offers surf and SUP lessons, plus boards and mountain bikes (half-day $30) for hire.

🛏 Sleeping

YHA Eco Beach   HOSTEL $
(☑03-5237 7899; www.yha.com.au; 5 Pascoe St; dm/d/f from $29/75/112; @🛜) 🍴 This multi-million dollar, architect-designed hostel is an outstanding place to stay, with eco-credentials, great loungeroom areas, kitchens, a boules pit and rooftop terraces. Rooms are generic but spotless. It's a block behind the beach.

Pisces Big4 Apollo Bay   CAMPGROUND $
(☑03-5237 6749; www.piscespark.com.au; 311 Great Ocean Rd; unpowered/powered sites from $34/42, cabins from $99; 🛜☒) It's the unbeatable views from the oceanfront villas (from $190) that set this family-oriented park apart from the others.

★ Beacon Point
Ocean View Villas   VILLA $$$
(☑03-5237 6218, 03-5237 6411; www.beaconpoint.com.au; 270 Skenes Creek Rd; r incl breakfast $200-350; ☒🛜) With a commanding hill location among the trees, this wonderful collection of comfortable one- and two-bedroom villas is a luxurious yet affordable bush retreat. Most villas have sensational coast views, balcony and wood-fired heater. There's also a popular restaurant

WALKING THE GREAT OCEAN ROAD

The superb multiday **Great Ocean Walk** (www.greatoceanwalk.com.au) starts at Apollo Bay and runs all the way to the Twelve Apostles. It takes you through changing landscapes along spectacular clifftops, deserted beaches and forested Otway National Park.

It's possible to start at one point and arrange a pickup at another (public transport options are few and far between). You can do shorter walks or the whole 104km trek over eight days. Designated camp sites are spread along the Great Ocean Walk catering for registered walkers only; bring cooking equipment and tents (no fires allowed). Otherwise there are plenty of comfortable accommodation options from luxury lodges to caravan parks. Check out the helpful FAQ page on the website for all the info.

Walk 91 (☑03-5237 1189; www.walk91.com.au; 157-159 Great Ocean Rd, Apollo Bay; 3 day/4 night guided walks per person $800) can arrange your itinerary, transport and equipment hire, and can shuttle your backpack to your destination.

✖ Eating & Drinking

★ Chris's Beacon Point Restaurant
GREEK $$$

(☑03-5237 6411; www.chriss.com.au; 280 Skenes Creek Rd; mains from $34; ☺6pm-late daily, plus noon-2pm Sat & Sun; 🛜) Feast on memorable ocean views, deliciously fresh seafood and Greek-influenced dishes at Chris's hilltop fine-dining sanctuary among the treetops. Reservations recommended. You can also stay in its wonderful stilted villas (p555). It's accessed via Skenes Creek.

La Bimba
MODERN AUSTRALIAN $$$

(☑03-5237 7411; www.labimba.com.au; 125 Great Ocean Rd; mains $36-42; ☺8.30am-3pm & 5.30-9.30pm Wed-Mon) This upstairs Mod Oz restaurant is worth the splurge. It's a warm, relaxed smart-casual restaurant with ocean views and a good wine list. Try the chilli Portarlington mussels or the local lamb.

★ Great Ocean Road Brewhouse
MICROBREWERY

(☑03-5237 6240; www.greatoceanroadbrewhouse. com.au; 29 Great Ocean Rd; pots $5; ☺pub 11am-11pm Mon-Thu, to 1am Fri & Sat, Tastes of the Region noon-8pm Mon-Thu, noon-9pm Fri, 10am-9pm Sat, 10am-8pm Sun) Set up by renowned Otways brewery Prickly Moses, this new taphouse pours an impressive range of ales. It's divided into two entities: the front bar is more your classic pub and bistro with pool table; while through the back is their 'Taste of the Region' room, with 16 of their beers on tap to enjoy with platters of local produce.

Hello Coffee
COFFEE

(☑0438 443 489; www.hellocoffee.com.au; 16 Oak Ave; ☺7am-3pm Mon-Fri, 9am-2pm Sat; 🛜) Set up by a couple of local mates in a backstreet industrial estate is this roaster-cafe that does the best coffee in the region. They roast single-origin beans from around the world on-site, served as V60 pourovers, Chemex, nitro cold brew or classic espresso. It has a cosy lounge-room set up, and does good breakfasts and smoked pulled-pork rolls etc.

ℹ Information

Great Ocean Road Visitor Centre (☑1300 689 297; www.visitapollobay.com; 100 Great Ocean Rd; ☺9am-5pm; 🛜) Modern and professional tourist office with a heap of info for the area, and an 'eco-centre' with displays. It has free wi-fi and can book bus tickets, too.

ℹ Getting There & Away

From Melbourne the fastest route is inland via the Geelong bypass that leads through to Birregurra and Forrest, a 200km drive. If taking the scenic route along the Great Ocean Road (highly recommended) count on a 4½-hour drive.

Apollo Bay is easily reached by public transport from Melbourne via train to Geelong and transferring to a connecting bus ($27.20, 3½ hours). There are three daily services during the week, and twice on weekends; stops include Torquay ($15.40, two hours), Anglesea ($11.20, 1¾ hours) and Lorne ($5, one hour), among others.

Cape Otway

Cape Otway is the second-most-southerly point of mainland Australia (after Wilsons Promontory) and one of the wettest parts of the state. This coastline is particularly beautiful, rugged and historically treacherous for passing ships. The turn-off for Lighthouse Rd, which leads 12km down to the lighthouse, is 21km from Apollo Bay. It's a beautiful forested road with towering trees, which are home to a sizeable population of koalas.

◎ Sights

Cape Otway Lightstation   LIGHTHOUSE
(☑03-5237 9240; www.lightstation.com; Lighthouse Rd; adult/child/family $19.50/7.50/49.50; ◷9am-5pm) Cape Otway Lightstation is the oldest surviving lighthouse on mainland Australia and was built in 1848 by more than 40 stonemasons without mortar or cement. The **Telegraph Station** has fascinating displays on the 250km undersea telegraph cable link with Tasmania, laid in 1859. It's a sprawling complex with plenty to see, from Aboriginal cultural sites to WWII bunkers.

⌅ Sleeping

★Bimbi Park   CARAVAN PARK $
(☑03-5237 9246; www.bimbipark.com.au; 90 Manna Gum Dr; unpowered sites $20-40, powered sites $25-45, dm $20, cabins $100-145; ☏) ⌀ Down a dirt road 3km from the lighthouse is this character-filled caravan park with bush sites, cabins, dorms and old-school caravans. It's a fantastic option for families, and also for hikers on the Great Ocean Walk. There's plenty of wildlife about, including koalas, plus horse rides (adult/child $65/55 per hour) and a rock-climbing wall. Good use of water-saving initiatives too.

Blanket Bay   CAMPGROUND $
(☑13 19 63; www.parkweb.vic.gov.au; sites from $28.70) Blanket Bay is one of those 'secret' camping grounds that Melburnians love to lay claim to discovering. It's serene (depending on your neighbours) and the nearby beach is beautiful. It's not really a secret; in fact it's so popular during summer and Easter holidays that it regularly books out.

★Great Ocean Ecolodge   LODGE $$$
(☑03-5237 9297; www.greatoceanecolodge.com; 635 Lighthouse Rd; r incl activities from $380; ☻) ⌀ Reminiscent of a luxury African safari lodge, this mud-brick homestead stands in pastoral surrounds with plenty of wildlife. It's all solar-powered and rates go towards the on-site **Centre for Conservation Ecology** (www.conservationecologycentre.org). It also serves as an animal hospital for local fauna and has a captive tiger quoll breeding program, which you'll visit on its dusk wildlife walk with an ecologist.

Cape Otway Lightstation   B&B $$$
(☑03-5237 9240; www.lightstation.com; Lighthouse Rd; d incl entry to lighthouse $240-450) There's a range of options at this romantic and historic windswept spot. You can book out the whole Head Lightkeeper's House (sleeps 16), or the smaller Manager's House (sleeps two). Prices are halved if you stay a second night.

Port Campbell National Park

East of the Otways, the Great Ocean Road levels out and enters narrow, flat scrubby escarpment lands that fall away to sheer, 70m-high cliffs along the coast between Princetown and Peterborough – a distinct change of scene. This is Port Campbell National Park, home to the Twelve Apostles, and the most famous and most photographed stretch of the Great Ocean Road.

None of the beaches along this stretch are suitable for swimming because of strong currents and undertows.

◎ Sights

★Twelve Apostles   LANDMARK
(Great Ocean Rd) The most iconic sight and enduring image for most visitors to the Great Ocean Road, the Twelve Apostles provide a fitting climax to the journey. Jutting out from the ocean in spectacular fashion, these rocky stacks stand as if they've been abandoned to the ocean by the retreating

---

WORTH A TRIP

OTWAY FLY

Twenty kilometres inland from the logging town of Lavers Hill on the Colac Rd (C155) is the popular **Otway Fly** (☑1800 300 477, 03-5235 9200; www.otwayfly.com; 360 Phillips Track; treetop walks adult/child $25/15, zipline tours $120/85; ◷9am-5pm, last entry 4pm). It's an elevated steel walkway suspended among the forest canopy, and includes a swaying lookout tower, 50m above the forest floor. Kids will enjoy the 'prehistoric path' loaded with dinosaurs, and everyone can test their bravery on the guided 2½-hour zipline tour – including a 120m run. You can also abseil down one of the giant trees.

TWELVE APOSTLES TRANSPORT & TOURS

Unless you're booked on a tour, having your own car is pretty much the only way to go in terms of exploring this area. The Apostles are located 15km from Port Campbell, with Loch Ard Gorge a little closer to town (around 12km).

Port Campbell Boat Charters (☑ 0428 986 366; www.portcampbellboatcharters.com.au; scenic tours/diving/fishing per person from $50/60/70) offers a unique way of viewing the Twelve Apostles, allowing you to see them from out on the water. Otherwise you can arrange a **scenic helicopter flight** (☑ 03-5598 8283; www.12apostleshelicopters.com.au; 15min flights $145) that'll take you over this dramatic stretch of coast.

From Port Campbell you can arrange a trip here with **Port Campbell Touring Company** (☑ 03-5598 6424, 0447 986 423; www.portcampbelltouring.com.au; half-day tours per person from $120, walks from $85). Otherwise the following tour operators make the trip here from Melbourne:

Go West Tours (p550)

Otway Discovery Tour (p550)

Ride Tours (p550)

headland. Today only seven 'apostles' can be seen from a network of viewing platforms connected by timber boardwalks around the clifftops.

There's pedestrian access to the viewing platforms from the car park at the Twelve Apostles Visitor Centre – more a kiosk and toilets than an info centre – via a tunnel beneath the Great Ocean Road.

The best time to visit is sunset, not only for optimum photographic opportunities and to beat the tour buses, but also to see little penguins returning ashore. Sightings vary, but generally they arrive 20 to 40 minutes after sunset. You'll need binoculars, which can be borrowed from the Port Campbell Visitor Centre.

Gibson Steps
BEACH

These 86 steps, hacked by hand into the cliffs by 19th-century landowner Hugh Gibson (and more recently replaced by safer concrete steps), lead down to wild Gibson Beach. You can walk along the beach here, but be careful not to get stranded by high tides.

ℹ️ Information

Twelve Apostles Visitor Centre Kiosk

(⏰ 10am-5pm Sun-Fri, to 5.30pm Sat) Based across the road from the iconic Twelve Apostles is this tourist information building with a kiosk, interpretative panels and toilets. To access the Twelve Apostles you'll need to park here, from where you can access the site via a tunnel that passes under the road.

Port Campbell

POP 618

This small, laid-back coastal town was named after Scottish Captain Alexander Campbell, a whaler who took refuge here on trading voyages between Tasmania and Port Fairy. It's a friendly town with some nice little eateries and drinking spots, which make for an ideal place to debrief after visiting the Twelve Apostles. Its tiny bay has a lovely sandy beach, one of few safe places for swimming along this tempestuous stretch of coast.

🛏️ Sleeping

Port Campbell Guesthouse Flashpackers
GUESTHOUSE $

(☑ 0407 696 559; www.portcampbellguesthouse.com; 54 Lord St; s/d without bathroom $50/80, r with bathroom from $100; ❄️🛜) A place for budget, independent-minded travellers who aren't into the whole hostel scene. Instead this homely guesthouse feels more like going around to a mate's place. Set up within a historic cottage are four cosy rooms, a comfy lounge and a country kitchen with filter coffee.

Port Campbell Hostel
HOSTEL $

(☑ 03-5598 6305; www.portcampbellhostel.com.au; 18 Tregea St; dm/s/d/tr/q from $38/80/130/175/240; @🛜) This modern purpose-built double-storey backpackers has rooms with western views, a huge shared kitchen and an even bigger lounge area. There's a range of clean mixed dorms and private rooms with en suites. It's a short stroll to the beach, and there are pizzas in the evenings ($10) and mountain-bike hire. Wi-fi only in the lounge area.

The opening of its new brewery **Sow and Piglets** (☺noon-late) is another reason to stay.

Sea Foam Villas APARTMENT $$
(☑03-5598 6413; www.seafoamvillas.com.au; 14 Lord St; r $185-570) Located directly across from the water, Sea Foam undoubtedly has the best views in town. It's only really worth it, however, if you can snag one of the bay-view apartments which are large, comfortable and luxurious.

✗ Eating & Drinking

★ **Forage on the Foreshore** CAFE $$
(☑03-5598 6202; 32 Cairns St; mains from $14; ☺9am-5pm; ☎) In the old post office is this seafront cottage cafe with wooden floorboards, art on the walls, an open fireplace and a vintage record player spinning vinyl. There's an all-day breakfast menu, burgers and curries for lunch, and items featuring fresh crayfish and abalone.

12 Rocks Cafe Bar CAFE $$
(☑03-5598 6123; www.12rocksbeachbar.com.au; 19 Lord St; mains $18-30; ☺9.30am-11pm) You can watch flotsam wash up on the beach from this busy eatery, which has perfect beachfront views. Try a local Otways beer with a pasta or seafood main, or just duck in for a coffee or ice cream from nearby Timboon.

ℹ️ Information

Port Campbell Visitor Centre (☑1300 137 255; www.visit12apostles.com.au; 26 Morris St; ☺9am-5pm) Stacks of regional and accommodation information and interesting relics from various shipwrecks – the anchor from the *Loch Ard* is out the front. Offers free use of binoculars, stargazer telescopes, cameras, GPS equipment and scavenger hunts for kids.

ℹ️ Getting There & Away

V/Line (p544) buses leave Geelong on Monday, Wednesday and Friday and travel through to Port Campbell ($32, five hours), but you'll need to transfer to a different bus in Apollo Bay ($11.20, two hours 15 minutes), which leaves a few hours later. There's also a bus to Warrnambool ($7.60, one hour 20 minutes).

Port Campbell to Warrnambool

Don't for a moment think that the Twelve Apostles are the end point of the Great Ocean Road, particularly given there's a whole string of iconic rock stacks on the road heading westward of Port Campbell. Some are arguably more scenic than the apostles themselves.

The drive continues through acres and acres of farming land here, passing through some laid-back towns. **Timboon**, about 16km inland from Peterborough, is best known for being surrounded by a number of wonderful places to sample local produce on the 12 Apostles Gourmet Trail. Here you'll be able to sample single-malt whiskeys, local homemade ice cream and chocolate, and fine wine and cheese.

HOW MANY APOSTLES?

The Twelve Apostles are not 12 in number and, from all records, never have been. From the viewing platform you can clearly count seven Apostles, but maybe some obscure others? We consulted widely with Parks Victoria officers, tourist-office staff and even the cleaner at the lookout, but it's still not clear. Locals tend to say, 'It depends where you look from', which really is true.

The Apostles are called 'stacks' in geologic parlance, and the rock formations were originally called the 'Sow and Piglets'. Someone in the 1960s (nobody can recall who) thought they might attract some tourists with a more venerable name, so they were renamed 'the Apostles'. Since apostles tend to come by the dozen, the number 12 was added sometime later. The two stacks on the eastern (Otway) side of the viewing platform are not technically Apostles – they're Gog and Magog.

The soft limestone cliffs are dynamic and changeable, with constant erosion from the unceasing waves – one 70m-high stack collapsed into the sea in July 2005 and the Island Archway lost its archway in June 2009.

⊙ Sights

London Bridge
LANDMARK

Just outside Port Campbell, en route to Peterborough, London Bridge has indeed fallen down. It was once a double-arched rock platform linked to the mainland, but in January 1990 the bridge collapsed leaving two terrified tourists marooned on the world's newest island – they were eventually rescued by helicopter. It remains a spectacular sight nevertheless. At dusk keep an eye out for penguins, who are often spotted on the beach.

Bay of Islands Coastal Park
VIEWPOINT

Past Peterborough (12km west of Port Campbell), the lesser-visited **Bay of Martyrs** and **Bay of Islands** both have spectacular lookout points of rock stacks and sweeping views comparable to the Twelve Apostles. Both have fantastic coastal walks, and there's a great beach at **Crofts Bay**.

The Arch
LANDMARK

Offshore from Point Hesse, the Arch is a rock formation worth stopping for. There's some good photo ops from the various viewing points looking down upon this intact bridgelike formation.

The Grotto
VIEWPOINT

A scenic stopover heading west from Port Campbell is the Grotto, where steep stairs lead down to a hollowed-out cavelike formation where waves crash through. It's approximately halfway between Port Campbell and Peterborough, a short drive from London Bridge.

Warrnambool

POP 33,979

Once a whaling and sealing station, these days Warrnambool is booming as a major regional commercial and whale-watching centre. While it's the whales that Warrnambool is most famous for, it has some great art galleries and historical sights to visit. Plus its sizeable population of uni students gives the town some spark, and you'll find some cool bars and cafes about.

⊙ Sights & Activities

★ Flagstaff Hill
Maritime Village
HISTORIC SITE

(☑03-5559 4600; www.flagstaffhill.com; 89 Merri St; adult/child/family $18/8.50/48; ⊙9am-5pm, last entry 4pm) The world-class Flagstaff Hill precinct is of equal interest for its shipwreck museum, heritage-listed lighthouses and garrison as it is for its reproduction of a historical Victorian port town. It also has the nightly **Shipwrecked** (adult/child/family $26/14/67), an engaging 70-minute sound-and-laser show telling the story of the *Loch Ard*'s plunge. The village is modelled on a pioneer-era Australian coastal port, with ye olde shoppes such as blacksmiths, candle makers and shipbuilders. If you're lucky the **Maremma dogs** (☑03-5559 4600; www.warrnamboolpenguins.com.au; adult/child $16/10) will be around for you to meet.

★ Warrnambool Art Gallery
GALLERY

(WAG; ☑03-5559 4949; www.thewag.com.au; 165 Timor St; ⊙10am-5pm Mon-Fri, noon-5pm Sat & Sun) **FREE** One of Australia's oldest art galleries (established in 1886), Warrnambool's collection of rotating permanent artworks showcases many prominent Australian painters. Its most famous piece is Eugene von Guérard's oil landscape *Tower Hill,* so detailed it was used by botanists as a historical record when regenerating the Tower Hill area to its original state. There's a contemporary component too, and several concurrent exhibitions on show.

Artery
GALLERY

(www.thefproject.org.au; 224 Timor St; ⊙10am-4pm Wed-Sun) Set up in a former funeral home by local art collective the F Project, this contemporary art gallery always has something interesting showing at its monthly exhibitions. There are also some cool street art murals outside. Its shop is another reason to visit, with some wonderful jewellery, accessories and artworks to pick up.

Reel Addiction
WHALE WATCHING

(☑0468 964 150; www.boatcharterswarrnambool.com.au; whale-watching trips per person $65, half-day fishing per person from $180) Runs morning and afternoon trips to see the whales when they're in town – usually from June to September – or otherwise to see the seal colony on Lady Julia Percy Island. Fishing trips are also their speciality.

⌂ Sleeping

Garrison Camp
CABIN $

(☑1800 556 111; www.flagstaffhill.com/accommodation; cabins with shared bathroom $50) Located within the Flagstaff Hill Maritime Village (p561) is this budget lodging in the Garrison Camp, a unique spot with replica

1870s Crimea-era British officer huts – small wooden A-frame bunk cabins. If you're around for longer they'll set up the bell tents (three-night minimum). It's BYO bedding or you can rent it for $15.

Warrnambool
Beach Backpackers HOSTEL $
(☑ 03-5562 4874; www.beachbackpackers.com.au; 17 Stanley St; per person camping $12, dm $28-36, d $80-90; @ ☎) A short stroll to the beach, this hostel has all backpackers' needs, with a huge living area, a kitchsy Aussie-themed bar, free wi-fi, a kitchen and free pick-up service. Its rooms are basic, but clean. As well as campers, 'vanpackers' can stay here for $12 per person. It hires out bikes, surfboards, SUPs, wetsuits, kayaks and fishing equipment, plus offers free use of boogie boards.

Flagstaff Hill
Lighthouse Lodge GUESTHOUSE $$
(☑ 1800 556 111; www.lighthouselodge.com.au; Flagstaff Hill; d/house incl dinner from $155/375; ❇☎) Once the former harbour master's residence, this charming weatherboard cottage can be rented as the entire house or separate rooms. It has a grassy area overlooking the Maritime Village and coastline. The rate includes entry to Flagstaff Hill Maritime Village, the Shipwrecked light show, dinner at Pippies restaurant and a bottle of wine, which makes it terrific value all up.

Hotel Warrnambool PUB $$
(☑ 03-5562 2377; www.hotelwarrnambool.com. au; cnr Koroit & Kepler Sts; d incl breakfast without/with bathroom from $110/140; ❇☎) Renovations to this historic 1894 hotel have seen rooms upgraded to the more boutique end of the scale, while keeping a classic pub-accommodation feel. Forget staying here on weekends if you're wanting peace and quiet.

✖ Eating & Drinking

Brightbird Espresso CAFE $
(☑ 03-5562 5749; www.brightbird.com.au; 157 Liebig St; mains from $12-20; ☺7.30am-4pm Mon-Fri, 8.30am-2pm Sat) Polished concrete floors, dangling light bulbs and single-origin coffees brewed by tattooed baristas brings a slice of inner-city Melbourne to the 'bool. All-day breakfasts encompass creative dishes, vegetarian sausage rolls and egg-and-bacon rolls.

Kermond's Hamburgers BURGERS $
(☑ 03-5562 4854; www.facebook.com/kermonds hamburgers; 151 Lava St; burgers $7.20-10; ☺9am-9.30pm) It seems likely not much has changed at this burger joint since it opened in 1949, with Laminex tables, wood-panelled walls and classic milkshakes served in stainless-steel tumblers. Its burgers are an institution.

Standard Dave PIZZA $$
(☑ 03-5562 8659; 218 Timor St; pizza $15-24; ☺5pm-late Tue-Sun, noon-2pm Fri) Standard Dave attracts a young indie crowd here for awesome pizzas, a drink and decent music. Its thin-crust pizzas use quality ingredients made from scratch or sourced locally. Be sure to head through next door to **Dart & Marlin** (216-218 Timor St; ☺5-11pm Wed-Fri, 2-11pm Sat & Sun).

Hotel Warrnambool PUB FOOD $$
(www.hotelwarrnambool.com.au; cnr Koroit & Kepler Sts; lunch mains $12-27, dinner $28-34; ☺noon-late; ☎) One of Victoria's best coastal pubs, Hotel Warrnambool mixes pub charm with bohemian character and serves wood-fired pizzas, among other gastro-pub fare.

Pickled Pig EUROPEAN $$$
(☑ 03-5561 3188; www.pickledpig.com.au; 78 Liebig St; dishes $17-37; ☺6-10pm Tue-Sat) Warrnambool's place to dress up, the Pickled Pig is smart dining with linen-clad tables and chandeliers. The food is seasonal contemporary European cuisine, which is best showcased in the chef's six-course tasting menu (per person $85); bookings are advised.

Lucy BAR
(www.facebook.com/thelucybar; 2/167 Koroit St, Ozone Walk; cocktails from $12; ☺3pm-late) A cool new dive bar tucked down a graffiti-splashed laneway. It's a tiny red-brick space, with a cassette deck for tunes and a drinks menu that specialises in local spirits produced by Victorian distilleries. They make a mean single-origin espresso Martini, and there are also gourmet jaffles, local wines, beers and ciders.

❶ Tourist Information
Warrnambool Visitor Centre (☑ 1800 637 725; www.visitwarrnambool.com.au; 89 Merri St; ☺9am-5pm) For the latest on whale sightings, local tours and accommodation bookings, plus bike and walking trail maps.

MELBOURNE & VICTORIA WARRNAMBOOL

❶ Getting There & Away

BUS

There are three V/Line buses a day along the Great Ocean Road to Apollo Bay ($21, two hours), as well as five daily buses to Port Fairy ($4.60, 35 minutes) and three to Portland ($12.40, 1½ hours). There's also a bus to Halls Gap ($27.20, three hours) four days a week via Dunkeld ($18.20, two hours) en route to Ararat ($32, three hours 40 minutes). There's a coach to Melbourne too via Ballarat ($18.20, two hours 50 minutes) departing Warrnambool at 7.15am Monday to Friday. Buses are run by **Christian's Bus Co** (☑ 03-5562 9432, 1300 734 441; www.christiansbus.com.au).

CAR

Warrnambool is an hour's drive west of Port Campbell on the Great Ocean Road, and about a three-hour drive from Melbourne on the Princes Hwy (A1).

TRAIN

V/Line (☑ 1800 800 007, 03-5562 9432; www.vline.com.au; Merri St) trains run to Melbourne ($34.60, 3¼ hours, three or four daily) via Geelong ($24.80, 2½ hours).

Tower Hill Reserve

Tower Hill, 15km west of Warrnambool, is a vast caldera born in a volcanic eruption 35,000 years ago. Aboriginal artefacts unearthed in the volcanic ash show that Indigenous people lived in the area at the time, and today the Worn Gundidj Aboriginal Cooperative operates the **Tower Hill Natural History Centre** (☑ 03-5565 9202, 0448 509 522; www.worngundidj.org.au; walks adult/child $22.95/10.65; ⏱ 10am-4pm).

The centre is housed within a UFO-like building designed by renowned Australian architect Robin Boyd in 1962. Bushwalks led by Indigenous guides depart daily at 11am and 1pm, and include boomerang-throwing and bush-tucker demonstrations. **Spotlighting night walks** (adult/child/family $28.95/14/65) are available too, with 24 hours' advance notice. The centre also sells handicrafts, artwork and accessories designed by the local Worn Gundidj community.

As well as the guided walks offered by the Tower Hill Natural History Centre, there are some other excellent walks, including the steep 30-minute **Peak Climb** with spectacular 360-degree views.

Port Fairy

POP 2835

Established as a whaling and sealing station in 1833, Port Fairy has retained its historic 19th-century maritime charm. Here it's all about heritage bluestone and sandstone buildings, whitewashed cottages, colourful fishing boats and wide, tree-lined streets.

❍ Sights

Wharf Area PORT

Back in the 1850s Port Fairy's port was one of the busiest in Australia, serving as the main departure point for ships heading to England loaded up with wool, gold and wheat. Today there's still plenty going on at this charming marina, from the luxury yachts to the weather-worn fishing boats moored here.

Battery Hill HISTORIC SITE

Located across the bridge from the picturesque harbour, Battery Hill is worthy of exploration, with cannons and fortifications positioned here in 1887 to protect the town from foreign warships. You'll also encounter resident black wallabies. It was originally used as a flagstaff, so the views are good.

Port Fairy History Centre MUSEUM

(☑ 03-5568 1266; www.historicalsociety.port-fairy.com; 30 Gipps St; adult/child/under 13yr $4/1/free; ⏱ 2-5pm Wed & Sat, 10.30am-12.30pm Sun) Housed in the old bluestone courthouse (complete with mannequins acting out a courtroom scene), this museum has shipping relics and old photos.

❋ Festivals & Events

★ **Port Fairy Folk Festival** MUSIC

(www.portfairyfolkfestival.com; tickets $250-300; ⏱ Mar) Australia's premier folk-music festival is held on the Labour Day long weekend in March. It includes an excellent mix of international and national acts, while the streets are abuzz with buskers. Accommodation can book out a year in advance.

⌂ Sleeping

Port Fairy YHA HOSTEL $

(☑ 03-5568 2468; www.portfairyhostel.com.au; 8 Cox St; dm $26-30, s/tw/d from $41.50/70/75; @ 🛜) Easily the best budget option in town, in the rambling 1844 home of merchant William Rutledge, is this friendly, well-run hostel with a large kitchen, a pool table, free cable TV and peaceful gardens.

Seacombe House GUESTHOUSE **$$**
(☑ 03-5568 1082; www.seacombehouse.com.au; 22 Sackville St; r without/with bathroom from $90/160, cottages $200; ❊ 🐾) Built in 1847, historic Seacombe House has cosy (OK, tiny) rooms, but it offers all the atmosphere and romance you'd hope for from this seafaring town. Modern motel rooms are available in its rear wing. It's above the acclaimed Fen restaurant.

Merrijig Inn HOTEL **$$**
(☑ 03-5568 2324; www.merrijiginn.com; 1 Campbell St; d from $120; 🐾) At the heritage-listed Merrijig, one of Victoria's oldest inns, you can make your choice between the quaint doll's house 'attic' rooms upstairs, and roomier, more comfortable rooms downstairs. There's a wonderful back lawn with veggie garden and silkie bantam chickens, plus comfy lounges with fireplaces throughout.

⭐ **Drift House** BOUTIQUE HOTEL **$$$**
(☑ 0417 782 495, 03-5568 3309; www.drifthouse.com.au; 98 Gipps St; d from $375; ❊🐾) An intriguing mix of 19th-century grandeur and 21st-century design, Drift House is a must for architecture lovers. Its grand frontage is the original 1860 double terrace, yet rooms open up to ultra-slick open-plan designs, decked out with boutique fittings. It's won a bunch of awards, and is undoubtedly *the* spot to treat yourself in town.

🍴 Eating

Farmer's Wife CAFE **$**
(☑ 03-5568 2843; www.facebook.com/farmerswifeportfairy; 47a Sackville St; mains $10-20; ⊘ 8am-2.30pm) Hidden down a walkway in a modern lot, Farmer's Wife doesn't need a heritage building to impress, and instead lets its food do the talking. Overseen by the chef previously from acclaimed Stag, the seasonal brunch menu features tempting items such as pork belly Benedict brioche, chilli fried eggs with pork quesadilla and salsa, and sourdough fruit toast.

⭐ **Coffin Sally** PIZZA **$$**
(www.coffinsally.com.au; 33 Sackville St; pizzas $13-20; ⊘ 4-11pm) This historic building was once used as a coffin makers; today it's well regarded for traditional thin-crust pizzas, cooked in an open kitchen and wolfed down on streetside stools or in the dimly lit dining

nooks out back next to an open fire. Its bar is also a good spot for a drink.

⭐ **Fen** MODERN AUSTRALIAN **$$$**
(☑ 03-5568 3229; www.fenportfairy.com.au; 22 Sackville St; mains $39, 5-course degustation menu $110, tasting menu for $150; ⊘ 6-11pm Tue-Sat) One of coastal Vic's best restaurants, this husband-and-wife-run operation earned itself two chef's hats in 2017. Set up inside a heritage bluestone building, the decor is minimalist and relaxed, while the menu showcases seasonal local produce from southwestern Victoria. Expect local lamb, seafood and duck dishes, infused with indigenous flavours.

Merrijig Kitchen MODERN AUSTRALIAN **$$$**
(☑ 03-5568 2324; www.merrijiginn.com; 1 Campbell St; mains $28-38; ⊘ 6-9pm Thu-Mon; 🐾) Here at Port Fairy's most atmospheric restaurant you can warm yourself by the open fire and enjoy superb dining with a menu that changes daily according to what's seasonal. It has a kitchen garden, cures meats, smokes fish and features an award-winning wine list. Delectable food with great service.

ℹ️ Information

Port Fairy Visitor Centre (☑ 03-5568 2682; www.portfairyaustralia.com.au; Bank St; ⊘ 9am-5pm; 🐾) Provides spot-on tourist information, walking-tour brochures (20 cents), free wi-fi, V/Line tickets, tourism brochures and publications. There's also bike hire (half-/full day $15/25).

ℹ️ Getting There & Away

Port Fairy is 20 minutes' drive west of Warrnambool on the A1. If coming from Melbourne it's a 288km journey, with the most direct route being along the B140 highway from Geelong.

Catch a train to Warrnambool, from where **V/Line** (☑ 1800 800 007; www.vline.com.au) run four to five buses a day to Port Fairy ($4.60, 35 minutes). The bus also heads to Tower Hill ($3.20) and Koroit ($3.20). There's also a bus from Port Fairy to Portland ($8.60, 55 minutes).

Portland

POP 10,700

Portland's claim to fame is as Victoria's first European settlement, founded as a whaling and sealing base in the early 1800s. Despite its colonial history, attractive architecture and beaches, blue-collared Portland feels much more like a regional hub than a tourist town.

Though with that said, there's a lot on offer. The Great Southwest Walk is a big attraction, as are seafood and fishing, whale-watching in winter, plus some good surf breaks outside town.

⊙ Sights

Historic Waterfront
WATERFRONT

(Cliff St) The grassy precinct overlooking the harbour has several heritage bluestone buildings. **Customs House** (1850) is still a working office, but you can ask to see its fascinating display of confiscated booty in the cellar, including a stuffed black bear among other random items. Also here is the 1845 **courthouse**, and the 1886 **Rocket Shed** with a display of ship rescue equipment.

Portland Maritime Discovery Centre
MUSEUM

(☑1800 035 567; Lee Breakwater Rd; adult/child under 15yr $7.50/free; ⊙9am-5pm) Excellent displays on shipwrecks and Portland's whaling history, plus a sperm whale skeleton that washed ashore and an original 1858 wooden lifeboat. There's also a **cafe** (☑03-5521 7341; mains from $17; ⊙9.30am-4.30pm) here with one of the best views in town.

⌂ Sleeping & Eating

Hotel Bentinck
HISTORIC HOTEL $$

(☑03-5523 2188; cnr Bentinck & Gawler Sts; motel s/d $70/90, hotel r incl breakfast $115-217; ❄️🖧) An attractive historic hotel (c 1856) on the main street, Bentinck's rooms offer local character, comfort and overall good value. Room 27 is the pick with water views, spa bath and chesterfield couches. There are also motel rooms around the back, which are generic, but get the job done if you're on a budget.

Annesley House
BOUTIQUE HOTEL $$

(☑0429 852 235; www.annesleyhouse.com.au; 60 Julia St; r $200-280; ❄️🖧) This restored former doctor's mansion (c 1878) has six very different self-contained rooms, some featuring claw-foot baths and lovely views. All have a unique sense of style, and they come with complimentary port wine.

Clifftop Accommodation
GUESTHOUSE $$

(☑03-5523 1126; www.portlandaccommodation. com.au; 13 Clifton Ct; d from $140; ❄️🖧) The panoramic ocean views from the balconies here are incredible. Three self-contained rooms are huge, with big brass beds, telescopes and a modern maritime feel.

Deegan Seafoods
FISH & CHIPS $

(☑03-5523 4749; 106 Percy St; fish from $6; ⊙9am-6pm Mon-Fri) This fish and chip shop famously serves up the freshest fish in Victoria. Whether you go the flake or the calamari rings, you're in for a serious treat.

Cafe Bahloo
CAFE $$

(www.cafebahloo.com.au; 85 Cliff St; mains $12-29; ⊙7.30am-3pm Tue-Thu, 7.30am-10pm Fri, 8am-late Sat, 8am-2pm Sun; 🖧) Housed in the original bluestone watchkeeper's house, across from the harbour, vibrant and arty Bahloo serves all-day breakfasts, toasties, Mt Gambier–roasted single-origin coffees and juices, and has a well-stocked bar.

ⓘ Information

Portland Visitor Centre (☑1800 035 567; www.visitportland.com.au; Lee Breakwater Rd; ⊙9am-5pm) In a modern building on the waterfront, this excellent information centre has a stack of suggestions for things to do and see.

ⓘ Getting There & Away

Portland is a one-hour drive west of Port Fairy on the Princes Hwy (A1).

V/Line buses connect Portland with Port Fairy (from $8.60, 50 minutes) and Warrnambool

---

DON'T MISS

CAPE BRIDGEWATER

Home to one of Australia's finest stretches of white-sand surf beach, Cape Bridgewater makes for an essential 21km detour off the Portland–Nelson Rd. Its powdery white sands and turquoise waters resemble Queensland more than a remote Victorian beach. Though the beach is the main drawcard, there are also a number of walks featuring some dramatic scenery and an opportunity to swim with **Australian fur seals** (☑03-5526 7247; www.sealsbyseatours.com.au; Bridgewater Rd; 45min tours adult/child $40/25, cage dives $60/30; ⊙Sep-May), which makes this destination one of the coast's best-kept secrets.

GREAT SOUTH WEST WALK

The 250km signposted loop that is the Great South West Walk begins and ends at Portland's visitor centre. It takes in some of the southwest's most stunning natural scenery: from the remote, blustery coast, through the river system of the Lower Glenelg National Park, and back through the hinterland to Portland. The whole loop would take at least 10 days, but it can be done in sections, and parts can be done as day walks or even a two-hour loop. Maps are available from visitor centres in Portland and Nelson.

Visit www.greatsouthwestwalk.com for all information, FAQs and registration details.

(from $12.40, one hour 40 minutes) three times daily on weekdays, and once a day on weekends. Buses depart from Henty St.

Nelson

POP 311

Tiny Nelson is the last vestige of civilisation before the South Australian border – just a general store, a pub and a handful of accommodation places. It's a popular holiday and fishing spot at the mouth of the Glenelg River, which flows through Lower Glenelg National Park. It's pretty much the halfway mark between Melbourne and Adelaide, and likes to think of itself as the beginning of the Great Ocean Road. Note that Nelson uses South Australia's 08 telephone area code.

🏃 Activities

★ **Nelson Canoe Hire**   CANOEING
(📱 0409 104 798; www.nelsonboatandcanoehire. com.au; canoe hire per half-/full day $40/65, kayak hire per half-/full day $25/60) Exploring the 65km stretch of scenic river along Lower Glenelg National Park on a multiday canoe trip is one of Victoria's best hidden secrets. This outfit can rig you up for leisurely paddles or serious river-camping expeditions – three days including waterproof barrels. There's no office but they'll deliver you all the gear; BYO tent and supplies.

★ **Nelson Boat Hire**   BOATING
(📱 0427 571 198, 08-8738 4048; www.nelson boatandcanoehire.com.au; dinghies per 4hr $115, motorboat per hr $55, houseboats per night $410-480; ⊙ Sep-Jul) Whether you head out for a few hours' fishing or hire a self-contained houseboat, cruising along the scenic waters of Lower Glenelg National Park will likely be the most relaxing time of your trip. The best bit is you don't need a boat licence. Houseboats, which sleep six, come with bathroom,

fridge and kitchen, and have a two-night minimum hire period.

Nelson River Cruises   CRUISE
(📱 0448 887 1225, 08-8738 4191; www.glenelgriver cruises.com.au; cruises adult/child $32.50/10; ⊙ Sep-Jun) These leisurely 3½-hour cruises head along the Glenelg River, departing Nelson at 1pm on Wednesday and Saturday, or daily during school holidays; check the website for the schedule. Tours include the impressive **Princess Margaret Rose Cave** (📱 08-8738 4171; www.princessmargaretrosecave. com; Princess Margaret Rose Caves Rd, Mumbannar, Lower Glenelg National Park; adult/child/family $20/13/44; ⊙ tours depart 10am, 11am, noon, 1.30pm, 2.30pm, 3.30pm & 4.30pm, reduced hours winter), with its gleaming underground formations; tickets for the cave cost extra.

🛏 Sleeping

Kywong Caravan Park   CAMPGROUND $
(📱 08-8738 4174; www.kywongcp.com; 92 North Nelson Rd; unpowered sites $23-28, powered sites $28-35, cabins d from $70; ❄ 🐾) Set 1km north of town, this 10 hectare park is next to the national park and Glenelg River, with plenty of wildlife (including bandicoots) and great birdwatching.

Nelson Cottage   COTTAGE $
(📱 08-8738 4161; www.nelsoncottage.com.au; cnr Kellett & Sturt Sts; s/d with shared bathroom & breakfast $70/90; 🐾) This 1882 cottage, once used as a police station, has old-fashioned rooms with clean shared amenities. The owners are keen travellers so call ahead first to check if they're around.

🍴 Eating & Drinking

★ **Nelson Hotel**   PUB
(📱 08-8738 4011; www.nelsonhotel.com.au; Kellett St; ⊙ 11am-late; 🐾) As real as outback pubs come, the Nelson Hotel (established in 1855) is an essential stop for a beer and a friendly

WORTH A TRIP

CAPE NELSON LIGHTHOUSE

Head up to the top of the still-operational **Cape Nelson Lighthouse** (☑ 0428 131 253; www.capenelsonlight house.com.au; adult/child/family $15/10/40; ⊙ tours 11am & 2pm), built in 1884 for fantastic views overlooking the edge of the world. You'll also get shown around the premises while hearing tales of shipwrecks and the history of the area. The **accommodation** (1-/2-bedroom cottages incl breakfast $200/270; ❄ 🛜) here is the perfect opportunity to indulge in that fantasy of living in a remote, windswept lighthouse keeper's cottage.

yarn with locals. It's got a character-filled front bar, featuring a dusty stuffed pelican, and a bistro serving hearty meals (mains from $15).

There are basic rooms too, which, while in need of a refurb, are perfectly fine for the night (single/double with shared bathroom $45/65).

ℹ️ Information

Nelson Visitor Centre (☑ 08-8738 4051; www.nelsonvictoria.com.au; ⊙ 10am-12.30pm & 1.30-5pm; 🛜) Good info on both sides of the border; particularly helpful for the parks and the Great South West Walk. Also has wi-fi. During summer they have longer opening hours, otherwise they leave tourist packages for visitors after hours.

THE GOLDFIELDS & GRAMPIANS

History, nature and culture combine spectacularly in Victoria's regional heart. For a brief time in the mid-19th century, more than a third of the world's gold came out of Victoria and, today, the spoils of all that precious metal can be seen in the grand regional cities of Bendigo and Ballarat, and the charming towns of Castlemaine, Kyneton and Maldon. This is a fantastic region for touring, with a range of contrasting landscapes, from pretty countryside and green forests, red earth and granite country, to farmland, orchards and wineries.

Further west, there's a different type of history to experience at Grampians National Park, one of Victoria's great natural wonders. Some 80% of Victoria's Aboriginal rock-art sites are found here, and the majestic ranges are an adventurer's paradise, lording it over the idyllic Wartook Valley and the towns of Halls Gap and Dunkeld.

Ballarat

POP 93,501

Ballarat was built on gold and it's easy to see the proceeds of those days in the grand Victorian-era architecture around the city centre. The single biggest attraction here is the fabulous, re-created gold-mining village at Sovereign Hill, but there's plenty more in this busy provincial city to keep you occupied, including grand gold-mining-era architecture, art galleries and microbreweries. Rug up if you visit in the winter months – Ballarat is renowned for being chilly.

👁️ Sights

⭐ **Sovereign Hill**   HISTORIC SITE
(☑ 03-5337 1100; www.sovereignhill.com.au; Bradshaw St; adult/child/family $54/24.50/136; ⊙ 10am-5pm, until 5.30pm during daylight saving) You'll need to set aside at least half a day to visit this fascinating re-creation of Ballarat's 1860s gold-mining township. The site was mined in the gold-rush era and much of the equipment is original, as is the mine shaft. Kids love panning for gold in the stream, watching the hourly gold pour and exploring the old-style lolly shop.

⭐ **Art Gallery of Ballarat**   GALLERY
(☑ 03-5320 5858; www.balgal.com; 40 Lydiard St Nth; ⊙ 10am-5pm, tour 2pm) FREE Established in 1884 and moved to its current location in 1890, the Art Gallery of Ballarat is the oldest provincial gallery in Australia. The architectural gem houses a wonderful collection of early colonial paintings, combined with modern art, with works from noted Australian artists (including Tom Roberts, Sir Sidney Nolan, Russell Drysdale, Albert Tucker, Fred Williams and Howard Arkley) along with contemporary works. There are free guided tours at 2pm daily.

Museum of Australian Democracy at Eureka   MUSEUM
(MADE; ☑ 1800 287 113; www.made.org; 102 Stawell St; adult/child/family $12/8/35; ⊙ 10.30am-3.30pm Mon-Fri, 9.30am-4.30pm Sat & Sun)

Standing on the site of the Eureka Rebellion, this fine museum opened in May 2013 and has already established itself as one of Ballarat's top attractions. Taking the Eureka Rebellion as its starting point – pride of place goes to the preserved remnants of the original Eureka flag and multimedia displays that re-create the events of 1854 – the museum then broadens out to discuss democracy in Australia and beyond through a series of interactive exhibits.

Botanic Gardens   GARDENS
(Wendouree Pde; ☉sunrise-sunset) **FREE** On the western side of the lake, Ballarat's beautiful and serene gardens were first planted in 1858. Stroll through the 40 hectares of immaculately maintained rose gardens, wide lawns and colourful conservatory. Visit the cottage of poet Adam Lindsay Gordon or walk along the Prime Ministers' Avenue, a collection of bronze busts of all of Australia's prime ministers.

Ballarat Wildlife Park   ZOO
(☑03-5333 5933; www.wildlifepark.com.au; cnr York & Fussell Sts; adult/child/family $33/18.50/90; ☉9am-5pm, tour 11am) Ballarat's tranquil wildlife park is strong on native fauna: Tasmanian devils, cassowaries, dingoes, quokkas, snakes, eagles and crocs. There are also animals from nearby neighbouring countries such as tree kangaroos from PNG and a komodo dragon. There's a daily guided tour, as well animal encounters throughout the day – check the website for the schedule.

Lake Wendouree   LAKE
Lake Wendouree, a large artificial lake used for the 1956 Olympics rowing events, is a natural focal point for the town. Old timber boat sheds spread along the shore, and a popular walking and cycling track encircles the lake. Alongside the lake are restaurants, the botanical gardens and a **tourist tramway** (☑03-5334 1580; www.btm.org.au; Gillies St North; rides adult/child $4/2; ☉12.30-5pm Sat & Sun, daily during holidays).

🏃 Activities

If youwant to head out prospecting you're free to chance your luck if you pick up a Miners Right licence – available online ($23.70 – valid for 10 years...). But unless you know what you're doing, sign up for a tour with **Gold & Relics** (☑1300 882 199; www.goldandrelics.com.au; per person $247; ☉8.30am-5.30pm).

Goldfields Bike Tours   CYCLING
(☑0418 303 065; www.goldfieldsbiketours.com.au; 1845 Sturt St, Bell Tower Inn; per day bike rental $50, electric bike $80) As well as offering a number of wonderful bike tours in the region, this is the spot to pick up any number of bikes (including handy e-bikes) to tackle the **Ballarat-Skipton Rail Trail** (www.ballaratskiptonrailtrail.com). Bikes are available for pick up from the Bell Tower Inn at the beginning of the trail, but you'll need to book ahead.

Gold Shop   OUTDOORS
(☑03-5333 4242; www.thegoldshop.com.au; 8a Lydiard St North; ☉10am-5pm Mon & Wed-Fri, 10am-3pm Sat) Hopeful prospectors can pick up miners' rights and rent metal detectors at the Gold Shop in the historic Mining Exchange. It also has gold nuggets and jewellery for sale, and its owner Cornell is a wealth of knowledge on everything gold in the region.

✨🎭 Festivals & Events

White Night Ballarat   CULTURAL
(www.whitenightballarat.com.au; ☉7pm-7am Mar) **FREE** Ballarat is the latest city in the world to be blessed by this wonderful all-night arts festival. It features a packed program of performances, exhibitions and patterned projections over its historical streetscape.

🛏 Sleeping

Ballarat Backpackers Hostel   HOSTEL $
(Eastern Hotel; ☑0427 440 661; www.ballaratbackpackers.com.au; 81 Humffray St Nth; dm/s/d $35/40/70; ☎) In the old Eastern Station Hotel (1862), this refurbished hostel is also a decent corner pub with occasional live music. Rooms are simple but decent value.

Big4 Ballarat
Goldfields Holiday Park   CAMPGROUND $
(☑1800 632 237, 03-5330 8000; www.ballaratgoldfields.com.au; 108 Clayton St; powered sites from $40, cabins $85-185; ❈@🛜🏊) Only a 300m walk to Sovereign Hill (and 1.5km from town), this caravan park offers a good holiday atmosphere with a heap of play areas and activities for kids. There's a good mix of cabins, houses and en-suite camp sites. In winter there's an indoor pool and heated toilet floors.

Quest Ballarat   APARTMENT $$
(☑03-5309 1200; www.questballarat.com.au; 7-11 Dawson St North; studio from $165, 1-/2-bed apt from $175/285; ❈☎) Housed behind the

Ballarat

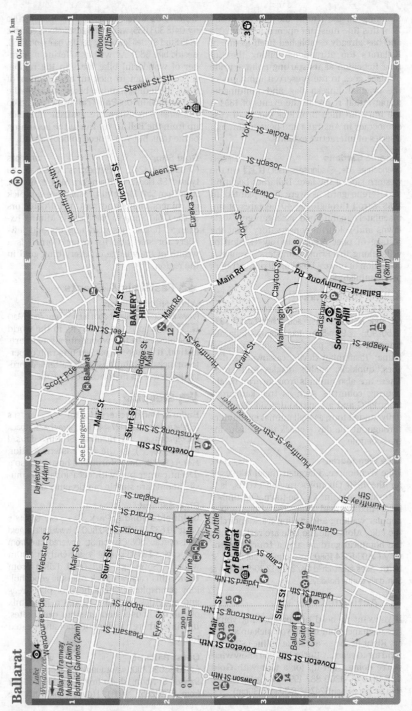

Stawell St Sth

Melbourne (115km)

Humffray St Nth

Victoria St

Queen St

Eureka St

York St

Main Rd

Main Rd

Mair St

Peel St Nth

BAKERY HILL

Bridge St Mall

Scott Pde

Ballarat

See Enlargement

Mair St

Sturt St

Daylesford (44km)

Doveton St Sth

Armstrong St Sth

Raglan St

Errard St

Drummond St

Webster St

Mair St

Sturt St

Ripon St

Eyre St

Pleasant St

Humffray St Sth

Yarrowee River

Grant St

Humffray St

Clayton St

Wainwright St

Bradshaw St

Magpie St

Sovereign Hill

Ballarat–Buninyong Rd

Buninyong (8km)

York St

Joseph St

Otway St

Rodier St

Stawell St Sth

Ballarat Tramway Museum (1.6km); Botanic Gardens (2km)

Wendouree Pde

Lake Wendouree

See Enlargement

Art Gallery of Ballarat

V/Line Ballarat

Airport Shuttle

Lydiard St Nth

Camp St

Grenville St

Sturt St

Lydiard St Sth

Ballarat Visitor Centre

Mair St

Armstrong St Nth

Doveton St Nth

Dawson St Nth

0   200 m
0   0.1 miles

0   1 km
0   0.5 miles

Ballarat

facade of a stately red-brick building (the historic Loreto Girls College), are these large and modern apartments, with friendly, professional staff.

Sovereign Hill Hotel   HISTORIC HOTEL **$$**
(☑ 03-5337 1159; www.sovereignhill.com.au/sovereign-hill-hotel; 39-41 Magpie St; r $175-195; ✱ ☞) Formerly the Comfort Inn, is this handily located hotel, a stone's throw from Sovereign Hill itself, with bright, modern rooms. Ask about its accommodation and entertainment packages.

Craig's Royal Hotel   HOTEL **$$$**
(☑ 03-5331 1377; www.craigsroyal.com; 10 Lydiard St South; s/d from $230/280) The best of the grand old pubs was so named after it hosted visits by the Prince of Wales and Duke of Edinburgh, as well as literary royalty in Mark Twain. It's a wonderful Victorian-era build-ing full of old-fashioned opulence – including a grand staircase and an elegant 1930s elevator – and the rooms have been beau-tifully refurbished with king beds, heritage furnishings and marble bathrooms.

✖ Eating

Fika Coffee Brewers   CAFE **$**
(☑ 0427 527 447; www.fikacoffeebrewers.com.au; 36a Doveton St North; dishes $8-20; ⊙ 7am-4pm Mon-Fri, 8am-3pm Sat) Ballarat's best cafe for food is this smart, urban-chic space with dangling light bulbs and wood-panelled walls. Here you can expect the likes of 'ca-cao pops' with almond milk and banana; peanut butter-and-tomato on sourdough; or pulled-pork bagels with cheddar and chilli. They don't roast their own beans, but its baristas know how to make a decent cuppa coffee.

Saltbush Kitchen   AUSTRALIAN **$**
(☑ 1800 287 113; www.made.org/visit/saltbush-kitchen; 102 Stawell St South; mains from $12.50; ⊙ 10:30am-3.30pm Mon-Fri, 9.30am-4pm Sat & Sun) A rare opportunity to sample indige-nous flavours is this cafe that's within the Museum of Australian Democracy at Eureka (p566). Its menu features contemporary everyday cafe fare infused with native ingre-dients such as mountain pepper, finger lime, saltbush, lemon myrtle and wattleseed. Also try their cocktails, including a white rum with roasted wattleseed.

★ Catfish   THAI **$$**
(☑ 03-5331 5248; www.catfishthai.com.au; 42-44 Main Rd; mains $18-34; ⊙ 6pm-late Tue-Sat, noon-2pm Sun) Run by chef Damien Jones, Catfish is Ballarat's most acclaimed restaurant, fea-turing a salivating menu of contemporary yet authentic Thai dishes to share. They're probably the only hatted restaurant in Aus-tralia to do takeaway too, a recommended option if they're booked out.

On Saturday mornings (10.30am) they of-fer a Thai cooking class for $165 per person, which run for four hours; advance bookings essential.

L'Espresso   ITALIAN **$$**
(☑ 03-5333 1789; www.facebook.com/lespresso ballarat; 417 Sturt St; mains $13.50-20; ⊙ 7.30am-6pm Sat-Thu, to late Fri) A mainstay on Ballarat's cafe scene for over 30 years is this old-school European-style cafe that doubles as a cool record shop – choose from their fine taste of indie, jazz, blues and world vinyl while you

THE EUREKA REBELLION

Life on the goldfields was a great leveller, erasing social distinctions as doctors, merchants, ex-convicts and labourers toiled side by side in the mud. But as the easily won gold began to run out, the diggers recognised the inequalities between themselves and the privileged few who held land and the government.

The limited size of claims and the inconvenience of licence hunts, coupled with police brutality and taxation without political representation, fired the unrest that led to the Eureka Rebellion.

In September 1854 Governor Hotham ordered the hated licence hunts to be carried out twice weekly. In the following October a miner was murdered near a Ballarat hotel after an argument with the owner, James Bentley. Bentley was found not guilty by a magistrate (and business associate), and a group of miners rioted and burned his hotel. Bentley was retried and found guilty, but the rioting miners were also jailed, which fuelled their distrust of authority.

Creating the Ballarat Reform League, the diggers called for the abolition of licence fees, a miner's right to vote and increased opportunities to purchase land.

On 29 November 1854 about 800 miners, led by Irishman Peter Lalor, burnt their licences at a mass meeting and built a stockade at Eureka, where they prepared to fight for their rights.

On 3 December the government ordered troopers to attack the stockade. There were only 150 diggers within the barricades at the time and the fight lasted only 20 minutes, leaving 30 miners and five troopers dead.

The short-lived rebellion was ultimately successful. The miners won the sympathy of Victorians and the government chose to acquit the leaders of the charge of high treason.

The licence fee was abolished. A miner's right, costing £1 a year, gave the right to search for gold and to fence in, cultivate and build a dwelling on a moderate-sized piece of land – and to vote. The rebel leader Peter Lalor became a member of parliament some years later.

wait for your espresso or Tuscan bean soup. Fabulous risotto and house-made pastas.

Craig's Royal Hotel   MODERN AUSTRALIAN **$$$**
(☑ 03-5331 1377; www.craigsroyal.com.au; 10 Lydiard St South; mains $20-45; ⊘7am-10pm; 🛜) Even if you can't afford to stay here, you can experience some royal treatment dining in the Gallery Bistro, a sumptuous light-filled dining room serving European-inspired cuisine. Otherwise, come for a cocktail in the historic, wood-panelled Craig's Bar. On Sundays the hotel hosts high tea ($60) in its elegant Victorian banquet room with silverware; reservations essential.

🍸 Drinking & Nightlife

⭐**Hop Temple**   BEER HALL
(☑ 03-5317 7158; www.hoptemple.com.au; rear of 24-28 Armstrong St North; ⊘4-11pm Wed-Fri, noon-11pm Sat, noon-9pm Sun) Symbolic of the Rat's meteoric rise from bogan country town to cool happening city is this massive converted red-brick warehouse tucked down a laneway. There are 16 craft beers on tap (plus 200 kinds in the fridge), along with

artisan cocktails, to go with a menu of buttermilk fried chicken po' boys, smoked BBQ meats and mac 'n' cheese.

⭐**Mitchell Harris**   WINE BAR
(☑ 03-5331 8931; www.mitchellharris.com.au; 38 Doveton St North; ⊘11am-9pm Mon-Wed, to 11pm Thu-Sat, to 6pm Sun) A stylish wine bar without a hint of pretension is this attractive red-brick space set up by local winemakers Mitchell Harris. It not only showcases their own range, but wines from the entire Victorian Pyrenees. As well as tastings ($10 for four wines), there's wine by the glass to go with a menu of local produce.

The Mallow Hotel   PUB
(☑ 03-5331 1073; www.themallow.com.au; 20 Skipton St; ⊘noon-6pm Wed-Sun) One of the first pubs in town to start serving decent beer, the Mallow remains a much cherished local. It has 12 beers and ciders on tap, featuring predominately Victorian microbreweries. Food is good too, from craft-beer-battered fish-and-chips and pulled pork spring rolls to its signature Mallow burger.

Athletic Club Brewery MICROBREWERY
(☎03-5332 7031; www.athleticclubbrewery.com.
au; 47 Mair St; ⊙11am-late) One of Ballarat's
best new spots for quality ales is this microbrewery that does a great range of craft
beers on tap. Its taproom overlooks the
brewing equipment, and the passionate
owner-brewer is good for a chat. It shares
space with a restaurant next door, and you
can order food in.

★ Entertainment

★Karova Lounge LIVE MUSIC
(☎03-5332 9122; www.karovalounge.com; 15
Field St; ⊙9pm-late Wed-Sat) One of Ballarat's
best original live-music venues showcases
local and touring bands in a grungy, industrial style.

Her Majesty's Theatre THEATRE
(☎03-5333 5888; www.hermaj.com; 17 Lydiard
St South) Ballarat's main venue for the performing arts since 1875, 'Her Maj' is in a
wonderful Victorian-era building and features theatre, live music, comedy and local
productions. Check the website for a calendar of shows.

❶ Information

Ballarat Visitor Centre (☎1800 446 633,
03-5337 4337; www.visitballarat.com.au; 225
Sturt St, Town Hall; ⊙9am-5pm; ☎) Inside the
town hall is this modern and well-equipped info
centre that sells the Ballarat Pass, stocks free
self-guided walking maps and offers complimentary internet access.

❶ Getting There & Away

Ballarat is 116km west from Melbourne (1½
hours), accessed via the Western Hwy.
Airport Shuttle Bus (☎03-5333 4181; www.
airportshuttlebus.com.au; Ballarat Railway
Station; ⊙office 8.30am-5.30pm Mon-Fri,
9am-1pm Sat) Goes direct from Melbourne
Airport to Ballarat train station (adult/
child $35/17, 1½ hours, 12 daily, seven on
weekends).
Firefly (☎1300 730 740; www.fireflyexpress.
com.au) Buses between Adelaide ($60, 8¾
hours, departs Adelaide 8.15pm) and Melbourne ($50, 1¾ hours), stopping in Ballarat if
you ask the driver.
V/Line (☎1800 800 007; www.vline.com.au)
Has frequent direct trains between Melbourne
(Southern Cross Station) and Ballarat (from
$14.42, 1½ hours, 28 daily) and at least three
services from Geelong ($10.20, 1½ hours).

Bendigo
POP 92,888
Bendigo is a city to watch. New hotels, a
dynamic dining scene and a stunning re-
imagining of historic spaces have joined
an already formidable array of attractions
that range from gold-rush-era architecture
and a fine art gallery to the Chinese dragons that awaken for the Easter Festival. Sitting as it does in the heart of goldfield and
wine-growing country, the only question is
why Bendigo has taken so long to take off.

◉ Sights & Activities

**★Golden Dragon
Museum & Gardens** MUSEUM
(☎03-5441 5044; www.goldendragonmuseum.
org; 1-11 Bridge St; adult/child/family $11/6/28;
⊙9.30am-5pm Tue-Sun) Bendigo's Chinese
heritage sets it apart from other goldfields
towns, and this fantastic museum is the
place to experience it. Walk through a huge
wooden door into an awesome chamber
filled with dragons and amazing Chinese
heritage items and costumes. The highlight
for many are the imperial dragons, including Old Loong (the oldest in the world) and
the soon-to-be-retired Sun Loong (the longest in the world at over 100m).

★Bendigo Talking Tram LANDMARK
(☎03-5442 2821; www.bendigotramways.com; 1
Tramways Ave; adult/child/family $17.50/11/51;
⊙10am-4pm) For an interesting tour of the
city, hop aboard one of the restored vintage
'talking' trams. The hop-on, hop-off trip runs
from the Central Deborah Goldmine to the
Tramways Depot every half-hour, making
half-a-dozen stops, including at the Golden
Dragon Museum and Lake Weeroona. Tickets are valid for two days.

★Bendigo Art Gallery GALLERY
(☎03-5434 6088; www.bendigoartgallery.com.
au; 42 View St; free to $25; ⊙10am-5pm Tue-Sun,
tour 2pm) One of Victoria's finest regional
galleries (founded in 1887), the permanent collection here includes outstanding
colonial and contemporary Australian art.
It showcases works by the likes of Russell
Drysdale, Arthur Boyd, Brett Whiteley and
Fred Williams. Aim to visit at 2pm for free
tours of the gallery. Its impressive temporary exhibitions are cutting edge and
have been an important part of Bendigo's
renaissance.

Bendigo Pottery
ARTS CENTRE

(☑03-5448 4404; www.bendigopottery.com.au; 146 Midland Hwy; ☉9am-5pm) **FREE** Australia's oldest pottery works, the Bendigo Pottery was founded in 1857 and is classified by the National Trust. The historic kilns are still used; watch potters at work, admire the gorgeous ceramic pieces (all for sale) or throw a pot yourself (per 30 minutes $18, an extra $10 to glaze and post home). The attached **museum** (adult/child $8/4) tells the story of pottery through the ages. It's just over 4km north of the town centre.

Sacred Heart Cathedral
CHURCH

(cnr Wattle & High Sts) You can't miss the soaring steeple of this magnificent cathedral. Though construction began in the 19th century it was only completed in 2001 with the installation of bells from Italy in the belfry. Inside, beneath the high-vaulted ceiling, there's a magnificently carved bishop's chair, some beautiful stained-glass windows, and wooden angels jutting out of the ceiling arches.

Victoria Hills Historic Mining Site
HISTORIC SITE

(24-32 Happy Valley Rd) **FREE** Back in the day this sprawling site was the world's deepest gold mine. Today you can wander by its relics and open-cut mines that date to the 1850s, and climb up the poppet head for wonderful views. In 100 years of operation Victoria Hills yielded the equivalent of $8 billion in today's money.

Sandhurst Gaol
HISTORIC BUILDING

(HM Prison Bendigo; ☑1800 813 153; www.bendigotourism.com/tours/bendigo/sandhurst-gaol-tour; adult/child $15/10; ☉tours 11am Tue & 2pm Sun) Originally opened in 1863, this Pentonville-designed prison (decommissioned in 2005) has recently been converted into the slick **Ulumbarra Theatre** (☑03-5434 6100; www.ulumbarratheatre.com.au; 10 Gaol Rd). To visit you'll need to sign up for its twice-weekly tours to see its very intact cells and learn of its notorious inmates and executions that took place here. Book online or through the visitor centre.

Great Stupa of Universal Compassion
BUDDHIST SITE

(☑03-5446 7568; www.stupa.org.au; 25 Sandhurst Town Rd, Myers Flat; by donation; ☉9am-5pm Mon-Fri, 10.30am-5pm Sat & Sun) In Myers Flat, just beyond Bendigo's city limits, this Buddhist stupa, surrounded by gum trees, promises to be the largest stupa in the Western world (with its 50m base and a height of 50m). When completed it will house a massive Buddha statue (also the world's largest) carved from jade.

Central Deborah Goldmine
HISTORIC SITE

(☑03-5443 8255; www.central-deborah.com; 76 Violet St; adult/child/family mine experience $30/16/83; ☉9.30am-5pm) For a very deep experience, descend into this 500m-deep mine with a geologist. The mine has been worked on 17 levels, and about 1 tonne of gold has been removed. After donning hard hats and lights, you're taken down the shaft to inspect the operations, complete with drilling demonstrations. The 'Mine Experience' tours are the main option with four tours a day that last about 75 minutes.

Rosalind Park
PARK

In the city centre, this lovely green space is reminiscent of a London park with lawns, grand old trees, fernery, 19th-century statues and the fabulous Cascades Fountain, which was excavated after being buried for 120 years. Climb to the top of the poppet head lookout tower at the back of the Bendigo Art Gallery for sensational 360-degree views or wander through the Conservatory Gardens. You can download a walking tour map from Bendigo Tourism's website (www.bendigotourism.com).

O'Keefe Rail Trail
CYCLING

(www.railtrails.org.au) Completed in 2015 is this rail trail bike path that follows a disused railway line for 49km from Lake Weeroona to Heathcote. There's a heap of wineries and eateries along the way; the Bendigo tourism website (www.bendigotourism.com) has a useful map. Bikes and tours can be arranged through **Goldfields Bike Tours** (☑0418 303 065; www.goldfieldsbiketours.com.au; Bendigo Lakeview Motor Inn, 286 Napier St; per day bike rental $50, electric bikes $80, tours per person from $140).

★ Festivals & Events

Vesak Festival of Light
CULTURAL

(☉May) Held at the Great Stupa of Universal Compassion is this annual festival celebrating Buddha's birthday, culminating in a spectacular light show and fireworks display. During the day there are tours of the stupa, meditation classes and chanting by Tibetan monks, along with vegetarian food and multicultural **performances**.

Bendigo

Bendigo

◎ Top Sights
1 Bendigo Art Gallery B2
2 Bendigo Talking Tram A4
3 Golden Dragon Museum & Gardens C1

◎ Sights
4 Central Deborah Goldmine A4
5 Lookout Tower B2
6 Post Office Gallery C2
7 Rosalind Park B2
8 Sacred Heart Cathedral A3
9 Sandhurst Gaol C1
10 Tramways Depot D1

🛏 Sleeping
11 Allawah Bendigo B2
12 Bendigo Backpackers B3
13 Shamrock Hotel C2

🍴 Eating
14 Brewhouse Coffee Roasters B3
15 El Gordo C2
16 GPO Bar & Grill C2
17 Mason's of Bendigo C3
18 Mr Beebe's Eating House & Bar B2
19 Toi Shan C3
Wine Bank .... (see 11)
20 Woodhouse C3

🍸 Drinking & Nightlife
21 Dispensary Bar & Diner C2
Get Naked Espresso .... (see 19)
Handle Bar .... (see 19)

★ Entertainment
Ulumbarra Theatre .... (see 9)

🛏 Sleeping

Bendigo Backpackers
HOSTEL $

(📞 03-5443 7680; www.bendigobackpackers.com.au; 33 Creek St South; dm/d/f with shared bathroom $35/55/70; ❄🛜) This small and friendly hostel is in a homely weatherboard cottage with a handy central location. It has bright cheery rooms with all the usual amenities plus a few extras and a lovely courtyard.

★ The Schaller Studio
BOUTIQUE HOTEL $$

(📞 03-4433 6100; www.artserieshotels.com.au/schaller; cnr Bayne & Lucan Sts; d from $112; 🅿❄🛜) At the forefront of Bendigo's style makeover, the Schaller Studio is part of the classy Art Series hotel chain that has won plaudits in Melbourne. The hotel takes as its inspiration the studio of Australian artist Mark Schaller, with his signed works in all their colourful glory. Public areas are edgy and cool, while most of the rooms have an almost playful energy.

★ Allawah Bendigo
APARTMENT $$

(📞 03-5441 7003; www.allawahbendigo.com; 45 View St; r $125-210; ❄🛜) Allawah offers two lovely options in the heart of Bendigo's historic centre, both in former heritage bank buildings. The maisonette rooms at the rear of the stunning Wine Bank are the more affordable choice, while its more boutique Fountain Suites are across the road in a splendid 19th-century building. For both, check-in is at the Wine Bank.

Shamrock Hotel
HOTEL $$

(📞 03-5443 0333; www.hotelshamrock.com.au; cnr Pall Mall & Williamson St; d incl breakfast $130-200, ste $200-285; ❄🛜) One of Bendigo's historic icons, the Shamrock is a stunning Victorian building with stained glass, original paintings, fancy columns and a *Gone with the Wind*–style staircase. The refurbished upstairs rooms range from small standard rooms to spacious deluxe and spa suites.

🍴 Eating

Brewhouse Coffee Roasters
CAFE $

(📞 03-5442 8224; www.brewhousecoffee.com.au; 402 Hargreaves St; mains $11-22; ⏱6am-5pm; 🛜) One of Bendigo's best spots for coffee is this Melbourne-like warehouse space that sources its beans globally and roasts locally. Great breakfasts segue nicely into lunchtime pizzas, sandwiches and dishes such as soft-shell crab burgers or Guinness-braised lamb shanks.

Toi Shan
CHINESE $

(📞 03-5443 5811; www.toishan.com.au; 65 Mitchell St; mains $13-23, buffet $13-16; ⏱11.30am-9.30pm Sun-Thu, to 10.30pm Fri & Sat) Opening its doors in 1892, cheap and cheerful Toi Shan has been around since the gold rush – reportedly Australia's oldest Chinese restaurant. Fill up on an excellent-value lunchtime smorgasbord ($13). BYO booze.

★ Mason's of Bendigo
MODERN AUSTRALIAN $$

(📞 03-5443 3877; www.masonsofbendigo.com.au; 25 Queen St; small plates $10-18, large plates $28-36; ⏱noon-2.30pm & 6-8.30pm Tue-Sat) Casual yet sophisticated, the menu at hatted Mason's is dominated by local produce to create an agreeable mix of fine food and great atmosphere. Order a bunch of tasting plates such as duck spring rolls or gin-and-tonic cured salmon with yabbie tails to go with a larger shared dish such as its signature roast lamb loin with crispy belly and rolled shoulder.

El Gordo
SPANISH $$

(📞 0401 412 894, 0466 432 156; www.elgordobendigo.com; Shop 3/70 Chancery Lane; dishes $8-18; ⏱8am-4pm Tue-Sat, 6-10pm Fri & Sat) Hidden down a city laneway is this Spanish cafe doing authentic tapas such as patatas bravas as well as soft-shell crab *bocadillos* (baguette) with jalapenos and aioli. There's also a good menu of *raciones* and Western brunch items, to go with Spanish beers, sangria and Industry Beans (p503) coffee from Melbourne.

Wine Bank
BISTRO $$

(📞 03-5444 4655, 0409 804 032; www.winebankonview.com; 45 View St; breakfast $9-22, mains $25-44; ⏱8am-11pm Mon-Thu, 8am-1am Fri, 8.30am-1am Sat, 8.30am-4pm Sun) Wine bottles line the walls in this beautiful former bank building (1876), which serves as a wine shop and bar specialising in central Victorian wines, and an atmospheric Italian-style cafe serving breakfasts, tapas and platters.

Mr Beebe's Eating House & Bar
MODERN AUSTRALIAN $$

(📞 03-5441 5557; www.mrbeebes.com.au; 17 View Point; small/large plates from $10/20, tasting menu 5/6 dishes $52/62; ⏱11am-11pm) Another eatery inside an elegant old bank building (like most restaurants in this area) is the casual-chic Mr Beebe's. It does a delicious range of inventive shared plates, but the chef's tasting plate is a good choice. Otherwise pop in for its tasty bar food with an awesome (and well-priced) choice of beers on tap and local wines by the glass.

GPO Bar & Grill
MEDITERRANEAN $$
(📞03-5443 4343; www.gpobendigo.com.au; 60-64 Pall Mall; tapas from $11, pizzas from $18, mains $21-37; ⏰11.30am-late; 🛜) Rated highly by locals, the food and atmosphere here is superb. Its porterhouse brioche rolls and Moroccan pulled-lamb pizzas are terrific lunch orders. The bar is a chilled place for a drink with an impressive wine and cocktail list.

Woodhouse
STEAK $$$
(📞03-5443 8671; www.thewoodhouse.com.au; 101 Williamson St; pizza $20-25, mains $38-65; ⏰noon-2.30pm & 5.30pm-late Tue-Fri, noon-late Sat) In a warehouse-style space clad in warm brick tones, Woodhouse has some of the finest steaks you'll find anywhere in regional Victoria – all cooked on a red gum wood-fired grill. The Wagyu Tasting Plate ($68) is pricey but close to heaven for dedicated (and hungry) carnivores. Its $22 lunch special gets you pizza and a glass of wine or craft beer.

🍷 Drinking & Nightlife

★ Goldmines Hotel
PUB
(📞03-5442 2453; www.thegoldmineshotel.weebly.com; 49-57 Marong Rd; ⏰4-11pm Tue & Wed, noon-11pm Thu & Fri, 11am-11pm Sat & Sun) Just outside the CBD in the west of town is this old local watering hole in a grand old mansion (1857). It's famous for its leafy beer garden that keeps on going and going. It has a bunch of craft beers on tap, live blues bands in its wine cellar on Fridays, and a menu of pulled-pork tacos, po' boys and pub classics.

★ Dispensary Bar & Diner
BAR
(📞03-5444 5885; www.dispensarybendigo.com; 9 Chancery Lane; ⏰noon-late Tue-Fri, 8.30am-late Sat, 8.30am-5pm Sun) With its sneaky laneway location and intimate den-like space, the Dispensary is equal to any of Melbourne's hip inner-city bars. They have a selection of 90 craft beers, 40 gins and 60 whiskies, along with quality cocktails. Food is of equal attraction, whether a plate of steamed buns or larger dishes such as Roast Aylesbury duck.

Cambrian Hotel
PUB
(📞03-5443 3363; www.cambrianhotel.com.au; 200 Arnold St, North Bendigo; ⏰3pm-late Tue & Wed, noon-late Thu-Sun) A must for lovers of craft beer, this laid-back country-style pub

has eight Victorian microbreweries on tap. It has a casual backyard beer garden with retro couches and large projector screen. Its food is another reason to visit with 12-hour smoked meats and Caribbean-style curries.

Get Naked Espresso
CAFE
(📞0411 950 044; www.getnakedespressobar.com; 73 Mitchell St; ⏰6.30am-2pm; 🛜) A cool little city cafe bar, Get Naked Espresso is a great spot to hang out and taste quality Mt Beauty roasted coffee. They also have a second cafe across from the Bendigo Art Gallery.

For booze head out back to its **Handle Bar** (📞0417 477 825; www.facebook.com/handle-barbendigo; ⏰noon-11pm Thu-Sun).

ℹ️ Information

Bendigo Visitor Centre (📞1800 813 153, 03-5434 6060; www.bendigotourism.com; 51-67 Pall Mall; ⏰9am-5pm) In the historic former post office this helpful visitor centre can book tickets for sights and tours, provide accommodation referrals and has a bazillion brochures. Also here is the **Post Office Gallery** (📞03-5434 6179; www.bendigoartgallery.com.au; 51-67 Pall Mall; gold coin donation; ⏰9am-5pm).

ℹ️ Getting There & Away

Bendigo Airport Service (📞03-5444 3939; www.bendigoairportservice.com.au; adult one way/return $45/83, child $22/44; ⏰office 9am-5pm Mon-Fri) Runs direct between Melbourne's Tullamarine Airport and Bendigo train station. Bookings essential.

V/Line (📞1800 800 007; www.vline.com.au) Has frequent trains between Melbourne (Southern Cross Station) and Bendigo (from $21.84, two hours, around 20 daily) via Castlemaine ($4.80, 20 minutes) and Kyneton ($7.84, 40 minutes).

Kyneton
POP 6629
Kyneton, established a year before gold was discovered, was the main coach stop between Melbourne and Bendigo and the centre for the farmers who supplied the diggings with fresh produce. Today its historic Piper St is a destination in itself, as Melbourne foodies flock here on the weekends to sample its string of quality restaurants and cafes in a precinct lined with heritage buildings. The rest of Kyneton remains blue collar, with a built-up shopping area around Mollison and High Sts.

✖ Eating

Kyneton's eat street is along historic Piper St, with its quarter-mile strip showcasing some of the region's best eateries and bars.

Dhaba at the Mill
INDIAN $

(☏ 03-5422 6225; www.dhaba.com.au; 18 Piper St; mains $12-16; ⊙ 5-9pm Thu-Sat, noon-2.30pm & 5-9pm Sun; ☏) Behind the heavy wooden doors at the old bluestone steam mill, you can tuck into authentic, affordable curries – classics such as butter chicken, palak paneer and lamb vindaloo. It's an appealing space decked out in retro Bollywood film posters and jars of spices.

La Bontà
ITALIAN $$

(☏ 03-5422 3683; www.labonta.com.au; 12-14 Piper St; mains $16-34, 5-course set menu per person $74; ⊙ noon-2.30pm & 6-10pm Tue-Sat) Slotting in nicely along epicurean Piper St is this contemporary Italian restaurant serving inventive dishes with authentic flavours. Expect to be wowed by the likes of *risotto asticino* (Moreton Bay bug poached in tomato butter on saffron risotto) or *gnocchi di zucca* (pumpkin gnocchi in burnt butter and sage with cider-braised duck), alongside a selection of mozzarellas and all-regional wine list.

Royal George
MODERN AUSTRALIAN $$

(☏ 03-5422 1390; www.royalgeorge.com.au; 24 Piper St; pizzas $12, mains $22-35; ⊙ noon-late Fri-Mon, 4-9.30pm Tue-Thu) The historic Royal George hotel has a wonderful relaxed country pub atmosphere, but with an added bonus of 16 craft beers on tap and awesome food. The menu is wide-ranging, from $12 prosciutto pizzas or a Kyneton Fried Chicken burger, to 12-hour roasted lamb shoulder with jus and roast veggies.

★ Source Dining
MODERN AUSTRALIAN $$$

(☏ 03-5422 2039; www.sourcedining.com.au; 72 Piper St; mains $36-40; ⊙ noon-2.30pm & 6-9pm Thu-Sat, noon-2.30pm Sun) One of central Victoria's best restaurants, this fine place has a menu that changes with the seasons and dish descriptions that read like a culinary short story about regional produce and carefully conceived taste combinations.

★ Mr Carsisi
MIDDLE EASTERN $$$

(☏ 03-5422 3769; www.mrcarsisi.com; 37c Piper St; mezze $5-15.50, mains $32.50-38.50; ⊙ 11.30am-late Fri-Tue) For the moment, Turkish tastes and Middle Eastern mezze dominate the menu at the well-regarded Mr Carsisi. It does a faultless job of combining foreign flavours with local produce – the honey-and-cardamom Milawa duck breast is typical of the genre. There are plans to overhaul its menu, however, so expect a possible shift in direction.

ℹ Information

Kyneton Visitor Centre (☏ 1800 244 711, 03-5422 6110; www.visitmacedonranges.com; 127 High St; ⊙ 9am-5pm) On the southeastern entry to town, with a large selection of brochures, including self-guided town and nature walks, and scenic driving routes.

ℹ Getting There & Away

Kyneton is just off the Calder Hwy about 90km northwest of Melbourne.

Regular **V/Line** (www.vline.com.au) trains on the Bendigo line run here from Melbourne (from $11.62, 1¼ hours). The train station is 1km south of the town centre.

Castlemaine

POP 9730

At the heart of the central Victorian goldfields, Castlemaine is a picturesque historic town home to some stirring examples of late-19th-century architecture and gardens. A rewarding working-class town, in recent years it's seen an influx of Melburnians – known locally as 'latte sipping blow-ins' (LSBIs) – and is popular with artists and tree-changers bringing with them inner-city style, bars and live music venues.

◉ Sights & Activities

★ The Mill
HISTORIC BUILDING

(www.millcastlemaine.com.au; 1/9 Walker St) Originally the Castlemaine Woollen Mills (1875), this red-brick industrial complex has been developed into one of the town's coolest precincts. It's worth dropping in for a look around; a number of local businesses have set up since 2014, including a brewery, vintage stores, an artisan ice-cream shop, an Austrian-inspired coffee house and even a winery.

★ Castlemaine Art Gallery & Historical Museum
GALLERY

(☏ 03-5472 2292; www.castlemainegallery.com; 14 Lyttleton St; adult//child $10/free; ⊙ 10am-5pm Mon & Wed-Fri, noon-5pm Sat & Sun) A superb art deco building houses this gallery, which features colonial and contemporary Australian art, including works by well-known Australian artists such as Frederick McCubbin, Russell Drysdale, Fred Williams and Sir Sidney Nolan. There's a guided tour each Saturday at 2pm.The museum, in the basement, provides an insight into Indigenous and colonial history, period costumes, porcelain, silverware and gold-mining relics.

Old Castlemaine Gaol MUSEUM
(☑ 03-5472 3749; www.oldcastlemainegaol.com.au; 36-48 Bowden St; adult/concession/child $20/15/free, self-guided tour $10; ⊙ guided tours 2pm Fri, 10am & 2pm Sat & Sun, self-guided tours 9am-4pm daily) Built in 1861, the last prisoners moved out of the imposing Pentonville-style Old Castlemaine Gaol in 1990. Today you can take a guided tour of the old cells, gallows and watchtowers, and hear tales of executions and notable inmates. At other times you can do a self-guided tour ($10).

The space is also used for live music – see its website for upcoming gigs – as well as a **cafe** (breakfast & lunch $8-22, dinner $20-38; ⊙ 8am-4pm Mon & Thu, 8am-11pm Fri & Sat, 8am-5pm Sun).

🛏 Sleeping

**Big4 Castlemaine
Gardens Holiday Park** CARAVAN PARK $
(☑ 03-5472 1125, 1300 472 762; www.big4.com.au; 1 Doran Ave; unpowered/powered sites from $38/40, cabins $105-155; ❋ 🛜) Beautifully situated next to the botanical gardens and public swimming pool (adult/child $5/4), this leafy park has a camp kitchen, barbecues, recreation hut and a heap of stuff for kids.

★ The Newnorthern BOUTIQUE HOTEL $$
(☑ 03-5472 3787; www.newnorthern.com.au; 359 Barker St; r with shared/private bathroom incl breakfast from $164/240; ❋ 🛜) The old Northern Hotel (c 1870) has been beautifully restored and decorated by renowned furniture maker/artist Nicholas Dattner. Rooms are spacious, comfortable and feature art works, antiques and furniture. Though not all rooms are en suite, each room is allocated its own private bathroom. It has a lovely lounge and bar downstairs, where breakfast is served.

The Empyre HISTORIC HOTEL $$$
(☑ 03-5472 5166; www.empyre.com.au; 68 Mostyn St; d incl breakfast from $265; ❋ 🛜) A beautifully restored 19th-century hotel done out in an elegant period style, and with a location perfect for the theatre and restaurants.

🍴 Eating & Drinking

Johnny Baker BAKERY $
(☑ 03-5470 5695; www.johnnybaker.com.au; 359 Barker St; pies & pastries from $5; ⊙ 6.30am-4pm) Not your usual country bakery, here it's all about hand-rolled croissants baked with Belgian butter, among other mind-blowing sugary pastries. Its pies are equally as popular, with favourites including the vegetarian lentil-and-eggplant shepherd's pie, or minted lamb and pea, which you can wolf down on the milk crate seating out the front.

★ Public Inn MODERN AUSTRALIAN $$$
(☑ 03-5472 3568; www.publicinn.com.au; 26a Templeton St; 2-/3-course meal $55/69, cafe $15/26; ⊙ restaurant 6-10pm daily, noon-3pm Sat & Sun, cafe 8am-10pm) A rustic facade of what was Castlemaine's former fire station opens to a slick yet casual restaurant and bar space with a 'barrel wall', where local wines are dispensed. Food is a set menu of highly seasonal, high-end contemporary fare.

Next door is its more casual **Cafe re-Public** with an all-day breakfast menu, pork-and-pinenut sausage hot dogs and veggie pakora burgers.

Castlemaine Brewing Co. BREWERY
(☑ 0438 042 901, 0425 323 005; www.castlemaine brewing.com; 9 Walker St, The Mill; ⊙ noon-6pm Tue & Wed, to 8pm Thu & Sun, to 10pm Fri & Sat) It's been a long time in between drinks, but finally Castlemaine has got a brewery back in town. It's a good one too, set up within the Mill complex, with 10 of its beers on tap and a bar looking on to its vats. There are pizzas and platters to go with its IPAs, pale, red and golden ales, ginger beer and cider.

☆ Entertainment

Bridge Hotel LIVE MUSIC
(☑ 03-5470 6426; www.facebook.com/thebridge castlemaine; 21-23 Walker St; ⊙ noon-late) One of regional Victoria's best live-music venues, the Bridge books a solid lineup of rock 'n' roll and indie bands, such as King Gizzard and the Lizard Wizard, and a few internationals. They also do great burgers and have a killer beer garden.

ℹ Information

Castlemaine Visitor Centre (☑ 03-5471 1795; www.maldoncastlemaine.com; 44 Mostyn St; ⊙ 9am-5pm) In the old Castlemaine Market is this handy tourist info office with a bunch of brochures, books, downloadable walking tours and bikes for rent (half-/full-day $20/30).

ℹ Getting There & Away

V/Line (www.vline.com.au) trains run hourly between Melbourne and Castlemaine (from $15.96, 1½ hours) and continue on to Bendigo ($4.48, 30 minutes).

Bendigo Airport Service (☑ 03-5444 3939; www.bendigoairportservice.com.au; adult one-way/return $45/83, child $22/44) runs direct between Melbourne's Tullamarine Airport and Castlemaine station. Bookings essential.

The Grampians

Rising up from the western Victorian plains, and acting as a haven for bushwalkers, rock climbers and nature lovers, the Grampians are one of the state's most outstanding natural and cultural features. The rich diversity of wildlife and flora, unique rock formations, Aboriginal rock art, spectacular viewpoints and an extensive network of trails and bush camp sites offers something for everyone. The local Indigenous Jardwadjali people called the mountains Gariwerd – in the local language *'gari'* means 'pointed mountain', while *'werd'* means 'shoulder'. Explorer Major Thomas Mitchell named the ranges the Grampians after the mountains in Scotland.

Grampians National Park (Gariwerd)

It's one thing to appreciate the Grampians' spectacular backdrop from afar – ie from Halls Gap with glass of wine in hand – but don't leave the region without getting out into the national park itself. With more than 150km of well-marked walking tracks, ranging from half-hour strolls to overnight treks through difficult terrain, there's something here to suit all levels. Along with scenic drives and adventure activities such as abseiling and rock climbing, there are many ways to experience the park.

In mid-January 2014, a series of bushfires swept through the Grampians region, with the northern region the hardest hit. Homes were lost around Wartook and Brimpaen, while large swathes of forest turned to ash in the areas around Mt Difficult. In spite of the fires, the Grampians remain very much open for business – check with the various visitors centres and Parks Victoria to see which, if any, trails are closed.

The four greatest mountain ranges of the Grampians are the **Mt Difficult Range** in the north, **Mt William Range** in the east, **Serra Range** in the southeast and **Victoria Range** in the southwest. They spread from Ararat to the Wartook Valley and from Dunkeld almost to Horsham. **Halls Gap**, the main accommodation base and service town, lies in the Fyans Valley. The smaller **Wonderland Range**, close to Halls Gap, has some of the most splendid and accessible outlooks, such as those that go to the Pinnacles or Silverband Falls.

◎ Sights & Activities

One of the most popular sights is spectacular **MacKenzie Falls**. From the car park the steep 600m path leads to the base of the falls and a large plunge pool (no swimming). Other popular places include: **Boroka Lookout**, with excellent views over Halls Gap and Lake Bellfield, and **Reed Lookout**, with its short walk to the **Balconies** and views over Lake Wartook.

ℹ Information

Parks Victoria (☑ 03-5361 4000, 13 19 63; www.parkweb.vic.gov.au; 277 Grampians Tourist Rd, Brambuk Cultural Centre, Halls Gap) The Brambuk Cultural Centre at Halls Gap is the place for park maps and advice about where to go, where to camp and what you might see. They also issue camping permits and fishing permits required for fishing in local streams.

Halls Gap

POP 613

Nudging up against the craggy Wonderland Range, Halls Gap is a pretty little town – you might even say sleepy if you visit midweek in winter, but boy does it get busy during holidays. This is the main accommodation base and easiest access for the best of the Grampians. The single street through town has a neat little knot of shops, a supermarket, adventure-activity offices, restaurants and cafes.

There are plenty of kangaroos about its grassy surrounds, with the football oval being a particular favourite hangout. Emus are also often spotted.

◎ Sights & Activities

★ **Brambuk Cultural Centre**   CULTURAL CENTRE (☑ 03-5361 4000, 03-8427 2311; www.brambuk. com.au; 277 Grampians Rd; gold coin donation; ⊙ 9am-5pm) 🅵 **FREE** Don't leave Halls Gap without missing the superb cultural centre

The Grampians (Gariwerd)

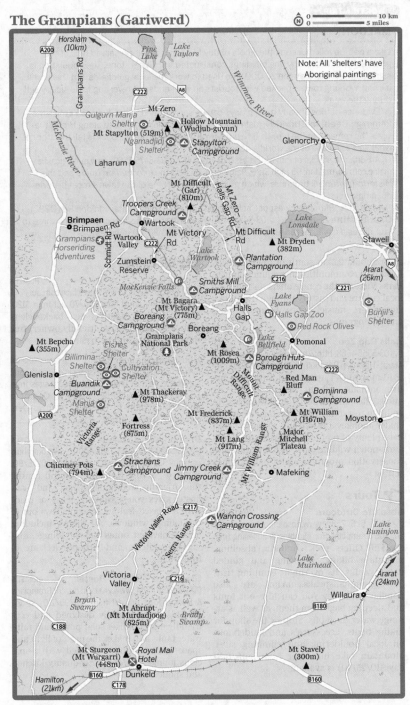

WORTH A TRIP

MALDON

Like a pop-up folk museum, the whole of tiny Maldon is a well-preserved relic of the gold-rush era, with many fine buildings constructed from local stone. The population is significantly lower than the 20,000 who used to work the local goldfields, but this is still a living, working town – packed with tourists on weekends but reverting to its sleepy self during the week.

Evidence of those heady mining days can be seen around town – you can't miss the 24m-high **Beehive Chimney**, just east of Main St. A short trip south along High St reveals the remains of the **North British Mine**, where interpretive boards tell the story of what was once one of the world's richest mines.

Among the stacks of info at the **visitor centre** (☑03-5475 2569; www.maldoncastle maine.com.au/maldon; 95 High St; ☺9am-5pm), pick up the *Information Guide* and the *Historic Town Walk* brochure, which guides you past some of the town's most historic buildings.

Maldon is 19km northwest of Castlemaine along the Bridgewater-Maldon Rd (C282). **Castlemaine Bus Lines** (☑03-5472 1455; www.castlemainebuslines.com.au) runs three to four buses a day between Maldon and Castlemaine ($3.20, 20 minutes).

at Brambuk, 2.5km south of town. Run by five Koori communities in conjunction with Parks Victoria, the centre offers insights into local culture and history through traditional stories, art, music, dance, weapons, tools and photographs.

Halls Gap Zoo   ZOO
(☑03-5356 4668; http://hallsgapzoo.com.au; 4061 Ararat–Halls Gap Rd; adult/child/family $28/14/70; ☺10am-5pm) Get up close to Australian native animals such as wallabies, dingoes, quolls, Tasmanian devils and wombats, in addition to exotic critters such as meerkats, spider monkeys, bison and tamarin. They have plenty of reptiles and birds too. This is a top-notch wildlife park with breeding and conservation programs and a natural bush setting.

☞ Tours

Absolute Outdoors   ADVENTURE
(☑1300 526 258; www.absoluteoutdoors.com. au; 105 Grampians Rd; climbing & abseiling half-day $75) Offers rock climbing, abseiling, mountain biking, canoeing and guided nature walks. Its overnight camping trips (www.grampianspeaks.com.au) are also popular, and they you can hire out tents and sleeping bags from them, as well as arrange water drop-offs. Stop by the shop for hiking boots, accessories and guidebooks on local bouldering and climbing sites. Mountain bike hire (per hour/half-/full-day $10/25/40) is available.

🛏 Sleeping

Tim's Place   HOSTEL $
(☑03-5356 4288; www.timsplace.com.au; 44 Grampians Rd; dm/d from $30/70; apt from $120; @🛜) Friendly, spotless eco backpackers with a homely feel and friendly owner; free mountain bikes and herb garden.

Halls Gap Caravan Park   CAMPGROUND $
(☑03-5356 4251; www.hallsgapcaravanpark.com. au; 26 School Rd; unpowered/powered sites from $32/40, cabins $120-195; ❄🛜) Camping and cabins right in the town centre. Gets crowded at peak times.

Brambuk Backpackers   HOSTEL $
(☑03-5356 4250, 03-5361 4000; www.brambuk. com.au; 332 Grampians Rd; dm/d/tr $30/75/90; ❄🛜) 🍃 Across from the cultural centre, this friendly Aboriginal-owned and -run hostel gives you a calming sense of place with a relaxed feel and craggy views out of the lounge windows. All rooms, including dorms, have en suites and the lounge, dining room, kitchen and barbecue deck are all top-notch.

Grampians YHA Eco-Hostel   HOSTEL $
(☑03-5356 4544; www.yha.com.au; cnr Grampians & Buckler Rds; dm/d/f from $31/95/110; @🛜) 🍃 This architecturally designed and eco-friendly hostel utilises solar power and rainwater tanks and makes the most of light and space. It's beautifully equipped with a spacious lounge, a *MasterChef*-quality kitchen and spotless rooms.

★ **D'Altons Resort** COTTAGE $$
(☑ 03-5356 4666; www.daltonsresort.com.au; 8 Glen St; studio/deluxe/family cottages from $110/125/160; ❄ 🛜 🏊) These delightful timber cottages, with cute verandahs and log fires, spread up the hill from the main road between the gums and kangaroos. They're immaculately kept, the friendly owners are a mine of local information, and there's even a tennis court and a saltwater pool.

Pinnacle Holiday Lodge MOTEL $$
(☑ 03-5356 4249; www.pinnacleholiday.com.au; 21-45 Heath St; 1-/2-bedroom unit from $99/163, d with spa from $140; ❄ 🛜 🏊) Right in the centre of Halls Gap, this gorgeous property behind the Stony Creek shops has a spectacular mountainous backdrop and plenty of kangaroos. The spacious grounds have a bucolic feel with barbecue areas, an indoor pool and tennis courts. Modern self-contained units, two-bedroom family apartments and a swanky spa suite feature gas log fires.

Mountain Grand Guesthouse GUESTHOUSE $$
(☑ 03-5356 4232; www.mountaingrand.com.au; Grampians Rd; s/d incl breakfast $146/166; ❄ 🛜) This gracious timber guesthouse prides itself on being a traditional old-fashioned lodge where you can take a pre-dinner port in one of the lounge areas and mingle with other guests. The rooms are still quaint but with a bright, fresh feel. The **Balconies Restaurant** here is well regarded.

Aspect Villas VILLA $$$
(☑ 03-5356 4457; www.aspectvillas.com.au; off Mackey's Peak Rd; d $520; ❄ 🛜) These two luxury villas are situated close to town, but seem a world away when you're reclining on your bed or by the log fire, taking in views of the Wonderland Range through floor-to-ceiling windows. They make the most of local building materials such as Grampians stone, and sit on a secluded property complete with its own lagoon.

🍴 Eating

Brambuk Bushfood Cafe AUSTRALIAN $
(☑ 03-5361 4000; www.brambuk.com.au; Brambruk Cultural Centre, 277 Grampians Rd; mains $8.50-22; ⏱ 9am-4pm) Within the Brambuk Cultural Centre, this cafe is a must if you want to sample native Australia flavours such as wattleseed, lemon myrtle and bush tomato. Expect also saltbush lasagne, kangaroo pies and grilled emu. The bushfood platter ($22) is a good way to sample a bit of everything.

Livefast Lifestyle Cafe CAFE $
(☑ 03-5356 4400; www.livefast.com.au; Shop 5, Stony Creek Stores; breakfast $8-17, lunch $15-19; ⏱ 7am-4pm Mon-Fri, to 5pm Sat & Sun; 🛜) Halls Gap's best coffee and a sunny atmosphere are the hallmarks of this cafe. It does interesting breakfasts, including Spanish- and Japanese-influenced dishes, and fresh and tasty lunches such as Vietnamese tofu salad with noodles and rosemary beef burgers. Great selection of craft beers and Grampian wines.

Harvest CAFE $$
(☑ 03-5356 4782; www.harvesthg.com.au; 2 Heath St; day menu $9.80-16.50, dinner $22-32; ⏱ 8am-4pm Mon-Thu & Sun, to 10pm Fri & Sat) Utilising the rich bounty of produce in the region, Harvest's cafe menu specialises in locally grown food and wine. It does all-day gourmet breakfasts (Mexican baked eggs) and bites like sourdough steak sandwiches for lunch. On Friday and Saturday they stay open for dinner, with a tasty menu of small and large sharing plates.

Spirit of Punjab INDIAN $$
(☑ 03-5356 4234; www.spiritofpunjabrestaurant. com; 161-163 Grampians Rd; mains $13.50-25; ⏱ noon-2.30pm & 5-9pm) For a taste of the subcontinent in an Aussie bush setting head to this excellent Punjabi restaurant, which features some fairly bizarre folk sculpture out front. They do an array of dishes with authentic flavours, including a good tandoori selection. There's cheap bottles of wine, and an outdoor deck overlooking a natural clearing often frequented by roos.

Kookaburra Hotel MODERN AUSTRALIAN $$
(☑ 03-5356 4222; www.kookaburrahotel.com.au; 125-127 Grampians Rd; mains $18-36; ⏱ 6-9pm Tue-Fri, noon-3pm & 6-9pm Sat & Sun) This Halls Gap institution is famed for its excellent pub food, such as the sublime crispy-skin duck and Aussie dishes such as barramundi and kangaroo fillet (cooked rare or medium-rare only, as it should be). The wine list features mostly Grampians area wines, and there's beer on tap at the convivial bar.

ℹ Information

Halls Gap Visitor Centre (☑ 1800 065 599; www.visithallsgap.com.au; 117-119 Grampians Rd; ⏱ 9am-5pm; 🛜) The staff here are helpful and can book tours, accommodation and activities. They also sell detailed maps ($3.50) and info on walks and drives in the park.

ROCK ART

Traditional Aboriginal owners have been occupying Gariwerd for more than 20,000 years and this is the most accessible place in Victoria to see Indigenous rock art. Sites include **Bunjil's Shelter**, near Stawell, one of Victoria's most sacred Indigenous sites, best seen on a guided tour from the **Brambuk Cultural Centre** (☑ 03-5356 4452; www.brambuk.com.au; Grampians Rd; 3/5hr tours $70/140). Other rock-art sites in the west of the park are the **Manja Shelter**, reached from the Harrop Track car park, and the **Billimina Shelter**, near the Buandik camping ground. In the north is the **Ngamadjidj Shelter**, reached from the Stapylton camping ground.

These paintings, in protected rock overhangs, are mostly handprints, animal tracks and stick figures. They indicate the esteem in which these mountains are held by local Indigenous communities and should be treated with respect.

ⓘ Getting There & Away

Halls Gap is located 254km from Melbourne along the Western Hwy (three hours), passing through Ballarat (142km) at the halfway mark. If coming from the Great Ocean Road it's 156km north of Port Fairy.

Halls Gap is well linked by public transport. V/Line connects it with Melbourne ($33.20, 3½ hours) and Ballarat ($17.20, two hours); connecting buses await at Ararat or Stawell stations. There's also a bus from Warrnambool ($28.20, three hours) on Tuesday, Friday and Sunday.

Dunkeld & Around

The southern point of access for the Grampians, Dunkeld (population 461) is a sleepy little town with a very big-name restaurant, the **Royal Mail Hotel** (☑ 03-5577 2241; www.royalmail.com.au; 98 Parker St; bistro $24-42, lunch $75-95, dinner $95-165; ☺ bar & bistro noon-3pm & 6-9pm, restaurant noon-2.30pm Thu-Sun & 6-10pm Wed-Sun) – long regarded as one of the finest in the state. The setting of the town is superb, with Mt Abrupt and Mt Sturgeon to the north, while the Grampians Tourist Rd to Halls Gap gives you a glorious passage into the park, with the cliffs and sky opening up as you pass between the Serra and Mt William Ranges. Dunkeld is 64km south of Halls Gap.

NORTHWEST OF THE GRAMPIANS

Horsham

POP 15, 894

The major town to the northwest of the Grampians and the capital of the Wimmera region, Horsham makes a convenient base for exploring the surrounding national parks and Mt Arapiles. The newly revamped Horsham Regional Art **Horsham Regional Art Gallery** (☑ 03-5382 9575; www.horshamartgallery.com.au; 80 Wilson St; ☺ 10am-5pm Tue-Fri, 11am-4.30pm Sat, 1-4.30pm Sun) FREE, within the historic art deco town hall, is a must for art lovers. Its downstairs space exhibits interesting contemporary shows, while upstairs has a permanent collection of photography featuring quality works by Bill Henson, Frank Hurley and Wolfgang Sievers. Also upstairs are paintings by Sidney Nolan, John Bracks, Fred Williams and Brett Whiteley.

ⓘ Information

Horsham & Grampians Visitors Centre (☑ 03-5382 1832; www.visithorsham.com.au; 20 O'Callaghan's Pde; ☺ 9am-5pm) Very helpful centre for information on Horsham and the surrounding area, including walking maps and art trails.

ⓘ Getting There & Away

Horsham is 300km from Melbourne along the Western Hwy, passing through Ballarat en route. The Little Desert National Park (74km) is just over an hour's drive, while Halls Gap (73km) in the Grampians is just under an hour.

From Melbourne's Southern Cross Station there's a daily train-coach service to Horsham ($39, four hours) with a transfer in Ararat.

Mt Arapiles State Park

Mt Arapiles is Australia's premier rock-climbing destination. Topping out at 369m, it's not the world's biggest mountain, but with more than 2000 routes to scale, it attracts salivating climbers from around the world. Popular climbs include the Bard Buttress, Tiger Wall and the Pharos. In the tiny nearby town of Natimuk, a community of avid climbers has set up to service visitors, and the town has also developed into a bit of an artists centre.

🏃 Activities

Arapiles Climbing Guides CLIMBING
(☑ 03-5384 0376; www.arapiles.com.au; Natimuk) Climbing instruction and guiding around Mt Arapiles.

Natimuk Climbing Company CLIMBING
(☑ 0400 871 328, 03-5387 1329; www.climbco.com.au) Offers climbing, bouldering and abseiling instruction.

Arapiles Mountain Shop CLIMBING
(☑ 03-5387 1529, 0428 871 529; www.facebook.com/arapilesresoles; 67 Main St, Natimuk; ⊙ 1-5.30pm Mon & Fri, 4.30-6pm Tue & Thu, 11am-5.30pm Sat, noon-5.30pm Sun) Sells and hires climbing equipment.

🛏 Sleeping & Eating

Centenary Park Campground CAMPGROUND $
(☑ 13 19 63; www.parkweb.vic.gov.au; Centenary Park Rd, Mt Arapiles; camp sites per person $5.30) Most climbers head for this popular camping ground at the base of the mountain with three separate sites – the Lower Gums, the Pines and Upper Gums areas. There are toilets, communal fireplaces and picnic tables, but you'll need to bring your own drinking water and firewood.

Duffholme Cabins CABIN $
(☑ 0421 442 050; 1859 Natimuk Frances Rd, Mitre; camping $10, d incl breakfast $100) A self-contained cottage and camp site (with toilets and shower) surrounded by wildlife and with views of Mt Arapiles. Ring to make arrangements (it's not staffed).

ℹ Getting There & Away

Mt Arapiles is 37km west of Horsham and 12km west of Natimuk.

Wimmera Roadways (☑ coach pickup 0428 861 160, office 08-8762 2962; www.wimmeraroadways.com.au) runs a bus service from Horsham to Mt Arapiles ($6, 30 minutes) from Monday to Friday passing through Natimuk ($4.80). It's essential to phone ahead to request Mt Arapiles as a stop. It leaves Mt Arapiles at 9.40am and Horsham at 2.40pm.

Little Desert National Park

While you shouldn't expect rolling sand dunes, this arid park does cover a huge 1320 sq km and is rich in flora and fauna that thrive in the dry environment. There are over 670 indigenous plant species here, and in spring and early summer the landscape is transformed into a colourful wonderland of wildflowers. The best-known resident is the Malleefowl, an industrious bird that can be seen in an aviary at the Little Desert Nature Lodge.

The Nhill–Harrow Rd through the park is sealed and the road from Dimboola is gravel, but in the park the tracks are mostly sand and only suitable for 4WD vehicles or walking. Some are closed to 4WDs in the wet season (July to October).

🛏 Sleeping

⭐ Little Desert
Nature Lodge CAMPGROUND, RESORT $
(☑ 03-5391 5232; www.littledesertlodge.com.au; camp sites $35, bunkhouse d $56, motel r $130; ❄) 🅿 On the northern edge of the desert, 16km south of Nhill, this well-equipped and friendly bush retreat is a superb base for exploring the park. With a spacious camping ground, bunkhouse and comfortable en-suite motel-style rooms there's something for everyone. A key attraction here is the tour of the Malleefowl aviary ($30), where you can see these rare birds in a breeding program.

Camping Grounds CAMPGROUND $
(☑ 13 19 63; www.parkweb.vic.gov.au; sites from $27.40) There are several camping grounds in the national park, with the most popular being in the eastern block at **Horseshoe Bend** and **Ackle Bend** – both on the Wimmera River south of Dimboola. They have toilets, picnic tables and fireplaces. Otherwise, there's free bush camping in the more remote central and western blocks where there are designated sites.

ℹ Information

Little Desert Park Office (☑ 13 19 63, 03-8427 2129; www.parkweb.vic.gov.au; Nursery Rd, Wail Nursery; ⊙ 9am-5pm Mon-Fri) Now that all info and bookings are online there's little reason to stop by here, but rangers can offer advice on camping inside the park.

Nhill

Nhill is the base for the northern entrance to the Little Desert National Park and Kiata campground. It's a big town for this part of the world – the main industries here are wheat farming and producing ducks for Victorian restaurant tables. Nhill is an

Aboriginal word meaning 'mist over the water' – check out the artificial **Lake Nhill** and surrounding wetlands to see if there's any water. It has a sizeable community of Karen refugees who have been settled here after spending decades in camps along the Thai-Burma border.

Hindmarsh Visitors Centre (☑ 03-5391 3086; www.wimmeramalleetourism.com.au; Victoria St; ⊙ 9am-5pm Mon-Fri) In Goldsworthy Park in the town centre, has plenty of information on the park and local sights and accommodation.

WILSONS PROMONTORY & GIPPSLAND

The Great Ocean Road may get the crowds, but Gippsland hides all the secrets. Gippsland is one region where it pays to avoid the cities – the towns along the Princes Hwy are barely worth a traveller's glance. But beyond the highway are some of the state's most absorbing, unspoiled and beautiful wilderness areas and beaches.

Along the coast there's Wilsons Promontory National Park, a fabulous destination for hikers and sightseers alike. This is only the start when it comes to stirring beaches. Epic Ninety Mile Beach yields to Cape Conran Coastal Park and Croajingolong National Park. Put them together and it's one of the wildest, most beautiful coastlines on Earth.

Inland, the Buchan Caves are a must-see attraction, while the national parks at Snowy River and Errinundra are as deeply forested, remote and pristine as any in the country.

Koonwarra & Fish Creek

Tucked away in rolling dairy country along the South Gippsland Hwy is the tiny township of Koonwarra that's built itself a rep-

Gippsland

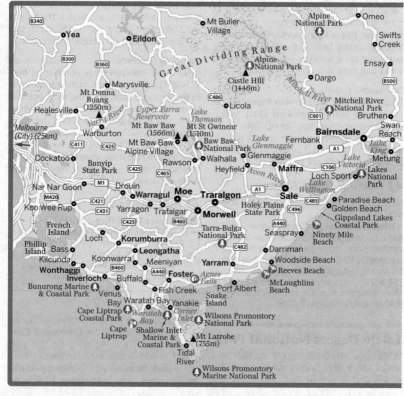

utation as something of a niche foodie destination. It has a cooking school, renowned farmers market and produce store, plus wineries nearby.

Travellers in the know have been stopping for a bite to eat at Fish Creek on their way to the coast or the Prom for years. These days it has developed into a little bohemian artists community with craft shops, galleries, studios, bookshops and some great cafes. The **Great Southern Rail Trail** (www.railtrails.org.au) passes through too.

⊙ Sights

Celia Rosser Gallery
GALLERY

(☑ 03-5683 2628, 0455 777 334; www.celiarossergallery.com.au; Promontory Rd; ⊙ 10am-4pm Fri-Sun) **FREE** A bright art space featuring the works of renowned botanical artist Celia Rosser who's most famous for her banksia watercolours. The *Banksia rosserae* was named after her; Queen Victoria is the only other woman to have a banksia in her name.

🛏 Sleeping & Eating

The Wine Farm
B&B **$$**

(☑ 03-5664 3204; www.thewinefarm.com.au; 370 Koonwarra–Inverloch Rd; d $150; ✳) Set on a 15-acre family-run boutique winery is this three-bedroom self-contained weatherboard cottage that's excellent value for couples and groups ($25 per extra person). It's a must for wine-lovers; South African vintner Neil Hawkins impresses with his range of 10 cool-climate varieties.

It's a two-night minimum stay, and can be used a base for day trips into the Prom, a one-hour drive away.

Fish Creek Hotel
PUB **$**

(☑ 03-5683 2404; www.fishcreekhotel.com.au; 1 Old Waratah Rd; mains $16-30, d with shared/private bathroom $85/100; ⊙ noon-2pm & 6-9pm) The striking art deco Fish Creek Hotel, universally known as the Fishy Pub, is not only an essential stop for a beer or bistro meal,

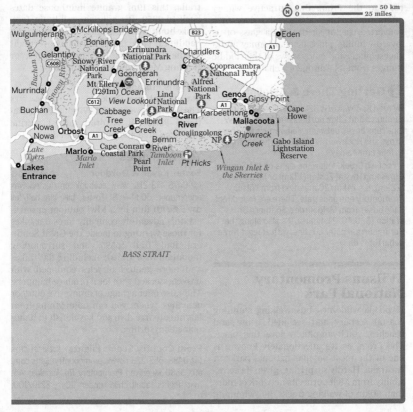

MELBOURNE & VICTORIA KOONWARRA & FISH CREEK

but also serves as a handy base for trips into Wilsons Prom. There's a choice of upstairs comfortable pub rooms (no TV or kettle) with shared bathrooms, and self-contained motel accommodation at the back.

★ **Koonwarra Store**   CAFE $$
(☑ 03-5664 2285; www.koonwarrastore.com.au; 2 Koonwarra-Inverloch Rd; mains $12-26; ⊙ 8.30am-4pm; ☞) Local produce and wines are on sale in this renovated timber building. It's also a renowned cafe that serves simple food with flair, priding itself on using organic, low-impact suppliers and products – go the Koonie burger with all-Gippsland ingredients. Soak up the ambience in the wooded interior, or relax at a table in the gardens with local ice cream, regional wines and a cheese paddle.

🍷 Drinking & Nightlife

Waratah Hills Vineyard   WINERY
(☑ 03-5683 2441; www.waratahhills.com.au; 20 Cottmans Rd; ⊙ 11am-4pm Fri-Sun, daily Jan) A five-minute drive out of Fish Creek on the road to the Prom, this attractive winery offers free tastings at its cellar door in a converted tractor shed. Grab a glass of its award-winning pinot or chardonnay and a cheese plate, and enjoy views of the Hoddle Ranges from its Adirondack chairs.

ⓘ Getting There & Away

By road Koonwarra is 32km southwest of Korumburra and 21km northeast of Inverloch. V/Line runs buses between Melbourne's Southern Cross and Koonwarra ($17.20, 2½ hours) three to four times a day.

For Fish Creek, follow the signs off the South Gippsland Hwy at Foster (13km) or Meeniyan (28km). It's 24km (20 minutes) from Wilsons Promontory entrance gate. There are four direct daily buses from Melbourne's Southern Cross station ($20.40, 2¾ hours). It's also along the Korumburra–Foster bus line, with at least three departures daily.

Wilsons Promontory National Park

If you like wilderness bushwalking, stunning coastal scenery and secluded white-sand beaches, you'll absolutely love this place. The Prom, as it's affectionately known, is one of the most popular national parks in Australia. Hardly surprising, given its accessibility from Melbourne, its network of more than 80km of walking tracks, its swimming and surf beaches and the abundant wildlife. The southernmost part of mainland Australia, the Prom once formed part of a land bridge that allowed people to walk to Tasmania.

Tidal River, 30km from the park entrance, is the hub, although there's no fuel to be had here. It's home to the Parks Victoria office, a general store, a cafe and accommodation. The wildlife around Tidal River is incredibly tame, but to prevent disease do not feed the animals or birds.

⊙ Sights

Norman Beach   BEACH
(Tidal River) The Prom's most popular beach is this beautiful stretch of golden sand, perfect for swimming and surfing, conveniently located at Tidal River campground.

Wilsons Promontory Lighthouse   LIGHTHOUSE
(Wilsons Promontory National Park) Close to being the southernmost tip of mainland Australia, this 19m granite lighthouse dates back to 1859. It's only accessibly on foot, a six-hour walk (18.3km) from Telegraph Saddle car park, hence most stay overnight at the Lighthouse Keepers' Cottages, or Roaring Meg campsite, 5.2km away.

Wilsons Promontory Marine National Park   NATIONAL PARK
The offshore version of Wilsons Prom National Park. It's Victoria's largest marine protected area and popular with divers.

🏃 Activities

Foster Kayak & Outdoor   OUTDOORS
(☑ 0475 473 211; www.facebook.com/fosterkayakandoutdoor; 50 Main St, Foster; bike hire half/full day $35/70) Run by a Kiwi outdoor enthusiast, this adventure company hires out bikes for those wanting to tackle the Great Southern Rail Trail (p585; and surrounding mountain-bike trails); including 'fat' bikes and more genteel bicycles equipped with baskets stocked with local produce hampers. They also offer a range of innovative outdoor activities, where you can do anything from learning to free dive and kayak-fish to handplane bodysurfing.

Prom Country Scenic Flights   SCENIC FLIGHTS
(☑ 0488 555 123; www.promcountryflights.com.au; 3680 Meeniyan Promontory Rd, Yanakie; 45-min flights adult/child under 10yr $210/100;

Wilsons Promontory National Park

N 0 — 5 km
0 — 2.5 miles

Fish Creek (16km);
Foster (25km)

C444 Yanakie

Millar Rd

Foster-Promontory Rd

Dalgleish Rd

Duck Point

Limosa Rise

Yanakie Beach

Foley Rd

Black Cockatoo Cottages

Park Entrance Booth

Wilsons Promontory Rd

Long Island

Corner Inlet

Corner Inlet Marine National Park

Shelter Cove

Freshwater Cove

Mt Singapore (147m)

Snake Island

Entrance Point

Tin Mine Cove

Mt Hunter (347m)

Hunter Point

Chinaman Long Beach

Lighthouse Point

Bennison Island

Mt Margaret (218m)

Tin Mine Track

Three Mile Beach

Chinamans Knob

Three Mile Point

Mt Roundback (316m)

Chinaman Creek

Johnnie Souey Cove

Millers Landing

Barry Creek

Johnny Souey Track

Five Mile Rd

St Kilda Junction

Five Mile Beach

Monkey Point

Vereker Lookout

Vereker Range

Cotters Beach

Emergencies Only

Mt Vereker (586m)

Shellback Island

Darby Bay

Lookout Rocks

Darby Beach

Darby Creek

Mt Leonard (556m)

Latrobe Range

Tidal River

Sealers Creek

Mt Latrobe (754m)

The Cathedral

Tongue Point

Sparkes Lookout

Mt Bishop (319m)

Whisky Bay

Picnic Bay

Norman Island

Leonard Point

Squeaky Beach

Mt Ramsay

Sealers Cove Walk

Horn Point

Hobbs Head

Sealers Cove

Norman Bay

Tidal River

Telegraph Saddle

Wilsons Range

Refuge Cove

Brown Head

Mt Oberon (558m)

Norman Point

Great Prom Walk Return Loop

Mt Wilson (705m)

Kersops Peak

Little Oberon Bay

Growler Creek

Oberon Bay

Fraser Creek

Mt Boulder (501m)

Little Waterloo Bay

Waterloo Bay

Cape Wellington

Great Glennie Island

Oberon Point

Telegraph Track

Mt Norgate (419m)

Waterloo Point

Great Prom Walk

Dannevig Island

Wilsons Promontory Marine National Park

Boulder Range

Lighthouse

McHugh Island

Citadel Island

South West Point

Roaring Meg Creek

Lighthouse Keepers' Cottages

Anser Island

Wattle Island

South Point

South-East Point

BASS STRAIT

9am-5pm) Head to the skies for spectacular Prom views with these 45-minute flights over the coast, lighthouse and bushland. They're based just past the Yanakie General Store on the road into the park.

Sleeping

Tidal River

Situated on Norman Bay and a short walk to a stunning beach, Tidal River is incredibly popular. Book accommodation online well in advance through Parks Victoria, especially for weekends and holidays.

Of Tidal River's 484 camp sites, only 20 are powered sites – so you'll need to book well in advance to secure these. For the Christmas school holiday period there's a ballot for sites (apply online by 30 June through Parks Victoria).

There are also wooden huts with bunks and kitchenettes, comfortable self-contained units and spacious safari-style tented camping with en-suite bathrooms.

Park Cabins – Tidal River   CABIN $$
(13 1963, 03-8427 2122; www.parkstay.vic.gov. au; Tidal River, Wilsons Promontory National Park; 6-bed cabins from $234.50) These spacious and private self-contained cabins with fully equipped kitchen (but no TV) sleep up to six people. They have large, sliding-glass doors and a deck, and overlook the bush or river.

★ **Lighthouse Keepers' Cottages**   COTTAGE $$$
(13 19 63, 03-5680 9555; www.parkweb.vic.gov. au; Wilsons Promontory National Park; d cottages $352-391, 12-bed cottages per person $127-141) These isolated, heritage-listed 1850s cottages, attached to a working light station on a pimple of land that juts out into the wild ocean, are a real getaway. Kick back after the 19km hike (around six hours) from Tidal River and watch ships or whales passing by. The cottages have thick granite walls and shared facilities, including a fully equipped kitchen.

Wilderness Retreat – Tidal River   TENTED CAMP $$$
(www.wildernessretreats.com.au; Tidal River, Wilsons Promontory National Park; d $318.50, extra person $26.20) Nestled in bushland at Tidal River, these large safari tents, each have their own deck, bathroom, queen-sized beds, fridge and heating, and there's a communal

tent kitchen. Tents sleep up to four people and are pretty cool. It's like being on an African safari with a kookaburra soundtrack.

Yanakie & Foster

The tiny settlement of Yanakie offers the closest accommodation – from cabins and camping to luxury cottages – outside the park boundaries. Foster, the nearest main town, has a backpackers and several motels.

Top of the Prom at Promview Farm   COTTAGE $$
(03-5687 1232, 0407 804 055; 4295 Meeniyan Promontory Rd, Yanakie; d $140-155, per extra person $20;) Only 200m from the park entrance, this two-bedroom dairy cottage is the closest private accommodation to the Prom. It has a kitchen, wi-fi, a DVD player and views over the paddocks; BYO linen and towel.

Black Cockatoo Cottages   COTTAGE $$
(03-5687 1306; www.blackcockatoo.com; 60 Foley Rd, Yanakie; d $150-250, 6-person houses $295-450) You can take in glorious views of the national park without leaving your very comfortable bed – or breaking the bank – in these private, stylish, timber cottages. There are three modern cottages painted in a cool 'yellow-tailed black cockatoo' colour scheme, as well a 1970s-style brown-brick three-bedroom house.

★ **Limosa Rise**   COTTAGE $$$
(03-5687 1135; www.limosarise.com.au; 40 Dalgleish Rd, Yanakie; d $295-400;) The views are stupendous from these luxury, self-contained cottages near the Prom entrance. The three tastefully appointed cottages (a studio, one bedroom and two bedroom) are fitted with wood-fire heaters, and full-length glass windows to take complete advantage of sweeping views across Corner Inlet, farmland and the Prom's mountains. Two-night minimum.

Eating

The **General Store** (03-5680 8520; Tidal River; mains $5-24; 9am-5pm Mon-Fri, to 6pm Sat, to 4pm Sun) in Tidal River stocks grocery items (but no alcohol), some camping equipment and a cafe. If you're hiking, or here for a while, it's cheaper to stock up in Foster. There's also a general store in Yanakie which is handy for food supplies, cold beer and Gippsland wines.

TOP PROM WALKS

During school holidays and on weekends from Christmas to Easter, a free shuttle bus operates between the Tidal River visitor car park and the **Telegraph Saddle car park** – a nice way to start the Great Prom Walk. They run every 30 minutes from 8.30am to 5.45pm, with a break for lunch at 1pm. For the overnight walks you'll need to arrange a hiking permit beforehand, as well as payment for campsites and or other accommodation.

Great Prom Walk The most popular long-distance hike is a moderate 45km circuit across to Sealers Cove from Tidal River, down to Refuge Cove, Waterloo Bay and the lighthouse, returning to Tidal River via Oberon Bay. Allow three days and coordinate your walk with tide times, as creek crossings can be hazardous. It's possible to visit or stay at the lighthouse by prior arrangement with the parks office.

Sealers Cove Walk The best overnight hike, this two-day walk starts at Telegraph Saddle and heads down Telegraph Track to stay overnight at beautiful Little Waterloo Bay (12km, 4½ hours). The next day, walk on to Sealers Cove via Refuge Cove and return to Telegraph Saddle (24km, 7½ hours).

Lilly Pilly Gully Nature Walk An easy 5km (two-hour) walk through heathland and eucalyptus forests, with lots of wildlife.

Mt Oberon Summit Starting from the Mt Oberon car park, this moderate-to-hard 7km (2½-hour) walk is an ideal introduction to the Prom with panoramic views from the summit. The free Mt Oberon shuttle bus can take you to the Telegraph Saddle car park and back.

Little Oberon Bay An easy-to-moderate 8km (three-hour) walk over sand dunes covered in coastal tea trees with beautiful views over Little Oberon Bay.

Squeaky Beach Nature Walk An easy 5km return stroll through coastal tea trees and banksias to a sensational white-sand beach.

Prom Wildlife Walk This short 2.3km (45 minute) loop trail yields good kangaroo, wallaby and emu sightings. It's located off the main road about 14km south of the park entrance.

ⓘ Information

Prom Country Visitor Information Centre (cnr McDonald & Main St, Foster; ⊙9am-5pm) Helpful info for those heading into Wilsons Prom, as well as ideas for the surrounding region.

Tidal River Visitors Centre (☑03-5680 9555, 03-8427 2122, 13 19 63; www.parkweb.vic.gov. au; ⊙8.30am-4.30pm, to 4pm in winter) The helpful visitor centre at Tidal River books all park accommodation (including permits for camping away from Tidal River), and offers info for all hiking options in the area.

ⓘ Getting There & Away

Tidal River lies approximately 224km southeast of Melbourne. There is no fuel here; the closest petrol station is at Yanakie.

There's no direct public transport between Melbourne and the Prom. The closest towns accessible by V/Line buses are Fish Creek ($20.40, 2¾ hours) and Foster ($23, three hours, four daily) via Dandenong and Koo Wee Rup.

Walhalla

POP 12

Tiny Walhalla lies hidden high in the green hills and forests at the foot of Baw Baw National Park. It's a postcard-pretty collection of sepia-toned period cottages and other timber buildings (some original, but mostly reconstructed). The setting is gorgeous, strung out along a deep, forested valley with Stringers Creek running through the centre of the township.

Gold was discovered here on 26 December 1862, although the first find was not registered until January 1863, which is when the gold rush really began. In its gold-mining heyday, Walhalla's population was 5000, today it's just 12!

Like all great ghost towns, the dead that are buried in the stunningly sited cemetery vastly outnumber the living.

⊙ Sights

The historical sights, including museums and a gold mine, are the main attraction in town. There's also a walk to extraordinary **Walhalla Cemetery** (20 minutes return), where the gravestones cling to the steep valley wall. Their inscriptions tell a sombre, yet fascinating, story of the town's history.

Post & Telegraph Office Museum   MUSEUM
(📞 0400 276 004; www.walhallaboard.org.au; Main Rd; gold coin donation; ⊙ 10am-4pm Sat & Sun) The last of Walhalla's original, unrenovated buildings is the old post office. Dating to 1886, it has been preserved as a museum open on weekends; literally nothing seems changed once you walk through its doors.

Walhalla Historical Museum   MUSEUM
(📞 03-5165 6250; www.victoriancollections.net. au/organisations/walhalla-museum#collection-records; 41 Main Rd; gold coin donation; ⊙ 10am-4pm) In a restored historic building along the main street, Walhalla Historical Museum displays artefacts from its bygone era, as well as acting as an information centre, souvenir shop and post office.

Long Tunnel Extended Gold Mine   MINE
(📞 03-5165 6259; www.walhallaboard.org.au; off Walhalla-Beardmore Rd; adult/child/family $20/15/50; ⊙ tours 1.30pm daily, plus noon & 3pm Sat, Sun & holidays) Relive the mining past with guided tours exploring Cohens Reef, once

---

DON'T MISS

TINAMBA HOTEL

The **Tinamba Hotel** (📞 03-5145 1484; www.tinambahotel.com.au; 4-6 Tinamba Seaton Rd, Tinamba; 2-/3-course lunch incl drink $30/39.50, dinner mains $35-39; ⊙ noon-2pm & 6-8pm Wed-Sat, noon-2pm Sun) in the small township of Tinamba, 10km west of Maffra, is a classy restaurant that's well known for its delectable menu using local, seasonal produce. Its dining room with piano and Chesterfield couches is in keeping with the lavishly presented cuisine centred around slow-cooked meats, Gippsland steaks and local seafood, accompanied by great local wines.

---

one of Australia's top reef-gold producers. Almost 14 tonnes of gold came out of this mine.

🏃 Activities

Walhalla Goldfields Railway   RAIL
(📞 03-5165 6280; www.walhallarail.com; adult/child/family return $20/15/50; ⊙ from Walhalla station 11am & 1pm, from Thomson Station 11.40am & 1.40pm Wed, Sat, Sun & public holidays) A star attraction is the scenic Walhalla Goldfields Railway, which offers a 20-minute ride between Walhalla and Thomson Stations (on the main road, 3.5km before Walhalla). The train snakes along Stringers Creek Gorge, passing lovely, forested gorge country and crossing a number of trestle bridges. There are daily departures during school holidays.

☞ Tours

Walhalla Ghost Tours   TOURS
(📞 03-5165 6250; www.walhallaghosttour.info; adult/child/family $25/20/75; ⊙ 7.30pm Sat, 8.30pm during daylight saving) Locals lead rather spooky ghost tours through this real-life ghost town on Saturday nights. Book through the Walhalla Historical Museum.

🛏 Sleeping & Eating

Walhalla Star Hotel   HISTORIC HOTEL $$
(📞 03-5165 6262; www.starhotel.com.au; Main Rd; d incl breakfast $189-249; ❋ @ 🛜) The rebuilt historic Star offers stylish boutique accommodation with king-sized beds and simple but sophisticated designer decor, making good use of local materials such as corrugated-iron water tanks. Guests can dine at the upmarket house restaurant; others need to reserve in advance. Or you can get good breakfasts, pies, coffee and cake at the attached **Greyhorse Cafe** (dishes from $5; ⊙ 10am-2pm).

ⓘ Information

There's tourist information at the Walhalla Historical Museum, and ww.walhalla.org.au is another helpful resource.

ⓘ Getting There & Away

Walhalla lies approximately 180km east of Melbourne. There's no public transport. By road, the town can be reached along a lovely, winding forest drive from Moe or Traralgon. If coming down the summit from Mt Baw Baw it's around an hour's drive for the slow, twisting 48km journey.

Lakes District

The Gippsland Lakes form the largest inland waterway system in Australia, with the three main interconnecting lakes – Wellington, King and Victoria – stretching from Sale to beyond Lakes Entrance. The lakes are actually saltwater lagoons, separated from the ocean by the Gippsland Lakes Coastal Park and the narrow coastal strip of sand dunes known as Ninety Mile Beach. Apart from the beach, the highlights here involve hanging out at the pretty seaside communities.

Sale

Gateway to the Lakes District, Sale is a regional centre with little charm of its own, but it has plenty of accommodation, shops, restaurants and pubs, making it a convenient base from which to explore Ninety Mile Beach.

Wellington Visitor Information Centre (☑03-5144 1108; www.tourismwellington.com.au; 8 Foster St; ⊙9am-5pm; ❡) has a ton of brochures, wi-fi access and a free accommodation booking service. From late 2017 it will be relocating to a new address at the Civic Centre, sharing space with the new **Gippsland Art Gallery** (☑03-5142 3500; www.gippslandartgallery.com; 68 Foster St, Civic Centre; ⊙10am-5pm Mon-Fri, to 4pm Sat & Sun) and library.

Ninety Mile Beach

To paraphrase the immortal words of Crocodile Dundee...that's not a beach, *this* is a beach. Isolated Ninety Mile Beach is a narrow strip of sand backed by dunes, featuring lagoons and stretching unbroken for more or less 90 miles (150km) from near McLoughlins Beach to the channel at Lakes Entrance. The area is great for surf fishing, camping and long beach walks, though the crashing surf can be dangerous for swimming, except where patrolled at Seaspray, Woodside Beach and Lakes Entrance.

The main access road to Ninety Mile Beach is the South Gippsland Hwy from Sale or Foster, turning off to Seaspray, Golden Beach and Loch Sport.

Metung

POP 1222

Curling around Bancroft Bay, little Metung is one of the prettiest towns in the Lakes District. Besotted locals call it the Gippsland Riviera, and with its absolute waterfront location and unhurried village charm, it's hard to argue.

◉ Sights & Activities

Riviera Nautic BOATING
(☑03-5156 2243; www.rivieranautic.com.au; 185 Metung Rd; 2½hr tours adult/child/under 6yr $45/20/free, boat hire per 2hr/day $85/175, yachts & cruisers for 3 days from $1065; ⊙tours 2.30pm Tue, Thu, Sat) Getting out on the water is easy in Metung, with Riviera Nautic hiring out boats and yachts for cruising, fishing and sailing on the Gippsland Lakes. There are also sightseeing cruises three times a week, with regular sightings of seals and dolphins. The liveaboard boats and motorised yachts offer a unique form of accommodation, and good value if you have a group. No boat licence required.

🛌 Sleeping

McMillans of Metung RESORT $$
(☑03-5156 2283; www.mcmillansofmetung.com.au; 155 Metung Rd; cottages/villas from $110/160; ❋❡❂) This swish lakeside resort has won stacks of tourism awards for its complex of English country–style cottages set in 3 hectares of manicured gardens, as well its modern villas, private marina and spa centre.

Moorings at Metung APARTMENT $$$
(☑03-5156 2750; www.themoorings.com.au; 44 Metung Rd; apt $160-390; ❡❂) At the end of the road in Metung, and with water views to either Lake King or Bancroft Bay, this contemporary complex has a range of apartments from spacious studios to two-bedroom, split-level town houses. The complex has a tennis court, indoor and outdoor pools, a spa and a marina. Outside peak season it's good value.

✗ Eating

★ Nautica MODERN AUSTRALIAN $$
(☑03-5156 2345; www.facebook.com/nauticametung; 50 Metung Rd; breakfasts from $10, mains from $19; ⊙8am-2pm & 6pm-late Wed-Sat, 8am-3pm Sun) A classy affair with smart polished wooden floorboards, open fire and views out to the water, Nautica is one not to miss in Metung. Start the day by treating yourself to a breakfast brioche roll filled with double bacon and Swiss cheese, while for lunch go the panko calamari or oysters. Dinner is anything from slow-cooked lamb shoulder to crispy-skin barramundi.

WORTH A TRIP

KROWATHUNKOOLONG KEEPING PLACE

Krowathunkoolong Keeping Place (☏ 03-5152 1891, 03-5150 0737; www.batalukculturaltrail.com.au; 37-53 Dalmahoy St; adult/child $3.50/2.50; ☺ 9am-5pm Mon-Fri) is a stirring and insightful Koorie cultural exhibition space that explores Kurnai life from the Dreaming until after European settlement. The exhibition traces the Kurnai clan from their Dreaming ancestors, Borun the pelican and his wife Tuk the musk duck, and covers life at Lake Tyers Mission, east of Lakes Entrance, now a trust privately owned by Aboriginal shareholders. The massacres of the Kurnai from 1839 to 1849 are also detailed.

★ **Metung Hotel** PUB FOOD $$
(☏ 03-5156 2206; www.metunghotel.com.au; 1 Kurnai Ave; mains $25-40; ☺ kitchen noon-2pm & 6-8pm, pub 11am-late; ☎) You can't beat the location overlooking Metung Wharf, and the big windows and outdoor timber decking make the most of the water views. The bistro serves top-notch pub food with a focus on fresh local seafood. The hotel also has the cheapest rooms in town ($85).

ℹ Information

Metung Visitor Centre (☏ 03-5156 2969; www.metungtourism.com.au; 3/50 Metung Rd; ☺ 9am-5pm) Accommodation-booking and boat-hire services. Also has a gift shop with local produce.

ℹ Getting There & Away

Metung lies south of the Princes Hwy along the C606; the turn-off is signposted at Swan Reach. The nearest major towns are Bairnsdale (28km) and Lakes Entrance (24km). The nearest inter-city rail services are at Bairnsdale.

Lakes Entrance

POP 4569

With the shallow Cunninghame Arm waterway separating the town from the crashing ocean beaches, Lakes Entrance basks in an undeniably pretty location. In holiday season it's a packed-out tourist town with a graceless strip of motels, caravan parks, minigolf courses and souvenir shops lining The Esplanade. Still, the bobbing fishing boats, fresh seafood, endless beaches and cruises out to Metung and Wyanga Park Winery should win you over.

🏃 Activities

Venture Out ADVENTURE SPORTS
(☏ 0427 731 441; www.ventureout.com.au; 347 The Esplanade; bike hire per hr/day $18/50, SUPs & kayaks per 2hr $25, tours from $45; ☺ 10am-5pm, or call for bookings) Rents out bicycles, sea kayaks and stand-up paddleboards (SUPs), as well as running mountain-biking tours on single tracks through the surrounding forest.

Sea Safari CRUISE
(☏ 0458 511 438; www.lakes-explorer.com.au; Post Office Jetty; 1¼hr cruises adult/child/family $15/10/40) ✐ These safaris aboard the *Lakes Explorer* have a focus on research and ecology, identifying and counting seabirds, testing water for salinity levels and learning about marine life.

Lonsdale Eco Cruises CRUISE
(☏ 0413 666 638; www.lonsdalecruises.com.au; Cunningham Quay; 3hr cruises adult/child/family $50/25/120; ☺ 1pm Thu-Tue) ✐ Scenic cruises out to Metung and Lake King on a former Queenscliff–Sorrento passenger ferry, with common dolphin sightings.

🛏 Sleeping

Eastern Beach Tourist Park CARAVAN PARK $
(☏ 03-5155 1581, 1800 761 762; www.easternbeach.com.au; 42 Eastern Beach Rd; unpowered sites $28-50, powered sites $35-69, cabins $118-285; @ 🐾 🖈 🐕) Most caravan parks in Lakes pack 'em in, but this one has space, grassy sites and a great location away from the hubbub in a bush setting back from Eastern Beach. A walking track takes you into town (30 minutes). New facilities are excellent, including a camp kitchen, barbecues and a kids' playground. Sells beers at reception, too.

Bellevue on the Lakes HOTEL $$
(☏ 03-5155 3055; www.bellevuelakes.com; 201 The Esplanade; d from $189, 2-bedroom apt from $249; 🖈 🐾 🖈) Right in the heart of the Esplanade, Bellevue has neatly furnished rooms in earthy tones, most with water views. For extra luxury, go for the spacious spa suites or two-bedroom self-contained apartments.

Goat & Goose B&B $$
(☏ 03-5155 3079; www.goatandgoose.com; 27b McCrae St; d from $120-200) Bass Strait views are maximised at this wonderfully unusual, multistorey, timber pole–framed house, with quaint rooms featuring spas.

✕ Eating

★ **Ferryman's Seafood Cafe**   SEAFOOD $$
(☑ 03-5155 3000; www.ferrymans.com.au; Middle Harbour, The Esplanade; mains lunch $18-24, dinner $21-45; ⊙ 10am-late) It's hard to beat the ambience of dining on the deck of this floating cafe-restaurant (an old Paynesville to Raymond Island passenger ferry), which will fill you to the gills with fish and seafood dishes. The fisherman's basket for lunch and seafood platter for dinner are popular orders. Downstairs you can buy fresh seafood, including prawns and crayfish.

Sparrows Nest   CAFE $$
(www.facebook.com/sparrowsnestlakesentrance; 581 The Esplanade; meals $11-21; ⊙ 7.30am-4pm; 🛜) Bringing a bit of urban style to Lakes Entrance is this cool spot doing single-origin coffees and house-made crumpets spread with Raymond Island honeycomb-butter speckled with bacon bits for breakfast. Lunches are good too, with the likes of pulled-pork baguettes and craft beer by **Sailors Grave Brewing** (☑ 0466 331 936; www.sailorsgravebrewing.com; 7 Forest Rd; ⊙ by appointment) in Marlo.

ℹ Information

Lakes Entrance Visitor Centre (☑ 1800 637 060, 03-5155 1966; www.discovereast gippsland.com.au; cnr Princes Hwy & Marine Pde; ⊙ 9am-5pm; 🛜) Free accommodation- and tour-booking services. Also check out www.lakesentrance.com.

ℹ Getting There & Away

Lakes Entrance lies 314km from Melbourne along the Princes Hwy.
V/Line (☑ 1800 800 007; www.vline.com.au) runs a train-bus service from Melbourne to Lakes Entrance via Bairnsdale ($39.80, 4½ hours, three daily).

East Gippsland & the Wilderness Coast

Beyond Lakes Entrance stretches a wilderness area of spectacular national parks and old-growth forest. Much of this region has never been cleared for agriculture and it contains some of the most remote and pristine national parks in the state, making logging in these ancient forests a hot issue.

Buchan

POP 385

The sleepy town of Buchan, in the foothills of the Snowy Mountains, is famous for the spectacular and intricate limestone cave system at the Buchan Caves Reserve, open to visitors for almost a century. Underground rivers cutting through ancient limestone rock formed the caves and caverns, and they provided shelter for Aboriginal people as far back as 18,000 years ago.

Buchan has huge potential as an outdoor adventure destination, with some 600 caves in the area – however only five remain open to the public. There are also swimming holes, mountain-biking trails, bushwalks and white-water rafting; see www.buchan.vic.au for more info.

Buchan has huge potential as an outdoor adventure destination, with some 600 caves in the area – however only five remain open to the public. There are also swimming holes, mountain-biking trails, bushwalks and white-water rafting; see www.buchan.vic.au for more info.

◉ Sights

★ **Buchan Caves**   CAVE
(☑ 131963; www.parks.vic.gov.au; tours adult/child/family $22/12.90/60.90, 2 caves $33/19.10/90.90; ⊙ tours 10am, 11.15am, 1pm, 2.15pm & 3.30pm, hours vary seasonally) Since it was unveiled to Melburnians as a blockbuster sight in the

---

WORTH A TRIP

RAYMOND ISLAND

For one of the best places in Victoria to see koalas, drop down off the Princes Hwy to the relaxed lakeside town of Paynesville. Agreeable in its own right, Paynesville is the departure point for a five-minute ferry crossing to Raymond Island. There's a large colony of koalas here, mostly relocated from Phillip Island in the 1950s. Kangaroos and echidnas are also regularly spotted.

The flat-bottom car-and-passenger ferry operates every 20 minutes from 6.40am to midnight and is free for pedestrians and cyclists. Cars cost $12 and motorcycles $5.

early 1900s, the Buchan Caves has been dazzling visitors with its fantasy world of glistening calcite formations. Parks Victoria runs guided cave tours daily, alternating between **Royal** and **Fairy Caves**. They're both impressive: Royal has more colour, a higher chamber and dripping candle-like formations; Fairy has more delicate decorations and potential fairy sightings.

🛏 Sleeping

Buchan Caves Motel   LODGE $$
(🖉 03-5155 9419; www.buchanmotel.com.au; 67 Main Rd; d $130, tr & q $150) Enjoy views of the bucolic countryside from your balcony at this comfortable hilltop lodge with modern rooms featuring boutique touches. The friendly, young, enthusiastic owners are a wealth of knowledge on the area and have grand plans to capitalise on Buchan's tourism potential.

Buchan Caves Reserve   CAMPGROUND $$
(🖉 13 19 63; www.parks.vic.gov.au; unpowered/ powered sites from $46/51, d cabins from $90, wilderness retreats d $191; ✳ ⊠) You can stay right by the caves at this serene Parks Victoria camping ground edged by state forest. Though its campsites are exorbitantly priced, there are a couple of decent value cabins, plus safari-style tents providing a 'luxury' wilderness experience, with comfortable queen-sized bed and air-conditioning. In summer there's a freshwater pool.

🍷 Drinking & Nightlife

Buchan Caves Hotel   PUB
(🖉 03-5155 9203; www.facebook.com/buchan caveshotel; 49 Main Rd; ⊙ 11am-late) Rising from the ashes, the 125-year-old Buchan pub is back in business after burning to the ground in 2014. It came about via the world's first crowd-funding campaign to build a pub, with funds raised from around the globe. It reopened its doors in December 2016. Be sure to celebrate its return by stopping in for a chicken parma and a cold frothy.

ℹ Getting There & Away

Buchan is an easy drive 56km north of Lakes Entrance. **Dyson's** (🖉 03-5152 1711) runs a bus service on Wednesday and Friday from Bairnsdale to Buchan ($16, two hours). It meets the train at Bairnsdale. At other times you'll need your own transport.

Snowy River National Park

Northeast of Buchan, this is one of Victoria's most isolated and spectacular national parks, dominated by deep gorges carved through limestone and sandstone by the Snowy River on its route from the Snowy Mountains in NSW to its mouth at Marlo. The entire park is a smorgasbord of unspoiled, superb bush and mountain scenery. It covers more than 950 sq km and includes a huge diversity of vegetation, ranging from alpine woodlands and eucalyptus forests to rainforests.

Walking and canoeing are the most popular activities, but you need to be well prepared for both – conditions can be harsh and subject to sudden change.

The classic canoe or raft trip down the Snowy River from McKillops Bridge to a pull-out point near Buchan takes at least four days and offers superb scenery: rugged gorges, raging rapids, tranquil sections and excellent camping spots on broad sandbars. The hilly and difficult Silver Mine Walking Track (15km, six hours) also starts at the eastern end of McKillops Bridge.

👉 Tours

Snowy River Expeditions   ADVENTURE
(🖉 03-5155 0220; www.karoondapark.com; Karoonda Park; tours per day $110-275) Snowy River Expeditions is a well-established company operating out of Karoonda Park, running adventure tours including one-, two- or four-day rafting trips on the Snowy. Half- or full-day abseiling, caving and horse-riding trips are also available. Costs include transport, meals and camping gear.

🛏 Sleeping

McKillops Bridge   CAMPGROUND $
(🖉 13 19 63; www.parkweb.vic.gov.au; camp sites free) The most popular of the free camping grounds in the area is this beautiful spot along the Snowy River. Sites have nonflush toilets and fireplaces. It's a popular launching site for canoeists, and a range of hikes start out from here.

Karoonda Park   FARMSTAY $
(🖉 03-5155 0220; www.karoondapark.com; 3558 Gelantipy Rd; dm/s/d/tr $35/50/70/90; ✳ @ 🛜 ⊠) Just south of Gelantipy, 40km north of Buchan on the road to Snowy River National Park, is this 1800-acre cattle-and-sheep property with comfortable backpacker and cabin digs. Meals are available with prior notice,

and there's also a kitchen. They can arrange activities such as abseiling, horse riding, caving and white-water rafting.

ℹ️ Getting There & Away

The two main access roads to the park are the Buchan-Jindabyne Rd from Buchan, and the Bonang Rd north from Orbost. These roads are joined by McKillops Rd (also known as Deddick Valley Rd), which runs across the northern border of the park. Various minor access roads and scenic routes run into and alongside the park from these three main roads. The 43km Deddick Trail, which runs through the middle of the park, is only suitable for 4WDs.

Dyson's (☑ 03-5155 0356) operates a bus service from Bairnsdale to Gelantipy (via Buchan) on Wednesday and Friday ($21.80, 2¾ hours), which can drop folks off at Karoonda Park.

Errinundra National Park

Errinundra National Park contains Victoria's largest cool-temperate rainforest and is one of east Gippsland's most outstanding natural areas.

The national park covers an area of 256 sq km and has three granite outcrops that extend into the cloud, resulting in high rainfall, deep, fertile soils and a network of creeks and rivers that flow north, south and east. The park has several climatic zones – some areas of the park are quite dry, while its peaks regularly receive snow. This is a rich habitat for native birds and animals, which include many rare and endangered species such as the potoroo.

Nestled by the edge of the national park is tiny **Goongerah** (population 50), a thriving community for conservationists.

You can explore the park with a combination of scenic drives and short- and medium-length walks. **Mt Ellery** has spectacular views; **Errinundra Saddle** has a rainforest boardwalk; and from **Ocean View Lookout** there are stunning views down the Goolengook River as far as the town of Bemm River. The park also has **mountain plum pines**, some of which are more than 400 years old and easily accessible from Goonmirk Rocks Rd.

🛏️ Sleeping

Tin Chalet   COTTAGE $
(☑ 03-5154 0145; Goongerah; houses $90) 🍃 A genuine rustic getaway is this solar-powered, double-storey cottage constructed from corrugated iron. It features a charming inte-

rior with wood-fire stove, reclaimed timber and plenty of character. By the river and surrounded by forest, it's set on an organic farm and orchard run by Jill Redwood, a well-known environmentalist who set up **Environment East Gippsland** (☑ 03-5154 0145; www.eastgippsland.net.au; Goongerah) 🍃.

Goongerah Camp Site   CAMPGROUND $
The most accessible of the free camping grounds on the park's edges is Goongerah, a 1½ hour's drive north of Orbost. It's within a state forest on the edge of the park, set along the Brodribb River, from which you are able to drink.

Frosty Hollow Camp Site   CAMPGROUND $
(☑ 13 19 63; www.parkweb.vic.gov.au; sites free) This is the only camping area within the national park, with basic sites (nonflush toilets, no fireplaces) along the eastern side. The only way to reach the campsite is along unsealed tracks into the park off the Bonang Rd north of Goongerah.

ℹ️ Getting There & Away

Errinundra National Park lies approximately 490km east of Melbourne. The main access roads to the park are Bonang Rd from Orbost and Errinundra Rd from Club Terrace. Bonang Rd passes along the western side of the park, while Errinundra Rd passes through the centre. Roads within the park are all unsealed, but are 2WD accessible. Road conditions are variable. Expect seasonal closures between June and November, though roads can deteriorate quickly at any time of year after rain and are often closed or impassable after floods (check Parks Victoria in Orbost or Bendoc first). Also watch out for logging trucks when driving.

Cape Conran Coastal Park

This blissfully undeveloped part of the coast is one of Gippsland's most beautiful corners, with long stretches of remote white-sand beaches. The 19km coastal route from Marlo to Cape Conran is particularly pretty, bordered by banksia trees, grass plains, sand dunes and the ocean.

🏃 Activities

Cape Conran is a fabulous spot for walking. One favourite is the nature trail that links up with the East Cape Boardwalk, where signage gives you a glimpse into how Indigenous peoples lived in this area. Following an indigenous theme, take the West Cape Rd off Cape Conran Rd to **Salmon Rocks**, where there's an Aboriginal **shell midden** dated at more than 10,000 years old.

For some relaxed swimming, canoeing and fishing, head to the Yerrung River, which shadows the coast east of the cape and can be reached along Yerrung River Rd. There's good surfing at West Cape Beach, extending northwest from the cape and accessible from West Cape Rd. For qualified divers, Marlo-based **Cross Diving Services** (☑03-5154 8554, 0407 362 960; www.crossdiving.com.au; 20 Ricardo Dr; ⊙shore dives with/without equipment hire $80/15, boat dives $100/150, 4-day open course $550) offers dives on most weekends.

🛏 Sleeping

Parks Victoria has three excellent privately managed accommodation options in Cape Conran Coastal Park – offering camping, cabins and safari-style tented camping, which are all privately managed.

Banksia Bluff Camping Area   CAMPGROUND $
(☑03-5154 8438; www.conran.net.au; Marlo-Conran Rd; unpowered sites $35.90-39.90) Run by Parks Victoria, this excellent privately managed camping ground is right by the foreshore. Its generous sites are surrounded by banksia woodlands offering shade and privacy. It has flush toilets, cold showers and a few fireplaces, but you'll need to bring drinking water. A ballot is held for using sites over the Christmas period.

**Cape Conran
Wilderness Retreat**   TENTED CAMP $$
(☑03-5154 8438; www.conran.net.au; d $191.20) Nestled in the bush by the sand dunes, these stylish safari tents are a great option, offering all the simplicity of camping, but with comfortable beds and a deck outside your flywire door. Two-night minimum stay on weekends.

Cape Conran Coastal Park Cabins   CABIN $$
(☑03-5154 8438; www.conran.net.au; cabins $171.70-237.20) These self-contained cabins, which can sleep up to eight people, are surrounded by bush and just 200m from the beach. Built from local timbers, the cabins are like oversized cubby houses, with lofty mezzanines for sleeping.

West Cape Cabins   CABIN $$
(☑03-5154 8296; www.westcapecabins.com; 1547 Cape Conran Rd; d $195-255) Crafted from local or recycled wood, these self-contained cabins a few kilometres from the park are works of art. The timbers are labelled with their species, and even the queen-sized beds are made from tree trunks. The outdoor spa baths add to the joy. The larger cottage sleeps eight. It's a 15-minute walk through coastal bush to an isolated beach.

ⓘ Getting There & Away

Cape Conran Coastal Park lies south of the Princes Hwy, 405km from Melbourne. The well-signposted turn-off from the highway lies just east of the small settlement of Cabbage Tree. The park is around 15km south of the turn-off along Cabbage Tree–Conran Rd.

Mallacoota

POP 1032

One of Gippsland's, and indeed Victoria's, little gems, Mallacoota is the state's most easterly town, snuggled on the vast Mallacoota Inlet and surrounded by the tumbling hills and beachside dunes of beautiful Croajingolong National Park. Those prepared to come this far are treated to long, empty, ocean-surf beaches, tidal estuaries and swimming, fishing and boating on the inlet.

It's a good place for wildlife too with plentiful kangaroos, koalas and echidnas.

⦾ Sights & Activities

The calm estuarine waters of Mallacoota Inlet have more than 300km of shoreline – hiring a boat is the best way to explore, and there are plenty of great walks along the water's edge.

For good surf, head to Bastion Point or Tip Beach. Get in touch with Surf Shack for board rental and surf classes. There's swimmable surf and some sheltered water at Betka Beach, which is patrolled during Christmas school holidays. There are also good swimming spots along the beaches of the foreshore reserve, at Bastion Point (patrolled by a surf life-saving club) and at Quarry Beach.

Gabo Island   ISLAND
On Gabo Island, 14km offshore from Mallacoota, the windswept 154-hectare **Gabo Island Lightstation Reserve** is home to seabirds and one of the world's largest colonies of little penguins, far outnumbering those on Phillip Island. Whales, dolphins and fur seals are regularly sighted offshore. The island has an operating lighthouse, built in 1862 and the tallest in the southern hemisphere – you can stay in the old keepers' cottages here.

Transport out here however is an issue, with boat access often restricted due to bad

MELBOURNE & VICTORIA MALLACOOTA

weather; **Wilderness Coast Ocean Charters** (☏ 0417 398 068, 03-5158 0701) and **Gabo Island Escapes** (☏ 0437 221 694, 03-5158 0605; per person $100) are your best bet.

While there no longer direct flights offered to Gabo Island from Mallacoota, **Merimbula Air Services** (☏ 02-6495 1074; www.mairserv.com.au) can arrange a drop-off and pickup service, but unless you have a group, it certainly ain't cheap (four seater one-way $775).

Mallacoota Equipment Hire   ADVENTURE SPORTS
(☏ 0488 329 611; www.mallacootahire.com.au; Buckland Dr, Mallacoota Foreshore Caravan Park; per hr/day bike hire from $10/40, kayaks $15/75; ☺ 9am-5pm) Hires bikes, kayaks and fishing gear, and has plenty of ideas for trails and itineraries. Can deliver bikes to where you're staying.

Mallacoota Hire Boats   BOATING
(☏ 0438 447 558; www.mallacootahireboats.com; 10 Buckland Dr; motorboats per 2/8hr $70/160, kayaks 1/2 people per 2hr $30/50) Hires out kayaks, motorboats, pedal boats and fishing equipment. No boat licence required; cash only. They're based out of Mallacoota Foreshore Holiday Park.

🛏 Sleeping

Mallacoota Foreshore Holiday Park   CARAVAN PARK $
(☏ 03-5158 0300; cnr Allan Dr & Maurice Ave; unpowered sites $16.60-33, powered sites $23.70-53; 🛜) Curling around the waterfront, the grassy sites here morph into one of Victoria's most scenic caravan parks, with sublime views of the inlet and its resident population of black swans and pelicans. No cabins, but the best of Mallacoota's many parks for campers. Reception is across the road in the same building as the visitor information centre.

★**Adobe Abodes**   APARTMENT $$
(☏ 0499 777 968; www.adobeabodes.com.au; 17-19 Karbeethong Ave; d $95-145, extra person $15) 🌿 These unique mud-brick self-contained units in Karbeethong are something special. With an emphasis on recycling and eco-friendliness, the flats have solar hot water and guests are encouraged to compost their kitchen scraps. The array of whimsical apartments are comfortable and well equipped, and come with welcome baskets of wine and chocolate, and wonderful views.

★**Karbeethong Lodge**   GUESTHOUSE $$
(☏ 03-5158 0411; www.karbeethonglodge.com.au; 16 Schnapper Point Dr; r incl breakfast $100-150) It's hard not to be overcome by a sense of serenity as you rest on the broad verandahs of this early 1900s timber guesthouse, which give uninterrupted views over Mallacoota Inlet and the expansive gardens. The large guest lounge and dining room have an open fire and period furnishings, there's a mammoth kitchen and the pastel-toned bedrooms are small but tastefully decorated.

Gabo Island Lighthouse   COTTAGE $$
(☏ 03-8427 2123, Parks Victoria 13 19 63; www.parkweb.vic.gov.au; up to 8 people $323.70-359.70) For a truly wild experience head out to stay at this remote lighthouse. Accommodation is available in the historic three-bedroom assistant lighthouse keeper's residence. There's a two-night minimum stay and a ballot for use during the Christmas and Easter holidays; take note there's no refunds if you're unable to reach the island (or get stranded there) during inclement weather.

Mallacoota Wilderness Houseboats   HOUSEBOAT $$$
(☏ 0409 924 016; www.mallacootawildernesshouseboats.com.au; Karbeethong Jetty; 4 nights midweek from $800, weekly from $1250) These six-berth houseboats are not as luxurious as the ones you'll find on the Murray, but they are the perfect way to explore Mallacoota's waterways, and they are economical for a group or family. They're fully self-contained with kitchen, fridge and hot-water showers. There's a $500 deposit from which fuel costs are deducted upon return. No boat licence required.

🍴 Eating & Drinking

★**Lucy's**   ASIAN $$
(☏ 03-5158 0666; 64 Maurice Ave; mains $8-28; ☺ 8am-8pm) Lucy's is popular for delicious and great-value homemade rice noodles with chicken, prawn or abalone, as well as dumplings stuffed with ingredients from the garden. It's also good for breakfast.

Mallacoota Hotel   PUB
(☏ 03-5158 0455; www.mallacootahotel.com.au; 51-55 Maurice Ave; ☺ noon-10pm) The local pub is a popular spot for a drink with a cosy indoor bar and a wonderful outdoor beer garden full of palm trees. Its bistro serves hearty meals (mains $20 to $40) from its varied menu, with reliable favourites being

the chicken parma, Gippsland steak and pale ale fish and chips. Bands play regularly in summer.

ⓘ Information

Mallacoota Visitor Centre (☏ 03-5158 0800, 03-5158 0116, 0408 315 615; www.visitmalla coota.com.au; cnr Allan Dr & Maurice Ave; ☉ 9am-5pm; ☏) On the main strip across from the water is this extremely helpful tourist centre with a ton of info on the area and its walking trails, and a handy booklet on local sights ($1). Has wi-fi and internet access too.

ⓘ Getting There & Away

Mallacoota is 23km southeast of Genoa (on the Princes Hwy), which is 492km from Melbourne. Take the train to Bairnsdale (3¾ hours), then the V/Line bus to Genoa ($51.80, 3½ hours, one daily). The Mallacoota–Genoa bus meets the V/Line coach on Monday, Thursday and Friday, plus Sunday during school holidays, and runs to Mallacoota ($3.20, 30 minutes).

Croajingolong National Park

Croajingolong is one of Australia's finest coastal wilderness national parks, recognised by its listing as a World Biosphere Reserve by Unesco (one of 14 in Australia). The park covers 875 sq km, stretching for about 100km from the town of Bemm River to the NSW border. Magnificent, unspoiled beaches, inlets, estuaries and forests make it an ideal park for camping, walking, swimming and surfing. The five inlets, Sydenham, Tamboon, Mueller, Wingan and Mallacoota (the largest and most accessible), are popular canoeing and fishing spots.

Two sections of the park have been declared wilderness areas (which means no vehicles, access to a limited number of walkers only and permits required): the Cape Howe Wilderness Area, between Mallacoota Inlet and the NSW border, and the Sandpatch Wilderness Area, between Wingan Inlet and Shipwreck Creek.

Point Hicks was the first part of Australia to be spotted by Captain Cook and the *Endeavour* crew in 1770, and was named after Lieutenant Zachary Hicks. There's a **lighthouse** (☏ 10am-3pm Mon-Fri; ☏ 03-5158 4268; www.pointhicks.com.au; Lighthouse Track, Tamboon; adult/child/family $7/4/20; ☉ tours 1pm, Fri-Sun) here and accommodation in the old cottages. You can still see remains of the SS *Saros,* which ran ashore in 1937, on a short walk from the lighthouse.

🛏 Sleeping

Mueller Inlet   CAMPGROUND $
(☏ 03-5158 4268; www.pointhicks.com.au; unpowered sites from $25) The calm waters here are fantastic for kayaking and swimming, and the camp sites are only a few metres away. It has eight sites, three of them walk-in, but no fireplaces. There's no vegetation to provide privacy, but outside Christmas and Easter holidays it's usually quiet. Bookings are made through Point Hicks Lighthouse.

Shipwreck Creek   CAMPGROUND $
(☏ 13 19 63; www.parkweb.vic.gov.au; unpowered sites from $26.50) Only 15km from Mallacoota, this is a beautiful camping ground set in forest above a sandy beach. It's a small area with just five sites, drop toilets and fireplaces (BYO wood) and there are lots of short walks to do here. Bookings through Parks Victoria.

Wingan Inlet   CAMPGROUND $
(☏ 13 19 63; www.parkweb.vic.gov.au; unpowered sites from $25.80) This serene and secluded camping ground has 24 sites among superb sandy beaches and great walks. The Wingan River Walk (5km, 2½ hours return) through rainforest has great waterholes for swimming. Bookings though Parks Victoria.

Point Hicks Lighthouse   COTTAGE $$
(☏ 03-5156 0432; www.pointhicks.com.au; bungalows $120-150, cottages $360-550) This remote lighthouse has two comfortable, heritage-listed cottages and one double bungalow, which originally housed the assistant lighthouse keepers. The cottages sleep six people, and have sensational ocean views and wood-burning fireplaces. Bring along your own bedding and towels, or you can hire it for $15 per person. To get here you'll need to walk 2.2km from the car park.

ⓘ Getting There & Away

Croajingolong National Park lies 492km east of Melbourne. Unsealed access roads of varying quality lead south off Princes Hwy and into the park from various points between Cann River and the NSW border. Among these are tracks leading to camping grounds at Wingan Inlet, Mueller Inlet, Thurra River and Shipwreck Creek.

Apart from Mallacoota Rd, all of the access roads are unsealed and can be very rough in winter, so check road conditions with Parks Victoria in **Cann River** (☏ 13 19 63, 03-5158 6351; www.parkweb.vic.gov.au; Cann River) or **Mallacoota** (☏ 13 19 63, 03-8427 2123; www.parkweb.vic.gov.au; Mallacoota) before venturing on, especially during or after rain.

THE HIGH COUNTRY

Mansfield

POP 4360

Mansfield is the gateway to Victoria's largest snowfields at Mt Buller, but also an exciting all-seasons destination in its own right. There's plenty to do here, with horse riding and mountain biking popular in summer, and a buzzing atmosphere in winter.

Sights & Activities

Mansfield Zoo ZOO
(☑ 03-5777 3576; www.mansfieldzoo.com.au; 1064 Mansfield Woods Point Rd; adult/child $15/13.50; ⊙10am-5.30pm, to 6.30pm or sunset summer) Located 10km south of Mansfield is this surprisingly good wildlife park with lots of native fauna and some exotics, including lions, which are fed at 1.30pm. You can sleep in the paddocks in a tent or swag (adult/child $65/45, including zoo entry for two days) and wake to the dawn wildlife chorus.

All Terrain Cycles MOUNTAIN BIKING
(☑ 03-5775 2724; www.allterraincycles.com.au; 58 High St; bicycle hire per half/full day $30/40) Hires out hybrid bicycles and equipment, and has info on trails in the area. Also runs tours and transfers for the **Great Victorian Rail Trail** (www.greatvictorianrailtrail.com.au).

Watson's Mountain Country Trail Rides HORSE RIDING
(☑ 03-5777 3552; www.watsonstrailrides.com.au; 296 Three Chain Rd, Booroolite; 1hr/2hr/full-day ride $50/90/175) A peaceful property where children can learn with pony rides or short trail rides, or take off on overnight rides. One of the highlights is the view from Kate Cameron's Peak, looking down the steep run featured in *The Man from Snowy River*.

High Country Horses HORSE RIDING
(☑ 03-5777 5590; www.highcountryhorses.com.au; 10 McCormacks Rd, Merrijig; 2hr/half-day/full-day ride $100/130/300, overnight from $640; ⊙Oct-May) Based at Merrijig on the way to Mt Buller, High Country Horses offers everything from a short trot to overnight treks to Craig's Hut, Howqua River and Mt Stirling.

Sleeping

Delatite Hotel PUB $
(www.thedelatitehotel.com.au; 95 High St; r $100-110, s/d with shared bathroom $80/90; 🖂) Run by a friendly owner who also runs the Mans-

field Regional Produce Store (p600), this country hotel on the main road has pub accommodation upstairs. Rooms are basic, but they're spacious and adequate for those on a budget. Downstairs has an atmospheric bistro with local beers – go for the Mansfield pale ale.

Mansfield Travellers Lodge HOSTEL, MOTEL $
(☑ 03-5775 1800; www.mansfieldtravellerslodge. com.au; 116 High St; s & dm from $40, r/f from $120/180; 🖂🖀) Located close to the centre of town, this long-time favourite for backpackers and families is run by the enthusiastic owner, Jed. The spacious dorms, in a restored heritage building, are often booked as private singles, while the motel section features spotless one- and two-bedroom units. Facilities include a kitchen, games rooms, laundry and drying room.

Highton Manor B&B $$
(☑ 03-5775 2700; www.hightonmanor.com.au; 140 Highton Lane; d stable/tower $130/365; 🖂🖀) Built in 1896 for Francis Highett, who sang with Dame Nellie Melba, this stately two-storey manor has style and romance but doesn't take itself too seriously. There's group accommodation in the shared room, modern rooms in the converted stables and lavish period rooms in the main house. If you want the royal treatment, choose the tower room, which includes breakfast.

Eating & Drinking

★ **Mansfield Coffee Merchant** CAFE $$
(☑ 03-5779 1703; www.mansfieldcoffeemerchant. com.au; 23 Highett St; mains $14-19; ⊙6.30am-4pm) This roaster setup within a cavernous, slick space is the place for coffee lovers. It also does contemporary fare such as brekky

---

CRAIG'S HUT

Cattlemen built huts throughout the High Country from the 1850s onwards, but the most iconic is Craig's Hut, built in 1981 for the film *The Man from Snowy River*. It was converted from a film set into a visitor centre 10 years later, then rebuilt in 2003. In 2006 it burned down in bushfires, before being rebuilt (again) in 2007. It's on Mt Stirling in the Alpine National Park about 53km east of Mansfield. The last 1.2km is accessible only by walking or 4WD, but it's worth it for the breathtaking views.

MELBOURNE & VICTORIA MANSFIELD

burgers, tempura-prawn rolls and smoked-lamb ribs. All of its single-origin beans are roasted on site, and prepared as siphon, V60 pour overs or machine coffee. Otherwise pop in for a local wine or ale.

Mansfield Regional Produce Store CAFE $$
(☑ 03-5779 1404; www.theproducestore.com.au; 68 High St; mains $12-24; ☺ 9am-5pm Sat-Thu, to 9pm Fri) Wildly popular with folk for breakfast and brunch is this rustic store-cafe with mismatched furniture that stocks an array of local produce and wine. The ever-changing menu offers full breakfasts, locally made sourdough baguettes and coffee.

Bos Taurus STEAK $$$
(☑ 03-5775 1144; www.bostaurus.com.au; 13-15 High St; mains from $35; ☺ 2.30-9.30pm Mon-Fri, from 11.30am Sat & Sun) A must for carnivores is this steakhouse specialising in premium pasture-fed chargrilled Angus fillets cut to size. The upper deck is a wonderful spot to enjoy a drink and a meal when the sun's out.

Social Bandit Brewing Co MICROBREWERY
(☑ 03-5775 3281; www.facebook.com/socialbandit brewing; 223 Mt Buller Rd; pizzas from $18; ☺ 11am-9pm Thu-Sun) In a commercial estate on Mansfield's outskirts, this boutique brewery is on the road to Mt Buller. It has taps to sample the numerous beers produced on site, including American and Australian pale ales, accompanied by pizzas and pretzels. Grab a few bottles to enjoy up on the mountain.

❶ Information

Mansfield & Mt Buller High Country Visitor Centre (☑ 1800 039 049; www.mansfieldmt buller.com.au; 173 High St; ☺ 9am-5pm) In a modern building next to the town's original railway station, the visitor centre books accommodation for the region and sells lift tickets.

❶ Getting There & Away

Mansfield is 209km northeast of Melbourne, but allow at least 2½ hours if you're driving; take the Tallarook or Euroa exits from the Hume Hwy.

V/Line (☑ 1800 800 007; www.vline.com. au) coaches run between Melbourne's Southern Cross station and Mansfield ($28.20, three hours) at least once daily, with more frequent departures during the ski season.

Mt Buller

Victoria's largest and busiest ski resort is also the closest major resort to Melbourne, so it buzzes all winter long. It's also developing into a popular summer destination for mountain bikers and hikers, with a range of cross-country and downhill trails. The downhill-skiing area covers 180 hectares, with a vertical drop of 400m.

There are plenty of outlets spread across Mansfield and Mt Buller that rent ski and other equipment – check out www.mtbuller. com.au for a full list of options.

🛏 Sleeping

There are over 7000 beds on the mountain. Rates vary throughout the ski season, with cheaper rates midweek. A handful of places are open year-round. **Mt Buller Alpine Reservations** (☑ 03-5777 6633; www.mtbuller reservations.com.au) books accommodation; there's generally a two-night minimum stay on weekends.

Buller Backpackers HOSTEL $
(☑ 1800 810 200; www.bullerbackpackers.com.au; Village Sq; dm $55-90; ☺ Jun-Sep) Only open during the ski season, this busy backpackers is one of Bulla's best budget choices. Dorms are the only option, all with en suite. While there's nowhere to hang out and no cooking facilities, it's right in the heart of the village with prime access to eateries and the chairlift.

Hotel Enzian CHALET $$$
(☑ 03-5777 6996; www.enzian.com.au; 69 Chamois Rd; r from $230-390; 🐾) Enzian has a good range of lodge rooms and apartments (sleeping up to 10) with all the facilities, alpine charm and an in-house restaurant and bar. Breakfast is included for the rooms, but not the apartments that have cooking facilities.

Mt Buller Chalet CHALET $$$
(☑ 03-5777 6566, 1800 810 200; www.mtbuller chalet.com.au; 5 Summit Rd; d incl breakfast $283-760; ☺ Jun-Oct; 🐾🏊) With a central location, the Chalet offers a range of suites, a library with billiards table, well-regarded eateries, an impressive sports centre and a heated pool. It only opens during the ski season.

🍴 Eating & Drinking

Black Cockatoo MODERN AUSTRALIAN $$
(☑ 03-5777 6566; www.blackcockatoo.net.au; Mt Buller Chalet Hotel, 207 Summit Rd; small plates $6-24, large plates $22-65, tasting menu $90; ☺ 7-

11am & 6-9pm June-Sep) Only open in winter, Black Cockatoo is the best restaurant on the mountain doing shared plates in its architecturally designed space. Expect dishes like Flinders Island saltgrass lamb shoulder, prawn toast *okonomiyaki* and smoked local rainbow trout.

Cattleman's Café　　　　CAFE, BISTRO **$$**
(☑ 03-5777 7970; Village Centre; mains $8-19; ⊘ 8am-9pm June-Sep) Open only during the ski season, Cattleman's Café is at the base of the Blue Bullet chairlift and is one of the best spots for breakfast, coffee or a bistro meal of steak, burgers or fish and chips.

Kooroora Hotel　　　　　　　PUB
(☑ 03-5777 6050; www.facebook.com/thekooro orahotel; Village Sq, 3-5 The Avenue; ⊘ 10am-3am June-Sep) Rocks hard and late during the ski season. There's live music on Wednesday night and most weekends. Serves good bistro meals.

ⓘ Information

Mt Buller Resort Management Board (☑ 03-5777 6077; www.mtbuller.com.au; Community Centre, Summit Rd; ⊘ 8.30am-5pm Mon-Fri, 10am-4pm Sat & Sun) Also runs an information office in the village square clock tower during winter.

ⓘ Getting There & Away

Mansfield–Mt Buller Buslines (☑ 03-5775 2606; www.mmbl.com.au; 137 High St, Mansfield) runs a winter bus service from Mansfield (adult/child return $66/45).

In winter there are numerous shuttles from Melbourne; visit www.mtbuller.com.au for the current operators.

V/Line operates at least one daily bus between Melbourne and Mansfield ($28.20, three hours), but has no connecting service to Mt Buller; however, there's a shuttle (from $15) from the **Mirimbah Store** (☑ 03-5777 5529; www.mirim bah.com.au; per ride $15, daily $40; ⊘ 8am-4pm Thu-Sun Sep-May, daily winter), at the foot of the mountain, daily in January and weekends from February to the end of April.

King Valley

From Melbourne, turning east off the Hume Hwy near Wangaratta and onto the Snow Rd brings you to the King Valley, a prosperous cool-climate wine region and an important gourmet-food area. The valley extends south along the King River, through the tiny towns of Moyhu, Whitfield and Cheshunt, with a sprinkling of 20 or so wineries noted for Italian varietals and cool-climate wines such as sangiovese, barbera, prosecco and pinot grigio. The area used to be a tobacco-growing region until legislation closed down the industry, at which time many farmers turned to wine instead. Check out www.winesof thekingvalley.com.au.

🛏 Sleeping

There are a number of cottage B&Bs in the region, including rooms at several of the wineries and the Mountain View Hotel; see www.visitkingvalley.com.au for full listings. There's also **camping** (3741 Wangaratta-Whitfield Rd, Edi Cutting) **FREE** at designated sites along the King River.

✕ Eating

Food is a huge lure to the region, with a number of great restaurants and wineries using local produce. Here you'll find several Italian eateries, a gastropub and a dairy producing naturally cultured items. In mid-November the region's produce is showcased during **La Dolce Vita Wine & Food Festival** (www.winesofthekingvalley.com.au/events/la-dolce-vita).

★ **King Valley Dairy**　　　　　DELI **$**
(☑ 1300 319 766, 03-5727 9329; www.kingvalley dairy.com.au; 107 Moyhu-Meadow Creek Rd, Moyhu; ⊘ 10am-4pm) The old Butter Factory in Myrtleford has moved to Moyhu in the King Valley to produce its naturally cultured dairy products. Its deli sells things like buttermilk ricotta, gourmet-flavoured butters (such as black truffle, smoked salt, wild thyme and chocolate) and other local produce, so you can put together a hamper to enjoy on the farm or by the river.

Mountain View Hotel　　　PUB FOOD **$$**
(☑ 03-5729 8270; www.mvhotel.com.au; 4 King Valley Rd, Whitfield; mains $20-38, 5-/7-course degustation $95/115; ⊘ pub bistro 11am-late daily, restaurant noon-3pm & 6-10pm Wed-Sat, noon-3pm Sun) Smarter than your average country pub, this gastropub is definitely worth a look for its craft beers, quality menu and stellar beer garden. It has a few ales by local King River Brewing (p604), and items such as twice-cooked Milawa chicken, dry-aged Angus steaks, parmas and Bavarian-style dishes. There's also a fine-dining section doing a degustation menu paired with local wines.

High Country

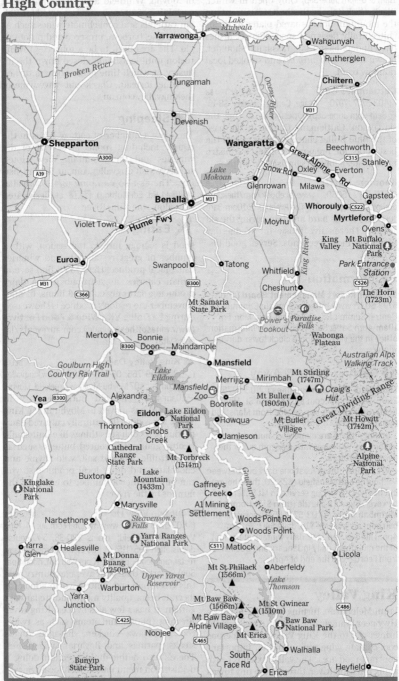

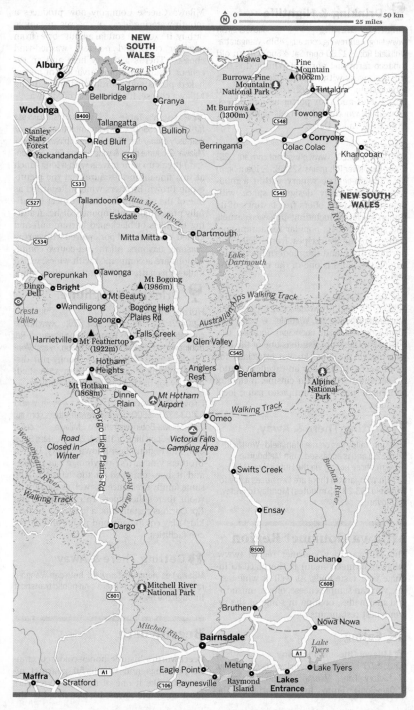

♟ Drinking & Nightlife

King River Brewing   MICROBREWERY
(www.kingriverbrewing.com.au; 4515 Wangaratta-Whitfield Rd; ⊙12.30-6pm Sat & Sun) On an old tobacco farm just north of Whitfield is this small brewery with its taphouse set inside a tobacco kiln. It has six beers on tap, doing an IPA, altbier and sour porter among others, as well as wood-fired pretzels using butter from King Valley Dairy.

Chrismont   WINERY
(☑03-5729 8220; www.chrismont.com.au; 251 Upper King River Rd; mains $28-38; ⊙10am-5pm) This Italian-centric winery within a modern, architecturally designed space with magnificent views offers free tastings of its Italian varietals including prosecco, arneis and sagrantino. Its popular restaurant specialises in family recipes from Sicily and northern Italy, and the modern guesthouse among the vines is one of the nicest in the region.

Dal Zotto Estate   WINERY
(☑03-5729 8321; www.dalzotto.com.au; 4861 Wangaratta-Whitfield Rd, Whitfield; ⊙cellar door 10am-5pm, restaurant noon-3pm Thu-Sun, plus 6-10pm Fri) Dal Zotto Estate is one of the best wineries in the area, known especially for its prosecco. It also has an excellent trattoria serving north Italian cuisine, including handmade pasta and antipasto using local produce.

ℹ Getting There & Away

The King Valley lies on the Mansfield–Whitfield Rd (C521) and is accessed from Melbourne (274km, three hours) via the Hume Hwy (M31).

From Wangaratta there are two buses a day to Whitfield ($3.20, 45 minutes) Monday to Friday, via Moyhu.

Milawa Gourmet Region

The Milawa/Oxley gourmet region (www.milawagourmet.com.au) is the place to indulge your taste buds. As well as wine tasting, you can sample cheese, olives, mustards and marinades, or dine in some of the region's best restaurants.

✗ Eating

★**Milawa Cheese Company**   CHEESE $
(☑03-5727 3589; www.milawacheese.com.au; 17 Factory Lane, Milawa; ⊙9am-5pm, meals 9.30am-3pm) From humble origins, the Milawa Cheese Company now produces a mouth-watering array of cheeses to sample or buy. It excels at soft farmhouse brie (from goat or cow) and pungent washed-rind cheeses. There's a bakery here and an excellent restaurant doing a variety of house-baked pizzas and sourdough toasties using Milawa cheese. It's 2km north of Milawa.

★**Patricia's Table**   MODERN AUSTRALIAN $$$
(☑03-5720 5540; www.brownbrothers.com.au/visit-us/victoria/eat; 239 Milawa-Bobinawarrah Rd, Milawa; 2-course meal & wine pairing $67; ⊙noon-3pm) Break up your travels with a long lunch at this fine-dining restaurant at the picturesque Brown Brothers winery. Regarded as one of the region's very best, expect beautifully presented, contemporary dishes featuring the likes of blackened barramundi and grilled honey-glazed pork paired with earthy seasonal flavours. All the set-course combinations are accompanied with wines, which makes this hatted restaurant excellent value.

♟ Drinking & Nightlife

Hurdle Creek Still   DISTILLERY
(☑0427 331 145, 0411 156 773; www.hurdlecreekstill.com.au; 216 Whorouly-Bobinawarrah Rd, Bobinawarrah; ⊙10am-5pm Sat & Sun, by app Mon-Fri) This rural, small-scale, family-run distillery produces all its gins from a tin shed; drop by for tastings and pick up a bottle.

Brown Brothers   WINERY
(☑03-5720 5500; www.brownbrothers.com.au; 239 Milawa-Bobinawarrah Rd, Milawa; ⊙cellar door 9am-5pm, 1hr tour 11am & 2pm Fri, 11am Sat & Sun) The region's best-known winery, Brown Brothers vineyard's first vintage was in 1889 and it has remained in the hands of the same family ever since. As well as the tasting room, there's the superb Patricia's Table and Epi.Curious restaurants, a gorgeous garden, kids' play equipment, and picnic and barbecue facilities.

ℹ Getting There & Away

Milawa lies along the Snow Rd, between Wangaratta and Myrtleford. There's no public transport through the region.

Beechworth

POP 3700
Beechworth's historic honey-coloured granite buildings and wonderful gourmet offerings make it one of northeast Victoria's most enjoyable towns. It's also listed by the

National Trust as one of Victoria's two 'notable' towns (the other is Maldon), and you'll soon see why.

⊙ Sights

★ Burke Museum MUSEUM

(☑ 03-5728 8067; www.burkemuseum.com.au; 28 Loch St; adult/child/family incl entry to Ned Kelly vault $8/5/16; ⊙ 10am-5pm) Dating to 1857 when it was the Beechworth Athenaeum, this is one of Australia's oldest museums. It was renamed in 1861 in tribute to the famous explorer Robert O'Hara Burke – police superintendent at Beechworth from 1854 to 1858 – following the ill-fated Burke and Wills expedition. It shows gold-rush relics and an arcade of shopfronts preserved as they were over 140 years ago. Highlights include a taxidermy thylacine (Tasmanian tiger), Charles Dickens' writing desk, Burke's pistol and 'trench art' bullets from WWI.

The ticket here includes entry to the excellent Ned Kelly Vault.

Ned Kelly Vault MUSEUM

(☑ 03-5728 8067; www.burkemuseum.com.au; 101 Ford St; adult/child/family incl entry to Burke Museum $8/5/16; ⊙ 11am-4pm) Within the original subtreasury building (c 1858) where gold was stored, is this exhibition space dedicated to Australia's most infamous bushranger, Ned Kelly. There's detailed info on the Kelly story, as well as one of his original death masks, an original Sir Sidney Nolan painting, rare photographs and an early manuscript of Peter Carey's *True History of the Kelly Gang*. There's also an exhibit on the iconic bulletproof suits, and a mask you can wear for a photo op.

Also on display are the original masks used in the films starring Heath Ledger and Mick Jagger. It's an annexe of the Burke Museum, which the admission also includes entry to.

Old Beechworth Gaol HISTORIC BUILDING

(www.oldbeechworthgaol.com.au; cnr Ford & Williams Sts; adult/child/family $15/10/40; ⊙ tours 11.45am Thu-Mon) In late 2016 a consortium of locals banded together to buy the historic 1860 Beechworth prison in order to save it from being developed. Join its 'Rogues, Rat Bags and Mongrel Dogs' tours, held most days during the week to hear tales of its most infamous inmates – namely Ned Kelly, his family and sympathisers; in more recent times Carl Williams spent time in here. You'll get to visit the cells and gallows where eight prisoners were executed.

Beechworth Courthouse HISTORIC BUILDING

(☑ 03-5728 8067; www.burkemuseum.com.au; 94 Ford St; adult/child/family $8/5/16; ⊙ 9.30am-5pm) The Beechworth Courthouse is notable for Ned Kelly's first court appearance; see the cell where Ned was held in the basement behind the Shire Hall. There are stories of other notable trials, and an interactive jury room where you can hand down a verdict. Entry here is included in the Golden Ticket.

Beechworth Asylum HISTORIC SITE

(Albert Rd) One for those into dark tourism is this old 'lunatic' asylum, decommissioned in 1995, which sits on Mayday Hill overlooking town. While a lot of the buildings have been redeveloped into hotels and residential properties (and a proposed artists' studio is on the cards), a lot remains abandoned and downright spooky. You can't go inside any of the buildings, unless you sign up with Asylum Ghost Tours, which operates historic tours by day and ghost tours by night.

✦ Activities

Beechworth Honey Experience FOOD

(☑ 03-5728 1433; www.beechworthhoney.com.au; 31 Ford St; electric bike per half/full day $35/55, bicycle $25/40; ⊙ 9am-5.30pm) FREE Beechworth Honey's passionate owners, a fourth-generation family of honey producers, take you into the world of bees with regular guided tours, a live hive, highly educational displays and honey tastings. Visit its Beechworth Honey Discovery (www.beechworthhoney.com.au/beechworth-honey-discovery; 87 Ford St; ⊙ 9am-5.30pm) FREE centre down the road for more food, cooking demos, a bee garden and tastings. It also hires out electric bikes and bicycles.

Walking Tours TOURS

(adult/child/family $10/7.50/25; ⊙ 10.15am & 1.15pm) Daily guided walking tours leave from the visitor centre and feature lots of gossip and interesting details. The Gold Rush tour starts at 10.15am, the Ned Kelly–themed tour at 1.15pm. The good-value Golden Ticket includes both walking tours in the price.

Asylum Ghost Tours TOURS

(☑ 0473 376 848; www.asylumghosttours.com; Mayday Hills Village; tours adult/child $35/20) Beechworth's most creepy outing is a trip up to the town's former asylum with plenty of eerie tales of murder and mayhem. Visit during the day for a history tour or at night for ghost tours (kids under eight years not permitted). There are also photography tours (from $45), paranormal investigations ($50), horror film nights ($15) and sleepovers.

Sleeping

Tanswell's Commercial Hotel PUB $
(☑ 03-5728 1480; www.tanswellshotelbeechworth. com.au; 50 Ford St; s/d with shared bathroom $60/82, apt $135; 🖭) In a town where accommodation ain't cheap, this historic main-street pub is here to save the day with its no-frills rooms that are perfectly placed for exploring Beechworth. It's worth staying for its beautifully restored downstairs bar and restaurant.

Lake Sambell Caravan Park CARAVAN PARK $
(☑ 03-5728 1421; www.caravanparkbeechworth. com.au; 20 Peach Dr; unpowered/powered sites from $24/32, cabins with/without bathroom $95/75; ✳🖭) This shady park next to beautiful Lake Sambell has great facilities, including a camp kitchen, playground, mountain-bike hire (half/full day $22/33) and canoe/kayak hire (from $45). The sunsets reflected in the lake are spectacular.

Old Priory GUESTHOUSE $$
(☑ 03-5728 1024; www.oldpriory.com.au; 8 Priory Lane; dm/s/d $50/70/100, cottages s $90, d $150-170, q $200; 🖭) This historic convent dating to 1904 is a spooky but charming old place. It's often used by school groups, but it's the best budget choice in Beechworth, with lovely gardens and a range of rooms, including beautifully renovated miners' cottages.

★ Freeman on Ford B&B $$$
(☑ 03-5728 2371; www.freemanonford.com.au; 97 Ford St; s/d incl breakfast from $250/275; ✳🖭🖭) In the 1876 Oriental Bank, this sumptuous but homely place offers five-star Victorian luxury in six beautifully renovated rooms,

---

> **ⓘ COMBINED TICKET**
>
> If you're going to visit more than a couple of Beechworth's museums, it's worth buying the combined **Golden Ticket** (adult/child/family $25/15/50), which can be bought online or in person through the **visitor centre**. It covers entry over four consecutive days to most of the major sights and includes two guided tours.

---

right in the heart of town. The owner, Heidi, will make you feel very special.

Eating

Project Forty Nine ITALIAN $
(☑ 03-5728 1599; www.projectfortynine.com.au; 46-48 Ford St; dishes $9-25; ⊙ 9am-5pm Wed-Mon, to 9pm Fri) Opened by the former sommelier of Melbourne's acclaimed Vue de Monde is this popular husband-and-wife-operated Italian deli/wine bar. It does a casual menu of cured meats, antipasti and a pasta to go with Italian wine by the glass, as well as its own locally produced chardonnay. It's opened up a bar in Collingwood (p492), Melbourne, too.

Beechworth Bakery BAKERY $
(☑ 1300 233 784; www.beechworthbakery.com.au; 27 Camp St; pies from $5; ⊙ 6am-7pm) This popular place is the original in a well-known, statewide bakery chain. It's great for pies and pastries, cakes and sandwiches. Its signature pie is the Ned Kelly, topped with an egg and bacon, but the veggie cauliflower pie is also a winner.

Blynzz Coffee Roasters CAFE $$
(☑ 0423 589 962; www.coffeeroastersbeechworth. com.au; 43 Ford St; mains from $15; ⊙ 8.30am-2pm Thu-Sun) This inner-city-chic micro-roastery cafe on Beechworth's main strip has polished concrete floors and designer fittings along with great breakfasts and brunches. However, it's best known for its coffee, roasting all of its single-origin beans on site, with awaiting hessian sacks of green beans stacked at the back.

★ Provenance MODERN AUSTRALIAN $$$
(☑ 03-5728 1786; www.theprovenance.com.au; 86 Ford St; 2-/3-course meals $68/88, degustation menu without/with matching wines $115/180; ⊙ 6.30-9pm Wed-Sun) In an 1856 bank building, Provenance has elegant but contemporary fine dining. Under the guidance of acclaimed local chef Michael Ryan, the innovative menu features modern Australian fare with Japanese influences, such as smoked wallaby tartare with umeboshi, egg yolk and miso sauce. If you can't decide, go for the degustation menu. Its wine list is highly renowned, too. Bookings essential.

Drinking & Nightlife

★ Bridge Road Brewers MICROBREWERY
(☑ 03-5728 2703; www.bridgeroadbrewers.com. au; Old Coach House Brewers Lane, 50 Ford St; pizza $15.50-22; ⊙ 11am-10pm) Hiding behind

Tanswell's Commercial Hotel, Beechworth's gem of a microbrewery produces some excellent beer (taste 10 for $15), with nine of them on tap. It goes beautifully with freshly baked pretzels, gourmet house-made pizzas, burgers etc. There's a brewery tour each Saturday at 11am ($15), which includes tastings. It also offers free bike hire!

Tanswell's Commercial Hotel PUB
(☑03-5728 1480; www.tanswellshotelbeechworth. com.au; 50 Ford St; mains $24-34; ⊙10.30am-late) A gold-rush-era pub dating to 1856, the imposing Tanswell's Hotel is very much a fixture along Beechworth's picturesque main street. Its front bar is done out elegantly with gleaming polished wood, black-and-white checkered tiles and a roaring fire, resembling an English pub more than an Aussie country hotel. There's also a fine-dining restaurant, live music, a billiards room and accommodation.

Local legend has it that Ned Kelly used to drink here regularly.

❶ Information

Beechworth Visitor Centre (☑1300 366 321; www.beechworthonline.com.au; 103 Ford St; ⊙9am-5pm) Information and an accommodation and activity booking service in the town hall.

❶ Getting There & Away

Beechworth is just off the Great Alpine Rd, 36km east of Wangaratta and 280km northeast of Melbourne.

V/Line runs a train/bus service between Melbourne and Beechworth ($36, 3½ hours, three daily), with a change at Wangaratta. There are direct buses from Wangaratta ($5, 35 minutes, five daily) and Bright ($4.80, 50 minutes, two daily).

Yackandandah

POP 950

An old gold-mining town nestled in beautiful hills and valleys east of Beechworth, 'Yack', as it's universally known, is original enough to be classified by the National Trust. Essentially a one-street town – bookended by two pubs (the Bottom Pub and the Top Pub) – its historic streetscape is one of the most charming you'll find in country Australia.

In a former bank building, the **Yackandandah Museum** (☑02-6027 0627; www. yackandandahmuseum.wordpress.com; 21 High St; gold coin donation; ⊙11am-4pm Wed-Sun, daily

school holidays) has changing historical exhibitions on Yackandandah. Out the back is an original 1850s cottage that's furnished in period style and includes a unique outdoor 'double dunny' (toilet). There's also a good selection of themed walking-tour maps in its gift shop.

On the 1½-hour **Karrs Reef Goldmine Tour** (☑0408 975 991; adult/child $25/20; ⊙10am, 1pm & 4pm Sat & Sun or by app) you'll don a hard hat and descend into the original tunnels of this gold mine that dates to 1857. Bookings can be made through the visitor centre.

🍴 Eating & Drinking

★**Star Hotel** PUB FOOD $$
(☑02-6027 1493; www.facebook.com/starhotel yack; 30 High St; mains $17-21; ⊙11am-late) Known locally as the 'Top Pub', this 1863 hotel does all the classic counter meals, but of more interest is its American-style BBQ using a red-gum smoker. It's also the place for craft beer, being the official home of Yack's very own Two Pot Brewing.

Saint Monday CAFE $$
(☑02-6027 1202; www.saintmondaycafe.com.au; 26 High St; mains $15-26; ⊙8am-4pm Wed-Sun; ☑) ✔ Deconstructed sushi and vegan doughnuts are definitely items you once couldn't order in Yackandandah, but those days are gone since the arrival of this lovely little cafe with art on the walls. The kitchen uses locally sourced ingredients to create delicious vegetarian and ethical cuisine.

Yackandandah Hotel PUB
(☑02-6027 1210; www.yackandandahhotel.com. au; 1 High St; s/d/tr $50/70/90; ⊙11am-late) Dating back to 1867, the 'Bottom Pub' is your quintessential country hotel with cold beer and pub grub, including its signature double schnitzel burger. There are budget rooms upstairs from $50 a night.

🔒 Shopping

★**Kirby's Flat Pottery** CERAMICS
(☑02-6027 1416; www.johndermer.com.au; 225 Kirby's Flat Rd; ⊙10.30am-5pm Sat & Sun or by app) The studio-cum-gallery-cum-shop of internationally renowned potter John Dermer, Kirby's Flat Pottery is a great place to pick up affordable, original pieces, or even just browse the gallery with its stunning collection of salt-glazed ceramics. It's

set in a lovely garden retreat 4km south of Yackandandah.

❶ Information

Yackandandah Visitor Centre (☑02-6027 1988; www.exploreyackandandah.com.au; 37 High St; ☺9am-5pm) Stocks a good selection of brochures, walking tours and accommodation for Yack and beyond. Also sells mining licences for those who fancy prospecting for gold.

❶ Getting There & Away

Yackandandah is 307km northeast of Melbourne – take the Hume Hwy to the Great Alpine Rd exit north of Wangaratta then follow the signs to Beechworth. From here it's a further 22km to Yackandandah.

On weekdays there are daily buses to/from Beechworth ($2.40) en route to Albury-Wodonga.

Chiltern

POP 1640

Like an old-time movie set, tiny Chiltern is one of Victoria's most historic and charming colonial townships. Its two main streets are lined with 19th-century buildings, antique shops and a couple of pubs – authentic enough that the town has often been used as a film set for period films, including the early Walt Disney classic *Ride a Wild Pony*. Originally called Black Dog Creek, it was established in 1851 and prospered when gold was discovered here in 1859.

◉ Sights

Pick up a copy of the Chiltern Touring Guide from the Chiltern Visitor Centre – it guides you around 20 historic sites scattered about the town.

Chiltern Athenaeum   MUSEUM
(☑03-5726 1280; www.chilternathenaeum.com. au; 57 Conness St; adult/child $2/free; ☺10am-3pm Tue-Fri, to 4pm Sat & Sun) Housed in the former historic town hall and library (1866) is this fantastic museum loaded with fascinating exhibits of yesteryear and local stories. Highlights include a gold-rush-era library, exquisite 19th-century gum-leaf paintings by Alfred William Eustace, a WWI horse saddle from the Battle of Beersheba and mementos from former primer minister John McEwen. It's volunteer run, so opening hours can be sporadic.

**Chiltern-Mt Pilot
National Park**   NATIONAL PARK
(Chiltern Box-Ironbark National Park; ☑13 19 63; www.parks.vic.gov.au) This important national park protects some of Victoria's last stands of Box-Ironbark forest in a patchwork of protected areas around the town. This is also one of the last Victorian refuges for the endangered Regent's Honeyeater, along with more than 200 other bird species. The Chiltern Visitor Centre has maps, a park information sheet, a brochure entitled *Bird Trails of Chiltern,* and information on the best places to see the Regent's Honeyeater.

To immerse yourself in the Ironbarks, consider the 8.5km **Whitebox Walking Track**, which completes a circuit in the area of the park south of Chiltern; ask at the visitor centre for directions.

Lake View House   HISTORIC BUILDING
(☑03-5726 1590, 03-9656 9889; www.national trust.org.au/places/lake-view-house; 18-22 Victoria St; adult/child $2/1; ☺11am-2pm Wed, 10am-1pm Sat, 1-4pm Sun) This was the home of local author Ethel Florence Richardson (better known by her pen name Henry Handel Richardson), who wrote about life here in the book *Ultima Thule* (1929), the third part of her trilogy *The Fortunes of Richard Mahony* (1930). Overlooking Lake Anderson, the house was built in 1870 and today is owned by the National Trust.

✖ Eating

★**Hub 62**   CAFE $
(☑03-5726 1207; www.hub62cafe.wixsite.com/cafe-gallery; 62 Main St; mains $10-19; ☺8am-4pm Mon & Wed-Fri, 7.30am-4pm Sat & Sun; 🐾) In the historic former Masonic Hall is this relaxed and vibrant, art-filled cafe that offers a distinct contemporary point of difference from the rest of ye olde town. As well as the best coffee in town, you can grab modern-style breakfasts and lunches.

Vine Chiltern   PUB FOOD $$
(☑0475 044 866; www.facebook.com/thevine chiltern; cnr Main & Conness Sts; mains $14-28; ☺5.30-9pm Wed & Thu, 5.30pm-late Fri & Sat, noon-4pm Sun) A pub way back in 1867, the Vine has brought this historic watering hole back to life with a menu of regional craft beers and wines to go with pizzas and burgers. It's named after the massive grapevine (the largest in Australia, possibly the world) in the courtyard next door, viewed from the alleyway.

ℹ️ Information

Chiltern Visitor Centre (☏ 03-5726 1611; www.chilternvic.com; 30 Main St; ⊘10am-4pm) Chiltern's helpful tourist office has information on the town and surrounding area, with useful tips on everything from birdwatching to gold prospecting.

ℹ️ Getting There & Away

Chiltern is 290km northeast of Melbourne and lies just off the Hume Hwy (M31).

Up to three **V/Line** (☏ 1800 800 007; www.vline.com.au) train services run daily from Melbourne's Southern Cross station to Chiltern ($36, 3¼ hours).

Rutherglen & Around

POP 2479

Rutherglen combines some marvellous gold-rush-era buildings (gold was discovered here in 1860) with northern Victoria's most celebrated winemaking tradition. The town itself has all the essential ingredients that merit a stopover, among them a great pie shop, antique dealers and classic country pubs to go with its changing face since the arrival of a swish new microbrewery and wine bar. It all adds up to an engaging destination in its own right and a good base for exploring the Murray River's Victorian hinterland.

🔘 Sights & Activities

An extension of the Murray to Mountains Rail Trail passes through Rutherglen and Wahgunyah and leads to some of the wineries. You can hire bicycles (half/full day $35/50), as well as tandem bikes (half/full day $50/85), from the Rutherglen Visitor Information Centre, which also has bicycle and walking trail maps of the area.

Big Wine Bottle LANDMARK
(45 Campbell St) In line with Australia's fine tradition of kitschy oversized monuments (the Big Prawn, Big Pineapple, Big Koala etc), Rutherglen has the Big Wine Bottle. It stands at 36m tall and is actually a historic brown-brick water tower (c 1900).

Rutherglen Wine Experience WINERY
(☏ 1800 622 871; www.rutherglenvic.com; 57 Main St; ⊘9am-5pm) FREE Set up inside the visitor information centre (p610) is the centrepiece for the region's wine industry. Here you'll get an overview of the local wineries and a map of the area, as well as free tastings of various fortified wines and locally made cordials.

👉 Tours

Behind the Scenes TOURS
(☏ 1800 622 871; www.rutherglenvic.com/behind-the-scenes-tours; ⊘2pm Mon, Wed & Thu, 11am Fri-Sun) FREE A few local wineries offer fantastic, free 'Behind the Scenes' winery tours that take you into the world of the wine-making process. Advance bookings are essential. Check the website to match your day with a winery, but it's best to pre-book through the visitor centre.

⭐ Festivals & Events

⭐ **Tastes of Rutherglen** FOOD & DRINK
(www.tastesofrutherglen.com.au; tickets $20, shuttle bus $27; ⊘Mar) A weekend of indulgence, this massive celebration of food and wine is held at dozens of vineyards and restaurants. There's a hop-on, hop-off shuttle bus linking the wineries.

⭐ **Winery Walkabout Weekend** WINE, MUSIC
(www.winerywalkabout.com.au; ⊘Jun) Australia's original wine festival, this huge events attracts 25,000 revellers to town for a weekend of merriment including music, barrel racing, food vans and probably some wine.

🛏️ Sleeping

Victoria Hotel HOTEL $
(☏ 02-6032 8610; www.victoriahotelrutherglen.com.au; 90 Main St; s/d without bathroom from $50/90, d with bathroom from $120, f from $200; ✽) A step up from your usual pub accommodation, this beautiful National Trust–classified pub is full of history, great bistro food and some very inviting guest rooms. It's a sprawling spot with plenty of choices, with the pick being the spruced-up en-suite rooms overlooking Main St. At $50 a night it's a great spot for budget travellers.

⭐ **Amberesque** B&B $$
(☏ 02-6032 7000; www.amberesque.com.au; 80 Main St; d from $180; ✽🕾) Named after host Amber, who, along with her husband, has set up this wonderful B&B in a historic bank in the heart of town. Upstairs rooms are lovely, with king-sized beds and spa baths, and a patio overlooking the garden. The highlight is the beautiful downstairs space where you can enjoy a lavish personalised breakfast, complimentary port and welcome cheese-and-wine platter.

Tuileries
BOUTIQUE HOTEL $$
(02-6032 9033; www.tuileriesrutherglen.com.au; 13 Drummond St; d $199, incl dinner $299; ❄☎☻) Looking out to the vineyards, all rooms at this luxurious place are individually decorated in bright contemporary tones. There's a guest lounge, tennis court, pool and fine-dining **restaurant** (lunch mains $16.50-19, dinner $31.50-40; ☺noon-2pm & 6.30-9pm) and cafe. Located next to Rutherglen Estates; rates include breakfast.

Carlyle House
B&B $$
(02-6032 8444; www.carlylehouse.com.au; 147 High St; r $160-195; ❄☎) Four traditional suites and modern garden apartments are beautifully presented in this lovingly restored home (c 1896), with lovely hosts Anthony and Sharyn. A choice of cafe-style cooked breakfasts is included in the rate.

✖️ Eating

✖️ Rutherglen

★ Parker Pies
BAKERY $
(02-6032 9605; www.parkerpies.com.au; 86-88 Main St; pies $5-9; ☺8.30am-5pm) If you think a pie is just a pie, this award-winning local institution might change your mind. Try the gourmet pastries – emu, venison, crocodile, buffalo or the lovely Jolly Jumbuck (a lamb pastry with rosemary and mint).

★ Taste @ Rutherglen
MODERN AUSTRALIAN $$$
(03-5728 1480; www.taste-at-rutherglen.com; 121b Main St; breakfast mains $7-20, mains $36-40, 5-/7-course degustation $80/100; ☺8-11am & 6-11pm Wed-Sun) Taste @ Rutherglen is the town's go-to place for fine dining, coffee and breakfast, while its attached brewpub is *the* spot for beer. Its evening menu offers options such as confit-duck spring rolls to go with hickory-smoked eye fillets, or there's a degustation menu with paired wines. For breakfast the Rutherglen pork sausage and poached egg on sourdough is a winner.

✖️ Wahgunyah

Pickled Sisters Café
MODERN EUROPEAN $$
(02-6033 2377; www.pickledsisters.com.au; Cofield Wines, Distillery Rd, Wahgunyah; mains $12-33; ☺10am-3pm Mon & Wed-Fri, 9am-4pm Sat & Sun) Attached to the Cofield winery, this popular little eatery does some interesting dishes such as honey-and-muscat-glazed confit

duck, and twice-baked Milawa goats-milk cheese soufflé, along with various platters to go with wine. There's also the opportunity to spend the night in a **luxury tent** (02-6033 3798; www.cofieldwines.com.au/glamping.aspx; Cofield Wines; d from $260).

★ Terrace Restaurant
MODERN EUROPEAN $$$
(02-6035 2209; www.allsaintswine.com.au/terrace-restaurant; All Saints Estate, All Saints Rd, Wahgunyah; 2-/3-course meal $60/80; ☺noon-3pm Wed-Fri & Sun, noon-3pm & 6-11pm Sat) One of the region's best restaurants, this classy bistro serves inventive and modern seasonal European cuisine, overlooking the stately grounds of All Saints wine estate.

🍷 Drinking & Nightlife

★ Thousand Pound
WINE BAR
(02-6035 2222; www.thousandpound.com.au; 82 Main St; mains from $24; ☺5pm-late Fri-Sun) If ever there was a place suited to a wine bar, it's Rutherglen's picturesque main street. Grab a stool at the long tiled bar, by the window or on the communal table to select from 140 local and international family-owned wineries. Its food is also a highlight with charcoal-grilled steaks, seafood and tapas dishes.

★ Rutherglen Brewery
MICROBREWERY
(02-6032 9765; www.rutherglenbrewery.com; 121b Main St; ☺11am-2.30pm & 5.30-10pm Wed-Sat) An awesome new addition to town is this nanobrewery that knocks up quality crafted ales from its back shed. It produces nine beers, with usually five on tap, along with a cider to go with a menu of smoked BBQ meats and pizzas. Plans are in place to start up a new distillery and speakeasy bar next door, which will no doubt be another hit.

ⓘ Information

Rutherglen Visitor Information Centre
(1800 622 871; 57 Main St; ☺9am-5pm) In the same complex as the Rutherglen Wine Experience; has good info on accommodation, wineries and sights. Also rents bikes and has wi-fi access.

ⓘ Getting There & Away

Rutherglen is 295km northeast of Melbourne. To get there by car, take the Hume Hwy (M31) and turn off at Chiltern.

V/Line (1800 800 007; www.vline.com.au) has a train and coach service between Melbourne and Rutherglen ($36, 3½ hours, eight

RUTHERGLEN REDS

Rutherglen's wineries produce superb fortifieds (port, muscat and tokay) and some potent durifs and shirazes – among the biggest, baddest and strongest reds. Many wineries date back to the 1860s, and are still run by fifth- or sixth-generation winemakers.

Most of the wineries don't distribute beyond the area, so it makes visiting all the more worthwhile. All (but one) offer free tastings. See www.winemakers.com.au for more information.

All Saints (☎ 02-6035 2222, 1800 021 621; www.allsaintswine.com.au; All Saints Rd, Wahgunyah; ⏱ 9am-5.30pm Mon-Sat, 10am-5.30pm Sun) With its aristocratic gardens and heritage-listed 19th-century castle, All Saints (established 1865) is a classy affair, which extends from its cheese-tasting room and cellar door to its fine-dining restaurant.

Buller Wines (☎ 02-6032 9660; www.buller.com.au; 2804 Federation Way; ⏱ 9am-5pm Mon-Fri, 10am-5pm Sat & Sun) Making fine shiraz since 1921; keep an eye out for its new restaurant.

Rutherglen Estates (☎ 02-6032 7999; www.rutherglenestates.com.au; Tuileries, 13-35 Drummond St; ⏱ 10am-5.30pm) Closest winery to town with shiraz, grenache and table red and white wines.

Stanton & Killeen Wines (☎ 02-6032 9457; www.stantonandkilleenwines.com.au; 440 Jacks Rd; ⏱ 9am-5pm Mon-Fri, 10am-5pm Sat & Sun) This century-old winery is known for its durif-shiraz blend, rosé and vintage ports.

Warrabilla Wines (☎ 02-6035 7242; www.warrabillawines.com.au; 6152 Murray Valley Hwy; ⏱ 10am-5pm) Run by a sixth-generation winemaker, this is one for those who like their reds big, brash and full of oak.

Morris (☎ 02-6026 7303; www.morriswines.com.au; 154 Mia Mia Rd; ⏱ 9am-5pm Mon-Sat, 10am-5pm Sun) Rutherglen's oldest winery (1859) with a dusty cellar door designed by esteemed architect Robin Boyd, looking out to wine barrels and the dirt production floor.

Pfeiffer (☎ 02-6033 2805; www.pfeifferwinesrutherglen.com.au; 167 Distillery Rd, Wahgunyah; ⏱ 9am-5pm Mon-Sat, 10am-5pm Sun) This atmospheric cellar door known for its gamay is run by a father-daughter winemaker team. It's on a river teeming with turtles and the occasional platypus.

Chambers Rosewood (☎ 02-6032 8641; www.chambersrosewood.com.au; Barkly St; ⏱ 9am-5pm Mon-Sat, 10am-5pm Sun) One of Rutherglen's originals, this ramshackle tin-shed cellar door's wine tasting is all self-serve.

Cofield Wines (☎ 02-6033 3798; www.cofieldwines.com.au; Distillery Rd, Wahgunyah; ⏱ 9am-5pm Mon-Sat, 10am-5pm Sun; 🍴) Stop by to sample Champagne-style sparkling wines, produced using a traditional method.

St Leonard's Vineyard (☎ 02-6035 2222; www.stleonardswine.com.au; 201 St Leonards Rd, Wahgunyah; ⏱ 10am-5pm Thu-Sun) Head through its dark (and kinda spooky) barrel room to enter a modern light-filled cellar door with grassy outdoors area and lagoon. Good food too.

Campbells Winery (☎ 02-6033 6000; www.campbellswines.com.au; 4603 Murray Valley Hwy; ⏱ 9am-5pm Mon-Sat, 10am-5pm Sun) Spanning five generation of winemakers, this well-respected family-owned winery is 3km west of Rutherglen. There are cheese and charcuterie platters to enjoy on its lawn.

Scion Vineyard (☎ 02-6032 8844; www.scionvineyard.com; 74 Slaughterhouse Rd; ⏱ 10am-5pm) A more contemporary affair than Rutherglen's more traditional offerings, this boutique cellar door is located close to town. Tastings are $5 and hampers can be pre-arranged.

Valhalla Wines (☎ 02-6033 1438; www.valhallawines.com.au; 163 All Saints Rd, Wahgunyah; ⏱ 10am-4pm Fri-Sun or by app) 🍴 Set up by a passionate winemaker, Valhalla adopts a modern approach using sustainable, renewable practices. Its cellar door is built entirely from straw bale.

weekly), with a change at Wangaratta. During festivals, bus transport to wineries can be organised through the **visitor centre** (p610).

The **Murray to Mountains Rail Trail** has an extension to Rutherglen, which means you can get here and around by bike.

Mt Buffalo National Park

Beautiful Mt Buffalo is an easily accessible year-round destination – in winter it's a tiny, family friendly ski resort with gentle runs, and in summer it's a great spot for bushwalking, mountain biking and rock climbing. Unlike the bigger ski resorts, there are no fees for visiting Mt Buffalo. You'll find granite outcrops, lookouts, streams, waterfalls, wildflowers and wildlife here.

It was named in 1824 by the explorers Hume and Hovell on their trek from Sydney to Port Phillip – they thought its bulky shape resembled a buffalo – and declared it a national park in 1898.

👁 Sights & Activities

The **Big Walk**, an 11km, five-hour ascent of the mountain, starts from Eurobin Creek picnic area, north of Porepunkah, and finishes at the Gorge day visitor area. A road leads to just below the summit of the Horn (1723m), the highest point on the massif. Nearby **Lake Catani** is good for swimming, canoeing and camping.

There are 14km of groomed **cross-country ski trails** starting out from the Cresta Valley car park, as well as a **tobogganing area**. In summer Mt Buffalo is a **hang-gliding** paradise, and the near-vertical walls of the Gorge provide some of Australia's most challenging **rock climbing** and **abseiling** – get in touch with Adventure Guides Australia.

Mt Buffalo Olives   FARM
(📞 03-5756 2143; www.mtbuffaloolives.com.au; 307 Mt Buffalo Rd, Porepunkah; ⊙11am-5pm Fri-Mon, daily school holidays) On the road up to Mt Buffalo from Porepunkah, this working olive grove has tastings and sales of olives, olive oils and other locally farmed products. It also has a lovely place to stay (Sunday to Thursday $195, Friday and Saturday $235, two-night minimum stay).

★**Adventure Guides Australia**   OUTDOORS
(📞 0419 280 614; www.adventureguidesaustralia. com) Set up by the extremely knowledgeable David Chitty (a former SAS officer), this established operator offers abseiling (beginner/adventure $90/110), including on the 300m multi-pitch North Wall. It also offers caving with glow-worms through an underground river system (from $120); check its website for scheduled trips. It hires out kayaks for Lake Catani and runs a cross-country snow-shoeing ski school in winter.

🛏 Sleeping

**Lake Catani
Campground**   CAMPGROUND $
(📞 13 19 63; www.parkweb.vic.gov.au; per site from $46.10; ⊙Nov-Apr) A popular summer camping ground on the lake shore, with 59 sites, flush toilets and showers. During winter there are also a few free camp sites available, but only non-flush toilet facilities. Book through Parks Victoria.

★**Kilns**   B&B $$$
(📞 0400 733 170, 0408 553 332; www.kilnhouse. com.au; Cavedons Lane, Porepunkah; d from $300; ❋🛜) Hidden away on an old tobacco farm in Porepunkah are these boutique luxury cottages converted from old tobacco kiln houses. Making for a unique stay, the architecturally designed self-contained houses feature stylish furniture, polished concrete floors and a wood-fire with views to Mt Buffalo. Each has a bicycle so you can pedal to the wineries. Minimum two-night stay.

🍷 Drinking & Nightlife

★**Feathertop Winery**   WINERY
(📞 03-5756 2356; www.feathertopwinery.com.au; 6619 Great Alpine Rd, Porepunkah; ⊙cellar door & cafe 10am-5pm daily, restaurant noon-3pm Fri-Mon) This winery-cafe-restaurant in Porepunkah, only 10km from Bright, is an essential stop along the Murray to Mountains Rail Trail. Its cellar door offers tastings of prosecco, pinot gris and shiraz, all grown on site, or you can enjoy a glass on the terrace. The cafe does homemade sausage rolls and sourdough baguettes, while the attached provedore can make up picnic hampers.

Porepunkah Pub   PUB
(📞 03-5756 2111; www.porepunkahpub.com.au; 13 Nicholson St, Porepunkah; mains from $15; ⊙noon-late daily, kitchen Thu-Sun) The 'Punka Pub' is all about craft beers, cocktails on tap and wine sourced exclusively from the immediate area. It does great food using local produce and also offers boutique, well-priced rooms ($140).

ⓘ Getting There & Away

The main access road is out of Porepunkah, between Myrtleford and Bright, from where it's around a one-hour drive to the summit. Porepunkah is 10km from Bright, and is on the **Murray to Mountains Rail Trail**.

Bright

POP 2165

Famous for its glorious autumn colours, Bright is a popular year-round destination in the foothills of the alps and a gateway to Mt Hotham and Falls Creek. Skiers make a beeline through Bright in winter, but it's a lovely base for exploring the Alpine National Park, paragliding, fishing and kayaking on local rivers, bushwalking and exploring the region's wineries. It's a big cycling destination, too, with the Murray to Mountains Rail Trail, as well as single track mountain-bike and alpine road trails. Plentiful accommodation and some sophisticated restaurants and cafes complete the rather-appealing picture.

◎ Sights & Activities

Bright is a base for all sorts of adventure activities, including fly-fishing, hiking, cycling and paragliding. The Murray to Mountains Rail Trail between Bright and Wangaratta starts (or ends) behind the old train station. Bikes, tandems and baby trailers can be rented from **Cyclepath** (☑ 03-5750 1442; www. cyclepath.com.au; 74 Gavan St; recreational bikes per hour/half-/full day from $25/30/38, mountain/ road bikes per day from $50/75; ⊘ 9am-5.30pm Mon-Fri, 9am-5pm Sat & Sun) or **Bright Electric Bikes** (☑ 03-5755 1309; www.brightelectricbikes. com.au; 2 Delany Ave; electric bike rental per hour/ half-/full day $22/45/65, bicycle from $15/25/35; ⊘ 9am-6pm daily Sep-May, 9am-6pm Fri-Sun Jun-Aug). The **Mystic MTB Park** (www.alpine communityplantation.com.au/mystic) is getting rave reviews from mountain-bikers. On weekends you can organise shuttles through **Blue Dirt Mountain Biking** (☑ 0409 161 903; www.bluedirt.com.au/village-bike-cafe; Slalom car park, Bogong High Plains Rd; bike rental per day $50-90, shuttle service 1/2 days $50/90; ⊘ Sat & Sun Nov-May, daily Jan) for $50 per day.

⮐ Courses

★ **Patrizia Simone**
Country Cooking School COOKING
(☑ 03-5755 2266; www.simonesbright.com.au; 98 Gavan St; per person $180) One of northeastern Victoria's most celebrated chefs, Patrizia

Simone runs fabulous four-hour cooking classes centred around Italian (especially Umbrian) cooking techniques using local ingredients. Her signature class is the 'Umbrian Experience', which touches on some of the recipes from Patrizia's cookbook, *My Umbrian Kitchen*.

🛏 Sleeping

Alpine Hotel Bright PUB $
(☑ 03-5755 1366; www.alpinehotelbright.com.au; 7-9 Anderson St; r $80-140) At the rear of this historic 1864 pub are refurbished motel-style rooms that offer excellent value for what's otherwise a pricey town accommodation-wise.

Bright Holiday Park CARAVAN PARK $
(☑ 1800 706 685, 03-5755 1141; www.brightholiday park.com.au; Cherry Lane; unpowered sites $33-50, powered sites $35-60, cabins $130-284; ❄ 🐾 ⓢ) Straddling pretty Morses Creek, this lovely park is five minutes' walk to the shops. The riverside spa cabins are very nice and feature pay TV channels. It's a great spot for families with a pool, minigolf and playground.

★ **Odd Frog** BOUTIQUE HOTEL $$
(☑ 0418 362 791; www.theoddfrog.com; 3 Mc-Fadyens Lane; d $150-195, q $250; ❄) 🐾 Designed and built by the architect/interior-designer owners, these contemporary, eco-friendly studios feature light, breezy spaces and fabulous outdoor decks with a telescope for star gazing. The design features clever use of the hilly site with sculptural steel-frame foundations and flying balconies.

Aalborg APARTMENT $$
(☑ 0401 357 329; www.aalborgbright.com.au; 6 Orchard Ct; r $220-250; ❄ 🐾) Clean-lined Scandinavian design with plenty of pine-and-white furnishings dominates this gorgeous place. Every fitting is perfectly chosen and abundant glass opens out onto sweeping bush views. There's a minimum two-night stay.

✖ Eating

Ginger Baker CAFE $
(☑ 03-5755 2300; www.gingerbaker.com.au; 127 Gavan St; mains $8-20; ⊘ 8am-3pm Sun-Thu, to 9pm Fri & Sat; 🐾) This rightfully popular cafe within a cute rustic weatherboard cottage opens up to an expansive garden with seating overlooking the river. Locally roasted coffee from Sixpence (p614) goes well with tasty hot breakfasts, while Bridge Road (p606) brewery beers on tap complement mains

such as buttermilk-fried chicken with aioli, prawn linguine or Mt Beauty lamb cutlets.

Tomahawks CAFE $$
(☑ 03-5750 1113; 15 Camp St; mains $16; ⊙ noon-11pm Wed-Fri, 9am-11pm Sat & Sun) A cool new kid in town, Tomahawks does a menu of urban fare from Korean sticky fried chicken and Old Bay spiced squid with charcoal mayo to a wagyu cheeseburger with habanero mustard, maple bacon and pickles. Also has a well-stocked bar, craft beers and single-origin coffees roasted in Mansfield.

Thirteen Steps MODERN AUSTRALIAN $$
(☑ 03-5750 1313; www.thirteensteps.com.au; 14 Barnard St; dishes $17-39; ⊙ 6-11pm Thu-Mon) Take 13 steps down to this atmospheric underground wine cellar and bistro where diners cram in to feast on local-produce plates or dishes ranging from modern Asian to American-style spare ribs.

★ Tani MODERN AUSTRALIAN $$$
(☑ 03-5750 1304; www.tanieatdrink.com.au; 100 Gavan St; 2-/3-/6-course meal $50/60/88; ⊙ 6-10pm Wed-Sun) Another star in regional Victoria's food scene, smart-rustic Tani offers understated class with its menu of local modern Australian food with plenty of indigenous and Asian twists. Its drinks list is an all-regional selection, and there's a distillery all set up to make gins on site from mid-2017.

🍸 Drinking & Nightlife

★ Bright Brewery BREWERY
(☑ 03-5755 1301; www.brightbrewery.com.au; 121 Gavan St; ⊙ 11am-10pm; 🛜) This boutique brewery produces a quality range of beers (sample six for $12) and beer-friendly food such as pizzas, Angus beef burgers and mezze boards. There's a guided tour and tasting on Monday, Friday and Saturday at 3pm ($18) and live blues on Sunday, or you can learn to be a brewer for a day ($360) – see the website for course dates.

Sixpence COFFEE
(☑ 0412 728 420; www.sixpencecoffee.com.au; 35 Churchill Ave; ⊙ 7.30am-2.30pm Mon-Fri) In an industrial estate a short drive from Bright's main strip is this micro-roastery that will excite coffee enthusiasts who love their Ethiopian beans. It's all roasted on site by Luke (formerly from Padre Coffee in East Brunswick, Melbourne) to be enjoyed on the garden tables, along with panini and fresh croissants. Sourdough bread is also baked, available most days.

ⓘ Information

Alpine Visitor Information Centre (☑ 03-5755 0584, 1800 111 885; www.brightvictoria.com. au; 119 Gavan St; ⊙ 9am-5pm; 🛜) Has a busy accommodation booking service, along with useful brochures, wi-fi access and attached cafe.

ⓘ Getting There & Away

Bright is 310km northeast of Melbourne, around a 3½-hour journey that's mostly via the Hume Hwy (M31).

V/Line (☑ 1800 800 007; www.vline.com. au) runs train/coach services from Melbourne ($37.60, 4½ hours, two daily) with a change at Wangaratta.

O'Connells Omeo Bus Service (☑ 0428 591 377; www.omeobus.com.au; Day Ave) has a handy year-round service three times a week that heads from Bright to Harrietville ($4.20, 15 minutes) and Mt Hotham ($5, one hour) en route to Omeo ($12.80, two hours).

During winter the **Snowball Express** (☑ 1300 656 546; www.snowballexpress.com.au) operates from Bright to Mt Hotham (adult/child return $52/44, 1½ hours).

Mt Beauty & the Kiewa Valley

Huddled at the foot of Victoria's highest mountain, Mt Bogong (1986m), on the Kiewa River, Mt Beauty and its twin villages of Tawonga and Tawonga South are the gateways to Falls Creek ski resort. It's reached by a steep and winding road from Bright, with some lovely alpine views.

⊙ Sights & Activities

The 2km **Tree Fern Walk** and the longer **Peppermint Walk** both start from **Mountain Creek Picnic Area**, on Mountain Creek Rd, off the Kiewa Valley Hwy (C531). Located about 1km south of Bogong Village (towards Falls Creek), the 1.5km return **Fainter Falls Walk** takes you to a pretty cascade. For information on longer walks in the area, visit the Mt Beauty Visitor Centre.

Kiewa Valley Historical Museum MUSEUM
(☑ 03-5755 0596; www.kiewavalleyhs.wixsite.com/kvhs-museum; 31 Bogong High Plains Rd; gold coin donation; ⊙ 9am-5pm) **FREE** Within the Mt Beauty Visitor Centre is this interesting little museum that covers the history of the Kiewa Valley and Bogong High Plains, from Indigenous groups through to the colonial highland cattlemen. There's a replica of an old

mountain hut, a historical background on skiing in the region and info on the **Bogong Power Station** (☑ 03-5754 3318; Bogong High Plains Rd; ☉ 10.30am-2.30pm Sun) **FREE**.

Bogong Horseback Adventures
HORSE RIDING

(☑ 03-5754 4849; www.bogonghorse.com.au; 52 Fredas Lane, off Mountain Creek Rd, Tawonga; 2/4hr ride $95/120, full day with lunch $250) Horse riders can experience this beautiful area on horseback on either short two-hour jaunts, day-long trips with a delicious lunch, or week-long pack-horse camping trips to remote alpine regions over Mt Bogong. It's 12km northwest of Tawonga, and includes the delightful Spring Spur homestay.

Big Hill MTB Park
MOUNTAIN BIKING

One of Victoria's first single-track mountain-bike trails, this downhill path will have you flying through scenic alpine forest. While it's more suited to experienced riders, its maze of trails has something for all levels.

🛏 Sleeping

Mt Beauty Holiday Centre
CARAVAN PARK $

(☑ 03-5754 4396; www.holidaycentre.com.au; 222-226 Kiewa Valley Hwy; unpowered/powered sites from $32/38, cabins & yurts $85-160; ❋ ❂) This family caravan park close to Mt Beauty town centre has river frontage, games and an interesting range of cabins, including hexagonal 'yurts'.

★ Spring Spur
HOMESTAY $

(☑ 03-5754 4849; www.springspurstay.com.au; 52 Fredas Lane, off Mountain Creek Rd, Tawonga; per person from $90; ☎) A wonderful place to soak up the High Country atmosphere is this family-run farm on a property known for its horseback tours. The well-designed, modern rooms (minimum two-night stay) have private verandahs looking out to Mt Feathertop and the Kiewa Valley. Meals are a highlight (set lunch or dinner $30), shared with the Baird family and featuring paddock-to-plate cuisine.

★ Dreamers
APARTMENT $$$

(☑ 03-5754 1222; www.dreamersmtbeauty.com.au; 218 Kiewa Valley Hwy, Mt Beauty; d $190-590; ❂❋) 🅿 Each of Dreamers' stunning self-contained eco apartments offers something special and architecturally unique. Sunken lounges, open fireplaces, loft bedrooms and balcony spas are just some of the highlights. Great views and a pretty lagoon complete a dreamily romantic five-star experience.

✗ Eating & Drinking

★ Å Skafferi
SWEDISH $$

(☑ 03-5754 4544; www.skafferi.com.au; 84 Bogong High Plains Rd, Mt Beauty; mains $16-23; ☉ 8am-4pm Thu-Mon) This cool Swedish pantry and foodstore is a fabulous place to stop. Try the grilled Milawa cheese sandwiches for breakfast and the Swedish meatballs or the sampler of herring and *knäckebröd* (crispbread) for lunch. It sells a range of local and Scandinavian produce.

Roi's Diner Restaurant
ITALIAN $$$

(☑ 03-5754 4495; 177 Kiewa Valley Hwy; mains from $30; ☉ 6.30-9.30pm Thu-Sun) It's hard to believe this unassuming timber shack on the highway 5km from Mt Beauty is an award-winning restaurant, specialising in exceptional modern northern Italian cuisine. Expect great risotto, eye fillet carpaccio, its signature roasted pork chops, homemade or imported pasta and handmade ice cream.

Sweetwater Brewing Company
MICROBREWERY

(☑ 03-5754 1881; www.sweetwaterbrewing.com.au; 211 Kiewa Valley Hwy; ☉ 1-7pm Fri, to 6pm Sat & Sun) This highway microbrewery in Mt Beauty utilises the fresh mountain water of the Kiewa River for its range of beers brewed on site – including a pale, golden, summer, IPA, wheat and porter. To sample its range, grab a tasting paddle, served on a cool, mini ski paddle.

❶ Information

Mt Beauty Visitor Centre (☑ 03-5755 0596, 1800 111 885; www.visitmountbeauty.com.au; 31 Bogong High Plains Rd; ☉ 9am-5pm) Has an accommodation booking service, and advice on local walks and mountain-bike trails. Its website is a wealth of info. It also has a lookout deck.

❶ Getting There & Away

V/Line (☑ 1800 800 007; www.vline.com.au) operates a train/bus service from Melbourne to Mt Beauty ($42.60, 5½ hours) on Monday, Wednesday and Friday, via Wangaratta and Bright.

In winter **Falls Creek Coach Service** (☑ 03-5754 4024; www.fallscreekcoachservice.com.au) operates daily direct buses from Melbourne to Mt Beauty (one way/return $85/134) and Falls Creek (one way/return $53/106) from 30 June to 17 September; prices include resort entry to Falls Creek. In early June and late September, there are less frequent services.

Falls Creek

ELEV 1780M

Victoria's glitzy, fashion-conscious resort, Falls Creek combines a picturesque alpine setting with impressive skiing and infamous après-ski entertainment. It offers some of the best downhill skiing, snowboarding and cross-country skiing in Victoria, and plenty of snow activities for non-skiers. Summer is also a good time to visit, with scenic hiking and a fast-emerging mountain-biking scene attracting outdoor enthusiasts in droves.

🛏 Sleeping

Howmans Gap YMCA   HOSTEL $
(☑ 03-5758 3228; www.camps.ymca.org.au/locate/howmans-gap.html; 2587 Bogong High Plains Rd; dm/s/d incl full board with shared bathroom $78/133/166; ⊘ Jun-Sep; 🖎) Only open to guests during winter, this YMCA lodge is a good budget option for those wanting to come to the snow. The room rates include three meals a day, which makes it a reasonable deal. It also manages the Falls Creek Nordic Centre for those wanting to do cross-country skiing.

Diana Alpine Lodge   LODGE $
(☑ 03-5758 3214; www.dianalodge.com; 6 Falls Creek Rd; per person incl breakfast $80-110; 🖎) One of the better-value choices in Falls Creek, Diana's has a mix of simple but homely rooms set over multiple levels with a classic alpine ambience. Lounge rooms have fireplaces, there's a tiny sauna and hot tub, and a cafe-bar with local beers and Mt Beauty–roasted coffee. Enquire about its glamping trips over summer.

QT Falls Creek   RESORT $$$
(☑ 03-5732 8000; www.qthotelsandresorts.com/falls-creek; 17 Bogong High Plains Rd; 1-bedroom apt $225-1025; 🖎) One of the few hotels that opens year-round, QT is a large-scale resort along the main road. Its self-contained apartments are modern and stylish, with wi-fi, pay TV, kitchen and a balcony with outdoor hot tub looking out to spectacular alpine views. Within the complex is a day spa, a pub and two restaurants.

🍴 Eating & Drinking

Milch Café   CAFE $$
(☑ 03-5758 3407; www.fvfallscreek.com.au/milchcafe/; 4 Schuss St; mains from $20; ⊘ 8am-late; 🖎) A vibrant, art-filled cafe run by a friendly owner, Milch does a good menu of breakfast rolls, house-baked breads and slow-cooked meats. Its bar is lined with a dangerous selection of schnapps bottles, and the coffee is specially roasted and best enjoyed on the AstroTurf terrace. It closes for a few months during the green season, so call ahead.

Huski   MODERN AUSTRALIAN $$
(☑ 03-5758 3863; www.huski.com.au/dining; 3 Sitzmark St; breakfast & lunch $10-25, dinner $21-44; ⊘ 10am-2.30pm & 5pm-late Thu-Sat, 10am-3pm Sun, daily winter) Falls Creek's best all-year restaurant, Huski does interesting breakfasts and lunches using local produce such as venison burgers on brioche buns, or Milawa fruit toast with Beechworth honey, ricotta, banana and berries. In the evening it serves up fusion sharing plates.

Summit Ridge   MODERN AUSTRALIAN $$$
(☑ 03-5758 3800; www.summitridge.com.au/resturant; 8 Schuss St; mains from $36; ⊘ 6-10pm mid-Jun–late Sep) One of the best restaurants for fine dining on the mountain, Summit Ridge does a menu of alpine-inspired modern Australian dishes using local produce, such as wild-boar terrine, scotch fillet with truffle mash and wild mushrooms, and Milawa cheese platters.

Man Hotel   PUB
(☑ 03-5758 3362; www.themanfallscreek.com; 20 Slalom St; ⊘ 4pm-late Jun-Sep) 'The Man' has been around forever, and is the heart of Falls' nightlife. It's only open in winter, when it fires up as a club, cocktail bar and live-music venue featuring popular Aussie bands. Good pub dinners and pizzas are available.

ℹ Information

For all the latest prices, packages and online tickets, visit www.fallscreek.com.au. Ski season daily resort entry is $49.50 per car, or $25 after 1pm and free after 4pm; however, it's cheaper to buy tickets online. One-day lift tickets per adult/child cost from $125/70. Combined adult lift-and-lesson packages cost from $195.

Falls Creek Resort Management (☑ 03-5758 1202; www.fallscreek.com.au; 1 Slalom St; ⊘ 9am-5pm Mon-Fri Nov-Jun, daily winter) Offers excellent information, as well as pamphlets on trails for skiing, hiking and mountain biking. Its website is useful too.

Activities Hotline (☑ 1800 204 424) Also handy for info on mountain activities.

ℹ Getting There & Away

Falls Creek is 375km from Melbourne, around a 4½-hour drive. The Hume Hwy (M31) to Wangaratta is the fastest route before heading through Milawa, Myrtleford, Bright and Mt Beauty. If coming from Gippsland way, note that the road to Omeo is only open when there's no snow – generally November (or December) to June.

During winter the **Falls Creek Coach Service** (☑ 03-5754 4024; www.fallscreekcoachservice.com.au) operates daily between Falls Creek and Melbourne (one way/return from $53/134) and also runs services to and from Albury and Mt Beauty. There's a reduced service in early June and late September. **Falls Bus** (☑ 1300 781 221; www.fallsbus.com.au; 🛜) also offers a service from Melbourne to Falls Creek (one way from $69, six hours) in winter.

If you've got camping gear you can hike here from Mt Hotham along the **Falls to Hotham Alpine Crossing** (www.parkweb.vic.gov.au; ☉Nov-Apr) trail.

Mt Hotham & Dinner Plain

ELEV 1868M

The conjoined-twin ski resort towns of Mt Hotham and Dinner Plain together provide the quintessential alpine experience, offering quality skiing mixed with a charming atmosphere. Serious hikers, skiers and snowboarders make tracks for Mt Hotham, which has some of the best and most challenging downhill runs in the country. Over at Dinner Plain, 10km from Hotham village and linked by a shuttle, there are excellent cross-country trails around the village, including the Hotham–Dinner Plain Ski Trail.

🛌 Sleeping

★**General Lodge**   LODGE $$$
(☑ 03-5759 3523; www.thegeneral.com.au; Great Alpine Rd, Mt Hotham; studio/1-/2-bedroom apt from $195/205/295; 🛜) Attached to the General pub are these modern and stylish fully self-contained apartments with lounge, gas fireplaces and kitchen, and fantastic views from the balcony. Note prices double in winter, when there's a two-night minimum stay.

Arlberg Resort   APARTMENT $$$
(☑ 03-5759 3618; www.arlberghotham.com.au; 1 Great Alpine Rd, Mt Hotham; 2 nights $460-920; ☉mid-Jun–mid-Sep; 🛜🏊) One of the largest resorts on the mountain, the Arlberg has a large range of apartments and motel-style rooms, plus restaurants, bars (including a brewery), ski hire and a heated pool. Ski season only.

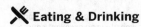

✖ Eating & Drinking

✖ Mt Hotham

★**Stone's Throw**   PUB FOOD $$
(☑ 03-5159 6324; www.hotelhighplains.com; Hotel High Plains, 185 Big Muster Dr, Dinner Plain; mains $19-28; ☉5pm-late) One of the best restaurants on the mountain, Stone's Throw specialises in produce from regional Victoria. The menu is seasonal, but expect the likes of peri peri Milawa chicken, Blizzard-beer-battered fish and chips and excellent gourmet wood-fired pizzas. It's located within the Hotel High Plains pub, which has local beers on tap, an open fire and accommodation (rooms $140) over summer.

★**The General**   PUB FOOD $$
(☑ 03-5759 3523; www.thegeneral.com.au; Great Alpine Rd, Mt Hotham; meals $15-24; ☉9.30am-late Mon-Sat, to 4pm Sun, open late Sun winter; 🛜) The ever-reliable 'Genny' is a popular watering hole with some good local beers and amazing views from its outdoor deck. There's a menu of pizzas, burgers and pub classics, plus good breakfasts and wi-fi. There's an attached grocery store selling fresh cheeses, meats and alcohol, while the accommodation here is also first-class.

✖ Dinner Plain

★**Blizzard Brewing Co**   MICROBREWERY
(☑ 0447 847 029; www.blizzardbrewing.com; 5 Cattle Pen Dr, Dinner Plain; ☉2-8pm Fri & Sat, to 6pm Sun Sep-May, noon-late daily Jun-Aug) An unexpected find in the outskirts of Dinner Plain alpine village is this awesome little brewery that produces all of its American-style craft beers on site. The warehouse setup has a taphouse pouring all of its range of core and seasonal ales, with the option of tasting paddles. There are no meals, but there is a menu of beer snacks and platters.

❶ Information

The ski-season admission fee is $46 per car per day, and $15 for bus passengers (this may be included in your fare). Lift tickets (peak) per adult/student/child cost $120/100/58. Passes are cheaper in September and there are packages that include gear hire and lessons. Lift tickets also cover Falls Creek.

Dinner Plain Visitor Centre (☑ 03-5755 0555; www.visitdinnerplain.com; Big Muster Dr, Dinner Plain; ☉10am-5pm Mon-Fri, 9am-5pm daily winter) In the Dinner Plain Alpine Village is this centre for chalet bookings, trail maps and general info. Its website is an excellent source of information too.

Mt Hotham Alpine Resort Management Board (☑ 03-5759 3550; www.mthotham. com.au; Great Alpine Rd, Mt Hotham; ⏰ 8am-4.30pm Mon-Fri, 7am-6pm daily winter) At the village administration centre, this visitor centre has a range of brochures with maps for short, eco, heritage and village walks. Also has an app with stop-off points for driving in the area.

Mt Hotham Central Guest Services (☑ 03-5759 4470) Can assist with general tourist info on the mountain, from ski lessons to bus timetables.

❶ Getting There & Away

Mt Hotham is 360km northeast of Melbourne. By car take the Hume Hwy to Wangaratta, then follow the Great Alpine Rd to Mt Hotham. Alternatively you can take the Princes Hwy to Omeo, before continuing on the Great Alpine Rd to Hotham via Dinner Plain.

In winter all vehicles must carry diamond-patterned snow chains, to be fitted at the designated fitting bays. During ski season all vehicles will need to purchase a resort pass (per day $46); if you're just passing through you're only permitted to stay for 30 minutes. The winding drive down to Harrietville is on a knife's edge so take it easy if there's snow on the road.

During the ski season, both **Hotham Bus** (☑ 1300 781 221; www.hothambus.com.au; 1-way/return from $50/114; ⏰ 24 Jun–11 Sep; 📶) and **Snowball Express** (☑ 1300 656 546; www.snowballexpress.com.au; 1-way/return from $70/120; ⏰ ski season) run buses here from Melbourne. **Omeo Bus Service** (☑ 0428 591 377; www.omeobus.com.au) has three buses a week connecting Mt Hotham and Dinner Plain with Bright ($6.40, two hours) and Omeo ($5 to $6.40, one hour); check its website for the schedule.

For hikers, there's the **Falls to Hotham Alpine Crossing** (p617), a two-night/three-day 37km trek that links Hotham with Falls Creek.

Omeo

POP 487

High in the hills, historic Omeo is a pretty town reached after the winding drive up from the coast or down from the mountains. It was a booming gold-mining town back in the day, with a population of nearly 10,000; today many of the grand buildings remain, yet its streets are ultra sleepy.

It's the southern access route to Mt Hotham and Falls Creek and the main town on the eastern section of the Great Alpine Rd. The road is sometimes snowbound in winter, so always check conditions before heading this way.

Back in the day, Omeo was one of Victoria's most lawless goldfield towns, and at the **Omeo Historical Park & Museum** (☑ 03-5159 1515; www.omeo.org.au/park; Day Ave; adult/child $4/1; ⏰ 10am-2pm) you can visit the site where troublemakers were dealt with. Guided tours take you through the original 1861 courthouse and the 'new' courthouse built in 1893, both of which have historical displays and photographs. Also here is the original log jail, a rather grim wooden cell dating from 1858, and remarkably used until 1981.

🛏 Sleeping & Eating

Snug as a Bug Motel   MOTEL $
(☑ 03-5159 1311, 0427 591 311; www.motelomeo. com.au; 188 Day Ave; s/d $120/130; ❄ 📶) Living up to its name, this quaint choice along the main strip has a range of rooms in lovely country-style historic buildings, with decor to match. Options include family motel rooms, the main guesthouse and a cute self-contained cottage.

Omeo Caravan Park   CARAVAN PARK $
(☑ 03-5159 1351; www.omeocaravanpark.com.au; Old Omeo Hwy; unpowered/powered sites $15/35, d cabins with shared/private bathroom $70/110; ❄ 📶) In a pretty valley alongside Livingstone Creek about 2km from town, this park has spacious, grassy sites.

Golden Age Hotel   HOTEL $
(☑ 03-5159 1344; www.goldenageomeo.com.au; Day Ave; s/d with shared bathroom $50/80, with private bathroom from $110/130; ⏰ kitchen noon-2.30pm & 6-8.30pm) This beautiful art deco corner pub (c 1854) dominates Omeo's main street. Upstairs has simple but elegant pub rooms, all with cooked breakfast, some with en suite and spa – the best rooms open onto the balcony. The welcoming restaurant (mains $25) serves plates piled high with steaks, salads and gourmet pizzas.

Homestead House Cafe   CAFE $
(☑ 03-5159 1511; 190 Day Ave; dishes from $12.50; ⏰ 8.30am-4pm) This smart and cheery little cafe on the main road does good coffee, roast-lamb rolls, wonderful homemade cakes and a daily changing menu of seasonal food.

❶ Information

Omeo Visitor Information Centre (☑ 03-5159 1455; www.omeoregion.com.au; 179 Day Ave;

⊙8.30am-5pm Mon-Fri, 10am-2pm Sat & Sun; ☎) Friendly visitor centre in the library with info on a bunch of walking trails in the area.

❶ Getting There & Away

Located 400km from Melbourne, Omeo is the gateway town to Mt Hotham (57km, 50 minutes) via Dinner Plain en route to Bright (108km, two hours) along the Great Alpine Rd. The road is open year-round but you'll need to attach car-tyre chains during the winter months. There's also a road to Falls Creek (C543), but it's only open during the warmer months (usually late November to May).

Omeo Bus Lines (☒ 0427 017 732; http://dysongroup.com.au/public-transport/regional; Day Ave) has a service to Omeo Monday to Friday from Bairnsdale ($16, two hours).

To get to the mountains, **O'Connells Omeo Bus Service** (p614) runs a year-round 'Alps Link' service to Dinner Plain ($5, 45 minutes), Mt Hotham ($6.40, one hour) and Bright ($12.80, two hours) three times a week.

THE MURRAY RIVER & AROUND

The mighty Murray River is Australia's longest and most important inland waterway, and arrayed along its banks are some of Victoria's most historic and captivating towns. The region is a stirring place of wineries and orchards, bush camping, balmy weather and river red gum forests. The Murray changes character constantly along its 2400km route. History looms large in towns such as Echuca; food and wine dominate proceedings around Mildura; and national parks enclose soulful desert expanses in the far northwest. It's a world of picturesque river beaches, of paddle steamers that were once the lifeblood of Victoria's inland settlements, and of unending horizons that serve as a precursor to the true outback not far away. It's an intriguing, if relatively far-flung mix, that enables you to follow in the footsteps of some of Australia's earliest explorers who travelled along the river.

Mildura

POP 51,800

Sunny, sultry Mildura is something of an oasis amid some very dry country, a modern town with its roots firmly in the grand old pastoralist era. Its calling cards include art deco buildings and some of the best dining in provincial Victoria. The hinterland, too, is worth exploring, from the nearby wilderness national parks to the Murray River, where activities include fishing, swimming, canoeing, waterskiing, houseboating, paddle-steamer cruising or riverside golf. The weather here is ideal – you can expect warm, sunny days even in midwinter.

⊙ Sights

★**Rio Vista &**
Mildura Arts Centre   HISTORIC BUILDING
(☒ 03-5018 8330; www.milduraartscentre.com.au; 199 Cureton Ave; ⊙10am-5pm) **FREE** The grand homestead of William B Chaffey (a Mildura founder), historic Queen Anne–style Rio Vista has been beautifully preserved and restored. Each room has a series of historical displays depicting colonial life in the 19th century, with period furnishings, costumes, photos and a collection of letters and memorabilia. The Mildura Arts Centre, in the same complex, combines a modern-art gallery with changing exhibitions and a theatre showing cutting-edge productions (thanks to its involvement on the regional performance circuit). There's a small cafe on-site.

Apex Beach   BEACH
This popular swimming and picnic spot is about 3km northwest of the centre, with a sandy river beach on the Murray. There's a good walking and cycling track from here to the Old Mildura Homestead.

Old Psyche Bend
Pump Station   HISTORIC SITE
(☒ 03-5024 5637; Kings Billabong; adult/family $3/8; ⊙1-4pm Tue & Thu, 10.30am-noon Sun) This station is where William B Chaffey, set up his system in 1891 to supply irrigation and drainage. The modern pumps are electric now and have been placed a bit further up the river. You can walk around the old centrifugal pumps and Chaffey's triple-expansion steam-engine pump.

Old Mildura Homestead   HISTORIC SITE
(Cureton Ave; by donation; ⊙9am-6pm) Along the river, near the historic Rio Vista & Mildura Arts Centre, this cottage was the first home of William B Chaffey. The heritage park here contains a few other historic log buildings, and has picnic and barbecue facilities.

Chateau Mildura   WINERY, MUSEUM
(☒ 03-5024 5901; www.facebook.com/chateaumil durawinery; 191 Belar Ave; museum adult/child $5/free; ⊙10am-4pm) Established in 1888 and

Murray River

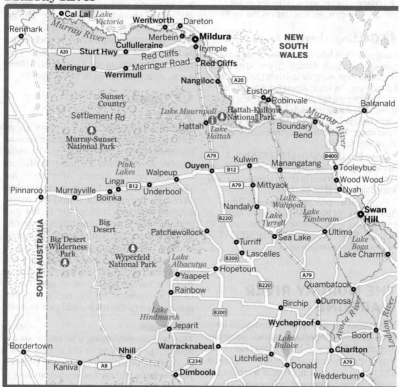

still producing table wines, Chateau Mildura is part vineyard and part museum, with wine tastings and historical displays.

🏃 Activities

★ Harry Nanya Tours
CULTURAL

(📞 03-5027 2076; www.harrynanyatours.com.au; tours adult/child $180/110) 🌿 Indigenous Australian guide Graham Clarke keeps you enchanted with stories of the Dreaming and his deep knowledge and understanding of the Mungo region. In summer (November to March) a spectacular sunset tour is offered. Minimum two people; Graham will pick up from central accommodation in Mildura.

Wild Side Outdoors
ADVENTURE

(📞 03-5024 3721, 0428 242 852; www.wildsideoutdoors.com.au; Canoes/kayaks/mountain bikes $35/25/25 per hr) 🌿 For more than 20 years this ecofriendly outfit has offered a range of activities, including a sunset kayaking tour at Kings Billabong ($120 for two people). Handily for independent travellers, they will support three-day river trips, supplying maps, gear and transport (from $450 for two people). Will deliver and collect gear too.

PS Melbourne
BOATING

(📞 03-5023 2200; www.paddlesteamers.com. au; 2hr cruises adult/child $30/14; ⊙ 10.50am & 1.50pm Sun-Thu) This is one of the original paddle steamers (built in 1925), and the only one still driven by steam power. Watch the operator stoke the original boiler with wood.

Mungo National Park Tours
TOURS

(📞 0408 147 330, 1800 797 530; www.murraytrek. com.au; day/sunset tours $145/175) Small-group day and sunset tours to Mungo National Park led by the experienced Trevor Hancock. Minimum two people.

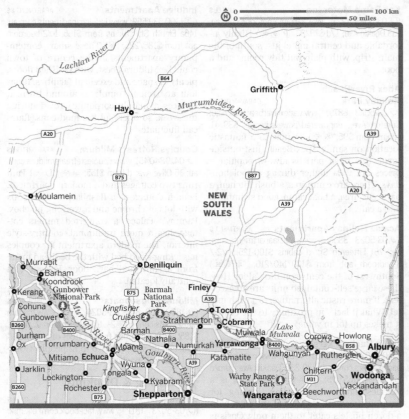

PV Rothbury BOATING
(☏ 03-5023 2200; www.paddlesteamers.com.au; cruises adult/child winery $70/35, dinner $70/35, lunch $35/17) Although it was built in 1881, *PV Rothbury* has a diesel engine and is one of the fastest paddle boats on the river. It heads through the lock on its twice-daily cruises on Fridays and Saturdays at 10.50am and 1.50pm, and also runs winery, lunch and dinner cruises on Tuesdays and Thursdays.

Sunraysia Cellar Door WINE
(☏ 03-5021 0794; www.sunraysiacellardoor.com. au; 125 Lime Ave; ☉ 9am-5pm Mon-Fri, 11am-5pm Sat & Sun) Sunraysia Cellar Door has free tastings and sales for around 250 local wines from 22 different wineries from the Murray–Darling region, as well as a handful of local craft beers and plenty of local edible products for purchase.

Moontongue Eco-Adventures KAYAKING
(☏ 0427 898 317; www.moontongue.com.au; kayak tours $35-65) 🌿 A sunset kayaking trip is a great way to see the river and its wildlife. Local guide Ian will tell you about the landscape and birdlife as you work those muscles in the magnificent, peaceful surroundings of Gol Gol Creek and the Murray. Note: operates by appointment only.

🛏 Sleeping

Mid City Motel MOTEL $
(☏ 03-5023 0317; www.midcityplantationmotel. com.au; 145 Deakin Ave; s/d from $75/90; 🅿 🛜 ❄) Rooms may be dated – the brick walls and brown carpets will beam you back into the 1970s – but this is one of Mildura's best-value options in terms of price. Some slightly more modern 'deluxe' rooms are available for around $20 more per person. Microwaves and toasters are useful touches and the owners are helpful.

Kar-Rama Motor Inn
MOTEL **$**

(📶 03-5023 4221; www.karramamotorinn.com.au; 153 Deakin Ave; s/d $78/83; P 🛜 🏊) Highly affordable and central motel just south of the main strip, with plain but tidy rooms and a pool.

Apex RiverBeach Holiday Park
CARAVAN PARK **$**

(📶 03-5023 6879; www.apexriverbeach.com.au; Cureton Ave; unpowered/powered sites $39/41, cabins from $95; ❄️ 🛜) Thanks to a fantastic location on sandy Apex Beach, just outside town, this bush park is always popular – prices are 25% higher during school holidays. There are campfires, a bush kitchen, a barbecue area, a boat ramp, good swimming and a cafe.

Acacia Holiday Apartments
APARTMENT **$**

(📶 03-5023 3855; www.acaciaapartments.com.au; 761 Fifteenth St; d cabins $100-125, 1-/2-/3-bedroom apt from $120/140/210; ❄️ 🛜 🏊) Southwest of the centre on the Calder Hwy, these large self-contained units are an excellent, if more rustic alternative, to a drab motel. What it lacks in proximity to the centre, it makes up for in value.

Oasis Backpackers
HOSTEL **$**

(📶 03-5022 8200, 0401 344 251; www.milduraoasis backpackers.com.au; 230-232 Deakin Ave; dm/d per week $165/175; ❄️ @ 🛜 🏊) Mildura is a big destination for travellers looking for fruit-picking work, so most of the city's half-a-dozen hostels cater to them only. Oasis is the best-equipped backpacker hostel, with a great pool and patio bar area, ultramodern kitchen and free internet. The owners can organise plenty of seasonal work. Minimum one-week stay.

★ Mildura Grand
HOTEL **$$**

(📶 03-5023 0511, 1800 034 228; www.milduragrand. com.au; Seventh St; s/d from $85/130; ❄️ 🛜 🏊) The standard rooms at the Grand aren't the most luxurious in town, but staying at this landmark hotel – Mildura's top address – gives you the feeling of being part of something special. Although cheaper rooms in the original wing are comfortable, go for one of the stylish suites with private spa.

Acacia Houseboats
HOUSEBOAT **$$**

(📶 0417 537 316, 1800 085 500; www.murrayriver. com.au/acacia-houseboats-949/fleet; 3 nights from $525) Has five houseboats, ranging from four to 12 berths, with everything supplied, except food and drink.

Indulge Apartments
APARTMENT **$$**

(📶 1300 539 559; www.indulgeapartments.com.au; 146a Eighth St; studios from $165, 1-/2-bedroom apt from $185/285; ❄️) These smart contemporary apartments in the centre of town could be Mildura's best, with polished floors, plenty of space and excellent facilities. It has four apartment complexes around town. It services a mainly corporate crowd during the week, so offers all the mod cons. Rates can fluctuate.

Couples Retreats Mildura
APARTMENT **$$**

(📶 0419 840 451; www.couplesretreatsmildura.com. au; 16 Olive Ave; d from $155; ❄️ 🛜) Local Pam runs two cottages and a modern apartment. Lemon Cottage is a flashback to the 1950s with lots of chrome and a working jukebox. Pammy's Palace, a converted miners cottage, has a more traditional, country-style interior. The modern apartment for couples has a king-sized bed with the bedhead made from a converted barn door. Eclectic and centrally located.

Mildura Houseboats
HOUSEBOAT **$$**

(📶 1800 800 842, 03-5024 7770; www.mildura houseboats.com.au; 2- to 6-berth for 7 nights $1850-2000) Choose from a fleet of around 15 houseboats sleeping two to 12 people. Gourmet and golf packages also offered.

✕ Eating & Drinking

Blk.Mlk
CAFE **$**

(📶 03-5023 1811; www.facebook.com/blk.mlk. specialty.coffee; 51 Deakin Ave; mains $10-20; ⏲ 7am-3pm) The deconstructed name might be a little pretentious (black milk, get it?) but the coffee and food are anything but. If you're like us, you'll find yourself sitting for a coffee and an hour later you will have polished off the likes of banana bread (served with edible flowers) or a pork belly salad. A great choice for gourmands and java hounds.

★ Black Stump
MODERN AUSTRALIAN **$$**

(www.theblackstump.com.au; 110-114 Eighth St; mains $20-36; ⏲ Tue-Sat) A hark back to its days as the Mildura Settlers Club, the Black Stump is one of the quirkiest and refreshingly different places to eat. To start with, it cleverly incorporates the historic building through its decor – vintage blue chairs, memorabilia and photos – while the kitchen, run by local chef Jim McDougall, serves Australian bistro meals with international influences.

Mildura

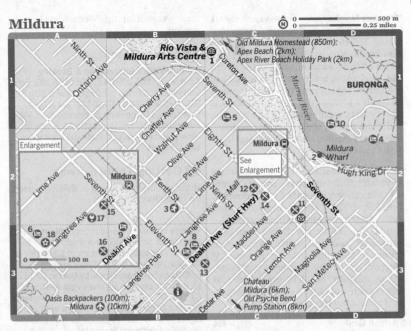

Mildura

◎ Top Sights
1 Rio Vista & Mildura Arts
Centre..C1

⊕ Activities, Courses & Tours
2 PS Melbourne D2
PV Rothbury ....(see 2)
3 Sunraysia Cellar Door B2

⊜ Sleeping
4 Acacia Houseboats..........................D2
5 Couples Retreats Mildura C1
6 Indulge Apartments.........................A3
7 Kar-Rama Motor Inn.........................B3
8 Mid City Motel B3
9 Mildura Grand B3

10 Mildura Houseboats........................D1

⊗ Eating
11 Black Stump C2
12 Blk.Mlk C2
13 Brass Monkey B3
14 Cider Tree C2
15 Spanish Grill A2
16 Stefano's Cafe A3
Stefano's Restaurant ....(see 9)

⊙ Drinking & Nightlife
17 Mildura Brewery A2

◉ Entertainment
18 Sandbar A3

★ **Stefano's Cafe**   CAFE **$$**
(☏ 03-5021 3627; 27 Deakin Ave; meals $14-22;
⊙ 7am-3pm Mon-Sat, 8am-noon Sun) Fresh
bread, Calabrese eggs, pastries and, of
course, good coffee – this casual daytime cafe
and bakery keeps things fresh and simple.
It's also a gourmet grocery store selling food-
stuffs and wines. Great egg breakfasts set off
the day and there's seating outdoors for the
summer months.

Cider Tree   PUB FOOD **$$**
(http://thecidertree.com.au; 56 Deakin Ave; mains
$20-28; ⊙ noon-late Mon-Sat) A no-nonsense
ale house and kitchen that does hefty
brews (there are 18 different ciders and
beers on tap, plus plenty more in bottles)
and hearty meals. It packs them in for specials, such as the Thursday Pot and Parmy
night (a pot of beer with every parmigiana
dish; $19.50).

★ **Brass Monkey**   MODERN AUSTRALIAN **$$$**
(☑ 03-50214769; www.facebook.com/brassmonkey mildura; 32 Carter Lane; share plates $10-20; ⊗ 6-11pm Tue-Thu, noon-3pm & 6-11pm Fri-Sun) Don't be put off by its location, south of the centre and overlooking a car park: Brass Monkey epitomises 'hidden gem'. It's cosy, buzzy and fun, with a hipster edge. A large communal table reflects a philosophy of share plates, and it delivers on the food front: fresh, refined street cuisine, creative ideas and wonderful presentation.

★ **Stefano's Restaurant**   ITALIAN **$$$**
(☑ 03-5023 0511; www.stefano.com.au; Quality Hotel Mildura Grand, Seventh St; 5-course dinner set menu $97; ⊗ 7-11pm Tue-Sat) Stefano de Pieri was a celebrity chef before the term was invented. The charismatic Italian-Australian introduced fresh and simple farm-to-plate cuisine to households via his popular TV program and at this delightful restaurant. It's an intimate, candlelit experience and very popular – book well in advance. After a brief break from the helm, he is back.

Spanish Grill   STEAK **$$$**
(☑ 03-5021 2377; www.stefano.com.au/the-span ish-grill; cnr Langtree Ave & Seventh St; mains $26-48; ⊗ 6-10pm Tue-Sat) In the Grand Hotel, this eatery re-opened late in 2016 under the stewardship of renowned local foodie Stefano de Pieri. Judging by his last results, it should be good, especially as the meat is sourced locally, and is cooked over gum and mallee-root coals.

★ **Mildura Brewery**   BREWERY
(☑ 03-5022 2988; www.mildurabrewery.com.au; 20 Langtree Ave; ⊗ noon-late) Set in the former Astor cinema, this is Mildura's trendiest drinking hole, and part of chef and restaurateur Stefano de Piera's stable. Shiny stainless-steel vats, pipes and brewing equipment make a great backdrop to the stylish lounge, and the beers brewed here – Honey Wheat and Mallee Bull among them – are superb. Good food, too (mains $24 to $36).

☆ **Entertainment**

Sandbar   LIVE MUSIC
(☑ 03-5021 2181; www.thesandbar.com.au; cnr Langtree Ave & Eighth St; ⊗ noon-late Tue-Sun) On a balmy evening locals flock to the fabulous beer garden at the back of this lounge bar in a classic art deco building. Local, national, original and mainstream bands play in the front bar regularly, or you can take to the stage yourself at the Wednesday karaoke session.

🛈 **Information**

Mildura Visitor Information & Booking Centre (☑ 1800 039 043, 03-5018 8380; www. visitmildura.com.au; cnr Deakin Ave & 12th St; ⊗ 9am-5.30pm Mon-Fri, to 5pm Sat & Sun) Free service for booking accommodation, with interesting displays, local produce, a cafe, a library, and very helpful staff who book tours and activities.

🛈 **Getting There & Away**

Mildura is 542km northwest of Melbourne along the Calder Hwy (A79).

AIR
Victoria's busiest regional airport, **Mildura Airport** (☑ 03-5055 0500; www.milduraairport. com.au; Alan Mathews Dr) is about 10km west of the town centre off the Sturt Hwy. Mildura–Melbourne flights are served by **Qantas** (☑ 13 13 13; www.qantas.com.au) and **Virgin Australia** (☑ 13 67 89; www.virginaustralia.com). **Regional Express Airlines** (Rex; ☑ 13 17 13; www.regional express.com.au) has flights to/from Melbourne, Sydney, Adelaide and Broken Hill.

BUS & TRAIN
V/Line (☑ 1800 800 007; www.vline.com.au) Combination train/coach services operate from the train station on Seventh St. There are no direct passenger trains to/from Mildura; change from V/Line trains to coaches at Ballarat, Bendigo or Swan Hill. Services ply the Mildura–Melbourne route ($50, seven to 10 hours, three to four daily).

NSW Trainlink (☑ 13 22 32; www.nswtrainlink. info) A coach/train combination covers the Mildura–Sydney route, with a coach to Cootamundra then Southern Express train to Sydney ($110, 13½ hours, once daily).

🛈 **Getting Around**

A paddle-steamer cruise here is a must. Mildura Paddlesteamers runs the three main vessels that paddle along: **PS Melbourne** (p620), **PV Rothbury** (p621) and **PV Mundoo** (the latter is for groups and weddings only). Check which services pass through the locks. You can enjoy sunset or even meal cruises.

Echuca
POP 14,000

One of the loveliest towns in rural Victoria, Echuca is the state's paddle-steamer capital and a classic Murray River town, bursting with history, nostalgia and, of course, riverboats. The Aboriginal name translates as 'meeting of the waters', as it's here that three great rivers meet: the Goulburn, the Campaspe and the Murray.

In the 1800s Echuca was an important crossing point between NSW and Victoria, and the ensuing river trade and transport ensured its success.

The highlight of Echuca is unquestionably its historic port area and the rivers themselves, best enjoyed on a riverboat cruise or a sunset stroll as cockatoos and corellas screech overhead.

◎ Sights

★ Port of Echuca
Discovery Centre
MUSEUM

(☑ 03-5481 0500; www.portofechuca.org.au; 74 Murray Esplanade; adult/child/family $14/8/45; ☻ 9am-5pm) At the northern end of Murray Esplanade, the stunning Port of Echuca Discovery Centre is your gateway to the Echuca wharf area. It presents excellent displays (some of them interactive) on the port's history, the paddle steamers and the riverboat trade. Informative and fun free guided tours set out from the discovery centre twice daily (11.30am and 1.30pm).

Great Aussie Beer Shed
MUSEUM

(☑ 03-5480 6904; www.greataussiebeershed.com.au; 377 Mary Ann Rd; adult/child/family $14/5/30; ☻ 9.30am-5pm Sat, Sun & holidays) This is a wall-to-wall shrine of more than 17,000 beer cans in a huge shed. It's the result of 30 years of collecting – one can dates back to Federation (1901). Guided tours will take you through the history of beer. Very Aussie.

National Holden Museum
MUSEUM

(☑ 03-5480 2033; www.holdenmuseum.com.au; 7 Warren St; adult/child/family $9.50/3.50/22.50; ☻ 9am-5pm) Car buffs should check out this museum dedicated to Australia's four-wheeled icon, with more than 40 examples of beautifully restored Holdens, from FJ to Monaro. There's also racing footage and memorabilia.

Echuca Historical Museum
MUSEUM

(☑ 03-5480 1325; www.echucahistoricalsociety.org.au; 1 Dickson St; adult/child $5/1; ☻ 11am-3pm) This historical museum is located in the old police station, which has been classified by the National Trust. It has a collection of local history items, charts and photos from the riverboat era and early records.

Also runs informative historic town walks on request ($12 per person).

Activities

River Country Adventours
CANOEING

(☑ 0428 585 227; www.adventours.com.au; half-/full-day safaris $65/100) For organised canoe safaris on the Goulburn River, this Kyabram-based team is the expert in this part of the world. It offers canoe and camping safaris around the Barmah and Goulburn regions, as well as on the Murray.

Brett Sands Watersports
WATER SPORTS

(☑ 03-5482 1851; www.brettsands.com; Merool Lane, Moama; half/full day $160/260) Several operators offer waterskiing trips and classes, but this outfit will teach you skills behind a boat for skis as well as wakeboard, kneeboard or barefoot. It also hires out gear.

Echuca Boat & Canoe Hire
BOATING

(☑ 03-5480 6208; www.echucaboatcanoehire.com; Victoria Park Boat Ramp) Hires out motor boats (one/two hours $50/75), 'barbie boats' with on-board BBQs (10 people from $120/180), kayaks ($20/30) and canoes ($20/30).

OFF THE BEATEN TRACK

THE MALLEE

Occupying the vast northwestern corner of Victoria, the Mallee appears as a flat horizon and endless, undulating, twisted mallee scrub and desert. The attractions – other than the sheer solitude – are the semi-arid wilderness areas, including Wyperfeld National Park and Big Desert Wilderness Park. Collectively these parks cover more than 750,000 hectares, and are notable for their abundance of native plants, spring wildflowers and birds. Nature lovers might delight in it, but much of it is inaccessible to all but experienced 4WD enthusiasts. Visiting this, the Victorian outback, is best avoided in the hot summer months.

The main route through the Mallee is the Sunraysia Hwy (B220), via the towns of Birchip and Ouyen, but if you want to explore the region's national parks, turn off to the historic farming towns of **Jeparit** (birthplace of Sir Robert Menzies and the jumping-off point for Lake Hindmarsh), **Rainbow**, **Yaapeet** and **Hopetoun**.

Echuca

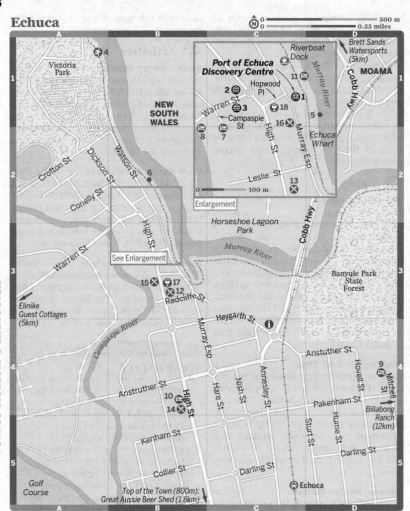

Multiday, self-guided 'campanoeing' trips, where you can arrange to be dropped upstream and canoe back, are also available.

🛏 Sleeping

High Street Motel MOTEL **$**
(☑03-5482 1013; www.highstreetmotelechuca. com.au; 439 High St; d $120; P✳🅿🛜) The current owners have done a good job at this motel makeover. Rooms are simple and as neat as a pin, and prices are fair for what you get. The decent mattresses will guarantee good slumber, and toasters and microwaves are handy for self-caterers. It's walking distance

to Echuca's centre and good cafes. Very friendly owners.

Christies Beach Camping CAMPGROUND **$**
About 5km east of town, Christies Beach is a free camping area on the banks of the Murray. There are pit toilets, but bring water and firewood.

Echuca Gardens GUESTHOUSE **$**
(☑0419 881 054; www.echucagardens.com; 103 Mitchell St; wagons $80-160, guesthouse r $120-200; P@🛜) Run by inveterate traveller Kym, this spot has some novel sleeping arrangements – two cosy 'gypsy wagons'

Echuca

that come complete with bathroom and kitchenette; a guesthouse (part of the owner's home, with private entry); or his entire home, which has a smart bathroom, a country kitchen and a TV room. The complex is surrounded by a pleasant garden with ponds, statues and fruit trees.

★ **Adelphi Boutique Apartments**　APARTMENT $$

(☑ 03-5482 5575; www.adelphiapartments.com. au; 25 Campaspe St; 1-/2-bedroom apt from $185/360; ☀) This semi-luxurious riverside accommodation, a block back from the main street, is a good choice, especially if you're willing to pay a little more for those apartments with a terrace overlooking the Campaspe River.

Elinike Guest Cottages　COTTAGE $$

(☑ 03-5480 6311; www.elinike.com.au; 209 Latham Rd; d $190-210; P☀☀) These rustic but romantic little self-contained cottages are set among rambling gardens on the Murray River around 5km northwest of town. They blend old-world style with modern conveniences and luxuries (such as double spas). The lilac cottage has a glass-roofed garden room.

★ **Cock 'n Bull Boutique Hotel**　BOUTIQUE HOTEL $$$

(☑ 03-5480 6988; www.cocknbullechuca.com; 17-21 Warren St; s/d from $150/250; P☀🛜☀) These luxury apartments add a touch of class to Echuca's central motel-style options. The building's older section (once a bustling pub from the 1870s) looks out over the Campaspe River while a newer, modern section

is at the rear. All apartments differ in mood and design, and all are tasteful.

Rich River Houseboats　HOUSEBOAT $$$

(☑ 03-5480 2444; www.richriverhouseboats.com. au; Riverboat Dock; per week $2500-$5200) These six beautiful boats are floating palaces. They cater mainly to larger groups, but bedding configurations can be altered to suit both couples and families.

🍴 Eating

★ **Fish in a Flash**　FISH & CHIPS $

(☑ 03-5480 0824; 602 High St; fish & chips from $9.90; ☺9am-8pm) Consistently ranked among the best fish-and-chip places in Victoria (the owner, Paul, has been frying for 27 years), Fish in a Flash does occasional river fish as well as the usual suspects, all dipped in the owner's secret batter. Great for a riverside picnic.

★ **Shebani's**　MEDITERRANEAN $$

(☑ 03-5480 7075; 535 High St; mains $17.50-20; ☺7.30am-4pm) Eating here is like taking a culinary tour of the Mediterranean – Greek, Lebanese and North African dishes all get a run with subtle flavours. The decor brings together Mediterranean tile work, Moroccan lamps and a fresh Aussie-cafe style.

Johnny & Lyle　CAFE $$

(☑ 03-5480 3133; www.facebook.com/johnnyand lyle; 433 High St; mains $12-25; ☺6am-2pm) This ticks the right boxes in terms of colour: not only the cups (an array of bright hues) but the lovely courtyard and the vibrant dishes – blueberry pancakes ($16.50), brekky burgers ($14) and fabulous lunch dishes including

MELBOURNE & VICTORIA ECHUCA

PADDLE-STEAMER CRUISES

A paddle-steamer cruise is almost obligatory. Six boats – wood-fired, steam-driven (one is electric diesel) with interesting commentary – offer trips operating at various times. Privately owned Murray River Paddle Steamers runs **PS Canberra** ([Z]03-5482 5244; www.murrayriverpaddlesteamers.com.au; adult/child/family $36/21/95), **PS Emmylou** (cruises 1hr adult/child/family $28.50/18/78, 2hr $36/21/95) and **PS Pride of the Murray** (adult/child/family $36/21/95); Echuca Paddlesteamers runs **PS Alexander Arbuthnot** ([Z]03-5482 4248, 1300 942 737; www.echucapaddlesteamers.net.au; adult/child/family $25/11/66), **PS Pevensey** (adult/child/family $25/11/66) and **PS Adelaide** (adult/child/family $25/11/66).

Buy tickets to any of these from the **Port of Echuca Discovery Centre** (p625), **Echuca Moama visitor information centre** or along **Murray Esplanade**. Note Murray River Paddle Steamers sells tickets only to the boats it runs. Your decision might be based on the boat's size, history and timetables – you can't really go wrong. Check timetables for lunch, dinner, twilight and sunset cruises.

pulled lamb with pumpkin hummus ($19) and steak sandwiches ($20). An excellent option and worth the slightly extra hike a few blocks south of the centre.

Star Hotel   BISTRO $$
([Z]03-5480 1181; www.starhotelechuca.com.au; 45 Murray Esplanade; pizzas $20-24, mains $20-32; ⊙11am-late) The historic 'Star Bar' is one of the liveliest places in town for a meal or a drink, especially on weekends when there's live music. Full cooked breakfasts and a reasonably priced lunch of calamari or chicken parma can be enjoyed on the front deck right beside the port. The wood-fired pizzas are easily the best in town.

Ceres   EUROPEAN $$$
([Z]03-5482 5599; www.ceresechuca.com.au; 554 High St; lunch $13-16, dinner $24-41; ⊙10am-late Mon-Fri, 9am-late Sat & Sun) In a beautifully converted 1881 brick flour mill, Ceres (named after the Roman goddess of agriculture) is forever reinventing itself; at the time of research new owners were at the helm. The jury's still out, but it's a relaxed place for lunch, with all-day coffee, and in the evenings the downstairs restaurant focuses on Italian cuisine and modern Australian dishes.

🍷 Drinking & Nightlife

Bordello Wine Bar   WINE BAR
([Z]03-5480 6902; www.rivergalleryinn.com.au; 578 High St; ⊙8.30-11pm) An ideal spot for fine local wines, with a fabulous range of 50-plus

world beers and Saturday-night live music. It attracts the over-30s crowd (read: despite the live music, you can have a conversation).

Henry's Bridge Hotel   PUB
([Z]03-5480 1000; 1 Hopwood Pl; ⊙8am-3.30pm Mon & Tue, to 11pm Wed-Sun) Formerly known as the Bridge Hotel, this historic spot and Echuca's oldest pub was built in 1859 by town-founder Harry Hopwood. At the time of research it was being renovated. Its new image is intended to be a family oriented cafe-restaurant-pub serving burgers, fish and chips, steaks and other pub-style meals. Should be worth checking out.

ℹ️ Information

Echuca Moama Visitor Information Centre
([Z]1800 804 446; www.echucamoama.com; 2 Heygarth St; ⊙9am-5pm; 🛜) In the old pump station; has helpful staff, brochures and offers booking services for accommodation and paddle steamers. Be sure to grab *Heritage Walk Echuca*, which points out historic buildings and sites.

ℹ️ Getting There & Away

Echuca lies 222km north of Melbourne. Take the Hume Fwy (M31) then the well-signposted turn-off to the B75, which passes through Heathcote and Rochester en route to Echuca.

V/Line ([Z]1800 800 007; www.vline.com.au) runs combined train and coach services between Melbourne and Echuca ($27.20, three to 3½ hours, regular departures) with a change at Bendigo, Shepparton or Murchison.

Tasmania

POP 516,900 / ♪02

Includes ➡

Why Go?

Some say islands are metaphors for the heart. Isolation mightn't be too good for romance, but Tasmania has turned remoteness into an asset. From the lichen-splashed granite of the east coast to the bleak alpine plateaus of Cradle Mountain–Lake St Clair National Park, Tasmania has a unique beauty. Tragic stories of the island's Indigenous and colonial history play out through this haunting, gothic landscape: the sublime scenery around Port Arthur only reinforces the site's grim convict past. It's just as easy to conjure-up visions of the raffish past in Hobart's Battery Point and atmospheric harbourside pubs. And then there's the food, the wine and the parties: Tasmania is seemingly custom-built for a driving holiday spent shuffling between farm-gate suppliers, boozy cellar doors and hip festivals. Yes, this is still Australia, but Tasmania is bewitchingly different.

Best Places to Eat

➡ Jackman & McRoss (p647)

➡ Templo (p646)

➡ Mrs Jones (p696)

➡ Lotus Eaters Cafe (p658)

➡ Geronimo (p685)

Best Places to Sleep

➡ Henry Jones Art Hotel (p645)

➡ Montacute (p645)

➡ The Shackeau (p661)

➡ Pumphouse Point (p711)

➡ Two Four Two (p683)

When to Go
Hobart

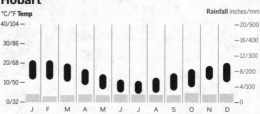

Feb–Mar Swim, bushwalk and mountain bike in the year's most settled weather.

Jun–Aug Embrace winter with affordable accommodation, minimal crowds and brooding gothic vibes.

Dec–Jan Enjoy the best of Hobart's festival season with food, wine, music, art and culture.

Tasmania Highlights

1 MONA (p639) Being inspired, turned on, appalled, educated and amused at Tasmania's unique art gallery.

2 Three Capes Track (p664) Ticking Tassie's superb new walking trail off your 'to do' list.

3 Port Arthur Historic Site (p664) Paying your respects to the past, both distant and recent, at these sombre ruins.

4 Wineglass Bay (p673) Sweating it out on the track to this distant bay, then cooling off in the sea once you get there.

5 Salamanca Market (p651) Losing yourself in the crowds at Hobart's local producers market.

100 km
50 miles

BASS STRAIT

Spirit of Tasmania Ferries
(Melbourne - Devonport)

Melbourne

King Island

Cape Wickham
Yambacoona
Naracoopa
Currie
King Island
Smithton
(130km)
Grassy
Stokes Point

King Island
(130km, see inset)

20 km
10 miles

Deal Island

Hunter Island
Woolnorth Point
Robbins Island
Three Hummock Island

The Nut
Stanley
Rocky Cape National Park
Smithton
Marrawah
Arthur River
Arthur River
Arthur Pieman Conservation Area
Sandy Cape

Wynyard
Somerset
Burnie
Penguin
Ulverstone
Devonport
Gunns Plains
Waratah
Savage River National Park
Savage River

Cape Frankland
Killiecrankie Bay
Emita
Whitemark
Flinders Island
Lackrana
Lady Barron
Strzelecki National Park
Cape Barren Island
Clarke Island
Cape Barren
Cape Portland

Bridport
Scottsdale
Gladstone
Derby
Pyengana
St Columba Falls
Lilydale
Launceston
Ben Lomond National Park
St Helens
St Marys
Binalong Bay
The Gardens
Eddystone Point
Mt William National Park
Bay of Fires
Musselroe Bay
Banks Strait

Beauty Point
George Town
Narawntapu National Park
Port Sorell
Beaconsfield
Exeter
Westbury
Deloraine
Mole Creek
Sheffield
Nietta
Latrobe
Gowrie Park

Tamar River
Tamar Valley

A3
B82
A8
A7
A10
A2
B18
1

6 Tamar Valley Wine Route (p686) Sampling sparkling wine and pinot noir at a series of ridiculously picturesque vineyards on both sides of the Tamar River.

7 Bruny Island (p655) Dropping in and out of mobile-phone reception for a couple of days while exploring the island's magical coastline.

8 Stanley (p702) Following the town's compact but richly rewarding heritage walking trail.

9 Overland Track (p710) Walking through World Heritage–listed landscape from Cradle Mountain to Lake St Clair.

10 Rafting the Franklin River (p708) Shooting the rapids on a rafting journey down Tasmania's wildest river.

Fingal

Bicheno

Perth

Douglas-Apsley National Park

Coles Bay ❹

Freycinet National Park

Wineglass Bay ❹

Schouten Island

Great Oyster Bay

Swansea

A4

Lake Leake

South Esk River

Campbell Town

Ross

Maria Island ❹ National Park

Maria Island National Park

Tooms Lake

Triabunna

Forestier Peninsula

Three Capes Track

Cape Pillar ❹

TASMAN SEA

Hobart International Airport

A9

Sorell ❹

Seven Mile Beach

Tasman National Park ❹

Tasman Peninsula ❷

Port Arthur ❸

Macquarie River

South Esk River

1

Oatlands

A3

Lake Dulverton

Lake Tiberius

Richmond

Bridgewater ❶ **MONA** ❺

Brighton

1

Hamilton

Storm Bay

Clifton Beach

Salamanca Market ❺

New Norfolk

HOBART ◎

Taroona

Kingston

Snug

Bruny Island ❼

Alonnah

South Bruny National Park ❹

Tasman Head

Great Western Tiers

B51

A5

Bothwell

Lake Sorell

Arthurs Lake

Great Lake

Central Plateau Conservation Area ❹

Miena

Walls of Jerusalem National Park ❹

Cradle Mountain–Lake St Clair National Park

Overland Track ❾

Mole Creek Karst National Park ❹

Tarraleah

A10

Maydena

Mt Field National Park

Derwent Bridge

Lake St Clair

Lake King William

Franklin River ❿

Franklin-Gordon Wild Rivers National Park

Strathgordon

Southwest Conservation Area

Southwest National Park ❹

Hartz Mountains National Park ❹

Huon River

Huonville

Geeveston

Cygnet

Dover

A6

D'Entrecasteaux Channel

Southport

South South East Cape

Rosebery

Zeehan

Queenstown

Strahan

Mersey River

River Forth

Cradle Valley

Franklin River

Gordon River

Olga River

Lake Gordon

Lake Pedder

South West Cape

Port Davey

Corinna

Pieman River

Cape Sorell

Macquarie Harbour

Lake Burbury

Arberg Bay

Hardwicke Bay

SOUTHERN OCEAN

South Cape

South West Cape

South East Cape

History

The first European to spy Tasmania was Dutch navigator Abel Tasman, who bumped into it in 1642. He named this new place Van Diemen's Land after the Dutch East Indies' governor. It's estimated there were between 5000 and 10,000 Indigenous people in Tasmania when Europeans arrived, living in 'bands' of around 50 people, each claiming rights over a specific area of land and being part of one of nine main language groups.

European sealers began to work Bass Strait in 1798, raiding tribal communities along the coast and kidnapping Aboriginal women to act as forced labour and sex slaves. The sealers were uninterested in Aboriginal land and eventually formed commercial relationships, trading dogs and other items.

In the late 1790s Governor King of NSW decided to establish a second settlement in Australia, south of Sydney Cove. Port Phillip Bay in Victoria was initially considered, but the site was rejected due to a lack of water on the Mornington Peninsula and, in 1803, Tasmania's Risdon Cove was chosen. A year later, the settlement was moved 10km south to the present site of Hobart on the other side of the Derwent River.

That same year 74 convicts were shipped out to Van Diemen's Land, with 71 soldiers, plus their 21 wives and 14 children, and by 1833 roughly 2000 convicts a year were sent to Tasmania as punishment for often-trivial crimes. The community quickly developed a very particular character: lawlessness and debauchery were rife.

Although it was ignored in the initial federal ministry, Tasmania became a state when Australia's Federation took place in 1901. For Tasmanians, as for mainlanders in the new Commonwealth of Australia, the first half of the 20th century was dominated by war.

The state's post-WWII economy was reassuringly buoyant, however, by the 1980s it had suffered a worrisome decline. Subsequent years saw economic unease reflected in climbing 'brain drain' levels to the mainland (especially among the under-30s) and falling birth rates.

Since the early 1970s, the key influence on Tasmanian history has been the ongoing battle between logging companies and environmental groups. In 1972, concerned groups got together to form the United Tasmania Group. Ten years later, thousands of people acted to stop the damming of the Franklin River. Leaders in these movements became a force in Australian federal politics – the Greens Party, under the leadership of Tasmanian Bob Brown, who was a senator from 1996 until 2012.

Tasmania is a state that's poorer and has less employment opportunities than mainland states, but it's also an island with world-class wilderness and scenic beauty. With these two contemporary markers of Tasmanian society, the ideological fault lines often evident in Tasmanian history are not difficult to trace back and understand.

Indigenous Tasmania

The culture of the Tasmanian Aboriginals diverged from the way people were living on the mainland, as they developed a sustainable, seasonal culture of hunting, fishing and gathering.

In 1803 Risdon Cove, on the Derwent River just north of Hobart, became the site of Australia's second British colony (after Sydney). One year later the settlement relocated to Sullivans Cove, the site of present-day Hobart, where the Hobart Rivulet offered a reliable water supply.

Despite initial friendly exchanges and trade, an unknown number of peaceable Aboriginal people were killed during this early period. In return Aboriginal people began to carry out their own raids. In 1816 Governor Thomas Davey produced his 'Proclamation to the Aborigines', which represented settlers and Indigenous Tasmanians living together amicably – in direct contrast to the realities of a brutal conflict.

By the 1820s these territorial disputes had developed into the so-called Black Wars, as Aboriginal people refused to surrender their lands, women and children without a fight. In 1828 martial law was declared by Lieutenant-Governor Arthur. Aboriginal groups were systematically murdered, arrested or forced at gunpoint from districts settled by whites – arsenic on bread and steel traps designed to catch humans were used. Many more succumbed to European diseases against which they had no immunity.

As the Black Wars continued, Lieutenant-Governor Arthur consented to George Augustus Robinson's plan to 'conciliate' the Aboriginal people. In effect Robinson enticed and cajoled virtually all of the Aboriginals in mainland Tasmania to lay down their arms, leave their traditional lands and accompany him to new settlements. There is strong historical evidence that the people of Oyster Bay followed him to a succession of settlements in the Furneaux Islands based on the promise of sanctuary and land. Instead, they were subjected to attempts to 'civilise' and Christianise them, and made to work for the government.

After enduring a number of moves, Tasmania's Indigenous inhabitants were finally settled at Wybalenna (Black Man's Houses) on Flinders Island. The people began to die from a potent mixture of despair, homesickness, poor food and respiratory disease. In 1847 survivors petitioned Queen Victoria, referring to the 'agreement' they thought Robinson had made with Lieutenant-Governor Arthur on their behalf. Wybalenna was eventually abandoned and the survivors transferred to mainland Tasmania. Of the 135 who had been sent to Flinders Island, only 47 lived to return. The new accommodation again proved to be substandard and within a decade, half of the 47 were dead.

National Parks

Tasmania's 19 national parks are awesome, in the truest sense of the word. Public access to the national parks is encouraged as long as safety and conservation regulations are observed. The golden rules: don't damage or alter the natural environment, and don't feed wild animals.

Fees

Visitor fees apply to all national parks, even when there's no rangers' office or roaming ranger on duty.

There are two main types of passes available for short-term visitors: 24-hour and holiday passes. A 24-hour pass costs $12/24 per person/vehicle; a holiday pass lasts for eight weeks and costs $30/60 per person/vehicle. Vehicle passes cover up to eight people. Annual passes ($96 per vehicle) and two-year passes ($123 per vehicle) are also available if you're a frequent visitor.

Passes are available at most park entrances, at many visitor centres, aboard the *Spirit of Tasmania* ferries, from **Service Tasmania** (Map p642; ☑ 1300 135 513; www.service.tas.gov. au; 134 Macquarie St, Hobart; ◷ 8.15am-5pm Mon-Fri) and online at www.parks.tas.gov.au.

🏃 Activities

Are you the outdoors type? If you're looking to do some bushwalking, fishing, rafting, sea kayaking, sailing, scuba diving or surfing, Tasmania could be your personal promised land! Your first ports of call:

Bureau of Meteorology (www.bom.gov. au/tas) Tasmanian weather can be fickle: check the forecast before you head into the wilds.

Canoe Tasmania (www.tas.canoe.org.au) Canoe and kayak club info around the state.

Inland Fisheries Service (www.ifs.tas. gov.au) Info on fishing regulations around the state.

Parks & Wildlife Service (www.parks.tas. gov.au) Click on 'Recreation' for oodles of bushwalking and camping info.

Royal Yacht Club of Tasmania (www.ryct. org.au) Swing the boom and hoist the spinnaker – sailing advice around the island.

Service Tasmania (www.service.tas.gov. au) For detailed bushwalking maps; outlets around the state.

Tasmanian Scuba Diving Club (www. tsdc.org.au) Get your goggles on and get underwater; scuba advice and events.

TASMANIAN WILDERNESS WORLD HERITAGE AREA

The internationally significant **Tasmanian Wilderness World Heritage Area** (☑ 03-6288 1283; www.parks.tas.gov.au/wha; ◷ 24hr) contains the state's four largest national parks – Southwest, Franklin–Gordon Wild Rivers, Cradle Mountain–Lake St Clair and Walls of Jerusalem – plus the Hartz Mountains National Park, the Central Plateau Conservation Area, the Adamsfield Conservation Area, a section of Mole Creek Karst National Park, the Devils Gullet State Reserve and part of the Liffey Falls State Reserve.

Unesco granted the region World Heritage status in 1982, acknowledging that these parks make up one of the planet's last great, temperate wilderness areas. An area nominated for World Heritage status must satisfy at least one of 10 criteria – the Tasmanian Wilderness World Heritage Area fulfilled a record seven categories! The area comprises a grand 15,840 sq km – around 20% of Tasmania.

In 1997 the **Macquarie Island World Heritage Area** – a remote sub-Antarctic island 1500km southeast of mainland Tasmania – was proclaimed for its outstanding geological and faunal significance.

Tassie Surf (www.tassiesurf.com) Daily surf photos and weather updates.

Tourism Tasmania (www.discovertasmania.com) Outdoor activity info; click on 'What to Do' then 'Outdoors & Adventure'.

⌲ Tours

Tasmanian Safaris   ADVENTURE
(☑1300 882 415; www.tasmaniansafaris.com) Multiday, eco-certified 4WD tours from Launceston heading to Hobart via the east coast, or Hobart to Launceston via the west coast. There's bushwalking, camping and lots of wilderness. Canoe trips also available.

Under Down Under   TOURS
(Tassie Day Tours; ☑1800 444 442; www.underdownunder.com.au) Offers pro-green, nature-based, backpacker-friendly trips. Tours from one to nine days, all over the state: Bruny Island, Port Arthur, Wineglass Bay, Richmond, Mt Wellington, Cradle Mountain...

Tasmanian Expeditions   OUTDOORS
(☑1300 666 856; www.tasmanianexpeditions.com.au) Offers an excellent range of activity-based tours: bushwalking, cabin-based walks, rafting, rock climbing, cycling and sea kayaking in remote parts of the state.

Adventure Tours   BUS
(☑1300 654 604; www.adventuretours.com.au) An Australia-wide company offering six-day tours around Tasmania, including hostel accommodation.

Jump Tours   BUS
(☑03-6288 7030; www.jumptours.com) Youth and backpacker-oriented one- to seven-day Tassie tours.

ⓘ Information

Parks & Wildlife Service (☑03-6165 4305; www.parks.tas.gov.au) Contact the Parks & Wildlife Service if you encounter injured wildlife.

Tasmanian Travelways (www.travelways.com.au) Online version of the tourist newspaper of the same name.

Tourism Tasmania (www.discovertasmania.com) Tasmania's official tourism promoters. The main Tasmanian Travel & Information Centre in Hobart is a helpful spot for planning statewide travel and can handle bookings of all sorts.

ⓘ Getting There & Away

There are no direct international flights to Tasmania. Visitors need to get to one of Australia's mainland cities and connect to a Tasmania-bound domestic flight to Hobart, Launceston or Devonport. Melbourne and Sydney (and, to a lesser extent, Brisbane) airports have the most frequent direct air links. Also popular is the *Spirit of Tasmania* passenger and car ferry, sailing between Melbourne and Devonport in Tasmania's north.

Flights, cars and tours can be booked online at lonelyplanet.com/bookings.

AIR

Jetstar (www.jetstar.com.au) Qantas' low-cost airline. Direct flights from Melbourne, Sydney and Brisbane to Hobart and Launceston.

Qantas (www.qantas.com.au) Direct flights from Sydney, Brisbane and Melbourne to Launceston, and from Sydney and Melbourne to Hobart. Also flies between Melbourne and Devonport.

Regional Express (Rex; www.regionalexpress.com.au) Flies from Melbourne to Burnie/Wynyard and to King Island.

Tiger Air (www.tigerair.com.au) Flies from Melbourne to Hobart.

Virgin Australia (www.virginaustralia.com.au) Direct flights from Melbourne, Sydney, Brisbane and Canberra to Hobart, and from Melbourne, Brisbane and Sydney to Launceston.

FERRY

Two big, red **Spirit of Tasmania** (☑03-6421 7209, 1800 634 906; www.spiritoftasmania.com.au) ferries ply Bass Strait nightly in each direction between Melbourne and Devonport on Tasmania's northwest coast. The crossing takes around 11 hours, departing either mainland Australia or Tasmania at 7.30pm and arriving at 6.30am. During peak periods, including Christmas, Easter and key holiday weekends, the schedule is ramped up to two sailings per day, departing at 9am and 9pm. Check the website for details.

Each ferry can accommodate 1400 passengers and around 650 vehicles and has restaurants, bars and games facilities. The ships' public areas have been designed to cater for wheelchair access, as have a handful of cabins.

ⓘ Getting Around

BICYCLE

Cycling Tasmania is one of the best ways to get close to nature (and, it has to be said, to log trucks, rain, hills, roadkill...). Roads are generally in good shape, and traffic outside the cities is light. If you're prepared for occasional steep climbs and strong headwinds, you should enjoy the experience immensely.

It's worth bringing your own bike, especially if you're coming via ferry: bike transport on the *Spirit of Tasmania* costs just $5 each way year-round. Or buy a bike in Hobart or Launceston and reselling it at the end of your trip – hit the bike shops or noticeboards at backpacker hostels.

Bike rental is available in the larger towns, or there are a number of operators offering multi-day cycling tours or experiences such as mountain biking down Mt Wellington in Hobart.

Bicycle helmets are compulsory in Tasmania, as are white front lights and red rear lights if you're riding in the dark. See www.biketas.org.au for more information.

BUS

Tassielink (☑ 03-6235 7300, 1300 300 520; www.tassielink.com.au) The main player, with extensive statewide services. From Hobart buses run south to Dover via the Huon Valley, southeast to Port Arthur, north to Richmond, to Launceston via the Midlands Hwy, to the east coast as far as Bicheno, and to Queenstown on the west coast via Lake St Clair.

Redline Coaches (☑ 1300 360 000; www.tasredline.com.au) The state's second-biggest operator. Services the Midland Hwy between Hobart and Launceston, and the north-coast towns between Launceston and Smithton. Shuttles to Hobart and Launceston airports also available.

CAR & MOTORCYCLE

Travelling with your own wheels gives you the freedom to explore to your own timetable, and you can crank up the music as loud as hell! You can bring vehicles from the mainland to Tasmania on the *Spirit of Tasmania* ferries, so renting may only be cheaper for shorter trips. Tasmania has the usual slew of international and local car-rental agencies.

Motorcycles are a hip way to get around the island, but be prepared for all kinds of weather in any season.

Rental

Before hiring a car, ask about any kilometre limitations and find out exactly what the insurance covers. Note that some companies don't cover accidents on unsealed roads, and hike up the excess in the case of any damage on the dirt – a considerable disadvantage as many of the top Tasmanian destinations are definitely off-piste! Some companies also don't allow their vehicles to be taken across to Bruny Island.

International company rates start at about $55 for a high-season, multi-day hire of a small car. Book in advance for the best prices. Small local firms rent cars for as little as $30 a day, depending on the season and the duration of the hire. The smaller companies don't normally have desks at arrival points, but can usually arrange for your car to be picked up at airports and the ferry terminal in Devonport.

Autorent-Hertz (☑ 1800 030 500; www.autorent.com.au) Also has campervans for hire and sale.

> ### TASMANIAN TRAIL
>
> The **Tasmanian Trail** (www.tasmaniantrail.com.au), a 480km multi-use route from Devonport to Dover, is geared towards walkers, horse riders and mountain bikers. Most of the trail is on forestry or fire trails and country roads. It passes farms, forests and towns en route, with camping spots every 30km or so (and lots of opportunities to sleep in a real bed!).

Avis (☑ 13 63 33; www.avis.com.au) Also has 4WDs.

Budget (☑ 1300 362 848; www.budget.com.au)

Europcar (☑ 1300 131 390; www.europcar.com.au)

Lo-Cost Auto Rent (☑ 03-6231 0550; www.locostautorent.com) Branches in Hobart and Launceston.

Rent For Less (☑ 1300 883 728; www.rentforless.com.au) Branches in Hobart and Launceston.

Selective Car Rentals (☑ 1300 729 230; www.selectivecarrentals.com.au) Branches in Hobart, Launceston and Devonport.

Thrifty (☑ 1300 367 227; www.thrifty.com.au)

Tasmanian Motorcycle Hire (☑ 0418 365 210; www.tasmotorcyclehire.com.au) Based in Launceston.

CAMPERVAN

Companies for campervan hire – with rates from around $90 (two-berth) or $150 (four-berth) per day, usually with minimum five-day hire and unlimited kilometres – include the following. For rate comparisons see www.fetchcampervanhire.com.au.

Apollo (p1074) Also has a backpacker-focused brand called Hippie Camper.

Britz (p1074) Campervan rental.

Cruisin' Tasmania (☑ 1300 664 485; www.cruisintasmania.com.au) Campervan rental.

Maui (p1074) Campervan rental.

Tasmanian Campervan Hire (☑ 0438 807 118; www.tascamper.com) Specialises in two-berth vans.

Tasmanian Campervan Rentals (☑ 03-6248 1867; www.tasmaniacampervanrentals.com.au) Campervan rental.

Tasmanian Motor Shacks (☑ 03-6248 4418; www.tassiemotorshacks.com.au) Campervan rental.

HOBART & AROUND

Australia's second-oldest city and southernmost capital, Hobart dapples the foothills of Mt Wellington, angling down to the slate-grey Derwent River. The town's rich cache of colonial architecture and natural charms are complemented by innovative festivals, eclectic markets and world-class food and drink experiences.

It's a gorgeous place, but until quite recently Hobart was far from cosmopolitan or self-assured – it's taken a while for Hobartians to feel comfortable in their own skins. Paralleling this shift (or perhaps driving it), the mainland Australian attitude to Hobart has changed from derision to delight: investors now recognise that Tasmania's abundant water, stress-free pace and cool climate are precious commodities.

Not far past the outskirts of town are some great beaches, alpine areas and historic villages. And don't miss MONA, Hobart's dizzyingly good Museum of Old and New Art, which has vehemently stamped Tasmania onto the global cultural map.

Hobart

POP 226,750

Hobart is a harbour town – a port city, where the world rushes in on the tide and ebbs away again, bringing with it influences from afar and leaving the locals buzzing with global zeitgeist. Or so the theory goes. And these days, Hobart's waterfront precinct is certainly buzzing, with old pubs alongside new craft-beer bars, myriad restaurants and cafes, museums, festivals, ferries, accommodation...and all of it washed with sea-salty charm and a sense of history. On a sunny afternoon there are few more pleasant places in Australia to find yourself.

◉ Sights

◉ Central Hobart

Penitentiary Chapel
Historic Site   HISTORIC SITE
(Map p638; ☑03-6231 0911; www.nationaltrust.org.au/places/the-tench; cnr Brisbane & Campbell Sts; tours adult/child/family $15/10/40; ☺tours 10am, 11.30am, 1pm & 2.30pm Mon-Fri, 1pm & 2.30pm Sat & Sun) The courtrooms, cells and gallows here at 'the Tench' had a hellish reputation in the 1800s: a stint here was to

be avoided at all costs. This perhaps goes some way towards explaining how these amazing old convict-built structures have survived in the middle of Hobart in original condition into the 21st century. Take the excellent National Trust–run tour, or the bookings-mandatory **Tench Ghost Tour** (https://nationaltrusttas.rezdy.com/43790/the-tench-ghost-tour; tours $25; ☺8pm Mon & Fri Jun-Aug, 9pm Mon & Fri Sep-May).

Gasworks Cellar Door   WINERY
(Map p642; ☑03-6231 5946; www.gasworkscellardoor.com.au; 2 Macquarie St; tastings from $2.50; ☺noon-4pm Sun-Wed, 11am-5pm Thu-Sat) If you don't have the time (or inclination) to visit Tasmania's wine regions to sip a few cool-climate drops, duck into the Gasworks Cellar Door at the bottom end of Macquarie St instead. Creatively crafted displays take you on a virtual tour, highlighting the best regional bottles (which you can buy here).

◉ Salamanca Place & the Waterfront

★Salamanca Place   HISTORIC SITE
(Map p642; www.salamanca.com.au) This picturesque row of three- and four-storey sandstone warehouses is a classic example of Australian colonial architecture. Dating back to the whaling days of the 1830s, Salamanca was the hub of Hobart's trade and commerce. By the mid-20th century many of the warehouses had fallen into ruin, before restorations began in the 1970s. These days Salamanca hosts myriad restaurants, cafes, bars and shops, and the unmissable Saturday morning Salamanca Market (p651).

★Mawson's Huts
Replica Museum   MUSEUM
(Map p642; ☑1300 551 422, 03-6231 1518; www.mawsons-huts-replica.org.au; cnr Morrison & Argyle Sts; adult/child/family $12/4/28; ☺9am-6pm Oct-Apr, 10am-5pm May-Sep) This excellent waterfront installation is an exact model of one of the huts in which Sir Douglas Mawson hunkered down on his 1911–14 Australasian Antarctic Expedition, which set sail from Hobart. Inside it is 100% authentic, right down to the matches, the stove and the bunks. A knowledgeable guide sits at a rustic table, ready to answer your Antarctic enquiries. Entry fees go towards the upkeep of the original huts at Cape Denison in Antarctica.

★**Tasmanian Museum**
& Art Gallery　　　　　　　　MUSEUM
(TMAG; Map p642; ☑03-6165 7000; www.tmag.
tas.gov.au; Dunn Pl; ⊙10am-4pm daily Jan-Mar,
10am-4pm Tue-Sun Apr-Dec) **FREE** Incorporating Hobart's oldest building, the Commissariat Store (1808), this revamped museum
features colonial relics and excellent Aboriginal and wildlife displays. The gallery cu-
rates a collection of Tasmanian colonial art.
There are free guided tours at 1pm and 2pm
from Wednesday to Sunday (hordes of school
kids might be a little less interested in proceedings than you are), plus special themed
tours at 11am: check the website or call to see
what's on. There's a cool cafe and shop, too.

Waterfront　　　　　　　　　　　AREA
(Map p642; off Davey St) Hobartians flock to
the city's waterfront like seagulls to chips.
Centred on **Victoria Dock** (a working fishing
harbour) and **Constitution Dock** (chock-
full of floating takeaway-seafood punts), it's
a brilliant place to explore. The obligatory
Hobart experience is to sit in the sun, munch
some fish and chips and watch the harbour
hubbub. If you'd prefer something with a
knife and fork, there are some superb restaurants here, too – head for **Elizabeth St Pier**.

◉ **Battery Point, Sandy Bay**
& South Hobart

★**Battery Point**　　　　　　HISTORIC SITE
(Map p642; www.batterypoint.net) An empty
rum bottle's throw from the waterfront, the
old maritime village of Battery Point is a
tight nest of lanes and 19th-century cottages,
packed together like shanghaied landlubbers in a ship's belly. Spend an afternoon
exploring: stumble up **Kelly's Steps** (Map
p642; Kelly St, via Salamanca Pl, Hobart) from
Salamanca Place and dogleg into **South St**,
where the red lights once burned night and
day. Spin around picturesque **Arthur Circus**,
refuel in the cafes on **Hampden Rd**, then ogle

HOBART IN...

One Day

Get your head into history mode with an amble around Battery Point, the storied precinct on the headland southeast of the city centre. Don't miss the photogenic cottages
on compact Arthur Circus, atmospheric South St, **St George's Anglican Church** on
Cromwell St, and the cafes on Hampden Rd. Stop for a pie or pastry at **Jackman &**
McRoss (p647). a neighbourhood favourite. After lunch, wander down Kelly's Steps
to the historic warehouses on Salamanca Place: check out the craft shops and galleries in the **Salamanca Arts Centre** (p650). Delve into Hobart's Antarctic heritage at
the **Mawson's Huts Replica Museum** on the waterfront near Constitution Dock, before feasting on fish and chips for dinner at **Flippers** (p647) or **Fish Frenzy** (p647).
If you have the energy after your seafood repast, head to Elizabeth Street Pier for
another tipple at upmarket **T-42°** (p649). Even more upmarket is the **Glass House**
(p649) in the floating Brooke Street Pier...or if you're feeling more earthy, try **Jack**
Greene (p649)back on Salamanca Place.

Two Days

On day two recuperate over a big breakfast and a couple of coffees at **Retro Café**
(p647) on Salamanca Place (if it's a Saturday, **Salamanca Market** (p651) will be
pumping). Afterwards, wander over to the floating Brook Street Pier and catch the
ferry out to **MONA** (p639) for an afternoon of saucy, subversive, mindful distraction.
There are eating options at MONA: try the delectable Source or the casual Museum
Cafe. Suitably fuelled, launch your foray into MONA's amazing subterranean spaces –
a multilevel maze of surprise encounters, quiet moments, hilarious installations and
dizzying undertakings. Expect to laugh, cry, gasp, turn away, stare and maybe even
bleed a little bit. After a drink at the bar, grab a cab back to North Hobart for Mexican
at **Pancho Villa** (p648) or steak at **Roaring Grill** (p648). Come down to earth after
your high-brow day with a wind-down drink and an evening out. For a craft beer or
three after dinner, try the bohemian, hipster **Winston** (p649), then see what's screening at the art-house **State Cinema** (p650) or wander down to **Republic Bar & Café**
(p650) for some live tunes.

Hobart

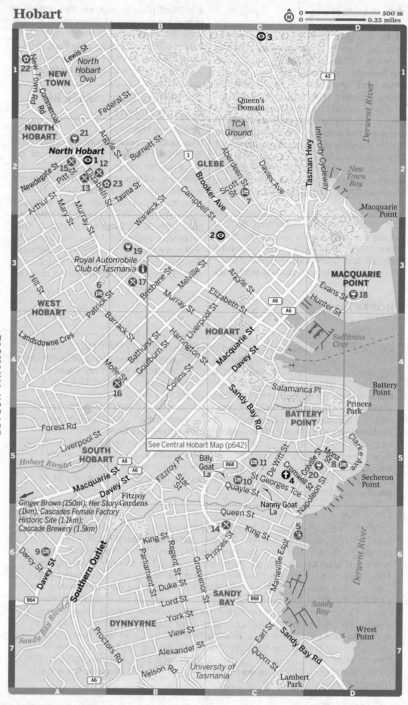

Hobart

◎ **Top Sights**
  1 North Hobart...A2

◎ **Sights**
  2 Penitentiary Chapel Historic Site.........C3
  3 Royal Tasmanian Botanical
     Gardens...C1
  4 St George's Anglican Church...............C5

◎ **Activities, Courses & Tours**
  5 Roaring 40s Kayaking...........................C6
     Tench Ghost Tour...........................(see 2)

◎ **Sleeping**
  6 Altamont House.....................................A3
  7 Corinda's Cottages...............................C2
  8 Grande Vue Private Hotel.....................D5
  9 Islington..A6
  10 Quayle Terrace.....................................C5
  11 St Ives Motel..C5

◎ **Eating**
  12 Annapurna...A2
  13 Burger Haus..A2

  14 Don Camillo...C6
  15 Pancho Villa...A2
  16 Pigeon Hole...B4
     Roaring Grill......................................(see 12)
  17 Templo...B3

◎ **Drinking & Nightlife**
  18 Hobart Brewing Company.....................D3
  19 Shambles Brewery.................................B3
  20 Shipwright's Arms Hotel.......................D5
     Willing Bros......................................(see 15)
  21 Winston..A2

◎ **Entertainment**
  22 Jokers Comedy Club..............................A1
  23 Republic Bar & Café..............................A2
     State Cinema....................................(see 21)

◎ **Shopping**
     State Cinema Bookstore................(see 21)

St George's Anglican Church (Map p638; ☑ 03-6223 2146; www.stgeorgesbatterypoint.org; 30 Cromwell St, Battery Point; ⊙ 9.15am-2.15pm Tue-Fri, service 10am Sun) on Cromwell St.

★ **kunanyi/ Mt Wellington** MOUNTAIN (mountwellington; ☑ 03-62384222; www.wellington park.org.au; Pinnacle Rd, via Fern Tree) Cloaked in winter snow, kunanyi/ Mt Wellington (1271m) towers over Hobart like a benevolent overlord. The citizens find reassurance in its constant, solid presence, while outdoorsy types find the space to hike and bike on its leafy flanks. And the view from the top is unbelievable! You can drive all the way to the summit on a sealed road; alternatively, the **Hobart Shuttle Bus Company** (☑ 0408 341 804; www.hobartshuttlebus.com; transfers & tours per adult/child from $30/20) runs daily two-hour tours to the summit.

★ **Cascade Brewery** BREWERY (☑ 03 6212 7800; www.cascadebrewery.com.au; 140 Cascade Rd; brewery tours adult/child 16-18yr $30/15, Cascade Story tour adult/child $15/5; ⊙ tours daily) Standing in startling, gothic isolation next to the clean-running Hobart Rivulet, Cascade is Australia's oldest brewery (1832) and is still pumping out superb beers. Ninety-minute tours involve plenty of history, with tastings at the end. Note that under-16s aren't permitted on the main brewery tour (take the family-friendly Cas-

cade Story tour instead), and that brewery machinery mightn't be running if you're here on a weekend (brewers have weekends, too). Bookings essential. To get here, take bus 446, 447, 448 or 449.

★ **Cascades Female Factory Historic Site** HISTORIC SITE (☑ 03-6233 6656; www.femalefactory.org.au; 16 Degraves St; adult/child/family $5/5/15, tour $15/10/40, 'Her Story' dramatisation $20/12.50/60; ⊙ 9.30am-4pm, tours hourly 10am-3pm (except noon), 'Her Story' dramatisation 11am) Enshrined by Unesco as a World Heritage historic site, this was where Hobart's female convicts were incarcerated and put to work. Rather amazingly, one in four convicts transported to Van Diemen's Land was a woman. Explore the site under your own steam, or book a guided tour or excellent 'Her Story' dramatisation to best understand the site, which looked very different back in the early 1800s. To get here by public transport, take bus 446, 447, 448 or 449.

◎ MONA & Northern Hobart

★ **MONA** MUSEUM, GALLERY (Museum of Old & New Art; ☑ 03-6277 9900; www. mona.net.au; 655 Main Rd, Berriedale; adult/child $25/free, Tasmanian residents free; ⊙ 10am-6pm daily Jan, 10am-6pm Wed-Mon Feb-Apr & Dec, 10am-5pm Wed-Mon May-Nov) Twelve kilometres north of Hobart's city centre, MONA occupies a saucepan-shaped peninsula jutting into the Derwent River. Arrayed across three underground levels, abutting a sheer rock face, the $75-million museum has been described by philanthropist owner David Walsh as 'a subversive adult Disneyland'. Ancient antiquities are showcased next to contemporary works: sexy, provocative, disturbing and deeply engaging. Don't miss it.

To get here catch the MR-1 ferry or MONA Roma shuttle bus from Hobart's Brooke Street Pier. Book everything online.

★ North Hobart
NEIGHBOURHOOD

(Map p638) Hobart at its most bohemian and multicultural, the Elizabeth St strip in North Hobart (or 'NoHo' to those with a sense of humour) is lined with dozens of cafes, restaurants, bars and pubs – enough to keep you coming back meal after meal after meal... Also here is the excellent art-house State Cinema (p650), and Hobart's best live music room, the Republic Bar & Café (p650).

Royal Tasmanian Botanical Gardens
GARDENS

(Map p638; ☑03-6166 0451; www.rtbg.tas.gov.au; Lower Domain Rd, Queens Domain; ◷8am-6.30pm Oct-Mar, to 5.30pm Apr & Sep, to 5pm May-Aug) FREE On the eastern side of the Queen's Domain, these small but beguiling gardens hark back to 1818 and feature more than 6000 exotic and native plant species. Picnic on the lawns, check out the Subantarctic Plant House or grab a bite at the restaurant or cafe. Across from the main entrance is the site of the former Beaumaris Zoo, where the last captive Tasmanian tiger died in 1936. Call to ask about guided tours.

🏃 Activities

★ Mt Wellington Descent
CYCLING

(☑1800 064 726; www.underdownunder.com.au/tour/mount-wellington-descent; adult/child $75/65; ◷10am & 1pm daily year-round, plus 4pm Dec-Feb) Take a van ride to the summit of Mt Wellington (1270m), and follow with 22km of downhill cruising (mostly – the last 5km are flat) on a mountain bike. It's terrific fun, with minimal energy output and maximum views! Tours start and end at 4 Elizabeth St on the Hobart waterfront, and last 2½ hours.

★ Roaring 40s Kayaking
KAYAKING

(Map p638; ☑0455 949 777; www.roaring40skayaking.com.au; Marieville Esplanade, Sandy Bay; adult/child $90/60; ◷10am daily Oct-Apr,

plus 4pm Nov-Mar) Hobart is perhaps at its prettiest when viewed from the water. Take a safe, steady, 2½-hour guided paddle with Roaring 40s, named after the prevailing winds at these latitudes. You'll cruise from Sandy Bay past Battery Point and into the Hobart docks for some fish and chips while you float, before returning to Sandy Bay.

Hobart Bike Hire
CYCLING

(Map p642; ☑0447 556 189; www.hobartbikehire.com.au; 35 Hunter St; bike hire per day/overnight from $25/35; ◷9am-5.30pm) Centrally located on Hobart's waterfront, and has lots of ideas for self-guided tours around the city or along the Derwent River to MONA. Kids' trailers and tandems also available; maps and helmets included. There's a second depot at Brooke St, near the MONA ferry.

Rockit Climbing
CLIMBING

(Map p642; ☑03-6234 1090; www.rockitclimbing.com.au; 54 Bathurst St; adult/child/family $25/12/60; ◷noon-9pm Mon-Fri, to 6pm Sat & Sun) Inside a converted warehouse, Rockit offers world-class climbing walls. Don your rubber shoes and harness (included in the admission price), chalk up your paws, and up you go.

👉 Tours

★ Pennicott Wilderness Journeys
BOATING

(Map p642; ☑03-6234 4270; www.pennicottjourneys.com.au; Dock Head Bldg, Franklin Wharf; tours adult/child from $225/155; ◷7am-6.30pm) Pennicott offers half-a-dozen outstanding boat trips around key southern Tasmanian sights, including trips to Bruny Island, Tasman Island, the Tasman Peninsula, D'Entrecasteaux Channel, and the Iron Pot Lighthouse south of Hobart. The Tasmanian Seafood Seduction (Map p642; ☑03-6234 4270; www.seafoodseduction.com.au) trip is a winner for fans of all things fishy.

Hobart Comedy Tours
CULTURAL

(www.hobartcomedytours.com; tours from adult/child $28/18) Laugh it up in Hobart's Franklin Sq with these very punny 'Horrible Hobart' tours (good for families; 11am and 2pm Thursday and Saturday), and more risque 'The (Un) fairer Sex' tours, looking at life as a working girl in old Hobart Town (adults only; 7pm Tuesday and Thursday). Bookings essential.

Gourmania
WALKING

(☑0419 180 113; www.gourmaniafoodtours.com.au; tours from $89) Fabulous, flavour-filled walking tours around Salamanca Place and central Hobart, with plenty of opportunities

HOBART FOR CHILDREN

Parents won't break the bank keeping the troops entertained in Hobart. The Salamanca Place area abounds in diversions, with the street performers, buskers and Saturday's **Salamanca Market** (p651) captivating kids of all ages. Free Friday-night Rektango (p649) music event in the courtyard at the Salamanca Arts Centre is also a family-friendly affair. And there's always something going on around the **waterfront** (p637) – fishing boats chugging in and out of Victoria Dock, yachts tacking in Sullivans Cove...and you can feed the tribe on a budget at the fish punts on Constitution Dock.

There are plenty of rainy-day attractions to satisfy your child (or inner child). The **Tasmanian Museum & Art Gallery** (p637) give kids the chance to understand Aboriginal history, get the low-down on the Tasmanian tiger, and ogle shiny stones, while the **Maritime Museum of Tasmania** (Map p642; ☑ 03-6234 1427; www.maritimetas.org; 16 Argyle St, Hobart; adult/child/family $10/8/20; ⊙ 9am-5pm) has shipwrecks, whaling, yachts, rusty anchors – if there's anything uninteresting at this museum, let us know. If need be, there's always **Mawson's Huts Replica Museum** (p636) for a taste of Antarctica – give the little blighters a concept of true hardship and see if their behaviour improves!

Babysitting If you're in need of a romantic dinner for two, contact the **Mobile Nanny Service** (☑ 0437 504 064, 03-6273 3773; www.mobilenannyservice.com.au).

Resources Pick up the free *LetsGoKids* magazine (www.letsgokids.com.au) at the Hobart Visitor Information Centre for activity ideas.

Transport Kids under five travel free on Metro Tasmania public buses; over-fives receive discounted fares (around 50% off).

to try local foods and chat to restaurant, cafe and shop owners.

Hobart Historic Tours WALKING
(☑ 03-6234 5550; www.hobarthistorictours.com.au; tours from $30) Informative, entertaining 90-minute walking tours of Hobart and historic Battery Point. There's also an Old Hobart Pub Tour, which sluices through some waterfront watering holes, and a three-hour Grand Hobart Walk. Call or see the website for times and bookings. Reduced winter schedule.

Her Story WALKING
(☑ 03-6233 6656, 1800 139 478; www.livehistoryhobart.com.au; 45min tour adult/child $20/12.50) Engaging tours of Hobart's female convict heritage at the Cascades Female Factory Historic Site (p639), interpreted through 'roaming theatre' with live actors. Tours depart midday daily (except Saturdays in winter).

Tasmanian Whisky Tours DISTILLERY
(☑ 0412 099 933; www.tasmanianwhiskytours.com.au; tours $249; ⊙ Tue, Fri & Sat) Tasmanian whisky has been getting plenty of press since Sullivans Cove Whisky won the coveted 'Best Single Malt' gong at the World Whisky Awards in 2014. Take a day tour with this passionate outfit, visiting three distilleries with tastings of top Tassie single malts. Minimum four passengers. Beer and wine tours also available.

Red Decker BUS
(☑ 03-6236 9116; www.reddecker.com.au; 20-stop pass adult/child/family 24hr $35/20/90, 48hr $40/25/100) Commentated sightseeing on an old London double-decker bus. Buy a 20-stop, hop-on-hop-off pass (valid for one or two days), or do the tour as a 90-minute loop. Pay a bit more and add a Cascade Brewery tour (adult/child $65/55) or Mt Wellington tour ($65/40) to the deal.

Lady Nelson BOATING
(Map p642; ☑ 03-6234 3348; www.ladynelson.org.au; Elizabeth St Pier; adult/child $30/15; ⊙ 11am & 1pm Sat & Sun) Sail around the harbour for 90 minutes on a replica of the surprisingly compact brig *Lady Nelson,* one of the first colonial ships to sail to Tasmania. Longer trips are occasionally on offer: check the website. There's an extra 3pm sailing on Saturday and Sunday from mid-December to April.

⚒ Festivals & Events

★ **Sydney to Hobart Yacht Race** SPORTS
(www.rolexsydneyhobart.com; ⊙ Dec) Maxiyachts competing in the world's most gruelling open-ocean race start arriving in Hobart

Central Hobart

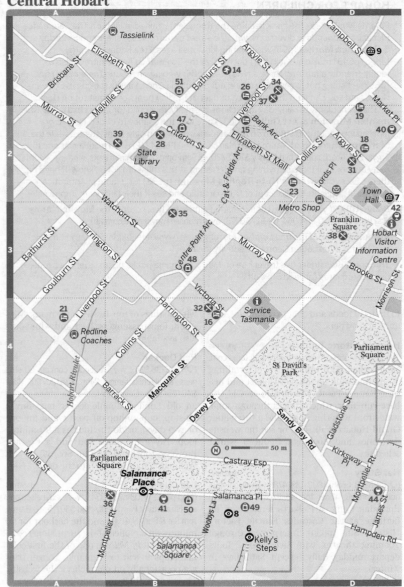

around 29 December – just in time for New Year's Eve! (Yachties sure can party...)

★ **Taste of Tasmania** FOOD & DRINK
(www.thetasteoftasmania.com.au; ☺ Dec-Jan) On either side of New Year's Eve, this week-long harbourside event is a celebration of Tassie's gastronomic prowess. The seafood, wines and cheeses are predictably fab, or branch out into mushrooms, truffles, raspberries... Stalls are a who's who of the Hobart restaurant scene. Live music, too. Just brilliant.

have included John Cale, Ava Mendoza and Nick Cave. Stirring stuff.

Hobart BeerFest BEER
(www.hobart.beerfestivals.com.au; ⊙ Jan) More than 200 brews from around Australia and the world, with brewing classes and lots of opportunities for waterfront snacking, foot tapping and imbibing.

**Australian Wooden
Boat Festival** CULTURAL
(www.australianwoodenboatfestival.com.au; ⊙ Feb) Biennial event (odd-numbered years) to co-incide with the Royal Hobart Regatta. The festival showcases Tasmania's boat-building heritage and maritime traditions.

Ten Days on the Island CULTURAL, ART
(www.tendays.org.au; ⊙ Mar) Tasmania's pre-mier cultural festival is a biennial event (odd-numbered years) celebrating Tasma-nian arts, music and culture at state-wide venues. Expect concerts, exhibitions, dance, film, theatre and workshops.

★**Dark MOFO** ART, MUSIC
(www.darkmofo.net.au) The sinister sister of MONA FOMA, Dark MOFO broods in the half-light of June's winter solstice. Expect to find live music, installations, readings, film noir, bonfires, red wine and midnight feasts, all mainlining Tasmania's gothic blood flow.

Falls Festival MUSIC
(www.fallsfestival.com.au; ⊙ 29 Dec-1 Jan) The Tasmanian version of the Victorian rock festival is a winner! Three nights and four days of live Oz and international tunes (Paul Kelly, Dan Sultan, Cold War Kids, Alt J) at Marion Bay, an hour east of Hobart.

🛏 Sleeping

🛏 Central Hobart

★**Alabama Hotel** HOTEL $
(Map p642; ☏ 0499 987 698; www.alabama hobart.com.au; L1, 72 Liverpool St; d/tw from $85/90; 🖥) Sweet home Alabama! This old art deco boozer – once a grim, sticky-carpet lush magnet – has been reborn as a bou-tique budget hotel. None of the 17 rooms has a bathroom, but the shared facilities are immaculate and plentiful. Decor is funky and colourful with retro-deco flourishes, and there's an all-day bar with a sunny bal-cony over the street.

MONA FOMA ART, MUSIC
(MOFO; www.mofo.net.au; ⊙ Jan) Acronyms ahoy! On the grounds of MONA, the won-derfully eclectic Festival of Music & Arts features a high-profile 'Eminent Artist in Residence' (EAR) every year. Previous EARs

Central Hobart

Nook HOSTEL $
(Map p642; ☑ 03-6135 4044; www.thenookback
packers.com.au; 251 Liverpool St; dm $24-30, s/d
from $50/75; P ☎) It's less of a nook, more
of a reconfigured old pub...but the Nook is
doing things right hostel-wise. Fourteen tidy
rooms extend above a sociable open-plan
kitchen space, with a neat BBQ deck area
out the back. A busy cleaning crew works
hard in the bathrooms: the vibe is, 'We spent
a lot on this place – don't mess it up!'

Tassie Backpackers HOSTEL $
(Map p642; ☑ 03-6234 4981, 0457 120 713; www.
brunswickhotelhobart.com.au; 67 Liverpool St;
dm from $29, d without bathroom from $114, d/tr
from $155/175; ✴☎) Upstairs at the vener-
able **Brunswick Hotel** (⊙11am-late) is one
of Hobart's better backpackers, with plenty

of shared spaces, a kitchen and a laundry.
Management also runs the pub downstairs.

Hobart Central YHA HOSTEL $
(Map p642; ☑ 03-6231 2660; www.yha.com.au; 9
Argyle St; dm from $31, d & tw with/without bath-
room from $143/123, f from $148; ☎) Attached
to a historic pub, this simple but clean YHA
offers bright, secure accommodation right in
the middle of town. Spread over three maze-
like levels are dorms of all sizes, including
nifty en suite rooms and family-sized rooms.
No parking, but you're walking distance
from everything here.

★ Astor Private Hotel HOTEL $$
(Map p642; ☑ 03-6234 6611; www.astorprivate
hotel.com.au; 157 Macquarie St; s/d with shared
bathroom from $89/110, d from $149, all incl

breakfast; 🛜) A rambling downtown 1920s charmer, the Astor retains much of its character: stained-glass windows, old furniture, lofty ceilings (with ceiling roses) and the irrepressible Tildy at the helm. Older-style rooms have shared facilities, which are plentiful, while the more recently refurbished rooms are en suite.

★ Old Woolstore
Apartment Hotel HOTEL $$
(Map p642; 📞1800 814 676, 03-6235 5355; www.oldwoolstore.com.au; 1 Macquarie St; d from $170, 1-/2-bedroom apt from $210/290; 🅿🛜) Oodles of parking and superfriendly staff are the first things you'll notice at this large, lavish hotel-apartment complex in a once-seedy area of Hobart known as Wapping in colonial times. You won't notice much wool lying around – it hasn't been a wool store for 100 years. Roomy apartments have kitchens and laundry facilities.

Quest Savoy
HOTEL $$
(Map p642; 📞03-6220 2300; www.questapartments.com.au; 38 Elizabeth St; d from $140, 1-/2-bedroom apt from $145/325; 🅿🛜) In a noble converted sandstone bank, the savvy Savoy offers 31 super-duper modern studios – all with kitchenettes and living-dining areas – smack bang in the middle of downtown Hobart. If you're travel weary, there's a day spa downstairs, with a pool and sundry rub and scrub treatments. Parking is off-site.

Mantra Collins Hotel
HOTEL $$$
(Map p642; 📞03-6226 1111; www.mantra.com.au; 58 Collins St; d from $250, 1-/2-bedroom apt from $290/540; 🛜) One of Hobart's newest hotels effortlessly shows up other places around town as a little old and weary. A youthful energy at reception flows through all 10 floors of spacious rooms and apartments, some with super views of Mt Wellington's gargantuan bulk. There's also a relaxed cafe-bar downstairs. No parking is the only drawback.

🛏 Salamanca Place & the Waterfront

★ Henry Jones Art Hotel
BOUTIQUE HOTEL $$$
(Map p642; 📞03-6210 7700; www.thehenryjones.com; 25 Hunter St; d from $340; 🅿🛜) Super-swish HJs is a beacon of sophistication. In the restored waterfront Henry Jones IXL jam factory, with remnant bits of jam-making machinery and huge timber beams, it oozes class but is far from snooty (this is Hobart, not Sydney). Modern art enlivens the walls, while facilities and distractions (bar, restaurant, cafe) are world class.

Somerset on the Pier
APARTMENT $$$
(Map p642; 📞1800 766 377, 03-6220 6600; www.somerset.com; Elizabeth St Pier; 1-/2-bedroom apt from $275/390; 🅿🛜) In a definitively Hobart location, on the upper level of the Elizabeth St Pier, this cool complex offers luxe apartments with beaut harbour views and breezy, contemporary design. You'll pay more for a balcony, but with these views you won't need to do any other sightseeing! Limited parking.

Salamanca Wharf Hotel
APARTMENT $$$
(Map p642; 📞03-6224 7007; www.salamancawharfhotel.com; 17a Castray Esplanade, Battery Point; r from $295; 🅿🛜) Filling a slender gap between historic sandstone ordnance stores just east of Salamanca Place, these 22 slick new one-bedroom apartments offer nifty kitchens, cool art, affable staff and an unbeatable location. Units at the front have balconies; those at the back have baths (take your pick). Cool cafe downstairs.

🛏 Battery Point, Sandy Bay & South Hobart

★ Montacute
HOSTEL $
(Map p642; 📞03-6212 0474; www.montacute.com.au; 1 Stowell Ave, Battery Point; dm/tw/d from $39/90/110; 🅿🛜) Many Hobart hostels are cheap remodellings of old pubs, but Montacute – a renovated house in Battery Point – sets the bar a mile higher, with immaculate rooms and shared bathrooms, nice art, quality linen and mattresses, a lovely lounge with open fire, bikes for guests, proximity to cafes, and gorgeous young internationalists swanning about the kitchen. Nice one!

★ Quayle Terrace
RENTAL HOUSE $$
(Map p638; 📞0418 395 543; www.quayleterrace.com.au; 51 Quayle St, Battery Point; d $225-250, extra person $20; 🅿🛜) Tracing the boundary between Battery Point and Sandy Bay, Quayle St features a long run of photogenic terrace houses (ignore the power lines and this could be 1900). Quayle Terrace is one such edifice – a two-storey, two-bedroom, tastefully renovated house with a cosy gas fire and mountain views from the shower. Free street parking; minimum three-night stay.

TASMANIA HOBART

St Ives Motel

MOTEL **$$**

(Map p638; ☑03-6221 5555; www.stivesmotel.
com.au; 67 St Georges Tce, Battery Point; d from
$185, 2-bedroom units from $260; P❄🐾🛜) Within
walking distance of Battery Point, Salamanca
and the city is this excellent option – a cur-
valicious '80s building with dozens of rooms,
all with kitchens. A recent flash makeover
has introduced the property to the 21st cen-
tury – pleased to meet you. Good last-minute
deals online; free parking and wi-fi.

★ Grande Vue Private Hotel

B&B **$$$**

(Map p638; ☑03-6223 8216; www.grande-vue-
hotel.com; 8 Mona St, Battery Point; 1-/2-bedroom
units from $225/350; P🐾🛜) 'Vues' from the best
rooms at this restored 1906 mansion take in
a broad sweep of Sandy Bay and the Derwent
River, or Mt Wellington in the other direction. Sleek new bathrooms, kitchenettes and
super-friendly service lift Grande Vue to the
top of the Battery Point B&B pile. Breakfast
(fresh muffins!) costs a very reasonable $15.

★ Islington

BOUTIQUE HOTEL **$$$**

(Map p638; ☑03-6220 2123; www.islingtonhotel.
com; 321 Davey St, South Hobart; d from $475;
P❄🐾🛜) At the top of Hobart's accommoda-
tion tree, classy Islington effortlessly merges
heritage architecture with antique furniture,
contemporary art and a glorious garden.
Service is attentive but understated, with
breakfast served in an expansive conserva-
tory. In the evening, wind down with a wine
in the guest library, music room or drawing
room. Exquisite private dinners also availa-
ble. No children under 15 years.

🛏 MONA & Northern Hobart

Altamont House

APARTMENT **$$**

(Map p638; ☑0427 842 140; www.airbnb.com.au/
rooms/5353814; 109 Patrick St, West Hobart; d $200,
extra adult/child $50/30; P❄🐾🛜) Are there rules
about how steep a street can be? The town
planners weren't paying attention when they
laid out Patrick St...but the views are great!
Occupying the ground floor of a gorgeous old
stone-and-slate house (1854), Altamont offers
a plush double suite with an extra room that
can be opened up as required.

Corinda's Cottages

B&B, COTTAGE **$$$**

(Map p638; ☑03-6234 1590; www.corindas
cottages.com.au; 17 Glebe St, Glebe; d incl breakfast
from $265; P🛜) Gorgeous Corinda, a reno-
vated Victorian mansion with meticulously
maintained parterre gardens, sits high on
the sunny Glebe hillside a short (steep!) walk

from town. Three self-contained cottages
(garden, coach house or servants' quarters)
provide contemporary comforts with none of
the twee, old-world guff in which too many
Tasmanian B&Bs wallow. Breakfast is DIY
gourmet (eggs, muffins, fresh coffee etc).

🍴 Eating

🍴 Central Hobart

★ Farm Gate Market

MARKET **$**

(Map p642; ☑03-6234 5625; www.farmgatemarket.
com.au; Bathurst St, btwn Elizabeth & Murray Sts;
⊙8.30am-1pm Sun) The waterfront Salamanca
Market has dominated for decades, but this
hyperactive foodie street-mart is giving it a
run for its money. Trading commences with
the ding of a big brass bell: elbow your way
in for the best fruit, veg, honey, wine, baked
goods, beer, smoked meats, coffee, cheese,
nuts, oils, cut flowers, jams... Terrific!

At the time of writing, a new Friday night
street-food market run by the Farm Gate folks
had just opened in Franklin Sq in the city,
called **Street Eats @ Franko** (Map p642; ☑03-
6234 5625; www.streeteatsfranko.com.au; Franklin
Sq, 70 Macquarie St, Hobart; ⊙5-9pm Fri).

★ Bury Me Standing

CAFE **$**

(Map p642; ☑0424 365 027; www.facebook.
com/burymestandinghobarttown; 104 Bathurst St;
bagels $5-10; ⊙6am-2.30pm Mon-Fri, 7am-2.30pm
Sat, coffee only 7am-1pm Sun) Run by a chipper
Minnesotan who ended up in Hobart acci-
dentally, this little coffee-and-bagel joint
is literally a hole in the wall of a car park.
Bagels are pot-boiled (a traditional method
ensuring a sticky outer and chewy inner) –
don't go past the Reuben version. Couple
of milk crates and dinky tables, and Dylan
piped through little speakers. Brilliant.

R Takagi Sushi

JAPANESE **$**

(Map p642; ☑03-6234 8524; 132 Liverpool St;
sushi from $4; ⊙10.30am-5.30pm Mon-Fri, to 4pm
Sat, 11.30am-3pm Sun) Hobart's best sushi spot
– a favourite of Hobart desk jockeys – makes
the most of Tasmania's great seafood. Udon
noodles and miso also make an appearance.
Gorgeous packaging to boot.

★ Templo

ITALIAN **$$**

(Map p638; ☑03-6234 7659; www.templo.com.au;
98 Patrick St; mains $24-32; ⊙noon-3pm & 6pm-
late Thu-Mon) Unpretentious little Templo, on a
nondescript reach of Patrick St, has assumed
the mantle of Hobart's 'must-do' restaurant.

With only about 20 seats (bookings essential), and only three or four Italian-inspired mains to choose from, Templo is an exercise in selectivity and sharing (your personal space, and your food). Survey the pricey-but-memorable wine list at the cute bar.

★**Pilgrim Coffee** CAFE **$$**

(Map p642; ✆03-6234 1999; www.pilgrimcoffee. com; 48 Argyle St; mains $15-20; ☻6.30am-4.30pm Mon-Fri, 8am-2pm Sat & Sun) With exposed bricks, timber beams and distressed walls, L-shaped Pilgrim is Hobart's hippest cafe. Expect wraps, panini and interesting mains – Bolivian breakfast bowl! – plus expertly prepared coffee. Fall into conversation with the locals at big shared tables. Down a laneway around the back is the **Standard** (Map p642; www.standard-burgers. com; Hudsons La, Hobart; burgers $7-12; ☻11am-10pm), a burger nook run by the same tattooed hipsters.

Urban Greek GREEK **$$**

(Map p642; ✆03-6109 4712; www.facebook.com/ urbangreek; 103 Murray St; small plates $12-19, large plates $26-35; ☻5-10pm Tue-Sun) Fancy Mediterranean offerings in a former garage, fitted out with bent copper lighting conduits, a timber bar, polished concrete floors and an intimidating Minotaur etched into the copper-plate wall. Expect generous Greek classics done to perfection (moussaka, saganaki, charcoal-grilled octopus), plus imported Greek beers and wines.

Franklin MODERN AUSTRALIAN **$$$**

(Map p642; ✆03-6234 3375; www.franklinhobart. com.au; 30 Argyle St; mains $19-41; ☻8.30am-late Tue-Sat) In a lofty industrial space (the former *Hobart Mercury* newspaper printing room – the papers would roll straight out the front window), Franklin is all concrete, steel beams, cowhide and curtains. Ignore the cheesy Eric Clapton soundtrack and have a drink at the bar, or settle in for a creative mod Oz meal cooked in the central kitchen.

✖ Salamanca Place & the Waterfront

★**Flippers** FISH & CHIPS **$**

(Map p642; ✆03-6234 3101; www.flippersfishand chips.com.au; Constitution Dock; meals $10-28; ☻9.30am-8.30pm) There are quite a few floating fish punts moored in Constitution Dock, selling fresh-caught seafood either uncooked or cooked. Our pick is Flippers, an enduring

favourite with a voluptuous fish-shaped profile. Fillets of flathead and curls of calamari – straight from the deep blue sea and into the deep fryer. The local seagulls will adore you.

★**Retro Cafe** CAFE **$**

(Map p642; ✆03-6223 3073; 31 Salamanca Pl; mains $11-17; ☻7.30am-6pm Mon-Fri, 8am-4pm Sat & Sun) So popular it hurts, funky Retro is ground zero for Saturday brunch among the market stalls (or any day, really). Masterful breakfasts, bagels, salads and burgers interweave with laughing staff, chilled-out jazz and the whirr and bang of the coffee machine. A classic Hobart cafe.

Fish Frenzy SEAFOOD **$$**

(Map p642; ✆03-6231 2134; www.fishfrenzy.com. au; Elizabeth St Pier; mains $15-35; ☻11am-9pm; ⊕🍴) A casual, waterside fish nook, overflowing with fish fiends and brimming with fish and chips, fishy salads (warm octopus with yoghurt dressing) and fish burgers. The eponymous 'Fish Frenzy' ($21) delivers a little bit of everything. Quality can be inconsistent, but good staff and buzzy harbourside vibes compensate. No bookings.

★**Aloft** MODERN AUSTRALIAN **$$$**

(Map p642; ✆03-6223 1619; www.aloftrestaurant. com; Brook St Pier; mains $34-35, Fri set lunch $30, banquets from $70; ☻6pm-late Tue-Sat) Staking a bold claim as Hobart's top restaurant, Aloft occupies a lofty eyrie in the floating Brook Street Pier. Menu hits include the likes of yellow fish curry with beetroot and fennel, and steamed oysters with fermented chilli. If you can drag your gaze away from the view, service and presentation are both excellent, in an unpretentious Hobart kinda way.

✖ Battery Point, Sandy Bay & South Hobart

★**Jackman & McRoss** BAKERY **$**

(Map p642; ✆03-6223 3186; 57-59 Hampden Rd, Battery Point; items $4-14; ☻7am-5pm Mon-Sat) Make sure you stop by this neighbourhood bakery-cafe, even if it's just to gawk at the display cabinet full of delectable pies, tarts, baguettes and pastries. Early-morning cake and coffee may evolve into a quiche for lunch, or perhaps a duck, cranberry and walnut sausage roll. Staff stay cheery despite being run off their feet. The city **branch** (Map p642; ✆03-6231 0601; 4 Victoria St, Hobart; items $4-14; ☻7am-4.30pm Mon-Fri) has parallel prices.

★ **Ginger Brown** CAFE $
(☑03-6223 3531; 464 Macquarie St, South Hobart; mains $10-20; ☺7.30am-4pm Mon-Fri, 8.30am-4pm Sat & Sun; ☑⛑) When a food business is this well run, the mood infects the entire room: happy staff, happy customers and happy vibes. Try the slow-cooked lamb panini with cornichons and hummus, or the signature kimchi pancake. Very kid- and cyclist-friendly, and the coffee is the best in South Hobart. Last orders 3pm.

Don Camillo ITALIAN $$$
(Map p638; ☑03-6234 1006; www.doncamillo restaurant.com; 5 Magnet Ct, Sandy Bay; mains $25-36; ☺6-9pm Tue-Sat) Just about the oldest restaurant in Hobart, little Don Camillo has been here forever and is still turning out a tight menu of classic Italian pastas, risottos and meat dishes (try the house-made ravioli). Look for the red Vespa parked out the front.

MONA & Northern Hobart

★ **Burger Haus** BURGERS $
(Map p638; ☑03-6234 9507; www.theburgerhaus. com.au; 364a Elizabeth St, North Hobart; mains $10-16; ☺11.30am-10pm) Blaring 1980s rock and boasting big beefy burgers and a little terrace on which to sit, chew and contemplate the moody hues of Mt Wellington...this place has got it all! The Haus Burger (with bacon, onion rings, caramelised pineapple and mustard mayo) reigns supreme.

★ **Pigeon Hole** CAFE $$
(Map p638; ☑03-6236 9306; www.pigeonhole cafe.com.au; 93 Goulburn St, West Hobart; mains $14-24; ☺7.30am-4.30pm Mon-Sat) This compact, friendly cafe is the kind of place every inner-city neighbourhood should have. A serious coffee attitude comes together with paddock-to-plate cafe food that's definitely a cut above. The freshly baked panini are the best you'll have, while the eggs *en cocotte* (baked eggs) with serrano ham is an absolute knockout.

Pancho Villa MEXICAN $$
(Map p638; ☑03-6234 4161; www.panchovilla. com.au; cnr Elizabeth & Pitt Sts, North Hobart; items $7-15; ☺5.30pm-late Mon-Wed, 11.30am-3.30pm & 5.30pm-late Thu-Sun) Cool renovation! A dour redbrick bank has become a super-moody tequila bar and restaurant (Day of the Dead skulls, pressed metal lanterns), where you order selections from the menu – creative tacos, enchiladas, quesadillas and corn and bean dishes – and knock them back with the aforementioned white spirit. 'Pancho Sundays' consume the courtyard: $5 tacos and tequila shots; $30 cocktail jugs (forget about work tomorrow...).

Annapurna INDIAN $$
(Map p638; ☑03-6236 9500; www.annapurna indiancuisine.com; 305 Elizabeth St, North Hobart; mains $16-18, banquets $22-32; ☺noon-3pm & 5-10pm Mon-Fri, 5-10pm Sat & Sun; ☑) It seems like half of Hobart lists Annapurna as their favourite eatery (you'd better book). Northern and southern Indian options are served with absolute proficiency: the *masala dosa* (south Indian crepe filled with curried potato) is a crowd favourite. Takeaways, too. Hard to top.

Roaring Grill STEAK $$$
(Map p638; ☑03-6231 1301; www.roaringgrill. com; 301 Elizabeth St, North Hobart; mains $27-35; ☺5pm-late Mon & Tue, noon-late Wed-Sun) Named for the 'Roaring 40s' winds that sweep across these southern latitudes, sassy Roaring Grill plates up the best Tasmanian fish and meat. It's a stylish split-level fit-out – exposed brickwork, dark wood tables and globular glassware – a far remove from the old foam mattress shop that was here for as long as anyone can remember.

🍸 Drinking & Nightlife

🍷 Central Hobart

★ **New Sydney Hotel** PUB
(Map p642; ☑03-6234 4516; www.newsydney hotel.com.au; 87 Bathurst St; ☺noon-10pm Mon, to midnight Tue-Sat, 4-9pm Sun) This low-key city pub is the best boozer in the CBD, with open fires, creative pub food (think duck tongue tortilla; mains $14 to $35) and a terrific 15-tap beer selection, including an ever-changing array of island craft beers (try the Seven Sheds Paradise Pale). Irish jam session 2pm Saturdays, if you're lucky.

Hope & Anchor PUB
(Map p642; ☑03-6236 9982; www.hopeandanchor. com.au; 65 Macquarie St; ☺11.30am-late) Depending on who you believe (don't listen to the barman at the Fortune of War in Sydney), this is the oldest continually licensed pub in Australia (1807). The interior is festooned with nautical knick-knacks (duck up the stairs to see the museum-like dining room). Not a bad spot for a cold Cascade or three.

Salamanca Place & the Waterfront

★ **Jack Greene** BAR
(Map p642; ☑ 03-6224 9655; www.jackgreene.
com.au; 49 Salamanca Pl; ⊙11.30am-late) The
gourmet burgers here nudge $20, but at-
mospheric Jack Greene (a European hunting lodge on the run?) is worthwhile if you're
a wandering beer fan. Glowing racks of bottled brews fill the fridges, and there are at
least 16 beers on tap from around Australia
and New Zealand. Occasional acoustic troubadours perch next to the stairs.

Hobart Brewing Company CRAFT BEER
(Map p638; ☑ 03-6231 9779; www.hobartbrewing
co.com.au; 16 Evans St; ⊙4-10pm Thu, to 11pm Fri,
2-11pm Sat, 11am-6pm Sun) In a big red shed on
Macquarie Point, fronted by the multivalent
Red Square community space, Hobart Brewing Company has been doing good things
with beer. There are plenty of creative brews
on tap (try the St Christopher cream ale, or
a $10 tasting paddle)...plus there's live music
most weekends and laughing staff.

Glass House COCKTAIL BAR
(Map p642; ☑ 0437 245 540; www.theglass.house;
Brooke St Pier; ⊙noon-10pm Mon & Tue, to midnight Wed-Sun) The very fancy Glass House
sits in the prow of the floating Brooke
Street Pier, a huge window-wall affording
uninterrupted views down the Derwent
River estuary. Put on your best duds, order
a Hobartian Sidecar and soak it all in. Fab
bar food, too (small plates $18 to $30). Is
Charlie, the quintessential Hobart barman,
working tonight?

Lark Distillery DISTILLERY
(Map p642; ☑ 03-6231 9088; www.larkdistillery.
com; 14 Davey St; ⊙10.30am-7pm Thu-Sun,
10.30am-late Fri & Sat) Lark Distillery was
a trailblazer in Tasmania's surge into the
world of single malt whisky. Stop by for a
drink, a tasting session ($20), or a two-hour
tour of the distillery ($75), a 20-minute drive
from the cellar door. Order a cheese board,
work your way along the whisky wall, or sip
a Moo Brew if you'd prefer.

T-42° BAR
(Map p642; ☑ 03-6224 7742; www.tav42.com.
au; Elizabeth St Pier; ⊙7.30am-late) Stylish
waterfront T-42° makes a big splash with
its food (mains $19 to $35), but also draws
well-dressed, late-week barflies with its minimalist interior, spinnaker-shaped bar and
ambient tunes. If you stay out late enough,
breakfast offers redemption from any nocturnal misdemeanours.

Battery Point, Sandy Bay & South Hobart

Shipwright's Arms Hotel PUB
(Map p638; ☑ 03-6223 5551; www.shipwrightsarms.
com.au; 29 Trumpeter St, Battery Point; ☎) Backstreet 'Shippies' is one of the best old pubs
in town. Soak yourself in maritime heritage
(and other liquids) at the bar, then retire to
your clean, above-board berth upstairs or
in the newer en-suited wing (doubles with/
without bathroom $150/90). Other bonuses
include pub meals and the delight in saying
you're having a drink on Trumpeter St.

Preachers BAR
(Map p642; ☑ 03-6223 3621; www.facebook.com/
preachershobart; 5 Knopwood St, Battery Point;
⊙noon-late) Grab a retro sofa seat inside this
1849 sailmaker's cottage, or adjourn to the
ramshackle garden bar – in which an old
Hobart bus is now full of beer booths – with
the hipsters. Lots of Tasmanian craft beers
on tap, plus cool staff and a resident ghost!
A steady flow of burgers and tapas keeps the
beer in check.

MONA & Northern Hobart

★ **Winston** PUB
(Map p638; ☑ 03-6231 2299; www.thewinston
bar.com; 381 Elizabeth St, North Hobart; ⊙4pm-
late) The grim old art deco Eaglehawk pub
has been transformed into the Winston, a
hipster-driven, US-style craft-beer alehouse.

TASMANIA HOBART

DON'T MISS

FRIDAY NIGHT FANDANGO

Some of Hobart's best live tunes get an
airing every Friday night at the **Salamanca Arts Centre Courtyard** (Map
p642; www.salarts.org.au/rektango; 77
Salamanca Pl; ⊙5.30-7.30pm Fri), just
off Woobys Lane. It's a free community
event that started in about 2000, with
the adopted name 'Rektango', borrowed
from a band that sometimes graces the
stage. Acts vary from month to month –
expect anything from African beats to
rockabilly, folk and gypsy-Latino. Drinks
essential (sangria in summer, mulled
wine in winter); dancing near-essential.

Grab a pint of the house stout from one of the beardy guys behind the bar and check out the wall of US registration plates near the pool table. Calorific bar food and live music, too.

★ **Shambles Brewery**   CRAFT BEER
(Map p638; ☑ 03-6289 5639; www.shambles brewery.com.au; 222 Elizabeth St, North Hobart; ☺ noon-late Wed-Sun) Excellent new brew-stuff just south of the NoHo strip, with minimalist interiors, concrete block bar and chunky Tasmanian oak tables. Tasting paddles are $12, or refill your 'growler' (1.9L bottle) to take home and savour. Terrific beery bar food, too: burgers, ribs, steak sandwiches and the like. Try the 'Dirty Copper' amber ale.

Willing Bros   WINE BAR
(Map p638; ☑ 03-6234 3053; www.facebook.com/willingbros; 390 Elizabeth St, North Hobart; ☺ 3pm-late Tue-Sun) Hey – a classy wine bar! Just what NoHo ordered. Pull up a window seat at the front of the skinny room and sip something hip from the tightly edited menu of reds, whites and bubbles. Food drifts from Moroccan fish cakes to spicy lamb *empanadas* – perfect fodder for a post-movie debrief.

☆ Entertainment

★ **Republic Bar & Café**   LIVE MUSIC
(Map p638; ☑ 03-6234 6954; www.republicbar.com; 299 Elizabeth St, North Hobart; ☺ 11am-late; ☎) The Republic is a raucous art deco pub hosting live music every night (often free entry). It's the number-one live-music pub around town, with an always-interesting line-up, including international acts. Loads of different beers and excellent food (mains $24 to $36; try the Jack Daniels–marinated scotch fillet!).

★ **State Cinema**   CINEMA
(Map p638; ☑ 03-6234 6318; www.statecinema.com.au; 375 Elizabeth St, North Hobart; ☺ 10am-late Mon-Fri, 9.30am-late Sat & Sun) Saved from the wrecking ball in the 1990s, the multiscreen State (built in 1913) shows independent and art-house flicks from local and international film-makers. There's a great cafe and bar on-site, plus a rooftop screen, a browse-worthy **bookshop** (☺ 10am-5pm Sun-Thu, 10am-late Fri & Sat) and the foodie temptations of North Hobart's restaurants right outside.

Theatre Royal   THEATRE
(Map p642; ☑ 03-6233 2299, 1800 650 277; www.theatreroyal.com.au; 29 Campbell St; ☺ box office 9am-5pm Mon-Fri) This venerable old stager

is Australia's oldest continuously operating theatre, with actors first cracking the boards here back in 1837 (the foundation stone says 1834, but it took them a few years to finish it). Expect a range of music, ballet, theatre, opera and university revues. Guided **tours** (1hr tour adult/child $15/10; ☺ tours 11am Mon, Wed & Fri) available.

Blundstone Arena   SPECTATOR SPORT
(Bellerive Oval; ☑ tickets 13 28 49, tours 03-6282 0433; www.blundstonearena.com.au; 15 Derwent St, Bellerive) Hobart's home of cricket and football is across the Derwent River from the city in Bellerive. The North Melbourne Kangaroos AFL football club (www.afl.com.au) plays three home games here a year, while cricket matches also pull good crowds. Guided arena tours (adult/child $10/2) run at 10am on Tuesdays. The **Tasmanian Cricket Museum** (adult/child $2/1, tours $10/2; ☺ 10am-3pm Tue-Thu, to noon Fri) is here, too.

Jokers Comedy Club   COMEDY
(Map p638; ☑ 0409 547 474; www.jokerscomedy.com.au; Polish Corner, cnr Elizabeth St & Augusta Rd, North Hobart; ☺ shows at 8pm Wed, bar from 6pm) Live weekly stand-up comedy at Hobart's Polish Club, just north of the main North Hobart strip. Cheap drinks and big laughs from Australian and overseas comics.

Federation Concert Hall   CLASSICAL MUSIC
(Map p642; ☑ 1800 001 190; www.tso.com.au; 1 Davey St; ☺ box office 10am-4pm Mon-Fri) Welded to the Hotel Grand Chancellor, this concert hall resembles a huge aluminium can leaking insulation from gaps in the panelling. Inside, the Tasmanian Symphony Orchestra does what it does best.

🛍 Shopping

★ **Fullers Bookshop**   BOOKS
(Map p642; ☑ 03-6234 3800; www.fullersbookshop.com.au; 131 Collins St; ☺ 8.30am-6pm Mon-Fri, 9am-5pm Sat, 10am-4pm Sun) Hobart's best bookshop has a great range of literature and travel guides, plus regular launches and readings, and the writerly **Afterword Cafe** in the corner. A real hub of the Hobart literary scene for around 70 years.

★ **Handmark Gallery**   ART
(Map p642; ☑ 03-6223 7895; www.handmark.com.au; 77 Salamanca Pl; ☺ 10am-5pm) A key tenant at the **Salamanca Arts Centre** (SAC; Map p642; ☑ 03-6234 8414; www.salarts.org.au; ☺ shops & galleries 9am-5pm), Handmark has been here for 30 years, displaying unique

ceramics, glass, woodwork and jewellery, plus paintings and sculpture – 100% Tasmanian.

Cool Wine WINE
(Map p642; ☑ 03-6231 4000; www.coolwine.com. au; shop 8, MidCity Arcade, Criterion St; ☺ 9.30am-6.30pm Mon-Sat) Excellent selection of Tasmanian wine, spirits and craft beers (plus a few global interlopers, if they're up to scratch). Open Sunday by appointment.

Hobart Twilight Market MARKET
(HTM; ☑ 0448 997 748; www.facebook.com/hobarttwilightmarket; Beach Rd, Lower Sandy Bay; ☺ 4-8.30pm Fri Sep-Mar) Filling the lawns behind Lower Sandy Bay Beach (aka Long Beach; about 5km south of central Hobart), the HTM is a relatively new and hugely popular phenomenon. The official line goes, 'eats, drinks, artisans, music' – add to that valet bike parking and heaps of dogs, and you get the picture. At Macquarie Pt near the waterfront every second week.

ℹ Information

EMERGENCY
Hobart Police Station (☑ 03-6230 2111, non-emergency assistance 13 14 44; www.police. tas.gov.au; 43 Liverpool St; ☺ 24hr) Hobart's main cop shop.

INTERNET ACCESS
State Library of Tasmania (☑ 03-6165 5597; www.linc.tas.gov.au; 91 Murray St; ☺ 9.30am-6pm Mon-Thu, to 8pm Fri, to 2pm Sat) Free pre-booked internet terminals.

MEDICAL SERVICES
Australian Dental Association Emergency Service (☑ 03-6248 1546; www.ada.org.au) Advice for dental emergencies.
My Chemist Salamanca (☑ 03-6224 9994; www.mychemist.com.au; 6 Montpelier Retreat; ☺ 8.30am-6pm Mon-Fri, to 5pm Sat, 10am-4pm Sun) Handy chemist just off Salamanca Place.
Royal Hobart Hospital (☑ 03-6222 8423; www.dhhs.tas.gov.au; 48 Liverpool St; ☺ 24hr) Accident and emergency, running round the clock.
Salamanca Medical Centre (☑ 03-6223 8181; www.doctors-4u.com/hobart/areas.htm; 5a Gladstone St; ☺ 8.30am-4pm Mon-Fri, 10am-3pm Sat, 10am-1pm Sun) General medical appointments, just off Salamanca Place.

MONEY
The major banks all have branches and ATMs around Elizabeth St Mall. There are also ATMs around Salamanca Place.

> **DON'T MISS**
>
> ## SALAMANCA MARKET
>
> Every Saturday morning since 1972, the open-air **Salamanca Market** (Map p642; ☑ 03-6238 2843; www.salamanca. com.au; Salamanca Pl; ☺ 8am-3pm Sat) has lured hippies and craft merchants from the foothills to fill the tree-lined expanses of Salamanca Place with their stalls. Fresh organic produce, secondhand clothes and books, tacky tourist souvenirs, ceramics and woodwork, cheap sunglasses, antiques, exuberant buskers, quality food and drink... It's all here, but people-watching is the real name of the game. Rain or shine – don't miss it!

POST
General Post Office (GPO; Map p642; ☑ 03-6236 3575; www.auspost.com.au; cnr Elizabeth & Macquarie Sts; ☺ 8.30am-5.30pm Mon-Fri, 9am-12.30pm Sat) Forget about the mail... check out the heritage architecture! It was built in 1905 in lavish Edwardian Baroque style.

TOURIST INFORMATION
Hobart Visitor Information Centre (Map p642; ☑ 03-6238 4222; www.hobarttravel centre.com.au; cnr Davey & Elizabeth Sts; ☺ 9am-5pm) Information, maps and state-wide tour, transport and accommodation bookings.

ℹ Getting There & Away

AIR
In an irony that doesn't elude the locals, Hobart's 'international' **airport** (☑ 03-6216 1600; www.hobartairport.com.au; Strachan St, Cambridge) has only domestic flights (perhaps we should commend the optimism?), with services operated by Qantas (p634), Virgin Australia (p634), Jetstar (p634) and Tiger Air (p634). Direct flights arrive from Melbourne, Sydney, Brisbane and sometimes Canberra. The airport is at Cambridge, 19km east of the city.

BUS
In the absence of passenger trains, buses are the mainstay of public transport to/from Hobart. There are two main intrastate bus companies operating here, **Redline Coaches** (Map p642; ☑ 1300 360 000; www.redlinecoaches. com.au; 230 Liverpool St; ☺ 8am-6pm) and **Tassielink** (Map p642; ☑ 1300 300 520; www. tassielink.com.au; 64 Brisbane St), and both run state-wide routes. Check online for fares, routes, arrival/departure locations and timetables. Tassielink buses leave Hobart from 64

Brisbane St and a temporary stop on Elizabeth St, across the road from the Hobart visitor information centre (a permanent bus depot is being planned – call or check the website for updates).

ⓘ Getting Around

TO/FROM THE AIRPORT

There's no public transport to Hobart airport.

A taxi into the city will cost around $50 and take about 20 minutes.

Pre-booked **Hobart Airporter** (✆1300 385 511; www.airporterhobart.com.au; one-way adult/child $19/14, return $35/25) shuttle buses meet every flight and can deliver you door-to-door.

BUS

The local bus network is operated by **Metro Tasmania** (✆13 22 01; www.metrotas.com.au), which is reliable but infrequent outside of business hours. The **Metro Shop** (Map p642; ✆13 22 01; www.metrotas.com.au; 22 Elizabeth St; ⊗8am-6pm Mon-Fri, 9.30am-2pm Sat) handles ticketing and enquiries: most buses depart from this section of Elizabeth St, or from nearby Franklin Sq.

TAXI

Maxi-Taxi Services (✆13 32 22; www.hobartmaxitaxi.com.au) Wheelchair-accessible vehicles, and taxis for groups.

Yellow Cab Co (✆13 19 24; http://hobart.yellowcab.com.au) Standard cabs (not all of which are yellow).

AROUND HOBART

Richmond & Around

POP 1610

Straddling the Coal River 27km northeast of Hobart, Richmond was once a strategic military post and convict station on the road to Port Arthur. Riddled with 19th-century buildings, it's arguably Tasmania's premier historic town, but businesses here do tend to err on the 'kitsch colonial' side of tourism.

That said, Richmond is certainly a picturesque little town and the kids will love chasing the ducks around the riverbanks. It's also quite close to the airport – a happy overnight option if you're on an early flight.

⊙ Sights

Richmond Bridge   BRIDGE

(Wellington St, Richmond) This chunky (but not inelegant) bridge still funnels traffic across the Coal River and is the town's proud centrepiece. Built by convicts in 1823 (making it

the oldest road bridge in Australia), it's purportedly haunted by the 'Flagellator of Richmond', George Grover, who died here in 1832.

★ Sullivans Cove Whisky   DISTILLERY

(✆03-6248 5399; www.sullivanscove.com; 1/10 Lamb Pl, Cambridge; tour/tasting per adult $30/30, combined $40; ⊗10am-4pm Mon-Fri) It doesn't look much from the outside, but this tin shed near the turn-off to Richmond managed to produce the best single malt whisky in the world, as adjudged at the 2014 World Whiskies Awards. And now there are a dozen distillers around Tasmania... Tours run on the hour; bookings advised.

Bonorong Wildlife Centre   WILDLIFE RESERVE

(✆03-6268 1184; www.bonorong.com.au; 593 Briggs Rd, Brighton; adult/child/family $28/14/77; ⊗9am-5pm) 🐾 The name 'Bonorong' derives from an Aboriginal word meaning 'native companion' – look forward to seeing Tasmanian devils, koalas, wombats, echidnas and quolls at this impressive operation. The emphasis here is on conservation, education and the rehabilitation of injured animals. Night tours also available (adult/child from $157/83). The centre is about 17km west of Richmond: take Middle Tea Tree Rd, turn left into Tea Tree Rd after 11km, then left again onto Briggs Rd once you get to Brighton.

Richmond ZooDoo Zoo   ZOO

(✆03-6260 2444; www.zoodoo.com.au; 620 Middle Tea Tree Rd, Richmond; adult/child $25/13; ⊗9am-5pm) Six kilometres west of Richmond on the road to Brighton (Middle Tea Tree Rd), ZooDoo has 'safari bus' rides, playgrounds, picnic areas and half of Dr Dolittle's appointment book, including tigers, llamas, Tasmanian devils, wallabies and a particularly imperious peacock. Hungry white lions chow down at regularly scheduled intervals.

🛏 Sleeping & Eating

BIG4 Hobart Airport
Tourist Park   CARAVAN PARK $

(✆03-6248 4551; www.hobartairporttouristpark.com.au; 2 Flight St, Cambridge; powered sites from $35, cabins from $150; 🛜) Filling a long-vacant void in the Hobart tourism sector is this newish caravan park near Hobart Airport – big, clean and grassy with excellent cabins, and perfectly located if you've got an early flight.

★ Daisy Bank Cottages   B&B $$

(✆03-6260 2390; www.daisybankcottages.com.au; 78 Middle Tea Tree Rd, Richmond; d from $160, extra person $30; 🛜) A rural delight: two spotless,

COAL RIVER VALLEY WINE REGION

Richmond and nearby Cambridge are at the centre of Tasmania's fastest-growing wine region, the Coal River Valley. Some operations here are sophisticated affairs with gourmet restaurants; others are small, family-owned vineyards with cellar doors open by appointment. See www.winesouth.com.au for more info.

Overlooking the Mt Pleasant Observatory, 9km southwest of Richmond, **Frogmore Creek** (☑03-6274 5844; www.frogmorecreek.com.au; 699 Richmond Rd, Cambridge; ☺10am-5pm, restaurant noon-4.30pm) has a smart restaurant serving lunch, along with excellent chardonnay, pinot noir and sticky botrytis riesling. Don't miss *Flawed History*, an in-floor jigsaw by local artist Tom Samek. Restaurant bookings recommended (mains $17 to $25).

Puddleduck Vineyard (☑03-6260 2301; www.puddleduck.com.au; 992 Richmond Rd, Richmond; ☺10am-5pm) is a small, family-run vineyard producing just 1500 cases per year: shoot for the riesling, pinot noir or 'Bubbleduck' sparkling white. Snaffle a cheese or vineyard platter ($25 to $34), or fire up the BBQs (BYO meat) for lunch by the lake with Lucky the duck and Polly the wine dog.

stylish self-contained units (one with spa) in a converted 1840s sandstone barn on a working sheep farm. There are loft bedrooms, views of the Richmond rooftops and plenty of bucolic distractions for kids. The surrounding farmland has interpretative walks and soaring birds of prey. Breakfast stuff provided on your first morning. Hard to beat.

★ **Richmond Bakery** BAKERY $
(☑03-6260 2628; 50 Bridge St, off Edward St, Richmond; items $3-8; ☺7.30am-6pm) Come for takeaway pies, pastries, sandwiches, croissants, muffins and cakes, or munch on them in the courtyard. Their version of the Tasmanian classic curried scallop pie more than passes muster. If the main street is empty, chances are everyone is in here.

Coal River Farm BISTRO $$
(☑1300 455 215; www.coalriverfarm.com.au; 634 Richmond Rd, Cambridge; mains $19-27; ☺9am-5pm; ▣) A snappy piece of hillside architecture, Coal River Farm is a family-friendly spot to try some artisan cheese, chocolate or grab some breakfast or lunch in the bistro – perhaps some smoked wallaby with white bean mash and spicy tomato and capsicum sauce. You can also pick strawberries, feed the goats and collect eggs from the chooks.

ⓘ Getting There & Away

Tassielink (☑1300 300 520; www.tassielink.com.au) runs buses from Hobart to Richmond ($7.60, 45 minutes) multiple times daily from Monday to Saturday.

Richmond Tourist Bus (Hobart Shuttle Bus; ☑0408 341 804; www.hobartshuttlebus.com/richmond-village.html; adult/child return

$30/20; ☺9am & 12.15pm Sun-Fri) runs services from Hobart, with three hours to explore Richmond (unguided) before returning. Call for bookings and pick-up locations. Extensions to Richmond ZooDoo Zoo also available.

Mt Field National Park & Around

Mt Field, 80km northwest of Hobart and 7km beyond Westerway, was declared a national park in 1916. It is famed for its alpine moorlands, lakes, rainforest, impressive waterfalls, walks, skiing and rampant wildlife. It's an accessible day trip from Hobart, or you can bunk down overnight. Either way, things can get mighty chilly here – bring a woolly hat!

⊙ Sights

Russell Falls WATERFALL
(www.parks.tas.gov.au; off Lake Dobson Rd, Mt Field National Park; ☺daylight hours) Don't miss the magnificently tiered, 45m-high Russell Falls, an easy 20-minute return amble from behind the Mt Field National Park visitor info centre. The path is suitable for prams and wheelchairs. National park entry fees apply.

★ **Two Metre Tall** BREWERY
(☑03-6261 1930, 0400 969 677; www.2mt.com.au; 2862 Lyell Hwy, Hayes; ☺cellar door 11am-3pm Tue-Thu, farm bar 11am-6pm Fri & noon-5pm Sun) One of Tassie's best craft-beer breweries (where the brewer ain't short) is open for tastings, plus 'Farm Bar' sessions every Friday and Sunday afternoon, featuring hand-pumped ales and ciders, with BBQs available (BYO meat). Hops and barley are sourced from

Two Metre Tall's own farm in the Derwent Valley. You'll find the brewery 12km north-west of New Norfolk, en route to Hamilton.

Salmon Ponds
FARM

(☑ 03-6261 5663; www.salmonponds.com.au; 70 Salmon Ponds Rd, Plenty; adult/child/family $8/6/22; ⊙ 9am-5pm, restaurant 9am-4pm Nov-Apr, 10am-3pm May-Oct) In 1864 rainbow and brown trout were bred for the first time in the southern hemisphere at this hatchery, 9km west of New Norfolk at Plenty. You can feed the fish in the display ponds, visit the hatchery and check out the angling museum. The **restaurant** (mains $11 to $21) specialises in sweet and savoury crepes (try the smoked salmon and camembert) plus Tasmanian wines and serves decent coffee.

🏃 Activities

★ Tassie Bound
CANOEING

(☑ 0417 008 422; www.tassiebound.com.au; per adult/family incl lunch $135/400) Take a small-group two-hour downstream canoe paddle on a scenic, serene section of the Derwent River, with lunch on the riverbank. Pick-ups from New Norfolk. Friday twilight paddles with a visit to the Two Metre Tall brewery are also available (adult/family $150/300, pick-ups from Bushy Park); plus five-hour paddles through sections of river rapids ($150/550).

Agrarian Kitchen
COOKING

(☑ 03-6261 1099; www.theagrariankitchen.com; 650 Lachlan Rd, Lachlan; classes per person from $385) Located in a 19th-century schoolhouse in the Derwent Valley village of Lachlan, about 45-minutes' drive from Hobart, is Tasmania's first hands-on, farm-based cookery school. The surrounding 5 acres provide sustainable, organically grown vegetables, fruit, berries and herbs for the classes. Other ingredients are sourced from local farmers, fishers and artisan producers.

Mt Mawson
SKIING

(☑ 03-6288 1149; www.mtmawson.info; off Lake Dobson Rd, Mt Field National Park; skiing adult/child full day $30/15, half-day $20/10, ski tow deposit $10; ⊙ 10am-4pm Sat & Sun mid-Jul-mid-Sep) Skiing was first attempted here on Mt Mawson in 1922. A low-key resort with clubby huts and rope tows has evolved, and when nature sees fit to offload some snow (infrequently in recent years) it makes a relaxed change from the commercial ski fields on mainland Australia. Check the website for snow reports and cams.

🛏 Sleeping & Eating

★ Duffy's Country Accommodation
COTTAGE $$

(☑ 03-6288 1373; www.duffyscountry.com; 49 Clark's Rd, Westerway; d $130-145, extra adult/child $25/15; 🐾) Overlooking a field of raspberry canes at Westerway (8km east of Mt Field National Park) are these great-value, immaculate self-contained cottages: one studio-style cabin for couples, and one two-bedroom relocated rangers' hut from Mt Field National Park for families. There are also a couple of cute two-bed bunkhouses where you can file the teenagers. Breakfast provisions available. Wallabies are a distinct possibility.

Possum Shed
CAFE $$

(☑ 03-6288 1364; www.thepossumshed.com. au; 1654 Gordon River Rd, Westerway; items $6-22; ⊙ 10am-4pm Wed-Fri, to 9am-5pm Sat & Sun, daily Dec-Feb) At Westerway, en route to Mt Field about 30km from New Norfolk, you'll find this vivacious riverside haunt, with outdoor seating, a resident platypus (sightings are not guaranteed – you have to be really quiet) and lunches and snacks (salads, burgers, pancakes, muffins, BLTs) with locally sourced ingredients. The coffee is good to go.

ℹ Information

Mt Field National Park Visitor Information Centre (☑ 1300 827 727, 03-6288 1149; www. parks.tas.gov.au; 66 Lake Dobson Rd, Mt Field National Park; park day pass per person/vehicle $12/24; ⊙ 8.30am-5pm Nov-Apr, 9am-4pm May-Oct) The Mt Field National Park Visitor Information Centre houses the Waterfalls Cafe and displays on the park's origins. It sells park day passes, and has reams of information on walks and ranger-led activities, held from late December until early February. There are excellent day-use facilities around the centre, including BBQs, shelters, lawns and a children's playground.

ℹ Getting There & Away

The 80km drive from Hobart to Mt Field through the Derwent River Valley and Bushy Park is an absolute stunner, with river rapids, hop fields, old oast houses, rows of poplars and hawthorn hedgerows. There's no public transport to the park, but some Hobart-based tour operators offer Mt Field day trips: try **Tours Tasmania** (☑ 1800 777 103; www.tourstas.com.au).

For nearby Westerway and Ellendale (and Fentonbury in between them), **Derwent Valley Link** (☑ 03-6261 4653; www.derwentvalleylink.com. au) run from Hobart once daily during school holidays to Westerway ($13.30, 1¾ hours) and Ellendale ($17.80, two hours) via New Norfolk.

Another Derwent Valley Link bus runs to Westerway and Ellendale once daily on school days, but leaves from Ogilvie High School in New Town, one of Hobart's northern suburbs.

THE SOUTHEAST

Still harbours, country villages and misty valleys – Tasmania's southeast has much to entice. The apple-producing heartland of the Apple Isle, this fertile area now also produces cherries, apricots, Atlantic salmon, wines, mushrooms and cheeses. The wide, tea-coloured Huon River remains the region's lifeblood. Courtesy of these southern latitudes and myriad waterways, the southeast is also known for its rainbows.

As you head south the fruity hillsides of the Huon Valley give way to the sparkling inlets of the D'Entrecasteaux Channel, with Bruny Island awaiting offshore. Hartz Mountains National Park is not far inland and, further south, the epic South Coast Track kicks off at magnificent Recherche Bay.

All sounding a bit French? French explorers Bruni d'Entrecasteaux and Nicolas Baudin charted much of the region's coastline in the 1790s and early 1800s, a good decade before the Brits hoisted the Union Jack at Risdon Cove near Hobart in 1803.

ⓘ Getting There & Away

Metro Tasmania (☎13 22 01; www.metrotas. com.au) Metro Tasmania buses run south from Hobart through Margate and Kettering to Woodbridge from Monday to Saturday. A bus tracks over the hill to Cygnet once daily on weekdays.

Tassielink (☎1300 300 520; www.tassielink. com.au) Tassielink runs daily buses along the Huon Hwy from Hobart through Huonville, Franklin and Geeveston to Dover, also extending from Huonville to Cygnet.

Bruny Island

POP 620

Bruny Island is almost two islands, joined by a narrow, 5km-long sandy isthmus called the Neck. Renowned for wildlife (little penguins, echidnas, mutton birds), it's a windswept, sparsely populated isle, blown by ocean rains in the south, and dry and beachy in the north. Access is via a short car-ferry chug from Kettering.

Bruny's coastal scenery is magical. There are countless swimming and surf beaches, plus good ocean and freshwater fishing.

South Bruny offers the steep, forested South Bruny National Park, with beautiful walking tracks, especially around Labillardiere Peninsula and Fluted Cape.

Tourism is increasingly important to the island's economy but remains low-key. There are (as yet) no homogenised resorts, just plenty of beachy cottages and houses. Too many visitors cram their Bruny experience into one day: if you can handle the peace and quiet, stay a few days. Bruny Island takes hold slowly, then tends not to let go.

◉ Sights

The Neck NATURE RESERVE, VIEWPOINT
(www.brunyisland.org.au/about-bruny-island/the-neck; Bruny Island Main Rd; ⊙24hr) **FREE** Park halfway across the isthmus – aka the Neck – between North and South Bruny and climb the 279 steps (count them!) to the **Truganini Memorial** for broad views of both ends of the island. Another timber walkway crosses the Neck to the beach on the other side. Keep to the boardwalk in this area: mutton birds and little (fairy) penguins nest here. Your best chance of seeing the penguins is at dusk in the warmer months.

South Bruny National Park NATIONAL PARK
(☑03-6293 1419; www.parks.tas.gov.au; via Adventure Bay & Lunawanna, South Bruny; park day pass per person/vehicle $12/24; ⊙24hr) South Bruny National Park comprises extensive coastal and wooded hinterland areas. At **Fluted Cape** near Adventure Bay, an easy trail leads to the old whaling station at **Grass Point** (1½ hours return). From here, **Penguin Island** is accessible at low tide, or tackle the challenging **Cape Circuit** (2½ hours return).

The park's southwestern portion comprises the **Labillardiere Peninsula**, featuring jagged coastal scenery and **Cape Bruny Lighthouse** (☑03-6293 1419; www.parks.tas. gov.au; Lighthouse Rd, South Bruny; park day pass per person/vehicle $12/24; ⊙reserve access vehicles 9.30am-4.30pm, pedestrians 24hr). Walks here range from leisurely beach meanderings to a seven-hour peninsula circuit.

Bligh Museum of Pacific
Exploration MUSEUM
(☑03-6293 1117, 0407 689 877; www.southcom.com. au/~jontan/index.html; 876 Adventure Bay Rd, Adventure Bay; adult/child/family $4/2/10; ⊙10am-4pm) This curio-crammed, windowless, brick museum details the local exploits of explorers Bligh, Cook, Furneaux, Baudin and, of course,

Bruni d'Entrecasteaux. The engaging collection includes maps, charts and manuscripts, many of them originals or first editions.

🏃 Activities

Bruny Island Cycle Tours & Hire   CYCLING
(📱 0477 495 339; www.brunyislandcycletoursand hire.com.au; 66 Ferry Rd, Kettering; hire per day mountain/e-bike $40/65, 2 days $75/120; ⊗ 9am-5pm) Take a self-guided tour of Bruny on a nifty 'e-bike', which can give you a boost of up to 25km/h courtesy of a little rechargeable electric motor. Pick-up in Kettering across the road from the ferry. See the website for suggested touring routes. Regular mountain and road bikes also available.

👉 Tours

★ Bruny Island Cruises   BOATING
(Pennicott Wilderness Journeys; 📱 03-6234 4270; www.brunycruises.com.au; 915 Adventure Bay Rd, Adventure Bay; adult/child/family $135/85/430) Run by Pennicott Wilderness Journeys, this excellent three-hour tour of the island's awesome southeast coastline takes in rookeries, seal colonies, bays, caves and towering sea cliffs. Trips depart Adventure Bay jetty at 11am daily, with an extra 2pm cruise in summer – make your own way there.

Bruny Island Safaris   TOURS
(📱 0437 499 795; www.brunyislandsafaris.com.au; per person $149, lighthouse tour only adult/child/family $10/5/35) Full-day tours departing Hobart, focusing on Bruny's history and landscapes. Look forward to sampling the island's culinary bounty, including oysters, salmon, cheese, wine and berries, and a visit to the old Cape Bruny Lighthouse. If you're already on the island, you can meet the tour at the lighthouse for a look inside (see www.brunyislandlighthousetours.com.au).

🛏️ Sleeping

★ Red Gate Cottage   RENTAL HOUSE $$
(📱 0411 030 445; www.redgatecottage.weebly.com; 178 Nebraska Rd, Dennes Point; d from $185, extra person $30) A charismatic old shiplap-board beach shack on Dennes Point dunes, with a red gate leading to the west-facing beach (great sunsets). 'Retro-shack-classic' would best describe the architecture, but inside it's all thoroughly comfortable, with a kitchen that's entirely new-century. Sleeps four in two bedrooms, plus a couple of spare mattresses for extra bods.

★ 43 Degrees   APARTMENT $$
(📱 03-6293 1018; www.43degrees.com.au; 1 Lumeah Rd & 948 Adventure Bay Rd, Adventure Bay; d/apt $190/240, extra person $40) At 43°S latitude, the accommodation here neatly bookends Adventure Bay beach: there are three tidy, roll-roofed studios (sleeping two) at the western end; and two similarly styled apartments (sleeping four) at the eastern end near the jetty. Double-glazing keeps the heat out/in, depending on the season.

Satellite Island   RENTAL HOUSE $$$
(📱 0400 336 444; www.satelliteisland.com.au; Satellite Island, via Alonnah or Middleton; d/extra person from $1200/200) An island, off an island, off an island... Adrift in the D'Entrecasteaux Channel, this amazing private-island lodge (boatshed-chic) offers self-contained accommodation for up to eight castaways. Kayaks and fishing rods for distraction; walking trails and oyster-clad rocks for exploring. Private-boat access from Alonnah on Bruny Island or Middleton on the Tasmanian 'mainland'. Two-night minimum (though you'll want to stay longer).

🍴 Eating & Drinking

★ Bruny Island Cheese Co   CHEESE $
(📱 03-6260 6353; www.brunyislandcheese.com.au; 1807 Bruny Island Main Rd, Great Bay; tastings free, meals from $12; ⊗ 9.30am-5pm) Hankering for a quivering sliver of cheese? Head to the Bruny Island Cheese Co, where Kiwi cheesemaker Nick Haddow draws inspiration from time spent working and travelling in France, Spain, Italy and the UK. Bruny Island Beer Co operates under the same auspices: try the Oxymoron dark pale ale, or some artisan wood-fired sourdough bread with your cheese platter.

★ Get Shucked Oyster Farm   SEAFOOD $$
(📱 0439 303 597; www.getshucked.com.au; 1735 Bruny Island Main Rd, Great Bay; 12 oysters unshucked/shucked from $10/16; ⊗ 9.30am-6.30pm, reduced winter hours) Get Shucked cultivates the 'fuel for love' in chilly Great Bay. Visit the tasting room and wolf down a briny dozen with lemon juice and Tabasco and a cold flute of Jansz bubbles. Shucking brilliant.

Bruny Island House of Whisky   BAR
(📱 03-6260 6344; www.tasmanianhouseofwhisky.com.au; 360 Lennon Rd, North Bruny; ⊗ 9.30am-5.30pm, reduced winter hours) Stand in awe before this lustrous, dazzling bar, full of bottles containing Tasmania's best single-malt whis-

The Southeast

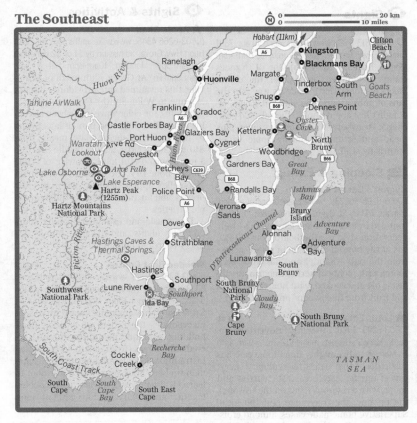

kies (there are a lot of them these days, including the house Trappers Hut whisky). Gourmet platters also available. Don't blame us if you miss the last ferry back to Kettering...

ℹ️ Information

Bruny D'Entrecasteaux Visitor Information Centre (☑ 03-6267 4494; www.brunyisland accommodationandtours.com; 81 Ferry Rd, Kettering; ☉ 9am-5pm) The Bruny Island visitor centre is at the Kettering ferry terminal – it's the best place for info on accommodation and services on Bruny, including walking maps and driving advice. There's a cafe here, too.

ℹ️ Getting There & Away

Bruny Island Ferry (☑ 03-6273 6725; www. brunyislandferry.com.au; Ferry Rd, Kettering; car return $33-38, motorcycle/bike/foot passenger return $6/6/free) Shuttles cars and passengers from Kettering to Roberts Point on North Bruny, with at least 10 services daily each way (20 minutes) on two boats. The

first ferry leaves Kettering at 6.30am (7.30am Sunday); the last one at 7pm. The first ferry from Bruny sails at 7am (8.30am Sunday); the last one at 7.15pm. No bookings – queue up at the jetties.

Cygnet

POP 1460

Groovy Cygnet was originally named Port de Cygne Noir (Port of the Black Swan) by Bruni d'Entrecasteaux, after the big *noir* birds that cruise around the bay. Youthfully reincarnated as Cygnet (a baby swan), the town has evolved into a dreadlocked, artsy enclave, while still functioning as a major fruit-producing centre. Weathered farmers and banjo-carrying hippies chat amiably in the main street and prop up the bars of the town's pubs. To the south, the **Randalls Bay** and **Verona Sands** beaches aren't far away.

Sights

Pagan Cider
BREWERY

(☑ 0448 813 988; www.pagancider.com.au; 7891 Channel Hwy, Cradoc; tastings free; ⊙ 11am-4pm Mon-Fri, 11am-5pm Sat & Sun) One of Cygnet's claims to fame is Pagan Cider, the 'champagne of ciders' that's made its way into the taps of pubs around the state. At Pagan, cider ain't just about apples: they also do pear, cherry, strawberry and blueberry cider, plus mead and scrumpy (punchy apple wine). Surprising stuff.

🛏 Sleeping & Eating

Cygnet's Secret Garden
B&B $$

(☑ 03-6295 0223; www.cygnets-secret-garden. com.au; 7 Mary St, Cygnet; d from $180; 🛜) Surrounded by a flower-filled garden, this lovely Federation-style weatherboard house (1913) sits at the bottom of the main street (across from the pub – handy) and has three B&B rooms with plenty of heritage charm. Breakfast is big and cooked, with homemade jams and fruit from the owners' orchard.

★ Lotus Eaters Cafe
CAFE $$

(☑ 03-6295 1996; www.thelotuseaterscafe.com. au; 10 Mary St, Cygnet; mains $12-25; ⊙ 9am-4pm Fri-Mon; 🖋) This mighty-fine hippie cafe has rustic decor that belies real culinary savvy: expect terrific eggy breakfasts, curries and soups, with a rigorous focus on the seasonal, the organic, the free-range and the local. Superlative homemade cakes, almond croissants and coffee. Head for the chunky timber tables outside in the sun.

Huonville & Around

The biggest town in the southeast, agrarian Huonville flanks the Huon River 35km south of Hobart, not far from some lovely vineyards and small villages. Having made its name as Tasmania's apple-growing powerhouse, it remains a functional, working town – low on charm but with all the services you need.

The Huon Hwy traces the Huon River south, passing the settlements of Franklin, Castle Forbes Bay and Port Huon. These were once important shipping ports for apples, but nowadays the old wharves and packing sheds are decaying like old fruit. Nearby Ranelagh is an agricultural hub, while strung-out Franklin is the oldest town in the Huon Valley. The wide, reedy riverscape here is one of Australia's best rowing courses.

Sights & Activities

★ Apple Shed
MUSEUM

(☑ 03-6266 4345; www.williesmiths.com.au; 2064 Huon Hwy, Grove; admission by $1 or $2 donation; ⊙ 10am-5pm Mon-Thu, 10am-6pm Sat & Sun, 10am-9pm Fri) At Grove, 6km north of Huonville, this revamped cafe-providore-museum is home to Willie Smith's Organic Apple Cider, riding the cider wave that's been sweeping Australia's pubs and bars of late. Swing by for a coffee, a cheese plate, meals (from $10 to $28), a cider tasting paddle ($12), or a more purp oseful 1.89L 'growler' of Willie Smith's Bone Dry. The museum zooms in on Huonville's appley heritage, with old cider presses and an amazing wall of different apple varieties.

Live music and extended opening hours on Friday nights...and the apple brandy distillery is up and bubbling!

Wooden Boat Centre
MUSEUM

(☑ 03-6266 3586; www.woodenboatcentre.com; 3333 Huon Hwy, Franklin; adult/child/family $15/5/30; ⊙ 9.30am-4.30pm Mon-Fri, 10.30am-4pm Sat & Sun) This engaging, sea-centric spot incorporates the School of Wooden Boatbuilding, a unique institution running accredited courses (from one to seven weeks) in traditional boat building, using Tasmanian timbers. Stick your head in the door to learn all about it, watch boats being cobbled together and catch a glorious whiff of Huon pine.

Huon Valley Bicycle Hire
CYCLING

(☑ 0447 270 669; www.huonvalleybicyclehire.com; 105 Wilmot Rd, Huonville; bike hire per half-/full day $25/35; ⊙ 10am-6pm Fri-Tue) Saddle up on a vintage, retro or mountain bike and go exploring around Huonville. See the website for some ideas on local routes to follow, from 12km to 32km.

🛏 Sleeping & Eating

Huon Valley Caravan Park
CARAVAN PARK $

(☑ 0438 304 383; www.huonvalleycaravanpark. com.au; 177 Wilmot Rd, Ranelagh; unpowered sites $35, powered sites $39-45, en-suite sites $65) At the junction of the Huon and Mountain Rivers is this lush, grassy patch, filling a budget-shaped gap in the local accommodation market. There are no cabins here (yet), but there's a fabulous camp kitchen with a pizza oven, tidy amenities and nifty powered sites with elevated, brightly painted en suites. And you can cast a fly into Mountain River.

★Huon Bush Retreats
CABIN $$

(☑ 03-6264 2233; www.huonbushretreats.com; 300 Browns Rd, Ranelagh; unpowered sites $30, tepees $105-145, 1- & 2-bedroom cabin d $185-420, extra person $40) 🍃 This private, wildlife-friendly retreat dapples the flanks of not-so-miserable Mt Misery. On site are five modern, self-contained cabins, luxury tepees, tent and campervan sites, plus 5km of walking tracks and a fantastic BBQ camp kitchen. Superb blue wrens flit through the branches. Check the website for directions – it's 12km from Huonville (beware: steep dirt road!).

★Ranelagh General Store
CAFE $

(☑ 03-6264 2316; www.facebook.com/ranelagh generalstore; 31 Marguerite St, Ranelagh; mains $12-15; ◷8am-5pm Mon-Thu, 8am-8pm Fri-Sun) The dodgy old Ranelagh General Store has been reborn as a cafe. Burgers are the main deal, plus coffee, smoothies, sundaes and racks full of Huon Valley produce to go. The 'Dennis' burger (Bruny Island wallaby, beetroot jam, Tabasco sauce, parsley and aioli) is an absolute winner.

★Summer Kitchen Bakery
BAKERY, CAFE $

(☑ 03-6264 3388; summerkitchen@aanet.com.au; 1 Marguerite St, Ranelagh; items $4-7; ◷7.30am-4pm Tue-Fri, 8am-4pm Sat) Locals come from miles around just for a loaf of bread from this excellent little bakery, on a street corner in Ranelagh a few kilometres out of Huonville. Organic wood-fired sourdough, sprouted-rye sourdough, organic beef-and-wallaby pies, pastries, fiendishly good chocolate croissants and the best coffee in the Huon. Just terrific.

❶ Information

Huon Valley Visitor Information Centre (☑ 03-6264 0326; www.southerntrove.com.au; 2273 Huon Hwy, Huonville; ◷9am-5pm) Southeast tourist information on the way into town from Hobart. Check out the live bee hive out the back.

Geeveston & Around

POP 1430

A rugged but photogenic town 31km south of Huonville, Geeveston was built by bushmen who came to extract timber from the surrounding forests. It's a utilitarian sort of place, but offers accommodation close to Hartz Mountains National Park and Tahune AirWalk along the Arve Rd.

Geeveston was founded in the mid-19th century by the Geeves family, whose descendants still have fingers in lots of local pies. In the 1980s the town was the epicentre of an intense battle over logging the Farmhouse Creek forests. At the height of the controversy, conservationists spent weeks living in the tops of 80m-tall eucalypts to prevent them being felled. The conservation movement ultimately won: Farmhouse Creek is now protected from logging.

More recently, Geeveston was the filming location for the fictional town of 'Rosehaven' for the 2016 ABC TV comedy series of the same name – a quirky and surprisingly tender insight into small-town Tasmania.

◉ Sights & Activities

★Hartz Mountains National Park
NATIONAL PARK

(☑ 03-6121 7026; www.parks.tas.gov.au; via Arve Rd, Geeveston; park day pass per person/vehicle $12/24; ◷24hr) The 65-sq-km Hartz Mountains alpine wilderness, part of the Tasmanian Wilderness World Heritage Area, is only 84km from Hobart – easy striking distance for day trippers and weekend walkers. The park is renowned for its jagged peaks, glacial tarns, gorges and alpine moorlands, where fragile cushion-plant communities hunker down in the cold, misty airs. Rapid weather changes bluster through – even day-walkers should bring waterproofs and warm clothing.

Tahune AirWalk
WALKING

(☑ 03-6251 3903, 1300 720 507; www.tahuneair walk.com.au; Arve Rd, Geeveston; adult/child/family $29/14.50/58; ◷9am-5pm Oct-Mar, 10am-4pm Apr-Sep) About 29km west of Geeveston, Tahune Forest has 600m of wheelchair-accessible steel walkways suspended 20m above the forest floor. One 24m cantilevered section is designed to sway disconcertingly with approaching footsteps. Vertigo? Ground-level walks include a 20-minute riverside stroll through stands of young Huon pine. There's also a **cafe** (mains $12 to $30) here and lodge **accommodation** (dorms/doubles/families/cabins $60/121/152/180).

🛏 Sleeping & Eating

Cambridge House
B&B $$

(☑ 03-6297 1561; www.cambridgehouse.com.au; 2 School Rd, Geeveston; d incl breakfast $140-165, extra person $44) This photogenic 1870s B&B – cottagey but not kitsch – offers three bedrooms upstairs with shared facilities (good for families), and two downstairs en-suite rooms. The timber staircase and Baltic pine ceilings are wonders. If you're quiet, you might spy a platypus in the creek at the bottom of the garden. Cooked breakfast.

★**Masaaki's Sushi** JAPANESE $
(☑ 0408 712 340; 20b Church St, Geeveston; sushi $9-20; ⊙ 11.30am-3pm Fri & Sat) What a surprise! Tasmania's best sushi – including fresh Tasmanian wasabi – is in sleepy Geeveston. Opening hours are disappointingly limited (and he usually sells out by 2pm), but you'll also find Masaaki (from Osaka) and his outstanding sushi at Hobart's Sunday morning Farm Gate Market (p646).

❶ Information

Geeveston Visitor Information Centre (☑ 03-6297 1120; www.facebook.com/geeveston visitorcentre; 15 Church St, Geeveston; ⊙ 9am-5pm, reduced winter hours) In Geeveston's old redbrick town hall, this unofficial visitor centre sells tickets to the Tahune Forest AirWalk and Hastings Caves & Thermal Springs further south. Hartz Mountains National Park info and tickets, too.

Dover
POP 960

A Port Esperance fishing town with a beach and a pier (but sadly no pub at the moment – it burned down in 2013), Dover is a chilled-out spot to while away a few deep-south days. The town was originally called Port Esperance after a ship in Bruni d'Entrecasteaux's fleet, but that moniker now only applies to the bay. The bay's three small islands are optimistically called Faith, Hope and Charity.

In the 19th century this was timber territory. Huon pine and local hardwoods were milled and shipped from here (and also from nearby Strathblane and Raminea),

heading to China, India and Germany for use as railway sleepers. Today the major industries are fruit growing and aquaculture, with Atlantic salmon reared here then exported throughout Asia.

🛏 Sleeping & Eating

Fisherman's Wife COTTAGE $$
(☑ 0428 981 574, 03-6298 1441; www.chapellane hall.com/fishermans-wife; 7059 Huon Hwy, Dover; d from $190) Any closer to the water and this little old roadside cottage would be a boat. Encircled by lush lawns, it's a classic deep-south holiday shack with a wood heater, sunny deck and cute country kitchen – call it retro, with a contemporary twist. A little private jetty juts into Port Esperance. Minimum two-night stay; sleeps four.

★**The Peninsula Experience** RENTAL HOUSE $$$
(☑ 03-6298 1441; www.peninsulatas.com; Blubber Head Rd, Dover; d from $475, extra bedroom $150; 🛜) Poised on a private peninsula beyond some steely gates and a long wiggly driveway, this stately 19th-century farmhouse now exudes 21st-century luxury. Asian-chic design infuses the three bedrooms (it sleeps six) and the elegant kitchen. At dusk, pademelons, wallabies and echidnas patrol the grounds. The Boat House is here too – a slick little waterside cottage for two.

★**Post>Office 6985** PIZZA $$
(☑ 03-6298 1905; 6985 Huon Hwy, Dover; mains $12-27; ⊙ 4-8pm Wed-Sat) Leonard Cohen and alt-country on the stereo, cool decor, foodie magazines... And that's before you get to the menu, which features excellent wood-fired pizzas (try the scallop, caramelised onion and pancetta version). An evening here will probably have you asking your accommodation if you can stay an extra night. Sterling beer and wine list, too.

DON'T MISS

HASTINGS CAVES & THERMAL SPRINGS

A 7.5km drive inland from the Southport turnoff on the Huon Hwy are the amazing **Hastings Caves & Thermal Springs** (☑ 03-6298 3209; www.parks.tas.gov.au/reserves/hastings; 754 Hastings Caves Rd, Hastings; caves & pool adult/child/family $24/12/60, pool only $5/2.50/12; ⊙ 9am-5pm Jan, 10am-4pm Feb-Apr & Oct-Dec, 10.30am-4pm May-Sep) and their adjunct thermal springs. Admission is via guided tour, leaving roughly hourly (call or check the website). Tours (45 minutes) take you into the impressive dolomite **Newdegate Cave**, followed by a dip in the **thermal pool** behind the visitor centre, filled with 28°C spring water. The **cafe** (mains $10 to $20) at the visitor centre also sells BBQ packs and picnic hampers.

COCKLE CREEK & RECHERCHE BAY

Australia's most southerly drive is the 19km gravel stretch from Ida Bay past the lulling waves of Recherche Bay to Cockle Creek. A grand grid of streets was once planned for Cockle Creek, but dwindling coal seams and whale numbers poured cold water on that idea.

This is epic country, studded with craggy, clouded mountains, sigh-inducing beaches and (best of all) hardly any people – perfect for camping and bushwalking.

The challenging **South Coast Track** starts (or ends) at Cockle Creek, tracking between here and Melaleuca in the **Southwest National Park** (www.parks.tas.gov. au; vehicle/person per day $24/12). Combined with the **Port Davey Track** you can walk all the way to Lake Pedder. Shorter walks from Cockle Creek include ambles along the shoreline to the lighthouse at **Fishers Point** (two hours return), and a section of the South Coast Track to **South Cape Bay** (four hours return). National park entry fees apply; self-register at Cockle Creek.

Southport & Around

Originally Southport was called Baie des Moules (Bay of Mussels), one of several names it's had over the years. Many travellers don't take the 2km detour off the main road to visit the town, but it's a worthy diversion if only to stay in its B&Bs, which make good use of the waterside locale. Nearby, the Hastings Caves & Thermal Springs reserve and quirky Ida Bay Railway at Lune River are worthwhile detours. Unfortunately, public transport won't get you here.

🏃 Activities

Ida Bay Railway RAIL
(☑ 03-6298 3110, 0459 984 246; www.idabayrail way.com.au; 328 Lune River Rd, Lune River; adult/child/family $32/17/75; ⏰ 10am, noon, 2pm & 4pm Jan, 10am, noon & 2pm Feb-May, 10am & 12.30pm Jun-Dec) Australia's southernmost railway tracks a scenic 14km, 1½-hour narrow-gauge course through native bush from Lune River to Deep Hole Bay: take a picnic, explore the beach then rattle back to Lune River. Trains run daily October to April, and Thursday to Sunday only from May to September.

🛏 Sleeping

★ Jetty House B&B $$
(☑ 03-6298 3139; www.southportjettyhouse.com; 8848 Huon Hwy, Southport; s/d/f incl breakfast from $120/185/265, entire house $380-500; 🔊🐾) Perfect for your post–South Coast Track recovery, this family-run guest house near the wharf is a rustic, verandah-encircled homestead built in 1876 for the local sawmill boss. Rates include full cooked breakfast and after-

noon tea. Open fires, interesting art and the total absence of doilies complete the package. Dinner by arrangement; cheaper long-stay rates. Kids and pets welcome. Lovely!

★ The Shackeau RENTAL HOUSE $$$
(☑ 03-6298 1441; www.shackeau.com; 223 Kingfish Beach Rd, Southport; d from $280) The name sounds goofy (a nod to local French history?), but this lovely, absolute-waterfront cottage is anything but. The last in a long row of quirky little beach shacks right above the waterline, it's a cream-coloured weatherboard affair, with mod, beachy interiors, a fabulous deck and an infinity-edge spa pool with unbeatable views. Sleeps four.

TASMAN PENINSULA & PORT ARTHUR

Just an hour from Hobart lie the staggering coastal landscapes, sandy beaches and historic sites of the Tasman Peninsula. Bushwalking, surfing, sea-kayaking, scuba-diving and rock-climbing opportunities abound – all good reasons to extend your visit beyond a hurried day trip from Hobart.

Don't miss visiting the peninsula's legendary 300m-high sea cliffs – the tallest in the southern hemisphere – which will dose you up on natural awe. Most of the cliffs are protected by Tasman National Park, a coastal enclave embracing chunky offshore islands and underwater kelp forests. Within the national park, the fabulous new Three Capes Track is enticing hikers from across the planet to experience this amazing landscape.

Waiting portentously at the end of Arthur Hwy is Port Arthur, the infamous and allegedly escape-proof penal colony dating from the early 19th century. Today kids kick footballs and dads poke sausages on BBQs there, but it's impossible to totally blank out the tragedy of this place, both historically and more recently.

👉 Tours

Under Down Under TOURS
(📞1800 444 442; www.underdownunder.com.au; per person $115) Guided backpacker-style day trips to Port Arthur, including accommodation pick-up, admission fees, a guided walk and a harbour cruise. There's also a quick look at Richmond en route.

Tours Tasmania TOURS
(📞1800 777 103; www.tourstas.com.au; per person $125) Good-value, small-group day tours to Port Arthur (including admission fees, walking tour and harbour cruise) via Richmond, Devil's Kitchen and Tasman Arch. Backpacker focused.

Dunalley

POP 310

The thickly timbered Forestier Peninsula – the precursor peninsula you'll cross en route to the Tasman Peninsula – is connected to mainland Tasmanian soil by the isthmus town of Dunalley. Much of the area was ravaged by bushfires in 2013, but is greening up again nicely. At Dunalley itself, the Denison Canal (1905) bisects the isthmus, providing a short cut for small boats. There's not a whole lot to do here, nor anywhere outstanding to stay, but there are a couple of good foodie haunts if you're hungry.

🍴 Eating

★Bangor Wine & Oyster Shed SEAFOOD $$
(📞03-6253 5558; www.bangorshed.com.au; 20 Blackman Bay Rd, Dunalley; 12 oysters from $24, mains $18-32; ⏱10am-5pm, reduced winter hours; 🐾) Turn left 1km beyond the Denison Canal to discover this excellent new foodie haunt. It's a black-stained timber shed, hosting a winery cellar door (the cool-climate pinot noir rocks) and restaurant, where you can sample the local oysters (try the red wine vinegar, shallots and pepper dressing), a tasting platter, or more substantial mains (sautéed abalone, calamari salad). Nice one.

★Dunalley Waterfront Café & Gallery CAFE $$
(📞03-62535122;www.dunalleywaterfrontcafe.com; 4 Imlay St, Dunalley; mains $13-30; ⏱9am-4pm Mon, Wed, Thu & Sun, 9am-9pm Fri & Sat, reduced winter hours) With its broad outdoor deck and views across the water, this bright, airy cafe is a Dunalley culinary hotspot. The menu ranges from seafood pie with potato gratin to a pulled-pork sandwich with fennel slaw and chilli aioli. Homemade cakes, pizzas, brilliant coffee and Tasmanian wines are further excuses to linger. The funky gallery showcases local artists.

Eaglehawk Neck to Port Arthur

Eaglehawk Neck is the second isthmus you'll cross heading south to Port Arthur, this one connecting the Forestier Peninsula to the Tasman Peninsula. Its historical importance harks back to the convict days, when the 100m-wide Neck had a row of ornery dogs chained across it to prevent convicts from escaping – the infamous Dogline. Timber platforms were also built in narrow Eaglehawk Bay to the west, and stocked with yet more ferocious dogs to prevent convicts from wading around the Dogline. To discourage swimming, rumours were circulated that the waters were shark infested – the occasional white pointer does indeed shimmy through these waters, but 'infested' is an overstatement. Remarkably, despite these measures, several convicts made successful bids for freedom.

Eaglehawk Neck is the northern access point to Tasman National Park. The natural landscape around here is astonishing, with huge stone arches, blowholes, cliffs, craggy shoreline terraces and a superb surf beach.

⊙ Sights

★Tasman National Park NATIONAL PARK
(📞03-6250 3980; www.parks.tas.gov.au; via Fortescue Bay or Eaglehawk Neck, Tasman Peninsula; park day pass per person/vehicle $12/24; ⏱24hr) Tasman National Park embraces the sky-high sea cliffs around Cape Raoul, Cape Hauy, Cape Pillar, Tasman Island and the craggy coast near Eaglehawk Neck. Bushwalking here is superb: hike the day trails from Fortescue Bay, or tackle the four-day Three Capes Track (p664), checking the three above-mentioned capes off your list en

Tasman Peninsula

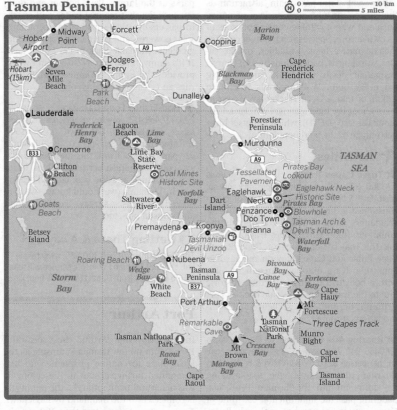

N 0 — 10 km
0 — 5 miles

route to Fortescue Bay. You can **camp** (☑03-6250 2433; Fortescue Rd, Fortescue Bay; unpowered sites per two people/family $13/16, extra adult/child $5/2.50) at Fortescue Bay, too. Another lovely walk extends to **Waterfall Bay** (off Blowhole Rd, Doo Town; park day pass per person/vehicle $12/24; ⊘24hr) in the park's north, starting at Devil's Kitchen near Eaglehawk Neck.

Blowhole, Tasman Arch & Devil's Kitchen
LANDMARK

(www.eaglehawkneck.org/attractions; off Blowhole Rd, Doo Town; ⊘24hr) **FREE** For a close-up look at the spectacular coastline just south of Eaglehawk Neck, follow the signs to the **Blowhole**, **Tasman Arch** (a cavern-like natural bridge) and **Devil's Kitchen** (a rugged 60m-deep cleft). Watch out for sporadic bursts at the Blowhole, and keep behind the fences at the other sites – the cliff edges tend to decay. On the road to the Blowhole, look for the signposted 4km gravel road

leading to **Waterfall Bay**, which has further camera-conducive views.

Coal Mines Historic Site
HISTORIC SITE

(☑1800 659 101; www.coalmines.org.au; Coal Mine Rd, via Saltwater River; ⊘daylight hours) **FREE** At Premaydena, take the signposted turn-off (the C431) 13km northwest to Saltwater River and the Coal Mines Historic Site, a powerful reminder of the colonial past. Excavated in 1833, the coal mines were used to punish the worst convicts, who worked here in abominable conditions. The poorly managed mining operation wasn't economically viable, and in 1848 it was sold to a private enterprise. Within 10 years it was abandoned. Some buildings were demolished; fire and weather put paid to the rest.

Tasmanian Devil Unzoo
WILDLIFE RESERVE

(☑1800 641 641; www.tasmaniandevilunzoo.com.au; 5990 Arthur Hwy, Taranna; adult/child/family $33/18/79, tour incl admission $79/39/190;

⊘9am-5pm) Taranna's main attraction is this 'unzoo', an unfenced enclave of native bushland where wildlife comes and goes of its own accord. Species you might encounter include native hens, wallabies, quolls, eagles, wattlebirds, pademelons and, of course, Tasmanian devils, which you can see being fed every hour. Walking trails extend to 2.5km, or take a Devil Tracker 4WD tour to learn about the fight against Devil Facial Tumour Disease (DFTD), which afflicts a huge percentage of the wild population.

🏃 Activities

★ Three Capes Track   HIKING
(☑1300 827 727; www.threecapestrack.com.au; adult/child $495/396) The latest project to consume the hearts, minds and money of Tasmania's Parks & Wildlife Service is the ambitious 46km Three Capes Track, traversing the majestic clifftops of Cape Raoul, Cape Pillar and Cape Hauy on the Tasman Peninsula. It's a four-day, three-night hike, with a boat trip from Port Arthur Historic Site to the trailhead, a bus ride back to Port Arthur at the end, and excellent hut accommodation en route.

★ Roaring 40s Kayaking   KAYAKING
(☑0455 949 777; www.roaring40skayaking.com. au; per person $220; ⊘8am Mon & Fri Nov-Apr) Roaring 40s conducts epic sea-kayaking day tours around the Tasman Peninsula, paddling past the monumental coastline of Cape Hauy in Tasman National Park. Prices include equipment, lunch and transfers from Hobart. Minimum age 16.

🛏 Sleeping & Eating

★ Larus Waterfront
Cottage   RENTAL HOUSE $$
(☑0457 758 711; www.larus.com.au; 576 White Beach Rd, White Beach; d from $230) Contemporary design, a marine colour scheme, audacious views and all mod-cons (big-screen TV, gas cooking, flash barbecue) equate to a great bolthole. It's in a quiet spot with just a narrow strip of scrub between you and the sea. You'll be spending a lot of time sitting, sipping and admiring the sunset from the wraparound deck. Sleeps four.

★ Cubed   CAFE $
(☑0439 001 588; www.facebook.com/cubedespresso; Pirates Bay Lookout, Pirates Bay Dr, Eaglehawk Neck; snacks from $3.50; ⊘9am-4pm Thu-Mon, closed Jun-Aug) 🍃 This restored 1957 caravan

parks at the Pirates Bay Lookout and doles out fastidiously prepared coffee and snacks to passers-by. It's a sustainable operation – solar powered, and using milk, coffee and ingredients traceable back to local farm level. If it's sunny, the cheery NZ-German owners provide a telescope to amuse and Persian rugs and cushions to perch on.

★ Doo-Lishus Food Caravan   FAST FOOD $
(☑0437 469 412; www.tasmanregion.com.au/doolishus; Blowhole Rd, Doo Town; meals $5-17; ⊘8.45am-6pm late Sep-Apr) At the Blowhole car park in Doo Town, this unexpected caravan dishes up fresh berry smoothies, beaut fish and chips and the best curried scallop pies in Tasmania (we should know – we conducted an extensive survey). Excellent rabbit and venison pies, too.

❶ Getting There & Away

The **Tassielink** (☑1300 300 520; www.tassielink.com.au) Tasman Peninsula service will take you to Dunalley from Hobart ($14, one hour).

Port Arthur

POP 250

In 1830 Governor Arthur chose beautiful Port Arthur on the Tasman Peninsula as the ideal place to confine prisoners who had committed further crimes in the colony. It was a 'natural penitentiary' – the peninsula is connected to the mainland by Eaglehawk Neck, a strip of land less than 100m wide, where ferocious guard dogs and tales of shark-infested waters deterred escape.

Despite its redemption as a major tourist site (the ruins here are undeniably amazing), Port Arthur remains a sombre place. Don't expect to remain unaffected by what you see: there's a sadness here that's palpable, and a Gothic pall of woe that can cloud your senses on even the sunniest of days. Compounding this, in April 1996 a young gunman fired bullets indiscriminately at the community, murdering 35 people and injuring 37 more. After burning down a guesthouse, he was finally captured and remains imprisoned north of Hobart.

⊙ Sights

★ Port Arthur Historic Site   HISTORIC SITE
(☑03-6251 2310, 1800 659 101; www.portarthur. org.au; 6973 Arthur Hwy, Port Arthur; adult/child/family from $39/17/99; ⊘tours & buildings 9am-5pm, grounds 9am-dusk) This amazing Unesco

World Heritage–listed convict site is one of Tasmania's big-ticket attractions. The dozens of structures here are best interpreted via guided tour (included with admission). The feared **Separate Prison** was built to punish prisoners through isolation and sensory deprivation (…bad vibes? What bad vibes?). The 1836 **church** burned down in 1884; the **penitentiary** was originally a granary. The shell of the Broad Arrow Café, scene of some of the 1996 shootings, has been preserved as a **memorial garden**.

Inside the main entrance is a daytime **cafe**, which becomes Felons Bistro (www.port arthur.org.au/planner/felons-bistro; mains $25-36; ⊗5.30pm-late) at night, and a gift shop, which stocks some interesting convict-focused publications. Downstairs is an interpretative gallery where you can follow the convicts' journey from England to Tasmania.

A guided walking tour of the site plus a short harbour cruise are included in admission prices. Additional tours include those to the **Isle of the Dead Cemetery** (www.port arthur.org.au/activities/isle-of-the-dead-cemetery-tour; combined site entry & tour adult/child/family $59/27/144), **Point Puer Boys' Prison** (www.portarthur.org.au/tickets/site-entry-point-puer-boys-prison-tour; combined site entry & tour adult/child/family $59/27/144) and after-dark **ghost tours** (www.portarthur.org.au/activities/port-arthur-ghost-tour; adult/child/family $26.50/15/75; ⊗dusk).

Buggy transport around the site can be arranged for people with restricted mobility – ask at the information counter. The ferry is also wheelchair accessible.

Note that at the time of writing a major overhaul of the main entrance building was being planned (expect some building works!).

Tours

★**Tasman Island Cruises**   BOATING
(Pennicott Wilderness Journeys; ☎03-6250 2200; www.tasmancruises.com.au; 6961 Arthur Hwy, Port Arthur; adult/child/family $135/85/430; ⊗9.15am year-round, plus 1.15pm mid-Dec–mid-Apr) Boat trips departing Pennicott Wilderness Journeys' office near Port Arthur, incorporating a three-hour adventure cruise past the Tasman Peninsula's most spectacular coastal scenery, plus Port Arthur admission. You can also start the tour at Hobart, taking the tour bus down to Port Arthur, then back again after the boat ride (adult/child $225/165 not including Port Arthur admission, $260/180 including Port Arthur).

REMARKABLE CAVE

About 7.5km south of Port Arthur is **Remarkable Cave** (www.eaglehawk neck.org/gateway-to/remarkable-cave; Safety Cove Rd; ⊗24hr), a long tunnel eroded from the base of a collapsed gully, under a cliff and out to sea. The waves surge through the tunnel and fill the gully with sea spray (and sometimes water – watch out!). A boardwalk and 115 steps (count 'em) provide access to a metal viewing platform. Believe it or not, hardcore surfers often brave the cave, paddling out through the opening to surf the offshore reefs beyond.

🛏 Sleeping & Eating

Port Arthur Holiday Park   CARAVAN PARK $
(☎1800 607 057, 03-6250 2340; www.portarthur hp.com.au; Garden Point Rd, Port Arthur; unpowered/powered/en-suite sites from $30/37/48, cabins from $120; ❄🐾) Spacious and with plenty of greenery and sing-song bird life, this park is 2km before Port Arthur within Stewarts Bay State Reserve, not far from a sheltered beach. Facilities are abundant, including a camp kitchen, wood BBQs, petrol pump and shop. The best (and only) budget option around these latitudes.

★**Brick Point Cottage**   RENTAL HOUSE $$
(☎0438 070 498; www.brickpointcottage.com.au; 241 Safety Cove Rd, Port Arthur; up to 4 people from $200) Fronted by a dinky little white garage and some mysterious crumbling ruins (convict bricks?), Brick Point Cottage is an old-school Tassie shack with two bedrooms, compact kitchen, wood heater, sunny deck and lawn arcing down to a sheltered reach of Carnarvon Bay. There are few more unpretentious, un-touristy and affordable places to stay on the whole Tasman Peninsula.

Stewarts Bay Lodge   RESORT $$
(☎03-6250 2888; www.stewartsbaylodge.com.au; 6955 Arthur Hwy, Port Arthur; d from $170, 2-/3-bedroom units from $236/368; ❄🐾) Arrayed around a gorgeous hidden cove – seemingly made for swimming and kayaking – Stewarts Bay Lodge combines older, rustic log cabins with newer deluxe units, some with private spa baths. You can cook in your contemporary kitchen, but you'll probably

spend more time in the sleek **Gabriel's on the Bay** (mains lunch $13-25, dinner $27-46; ⊘8-10am & noon-2pm daily, 5.30-8.30pm Thu-Mon) restaurant (on the bay).

Port Arthur Lavender   CAFE **$$**
(☑03-6250 3058; www.portarthurlavender.com.au; 6555 Arthur Hwy, Port Arthur; mains $13-26; ⊘9am-8pm Jan & Feb, 10am-4pm Mar-Dec) This contemporary shed just north of Port Arthur is part lavender farm, part lavender distillery, part lavender shop...but is mostly worth a stop for its all-day cafe. Expect the likes of seafood chowder, chilli-soy marinated squid, and deep-fried Tasmanian camembert with cucumber, beetroot and mint salad. Buy some lavender-infused hand cream afterwards if you must.

❶ Getting There & Away

Tassielink (☑1300 300 520; www.tassielink.com.au) runs a weekday afternoon bus from Hobart to Port Arthur ($24.20, 2¼ hours) during school terms (reducing to Monday, Wednesday and Friday afternoons during school holidays), plus a morning and afternoon bus on Saturday. No bus on Sunday. Buses stop at the main towns en route.

THE MIDLANDS

Tracking north–south between Launceston and Hobart, the convict-built Midland Hwy has been Tasmania's main thoroughfare since it opened to horse-and-carriage traffic in 1821. The towns along this route – now also nostalgically known as the 'Heritage Hwy' – were established as garrisons for prisoners and guards, protecting travellers from the menace of bushrangers. These days there are plenty of places to stop and eat, drink and absorb the history here, with some amazing old bridges, homesteads and convict remnants to see.

Learn more on www.heritagehighway.com.au.

❶ Getting There & Away

Redline Coaches (☑1300 360 000; www.tasredline.com.au) buses power between Hobart and Launceston ($41.50, 2¾ hours) two to four times daily, via Kempton, Oatlands, Ross and Campbell Town. **Tassielink** (☑1300 300 520; www.tassielink.com.au) plies the same route as an express service, so doesn't stop at the Midlands towns.

Oatlands & the Southern Midlands

POP 860

Oatlands contains Australia's largest single collection of Georgian architecture. On the stately main street alone (which feels like a film set) there are 87 historic buildings.

The town's site was chosen in 1821 as one of four military posts on the Hobart–George Town road, but it was slow to develop. In 1832 an optimistic town surveyor marked out 80km of streets on the assumption Oatlands would become the Midlands' capital. Many folks made the town home in the 1830s, erecting solid buildings with the help of former convicts and soldiers who were skilled carpenters and stonemasons.

These days the town has a few decent places to stay and eat, and makes for a history-soaked stopover.

◉ Sights

Callington Mill   HISTORIC BUILDING
(☑03-6254 1212; www.callingtonmill.com.au; 1 Mill Lane, Oatlands; tours adult/child/family $15/8/40; ⊘9am-5pm) 🖉 Spinning above the Oatlands rooftops, the Callington Mill was built in 1837 and ground flour until 1891. After decades of neglect, with the innards collecting pigeon poo and the stonework crumbling, it's been fully restored and is once again producing high-grade organic flour. It's an amazing piece of engineering – the only working Lincolnshire-style windmill in Australia – fully explained on guided tours leaving hourly from 10am to 3pm.

Redlands Distillery   DISTILLERY
(☑03-6259 3058; www.redlandsdistillery.com.au; 26 Main St, Kempton; tours with/without tastings $30/10; ⊘10am-4pm) Redlands set up shop in 2012 at the old Redlands estate near New Norfolk, but has relocated to the equally gorgeous Dysart House (1842) in Kempton. Pull off the highway for a whisky tasting ($8 to $24), a bite to eat in the cafe, or a guided tour of the distillery and lovely old homestead (11am and 1.30pm).

Nant Distillery   DISTILLERY
(☑1800 746 453, 03-6128 3105; www.nant.com.au; 254 Nant La, Bothwell; tour/tasting $15/25, combined $35; ⊘10am-4pm daily, closed Mon & Tue Jun-Aug, tours 11am & 3pm) A key component of Bothwell's mini-Scotland ambience is this distillery, where superb single malt whisky is crafted in an 1820s flour mill. Tours and

tastings were running when we visited, but the restaurant – a piece of architecture that contrasts beautifully with older structures, including the estate's original convict-built homestead – was undergoing redevelopment. Call for tour times and bookings.

Ratho Farm GOLF
(☑0497 644 916, 03-6259 5553; www.rathofarm. com; 2122 Highland Lakes Rd, Bothwell; 9/18 holes $25/40, club/trolley hire $10/5; ⊙8am-dusk) Australia's oldest golf course was conjured out of the dust in 1822 by the Scottish settlers who built Bothwell. It's an eccentric course: be sure to watch out for sheep, hedges and hay bales.

There's also **accommodation** (s/d from $135/170, 2-bedroom units from $295; ❄ 🕸) here now, if you feel like a snooze after tackling the course.

🛏 Sleeping & Eating

Blossom's Cottage B&B $
(☑0499 844 512, 03-6254 1516; www.blossoms cottageoatlands.com.au; 116 High St, Oatlands; d incl breakfast $110; 🕸) In a self-contained garden studio, Blossom's is bright and cheerful, with a cast-iron bed, blackwood timber floors, leadlight windows, a small kitchenette and a couple of easy chairs under a silver birch. Great value. Fulsome breakfast basket provided.

Feisty Hen Pantry Cafe CAFE $
(☑0411 232 776; www.feistyhenpantry.com.au; 94 High St, Oatlands; mains $6-15; ⊙9am-3.30pm) How sweet! This diminutive stone cottage out the back of Oatlands Lodge B&B houses a European-style deli-cafe, serving all-day breakfasts, afternoon Devonshire teas, toasted sandwiches, slabs of quiche and slices of carrot cake – using all local, all seasonal ingredients. Good coffee too. There's a scatter of sunny tables out the front if the Midlands wind isn't howling.

ℹ Information

Oatlands Visitor Information Centre (☑03-6254 1212; www.heritagehighwaytasmania. com.au; Callington Mill, 1 Mill Lane, Oatlands; ⊙9am-5pm) Proffers general info and handles accommodation bookings. Pick up the free *Welcome to Oatlands* series of brochures, which include a self-guided town tour and leaflets on the old town gaol, supreme court and military precinct; and the *Lake Dulverton & Dulverton Walkway Information Guide,* for explorations around the lake.

Ross
POP 430

Another tidy (nay, immaculate) Midlands town, Ross was established in 1812 to protect Hobart–Launceston travellers from bushrangers. The town became an important coach-staging post at the centre of Tasmania's burgeoning wool industry and, before the famous Ross Bridge was built in 1836, a fording point across the Macquarie River.

These days the town's elm-lined streets are awash with colonial charm. Plenty of tourist accommodation keeps the town buzzing.

◉ Sights

Ross Bridge BRIDGE
(Bridge St, Ross; ⊙24hr) FREE The oft photographed 1836 Ross Bridge is the third-oldest bridge in Australia. Designed by colonial architect John Lee Archer, it was built by two convict stonemasons, Messrs Colbeck and Herbert, who were granted pardons for their efforts. Herbert chiselled the 186 intricate carvings decorating the arches, including Celtic symbols, animals and notable people (including Governor Arthur and Anglo-Danish convict Jorgen Jorgensen, the farcical ex-king of Iceland).

Ross Female Factory HISTORIC SITE
(☑03-6381 5466; www.parks.tas.gov.au; cnr Bond & Portugal Sts, Ross; ⊙9am-5pm) FREE This barren site was once one of Tasmania's five female convict prisons (the others were in Hobart, Launceston, George Town and Cascades on the Tasman Peninsula). Only one cottage remains, full of interesting historical info, but archaeological excavations below the sunburnt grass have revealed much. Descriptive panels provide insight into the hard lives these women led. Pick up the *Ross Female Factory* brochure from the visitor centre, then traverse the track from the top of Church St to get here.

🛏 Sleeping & Eating

★ The Stables COTTAGE $$
(☑03-6381 5481, 0438 250 161; 21 Church St, Ross; d from $140; @ 🕸) Nooked in behind a larger accommodation business on the main street is this cosy little gem – stylishly renovated, two-room former stables sleeping just two. Contemporary art, a mod kitchen, bedroom nook and exposed stone walls give the place oodles more charisma than a motel room.

★ Ross Village Bakery
BAKERY $

(☑ 03-6381 5246; www.rossbakery.com.au; 15 Church St, Ross; pies $5-9, mains $10-24; ☺ 9am-4pm Wed-Mon; 🔊) Overdose on savoury carbs, pies and astonishingly tall vanilla slices, plus virtuous soups and salads of all kinds. The owners get up before dawn every day to set the 1860 wood oven blazing. Wood-fired pizzas on Saturday nights in summer.

❶ Information

Ross Visitor Information Centre (☑ 03-6381 5466; www.visitross.com.au; 48 Church St, Ross; ☺ 9.30am-5pm Mon-Fri, 10am-5pm Sat & Sun) Inside the Tasmanian Wool Centre.

Campbell Town
POP 1000

Campbell Town, 12km north of Ross, is another former garrison and convict settlement. Unlike in Oatlands and Ross, the Midland Hwy still trucks right on through town, making it a handy pit stop. Along High St, rows of red bricks set into the footpath detail the crimes, sentences and arrival dates of convicts such as Ephram Brain and English Corney, sent here for crimes as various as stealing potatoes, bigamy and murder.

After convict transportation ended, Campbell Town's first white settlers were Irish timber workers who spoke Gaelic and had a particularly debauched reputation. Today, Campbell Town is ground zero for Tasmania's cattle- and sheep-farming industries.

◉ Sights

Red Bridge
BRIDGE

(High St, Campbell Town; ☺ 24hr) FREE The convict-built bridge across the slow-roaming Elizabeth River at Campbell Town was completed in 1838, making it almost as venerable as the Ross Bridge. Locals call it the Red Bridge because it was built from more than 1.5 million red bricks, baked on site.

✕ Eating

★ Zeps
CAFE $$

(☑ 03-6381 1344; www.zeps.com.au; 92 High St, Campbell Town; meals $10-31; ☺ 7am-8pm Mon-Fri, 8am-8pm Sat & Sun) A top spot is the hyperactive Zeps, serving brekky, pasta, fat pies and good coffee throughout the day, plus impressive pizzas and more substantial mains in the evening. This ain't no blow-through truck stop...try the sticky soy pork belly with spicy roast pumpkin and Asian greens.

❶ Information

Campbell Town Visitor Information Centre (☑ 03-6381 1353; www.campbelltowntasmania.com; Town Hall, 75 High St, Campbell Town; ☺ 10am-3pm Mon-Sat) Local info, plus **Campbell Town Museum** (www.discovertasmania.com.au/attraction/campbelltownmuseum andvisitorinformationcentre; ☺ 10am-3pm Mon-Fri). The centre is volunteer-run so hours may vary. Pick up the *Campbell Town – Historic Heart of Tasmania* brochure.

THE EAST COAST

White sand, gin-clear water, high blue skies... now strip off and plunge in! But don't stay in for too long – even in summer the water temperatures here can leave you breathless.

Tasmania's east coast is sea-salted and rejuvenating – a land of quiet bays and sandy shores, punctuated by granite headlands splashed with flaming orange lichen. The whole coast is fringed with forests, national parks and farmland.

Tasmania's west coast cops all the rain – by the time the clouds make it out here they're virtually empty! No surprise, then, that this is prime holiday terrain for Tasmanians, with plenty of opportunities to hike, bike, kayak, surf, dive and fish – set up your beachside camp and get into it. At the end of the day, fish and chips on the beach is a sure-fire winner. Or, if luxury is more your thing, you'll find hip lodges and top-flight eateries aplenty.

❶ Getting There & Away

Calow's Coaches (☑ 0400 570 036, 03-6376 2161; www.calowscoaches.com.au) Calow's Coaches runs from St Helens to Launceston ($33, three hours) via Scamander, St Marys and Fingal, connecting with Tassielink (☑ 1300 300 520; www.tassielink.com.au) buses at Conara, on the Midlands Hwy, for the run to Hobart ($56, four hours). Calow's also runs from St Helens to Bicheno ($12, two hours).

Tassielink (☑ 1300 300 520; www.tassielink.com.au) Tassielink buses run up the east coast from Hobart as far as Bicheno, stopping at all the towns along the way.

Maria Island National Park

Captivating Maria Island (pronounced 'Muh-rye-ah'), with its jagged peaks, rises up like a fairy-tale castle across Mercury Passage, which separates it from the mainland. It's a

East Coast

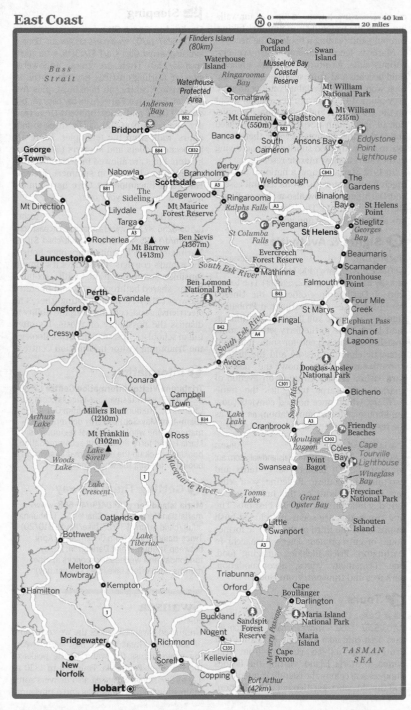

carefree, car-free haven – a top spot for walking, wildlife-watching, mountain biking, camping and reading a book on the beach.

Maria is laced with impressive scenery: curious cliffs, fern-draped forests, squeaky-sand beaches and azure seas. Forester kangaroos, wombats and wallabies wander around; grey-plumed Cape Barren geese honk about on the grasslands; and an insurance population of Tasmanian devils has been released and is thriving. Below the water there's also lots to see, with good snorkelling and diving in the clear, shallow marine reserve.

In 1972 Maria became a national park, as much for its history as for its natural assets, and Darlington is now also a Unesco World Heritage–listed site. The island doesn't have any shops: BYO food and gear.

◉ Sights & Avctivities

Darlington HISTORIC SITE
(☑03-6257 1420; www.parks.tas.gov.au; Darlington; park day pass per person $12; ⊙24hr) The township of Darlington – officially the Unesco World Heritage–listed Darlington Probation Station – is where you'll start your time on the island. Close to the ferry jetty are some amazing old **silos** (good for some midnight monastic chanting inside) and the historic **commissariat store**, now the national park visitor centre. Through an avenue of gnarled macrocarpa trees, lies the **penitentiary**, which once housed convicts (now bunkhouse-style accommodation) as well as the restored **Coffee Palace** and **mess hall**.

Maria Island Walk HIKING
(☑03-6234 2999; www.mariaislandwalk.com.au; per person $2450) Blisters, soggy tents and two-minute noodles? Redefine your concept of bushwalking on this luxury guided four-day hike through Maria's best bits. The first two nights are spent at secluded bush camps, with the third at the historic former home of entrepreneur Diego Bernacchi in Darlington. Price includes amazing food, fine Tasmanian wines, accommodation, park fees and transport from Hobart.

ⴳ Tours

East Coast Cruises CRUISE
(☑03-6257 1300; www.eastcoastcruises.com.au; tours adult/child from $195/65) ⌀ East Coast Cruises runs full-day ecotours from Triabunna to Maria Island, visiting the Ile des Phoques seal colony, the island's Painted Cliffs and the old convict settlement at Darlington.

🛏 Sleeping

Darlington Camp Site CAMPGROUND $
(☑03-6257 1420; www.parks.tas.gov.au; Darlington; unpowered sites s/d/f $7/13/16, extra adult/child $5/2.50) There are grassy unpowered sites at Darlington (fees payable at the island visitor centre; no bookings), plus free sites at **French's Farm** (park day pass per person $12) **FREE** and **Encampment Cove** (park day pass per person $12) **FREE** three-to-four hours' walk from the ferry pier. There are barbecues, toilets and showers ($1) at Darlington. Fires are allowed in designated fireplaces (often banned in summer). French's Farm and Encampment Cove have limited tank water – bring your own.

Penitentiary LODGE $
(☑03-6256 4772; www.tasmaniaseastcoast.com.au; dm/d/f $25/44/50, extra adult/child $10/5) Darlington's brick penitentiary once housed the island's convicts. These days it's simple, sensible accommodation, with six-bunk rooms, shared bathrooms and coin-operated showers ($1). BYO linen, lighting (there's no electricity), food, cooking gear and ability to dismiss the possibility of ghosts. It's often full of school groups, so plan ahead. Book via the Triabunna Visitor Information Centre.

ⓘ Information

Triabunna Visitor Information Centre (☑03-6257 4772; www.tasmaniaseastcoast.com.au; Charles St, Triabunna; ⊙9am-5pm Oct-Apr, 10am-4pm May-Sep) Cheerily delivered information on the whole east coast region, plus Maria Island ferry tickets and accommodation bookings. Pick up the handy *Great Eastern Drive* booklet, covering the whole coast.

ⓘ Getting There & Away

Maria Island Ferry (☑0419 746 668; www.mariaislandferry.com.au; Charles St, Triabunna; adult/child return $37/27, bike/kayak $10/20) Twice-daily service from December to April between Triabunna and Darlington; Friday-to-Monday and Wednesday services in other months. Also offers bike hire ($35 per day).

Swansea

POP 780

Unhurried Swansea graces the western shore of sheltered Great Oyster Bay, with sweeping views across the water to the peaks of the Freycinet Peninsula. Founded in 1820 as 'Great Swanport', Swansea also delivers some interesting historic buildings and a museum.

The town's revival since the doldrums of the 1980s has paralleled the boom in tourism across the state, though it manages to retain a laid-back holiday vibe. There are plenty of enticements for visitors in and around town, including myriad accommodation options, beaches, restaurants, cafes and some impressive wineries to the north. Swansea gets busy as a beaver (or perhaps a platypus?) in summer, so book ahead.

Sights & Activities

★Devil's Corner   WINERY
(☑03-6257 8881; www.brownbrothers.com.au; Sherbourne Rd, Apslawn; ☺10am-5pm) Below a devilishly tight turn on the Tasman Hwy, Devil's Corner is one of Tasmania's largest vineyards, run by the estimable Brown Brothers company. The mod cellar door here overlooks Moulting Lagoon, beyond which is Freycinet Peninsula. Even if you're not into wine, stop by to check out the jaunty lookout tower, or to grab a coffee, a sorbet, some oysters or fish and chips from the **food outlets** here, housed in styled-up shipping containers (mains $12 to $25).

★Spiky Bridge   BRIDGE
(off Tasman Hwy, Swansea; ☺24hr) **FREE** About 7km south of Swansea is the rather amazing Spiky Bridge, built by convicts in the early 1840s using thousands of local fieldstones (yes, they're spiky). The main east-coast road used to truck right across it, but these days it's set beside the highway. Nearby **Kelvedon Beach**, **Spiky Beach** and **Cressy Beach** have deep golden sand and rarely a footprint.

East Coast Heritage Museum   MUSEUM
(☑03-6256 5072; www.eastcoastheritage.org.au; 22 Franklin St, Swansea; entry by donation; ☺10am-4pm) **FREE** Inside Swansea's original schoolhouse – now also home to the Swansea Visitor Information Centre – this engaging little museum covers Aboriginal artefacts, colonial history, schooling in the early days and the plight of the thylacine.

Tours

Swansea Cycle Tours   CYCLING
(☑0400 899 956; www.swanseacycletours.com.au; 17 Old Spring Bay Rd, Swansea; tours per person guide/unguided from $100/60; ☺9am-5pm) Saddle up for one of seven customised bike tours around super-scenic, private east-coast farmland, visiting vineyards, oyster beds, lagoons and rivers. Bike hire also available ($15/25 per half-/full day).

Sleeping & Eating

Swansea Backpackers   HOSTEL $
(☑03-6257 8650; www.swanseabackpackers.com.au; 98 Tasman Hwy, Swansea; unpowered & powered sites $25-35, dm/d/tr/q from $39/85/85/90; ☎) This hip backpackers, next door to the Bark Mill, was purpose-built a few years ago, and is still looking sharp. Inside are smart, spacious public areas and a shiny stainless-steel kitchen. Rooms surround a shady deck and are clean and shipshape. More than a little fortuitously, the bar and bottle shop are right next door.

★Schouten House   B&B $$
(☑03-6257 8564; www.schoutenhouse.com.au; 1 Waterloo Rd, Swansea; d incl breakfast from $185; ☎) This brick-and-sandstone 1844 mansion was built by convicts, and was the centre of 'Great Swanport' before the action shifted a little further north. Decorated in simple, masculine Georgian style (no frills), its huge rooms now house antique beds and bathrooms. The history-buff owners do a mean pancake breakfast, and have perfected the art of making shortbread.

★Piermont   COTTAGE $$$
(☑03-6257 8131; www.piermont.com.au; 12990 Tasman Hwy, Swansea; 1-/2-bedroom cottages from $355/415; ☎▣) Down a hawthorn-hedged driveway, 5km south of Swansea, these 21 stylish stone cabins array out from an old farmhouse close to the sea. Each unit has a fireplace and a spa. There's also a pool, tennis court, free bikes and kayaks, and an eponymous **restaurant** (1-/2-/3-courses $45/65/75, degustation with/without wine $120/150; ☺6-8pm) that's been getting positive press. Big on weddings (so book ahead).

★Melshell Oysters   SEAFOOD $$
(☑0428 570 334, 03-6257 0269; www.melshelloysters.com.au; 1 Yellow Sandbanks Rd, Dolphin Sands; 12 oysters shucked/unshucked from $20/12; ☺10am-4pm) In the soupy back reaches of Moulting Lagoon, about 16km northeast of Swansea off Dolphin Sands Rd (itself off Swan River Rd – follow the signs), Melshell is a quirky caravan behind the dunes selling local Pacific oysters (and sometimes mussels). We like 'em natural, or with a little splash of Tabasco sauce.

Bark Mill Tavern & Bakery   CAFE $$
(☑03-6257 8094; www.barkmilltavern.com.au; 96 Tasman Hwy, Swansea; mains bakery $5-15, tavern $17-41; ☺bakery 6am-4pm, tavern noon-2pm &

5.30-8pm) The Bark Mill has two foodie faces: a busy bakery-cafe and a pubby tavern, both doing a roaring trade (to the exclusion of many other businesses in town, it seems). The bakery serves cooked breakfasts, stuffed rolls, sweet temptations, neat quiches and good coffee; the tavern does pizzas and voluminous mains (try the kangaroo and cheese sausage).

❶ Information

Swansea Visitor Information Centre (☑ 03-6256 5072; www.tasmaniaseastcoast.com.au; 22 Franklin St, Swansea; ◐ 9am-5pm; ☎) In the old school building on the corner of Noyes St (sharing space with the East Coast Heritage Museum).

Coles Bay & Freycinet National Park

POP 310

Coles Bay township sits on a sweep of sand at the foot of the dramatic pink-granite peaks of the Hazards on the Freycinet Peninsula. It's a laid-back holiday town with plenty of accommodation (though book well ahead in summer) and some active tour options. The sublime Freycinet National Park is the reason everyone is here: a wild domain of sugar-white beaches and utterly transparent water. In the coastal heath and forests, wild flowers and native critters hold sway.

The park encompasses the whole of the peninsula south of Coles Bay, including Schouten Island to the south, and a stretch of coastal scrub around the Friendly Beaches further north. The park's big-ticket sight is Wineglass Bay. Take the steep hike up to the saddle and grab your photo opportunity, or continue down to the sand on the other side for a (decidedly nippy) dip in the sea.

◉ Sights

★ **Friendly Beaches**   BEACH
(☑ 03-6256 7000; www.parks.tas.gov.au; Friendly Beaches Rd, Freycinet National Park; parks day pass per person/vehicle $12/24; ◐ 24hr) This wind-swept ocean beach is signposted from the main road about 26km north of Coles Bay. A five-minute walk leads from the car park to a vantage point: tumbling surf, an abandoned stretch of sand and views seemingly (if you squint, actually?) all the way to New Zealand.

Cape Tourville   LANDMARK
(☑ 03-6256 7000; www.parks.tas.gov.au; via Cape Tourville Rd, Freycinet National Park; parks day pass per person/vehicle $12/24; ◐ 24hr) There's an easy 20-minute circuit here for eye-popping panoramas of Freycinet Peninsula's eastern coastline. You can even get a wheelchair or a pram along here. Also here is **Cape Tourville Lighthouse**, which is totally spectacular when the sun cracks a smile over the horizon at dawn.

☞ Tours

★ **Freycinet Adventures**   KAYAKING
(☑ 03-6257 0500; www.freycinetadventures.com.au; 2 Freycinet Dr, Coles Bay; tour per adult/child $98/88; ◐ tours 8.30am Oct-Apr, 9am May-Sep; ♿) Get an eyeful of the peninsula from the sheltered waters around Coles Bay on these terrific three-hour paddles. There are also daily twilight tours available, setting off three hours before sunset. No experience necessary. Kayak hire is also available ($55 per person per day, including safety gear). Ask about overnight and multiday trips, too.

Freycinet Experience Walk   WALKING
(☑ 03-6223 7565, 1800 506 003; www.freycinet.com.au; adult/child $2400/2100; ◐ Nov-Apr) 🌿 For those who like their wilderness more mild, less wild, Freycinet Experience Walk offers a four-day, fully catered exploration of the peninsula. Walkers return each evening to the secluded, environmentally attuned Friendly Beaches Lodge for superb meals, local wine, hot showers and comfortable beds. The walk covers around 37km.

Wineglass Bay Cruises   BOATING
(☑ 03-6257 0355; www.wineglassbaycruises.com; Jetty Rd, Coles Bay; adult/child $40/90; ◐ 10am daily Sep-May, Tue, Thu & Sat only Jun-Aug) Sedate, four-hour cruises from Coles Bay to Wineglass Bay, including a gourmet chef-cooked lunch. The boat chugs around the southern end of the peninsula, passing Hazards Beach and Schouten Island en route. You're likely to see dolphins, sea eagles, seals, penguins and perhaps even migrating whales in the right season. Book ahead.

🛏 Sleeping

BIG4 Iluka on Freycinet Holiday Park   CARAVAN PARK, HOSTEL $
(☑ 03-6257 0115, 1800 786 512; www.big4.com.au; end of Reserve Rd, Coles Bay; unpowered sites $30, powered sites $36-40, hostel dm/tw/d $30/78/78, cabins & units $120-195; ☎) Iluka is a big, rambling park that's been here forever and is an unfaltering favourite with local holidaymakers – book well ahead. The backpackers section is managed by YHA; there's room

for only 32 (refreshingly small) in dorms, twins and doubles, and a predictably decent kitchen. The local shop, bakery and tavern are a short stroll down the hill.

Freycinet Rentals ACCOMMODATION SERVICES $$
(☑ 03-6257 0320; www.freycinetrentals.com; 5 East Esplanade, Coles Bay; rental houses $180-275) This is your hub for renting (mostly older-style) holiday houses and beach 'shacks' in and around Coles Bay. Prices swing wildly between summer and winter, and minimum stays apply for long weekends and Christmas holidays. One option, **81 On Freycinet**, has heaps of charm – the stone-and-timber house has three bedrooms, a spiral staircase and Hazards views (doubles $190).

★ **Saffire Freycinet** RESORT $$$
(☑ 1800 723 347, 03-6256 7888; www.saffire-freycinet.com.au; 2352 Coles Bay Rd, Coles Bay; d incl meals from $2100; ✿@☎) Saffire is an architectural and gastronomic marvel that sets the bar for top-notch Tasmanian hospitality. There are 20 luxe suites here, with the curvilicious main building housing a swanky restaurant, self-serve bar, library, art gallery and spa. There's also a menu of activity options, many included in the price. A two-night minimum stay often applies.

✗ Eating

★ **Tombolo Freycinet** CAFE, PIZZA $$
(☑ 03-6257 0124; www.tombolofreycinet.com.au; 6 Garnet Ave, Coles Bay; mains $17-25; ☺ 8am-8pm, to 9pm Dec-Feb) Local wines and seafood, superb wood-fired pizzas (try the Salty Sea Dog version) and the best coffee in town (Villino, roasted in Hobart), all served on a trim little deck overlooking the main street with views to the Hazards. Ooh, look – poached pear and frangipane tarts! Also has an outlet at Devil's Corner (p671) winery north of Swansea.

★ **Freycinet Marine Farm** SEAFOOD $$
(☑ 03-6257 0140; www.freycinetmarinefarm.com; 1784 Coles Bay Rd, Coles Bay; plates $15-25; ☺ 9am-5pm Sep-May, 10am-4pm Jun-Aug) Super-popular Freycinet Marine Farm grows huge, succulent oysters (a dozen shucked/unshucked $20/10) in the tidal waters of Moulting Lagoon. Also for your consideration are mussels, rock lobsters, scallops and abalone. Sit on the deck among the cray pots, sip some chardonnay and dig into your seafood picnic, as fresh as Freycinet.

DON'T MISS

WINEGLASS BAY WALK

This **route** (☑ 03-6256 7000; www.parks.tas.gov.au; Freycinet National Park; park day pass per person/vehicle $12/24; ☺ 24hr) is deservedly one of the most popular walks in Tasmania. You can make the steep climb to the **Wineglass Bay Lookout** (1½ hours return) for a super view over the bay and peninsula, but if you want to hear the beach squeak beneath your feet, you're in for a longer walk. The steep descent from the lookout to the bay takes another 30 minutes, making the out-and-back trip from the car park 2½ to three hours.

Bring your bathers if you want to take a dip in the brine once you make it to Wineglass.

❶ Information

Freycinet National Park Visitor Information Centre (☑ 03-6256 7000; www.parks.tas.gov.au; Freycinet Dr, Freycinet National Park; ☺ 8am-5pm Nov-Apr, 9am-4pm May-Oct) At the park entrance; get your parks passes here (day passes are popular, or there's a two-month holiday pass for not much more). Ask about free ranger-led activities December to February.

❶ Getting There & Away

Coles Bay is 31km from the Tasman Hwy turn-off. Traverse this stretch slowly between dusk and dawn to avoid hitting any wildlife on the road.

Calow's Coaches (☑ 0400 570 036, 03-6376 2161; www.calowscoaches.com.au) runs buses from Bicheno into Coles Bay ($12, 45 minutes). These buses also pick up passengers from **Tassielink** (☑ 1300 300 520; www.tassielink.com.au) east coast buses at the Coles Bay turn-off (from Hobart $36, three hours).

Bicheno

POP 860

Unlike upmarket Swansea and Coles Bay, Bicheno (*bish*-uh-no) is still a functioning fishing port. With brilliant ocean views and lovely beaches, it's also madly popular with holidaymakers, but the town has never sold its soul to the Tourism Devil and remains rough-edged and unwashed. A busy fishing fleet still comes home to harbour in the Gulch with pots of lobsters and scaly loot. Food and accommodation prices here will seem realistic if you're heading north from Freycinet.

European settlement began here when whalers and sealers came to the Gulch in 1803. The town became known as Waubs Bay Harbour, after an Aboriginal woman, Waubedebar, rescued two drowning men when their boat was wrecked offshore. After her death in 1832, the settlement bore her name until the 1840s when it was renamed to honour James Ebenezer Bicheno, once colonial secretary of Van Diemen's Land.

◎ Sights

★ Bicheno Motorcycle Museum   MUSEUM
(☑ 03-6375 1485; 35 Burgess St, Bicheno; adult/child $9/free; ◔ 9am-5pm Mon-Fri, 9am-4pm Sat, 9am-2pm Sun, closed Sun Jun-Aug) Andrew Quin got his first Honda at age four, and has been hooked on motorbikes ever since. You don't have to be an aficionado, though, to visit his wonderful museum out the back of his bike-repair shop. It's all shiny chrome and enamel under bright lights, with 60-plus immaculately restored bikes on display, including the rare Noriel 4 Café Racer – the only one of its kind in the world. East coast bikers wheel in for an oil top-up.

Diamond Island   ISLAND
(Redbill Beach, off Gordon St, Bicheno; ◔ 24hr) FREE Off the northern end of Redbill Beach is this photogenic granite outcrop, connected to the mainland via a short, semi-submerged, sandy isthmus, which you can wade across. Time your expedition for low tide – otherwise you might end up chest-deep in the waves trying to get back!

Natureworld   ZOO
(☑ 03-6375 1311; www.natureworld.com.au; 18356 Tasman Hwy, Bicheno; adult/child/family $25/12/65; ◔ 9am-5pm) About 7km north of Bicheno, this wildlife park is overrun with native and non-native wildlife, including Tasmanian devils, wallabies, quolls, snakes, wombats and enormous roos. There are devil feedings daily at 10am, 12.30pm and 3.30pm, and a devil house where you can see these little demons up close. There's a cafe here, too.

☆ Activities

★ Foreshore Footway   WALKING
(via Gordon St, Bicheno; ◔ 24hr) FREE This lovely 3km seaside stroll extends from Redbill Beach to the Blowhole (off Esplanade) via Waubedebar's Grave (off Old Tram Rd) and the Gulch (off Esplanade). When the

sea is angry (or just a bit annoyed), huge columns of foamy seawater spurt spectacularly into the air at the Blowhole. Don't get too close: even on calm days you can be unexpectedly drenched. Return along the path up Whalers Hill (off Foster St), which offers broad views over town. In whaling days, passing sea giants were spotted from here.

☞ Tours

Bicheno Penguin Tours   BIRDWATCHING
(☑ 03-6375 1333; www.bichenopenguintours.com.au; Tasman Hwy, Bicheno; adult/child $35/15; ◔ dusk nightly, booking office 9am-5.30pm Mon-Fri, 10am-5pm Sat & Sun) Bicheno is one of the top spots in Tasmania to see penguins: spy them on these one-hour dusk tours as they waddle back to their burrows. Expect a sincere nature experience: no cafes or souvenirs (and no photography allowed). Departure times vary year-round, depending on when dusk falls. Penguin numbers peak from November to January. Bookings essential.

Bicheno's Glass Bottom Boat   BOATING
(☑ 0407 812 217, 03-6375 1294; www.facebook.com/bichenoglassbottomboat; Esplanade, the Gulch; adult/child $25/10; ◔ 10am, noon & 2pm) This 40-minute trip will give you a watery perspective on Bicheno's submarine wonders. Tours run October to May from the Gulch, weather permitting (bookings advised in January).

⌨ Sleeping & Eating

Bicheno Backpackers   HOSTEL $
(☑ 03-6375 1651; www.bichenobackpackers.com; 11 Morrison St, Bicheno; dm/s/tw/d/houses from $30/55/70/78/130; ☏) This congenial backpackers has dorms spread across two mural-painted buildings, plus a 12-berth self-contained house nearby, set up as six doubles. The communal kitchen is the place to be. There's also free luggage storage, and a walking track to a lookout at the top of the street. Is the new wine centre next door open yet?

★ Beach Path House   RENTAL HOUSE $$
(☑ 03-6375 1583, 03-6375 1400; www.beachpathhouse.com.au; 2 Gordon St, Bicheno; d $195-380, weekly $950-1860; ☒) Painted cream and navy, this mid-century beach shack has been reborn as a contemporary holiday house, with three bedrooms, flower-filled gardens, an open fire and a little deck from where you can hear the surf. A couple of old cray pots are strewn

about for good nautical measure. Sleeps eight. Prices swing wildly with the seasons.

★ Pasinis
ITALIAN, CAFE **$$**

(☑ 03-6375 1076; 70 Burgess St, Bicheno; mains breakfast $8-20, lunch & dinner $13-33; ⊙ 9am-8pm Tue-Sat, 9am-3pm Sun) This expertly managed outfit does Italian staples such as antipasto plates, wood-fired pizzas and lasagne – but oh, so much better than most. The breakfasts border on artisanal, the pastas and gnocchi are homemade and the coffees ('Oomph' brand, roasted in Hobart) are richly delicious. Takeaways, east coast beers and wines, oysters and sumptuous sandwiches also make the cut. Winner!

ℹ Information

Bicheno Visitor Information Centre (☑ 03-6256 5072; www.eastcoasttasmania.com; 41b Foster St, Bicheno; ⊙ 9am-5pm Oct-Apr, 10am-4pm May-Sep) Local information and accommodation bookings.

St Helens

POP 2180

On the broad, protected sweep of Georges Bay, St Helens began life as a whaling and sealing settlement in the 1830s. Soon the 'swanners' came to plunder, harvesting the bay's black swans for their downy underfeathers. By the 1850s the town was a permanent farming settlement, which swelled in 1874 when tin was discovered nearby. Today, St Helens is a pragmatic sort of town, harbouring the state's largest fishing fleet. This equates to plenty for anglers to get excited about; charter boats will take you out to where the big game fish play. For landlubbers there are plenty of places to eat, sleep and unwind, and good beaches nearby.

◉ Sights

St Helens History Room
MUSEUM

(☑ 03-6376 1479, 0419 731 452; www.sthelens historyroom.com; 61 Cecilia St, St Helens; adult/family $3/5; ⊙ 9am-5pm) Out the back of the town visitor centre is this unexpected little museum, cataloguing the town's social and natural history. Farming, exploring, schooling, whaling, fishing, mining, shells and east-coast wildlife all get a once-over (is that thylacine's head life-sized?), all to the tick-tick-tick of an antique clock. Don't miss the amazing old funeral buggy, and the cheesy-but-interesting film introducing the

Trail of the Tin Dragon, focusing on Chinese tin mining in the northeast.

🏃 Activities

Gone Fishing Charters
FISHING

(☑ 03-6376 1553, 0419 353 041; www.breamfishing.com.au) Hook a bream or two on a close-to-shore fishing trip with an expert local guide. Call to talk times and prices. No fish, no pay (you have to admire the confidence).

🛏 Sleeping

BIG4 St Helens Holiday Park
CARAVAN PARK **$**

(☑ 1300 559 745; www.sthelenscp.com.au; 2 Penelope St, St Helens; powered/unpowered sites from $37/35, cabin & villa d $110-210, extra person $25; ❄ 🖥 🐾) This efficiently run park rolls itself across a green hillside 1.5km south of town and has plenty of family-centric amenities (games room, jumping pillow, playground, swimming pool). Shoot for one of the smart row of blue-and-cream villas running up the hill. Decent camp kitchen. Venture to the top of the slope to find a flat patch for your tent.

★ The French House
B&B **$$**

(☑ 0414 264 258, 03-6376 2602; www.thefrench housesthelens.com.au; 197 Ansons Bay Rd, St Helens; d $140-170; ❄ 🖥) About 4km from St Helens, this B&B, built 20 years ago by a Frenchman homesick for his country home, exudes Gallic charm. Upstairs are four compact en-suite rooms with TV and fridge; downstairs is a country kitchen and guest lounge with herringbone timber floor. Not frilly or kitsch, just simple and stylish. Breakfasts are generous cooked affairs. *Oui, oui!*

✕ Eating & Drinking

Mohr & Smith
CAFE **$$**

(☑ 03-6376 2039; www.mohrandsmith.com.au; 55-59 Cecilia St, St Helens; breakfast & lunch mains $16-22, dinner $28-40; ⊙ 10am-8pm Tue-Sat) Oh look! A slick urban nook! With a sunny front terrace, snug open-fire lounge area, chilled tunes and sexy staff, M&S would feel right at home on Salamanca Place in Hobart. Order a pulled-pork quesadilla or a Japanese pancake with chilli jam and coriander for lunch and see what the afternoon brings. Good for an evening drink, too.

★ Crossroads Wine Bar & Cafe
BAR

(☑ 0414 719 490; www.crossroadswinebar.com.au; 5/34 Quail St, St Helens; bar food $10-15; ⊙ 4pm-late Wed, 7pm-late Fri & Sat; 🔊) Named after the Robert Johnson blues classic, this surprising find is one of the east coast's only regular live music venues: there are blues, country and rock gigs most Friday nights. On other evenings, the owners usually fire up some music DVDs to complement a few cold ones (sports-free zone here). Open more often during summer.

ℹ Information

St Helens Visitor Information Centre (☑ 03-6376 1744; www.eastcoasttasmania.com; 61 Cecilia St, St Helens; ⊘ 9am-5pm) Just off the main street behind the library. Sells national parks passes. The St Helens History Room is here too.

Binalong Bay & the Bay of Fires

POP 210

The Bay of Fires is a 29km-long sweep of powder-white sand and crystal-clear seas that's featured on plenty of 'Most Beautiful Beaches in the World' lists recently. To refer to the Bay of Fires as a single beach, though, is a mistake: it's actually a string of superb beaches, punctuated by lagoons and rocky headlands, backed by coastal heath and bush.

There's no road that runs the length of the bay: the C850 heads out of St Helens to the gorgeous beachside holiday settlement of Binalong Bay, which marks the southern end of the bay. In the bay's northern end are **Ansons Bay**, a quiet holiday hamlet, and the southern sections of Mt William National Park (p676).

Eddystone Point, just north of Ansons Bay, within Mt William National Park, marks the Bay of Fires' northern extremity, the tall **Eddystone Point Lighthouse** (www.lighthouses.org.au; via Eddystone Point Rd, Mt William National Park; ⊘ 24hr) FREE standing as a symbolic exclamation mark.

⊙ Sights

Mt William National Park NATIONAL PARK
(☑ 03-6387 5510; www.parks.tas.gov.au; via St Helens or Gladstone; parks pass per person/vehicle $12/24, camping d/f $13/16, extra adult/child $5/2.50; ⊘ 24hr) Little-known, isolated Mt William National Park features long sandy beaches, low ridges and coastal heathlands; visit during spring or early summer when the wild flowers are bloomin' marvellous. The highest point, Mt William (1½-hour return walk), stands only 216m tall, yet projects your gaze over land and sea. The area was declared a national park in 1973, primarily to protect Tasmania's remaining Forester (eastern grey) kangaroos, which faced extinction in the 1950s and '60s (they've been breeding themselves silly ever since).

🏃 Activities & Tours

Bay of Fires Lodge Walk WALKING
(☑ 03-6392 2211; www.bayoffires.com.au; tour from $2300; ⊘ Oct-May) A four-day, three-night guided adventure through this glorious wave-washed domain. A maximum of 10 guests beachcomb the coastline, led by knowledgable guides. The first night is spent at a secluded tented beach camp, with the next two at the sublime Bay of Fires Lodge. Fine food and wine included. Magic!

Bay of Fires Eco Tours BOATING
(☑ 0499 209 756; www.bayoffiresecotours.com.au; Main Rd, Binalong Bay; 2½hr tour per adult/child/family $135/85/380) 🚤 Even with a 4WD it's impossible to access about 60% of the Bay of Fires coastline...so take a boat trip instead! Based in a little 1935 shack on the Binalong Bay waterfront, this outfit will get you out on the water to see dunes, dolphins, Aboriginal sites and the lichen-covered coast between Binalong Bay and Eddystone Point.

🛏 Sleeping & Eating

Kingfisher Cottage RENTAL HOUSE $$
(☑ 0467 808 738; www.stayz.com.au; 74 Main Rd, Binalong Bay; house from $195; ✳🛜) We like this one: not gregarious, not making a statement, not flashy or pretentious – just the perfect little beach house in a primo location, right in the sandy heart of Binalong Bay, next to the restaurant and a pebble's toss from the beach (the best bit for swimming). Sleeps six in two bedrooms.

Bay of Fires Bush Retreat TENTED CAMP $$
(☑ 0439 343 066; www.bayoffiresbushretreat.com.au; 795 Reids Rd, Binalong Bay; safari tent d & tw from $145; 🛜) Heading north from Binalong Bay into the Bay of Fires, this rustic, hippie-goes-boutique bush camping set-up involves interesting 'bell tents' with shared bathrooms and cooking facilities. Gourmet platters and breakfast hampers are available if you don't feel like cooking for yourself (order when you book). The vibe is chilled-out and wholesome.

★ Moresco Restaurant CAFE $$
(☑ 03-6376 8131; www.morescorestaurant.com.au; 64a Main Rd, Binalong Bay; mains $15-24; ⊘ noon-3pm & 6-8pm, closed Mon & Tue Jun-Aug)

TASMANIA BINALONG BAY & THE BAY OF FIRES

Binalong Bay's only food business means business: a fantastic food room overlooking the water, serving top-flight meals. Roll in for some Huon Valley mushrooms on toast with Tasmanian truffle oil for lunch, hit the surf, then come back for a vat of seafood broth (local fish) with toasted sourdough for dinner. Great coffee; even greater wine list.

ℹ️ Getting There & Away

At the southern end of the Bay of Fires is Binalong Bay, an easy 10-minute drive from St Helens. The northern end of the bay is flagged by Ansons Bay and Eddystone Point Lighthouse, both accessed via Ansons Bay Rd tracking north from St Helens. In between, other than the unsealed road from Binalong Bay to the Gardens holiday settlement, there's no road access, and certainly no public transport.

Derby & Around

POP 210

For much of the year, Derby (dur-bee) seems a rather forlorn little town nooked into the Ringarooma River valley, clinging grimly to its tin mining history, dating back to the 1870s. The tin mines closed in the 1940s, causing an exodus that has never really stopped.

But there's a transformation underway, courtesy of a network of brilliant mountain biking trails in the surrounding hills. The Australian Cross Country Marathon Mountain Bike Championships (www.mtba.asn.au) happened here in 2015 and 2016, and at the time of writing, a 2017 Enduro World Championships (www.enduroworldseries.com) event was about to transpire. When the mountain bikers are in town the place goes berserk, and accommodation is booked out from here to St Helens. About 8km west of Derby is **Branxholm** (population 210) with further sleeping and eating options.

If you're driving into Derby from Weldborough, check out the gigantic trout mural splashed across the cliffs near the bridge into town.

⊙ Sights

Tin Centre   MUSEUM
(☑ 03-6354 1062; www.trailofthetindragon. au/derby; 55 Main St, Derby; adult/child/family $9/4/20; ⊙ 9am-5pm, reduced winter hours) Derby's tin-mining heritage is on display in this architecturally impressive museum, part of the **Trail of the Tin Dragon** tourist route. The centrepiece is its multimedia presenta-

tion, *Small Town, Big History*, documenting the life and times of miners and mining in the northeast's tin-mining boom days. Call ahead in winter to ensure it's open. The **Crank It Cafe** (www.crankitcafederby.com; mains $6-14; ⊙ 9am-4pm Sun-Fri, 9am-5pm Sat) is here too.

Bridestowe Lavender Estate   FARM
(☑ 03-6352 8182; www.bridestowelavender.com. au; 296 Gillespies Rd, Nabowla; admission free Feb-Nov, per person $10 Dec & Jan; ⊙ 9am-6pm) Near Nabowla, 22km west of Scottsdale, is the turn-off to the largest lavender farm in the southern hemisphere, producing lavender oil for the perfume industry. The purple fields in flowering season (mid-December to late January) are unforgettable. There's also a **cafe** and **gift shop** that sells all things lavender: drawer scenters, fudge, ice cream and 'Bobbie Bears' – lavender-stuffed toys that (inexplicably) sell by the thousands.

🏃 Activities

**Blue Derby Mountain
Bike Trails**   MOUNTAIN BIKING
(☑ 03-6352 6500; www.ridebluederby.com.au; off Tasman Hwy, Derby; ⊙ 24hr) **FREE** Derby has become Tasmania's mountain biking mecca, with the Blue Derby network of 25 trails at the fore. Trails range from easy to extremely difficult, and from 1km to 40km (the latter being the three-stage track between the Blue Tier and Derby). Check out the signboards at the southern end of town for info, or download maps from the website.

Vertigo MTB   MOUNTAIN BIKING
(☑ 0488 463 448, 0409 702 875; www.vertigomtb. com.au; 66 Main St, Derby; bike hire per day incl equipment from $99; ⊙ 8am-5pm) One-stop shop for all your MTB needs in Derby: bike hire, trail info, repairs and maintenance, shuttles to trail heads, even advice on places to eat and accommodation. There are all kinds of shuttle-and-ride combos available: for example, Derby to the 24km Blue Tier track return with a lunch stop at the Weldborough Hotel is $79.

🛌 Sleeping & Eating

⭐ **Weldborough Hotel**   PUB $
(☑ 03-6354 2223; www.weldborough.com.au; 12 Main Rd, Weldborough; unpowered & powered sites $20, d/f without bathroom from $100/150; ⊙ 11.30am-late) The hub of town life, the 1876 Weldborough Hotel is a characterful lunch stop or overnighter. Beer boffins rejoice:

product from every Tasmanian craft brewery is on hand! The kitchen delivers excellent food (mains $13 to $32) and there's pub accommodation if you've had too many ales to drive. There are also verdant camp sites and hot showers out the back.

Branxholm Lodge   LODGE $

(☑ 0447 041 418; www.branxholmlodge.com.au; 32 Albert St, Branxholm; d $100, extra person $15) Breathing new life into what was once the Branxholm Primary School, this budget lodge is set-up well for mountain bikers, with dorm bunks for up to 12 people, bike storage, maintenance and wash-down areas, a kitchen, a laundry, multiple toilet areas and plenty of heaters for chilly northeastern nights.

Tin Dragon Trail Cottages   COTTAGE $$

(☑ 03-6354 6210, 0407 501 137; www.tindragon trailcottages.com.au; 3 Cox's La, Branxholm; d from $170, extra person $70) ✿ These five neat, sustainably built cottages sit near the Ringarooma River on a property that has an interesting story to tell from the Chinese mining past. Two interpretative walks here follow some of the original (now dry) mining races built by Chinese miners. More contemporary is the amazing 'micro-hydro' station the owners have built, powering the whole property. Two-night minimum.

Imperial Hotel   PUB FOOD $$

(☑ 03-6354 6121; www.myspace.com/branxholm imperial; 5-7 Stoke St, Branxholm; mains $16-26; ☺ bar 11am-late, meals noon-1.30pm daily, 6-7.30pm Mon-Sat) Locals in the know say Branxholm's 113-year-old country pub is the best place for a feed within miles. Expect country-sized plates of steak, seafood, pork chops, surf 'n' turf, schnitzels and roast-of-the-day, plus endless cold beer. There's basic pub-style accommodation upstairs, too, from $35 per person.

❶ Getting There & Away

Sainty's North East Bus Service (☑ 0400 791 076, 0437 469 186; www.saintysnortheastbus service.com.au) Runs between Launceston and Derby ($22, 2½ hours) once daily (Monday to Friday) in each direction.

Flinders Island

POP 700

There's more than one island here, adrift in Bass Strait off the northeastern corner of Tasmania: Flinders is just one of 51 islands in the Furneaux Group archipelago. These rocky, mountainous isles are all that remains of the land bridge that connected Tasmania with mainland Australia 10,000 years ago.

Sparsely populated and naturally gorgeous, Flinders is a rural community that lives mostly from fishing and agriculture. For visitors there's great bushwalking, wildlife spotting, fishing, kayaking, snorkelling, diving and safe swimming in its curvaceous bays. Or you can spend a few leisurely hours combing the beaches for elusive Killiecrankie diamonds (topaz, technically) and nautilus shells.

For online inspiration, see www.visit flindersisland.com.au.

◉ Sights

Furneaux Museum   MUSEUM

(☑ 03-6359 8434; www.flinders.tas.gov.au/furn eaux-museum; 8 Fowlers Rd, Emita; adult/child $4/ free; ☺ 1-5pm Sat & Sun Dec-Apr, 1-4pm Sat & Sun May-Nov) The grounds around the volunteer-run Furneaux Museum are strewn with whalebones, blubber pots and rusty wrecks. Inside are Aboriginal artefacts (including beautiful shell necklaces), plus sealing, sailing and mutton-bird industry relics.

Wybalenna Historic Site   HISTORIC SITE

(☑ 03-6359 5002; www.visitflindersisland.com.au/ places/wybalenna; Port Davies Rd, Emita; ☺ daylight hours) [FREE] A few piles of bricks, the chapel and cemetery are all that remain of this misguided settlement built to 'care for' relocated Tasmanian Aboriginal people, operating between 1829 and 1834. Eighty-seven people died here from poor food, disease and despair – among them was Manalargena, chief of the Ben Lomond tribe, whose headstone can be seen here. The site is on Aboriginal land: be respectful.

🏃 Activities

There's great **bushwalking** on Flinders. The highlight is a well-signposted track to the peak of **Mt Strzelecki** (756m, five hours return) for poetry-inspiring views. At the disarmingly named **Trousers Point** there's a terrific 1.9km coastal circuit walk. Keen for more? Source a copy of *A Walking Guide to Flinders Island and Cape Barren Island,* by Doreen Lovegrove and Steve Summers, or *Walks of Flinders Island,* by Ken Martin. Multiday guided hiking packages are available.

It's easy to find your own private beach for **swimming**. A local secret is the **Docks** below Mt Killiecrankie, where granite boulders protect white-sand coves. **Trousers Point**

Beach is the classic Flinders swimming spot, with picnic tables, BBQs, toilets and unpowered camp sites under the she-oaks; national park entry fees ($12/24 per person/vehicle per day) apply here. **Fishing, snorkelling** and **diving** possibilities also abound.

The granite faces of Mt Killiecrankie (319m) offer challenging **rock climbing**. There's also a climbable 200m granite wall on Mt Strzelecki.

Flinders Island Adventures   FISHING, WALKING
(✆03-6359 4507; www.flindersisland.com.au) Book a fishing charter with this local outfit, which also runs land-based walking tours (five-day all-inclusive guided walks per person from $2415). A two-night fishing package (with breakfast, lunch, accommodation at Lady Baron and transfers) costs $695 per person.

🛏 Sleeping & Eating

Furneaux Tavern   MOTEL $$
(✆03-6359 3521; www.furneauxtavern.com.au; 11 Franklin Pde, Lady Barron; s/d/f from $90/120/150; 🛜) An array of nicely updated motel-style cabins with wraparound decks, set amid native gardens. The fish-focused **Shearwater Restaurant** (✆03-6359 3521; www.furneauxtavern.com.au; Furneaux Tavern, 11 Franklin Pde, Lady Barron; mains $16-33; ⊗ noon-1.30pm & 6-7.30pm) is here, too, and you can bend an elbow over the pool table in the bar.

West End Beach House   RENTAL HOUSE $$$
(✆0488 089 955; www.westendbeachhouse.com.au; 801 West End Rd, Leeka; house $260-345) 🏖 Architect-designed to have a minimal environmental footprint, this fabulous, roll-roofed holiday house en route to Mt Tanner has a very Australian vibe: corrugated iron, lots of fold-back glass, sunny decks, outdoor post-beach shower and a short stroll to the sand. And the sunken bath is something to cherish! Two-night minimum stay.

A Taste of Flinders   DELI $
(✆0474 889 236; www.tasteofflinders.com.au; 3 Walker St, Whitemark; ⊗ 8am-4pm Mon-Fri, 9am-noon Sat) This savvy cafe-deli does the best coffee on the island, and has shelves full of fresh island produce: bread, vegetables, jams, bottled water, wine, honey. Food on your plate includes the likes of quiches, cakes and virtuous salads.

ℹ Information

Flinders Island Visitor Information Centre
(✆03-6359 5002; www.visitflindersisland.

com.au; 4 Davies St, Whitemark; ⊗ 9am-5pm Mon-Fri) The main hub for island advice.

ℹ Getting There & Around

Sharp Airlines (✆1300 556 694; www.sharpairlines.com; Flinders Island Airport, Palana Rd, Whitemark) Flies between Melbourne (Essendon Airport) and Flinders Island Airport at Whitemark (one-way $252), and between Launceston and Flinders Island (one-way $185). Fly-drive packages start at $463.

Flinders Island Car Rentals (✆03-6359 2168, 0415 505 655; www.ficr.com.au; 21 Memana Rd, Whitemark) Flinders Island Car Rentals has sedans and minivans from $77 per day, and operates an electricity-powered(!) airport shuttle between the airport and your accommodation (one-way from $10).

Flinders Island Travel (✆1800 674 719; www.flindersislandtravel.com.au) Offers package deals (flights, accommodation and car rental).

LAUNCESTON & AROUND

It's hard to imagine a pocket-sized city more appealing than Launceston. 'Lonnie', as the locals call it, is certainly large enough for some urban buzz, but small enough for country congeniality to be the rule rather than the exception. The city melds the historic with the contemporary, bolstered by vibrant arts and food scenes. Surrounded by bush, amazing Cataract Gorge brings the wilds into the heart of town, and those who want to travel a little further out have plenty of choices: following the Tamar Valley Wine Route delivers scenery in spades and gives the opportunity to taste world-class pinot noirs; visiting historic pastoral estates such as Woolmers and Clarendon hits all the heritage high notes; and national parks at Narawntapu and Ben Lomond offer plenty of opportunities to get up close to unspoiled nature.

Launceston

POP 74,090

Tasmania's second city has forever been locked in rivalry with big-smoke Hobart to the south. Launcestonians argue that their architecture is more elegant, their parks more beautiful, their surrounding hills more verdant and their food scene zestier. And on many of these points it's hard to argue. This is a city where art and design are highly valued, where the locals embrace the outdoors and where food and coffee culture thrives. It's an easy and endearing base for those exploring the Tamar Valley or other parts of the north.

Sights

★ Queen Victoria Museum
MUSEUM

(QVMAG; Map p682; ☑ 03-6323 3777; www.qvmag.tas.gov.au; 2 Invermay Rd, Invermay; ⊙10am-4pm, planetarium shows noon & 2pm Tue-Fri, 2pm & 3pm Sat) FREE The natural, social and technology-focused collections of the Queen Victoria Museum and Art Gallery (QVMAG) are exhibited in this annex housed in historic workshops in the the restored and reinvented Inveresk Railyards precinct. The building itself is half the attraction. Inside, the zoology, botany and geology collections are extensive and the planetarium (adult/child/family $6/4/16) is perennially popular. There's also a cafe and a museum shop on site. Get here on the Free Tiger Bus (p686).

★ Queen Victoria Art Gallery
MUSEUM, GALLERY

(QVMAG; Map p682; ☑ 03-6323 3777; www.qvmag.tas.gov.au; 2 Wellington St; ⊙10am-4pm) FREE Colonial paintings, including works by John Glover, are the pride of the collection at this art gallery in a meticulously restored 19th-century building on the edge of Royal Park. Other works cover the gamut of Australian painting from Tom Roberts to Fred Williams and Bea Maddock. There's also an impressive collection of decorative arts, a popular cafe and a gallery shop.

★ Cataract Gorge
PARK

(Map p681; ☑ 03-6331 5915; www.launceston cataractgorge.com.au; via Cataract Walk, Trevallyn; chairlift one way adult/child $12/8, return $15/10; ⊙gorge 24hr, chairlift 9am-5.30pm Dec-Feb, till 5pm Mar-May & Sep-Nov, till 4.30pm Jun-Aug) At magnificent Cataract Gorge, the bushland, cliffs and ice-cold South Esk River feel a million miles from town. At First Basin there's a free outdoor **swimming pool** (November to March), the world's longest single-span **chairlift** and Victorian-era gardens. Elsewhere, there are walking and cycling tracks as well as lookouts. Eating options include two cafes and a BBQ area. The whole shebang is impressively floodlit at night.

Boag's Brewery
BREWERY

(Map p682; ☑ 03-6332 6300; www.boags.com.au; 39 William St; tours adult/child $33/15; ⊙9.30am-5pm Mon-Fri, 10.30am-5pm Sat & Sun) James Boag's beer has been brewed on William St since 1881. See the amber alchemy in action on 90-minute guided tours (11am, 1pm and 3pm daily); these include a beer and cheese tasting. Alternatively, order a beer paddle ($10) and afterwards take a wander through the free on-site museum, which sheds further light on brewing history (old TV ads, beer labels and photographs aplenty).

Activities

Rock Climbing Tasmania
CLIMBING

(☑0447 712 638; http://rockclimbingtasmania.com.au) Offers half-day climbs and abseils in Cataract Gorge ($150 per person, minimum two people) with a qualified guide. Includes all equipment.

Cable Hang Gliding
ADVENTURE SPORTS

(☑0419 311 198; www.cablehanggliding.com.au; Reatta Rd, Trevallyn State Recreation Area, Trevallyn; adult/child/tandems/family $20/15/30/60; ⊙10am-5pm daily Dec-Apr, Sat & Sun during May-Nov school holidays; ⊕) Make like a condor with a spot of cable hang gliding in the Trevallyn Nature Recreation Area. You'll hurtle over the edge of a cliff and glide down a 200m-long cable, suspended under wide wings. Stomach-in-your-mouth stuff. Head west along Paterson St and from King's Bridge follow the signs. Closed on windy days.

Tours

Tamar River Cruises
BOATING

(Map p682; ☑03-6334 9900; www.tamarriver cruises.com.au; Home Point Pde) Hop aboard the 1890s-style *Lady Launceston* for a 50-minute Cataract Gorge cruise (adult/child/family $29/12/70), or opt for a longer exploration of the gorge and the riverfront on the modern *Tamar Odyssey* (adult/child/family $79/35/179). Four-hour cruises on the same boat take you downstream to Batman Bridge and back and include a light lunch (adult/child/family $125/60/290). Check the website for sailing times.

Launceston Historic Walks
WALKING

(Map p682; ☑03-6331 2213; www.1842.com.au/launceston-historic-walks; per person $15; ⊙tour at 4pm Mon, 10am Tue-Sat) Get your historical bearings with a 1½-hour walking journey through the Georgian, Victorian and modern architecture of the city. Walks depart from the '1842' building, on the corner of St John and Cimitiere Sts. Discounted family tickets can be arranged.

Launceston

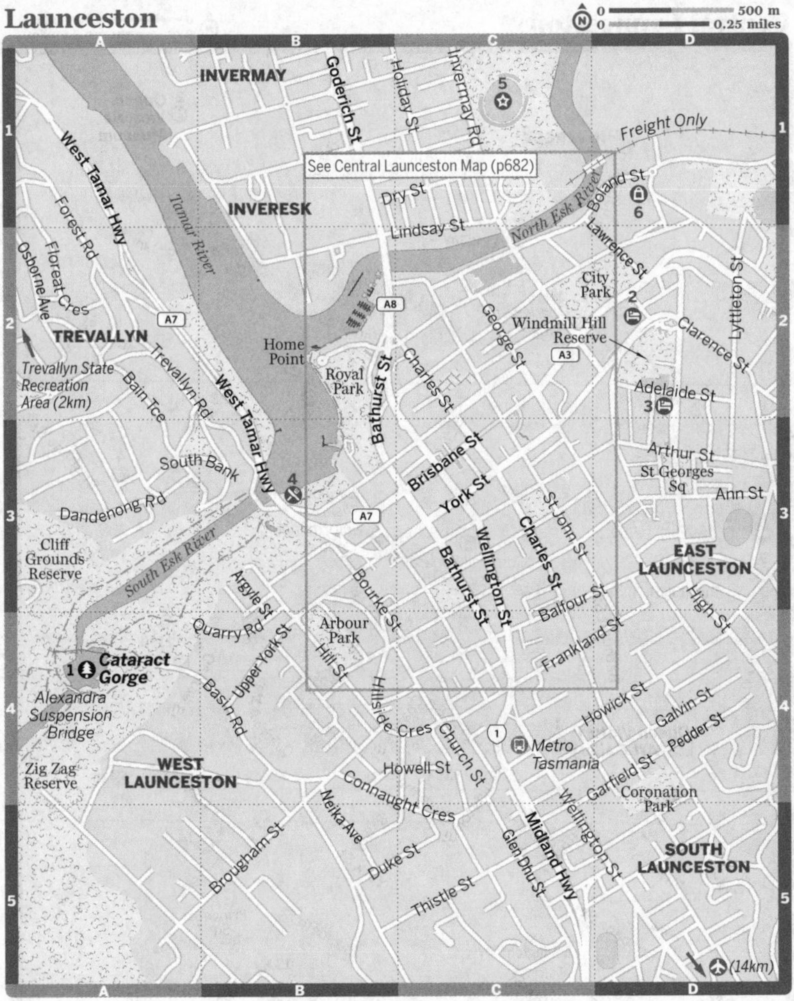

Mountain Bike Tasmania MOUNTAIN BIKING
(☎0447 712 638; www.mountainbiketasmania.com.au) Runs guided rides along the North Esk River ($100), through the Trevallyn Nature Recreation Area ($120) and down the slopes of Ben Lomond ($225) – a downhill rush shedding 1050m in altitude. Derby tours ($250) are also available, as is an off-road descent of Mt Wellington in Hobart ($225). Child riders receive a $20 discount.

Launceston Explorer BUS
(Map p682; ☎1800 651 827; adult/concession/child $50/45/40; ⏲Jan-Apr) Departing from the Launceston Visitor Information Centre, these

Launceston

Top Sights
1 Cataract Gorge....A4

Sleeping
2 Hi George....D2
3 Kurrajong House....D2

Eating
4 Stillwater....B3

Entertainment
5 York Park....C1

Shopping
6 Autobarn....D1

Central Launceston

0 — 200 m
0 — 0.1 miles

INVERESK

Dry St
Holiday St
Lindsay St
Goderich St
Lindsay St
Invermay Rd

Queen Victoria Museum
2

Victoria Bridge
Boland St

Charles St Bridge
North Esk River
Esplanade

Lindsay St

Shields St
William St
3
George St
Tamar St
22

Cimitiere St
City Park
Cimitiere St
4
Brisbane St

Seaport
Home Point Pde
William St
St John St
23
Cornwall Square Transit Centre
6
5
Launceston Visitor Information Centre
Cameron St
Cameron St
Tamar St

Royal Park

Civic Square

Paterson St
16
19
21
17
Earl St
York St

Cameron St
Paterson St
Charles St
St John St
Brisbane St
Quadrant Mall
George St

Queen Victoria Art Gallery
1
24
25
Wellington St
Brisbane St
Kingsway
18
20
14
15
Vincent St

Park St
Barrow St
York St
York St

Kings Park
Paterson St
Brisbane St
Bathurst St

Elizabeth St
Prince's Sq
13
St John St
George St

Babington St
West Tamar Hwy
Middle St
York St
Frederick St
Charles St

WEST LAUNCESTON

Canning St
Wellington St

Brickfields Reserve
Margaret St
8
Stone St
9
12
11
Balfour St

Arbour Park
Hill St
Hillside Cres
Bourke St
Upton St
Alice Pl
Rocher St
10
Frankland St
SOUTH LAUNCESTON

Tamar River

TASMANIA LAUNCESTON

Central Launceston

two-hour city-highlight bus tours pass by 40-or-so sights on their loop through the city.

🎊 Festivals & Events

Junction Arts Festival ART
(☑ 03-6331 1309; www.junctionartsfestival.com.au; ☺ Sep) Five days of offbeat and interesting arts performances, installations and gigs in or around Launceston's Prince's Sq.

Festivale FOOD, ART
(www.festivale.com.au; ☺ Feb) Three festive days in City Park, with eating, drinking, arts and live music (everything from country to cool jazz). Tasmanian food and wine get an appropriate airing. An entry ticket must be purchased.

Esk BeerFest BEER
(www.eskbeerfestivals.com.au; ☺ Jan) A two-day celebration of craft beer, cider, spirits and local produce; held on the Esplanade. An entry ticket must be purchased.

🛏 Sleeping

Launceston Backpackers HOSTEL $
(Map p682; ☑ 03-6334 2327; www.launcestonback packers.com.au; 103 Canning St; dm $25, s/tw/tr $55/58/78, d with/without bathroom $70/60; P 🛜) Overlooking Brickfields Reserve, this large Federation-era house has been gutted

to make way for a cavernous but comfortable hostel. Freshly painted dorms have air-conditioning and a mix of bunk and single beds; en-suite doubles have comfortable beds but no air-conditioning. There's a lounge with TV and DVD player, a clean and well-equipped communal kitchen and lovely dining room. Wi-fi costs $1 per 200MB.

Sportsmans Hall Hotel PUB $
(Sporties; Map p682; ☑ 03-6331 3968; www. sportieshotel.com.au; cnr Charles & Balfour Sts; s $50-75, d $60-100; P 🛜) On the main Charles St entertainment strip, 'Sporties' is a bit of a local institution. The nine upstairs rooms have queen beds and a TV: some have en suites and others have their own private bathrooms down the hallway. Light sleepers should ask for a room away from the bar on a Friday, Saturday or Sunday night (live bands).

⭐ Two Four Two APARTMENT $$
(Map p682; ☑ 03-6331 9242; www.twofourtwo. com.au; 242 Charles St; studio d $220-240, apt d $250; P 🅿❄🛜) Launceston's best self-catering accommodation, super-stylish Two Four Two is on the Charles St cafe strip, making a perfect base for a city sojourn. Two double studios and an apartment sleeping up to four feature fully equipped kitchens with coffee machines, spacious bathrooms and comfortable beds sheathed in quality

linen. Owner Pam has kitted out each space with books, DVDs and art.

★ **Kurrajong House** B&B $$
(Map p681; ☑03-6331 6655; www.kurrajong house.com.au; cnr High & Adelaide Sts; r $165-199, cottages $209; [P] [P] 🎅) Owned by a Scottish-Australian couple, this well-run B&B in a handsome 1887 house near Windmill Hill Reserve offers three rooms in the main house and a self-contained cottage in the garden. Angling for a mature clientele (over 21s only), it is made exceptional through attention to detail – fresh flowers, fresh milk for in-room tea, homemade jam with breakfast.

Hi George B&B $$
(Map p681; ☑03-6331 2144; www.higeorge.com. au; 64 York St; r $140; 🎅) This B&B in a quaint 1880 brick house on the York St hill is operated by David and Fiona, who have been in the business for decades and know what guests want – a clean, comfortable and well-located base. No frills, but no fuss either. And when it comes to B&Bs, that can be a blessing.

Auldington BOUTIQUE HOTEL $$
(Map p682; ☑03-6331 2050; www.auldington. com.au; 110 Frederick St; r $100-200, f $140-240; [P] 🍴 ❄ 🎅) Built in the late 19th century, this former convent perched high on Frederick St offers 18 frills-free rooms with comfortable beds, kettles, TVs and DVD players. It's a safe if unremarkable choice.

★ **Mantra Charles Hotel** HOTEL $$$
(Map p682; ☑03-6337 4100; www.hotelcharles. com.au; 287 Charles St; d $159-399, studio $169-319, apt $239-499; [P] 🍴 ❄ @ 🎅) Once a hospital, the Mantra Charles has been given a fresh and funky internal facelift and now rightfully claims the title of Launceston's best business hotel. There are a number of room types, including king rooms, apartments and studios with kitchenette. All are spacious and extremely comfortable. The ground-floor bar and restaurant are particularly popular with corporate travellers.

✖ Eating

★ **Sweetbrew** CAFE $
(Map p682; ☑0438 509 022; 93a George St; brunch dishes $13.50-18.50; ⊙7am-5pm Mon-Fri, 8am-3pm Sat & Sun; 🎅) Serving Melbourne's Five Senses coffee and cooking up an interesting and very yummy vegetarian brunch menu (including Manu pastries), this is the best cafe in the city centre. The sunny

booth room out the back offers free wi-fi and plenty of design magazines to read – bravo!

★ **Milkbar** CAFE $
(Map p682; ☑0457 762 378; www.themilkbar cafe.com.au; 139 St John St; mains $8-12; ⊙8am-4pm Mon-Fri; 🎅) 🍴 Sixties retro cool and 21st-century hipster chic collide at Milkbar, which serves excellent coffee made with Ritual beans, organic tea, huge milkshakes, delicious sandwiches and homestyle cakes (love the jaffa slice!). All of the produce is as local and sustainable as possible. There's also a little shop section selling vintage-inspired crafts and knitting gear.

Pasta Merchant ITALIAN $
(Map p682; ☑03-6334 7077; www.thepasta merchant.org; 248b Charles St; small/large pastas $7.80/10.40; ⊙8.30am-9pm Mon-Fri, 9am-9pm Sat) Look forward to wonderful fresh pasta with authentic sauces, all made on-site at this pint-sized operation. Pull up a bar stool and tuck into a spaghetti, fettucine, ravioli or lasagne dish – there are loads to choose from. It also serves house-made cakes and gelato. Takeaway pasta and sauces, too.

★ **Pierre's** FRENCH $$
(Map p682; ☑03-6331 6835; www.pierres.net. au; 88 George St; breakfast dishes $8-23, lunch mains $23-25, dinner mains $28-41; ⊙8.30am-3pm & 5.30pm-late Tue-Thu, 8.30am-late Fri & Sat) Pierre's Studio 54–style decor (striped velour walls, burnished mirrors, upholstered ceiling with gold stars) has gone from being dated to deliciously retro in recent years. It offers a menu of well-cooked classics (bluecheese tart, pork rillette, duck confit, steak tartare), an impressive wine list by glass and bottle, good coffee and professional service. The lunch menu is excellent value.

Pickled Evenings INDIAN $$
(Map p682; ☑03-6331 0110; www.pickledevenings. com.au; 135 George St; mains $19-23; ⊙5.30-9.30pm Tue-Sun; 🍴) Pickled evenings and holidays go hand in hand, but a visit to this excellent Indian restaurant will not (necessarily) involve excessive drinking. What you're here for are the traditional curries, which are generous, spicy and well priced. Good vegetarian options and takeaways available.

Stillwater MODERN AUSTRALIAN $$
(Map p681; ☑03-6331 4153; www.stillwater.net. au; 2 Bridge Rd, Ritchie's Mill; breakfast $9-23, lunch dishes $20-30, dinner dishes $22-45; ⊙8.30-11.30am, noon-3pm & 6-9pm Tue-Sat, 8.30-11.30am

& noon-3pm Sun; ⬛) Still waters run deep here – deep into the realm of Mod Oz cuisine, that is. In an historic flour mill on the Tamar (parts of which date back to 1832), it serves laid-back breakfasts and lunches... then puts on the Ritz for dinner. The menu changes with the seasons and both it and the thoughtful wine list concentrate on local produce.

★ **Geronimo**   MODERN AUSTRALIAN **$$$**

(Map p682; ✉03-6331 3652; www.geronimorestaurant.com.au; 186 Charles St; small plates $14-22, large plates $30-37, pizzas $21-27; ⊙5-10pm Mon-Thu, 10.30am-late Fri & Sat, 10.30am-6pm Sun; ⬛) Launceston's most sophisticated eatery, with an up-to-the-moment menu of shared plates and an impressive list of wines by glass and bottle. The food is beautiful to look at and even better to taste – flavours are Middle Eastern, Asian and Mediterranean and the execution is faultless. There's also a menu of snacks ($5 to $15.50) to enjoy during the aperitivo hour.

🍷 Drinking & Nightlife

★ **Saint John**   BAR

(Map p682; ✉03-6333 0340; www.saintjohncraftbeer.com.au; 133 St John St; ⊙noon-late Mon-Sat, 2pm-late Sun) The taps here are in constant use, pouring a huge range of craft beers for regular customers of every age and type. Out the back is an unexpected little food van plating up crispy chicken wings, lamb burgers and quinoa-and-chia rosti that you can order and eat in the bar after 5pm. The perfect symbiosis!

Bakers Lane   BAR

(Map p682; ✉03-6334 2414; www.bakerslanebar.com; 81 York St; ⊙11.30am-10.30pm Tue-Thu, till 4am Fri & Sat) The town's hipster hangout and coolest venue, this place delivers dude food (tacos, BBQ brisket, gumbo), cocktails and craft beer, live acoustic acts on Thursday after 9pm and DJs on Friday and Saturday. It also stays open later than most venues in town.

Red Brick Road Ciderhouse   BAR

(Map p682; ✉03-6334 8915; www.redbrickroadcider.com.au; 63a Brisbane St; ⊙5pm-late Mon-Fri, 4pm-late Sat & Sun) An outlet for Red Brick Road's handcrafted ciders and perries, this small bar features rustic wood panelling straight from an apple packing shed. Try the dry hopped cider, sparkling cider, scrumpy or perry. There's an open mic night every third Wednesday of the month at 8pm (entry $5).

☆ Entertainment

Princess Theatre   THEATRE

(Map p682; ✉03-6323 3666; www.theatrenorth.com.au; 57 Brisbane St; ⊙box office 9am-5pm Mon-Fri, 10am-1pm Sat) Built in 1911 and incorporating the smaller Earl Arts Centre out the back, the old Princess stages an eclectic schedule of drama, dance and comedy, drawing acts from across Tasmania and the mainland.

York Park   SPECTATOR SPORT

(University of Launceston Stadium; Map p681; www.aurorastadiumlaunceston.com.au; Invermay Rd, Invermay) If you're in town during football season (April to August), come here to see the big men fly – Melbourne-based AFL team Hawthorn plays a handful of home games here each season.

🛍 Shopping

★ **Design Tasmania Shop**   ARTS & CRAFTS

(Map p682; ✉03-6331 5506; www.designtasmania.com.au/shop; cnr Brisbane & Tamar Sts; ⊙9.30am-5.30pm Mon-Fri, 10am-2pm Sat & Sun) Seeking to snaffle a souvenir to take home? The wonderful shop at the **Design Centre Tasmania** (Map p682; adult/student/child/family $6/4/free/12; ⊙9.30am-5.30pm Mon-Fri, 10am-4pm Sat & Sun Oct-Apr, 10am-4pm Mon-Fri & 10am-2pm May-Sep) stocks a huge array of artisan-made objects, with a particular emphasis on furniture and homewares made from locally sourced wood – it's a veritable hymn to Huon pine. Also stocks jewellery and clothing.

★ **Harvest**   MARKET

(Map p682; ✉0417 352 780; www.harvestmarket.org.au; Cimitiere St car park; ⊙8.30am-12.30pm Sat) 🍃 Excellent weekly gathering of organic producers and sustainable suppliers from around northern and western Tasmania. Craft beer and cider, artisan baked goods (including locally baked Manu bread), cheese, Mt Direction olives, salmon from 41° Degrees South, honey and veggies are all on offer, and food trucks and stalls sell treats including *okonomiyaki* (Japanese pancakes, $10).

ⓘ Information

Launceston General Hospital (✉03-6777 6777; www.dhhs.tas.gov.au; 287-289 Charles St; ⊙24hr) Accident and emergency is open 24 hours.

Launceston Visitor Information Centre (Map p682; ☑ 03-6323 3082, 1800 651 827; www. visitlauncestontamar.com.au; 68-72 Cameron St; ⊙ 9am-5pm Mon-Fri, to 1pm Sat & Sun) Extremely helpful tourist office that can book accommodation and tours, supply a city map and offer other information about the city and region. Extended weekend hours from December to March.

ⓘ Getting There & Away

AIR

Jetstar (www.jetstar.com) Direct flights to Brisbane, Sydney and Melbourne.

Qantas (www.qantas.com.au) Direct flights to Melbourne.

Virgin Australia (www.virginaustralia.com) Direct flights to Melbourne and Sydney.

BUS

Calow's Coaches (Map p682; ☑ 03-6376 2161, 0400 570 036; www.calowscoaches.com) Services the east coast (St Marys, St Helens, Bicheno) from Launceston. Also runs into Coles Bay and Freycinet National Park, connecting with Tassielink buses to/from Hobart at the Coles Bay turn-off.

Cornwall Square Transit Centre (Map p682; 200 Cimitiere St) The depot for most Launceston bus services.

Redline Coaches (Map p682; ☑ 1300 360 000; www.tasredline.com.au) From Launceston west to Westbury, Deloraine, Mole Creek, Devonport, Ulverstone, Penguin, Burnie, Wynyard, Stanley and Smithton. Also south to Hobart via Campbell Town, Ross, Oatlands and Kempton.

Sainty's North East Bus Service (Map p682; ☑ 0400 791 076, 0437 469 186; www. saintysnortheastbusservice.com.au) Buses between Launceston and Lilydale, Scottsdale, Derby and Bridport.

Tassielink (Map p682; ☑ 1300 300 520; www.tassielink.com.au) West coast buses via Devonport and Cradle Mountain, and an express service from the Devonport ferry terminal to Hobart via Launceston. Also runs from Launceston to Evandale and Longford.

ⓘ Getting Around

TO/FROM THE AIRPORT

Launceston Airport (☑ 03-6391 6222; www. launcestonairport.com.au; 201 Evandale Rd, Western Junction) On the road to Evandale, 15km south of the city. The **Launceston Airporter** (☑ 1300 38 55 22; www.airporter launceston.com.au; adult/child one way $18/14, return $32/25) shuttle bus runs door-to-door services. A taxi into the city costs about $35.

BUS

Free Tiger Bus (☑ 03-6323 3000; www.launces ton.tas.gov.au) Free bus service running in a loop from the Inveresk QVMAG on two routes every 30 minutes. The **City Explorer** goes to Civic Sq, Prince's Sq, Launceston General Hospital, Windmill Hill Reserve and City Park between 10am and 3pm weekdays. The **River Explorer** goes to Civic Sq, the QVMAG in Paterson St and Home Point between 10.30am and 3.30pm.

Metro Tasmania (Map p681; ☑ 13 22 01; www.metrotas.com.au; 186 Wellington St) runs Launceston's suburban bus network. One-way fares vary with distances ('sections') travelled (from $3.30 to $4.60). Buses depart from the two blocks of St John St between Paterson and York Sts. Many routes don't operate in the evenings or on Sundays. Route maps and timetables can be found on the Metro website.

TAXI

Taxi Combined (☑ 131 008, 132 227)

AROUND LAUNCESTON

Tamar Valley

A terrain of undulating emerald hills covered with vineyards, orchards and stands of native forest, this valley is intersected by the wide Tamar River, a tidal waterway running 64km north from Launceston towards Bass Strait. On the river's eastern bank is Launceston's ocean port, Bell Bay, near George Town. The western bank is home to a string of laid-back country hamlets that are popular weekend and summer escapes for Launcestonians. The Batman Bridge unites the two shores near Deviot.

☞ Tours

Tamar Valley Winery Tours   WINE
(☑ 0447 472 177; www.tamarvalleywinerytours. au; tours per person $125) Highly regarded small-group tours that pick up/drop off in Launceston and visit four cellar doors on a half-day tour. Includes lunch.

ⓘ Information

Tamar Visitor Information Centre (☑ 1800 637 989, 03-6394 4454; www.wtc.tas.gov.au; cnr West Tamar Hwy & Winkleigh Rd, Exeter; ⊙ 8.30am-5pm Mon-Fri, 9am-5pm Sat & Sun daylight savings, 9am-4pm rest of year) This extremely helpful information centre sells the Tamar Triple Pass and national parks passes, stocks an array of brochures and offers free wi-fi.

Around Launceston

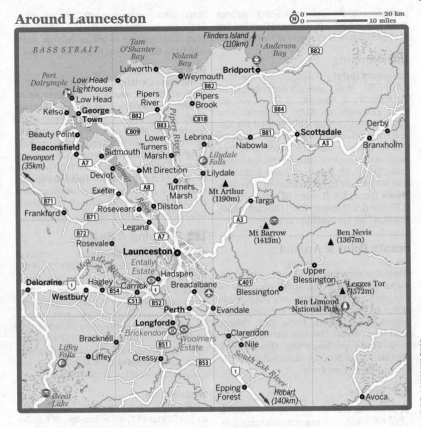

❶ Getting There & Away

Lee's Coaches (Map p682; ☎ 0400 937 440; www.leescoaches.com) Services the East Tamar Valley region from Launceston. Buses stop on Brisbane St.

Manions' Coaches (Map p682; ☎ 03-6383 1221; www.manionscoaches.com.au) Services the West Tamar Valley region from Launceston. Buses stop on Brisbane St.

Legana & Rosevears

POP 3220 (COMBINED)

These two hubs offer the first pit stops heading north out of Launceston along the West Tamar Hwy (A7) – they're almost suburbs of Launceston, they're so darn proximal. Legana is right on the highway; Rosevears adheres to narrow Rosevears Dr, running along the water past moored yachts and swaying reed beds. This is vineyard territory, so bring your downloaded map of the **Tamar Valley Wine Route** (www.tamarvalleywineroute.com.au).

◉ Sights

Tamar Ridge   WINERY
(☎ 03-6330 0300; www.tamarridge.com.au; 1a Wald-horn Dr, Rosevears; ⊙10am-5pm) Tamar Ridge is best known for its quaffable Pirie sparkling wine. Begin with a free tasting at the counter, choose a bottle to buy then hit the scenic terrace, which overlooks the Tamar, to enjoy a platter (terrine, salmon or cheese, $20 to $25). The kids can spin hula hoops on the lawn, or scrawl on the blackboard wall.

Vélo Wines   WINERY
(☎ 03-6330 3677; www.velowines.com.au; 755 West Tamar Hwy, Legana; ⊙11am-5pm) This is the first of the West Tamar wineries that you'll see if coming from Launceston. Its ownership recently changed, and the opening hours have been under review – check the website. When we visited, tastings were $5 per person, redeemable with purchase of a bottle. The onsite **Timbre Kitchen** (www.timbrekitchen.com;

small plates $3-20, large plates $32-36, set-price dinner $40; ⊙11am-3pm Sun-Thu, till 11pm Fri & Sat; P🍴) restaurant is the main attraction here.

🛏 Sleeping

Rosevears Hotel HOTEL $$
(☑03-6394 4074; www.rosevearshotel.com.au; 215 Rosevears Dr, Rosevears; d $195, d with spa $255, 2-bedroom ste $245) Recently constructed, these stylish units behind the Rosevears Hotel come in various permutations: choose from a standard room, premium room with outdoor spa, or two-bedroom suite. The suite, premium room and some standard rooms have river-facing balconies. **Meals** (pizzas $19-21, mains $23-45; ⊙8-11am, 11.30-2pm & 5.30-8pm Fri-Sun, 11.30-2pm & 5.30-8pm Mon-Thu) are available at the hotel.

Beauty Point & Around

POP 1210

While the surrounding hillsides and riverscapes are certainly beautiful, the name of this town actually derives from pulchritude of the bovine variety: a now-immortalised bullock called Beauty. These days, visitors head here to visit Platypus House and Seahorse World on Inspection Head Wharf. It's also a good base for those following the Tamar Valley Wine Route.

◉ Sights

★ Seahorse World AQUARIUM
(☑03-6383 4111; www.seahorseworld.com.au; Inspection Head Wharf, 200 Flinders St, Beauty Point; adult/concession/child/family $22/19.80/9.50/55; ⊙9.30am-4pm Dec-Apr, 10am-3pm May-Sep, 10am-4pm Oct & Nov) At coo-inducing Seahorse World, eight species of seahorses are raised to supply aquariums worldwide. Access is via 45-minute guided tours, which run on the hour and take you through the aquarium, which is populated with many bizarre sea creatures from the Southern Ocean and includes a touch pool, and well as the seahorse farm and a display showcasing the wonderful diversity of the species.

Platypus House ZOO
(☑03-6383 4884; www.platypushouse.com.au; Inspection Head Wharf, 200 Flinders St; adult/concession/child/family $24.50/22/10/59; ⊙9.30am-4.30pm Nov-Apr, 10am-3.30pm May-Oct) Housed in a huge wharf shed, Platypus House puts the world's only two monotremes – the platypus and the echidna – on display for your viewing pleasure. Platypuses gambol in glass-sided tanks and transparent 'burrows', while in the echidna room you can walk among the trundling creatures as guides dish out scientific facts. Guided tours depart on the hour.

**Beaconsfield Mine
& Heritage Centre** MUSEUM
(☑03-6383 1473; www.beaconsfieldheritage.com.au; West St, Beaconsfield; adult/concession/child/family $15/12/5/38; ⊙9.30am-4.30pm) This centre offers plenty of opportunities to learn about Beaconsfield's fascinating mining heritage. An interactive experience, it includes plenty of buttons to push, levers to pull and tunnels to crawl through. There are special exhibitions about the 2006 mine rescue, and it's possible to wander through the historic Grubb Shaft Engine and Boiler Houses.

🛏 Sleeping & Eating

★ Jensens Bed & Breakfast B&B $$
(☑0410 615 678; 77 Flinders St; r $180-220; P🛜) If only all B&Bs could be like this. Occupying a handsome Federation-style house surrounded by apple trees and a manicured garden, Jensens has a gracious communal lounge with open fire, two stylishly presented en-suite rooms and a large verandah with distinctive rotunda and spectacular river views. Helpful host Carol cooks her guests a full breakfast in the morning.

★ River Cafe CAFE $$
(☑03-6383 4099; 225 Flinders St; panini $16, pizzas $10-24, mains $21-38; ⊙9am-4pm, till 9pm Dec & Jan school holidays; 🛜🍴) On sunny days at the River Cafe the windows fold right back and the water feels so close you could touch it. The menu tempts with all-day breakfasts ($10 to $22), gourmet panini, pastas and a delectable array of local seafood – try the signature seafood platter ($38) with a glass of Tamar Valley wine. Takeaway pizzas, too.

George Town

POP 4310

George Town stands sentinel on the Tamar River's eastern shore, close to where it empties into Bass Strait. Originally the territory of the Leterremairrener or Port Douglas people, it was settled by Europeans in 1804 as part of the British attempt to stave off settlement by the French, who had been reconnoitring the area. It was the third British town settled in the new colony after Sydney and Hobart. A number of buildings in the town centre date from the 1830s and 1840s, when George

Town prospered as the port linking Tasmania with Victoria. Today it's in the economic doldrums as a result of employment losses at the nearby Bell Bay Smelter and TEMCO steel plant. It's a rewarding stop for history buffs, and also has some pleasant beaches.

⊙ Sights

★ Bass & Flinders Centre   MUSEUM
(☑ 03-6382 3792; www.bassandflinders.org.au; 8 Elizabeth St; adult/concession/child/family $10/8/4/24; ☺ 10am-4pm) Undoubtedly the highlight of a visit to George Town, this small museum in a former cinema houses a red-sailed replica of the *Norfolk,* the sloop used by Bass and Flinders for their 1897 circumnavigation of Van Diemen's Land. There are other old wooden boats here, too, including a replica of *Tom Thumb,* the cramped whaleboat that carried Bass, Flinders and an assistant up the Georges River in NSW – it's altogether a rather fabulous collection. There's also a **cafe** (lunch dishes $6-7, cakes $4.50; ☺ 10am-4pm Mon-Fri).

⊨ Sleeping

★ Peppers Tamar Cove   HOTEL, APARTMENT $$
(☑ 03-6382 9900; www.peppers.com.au/york-cove; 2 Ferry Blvd; r $159-199, 1-/2-bedroom apt from $199/239; ⓟ �ⓢ ⓩ) This corporate waterfront resort is making waves on the Tamar. It offers generously sized hotel rooms with kitchenettes at the rear of the main building (some with spa, but none with views), but the headline acts are the river-facing apartments, which are huge and facility-rich (laundry, full kitchen, lounge and balcony). Wi-fi is only available in the main building.

❶ Information

George Town Visitor Information Centre
(☑ 03-6382 1700; www.provincialtamar.com.au; 92-96 Main Rd; ☺ 9am-4pm daylight savings, till 3pm rest of the year) This volunteer-manned centre is located on the main road as you enter from the south. It supplies brochures and maps, makes accommodation bookings and has public toilets.

Low Head

POP 440

Low Head and George Town are barely divided – you won't notice leaving one before arriving in the other. Historic Low Head is in a spectacular setting though, looking out over the swirling – and treacherous – waters of the Tamar as it empties into the sea. There's good

HOLLYBANK TREETOPS ADVENTURE

Various adventure experiences are offered at **Hollybank Treetops Adventure** (☑ 03-6395 1390; www.treetopsadventure.com.au; 66 Hollybank Rd, Underwood; ☺ 9am-5pm), 7km south of Lilydale. Climb, scramble and balance through pine trees at height on a supervised two-hour **Ropes Course** (various levels of difficulty, adult/student/child eight to 17 years / child four to seven years $45/40/35/25), or take a guided three-hour **Treetops Canopy Tour** (adult/student/child three to 16 years $125/112.50/90) where you'll fly through native wet forest on ziplines.

You can also take a 1.5km guided exploration of a forest reserve on a Segway ($100) or hire a hard-tail bike (adult standard/superior bike $30/60 for two hours, child $30) to use in the on-site **mountain bike park**.

surf at **East Beach** on Bass Strait, and safe swimming at **Lagoon Beach** on the Tamar.

⊙ Sights & Activities

Low Head Maritime Museum   MUSEUM
(Low Head Pilot Station Museum; ☑ 03-6382 1143; www.lowheadpilotstation.com; 399 Low Head Rd; adult/child/family $5/3/15; ☺ 10am-4pm) In the Low Head Historic Precinct, this museum occupies the whitewashed pilot station, which is Australia's oldest (1805). A series of rooms contains a weird and wonderful array of exhibits about the maritime history of this part of Tasmania. Though dusty, they're quite fascinating. There's a **cafe** (☑ 03-6382 2826; sandwiches $6.50, mains $9.50-18.50; ☺ 10am-4pm Apr–mid-Dec, 9am-5pm mid-Dec–Mar; ☎) next door, and **accommodation** (☑ 0467 822 826; d $130-240, extra adult/child $20/10; ⓟ) in a number of cottages in the precinct.

Low Head Penguin Tours   BIRDWATCHING
(☑ 0418 361 860; www.penguintours.lowhead.com; 485 Low Head Rd; adult/child $20/10; ☺ sunset) Check out the little penguins that live around the Low Head Lighthouse. Wheelchair-friendly guided tours leave nightly at sunset from a signposted spot beside Low Head Rd just south of the lighthouse. Bookings advised.

Longford & Around

POP 3053

Longford was founded in 1807 when free landholding farmers were moved to Van Diemen's Land from Norfolk Island. It's one of the few Tasmanian towns not established by convicts. Two farming estates on the far edge of town, **Woolmers Estate** and **Brickendon**, are included on the list of the 11 Unesco World Heritage Australian Convict Sites and should be on your must-see list when visiting this neck o' the woods.

◎ Sights

★ **Woolmers Estate** HISTORIC SITE
(☑03-6391 2230; www.woolmers.com.au; 658 Woolmers Lane; tours adult/concession/child/family $20/17/7/45; ☺9.30am-4pm) This pastoral estate on the Macquarie River was built by Thomas Archer in 1817 and remained in the ownership of the Archer family until 1994. Admission to the homestead is via guided tours at 11.15am, 12.30pm and 2pm daily. Wandering through the rooms, which are still furnished with the family's possessions, is a fascinating experience. There are also farm outbuildings and a noted rose garden.

It's possible to overnight in self-contained **cottages** (d from $145, extra adult/child $35/30; P☺) on the site. Be sure to visit the shearing shed (the oldest in Australia still in use) and take the picturesque 2.8km **Convict Trail Walk** to Brickendon across the river.

Note that Woolmers' sleek new visitor centre was due to open in 2017 and will include a cafe, two galleries and gift shop.

Brickendon HISTORIC SITE
(☑03-6391 1383; www.brickendon.com.au; 236 Wellington St; adult/child/family $12.50/5/38; ☺9.30am-5pm Tue-Sun Oct-May, to 4pm Jun-Sep) Brickendon was established in 1824, and is still occupied by by the Archer family, so you can't see inside, but you can explore the gorgeous old gardens and the farm village, and take the 2.8km Convict Trail Walk to Woolmers. There's animal feeding for the kids at 10.15am, and on-site **accommodation** (d from $190, extra person $45; P☏☎☎) is on offer.

🛏 Sleeping & Eating

★ **Quamby Estate** BOUTIQUE HOTEL $$$
(☑03-6392 2135; www.quambyestate.com.au; 1145 Westwood Rd, Hagley; d $169-398, breakfast $15-30, 2-/3-course dinner $60/75; P☺❉☎) Few hotels can match the setting and surrounds on offer at this classy country-house hotel. In a pastoral homestead dating from 1828, it offers 10 stylish en-suite rooms (opt for a downstairs deluxe king suite). Relax in the gorgeous garden or sitting rooms, dine in the ballroom, play a round of golf and pretend you're 'to the manor born'.

You'll find it off Meander Valley Rd, between Carrick and Westbury.

★ **Red Feather Inn** BOUTIQUE HOTEL $$$
(☑03-6393 6506; www.redfeatherinn.com.au; 42 Main St, Hadspen; d/q incl breakfast from $250/450; P☺❉☎) The unreservedly gorgeous 1852 Red Feather Inn offers French Provincial–style boutique accommodation, gourmet in-house dining and a well-regarded cooking school. Rooms range from attic doubles to

---

DON'T MISS

PIPERS RIVER WINE REGION

Don't miss a long afternoon putting your palate to work at the cellar doors in this wine region, which is an easy day trip north of Launceston. Online see www.tamarvalleywineroute.com.au.

Pipers Brook Vineyard (☑03-6382 7527; www.pipersbrook.com.au; 1216 Pipers Brook Rd, Pipers Brook; dishes $15.50-28; ☺10am-5pm, cafe 11am-3pm, earlier closing Jun-Aug) is the Tamar's best-known vineyard, home to Pipers Brook, Ninth Island and Kreglinger wines (the Kreglinger sparkling is particularly impressive). There's a tasting room (three Ninth Island/Pipers Brooks/Kreglinger wines $5/7/10) and a cafe serving simple foods such as chicken baguettes ($18.50) and cheese boards ($28). The tasting fee is waived if you buy a bottle.

Located next door to Pipers Brook, **Jansz Wine Room** (☑03-6382 7066; www.jansz.com.au; 1216b Pipers Brook Rd, Pipers Brook; ☺10am-4.30pm), named after explorer Abel Jansz Tasman, was originally in partnership with Louise Roederer, so it's not surprising that its *Méthode Tasmanoise* is a more-than-quaffable drop. Ask for a picnic blanket and head outside to enjoy a cheese platter plus two flutes of the sparking stuff ($40). There are free tastings, too.

a cottage sleeping eight – the Library Suite and Garden Suite are particularly attractive. Full-day **cooking classes** (from $195) are held in the country kitchen, which also services the in-house **restaurant** (three courses $85).

★**Hubert & Dan**   MODERN AUSTRALIAN **$$**
(☑0458 822 308; www.hubertanddan.com.au; 59 Wellington St; lunch mains $15-26, set 3-course dinner $60; ◷9am-4.30pm Tue, Wed & Fri, 9am-4.30pm & 6-8pm Thu) Predominantly a catering operation, Hubert & Dan is known throughout northern Tasmania for the quality of its French-accented modern Australian food. Its small and stylish cafe serves coffee made with Ritual beans and a daily-changing menu of breakfast favourites, light lunch dishes, cakes, biscuits and slices. The Thursday night dinners are enthusiastically subscribed – book well ahead.

❶ Getting There & Away

Tassielink (☑1300 300 520; www.tassielink. com.au) From Monday to Saturday, operates three daily buses to Launceston ($7.30, 50 minutes) via Evandale ($6.10, 25 minutes). The buses stop along Marlborough and Wellington Sts.

Evandale
POP 1086

Walk down the main street in Evandale and you'll feel like you've time-warped back a century...precisely why the entire town is National Trust listed. It's a ridiculously photogenic place, and well worth a visit. Allow a few hours so you can admire its historic streetscapes, browse a few boutiques and take a break in the excellent Ingleside Bakery Cafe. If you visit on a Sunday, don't miss the Evandale Market.

◉ Sights

★**Clarendon**   HISTORIC BUILDING
(☑03-63986220;www.nationaltrust.org.au/places/ clarendon; 234 Clarendon Station Rd; adult/concession/child $15/10/free; ◷10am-4pm Thu-Sun Sep-Jun) Located next to the South Esk River, this 1838 mansion was built for wealthy wool grower and merchant James Cox. A Georgian gem, it looks like it's stepped straight out of *Gone with the Wind*. Long the grandest house in the colony, it is now owned by the National Trust. Visitors can take a self-guided tour of the house, which is furnished with antiques, and also visit its outbuildings

– one of these houses the **Australian Fly Fishing Museum** (www.affm.net.au).

🛏 Sleeping & Eating

Wesleyan Chapel   COTTAGE **$$**
(☑0417 641 536; 28 Russell St; d incl breakfast from $150, extra person $25; ❀) Built in 1836, this tiny brick chapel has since been used variously as a druids hall, an RSL hall and a scout hall. Now it's self-contained accommodation for up to four people. There's a washing machine and fully equipped kitchen in which guests will find homemade breakfast provisions (even the honey is hand produced).

Ingleside Bakery Cafe   CAFE **$**
(☑03-6391 8682; 4 Russell St; pies $8.50-$10, sandwiches & wraps $13-23; ◷8.30am-4.30pm Mon-Fri, to 4pm Sat, to 3.30pm Sun; ❀) Sit in the flowery walled courtyard or under the high ceiling inside this former council chambers (1867), where fresh-baked aromas waft from the wood oven. Expect delicious pies and pasties, a hefty ploughman's lunch and all manner of sweet treats, including Devonshire teas. The providore shelves are packed with Tasmanian products.

❶ Information

Evandale Visitor Information Centre (☑03-6391 8128; www.evandaletasmania.com; 18 High St; ◷10am-4pm) Local info and accommodation bookings. Stocks the *Evandale Heritage Walk* pamphlet ($3), detailing the town's historic riches. The **history room** here has a display on Victoria Cross–winning WWI soldier Harry Murray, who is commemorated with a statue on Russell St. When we last visited, free wi-fi was on its way.

❶ Getting There & Away

Tassielink (☑1300 300 520; www.tassielink. com.au) From Monday to Saturday, three daily buses travel between Launceston and Evandale ($6.10, 40 minutes), continuing to Longford ($6.10, 25 minutes). The bus stop is located on Scone St.

Ben Lomond National Park

Home to Tassie's best-equipped ski field, this 181-sq-km park takes in the whole of the Ben Lomond massif: a craggy alpine plateau whose highest point, Legges Tor (1572m), is the second-highest spot on the island (the highest is 1617m Mt Ossa). Bushwalkers traipse across the mountain plateau when the snow melts, swooning over alpine wildflowers during spring and summer, marvelling at the views from the precipitous escarpments and spotting native animals, including Bennett's wallabies, wombats, pademelons and Eastern quolls.

✦ Activities

Ben Lomond is considered Tasmania's Aspen – well, not quite, but when the snow does fall the lifts grind into action and you can ski here. The snow can be fickle, but the ski season generally runs from early July to late September. Two 'snow guns' top up the natural snow. Full-day ski-lift passes cost $70/50/30 per adult/teenager/child, while half-day passes cost $45/35/20. Under sevens and over 70s ride free. There are three T-bars and four poma lifts. For snow reports and cams, see www.benlomond.org.au.

Ben Lomond Snow Sports (☑03-6390 6185; www.skibenlomond.com.au; Ben Lomond Rd, Ben Lomond National Park; ⊙9am-4.30pm in ski season) runs a kiosk selling takeaway fare and a shop doing ski, snowboard and toboggan rental, and associated gear. Skis, boots, poles and a lesson cost $90/75 per adult/child; just skis, boots and poles costs $60/45.

You must have a valid national parks pass to access the snowfields.

ⓘ Getting There & Away

There's no public transport to the mountain, so driving is your only option.

Note that the road up to the plateau is unsealed and includes Jacob's Ladder, a sensationally steep climb with six white-knuckle hairpin bends and no safety barriers. During the snow season, chains are standard issue – hire them from **Skigia** (Map p642; ☑03-6234 6688; www.skigia.com.au; 123 Elizabeth St, Hobart; ⊙9.30am-6pm Mon-Fri, to 4pm Sat) in Hobart or **Autobarn** (Map p681; ☑03-6334 5601; www.autobarn.com.au/stores/launceston; 6 Innes St; ⊙8am-5.30pm Mon-Fri, 9am-5pm Sat, 9am-4pm Sun) in Launceston (around $40 per day, plus $60 deposit). Don't forget antifreeze.

During the ski season, Ben Lomond Snow Sports runs a shuttle bus ($15 each way) from the bottom car park at the Parks and Wildlife Service registration booth, 7km from the ski field. If you're catching the shuttle, you don't need to hire chains for your car. Call for pick-ups.

DEVONPORT & THE NORTHWEST

Tasmania's northwest is the island in a nutshell – wild and untramelled in parts, quietly sophisticated in others. Home to two national parks (Rocky Cape and Savage River) as well as the spectacular Arthur-Pieman Conservation Area, this part of the island is rich in wilderness and poor in tourists – you'll have many sites, landscapes and beaches to yourself when here, ensuring a truly relaxing stay. Little-visited areas include the ancient rainforests of the Tarkine wilderness and the remote beaches in the northwest tip, which are swept by the winds of the Roaring Forties and are famed as having the cleanest air on earth. Here also are some of the best places in Australia to see platypuses and penguins and to enjoy rustic meals featuring world-class local produce. Rest assured: the sense of exploring this, one of the world's last unspoiled corners, will linger long after you leave.

Devonport

POP 22,770

Tasmania's third-largest city is the port for the *Spirit of Tasmania I* and *II*, the red-and-white ferries that connect the island state with the mainland. It's quite an evocative sight when, after three deep blasts of the horn, these huge ships cruise past the end of the main street to begin their voyage north. After disembarking, most passengers scatter to other destinations on the island and Devonport slips back into obscurity. Before you do the same, consider popping into town to visit its excellent maritime museum and regional gallery and have a meal at one of the eateries overlooking Mersey Bluff Beach.

◉ Sights & Activities

★**Bass Strait Maritime Centre**   MUSEUM (☑03-6424 7100; www.bassstraitmc.com.au; 6 Gloucester Ave; adult/child/family $10/5/25; ⊙10am-5pm) Housed in the former harbour master's residence (c 1920), this small but impressive museum is home to displays about the geology and maritime history of Bass Strait. Its large collection of ship and ferry models is a crowd-pleaser, but the knock-out exhibit is the interactive simulator ($2) that allows museum-goers to steer a steamer along the Mersey River or through Port Phillip Heads. Also of note is a cleverly presented and informative exhibit on the history of container ships.

★**Devonport Regional Gallery** GALLERY
(☑03-6424 8296; www.devonportgallery.com; 45-47 Stewart St; by donation; ☺10am-5pm Mon-Fri, noon-5pm Sat, 1-5pm Sun) Currently housed in a decommissioned 1904 Baptist church with a stunning wooden vaulted ceiling, this small but well-curated gallery is slated to move into the new contemporary arts hub within the Devonport Entertainment & Contention Centre in 2018. One of the new venue's first exhibitions is likely to be the excellent biannual City of Devonport National Art Award (aka Tidal), which attracts entries from prominent Australian visual artists. Otherwise, the exhibition program tends to focus on local work.

Narawntapu National Park NATIONAL PARK
(☑03-6428 6277; www.parks.tas.gov.au; parks pass vehicle/person per day $24/12; ☺ranger station 9am-4pm Dec-Apr, to 3pm May-Nov) There's wildlife aplenty in this coastal park 78km north of Launceston and 41km east of Devonport. Visit just on dusk and you'll see Forester kangaroos, foraging wombats, wallabies and pademelons. There's plenty to do during the day, too. You can follow a walking trail, beachcomb, swim or horse ride. Rangers run guided walks and activities in summer and there's a **visitor centre** and full picnic and toilet facilities at Springlawn.

★**The Julie Burgess** CRUISE
(☑03-6424 7100; http://bassstraitmaritimecentre.com.au/julie-burgess; per person $40; ☺Wed & Sun) Purpose-built in 1936 to harvest the rich crayfish fields of Bass Strait and Tasmania, this fishing ketch has recently been meticulously restored and now offers two-hour cruises out the mouth of the Mersey River into Bass Strait towards Don Heads. Tickets should be booked in advance at the Bass Strait Maritime Centre; tours only operate with minimum numbers and in favourable weather conditions.

🛏 Sleeping

Tasman Backpackers HOSTEL $
(☑03-6423 2335; www.tasmanbackpackers.com.au; 114 Tasman St; dm $21-23, tw/d/tr with shared bathroom $52/54/72; ☺Oct-Jun; P⊜@) This sprawling building once housed nurses from Devonport's hospital, but it's now a well-run hostel that is popular with Asian backpackers doing visa-related farm work. Its six single-sex dorms and variety of twin, double

and triple rooms are worn but clean. Facilities include a good kitchen, BBQ courtyard, locker room, pool table, lounge and cinema room. Advance bookings are recommended.

Mersey Bluff Caravan Park CARAVAN PARK $
(☑03-6424 8655; www.merseybluff.com.au; 41 Bluff Rd; unpowered sites per person $15, powered sites per 2 adults $34, on-site caravan d $80-100; P🐾) Nestled behind a stand of Norfolk Pines on Mersey Bluff, this pleasantly green park is just steps from the main swimming beach and is immaculate. There's a campers' kitchen, laundry and excellent ablutions blocks. Though popular with grey nomads (book ahead), its proximity to the patrolled beach and a wonderful children's playground make it popular with families too.

Inspire Boutique Apartment 1 APARTMENT $$
(☑0400 012 231; 134 James St; d $160-180; P⊜) Planning on self-catering? If so, this apartment near Coles Beach is the best option in town. Located on the ground floor of a three-storey property, it offers a large lounge and dining area with TV and DVD, courtyard with barbecue, kitchenette with coffee machine, washing machine, bedroom with queen-size bed and secure off-street parking. Bookings can also be made through the Devonport Visitor Information Centre (p696).

★**The Grand on Macfie** B&B $$$
(☑03-6424 2000; www.thegrandonmacfie.com.au; 44a Macfie St; r $150-245; P⊜🐾🛜) Built over a century ago, the Grand is just that – a well-located, large and extremely handsome mansion offering five elegant antique-filled rooms, a guest lounge, a balcony with panoramic views and a dining room where a full cooked breakfast is served. On weekend afternoons, a high tea ($39.50) is offered. Guest feedback is extremely positive about hosts Paul and Brendan.

🍴 Eating & Drinking

Laneway CAFE $$
(☑03-6424 4333; www.lane-way.com.au; 2/38 Steele St; breakfast dishes $17-24, panini $14-18; ☺6.30am-5pm Mon-Fri, to 4pm Sat & Sun; 🛜💺) Occupying a former bakery, this cafe on Rooke Lane is as hip as Devonport gets. Large all-day breakfast plates (eggs, beans, waffles, coconut chia pudding) are the order of choice for a loyal local clientele, accompanied by well-made coffee, T2 tea or freshly squeezed fruit juice. Evening events with

The Northwest

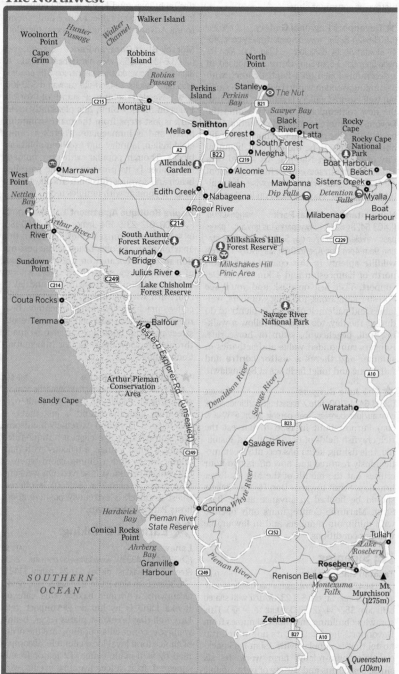

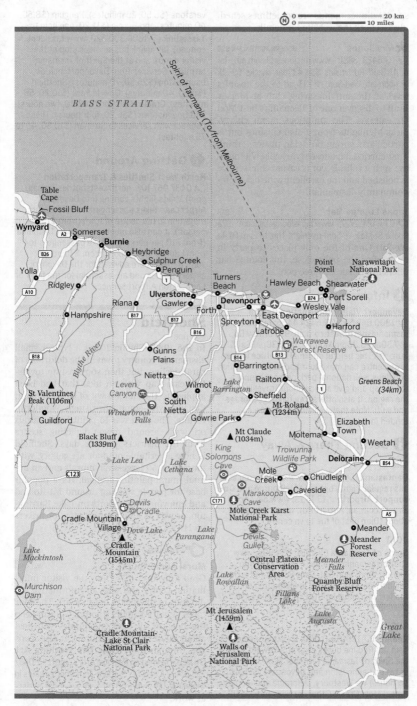

special dinner menus are sometimes scheduled – check the website for details.

⭐ **Mrs Jones** MODERN AUSTRALIAN **$$$**
(☎03-6423 3881; www.mrsjonesrbl.com.au; 1st fl, 41 Bluff Rd; mains $34-43, bar snacks $9-26; ☺noon-late Wed-Sun; 🖥) Head to the upstairs level of the surf lifesaving club at Mersey Bluff to discover one of Tasmania's best Mod Oz eateries. The ambitious menu cherry-picks highlights from global cuisines but is particularly strong on Asian dishes – think Thai curries, Japanese-style grills, Vietnamese spring rolls. Decor is casual chic, service is polished and the excellent wine list is predominantly Tasmanian.

Tapas Lounge Bar BAR
(☎03-6424 2727; www.tapasloungebar.com; 97a Rooke St Mall; ☺5pm-midnight Thu, to 2am Fri, to late Sat) One of the only places to party in town after the pubs close, this lounge bar offers live music and free pool.

ℹ️ Information

Devonport Visitor Information Centre
(☎1800 649 514, 03-6424 4466; http://tasmaniasnorthwest.com.au; 92 Formby Rd; ☺7.30am-3.30pm Mon-Fri, to 11.30pm Sat & Sun; 🖥) This helpful information office in the town centre can make tour and accommodation bookings, sell national park passes, supply a town map and give advice about travelling in the region. It also offers free baggage storage and wi-fi. Note that weekend hours are extended in summer.

ℹ️ Getting There & Away

AIR

QantasLink (☎13 13 13; www.qantas.com.au) has regular flights between Melbourne and **Devonport Airport** (☎13 13 13; www.devonportairport.com.au; Airport Rd), which is located about 10km east of the town centre.

BOAT

Spirit of Tasmania (☎1800 634 906; www.spiritoftasmania.com.au; ☺customer info 8am-8.30pm Mon-Sat, 9am-8pm Sun) Ferries sail between Station Pier in Melbourne and the ferry terminal on the Esplanade in East Devonport.

BUS

Redline (☎1300 360 000; www.tasredline.com.au) Redline buses stop at 9 Edward St and the *Spirit of Tasmania* terminal. Buses travel between Launceston and Devonport ($25.40, 1½ hours) via Westbury, Deloraine and (sometimes) Mole Creek. Other services include Ul-

verstone ($6.50, 25 minutes), Penguin ($8.50, 40 minutes) and Burnie ($11.20, one hour).

Tassielink (☎1300 300 520; www.tassielink.com.au) Tassielink bus services stop at the visitor centre and at the Spirit of Tasmania terminal. Services from Devonport include Launceston ($25.50, 70 minutes), Sheffield ($5.60, 40 minutes), Gowrie Park ($10.20, 55 minutes), Cradle Mountain ($42.40, two hours) and Queenstown ($56.20, four hours). These connect with services to Strahan ($10.60, 45 to 75 minutes).

ℹ️ Getting Around

North West Shuttles & Transportation
(☎0437 067 108; northwestshuttles@gmail.com) Meets flights coming into Devonport Airport and takes passengers to their accommodation in the centre of town (from $15 per person). It can also meet the Spirit of Tasmania (from $10 per person) or take passengers to/from Launceston Airport (from $75 per person). Bookings are advised for the Devonport airport service and are essential for the ferry or Launceston Airport services.

Sheffield

POP 1108

In the 1980s Sheffield was a typical small Tasmanian country town in the doldrums of rural decline. But then some astute townsfolk came up with an idea that had been applied to the small town of Chemainus in Canada, with some surprisingly wonderful results. The plan was to paint large murals on walls around town, depicting scenes from the district's pioneer days. Sheffield is now a veritable outdoor art gallery, with more than 50 large-scale murals and an annual mural-painting festival. It's a popular base for people walking around Mt Roland and enjoying water sports on Lake Barrington, as well as a popular pit stop for drivers on Hwy 1.

🧭 Tours

Mural Audio Tours WALKING
Grab a headset ($7) from the visitor information centre and take an informative audio tour of Sheffield's outdoor art. The tour takes about 1½ hours (though you can keep the headset all day) and guides you past about 20 of the town's murals. It also leads you through the **TRAK: The Working Art Space** (Tasmanian Regional Arts Kentish; ☎0437 795 374; 2 Albert St; ☺10am-4pm, shorter hours in winter) **FREE**, where you can see local artists at work.

🛏 Sleeping & Eating

Acacia B&B
B&B $$

(📞 0413 149 691, 0437 911 502; www.acacia-bandb.
com.au; cnr High & Tarleton Sts; tw $130, d & f
$150-160; 🅿🛜) Ann and Nigel Beeke are
justifiably proud of their quiet and metic-
ulously maintained B&B. There are four
rooms on offer (the king room with its four-
poster bed is the best). The family room has
an en suite bathroom and the others have
dedicated bathrooms in other parts of the
house. A generous continental breakfast is
served.

The Old Scone Shop & Cafe
CAFE $

(📞 0419 890 367; 72 Main St; pies $10.50-13.50,
sandwiches $5-5.50, scones $3; ⊙ 9am-4pm) A
visit here is akin to a time-travel experience,
with doiley-adorned tables and a menu that
the Country Women's Association would
wholeheartedly endorse. And the good news
is that the food is cheap and tasty – favour-
ites include lamb shank soup, chunky beef
pies, hot lamb and pork rolls with gravy,
plus sweet and savoury scones.

ℹ Information

Kentish Visitor Information Centre (📞 03-
6491 1179; www.sheffieldcradleinfo.com.au;
5 Pioneer Cres; ⊙ 9am-5pm Oct-Apr, to 4pm
May-Sep) Sheffield's helpful tourism informa-
tion centre supplies information on Sheffield,
Latrobe and the greater Kentish region. It also
provides maps and can make accommodation
and tour bookings.

ℹ Getting There & Away

Tassielink (📞 1300 300 520; www.tassielink.
com.au) Tassielink buses stop directly outside
the visitor information centre. Services to/
from Sheffield include Launceston ($31.20, 2¼
hours), Devonport ($5.60, 40 minutes), Cradle
Mountain ($27.60, one hour) and Queenstown
($49.70, 3¾ hours). Change at Queenstown for
Strahan.

Deloraine

POP 2333

Nestled at the foot of the Great Western
Tiers, Deloraine commands wonderful
views at almost every turn. The town itself
is bisected by the winding and very pretty
Meander River, and Georgian and Victorian
buildings are scattered around the main
street, Emu Bay Rd. There's a vibrant, artsy
feel here, with several good eateries and
craft studios to visit.

⊙ Sights

★ 41° South Tasmania
FARM

(📞 03-6362 4130; www.41southtasmania.com; 323
Montana Rd; ⊙ 9am-5pm Nov-Mar, to 4pm Apr-
Oct) 🌿**FREE** Salmon are reared in raised
tanks and a wetland is used as a natural
biofilter at 41° South Tasmania. This no-
waste, no-chemical method of fish farming
is the cleanest way of raising fish – and also
supplies the base for superb hot-smoked
salmon, which you can enjoy in a free tast-
ing or enjoy over lunch in the terrace **cafe**
(small/large tasting platter $12/40). The
farm is 6km out of town towards Mole Creek
(signed down Montana Rd).

Deloraine Museum
MUSEUM

(YARNS: Artwork in Silk; 📞 03-6362 5280; www.
greatwesterntiers.net.au; 98-100 Emu Bay Rd;
adult/concession/child/family $8/6/2/18; ⊙ 9am-
5pm, to 6pm Jan-Mar, 9.30am-4.30pm Sat & Sun
Jun-Aug) The centrepiece of this museum
is an exquisite four-panel, quilted and ap-
pliquéd depiction of the Meander Valley
through a year of seasonal change. It's an
astoundingly detailed piece of work that
was a labour of love for 300 creative local
men and women. Each of the four panels
entailed 10,000 hours of labour, and the
whole project took three years to complete.
It's now housed in a purpose-built audito-
rium, where you can witness a presentation
explaining the work every half-hour.

🛏 Sleeping & Eating

★ Bluestone Grainstore
B&B $$

(📞 03-6362 4722; www.bluestonegrainstore.com.
au; 14 Parsonage St; s $150, d $170-185, f $240;
🛜) 🌿 A 150-year-old warehouse has been
renovated with great style here: think white-
washed stone walls, hard-carved wooden
furniture, comfortable beds with crisp
linen and ultra-sleek bathrooms. There's a
mini-cinema with plenty of films to choose
from and a 24-hour hot-drink station. The
gourmet breakfasts provided draw on local
produce and are served in the main downstairs lounge and dining room.

★ Cycles @ The Empire
AUSTRALIAN $$

(📞 03-6362 1029; http://theempiredeloraine.com.
au; 19 Emu Bay Rd; breakfast dishes $4-18, mains
lunch $16-23, dinner $21-33; ⊙ 9am-9pm Tue-Fri,
10am-9.30pm Sat,10am-3pm Sun) Housed in a for-
mer bicycle factory attached to the heritage-
listed **Empire Hotel** (⊙ 9am-10pm Tue-Thu,
9am-midnight Fri & Sat, 9am-10pm Sun), Cycles

epitomises Australian country pub dining – hearty food served with a drink and a smile. The differences are the cafe-style vibe (coffee is available all day) and the ambitious menu, with treats including chicken curry and truffled mushroom risotto interspersed among the usual parmas, shanks and salt-and-pepper squid.

ⓘ Information

Great Western Tiers Visitor Information Centre (☑ 03-6362 5280; www.greatwestern tiers.net.au; 98-100 Emu Bay Rd; ☺ 8am-6pm Mon-Fri, 9am-5pm Sat & Sun Jan-Mar, 9am-5pm daily Apr, May & Sep-Dec, 9am-5pm Mon-Fri, 9.30am-4.30pm Sat & Sun Jun-Aug) Shares premises with the Deloraine Museum. Staff are helpful and can supply plenty of information about activities in the region as well as book accommodation.

ⓘ Getting There & Away

Redline (☑ 1300 360 000; www.tasredline. com.au) Redline buses run to Launceston ($14.30, one hour, three daily), Devonport ($8.50, 45 minutes, two daily) and Mole Creek ($6.50, 30 minutes, one daily).

Tassielink (☑ 1300 300 520; www.tassielink. com.au) Tassielink doesn't drop off passengers in Deloraine but it does pick-up passengers en route to Cradle Mountain ($61.50, 2½ hours, at least twice weekly) and Queenstown ($74.80, 5½ hours, twice weekly). From Queenstown, there are connecting services to Strahan ($10.60, 45 to 75 minutes). Buses leave from the stop outside Sullivans Restaurant on West Parade.

Mole Creek

POP 230

Diminutive Mole Creek, around 23km west of Deloraine, is a quiet rural town with beautiful mountain views. It's also a great base for those wanting to go bushwalking or caving in the nearby national parks. There's a good chance of seeing platypuses in the town's waterways – keep an eye out just after sunrise and just before sunset.

⊙ Sights

★ **Mole Creek Karst National Park**   NATIONAL PARK
(☑ 03-6363 5182; www.parks.tas.gov.au; daily national parks pass per person/car $12/24) The major draws in this national park are the **Marakoopa** (330 Mayberry Road, Mayberry) and the **King Solomons Caves** (Liena Rd, Liena; adult/child/family $19/9.50/47.50; ☺ regu-

lar departures 10.30am-4.30pm Dec-Apr, 11.30am-3.30pm May-Nov). These can be visited on tours operated by the Tasmanian Parks & Wildlife Service. Other caves in the park can be visited by experienced cavers or in a guided tour operated by **Wild Cave Tours** (☑ 03-6367 8142; www.wildcavetours.com; half-/full-day tours $130/260). Note that visitors who purchase a ticket for a PWS caves tour do not need a national parks pass. Those exploring elsewhere in the park do.

Trowunna Wildlife Park   WILDLIFE RESERVE
(☑ 03-6363 6162; www.trowunna.com.au; 1892 Mole Creek Rd; adult/child/concession/family $26/16/22/75; ☺ 9am-5pm, guided tours 11am, 1pm & 3pm) Home to Tasmanian devils, wombats, quolls, kangaroos, wallabies and pademelons, this privately owned wildlife park focuses on conservation and education and is a great stop for those headed to/from Cradle Mountain. During the informative tour you'll get to pat a wombat and see devils being fed. While there, don't miss the interactive **Devil Education & Research Centre**. The park is just off the highway – look for the big Tasmanian devil by the side of the road.

🛏 Sleeping & Eating

Mole Creek Guest House   B&B $$
(☑ 03-6363 1399; www.molecreekguesthouse.com. au; 100 Pioneer Dr; r $155-175, cottage d $155, house d $200, extra adult/child $50/20, all incl breakfast; ☎) 🍴 The owners here are justifiably proud of their spick-and-span guesthouse, which has six somewhat fussily decorated rooms above the **Pepperberry Cafe** (pizzas $16-20, mains $18-25; ☺ 9am-4pm Sun-Thu, to 9pm Fri & Sat; ☎🍴), one off the garden and a communal lounge with fireplace and kitchenette. There are also attractively presented houses sleeping five and nine for those wanting to self-cater. Breakfast provisions are included in the rates.

ⓘ Information

Mole Creek Community & Information Centre (☑ 03-6363 2030; http://molecreek. info; Mole Creek Rd; ☺ 10am-4pm; ☎) This small community and information centre offers wi-fi ($2 for 500MB) and free internet access on fixed computers. Staff can help with information about bushwalking in the area – particularly at the Walls of Jerusalem – and visiting the area's many caves. It also stocks a small range of tourist brochures and maps.
Parks & Wildlife Tasmania Mole Creek Caves Office (☑ 03-6363 5182; www.parks.tas.gov. au; Marakoopa Cave, 330 Mayberry Rd, May-

berry) Tour tickets for the Marakoopa Cave and information about Tasmania's national parks and reserves are available at this helpful office close to the cave entrance.

❶ Getting There & Away

Redline (☑ 1300 360 000; www.tasredline. com.au) One daily Redline bus service travels between Mole Creek and Launceston ($22.30, 1½ hours) and Deloraine ($6.50, 30 minutes) and via Westbury ($8.50, 45 minutes).

Walls of Jerusalem National Park

The **Walls of Jerusalem National Park** (www.parks.tas.gov.au; daily parks pass per person/vehicle $12/24) is one of Tasmania's most beautiful parks. It's a glacier-scoured landscape of spectacularly craggy dolerite peaks, alpine tarns and forests of ancient pines. The park adjoins the lake-spangled wilderness of the Central Plateau and is part of the Tasmanian Wilderness World Heritage Area. Several walking tracks lead through it, and also join with hikes in Cradle Mountain–Lake St Clair National Park.

🏃 Activities

A steep walking track leads up from the car park at Lake Rowland to **Trappers Hut** (two hours). From Trappers Hut, it is two hours to the **Wild Dog Creek** camping area and nearby **Herods Gate**, the start of the alpine region. From Wild Dog Creek it's three hours return to **Solomon's Throne** or 3½ hours return to the **Dixons Kingdom** camping area, which is surrounded by hauntingly beautiful pencil-pine forests. From Dixons Kingdom, the walk to the top of **Mt Jerusalem** takes 2½ hours return. You'll need to camp overnight if you plan to walk to Dixons Kingdom or Mt Jerusalem.

Note that major flooding in mid-2016 washed away the main access road to the park, making it impossible to access Lake Rowland by vehicle. As of February 2017, access was via Higgs Track at the back of Western Creek, where walkers can follow a track to Lake Ada. Contact the Parks & Wildlife Tasmania Mole Creek Caves Office for updates.

Be prepared for harsh weather conditions: it snows a substantial amount here, and not only in winter. Walks across the park are described in *Cradle Mountain Lake St Clair and Walls of Jerusalem National Parks,* by John Chapman and John Siseman.

Tasmanian Expeditions WALKING (☑ 1300 666 856; www.tasmanianexpeditions.com. au) Tasmanian Expeditions conducts a four-day Walls of Jerusalem experience ($1295), taking in the park's highlights and camping each night at a base camp near a cluster of alpine tarns known as Solomons Jewels. It also offers a truncated three-day self-guided version ($995).

❶ Getting There & Away

Cradle Mountain Coaches (☑ 03-6427 7626, 0448 800 599; www.cradlemountaincoaches. com.au) This shuttle service operated by Devonport-based Merseylink runs bushwalker shuttle services between Launceston or Devonport and Higgs Track ($260 for a private shuttle or $65 per person for four or more passengers). It can also transport passengers between Walls of Jerusalem and Cradle Mountain for the same cost. The shuttles collect passengers from Launceston or Devonport airport, the *Spirit of Tasmania* terminal or their accommodation.

Penguin

POP 3159

A large example of Australia's strange obsession with 'big' things stands between the main beach and shopping strip of this pretty town on Tasmania's north coast. This 3m high penguin signals the fact that this part of the coast is where the world's smallest penguin *(Eudyptula minor)* comes ashore during its breeding season. Many people head here to see these cute critters in the flesh (or should that be in the feather?), but the vibrant cafe culture and safe, sandy beach in the town centre are even greater attractions.

◎ Sights

True to its name, Penguin is a base for the little (or fairy) penguins that come ashore along the coast from mid-September or October to March or April. There are three places to see them. **Lalico Beach**, 22km east of Penguin, is where the largest breeding colony arrives around sunset. There's a viewing platform and, on most nights in season, there's a park ranger in residence to answer any questions. Contact Penguin's visitor information centre (p700) for more details. A smaller colony comes ashore at **Sulphur Creek**, 4km west of Penguin, and at **West Beach** in Burnie, behind the Makers' Workshop (19km west of Penguin).

📖 Sleeping & Eating

⭐ Penguin Beachfront Apartments
APARTMENT $$

(📞 0411 278 473; www.penguinbeachfront.com.au; 52 Main rd; d apt $150-190, extra person $30; 🅿️❄️🛜🐾) Penguin is high on the holiday wish list for families, and these five apartments are perfect choices for those travelling with children as they are located opposite the beach, sleep between four and six, and have excellent kitchens as well as laundry facilities. Couples like them too – especially the two downstairs apartments with their huge lounge areas and beachfront terraces.

⭐ The Madsen
BOUTIQUE HOTEL $$$

(📞 03-6437 2588, 0400 842 863; www.themadsen.com; 64 Main Rd; d $165, penthouse d $300, extra adult/child $40/20; 😊@🛜) Housed in a grand former bank building on the beachfront, this friendly and well-managed boutique hotel offers six well-sized rooms with comfortable beds. All are decorated tastefully – the luxurious penthouse and beachfront spa suites are the most impressive. A cooked breakfast is served in the downstairs lounge, which has an honour bar and tea-and-coffee station, or in your room.

⭐ Jo & Co Cafe
CAFE $$

(📞 03-6437 2101; www.facebook.com/joandcocafe; 74 Main Rd; breakfast dishes $14-19, burgers $15.50-17, dinner mains $15-20; 😊 8.30am-3pm Sat-Thu, to 10pm Fri; 🛜🐾) This ultra-friendly cafe has a retro decor, quirky vibe and menu that caters to vegetarians, vegans and the gluten-free. It's a winning combination. Breakfast involves everything from smashed avocado to the full cooked production, lunch focuses on burgers and salad, and the Friday night dinners are themed by cuisine or food style.

ℹ️ Information

Penguin Visitor Information Centre (📞 03-6437 1421; www.coasttocanyon.com.au; 78 Main Rd; 😊 9am-4pm Mon-Fri, to 3.30pm Sat & Sun Oct-Mar, 9.30am-3.30pm Mon-Fri, 9am-12.30pm Sat, 9am-3.30pm Sun Apr-Sep) Staffed by volunteers, the friendly Penguin visitor centre supplies brochures and advice about visiting nearby attractions. There are public toilets next door.

ℹ️ Getting There & Away

Redline (📞 1300 360 000; www.tasredline.com.au) buses go to Burnie ($6.50, 15 minutes) and Devonport ($8.50, 40 minutes) twice daily. The stop is at Johnsons Beach, opposite the Penguin Caravan Park.

Burnie
POP 19,819

Long dismissed as the island's ugly-duckling city, once-industrial Burnie is trying hard to reinvent itself as a 'City of Makers', referring both to its heavy manufacturing past and its present creative flair. The things being made here these days include paper, cheese and whisky – an unusual but interesting mix. Most visitors are here for business, but its Regional Museum and Penguin Centre are well worth a visit if you're on the north coast.

👁 Sights

⭐ Burnie Regional Museum
MUSEUM

(Pioneer Village Museum; 📞 03-6430 5746; www.burnieregionalmuseum.net; Little Alexander St; adult/concession/child/family $8/5/3/16; 😊 10am-4.30pm Mon-Fri, 1.30-4pm Sat & Sun) The centrepiece of this absorbing museum is a lovingly crafted re-creation of a 1900 Burnie streetscape – including blacksmith's forge and farriers shop, wash house, general store, post and telegraph office, stagecoach depot, inn, dentist's surgery, newspaper office and bootmaker. Each is based on an actual business that once existed in Burnie, incorporates multimedia elements and features excellent interpretative panels. Interesting temporary exhibitions are shown in an adjoining room.

Makers' Workshop
MUSEUM

(📞 03-6430 5831; www.discoverburnie.net; 2 Bass Hwy; 😊 9am-5pm) **FREE** Part museum and part arts centre, this dramatic structure dominates the western end of Burnie's main beach and is a good place to get acquainted with this city's creative heart. The life-size **paper people** you'll find in odd corners of the workshop's cavernous contemporary interior are the work of **Creative Paper** (makersworkshop@burnie.net; tours adult/concession/child/family $15/12/8/40; 😊 tours 9.15am-4.30pm), Burnie's handmade-paper producers. Its tours take you through the production process of making paper from such unusual raw materials as kangaroo poo, apple pulp and rainforest leaves.

Hellyers Road Distillery
DISTILLERY

(📞 03-6433 0439; www.hellyersroaddistillery.com.au; 153 Old Surrey Rd; tours $17.50; 😊 10am-4.30pm) Henry Hellyer was the first white settler in Emu Bay, and this respected distillery does his memory proud. You can tour the distillery to see how its golden single malt is made, and afterwards take a tasting (half/full nip $3/4). Tours depart at 10.30am, 11.30am, 2pm and 3pm daily.

🏃 Activities

★ Burnie Penguin Centre   BIRDWATCHING
(☑0437 436 803; by donation) A boardwalk on the foreshore leads from Burnie Beach to this centre, skirting the Makers' Workshop along the way. From October to March you can take a free Penguin Interpretation Tour about one hour after dusk when the penguins emerge from the sea and waddle back to their burrows. Volunteer wildlife guides are present to talk about the penguins and their habits. Wear dark clothing.

🛏 Sleeping & Eating

★ Ikon Hotel   BOUTIQUE HOTEL $$
(☑03-6432 4566; www.ikonhotel.com.au; 22 Mount St; d $175-230, tr $205-245, all incl breakfast; 🅿❋✿) Boutique hotel chic comes to Burnie at this centrally located hotel. Located on the 1st floor of a heritage hotel in the city centre, it offers extremely spacious and stylish suites with compact kitchenettes and sleek bathrooms. Breakfast provisions are modest.

Duck House   COTTAGE $$
(☑03-6431 1712; www.duckhousecottage.com. au; 26 Queen St; s/d $120/160, extra adult/child $40/20, all incl breakfast; 🅿➥✿) Named after Salvation Army stalwarts Bill and Winifred Duck, who lived here for 30 years, this charming little self-contained two-bedroom cottage sleeps up to five. The decoration, rather predictably, has an emphasis on ducks. A three-bedroom property next door, **Mrs Philpott's**, sleeps up to seven and a third house, **Amelia's**, has three bedrooms and is located nearby at 1 Princes St.

★ Fish Frenzy   SEAFOOD $
(☑03-6432 1111; www.fishfrenzy.com.au; 2 North Tce; fish, chips & salad $14-16, half-dozen oysters $16; ⊗8am-11pm summer, 11am-10pm rest of year; 🖟) This fish 'n' chippery breadcrumbs its super-fresh fish or dowses it in a tempura batter before frying, ensuring that its creations are a cut above the competition. A modern and bustling place right on the water, it also serves oysters and lavish seafood platters ($75 for two persons).

★ The Chapel   CAFE $$
(☑03-6432 3460; www.chapelcafe.com.au; 50 Cattley St; breakfast $6-18, lunch $13-17; ⊗7.30am-3pm Mon-Thu, 7.30am-3pm & 7pm-late Fri, 8am-3pm Sat) This hipsterish cafe is housed in a handsome decommissioned chapel and the quality of the food certainly matches the surrounds. The best cafe in Burnie (and probably the best on the north coast), it serves excellent house-roasted coffee, house-made chai and simply sensational toasted sandwiches made with freshly baked bread. There are some good pastries, muffins and cakes too.

ℹ Information

Visitor Information Centre (☑03-6430 5831; www.discoverburnie.net; 2 Bass Hwy; ⊗9am-5pm) A desk in the foyer of the Makers' Workshop, this volunteer-staffed information centre can provide advice, brochures and a city map.

ℹ Getting There & Away

Burnie/Wynyard airport (☑03-6442 1133; www.burnieairport.com.au; 3 Airport St, Wynyard), known as either Burnie or Wynyard airport, is located in Wynyard, 20km northwest of Burnie. Regular flights travel to/from Melbourne (75 minutes) with **Regional Express Airlines** (REX; www.regionalexpress.com.au), and to/from King Island (40 minutes) with **Sharp Airlines** (☑1300 556 694; www.sharp airlines.com).

Metro (☑13 22 01; www.metrotas.com.au) Regular local buses to Penguin ($6.40, 30 minutes), Ulverstone ($8.30, 55 minutes), and Wynyard ($6.40, 30 minutes), departing from the bus interchange on Cattley St, beside Harris Scarfe department store.

Redline (☑1300 360 000; www.tasredline. com.au) Redline buses stop on Wilmot St,

---

DON'T MISS

BOAT HARBOUR BEACH

This may well be paradise. Picture-perfect Boat Harbour Beach has the kind of pristine white sand and sapphire-blue waters that make you feel like you've taken a wrong turn off the Bass Hwy and ended up in the Caribbean. The usually calm seas are patrolled in summer and perfect for kids, and one of the north coast's best casual eateries is located in the surf lifesaving club. The beach is located 4.5km west of the small settlement of Boat Harbour, off the Bass Hwy.

opposite the Metro Cinemas. Useful destinations include Devonport ($11.20, one hour), Launceston ($39.30, 2½ hours) and Smithton ($24, 1½ hours).

Stanley

POP 481

Stanley is little more than a scatter of brightly painted heritage cottages sheltering in the lee of an ancient volcano, the Nut (also known as Circular Head). But boy oh boy, it's atmospheric. Fishing boats piled high with cray pots and orange buoys bob in the harbour, locals chat on door stoops and the blast of the Roaring Forties ensures that the air is exhilaratingly clear. With a couple of top-drawer tourist attractions (Highfield and the Nut), an array of excellent accommodation options and a few good eateries, it's an understandably popular place to while away a day or two.

Sights & Activities

The Nut   LANDMARK
Known to the area's Indigenous people as Monatteh and labelled 'Circular Head' by Matthew Flinders, this striking 143m-high, 12-million-year-old core of an extinct volcano can be seen for kilometres around. To get to the summit it's a steep 20-minute climb or a ride on the chairlift (☑03-6458 1482; info@ thenutchairlift.com.au; adult one way/return $10/16, child $5/10, family $30/45; ☺9.30am-4.15pm Oct-May). The best lookout is a five-minute walk to the south of the chairlift. When at the top you can take a 2km walk (about 35 minutes) on a dedicated path.

★ **Highfield**   HISTORIC BUILDING
(☑03-6458 1100; www.historic-highfield.com.au; Green Hills Rd; adult/concession/child/family $12/10/6/30; ☺9.30am-4.30pm daily Sep-May, Mon-Fri Jun-Aug) Built in 1835 for the chief agent of the Van Diemen's Land Company, this homestead 2km north of town is an exceptional example of domestic architecture of the Regency period in Tasmania. Managed by the Tasmanian Parks & Wildlife Service, it can be visited on a self-guided tour that covers the house, pretty garden and outbuildings including stables, grain stores, workers' cottages and the chapel.

Rocky Cape National Park   NATIONAL PARK
(www.parks.tas.gov.au; day admission vehicle/ person $24/12) Tasmania's smallest national park stretches 12km along Bass Strait's shoreline. Known to Aboriginal Tasmanians as Tangdimmaa, or Tang Dim Mer, it has great significance to the local Indigenous people, who made their homes in the sea caves here 8000 years before European occupation. Inland the park is made up of coastal heathland and rare *Banksia serrata* forests. On Rocky Cape itself, you can drive out to a squat lighthouse and enjoy fine Bass Strait views. Parks passes are available at the Sisters Beach General Store.

Stanley Seal Cruises   BOATING
(☑0419 550 134, 03-6458 1294; www.stanleyseal cruises.com.au; Fisherman's Dock, Wharf Rd; adult/ child 5-15yr/child under 5yr $55/18/10; ☺Sep-mid-Jun) These excellent 75-minute cruises on the MC *Sylvia C* take passengers to see up to 500 Australian fur seals sunning themselves on Bull Rock on the Bass Strait coast. Departures are at 10am and 3pm from September to April, and at 1pm from May to mid-July, sea conditions permitting – book ahead to make sure they're running.

Sleeping & Eating

Stanley Cabin & Tourist Park   CARAVAN PARK $
(☑03-6458 1266; www.stanleycabinpark.com.au; Wharf Rd; powered/unpowered sites per 2 people $33/25, dm $26, cabins d $90-160; ☑📶) Commanding expansive views of Sawyer Bay in one direction and the Nut on the other, this park offers waterfront camp sites, a camp kitchen and laundry, a games room with ping-pong, neat but basic self-contained cabins and a well-maintained backpacker hostel comprising four twin rooms, lounge with TV and communal kitchen. Linen is supplied, but it's BYO towels.

★ **Cable Station Accommodation**   B&B $$
(☑0405 819 728, 03-6458 1312; www.cablestation stanley.com.au; d $155, tr $185; 📶🍳❄📶📶) Perched on a windswept plateau close to Perkin's Bay, this 1930s building was constructed to carry Tasmania's first telephone link to the mainland. It now houses two delightful guest units sleeping two or three; each has a TV and large modern bathroom. The helpful managers supply breakfast provisions including freshly baked bread and homemade jams.

★ **@VDL**   BOUTIQUE HOTEL $$$
(☑0437 070 222, 03-6458 2032; www.atvdlstanley. com.au; 16 Wharf Rd; ste $200-250, loft $285-350; 📶📶) What's been done within the bluestone walls of this 1840s warehouse on the seafront

is quite incredible. This ultra-hip boutique offering has two suites and a self-contained loft apartment. Their decor and amenities are top class, featuring designer furniture, contemporary art, sleek bathrooms and coffee machines.

★ Nut Café
CAFE $

(☑ 03-6458 1186; The Nut; breakfast $8.50-19.50, lunch $10-23, 1/2 scones $6.50/8.50; ⊙ 9.30am-3pm Sep-May) Cafes at popular tourist attractions are often sub-standard, but that's decidedly not the case here. Stanley's best eatery by a long shot, the Nut Café serves gourmet breakfasts, delicious lunches and the best Devonshire tea on the island (and that's really saying something). Be sure to purchase some of the homemade jam to take home.

❶ Information

Stanley Visitor Information Centre (☑ 1300 138 229, 03-6458 1330; www.stanley.com.au; 45 Main Rd; ⊙ 9.30am-5pm Oct-May, 10am-4pm Jun-Sep; ☏) A mine of information on Stanley and surrounding areas. Offers bicycle hire (adult/child $22/15 for three hours) and free wi-fi.

❶ Getting There & Away

Redline (☑ 1300 360 000; www.tasredline. com.au) Redline buses stop at the visitor centre en route to/from Burnie ($21.10, 75 minutes, daily) and Smithton ($6.10, 25 minutes, daily).

Marrawah

POP 371

Untamed and unspoilt, Marrawah is a domain of vast ocean beaches, mind-blowing sunsets and green, rural hills. The power of the ocean here is astounding, and the wild beaches, rocky coves and headlands have changed little since they were the homeland of Tasmania's first people. This coast is abundant with signs of Aboriginal Tasmania – especially in the fascinating Preminghana Indigenous Protected Area just north of town. Sometimes the Southern Ocean throws up the remains of long-forgotten shipwrecks here – things tumble in on waves that sometimes reach more than 10m in length. Experienced surfers and windsurfers also come here for the challenging breaks.

🛌 Sleeping

Marrawah Beach House
RENTAL HOUSE $$

(☑ 03-6457 1285, 0428 571 285; www.marrawah beachhouse.com.au; d $140-170, extra person $25;

ℙ) Perched on the slopes of a working farm overlooking the wild Southern Ocean, these two self-contained cabins are extremely well maintained and are great options for those wanting a beach break. One sleeps four in two bedrooms, the second is a studio sleeping two. Both command magnificent views. You'll find them just up the hill from Green Point Beach. No wi-fi or TV reception.

King Island

POP 1565

King Island (or 'KI', as locals call it) is the kind of place where the only traffic control is a leisurely wave of the hand from a local as you pass by. A skinny sliver of land 64km long and 27km wide, it's a laid-back place where everyone knows everyone. The island's green pastures produce a rich dairy bounty (you'll be testing how much cheese it's actually possible to ingest over the space of a few days) and its seas supply fabulously fresh seafood, including crayfish. The island's main settlement is the town of Currie (population 687) on the west coast, and there are east coast settlements at Grassy (population 277) and Naracoopa (population 200).

⊙ Sights

King Island Dairy
DAIRY

(☑ 1800 677 852, 03-6462 0947; www.kingisland dairy.com.au; 869 North Rd, Loorana; ⊙ 10am-5pm) **FREE** Low-key but top quality, King Island Dairy's Fromagerie is 8km north of Currie (just beyond the airport). Taste its award-winning bries, cheddars and feisty blues, watch a 15-minute video about the cheesemaking process and then stock up in its shop on cheeses that are budget priced – only here – to fuel your King Island exploring.

King Island Museum
MUSEUM

(☑ 03-6462 1512; Lighthouse St, Currie; adult/child $8/2; ⊙ 2-4pm, closed Jul-Sep) Exhibits on lightkeeping, shipwrecks, local monuments and the island's soldier settlement history.

🏃 Activities

Being an island, the wind is off-shore somewhere every day, ensuring excellent **surfing**. Indeed, the break at Martha Lavinia is often described as one of the best in Australia. Named after an 1852 shipwreck, it is located just outside Currie. Other stellar breaks can be found at Phoques Bay on the northwest coast; Red Hut Point, south of the Island;

Porky Beach, behind the King Island Dairy; and British Admiral Beach near the Kelp Industries in Currie.

Surf and freshwater **fishing** almost guarantee a good catch, and you can **swim** at many of the island's unpopulated beaches (beware rips and currents) and freshwater lagoons. Bring your own gear for the legendary snorkelling and diving here.

For **hiking**, pick up a map from King Island Tourism and go independently, or take a guided walk. Tour companies are listed on the King Island Tourism website.

You don't even need to get out on foot for **wildlife spotting** on KI: it's just about everywhere you look. There are rufus and Bennett's wallabies, pademelons, snakes, echidnas and platypuses, and you may even glimpse seals. The island has 78 bird species and, on summer evenings, little penguins come ashore around the Grassy breakwater.

Sleeping & Eating

Island Breeze Motel
MOTEL $$

(☑03-6462 1260, 0475 351 807; www.islandbreezemotel.com.au; 95 Main St, Currie; d $170, cabin d $180, all incl breakfast; ⓟ☺) Popular with those playing at the nearby Cape Wickham Golf Course, this motel offers attractive, well-heated rooms with comfortable beds and tea- and coffee-making facilities. There are also two self-catering cabins with three bedrooms. The friendly and efficient manager can supply plenty of advice about touring the island. A continental breakfast is included in the price.

King Island
Accommodation Cottages
RENTAL HOUSE $$

(☑0427 002 397, 03-6461 1326; www.kingislandaccommodationcottages.com.au; 125 Esplanade, Naracoopa; 1-/2-bedroom cottages from $130/140; ⓟ☺🛰) Right on the coast and beautifully maintained, these quiet self-catering cottages are an excellent choice. If they were on the mainland, they'd cost double this price. Wi-fi in public areas only.

Wild Harvest
MODERN AUSTRALIAN $$$

(☑03-6461 1176; www.wildharvestkingisland.com.au; 4 Bluegum Dr, Grassy; mains $28-55; ☺6-9.30pm) Sea to table, paddock to plate – most of the produce used by the chefs at this eatery overlooking Grassy Harbour is local, seasonal and fresh. The result is a menu of tasty dishes with global accents accompanied by Tasmanian wines. Winter meals here are

enjoyed in front of a roaring log fire; in summer guests can dine outside.

ⓘ Information

King Island Tourism (☑03-6462 1355, 1800 645 014; www.kingisland.org.au; 5 George St, Currie; ☺10.30am-5pm Mon-Fri, 10am-noon Sat) Supplies brochures outlining the King Island Grazing Trail and Maritime Trail at both the airport and its office in town. Its website is an excellent pre-trip planning resource, with suggested itineraries and loads of information about activities, tours and accommodation.

ⓘ Getting There & Away

Three airlines fly into King Island's small airport at Loorana, 8km northeast of Currie. **King Island Airlines** (☑Currie 03-6462 1000, Moorabbin 03-9580 3777; www.kingislandair.com.au) flies to/from Melbourne's Moorabbin airport (one hour) once or twice daily; **Regional Express** (REX; ☑13 17 13; www.regionalexpress.com.au) flies daily to/from Melbourne's Tullamarine airport (55 minutes); and **Sharp Airlines** (☑1300 55 66 94; www.sharpairlines.com) flies to/from Melbourne's Essendon airport (45 minutes, twice daily) and from Launceston (1¾ hours, twice daily) via Burnie (40 minutes, daily).

ⓘ Getting Around

In Currie, **King Island Car Rental** (☑1800 777 282; kicars2@bigpond.com; 2 Meech St, Currie; ☺ per day from $73) and **P&A Car Rental** (☑03-6462 1603; admin@pacars.com.au; 2a Meech St, Currie; per day from $80) offer car hire.

The Tarkine Wilderness

The Tarkine is a 447,000-hectare stretch of temperate rainforest between the Arthur River in the north, the Pieman River in the south, the Murchison Hwy to the east and the Southern Ocean to the west. It's a globally significant ecosystem that encompasses vast forests of myrtle, leatherwood and pine trees, endless horizons of buttongrass plains, savage ocean beaches, sand dunes and extensive coastal heathland. It's also believed to be one of the oldest rainforests in Australia, and is home to several endangered species and extensive, ancient archaeological sites. Because of its remoteness, ferocious weather and isolation, the Tarkine survived almost untouched by modernity well into the 20th century and the region still offers a frontier-style experience for those keen to explore it.

There is no public transport within the Tarkine. You'll need a 4WD to drive on tracks and minor roads.

🏃 Activities

⭐ Tarkine Forest
Adventures   ADVENTURE SPORTS
(📞03-6456 7138; www.dismalswamptasmania.com.au; 26,059 Bass Hwy, Togari; adult/child $20/10, plus serpent slide $2; ⊙9am-5pm Dec & Jan, 10am-4pm Feb-May & Sep-Nov) Formerly known as Dismal Swamp, this forest adventure centre 32km southwest of Smithton (off the A2) is home to a 110m-long 'serpent slide' that provides a thrilling descent through the dense blackwood canopy to boardwalks down on the forest floor – sliders must be over eight years of age and at least 90cm tall. You'll see pandemelons, birds, rare funghi and orchids. There's also a cafe and an interpretation centre.

⭐ Tarkine Trails   WALKING
(📞0405 255 537; www.tarkinetrail.com.au) Tarkine Trails takes bushwalkers on a number of different adventures. Trips include the full-forest-immersion, six-day Tarkine Trail ($1950 per person), four-day Tarkine Rainforest Walk ($1800) or the six-day Tarkine Coast Trail ($1950) from Sandy Cape to Pieman Heads.

Corinna & the Pieman River

In the rip-roaring gold-rush days Corinna was a humming mining settlement with two hotels, a post office, plenty of shops and a population that numbered 2500 souls. These days, it's a tranquil place with only one business: Corinna Wilderness Experience. An outfit offering visitors the chance to experience a sense of adventure and immersion in the rainforest without forsaking too many comforts, it offers accommodation in camp sites and cabins, a restaurant and cafe-bar, cruises down the Pieman River and kayak hire.

🏃 Activities

Pieman River Cruises   BOATING
(📞03-6446 1170; www.corinna.com.au/river-cruises; ⊙Pieman River Cruise adult/child under 12yr $90/50, Sweetwater Cruise per person $30) When in Corinna, be sure to take one of these cruises. The 4½-hour Pieman River Cruise departs at 10am daily and sails downstream to where the Pieman River meets the Southern Ocean. Morning tea and a packed lunch is included. Also on offer is a one-hour Sweetwater Cruise to Lovers Falls and the SS *Croydon* shipwreck, which departs at 3pm. Book well ahead.

🛏 Sleeping & Eating

Corinna Wilderness Experience   COTTAGE $$
(📞03-6446 1170; www.corinna.com.au; camp sites $40, cottage d $165-220, f $270) Corinna's tranquil wilderness village offers accommodation in one- and two-bedroom timber cottages scattered in the attractive rainforest above the riverside lodge. These sleep up to five and are solar powered; all have a kitchen or kitchenette, a wood stove or fire, a simple bathroom and a deck. There are also camp sites and a camp kitchen with BBQ.

The lodge has a cafe-bar and the **Tannin Restaurant** (mains lunch $10-18, dinner $22-37; ⊙noon-2pm & 6-8pm) offers hearty meals.

CRADLE COUNTRY & THE WEST

Welcome to the island's wild west, a land of endless ocean beaches, ancient mossy rainforests, tannin-tinted rivers, glacier-sculpted mountains, wildflower-strewn high plains and boundless horizons where you'll often feel like you are the only soul on earth. This is Tasmania's vast outdoor playground, an area replete with national parks, conservation reserves and World Heritage–protected wilderness, and where your options for adventure are varied and plentiful.

Come here for the toughest multiday hikes (or gentle rainforest wanders); come to shoot rapids on untamed rivers (or cruise mirror-calm waters); and come to kayak into some of the last untouched temperate wilderness on earth (or fly over it all in a light plane). You can visit independently or with a guided group – however you choose to arrive, one thing is sure: you won't want to leave.

Queenstown

POP 1975

Most of Western Tasmania is green. Queenstown is orange or red. The winding descent into Queenstown from the Lyell Hwy is unforgettable for its moonscape of bare hills and eroded gullies where rainforest once proliferated. Copper was discovered here in the 1890s and mining has continued ever since, but today – thankfully – pollution is closely monitored and sulphur emissions are controlled. The town retains a rough-and-ready pioneer feel and though suffering the economic aftershocks of mine closures it is trying hard to reinvent itself as a tourism destination.

Sights

Iron Blow Lookout
VIEWPOINT

On top of Gormanston Hill on the Lyell Hwy, just before the final descent along hairpin bends into Queenstown, is a sealed side road leading to an utterly spectacular lookout over the geological wound of Iron Blow. This decommissioned open-cut mine, where Queenstown's illustrious mining career began, is awesomely deep and is now filled with emerald water. You can get an eagle's-eye view from the 'springboard' walkway projecting out into thin air above the mine pit.

Tours

Queenstown Heritage Tours
HISTORY

(0407 049 612; www.queenstownheritagetours.com; power plant tour adult/child $45/30; by appointment) Operated by the knowledgeable Anthony Coulson, this company offers industrial heritage buffs the opportunity to visit an early 20th-century hydroelectric power plant on Lake Margaret, but its most popular offering is a 'Lost Mines, Ancient Pines' tour (adult/child $80/40), which goes underground at old copper and gold mines and visits a commercial sawmill and stand of Huon pine rainforest.

Sleeping & Eating

★ Mt Lyell Anchorage
B&B $$

(03-6471 1900; www.mtlyellanchorage.com; 17 Cutten St; s $140-150, d $160-180; P 🐾 🕾) Though you wouldn't guess it from the outside, this 1890s weatherboard home has been transformed into a welcoming guesthouse with comfortable rooms featuring excellent beds. Three of the rooms have stylish bathrooms (a fourth has private facilities across the hall) and there's a shared fully equipped kitchen next to a comfortable communal lounge. Owner Joy is a mine of local information.

★ Penghana
GUESTHOUSE $$

(03-6471 2560; www.penghana.com.au; 32 Esplanade; d $180-195, d with shared bathroom $160, all incl breakfast; P 🕾) Built in 1898 for the general manager of the Mt Lyell Mining & Railway Co, this National Trust–owned mansion is located on a hill above town amid a beautiful garden. The views from here are magnificent. The new managers are gradually refurbishing all six rooms in great style – the Owen and Lyell rooms have en suites and are the pick of the bunch.

Empire Hotel
PUB FOOD $$

(03-6471 1699; www.empirehotel.net.au; 2 Orr St; mains lunch $12-16, dinner $18-35; bar 11am-10pm Mon-Sat, to 9pm Sun, dining room noon-2pm & 5.30-8pm) This old miners' pub has survived the ages and includes an atmospheric heritage dining room serving a changing menu of hearty pub standards, including well-cooked parmas, pastas and steaks. The menu focuses on meat dishes, but vegetarians are catered for with a massive veggie stack.

Information

West Coast Community Services Hub (03-6495 1530; westcoasthub@education.tas.gov.au; 9-13 Driffield St; 9.30am-5pm Mon-Fri; 🕾) There's no tourist information centre in Queenstown, but this excellent community services hub offers a library with free wi-fi and internet access. You can also access information, charge your phone and read Tasmanian and mainland newspapers here. An on-site Service Tasmania (1300 135 513; 9-13 Driffield St; 9.30am-4.30pm Mon-Fri) office sells good maps of the nearby national park.

Getting There & Away

Tassielink (1300 300 520; www.tassielink.com.au) Buses arrive at and depart from the West Coast Wilderness Railway Station on Driffield St. Services travel to/from Hobart ($67.60, 5½ hours) via Derwent Bridge and Lake St Clair three times weekly, and to/from Launceston ($74.80, six hours) via Cradle Mountain and Devonport at least twice weekly; all services connect with buses to Strahan ($10.60, 45 minutes).

Strahan
POP 660

The *Chicago Tribune* newspaper once dubbed Strahan 'the best little town in the world' and it's easy to image why it did so. The town's pure air, friendly locals and picturesque location nestled between the waters of Macquarie Harbour and the rainforest combines with top-drawer tourist attractions – Gordon River cruises and the West Coast

Wilderness Railway – to make it one of Tasmania's most popular and family-friendly tourist destinations.

◎ Sights

Ocean Beach BEACH

Head six kilometres west of Strahan's town centre to find Ocean Beach, awesome as much for its 40km length as for the strength of the surf that pounds it. This stretch of sand and sea runs uninterrupted from Trial Harbour in the north to Macquarie Heads in the south and is an evocative place to watch the orange orb of the sun melt into the sea. The water is treacherous: don't swim here.

West Coast Reflections MUSEUM

(Esplanade; adult/child/family $2/1/5; ⊙ 10am-6.30pm Oct-May, noon-5pm Jun-Sep) The Strahan Visitor Centre (p708) is home to this creative and thought-provoking display on the history of the west coast. It includes a refreshingly blunt appraisal of the region's environmental disappointments and achievements, including the Franklin Blockade, the 1982 protest against the damming of the Franklin River.

☞ Tours

World Heritage Cruises BOATING

(☑ 03-6471 7174; www.worldheritagecruises.com.au; 19 Esplanade; adult $115-160, child $60-90, family $290-370; ⊙ 9am mid-Aug–mid-Jul) The Grining family have been taking visitors to the Gordon since 1896 and they are true river experts. Join them aboard their low-wash, environmentally sensitive catamaran, the *Harbourmaster,* for a six-hour cruise through Macquarie Harbour and out through Hells Gates, to Sarah Island and up the Gordon River. Prices vary depending on whether you take a window seat (premium, or, if on the upper deck, gold) or one in the centre (standard).

Gordon River Cruises CRUISE

(☑ 03-6471 4300; www.gordonrivercruises.com.au; Strahan Activity Centre, The Esplanade; Gordon River cruise adult $115-230, child $62-230, family from $280) Operated by the Royal Automobile Club of Tasmania, the 5½-hour Gordon River Cruise departs at 8.30am and sails up the Gordon as far as Heritage Landing, stopping at Sarah Island en route. Prices depend on whether you opt for the standard package, premium window seating or the lavishly catered 'upper deck' experience. Advanced bookings are recommended.

DON'T MISS

WEST COAST WILDERNESS RAILWAY

Hop on board this **historic railway service** (☑ 03-6471 0100; www.wcwr.com.au; Queenstown Station, 1 Driffield St; Rack & Gorge journey standard carriage adult/child/family $100/50/240, wilderness carriage adult/child $165/95; ⊙ ticket office 8am-3.30pm Mon-Thu & Sat, 9am-3.30pm Fri & Sun) and take an unforgettable journey through the majestic rainforest that stretches between Strahan and Queenstown. The half-day Rack & Gorge trip departs from Queenstown station twice daily in high season and once daily at other times of the year, looping through the King River Gorge to Dubbil Barril and then returning to Queenstown.

West Coast Yacht Charters BOATING

(☑ 03-6471 7422; www.westcoastyachtcharters.com.au; 59 Esplanade, The Crays; Upper Gordon cruise adult/child $320/160; ⊙ Oct-Apr) If you'd like your Gordon River experience with a little adventure (and fewer people), sailing on the *Stormbreaker* may be the way to go. This 20m ketch has the only licence to cruise the Upper Gordon; it departs at 1pm and returns at noon the next day (minimum numbers apply, meals and accommodation included).

⌂ Sleeping & Eating

Strahan Holiday Retreat CARAVAN PARK $

(☑ 03-6471 7442; www.strahanretreat.com.au; 10 Innes St; unpowered sites $15, powered sites $30-45, cabins $105-160, cottages from $140; ℗⊛) Close to Strahan's West Beach, this well-maintained park offers camp and caravan sites, self-contained cabins and multi-room cottages. There's not much grass and accommodation is cheek-by-jowl, but the facilities, including a camp kitchen, BBQs, laundries and a games room, compensate. The retreat also offers kayak/sand board/bicycle hire ($45/8/35 per day).

Strahan Bungalows APARTMENT $$

(☑ 0412 870 684, 03-6471 7268; www.strahanbungalows.com.au; cnr Andrew & Harvey Sts; d $140-240; ℗⊛) Decorated with a nautical theme, these two-bedroom bungalows are clean, well maintained and equipped with everything you need for a self-contained stay. They sleep up to five persons but are compact, so things would be cramped for larger groups. The location is reasonably close to the beach and the golf course, and less than a 15-minutes walk from the town centre.

★ **Wheelhouse Apartments** RENTAL HOUSE $$$
(☑ 0429 356 117, 03-6471 7777; www.wheelhouse apartments.com.au; 4 Frazer St; d $240-320; P ❋) Talk about a room with a view! Perched high above the town centre, this pair of swish two-bedroom townhouses have seamless walls of glass framing a jaw-dropping view over Macquarie Harbour. They feature a well-equipped kitchen with oven and espresso machine, lounge with huge TV, downstairs bedroom and bathroom, and a spiral staircase leading to a master bedroom with spa.

★ **Union Takeaway** FISH & CHIPS $
(☑ 03-6471 7500; 23-25 Esplanade; oysters per piece $2, seafood & chips $13-22; ☺ noon-8pm daylight savings, 5-8pm Tue-Sat rest of the year) You're at the beach, so eating fish and chips at least once is obligatory. And in Strahan, the best place for a fishy fry-up is this takeaway joint on the main street. As well as whiting, flake or scallops with chips, it offers fresh oysters.

★ **Bushman's Bar & Cafe** MODERN AUSTRALIAN $$$
(☑ 03-6471 7612; www.bushmanscafe.com.au; 1 Harold St; mains lunch $13-25, dinner $35-45; ☺ 7.30am-8pm high season, 11am-8pm Mon-Fri, 5-8pm Sat rest of year) A focus on local produce, including Petuna salmon, Spring Bay scallops and Sassafras lamb, is the defining feature of the menu at Strahan's best restaurant. Lunch is a laid-back affair featuring homemade pies, salads, pasta dishes and burgers. Dinner is a more sophisticated proposition, featuring dishes such as slow-cooked pork belly, paillard of salmon and rack of lamb. Book ahead for dinner.

☆ **Entertainment**

★ **The Ship That Never Was** THEATRE
(www.roundearth.com.au/ship; West Coast Visitor Centre, Esplanade; adult/student/child $20/10/2; ☺ 5.30pm Sep-May, box office from 5pm) Presented in a small amphitheatre attached to the West Coast Visitor Centre, this 1½-hour, two-performer play tells the picaresque tale of a group of convicts who escaped from Sarah Island in 1834 by hijacking a ship they were building. A Strahan institution (it's been staged for over two decades), the entertaining performance involves audience participation and is suitable for all age groups.

ℹ **Information**

West Coast Visitor Centre (☑ 03-6472 6800; www.westcoast.tas.gov.au; The Esplanade; ☺ 10am-6.30pm Christmas-Mar, to 5.30pm Apr & May, noon-5pm Jun-Sep, noon-5.30pm Oct-Christmas) This extremely friendly and helpful visitor centre supplies information about Strahan and other destinations on the West Coast. Staff can also make tour and accommodation bookings.

ℹ **Getting There & Away**

Tassielink (☑ 1300 300 520; www.tassielink. com.au) operates weekday bus services to Queenstown ($10.60, 75 minutes) during the school term, departing at 7.30am. Outside these periods services depart Monday to Thursday at 8.15am. Many connect with services heading to Launceston ($74.80, six hours) and Hobart ($67.60, 5¼ hours). Services arrive at and depart from the Strahan Activities Centre.

Franklin-Gordon Wild Rivers National Park

Named after the wild rivers that twist and cascade their way through its infinitely rugged landscapes, this magnificent national park is part of the Tasmanian Wilderness World Heritage Area and encompasses the catchments of the Franklin, Olga and Gordon Rivers. It was proclaimed a national park in 1981 after the failed campaign to stop the flooding of precious Lake Pedder under the Pedder-Gordon hydroelectric dam scheme and is now a popular destination for bushwalkers, rafters and 4WD enthusiasts. The park's most significant peak is Frenchmans Cap (1443m), with a white-quartzite top formed by glacial action.

🏃 **Activities**

Rafting the Franklin River is about as wild and thrilling a journey as it's possible to make in Tasmania. This is really extreme adventure and a world-class rafting experience. Experienced rafters can tackle it independently if they're fully equipped and prepared, but for anyone who's less than completely river savvy (and that's about 90% of all Franklin rafters), there are tour companies offering complete rafting packages.

If you go with an independent group you must contact the park rangers at the **Queenstown Parks & Wildlife Service** (Queenstown Field Centre; ☑ 03-6471 5920; www.parks.tas.gov. au; Penghana Rd; ☺ sporadic hours) for current information on permits, regulations and environmental considerations. You should also check out the Franklin rafting notes on the Parks & Wildlife Service website. All expeditions should register at the booth at the point where the Lyell Hwy crosses the Collingwood River, 49km west of Derwent Bridge.

The trip down the Franklin, starting at Collingwood River and ending at Sir John Falls, takes between eight and 14 days, depending on river conditions. Shorter trips on certain sections of the river are also possible. From the exit point at Sir John Falls, you can be picked up by a **Strahan Helicopter** (🖉0419 656 974; www.strahanhelicopters.com.au; Esplanade; ☺Nov-May), or by the West Coast Yacht Charters (p707) yacht, *Stormbreaker*, for the trip back to Strahan.

The upper Franklin, from Collingwood River to the Fincham Track, passes through the bewitchingly beautiful Irenabyss Gorge and you can scale Frenchmans Cap as a side trip. The lower Franklin, from the Fincham Track to Sir John Falls, passes through the wild Great Ravine.

Franklin River Rafting   RAFTING
(🖉0422 642 190; www.franklinriverrafting.com; 8-/10-day trip $2860/3190; ☺Oct-Apr) Excellent eight- and 10-day guided and fully catered trips from Collingwood Bridge, with the final leg to Strahan on the *Stormbreaker*. The longer trip includes climbing Frenchmans Cap. Both trips include pick-up in Hobart.

Water By Nature   RAFTING
(🖉0408 242 941, 1800 111 142; www.franklinrivertasmania.com; 5-/7-/10-day trips $2090/2690/3180) This outfit provides five-, seven- and 10-day guided and fully catered trips down the Franklin. The 10-day trip includes an optional climb of Frenchmans Cap. Trips start and end in Hobart and include a final leg aboard the *Stormbreaker*.

Cradle Mountain-Lake St Clair National Park

Part of the World Heritage–listed Tasmanian Wilderness, this 1262-sq-km national park incorporates glacier-sculpted mountain peaks, river gorges, lakes, tarns and tracts of wild alpine moorland. Though it extends all the way from the Great Western Tiers in the north to Derwent Bridge in the south, its most beloved landscapes and walks – including parts of the world-renowned 65km Over-land Track – are around Cradle Mountain. The park encompasses Mt Ossa (1617m), Tasmania's highest peak, and Lake St Clair, the deepest (200m) lake in Australia. Within the park's boundaries are plenty of wildlife-watching opportunities – sightings of wombats, Bennett's wallabies and pademelons are almost guaranteed, and Tasmanian devils and platypuses are often spotted. The main tourist hubs are Cradle Mountain Village, a tourist settlement scattered along Cradle Mountain Rd, and the smaller Derwent Bridge near Cynthia Bay on Lake St Clair.

⊙ Sights

Devils@Cradle   WILDLIFE RESERVE
(🖉03-6492 1491; www.devilsatcradle.com; 3950 Cradle Mountain Rd; adult/child $18/10, family $45-60, night feeding tours adult/child $27.50/15, family $70-90; ☺10am-4pm, to 5pm daylight savings, tours 10.30am, 1pm & 3pm, night tours 5.30pm year-round & 8.30pm daylight savings) A refuge for Tasmanian devils, this excellent wildlife sanctuary also plays host to occasional eastern and spotted-tail quolls. Though open all day for self-guided visits, try to sign up for a tour (preferably at night, as this is when the mainly nocturnal animals are best observed). Day tours take 45 minutes and night tours 75 minutes. Extra information about the animals is given in an interesting DVD presentation.

🏃 Activities

Cradle Valley Walks

Cradle Valley has some of the most accessible trailheads in the park. The following is by no means an exhaustive list.

Knyvet Falls (45 minutes return) Begins opposite Cradle Mountain Lodge and follows Pencil Pine Creek to a lookout over the falls.

Crater Lake (two to three hours return) Climb up to this lake-filled crater from the Ronny Creek car park.

Cradle Valley Walk (two hours one-way) An easy 8.5km walk from the interpretation centre to Dove Lake. It's boardwalked as far as Ronny Creek (5.5km); the rest of the track to Dove Lake can get quite muddy and is sometimes closed after heavy rain.

Main Dove Lake Circuit (two- to three-hour loop) Go all the way around the lake from Dove Lake car park, with near-constant Cradle Mountain views.

Cradle Mountain Summit (six to eight hours return) A tough but spectacular climb with incredible views in fine weather; not recommended in bad visibility or when it's snowy and icy in winter. Begin at either Dove Lake car park or Ronny Creek.

Cynthia Bay Walks

If you're at the southern, Lake St Clair end of the national park, these are our top picks of the day hikes on offer. Always check weather and other conditions with the Lake St Clair Visitor Information Centre (p712) at Cynthia Bay before setting out.

Larmairremener tabelti (one hour return) Aboriginal cultural-interpretative walk that winds through the traditional lands of the Larmairremener, the Indigenous people of the region who know Lake St Clair as Leeawuleena ('Sleeping Water'). The walk starts at the visitor information centre and loops through the lakeside forest before heading along the shoreline back to the centre.

Platypus Bay Circuit (one hour return) From Watersmeet, near the visitor information centre, to the lake shore, from where uninterrupted views across the lake to the Traveller Range can be enjoyed.

Shadow Lake Circuit (four to five hours return) Mixture of bush tracks and boardwalks through rainforest, stringybark trees and subalpine forests.

Mt Rufus Circuit (seven to eight hours return) Climbs Mt Rufus through alpine meadows and past lakes and sandstone outcrops with fine views over Lake St Clair.

Lake St Clair Lakeside Walk Catch the ferry to Echo Point (three to four hours back to Cynthia Bay) or Narcissus Hut (five to seven hours back to Cynthia Bay) and walk back along the lakeshore.

Tours

Cradle Mountain Huts WALKING
(☑ 03-6392 2211; www.cradlehuts.com.au; Quamby Estate, 1145 Westwood Rd, Hagley; walks from $2350; ⊙ Oct-May) This well-regarded company based at historic Quamby Estate in Hagley offers six- and four-day guided walks along the Overland Track staying in private huts equipped with hot showers and drying rooms.

Tasmanian Expeditions WALKING
(☑ 1300 666 856; www.tasmanianexpeditions.com.au; 6-day hike from $2095; ⊙ Oct-early May) This long-operating company offers a range of walks and adventures, including a six-day guided Overland Track hike with accommodation in huts or tents.

THE OVERLAND TRACK

This is Tasmania's iconic alpine journey: a 65km, five- to seven-day odyssey with backpack through incredible World Heritage–listed mountainscapes from Ronny Creek, near Cradle Mountain, to Lake St Clair. The track ends on the northern shore of Lake St Clair – from here you can catch the ferry, or walk the 15km Lakeside Track back to civilisation. If you have experience with camping and multiday hikes, good fitness and are well prepared for Tasmania's erratic weather, it's a very achievable independent adventure. Inexperienced walkers should consider joining a guided group.

Most hikers walk the Overland Track during summer when alpine plants are fragrantly in flower, daylight hours are long and you can work up enough heat to swim in one of the frigid alpine tarns. The track is very busy at this time and is subject to a crowd-limiting permit system. In winter, the track is quiet and icily beautiful for experienced walkers. Spring and autumn have their own charms, and fewer walkers than in summer (though the permit system still applies).

Apart from the permit season, when a north–south walking regulation is enforced, the track can be walked in either direction. The trail is well marked for its entire length. Side trips lead to features such as Mt Ossa, and some fantastic waterfalls – so it's worth budgeting time for some of these. You can expect to meet many walkers each day except in the dead of winter. The walk itself is extremely varied, negotiating high alpine moors, rocky scree, gorges and tall forest. You can get all the latest on the track and walk planning at www.parks.tas.gov.au.

Lake St Clair Scenic Cruise CRUISE
(☑ 03-6289 1137; www.lakestclairlodge.com.au/
about-lake-st-clair/lake-st-clair-ferry; adult/child
$60/30; ⊘ 9am & 3pm during daylight savings)
Hop aboard the *Ida Clair* for a 1½-hour ferry
trip from Cynthia Bay to Echo Point and Narcissus Bay and back, admiring pristine Lake
St Clair and the peaks of Mt Hugel, Mt Olym-
pus, Mt Orthys, Mt Byron and Mt Ida along
the way. Advance bookings are advised.

🛏 Sleeping & Eating

🛏 Cradle Valley
Discovery Holiday Parks
Cradle Mountain CAMPGROUND $
(☑ 03-6492 1395; www.discoveryholidayparks.
com.au; 3832 Cradle Mountain Rd; unpowered
sites for 2 $36-42, powered sites for 2 $50-53, dm
$37, cabin d $150-$270; ℗) There are options
aplenty at this well-run holiday park. Camp
sites are well spaced; single-sex dorms are
set in bushland and sleep four; basic cabins
include kitchens and small bathrooms; and
larger versions have gas fires and TVs with
DVD player and Playstation. Communal
facilities include a laundry, squeaky clean
ablutions blocks and camp kitchens with
stoves, BBQs and pizza ovens.

Cradle Mountain Highlanders CABIN $$
(☑ 03-6492 1116; www.cradlehighlander.com.au;
3876 Cradle Mountain Rd, Cradle Mountain; d $136-
300; ℗ 🛜) The friendly hosts at this rustic
retreat opposite the Cradle Mountain Visitor
Information Centre offer 16 immaculately
kept timber cottages sleeping between two
and seven people. All have wood or gas fires,
electric blankets, TV and DVD and equipped
kitchens. Four cabins include a spa, and
all are serviced daily. There's a commu-
nal BBQ area and laundry. On-site wi-fi is
intermittent.

★Cradle Mountain
Wilderness Village CABIN $$$
(☑ 03-6492 1500; www.cradlevillage.com.au; 3816
Cradle Mountain Rd, Cradle Mountain; d cabins $190-
370; ℗ 😊 🛜) Cleverly camouflaged in the
bushland, the 44 cabins here are clean, comfortable, well equipped and extremely family-
friendly – all have TV with DVD player and
there's a purpose-built children's playground
next to the BBQ shelter. The elevated premium chalets are the best of the bunch, with
the romantic spa cottage a strong runner-up.
Wi-fi is available in the main building only.

★Hellyers Restaurant MODERN AUSTRALIAN $$$
(☑ 03-6492 1320; www.cradlevillage.com.au;
Cradle Mountain Wilderness Village, 3816 Cradle
Mountain Rd; mains $30-42; ⊘ from 5.30pm;
℗ 🛜) Head to this restaurant in the Cradle
Mountain Wilderness Villag to enjoy the
mountain's best food and friendliest service.
Serves are enormous and extremely tasty,
with steaks and Mediterranean dishes fea-
turing. Large windows look out onto bush
and there's a big open fire to keep guests
warm in winter. Advance bookings essential.

🛏 Cynthia Bay & Derwent Bridge
Derwent Bridge Chalets
& Studios COTTAGE $$
(☑ 03-6289 1000; www.derwent-bridge.com; 15,478
Lyell Hwy, Derwent Bridge; studio d $175, chalet
d $210-245; ℗ 🛜) There's a wide range of
closely located studios and small chalets
on offer here. All are well maintained and
equipped, five have wood fires, two have
spas and one is set up for guests with disabilities. Some have a kitchenette, others have
a full kitchen. The on-site guest laundry and
free wi-fi are welcome added-extras.

★Pumphouse Point BOUTIQUE HOTEL $$$
(☑ 0428 090 436; www.pumphousepoint.com.au;
1 Lake St Clair Rd; shorehouse r $280-420, pum-
phouse r $460-570; ℗ 😊) One of Australia's
most unique and impressive hotels occupies
a five-storey hydroelectric pumphouse built
in 1940 on Lake St Clair, accessed via a nar-
row walkway, as well as a smaller art-deco
substation on the shoreline. Pumphouse
rooms are best. The location, interior fit-out
and level of service are world-class, offering
guests the experience of a lifetime.

Hungry Wombat Café CAFE $
(☑ 03-6289 1125; 15488 Lyell Hwy, Derwent Bridge;
pies $5, sandwiches $12, burgers $10-16; ⊘ 8am-
6pm summer, 9am-5pm winter) The food is
homemade and served with pride at this
ultrafriendly cafe inside the service station
on the highway. The hearty breakfasts are
sure to keep bushwalkers going all day, and
sandwiches, pies, burgers and sweet slices
are available at other times. There's a small
grocery section too.

ℹ Information
Cradle Mountain Visitor Information Cen-
tre (☑ 03-6492 1110; www.parks.tas.gov.au;
4057 Cradle Mountain Rd, Cradle Mountain;

⊙8am-5pm, shorter hours in winter; 🛜) Located just outside the park boundary, this visitor information centre sells park passes and some bushwalking clothing and equipment; offers free wi-fi; hires personal locator beacons; and supplies detailed bushwalking information and maps. The helpful staff can also provide weather condition updates and advice on bush safety and etiquette. An on-site cafe (Visitor Information Centre, 4057 Cradle Mountain Rd; pies $9.50, sandwiches $12.50; ⊙9am-4.30pm, longer hours in daylight saving) and petrol station sells bottled water and snacks.

Lake St Clair Visitor Information Centre
(📋03-6289 1172; www.parks.tas.gov.au; Cynthia Bay; ⊙9am-4pm, 8am-5pm in daylight saving) Located at Cynthia Bay, on the southern boundary of the park. Helpful rangers provide park and walking information and a small shop sells a limited range of bushwalking equipment and clothing. There are also displays on the area's geology, flora and fauna and Aboriginal heritage. An attached privately operated cafes offers coffee and meals of average quality at relatively hefty prices.

ℹ️ Getting There & Away

Cradle Mountain Coaches (📋03-6427 7626, 0448 800 599) Operated by Devonport-based Merseylink, these bushwalker shuttle services run between Launceston and Cradle Mountain or Lake St Clair ($320 or $80 per person for four or more passengers), Devonport and Cradle Mountain ($260/$65) and Cradle Mountain and Lake St Clair ($400/$100).

Tassielink (📋1300 300 520; www.tassielink. com.au) Tassielink buses travel between Launceston ($61.50, 3¼ hours) and the transit centre next to the Cradle Mountain tourist information centre four times per week, stopping at the *Spirit of Tasmania* dock in East Devonport, stopping at the *Spirit of Tasmania* dock in East Devonport, at the Devonport town centre and in Sheffield en route. They continue to Queenstown ($74.80, six hours) twice weekly, where there are connections to Strahan.

THE SOUTHWEST

The wild southwest corner of this island state is an edge-of-the-world domain made up of primordial forests, rugged mountains and endless heathland, all fringed by untamed beaches and turbulent seas. This is among the last great wilderness areas on earth: an isolated place that's perfect for adventure and for marveling at the majesty of the natural world.

Just one road enters the 600,000-plus-hectare Southwest National Park, the largest national park in Tasmania and part of the Unesco-listed Tasmanian Wilderness World Heritage Area, and this only goes as far as the hydroelectric station on the Gordon Dam. Otherwise, all access is by light plane to the gravel airstrip at Melaleuca, by sailing boat around the tempestuous coastline, or on foot.

Tours

Par Avion　　　　　　　SCENIC FLIGHTS
(📋03-6248 5390; www.paravion.com.au; adult/child half day $395/345, full day $495/445) You can swoop over the southwest on a scenic small-plane flight with this Cambridge-based operator. On a clear day you can see the whole of this corner of Tasmania as you buzz over wild beaches and jagged peaks before landing at Melaleuca and heading out onto Bathurst Harbour on a boat. Half- and full-day tours are available.

Tasmanian Expeditions　　　　WALKING
(📋1300 666 856; www.tasmanianexpeditions. com.au) Tasmanian Expeditions offers numerous walking-tour options in the southwest, including the five-day Mt Anne Circuit ($1795 per person), the seven-day Port Davey Track ($2495), the nine-day South Coast Track ($2295) and 16-day Port Davey and South Coast Track ($4495). It also offers a seven-day kayaking trip on Bathurst Harbour and Port Davey ($3250).

Roaring 40s Kayaking　　　　KAYAKING
(📋0455 949 777; www.roaring40skayaking.com. au; 3-/7-day trip $2250/3250) To experience this wilderness area from the water, consider a sea-kayaking adventure. From November to early April, Hobart-based Roaring 40s Kayaking offers camp-based kayaking trips exploring Port Davey and Bathurst Harbour with access by light plane to/from Hobart.

Lake Pedder & Strathgordon

This vast flooded valley system at the northern edge of the southwest wilderness covers the area that once cradled the original Lake Pedder, a spectacularly beautiful natural lake that was the region's ecological jewel. The largest glacial outwash lake in the world, its shallow, whisky-coloured waters covered 3 sq km. The lake was home to several endangered species and considered so important that it was the first part of the southwest to be protected within its own national park. But even this status ultimately failed to preserve it and Lake Pedder disappeared beneath the waters in 1972.

These days, the man-made replacement is 242 sq km and is the largest freshwater lake in Australia. At its northern tip is the tiny settlement of Strathgordon.

🏃 Activities

Aardvark Adventures   ADVENTURE SPORTS
(📞 03-6273 7722; www.aardvarkadventures.com. au; per person $210) You can abseil over the edge of the Gordon Dam wall with Hobart-based Aardvark Adventures, which organises abseiling trips here (suitable for beginners, minimum two people). It's claimed to be the highest commercial abseil in the world.

🛏 Sleeping

There are two camping grounds near the lake's southern shore, the **Edgar Camping Ground** (off Scotts Peak Rd) and the **Huon Campground** (off Scotts Peak Rd). Both have pit toilets and fireplaces stocked with firewood. **Ted's Beach Campground** (Gordon River Rd), near Strathgordon, has toilets, non-treated drinking water, picnic facilities, shelters and electric BBQs. All three camp sites are free and no advance bookings can be made.

Pedder Wilderness Lodge (Lake Pedder Chalet; 📞 03-6280 1166; www.pedderwilderness lodge.com.au; Gordon River Rd; d $90-200, units $160-240, ste $370; 🅿🐾) in Strathgordon offers rooms and self-contained apartments.

❶ Getting There & Away

Strathgordon is accessed via the B61 highway. It isn't serviced by public transport. Note that no fuel is available past Maydena, and even there you may not have any luck – you are best off filling up at Westerway.

Southwest National Park

The state's largest national park is made up of remote, wild country – forest, mountain, grassy plains and seascapes. Home to both the Huon pine, which lives for 3000 years, and the swamp gum, the world's tallest flowering plant, it also hosts about 300 species of lichen, moss and fern – some very rare. These festoon the rainforests, and the alpine meadows are replete with wildflowers and flowering shrubs. Through it all run wild rivers, their rapids tearing through deep gorges and their waterfalls plunging over cliffs. All of this, combined with majestic Mt Anne, the Frankland Range and the jagged crest of the Western Arthur Range, makes the park beloved of photographers, bushwalkers and nature enthusiasts.

🏃 Activities

The best-known walks in the southwest are the 70km **Port Davey Track**, between Scotts Peak Rd near Lake Pedder and Melaleuca, which takes four to five days, and the considerably more popular, 85km **South Coast Track**, between Melaleuca and Cockle Creek, near Southport close to the park's southeastern edge, which takes six to eight days.

When walking here, hikers should be prepared for weather that could bring anything from sunburn to snow flurries. **Par Avion** (📞 03-6248 5390; www.paravion.com.au) flies bushwalkers into or out of the southwest, landing at Melaleuca, and there's vehicle access to Cockle Creek. Detailed notes to the South Coast Track are available in Lonely Planet's *Walking in Australia,* and there's comprehensive track information at www. parks.tas.gov.au.

Of the more difficult walks that require a high degree of bushwalking skill, the shortest is the three-day circuit of the **Mt Anne Range**, a challenging walk with some difficult scrambling. The walk to **Federation Peak**, which has earned a reputation as the most difficult bushwalking peak in Australia, will take a highly experienced walker seven to eight days. The spectacular **Western Arthur Range** is an extremely difficult traverse, for which seven to 11 days are recommended.

❶ Information

Get your national parks pass and information about the southwest at the **Mt Field National Park Visitor Centre** (p654) in National Park, near Maydena.

❶ Getting There & Away

Only one road (the B61) enters the park, and this only goes as far as the hydroelectric station on the Gordon Dam. Otherwise, all access is by light plane to the gravel airstrip at Melaleuca, by sailing boat around the tempestuous coastline, or on foot. No public transport services the park.

Adelaide & South Australia

POP 1.7 MILLION / 🕿 08

Best Places to Eat

➜ Peel Street (p728)

➜ Gin Long Canteen (p729)

➜ Star of Greece (p747)

➜ Metro Bakery (p776)

➜ Dudley Wines Cellar Door (p755)

Best Places to Sleep

➜ Adabco Boutique Hotel (p725)

➜ Port Elliot Beach House YHA (p749)

➜ Dawes Point Cottage (p783)

➜ Mayfair Hotel (p726)

➜ Bethany Chapel B&B (p745)

Why Go?

Travellers both domestic and foreign are waking up to the diverse appeal of South Australia (SA), which has been long underrated. Its capital, Adelaide, beats the heat by celebrating life's finer things: fine landscapes, fine festivals, fine food, and (...OK, forget the other three) fine wine.

Further afield, there's plenty of scope for exploration. Highlights range from the legendary wine regions of the Barossa and Clare Valleys to the cliffs and caves of the Eyre Peninsula and pastoral scenes of the Yorke Peninsula, bisected by the mighty Murray River.

To cap it off, the Flinders Ranges and Stuart Hwy to the north are pure outback fantasy: cattle stations, Indigenous culture, red sand, unending straight-line roads and ochre-coloured peaks.

When to Go
Adelaide

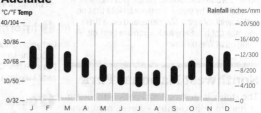

Feb–Mar SA's festival season hits its straps: the Adelaide Fringe and WOMADelaide are highlights.	**Mar–May** Beat the city heat in the shoulder season and benefit from autumn colours in the vineyards.	**Jun–Aug** Empty beaches, affordable accommodation and cosy fireside dining.

ADELAIDE

POP 1.34 MILLION

Sophisticated, cultured, neat-casual – the self-image Adelaide projects, a nod to the days of free colonisation without the 'penal colony' taint. Adelaidians may remind you of their convict-free status, but the stuffy, affluent origins of the 'City of Churches' did more to inhibit development than promote it. Bogged down in the old-school doldrums and painfully short on charisma, this was a pious, introspective place.

But these days things are different. Multicultural flavours infuse Adelaide's restaurants; there's a pumping arts and live-music scene; and the city's festival calendar has vanquished dull Saturday nights. There are still plenty of church spires here, but they're hopelessly outnumbered by pubs and a growing number of hip bars tucked away in lanes.

Just down the tram tracks is beachy Glenelg: Adelaide with its guard down and boardshorts up. Nearby Port Adelaide is slowly gentrifying but remains a raffish harbour 'hood with buckets of soul.

History

South Australia was declared a province on 28 December 1836, when the first British colonists landed at Holdfast Bay (current-day Glenelg). The first governor, Captain John Hindmarsh, named the state capital Adelaide, after the wife of the British monarch, William IV. While the eastern states struggled with the stigma of convict society, Adelaidians were free citizens – a fact to which many South Australians will happily draw your attention.

Adelaide has maintained a socially progressive creed: trade unions were legalised here in 1876; women were permitted to stand for parliament in 1894; and SA was one of the first places in the world to give women the vote, and the first state in Australia to outlaw racial and gender discrimination, legalise abortion and decriminalise gay sex.

⊙ Sights

⊙ Central Adelaide

★**Central Market**　　　　MARKET
(Map p724; ☑ 08-8203 7494; www.adelaidecentral
market.com.au; Gouger St; ☺7am-5.30pm Tue, 9am-5.30pm Wed & Thu, 7am-9pm Fri, 7am-3pm Sat) A tourist sight, or a shopping op? Either way, satisfy your deepest culinary cravings at the 250-odd stalls in superb Adelaide Central Market. A sliver of salami from the Mettwurst Shop, a crumb of English Stilton from the Smelly Cheese Shop, a tub of blueberry yoghurt from the Yoghurt Shop – you name it, it's here. Good luck making it out without eating anything. Adelaide's Chinatown is right next door. **Adelaide's Top Food & Wine Tours** (☑ 08-8386 0888; www.topfoodand
winetours.com.au) offers guided tours.

★**Art Gallery of South Australia**　GALLERY
(Map p724; ☑ 08-8207 7000; www.artgallery.
sa.gov.au; North Tce; ☺10am-5pm) **FREE**
Spend a few hushed hours in the vaulted, parquetry-floored gallery that represents the big names in Australian art. Permanent exhibitions include Australian, Aboriginal and Torres Strait Islander, Asian, European and North American art (20 bronze Rodins!). Progressive visiting exhibitions occupy the basement. There are free guided tours (11am and 2pm daily) and lunchtime talks (12.30pm every day except Tuesday). There's a lovely cafe out the back too.

South Australian Museum　　MUSEUM
(Map p724; ☑ 08-8207 7500; www.samuseum.
sa.gov.au; North Tce; ☺10am-5pm) **FREE** Dig into Australia's natural history with the museum's special exhibits on whales and Antarctic explorer Sir Douglas Mawson. An Aboriginal Cultures Gallery displays artefacts of the Ngarrindjeri people of the Coorong and lower Murray. Elsewhere, the giant squid and the lion with the twitchy tail are definite highlights. Free tours depart 11am weekdays and 2pm and 3pm weekends. The cafe here is a handy spot for lunch/recaffeination.

Adelaide Botanic Gardens　　GARDENS
(Map p724; ☑ 08-8222 9311; www.botanic
gardens.sa.gov.au; cnr North Tce & East Tce; ☺7.15am-sunset Mon-Fri, from 9am Sat & Sun) **FREE** Meander, jog or chew through your trashy airport novel in these lush city-fringe gardens. Highlights include a restored 1877 palm house, the water-lily pavilion (housing the gigantic *Victoria amazonica*), the First Creek wetlands, the engrossing **Museum of Economic Botany** and the fabulous steel-and-glass arc of the **Bicentennial Conservatory** (10am to 4pm), which recreates a tropical rainforest. Free 1½-hour **guided walks** depart the Schomburgk Pavilion at 10.30am daily. The classy **Botanic Gardens Restaurant** (Map p724; ☑ 08-8223 3526;

Adelaide & South Australia Highlights

1 Adelaide
(p715) Settling in for a cricket match or some AFL football at the magnificently revamped Adelaide Oval, then catching some live tunes in this Unesco 'City of Music'.

2 McLaren Vale
(p744) Swirling and quaffing your way through SA's most popular wine region.

3 Adelaide Hills
(p738) Day-tripping through Adelaide's backyard, with cellar doors, markets and historic towns.

4 Kangaroo Island
(p750) Listening to snorting seals and sampling seafood on 'KI'.

5 Flinders Ranges
(p785) Watching sunset colours shift across the rocky walls of 80-sq-km natural basin Ikara (Wilpena Pound).

6 Eyre Peninsula
(p781) Losing sight of yesterday (and tomorrow) in the wide open expanses of this western frontier.

7 Robe (p773)
Kicking back for a day or two of fine southeast wine and seafood.

8 Barossa Valley
(p759) Soaking up the German heritage in SA's seminal wine region.

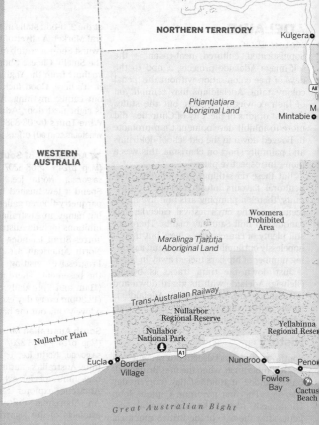

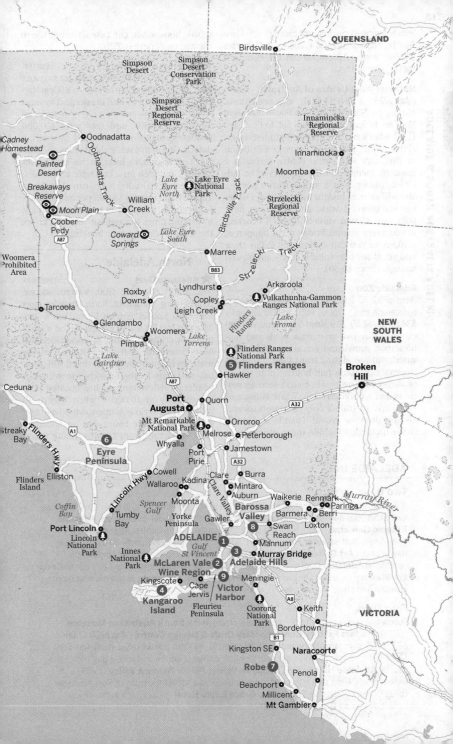

www.botanicgardensrestaurant.com.au; off Plane Tree Dr, Adelaide Botanic Gardens; 2-/3-courses $55/72; ⊗ noon-2.30pm Tue-Sun, 6.30-9pm Fri & Sat) is here too.

National Wine Centre of Australia   WINERY
(Map p724; ☑ 08-8313 3355; www.wineaustralia. com.au; cnr Botanic & Hackney Rds; ⊗ 8am-6pm Mon-Thu, to 9pm Fri, 9am-9am Sat, to 6pm Sun) FREE Check out the free self-guided, interactive Wine Discovery Journey exhibition at this very sexy wine centre (actually a research facility for the University of Adelaide, rather than a visitor centre per se). You will gain an insight into the issues winemakers contend with, and can even have your own virtual vintage rated. 'Uncorked' drinks every second Friday night happen at 4.30pm, or you can explore the Cellar Door and get stuck into some cleverly automated tastings (from $2.50).

Adelaide Zoo   ZOO
(Map p730; ☑ 08-8267 3255; www.zoossa.com. au/adelaide-zoo; Frome Rd; adult/child/family $34.50/19/88.50; ⊗ 9.30am-5pm) Around 1800 exotic and native mammals, birds and reptiles roar, growl and screech at Adelaide's wonderful zoo, dating from 1883. There are free walking tours half-hourly (plus a slew of longer and overnight tours), feeding sessions and a children's zoo. Wang Wang and Fu Ni are Australia's only giant pandas and always draw a crowd (panda-monium!). Other highlights include the nocturnal and reptile houses. You can take a river cruise to the zoo on Popeye (p722).

West Terrace Cemetery   CEMETERY
(Map p724; ☑ 08-8139 7400; www.aca.sa.gov.au; West Tce; ⊗ 6.30am-6pm Nov-Apr, to 8.30pm May-Oct) FREE Driven-by and overlooked by most Adelaidians, this amazing old cemetery (established in 1837, and now with 150,000 residents) makes a serene and fascinating detour. One of five self-guided tours, the 2km Heritage Highlights Interpretive Trail passes 29 key sites; pick up a brochure at the West Terrace gates. Guided tours run at 10.30am Tuesday and Sunday ($10/5 per adult/child). Night tours ($25/15) run twice every Friday, at varying times throughout the year; check the website. Call for tour bookings.

◉ North Adelaide

★ **Adelaide Oval**   LANDMARK
(Map p730; ☑ 08-8205 4700; www.adelaideoval. com.au; King William Rd, North Adelaide; tours adult/child $22/12; ⊗ tours 10am, 11am & 2pm daily, plus 1pm Sat & Sun) Hailed as the world's prettiest cricket ground, the Adelaide Oval hosts interstate and international cricket matches in summer, plus national AFL football and state football matches in winter. A wholesale redevelopment has boosted seating capacity to 50,000 – when they're all yelling, it's a serious home-town advantage! Guided 90-minute **tours** run on nongame days, departing from the Riverbank Stand

---

ADELAIDE IN...

Two Days

If you're here at Festival, WOMADelaide or Fringe time ('Mad March') lap it up. Otherwise, kick-start your day at the **Central Market** (p715) then wander through the **Adelaide Botanic Gardens** (p715), finishing up at the National Wine Centre. After a few bohemian beers at the **Exeter Hotel** (p732), have a ritzy dinner on Rundle St (p728). Next day, visit the **Art Gallery of South Australia** (p715) and then wander down to the revamped **Adelaide Oval** to check out the **Bradman Collection**. Grab a cab out to **Coopers Brewery** for a beer-tinged tour, then ride the tram to **Glenelg** for an evening swim and fish and chips on the sand.

Four Days

Follow the two-day itinerary – perhaps slotting in the **South Australian Museum** (p715) and **Jam Factory Contemporary Craft & Design Centre** (Map p724; ☑ 08-8231 0005; www.jamfactory.com.au; 19 Morphett St; ⊗ 10am-5pm Mon-Sat, noon-4pm Sun) FREE – then pack a picnic basket of Central Market produce and take a day trip to the nearby **Adelaide Hills** (p738), **McLaren Vale** (p743) or **Barossa Valley** (p759) wine regions. Next day, truck out to the museums and historic pubs of Port Adelaide (p719), then catch a live band at the **Grace Emily Hotel** (p732) back in the city, before dinner on **Gouger St** (p728).

(south entrance), off War Memorial Dr: call for bookings or book online.

Also here is the **Bradman Collection** (Map p730; ☑08-8211 1100; www.adelaideoval.com.au; War Memorial Dr, North Adelaide; ☺9am-4pm non-playing days) **FREE**, where devotees of Don Bradman, cricket's greatest batsman, can pore over the minutiae of his legend, on loan from the State Library of South Australia. Check out the bronze statue of 'the Don' cracking a cover drive out the front of the stadium. Also here is Roofclimb Adelaide Oval (p722), where you scale the giant roof scallops above the hallowed turf (amazing views!).

⊙ Inner Suburbs

Coopers Brewery BREWERY
(Map p720; ☑08-8440 1800; www.coopers.com.au; 461 South Rd, Regency Park; 1hr tours per person $27.50; ☺tours 1pm Tue-Fri) You can't possibly come to Adelaide without entertaining thoughts of touring Coopers Brewery. Tours take you through the brewhouse, bottling hall and history museum, where you can get stuck into samples of stouts, ales and lagers. Bookings required; minimum age 18. The brewery is in the northern suburbs; grab a cab, or walk 1km from Islington train station.

Penfolds Magill Estate Winery WINERY
(Map p720; ☑08-8301 5569; www.penfolds.com; 78 Penfolds Rd, Magill; tastings from $10; ☺9am-6pm) This 100-year-old winery is home to Australia's best-known wine – the legendary Grange. Taste the product at the cellar door; dine at the fab restaurant or bistro; take the Heritage Tour ($20); or steel your wallet for the Great Grange Tour ($150). Tour bookings essential.

⊙ Glenelg

Glenelg, or 'the Bay' – the site of SA's colonial landing – is Adelaide at its most LA. Glenelg's beach faces towards the west, and as the sun sinks into the sea, the pubs and bars burgeon with surfies, backpackers and sun-damaged sexagenarians. The tram rumbles in from the city, past the Jetty Rd shopping strip to the alfresco cafes around Moseley Sq.

The **Glenelg Visitor Information Centre** (Map p720; ☑08-8294 5833; www.glenelgsa.com.au; Glenelg Town Hall, Moseley Sq, Glenelg; ☺9am-5pm Mon-Fri, 10am-2pm Sat & Sun, reduced winter hours) has the local low-down, including information on diving and sailing opportunities. Pick up the *Kaurna yarta-ana* cultural map for some insights into Aboriginal heritage in the area.

From the city, take the tram or bus 167, 168 or 190 to get to Glenelg.

Bay Discovery Centre MUSEUM
(Map p720; ☑08-8179 9508; www.glenelgsa.com.au/baydiscover; Town Hall, Moseley Sq, Glenelg; admission by donation; ☺10am-5pm Oct-Mar, to 4pm Apr-Sep) This low-key museum in Glenelg's 1887 Town Hall building depicts the social history of Glenelg from colonisation to today, and addresses the plight of the local Kaurna people, who lost both their land and voice. Don't miss the relics dredged up from the original pier, and the spooky old sideshow machines.

⊙ Port Adelaide

Mired in the economic doldrums for decades, Port Adelaide – 15km northwest of the city – is slowly gentrifying, morphing its old redbrick warehouses into art spaces and museums, and its brawl-house pubs into boutique beer emporia. There's even an organic food market here now: the place has soul!

The helpful **Port Adelaide Visitor Information Centre** (Map p720; ☑08-8405 6560; 1800 629 888; www.portenf.sa.gov.au; 66 Commercial Rd, Port Adelaide; ☺9am-5pm; 🤶) stocks brochures on self-guided history, heritage-pub and dolphin-spotting walks and drives, plus the enticements of neighbouring Semaphore, a very bohemian beach burb. Activities include dolphin cruises and kayaking, plus downloadable walking-tour apps.

Adelaide's solitary tram line is rumoured to be extending to Port Adelaide at some stage. Until then, bus 150 will get you here from North Tce, or take the train.

South Australian Maritime Museum MUSEUM
(Map p720; www.samaritimemuseum.com.au; 126 Lipson St, Port Adelaide; adult/child/family $10/5/25; ☺10am-5pm daily, lighthouse 10am-2pm Sun-Fri) This salty cache is the oldest of its kind in Australia. Highlights include the iconic **Port Adelaide Lighthouse** ($1 on its own, or included in museum admission), busty figureheads made everywhere from Londonderry to Quebec, shipwreck and explorer displays, and a computer register of early migrants. Ask about tours to the nearby Torrens Island Quarantine Station.

Adelaide

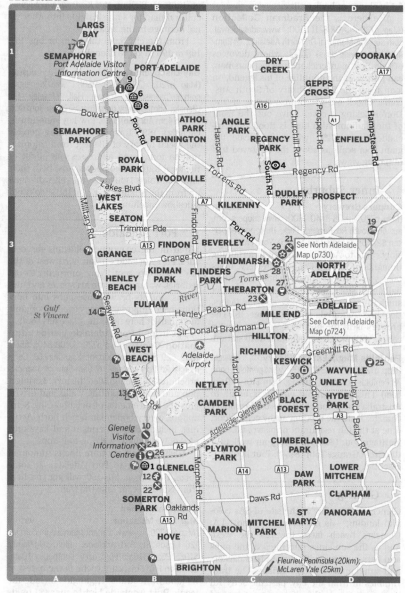

🏃 Activities

On the Land

Adelaide is a pancake-flat town – perfect for cycling and walking (if it's not too hot!). You can take your bike on trains if there's room (you'll need to buy a ticket for your bike), but not on buses or the tram.

Trails SA (www.southaustraliantrails.com) offers cycling- and hiking-trail info: pick up its *40 Great South Australian Short Walks* brochure, or download it from the website.

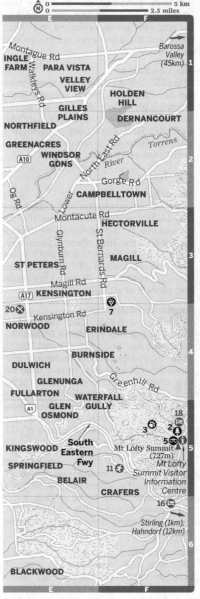

Adelaide

◎ Sights
1 Bay Discovery Centre	B5
2 Cleland Conservation Park	F5
3 Cleland Wildlife Park	F5
4 Coopers Brewery	C2
5 Mt Lofty Summit	F5
6 National Railway Museum	B1
7 Penfolds Magill Estate Winery	F3
8 South Australian Aviation Museum	B2
9 South Australian Maritime Museum	B1

◯ Activities, Courses & Tours
10 Adelaide Scuba	B5
11 Eagle Mountain Bike Park	F5
12 Glenelg Bicycle Hire	B5
13 Mega Adventure	B5

◯ Sleeping
14 Adelaide Luxury Beach House	A4
15 BIG4 Adelaide Shores	B4
16 Crafers Hotel	F6
Glenelg Beach Hostel	(see 1)
17 Largs Pier Hotel	A1
18 Mt Lofty YHA	F5
Port Adelaide Backpackers	(see 6)
19 Watson	D3

◯ Eating
20 Argo on the Parade	E4
Cleland Café	(see 3)
Good Life	(see 1)
21 Jarmer's Kitchen	C3
Low & Slow American BBQ	(see 9)
22 Mestizo	B5
Mt Lofty Summit Restaurant	(see 5)
23 Parwana Afghan Kitchen	C4
Zest Cafe Gallery	(see 26)
24 Zucca	B5

◯ Drinking & Nightlife
25 Earl of Leicester	D4
Lighthouse Wharf Hotel	(see 9)
26 Moseley	B5
27 Wheatsheaf	C3

◯ Entertainment
28 Adelaide Entertainment Centre	C3
29 Governor Hindmarsh Hotel	C3
Thebarton Theatre	(see 23)

◯ Shopping
30 Adelaide Farmers Market	D4

There are free guided walks in the Adelaide Botanic Gardens (p715). The riverside **Linear Park Trail** is a 40km walking/cycling path running from Glenelg to the foot of the Adelaide Hills, mainly along the River Torrens: pick up the two brochures covering the route from city to the hills, and the city to the beach, or download maps from www.southaustraliantrails.com. Another popular hiking trail is the steep **Waterfall Gully Track** (three hours return) up to Mt Lofty Summit and back.

To pick up an **Adelaide Free Bike** to explore for a day, contact Bicycle SA (p737).

Eagle Mountain Bike Park   MOUNTAIN BIKING
(Map p720; www.bikesa.asn.au/ridemapslist; Mt Barker Rd, Leawood Gardens; ⊙dawn-dusk) **FREE** Mountain bikers should wheel themselves to the Eagle Mountain Bike Park in the Adelaide Hills, pronto; it has 21km of gnarly trails. Check the website for directions.

Adelaide Bowling Club   BOWLING
(Map p724; ☑08-8223 5516; www.adelaidebowling club.com.au; 58 Dequetteville Tce; per person $15; ⊙noon-late Sun Oct-Mar) Trundle down for a few lawn bowls on Sunday Superbowlz sessions at this old club, just east of the CBD. Show up early for lunch and a few lubricative ales in the clubhouse.

Mega Adventure   ADVENTURE SPORTS
(Map p720; ☑1300 634 269; www.megaadventure. com.au; 4 Hamra Ave, West Beach; adult/child $55/48; ⊙11am-6pm Mon-Fri, 10am-6pm Sat & Sun, last entry 4pm) Behind the West Beach dunes you'll find this imposing steel-frame structure, festooned with ropes, ramps, swings, platforms and other precipitous mechanisms from which to dangle yourself at dangerous altitude. Fun for the fearless!

On & in the Water

Adelaide gets *reeally* hot in summer. Hit the beach at Glenelg, or try any other activity that gets you out on the water. Away from the beach, check out **Popeye** (Map p724; ☑0400 596 065; www.thepopeye.com.au; return adult/child $15/8, one-way $10/5; ⊙10am-4pm, reduced winter hours) cruises on the River Torrens and the little **Paddle Boats** (Map p724; ☑0400 596 065; www.facebook.com/popeyeade laide; Elder Park; hire per 30min $15; ⊙10am-5pm, reduced winter hours) nearby, run by the same folks. **Rymill Park Rowboats** (Map p724; ☑08-8232 2814; Rymill Park, East Tce; boats per 30min $10; ⊙8am-4.30pm Sat & Sun) on the east side of the CBD are another option.

Adventure Kayaking SA   KAYAKING
(☑08-8295 8812; www.adventurekayak.com.au; tours adult/child from $50/25, kayak hire per 3hr 1-/2-/3-seater $40/60/80) 🧭 Family-friendly guided kayak tours around the Port River estuary (dolphins, mangroves, shipwrecks). Also offers kayak and stand-up paddle-board hire, plus self-guided tours.

Adelaide Aquatic Centre   SWIMMING
(Map p730; ☑08-8203 7665; www.adelaideaquatic centre.com.au; Jeffcott Rd, North Adelaide; adult/ child/family $8.50/6.50/23; ⊙6am-9pm Mon-Fri, 7am-7pm Sat & Sun) The closest pool to the city, with indoor swimming and diving pools, and the usual gym, sauna, spa and coffee-afterwards stuff.

Adelaide Scuba   DIVING
(Map p720; ☑08-8294 7744; www.adelaidescuba. com.au; Patawalonga Frontage, Glenelg North; ⊙9am-5.30pm Mon-Fri, 8am-5pm Sat & Sun) Hires out snorkelling gear (per day $30) and runs local dives (single/double dive $50/100). There are also two-weekend learn-to-dive courses for $399.

🖝 Tours

★ **Adelaide City Explorer**   TOURS
(www.adelaidecityexplorer.com.au) Excellent new downloadable walking tours around the city, cosponsored by the Adelaide City Council and the National Trust (there's a definite architectural bias here...which we like!). There are 15 themed trails in all – art deco, pubs, North Tce, outdoor art, trees etc – get 'em on your phone and get walking.

RoofClimb Adelaide Oval   CLIMBING
(Map p730; ☑08-8331 5222; www.roofclimb. com.au; Adelaide Oval, King William Rd, North Adelaide; adult day/twilight $99/109, child $69/79) As per the Sydney Harbour Bridge and Brisbane's Story Bridge, you can now scale the lofty rooftops of the Adelaide Oval (p718). And the views are astonishing! Kids can climb too, but all climbers must be at least 120cm tall, and at most 136kg. Better yet, watch Port Adelaide play a quarter of AFL football from the roof for $225!

Escapegoat   MOUNTAIN BIKING
(☑0422 916 289; www.escapegoat.com.au) 🧭 Careen down the slopes of 727m Mt Lofty into Adelaide below ($99), or take a day trip through McLaren Vale by bike ($129). Extended Flinders Ranges MTB trips also available.

Bookabee Tours   CULTURAL
(☑08-8235 9954; www.bookabee.com.au) 🧭 Indigenous-run half-/full-day city tours ($180/255) focusing on Tandanya National Aboriginal Cultural Institute, the South Australian Museum and bush foods in the Adelaide Botanic Gardens. A great insight into Kaurna culture.

Haunted Horizons   TOURS
(☑0407 715 866; www.adelaidehauntedhorizons. com.au; per adult $35) Get spooked on these

ADELAIDE FOR CHILDREN

There are few kids who won't love the **tram ride** from the city to Glenelg (p719) (kids under five ride for free!). You may have trouble getting them off the tram – the lure of a splash in the shallows at the **beach** then some fish and chips on the lawn should do the trick.

During school holidays, the **South Australian Museum** (p715), **State Library of South Australia** (p736), **Art Gallery of South Australia** (p715), **Adelaide Zoo** (p718) and **Adelaide Botanic Gardens** (p715) run inspired kid- and family-oriented programs with accessible and interactive general displays. The Art Gallery also runs a **START at the Gallery** kids' program (tours, music, activities) from 11am to 3pm on the first Sunday of the month.

Down on the River Torrens there are **Popeye** (p722) river cruises and **Paddle Boats** (p722), which make a satisfying splash. **Rymill Park Rowboats** (p722) are along similar nautical lines.

In Port Adelaide, you can check out the **Maritime Museum** (p719), **National Railway Museum** (Map p720; www.natrailmuseum.org.au; 76 Lipson St, Port Adelaide; adult/child/family $12/6/32; ☺10am-4.30pm) or **South Australian Aviation Museum** (Map p720; www.saam.org.au; 66 Lipson St, Port Adelaide; adult/child/family $10/5/25; ☺10.30am-4.30pm), or set sail on a **dolphin-spotting cruise**.

The free monthly paper *Child* (www.childmags.com.au), available at cafes and libraries, is largely advertorial, but does contain comprehensive events listings.

Getting around town, Adelaide's buses and trains are straightforward to navigate with kids (through the tram is your best bet if you're pushing a pram). The city is 'flat as a tack', as they say – so getting around the streets with a pusher is easy. Baby-change facilities are available in some public toilets and large department stores: David Jones on Rundle Mall has a good one. For babysitters, try **Dial-an-Angel** (☏1300 721 111, 08-8338 3433; www.dialanangel.com.au; 6/202-208 Glen Osmond Rd, Fullarton).

---

two-hour, adults-only nocturnal tours of the old Adelaide Arcade, or a walking tour of the East End, digging up the dirt on Adelaide's macabre, murderous and mysterious past.

✪ Festivals & Events

Tour Down Under SPORTS
(www.tourdownunder.com.au) The world's best cyclists sweating in their lycra: six races through SA towns, with the grand finale in downtown Adelaide.

Adelaide Fringe PERFORMING ARTS
(www.adelaidefringe.com.au) This annual independent arts festival in February and March is second only to the Edinburgh Fringe. Funky, unpredictable and downright hilarious. Get into it!

Adelaide Festival PERFORMING ARTS
(www.adelaidefestival.com.au) Top-flight international and Australian dance, drama, opera, literature and theatre performances. Don't miss the Northern Lights along North Tce – old sandstone buildings ablaze with lights – and the hedonistic late-night club.

WOMADelaide MUSIC
(www.womadelaide.com.au; ☺Mar) One of the world's best live-music events, with more than 300 musicians and performers from around the globe. Perfect for families and those with a new-age bent.

Clipsal 500 SPORTS
(www.clipsal500.com.au) Rev-heads preen their mullets as Adelaide's streets become a four-day Holden-versus-Ford racing track in March. A massive rock gig coincides (past performers include Kiss, Cold Chisel and Mötley Crüe).

Tasting Australia FOOD & DRINK
(www.tastingaustralia.com.au; ☺May) SA foodie experiences around the city and its encircling wine regions. Expect classes, demonstrations, talks and plenty to put in your mouth.

Adelaide Cabaret Festival PERFORMING ARTS
(www.adelaidecabaretfestival.com; ☺Jun) The only one of its kind in the country. A bright, uplifting tonic in the deep and dark Adelaide winter June.

Central Adelaide

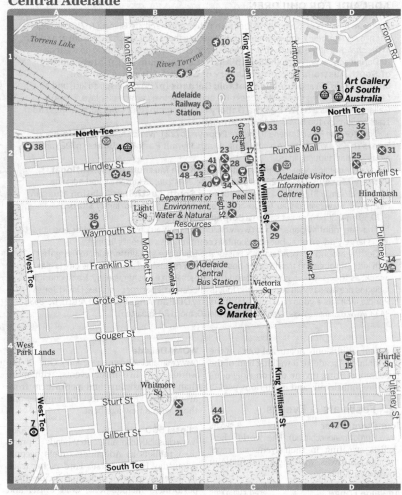

Adelaide Guitar Festival   MUSIC
(www.adelaideguitarfestival.com.au) Annual axe-fest with a whole lotta rock, classical, country, blues and jazz goin' on. Held in August (when there's not much else to do).

South Australian
Living Artists Festival   ART
(SALA; www.salafestival.com.au) Progressive exhibitions and displays across town in August (expired artists not allowed).

City to Bay   SPORTS
(www.city-bay.org.au) In September there's an annual 12km fun run from the city to Glenelg (aka 'the Bay'): much sweat and cardiac duress.

OzAsia Festival   CULTURAL
(www.ozasiafestival.com.au) Food, arts, conversation, music and the mesmerising Moon Lantern Festival. Two weeks in September/October.

Feast Festival   LGBT
(www.feast.org.au) Adelaide's big-ticket gay-and-lesbian festival happens over two weeks in October/November, with a carnival, theatre, dialogue and dance.

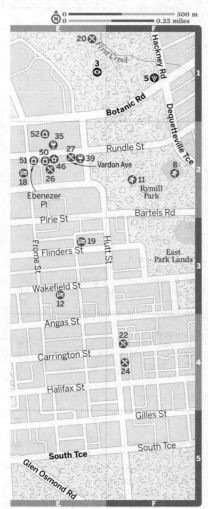

YHA isn't known for its gregariousness – you'll get plenty of sleep in the spacious and comfortable rooms here. This is a seriously schmick hostel with great security, a roomy kitchen and lounge area, and immaculate bathrooms. A real step up from the average backpacker places around town. Parking is around $10 per day....but the pancakes (Tuesday and Friday) are free!

Backpack Oz HOSTEL $
(Map p724; ☑ 08-8223 3551, 1800 633 307; www.backpackoz.com.au; cnr Wakefield & Pulteney Sts; dm $24-30, s/d/tw/tr $65/75/80/96; ❀ �"") It doesn't look flash externally, but this converted pub (the old Orient Hotel) strikes the right balance between party and placid. There are spacious dorms and an additional no-frills guesthouse over the road (good for couples; add $10 to these prices). Get a coldie and shoot some pool in the bar. Free breakfast, wi-fi, bikes, linen and Wednesday-night BBQ.

Hostel 109 HOSTEL $
(Map p724; ☑ 1800 099 318, 08-8223 1771; www.hostel109.com; 109 Carrington St; dm/s/tw/d/tr $30/65/75/90/105; ❀ @ "") A small, well-managed hostel in a quiet corner of town, with a couple of little balconies over the street and a cosy kitchen/communal area. Clean and friendly, with lockers, good security and gas cooking. The only negative: rooms open onto light wells rather than the outside world. Free on-street parking after 5pm.

★ Adabco Boutique Hotel BOUTIQUE HOTEL $$
(Map p724; ☑ 08-8100 7500; www.adabcohotel.com.au; 223 Wakefield St; d/f from $140/185; ❀ "") This excellent, stone-clad boutique hotel – built in 1894 in high Venetian Gothic style – has at various times been an Aboriginal education facility, a rollerskating rink and an abseiling venue! These days you can expect three levels of lovely rooms with interesting art and quality linen, plus complimentary breakfast, free wi-fi and smiling staff.

Soho Hotel HOTEL $$
(Map p724; ☑ 08-8412 5600; www.thesohohotel.com.au; 264 Flinders St; d from $159; P ❀ "" ⛆) Attempting to conjure up the vibe of London's Soho district, these plush suites in Adelaide's East End (some with spas, most with balconies) are complemented by sumptuous linen, 24-hour room service, Italian-marble bathrooms, a rooftop jet pool and a fab restaurant. Rates take a tumble midweek. Parking from $20; free wi-fi.

Christmas Pageant CULTURAL
(www.cupageant.com.au) An Adelaide institution for 70-plus years – kitschy old floats, bands and cheesy marching troupes occupy city streets for a day in (oddly) November.

🛏 Sleeping

🛏 Central Adelaide

Adelaide Central YHA HOSTEL $
(Map p724; ☑ 08-8414 3010; www.yha.com.au; 135 Waymouth St; dm from $31, d without/with bathroom $90/110, f from $121; P ❀ @ "") The

Central Adelaide

◉ Top Sights
| 1 | Art Gallery of South Australia | D1 |
| 2 | Central Market | C4 |

◉ Sights
3	Adelaide Botanic Gardens	E1
4	Jam Factory Contemporary Craft & Design Centre	B2
5	National Wine Centre of Australia	F1
6	South Australian Museum	D1
7	West Terrace Cemetery	A5

◉ Activities, Courses & Tours
8	Adelaide Bowling Club	F2
9	Paddle Boats	B1
10	Popeye	C1
11	Rymill Park Rowboats	F2

⊜ Sleeping
12	Adabco Boutique Hotel	E3
13	Adelaide Central YHA	B3
14	Backpack Oz	D3
15	Hostel 109	D4
16	Hotel Richmond	D2
17	Mayfair Hotel	C2
18	Roof Garden Hotel	E2
19	Soho Hotel	E3

⊗ Eating
20	Botanic Gardens Restaurant	E1
21	Café Troppo	B5
	Central Market	(see 2)
22	Chianti	F4
23	Gondola Gondola	C2
24	Good Life	F4
25	Jasmin Indian Restaurant	D2

26	Kutchi Deli Parwana	E2
27	Orana	E2
28	Peel Street	C2
29	Pizza e Mozzarella Bar	C3
30	Press	C3
31	Sukhumvit Soi.38	D2
32	Zen Kitchen	D2

◉ Drinking & Nightlife
33	2KW	C2
34	Clever Little Taylor	C2
35	Exeter Hotel	E2
36	Grace Emily Hotel	A3
37	Hains & Co	C2
38	HQ Complex	A2
	Maybe Mae	(see 28)
39	Nola	E2
40	Pink Moon Saloon	C2
41	Udaberri	C2
	Zhivago	(see 40)

◉ Entertainment
42	Adelaide Festival Centre	C1
43	Adelaide Symphony Orchestra	B2
44	Gilbert Street Hotel	C5
45	Jive	B2
46	Palace Nova Eastend Cinemas	E2

◉ Shopping
47	Gilles Street Market	D5
48	Imprints Booksellers	B2
49	Jurlique	D2
50	Midwest Trader	E2
51	Miss Gladys Sym Choon	E2
52	Streetlight	E2

Roof Garden Hotel
HOTEL **$$**

(Map p724; ☏1800 008 499, 08-8100 4400; www.majestichotels.com.au; 55 Frome St; d from $162; P❋@☞) Everything looks new in this central, Japanese-toned place. Book a room facing Frome St for a balcony and the best views (Rundle St is metres away), or take a bottle of wine up to the namesake rooftop garden to watch the sunset. Free wif-fi and good walk-in and last-minute rates. Parking from $20 per day.

Hotel Richmond
HOTEL **$$**

(Map p724; ☏08-8215 4444; www.hotelrichmond.com.au; 128 Rundle Mall; d from $165; P❋☞) This opulent hotel in a grand 1920s building in the middle of Rundle Mall has mod-minimalist rooms with king-sized beds, marble bathrooms, and American oak and Italian furnishings. Oh, and that hotel rarity – opening windows. Rates include movies and newspapers. Parking from $20 per day.

★Mayfair Hotel
HOTEL **$$$**

(Map p724; ☏08-8210 8888; www.mayfairhotel.com.au; 45 King William St; d from $215; P❋@☞) The gargoyles on Adelaide's 1934 Colonial Mutual Life insurance building guarded a whole lot of empty rooms for decades (has the money gone out of insurance?), but the old dame has been reborn as the very luxe Mayfair Hotel. It's a fabulous fit-out, with myriad bars, eateries and smiling, good-looking staff all over the place. Enjoy! Parking $20.

⌂ North Adelaide

Greenways Apartments
APARTMENT **$$**

(Map p730; ☏08-8267 5903; www.greenwaysapartments.com.au; 41-45 King William Rd, North Adelaide; 1-/2-/3-bedroom apt $132/175/250; P❋☞) These 1938 apartments ain't flash, but if you have a pathological hatred of slick, 21st-century open-plan 'lifestyles', then

Greenways is for you! And where else can you stay in apartments so close to town at these rates? A must for cricket fans, with the Adelaide Oval just a lofted hook shot away – book early for Test matches. New bathrooms.

Minima Hotel HOTEL **$$**

(Map p730; ☑ 08-8334 7766; www.majestichotels. com.au; 146 Melbourne St, North Adelaide; d from $100; P✱@⑤) The mural-clad Minima offers compact but stylish rooms, each decorated by a different SA artist, in a prize-winning Melbourne St location (wake up and smell the coffee). Limited parking from $10 per night.

O'Connell Inn MOTEL **$$**

(Map p730; ☑ 08-8239 0766; www.oconnellinn. com.au; 197 O'Connell St, North Adelaide; d/f from $175/200; P✱⑤) It's absurdly difficult to find a decent motel in Adelaide (most are mired in the '90s), but this one makes a reasonable fist of the new century, helped along by new bathrooms and vivid Aboriginal art. It's smallish, friendly, affordable and in a beaut location – handy for forays north to the Barossa, Clare, Flinders etc. Apartments also available.

Inner Suburbs

Adelaide Caravan Park CARAVAN PARK **$**

(Map p730; ☑ 08-8363 1566; www.aspenholiday parks.com.au/our-parks/adelaide-caravan-park; 46 Richmond St, Hackney; powered sites from $39, cabins & units from $112; P✱⑤☒) A compact, no-frills park on the River Torrens, rather surprisingly slotted in on a quiet street 2km northeast of the city centre. It's clean and well run, with a bit of green grass if it's not too far into summer (and a pool if it is).

Watson BOUTIQUE HOTEL **$$**

(Map p720; ☑ 08-7087 9666, 1800 278 468; www.artserieshotels.com.au/watson; 33 Warwick St, Walkerville; d from $165, 1-/2-bedroom ste from $216/280, B&B from $275; P✱⑤☒) The Watson (named after Indigenous artist Tommy Watson, whose works dazzle here) is a sassy, multilevel 115-unit complex 4km north of the CBD in Walkerville (an easy commute). Once upon a time these rooms were government Department of Infrastructure offices. There's a gym, a lap pool, 24-hour concierge, free bikes, free parking, car hire... Nice one!

Glenelg, Port Adelaide & Around

Glenelg Beach Hostel HOSTEL **$**

(Map p720; ☑ 08-8376 0007, 1800 359 181; www. glenelgbeachhostel.com.au; 1-7 Moseley St, Glenelg; dm/s/d/f from $25/60/70/110; ⑤) A couple of streets back from the beach, this beaut old terrace (1878) is Adelaide's budget golden child. Fan-cooled rooms maintain period details and are mostly bunk-free. There's cold Coopers in the basement bar (live music on weekends), open fireplaces, lofty ceilings, girls-only dorms, free on-street parking and a courtyard beer garden. Book *waaay* in advance in summer.

BIG4 Adelaide Shores CARAVAN PARK **$**

(Map p720; ☑ 08-8355 7320, 1800 444 567; www. adelaideshores.com.au; 1 Military Rd, West Beach; powered sites $40-55, eco-tents $109, 1-/2-bed cabins from $109/159; P✱⑤☒) Hunkered down behind the West Beach dunes, with a walking/cycling track extending to Glenelg (3.4km) in one direction and Henley Beach (3.5km) in the other, this vast holiday park is a choice spot in summer. There are lush sites, permanent 'eco-tents', snappy-looking cabins and passing dolphins.

Port Adelaide Backpackers HOSTEL **$**

(Map p720; ☑ 08-8447 6267; www.portadelaide backpackers.com.au; 24 Nile St, Port Adelaide; dm/s from $19/60, d without/with bathroom from $65/100; P✱⑤) We're unashamed fans of Port Adelaide, and it gladdens the heart to see this backpackers making a (rather casual) stand here. It's a reimagined brick seaman's lodge in Port Adelaide's historic hub. New bathrooms and laundry; free wi-fi and on-street parking.

★**Largs Pier Hotel** HOTEL **$$**

(Map p720; ☑ 08-8449 5666; www.largspierhotel. com.au; 198 Esplanade, Largs Bay; d/f/apt from $164/184/199; P✱⑤) Surprise! In the snoozy beach 'burb of Largs Bay, 5km north of Port Adelaide, is this gorgeous, 130-year-old, three-storey wedding-cake hotel with sky-high ceilings, big beds, taupe-and-chocolate colours and beach views. There's a low-slung wing of motel rooms off to one side; apartments are across the street. Pub trivia: AC/DC and Cold Chisel often played here in the bad old days.

Adelaide Luxury Beach House
RENTAL HOUSE **$$$**

(Map p720; ☑0418 675 339; www.adelaideluxury beachhouse.com.au; 163 Esplanade, Henley Beach; 3-/4-bedrooms $590/630; P ✳ ☎) Do you like to be beside the seaside? Adelaide's beaches face west, so there are brilliant sunsets. Sit on the terrace at this mod beach house with a sundowner and watch the big orange orb descend. It's a plush, three-tier, four-bedroom affair, with room for 12 bods. Pricey, but very lovely – and something different on the Adelaide accommodation scene.

✖ Eating

Foodies flock to West End hot spots like Gouger St (goo-jer), Chinatown and the food-filled Central Market. There are some great pubs here too. Arty/alternative Hindley St – Adelaide's dirty little secret – also has a smattering of good eateries. In the East End, Rundle St and Hutt St offer alfresco cafes and people watching. North Adelaide's Melbourne and O'Connell Sts have a healthy spread of bistros, cafes and pubs.

✖ Central Adelaide

★ Central Market
MARKET **$**

(Map p724; ☑08-8203 7494; www.adelaidecentral market.com.au; Gouger St; ⏰7am-5.30pm Tue, 9am-5.30pm Wed & Thu, 7am-9pm Fri, to 3pm Sat) This place is an exercise in sensory bombardment: a barrage of smells, colours and cacophonous stallholders selling fresh vegetables, breads, cheeses, seafood and gourmet produce. Cafes, hectic food courts, a supermarket and Adelaide's Chinatown are here too. Just brilliant.

Café Troppo
CAFE **$**

(Map p724; ☑08-8211 8812; www.cafetroppo adelaide.com; 42 Whitmore Sq; mains $10-17; ⏰7.30am-4pm Tue-Thu, to late Fri, 9am-late Sat, to 4pm Sun; ☎✐) ✐ Breathing vigour into Whitmore Sq, the least utilised of central Adelaide's five squares, corner-cafe Troppo has jaunty exposed timberwork and a sustainable outlook (local ingredients, recycling, organic milk, ecofriendly cleaning products etc). The coffee is fab, and so is the breakfast pizza and the black lentil, almond, cauliflower and tahini salad. Sandals, nose-rings, dreadlocks....

Zen Kitchen
VIETNAMESE **$**

(Map p724; ☑08-8232 3542; www.facebook. com/zenkitchenadelaide; unit 7, tenancy 2, Renaissance Arcade; mains $5-14; ⏰10.30am-4.30pm Mon-Thu, to 5pm Fri, 11am-3pm Sat) Superb, freshly constructed rice paper rolls, *pho* and super-crunchy barbecue-pork bahn mi, eat-in or take away. Wash it all down with a cold coconut milk or a teeth-grindingly strong Vietnamese coffee with sugary condensed milk. Authentic, affordable and absolutely delicious.

★ Peel Street
MODERN AUSTRALIAN, ASIAN **$$**

(Map p724; ☑08-8231 8887; www.peelst.com.au; 9 Peel St; mains $20-35; ⏰7:30am-10:30pm Mon & Wed-Fri, 7.30am-4:30pm Tues, 6-10:30pm Sat) Peel St itself – a long-neglected service lane in Adelaide's West End – is now Adelaide's after-dark epicentre, lined with hip bars and eateries, the best of which is this one. It's a super cool café/bistro/wine bar that just keeps packing 'em in: glam city girls sit at window seats nibbling parmesan-crumbed parsnips and turkey meatballs with preserved lemon. Killer wine list.

Pizza e Mozzarella Bar
ITALIAN **$$**

(Map p724; ☑08-8164 1003; www.pizzaemozza rellabar.com.au; 33 Pirie St; mains $18-32; ⏰noon-3pm Mon-Thu, to 9pm Fri, 5.30-9.30pm Sat) Everything at this split-level, rustic Italian eatery – adorned with breadbaskets and beautified by Italian staff – is cooked in the wood oven you see when you walk in the door. Pizzas are thin-based (Roma style); mozzarella plates come with wood-oven bread and meats (octopus, tuna, *salumi*). Super Italian/SA wine and beer list. Cooking classes monthly.

Jasmin Indian Restaurant
INDIAN **$$**

(Map p724; ☑08-8223 7837; www.jasmin.com. au; basement level, 31 Hindmarsh Sq; mains $17-29; ⏰noon-2.30pm Thu & Fri, 5.30-9pm Tue-Sat) Enter this basement wonderland for magical north Indian curries and consummately professional staff (they might remember your name from when you ate here in 2011). There's nothing too surprising about the menu, but it's done to absolute perfection. Bookings essential.

Gondola Gondola
ASIAN **$$**

(Map p724; ☑08-8123 3877; www.gondolagondola. com.au; 1 Peel St; small plates $9-18, big plates $19-32; ⏰noon-2.30pm Mon-Fri, 6-10pm Mon-Sat) When the late-night food attack hits, duck out of the bar and into Gondola Gondola – a bright, buzzy, fishbowl diner on the corner of Peel St and Hindley St. Go the salt-and-pepper eggplant, or the red steak: char-grilled sirloin with mixed herbs, heaps of chilli and peanuts. Then back to the bar.

Good Life
PIZZA $$

(Map p724; ☑08-8223 2618; www.goodlifepizza.com; 170 Hutt St; pizzas $20-39; ☺noon-2.30pm Mon-Fri, 6pm-late daily; ☑) ☞ At this brilliant organic pizzeria, thin crusts are stacked with tasty toppings like free-range roast duck, Spencer Gulf prawns and spicy Hahndorf salami. Ahhh, life is good... Also has a branch in **Glenelg** (Map p720; ☑08-8376 5900; level 1, cnr Jetty Rd & Moseley St, Glenelg; pizzas $20-39; ☺noon-2.30pm Tue-Fri & Sun, 6pm-late daily; ☑) ☞.

Sukhumvit Soi.38
THAI $$

(Map p724; ☑08-8223 5472; www.soi38.com.au; 54 Pulteney St; mains $14-25; ☺11.30am-2.30pm Mon-Fri, 5.30-9.30pm Mon-Sat) ☞ As the after-work brigades trudge between the East End pubs and the West End bars, sometimes they get hungry. That's where this street-food joint enters the fray: rapid-fire Thai snacks, soups, curries and stir-fries, take away or woofed down in the lavish black-and-gold dining room. Sustainable ingredients all the way.

★Press
MODERN AUSTRALIAN $$$

(Map p724; ☑08-8211 8048; www.pressfoodand wine.com.au; 40 Waymouth St; mains $16-46; ☺noon-late Mon-Sat) The pick of the restaurants on office-heavy Waymouth St. Super stylish (brick, glass, lemon-coloured chairs) and not afraid of offal (pan-fried lamb's brains, sweetbreads, grilled calf's tongue) or things raw (beef carpaccio, gravlax salmon). Tasting menu $68 per person. Book a table upstairs, or they'll fit you in downstairs near the bar, alongside journos from the *Advertiser* across the street.

Chianti
ITALIAN $$$

(Map p724; ☑08-8232 7955; www.chianti.net.au; 160 Hutt St; mains $34-44; ☺7.30am-late Mon-Fri, 8am-late Sat & Sun) Classy Chianti has been around since the '80s, but remains a fixture in the upper echelon of Adelaide fine dining. Step inside the welcoming, shady dining room in high summer and permit yourself some culinary respite: the house-made potato gnocchi with slow-cooked free-range goose and caramelised onion is a stunner. Breakfast too.

Orana
MODERN AUSTRALIAN $$$

(Map p724; ☑08-8232 3444; www.restaurant orana.com; upstairs, 285 Rundle St; tasting menus lunch/dinner $80/175, wine extra $75/150) Racking up plenty of 'Adelaide's Best Restaurant' awards, Orana is a secretive beast, with minimal signage and access via a black staircase at the back of Blackwood restaurant on Rundle St. Upstairs a fab tasting menu awaits: at least seven courses for lunch, and 18 for dinner (18!). Add wine to the experience to fully immerse yourself in SA's best offerings.

✕ North Adelaide

Bakery on O'Connell
BAKERY $

(Map p730; ☑08-8361 7377; www.bakeryono connell.com.au; 128-130 O'Connell St, North Adelaide; items $4-8; ☺24hr) Hunger pangs at 3am? Roll on into the Bakery on O'Connell for pizza slices, cakes, buns, pies, pasties and doughnuts as big as your face. Or perhaps a classic SA 'pie floater' is more to your taste (a meat pie floating in a bowl of pea soup, smothered in tomato sauce – awesome!).

★Gin Long Canteen
ASIAN $$

(Map p730; ☑08-7120 2897; www.ginlongcanteen. com.au; 42 O'Connell St, North Adelaide; small plates $9-15, mains $18-45; ☺noon-2.30pm Tue-Fri, 5.30pm-late Tue-Sat) This energetic food room is a winner. Chipper staff allocate you a space at the communal tables (bookings only for six or more) and take your order pronto. The food arrives just as fast: fab curries, slow-braised Thai beef and pork, netted spring rolls, Malay curry puffs... It's a pan-Asian vibe, bolstered by jumbo bottles of Vietnamese beer and smiles all round.

Ruby Red Flamingo
ITALIAN $$

(Map p730; ☑08-8267 5769; www.rubyredfla mingo.com; 142 Tynte St, North Adelaide; mains $22-30; ☺noon-2.30pm Wed-Fri, 5.30-9.30pm Wed-Sat) Fancy Italian on a North Adelaide side street, seated either in old-cottage confines, or out by the babbling fountain (a very Tuscan scene). The calamari-and-pea arancini balls and octopus carpaccio are utterly memorable. No bookings.

Lucky Lupitas
MEXICAN $$

(Map p730; ☑08-8267 3082; www.luckylupitas. com; Shop 1, 163 O'Connell St, North Adelaide; tacos $6-9, mains $17-25; ☺noon-2pm Sun, 5.30-9pm Mon-Thur & Sun, to 10pm Fri, 5-10pm Sat) Lucky Lupitas was holed-up in a humble southern-suburbs shopfront for years,

North Adelaide

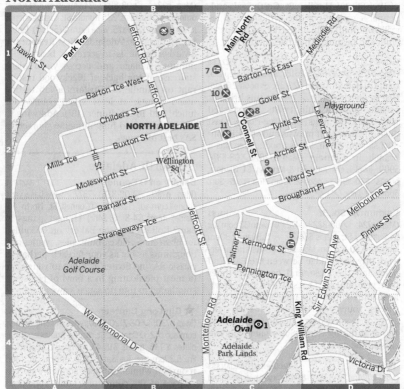

before a wrecking crew arrived to expand the adjacent highway. But now they're back in North Adelaide! Nifty plywood panelling, stacks of hot-sauce boxes by the door and unbelievably good spicy King George whiting tacos and beef brisket nachos. Cold *cerveza* by the gallon.

Inner Suburbs

★ Argo on the Parade
CAFE $

(Map p720; ☑ 08-8431 1387; www.facebook.com/argoespresso; 212 The Parade, Norwood; mains $8-22; ⏰ 7am-5.30pm Sat & Sun) The best cafe in affluent, eastern-suburbs Norwood is arguably the best cafe in Adelaide, too. It *is* in Norwood, so by default it's a bit thin on soul. But the food, coffee, service and quirky design all take the cake. As does the breakfast burrito. And the marinated tuna bowl. And the sweet potato fries...

Jarmer's Kitchen
CAFE $$

(Map p720; ☑ 08-8340 1055; www.jarmers kitchen.com.au; 18 Park Tce, Bowden; mains $12-36; ⏰ 7.30am-4pm Mon, to 9pm Tue-Fri, 8am-9pm Sat, to 4pm Sun) Jarmer's is a mainstay of rapidly redeveloping Bowden, a city-edge suburb once an industrial wasteland, now home to hundreds of hip new town houses with hip urbanites inside them. It's a fancy day/night affair in an old refurbished pub building, serving savvy sandwiches, filling pastas, burgers and substantial mains: try the pork-and-fennel sausages. Terrific wine list too.

Parwana Afghan Kitchen
AFGHANI $$

(Map p720; ☑ 08-8443 9001; www.parwana. com.au; 124b Henley Beach Rd, Torrensville; mains $14-25; ⏰ 6-10pm Tue-Thu & Sun, to 10.30pm Fri & Sat) Nutty, spicy, slippery and a little bit funky: Afghan food is unique, and this authentic restaurant, west of the CBD across the parklands, is a great place to try it. The

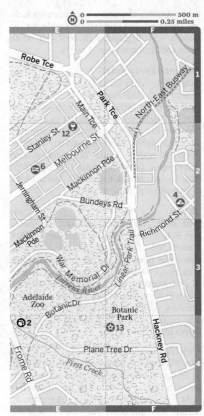

signature *banjaan borani* eggplant dish is a knockout. There's also a lunchtime branch just off Rundle St in the city called **Kutchi Deli Parwana** (Map p724; ☑ 08-7225 8586; 7 Ebenezer Pl; ☺ 11.30am-3pm Mon-Sat). BYO; cash only.

✕ Glenelg, Port Adelaide & Around

Zest Cafe Gallery　　　　　　　CAFE **$**
(Map p720; ☑ 08-8295 3599; www.zestcafegallery.com.au; 2a Sussex St, Glenelg; meals $9-17; ☺ 7.30am-6pm Mon-Sat, 8.30am-5pm Sun; ☒) Little sidestreet Zest has a laid-back vibe and brilliant breakfasts – more than enough compensation for any shortcomings in size. Baguettes and bagels are crammed with creative combos, or you can banish your hangover with some 'Hell's Eggs': baked in a ramekin with rosemary, tomato salsa,

cheese and Tabasco sauce. Great coffee, arty staff and regular vegetarian specials.

Zucca　　　　　　　　　　　　GREEK **$$**
(Map p720; ☑ 08-8376 8222; www.zucca.com.au; shop 5, Marina Pier, Holdfast Shores, Glenelg; meze $11-25, mains $24-29; ☺ noon-3pm & 6pm-late) Multicouloured tables, marina views, super service and a contemporary menu of mezze plates – you'd struggle to find anything this appealing on Santorini. The grilled Hindmarsh Valley halloumi with spiced raisins and the seared scallops with feta and pistachio are sublime.

Mestizo　　　　　　　　　　PERUVIAN **$$**
(Map p720; ☑ 08-8294 0295; www.mestizococinaperuana.com.au; 114 Partridge St, Glenelg South; mains $12-32; ☺ 12.30-3pm Fri, 5.30pm-late Tue-Fri, 1pm-late Sat & Sun) This endearing little plum-coloured eatery in the Glenelg South back blocks is Adelaide's best (only) Peruvian restaurant. The hard-working kitchen turns out fabulous pork ribs with spicy green *huacatay* sauce and *chimichurri*; or go on an Andean journey via the 'chef's selection' menu ($60 per person). Terrific South American wines too.

Low & Slow American BBQ   AMERICAN **$$**
(Map p720; ☑0402 589 722; www.lowand slowamericanbbq.com; 17 Commercial Rd, Port Adelaide; meals $10-29; ⊙noon-2.30pm Fri, 6-9pm Wed-Sun) Give your arteries something to do: this woody food room plates up succulent US-style BBQ meats, with a slew of slaws, beans, greens and grits on the side. Wash it all down with a Brooklyn Lager and a couple of Wild Turkey shots. Hip!

 Drinking & Nightlife

Rundle St has a few iconic pubs, while in the West End, Hindley St's red-light sleaze collides with the hip bars on Leigh and Peel Sts. Cover charges at clubs can be anything from free to $15, depending on the night. Most clubs close Monday to Thursday.

Central Adelaide

 ★**Exeter Hotel**   PUB
(Map p724; ☑08-8223 2623; www.theexeter. com.au; 246 Rundle St; ⊙11am-late) Adelaide's best pub, this legendary boozer attracts an eclectic brew of postwork, punk and uni drinkers, shaking the day off their backs. Pull up a bar stool or nab a table in the grungy beer garden and settle in for the evening. Original music nightly (indie, electronica, acoustic); no pokies. Book for curry nights in the upstairs restaurant (usually Wednesdays).

★**Maybe Mae**   BAR
(Map p724; ☑0421 405 039; www.maybemae. com; 15 Peel St; ⊙5pm-late Mon-Fri, 6pm-late Sat & Sun) Down some stairs down an alleyway off a laneway, Maybe Mae doesn't proclaim its virtues loudly to the world. In fact, if you can't find the door, you won't be the first

---

> **ⓘ PINT OF COOPERS PLEASE!**
>
> Things can get confusing at the bar in Adelaide. Aside from the 200ml (7oz) 'butchers' – the choice of old men in dim, sticky-carpet pubs – there are three main beer sizes: 285ml (10oz) 'schooners' (pots or middies elsewhere in Australia), 425ml (15oz) 'pints' (schooners elsewhere) and 568ml (20oz) 'imperial pints' (traditional English pints). Now go forth and order with confidence!

---

thirsty punter to wander back upstairs looking confused. But once you're inside, let the good times roll: classic rock, cool staff, booth seats and brilliant beers. Love it!

★**Grace Emily Hotel**   PUB
(Map p724; ☑08-8231 5500; www.graceemily hotel.com.au; 232 Waymouth St; ⊙4pm-late) Duking it out with the Exeter Hotel for the title of 'Adelaide's Best Pub' (it pains us to separate the two), the 'Gracie' has live music most nights (alt-rock, country, acoustic, open-mic nights), kooky '50s-meets-voodoo decor, open fires and great beers. Regular cult cinema; no pokies. Are the Bastard Sons of Ruination playing tonight?

★**Nola**   BAR
(Map p724; www.nolaadelaide.com; 28 Vardon Ave; ⊙4pm-midnight Tue-Thu, noon-2am Fri & Sat, 11am-midnight Sun) This hidden back-lane space was once the stables for the adjacent Stag Hotel. Out with the horse poo, in with 16 craft beers on tap, American and Australian whiskies (no Scotch!), Cajun cooking (gumbo, oysters, jambalaya, fried chicken) and regular live jazz. A saucy bit of Deep South in the East End.

Pink Moon Saloon   BAR
(Map p724; www.pinkmoonsaloon.com.au; 21 Leigh St; ⊙4pm-late Sat-Thu, noon-late Fri) Now this place is hip! Wedged into an impossibly tight alleyway space off Leigh St (seriously, it's only a couple of metres wide), Pink Moon Saloon has a bar in its front room, a little courtyard behind it, then a neat BBQ shack out the back. Cocktails and craft beer are why you're here. The same folks run Clever Little Taylor.

Hains & Co   BAR
(Map p724; ☑08-8410 7088; www.hainsco.com. au; 23 Gilbert Pl; ⊙4pm-late Tue-Fri & Sun, 6pm-late Sat) The nautical vibe might seem incongruous on a hot Adelaide night this far from the ocean (diving helmets, barometers, anchors etc) - but somehow it works. A really clever fit-out of a tight laneway space, with the focus on all things gin and rum. Get a few under your belt and belt out a sea shanty or three.

Clever Little Taylor   BAR
(Map p724; ☑0407 111 857; www.cleverlittletailor. com.au; 19 Peel St; ⊙4pm-late Mon-Sat) CLT was one of the vanguard which ushered in the new brigade of small bars in Adelaide's laneways. Good liquor is the thrust here, along

with fine SA wines and a hip brick-and-stone renovation (no prizes for guessing what this space used to be). Zippy bar food too.

Udaberri
BAR

(Map p724; ☑08-8410 5733; www.udaberri.com.au; 11-13 Leigh St; ☉4pm-late Tue-Fri, 6pm-late Sat & Sun) Laneway boozing at its best (in fact, this was one of Adelaide's first laneway bars), nouveau-industrial Udaberri is a compact bar on Leigh St, serving Spanish wines by the glass, good beers on tap and *pintxos* (Basque bar snacks) like oysters, cheeses, *jamón* and tortillas. The after-work crowd is cashed-up and city-savvy.

2KW
ROOFTOP BAR

(Map p724; ☑08-8212 5511; www.2kwbar.com.au; 2 King William St; ☉10am-late Mon-Fri, noon-late Sat & Sun) K2 on the China–Pakistan border is 8611m tall. 2KW is eight floors high – not quite as lofty, but it's an upmarket spot for a cocktail and eye-popping views out towards North Adelaide nonetheless. If you pass aesthetic muster (no running shoes; no logo-spangled T-shirts), access is via a *Get Smart*-like series of elevators.

Zhivago
CLUB

(Map p724; ☑08-8212 0569; www.zhivago.com.au; 54 Currie St; ☉9pm-late Fri-Sun) The pick of the West End clubs, Zhivago is all muscles and manscaping vs high heels and short skirts, with DJs pumping out everything from reggae and dub to quality house. Popular with the 18 to 25 dawn patrol.

HQ Complex
CLUB

(Map p724; ☑08-7221 1245; www.hqcomplex.com.au; 1 North Tce; ☉8pm-late Wed, Fri & Sat) Adelaide's heftiest club fills five big rooms with shimmering sound and light. Nighttime is the right time on Saturdays – the biggest (and trashiest) club night in town. Retro Wednesdays; live acts Fridays. Check the website for other gig listings.

North Adelaide

Kentish Hotel
PUB

(Map p730; ☑08-8267 1173; www.thekentish.com.au; 23 Stanley St, North Adelaide; ☉11.30am-11pm Mon-Thu, to midnight Fri & Sat, to 10pm Sun) They don't make 'em like they used to. Actually, these days, when it comes to handsome two-storey sandstone pubs, they don't make 'em at all. This backstreet beauty is great for a cold one on a hot afternoon, or gastronomic delights including a funky fish stew

and a 'Memphis Burger' with fried chicken and smoked bourbon barbecue sauce.

Inner Suburbs

★Wheatsheaf
PUB

(Map p720; ☑08-8443 4546; www.wheatsheafhotel.com.au; 39 George St, Thebarton; ☉1pm-midnight Mon-Fri, noon-midnight Sat, to 9pm Sun; ☜) A hidden gem under the flight path in industrial Thebarton, with an arty crowd of students, jazz musos, lesbians, punks and rockers. Tidy beer garden, eclectic live music out the back (acoustic, blues, country), open fires and food trucks parked out the front. Kick-ass craft beers to boot.

Earl of Leicester
PUB

(Map p720; ☑08-8271 5700; www.earl.com.au; 85 Leicester St, Parkside; ☉11am-late) Hidden in the suburban Parkside backstreets is this atmospheric old bluestone pub, serving a winning combo of abundant craft beers and the biggest schnitzels you're ever likely to bite into (mains $14 to $35). A mere 150 beers will see your name added to the 'Beer Legends' (dis)honour board.

🍸 Glenelg, Port Adelaide & Around

The Moseley
PUB

(Map p720; ☑08-8295 3966; www.themoseley.com.au; Moseley Sq, Glenelg; ☉11am-late Mon-Fri, 8am-late Sat & Sun) This old boozer was an Irish pub for years, but that's just *sooo* 2001... Reborn as the Moseley, a fancy refit has purged all the dark wood and replaced it with wicker. The upstairs balcony is where you want to be, sipping a G&T as the tram rumbles into Moseley Sq from the city. Classy pub mains $18 to $36.

Lighthouse Wharf Hotel
PUB

(Map p720; ☑08-8447 1580; www.thelighthousewharfhotel.com.au; 1 Commercial Rd, Port Adelaide; ☉10am-late Mon-Sat, 9am-11pm Sun) There are more raffish old pubs in Port Adelaide than hours in your afternoon. But if you're dry, swing into the 1935 Lighthouse Wharf Hotel for a quick Coopers, some whiting-and-chips or a bargain $11 weekday lunch.

☆ Entertainment

Arty Adelaide has a rich cultural life that stacks up favourably with much larger cities. For listings and reviews see *Adelaide*

Now (www.adelaidenow.com.au) and *Adelaide Review* (www.adelaidereview.com.au). Agencies for big-ticket event bookings include **BASS** (☎13 12 46; www.bass.net.au) and **Moshtix** (☎1300 438 849; www.moshtix.com.au).

Live Music

Adelaide knows how to kick out the jams! Top pub venues around town include the Wheatsheaf (p733), Grace Emily Hotel (p732) and Exeter Hotel (p732).

For gig listings check out the following:

➜ *Adelaide Review* (www.adelaidereview.com.au/guides)

➜ *Music SA* (www.musicsa.com.au)

➜ *jazz Adelaide* (www.jazz.adelaide.onau.net)

★ **Governor Hindmarsh Hotel**   LIVE MUSIC
(Map p720; ☎08-8340 0744; www.thegov.com.au; 59 Port Rd, Hindmarsh; ☺11am-late) Ground zero for live music in Adelaide, 'The Gov' hosts some legendary local and international acts. The odd Irish band fiddles around in the bar, while the main venue features rock, folk, jazz, blues, salsa, reggae and dance. A huge place with an inexplicably personal vibe. Good food too.

★ **Thebarton Theatre**   LIVE MUSIC
(Map p720; ☎08-8443 5255; www.thebartontheatre.com.au; 112 Henley Beach Rd, Torrensville) Now this old stager has got soul! Vaguely art deco, the 'Thebby' is an iconic Adelaide live-music venue with great acoustics and buckets of charm. Midsize acts like Rodriguez, Morrissey and the Black Crowes.

Gilbert Street Hotel   JAZZ
(Map p724; ☎08-8231 9909; www.gilbertsthotel.com.au; 88 Gilbert St; ☺11am-late) The best place in Adelaide to catch some live jazz (on Tuesday nights, at any rate) the Gilbert is a renovated old pub but continues to ooze soul. Order a *vin rouge* at the bar and dig the scene with the goatee-d regulars. Soul and acoustic acts Thursday and Sunday.

Jive   LIVE MUSIC
(Map p724; ☎08-8211 6683; www.jivevenue.com; 181 Hindley St) In a converted theatre spangled with a brilliant mural, Jive caters to an off-beat crowd of student types who like their tunes funky, left-field and removed from the mainstream. A sunken dance floor = great views from the bar. Top marks for endurance in an ever-changing world.

Adelaide Entertainment Centre   CONCERT VENUE
(Map p720; ☎08-8208 2222; www.theaec.net; 98 Port Rd, Hindmarsh; ☺box office 9am-5pm Mon-Fri) Around 12,000 bums on seats for everyone from the Wiggles to Keith Urban to Stevie Wonder.

Adelaide Symphony Orchestra   CLASSICAL MUSIC
(ASO; Map p724; ☎08-8233 6233; www.aso.com.au; 91 Hindley St; ☺box office 9am-4.30pm Mon-Fri) The estimable ASO, with gigs at various venues including the Grainger Studio on Hindley St, the Festival Theatre and Adelaide Town Hall. Check the website for performance info.

Cinemas

For cinema 'what's-on' listings: www.yourmovies.com.au/cinemas/city/adelaide and www.my247.com.au/adelaide/cinemas.

Palace Nova Eastend Cinemas   CINEMA
(Map p724; ☎08-8232 3434; www.palacecinemas.com.au; 250-51 Rundle St; tickets adult/child $19.50/15.50; ☺10am-late) Facing-off across Rundle St, both these cinema complexes screen 'sophisticated cinema': art-house, foreign-language and independent films as well as some mainstream flicks. Fully licensed too.

Moonlight Cinema   CINEMA
(Map p730; ☎1300 551 908; www.moonlight.com.au/adelaide; Botanic Park, Hackney Rd; tickets adult/child $20/15; ☺7pm daily Dec-Feb) In summer pack a picnic and mosquito repellent, and sprawl out on the lawn to watch old and new classics under the stars. 'Gold Grass' tickets, which cost a little more, secure you a prime-viewing beanbag.

Theatre & Comedy

See *Adelaide Theatre Guide* (www.theatreguide.com.au) for booking details, venues and reviews for comedy, drama and musicals.

At the time of writing, Adelaide's long-running comedy club the Rhino Room was scheduled to relocate to a new venue; check online to see if it's back in action.

Adelaide Festival Centre   PERFORMING ARTS
(Map p724; ☎08-8216 8600; www.adelaidefestivalcentre.com.au; King William Rd; ☺box office 9am-6pm Mon-Fri) The hub of performing arts in SA, this crystalline white Festival Centre opened in June 1973, four proud months before the Sydney Opera House! The *State*

Theatre Company (www.statetheatrecompany.com.au) is based here. Is it just us, or does the old dame need a bit of a spruce-up?

Sport

As most Australian cities do, Adelaide hangs its hat on the successes of its sporting teams. In the **Australian Football League** (www.afl.com.au), the Adelaide Crows and Port Adelaide Power have sporadic success and play at the Adelaide Oval. Suburban Adelaide teams compete in the confusingly named **South Australian National Football League** (www.sanfl.com.au). The football season runs from March to September.

In the **National Basketball League** (www.nbl.com.au), the Adelaide 36ers have been a force for decades (lately, not so much). In netball, the Adelaide Thunderbirds play in the **ANZ Championship** (www.anz-championship.com) with regular success. In soccer's **A League** (www.a-league.com.au), Adelaide United ('the Reds') won the championship in 2016.

In summer, under the auspices of **Cricket SA** (www.cricketsa.com.au), the Redbacks play state matches at the Adelaide Oval. The Redbacks rebrand as the Adelaide Strikers in the national **T20 Big Bash** (www.bigbash.com.au) competition. International cricket also happens at the Adelaide Oval (www.cricketaustralia.com.au).

🛍 Shopping

Shops and department stores line Rundle Mall. The beautiful old arcades running between the mall and Grenfell St retain their splendour, and house eclectic little shops. Rundle St and the adjunct Ebenezer Pl are home to boutique and retro clothing shops.

★ Streetlight   BOOKS, MUSIC

(Map p724; ☑ 08-8227 0667; www.facebook.com/streetlightadelaide; 2/15 Vaughan Pl; ☺ 10am-6pm Mon-Thu & Sat, to 9pm Fri, noon-5pm Sun) Lefty, arty and subversive in the best possible way, Streetlight is the place to find that elusive Miles Davis disc or Charles Bukowski poetry compilation.

★ Imprints Booksellers   BOOKS

(Map p724; ☑ 08-8231 4454; www.imprints.com.au; 107 Hindley St; ☺ 9am-6pm Mon-Wed, to 9pm Thu & Fri, to 5pm Sat, 11am-5pm Sun) The best bookshop in Adelaide is in the worst location (in the thick of the Hindley St strip-club fray). Still, jazz, floorboards, Persian

rugs and occasional live readings and book launches more than compensate. And a bit of sleaze has always been solid literary fuel.

Midwest Trader   FASHION & ACCESSORIES

(Map p724; ☑ 08-8223 6606; www.facebook.com/Midwest-Trader; Shop 1 & 2 Ebenezer Pl; ☺ 10am-6pm Mon-Thu & Sat, to 9pm Fri, noon-5pm Sun) Stocks a snarling range of punk, skate, vintage, biker and rockabilly gear, plus second-hand cowboy boots. Rock on! Check out its Facebook page for its latest wares.

Miss Gladys
Sym Choon   FASHION & ACCESSORIES

(Map p724; ☑ 08-8223 1500; www.missgladyssymchoon.com.au; 235a Rundle St; ☺ 9.30am-6pm Mon-Thu, to 9pm Fri, 10am-5.30pm Sat, 11am-5.30pm Sun) Named after a famed Rundle St trader from the 1920s (the first woman in SA to incorporate a business) this hip shop is the place for fab frocks, rockin' boots, street-beating sneakers and jewellery.

Adelaide Farmers Market   MARKET

(Map p720; ☑ 08-8231 8155; www.adelaidefarmersmarket.com; Adelaide Showground, Leader St, Wayville; ☺ 9am-1pm Sun) ✒ Don't mind dragging yourself out of bed too early on a Sunday and paying $8 for an organic parsnip? The Adelaide Farmers Market is for you! Actually, ignore our cynicism – the food offerings here are fabulous: fresh, organic, local and sustainable, take home or cooked into delicious things you can eat on the spot.

Gilles Street Market   MARKET

(Map p724; www.gillesstreetmarket.com.au; Gilles Street Primary School, 91 Gilles St; ☺ 10am-4pm 3rd Sun of the month, plus 1st Sun Oct-May) Kids' clothes, fashion, arts, crafts, buskers and general commercial hubbub consume an East End Adelaide school grounds.

Jurlique   COSMETICS

(Map p724; ☑ 08-8305 3000; www.jurlique.com.au; 100 Rundle Mall; ☺ 9am-6pm Mon-Thu, to 9pm Fri, to 5pm Sat, 11am-5pm Sun) An international success story, SA's own Jurlique sells fragrant skincare products that are pricey but worth every cent.

ⓘ Information

EMERGENCY

For ambulance, fire or police call ☑ 000
RAA Emergency Roadside Assistance ☑ 13 11 11

INTERNET ACCESS

State Library of South Australia (☎08-8207 7250; www.slsa.sa.gov.au; 1st fl, cnr North Tce & Kintore Ave; ☺10am-8pm Mon-Wed, to 6pm Thu & Fri, to 5pm Sat & Sun) Free internet access (book ahead), and kids' school-holiday programs.

MEDIA

Adelaide's daily tabloid is the parochial *Advertiser*, though the *Age*, *Australian* and *Financial Review* are also widely available.

Adelaide Review (www.adelaidereview.com. au) Highbrow articles, culture and arts. Free monthly.

Blaze (www.gaynewsnetwork.com.au) Gay-and-lesbian street press; free fortnightly.

CityMag (www.citymag.indaily.com.au) Food reviews, culture and urban happenings. Free quarterly.

Scenestr (www.scenestr.com.au/adelaide) Free monthly street press: music, fashion, clubbing and arts.

MEDICAL SERVICES

Emergency Dental Service (☎08-8222 8222; www.sadental.sa.gov.au) Sore tooth?

Midnight Pharmacy (☎08-8232 4445; 192-198 Wakefield St; ☺7am-midnight Mon-Sat, 9am-midnight Sun) Late-night presciptions.

Royal Adelaide Hospital (☎08-8222 4000; www.rah.sa.gov.au; 275 North Tce; ☺24hr) Emergency department (not for blisters!) and STD clinic.

Women's & Children's Hospital (☎08-8161 7000; www.cywhs.sa.gov.au; 72 King William Rd, North Adelaide; ☺24hr) Emergency and sexual-assault services.

MONEY

Travelex (☎08-8231 6977; www.travelex. com.au; shop 4, Beehive Corner, Rundle Mall; ☺8.30am-6pm Mon-Fri, 9am-3pm Sat, noon-5pm Sun) Foreign currency exchange.

POST

Adelaide General Post Office (GPO; Map p724; ☎13 13 18; www.auspost.com.au; 141 King William St; ☺9am-5.30pm Mon-Fri, to 12.30pm Sat) Adelaide's main (and rather stately) post office. There are also post offices just off **Rundle Mall** (Map p724; ☎13 13 18; www.auspost.com.au; 59 City Cross Arc; ☺8.30am-5pm Mon-Fri, 9am-12.30pm Sat, 11am-4pm Sun) and another on the **UniSA campus** (Map p724; ☎13 13 18; www.auspost. com.au; 61 North Tce; ☺9am-5pm Mon-Fri).

TOURIST INFORMATION

Adelaide Visitor Information Centre (Map p724; ☎1300 588 140; www.adelaidecity council.com; 9 James Pl, off Rundle Mall; ☺9am-5pm Mon-Fri, 10am-4pm Sat & Sun,

11am-3pm public holidays) Adelaide-specific information, plus abundant info on SA including fab regional booklets.

Department of Environment, Water & Natural Resources (DEWNR; Map p724; ☎08-8204 1910; www.environment.sa.gov.au; ground fl, 81-95 Waymouth St; ☺9am-5pm Mon-Fri) National parks information and bookings.

There are also helpful visitors centres in **Glenelg** (p719) and **Port Adelaide** (p719).

🛈 Getting There & Away

AIR

International, interstate and regional flights via a number of airlines service **Adelaide Airport** (ADL; ☎08-8308 9211; www.adelaideairport. au; 1 James Schofield Dr), 7km west of the city centre. Domestic services include:

Jetstar (www.jetstar.com.au) Direct flights between Adelaide and Perth, Darwin, Cairns, Brisbane, Gold Coast, Sydney and Melbourne.

Qantas (www.qantas.com.au) Direct flights between Adelaide and Perth, Alice Springs, Darwin, Cairns, Brisbane, Sydney, Canberra and Melbourne.

Regional Express (Rex; www.regionalexpress. com.au) Flies from Adelaide to regional centres around SA – Kingscote, Coober Pedy, Ceduna, Mount Gambier, Port Lincoln and Whyalla – plus Broken Hill in NSW and Mildura in Victoria.

Tiger Airways (www.tigerairways.com.au) Direct flights between Adelaide and Melbourne, Sydney and Brisbane.

Virgin Australia (www.virginaustralia.com. au) Direct flights between Adelaide and Perth, Alice Springs, Brisbane, Gold Coast, Sydney, Canberra and Melbourne.

BUS

Adelaide Central Bus Station (Map p724; ☎08 8221 5080; www.adelaidemetro.com. au/bussa; 85 Franklin St; ☺6am-9.30pm) is the hub for all major interstate and statewide bus services; see the website for routes and timetables. Note: there is no Adelaide–Perth bus service.

Firefly Express (☎1300 730 740; www. fireflyexpress.com.au) Runs between Sydney, Melbourne and Adelaide.

Greyhound Australia (☎1300 473 946; www.greyhound.com.au) Australia's main long-distance player, with services between Adelaide and Melbourne, Canberra, Sydney, Alice Springs and Darwin.

Premier Stateliner (☎1300 851 345; www. premierstateliner.com.au) Statewide bus services.

V/Line (☎1800 800 007; www.vline.com.au) Bus and bus/train services between Adelaide and Melbourne.

CAR & MOTORCYCLE

The major international car-rental companies have offices at Adelaide Airport and in the city. There's also a crew of local operators, including the following. Note that some companies don't allow vehicles to be taken to Kangaroo Island.

Acacia Car Rentals (☑ 08-8234 0911; www. acaciacarrentals.com.au; 91 Sir Donald Bradman Dr, Hilton; ☺ 8am-5pm Mon-Fri, to noon Sat) Cheap rentals for travel within a 100km radius of Adelaide; scooter hire available.

Access Rent-a-Car (☑ 08-8340 0400, 1800 812 580; www.accessrentacar.com; 464 Port Rd, West Hindmarsh; ☺ 8am-6pm Mon-Fri, to noon Sat & Sun) Kangaroo Island travel permitted; 4WDs available.

Cut Price Car & Truck Rentals (☑ 08-8443 7788; www.cutprice.com.au; cnr Sir Donald Bradman Dr & South Rd, Mile End; ☺ 7.30am-5pm Mon-Fri, to 3pm Sat & Sun) 4WDs available.

Koala Car Rentals (☑ 08-8352 7299; www. koalarentals.com.au; 41 Sir Donald Bradman Dr, Mile End; ☺ 7.30am-5pm Mon-Fri, 8am-3pm Sat & Sun)

Smile Rent-a-Car (☑ 08-8234 0655, 1800 891 002; www.smilerentacar.com.au; 315 Sir Donald Bradman Dr, Brooklyn Park; ☺ 8am-6pm)

The **Royal Automobile Association of South Australia** (RAA; ☑ 08-8202 4600; www.raa. com.au; 41 Hindmarsh Sq; ☺ 8.30am-5pm Mon-Fri, 9am-4pm Sat) provides auto advice (including road conditions in outback areas) and plenty of maps.

TRAIN

Interstate trains run by **Great Southern Rail** (☑ 1800 703 357, 08 8213 4401; www.great southernrail.com.au) grind into the **Adelaide Parklands Terminal** (Railway Tce, Keswick; ☺ 6am-5pm Mon & Fri, 6.30am-5.30pm Tue, 9am-5pm Wed, to 7pm Thu, 8.30am-1pm Sun), 1km southwest of the city centre. The following trains depart Adelaide regularly; backpacker discounts apply:

The Ghan to Alice Springs (from $799, 19 hours)

The Ghan to Darwin (from $1499, 47 hours)

The Indian Pacific to Perth (from $1189, 39 hours)

The Indian Pacific to Sydney (from $589, 25 hours)

The Overland to Melbourne (from $149, 11 hours)

ⓘ Getting Around

TO/FROM THE AIRPORT & TRAIN STATION

Prebooked private **Adelaide Airport Flyer** (☑ 08-8353 5233, 1300 856 444; www.adelaideairport flyer.com) minibuses run door-to-door between the airport and anywhere around Adelaide; get a quote and book online (into the city from the airport for one person costs $35). Public Adelaide Metro **JetExpress** (www.adelaidemetro.com.au/timetables-maps/special-services; $3.20-5.10; ☺ 6.30am-11pm Mon-Fri, 7.15am-11pm Sat & Sun) and **JetBus** (www.adelaidemetro.com.au/timetables-maps/special-services; $3.20-5.10; ☺ 6.30am-11pm Mon-Fri, 7.15am-11pm Sat & Sun) bus services – routes J1, J1X, J3, J7 and J8 – connect the airport with Glenelg and the CBD; standard Metro fares apply.

Taxis charge around $30 into the city from the airport (15 minutes); or about $15 from Adelaide Parklands Terminal (10 minutes). Many hostels will pick you up and drop you off if you're staying with them. Adelaide Transport (p738) also offers shuttle transfers.

BICYCLE

Adelaide is pizza-flat: great for cycling! With a valid passport or driver's licence you can borrow an **Adelaide Free Bike** from **Bicycle SA** (☑ 08-8168 9999; www.bikesa.asn.au; 53 Carrington St; ☺ 9am-5pm Mon-Fri, 8am-5pm Sat & Sun); helmet and lock provided. There are a couple of dozen locations around town: you can collect a bike at any of them, provided you return it to the same place. Multiday hires also available.

Down at the beach, hire a bike from **Glenelg Bicycle Hire** (Map p720; ☑ 08-8376 1934; www.glenelgbicyclehire.com.au; Norfolk Motel, 71 Broadway, Glenelg South; bikes per day $25, tandems per hour/day $25/50).

PUBLIC TRANSPORT

Adelaide Metro (☑ 1300 311 108; www. adelaidemetro.com.au; cnr King William & Currie Sts; ☺ 8am-6pm Mon-Fri, 9am-5pm Sat, 11am-4pm Sun) runs Adelaide's decent and integrated bus, train and tram network.

Tickets can be purchased on board, at staffed train stations and in delis and newsagents across the city. Ticket types include day trip ($10), two-hour peak ($5.30) and two-hour off-peak ($3.40) tickets. Peak travel time is before 9am and after 3pm. Kids under five ride free! There's also a three-day, unlimited-travel visitor pass ($26). If you're here for longer, save at least $1 per trip with a rechargable multitrip Metrocard.

Bus

Adelaide's buses are clean and reliable. Most services start around 6am and run until midnight.

Every 30 minutes daily, Adelaide Metro's **Free City Loop buses** (☑ 1300 311 108; www. adelaidemetro.com.au/timetables-maps/special-services; ☺ 9am-7.15pm Sat-Thu, to 9.15pm Fri) – routes 98A and 98C – run clockwise and anticlockwise around the CBD fringe, passing North Tce, Victoria Sq, Hutt St, the Central Market and winding through North Adelaide en route. The 99A and 99C buses ply the same route (minus

North Adelaide), Monday to Friday – the net effect is a free bus every 15 minutes Monday to Friday.

Adelaide Metro's **After Midnight buses** (www.adelaidemetro.com.au/timetables-maps/special-services; ⊙ midnight-5am Sat) run select standard routes but have an 'N' preceding the route number on their displays. Standard ticket prices apply.

Train

Adelaide's hokey old diesel trains are slowly being electrified. Trains depart from **Adelaide Station** (www.railmaps.com.au/adelaide.htm; North Tce), plying five suburban routes (Belair, Gawler, Grange, Noarlunga and Outer Harbour). Trains generally run between 6am and midnight (some services start at 4.30am).

Tram

Adelaide's state-of-the-art trams rumble to/from Moseley Sq in Glenelg, through Victoria Sq in the city and along North Tce to the Adelaide Entertainment Centre. Trams run approximately every 10 minutes on weekdays (every 15 minutes on weekends) from 6am to midnight daily. Standard Metro ticket prices apply, but the section between South Tce and the Adelaide Entertainment Centre is free. New route extensions are being discussed!

TAXI

Adelaide Independent Taxis (☎ 13 22 11; www.aitaxis.com.au) Regular and wheelchair-access cabs.

Adelaide Transport (☎ 08-8212 1861; www.adelaidetransport.com.au) Minibus taxis for four or more people, plus airport-to-city transfers.

Suburban Taxis (☎ 13 10 08; www.suburbantaxis.com.au) Taxis, all suburbs.

Yellow Cabs (☎ 13 22 27; www.yellowcabgroup.com.au) Regular cabs (most of which are white!).

ADELAIDE HILLS

When the Adelaide plains are desert-hot in the summer months, the Adelaide Hills (technically the Mt Lofty Ranges) are always a few degrees cooler, with crisp air, woodland shade and labyrinthine valleys. Early colonists built stately summer houses around Stirling and Aldgate, and German settlers escaping religious persecution also arrived, infusing towns like Hahndorf and Lobethal with European values and architecture.

The Hills make a brilliant day trip from Adelaide: hop from town to town (all with at least one pub), passing carts of fresh produce for sale, stone cottages, olive groves and wineries along the way.

Tours

Ambler Touring   TOURS
(☎ 0414 447 134; www.ambler.net.au; half-/full-day tours per person $99/155) See the Adelaide Hills in style with these personalised, locally run tours taking in Hahndorf, Mt Lofty Summit, Beerenberg Farm and plenty of other sights. Lots of wine, cheese, chocolate and arts.

✷✷ Festivals & Events

Crush   WINE
(www.crushfestival.com.au; ⊙ Jan) Celebrating all things good about life in the Adelaide Hills, with food and wine at the fore. Lots of cellar-door events and tastings.

Winter Reds   WINE
(www.winterreds.com.au; ⊙ Jul) 'Brrr, it's chilly. Pour me another shiraz.' Winter Reds celebrates the cold season in the Adelaide Hills, with winery tastings, hearty food and lots of open fires.

🛈 Getting There & Away

To best explore the Hills, BYO wheels. Alternatively, **Adelaide Metro** (www.adelaidemetro.com.au) runs buses between the city and most Hills towns. The 864 and 864F city–Mt Barker buses stop at Stirling, Aldgate and Hahndorf. The 823 runs from Crafers to Mt Lofty Summit and Cleland Wildlife Park; the 830F runs from the city to Oakbank, Woodside and Lobethal. Buses 835 and 835A connect Lobethal with Mt Barker. Standard Metro fares apply (one-way from $3.40).

Hahndorf

POP 2550

Like the Rocks in Sydney, and Richmond near Hobart, Hahndorf is a 'ye olde worlde' colonial enclave that trades ruthlessly on its history: it's something of a kitsch parody of itself.

That said, Hahndorf is undeniably pretty, with Teutonic sandstone architecture, European trees, and flowers overflowing from half wine barrels. And it *is* interesting: Australia's oldest surviving German settlement (1839), founded by 50 Lutheran families fleeing religious persecution in Prussia. Hahndorf was placed under martial law during WWI, and its name changed to 'Ambleside' (renamed Hahndorf in 1935). It's

Adelaide Hills

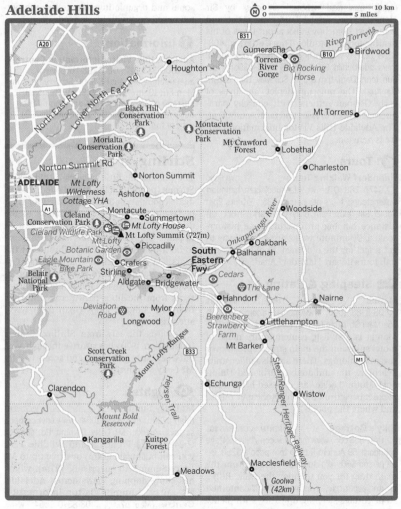

N 0 — 10 km
0 — 5 miles

also slowly becoming less kitsch, more cool: there are a few good cafes here now, and on a sunny day the main street is positively pumping.

◎ Sights

The Lane WINERY
(☎08-8388 1250; www.thelane.com.au; Ravenswood La; ◎10am-4pm) Camera-conducive views and contemporary varietals (viognier, pinot grigio, pinot gris), plus an outstanding restaurant (book for lunch: two/three courses $59/70, serving noon to 3pm). Tastings of entry-level wines free.

Beerenberg Strawberry Farm FARM
(☎08-8388 7272; www.beerenberg.com.au; Mount Barker Rd; strawberry picking per adult/child $4/free, strawberries per kg $10; ◎9am-5pm) Pick your own strawberries between November and April from this famous, family-run farm, also big-noted for its myriad jams, chutneys and sauces. Last entry for picking 4.15pm; open til 8.30pm Fridays in December and January. Strawberry ice cream to go.

Hahndorf Academy MUSEUM
(☎08-8388 7250; www.hahndorfacademy.org.au; 68 Main St; ◎10am-5pm) FREE This 1857 building houses an art gallery with rotating

exhibitions and original sketches by Sir Hans Heysen, famed landscape artist and Hahndorf homeboy – ask about tours of his nearby former studio, **The Cedars** (☑ 08-8388 7277; www.hansheysen.com.au; Heysen Rd; tours adult/child $10/free; ☺ 10am-4.30pm Tue-Sun, tours 11am, 1pm & 3pm Sep-May, 11am & 2pm Jun-Aug). The museum depicts the lives of early German settlers, with churchy paraphernalia, dour dresses and farm equipment. The Adelaide Hills Visitor Information Centre is here too.

Tours

Hahndorf Walking Tours
WALKING
(☑ 0477 288 011; www.facebook.com/hahndorf walkingtours; tours per person $33; ☺ tours 2pm Sat & Sat, plus 6pm daily Oct-Mar) Short on distance but big on insight, these history-soaked, 90-minute walks are a great way to get a feel for the old town. Bookings essential; tours depart Hahndorf Academy.

🛏 Sleeping & Eating

Manna
MOTEL, APARTMENTS **$$**
(☑ 08-8388 1000; www.themanna.com.au; 25 & 35a Main St; d/ste from $149/199; ❄🖰🅿) The Manna is a stylish, contemporary maze of motel suites on the main street, spread over several buildings. There are also older units nearby at the affiliated, refurbished Hahndorf Motor Lodge, an exposed-brick complex set back from the street (cheaper rates... and where the pool is).

Billy's Cottage
RENTAL HOUSE, B&B **$$$**
(☑ 0417 833 665; www.facebook.com/billyscottage hahndorf; 59 Auricht Rd; up to 4 people $250, extra person $60; ❄) Just far enough from the main drag for you to enjoy the walk, Billy's is an eccentric, renovated, self-contained stone cottage sleeping up to six, with plenty of beds and a weird stage platform in case an impromptu performance urge grabs you. Great value for groups or families.

★ Seasonal Garden Cafe
CAFE **$$**
(☑ 08-8388 7714; www.facebook.com/thesea sonalgardencafe; 100 Main St; mains $10-25; ☺ 7.30am-4.30pm Mon-Fri, to 5.30pm Sat & Sun; ☑) 🍴 Swimming against Hahndorf's mainstream currents – although slightly less earthy than it was, in its snappy new shopfront – this zero-waste cafe is adorned with wreaths, piles of pumpkins and strings of chubby chillies. Food-wise it's good coffee, grass-green smoothies and lots of local, sea-sonal and organic ingredients (try the potted baked eggs with house-made beans).

ℹ Information

Adelaide Hills Visitor Information Centre
(☑ 1800 353 323, 08-8388 1185; www. adelaidehills.org.au; 68 Main St; ☺ 9am-5pm Mon-Fri, 10am-4pm Sat & Sun) The usual barrage of brochures, plus accommodation bookings. The **Hahndorf Academy** (p739) is here too.

Stirling Area

The photogenic little villages of old-school Stirling (population 2950) and one-horse Aldgate (population 3350) are famed for their bedazzling autumn colours, thanks to the deciduous trees the early residents saw fit to plant. Oddly, Aldgate has also been home to both Bon Scott and Mel Gibson over the years. On a less rock 'n' roll tack, the 6km **Aldgate Valley Nature Walk** runs from Aldgate to nearby Mylor; follow the bandicoot signs from the little park across the road from the Aldgate shops (map from www. ahc.sa.gov.au).

Towards the city from Stirling, Crafers (population 1970) has a drive-through vibe but a seriously good pub...and access to lofty Mt Lofty Summit!

◉ Sights

Mt Lofty Summit
VIEWPOINT
(Map p720; ☑ 08-8370 1054; www.environment. sa.gov.au/parks; Mt Lofty Summit Rd, Crafers; ☺ 24hr) **FREE** From Cleland Wildlife Park you can bushwalk (2km) or drive up to Mt Lofty Summit (a surprising 727m), which has show-stopping views across Adelaide. **Mt Lofty Summit Visitor Information Centre** (Map p720; ☑ 08-8370 1054; www. mtloftysummit.com; ☺ 9am-5pm) has all the information you need on local attractions and walking tracks, including the steep Waterfall Gully Track (8km return, 2½ hours) and Mt Lofty Botanic Gardens Loop Trail (7km loop, two hours). The video of the Ash Wednesday bushfires of 16 February 1983 is harrowing. There's a snazzy **cafe/restaurant** (Map p720; ☑ 08-8839 2600; www.mountloftysummit.com; mains lunch $9-20, dinner $37-42; ☺ cafe 9am-5pm Mon-Fri, 8.30am-5pm Sat & Sun, restaurant 6pm-late Wed-Sat) here too.

Deviation Road
WINERY

(☑ 08-8339 2633; www.deviationroad.com; 207 Scott Creek Rd, Longwood; ⏰10am-5pm; 🚗) Nothing deviant about the wines here: sublime pinot noir, substantial shiraz, zingy pinot gris and a very decent bubbly, too. Grab a cheese platter and wind down in the afternoon in the sun. Unpretentious and lovely.

Mt Lofty Botanic Garden
GARDENS

(☑ 08-8222 9311; www.botanicgardens.sa.gov.au; gates on Mawson Dr & Lampert Rd, Crafers; ⏰8.30am-4pm Mon-Fri, 10am-5pm Sat & Sun) FREE From Mt Lofty, truck south 1.5km to the cool-climate slopes of the botanic garden. Nature trails wind past a lake, exotic temperate plants, native stringybark forest and eye-popping ranks of rhododendron blooms. Free guided walks depart the lower Lampert Rd car park at 10.30am every Thursday.

Cleland Wildlife Park
WILDLIFE RESERVE

(Map p720; ☑ 08-8339 2444; www.clelandwildlifepark.sa.gov.au; 365 Mt Lofty Summit Rd, Crafers; adult/child/family $25/12/56; ⏰ 9.30am-5pm, last entry 4.30pm) Within the steep **Cleland Conservation Park** (Map p720; ☑08-8278 5477; www.environment.sa.gov.au/parks; Mt Lofty Summit Rd, Crafers; ⏰24hr) FREE, this place lets you interact with all kinds of Australian beasts. There are keeper talks and feeding sessions throughout the day, plus occasional Night Walks (adult/child $50/40) and you can have your mugshot taken with a koala ($30; 2pm to 3.30pm daily, plus 11am to noon Sundays). There's a **cafe** (Map p720; www.environment.sa.gov.au/clelandwildlife; meals $5-15; ⏰9.30am-5pm) here too. From the city, take bus 864 or 864F from Grenfell St to Crafers for connecting bus 823 to the park.

🛏 Sleeping & Eating

Crafers Hotel
BOUTIQUE HOTEL, PUB $$

(Map p720; ☑08-8339 2050; www.crafershotel.com.au; 8 Main St, Crafers; d from $180; 🅿🛜) How marvellous: the seedy old Crafers Inn has been sandblasted, painted, gutted and refitted and has morphed from a sticky-carpet old-man's boozer into a boisterous craft-beer pub with seven stylish ensuite rooms upstairs. Crafers itself remains a loose affiliation of buildings with no civic heart...but perhaps this lovely old pub now fills this void.

Mt Lofty YHA
CABIN $$

(Map p720; ☑08-8414 3000; www.yha.com.au; Gate 25, Mt Lofty Summit Rd, Crafers; per night from $160) And now, for something completely different: a short detour off the road on the steep flanks of Mt Lofty, this 1880 stone cottage was originally a shepherd's hut. Today it's a simple, self-contained, three-bedroom cabin sleeping 10, with peek-a-boo views of Adelaide through the eucalyptuses. Pick up the keys from Adelaide Central YHA (p725) in the city.

★Stirling Hotel
BOUTIQUE HOTEL, PUB $$$

(☑08-8339 2345; www.stirlinghotel.com.au; 52 Mt Barker Rd, Stirling; d from $280; 🅿🛜) The owners spent so much money tarting up this gorgeous old dame, it's a wonder they can pay the staff. Upstairs are five guest suites: plush, contemporary and stylish. Downstairs is a free-flowing, all-day bistro (classy pub grub and pizzas) and a romantic restaurant (upmarket regional cuisine). The whole shebang is a runaway success story.

★Fred Eatery
CAFE $$

(☑08-8339 1899; www.fredeatery.com.au; 220 Mt Barker Rd, Aldgate; mains $11-26; ⏰7.30am-4pm Tue-Sun, plus 6-9pm Fri; 🚗) Build it, and they will come... For decades Aldgate eked-out a cafe lifestyle with no quality offerings. Then along came Fred, a rather urbane fellow, decked out in green, black and white, with a savvy cityside menu, killer coffee and great staff. The house bircher muesli makes a solid start to the day, while the bodacious Reuben sandwich is calorific heaven.

🔒 Shopping

Stirling Markets
MARKET

(☑0488 770 166; www.stirlingmarket.com.au; Druid Ave, Stirling; ⏰10am-4pm 4th Sun of the month, 3rd Sun in Dec) 'Bustling' is such a corny, overused adjective...but in this case it applies! Market stalls fill oak-lined Druid Ave: much plant-life, busking, pies, cakes, affluent locals with dogs and Hills knick-knackery (not many druids...).

Gumeracha, Birdwood & Lobethal

A scenic drive from Adelaide to Birdwood leads through the **Torrens River Gorge** to Gumeracha (gum-er-ack-a; population 1020), a hardy hillside town with a pub at the bottom (making it hard to roll home).

Nearby Birdwood (population 1300) marks the finishing line for September's Bay to Birdwood classic-car rally. The rest of the year it makes a perfectly soporific Hills detour, with an excellent automotive musuem.

Back towards Woodside, Lobethal (population 2350), was established by Lutheran Pastor Fritzsche and his followers in 1842. Like Hahndorf, Lobethal was renamed during WWI – 'Tweedale' was the unfortunate choice. It's still a pious sort of town: church life plays a leading role in many locals' day-to-day lives, though the local craft-beer brewery and some excellent wineries in the surrounding hills demand reverence of a different kind.

◉ Sights

Pike & Joyce   WINERY
(☏ 08-8389 8102; www.pikeandjoyce.com.au; 730 Mawson Rd, Lenswood; ⊙ 11am-5pm, to 4pm Jun-Aug) High on a hill behind Lenswood (itself behind Lobethal), Pike & Joyce is an architectural doozy, with rammed-earth walls, jaunty corrugated-iron roof pitches and mesmerising views over the vine-striped hillsides and apple orchards below. Sip some chardonnay or interesting Austrian gruner veltliner. There's a fancy restaurant here too (mains $28 to $32, serving noon to 3pm Thursday to Sunday).

National Motor Museum   MUSEUM
(☏ 08-8568 4000; www.nationalmotormuseum.com.au; Shannon St, Birdwood; adult/child/family $15.50/6.50/35; ⊙ 10am-5pm) Behind an impressive 1852 flour mill in Birdwood, the National Motor Museum has a collection of 300-plus immaculate vintage, modern and classic cars (check out the DeLorean!) and motorcycles.

Big Rocking Horse   MONUMENT
(☏ 08-8389 1085; www.thetoyfactory.com.au; 452 Torrens Rd, Gumeracha; $2; ⊙ 9am-5pm) Gumeracha's main attraction is climbing the 18.3m-high Big Rocking Horse, which doesn't actually rock, but is unusually tasteful as far as Australia's 'big' tourist attractions go. You can buy nifty wooden kids' toys at the shop below.

✦ Festivals & Events

Bay to Birdwood   SPORTS
(www.baytobirdwood.com.au) Come September, a convoy of classic cars chugs it's way up from Adelaide to Birdwood in the Adelaide Hills, crossing the finishing line at the National Motor Museum.

Lights of Lobethal   CHRISTMAS
(www.lightsoflobethal.com.au; ⊙ Dec) Dazzling Christmas lights festival, lighting up Lobethal's front yards. Expect bumper-to-bumper traffic.

🍷 Drinking & Nightlife

Lobethal Bierhaus   BREWERY
(☏ 08-8389 5570; www.bierhaus.com.au; 3a Main St, Lobethal; ⊙ noon-10pm Fri & Sat, to 6pm Sun) Repair to the quasi-industrial Lobethal Bierhaus for some serious craft-brewed concoctions (the Red Truck Porter will put hairs on your chest).

Mt Barker

POP 11,810

The biggest town in the Adelaide Hills and just a 35-minute commute to the city, Mt Barker began life as a small rural village. But these days it's booming, with 20,000 new residents predicted in the coming years as paddocks are subdivided apace. Mt Barker CBD can barely keep up, with shopping centres and new services being knocked together at a furious pace. There's still some small-town charm to be found on Gawler St, though, and some fab local businesses are keeping the new residents fed and watered.

◉ Sights

★ Prancing Pony   BREWERY
(☏ 08-8398 3881; www.prancingponybrewery.com.au; 42 Mt Barker Rd, Totness; ⊙ 10am-6pm Mon-Thu, to 10pm Fri & Sat, to 8pm Sun) Prize-winning craft beers, burgers, platters, bar snacks and live troubadours all make an appearance at this funky beer shed, on the road out of Mt Barker heading for Hahndorf. Something other than a pub or a winery in the Adelaide Hills was so long overdue it wasn't funny. But now we can all laugh, kicking back with an Amber Ale or three.

🛍 Shopping

Buzz Honey   FOOD
(☏ 08-8388 0274; www.buzzhoney.com.au; 42 Mount Barker Rd, Totness; ⊙ 8.30am-4.30pm Mon-Fri, 9.30am-4.30pm Sat) In Mt Barker's industrial zone, Buzz Honey has been generating quite a buzz of late, selling superb Adelaide Hills honey from its nondescript shopfront. Learn

about the process, taste some, then buy some (the local Blue Gum is a classic).

FLEURIEU PENINSULA

Patterned with vineyards, olive groves and almond plantations running down to the sea, the Fleurieu (*floo*-ree-oh) is Adelaide's weekend playground. The McLaren Vale wine region is booming, producing gutsy reds (salubrious shiraz) to rival those from the Barossa Valley (actually, we think McLaren Vale wins hands down). Further east, the Fleurieu's Encounter Coast is an engaging mix of surf beaches, historic towns and whales cavorting offshore.

❶ Getting There & Away

Your own vehicle is the best way to explore the Fleurieu, but several bus companies service the towns here.

Adelaide Metro (www.adelaidemetro.com. au) suburban trains run between Adelaide and Seaford (one hour). From here, bus 751 runs to McLaren Vale and Willunga (45 minutes). Regular Adelaide Metro ticket prices apply (from $3.40). **Southlink** (🖉 08 8186 2888; www.southlink.com.au) buses also service the Fleurieu Peninsula, working in conjunction with Adelaide Metro service.

LinkSA (www.linksa.com.au) runs daily buses from Adelaide to Victor Harbor ($26, one hour), continuing on to Port Elliot and Goolwa for the same fare.

On the Gulf St Vincent coast, the Kangaroo Island ferry company **SeaLink** (www.sealink. com.au) runs daily buses between Adelaide and Cape Jervis on the Fleurieu, from where the ferry departs. The bus can drop you off in Yankalilla or Normanville en route ($19, 1¼ hours).

On the first and third Sundays from June to November inclusive, **SteamRanger Heritage Railway** (🖉 08-8263 5621, 1300 655 991; www. steamranger.org.au) operates the *Southern Encounter* (adult/child return $71/37) tourist train from Mt Barker in the Adelaide Hills to Victor Harbor via Strathalbyn, Goolwa and Port Elliot. The *Cockle Train* (adult/child return $29/15) runs along the Encounter Coast between Victor Harbor and Goolwa via Port Elliot every Sunday and Wednesday, and daily during school holidays.

McLaren Vale

POP 3870

Flanked by the wheat-coloured Willunga Scarp and striated with vines, McLaren Vale is just 40 minutes south of Adelaide. Servicing the wine industry, it's an energetic, utilitarian town that's not much to look at – but it has some great eateries and offers easy

Fleurieu Peninsula

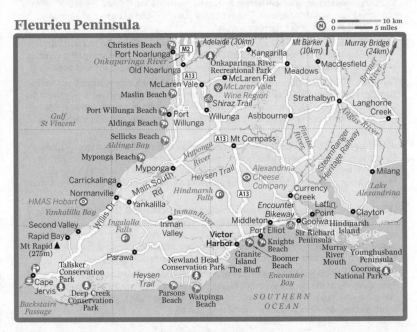

access to some truly excellent winery cellar doors.

◉ Sights & Activities

Most people come to McLaren Vale to cruise the 80-plus wineries here: you could spend days doing nothing else! Pick up a winery map at the visitor information centre.

Goodieson Brewery   BREWERY
(☑0409 676 542; www.goodiesonbrewery.com. au; 194 Sand Rd, McLaren Vale; tastings $5; ☉11am-5.30pm) There sure are a lot of wineries around here... Anyone for a beer? This family-run outfit brews a pale ale, pilsner, wheat beer and brown ale, plus brilliant seasonal beers. Sip a few on the sunny terrace.

Shiraz Trail   CYCLING, WALKING
(www.walkingsa.org.au; ☉24hr) You can get the McLaren Vale vibe on this 8km walking/ cycling track, along an old railway line between McLaren Vale and Willunga. If you're up for it, the trail continues another 29km

to Marino Rocks as the **Coast to Vines Rail Trail**. Hire a bike from **Oxygen Cycles** (☑08-8323 7345; www.oxygencycles.com; 143 Main Rd; bike hire per half-day/full day/overnight $15/25/40; ☉10am-6pm Tue-Fri, 9am-5pm Sat, plus Sun & Mon Dec-Feb); ask the visitor information centre for a map.

☞ Tours

Off Piste 4WD Tours   TOURS
(☑0423 725 409; www.offpistetours.com.au; half-/full-day tours $199/299) Full- or half-day 4WD adventure tours around the Fleurieu for two to 10 folks, with lots of wilderness, wine, beer and beaches. A really great insight into the region, getting away from the well-trodden trail.

Adelaide's Top Food & Wine Tours   FOOD & DRINK
(☑08-8386 0888; www.topfoodandwinetours.com. au) Either a full-day winery tour ex-Adelaide ($160 per person), or a more cheese-and-wine trail through the Vale ($320).

DON'T MISS

MCLAREN VALE WINERIES

If the Barossa Valley is SA wine's old school, then McLaren Vale is the upstart teenager smoking cigarettes behind the shed and stealing nips from mum's sherry bottle. The luscious vineyards around here have a Tuscan haze in summer, rippling down to a calm coastline that's similarly Ligurian. This is shiraz country – solid, punchy and seriously good. Quaff some at five of the region's best:

Alpha Box & Dice (☑08-8323 7750; www.alphaboxdice.com; 8 Olivers Rd, McLaren Vale; ☉11am-5pm Mon-Fri, 10am-6pm Sat & Sun) One out of the box, this refreshing little gambler wins top billing for interesting blends, retro furnishings, quirky labels and laid-back staff.

Coriole (☑08-8323 8305; www.coriole.com; Chaffeys Rd, McLaren Vale; ☉10am-5pm Mon-Fri, 11am-5pm Sat & Sun) Take your regional tasting platter out into the garden of this beautiful cottage cellar door (1860) to share kalamata olives, homemade breads and Adelaide Hills' Woodside cheeses, made lovelier by a swill of the Redstone shiraz or the flagship chenin blanc.

d'Arenberg (☑08-8329 4888; www.darenberg.com.au; Osborn Rd, McLaren Vale; ☉10am-5pm) 'd'Arry's' relaxes atop a hillside with mighty fine views. The wine labels are part of the character of this place: the Dead Arm shiraz and the Broken Fishplate sauvignon blanc are our faves. Book for lunch at the excellent d'Arry's Verandah restaurant (mains $34 to $40).

Wirra Wirra (☑08-8323 8414; www.wirrawirra.com; cnr McMurtrie & Strout Rds, McLaren Vale; ☉10am-5pm Mon-Sat, 11am-5pm Sun) Fancy some *pétanque* with your plonk? This barnlike, 1894 cellar door has a grassy picnic area, and there's a roaring fire inside in winter. Sample reasonably priced stickies (dessert wines) and the super-popular Church Block blend. Whites include a citrusy viognier and an aromatic riesling.

SC Pannell (☑08-8323 8000; www.pannell.com.au; 60 Olivers Rd, McLaren Vale; ☉11am-5pm) With one of the best views in the business, SC Pannell (Steve, to his mates) produces excellent reds you can drink young. Cellar them if you want, but really, life's too short. Kitchen open noon to 4pm Thursday to Sunday.

Chook's Little Winery Tours
TOURS

(☑ 0414 922 200; www.chookslittlewinerytours. com.au; per person from $100) Small-group tours visiting some of the lesser-known boutique McLaren Vale wineries, ex-Adelaide, run by the irrepressible Chook McCoy.

✿✿ Festivals & Events

Sea & Vines Festival
FOOD & DRINK

(www.seaandvines.com.au) It seems like most of Adelaide gets tizzed-up and buses down to the annual Sea & Vines Festival over the June long weekend. Local wineries cook up seafood, splash wine around and host live bands. Can get messy later in the evening.

🛏 Sleeping

McLaren Vale Backpackers
HOSTEL $

(☑ 08-8323 0916; www.mclarenvalebackpackers. com.au; 106 Main Rd; dm $28, s & d from $70; ✳@✿) McLaren Vale's boisterous backpackers fills an old heath club on the main street, with winery workers' beds in the old squash courts and regular dorms and private rooms out the front. Plus there's a sauna, spa and plunge pool! Good weekly rates.

★ Bethany Chapel B&B
B&B $$

(☑ 0416 342 470; www.bethanychapelbnb.com; 219 Strout Rd; d $155-195; ✳) Rest in peace in this lovely split-level conversion of an 1854 Wesleyan chapel, with honey-coloured floorboards, a sunny rear deck and wide views across the vines (and the old cemetery – the residents therein also resting in peace). Terrific value for your own private, self-contained church (worship your complimentary bottle of Wirra Wirra on arrival).

Red Poles
B&B $$

(☑ 08-8323 8994; www.redpoles.com.au; 190 McMurtrie Rd; d with/without bathroom $125/115; ✳✿) Bushy, eccentric Red Poles is a great place to stay (and eat!). Aim for the rustic ensuite room (bigger than its two counterparts). Order some gnocchi with goats curd (mains from $10 to $30, serving 9am to 4.30pm) and check out some local artwork while you wait. Live music Sunday afternoons, and tastings of McLaren Vale Beer Company (www.mvbeer.com) ales.

McLaren Eye
RENTAL HOUSE $$$

(☑ 08-8383 7122; www.mclareneye.com.au; 36a Peters Creek Rd, Kangarilla; 1-/2-bedroom $450/800; ✳) Super-luxe hillside architectural splendour with an outlook from here to eternity, McLaren Eye has everything you need for a decadent stay – and every room has a view, even the bathroom (slip into the fancy two-person bath). In Kangarilla, 13km from McLaren Vale township. Two-night minimum.

✗ Eating

★ Blessed Cheese
CAFE, DELI $

(☑ 08-8323 7958; www.blessedcheese.com.au; 150 Main Rd; mains $11-18; ⊙8am-4pm Mon-Fri, to 5pm Sat, 9am-4pm Sun) The staff at this blessed cafe crank out great coffee, croissants, wraps, salads, tarts, burgers, cheese platters, massive cakes and funky sausage rolls. The menu changes every couple of days, always with an emphasis on local produce. Sniff the aromas emanating from the cheese counter – deliciously stinky! Love the lime citrus tarts and Spanish baked eggs.

Salopian Inn
MODERN AUSTRALIAN $$$

(☑ 08-8323 8769; www.salopian.com.au; cnr Main & McMurtrie Rds; mains $30-33; ⊙noon-3.30pm daily, 6pm-late Thu-Sat) This old vine-covered inn has been here since 1851 (!). Its latest incarnation features super Mod Oz offerings with an Asian twist: launch into the Berkshire pork buns or blue swimmer crab and prawn dumplings, with a bottle of something local which you can hand-select from the cellar. And there are 170 gins with which to construct your G&T!

❶ Information

McLaren Vale & Fleurieu Visitor Information Centre (☑ 1800 628 410, 08-8323 9944; www. mclarenvale.info; 796 Main Rd; ⊙9am-5pm Mon-Fri, 10am-4pm Sat & Sun) At the northern end of McLaren Vale's main strip. Winery info, plus accommodation assistance and Sealink bus/ferry bookings for Kangaroo Island. Pick up the *McLaren Vale Heritage Trail* brochure for an historic walk around the main street.

Willunga
POP 2420

A one-horse town with three pubs (a winning combo!), arty Willunga took off in 1840 when high-quality slate was discovered nearby and exported across Australia (used for everything from flagstones to billiard tables). Today, the town's early buildings along High St are occupied by some terrific eateries, B&B accommodation and galleries. The **Kidman Trail** (www.kidmantrail.org.au)

kicks off here, winding north to beyond the Barossa Valley.

Sights

★ **Willunga Farmers Market**   MARKET

(☑08-8556 4297; www.willungafarmersmarket.
com; Willunga Town Sq; ◷8am-12.30pm Sat)
Heavy on the organic, the bespoke and the
locally sourced, Willunga Farmers Market
happens every Saturday morning, on the
corner of High St and Main Rd. Buskers,
coffee, breakfast and hamper-filling goodies.
Brilliant.

Festivals & Events

Fleurieu Folk Festival   MUSIC

(www.fleurieufolkfestival.com.au) Willunga Recreation Park hosts the annual FFF over
a hyperactive weekend in October: more
acoustic guitars than you've ever seen in one
town before.

Sleeping & Eating

Willunga House B&B   B&B $$

(☑08-8556 2467; www.willungahouse.com.au; 1 St
Peters Tce; d incl breakfast from $200; ❉ 🛜 ☀) If
you're looking for a real treat, this graceful,
two-storey 1850 mansion off the main street
is for you: Baltic-pine floorboards, Italian
cherrywood beds, open fires, Indigenous art
and a swimming pool. Breakfast is a feast
of organic muesli, fruit salad and poached
pears, followed by cooked delights.

The Farm   B&B $$$

(☑08-8328 2140, 0434 125 172; www.thefarm
willunga.com.au; 11 Martin Rd; d from $290; ❉ 🛜)
High on the hill behind Willunga (great
views!), The Farm is a cafe/providore and
working organic farm, with two ritzy accommodation suites out the back, one
atop the other. You'll pay a bit more to be
upstairs, but really, both suites are stylish,
contemporary and utterly comfortable. DIY
breakfast from the fridge, or have it cooked
in the cafe.

Russell's Pizza   PIZZA $$

(☑08-8556 2571; 13 High St; pizzas from $24;
◷6-11.30pm Fri & Sat) It may look like a rus-
tic, ramshackle chicken coop, but Russell's is
the place to be on weekends for sensational
wood-fired pizza. No one minds the wait for
a meal (which could be an hour) – it's all
about the atmosphere. It's super popular, so
book way ahead.

Gulf St Vincent Beaches

There are some ace swimming beaches (but
no surf) along the Gulf St Vincent coastline
from suburban **Christies Beach** onto **Mas-
lin Beach**, the southern end of which is a
nudist and gay hang-out. Maslin is 45 min-
utes from Adelaide by car – just far enough
to escape the sprawling shopping centres
and new housing developments trickling
south from the city.

Port Willunga is the closest sand to
McLaren Vale and is the best swimming spot
along this stretch of coast. There's a superb
cafe on the clifftops here, with the remnant
piers of what once was a 145m-long jetty
down below.

Keep trucking south to cute little My-
ponga (population 540), where the craft
beers at **Smiling Samoyed Brewery** (☑08-
8558 6166; www.facebook.com/mypongabrewery;
46 Main South Rd, via Hansen St, Myponga; ◷11am-
6pm Fri-Sun) will have you smiling like a
hound. There are four main brews to try –
a *Kölsch,* an APA, IPA and a dark ale – plus
seasonal efforts.

Further south is soporific Yankalilla
(population 1020), which has the regional
**Yankalilla Bay Visitor Information Cen-
tre** (☑08-8558 0240, 1300 965 842; www.
yankalilla.sa.gov.au; 163 Main South Rd, Yanka-
lilla; ◷9am-5pm Mon-Fri, 10am-4pm Sat & Sun;
🛜). There's a small local history **museum**
(☑1300 965 842; www.yankalilla.sa.gov.au; 169
Main South Rd, Yankalilla; museum adult/child/
family $5/1/12; ◷9am-5pm Mon-Fri, 10am-4pm
Sat & Sun) out the back; look for the radar
antenna from the scuttled *HMAS Hobart*
(www.exhmashobart.com.au), now a nearby
dive site offshore.

About 60km south of Adelaide is Carrick-
alinga (population 290), which has a gor-
geous arc of white sandy beach: it's a very
chilled spot with no shops. For supplies
and accommodation, head to neighbour-
ing **Normanville** (population 1360). Here
you'll find a rambling pub, a supermarket
and a couple of caravan parks. About 10km
out of Normanville along Hay Flat Rd are
the picturesque little **Ingalalla Falls** (follow
the signs from the Yankalilla side of town).
Along similar lines, the **Hindmarsh Falls**
are off Hindmarsh Tiers Rd, inland from
Myponga.

About 14km south of Normanville is Sec-
ond Valley (population 500). The beach here
is good for a sheltered swim. Another 5km

south is the turn-off to **Rapid Bay**, an eerie semi-ghost-town with a *looong* fishing jetty.

There's not much at **Cape Jervis**, 107km from Adelaide, other than the Kangaroo Island ferry terminal, and the start point for the **Heysen Trail** (www.heysentrail.asn.au). Nearby, **Deep Creek Conservation Park** (☑ 08-8598 0263; www.environment.sa.gov.au; via Main South Rd, Deep Creek; per car $10; ☺24hr) has sweeping coastal views, a wicked waterfall, man-size yakkas *(Xanthorrhoea semiplana tateana)*, sandy beaches, kangaroos, kookaburras and popular bush-camping areas (per car $9 to $25).

☞ Tours

Adventure Kayaking SA   KAYAKING
(☑ 08-8295 8812; www.adventurekayak.com.au; tours from $180) ✒ Runs six-hour paddling trips around the Rapid Bay coastline, checking out sea caves, beaches and wildlife.

🛏 Sleeping & Eating

Jetty Carvan Park   CARAVAN PARK $
(☑ 08-8558 2038; www.jettycaravanparknormanville.com.au; 34 Jetty Rd, Normanville; unpowered/powered sites $34/42, cabins with/without bathroom from $121/82; ❄🐾) The pick of the two caravan parks in 'Normy', split into two sections either side of the Bungala River, Jetty CP has grassy sites, towering Norfolk Island pines and trim cabins. The beachfront kiosk across the car park does a mean fish and chips.

Ridgetop Retreats   COTTAGE $$
(☑ 08-8598 4169; www.southernoceanretreats.com.au; Tapanappa Rd, Deep Creek; d $225, extra adult/child $35/25) Off the road to Deep Creek Conservation Park are the curved roofs of the superb Ridgetop Retreats, designed by estimable SA architect Max Pritchard: three corrugated iron-clad, self-contained luxury units in the bush, with wood heaters, leather lounges and stainless-steel benchtops. See the website for less-pricey local options.

Victory Hotel   PUB FOOD $$
(☑ 08-8556 3083; www.victoryhotel.com.au; Main South Rd, Sellicks Beach; mains $17-33; ☺noon-2.30pm & 6-8.30pm) On the highway near Sellicks Beach is a rowdy, 1858 pub, the Victory. There are awesome views of the silvery gulf, a cheery, laid-back vibe and a beaut beer garden. Factor in inspired meals, an impressive cellar and wines by the glass and you'll be feeling victorious. Three cabins available too (doubles $150, or $165 including breakfast).

★ **Star of Greece**   MODERN AUSTRALIAN $$$
(☑ 08-8557 7420; www.starofgreececafe.com.au; 1 The Esplanade, Port Willunga; mains $29-38; ☺noon-3pm Wed-Sun, 6pm-late Fri & Sat, daily Jan) Port Willunga hosts the eternally busy, cliff-top seafood shack the Star of Greece, named after a shipwreck; it has funky decor, great staff and a sunny patio. We asked the waiter where the whiting was caught: he gazed across the bay and said, 'See that boat out there?'. There's a takeaway kiosk too (snacks $7 to $15, open weekends and school holidays).

Victor Harbor

POP 15,200

The biggest town on the Encounter Coast is Victor Harbor (yes, that's the correct spelling: blame one of SA's poorly schooled early Surveyor Generals). It's a raggedy, brawling holiday destination with three huge pubs and migrating whales offshore. 'Another day in paradise,' says a pony tailed pensioner to no-one in particular, as he shuffles along Ocean St in the sun.

⊙ Sights

South Australian Whale Centre   MUSEUM
(☑ 08-8551 0750; www.sawhalecentre.com; 2 Railway Tce; adult/child/family $9/4.50/24; ☺10.30am-5pm) Victor Harbor is on the migratory path of southern right whales (May to October). The multilevel South Australian Whale Centre has impressive whale displays (including a big stinky skull) and can give you the low-down on where to see them. Not whale season? Check out the big mammals in the 3D-cinema, and the new exhibit on Aboriginal whale stories. For whale sightings info, call the **Whale Information Hotline** (☑ 1900 942 537).

Encounter Coast Discovery Centre & Museum   MUSEUM
(☑ 08-8552 4440; www.nationaltrust.org.au/sa; 2 Flinders Pde; adult/child/family $6/4/16; ☺1-4pm) Inside Victor's 1866 Customs House on the foreshore, this National Trust museum has interesting local-history displays from pre-European times to around 1900: whaling, railways, shipping and local Aboriginal culture. Good for a rainy day.

🏃 Activities

Horse-Drawn Tram
OUTDOORS

(☑ 08-8551 0720; www.horsedrawntram.com.au; Foreshore; return adult/child/family $9/7/25; ☺ hourly 10.30am-3.30pm) Just offshore is the boulder-strewn **Granite Island**, connected to the mainland by a 632m causeway built in 1875. You can walk to the island, but it's much more fun to take the 1894 double-decker tram pulled by a big Clydesdale. It's the definitive Victor Harbor experience. Tickets are available from the driver or visitor information centre.

Encounter Bikeway
CYCLING

(☑ 08-8551 0777; www.victor.sa.gov.au/webdata/resources/files/bikeway.pdf) The much-wheeled Encounter Bikeway extends 30km from Victor Harbor to Laffin Point beyond Goolwa, past beaches, lookouts and the odd visiting whale. The visitors centre stocks maps (or download one); hire a bike from **Victor Harbor Cycle Skate Bay Rubber** (☑ 08-8552 1417; www.victorharborcycles.com; 73 Victoria St; bike hire per 4/8hr $30/40; ☺ 9am-5pm Mon-Fri, 10am-3pm Sat, 11am-3pm Sun).

☞ Tours

Big Duck
BOATING

(☑ 08-8555 2203; www.thebigduck.com.au; Granite Island Causeway; 45min tour adult/child/family $35/25/110, 90min $60/50/195) Do a lap of Granite Island and cruise along the coast to check out seals, dolphins and whales (in season) on the rigid inflatable Big Duck boat. Call or go online for times and bookings. Strict guidelines about proximity to whales are adhered to.

🎊 Festivals & Events

Schoolies Festival
MUSIC

(www.encounteryouth.com.au/schoolies-festival) Beware: come November, Victor Harbor's grassy foreshore runs rampant with teenage school-leavers blowing off steam. Accommodation dries up.

🛏 Sleeping & Eating

Anchorage
GUESTHOUSE $

(☑ 08-8552 5970; www.anchorageseafronthotel.com; 21 Flinders Pde; s/d/tr/apt from $65/90/135/260; ✴🤶) This grand old guesthouse exudes seaside charm. Immaculately maintained, great-value rooms open off long corridors. Most rooms face the beach, and some have a balcony (you'd pay through the nose for this in Sydney!). The cheapest rooms are view-free and share bathrooms. The **cafe-bar** (breakfast mains $5-17, lunch & dinner $12-30; ☺ 8am-late) downstairs is a winner.

Victor Harbor City Inn
MOTEL $$

(☑ 08-8552 2455; www.victorharborcityinn.com.au; 51 Ocean St; d/2-bedroom unit from $115/135; ✴🤶) Smack dab in the middle of town, this old '70s motel has been on the receiving end of much renovation recently: new beds, new linen, new bathrooms, new paint... It's a modest, 15-room affair – great value for money and brilliantly located.

Nino's
CAFE, ITALIAN $$

(☑ 08-8552 3501; www.ninoscafe.com.au; 17 Albert Pl; mains $19-38; ☺ 9.30am-late) Nino's cafe has been here since 1974 (and the building a lot longer) but it manages to put a contemporary sheen on downtown VH. Hip young staff and a mod interior set the scene for gourmet pizzas, burgers, pasta, salads, risottos and meaty Italian mains. Good coffee, cakes and takeaways too.

🔒 Shopping

Alexandrina Cheese Company
CHEESE

(☑ 08-8554 9666; www.alexandrinacheese.com.au; Sneyd Rd, Mt Jagged; tastings free, cheese platters from $15; ☺ noon-5pm Mon-Fri, 10am-4.30pm Sat & Sun) On the road to Mt Compass, 18km north of Victor Harbor, this Fleurieu success story opens its doors to cheese fans and milkshake mavens. You can have a taste of the gouda, the edam and the feta, then buy a block of the powerful vintage cheddar to go.

ℹ Information

Victor Harbor Visitor Information Centre
(☑ 08-8551 0777; www.tourismvictorharbor.com.au; Foreshore; ☺ 9am-5pm) Handles tour and accommodation bookings. Stocks the *Beaches on the South Coast* brochure for when you feel like a swim, and when you don't, the *Victor Harbor Historic Markers Discovery Trail* walking-tour brochure.

Port Elliot
POP 3100

About 8km east of Victor Harbor, historic (and today, rather affluent) Port Elliot is set back from **Horseshoe Bay**, a gorgeous orange-sand arc with gentle surf and good swimming. Norfolk Island pines reach for the sky, and there are whale-spotting updates posted on the pub wall. If there are whales around, wander out to **Freemans Knob** lookout at the end of the Strand and peer through the free telescope.

🏃 Activities

Port Elliot Bike & Leisure Hire　　CYCLING
(📞0448 370 007; www.portelliotbikeleisurehire.
myob.net; 85-87 Hill St; per day from $40; ⏰9am-5pm Mon-Sat, from 10.30am Sun) Grab a mountain bike and hit the Encounter Bikeway (p748), running through Port Elliot to Goolwa (15km east) and Victor Harbor (7km west).

Surfing

Commodore Point, at the eastern end of Horseshoe Bay, and nearby **Boomer Beach** and **Knights Beach**, have reliable waves for experienced surfers, with swells often holding around 2m. The beach at otherwise-missable **Middleton**, the next town towards Goolwa, also has solid breaks. Further afield, try wild **Waitpinga Beach** and **Parsons Beach**, 12km southwest of Victor Harbor.

The best surfing season is March to June, when the northerlies doth blow. See www.southaustralia.com for info, and www.surfsouthoz.com for surf reports. There are a few good surfing schools in Middleton.

Surf & Sun　　SURFING
(📞1800 786 386; www.surfandsun.com.au; 44 Victor Harbor-Goolwa Rd, Middleton; 🚗) Offers board/wetsuit hire (per half-day $20/10), and surfing lessons ($55 for a two-hour lesson, including gear). Very kid friendly (two-hour family lessons $240).

🛏 Sleeping & Eating

⭐**Port Elliot Beach House YHA**　　HOSTEL $
(📞08-8554 1885; www.yha.com.au; 13 The Strand; dm/tw/d/f from $30/91/110/125; ❄@🌐) Built in 1910 (the old Arcadia Hotel), this sandstone beauty has sweeping views across the Port Elliot coastline. Drag your eyes away from the scenery and you'll find polished floorboards, new ensuite rooms, nice linen and contemporary colour schemes: a million-dollar fit-out. Surf lessons are almost mandatory, and the fab Flying Fish Cafe is 200m away.

BIG4 Port Elliot Holiday Park　　CARAVAN PARK $
(📞1800 008 480, 08-8554 2134; www.portelliotholidaypark.com.au; Victor Harbor-Goolwa Rd; powered sites/cabins/units/cottages from $35/90/115/145; ❄🌐) In an unbeatable position behind the Horseshoe Bay dunes (it can be a touch windy), this grassy, 5-hectare park has all the requisite facilities, including a shiny camp kitchen and all-weather barbecue area. Lush grass and healthy-looking trees. Prices plummet in winter.

⭐**Flying Fish Cafe**　　MODERN AUSTRALIAN $$
(📞08-8554 3504; www.flyingfishcafe.com.au; 1 The Foreshore; mains cafe $6-20, restaurant $28-45; ⏰cafe 9am-4pm daily, restaurant noon-3pm daily & 6-8pm Fri & Sat; 🚗) Sit down for a cafe breakfast and you'll be here all day – the views of Horseshoe Bay are sublime. Otherwise, grab some takeaway Coopers-battered flathead and chips and head for the sand. At night things get classy, with à la carte mains focusing on independent SA producers. One of SA's must-visit foodie haunts.

Goolwa
POP 2200

Much more low-key and elegant than kissing-cousin Victor Harbor, historic Goolwa is an unassuming river port where the rejuvenated Murray River empties into the sea. Beyond the dunes is a fantastic beach with ranks of breakers rolling in from the ocean, same as it ever was...

◉ Sights & Activities

Steam Exchange Brewery　　BREWERY
(📞08-8555 3406; www.steamexchange.com.au; 1 Cutting Rd, Goolwa Wharf; ⏰11.30am-5pm Wed-Sun) Down on the wharf, the Steam Exchange Brewery is a locally run brewery, turning out stouts and ales. Sip a Southerly Buster Dark Ale and look out over the rippling river. And SA's only single malt whiskey distillery is here! Small tasting fee; group tours by arrangement.

👉 Tours

Canoe the Coorong　　CANOEING
(📞0424 826 008; www.canoethecoorong.com; tours adult/child $135/85) 🛶 Full-day paddles around the Coorong and Murray River mouth, departing Goolwa. Includes lunch and a bush-tucker walk through the dunes. Three-hour sunset tours and overnight expeditions also available.

Spirit of the Coorong　　CRUISE
(📞08-8555 2203, 1800 442 203; www.coorongcruises.com.au; Goolwa Wharf) 🛶 Eco-cruises on the Murray and into the Coorong National

Park, including lunch and guided walks. The four-hour Coorong Discovery Cruise (adult/child $95/69) runs on Thursdays all year, plus Mondays from October to May. The six-hour Coorong Adventure Cruise ($110/76) runs on Sundays all year, plus Wednesdays from October to May. Bookings essential.

Cruise the Coorong CRUISE
(✆0410 488 779; www.cruisethecoorong.com.au; Goolwa Wharf; adult/child $130/100) Small-boat, 6½-hour Coorong Ultimate cruises with walks, bush tucker, seal spotting and digging for *pipis* (shellfish) on the beach. Lunch and snacks included. Shorter Coorong Highlights tours also available during school holidays (adult/child $60/50).

✪ Festivals & Events

**South Australian Wooden
Boat Festival** SPORTS
(www.woodenboatfestival.com.au) Wooden boats of all sizes, configurations and degrees of quaintness make a splash in the Murray in April in odd-numbered years.

🛏 Sleeping & Eating

Captains Quarters B&B $$
(✆0402 254 742; www.facebook.com/captains quartersgoolwa; 15 Wildman St; d from $150) It looks like an oldie, but it's actually a newie. Built in 2010, Captains Quarters is a super cute cottage in the Goolwa backstreets, just a short walk from the shops and cafes. Sleeps six in three bedrooms – a very clever use of space on a tight block of land.

★Boathouse Retreat B&B $$$
(✆08-8555 0338; www.birksharbour.com.au/stay/boathouse; 138 Liverpool Rd; d from $325; ❄☎) Around the riverfront from downtown Goolwa, the Boathouse is a photogenic, woody boat shed (minus the boat), with a sunny deck and private marina out the front full of bobbing boats. It's a two-person affair, angled towards the romantically inclined. DIY breakfast goodies in the fridge.

Australasian BOUTIQUE HOTEL $$$
(✆08-8555 1088; www.australasian1858.com; 1 Porter St; d incl breakfast from $395; ❄☎) This gorgeous 1858 stone hotel at the head of Goolwa's main street has been reborn as a B&B, with a sequence of Japanese-inspired decks and glazed extensions, and an upmarket dining room. The five suites all have views, and the breakfast will make you want to wake up here again. Two-night minimum.

Bombora CAFE $$
(✆08-8555 5396; www.bomboragoolwa.com; Goolwa Beach Car Park, Beach Rd; mains $10-28; ⏱8am-5pm Fri-Mon, closed mid-May–mid-Jul) Down at the Goolwa surf beach, this modest little brick bunker has a big rep, serving baguettes, burgers, salads, brilliant bacon-and-egg damper with homemade chutney and Goolwa cockles. Sit in the adjunct raised pavilion for surf views, or just grab an ice cream to go. Open daily during school holidays, and for dinner in summer.

Motherduck CAFE $$
(✆08-8555 1462; www.motherduckcafe.com.au; 1/13 Cadell St; mains breakfast $8-21, lunch $13-27; ⏱8am-4pm Tue-Sun; 🐾) A buzzy highlight of the Goolwa shopping strip is this crafty little cafe, which always seems busier than anywhere else in Goolwa. Exposed stone walls, bravely strong coffee, Spanish-style baked eggs, Langhorne Creek wines, curries, pancakes and Jack Johnson on the stereo – the perfect small-town cafe?

ⓘ Information

Goolwa Visitor Information Centre (✆1300 466 592, bike hire 0402 814 541; www.visit alexandrina.com; 4 Goolwa Tce; ⏱9am-5pm Mon-Fri, 10am-4pm Sat & Sun) Inside an 1857 post office, with detailed local info (including accommodation). Bike hire also available, if you feel like tackling the **Encounter Bikeway** (✆1300 466 592; www.victor.sa.gov.au/web data/resources/files/bikeway.pdf).

KANGAROO ISLAND

From Cape Jervis, car ferries chug across the swells of the Backstairs Passage to Kangaroo Island (KI). Long devoid of tourist trappings, the island these days is a booming destination for wilderness and wildlife fans – it's a veritable zoo of seals, birds, dolphins, echidnas and (of course) kangaroos. Still, the island remains rurally paced and underdeveloped – the kind of place where kids ride bikes to school and farmers advertise for wives on noticeboards. Island wine and produce is a highlight.

History

Many KI place names are French, attributable to explorer Nicholas Baudin who surveyed the coast in 1802 and 1803. Baudin's English rival, Matthew Flinders, named the island in 1802 after his crew feasted

Kangaroo Island

20 km
10 miles

Rapid Head

Victor Harbor (50km);
McLaren Vale (75km)

Cape Jervis

Backstairs Passage

Antechamber Bay

Cape
Willoughby

Hog Bay

28

19

Dudley
Peninsula

26

Dudley
Peninsula
Conservation
Park

Penneshaw

Eastern
Cove

Baudin
Beach

American
River

Island
Beach

Browns
Beach

Pelican
Lagoon

Pennington
Bay

Nepean Bay

SOUTHERN
OCEAN

29

D'Estrees
Bay

Point
Marsden

Natural
Resources
Centre

Kingscote

Brownlow

Western
Cove

Bay of
Shouls

Hog Bay Rd

4

Cape
Cassini

Emu
Bay

Emu Bay

North Coast Rd

Cygnet
River

Kingscote
Airport

Cygnet River

20

5

7

6

Parndana

Timber Creek

Cape Gantheaume
Conservation Park

Cape
Gantheaume

Eleanor River

9 10

14

Stokes
Bay

Middle
River

15

23

Cygnet River

Investigator Strait

Western River
Conservation
Park

Snug
Cove

Playford Hwy

Vivonne

Vivonne
Bay

Vivonne
Bay

16

Vivonne Bay
Conservation
Park

18 30

Karatta

South Coast Rd

West End Hwy

Flinders Chase
Visitor
Information
Centre

Hanson
Bay

21

8

25

Flinders Chase
National Park

13

Snake
Lagoon

24

Maupertius
Bay

1   12

Cape du
Couedic

Harvey's Return

Cape
Borda

2

22

11

27

West Bay

Kangaroo Island

on kangaroo meat here. By this stage the island was uninhabited, but archaeologists think Indigenous Australians lived here as recently as 2000 years ago. Why they deserted KI is a matter of conjecture, though the answer is hinted at in the Indigenous name for KI: Karta (Land of the Dead). In the early 1800s an Indigenous presence (albeit a tragically displaced one) was re-established on KI when whalers and sealers abducted Aboriginal women from Tasmania and brought them here.

🏃 Activities

The safest **swimming** is along the north coast, where the water is warmer and there are fewer rips. Try Emu Bay, Stokes Bay, Snelling Beach or Western River Cove.

For **surfing**, hit the swells along the south coast. Pennington Bay has strong, reliable breaks; Vivonne Bay and Hanson Bay in the southwest also serve up some tasty waves. Pick up the *Kangaroo Island Surfing Guide* brochure from visitor information centres, or do a web search for 'Kangaroo Island Surfing Guide' and follow the download link on www.tourkangarooisland.com.au.

There's plenty to see under your own steam on KI, including **bushwalking** trails ranging from 1km to the epic 61km, five-day Kangaroo Island Wilderness Trail (p759).

Check out www.tourkangarooisland.com.au/experiences for more trail info.

The waters around KI are home to 230 species of fish, plus coral and around 60 shipwrecks – great **snorkelling** and **diving**! **Kangaroo Island Dive & Adventures** (☎08-8346 3422) runs diving trips and offers gear and kayak hire; call for current prices.

There's good **fishing** around the island, including jetties at Kingscote, Penneshaw, Emu Bay and Vivonne Bay. Fishing charter tours (half-/full day per person from $150/250) include tackle and refreshments, and you keep what you catch. Try **KI Fishing Charters** (☎0401 727 234; www.kiboathire.com.au; 5 people per half-/full-day $550/950) or **Kangaroo Island Fishing Adventures** (☎08-8559 3232; www.kangarooislandadventures.com.au).

👉 Tours

Groovy Grape TOURS
(☎08-8440 1640, 1800 059 490; www.groovygrape.com.au) Two-day, all-inclusive, small-group wildlife safaris ($435, or $390 in winter) ex-Adelaide, with sandboarding, swimming, campfires and all the main sights.

Adventures Beyond ADVENTURE
(☎1300 736 014; www.adventuresbeyond.com.au; 1-/2-day tours $275/435) All-inclusive two-day island wildlife tours (small backpacker groups), departing Adelaide, with lots of

activities (sandboarding, snorkelling, hiking and farm-stay accommodation...). One-day tours also available.

Kangaroo Island Adventure Tours TOURS (📞 08-8202 8678; www.kiadventuretours.com.au) Two-day, all-inclusive tours ex-Adelaide (from $445 with dorm accommodation, a little bit more for private rooms – both at Vivonne Bay Lodge) with a backpacker bent and plenty of activities.

🛏 Sleeping

KI accommodation is expensive, adding insult to your wallet's injury after the pricey ferry ride. Self-contained cottages, B&Bs and beach houses start at around $160 per night per double (usually with a two-night minimum stay). There are, however, some great camp sites around the island, plus a few midrange motels and unsophisticated hostels. Quality caravan parks are scarce.

There are a few agencies which can help book accommodation on the island:

Gateway Visitor Information Centre (📞 1800 811 080; www.tourkangarooisland.com. au/accommodation)

Kangaroo Island Holiday Accommodation (📞 08-8553 9007; www. kangarooislandholidayaccommodation.com.au)

SeaLink (📞 13 13 01; www.sealink.com.au/ kangaroo-island-accommodation)

ℹ Information

Kangaroo Island Hospital (📞 08-8553 4200; www.countryhealthsa.sa.gov.au; 3 Esplanade; ⏱ 24hr) is in Kingscote.

There are ATMs in Kingscote and Penneshaw.

Mobile phone reception can be patchy outside the main towns (reception is best with Telstra).

The main **Gateway Visitor Information Centre** (p755) is in Penneshaw.

ℹ Getting There & Away

AIR

Kingscote Airport (📞 13 17 13; www.kangaroo island.sa.gov.au/airport) is 14km from Kingscote. **Regional Express** (Rex; www.regionalexpress. com.au) flies daily between Adelaide and Kingscote (return from $280).

Car-hire companies and some accommodation providers will meet you when you land. **Kangaroo Island Transfers** (📞 0427 887 575; www. kitransfers.com.au) connects the airport with Kingscote (per person $25), American River ($70 for one or two people) and Penneshaw ($90 for one or two people). Bookings essential.

BUS

SeaLink (📞 13 13 01; www.sealink.com.au) runs daily buses (return adult/child $48/24, 2¼ hours one way) between Adelaide and Cape Jervis on the Fleurieu Peninsula, where the ferry departs.

FERRY

SeaLink operates the car ferry between Cape Jervis and Penneshaw on KI, with at least three ferries each way daily (return adult/ child from $98/50, bicycles/motorcycles/cars $22/66/282, 45 minutes one-way). One driver is included with the vehicle price (cars only, not bikes).

ℹ Getting Around

Forget public transport: you're gonna need some wheels. The island's main roads are sealed, but the rest are gravel, including those to Cape Willoughby, Cape Borda and the North Coast Rd (take it slowly, especially at night). There's petrol at Kingscote, Penneshaw, American River, Parndana and Vivonne Bay.

BUS

SeaLink (p753) coaches run from Penneshaw to American River and Kingscote (one-way adult/child $16.50/9 and $19.50/11 respectively). Call for times and booking.

Rockhopper (📞 08-8553 4500; www.kangaroo island.sa.gov.au/rockhopper) is a community

---

ALL CREATURES GREAT & SMALL

You bump into a lot of wildlife on KI (sometimes literally). Kangaroos, wallabies, bandicoots and possums come out at night, especially in wilderness areas such as Flinders Chase National Park. Koalas and platypuses were introduced to Flinders Chase in the 1920s when it was feared they would become extinct on the mainland. Echidnas mooch around in the undergrowth, while goannas and tiger snakes keep KI suitably scaly.

Of the island's 267 bird species, several are rare or endangered. One notable species – the dwarf emu – has gone the way of the dodo. Glossy black cockatoos may soon follow it out the door due to habitat depletion.

Offshore, dolphins and southern right whales are often seen cavorting, and there are colonies of little penguins, New Zealand fur seals and Australian sea lions here too.

KANGAROO ISLAND TOUR PASS

If you plan on seeing most of the main sights, save some cash with a **Kangaroo Island Tour Pass** (☑08-8553 4444; www.environment.sa.gov.au/parks/entry-fees/parks-passes; adult/child/family $70/43/191), which covers all KI park and conservation area entry fees, plus ranger-guided tours at Seal Bay, Kelly Hill Caves, Cape Borda and Cape Willoughby. Available online, at visitor centres or at most sights.

bus service traversing eastern and western routes from Kingscote. The eastern service runs three times each way on Wednesdays, stopping at American River and Penneshaw; the western service runs twice daily on Tuesdays and Fridays, visiting Cygnet River, Parndana and Vivonne Bay. Flat-rate fares are one-way adult/child $10/5. Call for bookings.

CAR HIRE

Not all Adelaide car-rental companies will let you take their cars onto KI. **Budget** (www.budget.com.au) and **Hertz** (www.hertz.com.au) supply cars to Penneshaw, Kingscote and Kingscote Airport.

Penneshaw & Dudley Peninsula

Looking across Backstairs Passage to the Fleurieu Peninsula, Penneshaw (population 300), on the north shore of the Dudley Peninsula, is the ferry arrival point and KI's second-biggest town. The passing tourist trade lends a transience to the businesses here, but the pub and the backpacker joints remain authentically grounded.

Sights

Kangaroo Island Farmers Market　MARKET
(☑08-8553 1217; www.facebook.com/pg/kangaroo islandfarmersmarket; Lloyd Collins Reserve, 99 Middle Tce, Penneshaw; ⊙9am-1pm 1st Sun of the month) Baked goods, chutneys, seafood, olive oil, honey, eggs, cheese, yoghurt...and of course buskers and wine! SeaLink (p753) offers dedicated passenger-only return tickets (adult/child $41/31) from the mainland if you'd just like to visit the market for the day.

Cape Willoughby Lightstation　LIGHTHOUSE
(☑accommodation 08-8553 4410; www.environ ment.sa.gov.au/parks; Cape Willoughby Rd, Cape

Willoughby; tours adult/child/family $16/10/42, self-guided tour not incl lighthouse $3; ⊙guided tours 11.30am, 12.30pm & 2pm) About 28km southeast of Penneshaw (unsealed road) on a treeless headland, this tidy white turret started shining out in 1852 (SA's first lighthouse) and is now used as a weather station. Inside is lots of shipwreck info, with basic cottage accommodation adjacent (doubles from $170, extra person $30). Extra tours at 3pm and 4pm during school holidays.

Tours

Nocturnal Tour　WILDLIFE
(☑0448 575 801; www.kiwildlifesafari.net; tours adult/child $65/50) Two-hour after-dark tours ex-Penneshaw, looking for kangaroos, possums and wallabies under a great spangle of southern stars.

Kangaroo Island Ocean Safari　ADVENTURE
(☑0419 772 175; www.kangarooislandoceansafari. com.au; tours adult/child $77/55) Hop aboard this buoyant 12-seater for a 75-minute nautical tour ex-Penneshaw, spying seals, dolphins, birds and (sometimes) whales.

Sleeping

Antechamber Bay South Campground　CAMPGROUND $
(☑08-8204 1910; www.environment.sa.gov.au/parks; off Creek Bay Rd, Antechamber Bay; unpowered sites per person/car $9/15) Within Lashmar Conservation Park where the Chapman River runs into Antechamber Bay, these dozen refreshingly low-key camp sites are right on the riverbank, with fire pits, a BBQ hut and silvery bream in the water. There are more sites on the north bank of the river.

Kangaroo Island Backpackers　HOSTEL $
(☑0439 750 727; www.kangarooislandbackpackers. com; 43 North Tce, Penneshaw; dm/s/tw/d/f from $28/38/55/80/130; ❄) A tidy, affable independent hostel a short wander from both the pub and the ferry dock – proximity is the main asset here. It's a simple, compact set-up, but hey, you're on holiday on an island – who needs interior design? Dangle a line off the jetty instead.

Wallaby Beach House　RENTAL HOUSE $$
(☑08-8362 5293; www.wallabybeachhouse.com. au; off Hog Bay Rd, Browns Beach; d from $180, extra person $25) A secluded, self-contained three-bedroom beach house, 13km west of Penneshaw on unpeopled Browns Beach. Simple beachy decor, with broad sunset

views and passing seals, dolphins and penguins to keep you company. Sleeps six.

✗ Eating

★ Dudley Wines Cellar Door   CAFE $$
(☑ 08-8553 1333; www.dudleywines.com.au; 1153 Cape Willoughby Rd, Cuttlefish Bay; mains $15-32; ⊙ 10am-5pm) About 12km east of Penneshaw, KI's pioneering winery has a superb cellar door (doubling in size when we visited). It's a fancy corrugated-iron shed, with astonishing views back to the mainland and serving superb pizzas (try the King George whiting version), oysters and buckets of prawns – perfect with a bottle of chardonnay on the deck.

Fish   SEAFOOD $$
(☑ 0439 803 843; www.2birds1squid.com; 43 North Tce, Penneshaw; mains $13-24; ⊙ 4.30-8pm mid-Oct–Apr) Takeaway fish and chips like you ain't never had before – grilled, beer-battered or crumbed whiting and garfish – plus giant KI scallops, marron (freshwater crayfish), lobster medallions, prawns and oysters. Dunk them in an array of homemade sauces. Hours can vary; call in advance.

ℹ Information

Gateway Visitor Information Centre (☑ 1800 811 080, 08-8553 1185; www.tourkangaroo island.com.au; 3 Howard Dr, Penneshaw; ⊙ 9am-5pm Mon-Fri, 10am-4pm Sat & Sun; ☏) Just outside Penneshaw on the road to Kingscote; brimming with brochures and maps. Also books accommodation, and sells park entry tickets and **Kangaroo Island Tour Pass**.

American River

POP 230

Between Penneshaw and Kingscote, on the way to nowhere in particular, American River squats redundantly by the glassy **Pelican Lagoon**. The town was named after a crew of American sealers who built a trading schooner here in 1804. Today, there's just a general store and a pod of pelicans.

🛏 Sleeping & Eating

American River Camping Ground   CAMPGROUND $
(☑ 08-8553 4500; www.kangarooisland.sa.gov.au/camping; Tangara Dr; unpowered/powered sites per 2 people $15/25, extra person $5) Shady, council-run camping by the lagoon, with fire pits, showers, toilets and a nifty BBQ hut. Pay via self-registration.

Mercure Kangaroo Island Lodge   LODGE $$
(☑ 1800 355 581, 08-8553 7053; www.kilodge.com. au; 201-216 Scenic Dr; d from $160; ❄ ☏ ☒) Up-to-scratch motel-style suites overlooking either the pool or lagoon (the rammed-earth wing has the best rooms). The restaurant plates up buffet breakfasts and dinners featuring lots of local seafood (mains $28 to $36, serving 7.30am to 9am and 6pm to 8pm).

Oyster Farm Shop   SEAFOOD $
(☑ 08-8553 7122; www.facebook.com/oysterfarm shop; 486 Tangara Dr, American River; meals $5-20; ⊙ 11am-3pm) Run by a local oyster farm, this little shack acts as an outlet for sustainable seafood producers from all over KI. Oysters, marron, abalone, King George whiting...even barramundi, cooked into meals or take away uncooked. Get change from $10 for a dozen fresh unshucked oysters.

★ KI Tru Thai   THAI $$
(☑ 0408 848 211; Willowbrook, 148 Old Salt Lake Rd, Haines; mains $9-18, four dishes $30; ⊙ 5.30-8.30pm Thu) Hungry? Thursday night? If it's 'affirmative' to all of the above, wander over to this big steel farm shed (a couple of kilometers down a dirt road across from the American River turn-off) for some brilliant home-cooked Thai curries and stir-fries. Live music, kitsch Thai paintings, bark-chip floor – it's a great fun night!

Kingscote

POP 2040

Once slated as the future capital city of the South Australian colony, snoozy Kingscote (kings-coat) is the main settlement on KI, and the hub of island life. It's a photogenic town with swaying Norfolk Island pines, a couple of pubs and some decent eateries.

◉ Sights

Kangaroo Island Brewery   BREWERY
(☑ 0409 264 817; www.kangarooislandbrewery. com.au; 61 North Coast Rd; ⊙ 11am-7pm Sat & Sun) Here a brewery, there a brewery... Seems you can't go anywhere in Australia these days without being tempted by craft beer, and KI is no exception. This neat, black roadside shack pours some tasty drops, including a ginger wheat bear and Sheoak Stout.

Kangaroo Island Spirits   DISTILLERY
(KIS; ☑ 08-8553 9211; www.kispirits.com.au; 856 Playford Hwy, Cygnet River; tastings free, bottles from $42; ⊙ 11am-5pm Wed-Mon, daily during

school holidays) This fiesty little moonshiner makes small-batch gin with KI native juniper berries, plus vodka, brandy and liqueurs (pray the organic honey-and-walnut version hasn't sold out).

Island Pure Sheep Dairy   DAIRY
(☑08-8553 9110; www.islandpure.com.au; 127 Gum Creek Rd, Cygnet River; tours adult/child/family $6.50/5.50/22; ☺11am-4pm) Near Cygnet River, 12km from Kingscote, this dairy features 1500 sheep lining up to be milked (from 2pm daily). Take a tour of the factory, which includes yoghurt and cheese tastings (the halloumi is magic).

Island Beehive   FARM
(☑08-8553 0080; www.island-beehive.com.au; 59 Playford Hwy; tours adult/child/family $5/4/15; ☺9am-5pm, tours every 30min 9.30am-3.30pm) Runs 20-minute factory tours where you can study up on hard-working Ligurian bees and bee-keeping, then stock up on by-products (bee-products?) including delicious organic honey and honeycomb ice cream.

🏃 Activities

Pelican Feeding   BIRDWATCHING
(☑08-8553 3112; www.kipenguincentre.com.au/pelican-feeding.php; Kingscote Wharf; adult/child $5/3; ☺5pm) Pull up a pew and watch the daily feeding frenzy of 20-something ravenous pelicans at Kingscote Wharf. The host is well protected – hatted, gloved and booted – and mic'd-up so you can hear the spiel above the voraciously snapping beaks.

👉 Tours

Kangaroo Island Marine Adventures   TOURS
(☑0427 315 286, 08-8553 3227; www.kimarineadventures.com.au) One-hour north coast boat tours (adult/child $60/45) and longer three-hour jaunts (adult/child $190/110), spotting dolphins, seal colonies and eagles and visiting remote areas of KI. You can swim with the dolphins – and these guys adhere to a rigorous marine-mammal interaction policy – but be aware that natural behaviours and breeding patterns may be affected by such interactions.

🛏 Sleeping & Eating

**Kangaroo Island Central
Backpackers**   HOSTEL $
(☑08-8553 2787; www.kicentralbackpackers.com; 19 Murray St; dm/s/d/cabins from $27/65/65/80; ❋⊚) Just a couple of blocks from Kingscote's main strip, this small, innocuous hostel is clean and affordable, and has a cosy lounge, lush lawns and a beaut ensuite double cabin out the back. It feels like staying at someone's house – good or bad, depending on how sociable you're feeling.

Haven Cottage   RENTAL HOUSE $$
(☑0447 062 867; www.sealink.com.au/kangaroo-island-accommodation/487-haven-cottage; cnr Ayliffe St & Telegraph Rd; f from $180, extra person $25; ⊚) Fronted by standard roses, a lush patch of lawn and a wisteria-hung arbour, Haven Cottage is an old iron-clad house with a refreshing dearth of lace and 'ye olde' affectation (cast-iron beds are about as twee as things get). Three bedrooms; sleeps six (bunk beds for the kids). Two-night minimum.

Aurora Ozone Hotel   HOTEL $$
(☑08-8553 2011; www.ozonehotelki.com.au; 67 Chapman Tce; d $170-220, 1-/2-bedroom apt from $250/420; ❋⊚⊛) Opposite the foreshore with killer views, the 100-year-old Ozone pub has quality pub rooms upstairs, motel rooms, and stylish deluxe apartments in a new wing across the street. The eternally busy bistro (mains $18 to $42) serves meaty grills and seafood, and a range of KI wines at the bar.

Bella   ITALIAN $$
(☑08-8553 0400; 54 Dauncey St; pizzas $14-41, mains lunch $11-25, dinner $29-34; ☺10am-8.30pm Mon-Sat, 4-8pm Sun) Sit inside or on the pavement, al fresco, at Bella, a cheery Italian cafe/restaurant/pizza bar. Pizzas start around lunchtime (eat in or take away); dinner is à la carte (or pizzas), featuring American River oysters, Island Pure halloumi, local juniper-spiced roo and KI whiting.

North Coast Road

Exquisite beaches (calmer than the south coast), bushland and undulating pastures dapple the North Coast Rd, running from Kingscote along the coast to the Playford Hwy 85km west. There's not a whole lot to do here other than swan around on the beach – sounds good!

👁 Sights

About 18km from Kingscote, **Emu Bay** is a holiday hamlet with a 5km-long, white-sand beach flanked by dunes – one of KI's best swimming spots. Around 36km further west, **Stokes Bay** has a penguin rookery and broad rock pool, accessible by scrambling through a 20m tunnel in the cliffs at the bay's eastern end (mind your head!). Beware the rip outside the pool.

Further west along North Coast Rd, the view as you look back over Snelling Beach from atop Constitution Hill is awesome! Continue 7km west and you'll hit the turn-off to **Western River Cove**, where a small beach is crowded in by sombre basalt cliffs. The ridge-top road in is utterly scenic (and steep).

Snelling Beach BEACH
(off North Coast Rd, Middle River) The best swimming beach on the north coast, with a lovely arc of powdery sand and sheltered shallows. There's not much else at Snelling by way of facilities but that's all part of its charm.

Emu Bay Lavender FARM
(☑08-8553 5338; www.emubaylavender.com.au; 75 Emu Bay Rd, Wisanger; ⊙10am-4.30pm Wed-Sun mid-Sep–mid-May, daily during school holidays) FREE Lavender is yet another species that thrives in KI's Mediterranean climate. Follow the purple haze to this cute little roadside farm, where you can sniff out some gifts (oils, soaps, fumigating lavender bags) or grab a coffee and a lavender-infused snack.

🛏 Sleeping & Eating

Discovery Lagoon Caravan & Camping Grounds CARAVAN PARK $
(☑08-8553 5220; www.discoverycamping.com. au; 948 North Coast Rd, Emu Bay; unpowered sites $23-28, cabins $65) Not far along the road into Emu Bay after you turn off the North Coast Rd, this campground has lots of grass and shade, a neat camp kitchen and toilets, and the lake itself (or rather, lagoon) to look at, with ghostly white trunks emerging from the waters. Check in at 948 North Coast Rd.

Lifetime Private Rentals RENTAL HOUSE $$$
(www.life-time.com.au; North Coast Rd, Snelling Beach, Middle River; d from $430, extra person $25; ❄) Pricey but worth every penny, these four gorgeous stone-and-timber houses dot the hillsides above beautiful Snelling Beach (actually, they're not that pricey for groups from $570 for six people in three bedrooms). Expect decks, big windows, quirky art and knock-out views. Food-and-accommodation packages also available, including lunch with Hannaford & Sachs.

Rockpool Café CAFE $$
(☑08-8559 2277; www.facebook.com/therockpool cafe; off North Coast Rd, Stokes Bay; mains $15-28; ⊙11am-5pm mid-Sep–mid-May) Don't worry about sandy feet at this casual, al fresco joint by the beach in Stokes Bay. 'What's the house special?', we asked. 'Whatever I feel like doin'!', said the chef (usually seafood, washed down with local wines and decent espresso).

★**Hannaford & Sachs** MODERN AUSTRALIAN $$$
(☑08-8559 2236; www.hannafordandsachs. au; 5997 North Coast Rd, Middle River; lunch $115; ⊙noon-3pm Tue-Sun Dec-Mar) Beneath the sun-dappled boughs of a 150-year-old fig tree, Rachel Hannaford and Sasha Sachs deliver a unique gourmet lunch experience: canapes, entrees, mains, desserts and accompaniments, with global influences from Lebanon and India to Thailand and Mexico. And of course, fine wine. Bookings essential.

South Coast Road

Tracking from Kingscote to Flinders Chase National Park, the South Coast Rd doesn't often come close to the coast (at it's eastern end, at any rate). But if it did, you'd see that the wave-swept shores here are much less sheltered than those on the northern side of KI. This is wild country, and a great place to meet some island wildlife. And don't miss Vivonne Bay, one of SA's most beautiful beaches.

👁 Sights

Clifford's Honey Farm FARM
(☑08-8553 8295; www.cliffordshoney.com.au; 1157 Elsegood Rd, Haines; ⊙9am-5pm) FREE It's almost worth swimming the Backstairs Passage for the honey ice cream (sourced from a colony of rare Ligurian bees) at this charming, uncommercial farm, which is a bit off the tourist radar (again, charming). Honey-infused drinks, biscuits, mead, cosmetics and candles are also available in the cute shop. Look for the queen bee in the glass-fronted beehive.

Seal Bay Conservation Park NATURE RESERVE
(☑08-8553 4463; www.sealbay.sa.gov.au; Seal Bay Rd, Seal Bay; guided tours adult/child/family $35/20/85; ⊙tours 9am-4pm plus twilight year-round, extra tours Dec-Feb) 🐾 'Observation, not interaction' is the mentality here. Guided tours stroll along the beach (or boardwalk on self-guided tours; adult/child/family $16/10/42) to a colony of Australian sea lions: book in advance for both. Twilight beach tours (adult/child/family $60/38/165) run year-round on Monday, Wednesday and Friday; call for departure times and bookings.

Raptor Domain ZOO

(☑08-8559 5108; www.kangarooislandbirdsofprey.
com.au; cnr South Coast & Seal Bay Rds, Seal Bay;
adult/child/family birds of prey $18/12/55; reptiles
$12/10/35; ⏰10am-4pm) Check out some KI
wedge-tailed eagles, barn owls and kookaburras at a one-hour birds-of-prey display
(11.30am and 2.30pm), or go scaly at a one-
hour lizards and snakes show (1pm).

Little Sahara NATURE RESERVE

(off South Coast Rd, Vivonne Bay; ⏰24hr) **FREE** A
turn-off 6km west of Seal Bay Rd leads to
a rolling white dunescape looming above
the surrounding scrub. Amazing! You can
hire sandboards from **Kangaroo Island
Outdoor Action** (☑08-8559 4296; www.kiout
dooraction.com.au; 188 Jetty Rd, Vivonne Bay).

Kelly Hill Conservation Park NATURE RESERVE

(☑08-8553 4464; www.environment.sa.gov.au/
parks; South Coast Rd, Hanson Bay; tours adult/
child/family $18/10/45, adventure caving adult/
child $70/40; ⏰10.15am-4.30pm) This series
of dry limestone caves was 'discovered' in
the 1880s by a horse named Kelly, who fell
into them through a hole. Take the standard
show cave tour (10.30am, then hourly 11am
to 4pm), or add on an **adventure caving
tour** (2.15pm; bookings essential). The **Hanson Bay Walk** (9km one-way) runs from the
caves past freshwater wetlands. There are extra show cave tours during school holidays.

Activities

Tiger Trails HORSE RIDING

(☑0427 392 030; www.tiger-trails-kangarooisland.
com; 2492 East West Two Hwy, Newland; 30min/
1hr/2hr rides per person $30/60/100) Horse and
pony rides long and short, along the Harriet
River at Newland in the middle of the island.
Bookings essential.

🛏 Sleeping & Eating

Flinders Chase Farm HOSTEL, CABINS $

(☑0447 021 494; www.flinderschasefarm.com.au;
1561 West End Hwy, Karatta; dm/cabins/d/f from
$28/80/110/120) A working farm with charm,
a short drive from Flinders Chase National
Park. Accommodation includes tidy dorms,
a couple of cosy cabins and ensuite rooms in
a lodge. There's also a terrific camp kitchen,
fire pits and 'tropical' outdoor showers.

SupaShak RENTAL HOUSE $$

(☑08-8410 4557; www.sealink.com.au/kanga
roo-island-accommodation/470-supashak; Flinders
St, Vivonne Bay; d $190-310, extra person $25)
Oh look – a lunar landing pod has touched
down in the Vivonne Bay dunes... This angular architectural craft is future-fantastic,
responding to the bushfire-prone locale with
steel and fibre-cement construction and lots
of water storage. Geared towards longer
stays (minimum three nights), with room
for six bods. The wood fire cranks in winter.

★ Southern Ocean Lodge LUXURY HOTEL $$$

(☑08-8559 7347; www.southernoceanlodge.com.
au; Hanson Bay Rd, Hanson Bay; d per night from
$1100; ❉@🅟🅢🅦) Looking for a place to your
woo your sweetheart? The shining star in the
SA tourism galaxy is Southern Ocean Lodge,
a sexy, low-profile snake tracing the Hanson
Bay cliff-top – a really lovely piece of architecture, and a great place to stay. Two-night
minimum; prices include airport transfers,
all meals and drinks, and guided tours of KI.

Marron Café MODERN AUSTRALIAN $$

(☑08-8559 4114; www.andermel.com.au; 804
Harriet Rd, Central Kangaroo Island; mains $18-46;
⏰11am-4.30pm Sep-Apr, noon-3.30pm May-Aug)
Around 15km north of Vivonne Bay you can
check out marron in breeding tanks, then eat
some! It's a subtle taste, not always enhanced
by the heavy sauces issued by the kitchen...
There are salads, steak and chicken dishes
too, for the crustacean-shy. Last orders 30
minutes before closing. **Two Wheeler Creek**
winery cellar door is here too.

Flinders Chase National Park

Occupying the western end of the island,
Flinders Chase National Park is one of SA's
top national parks. Much of the park is
mallee scrub, and there are also some beautiful, tall sugar-gum forests, particularly
around Rocky River and the Ravine des Casoars, 5km south of Cape Borda. Sadly, around
100,000 acres of bush were burned out by
bushfires in 2007, but the park is making a
steady recovery. Kooky rock formations and
brilliant bushwalks are the highlights. Pay
your park entry fees at the Flinders Chase
Visitor Information Centre.

◉ Sights

Once a farm, **Rocky River**, the area around
the visitor centre, is now full of wildlife, with
kangaroos, wallabies and Cape Barren geese
competing for your affections. A slew of walks
start behind the visitors centre, including the

Rocky River Hike (9km loop, three hours), on which you might spy a platypus. There's camping and accommodation here.

From Rocky River, a road runs south to a remote 1906 lighthouse atop wild Cape du Couedic (de *coo*-dick). You can't access the lighthouse, but it's nice to look at! There's cottage accommodation here too. Not far away, a boardwalk weaves down to Admirals Arch, a huge archway ground out by heavy seas, and passes a colony of New Zealand fur seals (sweet smelling they ain't...).

At Kirkpatrick Point, a few kilometres east of Cape du Couedic, the Remarkable Rocks are a cluster of hefty, weather-gouged granite boulders atop a rocky dome that arcs 75m down to the sea.

On the northwestern corner of the island, the square 1858 Cape Borda Lightstation (☑ 08-8559 3257; www.environment.sa.gov.au/parks; tours adult/child/family $16/10/42, self-guided tour $3; ◷ 9am-5pm, tours 11am, 12.30pm & 2pm) stands tall above the Southern Ocean. There are walks here from 1.5km to 9km, and extra tours at 3.15pm and 4pm during summer holidays. The cannon is fired at 12.30pm! There's accommodation here too.

At nearby Harvey's Return a cemetery speaks poignant volumes about the reality of isolation in the early days. From here you can drive to Ravine des Casoars (literally 'Ravine of the Cassowaries', referring to the now-extinct dwarf emus seen here by Baudin's expedition). The challenging Ravine des Casoars Hike (8km return, four hours) tracks through the ravine to the coast.

🏃 Activities

★ Kangaroo Island
Wilderness Trail   HIKING
(☑ 08-8553 4410; www.kangarooislandwilderness
trail.sa.gov.au/home; Flinders Chase Visitor Information Centre, South Coast Rd, Flinders Chase; adult/child $161/96) The big-ticket bushwalk in Flinders Chase NP is this five-day, four-night wilderness trail – an excellent 61km adventure through the park wilds, with dedicated campsites or beds off-trail if you're in need of some comfort. The trail starts at the park visitors centre and ends at Kelly Hill Conservation Park on the south coast. Maximum numbers apply; book online.

🛏 Sleeping

Within the park there are campgrounds at Rocky River (per vehicle $30), Snake Lagoon (per vehicle $15), West Bay (per vehicle $15) and Harvey's Return (per vehicle $15). You'll need a 4WD to get to Harvey's Return and West Bay.

There's also refurbished cottage accommodation at Rocky River – the budget Postman's Cottage (d $75, extra person $26) and family-friendly May's Homestead (d $176, extra adult/child $30/15) – and lightkeepers' cottages at Cape du Couedic (d $225, extra adult/child $30/15) and Cape Borda (d $50-225, extra adult/child $30/15).

For all park accommodation, book online before you go at www.environment.sa.gov.au/parks/booking, through the Flinders Chase Visitor Information Centre, or at the Natural Resources Centre (☑ 08-8553 4444; www.naturalresources.sa.gov.au/kangaroo island; 37 Dauncey St; ◷ 9am-5pm Mon-Fri) in Kingscote.

🍴 Eating

Chase Cafe   CAFE $$
(☑ 08-8559 7339; www.thechasecafe.net; 442 Cape du Couedic Rd, Flinders Chase National Park; meals $7-30; ◷ 9am-5pm) On the food front, if you're not self-catering the only option within Flinders Chase National Park is the buzzy, daytime Chase Cafe at the visitor centre, serving burgers, wraps, soup, pizzas, big salads, coffee and wines by the glass.

ℹ Information

Flinders Chase Visitor Information Centre
(☑ 08-8553 4470, accommodation 08-8553 4410, camping 08-8553 4471; www.environ ment.sa.gov.au/parks; Cape du Couedic Rd, Flinders Chase; park entry adult/child/family $11/6/28; ◷ 9am-5pm) Info, park passes, maps and camping/accommodation bookings, plus the Chase Cafe and displays on island ecology.

BAROSSA VALLEY

With hot, dry summers and cool, moderate winters, the Barossa is one of the world's great wine regions – an absolute must for anyone with even the slightest interest in a good drop. It's a compact valley – just 25km long – yet it manages to produce 21% of Australia's wine, and it makes a no-fuss day trip from Adelaide, which is 65km southwest of the region.

The local towns have a distinctly German heritage, dating back to 1842. Fleeing religious persecution in Prussia and Silesia, settlers (bringing their vine cuttings with them) created a Lutheran heartland where German traditions endure today. The physical remnants of colonisation – Gothic church steeples and stone cottages – are everywhere. Cultural legacies of the early days include a dubious passion for oom-pah bands, and an appetite for wurst, pretzels and sauerkraut.

Tours

Barossa Explorer TOURS
(☑ 0423 376 155; www.barossaexplorer.com; per person/family $30/100; ☺ 10am-5pm Thu-Sun) Jump aboard this hop-on/hop-off tourist bus, which loops past nine handy Barossa sites, including the Barossa Valley Brewery, Maggie Beer's Farm Shop and the visitor centre in Tanunda. Do the whole loop in an hour, or take your own sweet time about it. Tickets are valid for 24 hours.

Uber Cycle Adventures CYCLING
(☑ 08-8563 1148; www.ubercycle.com.au; 2hr/half-day/full-day tours $95/145/195) Get on your bike and see the Barossa on two wheels, with lots of native flora and fauna en route (oh, and some wine!).

Groovy Grape TOURS
(☑ 1800 059 490, 08-8440 1640; www.groovy grape.com.au; full-day tours $99) Backpacker-centric day tours ex-Adelaide with a pizza lunch: good value, good fun. Tours run Monday, Friday, Saturday and Sunday.

Festivals & Events

Barossa Vintage Festival FOOD & DRINK
(www.barossavintagefestival.com.au) A week-long festival with music, maypole dancing, tug-of-war contests etc; around Easter (harvest time – very atmospheric) in odd-numbered years.

Barossa Gourmet Weekend FOOD & DRINK
(www.barossagourmet.com) Fab food matched with winning wines at select wineries; usually happens in September. The number-one event in the valley (book your beds way in advance).

❶ Getting There & Away

The Barossa Valley makes an easy day-trip from Adelaide, just 65km southwest of the region. If you're driving, consider the slightly longer route through the Adelaide Hills, which is super-scenic.

Adelaide Metro (www.adelaidemetro.com.au) runs regular daily trains from Adelaide to Gawler ($5.30, one hour), from where **LinkSA** (www.linksa.com.au) buses run to Tanunda ($10.10, 45 minutes), Nuriootpa ($12.80, one hour) and Angaston ($15.60, 1¼ hours).

❶ Getting Around

BICYCLE

The 27km **Jack Brobridge Track** runs from Gawler to Tanunda, with a 14km **rail trail** through Nuriootpa to Angaston, passing many wineries. It's part of the 40km north–south **Barossa Trail**. Pick up the *Barossa by Bike* brochure at the **Barossa Visitor Information Centre** (p762) in Tanunda, or download from its website.

Based in Nuriootpa, **Barossa Bike Hire** (☑ 0400 537 770; www.barossabikehire.com; 5 South Tce; ☺ 9am-5pm) rents out quality cycles/tandems from $40/70 per day (pick-up price: bikes can be delivered for $10/20 extra). Electric bikes, foodie hampers and guided half-day bike tours also available. In Tanunda, run by the visitor centre, the **Barossa Cycle Hub** (☑ 08-8563 0600, 1300 852 982; www.barossa.com; 70 Murray St; ☺ 9am-5pm Mon-Fri, to 4pm Sat, 10am-4pm Sun) has bikes per half/full-day for $30/44. **Angaston Hardware** (☑ 08-8564 2055; www. angastonhardware.com.au; 5 Sturt St; ☺ 8.30am-5.30pm Mon-Fri, 9am-4pm Sat, 10am-4pm Sun) also rents out bikes for $25/35 per half/full day.

Tanunda

POP 4680

At the centre of the valley both geographically and socially, Tanunda is the Barossa's main tourist town. Tanunda manages to morph the practicality of Nuriootpa with the charm of Angaston without a sniff of self-importance. There are some great eateries around town, but the wineries are what you're here for – sip, sip, sip!

◉ Sights

Mengler's Hill Lookout VIEWPOINT
(Menglers Hill Rd) From Tanunda, take the scenic route to Angaston via Bethany for hazy valley views (just ignore the naff sculptures). The road tracks through beautiful rural country, studded with huge eucalyptuses.

Keg Factory FACTORY
(☑ 08-8563 3012; www.thekegfactory.com.au; 25 St Hallett Rd; ☺ 8am-4pm Mon-Fri, 11am-4pm Sat & Sun) FREE Watch honest-to-goodness coopers make and repair wine barrels, 4km south of town. Amazing!

☐ Sleeping

Discover Holiday Parks
Barossa Valley CARAVAN PARK $
(☑ 08-8563 2784, 1800 991 590; www.discovery holidayparks.com.au; Barossa Valley Way; unpowered/powered sites from $30/38, cabins with/

Barossa Valley

Barossa Valley

⊙ Sights
1 Keg Factory	A4
2 Mengler's Hill Lookout	C3
3 Penfolds	C1
4 Peter Lehmann Wines	B2
5 Rockford Wines	B4
6 St Hallett	A4

🛏 Sleeping
7 Barossa Backpackers	B3
8 Discover Holiday Parks Barossa Valley	B3
9 Kirche @ Charles Melton	B4
10 Louise	A1
11 Marble Lodge	D2

⊗ Eating
12 Casa Carboni	D2
13 Ferment Asian	B3
14 Fino Seppeltsfield	A2
15 Maggie Beer's Farm Shop	B1
16 Red Door Espresso	B3
17 Vintners Bar & Grill	D2

⊙ Drinking & Nightlife
18 Barossa Valley Brewing	B3
19 Stein's Taphouse	C1

⊙ Shopping
Barossa Farmers Market	(see 17)
Barossa Valley Cheese Company	(see 12)

without bathroom from $145/110, villas from $240; ❋ 🛜 🛋) This spacious park just south of town is dotted with mature trees offering a little shade to ease your hangover. Facilities include a playground, barbecues, a laundry and bike hire for guests (per day $35). The flashy villas sleep up to six and have a two-night minimum stay.

Barossa Backpackers   HOSTEL $
(☑ 08-8563 0198; www.barossabackpackers.com.
au; 9 Basedow Rd; dm/s/d from $28/80/80; @ 🛜) Occupying a converted, U-shaped winery office building 500m from Tanunda's main street, Barossa Backpackers is a clean, secure and shipshape affair (if a little soulless) with good weekly rates. Management can help you find picking/pruning work.

★ **The Kirche @ Charles Melton**   B&B $$$
(☑ 08-8563 3606, 0409 838 802; www.thekirche.
com.au; 192 Krondorf Rd; d $515, extra adult/child $75/40; ❄ 🛜) Knocked together in 1964, this old stone Lutheran church – the Zum Kripplein Christi church, in fact – is now a fabulous boutique B&B. It's a few minutes' drive south of central Tanunda, on the same road as a string of good wineries. Inside you'll find black leather couches, a marble-tiled bathroom, two bedrooms and a cranking winter wood-heater. Two-night minimum.

✕ Eating

★ **Red Door Espresso**   CAFE $$
(☑ 08-8563 1181; www.reddoorespresso.com; 79 Murray St; mains breakfast $8-26, lunch $12-30; ☺ 7.30am-4pm Mon, to 5pm Wed-Sat, 9.30am-4pm Sun; 🛜 👶) A decent cafe shouldn't be hard to create, but it's rare in the Barossa for good food, coffee, staff, music and atmosphere to come together this well. The avocado and basil-infused eggs Benedict is a winner, best consumed with an eye-opening coffee in the pot-planted courtyard. Live music over weekend brunch; wine, cheese and antipasto in the afternoons.

Ferment Asian   SOUTHEAST ASIAN $$
(☑ 08-8563 0765; www.fermentasian.com.au; 90 Murray St; mains $26-34; ☺ noon-2pm Thu-Sun, 6-8.30pm Wed-Sat) In a lovely old stone villa fronting onto Tanunda's main street at a jaunty angle, Ferment always does things a little differently. What sounds exotic is actually refreshingly simple: *cari rau* (yellow vegetable curry); *tom nuong va boi* (citrus and prawn salad). Chef Tuoi Do really knows how to put it all together.

★ **Fino Seppeltsfield**   MODERN AUSTRALIAN $$$
(☑ 08-8562 8528; www.fino.net.au; 730 Seppeltsfield Rd, Seppeltsfield; small/large plates from $22/46; ☺ noon-3pm daily, 6-8.30pm Fri & Sat) From humble beginnings in a little stone cottage on the Fleurieu Peninsula, Fino has evolved into one of Australia's best restaurants, now ensconced in the gorgeous 1851

Seppeltsfield estate west of Tanunda. Food from the understated, deceptively simple menu highlights local ingredients, and is designed to be shared. Try the braised lamb with sherry, fennel, orange and chilli.

🍷 Drinking & Nightlife

Barossa Valley Brewing   CRAFT BEER
(☑ 08-8563 0696; www.bvbeer.com.au; 2a Murray St; ☺ noon-9pm Sun, Mon & Thu, to 6pm Tue & Wed, to 10pm Fri & Sat) Beer! Real beer, here amongst all the wine! If only for variety, pay a visit to BVB on the southern fringes of Tanunda – there's a paved terrace beneath some astoundingly big eucalypts, just made for an afternoon with a few easy-drinking IPAs. You can also peer at the stout steel tanks in the brewery, or grab a bite to eat.

❶ Information

Barossa Visitor Information Centre (☑ 1300 852 982, 08-8563 0600; www.barossa.com; 66-68 Murray St; ☺ 9am-5pm Mon-Fri, to 4pm Sat, 10am-4pm Sun; 🛜) The low-down on the valley, plus internet access, bike hire and accommodation and tour bookings. Stocks the *A Town Walk of Tanunda* brochure.

Nuriootpa

POP 5705

Along an endless main street at the northern end of the valley, Nuriootpa is the Barossa's commercial centre. It's not as endearing as Tanunda or Angaston, but has a certain agrarian simplicity. Lutheran spirit runs deep in 'Nuri': a sign says, 'God has invested in you – are you showing any interest?'.

🛏 Sleeping & Eating

The Louise   BOUTIQUE HOTEL $$$
(☑ 08-8562 2722; www.thelouise.com.au; 375 Seppeltsfield Rd, Marananga; d from $600; ❄ @ 🛜 ☲) Top of the accommodation tree in the BV, the Louise does everything with consummate style, from the architecture and the linen to the in-house restaurant Appellation and the smile at the front desk. Louise might stretch your wallet, but is worth every penny. Marananga (less a town, more an area) is equidistant from Nuriootpa and Tanunda.

Maggie Beer's Farm Shop   DELI $
(☑ 08-8562 4477; www.maggiebeer.com.au; 50 Pheasant Farm Rd; items $5-20, picnic baskets from $16; ☺ 10.30am-5pm) Celebrity SA gourmet Maggie Beer has been hugely successful

DON'T MISS

BAROSSA VALLEY WINERIES

The Barossa is best known for shiraz, with riesling the dominant white. There are around 80 vineyards here and 60 cellar doors, ranging from boutique wine rooms to monstrous complexes. The long-established 'Barossa Barons' hold sway – big, ballsy and brassy – while spritely young boutique wineries are harder to sniff out. The pick of the bunch:

Henschke (☑ 08-8564 8223; www.henschke.com.au; 1428 Keyneton Rd, Keyneton; ⏰ 9am-4.30pm Mon-Fri, to noon Sat) Detour about 10km southeast of Angaston to the Eden Valley, where old-school Henschke is known for its iconic Hill of Grace red...but most of the wines here are classics.

Rockford Wines (☑ 08-8563 2720; www.rockfordwines.com.au; 131 Krondorf Rd, Tanunda; ⏰ 11am-5pm) One of our favourite boutique Barossa wineries, this 1850s cellar door sells traditionally made, small-range wines, including sparkling reds. The Black Shiraz is a sparkling, spicy killer.

Penfolds (☑ 08-8568 8408; www.penfolds.com; 30 Tanunda Rd, Nuriootpa; ⏰ 9am-5pm) You know the name: Penfolds is a Barossa legend. Book ahead for the Make Your Own Blend tour ($65), or the Taste of Grange tour ($150), which allows you to slide some luscious Grange Hermitage across your lips.

Peter Lehmann Wines (☑ 08-8565 9555; www.peterlehmannwines.com.au; Para Rd, Tanunda; ⏰ 9.30am-5pm Mon-Fri, 10.30am-4.30pm Sat & Sun) The shiraz and riesling vintages here (oh, and the semillon) are probably the most consistent, affordable and widely distributed wines in the Barossa.

St Hallett (☑ 08-8563 7070; www.sthallett.com.au; St Hallett Rd, Tanunda; ⏰ 10am-5pm) Using only Barossa grapes, improving St Hallett produces reasonably priced but consistently good whites (try the Poacher's Blend) and the excellent Old Block Shiraz. Unpretentious and great value for money.

with her range of condiments, preserves and pâtés (and TV appearances!). The vibe here isn't as relaxed as it used to be, but stop by for some gourmet tastings, an ice cream, a cooking demo (2pm daily) or a takeaway hamper of delicious bites. Off Samuel Rd.

🍷 Drinking & Nightlife

⭐ **Stein's Taphouse**   CRAFT BEER, BAR
(☑ 08-8562 2899; www.steinstaphouse.com.au; 18-28 Barossa Valley Way; ⏰ noon-late) Inside the old Provenance Building in the Penfolds complex is this excellent craft beer bar (sacrilege?), also serving artisan spirits, small-production SA wines and food that pairs up nicely with all three (burgers, pork ribs, chilli con carne). There are a dozen beer taps: study the blackboard behind the bar and see what takes your fancy. Live music occasionally, too.

Angaston

POP 1910

Photo-worthy Angaston was named after George Fife Angas, a pioneering Barossa pastoralist. An agricultural vibe persists, as

there are few wineries on the town doorstep: cows graze in paddocks at end of the town's streets, and there's a vague whiff of fertiliser in the air. Along the photogenic main drag are two pubs and some terrific eateries.

🛏 Sleeping & Eating

Marble Lodge   B&B $$$
(☑ 08-8564 2478; www.marblelodge.com.au; 21 Dean St; d $225-250; ❋ 🛜) A grandiose 1915 Federation-style villa on the (reasonably steep!) hill behind the town, built from local pink and white granite. Accommodation is in two plush suites behind the house (high-colonial or high-kitsch, depending on your world view). Breakfast is served in the main house – a candlelit, buffet-style experience.

Casa Carboni   ITALIAN $$
(☑ 0415 157 669; www.casacarboni.com.au; 67 Murray St; meals from $25; ⏰ 9am-3pm Thu-Sun, 6pm-late Fri, closed Jul) Part Italian cooking school, part *enoteca* (wine bar/restaurant), Casa Carboni is run by real-life Italian Matteo Carboni, who visited the Barossa for a month in 2012 and has been here ever since. Sign up for a pasta master class, or just enjoy the spoils

of the kitchen and some fine Italian wine (if you've had enough of Barossa red).

Vintners Bar & Grill MODERN AUSTRALIAN $$$
(208-8564 2488; www.vintners.com.au; cnr Stockwell & Nuriootpa Rds; mains $36-40; ☉noon-2.30pm daily, 6.30-9pm Mon-Sat) One of the Barossa's landmark restaurants, Vintners stresses simple elegance in both food and atmosphere. The dining room has an open fire, vineyard views and bolts of crisp white linen; menus concentrate on local produce (the seared chicken livers with potato, muscat and burnt onion is a flavour sensation).

🅰 Shopping

Barossa Farmers Market MARKET
(20402 026 882; www.barossafarmersmarket.com; cnr Stockwell & Nuriootpa Rds; ☉7.30-11.30am Sat) Happens in the big farm shed behind Vintners Bar & Grill every Saturday. Expect hearty Germanic offerings, coffee, flowers and lots of local produce.

Barossa Valley Cheese Company CHEESE
(208-8564 3636; www.barossacheese.com.au; 67b Murray St; ☉10am-5pm Mon-Fri, to 4pm Sat, 11am-3pm Sun) The Barossa Valley Cheese Company is a fabulously stinky room, selling handmade cheeses from the milk of local cows and goats. Tastings are free, but it's unlikely you'll leave without buying a wedge of the Washington Washed Rind. Plenty of tourist brochures and maps, too.

CLARE VALLEY

At the centre of the fertile midnorth agricultural district, two hours north of Adelaide, the slender Clare Valley produces world-class, sweet scented rieslings and mineral-rich reds. This is gorgeous countryside, with open skies, rounded hills, stands of large gums and wind rippling over wheat fields. Towns here date from the 1840s; many were built to service the Burra copper mines.

You can tackle the Clare Valley as a day trip from Adelaide, but when the wine and food are this good, why rush? Spend a few days in old-fangled towns, cycling between cellar doors, eating an dexploring.

☞ Tours

Clare Valley Tours TOURS
(20418 832 812; www.clarevalleytours.com; tours from $145) Interesting valley tours with a local guide, 'Mr Wilson', taking you along the back roads and delivering some Indigenous Ngadjuri insights along with all the wine and colonial history. Ex-Clare Valley.

Clare Valley Grape Express TOURS
(208-8842 3098, 0428 055 590; david@clarevalleytaxis.com.au; tours $85) Quick-fire (four hour), affordable winery tours for those short on time, run by a local taxi company.

★☆ Festivals & Events

Clare Valley Gourmet Weekend FOOD & DRINK
(www.clarevalley.com.au; ☉May) A fab frenzy of Clare Valley wine, food and music in May. LinkSA (www.linksa.com.au) buses get involved, with shuttles to/from Adelaide.

ℹ Getting There & Around

In Auburn and Clare you can hire a bike to pelt around the wineries. Rates are around $25/40 per half-/full day.

Clare Valley Taxis (208-8842 1400, 13 10 08; www.131008.com) will drop-off/pick-up anywhere along the Riesling Trail.

Yorke Peninsula Coaches (208-8821 2755; www.ypcoaches.com.au) Runs Adelaide to Auburn ($34, 2¼ hours) and Clare ($42, 2¾ hours) on Monday, Wednesday, Friday and Sunday (also running in the opposite direction on these days). Services extend to Burra ($42, 3¼ hours) on Wednesday only.

Auburn
POP 600

Sleepy Auburn (1849) – the Clare Valley's southernmost village – is a leave-the-back-door-open-and-the-keys-in-the-ignition kinda town, with a time-warp vibe that makes you feel like you're in an old black-and-white photograph. The streets are defined by beautifully preserved stone buildings; cottage gardens overflow with untidy blooms. Pick up a copy of the *Walk with History at Auburn* brochure from the Clare Valley Visitor Information Centre (p767).

Now on the main route to the valley's wineries, Auburn initially serviced bullock drivers and South American muleteers whose wagons – up to 100 a day – trundled between Burra's copper mines and Port Wakefield.

🛏 Sleeping

Bed in a Shed APARTMENT, B&B $$
(20418 346 836; www.vineartstudio.com; cnr Leasingham Rd & Blocks Rd, Leasingham; d from $200; ❄🤶) Around 7km north of Auburn in little Leasingham, Bed in a Shed puts a

DON'T MISS

CLARE VALLEY WINERIES

The Clare Valley's cool microclimate, cool airs circulating around rivers, creeks and gullies, noticeably affect the local wines, enabling whites to be laid down for long periods and still be brilliant. The valley produces some of the world's best riesling, plus grand semillon and shiraz. Five of our favourites:

Skillogalee (☑ 08-8843 4311; www.skillogalee.com.au; 23 Trevarrick Rd, Sevenhill; ⊙7.30am-5pm) Skillogalee is a small family outfit known for its spicy shiraz, fabulous food and top-notch riesling (a glass of which is like kissing someone gorgeous on a summer afternoon). Kick back with a long, lazy lunch on the verandah (breakfast mains $17 to $19, lunch $24 to $49; book ahead). This place just might be heaven.

Pikes (☑ 08-8843 4370; www.pikeswines.com.au; Polish Hill River Rd, Sevenhill; ⊙10am-4pm) The industrious Pike family set up shop in the Polish Hill River sub-region of the Clare Valley in 1984, and have been producing show-stopping riesling ever since (and shiraz, sangiovese, pinot grigio, viognier...). It also bottles up the zingy Oakbank Pilsener, if you're parched.

Knappstein (☑ 08-8841 2100; www.knappstein.com.au; 2 Pioneer Ave, Clare; ⊙9am-5pm Mon-Fri, 11am-5pm Sat, to 4pm Sun) Taking a minimal-intervention approach to wine making, Knappstein has built quite a name for itself. Shiraz and riesling steal the show, but they also make a mighty fine semillon-sauvignon blanc blend (and beer!).

Sevenhill Cellars (☑ 08-8843 4222; www.sevenhill.com.au; 111c College Rd, Sevenhill; ⊙10am-5pm) Like a little religion with your drink? This place was established by Jesuits in 1851, making it the oldest winery in the Clare Valley (check out the incredible 1866 St Aloysius Church). Oh, and the wine is mighty fine too!

Shut The Gate (☑ 08-8843 0111; www.shutthegate.com.au; 2 Horrocks Hwy, Watervale; ⊙10am-4.30pm) Across a little creek and through a white gate (no need to shut it), this upbeat little cellar door has been making a few 'Best New Wineries' lists of late. Taste some of their good stuff inside the old duck-your-head cottage, or outside at the rather abstract collection of tables. Winning riesling.

different spin on the Clare Valley B&B: a rustic (but very well insulated) corrugated-iron farm shed decked out with cool art, woody built-in shelves, recycled timbers, quirky furnishings and a fridge full of breakfast stuff. Not a floral bedspread or lace curtain in sight! Nice one.

The Loft at Cobbler's Rest APARTMENT **$$**
(☑ 0424 784 572; www.theloftclarevalley.com.au; 24 Horrocks Hwy; d/q from $170/290; ﹡) Upstairs in a beautiful stone building in the heart of Auburn, the Loft is a compact apartment comprising two double bedrooms, kitchen/dining and a big bathroom. There's just enough of a 'cottage' vibe for the whole set-up to feel authentic, without overdoing it. Sleeps four; breakfast provisions provided.

✗ Eating

Rising Sun Hotel PUB FOOD **$$**
(☑ 08-8849 2015; www.therisingsunhotel.com.au; 19 Horrocks Hwy; mains $18-33; ⊙noon-2pm & 6-8pm, bar open 11am; ☏) This classic 1850 pub has a huge rep for its atmosphere, food and

accommodation. The seasonal pub food is inventive with plenty of local wines to try. Accommodation takes the form of ensuite pub rooms and cottage mews rooms out the back (doubles including breakfast $100 to $160).

★ **Terroir** MODERN AUSTRALIAN **$$$**
(☑ 08-8849 2509; www.terroirauburn.com.au; 21 Horrocks Hwy; mains from $35; ⊙2-5.30pm Fri & Sat, noon-4pm Sun, 6-8.30pm Wed-Sat; ☑) ✿ 'Terroir' – a word often associated with the wine trade – defines the nature of a place: its altitude, its soil, its climate, its vibe. At this excellent restaurant it applies to ingredients, sourced seasonally from within 100 miles, and cooked with contemporary savvy. The menu changes weekly (pray for the house halloumi). Love the Mintaro-slate floor.

Mintaro

POP 370

Heritage-listed Mintaro (min-*tair*-oh; founded 1849) is a stone village that could have been lifted out of the Cotswolds and plonked into the Australian bush. There are few architectural intrusions from the 1900s – the whole place seems to have been largely left to its own devices. A fact for your next trivia night: Mintaro slate is used internationally in the manufacture of billiard tables.

Pick up the *Historic Mintaro* pamphlet around the valley.

Sights & Activities

★ Martindale Hall
HISTORIC BUILDING

(☑ 08-8843 9088; www.martindalehall.com; 1 Manoora Rd, Mintaro; adult/child $12/8; ⊙11am-4pm Wed-Mon, daily during school holidays) Martindale Hall is an astonishing 1880 manor 3km from Mintaro. Built for young pastoralist Edmund Bowman Jnr, who subsequently partied away the family fortune (OK, so drought and plummeting wool prices played a part... but it was mostly the partying), the manor features original furnishings, a magnificent blackwood staircase, Mintaro-slate billiard table and an opulent, museum-like smoking room. The hall starred as Appleyard College in the 1975 film *Picnic at Hanging Rock*, directed by Peter Weir. *Mirandaaa...*

Mintaro Maze
OUTDOORS

(☑ 08-8843 9012; www.mintaromaze.com.au; Jacka Rd; adult/child $12/8; ⊙10am-4pm Wed-Mon, daily school holidays, closed Feb) Hedge your bets at the Mintaro Maze as you try to find your way into the middle and back out again. There's a little cafe here too.

Sleeping & Eating

★ Reilly's
MODERN AUSTRALIAN $$

(☑ 08-8843 9013; www.reillyswines.com.au; cnr Hill St & Leasingham Rd; mains $24-30; ⊙10am-4pm) Reilly's started life as a cobbler's shop in 1856. An organic veggie garden out the back supplies the current restaurant, which is decorated with local art and serves creative, seasonal Mod Oz food (antipasto, rabbit terrine, platters) and Reilly's wines. The owners also rent out four gorgeous old stone cottages on Hill St (doubles from $175, including cook-your-own breakfast).

Clare
POP 3280

Named after County Clare in Ireland, this town was founded in 1842 and is the biggest in the valley. Strung out along the Horrocks Hwy, it's more practical than charming. All the requisite services are here (post, supermarket, fuel, pubs), but you'll have a more interesting Clare Valley experience sleeping out of town.

Sleeping & Eating

Bungaree Station
FARMSTAY $

(☑ 08-8842 2677; www.bungareestation.com.au; 431 Bungaree Rd; per person per night $59-99; ✺) About 12km north of Clare is this beautiful, 175-year-old homestead – once with 50 staff, a church and a school! It's still a 3000-acre working farm, with accommodation in simple, renovated heritage buildings, sleeping two to 10, some with shared bathrooms. You can also feed farm animals, walk a history trail (per adult/child $15/7.50) or have a dip in the pool.

Riesling Trail &
Clare Valley Cottages
B&B $$

(☑ 0427 842 232; www.rtcvcottages.com.au; 9 Warenda Rd; 1-/2-/3-bedroom cottage incl breakfast from $160/195/390; ✺) A well-managed outfit offering seven contemporary cottages, encircled by country gardens and

---

THE RIESLING TRAIL

Following the course of a disused railway line between Auburn and Barinia, north of Clare, the fabulous Riesling Trail is 33km of wines, wheels and wonderment. It's primarily a cycling trail, but the gentle gradient means you can walk or push a pram along it just as easily. It's a two-hour dash end to end on a bike, but why hurry? There are three loop track detours and extensions to explore, and dozens of cellar doors to tempt you along the way. The **Rattler Trail** continues for another 19km south of Auburn to Riverton.

For bike hire, check out **Clare Valley Cycle Hire** (☑ 0418 802 077; www.clarevalleycyclehire.com.au; 32 Victoria Rd; bike hire per half-/full day $20/30; ⊙9am-5pm) or **Riesling Trail Bike Hire** (☑ 0418 777 318; www.rieslingtrailbikehire.com.au; 10 Warenda Rd; bike hire per half-/full day $25/40, tandems $40/60; ⊙8am-6pm Fri-Mon, other times by appointment) in Clare, or **Cogwebs Hub Cafe** (☑ 08-8849 2380, 0400 290 687; www.cogwebs.com.au; 30 Horrocks Hwy; bike hire per half-/full day $25/40, tandems $35/60; ⊙10am-5pm; ☎) in Auburn.

right on the Riesling Trail (Riesling Trail Bike Hire is across the street). The biggest cottage sleeps six; there are good deals on multinight and midweek stays.

★ Little Red Grape
BAKERY $
(☑ 08-8843 4088; www.thelittleredgrape.info; 148 Horrocks Hwy, Sevenhill; items $3-6; ⊙ 7am-5pm) There's a cellar door here, focusing on small-production local vineyards, but most folks are here for the bakery, serving excellent pies, cakes, big donuts, toasted bacon-and-egg Turkish bread sandwiches and wake-you-up coffee. The saltbush-lamb and rosemary pie is hard to top. It's at Sevenhill, 7km south of Clare.

ⓘ Information

Clare Valley Visitor Information Centre
(☑ 1800 242 131, 08-8842 2131; www.clare valley.com.au; cnr Horrocks Hwy & Spring Gully Rd; ⊙ 9am-5pm Sat-Thu, to 7pm Fri; ☜) Local info, valley-wide accommodation bookings and the *Clare History Walk* brochure. Local produce for sale too.

MURRAY RIVER

On the lowest gradient of any Australian river, the slow-flowing Murray hooks through 650 South Australian kilometres. Tamed by weirs and locks, it irrigates the fruit trees and vines of the sandy **Riverland** district to the north, and winds through the dairy country of the **Murraylands** district to the south. Raucous flocks of white corellas and pink galahs launch from cliffs and river red gums, darting across lush vineyards and orchards.

Prior to European colonisation, the Murray was home to Meru communities. Then came the paddle-steamers, carrying wool, wheat and supplies from Murray Bridge as far as central Queensland along the Darling River. With the advent of railways, river transport declined. These days, waterskiers, jet skis and houseboats crowd the river, especially during summer. If your concept of riverine serenity doesn't include the roar of V8 inboards, then sidestep the major towns and caravan parks during holidays and weekends.

ⓘ Getting There & Away

As with most places in regional SA, having your own vehicle will give you the most flexibility when exploring the Murray River towns. But if you are bussing it, there are a couple of options.

LinkSA (☑ 08 8532 2633; www.linksa.com. au) runs several daily bus services between Adelaide and Murray Bridge ($22.50, 1¼ hours) sometimes via a bus change at Mt Barker in the Adelaide Hills; plus Murray Bridge to Mannum ($7.50, 30 minutes) from Monday to Friday.

Premier Stateliner (www.premierstateliner. com.au) runs daily Riverland buses from Adelaide, stopping in Waikerie ($47.50, 2½ hours), Barmera ($59, 3¼ hours), Berri ($59, 3½ hours) and Renmark ($59, four hours). Change at Kingston-on-Murray for buses to Loxton ($59, 3¾ hours).

Murray Bridge

POP 17,920

SA's largest river town and a rambling regional hub (the fifth-biggest town in SA), Murray Bridge has lots of old pubs, an underutilised riverfront, a huge prison and charms more subtle than obvious.

◉ Sights

Monarto Zoo
ZOO
(☑ 08-8534 4100; www.monartozoo.com.au; Old Princes Hwy, Monarto South; adult/child/family $34.50/19/88.50; ⊙ 9.30am-5pm, last entry 3pm) About 14km west of Murray Bridge, this excellent open-range zoo is home to Australian and African beasts including cheetahs, meerkats, rhino, zebras and giraffe (and the photogenic offspring thereof). A hop-on/hop-off bus tour is included in the price; keeper talks happen throughout the day. There's a cafe here too, if you forget your sandwiches/thermos.

Murray Bridge Regional Gallery
GALLERY
(☑ 08-8539 1420; www.murraybridgegallery.com. au; 27 Sixth St; ⊙ 10am-4pm Tue-Sat, 11-4pm Sun) **FREE** This is the town's cultural epicentre, a great little space housing touring and local exhibitions: paintings, ceramics, gorgeous glassware, jewellery and prints. A terrific diversion on a rainy river afternoon.

ⓘ Information

Murray Bridge Visitor Information Centre
(☑ 08-8339 1142, 1800 442 784; www.murray bridge.sa.gov.au; 3 South Tce; ⊙ 9am-5pm Mon-Fri, 10am-4pm Sat & Sun) Stocks the Murray Bridge *Accommodation Guide* and *Dining Guide* brochures, and history walk and drive pamphlets. Also has information on river-cruise operators.

Mannum

POP 2570

About 30km upstream from Murray Bridge, clinging to a narrow strip of riverbank, improbably cute Mannum is the unofficial houseboat capital of the world! The *Mary Ann,* Australia's first riverboat, was knocked together here in 1853 and made the first paddle-steamer trip up the Murray.

◉ Sights

Mannum itself, clinging to the crumbling riverbanks, is quite a sight! The Mannum Visitor Information Centre incorporates the **Mannum Dock Museum of River History** (☑ 08-8569 1303, 1300 626 686; www.psmarion. com; 6 Randell St; adult/child/family $7.50/4/20; ☉ 9am-5pm Mon-Fri, 10am-4pm Sat & Sun), featuring info on local Ngarrindjeri Aboriginal communities, an 1876 dock and the restored 1897 paddle steamer *PS Marion,* on which you can occasionally chug around the river.

About 9km out of Mannum on the way to Murray Bridge, **Mannum Waterfalls** (off Cascade Rd; ☉ 24hr) FREE surge impressively over granite boulders after it's been raining (not much action in February). Head to the top car park for the best access.

From Mannum heading north to Swan Reach, the eastern riverside road often tracks a fair way east of the river, but lookouts en route help you scan the scene. Around 9km south of Swan Reach, the Murray takes a meander called **Big Bend**, a sweeping river curve with pock-marked, ochre-coloured cliffs.

Sedentary old Swan Reach (population 850), about 80km north of Mannum, is a bit of a misnomer: there's an old pub, a museum and plenty of pelicans here, but not many swans.

🏃 Activities

Breeze Holiday Hire   CANOEING
(☑ 0439 829 964; www.murrayriver.com.au/breeze-holiday-hire-1052) Hires out canoes and kayaks (per day $75), dinghies with outboards (per day $95) and fishing gear (per day $15), and can get you waterskiing too. Based in Mannum.

🛏 Sleeping & Eating

River Shack Rentals   ACCOMMODATION SERVICES
(☑ 0447 263 549, 08-8569 1958; www.rivershackrentals.com.au) Offers a raft of riverside properties (doubles from $100) to rent

from Murray Bridge, Mannum and further upstream, sleeping two to 20 bods. Most of them are right on the water: 36 River Lane is a solid Mannum-centric option with room for 10 (from $450). Houseboats also available.

Pretoria Hotel   PUB FOOD $$
(☑ 08-8569 1109; www.pretoriahotel.com.au; 50 Randell St; mains $20-34; ☉ 11.30am-2.30pm & 5.30-8.30pm) The family-friendly Pretoria (built 1900) has a vast bistro and deck fronting the river, and plates up big steaks and salads, king prawn linguine and impressive parmas (amongst other things). When the 1956 flood swamped the town they kept pouring beer from the 1st-floor balcony!

ℹ Information

Mannum Visitor Information Centre (☑ 08-8569 1303, 1300 626 686; www.psmarion.com/visitor-centre; 6 Randell St; ☉ 9am-5pm Mon-Fri, 10am-4pm Sat & Sun) This is the place for cruise and houseboat bookings, the *Mannum Historic Walks* brochure and the **Mannum Dock Museum of River History** (p768). Bike hire also available (per half-/full-day $25/40).

Waikerie

POP 2720

A citrus-growing centre oddly festooned with TV antennas, Waikerie takes its name from the Aboriginal phrase for 'anything that flies'. Indeed, there's plenty of bird life around here, plus houseboats gliding past on the river. The Waikerie vibe is utilitarian and workaday – tourism runs a distant second to fruit.

◉ Sights

Nippy's   FACTORY
(☑ 08-8541 0600; www.nippys.com.au; 2 Ian Oliver Dr; ☉ 8am-noon & 12.30-4pm Mon-Fri) A long-running local fruit-juice company with factory-front sales. Its lip-nipping lemon juice is ace on a hot river afternoon.

🛏 Sleeping & Eating

★ **Wigley Retreat**   B&B $$
(☑ 0417 186 364; www.facebook.com/wigleyretreat; Wigley Flat Rd, Wigley Flat; d from $190; ❋) Some 27km east of Waikerie and a couple of kilometres off the Sturt Hwy, Wigley Retreat is a simple but stylish stone cottage right on the riverbank. It's a one-bedroom arrangement, with a well-stocked fridge and a table for

two by the water. Super-private, super-scenic. The perfect spot to destress for a couple of days.

★ **Waikerie Hotel Motel** HOTEL, MOTEL **$$**
(🖉 08-8541 2999; www.waikeriehotel.com; 2 McCoy St; d from $120; 🕸 🛜) Much of this huge pub burnt down in 2012, two days shy of its 100th birthday! The 19 rebuilt ensuite pub rooms upstairs are awesome: fancy linen, glowing bar fridges and big TVs, with leather and granite everywhere. The bistro does pub-grub classics (mains $14 to $27). Slightly cheaper are the updated motel rooms out the back. Bike hire available.

Waikerie Bakery BAKERY **$**
(🖉 08-8541 2142; 3 Peake Tce; items $4-8; ⏰ 8.30am-5.30pm Mon-Fri, to 1pm Sat) Hey, that rhymes! This simple little bakehouse does fabulous pumpkin-and-feta pasties, apricot chicken pies, jam tarts, pecan pies and bags of biscuits. Consume them on the sunny deck off to one side.

ℹ Information

Waikerie Visitor Information Centre (🖉 08-8541 0708; www.waikerie.com; Strangman Rd; ⏰ 9am-5pm Mon-Fri, 10am-4pm Sat & Sun) The modest little Waikerie Visitor Information Centre is on the big roundabout on the way into town. Old-building fans should look for the *Waikerie Heritage Walk* brochure.

Barmera & Around

On the shallow shores of Lake Bonney (upon which world land-speed record holder Donald Campbell unsuccessfully attempted to break his water-speed record in 1964), snoozy Barmera (population 3020) was once a key town on the overland stock route from NSW. These days the local passion for both kinds of music (country *and* western) lends a simple optimism to proceedings. **Kingston-On-Murray** (population 260; aka Kingston OM) is a tiny town nearby, en route to Waikerie.

◉ Sights

★ **Banrock Station** WINERY
(🖉 08-8583 0299; www.banrockstation.com.au; Holmes Rd, Kingston OM; tastings free, wetland walks by gold-coin donation; ⏰ 9am-4pm Mon-Fri, to 5pm Sat & Sun) 🌿 Overlooking regenerated wetlands off the Sturt Hwy at Kingston OM, carbon-neutral Banrock Station Wine & Wetland Centre is a stylish, rammed-earth

---

HOUSEBOATING ON THE MURRAY
••••••••••••••••••••••••••••••••••••
Houseboating is big business on the Murray. Meandering along the river is great fun – you just need to be over 18 with a current driving licence. Boats depart most riverside towns; book ahead, especially between October and April.

The **Houseboat Hirers Association** (🖉 1300 665 122, 08-8346 6655; www.houseboatbookings.com) is a reputable booking service, with boats available in most Murray River towns. For a three-night weekend, expect to pay anywhere from $750 for two people to $2700 for a luxury 10-bed boat. Most boats sleep at least two couples and there's generally a bond involved (starting at $200). Many provide linen – just bring food and fine wine. See also SA Tourism's *Houseboat Holidays* booklet for houseboat listings.

---

wine-tasting centre (love the tempranillo). The jazzy lunchtime **restaurant** (mains $25 to $33 – try the slow-cooked pork belly with Riverland fennel) uses ingredients sourced locally. There are three **wetland walks** here too: 2.5km, 4.5km and 8km.

Rocky's Hall of Fame Pioneers Museum MUSEUM
(🖉 0407 720 560; www.facebook.com/rockyscountrymusicmuseum; 4 Pascoe Tce, Barmera; $2; ⏰ 8.30am-noon Mon & Thu, 9am-4pm Tue & Wed, to 12.30pm Fri) Named after Dean 'Rocky' Page, local radio legend, Rocky's blares sincere rural twangings down the main. Inside is a wealth of country-and-western ephemera. Don't miss the 35m Botanical Garden Guitar out the back, inlaid with the handprints of 160 country musos: Slim Dusty to Kasey Chambers and everyone in between.

✦ Festivals & Events

South Australian Country Music Festival MUSIC
(www.riverlandcountrymusic.com) Country music is a big deal in Barmera, with the South Australian Country Music Festival held in each year in June. Bring your hat, your horse and your dusty old acoustic guitar and get into it.

🛏 Sleeping

**Discovery Holiday Parks
Lake Bonney**   CARAVAN PARK **$**

(☑ 08-8588 2234; www.discoveryholidayparks.com.au; Lakeside Dr, Barmera; unpowered/powered sites from $23/34, cabins from $99; ✳ 🐾 🏊) This keenly managed, facility-rich lakeside park has small beaches (safe swimming), electric barbecues, a camp kitchen, a laundry and plenty of room for kids to run amok. Lots of trees and waterfront camp sites too, plus tandems, canoes and paddle boats for hire.

🍴 Eating

Backyard Bread   CAFE **$**

(☑ 08-8588 2159; www.backyardbread.com.au; cnr Sturt Hwy & McKenzie Rd, Barmera; items $5-15; ⊙ 10am-4pm Fri-Mon) A rusty, iron-clad shopfront on the Waikerie side of Barmera, Backyard Bread is a deli/cafe baking 'bread bites': mouth-sized bits of flavour-packed bread, infused with local ingredients (red wine, olive oil, pumpkin, lemon myrtle etc). Try some on a tasting platter, or just duck in for a coffee and a slice of cake.

Overland Corner Hotel   PUB FOOD **$$**

(☑ 08-8588 7021; www.overlandcornerhotel.com.au; 205 Old Coach Rd, via Barmera; mains $17-28; ⊙ noon-2pm Tue-Sun, 6-8pm Thu-Sat) About 19km northwest of Barmera, this moody 1859 boozer is named after a Murray River bend where drovers used to camp. The pub walls ooze character and the meals are drover sized, plus there's a museum, resident ghosts, a beaut beer garden and four walking trails leading down to the river (pick up the *Historic Overland Corner* brochure in Barmera).

ℹ Information

Barmera Visitor Information Centre (☑ 08-8588 2289; www.barmeratourism.com.au; Barwell Ave, Barmera; ⊙ 9am-4pm Mon-Fri, 10am-1pm Sat & Sun) Can help with transport and accommodation bookings. Pick up the *Historic Overland Corner* and *Heritage Walk Barmera* walking trail brochures.

Loxton

POP 3780

Sitting above a broad loop of the slow-roaming Murray, Loxton proclaims itself the 'Garden City of the Riverland'. The vibe here is low-key, agricultural and untour-isty, with more tyre distributors, hardware shops and irrigation supply outlets than anything else. It's perhaps telling that the two most interesting things in town are ancient trees.

◎ Sights

Tree of Knowledge   LANDMARK

(Grant Schubert Dr) Down by the river near the caravan park, the Tree of Knowledge is marked with flood levels from previous years. The bumper flows of 1931, '73, '74, '75, and 2011 were totally outclassed by the flood-to-end-all-floods of 1956, marked about 4m up the trunk.

Loxton Pepper Tree   LANDMARK

(Allen Hosking Dr) This gnarled, weather-split, termite-ravaged old pepper tree dates back to 1878, allegedly planted by boundary rider William Charles Loxton, after whom the town was named. He lived near here in a little pine hut from 1878 to 1881.

🛏 Sleeping

Mill Cottage   B&B **$$**

(☑ 0439 866 990; www.millcottage.com.au; 2 Mill Rd; d from $177, extra person $35; ✳ 🐾) In an unlikely locale down a dead-end street in Loxton's industrial back streets, Mill Cottage is a dignified, genteel 1924 B&B option. Breakfast provisions (terrific eggs!) are included for your first two nights. The decor is a bit cottagey, but hey, it's a cottage. Sleeps six; two-night minimum.

Loxton Hotel   HOTEL, MOTEL **$$**

(☑ 1800 656 686, 08-8584 7266; www.loxtonhotel.com.au; 45 East Tce; d hotel/motel from $110/170; ✳ 🐾 🏊) With all profits siphoned back into the Loxton community, this large complex offers immaculate rooms with tasty weekend packages. The original pub dates from 1908, and it has been relentlessly extended. Bistro meals available for breakfast, lunch and dinner (mains $15 to $35 – order the Argentine beef brisket).

🍷 Drinking & Nightlife

Here's Your Beer   BAR

(☑ 0472 688 012; www.facebook.com/heresyourbeer; 2 Mill Rd; ⊙ 5-10pm Wed & Thu, 11am-10pm Fri, 10am-8pm Sun) In a big tin shed in Loxton's back blocks, this hipster haven pours craft beers and plates up beaut burgers to anyone who doesn't want to go to the local pub. The vibe is 'urbanish', says the owner. It's closed Saturdays (somewhat irritatingly).

ⓘ Information

Loxton Visitor Information Centre (☏1300 869 990, 08-8584 8071; www.loxtontourism. com.au; Bookpurnong Tce; ⊙9am-5pm Mon-Fri, to 4pm Sat, 10am-4pm Sun) A friendly place for accommodation, transport and national-park info, plus there's an art gallery and local dried fruits for sale (oh those peaches!). Has the *History Walk of Loxton* brochure been reprinted yet?

Berri

POP 4110

The name Berri derives from the Aboriginal term *berri berri*, meaning 'big bend in the river', and it was once a busy refuelling stop for wood-burning paddle steamers. These days Berri is an affluent regional hub for both state government and agricultural casual-labour agencies; it's one of the best places to chase down casual harvest jobs. The 'Big Orange' – one of Australia's iconic 'big' roadside tourist lures – awaits resuscitation on the edge of town.

⊙ Sights

Riverland Farmers Market   MARKET
(☏0417 824 648; www.riverlandfarmersmarket. org.au; Senior Citizens Hall, Crawford Tce; ⊙7.30-11.30am Sat) All the good stuff that grows around here in one place. A bacon-and-egg roll and some freshly squeezed orange juice will right your rudder.

ⓖ Tours

Canoe Adventures   CANOEING
(☏0421 167 645; www.canoeadventure.com.au; canoe hire per half-/full-day from $35/45, tours per adult/child half-day $95/60, full day $140/90) 🍃 Canoe hire, guided half- and full day canoe trips and camping expeditions ahoy! This outfit conducts the above from its Berri base, and can also deliver to most Riverland towns.

✦ Festivals & Events

Riverland Wine & Food Festival   FOOD & DRINK
(RWFF; www.riverlandwineandfood.com; ⊙Oct) Get festive on the banks of the Murray at the annual Riverland Wine & Food Festival, highlighting local produce and booze. It's a reasonably classy event – buy tickets in advance and dress up.

🍴 Sleeping & Eating

Berri Backpackers   HOSTEL $
(☏08-8582 3144; www.berribackpackers.com.au; 1081 Old Sturt Hwy; dm per night/week $35/160; ✱☏❄) This eclectic hostel is destination numero uno for work-seeking travellers, who chill out in quirky new-age surrounds after a hard day's manual toil. Rooms range from messy dorms to doubles, share houses, a tepee and a yurt – all for the same price. The managers can hook you up with harvest work (call in advance).

Sprouts Café   CAFE $
(☏08-8582 1228; www.sproutscafe.com.au; 28 Wilson St; mains $7-13; ⊙8.30am-4pm Mon-Fri, 9.30am-1pm Sat) A cheery cafe on the hill a few blocks back from the river, with a natty lime-green colour scheme. Serves soups, quiches, burgers, pasta, curries, wraps and mighty fine coffee. Homemade cakes, scones and chocolate pecan pudding too.

ⓘ Information

Berri Visitor Information Centre (☏08-8582 5511, 1300 768 582; www.berribarmera.sa.gov. au; Riverview Dr; ⊙9am-5pm Mon-Fri, to 2pm Sat, 10am-2pm Sun) Right by the river, with brochures, maps, waterproof canoeing guides ($10) and clued-up staff.

Renmark & Paringa

Renmark (population 7500) is the first major river town across from the Victorian border; about 254km from Adelaide. It's not a pumping tourist destination by any means, but has a relaxed vibe and a grassy waterfront, where you can pick up a houseboat. This is also the hub of the Riverland wine region: lurid signs on the roads into town scream 'Buy 6 Get 1 Free!' and 'Bulk port $5/litre!'.

On the other side of the river, 4km upstream, is Renmark's low-key satellite town, Paringa (population 950).

⊙ Sights

★**Twenty Third Street Distillery**   DISTILLERY
(☏08-8586 8500; www.23rdstreetdistillery.com. au; cnr 23rd St & Renmark Ave, Renmark; tour/tasting $15/15, combined $25; ⊙10am-4pm) Sip your way into some heady Riverland spirits at this fabulously renovated, art-deco factory on the road into Renmark. The old distillery here closed in 2002, buckling under market pressures, but it's made one helluva comeback. Gin, whisky and brandy are the

headliners: do a tasting, take a tour of the century-old copper stills, or both.

Tours

Murray River Walk
HIKING

(☑ 0418 808 475; www.murrayriverwalk.com.au; per person from $2300) ∅ Step out into the Murray River wilderness on this four-day, three-night guided hike, traversing private land through redgum forests and flood plain wetlands. Prices include all meals and houseboat accommodation, and a full day of river cruising on the final day. Ex-Renmark.

Canoe the Riverland
CANOEING

(☑ 0475 754 222; www.canoetheriverland.com; 835 Murtho Rd, Paringa; full-day tours adult/child $125/75) ∅ Slow-paced guided canoe tours on the Murray, departing Paringa, across the river from Renmark, with a picnic lunch of regional produce. Canoe/kayak hire (per day from $60/35) and sunset, moonlight and overnight camping tours also available.

🛏 Sleeping & Eating

BIG4 Renmark Riverfront Holiday Park
CARAVAN PARK $

(☑ 1300 664 612, 08-8586 8111; www.big4renmark. com.au; cnr Sturt Hwy & Patey Dr, Renmark; unpowered/powered sites from $41/48, cabins/villas from $115/155; ✳🛜🏊) Highlights of this spiffy riverfront park, 1km east of town, include a camp kitchen, canoe and paddleboat hire, splashy water park for kids and absolute waterfront cabins and powered sites. The newish corrugated-iron cabins are top notch, and look a little 'Riviera' surrounded by scraggy palms. The waterskiing fraternity swarms here during holidays.

Paringa Backpackers Resort
HOSTEL $

(☑ 0400 659 659; www.paringabackpackersresort. com.au; 11 Hughes Ave, Paringa; dm per night/week $35/130, d per week $300; ✳🛜🏊) Not a rancid laundry, dank bathroom or crummy kitchen in sight, Paringa's sparkling highway-side hostel really is a resort, with tidy ranks of bright ensuite dorms (8 or 10-bed maximum), palm trees, a gym, pool, games room, BBQ terrace... What's the catch? An almost complete absence of soul.

Renmark Hotel
HOTEL, MOTEL $$

(☑ 08-8586 6755, 1800 736 627; www.renmarkhotel. com.au; cnr Para St & Murray Ave, Renmark; d from $100; ✳🛜🏊) The sexy art deco curves of Renmark's humongous pub are looking good. Choose from older-style hotel rooms

and upmarket motel rooms. On a sultry evening it's hard to beat a cold beer and some grilled barramundi on the balcony at **Nanya Bistro** (mains $16 to $32, serving noon to 2.30pm and 5.30pm to 8.30pm).

Renmark Club
PUB FOOD $$

(☑ 08-8586 6611; www.renmarkclub.com.au; 160 Murray Ave, Renmark; mains $18-37; ⊙noon-2.30pm & 6-8.30pm; 🚼) Right on the river, this old pub/club has been reborn as a shiny mod bistro, serving upmarket pub food (rustic shank pie, seared Lyrup kangaroo with bush spices and quandong jus) with unbeatable water views.

🍷 Drinking & Nightlife

★ Woolshed Brewery
BREWERY

(☑ 08-8595 8188; www.aboverenmark.com.au; Wilkinson Rd, Murtho, via Paringa; ⊙11am-5pm) Amid the grapevines and orchards, 15km north of Renmark on a Murray River kink, the Woolshed is doing marvellous things. Part of the historic Wilkadene Homestead, the 100-year-old shed is now a craft-beer brewery, its broad riverside deck built from floorboards from Adelaide's demolished Centennial Hall (The Beatles stood here!). Dive into a tasting paddle and enjoy. Live weekend music.

ℹ Information

Renmark Paringa Visitor Information Centre (☑ 08-8586 6704, 1300 661 704; www.visit renmark.com; 84 Murray Ave, Renmark; ⊙9am-5pm Mon-Fri, 10am-2pm Sat & Sun) Has the usual local info, brochures and contacts for backpacker accommodation around town, plus an interpretive centre and bike hire (per half-/full day $25/40). The adjacent recommissioned 1911 paddle steamer *PS Industry* goes for a 90-minute chug on the first Sunday of the month (adult/child $20/10).

LIMESTONE COAST

The Limestone Coast – strung out along southeastern SA between the flat, olive span of the lower Murray River and the Victorian border – is a curiously engaging place. On the highways you can blow across these flatlands in under a day, no sweat – but around here the delight is in the detail. Detour off-road to check out the area's lagoons, surf beaches and sequestered bays. Also on offer are wine regions, photogenic fishing ports and snoozy agricultural towns. And what's *below* the road is even more amazing: a bizarre subterranean landscape of limestone caves, sinkholes and bottomless crater lakes – a broad, formerly volcanic area that's known as the Kanawinka Geopark.

Heading southeast, trace the Limestone Coast through the sea-salty Coorong, past beachy holiday towns to Mount Gambier, SA's second city. And, if you haven't already overdosed on wine in SA, the Coonawarra wine region awaits.

ⓘ Getting There & Away

The Dukes Hwy (A8) is the most direct route between Adelaide and Melbourne (729km), but the coastal Princes Hwy (B1; about 900km), adjacent to the Coorong National Park, is infinitely more scenic.

AIR

Regional Express (Rex; www.regionalexpress. com.au) flies daily between Adelaide and Mount Gambier (one-way from $176, 1¼ hours).

BUS

Premier Stateliner (www.premierstateliner. com.au) runs two bus routes – coastal and inland – between Adelaide and Mount Gambier ($83, six hours). From Adelaide along the coast (Wednesday, Friday and Sunday) via the Coorong, you can stop at Meningie ($42, two hours), Robe ($75, 4½ hours) and Beachport ($79, five hours). The inland bus runs Tuesday to Sunday via Naracoorte ($79, five hours) and Penola ($81, 5¾ hours).

Robe

POP 1020

Robe is a cherubic little fishing port that's become a holiday hotspot for Adelaidians and Melburnians alike. The sign saying 'Drain L Outlet' as you roll into town doesn't promise much, but along the main street you'll find quality eateries and boundless accommodation, and there are some magic beaches and lakes around town. Over Christmas and Easter, Robe is packed to the heavens – book *waaay* in advance.

◉ Sights

Robe Town Brewery　　　　BREWERY
(☑ 0415 993 693; www.robetownbrewery.com; 97 Millicent Rd; ⊙ noon-5pm Tue-Sun) Riding the crest of Australia's craft beer wave, Robe Town uses old-fangled methods to produce its hearty Shipwreck Stout and an excellent amber ale (among other creative brews). The brewery occupies a low-key shed in the

eastern outskirts of town. Is the Robe Beer Festival on here this September?

🏃 Activities

Steve's Place　　　　SURFING
(☑ 08-8768 2094; www.facebook.com/steves.place. 66; 26 Victoria St; ⊙ 9.30am-5pm Mon-Fri, to 1pm Sat, 10am-1pm Sun) Steve's Place has been here for 50 years (!) and rents out boards (per day $40), bodyboards ($20), paddleboards ($50) and wetsuits ($20). It's also the place for info on surfing lessons and the annual Robe Easter Classic in April, SA's longest-running surf comp (since 1968).

🛏 Sleeping

Rental agents with properties from as low as $100 per night in the off season include **Happyshack** (☑ 08-8768 2341, 0403 578 382; www. happyshack.com.au), **SAL Coastal Holidays** (☑ 08-8768 2737; www.bookrobeaccommodation. com.au; 25 Victoria St; ⊙ 9am-5pm Mon-Fri), **Ottson Holidays** (☑ 08-8768 2600; www.robe-holidayrentals.com.au) and **Robe Lifestyle** (☑ 1300 760 629; www.robelifestyle.com.au).

Lakeside Tourist Park　　CARAVAN PARK **$**
(☑ 08-8768 2193; www.lakesiderobe.com.au; 24 Main Rd; unpowered/powered sites from $36/37, cabins/villas from $80/140; ❄🐾) Right on Lake Fellmongery (a 'fellmonger' is a wool washer, don't you know) this abstractly laid-out, rather boutique park has heritage-listed pine trees and reception building (130-year-old former stables), plenty of grass, basic cabins and flashy villas. The closest camping to the town centre.

★ Caledonian Inn　　　　HOTEL **$$**
(☑ 08-8768 2029; www.caledonianinnrobe.com.au; 1 Victoria St; s/d without bathroom from $55/90, cottages/houses from $200/400; ❄🐾) This historic inn (1859) has a half-dozen bright and cosy upstairs pub rooms: shared bathrooms and no air-con, but great value. Out the back, 'tween pub and sea, are a row of lovely two-tier cottages and a three-bedroom rental house called Splash. The pub grub is classy too (mains $23 to $35, serving noon to 2pm and 6pm to 8pm).

Robe Harbour View Motel　　MOTEL **$$**
(☑ 08-8768 2155; www.robeharbourview.com. au; 2 Sturt St; d/f from $120/175; ❄🐾) At the quiet end of town (and a five-minute walk from the action), this tidy, well-run motel has namesake harbour views from the best half-dozen rooms at the front. The standard

rooms out the back don't have views but are perfectly decent (who needs views when you're asleep?). Expect nice linen, subtle colours and vamped-up bathrooms.

Eating

Union Cafe
CAFE $

(📞 08-8768 2627; 4/17-19 Victoria St; mains $7-18; ⊘8am-4pm; 🛜) Always busy, this curiously angled corner cafe has polished-glass fragments in the floor and surf art on the walls. Unionise your hangover with a big cooked breakfast, lashed with locally made hot sauce. Good coffee, pancakes, curries, salads and wraps. Hard to beat!

Vic St Pizza Project
PIZZA $$

(📞 08-8768 2081; www.facebook.com/pizzaproject robesa; 6 Victoria St; mains $17-25; ⊘11.30am-2pm & 5-8pm; 🍴) Go for something trad (Hawaiian, margarita, pepperoni) or something more daring (lamb souvlaki, squid and chorizo) – either way, the pizzas at this bright, roomy room are sure-fire crowd pleasers. Pastas, risottos and salads too. Open early for dinner when you've got hungry familiars in tow.

Sails
MODERN AUSTRALIAN $$$

(📞 08-8768 1954; www.sailsatrobe.com.au; 2 Victoria St; mains $28-44; ⊘noon-2.30pm & 6-9pm) Sails is Robe's classiest restaurant, and comes with a big rep for seafood (oh that Sicilian seafood stew!). Not in an undersea mood? Try the kangaroo fillets with beetroot fritters and horseradish, or the warm beetroot salad with roasted shallots and pecorino cheese. Lovely ambience; smooth service.

ℹ Information

Robe Visitor Information Centre (📞1300 367 144, 08-8768 2465; www.robe.com.au; Public Library, cnr Mundy Tce & Smillie St; ⊘9am-5pm Mon-Fri, 10am-5pm Sat & Sun) History displays, brochures and free internet. Look for the *Scenic Drive, Heritage Drive* and *A Walk Through History* pamphlets.

Meningie & Coorong National Park

The amazing **Coorong National Park** (📞08-8204 1910, 08-8575 1200; www.environ ment.sa.gov.au/parks; ⊘24hr) FREE is a fecund lagoon landscape curving along the coast for 145km from Lake Alexandrina towards

Kingston SE. A complex series of soaks and salt pans, it's separated from the sea by the chunky dunes of the **Younghusband Peninsula**. More than 200 waterbird species live here. *Storm Boy,* an endearing film about a young boy's friendship with a pelican (based on the novel by Colin Thiele), was filmed here.

In the 1860s when white settlers started to arrive, the resources of the Coorong were supporting a large Ngarrindjeri population. The Ngarrindjeri are still closely connected to the Coorong, and many still live here.

Bordering the Coorong on **Lake Albert** (a large arm of Lake Alexandrina), Meningie (population 940) was established as a minor port in 1866. These 'lower lakes' were soupy puddles for many years before returning to life after the 2011 Murray River floods. A momentary reprieve from climate change? Time will tell...

Activities

For a watery perspective, try Spirit of the Coorong (p749) or Cruise the Coorong (p750) cruises, or Canoe the Coorong (p749), all based in Goolwa on the Fleurieu Peninsula.

Sleeping

Coorong National Park Camp Sites
CAMPGROUND $

(📞08-8575 1200, 08-8204 1910; www.environment. sa.gov.au/parks; per vehicle $15) There are 18 bush/beach camp sites in Coorong National Park; you need a permit from the Department of Environment, Water & National Resources (DEWNR), available online.

Dalton on the Lake
B&B $$

(📞0428 737 161; www.facebook.com/daltonon thelake; 30 Narrung Rd, Meningie; d from $150; ❄) Generous in spirit and unfailingly clean, this lakeside B&B goes to great lengths to ensure your stay is comfortable. There'll be fresh bread baking when you arrive, jars of homemade biscuits, and bountiful bacon and eggs for breakfast. There's a modern self-contained studio off to one side, and a renovated stone cottage – book either, or both.

Coorong Cabins
RENTAL HOUSE $$

(📞0407 412 857; www.coorongcabins.com.au; 436 Seven Mile Rd, Meningie; d from $170, extra person $50; ❄) Two mod, self-contained rental houses – Pelican and Wren, sleeping four and two respectively – about 14km south of

DON'T MISS

NARACOORTE CAVES NATIONAL PARK

About 10km southeast of Naracoorte is World Heritage–listed **Naracoorte Caves National Park** (☑08-8762 2340; www.environment.sa.gov.au/naracoorte; 89 Wonambi Rd, Naracoorte; tours from adult/child/family $9/5.50/25, Wonambi Fossil Centre $13/8/36; ◷9am-5pm). The discovery of an ancient fossilised marsupial in these limestone caves raised palaeontological eyebrows around the world, and featured in the BBC's David Attenborough series *Life on Earth*. The 26 limestone caves here, including **Alexandra Cave**, **Cathedral Cave** and **Victoria Fossil Cave**, have bizarre stalactite and stalagmite formations.

Prospective Bruce Waynes should check out the **Bat Cave**, from which thousands of endangered southern bentwing bats exit en masse at dusk during summer. You can see the **Wet Cave** by self-guided tour (adult/child/family $9/5.50/25), but the others require ranger-guided tours. Single-cave tours start at adult/child/family $20/12.50/65; adventure caving starts at adult/child $60/35. The behind-the-scenes **World Heritage Tour** (per two people $280) gives you a scientific slant on the action. A new family-/wheelchair-friendly walkway is due to link the visitor centre with the main caves. There's also a self-registration **campground** (☑08-8760 1210; unpowered/powered sites $29/31) here, just past the turn-off to the caves.

The park visitor centre doubles as the impressive **Wonambi Fossil Centre** – a recreation of the rainforest that covered this area 200,000 years ago. Follow a ramp down past grunting, life-sized reconstructions of extinct animals, including a marsupial lion, a giant echidna, *Diprotodon australis* (koala meets grizzly bear), and *Megalania prisca* – 500kg of bad-ass goanna.

For more local info and tips on places to stay, contact **Naracoorte Visitor Information Centre** (☑1800 244 421, 08-8762 1399; www.naracoortelucindale.com; 36 MacDonnell St, Naracoorte; ◷9am-5pm Mon-Fri, 10am-4pm Sat & Sun) in Naracoorte.

---

town, but right on the waterfront within the national park. Decor is beachy-chi-chi, and there are bikes and kayaks available so you can explore the Coorong beyond where the road may take you.

✖ Eating

Cheese Factory Restaurant　PUB FOOD **$$**
(☑08-8575 1914; www.meningie.com.au; 3 Fiebig Rd, Meningie; mains $15-33; ◷noon-2pm daily, 6-8pm Wed-Sat) Lean on the front bar with the locals, or munch into steaks, schnitzels, Coorong mullet or a Coorong wrap (with mullet!) in the cavernous dining room of this converted cheese factory (you might have guessed). The very lo-fi **Meningie Cheese Factory Museum** (☑08-8575 1914; www.meningiecheesefactorymuseum.com; $5; ◷8.30am-5pm) is here too (butter churns, old typewriters, domestic knick-knackery).

❶ Information

Meningie Visitor Information Centre (☑08-8575 1770; www.meningie.com.au; 14 Princes Hwy, Meningie; ◷10am-4.30pm) The spot for local info, inside a craft shop.

Mount Gambier

POP 27,760

Strung out along the flatlands below an extinct volcano, Mount Gambier is the Limestone Coast's major town and service hub. 'The Mount' can sometimes seem a little short on urban virtues (though you can get a good coffee here these days!). But it's not what's above the streets that makes Mount Gambier special – it's the deep Blue Lake and the caves that worm their way though the limestone beneath the town. Amazing!

◉ Sights

Blue Lake　LAKE
(☑1800 087 187; www.mountgambierpoint.com.au/attractions/blue-lake; John Watson Dr; ◷24hr) **FREE** Mount Gambier's big-ticket item is the luminous, 75m-deep lake, which turns an insane hue of blue during summer. Perplexed scientists think it has to do with calcite crystals suspended in the water, which form at a faster rate during the warmer months. Consequently, if you visit between April and November, the lake will look much like any other – a steely grey. But in February, WOW!

Aquifer Tours (☑08-8723 1199; www.aquifer tours.com; cnr Bay Rd & John Watson Dr; adult/child/family $10/5/29; ☺tours hourly 9am-5pm Nov-Jan, to 2pm Feb-May & Sep-Oct, to noon Jun-Aug) runs hourly tours, taking you down near the lake shore in a glass-panelled lift. Or you can just wander around the rim of the lake along a 3.6km trail.

Riddoch Art Gallery   GALLERY
(☑08-8723 9566; www.riddochartgallery.org.au; Main Corner, 1 Bay Rd; ☺10am-5pm Mon & Wed-Fri, to 3pm Sat & Sun) **FREE** If Mount Gambier's famed Blue Lake isn't blue, don't feel blue – cheer yourself up at one of Australia's best regional galleries. There are three galleries housing touring and permanent exhibitions, contemporary installations and community displays. In the same Main Corner complex are heritage exhibits and a cinema screening local history flicks (11am and 1pm).

Cave Gardens   CAVE
(☑1800 087 187; www.mountgambierpoint.com.au/attractions/cave-gardens; cnr Bay Rd & Watson Tce; ☺24hr) **FREE** A 50m-deep sinkhole right in the middle of town, with the odd suicidal shopping trolley at the bottom. You can walk down into it, and watch the nightly **Sound & Light Show** (from 8.30pm) telling local Aboriginal Dreaming stories.

🛌 Sleeping

Old Mount Gambier Gaol   HOSTEL $
(☑08-8723 0032; www.theoldmountgambiergaol.com.au; 25 Margaret St; dm $30, d with/without bathroom $100/90, f from $180; ☎) If you can forget that this place was a prison until 1995 (either that or embrace the fact), these refurbished old buildings make for an atmospheric and comfortable stay. There are backpacker dorms available in old admin buildings, or you can up the spooky stakes and sleep in a former cell. There's a bar, too, in which to plot your next criminal exploit.

BIG4 Blue Lake
Holiday Park   CARAVAN PARK $
(☑08-8725 9856; www.bluelakeholidaypark.com.au; 100 Bay Rd; unpowered/powered sites $35/41, cabins/units/bungalows from $99/129/162; ☀☎ ☸) Adjacent to the Blue Lake, a golf course and walking and cycling tracks (but too far to walk into town), this amiable park has some natty grey-and-white cabins and well-weeded lawns. There are also spiffy contemporary, self-contained 'retreats' (from $199) that sleep four.

★**Colhurst House**   B&B $$
(☑08-8723 1309; www.colhursthouse.com.au; 3 Colhurst Pl; d from $170; ☀) Most locals don't know about Colhurst – it's up a laneway off a side street (Wyatt St), and you can't really see it from downtown Mount G. It's an 1878 mansion built by Welsh migrants, and manages to be old-fashioned without being overly twee. There's a gorgeous wrap-around balcony upstairs with great views over the rooftops. Cooked breakfast. Nice.

🍴 Eating

★**Metro Bakery & Cafe**   CAFE $$
(☑08-8723 3179; www.metrobakeryandcafe.com.au; 13 Commercial St E; mains $8-34; ☺8.30am-5pm Mon-Wed, to late Thu-Sat, 9am-3pm Sun) Ask a local where they go for coffee: chances are they'll say, 'the Metro, you fool!'. In the thick of things on the main drag, it's an efficient cafe with natty black-and-white decor, serving omelettes, salads, sandwiches, pastries and meatier mains (try the twice-cooked lamb rump salad). There's a wine bar here too, brimming with Coonawarra cabernets. Book for dinner.

Macs Hotel   PUB FOOD $$
(☑08-8725 2402; www.themacshotel.com.au; 21 Bay Rd; mains $17-35; ☺noon-2.30pm & 5.30-9pm) Char-grilled, chilli-and-garlic marinated calamari; pork belly with cauliflower puree and star anise glaze... Not your standard pub grub, but the old Macs is far from a standard pub these days. A super renovation has elevated it above the fray, attracting Mount Gambier's brightest young things by the dozen. Join them for a drink in the 'cider garden' before dinner.

ℹ️ Information

Mount Gambier Visitor Information Centre (☑1800 087 187, 08-8724 9750; www.mount gambiertourism.com.au; 35 Jubilee Hwy E; ☺9am-5pm Mon-Fri, 10am-4pm Sat & Sun) Has details on local sights, activities, transport and accommodation, plus *Heritage Walk* and *Historic Hotels* pamphlets and a town history movie. The **Lady Nelson Discovery Centre** (☑1800 087 187; www.mountgambier. sa.gov.au; Mount Gambier Visitor Information Centre, 35 Jubilee Hwy E; ☺9am-5pm Mon-Fri, 10am-4pm Sat & Sun) is here too. Bike hire available.

Penola & the Coonawarra Wine Region

A rural town on the way up (what a rarity!), Penola (population 1710) is the kind of place where you walk down the main street and three people say 'Hello!' to you before you reach the pub. The town is famous for two things: first, for its association with the Sisters of St Joseph of the Sacred Heart, cofounded in 1867 by Australia's first saint, Mary MacKillop; and second, for being smack-bang in the middle of the Coonawarra wine region (killer cabernets).

◎ Sights

**Mary MacKillop
Interpretive Centre** MUSEUM
(☑08-8737 2092; www.mackilloppenola.org.au; cnr Portland St & Petticoat Lane, Penola; adult/child $5/free; ☉10am-4pm) The centre occupies a jaunty building with a gregarious entrance pergola (perhaps not as modest as St Mary might have liked!). There's oodles of info on Australia's first saint here, plus the Woods MacKillop Schoolhouse, the first school in Australia for children from lower socio-economic backgrounds.

🛏 Sleeping

Penola Backpackers HOSTEL $
(☑08-8736 6170, 0428 866 700; www.penola backpackers.com.au; 59 Church St, Penola; dm/s/d/f from $40/50/140/160; 🛜) In a Spanish Mission–style house on the main street, this five-bedroom backpackers has found its niche in the Limestone Coast accommodation scene. There's a tidy and clean kitchen, roses and daffodils out the front and a BBQ terrace out the back. Air-con in some rooms. Ask about their beach house in Southend.

Alexander Cameron Suites MOTEL $$
(☑1800 217 011, 08-8737 2200; www.alexander cameronsuites.com.au; 23 Church St, Penola; s/d/tw/f from $145/145/160/190; ❋🛜) Looking much less bleak now that some trees have matured around it, this newish motel over on the Mount Gambier side of town offers stylish rooms, well-tended gardens and rural Australian architectural stylings. It's named after Penola's founder, a wiry Scottish pastoralist: you can check out his statue next to the pub. Three-bedroom house also available (one bedroom $180, extra bedroom $30).

DON'T MISS

COONAWARRA WINERIES

When it comes to spicy cabernet sauvignon, it's just plain foolish to dispute the virtues of the **Coonawarra wine region** (www.coonawarra.org). The *terra rossa* (red earth) soils here also produce irresistible shiraz and chardonnay. Five of the Coonawarra's best:

Majella Wines (☑08-8736 3055; www.majellawines.com.au; Lynn Rd, Coonawarra; ☉10am-4.30pm) The family that runs Majella are fourth-generation Coonawarrans, so they know a thing or two about gutsy reds (love 'The Musician' shiraz-cabernet).

Rymill Coonawarra (☑08-8736 5001; www.rymill.com.au; Riddoch Hwy, Coonawarra; ☉11am-5pm Mon-Sat, noon-5pm Sun) Rymill rocks the local boat by turning out some of the best sauvignon blanc you'll ever taste. The cellar door is fronted by a statue of two duelling steeds – appropriately rebellious.

Wynns Coonawarra Estate (☑08-8736 2225; www.wynns.com.au; 1 Memorial Dr, Coonawarra; ☉10am-5pm) The oldest Coonawarra winery, Wynns' cellar door dates from 1896 and was built by Penola pioneer John Riddoch. Top-quality shiraz, fragrant riesling and golden chardonnay are the mainstays.

Zema Estate (☑08-8736 3219; www.zema.com.au; Riddoch Hwy, Coonawarra; ☉9am-5pm Mon-Fri, 10am-4pm Sat & Sun) A steadfast, traditional winery started by the Zema family in the early '80s. It's a low-key affair with a handmade vibe infusing the shiraz and cab sav.

Balnaves of Coonawarra (☑08-8737 2946; www.balnaves.com.au; 15517 Riddoch Hwy, Coonawarra; ☉9am-5pm Mon-Fri, noon-5pm Sat & Sun) The tasting notes here ooze florid wine speak (dark seaweed, anyone?), but even if your nosing skills aren't that subtle, you'll enjoy the cab sav and chardonnay.

✗ Eating

★ **Pipers of Penola**   MODERN AUSTRALIAN $$$
(☑ 08-8737 3999; www.pipersofpenola.com.au; 58 Riddoch St, Penola; mains $35-40; ☺ 6-9pm Tue-Sat) A classy, intimate dining room tastefully constructed inside a 1908 Methodist church, with friendly staff and seasonal fare. The menu is studded with ingredients like truffled parsnip, mustard fruit and *labneh* (Lebanese yoghurt cheese) – serious gourmet indicators! The prices are lofty, but so is the quality. Superb wine list with lots of locals (the beer list could be craftier).

ⓘ Information

Penola Visitor Information Centre (☑ 1300 045 373, 08-8737 2855; www.wattlerange. sa.gov.au/tourism; 27 Arthur St, Penola; ☺ 9am-5pm Mon-Fri, 10am-4pm Sat & Sun) Services the Coonawarra region, with info about local cycling routes and winery tours. The **John Riddoch Centre** (☑ 08-8737 2855; www.wattlerange.sa.gov.au/tourism; 27 Arthur St, Penola; ☺ 9am-5pm Mon-Fri, 10am-4pm Sat & Sun) is also here. Pick up the *Walk With History* brochures, and the *Coonawarra Wineries Walking Trail* brochure detailing an easy 5km walk past five wineries.

YORKE PENINSULA

For history buffs, the northwestern end of boot-shaped 'Yorkes' – just under two hours northwest of Adelaide – has a trio of towns called the Copper Triangle: Moonta (the mine), Wallaroo (the smelter) and Kadina (the service town). Settled by Cornish miners, this area drove the regional economy following a copper boom in the early 1860s. In the big-sky peninsula country to the east and south, things are much more agricultural and laid-back, with sleepy holiday towns, isolated Innes National Park, remote surf breaks and empty coastline.

☞ Tours

Heading Bush   OUTDOORS
(☑ 08-8356 5501; www.headingbush.com; 3-day tours from $695) ✐ Explore Yorkes – wildlife, cliffs, beaches, Aboriginal culture and even a winery – on a three-day tour ex-Adelaide. Price includes dorm accommodation; single, double or twin accommodation is available at extra cost.

ⓘ Information

Copper Coast Visitor Information Centre (☑ 1800 654 991, 08-8821 2333; www.yorkepeninsula.com.au; 50 Mines Rd; ☺ 9am-5pm Mon-Fri, 10am-4pm Sat & Sun) Yorke Peninsula's main visitor info centre, stocked to the rafters with brochures: look for the *Walk the Yorke* pamphlet detailing a dozen interesting trails, short and long, all around the peninsula; and the *Kadina Walking Trail* map. The **Farm Shed Museum** (www.farmshed.net.au; Copper Coast Visitor Information Centre, 50 Mines Rd; adult/child/family $10/5/23, railway per ride $2; ☺ 9am-5pm Mon-Fri, 10am-4pm Sat & Sun, railway 1st & 3rd Sun of the month) is here too.

Yorke Peninsula Visitor Information Centre (☑ 08-8853 2600, 1800 202 445; www.visityorkepeninsula.com.au; 29 Main St, Minlaton; ☺ 9am-5pm Mon-Fri) In agricultural Minlaton, right in the middle of the southern Yorke Peninsula. It's a good source of info on the lower half of the peninsula (including shipwrecks!).

ⓘ Getting There & Away

Yorke Peninsula Coaches (☑ 08 8821 2755; www.ypcoaches.com.au) Daily buses from Adelaide to Kadina ($40, 2¼ hours), Wallaroo ($40, 2½ hours) and Moonta ($40, three hours), with another route running down the peninsula's east coast daily except Tuesday and Thursday, stopping at Port Vincent ($52, 3¼ hours), Stansbury ($52, 3½ hours) and Edithburgh ($54, four hours).

West Coast

Fronting Spencer Gulf, the Yorke Peninsula's west coast has a string of shallow swimming beaches, plus the 'Copper Triangle' historic mining towns of Kadina, Wallaroo and Moonta, all a short drive from each other. **Kernewek Lowender** (www.kernewek.org), aka the Copper Coast Cornish Festival, happens around here in May of odd-numbered years. Further south, Point Turton is a magical little spot with a beaut caravan park and hillside tavern.

Wallaroo

POP 3230
Still a major wheat port and fishing town, Wallaroo is on the way up: there's a huge new subdivision north of town, a new shopping complex inserted in the middle of the old town, and the shiny new Copper Cove Marina is full of expensive boats. There are plenty of pubs here, and the pubs are full of folks.

That said, the old town area retains a romantically weathered 'seen-better-days' vibe: wander around the compact little streets and old cottages in the shadows of the huge grain silos and soak up the atmosphere (the place to pen your next novel?).

Sights

Wallaroo Heritage & Nautical Museum
MUSEUM

(☏08-8823 3015; www.nationaltrust.org.au; cnr Jetty Rd & Emu St; adult/child $6/3; ⊙10am-4pm) Down by the water, the stoic 1865 post office now houses the Wallaroo Heritage & Nautical Museum. There are several of these little National Trust museums around Yorkes: in Port Victoria, in Ardrossan, in Milaton, in Edithburgh... But this is the best of them, with tales of square-rigged English ships and George the pickled giant squid.

Sleeping & Eating

Sonbern Lodge Motel
HOTEL, MOTEL $

(☏08-8823 2291; www.sonbernlodgemotel.com. au; 18 John Tce; d/f from $85/100; ❋) The old Sonbern – a 100-year-old grand temperance hotel – is looking a bit weather-beaten these days, but it remains an old-fashioned charmer, right down to the old wooden balcony and antique wind-up phone. There are basic pub-style rooms in the main building (with bathrooms), and newish motel units out the back. Breakfast available.

Coopers Alehouse
PUB FOOD $$

(☏08-8823 2488; www.wallaroomarinahotel.com; 11 Heritage Dr; mains $15-39; ⊙noon-2.30pm & 6-8.30pm) Head downstairs at the Wallaroo Marina Apartments (☏08-8823 4068; www. wallarooapartments.com.au; d/apt from $144/184; ❋⏾) and you'll find cold Coopers ales, bistro meals (mixed grills, Spencer Gulf prawns and flathead), seductive marina views and regular live bands. Glowing in the corner, the pizza oven looks like Luke Skywalker's uncle's house in Star Wars. Try the 'Colossus' beef burger.

Moonta

POP 2670

In the late 19th century, the Moonta copper mine was the richest in Australia. These days the town, which calls itself 'Australia's Little Cornwall', maintains a faded glory and a couple of decent pubs.

Sights

Moonta Mines Museum
MUSEUM

(☏08-8825 1891; www.moontatourism.org.au; Verran Tce; adult/child $8/4; ⊙1-4pm, from 11am during school holidays) This impressive 1878 stone edifice was once the Moonta Mines Model School and had 1100 students. These days it's the centrepiece of the sprawling Moonta Heritage Site, and captures mining life – at work and at home – in intimately preserved detail. A little tourist train chugs out of the museum car park at 2pm on Wednesday, and 1pm, 2pm and 3pm on weekends (adult/child $8/4; daily during school holidays).

Sleeping & Eating

Cottage by Cornwall
B&B $$

(☏0438 313 952; www.cottagebycornwall.com.au; 24 Ryan St; d from $160, extra adult/child $20/free; ❋) The classiest accommodation in Moonta by a country mile, this tizzied-up 1863 cottage has three bedrooms (sleeping six), plus fancy bedding, mod furnishings and a clawfoot bath. It's just a short stroll to the pub and the Cornish Kitchen bakery. Two-night minimum stay. Cooked and continental provisions supplied.

Cornish Kitchen
BAKERY $

(☏08-8825 3030; 10-12 Ellen St; items $4-10; ⊙9am-3pm Mon-Fri, to 2pm Sat) After a dirty day digging down the mine, swing your pick into the Cornish Kitchen for the ultimate Cornish pastie (the chunky steak and onion pies are pretty great too).

❶ Information

Moonta Visitor Information Centre (☏08-8825 1891; www.moontatourism.org.au; Old Railway Station, Blanche Tce; ⊙9am-5pm) Stocks a smattering of history pamphlets including the Moonta Walking Trail map, and details on the Moonta Heritage Site 1.5km east of town.

East Coast

About 24km south of Ardrossan is magical little Black Point, a holiday hot spot with a long row of shacks built right on the dunes above a protected, north-facing beach (perfect if you've got kids).

Further south, unpretentious Port Vincent (population 480) is the happening-est town on the east coast, with lots of accommodation, a waterfront pub and a busy marina, from where yachts dart across to Adelaide. Continuing south, Stansbury (population

Eyre Peninsula & Yorke Peninsula

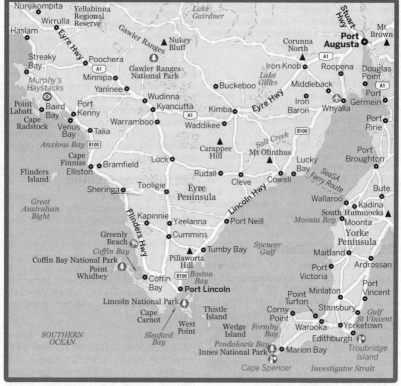

550; www.stansburysa.com) has a couple of motels and a beaut waterside pub.

Further south again, Edithburgh (population 400) has a free tidal swimming pool in a small cove. From the cliff tops here, views extend offshore to sandy **Troubridge Island Conservation Park** (☑ 08-8854 3200; www.environment.sa.gov.au/parks), home to much bird life including penguins, cormorants and terns. You can stay the night here at the old **lighthouse** (☑ 08-8852 6290; www.environment.sa.gov.au/parks; per adult/child incl transfers $120/60, min charge $480). The island is steadily eroding – what the sea wants, the sea will have...

South Coast & Innes National Park

At **Innes National Park** (☑ 08-8854 3200; www.environment.sa.gov.au/parks; via Stenhouse Bay Rd, Stenhouse Bay; per vehicle $10; ⊙ 24hr)

sheer cliffs plunge into indigo waters and rocky offshore islands hide small coves and sandy beaches. **Marion Bay** (www.marionbay.com.au), just outside the park, and **Stenhouse Bay** and **Pondalowie Bay**, both within the park, are the main local settlements. Pondalowie Bay has a bobbing lobster-fishing fleet and a gnarly surf beach. The rusty ribs of the 711-tonne steel barque *Ethel*, which foundered in 1904, arc forlornly from the sands just south of here.

Follow the sign past the Cape Spencer turn-off to the ghost-town of Inneston, a gypsum-mining village abandoned in 1930.

🛏 Sleeping

⭐ **Marion Bay Motel**   MOTEL $$
(☑ 08-8854 4044; www.marionbaymotel.com.au; Jetty Rd, Marion Bay; s/d/tr $120/150/170; ❄ 🐾) A highlight of tiny Marion Bay is this wing of five spiffy motel rooms (white walls, new TVs, nice linen) – a welcome surprise

if you've been camping or hanging out in sandy-floor beach shacks and are in need of a little sophistication. The **Marion Bay tavern** (📞 08-8854 4141; www.marionbaytavern. au; mains $16-38; ☉ bar 11am-late, meals noon-2pm & 6-8pm) is just next door.

★ **Yondah Beach House**　　RENTAL HOUSE $$$
(📞 0417 829 010; www.yondah.com.au; off South Coast Rd, Point Yorke; 1/2/3 bedrooms from $300/380/440; ❋ ☈ ❋) 🐾 One of the stars of the SA tourism scene, Yondah is a gorgeous, architect-designed, three-bedroom beach house, way over in the south-coast dunes east of Marion Bay. It's a wonderfully isolated spot, with lots of wildlife and luxe privacy by the bucketload. Good value for a group or a big family. And you can bring your dog!

EYRE PENINSULA & THE WEST COAST

The vast, straw-coloured triangle of Eyre Peninsula is Australia's big-sky country, and is the promised land for seafood fans. Meals out here rarely transpire without the option of trying the local oysters, tuna or whiting. Sublime national parks punctuate the coast along with world-class surf breaks and low-key holiday towns, thinning out as you head west towards the Great Australian Bight, the Nullarbor Plain and Western Australia.

The peninsula's photogenic wild western flank is an important breeding ground for southern right whales, Australian sea lions and great white sharks (the scariest scenes in *Jaws* were shot here). There are some memorable opportunities to encounter these submariners along the way.

🚩 Tours

Goin' Off Safaris　　TOURS
(📞 0428 877 488; www.goinoffsafaris.com.au; tours from $185) Check the big-ticket items off your Eyre Peninsula 'to-do' list – sharks, tuna, sea lions and seafood – with local guides. Day trips around Port Lincoln and Coffin Bay, plus overnight jaunts, seafood-focused trips and fishing expeditions.

❶ Getting There & Away

AIR
Regional Express (Rex; www.regionalexpress. com.au) operates daily flights from Adelaide to Whyalla (one way from $128), Port Lincoln (from $132) and Ceduna (from $189).

BOAT
The handy **SeaSA** (📞 08-8823 0777; www. seasa.com.au; 1 Heritage Dr, Wallaroo; one-way per adult/child/car from $35/10/140) car ferry running between Wallaroo on the Yorke Peninsula and Lucky Bay near Cowell on the Eyre Peninsula shaves 350km and several hours off the drive from Adelaide via Port Augusta. The voyage takes around two hours one way. Services have been sporadic over recent years: book in advance to guarantee your passage, and reconfirm a few days prior.

BUS
Premier Stateliner (www.premierstateliner.com. au) has daily buses from Adelaide to Port Augusta ($63, 4¼ hours), Whyalla ($70, 5½ hours), Port Lincoln ($126, 9¾ hours), Streaky Bay ($132, 10 hours) and Ceduna ($147, 11¼ hours).

TRAIN
The famous *Ghan* train connects Adelaide with Darwin via Port Augusta; the *Indian Pacific* (between Perth and Sydney) connects with the *Ghan* at Port Augusta. See www.greatsouthern rail.com.au for details.
Pichi Richi Railway (📞 1800 777 245; www.prr. org.au; Port Augusta Train Station, Stirling Rd; one-way adult/child/family $54/20/128) runs historic trains from Port Augusta to Quorn in the Flinders Ranges on most Saturdays, following the old *Ghan* train route.

Port Augusta

POP 13,900
From utilitarian, frontier-like Port Augusta – the 'Crossroads of Australia' – highways and railways roll west across the Nullarbor into WA, north to the Flinders Ranges or Darwin, south to Adelaide or Port Lincoln, and east to Sydney. Not a bad position! The old town centre has considerable appeal, with some elegant old buildings and a revitalised waterfront: locals cast lines into the blue as Indigenous kids backflip off jetties.

⊙ Sights

Australian Arid Lands Botanic Garden　　GARDENS
(📞 08-8641 9116; www.aalbg.sa.gov.au; 144 Stuart Hwy; guided tours adult/child $8/5; ☉ gardens 7.30am-dusk, visitor centre 9am-5pm Mon-Fri, 10am-4pm Sat & Sun) 🆓 Just north of town, the excellent (and free!) botanic garden has 250 hectares of sandhills, clay flats and desert fauna and flora (ever seen a Sturt's Desert Pea?). Explore on your own, or take a guided tour (10am Monday to Friday). There's a cafe here too.

🛏 Sleeping & Eating

Oasis Apartments APARTMENT **$$**
(☑ 08-8648 9000; www.majestichotels.com.au;
Marryatt St; d/f $160/260; 🅿❄🛜♨) Catering
largely to conventioneers, this group of 75
luxury units (from studios to two-bedroom)
with jaunty designs is right by the water. All
rooms have washing machines, dryers, TVs,
fridges, microwaves and flashy interior de-
sign. Fortress-like security might make you
feel like you're in some sort of elitist com-
pound... which you possibly are.

★ **Archers' Table** CAFE **$**
(☑ 08-7231 5657; www.archerstable.com.au; 11b
Loudon Rd; mains $9-12; ⊙8am-4pm Mon-Fri,
to 3pm Sat, to 2pm Sun) Beneath an attrac-
tive vine-hung awning across the gulf from
downtown PA, Archers is an urbane cafe
with small-town prices, serving interesting
cafe fare (beef, pumpkin and spinach lasa-
gne; spicy lentil and tomato soup; seafood
salad with walnuts, feta and lemon tahini
dressing). Great coffee, funky mural, open
seven days. We have a winner!

ℹ Information

Port Augusta Visitor Information Centre
(☑ 08-8641 9193, 1800 633 060; www.port
augusta.sa.gov.au; Wadlata Outback Centre,
41 Flinders Tce; ⊙9am-5.30pm Mon-Fri,
10am-4pm Sat & Sun) This is the major
information outlet for the Eyre Peninsula,
Flinders Ranges and the outback. It's part of
the **Wadlata Outback Centre** (www.wadlata.
sa.gov.au; 41 Flinders Tce; adult/child/family
$21/12/46; ⊙9am-5.30pm Mon-Fri, 10am-
4pm Sat & Sun).

Port Lincoln

POP 16,150

Prosperous Port Lincoln, the 'Tuna Capital
of the World', overlooks broad Boston Bay
on the southern end of Eyre Peninsula. It's
a raffish fishing town a long way from any-
where, but the vibe here is energetic (dare
we say progressive!).

If not for a lack of fresh water, Port Lin-
coln might have become the South Aus-
tralian capital. These days it's salt water
(and the tuna therein) that keeps the town
ticking. The grassy foreshore is a busy
promenade, and there are some good pubs,
eateries and aquatic activities here to keep
you out of trouble.

⊙ Sights

Lincoln National Park NATIONAL PARK
(☑ 08-8688 3111; www.environment.sa.gov.au/
parks; via Proper Bay Rd; per vehicle $11; ⊙24hr)
Lincoln National Park is 13km south of Port
Lincoln. You'll find roaming emus, roos and
brush-tailed bettongs, safe swimming coves,
vast dunes and pounding surf beaches. En-
try is via self-registration on the way in. The
Port Lincoln Visitor Information Centre can
advise on bush camping (per vehicle $12)
and **cottage accommodation** (☑ 0419 302
300; www.visitportlincolnaccommodation.net.au/
donington-cottage; per night $100) within the
park, including camping grounds at Fish-
erman's Point, Memory Cove, September
Beach and Surfleet Cove.

⊙ Tours

Tasting Eyre TOURS
(☑ 08-8687 0455; www.tastingeyre.com.au; adult/
child $99/79) Scenery, wildlife and fishing are
the names of the games on this well-planned
day tour around Port Lincoln, including
a walk in Lincoln National Park, a visit to
Whalers Way and seafood tasting at the
Fresh Fish Place.

Adventure Bay Charters BOATING
(☑ 08-8682 2979; www.adventurebaycharters.
com.au; 2 South Quay Blvd) Carbon-neutral Ad-
venture Bay Charters takes you swimming
with sea lions (adult/child $205/145) and
cage diving with great white sharks (ob-
server $395/285 – add $125 if you want to
actually get in the water, or view through
a submerged 'aqua sub'). Multiday ocean
safaris also available. Note that research
suggests that human interaction with sea
mammals potentially alters their behav-
ioural and breeding patterns.

Calypso Star Charters ADVENTURE
(☑ 08-8682 3939; www.sharkcagediving.com.
au; 3/10 South Quay Blvd; 1-day dive adult/child
$495/345) Runs submerged cage dives to
see great white sharks around the Neptune
Islands. Book in advance (cheaper if you're
just watching nervously from the boat).
Also runs four-hour swimming with sea li-
ons trips (adult/child/family $190/130/540).
Note that research suggests that human
interaction with sea mammals potentially
alters their behavioural and breeding
patterns.

✣ Festivals & Events

Tunarama Festival　　　CULTURAL
(www.tunarama.net) The annual Tunarama Festival on the Australia Day weekend in January celebrates every finny facet of the tuna-fishing industry (including the ethically questionable 'tuna toss').

🛏 Sleeping

★ Port Lincoln YHA　　　HOSTEL $
(☑ 08-8682 3605; www.yha.com.au; 26 London St; dm $24-35, tw/d/f from $80/100/125; ✳@🛜)
Run by a high-energy couple who have spent a fortune renovating the place, this impressive 84-bed hostel occupies a former squash court complex. Thoughtful bonuses include chunky sprung mattresses, reading lights, a cafe/bar and power outlets in lockers. Outrageously clean, and with 300 movies for a rainy day (including *Jaws*). Staff can help with activities bookings too.

★ Tanonga　　　B&B $$$
(☑ 0427 277 417; www.tanonga.com.au; Pope Dr, Charlton Gully; d incl breakfast from $340; ✳)
🌿 Two plush, solar-powered, architect-designed ecolodges, standing in stark-white modernist isolation in the hills behind Port Lincoln. They're both super-private and surrounded by native bush, bird life and walking trails. Roll into town for dinner, or order a DIY pack of local produce. Truly unique and absolutely glorious.

✕ Eating

★ Fresh Fish Place　　　SEAFOOD $
(☑ 08-8682 2166; www.portlincolnseafood.com.au; 20 Proper Bay Rd; meals $9-20; ⊙8.30am-6pm Mon-Fri, to 2pm Sat) Check the 'fish of the day' on the blackboard out the front of this fabulous seafood shack. Inside you can buy fresh local seafood straight off the boats (King George whiting, tuna, kingfish, flathead, squid etc), plus Coffin Bay oysters for $12 a dozen and superb fish and chips. Not to be missed! Seafood tasting tours and cooking classes also available.

ℹ Information

Port Lincoln Visitor Information Centre
(☑ 1300 788 378, 08-8683 3544; www.visitportlincoln.net; 3 Adelaide Pl; ⊙9am-5pm Mon-Fri, 10am-4pm Sat & Sun) This mega-helpful place books accommodation, has national-parks information and passes, and stocks the *Port Lincoln & District Cycling Guide*,
and the *Parnkalla Walking Trail* map, tracing a course around the Port Lincoln coastline.

Coffin Bay

POP 650

Oyster lovers rejoice! Deathly sounding Coffin Bay (named in 1802 by English explorer Matthew Flinders after his buddy Sir Isaac Coffin) is a snoozy fishing village basking languidly in the warm sun...until a 4000-strong holiday horde arrives every January. Slippery, salty oysters from the nearby beds are exported worldwide – superb!

◉ Sights

Coffin Bay National Park　　　NATIONAL PARK
(☑ 08-8688 3111; www.environment.sa.gov.au/parks; via Coffin Bay Rd; per vehicle $10; ⊙24hr)
Along the ocean side of Coffin Bay is wild, coastal Coffin Bay National Park, overrun with roos, emus and fat goannas. Access for conventional vehicles is limited: you can get to picturesque Point Avoid (coastal lookouts, rocky cliffs, good surf and whales passing between May and October) and Yangie Bay (arid rocky landscapes and walking trails), but otherwise you'll need a 4WD. There are some isolated camp sites within the park (per vehicle $12), generally with dirt-road access.

🛏 Sleeping & Eating

★ Dawes Point Cottage　　　RENTAL HOUSE $$
(☑ 0427 844 568; www.coffinbayholidayrentals.com.au/properties/dawes-point; 5 Heron Ct; per night from $180; ✳) This old-fashioned fishing shack (Aussie author Tim Winton would call it 'fish deco') was won by the present owners in a card game! Now a million-dollar property, it maintains its modesty despite sitting right on the water. There are three bedrooms and a beaut little deck above the gin-clear bay. Sleeps six.

1802 Oyster Bar & Bistro　　　BISTRO $$
(☑ 08-8685 4626; www.1802oysterbar.com.au; 61 Esplanade; mains $18-33; ⊙noon-2.30pm Tue-Sun, 6-8.30pm Thu-Sat) This snappy-looking place on the way into town, with its broad deck and rammed-earth walls, looks out across the boat-filled harbour. Order a bluefin tuna steak, some lamb cutlets with parsnip *skordalia*, or a bowl of seafood chowder to go with your crafty 1802 Cutters Dredge Lager (on tap). Pizzas and (of course) oysters also available.

ADELAIDE & SOUTH AUSTRALIA STREAKY BAY & AROUND

Streaky Bay & Around

POP 1630

This endearing little seasider (actually on Blanche Port) takes its name from the streaks of seaweed Matt Flinders spied in the bay as he sailed by. Visible at low tide, the seagrass attracts ocean critters and the bigger critters that eat them – first-class fishing.

The town itself has a terrific pub, plenty of accommodation and a couple of good eateries: a lovely spot to dream away a day or three.

◉ Sights

Murphy's Haystacks   LANDMARK
(www.nullarbornet.com.au/themes/murphys haystacks.html; off Flinders Hwy, Point Labbatt; per person/family $2/5; ☺ daylight hours) A few kilometres down the Point Labatt road are the globular Murphy's Haystacks, an improbable congregation of 'inselbergs' – colourful, weather-sculpted granite outcrops, which are an estimated 1500 million years old (not much chance of them eroding while you prep your camera – take your time).

⌫ Sleeping & Eating

Streaky Bay Motel & Villas   MOTEL **$$**
(☑ 08-8626 1126; www.streakybaymotelandvillas. com.au; 11-13 Alfred Tce; motel s/d/f from $110/130/160, villas $170-260; ☲☂☲) A tidy row of bricky, older-style motel units (with a facelift), plus an ever-expanding complex of family-size villas that are much more 'now' (spiky pot plants, mushroom-hued render, lime-coloured outdoor furniture). Good off-season rates and three-bedroom houses also available. There's a pool, too, if you don't fancy the shark-proof swimming enclosure down at the jetty.

Bay Funktion   CAFE **$**
(☑ 0428 861 242; www.bayfunktion.com.au; cnr Wells St & Bay Rd; mains $7-12; ☺ 8am-5pm Mon-Fri, to 2pm Sat) In a lovely old brick-and-stone shopfront on the main street, funky Bay Funktion is part cafe, part gift shop, part wedding planner (hence the slightly odd name). But as a cafe, it's great! Baguettes, pizzas, focaccias, breakfast wraps, slabs of cake and killer coffee, often served from the hip coffee van parked out the front. Also open Sundays during summer.

ⓘ Information

Streaky Bay Visitor Information Centre
(☑ 08-8626 7033; www.streakybay.com.au; 21 Bay Rd; ☺ 9am-12.30pm & 1.30-5pm Mon-Fri) For the local low-down, swing by the visitor info centre.

Ceduna

POP 2290

Despite the locals' best intentions, Ceduna remains a raggedy fishing town that just can't shake its tag as a sand-blown, edgy pit stop en route to WA (there are *five* caravan parks here). But the local oysters love it! And if you're heading west in whale season (May to October), Ceduna is the place for updates on sightings at Head of Bight.

◉ Sights

Thevenard   AREA
(Thevenard Rd; 24hr) For a dose of hard-luck, weather-beaten atmospheria, take a drive out to Thevenard, Ceduna's photogenic port suburb on the peninsula south of town. Boarded-up shops, a pub with barred windows, dusty old iron-clad shacks... all loomed-over by the massive silos next to the pier. If you're a painter or writer, this is fertile fuel for the imagination!

✦ Festivals & Events

Oysterfest   FOOD
(www.ceduna.sa.gov.au/oysterfest) If you happen to be passing through Ceduna in late September/early October, check out Oysterfest, the undisputed king of Australian oyster parties.

⌫ Sleeping & Eating

Ceduna Foreshore Hotel/Motel   MOTEL **$$**
(☑ 08-8625 2008; www.cedunahotel.com.au; 32 O'Loughlin Tce; d $150-195; ☲☂) Clad in aquamarine tiles, the 54-room Foreshore is the most luxurious option in town, with water views and a bistro focused on west-coast seafood (mains $18 to $38, serving 6.30am to 9am, noon to 2pm and 6pm to 8.30pm). The view from the outdoor terrace extends through Norfolk Island pines and out across the bay.

★ Ceduna Oyster Bar   SEAFOOD **$$**
(☑ 08-8626 9086; www.facebook.com/oysterbar ceduna; Eyre Hwy; 12 oysters $12, meals $14-22; ☺ 10am-7.30pm) Pick up a box of freshly shucked molluscs and head for the foreshore, or sit up on the rooftop here under an umbrella and watch the road trains rumble in from WA. Fresh as can be.

ℹ️ Information

Ceduna Visitor Information Centre (☎1800 639 413, 08-8625 2780; www.cedunatourism. com.au; 58 Poynton St; ⊙9am-5.30pm Mon-Fri, to 4pm Sat & Sun) The Ceduna Visitor Information Centre can help with local info and current whale-sighting stats.

Ceduna to the Western Australia Border

It's 480km from Ceduna to the WA border. Along this stretch you can get a bed and a beer at Penong (72km from Ceduna), Fowlers Bay (141km), Nundroo (151km), the Nullarbor Roadhouse (295km) near Head of Bight, and at Border Village on the border itself.

Wheat and sheep paddocks line the road to Nundroo, after which you're in mallee scrub for another 100km. Around 20km later, the trees thin to low bluebush as you enter the true Nullarbor (Latin for 'no trees'). Road trains, caravans and cyclists of questionable sanity are your only companions as you put your foot down and careen towards the setting sun.

◉ Sights & Activities

Head of Bight   LANDMARK
(☎08-8625 6201; www.headofbight.com.au; off Eyre Hwy; adult/child/family Jun-Oct $15/6/35, Nov-May $7/5/14; ⊙8am-5pm Jun-Oct, 8.30am-4pm Nov-May) The viewing platforms and boardwalks at Head of Bight overlook a major southern-right-whale breeding ground. Whales migrate here from Antarctica, and you can see them cavorting from May to October. The breeding area is protected by the **Great Australian Bight Commonwealth Marine Reserve** (☎1800 069 352; www.environ ment.gov.au), the world's second-largest marine park after the Great Barrier Reef. The info centre here has snacks.

Cactus Beach   SURFING
(☎08-86251036; www.nullarbornet.com.au/towns/ cactusbeach.html; off Point Sinclair Rd, via Penong) Turn off the highway at Penong, and follow the 21km dirt road to Point Sinclair and Cactus Beach, which has three of Australia's most famous surf breaks. Caves is a wicked right-hand break for experienced surfers (locals don't take too kindly to tourists dropping in). There's basic camping on private property close to the breaks (per vehicle $15); BYO drinking water.

GULLIVER'S TRAVELS IN CEDUNA?

According to coordinates in Jonathan Swift's famous 1726 novel *Gulliver's Travels*, the islands of St Peter and St Francis, a few kilometres off the coast of Ceduna in the Nuyts Archipelago, are where the tiny folk of Lilliput reside. While we can neither confirm nor deny this possibility, it's likely Swift drew inspiration from the adventures of the 158 Dutch sailors aboard the *Gulden Zeepaert*, which sailed through these waters in 1627.

FLINDERS RANGES

Known simply as 'the Flinders', this ancient mountain range is an iconic South Australian environment. Jagged peaks and escarpments rise up north of Port Augusta and track 400km north to Mt Hopeless. The colours here are remarkable: as the day stretches out, the mountains shift from mauve mornings to midday chocolates and ochre-red sunsets.

Before Europeans arrived, the Flinders were prized by the Adnyamathanha peoples for their red ochre deposits, which had medicinal and ritual uses. Sacred caves, rock paintings and carvings abound throughout the region. In the wake of white exploration came villages, farms, country pubs and cattle stations, many of which failed under the unrelenting sun.

☞ Tours

Flinders Ranges By Bike   MOUNTAIN BIKING
(☎08-8648 0048; www.flindersrangesbybike. com.au; per person 1/2/3/4 days $35/40/45/50) Pedal your way along a 200km circuit through the best bits of the Flinders Ranges, starting (and ending) at Rawnsley Park Station (p789), south of Wilpena. Fees cover park entry and access to private properties en route; book your own accommodation. Luggage transfers also available.

Arkaba Walk   WALKING
(☎02-9571 6399, 1300 790 561; www.arkabawalk. com; per person $2200; ⊙mid-Mar–mid-Oct) Hike for four days through the Flinders in style. Prices include park entry fees, chef-cooked meals, luggage portage, deluxe camping and a night at the superplush Arkaba Station (p788). A once-in-a-lifetime treat!

Flinders Ranges

N
0 ——— 50 km
0 ——— 25 miles

Groovy Grape Tours OUTDOORS
(📞 1800 661 177, 08-8440 1640; www.groovy
grape.com.au) Small-group tours including
a four-day Adelaide to Coober Pedy return
trip via the Flinders Ranges ($445). Meals,
camping and national-park entry fees are
included.

ℹ Getting There & Away

Exploring the Flinders on a tour or under your
own steam is the only way to go (public transport is very limited).

Genesis Transport (📞 08-8552 4000; www.
genesistransport.com.au) runs an Adelaide-
to-Copley bus on Thursdays, via Laura, Melrose, Quorn, Hawker, Parachilna and Leigh
Creek, returning on Fridays in the other direction. Extensions to Wilpena and Blinman on
demand. See the website for times and fares.

Pichi Richi Railway (📞 1800 777 245; www.
prr.org.au; Flinders Ranges Visitor Information
Centre, Railway Tce, Quorn; one-way adult/
child/family $54/20/128) runs historic trains
from Port Augusta to Quorn in the Flinders
Ranges on most Saturdays, following the old
Ghan train route.

Southern Ranges

Port Pirie (population 14,050) is a big lead- and zinc-smelting town on the edge of the Southern Flinders Ranges; the Nyrstar smelter dominates the skyline. It's a good spot to stock up on supplies before heading north, and there are plenty of places to stay here too (motels, caravan parks).

You enter the Southern Ranges proper near Laura (population 800), which emerges from the wheat fields like Superman's Small-ville (all civic pride and 1950s prosperity). The long, geranium-adorned main street has a supermarket, chemist, bakery, bank, post office... even a shoe shop!

The oldest town in the Flinders (1853) is photogenic Melrose (population 410), snug in the elbow of the 960m Mt Remarkable (which comprises most of Mt Remarkable National Park). Melrose has the perfect mix of well preserved architecture, a crack-ing good pub, quality accommodation and parks with actual grass. There are some great mountain-biking trails around here too. Pick up the Melrose Historical Walk brochure for a history tour.

Peterborough (population 1490), 87km in-land from Melrose, is a characterful place: a former service town for SA Railways trains, with a time-tunnel main street lined with old shopfronts, rickety verandahs and huge stone pubs.

◎ Sights

Mt Remarkable National Park   NATIONAL PARK
(☑08-8841 3400; www.environment.sa.gov.au/parks; National Hwy 1, via Mambray Creek; per vehicle $10; ◎24hr) Bush boffins rave about the steep, jagged Mt Remarkable National Park, which straddles the Southern Flinders and rises above little Melrose like a protec-tive overlord. Wildlife and bushwalking are the main lures, with various tracks (includ-ing part of the Heysen Trail) meandering through isolated gorges. Remarkable!

Steamtown Heritage Rail Centre   MUSEUM
(☑08-8651 3355; www.steamtown.com.au; 1 Telford Ave, Peterborough; adult/child/family $17.50/8/35, sound-and-light show per person $20; ◎9am-5pm) Inside Peterborough's original rail depot, this excellent museum takes you back to the days of steam power, when 100 trains a day were shunting through this little town. Guided tours (90 minutes) run all day, with the last one at 3.30pm. There's also a sound-and-light show at 8.30pm (7.30pm in winter).

🏃 Activities

Over The Edge   MOUNTAIN BIKING
(☑08-8666 2222; www.otesports.com.au; 6 Stuart St, Melrose; ◎9am-5pm Wed-Mon) Mountain biking is big in Melrose: Over The Edge has spares, repairs, bike rental ($45 to $100 per day) and a little cafe.

🛏 Sleeping

Under The Mount   RENTAL HOUSE $
(☑0409 093 649; www.underthemount.com.au; 9-11 Jacka St, Melrose; d/8-bed dm $110/180; ❄) Run by some mountain-biking doyens, casual Under The Mount features six ensuite doubles, two eight-bed dorms and a commu-nal kitchen inside, and BBQs, fire areas, a bike workshop and hose-down areas out-side. It's part share-house, part hostel, with a common love of mountain-biking good times uniting guests.

★North Star Hotel   PUB $$
(☑08-8666 2110; www.northstarhotel.com.au; 43 Nott St, Melrose; d/trucks from $110/160; ❄🛜) As welcome as summer rain: the North Star is a noble 1854 pub renovated in city-meets-woolshed style. Sit under spinning ceiling fans at the bistro (mains $18 to $30) for lunch, dinner or just a cold beer. Accommodation comprises plush suites upstairs, Bundaleer Cottage next door (sleeps 16) and quirky cab-ins atop two old trucks out the back.

❶ Information

Port Pirie Regional Tourism & Arts Centre
(☑08-8633 8700; www.pirie.sa.gov.au; 3 Mary Elie St, Port Pirie; ◎9am-5pm Mon-Fri, to 4pm Sat, 10am-4pm Sun) Port Pirie's visitor centre also houses the excellent local art gallery, is chock-full of info on places to stay and proffers advice on where to get a good coffee. 'Out-side the Gates' town tours leave from here at 12.30pm on Monday, Wednesday and Friday (adult/child/family $13/5/28).

Quorn

POP 1210

Is Quorn a film set after the crew has gone home? With more jeering crows than peo-ple, it's a cinematographic little outback town with a pub-lined main street. Wheat farming took off here in 1875, and the town prospered with the arrival of the Great Northern Railway from Port Augusta. Quorn (pronounced 'corn') remained an important railroad junction until trains into the Flinders were cut in 1970.

◉ Sights

Kanyaka RUINS
(off Quorn-Hawker Rd; ⊙daylight hours) Out of town, derelict ruins litter the Quorn–Hawker Rd, the most impressive of which is Kanyaka, a once-thriving sheep station founded in 1851. From the ruins (41km from Quorn), it's a 20-minute walk to a waterhole loomed over by the massive **Death Rock**. The story goes that local Aboriginal people once placed their dying kinfolk here to see out their last hours.

⌷ Sleeping

★ **Quorn Caravan Park** CARAVAN PARK $
(☑ 08-8648 6206; www.quorncaravanpark.com.au; 8 Silo Rd; unpowered/powered sites $28/25, dm $40, van s/d $65/75, cabins $100-140; ❄) 🌱 Fully keyed-in to climate change, this passionately run park on Pinkerton Creek is hell bent on reducing emissions and re-storing native habitat. Features include spotless cabins, a backpacker cabin (sleeps six), a camp kitchen made from recycled timbers, shady sites, rainwater tanks everywhere and a few lazy roos lounging about under the red gums. Discounts for walkers and cyclists.

Savings Bank of South Australia RENTAL HOUSE $$
(SBSA; ☑ 0419 233 729, 0456 129 870; www.sbsa-quorn.com.au; 37 First St; up to 6 people $260; ❄) Bank on a good night's sleep at Quorn's lovely old red-brick bank, a two-storey, two-bathroom, three-bedroom conversion of this 1906 charmer. It's a terrific base for exploring the Flinders. Sleeps six; two-night minimum stay (good weekly rates).

✕ Eating

★ **Quorn Cafe** CAFE $
(☑ 08-8648 6368; www.quorncafe.com.au; 43 First St; mains $10-25; ⊙8am-4pm Mon, 9am-3pm Tue & Wed, 7.30am-4pm Thu-Sun; 🖉) The menu board at this unexpected, culturally displaced cafe is an old door hung on the wall, covered with brown-paper sandwich bags. Each bag has a menu item scribbled on it: vegetable frittata, warm chicken salad, egg and bacon sandwich... Everything is homemade and generous. Try the delicious goat curry. Quorn's best coffee, too.

ℹ Information

Flinders Ranges Visitor Information Centre
(☑ 08-8620 0510; www.flindersranges.com; Quorn Railway Station, Railway Tce; ⊙9am-5pm Mon-Fri, 10am-4pm Sat & Sun) Maps, brochures, internet access and advice – the main info hub for the Flinders Ranges. Check out the little history room out the back.

Hawker

POP 300

Hawker is the last outpost of civilisation before Ikara (Wilpena Pound), 59km to the north. Much like Quorn, Hawker has seen better days, most of which were when the old *Ghan* train stopped here. These days Hawker is a pancake-flat, pit-stop town with an ATM, a general store, a pub and the world's most helpful petrol station.

⌷ Sleeping

Arkaba Station BOUTIQUE HOTEL $$$
(☑ 02-9571 6399, 1300 790 561; www.arkabastation.com; Wilpena Rd, via Hawker; adult/child from $465/930; ❄🖳🛏) Flashy outback station accommodation in an 1850s homestead, between Hawker and Wilpena: it's an exercise in contemporary bush luxury. Rates include chef-cooked meals and daily guided wilderness safaris tailored to your interests. Scenic flights and transfers also available.

ℹ Information

Hawker Motors (☑ 08-8648 4014; www.hawkermotors.com.au; cnr Wilpena & Cradock Rds; ⊙7.30am-6pm) The town's petrol station (fill up if you're heading north) doubles as the visitor information centre.

Flinders Ranges National Park

One of SA's most treasured parks, **Flinders Ranges National Park** (Ikara; ☑ 08-8648 0048; www.environment.sa.gov.au/parks; via Wilpena; per vehicle $10; ⊙24hr) is laced with gorges, saw-toothed ranges, abandoned homesteads, Aboriginal sites, native wildlife and, after it rains, carpets of wild flowers.

◉ Sights

The park's big-ticket drawcard is the 80-sq-km natural basin **Ikara (Wilpena Pound)** – a sunken elliptical valley ringed by gnarled ridges (don't let anyone tell you it's a meteorite crater!).

The only vehicular access to see Ikara (Wilpena Pound) is via the Wilpena Pound Resort's **shuttle bus** (☑1800 805 802, 08-8648 0004; www.wilpenapound.com.au; Wilpena Pound Resort, Wilpena; return adult/child/family $5/3/12), which drops you about 1km from the old **Hills Homestead**, from where you can walk to **Wangarra Lookout** (another 300m). The shuttle runs at 9am, 11am, 1pm and 3pm. Otherwise, it's a three-hour, 8km return walk between the resort and lookout (guided walking tours available from the resort for $45 per person).

The 20km **Brachina Gorge Geological Trail** features an amazing layering of exposed sedimentary rock, covering 120 million years of the earth's history. Grab a brochure from the visitor centre.

The **Bunyeroo–Brachina–Aroona Scenic Drive** is a 110km round trip, passing by Bunyeroo Valley, Brachina Gorge, Aroona Valley and Stokes Hill Lookout. The drive starts north of Wilpena off the road to Blinman.

🏃 Activities

Bushwalking in the Flinders is unforgettable. Before you make happy trails, ensure you've got enough water, sunscreen and a massive hat, and tell someone where you're going. Pick up the *Bushwalking in Flinders Ranges National Park* brochure from the visitor information centre. Many walks kick off at Wilpena Pound Resort.

For a really good look at Ikara, the walk up to **Tanderra Saddle** (return 15km, six hours) on the ridge of **St Mary Peak** is brilliant, though it's a thigh-pounding scramble at times. The Adnyamathanha people request that you restrict your climbing to the ridge and don't try to climb St Mary Peak itself, due to its traditional significance to them.

The quick, tough track up to **Mt Ohlssen Bagge** (return 6.5km, four hours) rewards the sweaty hiker with a stunning panorama. Good short walks include the stroll to **Hills Homestead** (return 6.5km, two hours), or the dash up to the **Wilpena Solar Power Station** (return 500m, 30 minutes).

Just beyond the park's southeast corner, a one-hour, 1km return walk leads to the **Sacred Canyon Cultural Heritage Site**, with Aboriginal rock-art galleries featuring animal tracks and designs.

ADNYAMATHANHA DREAMING

Land and nature are integral to the culture of the traditional owners of the Flinders Ranges. The people collectively called Adnyamathanha (Hill People) are actually a collection of the Wailpi, Kuyani, Jadliaura, Piladappa and Pangkala tribes, who exchanged and elaborated on stories to explain their spectacular local geography.

The walls of Ikara (Wilpena Pound), for example, are the bodies of two *akurra* (giant snakes), who coiled around Ikara during an initiation ceremony, eating most of the participants. The snakes were so full after their feast they couldn't move and willed themselves to die, creating the landmark.

🛏 Sleeping

★ Rawnsley Park Station
RESORT, CARAVAN PARK $$

(☑08-8648 0700; www.rawnsleypark.com.au; Wilpena Rd, via Hawker; unpowered/powered sites $26/36, hostel per adult/child $38/28, cabins/units/villas/houses from $100/160/410/550; ❄ 🛜 🛋) This homestead 35km from Hawker on the fringes of Flinders Ranges National Park offers everything from tent sites to luxe eco-villas, a 1950s self-contained house and a caravan park with cabins and dorms. Activities include mountain-bike hire (per hour $15), bushwalks, 4WD tours and scenic flights. The excellent on-site **Woolshed Restaurant** (mains $27-42; ⊙noon-2pm Wed-Sun, 6-8.30pm daily) does brilliant bush tucker, plus curries, seafood and pizzas. It's an atmospheric, rustic-chic spot for a cold sundowner, too...

Wilpena Pound Resort
RESORT $$

(☑08-8648 0004, 1800 805 802; www.wilpenapound.com.au; Wilpena Rd, via Hawker; unpowered/powered sites from $24/35, d/ste/safari tents from $193/263/320; ❄ 🛜 🛋) This far-flung resort has lost some of its sheen, but remains an interesting place to stay, with motel-style rooms, self-contained suite, and a popular camp site with plush safari tents (book way in advance over winter). Don't miss a swim in the pool, a drink at the bar and dinner at the **bistro** (mains $26 to $40 – try the roo!).

ℹ Information

Wilpena Pound Visitor Information Centre
(☑ 08-8648 0048; www.wilpenapound.com.
au/do/visitors-centre; Wilpena Pound Resort,
Wilpena; ⊙ 8am-6pm) At the resort's info
centre you'll find a shop, petrol, park and
bushwalking info and bike hire (per half-/full
day $35/65). Also handles bookings for scenic
flights and 4WD tours. Pay your park entry
fees here.

Blinman & Parachilna

About an hour north of Ikara on a sealed
road, ubercute Blinman (population 30)
owes its existence to the copper ore discovered here in 1859 and the smelter built
in 1903. But the boom went bust and 1500
folks left town. Today Blinman's main claim
to fame is as SA's highest town (610m above
sea level). There are interesting tours of the
old mines.

On the Hawker–Leigh Creek road, middle-
of-nowhere Parachilna (population between
four and seven) is an essential Flinders
Ranges destination. The drawcard here is
the legendary Prairie Hotel – a world-class
stay.

◉ Sights

Heritage Blinman Mine   HISTORIC SITE
(☑ 08-8648 4782; www.heritageblinmanmine.com.
au; Mine Rd, Blinman; tours adult/child/family
$28/11/65; ⊙ 9am-5pm, reduced hours Dec-Mar)
Much of Blinman's amazing, 150-year-old
copper mine has been redeveloped with
lookouts, audiovisual interpretation and information boards. Excellent one-hour tours
run at 10am, noon and 2pm.

🛏 Sleeping

★ Prairie Hotel   HOTEL $$$
(☑ 1800 331 473, 08-8648 4844; www.prairiehotel.
com.au; cnr High St & West Tce, Parachilna; powered
sites $35, budget cabins s/d/f $65/80/180, hotel
s/d/tr from $195/245/280; ❇ 🛜) The legend-
ary Prairie Hotel has slick suites out the
back, plus camping and basic cabins across
the street. Don't miss a pub meal (mains
breakfast $8 to $28, lunch and dinner $18
to $42): try the feral mixed grill (camel sau-
sage, kangaroo fillet, emu and bacon). 'Too
early for a beer!? Whose rules are those?',
said the barman at 10.42am.

Leigh Creek & Copley

In the early 1980s, the previously nonexist-
ent town of Leigh Creek (population 500
and shrinking) emerged from the northern
Flinders desert. It was built by the state
government to house people working at
the huge open-cut coal mine here, with a
school, a pub, a shopping centre...the whole
shebang. Population peaked at around 1000,
until in 2016 the mine shut down. What hap-
pens next is anyone's guess: a new natural-
gas project? The whole town up for sale? A
kooky resort? Swing by and check it out: at
least the pub is still open.

About 6km north of Leigh Creek is the
sweet meaninglessness of little Copley (pop-
ulation 80). There's not a whole to see or do
here, other than try a slice of quandong pie
at the cafe.

Further afield are the varied enticements
of the Aboriginal cultural centre Iga Warta,
Vulkathunha-Gammon Ranges National
Park and Arkaroola Wilderness Sanctuary.

◉ Sights

**Arkaroola Wilderness
Sanctuary**   WILDLIFE RESERVE
(☑ 08-8648 4848; www.arkaroola.com.au; Copley-
Arkaroola Rd, via Copley) ⚑ A privately operated
wildlife reserve–resort (unpowered/powered
sites $25/33, motel d $85-205, cottages f $149-230;
❇ 🏊) 129km east of Copley on unsealed
roads, Arkaroola Wilderness Sanctuary oc-
cupies a far-flung and utterly spectacular
part of the Flinders Ranges. The **visitor
centre** (open 9am to 5pm) has natural-
history displays, including a scientific ex-
planation of the tremors that often shake
things up hereabouts. The vertiginous 4WD
Ridgetop Tour (www.arkaroola.com.au/ridge
top.php; adult/child $155/55; ⊙ 8am & 1pm daily)
is a must!

**Vulkathunha-Gammon
Ranges National Park**   NATIONAL PARK
(☑ 08-8648 4829; www.environment.sa.gov.au/
parks; Copley-Arkaroola Rd, via Copley; ⊙ 24hr)
FREE Blanketing 1282 sq km of desert, this
remote national park has deep gorges, rug-
ged ranges, yellow-footed rock wallabies and
gum-lined creeks. Most of the park is diffi-
cult to access (4WDs are near-compulsory)
and has limited facilities. Bush camping is
$12 per vehicle (BYO everything); pick up

permits at the Balcanoona park HQ, 99km from Copley.

Iga Warta
CULTURAL CENTRE

(📞08-8648 3737; www.igawarta.com; Copley-Arkaroola Rd, via Copley; ⊙9am-5pm) Iga Warta, east of Copley en route to Vulkathunha-Gammon Ranges National Park, is an Indigenous-run cultural centre and bush camp, offering authentic Adnyamathanha experiences ($25 to $84 – bush foods, camp-fire story telling, artefact making) plus 4WD and bushwalking tours ($138). There's ac-commodation here too (unpowered sites $22, tents per person $36, cabins and safari tents $104 to $150).

🛏 Sleeping

Copley Caravan Park
CARAVAN PARK **$**

(📞08-8675 2288; www.copleycaravan.com.au; Lot 100 Railway Tce W; unpowered/powered sites $30/40, cabins with/without bathroom from $110/80; ❄) Copley Caravan Park is a going concern: a small, immaculate park (not a whole lotta shade, but hey, this is the desert) and regular bonfire cook-ups for guests. The **Quandong Cafe** (items $5-12; ⊙8am-5pm) is here too.

THE OUTBACK

The area north of the Eyre Peninsula and the Flinders Ranges stretches into the vast, empty spaces of SA's outback – about 70% of the state! If you're prepared, travelling through this sparsely populated and harsh country is utterly rewarding.

Heading into the red heart of Australia, Woomera is the first pit stop, with its dark legacy of nuclear tests and shiny collec-tion of left-over rockets. Further north on the Stuart Hwy and along the legendary Oodnadatta and Strzelecki Tracks, eccen-tric outback towns such as William Creek, Innamincka and Coober Pedy emerge from the heat haze. This is no country for the faint-hearted: it's waterless, fly-blown and dizzyingly hot. No wonder the opal miners in Coober Pedy live underground!

☞ Tours

Sacred Earth Safaris
ADVENTURE

(📞08-8536 2234; www.sacredearthsafaris.com.au; tours per adult/child $4995/4795) Epic 10-day outback 4WD tours trundling along the big three desert tracks – Oodnadatta, Strzelecki

and Birdsville – plus Coober Pedy and the Flinders Ranges.

ⓘ Getting There & Around

AIR
Regional Express (Rex; 📞13 17 13; www.regionalexpress.com.au) flies most days between Adelaide and Coober Pedy (from $247, two hours).

BUS
Greyhound Australia (p736) runs a daily (overnight) bus from Adelaide to Pimba ($94, 6¾ hours) and Glendambo ($108, 8¼ hours), Coober Pedy ($167, 11¼ hours) and Marla ($228, 14¼ hours), continuing to Alice Springs.

CAR & MOTORCYCLE
The Stuart Hwy tracks from Port Augusta to Darwin. In SA, fuel and accommodation are available at Pimba (176km from Port Augusta), Glendambo (288km), Coober Pedy (542km), Cadney Homestead (693km) and Marla (775km). Pimba, Coober Pedy and Marla have 24-hour fuel sales.

The Oodnadatta, Birdsville and Strzelecki Tracks are subject to closure after heavy rains; check conditions with the **Royal Automobile Association** (p737) in Adelaide, online at www.dpti.sa.gov.au/outbackroads, or call the Outback Road Report on 📞1300 361 033.

TRAIN
Operated by Great Southern Rail (www.greatsouthernrail.com.au), the *Ghan* train runs through outback SA between Adelaide and Alice Springs, with a stop at Coober Pedy (or rather, near) a possibility; see the website for details.

Woomera & Around

A 6km detour off the Stuart Hwy from little truckstop Pimba (population 50; 481km north of Adelaide), Woomera (pop-ulation 220) emerged as a settlement in 1947 as HQ for experimental British rocket and nuclear tests at notorious sites like Maralinga. Local Indigenous tribes suf-fered greatly from the resulting nuclear fallout. These days Woomera is an eerie artificial town that's still an active Depart-ment of Defence test site.

Beyond Woomera, drive-through Glen-dambo and quirky Roxby Downs offer trav-ellers a different take on the outback-town experience.

🛏 Sleeping

**Glendambo Hotel-Motel
& Caravan Park** MOTEL **$**
(☑08-8672 1030; www.turu.com.au/parks/sa/
outback/glendambo-hotel-motel-and-caravan-park.
aspx; Stuart Hwy, Glendambo; unpowered/powered
sites $23/27, s/d/f from $94/99/140; 🅿🌫) If
your eyelids are drooping out on the highway, bunk down at the oasis-like Glendambo
Hotel-Motel, which has bars, a restaurant
and a bunch of OK motel units. Outside are
dusty camp sites; inside are meaty mains at
the bistro ($18 to $32, serving noon to 2pm
and 6pm to 8pm).

Eldo Hotel MOTEL **$$**
(☑08-8673 7867; www.facebook.com/eldo-hotel;
Kotara Pl, Woomera; d from $110; 🌫) Built to
house rocket scientists, the Eldo Hotel has
comfortable budget and motel-style rooms,
and serves à la carte meals in the urbane bis-
tro (mains $20 to $35, serving 7am to 9am,
noon to 2pm and 6pm to 8.30pm). Try the
meaty game plate.

ℹ Information

**Woomera Heritage & Visitor Information
Centre** (☑08-8673 7042; http://homepage.
powerup.com.au/~woomera/herit1.htm;
Dewrang Ave, Woomera; museum adult/
child $6/3; ☉9am-5pm Mar-Nov, 10am-2pm
Dec-Feb) Rocket into the info centre, with its
displays on Woomera's past and present (plus
a bowling alley!). Just across the car park is the
Lions Club Aircraft & Missile Park, studded
with jets and rocket remnants.

Coober Pedy

POP 3500

Coming into cosmopolitan Coober Pedy
(yes, cosmopolitan – there are 44 nation-
alities represented in this little town!) the
dry, barren desert suddenly becomes rid-
dled with holes and adjunct piles of dirt –
reputedly more than a million around the
township. The reason for all this rabid
digging is opals. Discovered here 100 years
ago, these gemstones have made this small
town a mining mecca. This isn't to say it's
also a tourist mecca – with swarms of flies,
no trees, 50°C summer days, cave-dwelling
locals and rusty car wrecks, you might think
you've arrived in a postapocalyptic waste-
land – but it sure is interesting! The name
derives from local Aboriginal words *kupa*
(white man) and *piti* (hole).

The surrounding desert is jaw-droppingly
desolate, a fact not overlooked by interna-
tional film-makers who've come here to
shoot end-of-the-world epics like *Mad Max
III, Red Planet, Ground Zero, Pitch Black*
and the slightly more believable *Priscilla,
Queen of the Desert.*

⊙ Sights

⭐**Old Timers Mine** MUSEUM
(☑08-8672 5555; www.oldtimersmine.com; 1
Crowders Gully Rd; self-guided tours adult/child/
family $12/5/40; ☉9am-5.30pm) This interest-
ing warren of tunnels was mined in 1916,
and then hidden by the miners. The mine
was rediscovered when excavations for a
dugout home punched through into the
labyrinth of tunnels. As well as the great
self-guided tunnel tours, there's a museum,
a re-created 1920s underground home,
and free mining-equipment demos daily
(9.30am, 1.30pm and 3.30pm).

⭐**Spaceship** SCULPTURE
(Hutchinson St) Check out this amazing left-
over prop from the film *Pitch Black*, which
has crash-landed on Hutchison St (...a minor
Millennium Falcon?).

Umoona Opal Mine & Museum MUSEUM
(☑08-8672 5288; www.umoonaopalmine.com.au;
14 Hutchison St; museum free, tours adult/child
$10/5; ☉8am-6pm) For a terrific introduction
to Coober Pedy – including history, fossils,
desert habitats, Aboriginal culture, ecology
and mining – take a wander through this
free museum, run by the Umoona shop.
Book yourself on a guided tour (10am, 2pm
and 4pm) if you want a deeper insight.

**Catholic Church
of St Peter & St Paul** CHURCH
(☑08-8672 5011; www.pp.catholic.org.au/about-
our-parishes/coober-pedy-est-1965-; cnr Halliday
Pl & Hutchison St; ☉10am-4pm, Mass 10am Sun)
Coober Pedy's first underground church
still has a sweet appeal, with statue-filled
nooks and hushed classical music.

⭑ Tours

Arid Areas Tours DRIVING
(☑0439 881 049, 08-8672 3008; www.aridareas
tours.com; 2/4/6hr tours per 2 people from
$120/240/320) Offers 4WD tours around
town, extending to the Breakaways. Full-day
tours to Lake Eyre, the Painted Desert and
the Oodnadatta Track also available.

Coober Pedy

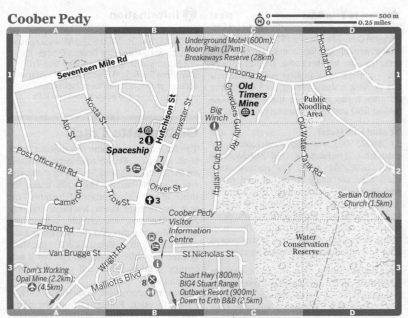

N 0 — 500 m
0 — 0.25 miles

Mail Run Tour DRIVING
(📞1800 069 911, 08-8672 5226; www.mailruntour.
com; tours per person $195) Coober Pedy–based
full-day mail-run tours, looping through the
desert and along the Oodnadatta Track between Oodnadatta and William Creek.

🛏 Sleeping

Riba's CAMPGROUND $
(📞08-8672 5614; www.camp-underground.com.au;
Lot 1811 William Creek Rd; underground sites $30,
above-ground unpowered/powered sites $20/28, s
& d $66; 🌐) Around 5km from town, Riba's
offers the unique option of underground
camping! Extras include an underground
TV lounge, cell-like underground budget
rooms and a nightly opal-mine tour (adult/
child $24/15; free for underground and
unpowered-site campers, discounted for
other guests).

Cadney Homestead CARAVAN PARK $
(📞08-7007 6591; www.turu.com.au/parks/sa/out
back/cadney-homestead-caravan-park.aspx; Stuart
Hwy, Cadney Park; unpowered/powered sites from
$20/30, d cabin/motel from $52/110; ❄@≋)
Cadney Homestead has caravan and tent
sites, serviceable motel rooms and basic
cabins (BYO towel), plus petrol, puncture repairs, takeaways, cold beer, an ATM, a swim-

Coober Pedy

⊙ Top Sights
1 Old Timers Mine C1
2 Spaceship B2

⊙ Sights
3 Catholic Church of St Peter &
    St Paul B2
4 Umoona Opal Mine & Museum B2

⊜ Sleeping
5 Desert Cave Hotel B2
6 Mud Hut Motel B3

⊗ Eating
7 John's Pizza Bar & Restaurant B2
8 Outback Bar & Grill B3
    Umberto's .... (see 5)

ming pool... On the Stuart Hwy, 151km north
of Coober Pedy.

Marla Travellers Rest CARAVAN PARK $
(📞08-8670 7001; www.marla.com.au; Stuart Hwy,
Marla; unpowered/powered sites $20/30, cabins
$40, d $110-140; ❄@≋) Marla Travellers Rest
has fuel, motel rooms, camp sites, a kidney-
shaped pool, a takeaway cafe, supermarket
and a vast tiled bar area (easy to hose out?).
On the Stuart Hwy at Marla, 234km north of
Coober Pedy.

★ **Down to Erth B&B** B&B **$$**
(☑ 08-8672 5762; www.downtoerth.com.au; Lot 1795 Wedgetail Cres; d incl breakfast $165; ☉☀) A real dugout gem about 3km from town: your own subterranean two-bedroom bunker (sleeps five – perfect for a family) with a kitchen/lounge area, a shady plunge pool for cooling off after a day exploring the earth, wood-fuelled BBQ and complimentary chocolates.

★ **Mud Hut Motel** MOTEL **$$**
(☑ 08-8672 3003; www.mudhutmotel.com.au; cnr Hutchison & St Nicholas Sts; s/d/f/2-bedroom apt $130/150/180/218; ☀☉) The rustic-looking walls here are made from rammed earth, and despite the grubby name this is one of the cleanest (and newest) places in town – and by far the best motel option if you don't want to sleep underground. The two-bedroom apartments sleep six (extra person $20) and have kitchens. Central location.

Desert Cave Hotel HOTEL **$$$**
(☑ 08-8672 5688; www.desertcave.com.au; Lot 1 Hutchison St; d above ground/underground $260/255; ☀☉☀) Top of the CP price tree, the Desert Cave brings a much-needed shot of luxury – plus a beaut pool, a daytime cafe, airport transfers and the excellent **Umberto's** (mains $28-43; ☉6-9pm) restaurant. Staff are supercourteous and can organise tours. Above-ground rooms cost a tad more (huge, but there are more soulful places to stay in town). Prices dive in summer.

✕ **Eating**

★ **Outback Bar & Grill** FAST FOOD **$$**
(☑ 08-8672 3250; www.facebook.com/shellcoober pedy; 454 Hutchison St; mains $7-25; ☉7am-9pm Mon-Sat, to 8pm Sun; ☉) It may sound a bit odd, but this brightly lit, petrol-station diner is one of the best places to eat in Coober Pedy! Roasts, pastas, burgers, lasagne, schnitzels…and an awesome Greek-style lamb salad that's a bold departure from trucker norms and expectations. You can get a beer here too, if you're dry from the highway.

John's Pizza Bar & Restaurant ITALIAN **$$**
(☑ 08-8672 5561; www.jpbr.com.au; Shop 24, 1 Hutchison St; mains $9-32; ☉10am-10pm) Serving up table-sized pizzas, hearty pastas and heat-beating gelato, you can't go past John's. Grills, salads, burgers, yiros, and fish and chips also available. Sit inside, order some takeaways, or pull up a seat with the bedraggled pot plants by the street.

ℹ **Information**

Coober Pedy Visitor Information Centre
(☑ 08-8672 4600, 1800 637 076; www.coober pedy.sa.gov.au/tourism; Council Offices, lot 773 Hutchison St; ☉8.30am-5pm Mon-Fri, 10am-1pm Sat & Sun) Free 30-minute internet access (prebooked), history displays and comprehensive tour and accommodation info.

Oodnadatta Track

The legendary, lonesome Oodnadatta Track is an unsealed, 615km road between Marla on the Stuart Hwy and Marree in the northern Flinders Ranges. The track traces the route of the old Overland Telegraph Line and the defunct Great Northern Railway. Along the way are remote settlements, quirky desert sights and the enormous Lake Eyre (usually dry). Bring a 4WD – the track is often passable in a regular car, but it gets bumpy, muddy, dusty and potholed (how exciting!).

You can traverse the Oodnadatta Track in either direction. Rolling in from the north, around 209km from Marla, Oodnadatta (population 170) is where the main road and the old railway line diverged. Here you'll find the **Pink Roadhouse** (☑ 08-8670 7822, 1800 802 074; www.pinkroadhouse.com.au; Lot 42 Ikartuka Tce, Oodnadatta; unpowered/powered sites from $22/32, cabins with/without bathroom from $120/70), a solid source of track info (they're big on maintaining correct tyre pressure) and meals (try the stultifying 'Oodnaburger'). The roadhouse also has an attached caravan park; options run from basic camping through to self-contained cabins.

In another 201km you'll hit William Creek (population six!), best experienced in the weather-beaten **William Creek Hotel** (☑ 08-8670 7880; www.williamcreekhotel.com; Oodnadatta Track, William Creek; unpowered/powered sites $25/30, d cabin/hotel $90/150; ☀), an iconic 1887 pub festooned with photos, business cards, old licence plates and money stapled to the walls. There's a dusty camping ground, and modest cabins and motel rooms. Also on offer are fuel, cold beer, basic provisions, all-day meals (mains $16 to $32) and spare tyres.

William Creek is also a base for **Wright-sair** (☑ 08-8670 7962; www.wrightsair.com.au; 1 Bill Rivers Ave, William Creek; flights per person from $260), which runs scenic flights over Lake Eyre (two-passenger minimum).

Some 130km shy of Marree, **Coward Springs Campground** (☑ 08-8675 8336; www.

cowardsprings.com.au; Oodnadatta Track, Coward Springs; unpowered sites adult/child $12.50/6.25) is the first stop at the old Coward Springs railway siding. You can soak yourself silly in a natural hot-spring tub made from old railway sleepers (adult/child $2/1), or take a six-day camel trek to Lake Eyre from here (from $1760...or you can buy a camel!).

Next stop is the lookout over the southern section of **Lake Eyre** (Kati Thanda; ☑08-8648 5300; www.environment.sa.gov.au/parks; ⊘24hr), the world's sixth-largest lake. It's usually dry but a couple of times in recent years has filled with flood waters running in from Queensland. When this happens (only once every decade or so) the explosion of bird life is astonishing! It's also the lowest point on the Australian continent, bottoming out at 15.2m below sea level.

Mutonia Sculpture Park – about 60km west of Marree – emerges from the desert haze unexpectedly. All sorts of wacky weldings stand mute and rusty in the heat, including several planes welded together with their tails buried in the ground to form *Planehenge*.

Marree (population 100) was once a vital hub for Afghan camel teams and the Great Northern Railway, and is the end (or start) of both the Oodnadatta and Birdsville Tracks. The big, stone 1883 **Marree Hotel** (☑08-8675 8344; www.marreehotel.com.au; Railway Tce S, Marree; unpowered sites free, hotel d without bathroom $120, cabins from $140; ✳❄☀) has decent pub rooms (shared bathrooms), smart ensuite cabins and free camp sites!

The folks at the Marree Hotel can also hook you up with a scenic flight. From the air you'll get a good look at **Marree Man**, a 4.2km-long outline of a Pitjantjatjara Aboriginal warrior etched into the desert near Lake Eyre. It was only discovered in 1998, and no one seems to know who created it. Eroding away to nothingness for many years, in 2016 it was reploughed into the dirt...and still no-one knows who's responsible!

From Marree it's 80km south to Lyndhurst, where the bitumen kicks back in, then 33km down to Copley at the northern end of the Flinders Ranges.

Birdsville & Strzelecki Tracks

These two iconic, historic outback stock routes tell stories of exploration and the opening up of the Australian continent...

but also of landscape: this is ancient terrain, crossed by Indigenous Australians for millenniums, from water source to water source. These days, if you pack plenty of H_2O in your 4WD, you won't need to rely on desert soaks and waterholes – but imagine doing it on foot!

For a detailed guide, pick up the interesting *Birdsville Strzelecki: Legendary Tracks of the Marree-Innamincka District* brochure from regional visitor centres.

Both of these tracks are hard-driving 4WD terrain – you'll need to keep your eyes on the dirt in front of you. But when you do stop to look around, the landscape here is dizzyingly bleak and beautiful, wildlife scurrying for shade and the desert air charged with ions. Completing either of these tracks is a real badge of honour – journeys into Australia's red heart that you won't hurriedly forget.

Birdsville Track

The Birdsville Track is an old droving trail running 517km from Marree in SA to Birdsville, just across the border in Queensland, passing between the Simpson Desert to the west and Sturt Stony Desert to the east. The track is one of Australia's classic outback routes, made famous by stockmen in the late 1800s who drove cattle from Queensland's Channel Country to the railway at Marree, from where they were shunted to boats at Port Augusta – about 1000km shorter than the route to the coast near Brisbane. More recently, the legendary outback mailman Tom Kruse (no, not that Tom Cruise) belted his mail truck along the track from 1936 until 1963.

Strzelecki Track

Meandering along through the sand hills of the **Strzelecki Regional Reserve** (☑08-8648 5300; www.environment.sa.gov.au/parks; Strzelecki Track), the Strzelecki Track spans 460km from Lyndhurst, 80km south of Marree, to the tiny desert outpost of Innamincka. The discovery of oil and gas at Moomba (closed to travellers) saw the upgrading of the road from a camel track to a decent dirt road, though heavy transport travelling along it has created bone-rattling corrugations. The newer **Moomba–Strzelecki Track** is better kept, but longer and less interesting than the old track, which follows Strzelecki Creek.

Darwin & the Northern Territory

POP 244.300 / ✆ 08

Best Places to Eat

➔ Marksies Camp Tucker (p835)

➔ Sounds of Silence (p872)

➔ Border Store (p825)

➔ Crustaceans (p808)

➔ Black Russian Caravan Bar (p834)

Best Places to Sleep

➔ Cicada Lodge (p837)

➔ Wildman Wilderness Lodge (p816)

➔ Hawk Dreaming Wilderness Lodge (p825)

➔ Anbinik Kakadu Resort (p825)

➔ Desert Gardens Hotel (p874)

Why Go?

The Top End is frontier country. It feels wild out here; time spent exploring the region's outer reaches will feel like exploring the Australia of childhood imaginings. This is the nation's most rewarding Indigenous homeland, a land of art centres, isolated communities and ancient rock art. It is also a world of iconic Aussie wildlife, from the jumping crocs of Mary River to the flood plains and wetlands of Kakadu. Darwin is an intriguing place with a steamy, end-of-Australia feel, excellent markets, restaurants and galleries of Indigenous art.

The remote and largely untamed chunk of the Northern Territory (NT) from Katherine to Uluru is where dreams end and adventure begins. If you enjoy off-road driving and meeting real characters of the Australian outback, then you've come to the right place. And, delighting travellers with its eccentric offerings, pioneering spirit and weathered mountain setting, Alice Springs is the city at the centre of a continent.

When to Go

Darwin

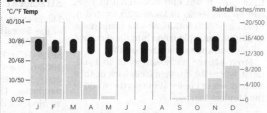

Apr–Sep Markets, fine weather and festivals. The south has mild temperatures but can be cold at night.

Oct & Nov The 'build-up' brings a chance of heavy rain and very humid conditions.

Dec–Mar The Wet brings monsoonal rains and fewer visitors. Many tours don't run during these months.

DARWIN

POP 135,000

Australia's only tropical capital city, Darwin gazes out confidently across the Timor Sea. It's closer to Bali than Bondi and can certainly feel removed from the rest of the country, which is just the way the locals like it.

Darwin has plenty to offer travellers. Chairs and tables spill out of streetside restaurants and bars, innovative museums celebrate the city's past, and galleries showcase the region's rich Indigenous art. Darwin's cosmopolitan mix – more than 50 nationalities are represented here – is typified by the wonderful markets held throughout the dry season.

History

Initial European attempts to settle the Top End were mainly due to British fears that the French or Dutch might get a foothold in Australia, but from the mid-1860s to 1895 huge amounts of livestock were overlanded to immense pastoral settlements, displacing Aboriginal Australians from their lands. Some Indigenous people had to take employment as stockmen or domestic servants on cattle stations, while others moved on to try to maintain their traditional lifestyle.

In the early 1870s, gold was discovered. A minor rush ensued, with an influx of Chinese prospectors. Though the gold finds were relatively insignificant, the searches for it unearthed a wealth of natural resources that would lead to mining becoming a major economic presence.

In 1966 a group of Aboriginal stockmen, led by Vincent Lingiari, went on strike on Wave Hill Station, to protest over the low wages and poor conditions that they received compared with white stockmen. The Wave Hill walk-off gave rise to the Aboriginal land-rights movement, and in 1976 the *Aboriginal Land Rights (Northern Territory) Act* was passed in Canberra. It handed over all reserves and mission lands in the NT to Aboriginal people and allowed Aboriginal groups to claim vacant government land if they could prove continuous occupation. Today, Aboriginal people own about half of the land in the NT, including Kakadu and Uluru-Kata Tjuta National Parks, which are leased back to the federal government. Minerals on Aboriginal land are still government property, though the landowners' permission is usually required for exploration and mining, and landowners are remunerated.

◉ Sights

◉ Central Darwin

★ **Crocosaurus Cove** ZOO
(Map p804; ☑ 08-8981 7522; www.crocosaurus cove.com; 58 Mitchell St; adult/child $32/20; ☻ 9am-6pm, last admission 5pm) If the tourists won't go out to see the crocs, then bring the crocs to the tourists. Right in the middle of Mitchell St, Crocosaurus Cove is as close as you'll ever want to get to these amazing creatures. Six of the largest crocs in captivity can be seen in state-of-the-art aquariums and pools, while an eco boat cruise (adult/child $14/7) takes you out on the water with them.

You can be lowered right into a pool with the crocs in the transparent **Cage of Death** (1/2 people $165/250). If that's too scary, there's another pool where you can swim with a clear tank wall separating you from some mildly less menacing baby crocs.

Aquascene AQUARIUM
(Map p804; ☑ 08-8981 7837; www.aquascene.com. au; 28 Doctors Gully Rd; adult/child/family $15/ 10/43; ☻ high tide, check website) At Doctors Gully, an easy walk from the Esplanade, Aquascene runs a remarkable fish-feeding frenzy at high tide. Visitors can hand-feed hordes of mullet, catfish, batfish and huge milkfish. Check the website for feeding times.

Bicentennial Park PARK
(Map p804; ☻ 24hr) Bicentennial Park (the Esplanade) runs the length of Darwin's waterfront and **Lameroo Beach** (Map p804): a sheltered cove popular in the '20s when it housed the saltwater baths, and traditionally a Larrakia camp area. Shaded by tropical trees, the park is an excellent place to stroll.

Mason Gallery GALLERY
(Map p804; ☑ 08-8981 9622; www.masongallery. com.au; Shop 7, 21 Cavenagh St; ☻ 9am-5pm Mon-Fri, 10am-3pm Sat & Sun) FREE This gallery features bold dot paintings from the Western and Central Desert regions, as well as other artworks from Arnhem Land and Utopia.

George Brown Botanic Gardens GARDENS
(Map p804; www.nt.gov.au/leisure/parks-reserves/ george-brown-darwin-botanic-gardens; Geranium St; ☻ 7am-7pm, information centre 8am-4pm) FREE These 42-hectare gardens showcase plants from the Top End and around the world – monsoon vine forest, the mangroves and coastal plants habitat, baobabs, and a mag-

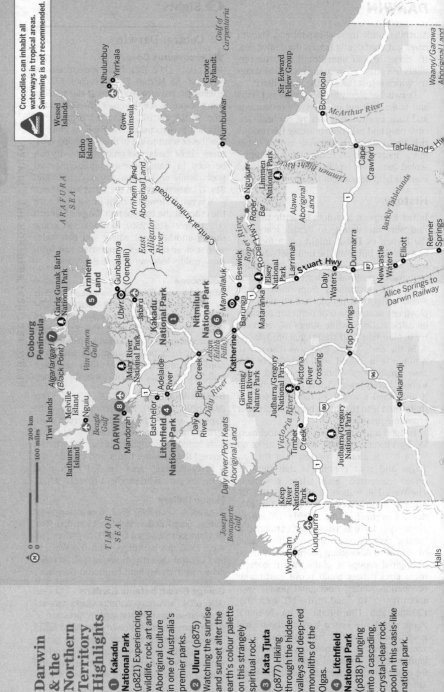

Darwin & the Northern Territory Highlights

1 Kakadu National Park
(p821) Experiencing wildlife, rock art and Aboriginal culture in one of Australia's premier parks.

2 Uluru (p875)
Watching the sunrise and sunset after the earth's colour palette on this strangely spiritual rock.

3 Kata Tjuta
(p877) Hiking through the hidden valleys and deep-red monoliths of the Olgas.

4 Litchfield National Park
(p818) Plunging into a cascading, crystal-clear rock pool in this oasis-like national park.

Crocodiles can inhabit all waterways in tropical areas. Swimming is not recommended.

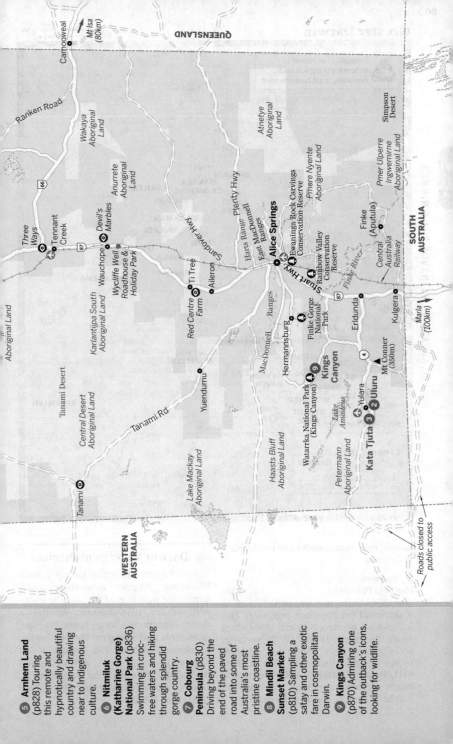

5 Arnhem Land (p828) Touring this remote and hypnotically beautiful country and drawing near to Indigenous culture.

6 Nitmiluk (Katharine Gorge) National Park (p836) Swimming in croc-free waters and hiking through splendid gorge country.

7 Cobourg Peninsula (p830) Driving beyond the end of the paved road into some of Australia's most pristine coastline.

8 Mindil Beach Sunset Market (p810) Sampling a satay and other exotic fare in cosmopolitan Darwin.

9 Kings Canyon (p870) Admiring one of the outback's icons, looking for wildlife.

Greater Darwin

Crocodiles can inhabit all waterways in tropical areas. Swimming is not recommended.

nificent collection of native and exotic palms and cycads.

Myilly Point
Heritage Precinct   HISTORIC SITE

(Map p804) At the northern end of Smith St is this small but important precinct of four houses built between 1930 and 1939 (which means they survived both WWII bombings and Cyclone Tracy!). They're now managed by the National Trust. One of them, **Burnett House** (☑08-8981 0165; www.national trust.org.au/places/burnett-house; $5; ⊙10am-1pm Mon-Sat, 3-5pm Sun), operates as a museum.

Darwin Waterfront Precinct

The bold redevelopment of the old Darwin Waterfront Precinct (www.waterfront.nt. gov.au) has transformed the city. The multimillion-dollar redevelopment features a cruise-ship terminal, luxury hotels, boutique restaurants and shopping, the Sky Bridge, an elevated walkway and elevator at the south end of Smith St, and a **Wave Lagoon** (Map p804; ☑08-8985 6588; www.waterfront. nt.gov.au; Wave Lagoon adult/child $9/6; ⊙Wave Lagoon 10am-6pm).

Greater Darwin

◎ Top Sights
1 Museum & Art Gallery of the
   Northern Territory A4

◎ Sights
2 Charles Darwin National Park B4
3 Crocodylus Park D3
4 East Point Reserve A3
5 Vesteys Beach.. A4

🛌 Sleeping
6 Casa on Gregory B4
7 Grungle Downs B&B D3

🍴 Eating
8 Darwin Ski Club A4
9 Laneway Specialty Coffee B4

Parap Fine Foods .... (see 9)
10 Pee Wee's at the Point A3

🍷 Drinking & Nightlife
Bogarts .... (see 9)
Darwin Sailing Club .... (see 5)
Darwin Ski Club .... (see 8)

🎭 Entertainment
11 Darwin Railway Club B4

🛍 Shopping
12 Nightcliff Market.................................... B2
Nomad Art Gallery.......................... (see 9)
Outstation Gallery .... (see 9)
Parap Village Market...................... (see 9)
Tiwi Art Network .... (see 9)

★ **Royal Flying Doctor Service** MUSEUM
(Map p804; ☎08-8983 5700; www.flyingdoctor.
org.au; Stokes Hill Wharf; adult/child/family
$26/16/70; ☻9.30am-6pm, last entry 5pm) This
outstanding new museum features a 55-seat
hologram cinema, virtual-reality glasses that
enable you to relive in vivid detail the 1942
Japanese bombing raid on Darwin Harbour, a decommissioned Pilatus PC-12 aircraft from the Royal Flying Doctor Service
(RFDS), a live map showing the current location of RFDS planes, and a series of touch
screens that take you through the story of
the RFDS and Darwin during WWII.

WWII Oil-Storage Tunnels TUNNEL
(Map p804; ☎08-8985 6322; www.darwintours.
com.au/ww2tunnels; self-guided tour per adult/
child $8/5; ☻9am-4pm May-Oct, to 1pm Nov-Apr)
You can escape from the heat of the day and
relive your Hitchcockian fantasies by walking through the WWII oil-storage tunnels.
They were built in 1942 to store the navy's oil
supplies (but never used); now they exhibit
wartime photos.

Indo-Pacific Marine Exhibition AQUARIUM
(Map p804; ☎08-8981 1294; www.indopacific
marine.com.au; 29 Stokes Hill Rd; adult/child/family
$24/10/58; ☻10am-4pm Apr-Oct, call for hours
Nov-Mar) This excellent marine aquarium at
the Waterfront Precinct (p800) gives you a
close encounter with the denizens of Darwin
Harbour. Each small tank is a complete ecosystem, with only the occasional extra fish
introduced as food for some of the predators,
such as stonefish or the bizarre angler fish.
   Also recommended here is the **Coral
Reef by Night** (Map p804; ☎08-8981 1294;

www.indopacificmarine.com.au; 29 Stokes Hill Rd;
adult/child $120/60; ☻6.30pm Wed, Fri & Sun),
which consists of a tour of the aquarium, a
seafood dinner and an impressive show of
fluorescing animals.

◎ Fannie Bay & Parap

★ **Museum & Art Gallery
of the Northern Territory** MUSEUM
(MAGNT; Map p800; ☎08-8999 8264; www.
magnt.net.au; 19 Conacher St, Fannie Bay; ☻9am-
5pm Mon-Fri, 10am-5pm Sat & Sun) **FREE** This
superb museum and gallery boasts beautifully presented galleries of Top End–centric
exhibits. The **Aboriginal art collection**
is a highlight, with carvings from the Tiwi
Islands, bark paintings from Arnhem Land
and dot paintings from the desert. An entire
room is devoted to 1974 natural disaster **Cyclone Tracy**, in a display that graphically il-
lustrates life before and after. You can stand
in a darkened room and listen to the whir-
ring sound of Tracy at full throttle – a sound
you won't forget in a hurry.

East Point Reserve GARDENS
(Map p800; ☻mangrove boardwalk 8am-6pm)
North of Fannie Bay, this spit of land is
particularly attractive in the late afternoon
when wallabies emerge to feed and you can
watch the sun set over the bay.
   Lake Alexander, a small, recreational
saltwater lake, was created so people could
enjoy a swim year-round without having
to worry about box jellyfish. There's a good
children's playground here and picnic areas
with BBQs. A 1.5km **mangrove boardwalk**
leads off from the car park.

Outer East

Crocodylus Park ZOO
(Map p800; www.crocodyluspark.com.au; 815 Mc-Millans Rd, Berrimah; adult/child \$40/20; ⊙9am-5pm) Crocodylus Park showcases hundreds of crocs and a minizoo comprising lions, tigers and other big cats, spider monkeys, marmosets, cassowaries and large birds. Allow about two hours to look around the whole park, and you should time your visit with a tour (10am, noon, 2pm and 3.30pm), which includes a feeding demonstration. Croc meat BBQ packs for sale!

The park is about 15km from the city centre. Take bus 5 from Darwin.

Activities

Beaches & Swimming
Darwin is no beach paradise – naturally enough the harbour has no surf – but along the convoluted coastline north of the city centre is a string of sandy beaches. The most popular are **Mindil** (Map p804) and **Vesteys** (Map p800) on Fannie Bay. Further north, a stretch of the 7km **Casuarina Beach** is an official nude beach. Darwin's swimming beaches tend to be far enough away from mangrove creeks to make the threat of meeting a crocodile very remote. A bigger problem is the deadly box jellyfish, which makes swimming decidedly unhealthy between October and March (and often before October and until May).

You can swim year-round without fear of stingers in the western part of **Lake Alexander**, an easy cycle from the centre at East Point Reserve (p801), and at the very popular Wave & Recreation Lagoons (p800), the centrepiece of the Darwin Waterfront Precinct (p800). At the Recreation Lagoon, nets provide a natural seawater swim.

Harbour Cruises

Darwin Harbour Cruises CRUISE
(Map p804; ☑08-8942 3131; www.darwinharbourcruises.com.au) Variety of cruises from Stokes Hill Wharf. The 20m schooner *Tumlaren* does a 'Tastes of the Territory' sunset cruise (adult/child \$74/45), and there are day and evening cruise options aboard the *Charles Darwin*, a tri-level catamaran.

Spirit of Darwin CRUISE
(Map p804; ☑0417 381 977; www.spiritofdarwin.com.au; tours per adult \$65) This fully licensed, air-con motor-catamaran does a two-hour sightseeing cruise at 2pm and a sunset cruise at 5.30pm daily from Stokes Hill Wharf.

Tours

★ Turtle Tracks TOURS
(Map p804; ☑1300 065 022; www.seadarwin.com; Stokes Hill Wharf; adult/child/family \$250/175/790; ⊙4pm May-Sep) This late-afternoon tour goes out beyond Darwin Harbour and Charles Point Lighthouse to beautiful Bare Sand Island, where you'll arrive around sunset. Guides will take you around the island, explaining its history, then take you by torchlight to watch the wonderful sight of turtles laying their eggs; come late in the season and you may see the hatchlings emerge.

★ Ethical Adventures TOURS
(☑0488 442 269; www.ethicaladventures.com) A cut above most of those offering day tours to Litchfield National Park from Darwin, Ethical Adventures runs sunrise-to-sunset tours that take in all of the main attractions, providing excellent food (including barbecued crocodile and buffalo) and good guides. Its focus on small groups, cultural engagement and ethical practices is a highlight.

★ Northern Territory Indigenous Tours CULTURAL TOUR
(☑1300 921 188; www.ntitours.com.au; day tours adult/child from \$249/124) Upmarket Indigenous tours to Litchfield National Park and Kakadu.

AAT Kings TOURS
(Map p804; ☑1300 228 546; www.aatkings.com; 52 Mitchell St) The big player in outback Australia, AAT Kings has loads of experience and plenty of tours to choose from, whether Darwin city tours or Kakadu and Litchfield. This is the antithesis of small-group travel, but it's still worth checking to see if it has a tour that suits.

Wallaroo Tours TOURS
(Darwin Tours; Map p804; ☑08-8981 6670; www.wallarootours.com; 50 Mitchell St; tours \$95-170) A collection of half- and full-day tours that include Mary River National Park and its wetlands (good for birding and croc spotting), the jumping crocs of Mary River, scenic flights, Litchfield day trips and Darwin city tours.

Sacred Earth Safaris ADVENTURE
(☑08-8536 2234; www.sacredearthsafaris.com.au; ⊙May-Oct) Multiday, small-group 4WD camping tours around Kakadu, Katherine and the Kimberley. The two-day Kakadu tour starts at \$850, while the five-day Top End National Parks Safari is \$2600.

Sea Darwin
OUTDOORS

(☎1300 065 022; www.seadarwin.com; 1hr tour adult/child/family $35/20/100) 🏄 Various eco tours around the city and Darwin Harbour, checking out mangroves, a crocodile trap, a shipwreck and (if you're lucky) dugongs and dolphins.

Darwin Walking Tours
WALKING

(Map p804; ☎08-8981 0227; www.darwinwalking tours.com; 50 Mitchell St; adult/child $25/free) 🏄 Two-hour guided history walks around the city, plus fishing, adventure and wildlife tours available from the Darwin Tours Shop.

Kakadu Dreams
TOURS

(☎1800 813 269; www.kakadudreams.com.au) Backpacker day tours to Litchfield ($149), and boisterous two-/three-day trips to Kakadu ($445/665).

✨ Festivals & Events

Darwin Festival
ART

(www.darwinfestival.org.au; ⊘Aug) This mainly outdoor arts and culture festival celebrates music, theatre, visual art, dance and cabaret and runs for 18 days in August. Festivities are centred in the large park next to Civic Sq, off Harry Chan Ave.

Darwin Aboriginal Art Fair
ART

(www.darwinaboriginalartfair.com.au) Held at the **Darwin Convention Centre** (Map p804; www.darwinconvention.com.au), this three-day August festival showcases Indigenous art from communities throughout the NT.

Darwin Fringe Festival
CULTURAL

(www.facebook.com/darwinfringefestival; ⊘Jul) Showcases eclectic, local performing and visual arts at venues including **Brown's Mart** (Map p804; ☎08-8981 5522; www.brown smart.com.au; 12 Smith St) theatre.

Beer Can Regatta
CULTURAL

(www.beercanregatta.org.au) An utterly insane and typically Territorian festival that features races for boats made out of beer cans. It takes place at Mindil Beach (p802) in July and is a good, fun day.

Darwin Cup Carnival
SPORTS

(www.darwinturfclub.org.au) The Darwin Cup racing carnival takes place in July and August at the Darwin Turf Club in Fannie Bay. The highlight of the eight-day program is the running of the Darwin Cup, along with the usual fashion and frivolities.

> **WORTH A TRIP**
>
> ## CHARLES DARWIN NATIONAL PARK
>
> **Charles Darwin National Park** (Map p800; ☎08-8946 5126; www.nt.gov. au/leisure/parks-reserves; ⊘8am-7pm) protects places of natural and cultural importance including part of Port Darwin wetland, one of the country's most significant wetland areas. The park is available for day use only. There's a lookout, some pleasant short walks and the bird-watching's good – watch for mangrove species such as the chestnut rail.

🛏 Sleeping

Darwin has a good range of accommodation, most of it handy to the CBD, but finding a bed in the peak May-to-September period can be difficult at short notice – book ahead, at least for the first night. Accommodation prices vary greatly with the season and demand; expect big discounts between November and March, especially for midrange and top-end places.

🛏 City Centre & Waterfront

Melaleuca on Mitchell
HOSTEL $

(Map p804; ☎1300 723 437; www.momdarwin. com; 52 Mitchell St; dm $32, d with/without bathroom $130/116; ❄@🛜🏊) If you stay here take note: 24-hour check-in and it's plonked right in the action on Mitchell St. So, sleeping...maybe not. Partying? Oh yes! The highlight is the rooftop island bar and pool area – complete with waterfall spa and big-screen TV. Party heaven! This modern hostel is immaculate with great facilities and it's very secure. Third floor female only.

Chilli's
HOSTEL $

(Map p804; ☎1800 351 313, 08-8980 5800; www. chillis.com.au; 69a Mitchell St; dm $32, tw & d without bathroom $90; ❄@🛜) Friendly Chilli's is a funky place with a small sun deck and spa (use the pool next door). There's also a pool table and a breezy kitchen/meals terrace overlooking Mitchell St. Rooms are compact but clean. There are nice touches to this place, such as pots with scented herbs hanging from the roof of the balcony.

Darwin YHA
HOSTEL $

(Map p804; ☎08-8981 5385; www.yha.com. au; 97 Mitchell St; dm $27-38, d $125; ❄@🛜🏊) This place gets good reports from travellers

Central Darwin

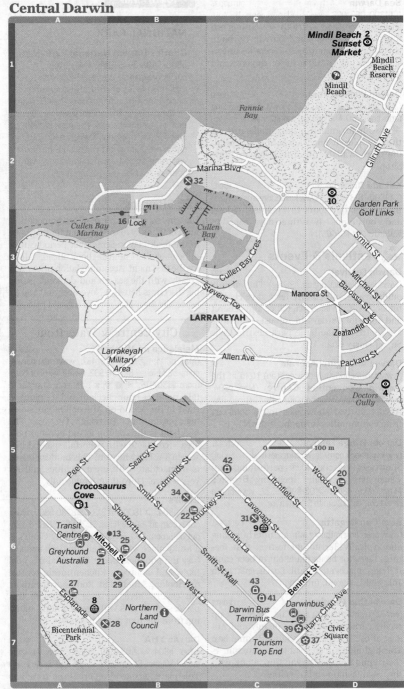

**Mindil Beach 2
Sunset
Market**

Mindil
Beach
Reserve

Mindil
Beach

10

Garden Park
Golf Links

*Fannie
Bay*

Marina Blvd

32

16 Lock

*Cullen Bay
Marina*

*Cullen
Bay*

Cullen Bay Cres

Stevens Tce

Manoora St

Smith St

Mitchell St

Barossa St

Zealandia Cres

LARRAKEYAH

*Larrakeyah
Military
Area*

Allen Ave

Packard St

*Doctors
Gully*

4

Peel St

Searcy St

Edmunds St

42

Litchfield St

Woods St

20

**Crocosaurus
Cove**

1

Smith St

Shadforth La

34

Knuckey St

22

Cavenagh St

31

9

Transit
Centre

13

25

Mitchell St

Greyhound
Australia

21

40

Austin La

29

Smith St Mall

27

West La

43

41

Esplanade

8

28

Northern
Land
Council

Darwin Bus
Terminus

Darwinbus

39

Harry Chan Ave

37

*Bicentennial
Park*

Tourism
Top End

Civic
Square

Bennett St

0 ——— 100 m

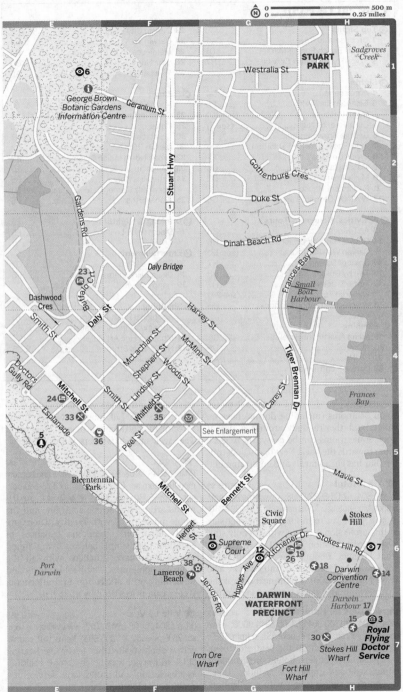

Central Darwin

DARWIN & THE NORTHERN TERRITORY DARWIN

(young and old). It's in a converted motel, so all 34 rooms (including dorms) have en suites, and they're built around a decent pool. Some rooms can be noisy; try to get a room towards the back. Next door Globetrotters Bar has cheap meals and entertainment.

★ **Vibe Hotel** HOTEL $$
(Map p804; ☑ 08-8982 9998; www.tfehotels.com/ brands/vibe-hotels; 7 Kitchener Dr; r $207-240; P ✳ @ ☎ ☎) You're in for an upmarket stay at this professional set-up with friendly staff and a great location at the Darwin Waterfront Precinct. Room prices creep upwards with more bed space and water views. The Wave Lagoon (p800) is right next door if the shady swimming pool is too placid for you.

Darwin Central Hotel HOTEL $$
(Map p804; ☑ 1300 364 263, 08-8944 9000; www. darwincentral.com.au; 21 Knuckey St; d from $220; P ✳ @ ☎ ☎ ☎) Right in the centre of town, this plush independent hotel oozes contemporary style and impeccable facilities. There is a range of stylish rooms with excellent ac-

cessibility for travellers with disabilities. Rack rates are steep, but internet, weekend, and three-night-stay discounts make it great value. The excellent breakfast caps things off nicely.

★ **Argus** APARTMENT $$$
(Map p804; ☑ 08-8925 5000; www.argusaccom modation.com.au; 6 Cardona Ct; 1-/2-/3-bedroom apt from $330/421/509; P ✳ @ ☎) Apartments are *very* spacious at Argus, and the whole place rings with quality. There are lovely bathrooms, generous expanses of cool floor tiles, simple balcony living/dining spaces and snazzy kitchens with all the requisite appliances. The pool is shady and welcoming on a sticky Top End afternoon. Wet-season prices drop by up to half.

★ **Villa La Vue** BOUTIQUE HOTEL $$$
(Map p804; ☑ 08-8942 3012; www.villalavue.com. au; 78 Esplanade; r $395-695) Beautiful rooms with a sophisticated but never overbearing old-world style, a gorgeous stone building as a backdrop, and professional service in a good central location. Put it all together and

you have one of Darwin's classiest and more intimate places to stay.

★ Adina Apartment Hotel
APARTMENT $$$

(Map p804; ☑ 08-8982 9999; www.tfehotels.com; 7 Kitchener Dr; apt $224-463) From the same people who brought the Vibe Hotel to Darwin, the Adina is a stylish place with contemporary apartments sporting clean lines and modern art on the walls. Most rooms have excellent views out over the water and waterfront precinct. You're close to restaurants and bars, and also within walking distance of downtown.

City Fringe & Suburbs

FreeSpirit Resort Darwin
CARAVAN PARK $

(Map p814; ☑ 08-8935 0888; www.darwinfreespiritresort.com.au; 901 Stuart Hwy, Berrimah; unpowered/powered camp sites from $45/52, cabins & units $95-245; ❋@�☕) An impressive highway-side park about a 10-minute drive from the city, with loads of facilities (including three pools). With a jumping cushion, a kidz corner, a bar and live music in the Dry, adults and kids are easily entertained.

Darwin City Edge
MOTEL $$

(Vitina Studio Motel; Map p804; ☑ 08-8981 1544; www.vitinastudiomotel.com.au; 38 Gardens Rd; d/ste $199/229; ⓟ❋@☕☕) We like this place: value-for-money rooms, friendly and efficient service, and a convenient Darwin location. It's a deal. Contemporary motel rooms and larger studios with kitchenettes are on offer. It's right on the city fringe convenient to the Gardens Park golf course, the Botanic Gardens (p797) and Mindil Beach (p802). Keep an eye on its website for discounts.

Grungle Downs B&B
B&B $$

(Map p800; ☑ 08-8947 4440; www.grungledowns.com.au; 945 McMillans Rd, Knuckey Lagoon; r incl breakfast $140-165, cottages $200-400; ❋☕☕) Set on a 2-hectare property, this beautiful rural retreat seems worlds away from the city (but it's only 13km). When it's hot outside, hang out in the guest lounge or by the pool. There are four lodge rooms (one with ensuite) and a gorgeous two-bedroom cottage.

Casa on Gregory
MOTEL $$

(Map p800; ☑ 08-8941 3477; www.casaongregory.com.au; 52 Gregory St, Parap; r $83-220; ❋❋☕) Describing itself as a 'boutique motel', this well-regarded Parap choice has motel-style rooms that are indeed a cut above your aver-

age motel with warm colour schemes and a hint of style in the decor.

✗ Eating

✗ City Centre & Waterfront

There are two large supermarkets in downtown Darwin: **Coles** (Map p804; www.coles.com.au; Mitchell Centre, 55-59 Mitchell St; ⊙6am-10pm) and **Woolworths** (Map p804; www.woolworths.com.au; cnr Cavenagh & Whitfield Sts; ⊙6am-10pm).

★ Aboriginal
Bush Traders Cafe
AUSTRALIAN $

(Map p804; ☑ 09-8942 4023; www.aboriginalbushtraders.com; cnr Esplanade & Knuckey St; mains & light meals $9.50-17; ⊙7.30am-2pm) In historic Lyons Cottage (p810), this fine little cafe has some really tasty dishes inspired by Aboriginal bush tucker from the desert. In addition to more conventional dishes such as gourmet toasted rolls, try the damper with jam (Kakadu plum or wild rosella jam), the kutjera (wild tomato) and aniseed myrtle feta damper, or the saltbush dukkah, avocado and feta smash.

Speaker's Corner Cafe
CAFE $

(Map p804; ☑ 08-8946 1439; www.karensheldoncatering.com.au/speakers; breakfast $5-20, mains $12-18; ⊙7.30am-4pm Mon-Fri) In the grounds of Darwin's **Parliament House** (Map p804; ☑ 08-8946 1512; www.nt.gov.au/lant; Mitchell St; ⊙8am-4.30pm) **FREE**, and part of a project for training young Indigenous workers for the hospitality industry, Speaker's Corner is a great spot for lunch. In addition to the usual cafe fare, try the Speaker's Corner laksa and wash it down with a Kakadu plum spritzer. There are also toasties, creative salads and homemade waffles.

Hanuman
INDIAN, THAI $$

(Map p804; ☑ 08-8941 3500; www.hanuman.com.au; 93 Mitchell St; mains $13-36; ⊙noon-2.30pm, dinner from 6pm; ☑) Ask locals about fine dining in Darwin and they'll usually mention

> ### ⓘ BOOKING SERVICE
>
> Track down the best Darwin deals through this professionally run booking service **More Than a Room** (☑ 0418 616 888; www.morethanaroom.com.au) – it can hook you up with apartments, hotel rooms, villas and holiday homes.

Hanuman. It's sophisticated but not stuffy. Enticing aromas of innovative Indian and Thai Nonya dishes waft from the kitchen to the stylish open dining room and deck. The menu is broad, with exotic vegetarian choices and banquets also available. Respect the sign on the door: 'we appreciate neat attire'.

Little Miss Korea
KOREAN $$

(Map p804; 09-8981 7092; www.littlemisskorea. com; Austin Lane; lunch mains $14-19, dinner mains $19-32; ⊙11.30am-2.30pm & 5.30pm-late Tue-Fri, 5.30pm-late Sat & Sun) Darwin's first real Korean barbecue place is a good one, with a dining area that manages to be classy, casual and contemporary all at once. Dishes are fresh and tasty and could include chargrilled pork belly or local tiger prawns with lemongrass. The laneway location, Darwin's first, is very cool.

Darwin RSL
INTERNATIONAL $$

(Map p804; 08-8981 5437; www.darwinrsl. com.au; 27 Cavenagh St; mains $14-30; ⊙10am-9pm;) If you've spent any time travelling in provincial Australian towns, you'll know the RSL (Returned Services League) clubs are a good deal. There's nothing pretentious here – the atmosphere's very casual and good for families (save for the constant hum of pokies). The food is similarly no-frills excellent, covering great burger choices, pasta, steak and seafood.

★ Crustaceans
SEAFOOD $$$

(Map p804; 08-8981 8658; www.crustaceans. net.au; Stokes Hill Wharf; mains $26-65; ⊙5.30-11pm;) This casual, licensed restaurant features fresh fish, Moreton Bay bugs, lobster, oysters, even crocodile, as well as succulent

---

PARAP VILLAGE

Parap Village is a foodie's heaven with several good restaurants, bars and cafes as well as the highly recommended deli **Parap Fine Foods**. However, it's the Saturday morning **market** (p810) that attracts locals like bees to honey. It's got a relaxed vibe as breakfast merges into brunch and then lunch. Between visits to the takeaway food stalls (most serving spicy Southeast Asian snacks) shoppers stock up on tropical fruit and vegetables – all you need to make your own laksa or rendang. The produce is local so you know it's fresh.

---

steaks. It's all about the location, perched right at the end of Stokes Hill Wharf with sunset views over Frances Bay. The cold beer and a first-rate wine list seal the deal.

Char Restaurant
STEAK $$$

(Map p804; 08-8981 4544; www.chardarwin. com.au; cnr Esplanade & Knuckey St; mains $29-69; ⊙noon-11pm Wed-Fri, 6-11pm Sat-Tue) Housed in the grounds of historic Admiralty House is Char, a carnivore's paradise. The speciality here is chargrilled steaks – aged, grain-fed and cooked to perfection – but there's also a range of clever seafood creations. It's an upmarket atmosphere so dress nicely.

✕ City Fringe & Suburbs

Parap Fine Foods
MARKET $

(Map p800; 08-8981 8597; www.parapfine foods.com; 40 Parap Rd, Parap; ⊙8am-6.30pm Mon-Fri, 8am-6pm Sat, 9am-1pm Sun) A gourmet food hall in Parap shopping centre, stocking organic and health foods, deli items and fine wine – perfect for a picnic.

Laneway Specialty Coffee
CAFE $

(Map p800; 08-8941 4511; www.facebook.com/ lanewayspecialtycoffee; 4/1 Vickers St, Parap; mains $12-18; ⊙8am-3pm Mon-Sat) The pared-back, industrial interior, corner location and powerhouse coffee here have locals wondering if they could be in Melbourne. Getting rave reviews, this place is fast becoming popular. Its well-prepared dishes use local and organic ingredients; the almost artistic bacon-and-egg roll is worth the trip here alone. For lunch the wagyu beef burger beckons.

★ Darwin Ski Club
MODERN AUSTRALIAN $$

(Map p800; 08-8981 6630; www.darwinskiclub. com.au; Conacher St, Fannie Bay; mains $18-28; ⊙noon-10pm) This place just keeps getting better. Already Darwin's finest location for a sunset beer (p809), it now does seriously good tucker too. The dishes are well prepared, and the menu is thoughtful and enticing. We had the red curry and were impressed. Highly recommended by locals.

★ Exotic North Indian Cuisine
INDIAN $$

(Map p804; 08-8941 3396; www.exoticnorth indiancuisine.com.au; Cullen Bay Marina; mains $14-23; ⊙5-10pm;) Offering outstanding value for quality Indian cuisine, this place has taken over the mantle of Darwin's best Indian restaurant. It's positioned right on the waterfront at Cullen Bay, making for extremely pleasant waterside dining in the evening. The service is attentive, there are high chairs for young 'uns and, unusually for Darwin, you can BYO wine.

Pee Wee's at the Point   MODERN AUSTRALIAN **$$$**
(Map p800; ☑ 08-8981 6868; www.peewees.com. au; Alec Fong Lim Dr, East Point Reserve; mains $41-68; ⊙ from 6.30pm) With Hahndorf venison striploin kicking in at $68 a serve, this is indeed a place for a treat. One of Darwin's finest restaurants, it is well worth shelling out for the experience. Enjoy your double-roasted duckling among tropical palms at East Point Reserve (p801), right on the waterfront.

🍷 Drinking & Nightlife

★Darwin Ski Club   PUB
(Map p800; ☑ 08-8981 6630; www.darwinskiclub. com.au; Conacher St, Fannie Bay; ⊙ noon-late) Leave Mitchell St behind and head for a sublime sunset at this laid-back waterski club on Vesteys Beach (p802). The view through the palm trees from the beer garden is a winner, and there are often live bands. Hands down the best venue for a sunset beer in Darwin.

Discovery & Lost Arc   CLUB
(Map p804; ☑ 08-8942 3300; www.discovery darwin.com.au; 89 Mitchell St; ⊙ noon-late) Discovery is Darwin's biggest nightclub and dance venue, with three levels featuring hip hop, techno and house, bars, private booths, karaoke, an elevated dance floor and plenty of partygoers. The Lost Arc is the classy chill-out bar opening on to Mitchell St, which starts to thaw after about 10pm.

Bogarts   BAR
(Map p800; ☑ 08-8981 3561; 52 Gregory St, Parap; ⊙ 4pm-late Tue-Sat) Bogarts is one of Darwin's best bars and well worth the trek out into the suburbs. The decor is old movie posters, cane furniture and animal-print lounges in a mishmash that, strangely enough, works beautifully. It has a low-key ambience and is a local favourite for the over-30s crowd.

Darwin Sailing Club   SPORTS BAR
(Map p800; ☑ 08-8981 1700; www.dwnsail.com. au; Atkins Dr, Fannie Bay; ⊙ noon-2pm & 5.30-9pm) More upmarket than the ski club (p809), the sailing club is always filled with yachties enjoying a sunset beer overlooking the Timor Sea. Tunes on the sound system are surprisingly un-yacht club (no Christopher Cross or Rod Stewart). Sign in as a visitor at the door (bring some ID).

☆ Entertainment

Off the Leash (www.offtheleash.net.au) magazine lists events happening around town.

★Deckchair Cinema   CINEMA
(Map p804; ☑ 08-8981 0700; www.deckchair cinema.com; Jervois Rd, Waterfront Precinct; adult/ child $16/8; ⊙ box office from 6.30pm Apr-Nov) During the Dry, the Darwin Film Society runs this fabulous outdoor cinema below the southern end of the Esplanade. Watch a movie while reclining under the stars. There's a licensed bar serving food or you can bring a picnic (no BYO alcohol). There are usually double features on Friday and Saturday nights (adult/child $24/12).

Happy Yess   LIVE MUSIC
(Map p804; www.happyyess.tumblr.com; Brown's Mart, 12 Smith St; ⊙ 6pm-midnight Thu-Sat) This venue is Darwin's leading place for live music. A not-for-profit venue for musicians run by musicians, you won't hear cover bands in here. Original, sometimes weird, always fun.

Darwin Railway Club   LIVE MUSIC
(Map p800; ☑ 08-8981 4171; 17 Somerville Gardens, Parap; ⊙ 4-11.30pm Mon-Fri, noon-2am Sat, noon-10pm Sun) Key to Darwin's live music scene, this place pulls in some class acts.

🔒 Shopping

★Outstation Gallery   ART
(Map p800; ☑ 08-8981 4822; www.outstation.com. au; 8 Parap Pl; ⊙ 10am-1pm Tue, 5pm Wed-Fri, 2pm Sat) One of Darwin's best galleries of Indigenous art, Outstation presents the works of nine different Aboriginal art centres from across the NT, from Arnhem Land to the Western Desert.

Nomad Art Gallery   ART
(Map p800; ☑ 08-8981 6382; www.nomadart. com.au; 1/3 Vickers St, Parap; ⊙ 10am-5pm Mon-Fri, 9am-2pm Sat) Around since 2005, this high-end gallery sells contemporary Indigenous art, including limited-edition paintings, textiles, carpets, bronze and jewellery.

Mbantua Fine Art Gallery   ART
(Map p804; ☑ 08-8941 6611; www.mbantua. com.au; 2/30 Smith St Mall; ⊙ 9am-5pm Mon-Sat) Vivid Utopian designs painted on everything from canvases to ceramics.

Aboriginal Bush Traders   ARTS & CRAFTS
(Map p804; ☑ 0487 007 070; www.aboriginal bushtraders.com; 74 Esplanade; ⊙ 9am-2pm) Inhabiting the fine old heritage building

DARWIN'S MAGICAL MARKETS

Mindil Beach Sunset Market (Map p804; www.mindil.com.au; off Gilruth Ave; ⊙5-10pm Thu, 4-9pm Sun May-Oct) Food is the main attraction here – from Thai, Sri Lankan, Indian, Chinese and Malaysian to Brazilian, Greek, Portuguese and more – all at around $6 to $12 a serve. But that's only half the fun – arts and crafts stalls bulge with handmade jewellery, fabulous rainbow tie-dyed clothes, Aboriginal artefacts, and wares from Indonesia and Thailand. **Mindil beach** (p802) is about 2km from Darwin's city centre; it's an easy walk or hop on buses 4 or 6, which go past the market.

Parap Village Market (Map p800; www.parapvillage.com.au; Parap Shopping Village, Parap Rd, Parap; ⊙8am-2pm Sat) This compact, crowded food-focused market is a local favourite. There's the full gamut of Southeast Asian cuisine, as well as plenty of ingredients to cook up your own tropical storm. It's open year-round.

Nightcliff Market (Map p800; www.nightcliffmarkets.com.au; Pavonia Way, Nightcliff; ⊙6am-2pm Sun) A popular community market north of the city in the Nightcliff Shopping Centre. You'll find lots of secondhand goods and designer clothing.

of **Lyons Cottage** (Map p804; ☑0488 329 933; FREE), this is a collection of artworks, carvings, weaving, jewellery and a small number of books and CDs. There's also a cafe (p807).

The Bookshop BOOKS
(Map p804; ☑08-8941 3489; www.bookshopdarwin. com.au; 1/30 Smith St Mall; ⊙9am-5pm Mon-Fri, 9am-3pm Sat, 10am-2pm Sun) Probably Darwin's best bookshop with a good general selection.

Darwin Art Trail ART
(www.darwinarttrail.com.au; ⊙10am-4pm 3rd Sun of month May-Sep) This online resource is a good way to get to know the lesser-known art galleries and artists around Darwin with around seven studios involved. Aside from the studios' normal opening hours, they all have monthly open days.

NT General Store SPORTS & OUTDOORS
(Map p804; ☑08-8981 8242; www.thentgeneral store.com.au; 42 Cavenagh St; ⊙8.30am-5.30pm Mon-Wed, 6pm Thu & Fri, 1pm Sat) This casual, corrugated-iron warehouse has shelves piled high with camping and bushwalking gear, as well as a range of maps.

Aboriginal Fine Arts Gallery ART
(Map p804; ☑08-8981 1315; www.aaia.com.au; 1st fl, cnr Mitchell & Knuckey Sts; ⊙9am-5pm Mon-Fri, 9am-3pm Sat, 10am-3pm Sun) Displays and sells art from Arnhem Land and the Central Desert region.

Tiwi Art Network ART
(Map p800; ☑08-8941 3593; www.ankaaa.org.au/ art-centre/tiwi-art-network-tiwi-islands; 3/3 Vickers St, Parap; ⊙10am-5pm Wed-Fri, to 2pm Sat)

✐ The office and showroom for three arts communities on the Tiwi Islands.

ⓘ Information

DANGERS & ANNOYANCES
➡ Darwin is a generally safe city to visit but the usual rules apply: petty crime can be a problem, particularly late at night, so avoid walking alone in unlit areas and don't leave valuables in your car.

➡ In response to several reports of drugged drinks, authorities are advising women to refuse drinks offered by strangers in bars and to drink bottled alcohol rather than from a glass.

➡ Always assume that there are crocodiles in waterholes and rivers in the Darwin area.

➡ Cyclones can happen from November to April, while heavy monsoon rains can curtail outdoor activities from December to March.

➡ **Fire** (☑000; www.pfes.nt.gov.au) For local fire services.

INTERNET ACCESS
Most accommodation in Darwin provides some form of internet access, and there's free wi-fi available in the Smith Street Mall.

Northern Territory Library (☑1800 019 155; www.dtc.nt.gov.au/arts-and-museums/ northern-territory-library; Parliament House, Mitchell St; ⊙10am-5pm Mon-Fri, 1-5pm Sat & Sun; ☎)

MEDICAL SERVICES
Ark Aid (☑0409 090 840; www.wildlifedarwin. org.au) The people to call if you come across injured wildlife.

Royal Darwin Hospital (☑08-8920 6011; www.health.nt.gov.au; 105 Rocklands Dr, Tiwi; ⊙24hr)

MONEY

There are 24-hour ATMs dotted around the city centre, and exchange bureaux on Mitchell St.

POST

General Post Office (Map p804; ☑ 13 13 18; www.auspost.com.au; 48 Cavenagh St; ⊘ 9am-5pm Mon-Fri, to 12.30pm Sat)

TOURIST INFORMATION

George Brown Botanic Gardens Information Centre (Map p804; ⊘ 8am-4pm)

Northern Land Council (Map p804; ☑ 08-8920 5100; www.nlc.org.au; 45 Mitchell St) Permits for Arnhem Land and other northern mainland areas.

Tiwi Land Council (Map p800; ☑ 08-8981 4898; www.tiwilandcouncil.com; 162/2 Armidale St, Stuart Park) Permits for the Tiwi Islands.

Tourism Top End (Map p804; ☑ 1300 138 886, 08-8980 6000; www.tourismtopend.com. au; cnr Smith & Bennett Sts; ⊘ 8.30am-5pm Mon-Fri, 9am-3pm Sat & Sun) Helpful office with hundreds of brochures; books tours and accommodation.

❶ Getting There & Away

AIR

Darwin International Airport (☑ 08-8920 1811; www.darwinairport.com.au; Henry Wrigley Dr, Marrara) is 12km north of the city centre, and handles both international and domestic flights. **Darwin City Airport Shuttle Service** (Map p800; ☑ 08-8947 3979; www.darwincity airportshuttleservice.com.au; per person $15) is one of a number of private airport shuttle companies who will pick up or drop off almost anywhere in the centre. When leaving Darwin book a day before departure. A taxi fare into the centre is about $40.

The following airlines operate from the airport: **Airnorth** (☑ 1800 627 474; www.airnorth.com. au), **Jetstar** (www.jetstar.com), **Qantas** (www. qantas.com.au) and **Virgin Australia** (www. virginaustralia.com).

BUS

Greyhound Australia (Map p804; ☑ 1300 473 946; www.greyhound.com.au) operates long-distance bus services from the **Transit Centre** (Map p804; www.enjoy-darwin.com/ transit-bus.html; 69 Mitchell St). There's at least one service per day up and down the Stuart Hwy, stopping at Pine Creek (from $62, three hours), Katherine ($75, four hours), Mataranka ($102, seven hours), Tennant Creek ($206, 14½ hours) and Alice Springs ($265, 22 hours).

For Kakadu, there's a daily return service from Darwin to Jabiru ($75, 3½ hours).

Backpacker buses and tours can also get you to out-of-the-way places.

CAR & CAMPERVAN

For driving around Darwin, conventional vehicles are cheap enough, but most companies offer only 100km per day free, which won't get you very far out of town. Rates start at around $40 per day for a small car with 100km per day.

There are also plenty of 4WD vehicles available in Darwin, through companies like **Britz** (☑ 1800 331 454; www.britz.com.au; 17 Bombing Rd, Winnellie), but you usually have to book ahead and fees/deposits are higher than for 2WD vehicles. Larger companies offer one-way rentals plus better mileage deals for more-expensive vehicles. Campervans are a great option for touring around the NT and you generally get unlimited kilometres even for short rentals. Prices start at around $60 a day for a basic camper or $100 to $120 for a three-berth hi-top camper, to $250-plus for the bigger mobile homes or 4WD bushcampers. Additional insurance cover or excess reduction costs extra.

Most rental companies are open every day and have agencies in the city centre. **Avis** (☑ 08-8936 0600; www.avis.com.au; 89 Smith St), **Budget** (☑ 08-8981 9800; www.budget.com.au; McLachlan St), **Hertz** (☑ 08-8941 0944; www. hertz.com.au; Shop 41, Mitchell Centre, 55-59 Mitchell St; ⊘ 8am-5pm Mon-Fri, to noon Sat & Sun) and **Thrifty** (☑ 08-8924 2454; www.renta-car.com.au; 50 Mitchell St) all have offices at the airport. Other car rental companies:

Europcar (☑ 08-8941 0300; www.europcar. com.au; 77 Cavenagh St; ⊘ 8am-5pm Mon-Fri, to noon Sat & Sun)

JJ's Car Hire (☑ 0427 214 229; www.jjscarhire. com.au; 7 Goyder Rd, Parap) A good local operator.

Mighty Cars & Campervans (www.mighty campers.com.au; 17 Bombing Rd, Winnellie)

Travellers Autobarn (☑ 1800 674 374; www. travellers-autobarn.com.au; 19 Bishop St)

For assistance or information try one of the following:

AANT Roadside Assistance (☑ 13 11 11; www. aant.com.au)

Automobile Association of the Northern Territory (AANT; ☑ 08 8925 5901; www.aant. com.au)

TRAIN

The legendary *Ghan* train, operated by Great Southern Rail (www.greatsouthernrail.com.au), runs weekly (twice weekly May to July) between Adelaide and Darwin via Alice Springs. The Darwin terminus is on Berrimah Rd, 15km/20 minutes from the city centre. A taxi fare into the centre is about $35, though there is a shuttle service to/from the **Transit Centre**.

ℹ️ Getting Around

BUS

Darwinbus (Map p804; ☎ 08-8944 2444; www.nt.gov.au/driving/public-transport-cycling) runs a comprehensive bus network that departs from the **Darwin Bus Terminus** (Map p804; Harry Chan Ave), opposite Brown's Mart.

A $3 adult ticket gives unlimited travel on the bus network for three hours (validate your ticket when you first get on). Daily ($7) and weekly ($20) travel cards are also available from bus interchanges, newsagents and the **visitor centre** (p811). Bus 4 (to Fannie Bay, Nightcliff, Rapid Creek and Casuarina) and bus 6 (Fannie Bay, Parap and Stuart Park) are useful for getting to **Aquascene** (p797), the **Botanic Gardens** (p797), **Mindil Beach** (p802), the **Museum & Art Gallery** (p801), **East Point Reserve** (p801) and the markets.

TAXI

Taxis wait along Knuckey St, diagonally opposite the north end of Smith St Mall, and are usually easy to flag down. Call **Darwin Radio Taxis** (☎ 13 10 08; www.131008.com).

AROUND DARWIN

In Darwin's hinterland you'll come across some real gems, particularly Litchfield National Park, the Mary River region, Pine Creek and the Tiwi Islands. You're never more than a couple of hours from the capital but, with the exception of the Tiwi Islands, we recommend doing more than just a day visit from Darwin – every one of these places is worth lingering over.

Tiwi Islands

The Tiwi Islands – Bathurst Island and Melville Island – lie about 80km north of Darwin, and are home to the Tiwi Aboriginal people. A visit here is one of the cultural highlights of the Top End. The Tiwis (We People) have a distinct culture and today are well known for producing vibrant art and the odd champion Aussie Rules football player. Tourism is restricted on the islands and for most travellers the only way to visit is on one of the daily organised tours from Darwin.

The main settlement on the islands is Wurrumiyanga in the southeast of Bathurst Island, which was founded in 1911 as a Catholic mission. On Melville Island the settlements are Pirlangimpi and Milikapiti.

☞ Tours

There's no public transport on the islands, so the best way to see them is on a tour. You can catch the Sealink ferry over to Wurrumiyanga and have a very quick (45-minute!) look around the town without taking a tour or buying a permit, but if you want to explore further you'll need a permit from the Tiwi Land Council (p811).

**Tiwi Tours Aboriginal
Cultural Experience**   CULTURAL
(☎ 1300 228 546; www.aatkings.com/tours/tiwi-tours-aboriginal-cultural-experience-by-ferry; adult/child $285/143) Runs fascinating day trips to the Tiwis, although interaction with the local community tends to be limited to your guides and the local workshops and showrooms. The tour is available by ferry (2½ hours each way Thursday and Friday).

Tiwi by Design   CULTURAL
(Map p804; ☎ 1300 130 679; www.sealinknt.com.au; adult/child $345/289; ⊙ 8am-5.45pm Thu & Fri Apr–mid-Dec, 8am-5.45pm Mon mid-Jun–Aug) Leaving from Cullen Bay ferry terminal, this tour to the Tiwi Islands includes permits, lunch and a welcome ceremony, as well as visits to a local museum, church and art workshop, where you get to create your own design. It's run by Sealink (p812), the ferry operator.

⭐ Festivals & Events

Tiwi Grand Final   SPORTS
(⊙ Mar) Held at the end of March on Bathurst Island, this sporting spectacular displays the Tiwis' sparkling skills and passion for Aussie Rules football. Thousands come from Darwin for the day, which coincides with the Tiwi Art Sale (www.tiwidesigns.com). Book your tour or ferry trip well in advance.

🛏️ Sleeping & Eating

Visitors are not allowed to stay on the island without permission and there are no hotels. Visit instead on a day trip from Darwin.

Some of the tour operators provide lunch, but otherwise there are no restaurants or supermarkets so you'll need to bring your own food.

ℹ️ Getting There & Away

Sealink (www.sealinknt.com.au; adult/child one-way $52.50/27.50, return $105/55) ferries operate from Darwin's Cullen Bay to the Tiwi Islands daily at noon (less often during the Wet); the journey takes 2½ hours and departs

TIWI ISLAND CULTURE

The Tiwis' island homes kept them fairly isolated from mainland developments until the 20th century, and their culture has retained several unique features. Perhaps the best known are the pukumani (burial poles), carved and painted with symbolic and mythological figures, which are erected around graves. More recently the Tiwis have turned their hand to art for sale: carving, painting, textile screen-printing, batik and pottery using traditional designs and motifs. The Bima Wear textile factory was set up in 1969 to employ Tiwi women, and today makes many bright fabrics in distinctive designs.

Most of the 2700 Tiwi Islanders live on Bathurst Island (there are about 900 people on Melville Island). Most follow a mainly nontraditional lifestyle, but they still hunt dugong and gather turtle eggs, and hunting and gathering usually supplements the mainland diet a couple of times a week. Tiwis also go back to their traditional lands on Melville Island for a few weeks each year to teach and to learn traditional culture. Descendants of the Japanese pearl divers who regularly visited here early last century also live on Melville Island.

Wurrumiyanga on the islands at 3.15pm. If you visit the islands on the public ferry, you'll only have 45 minutes to have a quick look around Wurrumiyanga.

Arnhem Highway

The Arnhem Highway (Rte 36) connects Darwin to Kakadu National Park – it branches off towards Kakadu 34km southeast of Darwin – and while many travellers stop for little more than petrol along the way, there are a number of worthwhile sights and activities if you have the time. These include river cruises and wetland birdwatching, as well as the small agricultural hub (and gloriously named) Humpty Doo where you can see The Big Boxing Crocodile.

◉ Sights

Djukbinj National Park   NATIONAL PARK
(Map p814; ☑08-8988 8009; www.nt.gov.au/leisure/parks-reserves) Flood plains and billabongs make for good birdwatching at this pretty park 80km southeast of Darwin off the Arnhem Hwy. This was once the hunting grounds for the Limilngan people who now comanage the park, and the waterbirds here can be epic in numbers, especially the magpie geese. There are lookouts at Scotts Creek, Little Sister Billabong and Twin Billabong, and a picnic area at Calf Billabong. The park is often inaccessible from December to March due to heavy rains.

Window on the
Wetlands Visitor Centre   WILDLIFE RESERVE
(Map p814; www.nt.gov.au/leisure/parks-reserves; Arnhem Hwy; ⊙8am-5.30pm) FREE Three kilometres past the Fogg Dam turn-off east

along the Arnhem Hwy is this dashing-looking structure full of displays explaining the wetland ecosystem, as well as the history of the local Limilngan-Wulna Aboriginal people. There are great views over the Adelaide River flood plain from the observation deck, and binoculars for studying the waterbirds on Lake Beatrice.

Fogg Dam
Conservation Reserve   NATURE RESERVE
(Map p814; www.foggdamfriends.org) Bring your binoculars – there are ludicrous numbers of waterbirds living at the fecund green Fogg Dam Conservation Reserve. The dam walls are closed to walkers (crocs), but there are a couple of nature walks (2.2km and 3.6km) through the forest and woodlands. Bird numbers are highest between December and July. The turn-off for the reserve is about 15km southeast along the Arnhem Hwy from Humpty Doo.

🏃 Activities

Adelaide River Cruises   WILDLIFE WATCHING
(Map p814; ☑08-8983 3224; www.adelaideriver cruises.com.au; tours adult/child/family $45/20/110; ⊙9am, 11am, 1pm & 3pm May-Oct) See the jumping crocodiles on a private stretch of river past the Fogg Dam turn-off. Also runs small-group full-day wildlife cruises.

Spectacular Jumping
Crocodile Cruise   WILDLIFE WATCHING
(Map p814; ☑08-8978 9077; www.jumpingcroc odile.com.au; tours adult/child $40/25; ⊙9am, 11am, 1pm & 3pm) Along the Window on the Wetlands (p813) access road, this outfit runs one-hour tours. Ask about trips ex-Darwin.

Around Darwin

DARWIN & THE NORTHERN TERRITORY ARNHEM HIGHWAY

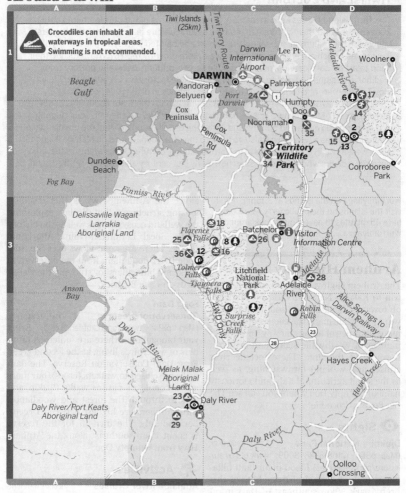

Adelaide River Queen   WILDLIFE WATCHING
(Map p814; ☑08-8988 8144; www.jumpingcroco
dilecruises.com.au; tours adult/child $45/30;
☺9am, 10am, 11am, 1pm, 2pm & 3pm Mar-Oct)
Well-established jumping-crocodile operator on the highway just before **Adelaide
River Crossing** (Map p814).

🛌 Sleeping & Eating

Humpty Doo Hotel   PUB FOOD $$
(Map p814; ☑08-8988 1372; www.humptydoo
hotel.net; Arnhem Hwy; mains $19-32; ☺10am-
9pm; ❄) Some people stop here because,
well, it's the sort of name you'd like to tell

your friends about when you're back home,
but there's more to this place than novelty.
The self-proclaimed 'world famous' Humpty
Doo Hotel is a popular local (even with Dar-
win locals) serving up big meals, big Sunday
sessions and Friday night bands.

There are unremarkable motel rooms and
cabins out the back (rooms $130 to $160).

❶ Getting There & Away

There's not much public transport along the
Arnhem Hwy, but most visitors either drive
or visit on a tour. There's a petrol station at
Humpty Doo.

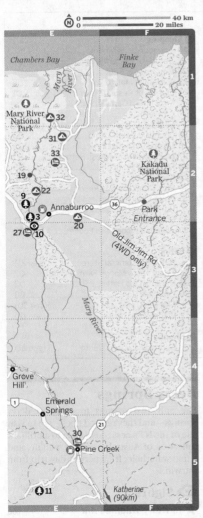

their glory. You're almost guaranteed to see saltwater crocs, as well as plenty of bird life. There are one-hour morning cruises (adult/child \$40/30) and lunch or sunset cruises along with full-day excursions from Darwin (adult/child \$130/100).

Pudakul Aboriginal Cultural Tours TOURS
(☑ 08-8984 9282; www.pudakul.com.au; adult/child/family \$99/55/250; ⊘ May-Oct) This fine small operator runs two-hour Indigenous cultural tours in the Adelaide River and Mary River regions, with Aboriginal guides taking you through everything from painting, spear-throwing and didgeridoo lessons to bush-tucker and bush-medicine guided walks.

🛏 Sleeping

Annaburroo Billabong CAMPGROUND $
(Map p814; ☑ 08-8978 8971; Arnhem Hwy; unpowered sites per adult/family \$10/22, cabins \$75-160) With a private billabong, bush camp sites, a wandering menagerie and friendly owners, this place seems a world away from the highway only 2km down the road, and is a great alternative to the roadhouses. The elevated African-style safari cabins with fridge and ensuite are cosy, and there are cabins, lodge rooms and immaculate tin-and-bamboo amenity blocks.

**★ Mary River
Wilderness Retreat** RESORT $$
(Map p814; ☑ 08-8978 8877; www.maryriverpark.com.au; Mary River Crossing, Arnhem Hwy; unpowered/powered sites \$30/43, cabins & safari tents \$145-220; ❀ 🛜 ⛱) Boasting 3km of Mary River frontage, this bush retreat has excellent poolside and bush cabins with decks surrounded by trees, as well as some fine safari tents. Pool cabins are the pick of the bunch with high ceilings, walk-in showers and more space to knock around in; both sleep up to three people. Camping on the grassy slopes here is delightful.

**Point Stuart
Wilderness Lodge** CAMPGROUND $$
(Map p814; ☑ 08-8978 8914; www.pointstuart.com.au; Point Stuart Rd; camping per adult/child \$17.50/6, safari tents s/d \$35/50, d \$130-195; ❀ ⛱) Accessible by 2WD and only 36km from the Arnhem Hwy, this remote-feeling lodge is part of an old cattle station and ideal for exploring the Mary River region. Accommodation ranges from camp sites and simple safari tents to budget rooms

Mary River Region

Often overlooked in the rush to Kakadu, Mary River is worth dedicating some time to, with the wetlands and wildlife of the Mary River National Park (p817), north of the Arnhem Hwy, the centrepiece.

🍴 Tours

**Wetland Cruises – Corroboree
Billabong** TOURS
(Map p814; ☑ 08-8985 5855; www.wetlandcruises.com.au; ⊘ Mar-Oct) These excellent boat excursions show the Mary River Wetlands in all

Around Darwin

and decent lodge rooms. Two-hour wetland cruises on croc-rich Rockhole Billabong cost $65/25 per adult/child, and boat hire is available.

★ **Wildman Wilderness Lodge** RESORT $$$
(Map p814; ☎ 08-8978 8955; www.wildmanwildernesslodge.com.au; Point Stuart Rd; safari tent/cabin half-board $615/769; ❄☀) One of the best places to stay in the Top End, Wildman Wilderness Lodge is an upmarket safari lodge with an exceptional program of optional tours and activities, not to mention some gorgeous, supremely comfortable accommodation in a beautiful and remote setting. There are just 10 air-conditioned, stylish, architect-designed cabins and 15 fan-cooled, clean-lined luxury tents.

ⓘ Getting There & Away

You'll need a 4WD to explore anywhere in the national park beyond the Arnhem Hwy, although a few park trails may be passable in a 2WD during the dry season. Petrol is available along the Arnhem Highway. Some accommodation places offer transfers from Darwin and elsewhere.

Berry Springs

The only two reasons to come to Berry Springs – and they're good ones – are to visit one of the NT's best zoos, home to a brilliant collection of Australia's native wildlife, and a fine waterhole. It's a perfect day trip from Darwin.

◉ Sights

★ **Territory Wildlife Park** ZOO
(Map p814; ☎ 08-8988 7200; www.territorywildlifepark.com.au; 960 Cox Peninsula Rd; adult/child/family $32/16/54.50; ☉9am-5pm) This excellent park, 60km from Darwin, showcases the best of Aussie wildlife. Pride of place must go to the aquarium, where a clear walk-through tunnel puts you among giant barramundi, stingrays, sawfish and saratogas, while a separate tank holds a 3.8m saltwater crocodile. To see everything you can either walk around the 4km perimeter road, or hop on and off the shuttle trains that run every 15 to 30 minutes and stop at all the exhibits.

Berry Springs Nature Park NATURE RESERVE
(Map p814; www.nt.gov.au/leisure/parks-reserves;
☺8am-6.30pm) This wonderful waterhole
is the closest to Darwin and very popular
with locals. It's a beautiful series of spring-
fed swimming holes shaded by paperbarks
and pandanus palms and serenaded by
abundant birds; native flowers bloom here
in March and April. Facilities include a kiosk, a picnic area with BBQs, toilets, changing sheds and showers. And there are large
grassed areas to lounge around on in between swims.

✖ Eating

★**Crazy Acres Mango Farm & Cafe** CAFE $
(Map p814; ☑08-8988 6227; www.crazyacres.
com.au; Reedbeds Rd; light meals $10-16; ☺9am-
5.30pm May-Sep) Homemade ice cream,
mango smoothies, local honey, Devonshire
teas and a range of light meals from mango
chicken (of course) to a gorgeous Farmer's
Platter – what's not to like about this lovely
little place just off Cox Peninsula Rd?

❶ Getting There & Away

The turn-off to Berry Springs is 48km down the
Stuart Hwy from Darwin; it's 10km from the
turn-off to the nature park, and a further 2km to
the wildlife park.

Batchelor
POP 336

The little town of Batchelor was once so
sleepy the government gave blocks of land
away for a time to encourage settlement.
That was before uranium was discovered
and the nearby Rum Jungle mine developed
(it closed in 1971 after operating for almost
20 years). These days, Batchelor is an important gateway and service centre for neighbouring Litchfield National Park (p818).

◉ Sights

From the Visitor Information Centre
(p818), pick up a copy of the photocopied
Batchelor Heritage Walk to guide your
steps. It provides a potted history of the
town and a self-guided route for a leisurely
amble with a focus on local history.

⌂ Sleeping & Eating

Litchfield Tourist Park CARAVAN PARK $
(Map p814; ☑08-8976 0070; www.litchfieldtourist
park.com.au; 2916 Litchfield Park Rd; camp sites
$38, bunkhouse $79, ensuite cabins from $148;
❋@🛰❄) Just 4km from Litchfield National Park (p818), there's a great range of
accommodation here and it's the closest option to the park. There's also a breezy, open-
sided bar-restaurant (all-day food $11 to $21,

DARWIN & THE NORTHERN TERRITORY BATCHELOR

DON'T MISS

MARY RIVER NATIONAL PARK

Mary River National Park (08-8978 8986; www.nt.gov.au/leisure/parks-reserves)
has an interesting mix of barramundi fishing, pretty landscapes and history, with good
bird life, saltwater crocodiles and paperbark-fringed swamps.

Bird Billabong (Map p814), just off the Arnhem Hwy a few kilometres before **Mary
River Crossing** (Map p814) if you're coming from the west, is a back-flow billabong,
filled by creeks flowing off the nearby Mt Bundy Hill during the Wet. It's 4km off the highway and accessible by 2WD year-round. The scenic loop walk (4.5km, two hours) passes
through tropical woodlands, with a backdrop of Mt Bundy granite rocks.

About another 2km along the same road is the emerald-green **Mary River Billabong**
(Map p814), with a BBQ area (no camping). From here the 4WD-only **Hardies Track**
leads deeper into the national park to **Corroboree Billabong** (25km) and **Couzens
Lookout** (Map p814; Mary River National Park; adult/child/family $3.30/1.65/7.70) (37km);
the sunsets are especially pretty from Couzens Lookout, where there's a camp site.

Further east and north of the Arnhem Hwy, the partly sealed Point Stuart Rd leads to
a number of riverside viewing platforms and to **Shady Camp** (Map p814; adult/child/
family $3.30/1.65/7.70). The causeway barrage here, which stops fresh water flowing into
saltwater, creates the ideal feeding environment for barramundi, and the ideal fishing
environment.

In the park's northern reaches, devotees of explorer history will not want to miss the
6km-return walk in Point Stuart Coastal Reserve out to **Stuart's Memorial Cairn** – it
marks the northernmost point reached by John McDouall Stuart in 1862.

open breakfast and dinner) where you can get a beer, a burger or a real coffee.

★ **Rum Jungle Bungalows** BUNGALOW **$$**
(Map p814; ☑ 08-8976 0555; 10 Meneling Rd; r $170; ❋ ☲) With more personality than most Batchelor places and rooms with warm and eclectic decor, Rum Jungle is an excellent choice. It's set in soothing and beautiful gardens and is open year-round.

Batchelor Butterfly Farm RESORT **$$**
(Map p814; ☑ 08-8976 0110; www.butterflyfarm.net. au; 8 Meneling Rd; d Aug-Sep $160, Oct-Mar $80-150; ❋ @ ☎ ☲) This compact, slightly eclectic retreat divides itself between a low-key tourist attraction and friendly tropical-style resort. There's a butterfly farm (adult/child $10/5), mini zoo (free for guests), ensuite cabins, a large homestay, and a busy all-day cafe-restaurant (mains $18 to $32) featuring Asian-inspired dishes. It's all a bit Zen with Buddha statues, chill music and wicker chairs.

Litchfield Motel RESORT **$$**
(Map p814; ☑ 08-8976 0123; www.litchfieldmotel. com.au; 37-49 Rum Jungle Rd; d Apr-Oct $195-215, Nov-Mar $150-170; ❋ ☎ ☲) On the edge of town, this sprawling orange-brick complex has decent motel rooms and energetic new managers. It's good for families, with bird feeding, two pools and two restaurants. There's also a bar and a grocery shop.

Batchelor General Store MARKET **$**
(Map p814; cnr Takarri Rd & Nurndina St; ⊙ 6am-6pm) Combines a well-stocked supermarket, takeaway, newsagent and post office.

🛍 Shopping

Coomalie Cultural Centre ARTS & CRAFTS
(Map p814; ☑ 08-8939 7404; www.facebook.com/ coomalieartcentre; cnr Awilla Rd & Nurndina St; ⊙ 10am-5pm Tue-Sat Apr-Sep, 10am-4pm Tue-Fri Oct-Mar) The community-based Coomalie Cultural Centre displays and sells a range of Indigenous art and crafts from throughout the NT, and runs an artist-in-residence program, so you'll often see artists at work.

❶ Information

Visitor Information Centre (Map p814; ☑ 08-8976 0444; Takarri Rd; ⊙ 8.30am-5pm)

❶ Getting There & Away

Batchelor is 98km south of Darwin and 14km west of the Stuart Highway along a sealed road. There's a **petrol station** (Map p814) in the town centre.

Litchfield National Park

It may not be as well known as Kakadu, but many Territory locals rate **Litchfield** (Map p814; ☑ 08-8976 0282; www.nt.gov.au/leisure/ parks-reserves) even higher. Our response? Why not visit both? The rock formations and the rock pools in cliff shadow here are simply stunning and Litchfield is smaller and more manageable than Kakadu. The 1500-sq-km national park encloses much of the spectacular Tabletop Range, a wide sandstone plateau mostly surrounded by cliffs. The waterfalls that pour off the edge of this plateau are a highlight of the park, feeding crystal-clear cascades and croc-free plunge pools.

The only downside is that, given its proximity to and ease of access from Darwin, it's often busy, and the only road through the park can be full of tour buses. Even so, it remains a beautiful place and certainly one of the best spots in the Top End for bushwalking, camping and especially swimming.

❍ Sights & Activities

About 17km after entering the park from Batchelor you come to what look like tombstones. But only the very tip of these **magnetic termite mounds** (Map p814) is used to bury the dead; at the bottom are the king and queen, with workers in between. They're perfectly aligned to regulate temperature, catching the morning sun, then allowing the residents to dodge the midday heat. Nearby are some giant mounds made by the aptly named cathedral termites.

Another 6km further along is the turn-off to **Buley Rockhole** (Map p814; 2km), where water cascades through a series of rock pools big enough to lodge your bod in. This turn-off also takes you to **Florence Falls** (5km), one of Litchfield's more agreeable waterholes and accessed by a 15-minute, 135-step descent to a deep, beautiful pool surrounded by monsoon forest. Alternatively, you can see the falls from a lookout, 120m from the car park. There's a walking track (1.7km, 45 minutes) between the two places that follows Florence Creek.

About 18km beyond the turn-off to Florence Falls is the turn-off to the spectacular **Tolmer Falls,** which are for looking at only. A 1.6km loop track (45 minutes) offers beautiful views of the valley. Tolmer Falls doesn't quite get the crowds because of the absence of swimming and we like it all the more for that.

It's a further 7km along the main road to the turn-off for Litchfield's big-ticket attraction, **Wangi Falls** (Map p814; *wong-guy*), 1.6km up a side road. The falls flow year-round, spilling either side of a huge orange-rock outcrop and filling an enormous swimming hole bordered by rainforest. Bring swimming goggles to spot local fish. It's immensely popular during the Dry (when there's a portable refreshment kiosk here, and free public wi-fi), but water levels in the Wet can make it unsafe; look for signposted warnings.

The park offers plenty of bushwalking, including the **Tabletop Track** (39km), a circuit of the park that takes three to five days to complete depending on how many side tracks you follow. You can access the track at Florence Falls, Wangi Falls and Walker Creek. You must carry a topographic map of the area, available from tourist and retail outlets in Batchelor. The track is closed late September to March.

🛏 Sleeping

There is excellent public camping (adult/child $6.60/3.30) with toilets and fireplaces at Florence Falls, Florence Creek, Buley Rockhole, Wangi Falls (better for vans than tents) and **Tjaynera Falls** (Sandy Creek; 4WD required). There are more-basic camp sites at **Surprise Creek Falls** (4WD required) and **Walker Creek** (Map p814).

Otherwise, most people who stay overnight do so in one of the motels or caravan parks in Batchelor or on the road into Litchfield.

Litchfield Safari Camp CAMPGROUND $
(Map p814; ☑ 08-8978 2185; www.litchfieldsafari camp.com.au; Litchfield Park Rd; unpowered/powered sites $25/35, dm $30, d safari tents $150; 🏊) Shady grassed sites make this a good alternative to Litchfield's bush camping sites, especially if you want power and to stay inside the park. The safari tents are great value as they comfortably sleep up to four folks. There's also a ramshackle camp kitchen, a kiosk and a pint-sized pool.

✕ Eating

Wangi Falls Centre CAFE $
(Map p814; www.wangifallscentre.com.au; mains from $10; ⊘10am-4pm Jun-Oct; 🛜) This busy cafe at Wangi Falls is arguably the best place in the park for a light meal. There are hot rolls and other bites to eat as well as a small

FLORENCE FALLS ALTERNATIVE ROUTE

An alternative to climbing the steep staircase up to the Florence Falls car park is Shady Creek Walk (950m), which begins by the waterhole and climbs gently through riverine monsoon forest then into the more open savannah woodland country. En route, watch for the shy short-eared rock wallaby.

souvenir shop. Try the smoothies made from local mangoes or the iced coffee.

Litchfield Cafe CAFE $$
(Map p814; Litchfield Park Rd; mains $14-36; ⊘noon-3pm & 6-8pm Apr-Sep, noon-3pm Oct-Mar) Filo parcels (try the chicken, mango and macadamia) make for a super lunch at this excellent licensed cafe, or you could go for a meal of grilled local barramundi or roo fillet, topped off with a good coffee and some wicked mango cheesecake.

ⓘ Getting There & Away

The two routes to Litchfield (115km south of Darwin) from the Stuart Hwy join up and loop through the park. The southern access road via Batchelor is all sealed, while the northern access route, off the Cox Peninsula Rd, is partly unsealed, corrugated and often closed in the Wet. Many travellers visit on a day tour from Darwin.

Daly River

POP 171

The Daly River is considered some of the best barramundi-fishing country in the NT and the hub is this small community. There's a shop and fuel here and visitors are welcome without a permit, but note that this is a dry community (no alcohol). Other than fishing, there's a fine art centre (p819) and a fine arts festival (p820). And don't be fooled by the river's enticing waters on a hot afternoon – crocs live here.

◉ Sights

Merrepen Arts GALLERY
(Map p814; ☑ 08-8978 2533; www.merrepenarts. com.au; ⊘8am-5pm Mon-Fri) FREE Around 20 artists work in a variety of traditional and contemporary media at this centre. Displays

WORTH A TRIP

MT BUNDY STATION

If you're into horse riding, fishing and country-style hospitality, **Mt Bundy Station** (Map p814; ☑ 08-8976 7009; www.mtbundy.com.au; Haynes Rd; unpowered/powered sites $22/30, s/d $70/100, cottage d from $140; ❄ ☀) is the perfect detour, 3km off the highway after Adelaide River. The original station buildings have become spotless guest accommodation, plus there are simple safari tents. There are 4WD tours and plenty of animals on the property – pony rides are available for kids.

may include etchings, screen prints, acrylic paintings, carvings, weaving and textiles.

Daly River Crossing　　　LANDMARK
(Map p814) Popular barramundi-fishing haunt and the crocs know it – ask about local conditions and advice before casting.

✯✰ Festivals & Events

Merrepen Arts Festival　　　CULTURAL
(www.merrepenfestival.com.au; adult/child $20/10) The excellent, three-day Merrepen Arts Festival celebrates arts and music from local communities, including Nauiyu, Wadeye and Peppimenarti, with displays, art auctions, workshops and dancing. The festival is held in Nauiyu, about 5km northwest of Daly River. It's usually held in May but it has moved around a little in recent years.

🛏 Sleeping & Eating

You can find basic supplies and takeaway food at the **petrol station** (Map p814) and general store.

Perry's　　　CAMPGROUND $
(Map p814; ☑ 08-8978 2452; www.dalyriver.com; Mayo Park; unpowered/powered sites $28/38, fisherman's hut $110; ☀) A very peaceful place with 2km of river frontage and gardens where orphaned wallabies bound around. Dick Perry, a well-known fishing expert, operates guided trips, and boat hire is available. The fisherman's hut has no air-con and is pretty basic with queen bed and bunks.

Daly River Mango Farm　　　CAMPGROUND $
(Map p814; ☑ 08-8978 2464; www.mangofarm. com.au; unpowered/powered sites $32/37, d $130-210; ❄ ☀) The camping ground here, on the

Daly River 9km from the crossing, is shaded by a magnificent grove of near-century-old mango trees. Other accommodation includes simple budget and self-contained cabins. Guided fishing trips and boat hire available.

❶ Getting There & Away

Daly River is 117km southwest of Hayes Creek, reached by a narrow sealed road off the Dorat Rd (Old Stuart Hwy; Rte 23), and 221km from Darwin.

Pine Creek

POP 380

A short detour off the Stuart Highway, Pine Creek is a small settlement that was once the scene of a frantic gold rush. The recent closing of the nearby iron-ore mine has dealt another blow to this boom-bust place, which somehow always seems to survive. It's a quietly pretty little town with a nice park in the centre and it's a good place to break up the journey, thanks to its good places to sleep and eat, and its proximity to the Kakadu Hwy turn-off.

◎ Sights

**Umbrawarra Gorge
Nature Park**　　　NATURE RESERVE
(Map p814; ☑ 08-8976 0282; www.nt.gov.au/leisure/parks-reserves) About 3km south of Pine Creek on the Stuart Highway is the turn-off to pretty Umbrawarra Gorge, with a safe swimming hole, a little beach and a basic camping ground (adult/child $3.30/1.65). It's 22km southwest on a rugged dirt road (just OK for 2WDs in the Dry; often impassable for everyone in the Wet). The walk along the water's edge is easy but will have you clambering over boulders every now and then. Bring plenty of water and mosquito repellent.

🛏 Sleeping & Eating

**Lazy Lizard Caravan
Park & Tavern**　　　CAMPGROUND $
(Map p814; ☑ 08-8976 1019; www.lazylizardpine creek.com.au; 299 Millar Tce; unpowered/powered sites $16/30, d cabins $120; ☀) The small, well-grassed camping area at the Lazy Lizard seems like an afterthought to the pulsing pub next door, but the sites are fine. The open-sided bar supported by carved ironwood pillars is a busy local watering hole with a pool table and old saddles slung across the rafters.

Pine Creek

Railway Resort BOUTIQUE HOTEL **$$**
(Map p814; ☑ 08-8976 1001; www.pinecreekrailway
resort.com.au; s/d $90/130, cabins $150-170;
❄ 🛜 🌊) This charming hotel uses raw iron,
steel and wood in its modern rooms, which
are easily the best for quite a distance in
any direction. The dining area has been de-
signed with romantic rail journeys of yore
in mind; it's a scene-stealer with pressed-tin
ceilings and elaborate chandeliers.

The menu (mains $21 to $30) is, however,
modern, with steaks, pasta, ribs and risotto
on offer.

Mayse's Cafe CAFE **$**
(Map p814; ☑ 08-8976 1241; Moule St; breakfast
$8-19, mains $9-13; ☉ 8am-3pm) Offering Pine
Creek's best lunches, Mayse's does sand-
wiches, homemade pies, fish burgers, steak
sandwiches and a mean lamb souvlaki in a
cavernous dining area that feels vaguely like
an American diner.

❶ Getting There & Away

The Kakadu Hwy (Rte 21) branches off the Stuart
Hwy here, connecting Pine Creek to Cooinda and
Jabiru. There's a **petrol station** (Map p814) in
the centre of town.

Greyhound buses (www.greyhound.com.
au) connect Pine Creek with Darwin (from $62,
three hours) and Katherine ($75, four hours)
twice daily.

KAKADU NATIONAL PARK

Kakadu (☑ 08-8938 1120; https://parksaus
tralia.gov.au/kakadu/; adult/child/family Apr-Oct
$40/20/100, Nov-Mar $25/12.50/65) is more
than a national park. It's also a vibrant, liv-
ing acknowledgement of the elemental link
between the Aboriginal custodians and the
country they have nurtured, endured and
respected for thousands of generations.
Encompassing almost 20,000 sq km (about
200km north–south and 100km east–west),
it holds within its boundaries a spectacu-
lar ecosystem, periodically scorched and
flooded, and mind-blowing ancient rock art.

In just a few days you can cruise on bil-
labongs bursting with wildlife, examine
25,000-year-old rock paintings with the help
of an Indigenous guide, swim in pools at the
foot of tumbling waterfalls and hike through
ancient sandstone escarpment country.

If Kakadu has a downside it's that it's very
popular – in the Dry at least. Resorts, camp-
ing grounds and rock-art sites can be very
crowded. But this is a vast park and with a
little adventurous spirit you can easily leave
the crowds behind.

Geography

The circuitous Arnhem Land escarpment,
a dramatic 30m- to 200m-high sandstone
cliff line, forms the natural boundary be-
tween Kakadu and Arnhem Land and winds
500km through eastern and southeastern
Kakadu.

Creeks cut across the rocky plateau and,
in the wet season, tumble off it as thunder-
ing waterfalls. They then flow across the
lowlands to swamp Kakadu's vast northern
flood plains. From west to east, the rivers
are the Wildman, West Alligator, South Al-
ligator and East Alligator (the latter form-
ing the eastern boundary of the park). The
coastal zone has long stretches of mangrove
swamp, important for halting erosion and
as a breeding ground for bird and marine
life. The southern part of the park is dry
lowlands with open grassland and eucalyp-
tuses. Pockets of monsoon rainforest crop
up throughout the park.

More than 80% of Kakadu is savannah
woodland. It has more than 1000 plant spe-
cies, many still used by Aboriginal people for
food and medicinal purposes.

---

❶ KAKADU PARK ADMISSION

Admission to the park is via a seven-day
Park Pass (adult/child/family Apr-Oct
$40/20/100, Nov-Mar $25/12.50/65).
Passes can be bought online (parks
australia.gov.au/kakadu/plan-your-trip/
passes-and-permits.html) or at vari-
ous places around the park, including
Bowali Visitor Information Centre
(p824) where you can pick up a pass,
along with the excellent *Visitor Guide*
booklet. Carry your pass with you at all
times as rangers conduct spot checks –
penalties apply for nonpayment.

Other places to buy the pass include:

➡ **Tourism Top End** (p811)

➡ **Cooinda Lodge & Campground**
(p827)

➡ **Katherine Visitor Information
Centre** (p835)

Kakadu National Park

N 0 ___ 40 km
0 ___ 20 miles

Crocodiles can inhabit all waterways in tropical areas. Swimming is not recommended.

Wildlife

Kakadu has more than 60 mammal species, more than 280 bird species, 120 recorded species of reptile, 25 species of frog, 55 freshwater fish species and at least 10,000 kinds of insect. Most visitors see only a fraction of these creatures (except the insects), since many of them are shy, nocturnal or scarce.

Rock Art

Kakadu is one of Australia's richest, most accessible repositories of rock art. There are more than 5000 sites, which date from

20,000 years to 10 years ago. The vast majority of these sites are off limits or inaccessible, but two of the finest collections are the easily visited galleries at Ubirr and Nourlangie.

The rock paintings have been classified into three roughly defined periods: Pre-estuarine, which is from the earliest paintings up to around 6000 years ago; Estuarine, which covers the period from 6000 to around 2000 years ago, when rising sea levels brought the coast to its present level; and Freshwater, from 2000 years ago until the present day.

For local Aboriginal people, these rock-art sites are a major source of traditional knowledge and represent their archives. Aboriginal people rarely paint on rocks anymore, as they no longer live in rock shelters and there are fewer people with the requisite knowledge. Some older paintings are believed by many Aboriginal people to have been painted by mimi spirits, connecting people with Creation legends and the development of lore.

As the paintings are all rendered with natural, water-soluble ochres, they are very susceptible to water damage. Drip lines of clear silicon rubber have been laid on the rocks above the paintings to divert rain. As the most accessible sites receive up to 4000 visitors a week, boardwalks have been erected to keep the dust down and to keep people at a suitable distance from the paintings.

⌖ Tours

★ **Guluyambi Cultural Cruise** CULTURAL
(☑ 1800 525 238; www.kakaduculturaltours.com; adult/child $76/49; ☺ 9am, 11am, 1pm & 3pm May-Nov) 🏊 Launch into an Aboriginal-led river cruise from the upstream boat ramp on the East Alligator River near Cahill's Crossing. Highly recommended by Darwin locals and a wonderful way to see crocodiles, see a little of Arnhem Land from the riverbank and listen to Indigenous stories as you go.

★ **Yellow Water Cruises** CRUISE
(☑ 1800 500 401; www.kakadutourism.com; per person $72-99) Cruise the South Alligator River and Yellow Water Billabong spotting wildlife. Purchase tickets from Cooinda Lodge, Cooinda; a shuttle bus will take you from here to the tour's departure point. Two-hour cruises depart at 6.45am, 9am and 4.30pm; 1½-hour cruises leave at 11.30am, 1.15pm and 2.45pm.

WATCHING WILDLIFE IN KAKADU

Species to watch out for include:

Saltwater crocodiles Cahill's Crossing over the East Alligator River – you can't miss them.

Dingoes At once elusive and possible everywhere; you may seem them at the flood plains stretching out from Ubirr, but they're also seen around Jabiru and along the Kakadu Hwy.

Black wallaroo This shy species is unique to Kakadu and Arnhem Land – look for them at Nourlangie Rock, where individuals rest under rocky overhangs.

Short-eared rock wallabies Can be spotted in the early morning around Ubirr.

Northern quoll Possible at night out the back of the Border Store and the surrounding area.

Northern brown bandicoot Find this and you've hit the jackpot; watch for it if you're driving at night.

Buffalo and wild horses Non-native species you might spot from the Yellow Water cruise.

★ **Kakadu Air** SCENIC FLIGHTS
(☑ 08-8941 9611, 1800 089 113; www.kakaduair. com.au; 30min flight adult/child $150/120, 60min flight $250/200, 45/60min helicopter flight adult $485/650) Offers both fixed-wing and helicopter scenic flights and both are a wonderful way to get a sense of the sheer scale and beauty of Kakadu and Arnhem Land. Note that flights are only available over Jim Jim Falls in the wet season – traditional owners request that the 'skies are rested' in the Dry.

★ **Arnhemlander Cultural & Heritage Tour** CULTURAL
(☑ 08-8979 2548; www.kakaduculturaltours.com. au; adult/child $269/215) 🏊 Aboriginal-owned and -operated tour into northern Kakadu and Arnhem Land. See ancient rock art, learn bush skills and meet local artists at Injalak Arts Centre (p830) in Oenpelli.

Ayal Aboriginal Tours CULTURAL
(☑ 0429 470 384; www.ayalkakadu.com.au; adult/child $220/99) 🏊 Full-day Indigenous-run tours around Kakadu, with former ranger

and local, Victor Cooper, shining a light on art, culture and wildlife.

Kakadu Animal Tracks   CULTURAL
(☑ 0409 350 842; www.animaltracks.com.au; adult/child $220/110; ☺ 1pm) 🏊 Based at Cooinda, this outfit runs seven-hour tours with an Indigenous guide combining a wildlife safari and Aboriginal cultural tour. You'll see thousands of birds, get to hunt, gather, prepare and consume bush tucker and crunch on some green ants.

ℹ️ Information

Bowali Visitor Information Centre (☑ 08-8938 1121; https://parksaustralia.gov.au/kakadu/plan-your-trip/visitor-centres.html; Kakadu Hwy, Jabiru; ☺ 8am-5pm) This excellent information centre has walk-through displays that sweep you across the land, explaining Kakadu's ecology from Aboriginal and non-Aboriginal perspectives. The helpful, staffed info window has 'Park Notes' flyers on all walks, with superb information about plants, animals and salient features you might encounter on each walk plus explanations of their uses and significance.

ℹ️ Getting There & Away

The Arnhem Hwy and Kakadu Hwy traverse the park; both are sealed and accessible year-round. The 4WD-only Old Jim Jim Rd is an alternative access from the Arnhem Hwy, joining the Kakadu Hwy 7km south of Cooinda. Fuel is available at Kakadu Resort, Cooinda and Jabiru.

Many people choose to access Kakadu on a tour, which shuffles them around the major sights with a minimum of hassle, but it's just as easy with your own wheels if you know what kinds of road conditions your trusty steed can handle (Jim Jim and Twin Falls, for example, are 4WD-access only).

Greyhound Australia (p811) runs a return coach service from Darwin to Jabiru ($75, 3½ hours).

Ubirr & Around

Magnificent Ubirr is one of the jewels in Kakadu's rather well-studded crown. Even if you know what to expect, coming here feels like wandering into a lost and beautiful world that is at once playful art gallery of the ancients and soulful history book of Kakadu's extraordinary human and natural history. There are real treasures here – the NT's best sunset, a rare and accessible depiction of the Rainbow Serpent, the intriguing and improbable representation of the thy-lacine (Tasmanian tiger) and mesmerising Ubirr rock art. It's a spiritual place, and very, very beautiful.

◉ Sights

⭐**Ubirr**   ROCK ART
(☺ 8.30am-sunset Apr-Nov, from 2pm Dec-Mar) Ubirr is 39km north of the Arnhem Hwy via a sealed road. It'll take a lot more than the busloads of visitors to disturb Ubirr's inherent majesty and grace. Layers of rock-art paintings, in various styles and from various centuries, command a mesmerising stillness.

Part of the main gallery reads like a menu, with images of kangaroos, tortoises and fish painted in X-ray, which became the dominant style about 8000 years ago. Predating these are the paintings of mimi spirits: cheeky, dynamic figures who, it's believed, were the first of the Creation Ancestors to paint on rock. (Given the lack of cherry-pickers in 6000 BC, you have to wonder who else but a spirit could have painted at that height and angle.) Look out for the yam-head figures, where the head is depicted as a yam on the body of a human or animal; these date back around 15,000 years.

The magnificent **Nardab Lookout** is a 250m scramble accessed from the main gallery. Surveying the exotic flood plain, watching the sun set in the west and the moon rise in the east like they're on an invisible set of scales gradually exchanging weight is humbling to say the least.

⭐**Cahill's Crossing**   RIVER
It may be small, but there can be few more dramatic frontiers in Australia. This shallow causeway, which is impassable when the tide's in, crosses the East Alligator River from Kakadu National Park on the west bank to Arnhem Land to the east. And watching you as you cross is the river's healthy and rather prolific population of saltwater crocs. Ask at Border Store (p825) for tide timings.

🏃 Activities

Manngarre Monsoon Forest Walk   WALKING
Mainly sticking to a boardwalk, this walk (1.5km return, 30 minutes, easy) starts by the boat ramp near the Border Store and winds through heavily shaded vegetation, palms and vines.

Bardedjilidji Sandstone Walk   WALKING
Starting from the upstream picnic-area car park, this walk (2.5km, 90 minutes, easy) takes in wetland areas of the East Alliga-

tor River and some interesting eroded sandstone outliers of the Arnhem Land escarpment. Informative track notes along the way point out features on this walk; watch for both rock wallabies and the chestnut-quilled rock pigeon (much prized among birders). This is a sacred place – no climbing on the rocks.

🛏 Sleeping & Eating

Merl Camping Ground CAMPGROUND $
(adult/child/family $15/7.50/38) The turn-off to this camping ground is about 1km before the Border Store. It is divided into a quiet zone and a generator use zone, each with a block of showers and toilets. It can get mighty busy at peak times and, be warned, the mosquitoes are diabolical. The site is closed in the Wet.

⭐ Hawk Dreaming
Wilderness Lodge LODGE $$$
(☑ 1800 525 238; www.kakaduculturaltours.com. au/hawk-dreaming-wilderness-lodge; s/d half-board $415/578) In a restricted area of the park (ie only guests and local Indigenous residents are allowed in), this deliciously remote lodge sits in the shadow of the stunning Hawk Dreaming sandstone escarpment and is as close to sweeping flood plains and billabongs as it is far from the clamouring crowds of Kakadu.

The safari tents are simple but nicely spread through shady grounds inhabited by wallabies, whistling kites and blue-winged kookaburras.

There's a small hot tub and rates include dinner and breakfast, transfers from the Border Store (p825) in Ubirr, sundowners and excursions to see local rock art that will be yours and yours alone to enjoy.

⭐ Border Store CAFE $$
(☑ 08-8979 2474; www.facebook.com/ubirrborder store/; mains $28; ⊙ 8.30am-8pm Jun-Oct) Run by Michael and Amm, charming little Border Store is full of surprises, including real coffee, sweet cakes and delicious Thai-cooked Thai food – a real treat. You can book a Guluyambi Cultural Cruise (p823) on the East Alligator River or a tour to Arnhem Land or browse the small selection of books and artwork.

❶ Getting There & Away

Ubirr is 39km north of the Arnhem Hwy via a sealed road.

Jabiru
POP 1200

It may seem surprising to find a town of Jabiru's size and structure in the midst of a wilderness national park, but it exists solely because of the nearby Ranger uranium mine. It's Kakadu's major service centre, with a bank, newsagent, medical centre, supermarket, bakery and service station. You can even play a round of golf here. It also has some good accommodation and simple restaurants, making it an agreeable if relatively unexciting base.

✯ Festivals & Events

Mahbilil Festival CULTURAL
(www.mahbililfestival.com; ⊙ Sep) A one-day celebration of Indigenous culture in Jabiru held in early September. There are exhibitions showcasing works by local artists as well as craft demonstrations, such as weaving and painting. Also on offer are competitions in spear throwing, didgeridoo blowing and magpie goose cooking. In the evening the focus is on Indigenous music and dance performances.

🛏 Sleeping

⭐ Anbinik Kakadu Resort CABIN $$
(☑ 08-8979 3144; www.kakadu.net.au; 27 Lakeside Dr; ensuite powered sites $42, bungalows/d/cabins $135/150/250; ❄ ≋) This Aboriginal-owned park is one of Kakadu's best, with a range of tropical-design bungalows set in lush gardens. The doubles share a communal kitchen, bathroom and lounge and also come equipped with their own TV and fridge. The 'bush bungalows' are stylish, elevated safari designs (no air-con) with private, open-air bathroom out the back and a nice verandah out front.

**Aurora Kakadu Lodge
& Caravan Park** RESORT $$
(☑ 08-8979 2422, 1800 811 154; www.aurorare sorts.com.au; Jabiru Dr; powered/unpowered sites $42/30, cabins from $275; ❄ 🛜 ≋) One of the best places to camp in town with lots of grass, trees and natural barriers between camping areas, creating a sense of privacy. This sprawling, impeccable resort/caravan park also boasts a lagoon-style swimming pool. The self-contained cabins sleep up to five people. The restaurant is a lovely place for outdoor meals overlooking the pool.

**Mercure Kakadu
(Crocodile Hotel)** HOTEL $$$
(☑ 08-8979 9000; www.accorhotels.com; 1 Flinders St; d from $275; 🕸 🌐 🏊) Known locally as 'the Croc', this hotel is designed in the shape of a crocodile, which, of course, is only obvious when viewed from the air. The rooms are clean and comfortable if a little pedestrian for the price (check their website for great deals). Try for one on the ground floor opening out to the central pool.

✗ Eating

Kakadu Bakery BAKERY $
(Gregory Pl; meals $4-19; ⏰ 6am-4pm Mon-Fri, 6.30am-3pm Sat, 8am-3pm Sun) Grab a made-to-order sandwich on home-baked bread to walk out the door. There are also mean burgers, slices, breakfast fry-ups, pizzas, cakes and basic salads. There are a few outdoor tables but it's mostly takeaway and we can think of plenty of places where we'd rather enjoy our burger out in the park.

Escarpment Restaurant INTERNATIONAL $$
(mains $22-38; ⏰ 7am-9pm) This restaurant inside the Mercure Kakadu gets very mixed reviews – some love it, others hate it and we lie somewhere in between. While probably Jabiru's best restaurant, it's pretty uninspiring but you won't leave hungry. Dishes on the regularly changing menu cover the usual meat and seafood staples (steaks, burgers, barra) with the occasional nod to local bush tucker tastes.

Jabiru Sports & Social Club PUB FOOD $$
(☑ 08-8979 2326; www.jabirusportsandsocialclub.com.au; Lakeside Dr; mains $16-35; ⏰ 6-8.30pm Mon-Sat, noon-2pm & 6-8.30pm Sun) Along with the golf club, this low-slung hangar is the place to meet locals over a beer or glass of wine. The bistro meals, such as steak, chicken parma or fish and chips, are honest and there's an outdoor deck overlooking the lake, a kids playground and sport on TV.

ℹ Information

Northern Land Council (☑ 1800 645 299, 08-8938 3000; www.nlc.org.au; 3 Government Bldg, Flinders St, Jabiru; ⏰ 8am-4.30pm Mon-Fri) Issues permits for Arnhem Land, including Gunbalanya (Oenpelli).

ℹ Getting There & Away

Jabiru lies 257km from Darwin along the Stuart and then Arnhem Hwys. There's no public transport out here, but nor is there any shortage of tours that can get you here.

Nourlangie

The sight of this looming outlier of the Arnhem Land escarpment makes it easy to understand its ancient importance to Aboriginal people. Its long red-sandstone bulk, striped in places with orange, white and black, slopes up from surrounding woodland to fall away at one end in stepped cliffs. Below is Kakadu's best-known collection of rock art.

◉ Sights

The name Nourlangie is a corruption of *nawulandja*, an Aboriginal word that refers to an area bigger than the rock itself. The 2km looped walking track (open 8am to sunset) takes you first to the **Anbangbang Shelter**, used for 20,000 years as a refuge and canvas. Next is the **Anbangbang Gallery**, featuring vivid Dreaming characters repainted in the 1960s. Look for the virile **Nabulwinjbulwinj**, a dangerous spirit who likes to eat females after banging them on the head with a yam. From here it's a short walk to **Gunwarddehwarde Lookout**, with views of the Arnhem Land escarpment.

🏃 Activities

Nawurlandja Lookout WALKING
This is a short walk (600m return, 30 minutes, medium) up a gradual slope, but it gives excellent views of the Nourlangie rock area and is a good place to catch the sunset.

Barrk Walk WALKING
This long day walk (12km loop, five to six hours, difficult) will take you away from the crowds on a circuit of the Nourlangie area. Barrk is a male black wallaroo and you might see this elusive marsupial if you set out early. Pick up a brochure from the Bowali Visitor Information Centre.

Nanguluwur Gallery WALKING
This outstanding rock-art gallery sees far fewer visitors than Nourlangie simply because it's further to walk (3.5km return, 1½ hours, easy) and has a gravel access road. Here the paintings cover most of the styles found in the park, including very early dynamic style work, X-ray work and a good example of 'contact art', a painting of a two-masted sailing ship towing a dinghy.

Anbangbang Billabong Walk   WALKING

This picturesque, lily-filled billabong lies close to Nourlangie and the picnic tables dotted around its edge make it a popular lunch spot. The track (2.5km loop, 45 minutes, easy) circles the billabong and passes through paperbark swamp. It's a lovely adjunct to the rock art.

🛏 Sleeping

Muirella Park   CAMPGROUND $

(Djarradjin; adult/child/family $15/7.50/38) Basic camping ground at Djarradjin Billabong, with BBQs, excellent amenities and the 5km-return Bubba Wetland Walk. Look for the turn-off from the Kakadu Hwy, about 7km south from the turn-off to Nourlangie.

ⓘ Getting There & Away

Nourlangie is well signposted at the end of a 12km sealed road that turns east off Kakadu Hwy.

Jim Jim Falls & Twin Falls

Remote and spectacular, these two falls epitomise the rugged Top End. **Jim Jim Falls**, a sheer 215m drop, is awesome after rain (when it can only be seen from the air), but its waters shrink to a trickle by about June. **Twin Falls** flows year-round (no swimming), but half the fun is getting here, involving a little boat trip (adult/child $15/free, 7.30am-5pm, last boat 4pm) and an over-the-water boardwalk.

🛏 Sleeping

Garrnamarr Camping Ground   CAMPGROUND $

(www.parksaustralia.gov.au/kakadu/plan-your-trip/camping-and-caravans.html; adult/child/family $15/7.50/38) Basic camping ground in a wonderful place and there's plenty of shade.

ⓘ Getting There & Away

These two iconic waterfalls are reached via a 4WD track that turns south off the Kakadu Hwy between the Nourlangie and Cooinda turn-offs. Jim Jim Falls is about 56km from the turn-off (the last 1km on foot) and it's a further five corrugated kilometres to Twin Falls. The track is open in the Dry only and can still be closed into late May; it's off limits to most rental vehicles (check the fine print). A couple of tour companies make trips here in the Dry.

Cooinda & Yellow Water

Cooinda is one of the main tourism hubs in Kakadu. A slick resort has grown up around the wetlands, which are known as Yellow Water, or to give it's rather challenging Indigenous name, *Ngurrungurrundjba*. The cruises, perferably around sunrise or sunset, are undoubted highlights of any visit to Kakadu.

◉ Sights

Warradjan Aboriginal Cultural Centre   MUSEUM

(www.kakadutourism.com/tours-activities/warradjan-cultural-centre/; Yellow Water Area; ⊙9am-5pm) FREE About 1km from the Cooinda resort (an easy 15 minutes' walk), the Warradjan Aboriginal Cultural Centre depicts Creation stories and has an excellent permanent exhibition that includes clap sticks, sugarbag holders and rock-art samples. You'll be introduced to the moiety system (the law of interpersonal relationships), languages and skin names, and there's a minitheatre with a huge selection of films from which to choose. A mesmeric soundtrack of chants and didgeridoos plays in the background.

🛏 Sleeping

Mardugal Park Campground   CAMPGROUND $

(www.parksaustralia.gov.au/kakadu/plan-your-trip/camping-and-caravans.html; camping per adult/child/family $15/7.50/38) Just south of the Kakadu Hwy, 2km south of the Cooinda turn-off, is the National Parks Mardugal Park campground – an excellent spot with shower and toilets.

Cooinda Lodge & Campground   RESORT $$

(☑1800 500 401; www.kakadutourism.com/accommodation/cooinda-lodge/; Cooinda; powered/unpowered sites $50/38, budget/lodge r from $159/189; ❄🅿🛜🛏) This sprawling place has a good variety of accommodation and is Kakadu's most popular resort – even with 380 camp sites, facilities can get very stretched. The budget air-con units share camping ground facilities and are compact and comfy enough. The lodge rooms are spacious and comfortable, sleeping up to four people.

There's a grocery shop, tour desk, fuel pump and the excellent open-air **Barra Bar & Bistro** (☑1800 500 401; www.kakadutourism.com/accommodation/cooinda-lodge/; Cooinda; mains $25-35; ⊙6.30am-9pm) here too.

Ask about the 'Flash Camp @ Kakadu', a semimobile camp of tents set up out in the bush with all the comforts of a tented camp.

❶ Getting There & Away

The turn-off to the Cooinda accommodation complex and Yellow Water wetlands is 47km down the Kakadu Hwy from the Arnhem Hwy intersection. It's then 4.5km to the Warradjan Aboriginal Cultural Centre, a further 1km to the Yellow Water turn-off and another 1km to Cooinda.

Southwestern Kakadu

Kakadu's southwestern reaches shelter two of Kakadu's most underrated attractions – the gorgeous waterhole at Maguk and the dramatic Gunlom. Both require a 4WD or high-clearance 2WD to get there and may be impassable in the Wet – all of which is precisely why you won't see any tour buses down here.

◉ Sights

★ **Maguk**   WATERFALL

(Barramundi Gorge) This southern section of Kakadu National Park sees far fewer tour buses. Though it's unlikely you'll have dreamy Maguk to yourself, you might time it right to have the glorious natural pool and falls between just a few of you. The walk in from the car park passes through monsoon forest rich in endemic anbinik trees and then opens out into a nicely bouldered river section.

The waterhole is 2km return walk from the car park (count on about an hour plus swimming time). Where the trail emerges from the forest into a broader valley and where the marked trail crosses the river to the right, stay on the left bank (or return here later) to climb up high above the falls for great views and a series of small rock pools to plunge into.

Wildlife here includes freshwater crocs (swimming is generally safe but check the signs) as well as birds such as rainbow pittas and emerald doves.

The track in here is a rough, 10km corrugated track lined with termite mounds.

★ **Gunlom**   WATERFALL

(Waterfall Creek) Gunlom is an utterly superb escarpment waterfall and plunge pool 40-odd kilometres south of Maguk and 37km along an unsealed, though easily doable,

gravel road. The reward is a gloriously large waterhole and drama-filled scenery, and that's just 200m through the paperbark forest from the car park. There's also a lovely picnic area here. If you're keen to explore a bit further, take the steep **Lookout Walk** (one hour, 1km), which affords incredible views.

❶ Getting There & Away

Both Maguk and Gunlom are clearly signposted off the Kakadu Hwy along unsealed tracks – Gunlom is easier to access in a 2WD. There's no public transport to either site and few tour operators come this way.

ARNHEM LAND

Arnhem Land is a vast, overwhelming and mysterious corner of the NT. About the size of the state of Victoria and with a population of only around 17,000, mostly Yolngu people, this Aboriginal reserve is one of Australia's last great untouched wilderness areas. Most people live on outstations, combining traditional practices with modern Western ones, so they might go out for a hunt and be back in time to watch the 6pm news. Travelling out here requires careful planning, but it's a small price to pay for visiting one of Australia's most ruggedly beautiful and culturally intriguing corners.

⛟ Tours

★ **Kakadu Cultural Tours**   CULTURAL

(☑ 1800 525 238; www.kakaduculturaltours.com.au; adult/child $269/215; ⊘ May-Nov) This eight-hour Arnhemlander 4WD Cultural Tour is outstanding. It takes you to ancient rock-art sites (hopefully it will include the Mountford site, but access depends on the age and mobility of the group), Inkiyu Billabong and Injalak art centre at Gunbalanya (Oenpelli). The tour leaves from Border Store (p825) at Ubirr in Kakadu National Park.

Outback Spirit   TOURS

(☑ 1800 688 222; www.outbackspirittours.com.au) This experienced operator has an epic 12-day traverse of Arnhem Land's north, from the Cobourg Peninsula to Yirrkala. Prices start at $10,995 per person.

Venture North Australia   TOURS

(☑ 08-8927 5500; https://venturenorth.com.au; 4-/5-day tours $2890/3290; ⊘ May-Oct) Four-wheel drive tours to remote areas and featuring expert guidance on rock art. The four-day Arnhem Land and Cobourg Peninsula Tour (per person $2890) is the pick of numerous Arnhem Land options. Also runs Cobourg Coastal Camp with safari-style tents overlooking the water near Smith Point on the Cobourg Peninsula for the use of tour guests.

Davidson's
Arnhemland Safaris　　　　　CULTURAL
(☑08-8979 0413; www.arnhemland-safaris.com) Experienced operator taking tours to Mt Borradaile, north of Oenpelli. Meals, guided tours, fishing and safari-camp ac-

commodation at its Safari Lodge (p829) are included in the daily price (from $750 per person); transfers from Darwin can be arranged.

🛏 Sleeping

★Davidson's Arnhemland
Safari Lodge　　　　　　LODGE $$$
(www.arnhemland-safaris.com; s/d cabins all-inclusive from $1025/1500; ▣) An oasis of good taste with high levels of comfort out in the wilds of western Arnhem Land, Davidson's has appealing cabins on stilts, good food and a lovely setting. It's generally worth paying a little extra for the deluxe cabins.

ARNHEM LAND PERMITS

Visits to Arnhem Land are strictly regulated through a permit system, designed to protect the environment, rock art and ceremonial grounds, as *balanda* (white people) are unaware of the locations of burial grounds and ceremonial lands.

Basically, you need a specific purpose for entering, usually to visit an arts centre, in order to be granted a permit. It's also worth remembering that some of the permits issued are transit permits (others are called recreational permits) that allow you to travel along certain roads but not either side of them – check when picking up your permit.

If you're travelling far enough to warrant an overnight stay, you'll need to organise accommodation (which is in short supply) in advance. It's easy to visit Gunbalanya (Oenpelli) and its arts centre on a day trip from Kakadu National Park, just over the border, either on a tour or independently. Elsewhere, it's best to travel with a tour, which will include the necessary permit(s) to enter Aboriginal lands.

If you're travelling independently, you'll need to arrange the following permits:

PLACE	ISSUED BY	COST	DURATION	PROCESSING TIME
Central Arnhem Highway	Northern Land Council (p811)	free	transit	10 days to issue
East Arnhem Land	Dhimurru Aboriginal Corporation (☑08-8939 2700; www.dhimurru.com.au; Arnhem Rd, Nhulunbuy)	$15/35/45	1 day/7 days/2 months	varies
Gunbalanya (Oenpili)	Northern Land Council (p811)	$16.50	1 day	issued on the spot
West Arnhem Land (incl Cobourg Peninsula & Garig Gunak Barlu National Park)	Northern Land Council (p811; transit permit); Parks & Wildlife Commission (☑08-8999 4555; parkmanagement.pwcnt@nt.gov.au; camping permit)	$88 (plus $232.10 per vehicle for camping permit)	5 days	10 days to issue

Excursions include billabong boat trips, hikes into the nearby escarpments and birdwatching.

Barramundi Lodge LODGE $$$
(☑ 08-8983 1544; www.barralodge.com.au; d from $550; ⭐) Out in the wilds of Arnhem Land, close to Maningrida, this lovely lodge is a haven for sport-fishers and birdwatchers from March to November. The safari-style tents are beautifully appointed in the finest African safari style with just canvas between you and the great outdoors but with high levels of comfort.

❶ Getting There & Away

Most visitors to Arnhem Land come as part of an organised tour.

Gunbalanya (Oenpelli)

POP 1200

Gunbalanya is a small Aboriginal community 17km into Arnhem Land across the East Alligator River from the Border Store in Kakadu. Home to one of the NT's best Indigenous art centres, Gunbalanya makes an excellent add-on to a visit to Kakadu.

The drive in itself is worth the trip, with brilliant green wetlands and spectacular escarpments lining the road. Road access is only possible between May and October: check the tides at Cahill's Crossing on the East Alligator River before setting out so you don't get stuck on the other side.

◉ Sights

★**Injalak Arts & Crafts Centre** GALLERY
(☑ 08-8979 0190; www.injalak.com; ◔ 8.30am-5pm Mon-Fri, 9am-2pm Sat) FREE At this centre, artists and craftspeople display traditional paintings on bark and paper, plus didgeridoos, pandanus weavings and baskets, and screen-printed fabrics; the shop is excellent and half of the sale price goes directly to the artists.

Take the time to wander around and watch the artists at work (morning only); the women usually make baskets out in the shade of the trees on the centre's west side, while the men paint on the verandah to the east. Some of the works come from remote outstations throughout Arnhem Land.

There are good views from the centre's grounds south towards the wetlands to the escarpment and Injalak Hill (Long Tom Dreaming).

Kakadu Cultural Tours (p828) and **Lord's Kakadu & Arnhemland Safaris** (☑ 0438 808 548; www.lords-safaris.com; adult/child $225/180) both offer excellent day tours that include a visit here.

☞ Tours

★**Rock Art Tours** TOURS
(☑ 08-8979 0190; www.injalak.com/rock-art-tours/; adult/child $110/33; ◔ 9am Mon-Sat Jun-Sep) Five kilometres south of the Injalak Arts & Crafts Centre (p830), Injalak Hill (Long Tom Dreaming) is one of Western Arnhem Land's best collections of rock art. To see it you'll need to join one of the three-hour tours run out of the arts centre.

✺ Festivals & Events

Stone Country Festival CULTURAL
This open day and cultural festival is held in August in Gunbalanya (Oenpelli). It has traditional music, dancing and arts and crafts demonstrations and is the only day you can visit Gunbalanya without a permit. Camping allowed; no alcohol.

❶ Getting There & Away

There is no public transport to Gunbalanya and most travellers visit as part of an organised tour. The road here from Cahill's Crossing is only partly sealed and is impassable in the Wet (usually from October or November to March).

Cobourg Peninsula

◉ Sights

★**Garig Gunak Barlu National Park** NATIONAL PARK
(https://nt.gov.au/leisure/parks-reserves; ◔ May-Oct) The entire wilderness of remote Cobourg Peninsula forms the Garig Gunak Barlu National Park which includes the surrounding sea. It's a stunning, isolated place and one of the loveliest spots on Australia's northern coast. You'll likely see dolphins and turtles and – what most people come for – a threadfin salmon thrashing on the end of your line.

Port Essington RUINS
(Victoria) On the shores of Port Essington are the stone ruins and headstones of Victoria settlement – Britain's 1838 attempt to establish a military outpost here to facilitate trade with Asia. It's an eerie place with

stone ruins and echoes a doomed dream to build a city in such remote country.

Activities

The Cobourg Peninsula is well-known among fisherfolk for its fabulous barramundi fishing in March, April, October and November, while wildlife-watching is excellent during the Dry season (note that the Peninsula is difficult to access at other times).

Wildlife Watching

The waters of Garig Gunak Barlu National Park are home to six different species of marine turtle: green, loggerhead, olive ridley, hawksbill, flatback and leatherback; some of these nest on remote beaches in the later months of the year. Watch out for the northern snake-necked turtle in the park's inland billabongs. Whales, dolphins, various shark species and saltwater crocodiles are all to be found in the waters off the coast – swimming here would be extremely dangerous.

Mammal species, though elusive, are always possible, especially around dawn, dusk and overnight. Species include dingoes, echidnas and northern brown bandicoots. The park is also home to more than 200 bird species.

Tours

Cobourg Fishing Safaris   FISHING
(☑ 08-8927 5500; www.cobourgfishingsafaris.com.au) These fishing safaris run by Venture North Australia (p828) are outstanding, with the fishing camps and food on offer a cut above others, not to mention excellent fishing guides.

Sleeping & Eating

There are two camping grounds in the park with showers, toilets, BBQs and limited bore water; generators are allowed in one area. Camping fees (per person per day $16.50) are covered by your vehicle permit. Other accommodation is available in pricey fishing resorts, while Cobourg Fishing Safaris has a tented safari camp for those on its tours at Smith Point.

You'll need to bring your own supplies, although **Garig Store** (☑ 08-8979 0455; Algarlarlgarl (Black Point); ⊘ 4-6pm Mon-Sat) sells basic provisions, fuel, ice and camping gas.

Wiligi Outstation   TENTED CAMP, CAMPING **$$$**
(☑ 08-8979 0069; www.wiligiarnhemland.com.au; camping per person $47, eco tents $275) On a remote outstation on the cusp of the Cobourg Peninsula's Garig Gunak Barlu National Park, Wiligi has some rather lovely eco tents, each with a private verandah looking out over Morris Bay, as well as some shady waterfront campsites. The eco tents in particular are a fine alternative to wild camping.

Getting There & Away

The quickest route here is by private charter flight, which can be arranged by accommodation providers. If you're driving, the track to Cobourg starts at Gunbalanya (Oenpelli) and is accessible by 4WD vehicles only from May to October. The 270km drive to Black Point from the East Alligator River takes about five hours.

Eastern Arnhem Land

The wildly beautiful coast and country of Eastern Arnhem Land (www.eastarnhemland.com.au) is really off the beaten track. About 4000 people live in the region's main settlement, Nhulunbuy, built to service the bauxite mine here. The 1963 plans to establish a manganese mine were hotly protested by the traditional owners, the Yolngu people; though mining proceeded, the case became an important step in establishing land rights. Some of the country's most respected art comes out of this region, too, including bark paintings, carved mimi figures, *yidaki* (didgeridoos), woven baskets and mats, and jewellery.

Sights

★ **Buku Larrnggay Mulka
Art Centre & Museum**   GALLERY
(☑ 08-8987 1701; www.yirrkala.com; Yirrkala; by donation; ⊘ 8am-4.30pm Mon-Fri, 9am-noon Sat) This museum, 20km southeast of Nhulunbuy in Yirrkala, is one of Arnhem Land's best. No permit is required to visit from Nhulunbuy or Gove airport.

Festivals & Events

★ **Garma Festival**   CULTURAL
(www.yyf.com.au; ⊘ Aug) A four-day festival in northeastern Arnhem Land. Garma is one of the most significant regional festivals, a celebration of Yolngu culture that includes performances, bushcraft lessons, a *yidaki* masterclass and an academic forum.

Serious planning is required to attend, so start early.

Sleeping & Eating

Walkabout Lodge
MOTEL **$$**

(☑08-8939 2000; www.walkaboutlodge.com.au; 12 Westal St, Nhulunbuy; s/d Aug & Sep $250/290, Oct-Jul $218/245) Air-conditioned, motel-style rooms in a leafy Nhulunbuy setting. They'd be overpriced elsewhere, but they're not bad value for here.

BanuBanu Wilderness Retreat
LODGE **$$$**

(☑08-8987 8085; www.banubanu.com; Bremer Island; d $720-1220) These eco tents on Bremer Island off the Gove Peninsula couldn't be closer to the beach – and it's the location (and the fishing) that is most memorable here. The tents are simple and the surrounding area a little bare and shadeless, but as you'll spend most of your day out fishing, this latter point may prove less significant.

Shopping

Nambara Arts & Crafts Aboriginal Gallery
ART

(Melville Bay Rd, Nhulunbuy; ☉10am-4pm Mon-Fri, 10am-2pm Sat) Sells art and crafts from northeast Arnhem Land and often has artists-in-residence.

Getting There & Away

Airnorth (☑1800 627 474; www.airnorth.com.au) and **Qantas** (p811) fly from Darwin to Gove Airport (for Nhulunbuy) daily.

Overland, it's a 10-hour 4WD trip and only possible in the Dry. The Central Arnhem Hwy to Gove leaves the Stuart Hwy (Rte 87) 52km south of Katherine.

KATHERINE

POP 10,766

Katherine is probably best known for the **Nitmiluk (Katherine Gorge) National Park** to the east; the town makes an obvious base, with plenty of accommodation. It also has a handful of interesting attractions to tempt you into staying an extra day or two.

Katherine is considered a big town in this part of the world, and you'll certainly feel like you've arrived somewhere if you've just made the long trip up the highway from Alice Springs; its namesake river is the first permanent running water on the road north of Alice Springs) or down from Darwin.

Sights

★ Top Didj Cultural Experience & Art Gallery
GALLERY

(☑08-8971 2751; www.topdidj.com; cnr Gorge & Jaensch Rds; cultural experience adult/child $70/45; ☉cultural experience 9.30am & 2.30pm Sun-Fri, 9.30am & 1.30pm Sat) Run by the owners of the now-onsite Katherine Art Gallery, Top Didj is a good place to see Aboriginal artists at work. The cultural experience is hands-on with fire sticks, spear throwing, painting and basket weaving, and is a somewhat more dynamic take on the Indigenous cultural experience.

Godinymayin Yijard Rivers Arts & Culture Centre
GALLERY

(☑08-8972 3751; www.gyracc.org.au; Stuart Hwy, Katherine East; ☉10am-5pm Tue-Fri, to 3pm Sat) This stunning arts and culture centre in Katherine is housed in a beautiful, contemporary building that is a real landmark. The centre is designed to be a meeting place for Indigenous and non-Indigenous people, and a chance to share cultures. Don't miss this place when you're in town.

Djilpin Arts
GALLERY

(☑08-8971 1770; www.djilpinarts.org.au; 27 Katherine Tce; ☉9am-4pm Mon-Fri) This Katherine gallery is Aboriginal owned and represents art from the Ghunmarn Culture Centre (p843) in the remote community of Beswick (Wugularr). Exhibits include paintings, weavings and termite-bored didgeridoos.

Katherine School of the Air
CULTURAL CENTRE

(☑08-8972 1833; www.ksa.nt.edu.au; Giles St; adult/child $12/free, VIP tour $20; ☉9am, 10am & 11am mid-Apr–Oct) At the School of the Air, 1.5km from the town centre, you can listen into a class and see how 170 kids from pre-school to Year 9 are educated in areas where there is no physical school – it is sometimes called the world's biggest classroom. The standard tour doesn't get much beyond the front room but is interesting nonetheless, while the 10am VIP tour takes you into the classrooms for a closer look at what goes on.

Tours

★ Nitmiluk Tours
TOURS

(☑1300 146 743, 08-8972 1253; www.nitmiluktours.com.au; 4/52 Katherine Terrace, Stuart Hwy) This excellent operator runs scenic flights, canoeing and boat cruises in Nitmiluk (Katherine Gorge) National Park and is a good place to begin as plan your time in the area.

Katherine

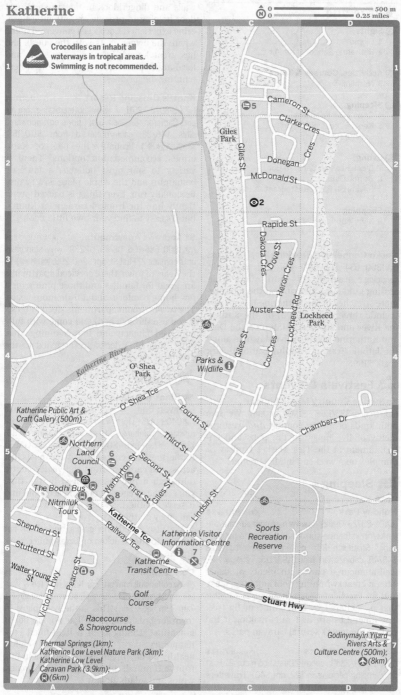

Crocodiles can inhabit all waterways in tropical areas. Swimming is not recommended.

0 — 500 m
0 — 0.25 miles

Cameron St
Clarke Cres
Cres
Giles Park
Giles St
Donegan
McDonald St
Rapide St
Dakota Cres
Dove St
Heron Cres
Lockheed Rd
Auster St
Cox Cres
Lockheed Park
Katherine River
O'Shea Park
Parks & Wildlife
Chambers Dr
O'Shea Tce
Fourth St
Katherine Public Art & Craft Gallery (500m)
Third St
Northern Land Council
6
Warburton St
Second St
4
First St
Giles St
The Bodhi Bus
Nitmiluk Tours
3
8
Katherine Tce
Railway Tce
Lindsay St
Shepherd St
Stutterd St
Walter Young St
Victoria Hwy
Pearce St
9
Katherine Visitor Information Centre
7
Katherine Transit Centre
Sports Recreation Reserve
Golf Course
Stuart Hwy
Racecourse & Showgrounds
Thermal Springs (1km);
Katherine Low Level Nature Park (3km);
Katherine Low Level Caravan Park (3.9km);
(6km)
Godinymayin Yijard Rivers Arts & Culture Centre (500m);
(8km)

Katherine

◉ Sights

✪ Activities, Courses & Tours

🛌 Sleeping

✗ Eating

⊙ Shopping

Gecko Canoeing & Trekking OUTDOORS
(☑1800 634 319, 0427 067 154; www.gecko canoeing.com.au) 🏄 This outfit offers exhilarating guided canoe trips on the more remote stretches of the Katherine River. Trips include three days ($1090) on the Katherine River and six days ($1895) on the Daly and Katherine Rivers. A five-day hike along the Jatbula Trail in Nitmiluk National Park costs $1895.

✷ Festivals & Events

Katherine Country Music Muster MUSIC
(adult/child $35/free; ☺May or Jun) 'We like both kinds of music: country *and* western.' Plenty of live music in the pubs and entertainment at the Tick Market Lindsay St Complex on a weekend in May or June.

🛌 Sleeping

**BIG4 Katherine
Holiday Park** CARAVAN PARK $
(☑08-8972 3962; www.big4.com.au/caravan-parks/nt/katherine-surrounds/katherine-holiday-park; Shadforth Rd; powered/unpowered sites $48/45, cabin/safari tent $198/115; ❋🀄🏊) A well-manicured park with plenty of shady sites, a great swimming pool adjoining a bar and an excellent bistro (mains $21 to $29) that is sheltered by a magnificent fig tree. The amenities are first rate, making it the pick of the town's several caravan parks.

Coco's Backpackers HOSTEL $
(☑08-8971 2889; coco@21firstst.com.au; 21 First St; camping per person $22, dm $40) Travellers love this place, with Indigenous art on the walls and didgeridoos in the tin shed next door helping to provide an authentic Katherine experience. Coco's is a converted home where the owner chats with the guests and has great knowledge about the town and local area. Aboriginal artists are often here painting didgeridoos.

Knott's Crossing Resort MOTEL $$
(☑08-8972 2511; www.knottscrossing.com.au; cnr Cameron & Giles Sts; powered/unpowered sites $46/28, cabin/motel d from $110/160; ❋@🀄🏊🐕) Probably the pick of Katherine's accommodation options. There is variety to suit most budgets, a fantastic restaurant and the whole place is very professionally run. Everything is packed pretty tightly into the tropical gardens at Knott's, but it's easy to find your own little nook.

St Andrews Apartments APARTMENT $$$
(☑1800 686 106, 08-8971 2288; www.standrews apts.com.au; 27 First St; apt $240-290; ❋🀄🏊) In the heart of town, these serviced apartments are great for families and those pining for a few home comforts and a little more space. The two-bedroom apartments sleep four (six if you use the sofa bed) and come with fully equipped kitchen and lounge/dining area. Nifty little BBQ decks are attached to the ground-floor units.

✗ Eating

★**Black Russian
Caravan Bar** INTERNATIONAL $
(☑0409 475 115; www.facebook.com/theblack russiancaravanbar/; Stuart Hwy; mains $7.80-12.50; ☺7am-1pm) Street food has arrived in Katherine! This cutesy little caravan sits just across the car park from the visitor centre (although it may have moved by the time you get there; check it out on Facebook) and it serves Katherine's best coffee, which you can enjoy on the lawn.

We also loved the cakes and thick-cut toasties (butter chicken or Texas pulled pork among others).

Coffee Club CAFE $$
(www.coffeeclub.com.au; cnr Katherine Tce & Warburton St; meals $13-19; ☺6.30am-3pm Mon-Fri, 7am-3pm Sat & Sun) This is the best place in town for breakfast, as well as a good bet at lunchtime. Dining is in a light-filled contemporary space. On offer is decent coffee, healthy all-day breakfast options including fruit and muesli, plus burgers, sandwiches, wraps and salads all day.

Savannah Bar & Restaurant   MODERN AUSTRALIAN $$

(📞 08-8972 2511; https://knottscrossing.com.au/facilities/#dining; Knott's Crossing Resort, cnr Giles & Cameron Sts; mains $25-35; ⏱ 6.30-9am & 6-9pm) Undoubtedly one of the best dining choices in Katherine. It's predominantly an outdoors garden restaurant, with a cool breeze wafting through the tropical vegetation. The menu includes steak, barramundi, croc croquettes and Venus Bay prawn dishes. There's even a suckling pig you can tuck into. Service is fast and friendly and the whole place is very well run.

★ Marksies Camp Tucker   AUSTRALIAN $$$

(📞 0427 112 806; www.marksiescamptucker.com.au; 363 Gorge Rd; adult/child $75/35; ⏱ 7pm Apr-Sep) Now here's something special. Head to this re-created stockman's camp 7km from town for a night of fabulous food and fun storytelling by Geoff Mark (Marksie), a warm and wily raconteur and one of Katherine's great characters.

The meal consists of a three-course set menu that might include crocodile, wild-caught barramundi, camel, buffalo and/or kangaroo, all leavened with bush spices and hilarious bush yarns. Bookings essential.

Marksies shares an entrance with Top Didj (p832).

☆ Entertainment

Katherine Outback Experience   LIVE PERFORMANCE

(📞 0428 301 580; www.katherineoutbackexperience.com.au; 115 Collins Rd, Uralla; adult/student/senior $50/25/45; ⏱ 4.30pm Mon, Thu & Fri, 5pm Wed, closed Nov-Mar) You get a little bit of everything for your money out here – the 90-minute show is about horse training and working station dogs, but don't be surprised if presenter Tom Curtain bursts into song at some stage during proceedings. Sometimes it falls a bit flat, but it's great when it works, which is often.

🛍 Shopping

★ Mimi Aboriginal Art & Craft   ARTS & CRAFTS

(📞 08-8971 0036; www.mimiarts.com; 6 Pearce St; ⏱ 8.30am-4.30pm Mon-Fri) Aboriginal-owned and not-for-profit, Mimi is arguably Katherine's best Indigenous art centre. It's a small but carefully chosen collection of works from the Katherine region, as well as the Tanami Desert and all the way up

to the Kimberleys. They also sell postcards and a small selection of books, music and didgeridoos.

ℹ Information

Katherine Wildlife Rescue Service (📞 0407 934 252; www.fauna.org.au) The place to call if you come across any injured wildlife.

Katherine Visitor Information Centre (📞 1800 653 142; www.visitkatherine.com.au; cnr Lindsay St & Stuart Hwy; ⏱ 8.30am-5pm daily in the Dry (mid-Apr-Sep), 8.30am-5pm Mon-Fri, 10am-2pm Sat & Sun in the Wet (Oct–mid-Apr)) Modern, air-con information centre stocking information on all areas of the Northern Territory. Pick up the handy *Katherine Region Visitor Guide*.

Northern Land Council (📞 08-8971 9899; www.nlc.org.au; 5/29 Katherine Tce) Permits for the Central Arnhem Hwy towards Gove.

Parks & Wildlife (📞 08-8973 8888; https://nt.gov.au/leisure/parks-reserves; 32 Giles St; ⏱ 8am-4.20pm) National park information and notes.

Katherine Hospital (📞 08-8973 9211; www.health.nt.gov.au; Giles St) About 3km north of town, with an emergency department.

ℹ Getting There & Away

Katherine is a major road junction: from here the Stuart Hwy tracks north and south and the Victoria Hwy heads west to Kununurra in WA.

AIR

Airnorth (📞 1800 627 474; www.airnorth.com.au) connects Katherine with Darwin, Alice Springs and Tennant Creek a few times a week.

BUS

Greyhound Australia (www.greyhound.com.au) has regular services between Darwin and Alice Springs, Queensland or Western Australia. Buses stop at **Katherine Transit Centre** (📞 08-8971 9999; 6 Katherine Tce). One-way fares from Katherine include: Darwin ($75, four hours), Alice Springs (from $175, 16 hours), Tennant Creek ($139, 8½ hours) and Kununurra ($108, six hours).

An alternative is the **Bodhi Bus** (📞 08-8971 0774; www.thebodhibus.com.au; 6/27 Katherine Tce), which travels to remote communities (including Borroloola and Timber Creek). It also services the Katherine–Darwin route ($70 one way, Monday, Thursday and Saturday) via Adelaide River ($50, 2½ hours) and Pine Creek ($50, one hour), dropping off passengers at the Palmerston bus exchange or Darwin airport.

TRAIN

The *Ghan* train, operated by **Great Southern Rail** (www.gsr.com.au), travels between

DON'T MISS

BARUNGA FESTIVAL

For three days over a long weekend in mid-June, Barunga, 80km east of Katherine, displays traditional arts and crafts, dancing, music and sporting competitions at the **Barunga Festival** (www.jawoyn.org/tourism/barunga-festival). Bring your own camping equipment; alternatively, visit for the day from Katherine.

Adelaide and Darwin twice a week, stopping at Katherine for four hours – enough for a whistle-stop tour to Katherine Gorge! **Nitmiluk Tours** (☑ 1300 146 743; www.nitmiluktours.com.au; Katherine Tce; ⊙ 9am-5pm Mon-Sat) runs shuttles between the station and town.

AROUND KATHERINE

The area around Katherine has plenty to keep you occupied, none more so than Nitmiluk (Katherine Gorge) National Park. The Indigenous community of Beswick (Wugularr) is a wonderful place to draw near to Aboriginal people and their culture.

Nitmiluk (Katherine Gorge) National Park

Spectacular **Katherine Gorge** (☑ 08-8972 1886, 08-8972 1253; https://nt.gov.au/leisure/parks-reserves/) forms the backbone of the 2920-sq-km Nitmiluk (Katherine Gorge) National Park, about 30km from Katherine. A series of 13 deep sandstone gorges have been carved out by the **Katherine River** on its journey from Arnhem Land to the Timor Sea. It is a hauntingly beautiful place – though it can get crowded in peak season – and a must-do from Katherine. In the Dry the tranquil river is perfect for a paddle, but in the Wet the deep still waters and dividing rapids are engulfed by an awesome torrent that churns through the gorge. Plan to spend at least a full day canoeing or cruising on the river and bushwalking.

The traditional owners are the Jawoyn Aboriginal people who jointly manage Nitmiluk with Parks & Wildlife. Nitmiluk Tours (p836) manages accommodation, cruises and activities within the park.

⊙ Sights & Activities

Leliyn (Edith Falls)   NATURE RESERVE
Reached off the Stuart Hwy 40km north of Katherine and 20km along a sealed road, Leliyn is an idyllic haven for swimming and hiking. The moderate **Leliyn Trail** (2.6km loop, 1½ hours; medium) climbs into escarpment country through grevillea and spinifex and past scenic lookouts (Bemang is best in the afternoon) to the Upper Pool, where the moderate **Sweetwater Pool Trail** (8.6km return, three to five hours) branches off.

The peaceful Sweetwater Pool has a small camping ground; overnight permits are available at the kiosk. The main Lower Pool – a gorgeous, mirror-flat swimming lagoon – is a quick 150m dash from the car park. The Parks & Wildlife **camping ground** (☑ 08-8975 4869; adult/child $12/6) next to the car park has grassy sites, lots of shade, toilets, showers, a laundry and facilities for travellers with disabilites. Fees are paid at the **kiosk** (⊙ 8am-6pm May-Oct, 9.30am-3pm Nov-Apr), which sells snacks and basic supplies. Nearby is a picnic area with BBQs and tables.

★ **Nitmiluk Tours**   CRUISE
(☑ 08-8972 1253, 1300 146 743; www.nitmiluktours.com.au; 2hr cruise per adult/child $89/44.50, 4hr cruise adult/child $129/63.50) An easy way to see far into the gorge is on a cruise. Bookings on some cruises can be tight in the peak season; make your reservation at least a day in advance. The two-hour cruise goes to the second gorge and visits a rock-art gallery (including an 800m walk). Departures are at 9am, 11am, 1pm and 3pm daily year-round depending on river level.

The four-hour cruise goes to the third gorge and includes a chance to swim. This cruise leaves at 9am daily from April to July, plus at 11am and 1pm May to August. There's also a more leisurely two-hour breakfast cruise, leaving at 7am April to November (adult/child $94/48), and a sunset cruise, sailing at 4.30pm, nightly from May to October, with a candlelit buffet dinner and champagne (adult/child $164.50/119).

There's wheelchair access to the top of the first gorge only.

Jatbula Trail   WALKING
This renowned walk (66km one way, five days, difficult) to Leliyn (Edith Falls) climbs the Arnhem Land escarpment, passing the swamp-fed Biddlecombe Cascades, Crystal Falls, the Amphitheatre and Sweetwater

Pool. This walk can only be done one way (ie you can't walk from Leliyn to Katherine Gorge), is closed from October to April and requires a minimum of two walkers.

A ferry service takes you across the gorge to kick things off.

Nitmiluk Tours SCENIC FLIGHTS
(☑1300 146 743; www.nitmiluktours.com.au) Nitmiluk Tours offers a variety of flights ranging from an eight-minute buzz over the first gorge (per person $104) to a 20-minute flight over all 13 gorges ($226). There are broader tours that take in Aboriginal rock-art sites and Kakadu National Park. Book at the Nitmiluk Visitor Centre (p840).

Nitmiluk Tours CANOEING
(☑1300 146 743, 08-8972 1253; www.nitmiluktours.com.au) From April to November, Nitmiluk Tours hires out single/double canoes for a half-day ($57/91 plus $50 deposit, departing 8am and 12.30pm), including the use of a splash-proof drum for cameras and other gear (it's not fully waterproof), a map and a life jacket.

Butterfly Gorge WALKING
A challenging, shady walk (12km return, 4½ hours, difficult) through a pocket of monsoon rainforest, often with butterflies, leads to midway along the second gorge and a deep-water swimming spot.

Jawoyn Valley WALKING
A difficult (40km loop, overnight) wilderness trail leading off the Eighth Gorge walk into a valley with rock outcrops and rock-art galleries.

Barrawei (Lookout) Loop WALKING
Starting with a short, steep climb, this walk (3.7km loop, two hours, moderate difficulty) provides good views over the Katherine River.

🛏 Sleeping

Nitmiluk National Park
Campground CAMPGROUND $
(☑1300 146 743, 08-8972 1253; www.nitmiluktours.com.au; powered/unpowered sites $49.50/37, safari tents $160; 🛜🏊) Plenty of grass and shade, hot showers, toilets, BBQs, a laundry and a kiosk by the good-lookin' swimming pool. Wallabies, goannas and night curlews are frequent visitors. There's a 'tent village' here with permanent safari tents sleeping two people. Book at the Nitmiluk Visitor Centre (p840).

★ Cicada Lodge BOUTIQUE HOTEL $$$
(☑1800 242 232, 08-8974 3100; www.cicadalodge.com.au; Nitmiluk National Park; d incl breakfast $750; 🅿❄@🛜🏊) This luxury lodge has been architecturally designed to meld modern sophistication and traditional Jawoyn themes. It has just 18 luxury rooms overlooking the Katherine River. Decor is tasteful and stylish and features include full-length louvred doors that open onto private balconies. Indigenous artworks decorate the walls. Breakfast included.

Nitmiluk Chalets CABIN $$$
(☑1300 146 743, 08-8972 1253; www.nitmiluktours.com.au; 1-/2-bedroom cabins $218/275; 🅿🛜🏊) Next door to the caravan park, these cabins are a serviceable choice if you'd rather have a solid roof over your head (and a flat-screen TV). Has access to all the caravan park facilities (pool, BBQs, kiosk etc).

🍴 Eating

Sugarbag Café CAFE $$
(Nitmiluk Visitor Centre; salads $12-20, mains $17-22, breakfast buffet adult/child $26/11, lunch buffet $26/21; ⏱7am-3pm) The food here at the visitor centre is excellent, with highlights including the Nitmiluk burger or the lemon-myrtle barra bites. It also does breakfast and lunch buffets from April to October. The elevated deck looking out over the river and

---

WORTH A TRIP

CUTTA CUTTA CAVES NATURE PARK

About 30km south of Katherine, turn your back on the searing sun and dip down 15m below terra firma into this mazelike limestone cave system. The 1499-hectare **Cutta Cutta Caves Nature Park** (☑1300 146 743, 08-8972 1940; https://nt.gov.au/leisure/parks-reserves; tours adult/child $20/10; ⏱8.30am-4.30pm guided tours 9am, 10am, 11am, 1pm, 2pm and 3pm) has a unique ecology and you'll be sharing the space with brown tree snakes and pythons, plus the endangered ghost bats and orange horseshoe bats that they feed on. Cutta Cutta is a Jawoyn name meaning 'many stars'; it was taboo for Aboriginal people to enter the cave, which they believed was where the stars were kept during the day. Admission is by guided tour only.

ALAN COPSON/GETTY IMAGES ©

Ultimate Outback

'Outback' means different things to different people and in different parts of Australia – deserts, tropical savannah, wetlands... But what's consistent is the idea that it's far from the comforts of home. The outback is 'beyond the black stump' and holds many surprises.

Uluru (Ayers Rock)

Uluru-Kata Tjuta National Park is the undisputed highlight of central Australia. There's not much that hasn't been said about Uluru, and not many parts of it that haven't been explored, photographed and documented. Still, nothing can prepare you for its almighty bulk, spiritual stories, remarkable textures and camera-worthy colours.

Kata Tjuta (The Olgas)

The tallest dome of Kata Tjuta is taller than Uluru (546m versus 348m), and some say exploring these 36 mounded monoliths is a more intimate, moving experience. Trails weave in amongst the red rocks, leading to pockets of silent beauty and spiritual gravitas.

1. Uluru (Ayers Rock; p875) **2.** Kata Tjuta (The Olgas; p877)
3. Kings Canyon (p870)

Watarrka National Park

In Watarrka National Park, about 300km north of Uluru by road, Kings Canyon is the inverse of Uluru – as if someone had grabbed the big rock and pushed it into the desert sand. Here, 270m-high cliffs drop away to a palm-lined valley floor, home to 600 plant species and delighted-to-be-here native animals. The 6km canyon rim walk is four hours well spent.

MacDonnell Ranges

The 'Macs' stretch east and west of Alice Springs. In their ancient folds are hidden worlds where rock wallabies and colourful birds can find water even on the hottest days.

filled with blue-faced honeyeaters is a fine place to rest after a walk or cruise.

Information

The **Nitmiluk Visitor Centre** (☑ 1300 146 743, 08-8972 1253; www.nitmiluktours.com.au; ⊙ 6.30am-5.30pm) has excellent displays and information on the park's geology, wildlife, the traditional owners (the Jawoyn) and European history. The **Sugarbag Cafe** (p837) is also here and a desk for Parks & Wildlife, which has information sheets on a wide range of marked walking tracks that start here and traverse the picturesque country south of the gorge. Registration for overnight walks and camping permits ($3.30 per night) is from 8am to 1pm; canoeing permits are also issued.

ⓘ Getting There & Away

It's 30km by sealed road from Katherine to the Nitmiluk Centre, and a few hundred metres further to the car park, where the gorge begins and the cruises start.

Daily transfers between Katherine and the gorge are run by **Nitmiluk Tours** (p836), departing the Nitmiluk Town Booking Office and also picking up at local accommodation places on request. Buses leave Katherine three times daily.

Katherine to Western Australia

The sealed Victoria Hwy – part of the Savannah Way – stretches 513km from Katherine to Kununurra in WA. A 4WD will get you into a few out-of-the-way national parks accessed off the Victoria Hwy or you can meander through semiarid desert and sandstone outcrops until bloated baobab trees herald your imminent arrival in WA. All fruits, vegetables, nuts and honey must be left at the quarantine inspection post on the border.

Victoria River Crossing

The red sandstone cliffs surrounding the spot where the highway crosses the Victoria River (194km west of Katherine) create a dramatic setting. Much of this area forms the eastern section of Judbarra / Gregory National Park.

⊙ Sights & Activities

Wander down to **Victoria River Crossing** and the old bridge for lovely river views and good birding; watch the tall grass for the prized purple-crowned fairy wren, as well as other bird species such as the star finch, chestnut-breasted mannikin and the blue-winged kookaburra.

As you continue west of Victoria River in the direction of Timber Creek, you'll pass through some lovely escarpment country where the river cuts its way through. A number of signposted walks head off up into the hills around here, while the old river crossing (signposted) is a gorgeous spot.

🛏 Sleeping

Victoria River Roadhouse Caravan Park CAMPGROUND $
(☑ 08-8975 0744; Victoria Hwy; powered/unpowered sites $25/20, r $50-150; @) Well-run camping ground behind the roadhouse with very good facilities and a range of cabins from the budget variety with shared bathrooms to more expansive options. It also has a shop, a bar and can provide meals ($10 to $37). It's on a rise on the west side of the bridge over the river.

ⓘ Getting There & Away

The **Bodhi Bus** (p835) that runs between Katherine ($60, 2½ hours) and Wyndham ($50, 3½ hours) passes through the Victoria River Crossing – make sure that the driver knows that this is as far as you're going.

Timber Creek

POP 232

Tiny Timber Creek is the only town between Katherine and Kununurra. It has a pretty big history for such a small place, with an early European exploration aboard the *Tom Tough* requiring repairs to be carried out with local timber (hence the town's name). The expedition's leader, AC Gregory, inscribed his arrival date into a baobab; it is still discernable (and is explained in detail through interpretive panels) at **Gregory's Tree**; 15km northwest of town. The tree is off the Victoria Hwy down a 3km unsealed road, which can become corrugated.

Other worthwhile detours just out of town include tracks to achingly pretty **Policeman's Point** (2km) and **Escarpment Lookout** (5km), the latter has fine views over town and the surrounding country.

ⓕ Tours

A highlight of Timber Creek is the **Victoria River Cruise** (☑ 0427 750 731; www.victoriarivercruise.com.au; sunset cruises adult/child $95/50;

⊘4pm daily Apr-Sep), which takes you 40km downriver spotting wildlife and returning in time for a fiery sunset.

🛏 Sleeping

There are a couple of caravan parks along the main road through town.

Basic meals and takeaway food are possible along the main road – that's about as good as it gets.

**Timber Creek Hotel
& Circle F Caravan Park** CARAVAN PARK **$**
(☑08-8975 0722; www.timbercreekhotel.com.au; Victoria Hwy; powered/unpowered sites $33/29, s/d $80/110; ❄❄) The town is dominated by this roadside hotel and caravan park. Enormous trees shade parts of the camping area, which is next to a small creek where there's croc feeding every evening (5pm). The complex includes the Timber Creek Hotel (pub) and a small supermarket.

ℹ Getting There & Away

The Bodhi Bus has a daily service to/from Katherine ($60, 3¼ hours) on its way through to Kununurra and Wyndham.

Judbarra / Gregory National Park

The rugged wilderness of the little-visited Judbarra / Gregory National Park (☑08-8975 0888; https://nt.gov.au/leisure/parks-re serves) will swallow you up – this is right off the beaten track and ripe for 4WD exploration. Covering 12,860 sq km, it sits at the transitional zone between the tropical and semiarid regions. The park consists of old cattle country and is made up of two separate sections: the eastern (Victoria River) section and the much larger Bullita section in the west.

This is croc country; swimming isn't safe. You'll need a 4WD vehicle to explore the park.

🛏 Sleeping & Eating

You'll need to bring your own food. There are basic supplies in the small grocery stores in Timber Creek.

Big Horse Creek CAMPGROUND **$**
(adult/child $3.30/1.75) There's accessible bush camping at Big Horse Creek, 10km west of Timber Creek.

ℹ Information

Parks & Wildlife (☑08-8975 0888; https:// nt.gov.au/leisure/parks-reserves; Timber

Creek; ⊘7am-4.30pm) in Timber Creek has park and 4WD notes. It can also provide a map featuring the various walks, camping spots, tracks and the historic homestead and ruggedly romantic original stockyards – a must before heading in.

Keep River National Park

The remote **Keep River National Park** (☑08-9167 8827; https://nt.gov.au/leisure/parks-reserves) is noted for its stunning sandstone formations, beautiful desolation and rock art.

Pamphlets detailing walks are available at the start of the excellent trails. Don't miss the **rock art walk** (5.5km return, two hours) near Jarnem and the **gorge walk** (3km return, two hours) at Jinumum.

🛏 Sleeping

There are basic, sandstone-surrounded camping grounds (adult/child $3.30/1.65) at Gurrandalng (18km into the park) and Jarnem (32km). Tank water is also available at Jarnem.

ℹ Getting There & Away

The park entrance is just 3km from the WA border. You can reach the park's main points by conventional 2WD vehicle during the Dry.

Mataranka

POP 244

With soothing, warm thermal springs set in pockets of palms and tropical vegetation, you'd be mad not to pull into Mataranka for at least a few hours to soak off the road dust. The small settlement regularly swells with towel-toting visitors to the thermal pool. But Mataranka has more calling cards than most roadside outback towns: nearby spring-fed **Elsey National Park** (☑08-8975 4560; www. nt.gov.au/leisure/parks-reserves) and a history linked to one of Australia's most enjoyable outback tales, not to mention the welcoming tree-lined road through town, add considerable appeal to a stop here.

⊙ Sights & Activities

★**Elsey Cemetery** CEMETERY
This lonely cemetery under the eucalypts is a poignant footnote to *We of the Never Never*, with so many of the larger-than-life characters from the book buried here, among them Aeneas Gunn (alongside a memorial to his wife), Henry Peckham, John MacLennan

WE OF THE NEVER NEVER

Few outback stories have captured the national imagination quite like *We of the Never Never*, Jeannie Gunn's account of life on Elsey Station at Mataranka.

Originally from Melbourne, where she ran a girls' school, Gunn arrived in the Northern Territory in 1902 with her husband, Aeneas, who had already spent time there and was returning to take up the manager's position at Elsey Station at Mataranka, south of Katherine.

At that time there were very few white women living in the NT, especially on isolated cattle stations. Station life was tough, but Jeannie adapted and interacted with the local Najig and Guyanggan Nganawirdbird Aboriginal people, a number of whom worked on the station.

Only a year after their arrival at Elsey, Aeneas contracted malarial dysentery and died. Jeannie returned to Melbourne and recorded her Top End experiences in the novel, which was published in 1908. She was a keen observer of the minutiae of station life and managed to spark the interest of people down south who led such a different existence. These days, however, her depiction of Aboriginal people seems naive and patronising.

Jeannie was awarded an OBE in 1939 for her contribution to Australian literature and died in Melbourne in 1961 at the age of 91. *We of the Never Never* was made into a film in 1981. Interestingly, in 2012 native title to Mataranka was granted to the Najig and Guyanggan Nganawirdbird Aboriginal groups, represented in court by Jessie Roberts, who played Nellie in the film.

A number of sites around Mataranka pay tribute to this history, most notably **Elsey Cemetery** (p841), the replica of **Elsey Station Homestead** (p842) and the **Never Never Museum** (120 Roper Tce; adult/child $4/2; ☉9am-4.30pm Mon-Fri). In the park along the Stuart Hwy in the centre of town, there are life-sized figures meant to represent the story's main characters.

and Tom Pearce. The last remains of the homestead (destroyed during roadworks in the 1940s) lie 300m to the southeast at the end of the gravel track.

The cemetery is around 20km south of Mataranka and signposted off the Stuart Hwy.

Elsey Station Homestead HISTORIC BUILDING
(admission by donation; ☉daylight hours) Outside the entrance to the Mataranka Homestead Resort (p842) is a replica of the Elsey Station Homestead, constructed for the filming of *We of the Never Never*, which is screened daily at noon in the resort bar. The low-lying and overgrown ruins of the actual site are a few hundred metres past the Elsey Cemetery.

Mataranka Thermal Pools THERMAL BATHS
Mataranka's crystal-clear thermal pool, shrouded in rainforest, is 10km from town beside the Mataranka Homestead Resort. The warm, clear water, dappled by light filtered through overhanging palms, rejuvenates a lot of bodies on any given day; it's reached via a boardwalk from the resort and can get mighty crowded.

🛏 Sleeping & Eating

**Territory Manor Motel
& Caravan Park** MOTEL $
(☏08-89754516; www.matarankamotel.com; Martin Rd; powered/unpowered sites $30/26, s/d $110/120; ❄@🏊) Mataranka's best caravan park is well positioned and a class act – no surprise it's also popular. Smallish motel rooms are well decked out and have good-sized bathrooms, and the grounds are well shaded for camping. In the licensed bistro (mains $22 to $35) they serve barramundi, along with steaks, salad, lamb chops with a honey mint glaze and other surprises.

**Mataranka
Homestead Resort** CAMPGROUND $
(☏08-8975 4544; www.matarankahomestead.com.au; Homestead Rd; powered/unpowered sites $30/26, d/cabins $89/115; ❄🏊) Only metres from the main thermal pool and with a range of accommodation, this is a *very* popular option. The large camping ground is dusty but has a few shady areas and decent amenities. The rudimentary air-con motel rooms have fridge, TV and bathroom, while the cabins have a kitchenette and sleep up to six people. Book ahead.

Bitter Springs Cabins
CABIN $$

(☑ 08-8975 4838; www.bittersspringscabins.com.au; 4705 Martin Rd, Bitter Springs; powered/unpowered sites $35/30, cabins $130; ❄ @ 🛜 🐾) On the banks of the Little Roper River, only a few hundred metres from Bitter Springs thermal pool, this quiet bush setting has some amazing termite mounds adorning the front paddock. The TV-equipped, open-plan cabins have a balcony with bush views. Pets welcome.

★ Stockyard Gallery
CAFE $

(☑ 08-8975 4530; Stuart Hwy; snacks & light meals $6-13; ⊙ hours vary) This casual cafe is a little gem and the lovely shaded garden area is a great respite from the heat and dust. There's a delicious range of homemade snacks (sandwiches and kebabs) plus fresh espresso coffee and divine mango smoothies. The art gallery here sells Aboriginal art, books and souvenirs. The only problem is that the opening hours change regularly.

❶ Getting There & Away

Mataranka lies 108km south of Katherine and 568km north of Tennant Creek along the Stuart Hwy. Daily **Greyhound buses** (p835) connect Mataranka with Katherine ($37, 1¼ hours) and Tennant Creek ($126, 7½ hours).

Beswick (Wugularr)

If you're interested in seeing genuine Aboriginal art produced by local communities, it's worth detouring off the Stuart Hwy to the remote cultural centre and small community of Beswick (Wugularr). It's an opportunity to draw near to the great artistic traditions of Arnhem Land, without straying down detours along long and lonely dirt tracks.

◎ Sights

★ Ghunmarn Culture Centre
GALLERY

(Djilpin Arts; ☑ 08-8977 4250; www.djilpinarts.org.au; Beswick; ⊙ 9.30am-4pm Mon-Fri Apr-Nov) The Ghunmarn Culture Centre, opened in 2007, displays local artworks, prints, carvings, weavings and didgeridoos from western Arnhem Land. The centre also features the Blanasi Collection, a permanent exhibition of works by elders from the western Arnhem Land region. Visitors are welcome to visit the centre without a permit; call ahead to check that it's open.

✦ Festivals & Events

Walking With Spirits
CULTURAL

(www.djilpinarts.org.au; ⊙ Jul) A two-day Indigenous cultural festival in July at Beswick Falls, 130km from Katherine. In a magical setting, traditional dance and music is combined with theatre, films and a light show. Camping is allowed at the site (only during the festival). A 4WD is recommended for the last 20km to the falls; alternatively, a shuttle bus runs from Beswick.

🍴 Sleeping & Eating

Beswick has a general store with limited supplies.

★ Djakanimba Pavilions
GUESTHOUSE $$

(☑ 08-8977 4250; www.djilpinarts.org.au/djakanimba-pavillions-beswick/; Cameron Rd, Beswick; d $140-180, 2-night all-inclusive package $880; ❄) These four attractive guestrooms attached to the impressive Djilpin Arts complex in Beswick are a wonderful chance to sleep overnight in a predominantly Aboriginal community. The accommodation, on stilts and with a contemporary Outback aesthetic with louvred windows to catch the breeze, is simple but stylish – an excellent choice.

❶ Getting There & Away

Beswick, reached via the sealed Central Arnhem Hwy, is 56km east of the Stuart Hwy on the southern fringes of Arnhem Land.

BARKLY TABLELAND & GULF COUNTRY

East of the Stuart Hwy lies some of the NT's most remote cattle country, but parts are accessible by sealed road and the rivers and inshore waters of the Gulf coast are regarded as some of the best fishing in the country. Other than the fishing, the reason to venture out here is to immerse yourself in the silence of this remote land – the last time we passed this way, we encountered two cars and one road train in the entire 390km from Daly Waters to Borroloola. Just the way we like it.

Roper Highway

Not far south of Mataranka on the Stuart Hwy, the mostly sealed single-lane Roper Hwy strikes 175km eastwards to **Roper Bar**, crossing the paperbark- and pandanus-lined

Roper River, where freshwater meets salt-water. It's passable only in the Dry.

◉ Sights

★ **Limmen National Park** NATIONAL PARK
(☑ 08-8975 9940; https://nt.gov.au/leisure/parks-reserves) A vast and rugged landscape, this 9608-sq-km national park is in the heart of tropical savannah country and appeals particularly to fisherfolk and 4WD enthusiasts. This is home to some of the most striking sandstone-escarpment country in southern Arnhem Land and the 'lost cities', upthrusts of rocky pinnacles that are simply spectacular and worth exploring on foot. For an aerial view, contact Heartbreak Hotel along the Carpentaria Highway.

There are two 'lost cities'. The first if you're coming from the north is **Southern Lost City**, 35km south of the Nathan River Ranger Station; a 2.5km walking track loops among the rocks. More difficult to access (you'll need a high-clearance 4WD), the **Western Lost City** lies at the end of a rough 28km track that begins just northwest of the Ranger Station (where you'll need to get the access code to unlock the gate; it's posted on the whiteboard).

★ **Ngukurr Arts Centre** GALLERY
(☑ 08-8975 4260; www.ngukurrarts.net; ⊙ 10am-4pm Mon-Fri) This community-owned and -run Indigenous arts centre is well worth the trip out here, showcasing works by artists from local Alawa, Mara, Ngalakan, Ngandi, Nunggubuyu, Rittarrngu and Wandarang clans; 60% of sales go back to the artist.

☷ Sleeping & Eating

Roper Bar Store has some takeaway meals and sells basic groceries, but you'll otherwise need to bring all of your food with you.

Roper Bar Store CARAVAN PARK $
(☑ 08-8975 4636; www.roperbar.com.au; unpowered sites per adult/child $15/10, s/d $115/135; ☏) You can't be choosy out here; rooms are simple and would be overpriced anywhere else. The nearby campground has plenty of shade and sits next to the river. Takeaway food is available at the general store.

❶ Getting There & Away

Roper Bar is a 4WD-only access point to Borroloola, a more beautiful but more rugged alternative to the route via the sealed Stuart and Carpentaria Hwys. Not deterred? Head south along the rough-going Nathan River Rd through Limmen

National Park – high-clearance with two spares required – and across southeastern Arnhem Land. They sell petrol at the Roper Bar Store.

The **Bodhi Bus** (p835) runs a dry-season service from Katherine to Numbulwar ($130, eight hours, Monday and Thursday) that only goes as far as Ngukurr ($90, 4½ hours, Tuesday and Friday) in the Wet. It stops at Roper Bar on request.

Carpentaria & Tablelands Highways

The Carpentaria Hwy connects the deserts of the outback with the subtropical hinterland of the Gulf of Carpentaria and it's one of the NT's most remote stretches of tarmac. Part of the Savannah Way (a loose network of highways from Broome to Cairns), it runs for 390km from Daly Waters on the Stuart Hwy to Borroloola. The only 'town' en route is Cape Crawford, which is little more than a roadhouse and petrol station.

⛷ Activities

★ **Scenic Flights** SCENIC FLIGHTS
(Heartbreak Hotel, Cape Crawford; 15/20/30min flights $155/210/315) You just expect to find helicopter scenic flights out here, but we're very glad that you do. Flights zip out over Limmen National Park and its dramatic rock formations known as 'lost cities' – you'll need to take the longer flights to get that far, while the shorter trips take in smaller versions of same.

☷ Sleeping

Heartbreak Hotel HOTEL $
(☑ 08-8975 9928; www.heartbreakhotel.com.au; cnr Carpentaria & Tablelands Hwys, Cape Crawford; powered/unpowered sites $28/20, s/d $75/90. deluxe cabins $165; ❄) The Heartbreak Hotel, a fairly standard Outback roadhouse and fuel stop, is 267km west of Daly River, 123km short of Borroloola and 374km from the Barkly Homestead Roadhouse...yes, you're in the middle of nowhere. Pitch the tent on the shaded grassy lawn and then nurse a cold beer on the wide verandah.

★ **Barkly Homestead Roadhouse** CARAVAN PARK $$
(☑ 08-8964 4549; www.barklyhomestead.com.au; powered/unpowered sites $36/28, cabins & motel d $150; ❄ ☒) You're a *long* way from anywhere out here; from Cape Crawford it's a desolate 374km south across the Barkly Tableland along the Tablelands Hwy (Rte 11), 210km

west to Tennant Creek or 252km east to the Queensland border. And yet it's here you'll find one of the NT's best roadhouses.

ℹ️ Getting There & Away

The only public transport along the Carpentaria Hwy is the daily Bodhi Bus (www.thebodhibus.com.au) from Katherine to Borroloola.

Borroloola

POP 926

On the McArthur River out near the Gulf of Carpentaria, Borroloola has a wonderful end-of-the-road feel to it – it's a sleepy, slightly neglected place that revels in its remoteness. There's a good Indigenous art centre, some fine wildlife and conservation reserves in neighbouring country and fabulous barramundi fishing.

The town isn't actually on the Gulf of Carpentaria – it's a further 59km to the Bing Bong port loading facility, from which you'll have obscured views of the Gulf of Carpentaria. The nearby Macarthur River zinc mine is the town's lifeblood.

◉ Sights

★ **Waralungku Arts Centre**   ARTS CENTRE
(☑ 08-8975 8677; www.waralungku.com; Robinson Rd, opposite Macarthur River Caravan Park; ◷ 8.30am-4pm Mon-Fri, 10am-1pm Sat May-Oct) This relaxed art centre on the main road through town showcases work by artists from the four different Indigenous-language groups in the area; the Yanyuwa, Garrwa, Marra and Gudanji people. Unlike the dot-painting styles of the Western Desert or the bark paintings of Arnhem Land, the paintings here have a style all their own, with a more figurative style.

There are also locally made screen prints and baskets. Ask about the 'Craft & Culture Experiences', a fine program that offers immersion into local culture and which may include painting, weaving, making didgeridoos, lessons in bush tucker and bush medicine and traditional dance and singing. Advance reservations essential.

Borroloola Museum   MUSEUM
(www.nationaltrust.org.au/places/old-police-station-borroloola/; Robinson Rd; $5; ◷ 8am-5pm Mon-Fri May-Sep) About three-quarters of the population of Borroloola is Indigenous and the town's colourful history is displayed at the Borroloola Museum, alongside mining

WORTH A TRIP

LORELLA SPRINGS

One of our favourite places to stay in the entire Gulf region, **Lorella Springs Wilderness Park** (☑ 08-8975 9917; www.lorellasprings.com.au/accommodation; camping per adult/child $20/5, s $130-230, d $130-250; ◷ Apr-Sep) has a marvellously isolated setting, a thermal spring and river frontage, a restaurant and bar as well as self-contained air-con cabins, rooms with ceiling fans and camp sites. Activities include fishing, swimming, birdwatching, bushwalking, 4WD expeditions and even helicopter scenic flights.

Lorella Springs is 130km from Cape Crawford, 180km from Borroloola and 275km from Roper Bar close to the Gulf of Carpentaria coast. You'll need a 4WD, unless you have your own plane.

memorabilia, within the 1887 police station. If you find it closed, ask any of the businesses around town and someone should be able to track down the key.

🏃 Activities

Borroloola is big news for fishing fans and bagging a barramundi in these parts is the stuff of fishing legend. The barramundi season is from February to April, but October and November can also be good. Whereas the big fishing charter companies dominate up in Arnhem Land, things can be a little more low-key here. The following companies can arrange for boat and equipment hire:

J & A Charters & Tours (☑ 0448 804 855)

KAB Fishing Club (☑ 0448 804 855)

🎊 Festivals & Events

Malandarri Festival   CULTURAL
(☑ 08-8941 1444, 08-8975 8677; www.artbacknt.com.au/index.php/itdp/dancesite/; per day $5; ◷ Oct) This two-day event in October is Borroloola's biggest celebration, with traditional dance the focal point alongside artworks, markets, workshops and other activities.

🛏️ Sleeping

Borroloola Hotel Motel   MOTEL $
(☑ 08-8975 8766; www.borroloolahotelmotel.com.au; Robinson Rd; r $75-110; ❄️) Simple rooms at the pub are nothing to write home about, but there is a large saltwater swimming pool.

CARANBIRINI CONSERVATION RESERVE

Just off the Carpentaria Hwy, 46km south of Borroloola, the fine **Caranbirini Conservation Reserve** (☎08-8975 8792; www.nt.gov.au/leisure/parks-reserves) is good for wildlife – including euros (wallaroos), agile wallabies and water goannas – and birdwatching (prize species include the Gouldian finch, Carpentaria grasswren and sandstone rockthrush) and plays an important role in many Aboriginal Dreaming stories. But Caranbirini is also remarkable for the drama of its sandstone spires and pinnacles – this is the most accessible of all of the 'lost-city' rock formations for which the area is renowned.

A number of walks take you into the heart of the pinnacles and surrounding country. From the car park, a 150m trail goes to the **waterhole** where a bird hide overlooks the billabong. The **Barrawulla Loop** (2km, one to two hours, easy) gets you into the heart of the rocky outcrops, while the **Jagududgu Loop** (5km, three hours, easy to medium) ranges further afield with some good views before joining the Barrawulla Loop.

McArthur River Caravan Park
CARAVAN PARK **$**

(☎08-89758734; www.mcarthurcaravanpark.com.au; powered/unpowered site $30/25, budget unit s/d $100/110, self-contained unit s/d $130/140) This fairly simple camp site and caravan park on the main road into town is a little dusty during the Dry, but the owners are keen fishers and it's a good place to stay if that's why you're here. Ask for one of the newer cabins that are much better than their older counterparts.

Savannah Way Motel
MOTEL **$**

(☎08-8975 8883; www.savannahwaymotel.com.au; Robinson Rd; r & cabins $80-130; ❄☎❄) This motel, close to the airstrip on the main road through town, is clean and comfortable, with cabins and guesthouse rooms set in tropical gardens. It's often full so book ahead.

✖ Eating

Carpentaria Grill AUSTRALIAN **$$**
(☎08-8975 8883; Savannah Way Motel, Robinson Rd; mains $17-37; ⏱5.30-10pm) Easily the best place to eat in town, the Carpentaria Grill does Aussie pub staples, but the best choice is always the barra – served with garlic prawns or on its own cooked just the way you like it. There are special nights: Monday is steak night, Fridays is all about barra, while Sunday is roasts.

Borroloola Hotel AUSTRALIAN **$$**
(166 Robinson Rd; meals $12-32; ⏱noon-2pm & 5.30-10pm) Borroloola Hotel serves the usual pub fare of burgers, chops and mixed grills within a lounge bar that's heavily reinforced with steel mesh.

❶ Getting There & Away

Airnorth (p811) has up to two daily flights between Darwin and the Macarthur River Mine Airport (70km from Borroloola) for $579, but it's mainly for miners. Tour companies sometimes use Borroloola's in-town air strip.

Bodhi Bus (☎in Katherine 08-8971 0774) has a daily bus service between Borroloola and Katherine ($120, 8½ hours), which runs via Mataranka, Larrimah, Daly Waters and Cape Crawford. Borroloola's stop is outside the Malandari General Store.

Under normal conditions, it's a 5½-hour drive (390km) from Daly Waters to Borroloola. In the other direction, it's 479km along a mostly unsealed road to Burketown in Queensland; parts of this latter route are impassable in the Wet.

CENTRAL NORTHERN TERRITORY

Central NT (basically the Stuart Hwy from Katherine to Alice Springs) is still referred to as 'the Track' – as it has been since WWII when it was literally a dirt track connecting the NT's two main towns, roughly following the Overland Telegraph Line. It's dead straight most of the way and gets progressively drier and flatter as you head south, but there are quite a few notable diversions.

Daly Waters
POP 50

The tiny community of Daly Waters is home to one of the NT's great outback pubs. It was an important staging post in the early days of aviation – Amy Johnson landed here on her epic flight from England to Australia in

1930. High on novelty value, it's worth the detour off the highway.

🛏 Sleeping

Daly Waters Pub   CARAVAN PARK **$**
(☑ 08-8975 9927; www.dalywaterspub.com; powered/unpowered sites $28/16, d $70-110, cabins $135-175; ❄ ☀) Decorated with business cards, bras, banknotes and memorabilia from passing travellers, this pub claims to be the oldest in the NT (its liquor licence has been valid since 1893). Beside the pub is a dustbowl camping ground with a bit of shade; book ahead or arrive early to secure a powered site.

Accommodation ranges from basic dongas (small, transportable buildings) to spacious self-contained cabins.

The pub has become a bit of a legend along the Track. Every evening from April to September there's the popular beef 'n' barra barbecue, along with entertainment some nights from a visiting country muso. Otherwise, hearty meals (mains $11 to $30), including the barra burger, roast beef rolls, kangaroo loin and home-made damper bread are served.

ⓘ Getting There & Away

Daly Waters is 3km off the highway; the turn-off is 160km south of Mataranka or 407km north of Tennant Creek. The petrol station here is expensive – fill up instead at the one out on the main highway at the junction of the Stuart and Carpentaria Hwys.

Tennant Creek

POP 3062

Tennant Creek is the only town of any size between Katherine, 680km to the north, and Alice Springs, 511km to the south, and is the NT's fifth-largest town (which says more about the NT's small population than it does about Tennant Creek). It's a good place to break up a long drive and check out the town's few attractions. Tennant Creek is known as Jurnkurakurr to the local Warumungu people and almost half of the population is of Aboriginal descent.

◉ Sights

★ **Nyinkka Nyunyu**   GALLERY
(☑ 08-8962 2699; www.nyinkkanyunyu.com.au; Paterson St; guided tour $15; ⊙ 9am-5pm Mon-Fri, 10am-2pm Sat & Sun Oct-Apr, 8am-6pm Mon-Sat, 10am-2pm Sun May-Sep) This innovative museum and gallery highlights the dynamic art and culture of the local Warumungu people. The absorbing displays focus on contemporary art, traditional objects (many returned from interstate museums), bush medicine and regional history. The diorama series, or bush TVs as they became known within the community, are particularly special.

Battery Hill Mining Centre   MINE
(☑ 08-8962 1281; www.barklytourism.com.au; Peko Rd; adult/child $30/20; ⊙ 9am-5pm) Experience life in Tennant Creek's 1930s gold rush at this mining centre, which doubles as the Visitor Information Centre, 2km east of town. There

DARWIN & THE NORTHERN TERRITORY TENNANT CREEK

WORTH A TRIP

PUNGALINA-SEVEN EMU WILDLIFE SANCTUARY

Pungalina-Seven Emu Wildlife Sanctuary (www.australianwildlife.org/sanctuaries/pungalina-seven-emu-sanctuary.aspx) represents a groundbreaking collaboration between the Australian Wildlife Conservancy and local traditional owners, merging wildlife conservation with a working cattle station in an area rich in coastal rainforest, mangroves, eucalypt woodlands, wetlands and thermal springs.

The sanctuary is home to a recorded 292 bird species and 48 mammals, among them little-known species such as the Carpentarian Pseudantechinus (small carnivorous marsupial), along with northern brown bandicoots, dingoes and a host of wallaby and rock wallaby species. Birds to watch out for include the Gouldian finch, red goshawk and purple-crowned fairy wren.

The sanctuary covers 3060 sq km and includes 55km of Gulf shoreline and 100km of the Calvert River. A good base is **Seven Emu Station** (☑ 08-8975 8307, 08-8975 9904; www.sevenemustation.com.au; camping per vehicle $50), deep in the heart of Gulf country and on the doorstep of Pungalina. It's a remote, working cattle station which offers a unique package of fishing, remote camping and wildlife watching. The campsites are in the stockman tradition, with shelter sheds, fire pits and long-drop loos-with-a-view.

DON'T MISS

LARRIMAH

Tiny roadside Larrimah, 185km south of Katherine, offers a couple of reasons to pull over:

Pink Panther (Larrimah) Hotel (☑08-8975 9931; https://larrimahwaysideinn.wordpress.com; powered/unpowered sites $25/18, r $65-100; ❉ ⛅) Originally a WWII officers' mess, now a cheerfully rustic and quirky pub offering basic rooms, meals (mains $12 to $34) and a small menagerie of animals. Its specialities are the homemade pies (which often sell out by midafternoon) and excellent burgers. The atmosphere is a cross between a cheerfully dishevelled forgotten outpost of the outback and an ageing art installation.

Fran's Devonshire Teahouse (Stuart Hwy; meals $6-20; ⊙8am-4pm) Fran's Devonshire Teahouse is in Fran's house, where she cooks up legendary pies and pastries. This is the place to stop for a filling camel or buffalo pie, roast lamb with damper or just a Devonshire tea (no, you couldn't be further from Exeter) or fresh coffee.

---

are **underground mine tours** and audio tours of the 10-head **battery**. In addition there is a superb **Minerals Museum** and you can try your hand at gold panning.

🏃 Activities

Kelly's Ranch HORSE RIDING (☑08-8962 2045; www.kellysranch.com.au; 5 Fazaldeen Rd; trail rides/lesson per person $150/50) Experience the Barkly from the back of a horse with local Warumungu man Jerry Kelly. His two-hour trail rides start with a lesson and then a ride through some superb outback scenery with bush-tucker stops along the way. Jerry entertains with stories about Aboriginal culture and life on the cattle stations.

🛌 Sleeping

Outback Caravan Park CAMPGROUND $ (☑08-8962 2459; 71 Peko Rd; powered/unpowered sites $36/30, cabins $70-150; ❉ ⛅) In a town that often feels parched, it's nice to be in the shade of this grassy caravan park about 1km east of the centre. There's a well-stocked kiosk, camp kitchen and fuel. You may even

be treated to some bush poetry and bush tucker, courtesy of yarn spinner Jimmy Hooker, at 7.30pm ($10). Decent outdoor bar area, but be quick, it closes early.

Bluestone Motor Inn MOTEL $ (☑08-8962 2617; www.bluestonemotorinn.com.au; 1 Paterson St; standard/deluxe d $100/123; 🛜 ⛅) At the southern end of town, this 3½-star motel has comfortable standard rooms in leafy surrounds. In addition there are spacious hexagonal deluxe rooms with queen-size beds and a sofa. There are also wheelchair-accessible units and a restaurant.

Safari Lodge Motel MOTEL $$ (☑08-8962 2207; www.arrahotels.com.au/safari-lodge-motel; Davidson St; s/d $110/130; ❉ @ 🛜) 🖋 You should book ahead to stay at this family-run motel. Safari Lodge is centrally located next to the best restaurant in town and has clean, fairly standard rooms with phone, fridge and TV.

🍴 Eating

Top of the Town Cafe CAFE $ (☑08-8962 1311; www.facebook.com/TopOfTownCafe/; 163 Paterson St; breakfast $7-15; ⊙7am-3pm Mon-Fri, 7am-2pm Sat) Home of pinkmolly cupcakes, this little gem is slightly twee. It's cute, quirky and a little cramped inside, but there are tables and chairs on the footpath, too. There are a range of toasties and bacon-and-egg options for brekky, making it the best place in town for breakfast.

**Tennant Creek
Memorial Club** AUSTRALIAN $$ (www.tennantcreekmemorialclub.com/dining; 48 Schmidt St; mains $16-32; ⊙noon-2pm & 6-9pm) In a town where eating rarely rises above the mediocre, the Memorial Club is a reliable if generally unexciting option. It has standard rural club fare, with oysters, burgers, steaks, pasta, curry, Asian noodle dishes... It's also a friendly place with a courtesy bus back to your hotel.

ℹ️ Information

Tennant Creek Hospital (☑08-8962 4399; Schmidt St)

Police Station (☑08-8962 4444; Paterson St)

Central Land Council (☑08-8962 2343; www.clc.org.au; 63 Paterson St, Tennant Creek)

Visitor Information Centre (☑1800 500 879; www.barklytourism.com.au; Peko Rd; ⊙9am-5pm Mon-Fri, 9am-1pm Sat)

ⓘ Getting There & Around

All long-distance buses stop at the **Transit Centre** (☑ 08-8962 2727; 151 Paterson St; 9am-5pm Mon-Fri, 8.30-11.30am Sat), where you can purchase tickets. **Greyhound Australia** (☑ 1300 473 946; www.greyhound.com.au) has daily buses from Tennant Creek to Alice Springs ($115, six hours), Katherine ($145, 8½ hours), Darwin (from $135, 14 hours) and Mount Isa ($163, eight hours). As few of the buses originate in Tennant Creek, departure times are sometimes 3.15am.

The weekly *Ghan* rail link between Alice Springs and Darwin can drop off passengers in Tennant Creek, although cars can't be loaded or offloaded. The train station is about 6km south of town so you will need a **taxi** (☑ 08-8962 3626).

Car hire is available from **Thrifty** (☑ 08-8962 2207, 1800 891 125; www.thrifty.com.au; Davidson St, Safari Lodge Motel) and there's a **petrol station** (☑ 08-8962 2626; 218 Paterson St) in the town centre.

Devil's Marbles & Around

The Stuart Hwy between Tennant Creek and Alice Springs is a long and lonely stretch of tarmac. The standout attractions are the Devils Marbles; otherwise, roadside roadhouses, no matter how basic, can seem like oases amid the great emptiness.

◉ Sights

★**Devil's Marbles** RELIGIOUS SITE
(www.nt.gov.au/leisure/parks-reserves) The gigantic granite boulders piled in precarious piles beside the Stuart Hwy, 105km south of Tennant Creek, are known as the Devil's Marbles (or Karlu Karlu in the local Warumungu language) and they're one of the more beautiful sights along this road. The Marbles are a sacred site to the traditional Aboriginal owners of the land, who believe the rocks are the eggs of the Rainbow Serpent.

🛏 Sleeping & Eating

Camping Ground CAMPGROUND $
(☑ 08-8962 4599; https://nt.gov.au/leisure/parks-reserves; adult/child $3.30/1.65) Basic camping available.

Barrow Creek Hotel PUB $
(☑ 08-8956 9753; Stuart Hwy; powered camp sites $24, s/d $65/80) The Barrow Creek Hotel is one of the highway's oddball outback pubs. In the tradition of shearers who'd write their name on a banknote and pin it to the wall to ensure they could afford a drink when next they passed through, travellers have left notes, photos, bumper stickers and knick-knacks. Dinner, basic motel-style rooms and campsites are available.

Wycliffe Well Roadhouse & Holiday Park CARAVAN PARK $
(☑ 1800 222 195, 08-8964 1966; powered/unpowered sites $38/35, budget s/d from $65/75, s/d cabins with bathroom $130/150; ☺ 6.30am-9pm; ✺ @ 🏊) At Wycliffe Well Roadhouse & Holiday Park, 17km south of Wauchope, you can fill up with fuel and food (mains $14 to $29; open 7am to 9pm) or stay and spot UFOs that apparently fly over with astonishing regularity. The park has a pleasant lawn camping ground, a kids' playground, an indoor pool, a cafe and a range of international beer.

The place is decorated with alien figures and newspaper clippings ('That UFO Was Chasing Us!').

Aileron Hotel Roadhouse MOTEL, CAMPGROUND $
(☑ 08-8956 9703; www.aileronroadhouse.com.au; Stuart Hwy; powered/unpowered sites $18/15, dm $40, s/d $120/130; ☺ 5am-9pm; ✺ 🏊) Aileron Hotel Roadhouse has camp sites (power available until 10pm), a 10-bed dorm and decent motel units. There's an ATM, a bar, shop and licensed restaurant. The owner's collection of Namatjira watercolours (at least 10 by Albert) is displayed around the roadhouse's bar and dining area – quite a find in this otherwise standard roadside roadhouse.

ROADSIDE STOPS

Threeways Roadhouse (☑ 08-8962 2744, 1800 448 163; www.threewaysroadhouse.com.au; Stuart Hwy; powered/unpowered sites $32/24, d $115; ✺ @ 🏊) Threeways Roadhouse, 537km north of Alice Springs at the junction of the Stuart and Barkly Hwys, is a potential stopover with a bar and restaurant. Rooms are simple but better than most roadhouse stops.

Banka Banka (☑ 08-8964 4511; adult/child $12/6) Banka Banka is a historic cattle station 100km north of Tennant Creek, with a grassy camping area (no power), marked walking tracks (one leading to a tranquil waterhole), a mudbrick bar and a small kiosk selling basic refreshments.

Devils Marbles Hotel HOTEL $
(☑ 08-8964 1963; www.wauchopehotel.com.au; Stuart Hwy; powered/unpowered sites $30/10, budget s/d $70/130; ✴ ✇) At Wauchope (*war*-kup), 8km south of the Devil's Marbles, are the well-kept rooms of the Wauchope Hotel. The budget rooms are dongas (small, transportable buildings); the more expensive rooms are more spacious, with ensuite. Meals from the **restaurant** (breakfast $10-32, mains $18-33) are more than satisfactory.

ℹ Getting There & Away

Greyhound buses run up and down the Stuart Hwy, stopping off in the major towns along the way. The road is tarmac and, at the time of writing, there were no speed limits between Tennant Creek and Alice Springs, part of an experiment by the local authorities – do check whether this remains the case before you put your foot to the floor.

Tanami Track

Welcome to one of the longest short cuts on the planet. Synonymous with isolated outback driving, the 1055km Tanami Rd connects Alice Springs with Halls Creek, the Red Centre with the Kimberley. The Tanami Desert and surrounding country are the homeland of the Warlpiri, Arrente, Luritja and Pintubi peoples and much of the land has reverted to their traditional ownership. The only real attractions along the way are the important Indigenous settlement of Yuendemu and Wolfe Creek Crater (on the Western Australian side of the border). It's a long haul and only occasionally beautiful; watch for the termite mounds, up to 800 per hectare in places. Crossing the Tanami does have huge cachet and is a journey to remember.

◉ Sights

The NT section is wide and usually well graded and starts 20km north of Alice Springs. The road is sealed to **Tilmouth Well** (☑ 08-8956 8777; www.tilmouthwell.com; powered/unpowered sites $40/30, cabins without bathroom $80; ✴ @ ✇) on the edge of Napperby Station, which bills itself as an oasis in the desert with a sparkling pool and lush, sprawling lawns.

The next fuel stop is at Yuendumu, the largest remote community in the region and home to the Warlpiri people who featured in the 2001 *Bush Mechanics* documentary. It's worth popping in to the **Warlukurlangu**

Art Centre (☑ 08-8956 4133; www.warlu.com; ⊙ 9am-4pm Mon-Fri), a locally owned venture specialising in acrylic paintings.

From here there is no fuel for another 600km until you cross the WA border and hit the community of **Billiluna** (08-9168 8076). Note, Rabbit Flat Roadhouse has closed permanently. Another 170km will have you resting your weary bones in Halls Creek.

ℹ Getting There & Away

In dry conditions it's possible to make it through the unsealed dust and corrugations in a well-prepared 2WD. Stay alert, as rollovers are common, and carry fuel, tyres, food and water.

ALICE SPRINGS

POP 28,667

Alice Springs wouldn't win a beauty contest, but there's a lot more going on here than first meets the eye. It has a lot to offer travellers, from the inspirational (excellent museums, a fine wildlife park and outstanding galleries of Indigenous art) to the practical (a wide range of accommodation, some good dining options and travel connections).

It serves as the gateway to some of central Australia's most stirring landscapes: Uluru-Kata Tjuta National Park is a relatively short four-hour drive away, while closer still, the ruggedly beautiful MacDonnell Ranges stretch east and west from the town centre; you don't have to venture far to find yourself among ochre-red gorges, pastel-hued hills and ghostly white gum trees.

Alice is also a key touchstone for understanding Aboriginal Australia in all its complexity (where else can you hear six uniquely Australian languages in the main street?) and present-day challenges.

◉ Sights

★**Alice Springs
Desert Park** WILDLIFE RESERVE
(☑ 08-8951 8788; www.alicespringsdesertpark.com. au; Larapinta Dr; adult/child $32/16, nocturnal tour adult/child $44/28; ⊙ 7.30am-6pm, last entry 4.30pm, nocturnal tour 7.30pm Mon-Fri) If you haven't glimpsed a spangled grunter or marbled velvet gecko on your travels, head to Desert Park where the creatures of central Australia are all on display in one place. The predominantly open-air exhibits recreate the animals' natural environments in a series of habitats: inland river, sand country and

woodland. It's an easy 2.5km cycle to the park. Pick up a free audioguide (available in various languages) or join one of the free ranger-led talks throughout the day.

Araluen Arts Centre   GALLERY
(Map p852; ✆08-8951 1122; www.araluenarts centre.nt.gov.au; cnr Larapinta Dr & Memorial Ave; ⊙10am-4pm) For a small town, Alice Springs has a thriving arts scene and the Araluen Arts Centre is at its heart. There is a 500-seat **theatre** (Map p852; ✆08-8951 1122; www.araluenartscentre.nt.gov.au; Larapinta Dr), and four galleries with a focus on art from the Central Desert region. The Albert Namatjira Gallery features works by the artist, who began painting watercolours in the 1930s at Hermannsburg. The exhibition draws comparisons between Namatjira and his initial mentor, Rex Battarbee, and other Hermannsburg School artists.

Olive Pink Botanic Garden   NATURE RESERVE
(Map p852; ✆08-8952 2154; www.opbg.com.au; Tuncks Rd; by donation; ⊙8am-6pm) A network of meandering trails leads through this lovely arid zone botanic garden, which was founded by the prominent anthropologist Olive Pink. The garden has more than 500 central Australian plant species and grows bush foods and medicinal plants like native lemon grass, quandong and bush passionfruit.

Royal Flying Doctor Service Base   MUSEUM
(RFDS; Map p856; ✆08-8958 8411; www.rfdsalice springs.com.au; Stuart Tce; adult/child $16/9; ⊙9am-5pm Mon-Sat, 1-5pm Sun, cafe 8.30am-4.30pm Mon-Sat) A $3 million facelift, which includes interactive information portals, has given this excellent museum a new lease of life. It is the home of the Royal Flying Doctor Service, whose dedicated health workers provide 24-hour emergency retrievals across an area of around 1.25 million sq km. State-of-the-art facilities includes a hologram of John Flynn (the RFDS founder) and a look at the operational control room, as well as some ancient medical gear and a flight simulator. Guided tours leave every half-hour, with the last at 4pm.

Araluen Cultural Precinct   CULTURAL CENTRE
(Map p852; ✆08-8951 1122; https://dtc.nt.gov. au/arts-and-museums/araluen-cultural-precinct; cnr Larapinta Dr & Memorial Ave; precinct pass adult/child $15/10) The Araluen Cultural Precinct is Alice Springs' cultural hub; leave at least an afternoon aside for exploration of its excellent sights. You can wander around freely outside, accessing the cemetery and grounds, but the 'precinct pass' provides entry to the exhibitions and displays for two days (with 14 days to use the pass).

Grave of John Flynn   CEMETERY
On the western edge of Alice on the road to the West MacDonnell Ranges, the grave of John Flynn is topped by a boulder donated by the Arrernte people (the original was a since-returned Devil's Marble). Opposite the car park is the start of the sealed cycling track to Simpsons Gap, a recommended three- to four-hour return ride.

Alice Springs Reptile Centre   ZOO
(Map p856; ✆08-8952 8900; www.reptilecentre. com.au; 9 Stuart Tce; adult/child $17/9; ⊙9.30am-5pm) It may be small, but this reptile centre packs a poisonous punch with its impressive collection of venomous snakes, thorny devils and bearded dragons. Inside the cave room are 11 species of NT geckos and outside there's Terry, a 3.3m saltwater croc, plus Bub, a magnificent perentie, Australia's largest lizard. The enthusiastic guides will happily plonk a python around your neck during the handling demonstrations (11am, 1pm and 3.30pm) or let you pet a blue-tongued lizard.

Anzac Hill   LANDMARK
(Map p852) For a tremendous view, particularly at sunrise and sunset, take a hike (use Lions Walk from Wills Tce) or a drive up to the top of Anzac Hill, known as Untyeyetweleye in Arrernte. From the war memorial there is a 365-degree view over the town down to Heavitree Gap and the MacDonnell Ranges.

Telegraph Station Historical Reserve   PARK
(Map p852; ✆08-8952 1013; https://nt.gov.au/ leisure/parks-reserves; adult/child $9/4.50; ⊙reserve 8am-9pm, building 9am-5pm) The old Telegraph Station, which used to relay messages between Darwin and Adelaide, offers a fascinating glimpse of the town's European beginnings. It's an easy 4km walk or cycle north from Todd Mall; follow the path on the riverbed's western side. Nearby is the original 'Alice' spring (Thereyurre to the Arrernte Aboriginal people), a semipermanent waterhole in the Todd River after which the town is named.

Museum of Central Australia   MUSEUM
(Map p852; ✆08-8951 1121; https://dtc.nt.gov. au/arts-and-museums/araluen-cultural-precinct/ museum-of-central-australia; cnr Larapinta Dr &

Alice Springs

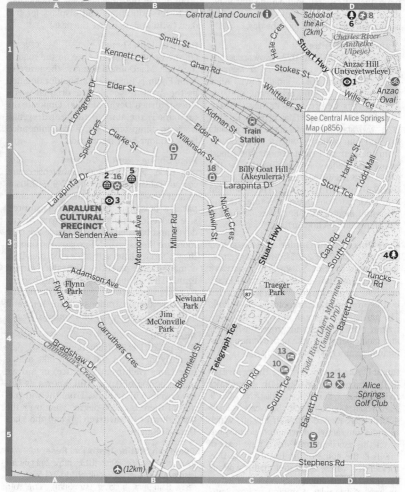

Memorial Ave; ⊙10am-5pm Mon-Fri) The natural history collection at this compact museum recalls the days of megafauna – when hippo-sized wombats and 3m-tall flightless birds roamed the land. In the geological displays are meteorite fragments and fossils. There's a free audio tour, narrated by a palaeontologist, which helps bring the exhibition to life.

Upstairs is the **Strehlow Research Centre** (Map p852; http://artsandmuseums.nt.gov.au/araluen-cultural-precinct; cnr Larapinta Dr & Memorial Ave) with a display on the work of Professor TGH Strehlow, a linguist, anthropologist and avid collector of Indigenous artefacts.

School of the Air   MUSEUM
(☑08-8951 6834; www.assoa.nt.edu.au; 80 Head St; adult/child $9/7; ⊙8.30am-4.30pm Mon-Sat, 1.30-4.30pm Sun) Started in 1951, this was the first school of its type in Australia, broadcasting lessons to children over an area of 1.3 million sq km. While transmissions were originally all done over high-frequency radio, satellite broadband internet and webcams now mean students can study in a virtual classroom. The guided tour of the centre includes a video. The school is about 3km north of the town centre.

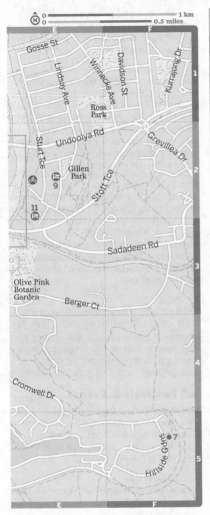

Alice Springs

◎ Sights
1 Anzac Hill	D1
2 Araluen Arts Centre	B2
3 Araluen Cultural Precinct	B3
Museum of Central Australia	(see 5)
4 Olive Pink Botanic Garden	D3
5 Strehlow Research Centre	B2
6 Telegraph Station Historical Reserve	D1

◉ Activities, Courses & Tours
7 Dreamtime Tours	F5
8 Outback Cycling	D1

⬤ Sleeping
9 Alice Lodge Backpackers	E2
10 Alice on Todd	C4
11 Alice's Secret Traveller's Inn	E2
12 Doubletree by Hilton	D4
13 Quest Alice Springs	C4

⊗ Eating
Bean Tree Cafe	(see 4)
14 Hanuman Restaurant	D4

⊙ Drinking & Nightlife
15 Juicy Rump	D5

⊛ Entertainment
16 Araluen Arts Centre	B2

⬚ Shopping
17 Ngurratjuta Iltja Ntjarra	B2
18 Tjanpi Desert Weavers	C2

Lone Dingo Adventure   HIKING
(Map p856; ☑08-8953 3866; www.lonedingo.com.au; cnr Todd Mall & Gregory Tce; ☺9am-5.30pm Mon-Fri, 9am-4pm Sat, 10am-3pm Sun) If you're keen to tackle part of the Larapinta Trail but don't have your own equipment, Lone Dingo Adventure can put together packs of camping and hiking gear for hire, as well as GPS and EPIRB (Emergency Positioning Indicating Radio Beacon) equipment.

Camel Riding

Pyndan Camel Tracks   CAMEL TOURS
(☑0416 170 164; www.cameltracks.com; Jane Rd; 1hr rides adult/child $70/40; ☺noon, 2.30pm & sunset) Local cameleer Marcus Williams offers one-hour rides at his base 17km southwest of Alice.

Cycling & Mountain Biking

Bikes are the perfect way to get around Alice Springs. There are cycle paths along the Todd River to the Telegraph Station, west to the Alice Springs Desert Park and further

🏃 Activities

Bushwalking

Experience the bush around Alice with several easy walks radiating from the Olive Pink Botanic Garden (p851) and the Telegraph Station (p851), which marks the start of the first stage of the Larapinta Trail.

Central Australian Bushwalkers   WALKING
(https://centralaustralianbushwalkers.com; walks $5) A group of local bushwalkers that schedules a wide variety of walks in the area, particularly the West MacDonnell Ranges, from March to November.

out to Simpsons Gap. For a map of cycling and walking paths go to the visitor information centre (p862).

Mountain-bike trails are easily accessed from town or meet up for a social sunset ride with the **Central Australian Rough Riders' Club** (208-8952 5800; www.central australianroughriders.asn.au; rides $5).

Outback Cycling CYCLING
(Map p852; 208-8952 3993; www.outbackcycling. com/alice-springs/; Alice Springs Telegraph Station; hire per day/week from $40/160) Bike hire with urban and mountain bikes available, as well as baskets, kids' bikes and baby seats. Also offer cycling tours of Alice and at Uluru.

Tours

★**Earth Sanctuary** TOURS
(208-8953 6161; www.earth-sanctuary.com.au; astronomy tour adult/child $36/25) See the stars of central Australia in the desert outside Alice with Earth Sanctuary's terrific nightly Astronomy Tours. Tours last for an hour and the informative guides have high-powered telescopes to get you up close and personal with the stars. You'll need to ring ahead – they'll know by 4pm if clear skies are forecast.

They also run food-themed events and tours like outback dinners and bush-tucker tours.

★**Wayoutback Desert Safaris** DRIVING
(208-8952 4324, 1300 551 510; www.wayoutback. com) Numerous small group, 4WD safari tours including the chance for remote desert camping near Uluru. There are also three-day safaris that traverse 4WD tracks to Uluru and Kings Canyon for $795 and five-day safaris that top it up with the West MacDonnell Ramges for $1195.

★**Trek Larapinta** HIKING
(21300 133 278; www.treklarapinta.com.au; 3/6 days from $1295/2695) ✐ Guided multiday walks along sections of the Larapinta Trail. Also runs volunteer projects involving trail maintenance, and bush regeneration on Aboriginal outstations.

Rainbow Valley Cultural Tours TOURS
(208-8956 0661; www.rainbowvalleyculturaltours. com; afternoon walking tours adult/child $90/50; ☉2pm-sunset Mon, Wed & Fri) Tour beautiful Rainbow Valley with a traditional owner and visit rock art sites not open to the general public. Tours can include overnight camping and dinner for an extra $20 per person. They also run birdwatching tours at the site upon request. You'll need your own transport to get there.

Dreamtime Tours CULTURAL
(Map p852; 208-8955 5095; 72 Hillside Garden; adult/child $85/42, self-drive $66/33; ☉8.30-11.30am) Runs the three-hour Dreamtime & Bushtucker Tour, where you meet Warlpiri Aboriginal people and learn a little about their traditions. As it caters for large bus groups it can be impersonal, but you can tag along with your own vehicle.

Emu Run Experience TOURS
(Map p856; 208-8953 7057, 1800 687 220; www. emurun.com.au; 72 Todd St) Operates day tours to Uluru ($226) and two-day tours to Uluru and Kings Canyon ($536). Prices include park entry fees, meals and accommodation. There are also recommended, small-group day tours through the West MacDonnell Ranges (from $119).

RT Tours TOURS
(208-8952 0327; www.rttoursaustralia.com; tours $160) Chef and Arrernte guide Bob Taylor runs a popular lunch and dinner tour at Simpsons Gap or the Telegraph Station Historical Reserve, where he whips up a bush-inspired meal. Other tours available.

Festivals & Events

Alice Springs Cup Carnival SPORTS
(www.alicespringsturfclub.org.au) On the first Monday in May, don a hat and gallop down to the Pioneer Park Racecourse for the main event of this five-day carnival.

Uluru Camel Cup SPORTS
(www.uluruoutbackfest.com.au) Over two days in May, Yulara hosts camel racing against a desert backdrop.

Finke Desert Race SPORTS
(www.finkedesertrace.com.au; ☉Jun) Motorcyclists and buggy drivers vie to take out the title of this crazy race 240km from Alice along the Old South Rd to Finke; the following day they race back again. Spectators camp along the road to cheer them on.

Alice Springs Beanie Festival ART
(www.beaniefest.orgThis four-day festival in June/July, held at the Araluen Art Centre, celebrates the humble beanie (knitted woollen hat), handmade by women throughout the Central Desert.

WORTH A TRIP

LARAPINTA TRAIL

The 230km Larapinta Trail extends along the backbone of the West MacDonnell Ranges and is one of Australia's great long-distance walks. The track is split into 12 stages of varying difficulty, stretching from the Telegraph Station in Alice Springs to the craggy 1380m summit of Mt Sonder. Each section takes one to two days to navigate and the trail passes many of the attractions in the West MacDonnell Ranges.

Section 1 Alice Springs Telegraph Station to Simpsons Gap (23.8km)

Section 2 Simpsons Gap to Jay Creek (24.5km)

Section 3 Jay Creek to Standley Chasm (13.6km)

Section 4 Standley Chasm to Birthday Waterhole (17.7km)

Section 5 Birthday Waterhole to Hugh Gorge (16km)

Section 6 Hugh Gorge to Ellery Creek (31.2km)

Section 7 Ellery Creek to Serpentine Gorge (13.8km)

Section 8 Serpentine Gorge to Serpentine Chalet Dam (13.4km)

Section 9 Serpentine Chalet Dam to Ormiston Gorge (28.6km)

Section 10 Ormiston Gorge to Finke River (9.9km)

Section 11 Finke River to Redbank Gorge (25.2km)

Section 12 Redbank Gorge to Mt Sonder (15.8km return)

Trail notes and maps are available from Parks & Wildlife. Walking groups of eight or more should contact **Parks & Wildlife** (p859) with a trip plan.

There's no public transport out to this area, but transfers can be arranged through the **Alice Wanderer** (☑1800 722 111, 08-8952 2111; www.alicewanderer.com.au); see the website for the various costs. For guided walks, including transport from Alice Springs, go through **Trek Larapinta** (p854).

★**Camel Cup**   SPORTS
(www.camelcup.com.au; ⊙mid-Jul) A carnival atmosphere prevails during the running of the Camel Cup at Blatherskite Park in mid-July.

★**Henley-on-Todd Regatta**   SPORTS
(www.henleyontodd.com.au; ⊙3rd Sat in Aug) These boat races in September on the dry bed of the Todd River are a typically Australian, light-hearted denial of reality. The boats are bottomless; the crews' legs stick through and they run down the course.

Alice Desert Festival   ART
(www.alicedesertfestival.com.au; ⊙late Aug) A cracker of a festival, including a circus program, music, film and comedy. A colourful parade down Todd Mall marks the beginning of the festival. It's held in September. The festival didn't run in 2016 but was expected to return in 2017.

Desert Song Festival   MUSIC
(☑0409 003 004; www.desertsong.com.au) Held over ten days in September with choirs from across central Australia and occasional international acts performing in venues across Alice.

🛏 Sleeping

Alice's Secret Traveller's Inn   HOSTEL $
(Map p852; ☑08-8952 8686; www.asecret.com.au; 6 Khalick St; dm $25-27, d from $65; ❄@🛖) Get the best accommodation deals here by booking your tour to Uluru through the inn. One of our favourite hostels in Alice, just across the Todd River from town, this place gets a big thumbs up for cleanliness and the helpful, friendly owner. Relax around the pool, blow on a didgeridoo or lie in a hammock in the garden.

Alice Lodge Backpackers   HOSTEL $
(Map p852; ☑08-8953 1975, 1800 351 925; www.alicelodge.com.au; 4 Mueller St; dm $27-30, d $74-105; ❄@🛜🛖) Alice Lodge gets great feedback from travellers, particularly for the friendly and helpful management. An easy 10-minute walk from town, this is a small, highly recommended, low-key hostel.

Central Alice Springs

MacDonnell Range Holiday Park

CARAVAN PARK $

(☑1800 808 373, 08-8952 6111; www.macrange. com.au; Palm Pl; powered/unpowered sites $48/42, cabins d $100-250; ❋@☎☎) Probably Alice's biggest and best kept, this caravan park has grassy sites and spotless amenities. Accommodation ranges from simple cabins with shared bathroom to self-contained, two-bedroom villas. Kids can cavort in the adventure playground, on the BMX track and on the basketball court.

Quest Alice Springs

APARTMENT $$

(Map p852; ☑08-8959 0000; www.questapart ments.com.au; 10 South Tce; d studio/1-bedroom apt from $135/196; P❋☎☎) These stylish modern apartments just across the road from the Todd River are an excellent choice. The Quest chain is reliably comfortable and well run and the quality of the rooms is well above most Alice choices.

Doubletree by Hilton

HOTEL $$

(Map p852; ☑1300 666 545, 08-8950 8000; www.doubletree3.hilton.com; Barrett Dr; d from $150, ste $175-350; ❋@☎☎) With its spacious resort-style facilities, this is widely considered one of Alice's top hotels. Choose from the garden-view rooms or the better mountain range–view rooms – they're decked out with floor-to-ceiling windows, cane furniture and pastel colours. There's a lovely pool and spa, well-equipped gym and sauna, tennis courts and a house peacock.

Alice on Todd

APARTMENT $$

(Map p852; ☑08-8953 8033; www.aliceontodd. com; cnr Strehlow St & South Tce; studio/1-bed apt $135/158; ❋@☎☎) This place has a great set-up, with friendly and helpful staff. It's an attractive and secure apartment complex on the banks of the Todd River offering one- and two-bedroom self-contained units with kitchen and lounge. There are also studios.

Central Alice Springs

The balconied units sleep up to six so they're a great option for families.

Chifley Alice Springs   HOTEL **$$**
(Map p856; ☑08-8951 4545; www.silverneedle hotels.com/chifley; 34 Stott Tce; standard/superior/deluxe d $139/155/179; ❄@�⊠) With a circle of double-storey buildings arranged around a swath of lawns and gum trees, the Chifley has a relaxed country club vibe. Go for the recently refurbished superior and deluxe accommodation overlooking the Todd River. There's an attractive pool area with a swim-up bar, plus a seafood restaurant.

Bond Springs Outback Retreat   B&B **$$**
(☑08-8952 9888; www.outbackretreat.com.au; cottage d $231; ❄⊠) Experience a taste of outback station life at this retreat, about 25km north of town. The private self-contained cottage is a refurbished stockman's quarters. A full breakfast is included but other meals are self-catering. Have a game of tennis or mooch around the enormous property including the original station school, which operated through the School of the Air.

✖ Eating

★Piccolo's   CAFE **$**
(Map p856; ☑08-8953 1936; Shop 1, Cinema Complex 11, Todd Mall; breakfast from $12; ☺7am-3pm Mon-Fri, 7am-2pm Sat, 8am-noon Sun) This modern cafe is popular with locals for its excellent food and probably Alice's best coffee. Try the toasties or one of the breakfast rolls.

★Montes   MODERN AUSTRALIAN **$$**
(Map p856; ☑08-8952 4336; www.montes.net.au; cnr Stott Tce & Todd St; mains $13-26; ☺11am-late; �) Travelling circus meets outback

homestead. It's family friendly with a play area for kids, and the food ranges from gourmet burgers, pizzas and tapas to curries and seafood. Sit in the leafy beer garden (with a range of beers) or intimate booth seating. Patio heaters keep patrons warm on cool desert nights.

★Hanuman Restaurant   THAI **$$**
(Map p852; ☑08-8953 7188; www.hanuman.com.au/alice-springs; Doubletree by Hilton, 82 Barrett Dr; mains $25-36; ☺noon-10pm Mon-Fri, 6pm-midnight Sat, 6-10pm Sun; �) You won't believe you're in the outback when you try the incredible Thai- and Indian-influenced cuisine at this stylish restaurant. The delicate Thai entrees are a real triumph as are the seafood dishes, particularly the Hanuman prawns. Although the menu is ostensibly Thai, there are enough Indian dishes to satisfy a curry craving.

Epilogue Lounge   TAPAS **$$**
(Map p856; ☑08-8953 4206; www.facebook.com/epiloguelounge/; 58 Todd Mall; mains $16-25; ☺8am-11.30pm Wed-Sat, 8am-3pm Sun & Mon) This urban, retro delight is definitely the coolest place to hang in town. With a decent wine list, food served all day and service with a smile, it is a real Alice Springs standout. Expect dishes like halloumi burgers or steak sandwiches and a cooling breeze under the shade cover. They also have live music some nights.

Red Dog Cafe   CAFE **$$**
(Map p856; ☑08-8953 1353; 64 Todd Mall; breakfast $5-17, mains $15-18.50; ☺7am-5pm) With tables and chairs strewn out over Todd Mall, this place is good for people watching,

hearty breakfasts and fresh, well-brewed coffee. Lunch is all about burgers, with a few veggie options thrown in. We enjoyed the kangaroo salad.

Bean Tree Cafe　　　　　CAFE **$$**
(Map p852; ☑08-8952 0190; www.opbg.com.au/bean-tree-cafe; Olive Pink Botanic Garden, Tuncks Rd; breakfast $7-18, mains $15-19; ⊗8am-4pm) Breakfast with the birds at this superb outdoor cafe tucked away in the Olive Pink Botanic Garden. It's a relaxing place to sit and the wholesome, homestyle dishes, such as the roo burger or kangaroo salad in a smoked native pepperberry sauce, are well worth the wait.

Overlanders Steakhouse　　　　STEAK **$$$**
(Map p856; ☑08-8952 2159; 72 Hartley St; mains $32-55; ⊗6pm-late) The place for steaks, big succulent cuts of beef – and crocodile, camel, kangaroo or emu. Amid the cattle station decor you can try Stuart's Tucker Bag: a combo of croc, kangaroo, emu and camel.

The 'Drovers Blowout' set menu will satisfy your need to eat as many local animalsas possible in one go, it features all of the meats and you'll never want to eat meat again.

Red Ochre Grill　　MODERN AUSTRALIAN **$$$**
(Map p856; ☑08-8952 9614; www.alicesprings aurora.com.au/red-ochre-grill; Todd Mall; mains $18.50-39; ⊗10am-9pm) Offering innovative fusion dishes with a focus on outback cuisine, the menu here usually features tradiitional meats plus locally bred proteins, such as kangaroo and emu, matched with native herbs such as lemon myrtle, pepperberries and bush tomatoes. Keep an eye out for special deals such as tapas with a bottle of wine or discounts for an early-bird dinner.

🍷 Drinking & Nightlife

Rock　　　　　　　BAR
(Map p856; ☑08-8953 8280; 78 Todd St; ⊗noon-2am) There is an excellent beer selection at this Alice classic. It's blessed with a beer garden and is ideal for a cold drink by the windows that open onto the street. The Rock pulls in a good mix of locals and tourists, although it can get seedy in the evenings.

Juicy Rump　　　　　　BAR
(Map p852; 93 Barrett Dr; ⊗10am-late) Not as bad as the name suggests but still an acquired taste, this is the late-night favourite if you want to have a dance to cheesy R&B or watch a big sporting event on the town's

largest plasma screen. Also has a deck with a view to the ranges, lovely for sunset drinks.

☆ Entertainment

★ Sounds of Starlight Theatre　　LIVE MUSIC
(Map p856; ☑08-8953 0826; www.soundsof starlight.com; 40 Todd Mall; adult/concession/family $30/25/90; ⊗8pm Tue, Fri & Sat) This atmospheric 1½-hour musical performance evoking the spirit of the outback with didgeridoos, drums and keyboards, plus wonderful photography and lighting, is an Alice institution. Musician Andrew Langford also runs free didgeridoo lessons (11am Monday to Friday). You can add dinner to the mix or just see the show.

🔒 Shopping

Alice is the centre for Aboriginal arts from all over central Australia. The places owned and run by community art centres ensure that a better slice of the proceeds goes to the artist and artist's community. Look for the black-over-red Indigenous Art Code (www.indigenousartcode.org) displayed by dealers dedicated to fair and transparent dealings with artists.

★ Papunya Tula Artists　　　　ART
(Map p856; ☑08-8952 4731; www.papunyatula.com.au; Todd Mall; ⊗9am-5pm Mon-Fri, 10am-2pm Sat) This stunning gallery showcases artworks from the Western Desert communities of Papunya, Kintore and Kiwikurra – even if you're not buying, it's worth stopping by to see the magnificent collection.

Talapi　　　　　　　ART
(Map p856; ☑08-8953 6389; www.talapi.com.au; 45 Todd Mall; ⊗9am-6pm Mon-Fri, 10am-5pm Sat) Talapi is a beautiful space in the heart of Alice Springs, exhibiting and promoting Central Desert Indigenous art. It sources its artworks directly from Aboriginal-owned art centres and is a member of the Indigenous Art Code. Drop in to ask about upcoming exhibitions.

Mbantua Gallery　　　　　ART
(Map p856; ☑08-8952 5571; www.mbantua.com.au; 64 Todd Mall; ⊗9am-6pm Mon-Fri, 9am-3pm Sat, 10am-2pm Sun) This privately owned gallery includes extensive exhibits of works from the renowned Utopia region, as well as watercolour landscapes from the Namatjira school. Collectors should ask to see their collection of bark paintings, old boomerangs and high-end works out the back.

Tjanpi Desert Weavers ART
(Map p852; ☑ 08-8958 2377; www.tjanpi.com.au; 3 Wilkinson St; ⊙ 10am-4pm Mon-Fri) This small enterprise employs and supports Central Desert weavers from 18 remote communities. The shop is well worth a visit to see the magnificent woven baskets and quirky sculptures created from grasses collected locally.

Ngurratjuta Iltja Ntjarra ART
(Map p852; ☑ 08-8951 1953; www.ngurart.com. au; 29 Wilkinson St; ⊙ 9am-3.30pm Mon-Fri) The 'many hands' art centre is a small gallery and studio for visiting artists from all over central Australia. Watercolour and dot paintings are reasonably priced and you buy directly from the artists. You can see artists at work from 10am to 3pm Monday to Thursday.

Red Kangaroo Books BOOKS
(Map p856; ☑ 08-8953 2137; www.redkangaroo books.com; 79 Todd Mall; ⊙ 9am-5pm Mon-Fri, 9am-3pm Sat & Sun) Excellent bookshop specialising in central Australian titles: history, art, travel, novels, guidebooks and more. It also has small but excellent wildlife section.

Jila Arts ART
(Map p856; ☑ 08-8953 3005; www.jilaarts.com. au; 63 Todd Mall; ⊙ 9am-5pm Mon-Fri, 9am-3pm Sat, 10am-2pm Sun) One of the better galleries selling original works; a focus on contemporary paintings from the Western Desert.

ⓘ Information

DANGERS & ANNOYANCES
Avoid walking alone at night anywhere in town. Catch a taxi back to your accommodation if you're out late.

MEDICAL SERVICES
Alice Springs Hospital (☑ 08-8951 7777; Gap Rd)
Alice Springs Pharmacy (☑ 08-8952 1554; shop 19, Yeperenye Shopping Centre, 36 Hartley St; ⊙ 8.30am-7.30pm)
Ambulance (☑ 000)

MONEY
Major banks with ATMs, such as ANZ, Commonwealth, National Australia and Westpac, are located in and around Todd Mall in the town centre.

POST
Main Post Office (Map p856; ☑ 13 13 18; https://auspost.com.au; 31-33 Hartley St; ⊙ 8.15am-5pm Mon-Fri)

TOURIST INFORMATION
Central Land Council (Map p852; ☑ 08-8951 6211; www.clc.org.au; PO Box 3321, 27 Stuart Hwy, Alice Springs; ⊙ 8.30am-noon & 2-4pm) For Aboriginal land permits and transit permits.
Parks & Wildlife (☑ 08-8951 8250, 08-8999 4555; www.nt.gov.au/leisure/parks-reserves; Arid Zone Research Institute, off Stuart Hwy) Information on national parks and for the Larapinta Trail.
Tourism Central Australia Visitor Information Centre (p862) This helpful centre can load you up with stacks of brochures and the free visitors guide. Weather forecasts and road conditions are posted on the wall. National parks information is also available. Ask about the unlimited kilometre deals if you are thinking of renting a car.
Wildcare Inc Alice Springs (☑ 0419 221 128; www.fauna.org.au) The people to call if you find injured wildlife

ⓘ Getting There & Away

AIR
Alice Springs is well connected, with **Qantas** (☑ 13 13 13, 08-8950 5211; www.qantas.com.au) and **Virgin Australia** (☑ 13 67 89; www.virgin australia.com) operating regular flights to/from capital cities. Airline representatives are based at Alice Springs airport.

BUS
Greyhound Australia (Map p856; ☑ 1300 473 946; www.greyhound.com.au; Shop 3, 113 Todd St) has regular services from Alice Springs (check the website for timetables and discounted fares). Buses arrive at, and depart from, the Greyhound office in Todd St. The following are Flexi Fares:

DESTINATION	ONE-WAY FARE ($)	DURATION (HR)
Adelaide	155	20
Coober Pedy	145	8
Darwin	185	22
Katherine	175	16½
Tennant Creek	115	6

Emu Run (p854) runs cheap daily connections between Alice Springs and Yulara (one way $120). **Gray Line** (Map p856; ☑ 1300 858 687; www.grayline.com; Capricornia Centre 9, Gregory Tce) also runs between Alice Springs and Yulara (one way $120).

Backpacker buses roam to and from Alice providing a party atmosphere and a chance to see some of the sights along the way. **Groovy Grape Getaways Australia** (☑ 1800 661 177; www.groovygrape.com.au) plies the route from

Indigenous Art & Culture

The intricate and mesmerising art, stories and dances of Australia's Aboriginal peoples resonate with a deep association with the land itself. The Top End and the outback are the best places to engage with Aboriginal culture: take a cultural tour, hear spoken stories of the Dreaming, see galleries of ancient rock art or check out some contemporary canvasses in modern acrylics.

Cultural Tours

There's a proliferation of Indigenous-owned and -operated cultural tours across outback Australia – a chance to learn about the outback from the people who know it best. Sign up for a cultural tour in Darwin, Kakadu National Park and Arnhem Land in the tropical north; and Alice Springs and Uluru-Kata Tjuta National Park in the Red Centre.

Rock Art

Evidence of Australia's ancient Indigenous culture can be found at the outdoor rock-art sites scattered across the outback. Highlights include the 5000-plus sites in Kakadu National Park that document a timeline of spirits from the Dreaming, extinct fauna, and remarkable 'contact art', portraying the interaction between Indigenous Australians, Macassan fishermen and early European settlers. Standout Kakadu sites include Ubirr and Nourlangie. More rock art can easily be seen at Nitmiluk (Katherine

1. Aboriginal dancers at Barunga Festival (p836)

2. Mbantua Gallery (p858)

3. Detail of artwork on a didgeridoo

Gorge) and Keep River National Parks, the MacDonnell Ranges near Alice, and Uluru (Ayers Rock).

Contemporary Indigenous Art

Contemporary Australian Indigenous art – the lion's share of which is produced in outback communities – has soared to global heights of late. Traditional methods and spiritual significance are fastidiously maintained, but often find a counterpart in Western materials – the results can be wildly original interpretations of traditional stories and ceremonial designs. Dot paintings (acrylic on canvas) are the most recognisable form, but you may also see synthetic polymer paintings, weavings, bark paintings, weapons, boomerangs and sculptures.

Indigenous Festivals

For an unforgettable Aboriginal cultural experience, time your outback visit to coincide with a traditional Indigenous festival. These celebrations offer visitors a look at Aboriginal culture in action. Witnessing a timeless dance and feeling the primal beats is a journey beyond time and place. The Northern Territory plays host to several Indigenous festivals and events, including the popular Walking With Spirits in Beswick, Barunga Festival near Katherine, Merrepen Arts Festival at Daly River, and Arnhem Land's Stone Country Festival.

Alice to Adelaide on a seven-day, backpacker camping jaunt for $975.

CAR & MOTORCYCLE

Alice Springs is a long way from everywhere. It's 1180km to Mt Isa in Queensland, 1490km to Darwin and 441km (4½ hours) to Yulara (for Uluru). Although the roads to the north and south are sealed and in good condition, these are still outback roads and it's wise to have your vehicle well prepared, particularly as you won't get a mobile phone signal outside Alice or Yulara. Carry plenty of drinking water and emergency food at all times.

All the major car-hire companies have offices in Alice Springs and many have counters at the airport. Prices drop by about 20% between November and April, but rentals don't come cheap, as most firms offer only 100km free per day, which won't get you far. Talk to the **Tourism Central Australia Visitor Information Centre** (Map p856; ☑1800 645 199, 08-8952 5800; www.discovercentralaustralia.com; cnr Todd Mall & Parsons St; ☺8.30am-5pm Mon-Fri, 9.30am-4pm Sat & Sun; ☎) about its unlimited kilometres deal before you book. A conventional (2WD) vehicle will get you to most sights in the MacDonnell Ranges and out to Uluru and Kings Canyon via sealed roads. If you want to go further afield, say to Chambers Pillar, Finke Gorge or even the Mereenie Loop Rd, a 4WD is essential.

TRAIN

A classic way to enter or leave the NT is by the *Ghan*, which can be booked through **Great Southern Rail** (☑13 21 47; www.greatsouthern rail.com.au). Discounted fares are sometimes offered, especially in the low season (February to June). Bookings are essential.

The train station is at the end of George Cres off Larapinta Dr.

ℹ Getting Around

BUS

The public bus service, **Asbus** (☑08-8944 2444), departs from outside the Yeperenye Shopping Centre. Buses run about every 1½ hours Monday to Friday and Saturday morning. There are three routes of interest to travellers: 400/401 has a detour to the cultural precinct, 100/101 passes the School of the Air, and 300/301 passes many southern hotels and caravan parks along Gap Rd and Palm Circuit. The visitor information centre has timetables.

TAXI

Taxis congregate near the visitor information centre. To book one, call 13 10 08 or 08-8952 1877.

MACDONNELL RANGES

The beautiful, weather-beaten MacDonnell Ranges, stretching 400km across the desert, are a hidden world of spectacular gorges, rare wildlife and poignant Aboriginal heritage all within a day from Alice.

East MacDonnell Ranges

Although overshadowed by the more popular West Macs, the East MacDonnell Ranges are extremely picturesque and, with fewer visitors, can be a more enjoyable outback experience. With gorges, some stunning scenery (especially around sunset or sunrise) and the old gold-mining ruins of Arltunga, there's enough to fill a day trip from Alice.

◉ Sights

★ Arltunga Historical Reserve   HISTORIC SITE

At the eastern end of the MacDonnell Ranges, 110km east of Alice Springs, the old gold-mining ghost town of Arltunga (33km on an unsealed road from the Ross Hwy) has lonely ruins and a wonderful end-of-the-road feel. Old buildings, a couple of cemeteries and the many deserted mine sites in this parched landscape give visitors an idea of what life was like for the miners.

★ Trephina Gorge Nature Park   NATURE RESERVE

If you only have time for a couple of stops in the East MacDonnell Ranges, make Trephina Gorge Nature Park (75km from Alice) one of them. The play between the pale river beds, the red and purple gorge walls, the white tree trunks, the eucalyptus-green foliage and the blue sky is spectacular. Depending on the time of year, you'll also find deep swimming holes and abundant wildlife. There's a **rangers station** (☑08-8956 9765) and **camping grounds** (Trephina Gorge Nature Park; adult/child $3.30/1.65) with barbecues, water and toilets.

N'dhala Gorge Nature Park   NATURE RESERVE

Just southwest of the Ross River Resort, a strictly 4WD-only track leads 11km south to N'Dhala Gorge. More than 5900 ancient Aboriginal rock carvings (some date back 10,000 years) and some rare endemic plants decorate a deep, narrow gorge, although the art isn't easy to spot. There's a small, exposed **camping ground** (N'Dhala Gorge; adult/child $3.30/1.65) without reliable water. From the car park, there's a 1.5km (one hour) return walk to the gorge with some signposts to rock art walls.

Ruby Gap Nature Park NATURE RESERVE

This remote park rewards visitors with wild and beautiful scenery. The sandy bed of the Hale River sparkles with thousands of tiny garnets. It's an evocative place and is well worth the considerable effort required to reach it – by high-clearance 4WD. **Camping** (adult/child $3.30/1.65) is permitted anywhere along the river; make sure to BYO drinking water and a camp cooker. Allow two hours each way for the 44km trip from Arltunga.

Emily & Jessie Gaps
Nature Park NATURE RESERVE

Both of these gaps in the rock wall of the East MacDonnells are associated with the Eastern Arrernte Caterpillar Dreaming trail. Emily Gap, 16km out of Alice, has stylised rock paintings and a fairly deep waterhole in the narrow gorge. The gap is a sacred site with some well-preserved paintings on the eastern wall, although some of the paintings have been vandalised. Jessie Gap, 8km further on, is usually much quieter. Both sites have toilets, but camping is not permitted.

Corroboree Rock
Conservation Reserve HISTORIC SITE

Corroboree Rock, 51km from Alice Springs, is one of many strangely shaped dolomite outcrops scattered over the valley floor. Despite the name, it's doubtful the rock was ever used as a corroboree area, but it is associated with the Perentie Dreaming trail. The perentie lizard, Australia's largest, grows in excess of 2.5m and takes refuge within the area's rock falls. There's a short walking track (15 minutes) around the rock.

🛏 Sleeping

Most people visit on a day trip from Alice, but there are basic campsites at Arltunga, Trephina Gorge, John Hayes Rockhole, Arltunga, Ruby Gap Nature Park and N'Dhala Gorge, as well as two fine options, one at Ross River, the other along the Arltunga Tourist Drive.

Arltunga Bush Hotel CAMPGROUND $

(☑ 08-8956 9797; sites per person $5, dm $10, family cottage $50; ☺ Mar-Nov) Arltunga Bush Hotel, close to the entrance of the Arltunga Historical Reserve, has a camping ground with showers, toilets, barbecue pits and

> ### CATERPILLAR DREAMING
>
> Known to the Arrernte as Anthwerrke, Emily Gap in the East MacDonnell Ranges is one of the most important Aboriginal sites in the Alice Springs area; it was from here that the caterpillar ancestral beings of Mparntwe originated before crawling across the landscape to create the topographical features that exist today.

picnic tables. Fees are collected in the late afternoon. It's a lovely spot with plenty of shade and nicely spaced sites.

★ Hale River Homestead
at Old Ambalindum FARMSTAY $$

(☑ 08-8956 9993; www.haleriverhomestead.com.au; powered/unpowered sites from $35/30, dm $60-80, d cottage/homestead $190/240; ❄ ☀) This remote spot run by NT veterans Sean and Lynne offers a great range of accommodation including a nicely renovated homestead, a cottage sleeping five people, simple bunkhouses and lovely campsites, all on a working cattle station. Bookings are essential and ring ahead to ask whether you need to bring your own food.

It's on the Arltunga Tourist Dr, which runs from Arltunga to the Stuart Hwy, about 50km north of Alice Springs.

Ross River Resort CARAVAN PARK $$

(☑ 08-8956 9711; www.rossriverresort.com.au; Ross Highway; powered/unpowered sites $33/25, bunkhouse with/without linen $35/30, d/f cabin $135/160; ❄ ☎ ☀) Nine kilometres along the continuation of the Ross Hwy past the Arltunga turn-off (coming from Alice Springs) is the secluded Ross River Resort. Built around a historic stone homestead, timber cabins encircle a swimming pool.

There's a store with fuel and it's worth stopping to check out the old homestead and maybe grab lunch (mains $17 to $25) or a beer in the Stockman's Bar. Ring first to check that the restaurant is open.

ℹ Getting There & Away

The sealed Ross Hwy runs 100km along the Ranges. Arltunga is 33km off the Ross Hwy along an unsealed road that is usually OK for 2WD vehicles; the first 13km off the Ross Hwy require careful driving as the road bucks and weaves through the hills, but the final 20km into Arltunga cross more open floodplains.

You'll need a 4WD to access John Hayes Rockhole (in Trephina Gorge Nature Park), N'Dhala Gorge and Ruby Gap.

From Arltunga it's possible to loop back to Alice along the Arltunga Tourist Dr, which pops out at the Stuart Hwy about 50km north of town.

West MacDonnell Ranges

With their stunning beauty and rich diversity of plants and animals, the West MacDonnell Ranges are not to be missed. Their easy access by conventional vehicle makes them especially popular with day-trippers. Although it is possible to visit all of the sights in the West MacDonnells in one very long day, we recommend spreading it out over two, allowing you time to linger at special places like Simpsons Gap, Ormiston Gorge, Hermannsburg and Palm Valley. Most sites in the West MacDonnell Ranges lie within the Tjoritja/West MacDonnell National Park, except for Standley Chasm, which is privately owned.

Sights

If you choose Namatjira Dr, one of your first stops might be **Ellery Creek Big Hole**, 91km from Alice Springs and with a large permanent waterhole – a popular place for a swim on a hot day (the water is usually freezing). It's good for wildlife and birdwatching, too. About 11km further west along Namatjira Dr, a gravel track leads to narrow, ochre-red

Serpentine Gorge, which has a lovely waterhole blocking the entrance and a lookout at the end of a short, steep track (30 minutes return), where you can view ancient cycads.

The **Ochre Pits** line a dry creek bed 11km west of Serpentine and were a source of pigment for Aboriginal people. The various coloured ochres – mainly yellow, white and red-brown – are weathered limestone, with iron-oxide creating the colours.

The car park for the majestic **Ormiston Gorge** is 25km beyond the Ochre Pits. It's the most impressive chasm in the West MacDonnells. There's a waterhole shaded with ghost gums, and the gorge curls around to the enclosed Ormiston Pound. It's a haven for wildlife (dingo, red kangaroo and euro are all possible, and look for the fat-tailed false antechinus near sunrise) and birds (western bowerbird, rufous-crowned emu-wren and spinifex pigeon among others). The only drawback? It's also the busiest site along Namatjira Dr. There are some excellent walking tracks – take one and you'll soon leave the crowds behind – including the Ghost Gum Lookout (20 minutes), which affords brilliant views down the gorge, and the excellent, circuitous Pound Walk (three hours, 7.5km). There's a small **visitor centre** (☑08-8956 7799; ⊙10am-4pm), a kiosk (open 10am to 4pm) and camping ground.

About 2km further is the turn-off to **Glen Helen Gorge**, where the Finke River cuts through the MacDonnells. Only 1km past Glen Helen is a good **lookout** over Mt Sonder; sunrise and sunset here are particularly impressive.

If you continue northwest for 25km you'll reach the turn-off (4WD only) to multi-hued, cathedral-like **Redbank Gorge**. This permanent waterhole runs for kilometres through the labyrinthine gorge and makes for an incredible swimming and scrambling adventure on a hot day. Namatjira Dr then heads south and is sealed as far as Tylers Pass Lookout.

Tylers Pass Lookout   VIEWPOINT
Tylers Pass Lookout provides a dramatic view of **Tnorala (Grosse Bluff)**, the legacy of an earth-shattering comet impact. It's a 30- to 40-minute drive beyond Glen Helen Gorge.

Standley Chasm   GORGE
(☑08-8956 7440; www.standleychasm.com.au; adult/concession/family $12/10/30; ⊙8am-5pm, last chasm entry 4:30pm) Standley Chasm is

---

WEST MACDONNELL WILDLIFE

The West MacDonnell Ranges offer some fine possibilities when it comes to native Australian wildlife. The main species to watch out for include:

Black-footed rock wallaby Most easily seen at Simpsons Gap.

Common brushtail possum Any riverine woodland across the range.

Dingo Possible at Ormiston Gorge or Ellery Creek Big Hole.

Euro or common wallaroo Simpsons Gap or Ormiston Gorge.

Fat-tailed false Antechinus Small, rodent-like marsupial sometimes seen early morning around Ormiston Gorge.

Red kangaroo Around Simpsons Gap, along Larapinta Dr around sunset and Ormiston Gorge.

owned and run by the local Iwupataka community. The narrowest of the West Macdonnell defiles, Standley Chasm is a stunning spot with sheer rock walls rising 80m from the canyon floor. A rocky path into the gorge (20 minutes, 1.2km) follows a creek bed lined with ghost gums and cycads. There's a kiosk, camping (per person $18.50; ☎), picnic facilities and toilets.

Although it may not look like there's a lot of water, this is one of eight permanent water sources in the ranges; note the many different rock types along the chasm floor, all carried here by water. Hikes radiate out from here, but the far end of the chasm is closed off as an Aboriginal sacred site lies beyond.

From 9am to 1pm on Thursdays (and at other times by appointment), you can take the Angkerle Cultural Experience (☑08-8956 7440; www.standleychasm.com.au; per person $85; ☺9am-1pm Thu), which includes a presentation about local cultural and natural history, an art workshop, morning tea and buffet lunch.

🛏 Sleeping

Ormiston Gorge
Campground CAMPGROUND $
(☑08-8954 6198; Ormiston Gorge; adult/child/family $10/5/25) Has showers, toilets, gas barbecues and picnic tables and is just far enough from the day visitor car park to offer a little privacy; we wouldn't leave anything of value lying around, however.

Glen Helen Resort HOTEL $
(☑08-8956 7489; www.glenhelen.com.au; Namatjira Dr; powered/unpowered sites $30/24, dm $35, r $160-175; ❋ ☎ ⊛) At the western edge of the West MacDonnell National Park is the popular Glen Helen Resort, which has an idyllic back verandah slammed up against the red ochre cliffs of the spectacular gorge. There's a busy restaurant-pub serving hearty meals (mains $29 to $42) and live music on the weekend. There are also 4WD tours available and helicopter flights (from $175).

Ellery Creek Campground CAMPGROUND $
(per adult/child $5/1.50) These simple camp sites in the Ellery Creek car park are not as good as those at Ormiston Gorge, but are otherwise fine.

❶ Getting There & Away

Heading west from Alice, Namatjira Dr turns northwest off Larapinta Dr 6km beyond Standley

---

RED CENTRE WAY & MEREENIE LOOP

The Red Centre Way is the 'back road' from Alice Springs to Uluru. It incorporates part of the West MacDonnell Ranges, an 'inner loop' comprising Namatjira and Larapinta Drs, plus the rugged Mereenie Loop Rd, the short cut to Kings Canyon. This dusty, heavily corrugated road is not to be taken lightly and hire-car companies won't permit their 2WDs to be driven on it.

To travel along this route, which passes through Aboriginal land, you need a Mereenie Tour Pass ($5), which is valid for one day and includes a booklet with details about the local Aboriginal culture and a route map. The pass is issued on the spot (usually only on the day of travel) at the visitor information centre in Alice Springs, Glen Helen Resort, Kings Canyon Resort and Hermannsburg service station.

Chasm and is sealed all the way to Tylers Pass. Beyond Tylers Pass, there is a 43km stretch of unsealed road – reports of this section being sealed (and hence closing the loop between Larapinta and Namatjira Drs) often circulate but funding was frozen at the time of our visit.

Hermannsburg

POP 624
The Aboriginal community of Hermannsburg (Ntaria), about 125km from Alice Springs, is famous as the one-time home of artist Albert Namatjira and as the site of the Hermannsburg Mission. It's an appealingly rundown and sleepy place which belies its significance as one of the most important Aboriginal communities in the area.

◉ Sights

Hermannsburg Mission HISTORIC SITE
(☑08-8956 7402; www.hermannsburg.com.au; adult/child $10/5; ☺9am-5pm Mon-Sat, 10.30am-5pm Sun) The whitewashed walls of the old mission are shaded by tall river gums and date palms. This fascinating monument to theNT's early Lutheran missionaries includes a school building, a church and various outbuildings. The 'Manse' houses an art gallery and a history of the life and times of Albert Namatjira (a one-time resident) as well as work of 39 Hermannsburg artists.

WORTH A TRIP

WALLACE ROCKHOLE

You'll be virtually guaranteed seclusion at the **Wallace Rockhole Tourist Park** (📞 08-8956 7993; www.wallacerock holetours.com.au; powered/unpowered sites $28/22, cabins $120; ❄), situated at the end of an 18km dirt road branching off Larapinta Dr. The park has a camping area with good facilities. Tours here include a 1½-hour rock art and bush medicine tour (adult/child $10/8) with billy tea and damper (advance booking essential).

✖ Eating

Kata-Anga Tea Rooms   CAFE $
(mains $8-15; ⊙9am-4pm) Within Hermannsburg Mission, Kata-Anga Tea Rooms, in the old missionary house, serves Devonshire teas, sandwiches and strudel, and displays historic photographs, plus a good range of traditional and watercolour paintings. There are ceramic works by the Hermannsburg potters on display and available for sale.

❶ Getting There & Away

There's no public transport to/from Hermannsburg.

Finke Gorge National Park

With its primordial landscape, the Finke Gorge National Park, south of Hermannsburg, is one of central Australia's premier wilderness reserves. It's hard going getting here and even harder getting around, but that also tends to keep the numbers of visitors down, which only adds to the park's already considerable appeal.

◉ Sights

★**Palm Valley**   GORGE
Top attraction Palm Valley is famous for its red cabbage palms (up to 12,000 of them!), which exist nowhere else in the world. These relics from prehistoric times give the valley a picture-book oasis feel. In Palm Valley, tracks include **Arankaia walk** (2km loop, one hour), which traverses the valley, returning via the sandstone plateau; the **Mpulungkinya track** (5km loop, two hours) through the gorge before joining the Arankaia walk; and the **Mpaara track** (5km loop, two hours).

🛏 Sleeping

There's a **camping ground** (adult/child $6.60/3.30) with basic facilities inside the national park.

❶ Getting There & Away

Access to the park follows the sandy bed of the Finke River and rocky tracks, so a high-clearance 4WD is essential. If you don't have one, several tour operators go to Palm Valley from Alice Springs. The turn-off to Palm Valley starts about 1km west of the Hermannsburg turn-off on Larapinta Dr.

NORTHERN TERRITORY'S FAR SOUTH

Most travellers clocking long desert kilometres along the Stuart and Lasseter Hwys often do so oblivious to the fact that some fascinating and dramatic sites lie off in the hinterland. You'd need a few days to see all of them, but possibilities for those with limited time include Rainbow Valley Conservation Reserve, Henbury Meteorite Craters, the views of Mt Connor and Australia's geographic centre.

Old South Road

The Old South Road, which runs close to the old *Ghan* railway line, is a pretty rough 4WD track that takes you about as far off the beaten track as you go this close to Alice Springs. Attractions, beyond that sense of being somewhere deliciously remote, are few, but you may end up at Australia's geographical centre if you go far enough.

◉ Sights

It's only 39km from Alice Springs to **Ewaninga**, where prehistoric Aboriginal petroglyphs are carved into sandstone. The rock carvings found here and at N'Dhala Gorge are thought to have been made by Aboriginal people who lived here before those currently in the region, between 1000 and 5000 years ago.

The eerie, sandstone **Chambers Pillar**, southwest of Maryvale Station, towers 50m above the surrounding plain and is carved with the names and visit dates of early explorers – and, unfortunately, some much less worthy modern-day graffiti. To the Aboriginal people of the area, Chambers Pillar is the remains of Itirkawara, a powerful gecko ancestor. Most photogenic at sunset and sunrise, it's best to stay overnight at the **camping ground** (adult/child $3.30/1.65). It's 160km from Alice Springs and a 4WD is required for the last 44km from the turn-off at Maryvale Station.

Back on the main track south, you eventually arrive at **Finke** (Aputula), a small Aboriginal community 230km from Alice Springs. When the old *Ghan* was running, Finke was a thriving town; these days it seems to have drifted into a permanent torpor, except when the Finke Desert Race (p854) is staged. Fuel and basic supplies are available here at Aputula Store.

Just 21km west of Finke, and 12km north of the road along a signposted track, is the **Lambert Centre**. The point marks Australia's geographical centre and features a 5m-high version of the flagpole found on top of Parliament House in Canberra.

✕ Eating

Basic supplies are available at the **Aputula Store** (☑ 08-8956 0968; ⊙ 9am-noon & 2-4pm Mon-Fri, 9am-noon Sat) in Finke, but we strongly recommend that you carry with you everything you're likely to need, as supplies sometimes run low and prices are high.

❶ Getting There & Away

You'll need a fully equipped, high-clearance 4WD to travel this route. The road begins south of Alice Springs, close to where the road branches to the newer Stuart Hwy. At the southern end, from Finke, you can turn west along the Goyder Stock Rte to join the Stuart Hwy at Kulgera (150km) or east to Old Andado station on the edge of the Simpson Desert (120km). (Expensive) fuel is sold at the Aputula Store.

Rainbow Valley Conservation Reserve

Visit this series of free-standing sandstone bluffs and **cliffs**, in shades ranging from cream to red, at sunset or sunrise and you'll encounter one of central Australia's more underrated sights. Visit in the middle of the day and you're likely to wonder what all the fuss is about, save for one thing – deep-desert silence will overwhelm you whatever time of day you are here. A walking trail takes you past claypans and in between the multihued outcrops to Mushroom Rock.

🛏 Sleeping

Rainbow Valley Camping Ground   CAMPGROUND $
(Rainbow Valley Conservation Reserve; adult/child/family $3.30/1.65/7.70) We love staying here, but there's barely a scrap of shade (apart from the picnic shelters), so set up late afternoon and pack up by midmorning – if you do this, you'll leave with fond memories of the silence and the wonderful sunrise and sunset views.

❶ Getting There & Away

The park lies 22km off the Stuart Hwy along a 4WD track; the turn-off is 77km south of Alice Springs. If it hasn't rained for a while, the track should be passable in a 2WD vehicle.

Ernest Giles Road

The Ernest Giles Rd heads off to the west of the Stuart Hwy, about 140km south of Alice, and is a shorter but much rougher route to Kings Canyon only recommended for 4WD vehicles. The main attraction, apart from the sense of adventure that comes from travelling such a remote and challenging route, is the chance to visit Henbury Meteorite Craters.

◉ Sights

Henbury Meteorite Craters   LANDMARK
Eleven kilometres west of the Stuart Hwy, a corrugated track leads 5km off Ernest Giles Rd to this cluster of 12 small craters, formed after a meteor fell to earth 4700 years ago. The largest of the craters is 180m wide and 15m deep. It's worth the detour: the road is fine for 2WDs if you proceed carefully and the craters are surrounded by some beautiful country.

There are no longer any fragments of the meteorites at the site, but the Museum of Central Australia (p851) in Alice Springs has a small chunk that weighs 46.5kg.

There are some pretty exposed **camp sites** (adult/child/family $3.30/1.65/7.70) available.

❶ Getting There & Away

The turn-off to the Ernest Giles Rd is 132km south of Alice Springs and 68km north of Erldunda. Even if you have a 4WD, remember that many car-rental companies won't allow you to travel this road and doing so without permission may mean that your insurance is invalid.

South of Alice Springs

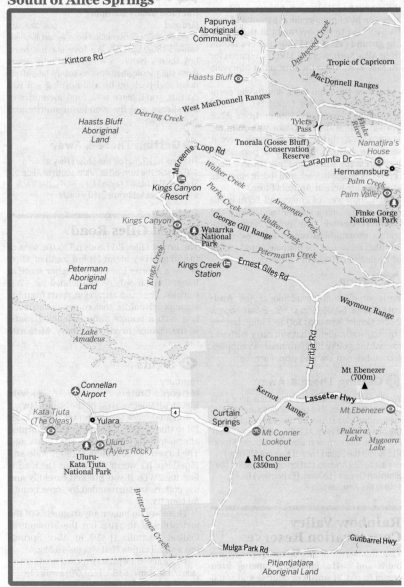

Lasseter Highway

The Lasseter Hwy connects the Stuart Hwy with Uluru-Kata Tjuta National Park, 244km to the west from the turn-off at Erldunda.

Much of the way it's fairly standard central Australian scenery with red sand, scrub and spinifex to the horizon, but there are two attractions: the first sighting of Uluru as you approach Yulara and free-standing Mt Conner.

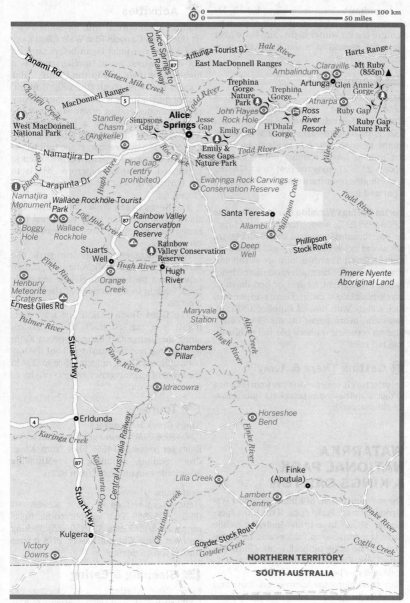

◉ Sights

Mt Conner MOUNTAIN

Mt Conner, the large mesa (tabletop mountain) that looms 350m out of the desert, is the outback's most photographed red herring – on first sighting many mistake it for Uluru.

It has great significance to local Aboriginal people, who know it as Atila. There's a signposted **lookout** around 20km east of Curtin Springs; from the lookout's summit, there are also views to the north over the salt pan, which often has standing water.

According to local Indigenous beliefs, Mt Connor is the home of the Ice Men, who venture out on winter nights and leave frost upon the ground as a sign that they have passed.

🛏 Sleeping

Desert Oaks Resort MOTEL $$
(☑08-8956 0984; www.desertoaksresort.com; Stuart Hwy, Erldunda; powered/unpowered sites $32/22, motel s/d from $115/149; ❋ 🛜 🐾) Motel rooms here are a good standard and look out onto a lovely red-dirt native garden. Rooms 23 to 27 enjoy the best views. There's a roadhouse restaurant (mains $10 to $16), a bar and fuel.

Curtin Springs Wayside Inn MOTEL $$
(☑08-8956 2906; www.curtinsprings.com; Lasseter Hwy; powered/unpowered sites $40/free, s/d with shared bathroom $90/130, r with private bathroom $180; ❋) There's a jolly air at this inn where they pride themselves on their friendliness. Pitch a tent for free or bed down in a well-maintained cabin. There's (expensive) fuel, a store with limited supplies and takeaway and bistro meals (mains $18 to $34), plus an eccentric outback bar full of history and tall tales.

❶ Getting There & Away

Lasseter Hwy is sealed all the way from Erldunda to Yulara (and beyond as far as Kata Tjuta inside the national park).

WATARRKA NATIONAL PARK & KINGS CANYON

The yawning chasm of Kings Canyon in Watarrka National Park is one of the most spectacular sights in central Australia. While there is a certain soulfulness and mystique to those two other outback icons, Uluru and Kata Tjuta, Kings Canyon impresses with its scale and raw beauty

Plan to explore the canyon on foot, and therefore to spend at least two nights here, so that you can go walking on a number of occasions in the cool of the morning or late afternoon.

Wildlife is another highlight out here, from native mammals (dingoes and red kangaroos) to feral camels and brumbies (wild horses) and around 100 bird species (watch for the handsome spinifex pigeon).

🏃 Activities

Walkers are rewarded with awesome views on the **Kings Canyon Rim Walk** (6km loop, four hours; you must begin before 9am on hot days), which many travellers rate as a highlight of their trip to the Centre. After a short but steep climb (the only 'difficult' part of the trail), the walk skirts the canyon's rim before descending down wooden stairs to the Garden of Eden: a lush pocket of ferns and prehistoric cycads around a tranquil pool. The next section of the trail winds through a swarm of giant beehive domes: weathered sandstone outcrops, which to the Luritja represent the men of the Kuniya Dreaming.

The **Kings Creek Walk** (2km return) is a short stroll along the rocky creek bed to a raised platform with views of the towering canyon rim.

About 10km east of the car park, the **Kathleen Springs Walk** (one hour, 2.6km return) is a pleasant, wheelchair-accessible track leading to a waterhole at the head of a gorge.

The **Giles Track** (22km one way, overnight) is a marked track that meanders along the George Gill Range between Kathleen Springs and the canyon; fill out the logbook at Reedy Creek rangers office so that in the event of an emergency, rangers can more easily locate you.

☞ Tours

Kings Creek Helicopters SCENIC FLIGHTS
(☑08-8956 7474; www.kingscreekstation.com.au; flights per person $60-460) Flies from Kings Creek Station, including a breathtaking 30-minute canyon flight (from $275).

Professional Helicopter Services SCENIC FLIGHTS
(PHS; ☑08-8956 2003; www.phs.com.au; flights per person 8/15/30mins $95/150/285) Picking up from Kings Canyon Resort, PHS buzzes the canyon on demand.

🛏 Sleeping & Eating

Kings Creek Station CAMPGROUND $$
(☑08-8956 7474; www.kingscreekstation.com.au; Luritja Rd; powered/unpowered sites for 2 people $51/45, safari cabins s/d incl breakfast $117/189, luxury safari tents all inclusive $950; @🐾) Located 35km before the canyon, this family-run station offers a bush camping experience among the desert oaks. Cosy safari-style cabins (small canvas tents on solid floors) share

Kings Canyon

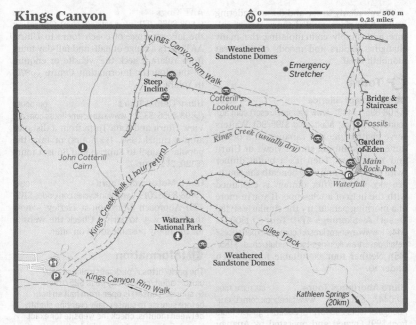

amenities and a kitchen-BBQ area, while the luxury glamping experience is very cool. You can also tear around the desert on a quad bike (one-hour ride $105).

Kings Canyon Resort RESORT $$$
(☑08-8956 7442, 1300 863 248; www.kingscanyon resort.com.au; Luritja Rd; powered/unpowered sites $50/42, dm $40, d $285-500; ❋@☎☒) Only 10km from the canyon, this well-designed resort boasts a wide range of accommodation, from a grassy camping area with its own pool and bar to deluxe rooms looking out onto native bushland. Eating and drinking options are as varied, with a bistro, the Thirsty Dingo bar and an outback BBQ for big steaks and live entertainment.

Under the Desert Moon AUSTRALIAN $$$
(www.kingscanyonresort.com.au/Under-A-Desert-Moon.aspx; per person $149; ☺6pm Apr-Oct) Dine out under the stars and around a campfire in great comfort and with fine food at the Kings Canyon Resort. There's a five-course set menu and the whole experience lasts from three to four hours.

ⓘ Getting There & Away

There are three routes to Kings Canyon from Alice Springs, but no public transport.

The only sealed route leaves the Stuart Hwy at Erldunda, 199km south of Alice Springs, then take the sealed Lasseter Hwy for 108km and then along the Luritja Rd for 169km. The other options are the 4WD-only Mereenie Loop or Red Centre Way from Hermannsburg and the unsealed Ernest Giles Rd.

ULURU-KATA TJUTA NATIONAL PARK

There are some world-famous sights touted as unmissable that end up being a let-down when you actually see them. And then there's Uluru: nothing can really prepare you for the immensity, grandeur, changing colour and stillness of 'the Rock'. It really is a sight that will sear itself onto your mind.

The World Heritage–listed icon has attained the status of a pilgrimage. Uluru, the equally impressive Kata Tjuta (the Olgas) and the surrounding area are of deep cultural significance to the traditional owners, the Pitjantjatjara and Yankuntjatjara Aboriginal peoples (who refer to themselves as Anangu). The Anangu officially own the national park, which is leased to Parks Australia and jointly administered.

There's plenty to see and do: meandering walks, bike rides, guided tours, desert culture and simply contemplating the many changing colours and moods of the great monolith itself.

👉 Tours

★ Sounds of Silence   TOURS
(☑08-8957 7448; www.ayersrockresort.com.au/sounds-of-silence; adult/child $195/96) Waiters serve champagne and canapés on a desert dune with stunning sunset views of Uluru and Kata Tjuta. Then it's a buffet dinner (with emu, croc and roo) beneath the southern sky, which, after dinner, is explained with the help of a telescope. If you're more of a morning person, try the similarly styled **Desert Awakenings 4WD Tour** (☑1300 134 044; www.ayersrockresort.com.au/experiences/detail/desert-awakenings-tour; adult/child $185/145). Neither tour is suitable for children under 10.

Uluru Aboriginal Tours   CULTURAL TOUR
(☑0447 878 851; www.facebook.com/Uluru-Aboriginal-Tours-248457278623328/; guided tours from $99) Owned and operated by Anangu from the Mutitjulu community, this company offers a range of trips to give you an insight into the significance of Uluru through the eyes of the traditional owners. Tours operate and depart from the cultural centre (p876), as well as from Yulara Ayers Rock Resort through AAT Kings and from Alice Springs.

Professional Helicopter Services   SCENIC FLIGHTS
(PHS; ☑08-8956 2003; www.phs.com.au; per person 15/30/120min scenic flight $150/285/950) Fabulous aerial views. The 120-minute option is part of a 4½-hour package that takes in Uluru, Kata Tjuta and Kings Canyon, including two hours' flying time.

Ayers Rock Helicopters   SCENIC FLIGHTS
(☑08-8956 2077; www.new.helicoptergroup.com/arh-index; 20/40/60min scenic flight per person $115/230/360) One of the most memorable ways to see Uluru; you'll need the 40-minute flight to also take in Kata Tjuta.

Seit Outback Australia   TOURS
(☑08-8956 3156; www.seitoutbackaustralia.com.au) This small-group tour operator has dozens of Uluru and Kata Tjuta tours, including sunset tours around Uluru and sunrise tours at Kata Tjuta. Food is increasingly a part of what they offer as well.

AAT Kings   TOURS
(☑08-8956 2171; www.aatkings.com) Operating the largest range of coach tours to Uluru, AAT offers a range of half- and full-day tours from Yulara. Check the website or enquire at the Tour & Information Centre (p875) in Yulara.

Uluru Camel Tours   OUTDOORS
(☑08-8956 3333; www.ulurucameltours.com.au) View Uluru and Kata Tjuta from a distance atop a camel ($80, 1½ hours) or take the popular Camel to Sunrise and Sunset tours ($129, 2½ hours).

Uluru Motorcycle Tours   TOURS
(☑08-8956 2019; www.ulurucycles.com; rides $119-429) Approach Uluru on a Harley – now that's the way to arrive! Check the website for the many possible tours on offer.

ℹ Information

The **park** (https://parksaustralia.gov.au/uluru/; adult/child 3-day pass $25/free; ☉sunrise-sunset) is open from half an hour before sunrise to sunset daily (varying slightly between months; check the website for exact times). Entry permits are valid for three days and are available at the drive-through entry station on the road from Yulara.

Yulara
POP 888

Yulara is the service village for the Uluru-Kata Tjuta National Park and has effectively turned one of the world's least hospitable regions into a comfortable place to stay. Lying just outside the national park, 20km from Uluru and 53km from Kata Tjuta, the complex is the closest base for exploring the park.

⊙ Sights & Activities

Wintjiri Arts & Museum   GALLERY
(Yulara Dr; ☉8.30am-5pm) A fascinating overview of local natural and cultural history, with plenty of artworks, an artist-in-residence and an excellent small shop. It's just north of reception for the Desert Gardens Hotel.

Mulgara Gallery   GALLERY
(Sails in the Desert Hotel; ☉8.30am-5pm) Wide range of quality, handmade Australian arts and crafts are displayed here, such as textiles, paintings and crafty Indigenous knick-knacks.

Yulara (Ayers Rock Resort)

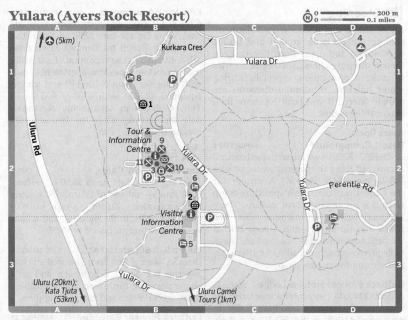

Yulara (Ayers Rock Resort)

◎ Sights
1 Mulgara Gallery	B1
2 Wintjiri Arts & Museum	B2

◑ Activities, Courses & Tours
3 AAT Kings	B2
Ayers Rock Helicopters	(see 3)
Professional Helicopter Services	(see 3)
Seit Outback Australia	(see 3)
Uluru Outback Sky Journey	(see 3)

⬤ Sleeping
4 Ayers Rock Resort Campground	D1
5 Desert Gardens Hotel	B3

6 Emu Walk Apartments	B2
7 Outback Pioneer Hotel & Lodge	D3
8 Sails in the Desert	B1

◎ Eating
9 Ayers Wok Noodle Bar	B2
Bough House	(see 7)
Geckos Cafe	(see 9)
10 Kulata Academy Cafe	B2
Outback Pioneer Barbecue	(see 7)
Walpa Lobby Bar	(see 8)
11 Yulara IGA Supermarket	B2

⬤ Shopping
12 Newsagency	B2

Uluru Outback Sky Journey STARGAZING
(☎08-8956 2563; Town Sq, Yulara; adult/child $45/free) Takes an informative one-hour look at the startlingly clear outback night sky with a telescope and an astronomer. Tours start at the Yulara Town Sq, 30 minutes after sunset.

✵ Festivals & Events

★ **Tjungu Festival** CULTURAL
(www.ayersrockresort.com.au/tjungu; ⊘ late Apr) A new festival that runs over four days in late April, hosted at Ayers Rock Resort and celebrating Indigenous culture. Food, art, film and music, plus plenty to keep the kids entertained.

Australian Outback Marathon SPORTS
(www.australianoutbackmarathon.com; ⊘ Jul) Yulara is abuzz in late July when runners converge on Ayers Rock Resort. The route of the outback marathon cuts an impressive path through the heart of Australia's Red Centre, taking in views of Uluru and Kata Tjuta.

🛏 Sleeping

All of the accommodation in Yulara, including the camping ground and hostel, is owned by the Ayers Rock Resort. Even though there are almost 5000 beds, it's wise to make a reservation, especially during school holidays. Substantial discounts are usually offered if you book for more than two or three nights.

Ayers Rock
Resort Campground   CAMPGROUND $
(☑ 08-8957 7001; www.ayersrockresort.com.au/arrcamp; off Yulara Dr; powered/unpowered sites $49/40, cabins $174; ✳@🌐🏊) A saviour for the budget conscious, this sprawling camp ground is set among native gardens. There are good facilities including a kiosk, free BBQs, a camp kitchen and a pool. During the peak season it's very busy and the inevitable predawn convoy heading for Uluru can provide an unwanted wake-up call.

Outback Pioneer Hotel & Lodge   HOSTEL $$
(☑ 1300 134 044; www.ayersrockresort.com.au/accommodation/outback-pioneer-hotel; Yulara Dr; dm/d from $42/198; ✳@🌐🏊) With a lively bar, barbecue restaurant and musical entertainment, this is the budget choice for noncampers. The cheapest options are the 20-bed YHA unisex dorms and squashy four-bed budget cabins with fridge, TV and shared bathroom. There are also more spacious motel-style rooms that sleep up to four people.

⭐ Desert Gardens Hotel   HOTEL $$$
(☑ 1300 134 044; Yulara Dr; r $192-480; ✳🌐🏊) One of Yulara's original hotels, the four-and-a-half-star Desert Gardens is undergoing gradual renovations – the updated rooms have a lovely Scandinavian minimalist look and are supremely comfortable. Some rooms have partial or distant Uluru views. Prices drop considerably, depending on the number of nights you stay.

Sails in the Desert   HOTEL $$$
(☑ 1300 134 044; www.ayersrockresort.com.au/sails; Yulara Dr; superior d from $404; ✳@🌐🏊) The rooms seem overpriced at the resort's flagship hotel, but they're still the most upmarket choice in Yulara. There's a lovely pool and surrounding lawn shaded by sails and trees. There are also tennis courts, several restaurants, a health spa and piano bar. The best rooms have balcony views of Uluru – request one when you make a booking.

Emu Walk Apartments   APARTMENT $$$
(☑ 1300 134 044; www.ayersrockresort.com.au/emu; Yulara Dr; apt from $258; ✳🌐🏊) The pick of the bunch for families looking for self-contained accommodation, Emu Walk has comfortable, modern apartments, each with a lounge room (with TV) and a well-equipped kitchen with washer and dryer. The one-bedroom apartments accommodate four people, while the two-bedroom version sleeps six.

🍴 Eating

Kulata Academy Cafe   CAFE $
(Town Sq, Yulara; light meals $6.50-10; ⊙ 8am-5pm) Run by trainees of Uluru's Indigenous training academy, Kulata is a good place to pick up a coffee in the morning and a light lunch (including pies) later in the day.

Yulara IGA Supermarket   SUPERMARKET $
(Town Sq, Yulara; ⊙ 8am-9pm) This well-stocked supermarket has a delicatessen and sells picnic portions, fresh fruit and vegetables, meat, groceries, ice and camping supplies.

Outback Pioneer Barbecue   BARBECUE $$
(Outback Pioneer Hotel & Lodge; burgers $20, meat $32, salad bar $18; ⊙ 6-9pm) For a fun, casual night out, this lively tavern is the popular choice for everyone from backpackers to grey nomads. Choose between kangaroo skewers, prawns, veggie burgers, steaks and emu sausages, and grill them yourself at the communal BBQs. The deal includes a salad bar.

Geckos Cafe   MEDITERRANEAN $$
(Town Sq, Yulara; mains $19-25; ⊙ noon-2.30pm & 6.30-9pm; 🍴) For great value, a warm atmosphere and tasty food, head to this buzzing licensed cafe. The wood-fired pizzas, pulled pork sliders and kangaroo burgers go well with a carafe of sangria, and the courtyard tables are a great place to enjoy the desert night air. There are several veggie and gluten-free options, plus meals can be made to takeaway.

Ayers Wok Noodle Bar   ASIAN $$
(Town Square, Yulara; stir-fried noodles $16; ⊙ 6-8.30pm) This takeaway-only joint does a reasonable job with stir-fries and is a good change of pace from the hotel restaurants.

Tali Wiru   AUSTRALIAN $$$
(☑ 02-8296 8010; www.ayersrockresort.com.au; per person $325; ⊙ Apr–mid-Oct) One way to combine creature comfort with the ruggedness of the central Australian landscape is

the Tali Wiru outdoor dining experience. Organised by the Ayers Rock Resort between April and October, it involves walking to a dune-top 'restaurant' to eat and drink as the sun sets over timeless Uluru.

★ **Bough House**   AUSTRALIAN $$$
(Outback Pioneer Hotel & Lodge; mains $35-45; ⊙6.30-10am & 6.30-9.30pm; 📶) This family-friendly, country-style place overlooks the pool at the Outback Pioneer. Intimate candle-lit dining is strangely set in a barnlike dining room. Bough House specialises in native ingredients such as lemon myrtle, kakadu plums and bush tomatoes. The entree or buffet dessert is free with your main course or you can opt for the whole three courses.

Walpa Lobby Bar   MODERN AUSTRALIAN $$$
(Sails in the Desert; mains $35; ⊙11am-10pm) if you want to treat yourself, this is the place to try. With a recent makeover, and the feel of a Hilton Hotel bar, the excellent food and friendly service make up for the slight sterility. Hot and cold seafood platters are a treat and most dishes feature Australian bush ingredients. Salads and antipasto are also available.

🛍 Shopping

Newsagency   BOOKS
(⊙8.30am-8pm) Excellent newsagents with magazines, a wide range of books with outback Australian themes and good maps.

ℹ Information

Visitor Information Centre (☑08-8957 7377; Town Square, Yulara; ⊙8.30am-4.30pm) Contains displays on the geography, wildlife and history of the region. There's a short audio tour ($2) if you want to learn more. It also sells books and regional maps.

Post Office (☑08-8956 2288; Resort Shopping Centre; ⊙9am-5pm Mon-Fri, 9am-noon Sat) An agent for the Commonwealth and NAB banks. Pay phones are outside.

Royal Flying Doctor Service Medical Centre (☑08-8956 2286; Yulara Dr; ⊙9am-noon & 2-5pm Mon-Fri, 10-11am Sat & Sun) The resort's medical centre and ambulance service.

ANZ bank (☑08-8956 2070; ⊙10am-noon & 12.30-3pm Mon-Thu, 10am-noon & 12.30-4pm Fri) Currency exchange and 24-hour ATMs.

ℹ Getting There & Away

Yulara is the gateway to the park and has an airport with flights from major Australian cities. There are also buses and tours from Alice Springs. If you're driving, the sealed route from

Alice Springs (447km) is via the Stuart and then Lasseter Hwys.

AIR
Yulara's **Connellan Airport** (☑08-8956 2266), serviced by a number of **Qantas** (☑13 13 13; www.qantas.com.au), **Virgin Australia** (☑13 67 89; www.virginaustralia.com) and **Jetstar** (www.jetstar.com) flights, is about 4km north from Yulara.

BUS
Emu Run (p854) runs cheap daily connections between Alice Springs and Yulara (one way adult/child $135/80).

CAR & MOTORCYCLE
One route from Alice to Yulara is sealed all the way, with regular food and petrol stops. It's 200km from Alice to Erldunda on the Stuart Hwy, where you turn west for the 245km journey along the Lasseter Hwy. The journey takes four to five hours.

There's a much longer route requiring a 4WD that goes via Hermannsburg and Kings Canyon.

Renting a car in Alice Springs to go to Uluru and back is an excellent way to see a little of the country en route if you have the time.

ℹ Getting Around

A free shuttle bus meets all flights (pick-up is 90 minutes before your flight) and drops off at all accommodation points around the resort. Another free shuttle bus loops through the resort – stopping at all accommodation points and the shopping centre – every 15 minutes from 10.30am to 6pm and from 6.30pm to 12.30am daily.

Uluru Express (☑08-8956 2152; www.uluruexpress.com.au; adult/child $45/15) falls somewhere between a shuttle-bus service and an organised tour. It provides return transport from the resort to Uluru and Kata Tjuta – see website for details.

Hiring a car will give you the flexibility to visit Uluru and Kata Tjuta whenever you want. Car-rental offices are at the **Tour & Information Centre** (☑08-8957 7324; Resort Shopping Centre; ⊙8am-7pm) and Connellan Airport.

Uluru (Ayers Rock)

The first sight of Uluru on the horizon will astound even the most jaded traveller. Uluru is 3.6km long and rises a towering 348m from the sandy scrubland (867m above sea level). If that's not impressive enough, it's believed that two-thirds of the rock lies beneath the sand. Closer inspection reveals a wondrous contoured surface concealing numerous sacred sites of particular significance to the Anangu. If your first sight of Uluru is during the afternoon, it appears as an ochre-brown colour, scored and pitted by dark shadows. As the sun sets, it illuminates the rock in burnished orange, then a series of deeper reds before it fades into charcoal. A performance in reverse, with marginally fewer spectators, is given at dawn.

◉ Sights

Uluru-Kata Tjuta Cultural Centre (☑08-8956 1128; www.parksaustralia.gov.au/uluru/do/cultural-centre.html; ◷7am-6pm) is 1km before Uluru on the road from Yulara and should be your first stop. Displays and exhibits focus on *tjukurpa* (Aboriginal law, religion and custom) and the history and management of the national park. The information desk in the Nintiringkupai building is staffed by park rangers who supply the informative *Visitor Guide,* leaflets and walking notes.

Walkatjara Art Centre (☑08-8956 2537; ◷9am-5.30pm) is a working art centre owned by the local Mutitjulu community. It focuses on paintings and ceramics created by women from Mutitjulu.

✦ Activities

Walking

There are walking tracks around Uluru, and ranger-led walks explain the area's plants, wildlife, geology and cultural significance.

All the trails are flat and suitable for wheelchairs. Several areas of spiritual significance are off limits to visitors; these are marked with fences and signs. The Anangu ask you not to photograph these sites.

The excellent *Visitor Guide & Maps* brochure, which can be picked up at the Cultural Centre (p876), gives details on a few self-guided walks.

Base Walk   WALKING
This track (10.6km, three to four hours) circumnavigates the rock, passing caves, paintings and sandstone folds along the way.

Kuniya Walk   WALKING
A short walk (1km return, 45 minutes) from the car park on the southern side leads to the most permanent waterhole, Mutitjulu, home of the ancestral water snake. Great birdwatching and some excellent rock art are highlights of this walk.

Liru Walk   WALKING
Links the Cultural Centre with the start of the Mala walk and climb, and winds through strands of mulga before opening up near Uluru (4km return, 1½ hours).

Mala Walk   WALKING
From the base of the climbing point (2km return, one hour), interpretive signs explain

Uluru (Ayers Rock)

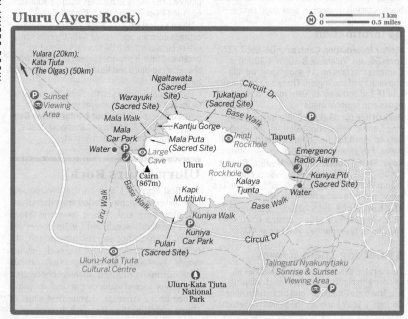

the *tjukurpa* (Aboriginal law, religion and custom) of the Mala (hare-wallaby people), which is significant to the Anangu. There are also fine examples of rock art. A ranger-guided walk (free) along this route departs at 10am (8am from October to April) from the car park.

Cycling

Bike Hire at Uluru   CYCLING
(📱 0437 917 018; http://outbackcycling.com/uluru; 3hr hire adult/child $45/30; ⏰ Feb-Nov) Adult and kids' bikes as well as toddler seats and tag-alongs for hire to ride around the base of Uluru. It's a terrific way to experience Uluru, especially if you want to do so a bit quicker than on foot.

🛏 Sleeping & Eating

The only places to stay close to Uluru are at Yulara, around 20km away, with all accommodation run by Ayers Rock Resort.

The only places to eat inside the park are the kiosk/cafe at the Uluru-Kata Tjuta Cultural Centre or the numerous wonderful places for a picnic (bring your own food). Otherwise, there are plenty of restaurants and a good supermarket at Yulara.

❶ Getting There & Away

It's around 20km from Uluru to Yulara and 51km to Kata Tjuta. Unless you're here on a tour, take the **Uluru Express** (📱 08-8956 2152; www.uluruexpress.com.au; adult/child $45/15), you'll need your own wheels.

Kata Tjuta (The Olgas)

No journey to Uluru is complete without a visit to Kata Tjuta (the Olgas), a striking group of domed rocks huddled together about 35km west of the Rock. There are 36 boulders shoulder to shoulder forming deep valleys and steep-sided gorges. Many visitors find them even more captivating than their prominent neighbour, but why choose? The tallest rock, **Mt Olga** (546m, 1066m above sea level) is approximately 200m higher than Uluru. Kata Tjuta means 'many heads' and is of great *tjukurpa* significance (relating to Aboriginal law, religion and custom), particularly for Indigenous men, so stick to the tracks.

There's a picnic and sunset-viewing area with toilet facilities just off the access road, a few kilometres west of the base of Kata

Kata Tjuta (The Olgas)

Tjuta. Like Uluru, Kata Tjuta is at its glorious, blood-red best at sunset.

🏃 Activities

The 7.4km **Valley of the Winds** loop (two to four hours) is one of the most challenging and rewarding bushwalks in the park. It winds through the gorges giving excellent views of the surreal domes and traversing varied terrain. It's not particularly arduous, but wear sturdy shoes and take plenty of water. Starting this walk at first light often rewards you with solitude, enabling you to appreciate the sounds of the wind and bird calls carried up the valley. When the weather gets too hot, trail access is often closed by late morning.

The short signposted track beneath towering rock walls into pretty **Walpa Gorge** (2.6km return, 45 minutes) is especially beautiful in the afternoon, when sunlight floods the gorge. Watch for rock wallabies in the early morning or late afternoon.

🛏 Sleeping & Eating

The nearest accommodation is at Yulara, 53km away.

There are, of course, no restaurants out here. Bring your own food for a picnic lunch or head to Yulara.

❶ Getting There & Away

Unless you're here on a tour, you'll need your own wheels to reach Kata Tjuta. The road is paved all the way from Uluru (51km) and Yulara (53km).

Perth & Western Australia

POP 2.6 MILLION / ☑ 08

Best Places to Eat

➡ Long Chim (p892)

➡ Bread in Common (p908)

➡ Rustico at Hay Shed Hill (p937)

➡ Piari & Co (p931)

➡ Pepper & Salt (p948)

Best Places to Sleep

➡ Burnside Organic Farm (p938)

➡ Gnaraloo Station (p972)

➡ Como The Treasury (p887)

➡ Beach House at Bayside (p951)

➡ Karijini Eco Retreat (p991)

Why Go?

Larger than most of the world's countries, Western Australia (WA) is Australia's last frontier, a place known for its epic scale and isolation. Up north in the Kimberley, you'll encounter wide open spaces that shrewdly conceal striking gorges, waterfalls and ancient rock formations. At the other end of the state, the south is a playground of white-sand beaches, expanses of springtime wildflowers, lush green forests and world-class wineries.

But WA is more than just its seemingly unending coastline, dramatic outback landscapes, fascinating wildlife and strong Indigenous culture. The continued development of the Margaret River wine region and a renewed appreciation for boom-town Perth, raffish, arty Fremantle and meltingpot Broome are attracting growing numbers of visitors to the region.

When to Go
Perth

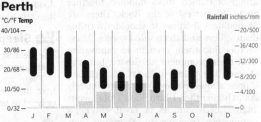

Dec–Mar In the south the weather is at its hottest and driest, while in the north, this is the wet (low) season.	Apr, May & Sep–Nov The best time to visit the north. Wildflowers, humpback whales and whale sharks.	Jun–Aug Coolest time in the south. High season for the Coral Coast, the Pilbara, Broome and the Kimberley.

PERTH

POP 2.02 MILLION / ✏ 08

Laid-back, liveable Perth has wonderful weather, beautiful beaches and an easygoing character. About as close to Bali as to some of Australia's eastern state capitals, Perth combines big-city attractions and relaxed, informal surrounds, providing an appealing lifestyle for locals and lots to do for visitors. It's a sophisticated, cosmopolitan city, with myriad bars, restaurants and cultural activities all vying for attention. When you want to chill out, it's easy to do so. Perth's pristine parkland, nearby bush, and river and ocean beaches – along with a good public-transport system – allow its inhabitants to spread out and enjoy what's on offer.

History

The discovery of stone implements near the Swan River suggests that Mooro, the site on which the city of Perth now stands, has been occupied for around 40,000 years. Modern Perth was founded in 1829 when Captain James Stirling established the Swan River Colony, and named the main settlement after the Scottish home town of the British Secretary of State for the Colonies. At the time Mooro belonged to a Wadjuk leader called Yellagonga and his people. Relations were friendly at first, the Noongar believing the British to be the returned spirits of their dead, but competition for resources led to conflict. Yellagonga moved his camp first to Lake Monger, but by the time he died in 1843 his people had been dispossessed of all of their lands and were forced to camp around swamps and lakes to the north.

Life for the settlers was much harder than they had expected. The early settlement grew very slowly until 1850, when convicts alleviated the labour shortage and boosted the population. Convicts constructed the city's substantial buildings, including Government House and the Town Hall. Yet Perth's development lagged behind that of the cities in the eastern colonies until the discovery of gold inland in the 1890s. Perth's population increased by 400% within a decade and a building bonanza commenced.

WA's 21st-century mining boom has cooled slightly in recent years, but there are still plenty of Aussie dollars awash in the state's economy, and Perth continues to blossom like WA's wildflowers in spring. Major civic works include a new football stadium, and visitors to Perth can witness ongoing work on two major reboots of the central city's urban landscape.

Largely excluded from this race to riches have been the Noongar people. In mid-2015, a $1.3-billion native-title deal was settled by the WA government recognising the Noongar people as the traditional owners of the southwest. Covering over 200,000 sq km, the settlement region stretches from Jurien Bay to Ravensthorpe, and includes the Perth metropolitan area.

◉ Sights

Many of Perth's main attractions are within walking distance of the inner city, and several are in the Perth Cultural Centre precinct past the railway station in Northbridge.

★**Kings Park & Botanic Garden**　PARK
(Map p898; ✏ 08-9480 3600; www.bgpa.wa.gov.au; ⊙ guided walks 10am, noon & 2pm) **FREE** Rising above the Swan River on the city's western flank, the 400-hectare, bush-filled expanse of Kings Park is Perth's pride and joy. At the park's heart is the 17-hectare Botanic Garden, containing over 2000 plant species indigenous to WA. In spring there's an impressive display of the state's famed wildflowers. A year-round highlight is the **Lotterywest Federation Walkway** (Map p884; ⊙ 9am-5pm), a 620m path including a 222m-long glass-and-steel bridge that passes through the canopy of a stand of eucalypts.

★**Art Gallery of Western Australia**　GALLERY
(Map p888; ✏ 08-9492 6622; www.artgallery.wa.gov.au; Perth Cultural Centre; ⊙ 10am-5pm Wed-Mon) **FREE** Founded in 1895, this excellent gallery houses the state's pre-eminent art collection. It contains important post-WWII works by Australian luminaries such as Arthur Boyd, Albert Tucker, Grace Cossington Smith, Russell Drysdale, Arthur Streeton and Sidney Nolan. The Indigenous art galleries are also very well regarded: work ranges from canvases to bark paintings and sculpture, and artists include Rover Thomas, Angilya Mitchell, Christopher Pease and Phyllis Thomas. Check the website for info on free tours running most days at 11am and 1pm.

Aquarium of Western Australia　AQUARIUM
(AQWA; ✏ 08-9447 7500; www.aqwa.com.au; Hillarys Boat Harbour, 91 Southside Dr; adult/child $30/18; ⊙ 10am-5pm) Dividing WA's vast coastline into five distinct zones (Far North,

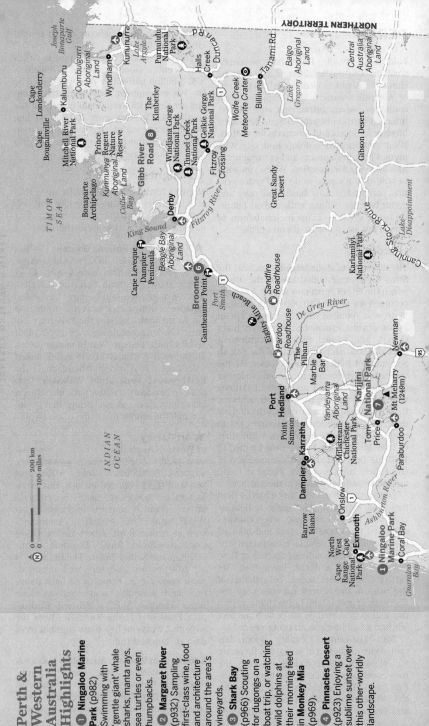

Perth & Western Australia Highlights

1 Ningaloo Marine Park (p982) Swimming with 'gentle giant' whale sharks, manta rays, sea turtles or even humpbacks.

2 Margaret River (p932) Sampling first-class wine, food and architecture around the area's vineyards.

3 Shark Bay (p966) Scouting for dugongs on a boat trip, or watching wild dolphins at their morning feed in **Monkey Mia** (p969).

4 Pinnacles Desert (p923) Enjoying a sublime sunset over this other-worldly landscape.

SOUTH AUSTRALIA

5 Perth & Fremantle

Taking in sophisticated restaurants and chic cocktail bars in flashy **Perth** (p879), or sipping craft brews in lively port **Fremantle** (p903).

6 Broome (p992)

Watching the sun set into the Indian Ocean behind a line of camels, at one of the world's greatest cultural melting pots.

7 Karijini National Park (p991)

Descending into the 'centre of the earth' on an adventure tour through the gorges.

8 Gibb River Road

(p1006) Tackling the notorious road through the Kimberley on a 4WD adventure.

Coral Coast, Shipwreck Coast, Perth and Great Southern), AQWA features a 98m underwater tunnel showcasing stingrays, turtles, fish and sharks. (The daring can snorkel or dive with the sharks with the aquarium's in-house dive master.) By public transport, take the Joondalup train to Warwick station and then transfer to bus 423. By car, take the Mitchell Fwy north and exit at Hepburn Ave.

Elizabeth Quay
AREA
(Map p888; www.elizabethquay.com.au) A vital part of the city's urban development is the Elizabeth Quay area taking shape at the bottom of Barrack St. Luxury hotels and apartments are under construction, joining recently opened waterfront restaurants. With a busport, train station and ferry terminal, the area is also developing as a transport hub. Current highlights include the spectacular Elizabeth Quay pedestrian bridge.

Bell Tower
LANDMARK
(Map p888; ☑08-6210 0444; www.thebelltower.com.au; Barrack Sq; adult/child $18/9; ☉10am-4pm, ringing noon-1pm Sat-Mon & Thu) This pointy glass spire fronted by copper sails contains the royal bells of London's St Martin-in-the-Fields, the oldest of which dates to 1550. The bells were given to WA by the British government in 1988, and are the only set known to have left England. Clamber to the top for 360-degree views of Perth by the river.

Perth Mint
HISTORIC BUILDING
(Map p888; ☑08-9421 7222; www.perthmint.com.au; 310 Hay St; adult/child $19/8; ☉9am-5pm) Dating from 1899, the compelling Mint displays a collection of coins, nuggets and gold bars. You can caress a bar worth over $200,000, mint your own coins and watch gold pours (on the half-hour, from 9.30am to 3.30pm). The Mint's Gold Exhibition features a massive 1 tonne gold coin worth a staggering $50 million.

Perth Institute of Contemporary Arts
GALLERY
(PICA; Map p888; ☑08-9228 6300; www.pica.org.au; Perth Cultural Centre; ☉10am-5pm Tue-Sun) FREE PICA (*pee*-kah) may look traditional – it's housed in an elegant 1896 red-brick former school – but inside it's one of Australia's principal platforms for contemporary art, including installations, performance, sculpture and video. PICA actively promotes new and experimental art, and it exhibits graduate works annually.

From 10am Tuesday to Sunday, the PICA Bar is a top spot for a coffee or cocktail, and has occasional live music.

Nostalgia Box
MUSEUM
(Map p888; ☑08-9227 7377; www.thenostalgiabox.com.au; 16 Aberdeen St; adult/child/family $15/10/45; ☉10.30am-5pm) Ease into poignant low-pixel childhood memories of Atari, Nintendo and Super Mario at this surprisingly interesting collection of retro 1970s and 1980s gaming consoles and arcade games. Along the way, you'll learn about the history of gaming, and there are plenty of consoles to jump onto and see if the old skills are still there from a few decades back.

Perth Zoo
ZOO
(Map p884; ☑08-9474 0444; www.perthzoo.wa.gov.au; 20 Labouchere Rd; adult/child $29/14; ☉9am-5pm) Part of the fun of a day at the zoo is getting there – taking the ferry across the Swan River from Elizabeth Quay Jetty to Mends Street Jetty (every half-hour) and walking up the hill. Zones include Reptile Encounter, African Savannah (rhinos, cheetahs, zebras, giraffes and lions), Asian Rainforest (elephants, tigers, sun bears, orangutans) and Australian Bushwalk (kangaroos, emus, koalas, dingos). Another transport option is bus 30 or 31 from Elizabeth Quay Busport.

🏖 Beaches

Run by the Surf Life Saving Club of WA, the website www.mybeach.com.au has a profile of all the city beaches, including weather forecasts and information about buses, amenities and beach patrolling. Note that many beaches can be rough, with strong undertows and rips – swim between the flags.

Port Beach and **Leighton Beach** are popular for surfing. The Port (south) end is slightly better for swimming and has some eateries. Leighton Beach is a short walk from North Fremantle train station.

Hamersley Pool, North, Watermans and **Sorrento Beaches** are excellent for swimming and have picnic areas, BBQs and a bike path through scrub.

Cottesloe Beach
BEACH
(Map p884; Marine Pde) The safest swimming beach, Cottesloe has cafes, pubs, pine trees and fantastic sunsets. From Cottesloe train station (on the Fremantle line) it's 1km to the beach. Bus 102 ($4.60) from Elizabeth Quay Busport goes straight to the beach.

Swanbourne Beach
BEACH

(Map p884; Marine Pde) Safe swimming, and an unofficial nude and gay beach. From Grant St train station it's a 1.5km walk to the beach (2km from Swanbourne station). Catch bus 102 from Wellington St station and get off at Marine Pde. The recently opened Shorehouse restaurant has excellent ocean views.

City Beach
BEACH

(Map p884; Challenger Pde) Swimming, surfing, lawn and amenities. Several new cafes and restaurants have opened here recently. Take bus 82 from Perth Busport.

Floreat Beach
BEACH

(Map p884; West Coast Hwy) A generally uncrowded beach, but it can sometimes be windy. There's good swimming, surfing, cafes and a playground. Catch bus 82 from Perth Busport to City Beach and walk north 800m.

Scarborough Beach
BEACH

(Map p884; The Esplanade) This is a popular young surfers' spot, so be sure to swim between the flags, as it can be dangerous. There are lots of shops and eateries, and the beachfront is being developed to make it more pedestrian- and bike-friendly, with new restaurants and cafes. Catch a Joondalup-line train from Esplanade to Stirling, and then bus 421 to the beach.

🏃 Activities

Whale Watching
Mills Charters
WHALE WATCHING

(☑08-9246 5334; www.millscharters.com.au; adult/child $80/65; ☺9am & 1.30pm Sat & Sun mid-Sep–Nov) Informative three- to four-hour trips departing from Hillarys Boat Harbour.

Oceanic Cruises
WHALE WATCHING

(Map p888; ☑08-9325 1191; www.oceaniccruises.com.au; adult/child $75/29) Departs Perth's Barrack Street Jetty or Fremantle's B Shed.

Cycling

Cycling is an excellent way to explore Perth. Kings Park has some good bike tracks and there are cycling routes along the Swan River, running all the way to Fremantle, and along the coast. Bikes can be taken free of charge on ferries at any time and on trains outside of weekday peak hours (7am to 9am and 4pm to 6.30pm) – with a bit of planning you can pedal as far as you like in one direction and return via public transport. Bikes can't be taken on buses at any time, except some regional coaches (for a small charge). For route maps, see www.transport.wa.gov.au/cycling/ or call into a bike shop.

Spinway WA
CYCLING

(www.spinwaywa.bike/; from $11 per hour) Spinway WA has 17 self-serve bicycle-hire kiosks in city hot spots. Bikes, costing $11 for one hour, $22 for four hours, or $33 for 24 hours, can be rented in central Perth, Kings Park, South Perth, Scarborough and Fremantle.

Other Activities
Australasian Diving Academy
DIVING

(Map p884; ☑08-9389 5018; www.ausdiving.com.au; 142 Stirling Hwy) Hires diving gear (per day/week $75/200) and offers diving courses (four-day open-water $495). There are a variety of sites in the vicinity, including several around Rottnest Island, and four wrecks.

Surfschool
SURFING

(Map p884; ☑08-9447 5637; www.surfschool.com; Scarborough Beach; from $60; ☺Oct–May) Two-hour lessons at Scarborough Beach

---

PERTH & FREMANTLE IN...

Two Days

Have a leisurely breakfast in **Mt Lawley** (p893) or the **City Centre** (p891) and then spend your first morning exploring the art galleries of the **Perth Cultural Centre** (p879). Grab lunch and go shopping in the hip **Leederville** (p901) neighbourhood before exploring verdant and view-friendly **Kings Park** (p879). The following day, discover the lustrous riches of the **Perth Mint** (p882) before catching the **Little Ferry Co** (p886) from **Elizabeth Quay** to Claisebrook Cove to enjoy riverside eating and drinking.

Four Days

Follow the two-day itinerary and also make time to take excursions to the best of Perth's beaches – maybe pick up provisions for a picnic at **Cottesloe** or **City Beach** (p883). Take a trip north to the **Aquarium of Western Australia** (p879) and spend the evenings hunting out hidden bars and good eating around **Northbridge** (p892).

Greater Perth

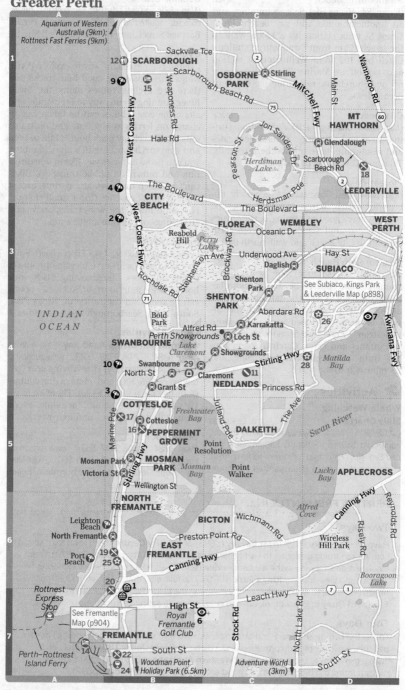

Aquarium of Western
Australia (9km);
Rottnest Fast Ferries (9km)

Sackville Tce

SCARBOROUGH

12

9

15

Scarborough Beach Rd

Weaponess Rd

Hale Rd

West Coast Hwy

OSBORNE PARK

Stirling

75

Jon Sanders Dr

Pearson St

*Herdsman
Lake*

Main St

Mitchell Fwy

Wanneroo Rd

60

MT HAWTHORN

Glendalough

Scarborough
Beach Rd

18

2

LEEDERVILLE

The Boulevard

CITY BEACH

4

2

West Coast Hwy

Reabold
Hill

*Perry
Lakes*

Stephenson Ave

Rochdale Rd

The Boulevard

Herdsman Pde

FLOREAT

Brockway Rd

Oceanic Dr

WEMBLEY

Underwood Ave

Daglish

WEST PERTH

Hay St

SUBIACO

See Subiaco, Kings Park
& Leederville Map (p898)

Shenton
Park

SHENTON PARK

71

*Bold
Park*

Alfred Rd

Perth Showgrounds

*INDIAN
OCEAN*

SWANBOURNE

*Lake
Claremont*

10

Swanbourne

North St

29

3

Grant St

COTTESLOE

Karrakatta

Loch St

Showgrounds

Aberdare Rd

26

7

Stirling Hwy

28

*Matilda
Bay*

Claremont

11

NEDLANDS

Princess Rd

*Freshwater
Bay*

Jutland Pde

The Ave

Swan River

17

Cottesloe

16

PEPPERMINT GROVE

Marine Pde

Point
Resolution

DALKEITH

Mosman Park

Victoria St

Stirling Hwy

MOSMAN PARK

*Mosman
Bay*

Point
Walker

Wellington St

NORTH FREMANTLE

Leighton
Beach

North Fremantle

Port
Beach

19

25

BICTON

Wichmann Rd

EAST FREMANTLE

Preston Point Rd

Canning Hwy

*Alfred
Cove*

*Lucky
Bay*

APPLECROSS

Canning Hwy

Reynolds Rd

Wireless
Hill Park

Risely Rd

20

1

5

High St

Royal
Fremantle
Golf Club

6

Leach Hwy

Stock Rd

North Lake Rd

7

1

*Booragoon
Lake*

Rottnest
Express
Stop

See Fremantle
Map (p904)

FREMANTLE

Perth–Rottnest
Island Ferry

14

22

24

South St

*Woodman Point
Holiday Park (6.5km)*

*Adventure World
(3km)*

South St

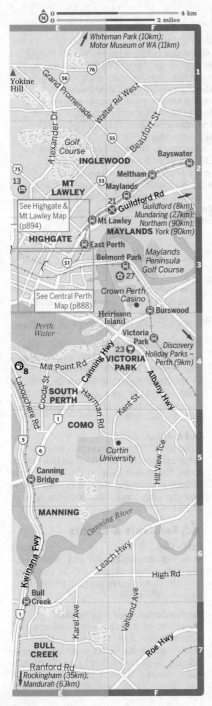

Greater Perth

⊙ Sights
1 Army Museum of WA	B6
2 City Beach	B3
3 Cottesloe Beach	B4
4 Floreat Beach	B2
5 Fremantle Arts Centre	B7
6 Fremantle Cemetery	B7
7 Lotterywest Federation Walkway	D4
8 Perth Zoo	E4
9 Scarborough Beach	B1
10 Swanbourne Beach	B4

⊕ Activities, Courses & Tours
11 Australasian Diving Academy	C4
12 Surfschool	B1

⊜ Sleeping
13 Above Bored	E2
14 Be.Fremantle	A7
15 Western Beach Lodge	B1

⊗ Eating
16 Boatshed Market	B5
Canvas	(see 5)
17 Cott & Co Fish Bar	B5
18 Divido	D2
19 Flipside	B6
Il Lido	(see 17)
20 Mantle	B7
21 Mrs S	F2
New Norcia Bakery	(see 18)
22 Ootong & Lincoln	B7
Propeller	(see 19)

⊜ Drinking & Nightlife
23 Dutch Trading Co	F4
Mrs Browns	(see 19)
24 Percy Flint's Boozery & Eatery	B7
Swallow	(see 21)

⊕ Entertainment
25 Mojos	B6
26 Moonlight Cinema	D4
27 Perth Stadium	F3
28 Somerville Auditorium	D4

⊜ Shopping
29 æ'lkemi	B4
Found	(see 5)

(at the end of Manning St), including boards and wetsuits. Bookings essential. From June to September the operation moves to Leighton Beach just north of Fremantle.

WA Skydiving Academy ADVENTURE SPORTS
(☑1300 137 855; www.waskydiving.com.au)
Tandem jumps from 6000/8000/10,000/12,000ft from \$260/300/340/380. Drop-zone options include Perth, Mandurah and Pinjarra.

PERTH FOR CHILDREN

With a clement climate and plenty of open spaces and beaches to run around in, Perth is a great place to bring children. Of the beaches, **Cottesloe** (p882) is the safest and a family favourite. With older kids, arrange two-wheeled family expeditions along Perth's riverside and coastal bike paths. **Kings Park** (p879) has playgrounds and walking tracks.

The **Perth Royal Show** (www.perthroyalshow.com.au; Claremont Showground; ☺ late Sep-early Oct), held late September, is an ever-popular family outing, with sideshow rides, show bags and proudly displayed poultry. Many of Perth's big attractions cater well for young audiences, especially the **Aquarium of Western Australia,** (p879) **Perth Zoo** (p882) and the **Art Gallery of Western Australia** (p879).

Scitech (Map p898; ☎08-9215 0700; www.scitech.org.au; City West Centre, Sutherland St; adult/child $19/12; ☺9.30am-4pm Mon-Fri, 10am-5pm Sat & Sun) is a good rainy-day option, with more than 160 hands-on, large-scale science and technology exhibits.

Adventure World (☎08-9417 9666; www.adventureworld.net.au; 351 Progress Dr; adult/child/family $58/48/180; ☺10am-5pm Thu-Mon late Sep-early May, daily school holidays & Dec) has exciting rides such as the G-force-defying 'Black Widow' and the 'Abyss' roller coaster, as well as pools, water slides and a castle.

Rottnest Air Taxi SCENIC FLIGHTS
(☎1300 895 538; www.rottnest.aero) Thirty-minute joy flights over the city, Kings Park and Fremantle (per person $149), leaving from Jandakot airport.

Tours

Food Loose Tours FOOD & DRINK
(www.foodloosetours.com.au; ☺from $42) Fun and informative walking tours negotiating flavour-packed routes taking in restaurants, ethnic eateries and hard-to-find small bars in Perth and Fremantle.

Indigenous Heritage Tour CULTURAL
(☎0405 630 606; www.indigenouswa.com; adult/child $50/15; ☺1.30pm Mon-Fri) A 90-minute Indigenous-themed stroll around Kings Park. Bookings (essential) can be made online or through the WA Visitor Centre (p902).

Little Ferry Co BOATING
(Map p888; ☎0488 777 088; www.littleferryco.com.au; adult/child single $10/12, return $22/16; ☺9.30am-5.30pm) This heritage-style electric ferry travels between the Elizabeth Quay terminal and the cafes and restaurants of Claisebrook Cove. Either take a return trip or return by free Central Area Transit (CAT) bus to the city. Friendly skipper Kevyn provides an interesting commentary, and when the new Perth Stadium opens in early 2018 he hopes to offer transport linking the city and the venue.

Two Feet & a Heartbeat WALKING
(☎1800 459 388; www.twofeet.com.au; per person $35-55) Daytime walking tours of Perth with an emphasis on heritage, culture and archi-

tecture, and a popular after-dark 'Small Bar Tour'.

Beer Nuts BREWERY
(☎08-9295 0605; www.beernuts.com.au; per person from $70; ☺Wed-Sun) Tours visit Swan Valley microbreweries and a rum distillery.

Captain Cook Cruises CRUISE
(Map p888; ☎08-9325 3341; www.captaincook cruises.com.au; adult/child from $40/23) Cruises to the Swan Valley or Fremantle, with an array of add-ons such as meals, craft beer, wine tastings and tram rides. Departures are from Barrack Street Jetty.

Out & About WINE
(☎08-9377 3376; www.outandabouttours.com.au; per person from $85) Wine-focused tours of the Swan Valley and historic Guildford. Some include river cruises, breweries, and cheese and chocolate stops. Also runs day trips to Margaret River.

Festivals & Events

Perth Cup SPORTS
(www.perthracing.org.au; ☺1 Jan) New Year's Day sees Perth's biggest day at the races, with the party people heading to 'Tentland' for DJs and daiquiris.

Perth International Arts Festival ART
(www.perthfestival.com.au; ☺mid-Feb–early Mar) Artists such as Laurie Anderson, Dead Can Dance and Sleater-Kinney perform alongside top local talent. Held over 25 days, it spans theatre, classical music, jazz, visual arts, dance, film and literature. Worth

scheduling a trip around, especially for nocturnal types.

Kings Park Festival
CULTURAL

(www.kingsparkfestival.com.au) Held throughout September to coincide with the wildflower displays, the festival includes live music every Sunday, guided walks and talks.

🛏 Sleeping

Hotel options have improved recently, especially around Northbridge – and new luxury international hotels from Westin and Ritz-Carlton are scheduled to open in the CBD and at Elizabeth Quay in 2017 and 2018.

Both the CBD and Northbridge are close to public transport, making hopping out to inner-city suburbs such as Leederville and Mt Lawley straightforward.

🛏 City Centre

Perth City YHA
HOSTEL $

(Map p888; ☑ 08-9287 3333; www.yha.com.au; 300 Wellington St; dm $33-36, r $125, with shared bathroom $100; ❋ @ 🛜 ≋) Occupying an impressive 1940s art-deco building by the train tracks, the centrally located YHA has a slight boarding-school feel in the corridors, but the rooms are clean and there are good facilities including a gym and a bar. Like many Perth hostels, it's popular with FIFO ('fly-in, fly-out') mine workers, so the traditional YHA travellers' vibe has been diminished.

Riverview 42 Mt St Hotel
APARTMENT $$

(Map p898; ☑ 08-9321 8963; www.riverview perth.com.au; 42 Mount St; apt $130-229; ❋ @ 🛜) There's a lot of brash new money up here on Mount St, but character-filled Riverview stands out as the best personality on the block. Its refurbished 1960s bachelor pads sit neatly atop a modern foyer and a relaxed cafe. Rooms are sunny and simple; the front ones have river views, while the back ones are quieter.

Pensione Hotel
BOUTIQUE HOTEL $$

(Map p888; ☑ 08-9325 2133; www.pensione.com. au; 70 Pier St; d from $182; ❋ 🛜) Formerly the budget-oriented Aarons, this central-city 98-room property now features a boutique sheen as the Pensione Hotel. The standard rooms definitely veer to cosy and (very) compact, but classy decor and a good location are two definite pluses in an expensive city. A few carpets are looking a tad worn, though.

★ Como The Treasury
BOUTIQUE HOTEL $$$

(Map p888; ☑ 08-6168 7888; www.comohotels. com/thetreasury; State Buildings, 1 Cathedral Ave; r from $491; ❋ ❋ ≋) Judged the world's second-best hotel in late 2016 by the readers of *Condé Nast Traveler* magazine – just a few months after opening – Como The Treasury has 48 luxury rooms that fill the heritage splendour of the 140-year-old State Buildings. Despite the historic backdrop, the property is wonderfully understated and contemporary, with a superb spa and indoor pool.

Terrace Hotel
BOUTIQUE HOTEL $$$

(Map p888; ☑ 08-9214 4444; www.terracehotelperth. com.au; 237 St Georges Tce; d from $319; ❋ 🛜) The Terrace Hotel fills a heritage-listed terrace house in Perth's historic West End. There are 15 deluxe rooms and suites, all with a clubby, luxurious ambience. Modern accoutrements include huge flat-screen TVs, Apple TV and iPads, and king-sized four-poster beds with Egyptian-cotton linen. The downstairs restaurant is popular for high tea and hosts regular events for Perth's movers and shakers.

🛏 Northbridge

Most of Perth's hostels are in Northbridge, and it's possible to walk around and inspect rooms before putting your money down. Note that many hostels have long-term residents working in Perth, and this can alter the ambience for short-term visitors and travellers. Northbridge also has a few new boutique hotels, which are convenient for the area's good restaurants, bars and nightlife.

Witch's Hat
HOSTEL $

(Map p894; ☑ 08-9228 4228; www.witchs-hat. com; 148 Palmerston St; dm $24-30, tw & d $75; ❋ @ 🛜) Witch's Hat is like something out of a fairy tale. The 1897 building itself could be mistaken for a gingerbread house, and the witch's hat (an Edwardian turret) stands proudly out the front, beckoning the curious to step inside. Dorms are light and uncommonly spacious, and there's a red-brick barbecue area out the back.

Emperor's Crown
HOSTEL $

(Map p888; ☑ 08-9227 1400; www.emperors crown.com.au; 85 Stirling St; dm $24-28, r from $95, with shared bathroom from $90; ❋ @ 🛜) One of Perth's best hostels has a great position (close to the Northbridge scene without being in the thick of it), friendly staff and high housekeeping standards. It's a bit pricier than most, but it's worth it.

Central Perth

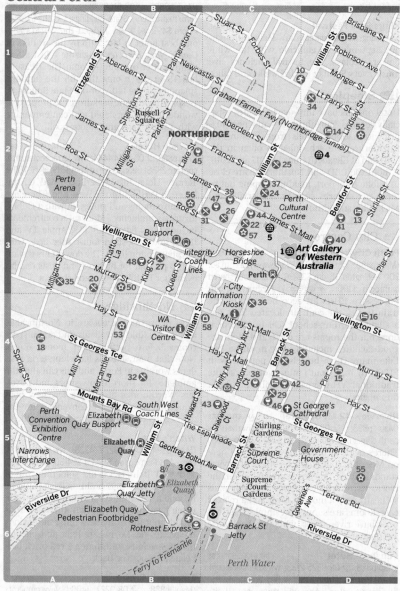

PERTH & WESTERN AUSTRALIA PERTH

Nest on Newcastle   BOUTIQUE HOTEL **$$**
(Map p888; ☑08-6151 4000; www.theneston
newcastle.com.au; 172 Newcastle St; r $190-220;
✷ 🛜) Combining a convenient Northbridge
location and rooms with design influences
as diverse as 'Bali', 'New York' and 'Audrey
Hepburn', Nest on Newcastle is one of Perth's
newest boutique hotels. Gleaming white tiles
make the bathrooms shine and some rooms
have compact balconies. Mod cons include
Nespresso coffee machines and smart TVs,
and there's a rooftop terrace with good views.

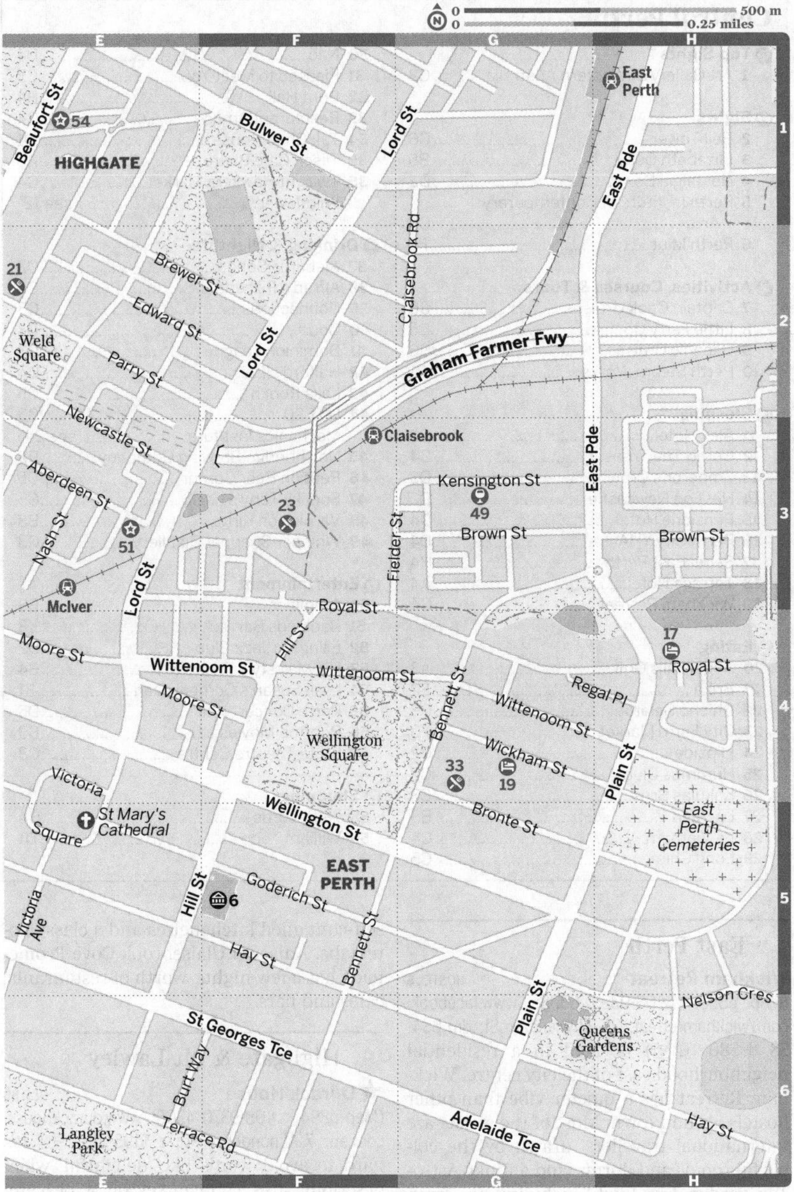

Alex Hotel BOUTIQUE HOTEL **$$**
(Map p888; ☎08-6430 4000; www.alexhotel.com.au; 50 James St; d from $209; ❄@☕) The Alex Hotel is stylish evidence of the reinvention of Northbridge as a happening neighbourhood. Classy and compact rooms are decked out in neutral colours, and stacked with fine linen and electronic gear. Relaxed shared spaces include a hip mezzanine lounge, and the roof terrace has great city views. Shadow Wine Bar, the Alex's street-front restaurant, channels a European bistro.

Central Perth

East Perth

Wickham Retreat   HOSTEL $
(Map p888; ☑ 08-9325 6398; www.facebook.
com/wickhamretreat; 25-27 Wickham St; dm $34-
38, d $80; @ ⊠) Located in a residential
neighbourhood east of the city centre, Wickham Retreat has a quieter vibe than other
hostels around town. Most of the guests are
international travellers, drawn by the colourful rooms and dorms, and a funky Astro-
Turf garden. Free food – including rice, fresh
bread and vegies – extends travel budgets
eroded by Perth's high prices.

Sebel East Perth   APARTMENT $$$
(Map p888; ☑ 08-9223 2500; www.accor
hotels.com.au; 60 Royal St; apt from $300;
❊ ⊠) Modern and chic apartments with
self-contained kitchenettes and a classy ho-
tel vibe. Adjacent Claisebrook Cove Prome-
nade has a few nights' worth of restaurants,
cafes and bars.

Highgate & Mt Lawley

★ **Durack House**   B&B $$
(Map p894; ☑ 08-9370 4305; www.durackhouse.
com.au; 7 Almondbury Rd; r $195-215; ⊠) It's
hard to avoid words like 'delightful' when
describing this cottage, set on a peaceful
suburban street behind a rose-adorned
white picket fence. The three rooms have
plenty of old-world charm, paired with thoroughly modern bathrooms. It's only 250m
from Mt Lawley station; turn left onto Railway Pde and then take the first right onto
Almondbury Rd.

Above Bored
B&B **$$**

(Map p884; ☑ 08-9444 5455; www.abovebored. com.au; 14 Norham St; d $190-200; ❀ ❤) In a quiet residential neighbourhood, this 1927 Federation house is owned by a friendly TV scriptwriter. The two themed rooms in the main house have eclectic decor, and in the garden there's a cosy self-contained cottage with a kitchenette. In an expensive town for accommodation, Above Bored is great value. Northbridge and Mt Lawley are a short drive away.

Subiaco & Kings Park

Sage Hotel
DESIGN HOTEL **$$**

(Map p898; ☑ 08-6500 9100; www.snhotels. com/sage/west-perth; 1309 Hay St; r $149-246; ❀ ❤) Handily placed for both the CBD and Kings Park, the newly opened Sage offers modern rooms with iPod docking stations, 48in TVs and cleverly designed bathrooms and work stations. Amenities include a gym, and downstairs is a good Italian restaurant located in a 100-year-old heritage residence.

Richardson
HOTEL **$$$**

(Map p898; ☑ 08-9217 8888; www.therichardson. com.au; 32 Richardson St; r/ste from $295/395; ❀ ❤ ▤) Ship-shaped and shipshape, the Richardson offers luxurious, thoughtfully designed rooms, some with sliding doors to divide them into larger suites. The whole complex has a breezy, summery feel, with pale marble tiles, creamy walls and interesting art. There's an in-house spa centre if you require additional pampering.

Beaches

If you care most for the beach, consider staying at Cottesloe or Scarborough, as public transport to this part of town can be time-consuming.

Western Beach Lodge
HOSTEL **$**

(Map p884; ☑ 08-9245 1624; www.westernbeach. com; 6 Westborough St, Scarborough; dm $34, d with shared bathroom $75; @ ❤) A real surfer hang-out, this sociable, homey hostel has a good, no-frills feel. Discounts kick in for stays of three nights or longer. Surfboards and boogie boards are available.

Trigg Retreat
B&B **$$**

(☑ 08-9447 6726; www.triggretreat.com; 59 Kitchener St, Trigg; r $175; ❀ @ ❤) This classy three-room B&B offers attractive and supremely comfortable queen bedrooms in a modern

house a short drive from Trigg Beach. Each has fridge, TV, DVD player and tea- and coffee-making facilities, and there's also a compact guest kitchen. A full cooked breakfast is provided. Also available is a nearby cottage ($240) accommodating up to four people.

✖ Eating

✖ City Centre

Twilight Hawkers Market
STREET FOOD **$**

(Map p888; www.twilighthawkersmarket.com; Forrest Chase; snacks & mains around $10; ⊙ 4.30-9pm Fri mid-Oct–late Apr) Ethnic food stalls bring the flavours and aromas of the world to central Perth on Friday night in spring and summer. Look forward to combining your Turkish *gözleme* (savoury crepe) or Colombian empanadas (deep-fried pastries) with regular live music from local Perth bands.

Le Vietnam
VIETNAMESE **$**

(Map p888; ☑ 08-6114 8038; www.facebook.com/ LeVietnamCafe; 1/80 Barrack St; snacks $7; ⊙ 6am-3pm Mon-Fri, 8.30am-2pm Sat; ☑) The best *banh mi* (Vietnamese baguettes) in town are served in this narrow, centrally located spot. Classic flavour combos blend chicken, pâté, chilli and lemon grass, while newer spins feature pulled pork, roast pork and crackling. Interesting drinks include Vietnamese coffee and lychee lemonade, and a hearty breakfast or lunch will only cost around 10 bucks.

Nao
JAPANESE **$**

(Map p888; ☑ 08-9325 2090; www.naojapanese restaurant.com.au; Equus Arcade, Shop 191/580 Hay St; mains $11-14; ⊙ 11.30am-6pm Mon-Thu, 11.30am-9pm Fri, noon-5pm Sun) Asian students, CBD desk jockeys and savvy foodies all gravitate to this spot serving the best ramen in town. At peak times you'll need to battle a small queue, but the silky combinations of broth, roast chashu pork and noodles are definitely worth the wait.

Angel Falls Grill
VENEZUELAN **$$**

(Map p888; ☑ 08-9481 6222; www.angelfalls grill.com.au; Shop 16, Shafto Lane; mains $14-27; ⊙ 7am-10pm Mon-Fri, 8am-11pm Sat, 9am-10pm Sun) The pick of Shafto Lane's ethnic eateries, Angel Falls Grill brings a taste of South America to Western Australia. Salads and meat dishes are served with *arepas* (flat breads), and appetisers include empanadas and savoury-topped plantains. Grilled meat dishes from the *parrillada* (barbecue) are packed with flavour, and surprising breakfast options also make Angel Falls a great place to start the day.

La Veen
CAFE $$

(Map p888; ☑ 08-9321 1188; www.laveencoffee.com.au; 90 King St; mains $13-25; ⊙7am-3pm Mon-Sat, 7am-1pm Sun) La Veen's sunny brick-lined space showcases some of the city's best breakfast and lunch dishes. This being Australia, of course *shakshuka* (baked eggs) is on the menu, but La Veen's version, topped with *dukkah* and yoghurt and served with ciabatta toast, is one of Perth's best. It's a worthy coffee stop while browsing nearby fashion and design stores too.

Tiisch Cafe Bistro
CAFE $$

(Map p888; www.tiisch.com.au; 938 Hay St; mains $14-24; ⊙7am-3pm Mon-Fri) High ceilings inspire a European ambience at this recent CBD opening. A serious approach to drinks includes cold-brew coffee, matcha and green

---

SELF-CATERING

The pick of the self-catering crop:

Boatshed Market (Map p884; ☑ 08-9284 5176; www.boatshedmarket.com.au; 40 Jarrad St; ⊙6.30am-8pm) Excellent deli and provedore.

Chez Jean-Claude Patisserie (Map p898; ☑ 08-9381 7968; www.chezjean-claudepatisserie.com.au; 333 Rokeby Rd; snacks $3-8; ⊙6am-6pm Mon-Fri) Brioche and baguettes.

City Farm Market (Map p888; ☑ 08-9221 7300; www.perthcityfarm.org.au; 1 City Farm Pl; mains $12-15; ⊙8am-noon Sat, cafe 7am-3pm Mon-Fri, to noon Sat) Organic eggs, fruit, vegetables and bread, plus an excellent cafe.

Kailis Bros (Map p898; ☑ 08-9443 6300; www.kailisbrosleederville.com.au; 101 Oxford St; ⊙shop 8am-6pm, cafe 7am-late) Fresh seafood and a cafe.

Kakulas Bros (Map p888; ☑ 08-9328 5285; www.kakulasbros.com.au; 183 William St; ⊙8am-5pm Mon-Sat, 11am-4pm Sun; ☑) Deli and provisions store.

Subiaco Farmers Market (Map p898; ☑ 0406 758 803; www.subi-farmersmarket.com.au; Subiaco Primary School, 271 Bagot Rd; snacks & meals $7-12; ⊙8am-noon Sat) Street eats, organic produce and family entertainment.

---

tea, and the breakfast and lunch menus are equally tasty and on trend. Start the day with macadamia-nut granola with coconut *labneh*, or drop by at lunch for the wagyu beef burger with chilli and provolone cheese.

★ Long Chim
THAI $$$

(Map p888; ☑ 08-6168 7775; www.longchimperth.com; State Buildings, cnr St Georges Tce & Barrack St; mains $28-45; ⊙noon-late; ☑) Australian chef David Thompson is renowned for respecting the authentic flavours of Thai street food, and with dishes like a fiery chicken *laap* (warm salad with fresh herbs) and roast curry of red duck, there's definitely no dialling back on the flavour for Western palates. The prawns with toasted coconut and betel leaves may well be the planet's finest appetiser.

★ Wildflower
MODERN AUSTRALIAN $$$

(Map p888; ☑ 08-6168 7855; www.wildflowerperth.com.au; State Buildings, 1 Cathedral Ave; mains $36-49, 5-course tasting menu without/with wine $145/240; ⊙noon-3pm & 6pm-late Tue-Fri, 6pm-late Sat) Filling a glass pavilion atop the restored State Buildings, Wildflower offers seasonal menus inspired by the six seasons of the Indigenous Noongar people of southwestern WA. There's a passionate focus on Western Australian produce: dishes often include Shark Bay scallops or kangaroo smoked over jarrah embers, as well as indigenous herbs and bush plants like lemon myrtle and wattle seed.

Print Hall
MODERN AUSTRALIAN $$$

(Map p888; ☑ 08-6282 0000; www.printhall.com.au; 125 St Georges Tce; shared plates $14-36, mains $25-36; ⊙11.30am-midnight Mon-Fri, 4pm-midnight Sat) This sprawling complex in the Brookfield Pl precinct includes The Apple Daily, featuring Southeast Asian–style street food, and the expansive Print Hall Bar, with an oyster bar and grilled WA meat and seafood. Don't miss having a drink and Spanish tapas in the rooftop Bob's Bar, named after Australia's larrikin former prime minister Bob Hawke.

✕ Northbridge

Chicho Gelato
GELATO $

(Map p888; www.chichogelato.com; 180 William St; from $5; ⊙noon-10pm Sun-Wed, to 11pm Thu-Sat) 'New-style gelato', the owners reckon, and with innovative flavours like lavender and honeycomb, and smoky Mexican chocolate they certainly have a point. Expect queues in the evening – don't worry, the line moves quickly – and ask about current collaborations with Perth and Fremantle chefs.

Tak Chee House
MALAYSIAN $

(Map p888; ☑08-9328 9445; 1/364 William St; mains $11-18; ⊙11am-3pm & 5-9pm Tue-Sun) With Malaysian students crammed in for a taste of home, Tak Chee is one of the best Asian cheapies along William St. If you don't have a taste for satay, Hainan chicken or *char kway teo* (fried noodles), Thai, Vietnamese, Lao and Chinese flavours are all just footsteps away. Cash only; BYO wine or beer.

Chu Bakery
CAFE, BAKERY $

(Map p894; ☑08-9328 4740; www.facebook.com/Chu-Bakery-492284474260141; 498 William St; snacks from $5; ⊙7am-4pm Tue-Sun) Chu makes a great stop before or after exploring nearby Hyde Park. The coffee is excellent, the doughnuts superb, and the sourdough bread recommended if you're planning a beachy picnic out at Cottesloe or City Beach. For lunch, a favourite Hyde Park outdoor combo is a takeaway espresso and toast topped with creamy avocado, whipped feta and *sriracha* sauce.

★ Brika
GREEK $$

(Map p888; ☑0455 321 321; www.brika.com.au; 3/177 Stirling St; meze & mains $9-27; ⊙noon-3pm & 5pm-late Fri-Sun, 5pm-late Mon-Thu) Presenting a stylish spin on traditional Greek cuisine, Brika is one of Perth's most appealing restaurants. The whitewashed interior is enlivened by colourful traditional fabrics, and menu highlights include creamy smoked-eggplant dip, slow-cooked lamb, and prawn*s* with saganaki. Definitely leave room for a dessert of *loukoumades* (Greek doughnuts).

If you're pushed for time, grab an espresso, baklava and a souvlaki wrap from Brika's new Filos + Yiros hole-in-the-wall option (open 7.30am to 4pm daily). There's a pleasant park just across the road to sit while you eat.

Hummus Club
MIDDLE EASTERN $$

(Map p888; ☑08-9227 8215; www.thehummusclub.com; 258 William St; mains $14-18; ⊙5-10pm Tue-Sun; ✍) Formerly operating at markets around Perth, Hummus Club is now all grown up and, following a successful crowd-funding campaign, has graduated to a bricks-and-mortar location in Northbridge. Creamy hummus is served with pitta bread, and other dishes include lamb kofta, felafel and good salads. Cocktails with Perth craft spirits and Lebanese Almaza beer complement a fun vibe.

Pleased to Meet You
BISTRO, BAR $$

(Map p888; ☑08-9227 9238; www.pleasedtomeetyou.com.au; 38 Roe St; shared plates $9-20; ⊙5pm-late Mon-Thu, noon-late Fri-Sun) Ticking all the hipster culinary boxes with its dedication to Asian and South American street food, Pleased to Meet You presents bold flavours in a menu that's perfect for sharing over a few cocktails, WA wines or craft beers. Grab a spot at the shared tables and tuck into flavour hits such as coconut ceviche, duck tacos and grilled garlic oysters.

✗ East Perth

★ Restaurant Amusé
MODERN AUSTRALIAN $$$

(Map p888; ☑08-9325 4900; www.restaurantamuse.com.au; 64 Bronte St; degustation without/with wine pairing $130/210; ⊙6.30pm-late Tue-Sat) The critics are certainly amused by this degustation-only establishment, regularly rated as one of Australia's finest. Ongoing accolades include being dubbed WA's number-one eatery by *Gourmet Traveller* magazine every year since 2010. Book well ahead and come prepared for a culinary adventure.

✗ Highgate, Mt Lawley & Maylands

Veggie Mama
VEGETARIAN $

(Map p894; ☑08-9227 1910; www.facebook.com/veggiemama01; cnr Beaufort & Vincent Sts; mains $10-20; ⊙8am-7pm Mon & Tue, 8am-9pm Wed-Fri, 9am-5pm Sat & Sun; 🛜✍) 🌱 Loads of vegan and gluten-free options shine at this cute corner cafe where flavour is definitely not compromised. The menu includes delicious salads, smoothies, vegie curries and burgers; weekend breakfasts are very popular.

El Público
MEXICAN $$

(Map p894; ☑0418 187 708; www.elpublico.com.au; 511 Beaufort St; snacks & shared plates $9-18; ⊙5pm-midnight Mon-Fri, from 4pm Sat & Sun) Look forward to interesting and authentic spins on Mexican street food, all served as small plates that are perfect for sharing. Menu standouts include duck *carnitas* tacos, grilled octopus, and a sweetcorn sundae with coconut and popcorn for dessert. Bring along a few friends and groove to the occasional DJs over mezcal and great cocktails.

Mrs S
CAFE $$

(Map p884; ☑08-9271 6690; www.mrsscafe.com.au; 178 Whatley Cres; mains $11-23; ⊙7am-4pm Tue-Fri, 8am-4pm Sat & Sun) Mrs S has a quirky

Highgate & Mt Lawley

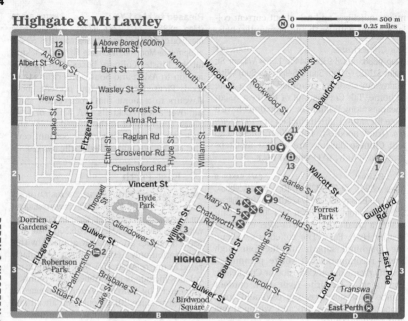

retro ambience, the perfect backdrop for excellent homestyle baking or a lazy brunch. Menus – presented in Little Golden children's books – feature loads of innovative variations on traditional dishes. Weekends are *wildly* popular, so try to visit on a weekday.

Mary Street Bakery　　　　　CAFE $$
(Map p894; ☑08-499-509-300; www.facebook.com/marystreetbakery; 507 Beaufort St; mains $12-24; ⊙7am-4pm) Crunchy and warm wood-fired baked goods, artisan bread and interesting cafe fare combine with what are quite probably Perth's best chocolate-filled doughnuts at this spacious, sunny addition to the competitive dining scene in Mt Lawley. It's a good way to start the day before exploring the area's retail scene. At lunchtime a concise wine and beer selection also features.

St Michael 6003　　MODERN AUSTRALIAN $$$
(Map p894; ☑08-9328 1177; www.stmichael6003.com.au; 483 Beaufort St; 3/7 small plates per person $59/89; ⊙6-10pm Tue-Sat, plus noon-3pm Fri) Welcome to one of the city's classiest and most elegant eateries. Like the rest of Perth, the emphasis here is on smaller shared plates, but there's some serious culinary wizardry in the kitchen. Menu highlights could include WA marron (freshwater lobster), scallops,

quail and trout. Sign up for the seven-course menu for a leisurely treat.

Must Winebar　　　　　FRENCH $$$
(Map p894; ☑08-9328 8255; www.must.com.au; 519 Beaufort St; bar snacks $9-24, mains $39-46; ⊙noon-midnight) One of Perth's best wine bars, Must is also one of the city's best restaurants. The Gallic vibe is hip, slick and a little bit cheeky, and the menu marries classic French bistro flavours with the best local produce. Oysters, bar snacks and charcuterie plates are more informal, but equally tasty, distractions.

Mt Hawthorn & Leederville

New Norcia Bakery　　　BAKERY, CAFE $
(Map p884; www.newnorciabaker.com.au; 163 Scarborough Beach Rd; mains $14-18; ⊙6.30am-5.30pm) With Perth's best bread, delicious pastries and a bright cafe as well, this place gets crammed on the weekends. There's another more central **branch** (Map p898; The Cloisters, Bagot Rd; ⊙7am-5.30pm Mon-Sat, 7.30am-2.30pm Sun) in Subiaco for takeaway goodies.

Market Juicery　　　　　CAFE $
(Map p898; ☑0458 877 000; www.facebook.com/Themarketjuicery; Shop 2, 139-141 Oxford St; salads $10-12, juices & smoothies $8-9; ⊙7am-

Highgate & Mt Lawley

🛏 Sleeping
1 Durack House	D2
2 Witch's Hat	A3

🍴 Eating
3 Chu Bakery	B3
4 El Público	C2
5 Mary Street Bakery	C2
6 Must Winebar	C2
7 St Michael 6003	C3
8 Veggie Mama	C2

🍷 Drinking & Nightlife
9 Five Bar	C2
10 Flying Scotsman	C2
Must Winebar	(see 6)

🎭 Entertainment
11 Astor	C2

🛍 Shopping
12 Future Shelter	A1
13 Planet Books	C2

3pm Mon-Fri, 8am-2pm Sat; 🖪) ⛟ Superfood smoothies, cold-pressed juices and zingy salads all feature at this good-value lunch stop amid the funky retailers of Leederville. Wraps and bagels are also appealing. You'll the find the Juicery down an arcade behind the magazine store.

Sayers ⠀⠀⠀⠀⠀⠀⠀⠀⠀⠀⠀⠀⠀⠀⠀⠀CAFE **$$**
(Map p898; 🖪 08-9227 0429; www.sayersfood. com.au; 224 Carr Pl; mains $12-28; ⏰7am-4pm) This classy Leederville cafe has a counter groaning under the weight of its cake selection. The breakfast menu includes poached eggs with potato rosti, while lunch highlights include harissa-spiced lamb shoulder with a Lebanese couscous salad and tahini *labneh*. Welcome to one of Perth's best cafes.

Low Key Chow House ⠀⠀⠀⠀⠀⠀⠀ASIAN **$$**
(Map p898; 🖪 08-9443 9305; www.keepitlowkey. com.au; 140 Oxford St; mains $24-30; ⏰5.30-10.30pm Tue-Fri, noon-3pm & 5.30-10.30pm Sat & Sun) Noisy and bustling – just like the Southeast Asian street-food eateries it references – eating at Low Key Chow House is a fun experience best shared with a group. Sip cold Singha beer or punchy Asian cocktails, and order up a storm from a menu featuring the best of Malaysia, Vietnam, Thailand, Cambodia and Laos.

Divido ⠀⠀⠀⠀⠀⠀⠀⠀⠀⠀⠀⠀⠀⠀⠀ITALIAN **$$$**
(Map p884; 🖪 08-9443 7373; www.divido.com.au; 170 Scarborough Beach Rd; mains $38-38, 5-course degustation $79; ⏰11am-late Mon-Sat) Italian but not rigidly so (the chef's of Croatian extraction, so Dalmatian-style doughnuts are served as dessert), this romantic restaurant serves handmade pasta dishes and expertly grilled mains. The five-course degustation menu is highly recommended for a night of culinary adventure. A two-course special for $39.50 is good value and the roast lamb for two diners ($85) is stellar.

🍴 Subiaco

Boucla ⠀⠀⠀⠀⠀⠀⠀⠀⠀⠀⠀⠀⠀⠀⠀⠀⠀CAFE **$**
(Map p898; 🖪 08-9381 2841; 349 Rokeby Rd; mains $11-24; ⏰7am-5pm Mon-Fri, to 3.30pm Sat) A locals' secret, this Greek- and Levantine-infused haven is pleasingly isolated from the thick of the Rokeby Rd action. Baklava and cakes tempt you from the corner, and huge tarts filled with blue-vein cheese and roast vegetables spill off plates. The salads are great too.

Meeka ⠀⠀⠀⠀⠀⠀⠀⠀MIDDLE EASTERN **$$$**
(Map p898; 🖪 08-9381 1800; www.meekares taurant.com.au; 361 Rokeby Rd; meze $15-18, mains $31-39; ⏰6pm-late Tue-Sun) In Subiaco's Rokeby Rd restaurant enclave, Meeka combines Modern Australian cuisine with the flavours of the Middle East and North Africa. Standout shared meze dishes include Tasmanian-smoked-salmon terrine, and the seafood tagine with prawn, squid and Pernod sauce integrates French and Moroccan influences. Try the doughnuts with Turkish-delight marshmallow for dessert.

🍴 Cottesloe

Cott & Co Fish Bar ⠀⠀⠀⠀⠀⠀⠀⠀SEAFOOD **$$**
(Map p884; 🖪 08-9383 1100; www.cottandco. com.au; 104 Marine Pde; bar snacks & oysters $12-26, mains $28-36; ⏰11am-late) This sleek seafood restaurant and wine bar is part of the renovated and historic Cottesloe Beach Hotel. Settle in with a few local oysters and a glass of Margaret River wine, and ease into a relaxing reverie in front of an Indian Ocean sunset. The pub's formerly rowdy garden bar now channels a whitewashed Cape Cod vibe as The Beach Club.

Il Lido ⠀⠀⠀⠀⠀⠀⠀⠀⠀⠀⠀⠀⠀⠀⠀⠀ITALIAN **$$**
(Map p884; www.illido.com.au; 88 Marine Pde; mains $20-42; ⏰7am-late) Il Lido's alfresco area is popular with Cotteslocals and their

dogs, but the sunny interior of this self-styled 'Italian canteen' is arguably even better. Breakfast and coffee attract early-bird swimmers, and throughout the day antipasto plates, pasta and risottos, alongside a good beer and wine list, continue the culinary buzz. Maybe linger for cocktails and an Indian Ocean sunset.

Drinking & Nightlife

A local law change a few years ago has produced a salvo of quirky small bars that are distinctly Melbourne-ish in their hipness. They're sprouting all over the place, including in the formerly deserted-after-dark central city. Northbridge is also a happy hunting ground for more idiosyncratic drinking establishments.

City Centre

★ Petition Beer Corner — CRAFT BEER

(Map p888; ☑08-6168 7773; www.petitionperth. com/beer; State Buildings, cnr St Georges Tce & Barrack St; ⊘11.30am-late Mon-Sat, from noon Sun) Distressed walls provide the backdrop for craft brews at this spacious bar. There's a rotating selection of beers on tap – check out Now Tapped on Petition's website – and it's a great place to explore the more experimental side of the Australian craft-beer scene. Servings begin at just 150mL, so the curious beer fan will be in heaven.

Halford — COCKTAIL BAR

(Map p888; ☑08-9325 4006; www.halfordbar. com.au; State Buildings, cnr Hay St & Cathedral Ave; ⊘4pm-midnight Sun-Wed, to 2am Thu-Sat) Channeling a cosmopolitan 1950s vibe, Halford is where to come to sip Rat Pack–worthy cocktails, including expertly prepared martinis and other American bar classics. Halford's decor and furnishings have a tinge of retro style too, with shimmering fabrics, mood lighting, and vintage boxing pics lining the walls. Maybe this is the closest a remote Australian city comes to Vegas, baby.

Alfred's Pizzeria — BAR

(Map p888; www.alfredspizzeria.com.au; 37 Barrack St; ⊘3pm-midnight) Pizza by the slice, a dive-bar vibe (with a touch of *The Godfather*), and craft beer and Aussie wines all combine in this compact space in the CBD. Look forward to checking out the cool B&W photos of heritage NYC, and don't miss the wall-covering murals featuring Axl Rose as Jesus and Madonna as the Virgin Mary.

Lalla Rookh — WINE BAR

(Map p888; ☑08-9325 7077; www.lallarookh. com.au; Lower Ground Floor, 77 St Georges Tce; ⊘11.30am-midnight Mon-Fri, from 5pm Sat) Escape downstairs from the CBD to this cosy bar specialising in wine, craft beer and Italian food. Cocktails also come with a whisper of the Mediterranean, and the all-day menu encourages relaxed grazing over shared dishes (pizza from $18, shared plates from $15). Try the king-prawn pizza partnered with a zesty Feral Hop Hog Pale Ale from the Swan Valley.

Varnish on King — COCKTAIL BAR

(Map p888; ☑08-9324 2237; www.varnishonking. com; 75 King St; ⊘11.30am-midnight Mon-Fri, 4pm-midnight Sat) With interesting shopping, cafes and bars, lower King St is an emerging Perth hot spot. Amid the hipster barber shops and single-origin coffee is this brick-lined homage to American whisky. More than 100 are available, and a decent beer and wine list is partnered by grown-up party food such as Texan spiced octopus with squid, zucchini and tarragon.

Northbridge

Northbridge is the rough-edged hub of Perth's nightlife, with pubs and clubs around William and James Sts. Recent openings have lifted the tone of the area. Most pubs have lockouts, so you'll need to be in before midnight. You may need to present photo ID.

★ Sneaky Tony's — BAR

(Map p888; www.facebook.com/sneakytonys; Nicks Lane; ⊘4pm-midnight) On Friday and Saturday you'll need the password to get into this unmarked bar amid street art and Chinese restaurants – don't worry, it's revealed weekly on Sneaky Tony's Facebook page – but once inside park yourself at the long bar and order a rum cocktail. Try the refreshing Dark & Stormy with ginger beer and lime. The entrance is behind 28 Roe St.

Dominion League — BAR

(Map p888; ☑08-9227 7439; www.dominion league.com.au; 84 Beaufort St; ⊘noon-midnight Tue-Thu, to 2am Fri & Sat) In a quieter location in eastern Northbridge, the Dominion League – named after a 1929 movement pushing for WA to secede from Australia – is a thoroughly grown-up bar with a sophisticated European vibe. Leather sofas and brick walls hint at a gentlemen's-club ambience, while a stellar craft-beer selection combines with a serious wine and cocktail list.

Bar snacks are equally cosmopolitan – think grilled lamb shoulder with tahini yoghurt – and downstairs is a cosy whisky bar.

Alabama Song
BAR

(Map p888; www.facebook.com/alabamasongbar; Level 1, behind 232 William St; ⊙6pm-2am Wed-Sun) Featuring canned brews and over 100 American whiskies and bourbons, Alabama Song is a loads-of-fun, late-night destination down a back lane in Northbridge. Chicken wings and cheeseburgers feature on the bar menu, and on Friday and Saturday nights DJs and local bands rip through rockabilly, honky tonk and country classics. Don't forget your John Deere trucker cap.

LOT 20
BAR

(Map p888; ☑08-6162 1195; www.lot20.co; 198-206 William St; ⊙10am-midnight Mon-Sat, to 10pm Sun) LOT 20 is more evidence of the transformation of rough-and-ready Northbridge into the home of more intimate and sophisticated small bars. The brick-lined courtyard is perfect on a warm WA evening, and on cooler nights the cosy interior is best experienced with a few bar snacks, gourmet burgers and WA wine or Aussie craft beer. The entrance is on James St.

Northbridge Brewing Company
MICROBREWERY

(Map p888; ☑08-6151 6481; www.northbridge brewingco.com.au; 44 Lake St; ⊙8am-10pm Sun-Tue, to midnight Wed-Sat) The four beers brewed here are decent enough, but the real attractions are the occasional on-tap guest beers from around Australia. The outdoor bar adjoining the expanse of Northbridge Plaza is relaxed and easygoing, and various big screens dotted around the multilevel industrial space make this a good spot to watch live sport.

Mechanics Institute
BAR

(Map p888; ☑08-9228 4189; www.mechanics institutebar.com.au; 222 William St; ⊙noon-midnight Mon-Sat, to 10pm Sun) Negotiate the laneway entrance around the corner on James St to discover one of Perth's most down-to-earth small bars. Share one of the big tables on the deck or nab a stool by the bar. Craft beers are on tap, and you can even order in a gourmet burger from **Flipside** (Map p888; ☑08-9228 8822; www.flipsideburgerbar.com.au; burgers $11.50-15.50; ⊙11.30am-9.30pm Mon-Wed, 11.30am-late Thu-Sat, noon-9pm Sun) downstairs.

Highgate, Mt Lawley & Maylands

Swallow
WINE BAR

(Map p884; ☑08-9272 4428; www.swallowbar. com.au; 198 Whatley Cres; ⊙5-10pm Wed-Thu, 4pm-midnight Fri, noon-10pm Sat & Sun) Channeling an art-deco ambience with funky lampshades and vintage French advertising, Swallow is the kind of place you'd love as your local. Wine and cocktails are exemplary, and the drinks list includes Spanish lagers, New Zealand dark beers and WA ciders. Check the website for live music from Thursday to Sunday. Snacks ($10 to $19) are also available.

Five Bar
CRAFT BEER

(Map p894; ☑08-9227 5200; www.fivebar.com. au; 560 Beaufort St; ⊙noon-midnight Mon-Sat, to 10pm Sun) International and Australian craft

---

GAY & LESBIAN PERTH

Perth is home to all of Western Australia's gay and lesbian venues. Before you get excited, let's clarify matters: it has precisely two bars and one men's sauna. Many other bars, especially around Highgate and Mt Lawley, are somewhat gay friendly, but it's hardly what you'd call a bustling scene.

For a head's up on what's on, pick up the free monthly newspaper *Out in Perth* (www. outinperth.com). Pride WA (www.pridewa.com.au) runs PrideFest, a 10-day festival from mid-November culminating in the Pride Parade.

Court (Map p888; ☑08-9328 5292; www.thecourt.com.au; 50 Beaufort St; ⊙noon-midnight Sun-Thu, to 2am Fri & Sat) A large, rambling complex consisting of an old corner pub and a big, partly covered courtyard with a clubby atmosphere. Wednesday is drag night, with kings and queens holding court in front of a young crowd.

Connections (Map p888; ☑08-9328 1870; www.connectionsnightclub.com; 81 James St; ⊙8pm-late Wed-Sat) DJs, drag shows and the occasional bit of lesbian mud wrestling.

Perth Steam Works (Map p888; ☑08-9328 2930; www.perthsteamworks.com.au; 369 William St; $25; ⊙noon-1am Sun-Thu, to 2am Fri & Sat) Gay men's sauna. Entry on Forbes St.

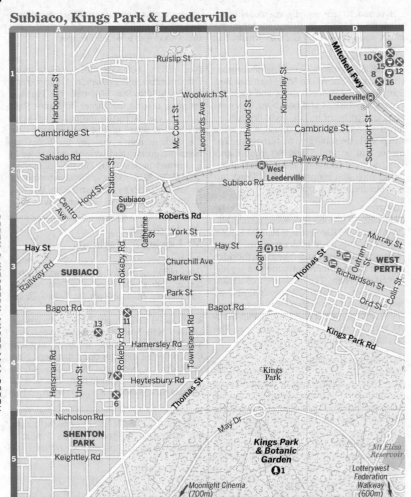

beers – including seasonal and one-off brews from WA's best – make Mt Lawley's Five Bar worth seeking out for the discerning drinker. Wine lovers are well catered for, and the menu leans towards classy comfort food.

Must Winebar   WINE BAR
(Map p894; ☑ 08-9328 8255; www.must.com.
au; 519 Beaufort St; ☉ noon-midnight) With cool French house music pulsing through the air (40 offerings by the glass, 500 on the list), Must is hard to beat. Upstairs is an exclusive, bookings-only Champagne bar.

Flying Scotsman   PUB
(Map p894; ☑ 08-9328 6200; www.facebook.com/
TheFlyingScotto; 639 Beaufort St; ☉ 11am-midnight) Old-style pub that attracts the indie crowd. A good spot for a drink before a gig up the road at the **Astor** (Map p894; ☑ 08-9370 1777; www.
astortheatreperth.com; 659 Beaufort St).

🍷 Leederville

Pinchos   BAR
(Map p898; ☑ 08-9228 3008; www.pinchos.me;
124 Oxford St; ☉ 7am-late) Look forward to Iberian-inspired good times at this corner

Other Areas

Dutch Trading Co   CRAFT BEER

(Map p884; ☑ 08-6150 8329; www.thedutchtrad ingco.com.au; 243 Albany Hwy; ⊙ 4-11pm Tue-Thu, noon-midnight Fri & Sat, noon-10pm Sun) Located in an up-and-coming eating-and-drinking strip, the Dutch Trading Co combines rustic bar leaners and repurposed sofas with tattooed and bearded bartenders slinging the best of Aussie craft beers. Besides the ever-changing taps, there's a fridge full of international brews, and bar snacks include croquettes with mustard, spicy buttermilk chicken and hearty steak sandwiches.

Hippocampus Metropolitan Distillery   DISTILLERY

(Map p898; ☑ 08-9212 6209; www.hippocampus md.com.au; 19 Gordon St; ⊙ 1-8pm Fri) Ten rounds of distillation in a gleaming copper still produce the excellent gin at this West Perth distillery, and on Friday afternoons it morphs into a surprising bar with cocktails and Australian craft beer. Try the infused vodkas or snack on an antipasto platter. (Be sure to pick up a duty-free bottle of Hippocampus gin at Perth Airport as you leave.)

Whipper Snapper Distillery   DISTILLERY

(Map p888; ☑ 08-9221 2293; www.whipper snapperdistillery.com; 139 Kensington St; tours & tastings $20-75; ⊙ 7am-5pm Mon-Fri, 8am-4pm Sat, 11am-4pm Sun) Look for the vintage aircraft logo on the exterior wall as you visit this combination of urban whisky distillery and sunny coffee shop. The whisky is crafted from 100% WA ingredients, something you'll hear a lot about on an entertaining and informative distillery tour.

☆ Entertainment

Live Music

Badlands Bar   LIVE MUSIC

(Map p888; ☑ 08-9225 6669; www.badlands. bar; 3 Aberdeen St; ⊙ 7pm-2am) Located on the fringes of Northbridge, Badlands has shrugged off its previous incarnation as a retro 1950s-inspired nightclub to be reborn as the city's best rock venue. The best WA bands are regulars, and if an up-and-coming international band is touring, Badlands is the place to see them before they become really famous. Check online for listings.

location amid Leederville's many cafes, restaurants and fast-food joints. Tapas with anchovies, chorizo or goats cheese are perfect drinking fodder with Spanish beer, wine and sherry, and larger shared plates include lamb and pork meatballs, Spanish tortilla and creamy salt-cod-and-saffron croquettes.

Leederville Hotel   PUB

(Map p898; ☑ 08-9202 8282; www.leedervillehotel. com; 742 Newcastle St; ⊙ 11am-late) Cool decor and good food ensure nights are huge at The Garden, the Leederville's decent stab at a 21st-century gastropub.

Subiaco, Kings Park & Leederville

Ellington Jazz Club
JAZZ

(Map p888; ☑08-9228 1088; www.ellingtonjazz. com.au; 191 Beaufort St; ☺6.30pm-1am Mon-Thu, to 3am Fri & Sat, 5pm-midnight Sun) There's live jazz nightly in this handsome, intimate venue. Standing-only admission is $10, or you can book a table (per person $15 to $20) for tapas and pizza.

Amplifier
LIVE MUSIC

(Map p888; ☑08-9321 7606; www.amplifiercapitol. com.au; rear 383 Murray St) The good old Amplifier is one of the best places for live (mainly indie) bands. (Part of the same complex is Capitol, used mainly for DJ gigs.)

Comedy

Lazy Susan's Comedy Den
COMEDY

(Map p888; ☑08-9328 2543; www.lazysusans. com.au; Brisbane Hotel, 292 Beaufort St; ☺8.30pm Tue, Fri & Sat) Shapiro Tuesday offers a mix of first-timers, seasoned amateurs and pros trying out new shtick (for a very reasonable $5). Friday is for more grown-up stand-ups, including some interstaters. Saturday is the Big Hoohaa – a team-based comedy wrassle.

Theatre & Classical Music

Check the *West Australian* newspaper for what's on. Book through www.ticketek.com. au or www.ticketmaster.com.au.

His Majesty's Theatre
THEATRE

(Map p888; ☑08-9265 0900; www.ptt.wa.gov. au/venues/his-majestys-theatre; 825 Hay St) The majestic home to the **West Australian Ballet** (☑08-9214 0707; www.waballet.com.au) and **West Australian Opera** (☑08-9278 8999; www.waopera.asn.au), as well as lots of theatre, comedy and cabaret.

Perth Concert Hall
CONCERT VENUE

(Map p888; ☑08-9231 9999; www.perthconcert hall.com.au; 5 St Georges Tce) Home to the **Western Australian Symphony Orchestra** (WASO; ☑08-9326 0000; www.waso.com.au).

State Theatre Centre
THEATRE

(Map p888; ☑08-6212 9200; www.ptt.wa.gov.au/ venues/state-theatre-centre-of-wa; 174 William St) This complex includes the 575-seat Heath Ledger Theatre and the 234-seat Studio Underground. It's home to the Black Swan State Theatre Company, Perth Theatre Company and the Barking Gecko young people's theatre (www.barkinggecko.com.au).

Cinema

Somerville Auditorium
CINEMA

(Map p884; ☑08-6488 2000; www.perthfestival. com.au; 35 Stirling Hwy; ☺Dec-Mar) A quintessential Perth experience, the Perth Festival's film program is held here on the University of WA's beautiful grounds surrounded by pines. Picnicking before the film is a must.

Rooftop Movies
CINEMA

(Map p888; ☑08-9227 6288; www.rooftopmovies. com.au; 68 Roe St; $16; ☺Tue-Sun late Oct-late Mar) Art-house and classic movies screen under the stars on the 6th floor of a Northbridge car park. Deckchairs, wood-fired pizza and craft beer all combine for a great night out. Booking ahead online is recommended and don't be surprised if you're distracted from the on-screen action by the city views.

Moonlight Cinema
CINEMA

(Map p884; www.moonlight.com.au; Synergy Parklands, Kings Park; ☺Dec-Easter) In summer, bring a picnic and a blanket and enjoy a romantic moonlit movie. Booking ahead online is recommended.

Sport

In WA 'football' means Aussie Rules, and during the Australian Football League (AFL) season it's hard to get locals to talk about anything but the two Western Australian teams: the **West Coast Eagles** (www.westcoasteagles.com.au) and the **Fremantle Dockers** (www.fremantlefc.com.au).

Perth Stadium STADIUM
(Map p884; www.perthstadium.com.au; Victoria Park Dr) Perth's new 60,000-seat riverside stadium is scheduled to open in March 2018 for the beginning of the AFL season. Big concerts and other international sport fixtures are also expected to be held there, and a new Perth Stadium transit station will be opening nearby. It's also envisaged there will be river transport from Elizabeth Quay to key events.

🔒 Shopping

Visit Northbridge for vintage and retro stores and hit up Leederville and North Perth for design shops and galleries. In the city, the William St mall offers major retailers, while King St is home to independent clothing designers.

78 Records MUSIC
(Map p888; 🖰08-9322 6384; www.facebook.com/78-Records-78432813221; 1st fl, 255 Murray St Mall; ⊙9.30am-5.30pm Mon-Sat, 11am-5pm Sun) Independent record shop. Also good for vinyl, and tickets to rock and indie gigs.

Future Shelter HOMEWARES
(Map p894; 🖰08-9228 4832; www.futureshelter.com; 56 Angove St; ⊙10am-5pm Mon-Sat, noon-3pm Sun) Quirky clothing, gifts and homewares designed and manufactured locally. Surrounding Angove St is an emerging hip North Perth neighbourhood with other cafes and design shops worth browsing.

William Topp DESIGN
(Map p888; www.williamtopp.com; 452 William St; ⊙10am-6pm Mon-Sat, 11am-4pm Sun) Cool designer knick-knacks.

Planet Books BOOKS, MUSIC
(Map p894; 🖰08-9328 7464; www.planetbooks.com.au; 636-638 Beaufort St; ⊙10am-9pm Sun-Thu, 11am-11pm Fri & Sat) Cool bookshop with prints, posters and a good range of Australian-themed titles.

Indigenart ART
(Map p898; 🖰08-9388 2899; www.mossensongalleries.com.au; 115 Hay St; ⊙11am-4pm Wed-Sat) Indigenous art from around Australia but with a focus on WA artists. Works include weavings, paintings on canvas, bark and paper, and sculpture.

Aboriginal Art & Craft Gallery ART
(Map p898; 🖰08-9481 7082; www.aboriginalgallery.com.au; Fraser Ave; ⊙10.30am-4.30pm Mon-Fri, 11am-4pm Sat & Sun) Work from around WA; more populist than high end or collectable.

Aspects of Kings Park ART, SOUVENIRS
(Map p898; 🖰08-9480 3900; www.aspectsofkingspark.com.au; Fraser Ave; ⊙9am-5pm) Australian art, craft and books.

æ'Ikemi CLOTHING
(Map p884; 🖰08-9284 2736; www.aelkemi.com; Times Sq Centre, 337 Stirling Hwy; ⊙10am-5pm Tue-Sun) Top WA designer's signature store, showcasing feminine frocks and distinctive prints. Adjacent Claremont Quarter is an extensive mall.

ℹ Information

INTERNET ACCESS

Perth City offers free wi-fi access in Murray St Mall between William St and Barrack St.

State Library of WA (www.slwa.wa.gov.au; Perth Cultural Centre; ⊙9am-8pm Mon-Thu, 10am-5.30pm Fri-Sun; 🛜) Free wi-fi and internet access.

MEDICAL SERVICES

Lifecare Dental (🖰08-9221 2777; www.lifecaredental.com.au; 419 Wellington St; ⊙8am-8pm) In Forrest Chase.

Royal Perth Hospital (🖰08-9224 2244; www.rph.wa.gov.au; Victoria Sq) In central Perth.

Travel Medicine Centre (🖰08-9321 7888; www.travelmed.com.au; 5 Mill St; ⊙8am-5pm Mon-Fri) Travel-specific advice and vaccinations.

Sexual Assault Resource Centre (🖰08-9340 1828, freecall 1800 199 888; www.kemh.health.wa.gov.au/services/sarc; ⊙24hr) Provides a 24-hour emergency service.

MONEY

ATMs are plentiful, and there are currency-exchange facilities at the airport and major banks in the CBD.

POST

Post Office (Map p888; 66 St Georges Tce; ⊙8am-5pm Mon-Fri, 9am-12.30pm Sat)

TOURIST INFORMATION

i-City Information Kiosk (Map p888; Murray St Mall; ⊙ 9.30am-4.30pm Mon-Thu & Sat, to 8pm Fri, 11am-3.30pm Sun) Volunteers here answer questions and run walking tours.

WA Visitor Centre (Map p888; ☑ 1800 812 808, 08-9483 1111; www.bestofwa.com.au; 55 William St; ⊙ 9am-5.30pm Mon-Fri, 9.30am-4.30pm Sat, 11am-4.30pm Sun) Excellent resource for information across WA.

ⓘ Getting There & Away

AIR

If you're coming to Australia from Europe, Asia or Africa you'll find it quicker to fly directly to Perth Airport, rather than via the east coast cities. If you do fly to the east coast first, there are frequent connecting flights to Perth from major cities. Port Hedland and Broome both welcome interstate flights, and there are weekend flights between Port Hedland and Bali.

Perth Airport (☑ 08-9478 8888; www. perthairport.com; George Wiencke Dr, Perth Airport) is the main international entry point. The following domestic airlines offer interstate services between WA and the rest of the country:

Jetstar (JQ; ☑ 13 15 38; www.jetstar.com)

Qantas (QF; ☑ 13 13 13; www.qantas.com.au)

Virgin Australia (VA; ☑ 13 67 89; www.virgin-australia.com)

BUS

Transwa (Map p894; ☑ 1300 662 205; www.transwa.wa.gov.au) operates services from the bus terminal at East Perth train station to/from many destinations around the state.

South West Coach Lines (Map p888; ☑ 08-9261 7600; www.southwestcoachlines.com.au) focuses on the southwestern corner of WA, running services from Elizabeth Quay Busport to most towns in the region.

Integrity Coach Lines (p1070) runs north-bound and southbound services linking Perth to Broome and stopping at key travellers' destinations en route. It also runs services between Perth and Port Hedland via Mt Magnet, Cue, Meekatharra and Newman.

CAR & MOTORCYCLE

Car-rental companies include **Bayswater** (☑ 08-9325 1000; www.bayswatercarrental.com.au; 160 Adelaide Tce), **Budget** (☑ 1300 362 848; www.budget.com.au; 960 Hay St), **Campabout** (☑ 08-9301 2765; www.campaboutoz.com.au), **Hertz** (☑ 13 30 39; www.hertz.com.au) and **Thrifty** (☑ 1300 367 227; www.thrifty.com.au). **Britz** (☑ 1800 331 454; www.britz.com.au) hires out fully equipped 4WDs fitted out as camper-vans, popular on the roads of northern WA; it has

offices in all the state capitals, as well as Perth and Broome, so one-way rentals are possible.

TRAIN

Transwa runs the following services from Perth railway station:
➡ Australind (twice daily) Perth to Pinjarra ($17.50, 1¼ hours) and Bunbury ($32, 2½ hours).
➡ AvonLink (daily) East Perth to Toodyay ($17.50, 1¼ hours) and Northam ($20.50, 1½ hours).
➡ Prospector (daily) East Perth to Kalgoorlie–Boulder ($89, seven hours).

ⓘ Getting Around

TO/FROM THE AIRPORT

Perth Airport (☑ 08-9478 8888; www.perthairport.com.au) is served by numerous airlines, including **Qantas** (QF; ☑ 13 13 13; www.qantas.com.au), and there are daily flights to and from international and Australian destinations. The airport's domestic and international terminals are 10km and 13km east of Perth respectively, near Guildford. Taxi fares to the city are around $45 from each terminal.

Connect (www.perthairportconnect.com.au; 1 way/return $15/30) runs shuttles to/from central accommodation and transport options in the city centre (one way/return $15/30, every 50 minutes). Pay the driver as you board. Bookings are recommended for groups.

Transperth buses 36, 37 and 40 travel to the domestic airport from St Georges Tce (stop 10121), near William St ($4.60, 40 minutes, every 10 to 30 minutes, hourly after 7pm). A free transfer bus links the domestic and international terminals.

CAR & MOTORCYCLE

Driving in the city takes a bit of practice, as some streets are one-way and many aren't sign-posted. There are plenty of car-parking buildings in the central city but no free places to park. For unmetered street parking you'll need to look well away from the main commercial strips and check the signs carefully.

A fun way to gad about the city is on a moped. **Scootamoré** (☑ 08-9380 6580; www.scootamore.com.au; 356a Rokeby Rd, Subiaco; day/3 days/week/month $45/111/200/400) hires 50cc scooters with helmets (compulsory) and insurance included (for those over 21; $500 excess).

PUBLIC TRANSPORT

Transperth (☑ 13 62 13; www.transperth.wa.gov.au) operates Perth's public buses, trains and ferries. There are Transperth information offices at Perth Station (Wellington St), Perth Busport (between Roe St and Wellington St), Perth underground station (off Murray St) and the Elizabeth Quay Busport (Mounts Bay Rd). There's a good online journey planner.

Bus

The Free Transit Zone (FTZ) is served by regular buses and is well covered during the day by the three free Central Area Transit (CAT) services. Pick up a copy of the free timetable (widely available on buses and elsewhere) for the exact routes and stops. Buses run every five to eight minutes during weekdays and every 15 minutes on weekends.

The metropolitan area is serviced by a wide network of Transperth buses. Pick up timetables from any of the Transperth information centres or use the online journey planner. Most buses leave from the city's new Perth Busport, located between the CBD and Northbridge.

Ferry

A ferry runs every 20 to 30 minutes between the new Elizabeth Quay Jetty and Mends Street Jetty in South Perth – use it to get to the zoo or for a bargain from-the-river glimpse of the Perth skyline. The **Little Ferry Co** (p886) runs services linking Elizabeth Quay and Claisebrook Cove.

Rottnest Express (Map p888; Pier 2, Barrack St Jetty; adult/child $105.50/58) runs ferries to Rottnest Island.

Train

Transperth operates five train lines from around 5.20am to midnight weekdays and until about 2am Saturday and Sunday. Your rail ticket can also be used on Transperth buses and ferries within the ticket's zone. You're free to take your bike on the train during non-peak times.

TAXI

Perth has a decent system of metered taxis, though the distances make frequent use costly and on busy nights you may have trouble flagging a taxi down in the street. The two main companies are **Swan Taxis** (☏ 13 13 30; www.swantaxis.com.au) and **Black & White** (☏ 13 10 08; www.bwtaxi.com.au); both have wheelchair-accessible cabs. Uber drivers are also common throughout the city.

FREMANTLE

POP 28,100

Creative, relaxed, open-minded: Fremantle's spirit is entirely distinct from Perth's. Perhaps it has something to do with the port and the city's working-class roots. Or the hippies, who first set up home here a few decades ago and can still be seen casually bobbling down the street on old bicycles. Or perhaps it's just that a timely 20th-century economic slump meant that the city retained an almost complete set of formerly grand Victorian and Edwardian buildings, creating a heritage precinct that's unique among Australia's cities today.

Whatever the reason, today's clean and green Freo makes a cosy home for performers, professionals, artists and more than a few eccentrics. There's a lot to enjoy here: fantastic museums, edgy galleries, pubs thrumming with live music and a thriving coffee culture. On weekend nights the city's residents vacate the main drag, leaving it to kids from the suburbs to party hard and loud.

History

This was an important area for the Wadjuk Noongar people, as it was a hub along trading paths. Some of these routes exist to this day in the form of modern roads. Before the harbour was altered, the mouth of the river was nearly covered by a sandbar and it was only a short swim from north to south.

Fremantle's European history began when the ship HMS *Challenger* landed in 1829. The ship's captain, Charles Fremantle, took possession of the whole of the west coast 'in the name of King George IV'. Like Perth, the settlement made little progress until convict labour was used.

As a port, Fremantle wasn't up to much until the engineer CY O'Connor created an artificial harbour in the 1890s, destroying the Wadjuks' river crossing in the process. This caused such disruption to their traditional patterns of life that it's said that a curse was placed on O'Connor; some took his later suicide at Fremantle as evidence of its effectiveness.

The port blossomed during the gold rush and many of its distinctive buildings date from this period. Economic stagnation in the 1960s and 1970s spared the streetscape from the worst ravages of modernisation. It wasn't until 1987, when Fremantle hosted the America's Cup, that it transformed itself from a sleepy port town into today's vibrant, artsy city. The cup was lost that year, but the legacy of a redeveloped waterfront remains.

◉ Sights

Fremantle boomed during the WA gold rush in the late 19th century, and many wonderful buildings remain that were constructed during, or shortly before, this period. High St, particularly around the bottom end, has some excellent examples, including several old hotels.

Fremantle

200 m
0.1 miles

Port Beach (1.7km)

Rous Head

Ferry to Rottnest Island (Wadjemup)

Swan River

Victoria Quay

Rottnest Express

Rottnest Island Visitor Centre

Western Australian Museum – Maritime 2

Arthur Head

Bathers Beach

INDIAN OCEAN

Western Australian Museum – Shipwreck Galleries 3

Fleet St

Cliff St

Mouat St

High St

Henry St

Pakenham St

Phillimore St

Victoria Quay Rd

Mantle (600m)

Mojos (1.8km); Flipside (2km); Mrs Browns (2km); Propeller (2km)

Elder Pl

Fremantle

Cantonment St

Adelaide St

Kings Square

Visitor Centre

William St

Market St

Bannister St

Collie St

Essex St

Norfolk St

Marine Tce

Fishing Boat Harbour

Fisherman's Wharf

Be. Fremantle (80m)

South Beach (1.5km)

Howard St

Suffolk St

Arundel St

Marine Tce

South Tce

Parry St

Fremantle Oval

Fremantle Prison 1

The Terrace

Holdsworth St

Queen St

Henderson St

High St

Ellen St

Parry St

Ord St

Canvas (400m); Found (400m); Fremantle Arts Centre (400m); Army Museum of WA (700m)

Knutsford St

War Memorial

Fremantle Cemetery (2km)

Swanbourne St

Stevens Reserve

Stevens St

Solomon St

Hampton Rd

Hampton Rd

Fothergill St

Attfield St

Alma St

Wray Ave

13

16

17

19

24

30

8

33

29

34

25

27

32

35

38

22

23

14

37

36

42

21

26

31

9

41

39

15

40

5

10

4

20

6

28

7

11

12

18

Fremantle

★**Fremantle Prison**   HISTORIC BUILDING
(☑ 08-9336 9200; www.fremantleprison.com.au;
1 The Terrace; single day tour adult/child $20/11,
combined day tours $28/19, Torchlight Tour $26/16,
Tunnels Tour $60/40; ⊙ 9am-5.30pm) With
its foreboding 5m-high walls, the old con-
vict-era prison still dominates Fremantle.
Daytime tour options include the Doing
Time Tour, taking in the kitchens, men's cells
and solitary-confinement cells. The Great
Escapes Tour recounts famous inmates and
includes the women's prison. Book ahead
for the Torchlight Tour, focusing on macabre
aspects of the prison's history, and the 2½-
hour Tunnels Tour (minimum age 12 years),
which includes an underground boat ride
and subterranean tunnels built by prisoners.

★**Western Australian
Museum – Maritime**   MUSEUM
(☑ 1300 134 081; www.museum.wa.gov.au; Victoria Quay; adult/child museum $15/free, subma-
rine $15/7.50, museum & submarine $25/7.50;
⊙ 9.30am-5pm) Housed in an intriguing sail-
shaped building on the harbour, just west
of the city centre, the maritime museum is
a fascinating exploration of WA's relation-

ship with the ocean. Well-presented displays
range from yacht racing to Aboriginal fish
traps and the sandalwood trade. If you're not
claustrophobic, take an hour-long tour of
the submarine HMAS *Ovens;* the vessel was
part of the Australian Navy's fleet from 1969
to 1997. Tours leave every half-hour from
10am to 3.30pm. Booking is recommended.

★**Western Australian Museum –
Shipwreck Galleries**   MUSEUM
(☑ 1300 134 081; www.museum.wa.gov.au; Cliff St;
admission by donation; ⊙ 9.30am-5pm) Located
within an 1852 commissariat store, the Shipwreck Galleries are considered the finest display of maritime archaeology in the southern
hemisphere. The highlight is the **Batavia
Gallery**, where a section of the hull of Dutch
merchant ship *Batavia*, wrecked in 1629,
is displayed. Nearby is a large stone gate,
intended as an entrance to Batavia Castle,
which was being carried when the ship sank.

Round House   HISTORIC BUILDING
(☑ 08-9336 6897; www.fremantleroundhouse.
com.au; Captains Lane; admission by donation;
⊙ 10.30am-3.30pm) Built from 1830 to 1831,
this 12-sided stone prison is WA's oldest

surviving building. It was the site of the colony's first hangings, and was later used for holding Aboriginal people before they were taken to Rottnest Island. On the hilltop outside is the Signal Station, where at 1pm daily a time ball and cannon blast were used to alert seamen to the correct time. The ceremony is re-enacted daily; book ahead if you want to fire the cannon.

Bathers Beach Art Precinct ARTS CENTRE
(www.facebook.com/bathersbeachartsprecinct; Captains Lane; ⊙ opening hours vary) Part of the redevelopment of the Bathers Beach area has been the opening of artists' galleries and studios in heritage cottages and warehouses stretching from near the Round House north and west towards the Western Australian Museum – Maritime (p905).

**Walyalup Aboriginal
Cultural Centre** CULTURAL CENTRE
(☑ 08-9430 7906; www.fremantle.wa.gov.au/wacc; 12 Captains Lane; ⊙ 2.30-6.30pm Tue, 10am-2pm Wed-Sat) Various classes and workshops, including language, art and crafts, are held at this interesting cultural centre. Booking ahead for most is encouraged, so check the program online. As it's part of the Bathers Beach Art Precinct there are also regular Indigenous art exhibitions, with works available for purchase and proceeds going directly to the artists.

Fremantle Arts Centre GALLERY
(Map p884; ☑ 08-9432 9555; www.fac.org.au; 1 Finnerty St; ⊙ 10am-5pm) **FREE** An impressive neo-Gothic building surrounded by lovely elm-shaded gardens, the Fremantle Arts Centre was constructed by convict labourers as a lunatic asylum in the 1860s. Saved from

---

FREMANTLE FOR CHILDREN
••••••••••••••••••••••••••••••••••••••

You can let the littlies off the leash at **Esplanade Reserve**, watch buskers at the **markets**, make sandcastles at **Bathers Beach** or have a proper splash about at **South Beach** or **Port Beach**. Older kids might appreciate the creepier aspects of the **prison** (p905) and the innards of the submarine at the **Maritime Museum** (p905), where they can also poke about on actual boats. **Adventure World** (p886) is nearby for funfair rides. Finish up with fish and chips at Fishing Boat Harbour.

---

demolition in the 1960s, it houses interesting exhibitions and the excellent Canvas (p909) cafe. During summer there are concerts, courses and workshops.

Fremantle Markets MARKET
(www.fremantlemarkets.com.au; cnr South Tce & Henderson St; ⊙ 8am-8pm Fri, to 6pm Sat & Sun) **FREE** Originally opened in 1897, these colourful markets were reopened in 1975 and today draw slow-moving crowds combing over souvenirs. A few younger designers and artists have introduced a more vibrant edge. The fresh-produce section is a good place to stock up on snacks and there's an excellent food court featuring lots of global street eats.

Army Museum of WA MUSEUM
(Map p884; ☑ 08-9430 2535; www.armymuseum wa.com.au; Burt St; adult/child $10/7; ⊙ 10.30am-1pm Wed-Sun) Situated within the imposing Artillery Barracks, this little museum pulls out the big guns, literally. Howitzers and tanks line up outside, while inside you'll find cabinets full of uniforms and medals. The WWI galleries were completely redeveloped for the centenary of the war in 2014. Photo ID is required at entry.

PS Arts Space ARTS CENTRE
(☑ 08-9430 8145; www.facebook.com/pg/Paken hamStreetArtSpace; 22 Pakenham St; ⊙ gallery 10am-5pm Tue-Sat) Independent WA artists display often-challenging work in this repurposed heritage warehouse. Occasional events, including pop-up opera, fashion shows and concerts, fill the spacious interior after dark. Drop by or check the Facebook page for what's on.

Bon Scott Statue STATUE
The most popular of Fremantle's public sculptures is Greg James's statue of Bon Scott (1946–80), strutting on a Marshall amplifier in Fishing Boat Harbour. The AC/DC singer moved to Fremantle with his family in 1956 and his ashes are interred in **Fremantle Cemetery** (Map p884; Carrington St). Enter the cemetery near the corner of High and Carrington Sts. Bon's plaque is on the left around 15m along the path.

🏝 Beaches & Parks

Green spaces around Fremantle include **Esplanade Reserve** (Marine Tce), shaded by Norfolk Island pines and dividing the city from Fishing Boat Harbour. Nearby **Bathers Beach** has recently been revitalised with a good waterfront restaurant and an arts precinct with galleries and studios. Down in South Freo, **South Beach** (Ocean Dr) is sheltered, swimmable, only 1.5km from the city centre and on the free CAT bus route. The next major beach is **Coogee Beach** (Cockburn Rd), 6km further south.

👉 Tours

Two Feet & a Heartbeat   WALKING
(📞 1800 459 388; www.twofeet.com.au; per person $45-60; ⊙ 10am) Operated by a young, energetic crew, tours focus on Fremantle's often-rambunctious history. The three-hour 'Sailors' Guide to Fremantle' option includes a couple of drink stops.

**Fremantle Indigenous
Heritage Tours**   WALKING
(📞 0405 630 606; www.indigenouswa.com; adult/child $35/15; ⊙ 10.30am & 1.30pm Thu & Sat) Highly regarded tour covering the history of Fremantle and the Noongar and Wadjuk people. Book online or through the Fremantle visitors centre.

Oceanic Cruises   WHALE WATCHING
(📞 08-9325 1191; www.oceaniccruises.com.au; B Shed, Victoria Quay; adult/child $75/29; ⊙ mid-Sep–mid-Nov) Departs at 10.15am for a two-hour tour. Days of operation vary by month, so check the website.

STS Leeuwin II   BOATING
(📞 08-9430 4105; www.sailleeuwin.com; Berth B, Victoria Quay; adult/child $99/69; ⊙ Nov–mid-Apr) Take a three-hour trip on a 55m, three-masted tall ship; see the website for details of morning, afternoon and twilight sails. Sailings are usually Saturday and Sunday, but dates vary, so check online.

🎊 Festivals & Events

Laneway   MUSIC
(www.fremantle.lanewayfestival.com; ⊙ early Feb) WA's skinny-jean hipsters party to the planet's up-and-coming indie acts. The ubercool festival takes place around Fremantle's West End and Esplanade Reserve.

Blessing of the Fleet   RELIGIOUS
(www.facebook.com/fremantle.blessingfleet; Fishing Boat Harbour, Esplanade Reserve) An October tradition since 1948, this event was brought to Fremantle by immigrants from Molfetta, Italy. It includes the procession of the Molfettese *Our Lady of Martyrs* statue (carried by men) and the Sicilian *Madonna di Capo d'Orlando* (carried by women) from St Patrick's Basilica (47 Adelaide St) to Fish-

ing Boat Harbour, where the blessing takes place.

Fremantle Festival   CULTURAL
(www.fremantle.wa.gov.au/festivals; ⊙ late Oct-early Nov) In spring the city's streets and concert venues come alive with parades and performances in Australia's longest-running festival.

🛏 Sleeping

Fremantle Prison YHA Hostel   HOSTEL $
(📞 08-9433 4305; www.yha.com.au; 6a The Terrace; dm $26-29, d & tw from $76; ❈ �🖥) Opened in early 2015, Fremantle's former women's prison is now a hostel with dorm-style accommodation and private rooms. Slightly more upmarket options include bathroom, and there are excellent shared spaces often drenched in sun. Interesting photo boards telling the fascinating stories of inmates and the prison are dotted throughout the halls.

Fremantle Beach Backpackers   HOSTEL $
(📞 08-6219 5355; www.freobackpackers.com.au; 39 High St; dm $29-40, r $100; ❈ @ �🖥) This recently opened backpackers in an old pub is getting good reviews from guests. Rates include a (very) simple breakfast, and quiz nights, movie nights and shared dinners all reinforce a social vibe. Though it's smack-bang in Freo's historic West End, it's a bit of stretch to include 'Beach' in the name...

★ Fremantle Apartment   APARTMENT $$
(www.thefremantleapartment.com; 7 Leake St; apt $110-160; ❈ �🖥) Arrayed across three floors and featuring a New York-loft vibe, this spacious apartment is located right in Fremantle's heritage precinct. A massive leather couch and big-screen TV combine with a well-equipped kitchen, and the fridge is usually stocked with a few complimentary chocolate nibbles. Friendly owners Cam and Terri have plenty of ideas on how best to enjoy Fremantle.

Fremantle Colonial Cottages   COTTAGE $$
(📞 08-9433 4305; www.fremantlecottages.com.au; 6a The Terrace; cottages $250) Located on a grassy terrace with views of Fremantle, these heritage cottages were originally occupied by wardens at the Fremantle women's prison (now the YHA hostel. With bedrooms and bunks, each of the three cottages can accommodate up to six people, and fully equipped kitchens make them a good choice for self-caterers. Wooden floors also make them good for families.

Hougoumont Hotel BOUTIQUE HOTEL $$
(📞 08-6160 6800; www.hougoumonthotel.com.au; 15 Bannister St; d $194-260) Standard 'cabin' rooms are definitely compact, but they're very stylish and efficiently designed, and you can't beat the central location of this recently opened boutique hotel. Top-end toiletries, a hip, breezy ambience, and complimentary late-afternoon wine and snacks for guests reinforce the Hougoumont's refreshingly different approach to accommodation. Service from the multinational team is relaxed but professional.

Fothergills of Fremantle B&B $$
(📞 08-9335 6784; www.fothergills.net.au; 18-22 Ord St; r $195-245; 🕸🛜) Naked bronze women sprout from the front garden, while a life-size floral cow shelters on the verandah of these neighbouring mansions on the hill. Inside, the decor is in keeping with the buildings' venerable age (constructed 1892), including wonderful Aboriginal art and a superb collection of heritage maps of Australia. Breakfast is served in a sunny conservatory.

Lodging APARTMENT $$$
(📞 08-9430 6568; www.thelodging.co; 215 High St; ste $199-299; 🕸@) Formerly colonial accommodation with chintzy heritage decor, the Lodging has undergone a sleek designer makeover to re-emerge as a cool and sophisticated place to stay. The four suites now feature minimalist white decor enlivened by big-format B&W photos and colourful rugs, and the spotless bathrooms incorporate subtle art-deco touches. A communal kitchen includes a shared Nespresso machine.

Be.Fremantle APARTMENT $$$
(Map p884; 📞 08-9430 3888; www.befremantle.com.au/; Challenger Harbour, Mews Rd; apt from $250; 🕸🛜) At the end of a wharf, these sandstone one- to three-bedroom apartments have recently had a stylish makeover to reopen as the Be.Fremantle complex. The more expensive Marina View apartments enjoy the best vistas, and bikes are available for guests to explore Fremantle. A further 24 new apartments opened in mid-2017, so ask about scoring one of those.

✖️ Eating

Although it doesn't have Perth's variety of fine-dining places, eating and drinking your way around town are two of the great pleasures of Freo. People watching from outdoor tables on South Tce is a legitimate lifestyle

choice. The Fremantle Markets (p906) are a good place to stock up on fruit and picnic items and have a decent selection of international street eats.

⭐Ootong & Lincoln CAFE $
(Map p884; 📞 08-9335 6109; www.ootongandlincoln.com.au; 258 South Tce; mains $12-23; ⏱6am-5pm; 🚗) Catch the free CAT bus to South Fremantle for a top breakfast spot. Join the locals grabbing takeaway coffee or beavering away on their laptops, and start the day with macadamia-and-*dukkah* porridge or pop in from noon for Mexican corn croquettes. Vintage 1960s furniture and loads of space make it a great place to linger.

Leake St Cafe CAFE $
(www.facebook.com/pg/leakestcafeteria; Leake St; mains $10-15; ⏱7.30am-3.30pm; 🚗) 🍃 Access this compact courtyard space by walking through the **Kakulas Sister deli** (📞 08-9430 4445; www.kakulassister.com.au; 29-31 Market St; ⏱9am-5.30pm Mon-Sat, 11.30am-5pm Sun; 🚗), and look forward to some of Freo's best coffee and an ever-changing menu designed by Wade Drummond, a former contestant on Australian *MasterChef*. Healthy flavours could include a salad of roasted eggplant, chickpeas and toasted almonds, sourdough sandwiches, or good-value brown-rice bowls overflowing with Asian spiced chicken.

Little Concept CAFE $
(📞 08-6323 1531; www.facebook.com/TheLittleConcept; 7 Wray Ave; snacks & mains $10-18; ⏱6.30am-5pm Mon-Sat, 7.30am-3pm Sun; 🚗) 🍃 Part of the emerging Wray Ave cafe scene, the Little Concept is popular with Freo locals popping in for smoothies, excellent breakfast wraps and stonking slabs of frittata. If you're feeling a tad coffeed out, come here to try a wide range of flavoured teas and chais. Lots of raw and vegan options make this a healthy choice too.

⭐Bread in Common BISTRO, BAKERY $$
(📞 08-9336 1032; www.breadincommon.com.au; 43 Pakenham St; shared platters $15-21, mains $19-26; ⏱9am-10pm Sun-Thu, to 11pm Fri & Sat) Be lured by the comforting aroma of the in-house bakery before staying on for cheese and charcuterie platters, or larger dishes such as lamb ribs, octopus or pork belly. The focus is equally on comfort food and culinary flair, while big shared tables and a laid-back warehouse ambience encourage conversation over WA wines and Aussie craft beers and ciders.

★**Manuka Woodfire Kitchen** BARBECUE, PIZZA **$$**
(⌨08-9335 3527; www.manukawoodfire.com.au; 134 High St; shared plates $11-38, pizzas $19-21; ⊙5-9pm Tue-Fri, noon-3pm & 5-9pm Sat & Sun) Centred on a wood-fired oven, the kitchen at Manuka is tiny, but it's still big enough to turn out some of the tastiest food in town. Pretty well everything is cooked in the oven and the seasonal menu could include Esperance octopus, roast chicken with miso sauce or peppers and basil pesto. The pizzas are also very good.

A proudly local drinks menu includes Margaret River wine, cocktails using craft gin from Perth, and beers from WA's Nail Brewing. The Red Ale is a hoppy marvel.

Raw Kitchen VEGETARIAN **$$**
(⌨08-9433 4647; www.therawkitchen.com.au; 181a High St; mains $19-28; ⊙11.30am-3.30pm Mon-Thu, to 9pm Fri-Sun; ⌨) 🍃 Vegan, organic and sustainable, and therefore *very* Freo. Reset your chakra and boost your energy levels with the super-healthy but still very tasty food in this funky, brick-lined warehouse. A lot (but not all) of the menu showcases raw ingredients, but taste is never sacrificed. Gluten-free beer and sustainably produced wine mean you don't have to be *too* virtuous.

Canvas CAFE **$$**
(Map p884; ⌨08-9335 5685; www.canvasat fremantleartscentre.com; Fremantle Arts Centre; mains $15-27; ⊙8am-4pm; ⌨) Freo's best cafe is in the shaded courtyard of the Fremantle Arts Centre, with a menu channelling Middle Eastern, Spanish and North African influences. Breakfast highlights include baked-egg dishes – try the Israeli-style Red Shakshuka – and lunch presents everything from jerk-chicken wraps to bouillabaisse and Tasmanian salmon. The concise drinks list includes craft beer, ciders and wine.

Mantle SOUTH AMERICAN **$$**
(Map p884; www.themantle.com.au; cnr Beach & James Sts; mains $18-30; ⊙4.30-11pm Tue-Fri, 11am-11pm Sat & Sun) Filling a heritage warehouse, the Mantle's three businesses make it worth the 1.5km schlep from central Fremantle. Don Tapa combines South American and Asian flavours, Magna Pizza creates good wood-fired pizza amid the Mantle's rustic industrial ambience, and Alter Ego's hipster bar crew concocts inventive cocktails and serves up frosty craft beer best enjoyed in the raffish, compact courtyard.

Propeller CAFE **$$**
(Map p884; ⌨08-9335 9366; www.propeller northfreo.com.au; 222 Queen Victoria St; shared plates & mains $12-28, pizzas $16-26; ⊙8am-late) Echoes of Fremantle's maritime heritage fill this sunny cafe and bistro in North Fremantle, but the food is anything but old-fashioned and stuffy. Middle Eastern flavours inform dishes including Moorish skewers, a refreshing fennel-and-blood-orange salad, and rustic wood-fired *manoushe* (Lebanese flat breads). Out the front, good coffee is dispensed from a converted shipping container around a sunny courtyard.

Some of Fremantle's more interesting breakfast dishes are served with bloody Mary or Mimosa cocktails.

Bathers Beach House MODERN AUSTRALIAN **$$$**
(⌨08-9335 2911; www.bathersbeachhouse.com. au; 47 Mews Rd; mains $32-42, shared platters $42-72; ⊙11am-late; ⌨) This grand building overlooking Bathers Beach has been reborn as a bustling bistro, with a seafood-heavy menu and chilled wine and craft beer. Oysters come three ways, barramundi partners linguini, and pork belly or wagyu rump are robust meaty options. The deck is Fremantle's best place for a sunset drink, and an adjacent playground is handy for travelling families.

🍸 **Drinking & Nightlife**

Most of Fremantle's big pubs are lined up along South Tce and High St. A couple of interesting smaller bars also lurk in North and South Fremantle, and it's a good destination for fans of craft beer.

★**Norfolk Hotel** PUB
(⌨08-9335 5405; www.norfolkhotel.com.au; 47 South Tce; ⊙11am-midnight Mon-Sat, to 10pm Sun) Slow down to Freo pace at this 1887 pub. Interesting guest beers create havoc for the indecisive drinker, and the food and pizzas are very good. The heritage limestone courtyard is a treat, especially when sunlight peeks through the elms and eucalypts. Downstairs, the Odd Fellow channels a bohemian small-bar vibe and has live music Wednesday to Saturday from 7pm.

Strange Company COCKTAIL BAR
(www.strangecompany.com.au; 5 Nairn St; ⊙noon-midnight) Excellent cocktails – try the spiced daiquiri – WA craft beers and smart bar food make Strange Company a sophisticated alternative to the raffish pubs along South

Tce. It's still very laid-back, though – this is Freo, after all – and after-work action on the sunny terrace segues into after-dark assignations in Strange Company's cosy interior booths.

Percy Flint's Boozery & Eatery
BAR

(Map p884; ☑08-9430 8976; www.facebook.com/percyflintsouthfreo; 211 South Tce; ⏰4pm-midnight Tue-Thu, noon-midnight Fri-Sun) A relaxed neighbourhood watering hole, Percy Flint is very popular with locals. The tap-beer selection is one of Freo's most interesting, with brews from around WA, and shared plates with Mediterranean or Asian flavours are best enjoyed around the big tables in the garden courtyard.

Monk
MICROBREWERY

(☑08-9336 7666; www.themonk.com.au; 33 South Tce; ⏰noon-midnight Mon-Thu, 11am-midnight Fri & Sat, 11am-10pm Sun) Park yourself on the spacious front terrace or in the chic interior, partly fashioned from recycled railway sleepers, and enjoy the Monk's own brews (*kolsch,* mild, wheat, porter, *rauch,* pale ale). The bar snacks and pizzas are also good, and guest beers and regular seasonal brews always draw a knowledgable crowd of local craft-beer nerds.

Mrs Browns
BAR

(Map p884; ☑08-9336 1887; www.mrsbrownbar.com.au; 241 Queen Victoria St; ⏰4.30pm-midnight Tue-Thu, noon-midnight Fri-Sun) Exposed bricks and a copper bar combine with retro and antique furniture to create North Fremantle's most atmospheric drinking den. The music could include all those cult bands you thought were *your* personal secret, and an eclectic menu of beer, wine and tapas targets the more discerning, slightly older bar hound. And you can order in burgers from Flipside (Map p884; ☑08-9433 2188; www.flipsideburgers.com.au; 239 Queen Victoria St; burgers $11.50-14.50; ⏰11.30am-9pm) next door.

Little Creatures
BREWERY

(☑1800 308 388; www.littlecreatures.com.au; Fishing Boat Harbour, 40 Mews Rd; ⏰10am-midnight) Try the Little Creatures Pale Ale and Pilsner, and other beers and ciders under the White Rabbit and Pipsqueak labels. Keep an eye out for one-off Shift Brewers' Stash beers. It's chaotic at times, but the wood-fired pizzas ($19 to $24) are worth the wait. More substantial shared plates ($8 to $24) include kangaroo with tomato chutney and marinated octopus. No bookings.

☆ Entertainment

Fly by Night Musicians Club
LIVE MUSIC

(☑08-9430 5208; www.flybynight.org; 179 High St) Variety is the key at Fly by Night, a not-for-profit club that's been run by musos for musos for years. All kinds perform here, and many local bands made a start here.

Mojos
LIVE MUSIC

(Map p884; ☑08-9430 4010; www.mojosbar.com.au; 237 Queen Victoria St; ⏰7pm-late) Local and national bands (mainly Aussie rock and indie) and DJs play at this small place, and there's a sociable beer garden out the back. First Friday of the month is reggae night; every Monday is open-mic night.

Metropolis Fremantle
LIVE MUSIC

(☑08-9336 1880; www.metropolisfremantle.com.au; 58 South Tce) A great space to watch a gig, Metropolis turns into a nightclub on the weekends. International and popular Australian bands and DJs perform here.

Newport Hotel
LIVE MUSIC

(☑08-9335 2428; www.thenewport.com; 2 South Tce; ⏰noon-midnight Mon-Sat, to 10pm Sun) Local bands and DJs gig from Friday to Sunday. The Tiki Beat Bar is worth a kitsch cocktail or two.

🛍 Shopping

The bottom end of High St features interesting and quirky shopping. Fashion stores run along Market St, towards the train station. Queen Victoria St in North Fremantle is the place to go for antiques. Don't forget Fremantle Markets (p906) for clothes and souvenirs.

Common Ground Collective
DESIGN

(☑0418 158 778; www.facebook.com/cmmngrnd; 82 High St; ⏰9am-5pm Mon-Sat, 10am-4pm Sun) An eclectic showcase of jewellery, apparel and design, mainly from local Fremantle artisans and designers. The coffee at the in-house cafe is pretty damn good too.

Didgeridoo Breath
ARTS & CRAFTS

(☑08-9430 6009; www.didgeridoobreath.com; 6 Market St; ⏰10.30am-5pm) The planet's biggest selection of didgeridoos, Indigenous Australian books and CDs, and how-to-play lessons ranging from one hour to four weeks. You'll probably hear the shop before you see it.

Aboriginart
ART

(☑08-9336 1739; www.aboriginart.com.au; 6 Elder Pl; ⏰10am-4pm Tue-Sun) Contemporary and collectable art ethically sourced from

Indigenous artists living in Australia's Central and Western Desert areas.

Found
ARTS & CRAFTS

(Map p884; ☑ 08-9432 9555; www.fac.org.au; Fremantle Arts Centre, 1 Finnerty St; ☉ 10am-5pm) The Fremantle Arts Centre (p906) shop stocks an inspiring range of WA art and craft.

Japingka
ART

(☑ 08-9335 8265; www.japingka.com.au; 47 High St; ☉ 10am-5.30pm Mon-Fri, noon-5pm Sat & Sun) Specialising in Aboriginal fine art from WA and beyond. Purchases come complete with extensive notes about the works and the artists who created them.

Record Finder
MUSIC

(☑ 08-9335 2770; www.facebook.com/The-Record-Finder-232286070119578/; 87 High St; ☉ 10am-5pm) A treasure trove of old vinyl, including rarities and collectables.

Bodkin's Bootery
SHOES

(☑ 08-9336 1484; www.bodkinsbootery.com; 72 High St; ☉ 9am-5pm Mon-Sat, noon-5pm Sun) Handcrafted men's and women's boots and hats. Aussie as.

New Edition
BOOKS

(☑ 08-9335 2383; www.newedition.com.au; cnr High & Henry Sts; ☉ 9am-6pm) Celebrating a sunny corner location, this bookworm's dream has comfy armchairs for browsing, and a superb collection of Australian fiction and non-fiction tomes for sale.

Mills Records
MUSIC

(☑ 08-9335 1945; www.mills.com.au; 22 Adelaide St; ☉ 9am-5.30pm Mon-Sat, noon-5pm Sun) Music, including some rarities, and concert tickets. Check out the 'Local's Board' for recordings by Freo and WA acts.

ℹ Information

INTERNET ACCESS

For free wi-fi, try **Moore & Moore** (☑ 08-9335 8825; www.mooreandmoorecafe.com; 46 Henry St; mains $13-22; ☉ 7am-4pm; 🛜), or the FREbytes hot spot in the vicinity of the Town Hall and **library** (☑ 08-9432 9766; www.frelibrary. wordpress.com; Town Hall, Kings Sq; ☉ 9.30am-5.30pm Mon, Fri & Sat, to 8pm Tue-Thu; 🛜).

TOURIST INFORMATION

See www.fremantlestory.com.au for visitor information. Online www.lovefreo.com is a good source of information on local openings and events.

Rottnest Island Visitor Centre (p917) Book bikes and excursions here before you depart Fremantle.

Visitor Centre (☑ 08-9431 7878; www.visitfre mantle.com.au; Town Hall, Kings Sq; ☉ 9am-5pm Mon-Fri, 9am-4pm Sat, 10am-4pm Sun) Accommodation and tour bookings, and bike rental.

ℹ Getting There & Away

A taxi fare from **Perth Airport** (☑ 08-9478 8888; www.perthairport.com.au) is $65 to $70.

Fremantle sits within zone 2 of **Transperth** (p902), the Perth public-transport system, and is only 30 minutes from Perth by train. There are numerous buses between Perth's city centre and Fremantle, including routes 103, 106, 107, 111 and 158.

Another very pleasant way to get here from Perth is by taking the 1¼-hour river cruise run by **Captain Cook Cruises** (p886).

ℹ Getting Around

There are numerous one-way streets and parking meters in Freo. It's easy enough to travel by foot or on the free CAT bus service, which takes in all the major sights on a continuous loop every 10 minutes from 7.30am to 6.30pm Monday to Thursday, till 9pm Friday, and 10am to 6.30pm on the weekend.

Bicycles (Fremantle Visitor Centre, Kings Sq; ☉ 9am-5pm Mon-Fri, 9am-4pm Sat, 10am-4pm Sun) can be rented for free at the visitor centre and are an ideal way to get around Freo's storied streets. A refundable bond of $200 applies.

Car rental is available through **Backpacker** (☑ 08-9430 8869; www.backpackercarrentals. com.au; 235 Hampton Rd).

Ferries depart Fremantle for Rottnest Island from stops at Victoria Quay and Rous Head.

AROUND PERTH

Rottnest Island (Wadjemup)

POP 475

'Rotto' has long been the family-holiday playground of choice for Perth locals. Although it's only about 19km offshore from Fremantle, this car-free, off-the-grid slice of paradise, ringed by secluded beaches and bays, feels a million miles away.

Cycling around the 11km-long, 4.5km-wide island is a real pleasure, and it's easy to discover your own sandy beach. You're bound to spot quokkas, the island's only native land mammals. Also relatively common are New Zealand fur seals off magical **West End**, dolphins, and – in season – whales. King skinks are also regularly seen sunning themselves on the roads.

Snorkelling, fishing, surfing and diving are also all excellent on the island. There's not a lot to do here that's not outdoors, so postpone your day trip if the weather is bad. It can be quite unpleasant when the wind really kicks up.

History

The island was originally called Wadjemup (place across the water), but Wadjuk oral history recalls that it was joined to the mainland before being cut off by rising waters. Modern scientists date that occurrence to before 6500 years ago, making these memories some of the world's oldest.

Dutch explorer Willem de Vlamingh claimed discovery of the island in 1696 and named it Rotte-nest ('rat's nest' in Dutch) because of the king-sized 'rats' (which were actually quokkas) he saw there.

From 1838 the island was used as a prison for Aboriginal men and boys from all around the state. At least 3670 people were incarcerated here, in harsh conditions, with around 370 dying. Although there were no new prisoners after 1903, some existing prisoners served their sentences here until 1931. Even before the prison was built, Wadjemup was considered a 'place of the spirits', and it's been rendered even more sacred to Indigenous people because of the hundreds of their own, including prominent resistance leaders, who died here. Many avoid it to this day.

During WWI, approximately a thousand men of German or Austrian extraction were incarcerated here, their wives and children left to fend for themselves on the mainland. Internment resumed during WWII, although at that time it was mainly WA's Italian population that was imprisoned.

There's an ongoing push to return the island to its original name. One suggested compromise is to adopt a dual name, Wadjemup/Rottnest.

◉ Sights

Most of Rottnest's historic buildings, built mainly with the labour of Aboriginal prisoners, are grouped around Thomson Bay, where the ferry lands.

Salt Store HISTORIC BUILDING
(Colebatch Ave; ⊙10am-3pm) **FREE** A photographic exhibition in this 19th-century building looks at a different chapter of local history: when the island's salt lakes provided all of WA's salt (between 1838 and 1950). It's also the meeting point for walking tours.

Vlamingh's Lookout VIEWPOINT
Not far away from Thomson Bay (go up past the old European cemetery), this unsigned vantage point offers panoramic views of the island, including its salt lakes. It's on View Hill, off Digby Dr.

Quod HISTORIC SITE
(Kitson St) Built in 1864, this octagonal building with a central courtyard was once the Aboriginal prison block but is now part of the Rottnest Lodge hotel. During its time as a prison several men would share a 3m by 1.7m cell, with no sanitation (most of the deaths here were due to disease). The only part of the complex that can be visited is a small whitewashed chapel. A weekly Sunday service is held at 9.30am.

Aboriginal Burial Ground CEMETERY
Adjacent to the Quod is a wooded area where hundreds of Aboriginal prisoners are buried in unmarked graves. Until relatively recently, this area was used as a camping ground, but it's now fenced off with signs asking visitors to show respect for what is regarded as a sacred site. Plans are under consideration to convert the area into a memorial, in consultation with Aboriginal elders.

Rottnest Museum MUSEUM
(Kitson St; admission by gold-coin donation; ⊙11am-3.30pm) Housed in the old hay-store building, this little museum tells the island's natural and human history, warts and all, including dark tales of shipwrecks and incarceration.

🏃 Activities

Most visitors here come for Rottnest's beaches and aquatic activities. **The Basin** is the most popular beach for family-friendly swimming as it's protected by a ring of reefs. Other popular spots are **Longreach Bay** and **Geordie Bay**, though there are many smaller secluded beaches such as **Little Parakeet Bay**.

Excellent visibility, temperate waters, coral reefs and shipwrecks make Rottnest a top spot for scuba diving and snorkelling. There are snorkel trails with underwater

Around Perth

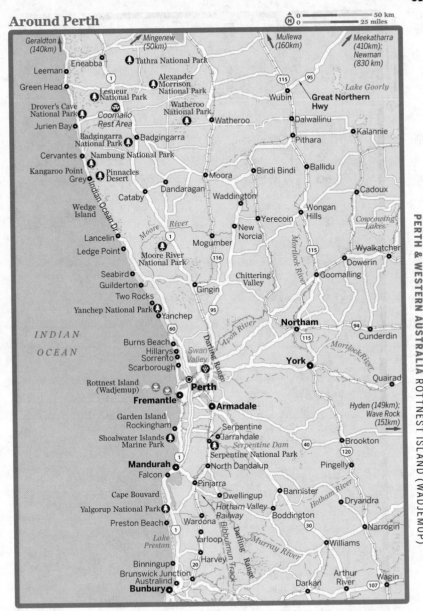

plaques at Little Salmon Bay and Parker Point. The Basin, Little Parakeet Bay, Longreach Bay and Geordie Bay are also good. Rottnest Island Bike Hire (p917) hires out masks, snorkels and fins, as well as kayaks, surfboards, paddleboards and scooters. The only wreck that's accessible to snorkellers without a boat is at Thomson Bay.

The Australasian Diving Academy (p883) organises wreck-diving here. The best surf breaks are at Strickland, Salmon and Stark Bays, towards the western end of the island.

Rottnest Island (Wadjemup)

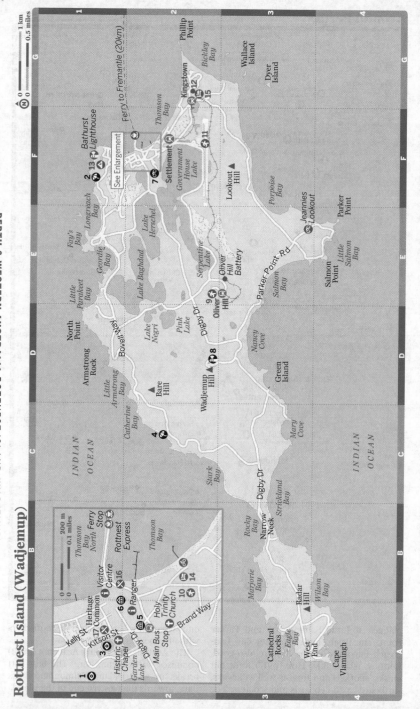

Rottnest Island (Wadjemup)

Rottnest is ideal for twitchers because of the varied habitats: coast, lakes, swamps, heath, woodlands and settlements. Coastal birds include pelicans, gannets, cormorants, bar-tailed godwits, whimbrels, fairy terns, bridled terns, crested terns, oystercatchers and majestic ospreys. For more, grab a copy of *A Bird's Eye View of Rottnest Island* from the visitor centre (p917).

Skydive Geronimo SKYDIVING
(☑ 1300 449 669; www.skydivegeronimo.com.au; Rottnest Airport; 10,000/14,000/15,000ft $389/ 489/539; ◷ 8am-3pm Sat & Sun, by appointment weekdays) Take an island leap of faith and land on the beach. Bookings essential; minimum age 12.

Oliver Hill Train & Tour RAIL
(☑ 08-9432 9300; www.rottnestisland.com; adult/ child $29/16.50) This trip (departing from the train station at 1.30pm) takes you by train to historic **Oliver Hill battery** and includes the Gun & Tunnels tour run by Rottnest Voluntary Guides.

Scenic Joy Flights SCENIC FLIGHTS
(☑ 1300 895 538, 0411 264 547; www.rottnest. aero/scenic-rottnest; 10/20/35min $45/75/110) Spectacular flights over the island, departing from Rottnest Airport.

☞ Tours

Check times online at www.rvga.asn.au or at the Salt Store (p912), or call the visitor centre.

Grand Island Tour BUS
(☑ 08-9432 9300; www.rottnestisland.com/tours; adult/child incl lunch $69/55; ◷ departs 11am) A 3½-hour in-depth exploration of the island that includes lunch. Book online or at the visitor centre when you arrive. Buses depart from the main bus stop in Thomson Bay.

Island Explorer Tour BUS
(☑ 08-9432 9300; www.rottnestisland.com; adult/ child/family $20/12/50; ◷ departs every 1¼hr 8.45am-3pm) Handy hop-on, hop-off coach service stopping at 18 locations around the island. Includes a limited commentary and is a great way to get your bearings when you first arrive.

Segway Tours TOURS
(☑ 1300 808 180; www.segwaytourswa.com.au; Kingstown Barracks, cnr Kingstown Rd & Hospital Lane; 1hr/90min $79/115; ◷ tours depart 9am, 11am, 12.30pm & 2.30pm) Choose from the popular 90-minute off-road Fortress Adventure Tour or the 60-minute Settlement Explorer Tour taking in the history of Rottnest's original settlement. If you just want to zip around on a Segway, sign up for 25 minutes ($40) in the Segway Experience Zone. Participants must be at least nine years old.

Charter 1 BOATING
(☑ 0428 604 794; www.charter1.com.au; adult/ child $229/149; ◷ mid-Sep–Apr) Briny excursions departing from Fremantle include full-day sails incorporating kayaking and snorkelling.

Rottnest Voluntary Guides WALKING
(☑ 08-9372 9757; www.rvga.asn.au) FREE Free, themed walks leave from the central Salt Store daily, with topics including History, Reefs, Wrecks and Daring Sailors, Vlamingh Lookout and Salt Lakes, and the Quokka Walk. It also runs tours of Wadjemup Lighthouse (adult/child $9/4) and Oliver Hill Gun & Tunnels (adult/child $9/4); you'll need to make your own way there for the last two.

PERTH & WESTERN AUSTRALIA ROTTNEST ISLAND (WADJEMUP)

QUOKKAS

These cute little docile bundles of fur have suffered a number of indignities over the years. First Willem de Vlamingh's crew mistook them for rats as big as cats. Then the British settlers misheard and mangled their name (the Noongar word was probably *quak-a* or *gwaga*). But, worst of all, a cruel trend of 'quokka soccer' by sadistic louts in the 1990s saw many kicked to death before a $10,000 fine was imposed; occasional cases are still reported. On a more positive note, the phenomenon of 'quokka selfies' briefly illuminated the internet in 2015 with various Rottnest marsupials achieving minor global fame on Instagram. Google 'Rottnest quokka selfies' to see the best of #quokkaselfie.

These marsupials of the macropod family (relatives of kangaroos and wallabies) were once found throughout the southwest but are now confined to mainland forests and a population of 8000 to 10,000 on Rottnest Island. Don't be surprised if one approaches looking for a titbit. Just say no, as human food isn't good for them.

✾ Festivals & Events

Rotto is the site of annual school leavers' and end-of-uni-exams parties, a time when the island is overrun by kids 'getting blotto on Rotto'. Depending on your age, it's either going to be the best time you've ever had or the worst – check the calendar before proceeding.

Rottofest   MUSIC

(www.rottofest.com.au; ☉Sep) The annual Rottofest immerses the island in a day of music, film and comedy.

🛏 Sleeping & Eating

Rotto is wildly popular in summer and during school holidays, when accommodation is booked out for months in advance. Prices can rise steeply at these times. Check websites for off-peak deals combining transport to the island, especially for weekday visits.

Most visitors to Rotto self-cater. The **general store** (☑08-9292-5017; www.rottnestgeneral store.com.au; Thomson Bay; ☉8am-6pm) is a small supermarket (and also stocks liquor), but if you're staying a while, it's better to bring supplies with you. Another option is to pre-order food from the general store, and they'll equip your accommodation with food and drinks before your arrival. Rottnest's small township has cafes and a good bakery.

Kingstown Barracks
Youth Hostel   HOSTEL $

(☑08-9432 9111; www.rottnestisland.com; Kingstown Rd; dm/f $53/117) This hostel is located in old army barracks that still have a rather institutional feel and few facilities. Check in at the visitor centre before you make the 1.8km walk, bike or bus trip to Kingston.

Allison Tentland   CAMPGROUND $

(☑08-9432 9111; www.rottnestisland.com; Thomson Bay; sites $38) Camping on the island is restricted to this leafy camping ground with barbecues. Be vigilant about your belongings, especially your food – cheeky quokkas have been known to help themselves.

Rottnest Island
Authority Cottages   COTTAGE $$

(☑08-9432 9111; www.rottnestisland.com; cottages $189-322) There are more than 250 villas and cottages for rent around the island. Some have magnificent beachfront positions and are palatial; others are more like beach shacks. Prices rise by around $60 for Friday and Saturday, and they increase by up to $120 in peak season (late September to April). Check online for the labyrinthine pricing schedule.

Karma Rottnest Lodge   HOTEL $$

(☑1300 7688 6378; www.karmagroup.com; Kitson St; r $210-320; 🖶🅿🌊) It's claimed there are ghosts in this complex, which is based around the former Quod (p912) prison building and boys' reformatory school. If that worries you, ask for a room in the new section, looking onto a salt lake. Older rooms are comfortable but fairly compact and basic. Services and amenities include bar, restaurant and spa treatments. Rates are best midweek.

Hotel Rottnest   HOTEL $$$

(☑08-9292 5011; www.hotelrottnest.com.au; 1 Bedford Ave; r $270-320; 🖶🅿) Based around the former summer-holiday pad for the state's governors (built in 1864), the former Quokka Arms has been transformed by a stylish renovation. The whiter-than-white rooms in an adjoining building are smart and modern, if a tad pricey. Some have beautiful sea views.

Hotel Rottnest
PUB FOOD **$$**

(☎ 08-9292 5011; www.hotelrottnest.com.au; 1 Bedford Ave; mains $23-37, pizzas $20-26; ◷ 11am-late) It's hard to imagine a more inviting place for a sunset pint of Little Creatures than the AstroTurf 'lawn' of this chic waterfront hotel. A big glass pavilion creates an open and inviting space, and bistro-style food and pizzas are reasonably priced given the location and ambience. Bands and DJs regularly boost the laid-back island mood during summer.

Aristos
SEAFOOD **$$$**

(☎ 08-9292 5171; www.aristosrottnest.com.au; Colebatch Ave; breakfast $10-23, lunch & dinner mains $27-46; ◷ 8am-late) An upmarket but pricey option for seafood, steaks and salads, fish and chips, burgers, ice cream or excellent coffee. Push the boat (way) out with a seafood platter for two people ($155).

❶ Information

At the Thomson Bay settlement, behind the main jetty, there's a shopping area with an ATM. **Visitor Centre** (☎ 08-9372 9732; www.rottnest island.com; Thomson Bay; ◷ 7.30am-5pm Sat-Thu, to 7pm Fri, extended hours summer) Handles check-ins for all of the island authority's accommodation. There's a bookings counter at the **Fremantle office** (☎ 08-9432 9300; www. rottnestisland.com; E Shed, Victoria Quay), near where the ferry departs.
Ranger (☎ 08-9372 9788) For fishing and boating information.

❶ Getting There & Away

There is a fee per adult/child/family of $18/6.50/42.50 to visit the island. This fee is included in ferry costs but payable separately if you're visiting the island on a private boat.

AIR
Rottnest Air-Taxi (☎ 1300 895 538; www.rott nest.aero) Flies from Jandakot airport. Prices for whole planes cost from $250, working out to around $83 per person.

BOAT
Ferry services to the island:
Rottnest Express (☎ 1300 467 688; www. rottnestexpress.com.au) Ferries from Perth's **Barrack Street Jetty** (p903; 1¾ hours, once daily), **Fremantle** (30 minutes, five times daily) and North Fremantle (30 minutes, three times daily). Packages including bike hire, snorkelling equipment, meals, accommodation and tours are all available. Services increase in summer and during school holidays. The Perth and Fremantle departure points are handy to train stations.

Rottnest Fast Ferries (☎ 08-9246 1039; www.rottnestfastferries.com.au; adult/child $85.50/48.75) Departs from Hillarys Boat Harbour (40 minutes; three times daily), around 40 minutes' drive north of Perth. See www.hillarys boatharbour.com.au for public-transport details. An additional 6pm ferry departs on Friday night in summer. Packages also available.

❶ Getting Around

BICYCLE
Rottnest is just big enough (and has just enough hills) to make a day's ride good exercise. Electric bikes (half-/full-day $40/60) are also available.

Bikes can be booked in advance online or on arrival through **Rottnest Island Bike Hire** (☎ 08-9292 5105; www.rottnestisland.com; cnr Bedford Ave & Welch Way; bikes per half-/full-day from $16/30; ◷ 8.30am-4pm, to 5.30pm summer). Photo ID must be shown.

The ferry companies also hire bikes as part of an island package, and they have them waiting for visitors on arrival. The visitor centre hires bikes, too.

BUS
A free shuttle runs between Thomson Bay, the main accommodation areas and the airport, departing roughly every 35 minutes, with the last bus at 8pm.

The **Island Explorer** (p915) is a handy hop-on, hop-off coach service stopping at 18 locations around the island. It includes a commentary and is a great way to get your bearings when you first arrive. Between Geordie Bay and Thomson Bay it's free.

Rockingham & the Peel District

Taking in swaths of jarrah forest, historic towns and the increasingly glitzy coastal resort of Mandurah, the Peel Region can easily be tackled as a day trip from Perth or as the first stopping point of a longer expedition down the South Western Hwy (Rte 1).

As you enter the Peel, you'll pass out of Wadjuk country and into that of their fellow Noongar neighbours, the Pinjarup (or Binjareb) people.

Rockingham
POP 135,000

Just 46km south of Perth, Rockingham has good beaches and the Shoalwater Islands Marine Park (p918), where you can observe dolphins, sea lions and penguins in the wild.

Rockingham was founded in 1872 as a port, although this function was taken over by Fremantle in the 1890s. There's still a substantial industrial complex to the north, at Kwinana.

Most places of interest are stretched along Rockingham Beach.

◉ Sights & Activities

**Shoalwater Islands
Marine Park**   NATURE RESERVE
(www.parks.dpaw.wa.gov.au/park/shoalwater-islands; ⊙ closed for nesting Jun–mid-Sep) ✿ Just a few minutes' paddle, swim or boat ride away from the shore is strictly protected **Penguin Island**, home to penguins, silver gulls, boardwalks, swimming beaches and picnic tables. Apart from birdwatching (pied cormorants, pelicans, crested and bridled terns, oystercatchers), day visitors can also swim and snorkel.

The **Penguin Island ferry** is run by Rockingham Wild Encounters. Tickets that combine the ferry with entry to the penguin feeding at the island's **discovery centre** (adult/child $23/18.50) are available.

West Coast Dive Park   DIVING
(✆ 08-9592 3464; www.westcoastdivepark.com.au; permits per day/week $25/50) Diving within the Shoalwater Islands Marine Park became even more interesting after the sinking of the *Saxon Ranger*, a supposedly jinxed 400-tonne fishing vessel. Permits to dive at this site are available from the visitor centre (p918). Contact the Australasian Diving Academy (p883) about expeditions here and to the wrecks of three other boats, two planes and various reefs in the vicinity.

Rockingham Wild Encounters   WILDLIFE
(✆ 08-9591 1333; www.rockinghamwildencounters.com.au; cnr Arcadia Dr & Penguin Rd; ⊙ Sep-May) ✿ The only operator licensed to take people to Penguin Island near Rockingham, this outfit also runs other low-impact tours. The most popular is the **dolphin swim** (per person $205 to $225), which lets you interact with wild bottlenose dolphins. Swimming with dolphins can disturb them, so an alternative is the two-hour **dolphin-watch tour** (adult/child $85/50).

Capricorn Seakayaking   KAYAKING
(✆ 0427 485 123; www.capricornseakayaking.com.au; per person $180; ⊙ late Sep–late Apr) Runs full-day sea-kayaking tours around Penguin and Seal Islands. Also includes wildlife watching and snorkelling.

✗ Eating

★ Ostro Eatery   CAFE $$
(✆ 08-9592 8957; www.ostroeatery.com.au; 11a Rockingham Beach Rd; mains $15-28; ⊙ 7.30am-3pm Mon-Wed, 7.30am-late Thu-Sun) This weekday cafe with shared tables morphs into a sociable evening option later in the week. The blue-swimmer-crab omelette is a great way to start the day, and from Thursday to Sunday there are sophisticated dinner options, including Exmouth prawns and beef-cheek ravioli. Cold-pressed juices and house-made sodas complement a concise selection of beer and wine.

Rustico   CAFE $$
(✆ 08-9528 4114; www.rusticotapas.com.au; 61 Rockingham Beach Rd; shared plates $14-26, pizzas $17; ⊙ 4-9pm Tue, noon-10pm Wed-Sun) This stylish cafe is renowned for its authentic Spanish-style food. Sit on the corner terrace with ocean views, and tuck into sweetcorn-and-cheese croquettes or pan-seared squid. A six-course degustation (per person $59) showcases salmon, scallops and pork belly, and wines are also available to partner each course. Cocktails, sangria and craft beer all contribute to a fun vibe.

ⓘ Information

Visitor Centre (✆ 08-9592 3464; www.rockinghamvisitorcentre.com.au; 19 Kent St; ⊙ 9am-5pm) Has accommodation listings.

ⓘ Getting There & Around

Rockingham sits within zone 5 of the Perth public-transport system, **Transperth** (p902). Regular trains depart from Rockingham station, via the Mandurah line, to Perth Underground/Esplanade ($8.10, 34 minutes) and Mandurah ($5.50, 18 minutes).

Rockingham station is around 4km southeast of Rockingham Beach and around 6km east of Mersey Point, from where the **Penguin Island Ferry** (Mersey Point Jetty; adult/child $15/12.50; ⊙ hourly 9am-3pm mid-Sep–May) departs; catch bus 551 or 555 to the beach or stay on the 551 to Mersey Point.

Mandurah

POP 84,537

Shrugging off its fusty retirement-haven image, Mandurah has made concerted efforts to reinvent itself as an upmarket beach resort, taking advantage of its new train link to Perth's public-transport network. And, although its connected set of redeveloped 'precincts' and 'quarters' may sound a little pretentious, the overall effect is actually pretty cool. You can wander along the waterfront from the Ocean Marina (boats, cafes and the Dolphin Quay indoor market), past the Venetian Canals (glitzy apartments linked by Venetian-ish sandstone bridges), through the Boardwalk and Cultural Precinct (more eateries, visitor centre, cinema, arts centre) to the Bridge Quarter (still more restaurants and bars).

Mandurah Bridge spans the Mandurah Estuary, which sits between the ocean and the large body of water known as the Peel Inlet. It's one of the best places in the region for fishing, crabbing, prawning (March and April) and dolphin spotting.

◉ Sights & Activities

Several beautiful beaches are within walking distance of the Mandurah waterfront. Town Beach is just across from the marina, at the southern end of Silver Sands resort. It's perhaps the best of the ocean beaches. There's a boat-free swimming area on the far side of the estuary, just north of Mandurah Bridge. Here dolphins have been known to swim up to kids for a frolic. West of the mouth of the estuary is family-friendly Doddi's Beach, facing the ocean.

Mandurah Cruises CRUISE
(☑ 08-9581 1242; www.mandurahcruises.com.au; Boardwalk) Take a one-hour Dolphin & Scenic Canal Cruise (adult/child $28/14; departs on the hour from 10am to 4pm), a half-day Murray River Lunch Cruise ($89/55; Wednesday and Saturday) and, through December, a one-hour Christmas Lights Canal Cruise ($33/18), that gawps at millionaires' mansions under the pretence of admiring their festive displays.

**Mandurah Boat
& Bike Hire** BOATING, CYCLING
(☑ 08-9535 5877; www.mandurahboatandbikehire. com.au; Boardwalk) Chase the fish on a four-seat dinghy or six-seat pontoon (per hour/ day from $55/350). Also hires out bikes (per hour/day $10/40). If you're keen to get active on the water, ask about kayak and SUP (stand-up paddleboard) hire.

⊨ Sleeping & Eating

Restaurants and cafes abound on the Boardwalk, at Dolphin Quay, and back in the older, more established area of Mandurah.

Dolphin Point B&B B&B $$
(☑ 08-9581 5813; www.dolphinpointbandb.com.au; 26 Bermuda Pl, Halls Head; ste/apt from $170/270; ❄ ⸙) With a waterfront location right in the heart of Mandurah's famed canals, Dolphin Point B&B is a great place to wind down and wave at the excursion boats as they putter past. Options include a comfortable suite and a self-contained apartment with a full kitchen. Both have water views, and the apartment also has a barbecue for relaxed evening meals.

Seashells Resort RESORT $$
(☑ 08-9550 3000; www.seashells.com.au; 16 Dolphin Dr; apt from $195; ❄ ⸙ ⸙) Seashells' apartments are cool and spacious, and there's a beach on its doorstep and a lovely infinity-lipped pool just metres away. Check into one of the luxury beachfront villas and you may not want to leave.

Mandurah Ocean Marina Chalets MOTEL $$
(☑ 08-9535 8173; www.marinachalets.com.au; 6 The Lido; studios & chalets $117-175; ❄ ⸙) The ambience is a bit like a British holiday camp, but the chalets and motel units are spotless and modern, with fully equipped kitchens. There's a shared barbecue area and crab-cooking facility, and the canals and restaurants of Ocean Marina and Dolphin Quay are a short walk away.

★Flic's Kitchen MODERN AUSTRALIAN $$
(☑ 08-9535 1661; www.flicskitchen.com; 3/16 Mandurah Tce; breakfast $10-23, shared plates $16-24; ☺ 8am-late Wed-Sat, to 3pm Sun; ⸙) Perfectly located to catch the afternoon sun, this recent opening infused with cosmopolitan cool has outdoor seating and a menu covering breakfast, lunch and dinner. Highlights include corn hotcakes with chipotle-spiced chicken for brunch, and Mandurah-crab croquettes as the sun goes down. Expect a good beer and wine list and vegan and paleo menu options.

Peninsula BISTRO $$
(☑ 08-9534 9899; www.thepenmandurah.com. au/; 1 Marco Polo Dr; mains $22-40, bar snacks $10-24; ☺ 11am-9.30pm) There's been a pub on this spot since 1911, but 'The Pen's' latest 2016 reincarnation has turned it into a sleek 21st-century watering hole. Huge picture windows allow brilliant marine views from the restaurant serving upscale mains, while the absolute waterside beer garden is great for frosty pints of Tiger beer and crab tacos with daikon and *sriracha* dressing.

🍷 Drinking & Nightlife

DPM Cafe   CAFE
(☎0459 982 710; www.facebook.com/dawnpatrol
mobilecafe; 14 Mandurah Tce; ⊙6am-4pm Mon,
Tue, Thu & Fri, 6am-noon Wed, 7am-noon Sat &
Sun) The best coffee in town is at this funky
hole-in-the-wall place a short stroll from the
estuary. Partner it with a toasted sourdough
sandwich for a good-value lunch.

Brighton Hotel   PUB
(☎08-9534 8864; www.brightonmandurah.com.
au; 10-12 Mandurah Tce; ⊙10am-late Mon-Sat, to
10pm Sun) Watch the sun set over the estuary
with a glass of wine, and return after 8pm
at the weekend to move to the DJs. Decent
meals for lunch and dinner complete the
picture for a classic Aussie pub.

ⓘ Information

Visitor Centre (☎08-9550 3999; www.visit
peel.com.au; 75 Mandurah Tce; ⊙9am-5pm)
On the estuary boardwalk.

ⓘ Getting There & Away

Mandurah is 72km from central Perth; take the
Kwinana Fwy and follow the signs.

Mandurah sits within the outermost zone (7)
of the Perth public-transport system and is the
terminus of Transperth's Mandurah line. There
are direct trains from Mandurah to Perth Un-
derground/Esplanade ($10.70, 50 minutes) and
Rockingham ($8.10, 18 minutes).

Transwa (☎1300 662 205; www.transwa.
wa.gov.au) coach routes include the following:
➡ SW1 (12 per week) to East Perth ($17.50, 1½
hours), Bunbury ($17.50, two hours), Busselton
($27, 2¾ hours), Margaret River ($35, four
hours) and Augusta ($38, 4¾ hours).
➡ SW2 (three times weekly) to Balingup ($29,
three hours), Bridgetown ($32, 3½ hours) and
Pemberton ($44, 4½ hours).
➡ GS3 (weekly) to Denmark ($69, 7¼ hours)
and Albany ($75, eight hours).

Hyden & Wave Rock

Large granite outcrops dot the Central and
Southern Wheat Belts, and the most famous
of these is Wave Rock. The nearest town is
Hyden, a sleepy bush settlement including
motel, cafe, bakery and petrol station.

This area is best explored with your own
vehicle, ideally on the way to somewhere
else. If heading to/from the Nullarbor,
take the 300km unsealed direct Hyden–
Norseman Rd, which will save 100km or
so. Look for the brochure *The Granite and
Woodlands Discovery Trail* at the Norseman or Wave Rock visitor centres.

Transwa (☎1300 662 205; www.transwa.
wa.gov.au) runs bus GE2 from East Perth to
Hyden ($55, five hours) and on to Esperance
($53, five hours) every Tuesday, returning on
Thursday. **Western Travel Bug** (☎08-9486
4222; www.travelbug.com.au; adult/child $185/135;

WORTH A TRIP

DWELLINGUP

Dwellingup is a small, forest-shrouded township with character, 100km south of Perth.
Its reputation as an activity hub has been enhanced by the hardy long-distance walk-
ers and cyclists passing through on the **B**ibbulmun Track (p951) and the Munda
Biddi Trail respectively.

Visit the **Forest Heritage Centre** (☎08-9538 1395; www.forestheritagecentre.com.au;
1 Acacia St; adult/child $5.50/3.50; ⊙10am-3pm) for displays on local flora and fauna and
a shop selling pieces crafted by the resident woodwork artists. The **Hotham Valley
Railway** (☎08-6278 1111; www.hothamvalleyrailway.com.au; Forest Train adult/child $28/14,
Restaurant Train $92, Steam Ranger $40/20; ⊙Forest Train departs 10.30am & 2pm Sat & Sun,
Restaurant Train 7.45pm Sat, Steam Ranger 10.30am & 2pm Sun May-Oct) chugs along 8km of
forest track on a 90-minute return trip, and **Dwellingup Adventures** (☎08-9538 1127;
www.dwellingupadventures.com.au; cnr Marrinup & Newton Sts; 1-person kayaks & 2-person canoes per 3hr $30; ⊙8.30am-5pm) can arrange bike, kayak and canoe rental, and also book
self-guided canoeing and mountain-biking excursions, and guided white-water-rafting
tours (per person $150, from June to October).

Pop into the **Blue Wren Cafe** (☎08-9538 1234; www.facebook.com/DwellingupBlue
WrenCafe; 53 McLarty St; mains $15-18; ⊙8am-7pm Tue-Sun, to 5pm Mon) for excellent home-
made pies, and consider **Lewis Park Chalets'** (☎08-9538 1406; www.lewisparkchalets.
com.au; 99 Irwin Rd; d $150) rural ambience for an overnight stay.

⊘ Tue, Thu & Sat) offers a very long one-day tour from Perth three times a week.

Wave Rock
LANDMARK

The multicoloured cresting swell of Wave Rock is 350km from Perth. Formed some 60 million years ago by weathering and water erosion, the granite outcrop is streaked with colours created by run-off from local mineral springs. To get the most out of Wave Rock, obtain the *Walk Trails at Wave Rock and The Humps* brochure from the visitor centre.

Mulka's Cave & the Humps
CAVE

The superb Mulkas Cave is an important rock-art site, with 450 stencils and handprints. The more adventurous can choose from two walking tracks. The Kalari Trail (1.6km return) climbs onto a huge granite outcrop (one of the Humps) with excellent views, somehow wilder and more impressive than Wave Rock, while the Gnamma Trail (1.2km return) stays low and investigates natural waterholes with panels explaining Noongar culture. The site is 16km from Wave Rock.

Wave Rock Cabins & Caravan Park
CABIN $

(☑ 08-9880 5022; www.waverock.com.au; unpowered/powered sites from $30/48, cabins & cottages from $140; ❋ ⊛) Accommodation can fill up quickly, so phone ahead for a spot amid the gum trees here.

Wave Rock Motel
MOTEL $$

(☑ 08-9880 5052; www.waverock.com.au; 2 Lynch St, Hyden; s/d from $105/150; ❋ ⊛) In Hyden, 4km east of Wave Rock, this motel has well-equipped rooms, a comfy lounge with fireplace, and a bistro where you can barbecue steaks and chicken on an indoor grill.

Visitor Centre
TOURIST INFORMATION

(☑ 08-9880 5182; www.waverock.com.au; Wave Rock; ⊘9am-5pm) Also has a good cafe and quirky local souvenirs.

The Avon Valley

The lush, green Avon Valley – with its atmospheric homesteads featuring big verandahs, rickety wooden wagons and moss-covered rocks – was settled just a year after Perth was founded, and many historic stone buildings still stand proudly in the towns and countryside in the area.

This country traditionally belongs to the Balardung, one of the Noongar peoples.

York
POP 2100

York is the most atmospheric spot in the Avon Valley and is a wonderful place to while away a couple of hours. Avon Tce is lined with heritage buildings, and the entire town has been classified by the National Trust.

The settlers here saw similarities between the Avon Valley and their native Yorkshire, so Governor Stirling bestowed the name York. The town prospered during the gold rush, servicing miners who were heading to Southern Cross, a goldfields town 273km to the east. Most buildings date from this time.

Residency Museum
MUSEUM

(☑ 08-9641 1765; www.theyorksociety.com/residency-museum; Brook St; adult/child $5/3; ⊘1-3pm Tue, Wed & Thu, 11am-3.30pm Sat & Sun) Built in 1858, this museum houses some intriguing historical exhibits and poignant old black-and-white photos of York.

Motor Museum
MUSEUM

(☑ 08-9641 1288; www.yorkmotormuseum.com; 116 Avon Tce; adult/child $9/4; ⊘9.30am-3pm) A must for vintage-car enthusiasts.

Skydive Express
SKYDIVING

(☑ 08-9444 4199; www.skydive.com.au; 3453 Spencers Brook Rd; tandem jumps 8000/14,000ft $259/399) The Avon Valley is WA's skydiving centre; the drop zone is about 3km from town. Weekdays usually offer the best rates.

Faversham House
B&B $$

(☑ 08-9641 1366; www.favershamhouse.com.au; 24 Grey St; r $125-255; ❋ ☏) If you've ever wished you were 'to the manor born', indulge your fantasies in this grand stone mansion (1840). The rooms in the main house are large, TV-free and strewn with antiques; some have four-poster beds. All have smallish bathrooms. The cheaper rooms are in the old servants' quarters (naturally). Breakfast often features poached fruit and croissants with homemade jam.

Jules Cafe
CAFE $

(☑ 08-9641 1832; 121 Avon Tce; snacks & mains $10-18; ⊘8am-4pm Mon-Sat; ☏) 🍴 Putting a colourful spin on heritage York since 1990, Jules Cafe channels a Lebanese heritage for top-notch kebabs, falafel and Middle Eastern sweets. A funky new-age accent is introduced with organic, veggie and gluten-free options, and juices and fruit smoothies are perfect in summer.

WORTH A TRIP

DRYANDRA WOODLAND

With small populations of threatened numbats, woylies and tammar wallabies, this isolated remnant of eucalypt forest 164km southeast of Perth hints at what the wheat belt was like before large-scale land clearing and feral predators wreaked havoc on ecosystems. With numerous walking trails, it makes a great getaway from Perth.

The excellent **Barna Mia Animal Sanctuary** (adult/child/family $20/10/50), home to endangered bilbies, boodies, woylies and marla, conducts 90-minute after-dark torchlight tours, providing a rare opportunity to see these creatures up close. Book through **Parks & Wildlife** (✆08-9881 9222; www.parks.dpaw.wa.gov.au; 7 Wald St, Narrogin; ◷8.30am-4pm) for postsunset tours on Monday, Wednesday, Friday and Saturday and book early for peak periods.

The **Lions Dryandra Village** (✆08-9884 5231; www.dryandravillage.org.au; adult/child $30/15, 2-/4-person cabins $70/90, 8- to 12-person cabins $130) is a 1920s forestry camp with self-contained renovated woodcutters' cabins and the attention of nearby grazing wallabies.

Dryandra Woodland can only be reached with private transport.

ℹ Information

Visitor Centre (✆08-9641 1301; www.avonvalleywa.com.au; Town Hall, 81 Avon Tce; ◷10am-4pm)

Transwa (✆1300 662 205; www.transwa.wa.gov.au) Transwa coach routes include the following: GE2 (three per week) to East Perth ($17.50, 1½ hours), Mundaring ($14, 47 minutes), Hyden ($42, 3¼ hours) and Esperance ($85, 8½ hours), and GS2 to Northam ($8, 33 minutes, six per week), Mt Barker ($58, 5¼ hours, four per week) and Albany ($63, six hours, four per week).

New Norcia

POP 70

The idyllic monastery settlement of New Norcia, 132km from Perth, consists of a cluster of ornate, Spanish-style buildings set incongruously in the Australian bush. Founded in 1846 by Spanish Benedictine monks as an Aboriginal mission, the working monastery today holds prayers and retreats, alongside a business producing boutique breads and gourmet goodies.

New Norcia Museum & Art Gallery
MUSEUM, GALLERY

(✆08-9654 8056; www.newnorcia.wa.edu.au; Great Northern Hwy; combined museum & town tours adult/family $25/60; ◷10am-4.30pm) New Norcia Museum & Art Gallery traces the history of the monastery and houses impressive art, including contemporary exhibitions and one of the country's largest collections of post-Renaissance religious art. The gift shop sells souvenirs, honeys, preserves, and breads baked in the monks' wood-fired oven.

Abbey Church
CHURCH

Inside the abbey church, try to spot the native wildlife in the sgraffito artworks that depict the Stations of the Cross. Look hard, as there's also an astronaut.

Town Tours
TOURS

(✆08-9654 8056; www.newnorcia.wa.edu.au; adult/child $15/10; ◷11am & 1.30pm) Guided two-hour town tours offer a look at the abbey church and the frescoed college chapels; purchase tickets from the museum.

New Norcia Hotel
HOTEL $

(✆08-9654 8034; www.newnorcia.wa.edu.au; Great Northern Hwy; s/d with shared bathroom incl breakfast from $80/100; ◷11am-2pm & 6-8.30pm) New Norcia Hotel harks back to a more genteel time, with sweeping staircases, high ceilings, understated rooms and wide verandahs. An international menu ($15 to $36) is available at the bar or in the elegant dining room. Be sure to try the selection of dips served with New Norcia's own wood-fired sourdough bread.

Monastery Guesthouse
GUESTHOUSE $

(✆08-9654 8002; www.newnorcia.wa.edu.au; full board suggested donation $80) The abbey offers lodging in the Monastery Guesthouse, within the walls of the southern cloister. Guests can join in prayers with the monks (and men can dine with them).

Sunset & Turquoise Coasts

The Indian Ocean Drive connects Perth to a succession of beautiful beaches, sleepy fishing villages, extraordinary geological formations, rugged national parks and incredibly diverse flora.

ⓘ Getting There & Away

Integrity (☑ 1800 226 339; www.integrity coachlines.com.au) runs three times a week along the coast between Perth and Geraldton and on to Exmouth and Broome.

Lancelin
POP 670

Afternoon offshore winds, protective coral and limestone reef and mountainous soft, white dunes make Lancelin perfect for windsurfing, kitesurfing, snorkelling and sandboarding, attracting action seekers from around the world. In January wind worshippers descend for the Lancelin Ocean Classic windsurfing race, starting at Ledge Point to the south.

Makanikai Kiteboarding KITESURFING
(☑ 0406 807 309; www.makanikaikiteboarding. com; lessons from $200) Run lessons in the art of kiteboarding and hires out gear; accommodation packages are also available.

Have a Chat General Store OUTDOORS
(☑ 08-9655 1054; 104 Gingin Rd; sandboard hire per 2hr $10; ⊙ 7am-6pm) Hires sandboards.

Lancelin Ocean Classic SPORTS
(☑ 08-9314 3820; www.lancelinoceanclassic.com.au; ⊙ Jan) Thousands flock to tiny Lancelin each year for this world-famous windsurfing event. Held over four days, the event covers wave sailing on the Thursday and Friday, the marathon on Saturday and the Sunday slalom.

★ Lancelin Lodge YHA HOSTEL $
(☑ 08-9655 2020; www.lancelinlodge.com.au; 10 Hopkins St; dm/d/f $33/90/130; @ 🛜 🗷) This laid-back hostel is well equipped and welcoming, with wide verandahs and lots of communal spaces. The excellent facilities include big kitchen, barbecue, wood-fired pizza oven, swimming pool, ping-pong table, volleyball court and free use of bikes and boogie boards. New owners have effortlessly maintained the standards of previous years. This is still one of WA's best hostels.

Ledge Point Holiday Park CARAVAN PARK $
(☑ 1300 856 088; www.lphp.com.au; 742 Ledge Point Rd; 2-person sites $45, chalets & studios $115-180; @ 🛜) About 10 minutes' drive south of Lancelin, with excellent facilities and spotless accommodation ranging from caravan and camping sites to chalets and studios.

Lots of family-friendly attractions include pedal carts and a jumping pillow. Ledge Point's beach – good for fishing and swimming – is around 500m away.

Windsurfer Beach Chalets APARTMENT $$
(☑ 08-9655 1454; www.lancelinaccommodation. com.au; 1 Hopkins St; d from $170) These self-contained two-bedroom chalets are near the windsurfing beach and are a good choice for groups of friends and families (each chalet sleeps up to six). They're functional and well equipped, and have a sun terrace backing onto a grassy area. The operators can also arrange accommodation in Lancelin and nearby Ledge Point in a variety of self-contained holiday homes.

★ Endeavour Tavern PUB FOOD $$
(☑ 08-9655 1052; www.endeavourtavern.com.au; 58 Gingin Rd; mains $23-32; ⊙ 10.30am-10pm Sun-Thu, to midnight Fri & Sat) A classic beachfront Aussie pub with a beer garden overlooking the ocean. The casual eatery serves pub-grub classics and tasty burgers and salads. Naturally, the seafood is popular and very good.

ⓘ Getting There & Away

From Lancelin, Integrity buses leave from Lancelin Lodge YHA at 11.30pm on Tuesday and Thursday to Cervantes ($34, one hour), Jurien Bay ($34, 1¼ hours) and Geraldton ($50, four hours). Heading south, buses travel to Perth ($34, two hours), leaving Lancelin at 4.55am on Saturday and Monday mornings.

Cervantes & Pinnacles Desert
POP 480

The laid-back crayfishing town of Cervantes, 198km north of Perth, makes a pleasant overnight stop for enjoying the Pinnacles Desert and a good base for exploring the flora of the Kwongan (p925), the inland heathland of Lesueur National Park (p924) and Badgingarra National Park. There are also lovely beaches on which to while away the time.

◉ Sights

Just south of Cervantes, turn off for Lake Thetis, where living stromatolites – the world's oldest organisms – inhabit the shoreline. Nearby Hansen Bay Lookout has excellent views across the coast.

★ Nambung National Park NATIONAL PARK
(per car $12) Situated 19km from Cervantes, Nambung is home to the spectacular **Pinnacles Desert**, a vast, alien-like plain studded

with thousands of limestone pillars. Rising eerily from the desert floor, the pillars are remnants of compacted seashells that once covered the plain and, over millennia, subsequently eroded. A loop road runs through the formations, but it's more fun to wander on foot, especially at sunset, full moon or dawn, when the light is sublime and the crowds evaporate.

Lesueur National Park NATIONAL PARK
(per car $12) This botanical paradise, 50km north of Cervantes, contains a staggering 820 plant species, many of them rare and endemic, such as the pine banksia (*Banksia tricupsis*) and Mt Lesueur grevillea (*Grevillea batrachioides*). Late winter sees the heath erupt into a mass of colour, and the park is also home to the endangered Carnaby's cockatoo. An 18km circuit drive is dotted with lookouts and picnic areas. Flat-topped **Mt Lesueur** (4km return walk) has panoramic coastal views.

🏃 Activities

Many Perth-based companies offer day trips to the Pinnacles.

Pinnacle Helicopter Flights SCENIC FLIGHTS
(📞 0428 880 066; www.pinnaclehelicopterflights. com.au; Pinnacles Discovery Centre, Nambung National Park; per person $135-300) Spectacular flights allow you to see the beauty of the Pinnacles and the WA coastline from the air.

🛏 Sleeping & Eating

⭐ **Cervantes Lodge &**
Pinnacles Beach Backpackers HOSTEL $
(📞 1800 245 232; www.cervanteslodge.com.au; 91 Seville St, Cervantes; dm $33, d $135, d with shared bathroom $90; @🛜) This relaxing hostel has a wide verandah, small and tidy dorms, a nice communal kitchen and a cosy lounge area. Bright, spacious en-suite rooms, some with views, are next door in the lodge. There's a good on-site cafe too – open to outside guests during the day – and affable co-owner Tony is always up for a chat.

RAC Cervantes Holiday Park CARAVAN PARK $
(📞 08-9652 7060; www.parksandresorts.rac.com. au/park/cervantes-holiday-park; 35 Aragon St, Cervantes; sites $30-32, cabins & units $90-225; 🛜🏊) Fantastic location right behind the dunes with plenty of shady, grassy sites and an on-site cafe. New chalets and a swimming pool and rec room opened in early 2017.

⭐ **Amble Inn** B&B $$
(📞 0429 652 401; www.amble-inn.com.au; 2150 Cadda Rd, Hill River; d from $160; ❄🛜) High up on the heathland, about 25km east of Cervantes, this hidden gem of a B&B has beautiful thick stone walls, wide verandahs and superbly styled rooms. Watch the sunset over the coast from the nearby hill with a glass of your complimentary wine.

Cervantes Bar & Bistro PUB FOOD $$
(📞 08-9652 7009; www.facebook.com/cervantes barandbistro; 1 Cadiz St, Cervantes; mains $21-35; ⏰11am-midnight Mon-Sat, to 10pm Sun) This welcoming pub offers meals that are a cut above the fare in most other regional WA towns. Local seafood is the star – lobster, squid, mussels and oysters all feature – and a decent array of tap beers goes well with Aussie culinary classics, including steak sandwiches and chicken parmigiana.

Lobster Shack SEAFOOD $$
(📞 08-9652 7010; www.lobstershack.com.au; 11 Madrid St, Cervantes; ⏰shop 8am-5pm, cafe 11am-3pm, tours noon-3pm) Craving crayfish? They don't come much fresher than at this lobster-factory-turned-lunch spot, where half a delicious grilled cray, chips and salad will set you back around $40. Cheaper lobster and octopus burgers ($20) and fish and chips are also on offer. Self-guided factory tours and takeaway frozen seafood are also available.

ℹ Information

Post Office and Visitor Centre (📞 08-9652 7700, freecall 1800 610 660; www.visit pinnaclescountry.com.au; Cadiz St, Cervantes; ⏰9am-5.30pm Mon-Fri, to 5pm Sat & Sun) Grab a copy of the *Turquoise Coast Self Drive Map* from Cervantes' combined post office and visitor centre, which also supplies accommodation and tour information.

ℹ Getting There & Away

Integrity (p923) runs three times weekly to Perth ($44, three hours), Dongara ($34, two hours), Geraldton ($42, three hours) and Exmouth ($183, 14 hours). **Transwa** runs twice weekly to Perth ($34, three hours), Dongara ($22, two hours) and Geraldton ($40, three hours).

Jurien Bay

POP 1500

The largest town on the Turquoise Coast is likely to become quite a lot bigger after being selected as a regional 'Super Town'. Home to

KWONGAN WILDFLOWERS

Take any road inland from the Turquoise Coast and you'll soon enter the Kwongan heathlands, where, depending on the season, the roadside verges burst with native wildflowers such as banksia, grevillea, hakea, calothamnus, kangaroo paw and smokebush. While Lesueur National Park (p924) is an obvious choice for all things botanical, consider some of the following options.

Badgingarra National Park Three-and-a-half kilometres of walking trails, kangaroo paws, banksias, grass trees, verticordia and a rare mallee. The back road linking Badgingarra and Lesueur is particularly rich in flora. Obtain details from the Badgingarra Roadhouse. There's also a picnic area on Bibby Rd.

Alexander Morrison National Park Named after WA's first botanist. There are no trails, but you can drive through slowly on the Coorow Green Head Rd, which has loads of flora along its verge all the way from Lesueur. Expect to see dryandra, banksia, grevillea, smokebush, leschenaultia and honey myrtle.

Tathra National Park Tathra has similar flora to Alexander Morrison National Park, and the drive between the two is rich with banksia, kangaroo paw and grevillea.

Coomallo Rest Area Orchids, feather flowers, black kangaroo paws, wandoo and river red gums can be found upstream and on the slopes of the small hill.

Brand Hwy (Rte 1) The route's not exactly conducive to slow meandering, but the highway verges are surprisingly rich in wildflowers, especially either side of Eneabba.

If you're overwhelmed and frustrated by not being able to identify all these strange new plants, consider staying at Western Flora Caravan Park (☑08-9955 2030; wflora cp@activ8.net.au; Brand Hwy, North Eneabba; unpowered/powered sites $28/32, d $65, on-site vans $80, chalets $130), where the enthusiastic owners run free two-hour wildflower walks across their 65-hectare property every day at 4.30pm.

a hefty fishing fleet and lots of big houses, it's already rather spread out; however, there's a nice long swimming beach and great snorkelling and diving opportunities. Anglers have a choice of jetties and the lengthy foreshore walkway links several pleasant parks.

🏃 Activities

Snorkelling Trail SNORKELLING
(☉Sep-May) FREE Around 25m off the beach near the piles of the old jetty, this underwater trail marked by buoys guides snorkellers around a reef slowly becoming inhabited by marine flora and fauna. The water is around 2m to 3m deep, and interpretive plinths on the sea floor provide information.

Skydive Jurien Bay SKYDIVING
(☑08-9652 1320, 1300 293 766; www.skydivejurien bay.com; 65 Bashford St; 8000/10,000/14,000ft jumps $300/350/450) To see the coastline from the air and land on the beach, see the team at Skydive Jurien Bay.

Turquoise Safaris FISHING, SNORKELLING
(☑0458 905 432; www.turquoisesafaris.com.au; Shop 1, Roberts St Arcade; fishing half-/full-day per person $150/220, snorkelling & sea lions adult/ child $90/60) Offers half- and full-day fishing charters and trips viewing sea lions and then time spent snorkelling. Turquoise Safaris also has a handy 4WD-recovery service if you get stuck in the sand or in WA's red dirt.

Jurien Bay Adventure Tours ADVENTURE
(☑1300 462 383; www.jurienbayadventuretours. com.au; tours per person $39-99) Versatile one-stop shop for hire of bikes, sandboards, paddleboards and snorkelling gear, and guided tours covering everything from the Pinnacles and the crayfishing industry south at Cervantes, to exploring the nearby Stockyard Gully caves or Mt Lesueur, or going by 4WD to the best sandboarding spots in the area. All tours depart from the visitor centre (p926).

🛏 Sleeping & Eating

Jurien Bay Tourist Park CARAVAN PARK $
(☑08-9652 1595; www.jurienbaytouristpark.com. au; Roberts St; sites $38, chalets $145-170; ☎) There are comfortable chalets right behind the beach, although the tent sites are set back against the main road. A $20 single-night surcharge applies to the chalets.

Jurien Bay Holidays
ACCOMMODATION SERVICES $$$

(☑08-9652 2055; www.jurienbayholidays.com; Shop 1a, 34 Bashford St) Check here for holiday rentals.

Jetty Cafe
CAFE $

(☑08-9652 1999; 1 Roberts St; meals $10-19; ⊗7.30am-5pm) In a great position next to the caravan park, Jetty serves up decent brekkies, burgers and grilled fish.

Beach Bistro
CAFE $$

(☑08-9652 1513; www.beachbistro.com.au; 2/1 Roberts St; lunch $15-22, dinner $21-36; ⊗11am-8pm Wed-Mon) For a beer or wine with lunch or dinner, try the eclectic international menu at the laid-back Beach Bistro. Quiz night from 7pm on occasional Thursdays is always fun, and the $20 beer-and-a-burger deal on a Monday night is good value.

❶ Information

Turquoise Coast Visitor Centre (☑08-9652 0870; www.facebook.com/TurquoiseCoastWA; 67 Bashford St; ⊗9am-5pm Mon-Fri, to 1pm Sat) The excellent new Turquoise Coast Visitor Centre can advise on activities, transport and accommodation in Jurien Bay and the surrounding Dandaragan Shire.

GEOGRAPHE BAY

Turquoise waters and 30km of excellent swimming beaches define this gorgeous bay. Positioned between the Indian Ocean and a sea of wine, the beachside towns of Busselton and Dunsborough attract hordes of holidaymakers. By WA standards, attractions are close together, making it perfect for leisurely touring. Accommodation prices can rise around 30% during summer and school holidays.

For 55,000 years the area from Geographe Bay to Augusta was inhabited by the Wardandi, one of the Noongar peoples. They lived a nomadic life linked to the seasons, heading to the coast in summer to fish, and journeying inland during the wet winter months.

The French connection to many of the current place names dates from an early-19th-century expedition by the ships *Le Géographe* and *Naturaliste*. Thomas Vasse, a crewman who was lost at sea, is remembered in the name of a village, river, inlet and Margaret River winery.

Bunbury
POP 67,090

The southwest's only city is morphing from an industrial port into a seaside holiday destination. From Bunbury, the main route south branches to the Bussell Hwy (for Margaret River), and the South Western Hwy (to the southern forests and south coast). It's also the southernmost stop on the train network and a hub for regional buses.

The town centre has basically one main street (Victoria), and a few blocks to the west lies the beach. Immediately to the north, the redeveloped port features waterside restaurants.

The city lies at the western end of Leschenault Inlet. The area was named Port Leschenault after the botanist on Nicolas Baudin's ship *Le Géographe* in 1803, but British Governor James Stirling renamed it Bunbury after a lieutenant in charge of the original military outpost. The first British settlers arrived in 1838.

◉ Sights & Activities

Bunbury Wildlife Park
ZOO

(☑08-9721 8380; www.bunburywildlifepark.com.au; Prince Philip Dr; adult/child $9.80/5; ⊗10am-5pm) Parrots, kangaroos, wallabies, possums, owls and emus all feature. Across the road, the **Big Swamp** wetlands has good walking tracks and stops for birdwatching. Head south on Ocean Dr, turn left at Hayward St and continue through the roundabout to Prince Philip Dr.

Dolphin Discovery Centre
WILDLIFE RESERVE

(☑08-9791 3088; www.dolphindiscovery.com.au; Koombana Beach; adult/child $10/5; ⊗9am-2pm May-Sep, 8am-4pm Oct-Apr) Around 60 bottlenose dolphins live in the bay year-round, their numbers increasing to 260 in summer. This centre has a beachside zone where dolphins regularly come to interact with people in the shallows and you can wade in alongside, under the supervision of trained volunteers.

If you want to up your chances, there are 1½-hour **Eco Cruises** (1½hr cruise adult/child $54/40; ⊗11am mid-Oct–Apr, 11.30am May–mid-Oct) and three-hour **Swim Encounter Cruises** (3hr cruises $165; ⊗7.30am mid-Oct–mid-Dec & Feb-Apr, 7.30am & 11.30am mid-Dec–Jan).

Bunbury Regional Art Galleries
GALLERY

(☑08-9792 7323; www.brag.org.au; 64 Wittenoom St; ⊗10am-4pm) FREE Housed in a restored pink convent (1897), this excellent gallery

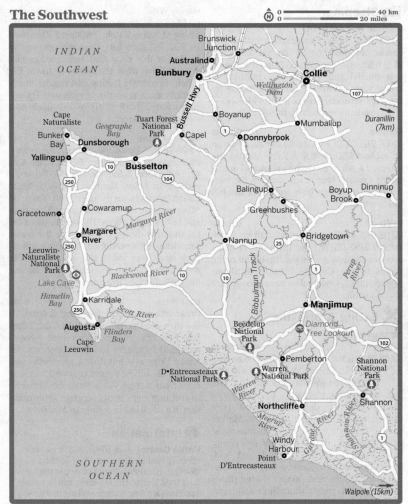

has a collection that includes works by Australian art luminaries Arthur Boyd and Sir Sidney Nolan.

St Mark's (Old Picton) Church   CHURCH
(cnr Charterhouse Cl & Flynn St, East Bunbury) Built in 1842 using wattle and daub construction, this is WA's second-oldest church.

Mangrove Boardwalk   WALKING
Mangrove Boardwalk (enter off Koombana Dr) meanders through the most southerly mangroves in WA, rich with more than 70 species of bird. Interpretive signs provide information about this 2500-year-old ecosystem.

👉 Tours

Ngalang Wongi Aboriginal Cultural Tours   CULTURAL
(📞0457 360 517; www.ngalangwongi.com.au; adult/child from $50/25) Local man Troy Bennell shares his Noongar culture and heritage on a town tour incorporating the Indigenous history of the Bunbury area, and a walking tour around the Mangrove Boardwalk and Koombana Bay finishing at the Dolphin Discovery Centre.

🛏 Sleeping

Dolphin Retreat YHA
HOSTEL $

(📞 08-9792 4690; www.dolphinretreatbunbury.com.au; 14 Wellington St; dm/s/d $31/57/82; @🤫) Around the corner from the beach, this small hostel is in a labyrinthine old house with hammocks and a barbecue on the back verandah. It's popular with longer-term residents working in the area.

Mantra
APARTMENT $$

(📞 08-9721 0100; www.mantra.com.au; 1 Holman St; apt from $210; ❄@🤫❄) The Mantra has sculpted a set of modern studios and apartments around four grain silos by the harbour. Deluxe rooms have spa baths and full kitchens.

Clifton
MOTEL $$

(📞 08-9721 4300; www.theclifton.com.au; 2 Molloy St; r $150-275; 🤫) For luxurious heritage accommodation, go for the top-of-the-range rooms in the Clifton's historic Grittleton Lodge (1885). Good-value motel rooms are also available.

🍴 Eating & Drinking

⭐Market Eating House
MODERN AUSTRALIAN $$

(📞 08-9721 6078; www.marketeatinghouse.com.au; 9 Victoria St; shared plates $12-18, mains $35-42; ⏲5.30pm-late Wed-Thu, noon-late Fri & Sat, 9am-4pm Sun) More evidence that Bunbury's dining scene has definitely become more interesting across recent years, the Market Eating House focuses on a custom-made wood-fired grill that is used for everything from chicken and fish to pork and beef. Turkish and Middle Eastern flavours underpin many dishes, and smaller shared plates include plump ricotta dumplings and hummus topped with lamb.

Café 140
CAFE $$

(📞 08-9721 2254; www.cafe140.com.au; 140 Victoria St; mains $13-32; ⏲7am-4.30pm Mon-Thu, to midnight Fri, 8am-2pm Sat & Sun) Hip, on-to-it staff make the funky Café 140 a top spot for a leisurely Bunbury breakfast. Try the Indian-inspired salmon kedgeree omelette. Later in the day, gourmet burgers, charcuterie platters and grilled Turkish sandwiches combine with a concise beer and wine list. Pop next door to the recently added wood-fired bakery for crunchy and still-warm sourdough loaves and great doughnuts.

Happy Wife
CAFE $$

(📞 08-9721 7706; www.thehappywife.com.au; 98 Stirling St; mains $11-24; ⏲6.30am-3.30pm Mon-Fri, 7.30am-2.30pm Sat) Grab a spot in the garden of this Cape Cod–style cottage just a short drive from the centre of town. Excellent homestyle baking and regular lunch specials make it worth seeking out. Try the slow-roasted pork salad or the duck and sweet potato parcel.

Yours or Mine
BAR

(📞 08-97918884; www.facebook.com/yoursormine1; 26 Victoria St; shared plates $18-28, mains $24-42; ⏲noon-3pm & 5pm-midnight Mon-Thu, noon-midnight Sat & Sun) Bunbury's Monday-night dining scene is pretty quiet, but Yours or Mine comes to the rescue with small-bar style and tasty shared plates. The service was a bit hit-and-miss during our visit, but the South American–influenced food, including pulled-pork tacos, was worth the wait. Check the website for nightly specials and occasional Sunday-afternoon live music.

Lost Bills
BAR

(www.facebook.com/pg/lostbillsishere; 41 Victoria St; ⏲4-11pm Wed-Thu, 3pm-midnight Fri & Sat, 2-8pm Sun) Lost Bills' compact brick-lined space is enlivened by quirky artwork – look out for Snoop Dogg as a hot dog. A good wine and cocktail list and four guest taps with beer and cider from around WA are also valid reasons to visit Bunbury's pretty accurate approximation of a small bar in Sydney or Melbourne.

ℹ Information

Visitor Centre (📞 08-9792 7205; www.visitbunbury.com.au; Carmody Pl; ⏲9am-5pm Mon-Sat, 10am-2pm Sun) Located in the historic train station (1904). Bikes can be rented and there are free historic walking tours every Wednesday at 10am.

ℹ Getting There & Away

Coaches stop at the **central bus station**, next to the visitor centre, or at the **train station**.

Transwa (www.transwa.wa.gov.au) routes:

➡ SW1 (12 weekly) to East Perth ($32.45, 3¼ hours), Mandurah ($17.50, two hours), Busselton ($9.90, 43 minutes), Margaret River ($17.50, two hours) and Augusta ($26.50, 2½ hours).

➡ SW2 (three weekly) to Balingup ($14.45, 53 minutes), Bridgetown ($17.50, 1¼ hours) and Pemberton ($29.40, 2¼ hours).

➡ GS3 (daily) to Walpole ($47, 4½ hours), Denmark ($52, 5½ hours) and Albany ($60, six hours).

South West Coach Lines (☑08-9261 7600; www.southwestcoachlines.com.au) Runs services to/from Perth's Elizabeth Quay Busport ($35, 2½ hours, three daily), Busselton ($12, 1¼ hours, four daily), Dunsborough ($21, 1¾ hours, daily) and Bridgetown ($19, 1¾ hours, daily).

TransBunbury Runs buses (30 minutes) between the central bus station and train station ($2.90; no Sunday service). Look for bus number 827.

Bunbury is the terminus of the **Transwa** (www.transwa.wa.gov.au) Australind train line, with two daily services to Perth ($31.45, 2½ hours) and Pinjarra ($17.50, 1¼ hours).

Busselton

POP 31,767

Unpretentious and uncomplicated, Busselton is what passes for the big smoke in these parts. Surrounded by calm waters and white-sand beaches, its outlandishly long jetty is its most famous attraction. Other than that, the family-friendly town has plenty of diversionary activities for lively kids, including sheltered beaches, water slides and animal farms.

◉ Sights & Activities

Busselton Jetty   LANDMARK
(☑08-9754 0900; www.busseltonjetty.com.au; adult/child $3/free, return train adult/child $13/6.50, Interpretive Centre free; ☺Interpretive Centre 8.30am-5pm Sep-Apr, 9am-5pm May-Aug) Busselton's 1865 timber-piled jetty – the southern hemisphere's longest (1841m) – reopened in 2011 following a $27-million refurbishment. A little **train** chugs along to the **Underwater Observatory** (Map p934; adult/child incl train $33/16.50; ☺9am-4.25pm), where tours take place 8m below the surface; bookings are essential. There's also an Interpretive Centre, an attractive building in the style of 1930s bathing sheds, about 50m along the jetty. A new option to explore the underwater world around the jetty's historic piles, offered by Dive Busselton Jetty, is wearing a self-contained breathing apparatus called a SeaTREK helmet.

ArtGeo Cultural Complex   GALLERY
(☑08-9751 4651; www.artgeo.com.au; 6 Queen St; ☺10am-4pm) Grouped around the old courthouse (1856), this complex includes tearooms, wood turners, an artist-in-residence and the Busselton Art Society's gallery, selling works by local artists.

Capel Vale   WINE
(☑08-9727 1986; www.capelvale.com.au; Mallokup Rd; ☺cellar door 10am-4.30pm, restaurant 11.30am-3pm Thu-Mon) Geographe Bay wine region's best-known winery is conveniently located halfway between Bunbury and Busselton. Capel Vale offers free tastings and Match restaurant overlooking the vines. It's located off the Bussell Hwy on the opposite side of the highway from Capel village.

Dive Busselton Jetty   DIVING
(☑1800 994 210; www.divebusseltonjetty.com.au; underwater walks $165, snorkelling/diving from $29/99; ☺underwater walks Dec-Apr) Offers snorkelling and dive trips around the jetty, and also a walk along the ocean floor around Busselton Jetty's wooden piles while wearing a self-contained breathing helmet called a SeaTREK apparatus. The experience is open to everyone – you can leave your glasses on and your hair won't get wet – and the underwater view includes coral and fish. Book ahead for the popular underwater walks.

Southwest Eco Discoveries   ECOTOUR
(☑0477 030 322, 0477 049 722; www.southwestecodiscoveries.com.au; tours $45-95) Brothers Ryan and Mick White run tours exploring around Geographe Bay and Cape Naturaliste. Options include morning tours discovering the stunning coastline, afternoon tours with a wine and gourmet focus, and evening outings to see endangered woylies and other nocturnal marsupials. Tour pick-ups can be made from accommodation in Busselton, Dunsborough and Cowaramup, and from Margaret River by availability and arrangement.

✵✵ Festivals & Events

CinéfestOZ   FILM
(www.cinefestoz.com; ☺late Aug) Busselton briefly morphs into St-Tropez with this oddly glamorous festival of French and Australian cinema, including lots of Australian premieres and the odd Aussie starlet.

Southbound   MUSIC
(www.southboundfestival.com.au; ☺late Dec) Celebrate the end of the year with three days of alternative music and camping just after Christmas.

🛏 Sleeping

Accommodation sprawls along the beach for several kilometres either side of the town centre, so check the location if you don't have transport. During school holidays, the population increases fourfold and accommodation prices soar.

Beachlands Holiday Park
CARAVAN PARK $

(Map p934; ☑08-9752 2107; www.beachlands.com.au; 10 Earnshaw Rd, West Busselton; sites per 2 people $51, chalets from $156; ❋ ❀ ❀) This excellent family-friendly park offers a wide range of accommodation amid shady trees, palms and flax bushes. Deluxe spa villas ($185) have corner spas, huge TVs, DVD players and full kitchens.

Observatory Guesthouse
B&B $$

(☑08-9751 3336; www.observatoryguesthouse.com; 7 Brown St; d $150; ❋ ❀) A five-minute walk from the jetty, this friendly B&B has four bright, cheerful rooms. They're not overly big, but you can spread out on the communal sea-facing balcony and front courtyard.

Aqua
DESIGN HOTEL $$$

(Map p934; ☑08-9750 4200; www.theaquaresort.com.au; 605 Bussell Hwy; apt from $480; ❋ ❀ ❀) Down a driveway framed by peppermint trees and with direct beach access, the luxury beach houses at Aqua are a grand option for families or a pair of couples travelling together. Bedrooms and bathrooms are stylish and understated, but the real wow factor comes in the stunning lounges and living areas. Facilities include a beachfront infinity pool and a spa and sauna.

✖ Eating & Drinking

Laundry 43
CAFE $$

(☑08-9754 1503; www.laundry43.com.au; 43 Prince St; shared plates $14-29; ⊙4pm-late Tue-Thu, 11am-late Fri & Sat) Brick walls and a honey-coloured jarrah bar form the backdrop for Margaret River beers and wines, great cocktails, and classy shared plates and bigger dishes. Definitely get ready to linger longer than you planned. Ask about occasional special degustation menus.

Goose
CAFE $$

(☑08-9754 7700; www.thegoose.com.au; Geographe Bay Rd; breakfast $13-22, shared plates & mains $11-35; ⊙7am-10pm; ❀) Near the jetty, stylish Goose is a cool and classy cafe, bar and bistro. The drinks list bubbles away with WA craft beer and wine, and a versatile menu kicks off with eggy breakfasts, before graduating to shared plates including Vietnamese pulled-pork sliders, and larger dishes such as steamed mussels and seafood chowder.

Fire Station
CRAFT BEER

(☑08-9752 3113; www.firestation.bar; 68 Queen St; ⊙4-11pm Tue-Wed, 11.30am-midnight Thu-Sat, 11.30am-10pm Sun) Park yourself in the cosy interior or outside under the market umbrellas and enjoy one of the southwest's best selections of wine and craft beer. The tasty food menu includes classic drinking dishes like spicy chicken wings and cheese and chilli croquettes, and weekly specials include Thursday's Bao & Beer deal with $7 pints and Asian steamed buns from 4pm.

❶ Information

Visitor Centre (☑08-9752 5800; www.margaretriver.com; end of Queen St, Busselton foreshore; ⊙9am-5pm Mon-Fri, to 4.30pm Sat & Sun) On the waterfront near the pier. Bikes can be rented for exploring Busselton's foreshore.

❶ Getting There & Away

Buses link Busselton to the north and south.

South West Coach Lines (☑08-9753 7700; www.southwestcoachlines.com.au; Peel Tce) Runs services to/from Perth's Elizabeth Quay Busport ($40, 3¾ hours, three daily), Bunbury ($12, one hour, three daily), Dunsborough ($12, 30 minutes, three daily) and Margaret River ($12, 50 minutes, three daily).

Transwa (☑1300 662 205; www.transwa.wa.gov.au) The SW1 service (12 weekly) stops on Peel Tce heading to/from East Perth ($38, 4¼ hours), Bunbury ($9.90, 43 minutes), Dunsborough ($8.25, 28 minutes), Margaret River ($14.45, 1½ hours) and Augusta ($17.50, 1¾ hours).

Following a recent expansion of Busselton airport, interstate flights are expected to launch in 2018.

Dunsborough

POP 3400

Smaller and less sprawling than Busselton, Dunsborough is a relaxed, beach-worshipping town that goes bonkers towards the end of November when about 7000 'schoolies' descend. When it's not inundated with drunken, squealing teenagers, it's a thoroughly pleasant place to be. The beaches are better than Busselton's, but accommodation is more limited.

The name Dunsborough first appeared on maps in the 1830s, but to the Wardandi people it was always Quedjinup, meaning 'place of women'.

🏃 Activities

Naturaliste Charters
WHALE WATCHING

(📞 08-9750 5500; www.whales-australia.com; 25/27 Dunn Bay Rd; adult/child $90/50; ☺10am & 2pm Sep–mid-Dec) Two-hour whale-watching cruises from September to early December. From December to January, the emphasis switches to an **Eco Wilderness Tour** showcasing beaches, limestone caves with Indigenous art, and wildlife, including dolphins and New Zealand fur seals. Tours also run out of Augusta from late May to August.

Cape Dive
DIVING

(📞 08-9756 8778; www.capedive.com; 222 Naturaliste Tce; ☺9am-5pm) There is excellent diving in Geographe Bay, especially since the decommissioned Navy destroyer HMAS *Swan* was purposely scuttled in 1997 for use as a dive wreck. Marine life has colonised the ship, which lies at a depth of 30m, 2.5km offshore.

🛏 Sleeping

As well as motels and a hostel, there are many options for self-contained rentals in town depending on the season. The visitor centre has listings.

Dunsborough Beachouse YHA
HOSTEL $

(📞 08-9755 3107; www.dunsboroughbeachouse. com.au; 205 Geographe Bay Rd; dm $34-36, s/d $60/92; @🖥) On the Quindalup beachfront, this friendly hostel has lawns stretching languidly to the water's edge. It's an easy 2km cycle from the town centre.

Dunsborough Central Motel
MOTEL $$

(📞 08-9756 7711; www.dunsboroughmotel.com. au; 50 Dunn Bay Rd; r $130-175; 🖥🖨) Centrally located in Dunsborough town, this well-run motel is good value, especially if you can snare an online midweek discount, which leaves more of your travel budget to enjoy the nearby wineries and breweries.

🍴 Eating

Wild & Woods
CAFE $$

(📞 08-9755 3308; www.wildandwoods.com.au; 2/237 Naturaliste Tce; mains $12-25; ☺8am-4pm Tue-Fri, to 3pm Sat, to 2pm Sun) Wild & Woods' Australia-meets-Scandinavia decor is a relaxing backdrop for good cafe fare – try the apricot and macadamia muesli for breakfast – and interesting counter food like felafel wraps. There's a handy providore section for picking up local gourmet produce, and juices and smoothies provide a healthy balance to the region's vineyards and craft breweries.

Pourhouse
BISTRO $$

(📞 08-9759 1720; www.pourhouse.com.au; 26 Dunn Bay Rd; mains $19-34; ☺4pm-late) Hip but not pretentious, with comfy couches, weekend DJs and an upstairs terrace for summer. The pizzas are excellent, and top-notch burgers come in a locally baked sourdough bun. A considered approach to beer includes rotating taps from the best of WA's craft breweries and lots of bottled surprises. Check the Facebook listing to see what's pouring. Two-for-one burgers on Wednesdays.

★ Piari & Co
BISTRO, BAR $$$

(📞 08-9756 7977; www.piariandco.com.au; 5/54 Dunn Bay Rd; small plates $21-23, mains $34-42; ☺5-11pm Tue-Sat) This relaxed and stylish bistro has a strong emphasis on local and seasonal produce. Small plates include Shark Bay prawns wrapped in ham, and a punchy combination of beef tartare and horseradish. Mains such as lamb rump and fish go well with a drinks list proudly showcasing Margaret River wines and craft beer. Bookings recommended.

ℹ Information

Visitor Centre (📞 08-9752 5800; www.margaretriver.com; 1/31 Dunn Bay Rd; ☺9am-5pm Mon-Fri, 9.30am-4.30pm Sat & Sun) Information and bookings.

ℹ Getting There & Away

Buses link Dunsborough north to Perth and further south through Margaret River to Albany and the southwest.

South West Coach Lines (📞 08-9753 7700; www.southwestcoachlines.com.au; Seymour Blvd) Runs services to/from Perth's Elizabeth Quay Busport ($46, 4½ hours, daily), Bunbury ($21, 1¾ hours, daily) and Busselton ($12, 30 minutes, three daily).

Transwa (📞 1300 662 205; www.transwa. wa.gov.au; Seymour Blvd) The SW1 (12 weekly) service stops at the visitor centre, heading to/from East Perth ($41.25, 4½ hours), Bunbury ($14.45, 1¼ hours), Busselton ($8.25, 28 minutes), Margaret River ($9.90, 49 minutes) and Augusta ($17.50, 1¼ hours).

Cape Naturaliste

Northwest of Dunsborough, Cape Naturaliste Rd leads to the excellent beaches of **Meelup**, **Eagle Bay** and **Bunker Bay**, and on to Cape Naturaliste. There are walks and lookouts along the way; pick up brochures from Dunsborough's visitor centre before heading out. Whales and hammerhead sharks like to hang out on the edge of Bunker Bay, where the continental shelf drops 75m. There's excellent snorkelling on the edge of the shelf at Shelley Cove.

Bunker Bay is home to **Bunkers Beach Cafe** (Map p934; ☑ 08-9756 8284; www.bunkers beachcafe.com.au; Farm Break Lane; breakfast $14-25, lunch $29-38; ⊙ 8.30am-4pm), serving an adventurous menu with Asian and Mediterranean flavours just metres from the sand.

The **Cape Naturaliste lighthouse** (Map p934; ☑ 08-9780 5911; www.margaretriver.com; adult/child $14/7; ⊙ tours every 30min 9.30am-4pm) can be visited on tours and there's also a free museum and a cafe. Above and Below (adult/child $30/15) packages are available, combining entry to Ngilgi Cave.

Leeuwin-Naturaliste National Park NATIONAL PARK
(Map p934; Caves Rd) Despite the vast areas of aridity it contains, Western Australia also boasts a startling variety of endemic wildflowers. The Leeuwin-Naturaliste National Park explodes with colour in the spring months. The leached, sandy soils of Western Australia produce a surprising variety of vividly coloured wildflowers.

Cape to Cape Track WALKING
(Map p934; www.capetocapetrack.com.au) Stretching from Cape Naturaliste to Cape Leeuwin, the 135km Cape to Cape Track passes through the heath, forest and sand dunes of the Leeuwin-Naturaliste National Park (p932), all the while providing Indian Ocean views. Most walkers take about seven days to complete the track, staying in a combination of national-park camp sites and

---

RED TAILS IN THE SUNSET

Between Cape Naturaliste and Cape Leeuwin is the most southerly breeding colony of the red-tailed tropicbird (*Phaethon rubricauda*) in Australia. From September to May, look for it soaring above Sugarloaf Rock, south of Cape Naturaliste. The viewpoint can be reached by a 3.5km boardwalk from the Cape Naturaliste lighthouse or by Sugarloaf Rd.

The tropicbird is distinguished by its two long, red tail streamers – almost twice its body length. Bring binoculars to watch this small colony soar, glide, dive and then swim with their disproportionately long tail feathers cocked up.

---

commercial caravan parks along the way, but you can walk it in five days or break up the route into day walks.

Cape to Cape Tours WALKING
(☑ 0459 452 038; www.capetocapetours.com.au; per couple from $1300) Negotiate the entire route or just parts of the stunning Cape to Cape coastal walk on self-guided and guided itineraries. Trips include camping or lodge accommodation and excellent meals, and options from three to eight days are available. Various day tours exploring the Margaret River region are also offered.

MARGARET RIVER WINE REGION

With vineyard restaurants, artisan food producers, and some of Australia's most spectacular surf beaches and rugged coastline, the Margaret River wine region packs attractions aplenty into a compact area. Sleepy Yallingup conceals excellent beaches, restaurants and luxe accommodation, Margaret River township is the region's bustling foodie heart, and the best of the area's wineries are focused around Cowaramup and Wilyabrup. Throughout the area, an excellent craft-beer scene bubbles away, and the road further south to the windswept Cape Leeuwin Lighthouse at Augusta is studded with spectacular underground caves.

👉 Tours

Margaret River Brewery Tours FOOD & DRINK
(☑ 0458 450 120; www.mrbt.com.au; tours $70-110; ⊙ noon-6pm) Four craft breweries are visited on these small-group minibus tours helmed by the super-friendly Jules. The $70 'Mid Strength' option allows participants to buy their own drinks as they go, while the $110 'Full Strength' tour includes a six-brew tasting paddle at each stop. Both options include an excellent lunch, and cider drinkers can also be catered for.

Taste the South WINE
(☑ 0438 210 373; www.tastethesouth.com.au; per person from $95) Wine and craft-beer tours. Up to five breweries can be visited, and the special Hits with Kids tour combines children-friendly vineyards with activities, including lamb feeding, sheep shearing and a chocolate factory.

Wine for Dudes WINE

(☑0427 774 994; www.winefordudes.com; tours $105) Includes a brewery, a chocolate factory, four wineries, a wine-blending experience and lunch.

⚜ Festivals & Events

**Margaret River
Gourmet Escape** FOOD & DRINK

(www.gourmetescape.com.au; ☉late Nov) From Rick Stein, Nigella Lawson and Heston Blumenthal to MasterChef's George Calombaris and Matt Preston, the Gourmet Escape food and wine festival attracts the big names in global and Australian cuisine. Look forward to three days of food workshops, tastings, vineyard events and demonstrations.

❶ Getting There & Away

Margaret River is easily reached by bus from Perth. To drive from Perth to Margaret River township takes around three hours.

South West Coach Lines (☑08-9261 7600; www.southwestcoachlines.com.au) Runs services between Busselton and Augusta, stopping at Cowaramup and Margaret River, and linking with Perth on the weekends.

Transwa (☑1300 662 205; www.transwa. wa.gov.au) The SW1 service (12 weekly) from Perth to Augusta stops at Yallingup and Margaret River, with three coaches weekly continuing to Pemberton.

Yallingup & Around

POP 1070

Beachside Yallingup is a mecca for both surfers and wine aficionados. You're permitted to let a 'wow' escape when the surf-battered coastline first comes into view. For romantic travellers, Yallingup means 'place of love' in the Wardandi Noongar tongue.

Beautiful walking trails follow the coast between here and Smiths Beach. Canal Rocks, a series of rocky outcrops forming a natural canal, are just past Smiths Beach.

◉ Sights & Activities

Ngilgi Cave CAVE

(Map p934; ☑08-9755 2152; www.margaretriver. com; Yallingup Caves Rd; adult/child $22.50/12; ☉9am-5pm) Between Dunsborough and Yallingup, this 500,000-year-old cave is associated in Wardandi spirituality with the victory of the good spirit Ngilgi over the evil spirit Wolgine. To the Wardandi people it became a kind of honeymoon location.

A European man first stumbled upon it in 1899 while looking for his horse. Formations include the white **Mother of Pearl Shawl** and the equally beautiful **Arab's Tent** and **Oriental Shawl**. Tours depart every half-hour. Check online for other options.

**Wardan
Aboriginal Centre** CULTURAL CENTRE, GALLERY

(Map p934; ☑08-9756 6566; www.wardan.com. au; Injidup Springs Rd, Yallingup; experiences adult/child $20/10; ☉10am-4pm daily mid-Oct–mid-Mar, 10am-4pm Mon, Wed-Fri & Sun mid-Mar–mid-Jun & mid-Aug–mid-Oct, experiences Sun, Mon, Wed & Fri) ✦ Offers a window into the lives of the local Wardandi people. There's a gallery (free admission), an interpretive display on the six seasons that govern the Wardandi calendar (adult/child $8/3), and the opportunity to take part in various experiences, including making stone tools and throwing boomerangs and spears. A guided bushwalk explores Wardandi spirituality and the uses of various plants for food, medicine and shelter.

Koomal Dreaming TOURS

(☑0413 843 426; www.koomaldreaming.com.au; adult/child from $55/25) Yallingup local and Wardandi man Josh Whiteland runs tours showcasing Indigenous food, culture and music, usually also including bushwalking and exploration of the Ngilgi Cave.

🛏 Sleeping

**Yallingup Beach
Holiday Park** CARAVAN PARK $

(☑08-9755 2164; www.yallingupbeach.com.au; Valley Rd; sites per 2 people $40, cabins $115-165; ☎) You'll fall asleep to the sound of the surf here, with the beach just across the road.

Caves House HOTEL $$

(Hotel Yallingup; ☑08-9750 1888; www.caves househotelyallingup.com.au; 18 Yallingup Beach Rd; d $170, ste $280-410; ☎) Sunday to Thursday rates at this restored heritage hotel are good value, and it's an atmospheric spot for a drink, with live gigs from 5pm on Friday and Sunday afternoons. Over summer, some of Australia's biggest touring bands sometimes drop by, and outdoor movies add to a laid-back holiday vibe.

★Wildwood Valley Cottages COTTAGE $$$

(Map p934; ☑08-9755 2120; www.wildwoodvalley. com.au; 1481 Wildwood Rd; cottages from $250; ☎) Luxury cottages trimmed by native bush are arrayed across 120 acres, and the property's main house also hosts the **Wildwood Valley**

Margaret River Wine Region

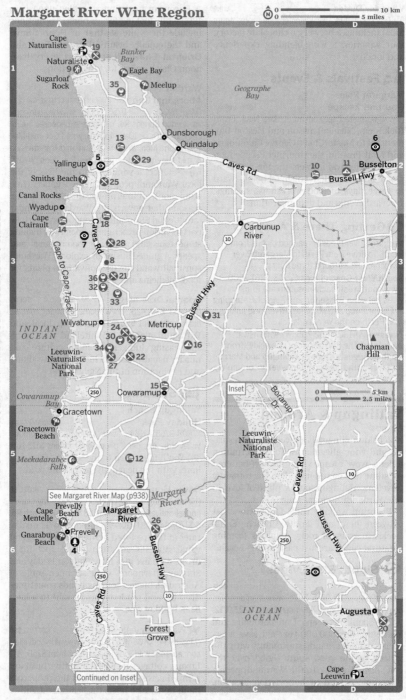

Margaret River Wine Region

⊙ **Sights**
1 Cape Leeuwin Lighthouse D7
2 Cape Naturaliste Lighthouse A1
3 Jewel Cave D6
4 Leeuwin-Naturaliste National Park A6
5 Ngilgi Cave A2
6 Underwater Observatory D2
7 Wardan Aboriginal Centre A3

✪ **Activities, Courses & Tours**
8 Cape Lodge A3
9 Cape to Cape Track A1

🛏 **Sleeping**
10 Aqua D2
11 Beachlands Holiday Park D2
12 Burnside Organic Farm B5
13 Empire Retreat & Spa B2
14 Injidup Spa Retreat A3
15 Noble Grape Guesthouse B4
16 Taunton Farm Holiday Park B4
17 Wharncliffe Mill Bush Retreat B5
18 Wildwood Valley Cottages A3

🍴 **Eating**
19 Bunkers Beach Cafe A1
20 Colourpatch Café D7
21 Knee Deep in Margaret River B3
22 Margaret River Nougat Company B4
23 Providore B4
24 Rustico at Hay Shed Hill B4
25 Studio Bistro A2
26 Temper Temper B6
27 Vasse Felix B4
28 Wills Domain B3
29 Yallingup Woodfired Bread B2

🍷 **Drinking & Nightlife**
30 Ashbrook B4
31 Beer Farm B4
32 Black Brewing Co A3
33 Bootleg Brewery B3
34 Cheeky Monkey Brewery B4
35 Eagle Bay Brewing Co B1
36 Stormflower Vineyard A3

Cooking School (per person $140; ⊙Dec-Mar) with Sioban and Carlo Baldini. Look out for grazing kangaroos as you meander up the unsealed road to reception.

Empire Retreat & Spa   SPA HOTEL $$$
(Map p934; ☑08-9755 2065; www.empireretreat. com; Caves Rd; ste $295-575; ❈ 🐾) Everything about the intimate Empire Retreat is stylish, from the cool Scandi-inspired design to the attention to detail and service. The rooms are built around a former farmhouse, and a rustic but sophisticated ambience lingers. Check online for good packages combining accommodation and spa treatments.

Injidup Spa Retreat   BOUTIQUE HOTEL $$$
(Map p934; ☑08-9750 1300; www.injidupspa retreat.com.au; Cape Clairault Rd; ste from $650; ❈ 🐾) 🌿 The region's most stylish and luxurious accommodation, Injidup perches atop an isolated cliff south of Yallingup. A striking carved concrete and iron facade fronts the car park, while inside there are heated polished-concrete floors, 'eco' fires and absolute sea views. Each of the 10 suites has its own plunge pool. It's off Wyadup Rd.

🍴 Eating

Yallingup Woodfired Bread   BAKERY $
(Map p934; 189 Biddle Rd; bread from $4; ⊙7am-6pm Mon-Sat) Look out for excellent sourdough, rye bread and fruit loaves at local shops and the Margaret River Farmers Market, or pick up some still-warm loaves at the bakery near Yallingup.

Wills Domain   BISTRO $$$
(Map p934; ☑08-9755 2327; www.willsdomain. com.au; cnr Brash & Abbey Farm Rds; mains $31-42, 5-/7-course degustation $85/99; ⊙tastings 10am-5pm, lunch noon-3pm) Restaurant, gallery and wonderful hilltop views over vines. An innovative seven-course tasting menu (with/without wine match $139/99) is also available.

Studio Bistro   MODERN AUSTRALIAN $$$
(Map p934; ☑08-9756 6164; www.thestudiobistro. com.au; 7 Marrinup Dr; small plates $15-20, mains $28-39, degustation menu with/without wine matches $135/95; ⊙10am-5pm Wed-Mon, 6pm-late Sat; 🌿) 🌿 Studio Bistro's gallery focuses on Australian artists, while the garden restaurant showcases subtle dishes such as pan-fried fish with cauliflower cream, radicchio, peas and crab meat. Five-course degustation menus are offered on Friday and Saturday nights. Bookings recommended.

Cowaramup & Wilyabrup
POP 988

Cowaramup (Cow Town to some) is a couple of blocks of shops lining Bussell Hwy. Wilyabrup to the northwest is where the Margaret River wine industry began in the 1960s. This area has the highest concentration of wineries, and pioneers Cullen Wines and Vasse Felix are still leading the way.

Courses

Cape Lodge
COOKING

(Map p934; ☑08-9755 6311; www.capelodge. com.au; 3341 Caves Rd, Wilyabrup; $145) Cooking classes with renowned chef Michael Elfwing take place at this lovely country lodge around every second Saturday. Menus harnessing WA produce have a seasonal focus, and the experience includes a three-course lunch. Check the website for what's coming up and consider booking an overnight accommodation package as well (from $395).

🛌 Sleeping

Taunton Farm Holiday Park
CARAVAN PARK $

(Map p934; ☑1800 248 777; www.tauntonfarm. com.au; Bussell Hwy, Cowaramup; sites $45, cottages $130-160; 🐾) There are plenty of farm animals for the kids to meet at one of Margaret River's best family-oriented camping grounds. For caravan and tenting buffs, the ameni-

ties blocks are spotless, and farm-style self-contained cottages are also scattered about.

Noble Grape Guesthouse
B&B $$

(Map p934; ☑08-9755 5538; www.noblegrape. com.au; 29 Bussell Hwy, Cowaramup; s $140-160, d $150-190; ❄🐾) Noble Grape is more like an upmarket motel than a traditional B&B. Rooms offer a sense of privacy and each has a verdant little garden courtyard.

Eating

Margaret River Nougat Company
SWEETS $

(Map p934; ☑08-9755 5539; www.margaretriver nougat.com.au; cnr Tom Cullity Dr & Miamup Rd, Cowaramup; ⊙9.30am-5pm) Visit the modern lakeside tasting room for award-winning French-style nougat. Our favourite flavours are the salted caramel and liquorice. Wines can also be sampled and purchased.

Providore
DELI $

(Map p934; ☑08-9755 6355; www.providore. com.au; 448 Tom Cullity Dr, Wilyabrup; ⊙9am-5pm) Voted one of Australia's Top 100 Gour-

---

GETTING CRAFTY IN MARGARET RIVER

The Margaret River region's wine credentials are impeccable, but the area is also a destination for craft-beer fans. Many breweries serve bar snacks and lunch.

Eagle Bay Brewing Co (Map p934; ☑08-9755 3554; www.eaglebaybrewing.com.au; Eagle Bay Rd, Dunsborough; ⊙11am-5pm) A lovely rural outlook; interesting beers and wines served in modern, spacious surroundings; and excellent food, including crisp wood-fired pizzas ($20 to $25). Keep an eye out for Eagle Bay's Single Batch Specials.

Black Brewing Co (Map p934; ☑08-9755 6500; www.blackbrewingco.com.au; 3517 Caves Rd, Wilyabrup; 4-beer tasting paddle $20; ⊙11am-late) Black Brewing's well-made beers are approachable for beginner craft-beer fans – just don't expect any bold hop bombs – and brews like the crisp and citrusy extra pale ale (XPA) and rich milk stout go well with dishes inspired by Asian street food. Also sharing the spectacular location on a private lake is Vintner Black winery, specialising in chardonnay and cabernet sauvignon.

Cheeky Monkey Brewery (Map p934; ☑08-9755 5555; www.cheekymonkeybrewery.com. au; 4259 Caves Rd, Margaret River; ⊙10am-6pm) Set around a pretty lake, Cheeky Monkey has an expansive restaurant and lots of room for the kids to run around. Try the Hatseller Pilsner with bold New Zealand hops or the Belgian-style Hagenbeck Pale Ale. Decent food and apple and pear ciders mean you'll make a day of it.

Beer Farm (Map p934; ☑08-9755 7177; www.beerfarm.com.au; 8 Gale Rd, Metricup; ⊙noon-5pm Mon-Thu, to 7pm Fri-Sun) Located in a former milking shed down a sleepy side road, the Beer Farm is Margaret River's most rustic brewery. Loyal locals crowd in with their children and dogs, supping on the Beer Farm's own brews – try the hoppy Rye IPA – and there's a food truck and plenty of room for the kids (and dogs) to run around.

Bootleg Brewery (Map p934; ☑08-9755 6300; www.bootlegbrewery.com.au; Puzey Rd, off Yelverton Rd, Wilyabrup; ⊙11am-6pm) More rustic than some of the area's flashier breweries, but lots of fun with a pint in the sun – especially with live bands on Saturday. Try the award-winning Raging Bull Porter – a West Australian classic – or the US West Coast–style Speakeasy IPA. The food is also very good.

met Experiences by *Australian Traveller* magazine – given its amazing range of artisan produce, including organic olive oil, tapenades and preserved fruits, we can only agree. Look forward to loads of free samples.

★**Rustico at Hay Shed Hill** TAPAS $$$
(Map p934; ☑08-9755 6455; www.rusticotapas.com.au; 511 Harmans Mill Rd, Wilyabrup; shared plates $17-28, pizzas $27-29, degustation from $85; ◷11am-5pm) Vineyard views from Rustico's deck are the background for a Spanish-influenced menu using the best of southwest Australian produce. Albany rock oysters are paired with Margaret River riesling, pork belly comes with Pedro Ximinéz sherry, and paella is crammed with chicken from Mt Barker and local seafood. Consider a leisurely six-course degustation with wine matches.

Vasse Felix BISTRO $$$
(Map p934; ☑08-9756 5050; www.vassefelix.com.au; cnr Caves Rd & Tom Cullity Dr, Cowaramup; mains $37-39, five-course menu $95; ◷cellar door 10am-5pm, restaurant 10am-3pm) Vasse Felix winery is considered by many to have the best fine-dining restaurant in the region, the big wooden dining room reminiscent of an extremely flash barn. The grounds are peppered with sculptures, while the gallery displays works from the Holmes à Court collection.

Knee Deep in Margaret River BISTRO $$$
(Map p934; ☑08-9755 6776; www.kneedeepwines.com.au; 61 Johnson Rd, Wilyabrup; mains $34-40, 4-course menu $70; ◷cellar door 10am-5pm, lunch noon-3pm) ✍ Small and focused could be the motto here. Only a handful of mains are offered – crafted with locally sourced, seasonal produce – and the open-sided pavilion provides a pleasantly intimate vineyard setting. The $70 'Trust the Chef' four-course option is worth the splurge.

🍷 Drinking & Nightlife

Stormflower Vineyard WINERY
(Map p934; www.stormflower.com.au; 3503 Caves Rd, Wilyabrup; ◷11am-5pm) A rustic, relaxed but modern alternative to some of Margaret River's more grandiose tasting rooms and formal wine estates. The compact organic vineyard is just 9 hectares, and Stormflower's cabernet shiraz is highly regarded.

Ashbrook WINERY
(Map p934; ☑08-9755 6262; www.ashbrookwines.com.au; 379 Tom Cullity Dr, Wilyabrup; ◷10am-5pm) Ashbrook grows all of its grapes on-site. Its award-winning rieslings are rightly lauded.

Margaret River
POP 4500

Although tourists usually outnumber locals, Margaret River still feels like a country town. The advantage of basing yourself here is that after 5pm, once the wineries shut up shop, it's one of the few places with any vital signs. Plus, it's close to the incredible surf of Margaret River Mouth and Southside, and the swimming beaches at Prevelly and Gracetown.

Margaret River spills over with tourists every weekend and gets very, *very* busy at Easter and Christmas (when you should book weeks, if not months, ahead). Accommodation prices tend to be cheaper midweek.

🛏 Sleeping

**Wharncliffe Mill
Bush Retreat** GUESTHOUSE $
(Map p934; ☑08-9758 8227; www.wharncliffemill.com.au; McQueen Rd, Bramley National Park; sites $34, dm $25-30, safari tents & cabins $95-180; @☎) ✍ Set amid shaded forests and around a former timber mill, Wharncliffe has accommodation ranging from simple shared dorms to safari tents and cosy wooden cabins. Solar power and sustainable environmental practices are encouraged, and there's plenty of excellent advice on local opportunities for bushwalking and mountain biking. Margaret River township is just 2km away, and mountain bikes can be hired (half-/full-day $15/25).

Margaret River Lodge HOSTEL $
(Map p938; ☑08-9757 9532; www.margaretriverbackpackers.com.au; 220 Railway Tce; dm $30-32, r with/without bathroom $87/76; @☎☒) About 1.5km southwest of the town centre, this clean, well-run hostel has a pool, volleyball court and football field. Dorms share a communal kitchen, and a quieter area with private rooms has its own little kitchen and lounge.

Edge of the Forest MOTEL $$
(Map p938; ☑08-9757 2351; www.edgeoftheforest.com.au; 25 Bussell Hwy; r $165-175; ❉☎) Just a pleasant stroll from Margaret River township, the rooms here have stylish bathrooms and a chic Asian theme. The friendly owners have lots of local recommendations, and the leafy shared garden is perfect for an end-of-day barbecue. The spacious front unit is a good option for families.

Margaret River

Margaret River

🛏 Sleeping
1	Edge of the Forest	C1
2	Margaret River Lodge	B4

🍴 Eating
3	Larder	C2
4	Margaret River Bakery	C2
5	Margaret River Farmers Market	C3
6	Miki's Open Kitchen	C3
7	Swings Taphouse	C2

🍸 Drinking & Nightlife
8	Brewhouse	C1
9	Margaret River Distilling Company	C1

🛍 Shopping
10	Margaret River Artisan Store	C2

★ **Burnside Organic Farm**   BUNGALOW $$$
(Map p934; ☑08-9757 2139; www.burnside
organicfarm.com.au; 287 Burnside Rd; d $350;
❄☎) Welcome to the perfect private re-
treat after a day cruising the region's wine,
beer and food highlights. Bungalows made
from rammed earth and limestone have
spacious decks and designer kitchens, and
the surrounding farm hosts a menagerie of
animals and organic orchards. Guests can
pick vegetables from the garden. Minimum
two-night stay.

✖ Eating

Margaret River Farmers Market   MARKET $
(Map p938; ☑0438 905 985; www.margaretriver
farmersmarket.com.au; Lot 272 Bussell Hwy, Marga-
ret River Education Campus; ⊗8am-noon Sat)
The region's organic and sustainable artisan
producers come to town every Saturday. It's

a top spot for breakfast. Check the website for your own foodie hit list.

Margaret River Bakery
CAFE $

(Map p938; ☑08-9757 2755; 89 Bussell Hwy; mains $10-18; ⊙7am-4pm Mon-Sat; ☑) ✐ Elvis on the stereo, retro furniture and kitsch needlework art – the MRB has a rustic, playful interior. It's the perfect backdrop to the bakery's honest homestyle baking, often with a veg or gluten-free spin. Soak up the previous day's wine tasting with terrific burgers and pies.

Swings Taphouse
BISTRO, WINE BAR $$

(Map p938; ☑08-9758 7155; www.swings.com. au; 85 Bussell Hwy; shared plates $13-32 pizzas $22-25; ⊙7am-late) Local wine served from taps, craft beer, shared tapas plates and gourmet pizzas combine at this cosmopolitan spot at the northern end of Margaret River township. It's also a good spot for a leisurely breakfast. Try the house-smoked salmon, carrot, quinoa and orange blossom. Bloody Marys and Mimosas kick off at 10am for a restorative hair of the dog.

Larder
DELI $$

(Map p938; ☑08-9758 8990; www.larder.biz; 2/99 Bussell Hwy; ⊙9.30am-6pm Mon-Sat, 10.30am-4pm Sun) Showcasing local Margaret River produce and gourmet foods, the Larder also sells takeaway meals ($15 to $18) – a good option for dinner – and comprehensive breakfast packs, picnic hampers and barbecue fixings ($50 to $95). Occasional cooking classes complete the tasty menu.

Miki's Open Kitchen
JAPANESE $$$

(Map p938; ☑08-9758 7673; www.facebook. com/mikisopenkitchen; 131 Bussell Hwy; small plates $12-17, large plates $31-36; ⊙6pm-late Tue-Sat) Secure a spot around the open kitchen and enjoy the irresistible theatre of the Miki's team creating innovative Japanese spins on the best of WA seafood and produce. Combine a Margaret River wine with the $60 multi-course tasting menu for the most diverse experience, and settle in to watch the laid-back Zen chefs work their tempura magic. Bookings recommended.

🍷 Drinking & Nightlife

Brewhouse
MICROBREWERY

(Map p938; ☑08-9757 2614; www.brewhouse margaretriver.com.au; 35 Bussell Hwy; ⊙11am-7pm Mon-Sat, to 10pm Sun) Finally, a craft-beer place you can walk to from Margaret River township. Around 900m north of town, the Brewhouse is nestled amid karri forest with a rustic bar and restaurant serving three guest beers and six of its own brews. Try the Inji Pale Ale with the chilli salt squid, and check out live music on Sundays from 4pm.

Margaret River Distilling Company
DISTILLERY

(Map p938; ☑08-9757 9351; www.distillery.com. au; Maxwell St, off Carters Rd; ⊙10am-7pm) Limeburners Single Malt whisky, Tiger Snake Sour Mash, Great Southern Gin and White Shark Vodka can all be sampled at this edge-of-the-forest tasting room. There are also local beers to go with pizzas and shared platters.

🛍 Shopping

★Temper Temper
SWEETS

(Map p934; ☑08-9757 3763; www.tempertemper. com.au; 2 Rosa Brook Rd; ⊙9am-5pm) This colourful shrine to chocolate features a tasting area where you can try loads of free samples showcasing the difference between cacao from Cuba, Venezuela, Sumatra and Madagascar, and also enticingly rich slabs with thoroughly adult and addictive flavours like pink peppercorn or liquorice. If you're buying souvenirs for the folks back home, you could certainly do worse.

Margaret River Artisan Store
ARTS & CRAFTS

(Map p938; ☑0448 733 799; www.margaretriver artisanstore.com; 2/110 Bussell Hwy; ⊙10am-5pm Mon-Sat & to 1pm Sun) Clothing, design and arts all feature at this eclectic shop where the majority of items are sourced from local Margaret River designers, jewellers and artists.

ℹ Information

Visitor Centre (Map p938; ☑08-9780 5911; www.margaretriver.com; 100 Bussell Hwy; ⊙9am-5pm) Bookings and information plus displays on local wineries.

ℹ Getting Around

Margaret River Beach Bus (☑08-9757 9532; www.margaretriverbackpackers.com.au) Minibus linking the township and the beaches around Prevelly ($10, three daily); summer only, bookings essential.

Augusta & Around

POP 1700

Augusta is positioned at the mouth of the Blackwood River, 5km north of Cape Leeuwin, and quite separate from the main wine

ACTIVE MARGARET RIVER

Much of the Margaret River experience is based around sybaritic pleasures, but to balance the virtue-vs-vice ledger, get active amid the region's stunning scenery. Surfing, swimming and walking are obvious choices, but there's also caving, diving and kayaking – to name a few.

Cape to Coast (📞 0418 808 993; www.capestocoast.com.au; half-/full-day $80/160) Mountain biking, reef snorkelling and 'coasteering' – a combination of rock climbing, shore scrambling and leaping off cliffs into the ocean – all combine in these fun and active tours.

Dirty Detours (📞 08-9758 8312; www.dirtydetours.com; tours $80-105) Runs guided mountain-bike rides, including through the magnificent Boranup Forest, as well as a Sip 'n' Cycle cellar-door tour. Multiday tours are also available.

Dirt Skills (📞 0402 305 104; www.dirtskillsmargaretriver.com; per person $65-70; ☉Sat) If you're serious about getting active amid Margaret River's growing mountain-biking scene, consider a training hook-up with these guys. Beginner and intermediate riders are all welcome, and if there's at least two of you, a special Trail Guiding session will help you find the region's best tracks. Bikes can also be hired.

Margaret River Climbing (📞 0415 970 522; www.margaretriverclimbingco.com.au; half-/full-day $130/250) Caving, rock climbing and abseiling.

Margaret River Surf School (📞 0401 616 200; www.margaretriversurfschool.com; group/individual lessons from $50/120, 3-/5-day course from $120/185) Group and individual lessons for both surfing and stand-up paddleboarding. Three- and five-day courses are the best option if you're serious about learning to surf.

region. There are a few vineyards, but the vibe here is less epicurean and more languid.

Sights & Activities

Operators running boat trips up the Blackwood River include **Absolutely Eco River Cruises** (📞 0419 975 956; cdragon@westnet.com.au; Victoria Pde; adult/child $30/15; ☉Oct-May) and **Miss Flinders** (📞 0409 377 809; Victoria Pde; adult/child $30/15; ☉Oct-May).

Cape Leeuwin Lighthouse   LIGHTHOUSE
(Map p934; 📞 08-9780 5911; www.margaretriver.com; adult/child $8/5; ☉9am-4.30pm) Wild and windy Cape Leeuwin, where the Indian and Southern Oceans meet, is the most southwesterly point in Australia. It takes its name from a Dutch ship that passed here in 1622. The lighthouse (1896), WA's tallest, offers magnificent views of the coastline. Tours leave every 40 minutes from 9am to 4.20pm (adult/child $20/13) – expect a short wait during the holiday season. The Augusta Icons Pass (adult/child $36/12) combines admission to the lighthouse with Jewel Cave.

Jewel Cave   CAVE
(Map p934; 📞 08-9780 5911; www.margaretriver.com; Caves Rd; adult/child $22.50/12; ☉tours hourly 9.30am-3.30pm) The most spectacular of the region's caves, Jewel Cave has an impressive 5.9m straw stalactite, so far the longest seen in a tourist cave. Fossil remains of a Tasmanian tiger (thylacine), believed to be 3500 years old, were discovered here. It's located near the south end of Caves Rd, 8km northwest of Augusta. The interesting interpretive galleries of the Jewel Cave Preservation Centre have been recently added. Access to the cave is by guided tours only.

Naturaliste Charters   WHALE WATCHING
(📞 08-9750 5500; www.whales-australia.com.au; adult/child $90/$50; ☉whale watching mid-May–Aug) 🐋 Runs two-hour whale-watching cruises departing Augusta from mid-May to August. During May, the emphasis switches to an Eco Wilderness Tour showcasing beaches and wildlife, including dolphins, New Zealand fur seals and lots of seabirds.

Sleeping & Eating

Baywatch Manor   HOSTEL $
(📞 08-9758 1290; www.baywatchmanor.com.au; 9 Heppingstone View; dm $8, d $130, d without bathroom $100; @ 🛜) Clean, modern rooms with creamy brick walls and pieces of antique furniture. There is a bay view from the deck and, in winter, a roaring fire in the communal lounge. Some doubles have compact balconies.

Colourpatch Café CAFE $
(Map p934; ☑08-9758 1295; 38 Albany Tce; snacks & mains $10-20; ⊙9am-3pm, to 7pm for takeaways) Watch the Blackwood River meet the waters of Flinders Bay at the self-styled 'last eating house before the Antarctic', which sells fish from the ocean across the road.

⊙ Information

Visitor Centre (☑08-9780 5911; www.mar garetriver.com; cnr Blackwood Ave & Ellis St; ⊙9am-5pm) Information and bookings. Ask about seeing local wildflowers around September to November.

SOUTHERN FORESTS

The tall forests of WA's southwest region are simply magnificent, with towering gums (karri, jarrah, marri) sheltering cool undergrowth. Between the forests, small towns bear witness to the region's history of logging and mining. Many have redefined themselves as small-scale tourist centres where you can take walks, wine tours, canoe trips and trout- and marron-fishing expeditions.

⊙ Getting There & Away

Transwa (☑1300 662 205; www.transwa. wa.gov.au) coach routes include the following:
→ SW1 (three weekly) to Nannup and Pemberton from East Perth, Bunbury, Busselton, Margaret River and Augusta.
→ SW2 (three weekly) to Balingup, Bridgetown, Manjimup and Pemberton from East Perth, Mandurah and Bunbury.
→ GS3 (daily) to Balingup, Bridgetown, Manjimup and Pemberton from Perth, Bunbury, Walpole, Denmark and Albany.

South West Coach Lines (☑08-9261 7600; www.southwestcoachlines.com.au) runs services to the following:
→ Nannup from Busselton (twice weekdays) and Bunbury (weekdays).
→ Balingup, Bridgetown and Manjimup from Bunbury, Mandurah and Perth (daily).

Nannup

POP 500

Nannup's historic weatherboard buildings and cottage gardens have an idyllic bush setting on the Blackwood River. The Noongar-derived name means 'a place to stop and rest'; it's also a good base for bushwalkers and canoeists.

Sporadic but persistent stories of sightings of a striped wolflike animal, dubbed the Nannup tiger, have led to hopes that a Tasmanian tiger may have survived in the surrounding bush (the last known Tasmanian tiger, or thylacine, died in Hobart Zoo in 1936).

Blackwood River Canoeing (☑08-9756 1209; www.blackwoodrivercanoeing.com; hire per day from $25) runs trips which access the largely untouched jarrah forests framing southwest Australia's longest river, and multiday expeditions which incorporate overnight camping. It provides equipment, basic instruction and transfers for canoeing paddles and longer expeditions. The best time to paddle is in late winter and early spring, when the water levels are up.

In early autumn, Nannup holds the **Nannup Music Festival** (☑08-9756 1511; www.nannupmusicfestival.org; ⊙early Mar), focusing on folk and world music. Buskers are encouraged. Check the website for ridesharing opportunities if you don't have your own transport.

⌨ Sleeping & Eating

Holberry House B&B $$
(☑08-9756 1276; www.holberryhouse.com; 14 Grange Rd; r $165-220; ☃☀) The decor might lean towards granny-chic, but this large house on the hill has charming hosts and comfortable rooms. It's surrounded by large gardens dotted with quirky sculptures (open to nonguests for $4).

Pickle & O CAFE $
(☑08-9756 1351; 16 Warren Rd; snacks $7-12; ⊙9.30am-4pm Sun-Fri, to 3pm Sat; ☃☀) ⌀ Good fair-trade coffee, huge slabs of cheesecake, and smoked trout kebab wraps are all tasty reasons to stop in at this quirky combination of health-food store and organic, sustainable cafe. An associated gift shop next door was acting as the local information office at the time of writing.

Nannup Bridge Cafe CAFE $$
(☑08-9756 1287; www.facebook.com/nannup bridgecafe; 1 Warren Rd; breakfast & lunch $9-24, dinner $16-34; ⊙9am-2pm Tue-Sun, 6-8pm Thu-Sat) This riverfront cafe morphs into a bistro at night from Thursday to Saturday. Standout dishes include the pork belly and the sticky-date pudding.

Bridgetown

POP 2400 / ✆ 08

Lovely Bridgetown is surrounded by karri forests and farmland, and spread around the Blackwood River. Weekends are busy, and the popular **Blues at Bridgetown Festival** (✆ 08-9761 2921; www.bluesatbridgetown. com.au) occurs annually on the second weekend of November.

Bridgetown's old buildings include **Bridgedale House** (Hampton St; gold-coin donation; ✆ 10am-2pm Sat & Sun), built of mud and clay by the area's first settler in 1862, and since restored by the National Trust.

🛏 Sleeping & Eating

Bridgetown Riverside Chalets CHALET $$
(✆ 08-9761 1040; www.bridgetownchalets.com. au; 11347 Brockman Hwy; chalets from $150) On a rural riverside property, 5km up the road to Nannup, these four stand-alone wooden chalets (complete with pot-bellied stoves and washing machines) sleep up to six in two bedrooms.

Barking Cow CAFE $$
(✆ 08-9761 4619; 88 Hampton St; breakfast $11-18, lunch $13-21; ✆ 8am-2.30pm Mon-Sat; ✐) Colourful, cosy, and serving the best coffee in town, the Barking Cow is also worth stopping at for daily vegetarian specials and world-famous-in-Bridgetown gourmet burgers.

Cidery CAFE $$
(✆ 08-9761 2204; www.thecidery.com.au; 43 Gifford Rd; mains $10-25; ✆ 11am-4pm Sat-Thu, to 8pm Fri) Craft beer from the Blackwood Valley Brewing Company, cider and light lunches are all enjoyed on outdoor tables. On Friday nights from 5.30pm there's live music. Our favourite brew is the easy-drinking mid-strength Summer Ale.

ℹ Information

Visitor Centre (✆ 08-9761 1740; www.bridge town.com.au; 154 Hampton St; ✆ 9am-5pm Mon-Fri, 10am-3pm Sat, 10am-1pm Sun) Includes apple-harvesting memorabilia and a surprisingly interesting display of jigsaws from around the world in the attached heritage museum.

Manjimup

POP 4300 / ✆ 08

Surrounded by spectacular forest, Manjimup is at the heart of WA's timber industry. For foodies it's known for something very different: truffles. During August especially, Manjimup's black Périgord truffles make their way onto top Australian menus.

◉ Sights

★ Truffle & Wine Co FARM
(✆ 08-9777 2474; www.truffleandwine.com.au; Seven Day Rd; ✆ 10am-4pm, cafe 11am-3pm) To discover how the world's most expensive produce is harvested, follow your snout to the Truffle & Wine Co. Join a 2½-hour truffle hunt with the clever truffle-hunting Labradors from Friday to Sunday from June to August (adult/child $90/81; definitely book ahead). Throughout the year there are plenty of truffle products to sample, and the attached provedore and cafe serves up tasting plates ($10 to $15) and truffle-laced mains ($25 to $40), including seafood ravioli and mushroom risotto.

Four Aces FOREST
(Graphite Rd) These four 300-plus-year-old karri trees sit in a straight line; stand directly in front and they disappear into one. There's a short loop walk through the surrounding karri glade, or a 1½-hour loop bushwalking trail from the Four Aces to One Tree Bridge.

Diamond Tree Lookout VIEWPOINT
Nine kilometres south of Manjimup along the South Western Hwy is the Diamond Tree Lookout. Metal spikes allow you to climb this 52m karri, and there's a nature trail nearby.

🛏 Sleeping & Eating

Diamond Forest Cottages COTTAGE $$
(✆ 08-9772 3170; www.diamondforest.com.au; 29159 South Western Hwy; chalets $180-220; ❋🗢) South of Manjimup, before the turn-off to Pemberton, is this collection of well-equipped wooden chalets with decks, scattered around a farm. Turkeys and sheep wander around, and it has a petting zoo and daily animal-feeding for the kids. Sunday to Thursday stays offer the best rates.

★ Tall Timbers BISTRO $$
(✆ 08-9777 2052; www.talltimbersmanjimup.com. au; 88 Giblett St; tapas $10-19, mains $19-44; ✆ 9am-10pm Mon-Fri, from 8am Sat & Sun) Tall Timbers' upscale pub food stretches from gourmet burgers to confit duck, but its real point of difference is wines from all south-west Australia. More than 40 wines are available, many from boutique vineyards that don't have cellar doors, and a special dispensing system allows visitors to pur-

chase samples from just 25ml and pair them with tapas or cheese platters.

❶ Information

Visitor Centre (☑ 08-9771 1831; www.manjim upwa.com; Giblett St; ⊙ 9am-5pm) Located in Manjim Park and offering accommodation and transport bookings.

Pemberton

POP 760

Hidden deep in the karri forests, drowsy Pemberton produces excellent wine. If Margaret River is WA's Bordeaux, Pemberton is its Burgundy – producing excellent chardonnay and pinot noir, among other varietals. Wine tourism isn't as developed here, with some of the better names only offering tastings by appointment. Grab a free map listing cellar-door opening hours from the visitor centre (p944).

The national parks circling Pemberton are impressive. Aim to spend a day or two driving the well-marked Karri Forest Explorer tracks, walking the trails and picnicking in the green depths.

◉ Sights & Activities

Big Brook Arboretum NATURE RESERVE
FREE Showcase of big trees from all around the world. Pick up a Karri Forest Explorer map from the Pemberton visitor centre.

Fine Woodcraft Gallery ARTS CENTRE
(☑ 08-9776 1741; www.facebook.com/Pemberton FineWoodcraftGallery; Dickinson St; ⊙ 9am-5pm) In lush gardens, the Fine Woodcraft Gallery has truly beautiful pieces, all mastercrafted from salvaged timber. It also has a good cafe offering hearty breakfasts and lunches and the opportunity to purchase house-made smoked meats and charcuterie from Pemberton's Holy Smoke. Try the excellent tasting platter for $32.

Pemberton Tramway RAIL
(☑ 08-9776 1322; www.pemtram.com.au; adult/child $28/14; ⊙ 10.45am & 2pm Mon-Sat; ⊙) Built between 1929 and 1933, the tram route travels through lush karri and marri forests to Warren River. A commentary is provided and it's a fun – if noisy – 1¾-hour return trip.

Pemberton Pool SWIMMING
(Swimming Pool Rd) **FREE** Surrounded by karri trees, this natural pool is popular on a hot day – despite the warning sign (currents,

venomous snakes). They breed them tough around here. Nearby is the trailhead for tracks making up the **Pemberton Mountain Bike Park** (www.pembertonvisitor.com.au/pages/pemberton-mountain-bike-park).

Pemberton Wine Centre WINE
(☑ 08-9776 1211; www.pembertonwine.com.au; 388 Old Vasse Rd; ⊙ noon-5pm) At the very heart of Warren National Park, this centre offers tastings of local wines and can compile a mixed case of your favourites.

☞ Tours

Pemberton Hiking & Canoeing HIKING, CANOEING
(☑ 08-9776 1559; www.hikingandcanoeing.com. au; half-/full-day $50/100) ⊘ Environmentally sound tours in Warren and D'Entrecasteaux National Parks and to the Yeagarup sand dunes. Specialist tours (wildflowers, frogs, rare fauna) are also available, as are night canoeing trips ($50) to spot nocturnal wildlife.

Donnelly River Cruises BOATING
(☑ 08-9777 1018; www.donnellyrivercruises.com. au; adult/child $65/35) ⊘ Cruises through 12km of D'Entrecasteaux National Park to the cliffs of the Southern Ocean.

Pemberton Discovery Tours TOURS, MOUNTAIN BIKING
(☑ 08-9776 0484; www.pembertondiscoverytours. com.au; 12 Brockman St; adult/child $155/55; ⊙ 10am-5pm Mon-Sat, to 2pm Sun) ⊘ Half-day 4WD tours to the Yeagarup sand dunes and the Warren River mouth. Other tours focus on local vineyards, breweries and cideries, and the wild coastal scenery of D'Entrecasteaux National Park. Visit its central Pemberton location for local information and mountain-bike hire, including details of nearby tracks and recommended rides.

⌂ Sleeping

Pemberton Backpackers YHA HOSTEL $
(☑ 08-9776 1105; www.yha.com.au; 7 Brockman St; dm/s/d $33/70/77; @ ⊚) The main hostel in Pemberton's main street is given over to seasonal workers, but you'll need to check in there for a room in the separate cottage (8 Dean St) that's set aside for travellers. It's cute and cosy, but book ahead as it only has three rooms, one of which is a six-person dorm.

Marima Cottages COTTAGE $$
(☑ 08-9776 1211; www.marima.com.au; 388 Old Vasse Rd; cottages $200-225) Right in the middle of Warren National Park, these four

country-style rammed-earth-and-cedar cottages with pot-bellied stoves and lots of privacy are luxurious getaways. Look forward to marsupial company at dusk.

Pump Hill Farm Cottages
COTTAGE $$

(☑ 08-9776 1379; www.pumphill.com.au; Pump Hill Rd; cottages $150-205; ☜) Families love this farm property, where kids are taken on a daily hay ride to feed the animals. Child-free folk will enjoy the ambience of the private, well-equipped cottages too.

Foragers
COTTAGE $$$

(☑ 08-9776 1580; www.foragers.com.au; cnr Roberts & Northcliffe Rds; cottages $270-290; ✴) 🍃 Choose between very nice, simple karri cottages, or leap to the top of the ladder with the luxury eco-chalets. The latter are light and airy, with elegant, contemporary decor, eco-conscious waste-water systems and a solar-passive design. You're also right on hand to enjoy culinary treats at the adjacent Foragers Field Kitchen.

✗ Eating & Drinking

Millhouse Cafe
CAFE $$

(☑ 08-9776 1776; www.facebook.com/Pemberton millhousetearooms; 14 Brockman St; breakfast $10-21, lunch $10-16; ☀ 8am-4pm) Now under new management, this cafe is situated in a cosy heritage cottage with wraparound verandahs and provides good coffee and surprising spins on breakfast. Regular marron specials and trout are on offer for lunch, and local art is displayed on the walls. On Thursdays, Thai meals ($19 to $22) are often available in the cafe until 3pm and for takeaway until 6pm.

Foragers Field Kitchen
INTERNATIONAL $$$

(☑ 08-9776 1580; www.foragers.com.au; cnr Roberts & Northcliffe Rds; dinner $80, cooking classes $85; ☀ dinner 7pm Sat) 🍃 Join renowned chef Sophie Zalokar at one of her regular four-course Saturday-night set dinners – menus always include seasonal and local southwest WA produce – or sign up for one of her monthly cooking classes (usually on a Friday night). Check the website's events calendar for dates. Booking at least 48 hours ahead is preferred.

Jarrah Jacks
CRAFT BEER

(☑ 08-9776 1333; www.jarrahjacks.com.au; Lot 2 Kemp Rd; ☀ 11am-5pm Thu-Sun) Reopened under new ownership, this craft brewery features vineyard views, six craft beers and tasty locally sourced food from a seasonal menu. Try the Swinging Axe Ale, a robust 6% Red Ale, or take it easy with the mid

strength 2.9% Arthur's Hop Ale. Sampling trays are also available for hoppy variety, and you can also try wines from Pemberton's Woodsmoke Estate.

ℹ Information

Department of Parks & Wildlife (☑ 08-9776 1207; www.dpaw.wa.gov.au; Kennedy St; ☀ 9am-4.30pm) Information on local parks and bushwalks.

Visitor Centre (☑ 08-9776 1133; www.pember tonvisitor.com.au; Brockman St; ☀ 9am-4pm) Includes a pioneer museum and karri-forest discovery centre.

SOUTHERN WA

Walpole & Nornalup

POP 320 & 50

The peaceful twin inlets of Walpole (population 320) and Nornalup (population 50) make good bases from which to explore the heavily forested Walpole Wilderness Area – an immense wilderness incorporating a rugged coastline, several national parks, marine parks, nature reserves and forest conservation areas – covering a whopping 3630 sq km. Walpole is the bigger settlement, and it's here that the South Western Hwy (Rte 1) becomes the South Coast Hwy.

◉ Sights

Walpole-Nornalup
National Park
NATIONAL PARK

(www.parks.dpaw.wa.gov.au) Giant trees include red, yellow and Rate's tingles (all types of eucalypt, or gum, trees). Good **walking tracks** include a section of the Bibbulmun Track, which passes through Walpole to Coalmine Beach. **Scenic drives** include the Knoll Drive, 3km east of Walpole; the Valley of the Giants Rd; and through pastoral country to Mt Frankland, 29km north of Walpole. Here you can climb to the summit for panoramic views or walk around the trail at its base.

★ Valley of the Giants
NATURE RESERVE

(☑ 08-9840 8263; www.valleyofthegiants.com.au; Valley of the Giants Rd; Tree Top Walk adult/child $21/10.50; ☀ 9am-5pm) In the Valley of the Giants is the spectacular Tree Top Walk. A 600m-long ramp rises from the valley, allowing visitors access high into the canopy of the giant tingle trees. At its highest point, the ramp is 40m above the ground. It's on a gentle incline so it's easy to walk and is accessible by assisted wheelchair. At ground level, the Ancient Empire boardwalk (admission free) meanders through veteran red tingles, up to 16m in circumference and 46m high.

Conspicuous Cliffs   LANDMARK
Midway between Nornalup and Peaceful Bay, Conspicuous Cliffs is a good spot for whale watching from July to November. It features a hilltop lookout and a steepish 800m walk to the beach.

☞ Tours

★ WOW Wilderness Ecocruises   CRUISE
(☑ 08-9840 1036; www.wowwilderness.com.au; adult/child $45/15) ❂ The magnificent landscape and its ecology are brought to life with anecdotes about Aboriginal settlement, salmon fishers and shipwrecked pirates. The 2½-hour cruise through the inlets and river systems leaves at 10am daily; book at the visitor centre.

Naturally Walpole Eco Tours   ECOTOUR
(☑ 08-9840 1111; Walpole Visitor Centre) ❂ Half-day tours exploring the Walpole Wilderness (adult/child $70/35) and the Tree Top Walk ($80/40).

🛏 Sleeping

As well as hostels, campgrounds and chalets, there are bush camping sites in the Walpole Wilderness Area, including at Crystal Springs and Fernhook Falls.

Tingle All Over YHA   HOSTEL $
(☑ 08-9840 1041; www.yha.com.au; 60 Nockolds St, Walpole; dm/s/d $31/54/74; @ 🛜) Help yourself to lemons and chillies from the garden of this clean, basic option near the highway. Lots of advice on local walks is on offer and the owners are super-friendly.

Rest Point Holiday Village   CARAVAN PARK $
(☑ 08-9840 1032; www.restpoint.com.au; Rest Point; 2-person sites $32, cabins $115-140) Set on wide lawns with direct water frontage, this spacious holiday park has shade for campers and a range of self-contained accommodation.

Nornalup Riverside Chalets   CHALET $$
(☑ 08-9840 1107; www.nornalupriversidechalets. com.au; Riverside Dr, Nornalup; chalets $115-190) Stay a night in sleepy Nornalup in these comfortable, colourful self-contained chalets, just a rod's throw from the fish in the Frankland River. The chalets are well spaced out, giving a feeling of privacy.

Riverside Retreat   CHALET $$
(☑ 08-9840 1255; www.riversideretreat.com.au; South Coast Hwy, Nornalup; chalets $150-210) On the banks of the beautiful Frankland River, these well-equipped chalets are great value, with pot-bellied stoves for cosy winter warmth, and tennis and canoeing as outdoor pursuits. Expect frequent visits from the local wildlife.

🍴 Eating

Nornabar   BISTRO $$
(☑ 08-9840 1407; 6684 South Coast Hwy; tapas $10-13, mains $23-34; ☺ 8am-late Wed-Sat & 8am-3pm Tue & Sun) Nornalup's former tearooms have been reborn as a light, sunny bar and cafe soundtracked with cool jazz and enlivened by colourful local art. There's a concise selection of local Great Southern wines available, and the menu stretches from chicken, ricotta and tarragon meatballs to a delicate salad of poached WA tiger prawns. A compact beer garden completes a versatile offering.

Thurlby Herb Farm   CAFE $$
(☑ 08-9840 1249; www.thurlbyherb.com.au; 3 Gardiner Rd; snacks & mains $8-24; ☺ 9am-5pm Mon-Fri) Thurlby offers light lunches and cakes accompanied by fresh-picked herbal teas, as well as other herb-based products including soap and aromatherapy treatments. It's north of Walpole on the way to Mt Frankland National Park.

❶ Information

Visitor Centre (☑ 08-9840 1111; www.walpole. com.au; South Coast Hwy, Walpole; ☺ 9am-5pm) In the Pioneer Cottage.

❶ Getting There & Away

Departing from the visitor centre, **Transwa** (☑ 1300 662 205; www.transwa.wa.gov.au)

THE ROAD TO MANDALAY

About 13km west of Walpole, at Crystal Springs, is an 8km gravel road to **Mandalay Beach**, where the *Mandalay*, a Norwegian barque, was wrecked in 1911. The wreck eerily appears every 10 years or so after storms. See the photos at Walpole **visitor centre**. The beach is glorious, and accessed by a boardwalk across sand dunes and cliffs. It's part of D'Entrecasteaux National Park.

South Coast

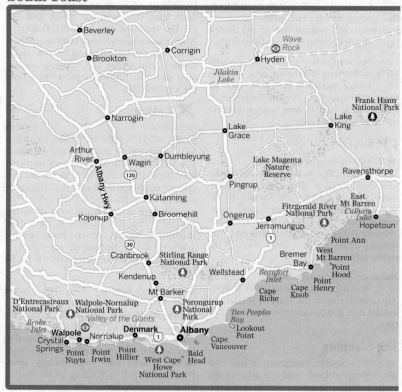

bus GS3 heads daily to/from Bunbury ($47, 4½ hours), Bridgetown ($26.50, 3¼ hours), Pemberton ($20.50, 1¾ hours), Denmark ($14.45, 42 minutes) and Albany ($23, 1½ hours).

Denmark

POP 2800

Denmark's beaches and coastline, river and sheltered inlet, forested backdrop and hinterland have attracted a varied, creative and environmentally aware community. Farmers, ferals, fishers and families all mingle during the town's four market days each year.

Denmark was established to supply timber to the early goldfields. Known by the Minang Noongar people as Koorabup (place of the black swan), there's evidence of early Aboriginal settlement in the 3000-year-old fish traps found in Wilson Inlet.

Sights & Activities

Surfing & Fishing

Surfers and anglers should head to ruggedly beautiful **Ocean Beach**.

Surf Lessons   SURFING
(☑ 0401 349 854; www.southcoastsurfinglessons.com.au; 2hr lessons incl equipment from $60) Surfing lessons from Mike Neunuebel on Ocean Beach. October to June is the best time to learn.

Walking

To get your bearings, walk the **Mokare Heritage Trail** (a 3km circuit along the Denmark River), or the **Wilson Inlet Trail** (12km return, starting at the river mouth), which forms part of the longer **Nornalup Trail**. The **Mt Shadforth Lookout** has fine coastal views, and lush **Mt Shadforth Rd**, running from town to the South Coast Hwy west of town, makes a great scenic drive. A longer

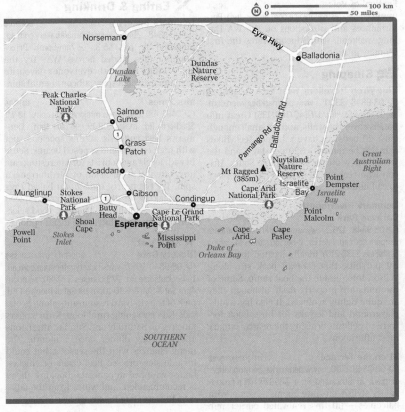

pastoral loop is via **Scotsdale Rd**. Attractions include alpaca farms, wineries, dairy farms, and arts-and-crafts galleries.

Swimming

William Bay National Park, about 20km west of town, offers sheltered swimming in gorgeous **Greens Pool** and **Elephant Rocks**, and has good walking tracks. Swing by **Bartholomews Meadery** (☑08-9840 9349; www.honeywine.com.au; 2620 South Coast Hwy; ice cream from $5; ☺9.30am-4.30pm) for a post-beach treat of mead (honey wine) or delicious home-made honey-rose-almond ice cream ($5).

☞ Tours

Poornati Aboriginal Tours   CULTURAL
(☑0415 840 216, 0412 786 588; www.poornarti. com.au; adult/child $150/60) Day tours focus on the Noongar Indigenous cultural history of Kinjarling (Albany) and Kwoorabup

(Denmark) and include foraging and tasting bush tucker, as well as local art and traditional song and dance. Vibrational healing day tours are also available, incorporating ancient Noongar healing techniques.

Denmark Wine Lovers Tour   WINE
(☑0427 482 400; www.denmarkwinelovers.com. au; half-/full-day per person from $70/88) Full-day and half-day tours taking in Denmark wineries or heading further afield to Porongurup or Mt Barker. Check out the website to see which vineyards can be included in the mix. Ice cream and craft beer can also be included as stops on Denmark tours.

✲ Festivals & Events

Market Days   FAIR
(www.denmarkarts.com.au) Four times a year (mid-December, early and late January and Easter) Denmark hosts riverside market days with craft stalls, music and food.

Festival of Voice
MUSIC

(www.denmarkfestivalofvoice.com.au; ☺Jun) Performances and workshops on the WA Day long weekend, which incorporates the first Monday in June.

🛏 Sleeping

Blue Wren Travellers' Rest YHA
HOSTEL $

(☑08-9848 3300; www.denmarkbluewren.com.au; 17 Price St; dm/d/f $40/100/135) Great info panels cover the walls, and it's small enough (just 20 beds) to have a homey feel. Bikes can also be rented – $20 per day – and the friendly new owner is an affable South African who reckons Denmark is a great place to call home.

Denmark Rivermouth Caravan Park
CARAVAN PARK $

(☑08-9848 1262; www.denmarkrivermouthcaravanpark.com.au; Inlet Dr; 2-person sites $34, cabins & chalets $135-210) Ideally located for nautical pursuits, this caravan park sits along Wilson Inlet beside the boat ramp. Some of the units are properly flash, although they are quite tightly arranged. It also has a kids' playground and kayaks for hire. Look forward to pelicans cruising the nearby estuary most afternoons.

31 on the Terrace
BOUTIQUE HOTEL $$

(☑08-9848 1700; www.denmarkaccommodation.com.au; 31 Strickland St; r $85-175; 🕸) Good-value, stylish en-suite rooms – some with balconies – fill this renovated corner pub in the centre of town. Compact apartments sleep up to five people.

★Cape Howe Cottages
COTTAGE $$$

(☑08-9845 1295; www.capehowe.com.au; 322 Tennessee Rd S; cottages $180-290; 🕸) For a remote getaway, these five cottages in bushland southeast of Denmark really make the grade. They're all different, but the best is only 1.5km from dolphin-favoured Lowlands Beach and is properly plush – with a BBQ on the deck, a dishwasher in the kitchen and laundry facilities.

Celestine Retreat
CHALET $$$

(☑08-9848 3000; www.celestineretreat.com; 413 Mt Shadforth Rd; d $239-289; 🕸) With just four spa chalets scattered over 13 hectares, there are stunning ocean and valley views at this luxury retreat. Romance is also on the agenda, with private spas, fluffy bathrobes and high-end bathroom goodies. There is usually a two-night stay minimum.

🍴 Eating & Drinking

Denmark Bakery
BAKERY $

(☑08-9848 2143; www.denmarkbakery.com.au; Strickland St; pies $6-8; ☺7am-5pm) Prize-winning pies lauded across WA. Try the spicy Vinda-Roo with everyone's favourite marsupial given a spicy subcontinental spin.

Mrs Jones
CAFE $$

(☑0467 481 878; www.mrsjonescafe.com; 12 Mt Shadforth Rd; mains $12-19; ☺7am-4pm) Denmark's best coffee is at this spacious spot with high ceilings and exposed beams. Settle in with locals and tourists for interesting cafe fare, often with an Asian or Mediterranean spin. Try the hearty *shakshuka* baked eggs for breakfast or the robust harissa-spiced lamb burger for lunch. There's a good selection of vegan and gluten free menu options.

★Kirby's at Rickety Gate
MODERN AUSTRALIAN $$$

(☑08-9840 9967; www.ricketygateestate.com.au; 1949 Scotsdale Rd; 2/3 courses $70/80; ☺noon-4pm Sat & Sun & 6.30-10pm 1st Sat of month) Our pick of the vineyard restaurants along Scotsdale Rd's easygoing rural loop, Kirby's offers lunches on Saturday and Sunday afternoons and Saturday dinner once a month. The menu changes with the seasons, but could include slow-braised beef cheek or chicken breast wrapped in pancetta. Booking ahead is recommended, and wines from the adjacent Rickety Gate Estate are also available.

★Pepper & Salt
MODERN AUSTRALIAN, ASIAN $$$

(☑08-9848 3053; www.pepperandsalt.com.au; 1564 South Coast Hwy, Forest Hill Vineyard; mains $39-44; ☺noon-3pm Thu-Sun, from 6pm Fri) With his Fijian-Indian heritage, chef Silas Masih's knowledge of spices and herbs is wonderfully showcased in his fresh and vibrant food. Highlights include king prawns with chilli popcorn and lime mayonnaise, or the excellent tapas platter ($69), which effortlessly detours from Asia to the Middle East. Bookings essential.

★Boston Brewery
CRAFT BEER

(☑08-9848 1555; www.willoughbypark.com.au; Willoughby Park Winery, South Coast Hwy; pizzas $17-18, mains $25-38; ☺10am-7pm Mon-Thu, to 10pm Fri & Sat, to 9pm Sun) The industrial chic of the brewery gives way to an absolute edge-of-vineyard location, where wood-fired pizzas, meals and bar snacks go well with Boston's core portfolio of seven beers. The Willoughby Park Winery is also on site, and there's live music from 4pm to 8pm every second Saturday. See if any seasonal brews are available.

ℹ️ Information

Visitor Centre (📋 08-9848 2055; www. denmark.com.au; 73 South Coast Hwy; ⏱9am-5pm) Information, accommodation bookings, and a display on the local wine scene. Bikes (half/full day $22/33) and body boards can also be hired of you're feeling active.

ℹ️ Getting There & Away

Transwa (📋 1300 662 205; www.transwa. wa.gov.au; Holling Rd) Transwa bus service GS3 heads daily to/from Bunbury ($53, 5½ hours), Bridgetown ($35, 4¾ hours), Pemberton ($29, 2¾ hours), Walpole ($14, 42 minutes) and Albany ($10, 42 minutes).

Albany

POP 37,233

Established shortly before Perth in 1826, the oldest European settlement in the state is now the bustling commercial centre of the southern region. Albany is a mixed bag comprising a stately and genteel decaying colonial quarter, a waterfront in the midst of sophisticated redevelopment and a hectic sprawl of malls and fast-food joints. Less ambivalent is its spectacular coastline, from Torndirrup National Park's surf-pummelled cliffs to Middleton Beach's white sands and the calm waters of King George Sound.

The town is in an area that's seen the violence of weather and whaling. Whales are still a part of the Albany experience, but these days are hunted with a camera lens.

The Bibbulmun Track (p951) ends (or starts) here, just outside the visitor centre.

History

The Minang Noongar people called this place Kinjarling (the place of rain) and believed that fighting Wargals (mystical giant serpents) created the fractured landscape.

Initial contacts with Europeans were friendly, with over 60 ships visiting between 1622 and 1826. The establishment of a British settlement was welcomed as it regulated the behaviour of sealers and whalers, who had been kidnapping, raping and murdering Minang people. Yet by the end of the 19th century, every shop in Albany refused entry to Aboriginal people, and their control over every aspect of their lives (including the right to bring up their own children) had been lost.

For the British, Albany's raison d'être was its sheltered harbour, which made it a whaling port right up to 1978. During WWI it was the mustering point for transport ships for Australian and New Zealand Army Corps (Anzac) troops heading for Egypt and the Gallipoli campaign.

In late 2014, Albany commemorated the centenary of the departure of over 40,000 Anzac soldiers to the Great War, and the opening of the National Anzac Centre has seen the city develop into an important destination for travellers interested in WWI history.

◎ Sights

Albany Heritage Park   PARK
(www.nationalanzaccentre.com.au/visit/albany-heritage-park; 67 Forts Rd) Inaugurated in 2014, the Albany Heritage Park incorporates the National Anzac Centre, Princess Royal Fortress, Padre White Lookout, Desert Mounted Corps Memorial and the Ataturk Memorial.

➡ **National Anzac Centre**
(📋 08-6820 3500; www.nationalanzaccentre.com. au; adult/child $24/10; ⏱9am-5pm) Opened for Albany's Anzac centenary commemorations in late 2014, this superb museum remembers the men and women who left by convoy from Albany to fight in WWI. Excellent multimedia installations provide realism and depth to the exhibitions, and there is a profound melancholy in the museum's location overlooking the same expansive body of water the troop ships left from.

➡ **Princess Royal Fortress**
(Forts Rd; incl with entry to National Anzac Centre; ⏱9am-5pm) As a strategic port, Albany was historically regarded as being vulnerable to attack. Built in 1893 on Mt Adelaide, this fort was initially constructed as a defence against potential attacks from the Russians and French, and the restored buildings, gun emplacements and views are very interesting. From the fortress take the Convoy Walk for excellent views of King George Sound and signage showing where each ship was anchored before its departure to the Egypt and Gallipoli campaigns of WWI.

➡ **Desert Mounted Corps Memorial**
Memorial to WWI soldiers who fought at the Nek in the Gallipoli campaign of 1915. The memorial was originally erected in Port Said, Egypt. However, it was irreparably damaged during the Suez crisis in 1956, and this copy was made from salvaged masonry. Excellent views over King George Sound.

Albany

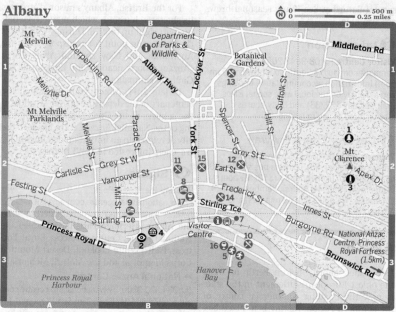

Albany

Sights
1 Albany Heritage Park D2
   Albany Residency Museum ....(see 4)
2 Brig Amity B3
3 Desert Mounted Corps Memorial D2
4 Western Australian Museum –
   Albany...B3

Activities, Courses & Tours
5 Albany Ocean Adventures C3
6 Albany Whale Tours C3
7 Busy Blue Bus C3

Sleeping
8 1849 Backpackers B2

9 Albany Harbourside B2

Eating
10 Albany Boatshed Markets.....................C3
11 Albany Farmers Market.........................B2
12 Earl of Spencer C2
13 Lime 303..C1
14 White Star Hotel C2
15 York Street Cafe C2

Drinking & Nightlife
16 Due South...C3
17 Liberté...B2

Western Australian Museum – Albany

MUSEUM

(www.museum.wa.gov.au; Residency Rd; by donation; ☺10am-4.30pm) This branch of the state museum is split between two neighbouring buildings. The newer Eclipse building has a childrens' discovery section, a lighthouse exhibition and usually excellent visiting displays. The restored 1850s home of the resident magistrate illuminates Minang Noongar history, local natural history and seafaring stories.

Brig Amity

SHIP

(adult/child $5/2; ☺10am-4.30pm) This full-scale replica of the brig that carried Albany's first British settlers from Sydney in 1826 was completed for the city's 150th anniversary. Around the brig is a heritage area worth exploring.

Albany Residency Museum

MUSEUM

(☎08-9841 4844; www.museum.wa.gov.au; Residency Rd; by donation; ☺10am-5pm) One of Albany's most impressive buildings how houses the Albany Residency Museum. Built in the 1850s as the home of the resident magistrate, the museum has displays telling seafaring stories, explaining local natural history, and showing Aboriginal artefacts.

Great Southern Distillery
DISTILLERY

(☑08-9842 5363; www.distillery.com.au; 252 Frenchman Bay Rd; tours $15; ⊙cellar door 10am-5pm) Limeburners Single Malt whisky is the star at this waterfront distillery, but brandy, gin, absinthe and grappe also feature. Tours on weekends – phone to check on timing and availability – include tastings, and there's a cafe offering tapas, local beer and snacks.

🏖 Beaches

East of town, the beautiful Middleton and Emu Beaches face King George Sound and share one long stretch of family-friendly sand. In winter, you'll often see pods of mother whales and their calves here. Head around Emu Point to Oyster Harbour for swimming pontoons and even calmer waters.

A clifftop walking track hugs much of the waterfront between the town centre and Middleton Beach. Boardwalks continue along Emu Beach.

🏃 Activities

For the ultimate views of the area, **Skyhook Helicopters** (☑08-9844 4019; www.skyhookhelicopters.com.au; flights from $140) run 10-minute scenic flights around Albany harbour or longer options taking in Albany's stunning coastal scenery and landing at the lighthouse on historic Breaksea Island, around 8km from Albany in King George Sound.

Albany Ocean Adventures (☑0428 429 876; www.whales.com.au; 5a Toll Pl; adult/child $88/50; ⊙Jul-Oct) and **Albany Whale Tours** (☑08-9845 1068; www.albanywhaletours.com.au; Albany Waterfront Marina, cnr Princess Royal Dr & Toll Pl; adult/child $95/55; ⊙Jun-Oct) run regular whale-watching trips in season.

Hiking

Bibbulmun Track
HIKING

(www.bibbulmuntrack.org.au) Taking around eight weeks, the 963km Bibbulmun Track goes from Kalamunda, 20km east of Perth, through mainly natural environment to Walpole and Albany. Terrain includes jarrah and marri forests, wildflowers, granite outcrops, coastal heath country and spectacular coastlines. Comfortable camp sites are spaced regularly along the track, and the best time to do it is from August to October.

👉 Tours

Busy Blue Bus
BUS

(☑08-9842 2133; www.busybluebus.com.au; ⊙adult/child from $135/108) Full- and half-day tours taking in Albany's Anzac history, the city's whaling heritage, or further afield to the Great Southern vineyards or Castle Rock and the Granite Skywalk in the Porongurup National Park.

Kalgan Queen
BOATING

(☑08-9844 3166; www.albanyaustralia.com; Emu Point; adult/child $85/50; ⊙9am Sep-Jun) Four-hour cruises up the Kalgan River in a glass-bottomed boat explain the history and wildlife of the area.

🛏 Sleeping

1849 Backpackers
HOSTEL $

(☑08-9842 1554; www.albanybackpackersaccommodation.com.au; 45 Peels Pl; dm/s/d $30/63/80; @🛜) Big flags from many nations provide a colourful international welcome at this well-run hostel. A huge, modern kitchen, sunny rooms and a laid-back social ambience make this one of Western Australia's best places to stay for budget travellers. Make sure you book in for 1849's free barbecue on Sunday night.

Emu Beach Holiday Park
CARAVAN PARK $

(☑08-9844 1147; www.emubeach.com; 8 Medcalf Pde, Emu Point; sites $40, chalets $140-200; ❄) Families love the Emu Beach area, and this friendly holiday park includes a BBQ area and a kids' playground.

Albany Harbourside
APARTMENT $$

(☑08-9842 1769; www.albanyharbourside.com.au; 8 Festing St; d $169-239; ❄🛜) Albany Harbourside's portfolio includes spacious and spotless apartments on Festing St, and three other self-contained options arrayed around central Albany. Decor is modern and colourful, and some apartments have ocean views.

Coraki Holiday Cottages
RENTAL HOUSE $$

(☑08-9844 7068; www.corakicottages.com.au; 16 Nanarup Rd; cottages from $125) On the edge of Oyster Bay, between the King and Kalgan Rivers, these light, bright, private cottages with bush surrounds are great value.

⭐ Beach House at Bayside
BOUTIQUE HOTEL $$$

(☑08-9844 8844; www.thebeachhouseatbayside.com.au; 33 Barry Ct, Collingwood Park; r $280-375; ❄🛜) Positioned right by the beach and the golf course in a quiet cul-de-sac, midway between Middleton Beach and Emu Point, this

ALBANY TO ESPERANCE ALTERNATIVES

The rural 480km of South Coast Hwy (Rte 1) between Albany and Esperance is a relatively unpopulated stretch. Break up the first leg by taking the Albany Hwy (Rte 30) to Mt Barker, and then head east to Porongurup. Then travel north through the Stirling Ranges, and turn east again through Ongerup, and rejoin the highway at Jerramungup. This route adds 57km to the trip.

At Ongerup, the **Yongergnow Malleefowl Centre** (☑ 08-9828 2325; www.yongergnow.com.au; adult/child $10/5; ⊙10am-4pm Tue-Sat) is devoted to the conservation of a curious endangered bird that creates huge mounds to incubate its chicks.

Near Jerramungup is **Fitzgerald River National Park** – base yourself at Hopetoun or Bremer Bay to explore the national park. Note that Bremer Bay is best reached by taking the South Coast Hwy from Albany.

modern accommodation offers wonderful service. Rates include breakfast, afternoon tea, and evening port and chocolates. The friendly owners have their fingers on the pulse of Albany's dining scene, and a second property a few doors away is equally comfortable.

🍴 Eating & Drinking

Albany Boatshed Markets MARKET $
(☑ 0458 433 248; www.albanyboatshedmarkets. com; Princess Royal Dr, the Boatshed; ⊙10am-1pm Sun) Local produce, arts and crafts, and wines from around the Great Southern area.

Albany Farmers Market MARKET $
(☑ 0417 983 428; www.albanyfarmersmarket.com. au; Collie St; ⊙8am-noon Sat) Weekly market with gourmet food and local artisan produce.

White Star Hotel PUB FOOD $$
(☑ 08-9841 1733; www.whitestarhotel.com.au; 72 Stirling Tce; mains $21-39; ⊙11am-late) With good beers on tap, excellent pub grub, a beer garden and lots of live music, this old pub gets a gold star. Sunday-night folk and blues gigs are a good opportunity to share a pint with Albany's laid-back locals. The sur-

rounding Stirling Tce area has other good cafes and restaurants, with outdoor seating during spring and summer.

York Street Cafe CAFE $$
(☑ 08-9842 1666; www.184york.com; 184 York St; mains $12-22; ⊙7am-4pm; 🐾) The food is excellent at this cosmopolitan and versatile cafe on the main strip. Breakfast options include a terrific egg, bacon and hash-brown wrap and an Asian-style omelette, while Thai fishcakes and gourmet burgers are lunchtime highlights.

Earl of Spencer PUB FOOD $$
(☑ 08-9847 4262; www.facebook.com/TheEarlOf Spencer; cnr Earl & Spencer Sts; mains $23-36; ⊙11.30am-late) Locals crowd in for the Earl's famous pie-and-pint deal or hearty lamb shanks. There are regular live bands on weekends, often with a jaunty Irish brogue. Occasional guest taps from WA craft brewers make it a good destination for travelling beer fans.

Lime 303 MODERN AUSTRALIAN $$$
(☑ 08-9841 1400; www.dogrockmotel.com.au; 303 Middleton Rd; mains $32-42; ⊙dinner 6pm-late, tapas 4.30-9pm) Pretty flash for regional WA, Lime 303 showcases local produce in dishes such as spiced aubergine moussaka, confit duck leg and hearty lamb rump with artichoke hash. More informal bar tapas are available from 4.30pm.

Due South PUB
(☑ 08-9841 8526; www.duesouthalbany.com.au; 6 Toll Pl; ⊙11am-late) Due South's bar is nattily concealed in a colourful shipping container, and the best place for a sunset drink is this bustling waterfont tavern's outdoor deck. There are decent craft beers on tap and local Albany wines, and the pub food menu is available throughout the day – handy in a town where many places take a break between lunch and dinner.

Liberté WINE BAR
(☑ 08-9847 4797; www.facebook.com/Libertebar; 162 Stirling Tce; ⊙noon-midnight Mon-Sat) Housed in the corner bar of a heritage pub, Liberté is a surprisingly hip addition to Albany's eating and drinking scene. The ragtag decor channels a louche Parisian cafe and velvet-trimmed speakeasy, while top cocktails, Great Southern wines and craft beers partner interesting French-Vietnamese bar food, such as steamed buns with soft shell crab, truffled egg and Sri Racha mayonnaise.

ℹ Information

Department of Parks & Wildlife (☑ 08-9842 4500; www.parks.dpaw.wa.gov.au; 120 Albany Hwy; ⊙ 8am-4.30pm Mon-Fri) For national park information.

Visitor Centre (☑ 08-9841 9290; www. amazingalbany.com; Proudlove Pde; ⊙ 9am-5pm) In the old train station.

ℹ Getting There & Away

Transwa (☑ 1300 662 205; www.transwa. wa.gov.au) State-wide WA bus services stop at the visitor centre.

Around Albany

Torndirrup National Park   NATIONAL PARK
(Frenchman Bay Rd; per motorcycle/car $6/12) Covering much of the peninsula enclosing the southern reaches of Princess Royal Harbour and King George Sound, this national park features windswept, ocean-bashed cliffs. **The Gap** is a natural cleft in the rock, channelling surf through walls of granite. A spectacular new viewing platform provides superb access. Close by is the **Natural Bridge**. National park fees apply and there is a kiosk for paying by credit card. Alternatively passes are available at Albany's visitor centre.

Discovery Bay   MUSEUM
(☑ 08-9844 4021; www.discoverybay.com.au; 81 Whaling Station Rd; adult/child/family $32/12/75; ⊙ 9am-5pm) When the Cheynes Beach Whaling Station ceased operations in November 1978, few could have guessed that the formerly gore-covered decks would eventually be covered in tourists discovering the area's bleakly fascinating story. An attached museum screens films about sharks and whales, and displays giant skeletons, harpoons, whaleboat models and scrimshaw (etchings on whalebone). Outside there's the rusting *Cheynes IV* whale chaser and station equipment to inspect. Free guided tours depart on the hour from 10am to 3pm.

Two Peoples Bay   NATURE RESERVE
(Two Peoples Bay Rd) Around 20km east of Albany, Two Peoples Bay is a scenic 46-sq-km nature reserve with a good swimming beach.

Porongurup National Park

The 24-sq-km, 12km-long Porongurup National Park has 1100-million-year-old granite outcrops, panoramic views, beautiful scenery and some excellent bushwalks. Porongurup is also part of the Great Southern wine region and there are 11 wineries in the vicinity. See www.porongurup.com.

Porongurup National Park   NATIONAL PARK
(entry per car/motorcycle $12/6) Bushwalks range from the 100m **Tree-in-the-Rock** stroll to the harder **Hayward and Nancy Peaks** (5.5km loop). The **Devil's Slide** (5km return) passes through karri forest to the stumpy vegetation of the granite zone. These walks start from the main day-use area (Bolganup Rd). **Castle Rock Trail to Balancing Rock** (3km return) starts further east, signposted off the Mt Barker–Porongurup Rd.

The **Castle Rock Granite Skywalk Trail** (4.4km return, two hours) negotiates a steep and spectacular path up the rock. The final 200m ascent to the summit incorporates a steep rocky scramble and a vertical 7m ladder.

PERTH & WESTERN AUSTRALIA AROUND ALBANY

Porongurup National Park

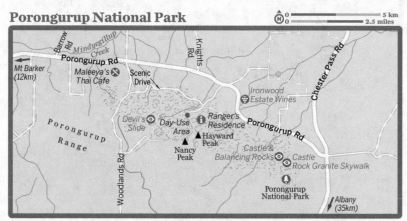

🛏 Sleeping & Eating

There is limited accommodation around the national park. See www.porongurup.com for listings of a caravan park and B&Bs. Most visitors stay in Mt Barker, a short drive away, or make the 54km trip from Albany.

Nomads Guest House   GUESTHOUSE $
(☑ 08-9851 2131; www.nomadsguesthousewa.com.au; 12 Morpeth St, Mt Barker; s/d/yurts/chalets $70/90/100/110; 🛜) A surprising sight is the authentic Mongolian yurt (felt tent) and gallery of Mongolian and Chinese art in the grounds of Nomads Guest House. The owners frequently rescue orphaned kangaroos, so don't be surprised to see a few temporary marsupial visitors in the main house.

★ Maleeya's Thai Cafe   THAI $$
(☑ 08-9853 1123; www.maleeya.com.au; 1376 Porongurup Rd; mains $25-33; ⊙11.30am-3pm & 6-9pm Fri-Sun; 🖉) 🍴 Foodies and chefs venture to Porongurup for some of WA's most authentic Thai food. Curries, soups and stir-fries all come punctuated with fresh herbs straight from Maleeya's garden, and other ingredients are organic and free range.

Ironwood Estate Wines   WINERY
(☑ 08-9853 1126; www.ironwoodestatewines.com.au; 2191 Porongurup Rd; ⊙11am-5pm Wed-Mon) Bailey, the friendly labradoodle, usually welcomes visitors who come to enjoy the stunning Porongurup views at Ironwood's tasting room and cafe. Our favourite wine is the flinty and fruity Riesling. Light meals ($12 to $15), including salmon quiche, are available along with coffee, tea and cakes.

Plantagenet Wines   WINERY
(☑ 08-9851 3111; www.plantagenetwines.com; Albany Hwy; ⊙10am-4.30pm) Plantagenet Wines' cellar door is conveniently situated in the middle of Mt Barker town.

Stirling Range National Park

Rising abruptly from surrounding flat and sandy plains, the Stirling Range's propensity to change colour through blues, reds and purples captivates photographers during the spectacular wildflower season from late August to early December. It's also recognised by the Noongar people as a place of special significance – a place where the spirits of the dead return. Every summit has an ancestral being associated with it, so it's appropriate to show proper respect when visiting.

This 1156-sq-km **national park** (⊙entry per car/motorcycle $12/6) consists of a single chain of peaks pushed up by plate tectonics to form a range 10km wide and 65km

Stirling Range National Park

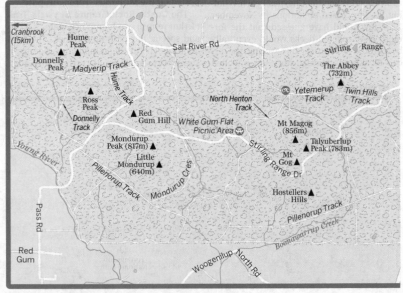

long. Running most of its length are isolated summits, some knobbly and some perfect pyramids, towering above broad valleys covered in shrubs and heath. Bluff Knoll (Bular Mai), at 1095m, is the highest point in the southwest.

Park fees are charged at the start of Bluff Knoll Rd.

The Stirlings are renowned for serious **bushwalking**. Keen walkers can choose from **Toolbrunup** (for views and a good climb; 1052m, 4km return) and **Bluff Knoll** (a well-graded tourist track; 1095m, 6km return). **Mt Hassell** (848m, 3km return) and **Talyuberlup** (783m, 2.6km return) are popular half-day walks.

Challenging walks cross the eastern sector include those from **Bluff Knoll to Ellen Peak** (three days), or the shorter traverse from **The Arrows to Ellen Peak** (two days).

Stock up on food in Mt Barker or Albany if you're camping. If you're staying at the Lily (p955), evening meals are available for in-house guests.

Stirling Range Retreat CARAVAN PARK **$**
(☑08-9827 9229; www.stirlingrange.com.au; 8639 Chester Pass Rd; unpowered/powered 2-person sites $32/36, cabins $95-149, units $160-195; ❄@❁) On the park's northern boundary, this shaded area offers camp sites, cabins and vans, and self-contained, rammed-earth units. Wildflower and orchid bus tours and walkabouts (three hours, $49 per person) are conducted from mid-August to the end of October. The swimming pool only opens from November to April.

Mount Trio Bush Camping & Caravan Park CARAVAN PARK **$**
(☑08-9827 9270; www.mttrio.com.au; Salt River Rd; unpowered/powered sites per person $14/18) Rustic bush campground on a farm property close to the walking tracks, north of the centre of the park. It has hot showers, a kitchen, free gas BBQs and a campfire pit. Guided walks, from 90 minutes to one day in length, are on offer.

★**Lily** COTTAGE **$$**
(☑08-9827 9205; www.thelily.com.au; Chester Pass Rd; cottages $159-189) These cottages, 12km north of the park, are grouped around a working windmill. Accommodation is self-contained, and meals are available for guests at the neighbouring restaurant. Call to enquire which nights the restaurant is open to the public and to arrange mill tours ($50, minimum of four people). There's also private accommodation in a restored 1944 Dakota DC3 aircraft ($249).

PERTH & WESTERN AUSTRALIA STIRLING RANGE NATIONAL PARK

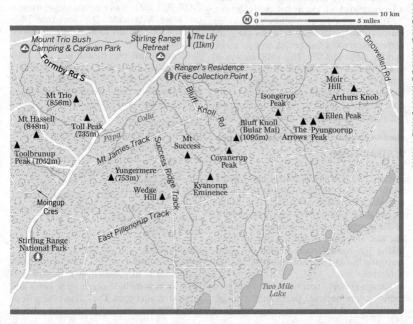

Fitzgerald River National Park

Midway between Albany and Esperance, this gem of a national park (entry per car/motorcycle $12/6) has been declared a Unesco Biosphere Reserve. Its 3300 sq km contain half of the orchid species in WA (more than 80, 70 of which occur nowhere else), 22 mammal species, 200 species of bird and 1700 species of plant (20% of WA's described flora species).

Walkers will discover beautiful coastline, sand plains, rugged coastal hills (known as 'the Barrens') and deep, wide river valleys. In season, you'll almost certainly see whales and their calves from the shore at **Point Ann**, where there's a lookout and a heritage walk that follows a short stretch of the 1164km **No 2 rabbit-proof fence**.

Bookending the park are the sleepy coastal settlements of Bremer Bay and Hopetoun, both with white sand and shimmering waters.

You'll need your own transport. A 4WD vehicle is strongly recommended. The three main 2WD entry points to the park are from the South Coast Hwy (Quiss Rd and Pabelup Dr), Hopetoun (Hamersley Dr) and Bremer Bay (along Swamp and Murray Rds). All roads are gravel, and likely to be impassable after rain, so check locally before you set out.

An accommodation option is **Quaalup Homestead** (08-9837 4124; www.whalsand wildflowers.com.au; 1 Gairdner Rd; sites per person from $12, cabins $115-125). This 1858 homestead is secluded deep within the park's southern reaches. Electricity is solar generated, and forget about mobile-phone coverage. Accommodation includes a bush camp site with gas BBQs and cosy units and chalets.

Esperance

POP 9600 / 08

Framed by aquamarine waters and pristine white beaches, Esperance sits in solitary splendour on the Bay of Isles. But despite its isolation, families still travel from Perth or Kalgoorlie just to plug into the easygoing vibe and great beach life. For travellers taking the coastal route across the continent, it's the last sizeable town before the Nullarbor.

Picture-perfect beaches dot the even more remote national parks to the town's southeast, and the pristine environment of the 105 islands of the offshore Recherche Archipelago are home to fur seals, penguins and sea birds.

History

Esperance's Indigenous name, Kepa Kurl (water boomerang), refers to the shape of the bay. Archaeological finds on Middle Island suggest that it was occupied before the last Ice Age, when it was still part of the mainland.

Esperance received its current name in 1792 when the *Recherche* and *Espérance* sailed through the archipelago and into the bay to shelter from a storm. In the 1820s and 1830s the Recherche Archipelago was home to Black Jack Anderson – Australia's only pirate. From his base on Middle Island he raided ships and kept a harem of Aboriginal women, whose husbands he had killed. He was eventually murdered in his sleep by one of his own men.

Although the first settlers came in 1863, it wasn't until the gold rush of the 1890s that the town really became established as a port. Since the 1950s Esperance developed as an agricultural centre, and it continues to export grain and minerals.

◉ Sights & Activities

Esperance Museum MUSEUM
(08-9071 1579; www.esperancemuseum.com.a; cnr James & Dempster Sts; adult/child $8/3; 1.30-4.30pm) Glass cabinets are crammed with quirky collections of sea shells, frog ornaments, tennis rackets and bed pans. Bigger items include boats, a train carriage and the remains of the USA's spacecraft *Skylab*, which made its fiery re-entry at Balladonia, east of Esperance, in 1979.

Museum Village HISTORIC BUILDING
(cnr Dempster & Kemp Sts) The museum consists of galleries and cafes occupying various restored heritage buildings; markets are held here every second Sunday morning. Aboriginal-run **Kepa Kurl Art Gallery** (08-9072 1688; www.kepakurl.com.au; 10.30am-3.30pm Tue-Fri, market Sun) has reasonably priced works by local and Central Desert artists.

Lake Warden Wetland System NATURE RESERVE
Esperance is surrounded by extensive wetlands, which include seven large lakes and over 90 smaller ones. The 7.2km-return **Kepwari Wetland Trail** (off Fisheries Rd) takes in

Lake **Wheatfield** and **Woody Lake**, with boardwalks, interpretive displays and good birdwatching. **Lake Monjingup**, 14km to the northwest along the South Coast Hwy, is divided by Telegraph Rd into a conservation area (to the west) and a recreation area (to the east). It has recently been temporarily closed due to bushfire damage; check its current status before visiting.

Great Ocean Drive   SCENIC DRIVE

Many of Esperance's most dramatic sights can be seen on this well-signposted 40km loop. Starting from the waterfront, it heads southwest along the breathtaking stretch of coast that includes a series of popular surfing and swimming spots, including **Blue Haven Beach** and **Twilight Cove**. Stop at rugged **Observatory Point** and the lookout on **Wireless Hill**. A turn-off leads to the **wind farm**, which supplies about 23% of Esperance's electricity. Walking among the turbines is surreal when it's windy.

Tours

Esperance Island Cruises   BOATING

(☑ 08-9071 5757; www.esperancecruises.com.au; 72 The Esplanade; adult/child $100/65; ⊙ 9am-12.30pm) Scenic wildlife cruises for spotting sea lions, New Zealand fur seals, dolphins, Cape Barren geese and sea eagles. Snorkelling equipment and a light morning tea are also provided.

Eco-Discovery Tours   DRIVING

(☑ 0407 737 261; www.esperancetours.com.au) Runs 4WD tours along the sand to Cape Le Grand National Park (half/full day $105/195, minimum of two/four people) and two-hour circuits of Great Ocean Dr (adult/child $60/45).

Woody Island Tours   BOATING

(☑ 0484 327 580; www.woodyisland.com.au; full-day ferry adult/child $40/30, half-day guided trip adult/child $65/55; ⊙ mid-Dec–Jan, mid-Apr–early May) Half-day boat trips incorporating a guided island walk, snorkelling, morning tea and the opportunity to spot local wildlife, including fur seals, sea lions, dolphins and Cape Barren geese. Alternatively, for independent fishing, swimming and bush-walking on the island, catch a ferry at 7am and return at 3pm.

Esperance Diving & Fishing   DIVING, FISHING

(☑ 08-9071 5111; www.esperancedivingandfishing. com.au; 72 The Esplanade) Takes you wreck diving on the *Sanko Harvest* (two-tank dive including all gear $260) or charter fishing throughout the archipelago. Also gear hire and dive courses.

Sleeping

Woody Island Eco-Stays   CAMPGROUND $

(☑ 0484 327 580; www.facebook.com/woodyisland ecotours; ⊙ mid-Dec–Jan, mid-Apr–early May) At the time of writing, accommodation on this nature reserve island was closed for renovation but was due to open again in late 2017. Options will include leafy camp sites and canvas-sided bush huts. Power is mostly solar, and rainwater supplies the island – both are highly valued. Allow for an $80 return ferry transfer as well.

Check the website to get the latest information on Woody Island's reopening.

Blue Waters Lodge YHA   HOSTEL $

(☑ 08-9071 1040; www.yha.com.au; 299 Goldfields Rd; dm/d/tr $33/67/91) On the beachfront about 1.5km from the town centre, this rambling place feels institutional, and many of the guests are long-stay residents working in the area. Bikes can be hired to ride along the beach.

★**Esperance B&B by the Sea**   B&B $$

(☑ 08-9071 5640; www.esperancebb.com; 34 Stewart St; s/d $130/190; ❋) This great-value beachhouse has a private guest wing and the views from the deck overlooking Blue Haven Beach are breathtaking, especially at sunset. It's just a stroll from the ocean and a five-minute drive from central Esperance.

Driftwood Apartments   APARTMENT $$

(☑ 0428 716 677; www.driftwoodapartments.com. au; 69 The Esplanade; apt $165-220; ❋) Each of these seven smart blue-and-yellow apartments, right across from the waterfront, has its own BBQ and outdoor table setting. The two-storey, two-bedroom units have decks and a bit more privacy.

Eating & Drinking

★**Fish Face**   SEAFOOD $$

(☑ 08-9071 1601; www.facebook.com/FishFaceEs-perance; 1 James St; mains$15-20; ⊙ 4.30-8.30pm Thu-Tue) Seafood is the star at Fish Face, with superior fish and chips, grilled prawns and squid, and scallops and oysters served up in stylish surroundings. Good sides include caesar salads, tasty buckwheat noodles with a ponzu dressing, and a healthy carrot and quinoa salad. Specials could include surf and turf, seafood risotto or Tasmanian salmon.

Taylor's Beach Bar & Cafe
CAFE $$

(☑08-9071 4317; Taylor St Jetty; mains $16-34; ⊙8am-10pm Wed-Sun; ☎) This sprawling cafe by the jetty serves cafe fare, burgers, seafood and salads. Locals hang out at the tables on the grass or read on the covered terrace. Focaccia sandwiches are good value and it's good for a glass of wine or chilled pint of Lucky Bay Brewing's refreshing *Kölsch*-style beer. Ask about occasional live music – usually on Sunday afternoons.

Pier Hotel
PUB FOOD $$

(☑08-9071 1777; www.thepierhotelesperance.com; 47 The Esplanade; mains $22-38; ⊙11.30am-late) Lots of beers on tap, wood-fired pizzas and good-value bistro meals conspire to make the local pub a firm favourite with both locals and visitors. The Pale Ale from Esperance's very own Lucky Bay Brewing is usually on tap, and there's live music most weekends.

Lucky Bay Brewery
MICROBREWERY

(☑0447 631 115; www.facebook.com/luckybay brewing; Barook Rd; tastings $10; ⊙2-5.30pm Fri-Sun) Look for Lucky Bay's beers in bars around Esperance – watch for the kangaroo tap badge – or make the journey 12km west to their simple brewery and tasting room. Two-litre growlers are available for takeaway, and Nigel the friendly brewmaster will guide you through beers, including the refreshing *Kölsch*-style Skippy Rock, Belgian-style Homestead *saison* or hoppy Cyclops India pale ale (IPA).

Coffee Cat
CAFE

(☑0417 968 177; ⊙7am-2pm Mon-Fri) Parked up near Esperance's Tanker Jetty, WA's hippest mobile coffee caravan also serves up yummy home-baked cakes and muffins. Grab an early-morning java to fuel a stroll along Esperance's recently redeveloped and very impressive esplanade. During summer the surrounding area often attracts a few other food trucks.

❶ Information

Visitor Centre (☑08-9083 1555; www.visit esperance.com; cnr Kemp & Dempster Sts; ⊙9am-5pm Mon-Fri, to 4pm Sat, to 2pm Sun) In the museum village with a handy 24-hour information touch screen also.

Parks & Wildlife (☑08-9083 2100; www. parks.dpaw.wa.gov.au; 92 Dempster St; ⊙8am-4.40pm Mon-Fri) National parks information.

❶ Getting There & Away

Esperance Airport (Coolgardie-Esperance Hwy) is 18km north of the town centre. **Rex** (Regional Express; ☑13 17 13; www.rex.com. au) flies between Perth and Esperance.

Transwa (☑1300 662 205; www.transwa. wa.gov.au) services stop at the visitor centre.

➸ GE1 to/from East Perth ($95, 10¼ hours, three weekly).

➸ GE2 to/from East Perth ($95, 10 hours), Mundaring ($93, 9¼ hours), York ($85, 8½ hours) and Hyden ($60, five hours) – all three times weekly.

➸ GE3 to/from Kalgoorlie ($60, five hours, three weekly), Coolgardie ($58, 4¾ hours, weekly) and Norseman ($32, 2¼ hours, three weekly).

❶ Getting Around

Rent a car from **Avis** (☑08-9071-3998; www. avis.com.au; 63 The Esplanade; ⊙8.30am-5pm Mon-Fri & to noon Sat) if you wish to explore Cape Le Grand National Park or the spectacular Great Ocean Drive. There is a branch at the Esperance airport too.

Around Esperance

Cape Le Grand National Park   NATIONAL PARK
(entry per car/motorcycle $12/6, sites adult/child $10/2.20) Good fishing, swimming and camping can be found at **Lucky Bay** and **Le Grand Beach**, and day-use facilities at gorgeous **Hellfire Bay**. Make the effort to climb **Frenchman Peak** (a steep 3km return, allow two hours), as the views from the top and through the rocky 'eye', especially during the late afternoon, are superb.

The 15km Le Grand Coastal Trail links the bay, or you can do shorter stretches between beaches.

Cape Arid National Park   NATIONAL PARK
(entry per car/motorcycle $12/6, sites adult/child $10/2.20) Whales (in season), seals and Cape Barren geese are seen regularly here. Most of the park is 4WD-accessible only, although the Thomas River Rd leading to the shire camp site suits all vehicles. There's a challenging walk to the top of Tower Peak on Mt Ragged (3km return, three hours).

Lucky Bean Cafe   CAFE
(☑0418 913 414; www.facebook.com/luckybean cafe; Lucky Bay; ⊙9.30am-4pm Thu-Mon Oct-Apr, open daily in school holidays) This spring-and-summer-only beachfront caravan may be the most spectacular place you ever have a coffee

and a muffin. You may even get lucky and see marsupial visitors on Lucky Bay's glorious sandy arc while sipping your 'Kangacino'.

BATAVIA COAST

From tranquil Dongara-Port Denison to the remote, wind-scoured Zutydorp Cliffs stretches a dramatic coastline steeped in history, littered with shipwrecks and rich in marine life. While the region proved the undoing of many early European sailors, today modern fleets make the most of a lucrative crayfish industry, and travellers hunt down empty beaches.

Geraldton

POP 40,000

Capital of the midwest, sun-drenched 'Gero' is surrounded by excellent beaches offering myriad aquatic opportunities – swimming, snorkelling, surfing and, in particular, windsurfing and kitesurfing. The largest town between Perth and Darwin has huge wheat-handling and fishing industries that make it independent of the fickle tourist dollar, and seasonal workers flood the town during crayfish season.

In parts, Geraldton is still something of a work in progress, as the town's focus shifts to the waterfront and leaves a few empty lots ripe for development. The fantastically revamped waterfront is a masterclass in creating fun public spaces, and Gero blends big-city sophistication with small-town friendliness, offering a strong arts culture and a blossoming foodie scene.

Sights

★ **Foreshore**   WATERFRONT

Geraldton's foreshore is a great example of waterfront redevelopment: loads of beach space and grassy spots, walking paths, picnic shelters, free barbecues, playgrounds (including a water-play park), cafes and event spaces. Check out the fun 'Rubik's cube' public toilets at the northern end, and the wonderful 'emu eggs' art sculpture from local Indigenous artists.

★ **HMAS Sydney II Memorial**   MONUMENT

(www.hmassydneymemorial.com.au; Gummer Ave; ⊘24hr) FREE Commanding the hill overlooking Geraldton is this moving, multifaceted memorial to the 1941 loss of the *Sydney* and its 645 men after a skirmish with the German raider *Kormoran*. Note the cupola over the pillared sanctuary – it comprises 645 steel gulls, representing the lives lost. Free guided tours are available at 10.30am daily.

★ **Western Australian Museum – Geraldton**   MUSEUM

(☏08-9431 8393; www.museum.wa.gov.au; 2 Museum Pl; by donation; ⊘9.30am-3pm) At one of the state's best museums, intelligent multimedia displays relate the area's natural, cultural and Indigenous history. The Shipwreck Gallery documents the tragic story of the *Batavia*, while 3D video footage reveals the sunken wrecks of HMAS *Sydney II* and the *Kormoran*. A highlights tour is offered daily at 11.30am.

Cathedral of St Francis Xavier Church   CHURCH

(☏08-9921 3221; www.geraldtondiocese.org.au; Cathedral Ave; ⊘generally 8am-5pm) Geraldton's cathedral, built between 1916 and 1938, is arguably the finest example of the architectural achievements of the multi-skilled Monsignor John Hawes. The cathedral's striking features include imposing twin towers with arched openings, a central dome, Romanesque columns and boldly striped walls.

The cathedral is generally open for visitors from about 8am (after Mass at 7am) until 5pm (6pm on weekends, before a 6pm Mass). Tours are held at 10am Monday and Friday, and 4pm Wednesday.

Geraldton Regional Art Gallery   GALLERY

(☏08-9964 7170; artgallery.cgg.wa.gov.au; 24 Chapman Rd; ⊘10am-4pm Mon-Sat) FREE With an excellent permanent collection, including paintings by Norman Lindsay and Elizabeth Durack, this petite gallery also presents provocative contemporary work and regular touring exhibitions.

Activities

Most activities are water-based, but there is also a network of bike paths, including the 10km-long coastal route from **Tarcoola Beach to Chapman River**. Grab the Local Travelsmart map from the visitor centre (p962). Bikes can be hired from **Revolutions** (☏08-99641399; www.revolutionsgeraldton.com.au; 268 Marine Tce; bike hire per half/full day $25/30; ⊘9am-5.30pm Mon-Fri, to 2pm Sat, 10am-2pm Sun), right by the foreshore.

The best surfing conditions are from April to October, when there is little wind and

Geraldton

PERTH & WESTERN AUSTRALIA GERALDTON

Geraldton

ideal swell. The windy season is roughly November to April – this is when wind-based water sports are at their best.

One of the best activities is a tour to the beautiful Abrolhos Islands (p963), 60km offshore.

Companies offering flights to the islands also offer scenic flights around the Geraldton area. See **G-Spot Xtreme** (☏ 0428 122 726; www.gspotxtreme.com.au), **KiteWest** (☏ 0449 021 784; www.kitewest.com.au; lessons per hr from $70) and **Midwest Surf School** (☏ 0419 988

756; http://surf2skool.com; lessons from $60, board hire from $20) for above-water action, while the **Batavia Coast Dive Academy** (☑08-9921 4229; www.facebook.com/bataviacoastdive; 118 North West Coastal Hwy; local dives $200; ☺8.30am-5pm Mon-Fri, 8am-2pm Sat, 10am-noon Sun) can arrange PADI courses and chartered trips to the Houtman Abrolhos Islands.

🎊 Festivals

Sunshine Festival CULTURAL
(www.sunshinefestival.com.au) It started in 1959 as a tomato festival, but now Geraldton's celebrations include dragon-boat races, parades, sand sculptures and parties. It's held over a week in early October.

🛏 Sleeping

⭐**Foreshore Backpackers** HOSTEL $
(☑08-9921 3275; www.foreshorebackpackers.com. au; 172 Marine Tce; dm/s/d without bathroom $35/55/75; @🗢) This rambling central hostel is full of hidden nooks, sunny balconies and world-weary travellers. It's very close to beaches, bars and cafes, and a good place to find a job, lift or travel buddy. It's well run, too, with bright, fresh decor that's a cut above. Discounts for stays longer than one night.

Sunset Beach Holiday Park CARAVAN PARK $
(☑1800 353 389; www.sunsetbeachpark.com.au; 4 Bosley St; powered sites $38, cabins $110-152; 🗢) About 6km north of the CBD, Sunset Beach has roomy, shaded sites just a few steps from a lovely beach, and an ultramodern camp kitchen with a huge TV. Decor in some of the cabins is pretty dated.

Ocean West APARTMENT $$
(☑08-9921 1047; www.oceanwest.com.au; 1 Hadda Way; 1-/2-/3-bedroom apt from $140/195/245; ❄🗢❄) Don't let the '60s brick put you off; these fully self-contained units have all been renovated in fresh monochrome, making them one of the better deals in town (especially for families or groups). Facilities are excellent; the wildly beautiful back beach is just across the road.

Mantra Geraldton APARTMENT $$
(☑08-9956 1300; www.mantra.com.au; 221 Foreshore Dr; 1-/2-bedroom apt from $189/239; ❄🗢❄) The pick of the upmarket options, for its marina-side location and proximity to museums, the foreshore and town centre. It offers a selection of modern apartments (one- to three-bedroom, all with balcony, kitchen and laundry), polished facilities and

Skeetas (☑08-9964 1619; www.skeetas.com. au; 3/219 Foreshore Dr; mains $20-46; ☺7am-9.30pm) restaurant downstairs.

🍴 Eating

Quiet Life CAFE $
(☑0484 314 364; www.quietlifecoffee.com.au; 287 Marine Tce; bagels $8-12; ☺7am-4pm Thu-Tue) Sit outside under the grapevine at this sweet old cottage, now a hipster-fied cafe serving up outstanding speciality coffee and delicious filled bagels (the chicken with slaw and bacon jam is top-notch). There's an additional brunch menu from Thursday to Sunday; keep an eye out for Friday-night 'After Dark' events.

Jaffle Shack CAFE $
(☑08-9949 9755; www.facebook.com/TheJaffle Shack; 188 Marine Tce; jaffles $6-12; ☺7am-3pm) The humble jaffle (toasted sandwich) is showcased at this rustic, surfer-chic cafe. Fillings range from classic Aussie combos such as Vegemite and cheese or baked beans, to prosciutto with garlic mushrooms. Leave room for a dessert jaffle (like apple with almond and ricotta). Ice-cream milkshakes and damn fine coffee too. There's a second **shack** (Foreshore Dr; jaffles $6-12; ☺7.30am-4pm) on the foreshore.

⭐**Saltdish** CAFE $$
(☑08-9964 6030; 35 Marine Tce; breakfast $8-25, lunch $22-30; ☺7am-4pm Mon-Fri, plus 6-9pm Fri & Sat) The hippest cafe in town serves innovative, contemporary brekkies, light lunches and industrial-strength coffee, plus home-baked sweet treats. The menu is an ode to local produce and accomplished cooking, from Exmouth prawn and spring-pea risotto to tempura-fried Atlantic cod. It's also open for dinner on Friday and Saturday nights (two courses for $55). BYO wine or beer.

⭐**The Provincial** MODERN AUSTRALIAN $$
(☑08-9964 1887; 167 Marine Tce; pizza $13-20, mains $18-34; ☺4.30pm-late Tue-Sat) Stencil art adorns this cool little taste of the city, an atmospheric bar serving up tasty share plates, wood-fired pizzas and more. It's a loungey spot with smooth tunes, outdoor courtyard, cocktail specials, and live music most Friday and Saturday nights.

🍸 Drinking & Nightlife

There's an assortment of pubs offering live music on weekends (local artists plus visiting Perth bands) and various cheap meal deals to lure in the punters. See Facebook pages to see what live music is on offer. And check out The Provincial (p961), too, for a smooth lounge-bar vibe.

Geraldton Hotel
PUB

(☑ 08-9921 3700; www.geraldtonhotel.com.au; 19 Gregory St; ⊙ 10am-10pm Sun-Thu, to midnight Fri & Sat) Winning features of this landmark old pub (dating from 1860) include a huge palm-tree-lined courtyard, $10 meal deals, and live music on weekends, including popular Sunday-afternoon sessions.

Freemasons Hotel
PUB

(☑ 08-9964 3457; www.thefreemasonshotel.wixsite. com/home#; cnr Marine Tce & Durlacher St; ⊙ 5.30-9pm Mon-Tue, 11am-9pm Wed-Thu, 11am-10pm Fri-Sun) The heritage-listed Freo has been serving beer to thirsty travellers since the 1800s. Nowadays it's a popular hang-out, with live music, DJs and open-mic nights complemented by a good range of bar meals.

ⓘ Information

Visitor Centre (☑ 08-9956 6670; www.visit geraldton.com.au; 246 Marine Tce; ⊙ 9am-5pm Mon-Fri, to 1pm Sat & Sun) Top location at the foreshore, with helpful staff. Accommodation, tour and transport bookings.

ⓘ Getting There & Around

Geraldton is 420km north of Perth.

Virgin Australia and Qantas both fly daily between Perth and Geraldton. The airport is 12km east of the city centre, on the road to Mullewa and Mt Magnet.

The long-distance bus station is at the old railway station on Chapman St; a Transwa booking office is here.

WORTH A TRIP

PINK LAKE

More commonly referred to as 'Pink Lake', **Hutt Lagoon** is an arresting sight near the seaside villages of Horrocks and Port Gregory. Yes, the saltwater here is pink, due to the presence of the algae *Dunaliella salina*. The algae is a source of beta-carotene, which is harvested here and used in food colouring and make-up.

You can see the lake from George Grey Dr (the road south of Kalbarri), but take the turn-off to Port Gregory for the best viewpoints. You can also take popular sightseeing flights over the lake from Kalbarri and Geraldton.

Transwa (www.transwa.wa.gov.au) runs buses between Perth and Geraldton ($66, six to 8½ hours) taking one of four possible routes. The twice-weekly coastal option runs via Indian Ocean Drive. Inland options run via Rte 1, Rte 115, or Rtes 95 and 116. The most frequent service is via the Brand Hwy (Rte 1); it offers connection to Kalbarri ($30; 2½ hours) three times a week. Transwa also has a twice-weekly service from Geraldton to Meekatharra ($79, seven hours).

Integrity (www.integritycoachlines.com.au) Runs three bus services per week linking Geraldton to Perth ($63, six hours), Carnarvon ($115, 6½ hours) and Exmouth ($156, 11½ hours). All fares listed are one way.

Kalbarri

POP 2000

Magnificent sandstone cliffs terminate at the Indian Ocean. The beautiful Murchison River snakes through tall, steep gorges before ending treacherously at Gantheaume Bay. Wildflowers line paths frequented by kangaroos, emus and thorny devils, while whales breach just offshore, and rare orchids struggle in the rocky ground. To the north, the towering line of the limestone Zuytdorp Cliffs remains aloof, pristine and remote.

Kalbarri is surrounded by stunning nature, and there's great surfing, swimming, fishing, bushwalking, horse riding and canoeing both in town and in Kalbarri National Park (p965). While its vibe is mostly low-key, Kalbarri is stretched to the limit in school holidays.

◉ Sights

Aside from the beaches, Kalbarri's biggest drawcards lie in the national park (p965) that surrounds the town to the northeast and the south. Be sure to admire the views from lookouts at coastal cliffs and river gorges.

Foreshore
WATERFRONT

In town, the river foreshore is lovely for a stroll or cycle – it has children's playgrounds (behind the town beach and by the jetty), picnic tables, barbecues, and fine swimming areas at the west end of town.

Rainbow Jungle
BIRD SANCTUARY

(☑ 08-9937 1248; www.rainbowjunglekalbarri.com; Red Bluff Rd; adult/child/family $16/8/42; ⊙ 9am-5pm Mon-Sat, to 4pm Sun) Bird fans (and kids) will enjoy this bird park south of town – it's an Australian parrot breeding centre, and there's all manner of colourful feathered

HOUTMAN ABROLHOS ISLANDS

Better known as 'the Abrolhos', this archipelago of 122 islands and coral reefs 60km off the coast of Geraldton is home to amazing wildlife, including sea lions, green turtles, carpet pythons, seabirds and the Tammar wallaby.

The name Abrolhos is thought to derive from the Portuguese expression Abre os olhos, meaning 'keep your eyes open'. These reefs have claimed many ships over the years, including the ill-fated Dutch East India Company's vessels Batavia (1629), and Zeewijk (1727). You can dive on some wreck sites, as well as follow a number of self-guided dive trails.

Much of the flora is rare, endemic and protected, and the surrounding reefs offer great diving and snorkelling thanks to the warm Leeuwin Current, which allows tropical species such as Acropora (staghorn) coral to flourish further south than normal. In fact, the Abrolhos Islands are the southernmost coral reefs in the Indian Ocean; they are clustered into three main groups (Wallabi, Easter and Pelsaert) and spread from north to south across 100km of ocean.

How to Visit

Unless you have your own boat, you'll need to take a tour. Because the general public can't stay overnight, divers (and surfers and fishers) normally need a multi-day boat charter. If you're content with a day trip where you can bushwalk, picnic and snorkel, then flying in is your best bet (and the aerial views are truly spectacular).

Tours generally depart from Geraldton. Two airlines offer tours and day trips: **Shine Aviation** (⌨08-9923 3600; www.shineaviation.com.au; Geraldton Airport; 4/6hr Abrolhos tour $235/255) and **Geraldton Air Charter** (⌨08-9923 3434; www.geraldtonaircharter.com.au; Geraldton Airport; 4/6hr Abrolhos tour $240/260) fly from the Geraldton airport 12km east of town and offer similar services and prices. The most popular tour is to land on East Wallabi Island and snorkel off the pristine beach here – four- and six-hour tours are available. Shorter, cheaper flights (flightseeing only, no landing; $215 for 90 minutes) are possible, or you can combine a visit to East Wallabi Island with flightseeing over Kalbarri and Hutt Lagoon (aka Pink Lake; from $455).

Kalbarri Scenic Flights (⌨08-9937 1130; www.kalbarriaircharter.com.au; Kalbarri Airport, off Ajana-Kalbarri Rd; flights & tours $84-315) offers flightseeing ($245) or a five-hour tour including landing ($255), departing from Kalbarri.

Divers should contact Batavia Coast Dive Academy (p961) in Geraldton, which can help get a boat together (from $300 per person per day).

Eco Abrolhos (⌨08-9964 5101; www.ecoabrolhos.com.au; 3-/5-day cruise incl meals from $1176/1960) is run by a crayfisherman with longstanding connections to the Abrolhos. The company offers liveaboard boat tours, departing from Geraldton between March and October and taking in snorkelling, diving, fishing, wildlife spotting and shore excursions around the islands. The vessel can accommodate 38 passengers in air-con cabins with en suite bathrooms.

creatures to admire (local lorikeets and cockatoos, but also South American macaws). It has a walk-through aviary, a lookout tower to climb and a small cafe. Look for outdoor movie evenings at the park's Cinema Parrotiso (adult/child $18/10), held in the school holidays.

Pelican Feeding WATERFRONT
(Foreshore; ⏱8.45-9.15am) **FREE** Kalbarri's most popular attraction takes place every morning on the waterfront. Look for the compact wooden viewing area and wait for the hungry birds to rock up.

 Activities

Just south of town are turn-offs to a string of **beaches** (all are great for sunset-watching), connected by the 8km **Melaleuca Cycle-Walk Trail**.

Blue Holes is the best place for snorkelling, while **Jakes Bay** draws surfers (Jakes Point is an elevated area for watching the surfers and any visiting dolphins). **Wittecarra Beach** draws fishing fans, and **Red Bluff Beach** is ideal for swimming. South of here is Red Bluff itself, the start of the southern section of Kalbarri National Park (p965).

Kalbarri

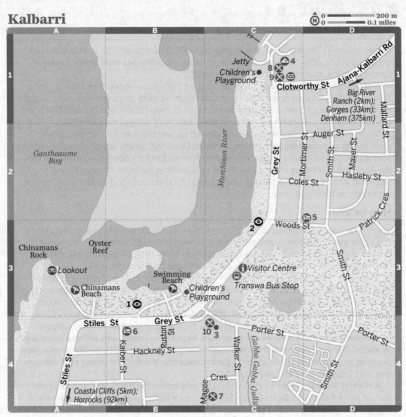

Kalbarri

◎ Sights
1 Foreshore B3
2 Pelican Feeding C3

☉ Activities, Courses & Tours
3 Reefwalker Adventure Tours C4

⌂ Sleeping
4 Anchorage Caravan Park C1

5 Kalbarri Backpackers YHA D2
6 Pelican Shore Villas B4

⊗ Eating
7 Finlay's Fresh Fish BBQ C4
8 Gorges Café C1
9 Jetty Seafood Shack C1
10 Restaurant Upstairs C4

Wildflowers bring visitors in spring – with the right conditions, the season can last from mid-June into November. Look for wildflowers along Stiles Rd, the Ajana-Kalbarri Rd, and near the airport. The visitor centre publishes wildflower updates.

⌲ Tours

Kalbarri is an outdoor adventure hub and excursions on offer include **Kalbarri Quad-bike Safaris** (☎08-9937 1011; www.kalbarri quadsafaris.com.au; off Ajana-Kalbarri Rd; driver/passenger from $80/40), whale watching with **Reefwalker Adventure Tours** (☎08-9937 1356; www.reefwalker.com.au; office: Porter St; whale-watching tour adult/child $85/55) (from June to November), and abseiling in the gorges of Kalbarri National Park with **Kalbarri Abseil** (☎08-9937 1618; www.kalbarriabseil.com; adult/child $90/80).

For interesting full- and half-day tours combining canoeing, bushwalking and swimming, contact **Kalbarri Adventure Tours** (☑08-9937 1677; www.kalbarritours.com.au; adult/child from $75/50).

Ask at the visitor centre also about canoeing, boat rental, horse riding, wilderness cruises and scenic flights.

🛏 Sleeping & Eating

Anchorage Caravan Park   CARAVAN PARK $
(☑08-9937 1181; www.kalbarrianchorage.com.au; cnr Anchorage Lane & Grey St; sites $35-45, cabins $80-90; ☒) The best option for campers, Anchorage has roomy, nicely shaded sites that overlook the rivermouth. Standard cabins have a kitchen and are family-sized, but they're budget affairs (no bathroom, BYO linen or hire it).

Kalbarri Backpackers YHA   HOSTEL $
(☑08-9937 1430; www.kalbarribackpackers.com; cnr Woods & Mortimer Sts; dm/d $29/77; @☎☒) The great location (one block back from the beach) and the friendly hosts win brownie points; the facilities themselves are a bit rundown. Still, there's a pool, a barbecue and an outdoor kitchen, and you can hire bikes ($20 per day), snorkels and boogie boards.

Pelican Shore Villas   APARTMENT $$
(☑08-9937 1708; www.pelicanshorevillas.com.au; cnr Grey & Kaiber Sts; villas $150-207; ❋☎☒) This complex of 18 modern and stylish villas have the best view in town and lovely grounds. All units have full kitchen and laundry; choose from two- or three-bedroom options.

Jetty Seafood Shack   FISH & CHIPS $
(☑08-9937 1067; Grey St; meals $11-25, burgers $9-14; ☺4.30-8.30pm) Excellent fish and chips, bumper burgers and takeaway salads (to make you feel at least slightly healthy). Pop across the road and dine at one of the outdoor picnic tables.

★Finlay's Fresh Fish BBQ   SEAFOOD $$
(☑08-9937 1260; www.finlaysfreshfishbbq.com; 24 Magee Cres; mains $15-45; ☺5.30-10pm Tue-Sun) Fresh local seafood comes simply prepared at this quirky Kalbarri institution, and often with piles of chips and salads lashed with mayonnaise. Don't miss the walls packed with a few decades' of kitsch Australiana and Oz popular culture. It's not all seafood – steak and burgers available too. BYO drinks.

★Gorges Café   CAFE $$
(☑08-9937 1200; 166 Grey St; meals $10-30; ☺7am-2pm Wed-Mon) Just opposite the jetty, Gorges has excellent breakfasts and lunches,

and bright friendly service. Look forward to the best coffee in town, ace eggy breakfasts and delicious lunchtime dishes like fish cakes, Thai beef salad or club sandwiches.

Restaurant Upstairs   MODERN AUSTRALIAN $$$
(☑08-9937 1033; 2 Porter St, upstairs; mains $27-44; ☺6pm-late Wed-Mon) Stick to the core menu of seafood and Asian-influenced mains, and you'll be satisfied at the classiest dining spot in town. Book ahead and ask for a spot on the balcony. Good desserts and a decent wine list seal the deal. Small kids not welcome.

ℹ Information

There are ATMs at the shopping centre on Porter St, and by the post office opposite the jetty on Grey St.

Visitor Centre (☑08-9937 1104; www.kalbarri.org.au; Grey St; ☺9am-5pm Mon-Sat, to 1pm Sun) Books accommodation, tours and bus tickets.

Kalbarri National Park

With its magnificent river red gums and Tumblagooda sandstone, rugged Kalbarri National Park (www.parks.dpaw.wa.gov.au/park/kalbarri; admission per car $12) contains almost 2000 sq km of wild bushland, stunning river gorges and savagely eroded coastal cliffs. It contains abundant wildlife, including 200 species of birds, and spectacular wildflowers between July and November.

There are two faces to the park: coastal cliffs line the coast south of Kalbarri, with great lookouts and walking trails connecting them. Inland are the river gorges.

◉ Sights

Coastal Cliffs

A string of lookouts dot the coast south of Kalbarri (accessed from George Grey Dr). Most lookouts are just a short walk from car-parking areas; a few have trails down to small beaches below. From July to November, you may spot migrating whales.

For an invigorating walk, take the **Bigurda Trail** (8km one way) following the clifftops between Natural Bridge and Eagle Gorge.

Closer to town are Pot Alley, Rainbow Valley, Mushroom Rock and Red Bluff. **Red Bluff** is the closest part of the park to town, and is accessible via a walking trail from Kalbarri (5.5km one way). From the lookout there are wonderful views of the Zuytdorp Cliffs to the north, and sunsets here are stunning.

River Gorges

The river gorges are east of Kalbarri, accessed from the Ajana-Kalbarri Rd. Roads travel to car-park areas with shaded picnic facilities, basic toilets and short walking paths (from 200m to 1.2km return) to dramatic lookouts.

Travel east of town for 11km to reach the first park turn-off. After a period of disruptive closures (from December 2016 to July 2017), a newly sealed, 20km road grants access to the park's favourite sites.

At the T-intersection, turn left to reach **West Loop Lookout** (where a new **Skywalk** was under construction at the time of research) and the Loop Lookout. From the Loop Lookout, a 1km return path leads to the park's most iconic attraction, the superb **Nature's Window** (a rock formation that perfectly frames the Murchison River below).

Bring lots of water if you want to walk the unshaded **Loop Trail** (9km return), accessed from Nature's Window.

Turning right at the T-intersection leads to **Z-Bend** with a breathtaking lookout (1.2km return), or you can continue steeply down to the gorge bottom (2.6km return).

Head back to Ajana-Kalbarri Rd and travel a further 24km east to reach the second set of sights. Turn off the road and you'll quickly reach the **Ross Graham Lookout**, where you can access the river's edge (1.4km return). Nearby **Hawks Head** has more great views – it's named after the shape of the rock structure seen from the lookout.

ℹ Information

For information, visit the Kalbarri **visitor centre** (p965) or the Department of Parks & Wildlife website (www.parks.dpaw.wa.gov.au). The Kalbarri tourist brochure (published annually) has excellent maps and details of all the walks.

Take water if you're visiting the gorges, and note that temperatures in this part of the park can be high – hike in the early part of the day.

SHARK BAY

The World Heritage–listed area of Shark Bay, stretching from Kalbarri to Carnarvon, consists of more than 1500km of dazzling coastline: turquoise lagoons, barren finger-like peninsulas, hidden bays, white-sand beaches, towering limestone cliffs and numerous islands. It's the westernmost part of the Australian mainland, and one of WA's most biologically rich habitats, with an array of plant and animal life found nowhere else on earth. Lush beds of sea-grass and sheltered bays nourish dugongs, sea turtles, humpback whales, dolphins, stingrays, sharks and more.

On land, Shark Bay's biodiversity has benefited from Project Eden, an ambitious ecosystem-regeneration program that has sought to eradicate feral animals and reintroduce endemic species. Shark Bay is also home to the amazing stromatolites of Hamelin Pool.

The Malgana, Nhanda and Inggarda peoples originally inhabited the area, and visitors can take Indigenous cultural tours to learn about 'Country'.

Shark Bay played host to early European explorers (and shipwrecks), and many geographical names display this legacy. In 1616, Dutch explorer Dirk Hartog nailed a pewter dinner plate (now in Amsterdam's Rijksmuseum) to a post on the island that now bears his name.

ℹ Getting There & Away

Shark Bay airport is located between Denham and Monkey Mia. **Skippers Aviation** (www.skippers.com.au) flies to/from Perth a handful of times weekly.

Integrity (www.integritycoachlines.com.au) buses run along the coast between Perth and Broome a few days a week, but don't make it up to Denham or Monkey Mia. They do, however, stop at the Overlander Roadhouse on the North West Coastal Hwy, 130km from Denham. **Shark Bay Car Hire** (☑08-9948 3032, 0427 483 032; www.carhire.net.au/shuttle-service/; 65 Knight Tce, Denham; shuttle $72, car/4WD hire per day from $95/185) runs a connecting shuttle service (book at least 24 hours ahead). It also has cars and 4WDs for hire.

If you're visiting without your own wheels, **Shark Bay Coaches & Tours** (☑0429 110 104; www.sharkbaycoaches.com) provides useful transfers between Denham and Monkey Mia ($15), plus links to the airport. The **Monkey Mia Dolphin Resort** (p970) can also arrange airport transfers for its guests.

Overlander Roadhouse to Denham (Shark Bay Rd)

It can feel like a long stretch driving the 130km from the North West Coastal Hwy (at Overlander Roadhouse) to Denham, a road known as Shark Bay Rd or, in marketing speak, World Heritage Drive. There are some excellent reasons to break the journey.

Turn-offs lead to great natural attractions, including the 'living fossils' at Hamelin Pool and the stunning Shell Beach. With some preparation and a 4WD, you can explore the Australian mainland's most westerly tip.

★ Hamelin Pool   MARINE RESERVE

Twenty-nine kilometres along Shark Bay Rd from the Overlander Roadhouse is the turn-off for Hamelin Pool, a marine reserve with the world's best-known colony of **stromatolites**. These coral-like formations consist of cyanobacteria almost identical to organisms that existed 3.5 billion years ago; through their use of photosynthesis they are considered largely responsible for creating our current atmosphere, paving the way for more complex life. There's an excellent boardwalk with information panels, best seen at low tide.

Steep Point   LANDMARK

The Australian mainland's most westerly point, accessed by 4WD via Useless Loop Rd off Shark Bay Rd.

Shell Beach   BEACH

Inside the vermin-proof fence, and 55km past the Hamelin turn-off, is the road to deserted Shell Beach, where tiny cockle shells, densely compacted over time, were once quarried as building material for places such as the Old Pearler Restaurant in Denham. For swimmers, the water is often warm, but quite salty.

★ Eagle Bluff   VIEWPOINT

About 25km south of Denham, take the turn-off 4km to this brilliant viewpoint, where a boardwalk allows you vistas that meld pinky-orange cliffs with the azure lagoon below. You may spot turtles, sharks or manta rays in the clear waters.

★ Hamelin Outback
Station Stay   FARMSTAY $

(✆08-9948 5145; www.hamelinstationstay.com.au; sites per person $14, d without bathroom from $90; ☺mid-Mar–Oct) ✦ Far and away the nicest place to stay along Shark Bay Rd, Hamelin Station is a former pastoral property transformed into a 202,000-hectare conservation reserve by its new owners (since 2015), the NGO Bush Heritage Australia. The rooms in the converted shearers' quarters are lovely and the amenities (including the communal kitchen-dining area) are top-notch; the bush camping sites are all unpowered.

Denham

POP 1000

Beautiful, laid-back Denham, with its aquamarine sea and palm-fringed beachfront, makes a great base for trips to the surrounding Shark Bay Marine Park, nearby Francois Peron and Dirk Hartog Island National Parks, and Monkey Mia, 26km away.

Australia's westernmost town originated as a pearling base, and the streets were once paved with pearl shell. The recently revamped Denham foreshore might not be quite that flash, but it's a lovely place for a barbecue, picnic, stroll or swim. Opposite the visitor centre is cracker ship-themed playground that kids will love.

◉ Sights

★ Ocean Park   AQUARIUM

(✆08-9948 1765; www.oceanpark.com.au; Shark Bay Rd; adult/child $25/18; ☺9am-5pm; ⊕) ✦ On a spectacular headland 8km south of Denham, this family-friendly attraction features an artificial lagoon where you can observe shark feedings, plus tanks filled with turtles, stingrays and fish (many of them being rehabilitated after rescue). It's all revealed on a well-done, 60-minute guided tour. The park also has a range of diving opportunities (including diving with the park's sharks), plus 4WD and boat tours. It also has a good restaurant (p968) and there are plans for luxury accommodation.

★ Little Lagoon   LAGOON

Idyllic Little Lagoon, 4km from town, has picnic tables and barbecues, and is good for a walk or swim. Don't be surprised if an emu wanders by.

Shark Bay World
Heritage Discovery Centre   MUSEUM

(✆08-9948 1590; www.sharkbayvisit.com; 53 Knight Tce; ☺9am-5pm Mon-Fri, 10am-4pm Sat & Sun) There are two sides to this centre, which is home to Shark Bay's helpful visitor centre. A gallery (free to enter) that houses stunning aerial photos of the Shark Bay area will have you itching to book a scenic flight. The main part of the centre is dedicated to a museum (adult/child $11/6), which has informative and evocative displays of Shark Bay's ecosystems, marine and animal life,

DIRK HARTOG NATIONAL PARK

The wind-raked island, which runs parallel to the Peron Peninsula, once attracted Dutch, British and French explorers (who left pewter plates nailed to posts as calling cards), but until recently its visitors were mostly fisherfolk and sheep. Now WA's largest island has become a national park (https://parks.dpaw.wa.gov.au/park/dirk-hartog-island) and is slowly opening itself up to tourism (although access is not easy, and is very expensive).

Only 20 4WD vehicles are allowed on the island at any one time, so bookings are necessary. The drawcards are isolation, natural beauty, wildlife (from loggerhead turtles to dugongs) and history – a winning combination.

4WD excursions, camping tours and scenic flights can be booked in Denham.

Indigenous culture, early explorers, settlers and shipwrecks.

Tours

Ocean Park Tours   ADVENTURE
(☑ 08-9948 1765; www.oceanpark.com.au; Ocean Park Rd) As well as its fun aquarium, Ocean Park (p967) has some great diving excursions (and PADI courses) and boat tours, plus a range of 4WD tours. Dive excursions head west to Steep Point or Dirk Hartog Island (from $275, non-divers welcome for $175). Boat cruises are also available to the same areas, and there are whale-watching trips from August to October ($175).

Shark Bay Scenic Flights   SCENIC FLIGHTS
(☑ 08-9948 1773; www.sharkbayair.com.au; Shark Bay airport; flights from adult/child $120/60) Flights range from a 15-minute Monkey Mia flyover to a sensational 40-minute trip over Steep Point and the Zuytdorp Cliffs (adult/child $195/98). From the air, the region looks like a piece of art, vibrant with colour. There are also tours available to Dirk Hartog Island, Coral Bay or Mt Augustus.

Sleeping & Eating

Expect school-holiday surcharges for accommodation, and possible minimum night stays (two or three nights is the norm). Compared with Monkey Mia, choices are wider and prices are lower.

Denham Seaside Tourist Village   CARAVAN PARK $
(☑ 08-9948 1242; www.sharkbayfun.com; Knight Tce; sites $33-54, cabins & villas $85-170; ☜) This lovely, shady park on the water's edge is the best of the three parks in Denham, though you will need to borrow the drill for your tent pegs. Accommodation ranges from small five-bed cabins without bathroom through to two-bedroom villas. A handy supermarket is across the road.

Bay Lodge   LODGE $
(☑ 08-9948 1278; www.baylodge.info; 113 Knight Tce; dm $36, d $80-140; ❈☜❤) Every room (including dorm rooms) at this lodge has its own en suite, kitchenette and TV/DVD, and there are motel-style rooms, family-size apartments, and beachfront units to choose from. Ideally located across from the beach, it also has a pool and a large common outdoor kitchen. There's a two-night minimum stay during school holidays.

Oceanside Village   APARTMENT $$
(☑ 08-9948 3003; www.oceanside.com.au; 117 Knight Tce; villas $160-215; ❈☜❤) This complex of neat self-catering cottages is perfectly located opposite the beach. Choose from one- or two-bedroom, beachfront or elevated. Facilities are top-notch.

Ocean Restaurant   CAFE $$
(☑ 08-9948 1765; www.oceanpark.com.au; Ocean Park Rd; mains $14-34; ⊙ 9am-3pm) The most refined lunch in Denham also comes with the best view. At Ocean Park (p967), overlooking aquamarine waters, breakfast is served until 11am, and you can partner beer and wine with lunches of local seafood and more. The platter for two people ($58) is good value.

Shark Bay Hotel   PUB $$
(☑ 08-9948 1203; www.sharkbayhotelwa.com.au; 43 Knight Tce; dinner mains $20-38; ⊙ 10am-late) Sunsets are dynamite from the front beer garden of Australia's most westerly pub, lovingly called 'the Oldie' by locals. It has a decent menu of pub classics (served noon to 2pm, and 6pm to 9pm), plus occasional live music.

Old Pearler Restaurant   SEAFOOD $$$
(☑ 08-9948 1373; 71 Knight Tce; mains $30-61; ⊙ from 5pm Mon-Sat) Built from shell bricks, this atmospheric nautical haven serves fantastic seafood. The menu and interior is decidedly old-school and there are no out-

door tables or view, but the fresh fishy fare is great – the hefty seafood platter ($115 for two people) features local snapper, whiting, crayfish, oysters, prawns and squid – all grilled, not fried. BYO drinks; bookings recommended.

ℹ️ Information

For information, interactive maps and downloadable permits, check out www.sharkbay.org.au. There's more info at www.sharkbayvisit.com.au and www.experiencesharkbay.com.

Department of Parks & Wildlife (📞 08-9948 2226; www.parks.dpaw.wa.gov.au; 61 Knight Tce; ⊙ 8am-5pm Mon-Fri) Park passes, maps and information about Edel Land, Dirk Hartog Island and Francois Peron National Park.

Shark Bay Visitor Centre (📞 08-9948 1590; www.sharkbayvisit.com; 53 Knight Tce; ⊙ 9am-5pm Mon-Fri, 10am-4pm Sat & Sun) Accommodation, tour bookings and bush-camping permits for South Peron. Located inside the Shark Bay World Heritage Discovery Centre.

Monkey Mia

Watching the wild dolphins turning up for a feed each morning in the shallow waters of Monkey Mia, 26km northeast of Denham, is a highlight of every traveller's trip to the region.

There's not much to the place (Monkey Mia is little more than a beach and resort), but you don't need to rush off after the early feeding – the beach is lovely, and there are some excellent tour experiences too.

◉ Sights

★ Monkey Mia Marine Reserve   BAY
(adult/child/family $12/4.50/28.50; ⊙ feeding at 7.45am; 🅿️) 🌊 It's hard not to smile as Indo-Pacific bottlenose dolphins start arriving for a breakfast snack. Note that during feedings, visitors are restricted to the edge of the water, and only a lucky few people per session are selected to wade in and help feed the dolphins. The pier makes a good vantage point for it all. Rangers talk you through the history of the dolphin encounters. It may seem a little touristy, but there's no denying its charm, or the loveliness of the setting.

🧭 Tours

★ Wula Guda Nyinda Eco
Adventures   ECOTOUR
(📞 0432 029 436; www.wulaguda.com.au; 2hr sunset tour adult/child $70/35) 🌊 Learn how to let the Country talk to you on these excellent tours led by local Aboriginal guide Darren 'Capes' Capewell, including the secrets of bush survival and bush tucker. The campfire-at-sunset 'Didgeridoo Dreaming' tours are magical. There are also snorkelling and kayak tours (adult/child $199/145) and exciting 4WD adventures into Francois Peron National Park ($199/140).

Wildsights   ADVENTURE
(📞 1800 241 481; www.monkeymiawildsights.com.au; 2½hr cruise adult/child $89/45) On the small *Shotover* catamaran you're close to the action for the 2½-hour wildlife cruise. There are also 1½-hour sunset cruises ($49, bring your own

PERTH & WESTERN AUSTRALIA MONKEY MIA

WORTH A TRIP

FRANCOIS PERON NATIONAL PARK

Covering the whole peninsula north of Denham, this 520-sq-km **national park** (https://parks.dpaw.wa.gov.au/park/francois-peron; admission per car $12) is a spectacular area of low scrub, salt lagoons and sandy dunes, and is home to the rare bilby, mallee fowl and woma python. Rust-red cliffs, white-sand beaches and blue waters all interplay, but you'll need to join a tour in Denham or Monkey Mia, or have a high-clearance 4WD.

2WD vehicles can only travel as far as the **'Peron Heritage Precinct'** (7km from the main road), where the old **Peron Homestead** houses museum displays. There's a walking trail around the shearing sheds, and a rustic, artesian-bore hot tub for visitors who'd like a soak. Further north, swim, kayak or stand-up paddleboard at the **Big Lagoon**, where there is also an excellent campsite. At the tip of the peninsula, the fantastic **Wanamalu Trail** (3km return) follows the clifftop between Cape Peron and Skipjack Point. Spot marine life in the crystal waters below.

The turn-off to the park is just past **Little Lagoon** on the road to Monkey Mia. Beyond the heritage precinct, the sandy road becomes passable only to high-clearance 4WD vehicles. Near the homestead, there's a tyre station to reduce tyre pressure to 20psi (or reinflate, as you exit). Caravans are not recommended; you'll need an off-road camper trailer.

drinks and snacks), and a full-day 4WD trip to Francois Peron National Park ($195); discounts are available for multiple trips.

🛏 Sleeping & Eating

Monkey Mia Dolphin Resort   RESORT $$
(📞1800 871 570; www.monkeymia.com.au; unpowered/powered sites from $37/54, backpacker dm/d $35/139, d from $267; 🅿🛜💺) With a stunning location, the only accommodation option in Monkey Mia caters to campers, backpackers, package and top-end tourists. The staff are friendly, and the backpacker rooms are good value (two rooms share a bathroom), but the top-end rooms are expensive, and it can get crowded. The grounds are home to a restaurant, bar, pool, store and tour booking office.

★ Boughshed   MODERN AUSTRALIAN $$
(Monkey Mia Resort; lunch $15-24, dinner mains $27-41; ⊘7am-8pm) The setting is fabulous, the views are grand (and visiting birdlife is prolific – don't leave your food unattended!). The Boughshed has a fresh, stylish interior and plenty of areas in which to nurse a coffee or drink (happy hour is 4pm to 5pm). Menus range from buffet or a la carte breakfast to light lunches and creative dinner options.

Monkey Bar   BAR
(Monkey Mia Resort; pizzas & meals $16-23; ⊘4-10pm) A relaxed and informal option closer to the backpacker section of the resort, the Monkey Bar has a pool table, happy hour from 5pm to 6pm, and a menu of pizzas and pub-style grub (fish and chips, lasagne, burgers). There are children's options too. It's open from noon during school holidays.

ℹ Information

Monkey Mia Visitor Centre (📞08-9948 1366; ⊘7am-3.30pm) Information about the area, plus tour bookings. It's on the beach, close to where the dolphin feeding takes place.

Volunteer Coordinator (📞08-9948 1366; monkeymiavolunteers@westnet.com.au) Contact for volunteering at Monkey Mia.

GASCOYNE COAST

This wild, rugged, largely unpopulated coastline stretches between two World Heritage–listed areas, Shark Bay and Ningaloo Reef, and offers excellent fishing and waves that attract surfers from around the world.

Subtropical Carnarvon, the region's hub, is an important fruit- and vegetable-growing district, and farms are often looking for seasonal workers. For travellers, it's usually seen as a handy place to restock, but not much more – but with time up your sleeve and a desire to get well off the beaten path, consider the option of heading north from Carnarvon along the Quobba coast.

Carnarvon

POP 6900
On Yinggarda country at the mouth of the Gascoyne River, fertile Carnarvon, with its fruit and vegetable plantations and fishing industry, makes a decent stopover between Denham and Exmouth.

It's a friendly place without the tourist focus of other coastal towns, but it has a few quirky attractions, decent accommodation, well-stocked supermarkets and great local produce. The tree-lined CBD exudes a tropical feel, and the palm-fringed waterfront is a relaxing place to amble. The long picking season from March to January ensures plenty of seasonal work.

👁 Sights

You can walk or cycle 2.5km along the old tramway to the **Carnarvon Heritage Precinct** on Babbage Island, once the city's port. **One Mile Jetty** (off Babbage Island Rd; adult/child $5/free) provides great fishing and views; walk or take the quirky Coffee Pot Train to the end. The nearby **Lighthouse Keepers Cottage** (off Babbage Island Rd; ⊘10am-1pm) **FREE** has been painstakingly restored; don't miss the view from the top of the creaky water tower in the **Railway Station Museum** (off Babbage Island Rd; ⊘9am-5pm). There's a cafe here, housing interpretive displays on the HMAS Sydney shipwreck in 1941.

Carnarvon Space & Technology Museum   MUSEUM
(www.carnarvonmuseum.org.au; Mahony Ave; adult/child/family $10/6/25; ⊘9am-4pm Apr-Sep, 10am-2pm Oct-Mar; 🅿) Established jointly with NASA in 1966, the **OTC Satellite Earth Station** (or OTC Dish) at the edge of town tracked the Gemini and Apollo space missions, as well as Halley's Comet, before closing in 1987. The Space & Technology Museum is here, with its fascinating, family-friendly assortment of space paraphernalia (including handprints from visitors like Buzz Aldrin and Australian astronaut Andy Thomas).

🛏 Sleeping & Eating

A good way to enjoy the local seafood is to cook your own on the free barbecues along the Fascine and at Baxter Park. Self-caterers should check out the produce at the **Gascoyne Arts, Crafts & Growers Market** (www.gascoynefood.com.au/growers-market; Civic Centre car park; ⊙ 8-11.30am Sat late May-early Oct), or stop at various orchards around town.

With a few notable exceptions, the dining scene doesn't exactly shine, but there are takeaways and a handful of pubs.

Coral Coast Tourist Park   CARAVAN PARK $
(☑ 08-9941 1438; www.coralcoasttouristpark.com.au; 108 Robinson St; powered sites $37-43, cabins & units $79-215; ❄ 🐾 🏊) This pleasant, shady park, with a pool and grassy sites, is close to the town centre. It has a variety of well-appointed cabins, a decent camp kitchen and excellent bathrooms, plus bicycles for hire ($25/75 per day/week).

Fish & Whistle   HOSTEL $
(☑ 08-9941 1704; Beardaj@highway1.com.au; 35 Robinson St; s/d/tw $55/70/70, motel r $120; ❄ @ 🐾) Travellers love this big, breezy backpackers with its wide verandahs, bunk-free rooms and excellent kitchen. There are air-con motel rooms out the back and the Port Hotel downstairs. The owners can help guests find seasonal jobs and provide transport to orchards and farms; there are discounted rates for longer stays.

Best Western Hospitality Inn   MOTEL $$
(☑ 08-9941 1600; www.hospitalityinncarnarvon.com.au; 6 West St; d $159-179; ❄ 🐾 🏊) Don't mind the dated exterior – this is the best of the motels in town, with fresh, modern rooms and good service. The on-site restaurant, Sails, is highly regarded.

⭐ Bumbak's   MARKET $
(☑ 0409 377 934; www.facebook.com/bumbaks; 449 North River Rd; smoothies $8; ⊙ 9am-4pm Mon-Fri, 10am-4pm Sat & Sun) Bumbak's, a working banana and mango plantation about 10km north of town (signposted off the highway), sells a variety of fresh and dried fruit, preserves and delicious homemade ice cream. On the must-try list: mango smoothies, caramelised-fig ice cream and choc-coated bananas.

Sails Restaurant   MODERN AUSTRALIAN $$
(☑ 08-9941 1600; www.hopitalityinncarnarvon.com.au; 6 West St; mains $25-45; ⊙ 6-9pm) Ask a local for a smart food recommendation and this is it: the town's most upmarket choice, at the Hospitality Inn. The kitchen team is led by a bona-fide French chef, and the output is high quality: spicy seafood laksa, honey-glazed spatchcock, parmesan-crusted barramundi and some tropical-minded desserts. Reservations recommended.

Port Hotel   CAFE $$
(☑ 08-9941 1704; 35 Robinson St; meals $14-42; ⊙ 8.30am-2pm Mon-Sat, 6-8.30pm Tue-Sat) There's a relaxed cafe feel to this revamped corner pub on the main drag, and the kitchen's daytime output ranges from eggs Benedict to lunchtime caesar salad and panini (good coffee, too). The evening menu highlights seafood, burgers and tacos.

ℹ Information

Visitor Centre (☑ 08-9941 1146; www.carnarvon.org.au; Civic Centre, 21 Robinson St; ⊙ 9am-5pm Mon-Fri, to noon Sat) Information, internet, maps and booking service. Open Sunday mornings May to October.

ℹ Getting There & Away

Integrity (www.integritycoachlines.com.au) Runs three times a week to Exmouth ($92, 4¾ hours), Geraldton ($115, six hours) and Perth ($167, 11¾ hours). Buses arrive and depart from the visitor centre.

Quobba Coast

While the North West Coastal Hwy heads inland, the coast north of Carnarvon is wild, rugged and desolate, and a favourite haunt of surfers and fisherfolk. Not many make it this far, but those who do are rewarded by huge winter swells, high summer temperatures, relentless winds, amazing marine life, breath-taking scenery and some truly magical experiences. Red Bluff is the southern point of the majestic Ningaloo Reef.

Two large, remote stations are found along the Quobba coastline, each offering beachside campgrounds and self-contained cottages. The beaches, sunsets, snorkelling, fishing and surfing possibilities are outstanding – as is the feeling that you've really stumbled across a secret, secluded destination.

From the turn-off on the North West Coastal Hwy (about 12km north of the bridge over the Gascoyne River), it's 49km on a sealed road to reach the blowholes. Heading north from here takes you 75km to Gnaraloo Station, passing a couple of coastal sites and campgrounds en route. You'll need to retrace your steps to join the highway again (you can't travel north of Gnaraloo to Coral Bay).

Ask locally for advice about road conditions – north of the blowholes, the road is unsealed and often quite sandy, and a 4WD is recommended. The website www.gnaraloo.com/getting-here has useful info to read before setting out.

Blowholes
LANDMARK

From the turn-off on the North West Coastal Hwy, it's 49km (on sealed road) to this natural phenomenon. Big swells force sprays of water through sea caves and up out of narrow chimneys in the rocks.

Just south of here (turn left at the 'King Waves Kill' sign and travel a kilometre or two) is Point Quobba, home to a gorgeous swimming and snorkelling lagoon known locally as the Aquarium, plus some beach shacks, excellent fishing and rough campsites.

Gnaraloo Turtle Conservation Program
VOLUNTEERING

(GTCP; ☑08-9315 4809; www.gnaraloo.com; Quobba Coast via Carnarvon; ☉Oct-May) ✦ Science graduates (any discipline) prepared to commit for six months can apply to GTCP, where food, accommodation, transport and training are supplied.

Quobba Station Homestead
CAMPGROUND, COTTAGE $

(☑08-9948 5098; www.quobba.com.au; unpowered/powered sites per person $13/16, cottages & chalets per person $40-75) ✦ Ten kilometres north of the blowholes is Quobba Station, a huge, ocean-front pastoral property with plenty of rustic self-catering accommodation, campsites (including some generator-powered sites), a small store and legendary fishing. The family-sized chalets are the pick for non-campers.

Red Bluff
CAMPGROUND $

(☑08-9948 5001; www.quobba.com.au; unpowered sites/shacks per person $15/20, eco-tents from $200) ✦ On Quobba Station property but 60km north of the homestead, Red Bluff is a spectacular headland with a wicked surf break and excellent fishing, and is the southern boundary of Ningaloo Marine Park. Accommodation comes in all forms, from exposed campsites and palm shelters, to eco-safari tents with balconies and superb views. It's 10km off the road (4WD recommended).

★ Gnaraloo Station
CAMPGROUND, COTTAGE $$

(☑08-9942 5927; www.gnaraloo.com; unpowered sites per person $18-25, cottage d $70-210; ☎) ✦ At the end of the road around 150km from Carnarvon, Gnaraloo Station is the jewel in the crown of the Gascoyne Coast. Surfers from around the world come every winter to ride the notorious Tombstones, while summer brings turtle monitoring and windsurfers trying to catch the Carnarvon Doctor, the strong afternoon sea breeze.

You can stay in campsites next to the beach at 3-Mile Camp (there's a small store here), or there's a range of options up at the homestead (5km further north of the 3-Mile turn-off). The nicest homestead options are the self-contained stone cabins with uninterrupted ocean views – great for spotting migrating whales (between June and November) and sea eagles. Don't leave without visiting the pristine Gnaraloo Bay, 7km from the homestead. Here and around 3-Mile Camp, there's excellent snorkelling close to shore.

Gnaraloo is dedicated to sustainability and has implemented a number of visionary environmental programs. The station is always looking for willing workers. Just be aware that this is a working station in the Australian outback, not a luxury resort

NINGALOO COAST & THE PILBARA

❶ Getting There & Away

AIR

Learmonth airport (south of Exmouth) is the primary hub for Ningaloo, while there are airports enabling the ferrying of workers between Perth and the Pilbara mining towns of Port Hedland, Karratha, Paraburdoo and Newman.

Several airlines service the Ningaloo region and the Pilbara, primarily out of Perth. Qantas (☑13 13 13; www.qantas.com.au) covers the biggest network: it flies from Perth to Learmonth, Karratha, Newman, Port Hedland and Paraburdoo. It has codeshare flights from Karratha to Broome and Port Hedland. Qantas also has direct flights from Melbourne and Brisbane to Port Hedland.

Virgin Australia (☑13 67 89; www.virgin australia.com) covers some Perth-to-Pilbara routes. Alliance Airlines (☑1300 780 970; www.allianceairlines.com.au) is a smaller player, with limited Pilbara destinations.

BUS

Integrity (☎1800 226 339; www.integrity coachlines.com.au) operates twice-weekly departures from Perth to Broome, stopping at Coral Bay, Exmouth, Karratha, Roebourne and Port Hedland. A weekly departure from Perth runs to Port Hedland via Coral Bay, Exmouth, Paraburdoo and Tom Price. A fourth service runs from Perth to Port Hedland via Meekatharra and Newman.

From April to October, Integrity works with the Flying Sandgroper to offer connections to Karijini National Park.

Integrity's hop-on, hop-off passes are good value – 1500/3000km over 12 months for $265/395.

Coral Bay

POP 255

Beautifully situated just north of the Tropic of Capricorn, the tiny, chilled-out seaside village of Coral Bay is one of the easiest locations from which to access the exquisite Ningaloo Marine Park (p982). Consisting of only one street and a sweeping white-sand beach, the town is small enough to enjoy on foot, making it popular with families.

Coral reefs lie just off the town beach, making it brilliant for snorkelling, swimming and sunbathing. It's also a great base for outer-reef activities such as scuba diving, fishing and whale watching (June to November), and swimming with whale sharks (April to July) and manta rays.

Development is strictly limited, so expect higher prices for food and accommodation. Exmouth, 152km away, has more options. The town is busy from April to October.

◎ Sights & Activities

★ Bill's Bay   BEACH
(🏛) Bill's Bay is the perfectly positioned town beach, at the end of Robinson St. Easy access and sheltered waters make this a favourite with everyone, from families to snorkellers. Keep to the southern end when snorkelling; the northern end (Skeleton Bay) is a breeding ground for reef sharks.

Purdy Point   SNORKELLING
Walk 500m south from Bill's Bay along the coast until the 8km/h marker. Snorkelling from this point allows access to some fantastic coral bommies, and you can drift with the current back to the bay. Hire snorkel gear anywhere in town.

☞ Tours

Popular tours from Coral Bay include snorkelling with whale sharks or manta rays (reduced price for observers), boat tours to spot marine life (most with snorkelling offered; diving also possible), coral viewing from glass-bottom boats, and quad-bike trips. Fishing charters and scenic flights are also possible. Book through tour offices at the shopping centre and caravan parks, and check for advance discounts.

Families are catered for with family rates. 'Observers' on whale-shark tours are welcome, and pay a reduced rate compared to swimmers.

Sail Ningaloo   SAILING
(☎1800 197 194; www.sailningaloo.com.au; 4 days per person from $1800; ⊗Mar-Dec) ✒ Sailing from Coral Bay, the *Shore Thing* is a luxury catamaran that offers liveaboard trips sailing the Ningaloo Reef (maximum of 10 passengers). Trips include four-, six- or 10-day options. Guided snorkelling, diving, kayaking and fishing are included, as are all meals.

Ningaloo Reef Air   SCENIC FLIGHT
(☎08-9942 5824; www.ningalooreefdive.com/package/scenic-flights; Shopping Centre, Robinson St; per tour from $220) Bookable through Ningaloo Reef Dive & Snorkel (p975), these scenic flights are in a small aircraft primarily used for spotting whale sharks and manta rays, so the pilots know these waters well, and the views from the air (and the wildlife-watching potential) are spectacular. Prices are per flight, not per person; three passengers can be taken. Departures are from the local airfield, not far out of town.

Coastal Adventure Tours   ADVENTURE
(☎08-9948 5190; www.coralbaytours.com.au; Shopping Centre, Robinson St; quad bike tour $110-130, sunset sail $75) More a booking service than an individual operator, with the prime offering being a combined quad-bike and snorkelling trip (which gets rave reviews). You can also book sailing excursions on the *Coral Breeze* catamaran, glass-bottom boat tours and manta-ray interaction.

Ningaloo Marine
Interactions   BOATING, SNORKELLING
(☎08-9948 5190; www.mantaraycoralbay.com.au; Shopping Centre, Robinson St) ✒ Informative and sustainably run tours to the outer

Coral Coast & the Pilbara

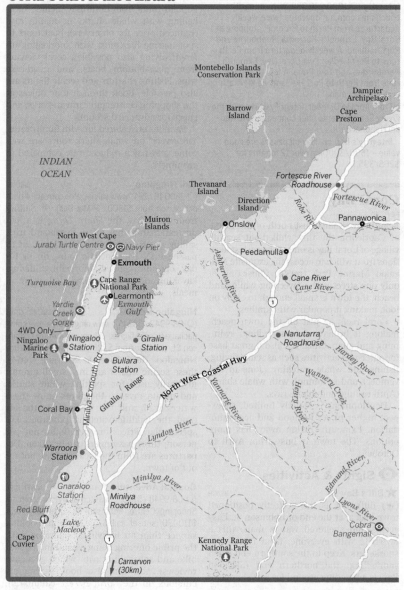

reef include two-hour whale-watching (seasonal; $75), half-day manta-ray interaction (year-round; $170) and six-hour wildlife-spotting cruise with snorkelling ($210). Child prices and family deals too.

Coral Coast Tours ADVENTURE
(☎ 0427 180 568; www.coralcoasttours.com.au; Shopping Centre, Robinson St) A mixed back of adventure trips: a four-day exploration of Karijini National Park ($685); fun 4x4 buggies for tours over dunes and along

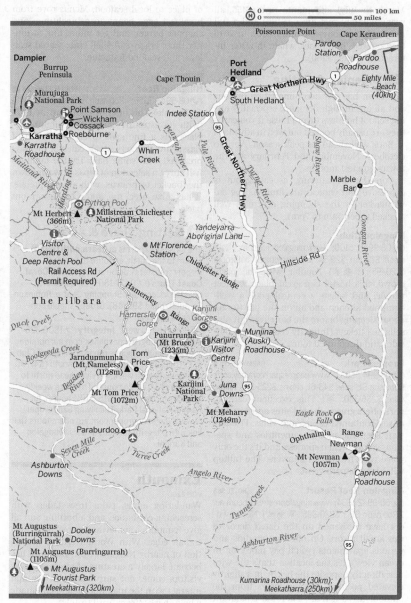

beach tracks (can be combined with snorkelling; tours $125 to $145); and snorkelling from the Aqua Rush RIB (rigid-inflatable 12-seater boat). The company also arranges airport transfers ($95) continuing on to Exmouth ($135).

**Ningaloo Reef
Dive & Snorkel** DIVING, SNORKELLING
(☎ 08-9942 5824; www.ningalooreefdive.com; Shopping Centre, Robinson St) 🖉 This highly regarded PADI and eco-certified dive crew offers snorkelling with whale sharks ($380,

March to July) and manta rays ($155, all year), half-day reef dives ($180) and a full range of dive courses (from $300). In 2016 they offered 'humpback whale in-water interaction' tours ($260).

Sleeping & Eating

The town has few accommodation options and all are in high demand, especially during school holidays (avoid these if you can – they are usually booked out well in advance).

Book well ahead for peak season (April to October). November and February are the town's quietest months.

Consider self-catering, as eating out is expensive and choices are limited. The supermarket in the shopping centre is well stocked (open 7am to 7pm).

Ningaloo Club   HOSTEL $

(☑08-9948 5100; www.ningalooclub.com; Robinson St; dm $29-34, d with/without bathroom $120/95; ❉@❉) Popular with the party crowd, this hostel is a great place to meet people, and boasts a central pool, a well-equipped kitchen and an on-site bar (forget about sleeping before the bar closes). It also sells bus tickets (Integrity coaches stop outside) and discounted tours.

Peoples Park   CARAVAN PARK $

(☑08-9942 5933; www.peoplesparkcoralbay.com; Robinson St; sites $43-61, cabins $225-286, hilltop villas $266-330; ❉) This excellent caravan park offers grassy, shaded sites and a variety of self-contained cabins and villas. Friendly staff keep the modern amenities and spacious camp kitchen spotless, and it's the only place with freshwater showers. The hilltop villas have superb views.

Ningaloo Reef Resort   HOTEL $$$

(☑08-9942 5934; www.ningalooreefresort.com.au; 1 Robinson St; r $220-395; ❉🛜❉) New owners have freshened up the dated decor of this small resort. On offer are studios and various apartments (you'll pay more for an ocean view). It's the location that's the winner: directly opposite the beach, in a slightly elevated position, making views from the outdoor areas a treat. There's a restaurant and bar here too.

★Fin's Cafe   SEAFOOD $$

(☑08-9942 5900; www.facebook.com/finscafecb; Robinson St; dinner mains $26-42; ⊙8am-9.30pm) Out front of Peoples Park, Fin's is a super-casual outdoor place with an ever-changing blackboard menu giving pride of place to local seafood. Menus rove from breakfast eggs benny to a lunchtime king snapper burger, and get interesting at dinner time: crispy soft-shell crab, seared scallops, and seafood fettucine.

Bill's on the
Ningaloo Reef   MODERN AUSTRALIAN $$

(☑08-9948 5156; Robinson St; mains $16-40; ⊙11am-late) The interior courtyard at Bill's (with its astroturf carpet and inbuilt fireplaces) is a fine spot to enjoy a menu of classic hits (burgers, steak, catch of the day) prepared with some flair. Try the fabulous fish curry, a selection of tapas or wash down the 'bucket of prawns' with a boutique ale. It has a bar area, too, and a bottleshop out back.

❶ Getting There & Away

The closest airport is at **Learmonth** (p980), 116km to the north, en route to Exmouth. Airport transfers can be arranged with **Coral Coast Tours** (☑0427 180 568; www.coral coasttours.com.au; Shopping Centre, Robinson St; adult/child $95/48). Groups should consider hiring a car.

Three times a week, **Integrity** (☑1800 226 339; www.integritycoachlines.com.au; outside Ningaloo Club) coaches run from Ningaloo Club to Perth ($203, 16 hours) and Exmouth ($47, 90 minutes); twice a week, services head north to Broome ($240, 18½ hours). There are weekly services to Tom Price ($162, 10½ hours), for Karijini National Park. The Flying Sandgroper (www.flyingsandgroper.com.au) offers tours that link with Integrity services and visit Ningaloo and Karijini.

Exmouth

POP 2200

Wandering emus, palm trees laden with screeching cockatoos, and a burning sun all give Exmouth a somewhat surreal, very Australian edge. With World Heritage protection of nearby Ningaloo Reef, Exmouth has become largely a creature of tourism. Many visitors come, not surprisingly, to see and interact with the magnificent and enigmatic whale sharks (from April to July).

Peak season stretches from April to October and sees this laid-back town stretched to epic proportions, but don't be put off: it's still the perfect base to explore nearby Ningaloo Marine and Cape Range National Parks. Alternatively, just relax, wash away the road dust and enjoy the local wildlife.

Exmouth

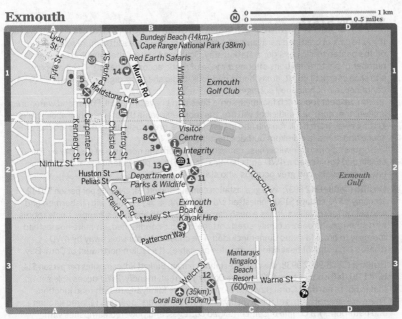

Exmouth

⊚ Sights
1 Ningaloo Centre	B2
2 Town Beach	D3

⊕ Activities, Courses & Tours
3 Exmouth Adventure Co	B2
4 Kings Ningaloo Reef Tours	B2
5 Ocean Eco Adventures	A1
6 Three Islands Whale Shark Dive	A1

⊜ Sleeping
7 Exmouth Cape Holiday Park	B2

8 Exmouth Ningaloo Caravan & Holiday Resort	B2
9 Ningaloo Lodge	B1

⊗ Eating
BBqFather	(see 8)
10 See Salt	A1
11 Short Order Local	B2
12 Whalers Restaurant	C3

⊜ Drinking & Nightlife
13 Cadillacs	B2
14 Potshot Hotel	B1

⊙ Sights & Activities

Ningaloo Centre MUSEUM
(Murat Rd) Due for completion in September 2017, Exmouth's brand-new showpiece is expected to house the expanded visitor centre, the relocated town library, and lots of first-rate interactive displays on the region's history and stunning surrounds, from reef to range. Plans are afoot for an aquarium; expect an admission fee to some displays.

Town Beach BEACH
(end of Warne St) A relatively short walk from town, this beach is popular with kitesurfers when an easterly is blowing. There are barbecues and picnic tables.

Exmouth Boat & Kayak Hire BOATING, FISHING
(☑ 0438 230 269; www.exmouthboathire.com; 7 Patterson Way) Tinnies (small dinghies) or something larger (including a skipper!) can be hired from $100 per day. You can also hire kayaks (from $50 per day), fishing gear, camping gear and 4WDs, or arrange highly regarded fishing charters.

⊕ Tours

Swim with whale sharks or humpbacks, dive, snorkel, kayak, surf and fish to your heart's content – the excellent visitor centre (p980) has the full list of tours available, along with

STATION STAYS

If you're sick of cramped caravan parks and want somewhere a little more relaxed and off the beaten track, consider a station stay. Scattered around the Ningaloo coast are a number of pastoral stations offering a range of rustic accommodation – be it an exquisite slice of empty coast, dusty home paddock, basic shearers' digs or fully self-contained, air-conditioned cottages.

Don't expect top-notch facilities; some sites don't have any at all. Power and water are limited; the more self-sufficient you are, the more enjoyable the stay – remember, you're getting away from it all. You will find loads of wildlife, previously unseen stars, oodles of space and some fair-dinkum outback hospitality.

Some stations offer wilderness camping away from the homestead (usually by the coast) and you'll need a 4WD and chemical toilet. These places tend to cater for fisher-types with boats, and grey nomads who stay by the week.

Giralia (☑08-9942 5937; www.giraliastation.com.au; Burkett Rd; camping per person $10-12, economy s $70, cottage $160, homestead s/d $220/300; ❄❢) Popular with fishermen and well set up for travellers. It has a bush camping area with amenities, simple single rooms with shared bathroom, a family-sized cottage, and air-conditioned, en-suite homestead rooms with breakfast and dinner included. The coast is 40 minutes away by 4WD (there's a handful of beachside campsites available). It's 110km northwest of Coral Bay.

Bullara (☑08-9942 5938; www.bullara-station.com.au; Burkett Rd; campsites per person $14, tw/d $110/140, cottage from $220; ⊘Apr-Oct; ❄) A great, friendly, 2WD-accessible set-up that is 65km north of Coral Bay, and 6km east of the Minilya-Exmouth road junction. There are several rooms in the stylishly renovated shearers' quarters (shared kitchen and bathrooms), a couple of self-contained cottages, and powered campsites with amenities (including laundry and open-air showers).

Warroora (☑08-9942 5920; www.warroora.com; Minilya-Exmouth Rd; camping per person per day/week $10/50, budget r per person $35, cottages $150-270) South of Coral Bay, Warroora offers wilderness campsites along the coast (some 2WD accessible), cheap twin-share rooms in the shearers' quarters, as well as a couple of large, self-contained homes. There are two access points off the main road – both are OK for 2WD. Chemical toilets are compulsory for campers, and available for hire.

all the details and forthcoming availability, and can book everything. Booking offices for individual operators are primarily found at the shopping centre, with a handful at Exmouth Ningaloo Caravan & Holiday Resort.

Outside whale-shark season (from around mid-March to August), marine tours focus on humpbacks (August to October) and manta rays (year-round, but in summer these are done out of Coral Bay). To get the most from the tours, you need to be a capable snorkeller and swimmer. Be wary of snorkelling on what may essentially be a dive tour – the action may be too deep. Ask the operators for advice. It's normally 30% cheaper if you don't swim and board as an 'observer'.

Many reef tours depart from **Tantabiddi** on the western cape and include free transfers from Exmouth; some may require you to make your own way to the departure point. Check conditions carefully regarding 'no sighting' policies and cancellations.

Birds Eye View　　　　SCENIC FLIGHTS
(☑0427 996 833; www.birdseyeview.net.au; Exmouth Aerodrome; 30/60/90min flight $199/299/399) Don't want to get your feet wet but still after adrenaline? Get some altitude on these incredible microlight flights over the Cape and (longer flights only) Ningaloo Reef.

Ocean Eco Adventures　　　SNORKELLING
(☑08-9949 1208; www.oceanecoadventures.com.au; Exmouth Shopping Centre; whale-shark swim/observation $410/200) ✦ A well-set-up operator with luxurious vessel; the rate includes breakfast and tour photographs. The whale-shark swim months are followed by humpback interaction and whale-watching tours.

Dive Ningaloo　　　　DIVING
(☑0456 702 437; www.diveningaloo.com.au; 2 dives from $200) A small, local company garnering a big reputation, Dive Ningaloo offers try dives, PADI courses, snorkelling trips (including with small Sea-Doo scooters),

whale-watching cruises and great dive options, including visits to Navy Pier (p981) and the Muiron Islands. You can also sign up for four-dive overnight trips.

Three Islands
Whale Shark Dive
SNORKELLING

(☑1800 138 501; www.whalesharkdive.com; 1 Kennedy St; whale-shark swim/observation $385/225) 🏊 This well-respected outfit consistently wins awards for its whale-shark tours, which run from mid-March to July. From August to October 2016, it also offers humpback tours ($325). The rest of the year, there are full-day snorkelling tours of the reef or Muiron Islands ($185). From August to October, there are sunset whale-watching cruises ($80).

Exmouth Adventure Co
KAYAKING

(☑0477 685 123; www.exmouthadventureco. au; Murat Rd, Exmouth Ningaloo Caravan & Holiday Resort; half-/1-/2-/5-day tour $99/179/665/1650) Newly rebranded (formerly Capricorn Kayak Tours), this company has an expanding range, including multiday kayaking, snorkelling and hiking adventures (including to Karijini). You can also take surfing and stand-up paddleboarding lessons. Its original offerings are excellent: a half- ($99) or full-day ($199) kayaking and snorkelling in pristine waters.

Kings Ningaloo Reef Tours
SNORKELLING

(☑08-9949 1764; www.kingsningalooreeftours. com.au; Murat Rd, Exmouth Ningaloo Caravan & Holiday Resort; whale-shark swim/observation $395/285) 🏊 Long-time player Kings gets rave reviews for its whale-shark tours. It's renowned for staying out longer than everyone else, and has a 'next available tour' no-sighting policy. In 2016 it also offered humpback interaction.

🛏 Sleeping

Accommodation is limited, so book ahead, especially for the peak season (April to October).

Exmouth Cape Holiday Park
CARAVAN PARK $

(☑1800 871 570; www.parksandresorts.rac.com. au/park/exmouth/; 3 Truscott Cres; unpowered/powered sites $39/53, dm/d $34/105, cabins from $135; ❄️🐾🛜🏊) Under new ownership, this large park is getting a spruce-up and offers good facilities for campers, backpackers (its rooms are known as Blue Reef Backpackers), families and more. Lots of cabin options, too, from simple (some kitchen facilities, no bathroom) to deluxe family-sized units. Bike hire available.

Exmouth Ningaloo Caravan & Holiday Resort
CARAVAN PARK $

(☑08-9949 2377; www.exmouthresort.com; Murat Rd; unpowered/powered sites $40/50, dm/d $40/84, chalets from $205; ❄️🐾🛜🏊) Across from the visitor centre, this friendly, spacious park has grassy sites, self-contained chalets, backpacker dorms and doubles (shared bathrooms; known as Winston's Backpackers), an on-site restaurant and even a pet section.

Ningaloo Lodge
GUESTHOUSE $$

(☑08-9949 4949; www.ningaloolodge.com.au; Lefroy St; d $160; ❄️🐾🛜🏊) One of the better deals in town. Rooms at this lodge are compact but clean and well-appointed, and the bathrooms are somewhat dated, but the extras are great: a modern communal kitchen and laundry, barbecue, shady pool and courtyard, and quite possibly the best wi-fi in town.

★ Mantarays Ningaloo
Beach Resort
RESORT $$$

(☑08-9949 0000; www.mantaraysningalooresort. com.au; Madaffari Dr; d/apt from $325/377; ❄️@🛜🏊) At the marina, this newly rebranded resort (formerly a Novotel) is at the pointy end of sophistication (and expense) in Exmouth. The tasteful rooms are spacious and well-equipped and all have balconies. They range from standard rooms to two-bedroom self-contained bungalows with ocean views. Grounds, pool, beach access and **restaurant** (lunch $17-30, dinner mains $28-43; ⊙6.30am-late) are all top-notch.

🍴 Eating & Drinking

Cadillacs (Grace's Tavern; ☑08-9949 1000; www.cadillacsbar.com.au; cnr Murat Rd & Pelias St; ⊙8am-10pm), at Grace's Tavern, and the bars of **Potshot Hotel** (☑08-9949 1200; www.potshot resort.com; Murat Rd; ⊙10am-late) are your drinking options, and both serve decent pub meals. Mantaray's at Mantarays Ningaloo Beach Resort is a great spot for a sundowner cocktail.

Rumour has it that a new microbrewery will be opening on Kennedy St, behind the shopping centre.

★ Short Order Local
CAFE $

(☑0421 777 864; www.facebook.com/theshortorder local; 3 Truscott Cres; snacks $5-10; ⊙6.30-11.30am Mon-Sat) Cute as a button, this pastel-striped food van is parked at the entry to Exmouth Cape Holiday Park and rewards early risers with great coffee, toasties and fresh muffins to early risers. It has a sweet array of timber tables and chairs scattered around, and occasional emu visitors dropping by.

BBqFather BARBECUE, ITALIAN $$
(Pinocchio's; ☑08-9949 4905; www.thebbqfather.com.au; Murat Rd, Exmouth Ningaloo Caravan & Holiday Resort; mains $18-40; ☺6-9pm Mon-Sat; 🖤) This popular, licensed alfresco *ristorante* changed its name and went barbecue crazy, serving up huge, succulent, smoky slabs of meat. After local outcry, the Italian owners returned their much-loved pizzas and homemade pastas to the menu – so these days, the options are wide, and crowd-pleasing. The servings are as legendary as ever. Locals still call it Pinocchio's. BYO wine.

See Salt CAFE $$
(☑08-9949 1400; www.seesalt.com.au; 3 Thew St; meals $9-30; ☺7am-4pm daily, plus 6-8.30pm Thu-Sun Apr-Oct; 🖤☑) Easy-breezy daytime options, expanding to dinners later in the week during the peak season. Kickstart your morning with chilli eggs or a bowl of Vietnamese *pho* (beef and rice-noodle soup), or keep it sweet with banana pikelets. Lunch might roam from Mexican fish burrito to Sri Lankan chicken curry. Joy for vegetarians, and decent coffee and smoothies too.

★ **Whalers Restaurant** SEAFOOD $$$
(☑08-9949 2416; whalersrestaurant.com.au; 27 Murat Rd, inside Exmouth Escape; mains $30-40; ☺5.30pm-late; 🖤) This Exmouth institution has a pretty poolside location, smart service and a mega-seafood menu (but vegetarians and vegans get some loving too). Don't miss the signature New Orleans gumbo, or spread your wings to the blackened fish tacos or Indian seafood curry. Die-hard bug aficionados need look no further than the towering seafood medley. Bookings recommended.

ℹ Information

For information on environmental projects around the cape, check out the Cape Conservation Group's Facebook page.

Department of Parks & Wildlife (DPaW; ☑08-9947 8000; www.dpaw.wa.gov.au; 20 Nimitz St; ☺8am-5pm Mon-Fri) Supplies maps, brochures and permits for Ningaloo, Cape Range and Muiron Islands, including excellent wildlife guides. Can advise on turtle volunteering.

Visitor Centre (☑08-9949 1176; www.visitningaloo.com.au; Murat Rd; ☺9am-5pm Apr-Oct, 9am-5pm Mon-Fri, to 1pm Sat & Sun Oct-Mar; ☎) Tour bookings, bus tickets, accommodation service and parks information. It's a great first port-of-call, with boards and folders outlining all the tour options in the area, and friendly helpful staff. You can hire snorkel gear here too. It's moving from its old location to the new Ningaloo Centre from April 2017.

ℹ Getting There & Away

Learmonth Airport (www.exmouth.wa.gov.au) is 36km south of town and has regular links with Perth courtesy of Qantas.

The **airport shuttle bus** (☑08-9949 4623) must be prebooked; it costs adult/child $35/25 between Learmonth and Exmouth town.

Three times a week, **Integrity** (☑1800 226 339; www.integritycoachlines.com.au) coaches run from the visitors centre to Perth ($240, 17½ hours) and Coral Bay ($47, 90 minutes); twice a week, services head north to Broome ($240, 16¾ hours). There are weekly services to Tom Price ($146, 8½ hours), for Karijini National Park. The **Flying Sandgroper** (p991) offers tours that link with Integrity services and visit Ningaloo and Karijini.

Red Earth Safaris (☑1800 827 879; www.redearthsafaris.com.au) operates a weekly tour out of Perth, which reaches Exmouth over six days ($785, including dorm accommodation and most meals). On Sundays it departs Exmouth from the Potshot Hotel Resort at 7am, returning to Perth over two days ($200, 30 hours; price includes meals and an overnight stop).

ℹ Getting Around

Budget, Avis and Europcar have agents around town, with car rental starting at around $90 per day. They can arrange car rental from the airport. **Allens** (☑08-9949 2403; alscarhire@bigpond.com; 24 Nimitz St; per day from $45) is a cheaper local option, with older cars; 4WDs and airport transfers also available. **Exmouth Camper Hire** (☑08-9949 4050; www.ningalooexcape.com.au; 16 Nimitz St; 4 nights from $575) has campervans and motor homes with everything you need to spend time in Cape Range National Park, including solar panels. There's a minimum four-night hire.

To zip around town, you only need a car licence for the 50cc scooters hired out by **Ningaloo Salty's Scooters** (☑0448 997 906; www.ningaloosaltyscooters.com.au; 77 Maidstone Cres; 1/3/7 days $70/150/240). They're considerably cheaper by the week. Its base is behind the Caltex petrol station.

Bikes can be hired from **Exmouth Cape Holiday Park** (p979).

For a taxi, contact **Cabs on Call** (☑0408 449 944). Airport transfers are possible, but must be booked.

NINGA TURTLE TRACKERS

Along the northwest coast each year between October and March, volunteer turtle-monitoring programs provide exciting opportunities for active involvement in local conservation. Expect strange hours, some uncomfortable conditions and immense satisfaction. Applications usually open around August, but check individual programs.

Ningaloo Turtle Program (NTP; www.ningalooturtles.org.au; Exmouth; 5 weeks $1300; ☻ Dec-Jan) Volunteers must commit to a five-week period, and some of that time is spent camping at a remote Ningaloo base (some is in Exmouth). Work from sunrise for five hours collecting data on turtle nesting, habitat and predation, then the rest of the day is free. Your fee covers all training and equipment, some meals, accommodation and transport from Exmouth.

Pendoley Environmental (☑ 08-9330 6200; www.penv.com.au; ☻ Nov-Jan) Pendoley is a marine conservation consultancy working with the oil and gas industry at Pilbara sites such as Barrow Island, offshore from Onslow. Typical program placements are for 17 days with all expenses covered; there's a strict selection process.

Care for Hedland (☑ 0447 907 661; www.careforhedland.org.au; Port Hedland; ☻ Oct-Mar) Grass-roots environmental group runs volunteer monitoring programs of flatback turtles on Port Hedland beaches from October to March.

Gnaraloo Turtle Conservation Program (p972) Science graduates (any discipline) prepared to commit for six months can apply to GTCP, which supplies food, accommodation, transport and training. The base is remote Gnaraloo Station, 150km north of Carnarvon.

Around Exmouth

North of Exmouth, the main road skirts the top of the **North West Cape** before turning and running south, passing glorious beaches until it reaches the entry to Cape Range National Park (p984).

Head north past Harold E Holt Naval Communication Station to an intersection before the VLF antenna array. Continue straight on for Bundegi Beach or turn left onto Yardie Creek Rd for the magnificent beaches and bays of the western cape and Ningaloo Reef.

◉ Sights & Activities

Bundegi Beach   BEACH
(Murat Rd) In the shadow of the VLF antenna array, and within cycling range of Exmouth (which is 13km to the south), the calm, sheltered waters of Bundegi Beach and accompanying reef provide pleasant swimming, snorkelling, diving, kayaking and fishing.

★ Navy Pier   DIVING
(☑ 0456 702 437; www.diveningaloo.com.au; Point Murat; 1-/2-dive tours $130/200) Point Murat, named after Napoleon's brother-in-law, is home to one of the world's very best shore dives, under the Navy Pier. There's a fan-tastic array of marine life including nudibranchs, scorpion fish, moray eels and reef sharks. As it's on Defence territory, there are strict visitation rules and you'll need to join a tour operated by Dive Ningaloo (p978).

SS Mildura Wreck   SHIPWRECK
(Mildura Wreck Rd) Follow the signpost from Yardie Creek Rd to find the 1907 cattle steamer shipwreck that ran aground on the reef. It's visible from shore.

★ Vlamingh Head Lighthouse   LIGHTHOUSE, VIEWPOINT
(off Yardie Creek Rd) It's hard to miss this hill-top lighthouse built in 1912. Spectacular views of the entire cape make it a great place for whale spotting and sunset watching, and info panels give you excellent overviews of what makes the area special.

Exmouth Kite Centre   KITESURFING
(☑ 0467 906 091; www.exmouthkitecentre.com.au; Yardie Creek Rd, Ningaloo Lighthouse Caravan Park; 1/3hr kitesurf lessons $100/290) Learn to kitesurf, surf or stand-up paddleboard (SUP) with this fun, expert crew based at the Ningaloo Lighthouse Caravan Park. You can take various lessons, SUP sunset tours or just rent the gear. Locations for lessons are determined based on weather and wind conditions.

Jurabi Turtle Centre VISITOR CENTRE
(JTC; www.ningalooturtles.org.au/jurabi.html; Yardie Creek Rd; ⊙24hr) 🖉 **FREE** Visit this unmanned interpretive centre by day to study turtle life cycles and obtain the Department of Parks and Wildlife pamphlet *Marine Turtles in Ningaloo Marine Park*. Return at night to observe nesting turtles and hatchlings (December to March), remembering to keep the correct distance and to never shine a light or camera flash directly at any animal. Guided evening **turtle-viewing tours** (www.ningalooturtles.org.au/datesjurabi.html; Jurabi Turtle Centre; adult/child $20/10; ⊙6.30pm Mon, Wed & Fri Dec-Feb) available.

❶ Getting There & Away

The Cape Range National Park (p984) entrance station is 40km from Exmouth, and the road south is navigable by all vehicles as far as Yardie Creek (a further 50km from the entrance station).

For exploration, cars, scooters and boats can be hired out of Exmouth.

Ningaloo Marine Park

You'll be hard-pressed to find words that do justice to the pristine, aquarium-like waters and pure sands of Ningaloo, Australia's largest fringing reef. The fact that it abuts the arid, rugged Cape Range National Park for much of its length simply adds to the appeal. World Heritage–listed Ningaloo Marine Park protects the full 300km length of Ningaloo Reef, from Bundegi on the eastern tip of the North West Cape to Red Bluff on Quobba Station far to the south. It's home to a staggering array of marine life – sharks, manta rays, humpback whales, turtles, dugongs, dolphins and more than 200 coral species and 500 fish species – and it's also easily accessible; in places it's only 100m offshore.

When to Go

December to March Turtles – three endangered species nest and hatch in the dunes. Best seen outside Exmouth.

March & April Coral spawning – an amazing event occurring seven days after the full moon.

Mid-March to mid-August Whale sharks – the biggest fish on the planet arrive for the coral spawning. Tours out of Exmouth and Coral Bay.

May to November Manta rays – present year-round; their numbers increase dramatically over winter and spring. Snorkelling and diving tours that interact with manta rays (ie, swim above them) leave from Exmouth and Coral Bay in winter, and from Coral Bay in summer.

June to November Humpback whales – breed in the warm tropics then head back south to feed in the Antarctic. Tours out of Exmouth and Coral Bay (whale watching, and also new interaction tours).

September to February Reef sharks – large numbers of harmless black tip reef sharks can be found inhabiting the shallow lagoons. Skeleton Bay near Coral Bay is a well-known nursery.

Aside from marine encounters, factors to consider: school holidays (you'll pay more, and have strong competition for accommodation) and weather. The region is dry and warm all year, but temperatures are high in summer (mid-30s to low 40s Celsius from November to March), and there is also moderate risk at this time of a tropical cyclone.

Hint: bring polarised sunglasses, which make it easier to spot marine life.

Wildlife

Over 220 species of hard **coral** have been recorded in Ningaloo, ranging from bulbous brain corals found on bommies (submerged offshore reefs), to delicate branching staghorns and the slow-growing massive coral. While less colourful than soft corals (which are normally found in deeper water on the outer reef), the hard corals have incredible formations. Spawning, where branches of hermaphroditic coral simultaneously eject eggs and sperm into the water, occurs after full and new moons between February and May, but the peak action is usually seven to 10 days after the March and April full moon.

It's this spawning that attracts the park's biggest drawcard, the solitary speckled **whale shark** (*Rhiniodon typus*). Ningaloo is one of the few places in the world where these gentle giants arrive like clockwork each year to feed on plankton and small fish, making it a mecca for marine biologists and visitors alike. The largest fish in the world, whale sharks can reach up to 18m long, and are believed to live for 70 to 100 years. Whale sharks encountered at Ningaloo are mostly between 3m and 12m (a 12m whale shark may weigh as much as 11 tonnes and have a mouth more than 1m wide).

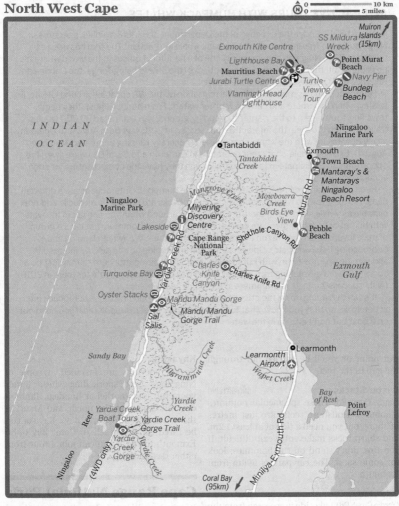

🏃 Activities

Snorkelling & Diving

Most travellers visit Ningaloo Marine Park to snorkel. Always stop first at Milyering Discovery Centre (p985) for maps and information on the best spots and conditions. Check the tide chart: currents can be dangerous, the area is remote, and there's no phone coverage or lifeguards. While not common, unseasonal conditions can bring dangerous 'smacks' of irukandji jellyfish. Milyering also rents and sells snorkelling equipment (as do many other places around Exmouth and Coral Bay).

Add a new dimension to your snorkelling or diving by collecting marine data in your own time, or volunteering for reef monitoring (courses available). Visit www.reefcheck australia.org for more information.

★ **Turquoise Bay**   SNORKELLING
(Yardie Creek Rd) Some 63km from Exmouth, this beautiful bay lives up to its name. The **Bay Snorkel Area** is suitable for all skill levels with myriad fish and corals just off the beach. The **Drift Snorkel Area** attracts stronger swimmers where the current carries you over coral bommies. Don't miss the

INTERACTIVE TOURS WITH HUMPACK WHALES

In August 2016, under the directive of the Department of Parks & Wildlife, operators in Ningaloo began trialling 'in-water humpback whale interaction'. The trial has been extended to 2017. Ningaloo becomes only one of a handful of places in the world where it's possible to interact in this way with humpbacks (the others being Tonga, the Dominican Republic and Queensland's Sunshine Coast).

Humpback whales make their annual migration up the WA coastline around late April to May, when they mate and calve in warmer waters. From about August, they begin travelling south again to their Antarctic feeding grounds. An estimated 30,000 whales travel through the area; the interactive tour season in 2016 was from August to October, nicely dovetailing with the whale-shark period (generally running about mid-March to August). Existing whale-shark tour operators in Exmouth and Coral Bay were given the opportunity to participate in the 2016 trial, given they have the correct set-up for such encounters.

Keen participants do need to be aware that the humpback interactions are a different beast (so to speak) to whale-shark swims. Humpbacks are not nearly as docile and predictable as whale sharks and there are more rules around when you can get in the water with humpbacks (not if there are calves present – which is common; not if it's a group of male juveniles, as they're too unpredictable; not if there is any tail-slapping and/or breaching behaviour, etc). Operators are still fine-tuning how to sell the interaction, and signing up for a 'swim with humpbacks' tour is not straightforward (it may just be a successful whale-watching trip). Overall, there was a 70% success rate for tours in 2016 (with 'success' defined as swimmers in the water near whales).

It's worth reading up on the prices and conditions surrounding these humpback interaction tours so that you know what to expect and don't feel disappointed if you head out on a boat but don't end up in the water.

exit point or you'll be carried out through the gap in the reef.

Oyster Stacks　　　　SNORKELLING

(Yardie Creek Rd) These spectacular bommies (submerged offshore reefs) are just metres offshore, but you need a tide of at least 1.2m, and sharp rocks make entry/exit difficult. If you tire, don't stand on the bommies; look for some sand. The car park is 69km from Exmouth.

Lakeside　　　　SNORKELLING

(Yardie Creek Rd) Lakeside is accessed from the road by Milyering Visitor Centre; it's 56km from Exmouth. Walk 500m south along the beach from the car park then snorkel out with the current before returning close to your original point.

Lighthouse Bay　　　　DIVING

(Yardie Creek Rd) There's great scuba diving at Lighthouse Bay (at the northern tip of the cape) at sites such as the Labyrinth, Blizzard Reef and Helga's Tunnels. Check out the DPaW book *Dive and Snorkel Sites in Western Australia* for other ideas. Dive operators in Exmouth can set you up and take you out.

Kayaking

Kayak moorings are installed at some of Ningaloo's best snorkelling sites. Tether your craft and snorkel at Bundegi, Tantabiddi and Osprey in the north, and Maud in the south (close to Coral Bay). Kayaks can be hired off the beach in Coral Bay or in Exmouth town, or you can join a tour from either destination.

Cape Range National Park

It's the coastline of Cape Range National Park (https://parks.dpaw.wa.gov.au/park/cape-range; admission per car $12) that gets most of the attention – after all, these are the spectacular beaches that give access to the pristine Ningaloo Marine Park (p982).

Still, the jagged limestone peaks and gorges of the rugged 510-sq-km park deserve some acclaim of their own – they offer relief from the otherwise flat, arid expanse of North West Cape, and are rich in wildlife, including the rare black-flanked rock wallaby, five types of bat and over 200 species of bird. Spectacular deep canyons cut dramatically into the range, before emptying out onto the wind-blown coastal dunes and turquoise waters of Ningaloo Reef.

◎ Sights & Activities

Charles Knife Canyon GORGE
(Charles Knife Rd) On the east coast, an incredibly scenic and at times dramatic road (11km in length) ascends a knife-edge ridge via rickety corners, necessitating frequent photo stops to make the most of the breathtaking views. A rough track continues to **Thomas Carter lookout** (at 311m, with great views). From the lookout area, in the cooler months you can walk the 8km **Badjirrajirra loop trail** through spinifex and rocky gullies; there's no shade or water. Under no circumstances attempt this during summer.

Yardie Creek Gorge GORGE
(end of Yardie Creek Rd) A couple of walking trails give access to excellent views above this water-filled gorge: the gentle Nature Walk is 1.2km return, or the longer trail is 2km return and takes you high above the creek. There's also the option of a more relaxing boat tour (p985).

Yardie Creek is 50km from the park entry (and accessible to all vehicles).

Mandu Mandu Gorge GORGE
(Yardie Creek Rd) There's a small car park off the main road 14km south of the Milyering Discovery Centre, and from here there's a pleasant, occasionally steep 3km return walk onto the gorge rim.

Yardie Creek Boat Tours BOATING
(☑08-9949 2920; www.yardiecreekboattours. com.au; adult/child/family $35/15/80; ⊙11am & 12.30pm on scheduled days; ☀) A relaxing one-hour cruise up the short, sheer Yardie Creek Gorge, where you might spot rare black-flanked rock wallabies. It's worth checking operating days – with the company, or with Exmouth visitor centre (p980) – as these vary with season. There are no cruises from early January to late March.

🛏 Sleeping

Sal Salis TENTED CAMP $$$
(☑08-9949 1776; www.salsalis.com; South Mandu, off Yardie Creek Rd; per person per night $750-1080; ⊙mid-Mar–Oct) ⚑ Want to watch that crimson Indian Ocean sunset from between 500-threadcount sheets? Pass the chablis! For those of you who want their camp without the cramp, this exclusive tented camp has a minimum two-night stay, 16 en-suite tents, three gourmet meals a day, a free bar (!) and the same things to do as the folks staying over the dune in the pop-up camper.

ℹ Information

Milyering Discovery Centre (☑08-9949 2808; Yardie Creek Rd; ⊙9am-3.45pm; ☀) Serving both Ningaloo Marine Park and Cape Range National Park, this visitor centre has informative natural and cultural displays, maps, tide charts, campsite photos and publications. Check here for road and water conditions. It rents out snorkelling gear (day/overnight $10/15), and sells drinks and ice creams.

PERTH & WESTERN AUSTRALIA CAPE RANGE NATIONAL PARK

ℹ CAMPING IN CAPE RANGE NATIONAL PARK

The campgrounds (adult/child $10/2.20) are run by the Department of Parks & Wildlife, and from April to October sites must be prebooked (up to 180 days before arrival). All peak-season bookings are done online, where you can also see the location and facilities of each campground: https://parkstay.dpaw.wa.gov.au.

Off-peak, sites operate on a first-come, first-served basis, and info is available at the park's entrance station as well as the visitor centre.

The park campgrounds stretch from Neds Camp in the north to Yardie Creek in the south (note: there is no campground at Turquoise Bay).

Facilities and shade are minimal at the sandy grounds, though most have eco-toilets (no showers, no water) and some shelter from prevailing winds, plus possibly a picnic shelter or two. No campfires are allowed; bring your own camp stove. There are no powered sites; seek a generator-free area if you're after peace and quiet. Most camps have resident caretakers during peak season. Our pick: the redeveloped grounds at Osprey Bay, or beachside North Kurrajong.

Pilbara Coast

Karratha

POP 19,250

In the past, most travellers to Karratha ran their errands – banking, restocking, repairing stuff etc – and then got out of town before their wallet ignited. That did the town a small disservice. It's the primary base for mining and industry in the region, and while it won't win any awards for prettiest town, it certainly has a few things worth sticking around to investigate – from tours to ancient rock art to cafes that wouldn't look out of place in the coolest parts of Perth.

◉ Sights & Activities

Miaree Pool   LAKE

(North West Coastal Hwy) Yeah, it gets hot up here. You might have noticed. Cool off at this shady waterhole, popular with locals for picnicking and swimming. It's 30km southwest of the Karratha turn-off, on the North West Coastal Hwy (Hwy 1).

Yaburara Heritage Trail   WALKING

From behind the visitor centre, a series of trails (the longest of which is 3.5km one way) wind through significant traditional sites, detailing the displacement and eventual extinction of the Yaburara people. Sites include rock art, stone quarries and shell middens, plus excellent lookout points. Bring plenty of water and start your walks early.

★ Ngurrangga Tours   CULTURAL

(☑ 08-9182 1777; www.ngurrangga.com.au; half-day adult/child $132/66; ☺ Feb-Nov) Clinton Walker, Ngarluma man, runs cultural tours that garner rave reviews from travellers. His half-day Murujuga National Park tour explores rock-art petroglyphs on the Burrup Peninsula near Dampier, while his day tours explore the culturally significant areas of Millstream Chichester National Park (adult/child $300/150). Three-day Millstream camping tours are also available ($800/400). Departures from the Karratha visitor centre.

✦ Festivals & Events

Red Earth Arts Festival   CULTURAL

(www.reaf.com.au) Over 10 days in mid-September, Karratha and the surrounding coastal Pilbara towns come alive for this festival, an eclectic mix of live music (all genres), theatre, comedy, visual arts and storytelling.

🛏 Sleeping & Eating

The Ranges   APARTMENT $$

(☑ 1300 639 320; www.therangeskarratha.com.au; De Witt Rd; d $195-285; ☀ ❄) This swank complex of deluxe self-contained apartments offers a surprising level of sophistication, with king-sized beds and smart kitchen appliances. Outside are manicured grounds and a big pool and barbecue area. Service is first-rate. It's about 1km south of the visitor centre, on the road into town.

★ Empire 6714   CAFE $$

(☑ 0427 654 045; www.empire6714.com.au; Warambie Rd; meals $13-28; ☺ 6am-4pm; ☑) Sure, you can get your standard bacon and eggs here, but why wouldn't you go for coconut flour pancakes with berries or fig and fennel fruit loaf? There's lots of organic, hard-to-source goodness on the menu, but we like how it's not one-sided (raw pizza is on the lunch menu, alongside steak sandwich). There are also impeccable smoothies, cold-pressed juices, coffee and kombucha (fermented tea drink).

Soul   CAFE, BAR $$

(☑ 08-91838278; www.facebook.com/soulkarratha; Warambie Rd, Pelago Centre; dishes $10-33; ☺ 6am-10pm Mon-Sat, 7am-3pm Sun) City-style sophisticated breakfasts (until 11am) are followed by an all-day menu of crowd-pleasers, from gourmet burgers to tempting share plates (sliders, quesadillas, antipasto platters). It delivers top-notch coffee, too, from its cute, bright-blue Elektra coffee machine.

ⓘ Information

Karratha Visitor Centre (☑ 08-9144 4600; www.karrathavisitorcentre.com.au; De Witt Rd; ☺ 8.30am-5pm Mon-Fri, 9am-2pm Sat & Sun Apr-Sep, 9am-4pm Mon-Fri, 10am-1pm Sat Oct-Mar; ☀) Has local maps and info, supplies rail access road permits (for the most direct route to Tom Price), books tours (including to mining infrastructure) and may find you a room.

ⓘ Getting There & Away

Karratha Airport (www.karrathaairport.com.au) located halfway between Karratha and Dampier, is well connected to Perth courtesy of Virgin Airlines, Qantas and Alliance Airlines.

Integrity (☑ 1800 226 339; www.integrity coachlines.com.au) operates twice-weekly bus services from Perth to Broome, stopping at Coral Bay, Exmouth, Karratha, Roebourne and Port Hedland.

Fares from Karratha include Perth ($282, 24 hours), Exmouth ($164, 6½ hours), Port Hedland ($89, 3½ hours) and Broome ($187, 10 hours).

Buses arrive and depart from the bus stop on Welcome Rd (opposite the church) in the centre of the shopping area.

Around Karratha

Practically a suburb of Karratha, **Dampier** is the region's main port and is home to heavy industry. It's spread around King Bay 20km northwest of Karratha. Its most famous resident is Red Dog (who has had books written about him, and movies made), a much-loved dog that roved the town and surrounds in the 1970s. A statue of him is at the entry to town.

Sitting on Ngaluma country, 40km east of Karratha, **Roebourne** is the oldest (1866) Pilbara town still functioning. It's home to a large Aboriginal community; Yindjibarndi is the dominant language group. There are some beautiful old buildings and a thriving Indigenous art scene (www.roebourneart. com.au). The **Yinjaa-Barni** (☑08-9182 1959; www.yinjaa-barni.com.au; Lot 3 Roe St; ⊙vary) Indigenous-run gallery showcases gifted Millstream artists.

In good news for the town, the old Victoria Hotel (built in 1866, but shuttered since 2006) is slated for restoration, to return it to its architectural glory. Once restored, the plan is to make it a tourism and cultural hub for the local community.

★**Murujuga National Park**   NATIONAL PARK
(parks.dpaw.wa.gov.au/park/murujuga; Burrup Peninsula Rd) FREE Murujuga is home to the world's largest concentration of rock art (dating back more than 30,000 years), stretched out along the rocky hills of the heavily industrialised Burrup Peninsula. The most accessible are at **Deep Gorge**, near Hearson's Cove. Devastatingly, some sites have been vandalised. The engravings depict fish, turtles, kangaroos and even a Tasmanian tiger.

The best way to see and appreciate the importance of this art is through a half-day tour with Ngurrangga Tours.

Dampier Archipelago   NATURE RESERVE
(https://parks.dpaw.wa.gov.au/park/dampier-archipelago) Offshore from Dampier, the coral waters and pristine islands of the Dampier Archipelago support a wealth of marine life and endangered marsupials (25 of the 42 islands are nature reserves). It's a recreational fishing and boating mecca, and plenty of boat-owning locals head here for R&R. Enquire at Karratha visitor centre about fishing charters and cruises.

OFF THE BEATEN TRACK

MARBLE BAR

Marble Bar, a long way off everybody's beaten track, burnt itself into the Australian psyche as the country's hottest town when, back in summer of 1923–24, the mercury reached 37.8°C (100°F) for 160 consecutive days. The town was (mistakenly) named after a bar of jasper beside a pool on the Coongan River, 5km southwest of the town centre.

Most days there's not much to do. Pore over the minerals at the **Comet Gold Mine,** (☑08-9176 1015; Hillside Rd; $3; ⊙9am-4pm) 8km out of town, or prop yourself up at the bar and have a yarn with Foxie at the **Ironclad Hotel** (☑08-9176 1066; 15 Francis St; mains $17-45; ⊙noon-close). This classic outback pub offers comfy rooms, decent meals, and a warm welcome. If the temperature's climbing, head for the town's swimming pool.

Come the first weekend in July, the sleepy town swells to 10 times its normal size for a weekend of drinking, gambling, fashion crime, country music, nudie runs and horse racing known as the **Marble Bar Cup** (www.marblebarraces.com; ⊙early Jul). The **holiday park** (☑08-9176 1569; Contest St; unpowered/powered sites $20/38) overflows and the Ironclad is besieged as punters from far and wide come for a bit of an outback knees-up.

Marble Bar is 200km from Port Hedland via Rte 138 (a sealed road). To carry on to Newman is 300km on an unsealed road that sees little traffic, but is usually OK for 2WDs (check locally; carry plenty of water).

The East Pilbara shire runs a bus between Port Hedland and Marble Bar ($29, 3¼ hours) a couple of times a week (twice in either direction). See www.eastpilbara.wa.gov. au for details.

Hearson's Cove BEACH

(Hearson Cove Rd) A fine swimming beach and picnic spot, providing Staircase to the Moon viewing (March to October) and great mud-flat exploring at low tide.

Port Hedland

POP 16,000

Port Hedland ain't the prettiest place. A high-visibility dystopia of railway yards, iron-ore stockpiles, salt mountains, furnaces and a massive deep-water port confront the passing traveller. Yet under that red dust lurks a colourful 130-year history of mining booms and busts, cyclones, pearling and WWII action. Several pleasant hours may be spent exploring Hedland's thriving art and cafe (real coffee!) scene, historic CBD and scenic foreshore.

◎ Sights & Activities

Collect the brochure entitled *Adventure Awaits: Your Guide to Port Hedland* from the visitor centre and take a self-guided tour around the CBD and foreshore.

Goode St, near Pretty Pool, is handy to observe Port Hedland's **Staircase to the Moon** (on full-moon nights from March to October), where water caught in sand ripples reflects the moonlight, creating the effect of a staircase to the moon.

★**Courthouse Gallery** GALLERY

(☑08-9173 1064; www.courthousegallery.com.au; 16 Edgar St; ⊙9am-4.30pm Mon-Fri, 9am-3pm Sat) More than a gallery, this leafy arts HQ is the centre of all goodness in Port Hedland. Inside are stunning, curated local contemporary and Indigenous exhibitions, while the shady surrounds host sporadic craft markets. If something is happening, these folks will know about it.

Spinifex Hill Studios GALLERY

(☑08-9172 1699; www.spinifexhillstudio.com.au; 18 Hedditch St, South Hedland; ⊙9am-5pm Tue-Fri, 10am-2pm Sun) A great initiative showcasing Aboriginal artists from Port Hedland and across the Pilbara. Saturday is the best time to visit, with artists at work and coffee offered (a kind of 'open house'). It's generally open other times, but call before visiting.

Pretty Pool SWIMMING

(off Matheson Dr) A popular picnicking and swimming spot (beware of stonefish and backpackers), 7km east of the town centre. The best swimming spots depend on the tides – follow the locals' lead.

⛵ Tours

Harbour Tour TOURS

(☑08-9173 1315; www.phseafarers.org; cnr Wedge & Wilson Sts; adult/child $55/30; ⊙9.30am Mon-Sat, 1.30pm Sun) Run by the Seafarers Centre, this hour-long tour covers the facts and figures of the port, and includes a boat tour around the harbour. Tour times may vary, so it pays to check.

BHP Billiton Iron Ore Tour TOURS

(adult/child $45/30; ⊙1pm Tue & Thu) Popular one-hour guided tour of an iron-ore plant. Book through the visitor centre, from which the tour departs. It's free for kids under 10 years.

🛏 Sleeping & Eating

The visitor centre can help with information or bookings.

If you prefer somewhere on the beach, away from town and mines, better to plan a stay at Eighty Mile Beach en route north, or Point Samson south.

Discovery Parks Port Hedland CARAVAN PARK $

(☑08-9173 1271; www.big4.com.au; cnr Athol & Taylor Sts; powered sites $38-55, backpacker d $60, unit d from $119; ❊ᚎ⏾❄) At the town's eastern end, this park offers lots of cabin options, backpacker rooms (with shared kitchen and bathroom) and well-maintained amenities. There's a nice view over the mangroves.

Esplanade Hotel HOTEL $$

(☑08-9173 9700; www.theesplanadeporthedland. com.au; 2-4 Anderson St; d incl breakfast weekend/ weekday from $165/215; ❊@ᚎ) Previously one of the roughest pubs in Port Hedland, the 'Nard' is now an exclusive 4½-star resort with 98 smart, well-equipped guest rooms (though they're petite and quite pricey). It's a favourite with business travellers, making the weekend rates considerably cheaper. It has good food and drink on-site.

★**Esplanade Hotel** MODERN AUSTRALIAN $$

(☑08-9173 9700; www.theesplanadeporthedland. com.au; 2-4 Anderson St; bar mains $20-30, restaurant mains $20-45; ⊙5.30am-midnight) There's a surprising air of sophistication about this old hotel. Breakfast until 11.30am is good value, then the Empire Bar's all-day menu blends old classics with new (Vietnamese poached chicken salad, scotch fillet steak). There's an evening restaurant too, with surprises like jerk chicken with wild rice or goat vindaloo.

MILLSTREAM CHICHESTER NATIONAL PARK

Among the arid, spinifex-covered plateaus and basalt ranges between Karijini and the coast, the tranquil waterholes of the Fortescue River form cool, lush oases in Millstream Chichester National Park (https://parks.dpaw.wa.gov.au/park/millstream-chichester; admission per car $12). In the park's north are the stunning breakaways and eroded mesas of the Chichester Range. As a lifeline for local flora and fauna, the park is one of the most important Aboriginal sites in WA.

Millstream Homestead Visitor Centre (⊘8am-4pm) Once the station homestead, the unmanned visitor centre houses historical, ecological and cultural displays. It's 22km west of the Karratha-Tom Price Rd.

Python Pool Just off the road that traverses the Chichester Range (19km east of the Karratha-Tom Price Rd), this plunge pool sits photogenically at the base of a cliff. The water is normally fine for swimming, though check for algae bloom before sliding in.

Deep Reach Pool (Millstream; 🖑) Some 4km from the visitor centre, shady picnic tables and barbecues back onto a perfect swimming hole (Nhanggangunha in the local language) believed to be the resting place of the Warlu (creation serpent). The water is deep and the banks can be steep, so use the steps here.

Mt Herbert A 10-minute climb from the car park (arrowed off the road to Roebourne) reveals a fantastic panorama of the ragged Chichester Range.

Jirndarwurrunha Pool (Millstream) A short stroll from the visitor centre, beautiful lily- and palm-fringed Jirndarwurrunha is deeply significant to the traditional Yindjibarndi owners. An easy half-hour walk leads through the wetlands area; swimming is not permitted.

ⓘ Information

Visitor Centre (📞 08-9173 1711; www.visit porthedland.com; 13 Wedge St; ⊘9am-5pm Mon-Fri & to 2pm Sat; 📶) This excellent centre sells travel books, publishes shipping times, arranges iron-ore plant tours, and helps with accommodation and turtle monitoring (November to February). Open Sundays (9am to 2pm) April to September.

ⓘ Getting There & Away

Port Hedland International Airport (www.porthedlandairport.com.au) is about 12km south of town and has good connections. Virgin and Qantas both fly to Perth daily, and Qantas also has a weekly direct flight to Brisbane and Melbourne. Virgin has handy weekend flights to Bali.

The large car-hire companies (Hertz, Avis, Budget etc) offer car rental from the airport. A **taxi** (📞 08-9173 1010; www.hedlandtaxis.com.au) to the town centre costs $35 to $40.

Integrity (📞 1800 226 339; www.integrity coachlines.com.au) operates two weekly bus services north to Broome ($129, 6½ hours). There are four services south to/from Perth ($274 to $293, 21¼ to 28¼ hours) taking various routes, coastal and inland.

Buses arrive and depart from the Port Hedland visitor centre and South Hedland shopping centre.

Karijini National Park

The narrow, breathtaking gorges, hidden pools and spectacular waterfalls of Karijini National Park (https://parks.dpaw.wa.gov.au/park/karijini; admission per car $12) form one of WA's most impressive attractions. Adventurers and nature lovers flock to the rocky red ranges and deep, dark chasms, home to abundant wildlife and over 800 different plant species.

Kangaroos, snappy gums and wildflowers dot the plains, rock wallabies cling to sheer cliffs and endangered olive pythons lurk in giant figs above quiet pools. The park also contains WA's three highest peaks: Mt Meharry, Punurrunha (Mt Bruce) and Mt Frederick.

Summer temperatures reach extremes in the park, so carry plenty of water. Winter nights are cold. At any time of year, choose walks wisely, dress appropriately and never enter a restricted area without a certified guide. Avoid the gorges during and after rain, as flash flooding does occur.

⊙ Sights & Activities

Generally, within the park, roads lead to car parks from where there are short, relatively easy walks to scenic lookouts that peer into a gorge. There are a few flat walking trails

Karijini National Park

Millstream Chichester
National Park (145km)

Hamersley
Gorge (14km)

Nanutarra–Munjina Rd

Range Gorge

Bee Gorge

Joffre Creek

Fortescue River

Chichester Range

Mt King
(1031m)

Oxer Lookout

Weano Rd

Weano
Gorge

Red Gorge

Hancock Gorge

Joffre Gorge

Karijini
Eco Retreat

Knox Lookout

Knox Gorge

Joffre Falls

4WD
Only

Joffre Creek

Joffre
Falls Rd

Banjima Dr West

Kalamina
Gorge

Kalamina Gorge

Yampire Gorge

Nanutarra–Munjina Rd

Port Hedland
(260km)

Munjina
(Auski)
Roadhouse

Mt George
(832m)

Circular
Pool

Kalamina Rd

Visitor
Centre

Dales Gorge

Banjima Dr North

Fortescue
Falls

Fern
Pool

Mt Vigors
(1161m)

Entrance
Station

Mt Oxer
(1192m)

Karijini
National
Park

Entrance
Station

Banjima Dr East

Tom Price
(50km)

Punurrunha
(Mt Bruce)
(1235m)

Karijini Dr

Marandoo

Mt Windell
(1107m)

Karijini Dr

Great Northern Hwy

Mt Howieson
(1113m)

Newman (156km)

> Unsealed roads can vary
> from excellent to impassable,
> depending on many factors

PERTH & WESTERN AUSTRALIA KARIJINI NATIONAL PARK

along gorge-rim paths, plus longer and more difficult trails (some via steps or ladders) that descend to gorge floors and pools.

The best swimming is at Fortescue Falls and Fern Pool (in Dales Gorge in the park's east), and at Hamersley Gorge (tucked away in the park's northwest). Other gorge pools are beautiful, but many are sheltered from the sun and the water is often chilly.

★ **Dales Gorge** GORGE
(accessed from Banjima Dr East; 🚻) From the Fortescue Falls car park (just south of Dales Campground), a trail descends steeply via a long staircase to stunning **Fortescue Falls** (the park's only permanent waterfall) and a swimming hole, behind which a leafy 300m stroll upstream reveals beautiful **Fern Pool**.

You can enjoy a 2km **gorge-rim trail** from the start of the Fortescue Falls track to Circular Pool lookout, with great views into

Dales Gorge. The Circular Pool lookout is also connected to Dales Campground by an easy walking trail.

★ **Hamersley Gorge** GORGE
(off Nanutarra-Munjina Rd; 🚻) Away in Karijini's northwest corner, this idyllic swimming hole makes a lovely stop if you're heading north towards the coast or Millstream (it can't be accessed from Banjima Dr). It's about 67km from Tom Price: head north on Bingarn Rd for 26km, and turnw right at the T-junction, carrying on another 41km (unsealed). Turn at the sign for Hamersley Gorge, not Hamersley Range.

★ **Fern Pool** LAKE
(Jubura) Swim quietly and with respect at this lovely, shady pool – it has special significance to the local Indigenous people. It's a 300m walk upstream from Fortescue Falls.

Hancock Gorge
GORGE

(Weano Rd, accessed from Banjima Dr West) At Hancock Gorge, a steep descent (partly on ladders) brings you to the sunny **Amphitheatre**. Follow the slippery **Spider Walk** to sublime **Kermits Pool**.

Oxer Lookout
VIEWPOINT

(Weano Rd, accessed from Banjima Dr West) The final 13km drive (past the Karijini Eco Retreat) to the breathtaking Oxer Lookout can be rough, but it's worth it for the magnificent views of the junction of the Red, Weano, Joffre and Hancock Gorges some 130m below. The lookout is a short walk from the car park.

Joffre Gorge
GORGE

(Joffre Falls Rd, accessed from Banjima Dr West) When not trickling, **Joffre Falls** are spectacular, but the frigid pools below are perennially shaded. The gorge lookout is 10 minutes' walk from the parking area; there's a 1.3km-return trail down to the pool. There's also a walking track to the falls from the nearby Karijini Eco Retreat.

Weano Gorge
GORGE

(Weano Rd, accessed from Banjima Rd West) The upper gorge is dry, but the steep track winding down from the car park to the lower gorge narrows until you reach the perfect, surreal bowl of **Handrail Pool**.

Kalamina Gorge
GORGE

(Kalamina Gorge Rd, accessed from Banjima Dr North; 🐾) Wide, easy gorge with a small, tranquil pool and falls. You'll need a 4WD to access it, as it lies north of Banjima Dr North.

Punurrunha
HIKING

(Mt Bruce) Gorged out? Go and grab some altitude on WA's second-highest mountain (1235m), a superb ridge walk with fantastic views all the way to the summit. Start early, carry lots of water and allow six hours (9km return). The access road is off Karijini Dr opposite Banjima Dr West.

👉 Tours

★ West Oz Active Adventure Tours
ADVENTURE

(📱0438 913 713; www.westozactive.com.au; Karijini Eco Retreat; tour $285; ☻Apr-Oct) Based at Karijini Eco Retreat, this highly regarded company offers action-packed day trips through the restricted gorges of the park and combines hiking, swimming, floating on inner tubes, climbing, sliding off water-falls and abseiling. All equipment and lunch provided. The minimum age for tours is 14.

★ Flying Sandgroper
TOURS

(📱0438 913 713; www.flyingsandgroper.com.au; ☻Apr-Oct) The Flying Sandgroper's aim is to overcome the huge distances and costs of visiting the northwest, so it is set up to offer multi-day tours that take in Karijini (and Ningaloo too), with the choice of bus-in bus-out and fly-in-fly-out packages, depending on your budget. It's affiliated with the excellent West Oz Active Adventure Tours, and based at Karijini Eco Retreat.

🛏 Sleeping & Eating

Dales Gorge Campground
CAMPGROUND $

(sites adult/child $10/2.20) Though somewhat dusty, this large Department of Parks and Wildlife campground offers shady, spacious sites with nearby toilets, gas barbecues and picnic tables. Forget tent pegs – you'll be using rocks as anchors. It's first come, first served (no bookings). The camping ground is 17km on sealed road from the eastern entrance station.

★ Karijini Eco Retreat
RESORT $$$

(📱08-9425 5591; www.karijiniecoretreat.com.au; Weano Rd, accessed from Banjima Dr West; sites per person $20, deluxe tent d low/high season $189/349) 🌿 This 100% Indigenous-owned retreat is a model for sustainable tourism, and the on-site restaurant (dinner mains $18-39; ☻7am-8pm) has fantastic food, with the chefs offering high-quality dishes that are often accented by bush-tucker ingredients (bush tomatoes, wild herbs, wattleseed). To be this far from 'civilisation' but able to dine on salmon on soba noodles or scotch fillet steak is pretty wondrous. Breakfast and lunch are also served.

The deluxe eco-tents have en suites; there are also cheaper tents and cabins with shared bathrooms. Campers get access to hot showers and the same rocks as elsewhere in the park. The setting, close to Joffre Gorge, is beautiful.

ℹ Information

Visitor Centre (📱08-9189 8121; https:// parks.dpaw.wa.gov.au/park/karijini; Banjima Dr North; ☻9am-4pm mid-Feb–mid-Dec) An Indigenous-managed centre with excellent interpretive displays highlighting Banyjima, Yinhawangka and Kurrama culture, as well as displays on park wildlife, good maps and walks information, a public phone, cold drinks and souvenirs for sale, and really great air-con. In a separate building are toilets, plus showers ($4).

It's accessible on a sealed road, 10km from the eastern entrance. West of here, the road is unsealed.

❶ Getting There & Away

Bring your own vehicle or join a tour. Check out the excellent options from the **Flying Sandgroper** (p991) to make a visit more accessible.

The closest airports are Paraburdoo (101km) and Newman (201km).

Integrity (📞1800 226 339; www.integrity coachlines.com.au) operates a weekly bus service between Perth and Port Hedland along the coast, heading inland from Exmouth on Rte 136 and stopping at Paraburdoo and Tom Price, where you can pick up a tour to the park.

THE KIMBERLEY

Broome

POP 16,500

Like a paste jewel set in a tiara of natural splendours, Broome clings to a narrow strip of red pindan on the Kimberley's western edge, at the base of the pristine Dampier Peninsula. Surrounded by the aquamarine waters of the Indian Ocean and the creeks, mangroves and mudflats of Roebuck Bay, this Yawuru country is a good 2000km from the nearest capital city.

Cable Beach, with its luxury resorts, hauls in the tourists during high season (April to October), with romantic notions of camels, surf and sunsets. Magnificent, sure, but there's a more to Broome than postcards, and tourists are sometimes surprised when they scratch the surface and find pindan just below.

The Dry is a great time to find casual work, while in the Wet (low season) prices plummet.

Each evening, the whole town collectively pauses, drinks in mid-air, while the sun slinks slowly towards Madagascar.

◉ Sights

★ **Cable Beach**   BEACH
(Map p999; 🅿️🚻) Western Australia's most famous landmark offers turquoise waters and beautiful white sand curving away to the sunset. Clothing is optional north of the rocks, while south of them, walking trails lead through the red dunes of **Minyirr Park**, a spiritual place for the Yawuru people. Ca-

ble Beach is synonymous with camels, and an evening ride along the sand is a highlight for many visitors. Locals in their 4WDs swarm north of the rocks for sunset drinks. Stingers are common in the Wet.

Gantheaume Point
& Dinosaur Prints   VIEWPOINT
(🅿️🚻) Beautiful at dawn or sunset when the cliffs turn scarlet and the Indian Ocean brilliant turquoise, this lookout holds a 135-million-year-old secret. Nearby lies one of the world's most varied collections of dinosaur footprints, impossible to find except at very low tides. Grab the map from the visitor centre (p1000) and beware of slippery rocks. Look out for the ospreys returning to their nests on the lighthouse.

Sun Pictures   HISTORIC BUILDING
(Map p996; 📞08-9192 1077; www.sunpictures. com.au; 27 Carnarvon St; movies adult/child $17/12, history tour $5; ⏰history tour 10.30am & 1pm; 🚻) Sink back in a canvas deck chair in the world's oldest operating picture gardens, dating from 1916. The history of the Sun building is the history of Broome itself; it has witnessed war, floods, low-flying aircraft (it's still on the airport flight path) and racial segregation. There's a short 15-minute history tour during the Dry.

Bungalow   GALLERY
(Map p996; 📞08-9192 6118; www.shortstgallery. com; 3 Hopton St, Town Beach; ⏰10am-3pm Mon-Sat, shorter hours wet season) Short St Gallery's Hopton St stock room at Town Beach holds a stunning collection of canvasses from across the Kimberley and beyond.

Broome Bird Observatory   NATURE RESERVE
(📞08-9193 5600; www.broomebirdobservatory. com; Crab Creek Rd; by donation, camping per person $18, unit with shared bathroom s/d/f $45/60/85, chalets $165; ⏰8am-4pm; 🅿️) 🍃 The tidal mudflats of Roebuck Bay are a vital staging post for migratory birds, some coming from as far away as Siberia. In a peaceful coastal setting 25km from Broome, the 'Bird Obbie' offers quiet walking trails, secluded bush camp sites and a choice of low-key rooms. There's a number of tours ($70, 2½ hours) and courses ($1400, five days) available as well as volunteering opportunities.

Broome Museum   MUSEUM
(Map p996; 📞08-9192 2075; www.broomemu seum.org.au; 67 Robinson St; adult/child $6/1; ⏰10am-4pm Mon-Fri, to 1pm Sat & Sun dry season,

to 1pm daily wet season; **P**) Discover Cable Beach and Chinatown's origins through exhibits devoted to the area's pearling history and WWII bombing in this quirky museum, occupying the former Customs House.

WWII Flying Boat Wrecks HISTORIC SITE
(Map p996) On a very low tide it's possible to walk out across the mudflats from **Town Beach** (Map p996; **P**) to the wrecks of Catalina and Dornier flying boats attacked by Japanese 'Zeroes' during WWII. The planes had been evacuating refugees from Java and many still had passengers aboard. Over 60 people and 15 flying boats (mostly Dutch and British) were lost. Only six wrecks are visible, with the rest in deep water.

Nagula Jarndu Women's
Resource Centre ARTS CENTRE
(☑ 0499 330 708; www.nagulajarndu.com.au; 3/12 Gregory St; ⊙ 9.30am-4pm Mon-Fri) Beautiful screen- and block-printed textiles and other crafts are on show (and sale!) at this studio/gallery run by Yawuru women. Enter via Pembroke Rd.

Cemeteries

A number of cemeteries testify to Broome's multicultural past. The most striking is the **Japanese Cemetery** (Port Dr) with 919 graves (mostly pearl divers). Next to this, the **Chinese Cemetery** (Frederick St) has over 90 graves and monuments. The small **Muslim Cemetery** (Frederick St) honours Malay pearl-divers and Afghan cameleers.

A couple of kilometres southeast, the small **Pioneer Cemetery** (Map p996; **P**) overlooks Roebuck Bay at Town Beach.

🏃 Activities

Odyssey Expeditions DIVING
(www.odysseyexpeditions.com.au; 8-day tour from $3495; ⊙ Sep-Oct) Runs several eight-day, liveaboard diving tours from Broome each spring to the **Rowley Shoals Marine Park**. You need to be an experienced diver with your own gear (though some gear may be hired in Broome).

Turtle Monitoring WILDLIFE
(☑ 08-9195 5500; Yawuru.Rangers@dpaw.wa.gov. au; Cable Beach; ⊙ Nov-Feb; ⛟) 🖢 **FREE** Stuck in Broome over the Wet? Volunteers walk 4km along Cable Beach in the morning and record the previous night's turtle activity. Free training provided.

OFF THE BEATEN TRACK

ROWLEY SHOALS MARINE PARK
....

These three coral atolls lie approximately 300km from Broome in the Indian Ocean, on the edge of Australia's continental shelf, and have a reputation for some of the best diving in the country. Protected by a marine park, there's over 600 species of fish and 200-plus different varieties of coral. At a good 12-hour cruise from land, the shoals only see a minute number of visitors each year. Several Broome operators offer multinight cruises for experienced divers.

Broome Aviation SCENIC FLIGHTS
(☑ 08-9192 1369; www.broomeaviation.com.au; half-/full-day flights from $640/1090) Half-day flights to Cape Leveque and the Horizontal Falls (p1004). Full-day tours add-on the Devonian Reef National Parks, Bell Gorge (p1007) and Mt Hart or Mitchell Falls.

King Leopold Air SCENIC FLIGHTS
(☑ 08-9193 7155; www.kingleopoldair.com.au; half-/full-day tours from $595/1060) Flights over the Dampier Peninsula (half-day) and to Mitchell Falls or Devonian Reef National Parks (full day). Also has a 30-minute flight over Broome's beaches (per person two passengers/three to five passengers $240/150).

👉 Tours

Camel Tours

Broome Camel Safaris OUTDOORS
(Map p999; ☑ 0419 916 101; www.broomecamel safaris.com.au; Cable Beach; adult/child morning $65/45, afternoon $45/30, sunset $85/65; ⛟) Run by Alison 'the Camel Lady', Broome Camel Safaris (with animals sporting blue camel blankets) offers 45-minute morning, 30-minute afternoon (3pm) and one-hour sunset camel rides along Cable Beach (p992).

Red Sun Camels OUTDOORS
(Map p999; ☑ 1800 184 488; www.redsuncamels. com.au; Cable Beach; adult/child morning $65/45, afternoon $45/30, sunset $90/65) Morning (40-minute), afternoon (30-minute) and sunset (one-hour) camel rides along Cable Beach on red-blanketed camels.

Sundowner Camel Tours OUTDOORS
(Map p999; ☑ 0477 774 297; www.sundowner cameltours.com.au; Cable Beach; adult/child afternoon $40/30, sunset $90/60) Yellow-blanketed

The Kimberley

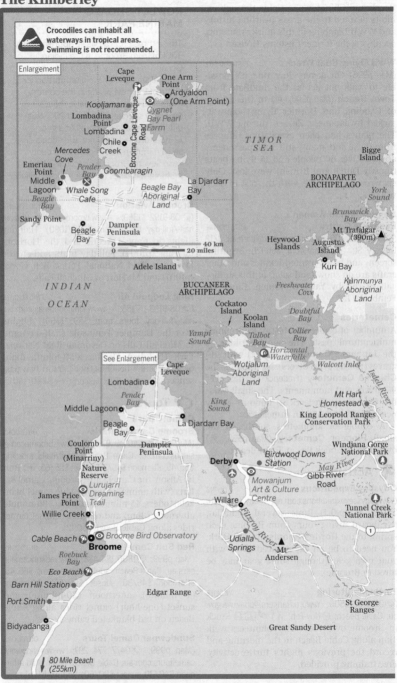

Crocodiles can inhabit all waterways in tropical areas. Swimming is not recommended.

Enlargement

Cape Leveque
One Arm Point
Kooljaman
Ardyaloon (One Arm Point)
Cygnet Bay Pearl Farm
Lombadina Point
Lombadina
Chile Creek
Mercedes Cove
Pender Bay
Emeriau Point
Goombaragin
Middle Lagoon
Whale Song Cafe
Beagle Bay Aboriginal Land
La Djardarr Bay
Beagle Bay
Sandy Point
Beagle Bay
Dampier Peninsula
Broome Cape Leveque Road

0   40 km
0   20 miles

Adele Island

TIMOR SEA

Bigge Island

BONAPARTE ARCHIPELAGO

York Sound

Brunswick Bay
Mt Trafalgar (390m)

Heywood Islands
Augustus Island
Kuri Bay

Kunmunya Aboriginal Land

INDIAN

OCEAN

BUCCANEER ARCHIPELAGO

Freshwater Cove

Cockatoo Island
Koolan Island

Doubtful Bay

Collier Bay

Yampi Sound

Talbot Bay

Horizontal Waterfalls

Walcott Inlet

Isdell River

See Enlargement

Cape Leveque

Lombadina

Pender Bay

Wotjalum Aboriginal Land

King Sound

Middle Lagoon

Beagle Bay

La Djardarr Bay

Dampier Peninsula

Mt Hart Homestead

King Leopold Ranges Conservation Park

Windjana Gorge National Park

Coulomb Point (Minarriny)
Nature Reserve

Derby

Birdwood Downs Station

May River

Gibb River Road

Lurujarri Dreaming Trail

James Price Point

Mowanjum Art & Culture Centre

Willare

Tunnel Creek National Park

Willie Creek

Cable Beach
Broome Bird Observatory

Broome

Roebuck Bay

Eco Beach

Fitzroy River

Udialla Springs

Mt Andersen

Barn Hill Station

Port Smith

Edgar Range

St George Ranges

Bidyadanga

Great Sandy Desert

80 Mile Beach (255km)

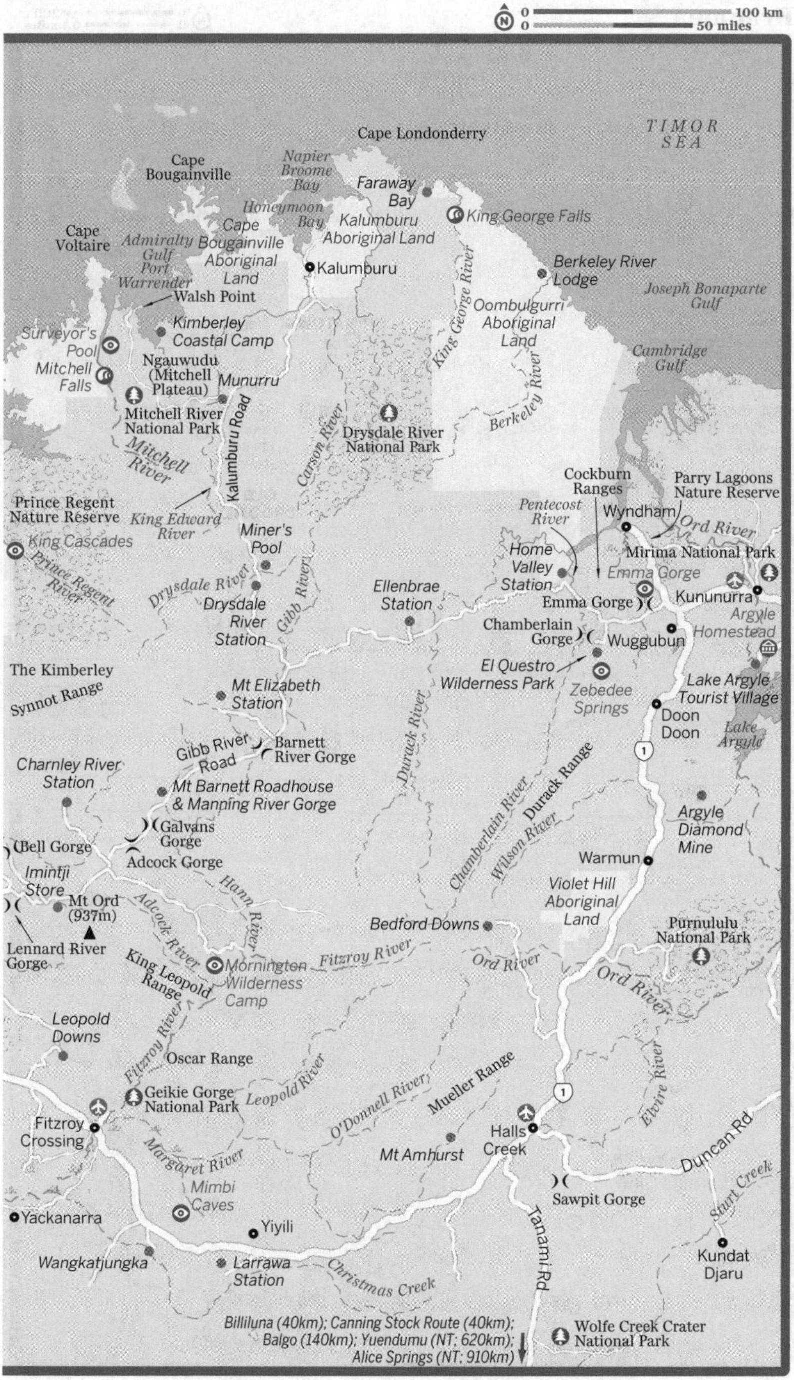
0 100 km
0 50 miles
TIMOR SEA
Cape Londonderry
Cape Bougainville
Napier Broome Bay
Faraway Bay
Honeymoon Bay
Kalumburu Aboriginal Land
King George Falls
Cape Voltaire
Admiralty Gulf
Cape Bougainville Aboriginal Land
Port Warrender
Walsh Point
Kalumburu
Berkeley River Lodge
Joseph Bonaparte Gulf
King George River
Oombulgurri Aboriginal Land
Surveyor's Pool
Kimberley Coastal Camp
Mitchell Falls
Ngauwudu (Mitchell Plateau)
Munurru
Cambridge Gulf
Mitchell River National Park
Kalumburu Road
Carson River
Drysdale River National Park
Berkeley River
Mitchell River
Cockburn Ranges
Parry Lagoons Nature Reserve
Prince Regent Nature Reserve
King Edward River
Pentecost River
Wyndham
Ord River
King Cascades
Miner's Pool
Home Valley Station
Mirima National Park
Prince Regent River
Drysdale River
Gibb River
Ellenbrae Station
Emma Gorge
Emma Gorge
Kununurra
Drysdale River Station
Argyle Homestead
Chamberlain Gorge
Wuggubun
El Questro Wilderness Park
Zebedee Springs
The Kimberley
Lake Argyle Tourist Village
Synnot Range
Mt Elizabeth Station
Doon Doon
Gibb River Road
Barnett River Gorge
Durack River
Lake Argyle
1
Durack Range
Charnley River Station
Mt Barnett Roadhouse & Manning River Gorge
Chamberlain River
Wilson River
Argyle Diamond Mine
Galvans Gorge
Bell Gorge
Adcock Gorge
Warmun
Imintji Store
Hann River
Violet Hill Aboriginal Land
Mt Ord (937m)
Adcock River
Bedford Downs
Purnululu National Park
Lennard River Gorge
Fitzroy River
Ord River
King Leopold Range
Mornington Wilderness Camp
Ord River
Leopold Downs
Fitzroy River
Elvire River
Oscar Range
Mueller Range
Geikie Gorge National Park
Leopold River
O'Donnell River
1
Fitzroy Crossing
Halls Creek
Duncan Rd
Margaret River
Mt Amhurst
Sturt Creek
Mimbi Caves
Sawpit Gorge
Yackanarra
Yiyili
Tanami Rd
Kundat Djaru
Wangkatjungka
Larrawa Station
Christmas Creek
Billiluna (40km); Canning Stock Route (40km); Balgo (140km); Yuendumu (NT; 620km); Alice Springs (NT; 910km)
Wolfe Creek Crater National Park

Broome

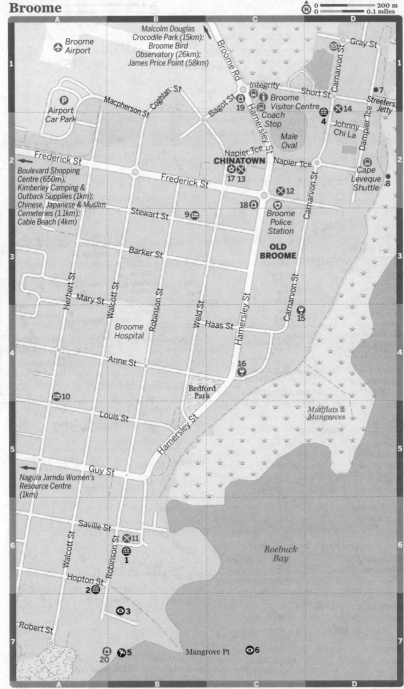

Malcolm Douglas Crocodile Park (15km); Broome Bird Observatory (26km); James Price Point (58km)

Broome Airport

Airport Car Park

Macpherson St

Coghlan St

Broome Rd

Gray St

Carnarvon St

Short St

Integrity
Broome
Visitor Centre
Coach Stop

Streeters Jetty

Dampier Tce

Johnny Chi La

Male Oval

Frederick St

Boulevard Shopping Centre (650m); Kimberley Camping & Outback Supplies (1km); Chinese, Japanese & Muslim Cemeteries (1.1km); Cable Beach (4km)

Bagot St

Hamersley St

Napier Tce

CHINATOWN

Napier Tce St

Cape Leveque Shuttle

Frederick St

Stewart St

Barker St

Broome Police Station

OLD BROOME

Herbert St

Walcott St

Mary St

Robinson St

Weld St

Haas St

Carnarvon St

Broome Hospital

Anne St

Louis St

Bedford Park

Mudflats & Mangroves

Hamersley St

Guy St

Nagula Jarndu Women's Resource Centre (1km)

Saville St

Robinson St

Roebuck Bay

Hopton St

Robert St

Mangrove Pt

Broome

camels hit Cable Beach (p992) in the afternoon (3pm) and at sunset.

Non-camel Tours

Other options around Broome include kayaking, stargazing, birdwatching, historical walking tours, dolphin and marine wildlife spotting, and hovercraft tours.

★ Lurujarri Dreaming Trail   WALKING
(☑ Frans 0423 817 925; www.goolarabooloo.org.au; adult/student $1600/900; ⊗ May-Jul but can vary; ◉) This incredible 82km walk follows a section of ancient songline north along the coast from Gantheaume Point (p992) (Minyirr) to Coulomb Point (Minarriny). The Goolarabooloo organise several guided nine-day walking trips each dry season, staying at traditional camp sites. There is a strong emphasis on sharing Indigenous culture with activities like spear-making, bushtucker hunting, fishing, mud-crabbing and native jewellery making.

★ Jetty to Jetty   WALKING
(Map p996; www.yawuru.com; ◉◉) FREE
This self-guided walking tour from the local Yawuru people comes with a fantastic audio accompaniment (download the free Jetty to Jetty smartphone app), taking you past 13 points of historical and cultural significance between Chinatown's Streeter's Jetty and the Town Beach (p993). The 2.8km walk (with stops) should take around two hours.

Narlijia Cultural Tours   CULTURAL
(Map p996; ☑ 08-9195 0232; www.narlijiacultural tours.com.au; Chinatown; adult/child mangroves $75/35, history $55/25; ⊗ May–mid-Oct; ◉) Yawuru local Bart Pigram runs two-hour cultural tours around the mangroves and historical buildings of Chinatown.

✦ Festivals & Events

Festival timings vary from year to year so check with the visitor centre (p1000).

Sea Grass Monitoring   ENVIRONMENTAL
(☑ 08-9192 1922; www.facebook.com/broome.seagrass; Roebuck Bay; ⊗ hours vary Mar, Jun, Aug & Dec; ◉) ✦ FREE Every three months or so volunteers walk out onto the mudflats of Roebuck Bay to monitor the sea grass that marine creatures such as dugongs and turtles depend on. All are welcome and no experience is necessary. Bring a hat, water bottle and closed shoes.

A Taste of Broome   FOOD & DRINK
(www.goolarri.com; Goolarri Amphitheatre, Blackman St, Old Broome) Indigenous flavours, dance and music caress the senses at this ticketed event held monthly during the Wet.

Kullarri Naidoc Week   CULTURAL
(www.goolarri.com; ⊗ late Jun–mid-Jul) Celebration of Aboriginal and Torres Strait Islander culture.

Corrugated Lines   LITERATURE
(www.facebook.com/corrugatedlines; ⊗ Aug) Three-day festival of the written word with various workshops and talks around town.

Shinju Matsuri Festival of the Pearl   CULTURAL
(www.shinjumatsuri.com.au; ⊗ Aug/Sep; ◉) Broome's homage to the pearl includes a week of parades, food, art, concerts, fireworks and dragon-boat races.

STAIRCASE TO THE MOON

The reflections of a rising full moon rippling over exposed mudflats at low tide create the optical illusion of a **golden stairway** (Town Beach; ⊙Mar-Oct; 🚻🖼️) leading to the moon. Between March and October Broome buzzes around the full moon, with everyone eager to see the spectacle. At **Town Beach** (p993) there's a lively **evening market** (Map p996; ⊙Mar-Oct) with food stalls, and people bring fold-up chairs, although the small headland at the end of Hamersley St has a better view.

While Roebuck Bay parties like nowhere else, this phenomenon happens across the Kimberley and Pilbara coasts – anywhere with some east-facing mudflats. Other good viewing spots are **One Arm Point** at Cape Leveque, **Cooke Point** in Port Hedland, **Sunrise Beach** at Onslow, **Hearson Cove** near Dampier and the lookout at **Cossack**. Most visitor centres publish the dates on their websites.

🛏️ Sleeping

Accommodation is plentiful, but either book ahead or be flexible. If you're travelling in a group, consider renting an apartment. Prices plummet in the Wet.

⭐ Beaches of Broome   HOSTEL $

(Map p999; ☎1300 881 031; www.beachesof broome.com.au; 4 Sanctuary Rd, Cable Beach; dm $32-45, motel d without/with bathroom $140/180; 🅿️❄️@🛜🖼️) More resort than hostel, spotless, air-conditioned rooms are complemented by shady common areas, a poolside bar and a modern self-catering kitchen. Dorms come in a variety of sizes (and include female-only rooms), and the motel rooms are beautifully appointed. Both the continental breakfast and wi-fi are free.

Tarangau Caravan Park   CARAVAN PARK $

(Map p999; ☎08-9193 5084; www.tarangau caravanpark.com; 16 Millington Rd, Cable Beach; unpowered/powered sites $38/48; 🅿️🖼️) A quieter alternative to the Cable Beach caravan parks, Tarangau has pleasant, grassy sites 1km from the beach.

⭐ McAlpine House   B&B $$$

(Map p996; ☎08-9192 0588; http://mcalpine house.com.au; 55 Herbert St; d $185-420; 🅿️❄️🛜🖼️) Lord McAlpine made this stunning house, a former pearl master's lodge, his Broome residence during the '80s. Now renovated to its former glory, there are lovely airy rooms, open communal areas, shady tropical verandahs and a lush canopy of mango trees, tamarind and frangipanis. Escape from the heat by the pool, or travel back through time in the library.

Bali Hai Resort & Spa   SPA HOTEL $$$

(Map p999; ☎08-9191 3100; www.balihairesort. com; 6 Murray Rd, Cable Beach; r from $228, cafe mains $29-42; ⊙cafe 3.30pm-late Wed-Sun; 🅿️➰❄️🛜🖼️) Lush and tranquil, this beautiful small resort has gorgeously decorated studios and villas, each with individual outside dining areas and open-roofed bathrooms. The emphasis is on relaxation, and the on-site spa offers a range of exotic therapies. There's also an Asian-themed cafe showcasing fresh WA produce. The off-season prices are a bargain.

Broome Town B&B   B&B $$$

(Map p996; ☎08-9192 2006; www.broometown. com.au; 15 Stewart St, Old Broome; r $285; 🅿️❄️🛜🖼️) This delightful, boutique-style B&B epitomises Broome-style architecture, with high-pitched roofs, wooden louvres, jarrah floors, tasteful rooms, an open communal guest lounge and lots of tropical shade.

🍴 Eating

Be prepared for 'Broome prices' (exorbitant), 'Broome time' (should be open but it's closed) and surcharges (credit cards, public holidays, bad karma). Service fluctuates wildly, as most staff are just passing through. Most places close in low season.

You'll find cafes along Carnarvon St in Chinatown, while many resorts have in-house restaurants, though often you're just paying for the view.

Cable Beach General
Store & Cafe   CAFE $

(Map p999; ☎08-9192 5572; www.cablebeach store.com.au; cnr Cable Beach & Murray Rds; snacks $6-19; ⊙6am-8pm; 🅿️🛜🚻) Cable Beach unplugged – a typical Aussie corner shop with egg breakfasts, barramundi burgers, pies, internet and no hidden charges. You can even play a round of minigolf (adult/child/family $12/8/20).

Cable Beach

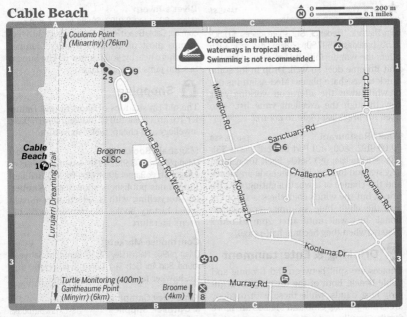

N ⬆ 0 — 200 m
0 — 0.1 miles

Coulomb Point
(Minarriny) (76km)

Crocodiles can inhabit all
waterways in tropical areas.
Swimming is not recommended.

Cable
Beach
1

Broome
SLSC

Cable Beach Rd West

Lurujarri Dreaming Trail

Millington Rd

Sanctuary Rd

Challenor Dr

Koolama Dr

Koolama Dr

Murray Rd

Lullfitz Dr

Sayonara Rd

Turtle Monitoring (400m);
Gantheaume Point
(Minyirr) (6km)

Broome
(4km)

PERTH & WESTERN AUSTRALIA BROOME

Yuen Wing   MARKET $
(Map p996; ☎08-9192 1267; 19 Carnarvon St;
⏰8.30am-5.30pm Mon-Fri, to 2pm Sat & Sun) This
friendly grocery is your best bet for spices,
noodles and all things Asian. Also stocks
beach and camping gear.

★**18 Degrees**   MODERN AUSTRALIAN $$
(Map p996; ☎08-9192 7915; www.18degrees.
com.au; Shop 4, 63 Robinson St; share plates $8-
34; ⏰meals 4-9pm Tue-Sat, snacks 9-11pm Thu-
Sat; P) Exquisite share plates (serving two)
and the best cocktails in town await you at
Broome's newest, hippest nightspot. The
more daring can try the squid ink, tentacles
and chorizo with beetroot aioli, while the
meeker can safely opt for grapefruit-glazed

chicken breast. The desserts are brilliant,
and the bar list runs for nine pages.

★**Good Cartel**   CAFE $$
(Map p996; ☎0499 335 949; 3 Weld St; breakfast
$7-19, burgers $15-20; ⏰5am-noon Mon-Fri, to 2pm
Sat & Sun; P🎨🐾) 🌿 What started as a pop-up
cafe is now *the* place in town to grab a great
coffee, healthy juice and Mexican-themed
breakfasts. Burgers appear weekend lunch-
times and Friday nights (5pm to 9pm). Follow
the line of cars behind the **Twin Cinema** (Map
p996; ☎08-9192 3199; http://broomemovies.
com.au; 3 Weld St; adult/child/family $17/12/55;
⏰10am-midnight or end of last movie; 👶) in the
business park. Doggies more than welcome as
the cafe is active in rehabilitating strays.

★ **Aarli** TAPAS $$

(Map p996; ☑08-9192 5529; www.facebook. com/theaarli; Frederick St; share plates $11.50-21.50, breakfast $5-17.50; ☺8am-late; ℗) Aarli offers the wonderful outdoor relaxed dining that Broome does so well. Drop in for some quick tapas share plates (Med-Asian fusion) or while away the afternoon working your way through the excellent wine list. Also open for breakfast (8am to noon).

Wharf Restaurant SEAFOOD $$$

(☑08-9192 5800; 401 Port Dr, Port; mains $31-120; ☺10am-late; ℗) Settle back for a long, lazy seafood lunch with waterside ambience and the chance of a whale sighting. OK, it's pricey, but the wine's cold, the sea stunning and the chilli blue swimmer crab sensational. Just wait until after 2pm to order oysters (when they become half-price).

🍸 **Drinking & Entertainment**

Choices are split between Old Broome and Cable Beach. Both of the town's pubs regularly host bands, while those with outdoor areas like the Bay Club and Matso's are more family friendly.

Matso's Broome Brewery PUB

(Map p996; ☑08-9193 5811; www.matsos.com. au; 60 Hamersley St; share plates $6-35, mains $20-39; ☺7am-midnight; 🖈) Get yourself a 50/50 chilli/ginger beer combo and a half-kilogram bucket of prawns then kick back to the lazy afternoon music on the shady verandah of Broome's finest brewery.

Bay Club BAR

(Mangrove Hotel; Map p996; ☑08-9192 1303; www.mangrovehotel.com.au; 47 Carnarvon St; mains $19-38; ☺11am-10pm) The Mangrove Hotel's casual outdoor bar is perfect for a few early bevvies while contemplating Roebuck Bay. Decent bistro meals and live music complement excellent Staircase to the Moon (p998) viewing. On Sundays, parents can drop their kids at the bouncing castle.

Sunset Bar & Grill BAR

(Map p999; ☑08-9192 0470; www.cablebeach club.com; Cable Beach Club Resort, Cable Beach Rd; ☺breakfast 6.30-10.30am, bar 4-9pm, dinner 5.30-9pm) Arrive around 4.45pm, grab a front-row seat, order a drink and watch the show – backpackers, package tourists, locals, camels and a searing Indian Ocean sunset shaded by imported coconut palms.

Diver's Tavern LIVE MUSIC

(Map p999; ☑08-9193 6066; www.diverstavern. com.au; Cable Beach Rd; ☺11am-midnight) Diver's pumps most nights, and if you're camped anywhere nearby, you'll know it. The Sunday Session jams are legendary.

🛍 **Shopping**

The old tin shanties of Short St and Dampier Tce are chock-full of Indigenous art, pearl jewellery and cheap, tacky souvenirs.

Magabala Books BOOKS

(Map p996; ☑08-9192 1991; www.magabala.com; 1 Bagot St; ☺9am-4.30pm Mon-Fri; 🖈) Brilliant Indigenous publishers showcasing Kimberley storytelling with a selection of novels, social history books, biographies and children's literature.

Courthouse Markets MARKET

(Map p996; Hamersley St; ☺8am-1pm Sat year-round, Sun Apr-Oct; 🖈) Local arts, crafts, music, hawker food and general hippie gear.

Kimberley Camping & Outback Supplies SPORTS & OUTDOORS

(☑08-9193 5909; www.kimberleycamping.com.au; cnr Frederick St & Cable Beach Rd; ☺8.30am-5pm Mon-Fri, to 1.30pm Sat, 9am-1pm Sun) Jerrycans, Akubra hats, tent pegs and everything else you need for a Kimberley expedition.

ℹ **Information**

Broome Visitor Centre (Map p996; ☑08-9195 2200; www.visitbroome.com.au; 1 Hamersley St; ☺8.30am-5pm Mon-Fri, to 4.30pm Sat & Sun, shorter hours during wet season) Great for info on road conditions, **Staircase to the Moon** (p998) viewing, **dinosaur footprints** (p992), **WWII wrecks** (p993), tide times and souvenirs. Books accommodation and tours for businesses registered with it, and is also the long-haul coach stop. It's on the roundabout entering town, opposite Male Oval.

ℹ **Getting There & Away**

The easiest way into Broome is by air. **Broome Airport** (Map p996; ☑08-9194 0600; www. broomeair.com.au; Macpherson St) is centrally located and serviced by **Qantas** (☑13 13 13; www.qantas.com.au), Skippers (www. skippers.com.au), **Virgin** (☑13 67 89; www. virginaustralia.com) and **Airnorth** (☑08-8920 4001; www.airnorth.com.au). A **shuttle** (Airport Shuttle; ☑08-9192 5252; www.broometaxis. com; Broome/Cable Beach hotels $7/11) service meets flights and drops off passengers at most Broome hotels and Cable Beach resorts.

Long-distance **Integrity** (Map p996; ☑ 08-9274 7464; www.integritycoachlines.com.au) buses run to Perth and **Greyhound** (☑ 1300 473 946; www.greyhound.com.au) to Darwin. A local **bus** (p1005) goes to Derby and there's a daily **shuttle** (p1002) to Cape Leveque as well as the thrice-weekly **mail run** (p1002).

Britz (☑ 08-9192 2647; www.britz.com; 10 Livingston St; minimum 5-day hire van/4WD from $1000/1600) hires campervans, motorhomes and rugged 4WDs, the latter being essential for the Gibb River Road.

ℹ️ Getting Around

Broome's attractions are fairly spread out; don't underestimate distances or the heat. Most hostels will rent out bicycles and/or scooters.

Town Bus Service (☑ 08-9193 6585; www.broomebus.com.au; adult $4, day pass $10; ⊙ 7.23am-6.23pm dry season, 8.53am-5.53pm Mon-Sat, from 10.53am Sun wet season; ♿) links Town Beach, Chinatown and Cable Beach every 30 minutes during the Dry and every hour during the Wet.

Broome Broome (☑ 08-9192 2210; www.broomebroome.com.au; 3/15 Napier Tce; car/4WD/scooter per day from $65/155/35) is the only rental car company that can offer unlimited kilometres. Scooter hire is $35 per day.

Broome Cycles (☑ 08-9192 1871; www.broomecycles.com.au; 2 Hamersley St; per day/week $30/100, deposit $150; ⊙ 8.30am-5pm Mon-Fri, to 2pm Sat) hires mountain bikes out by the day ($30) or week ($100) from Chinatown, and from a trailer at **Cable Beach** (☑ 0409 192 289; cnr Cable Beach & Sanctuary Rds, Cable Beach; ⊙ 9am-noon May-Oct) when in season.

For a taxi, try **Broome Taxis** (☑ 13 10 08), **Chinatown Taxis** (☑ 1800 811 772) or **Pearl Town Taxis** (☑ 13 13 30).

Dampier Peninsula

Stretching north from Broome, the red pindan of the Dampier Peninsula ends abruptly above deserted beaches, secluded mangrove bays and cliffs burnished crimson by the setting sun. This remote and stunning country is home to thriving Indigenous settlements of the Ngumbarl, Jabirr Jabirr, Nyul Nyul, Nimanburu, Bardi Jawi and Goolarabooloo peoples. Access is by 4WD, along the largely unsealed 215km-long Cape Leveque Rd.

The Manari Road (p1003) turn-off, home to Broome's northern beaches and bush camp sites, is reached after 15km.

If you wish to visit Aboriginal communities, you must *always* book ahead (ideally directly with your community hosts, though the Broome Visitor Centre may help); check if permits and/or payments are required. Look for the informative booklet *Ardi–Dampier Peninsula Travellers Guide* ($5). You need to be self-sufficient, though limited supplies are available.

Beagle Bay

Beagle Bay Church CHURCH
(☑ 08-9192 4913; by donation) Around 110km from Broome, Beagle Bay is notable for the extraordinarily beautiful mother-of-pearl altar at Beagle Bay church, built by Pallottine monks in 1918. Fuel is available at the community store (weekdays only).

Ngarlan Yarnin' HISTORY
(☑ 0438 118 578; Beagle Bay; 2 people/family $25/40; ⊙ tours 9am, 10.30am, noon, 1.50pm & 5pm Mon-Sat) Mena Lewis, a local Nyul Nyul and Bardi woman, holds fascinating one-hour story tellings on the history of the Sacred Heart Church, Beagle Bay and the community itself. Cash only.

Pender Bay

Exquisitely remote, this pristine **bay** (☑ 0429 845 707; day use/camp sites per person $10/15; ♿) is an important calving ground for humpback whales and many can be seen offshore from May to November. The easiest access is from either Whale Song Cafe, if open, or via the small Pender Bay camping ground (between Mercedes Cove and Whale Song), where clifftop vantage points provide exceptional viewing. Simple bush camp sites are available.

Goombaragin Eco Retreat CAMPGROUND $$
(☑ 0429 505 347; www.goombaragin.com.au; Pender Bay; site per person $18, tent with/without bathroom $175/80, chalets $220; ⊙ Apr-Oct; 🐕) With a superb location overlooking the scarlet pindan cliffs and turquoise waters of Pender Bay, this eco-retreat offers several unpowered camp sites, a range of safari tents and a self-contained chalet. There's a nightly communal get-together around the fire.

★ Whale Song Cafe CAFE $$
(☑ 08-9192 4000; www.whalesongcafe.com.au; Munget, Pender Bay; light meals $11-29; ⊙ 9am-2pm Jun-Aug; 🐕) This exquisitely located ecocafe overlooking Pender Bay serves fabulous mango smoothies, homemade gourmet pizzas and the best coffee on the peninsula. There's a tiny bush camping ground (camp sites per person $20) with stunning views, a funky

outdoor shower and not a caravan in sight. Telstra mobile reception available.

Lombadina & Around

Between Middle Lagoon and Cape Leveque, **Lombadina** (☑08-9192 4936; www.lombadina.com; entry per car $10; ☼office 8am-noon & 1-4pm Mon-Fri) is 200km from Broome. This beautiful tree-fringed Indigenous community offers various tours (minimum three people), including fishing, whale watching, 4WD tours, mud-crabbing, kayaking and walking, which can be booked through the office. Accommodation is in backpacker-style rooms and self-contained cabins ($220 to $280 for four people), but there's no camping. Fuel is available on weekdays and there are lovely pieces for sale at the Arts Centre (open weekdays). Don't miss the paperbark church.

Ardi Festival
CULTURAL

(www.visitbroome.com.au; Lombadina; adult $20, under 15 free; ☼varies Jun-Sep) Annual celebration of Ardi culture featuring music, food and art at Lombadina community. Check the dates with the Broome Visitor Centre (p1000) as the timing of this fledgling festival varies each year. Drug and alcohol free.

Chile Creek
CAMPGROUND $

(☑08-9192 4141; www.chilecreek.com.au; Chile Creek, Lombadina; sites per adult/child $16.50/10, bungalows $95, family safari tents $185) Tiny mangrove-fringed Chile Creek, 10km from Lombadina down an eroded sandy track, offers basic bush camp sites, bungalows (shared bathroom) and en-suite safari tents (minimum two-night stay). There's great bird life and plenty of mud crabs, but BYO food (unless you plan to catch it!).

Cape Leveque & Around

Spectacular **Cape Leveque** (day access per person $5; ꙮ) 🗷, right on the tip of the Dampier Peninsula, has stunning red cliffs and gorgeous white beaches perfect for swimming and snorkelling. Access is via Kooljaman resort.

Brian Lee Tagalong Tours
TOURS

(☑08-9192 4970; www.brianleetagalong.com.au; Kooljaman; adult/child $98/45) Tag-along (in your own 4WD) with Bardi traditional owner Brian Lee as he reveals the culture and history surrounding Hunters Creek, where you'll get a chance to fish and hunt for mud crabs.

Bundy's Tours
CULTURAL

(☑09-9192 4970; www.bundysculturaltours.com.au; Kooljaman; adult $45-80, child $25-40) Bardi custodian Bundy offers a range of cultural tours providing an amazing insight into traditional customs, including bush tucker, night fishing and spear-making.

Gumbanan
CAMPGROUND $

(☑0499 330 169; www.kimberleyoutbackxposure.com.au; near One Arm Point; site per adult $15, child under 10 free, safari tent d/f $120/140) On an unspoiled mangrove coast, this small outstation between Cape Leveque and **Ardyaloon** (Bardi; ☑08-9192 4930; http://ardyaloon.org.au; per person $15, child free; ☼office 8am-noon & 1.30-4pm Mon-Thu, 8am-noon & 1.30-3pm Fri) offers quiet, unpowered sites and simple safari tents. Immerse yourself in traditional culture with spear-making ($85) or mud-crabbing ($95) courses, or jump on a quad bike for a tour of the Joowon marshes ($130).

Kooljaman
RESORT $$

(☑08-9192 4970; www.kooljaman.com.au; entry per adult $5, unpowered/powered sites $45/50, dome tents $85, beach shelters $120, cabin with/without bathroom $200/155, safari tents from $275; ꙮ🗷) Ecotourism award-winner Kooljaman offers a range of accommodation from grassy camp sites and budget dome tents to driftwood beach shelters, cabins with or without bathrooms, and hilltop safari tents with superb views. On-site restaurant Raugis (p1002) overlooks Western Beach and the smaller Dinkas Cafe (open March to September) is on the eastern side, or you can order BBQ packs.

Raugis
MODERN AUSTRALIAN $$

(☑08-9192 4970; Kooljaman Resort; mains $27-39, BBQ packs $25; ☼7.30-10am, 11.30am-2pm & 6-10pm Apr-Oct, 11.30am-2pm Nov-Mar; ꙮ) Overlooking the red pindan cliffs of Cape Leveque's Western Beach, this BYO restaurant at Kooljaman (p1002) resort opens for all meals (April to October) and serves up tasty, stylish fare. Or you can order a takeaway BBQ pack.

❶ Getting There & Away

The **Cape Leveque Shuttle** (Broome Transit; Map p996; ☑08-9192 5252; www.broometaxis.com; ☼one way/day return $70/120) runs daily (dependent on passenger numbers) from Broome to Beagle Bay, Cape Leveque (Kooljaman) and Cygnet Bay and back.

The **Cape Leveque Mail Run** (☑08-9193 7650; http://ahoybuccaneers.com.au; one way/return $70/140; ☼5am Mon, Wed & Fri) postie

MANARI ROAD: BROOME'S NORTHERN BEACHES

The beaches, headlands and red pindan cliffs along Manari Rd are one of Broome's best-kept secrets, frequented mainly by anglers, locals and adventurous travellers looking for something more than just Broome-time. Leaving the Cape Leveque Rd just 15km from the Great Northern Hwy, unsealed, sandy and sometimes corrugated Manari Rd runs roughly northwest through **Goolarabooloo Country**, parallel to the coastal **Lurujarri Songline** (an oral memory map of stories, song and dance that describes the landscape and is handed down from generation to generation).

Just 5km along you'll reach the turn-off to **Willie Creek** where there's a **pearl farm** (Wirrkinymirri; ☑ 08-9192 0000; www.thebroomeexperience.com.au; Willie Creek Rd; tours adult/child/family from $65/35/165; ☺ cafe 11am-3pm Apr-Sep; ℗) in a stunning location on a mangrove-lined inlet; the 7.5km sandy access track feels quite remote as you skirt a wide salt lake. Various tours are available and there's a cafe for lunch, but don't swim, as there are salties (saltwater crocodiles) in the creek.

Back on Manari Rd, there are bush camp sites (no facilities, maximum three-night stay) at **Barred Creek** (Nuwirrar; Manari Rd; ℗ 🏕) 🅵 **FREE**, **Quandong Point** (Kardilakan; Manari Rd; 🚻 🏕) **FREE**, **James Price Point** (Walmadan; Manari Rd; 🚾 🏕) 🅵 **FREE** and **Coulomb Point** (Minarinny; Manari Rd; 🚾 🏕) 🅵 **FREE**, where there is a nature reserve. You can swim at the beaches here, fish off the reefs and wander the rock platforms at low tide looking for dinosaur footprints and plant fossils, but don't take anything away other than rubbish.

Conventional vehicles should make it to **James Price Point**, in the middle of the Songline. Its crumbling, crimson pindan cliffs, once home to the proud warrior **Walmadan**, have in more recent years become both an icon and the frontline of the Kimberley's environmental movement. Whether or not you plan on camping, don't miss this spectacular location. Especially at sunset!

For more information about the area, see www.goolarabooloo.org.au and www.environskimberley.org.au.

can drop off and pick up passengers from Beagle Bay, Lombadina, Djarindjin, Gambanan (June to September only), Cape Leveque (Kooljaman) and Cygnet Bay on Monday, Wednesday and Friday.

A high-clearance 4WD is best, as the roads can become corrugated and washed out after rain.

Derby

POP 4000

Late at night while Derby sleeps, the boabs cut loose and wander around town, marauding mobs flailing their many limbs in battle against an army of giant, killer croc-people emerging from the mudflats... If only.

There *are* crocs hiding in the mangroves, but you're more likely to see birds, over 200 different varieties, while the boabs are firmly rooted along the two parallel main drags, Loch and Clarendon Sts. Derby is the departure point for tours to the Horizontal Waterfalls (p1004) and Buccaneer Archipelago, and the western terminus of the Gibb River Road (GRR).

Derby is West Kimberley's administrative centre, though the closure of the asylum seeker detention facility at nearby RAAF Curtin has seen a drop in contract workers, freeing up stretched accommodation resources.

◉ Sights

★ **Norval Gallery**   GALLERY
(☑ 0458 110 816; www.facebook.com/norval-gallery-676996675735315; 1 Sutherland St; ☺ varies) Kimberley art legends Mark and Mary Norval have set up an exciting gallery-cafe in an old tin shed on the edge of town. Featuring striking artworks, exquisite jewellery, decent coffee and 5000 vinyl records (brought out on themed nights), it's a delight to the senses.

Wharefinger Museum   MUSEUM
(cnr Elder & Loch Sts; by donation) Grab the key from the visitor centre (p1005) and have a peek inside the nearby museum, with its atmospheric shipping and aviation displays.

Jetty   LANDMARK
Check out King Sound's colossal 11.5m tides from the circular jetty, 1km north of town, a popular fishing, crabbing, bird-spotting and staring-into-the-distance haunt. Yep, there are crocs in the mangroves.

Kimberley School of the Air SCHOOL
(Marmion St; $10) Fascinating look at how school is conducted over the radio for children on remote stations. Opening times vary, so check with the visitor centre (p1005) first.

🏃 Activities & Tours

The Horizontal Waterfalls (p1004) are Derby's top draw and most cruises also include the natural splendours of remote King Sound and the Buccaneer Archipelago. There are many operators to choose from; ask at the visitor centre (p1005) for a full list. Most tours only operate during peak season.

★ Horizontal Falls
Seaplane Adventures SCENIC FLIGHTS
(☑ 08-9192 1172; www.horizontalfallsadventures.com.au; 6hr tours from Derby/Broome $745/795) If you do one tour in the Kimberley, make sure it's this one. Flights to Horizontal Waterfalls land on Talbot Bay before transferring to high-powered speedboats for an adrenalin-packed ride through both sets of falls. There's also an overnight-stay option (ex-Derby) from $895.

Depending on the tide, several runs are made through the falls, before a barramundi lunch is served on the base pontoon. For a different perspective, try the 10-minute chopper ride ($100). After lunch, there are a few more runs as the tide changes direction, before flying back over the Buccaneer Archipelago.

North West Bush Pilots SCENIC FLIGHTS
(☑ 08-9193 2680; www.northwestbushpilots.com.au; flights from $370) Horizontal Waterfalls (p1004), Buccaneer Archipelago and Walcott Inlet – you can look but not touch.

Kimberley Dreamtime
Adventure Tours CULTURAL
(☑ 08-9191 7280; www.kdat.com.au; adult/child 2-day $492/350, 3-day $710/565; ⊙ Mon & Wed Apr-Oct) Indigenous-owned and -operated cultural tours based in Nyikina Mangala country on Mt Anderson Station, 126km southeast of Derby. Camp under the stars, ride camels, fish, hunt, walk and learn about Aboriginal culture. Pick-ups from Broome, Willare or Derby.

Wandjina Tours CULTURAL
(☑ 1800 111 163; www.wandjinatours.com.au; Freshwater Cove; 2-/4-day tour $2600/3800) Immerse yourself in Worrorra culture at Freshwater Cove, a remote beach camp 200km north of Derby on the pristine West Kimberley coast. Experience rock art, sacred beaches, traditional artists and amazing seafood. Return over the Horizontal Waterfalls. Access is by air from Derby.

Uptuyu CULTURAL
(☑ 0400 878 898; www.uptuyu.com.au; Oongkalkada Wilderness Camp, Udialla Springs; per day from $450) In Nyikina country on the Fitzroy River, 50km from the Great Northern Hwy, Neville and Jo run 'designer' cultural tours taking in wetlands, rock art, fishing and Indigenous communities along the Fitzroy and further afield.

🎇 Festivals & Events

Boab Festival MUSIC, CULTURAL
(www.derbyboabfestival.org.au; ⊙ Jul) Concerts, mud footy, horse and mud-crab races, poetry readings, art exhibitions and street parades. Try to catch the Long Table dinner out on the mudflats.

HORIZONTAL WATERFALLS

One of the most intriguing features of the Kimberley coastline is the phenomenon known as 'horizontal waterfalls'. Despite the name, the falls are simply tides gushing through narrow coastal gorges in the Buccaneer Archipelago, north of Derby. What creates such a spectacle are the huge tides, often varying up to 11m. The water flow reaches an astonishing 30 knots as it's forced through two narrow gaps 20m and 10m wide – resulting in a 'waterfall' reaching 4m in height.

Many tours leave Derby (and some Broome) each Dry, by air, sea or a combination of both. It's become de rigueur to 'ride' the tide change through the gorges on a high-powered speedboat. There is a risk element involved, and accidents have occurred. Scenic flights are the quickest and cheapest option, and some seaplanes will land and transfer passengers to a waiting speedboat for the adrenalin hit. If you prefer to be stirred, not shaken, then consider seeing the falls as part of a longer cruise through the archipelago. Book tours at the Derby and Broome visitor centres.

🛏 Sleeping & Eating

Kimberley Entrance
Caravan Park   CARAVAN PARK $
(☑ 08-9193 1055; www.kimberleyentrancecaravan
park.com; 2 Rowan St; unpowered/powered sites
$34/40; ℗ 🐾) Not all sites are shaded,
though there's always room. Expect lots of
insects this close to the mudflats.

Desert Rose   B&B $$
(☑ 08-9193 2813; 4 Marmion St; d $225; 🐾) It's
worth booking ahead for the best sleep in
town, with spacious, individually styled
rooms, a nice shady pool, lead-light windows and a sumptuous breakfast. Host Anne
is a fount of local information.

Spinifex Hotel   RESORT $$
(☑ 08-9191 1233; www.spinifexhotel.com.au; 6 Clarendon St; donga/motel r $120/225; ℗ 🐾 @ 🛜 🐾)
Rising phoenix-like from the ashes of the old
Spini, this sleek resort has corporate-class
rooms (some with kitchenettes) and an on-
site restaurant (mains $22-42). Peak season
brings outdoor live music.

⭐ Neaps Bistro   MODERN AUSTRALIAN $$
(☑ 08-9193 2924; www.facebook.com/neaps
bistro; Derby Lodge, 15-19 Clarendon St; mains
$19-39; ⊘ 7-11am daily, 6-9pm Mon-Sat; 🐾) The
new favourite among Derby locals, with
a chef direct from the Barossa Valley. Dinners are succulent and draw from a wide
palette, while the breakfasts ($7 to $23) are
outstanding, showing a level of refinement
rarely seen outside of capital cities.

Jila Gallery   ITALIAN $$
(☑ 08-9193 2560; www.facebook.com/jilagallery;
18 Clarendon St; pizzas $20-28, mains $24-34;
⊘ 10.30am-2pm & 6pm-late Tue-Fri, 6pm-late Sat)
Jila's fortunes fluctuate with its chefs, who
turn out wood-fired pizzas, homemade
pastas and wonderful cakes, in a shady alfresco setting.

ℹ Information

Derby Visitor Centre (☑ 08-9191 1426; www.
derbytourism.com.au; 30 Loch St; ⊘ 8.30am-
4.30pm Mon-Fri, 9am-3pm Sat & Sun dry
season) Helpful centre with the low-down on
road conditions, accommodation, transport
and tour bookings.

ℹ Getting There & Away

Charter and sightseeing flights use Derby Airport (DRB), just past the Gibb turn-off. There are
currently no scheduled commercial services,
but if Perth flights are ever reinstated, they will
leave from Curtin Airport (DCN), 40km away.

All buses depart from the **visitor centre**.

Derby Bus Service (☑ 08-9193 1550; www.
derbybus.com.au; one way/return $50/90;
⊘ Mon, Wed & Fri) Leaves early for Broome (2½
hours), stopping at Willare Roadhouse (and basically anywhere else you ask the driver to stop
along the way), and returning the same day.

Greyhound (☑ 1300 473 946; www.greyhound.
com.au) Broome ($52, 2½ hours), Darwin
($261, 23 hours) and Kununurra ($134, 11
hours) daily (except Sundays).

Devonian Reef National Parks

Three national parks with three stunning
gorges were once part of a western 'great
barrier reef' in the Devonian era, 350 million
years ago. Windjana Gorge and Tunnel Creek
National Parks are accessed via the unsealed
Fairfield-Leopold Downs Rd (linking the
Great Northern Hwy with the Gibb River
Road), while Geikie Gorge National Park is
22km northeast of Fitzroy Crossing.

⊙ Sights

⭐ Tunnel Creek   NATIONAL PARK
(per car $712; ⊘ dry season; ℗) Sick of the
sun? Then cool down underground at Tunnel Creek, which cuts through a spur of
the Napier Range for almost 1km. It was
famously the hideout of Jandamarra (a
Bunuba man who waged an armed guerrilla
war against the police and white settlers for
three years before he was killed). In the Dry,
the full length is walkable by wading partly
through knee-deep water; watch out for bats
and bring good footwear and a strong torch.

There's rock art in the area around the far
entrance. Camping not permitted.

Geikie Gorge   NATIONAL PARK
(Darngku; ⊘ Apr-Dec; ℗) Don't miss this magnificent gorge near Fitzroy Crossing. The
self-guided trails are sandy and hot, so take
one of the boat cruises run by either **Department of Parks & Wildlife staff** (☑ 08-9191
5121; 1hr tour adult/child $45/12; ⊘ cruises from
8am May-Oct) or local Bunuba guides.

Windjana Gorge   NATIONAL PARK
(entry per car $12, camping adult/child $12/2.20;
⊘ dry season;7 ℗ 🛖) The walls of this gorge
soar 100m above the Lennard River, which
surges in the Wet but is a series of pools
in the Dry. Scores of freshwater crocodiles

lurk along the banks. Bring plenty of water for the 7km return walk from the camping ground. Swimming is not recommended due to croc numbers.

Tours

Darngku Heritage Tours   CRUISE
(☑ 0417 907 609; www.darngku.com.au; adult/child 2hr tour $70/60, 3hr $90/75, half-day $175/138; ☺ Apr-Dec; ♦) Local Bunuba guides introduce Indigenous culture and bush tucker on these amazingly informative cruises through Geikie (Darngku) Gorge (p1005). A shorter one-hour cruise (adult/child $35/7.50) operates during the shoulder seasons (April and October to December).

Bungoolee Tours   CULTURAL
(☑ 08-9191 5355; www.bungoolee.com.au; 2hr tour adult/child $60/20; ☺ 9am & 2pm Mon, Wed & Fri dry season) Bunuba lawman Dillon Andrews runs two-hour Tunnel Creek tours explaining the story of Jandamarra. Book through Fitzroy Crossing visitor centre (p1010).

Getting There & Away

You'll need your own vehicle to visit the three parks. **Geikie Gorge** (p1005) is easily accessed from Fitzroy Crossing, but if you only have a 2WD, check the condition of Fairfield-Leopold Downs Rd first (for **Windjana Gorge** (p1005) and **Tunnel Creek** (p1005)); there's at least one permanent creek crossing. Otherwise, consider taking a **day tour** (☑ 0499 336 967; www.windjana.com.au; adult/child $195/95; ☺ Tue, Thu & Sun May-Sep, also Fri Jun-Aug) from Derby.

Gibb River Road

Cutting a swath through the scorched heart of the Kimberley, the legendary Gibb River Road ('the Gibb' or GRR) provides one of Australia's wildest outback experiences. Stretching 660km between Derby and Kununurra, the largely unpaved road runs through endless seas of red dirt and open skies. Rough, sometimes deeply corrugated side roads lead to remote gorges, shady pools, waterfalls and million-acre cattle stations. Rain can close the road any time, and it's permanently closed during the Wet. This is true wilderness with minimal services, so good planning and self-sufficiency are vital.

A high-clearance 4WD (eg Toyota Land Cruiser) is mandatory, with two spare tyres, tools, emergency water (20L minimum) and several days' food in case of breakdown. Britz (p1001) in Broome is a reputable hire outfit. Fuel is limited and expensive, most mobile phones won't work, and temperatures can be life-threatening.

Tours

Adventure Tours   DRIVING
(☑ 03-8102 7800; www.adventuretours.com.au; from $1995) Nine-day Gibb River Road camping tours catering for a younger crowd.

Wundargoodie Aboriginal Safaris   CULTURAL
(☑ 0429 928 088; www.wundargoodie.com.au; tag-along per vehicle per day $250, women-only 11-day tour $3500; ☺ Apr-Sep; ♦) These insightful Indigenous-run 4WD tag-along tours (ie you bring your own vehicle) showcase local culture and rock art in the remote West Kimberley. The women-only tour is all-inclusive, camping at special sites and sharing experiences with Aboriginal women.

Kimberley Adventure Tours   DRIVING
(☑ 1800 171 616; www.kimberleyadventures.com.au; 9-day tour $1995) Small-group camping tours from Broome up the Gibb, with the nine-day tour continuing to Purnululu and Darwin. Also offers the reverse direction, starting in Darwin.

Kimberley Wild Expeditions   DRIVING
(☑ 1300 738 870; www.kimberleywild.com.au) Consistent award winner. Tours from Broome range from one ($239) to 14 days ($3995) on the Gibb River Road.

Information

Check out www.kimberleyaustralia.com or visit the **Derby** (p1005) and **Kununurra** (p1013) visitor centre websites. The visitor centres also sell *The Gibb River & Kalumburu Road Guide* ($5).

Mainroads Western Australia (MRWA; ☑ 13 81 38; www.mainroads.wa.gov.au; ☺ 24hr) Highway and Gibb River Road conditions.

Parks & Wildlife (www.dpaw.wa.gov.au) Park permits, camping fees and information. Consider a Holiday Pass ($44) if visiting more than three parks in one month.

Shire of Derby/West Kimberley (☑ 08-9191 0999; www.sdwk.wa.gov.au) Side-road conditions for the Western and Central Gibb.

Shire of Wyndham/East Kimberley (☑ 08-9168 4100; www.swek.wa.gov.au) Kalumburu/Mitchell Falls road conditions.

Derby to Imintji

Heading east from Derby, the first 100-odd kilometres of the Gibb River Road are now sealed. Don't miss **Mowanjum Art & Culture**

Centre (08-9191 1008; www.mowanjumarts. com; Gibb River Rd, Derby; 9am-5pm daily dry season, closed Sat & Sun wet season, closed Jan; P) **FREE**, only 4km along.

The Windjana Gorge turn-off at 119km is your last chance to head back to the Great Northern Highway. Windjana is an easy 22km off the Gibb and is a popular camp site. Back on the GRR, the scenery improves after crossing the **Lennard River** into Napier Downs Station as the **King Leopold Ranges** loom ahead. Just after **Inglis Gap** is the Mt Hart Homestead turn-off and another 7km brings the narrow **Lennard River Gorge**.

Despite its name, **March Fly Glen**, 204km from Derby, is a pleasant, shady picnic area ringed by pandanus and frequented by blue-faced honeyeaters. Don't miss stunning **Bell Gorge** (per car $12; P), with its waterfall and plunge pool. Refuel (diesel only), grab an ice cream and check your email at **Imintji Store** (08-9191 7227; www.imintji.com; 9am-5pm dry season, shorter hours wet season;).

Mt Hart Homestead   CAMPGROUND $
(08-9191 4645; www.kimberleyoutbacktours.com; sites per person $18, s/d incl dinner & breakfast $430/590, safari tents $590; dry season) Below Inglis Gap a rough 50km track leads to the remote Mt Hart Homestead with grassy camp sites, pleasant gorges, and swimming and fishing holes.

Full board is available in lovely restored rooms or modern safari tents, and campers may eat in the restaurant (breakfast/lunch/dinner $25/25/40). Diesel is available at Imintji (p1007) prices and there's an onsite bar, though nearby Sunset Hill across the airstrip is the appropriate venue for sundowners.

Birdwood Downs Station   FARMSTAY $
(08-9191 1275; www.birdwooddowns.com; camping $14.50, huts per person $86; P) About 20km from Derby, 2000-hectare Birdwood Downs offers rustic savannah huts, butterflies and basic camping. WWOOFers are welcome and it's also the home of the Kimberley School of Horsemanship, with lessons, riding camps and trail rides ($60 per hour).

There's also a 90-minute sunset ride ($105) complete with bubbly, and, for the more experienced rider, a three-hour journey across the marshes of King Sound ($180). If you prefer your horsepower under the hood, try the Savannah Eco Tour ($60), an informative 90-minute cruise around the property.

Imintji to Mt Elizabeth Station

Heading east from Imintji, it's only 25km to the Mornington turn-off and another 5km further to the entrance of **Charnley River Station** (08-9191 4646; www.australianwildlife. org; sites per person $20, entry per vehicle $25; P). If heading across the lonely savannah to exquisite Mornington Wilderness Camp, call first using the radio at the Gibb. Back on the GRR, most of the cattle you pass are from **Mount House Station**. Cross the **Adcock**, wave to Nev and Leonie as you pass Over the Range Repairs, then drop down to **Galvans Gorge** (Gibb River Rd; P) at the 286km mark.

Fuel up at Mt Barnett Roadhouse, 300km from Derby, and get your camping permit if choosing to stay at nearby **Manning River Gorge** (7km behind Mt Barnett Roadhouse; camp site per person $22.50; P), though there are better options further east. There's free camping on the **Barnett River** (29km east of Mt Barnett Roadhouse) **FREE** at the 329km mark, and if you've still got daylight, consider pushing on to the turn-off for historic **Mt Elizabeth Station** (08-9191 4644; sites per person $22, s/d incl breakfast & dinner $195/390; dry season) at the 338km mark.

Between Adcock and Galvans gorges, Nev and Leonie of **Over the Range Repairs** (08-9191 7887; 8am-5pm dry season) are your best – if not only – hope of mechanical salvation on the whole Gibb.

Groceries, diesel and unleaded petrol (most expensive on the Gibb) are found at **Mt Barnett Roadhouse** (08-9191 7007; 8am-5pm dry season, shorter hours wet season). Also camping permits for Manning River Gorge.

★ **Mornington**
Wilderness Camp   WILDLIFE RESERVE
(08-9191 7406; www.awc.org.au; entry per vehicle $25, camp sites per adult/child $20/10, full-board safari tents s/d $335/600; May–mid-Oct; P) Part of the Australian Wildlife Conservancy, the superb Mornington Wilderness Camp is as remote as it gets, lying on the Fitzroy River, an incredibly scenic 95km drive across the savannah from the Gibb's 247km mark. Nearly 400,000 hectares are devoted to conserving the Kimberley's endangered fauna and there's excellent canoeing, swimming, birdwatching and bushwalking.

Choose from shady camp sites with gas BBQs or raised tents (including full board) with verandahs and bathrooms. The bar and restaurant offer full dinner ($60), BBQ packs ($25) and the best cheese platter ($25) this side of Margaret River. **Sir John Gorge** in the late afternoon sun is sublime. Call ahead using the radio provided at the Gibb turn-off.

Kalumburu Rd to Wyndham/Kununurra

Four-hundred-and-six kilometres from Derby you reach the Kalumburu turn-off. Head right on the Gibb River Road, and continue through spectacular country, crossing the **Durack River** then climbing though the **Pentecost Ranges** to panoramic views of the Cockburn Ranges, Cambridge Gulf and Pentecost River. Shortly after is the turn-off to the lovely Home Valley Station.

Soon after Home Valley, at 589km from Derby, you'll cross the infamous **Pentecost River** – take care as water levels are unpredictable and saltwater crocs lurk nearby. The last section of the Gibb River Road is sealed. The turn-off to beautiful **Emma Gorge** (☉Apr-Sep; ℗) is 10km past El Questro. You'll cross **King River** 630km from Derby and, at 647km, you'll finally hit the Great Northern Highway – turn left for Wyndham (48km) and right to Kununurra (53km).

El Questro Wilderness Park   PARK
(☑08-9169 1777; www.elquestro.com.au; adult permit per day/week $12/20; ☉dry season; ℗▣) This vast 400,000-hectare former cattle station turned international resort incor-porates scenic gorges (Amelia, El Questro) and **Zebedee Springs** (☉7am-noon; ℗). Boat tours explore Chamberlain Gorge or you can hire your own boat ($100). There are shady camp sites and air-con bungalows at **El Questro Station Township** (☑08-9169 1777; www.elquestro.com.au; sites per person $20-28, station tent d $164, bungalow d from $329; ❄☎▣) and also an outdoor bar and upmarket steakhouse (mains $28 to $44).

Chamberlain Gorge Boat Tours   CRUISE
(adult/child $62/32; ☉3pm) Departing from El Questro Wilderness Park, boat tours explore massive Chamberlain Gorge.

★**Home Valley Station**   FARMSTAY $
(☑08-9161 4322; www.homevalley.com.au; camp sites adult/child $19.50/5, eco-tent d from $165, homestead d from $295; ☉May-Oct; ℗❄@☎▣) The privations of the Gibb are left behind after pulling into amazing Home Valley Station, an Indigenous hospitality training resort with a superb range of luxurious accommodation. There are excellent grassy camp sites and motel-style rooms, a fantastic open-air bistro (mains $28 to $45), tyre repairs and activities including trail rides, bushwalks, fishing and cattle mustering.

Great Northern Highway

One of the Kimberley's best-kept secrets is the vast subterranean labyrinth of Mimbi Caves, 90km southeast of Fitzroy Crossing,

---

OFF THE BEATEN TRACK

KALUMBURU

Kalumburu is a picturesque mission nestled beneath giant mango trees and coconut palms with two shops and fuel. There's some interesting rock art nearby, and the odd WWII bomber wreck. You can stay at the **Kalumburu Mission** (☑08-9161 4333; www.kalumburumission.org.au; sites per adult/child $20/8, donga s/d $125/175; ℗), which has a small **museum** (Fr Thomas Gill Museum; ☑08-9161 4333; www.kalumburumission.org.au; $10; ☉11am-1pm), or obtain a permit from the Kalumburu Aboriginal Community (KAC) office to camp at **Honeymoon Bay** (☑08-9161 4378; www.facebook.com/honeymoonbaywa; sites $20) or **McGowan Island** (☑08-9161 4748; www.facebook.com/pages/McGowan-Island/194876760642959; sites $20), 20km further out on the coast – the end of the road.

The road to Kalumburu deteriorates quickly after the Mitchell Plateau turn-off and eventually becomes very rocky. Fuel is available from the yard next to the **mission store** (☉7-11.30am & 1.30-4pm Mon-Fri, 9-11am Sat).

You'll need a permit from the **Department of Aboriginal Affairs** (DAA; ☑1300 651 077; www.daa.wa.gov.au) in Broome to visit Kalumburu and a Kalumburu Aboriginal Community (08-9161 4300, www.kalumburu.org) visitors' permit ($50 per vehicle, valid for seven days) upon entry, available from the **Community Resource Centre** (CRC, Visitor Centre; ☑08-9161 4627; www.kalumburu.org; ☉varies; ☎). Alcohol is banned at Kalumburu.

located within Mt Pierre Station on Gooni-yandi land. Nearby **Larrawa Station** (Bush Camp; ☑08-9191 7025; www.larrawabushcamp. com; Great Northern Hwy; camp sites per person $10; ☺Apr-Sep; @✿) makes a pleasant over-night stop, with hot showers, basic camp sites and shearers' rooms. Another 30km towards Halls Creek is tiny Yiyili with its Laarri Gallery.

Pushing on from Halls, the scenery be-comes progressively more interesting and just after the Ord River bridge you'll pass the Purnululu National Park (p1013) turn-off at 108km. Warmun (162km) has a road-house and an amazing gallery (p1009) in the nearby community. **Doon Doon Road-house** (☑08-9167 8004; Doon Doon; ☺7am-5.30pm), 91km from Warmun and 60km from the Victoria Hwy junction, is the only other blip on the landscape and your last chance to refuel before Kununurra or Wyn-dham. If heading to **Wuggubun** (☑08-9161 4040; http://wuggubuntourism.com; ☺Apr-Sep; ✿), the signposted turn-off is 4km south of the highway junction, just before Card Creek (if heading north).

◉ Sights

★ Mimbi Caves
CAVE

(Mt Pierre Station) One of the Kimberley's best-kept secrets, this vast subterranean lab-yrinth, 90km southeast of Fitzroy Crossing, on Gooniyandi land, houses a significant collection of Aboriginal rock art and some of the most impressive fish fossils in the south-ern hemisphere. Indigenous-owned Girloor-loo Tours runs trips here.

Warmun Arts
GALLERY

(☑08-9168 7496; www.warmunart.com; Great Northern Hwy, Warmun; ☺9am-4pm Mon-Fri; P) Between Kununurra and Halls Creek, War-mun artists create abstract works using ochres to explore Gija identity.

Laarri Gallery
GALLERY

(☑08-9191 7195; www.laarrigallery.com; Yiyili; ☺8am-4pm school days; P✿) This tiny not-for-profit gallery in the back of the community school has interesting contemporary and tra-ditional art and crafts detailing local history. It's 120km west of Halls Creek Phone ahead.

⌕ Tours

Girloorloo Tours
CULTURAL

(☑08-9191 5468; www.mimbicaves.com.au; 3hr tour adult/child $80/40; ☺10am & 2pm Mon-Thu & Sat Apr-Sep) Aboriginal-owned Girloorloo

MITCHELL FALLS & DRYSDALE RIVER
....

In the Dry, Kalumburu Rd is normally navigable as far as **Drysdale River Station** (☑08-9161 4326; www.drysdale river.com.au; camp sites per person $12-16, d from $150; ☺8am-5pm Apr-Oct; P✿), 59km from the Gibb River Road.

The **Mitchell Plateau** (Ngauwudu) turn-off is 160km from the Gibb, and within 6km a deep, rocky ford crosses the **King Edward River**, formidable early in the season. The turn-off to **Munurru Campground** (adult/child $7.50/2.20) is on the right, soon after the crossing.

From the Kalumburu Rd it's a rough 87km, past lookouts and forests of *Livistona* palms to the dusty camping ground at **Mitchell River National Park** (entry per vehicle $12, camping adult/child $10/2.20; ☺dry season; P✿). The park contains the stunning, multi-tiered **Mitchell Falls** (Punamii-unpuu), which can be seen on a lovely three-hour re-turn walk passing inviting, shady water-holes and incredible Aboriginal rock art.

Tours runs trips to the remarkable Mimbi Caves, a vast subterranean labyrinth hous-ing Aboriginal rock art and impressive fish fossils. The tours include an introduction to local Dreaming stories, bush tucker and traditional medicines. Book through Fitzroy Crossing (p1010) or Halls Creek (p1010) vis-itor centres.

Luridgii Tours
DRIVING

(Junama; ☑0438 080 291; http://luridgiitours. com.au; Doon Doon; per vehicle $150; ☺Sat & Sun; ✿) Be personally guided through Mir-iuwung country by the traditional own-ers on these weekend 4WD tag-alongs (ie you follow the guide in your own vehicle). Gorges, thermal pools and Dreaming stories abound, and there's the option of camping overnight. BYO food. Tours depart from Doon Doon Roadhouse on the Great North-ern Highway.

Fitzroy Crossing

POP 1300

Gooniyandi, Bunuba, Walmajarri, Nyikina and Wangkajungka peoples populate the small settlement of Fitzroy Crossing where the Great Northern Highway crosses the mighty Fitzroy River. It's a good access point for the Devonian Reef National Parks and has some fine art galleries.

Mangkaja Arts GALLERY
(☑ 08-9191 5833; www.mangkaja.com; 8 Bell Rd; ☺ 11am-4pm Mon-Fri) This gallery is where desert and river tribes interact, producing unique acrylics, prints and baskets.

Marnin Studio ARTS CENTRE
(Marninwarntikura Women's Resource Centre; ☑ 08-9191 5284; www.mwrc.com.au; Lot 284, Balanijangarri Rd; ☺ 8.30am-4.30pm Mon-Fri) Marnin is the Walmajarri word for women, and this studio uses crafts such as boab-nut painting, textile printing and bush-nut jewellery-making to bind together the women of the various local language groups.

Crossing Inn CAMPGROUND $
(☑ 08-9191 5080; www.crossinginn.com.au; Skuthorpe Rd; unpowered/powered sites $32/39, r from $179; ❄ @) The oldest pub in the Kimberley also has tidy rooms with views (continental breakfast included) and a small camping area. A true outback beer experience.

Fitzroy River Lodge RESORT $$
(☑ 08-9191 5141; www.fitzroyriverlodge.com.au; Great Northern Hwy; camping per person $17, tent d $180, motel d $230, studios $340-460; P ❄ @ ☂ ☸) Across the river from town, with comfortable motel rooms, safari tents, exclusive Riverview studios and grassy camp sites. The friendly bar (mains $22-42; ☺ 12-2pm, 5-8.30pm) has decent counter meals.

Grungaja Shop CLOTHING
(☑ 08-9191 5316; 1 Emmanuel Way; ☺ 10am-4.30pm Mon-Fri) If rodeo clothing is your thing, Grungaja stocks everything you need to ride a bull. You won't find better hats or boots. Opening hours vary so call ahead.

For tours (including Mimbi Caves), accommodation and bus tickets, head to the **Visitor Centre** (☑ 08-9191 5355; www.sdwk.wa.gov.au; ☺ 8.30am-4.30pm Mon-Fri year-round, 9am-1pm Sat dry season). **Greyhound** (☑ 1300 473 946; www.greyhound.com.au) also stops here. They run to Broome ($92, five hours), Derby ($62, 2½ hours), Halls Creek ($78, three hours), Kununurra ($120, 7½ hours) and Darwin ($257, 20 hours) Monday to Saturday.

Skippers (www.skippers.com.au) flies to Broome and Halls Creek three times weekly.

Halls Creek

POP 1700

On the edge of the Great Sandy Desert, Halls Creek is a small town with communities of Kija, Jaru and Gooniyandi peoples. The excellent visitor centre can book tours to the Bungles and tickets for Mimbi Caves. Across the highway, **Yarliyil Gallery** (☑ 08-9168 6723; http://yarliyil.com.au; Great Northern Hwy; ☺ 8am-4pm Mon-Fri; P) is definitely worth a look. The town regularly suffers water shortages.

Sawpit Gorge GORGE
(Duncan Rd; P ❄ ☸) **FREE** Great bushwalking, swimming and camp sites await the traveller prepared to cross the rocky Albert Edward Range in this gorge 50km from Halls Creek.

Palm Springs OASIS
(Lugangarna; Duncan Rd; ❄ ☸) **FREE** Soak your weary, corrugations-bashed body in this beautiful, permanent pool on the Black Elvire River, 45km from Halls Creek. Free, 24-hour camping allowed.

Northwest Regional Airlines SCENIC FLIGHTS
(☑ 08-9168 5211; www.northwestregional.com.au; Halls Creek Airport; flights per person 2/3/4 passengers from $535/360/275) Scenic flights from Halls Creek over **Wolfe Creek Meteorite Crater** (Kandimalal; Tanami) **FREE** and the Bungle Bungles.

Kimberley Hotel HOTEL $$
(☑ 08-9168 6101; www.kimberleyhotel.com.au; Roberta Ave; r from $220; P ❄ ☂ ☸) Comfortable rooms are complemented by a lovely pool, shady terrace bar and a kitchen open for breakfast, lunch ($14 to $20, noon to 2pm) and dinner ($18 to $46, 5.30pm to 8.30pm).

Russian Jack's BISTRO $$$
(☑ 08-9168 9600; www.hallscreekmotel.com.au; Halls Creek Motel; mains $26-45; ☺ 5-8.30pm) Probably the best food in Halls Creek with miner-sized helpings of bistro tucker. It's at the **Halls Creek Motel** (☑ 08-9168 9600; www.hallscreekmotel.com.au; s/d $165/225; ❄ ☂ ☸).

ⓘ Information

Visitor Centre (☑ 08-9168 6262; www.hallscreektourism.com.au; Great Northern Hwy; ☺ 8am-4pm; ☂) Can book tours (including Mimbi Caves) and arrange art-gallery visits.

Greyhound leaves from the roadhouse. Buses go to Broome ($120, nine hours), Derby ($95, six hours) and Fitzroy Crossing ($80, three hours) Sunday to Friday, and Kununurra ($104,

four hours), Katherine ($198, 11 hours) and Darwin ($236, 16 hours) Tuesday to Sunday.
Skippers (☑1300 729 924; www.skippers.com.au) flies to Broome and Fitzroy Crossing.
Aviair (☑08-9166 9300; www.aviair.com.au) flies to Kununurra three times weekly.

Kununurra

POP 6000

Kununurra, on Miriwoong country, is a relaxed town set in lush farmland and tropical fruit and sandalwood plantations, thanks to the Ord River irrigation scheme. With good transport and communications, excellent services and well-stocked supermarkets, it's every traveller's favourite slice of civilisation between Broome and Darwin.

Kununurra is also the departure point for most of the tours in the East Kimberley, and with all that fruit, there's plenty of seasonal work. Note the Northern Territory is in the Australian Central time zone, 90 minutes ahead of Australian Western Standard Time.

☉ Sights

Waringarri Aboriginal Arts Centre   GALLERY
(☑08-9168 2212; www.waringarriarts.com.au; 16 Speargrass Rd; ☉8.30am-4.30pm Mon-Fri, 10am-2pm Sat dry season, weekdays only wet season; ℗) This excellent Kununurra gallery-studio hosts local artists working with ochres in a unique abstract style. It also represents artists from Kalumburu.

Kelly's Knob   VIEWPOINT
(Kelly Rd; ℗☼) **FREE** The best view in Kununurra is from this outcrop on the town's northern edge. Great for sunrise or sunset.

Lily Creek Lagoon   LAKE
Across the highway from the township, Lily Creek Lagoon is a mini-wetlands with amazing bird life, boating and freshwater crocs.

Kununurra Historical Society Museum   MUSEUM
(www.kununurra.org.au; Coolibah Dr; gold coin donation; ☉10am-3pm; ℗) Old photographs and newspaper articles document Kununurra's history, including the story of a wartime Wirraway aircraft crash and the subsequent recovery mission. The museum is opposite the country club exit.

Mirima National Park   NATIONAL PARK
(per car $12; ℗🚻) Like a mini–Bungle Bungles, the eroded gorges of Hidden Valley are home to brittle red peaks, spinifex, boab trees and abundant wildlife. Several walking trails lead to lookouts, and early morning or dusk are the best times for sighting fauna.

🏃 Activities

Helispirit   SCENIC FLIGHTS
(☑1800 180 085; www.helispirit.com.au; 18/30/42min flights ex Bellbird $269/379/499) The Kimberley's largest chopper outfit offers scenic flights over the Bungles from Bellbird (inside the park) and Warmun (45 minutes $399). It also arranges flights over Mitchell Falls, Kununurra, King George Falls, Lake Argyle and anywhere else in the Kimberley.

Yeehaa Trail Rides   HORSE RIDING
(☑0417 957 607; www.yeehaatrailrides.com; Boab Park; 1-/6½hr rides $70/220) Trail rides and tuition to suit all skill levels, 8km from Kununurra. The sunset ride to Elephant Rock ($120, 2½ hours) is the perfect introduction to the Kimberley.

Go Wild   ADVENTURE SPORTS
(☑1300 663 369; www.gowild.com.au; 3-day canoe trips $220) Self-guided multiday canoe trips from Lake Argyle along the Ord River, overnighting at riverside camp sites.

OFF THE BEATEN TRACK

THE DUNCAN ROAD

The first 50km from Halls Creek is usually the roughest as you cross the Albert Edward Range and Caroline Pool at 15km, Palm Springs at 45km and Sawpit Gorge at 50km have some nice campsites. Nicholson Station no longer grants permission to camp at Morella Gorge. At Nicholson (174km) turn north and follow the ridges behind Purnululu and Lake Argyle (271km) to the Victoria Hwy. Kununurra is another 56km.

The latest conditions can be checked online at www.hallscreek.wa.gov.au (WA) and www.ntlis.nt.gov.au/road report (NT).

The **Zebra Rock Mine** (Wetland Safaris; ☑0400 767 650; www.zebrarockmine.com.au; sites per adult $10; ☉Apr-Sep; 🐾) is the only formal accommodation on Duncan Rd. It's 10km from the Victoria Hwy, and is technically in the Northern Territory. Travellers love the rustic vibe, and the sunset birdwatching tour ($100) is not to be missed.

PERTH & WESTERN AUSTRALIA KUNUNURRA

THE KIMBERLEY'S ART SCENE

The Indigenous art of the Kimberley is unique. Encompassing powerful and strongly guarded Wandjina, prolific and enigmatic Gwion Gwion (Bradshaws), bright tropical coastal X-rays, subtle and sombre bush ochres and topographical dots of the western desert, every work sings a story about Country. To experience it firsthand, visit some of these Aboriginal-owned cooperatives; most are accessible by 2WD.

Mowanjum Art & Culture Centre (p1006) This incredible gallery, shaped like a Wandjina image, features work by Mowanjum artists. Just 4km along the Gibb River Road from Derby.

Waringarri Aboriginal Arts Centre (p1011) This excellent Kununurra gallery-studio hosts local artists working with ochres in a unique abstract style. It also represents artists from Kalumburu.

Warmun Arts (p1009) Between Kununurra and Halls Creek, Warmun artists create beautiful works using ochres to explore Gija identity.

Laarri Gallery (p1009) This tiny not-for-profit gallery located in the back of the Yiyili community school depicts local history through interesting contemporary-style art. It's 120km west of Halls Creek and 5km from the Great Northern Highway. Phone ahead.

Mangkaja Arts (p1010) Respected Fitzroy Crossing gallery where desert and river tribes interact, producing unique acrylics, prints and baskets.

Warlayirti Artists Centre (☑ 08-9168 8960; www.balgoart.org.au; Balgo; ⊙ 9am-4pm Mon-Fri) This Balgo centre, 255km down the Tanami Rd, is a conduit for artists around the area and features bright acrylic dot-style works as well as lithographs and glass works. Phone first, before leaving the highway.

Bidyadanga Community Art Centre (☑ 08-9192 4885; http://desertriversea.com.au/art-centres/bidyadanga-community-art-centre; Bidyadanga Rd, Bidyadanga; ⊙ 9am-1pm Mon-Thu) South of Broome, this intriguing centre brings together both desert and coastal influences in WA's largest remote community.

For more information, look up www.desertriversea.com.au and download the *Kimberley Aboriginal Art Trail* map, or find it in a visitor centre.

Canoes, camping equipment and transport are provided; BYO food and sleeping bag. It also runs caving, abseiling and bushwalking trips.

✦ Festivals & Events

Ord Valley Muster   CULTURAL
(☑ 08-9168 1177; www.ordvalleymuster.com.au; ⊙) For 10 days each May, Kununurra hits overdrive with a collection of sporting, charity and cultural events culminating in a large outdoor concert under the full moon on the banks of the Ord River.

⛏ Sleeping

★ Wunan House   B&B $
(☑ 08-9168 2436; www.wunanhouse.com; 167 Coolibah Dr; r from $125; P ⊛ ❋ 🞳) Indigenous-owned and -run, this immaculate B&B offers light, airy rooms, all with en suites and TVs. There's free wi-fi, off-street parking and an ample continental breakfast.

Hidden Valley Tourist Park   CARAVAN PARK $
(☑ 08-9168 1790; www.hiddenvalleytouristpark.com; 110 Weaber Plains Rd; unpowered/powered sites $30/40, cabin d $135; @ ❋ 🞳) Under the crags of Mirima National Park, this excellent little spot has nice grassy sites and is popular with seasonal workers and roadtrippers. The self-contained cabins are good value.

Freshwater   APARTMENT $$
(☑ 08-9169 2010; www.freshwaterapartments.net.au; 19 Victoria Hwy; studios $224, 1-/2-/3-bedroom apt $255/339/399; P ❋ ❋ 🞳) Exquisite units with exotic open-roofed showers.

Kimberley Croc Motel   MOTEL $$
(☑ 08-9168 1411; www.kimberleycrocmotel.com.au; 2 River Fig Ave; budget/standard/deluxe d from $119/149/179; P ❋ ❋ 🞳) The old Croc lodge has reinvented itself as a sleek motel, offering a variety of newly renovated budget (basically four-bed dorms), standard and deluxe rooms, all with en suites and kitchenettes. Add on

the central location, mandatory pool, guests' kitchen and free wi-fi and you have a winner.

Lakeview Apartments APARTMENT $$

(☑08-9168 0000; www.lakeviewapartments.net; 31 Victoria Hwy; 1-/2-/3-bedroom apt $230/ 280/380; P⊖❄🛜🏊) These spacious, self-contained apartments across from Lily Creek Lagoon (p1011) have all the mod cons, fully equipped kitchens, free wi-fi and cable TV. There's a weekend minimum two-night stay.

✗ Eating & Drinking

Like other Kimberley and Top End towns, there are restrictions on where and when you can buy and consume takeaway alcohol. Kununurra and Wyndham have been trialling a Takeaway Alcohol Management System (TAMS), so if you're stocking up for the Gibb River Road, check the rules first.

★ Wild Mango CAFE $$

(☑08-9169 2810; www.wildmangocafe.com.au; 20 Messmate Way; breakfast $9-23, lunch $15-19; ⊙7am-4pm Mon-Fri, to 1pm Sat & Sun; P❄🍴) 🍃 The hippest, healthiest feed in town with breakfast burritos, succulent salads, mouth-watering pancakes, chai smoothies, real coffee and homemade gelato. The entrance is on Konkerberry Dr.

Ivanhoe Cafe CAFE $$

(☑0427 692 775; www.facebook.com/ivanhoe-cafe-549293358437140; Ivanhoe Rd; breakfast $9-23, lunch $11-22; ⊙8am-2pm Wed-Mon Apr-Sep; P🍴) Grab a table under the leafy mango trees and tuck into tasty wraps, salads and burgers, all made from fresh, local produce. Don't miss the signature mango smoothie.

★ PumpHouse MODERN AUSTRALIAN $$$

(☑08-9169 3222; www.thepumphouserestaurant. com; Lakeview Dr; mains lunch $18-27, dinner $32-42; ⊙4.30pm-late Tue-Fri, 8am-late Sat & Sun; P) Idyllically situated on Lake Kununurra (Diversion Dam; P🍴), the PumpHouse creates succulent dishes featuring quality local ingredients. Watch the catfish swarm should a morsel slip off the verandah, or just have a beer and watch the sunset.

🛍 Shopping

Bush Camp Surplus SPORTS & OUTDOORS

(☑08-9168 1476; www.facebook.com/bushcamp surplus; cnr Papuana St & Konkerberry Dr; ⊙8.30am-5pm Mon-Fri, to noon Sat) The biggest range of camping gear between Broome and Darwin.

Artlandish ART

(☑08-9168 1881; www.artlandish.com; cnr Papuana St & Konkerberry Dr; ⊙9am-4pm Mon-Fri, to 1pm Sat) Stunning collection of Kimberley ochres and Western Desert acrylics for all price ranges.

ℹ Information

Visitor Centre (☑1800 586 868; www.visit kununurra.com; Coolibah Dr; ⊙8.30am-4.30pm Apr-Sep, shorter hours Oct-Mar) Can help find accommodation, tours and seasonal work.

Parks & Wildlife Office (DPAW; ☑08-9168 4200; www.dpaw.wa.gov.au; Lot 248, Ivanhoe Rd; ⊙8am-4.30pm Mon-Fri) For park permits and publications.

ℹ Getting There & Away

Airnorth (TL; ☑1800 627 474; www.airnorth. com.au) flies to Broome and Darwin daily, and to Perth on Saturdays. **Virgin Australia** (VA; ☑13 67 89; www.virginaustralia.com.au) has four flights a week to Perth.

Greyhound (☑1300 473 946; www.greyhound. com.au) buses stop at the **BP Roadhouse** (☑08-9169 1188; 5 Messmate Way; ⊙24hr) and leave Sunday to Friday for Broome ($165, 13 hours) via Halls Creek ($104, four hours), Fitzroy Crossing ($121, 8½ hours) and Derby ($141, 10 hours). Buses for Darwin ($145, 12½ hours) via Katherine ($108, 7½ hours) leave Tuesday to Sunday.

Avis (☑08-9168 1999), **Budget** (☑08-9168 2033) and **Thrifty** (☑1800 626 515) all have offices at the airport. **Ordco** (Weaber Plains Rd; ⊙24hr) is a local co-op selling the cheapest diesel in Kununurra.

Purnululu National Park & Bungle Bungle Range

The bizarre, ancient, eroded sandstone domes of the Unesco World Heritage **Purnululu National Park** (per car $12; ⊙Apr-Nov; P🚶) will take your breath away. Known colloquially as the **Bungle Bungles**, these distinctive rounded rock towers are made of sandstone and conglomerates moulded by rainfall over millions of years. They are recognised as the finest example of cone karst sandstone in the world.

Their stripes are the result of oxidised iron compounds and algae. To the local Kidja people, *purnululu* means sandstone, with Bungle Bungle possibly a corruption of 'bundle bundle', a common grass.

Purnululu National Park

The park abounds with fauna and flora and several easy walks lead out of the baking sun into shady, palm-lined gorges. Sunsets here are sublime. Facilities in the park are refreshingly minimal and visitors must be totally self-sufficient. Temperatures can be extreme. Rangers are in attendance during the high season when the small visitor centre opens. There are two large, basic bush camping grounds at either end of the park.

Access is by a rough, unsealed, flood-prone 4WD-only track from the Great Northern Highway north of Halls Creek, or by air on a package tour from Kununurra or Warmun.

◉ Sights & Activities

Kungkalanayi Lookout   VIEWPOINT
(P ♿) Sunsets and sunrises are spectacular from this hill near Three Ways.

Piccaninny Gorge   GORGE
A 30km return trek (two to three days) from the southern car park to a remote and pristine gorge best suited for experienced hikers. There are plenty of opportunities for further exploration in the upper gorge. Take plenty of water, and go early in the season. You must register at the visitor centre first.

Echidna Chasm   GORGE
(P ♿) Look for tiny bats high on the walls above this palm-fringed, extremely narrow gorge in the northern park. The entrance is fringed by *Livistona* palms. Allow one hour for the 2km return walk.

Cathedral Gorge   GORGE
(P ♿) Aptly named, this immense and inspiring circular cavern is an easy 2km (return) stroll from the southern car park.

Bungle Bungle Guided Tours   WALKING
(☑ 1800 899 029; www.bunglebungleguidedtours.com.au; Bellburn Airstrip, Purnululu) Indigenous-run half-day walking tours to Cathedral Gorge and Echidna Chasm and a full-day helicopter ride/hike ($799) to Piccaninny Gorge. Tours depart from the park airstrip at Bellburn, and can be linked up with scenic flights from Kununurra, Warmun and Halls Creek.

⌂ Sleeping

Kurrajong Campsite   CAMPGROUND $
(sites per person $12; ⊙ Apr-Nov; P) In the northern end of Purnululu National Park, there are dusty camp sites with water, toilets and the odd picnic table, and thankfully no generators.

Walardi Campsite   CAMPGROUND $
(sites per person $12; ⊙ Apr-Nov; P) Fresh water, toilets and some generator-free areas in the southern park.

ℹ Information

Visitor Centre (☑ 08-9168 7300; ⊙ 8am-noon & 1-4pm Apr-Sep) Pay for your permit and grab a map. If closed, use the honesty envelopes.

ℹ Getting There & Away

If you haven't got a high-clearance 4WD, consider taking a tour instead. You can fly in from Kununurra, Warmun and Halls Creek.

Understand Australia

Australia Today

Australia seems caught between the populist disaffection sweeping Western countries and the innate optimism of its people – which will win? In the meantime, those touchstones and preoccupations of modern Australian life – the relationship between Indigenous and non-Indigenous Australians, the economy, the future of multicultural Australia – all still hold centre stage. If only the country's politicians could get their act together...

Best on Film

Crocodile Dundee (1986) Outback Australia hits the cinematic jackpot and Kakadu becomes famous.

Gallipoli (1981) Nationhood formed in the harsh crucible of WWI.

Mad Max (1979) Mel Gibson gets angry and creates an Aussie legend.

The Hunter (2011) Willem Dafoe goes hunting for the last Tasmanian Tiger.

Another Country (2015) Renowned actor David Gulpilil takes you on an arresting visit to his remote Arnhem Land community.

Best in Print

The Narrow Road to the Deep North (Richard Flanagan; 2014) From Hobart to the Thai-Burma Death Railway.

Dirt Music (Tim Winton; 2002) Guitar-strung Western Australian page-turner.

True History of the Kelly Gang (Peter Carey; 2000) Fictionalised re-creation of Australia's favourite bushranger.

The Secret River (Kate Grenville; 2005) A novel about 19th-century convict life around Sydney.

The Red Highway (Nicolas Rothwell; 2009) A lyrical exploration of Australia's interior.

Indigenous Australians

Australia's treatment of Indigenous Australians has come a long way since the days of *terra nullius* – the legal fiction that declared Australia devoid of human settlement and which the British empire used to prop up its colonisation – and needing a referendum to grant the most basic citizenship rights to its first inhabitants. Indigenous owners now own roughly half of the Northern Territory's land, for example, and many Aboriginal communities have negotiated lucrative royalty deals with mining companies working on traditional lands. But many Aboriginal communities remain in crisis – poorly governed and beset with problems of alcohol, petrol-sniffing, high crime levels and the concomitant high levels of incarceration. But the correct balance between self-determination and government intervention is one that no one in Australian policy circles has ever quite worked out.

In the meantime, there have been moves towards greater legal recognition: in 2017 both Victoria and South Australia began formal treaty negotiations with local Indigenous communities, and there appears to be bipartisan support for a formal referendum seeking constitutional recognition of Indigenous Australians as Australia's first people. But with Indigenous Australians suffering disproportionately when compared to non-Indigenous Australians – from life expectancy and key health indicators to unemployment and economic disadvantage – there remains a long way to go.

The Rise of Populism?

With the world still reeling from the rise of the UK's Brexit referendum and the election of US President Donald Trump, many Australians are wondering what their political future holds. While there appear to be no obviously Trump-like candidates with nationwide appeal ready and able to take up the mantle of populist anger, there are signs that disaffection with mainstream politics is growing. Independents are an increasingly powerful force in Australian politics. One Nation leader Pauline Hanson has returned to the fore, calling for a cap on immigration from Muslim countries and even a Royal Commission into Islam. Other names advocating a similar line include Tasmanian independent senator Jacqui Lambie and South Australian senator Cory Bernardi, who in early 2017 left the Liberal Party to form his own party, the Australian Conservatives. In the absence of an economic downturn, such views remain on the fringe (albeit with a vocal presence in parliament), but are increasingly a feature of the national conversation.

Revolving-Door Politics

After decades of stable governments and democratic transitions of power, the two major parties – the centre-left Australian Labor Party (ALP) and the centre-right Coalition of the Liberal and National Parties – have resorted to infighting and the politics of the revolving door. In 2010, Labor deputy Julia Gillard overthrew the sitting prime minister, Kevin Rudd, and the Labor Government never quite recovered; Rudd even returned the favour, unseating Gillard in 2013, only to remain in power for just three months. After the Coalition won power in elections later that year, they clearly hadn't learned from their opposition's mistake: in 2015, Malcolm Turnbull pulled a Gillard and unseated Prime Minister Tony Abbott.

Like Gillard, Turnbull barely survived the next election; at the time of writing, his government relies on the flimsiest majority to rule and appears to be fatally wounded. In the meantime, important issues such as economic reform, constitutional recognition for Indigenous Australians, same-sex marriage equality and the question of whether Australia should become a republic remain on the back burner for a government paralysed by fighting within its own ranks.

Economy & Environment

Australia's economy weathered the GFC with barely a blip, and the country continues to enjoy low unemployment, low inflation and generally high wages – though the cost of living has soared to levels that threaten to leave behind a generation of would-be home-owners and the great mining boom is definitely over. But for now at least, the economy is forging onwards and upwards.

Economists have, however, warned that storm clouds could be gathering unless governments undertake meaningful economic reform, while environmentalists worry that the government will continue to keep environmental protection as a low priority, with new coal mines in Queensland, policies that arguably pose serious threats to the Great Barrier Reef and the dismantling of the country's carbon tax.

POPULATION: **24,127,200**

AREA: **7,692,024 SQ KM**

GDP: **US$1.257 TRILLION**

GDP GROWTH: **2.9%**

INFLATION: **1.4%**

UNEMPLOYMENT: **5.8%**

if Australia were 100 people

79 would speak English at home
3 would speak Chinese at home
2 would speak Italian at home
1 would speak Vietnamese at home
1 would speak Greek at home
14 would speak another language at home

belief systems
(% of population)

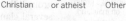

61 — Christian
23 — Agnostic or atheist
11 — Other

2 — Buddhist
2 — Muslim
1 — Hindu

population per sq km

AUS   NZ   USA

🚶 ≈ 3 people

History

The story of Australia is an epic where the New World meets the Old in a clash of two very different versions of history. It's only in recent years that the story of Indigenous Australians – here for more than 50,000 years before British colonisation – has come to occupy its rightful place at centre stage. It is a further sign, perhaps, that this dynamic, sometimes progressive and laid-back country is really starting to grow up.

First Australians

Human contact with Australia is thought by many to have begun around 60,000 years ago, when Aboriginal people journeyed across the straits from what is now Indonesia and Papua New Guinea. Aboriginal people, however, believe they have always inhabited the land. Undoubtedly, Indigenous life in Australia marked the beginning of the world's longest continuous cultural history.

Across the continent, Aboriginal peoples traded goods, items of spiritual significance, songs and dances, using routes that followed the paths of ancestors from the Dreaming, the complex system of country, culture and beliefs that defines Indigenous spirituality. An intimate understanding of plant ecology and animal behaviour ensured that food shortages were rare. Even central Australia's hostile deserts were occupied year-round, thanks to scattered permanent wells. Fire-stick farming was practised in forested areas, involving the burning of undergrowth and dead grass to encourage new growth, to attract game and reduce the threat of bushfires.

At the time of European contact the Aboriginal population was grouped into 300 or more different nations, with distinct languages and land boundaries. Most people did not have permanent shelters but moved within their territory and followed patterns of animal migration and plant availability. The diversity of landscapes in Australia meant that each nation varied in their lifestyles; although they were distinct cultural groups, there were also many common elements, and each nation had several clans or family groups who were responsible for looking after specific areas. For thousands of years Aboriginal people lived within a

In remote parts of Australia, and in centres like Alice Springs and Darwin, many Indigenous Australians still speak their traditional languages rather than English. Many people are multilingual – there were once over 300 Aboriginal language groups on mainland Australia.

TIMELINE	80 million years ago	50,000 years ago	1606
	After separating from the prehistoric Gondwana landmass about 120 million years ago, Australia breaks free from Antarctica and heads north.	The earliest record of Indigeneous Australians inhabiting the land. The country is home to lush forests, teeming lakes and giant marsupials – including a wombat the size of a rhinoceros.	Dutch seaman Willem Janszoon 'discovers' Cape York on a foray from the Dutch East Indies, although he mistakes it for part of New Guinea.

complex kinship system that tied them to the natural environment. From the desert to the sea Aboriginal people shaped their lives according to their environments and developed skills and a wide body of knowledge on their territory.

Intruders Arrive

In April 1770, Aboriginal people standing on a beach in southeastern Australia saw an astonishing spectacle out at sea. It was an English ship, the *Endeavour*, under the command of then-Lieutenant James Cook. His gentleman passengers were English scientists visiting the Pacific to make astronomical observations and to investigate 'new worlds'. As they sailed north along the edge of this new-found land, Cook began drawing the first British chart of Australia's east coast. This map heralded the beginning of conflicts between European settlers and Indigenous peoples.

A few days after that first sighting, Cook led a party of men onto a narrow beach. As they waded ashore, two Aboriginal men stepped onto the sand and challenged the intruders with spears. Cook drove the men off with musket fire. For the rest of that week, the Aboriginal people and the intruders watched each other warily.

Cook's ship *Endeavour* was a floating annexe of London's leading scientific organisation, the Royal Society. The ship's gentlemen passengers included technical artists, scientists, an astronomer and a wealthy botanist named Joseph Banks. As Banks and his colleagues strode about the Indigenous Australians' territory, they were delighted by the mass of new plants they collected. (The showy flowers called banksia – which look like red, white or golden bottlebrushes – are named after Banks.) The local Aboriginal people called the place Kurnell, but Cook gave it a foreign name: he called it 'Botany Bay'.

When the *Endeavour* reached the northern tip of Cape York, blue ocean opened up to the west. Cook and his men could smell the sea-route home. And on a small, hilly island ('Possession Island'), Cook raised the Union Jack. Amid volleys of gunfire, he claimed the eastern half of the continent for King George III.

Cook's intention was not to steal land from the Indigenous Australians. In fact he rather idealised them. 'They are far more happier than we Europeans,' he wrote. 'They think themselves provided with all the necessaries of Life and that they have no superfluities.' His patriotic ceremony was intended to contain the territorial ambitions of the French, and of the Dutch, who had visited and mapped much of the western and southern coast over the previous two centuries. Indeed, Cook knew the western half of Australia as 'New Holland'.

For an insight into the early days of British settlement and interaction with Aboriginal Australians, check the notebooks of William Dawes, officer of the First Fleet from 1787–88. These diaries – which are accessible online at www. williamdawes. org – contain the first recorded words and phrases of an Aboriginal language and relate aspects of traditional life, which he learned under the tutelage of a young Aboriginal woman named Patyegarang.

1616	1770	1788	1789
The Dutch trading route across the Indian Ocean to Indonesia utilises winds called 'the Roaring Forties'. These winds bring Dutch Captain Dirk Hartog to the Western Australian coast.	Captain James Cook is the first European to map Australia's east coast, which he names New South Wales. He returns to England having found an ideal place for settlement at Botany Bay.	The First Fleet brings British convicts and officials to the lands of the Eora people, where Governor Arthur Phillip establishes a penal settlement, which he calls Sydney.	An epidemic of smallpox devastates Indigenous peoples – who have no immunological resistance to it – around Sydney.

Convict Beginnings

In 1788, 18 years after Cook's arrival, the English were back to stay. They arrived in a fleet of 11 ships, packed with supplies including weapons, tools, building materials and livestock. The ships also contained 751 convicts and around 250 soldiers, officials and their wives. This motley 'First Fleet' was under the command of a humane and diligent naval captain, Arthur Phillip. As his orders dictated, Phillip dropped anchor at Botany Bay. But the paradise that had so delighted Joseph Banks filled Phillip with dismay. The country was marshy, there was little healthy water, and the anchorage was exposed to wind and storm. Just a short way up the coast his heart leapt as he sailed into the finest harbour in the world. There, in a small cove, in the idyllic lands of the Eora people, he established a British penal settlement on 26 January 1788. He renamed the place after the British Home Secretary, Lord Sydney.

The intruders set about clearing the trees and building shelters and were soon trying to grow crops. Phillip's official instructions urged him to colonise the land without doing violence to the local inhabitants, but the loss of their lands and water resources, and an epidemic of diseases, had a devastating effect. Smallpox killed around half of the Indigenous people who were native to Sydney Harbour.

A period of resistance occurred as Aboriginal people fought back to retain their land and way of life; as violence and massacres swept the country, many were pushed away from their traditional lands. Over a century, the Aboriginal population would be decimated by 90%.

In 1803 English officers established a second convict settlement in Van Diemen's Land (later called Tasmania). Soon, re-offenders filled the grim prison at Port Arthur, on the beautiful and wild southern coast near Hobart. In time, others would endure the senseless agonies of Norfolk Island prison in the remote Pacific Ocean.

So miserable were these convict beginnings that Australians long regarded them as a period of shame. But things have changed: today most white Australians are inclined to brag a little if they find a convict in their family tree. And there is a growing push among both Indigenous and non-Indigenous Australians to move the Australia Day holiday – celebrated on 26 January since 1994 – to a different day in recognition of the fact that this fateful date has long been referred to by many Indigenous Australians as 'Invasion Day'.

From Shackles to Freedom

At first, Sydney and Port Arthur depended on supplies brought in by ship. Anxious to develop productive farms, the government granted land to soldiers, officers and settlers. After 30 years of trial and error, the farms began

1804	1820s	1829	1835
In Van Diemen's Land (today Tasmania), David Collins moves the fledgling convict colony from Risdon Cove to the site of modern Hobart.	Indigeneous Australians and European settlers in Van Diemen's Land clash in the Black Wars. The bloody conflict devastates the Aboriginal population – few survive.	Captain James Stirling heads a private company that founds the settlement of Perth on Australia's west coast. The surrounding land is arid, slowing the development of the colony.	John Batman sails from Van Diemen's Land to Port Phillip and negotiates a land deal with elders of the Kulin Nation. The settlement of Melbourne is founded later that year.

BENNELONG

Among the Indigenous Australians Governor Philip used as intermediaries was an influential Eora man named Bennelong, who adopted many white customs and manners. After his initial capture, Bennelong learnt to speak and write English and became an interlocutor between his people and the British, both in Australia and on a trip to the United Kingdom in 1792. His 1796 letter to Mr and Mrs Philips is the first known text in English by an Indigenous Australian.

For many years after his return to Sydney, Bennelong lived in a hut built for him on the finger of land now known as Bennelong Point, the site of the Sydney Opera House. He led a clan of 100 people and advised then Governor Hunter. Although accounts suggest he was courageous, intelligent, feisty, funny and 'tender with children', in his later years Bennelong's health and temper were affected by alcohol. He died in 1813 and was buried in the orchard of his friend, brewer James Squire.

to flourish. The most irascible and ruthless of these new landholders was John Macarthur. Along with his spirited wife Elizabeth, Macarthur pioneered the breeding of merino sheep on his verdant property near Sydney.

Macarthur was also a leading member of the 'Rum Corps', a clique of powerful officers who bullied successive governors (including William Bligh of *Bounty* fame) and grew rich by controlling much of Sydney's trade, notably rum. But the Corps' racketeering was ended in 1810 by a tough new governor named Lachlan Macquarie. Macquarie laid out the major roads of modern-day Sydney, built some fine public buildings (many of which were designed by talented convict-architect Francis Greenway) and helped to lay the foundations for a more civil society.

By now, word was reaching England that Australia offered cheap land and plenty of work, and adventurous migrants took to the oceans in search of their fortunes. At the same time the British government continued to transport prisoners.

In 1825 a party of soldiers and convicts established a penal settlement in the territory of the Yuggera people, close to modern-day Brisbane. Before long this warm, fertile region was attracting free settlers, who were soon busy farming, grazing, logging and mining.

Two New Settlements: Melbourne & Adelaide

In the cooler grasslands of Tasmania, the sheep farmers were also thriving. In the 1820s they waged a bloody war against the island's Aboriginal people, driving them to the brink of extinction. Now these settlers were hungry for more land. In 1835 an ambitious young man named John

The website www.portarthur.org.au is a vital guide to Tasmania's World Heritage–listed Port Arthur Historic Site, whose grim history spans from 1830s convicts life to the tragic 1996 mass shooting that took place there.

1836	1851	1854	1861
Colonel William Light chooses the site for Adelaide on the banks of the River Torrens in the lands of the Kaurna people. Unlike Sydney and Hobart, settlers here are free and willing immigrants.	Prospectors find gold in central Victoria, triggering a great rush of youthful prospectors from across the world. At the same time, the eastern colonies exchange the governor's rule for democracy.	Angered by the hefty cost of licences, gold miners stage a protest at the Eureka Stockade near Ballarat. Several rebels are killed; others are charged with treason. Public opinion supports the rebels.	The explorers Burke and Wills become the first Europeans to cross the continent from south to north. Their expedition is an expensive debacle that claims several lives, including their own.

Batman sailed to Port Phillip Bay on the mainland. On the banks of the Yarra River, he chose the location for Melbourne, famously announcing 'This is the place for a village.' Batman persuaded local Indigenous Australians to 'sell' him their traditional lands (a whopping 250,000 hectares) for a crate of blankets, knives and knick-knacks, although some historians question whether the Indigenous parties to the treaty understood that they were signing away their ancestral lands.

At the same time, a private British company settled Adelaide in South Australia (SA). Proud to have no links with convicts, these God-fearing folks instituted a scheme under which their company sold land to well-heeled settlers and used the revenue to assist poor British labourers to emigrate. When these worthies earned enough to buy land from the company, that revenue would in turn pay the fare of another shipload of labourers. This charming theory collapsed in a welter of land speculation and bankruptcy, and in 1842 the South Australian Company yielded to government administration. By then miners had found rich deposits of silver, lead and copper at Burra, Kapunda and the Mt Lofty Ranges, and the settlement began to pay its way.

The Search for Land Continues

Each year, settlers pushed deeper into Aboriginal territories in search of pasture and water for their stock. These men became known as squatters – because they 'squatted' on Aboriginal lands – and many held this territory with a gun. To bring order and regulation to the frontier, from the 1830s the governments permitted the squatters to stay on these 'Crown lands' for payment of a nominal rent. Aboriginal stories tell of white men slaughtering groups of Indigenous Australians in reprisal for the killing of sheep or settlers. Later, across the country, people would also tell stories of black resistance leaders, including Yagan of Swan River, Pemulwuy of Sydney, and Jandamarra, the outlaw-hero of the Kimberley.

By the late 1800s most of the fertile land had been taken and most Indigenous Australians were living in poverty on the fringes of settlements or on land unsuitable for settlement. Aboriginal people had to adapt to the new culture, but had few to no rights. Employment opportunities were scarce and most worked as low-paid (or unpaid) labourers or domestic staff in order to remain on their traditional lands. This arrangement would continue in outback pastoral regions until after WWII.

The newcomers had fantasised about the wonders waiting to be discovered from the moment they arrived. Before explorers crossed the Blue Mountains west of Sydney in 1813, some credulous souls imagined that China lay on the other side. Then explorers, surveyors and scientists began trading theories about inland Australia. Most spoke of an

The tragic story of the ill-fated 1860s expedition of explorers Robert O'Hara Burke and William John Wills is well told in *The Dig Tree* (2010) by Sarah Murgatroyd. *The Aboriginal Story of Burke and Wills: Forgotten Narratives* (2016), by Dr Ian Clark and Fred Cahir, is a fascinating take on the subject. Burke & Wills Web (www.burkeand wills.net.au) is an accessible digital research archive of the expedition's records.

1880	1901	1915	1928
Police capture the notorious bushranger Ned Kelly at the Victorian town of Glenrowan. Kelly is hanged as a criminal – and remembered by the people as a folk hero.	The Australian colonies form a federation of states. The federal parliament sits in Melbourne, where it passes the *Immigration Restriction Act* – aka the 'White Australia policy'.	On 25 April the Australian and New Zealand Army Corps (the Anzacs) joins an ambitious British attempt to invade Turkey. The ensuing military disaster at Gallipoli spawns a nationalist legend.	Anthony Martin Fernando, the first Aboriginal activist to campaign internationally against racial discrimination in Australia, is arrested for protesting outside Australia House in London.

Australian Mississippi. Others predicted desert. An obsessive explorer named Charles Sturt (there's a fine statue of him looking lost in Adelaide's Victoria Sq) believed in an almost mystical inland sea.

The explorers' expeditions inland were mostly journeys into disappointment. But Australians made heroes of explorers who died in the wilderness (Ludwig Leichhardt, and the duo of Burke and Wills, are the most striking examples). It was as though the Victorian era believed that a nation could not be born until its men had shed their blood in battle – even if that battle was with the land itself.

Gold & Rebellion

Transportation of convicts to eastern Australia ceased in the 1840s. Soon after, in 1851, prospectors discovered gold in New South Wales (NSW) and central Victoria. The news hit the colonies with the force of a cyclone. Young men and some adventurous women from every social class headed for the diggings. Soon they were caught up in a great rush of prospectors, entertainers, publicans, 'sly-groggers' (illicit liquor-sellers), prostitutes and quacks from overseas.

In Victoria, the British governor was alarmed – both by the way the Victorian class system had been thrown into disarray, and by the need to finance law and order on the goldfields. His solution was to compel all miners to buy an expensive monthly licence, partly in the hope that the lower orders would be unable to afford it and return to their duties in town. But the lure of gold was too great. In the reckless excitement of the goldfields, the miners initially endured the thuggish troopers who enforced the government licence. After three years, however, the easy gold at Ballarat was gone, and miners were toiling in deep, water-sodden shafts. They were now infuriated by a corrupt and brutal system of law that held them in contempt. Under the leadership of a charismatic Irishman named Peter Lalor, they raised their own flag, the Southern Cross (which depicts a constellation of stars seen in the Australian night sky), and swore to defend their rights and liberties. They armed themselves and gathered inside a rough stockade at nearby Eureka, where they waited for the government to make its move.

In the pre-dawn of Sunday 3 December 1854, British troops attacked the stockade. It was all over in 15 terrifying minutes. The brutal and one-sided battle claimed the lives of 30 miners and five soldiers. But democracy was in the air and public opinion sided with the civilians. When 13 of the surviving rebels were tried for their lives, Melbourne juries set them free. Many Australians have found a kind of splendour in these events: the story of the Eureka Stockade is often told as a battle for nationhood and democracy – again illustrating the notion that any 'true' nation must be born out of blood. But these killings were tragically unnecessary. The

David Unaipon (Ngarrindjeri; 1872–1967), the 'Australian Leonardo da Vinci', is remembered as an advocate for Indigenous culture, a writer and an inventor. He took out 19 provisional patents, including drawings for a pre-WWI, boomerang-inspired helicopter. His portrait is on the Australian $50 note.

HISTORY GOLD & REBELLION

Two very different, intelligent introductions to Australian history: Stuart Macintyre's *A Concise History of Australia* (1999) and Geoffrey Blainey's *A Shorter History of Australia* (1994).

eastern colonies were already in the process of establishing democratic parliaments, with the full support of the British authorities. In the 1880s Peter Lalor himself became speaker of the Victorian parliament.

The gold rush had also attracted boatloads of prospectors from China. These Asian settlers sometimes endured serious hostility from whites, and were the victims of ugly race riots on the goldfields at Lambing Flat (now called Young) in NSW in 1860–1. Chinese precincts soon developed in the backstreets of Sydney and Melbourne, and popular literature indulged in tales of Chinese opium dens, dingy gambling parlours and brothels. But many Chinese went on to establish themselves in business and, particularly, market gardening. Today the busy Chinatowns of the capital cities and the presence of Chinese restaurants in towns across the country are reminders of the vigorous role of the Chinese in Australia since the 1850s.

Gold and wool brought immense investment and gusto to Melbourne and Sydney. By the 1880s they were stylish modern cities, with gaslights in the streets, railways, electricity and that great new invention: the telegraph. In fact, the southern capital became known as 'Marvellous Melbourne', so opulent were its theatres, hotels, galleries and fashions. But the economy was overheating. Many politicians and speculators were engaged in corrupt land deals, while investors poured money into wild and fanciful ventures. It could not last.

Meanwhile, in the West...

Western Australia (WA) lagged behind the eastern colonies by about 50 years. Though Perth was settled by genteel colonists back in 1829, their material progress was handicapped by isolation, resistance by Indigenous peoples and the arid climate. It was not until the 1880s that the discovery of remote goldfields promised to gild the fortunes of the isolated colony.

At the time, the west was just entering its own period of self-government, and its first premier was a forceful, weather-beaten explorer named John Forrest. He saw that the mining industry would fail if the government did not provide a first-class harbour, efficient railways and reliable water supplies. Ignoring the threats of private contractors, he appointed the brilliant engineer CY O'Connor to design and build each of these as government projects.

Growing Nationalism

By the end of the 19th century, Australian nationalists tended to idealise 'the bush' and its people. The great forum for this 'bush nationalism' was the massively popular *Bulletin* magazine: its politics were egalitarian, democratic and republican, and its pages were filled with humour and

1939	1941	1945	1948
Prime Minister Robert Menzies announces that Britain has gone to war with Hitler's Germany and that 'as a result, Australia is also at war'.	The Japanese attack Pearl Harbor and sweep through Southeast Asia. Australia discovers that it has been abandoned by traditional ally Britain. Instead, it welcomes US forces, based in Australia.	WWII ends. Australia adopts a new slogan, 'Populate or Perish'. Over the next 30 years more than two million immigrants arrive. One-third are British.	Cricketer Don Bradman retires with an unsurpassed test average of 99.94 runs. South African batsman Graeme Pollock is next in line, having retired in 1970 with a relatively paltry average of 60.97.

sentiment about daily life written by a swag of writers, most notably Henry Lawson and AB 'Banjo' Paterson.

The 1890s were also a time of great trauma. As the speculative boom came crashing down, unemployment and hunger dealt cruelly with working-class families in the eastern colonies. However, Australian workers had developed a fierce sense that they were entitled to share in the country's prosperity. As the depression deepened, trade unions became more militant in their defence of workers' rights. At the same time, activists intent on winning legal reform established the Australian Labor Party (ALP).

Nationhood

On 1 January 1901 the six colonies of Australia became a federation of self-governing states – the Commonwealth of Australia. When the be-whiskered members of the new national parliament met in Melbourne, their first aim was to protect the identity and values of a European Australia from an influx of Asians and Pacific Islanders. Their solution was a law that became known as the White Australia policy, which would act as a racial tenet of faith in Australia for the next 70 years.

For whites who lived inside the charmed circle of citizenship, this was to be a model society, nestled in the skirts of the British Empire. Just one year later, white women won the right to vote in federal elections (South Australia had led the world by allowing women to vote in 1895). In a series of radical innovations, the government introduced a broad social-welfare scheme and protected Australian wage levels with import tariffs. Its radical mixture of capitalist dynamism and socialist compassion became known as the 'Australian settlement'.

Meanwhile, most Australians continued to live on the coasts of the continent. So forbidding was the arid, desolate inland that the great dry Lake Eyre was given a grim nickname: 'the Dead Heart' of the country. But one prime minister in particular, the dapper Alfred Deakin, dismissed such talk – he and his supporters were determined to triumph over this tyranny of the climate. Even before Federation, in the 1880s, Deakin championed irrigated farming on the Murray River at Mildura. Soon the district was green with grapevines and orchards.

Entering the World Stage

Living on the edge of a dry and forbidding land and isolated from the rest of the world, most Australians took comfort in the knowledge that they were a dominion of the British Empire. When WWI broke out in Europe in 1914, thousands of Australian men rallied to the Empire's call. They had their first taste of death on 25 April 1915, when the Australian and New Zealand Army Corps (the Anzacs) joined thousands of other

Australia's first female prime minister – Labor's Julia Gillard – held the position from 2010 to 2013. In 1895, her home state of South Australia was the first colony to give women the right to run for parliament.

The most accessible version of the Anzac legend is Peter Weir's Australian epic film *Gallipoli* (1981), with a cast that includes a fresh-faced young Mel Gibson.

1956	1965	1967	1971
The Olympic Games are held in Melbourne. The Olympic flame is lit by running champion Ron Clarke, and Australia finishes third on the medal tally with an impressive 13 golds.	Prime Minister Menzies commits Australian troops to the American war in Vietnam, dividing national opinion. A total of 426 Australians were killed in action, with a further 2940 wounded.	White Australians vote to grant citizenship to Indigenous Australians. The words 'other than the Aboriginal race in any State' are removed from citizenship qualifications in the Australian Constitution.	The Aboriginal flag first flies on National Aborigines Day in Adelaide. Designed by Central Australian man Harold Thomas, the flag has become a unifying symbol of identity for Aboriginal people.

THE STOLEN GENERATIONS

When Australia became a Federation in 1901, a government policy known as the 'White Australia policy' was put in place. It was implemented mainly to restrict non-white immigration to Australia, but the policy also had a huge impact on Indigenous Australians. Assimilation into broader society was encouraged by all sectors of government, with the intent to eventually 'fade out' the Aboriginal race. A policy of forcibly removing Aboriginal and Torres Strait Islander children from their families was official from 1909 to 1969, although the practice happened both before and after those years. Although accurate numbers will never be known, it is estimated that around 100,000 Indigenous children – or one in three – were taken from their families.

A government agency, the Aborigines Protection Board, was set up to manage the policy, and had the power to remove children from families without consent, not even needing a court order. Many children never saw their families again; those who did manage to find their way home often found it difficult to maintain relationships. They became known as the Stolen Generations.

In the 1990s the Australian Human Rights Commission held an inquiry into the practice of removing Aboriginal children. *Bringing Them Home,* a nearly 700-page report that was tabled in parliament in May 1997, told of the devastating impact these policies had had on the children and their families. Government bureaus, church missions and welfare agencies all took part in the forced removal, and sexual and physical abuse and cruelty was found to be common in many of the institutions where children were placed. Today many of the Stolen Generations still suffer trauma associated with their early lives.

On 13 February 2008 Kevin Rudd, then prime minister of Australia, offered a national apology to the Stolen Generations. For many Indigenous people it was the start of a national healing process, and today there are many organisations working with the survivors of the Stolen Generations to bring healing and, in some cases, to seek compensation.

To learn more about the Stolen Generations and its impact upon countless Indigenous lives, the film *Rabbit-Proof Fence* (2002) and Archie Roach's classic song 'Took the Children Away' are good places to start.

British and French troops in an assault on the Gallipoli Peninsula in Turkey. It was eight months of fighting before the British commanders acknowledged that the tactic had failed – by then 8141 young Australians were dead. Before long the Australian Imperial Force was fighting in the killing fields of Europe. By the time the war ended, 60,000 Australian men had given their lives in military service. Ever since, on 25 April, Australians have gathered at war memorials around the country for the sad and solemn services of Anzac Day.

In the 1920s Australia embarked on a decade of chaotic change. Cars began to rival horses on the highway. Young Australians enjoyed

1972	1973	1974	1975
The Aboriginal Tent Embassy is set up on the lawns of Parliament House in Canberra to oppose the treatment of Indigenous people and the government's rejection of a proposal for Aboriginal Land Rights	After a conflict-ridden construction, which included the sacking of Danish architect Jørn Utzon, the Sydney Opera House opens for business. This iconic building was granted Unesco World Heritage status in 2007.	Cyclone Tracy tears through Darwin on Christmas Eve, demolishing 70% of the city's buildings and killing 71 people. Much of the city was rebuilt (with stronger construction) within four years.	Against a background of radical reform and uncontrolled inflation, Governor-General Sir John Kerr sacks Labor's Whitlam government and orders a federal election, which the conservatives win.

American movies in the new cinemas, and – in an atmosphere of sexual freedom not equalled until the 1960s – partied and danced to American jazz. At the same time, popular enthusiasm for the British Empire grew more intense, as if imperial fervour were an antidote to postwar grief. As radicals and reactionaries clashed on the political stage, Australia careered wildly through the 1920s until it collapsed into the abyss of the Great Depression in 1929. World prices for wheat and wool plunged; unemployment brought misery to one in three households. Once again working people experienced the cruelty of a system that treated them as expendable, though for those who were wealthy – or who had jobs – the Depression was hardly noticeable. (If anything, the extreme deflation of the economy enhanced the purchasing power of their money.)

Against the backdrop of the Depression and economic desperation experienced by many ordinary Australians, the escape offered by cricket was important than ever, and the 1932 Ashes series for a time unified the nation. The English team, under their captain Douglas Jardine, employed a violent new bowling tactic known as 'bodyline', its aim to unnerve Australia's star batsman, the devastatingly efficient Donald Bradman. The bitterness of the tour provoked a diplomatic crisis with Britain, and became part of Australian legend, but Bradman batted on. When he retired in 1948 he had an unsurpassed career average of 99.94 runs.

War With Japan

After 1933, the economy began to recover. The whirl of daily life was hardly dampened when Hitler hurled Europe into a new war in 1939. Though Australians had long feared Japan, they took it for granted that the British navy would keep them safe. In December 1941 Japan bombed the US fleet at Pearl Harbor. Weeks later, the 'impregnable' British naval base in Singapore crumbled, and before long thousands of Australians and other Allied troops were enduring Japanese prisoner-of-war camps.

During WWII, the Northern Territory's capital Darwin was the front line for Allied action against the Japanese in the Pacific – and in 1942, Japan launched a devastating air attack on the city, killing 243 people and laying waste to its port. It was the only Australian city ever bombed in the war; official reports of the time downplayed the damage to buoy morale.

As the Japanese swept through Southeast Asia and into Papua New Guinea, the British announced that they could not spare any resources to defend Australia. But the legendary US commander General Douglas MacArthur saw that Australia was the perfect base for American operations in the Pacific. In a series of fierce battles on sea and land, Allied forces gradually turned back the Japanese advance. Significantly, it was the USA – not the British Empire – that saved Australia. The days of the nation's alliance with Britain alone were numbered.

Best History Museums

Rocks Discovery Museum (Sydney, NSW)

Mawson's Huts Replica Museum (Hobart, Tasmania)

Museum of Sydney (Sydney, NSW)

Commissariat Store (Brisbane, Queensland)

1979	1987	1983	1992
Despite heated protests from environmental groups, the federal government grants authorisation for the Ranger consortium to mine uranium in the Northern Territory.	A Royal Commission investigates the high number of Aboriginal deaths in police custody and prisons. Aboriginal people are still over-represented in the criminal system today.	Tasmanian government plans for a hydro-electric dam on the wild Franklin River dominate a federal election campaign. Supporting a 'No Dams' policy, Labor's Bob Hawke becomes prime minister.	After 10 years in the courts, the landmark Mabo decision is delivered by the High Court. Effectively, this gives recognition to Indigenous land rights across the country and overturns the principal of terra nullius.

PHAR LAP'S LAST LAP

In the midst of the Depression-era hardship, sport brought escape to an Australia in love with games and gambling. A powerful chestnut-coloured horse called Phar Lap won race after race, culminating in an effortless and graceful victory in the 1930 Melbourne Cup (this annual event is still known as 'the race that stops a nation'). In 1932 the great horse travelled to the racetracks of America, where he mysteriously died. In Australia, the gossips insisted that the horse had been poisoned by envious Americans...and the legend grew of a sporting hero cut down in his prime.

Phar Lap was stuffed and can be seen as a revered exhibit at the Melbourne Museum. His skeleton was returned to his birthplace, New Zealand, where it is displayed in Wellington at the country's national museum.

Visionary Peace

When WWII ended, a new slogan rang through the land: 'Populate or Perish!' The Australian government embarked on an ambitious scheme to attract thousands of immigrants. With government assistance, people flocked from Britain as well as from non-English-speaking countries, including Greek, Italian, Slav, Serb, Croatian, Dutch and Polish migrants, and, later, people from Turkey, Lebanon and many others. These 'new Australians' were expected to assimilate into a suburban stereotype known as the 'Australian way of life'.

Many migrants found jobs in the growing manufacturing sector, in which companies such as General Motors and Ford operated with generous tariff support. In addition, the government embarked on audacious public works schemes, notably the mighty Snowy Mountains Hydro-Electric Scheme in the mountains near Canberra. Today, environmentalists point out the devastation caused by this huge network of tunnels, dams and power stations, but the Snowy scheme was an expression of a new-found postwar optimism and a testimony to the cooperation among the labourers of many nations who completed the project.

This era of growth and prosperity was dominated by Robert Menzies, the founder of the modern Liberal Party and Australia's longest-serving prime minister, with over 18 years in office. Menzies was steeped in British history and tradition, and liked to play the part of a sentimental monarchist; he was also a vigilant opponent of communism. As Asia succumbed to the chill of the Cold War, Australia and New Zealand entered a formal military alliance with the USA – the 1951 Anzus security pact. When the USA hurled its righteous fury into a civil war in Vietnam, Menzies committed Australian forces to the battle, introducing conscription for military service overseas. The following year Menzies retired, leaving his successors a bitter legacy – the antiwar movement would split Australia.

There was a feeling, too, among many artists, intellectuals and the younger generation that Menzies' Australia had become a rather dull, complacent country, more in love with American and British culture than with its own talents and stories. In an atmosphere of youthful rebellion and emerging nationalism, the Labor Party was elected to power in 1972 under the leadership of a brilliant, idealistic lawyer named Gough Whitlam. In just four short years his government transformed the country: he ended conscription and abolished all university fees, and he introduced a free universal health-care scheme, no-fault divorce, the principle of Aboriginal Australian land rights, and equal pay for women. The White Australia policy had been gradually falling into disuse, and under Whitlam it was finally abandoned altogether. By now, around one million migrants had arrived from non-English-speaking countries, and they had filled Australia with new languages, cultures, foods and ideas. Under Whitlam this achievement was embraced as 'multiculturalism'.

By 1975 the Whitlam government was rocked by a tempest of economic inflation and scandal. At the end of 1975 his government was controversially dismissed from office by the governor-general, the Queen's representative within Australia. But the general thrust of Whitlam's social reforms was continued by his successors. The principle of Indigenous land rights was expanded, and from the 1970s Asian immigration increased, and multiculturalism became a new national orthodoxy. Not only that, but China and Japan far outstripped Europe as major trading partners – Australia's economic future lay in Asia.

Modern Challenges

Today Australia faces new challenges. In the 1970s the country began dismantling its protectionist scaffolding. New efficiency brought new prosperity. At the same time, wages and working conditions, which were once protected by an independent tribunal, became more vulnerable as egalitarianism gave way to competition. And after two centuries of development, the strains on the environment were starting to show – on water supplies, forests, soils, air quality and the oceans.

Under the conservative John Howard, Australia's second-longest-serving prime minister (1996–2007), the country grew closer than ever to the USA, joining the Americans in their war in Iraq. The government's harsh treatment of asylum seekers, its refusal to acknowledge the reality of climate change, its anti-union reforms and the prime minister's lack of empathy with Indigenous Australians dismayed more liberal-minded Australians. But Howard presided over a period of economic growth that

British scientists detonated seven nuclear bombs at Maralinga in remote South Australia in the 1950s and early 1960s, with devastating effects on the local Maralinga Tjarutja people. Lesser known are the three nuclear tests carried out in the Monte-bello Islands in Western Australia in the '50s; a good read on the subject is Robert Drewe's *Montebello* (2012).

2009	2010	2010	2011
On 7 February Australia experiences its worst loss of life in a natural disaster when 400 bushfires kill 173 people in the countryside of Victoria – a day known thereafter as 'Black Saturday'.	Aboriginal leader Yagan is put to rest in a Perth park bearing his name. He was murdered in 1833 and his head sent to England. Aboriginal people have campaigned for decades to repatriate their people's remains.	Australia's first female prime minister, Julia Gillard, is sworn in. Born in Wales, Gillard emigrated to Australia's warmer climate as a child with her family due to her poor health.	Category 5 Tropical Cyclone Yasi makes landfall at Mission Beach on the north Queensland coast, causing mass devastation to property, infrastructure and crops.

RIGHTS & RECONCILIATION

The relationship between Indigenous Australians and other Australians hasn't always been an easy one. Over the years several systematic policies have been put in place, but these have often had underlying and often conflicting motives that include control over the land, decimating the population, protection, assimilation, self-determination and self-management.

The history of forced resettlement, removal of children, and the loss of land and culture can never be erased, even with governments addressing some of the issues. Current policies focus on 'closing the gap' and better delivery of essential services to improve lives, but there is still great disparity between Indigenous Australians and the rest of the population, including lower standards of education, employment, health and living conditions; high incarceration and suicide rates; and a lower life expectancy.

Throughout all of this, Aboriginal people have managed to maintain their identity and link to country and culture. Although there is a growing recognition and acceptance of Indigenous Australians' place in this country, there is still a long way to go. Aboriginal people have no real political or economic wealth, but their struggle for legal and cultural rights continues today and is always at the forefront of politics. Any gains for Aboriginal people have been hard-won and initiated by Aboriginal communities themselves.

emphasised the values of self-reliance and won him continuing support in middle Australia.

In 2007 Howard was defeated by the Labor Party's Kevin Rudd, an ex-diplomat who immediately issued a formal apology to Indigenous Australians for the injustices they had suffered over the past two centuries. Though it promised sweeping reforms in environment and education, the Rudd government found itself faced with a crisis when the world economy crashed in 2008; by 2010 it had cost Rudd his position. Incoming Prime Minister Julia Gillard, along with other world leaders, now faced three related challenges: climate change, a diminishing oil supply and a shrinking economy. This difficult landscape, shrinking popularity and ongoing agitations to return Rudd to the top job saw Gillard toppled and Rudd reinstated in 2013. Not three months later Rudd lost government to Tony Abbott's conservative Liberal-National Coalition in the 2013 federal election. With his own poll numbers slipping, Abbott fell to his Liberal Party colleague Malcolm Turnbull in 2015.

2012	2014	2015	2016
Australia wins just seven gold medals at the London Olympics, after 14 in Beijing 2008, 17 in Athens 2004, and 16 in Sydney 2000, denting national pride. (The Rio 2016 tally? Only eight.)	New conservative Prime Minister Tony Abbott commits RAAF combat aircraft and army special forces advisers to a multinational military operation against Islamic extremists in Iraq.	Malcolm Turnbull defeats Tony Abbott in a party-room ballot and becomes Australia's 29th prime minister. He is quoted as saying that 'there has never been a more exciting time to be an Australian'.	Prime Minister Turnbull narrowly wins a federal election and returns to power with a wafer-thin majority in parliament.

Aboriginal Culture

Aboriginal culture has evolved over thousands of years with strong links between the spiritual, economic and social lives of the people. This heritage has been kept alive from one generation to the next by the passing of knowledge and skills through rituals, art, cultural material and language. From the cities to the bush, there are opportunities to get up close with Australia's Indigenous people and learn from a way of life that has existed for over 50,000 years.

Indigenous Australians originally had an oral tradition, and language has played an important role in preserving Aboriginal cultures. Today there is a national movement to revive Aboriginal languages and a strong Aboriginal art sector; traditional knowledge is being used in science, natural resource management and government programs. Aboriginal culture has never been static, and continues to evolve with the changing times and environment. New technologies and media are now used to tell Aboriginal stories, and cultural tourism ventures, through which visitors can experience the perspectives of Indigenous peoples, have been established. You can learn about ancestral beings at particular natural landmarks, look at rock art that is thousands of years old, taste traditional foods or attend an Aboriginal festival or performance.

Government support for cultural programs is sporadic and depends on the political climate at the time. However, Aboriginal people are determined to maintain their links with the past and to also use their cultural knowledge to shape a better future.

The Land
Aboriginal culture views humans as part of the ecology, not separate from it. Everything is connected – a whole environment that sustains the spiritual, economic and cultural lives of the people. In turn, Aboriginal people have sustained the land over thousands of years, through knowledge passed on in ceremonies, rituals, songs and stories. Land is intrinsically connected to identity and spirituality; all land in Australia is reflected in Aboriginal lore, but particular places may be significant for religious and cultural beliefs. Some well-known sites are the Three Sisters in the Blue Mountains, and Warreen Cave in Tasmania, which has artefacts dated around 40,000 years old.

Sacred sites can be parts of rocks, hills, trees or water and are associated with an ancestral being or an event that occurred. Often these sites are part of a Dreaming story and link people across areas. The ranges

---

TORRES STRAIT ISLANDERS

Aboriginal society is a diverse group of several hundred sovereign nations. Torres Strait Islanders are a Melanesian people with a separate culture from that of Aboriginal Australians, though they have a shared history. Together, these two groups form Australia's Indigenous peoples.

Tasmania's Aboriginal people were separated from mainland Australia when sea levels rose after the last ice age. They subsequently developed their own entirely distinct languages and cultures.

around Alice Springs are part of the caterpillar Dreaming, with many sites including Akeyulerre (Billy Goat Hill), Atnelkentyarliweke (Anzac Hill) and rock paintings at Emily Gap. The most well known are Uluru (Ayers Rock) and Kata Tjuta (The Olgas), which is the home of the snake Wanambi – his breath is the wind that blows through the gorge. Pirla Warna Warna, a significant site in the Tanami Desert for Warlpiri people, is 270 miles northwest of Alice Springs (NT) and is where several Walpiri Dreaming stories meet.

Cultural tours to Aboriginal sites can provide opportunities to learn about plants and animals, hunting and fishing, bush food or dance.

Please note that many Indigenous sites are protected by law and are not to be disturbed in any way.

The Arts

Aboriginal art has impacted the Australian cultural landscape and is now showcased at national and international events and celebrated as a significant part of Australian culture. It still retains the role of passing on knowledge, but today is also important for economic, educational and political reasons. Art has been used to raise awareness of issues such as health and has been a primary tool for the reconciliation process in Australia. In many Indigenous communities art has become a major source of employment and income.

Visual Arts

Although there is no word in Indigenous Australian languages for 'art', visual imagery is a fundamental part of Aboriginal culture and life: a connection between the past, present and future, and between Indigenous people and their traditional homelands. The earliest forms of Indigenous visual cultural expression were rock carvings (petroglyphs), paintings on rock galleries, body painting and ground designs, with the earliest engraved designs known to exist dating back at least 40,000 years – perhaps older.

Rock Art

Rock art is the oldest form of human art: Indigenous rock art stretches back thousands of years and is found in every state of Australia. For Aboriginal people, rock art is a direct link with life before Europeans. The art and the process of making it are part of songs, stories and customs that connect the people to the land. There are a number of different styles of rock art across Australia. These include engravings in sandstone, and stencils, prints and drawings in rock shelters. Aboriginal people created rock art for several reasons, including as part of a ritual or ceremony and to record events.

Some of the oldest examples of engravings can be found in the Pilbara in Western Australia (WA) and in Olary in South Australia (SA), where there's an engraving of a crocodile – quite amazing as crocodiles are not found in this part of Australia. Rock art in the Kimberley (WA) rock art focuses on the Wandjina, the ancestral creation spirits. All national parks surrounding Sydney have rock engravings and are easily accessed and viewed. At Gariwerd (The Grampians) in Victoria, there are hand prints and hand stencils. There's also the Wangaar-Wuri painted rock art sites near Cooktown in Queensland.

In the Northern Territory (NT), many of the rock art sites have patterns and symbols that appear in paintings, carvings and other cultural material. Kakadu National Park has over 5000 recorded sites, but many more are thought to exist across the Arnhem Land Escarpment, some of which are over 20,000 years old. There's even a depiction of a thylacine

(Tasmanian tiger). World Heritage–listed Kakadu is internationally recognised for its cultural significance.

In central Australia, rock paintings still have religious significance. Here, Aboriginal people continue to retouch the art as part of ritual and to connect them to stories. In most other areas, people no longer paint rock images, but instead work on bark, paper and canvas.

If you visit rock-art sites, please do not touch or damage the art, and respect the sites and the surrounding areas.

Contemporary Indigenous Art

The contemporary Indigenous art industry started in a tiny community called Papunya (NT) in central Australia. It was occupied by residents from several language groups who had been displaced from their traditional lands. In 1971 an art teacher at Papunya school encouraged painting and some senior men took an interest. This started the process of transferring sand and body drawings onto modern mediums and the 'dot and circle' style of contemporary painting began. The emergence of dot paintings is one of the most important movements in 20th-century Australian art, and the Papunya Tula artists became a model for other Aboriginal communities.

The National Gallery of Australia (p254) in Canberra has a fantastic collection, but contemporary Aboriginal art can also be viewed at any public art gallery or in one of the many independent galleries dealing in Aboriginal work. Contemporary artists work in all media and Aboriginal art has appeared on unconventional surfaces such as a BMW car and a Qantas plane. The central desert area is still a hub for Aboriginal art and Alice Springs is one of the best places to see and buy art. Cairns is another hot spot for innovative Aboriginal art.

If you are buying art, make sure that provenance of the work is included. This tells the artist's name, the community and language group they come from and the story of the work. If it is an authentic work, all proceeds will go back to the artist. Australia has a resale royalty scheme.

Music

Music has always been a vital part of Aboriginal culture. Songs were important for teaching and passing on knowledge, and musical instruments were often used in healing, ceremonies and rituals. The most well-known instrument is the *yidaki* (didgeridoo), which was traditionally played in northern Australia, and only by men. Other instruments included clapsticks, rattles and boomerangs; in southern Australia, animal skins were stretched across the lap to make a drumming sound.

This rich musical heritage continues today with a strong contemporary music industry. Like other art forms, Aboriginal music has developed into a fusion of new ideas and styles mixed with strong cultural identity. Contemporary artists such as Dan Sultan and Jessica Mauboy have crossed over successfully into the mainstream, winning major music awards and seen regularly on popular programs and at major music festivals. Aboriginal radio (p1034) is the best and most accessible way to hear Aboriginal music.

Performing Arts

Dance and theatre are a vital part of Aboriginal culture. Traditional styles varied from one nation to the next; imitation of animals, birds and the elements is common across all nations, but arm, leg and body movements differed greatly. Ceremonial or ritual dances, often telling stories to pass on knowledge, were highly structured and were distinct from the social dancing at corroborees (Aboriginal gatherings). Like other Indigenous art forms, dance has adapted to the modern world, with contemporary

When Europeans first saw a corroborree they described it as a 'bush opera'. These festive social events combined music, dance and drama performances with body art. One of the first recorded corroborees was in 1791 at Bennelong Point, now rather appropriately the site of the Sydney Opera House.

THE IMPORTANCE OF STORYTELLING

Indigenous Australians historically had an oral culture, so storytelling was an important way to learn. Stories gave meaning to life and were used to teach the messages of the spirit ancestors. Although beliefs and cultural practices vary according to region and language groups, there is a common world-view that these ancestors created the land, the sea and all living things. This is often referred to as the Dreaming.

Through stories, the knowledge and beliefs are passed on from one generation to another, setting out the community's social mores and recording events from the past. Today artists have continued this tradition with new media such as film and literature. The first published Indigenous Australian was David Unaipon (1872–1967), a Ngarrindjeri man from South Australia who was a writer, a scientist and an advocate for his people, and the author of *Aboriginal Legends* (1927) and *Native Legends* (1929) – you can see Unaipon's portrait on the $50 note.

Other early published writers were Oodgeroo Noonuccal, Kevin Gilbert and Jack Davis. Contemporary writers of note include Alexis Wright, Kim Scott, Anita Heiss and Ali Cobby Eckerman. Award-winning novels to read are Kim Scott's *Deadman Dancing* (2010) and *Benang* (1999); Alexis Wright's *Carpentaria* (2006); and Ali Cobby Eckerman's *Little Bit Long Time* (2009) and *Ruby Moonlight* (2012).

dance groups bringing a modern interpretation to traditional forms. The most well-known dance company is the internationally acclaimed Bangarra Dance Theatre (p134).

Theatre also draws on the storytelling tradition, where drama and dance came together in ceremonies or corroborees, and this still occurs in many contemporary productions. Today, Australia has a thriving Aboriginal theatre industry and many Indigenous actors and writers work in or collaborate with mainstream productions. There are two major Aboriginal theatre companies – **Ilbijerri** (www.ilbijerri.com.au) in Melbourne and **Yirra Yakin** (www.yirrayaakin.com.au) in Perth – as well as several mainstream companies that specialise in Aboriginal stories and have had successful productions in Australia and overseas.

TV, Radio & Film

Aboriginal people have developed an extensive media network of radio, print and television services. There are over 120 Aboriginal radio stations and programs operating across Australia – in cities, rural areas and remote communities. Program formats differ from location to location: some broadcast only in Aboriginal languages or cater to specific music tastes. From its base in Brisbane, The **National Indigenous Radio Service** (NIRS; www.nirs.org.au) broadcasts four radio channels of Aboriginal content via satellite and over the internet. There's also **Radio Larrikia** (www.radiolarrakia.org) in Darwin (NT) and **Koori Radio** (www.kooriradio.com) in Sydney.

There's a thriving Aboriginal film industry and in recent years feature films such as *The Sapphires, Bran Nue Day, Samson and Delilah* and *Putuparri and the Rainmakers* have had mainstream success. Since the first Aboriginal television channel, **NITV** (www.nitv.org.au), was launched in 2007, there has been an increase in the number of filmmakers wanting to tell their stories.

Environment

by Tim Flannery

Australia's plants and animals are just about the closest things to alien life on earth. That's because Australia has been isolated from the other continents for a very long time: around 80 million years. Unlike those on other habitable continents that have been linked by land bridges, Australia's birds, mammals, reptiles and plants have taken their own separate and very different evolutionary journey. The result today is the world's most distinct natural realm – and one of the most diverse.

A Unique Environment

The first naturalists to investigate Australia were astonished by what they found. Here the swans were black – to Europeans this was a metaphor for the impossible – and mammals such as the platypus and echidna were discovered to lay eggs. It really was an upside-down world, where many of the larger animals hopped and where each year the trees shed their bark rather than their leaves.

If you are visiting Australia for a short time, you might need to go out of your way to experience some of the richness of the environment. That's because Australia is a subtle place, and some of the natural environment – especially around the cities – has been damaged or replaced by trees and creatures from Europe. Places like Sydney, however, have preserved extraordinary fragments of their original environment that are relatively easy to access. Before you enjoy them though, it's worthwhile understanding the basics about how nature operates in Australia. This is important because there's nowhere like Australia, and once you have an insight into its origins and natural rhythms, you will appreciate the place so much more.

There are two important factors that go a long way towards explaining nature in Australia: its soils and its climate. Both are unique.

Climate

In most parts of the world outside the wet tropics, life responds to the rhythm of the seasons – summer to winter, or wet to dry. Most of Australia experiences seasons – sometimes severe ones – yet life does not respond solely to them. This can clearly be seen by the fact that although there's plenty of snow and cold country in Australia, there are almost no trees that shed their leaves in winter, nor do many Australian animals hibernate. Instead there is a far more potent climatic force that Australian life must obey: El Niño.

El Niño is a complex climatic pattern that can cause major weather shifts around the South Pacific. The cycle of flood and drought that El Niño brings to Australia is profound. Our rivers – even the mighty Murray River, which is the nation's largest and runs through the southeast – can be miles wide one year, yet you can literally step over its flow the next. This is the power of El Niño, and its effect, when combined with Australia's poor soils, manifests itself compellingly.

Professor Tim Flannery is a scientist, explorer, activist, writer and the chief councillor of the independent Climate Council. He was a professor of science at Macquarie University in Sydney until 2013 and is currently a professorial fellow at Melbourne University. He was named Australian of the Year in 2007. He has written several award-winning books, including *The Future Eaters, Throwim Way Leg* (an account of his work as a biologist in New Guinea) and *The Weather Makers*.

Soils & Geology

In recent geological times, on other continents, processes such as volcanism, mountain building and glacial activity have been busy creating new soil. Just think of the glacier-derived soils of North America, north Asia and Europe. The rich soils of India and parts of South America were made by rivers eroding mountains, while Java in Indonesia owes its extraordinary richness to volcanoes.

All of these soil-forming processes have been almost absent from Australia in more recent times. Only volcanoes have made a contribution, and they cover less than 2% of the continent's land area. In fact, for the last 90 million years, beginning deep in the age of dinosaurs, Australia has been geologically comatose. It was too flat, warm and dry to attract glaciers, its crust too ancient and thick to be punctured by volcanoes or folded into mountains. Look at Uluru and Kata Tjuta. They are the stumps of mountains that 350 million years ago were the height of the Andes. Yet for hundreds of millions of years they've been nothing but nubs.

Under such conditions no new soil is created and the old soil is leached of all its goodness by the rain, and is blown and washed away. Even if just 30cm of rain falls each year, that adds up to a column of water 30 million kilometres high passing through the soil over 100 million years, and that can do a great deal of leaching! Almost all of Australia's mountain ranges are more than 90 million years old, so you will see a lot of sand here, and a lot of country where the rocky 'bones' of the land are sticking up through the soil. It is an old, infertile landscape and life in Australia has been adapting to these conditions for aeons.

In 2016, Unesco warned that the Great Barrier Reef may be placed on its Danger List, which covers those sites considered at risk unless action is taken. Bleaching of the coral, caused by a combination of climate change and increased human activity in the area, is considered the most serious risk to the future of the reef. For more on its beauty and vulnerability, watch the BBC's *Great Barrier Reef* (narrated by Sir David Attenborough) or visit www.attenboroughsreef.com.

Fauna & Flora

Mammals

Of all the continents, Australia has the worst record on the extinction of mammals, with an estimated 27 mammal species having become extinct since European settlement in 1788. And things aren't getting any better. The comprehensive 2014 *Action Plan for Australian Mammals* found that 55 Australian land-mammal species face a serious threat of extinction.

Kangaroos

Australia is, of course, famous as the home of the kangaroo (aka just plain 'roo') and other marsupials. Unless you visit a wildlife park, such creatures are not easy to see, as most are nocturnal. Their lifestyles, however, are exquisitely attuned to Australia's harsh conditions. Have you ever wondered why kangaroos, alone among the world's larger mammals, hop? It turns out that hopping is the most efficient way of getting about at medium speeds. This is because the energy of the bounce is stored in the tendons of the legs – much like in a pogo stick – while the intestines bounce up and down like a piston, emptying and filling the lungs without needing to activate the chest muscles. When you travel long distances to find meagre feed, such efficiency is a must.

Koalas

Marsupials are so energy-efficient that they need to eat one-fifth less food than equivalent-sized placental mammals (everything from bats to rats, whales and ourselves). But some marsupials have taken energy efficiency much further. If you visit a wildlife park or zoo, you might notice that faraway look in a koala's eyes. It seems as if nobody is home – and this, in fact, is near the truth.

Several years ago biologists announced that koalas are the only living creatures that have brains that don't fit their skulls. Instead they have a

World Heritage Wonders

Great Barrier Reef (Queensland)

South West Wilderness (Tasmania)

Uluru-Kata Tjuta National Park (NT)

Kakadu National Park (NT)

shrivelled walnut of a brain that rattles around in a fluid-filled cranium. Other researchers have contested this finding, however, pointing out that the brains of the koalas examined for the study may have shrunk because these organs are so soft. Whether soft-brained or empty-headed, there is no doubt that the koala is not the Einstein of the animal world, and we now believe that it has sacrificed its brain to energy efficiency – brains cost a lot to run. Koalas eat gum leaves, which are so toxic that they use 20% of their energy just detoxifying this food. This leaves little energy for the brain, but fortunately living in the treetops – where there are so few predators – means that they can get by with few wits at all.

Wombats

The peculiar constraints of the Australian environment have not made everything as dumb as the koala. The koala's nearest relative, the wombat (of which there are three species), has a large brain for a marsupial. These creatures live in complex burrows and can weigh up to 35kg, making them the largest herbivorous burrowers on earth. Because their burrows are effectively air-conditioned, they have the neat trick of turning down their metabolic activity when they are in residence. One physiologist, who studied wombats' thyroid hormones, found that biological activity ceased to such an extent in sleeping wombats that, from a hormonal point of view, they appeared to be dead!

Wombats can remain underground for a week at a time, and can get by on just one-third of the food needed by a sheep of equivalent size. One day, perhaps, efficiency-minded farmers will keep wombats instead of sheep; at the moment, however, that isn't possible – the largest of the wombat species, the northern hairy-nose, is one of the world's rarest creatures, with only around 196 surviving in a remote nature reserve in central Queensland.

Other Mammals

Among the more common marsupials you might catch a glimpse of in the national parks around Australia's major cities are the species of antechinus. These nocturnal, rat-sized creatures lead an extraordinary life. The males live for just 11 months, the first 10 of which consist of a concentrated burst of eating and growing. The day comes when their minds turn to sex, and in the antechinus this becomes an obsession. As they embark on their quest for females they forget to eat and sleep. By the end of August – just two weeks after they reach 'puberty' – every male is dead, exhausted by sex and by carrying around swollen testes.

Two unique monotremes (egg-laying mammals) live in Australia: the bumbling echidna, something akin to a hedgehog; and the platypus, a bit like an otter, with webbed feet and a duck-like bill. Echidnas are common along bushland trails, but platypuses are elusive, and only seen at dawn and dusk in quiet rivers and streams.

Reptiles

One thing you will see lots of in Australia are reptiles. Snakes are abundant, and they include some of the most venomous species known. Where the opportunities to feed are few and far between, it's best not to give your prey a second chance, hence the potent venom. Snakes will usually leave you alone if you don't fool with them. Observe, back quietly away and don't panic, and most of the time you'll be OK.

Some visitors mistake lizards for snakes, and indeed some Australian lizards look bizarre. One of the more abundant is the sleepy lizard. These creatures, which are found in the southern arid region, look like animated pine cones. They are the Australian equivalent of tortoises, and

---

Official Floral Emblems

Common heath (Victoria)

Cooktown orchid (Queensland)

Red and green kangaroo paw (WA)

Royal bluebell (ACT)

Tasmanian blue gum (Tasmania)

Sturt's desert pea (SA)

Sturt's desert rose (NT)

Waratah (NSW)

ENVIRONMENT FAUNA & FLORA

The Coastal Studies Unit at the University of Sydney has deemed there to be an astonishing 10,685 beaches in Australia! (They define a beach as a stretch of sand that's more than 20m long and remains dry at high tide.)

are harmless. Other lizards are much larger. Unless you visit the Indonesian island of Komodo you will not see a larger lizard than the desert-dwelling perentie. These creatures, with their leopardlike blotches, can grow to more than 2m long, and are efficient predators of introduced rabbits, feral cats and the like.

Feeling right at home in Kakadu National Park, the saltwater crocodile is the world's largest living reptile – old males can reach an intimidating 6m long.

Flora

Australia's plants can be irresistibly fascinating. If you happen to be in the Perth area in spring it's well worth taking a wildflower tour. The best flowers grow on the arid and monotonous sand plains, and the blaze of colour produced by the kangaroo paws, banksias and similar native plants can be dizzying. The sheer variety of flowers is amazing, with 4000 species crowded into the southwestern corner of the continent. This diversity of prolific flowering plants has long puzzled botanists. Again, Australia's poor soils seem to be the cause. The sand plain is about the poorest soil in Australia – it's almost pure quartz. This prevents any single fast-growing species from dominating. Instead, thousands of specialist plant species have learned to find a narrow niche and so coexist. Some live at the foot of the metre-high sand dunes, some on top, some on an east-facing slope, some on the west and so on. Their flowers need to be striking in order to attract pollinators, for nutrients are so lacking in this sandy world that even insects such as bees are rare.

If you do get to walk the wildflower regions of the southwest, keep your eyes open for the sundews. Australia is the centre of diversity for these beautiful, carnivorous plants. They've given up on the soil supplying their nutritional needs and have turned instead to trapping insects with the sweet globs of moisture on their leaves, and digesting them to obtain nitrogen and phosphorus.

Australia has seen some devastating bushfires in recent times: the 'Black Saturday' fires in Victoria in 2009 claimed 173 lives, while in 2013 fires in Tasmania killed a firefighter and destroyed hundreds of buildings. The 2015 Adelaide Hills (SA) fires burned 125 sq km and dozens of houses and outbuildings; bushfires along Victoria's Great Ocean Road the same year consumed over 100 homes, and fires wiped out the small NSW village of Uarbry in early 2017.

If you are very lucky, you might see a honey possum. This tiny marsupial is an enigma. Somehow it gets all of its dietary requirements from nectar and pollen, and in the southwest there are always enough flowers around for it to survive. But no one knows why the males need sperm larger even than those of the blue whale, or why their testes are so massive. Were humans as well endowed, men would be walking around with the equivalent of a 4kg bag of potatoes between their legs!

Environmental Challenges

The European colonisation of Australia, commencing in 1788, heralded a period of catastrophic environmental upheaval. The result today is that Australians are struggling with some of the most severe environmental problems to be found anywhere in the world. It may seem strange that a population of just 24 million, living in a continent the size of the USA (minus Alaska), could inflict such damage on its environment, but Australia's long isolation, its fragile soils and difficult climate have made it particularly vulnerable to human-induced change.

Environmental damage has been inflicted in several ways, some of the most important being the introduction of pest species, destruction of forests, overstocking range lands and interference with water flows.

Beginning with the escape of domestic cats into the Australian bush shortly after 1788, a plethora of vermin – from foxes to wild camels and cane toads – have run wild in Australia, causing extinctions in the native fauna. One out of every 10 native mammals living in Australia prior to European colonisation is now extinct, and many more are highly endangered. Extinctions have also affected native plants, birds and amphibians.

The destruction of forests has also had an effect on the environment. Most of Australia's rainforests have suffered clearing, while conservationists fight with loggers over the fate of the last unprotected stands of 'old growth'.

Many Australian range lands have been chronically overstocked for more than a century, the result being the extreme vulnerability of both soils and rural economies to Australia's drought and flood cycle, as well as the extinction of many native species. The development of agriculture has involved land clearance and the provision of irrigation; again the effect has been profound. Clearing of the diverse and spectacular plant communities of the Western Australia wheat belt began just a century ago, yet today up to one-third of that country is degraded by salination of the soils.

Just 1.5% of Australia's land surface provides over 95% of its agricultural yield, and much of this land lies in the irrigated regions of the Murray-Darling Basin. This is Australia's agricultural heartland, yet it too is under severe threat from salting of soils and rivers. Irrigation water penetrates into the sediments laid down in an ancient sea, carrying salt into the catchments and fields. The Snowy River in New South Wales and Victoria also faces a battle for survival.

Despite the enormity of the biological crisis engulfing Australia, governments and the community have been slow to respond. It was in the 1980s that coordinated action began to take place, but not until the '90s that major steps were taken. The establishment of **Landcare** (www.land careaustralia.com.au), an organisation enabling people to effectively address local environmental issues, and the expenditure of over $2 billion through the federal government program 'Caring for our Country' have been important national initiatives. Yet so difficult are some of the issues the nation faces that, as yet, little has been achieved in terms of halting the destructive processes.

So severe are Australia's environmental problems that it will take a revolution before they can be overcome, for sustainable practices need to be implemented in every arena of life – from farms to suburbs and city centres. Renewable energy, sustainable agriculture and water use lie at the heart of these changes, and Australians are only now developing the road map to sustainability that they so desperately need if they are to have a long-term future on the continent.

Uluru (Ayers Rock) is often thought to be the world's largest monolith, but in fact it only takes second prize. The biggest is Burringurrah (Mt Augustus) in Western Australia, which is 2½ times the size of Uluru.

ENVIRONMENT ENVIRONMENTAL CHALLENGES

Walk Among the Tall Timber

Valley of the Giants (WA)

Tahune Airwalk (Tasmania)

Otway Fly (Victoria)

Illawarra Fly Tree Top Walk (NSW)

ENVIRONMENT & CONSERVATION GROUPS

➡ The **Australian Conservation Foundation** (www.acf.org.au) is Australia's largest nongovernment organisation involved in protecting the environment.

➡ **Bush Heritage Australia** (www.bushheritage.org.au) and **Australian Wildlife Conservancy** (AWC; www.australianwildlife.org) allow people to donate funds and time to conserving native species.

➡ Want to get your hands dirty? **Conservation Volunteers Australia** (www.conser vationvolunteers.com.au) is a nonprofit organisation focusing on practical conservation projects such as tree planting, walking-track construction, and flora and fauna surveys.

➡ **Ecotourism Australia** (www.ecotourism.org.au) has an accreditation system for environmentally friendly and sustainable tourism in Australia, and lists ecofriendly tours, accommodation and attractions by state.

➡ The **Wilderness Society** (www.wilderness.org.au) focuses on protection of wilderness and forests.

The website of the Australian Museum (www.australianmuseum.net.au) holds a wealth of info on Australia's animal life from the Cretaceous period till now. Kids can get stuck into online games, fact files and movies.

Current Environmental Issues

Headlining the environmental issues facing Australia's fragile landscape at present are climate change, water scarcity, nuclear energy and uranium mining. All are interconnected. For Australia, the warmer temperatures resulting from climate change spell disaster to an already fragile landscape. A 2°C climb in average temperatures on the globe's driest continent will result in an even drier southern half of the country and greater water scarcity. Scientists also agree that hotter and drier conditions will exacerbate bushfire conditions and increase cyclone intensity.

Australia is a heavy greenhouse-gas emitter because it relies on coal and other fossil fuels for its energy supplies. The most prominent and also contentious alternative energy source is nuclear power, which creates less greenhouse gases and relies on uranium, in which Australia is rich. But the radioactive waste created by nuclear power stations can take thousands of years to become harmless. Moreover, uranium is a finite energy source (as opposed to even cleaner and also renewable energy sources such as solar and wind power) – and even if Australia were to establish sufficient nuclear power stations now to make a real reduction in coal-dependency, it would be years before the environmental and economic benefits were realised.

Uranium mining also produces polarised opinions. Because countries around the world are also looking to nuclear energy, Australia finds itself in a position to increase exports of one of its top-dollar resources. But uranium mining in Australia has been met with fierce opposition, not only because the product is a core ingredient of nuclear weapons, but also because much of Australia's uranium supplies sit beneath sacred Indigenous land. Supporters of increased uranium mining and export suggest that the best way to police the use of uranium is to manage its entire life cycle: that is, to sell the raw product to international buyers, and then charge a fee to accept the waste and dispose of it. Both major political parties consider an expansion of Australia's uranium export industry to be inevitable for economic reasons.

Birdlife Australia (www.birdlife.org.au) is the nation's peak birding body; it organises birding excursions and publishes a regular newsletter. Watch its website for updates on unusual sightings.

National & State Parks

Australia has more than 500 national parks – nonurban protected wilderness areas of environmental or natural importance. Each state defines and runs its own national parks, but the principle is the same

---

BIRDS IN BED

Australia has 898 recorded bird species, although an estimated 165 of these are considered to be vagrants, with only a handful of sightings (or occasionally even one!) recorded. Nearly half of all Australian birds are not found anywhere else on earth. A 2014 study by the Commonwealth Scientific and Industrial Research Organisation (CSIRO), warned that as many as 10% of Australia's birds could become extinct by the end of the century.

Relatively few of Australia's birds are seasonal breeders, and few migrate – instead, they breed when the rain comes. A large percentage are nomads, following the rain across the breadth of the continent.

So challenging are conditions in Australia that its birds have developed some extraordinary habits. Kookaburras, magpies and blue wrens (to name just a few) have developed a breeding system called 'helpers at the nest'. The helpers are the young adult birds of previous broods, which stay with their parents to help bring up the new chicks. Just why they should do this was a mystery until it was realised that conditions in Australia can be so harsh that more than two adult birds are needed to feed the nestlings. This pattern of breeding is very rare in places like Asia, Europe and North America, but it is common in many Australian birds.

A WHALE OF A TIME

Whaling, a driving economic force across much of southern Australia from the time of colonisation, was finally banned in Australia in 1979. The main species on the end of the harpoon were humpback, blue, southern right and sperm whales, which were culled in huge numbers in traditional breeding grounds such as Sydney Harbour, the Western Australia coast around Albany and Hobart's Derwent River estuary. The industry remained profitable until the mid-1800s, before drastically depleted whale numbers, the lure of inland gold rushes and the emergence of petrol as an alternative fuel started to have an impact.

Over recent years (and much to locals' delight), whales have made cautious returns to both Sydney Harbour and the Derwent River. Ironically, whale watching has emerged as a lucrative tourist activity in migratory hot spots such as Head of Bight in South Australia, Warrnambool in Victoria, Hervey Bay in Queensland and out on the ocean beyond Sydney Harbour.

throughout Australia. National parks include rainforests, vast tracts of empty outback, strips of coastal dune land and rugged mountain ranges.

Public access is encouraged as long as safety and conservation regulations are observed. In all parks you're asked to do nothing to damage or alter the natural environment. Camping grounds (often with toilets and showers), walking tracks and information centres are often provided for visitors. In most national parks there are restrictions on bringing in pets.

State parks and state forests are owned by state governments and have fewer regulations. Although state forests can be logged, they are often recreational areas with camping grounds, walking trails and signposted forest drives. Some permit horses and dogs.

Watching Wildlife

In the Rainforest

For those intrigued by the diversity of tropical rainforests, Queensland's World Heritage Sites are well worth visiting. Birds of paradise, cassowaries and a variety of other birds can be seen by day, while at night you can search for tree-kangaroos (yes, some kinds of kangaroo do live in the treetops). In your nocturnal wanderings you are highly likely to see curious possums, some of which look like skunks, and other marsupials that are restricted to a small area of northeast Queensland.

In the Desert

Australia's deserts are a real hit-and-miss affair as far as wildlife is concerned. If you're visiting in a drought year, all you might see are dusty plains, the odd mob of kangaroos and emus, and a few struggling trees. Return after big rains, however, and you'll encounter something close to a Garden of Eden. Fields of white and gold daisies stretch endlessly into the distance. The salt lakes fill with fresh water, and millions of water birds – pelicans, stilts, shags and gulls – can be seen feeding on the superabundant fish and insect life of the waters. It all seems like a mirage, and like a mirage it will vanish as the land dries out, only to spring to life again in a few years or a decade's time.

For a more reliable birdwatching spectacular, Kakadu is worth a look, especially towards the end of the dry season around November.

There are numerous guides to Aussie mammals on the market, but some are more suited to your reference library than your suitcase. One excellent exception is *A Field Guide to the Mammals of Australia* (3rd ed, 2011) by Peter Menkhorst and Frank Knight, with just enough detail, maps and fine illustrations.

SHARKY

Shark-phobia ruining your trip to the beach? Despite media hype spurred by five deaths in 2014, Australia has averaged just one shark-attack fatality per year since 1791. There are about 370 shark species in the world's oceans – around 160 of these swim through Australian waters. Of these, only a few pose any threat to humans: the usual suspects are oceanic white tip, great white, tiger and bull sharks.

It follows that where there are more people, there are more shark attacks. New South Wales, and Sydney in particular, have a bad reputation. Attacks in Sydney peaked between 1920 and 1940, but since shark-net installation began in 1937 there's only been one fatality (1963), and dorsal-fin sightings are rare enough to make the nightly news. Realistically, you're more likely to get hit by a bus – so get wet and enjoy yourself!

In the Ocean

The largest creatures found in the Australian region are marine mammals such as whales and seals, and there is no better place to see them than South Australia. During springtime southern right whales crowd into the head of the Great Australian Bight, which is home to more kinds of marine creatures than anywhere else on earth. You can readily observe them near the remote Aboriginal community of Yalata as they mate, frolic and suckle their young. Kangaroo Island, south of Adelaide, is a fantastic place to see seals and sea lions. There are well-developed visitor centres to facilitate the viewing of wildlife, and nightly penguin parades occur at some places where the adult blue penguins make their nest burrows. Kangaroo Island's beaches are magical places, where you're able to stroll among fabulous shells, whale bones and even jewel-like leafy sea dragons amid the sea wrack.

The fantastic diversity of Queensland's Great Barrier Reef is legendary, and a boat trip out to the reef from Cairns or Port Douglas is unforgettable.

In Tasmania

Some regions of Australia offer unique opportunities to see wildlife, and one of the most fruitful is Tasmania. The island is jam-packed with wallabies, wombats and possums, principally because foxes, which have decimated marsupial populations on the mainland, were slow to reach the island state – the first fox was found in Tasmania only as recently as 2001.

The island is also home to its eponymous Tasmanian devil. They're common on the island, and in some national parks you can watch them tear apart road-killed wombats. Their squabbling is fearsome, their shrieks ear-splitting – it's the nearest thing Australia can offer to experiencing a lion kill on the Masai Mara. Unfortunately, Tassie devil populations are being decimated by devil facial tumour disease (DFTD). Conservation projects, including establishing a disease-free population on Tasmania's Maria Island, and scientific projects aimed at building a vaccine, have offered hope that the devil may be saved, but the species remains classified as endangered.

Food & Drink

In a decade not so long ago, Australians proudly survived on a diet of 'meat and three veg'. Fine fare was a Sunday roast, and lasagne or croissants were considered exotic. Not any more. These days Australian gastronomy is keen to break rules, backed up by award-winning wines, world-class coffee, an organic revolution in the importance of fresh produce and a booming craft beer scene.

Modern Australian Cuisine

The phrase Modern Australian (or Mod Oz) has been coined to classify contemporary Australian cuisine: a melange of East and West; a swirl of Atlantic and Pacific Rim; a flourish of authentic French and Italian.

Immigration has been the key to this culinary concoction. An influx of immigrants since WWII, from Europe, Asia, the Middle East and Africa, introduced new ingredients and new ways to use staples. Vietnamese, Japanese, Fijian – no matter where it's from, there are expat communities and interested locals keen to cook and eat it. You'll find Jamaicans using Scotch bonnet peppers and Tunisians making *tajine*.

If all this sounds overwhelming, never fear. The range of food in Australia is a true asset. You'll find that dishes are characterised by bold and interesting flavours and fresh ingredients. All palates are catered for: the chilli-metre spans gentle to extreme, seafood is plentiful, meats are full-flavoured, and vegetarian needs are considered (especially in the cities).

Fresh Local Food

Australia is huge (similar in size to continental USA), and it varies so much in climate – from the tropical north to the temperate south – that at any time of the year there's an enormous array of produce on offer. Fruit is a fine example. In summer, kitchen bowls overflow with nectarines, peaches and cherries, and mangoes are so plentiful that Queenslanders get sick of them. The Murray River hinterland gives rise

Top Food Festivals

Taste of Tasmania
(Hobart, Tasmania)

Melbourne Food & Wine Festival
(Melbourne, Victoria)

Clare Valley Gourmet Weekend
(Clare Valley, SA)

Margaret River Gourmet Escape
(WA)

Oysterfest
(Ceduna, SA)

Tunarama Festival
(Port Lincoln, SA)

FOOD: WHEN, WHERE & HOW

➡ Budget eating venues usually offer main courses for under $15; midrange mains are generally between $15 and $30; and top-end venues charge over $30.

➡ Cafes serve breakfasts from around 8am on weekends – a bit earlier on weekdays – and close around 5pm.

➡ Pubs and bars usually open around lunchtime and continue till at least 10pm – later from Thursday to Saturday. Pubs usually serve food from noon to 2pm and 6pm to 8pm.

➡ Restaurants generally open around noon for lunch, 6pm for dinner. Australians usually eat lunch shortly after noon; dinner bookings are usually made between 7pm and 8pm, though in big cities some restaurants stay open past 10pm.

➡ Vegetarian eateries and vegetarian selections in nonveg places (including vegan and gluten-free menu choices) are common in large cities. Rural Australia continues its dedication to meat.

to orchards of citrus fruits, grapes and melons. Tasmania's cold climate makes its strawberries and stone fruits sublime. The tomatoes and olives of South Australia (SA) are the nation's best. Local supermarkets stock the pick of the bunch.

Seafood is always freshest close to the source; on this big island it's plentiful. Oysters are popular – connoisseurs prize Sydney rock oysters, a species that actually lives right along the New South Wales (NSW) coast; excellent oysters are grown in seven different regions in SA, such as Coffin Bay; and Tasmania is known for its Pacific oysters. Australia's southernmost state is also celebrated for its trout, salmon and abalone.

An odd-sounding delicacy from these waters is 'bugs' – shovel-nosed lobsters without a lobster's price tag (try the Balmain and Moreton Bay varieties). Marron are prehistoric-looking freshwater crayfish from Western Australia (WA), with a subtle taste that's not always enhanced by the

WINE REGIONS

All Australian states and mainland territories (except tropical and desert Northern Territory) sustain wine industries, some almost 200 years old. Many wineries have tastings for free or a small fee, often redeemable if you buy a bottle. Although plenty of good wine comes from big wineries with economies of scale on their side, the most interesting wines are often made by small producers. The following rundown should give you a head start.

New South Wales & the Australian Capital Territory
Dating from the 1820s, the Hunter Valley is Australia's oldest wine region. The Lower Hunter is known for shiraz and unwooded semillon. Upper Hunter wineries specialise in cabernet sauvignon and shiraz, with forays into verdelho and chardonnay. Further inland are award-winning wineries at Griffith, Mudgee and Orange. In the ACT, Canberra's surrounds also have a growing number of excellent wineries.

Queensland
High-altitude Stanthorpe and Ballandean in the southeast are the centres of the Queensland wine industry, though you'll find a few cellar doors at Tamborine Mountain in the Gold Coast hinterland.

South Australia
South Australia's wine industry is a global giant, as a visit to the National Wine Centre of Australia (p718) in Adelaide will attest. Cabernet sauvignon from Coonawarra, riesling from the Clare Valley, sauvignon blanc from the Adelaide Hills and shiraz from the Barossa Valley and McLaren Vale are bliss in a bottle.

Tasmania
Try the Pipers River region and the Tamar Valley in the north, and explore the burgeoning wine industry in the Coal River Valley around Richmond (p652) near Hobart. Cool-climate drops are the name of the game here: especially pinot noir, sauvignon blanc and sparkling whites (our favourite is the 'Méthode Tasmanoise' made by Jansz).

Victoria
Victoria has more than 500 wineries. The Yarra Valley produces excellent chardonnay and pinot noir, as does the Mornington Peninsula; both can be done as day trips from Melbourne. Wineries around Rutherglen produce champion fortified wines as well as shiraz and durif.

Western Australia
Margaret River in the southwest is synonymous with superb cabernets and chardonnays. Among old-growth forest, Pemberton wineries produce cabernet sauvignon, merlot, pinot noir, sauvignon blanc and shiraz. The south coast's Mt Barker is another budding wine region.

heavy dressings that seem popular. Prawns in Australia are incredible, particularly the school prawns or the eastern king (Yamba) prawns found along the northern New South Wales (NSW) coast. You can sample countless wild fish species, including prized barramundi from the Northern Territory (NT), but even fish that are considered run-of-the-mill (such as snapper, trevally and whiting) taste fabulous when simply barbecued.

There's a growing boutique cheese movement across the country's dairy regions – Tasmania alone now produces 50 cheese varieties.

Fine Dining

A restaurant meal in Australia is a relaxed affair. You'll probably order within 15 minutes and see the first course (called a starter or entrée) 15 minutes later. The main course will arrive about half an hour after that. Even at the finest restaurants a jacket is not required.

If a restaurant is BYO, you can bring your own alcohol. If it also sells alcohol, you can usually only bring your own bottled wine (no beer or cask or box wine) and a corkage charge is added to your bill. The cost is either per person or per bottle, and can be up to $20 per bottle in fine-dining places (do the sums in advance: you'll often be better off buying from the restaurant, even with their inflated prices).

Quick Eats

In the big cities, street vending is on the rise – coffee carts have been joined by vans selling tacos, burritos, baked potatoes, kebabs, burgers and more. Elsewhere around the cities you'll find fast-food chains, gourmet sandwich bars, food courts in shopping centres and market halls, bakeries, and sushi, noodle and salad bars. Beyond the big smoke the options are more limited and traditional, such as milk bars (known as delis in SA and WA) – these corner stores often serve old-fashioned hamburgers (with bacon, egg, pineapple and beetroot) and other takeaway foods.

There are more than a million Aussies with Italian heritage: it follows that pizza is (arguably) the most popular Australian fast food. Most home-delivered pizzas are of the American style (thick and with lots of toppings) rather than Italian style. However, thin, Neapolitan-style pizza cooked in a wood-fired oven can increasingly be found, even in country towns.

Fish and chips are still hugely popular, the fish is most often a form of shark (often called flake; don't worry, it's delicious), either grilled or dipped in batter and fried.

If you're at a rugby league or Aussie rules football match, downing a beer and a meat pie is as compulsory as wearing your team's colours and yelling loudly from the stands.

Eating with the Locals

Most Aussies eat cereal, toast and/or fruit for breakfast, often extending to bacon and eggs on weekends, washed down with tea and coffee. They generally favour sandwiches, salads and sushi for lunch, and then eat anything and everything in the evening.

The iconic Australian barbecue (BBQ or 'barbie') is a near-mandatory cultural experience. In summer locals invite their friends around at dinnertime and fire up the barbie, grilling burgers, sausages ('snags'), steaks, seafood, and vegie, meat or seafood skewers. If you're invited to a BBQ, bring some meat and cold beer. Year-round the BBQ is wheeled out at weekends for quick-fire lunches. There are plenty of free electric or gas BBQs in parks around the country, too – a terrific traveller-friendly option.

Cafes & Coffee

Coffee has become an Australian addiction. There are Italian-style espresso machines in virtually every cafe, boutique roasters are all the rage

BUSH TUCKER: AUSTRALIAN NATIVE FOODS

There are around 350 food plants that are native to the Australian bush. Bush foods provide a real taste of the Australian landscape. There are the dried fruits and lean meats of the desert; shellfish and fish of the coast; alpine berries and mountain peppers of the high country; and citrus flavours, fruits and herbs of the rainforests.

This cuisine is based on Indigenous Australians' expert understanding of the environment, founded in cultural knowledge handed down over generations. Years of trial and error have ensured a rich appreciation of these foods and mastery of their preparation.

The harvesting of bush foods for commercial return has been occurring for about 30 years. In central Australia it is mainly carried out by middle-aged and senior Aboriginal women. Here and in other regions, bush meats (such as kangaroo, emu and crocodile), fish (such as barramundi), and bush fruits (including desert raisins, quandongs, riberries, and Kakadu plums) are seasonally hunted and gathered for personal enjoyment, as well as to supply local, national and international markets.

– Dr Janelle White, *Adjunct Research Fellow at the Nulungu Research Institute.*

and, in urban areas, the qualified barista is ever present (there are even barista-staffed cafes attached to petrol stations).

Sydney and Melbourne, the two cities arguing it out for bragging rights as Australia's coffee capital, have given rise to a whole generation of coffee snobs. The cafe scene in Melbourne is particularly hipster; the best way to immerse yourself in it is by wandering the city centre's cafe-lined laneways. You'll also find decent places in the other big cities and towns, and there's now a sporting chance of good coffee in many rural areas.

Cafes in Australia generally serve good-value food: they're usually more casual than restaurants and you can get a decent meal for around $20, although many only open for breakfast and lunch. Children are usually more than welcome.

Pubs & Drinking

You're in the right country if you're in need of a drink. Long recognised as some of the finest in the world, Australian wines are one of the nation's top exports. As the public develops a more sophisticated palate, local craft beers are rising to the occasion. There's a growing wealth of microbrewed flavours and varieties on offer, challenging the nation's entrenched predilection for mass-produced lager. If you're into whisky, head to Tasmania: there are a dozen distillers there now, bottling-up superb single malts and racking up international awards.

Most Australian beers have an alcohol content between 3.5% and 5.5%, which is less than European beers but more than most in North America. Light beers contain under 3% alcohol and are a good choice if you have to drive (as long as you don't drink twice as much).

The terminology used to order beer varies state by state. In NSW you ask for a schooner (425mL) if you're thirsty, and a middy (285mL) if you're not quite so dry. In Victoria the 285mL measure is called a pot; in Tasmania it's called a 10-ounce. Pints can be either 425mL or 568mL, depending on where you are. Mostly you can just ask for a beer and see what turns up.

'Shouting' is a revered custom where people drinking together take turns to pay for a round of drinks. At a toast, everyone should touch glasses and look each other in the eye as they clink – failure to do so is purported to result in seven years' bad luck (whether you believe that or not, why not make eye contact just in case...?).

Pub meals (often referred to as counter meals) are usually hefty and good value: standards such as sausages and mashed potatoes or chicken schnitzel and salad go for $15 to $30.

Delicious is a monthly magazine published by the Australian Broadcasting Corporation (ABC) listing recipes, restaurant reviews, food and wine trends, and foodie-related travel articles. *Australian Gourmet Traveller* (www.gourmet traveller.com.au) is another fine magazine.

Sport

Whether they're filling stadiums, glued to a pub's big screen or on the couch in front of the TV, Australians invest heavily in sport – both fiscally and emotionally. The federal government kicks in more than $300 million every year – enough for Australia to hold its own against formidable international sporting opponents. Fuelled as it is by numerous stories of international success, however, it's the passion of the ordinary Aussie for sport that truly defines the country's sporting life.

Australian Rules Football

Australia's most attended sport, and one of the two most watched, is Australian Rules football (aka 'footy' or 'Aussie rules'). While traditionally embedded in Victorian state culture and identity, the Australian Football League (AFL; www.afl.com.au) has gradually expanded its popularity into all states, including rugby-dominated New South Wales and Queensland; South Australia and Western Australia needed no encouragement and have long been die-hard footy states. Long kicks, high marks and brutal collisions whip crowds into frenzies: the roar of 50,000-plus fans yelling 'Baaalll!!!' upsets dogs in suburban backyards for miles around.

The season runs from late March to September; tickets can usually be purchased online or at the stadiums on the day for all but the biggest games. In September, it all culminates in the AFL Grand Final at Melbourne's MCG stadium, one of Australia's most-watched sporting events. But footy is an obsession across the nation, and even in remote communities, it seems like the whole world stops whenever there's a big game on – the Tiwi Grand Final (p812) in March, on the Tiwi Islands off Darwin (and about as far away from Melbourne as you can get in Australia), is one memorable example.

Cricket

The pinnacle of Australian cricket is the biennial test series played between Australia and England, known as 'The Ashes'. The unofficial Ashes trophy is a tiny terracotta urn containing the ashen remnants of an 1882 cricket bail (the perfect Australian BBQ conversation opener: ask a local what a 'bail' is). Series losses in 2009, 2011 and 2013 to the arch-enemy caused nationwide misery. Redemption came in 2014, when Australia won back the Ashes 5–0, only the third clean-sweep in Ashes history, but

---

WOMEN'S FOOTY

Australian Rules Football has always had a firm following among female sports fans, but the participatory side of things has always been a male realm. In early 2017, the **Women's AFL** (www.afl.com.au/womens) finally got underway. The eight-team league kicked off with a sell-out match between Carlton and Collingwood (with a decisive victory by Carlton) – the capacity 24,000 crowd that turned up forced a rethink of future venues. Games are shorter (quarters last for 15 minutes) and the two teams have 16 instead of 18 players. However, for many the question lingers: why did it take so long for a women's league to happen?

'Footy' in Australia can mean a number of things. In NSW and Queensland it's rugby league; everywhere else it's Australian Rules football. Just to confuse you, 'football' can also mean soccer – the national governing body for soccer is called the Football Federation of Australia.

the pendulum shifted back in 2015 when England won a tight series 3–2. The next series is due to take place in the 2017–18 Australian summer.

Take the time to watch a match if you never have – such tactical cut-and-thrust, such nuance, such grace...! Despite the Australian cricket team's bad rep for 'sledging' (verbally dressing down one's opponent on the field), cricket is still a gentleman's game. Test cricket lasts for up to five days, while shorter versions of the game – one-day internationals or T20 – are probably a more accessible (and less boring) introduction.

Rugby

The **National Rugby League** (NRL; www.nrl.com.au) is the most popular football code north of the Murray River, the highlight being the annual State of Origin series between NSW and Queensland. To witness a game is to appreciate all of Newton's laws of motion – it's bone-crunching!

The national rugby union team, the Wallabies, won the Rugby World Cup in 1991 and 1999 and was runner-up in 2003 (to England) and 2015 (to eternal rivals New Zealand).

Teams from Australia, New Zealand, South Africa, Japan and Argentina compete in the super-popular **Super 15s** (www.superxv.com) competition, which includes five Australian teams: the Waratahs (Sydney), the Reds (Brisbane), the Brumbies (Australian Capital Territory, aka ACT), the Force (Perth) and the Rebels (Melbourne).

Soccer

Australia's national soccer team, the Socceroos, qualified for the 2006, 2010 and 2014 FIFA World Cups after a long history of almost-but-not-quite getting there. Results were mixed, but pride in the national team is sky-high (and actually reached the stratosphere when the Socceroos won the Asian Cup in 2015).

The national **A-League** (www.a-league.com.au) competition, with nine teams from around Australia and one from New Zealand, has enjoyed increased popularity in recent years, successfully luring a few big-name international players to bolster the home-grown talent pool.

Tennis

Every January in Melbourne, the **Australian Open** (www.australianopen.com; Melbourne Park, Olympic Blvd, Melbourne; ⊘Jan) attracts more people to Australia than any other sporting event. Get to a game there if you can.

The men's competition was last won by an Australian, Mark Edmondson, back in 1976. After an era dominated by the gentlemanly Pat Rafter (who won the US Open in 1997 and 1998) and the gutsy Lleyton Hewitt (who won the US Open in 2001 and Wimbledon a year later), Australia's male tennis fraternity doesn't quite know what to make of the mercurial and talented enfants terribles, Nick Kyrgios and Bernard Tomic.

In the women's game, Australian Sam Stosur won the US Open in 2011 and has been hovering in the top-20 player rankings ever since.

Swimming

Australia: girt by sea and pock-marked with pools – its population can swim. Australia's greatest female swimmer, Dawn Fraser, known simply as 'our Dawn', won the 100m freestyle gold at three successive Olympics (1956–64), plus the 4x100m freestyle relay in 1956. Australia's greatest male swimmer, Ian Thorpe (known as Thorpie or the Thorpedo), retired in 2006 at age 24, with five Olympic golds swinging from his neck. Since then, Australia's reputation as a nation of swimming world champions has taken a battering with disappointing performances at both the 2012 London and 2016 Rio Olympics.

Survival Guide

Deadly & Dangerous

Australia has a formidable list of things that can bite, sting or even eat you. But despite the horror stories, most such creatures (crocs aside) are as wary of humans as we are of them. Chances are that the worst you'll encounter are a few pesky flies and mosquitoes. Splash on some insect repellent and boldly venture forth!

Wildlife

Australia's profusion of dangerous creatures is legendary: snakes, spiders, sharks, crocodiles, jellyfish... Travellers needn't be alarmed, though – you're unlikely to see many of these creatures in the wild, much less be attacked by one.

Crocodiles

Around the northern Australian coastline, saltwater crocodiles (salties) are a real danger. They also inhabit estuaries, creeks and rivers, sometimes a long way inland. Observe safety signs or ask locals whether that inviting-looking waterhole or river is croc-free before plunging in. This is one of a few dangerous animals that sees people as food, rather than acting in self-defence.

Jellyfish

With venomous tentacles up to 3m long, box jellyfish (aka sea wasps or stingers) inhabit Australia's tropical waters. They're most common during the wet season (October to March) when you should stay out of the sea in many places. Stinger nets are in place at some beaches, but never swim unless you've checked. 'Stinger suits' (full-body Lycra swimsuits) prevent stinging, as do wetsuits. If you are stung, wash the skin with vinegar then get to a hospital.

The box jellyfish also has a tiny, lethal relative called an irukandji, though to date, only two north-coast deaths have been directly attributed to it.

Sharks

Despite extensive media coverage, the risk of shark attack in Australia is no greater than in other countries with extensive coastlines. Check with surf life-saving groups about local risks.

Snakes

Australia has some of the world's most venomous snakes. Most common are brown and tiger snakes, but few species are aggressive. Unless you're poking a stick at or accidentally standing on one, it's extremely unlikely that you'll get bitten. If you are bitten, prevent the spread of venom by applying pressure to the wound and immobilising the area with a splint or sling. Stay put and get someone else to go for help.

Spiders

Australia has several poisonous spiders, bites from which are usually treatable with antivenoms. The deadly funnel-web spider lives in New South Wales (including Sydney) – bites are treated as per snake bites (pressure and immobilisation before transferring to a

---

MAINTAINING PERSPECTIVE

There's about one fatal crocodile attack per year in Australia. In 2016 there were two fatal shark attacks (both in Western Australia) and 16 injuries. Blue-ringed octopus–sting deaths are rarer – only two in the last century. Jellyfish account for about two deaths annually, but you're 100 times more likely to drown. Spiders haven't killed anyone since 1979. Snake bites kill one or two people per year, as do bee stings, but you're about a thousand times more likely to perish on the nation's roads.

hospital). Redback spiders live throughout Australia; bites cause pain, sweating and nausea. Apply ice or cold packs, then transfer to hospital. White-tailed spider bites may cause an ulcer that's slow and difficult to heal. Clean the wound and seek medical assistance. The disturbingly large huntsman spider is harmless, though seeing one can affect your blood pressure and/or underpants.

Out & About

At the Beach

Check surf conditions and be aware of your own expertise and limitations before entering the waves. Patrolled, safe-swimming areas are indicated by red-and-yellow flags – swim between them. Undertows (rips) are a problem: if you find yourself being carried out to sea, swim parallel to the shore until you're out of the rip, then head for the beach.

Several people are paralysed every year by diving into shallow waves and hitting sand bars: look before you leap.

Bushfires

Bushfires happen yearly across Australia. In hot, dry and windy weather, and on total-fire-ban days, be extremely careful with naked flames (including cigarette butts) and don't use camping stoves, campfires or BBQs. Bushwalkers should delay trips until things cool down. If you're out in the bush and you see smoke, take it seriously: find the nearest open space (downhill if possible). Forested ridges are dangerous places to be.

Cold Weather

More bushwalkers in Australia die of cold than in bushfires. Even in summer, particularly in highland Tasmania, Victoria and New

South Wales (NSW), conditions can change quickly, with temperatures dropping below freezing and blizzards blowing in. Hypothermia is a real risk. Early signs include the inability to perform fine movements (eg doing up buttons), shivering and a bad case of the 'umbles' (fumbles, mumbles, grumbles, stumbles). Get out of the cold, change out of wet clothing immediately and into dry stuff, and eat and drink to warm up.

Crime

Australia is a relatively safe place to visit, but you should still take reasonable precautions. Avoid walking around alone at night, don't leave hotel rooms or cars unlocked, and don't leave valuables visible through car windows.

Some big-city pubs post warnings about drugged (or 'spiked') drinks: play it safe if someone offers you a drink in a bar.

Diseases

You'll be unlucky to pick any of these up in your travels, but the following diseases do crop up around Australia.

Dengue Fever

Dengue fever occurs in northern Queensland, particularly during the wet season. Causing severe muscular aches, it's a viral disease spread by a day-feeding species of mosquito. Most people recover in a few days, but more severe forms of the disease can occur.

Giardiasis

Giardia is widespread in Australian waterways. Drinking untreated water from streams and lakes is not recommended. Use water filters, and boil or treat this water with iodine to help prevent giardiasis. Symptoms consist of intermittent diarrhoea, abdominal bloating and wind. Effective treatment is available (tinidazole or metronidazole).

Hepatitis C

This is a growing problem among intravenous-drug users. Blood-transfusion services fully screen all blood before use.

Meningococcal Disease

A minor risk if you have prolonged stays in dormitory-style accommodation such as in hostels. A vaccine exists for some types of this disease (meningococcal A, C, Y and W), but there's no vaccine available for viral meningitis.

Ross River Fever

The Ross River virus is widespread in Australia, transmitted by marsh-dwelling mosquitoes. In addition to fever, it causes headache, joint and muscular pain, and a rash that resolves after five to seven days.

Tick Typhus

Predominantly occurring in Queensland and NSW, tick typhus involves a dark area forming around a tick bite, followed by a rash, fever, headache and lymph-node inflammation. The disease is treatable with antibiotics (doxycycline).

Viral Encephalitis

This mosquito-borne disease is most common in northern Australia (especially during the wet season), but poses minimal risk to travellers. Symptoms include headache, muscle pain and sensitivity to light. Residual neurological damage can occur and no specific treatment is available.

For more information on health, see p1056.

Directory A–Z

Accommodation

During the summer high season (December to February) and at other peak times, particularly school holidays and Easter, prices are usually at their highest. Outside these times you'll find useful discounts and lower walk-in rates. Notable exceptions include central Australia, the Top End and Australia's ski resorts, where summer is the low season and prices drop substantially.

B&Bs

Australian bed-and-breakfast options include restored miners' cottages, converted barns, rambling old houses, upmarket country manors and beachside bungalows. Tariffs are typically in the midrange bracket, but can be higher. In areas that attract weekenders – historic towns, wine regions, accessible forest regions such as the Blue Mountains in New South Wales and the Dandenongs in Victoria – B&Bs are often upmarket, charging small fortunes for weekend stays in high season.

Some places advertised as B&Bs are actually self-contained cottages with breakfast provisions supplied. Only in the cheaper B&Bs will bathroom facilities be shared. Some B&B hosts may also cook dinner for guests (usually 24 hours' notice is required).

Online resources:

Beautiful Accommodation (www.beautifulaccommodation. com) A select crop of luxury B&Bs and self-contained houses.

Bed & Breakfast Site (www. babs.com.au) B&Bs across the country.

Hosted Accommodation Australia (www.australianbed andbreakfast.com.au) Listings for B&Bs, farmstays, cottages and homesteads.

OZ Bed and Breakfast (www. ozbedandbreakfast.com) Nationwide website.

Camping & Holiday Parks

Camping in the bush is a highlight of travelling in Australia: in the outback and northern Australia you often won't even need a tent, and nights spent around a

campfire under the stars are unforgettable.

Seasons To avoid extremes of hot and cold weather, camping is best done during winter (the dry season) across the north of Australia, and during summer in the south.

Costs The nightly camping cost for two people in a privately run campground is usually between $22 and $35, slightly more for a powered site; prices can be higher in remote areas. Unless otherwise stated, prices for camp sites are for two people. Staying at designated camp sites in national parks normally costs between $3.50 and $15 per person.

Facilities Almost all caravan and holiday parks are equipped with hot showers, flushing toilets and laundry facilities, and frequently a pool. Most have cabins, powered caravan sites and tent sites. Cabin sizes and facilities vary, but expect to pay $80 to $100 for a small cabin with a kitchenette and up to $200 for a two- or three-bedroom cabin with a fully equipped kitchen, lounge room, TV and beds for up to six people.

Locations Note that most city camping grounds usually lie several kilometres from the town centre – only convenient if you have wheels. Caravan parks are popular in coastal areas: book well in advance during summer and Easter.

Resources Get your hands on **Camps Australia Wide** (www. campsaustraliawide.com), a

---

BOOK YOUR STAY ONLINE

For more accommodation reviews by Lonely Planet authors, check out http://lonelyplanet.com/hotels/. You'll find independent reviews, as well as recommendations on the best places to stay. Best of all, you can book online.

handy publication (and app) containing maps and information about camping grounds across Australia.

Permits Applications for national park camping permits are often handled online by state departments – check with the local national park service in the state you're visiting.

Major Chains If you're doing a lot of caravanning/camping, consider joining one of the chain organisations, which offer member discounts:

Big 4 Holiday Parks (www.big4.com.au)

Discovery Holiday Parks (www.discoveryholidayparks.com.au)

Top Tourist Parks (www.toptouristparks.com.au)

Farmstays

Country farms sometimes offer a bed for a night, while some remote outback stations allow you to stay in homestead rooms or shearers' quarters and try activities such as horse riding. Some let you kick back and watch workers raise a sweat; others rope you in to helping with day-to-day chores. Most accommodation is very comfortable – B&B-style in the main homestead (dinner on request), or in self-contained cottages. Some farms also provide budget outbuildings or shearers' quarters.

Remember, however, that some farmstays use their accommodation for its army of seasonal fruit pickers, while we've also heard reports of some who cut corners and others out to take advantage of those who stay. Make sure you lock in rates and any extras (such as laundry) before you agree to stay, and always check them for basic safety infrastructure, such as smoke alarms and fire escapes, before bedding in for the night.

Recommended websites:

Farmstay Camping Australia (www.farmstaycampingaustralia.com.au)

Hosted Accommodation Australia (www.australianbedandbreakfast.com.au)

Stayz (www.stayz.com.au/farm-accommodation)

Holiday Apartments

Holiday apartments are particularly common in coastal areas, with reservations often handled by local real estate agents or online booking engines.

Costs For a two-bedroom flat, you're looking at anywhere between $150 and $250 per night, but you will pay much more in high season and for serviced apartments in major cities.

Facilities Self-contained holiday apartments range from simple, studio-like rooms with small kitchenettes, to two-bedroom apartments with full laundries and state-of-the-art entertainment systems: great value for multinight stays. Sometimes they come in small, single-storey blocks, but in tourist hot spots such as the Gold Coast expect a sea of high-rises.

Hostels

Backpacker hostels are exceedingly popular in Australian cities and along the coast, but in the outback and rural areas you'll be hard pressed to find one. Highly social affairs, they're generally overflowing with 18- to 30-year-olds, but some have reinvented themselves to attract other travellers who simply want to sleep for cheap.

Costs Typically a dorm bed costs $28 to $40 per night, and a double (usually without bathroom) $80 to $100.

Facilities Hostels provide varying levels of accommodation, from the austere simplicity of wilderness hostels to city-centre buildings with a cafe-bar and en-suite rooms. Most of the accommodation is in dormitories (bunk rooms), usually ranging in size from four to 12 beds. Many hostels also provide twin rooms and doubles. Hostels generally have cooking facilities, a communal area with a TV, laundry facilities and sometimes travel offices and job centres.

Bed linen Often provided; sleeping bags are not welcome due to hygiene concerns.

HOSTEL ORGANISATIONS & CHAINS

The **Youth Hostels Association** (www.yha.com.au) has around 60 Australian hostels, offering dorms, twin and double rooms, and cooking and laundry facilities: the vibe is generally less 'party' than in independent hostels.

Nightly charges start at $25 for members; hostels also take non-YHA members for an extra $3. Australian residents can become YHA members for $42 for one year ($32 if you're aged between 18 and 25). Join online or at any YHA hostel. Families can also join: just pay the adult price, then kids under 18 can join for free.

The YHA is part of **Hostelling International** (www.hihostels.com). If you already have HI membership in your own country, you're entitled to YHA rates in Australia. Preferably, visitors to Australia should purchase an HI card in their country of residence, but once you're in Australia you can also buy

PRACTICALITIES

DVDs Australian DVDs are encoded for Region 4, which includes Mexico, South America, Central America, New Zealand, the Pacific and the Caribbean.

Newspapers Leaf through the daily *Sydney Morning Herald* (www.smh.com.au), Melbourne's *Age* (www.theage.com.au) or the national *Australian* broadsheet newspaper (www.theaustralian.com.au).

Radio Tune in to ABC radio; check out www.abc.net.au/radio for local frequencies.

Smoking Banned on public transport, in pubs, bars and eateries, and in some public outdoor spaces.

TV The main free-to-air TV channels are the government-sponsored ABC, multicultural SBS and the three commercial networks – Seven, Nine and Ten. Numerous free spin-off and local channels enrich the viewing brew.

Weights & measures Australia uses the metric system.

memberships online, at state offices or major YHA hostels.

Other international organisations with Australian hostels:

Base Backpackers (www.stayatbase.com)

Nomads (www.nomadsworld.com)

VIP Backpackers (www.vipbackpackers.com)

Hotels

Hotels in Australian cities or well-touristed places are generally of the business or luxury-chain variety (mid-range to top end): comfortable, anonymous, mod-con-filled rooms in multistorey blocks. For these hotels we quote 'rack rates' (official advertised rates – usually upwards of $160 a night), though significant discounts can be offered when business is quiet.

Lodges & Tented Camps

Out in the wilds of some national parks, safari-style lodges are slowly making their presence felt. Based around the same principles as African safari lodges, they inhabit fabulously remote

(sometimes fly-in) locations and they offer a mix of semi-luxurious four-walled cabins and elevated canvas tents with en-suite bathrooms. Rates usually include all meals and may also include all activities and excursions. Currently, such places are starting to appear in Kakadu National Park, Mary River National Park and Arnhem Land, all in the Northern Territory.

Motels

Drive-up motels offer comfortable midrange accommodation and are found all over Australia, often on the edges of urban centres. They rarely offer a cheaper rate for singles, so are better value for couples or groups of three. You'll mostly pay between $120 and $180 for a simple room with a kettle, fridge, TV, air-con and bathroom.

Pubs

Many Australian pubs (from the term 'public house') were built during boom times, so they're often among the largest, most extravagant buildings in town. Some have been restored, but generally rooms remain small

and weathered, with a long amble down the hall to the bathroom. They're usually central and cheap – singles/doubles with shared facilities from $60/100, more if you want a private bathroom. If you're a light sleeper, avoid booking a room above the bar and check whether a band is cranking out the rock downstairs that night.

Rental Accommodation

If you're in Australia for a while (visas permitting), then a rental property or room in a shared flat or house will be an economical option. Delve into the classified advertisement sections of the daily newspapers; Wednesday and Saturday are usually the best days. Noticeboards in universities, hostels, bookshops and cafes are also useful. Properties listed through a real-estate agent usually necessitate at least a six-month lease, plus a bond and first month's rent up front.

City Hobo (www.cityhobo.com) Matches your personality with your ideal big-city suburb, although it's aimed at those coming to live.

Couch Surfing (www.couchsurfing.com) Connects spare couches with new friends.

Flatmate Finders (www.flatmatefinders.com.au) Long-term share-accommodation listings.

Gumtree (www.gumtree.com.au) Classified site with jobs, accommodation and items for sale.

Stayz (www.stayz.com.au) Holiday rentals.

Children

If you can survive the long distances between cities, travelling around Australia with the kids can be a real delight. There's oodles of interesting stuff to see and do, both indoors and outdoors.

Lonely Planet's *Travel with Children* contains plenty of useful information.

Practicalities

Accommodation Many motels and the better-equipped caravan parks have playgrounds and swimming pools, and can supply cots and (sometimes) baby baths – motels may also have in-house children's videos and child-minding services. Top-end hotels and many (but not all) midrange hotels are well versed in the needs of guests with children. B&Bs, on the other hand, often market themselves as child-free.

Change rooms and breastfeeding All cities and most major towns have centrally located public rooms where parents can go to nurse their baby or change a nappy; check with the local tourist office or city council for details. Most Australians have a relaxed attitude about breastfeeding and nappy changing in public.

Child care Australia's numerous licensed child-care agencies offer babysitting services. Check under 'Baby Sitters' and 'Child Care Centres' in the *Yellow Pages* telephone directory, or phone the local council for a list. Licensed centres are subject to government regulations and usually adhere to high standards; avoid unlicensed operators.

Child safety seats Major hire-car companies will supply and fit child safety seats, charging a one-off fee of around $25 or a per-day rate. Call taxi companies in advance to organise child safety seats. The rules for travelling in taxis with kids vary from state to state: in most places safety seats aren't legally required, but must be used if available.

Concessions Child concessions (and family rates) often apply to accommodation, tours, admission fees and transport, with some discounts as high as 50% of the adult rate. However, the definition of 'child' varies from under 12 years to under 18 years. Accommodation concessions generally apply to children under 12 years sharing the same room as adults.

Health care Australia has high-standard medical services and facilities, and items such as baby formula and disposable nappies are widely available.

Eating with Children

Dining with children in Australia is relatively easy. At all but the flashiest places children are commonly seen. Kids are usually more than welcome at cafes, while bistros and clubs often see families dining early. Many fine-dining restaurants discourage small children (assuming that they're all ill behaved).

Most places that do welcome children don't have kids' menus, and those that do usually offer everything straight from the deep fryer – crumbed chicken and chips etc. You might be best finding something on the normal menu (say a pasta or salad) and asking the kitchen to adapt it to your child's needs.

The best news for travelling families is that there are often plenty of free or coin-operated barbecues in parks. Note that these will be in high demand at weekends and on public holidays.

Customs Regulations

For detailed information on customs and quarantine regulations, contact the **Department of Immigration and Border Protection** (☑02-6275 6666, 1300 363 263; www.border.gov.au).

When entering Australia you can bring most articles in free of duty provided that customs is satisfied they are for personal use and that you'll be taking them with you when you leave. Duty-free quotas per person (note the unusually low figure for cigarettes):

Alcohol 2.25L (over the age of 18)

Cigarettes 50 cigarettes (over the age of 18)

Dutiable goods Up to the value of $900 ($450 for people under 18)

Narcotics, of course, are illegal, and customs inspectors and their highly trained hounds are diligent in sniffing them out. Quarantine regulations are strict, so you must declare all goods of animal or vegetable origin on entering the country – wooden spoons, straw hats, the lot. Fresh food (meat, cheese, fruit, vegetables etc) and flowers are prohibited. There are often disposal bins located in airports where you can dump any questionable items if you don't want to bother with a customs inspection. You must declare currency in excess of $10,000 (including foreign currency).

Discount Cards

Travellers over the age of 60 with some form of identification (eg a state-issued seniors card or overseas equivalent) are sometimes eligible for concession prices for public transport.

The internationally recognised **International Student Identity Card** (ISIC; www.isic.org) is available to full-time students aged 12 years and over. The card gives the bearer discounts on accommodation, transport and admission to various attractions. The same organisation also produces the International Youth Travel Card (IYTC), issued to people under 26 years of age and not full-time students, and has benefits equivalent to the ISIC; also similar is the International Teacher Identity Card (ITIC), available to teaching professionals. All three cards are available online (from the ISIC website) and from student travel companies ($30).

Electricity

240V AC, 50Hz. Use a three-pin adaptor (different to British three-pin adaptors).

Type I
230V/50Hz

Food & Drink

See Food & Drink chapter, p1043.

LGBTIQ Travellers

Australia is a popular destination for gay and lesbian travellers, with the so-called 'pink tourism' appeal of Sydney especially big, thanks largely to the city's annual, high-profile and spectacular Sydney Gay & Lesbian Mardi Gras. In general, Australians are open-minded, but the further from the cities you get, the more likely you are to run into suspicion or hostility.

Throughout the country, but particularly on the east coast, there are tour operators, travel agents and accommodation places that make a point of welcoming the gay and lesbian community.

Same-sex acts are legal in all states, but the age of consent varies.

Resources

Major cities have gay-community newspapers, available from clubs, cafes, venues and newsagents. Lifestyle magazines include *DNA*, *Lesbians on the Loose (LOTL)* and the Sydney-based *SX*. In Melbourne look for *MCV*, in Queensland, *Queensland Pride*. Perth has the free *OutinPerth* and Adelaide has *Blaze*.

Gay & Lesbian Tourism Australia (Galta; www.galta.com.au) General information on gay-friendly businesses, places to stay and nightlife.

Gay Stay Australia (www.gaystayaustralia.com) A useful resource for accommodation.

Same Same (www.samesame.com.au) News, events and lifestyle features.

Festivals & Events

Midsumma Festival, Melbourne (www.midsumma.org.au; ⊙Jan-Feb)

Sydney Gay & Lesbian Mardi Gras, Sydney (www.mardigras.org.au; ⊙Feb-Mar)

Feast Festival, Adelaide (www.feast.org.au; ⊙Oct/Nov)

PrideFest, Perth (www.pridewa.com.au; ⊙Nov)

Brisbane Pride Festival (www.brisbanepride.org.au; ⊙Sep)

Health

Health-wise, Australia is a remarkably safe country in which to travel, considering that such a large portion of it lies in the tropics. Few travellers to Australia will experience anything worse than an upset stomach or a bad hangover and, if you do fall ill, the standard of hospitals and health care is high.

Before You Go

HEALTH INSURANCE

Health insurance is essential for all travellers. Remember that some policies specifically exclude some 'dangerous activities' listed in the policy. These might include scuba diving, skiing and even bushwalking. Make sure the policy you choose fully covers you for your activity of choice.

MEDICAL-KIT CHECKLIST

➡ paracetamol (acetaminophen) or aspirin

➡ antibiotics

➡ antidiarrhoeal drugs (eg loperamide)

➡ antihistamines (for hayfever and allergic reactions)

➡ anti-inflammatory drugs (eg ibuprofen)

➡ antibacterial ointment in case of cuts or abrasions

➡ steroid cream or cortisone (for allergic rashes)

➡ bandages, gauze, gauze rolls

➡ adhesive or paper tape

➡ scissors, safety pins, tweezers

➡ thermometer

➡ pocket knife

➡ DEET-containing insect repellent for the skin

➡ permethrin-containing insect spray for clothing, tents and bed nets

---

EATING PRICE RANGES

The following price ranges refer to a standard main course:

$ less than $15

$$ $15 to $30

$$$ more than $30

→ sunscreen

→ oral rehydration salts

→ iodine tablets or water filter (for water purification)

RESOURCES

There's a wealth of travel health advice on the internet: **Lonely Planet** (www.lonelyplanet.com) is a good place to start. The **World Health Organization** (www.who.int/ith) publishes *International Travel and Health*, revised annually and available free online. **MD Travel Health** (www.mdtravelhealth.com) provides complete travel-health recommendations for every country, updated daily. Government travel-health websites include the following:

Australia (www.smartraveller.gov.au)

Canada (www.hc-sc.gc.ca)

UK (www.nhs.uk/livewell/travelhealth/Pages/Travelhealthhome.aspx)

USA (www.cdc.gov/travel)

VACCINATIONS

Visit a physician four to eight weeks before departure. Ask your doctor for an International Certificate of Vaccination (aka the 'yellow booklet'), which will list the vaccinations you've received.

Upon entering Australia you'll be required to fill out a 'travel history' card detailing any visits to Ebola-affected regions within the last 21 days.

If you're entering Australia within six days of having stayed overnight or longer in a yellow-fever-infected country, you'll need proof of yellow-fever vaccination. For a full list of these countries visit **Centers for Disease Control & Prevention** (www.cdc.gov/travel).

The **World Health Organization** (www.who.int) recommends that all travellers should be covered for diphtheria, tetanus, measles, mumps, rubella, chicken pox and polio, as well as hepatitis

B, regardless of their destination. While Australia has high levels of childhood vaccination coverage, outbreaks of these diseases do occur.

In Australia

AVAILABILITY & COST OF HEALTH CARE

Facilities Australia has an excellent health-care system. It's a mixture of privately run medical clinics and hospitals alongside a system of public hospitals funded by the Australian government. There are also excellent specialised public-health facilities for women and children in major centres.

Medicare The Medicare system covers Australian residents for some health-care costs. Visitors from countries with which Australia has a reciprocal health-care agreement – New Zealand, the Republic of Ireland, Sweden, the Netherlands, Finland, Italy, Belgium, Malta, Slovenia, Norway and the UK – are eligible for benefits specified under the Medicare program. See www.humanservices.gov.au/customer/subjects/medicare-services.

Medications Painkillers, antihistamines for allergies, and skincare products are widely available at chemists throughout Australia. You may find that medications readily available over the counter in some countries are only available in Australia by prescription. These include the oral contraceptive pill, some medications for asthma and all antibiotics.

HEALTH CARE IN REMOTE AREAS

In Australia's remote locations it's possible there will be a significant delay in emergency services reaching you in the event of serious accident or illness. Do not underestimate the vast distances between most major outback towns; an increased level of self-reliance and preparation is essential. The **Royal Flying Doctor Service** (www.flyingdoctor.org.au) provides an important back-up for remote communities.

Consider taking a wilderness first-aid course, such as those offered by **Wilderness First Aid Consultants** (www.wfac.com.au). Take a comprehensive first-aid kit that is appropriate for the activities planned.

Ensure that you have adequate means of communication. Australia has extensive mobile-phone coverage, but additional radio communication (such as a satellite phone) is important for remote areas. A safety flare or beacon is also an essential piece of kit if you're really going off track.

Heat Exhaustion & Heatstroke

Symptoms of heat exhaustion include dizziness, fainting, fatigue, nausea or vomiting. The skin is usually pale, cool and clammy. Treatment consists of rest in a cool, shady place and fluid replacement with water or diluted sports drinks.

Heatstroke is a severe form of heat illness and is a true medical emergency, with heating of the brain leading to disorientation, hallucinations and seizures. Prevent heatstroke by maintaining an adequate fluid intake to ensure the continued passage of clear and copious urine, especially during physical exertion.

Insect-Borne Illnesses

Various insects in Australia may be the source of specific diseases (dengue fever, Ross River fever, viral encephalitis, Bairnsdale (Buruli) ulcer). For protection wear loose-fitting, long-sleeved clothing, and apply 30% DEET to all exposed skin.

Sun & Surf

Check with local surf lifesaving organisations and be aware of your own expertise and limitations before entering the surf.

The Australian sun is extremely powerful and generally burns far faster than most travellers are used to in their home countries. Always use SPF50+ sunscreen; apply it 30 minutes before going into the sun and repeat applications regularly.

Travellers Diarrhoea

All water other than tap water should be boiled, filtered or chemically disinfected (with iodine tablets) to prevent travellers diarrhoea and giardiasis.

If you develop diarrhoea (more than four or five stools a day), drink plenty of fluids – preferably an oral rehydration solution containing lots of salt and sugar. You should also begin taking an antibiotic (usually a quinolone drug) and an antidiarrhoeal agent (such as loperamide). If diarrhoea is bloody, persists for more than 72 hours, or is accompanied by fever, shaking, chills or severe abdominal pain, seek medical attention.

Drinking Water

Tap water is universally safe in Australia.

Insurance

Worldwide travel insurance is available at www.lonelyplanet.com/travel-insurance. You can buy, extend and claim online anytime – even if you're already on the road.

Level of Cover A good travel insurance policy covering theft, loss and medical problems is essential. Some policies specifically exclude designated 'dangerous activities' such as scuba diving, skiing and even bushwalking. Make sure the policy you choose fully covers you for your activity of choice.

Health You may prefer a policy that pays doctors or hospitals directly rather than requiring you to pay on the spot and claim later. If you have to claim later make sure you keep all documentation. Check that the policy covers ambulances and

emergency medical evacuations by air.

Internet Access

Wi-fi

Wi-fi is increasingly the norm in urban Australian accommodation (often free for guests). Cafes, bars and even some public gardens and town squares also provide wi-fi access. Local tourist offices should have details of public wi-fi hot spots.

Even so, there remain a surprising number of black spots without mobile or internet coverage. Most of these are in rural or outback areas. In such areas, hotel wi-fi may be your saviour.

Internet Cafes & Access

There are fewer internet cafes around these days than there were five years ago (thanks to the advent of iPhones, iPads and wi-fi), but you'll still find them in most sizeable towns. Most accommodation is phasing out internet terminals and kiosks in favour of wi-fi, although most hostels still have a public computer.

Most public libraries have internet access, but generally it's provided for research needs, not for travellers to check Facebook – so book ahead or find an internet cafe.

Legal Matters

Most travellers will have no contact with Australia's police or legal system; if they do, it's most likely to be while driving.

Driving There's a significant police presence on Australian roads, and police have the power to stop your car, see your licence (you're required to carry it), check your vehicle for roadworthiness and insist that you

take a breath test for alcohol (and sometimes illicit drugs).

Drugs First-time offenders caught with small amounts of illegal drugs are likely to receive a fine rather than go to jail, but the recording of a conviction against you may affect your visa status.

Visas If you remain in Australia beyond the life of your visa, you'll officially be an 'overstayer' and could face detention and then be prevented from returning to Australia for up to three years.

Legal Advice It's your right to telephone a friend, lawyer or relative before questioning begins. Legal aid is available only in serious cases and is subject to means testing; for Legal Aid info see www.nationallegalaid.org. However, many solicitors do not charge for an initial consultation.

Maps

Good-quality road and topographical maps are plentiful and readily available around Australia. State motoring organisations are a dependable source of road maps, while local tourist offices usually supply free town and region maps (though cartographic quality varies).

Bushwalking maps Bushwalkers and others undertaking outdoor activities for which large-scale maps are essential should browse the topographic sheets published by **Geoscience Australia** (☑1800 800 173; www.ga.gov.au). The more popular topographic sheets are usually available over the counter at shops selling specialist bushwalking gear and outdoor equipment.

Outback Driving Maps Hema Maps (www.hemamaps.com) publishes some of the best maps for desert tracks and regions. They're available online and from some bookstores.

GPS You can hire a GPS from the major car-hire companies (subject to availability), but they're pretty unnecessary if you're sticking to the main roads.

Money

ATMs & Eftpos

ATMs Australia's 'big four' banks – ANZ, Commonwealth, National Australia Bank and Westpac – and affiliated banks have branches all over Australia, plus a slew of 24-hour auto-mated teller machines (ATMs); you'll even find them in some outback roadhouses. Most ATMs accept cards issued by other banks (for a fee) and are linked to international networks.

Eftpos Most service stations, supermarkets, restaurants, cafes and shops have Electronic Funds Transfer at Point of Sale (Eftpos) facilities, allowing you to make purchases and some even allow you to draw out cash with your credit or debit card.

Fees Bear in mind that withdraw-ing cash through ATMs or Eftpos may attract significant fees – check the associated costs with your bank first.

Credit & Debit Cards

Credit cards such as Visa and MasterCard are widely accepted for everything from a hostel bed or a restaurant meal to an adventure tour, and are pretty much essen-tial (in lieu of a large deposit) for hiring a car. They can also be used to get cash advances over the counter at banks and from many ATMs, de-pending on the card, though these transactions incur immediate interest. Diners Club and American Express (Amex) are not as widely accepted.

Lost credit-card contact numbers:

American Express (✆1300 132 639; www.americanexpress. com.au)

Diners Club (✆1300 360 060; www.dinersclub.com.au)

MasterCard (✆1800 120 113; www.mastercard.com.au)

Visa (✆1800 450 346; www. visa.com.au)

Currency

Australia's currency is the Australian dollar, comprising 100 cents. There are 5c, 10c, 20c, 50c, $1 and $2 coins, and $5, $10, $20, $50 and $100 notes. Prices in shops are often marked in single cents then rounded to the nearest 5c when you come to pay.

Debit Cards

A debit card allows you to draw money directly from your home bank account using ATMs, banks or Eftpos machines. Any card con-nected to the international banking network – Cirrus, Maestro, Plus and Euro-card – should work with your PIN. Expect substantial fees.

Companies such as Trav-elex offer debit cards with set withdrawal fees and a balance you can top up from your personal bank account while on the road.

Exchanging Money

Changing foreign currency (or travellers cheques, if you're still using them) is usually no problem at banks throughout Australia, or at licensed moneychangers such as Travelex or Amex in cities and major towns.

Opening a Bank Account

If you're planning on staying in Australia a while (on a Working Holiday visa for instance), it makes sense to open a local bank account. This is easy enough for overseas visitors provided it's done within six weeks of arrival. Simply present your passport and provide the bank with a postal address and it'll open the account and send you an ATM card.

After six weeks it be-comes much more com-plicated. A points system operates and you need to score a minimum of 100 points before you can have the privilege of letting the bank take your money. Pass-ports and birth certificates are worth the most points, followed by an international driving licence with photo, then minor IDs such as credit cards. You must have at least one ID with a pho-tograph. Once the account is open, you should be able to have money transferred from your home account (for a fee, of course).

Before you arrive It's possible to set up an Australian bank account before you embark on your international trip and applications can be made online; check bank websites for details:

ANZ (www.anz.com.au)

Commonwealth Bank (www. commbank.com.au)

INTERSTATE QUARANTINE

When travelling within Australia, whether by land or air, you'll come across signs (mainly in airports and inter-state train stations and at state borders) warning of the possible dangers of carrying fruit, vegetables and plants from one area to another. Certain pests and diseases (fruit fly, cucurbit thrips, grape phylloxera...) are preva-lent in some areas, but not in others: authorities would like to limit their spread.

There are quarantine inspection posts on some state borders and occasionally elsewhere. While quarantine control often relies on honesty, many posts are staffed and officers are entitled to search your car for un-declared items. Generally they will confiscate all fresh fruit and vegetables, so it's best to leave shopping for these items until the first town past the inspection point.

National Australia Bank (NAB; www.nab.com.au)

Westpac (www.westpac.com.au)

Taxes & Refunds

Goods & Services Tax The GST is a flat 10% tax on all goods and services – accommodation, eating out, transport, electrical and other goods, books, furniture, clothing etc. There are exceptions, however, such as basic foods (milk, bread, fruit and vegetables etc). By law the tax is included in the quoted or shelf price, so all prices are GST-inclusive. International air and sea travel to/from Australia is GST-free, as is domestic air travel when purchased outside Australia by nonresidents.

Refund of GST If you purchase goods with a total minimum value of $300 from any one supplier no more than 30 days before you leave Australia, you are entitled under the Tourist Refund Scheme (TRS) to a refund of any GST paid. The scheme only applies to goods you take with you as hand luggage or wear onto the plane or ship. Also note that the refund is valid for goods bought from more than one supplier, but only if at least $300 is spent in each. Check out www.border.gov.au/Trav/Ente/Tour/Are-you-a-traveller for more details.

Income Tax Visitors pay tax on earnings made within Australia, and must lodge a tax return with the Australian Taxation Office (ATO). If too much tax was withheld from your pay, you will receive a refund. See the Australian Taxation Office (www.ato.gov.au) website for details. In 2016 the Australian Government introduced the so-called 'backpacker tax', whereby all 417 or 462 visa holders will, from 2017 on, be taxed at 15% for the first $37,000 earned.

Tipping

It's common but by no means obligatory to tip in restaurants and upmarket cafes if the service warrants it – a gratuity of between 5% and 10% of the bill is the norm. Taxi drivers will also appreciate you rounding up the fare. Tipping is not usually expected in hotels.

Travellers Cheques

➡ The ubiquity and convenience of internationally linked credit- and debit-card facilities in Australia means that travellers cheques are virtually redundant.

➡ Amex and Travelex will exchange their associated travellers cheques, and major banks will change travellers cheques also.

➡ In all instances you'll need to present your passport for identification when cashing them.

Opening Hours

Business hours vary from state to state, but the following is a guide. Note that nearly all attractions across Australia are closed on Christmas Day; many also close on New Year's Day and Good Friday.

Banks 9.30am-4pm Monday to Thursday; until 5pm on Friday.

Cafes All-day affairs opening from around 7am until around 5pm, or continuing their business into the night.

Petrol stations & roadhouses Usually 8am-10pm. Some urban service stations are open 24 hours.

Post offices 9am-5pm Monday to Friday; some also 9am-noon on Saturday. You can also buy stamps from newsagents and delis.

Pubs Usually serving food from noon-2pm and 6-8pm. Pubs and bars often open for drinking at lunchtime and continue well into the evening, particularly from Thursday to Saturday.

Restaurants Open around noon-2.30pm for lunch and 6-8pm for dinner. Eateries in major cities keep longer hours.

Shops & businesses 9am-5pm or 6pm Monday to Friday, and until either noon or 5pm on Saturday. In larger cities, doors stay open until 9pm.

Supermarkets Generally open from 7am until at least 8pm; some open 24 hours. Delis and general stores also open late.

Post

Australia Post (www.auspost.com.au) runs very reliable national and worldwide postal services; see the website for info on international delivery zones and rates. All post offices will hold mail for visitors: you need to provide some form of identification (such as a passport or driver's licence) to collect mail.

Public Holidays

Timing of public holidays can vary from state to state: check locally for precise dates. Some holidays are only observed locally within a state.

National

New Year's Day 1 January

Australia Day 26 January

Easter (Good Friday to Easter Monday inclusive) late March/early April

Anzac Day 25 April

Queen's Birthday Second Monday in June (last Monday in September in WA)

Christmas Day 25 December

Boxing Day 26 December

Australian Capital Territory

Canberra Day Second Monday in March

Bank Holiday First Monday in August

Labour Day First Monday in October

New South Wales

Bank Holiday First Monday in August

Labour Day First Monday in October

Northern Territory

May Day First Monday in May

Show Day (Alice Springs) First Friday in July; (Tennant Creek) second Friday in July; (Katherine) third Friday in July; (Darwin) fourth Friday in July

Picnic Day First Monday in August

Queensland

Labour Day First Monday in May

Royal Queensland Show Day (Brisbane) Second or third Wednesday in August

South Australia

Adelaide Cup Day Third Monday in May

Labour Day First Monday in October

Proclamation Day Last Monday or Tuesday in December

Tasmania

Regatta Day (Hobart) 14 February

Launceston Cup Day (Launceston) Last Wednesday in February

Eight Hours Day First Monday in March

Bank Holiday Tuesday following Easter Monday

King Island Show (King Island) First Tuesday in March

Launceston Show Day (Launceston) Thursday preceding second Saturday in October

Hobart Show Day (Hobart) Thursday preceding fourth Saturday in October

Recreation Day (Northern Tasmania) First Monday in November

Victoria

Labour Day Second Monday in March

Melbourne Cup Day First Tuesday in November

Western Australia

Labour Day First Monday in March

Foundation Day First Monday in June

School Holidays

➡ The Christmas and summer school holidays run from mid-December to late January.

➡ Three shorter school holiday periods occur during the year, varying by a week or two from state to state. They fall roughly from early to mid-April (usually including the Easter public holidays), late June to mid-July, and late September to early October.

Safe Travel

Australia is a relatively safe place to travel by world standards – crime- and war-wise at any rate – but natural disasters regularly wreak havoc. Bushfires, floods and cyclones decimate parts of most states and territories, but if you pay attention to warnings from local authorities and don't venture into affected areas, you should be fine.

➡ Swimming in far-northern Australia is often dangerous thanks to crocodiles – always check with locals.

➡ If driving on rural roads after dark, do so carefully and watch for wandering wildlife.

➡ For more on safety, see p1050.

Telephone

Australia's main telecommunication companies:

Optus (☎1800 780 219; www.optus.com.au)

Telstra (☎13 22 00; www.telstra.com.au)

Virgin (☎1300 555 100; www.virginmobile.com.au)

Vodafone (☎1300 650 410; www.vodafone.com.au)

Information & Toll-Free Calls

➡ Many businesses have either a toll-free ☎1800 number, dialled from anywhere within Australia for free, or a 13 or 1300 number, charged at a local call rate. None of these numbers can be dialled from outside Australia (and often can't be dialled from mobile phones within Australia).

➡ To make a reverse-charge (collect) call from any public or private phone, dial ☎1800 738 3773 or 12 550.

GOVERNMENT TRAVEL ADVICE

The following government websites offer travel advisories and information for travellers.

Australian Department of Foreign Affairs & Trade (www.smartraveller.gov.au)

Canadian Department of Foreign Affairs & International Trade (www.voyage.gc.ca)

French Ministère des Affaires Étrangères et Européennes (www.diplomatie.gouv.fr/fr/conseils-aux-voyageurs)

Italian Ministero degli Affari Esteri (www.viaggia resicuri.mae.aci.it)

New Zealand Ministry of Foreign Affairs & Trade (www.safetravel.govt.nz)

UK Foreign & Commonwealth Office (www.gov.uk/foreign-travel-advice)

US Department of State (www.travel.state.gov)

→ Numbers starting with 190 are usually recorded information services, charged at anything from 35c to $5 or more per minute (more from mobiles and payphones).

International Calls

From payphones Most payphones allow International Subscriber Dialling (ISD) calls, the cost and international dialling code of which will vary depending on which international phonecard provider you are using. International phone cards are readily available from internet cafes and convenience stores.

From landlines International calls from landlines in Australia are also relatively cheap, depending where you're calling, and quite often subject to special deals; rates vary with providers.

Codes When calling overseas you will need to dial the international access code from Australia (⏴0011 or 0018), the country code and then the area code (without the initial 0). So for a London telephone number you'll need to dial ⏴0011-44-20, then the number. In addition, certain operators will have you dial a special code to access their service. If dialling Australia from overseas, the country code is ⏴61 and you need to drop the 0 in state/territory area codes.

Local Calls

Local calls cost 50c from public phones, and 25c from private phones (although it depends on the provider) – there are no time limits. Calls to/from mobile phones cost more and are timed.

Long Distance Calls & Area Codes

Long-distance calls (over around 50km) are timed. Australia uses four Subscriber Trunk Dialling (STD) area codes. These STD calls can be made from any public phone and are cheaper during off-peak hours (generally between 7pm and 7am, and on weekends). The area codes are as follows.

STATE/ TERRITORY	AREA CODE
ACT	⏴02
NSW	⏴02
NT	⏴08
QLD	⏴07
SA	⏴08
TAS	⏴03
VIC	⏴03
WA	⏴08

Area-code boundaries don't necessarily coincide with state borders; for example some parts of NSW use the neighbouring states' codes.

Mobile Phones

Numbers Numbers with the prefix ⏴04 belong to mobile phones.

Networks Australia's digital network is compatible with GSM 900 and 1800 (used in Europe), but generally not with the systems used in the USA or Japan.

Reception Australia's mobile networks service more than 90% of the population, but leave vast tracts of the country uncovered.

Providers It's easy enough to get connected short-term: the main service providers (Telstra, Optus, Virgin and Vodafone) all have prepaid mobile systems. Buy a starter kit, which may include a phone or, if you have your own phone, a SIM card and a prepaid charge card. Shop around for the best offer.

Phonecards

A variety of phonecards can be bought at newsagents, hostels and post offices for a fixed-dollar value (usually $10, $20 etc) and can be used with any public or private phone by dialling a toll-free access number and then the PIN number on the card. Shop around.

Public Phones Most of the few public phones that remain use phonecards; some also accept credit cards. Old-fashioned coin-operated public phones are becoming increasingly rare (and if you do find one, chances are the coin slot will be gummed up or vandalised beyond function).

Time

Zones Australia is divided into three time zones: Western Standard Time (GMT/UTC plus eight hours), covering Western Australia; Central Standard Time (plus 9½ hours), covering South Australia and the Northern Territory; and Eastern Standard Time (plus 10 hours), covering Tasmania, Victoria, NSW, the ACT and Queensland. There are minor exceptions – Broken Hill (NSW), for instance, is on Central Standard Time.

Daylight saving Clocks are put forward an hour in some states during the warmer months (October to early April), but Queensland, Western Australia and the Northern Territory stay on standard time.

Toilets

→ Toilets in Australia are sit-down Western style (though you mightn't find this prospect too appealing in some remote outback pit stops).

→ See www.toiletmap.gov. au for public toilet locations, including disabled-access toilets.

Tourist Information

Tourism Australia (www. australia.com) is the national government tourist body and has a good website for pretrip research. The website also lists reliable travel agents in countries around the world that can help you plan your trip, plus visa, work and customs information.

Within Australia, tourist information is disseminated by various regional and local offices. Almost every major town in Australia has a tourist office of some type and they can be super helpful, with chatty staff (often retiree volunteers) providing local info not readily available from the state offices. If booking accommodation or tours from local offices, bear in mind that they often only promote businesses that are paying members of the local tourist association.

Travellers with Disabilities

Download Lonely Planet's free Accessible Travel guide from http://lptravel.to/AccessibleTravel.

➡ Levels of disability awareness in Australia are high and increasing.

➡ Legislation requires that new accommodation meets accessibility standards for mobility-impaired travellers, and discrimination by tourism operators is illegal.

➡ Many of Australia's key attractions, including many national parks, provide access for those with limited mobility and a number of sites also address the needs of visitors with visual or aural impairments. Contact attractions in advance to confirm the facilities.

➡ Tour operators with vehicles catering to mobility-impaired travellers operate from most capital cities.

➡ Facilities for wheelchairs are improving in accommodation, but there are still many older establishments where the necessary upgrades haven't been done.

Getting Around
AIR TRAVEL

Qantas entitles a disabled person with high-support needs and the carer travelling with them to a discount on full economy fares; contact **National Information Communication & Awareness Network** (Nican; ☏1300 655 535, 02 6241 1220; www.nican.com.

au) for eligibility info and an application form. Guide dogs travel for free on Qantas, Jetstar, Virgin Australia and their affiliated carriers. All of Australia's major airports have dedicated parking spaces, wheelchair access to terminals, accessible toilets, and skychairs to convey passengers onto planes via air bridges.

TRAIN TRAVEL

In NSW, CountryLink's XPT trains have at least one carriage (usually the buffet car) with a seat removed for a wheelchair, and an accessible toilet. Queensland Rail's *Tilt Train* from Brisbane to Cairns has a wheelchair-accessible carriage.

All of Australia's suburban rail networks are wheelchair-accessible and guide dogs and hearing dogs are permitted on all public transport.

In Victoria, **PTV** (Public Transport Victoria; ☏1800 800 007; www.ptv.vic.gov.au) offers a free travel pass to visually impaired people and wheelchair users for transport around Melbourne.

Resources
AUSTRALIAN

Deaf Australia (www.deaf australia.org.au)

e-Bility (www.ebility.com)

National Information Communication & Awareness Network (Nican; ☏1300 655 535, 02 6241 1220; www.nican.com.au) Australia-wide directory providing information on access, accommodation, sports and recreational activities, transport and specialist tour operators.

Vision Australia (☏1300 847 466; www.visionaustralia.org.au)

INTERNATIONAL

Mobility International USA (www.miusa.org) In the US, advising disabled travellers on mobility issues. It primarily runs educational exchange programs,

and some include Australian travel.

Society for Accessible Travel & Hospitality (www.sath.org) In the US; offers assistance and advice.

Visas

➡ All visitors to Australia need a visa – only New Zealand nationals are exempt, and even they sheepishly receive a 'special category' visa on arrival.

➡ There are several different visas available, depending on your nationality and what kind of visit you're contemplating.

➡ See the website of the **Department of Immigration & Border Protection** (☏02-6275 6666, 1300 363 263; www.border.gov.au) for info and visa application forms (also available from Australian diplomatic missions overseas and many travel agents).

eVisitor (651)

➡ Many European passport holders are eligible for a free eVisitor visa, allowing stays in Australia for up to three months within a 12-month period.

➡ eVisitor visas must be applied for online (www.border.gov.au). They are electronically stored and linked to individual passport numbers, so no stamp in your passport is required.

➡ It's advisable to apply at least 14 days prior to the proposed date of travel to Australia.

Electronic Travel Authority (601)

➡ Passport holders from eight countries that aren't part of the eVisitor scheme – Brunei, Canada, Hong Kong, Japan, Malaysia, Singapore, South Korea and the USA – can apply for either a visitor or business Electronic Travel Authority (ETA).

➡ ETAs are valid for 12 months, with stays of up to three months on each visit.

➡ You can apply for an ETA online (www.border.gov.au), which attracts a nonrefundable service charge of $20.

Visitor (600)

➡ Short-term Visitor visas have largely been replaced by the eVisitor and ETA. However, if you're from a country not covered by either, or you want to stay longer than three months, you'll need to apply for a Visitor visa.

➡ Standard Visitor visas allow one entry for a stay of up to three, six or 12 months, and are valid for use within 12 months of issue.

➡ Apply online at www.border.gov.au.

Working Holiday (417)

On a normal visa you're not allowed to work in Australia, but you may be eligible for a 12-month Working Holiday visa, which lets you supplement your travels with casual employment. People from 19 countries (including the UK, Canada, Korea, the Netherlands, Malta, Ireland, Japan, Germany, France, Italy, Belgium, Finland, Sweden, Norway and Denmark) are eligible, but you must be between 18 and 30 years of age at the time of lodging your application (the government was considering raising the eligible age to 35 years at the time of writing, although nothing was confirmed). A visa subclass is available to residents of Chile, Thailand, Turkey and the USA.

The emphasis on casual rather than full-time work means that you can only work for six months at a time with any one employer – but you are free to work for more than one employer within the 12 months. There's a limit on

the number of visas issued each year, so apply as early as possible to the Australian embassy in your home country before you leave.

Apply prior to entry to Australia (up to a year in advance) – you can't change from another tourist visa to a Working Holiday visa once you're in Australia. Conditions include having a return air ticket or sufficient funds for a return or onward fare.

Work & Holiday (462)

Nationals from Argentina, Bangladesh, Chile, Indonesia, Malaysia, Poland, Portugal, Spain, Thailand, Turkey, the USA and Uruguay aged between the ages of 18 and 30 years can apply for a Work and Holiday visa prior to entry to Australia.

Once granted this visa allows the holder to enter Australia within three months of issue, stay for up to 12 months, leave and re-enter Australia any number of times within that 12 months, undertake temporary employment to supplement a trip, and study for up to four months.

For details see www.border.gov.au.

Visa Extensions

If you want to stay in Australia for longer than your visa allows, you'll need to apply for a new visa via www.border.gov.au. Apply at least two or three weeks before your visa expires.

Volunteering

Lonely Planet's *Volunteer: A Traveller's Guide to Making a Difference Around the World* provides useful information about volunteering.

See also the following websites:

GoVolunteer (www.govolunteer.com.au) Thousands of volunteering opportunities around the country.

Responsible Travel (www.responsibletravel.com) Travel to

Australia and take up a fixed-term volunteering position when you arrive.

Volunteering Australia (www.volunteeringaustralia.org) State-by-state listings of volunteering opportunities around Australia.

Australian Volunteers International (www.australianvolunteers.com) Places skilled volunteers into Indigenous communities in northern and central Australia (mostly long-term placements). Occasional short-term unskilled opportunities too, helping out at community-run roadhouses.

Conservation Volunteers Australia (www.conservationvolunteers.com.au) Nonprofit organisation involved in tree planting, walking-track construction and flora and fauna surveys.

Earthwatch Institute Australia (www.earthwatch.org) Volunteer expeditions that focus on conservation and wildlife.

STA (www.statravel.com.au) Volunteer holiday opportunities in Australia – on the website, click 'Planning' then 'Volunteering'.

Willing Workers on Organic Farms (WWOOF: www.wwoof.com.au) WWOOFing is where you do a few hours of work each day on a farm in return for bed and board. Most hosts are concerned to some extent with alternative lifestyles and have a minimum stay of two nights. You can join online for $70. You'll get a membership number and a booklet listing participating enterprises ($5 overseas postage).

Women Travellers

Australia is generally a safe place for women travellers, although the usual sensible precautions apply.

Night-time Avoid walking alone late at night in any of the major cities and towns – keep enough money aside for a taxi back to your accommodation.

Pubs Be wary of staying in basic pub accommodation unless it looks safe and well managed.

Sexual harassment Rare, though some macho Aussie males still slip – particularly when they've been drinking.

Rural areas Stereotypically, the further you get from the big cities, the less enlightened your average Aussie male is probably going to be about women's issues. Having said that, many women travellers say that they have met the friendliest, most down-to-earth blokes in outback pubs and remote roadhouse stops.

Hitchhiking Hitching is not recommended for anyone. Even when travelling in pairs, exercise caution at all times.

Drugged drinks Some pubs in Sydney and other big cities post warnings about drugged or 'spiked' drinks. It's probably not cause for paranoia, but play it safe if someone offers you a drink in a bar.

Work

If you come to Australia on a tourist visa, you're not allowed to work for pay: you'll need a Working Holiday (417) or Work and Holiday (462) visa – see Visa section for details.

Finding Work

Backpacker magazines, newspapers and hostel noticeboards are good places to source local work opportunities. Casual work can often be found during peak season at the major tourist centres: places such as Alice Springs, Cairns and resort towns along the Queensland coast, and the ski fields of Victoria and NSW are all good prospects during holiday season. Other possibilities for casual employment include factory work, labouring, bar work, waiting tables, domestic chores at outback roadhouses, nanny work, working as a station hand and collecting for char-

ities. People with computer, secretarial, nursing and teaching skills can find work temping in the major cities by registering with a relevant agency.

See also the following websites, which are good for opportunities in metropolitan areas:

➡ **Career One** (www.careerone.com.au) General employment site; good for metropolitan areas.

➡ **Gumtree** (www.gumtree.com.au) Classified site with jobs, accommodation and items for sale.

➡ **Job Active – Harvest** (www.jobsearch.gov.au/harvest) Harvest job specialists.

➡ **National Harvest Labour Information Service** (☑1800 062 332) Info on when and where you're likely to pick up harvest work.

➡ **QITE** (www.qite.com) Nonprofit Queensland employment agency operating around Cairns, Innisfail and the Atherton Tablelands.

➡ **Seek** (www.seek.com.au) General employment site; good for metropolitan areas.

➡ **Travellers at Work** (www.taw.com.au) Excellent site for working travellers in Australia.

➡ **Workabout Australia** (www.workaboutaustralia.com.au) Gives a state-by-state breakdown of seasonal work opportunities.

Seasonal Work

Seasonal fruit-picking (harvesting) relies on casual labour – there's always something that needs to be picked, pruned or farmed somewhere in Australia all year round. It's definitely hard work, involving early morning starts, and you're usually paid by how much you pick (per bin, bucket, kilo etc). Expect to earn about $50 to $60 a day to start with, and more when your skills and speed improve.

Some work, such as pruning or sorting, is paid at around $15 per hour.

Note that due to the complexities of visa situations, many local visitor information centres and backpacker hostels are stepping away from assisting travellers in finding work. To avoid disappointment, never put a deposit down to reserve a fruit-picking job and never pay for fruit-picking accommodation in advance.

SEASONAL WORK HOT SPOTS

➡ **NSW** The NSW ski fields have seasonal work during the ski season, particularly around Thredbo. There's also harvest work around Narrabri and Moree, and grape picking in the Hunter Valley. Fruit picking happens near Tenterfield, Orange and Young.

➡ **NT** The majority of working-holiday opportunities in the NT for backpackers are in fruit picking, station handing, labouring and hospitality.

➡ **Queensland** Queensland has vast tracts of farmland and orchards: there's fruit-picking work to be found around Stanthorpe, Childers, Bundaberg and Cairns. Those looking for sturdier (and much-better-paying) work should keep an eye on mining opportunities in towns such as Weipa and Cloncurry.

➡ **SA** Good seasonal-work opportunities can be found on the Fleurieu Peninsula, in the Coonawarra region and Barossa Valley (wineries), and along the Murray River around Berri (fruit picking).

➡ **Tasmania** The apple orchards in the south, especially around Cygnet and Huonville, are your best bet for work in Tassie.

➡ **Victoria** Harvest work in Mildura and Shepparton.

➡ **WA** In Perth plenty of temporary work is available

in tourism and hospitality, administration, IT, nursing, child care, factories and labouring. Outside of Perth travellers can easily get jobs in tourism and hospitality, plus a variety of seasonal work. For grape-picking work, head for the vineyards around Margaret River.

Income Tax

TAX FILE NUMBER

If you're working in Australia, you should apply for a Tax File Number (TFN). Without it, tax will be deducted at the maximum rate from any wages you receive. Apply for a TFN online through the Australian Taxation Office (ATO; www.ato.gov.au); it takes up to four weeks to be issued.

PAYING TAX & TAX REFUNDS

Even with a TFN, nonresidents (including Working Holiday visa holders) pay a considerably higher rate of tax than most Australian residents. For a start, there's no tax-free threshold (Australians pay no tax on their first $18,200) – you pay tax on every dollar you earn.

Because you have been paid wages in Australia, you must lodge a tax return with the ATO – see the website for info on how to do this, including getting a Payment Summary (an official summary of your earnings and tax payments) from your employer, timing/dates for lodging your tax return, and how to receive your Notice of Assessment.

Bear in mind that you're not entitled to a refund for the tax you paid – you will only receive a refund if too much tax was withheld from your pay. If you didn't pay enough while you were working, you will have to pay more. You are, however, entitled to any superannuation that you have accumulated.

Transport

GETTING THERE & AWAY

Australia is a long way from just about everywhere – getting there usually means a long-haul flight. If you're short on time on the ground, consider internal flights – they're affordable (compared with petrol and car-hire costs), can usually be carbon offset, and will save you some long days in the saddle. Flights, tours and rail tickets can be booked online at www.lonelyplanet.com/bookings.

Entering the Country

Arrival in Australia is usually straightforward and efficient, with the usual customs declarations. There are no restrictions for citizens of any particular foreign countries entering Australia – if you have a current passport and visa, you should be fine.

Passport

There are no restrictions for citizens of any particular foreign countries entering Australia. If you have a current passport and visa, you should be fine.

Air

Airports & Airlines

Most major international airlines fly to/from Australia. Australia's international carrier is **Qantas** (☑13 13 13; www.qantas.com.au).

Australia has numerous international gateways, with Sydney and Melbourne being the busiest.

Adelaide Airport (ADL; ☑08-8308 9211; www.adelaide airport.com.au; 1 James Schofield Dr)

Brisbane Airport (www.bne.com.au; Airport Dr)

Cairns Airport (☑07-4080 6703; www.cairnsairport.com; Airport Ave)

Darwin International Airport (☑08-8920 1811; www.darwinairport.com.au; Henry Wrigley Dr, Marrara)

Gold Coast Airport (www.goldcoastairport.com.au; Longa Ave, Bilinga)

Melbourne Airport (MEL; ☑03-9297 1600; www.melbourne airport.com.au; Departure Rd, Tullamarine)

Perth Airport (☑08-9478 8888; www.perthairport.com.au)

Sydney Airport (☑02-9667 9111; www.sydneyairport.com.au; Airport Dr, Mascot)

Sea

It's possible (though by no means easy and not necessarily safe) to make your way between Australia and places such as Papua New Guinea, Indonesia, New Zealand and the Pacific islands by hitching rides or crewing on yachts – usually you have to at least contribute towards food. Ask

---

CLIMATE CHANGE & TRAVEL

Every form of transport that relies on carbon-based fuel generates CO_2, the main cause of human-induced climate change. Modern travel is dependent on aeroplanes, which might use less fuel per kilometre per person than most cars but travel much greater distances. The altitude at which aircraft emit gases (including CO_2) and particles also contributes to their climate change impact. Many websites offer 'carbon calculators' that allow people to estimate the carbon emissions generated by their journey and, for those who wish to do so, to offset the impact of the greenhouse gases emitted with contributions to portfolios of climate-friendly initiatives throughout the world. Lonely Planet offsets the carbon footprint of all staff and author travel.

around at marinas and sailing clubs in places such as Coffs Harbour, Great Keppel Island, Airlie Beach, the Whitsundays, Darwin and Cairns. April is a good time to look for a berth in the Sydney area.

Alternatively **P&O Cruises** (www.pocruises.com.au) operates holiday cruises between Brisbane, Melbourne or Sydney and destinations in New Zealand and the Pacific. Some freighter ships also allow passengers to travel on board as they ship cargo – check out websites such as www.freighter expeditions.com.au and www.freightercruises.com for options.

GETTING AROUND

Australia is the sixth-largest country in the world: how you get from A to B requires some thought.

Car Travel at your own tempo and visit regions with no public transport. Hire cars in major towns; drive on the left.

Plane Fast track your holiday with affordable, frequent, fast flights between major centres. It's possible to carbon offset your flights.

Bus Reliable, frequent long-haul services around the country. Not always cheaper than flying.

Train Slow, expensive and infrequent...but the scenery is great! Opt for a sleeper carriage rather than an 'overnighter' seat.

Air

Time pressures combined with the vastness of the continent may lead you to consider taking to the skies at some point in your trip. Both **STA Travel** (☑134 782; www. statravel.com.au) and **Flight Centre** (☑133 133; www.flight

centre.com.au) have offices throughout Australia, or you can book online. Try these:

➡ www.travel.com.au

➡ www.webjet.com.au

Airlines in Australia

Australia's main domestic airlines service the large centres with regular flights. The major players:

Jetstar (☑131 538; www. jetstar.com)

Qantas (☑13 13 13; www. qantas.com.au)

Tigerair (☑1300 174 266; www. tigerair.com)

Virgin Australia (☑13 67 89; www.virginaustralia.com)

A number of smaller regional airlines operate within smaller geographical parameters and flying into regional airports. Queensland in particular has several such airlines. A couple of the better-known airlines:

Airnorth (☑1800 627 474; www.airnorth.com.au) Northern Territory and northwestern West Australia.

Regional Express (REX; ☑13 17 13; www.rex.com.au) Eastern and southeastern Australia.

Air Passes

Qantas (☑13 13 13; www. qantas.com.au) offers a discount-fare **Walkabout Air Pass** (www.qantas.com/travel/ airlines/walkabout/us/en) for passengers flying into Australia from overseas with Qantas or American Airlines. The pass allows you to link up around 80 domestic Australian destinations for less than you'd pay booking flights individually.

Bicycle

Australia has much to offer cyclists, from bike paths winding through most ma-

jor cities, to thousands of kilometres of good country roads where you can wear out your sprockets. There's a lot of flat countryside and gently rolling hills to explore and, although Australia is not as mountainous as, say, Switzerland or France, mountain bikers can find plenty of forest trails and high country. If you're really keen, outback cycling might also be an option.

Hire Bike hire in cities is easy, but if you're riding for more than a few hours or even a day, it's more economical to invest in your own wheels.

Legalities Bike helmets are compulsory in all states and territories, as are white front lights and red rear lights for riding at night.

Maps You can get by with standard road maps, but to avoid low-grade unsealed roads, the government series is best. The 1:250,000 scale is suitable, though you'll need lots of maps if you're going far. The next scale up is 1:1,000,000 – widely available in map shops.

Weather In summer carry plenty of water. Wear a helmet with a peak (or a cap under your helmet), use sunscreen and avoid cycling in the middle of the day. Beware summer northerly winds that can make life hell for a northbound cyclist. Southeasterly trade winds blow in April, when you can have (theoretically) tail winds all the way to Darwin. It can get very cold in Victoria, Tasmania, the southern part of South Australia and the New South Wales mountains, so pack appropriate clothing.

Transport If you're bringing in your own bike, check with your airline for costs and the degree of dismantling or packing required. Within Australia, bus companies require you to dismantle your bike and some don't guarantee that it will travel on the same bus as you.

Buying a Bike

If you want to buy a reliable, new road or mountain bike, your bottom-level starting price will be around $600. Throw in all the requisite on-the-road equipment (panniers, helmet etc) and your starting point becomes around $1750. Secondhand bikes are worth checking out in the cities, as are the post-Christmas and midyear sales, when newish cycles can be heavily discounted.

To sell your bike (or buy a secondhand one), try hostel noticeboards or online at **Trading Post** (www.trading post.com.au) or **Gumtree** (www.gumtree.com.au).

Resources

Each state and territory has a cycling organisation that can help with cycling information and put you in touch with touring clubs. **Bicycles Network Australia** (www. bicycles.net.au) offers information, news and links.

Bicycle NSW (www.bicyclensw. org.au)

Bicycle Network Tasmania (www.biketas.org.au)

Bicycle Network Victoria (www. bicyclenetwork.com.au)

Bicycle Queensland (www. bq.org.au)

Bike SA (www.bikesa.asn.au)

Bicycle Transportation Alliance (www.btawa.org.au) In WA.

Cycling Northern Territory (www.nt.cycling.org.au)

Pedal Power ACT (www.pedal power.org.au)

Boat

There's a hell of a lot of water around Australia, but unless you're fortunate, skilled or well-connected enough to land a position crewing a yacht, it's not really a feasible way of getting around. Other than short-hop regional ferries (eg to Kangaroo Island in SA, Rottnest Island in WA, Bruny Island in Tasmania, North Stradbroke Island in Queensland), the only long-range passenger service is the high-speed, vehicle-carrying **Spirit of Tasmania** (☑1800 634 906; www. spiritoftasmania.com.au; ⊙customer info 8am-8.30pm Mon-Sat, 9am-8pm Sun) between Melbourne and Devonport on Tasmania's northwest coast.

Bus

Australia's extensive bus network is a reliable way to

Principal Bus Routes & Railways

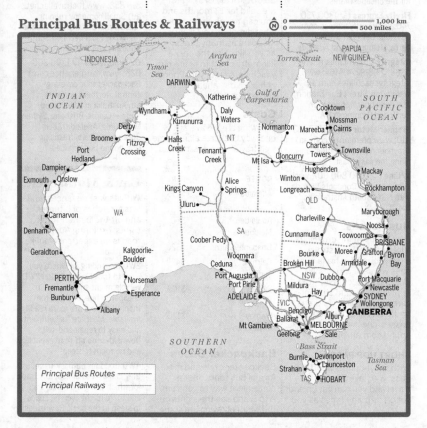

Principal Bus Routes ⎯⎯⎯⎯
Principal Railways ⎯⎯⎯⎯

get around, though bus travel isn't always cheaper than flying and it can be tedious over huge distances. Most buses are equipped with air-con, toilets and videos; all are smoke-free and some have wi-fi. There are no class divisions on Australian buses (very democratic), and the vehicles of the different companies all look similar.

Small towns eschew formal bus terminals for a single drop-off/pick-up point (it will be the post office, newsagent or corner shop).

Greyhound Australia (Map p258; ☑02-6211 8545; www. greyhound.com.au; 65 Northbourne Ave; ☉6am-6pm) Runs a national network (notably not across the Nullarbor Plain between Adelaide and Perth, nor Perth to Broome). Book online for the cheapest fares.

Firefly Express (☑1300 730 740; www.fireflyexpress.com. au) Runs between Sydney, Canberra, Melbourne and Adelaide.

Integrity Coach Lines (Map p888; ☑08-9274 7464; www. integritycoachlines.com.au; Wellington Street Bus Station) The main operator between Perth and Broome in WA.

Premier Motor Service (☑133 410; www.premierms.com.au) Greyhound's main competitor along the east coast.

V/Line (☑1800 800 007; www. vline.com.au) Connects Victoria with NSW, South Australia and the ACT.

Bus Passes

If you're planning on doing a lot of travel in Australia, a Greyhound Australia bus pass will save you money. Bus-pass discounts of 10% apply to YHA- and student-card holders, and children under 14. For a full list of passes, check out www.greyhound.com.au/passes.

SHORT HOP PASS

With Greyhound's Short Hop Pass, you have 30 days to travel and you can get on and get off as many times as you

like between two preselected major cities. Routes covered:

➡ Adelaide–Alice Springs ($229)

➡ Alice Springs–Darwin ($225)

➡ Melbourne–Brisbane ($235)

➡ Sydney–Brisbane ($139)

➡ Sydney–Byron Bay ($115)

➡ Sydney–Melbourne ($105)

HOP ON HOP OFF PASS

Greyhound's Hop On Hop Off Pass gives you 90 days to take long journeys in stages along a prescribed route.

KILOMETRE PASS

Greyhound's simplest passes, giving you specified amounts of travel starting at 1000km ($189), up to 25,000km ($2675). Passes are valid for 12 months and you can travel where and in what direction you please, stopping as many times as you like. Use the online kilometre chart to figure out which pass suits you. Phone at least a day ahead to reserve your seat.

Costs

Following are the average one-way bus fares along some well-travelled routes, booked online.

ROUTE	FARE
Adelaide–Alice Springs	$155
Adelaide–Melbourne	$60
Brisbane–Cairns	$320
Cairns–Sydney	$429
Sydney–Brisbane	$109
Sydney–Melbourne	$120

Backpacker Buses

Backpacker-style and more formal bus tours offer a convenient way to get from A to B and see the sights on the way. Following are some

multistate operators; there are also smaller companies operating within individual states and territories.

AAT Kings (☑1300 556 100; www.aatkings.com) Big coach company (popular with the older set) with myriad tours all around Australia.

Adventure Tours Australia (☑1300 654 604; www.adventuretours.com.au) Affordable, young-at-heart tours in all states.

Autopia Tours (☑03-9393 1333; www.autopiatours.com. au) One- to three-day tours from Melbourne, Adelaide and Sydney.

Groovy Grape Tours (☑1800 661 177, 08-8440 1640; www. groovygrape.com.au) Small-group operator running one-day to one-week tours ex-Adelaide, Melbourne and Alice Springs.

Nullarbor Traveller (☑1800 816 858; www.thetraveller.net. au) Small company running relaxed minibus trips across the Nullarbor Plain between South Australia and Western Australia.

Oz Experience (☑1300 300 028; www.ozexperience.com) Backpacker tour covering central, northern and eastern Australia in a U-shaped route – Cairns, Brisbane, Sydney, Melbourne, Adelaide, Alice Springs and Darwin – using Greyhound bus services.

Car & Motorcycle

With its vast distances, endless stretches of bitumen and off-the-beaten-track sights, exploring Australia by road is an experience unlike any other.

2WD Depending on where you want to travel, a regulation 2WD vehicle might suffice. They're cheaper to hire, buy and run than 4WDs and are more readily available. Most are fuel efficient and easy to repair and sell. Downsides: no off-road capability and no room to sleep!

4WD Good for outback travel as they can access almost any track for which you get a hankering, and there might even be space to sleep in the back. Downsides:

poor fuel economy, awkward to park and more expensive to hire or buy.

Campervan Creature comforts at your fingertips: sink, fridge, cupboards, beds, kitchen and space to relax. Downsides: slow and often not fuel-efficient, not great on dirt roads and too large for nipping around the city.

Motorcycle The Australian climate is great for riding, and bikes are handy in city traffic. Downsides: Australia isn't particularly bike-friendly in terms of driver awareness; there's limited luggage capacity, and exposure to the elements.

Auto Clubs

Under the auspices of the **Australian Automobile Association** (AAA; 02-6247 7311; www.aaa.asn.au) there are automobile clubs in each state, which is handy when it comes to insurance, regulations, maps and roadside assistance. Club membership (around $100 to $150) can save you a lot of trouble if things go wrong mechanically. If you're a member of an auto club in your home country, check if reciprocal rights are offered in Australia. The major Australian auto clubs generally offer reciprocal rights in other states and territories.

Automobile Association of the Northern Territory (AANT; 08 8925 5901; www.aant.com. au; 2/14 Knuckey St; 9am-5pm Mon-Fri, to 12.30pm Sat)

National Roads & Motorists Association (NRMA; 13 11 22; www.mynrma.com.au) NSW and the ACT

Royal Automobile Club of Queensland (RACQ; 13 19 05; www.racq.com.au)

Royal Automobile Club of Tasmania (RACT; Map p638; 03-6232 6300, roadside assistance 13 11 11; www.ract.com.au; cnr Murray & Patrick Sts, Hobart; 8.45am-5pm Mon-Fri)

Royal Automobile Club of Victoria (RACV; 13 72 28; www.racv.com.au)

Royal Automobile Club of Western Australia (RAC; 13 17 03; www.rac.com.au)

Driving Licences

To drive in Australia you'll need to hold a current driving licence issued in English from your home country. If the licence isn't in English, you'll also need to carry an International Driving Permit, issued in your home country.

Environmental Considerations

A few simple actions can help minimise the impact your journey has on the environment.

➡ Ensure your vehicle is well serviced and tuned.

➡ Travel lightly to reduce fuel consumption.

➡ Drive slowly – many vehicles use 25% more fuel at 110km/h than at 90km/h.

➡ Avoid hard acceleration and heavy braking.

Sydney to Melbourne via the Princes Hwy

Total Distance = 1041km

93 Distance (km) between towns

SYDNEY
93
[1]
Wollongong
28
Kiama
47
Nowra
68
Canberra (144km) — **Ulladulla**
48
[52] **Batemans Bay**
69
Narooma
Cooma (101km) — 77
[18]
Bega
35
Pambula — **Merimbula**
Eden
19
57
NSW
VICTORIA **Genoa**
Bombala (85km) — [B23] 47 → *Mallacoota (23km)*
Cann River
→ *Bemm River (23km)*
75
Orbost → *Marlo (15km) & Cape Conran (34km)*
59
Lakes Entrance → *Metung (10km)*
Omeo (120km) — [B500] 36
Bairnsdale
69
[A1]
Sale [A440] → *Yarram (72km)*
49
Traralgon [C482] → *Yarram (60km)*
31
Moe [B460]
28 → *Leongatha (56km)*
Warragul
72
Dandenong
34
MELBOURNE

Sydney to Brisbane via the Pacific Hwy

Total Distance = 940km

Distance (km) between towns
93

BRISBANE
106
M1
QUEENSLAND
NEW SOUTH WALES
Surfers Paradise
Coolangatta
Tweed Heads
24
Murwillumbah
81 7
Byron Bay
33
Lismore (35km) — 44 Ballina
130
Glen Innes (162km) — 38 Grafton
82
Armidale (169km) — 78 Coffs Harbour
62
Nambucca Heads
Macksville
56
Walcha (166km) — Kempsey
34 41
Port Macquarie
73
Taree
73
Bulahdelah
Singleton (109km) — 1
15 88
Newcastle
77
Gosford
71
Katoomba (94km) — 4 SYDNEY

→ Crank the air-con only when absolutely necessary.

→ Stay on designated roads and vehicle off-road tracks. Drive in the middle of tracks to minimise track widening and damage, don't drive on walking tracks and avoid driving on vegetation.

→ Cross creeks at designated areas.

→ Consider ride sharing where possible. For more info, see www.greenvehicleguide.gov.au.

Fuel

Fuel types Unleaded and diesel fuel is available from service stations sporting well-known international brand names. LPG (liquefied petroleum gas) is not always stocked at more remote roadhouses – if you're on gas, it's safer to have dual-fuel capacity.

Costs Prices vary from place to place, but at the time of writing, unleaded was hovering between $1.20 and $1.50 per litre. Out in the country, prices soar – in outback Northern Territory, South Australia, Western Australia and Queensland you can pay as much as $2 per litre.

Availability In cities and towns petrol stations proliferate, but distances between fill-ups can be long in the outback. That said, there are only a handful of tracks that require a long-range fuel tank. On main roads there'll be a small town or roadhouse roughly every 150km to 200km. Many petrol stations, but not all, are open 24 hours.

Hazards & Precautions
ANIMAL HAZARDS

→ Roadkill is a huge problem in Australia, particularly in the Northern Territory, Queensland, NSW, South Australia and Tasmania. Many Australians in rural areas avoid travelling once the sun drops because of the risks posed by nocturnal animals on the roads.

→ Kangaroos are common on country roads, as are cows and sheep in the unfenced outback. Kangaroos are most active around dawn and dusk and often travel in groups: if you see one hopping across the road, be sure to slow right down, as its friends may be just behind it.

→ If you hit and kill an animal while driving, pull it off the road, preventing the next car from having a potential accident. If the animal is only injured and is small – perhaps an orphaned joey (baby kangaroo) – wrap it in a towel or blanket and call the relevant wildlife rescue line:

Department of Environment & Heritage Protection (☏1300 264 625; www.ehp.qld.gov.au) Queensland

Department of Parks & Wildlife (☏Wildcare Helpline 08-9474 9055; www.parks.dpaw.wa.gov.au) Western Australia

Fauna Rescue of South Australia (☏08-8289 0896; www.faunarescue.org.au)

NSW Wildlife Information, Rescue & Education Service (WIRES;☏1300 094 737; www.wires.org.au)

Parks & Wildlife Service (☏03-6165 4305; www.parks.tas.gov.au) Tasmania

Wildcare Inc NT (☏0408 885 341; www.wildcarent.org.au)

Wildlife Victoria (☏1300 094 535; www.wildlifevictoria.org.au)

BEHIND THE WHEEL

Fatigue Be wary of driver fatigue; driving long distances (particularly in hot weather) can be utterly exhausting. Falling asleep at the wheel is not uncommon. On a long haul, stop and rest every two hours or so – change drivers or have a coffee.

Road trains Be careful overtaking road trains (trucks with two or three trailers stretching for as long as 50m); you'll need distance and plenty of speed. On single-lane roads get right off the road when one approaches.

Unsealed roads Unsealed road conditions vary wildly and cars perform differently when braking and turning on dirt. Don't exceed 80km/h on dirt roads; if you go faster, you won't have time to respond to a sharp turn, stock on the road or an unmarked gate or cattle grid.

Hire

Larger car-rental companies have offices in major cities and towns. Most companies require drivers to be over the age of 21, though in some cases it's 18 and in others 25.

Suggestions to assist in the process:

➡ Read the contract cover to cover.

➡ Some companies may require a signed credit-card slip as bond, while others may actually charge your credit card. If the latter is the case, find out when you'll get a refund.

➡ Ask if unlimited kilometres are included and, if not, what the extra charge per kilometre is.

➡ Find out what excess you'll have to pay if you have an accident, and if it can be lowered by an extra charge per day (this option will usually be offered to you whether you ask or not). Check if your personal travel insurance covers you for vehicle accidents and excess.

➡ Check for exclusions (hitting a kangaroo, damage on unsealed roads etc) and whether you're covered on unavoidable unsealed roads (eg accessing campsites). Some companies also exclude parts of the car from cover, such as the underbelly, tyres and windscreen.

➡ At pick-up inspect the vehicle for any damage. Make a note of anything on the contract before you sign.

Brisbane to Cairns via the Bruce Hwy

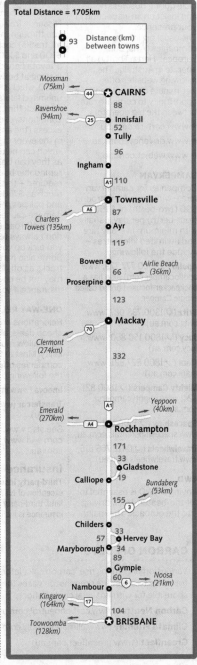

Total Distance = 1705km

93 Distance (km) between towns

Mossman (75km)
(44) ✪ CAIRNS
88
Ravenshoe (94km)
(25) ● Innisfail
52
● Tully
96
Ingham ●
(A1) 110
● Townsville
(A6) 87
Charters Towers (135km)
● Ayr
115
Bowen ●
Airlie Beach (36km)
66
Proserpine ●
123
● Mackay
(70)
Clermont (274km)
332
Emerald (270km)
(A1)
Yeppoon (40km)
(A4) ● Rockhampton
171
33
● Gladstone
Calliope ● 19
Bundaberg (53km)
155
(3)
Childers ●
33
57 ● Hervey Bay
Maryborough ● 34
89
● Gympie
Noosa (21km)
60 (6)
Nambour ●
Kingaroy (164km)
(17)
104
Toowoomba (128km)
✪ BRISBANE

→ Ask about breakdown and accident procedures.

→ If you can, return the vehicle during business hours and insist on an inspection in your presence.

The usual big international companies (Avis, Budget, Europcar, Hertz, Thrifty) all operate in Australia. The following websites offer last-minute discounts and the opportunity to compare rates between the big operators:

→ www.carhire.com.au

→ www.drivenow.com.au

→ www.webjet.com.au

CAMPERVAN

Companies for campervan hire – with rates from around $90 (two-berth) or $150 (four-berth) per day, usually with minimum five-day hire and unlimited kilometres – include the following:

Apollo (☑1800 777 779; www.apollocamper.com) Also has a backpacker-focused brand called Hippie Camper.

Britz (☑1300 738 087; www.britz.com.au)

Jucy (☑1800 150 850; www.jucy.com.au)

Maui (☑1800 827 821; www.maui.com.au)

Mighty Campers (☑1800 821 824; www.mightycampers.com.au)

Spaceships (☑1300 132 469; www.spaceshipsrentals.com.au)

Travelwheels (☑0412 766 616; www.travelwheels.com.au)

4WD

Having a 4WD is essential for off-the-beaten-track driving into the outback. The major

car-hire companies have 4WDs.

Renting a 4WD is affordable if a few people get together – something like a Nissan X-Trail (which can get you through most, but not all, tracks) costs between $100 and $150 per day; for a Toyota Landcruiser you're looking at between $150 and $200, which should include unlimited kilometres.

Check the insurance conditions, especially the excess (the amount you pay in the event of accident and which can be up to $5000), as they can be onerous. A refundable bond is also often required – this can be as much as $7500. The excess and policies might not cover damage caused when travelling off-road (which they don't always tell you when you pick up your vehicle). Some also name specific tracks as off-limits and you may not be covered by the insurance if you ignore this.

ONE-WAY RELOCATIONS

Relocations are usually cheap deals, although they don't allow much time flexibility. Most of the large hire companies offer deals, or try the following operators:

imoova (www.imoova.com)

Transfercar (www.transfercar.com.au)

See also www.hippiecamper.com and www.drivenow.com.au.

Insurance

Third-party insurance With the exception of NSW and Queensland, third-party personal-injury insurance is included in the

vehicle registration cost, ensuring that every registered vehicle carries at least the minimum insurance (if registering in NSW or Queensland you'll need to arrange this privately). We recommend extending that minimum to at least third-party property insurance – minor collisions can be amazingly expensive.

Rental vehicles When it comes to hire cars, understand your liability in the event of an accident. Rather than risk paying out thousands of dollars, consider taking out comprehensive car insurance or paying an additional daily amount to the rental company for excess reduction (this reduces the excess payable in the event of an accident from between $2000 and $5000 to a few hundred dollars).

Exclusions Be aware that if travelling on dirt roads you usually will not be covered by insurance for your rental vehicle unless you have a 4WD (read the fine print); some agreements even specify specific roads or tracks that you're not allowed to drive on. Also, many companies won't cover the cost of damage to glass or tyres.

Purchase

Buying your own vehicle to travel around in gives you the freedom to go where and when the mood takes you, and may work out cheaper than renting in the long run. Downsides include dealing with confusing and expensive registration, roadworthy certificates and insurance; forking out for maintenance and repairs; and selling the vehicle, which may be more difficult than expected.

If you're buying a second-hand vehicle, keep in mind the hidden costs: stamp duty, registration, transfer fee, insurance and maintenance.

PAPERWORK

Registration When you buy a vehicle in Australia, you need to transfer the registration into your own name within 14 days. Each state has slightly different requirements and different organisations that do this. Similarly, when

CARBON OFFSETS

Various organisations use 'carbon calculators' that allow travellers to offset the greenhouse gases they are responsible for with financial contributions.

Carbon Neutral (www.carbonneutral.com.au)

Climate Friendly (www.climatefriendly.com)

Greenfleet (www.greenfleet.com.au)

ROAD DISTANCES (KM)

	Adelaide	Albany	Alice Springs	Birdsville	Brisbane	Broome	Cairns	Canberra	Cape York	Darwin	Kalgoorlie	Melbourne	Perth	Sydney	Townsville
Albany	2649														
Alice Springs	1512	3573													
Birdsville	1183	3244	1176												
Brisbane	1942	4178	1849	1573											
Broome	4043	2865	2571	3564	5065										
Cairns	3079	5601	2396	1919	1705	4111									
Canberra	1372	4021	2725	2038	1287	5296	2923								
Cape York	4444	6566	3361	2884	2601	5076	965	3888							
Darwin	3006	5067	1494	2273	3774	1844	2820	3948	3785						
Kalgoorlie	2168	885	3092	2763	3697	3052	5234	3540	6199	4896					
Melbourne	728	3377	2240	1911	1860	4811	3496	637	4461	3734	2896				
Perth	2624	411	3548	3219	4153	2454	6565	3996	7530	4298	598	3352			
Sydney	1597	4246	3109	2007	940	5208	2634	289	3599	3917	3765	862	3869		
Townsville	3237	5374	2055	1578	1295	3770	341	2582	1306	2479	4893	3155	5349	2293	
Uluru	1559	3620	441	1617	2290	3012	2837	2931	3802	1935	3139	2287	3595	2804	2496

	Bicheno	Cradle Mountain	Devonport	Hobart	Launceston
Cradle Mountain	383				
Devonport	283	100			
Hobart	186	296	334		
Launceston	178	205	105	209	
Queenstown	443	69	168	257	273

These are the shortest distances by road; other routes may be considerably longer. For distances by coach, check the companies' leaflets.

selling a vehicle you need to advise the state or territory road-transport authority of the sale and change of name.

In NSW, Northern Territory, Queensland, Tasmania, Victoria and Western Australia, the buyer and seller need to complete and sign a Transfer of Registration form. In the ACT and South Australia there is no form, but the buyer and seller need to complete and sign the reverse of the registration certificate.

Roadworthy certificate
Sellers are required to provide a roadworthy certificate when transferring registration in the following situations:

➡ ACT – once the vehicle is six years old

➡ NSW – once the vehicle is five years old

➡ NT – once the vehicle is three years old

➡ Queensland – Safety Certificate required for all vehicles

➡ Victoria – Certificate of Roadworthiness required for all vehicles

➡ WA, SA & Tasmania – no inspections/certificates required in most circumstances. If the vehicle you're considering doesn't have a roadworthy certificate, it's worth having a roadworthiness check done before you buy it. This can cost upwards of $100 but can save you money on hidden costs. Road-transport authorities have lists of licensed vehicle testers.

Gas certificate In Queensland, if a vehicle runs on gas, a gas certificate must be provided by the seller in order to transfer the registration. In the ACT, vehicles running on gas require an annual inspection.

Immobiliser fitting In Western Australia it's compulsory to have an approved immobiliser fitted to most vehicles (not motorcycles) before transfer of registration; this is the buyer's responsibility.

Changing state of registration Note that registering a vehicle in a different state to the one it was previously registered in can be difficult, time-consuming and expensive.

Renewing registration Registration is paid annually Australia-wide, but most states and territories also give you the option of renewing it for six and sometimes three months.

ROAD TRANSPORT AUTHORITIES
For more information about processes and costs:

Access Canberra (☎13 22 81; www.accesscanberra.act.gov. au) ACT

Department of Planning, Transport & Infrastructure (☎1300 872 677; www.transport.sa.gov. au) South Australia

Department of State Growth – Transport (☎1300 135 513; www.transport.tas.gov.au) Tasmania

Department of Transport (☏1300 654 628; www.transport.nt.gov.au) Northern Territory

Department of Transport (☏13 11 56; www.transport.wa.gov.au) Western Australia

Department of Transport & Main Roads (☏13 23 80; www.tmr.qld.gov.au) Queensland

Roads & Maritime Services (☏13 22 13; www.rta.nsw.gov.au) NSW

VicRoads (☏13 11 71; www.vicroads.vic.gov.au) Victoria

WHAT TO LOOK FOR

It's prudent to have a car checked by an independent expert – auto clubs offer vehicle checks, and road transport authorities have lists of licensed garages – but if you're flying solo, here are some things to check:

➡ tyre tread

➡ number of kilometres

➡ rust damage

➡ accident damage

➡ oil should be translucent and honey-coloured

➡ coolant should be clean and not rusty in colour

➡ engine condition: check for fumes from engine, smoke from exhaust while engine is running, and engines that rattle or cough

➡ exhaust system should not be excessively noisy or rattly when engine is running

➡ windscreen should be clear with no cracks or chip marks

When test driving the car, also check the following:

➡ listen for body and suspension noise and changes in engine noise

➡ check for oil and petrol smells, leaks and overheating

➡ check instruments, lights and controls all work: heating, air-con, brake lights, headlights, indicators, seat belts and windscreen wipers

➡ brakes should pull the car up straight, without pulling, vibrating or making noise

➡ gears and steering should be smooth and quiet

BUYING FROM BACKPACKERS

Hostel noticeboards and the Thorn Tree travel forum at www.lonelyplanet.com are good places to find vehicles for sale. Tour desks also often have noticeboards.

BUYING FROM DEALERS

Licensed car dealers are obliged to guarantee that no money is owing on a car. Depending on the age of the car and the kilometres travelled, you may also receive a statutory warranty. You will need to sign an agreement for sale; make sure you understand what it says before you sign. Some dealers will sell you a car with an undertaking to buy it back at an agreed price, but don't accept verbal guarantees – get it in writing.

BUYING ONLINE

Private and dealer car sales are listed online on websites such as **Car Sales** (www.carsales.com.au), the **Trading Post** (www.tradingpost.com.au) and **Gumtree** (www.gumtree.com.au).

BUYING FROM PRIVATE SELLERS

Buying privately can be time consuming, and you'll have to travel around to assess your options. But you should expect a lower price than that charged by a licensed dealer. The seller should be able to provide you with a roadworthy certificate (if required in the state you're in), but you will not get a cooling-off period or a statutory warranty.

It's your responsibility to ensure the car isn't stolen and that there's no money owing on it: check the car's details with the **Personal Property Securities Register** (1300 007 777; www.ppsr.gov.au).

BUYING FROM TRAVELLERS' MARKETS

Cairns, Sydney, Darwin and Perth (cities where travellers commonly begin or finish their travels) are the best places to buy or sell a vehicle, especially Cairns. It's possible these cars have been around Australia several times, so it can be a risky option.

ROAD CONDITIONS

For up-to-date information on road conditions around the country, check out the following:

Australian Bureau of Meteorology (www.bom.gov.au) Weather information.

Department of Planning, Transport & Infrastructure (☏1300 872 677; www.transport.sa.gov.au) South Australian road conditions.

Live Traffic NSW (☏1300 131 122; www.livetraffic.com) NSW road conditions.

Main Roads Western Australia (☏13 81 38; www.mainroads.wa.gov.au) WA road conditions.

Road Report (☏1800 246 199; www.roadreport.nt.gov.au) Northern Territory road conditions.

Traffic & Travel Information (☏13 19 05; www.racq.com.au/cars-and-driving/safety-on-the-road/roadconditions) Queensland road conditions.

Road Rules

Australians drive on the left-hand side of the road and all cars are right-hand drive.

Give way An important road rule is 'give way to the right' – if an intersection is unmarked (unusual), and at roundabouts, you must give way to vehicles entering the intersection from your right.

Speed limits The general speed limit in built-up and residential areas is 50km/h. Near schools, the limit is usually 25km/h (sometimes 40km/h) in the morning and afternoon. On the highway it's usually 100km/h or 110km/h; in the NT it's either 110km/h or 130km/h. Police have speed radar guns and cameras and are fond of using them in strategic locations.

Seat belts & car seats It's the law to wear seat belts in the front and back seats; you're likely to get a fine if you don't. Small children must be belted into an approved safety seat.

Drink-driving Random breath tests are common. If you're caught with a blood-alcohol level of more than 0.05% expect a fine and the loss of your licence. Police can randomly pull any driver over for a breathalyser or drug test.

Mobile phones Using a mobile phone while driving is illegal in Australia (excluding hands-free technology).

Hitching & Ride Sharing

Hitching is never entirely safe in any country in the world, and we don't recommend it. Travellers who decide to hitch should understand that they are taking a small but potentially serious risk. People who do choose to hitch will be safer if they travel in pairs and let someone know where they are planning to go.

Ride sharing is a good way to split costs and environmental impact with other travellers. Noticeboards are good places to find ads; also check these online classifieds:

Catch a Lift (www.catch alift.com)

Coseats (www.coseats.com)

Need a Ride (www.need aride.com.au)

Local Transport

All of Australia's major towns have reliable, affordable public bus networks, and there are suburban train lines in Sydney, Melbourne, Brisbane, Adelaide and Perth. Melbourne also has trams (Adelaide has one!), Sydney and Brisbane have ferries and Sydney has a light-rail line. Taxis operate Australia-wide.

Train

Long-distance rail travel in Australia is something you do because you really want to – not because it's cheap, convenient or fast. That said, trains are more comfortable than buses, and there's a certain long-distance 'romance of the rails' that's alive and kicking. Shorter-distance rail services within most states are run by state rail bodies, either government or private.

These are most important long-distance rail links:

Great Southern Rail (☑08-8213 4401, 1800 703 357; www. greatsouthernrail.com.au) Operates the *Indian Pacific* between Sydney and Perth, the *Overland* between Melbourne and Adelaide, and the *Ghan* between Adelaide and Darwin via Alice Springs.

Queensland Rail (☑1300 131 722; www.queenslandrail travel.com.au) Runs the high-speed *Spirit of Queensland* service between Brisbane and Cairns.

NSW TrainLink (☑13 22 32; www.nswtrainlink.info) Trains

from Sydney to Brisbane, Melbourne and Canberra.

V/Line (☑1800 800 007; www. vline.com.au) Trains within Victoria, linking up with buses for connections into NSW, South Australia and the ACT.

Costs

Following are standard internet-booked one-way, high-season fares. Backpacker discounts are also available.

Adelaide–Darwin Adult/child $2329/2089

Adelaide–Melbourne Adult/child from $149/69

Adelaide–Perth Adult/child $1839/1649

Brisbane–Cairns Adult/child seated from $369/184; sleeper from $519/311

Sydney–Brisbane Adult/child seated from $66/66; sleeper from $216/179

Sydney–Canberra Adult/child seated from $40/28

Sydney–Melbourne Adult/child seated from $66/66; sleeper from $216/179

Sydney–Perth Adult/child $2599/2329

Train Passes

Queensland Rail offers the Queensland Coastal Pass allowing unlimited stopovers one-way between Cairns and Brisbane in either direction. A one-month Coastal Pass costs $209; two months is $289. The Queensland Explorer Pass is similar but extends over the entire state rail network. A one-month Explorer Pass costs $299; two months is $389.

NSW TrainLink has the Discovery Pass for both international visitors and Australians, allowing unlimited one-way economy travel around NSW, plus connections to Brisbane, the Gold Coast, Melbourne and Canberra. A 14-day/one-/three-/six-month pass costs $232/275/298/420; premium class upgrades are available.

Behind the Scenes

SEND US YOUR FEEDBACK

We love to hear from travellers – your comments keep us on our toes and help make our books better. Our well-travelled team reads every word on what you loved or loathed about this book. Although we cannot reply individually to your submissions, we always guarantee that your feedback goes straight to the appropriate authors, in time for the next edition. Each person who sends us information is thanked in the next edition – the most useful submissions are rewarded with a selection of digital PDF chapters.

Visit **lonelyplanet.com/contact** to submit your updates and suggestions or to ask for help. Our award-winning website also features inspirational travel stories, news and discussions.

Note: We may edit, reproduce and incorporate your comments in Lonely Planet products such as guidebooks, websites and digital products, so let us know if you don't want your comments reproduced or your name acknowledged. For a copy of our privacy policy visit lonelyplanet.com/privacy.

OUR READERS

Many thanks to the travellers who used the last edition and wrote to us with helpful hints, useful advice and interesting anecdotes:

Alan Taylor, Anastasia Papaioannou, Andrea Edwards, Andrew Walter, Cathy Sohler, Daniel Richard, Jane Rushworth, Kathrin Schad, Kersti Esbjörnsson, Mary Munro, Patricia Aufderheide, Pauline Dejoux, Sain Alizada, Shelagh O'Brien

WRITER THANKS

Brett Atkinson

Thanks to Tourism WA and visitor information centres and Parks and Wildlife offices throughout the state. Cheers to Western Australia's talented craft brewers for refreshment on the road, and special thanks to Tasmin Waby at Lonely Planet for another opportunity to explore my spectacular neighbour. Thanks also to my fellow authors, Carolyn and Steve, and the industrious in-house editors and cartographers. Final thanks to Carol for helping me devour the excellent Hippocampus gin and Temper Temper chocolate when I got home.

Anthony Ham

A very big thank you to Tasmin Waby for sending me out into some of Australia's most beautiful corners and for her commitment to good writing. Thanks also to Liam, Sticks, Mandy Dwyer and so many others who made my stay in the Northern Territory so memorable. And to my family who always keep the home fires burning – os quiero and I can't wait to take you there next time.

Paul Harding

Thanks to all those travellers and locals who helped with company and advice on my journey through Queensland's most remote corners, especially the helpful guys who got me out of vehicular trouble at Eliot Falls. Thanks to Tamara for coffee and a chat in Cairns, and to Tasmin at LP. But mostly to Hannah and Layla for being there.

Kate Morgan

Big thanks to Destination Editor Tasmin Waby for the opportunity to basically eat and drink my way around Melbourne's best neighbourhoods! Thank you to Caro Cooper for suggestions and being a drinking partner on occasion, and to my partner Trent for all your help and support.

Charles Rawlings-Way

Huge thanks to Tasmin for the gig, and to all the helpful souls I met and friends I reconnected with on the road in South Australia and Tasmania, who flew through my questions with the greatest of ease. Biggest thanks of all to Meg, who held the increasingly chaotic fort while I was busy scooting around in the sunshine ('Where's daddy?') – and made sure that Ione, Remy Liv and Reuben were fed, watered, schooled, tucked-in and read-to.

Andy Symington

As a prodigal Sydneysider returned for this project, I've had so much invaluable advice and help from friends about what's going on in town that I can't possibly thank them all. Tourist offices and more were helpful across the region. Particular gratitude, however, goes to Stephen Freiberg, Kate McGuinness, Hugh O'Keefe, Ben Hamilton, Matthew Beech, Iain and Amanda Ashley, Tasmin Waby and the LP team. And also, as ever, to my family.

Kate Armstrong

Particular thanks to Jacqui Loftus-Hills, Visit Victoria; Wendy Jones, Goulburn River Valley Tourism; Sue Couttie, Tourism Northeast; Marie Glasson, Greater Shepparton City Council; and Fran Martin, Echuca Visitor Information Centre. Finally, to my dear friends Sue Mulligan, Lou Bull and Emmo – with thanks.

Carolyn Bain

Covering such vast distances and calling to check on some astoundingly beautiful coastline was a joy – my thanks to Tasmin Waby for the commission, and to fellow WA scribes Brett Atkinson and Steve Waters for sharing info. In the west, sincere thanks to all those who guided me to find ancient rocks, manta rays, deserted beaches and breathtaking aerial panoramas, and also to those who shared a beer, a chat, travel tips and recommendations.

Cristian Bonetto

First and foremost, an epic thank you to Drew Westbrook for his hospitality and generosity. Sincere thanks also to Craig Bradbery, Tim Crabtree, Amy Ratcliffe, Leanne Layfield, Terese Finegan, Michael Flocke, Simon Betteridge, Annabel Sullivan, Garry Judd and the many locals who offered insight and insider knowledge along the way. At Lonely Planet, a huge thanks to Tasmin Waby for her support and encouragement.

Peter Dragicevich

Researching this guidebook was an absolute pleasure, especially because of the wonderful company that I had on the road. Special thanks go to Braith Bamkin, Peter van Gaalen, Marg Toohey and Jo Stafford for all their practical assistance in Melbourne, and to David Mills and Barry Sawtell for the Canberra Morrissey safari. And cheers to all my eating and drinking buddies along the way, especially Errol Hunt, Kim Shearman, Cristian Bonetto and Maryanne Netto.

Trent Holden

First up a massive thanks to Tasmin Waby for commissioning me to update the bulk of regional Victoria. Was an absolute honour to cover my home state. Totally blown away how much cool stuff there is to visit out here. Thanks to all the tourist visitor centres across the state, who are staffed by a fantastic team of volunteers who are doing a sensational job. Cheers to everyone else for giving me the time of day for a chat, and helping me put together this new edition. As per always lots of love to my family, particularly my partner Kate, who I had the great fortune of having accompany me this time round.

Virginia Maxwell

Staff at visitor information centres in Tasmania were almost universally knowledgeable, helpful and friendly. Particular thanks go to Jo in Wynyard, Bronwyn in Strahan and Michelle at Cradle Mountain. Thanks, too, to my travel companions Peter Handsaker and Catherine Hannebery, to Janni Soltys for first bringing Pumphouse Point to my attention and to Mandy Stroebel for her local insight.

Tamara Sheward

Sweaty Cairns hugs and hearty thanks to my friends, family, local experts and random ring-ins who helped me delve ever deeper into the wonders of my hometown and surrounds; it's always an eye-opener being a traveller/travel writer in one's own backyard. At LP, mega-thanks to Tasmin Waby for the gig, and for your eternal encouragement; and to chapter co-author Paul Harding. The biggest clink of the coconuts goes, as ever, to my favourite FNQers: my crazy crocodiles Dušan and Masha.

Tom Spurling

To Tasmin for choosing me to go around again! To Goose for riding shotgun to Rockhampton and making me go for a jog. To Lucy for sleeping in the backseat and showing no interest in cryptic crosswords. To the bar staff in Ravenswood for reminding me why I wanted this job in the first place. To the Whitsundays for being discovered. To the Town of 1770 for providing so many openings at dinner parties (a number? Really?). To my children for not missing me very much (I will never forget that slight, O and P).

Benedict Walker

Huge thanks to Tasmin Waby/Tamsin Maybe from LP for taking me on for this awesome roadie and for sticking by me when I struck a few potholes along the way. To my sometime co-pilot, the lovely Sarah Sabell, for teaching me to drive stick and not fighting with me even once! And to my beautiful mum Trish, and the Cooks, who let me go off to do my own thing at a time of family grief. I live a weird and wonderful life but without your love and support, I'd have nothing and be nobody.

Steve Waters

Thanks to Trace and Heath, Brodie, Abbie, Meika and Kaeghan for midnight arrivals, James, Toby, John, Sam, Lauren, Dana and the rest of MC for gorge love, Di for making us a cuppa during the grand final, Unruly Ted for getting that trivia question, Roz and Megan for caretaking and especially Hamish and Kaz for sharing all those sunsets and sunrises and drowning out the dust, heat and corrugations with grace, good humour and lashings of ginger Matsos.

BEHIND THE SCENES

Donna Wheeler
Love and gratitude to Juliette Claire for her inspiration and incredible regional knowledge. Thanks to ex-locals Peter Maclaine and Debbie Wheeler, especially for Pete's surfing expertise. Thanks to Harry in Broadbeach, to the Byron skydivers and to Amanda and Simon in Brunswick Heads for great hospo insights. Thanks also to Nic Wrathall for your company during some long research days and Brigid Healy and Andrew King, Kate Dale, Darryn Devlin for Sydney homecoming love. Finally thanks to Joe Guario. for everything.

ACKNOWLEDGEMENTS

Climate map data adapted from Peel MC, Finlayson BL & McMahon TA (2007) 'Updated World Map of the Köppen-Geiger Climate Classification', Hydrology and Earth System Sciences, 11, 163344.

Sydney Trains Network and Sydney Ferries Network maps © Transport for NSW 2017. Train and ferry maps courtesy of Transport for NSW. Maps current at time of printing.

Photograph p12, bottom: image courtesy of MONA Museum of Old and New Art, Hobart, Tasmania, Australia.

Photographs p20, bottom, and page 60, top right: images courtesy of Tourism NT, Australia.

Illustration pp72-3 by Javier Zarracina.

Cover photograph: Aerial image photographed near Broome in Western Australia, shannonstent/Getty.

THIS BOOK

This 19th edition of Lonely Planet's *Australia* guidebook was researched and written by Brett Atkinson, Anthony Ham, Paul Harding, Kate Morgan, Charles Rawlings-Way, Andy Symington, Kate Armstrong, Carolyn Bain, Cristian Bonetto, Peter Dragicevich, Trent Holden, Virginia Maxwell, Tamara Sheward, Tom Spurling, Benedict Walker, Steve Waters and Donna Wheeler. We would also like to thank the following people for their contributions to this guide: Dr Michael Cathcart, Cathy Craigie, Dr Tim Flannery and Dr Janelle White. This guidebook was produced by the following:

Destination Editor
Tasmin Waby

Product Editors Vicky Smith, Catherine Naghten

Senior Cartographer
Julie Sheridan

Book Designer
Nicholas Colicchia

Assisting Editors Sarah Bailey, Andrew Bain, Imogen Bannister, Michelle Bennett, Bridget Blair, Laura Crawford, Melanie Dankel, Andrea Dobbin, Bruce Evans, Victoria Harrison, Gabrielle Innes, Ali Lemer, Jodie Martire, Rosie Nicholson, Lauren O'Connell, Susan Paterson, Chris Pitts, Saralinda Turner, Simon Williamson

Assisting Cartographers
Julie Dodkins, James Leversha

Cover Researcher
Naomi Parker

Thanks to William Allen, Jennifer Carey, Hannah Cartmel, Heather Champion, Daniel Corbett, Megan Eaves, Shona Gray, Sandie Kestell, Anne Mason, Kate Mathews, MaSovaida Morgan, Claire Naylor, Karyn Noble, Jessica Ryan, Ross Taylor, Amanda Williamson, Clifton Wilkinson

Index

Map Pages **000**

Photo Pages **000**

Map Legend

Sights

- Beach
- Bird Sanctuary
- Buddhist
- Castle/Palace
- Christian
- Confucian
- Hindu
- Islamic
- Jain
- Jewish
- Monument
- Museum/Gallery/Historic Building
- Ruin
- Shinto
- Sikh
- Taoist
- Winery/Vineyard
- Zoo/Wildlife Sanctuary
- Other Sight

Activities, Courses & Tours

- Bodysurfing
- Diving
- Canoeing/Kayaking
- Course/Tour
- Sento Hot Baths/Onsen
- Skiing
- Snorkelling
- Surfing
- Swimming/Pool
- Walking
- Windsurfing
- Other Activity

Sleeping

- Sleeping
- Camping

Eating

- Eating

Drinking & Nightlife

- Drinking & Nightlife
- Cafe

Entertainment

- Entertainment

Shopping

- Shopping

Information

- Bank
- Embassy/Consulate
- Hospital/Medical
- Internet
- Police
- Post Office
- Telephone
- Toilet
- Tourist Information
- Other Information

Geographic

- Beach
- Gate
- Hut/Shelter
- Lighthouse
- Lookout
- Mountain/Volcano
- Oasis
- Park
- Pass
- Picnic Area
- Waterfall

Population

- Capital (National)
- Capital (State/Province)
- City/Large Town
- Town/Village

Transport

- Airport
- Border crossing
- Bus
- Cable car/Funicular
- Cycling
- Ferry
- Metro station
- Monorail
- Parking
- Petrol station
- Subway station
- Taxi
- Train station/Railway
- Tram
- Underground station
- Other Transport

Note: Not all symbols displayed above appear on the maps in this book

Routes

- Tollway
- Freeway
- Primary
- Secondary
- Tertiary
- Lane
- Unsealed road
- Road under construction
- Plaza/Mall
- Steps
- Tunnel
- Pedestrian overpass
- Walking Tour
- Walking Tour detour
- Path/Walking Trail

Boundaries

- International
- State/Province
- Disputed
- Regional/Suburb
- Marine Park
- Cliff
- Wall

Hydrography

- River, Creek
- Intermittent River
- Canal
- Water
- Dry/Salt/Intermittent Lake
- Reef

Areas

- Airport/Runway
- Beach/Desert
- Cemetery (Christian)
- Cemetery (Other)
- Glacier
- Mudflat
- Park/Forest
- Sight (Building)
- Sportsground
- Swamp/Mangrove

Benedict Walker

Southwest, Central & Outback New South Wales Ben was born in Newcastle, Australia, and grew up in the 'burbs spending weekends and long summers by the beach, whenever possible. Although he's drawn magnetically to the kinds of mountains he encountered in the Canadian Rockies and the Japan and Swiss Alps, beach life is in his blood. Japan was the first gig he got for Lonely Planet, in 2008, and he's been blessed to have been asked back three more times since then. He really is someone who is living his dreams, though life on the road can have its ups and downs. He's also written and directed a play, toured Australia managing the travel logistics for top-billing music festivals and is playing around with photography and film-making. Join him on his journeys on Instagram: @wordsandjourneys.

Steve Waters

Broome & the Kimberley Travel and adventure have always been Steve's life; he couldn't imagine a world without them. He's been using Lonely Planet guidebooks for more than 30 years in places as diverse as Iran, Central Asia, Kamchatka, Tuva, the Himalaya, Canada, Patagonia, the Australian Outback, NE Asia, Myanmar and the Sahara. Little wonder then that he finally got a gig with the company he was supporting! He's contributed to Iran and Indonesia guidebooks, and to the past four editions of Western Australia, and come any September you're likely to find him in a remote gorge somewhere in the Kimberley. His travel ethos:Travel gives you a unique view of the world. Patience, acceptance, resourcefulness and flexibility are all lessons well learnt. Plans change, where some people see obstacles, others see possibilities. Go with an open mind. But go!

Donna Wheeler

Central Coast New South Wales, Byron Bay & Northern New South Wales, the Gold Coast Donna has written guidebooks for Lonely Planet for 10 years, contributing to guides to Italy, Norway, Belgium, Africa, Tunisia, Algeria, France, Austria and Melbourne. She is the author of *Paris Precincts*, a curated photographic guide to the city's best bars, restaurants and shops and is a reporter for Italian contemporary art publisher My Art Guides. Donna's work on contemporary art, architecture and design, food, wine, wilderness areas and cultural history can be found in a variety of other publications. She became a travel writer after various careers as a commissioning editor, creative director, digital producer and content strategist.

Peter Dragicevich

Canberra, ACT & Snowy Mountains, Melbourne & Victoria After a successful career in niche newspaper and magazine publishing, both in his native New Zealand and in Australia, Peter finally gave into Kiwi wanderlust, giving up staff jobs to chase his diverse roots around much of Europe. Over the last decade he's written literally dozens of guidebooks for Lonely Planet on an oddly disparate collection of countries, all of which he's come to love. He once again calls Auckland, New Zealand his home – although his current nomadic existence means he's often elsewhere.

Trent Holden

Around Melbourne, Mornington Peninsula & Phillip Island, Great Ocean Road, Goldfields & Grampians, Wilsons Promontory & Gippsland, Victorian High Country A Geelong-based writer, located just outside Melbourne, Trent has worked for Lonely Planet since 2005. He's contributed to 30-plus guidebooks across Asia, Africa and Australia. With a penchant for megacities, Trent's in his element when assigned to cover a nation's capital – the more chaotic the better – to unearth cool bars, art, street food and underground subculture. On the flipside he also writes guides to idyllic tropical islands across Asia, in between going on safari to national parks in Africa and the subcontinent. When not travelling, Trent works as a freelance editor, reviewer and spending all his money catching live gigs. You can catch him on Twitter @hombreholden.

Virginia Maxwell

Launceston & Around, Devonport & Northwestern Tasmania, Cradle Country & Western Tasmania Although based in Australia, Virginia spends at least half of her year updating Lonely Planet destination coverage in Europe and the Middle East. The Mediterranean is her favourite place to travel, and she has covered Spain, Italy, Turkey, Syria, Lebanon, Israel, Egypt and Morocco for Lonely Planet guidebooks – there are only eight more countries to go! Virginia also writes about Armenia, Iran and Australia. Follow her @maxwellvirginia on Instagram and Twitter.

Tamara Sheward

Cairns & Around After years of freelance travel writing, rock'n'roll journalism and insalubrious authordom, Tamara leapt at the chance to join the Lonely Planet ranks in 2009. Since then, she's worked on guides to an incongruous jumble of countries including Montenegro, Australia, Serbia, Russia, the Samoas, Bulgaria and Fiji. She's written a miscellany of travel articles for the BBC, *The Independent*, *Sydney Morning Herald* et al; she's also fronted the camera as a documentary presenter for Lonely Planet TV, Nat Geo and Al-Jazeera. Tamara's based in far northern Australia, but you're more likely to find her roaming elsewhere, tattered notebook in one hand, the world's best-travelled toddler in the other.

Tom Spurling

Fraser Island & the Fraser Coast, Capricorn Coast, Whitsunday Coast, Townsville & Mission Beach, the Great Barrier Reef For this edition, Tom Spurling bumbled from Mission Beach to Fraser Island, but he grew up further south where fewer things can sting you. He has worked on 14 Lonely Planet titles, including *Central America*, *India*, *Turkey*, *Japan*, *South Africa* and *China*. When not pretending to be a twenty-something backpacker, he is a much older married man with two small children who discusses very grave matters with high school students in Hong Kong.

Charles Rawlings-Way
Queensland, Hobart & Tasmania, Adelaide & South Australia Charles is a veteran travel writer who has penned 30-something titles for Lonely Planet – including guides to Singapore, Toronto, Sydney, Tasmania, New Zealand, the South Pacific and Australia – and numerous articles. After dabbling in the dark arts of architecture, cartography, project management and busking for some years, Charles hit the road for LP in 2005 and hasn't stopped travelling since. 'What's in store for me in the direction I don't take?' (Kerouac).

Andy Symington
Sydney, South Coast NSW, Lord Howe Island Andy has written or worked on more than a hundred books and other updates for Lonely Planet (especially in Europe and Latin America) and other publishing companies, and has published articles on numerous subjects for a variety of newspapers, magazines and websites. He part-owns and operates a rock bar, has written a novel and is currently working on several fiction and non-fiction writing projects. Originally from Australia, Andy moved to northern Spain many years ago. When he's not off with a backpack in some far-flung corner of the world, he can probably be found watching the tragically poor local football side or tasting local wines after a long walk in the nearby mountains.

Kate Armstrong
The Murray Kate has spent much of her adult life travelling and living around the world. A full-time freelance travel journalist, she has contributed to around 40 Lonely Planet guides and trade publications and is regularly published in Australian and worldwide publications. She is the author of several books and children's educational titles. Over the years, Kate has worked in Mozambique, picked grapes in France and danced in a Bolivian folkloric troupe. A keen photographer, greedy gourmand and frenetic festival goer, she enjoys exploring off-the-beaten-track locations, restaurants and theatres. You can read more about her on www.katearmstrongtravelwriter.com and @nomaditis.

Carolyn Bain
Monkey Mia & the Central West, Ningaloo Coast & the Pilbara, Outback Western Australia A travel writer and editor for 16 years, Carolyn has lived, worked and studied in various corners of the globe, including London, Denmark, St Petersburg and Nantucket. She is regularly drawn north from her base in Melbourne, Australia to cover diverse destinations for Lonely Planet, from dusty outback Australia to luminous Greek islands, by way of Maine's lobster shacks and Slovenia's alpine lakes. The Nordic region stakes a large claim to her heart, with repeated visits to Iceland and Denmark for work and pleasure. Carolyn writes about travel and food for a range of publishers; see carolynbain.com.au for more.

Cristian Bonetto
Brisbane & Around, Noosa & the Sunshine Coast, Melbourne Cristian has contributed to more than 30 Lonely Planet guides to date, spanning cities, regions and countries across four continents, including his homeland, Australia. His musings on travel, food, culture and design have appeared in numerous publications and media outlets around the world. When not on the road, you'll find the reformed playwright and TV scriptwriter slurping espresso in his beloved hometown, Melbourne. You can follow Cristian's adventures on Instagram (rexcat75) and Twitter (@CristianBonetto).

OUR STORY

A beat-up old car, a few dollars in the pocket and a sense of adventure. In 1972 that's all Tony and Maureen Wheeler needed for the trip of a lifetime – across Europe and Asia overland to Australia. It took several months, and at the end – broke but inspired – they sat at their kitchen table writing and stapling together their first travel guide, *Across Asia on the Cheap*. Within a week they'd sold 1500 copies. Lonely Planet was born.

Today, Lonely Planet has offices in Franklin, London, Melbourne, Oakland, Dublin, Beijing and Delhi, with more than 600 staff and writers. We share Tony's belief that 'a great guidebook should do three things: inform, educate and amuse'.

OUR WRITERS

Brett Atkinson

Perth, Around Perth, Margaret River & the Southwest Coast, Southern WA For this edition, Brett uncovered new restaurants, bars and distilleries in Perth and Fremantle, and jumped from beach to forest and back to beach throughout Margaret River and the southwest. In Albany, a poignant highlight was the National Anzac Centre telling the story of brave WWI soldiers. Brett has contributed to Lonely Planet guidebooks spanning Europe, Africa, Asia, the United States and the Pacific, and covered over 60 countries as a food and travel writer. See www. brett-atkinson.net for his latest adventures.

Anthony Ham

Central Australia, Northern Territory Anthony is a freelance writer and photographer who specialises in Spain, East and Southern Africa, the Arctic and the Middle East. When he's not writing for Lonely Planet, Anthony writes about and photographs Spain, Africa and the Middle East for newspapers and magazines in Australia, the UK and US.

Paul Harding

Cairns & the Daintree, Cape York Peninsula, Gulf Savannah, Outback Queensland, As a writer and photographer, Paul has been travelling the globe for the best part of two decades, with an interest in remote and offbeat places, islands and cultures. He's an author and contributor to more than 50 Lonely Planet guides to countries and regions as diverse as India, Iceland, Belize, Vanuatu, Indonesia, New Zealand, Finland, Philippines and – his home patch – Australia.

Kate Morgan

Melbourne & Victoria Having worked for Lonely Planet for over a decade, Kate has been fortunate enough to cover plenty of ground working as a travel writer on destinations such as Shanghai, Japan, India, Zimbabwe, the Philippines and Phuket. She has done stints living in London, Paris and Osaka but these days is based in one of her favourite regions in the world – Victoria, Australia. In between travelling the world and writing about it, Kate enjoys spending time at home working as a freelance editor.

OVER PAGE
MORE WRITERS

Published by Lonely Planet Global Limited
CRN 554153
19th edition – Nov 2017
ISBN 978 1 78657 237 0
© Lonely Planet 2017   Photographs © as indicated 2017
10 9 8 7 6 5 4 3 2 1
Printed in Singapore

Although the authors and Lonely Planet have taken all reasonable care in preparing this book, we make no warranty about the accuracy or completeness of its content and, to the maximum extent permitted, disclaim all liability arising from its use.